American
Labor
Sourcebook

American
Labor
Sourcebook

Bernard and Susan Rifkin

McGraw-Hill Book Company

*New York   St. Louis   San Francisco   Auckland
Bogotá   Düsseldorf   Johannesburg   London
Madrid   Mexico   Montreal   New Delhi
Panama   São Paulo   Singapore
Sydney   Tokyo   Toronto*

Library of Congress Cataloging in Publication Data

Rifkin, Bernard.
    American labor sourcebook.

    Includes indexes.
    1. Industrial relations--United States--
Handbooks, manuals, etc.   2. Trade-unions--United
States--Handbooks, manuals, etc.   3. Labor and
laboring classes--United States--Handbooks,
manuals, etc.   4. Industrial relations--Handbooks,
manuals, etc.   I. Title.
HD8072.R53   331'.0973   79-16918
ISBN 0-07-052830-6

1234567890   BPBP   7865432109

*The editors for this book were Robert L. Davidson and Joseph Williams, and the production supervisor
was Thomas G. Kowalczyk. The cover was designed by Naomi Auerbach. It was set in Plantin by
Monotype Composition Company, Inc.*

Many of the sources used for this book are from government publications, particularly the Monthly
Labor Review. *A full list of sources is given on pp. xv–xvii.*

Printed and bound by The Book Press.

Contents

Preface   xiii

Sources   xv

Section 1   Labor in 1977 and 1978   **1-1**

Labor in 1977   1-3

Teamsters Settle with United Parcel • Safety Agency Issues Coke Emission
Standard • Job-Related Injuries Decline • Auto Workers Settle with Cat-
erpillar • Air Traffic Controllers Slowdown Averted • New York City
Schools Charged with Job Bias • Three U.S. Agencies Revise Job Test
Guidelines • NEA, State Employees Union Reach Accord • AFL-CIO Reac-
tivates Food and Beverage Unit • Gas Shortages Cause Numerous
Layoffs • Marshall Becomes Secretary of Labor • Oil Pacts Provide Initial
9-percent Raise • Fitzmaurice, Elected IUE President, Seeks Merger • Fraser
Endorsed by Auto Workers Leaders • Patrick to Seek UMW Presidency •
New York City to Keep Social Security Coverage • Meany Rejects Preno-
tification of Wage Increases • McBride Apparent Victor in Steelworkers
Contest • Winpisinger to Head Machinists • Auto Workers Sign Pact with
American Motors • Construction Unions Agree to Work Rule
Concessions • Fitzsimmons, Three Others Quit Pension Fund • Truce Ends
10-year Jurisdictional Dispute on Farms • Tobacco Workers Complete Bar-
gaining • New York City Defers Teacher Pay Increases • Newspaper Unions
Forgo First-Year Increase • Goodrich Proposes Binding Arbitration
Plan • Marshall Identifies Safety Administration Problems • Glass Bottle
Blowers Settle Early • TV Network Agrees to Promotion, Hiring
Goals • Steelworkers Win Enhanced Employment Security • Carter An-
nounces Anti-Inflation Program • AFL-CIO Rebuffed on Shoe Imports,
Situs Picketing • Eastern, Air Line Pilots Settle • Nursing Home Strike
Averted in New York City • Auto Workers Elect Fraser President • Bridges
Retires After 40 Years at Union Helm • OSHA Announces Benzene Stand-
ard • Wages Increased by Southern Textile Firms • Dock Container Dispute
Resolved • Florida Plumbers Local Agrees to Pay Cuts • AFL-CIO Questions
Carter's Economic Program • Law Firm Agrees to Affirmative Action Pro-
gram • Aluminum Accords Comparable to Steel Settlement • Miller Ap-
parent Victor in UMW Race • Bakery Accord Reached • Construction Set-
tlement Covers Three-State Region • First Grape Settlement Reached • U.S.
to Investigate Steelworkers' Election • Garment Workers Elect
Officers • Herman Elected ILWU President • Trustees Resign Coal Union's
Benefit Fund • Kennecott Settlements End Walkouts • Apparel Accord
Provides Wage Increase of $1.10 • Air Line Mechanics' Wages Tied to
Company Profits • Chrysler, UAW Announce Legal Service Plan • Gimbels'
Workers Win 3-year Contract • Paperworkers Settle • Texas Telephone
Workers Win Pay Increases • OSHA Streamlines Reporting Forms • Bias
Against Handicapped Charged • Boot and Shoe Workers Merge with Retail
Clerks • Telephone Accord Averts Strike • New York City Ties Wage
Increases to Productivity • Construction Hiring Goals for Women Un-
veiled • U.S. Delays Final Decision on Quitting ILO • AFGE Locals Veto
Organizing Military • Nabisco, Union Negotiate 2-year Contract • Union
Plumbers Reduce Pay Scales • AFL-CIO Executive Council Lists Priori-
ties • ITU Convention Appoints Merger Panel • United Farm Workers
Convene • Retail Clerks International President Dies • Steel Companies
Announce Layoffs • Federal Pay Increase • UAW Board Rejects Reaffiliation
Bid • UAW, American Motors Negotiate New Contract • AIW Delegates
Favor Merger with Molders • GM Charged with Labor Law Violations • New
Bargaining Group Formed for Truckers • U.S. Won't Seek New Mine

Workers' Election • Aerospace Workers Settle, Ending Walkout • Can Companies Settle • Mine Safety Act Signed • OSHA Proposes New Policy on Carcinogens • United States Leaves ILO • New Minimum Wage • Glass Workers Negotiate Wage Increase • Southern Apparel Workers Win Contract • Chicago Meat Cutters' Accord Ends Ban • New York City Bricklayers Accept Pay Cuts • California Wineries Settle • Transport Workers Convene • White Male Steelworkers Charge Bias • Maine to Texas Dock Strike Ends • Hawaiian Sugar Accord Reached • Carter Signs Social Security Tax Rise • Gotbaum Calls For Meany Resignation

Labor in 1978   1-46

Carter urges wage and price constraint • Farm Workers end longstanding boycott • NLRB requests injunction against Stevens • AFL-CIO forms unit for professionals • Physicians' union established • Musicians' president dies • Miners reject contract; Taft-Hartley invoked • Steelworkers win Southern shipyard vote • Sadlowski sues for election rerun • UAW wins 14-year representation fight • Goodrich proposes no-strike plan • U.S. sues pension fund officials • Service workers' strike averted • Coal strike ends • Black lung program made permanent • OSHA limits exposure to benzene • Porters and Railway Clerks merge • AFL-CIO Executive Council meets • EEOC announces new discrimination criteria • Mandatory retirement age raised to 70 • Laid-off workers win 'rule-of-65' pensions • Postal service accused of labor violations • Asbestos-stricken workers sue U.S. • President proposes Federal pay "cap" • Construction unions, contractors sign agreement • Kansas City Construction Committee formed • Aerospace workers win '55 and '30 retirement • Cement companies settle • NLRB, J. P. Stevens reach accord • California grape, citrus workers settle • AFL-CIO rebuffs Carter on wage increases • New York union merges with AFSCME • U.S. adopts construction hiring goals for women • More settlements in aerospace • East and Gulf Coast seamen settle • Trucking associations merge • New standards for cotton dust exposure • Southern textile firms announce wage increases • Electrical workers in New York settle • City workers in New York win pay increase • Stevens-NLRB settlement assailed • Contractors, unions sign cost-cutting pact • GE discrimination complaint settled • Postal accord retains 'no layoff' clause • Railroads, four unions reach agreement • State employees win wage increase • Philadelphia municipal employees end strike • New York City police accept 'third' agreement • Guild, New York newspaper accord ends strike • Hospital league and union settle • Plumbers' compensation surpasses $21 an hour • Hiring cuts begin in wake of 'Proposition 13' • Northwest pilots settle, ending walkout • Insurance agents end strike • West Coast dockworkers settle • AFL-CIO establishes safety department • Convention activities • New York City adopts 'residency' law • Paperworkers two officials indicted • Aribtrator awards higher pay to postal workers • Conrail, UTU announce settlement • New study on job-related cancers • Teacher strikes widespread • GM agrees to 'preferential hiring plan' • Stevens, NLRB reach agreement • Airlines reduce strike aid • Soccer players win union representation • Carter Administration's anti-inflation plan • Brewery workers win backpay • Volkswagen proposal modified after strike • Brewery workers win backpay • Steelworkers' income protection guidelines set • ACTWU approves merger with Shoe Workers • Carpenters assail 'open shop' trend • Union election results • Civil Service reorganization • Job safety task force report • Administration's anti-inflation plan revised • TWA and Machinists settle • Shoe workers get 2-year contracts • Teachers open drive to organize nurses

Section 2   Organized Labor in the United States   **2-1**

Structure of the Labor Movement   2-3
  The AFL-CIO   2-3

Railway Labor Executives' Association   2-6
Other Federations   2-6
Unaffiliated or Independent Unions   2-6
Internal Disputes Plan   2-6
Professional and State Employee Associations   2-7
AFL-CIO Paid Membership   2-7
Listings for American Federation of Labor and Congress of Industrial Organi-
zations   2-10
Executive Council   2-10
Standing Committees and Chairmen   2-10
Staff   2-11
Department of Organization and Field Services   2-11
Trade and Industrial Departments of the AFL-CIO   2-11
Other National Federations of Unions and Employee Associations   2-16
Listing of Labor Unions and Employee Associations   2-18
Finding Index   2-18
AFL-CIO State Labor Organizations   2-49
Labor Organizations' Dues and Fees   2-54
Decline in Labor Union and Employee Association Membership   2-59
Union Conventions Scheduled for 1979   2-64

Section 3   Labor on Politics and Foreign Affairs   **3-1**

Excerpts from the Speech of George Meany at the 12th Convention of the AFL-
CIO   3-3
AFL-CIO Positions on Legislation in the Senate   3-6
AFL-CIO Positions on Legislation in the House of Representatives   3-9
Labor and the World   3-12
Defense and Disarmament   3-12
Western Europe and NATO   3-12
Eastern Europe   3-13
Asia   3-12
Africa   3-14
Latin America   3-15
The International Labor Organization   3-17
Council Recommendation
African-American Labor Center   3-19
Asian-American Free Labor Institute   3-20
American Institute for Free Labor Development   3-21
Free Trade Union Institute   3-22
U.S. Unions Affiliated with International Trade Secretariats   3-23

Section 4   Federal Legislation Related to Labor   **4-1**

Federal Legislation Related to Labor Relations   4-3
Sherman Antitrust Act [July 2, 1890]   4-3
Clayton Antitrust Act [October 15, 1914]   4-3
The Railway Labor Act [May 20, 1926]   4-4
The Norris-LaGuardia (Anti-Injunction) Act [March 23, 1932]   4-6
Anti-Racketeering Act (Hobbs Act) [June 18, 1934]   4-7
Anti-Strikebreaker Law (Byrnes Act) [June 24, 1936]   4-7
Labor-Management Relations Act of 1947 (Taft-Hartley) [June 23, 1947]   4-8
Anti-Kickback Law and Copeland Act [June 25, 1948]   4-37
Labor-Management Reporting And Disclosure Act of 1959 (Landrum-Grif-
fin) [September 14, 1959]   4-37
Farm Labor Contractor Registration Act of 1963 [September 7, 1964]   4-44
Executive Order 11491—Labor-Management Relations in the Federal Serv-
ice [October 31, 1969]   4-44
Postal Reorganization Act of 1970 Applicability of Law [August 12, 1970] 4-51
The Employee Retirement Income Security Act of 1974 [September 2, 1974]   4-52

Federal Legislation Related to Labor Standards and Equal Employment Opportunity — 4-58

    Davis-Bacon Act [March 3, 1931] — 4-58

    Miller Act [August 24, 1935] — 4-60

    Walsh-Healey Public Contracts Act [June 30, 1936] — 4-60

    Fair Labor Standards Act of 1938 [June 25, 1938] — 4-62

    The 1977 Amendments to the Federal Minimum Wage Law — 4-67

    Portal to Portal Act of 1947 [May 4, 1947] — 4-70

    Equal Pay Act of 1963 [July 10, 1963] — 4-73

    Civil Rights Act of 1964 [July 2, 1964] — 4-73

    Urban Mass Transportation Act (Pertinent Provisions) [July 9, 1964] — 4-76

    National Foundation on the Arts and Humanities Act—Secs. 5(j)–(k) [September 16, 1965] — 4-77

    Executive Order 11246—Equal Employment Opportunity [September 24, 1965] — 4-78

    Executive Order 11247—Providing for the Coordination by the Attorney General of Enforcement of Title VI of the Civil Rights Act of 1964 [September 24, 1965] — 4-82

    Service Contract Act of 1965 [October 22, 1965] — 4-82

    Executive Order 11375—Amending Executive Order No. 11246, Relating to Equal Employment Opportunity [October 13, 1967] — 4-84

    Age Discrimination in Employment Act of 1967 [December 15, 1967] — 4-85

    Consumer Credit Protection Act (Garnishment) [May 28, 1968] — 4-86

    Executive Order 11478—Equal Employment Opportunity in the Federal Government [August 8, 1969] — 4-86

    Contract Work Hours and Safety Standards Act [August 9, 1969] — 4-87

    Rail Passenger Service Act of 1970 (Pertinent Provisions) [October 30, 1970] — 4-89

Federal Legislation Related to Employee Training, Benefits, and Safety and Health — 4-91

    Federal Employees' Compensation Act [September 7, 1916] — 4-89

    Longshoremen's and Harbor Workers' Compensation Act [August 23, 1958] — 4-91

    Federal Metal and Nonmetallic Mine Safety Act [September 16, 1966] — 4-92

    Federal Coal Mine Health and Safety Act of 1969 [December 30, 1969] — 4-92

    Occupational Safety and Health Act of 1970 [December 29, 1970] — 4-95

    Executive Order 11612—Occupational Safety and Health Programs for Federal Employees [July 28, 1971] — 4-100

    Comprehensive Employment and Training Act (CETA) [December 28, 1973] — 4-101

Section 5   Federal Agencies Related to Labor — 5-1

Department of Labor — 5-3

    International Affairs — 5-8

    Employment and Training Administration — 5-8

    Labor-Management Services Administration — 5-14

    Employment Standards Administration — 5-16

    Occupational Safety and Health Administration — 5-18

    Mine Safety and Health Administration — 5-18

    Labor Statistics — 5-18

    Sources of Information

International Labor Organization — 5-20

Council on Wage and Price Stability — 5-20

Federal Mediation and Conciliation Service — 5-21

Commission on Civil Rights — 5-22

Equal Employment Opportunity Commission — 5-23

Department of Health, Education, and Welfare — 5-25

    Office of Human Development Services — 5-31

    Education Division — 5-34

    Health Care Financing Administration — 5-35

    Social Security Administration — 5-36

    Sources of Information — 5-37

National Labor Relations Board | 5-39
National Mediation Board | 5-42
Occupational Safety and Health Review Commission | 5-43
Pension Benefit Guaranty Corporation | 5-45
Railroad Retirement Board | 5-47
Appendix: Standard Federal Regions | 5-49

Section 6 Unemployment Insurance and the Employment Service **6-1**

State Unemployment Insurance: Changes During 1978 | 6-3
Significant Provisions of State Unemployment Insurance Laws | 6-7
Benefit Data Under State Unemployment Insurance Programs | 6-12
The Employment Service in 1977 | 6-13
    The ES System Today | 6-14
    Public Policy Issues | 6-25

Section 7 Workers' Compensation **7-1**

Workers' Compensation Laws: Major Amendments in 1976 | 7-3
Workers' Compensation Laws: Significant Enactments in 1977 | 7-10
Workers' Compensation Laws—Key State Amendments in 1978 | 7-19
Research Summaries | 7-27

Section 8 State Labor Legislation **8-1**

State Labor Legislation Enacted in 1976 | 8-3
State Labor Legislation Enacted in 1977 | 8-17
State Labor Legislation Enacted in 1978 | 8-39

Section 9 Labor and the Courts **9-1**

Early Landmark Decisions on Labor | 9-3
Labor and the Supreme Court: Significant Decisions of 1976–77 | 9-6
Labor and the Supreme Court: Significant Decisions of 1977–78 | 9-12
Significant Decisions in Labor Cases | 9-19

Pregnancy Exclusion not Sexually Biased • Standing for the Rights of Others in Title VII • Free Speech in Employment • Equal Pay Act as Applied to States Upheld • Due Process Rights at Hearings • Religious Bias Charges to be Reconsidered • Warrantless Safety Inspections Under OSHA • Public Employee Rights as Citizens • Reasonable Requirements for Union Office • Antipathy to Women, or to a Woman? • No Arbitration of Interest Arbitration • Discrimination Against Widowers in Social Security • Exclusive Bargaining Absent State Authority • Challenge to Smokers • Work Preservation as Secondary Activity • Contract Construction (Employer Payments for Other Workers) • Duplicate Suits Under Title VII • Due Process Hearing Unnecessary When Truth is Not Denied • New York Bias Ban Not For Export • Death of a Bakery-Severance Pay Arbitration • Union Harassment and State Law • Captain's Authority Unabridged • Restitution For Rescue on the Sea • The Agency Shop in Government Agencies • Protection From Misleading Rhetoric in Representation Election • 'Bona Fide' Seniority and Racial Bias • The Bar Overturned on Union Representation • Saturday Services • Layoff Aid Denied During Strike of Others • Jobless Fathers Defined by State—Welfare Benefits • Union Bankruptcy to Avoid Damages • NLRB Extends Sovereignty to Commercial Activity of Foreign Governments • Women Prison Guards Under Title VII • Veterans Protection in Pensions • New 'BLS Method' Affirmed in CETA • Statistical Significance Under Title VII • The NLRB and Religion Clause of First Amendment • Searching For 'Probable Cause' Under OSHA • Supreme Court Opens New Term • Lawful Leverage by State on Collective Bargaining • 'Employ Me' Ads May Tell All • Disciplinary Latitude in Union Discharge • Assault of Supervisor and Job Rights

Labor and the Law	9-53
Title VII Seniority Decisions	9-54
National League of Cities v. Usery	9-56
NLRB v. Pipefitters	9-57
"Traditional" Labor Law Cases	9-58
Public Employees	9-60
Employment Discrimination	9-63
Landrum-Griffin Act	9-65
Taft-Hartley Trusts	9-65
Social Benefit Cases	9-65
Occupational Safety and Health Act	9-66
Veterans' Reemployment Rights	9-66
Federal Employee Reclassification	9-66

Section 10   History of American Labor   **10-1**

Chronology of American Labor	10-3
Two Hundred Years of Work in America	10-25
The Workers	10-27
Population Growth and Change	10-27
Changes in the Labor Force	10-30
Education and Training of Workers	10-35
The Changing Nature of Work	10-37
Economic Activity	10-37
Organization of Work	10-38
Occupations	10-39
Working Conditions	10-44
Earnings from Work	10-48
Money Wages	10-48
Real Earnings	19-50
Work and Security	10-55
Unemployment	10-55
Accidents and Sickness	10-59
Old Age	10-60
Conclusion	10-62

Section 11   Labor in the Public Sector—State and Local   **11-1**

The New York Taylor Law	11-7
Directory of Public Employment Relations Boards and Agencies	11-19
Union Security Provisions by Government Function (table)	11-48
Check Off Provisions by Government Function (table)	11-49
Grievance Procedures by Level of Government (table)	11-50
Grievance Arbitration Procedures by Level of Government	11-50
Work Stoppage Provisions by Level of Government (table)	11-50
Negotiation Impasse Procedures by Level of Government (table)	11-51
Municipal Pension Plans	11-52
Comparison of Average Salaries in Private and Federal Employment	11-61

Section 12   Labor in Other Countries   **12-1**

An Analysis of Unemployment in Nine Industrial Countries	12-3
Population and Labor Force, Selected Countries (table)	12-16
Labor Force, Employment and Unemployment in Selected Industrial Countries (table)	12-20
Estimated Compensation Per Hour Worked of Production Workers in Manufacturing, Selected Countries (table)	12-21
Work Stoppages and Time Lost Due to Industrial Disputes in Selected Countries (table)	12-22

Section 13   Sample Contract Clauses in Labor Agreements   **13-1**

Section 14   Glossary of Labor Terms   **14-1**

Section 15   Indexes of *Monthly Labor Review*   **15-1**

Index of *Monthly Labor Review*, 1971–1975 (vol. 94-98)   15-3
Index of *Monthly Labor Review*, 1976 (vol. 99)   15-23
Index of *Monthly Labor Review*, 1977 (vol. 100)   15-33
Index of *Monthly Labor Review*, 1978 (vol. 101)   15-41

Section 16   Labor Education   **16-1**

Academic Degrees for Labor Studies—A New Goal for Unions   16-3
George Meany Center for Labor Studies   16-9

Section 17   Directory of International Labor Press Association   **17-1**

General Information   17-3
Official AFL-CIO Publications   17-4
    Official Canadian Labour Congress Publication   17-4
    AFL-CIO Departmental Publications   17-4
    AFL-CIO National and International Publications   17-5
AFL-CIO State and Local Central Body Publications U.S. Local Union Publications   17-11
Canadian Labor Publications   17-29
Associate Members   17-31
Regional and Industrial Associations   17-31
Government Information Sources   17-32
Current ILPA Publications   17-34

Section 18   The Work Force   **18-1**

Employment status of the noninstitutional population 16 years and over, 1947 to date (table)   18-3
Employment status of the noninstitutional population 16 years and over by sex, 1967 to date (table)   18-4
Employment status of the noninstitutional population by sex, age, and race (table)   18-5
Employment status of the noninstitutional population, 16 years and over by sex, 1947 to date (table)   18-7
Employment status of the noninstitutional population by sex, age, and race (table)   18-8
Employees on nonagricultural payrolls by industry division, 1919 to date (table)   18-10
Employed persons by detailed occupation, sex, and race (table)   18-11

Section 19   Hours and Earnings   **19-1**

Statistics on Compensation Changes   19-3
Gross hours and earnings of production or nonsupervisory workers on private nonagricultural payrolls by industry division, 1957 to date (table)   19-7
Gross hours and earnings of production or nonsupervisory workers on private nonagricultural payrolls by industry (table)   19-8
Employment, hours, and indexes of earnings in the Executive Branch of the Federal Government (table)   19-24
Average hourly earnings excluding overtime of production workers on manufacturing payrolls by industry (table)   19-24
Annual percent increases in average hourly earnings for selected occupational groups in metropolitan areas (table)   19-25

Section 20   Consumer Price Index   **20-1**
Price Data   20-3
Tables   20-4

Index follows Section 20.

Preface

The years between the entry of the United States into the first world war and the advent of the Roosevelt administration found the American labor movement in a continuing process of decline. The nadir had been reached by 1933. The American Federation of Labor (AFL) had declined to a membership of below 3,000,000 and its earlier competitor, the Industrial Workers of the World (IWW), had practically ceased to exist. It was during this period of decline that the Rand School of Social Science, then the central educational institution of socialism in the United States, published the *American Labor Year Book*. From 1916 until 1933 the book appeared annually under the successive editorship of Alexander Trachtenberg, Solon DeLeon, and Nathan Fine. Perhaps because it was a labor of idealistic love, the book was both a profitable venture and consistent with its purpose of service to labor. The publication had a wide circulation and is still referred to by students interested in the subject matter of its time.

This publishing effort was somewhat anachronistic and printing ceased in 1933, just when the turning point in labor had been reached. Inspired by the legislation of the New Deal, and later by the formation of the aggressive and militant competition of the Congress of Industrial Organization (CIO), organized labor went through a period of unprecedented growth. World War II gave the final impetus, and by its close, membership in unions was more than five times as great as when Franklin Delano Roosevelt took his oath of office. Chapters in the *American Labor Year Book* on significant federal labor legislation were necessarily sparse. The plethora of court and administrative decisions and the large government bureaucracies concerned with labor relations and labor standards would have to await the passage of all the labor legislation resulting from the New Deal.

The American Labor Sourcebook is, quite frankly, an effort for a single-volume work to fill the void left by the demise of the *American Labor Year Book* more than 45 years ago. There is now an even greater need for a single volume that encompasses the subject matter of American labor. Our purpose in preparing this book is to fill that need. This volume cannot replace the excellent and timely publications of the Bureau of Labor Statistics of the Department of Labor from which so much of this material is drawn. It may, however, be of service to practitioners and students in the field of labor relations. The central effort has been to present the mass of significant material extant in a format readily available to users and to indicate where future search might be advantageous.

Eminently reputable publishing institutions now service labor and management organizations with annual, monthly, weekly, and even daily reports on everything of importance in the area of labor relations and standards. They appear as bulletins, pamphlets, bound books, and as looseleaf insertions to assure timeliness of the material. They are recommended to readers of this volume.

The American Labor Sourcebook is well beyond the generous allocations of pages made by the publisher. Nevertheless, we were forced to omit essential material to prevent the enlargement to more than prohibitive size. We are aware of some of the shortcomings of this volume and will be grateful for suggestions that might improve subsequent editions.

Bernard and Susan Rifkin

Sources

Section 1

Articles are picked up from the *Monthly Labor Review:* February 1977, pp. 86–89; March 1977, pp. 79–81; April 1977, pp. 84–85; May 1977, pp. 57–60; June 1977, pp. 62–65; July 1977, pp. 52–54; August 1977, pp. 52–55; September 1977, pp. 45–48; October 1977, pp. 74–76; November 1977, pp. 56–57; December 1977, pp. 71–73; January 1978, pp. 41–45; March 1978, pp. 53–54; April 1978, pp. 55–58; May 1978, pp. 69–71; June 1978, pp. 56–58; July 1978, pp. 43–45; August 1978, pp. 50–54; September 1978, pp. 63–65; October 1978, pp. 56–58; November 1978, pp. 44–46; December 1978, pp. 74–77; February 1979, pp. 67–68. Published by the Bureau of Labor Statistics, U.S. Department of Labor.

Section 2

"Structure of the Labor Movement": from *Directory of National Unions and Employee Associations*, 1975, published by the Bureau of Labor Statistics, August 1977 (updated as of February 1978).

"Internal Disputes Plan": from *Report of the Executive Council to the 12th Convention of the AFL-CIO*, December 1977.

"Labor Organizations' Fees and Dues," *Monthly Labor Review*, May 1977, pp. 19–24.

"Decline in Labor Union and Employee Association Membership," from Bureau of Labor Statistics, September 1977.

"Listings for AFL-CIO." Courtesy of AFL-CIO.

Section 3

"Excerpts from the Speech of George Meany": from *The American Federationist*, December 1977.

"AFL-CIO Position on Legislation in the Senate" and "The AFL-CIO Position on Legislation in the House of Representatives," *AFL-CIO News*, Nov. 26, 1977.

"Labor and the World," from the *Report of the Executive Council to the 12th Convention of the AFL-CIO*, December 1977.

"U.S. Unions Affiliated with International Trade Secretariats": from *Directory of National Unions and Employee Associations*, Bureau of Labor Statistics, 1977.

Section 4

Articles on selected laws were picked up from: *Federal Labor Laws and Programs*, U.S. Department of Labor, Employment Standards Administration, Division of Employment Standards; material from the Office of Employee Benefit Security, Labor-Management Services Administration, U.S. Department of Labor; material from the Employment and Training Administration; and *Compilation of Selected Labor Laws Pertaining to Labor Relations* and *Compilation of Selected Labor Laws Pertaining to Labor Standards* and Equal Employment Opportunity, Subcommittee on Labor of the Committee on Labor and Public Welfare, United States Senate.

"A Guide to Basic Laws and Procedures Under the National Labor Relations Act," prepared by the Office of the General Counsel, National Labor Relations Board, Washington, 1976.

"Handy Reference Guide to the Fair Labor Standards Act," Wage and Hour Division, Employment Standards Administration, U.S. Department of Labor, 1972, revised October 1978.

Section 5

U.S. Government Manual, 1977–78, Office of the Federal Register, National Archives and Records Service, and General Services Administration, U.S. Government Printing Office, Washington, D.C., 1978.

Section 6

"State Unemployment Insurance: Changes During 1978," *Monthly Labor Review,* February 1979, pp. 13–16.

"Significant Provisions of State Unemployment Insurance Laws," from Bureau of Labor Statistics.

"The Employment Service in 1977," from *Employment and Training Report by the President,* transmitted to Congress January 1977, pp. 71–87.

Section 7

"Workers' Compensation Laws: Major Amendments in 1976," *Monthly Labor Review,* February 1977, pp. 39–45.

"Workers' Compensation Laws—Significant Enactments in 1977," *Monthly Labor Review,* December 1977, pp. 25–35.

"Workers' Compensation Laws—Key State Amendments of 1978," *Monthly Labor Review,* pp. 43–50.

"Research Summaries," *Monthly Labor Review,* August 1977, pp. 41–43.

Section 8

"State Labor Legislation Enacted in 1976," *Monthly Labor Review,* February 1977, pp. 25–38.

"State Labor Legislation Enacted in 1977," *Monthly Labor Review,* December 1977, pp. 3–24.

"State Labor Legislation Enacted in 1978" *Monthly Labor Review,* January 1979, pp. 26–42.

Section 9

"Labor and the Supreme Court: Significant Decisions of 1976–77," *Monthly Labor Review,* pp. 12–17.

"Labor and the Supreme Court: Significant Decisions of 1977–78," *Monthly Labor Review,* pp. 51–56.

"Significant Decisions in Labor Cases," *Monthly Labor Review:* March 1977, pp. 73–76; April 1977, pp. 79–81; May 1977, pp. 51–53; June 1977, pp. 57–59; July 1977, pp. 46–48; August 1977, pp. 46–49; September 1977, pp. 39–42; October 1977, pp. 70–72; November 1977, pp. 51–53; December 1977, pp. 66–69.

"Labor and the Law," from *Report of the Executive Council to the 12th Convention of the AFL-CIO,* December 1977.

Section 10

"Two Hundred Years of Work in America," from *Employment and Training Report of the President,* submitted to Congress June 1976.

Section 11

"Binding Arbitration Laws," *Monthly Labor Review,* October 1978, pp. 36–39.

"The New York Taylor Law," New York State Public Employment Relations Board, 1973.

Directory of Public Employment Relations Boards and Agencies, U.S. Department of Labor, Labor-Management Services Administration, 1977. "Characteristics of Agreements in State and Local Governments," Bureau of Labor Statistics.

"Municipal Pension Plans: Provisions and Payments," *Monthly Labor Review,* November 1977, pp. 24–31.

"Comparison of Average Salaries in Private and Federal Employment," from *National Survey of Professional, Administrative, Technical and Clerical Pay,* Bureau of Labor Statistics, March 1977.

Section 12

"An Analysis of Unemployment in Nine Industrial Countries," *Monthly Labor Review*, April 1977, pp. 12–24.

Population tables are from the *Handbook of Labor Statistics*, published by the Bureau of Labor Statistics, 1977, pp. 327–331, 333, 338, and 339.

Section 15

Monthly Labor Review: Index of Volumes 94–98, U.S. Government Printing Office, Washington, 1976, pp. 1–20.

Monthly Labor Review, December 1976, pp. 101–110; December 1977, pp. 119–126; December 1978, pp. 126–136.

Section 16

"Academic Degrees for Labor Studies— A New Goal for Unions," *Monthly Labor Review*, June 1977, pp. 15–20.

"George Meany Center for Labor Studies," from the *Report of the Executive Council to the 12th Convention of the AFL-CIO*, December 1977.

Section 17

"Directory of the International Labor Press Association," from *ILPA Directory of Member Publications*, July 1977. Courtesy of the ILPA.

Section 20

Monthly Labor Review, February 1978, pp. 94–98.

American
Labor
Sourcebook

Labor in 1977 and 1978

Developments in Industrial Relations

Reported in *Monthly Labor Review*, January 1977.

Teamsters settle with United Parcel

Striking Teamsters voted to accept a 3-year contract with United Parcel Service on December 9, ending a walkout that began September 16. The strike, involving 18,000 workers, disrupted parcel delivery service in 15 States, from Maine to South Carolina, and caused backups in other States, where contracts were still in effect and workers remained on the job.

One of the major issues was resolved when United Parcel agreed to maintain the number of full-time positions in each building as of September 15. The company had wanted to reduce by attrition the number of full-time sorters. UPS did win the right to continue to exclude part-time workers from the union pension and health programs. They will remain instead in the company plan. Part-time workers won an additional $1 an hour in wages over the life of the contract to end a claimed pay disparity between such workers in the East and in other parts of the country.

The pact's other economic terms were similar to those the union had won in the trucking industry in April. Workers received an immediate 65-cent hourly wage increase and 50 cents in the second and third years. The pact also provides for unlimited cost-of-living adjustments in the second and third years; previously, there was a maximum of 11 cents on each adjustment. Additional health and welfare and pension contributions will total $17 per week. Other changes included an increased uniform allowance, air-conditioned truck cabs, the right to use Citizen Band radios, and up to $50 reimbursement for personal losses resulting from holdups.

Safety agency issues coke emission standard

The Department of Labor has issued standards for controlling exposure of workers to cancer-causing emissions from coke ovens. The Department's Occupational Safety and Health Administration (OSHA) said the standards are based on its conclusion that coke oven emissions "play a causal role in the induction of cancer of the lung and genito-urinary tract" among exposed workers. OSHA's ruling limits workers' exposure to "150 micrograms of benzene-soluble fraction of total particulate matter (BSFTPM) per cubic meter of air averaged over an 8-hour period."

Dr. Morton Corn, Assistant Secretary of Labor for OSHA, said that unlike other job health standards issued by OSHA in the past, the coke-oven emission standard mandates that affected employers implement specific engineering and work practice controls as soon as possible. Further, if these controls are not sufficient to reduce employee exposures to the concentration limit mentioned above, they "will nonetheless be used to reduce exposures to a level as low as possible." They are also to be supplemented by the use of respirators to further reduce exposures. Employers must also devise additional controls if employee exposures still exceed the stipulated concentration limit.

More specifically, provisions of the standard include the following:

- Establishment of a "regulated area" with access limited to authorized persons.
- Monitoring and measuring requirements that are to be repeated every 3 months or whenever there have been production, process, or control changes.
- Detailed engineering controls applicable during charging operations, including specified methods of charging, drafting, or aspirating the ovens; and volumetric controls to charge sufficient coal to permit gases to effectively move from the oven into collectors.
- Engineering controls during coking operations including a pressure control system on each coke-oven battery to maintain uniform collector main pressure, and ready access to one or more facilities capable of repair of doors.
- Work practice controls that include preparation of written inspection and cleaning procedures, and charging, coking, and pushing procedures.
- Provisions requiring that new and rehabilitated coke-oven batteries incorporate the best available engineering and work practice controls to achieve compliance with the 150-microgram limit.
- A requirement for a detailed written compliance

"Developments in Industrial Relations" is prepared by Leon Bornstein and other members of the staff of the Division of Trends in Employee Compensation, Bureau of Labor Statistics, and is largely based on information from secondary sources.

program specifying dates for installation of engineering and work practice controls, monitoring dates, technology considered in meeting the permissible exposure limit, and any other relevant information.

- Respirators to be furnished whenever controls do not reduce exposures sufficiently. Wearing of the respirators is voluntary for 1 year, and will be required afterward whenever the permissible exposure limit is exceeded.
- Requirements for protective clothing and equipment other than respirators where the possibility exists of repeated skin contact or of exposures to heat or flame generated by the coking process, or both.

OSHA estimated that increased costs to the steel industry resulting from compliance will be $200 million a year and will range from $1.50 to $13.29 per ton, based on a steel price of $291 per ton, or an increase in the Consumer Price Index of from 0.01 to 0.07 percent—an impact OSHA termed small and which "will not disrupt substantially the income and consumption patterns of the economy."

Coke is the product of the destructive distillation or carbonization of coal. It is used as a fuel and reducing agent in blast furnace operations and in foundries as a cupola fuel. Of the approximately 61 million tons of coke produced a year in the United States, 90 percent is made by the steel industry plants, 8 percent by foundries, and 1 percent by beehive ovens. This ruling took effect January 20.

Job-related injuries declined in 1975

The latest results of the Bureau of Labor Statistics' annual survey of job safety and health in the private economy show that job-related fatalities dropped 10 percent from 1974 to 1975, from 5,900 to 5,300, and that occupational injuries dropped 16 percent, from 5.7 million to 4.8 million. Recognized occupational illnesses were estimated to total 163,000 for 1975, compared with 200,400 for 1974. Other survey findings released on December 8 included the following:

- A decline in the number of lost worktime injury cases from 1.94 million to 1.77 million.
- A decline from 30.2 million to 29.8 million in workdays lost because of work-related injuries.
- A decline in injury rates from 10.0 in 1974 to 8.8 injuries per 100 full-time workers in 1975.

Bert M. Concklin, Deputy Assistant Secretary of Labor, Occupational Safety and Health Administration, said the reductions are part of a national downward trend. The survey findings were based on reports submitted during 1976 by a sample of employers in the private sector.

Auto Workers settle with Caterpillar

The Auto Workers negotiated a 3-year contract with Caterpillar Tractor Co. for 34,500 workers at seven plants in five States, thus ending the round of negotiations with the "Big Three" agricultural and construction equipment companies. Production workers approved the accord by a vote of 6,442 to 1,640, and the skilled trades workers approved it by 808 to 745. The settlement provided for terms generally similar to those the union negotiated at Deere & Co. and International Harvester Co. (See *Monthly Labor Review,* January 1977, pp. 29–30.)

The Caterpillar agreement calls for an initial wage increase of 34 to 60 cents an hour, and increases of 3 percent in both the second and third years. It also provides for incorporating into base rates the $1.26 in cost-of-living increases gained under the prior contract and for the continuation of the escalator formula, which calls for a 1-cent-an-hour quarterly adjustment for each 0.3-point movement in the CPI (1967=100). The first adjustment under the clause, effective December 6, 1976, was 8 cents.

The bonus hours program at Caterpillar differs from that at Deere. It provides that employees receive 1-1/2 hours paid time off for each week of full attendance, starting January 3, 1977. At Deere, workers receive 1 hour for each of the first 4 weeks of perfect attendance in a year and 1-1/2 hours for each week thereafter. At International Harvester, the program was abolished in return for increased paid time off under the regular vacation plan.

The Caterpillar contract also differs from the other pacts in the area of pensions. At Caterpillar, the normal benefit rate was raised to $17 a month for each year of credited service, compared with $16 at the other companies.

Meanwhile, the Auto Workers' union reached no decision on whether to return to the AFL-CIO after union leaders met with federation chief George Meany in early December to discuss a possible reaffiliation. Auto Workers' President Leonard Woodcock told reporters after the meeting that "we came to no conclusions." The UAW had pulled out of the AFL-CIO in 1968, primarily because of former President Walter Reuther's policy dispute with Meany over the future course of the federation. The auto union has reportedly been studying a reconciliation with the AFL-CIO since Woodcock assumed the UAW presidency in 1970 following the death of Reuther. UAW Secretary-Treasurer Emil Mazey, who joined Woodcock at the meeting, said he was not yet in favor of reaffiliation. According to Mazey, "We left the AFL-CIO for specific reasons and unless and until these conditions are corrected I would not be in favor of it."

Air traffic controllers slowdown averted

The Professional Air Traffic Controllers Organization (PATCO) accepted a Civil Service Commission decision on the classification of jobs and withdrew its threat of a work slowdown during the holiday season. PATCO President John Leyden said that the Civil Service Commission and the Federal Aviation Administration have "finally" responded "realistically to the needs of controllers."

Although Federal employee unions are not allowed to bargain on compensation, the controllers were seeking to raise job ratings from General Schedule grade 13 to grade 14 for jobs at heavily used airports and regional air traffic control centers. The controllers also sought the upgrading of some middle-level jobs at many other terminals and centers and a guarantee that there will be no downgradings. After a study, the Civil Service Commission staff recommended that no GS-14's be granted and that there be a substantial number of downgradings. PATCO and the Federal Aviation Administration appealed to the full Commission, which ordered its staff to establish GS-14 positions at some facilities, upgrade some of the middle-level jobs, and downgrade some jobs. At a press conference which had been set up to announce an impending slowdown, PATCO and the Civil Service Commission confirmed a compromise under which GS-14 ratings would be approved for eight terminals or centers, and possibly a ninth; that there would be middle-level upgradings in "at least 22" facilities, and that no more than 63 positions would be downgraded.

Leyden estimated that the job reclassifications would provide about 2,000 controllers with pay raises effective by January 15, 1977. The salary rate range for GS-14 is $28,725 to $37,347, varying with length of service, compared with $24,308 to $31,598 for GS-13. PATCO represents 14,000 of the 16,000 controllers and trainees.

New York City schools charged with job bias

The Federal Government charged New York City's public school system with bias against women and minority teachers in hiring, promotions, and assignments. Martin H. Gerry, director of the Department of Health, Education, and Welfare's Office for Civil Rights, said the school system's examinations for the hiring of teachers were discriminatory and that minority applicants who passed were too frequently assigned to schools in which most students were from minority groups. Gerry added, "We have also found the system denied women access to positions as principals and assistant principals, and paid women athletic coaches less than men." The Office for Civil Rights is charged with enforcing civil rights in all federally assisted health and social services programs.

The school system faces sanctions, including the loss of $22 million in Federal education funds, unless it acts within 90 days to develop an interim plan for compliance with the regulations. School Chancellor Irving Anker said, "The Board of Education is in compliance with State law, which mandates a competitive examination system for teachers." United Federation of Teachers President Albert Shanker said he found the report "sloppy and full of contradictions." The study stated although 66.8 percent of all students in New York City public schools are black or Americans of Spanish origin, only 13.2 percent of the city's teachers are members of these groups.

Three U.S. agencies revise job test guidelines

Three Federal agencies have initiated new job testing and hiring guidelines to protect the rights of minorities and women. The new rules affect the employment practices of the Federal Government and Federal contractors and subcontractors and are to be used to determine if tests given to workers are inherently discriminatory. Agencies initiating the new guidelines are the Departments of Labor and Justice and the U.S. Civil Service Commission.

The three agencies said the rules were needed because their existing guidelines weren't uniform throughout the Government and did not take into account recent psychological studies and legal rulings. They said the new rules were endorsed by the American Psychological Association as "concise, realistic, and much needed." A Labor Department official said the guidelines explain to employers in technical detail the procedures for ensuring that hiring tests are fair to all applicants and do not contain a built-in bias against women or minorities.

Civil rights groups and the Equal Employment Opportunity Commission (EEOC) objected to the new rules. The EEOC called them too lenient. Elizabeth B. Walsh, the EEOC's acting chairperson, said the new guidelines "certainly are weaker than our guidelines," adding the Commission would continue to use its own guidelines in monitoring job bias in the private sector. Although the three other agencies' rules apply only to the Federal

Government and contractors doing business with it, the EEOC handles civil cases involving most other employers.

NEA, State employees union reach accord

The 1.8-million member National Education Association (NEA) and the 750,000-member State, County and Municipal Employees (AFSCME) settled organizational disputes in Ohio and Colorado. The pacts are expected to be the forerunner of increased efforts by both the NEA and the AFSCME to organize jointly all school system employees.

The Colorado agreement essentially limits the NEA's organizational efforts to teachers, and the Ohio agreement allows the NEA to try to organize teacher aides, clerks, secretaries, and school nurses, as well as teachers. In both States, the AFSCME will concentrate on cafeteria workers, janitors, busdrivers, and other blue-collar school employees. NEA President John Ryor said, "I expect this to result in more joint organizing efforts." He said similar agreements were anticipated in New Mexico and possibly four or five other States. Both organizations are leading members of the six-member Coalition of American Public Employees, founded in 1971, and have worked together on political as well as labor issues.

Officials for both bodies said that among the aims of the accords was the prevention of costly battles between them. An AFSCME spokesman said, "In a few places over the past couple of years, we've found ourselves in jurisdictional conflicts with the NEA, and we want to keep that from happening."

The AFSCME and the 175,000-member American Federation of Teachers are both affiliated with the AFL-CIO. Albert Shanker, head of the Teachers union, expressed concern over the pact. Shanker's union is a rival of NEA. He said, "We're going to study their legality to see whether there are violations of AFL-CIO rules governing jurisdictional questions, and if there are, we would take appropriate action."

In an earlier development, the NEA announced plans to organize New York City teachers, who are members of the United Federation of Teachers, an affiliate of the AFT. In 1972, the NEA and AFT State organizations formed a joint body, the New York State United Teachers, with each wing having the right to affiliate with the AFT or NEA, or both. In March 1976, this organization voted to cut its ties with the NEA. (See *Monthly Labor Review,* May 1976, p. 54.)

The NEA said it would spend $500,000 in an initial organizing effort. In announcing the drive, NEA President Ryor criticized Shanker's proposal that city municipal unions suspend collective bargaining for the duration of the city's fiscal crisis. Shanker responded that Ryor "knows full well that all New York City employees have suffered contract losses, and that all new contracts bargained since the fiscal crisis began have resulted in employees making very small money gains but giving up very important benefits."

AFL-CIO reactivates food and beverage unit

The AFL-CIO reactivated the Food and Beverage Trades Department in a convention held in the AFL-CIO building in Washington, D.C. Unions representing 2 million workers in the industry participated, and elected James T. Housewright, head of the Retail Clerks, and Daniel E. Conway, chief of the Bakery and Confectionery Workers, as president and secretary-treasurer of the department. Housewright said that the department's primary activities would be legislation and organization. Other unions joining the department include the Meat Cutters, Hotel and Restaurant Employees, Distillery Workers, Grain Millers, Laundry and Dry Cleaning union, Service Employees, Operating Engineers, Plumbers, Seafarers, and the Retail, Wholesale and Department Store Union.

The department, which originally had been founded in December 1961, surrendered its charter in December 1965 because its activites had been "negligible" and it had ceased to function for 3 years. Since then, there has reportedly been an increased spirit of cooperation among the unions involved. Housewright said, "Everyone is willing and eager to work together. I am convinced that this will aid us in achieving legislation of concern to workers in the food and beverage industries. It will help in future organizing programs for all affiliated unions." □

Developments in Industrial Relations

Reported in *Monthly Labor Review*, March 1977

Gas shortages cause numerous layoffs

The severe January weather sent a chill through the labor force as shortages of natural gas caused temporary layoffs. An estimated 1.5 million workers had been idled by February 1, according to press reports. Hard-hit areas included:

- Ohio, where State officials estimated that 750,000 workers were idled after factories and other businesses were ordered closed to save gas.
- New Jersey, where a State official estimated that 300,000 to 400,000 workers had been laid off.
- Pennsylvania, where Governor Milton Shapp said 90,000 workers had been laid off.
- Florida, where 50,000 were jobless, including many farmworkers. Governor Reuben Askew said the number could rise to 100,000.

(The March 4 BLS report on unemployment, which covered a period in February when the weather had improved, showed an increase in national unemployment from 7.3 to 7.5 percent. On a national basis, the number of unemployed increased by 225,000 in February to 7.2 million, with the over-the-month rise resulting from job losses due to layoffs.)

Marshall becomes Secretary of Labor

F. Ray Marshall was sworn in as the Nation's 16th Secretary of Labor on January 27. The Senate had confirmed the nomination of the University of Texas labor economist by a 74 to 20 vote. Senator Harrison A Williams, D.–N.J., chairman of the Senate Labor Subcommittee, supported Marshall, saying that he had "an abundance of attributes" to make him a strong Secretary of Labor and that he was sensitive to the problems of working people and fully understood the "scandalous conditions" of the poor and the problems of urban centers. Some conservatives opposed his nomination, alleging that he was too closely allied with the goals of organized labor, particularly the repeal of State "right to work" laws.

"Developments in Industrial Relations" is prepared by Leon Bornstein and other members of the staff of the Division of Trends in Employee Compensation, Bureau of Labor Statistics, and is largely based on information from secondary sources.

Marshall, 48, prior to his appointment as Labor Secretary had also been director of the University of Texas' Center for the Study of Human Resources and president of the National Rural Center, a nonprofit organization. Marshall succeeded W. J. Usery, who had served a year as Labor Secretary.

Following his swearing in, Secretary Marshall announced a plan to create 200,000 jobs for unemployed Vietnam veterans. He said that the jobs program expressed President Carter's concern for the "Vietnam-era veterans who continue to bear a disproportionate share of the unemployment that exists today." Under the plan, special preferences will be given to veterans in the 20-to-24 age bracket, whose unemployment rate was 18 percent when the plan was announced. (In December, data compiled by the Bureau of Labor Statistics showed that there were 558,000 out-of-work Vietnam-era veterans in the 20-to-34 age bracket. Their jobless rate was 8.6 percent, compared with a national unemployment rate of 7.9 percent in December.) The plan's three major components were as follows:

- A program called HIRE, designed to induce private business to place 50,000 to 60,000 veterans in training jobs. The Federal Government is to pay an estimated $100 million training costs incurred by companies hiring the veterans. The plan, which would operate under the Comprehensive Employment and Training Act (CETA), would focus on disabled veterans first, then on all Vietnam-era veterans, and, if there are not enough eligible veterans in a given community, on "disadvantaged young jobseekers and the long-term unemployed."

- A request for an additional 290,000 public service jobs to be financed under CETA in 1977, and 125,000 more in 1978 under the economic recovery package the President is sending to the Congress. The President proposed that 145,000 of these jobs be allotted to veterans.

- Outreach units staffed by disabled Vietnam-era veterans within the employment services of the 100 largest cities, with at least one unit in each State. These veterans "will work as paraprofessionals in temporary, federally funded jobs" and would "concentrate on identifying disabled veterans in need of services and bringing them into the mainstream of the labor market, helping them to avail themselves of the programs and services to which they are entitled, including special consideration for public service jobs." The staff of these units would also be given responsibility for developing jobs in the private sector for disabled veterans.

Oil pacts provide initial 9-percent raise

The round of bargaining in the petroleum refining industry was concluded in January, as the Oil, Chemical and Atomic Workers union settled with various companies for the 60,000 workers it represents in the industry. The agreements were patterned after a 2-year contract with Gulf Oil Corp. reached on January 7 that averted an industrywide strike scheduled for the next day, when some 400 OCAW agreements expired. Among the firms settling were Shell Oil Co., Atlantic Richfield Co., Standard Oil Co. (Ohio), Texaco, Inc., and Mobil Oil Corp.

The Gulf contract provided for a wage increase of 9 percent effective immediately and 75 cents an hour in January 1978. The OCAW had been seeking the adoption of a wage escalator clause, but union President A. F. Grospiron said it had dropped its demand because the two wage increases were "such that we don't need [an escalator] unless the economy gets completely out of hand."

The shift premium for employees on the evening turn was increased from 20 to 45 cents an hour, effective immediately and to 50 cents in January 1978. The premium for those on the midnight turn was increased from 40 to 90 cents and $1 on the respective dates. Gulf agreed to increase its contribution for hospital and medical insurance by $4 a month in each year for single employees and by $12 in the first year and $10 in the second for workers with family coverage. The increases will bring the total company obligation to $30.50 a month for single employees and to $72 for those with families. The minimum pension rate was increased from $10 to $12 a month for each year of credited service for years the plan has been noncontributory (since 1970) and lower amounts for earlier years.

The accord also required Gulf to train five employees in each unit in occupational health practices and gave the union the right to investigate accidents involving its members.

Fitzmaurice, elected IUE president, seeks merger

David J. Fitzmaurice was elected to a 4-year term as president of the 275,000-member International Union of Electrical Workers (IUE). Fitzmaurice, 62, had been the union's president since mid-1976, when the IUE executive board selected him to succeed Paul Jennings, who resigned because of illness. Previously, Fitzmaurice had been the union's secretary-treasurer. Results released in late December showed Fitzmaurice defeating William Bywater by a vote of 43,018 to 34,462. The election received much press coverage because the U.S. Department of Labor monitored the balloting, at the request of the IUE, which wanted to avoid a repetition of the bitter 1964 contest, which Jennings won after the Labor Department found voting irregularities in favor of the apparent winner, James E. Carey.

Following the release of the unofficial 1976 vote tally, Fitzmaurice said he hoped "within the next year" to negotiate a merger with the 165,000-member United Electrical Workers (UE). The UE had been expelled by the Congress of Industrial Organizations (CIO) in 1949 on charges of Communist domination. The CIO then chartered the IUE to organize electrical workers. Fitzmaurice said that UE officials are "very desirous of putting the union back together."

Fraser endorsed by Auto Workers leaders

Auto Workers' Vice President Douglas A. Fraser was publicly endorsed by key UAW leaders to succeed President Leonard Woodcock as the 1.4 million member union's head. Woodcock is scheduled to retire in the spring, having reached the union's mandatory retirement age of 65. A successor will be chosen at the union's convention in May 1977. Fraser, 60, who heads the union's Chrysler Department, had been considered for the presidency of the UAW in 1970, after Walter Reuther, the incumbent president, died in an airplane crash. The executive board then chose Woodcock over Fraser by a 13 to 12 vote.

Fraser's succession seemed assured on January 3, when Woodcock announced that the three vice presidents most often mentioned as possible challengers were not planning to run. They were Ken Bannon, Irving Bluestone, and Duane (Pat) Greathouse. Woodcock said they had told him "they aren't pressing their candidacies and are supporting" Fraser. On January 11, the executive board unanimously recommended that Fraser succeed Woodcock in May. As a result, Fraser was two hurdles short of the presidency—endorsement by the national steering committee as the "administrative caucus candidate" in February and formal election at the May convention.

In a surprise move, the union's executive board also recommended that the UAW decide whether to reaffiliate with the AFL–CIO at a special convention to be held in September. Woodcock told reporters that the period from May to September would be devoted to "a full debate throughout all levels of the union" over a possible reaffiliation. After meeting with Federation chief George Meany in December, UAW leaders had reportedly come to no conclusions on reaffiliation. (*See Monthly Labor Review,* February 1977, p. 87.)

Patrick to seek UMW presidency

Harry Patrick, secretary-treasurer of the United Mine Workers Union (UMW), announced he would challenge incumbent Arnold Miller for the union's presidency. Patrick's differences with Miller became public shortly after the UMW convention in September. (See *Monthly Labor Review,* January 1977, pp. 58–61.) Patrick claimed that Miller had "surrounded himself with yes men, paper pushers, and payrollers," and asserted he reluctantly decided to challenge Miller because he could no longer stand by to see the union "torn apart by bitterness" and "inept" leadership. Lee Roy Paterson, the third announced candidate, was expected to benefit from the Patrick-Miller split. Paterson reportedly has the backing of Mike Trbovich, who joined with Miller and Patrick to form the ticket that overthrew the regime of W. A. (Tony) Boyle 4 years earlier, but who has since split with Miller over a variety of issues.

New York City to keep social security coverage

Mayor Abraham Beame disclosed that New York City had dropped its plan to withdraw its municipal employees from the social security system. In March 1976, the city had given the Federal Government the required 2 years' notice of intent to withdraw from the system. (See *Monthly Labor Review,* May 1976, p. 54.) Beame, in releasing his financial plan for the coming year, said that his Mayor's Management Advisory Board had recommended against a pullout because the cost of substitute pension and disability programs would offset any savings. The withdrawal, affecting more than 100,00 employees in agencies under the mayor's control, would have been the largest in the history of the social security system. A similarly notice to withdraw from the system had later been served by the New York City Transit Authority. (See *Monthly Labor Review,* December 1976, p. 56.) ☐

Developments in Industrial Relations

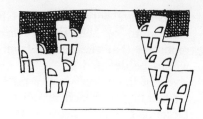

Reported in *Monthly Labor Review*, March 1977.

Meany rejects prenotification of wage increases

AFL-CIO President George Meany said the Federation did not intend to take part in President Carter's proposed anti-inflation program under which the Federal Government would be notified of union-negotiated wage increases before they are implemented. He said labor is "absolutely, completely opposed" to any such requirement because "it would destroy collective bargaining." Meany explained that a prenotification program would be "just a foot in the door" leading to voluntary wage guidelines, and "the first thing you know, wage and price controls." His February 21 comments were made during the midwinter meeting of the Federation's Executive Council, held in Bal Harbour, Fla.

Meanwhile, President Carter ruled out specific wage-price guidelines as "too restrictive." Speaking in Washington, D.C., he said he is "quite concerned about the pressure of inflation, but I think rigid guidelines are a mistake." He indicated that he was still interested in the idea of advance notification of major wage and price decisions "to the extent that I can arrive at a common understanding with industry and labor leaders that a certain amount of cooperation and information can be exchanged before a major proposal is made." He added, "I can't force it. It's got to be voluntary."

In other actions, the AFL-CIO Executive Council declared that existing laws frustrate union efforts to organize and represent workers and outlined some of the changes the Federation will press for in the National Labor Relations Act:

- Repeal of Section 14(B) of the Act, which permits States to ban the union shop.
- Expansion of the Act to cover public and farm employees.
- Acceleration of the procedures governing union representation elections and heavier penalties for employers found guilty of unfair labor practices.
- Adoption of the common-site picketing bill vetoed by President Ford. The bill would permit a single union which has a dispute with one contractor to close down an entire project.

McBride apparent victor in Steelworkers contest

Lloyd McBride appeared to have defeated insurgent Edward Sadlowski in the race to succeed I.W. Abel as president of the 1.4-million-member Steelworkers' union, but Sadlowski refused to concede defeat and filed a protest with the union's tellers, charging violations of Federal laws governing union elections. His chief assertion was that Abel and other officers had used staff employees to aid the McBride campaign. He also charged that there had been some voting irregularities. An unofficial tally showed 322,000 votes for McBride and 238,000 for Sadlowski. The tellers have until May 1 to rule on the protest. If they refuse to call for a new election, Sadlowski has 10 days to appeal to the union's executive board, which must make a decision by June 1. If it rules against Sadlowski, he could then appeal to the U.S. Department of Labor. At the request of the union, the Department had stationed advisers in each of the 22 union districts to help resolve any complaints arising during the balloting.

McBride, 60, had the backing of AFL-CIO President George Meany, who usually refrains from endorsing candidates in union elections. McBride began his career with the Steelworkers Organizing Committee in 1936 and was elected a local union president 2 years later at the age of 22. He has been director of the Steelworkers' St. Louis district since 1965. Sadlowski, 38, had resigned as director of the Chicago district to run for the union presidency. Abel, who had reached the union's mandatory retirement age of 68, was scheduled to leave office on June 1, but he had threatened to resign immediately if Sadlowski was elected.

On February 14, Abel opened talks with the major steel companies on renewal of agreements expiring August 1. As a capstone to his career, he is

---

"Developments in Industrial Relations" is prepared by Leon Bornstein and other members of the staff of the Division of Trends in Employee Compensation, Bureau of Labor Statistics, and is largely based on information from secondary sources.

hoping to gain a "lifetime security" plan for the nearly 500,000 workers the union represents at the major companies and smaller producers. Abel did not announce details of the proposal to be presented by the union, but he did define the goal as "a job for life with a decent, respectable income for life."

Winpisinger to head Machinists

William W. Winpisinger will become president of the Machinists (IAM) union on July 1, succeeding Floyd R. Smith, who was scheduled to retire. Smith, 64, has headed the 920,000-member union for the past 8 years. Winpisinger, 52, a Machinists vice president since 1967, and chief of the union's headquarters' staff for the past 4 years, emerged unopposed after a month-long nominating process. The union announced that no other person was nominated by 25 locals or more, as required by the union's constitution for an individual to be considered a candidate. Winpisinger is also president of the Institute of Collective Bargaining, an advisory member of the Federal Committee on Apprenticeship, and a trustee of the National Planning Association. He was also the first head of the union's transportation department. Secretary-Treasurer Eugene D. Glover and five incumbent vice presidents were also unopposed.

Auto Workers sign pact with American Motors

The Auto Workers union concluded its round of bargaining with automobile manufacturers on February 15, when it agreed to a 7-month contract tailored to improve the financial position of American Motors Corp., which had lost $46 million in fiscal 1976. Although the prior agreement had been scheduled to expire September 15, 1976, it had been extended pending the outcome of negotiations at Ford Motor Co., General Motors Corp., and Chrysler Corp., which settled on 3-year contracts in October and November. (See *Monthly Labor Review*, January 1977, pp. 28-29.)

The American Motors contract called for a 3-percent increase and a 17-cent-an-hour wage escalator increase, effective February 28. The settlements at the other companies had provided for a wage increase of 3 percent plus 20 cents an hour, effective earlier—October 18 at Ford and September 20 at General Motors and Chrysler. Employees of these companies had also received an 8-cent-an-hour quarterly wage escalator increase in December 1976 and may receive escalator adjustments in March,

June, and September of 1977. American Motors employees are eligible to receive these same 1977 escalator adjustments. Unlike the other companies, the American Motors agreement did not incorporate into base rates the $1.09 in escalator increases gained during the previous 3-year contract period. This tended to hold down the levels of those benefits—such as life insurance—that automatically rise with increases in an employee's base rate.

The final concession was that the agreement did not provide for any improvements in benefits. The "Big Three" contracts do provide for several benefit improvements in the first contract year, which ends on September 15, 1977, the same time the American Motors agreement expires, but most of their benefit improvements are effective in the second and third years.

Construction unions agree to work rule concessions

The Washington (D.C.) Building Trades Council reached a pact with the George Hyman Construction Co. under which the construction unions agreed to cost and work-rule concessions that cleared the way for the first phase of a private redevelopment project scheduled to include residential and commercial construction in a 100-acre area now consisting of old row houses, warehouses, and vacant land. The parties said the unions accepted the changes to "allow contractors to become more competitive in residential work, which has been going more and more to nonunion contractors . . . ." The Hyman firm had told the unions it would hire nonunion labor if such an agreement could not be worked out. Two of the Wasington area's 27 building trades unions—locals of the Ironworkers and Painters—reportedly refused to sign the agreement, but negotiations were continuing.

In addition to assuring the developer that the work would not be interrupted by labor disputes, the contract also called for standardized work hours, uniform holidays, and uniform overtime work schedules for all trades. It also eliminates formal coffee breaks, cuts overtime pay rates from double time to time-and-one-half, and gives the contractor the right to decide how many workers are required for given jobs.

Other cities in which unions recently have made concessions intended to spur hiring for rehabilitation projects have been New York City, Philadelphia, Baltimore, Boston, and Los Angeles. The concessions have included reduced pay rates and increased ratios of apprentices to experienced workers. □

Developments in Industrial Relations

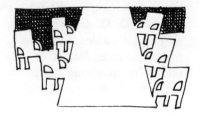

Reported in *Monthly Labor Review*, April 1977.

Fitzsimmons, three others quit pension fund

President Frank Fitzsimmons and three other Teamsters officials agreed to resign as trustees of the $1.4-billion Central States Pension Fund effective April 30, and the fund has agreed to turn over control of its assets to outside investment managers. The resignations were announced March 13 as part of an agreement with the Department of Labor and the Internal Revenue Service which set stringent conditions for future operations of the fund. The Federal Government has been investigating the fund since 1975 because of charges that it mismanaged its assets and maintained ties to organized crime. In October 1976, 11 of the 16 trustees resigned (joining one who had resigned earlier) at the behest of the Department of Labor (*Monthly Labor Review,* January 1977, p. 34).

On February 16, Secretary of Labor Ray Marshall requested the resignation of the four trustees and the transfer of the fund's investment management to outsiders. A week later, when these demands were not fully met, he ordered Federal attorneys to start preparing a suit against the fund. Shortly thereafter, the agreement was reached.

Marshall hailed the settlement, saying its provisions "significantly reform the structure and procedures of the fund respecting asset management." He added, "It now appears possible that we can avoid litigation, assuming the fund trustees make good progress in following up on their commitments." A spokesman for the Teamsters said that Fitzsimmons would not have any comment on the agreement.

In addition to averting a lawsuit, the agreement also provided for IRS restoration of the fund's unconditional tax-exempt status. Such status had been withdrawn in the summer of 1976 and had been restored on a continuing temporary basis since then, contingent on the outcome of the investigation. Loss of the tax exemption means that employer contributions are not deductible business expenses. The settlement stipulates that once the fund turns over its assets to outside managers, the IRS "shall issue a determination letter requalifying the fund" for a tax exemption retroactive to January 1, 1976. The accord also commits the Labor Department to "terminate that portion of its investigation that relates to procedures of the fund respecting asset management" once outside managers assume control. However, the Department is continuing its investigation of the Central States Fund's past activities, and is not waiving its right to go to court against former trustees over past actions that may have been illegal.

The agreement also called for the fund to commission an "independent review" of all transactions since February 1, 1965, and take any necessary remedial action.

In the wake of the settlement with the Government, Fitzsimmons announced that he will not resign as president of the Teamsters and that he will be a candidate for reelection when his current term of office expires in 1981.

In a separate development, the Twentieth Century Fund asserted that alleged Teamster pension abuses "hang over the entire pension field" and proposed that Federal labor laws be revised to give pension fund trustees greater autonomy. The report, part of a series of studies of conflicts of interest in the securities market, also called for trustees to be given stronger legal rights to pursue delinquent employers and for restraints on use of a union's pension funds to create jobs for the union's members. It estimated that pension funds control $35 billion in investments.

Truce ends 10-year jurisdictional dispute on farms

A 5-year jurisdictional agreement between the United Farm Workers and the Teamsters has apparently ended their decade-long dispute over organizing California's 250,000 farmworkers. The agreement, which also applied to organizing activities in 12 other Western States,[1] specified that Farm Workers' organizing efforts will be limited to firms primarily engaged in growing agricultural products,

---

"Developments in Industrial Relations" is prepared by Leon Bornstein and other members of the staff of the Division of Trends in Employee Compensation, Bureau of Labor Statistics, and is largely based on information from secondary sources.

and the Teamsters' efforts will be limited to firms primarily engaged in processing, preserving, and transporting the products. The agreement, which provides for compulsory binding arbitration of disputes between the unions, also specified that negotiations will be undertaken in 2 years on extending the contract to the entire country.

Cesar Chavez, president of the Farm Workers, said that the money the unions "spent in all these years of fighting can now be used to fight the growers for more union contracts." Teamsters' President Frank E. Fitzsimmons indicated that his union was motivated to settle the dispute to dispel the conception that it was working with the growers to suppress farmworkers. "We are now in the position where we are not accused," he said. "We are not the people suppressing the farmworkers."

Growers' reaction to the accord was mixed. Some said the agreement would stabilize labor-management relations in the industry and moderate labor-cost increases because each union will now be under less pressure to gain larger wage settlements than the other. Other growers feared that future strikes would have more severe impact on them because the unions will no longer cross each others' picket lines.

M. E. Anderson, director of the Western Conference of Teamsters, estimated his union will lose 10,000 to 12,000 members to the Farm Workers, and Chavez stated that he expected his union to have 40,000 members by year's end, up from the current 25,000. There are about 350,000 Teamsters members in California in all industries.

Since its inception in 1975 under the California Agricultural Labor Relations Act, the California Agricultural Labor Relations Board has conducted representation elections for fieldworkers. It has certified the Farm Workers as bargaining agent in 151 cases, the Teamsters in 41 cases, and set aside the results of 47 elections. The act, the first such State law in the Nation, permits fieldworkers to vote on union representation. Fieldworkers are not covered by the National Labor Relations Act, unlike the cannery workers and other employees the Teamsters will focus on organizing.

Tobacco Workers complete bargaining

Bargaining in the tobacco industry was concluded in March, when the Tobacco Workers union settled with various companies for approximately 26,500 workers it represents in the industry. Among the firms settling were American Tobacco Co.; Brown and Williamson Tobacco Corp.; Lorillard, division of Loews Theaters, Inc.; and Liggett and Myers Tobacco Co.

Terms of the agreements were generally similar to those in the Phillip Morris Co. accord, the first in the round of bargaining. That 3-year contract provided for a 50-cent-an-hour general wage increase effective February 1, 1977, 22 cents on February 1, 1978, and 23 cents on February 1, 1979. The existing 30-cent cost-of-living allowance was incorporated into base rates, and the escalator clause was modified to provide unlimited quarterly cost-of-living adjustments of 1 cent an hour for each 0.4-movement in the BLS Consumer Price Index. Previously, quarterly adjustments were limited to a total of 10 cents in each year. Other improvements included increased shift differentials; 3 weeks of paid vacation after 5 years (was 8), 4 weeks after 13 years (was 15), and 5 weeks after 22 years (was 25); an 11th paid holiday, the Friday before Memorial Day; and adoption of a dental plan.

New York City defers teacher pay increases

After more than 15 months of negotiations, the New York City Board of Education and the United Federation of Teachers (UFT) agreed to defer the scheduled effective dates of some salary provisions of their 1975–77 agreement and to extend it by 1 year, to September 1978. The new accord, which covered 55,000 teachers, was approved by the Emergency Financial Control Board on February 7. UFT President Albert Shanker said the deferrals—which were intended to aid the city's financial situation—paralleled contract modifications accepted by other city employee unions in 1975. (See *Monthly Labor Review,* October 1975, pp. 63–64.)

The deferral agreement, which was announced on December 17, provided for immediate retroactive payment of the following items originally scheduled for the October 1975-September 1976 school year:

- A $300 cost-of-living increase in annual salaries.
- A $50 increase in the school system's annual contribution to the union's welfare fund.

In addition, the following provisions covering the 1976–77 school year were agreed to:
- A salary increase of $750 for teachers who had attained 10 years of service during October 1, 1975, through October 1, 1976, and $1,500 for those who had attained 15 years of service. These increases which are retroactive to October 1, 1976, had originally been scheduled for the first year.
- A $300 cost-of-living increase for all other teachers.
- Resumption of the payment of salary differentials to teachers as they attain specified educational levels. These differentials, which existed prior to the original settlement, had been paid to teachers attaining eligibility in the 1975–76 school year but not to those attaining eligibility in the 1976–77 year, because of the deferral negotiations.

- Indefinite deferral of a scheduled further $50 increase in the school system's annual contribution to the welfare fund.

The third or "extension" year of the agreement provided for the following:

- A December 1977 cost-of-living increase, with the amount to be determined by the Control Board based on productivity savings or new revenue.
- Resumption of regular increases for teachers as they attain specified durations of service. These increases (which were in effect prior to the 1975–77 agreement) had been paid to teachers who became eligible in the 1975–76 school year but not those who became eligible in the 1976–77 year, because of the deferral negotiations.
- Conversion of 2 conference days per year into free time for teachers, in exchange for a provision permitting the administration to assign teaching duties for one period per week that is now a preparation period.

Newspaper unions forgo first-year increase

In another move to help *The Washington (D.C.) Star* return to profitability, members of 10 unions[2] ratified 3-year contracts with the newspaper that provide for no first-year wage increase. If the newspaper attains profitability, the employees are to receive cash bonuses from an allocation equal to 10 percent of pretax profits. Other provisions included $20 a week wage increases on the first and second anniversaries of the agreement, and an increase of $3.50 per week per employee in the company's contribution for health and welfare benefits over the contract term.

Joe L. Albritton, chairperson of the company's board of directors, said the 3-year contract term provides "the time necessary to work out long-range plans for a successful and profitable operation."

In April 1976, the unions had agreed to a wage moratorium and other contract concessions to aid the newspaper. (See *Monthly Labor Review,* July 1976, p. 59.)

Goodrich proposes binding arbitration plan

The B. F. Goodrich Co. proposed a binding arbitration plan intended to avert what it called the "trial by ordeal" of strikes. Peter J. Pestillo, Goodrich's vice president for employee relations, said the company's proposal would avert crippling strikes such as the Rubber Workers' 4-month walkout which ended in September 1976 (*Monthly Labor Review,* October 1976, pp. 50-51).

The plan, unveiled by Pestillo on February 22 in a speech to business executives at the University of Pennsylvania, included the following features:

- If no agreement is reached between Goodrich and its unions within 7 to 10 days of a contract's expiration date, each side would present to the other and an arbitrator two complete "final offers."
- 3 days, a hearing would be held with the arbitrator, with each side defending its positions.
- After another 3 days, the arbitrator would select one of the offers and impose it, unless the two sides decided to bargain another 3 days to try to reach an agreement on their own.

Rubber Workers' President Peter Bommarito said he was surprised at the proposal because of what he termed an "understanding" reached in a Washington meeting in January between representatives of the Rubber Workers and the Big Four tire producers. He asserted, "It was completely understood that all sides were opposed to binding arbitration. It was unethical to make that kind of statement in view of what we discussed at the Washington meeting." Bommarito stated he was "absolutely" opposed to binding arbitration. The proposal probably would require a change in the union's constitution and approval by Goodrich locals. Other Rubber Workers' leaders also opposed it. Matt Contese, president of Goodrich Local 5 in Akron, said the proposal "would take away the (union) negotiating committee's strength." There was no comment on the proposal from Goodyear, Firestone, and Uniroyal—the other members of the Big Four.

The Washington meeting was held because the September 1976 3-year agreement provided that the Big Four and the Rubber Workers would set up a committee to work toward improving bargaining. Pestillo, who attended the Washington meeting, said it was his understanding that binding arbitration was only ruled out on an industrywide scale but was left open for the individual companies to pursue if they so chose.

Marshall identifies safety administration problems

Secretary of Labor Ray Marshall, in a statement issued March 11, stated that after 6 weeks of review he has found administration of the Occupational Safety and Health Act of 1970 (OSHA) wrought with problems that are "even greater than I expected." He termed the act "a good piece of legislation," but stated that, "reviewing the history of OSHA, I realize that this was a program forced upon a reluctant Administration by Congress. The tangled history of its first 6 years illustrates what happens when people are asked to enforce legislation they don't believe in." Marshall cited "this lack of sympathy for the basic aspirations of the act," for the absence of "clear administrative guidelines" to be used by "those responsible for enforcing OSHA." In Marshall's words:

"The result has been chaos. Let me just identify some of the continuing problems. There is no continuity of leadership. One consequence has been that OSHA has changed its priorities and focus with alarming frequency. Another result has been a lack of clearcut enforcement strategy. The agency also has had difficulty in forming good relationships with the public. There has been inadequate cooperation with labor unions, business, the press, and the general public. In initial conferences, informal methods of correcting abuses have been infrequently utilized. Another problem is that the agency has suffered from a continuing shortage of enough technical staff. Related to this are the technical difficulties in determining the long-range health hazards caused by many chemicals and other toxic substances."

Secretary Marshall acknowledged that there is "much validity" to charges against OSHA by business, labor, and the general public. He stated he intended to consult closely with representatives of these groups to develop a strategy to change the agency's direction. He asserted, "Next to putting America back to work. . . . I believe that perhaps my most important responsibility is guaranteeing to the American workers an environment that is safe and healthful."

Glass Bottle Blowers settle early

Owens-Illinois Inc. and the Glass Bottle Blowers union settled in February on a contract covering 11,600 production and maintenance employees. The agreement was expected to set a pattern for 30,000 other employees the union represents in the industry. Owens-Illinois said the 3-year contract, settled almost 2 months in advance of the scheduled expiration date of the current agreement, would raise labor costs 30 percent.

Provisions included a 50-cent-an-hour wage increase retroactive to January 3 and 43-cent increases on April 1 of 1978 and 1979. The wage escalator clause, which had yielded 16 cents in wage increases since the prior settlement in April 1974, was terminated.

The number of paid holidays was increased to 11, from 10, and a sixth week of paid vacation was added for employees with 30 years of service or more. Life insurance coverage was increased by $2,000, bringing the range to $10,000–$12,000, depending on the employee's pay rate, and sickness and accident benefits to a $100–120 a week range, also depending on the pay rate. The pension rate was increased to a range of $11 to $14 a month for each year of credited service, from a flat $10, and the optional retirement age for 30-year employees was reduced to 55, from 58.

The company and union also agreed to a 3-year contract for 1,900 employees in the automatic machine department. It called for 50-, 25-, and 25-cent annual wage increases in each successive year, and for an additional immediate increase that varied according to the type of machine an employee operates. Benefit terms were similar to those for the other workers.

TV network agrees to promotion, hiring goals

The National Broadcasting Co. (NBC) agreed to a $2 million out-of-court settlement of a sex-bias suit brought by women employees of the broadcast network. The pact resulted from a class action suit which was filed in Federal District Court in Manhattan for 2,600 past and current women employees. Under the terms of the settlement, each woman is expected to receive cash payments estimated at $500 to $1,000.

The proposed settlement, which remains subject to modification and court approval, requires the network to make "good faith efforts" to promote women to a wide range of professional, managerial, and official positions. Specific goals include the provision that 15 percent of the top NBC positions below the rank of vice president would be filled by women, with the goals "to be achieved no later than December 31, 1981." The settlement also called for NBC to adjust the salaries of women who are promoted, so that they equal "the average annual salary of men" in similar positions who have 5 years of NBC service.

The agreement specifies goals for hiring women to fill vacancies in technical jobs and news positions over the next 5 years. One-third of the vacancies each year from now through 1981 for jobs in the union category of TV assistant 1A, which includes beginning camera operators, are to be filled by women. One-third of the vacancies for newswriters would also be allocated to women for each year of the 5-year period, with NBC agreeing "to make a good faith effort to assure that female newswriters are assigned to network news programs as well as other news shows." □

------FOOTNOTES------

[1] Washington, Oregon, Idaho, Montana, Wyoming, Colorado, Utah, Nevada, Arizona, New Mexico, Alaska, and Hawaii.

[2] The Mailers, Photoengravers, Pressmen, Newspaper Guild, Service Employees, Teamsters, Electrical Workers (IBEW), Operating Engineers, Machinists, and Firemen and Oilers.

Developments in Industrial Relations

Reported in *Monthly Labor Review*, May 1977.

Steelworkers win enhanced employment security

Operating under the bargaining procedures and deadlines of their Experimental Negotiating Agreement, the 10 Coordinating Committee Steel Companies and the United Steelworkers settled on April 8, almost 4 months in advance of the scheduled July 31 expiration date of their current labor contracts. The pressure for an early accord resulted from the ENA requirement that all unresolved national issues be submitted to binding arbitration on April 20, a route both parties wanted to avoid. But two ballots were necessary before the union's ratifying body approved the settlement, reflecting a continuing split in the union in the wake of the bitterly-fought contest for the union's presidency.

The chief issue in the 1977 negotiations was the Steelworkers' goal of "lifetime security" which retiring union president I. W. Abel had earlier defined as "a job for life with a decent, respectable income for life." President-elect Lloyd McBride, who participated in the negotiations, said that certain provisions of the new contract were "a start" toward that goal.

The new Employment and Income Security Program provides for the following benefits, which apply only to employees with 20 years of service, who reportedly make up almost 40 percent of the industry's work force.

- A maximum of 104 weeks of Supplemental Unemployment Benefits for laid-off workers, with no reduction in benefit levels or duration even if the fund is depleted.
- Increased SUB "short week" payments (paid to bring weekly pay to 32 hours when scheduled hours are less than 32) as a result of inclusion of incentive earnings in the computation.
- Earnings Protection Plan makeup payments to assure employees that their quarterly earnings will be 90 percent of their "base period rate"

and the payments will no longer be tied to the SUB fund.
- An additional 52 weeks of sickness and accident benefits coverage for employees who are temporarily disabled, bringing the duration to 104 weeks.
- Insurance coverage for the full 104 weeks' duration of SUB or sickness and accident benefits.
- A new early pension for those employees affected by plant shutdowns and extended layoffs whose age and years of service total at least 65. They will also receive a $300-a-month supplement until age 62.

Another major issue was contracting out of work, which the union contended had reduced job opportunities for the trade and craft workers in the industry. The accord established a Joint Steel Industry-Union Contracting Out Review Commission, headed by a neutral chairperson, to investigate the practice and report findings to the heads of the bargaining teams by September 1, 1979. Beginning August 1, 1977, and continuing until the Commission submits its report, trade and craft workers on layoff or short weeks will be guaranteed 40 hours of pay for each week contractors are performing trade and craft type work in their plant.

To receive this benefit, employees may be required to work outside their regular unit. The contract also calls for arbitration of any union charges that a company has failed to give the required notice of contracted-out work performed in its plants and for each company to begin notifying the union of work to be performed outside its plant on company-owned equipment.

Under the ENA, wage increases negotiated in 1977 for the 340,000 employees were guaranteed to be at least 3 percent in each contract year. The initial increase, on May 1, 1977, was 20 cents an hour, followed by an increase on August 1, 1977, consisting of a 20-cent general raise and a 0.4-cent increase in the increment between job grades. This will result in an increase ranging from 20 cents for employees in the lowest job grade to 32.8 cents for those in the highest grade of the 33-grade structure that prevails at most of the companies. The other

"Developments in Industrial Relations" is prepared by Leon Bornstein and other members of the staff of the Division of Trends in Employee Compensation, Bureau of Labor Statistics, and is largely based on information from secondary sources.

scheduled increases are 10 cents on February 1 of 1978 and 1979, and 10 to 19.6 cents (10 cents general increase and 0.3-cent increment increase) on August 1 of 1978 and 1979. All of the increases are included in the base rates used for calculating incentive earnings, which means that incentive employees will actually receive more than the indicated amounts. As specified in the ENA, all employees on the payroll on August 1, 1977, will receive a $150 bonus, payable in October.

ENA also guaranteed continuation of the cost-of-living wage escalator clause; it provides for quarterly adjustments of 1 cent an hour for each 0.3-point movement in the Consumer Price Index (1967 = 100). Since May 1, 1974, escalator increases have totaled $1.32, including a 13-cent increase effective May 1, 1977.

Other contract provisions included the following:

- An additional paid holiday, bringing the total to 11 a year.
- Pension improvements, including an increase in the minimum formula to $13.50 a month for each of the first 15 years of service, $15 for each of the next 15 years, and $16.50 for each year in excess of 30, and a 5-percent increase in benefits for employees who retire under the alternate basic formula, which provides for a benefit equal to 1.1 percent of average monthly pre-retirement earnings for each of the first 30 years of service and 1.2 percent for each additional year.
- Insurance improvements, including a $2,000 increase in life insurance for active employees, bringing the range to $10,000 to $12,500, depending on the employee's hourly wage rate, and a varying increase in retirees' coverage, bringing it to a uniform $3,000; a $39 to $52-a-week increase in sickness and accident benefits, bringing the range to $153 to $211; and establishment of a vision care plan for employees and their dependents.
- SUB improvements, including an increase in the maximum benefit to $125 for weeks when an employee on layoff is receiving State benefits and $170 for all other weeks (plus, in both cases, $1.50 per week for each dependent up to four); and a 3-cent increase in the employer's maximum financing rate, to 18 cents per hour.

In keeping with the increased degree of cooperation between the industry and union in recent years, the parties also established a program to instruct new employees in the history of the union, the industry, the collective bargaining relationship, the impact of imported steel, and the role of productivity in advancing the interests of the industry and its

employees. Financing will be at the rate of $500,000 a year from the union and a total of $500,000 a year from the companies.

The 10 companies party to the accord were U.S. Steel Corp.; Bethlehem Steel Corp.; Republic Steel Corp.; National Steel Corp.; Jones & Laughlin Steel Corp., a subsidiary of LTV Corp.; Armco Steel Corp.; Youngstown Sheet and Tube Co., a subsidiary of Lykes-Youngstown Corp.; Inland Steel Corp.; Wheeling-Pittsburgh Steel Corp.; and Allegheny Ludlum Industries, Inc.

Members of the union's Basic Steel Industry Conference first rejected the accord 148 to 143 in a "stand-up" vote but later approved it 193 to 98 in a roll call vote. The Conference, which consists of a representative from each steel local, plus some union officials, has final power to approve or reject steel settlements. Opposition to the accord was led by Edward Sadlowski, who had run against McBride for the union presidency on a platform that called for a more militant approach to bargaining, including termination of the ENA, (See *Monthly Labor Review,* April 1977, pp. 84-85.) (On April 24, the union's tellers rejected Sadlowski's charges of irregularities in the presidential election and announced that the official vote totals were 328,861 to 249,281 in favor of McBride. Despite this setback, Sadlowski said he will proceed with his efforts to overturn the election.)

Although the ENA approach came under more strain than when it was first used in the 1974 bargaining, the parties agreed to use it again in the 1980 bargaining round. As a result, the employees will be guaranteed another $150 bonus in 1980, there will be a 3-percent "floor" under the 1980, 1981, and 1982 wage increases, and automatic wage escalation will be continued, as will the right to strike over local issues and the use of binding arbitration to break any stalemate in the 1980 talks. Continuation of the ENA also means that there will be no industrywide strike over national issues in 1980; the last industrywide strike, which lasted 116 days, was in 1959.

The agreement with the 10 producers, which expires on July 31, 1980, was expected to set a pattern for later Steelworkers' settlements for more than 175,000 employees of other basic steel and steel fabrication companies and to influence settlements for 200,000 workers in other industries, such as containers, aluminum, and copper.

Carter announces anti-inflation program

On April 15, President Carter announced a 19-point program to reduce the Nation's inflation rate to 4 percent by the end of 1979. A keystone of the largely voluntary program was a cooperative effort by business, labor, and the Government. The President said that AFL-CIO President George Meany and Reginald Jones, chairperson of General Electric Co., had agreed to work with Council of Economic Advisers Chairperson Charles Schultze to develop "the more detailed arrangements" for implementing part of his program. The President described this "collaborative effort" as consisting of "working together to advise government on its objectives for our economy, for job creation, and inflation reduction. . . . and to monitor the results on a continuing basis."

In addition to "well-conceived monetary and fiscal policies," the President proposed a series of steps the Government could take to reduce inflationary pressures. Among the proposals are the following:

- Expansion of the Council on Wage and Price Stability's activities in providing detailed and timely analysis of economic conditions in those industries and markets which are most important to price stabilization.

- An early warning system under which the Council on Wage and Price Stability would develop "detailed industry studies to detect emerging bottlenecks, capacity shortages, and other problems that, if left unattended, would lead to significant price increases."

- Employment policies that stress job skills training, improved job placement services, and improved services to match job openings with available workers.

- A new program to restrain increases in hospital costs.

- Encouragement of increased productivity in business and agriculture.

AFL-CIO rebuffed on shoe imports, situs picketing

Organized labor attacked President Jimmy Carter's rejection of a recommendation by the International Trade Commission for a sharp boost in tariffs on foreign shoes. Instead, the President indicated he hoped to work out voluntary agreements during the next 90 days with Taiwan and South Korea to limit their shipments of low-cost shoes to the U.S. market.

AFL-CIO Secretary-Treasurer Lane Kirkland told a Federation conference on international trade and jobs, "Last week the shoe industry was served up" on the "holy altar of free trade." Steelworkers' Chief I.W. Abel said that if the agreements with the foreign shoe-exporting countries "aren't forthcoming or aren't satisfactory," it would "certainly be appropriate for the American trade union movement to ask the Congress to overrule the President's action." The AFL-CIO was particularly angered by the shoe decision because it followed other political disappointments this year.

In one major setback, the House of Representatives defeated by a vote of 217 to 205 a common situs picketing bill that the AFL-CIO and its Building and Construction Trades Department had labeled a major legislative goal in 1977. The bill would have allowed a single union which has a dispute with one contractor to close down an entire project. (Congress passed a similar measure 15 months earlier, but it had been vetoed by President Gerald R. Ford.)

Another setback was the Administration's proposal that the minimum wage be raised from $2.30 an hour to $2.50 on July 1, and then periodically adjusted thereafter to maintain it at a level of 50 percent of the average straight-time hourly earnings for production and nonsupervisory workers in the manufacturing sector, as measured by the Bureau of Labor Statistics. The Federation had called for a $3 minimum and for indexing at a 60-percent rate.

"The recent signs and portents lead us to wonder if our support [for the Carter candidacy] wasn't just another triumph of hope over experience," Kirkland stated. He added, "If the gross and compelling problems of the shoe industry fail to draw a sympathetic response from the President, what will?"

At a news conference on April 5, Secretary of Labor Ray Marshall defended the Administration's decision in the shoe case. He said that the route President Carter took to ameliorate difficulties in the shoe industry was "a fair way to handle it" and one that does not preclude a "more substantial kind of relief." He added he would favor some sort of tariff or import quota if a voluntary agreement cannot be reached.

Ladies' Garment Workers President Sol C. Chaikin, Amalgamated Clothing and Textile Workers President Murray H. Finley, and AFL-CIO President George Meany met with President Carter at the White House on April 3 to discuss the imports issue, while an estimated 300,000 members of their unions attended protest rallies in 150 cities and towns across the Nation. "He has given us a fair hearing," said Meany, "and indicated his mind is open." The unionists reportedly urged the President to cut in half the growth in annual textile and garment imports allowed under the Multifiber Textile Arrangement. The current arrangement allows an annual growth in imports of 6 percent a year. It expires December 31, when a new 5-year agreement between the United States and exporting Nations is to be negotiated. The labor leaders argued that because the growth of the domestic industry is only 3 percent a year, the President should seek to limit import growth to that level.

Finley said that in 1976 alone, between 25,000 and 45,000 jobs were lost in the Nation's men's apparel industry, and other union officials estimated that 150,000 jobs has been lost in the textile and apparel industry in the past 10 years. At a New York City rally, they said that 35 out of every 100 garments currently sold in the United States are imports, compared with 4 out of 100 a decade ago.

Eastern, Air Line Pilots settle

In March, members of the Air Line Pilots Association accepted an Eastern Airlines' proposal that part of their earnings be contingent on the company's profit level. Under the plan, which is effective July 2, 3.5 percent of each flight officer's monthly earnings will be withheld until year's end, when the money will be paid to the 4,300 workers if Eastern's annual profit amounts to 2 percent of sales. If it is more than 2 percent, the employees will receive the full amount that had been withheld plus an additional amount, ranging up to another 3.5 percent of earnings. If it is less than 2 percent, part of the withheld earnings will be paid to the workers, and the balance will be used to increase the profit level.

The new 27-month contract also provides for salary increases of 5.65 percent on July 2, 1977, and 4.2 percent on March 2, 1978, October 1, 1978, and June 1, 1979, for increased travel-expense payments, and for improved life insurance, hospital insurance, and pension benefits.

Earlier, a majority of Eastern's 14,000 nonunion employees had voted for a similar variable wage plan, although it has not yet been implemented. Negotiations were continuing with the Transport Workers for 4,000 flight attendants. Their previous agreement had expired January 1. Eastern's current agreement with the Machinists for 11,000 ground service workers does not expire until December 31, 1978.

In 1975, the three unions had rejected a company proposal for a temporary pay cut and the company then decided not to implement the cut for nonunion workers, who had accepted the proposal by a majority vote. In 1976, all employees accepted a delay in the effective date of a scheduled wage increase. This action, plus a nonrecurring credit of $11.1 million, aided the company in attaining a net income of $46.2 million. Without the credit, the profit level was less than 2 percent.

Nursing home strike averted in New York City

The Metropolitan New York Nursing Home Association and Service Employees' Local 144 reached agreement on April 15, just 2 hours before a scheduled strike that would have affected 15,000 patients. The provisions of the settlement, recommended by an arbiter, were accepted by the Association with the understanding that it could not meet its obligations without further State aid. At that point, the State offered to examine the operation of those homes that are in financial difficulty and recommend cost-reduction measures. If the changes do not enable the homes to meet the cost of the new contract, the State indicated that it would then consider raising the reimbursement to these homes under the Medicaid program. The Association has been pressing the State for larger reimbursements since 1975, when the State ended its practice of permitting nursing-home owners to be reimbursed automatically under Medicaid for labor-cost increases.

The new 3-year contract, which covers 11,500 employees, calls for a wage increase of $10 a week, payable beginning June 15 but retroactive to April 15, and for a $5 increase on January 1, 1978. Previously, wage rates ranged from $193.18 a week for aides, porters, and maids to $309 for registered nurses. The employers are also required to contribute a total of $6 million to the pension, welfare, and dental funds within 30 days of the contract date and to establish a training fund equal to 1 percent of payroll. The employers are $15 million in arrears in payments to the pension fund and the union has obtained court judgments, which are now on appeal, for the debts.   □

Developments in Industrial Relations

Reported in *Monthly Labor Review*, June 1977.

Auto Workers elect Fraser president

Delegates to the Auto Workers 25th convention elected Douglas A. Fraser president of the union, succeeding Leonard Woodcock, who had reached the mandatory retirement age of 65. Fraser, 60, became head of a UAW local at the age of 25, and was the late Walter Reuther's chief assistant for 8 years. When Reuther died in a plane crash in 1970, Fraser withdrew from a battle with Woodcock over succession to the UAW presidency to avoid turmoil within the union in what appeared to be a close contest. Fraser then resumed his post as vice president in charge of the UAW's Chrysler Department. In other actions, the delegates approved a measure permitting a special convention within the next 6 months to decide whether the UAW should reaffiliate with the AFL–CIO.

Bridges retires after 40 years at union helm

Harry Bridges closed the 22d biennial convention of the International Longshoremen's and Warehousemen's Union in Seattle by announcing his retirement, after a 40-year tenure as president of the 55,000-member union he helped found. Bridges, 75, was the last active member of the group of industrial union leaders including John L. Lewis, Philip Murray, David Dubinsky, and Sidney Hillman that achieved the organizing triumphs of the 1930's. Although Bridge's Marxist views kept him and his West Coast dock workers out of the mainsteam of organized labor (in particular the AFL–CIO), he was a leader in innovative and cooperative approaches to automation on the waterfront. Indicative of his alienation from the mainstream of American society was special legislation passed by Congress to force him out of the country, and attempts by the Roosevelt, Truman, and Eisenhower Administrations to have him deported as a Communist. When the Supreme Court ordered a stop to all such efforts in the early 1950's, Justice Frank Murphy denounced the Government's actions as a case study in "man's inhumanity to man."

Vice president and assistant to the president, William H. Chester, and secretary-treasurer Louis Goldblatt also retired. Bridges seconded the nomination of James Herman to succeed him. Herman, 52, is president of Local 34 in San Francisco. Johnny Parks, 55, of Portland, Ore., Northwest regional director of the union, opposed Herman in a June mail referendum.

OSHA announces benzene standard

On May 23, the Department of Labor asked a Federal court to lift an order blocking the Department's emergency standard, issued 2 weeks earlier, sharply reducing worker exposure to benzene. The order was issued at the request of several oil companies and two industry trade associations, which claimed that producers were not able to comply with the standard.

When the standard was announced, Eula Bingham, Assistant Secretary of Labor for Occupational Safety and Health, said that "a grave danger currently exists for over 150,000 working men and women who are exposed each day to benzene." Bingham explained that permissible worker exposure is being lowered from 10 parts to 1 part of benzene per million parts of air (PPM), based on an 8-hour average. The standard also reduces the present ceiling level of 25 PPM to 5 PPM and eliminates the peak level of 50 PPM for any 15-minute period during the 8-hour day. Emergency requirements include the measurement of employee exposure, personal protective equipment and clothing, employee training, medical surveillance, work practices, and recordkeeping. Benzene, which has been linked to leukemia and other blood abnormalities, is a clear, non-corrosive, highly flammable liquid used in the production of organic chemicals, detergents, and pesticides.

Bingham said the emergency standard will be replaced by a permanent standard within 6 months.

Wages increased by Southern textile firms

Burlington industries led off a round of wage increases in the Southern textile industry in April,

"Developments in Industrial Relations" is prepared by Leon Bornstein and other members of the staff of the Division of Trends in Employee Compensation, Bureau of Labor Statistics, and is largely based on information from secondary source.

when it announced a 9-percent increase for its 50,-000 hourly employees, effective June 13. J. P. Stevens & Co., with 35,000 employees in six States, and West Point Pepperell, with 19,000 employees in five States, announced unspecified wage increases, as did Cannon Mills, Spring Mills, and Thomaston Mills. Smaller firms in the industry usually follow the lead of the larger firms in granting wage increases. In the most recent previous increase in June 1976, workers received pay raises of about 10 percent.

The Amalgamated Clothing and Textile Workers Union, which claims to represent about 15 percent of the employees of Southern textile firms, held a Southern Wage Drive Conference in mid-March and called for a 15-percent pay increase to compensate for purchasing power lost because of inflation and to close the gap between wages in the Southern textiles and other domestic manufacturing industries. According to a union official, straight-time earnings of all production workers in the Southern textile industry averaged $3.65 an hour. At the end of May, the union had not yet reached agreement for any of the workers it represents in the industry.

Dock container dispute resolved

North Atlantic shipping employers and the International Longshoremen's Association (ILA) reached an agreement which restored the contract canceled in February because work rules regarding container handling had been invalidated by the National Labor Relations Board and the courts. The rules had been intended to preserve job opportunities for ILA members by, in effect, penalizing employers for packing and unpacking containers in off-dock areas. The union, which had been demanding other contract improvements to make up for this loss of job protection, struck seven shipping firms in April for 5 days, returning to work when it believed that some progress was being made in the dispute.

Under the revised provisions, the payment to the container royalty fund on van-size containers will be doubled to a range of 70 cents to $2 a ton, varying according to the type of vessel, retroactive to May 1. This fund has provided longshore workers with year-end bonuses of $400 to $600. The royalty is in addition to a $1-per-ton charge for all container freight, used to support fringe benefits, which was not changed. The parties also agreed to begin talks June 15 on a new master contract to replace the one scheduled to expire October 1. Any economic improvements will cover 35,000 workers from Boston, Mass., to Norfolk, Va.

Striker's benefits held illegal in New York

New York State's practice of paying unemployment benefits to striking workers was held unconstitutional by Federal District Court Judge Richard Owen. The case involved the New York Telephone Co., which filed suit after the State paid out about $49 million to striking employees during a 7-month strike against the company that began in 1971. In his decision, Judge Owen said that the 40-year-old law permitting the payments "is State intervention on behalf of the strikers, causes an employer to finance its own strikers, is in conflict with Federal labor-law policies and is therefore unconstitutional and void." The judge said further court arguments would be necessary before he could rule on whether the State must repay the money the company had contributed to the unemployment fund as a result of the strike.

A New York Telephone official said the decision "has restored an equilibrium to collective bargaining" and other business leaders asserted that it would help in retaining and attracting industry. Morton Bahr, a vice president of the Communications Workers, the union involved in the strike, said he was confident that the ruling would be reversed on appeal because the Supreme Court had previously held that the States have the right to pass unemployment insurance and welfare laws providing benefits to strikers. New York State Attorney General Louis J. Lefkowitz said the State would seek a stay of the decision pending an appeal.

At the time of Judge Owen's ruling, strikers were eligible for weekly benefits ranging up to $95, commencing with the ninth week of idleness. Rhode Island is the only other State that grants unemployment benefits to strikers.

Florida Plumbers local agrees to pay cuts

In an effort to reduce an unemployment rate of about 50 percent in the local, members of Plumbers Local 519 in Dade County (Miami), accepted a 1-year contract that calls for wage cuts and other concessions. The new pay rate for experienced plumbers is $8.34 an hour, down from $10.34, and there are also cuts in all pay steps for apprentices, who now start at $2.91, instead of $5. The local, which has 1,200 members, also agreed that overtime pay rates will apply only to hours worked in excess of 8 per day, rather than 7; to termination of travel pay, which ranged up to $6 a day for employees required to work beyond specified distances from Miami; to an increased ratio of apprentices to experienced workers; and to changes in grievance procedures intended to reduce the number of strikes.

AFL–CIO questions Carter's economic program

At its spring meeting, the AFL–CIO Executive Council asserted that President Carter's economic stimulus program "will not bring rapid economic growth and will not reduce the Nation's unemployment problem." President George Meany said he would reserve judgment on the Administration's record to date, but commented that "we're not very happy" with the President's position on minimum wage legislation, claiming it showed a lack of compassion for those in poverty.

The Council adopted a policy statement agreeing with the general objectives of the President's energy program but strongly opposing the taxing and pricing proposals because they would have a "significant inflationary and recessionary impact." The Council again asked Congress to revise the Hatch Act to increase political rights for Federal and postal employees, saying that Federal workers should have the same right as other Americans to participate in the Nation's political life.

In other actions, the Council reaffirmed its support of a consumer boycott of Coors beer and elected Operating Engineers' President J.C. Turner to the 35-member body, succeeding Hunter P. Wharton, who resigned. Wharton, 76, is president emeritus of the Operating Engineers.

Law firm agrees to affirmative action program

A sex discrimination suit against the New York City law firm of Sullivan & Cromwell was settled when it agreed to recruit, hire, and promote women attorneys on the same basis as men. Sullivan & Cromwell, which was represented by outside counsel, said it had not discriminated and had settled only because it would have been more expensive and burdensome to fight the case. Under the agreement, subject to approval by the Federal District Court Judge Constance Baker Motley, who heard the case, Sullivan & Cromwell will be required to:

- Appoint one of its partners to administer compliance with the terms of the settlement.
- Conduct job interviews annually at nine designated law schools and at least two of five other law schools, with the interviews to be conducted according to specified nondiscrimination guidelines.
- Revise written material distributed to law school placement offices to indicate the number of women who are associate members of the firm and its desire to hire "without regard to sex."
- Supply the plaintiff's attorney with information on the percentage of applicants, interviewees, and new hires who are women and on the duties, rate of promotion, and earnings of associate members of the firm.
- Assure women associates of equal access to all social functions sponsored by the firm.
- Pay for the arbitration of all disputes under the agreement, except when the arbitrator finds that the plaintiff's attorney has raised "frivolous" issues.

The case originated in 1971, when a job applicant charged before the Equal Employment Opportunity Commission that Sullivan & Cromwell had discriminated in not hiring her. The EEOC dismissed the case in 1974, noting that women attorneys then made up 12.5 percent of the firm's associates, compared with only 2 percent in 1970. The applicant then took the case to Federal District Court, where the judge permitted her to extend it to a class action on behalf of all other women who might have been similarly discriminated against. When the settlement was reached, Sullivan & Cromwell had 57 partners in New York and 2 overseas, none of them women, and 116 associates, including 26 women.

Developments in Industrial Relations

Reported in *Monthly Labor Review*, July 1977.

Aluminum accords comparable to steel settlement

The Aluminum Company of America and the Steelworkers reached a 3-year agreement on May 24, leading off a round of settlements in the aluminum industry that contained provisions comparable to those the union gained in April from steel producers (See *Monthly Labor Review,* June 1977, pp. 62–65.) Concurrently with the Alcoa accord, the Steelworkers settled with Reynolds Metals Co. and Kaiser Aluminum & Chemical Corp., and on May 27 the Aluminum Workers gained similar terms for the 30,-000 workers it represents at Alcoa and Reynolds. The three Steelworkers' contracts covered a total of 32,000 workers. Thus, contracts were reached at the larger companies in advance of the May 31 expiration date for the old agreements. Both unions had yet to negotiate agreements for workers at some smaller companies, where contracts expire after May 31.

The Alcoa-Steelworkers contract included a Job and Income Security Program based on the Employment and Income Security Program the union had negotiated with the steel companies. The major difference between the plans was that the aluminum program generally provided for graduated benefits for all employees with 2 or more years of service, and the steel plan provided for uniform benefits that applied only to employees with 20 years of service or more.

The Alcoa program calls for the following benefits:

- A maximum of 52 weeks of Supplemental Unemployment Benefits for laid-off "Tier I" workers (those with 2 to 10 years of service), a maximum of 78 weeks for those in Tier II (10 to 20 years of service), and a maximum of 104 weeks for those in Tier III (20 years of service or more). Previously, the maximum duration was 52 weeks for all laid-off employees with 2 years of service or more. In addition, maximum limits on the size of weekly benefits were increased or eliminated, the company's financial obligation to the SUB fund was increased, payment of benefits was guaranteed to laid-off Tier II and III employees, and Short Week benefits are now guaranteed and no longer charged against the fund.

- A new "rule-of-65" (age plus years of service total 65) pension for idled Tier III employees eligible under one of several criteria related to layoffs, permanent or prolonged shutdowns, and sickness. The monthly entitlement is calculated at the normal pension rate, and it will be supplemented by a $300 a month payment that will continue until age 62 or until the person obtains suitable long-term employment, whichever comes first.

- A 3-step increase in weekly sickness and accident benefits for employees in all tiers, bringing the range to $168 to $230, from $125 to $173.

- Continuation of all insurance coverage (except sickness and accident) for up to 1 year for employees in all tiers in the event of layoff. Previously, medical coverage was continued for up to 6 months for laid-off employees with 2 but less than 10 years of service and for up to 2 years for those with 10 years of service or more.

- Adoption of an income maintenance provision under which employees reassigned to lower rated jobs are guaranteed 85, 90, and 95 percent of their prior earnings rate if they are in Tiers I, II, or III, respectively. This is in addition to an existing provision that assures employees of their full pay rate for the first 8 working days on a lower rated job.

The Alcoa-Steelworkers accord provided for a May 30, 1977, general wage increase of 40 cents an hour and a 0.5-cent increase in the increment between the 27 job grades, which resulted in an overall increase ranging from 40 cents for employees in the lowest rated jobs to 53 cents for those in the highest. Other specified wage increases are 10-cent raises in December of 1977 and 1978, 10 cents to 23 cents in June 1978 (a 10-cent general increase plus a 0.5-cent increment increase) and 10 to 17.8 cents in June 1979 (a 10-cent general increase plus a 0.3-cent increment increase).

Employees also received a 15-cents-an-hour cost-of-living adjustment on May 30, 1977, as a result of the continuation of the wage escalator formula,

"Developments in Industrial Relations" is prepared by Leon Bornstein and other members of the staff of the Division of Trends in Employee Compensation, Bureau of Labor Statistics, and is largely based on information from secondary sources.

which calls for a 1-cent adjustment for each 0.3-point movement in the BLS Consumer Price Index (1967 =100). Escalator increases totaled $1.26 an hour during the previous contract. There was one change in application of the clause—the escalator allowance will apply to all hours employees are paid for, rather than only hours worked.

There were other pension changes in addition to introduction of the rule-of-65 benefit for Tier III employees. The normal benefit rate was increased by $1.75 on June 1, 1977, and by $1.50 on June 1, 1979, which will bring it to $14.25 a month per year of service for employees in job grades 1-4 and to $18.25 for those in grades 23 and above. The pension "cap," which had limited a retiree's combined pension and social security income to 85 percent of average annual preretirement income, was liberalized by providing for a percentage-point increase in the cap for each year of service from the 31st through the 45th. The provision for automatic annual cost-of-living adjustments in pensions adopted in the 1974 settlement was terminated, but retirees who had received the two adjustments, which totaled 10 percent, will continue to receive that amount.

Life insurance coverage for active employees was increased from $8,000 to $10,000, and coverage for retirees was increased by varying amounts, bringing the maximum to $10,000 prior to age 62 and the minimum to $3,000 at age 66 or over. A vision care plan was established for employees and dependents, and there were a number of improvements in hospital-medical-surgical and dental coverage. Other benefit changes included an 11th paid holiday, effective in the third year.

Miller apparent victor in UMW race

Arnold Miller was the apparent victor in the United Mine Workers June 14 presidential election, but the other candidates indicated that they would challenge the outcome. Of the ballots tallied as of mid-July, Miller had 55,236 votes, Lee Roy Patterson, a UMW Executive Board member, had 49,035 votes, and Harry Patrick, the union's secretary-treasurer, had 34,512 votes. In a call for unity, Miller asserted, "It is time now for wounds to be healed by all on the losing side in this democratic election. They should come forth and recognize who the enemy is, which is the mine operators."

Patterson declared, "The only reason I lost this election is because it was stolen from me. Personally, I feel compelled to challenge it." Under the union's constitution, challenges are filed with the 21-member Executive Board, which has the power to order a new election. In the months preceding the election,

the board had generally backed Patterson in various controversies with Miller over administrative and policy matters.

Patrick first announced he would not challenge the election but reversed his position on June 20, a few days after trustees of the UMWA Health and Retirement Fund announced cutbacks in medical benefits for miners and their families. In letters mailed to the 821,000 beneficiaries, the trustees said that beginning July 1, each family would be required to pay the first $250 of hospital costs and 40 percent of doctors' charges in a year, subject to an overall maximum family liability of $500 a year. Previously, the plan paid the entire cost. The trustees said that the change was necessary because of unauthorized work stoppages that have cost the funds $65 million in employer contributions since 1974 and because the severe winter had curtailed production and led to the loss of $20 million in contributions. The trustees are Harry Huge, selected by the union, C. W. Davis, selected by the industry, and Paul R. Dean, the neutral member. Immediately after their announcement, scattered protest walkouts erupted in the coal fields. On June 21, the Bituminous Coal Operators' Association (the industry's bargaining arm) estimated that the number of idle miners had reached 18,000. Patrick asserted that Miller and the fund trustees had delayed the announcement until after election so that Miller's reelection hopes would not be damaged. (Patrick later announced that he himself would not challenge the election but would support a new challenge filed by one of the union's tellers.)

Miller denied such a motive and attributed the need for the cutback to refusal by the BCOA to reallocate money among the four trusts that provide benefits for employees, retirees, and their dependents. According to Joseph Brennan, president of the BCOA, reallocation was not proper because it would weaken the position of the trusts from which money would be diverted and because it would "divert attention from the basic cause [of the benefit cutback], the wildcat strike." According to the coal operators, coal production lost because of wildcat strikes during the first 5 months of 1977 rose 89 percent compared with the same period of 1976, which deprived the trust funds of $15.9 million in employer contributions, compared with $8.8 million lost for the earlier period.

Bakery accord reached

The Bakery and Confectionary Workers union negotiated 2-year contracts with several major wholesale bread and cake companies on the East and West coasts. The West Coast accord was reached by the union's Pacific Coast Bargaining Conference, after a 3-day strike in May affecting 35 plants from San Diego to Seattle. The union said that it was the first conferencewide strike in the baking industry. A major issue in the dispute was the union's concern over the maintenance of medical and hospital benefits that it said were being eroded by increasing costs. (The union's East-Central States Bargaining Conference settled without a walkout.)

The settlements on both coasts raised the employers' hospital-medical insurance contribution by $1.05 a week for each worker in the first year. The agreements also raised pensions by $100 a month for 25-year employees retiring at age 65, bringing their benefit to $500. The firms also agreed to a $1-an-hour pay increase for all employees over the term and to an additional increase for workers who do not receive 2 consecutive days off during a workweek. The companies involved were ITT Continental Baking Co., Inter-state Brands, American Bakeries, Campbell-Taggart, and Oroweat.

Construction settlement covers three-state region

The National Constructors Association and the Laborers International Union of North America reached an agreement expected to cover union members engaged in industrial plant construction in Texas, Oklahoma, and New Mexico. The 2-year agreement covers both wages and working conditions and will be phased in to replace locally negotiated agreements now in effect. A no-strike clause provides for binding arbitration and overtime pay is limited to time-and-one-half, except for double time on Sundays and holidays. Employers are given the right to determine crew sizes, shut down projects in the event of work stoppages or slowdowns by one or more unions, and fire employees not complying with safety regulations. The agreement, which will affect as many as 23,000 union workers if all of the Association's 50-member companies sign it, was designed to promote stability in the industry by widening regional bargaining. Union leaders said they also hope the agreement will make union contractors more competitive and stop the recent trend toward nonunion construction. Wages and employer contributions for benefits established in the new agreement vary by State and by zones within the States. The agreement is subject to reopening April 1, 1978, on wages and benefit contributions.

First grape settlement reached

The United Farm Workers union led off its round of bargaining with California table grape growers by negotiating a 3-year contract for 1,100 field employees of David Freedman & Co., located in the Coachella Valley town of Thermal. Union President Cesar Chavez described the accord as "a pacesetter that will set the trend for the industry." The June agreement raises the basic wage from $2.70 an hour to $3.35 this season, to $3.55 in 1978, and to $3.76 the following year. It also provides for the industry's first paid vacation plan and for improvements in pensions and in the employer-financed hospital-medical plan. After the Freedman settlement, the union quickly reached similar agreements with two smaller growers.

David Freedman & Co. was the first table grape grower to sign a contract with the UFW in 1970 and was the only one to remain under contract with the UFW when other growers shifted to the Teamsters in 1973. Since then, the unions have signed an agreement giving the UFW the right to organize firms primarily engaged in growing agricultural products and giving the Teamsters the right to organize those engaged in processing, preserving, and transporting the products. (See *Monthly Labor Review,* May 1977, pp. 57–58.)

U.S. to investigate Steelworkers' election

The U.S. Department of Labor agreed to investigate Edward Sadlowski's claim of "massive violations" of Federal laws in the recent Steelworkers election. Sadlowski, who had exhausted all of the election appeals procedures within the union, said the chief cause of his loss to Lloyd McBride *(Monthly Labor Review,* April 1977, pp. 84–85) was that the union's staff had been mobilized against him. According to Sadlowski, "Electioneering became a full-time job and contributions a forced necessity" for the staff members.

McBride, who received 328,861 votes in the February contest compared with 249,281 for Sadlowski, assumed office June 1. He said the union would cooperate in the investigation, but described the complaint as "the biggest case of sour grapes in union electoral history."

The Labor Department, which must report its findings within 60 days of the complaint, could seek a court order for a new election if it finds violations deemed serious enough to have affected the outcome. If not, Sadlowski could sue the Department on grounds that the decision was arbitrary and capricious.

Garment workers elect officers

Sol C. Chaikin was elected to a full 3-year term as president of the Ladies' Garment Workers at the union's convention in Hollywood, Fla. Chaikin had held the combined post of president-secretary-treasurer since September 1975, following the resignation of President Louis Stulberg. Shelly Appleton, a vice-president since 1962, was elected to the reconstituted post of secretary-treasurer. The nearly 1,000 delegates also approved the creation of a second executive vice president's office and elected Frederick R. Siems to this position. Siems had been an ILGWU vice president since 1959 and also was director of the ILGWU's Central States Region. Other incumbent officers were reelected, and eight new vice presidents were elected to the executive board.

The convention also endorsed the union's ongoing program to consolidate a number of locals, district councils, and regions. "No longer are we cloakmakers, dressmakers, shirtmakers, etc.," the committee on jurisdiction told the delegates, "We are all garment workers striving together for decent wages and conditions." Along these lines, the convention called on the union's leadership to consider the development of a wage standard for all ILGWU members involved in garment production. The convention also approved increases in membership dues and the per capita tax. The union's leadership had requested this action to put the union on a sound financial footing.

Herman elected ILWU president

In balloting results announced June 23, James R. Herman, 52, won election as president of the International Longshoremen's and Warehousemen's Union, succeeding Harry Bridges, who had retired.

(See *Monthly Labor Review,* July 1977, p. 52.) Herman defeated G. Johnny Parks of the union's Portland, Oreg., office by a vote of 21,662 to 7,451. The new union chief had been president of Ship Clerk's Local 34 in the San Francisco Bay region since 1960.

Trustees resign coal union's benefit fund

The Department of Labor announced that three trustees of the Southern Labor Union's pension and welfare funds had agreed to resign and restore more than $50,000 in fund assets. The union, which has 3,000 members, all in coal mining, is a rival of the United Mine Workers. The agreement, part of a consent decree filed in Federal District Court in Knoxville, Tenn., settled a case in which the Government had charged the trustees with illegal acts, including failure to collect employer contributions, payment of improper benefits, and leasing airplanes at excessive cost from a firm partly owned by two of the trustees. The Government's suit was initiated in November 1976 under provisions of the Employee Retirement Income Security Act of 1974. The departing trustees are also required to collect a number of pension fund loans in default and to indemnify the funds for any amounts they are unable to collect. A Department of Labor official said the loans totaled about $120,000. One of the three departing trustees of the $5 million fund was Ted Q. Wilson, counsel of the union. Two other trustees continued to serve under court control pending union and management selection of their replacements. □

Developments in Industrial Relations

Reported in *Monthly Labor Review*, August 1977.

Kennecott settlements end walkouts

The Kennecott Copper Corp. and a coalition of 26 unions (led by the Steelworkers) reached a 3-year settlement shortly after walkouts began on June 30 at seven major copper producers. The agreement provided total raises of 85 cents hourly for 10,000 workers over the life of the contract. Shortly afterwards, a similar settlement was reached at Magma Copper Co. for 4,500 workers. Magma's settlement also resolved local issues and its workers immediately ended the walkout. Similar settlements were reached in late July at Cities Service, Inc., and Anaconda Co.

The Kennecott settlement provided general wage increases of 21 cents an hour on July 1, 1977, 1978, and 1979. In addition, workers will receive job increment increases between job classes of 0.43 cents per hour on each of those dates. The job classification system, to be revised in the second year, will result in an average 10 cents additional increase. The escalator clause, which provides quarterly cost-of-living adjustments of 1 cent for each 0.3 point change in the Consumer Price Index was continued, and 38 cents of the prior cost-of-living adjustments was incorporated into base rates. Basic pension benefits were raised to $13 a month for each of the first 15 years of service, $14.50 for each of the next 15 years, and $16 for each year in excess of 30.

Sickness and accident weekly benefits were increased by $10 in July 1977 and July 1978, and by $15 in July 1979. Kennecott's contribution to the Supplemental Unemployment Benefit fund was increased by 2 cents, raising the total to 5 cents hourly.

The Kennecott agreement did not end strikes against the company as walkouts continued over local issues in five States. By July 20, all 9,000 workers had returned as agreement was reached over the number of absentee days allowed at Kennecott's Arizona plant. (Local issues had already been resolved in Utah, Nevada, New Mexico, and Maryland.) In early August, workers were still on strike against

Phelps Dodge Corp., Asarco, Inc., Inspiration Consolidated Copper Co., and U.S. Metals Refining Co.

Apparel accord provides wage increase of $1.10

The Amalgamated Clothing and Textile Workers Union and the Clothing Manufacturers Association of the USA negotiated a 40-month contract for more than 80,000 workers in the men's and boys' tailored clothing industry. The June settlement, which involves about 700 companies throughout the country, provides for wage increases of 30 cents an hour on June 1, 1977, January 30, 1978, and October 2, 1978, and 20 cents on October 1, 1979. The revised cost-of-living formula provides for an adjustment up to 15 cents on October 2, 1978, calculated at 5 cents an hour for each percentage-point increase in the Consumer Price Index in excess of 7.5 percent between April 1977 and April 1978, and for an adjustment up to 10 cents on October 1, 1979, calculated at 5.3 cents for each percentage-point increase in the Index in excess of 6 percent between April 1978 and April 1979.

Employers will contribute an additional 2 percentage points of gross payroll to the pension fund to finance a three-step increase in the benefit rate, to $5.75 a month for each year of credited service, from $5, and to end a $200-a-month limit on pensions. This means that employers will pay a total of 6.9 percent of gross payroll to the pension fund. The agreement also provides for improved health insurance benefits, two additional holidays (bringing the total to 10), a reduction to 1,000 hours (from 1,200) in the work requirement to qualify for pay for the second and third weeks of vacation, guaranteed 5 hours' pay (instead of 4) for reporting to work, and a broadened definition of "immediate family" for bereavement pay purposes.

Airline mechanics' wages tied to company profits

Eastern Airlines' 11,300 mechanics have agreed to a plan tying a portion of their wages to the company's profits. The plan is similar to the earlier agreements between the airline and its pilots

"Developments in Industrial Relations" is prepared by Leon Bornstein and other members of the staff of the Division of Trends in Employee Compensation, Bureau of Labor Statistics, and is largely based on information from secondary sources.

and flight attendants (*Monthly Labor Review,* June 1977, p. 65). Nonunion employees agreed to the plan in October 1976. Under the agreement, 3.5 percent of an employees monthly wages are withheld until yearend when the money will be repaid if Eastern's annual profits amount to 2 percent of sales. If profits exceed 2 percent, employees could receive an additional amount ranging up to another 3.5 percent of earnings. If profits are less than 2 percent, some or all of the money could be used to boost the profit level. Pay deductions began July 4 for the plan which is scheduled to remain in effect for 5 years.

Chrysler, UAW announce legal service plan

The United Auto Workers' union and the Chrysler Corp. announced a new legal assistance program under which hourly paid Chrysler workers and retirees in the United States, their dependents, and surviving spouses can obtain personal legal services at no cost to the worker or his family through a group plan. The program will cover most legal services of a personal nature, including traffic violations, social security claims, divorces, wills, bankruptcies, property damage claims, and other personal services. Once approval is obtained from the Internal Revenue Service, pilot plans will start at Chrysler locals in selected areas. The UAW Legal Services Plan is expected to eventually cover about 150,000 UAW-Chrysler families in the United States (including retirees) and would be the largest such group legal services plan in the Nation.

The program will be financed by using a portion of the assets of the UAW-Chrysler SUB Reserve Fund. (During the 1974–75 recession, money from the reserve fund was used to pay for insurance protection for laid-off workers who would have lost that protection when the regular Chrysler SUB Fund became exhausted). The SUB plan was restructured in 1976, and Chrysler "has been trying to transfer this Reserve Fund into the regular SUB Fund, in order to reduce its contribution," according to the union. Vice President Marc Stepp (UAW director for Chrysler) asserted, "Rather than allow this, the UAW has now achieved this precedent-setting benefit through the use of assets from this fund."

The 1976 tax reform law encourages the formation of group legal plans by making money negotiated to finance such plans and benefits received from such plans tax exempt. (Although the plan would initially be financed by the SUB Reserve Fund, this tax exemption would apply to any future company or employee contributions if the Fund eventually becomes depleted.)

Gimbels' workers win 3-year contract

United Storeworkers Local 2 in New York negotiated a 3-year contract with Gimbels Bros., Inc. The agreement covers 6,000 employees at Gimbels' midtown Manhattan store and branches in Westchester, Long Island, New Jersey, and Connecticut. Wages were raised by $8 weekly in June 1977 with another $2 scheduled for December. In the second year, the union won its demand that wage increases match those of Storeworkers' Local 3 in 1978 bargaining with Bloomingdale Bros. In the third year, increases would be contingent on the results of an unrestricted reopener on wages and working conditions, with the union free to strike without cancellation of the contract. Among other provisions, Gimbels increased its contribution to the employee medical plan to 7 percent of the payroll (from 6.75 percent) effective June 10, 1977.

A major obstacle to a peaceful settlement was the union's insistence on a longer than 1-year contract. (Storeworkers questioned whether the company, now British owned, would stay in the area.) In view of Gimbels' insistence on a 1-year agreement, the concerned membership voted to strike if a longer agreement, along with a company statement that it had no intention of suspending operations, was not forthcoming. The deadline for a strike was set for June 7, 1 week after the prior agreement expired. The union members approved the 3-year package on the eve of the strike deadline after receiving a letter of intent to stay in operation from Gimbels. Martin S. Kramer, chairman of Gimbels' board of directors, stated that Brown and Williamson, Gimbels' parent company, had provided "assurance of complete financial support," and the New York division is "planning major improvements in its various stores."

Paperworkers settle

Members of the Paperworkers union ratified a 2-year agreement with the International Paper Co. The contract covered 10,000 paperworkers at plants in Mississippi, Alabama, Florida, Louisana, Arkansas, and South Carolina. The settlement provided for a 10.5-percent wage increase the first year, and 10 percent the second year. Minimum pension benefits increased from $7.50 a month for each year's credited service to $9, and the company agreed to repay contributions made by employees before the plan became noncontributory. The union estimated that about 8,000 workers would receive an average of $3,000 in three installments.

The contract also improved vacation schedules, shift differentials, meal allowances, and funeral leave provisions. The firm raised its contributions to the hospitalization and surgical plans by $10 a month to include coverage for dependents. Additional general wage adjustments ranging from 2 to 18.5 cents an hour were negotiated on a plant-by-plant basis for the 10 participating facilities.

Texas telephone workers win pay increases

The Communications Workers of America and the General Telephone Co. of the Southwest, San Angelo, Tex., negotiated a 3-year contract covering 6,000 employees. The agreement calls for hourly pay increases of 8.06 percent retroactive to May 18, and 2.31 percent in December 1977; 4.85 percent in May and 2.03 percent in December 1978; and 4.88 percent in May and 1.89 percent in December 1979. The contract also increased night shift differentials to 40 cents an hour (from 30 cents), and provided double-time pay for those working over 50 hours a week.

Vacation provisions were improved and, effective in 1978, a 10th paid holiday (floating) will be added. Major medical coverage was raised from $50,000 to $75,000, with the company now paying the full premium cost. A dental plan was established, as was optional life insurance for employee's dependents. The annual pension benefit was raised to 1.3 percent (from 1.25) of the average of the employee's highest 5 years of earnings.

OSHA streamlines reporting forms

Secretary of Labor Ray Marshall announced a reduction in the number of forms needed for job injury and illness recordkeeping and reporting requirements. Under the new format, businesses will use a simple check-off procedure rather than code numbers, and will summarize illness and injuries by using a "running total." The change will reduce the number of entries from 80 to 19 for 1.5 million businesses. For the Nation as a whole, this will result in a reduction of more than 91.5 million entries.

Noting President Carter's concern with reducing the burdens of government paperwork, Marshall said, "This Administration is committed to preserving the health and safety of American workers. But we don't believe OSHA has to be a burden on anyone's back."

Dr. Eula Bingham, Assistant Secretary for Occupational Safety and Health, said, "Any effort which streamlines and simplifies compliance serves to increase worker and health safety. The best way for businesses to reduce their paperwork burden is by reducing accidents and illnesses."

In related actions, the Department also disclosed a proposal giving workers access to job illness and injury data at their workplace, and OSHA and the Bureau of Labor Statistics announced that the number of firms required to participate in the BLS annual survey of occupational injuries and illnesses has been reduced to 332,000. When added to prior adjustments, this reduction represents a 50-percent cut from the 1972 sample size of 650,000. Also, businesses with 10 or fewer workers will be exempt from all recordkeeping requirements unless selected for the BLS annual survey.

Bias against handicapped charged

In the first reported cases of their kind, the U.S. Department of Labor threatened to withhold Federal contracts from two airlines and a Hawaiian construction firm accused of discriminating against handicapped workers. Acting under the Vocational Rehabilitation Act of 1973, which bars job discrimination against qualified handicapped workers, the Labor Department issued citations to United Air Lines, Trans World Airlines, and E. E. Black, Ltd. The companies have 20 days to respond and may request a hearing on the complaints.

The United Air Lines case involved a job repairing ticket and reservation computer terminals in Honolulu. The Labor Department said United denied an applicant the job, asserting high noise levels would aggravate a hearing problem, and moving equipment might injure a previously broken ankle. The Department's investigators found, however, that the job did not involve working in high noise areas, and the employee's ankle had healed completely. In Chicago, a United spokesperson said the carrier "is proud of the record of hiring qualified handicapped employees and doesn't believe it has failed to provide equal employment opportunities for them," and added that United would respond to the specific allegations after reviewing the citation.

TWA was accused of bias against a former pilot in Kansas City who, after recovering from a heart attack, was denied another job with the airline. By refusing to hire him in a different position TWA discriminated against a qualified handicapped worker, according to the Department. TWA responded that it had been unable to find a suitable position for the man, given his medical history and qualifications. However, a spokesperson said TWA was continuing to make an effort and would review the matter.

E. E. Black, a Honolulu-based construction firm, refused to employ a construction worker with a congenital spine deformity. The Labor Department charged the worker had been cleared for heavy labor by previous examinations and had already worked in the construction industry for 3 years. There was no immediate public comment from company officials.

Boot and Shoe Workers merge with Retail Clerks

Delegates to the 27th Boot and Shoe Workers convention approved a proposal to merge the 30,000-member union with the 700,000-member Retail Clerks International Association (RCIA). The action came after 5 years of talks between Boot and Shoe Workers and United Shoe Workers about a merger. When that effort was not successful, the focus of the talks shifted toward merging the two shoeworker unions into the Retail Clerks union. The Boot and Shoe Workers and the RCIA agreed to merger terms; but negotiations were continuing with the United Shoe Workers. (Meanwhile, the Retail Clerks union was involved in merger discussions with the Meat Cutters and Butcher Workmen and the Retail, Wholesale and Department Store Union.)

President John E. Mara, reelected at the Boot and Shoe Workers' convention, told the delegates that the "overwhelming benefits" to shoeworkers outweighed the "understandable sadness" of the occasion. He cited greater coordination of industrywide bargaining, increased political strength, stepped-up organizing campaigns, and added strength in negotiations as practical reasons for the merger. He stated, "We need the strength and the assurance of the Retail Clerks to win the thousands of unorganized shoeworkers still outside the pale." Under the terms of the merger agreement, Mara heads the shoe division within the Retail Clerks.

The delegates also heard from Retail Clerks' Secretary-Treasurer William Wynn and Vice President Jay Foreman on items of transition and administration involved in completing the merger, effective September 1. The Retail Clerks had approved the merger by a unanimous vote of the union's executive board following the Boot and Shoe Workers' convention. □

Developments in Industrial Relations

Reported in *Monthly Labor Review*, September 1977.

Telephone accord averts strike

More than 700,000 workers in the telephone industry were covered by settlements with American Telephone & Telegraph Co. that focused on the unions' demands for substantial wage increases and increased job security. The breakthrough in the 2 months of negotiations came in early August, only hours before a strike deadline, when the Communications Workers (representing 500,000 workers), the International Brotherhood of Electrical Workers (120,000), and the Telecommunications International Union (70,000) reached agreement with AT&T. In the next few days, bargaining was concluded on local issues, although there were brief scattered walkouts, three of which continued until mid-August. During this period, several of the companies within the Bell System negotiated similar contracts with other unions. Overall, the accords with all of the unions covered employees of the 24 operating companies in the Bell System, as well as some facilities of the Western Electric Co., Bell's manufacturing arm.

The CWA contract did not raise pay rates for the lowest progression step in each pay grade but all other steps were increased. The maximum increases, which applied to the final steps of grades with total progression periods of at least 48 months, were 8 percent on August 7, 1977, and 3 percent on August 6, 1978, and August 5, 1979. All employees—including those in the lowest step of each grade—were guaranteed a minimum increase of $5 a week on each of the dates.

The cost-of-living wage escalator clause was the same as in the prior contract, providing for adjustments on the first and second anniversaries of the contract each equal to 50 cents a week, plus 0.6 percent of each individual employee's weekly rate during the first contract year, for each 1-percent rise in the BLS Consumer Price Index. Communications Workers President Glenn E. Watts estimated that total compensation for CWA-represented employees would increase by 31 percent over the 3-year term, including wage escalator adjustments calculated on an assumed 6-percent annual rise in the Index. Watts said the three wage increases plus cost-of-living adjustments based on the assumed rise in the Index would average $75.33 a week for employees in the top step of 60-month progression schedules.

The changes in job security provisions reflected employees' concern over the possibility of further job cuts in the Bell System companies. From 1973 to the end of 1976, total employment declined from 1,040,000 to 938,000, chiefly because of advances in technology. The job security provisions included:

- A clause permitting employees to decline overtime work in excess of 10 hours a week (12 hours at Western Electric) during 7 specified months in both 1979 and 1980.

- Adoption of a Reassignment Pay Protection Plan providing loss-of-income protection for employees reassigned to lower paying jobs as a result of layoffs. Under the plan, the pay cut would be imposed in stages over a period ranging from 12 weeks for employees with up to 10 years of service to 64 weeks for those with 15 years or more.

- Adoption of a clause giving employees 1 day off with pay and 1 day without pay in 1978, 2 days with pay and 1 day without in 1979, and 3 days with and 2 days without in 1980.

- Adoption of a Supplemental Income Protection Plan available to employees who face layoffs or involuntary reassignments as a result of work force cuts or job relocations and who are eligible for retirement. Payments, ranging up to $250 a month (in addition to pension benefits) will continue until age 62 or eligibility for social security benefits.

- Adoption of a Savings and Security Plan for employees with 1 year of service or more, effective January 1, 1979. Participating employees will allot amounts ranging from $5 or $10 a week for those earning up to $200 a week and $5 to $20 for those earning $300 or more, with the company matching 50 percent of the amount with AT&T stock shares. Each employee will have several options on how the allotment will be invested and will be permitted to withdraw the full value of the account if employment is terminated.

"Developments in Industrial Relations" is prepared by Leon Bornstein and other members of the staff of the Division of Trends in Employee Compensation, Bureau of Labor Statistics, and is largely based on information from secondary sources.

• Adoption of moving expenses for involuntarily relocated employees, with application of the provision to be bargained locally.

There were a number of changes in pension benefits, including an improvement in normal basic benefits that, the union said, would result in a 28-percent increase in payments to those who retire in 1980. Benefits were also increased under the alternate formula for minimum benefits, by amounts ranging from $40 to $75 a month, depending on length of service.

A new maternity plan provides that pregnant employees will receive 6 weeks of leave paid at rates ranging from 50 percent of normal pay for those with 6 months but less than 2 years of service, to full pay for those with at least 5 years of service. Under the plan, employees disabled by birth complications at the end of the paid leave will be returned to the payroll and be eligible for regular disability benefits.

The new Long-Term Disability Plan, which covers all employees with 6 months of service, provides for the company to assure disabled employees 50 percent of their previous earnings.

The contracts, which expire August 9, 1980, also call for a number of improvements in life and health insurance, and for continuing local talks on "flex-itime" work schedules, and reimbursement of bargaining committee members in units where they are not already paid for time spent on union-management business.

New York City ties wage increases to productivity

In mid-August, New York City Mayor Abraham Beame announced a policy enabling municipal employees to receive additional wage increases in 1977 based on future productivity improvements in the work force. The agreement was reached with the Uniformed Sanitationmen's Association but the policy would apply to all municipal workers. The new policy was subject to approval by the Emergency Financial Control Board established by New York State to oversee the city's fiscal recovery. Under the plan, workers who agreed to work rules changes or other measures improving productivity would receive, as wage increases, at least part of the money saved in the process.

Previously, New York City employees were under a modified wage freeze and were entitled to cost-of-living adjustments paid out of productivity gains or from other revenues not originally in the city budget. The new policy would generate wage increases in addition to those tied to the cost-of-living. According to officials, the productivity-related saving would probably have to recur for the wage increase to be paid, but details have to be worked out.

Mayor Beame said, "This is a good labor-management policy. This gives an incentive to the workers to produce. It won't affect the budget. I believe this should be a universal policy."

At the same time, members of the Uniformed Sanitationmen's Association approved a 2-year contract providing for a cost-of-living payment of $304.50 in September 1977 in addition to the "gain sharing" productivity provision. The contract, which runs to July 1, 1978, did not provide for any other increases in the existing $15,371 base pay for the 8,500 employees.

After the sanitation workers accord, members of the Patrolmen's Benevolent Association also ratified a contract that contained the new gain-sharing provision. The police contract ended 2 years of negotiations on changes desired by the parties in an arbitrator's recommended terms. Under the new contract, effective for 2 years beginning July 1, 1976, police officers received a 6-percent salary increase retroactive to July 1, 1977—raising their base pay to $17,458 a year, from $16,470. Union president Samuel DeMilia said the PBA would continue its court suit to have the increase made retroactive to July 1, 1976. The previous contract had raised pay by 6 percent on July 1, 1975, but the city had suspended payment of the increase from July 1, 1976, to July 1, 1977, as part of a general plan to ease its financial crisis. (Members of other city employee unions had also suffered a 1-year suspension of their 6-percent increase, beginning in 1975.)

The new police contract also provided for a $200 cost-of-living pay adjustment on August 5 and for 248.8 days of work per year, compared with 253 days under the prior agreement. DeMilia said that all 56-hour "swings"—the time off between weekly tours of duty—would be eliminated and that there would now be forty-four 72-hour swings, three 64-hour swings, and three 80-hour swings a year. In return, police officers will work 2 hours of overtime at straight-time pay rates 16 times during a year. The city had previously paid overtime for all hours worked in excess of the normal 8 hours a day. Also, DeMilia said that the city had agreed to limit its experiment with one-officer police cars to 7 precincts until its effectiveness is determined.

Construction hiring goals for women unveiled

The U. S. Department of Labor has proposed that contractors on Federal projects establish goals and timetables for hiring women in the building trades. The proposal, subject to revision by the department after comments are received from interested parties, would require that women work at least 3.1 percent of a project's work hours the first year, 5 percent after 2 years, and 6.9 percent after 3 years. The goals would apply to a contractor's entire work force, regardless of which employees worked on construction involving Federal funds. Labor Department officials estimated that, based on the 1970 census, women constitute 1.2 percent of the available construction work force, or about 30,000 of the almost 3 million skilled construction workers.

In another action, the department also proposed changes that would abolish two types of Equal Employment Opportunity plans that are used in areas either where voluntary efforts have not been successful or where there are "high impact" projects, that is, large projects that offer significant employment opportunities. Included was the 1969 "Philadelphia Plan," which marked the first Federal efforts to establish minority hiring goals in construction. Other mandatory plans proposed for elimination included those for San Francisco, St. Louis, Atlanta, Chicago, and Camden, N.J. However, the agency would retain, with modifications, some 42 voluntary "hometown" minority hiring plans.

The proposed regulations specify the actions contractors would be expected to take "to ensure equal employment opportunity," including provision of a working environment free of "harassment, intimidation, and coercion," while maintaining a current file of minority and female recruitment sources and applicants, and actively participating in training programs for minorities and women.

An attorney for the League of Women Voters said the proposed regulations regarding employment of women were a "good beginning" but the League would not end its current suit against the department until the regulations are final, and implemented to the satisfaction of women. The League filed suit in 1976 to compel the department to establish such hiring goals.

U.S. delays final decision on quitting ILO

A Cabinet-level committee appointed by President Carter agreed to let stand, for the time being, a 1975 decision by the Ford Administration to terminate U.S. membership in the International Labor Organization (*Monthly Labor Review,* January 1976, p. 72). A Department of State official said a final recommendation would be made to President Carter before November 7, 1977, when the withdrawal would become effective. Among those involved in the decision were Secretary of State Cyrus R. Vance, National Security Affairs Adviser Zbigniew Brzezinski, Secretary of Labor Ray Marshall, AFL-CIO President George Meany, and former Chamber of Commerce President Charles Smith. Officials indicated that Meany had sought an immediate final decision to withdraw from the ILO but acceded to the wishes of Brzezinski and Vance, who recommended the delay. The withdrawal decision was reinforced in June 1977 when a coalition of Arab and Communist nations resurrected a resolution calling for an ILO investigation into working conditions for Arabs in Israeli-held territory.

AFGE locals veto organizing military

The American Federation of Government Employees announced that its members had rejected a proposal that the union organize uniformed members of the Armed Forces. The tally in the ballot was 151,582 to 38,764. Union president Kenneth T. Blaylock said that the membership action did not preclude the possibility of undertaking an organizing campaign in coming years. He stated that the poll results should not be "misconstrued as a rejection of the idea that military personnel need representation," and urged associations which represent the interests of military personnel to take stronger positions against the ". . . eroding conditions for military personnel—cutbacks in pay, medical benefits, subsistence, and many others. . . ."

The organizing issue first arose at the union's 1976 convention (*Monthly Labor Review,* November 1976, p. 59), when delegates revised the constitution to permit Armed Forces personnel to become members. Since then, there have been some moves in Congress to adopt a law prohibiting the organizing of members of the Armed Forces and the Department of Defense has issued a regulation prohibiting military commanders from engaging in collective bargaining with unions.

The 300,000-member AFGE is the largest union in the Federal civilian work force, representing a total of about 600,000 employees. However, it, and other Federal employee unions, have only an advisory role on pay and related benefits, which are set through presidential and legislative actions. □

Developments in Industrial Relations

Reported in *Monthly Labor Review*, October 1977.

Nabisco, union negotiate 2-year contract

More than 11,000 members of the Bakery and Confectionery Workers were covered by a new 2-year contract with Nabisco, Inc. The union estimated that the agreement, covering workers in 15 cities, would raise wage and benefit costs by $1.43 an hour over the term.

The contract, negotiated August 25, calls for a 50-cent-an-hour general wage increase on September 1 of 1977 and 1978 (with an additional 15 cents to maintenance and repair employees on those dates) and various job reclassification adjustments.

The company's contribution to the pension fund was increased to permit a $50-a-month raise in the basic normal benefit (age 65 after 30 years of service) on November 1, 1977, a $25-increase on September 1, 1978, and a $50-increase on March 1, 1979, bringing the benefit to $400 a month. Other contract provisions included a 15 cent-an-hour night shift premium (instead of 12 cents); 3 weeks of paid vacation after 5 years of service (was 7 years), 4 weeks after 15 years (was 17 years), and 5 weeks after 20 years (was 25 years); a $90-a-week sickness and accident benefit (up from $80); $600 maximum surgical coverage (up from $500), and $100 coverage of X-ray and laboratory fees (up from $50).

Union plumbers reduce pay scales

In an attempt to regain some residential work from nonunion plumbers, the United Association of Journeymen and Apprentices of the Plumbing and Pipe Fitting Industry and employer associations have adopted reduced pay scales for performing residential plumbing jobs. The 2-year agreement covered the State of Washington, except for the southeastern corner. According to a union official, nonunion contractors have performed about 90 percent of the residential work in recent years. The official said the new wage rate of $7.52 an hour plus $1.61 for benefits

would be "in the ballpark" of nonunion rates which he estimated at $7.50 to $12 an hour.

In the second year of the agreement, pay rates for plumbers on both residential and commercial jobs will be increased at least 50 cents an hour under an automatic wage escalator provision tied to the movement of the Bureau of Labor Statistics' Consumer Price Index. In the first year, the commercial rate is $16.23 an hour, including benefits.

AFL–CIO Executive Council lists priorities

At the midsummer meeting of the AFL–CIO Executive Council, in Washington, D.C., President George Meany said that the goal of the labor movement "can be summed up in perhaps one word—jobs. We don't want people unemployed. . . . The number one priority is jobs."

In the area of national affairs, the Executive Council took the following actions:

• Urged Congress and the Administration to develop policies and programs that would stimulate more rapid and sustained economic growth, and criticized President Carter's targets and timetables for reducing unemployment as "too timid."

• Affirmed its support for Mr. Carter's proposed revisions in Federal labor laws and urged prompt enactment by Congress.

• Asked for early congressional passage of the Administration's proposed requirement that a larger percentage of imported oil be shipped in tankers carrying the U.S. flag.

• Endorsed the Occupational Safety and Health Administration's "common sense" approach to enforcement of Federal job safety standards by concentrating on high risk industries and health hazards while reducing the required number of forms needed for recordkeeping and reporting.

• Assailed the Internal Revenue Service proposals to tax some of the fringe benefits of workers as income.

In other business, the Council elected three new members—Lloyd McBride, president of the Steelworkers; David J. Fitzmaurice, president of the Electrical Workers, and Kenneth T. Blaylock, president

"Developments in Industrial Relations" is prepared by Leon Bornstein and other members of the staff of the Division of Trends in Employee Compensation, Bureau of Labor Statistics, and is largely based on information from secondary sources.

of the American Federation of Government Employees. These members replaced I. W. Abel, former president of the Steelworkers, Paul Jennings, former president of the Electrical Workers, and the late Frances S. Filbey, former president of the Postal Workers.

ITU convention appoints merger panel

At the International Typographical Union's (ITU) 119th convention in Cincinnati, delegates authorized a committee to work out terms of a merger with the Newspaper Guild. (Earlier this year, the Newspaper Guild's convention had authorized a similar committee to negotiate with the ITU.) The convention also endorsed a merger proposal, approved earlier by the ITU executive council, for submission to the unaffiliated 3,000-member International Mailer's Union, and urged the council to continue talks "toward closer cooperation, liaison, and possible merger" with the Printing and Graphic Communications Union (PGCU) and the Paperworkers.

The merger actions followed calls for unity among publishing industry unions from ITU President A. Sandy Bevis, Guild President Charles A. Perlik, Jr., Mailers President Ralph H. Valero, and PGCU President Henry Segal. Both Bevis and Perlik pointed to the joint and cooperative efforts of the Guild and the ITU over the past 2 years in bargaining and organizing, which helped lay the groundwork for merging the two unions. They said that only a broad multitrade union would be able to properly represent industry employees because the introduction of new printing methods was blurring the jurisdictional lines of the various trades. A merger committee was directed to conclude the merger talks and present the results to the union's members in 1978.

United Farm Workers convene

In his opening address to the third constitutional convention of the United Farm Workers (UFW), in Fresno, Calif., President Cesar Chavez told 850 delegates that he would seek to build the union into a nationwide organization. Estimating that there are 200,000 unorganized farmworkers in California, Chavez said, "Our goal is to organize farmworkers in California as quickly as possible and then go elsewhere—to Florida and Texas, Arizona and New York, and other States where farmworkers want and need help." Chavez added that he believes the UFW should start "moving as quickly as possible to a major expansion in other States."

A theme of the convention was the union's concern over job losses resulting from the increasing mechanization of farming operations. Chavez contended that within 10 years mechanical harvesting equipment could lead to the elimination of 100,000 of the 250,000 farm jobs in California. The delegates approved a resolution calling for a moratorium on research in mechanization until there are assurances that the interests of farmworkers will be protected.

The delegates reelected Chavez as president. Other officers reelected included Secretary-Treasurer Gilbert Padilla, First Vice President Dolores Huerta, and Third Vice President Pete Velasco. Second Vice President Phillip Villacruz resigned and was succeeded by Elisco Medina.

Retail Clerks International president dies

James T. Housewright, president of the Retail Clerks International Union, and an AFL–CIO vice president, has died of cancer at age 55. AFL–CIO President George Meany and Secretary-Treasurer Lane Kirkland described Housewright as "an articulate, dedicated, hard-working trade unionist who earned respect for his union and the entire labor movement through his strong leadership and the high standards of conduct he set for himself." The union's executive board named William H. Wynn, 47, to succeed Housewright. Wynn, a vice president since 1972, was elected to a 5-year term as secretary-treasurer at the union's 1977 convention, succeeding Peter Hall who retired in 1976.

Housewright joined the union in 1947, became secretary-treasurer of a local in Indianapolis, moved through a series of increasingly responsible positions, and was first elected president of Retail Clerks International in 1968. Under his leadership the union almost doubled its membership to 700,000. At the time of death, Housewright was negotiating a merger with the 450,000-member Amalgamated Meat Cutters and Butcher Workmen of North America and the 118,000-member Retail, Wholesale and Department Store Union. The resulting union, with more than one million workers, would be one of the largest in the AFL–CIO. □

Developments in Industrial Relations

Reported in *Monthly Labor Review*, November 1977.

Steel companies announce layoffs

Citing declining sales attributed mainly to increasing competition from foreign producers, U.S. steel companies continue efforts to cut back employment and production.

In September, the Youngstown Sheet and Tube Co. announced the permanent closing of part of its operations in Youngstown, Ohio, at a cost of 5,000 jobs. Also, U.S. Steel Corp., the Nation's largest producer, announced plans to consolidate its operations in Youngstown, which may result in cuts in its 6,400-member work force.

In August, Bethlehem Steel Corp. announced the permanent closing of parts of its flood-damaged operations in Johnstown, Pa., and some of its operations in Lackawanna, N.Y., which would result in a combined loss of 7,300 jobs.

On September 28, a week after Youngstown Sheet and Tube announced its layoffs, the Department of Labor certified the affected workers as eligible for assistance under the Trade Act of 1974. Two days earlier, the department had announced that it was considering trade assistance benefits for the 3,500 Bethlehem Steel workers facing layoff at Lackawanna. The department said its investigation had shown that increased steel imports "contributed importantly" to the unemployment of workers at the Youngstown Sheet and Tube plants. Under the act, workers losing their jobs due to competition from imports are eligible for benefits—including State unemployment payments—equal to 70 percent of their prior average weekly wage, for up to 52 weeks. Benefits are not to exceed the national average weekly manufacturing wage. Laid-off workers are also eligible for up to 26 additional weeks of allowances to complete job retraining programs and for job testing, counseling, and placement, as well as relocation allowances.

The layoffs in the industry raised the possibility of a confrontation between the companies involved and the United Steelworkers over whether all of the laid-off workers will receive the benefits provided by the Employment Income Security Program established in the industry's April settlement (*Monthly Labor Review,* June 1977, pp. 62–63). The program, effective January 1, 1978, provides for special improvements in pensions, Supplemental Unemployment Benefits, insurance protection, and other benefits for employees with at least 20 years of service who are laid off or downgraded because of production cuts.

Also, in an effort to reduce labor costs, Bethlehem Steel has offered a bonus of 3 months' pay to any of "several thousand" salaried employees who are eligible to retire and do so before January 1, 1978. The bonus is in addition to the usual 13 weeks' pay that employees receive upon retirement at age 60 after at least 15 years of service, or after 30 years of service regardless of age.

At a White House meeting with management and union leaders in the steel industry, President Carter pledged to slow the flow of imported steel which was being "dumped" in the United States below production costs and hurting domestic steel production and employment. However, the President repeated his opposition to outright restrictions on steel imports explaining that the industry's problems will not all be solved if the "dumping" is halted and that it was an "erroneous thing to present to the American people that the simplistic, quick, painless solution to the steel industry's problems . . . is to erect trade barriers." The Council on Wage and Price Stability studied economic conditions in the steel industry and reported its findings to the President (*Monthly Labor Review* November 1977, p. 2).

Federal pay increase

Approximately 3.4 million Federal employees received a 7.05-percent salary increase in October as a result of President Carter's decision that this was the amount necessary for the 1.4 million white-collar employees under the General Schedule pay system to maintain pay comparability with equivalent jobs in

---

"Developments in Industrial Relations" is prepared by Leon Bornstein and other members of the staff of the Division of Trends in Employee Compensation, Bureau of Labor Statistics, and is largely based on information from secondary sources.

the private economy. The 2 million others—members of the Foreign Service, the medical and dental staff of the Veterans' Administration, and members of the Armed Forces—automatically received the same amount because their salary increases are linked to those of the General Schedule employees. (The increase for members of the Armed Forces was "reallocated" among base pay, quarters allowances, and subsistence payments.) The Federal Pay Comparability Act of 1970 provides for annual comparisons of General Schedule salaries with those in the private economy and specifies the role of the President, the Congress, and other officials and organizations involved in the pay-setting process.

The increase was the amount the President's "pay agent" (the Chairman of the Civil Service Commission, the Director of the Office of Management and Budget, and the Secretary of Labor) had recommended based on the Bureau of Labor Statistics' March 1977 survey of professional, administrative, technical, and clerical occupations in the private sector. The Federal Employees Pay Council, which consists of officials from various employee labor organizations, had recommended an 8.8-percent increase.

Some employees in the highest salary grades did not receive the increase or received only part of it because of a statute that limits their maximum salary to the current rate ($47,500 a year) for the lowest level of the Executive Schedule that applies to certain Presidential appointees.

Under the Executive Salary Cost-of-Living Adjustment Act of 1975, members of Congress, Executive Schedule personnel, and Federal judges would have automatically received a matching 7.05-percent salary increase in October, but earlier in 1977 the Congress had voted to forgo this year's increase. The vote came after the members of Congress, judges, and Executive Schedule employees had received salary increases based on the recommendations of a regular quadrennial Commission on Executive, Legislative, and Judicial Salaries.

UAW board rejects reaffiliation bid

The United Auto Workers' executive board unanimously voted not to call a special convention of the union's members to consider reaffiliation with the AFL-CIO. UAW President Douglas Fraser said that he and a majority of the board favored reaffiliation but informal polls of union members in October convinced them that a "clear majority" opposed reaffiliation, usually because they believed that it would result in a "loss of identity" for the UAW. Fraser said that rejoining the AFL-CIO would help unify

and strengthen the labor movement, "But we just don't have the votes in the union to win." He also indicated that the UAW would continue to cooperate with the AFL-CIO on legislative and other matters.

An AFL-CIO spokesman said the federation had no official comment on the action. The UAW left the federation in 1968 because UAW President Walter Reuther had differences with AFL-CIO President George Meany over policies regarding social issues.

UAW, American Motors negotiate new contract

American Motors Corp. and the United Auto Workers negotiated a 1-year contract tailored to improve the corporation's financial position by omitting or modifying some of the provisions of the union's current 3-year agreements with the other major automobile manufacturers. (See *Monthly Labor Review*, December 1976, p. 53.) (The previous American Motors agreement, which was for a 7-month term that expired September 15, also was intended to hold down labor costs, by providing for a wage increase but no improvements in benefits.) In the 9-month period ended June 30, American Motors continued to lose money on automobile manufacturing but reported net earnings of $5.3 million on the strength of profits from the manufacture of trucks, buses, and utility vehicles.

The September 16 contract, which covered 10,000 workers in Kenosha and Milwaukee, Wis., and Brampton, Ontario, Canada, provided for a 3-percent general wage increase and an additional 15 cents an hour for skilled employees. There also were some wage inequity adjustments at Milwaukee and Brampton and provision for settling inequity issues within 60 days at Kenosha.

Of the $1.62 wage escalator allowance, $1.09 was incorporated into base wage rates and the clause will continue to provide for quarterly adjustments of 1 cent an hour for each 0.3-point movement in the BLS Consumer Price Index (1967 = 100). This is the same formula as the other companies', except that their clauses call for the temporary diversion of some money from the allowance to finance a one-time lump-sum payment to retired employees.

The only benefit improvements in the American Motors accord were a $25-a-month increase, to $650, in the pension for 30-year employees, and a $1,500-a-year increase, to $4,500, in the amount a retiree can earn before suffering a reduction in pension.

The contract is scheduled to expire September 16, 1978, a year earlier than the contracts at the other companies.

AIW delegates favor merger with Molders

Delegates to the 21st Convention of the Allied Industrial Workers (AIW) approved continuing efforts to merge the 90,000-member union with the Molders and Allied Workers Union. Molders' President Carl W. Studenroth was enthusiastically received by the delegates when he declared that the two unions can do "constructive things together."

In his opening address, Allied Industrial Workers President Dominick D'Ambrosio said the AIW faced problems in growing "without merging with another union, . . . because there are few large industrial plants that have not been organized and the areas of work where we have traditionally organized are decreasing, not increasing." He added that the trend in the labor movement is toward merger, with the number of international unions affiliated with the AFL–CIO dropping from 130 to 106 in recent years.

In other business, the delegates voted to increase the international union's basic dues by $1.75 a month to $9, effective December 1, 1977.

GM charged with labor law violations

A National Labor Relations Board administrative law judge ruled that General Motors Corp. committed a series of labor law violations in opposing an Auto Workers' attempt to organize employees at a GM auto battery plant in Fitzgerald, Ga. The facility is one of eight plants GM has opened in the South in recent years, prompting UAW officials to accuse GM of devising a "Southern strategy" of locating new plants in the South where antiunion sentiments are sometimes strong, and then aggressively campaigning against unionization. The automaker denied such an intent but the union made it a priority issue in the 1976 national bargaining with GM and the resulting agreement included a clause which specified that GM would not engage in antiunion activities in future UAW organizing drives.

The administrative law judge, Walter H. Maloney, Jr., found that GM illegally fired two workers for union activities during the organizing drive and ordered them to be reinstated with back pay. He also held GM guilty of "coercively interrogating" workers about union activities, asking them to campaign against the union, and threatening to fire or demote workers if the union won the election.

The ruling can be appealed to the National Labor Relations Board and to the Federal courts. GM's initial response to the decision was that it had not yet decided whether to appeal.

The defeat at Fitzgerald in the summer of 1976 was the union's third straight unsuccessful attempt to organize a GM plant in the South. Earlier, the UAW had twice tried to organize an electrical parts plant in Clinton, Miss. (A Federal administrative law judge found GM guilty of violating Federal labor law during the Clinton organizing drive.) Later in 1976, after the "neutrality pledge" was negotiated, the UAW won the right to represent workers at a Monroe, La., parts facility.

New bargaining group formed for truckers

The trucking industry's united front in bargaining with the Teamsters and other unions suffered a blow when three top officers and seven other directors of its leading association, Trucking Employers, Inc. (TEI), resigned to form a new association. The three officers who assumed corresponding positions in the new association, Carrier Management, Inc. (CMI), were Chairman Arthur E. Imperatore, Vice Chairman Don McMorris, and Secretary-Treasurer Thomas Dwyer. CMI General Counsel Raymond Beagle, who also held the same position in TEI, said the major reason for forming the new association was to improve the collective bargaining process in the industry by providing "more direct attention" to the needs of individual firms during industry-union talks and to provide improved services to member companies.

Beagle declined to confirm reports of widespread dissatisfaction among employers over the cost of TEI settlements with the Teamsters and refused to speculate on whether CMI would accept the same terms as those negotiated by TEI in 1979 talks with the Teamsters or would attempt to set its own pattern. Although CMI is not soliciting new members, Beagle predicted that a large number of employers will join. Initial membership was 10 companies with 50,000 employees.

U.S. won't seek new Mine Workers' election

The Department of Labor announced it would not seek a court order for a rerun of the June election in which Arnold Miller retained the presidency of the United Mine Workers Union. Lee Roy Patterson, one of Miller's rivals, requested the investigation, charging that there had been voting irregularities. A Department of Labor official said the investigation did uncover some technical violations in the election, but nothing that would alter the outcome.

After the decision was announced in mid-October, Miller appealed to the union's 190,000 active members to unite behind his leadership. □

Developments in Industrial Relations

Reported in *Monthly Labor Review*, December 1977.

Aerospace workers settle, ending walkout

The first settlement in the 1977 round of bargaining in the aerospace industry came in mid-November when the Boeing Co. and the International Association of Machinists and Aerospace Workers negotiated a new contract covering 24,000 employees in the Puget Sound area, Portland, Oreg., Wichita, Kans., Cape Canaveral, Fla., and various missile sites. The agreement was ratified on November 17 and employees returned to work the next day, ending a strike that began on October 4.

The contract provided for an initial wage increase averaging 6.9 percent, which raised the rate for the lowest of the 11 pay grades to $6.41 an hour, and the rate for grade 11 to $9.10. Additional increases averaging 3 percent will be effective in the second and third years. The $1.04-an-hour cost-of-living wage escalator allowance was incorporated into base wage rates, and the escalator clause will continue to provide for quarterly pay adjustments of 1 cent for each 0.3-point movement in the BLS Consumer Price Index (1967 = 100).

Other terms included:

- three additional "one time" holidays in 1978, bringing the total of paid holidays to 41 during the contract term;

- a $14-a-month pension rate (up from $12) for each year of service accrued after January 1, 1978, a $12 rate (was $9) for service prior to January 1, 1975, and a change in the early retirement formula to permit retirees between the ages of 55 and 62 to receive 74 percent of the "normal" pension, instead of 56.51 percent;

- a company-financed major medical plan for early retirees that covers 80 percent of costs;

- a company-financed vision care plan that covers eye examinations, eyeglasses, frames, and contact lenses;

- an improved dental plan that no longer calls for deductibles; and

- an improved sickness and accident plan that increases benefit payments by $20 a week and now covers disability resulting from childbirth.

The union security clause—which has been a major bargaining issue in the industry in recent years —was revised to permit employees to withdraw from the union or cancel their agency shop obligation (to pay the equivalent of union dues), 10 days before the contract expires. Previously, they could take this action after 1 year of employment.

Boeing was still seeking a settlement covering 9,500 members of the Seattle Professional Engineering Employees Association. Elsewhere in the aerospace industry, bargaining continued between the Machinists union and Lockheed Corp., where 13,000 members continued a strike at various locations, while some members at the Missiles and Space Division in Sunnyvale, Calif., had returned to work after the local union accepted a company offer, despite an order by the international union that votes must be conducted on a companywide basis. Other negotiations involved the Machinists and Auto Workers unions and McDonnell Douglas Corp; the Auto Workers and Rockwell International Corp; and the Auto Workers and United Aircraft Corp.

Can companies settle

The United Steelworkers and four major can companies agreed to 40-month contracts providing for improvements in job and income security similar to those in the steel and aluminum accords. (See *Monthly Labor Review,* August 1977, pp. 52–53.) The October 31 settlement averted a strike scheduled for midnight of that day. The contracts covered 27,000 U.S. employees and 2,600 Canadian employees of American Can Co., National Can Corp., Continental Can Co., and Crown Cork and Seal Co. The union announced that it expects the same terms to be accepted in later settlements with smaller companies employing a total of 10,000 workers.

The initial wage increase of 23 cents an hour under the new settlement was retroactive to March 1, 1977,

"Developments in Industrial Relations" is prepared by Leon Bornstein and other members of the staff of the Division of Trends in Employee Compensation, Bureau of Labor Statistics, and is largely based on information from secondary sources.

as required in the August 1976 settlement that extended the then-current contract to October 31, 1977. In addition, the August 1976 settlement provided for a 17-to-23-cents-an-hour wage increase, also effective March 1, 1977.

Other wage terms of the October settlement include a 10-cent general increase on November 1, 1977, a 10-cent general increase plus a 0.4-cent increase in the increment between the 21 job grades on March 1, 1978, a 10-cent general increase on September 1, 1978, a 10-cent general increase plus a 0.5-cent increment increase on March 1, 1979, and a 34-cent general increase plus a 0.4-cent increment increase on March 1, 1980. The union said that certain job reclassifications raised labor costs 3.5 cents an hour, averaged over all employees.

The quarterly cost-of-living wage escalator adjustments will now be immediately added to each employee's base rate, rather than being carried in a separate "float" and incorporated annually. This eliminates the delay in increasing holiday pay and other benefits that are affected by changes in base rates. The escalator formula itself was not changed.

One improvement in job and income security was the adoption of a "two-tier" approach to Supplemental Unemployment Benefits under which laid-off workers with 10 years of service or more will be eligible for up to 260 weeks of benefits, with the first 104 weeks guaranteed and the balance dependent on the fund level. Those with less than 10 years of service will be eligible for 104 weeks of benefits, all dependent on the fund level. The companies agreed to raise the SUB fund to 80 percent of its maximum level by January 1, 1978, and to raise their contribution rate by 4 cents an hour (1 cent of this was a "contingent liability.")

Another improvement in income security was the establishment of retirement benefits for employees affected by plant closings or long-term layoffs, providing their age plus years of service total at least 65. Other pension changes included a $12.50- to $16.50-a-month benefit rate (varying according to preretirement pay rate) for each year of credited service, effective March 1, 1978, increasing to a $13.50 to $17.50 range a year later. The previous range was $11 to $15 a year.

Other benefit changes included an 11th annual paid holiday, beginning in 1979; a $10-increase in the $30-a-week vacation bonus (which is in addition to regular vacation pay); adoption of a vision care plan; and a $2,000-increase in employee life insurance coverage.

Mine safety act signed

In November, President Carter signed a bill intended to improve safety and health conditions for miners. Upon signing the Federal Mine Enforcement Safety and Health Act of 1977, the President said the legislation "goes far forward in protecting miners in the coal fields and previously uncovered miners." Stating that "in the past, enforcement of existing safety regulations has not been assured," he said the new law will permit "a more rapid enforcement of safety and health regulations when defects are found."

The legislation places both coal and hardrock miners under one safety and health law enforced by the Department of Labor. Previously, the Department of the Interior had primary responsibility for mine safety and health. The act, which replaces the 1966 Federal Metal and Nonmetallic Mine Safety Act, will be administered by a new Mine Safety and Health Administration under an assistant Secretary of Labor for Mine Safety and Health. Also created was an independent five-member Federal Mine Safety and Health Review Commission to carry out administrative and adjudicative functions.

The law provides for four inspections a year for underground mines and two inspections for others, permits a miners' representative to accompany Federal inspectors checking a mine, and prohibits reprisals against miners exercising their rights under the act.

Other provisions allow miners and their representatives to obtain an immediate inspection by giving written notice to the Secretary of Labor of any apparent violation or imminent danger; require minimum training periods for inexperienced miners; and provides for mine closures if the Secretary of Labor finds a pattern of violations affecting health or safety.

Secretary of Labor Ray Marshall said that "a major achievement of this legislation is to ensure that all miners will benefit equally from strong Federal legislation designed to safeguard them from occupational accidents and illnesses." He added that transferring mine safety jurisdiction from Interior to Labor "makes administrative sense" because his agency already enforces the Occupational Safety and Health Act of 1970.

OSHA proposes new policy on carcinogens

The Department of Labor proposed a new policy designed to improve the methods used by the Occuational Safety and Health Administration (OSHA) for identifying and protecting workers from cancer-causing substances. OSHA officials said they hoped the policy would eliminate much of the current administrative and legal delays under the current "substance-by-substance" approach to regulating carcinogens.

Under the new policy, OSHA will (1) define four categories of actual or suspected carcinogens and outline procedures for categorizing these substances, and (2) develop three standard approaches for regulating the substances (the approach used would depend on the category of the substance). OSHA officials said this means that when the agency acted on a substance the only issues to be resolved would be whether it had been correctly categorized and what the appropriate exposure limit should be.

Hearings on the proposal were scheduled for March 1978, and Labor Department officials said they hoped to put the policy into effect within a year.

Eula Bingham, Assistant Secretary of Labor for OSHA, said the new program is designed "to prevent cancer in the workplace." Noting that cancer claims close to 270,000 lives a year, she said many researchers attribute most of these cancer deaths to "environmental factors," such as chemicals, cigarette smoke, radiation, and asbestos.

United States leaves ILO

The United States officially withdrew from the International Labor Organization (ILO) on November 5. In 1975, the then Secretary of State, Henry A. Kissinger, had warned the United Nations agency that the United States had become dissatisfied with the ILO's policies and objectives and would withdraw unless changes were made within 2 years. (See *Monthly Labor Review,* December 1977, p. 2.)

New minimum wage

On November 1, President Carter signed a bill which will increase the minimum wage 45 percent by 1981. The current $2.30 an hour minimum rose to $2.65 on January 1, 1978, and will go to $2.90 on January 1, 1979, to $3.10 on January 1, 1980, and finally to $3.35 on the first day of 1981. (For additional details of the legislation, see pp. 9–11, this issue.)

Glass workers negotiate wage increase

Libby-Owens-Ford negotiated a 3-year contract with the United Glass and Ceramic Workers for 7,600 flat glass workers and the Glass Package Institute negotiated a 3-year contract with the American Flint Glass Workers for over 3,000 glass container workers.

The Libby-Owens-Ford agreement provided for immediate wage increases of 18 to 28 cents an hour, with additional increases ranging from 11 to 15 cents an hour in the second and third year of the contract. The automatic wage escalator formula was revised to provide for 1-cent-an-hour quarterly adjustments for each 0.3-point movement in the BLS Consumer Price Index (1967 = 100). Formerly, the formula was 1 cent for each 0.4-movement in the 1957–59 = 100

index. Seven cents will be diverted from the cost-of-living allowance to help meet the cost of various benefits and 2 cents will be diverted to raise the amount of the immediate increases at some of the plants.

Other provisions of the October settlement included a 15-cents-an-hour pay differential (was 9 cents) for the second shift and 25 cents (was 12 cents) for the third shift; a total of 31 paid holidays (was 27) during the contract term; $10,000 of company-paid life insurance for employees; $150 a week (was $100) sickness and accident benefits; extension of major medical and dental insurance to retirees (financed by the diversion from the cost-of-living pay allowance for active employees); and a $12.75-a-month pension rate (was $9) for each year of credited service.

Ending a month-long strike by 3,000 mold makers, the Glass Package Institute accord, also reached in October, provided for a 70-cent-an-hour wage increase retroactive to July 12, and for 40-cent increases in the second and third years. It also continued a cost-of-living wage escalator clause that provides for up to 20 cents an hour in pay increases in the second and third years, calculated at the rate of 1 cent for each 0.5-percent rise in the CPI. Other terms included increased employer contributions to the pension fund and improvements in insurance benefits.

The Glass Package Institute comprises 13 companies and is the successor to the Glass Container Manufacturers Institute which broke up in 1971 when several member companies decided to bargain independently with the Flint Glass Workers and the Glass Bottle Blowers Association which represents production workers.

Southern apparel workers win contract

The Ladies' Garment Workers' drive to organize nonunion apparel workers in the South gained strength in October, when the union negotiated an initial contract with Vanity Fair Mills for its Jackson, Ala., plant. Although the accord covered only 500 of the lingerie manufacturer's 8,000 employees, ILGWU President Sol C. Chaikin said it was a "foot in the door" and "just the beginning" of the union's organizing efforts among other Vanity Fair workers.

Under the 3-year agreement, incentive workers received 10-cent increases in their base rates effective immediately and on January 1, 1978, and 20-cent increases in base rates on January 1 of 1979 and 1980. Minimum hourly pay scales for craftworkers were increased by comparable amounts on the same dates. Other provisions included an eighth annual paid holiday, beginning in 1978; and improved health and welfare benefits, jury duty pay, and bereavement leave.

The workers voted for union representation in October 1976; however, bargaining did not start until after February 1977, when the National Labor Relations Board rejected the company's protest of the voting procedures.

In September, Vanity Fair announced a 10-cent-an-hour pay increase for hourly employees at its plants in Alabama and Northern Florida. The company said it granted the increase to offset an expected $7.40-a-month rise in employees' cost for hospital-surgical insurance and as a step toward adjusting to the January 1, 1978, rise in the Federal minimum wage.

Chicago Meat Cutters' accord ends ban

Termination of a ban in Chicago on the sale of fresh meats after 6 p.m., Sundays, and holidays was featured in an accord between five supermarket chains and the Meat Cutters. Under the new provision, fresh meat can be sold any time (except for 3 specified holidays) and employers can operate without a journeyman on duty during the added selling times. The agreement requires only voluntary service by union members during the new selling times, except on weekdays after 6 p.m., when journeymen may be assigned if there are no volunteers. Saturday night, Sunday, and holiday hours must be offered on a seniority basis within each classification starting with the head meat cutters, then the journeymen, then the wrappers, until the necessary volunteers are found. Pay rates are at time-and-a-half for all evenings and double-time for Sundays and holidays. In April, the union had eased the 25-year-old ban by permitting the sale of fresh meat as late as 9 p.m., as long as a meat cutter was present. At the time of the settlement, some members of the State Legislature were planning to introduce a bill that would prohibit all time-of-sale restrictions.

The 3-year contract, ratified October 27, covers approximately 5,000 union members. Head meat cutters and journeymen cutters will receive wage increases of $35 a week, retroactive to September 25; $15 on March 26, 1978; $12 on September 24, 1978; $10 on March 25, 1979; and $8 on September 23, 1979. Uncapped cost-of-living adjustments, based on an assumed 6.8-percent annual rise in the Consumer Price Index, are expected to yield $13.60 on September 24, 1978, and $16.40 on September 23, 1979. Under the prior contract, weekly scales were $344.63 for head meat cutters and $333.63 for meat cutters.

Changes in paid annual vacations, to be accomplished in stages, include 3 weeks after 5 years of service (was 8 years), 4 weeks after 12 years (was 15), and a maximum 6 weeks after 25 years (the former maximum was 5 weeks after 20 years).

Pension provisions call for past service to be "frozen" at a value of $11.42 a month for each year of credited service before October 1, 1977. The years of service after October 1, 1977, will be credited at $14.42, with the rate increasing to $17.42 on October 1, 1978, and to $20.42 on October 1, 1979. A prescription drug reimbursement plan became operative October 1, 1977, and optical and dental plans become operative on April 1, 1978. Sick leave was increased to 3 days a year, effective January 1, 1978, and to 4 days on January 1, 1979.

The five chains involved in the settlement were Jewel, A&P, Dominick's, Eagle Discount, and Kohl's. Negotiations were continuing with the Illinois Food Retailers Association, which consists of about 540 independent stores.

New York City bricklayers accept pay cuts

In hopes of increasing their employment opportunities, bricklayers in New York City agreed to a reduction in wages and fringe benefits beginning in 1978. The move will apply to all commercial construction performed by members of the New York City-Long Island District Council of the International Union of Bricklayers and Allied Craftsmen. The District Council has 5,000 members, but many are not working. Local 37, for example, has 1,000 members, but only 60 or 70 of them are currently employed.

The present agreement between the union and various contractors, which expires May 31, 1978, provides for a total hourly wage and benefit package of $16.27. Effective June 1, that amount will be reduced to $13.91 with the wage rate decreasing from the current $11.04 to $10. The new rates will remain in effect for 3 years.

California wineries settle

An uninterrupted flow of wine from the Central Valley of California was assured when members of the Distillery, Rectifying, Wine, and Allied Workers ratified a 3-year contract with the Winery Employers Association. The 4,000 workers had earlier authorized a strike, after rejecting two employer offers. Union officials said that the September accord covered 26 wineries that produce 90 percent of California's wine and that it was expected to set a pattern for settlements with independent producers.

Wages were increased by 8 percent, retroactive to August 1, 6 percent on August 1, 1978, and 5.5 percent on August 1, 1979. In addition, the wage escalator clause will continue to provide for quarterly adjustments of 1 cent an hour for each 0.5-point movement in the Bureau of Labor Statistics' Consumer Price Index (1967=100). The adjustments, which begin in the second contract year, will be limited to 12 cents each year, compared with the 10-cent limits for the corresponding years of the prior contract.

Other provisions included 3 weeks of paid vacation after 6 years of service (formerly 8 years), 4 weeks after 13 years (formerly 15 years), and introduction of a fifth week after 20 years; a $19-a-month increase in the employers' payment into the health and welfare benefits fund, bringing the payment to $87.50 (as in the prior contract, the payment is subject to increases of up to 25 percent in the second and third years if needed to maintain benefit levels); a $7.65-a-month increase in employers' financing of dental benefits; and provision for retirement at full benefit rates at age 62 after 25 years of service.

The contract, which expires July 31, 1980, covers operations from Bakersfield to the Oregon border.

Transport Workers convene

The Transport Workers union concluded its 15th convention, held in New York City, by re-electing its three top officers and adopting bargaining demands that included "substantial" economic gains for employees of the New York City Transit System; American, Pan American, and National airlines; and Consolidated Rail Corp. Matthew Guinan, Transport Workers president since 1966, was elected to a new 4-year term, as were Secretary-Treasurer Roosevelt Watts and Executive Vice President James F. Horst. The convention also named 13 vice presidents and 32 members of the executive board and changed the monthly dues payment to two times a member's hourly wage rate or $10.50 a month, whichever is greater.

White male steelworkers charge bias

A group of white male steelworkers filed suit against a program they claimed favors less qualified women and black employees. The group, American Male: Equality Now, was attempting to stop an affirmative action program established under consent agreement at Armco Steel Corp. in Ashland, Ky. The agreement was signed in 1974 by Armco, eight other major steel companies, and the United Steelworkers union after the U.S. Department of Justice and the Equal Employment Opportunity Commission filed suit alleging bias in the industry (*Monthly Labor Review,* June 1974, pp. 68–69).

A spokesman for the group said that hiring quotas and elimination of seniority in some departments as a result of the affirmative action program have resulted in bias against white males. He said that the suit, filed in the district court in Catlettsburg, Ky., asks for a permanent injunction to halt the affirmative action program and the new seniority system. The suit also asks compensation for wages and other benefits white male employees may have lost because of "reverse discrimination." The defendants are Armco Steel Corp., the Steelworkers union, and the union's Local 1865 at Ashland.

MAINE TO TEXAS DOCK STRIKE ENDS

Members of the International Longshoremen's Association on November 29 approved a settlement with associations of steamship companies, stevedoring companies, and terminal operators that ended a strike against containerized cargo in 34 ports from Maine to Texas. Dockworkers continued to load and unload conventional ships, except for brief periods in Baltimore and New Orleans when all shipping was struck. The ILA limited the strike to container cargo because the increasing use of the van-sized containers, along with other moves to increase the efficiency of cargo handling, had drastically cut work opportunities for its members.

Bargaining issues for the 50,000 ILA dockworkers are determined by a master agreement covering 35,000 of the workers negotiated by the Council of North Atlantic Shipping Associations and the ILA, which sets the basic contract pattern for the 15,000 South Atlantic and Gulf Coast workers, and by local agreements for each of the 34 ports. In the past, the CONASA-ILA master agreement has covered wages, hours, contract duration, container cargo, and contributions to pension and welfare funds. Items such as the level of Guaranteed Annual Income benefits and the supplementary items such as holidays and vacations have been negotiated locally. The 1977 negotiations were stalled for some time because the ILA wanted to include the Guaranteed Annual Income levels under the master contract. The parties finally agreed that GAI would continue to be a local issue and some of the local settlements provided for higher GAI levels.

Another problem was the funding of pension and welfare benefits. Increased containerization of cargo and a resulting decline in hours worked have caused financial difficulties in some ports because various benefits are financed by employer contributions for each hour worked. Under the new contract, the employers guaranteed that local pension and welfare funds will remain solvent.

The 3-year settlement also provided for wage increases of 80 cents an hour in each year, bringing the basic hourly rate to $10.40 on October 1, 1979. In some ports, the first 80 cents was retroactive to June 1, 1977. The employer contributions to the pension and welfare were increased by 54 and 47 cents an hour, respectively, over the term.

Benefits were also improved in some ports. For example, monthly pensions in the port of New York will rise to a range of $500 to $550, from a range of $450 to $500, for new retirees and pensions for current retirees were increased $25 per month. A paid holiday also was added for employees in this port, bringing the total to 15 a year.

HAWAIIAN SUGAR ACCORD REACHED

Ratification of a 15-month contract on November 21 ended a 20-day strike by 7,200 Hawaiian sugar workers. The pact provided members of the International Longshoremen's and Warehousemen's Union with a 30-cent-an-hour wage increase effective immediately and a 10 cent increase on July 1, 1978.

The 15 sugar companies also agreed to a 4-year pension agreement effective February 1, 1978, which will raise the benefit rate to $8.50 a month for each year of service to 35 years and $4.25 for each additional year. The prior formula was $7 a month for each year of service to 33½ years and $3 for each additional year.

The union won a key point when management agreed to procedures for discussing disputes resulting from the contracting out of work. All provisions were to be binding for the full contract term, even if a plantation ceases business.

CARTER SIGNS SOCIAL SECURITY TAX RISE

On December 20th President Carter signed into law a bill to secure the financing of the Social Security System. The fact sheet issued by the White House on the day of signing reads as follows:

FACT SHEET: H.R. 9346, SOCIAL SECURITY AMENDMENTS OF 1977

This bill strengthens the financing of the Social Security system by providing increases in tax rates and the wage base above those in current law, and by restricting the growth of future benefits.

Preliminary estimates indicate that under this bill the old-age, survivors and disability insurance system will shift from an annual deficit to a surplus position in fiscal year 1980. The cumulative surplus in the system for fiscal years 1978–1983 would be about $26 billion, compared to a cumulative deficit of about $62 billion under the present law.

In the long run, if current assumptions are correct, the system will shift back to a deficit position. However, the overall effect of this bill will decrease the long-range deficit from 8.20 percent of the taxable payroll to within 1.45 percent of the taxable payroll. If the system is within 2.0 percent of taxable payroll, the deficiency is not generally considered serious because the economic and demographic assumptions on which the financing is based cannot be reliably forecast for the full actuarial period—75 years ahead.

Tax Rates The bill increases the overall Social Security tax rate starting in 1979. The present overall tax rate is 5.85 percent of taxable earnings. In 1979 it will be 6.13 percent. Had the law not been changed, the tax would have reached its highest rate (7.45 percent of taxable earnings) in 2011. Under this bill, the highest tax rate will be 7.65 percent and it will be reached in 1990.

Wage Base The bill provides for increases in the wages on which Social Security taxes are paid. The present ceiling is $16,500. The bill will raise that level to $17,700 in 1978, and increase it gradually thereafter to a ceiling of $38,100 in 1985

Retirement Earnings The bill increases the annual amoun that persons over 65 may earn each year without forfeiting Social Security benefits. Under the old law, recipients began losing benefits when they earned more than $3,000 a year. The old law provided for some automatic increases in that ceiling: it was estimated that by 1982 the ceiling would have been $4,200. Under the bill the ceiling will be $6,000 in 1982 for persons between 65 and 72; the ceiling will be eliminated entirely for persons older than 70 [after 1982].

Wage Replacement Stabilization   The bill takes a series of steps to correct the unintended over-indexing effect of the automatic cost-of-living increase mechanisms adopted in 1972.

The bill has a number of other provisions, including one that will provide $187 million in fiscal relief for state and local welfare costs.

GOTBAUM CALLS FOR MEANY RESIGNATION

Victor Gotbaum, Director of AFSCME's largest affiliate (110,000 member public employee union in New York City), called upon George Meany to resign as president at the forthcoming convention of the AFL-CIO in Los Angeles. Gotbaum's statement called for an opening in the democracy of the labor federation.

Developments in Industrial Relations

Reported in *Monthly Labor Review*, March 1978.

Carter urges wage and price restraint

In an economic message to Congress following his January 19 State of the Union message, President Jimmy Carter announced a "voluntary" anti-inflation program, calling on labor and management to keep the wage and price increases in 1978 below the average of the last 2 years. (The Administration later clarified its position by indicating that 1978 labor contracts should provide for a lower average annual rate of increase in compensation than the parties' prior contract.)

The President, anticipating some resistance, stated "I recognize that not all wages and prices can be expected to decelerate at the same pace, . . . in exceptional cases, deceleration may not be possible at all."

Both labor and management criticized the plan. Although the President did not mention controls, AFL–CIO President George Meany said the plan could lead to guidelines, which he calls "a step down the road toward controls."

Jack Carlson, chief economist of the Chamber of Commerce, called the program "misdirected," saying that government, not business or labor, was the source of most current inflationary pressures.

At a press briefing, Council of Economic Advisers Chairman Charles L. Schultze said the anti-inflation program was based on the premise that wages and prices should rise by "significantly" smaller amounts in 1978 than in 1976 and 1977. But because one industry may have depressed profit margins while another industry has higher-than-usual material costs, there would be no effort under the plan to apply uniform standards or guidelines to the behavior of wages and prices.

The Administration announced that the Council on Wage and Price Stability and officials from the Department of Labor and the Council of Economic Advisers will meet informally with representatives of individual companies and groups of workers to discuss specific steps that could be taken toward deceleration.

"Developments in Industrial Relations" is prepared by Leon Bornstein and other members of the staff of the Division of Trends in Employee Compensation, Bureau of Labor Statistics, and is largely based on information from secondary sources.

Farm Workers end longstanding boycott

On January 31, Cesar Chavez, president of the United Farm Workers of America (UFW), announced that the union was calling off its longstanding boycott of table grapes, iceberg lettuce, and Gallo wines. Although Chavez did not cite a specific reason for ending the boycott, which industry officials contended had not been effective in the union's drive to organize the State's 250,000 farmworkers.

In his official statement, Chavez said that the UFW looked to 1978 with "cautious optimism" over the workings of California's Agricultural Labor Relations Act of 1975, which provided the machinery for farmworkers to select the union, if any, they want to represent them. Chavez said the law is "alive and functioning," and has yielded "some progress" in farm labor relations, adding that the UFW had signed agreements with over 100 growers since the law went into effect, while continuing bargaining with 100 more. He also said the union had won 43 representational elections, now awaiting certification by the Agricultural Labor Relations Board, which administers the act. However, the union chief left open the possibility the UFW might begin a boycott against the products of growers who "refuse to negotiate in good faith even after the workers have voted for the United Farm Workers in secret ballot elections."

Les Hubbard, a spokesman for the Western Growers Association which represents major vegetable producers in Southern California, viewed the UFW's move as a political "ploy to diminish interest in [possible] legislation to correct weaknesses and malfunctions of the law," adding that grower groups would push for changes in the law to modify what they view as provisions that are too pro-union. A spokesman for E&J Gallo winery in Modesto, Calif., said, "We have been unaware of any UFW boycott activity for several years, and the UFW has merely formalized their longstanding position."

NLRB requests injunction against Stevens

The National Labor Relations Board (NLRB) asked a Federal court to issue a nationwide injunction against J.P. Stevens & Co. to bar the textile producer from violating the law in its efforts to thwart union attempts to organize its employees. The injunction request was filed in U.S. District Court in New York City, where Stevens is headquartered. This is the first time a nationwide injunction has been sought against an employer since the National Labor Relations Act was passed 43 years ago. The injunction would apply to all of the firm's plants, except those in North and South Carolina, and two plants in Georgia, which were already covered by local injunctions.

NLRB counsel John S. Irving said the injunction petition was filed only after "extensive negotiations to settle or adjust" charges of unfair labor practices filed against the company by the Amalgamated Clothing and Textile Workers Union. The Board, in its petition, accused Stevens of engaging in a 15-year "massive, multi-State campaign to deny its employees their rights" under Federal law to be represented by unions. It added that the injunction was necessary to "restrain Stevens from a nationwide program of illegal activity and its contumacious conduct toward the National Labor Relations Act." The Board further asserted that Stevens "has committed unfair labor practices of unprecedented flagrancy and magnitude," saying that the textile firm had been found guilty 15 times of violating labor laws and had paid $1.3 million in fines and back wages since the early 1960's.

J.P. Stevens claimed that interim negotiations had resolved all issues except one, the demand by the NLRB that Stevens waive its right to defend itself against any future petition for an injunction. Stevens said any future petition would be a matter for the appropriate court to decide and that it could not waive that due-process right. The company said it was continuing its attempts to resolve the issue with the NLRB.

AFL-CIO forms unit for professionals

Organizing of professional employees was given higher priority by the AFL-CIO, as the federation announced the establishment of a Department for Professional Employees. Albert Shanker, president of the American Federation of Teachers, was elected president of the new department at its founding convention, held in December.

Shanker said that 20 years ago professional employees generally believed that their interests could not be served by unions, but this attitude had changed as more professionals became employed by large institutions and companies and the professionals realized that "isolationism" is self-defeating.

The new department replaces the former Council of AFL-CIO Unions for Professional Employees. The former director, Jack Golodner, retained the director's post in the new department.

Physicians' union established

Doctors employed by the Group Health Association, Inc., of Washington, D.C., have formed the Group Health Association Physicians Association, the first union of physicians in the Nation. The vote in the National Labor Relations Board election was 53 to 16 for union representation. Dr. Norman Lieberman, president of the newly formed union, said the primary objective in coming negotiations would be to improve patient care by examining issues such as staffing and the number of patients seen by each doctor. He said that the doctors were also seeking a cost-of-living increase in their salaries, which generally range from $50,000 to $55,000.

The Group Health Association, Inc., is a prepaid plan that provides medical care for 107,000 members.

Musicians' president dies

Hal C. Davis, president of the American Federation of Musicians since 1970, died of a heart attack at age 63. He had been a vice president of the 335,000-member union for 6 years, as well as president of a local in his native Pittsburgh before becoming president of the union. Davis also had been a member of the AFL–CIO Executive Council, a general vice president of the Federation's department for professional employees, and chairman of its arts entertainment, and media industries committee. Since 1974, he had served as president of the Inter-American Federation of Entertainment Workers, which represents all union activities in entertainment, recording, broadcasting, and movies in the Western Hemisphere. Victor Fuentealba, vice president of the Musicians' union, will succeed Davis as president.

Developments in Industrial Relations

Reported in *Monthly Labor Review*, April 1978.

Miners reject contract; Taft-Hartley invoked

On March 6, President Jimmy Carter moved to end the 92-day-old soft coal strike by invoking procedures of the Taft-Hartley Act. The action followed the miners' rejection of a February 24 accord with the Bituminous Coal Operators Association (BCOA). United Mine Workers (UMW) officials expressed doubt that a significant number of the 160,000-strikers would obey court orders to return to work.

The President said that "at least a million more Americans would be unemployed" if the walkout was permitted to continue for another month, and that, "My responsibility is to protect the health and safety of the American public, and I intend to do so." In an attempt to make the return to work more palatable for the miners, the President asked the coal operators to put into effect the $1-an-hour initial pay raise included in the rejected contract. The operators refused, but they did offer to pay any wage increase resulting from a new settlement retroactive to the date the miners obeyed the injunction and returned to work.

The first step in the Taft-Hartley procedures was completed on March 9 when a 3-member board of inquiry presented to the President its report on the dispute. President Carter then directed the Attorney General to seek Federal court orders requiring the miners and mine owners to resume production for 80 days, as provided in the Act. During the first 60 days, the parties are required to bargain. If an agreement is not reached, the miners will vote on management's final offer. If the final offer is rejected, then the miners are free to resume their strike.

In the March 6 announcement, President Carter declared that "collective bargaining . . . is at an impasse." This raised the possibility that some companies might break away from the BCOA and bargain independently with the UMW, because some Federal district courts have ruled that such with-drawals from multiemployer bargaining groups are permitted when an impasse occurs.

The miners' chief objections to the February 24 agreement focused on: (1) the provisions permitting employers to suspend or fine instigators of wildcat strikes; (2) the provision requiring employees and retirees to pay up to $700 a year per family toward hospital and medical costs; and (3) the provision under which employees who retired prior to 1976 would continue to receive smaller pensions than those who retired later. (In 1976, a UMW convention had decided that equalization of benefits for the earlier retirees should be a primary goal in 1977 negotiations.)

Bargaining setting. Federal and State government pressure on the BCOA and the UMW for a settlement had intensified after the union's 39-member bargaining council rejected a February 6 proposed accord. During this period, governors of Appalachian and Midwestern States, in particular, warned of severe electric power cutbacks and employee layoffs if the strike was not settled soon.

Throughout the talks, the union's bargaining ability was restricted by the bitter factionalism and the challenges to the leadership of Arnold Miller that have plagued the union in recent years. Apparently there were also some differences on bargaining strategy and goals among the 130 companies in the BCOA, because its negotiating team underwent several leadership changes during the talks.

The major development leading to the February 24 accord occurred February 20, when the union announced that it had reached agreement with the Pittsburgh & Midway Coal Mining Co., a subsidiary of Gulf Oil Corp. This was a shift from the UMW's usual practice of first settling with the BCOA, and then pressing independent companies (such as Pittsburgh & Midway) to accept the same terms. The Pittsburgh & Midway agreement—which later proved to be the pattern for the tentative BCOA agreement—was not acceptable to the BCOA at the time it was negotiated because it made concessions to the union on several of the items in the rejected February 6 BCOA-UMW accord.

"Developments in Industrial Relations" is prepared by Leon Bornstein and other members of the staff of the Division of Trends in Employee Compensation, Bureau of Labor Statistics, and is largely based on information from secondary sources.

These concessions included continuation of the automatic wage escalator clause; continuation of employer-paid royalties to the health and retirement fund for coal purchased from nonunion operators; exclusion of a requirement that new miners undergo a 30-day probationary period; exclusion of a provision for establishing "production incentives" to increase productivity; and exclusion of a requirement that miners be required to pay $20 to the health benefits fund for each of the first 10 days they participated in a wildcat strike, followed by possible termination of their health benefits.

After the BCOA rejected the Pittsburgh & Midway accord as a basis for settlement, Secretary of Labor Ray Marshall and Federal Mediation and Conciliation Service Director Wayne Horvitz increased their efforts to aid the parties in reaching agreement. The operators then agreed to some of the concessions included in the Pittsburgh & Midway agreement but this was still unacceptable to the union. Subsequently, the BCOA suggested that the dispute be settled through binding arbitration. This approach was also rejected by the UMW. The continuing impasse, coupled with the continuing decline of coal stockpiles, then led to the Government pressure on the BCOA that resulted in the February 24 agreement.

Provisions of rejected contract. The contract would have provided for a $1-an-hour wage increase effective on resumption of production and 40-cent increases in both the second and third years. After these increases, hourly rates would range from $8.32 to $9.96 for workers in deep mines, $9.34 to $10.73 for those in strip and auger mines, and $9.31 to $9.91 for employees of coal preparation plants and related facilities. (Deep miners are paid for 8 hours a shift while the others are paid for 7¼ hours.) In addition, all of the workers were to receive a $100 payment when they returned to work. The wage escalator clause (using the same formula as in the previous contract) provided for quarterly adjustments in the second and third contract years. The resulting allowance was not to exceed 30 cents in the second year and 60 cents in the third year.

The operators had agreed to guarantee health and retirement benefits for employees who retired prior to December 6, 1974, and to increase their contribution to the benefit funds for these retirees by about 70 percent. In a departure from past contracts, active employees, those who retired on or after December 6, 1974, and future retirees would have been covered by standard hospital-medical and life insurance plans maintained by their particular employer, rather than by the industry.

In another change from past contracts, all active and retired employees and their dependents would have been required to pay part of hospital and medical charges, up to specified annual family limits. The operators agreed to set up a special $5 million fund to reimburse employees and retirees for amounts they began paying out in July 1977, when fund trustees imposed deductibles to offset a decline in benefit fund income attributed to lost production resulting from wildcat strikes.

Pension payments were guaranteed by the operators. The benefit rate for employees retiring after the effective date of the contract was increased by $1 a month for each year of credited service, bringing it to $13.50 a month for each of the first 10 years of service, $14 for each of the next 10 years of service, $14.50 for each of the next 10 years, and $15 a month for each year in excess of 30. Retirement eligibility remained at age 55 after at least 10 years of service. Pensions would have been increased by $25 or $50 a month for those who had retired earlier.

Other provisions included a 20-cent-an-hour pay differential for second shift workers (formerly 15 cents) and 30 cents for the midnight shift (formerly 20 cents); liberalized clothing allowance; extension of the funeral leave to cover the death of stepchildren; accelerated and revised grievance procedures; and a specification that managment policies on absenteeism must be in accord with the contract.

The rejected contract included an article on "Work Force Stability and Industry Development" which permitted coal operators to fire or otherwise discipline employees who refuse to cross picket lines of wildcat strikers, as well as those instigating or participating in such strikes. Under the settlement, the employers could discipline "employees who picket or actively cause an unauthorized work stoppage" but "miners who honor picket lines will not be disciplined."

The article also provided for a Joint Union-Industry Development Committee to report within a year on labor relations and productivity. The Committee would study the grievance procedures, recommend ways "unauthorized" work stoppages may be eliminated, and visit coal mines to study "work practices, safety standards, and other factors which affect productivity." (Also, President Carter had announced that he would appoint an advisory commission "to find answers to the basic questions of health, safety, and productivity" in the coal mines.)

Steelworkers win Southern shipyard vote

The United Steelworkers won a National Labor Relations Board representation election at the Newport News Shipbuilding & Drydock Co. Union president Lloyd McBride described the win as "a significant advance for the cause of trade unionism in the South," referring to the continuing campaign by various international unions to organize Southern workers. The tally at the shipyard, which is the largest in the world and the largest private employer in Virginia, was 9,093 for the Steelworkers and 7,548 for the Peninsula Shipbuilders Association (PSA), a local independent union that had represented the yard's production and maintenance workers (currently numbering 19,000) since 1939. The PSA had rebuffed challenges by the Boilermakers union in 1956 and 1959 and by the Machinists union in 1972.

The company and the PSA announced that they would appeal the conduct of the election to the NLRB.

In another development, a NLRB administrative law judge ruled that Newport News Shipbuilding had refused to bargain in good faith with the Steelworkers on an initial contract for 1,200 designers and marine draftsmen the union has represented since it defeated the PSA in a 1976 NLRB election. Judge Robert Cohn held that the company had forced the employees to strike by insisting "to the point of impasse" that the union agree to remove some designers from the bargaining unit, which had been defined at the time of the representation election. Since the workers went on strike April 1, 1977, 300 have returned to work, about 40 replacements have been hired, and some work has been contracted out.

The company announced that it plans to appeal the decision to the NLRB. If the NLRB upholds Judge Cohn's decision, the company could be required to rehire all of the strikers, including those who were replaced and those whose jobs were terminated.

Sadlowski sues for election rerun

In mid-February, Edward Sadlowski and four other defeated insurgent candidates in the Steelworkers' union's 1977 election sued the Department of Labor in an effort to have the election rerun. Filed in Federal district court in Washington, D.C., the suit charged that the Department acted in an "arbitrary and capricious" manner when it decided there were insufficient grounds for seeking a rerun. The agency had ruled in November 1977 that although some violations did occur, they did not affect the election's outcome. Under Federal law, the Department of Labor is required to seek a court order for a new election only if it finds that violations "may have affected" the election's outcome.

The suit listed a series of alleged violations by the union on behalf of Lloyd McBride, Sadlowski's rival for the presidency. Included was the use of union resources to promote McBride's candidacy, efforts to require Steelworkers union staff representatives and department heads to contribute to McBride's campaign, and use of intimidating tactics against Sadlowski's supporters. Outgoing Steelworkers' President I.W. Abel had backed McBride in the election, held in February 1977 (*Monthly Labor Review,* April 1977, p. 84).

UAW wins 14-year representation fight

The United Auto Workers and the Monroe Auto Equipment Co. of Hartwell, Ga., agreed on an initial labor contract in February, ending a 14-year dispute over the union's right to represent the plant's 1,000 workers. The UAW had won a National Labor Relations Board election to represent the workers in 1966, but legal appeals by Monroe had been successful in averting unionization. The UAW's organizing campaign began in 1964 when Monroe was located in Michigan, and continued after the company moved to Georgia.

Between June 1964 and July 1977, the NLRB ordered three separate elections at Monroe, each of which was won by the UAW. The NLRB upheld the election results nine separate times and Monroe appealed the decisions five times to Federal courts. One of the appeals ended in the Supreme Court, which upheld the NLRB ruling.

The break in the stalemate came after Tenneco, Inc., acquired the shock absorber manufacturer in 1977 and started negotiating with the UAW. The resulting 3-year contract provided for 97 cents in wage increases over the term, and improved shift differentials and vacation, insurance, and pension provisions.

Goodrich proposes no-strike plan

The B.F. Goodrich Co. proposed a no-strike agreement with the United Rubber Workers union (URW) in return for a guarantee that Goodrich employees would receive the wage pattern set at other companies in the industry. Under the proposal, rubber industry economic issues and Goodrich noneconomic issues would be subject to arbitration, although local noneconomic issues would still be subject to strikes. Also, Goodrich would offer its wage employees a stock-purchase plan identical to one available to salaried employees and give each employee a $200-cash bonus upon ratification of a contract.

The proposed plan would extend the current Goodrich-URW agreement, scheduled to expire April 20, 1979, for 90 days. If the union strikes the other major tire companies—Goodyear Tire and Rubber Co., Firestone Tire and Rubber Co., and Uniroyal, Inc.—

Goodrich employees would continue to work, on the assumption that terms of an overall settlement would be reached before the Goodrich pact expired in July.

Peter Pestillo, vice president for employee relations at Goodrich, the No. 4 tiremaker, explained, " . . . we don't set the pattern . . ." and because neither Goodrich or URW members who work at the plant "control our economic destiny . . . our people . . . don't have anything to gain [by striking]." Goodrich has been struck every 3 years since 1967, including a 4-month strike in 1976. The URW did not comment on the plan, but, reportedly, both the company and the union have established committees to explore the proposal.

U.S. sues pension fund officials

In February, the Department of Labor sued Teamsters Union President Frank Fitzsimmons and 18 others affiliated with the union's $1.65 billion Central States Pension Fund to recover millions of dollars in losses due to alleged fund mismanagement. The civil suit, filed in Federal district court in Chicago, listed a series of questionable loan transactions which illustrated a "pattern of imprudent behavior" by the defendants, although the suit did not allege fraud on their part. Labor officials said that information concerning possible violations of the law has been turned over to the Department of Justice. Secretary of Labor Ray Marshall said the suit represents the second phase of a two-step initiative against the fund. Under the first phase, the Department secured the resignations of the fund's trustees and transferred control of the fund's assets to government-approved outsiders (*Monthly Labor Review,* May 1977, p. 57).

Under the Employee Retirement Income Security Act of 1974, a fund's trustees and officers can be held personally liable for losses. Francis X. Burkhardt, Assistant Secretary of Labor for Labor-Management Relations, indicated that the Department would consider efforts to settle the case out of court. Burkhardt said the fund's losses attributable to sloppy management would probably amount to millions of dollars, based on questionable loans totaling about $125 million.

The other Teamster officials named in the suit were Ray Williams, Robert Holmes, Donald Peters, Joseph W. Morgan, Frank H. Ranney, Walter W. Teague, Jackie Presser, and William Presser. Also named were the funds current executive director, Daniel Shannon, and Alvin Baron, a former asset manager. Former trustees who represented the trucking industry named were Albert D. Matheson, Thomas J. Duffey, John Spickerman, Herman A. Lueking, Jack A. Sheetz, William J. Kennedy, Bernard S. Goldfarb, and Andrew G. Massa.

Fitzsimmons reacted to the suit by saying it was "regrettable" that the Department of Labor singled out the Teamsters funds, but that he would "appear in court and fully answer the charges with every confidence that my performance as a trustee has met the highest of fiduciary standards."

Service workers' strike averted

A scheduled strike by 30,000 service employees against 2,500 commercial buildings in New York City was averted when the Realty Advisory Board on Labor Relations and the Service Employees union agreed to a 3-year contract.

The accord provided for a wage increase of $12 a week, retroactive to the January 1 termination date of the prior contract, a $12 increase on January 1, 1978, and $11 on January 1, 1979. The initial increase reportedly sets the average weekly wage at $237.

The employers' contributions to the pension fund was raised to $9 a week for all employees, from the $7.50 a week that applied for women represented by Local 32J, and the $8 a week for men represented by Local 32B. Prior to the settlement, the locals had merged. Trustees of the fund were authorized to commission an actuarial study to examine the feasibility of increasing the $250-a-month normal pension by $50, and granting a cost-of-living adjustment to current retirees.

Other benefit changes included a 12th annual paid holiday and employer reimbursement of up to 70 percent of an employee's unused allotment of 10 days sick leave per year (instead of 50 percent).

The employers' contribution to the health and welfare fund was expected to rise to about $660 a year for each employee, from $500, to cover the cost of benefit improvements, including a dental plan to be initiated in April 1979. ☐

Developments in Industrial Relations

Reported in *Monthly Labor Review*, May 1978.

Coal strike ends

On March 24, soft coal miners approved an agreement with the Bituminous Coal Operators Association (BCOA), ending one of the longest walkouts in the history of the industry. United Mine Workers (UMW) President Arnold Miller announced that with 87 percent of the union's locals reporting, the tally stood at 55,726 to 42,391. The strike began on December 6, when the previous contract expired.

Some miners returned to work on March 27, but several thousand stayed out, respecting scattered picket lines set up by some of the 10,000 mine construction workers. Later that day, negotiators for the construction workers and the Association of Bituminous Contractors reached an agreement patterned after the BCOA accord. The construction workers returned to work on April 5, after ratifying the agreement.

The March 14 agreement was the third accord reached by the BCOA and UMW. Earlier, the miners had rejected an agreement reached on February 24; the union's bargaining council had rejected a February 6 agreement. The rejection of the February 24 agreement led President Jimmy Carter to invoke the Taft–Hartley Act, which enabled the Government to obtain a temporary back-to-work order from Federal District Court Judge Aubrey Robinson. The order expired on March 18. Judge Robinson refused to extend it, explaining that the miners "are not paying attention to what I do anyhow." He ruled that the Government had failed to prove, as required by the act, that the impact of the strike had reached the point of threatening the health and safety of the Nation.

Below are some major differences between the new contract and the rejected February 24 agreement. (See *Monthly Labor Review*, April 1978, pp. 55–56, for other provisions of the February 24 agreement which were also included, without change, in the new contract.)

Health benefits. The annual maximum deductible per family was set at $150 for physicians' charges and $50 for prescription drugs for employees, and at $100 and $50, respectively, for retirees. There is no deductible for hospital charges. Under the February 24 agreement, the combined deductibles for the three types of coverage would have totaled as much as $700 a year for active employees and $450 for retirees. Under the 1974 contract, there were no deductibles.

Retirement benefits. The uniform $275-a-month pension to employees who retired prior to 1976 will be effective immediately, rather than in stages as called for by the rejected contract. Under the 1974 contract, these retirees received $225 a month if they were receiving Federal black lung benefits and $250 if they were not.

Industry development provisions. The provisions, as stated in the 1974 contract, were not changed. The February 24 agreement would have added a clause permitting employers to discharge or otherwise discipline employees leading unauthorized strikes. Arbitrators would have decided if disciplinary action was warranted but would not have been permitted to modify the penalties in cases where discipline was warranted.

Wages. The new contract provided for a $1-an-hour immediate wage increase and 70-cent increases in March of 1979 and 1980. The 70-cent increase each include a 30-cent "cost-of-living" increase that is not contingent on the movement of the Bureau of Labor Statistics' Consumer Price Index. The February accord had called for the same $1 immediate increase but the March 1979 and 1980 increases each would have consisted of a 40-cent set amount plus a wage escalator adjustment of up to 30 cents, depending on the movement of the CPI. Under the 1974 contract, employees received a total of 80 cents an hour in wage escalator adjustments, plus 10-, 4-, and 3-percent annual wage increases.

Vacations. Four paid "floating" days per year, to be selected by the individual employees, are to be granted. The February 24 agreement had called for

"Developments in Industrial Relations" is prepared by Leon Bornstein and other members of the staff of the Division of Trends in Employee Compensation, Bureau of Labor Statistics, and is largely based on information from secondary sources.

3 paid floating days, to be taken in conjunction with existing paid holidays to provide unbroken time off from Christmas through New Year's Day. Under the 1974 contract, employees received 2 floating holidays, of their choice. Both the February 24 and March 14 settlements revised the separate "graduated" vacation plan to provide for 1 day of paid time off after 6 years of service, 2 days after 7 years, up to a maximum of 13 days after 18 years of service. The 1974 contract had provided for 1 day after 7 years, 2 days after 8 years, up to a maximum of 13 days after 19 years.

Incentive production plans. Employers will be allowed to establish plans compensating employees according to output, subject to majority approval by members of the particular local union. The February 24 agreement and the 1974 agreements did not provide for such plans.

Despite the settlement, there was no easing of the bitter quarreling and factionalism within the United Mine Workers, as opponents of Miller vowed to continue their efforts to recall him from office and Miller said he was just as determined to retain the presidency. There also was speculation that the extreme difficulty of the BCOA and the UMW in reaching an agreement might cause some operators to withdraw from the BCOA and conduct future bargaining with the union on a regional or individual company basis.

Black lung program made permanent

On March 1, President Carter signed the Black Lung Benefits Reform Act, the result of a 4-year congressional effort to improve the black lung program. The legislation made the black lung benefits program permanent, by eliminating the scheduled 1981 termination date. The President said that the improved black lung compensation program will help "ensure that more coal miners and their families will receive benefits they deserve."

Secretary of Labor Ray Marshall called the amendment of the 1969 Federal Mine Health and Safety Act a "milestone in social legislation." The new legislation removes certain eligibility restrictions that have prevented many coal miners suffering from black lung disease from obtaining benefits. Many of the 240,000 persons whose claims for benefits had been denied will now get automatic reviews to determine if they qualify under the new provisions.

In addition to the provision for review of rejected claims, other provisions of the new law included:

- Redefining pneumoconiosis (black-lung disease) to include all respiratory and pulmonary impairment resulting from employment in or around coal mines. (Previously, it was defined as a chronic dust disease of the lungs resulting from coal mine employment.)
- Redefining the word "miner" to include (a) all individuals who work or have worked in or around a coal mine or in a facility engaged in the preparation or extraction of coal, (b) any individual who has worked in coal mine construction or transportation in or around a coal mine and is or was exposed to coal dust, and (c) self-employed miners. The previous definition limited eligibility to those employed in a coal mine (surface or underground) who performed duties in the preparation or extraction of coal.
- Accepting chest X-ray indications of physical impairment as valid evidence without further review.
- Removing certain time limits on miners, retirees, or survivors' applications for benefits.

The act also establishes a Black Lung Disability Trust Fund, supported by excise taxes on coal companies, to finance claims for eligible miners last employed prior to January 1, 1970, and for administrative expenses. If the miners' last employment was on January 1, 1970, or later, individual mine operators will be responsible for the monthly benefit payments to disabled miners or their survivors and for the related medical expenses. If the operator is out of business or cannot be identified, benefits for these miners will be paid from the new trust fund.

OSHA limits exposure to benzene

The Department of Labor's Occupational Safety and Health Administration (OSHA) issued a permanent standard limiting workers' exposure to benzene, a chemical that has been linked to leukemia. The new standard restricts workers' exposure to one part of benzene per million parts of air over an 8-hour period with a ceiling of 5 parts per million during a 15-minute period, with eye or repeated skin contact prohibited entirely. The new standard is a 90-percent reduction from OSHA's prior permanent standard for an 8-hour period. The agency estimated that the new rules would affect about 600,000 workers at 150,000 worksites and could cost employers about $450 million the first year.

The Nation produces 11 billion pounds of benzene each year. About 86 percent of the output is used in the production of organic chemicals which are used as intermediates to manufacture plastics, resins, disinfectants, and pharmaceuticals. The remainder is used primarily in the manufacture of detergents, pesticides, solvents, and paint removers.

In response to the new regulations, the American Petroleum Institute asserted that "OSHA has ignored the fact that there is no evidence that the former exposure standard for benzene is unsafe. Exposure to large amounts of benzene can be harmful, but the new standard is far too rigid and unnecessary." The Institute, joined by the National Petroleum Refiners Association, filed a petition in the Fifth Circuit Court of Appeals in New Orleans for a review of the new permanent standard. Later, the parties asked the same court for a temporary injunction to delay enforcement of the new benzene standard until it is reviewed. A temporary injunction was granted until the week of April 17, when a three-judge court of appeals was to decide whether to extend the injunction, pending a review of the new standard.

Porters and Railway Clerks merge

The Sleeping Car Porters Union, founded in 1925 by civil rights leader A. Philip Randolph, is now a division of the Brotherhood of Railway, Airline and Steamship Clerks (BRASC). In February, a special convention of the Sleeping Car Porters had unanimously approved the action. (The Railway Clerks' executive board had previously approved the merger.)

During the height of American railroad passenger service in the early 1940's, the Porters' membership peaked at 12,000, but subsequent changes in travel patterns resulted in a severe decline in membership to about 1,000. The Clerks' membership was 250,000 prior to the merger.

Under the merger agreement, Porters' President C. L. Dellums, who had been in poor health, retired. His position was abolished, but for 3 years he will serve as a consultant to BRASC. Leroy Shackelford, who had been vice president of the Porters, was designated general chairman of the new division.

AFL–CIO Executive Council meets

The AFL–CIO's Executive Council adopted a comprehensive statement on the state of the national economy at its midwinter meeting, held in Bal Harbour, Fla. The council declared that an economic stimulus program of $29.55 billion was needed in fiscal year 1979 to increase the growth rate of the economy and to create 2 million more jobs. While noting an improvement in job creation in 1977, the council said the existing programs must be expanded further "to prevent a stagnating unemployment rate." The council warned that the rising flood of imports was creating a major crisis and called for a wide range of congressional actions to stem the continuing loss of jobs.

The council also called on the Senate to pass "without any crippling amendments" a pending bill that would make a number of changes in existing labor laws. A similar bill had been approved by the House of Representatives in 1977. Provisions of the bill would (1) end "unnecessary delays in resolving unfair labor practice cases;" (2) provide adequate compensation for workers harmed by illegal employer actions; (3) assure "timely elections" when workers petition for union representation; and (4) deny Federal contracts to firms that "repeatedly and willfully violate employee rights."

In other actions, the council approved some name changes. The Doll & Toy Workers will now be known as the International Union of Allied Novelty Production Workers, and the Distillery Workers will be the Distillery, Wine & Allied Workers International Union. The council also elected Fred J. Kroll, president of the Brotherhood of Railway, Airline and Steamship Clerks to fill the vacancy on the council caused by the death of Musicians' Union President Hal C. Davis. Kroll, 42, has been president of BRASC since November 1976.

EEOC announces new discrimination criteria

The Equal Employment Opportunity Commission (EEOC) in mid-March announced six standards it will use in determining whether to take action against employers for race or sex discrimination. EEOC Chairperson Eleanor Holmes Norton said that while the standards were primarily intended for internal guidance of the Federal agency, they also are useful to employers in determining if their employment practices conflict with the position of the agency. According to the standards, enforcement actions will be aimed at employers who (1) maintain hiring policies that result in "low utilization of available minorities and women;" (2) employ members of minority groups and women at "substantially lower" pay rates than other employers who use such workers for comparable work; (3) pay minorities and women less than their other employees in comparable jobs; (4) maintain recruitment, hiring, job assignment, and other work policies that have "an adverse impact on minorities and women and are not justified by business necessity;" (5) maintain discriminatory practices that are likely to be emulated by other employers because of the company's size, influence in the community, or competitive position in the industry; and (6) have an opportunity to hire and promote more minorities and women because of expansion or high turnover rates but neglect such workers in filling the positions. □

Developments in Industrial Relations

Reported in *Monthly Labor Review*, June 1978.

Mandatory retirement age raised to 70

President Jimmy Carter signed legislation that raises the age at which private employers and State and local governments can require employees to retire. Effective January 1, 1979 (July 1, 1982, for university professors with tenure), employees can be required to retire at age 70, instead of age 65. For workers covered by collective bargaining agreements with compulsory retirement provisions, the law becomes effective at the expiration of the current agreement, or July 1, 1980, whichever comes first. The legislation also eliminates the age 70 limit that generally applied to Federal workers, effective October 1, 1978.

The measure amends the Age Discrimination in Employment Act of 1967. President Carter hailed the revision as a "historic event" that would provide "fairness and equity in protecting older workers from discrimination in employment," adding that "this will be a good example for the rest of the Nation to emulate." He called on State and local governments to follow the lead of the Federal Government.

The legislation does not alter the age requirements for social security benefits and does not apply to executives and "high policymaking employees" who are eligible for annual pension of $27,000 or more—they could still be required to retire at age 65. Certain Federal employees will also continue to be subject to retirement at earlier ages (for example, law enforcement personnel, firefighters, air traffic controllers, foreign service officers, and certain Central Intelligence Agency personnel). The amendments, and the 1967 Act, do not cover companies with 20 or fewer employees.

Opponents of the legislation asserted that it would disrupt employment practices, create more joblessness, keep minorities and women from jobs, and block the upward mobility of young workers. Also, university administrators expressed concern that older professors with tenure would remain at their posts, thereby reducing opportunities for younger professors. In a report on the amendments, the Department of Labor expressed "some concerns" over the impact of the measure on employment opportunities for young workers, women, and members of minority groups but concluded that the effect on the job market would not be substantial, estimating that only about 200,000 employees would work beyond age 65 in the first year after passage of the legislation. The Department also said that forced retirement of older workers was not the solution to problems of youth joblessness, because "this would be robbing one generation to pay another."

Laid-off workers win 'rule-of-65' pensions

An arbitration panel ruled that certain Steelworkers, laid off because of plant closings by Bethlehem Steel Corp. and Youngstown Sheet & Tube Co., were eligible for the "rule-of-65" pensions established in the 1977 settlements in the steel industry. Under the pension provision, laid-off workers whose age plus years of service equals 65 were eligible for a lifetime benefit plus a $300 monthly supplement until age 62.

The companies contended that because the new provision was not effective until January 1, 1978, employees laid off prior to that time were not eligible for the benefit. However, the arbitration panel ruled that "consistent past practice" in negotiating pension agreements in the steel industry had extended eligibility to workers who were laid off as long as 2 years before the effective date of a new benefit. The companies' liability, which had earlier been estimated at $36 million for Bethlehem Steel and $25 million for Youngstown Sheet & Tube, would be reduced if they could offer the laid-off employees "suitable long-term employment." Discussions were underway between the companies and the union on the meaning of this contract phrase, with the union contending that laid-off workers should not be forced to move from their current residences or to commute "unreasonable" distances to new jobs.

Law professor Benjamin Aaron headed the arbitration panel. Also serving were Sylvester Garrett,

"Developments in Industrial Relations" is prepared by Leon Bornstein and other members of the staff of the Division of Trends in Employee Compensation, Bureau of Labor Statistics, and is largely based on information from secondary sources.

the permanent arbitrator between the Steelworkers union and United States Steel Corp., and Ralph T. Seward, the permanent arbitrator for the union and Bethlehem Steel.

Postal Service accused of labor violations

The Department of Labor filed suit against the U.S. Postal Service, charging violation of overtime pay and other provisions of the Fair Labor Standards Act. The action came 3 days after the Postal Service had settled 11 suits filed by 80,000 former and current postal employees that also alleged the Postal Service had violated the Act. The Department of Labor's suit was filed on behalf of employees who were not plaintiffs in the 11 suits. Estimates varied widely on how many employees might actually be affected by the suit. The Postal Service has 600,000 employees.

The major postal unions had urged postal workers to join in the 11 suits and aided in preparing the cases, but the unions were not among the plaintiffs. Union officials estimated payments to individual postal workers would average about $650 and range as high as $1,300, depending on the number of unpaid overtime hours the individual had worked since May 1, 1974, the date when the Act was extended to cover Federal employees.

One of the key issues in all of the suits was the Postal Service's refusal to pay for overtime that appeared on employee time cards but was not specifically authorized. The suits charged that this was a violation of the Act's requirement that employers pay for overtime work they "suffer or permit."

Other allegations in the Department of Labor's suit (which also were similar to those in the settled suits) were that the Postal Service had failed to compensate employees for time they had spent learning delivery routes and for travel time in connection with training, and had failed to pay cost-of-living allowances to workers in certain areas, such as Alaska and Hawaii.

Asbestos-stricken workers sue U.S.

Nineteen present and former employees of the Newport News Shipbuilding & Drydock Co. filed suit against two Federal agencies for allegedly failing to warn or protect them from the dangers of working with asbestos. Each of the plaintiffs was seeking $1 million in damages, contending that each had contracted an asbestos-related disease because the Department of the Navy and the General Services Administration had not properly enforced safety regulations at the Virginia yard, which builds and overhauls ships for the Navy. The plaintiffs also filed suit against 15 asbestos manufacturers, accusing

them of not warning workers of the dangers of using asbestos.

In February, the Government agreed to pay an out-of-court settlement of $5.75 million to 445 former employees of a PPG Industries, Inc., asbestos plant in Tyler, Tex. These plaintiffs also had contended that they had been harmed because the Government failed to ensure safe working conditions. Under the settlement, the plaintiffs also received $8 million from PPG Industries, $5.2 million from three firms that supplied asbestos to the plant, and $1 million from UNARCO, the previous owner of the plant.

President proposes Federal pay 'cap'

President Jimmy Carter announced that he plans to hold the Federal white-collar salary increase to "about 5.5 percent this year, thereby setting the example for labor and industry to moderate wage and price increases." Earlier the President had appealed to labor and industry to hold increases to a level below the average rate of the last several years (*Monthly Labor Review*, March 1978, p. 53).

Federal white-collar employees had expected a 1978 pay raise of at least 6 percent, based on the projected amount the President had included in his January budget message to Congress. Under the Federal Pay Comparability Act of 1970, Government employees are supposed to receive salary increases each October to maintain comparability with occupations covered by surveys of similar private occupations; however, the President can delay or cut the increase because of a "national emergency or economic conditions affecting the general welfare." Members of the Armed Forces receive comparable increases because their salary rates are linked to those for Federal white-collar employees. (In 1977, the white-collar employees received a 7.05-percent raise.)

The President also called on governors and mayors to similarly hold down pay raises for their employees.

AFL-CIO President George Meany said that labor would cooperate in the anti-inflation fight, but that "under no circumstances will we take part in a process that sets up Government interference with collective bargaining." He also criticized the President's decision to impose the 5.5-percent cap on Federal salary increases, contending that it appeared to violate his promise not to impose wage and price controls. Kenneth T. Blaylock, president of the 300,000-member American Federation of Government Employees, said Mr. Carter's program "is really no program at all; it is a simple reconditioning of the ineffective discredited techniques used by Presidents Nixon and Ford."

Construction unions, contractors sign agreement

Construction unions and four contractors signed a national agreement designed to reduce labor-management strife at nuclear plant sites. President Carter described the agreement as a "superb example of how business and labor can cooperate to the mutual advantage of both sides of the bargaining table and at the same time be of great benefit to our country." The President also said the agreement would mean a "significant saving" in the cost of building a nuclear plant, lower utility bills, better profits for contractors, and better working conditions and pay for union workers.

Robert Georgine, president of the AFL-CIO Building and Construction Trades Department, estimated that the pact could cut as much as a year from the current 3- to 5-year construction time for building a nuclear generator. He added, however, that environmental and regulatory delays add another 5 to 7 years to the process, and the agreement does not address those delays.

In addition to a clause barring strikes or lockouts, the contract provides for greater flexibility in job assignments and calls for a committee of international union and contractor representatives to establish pay and benefits, under certain conditions.

All of the AFL-CIO's Building and Construction Trades Department unions were included in the agreement, except for the Sheet Metal Workers. The contractors were Bechtel Power Corp.; Stone & Webster Engineering Corp., a subsidiary of Stone & Webster, Inc.; United Engineers & Constructors, Inc., a subsidiary of Raytheon Co.; and Ebasco Services, Inc., a subsidiary of Enserch Corp.

Kansas City Construction Committee formed

In mid-April, the Department of Labor announced that 25 representatives of labor, industry, and government in the Kansas City area will work on "cooperative solutions" to construction industry problems. The plan, part of the Administration's efforts to bring employers and unions together to work out solutions to common problems, is expected to set a pattern for other areas.

The program will be operated by the Department of Labor's Labor-Management Services Administration, with voluntary Committee members serving without compensation. Under Secretary of Labor Robert J. Brown urged the new Kansas City Construction Committee to seek ways to solve persistent underlying problems of the industry so that employees, employers, and the general public will benefit. He said the Committee could work towards a number of goals, such as eliminating the awarding of large numbers of public construction contracts at the start and end of each fiscal year (which causes uneven labor market demands); encouraging government agencies to do construction and maintenance work during the winter, when possible; and finding ways to improve training. □

Developments in Industrial Relations

Reported in *Monthly Labor Review*, July 1978.

Aerospace workers win '55 and 30' retirement

A 3-year contract between the McDonnell Douglas Corp. and the Auto Workers featured a first for a major aerospace company. The mid-April agreement provides for retirement at age 55 after 30 years of service, without actuarial reduction. (The provision is based on those gained as early as 1973 in the automobile and farm and construction equipment industries where retirement at unreduced rates is permitted after 30 years of service, regardless of age.)

Under the provision, retirees will receive a lifetime pension of $12 a month for each year of credited service plus a supplemental amount to bring the total benefit to $600 a month. The supplemental portion of the $600 will terminate at age 62, when the retirees become eligible for social security benefits. Under the previous contract, a 30-year employee electing early retirement at age 55 received only a $176-a-month lifetime benefit because the normal benefit calculation rates of $10 a month for each year of credited service ($9 a month prior to 1975) were actuarially reduced.

The settlement ended an 11-week walkout by 8,000 employees in Long Beach and Compton, Calif.; Tulsa, Okla.; and Melbourne, Ark. The contract provides for 3-percent wage increases in each year, compared with increases of 6.9, 3, and 3 percent the Machinists union had gained in its settlement with the Boeing Co., the first in the current bargaining round in the aerospace industry. (See *Monthly Labor Review,* February 1978, p. 30.) Auto Workers officials indicated that they had accepted the smaller increases in return for introduction of the new type of pensions.

The wage escalator formula at McDonnell Douglas will continue at 1 cent for each 0.3-point movement in the Bureau of Labor Statistics' Consumer Price Index (1967 = 100), but the first 2 cents of each quarterly adjustment will be retained by the company to help offset the cost of the settlement. (This also differed from Boeing, where there was no provision for diversion from adjustments.) There also were a number of improvements in supplementary benefits.

Meanwhile, talks were continuing between McDonnell Douglas and the Machinists for 6,000 workers at five sites in California. Their contract also had expired in October, but the employees did not strike. McDonnell Douglas also was negotiating with the Machinists for 11,000 workers in St. Louis, where the contract expired on May 7.

Cement companies settle

General Portland, Inc., and Martin Marietta Corp. signed similar contracts with the Cement, Lime and Gypsum Workers. The 3-year agreements, reached in late April, covered 2,200 employees and are expected to set a pattern for subsequent settlements for 15,000 employees of other cement companies. The accords provide for a 60-cent-an-hour wage increase on May 1, 1978, and 20 cents on November 1, 1978, plus an increase in the wage increment between job grades. In addition, employees will receive automatic wage escalator increases of at least 50 cents an hour on May 1, 1979 and 1980. Other terms included a $1-increase in the pension rate in each contract year (bringing it to $17.50 a month for each year of credited service for employees retiring in 1980), a 12th paid holiday, and improved insurance benefits.

NLRB, J. P. Stevens reach accord

J. P. Stevens & Co. and the National Labor Relations Board announced an agreement under which the NLRB withdrew its request for a nationwide court injunction to end alleged antiunion activities by the company (*Monthly Labor Review,* March 1978, pp. 53–54). In return for termination of the action, the company agreed not to engage in tactics that would have been barred by the injunction and also agreed to rehire 11 workers the NLRB said were fired for engaging in union organizing activities.

J. P. Stevens also will withdraw reprimands and

"Developments in Industrial Relations" is prepared by Leon Bornstein and other members of the staff of the Division of Trends in Employee Compensation, Bureau of Labor Statistics, and is largely based on information from secondary sources.

disciplinary actions against employees for union activities, and will restore those who were demoted to their original grade. Further, the company will notify employees that it will not:

- Discriminate against them because they may have filed charges or testified against the company under the National Labor Relations Act.
- Threaten them with discharge, plant closure, harassment, or other reprisals because of union activities.
- Suggest to them that it will never recognize, bargain, or sign a contract with the Amalgamated Clothing and Textile Workers Union (ACTWU);
- Grant or promise benefits, or deny benefits, to discourage their union activities.
- Restrict, in any unlawful manner, the distribution of union literature or the solicitation of union authorization cards.
- Restrain or coerce them in the exercise of their right to self-organization, to join or assist the ACTWU, or to bargain collectively through representatives of their own choosing.

The settlement also provided that "upon reasonable cause to believe that the terms of this stipulation have been breached" or that a new violation of the National Labor Relations Act has occurred, the NLRB may refile its injunction petition.

An official of J. P. Stevens said that the company was "pleased" that an agreement had been signed, adding that the "terms of the settlement agreement are identical to the terms the company had offered before the suit was filed in the U.S. District Court in New York." (The NLRB was to hold hearings to determine the validity of the allegations in the lawsuit.) The official also noted that in signing the agreement the company had not admitted to unfair labor practices, explaining that "we believe the settlement of this suit was brought about by the NLRB's recognition of the voluntary efforts of Stevens to fully comply with all valid Federal labor laws." The firm invited the Clothing and Textile Workers union to conduct secret ballot elections to prove "representation claims."

The agreement applies to all company plants, except those in North Carolina and South Carolina and one in Dublin, Ga., which are covered by enjoining orders of other Federal courts.

California grape, citrus workers settle

Some 2,000 members of the United Farm Workers of America (UFW) were covered by settlements with seven table grape growers in the Delano, Calif., area. The union also announced a settlement with California's largest association of citrus growers.

The table grape agreements were the first since the Farm Workers regained bargaining rights for the grape workers in 1975 elections held under California's Agricultural Labor Relations Act. The grape growers had signed contracts with the International Brotherhood of Teamsters in 1973, after expiration of the UFW's 1970 pacts. The elections returned bargaining rights to the UFW.

The 3-year agreement guaranteed $3.50 an hour (formerly $3.15 to $3.25 per hour) in the first year and provided for improvements in vacations, holidays, and medical and pension plans.

The citrus settlements with the Coastal Growers Association, covering 1,100 employees of the 300 growers in the Ventura County area, ended a 5-week strike. The pact provides for piece rates of 59 cents per box the first year (formerly 53 cents), 62 cents in the second year, and 65 cents in the third. If a ladder is used, the rates are 60, 63, and 66 cents, respectively. Checkers on hourly rates will go from $3.85 to $4.30 an hour. The citrus growers also agreed to pay 16.5 cents an hour into the Robert F. Kennedy medical plan and 5 cents per hour to the Martin Luther King, Jr., fund for educational and economic development programs. There also were improvements in holiday and vacation provisions.

The Farm Workers gained the right to represent the citrus workers in a March 31, 1978, election after initiating a strike on March 29. The agricultural act provides for expedited elections when at least 50 percent of a work force walks out.

AFL–CIO rebuffs Carter on wage increases

The AFL–CIO Executive Council dealt a major blow to the Administration's anti-inflation program by rejecting President Carter's call for a "deceleration" of wage increases. The President had asked unions to hold 1978 compensation increases below the average annual rate of increase in the prior settlement. (*Monthly Labor Review*, March 1978, p. 53, and June 1978, p. 57.)

Despite the rejection of the "deceleration" principle, the leaders of AFL–CIO unions did pledge general cooperation with the anti-inflation program. AFL–CIO chief George Meany said the council supported "the heart of the President's program," but explained that "if we were to take the position that we're going to tie ourselves to something less than we got in the contract 2 or 3 years ago, we'd be tying ourselves to a fixed figure and we'd be ignoring what had taken place in the meantime." The council said the focus of the anti-inflation program should be on curtailing price rises, because wage increases "are an attempt to catch up and stay even," and that if the pace of price increases slowed, so would the rate of wage boosts.

The council suggested other anti-inflation measures, such as reducing interest rates, creating agricultural and raw material commodity reserves, continuing the regulation of natural gas, and enacting a hospital cost containment program. They also recommended rolling back the recent increase in social security contribution rates, continuing the emphasis on job-creating programs to reduce the level of unemployment, and reconsidering the decision to limit Federal white-collar and military personnel 1978 pay raises to 5.5 percent.

New York union merges with AFSCME

Membership in the American Federation of State, County and Municipal Employees union (AFSCME) passed 1 million in April, when the 260,000-member Civil Service Employees Association in New York State merged into the AFL–CIO affiliate. The association was founded in 1910 and is reportedly the oldest and largest unaffiliated union of public employees in the Nation.

William L. McGowan will continue to head the union, now designated as CSEA, Local 100, of the AFSCME. The merger increased AFSCME membership to 400,000 in New York State, including the 110,000 employees of New York City comprising District 37.

AFSCME President Jerry Wurf hailed the merger as "a historic event for the labor movement," adding that the move strengthens public employee unions "at a time when our rights are under attack."

U.S. adopts construction hiring goals for women

The Department of Labor has adopted regulations intended to assure employment opportunity for women on Federal and federally assisted construction projects. The regulations, proposed last year (*Monthly Labor Review*, October 1977, pp. 75–76), set nationwide goals for hiring women on construction projects ranging from 3.1 percent of a project's work hours in the first year to 6.9 percent in the third year. The regulations also established legal procedures for assuring compliance and stipulated the steps contractors must take in hiring and promoting minorities and women.

Secretary of Labor Ray Marshall said, "We are committed to strengthening equal employment opportunity and affirmative action under Executive Order 11246," adding that the regulations would "bring about greater uniformity in the construction compliance program," and more importantly "will mean increased job opportunities for women and minority group members in the construction industry." Under Executive Order 11246, Federal contractors and subcontractors are barred from employment discrimination based on race, color, sex, religion, or national origin. These employers are also required to take affirmative action to hire and promote women and minorities. The order, issued in 1965, is administered by the Department of Labor's Office of Federal Contract Compliance Programs in the Employment Standards Administration.

Prior to the issuance of the new regulations, affirmative action was implemented through three programs—hometown plans, special bid conditions, and imposed plans. Hometown plans are voluntary agreements between contractors, unions, and representatives of minority communities in local areas. Special bid conditions and imposed plans established goals and timetables for minority workers in specific geographic areas or on special construction projects. Under the new regulations, hometown plans stay in effect, but special bid conditions and imposed plans are eliminated. However, the goals and timetables for minority workers established by these plans were to remain in effect.

The 33 hometown plans currently in effect will be required to develop goals and timetables for women within 45 days after the regulations become effective. If acceptable goals are not submitted, the Department's approval would automatically be withdrawn, and the new nationwide goals for women would be imposed.

The regulations specify the required minimum effort necessary to fulfill affirmative action obligations. These specifications, which replace special bid conditions and imposed plans, require contractors to (1) ensure and maintain a working environment free of harassment, intimidation, and coercion at all sites and facilities which the contractor's employees are assigned to work, (2) establish and maintain a current list of minority and female recruitment sources, (3) develop on-the-job training opportunities or participate in training programs for the area which expressly include minorities and women, and (4) direct recruitment efforts to minority, female, and community organizations.

□

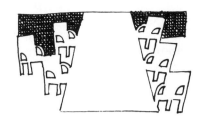

Developments in Industrial Relations

Reported in *Monthly Labor Review*, August 1978.

More settlements in aerospace

The round of bargaining in the aerospace industry continued as the Machinists union negotiated separate 3-year agreements with McDonnell Douglas Corp. in St. Louis, Mo., and Huntington Beach and Torrance, Calif., and with General Dynamics Corp. in San Diego, Calif.

Unlike the earlier settlement between McDonnell Douglas and the Auto Workers for operations in Long Beach, Calif., and other locations (see *Monthly Labor Review*, July 1978, p. 43), the McDonnell Douglas-IAM agreement for St. Louis employees did not provide for optional retirement at unreduced benefit rates at age 55 after 30 years of service. Instead, employees will be permitted to retire as early as age 55 with at least 10 years of service, with their pensions calculated on a scale ranging from 74 percent of the normal benefit rate for those retiring at age 55, to 100 percent for those retiring at 62. In addition, those retiring at age 60 or 61 will receive a $325-a-month pension supplement until age 62. Employees retiring at age 62 or later will receive monthly pensions calculated at 1.6 percent of the first $7,800 of future annual earnings and 2 percent of any excess plus $9 a month for each year of service from 1975 to 1978 and $8 for each earlier year.

Wage terms for the McDonnell Douglas-IAM employees in St. Louis included a 38-cent (average 6 percent) immediate increase and 3 percent increases in the second and third years. The 11,000 workers also will receive wage increases as a result of the continuation of the wage escalator clause, which provides for a 1-cent-an-hour adjustment for each 0.3-point movement in the BLS Consumer Price Index (1967 = 100).

The agreement for 4,800 workers at the Huntington Beach and Torrance plants followed the UAW lead by adopting the "30 and 55" pension provision in return for the same union concession on wage gains.

The General Dynamics Corp.-IAM agreement, which covered 3,200 workers, called for a 6-percent wage increase in the first year and 3 percent increases in the second and third years. Eighty-eight cents of the cost-of-living allowance was incorporated into base wage rates and the escalator clause will continue to provide for semiannual adjustments. The normal pension rate for employees retiring on or after May 1, 1978, was increased to $12 for each year of past and future credited service.

All of the May settlements in the industry also provided for improvements in insurance and other supplementary benefits, as well as the improvements in pensions.

Elsewhere in the industry, the UAW was bargaining with Rockwell International Corp. for 12,000 workers in Southern California and other locations and with Teledyne-Ryan Aeronautical Co. for 1,000 workers in San Diego, Calif. The prior contracts had expired on October 1, 1977, and June 10, 1978.

East and Gulf Coast seamen settle

The National Maritime Union negotiated 3-year contracts with the Maritime Service Committee and the Tanker Service Committee, covering 35,000 unlicensed crew members of about 250 ships that operate out of East and Gulf Coast ports. The agreements, effective June 16, provide for wage increases of 7.5 percent in each of the 3 years, semiannual cost-of-living reviews beginning in December 1979, and additional wage increases for crews aboard vessels which have a power tonnage (gross weight plus horsepower) in excess of 38,000. Vacation bonuses will be increased each year by $15, $25, and $35 for entry, middle, and key ratings, respectively. Presently, the bonuses are $90 a month for entry ratings, $150 for middle, and $210 for key ratings.

Effective June 16, 1978, pensions were increased by $20 month for each year of service in excess of 25 years. The break-in-service rule was also liberalized to allow seamen an additional 10 years in which to earn a pension. Thus, a monthly $250 pension at age 55 with 20 years of service can now be achieved over a 30-year period. Improvements were made to the dental plan and death benefits, contributions to the Upgrading and Retraining

"Developments in Industrial Relations" is prepared by Leon Bornstein and other members of the staff of the Division of Trends in Employee Compensation, Bureau of Labor Statistics, and is largely based on information from secondary sources.

School will increase by 40 cents per employee per day over the contract, and contributions to the Joint Employment Committee will increase by 25 cents.

The two employer associations also announced that they had reached a similar agreement with the Marine Engineers Association, subject to employee ratification.

Trucking associations merge

Members of Trucking Employers, Inc., and Carrier Management, Inc., formed a new association, Trucking Management, Inc., ending an 8-month division among the industry's major employer associations. The split occurred last September when several officers and directors of Trucking Employees Inc. resigned their posts to form Carrier Management, Inc., saying they were dissatisfied with bargaining and contract administration services (Monthly Labor Review, December 1977, p. 73).

J. Curtis Counts, president of the new association, said there is no guarantee the industry will remain unified during 1979 contract negotiations. He also said that the structure of the new organization cannot be interpreted as a victory by either faction because the merger was unanimously approved by members of the two organizations.

New standards for cotton dust exposure

Secretary of Labor Ray Marshall announced that the Occupational Safety and Health Administration (OSHA) was issuing final rules which he said would greatly reduce the hazard of lung disease for the 600,000 workers exposed to cotton dust. Cotton dust exposure has long been recognized as the cause of byssinosis or "brown lung" disease and has also been linked to increased risk of chronic bronchitis and emphysema. Marshall said the standard would provide significant additional protection to workers in the cotton industry without placing unreasonable economic burdens on employers who must comply with the new regulations.

The final standard sets varying requirements among the various segments of the industry. The limit of exposure for yarn manufacturing, the most hazardous segment of the textile manufacturing, was set at 200 micrograms of lint-free respirable cotton dust per cubic meter of air averaged over 8 hours, instead of the prior 1,000 micrograms. For operations where the toxic ingredients were less hazardous, higher limits were allowed—750 milligrams for slashing and weaving operations, and 500 for nontextile industries such as cottonseed oil mills and mattress and bedding manufacturers.

The new standard does not apply to the harvesting of cotton, to dust generated solely from the handling of woven and knitted materials, to fabric manufacturing using cotton yarn, or to processing washed cotton. If employers can demonstrate effective alternatives to the procedures required by the new standard, they may ask OSHA for a variance. The new standard becomes effective in September. Employers are required to develop a written compliance plan within a year and that plan must be completely implemented within 4 years.

Both organized labor and management criticized the new standards. Murray H. Finley, president of the Amalgamated Clothing and Textile Workers Union said, "we are deeply disappointed in the terms of this standard," adding, "they failed to protect the health of more than half a million textile workers exposed to cotton dust in the United States." Robert S. Small, president of the American Textile Manufacturers Institute, said, "It is apparent that the standard as outlined to us by OSHA will have overwhelming financial implications for the entire cotton industry, not to mention boosting the price of any product containing cotton."

Southern textile firms announce wage increases

A number of the major textile companies in the South announced wage increases for their employees generally effective in late June or early July. The companies did not disclose the size of the increases, but indicated that they varied among plants. (The previous round of wage increases was effective in June 1977 and reportedly averaged about 9 percent.)

Several companies indicated that increases in employee compensation included a wage increase and improvements in supplementary benefits. An example was Burlington Industries, Inc., which granted 47,000 employees an additional paid holiday as well a wage increase. Other companies granting wage increases were Cannon Mills, Inc. (for 20,000 workers), Dan River, Inc. (15,000), Cone Mills, Inc. (15,000), Spring Mills, Inc. (13,000), Riegel Textile Corp. (6,000), and Abney Mills, Inc. (3,000). In April, several small mills had granted increases, including Textiles, Inc., and Parkdale Mills, where the increases reportedly ranged from 8 to 9 percent.

Electrical workers in New York settle

A novel accord ended an 8-week strike by electrical workers in New York City. The contract featured a work-sharing plan designed to deal with the problem of high unemployment in the area, and involved local 3 of the International Brotherhood of Electrical Workers, representing about 5,000 electricians, and the New York Electrical Contractors Association, the Empire Electrical Contractors Association, and the Association of Electrical Contractors.

The electricians had been without a contract since June 30, 1977, although an agreement was made to freeze wages for 1 year from that date. Difficulty at arriving at a new contract centered on a union-sought work-sharing plan which would help to alleviate the near 50-percent unemployment rate of electricians in the area. When the contractors balked at the plan, the union began a selective, then a general, strike in March.

Under the new plan, contractors will be permitted to retain a "base work force" of employees not subject to layoff. However, these workers are required to take annual unpaid vacations, or "furloughs" which could be as long as 8 weeks, depending on economic conditions. Additional workers required by the contractors will be assigned on a temporary basis, and rotated so that no worker is laid off for more than 26 weeks at a time. In addition to the work-sharing plan, the new agreement provides for wage increases of 60 cents an hour in each year of the 2-year agreement, and increases the number of apprenticeships by 1,000.

City workers in New York win pay increase

A 2-year agreement was concluded between New York City and a coalition of municipal labor unions representing about 225,000 employees. The settlement was reached on the eve of an appearance by Mayor Edward I. Koch before the Senate Banking Committee to ask for continued Federal assistance in the city's fiscal recovery. The accord was viewed as a key element in the recovery plan because Senator William Proxmire (D–Wis.), chairman of the committee, had stated that the city's chances for continued Federal aid would be reduced if a settlement was not reached.

The settlement specified the provisions to be included in the separate contracts to be drawn up by the city and each of the 50 unions in the coalition. These contracts were to be effective immediately after the termination dates of the prior contracts. (Termination dates ranged from Dec. 31, 1977, to Oct. 1, 1978.)

The settlement called for the following wage provisions to be included in each contract:

1. Existing cost-of-living wage escalator allowances of up to $441 a year (varying by job classification) were to be incorporated into base annual salaries, beginning on the effective date of the contract. On the first anniversary of the contract, the amount was to be a uniform $441 for all employees.

2. An immediate lump-sum payment equal to the amount that had been accrued under the cost-of-living wage escalator provisions of the 1976–78 agreements, but not paid because the city contended that the cost increase had not been offset by required improvements in productivity. For members of District Council 37 of the State, County and Municipal Employees, the largest union unit involved in the bargaining, the total payment was $672.

3. A $750 increase in base annual salaries, in return for termination of wage escalator provisions.

4. Four percent (minimum $400) increases in annual salaries effective at the beginning of the 4th and 16th months of the contract. The increases were to be calculated on each employee's current base annual salary, excluding the portion resulting from items (1) and (3).

5. Arbitration of the issue of whether the city must now pay the portion of a scheduled 1975 wage increase of 6 percent that employees had agreed to defer to aid the city. (See *Monthly Labor Review,* October 1975, pp. 62–63.) At that time, the city had promised to pay the deferred amounts by June 30, 1978, if it could attain a balanced budget by that date. The city's position was that this goal had not been reached and, therefore, it was completely relieved of the obligation.

The unions said they were cheered by the fact that the agreement did not contain "give-backs" of some fringe benefits that management considered wasteful and had sought to modify or eliminate. Victor Gotbaum, head of District 37, conceded that "there won't be dancing in the streets," because "we are settling for considerably less than what others in the private sector are getting. But. . . we are emerging with some important gains. We have effectively ended the era of 'no-cost' agreements and city employees will no longer carry the load of the fiscal crisis. And we have ended the nonsense of having to show productivity savings for every penny we receive."

After the municipal employees' settlement, 31,000 members of the Transport Workers Union (TWU) began voting on an April 1 settlement with the New York City Transit Authority. The union had delayed the vote because the Transit Authority had agreed that talks could be resumed if the municipal workers gained a larger wage and benefit package.

The TWU contract (and a similar accord for 2,000 members of the Amalgamated Transit

Union) provided for a 6-percent wage increase effective July 1, an immediate lump-sum payment of $250 to each worker, and a cost-of-living increase of up to $500, depending on the movement of the Consumer Price Index for the New York City–Northeastern N.J. area. Transit officials said that the cost-of-living increase would be paid only to the extent that the cost could be recovered through improvements in productivity.

The authority gained the right to hire 200 part-time employees to operate fare booths during rush hours. These workers will receive only basic pay, not cost-of-living allowances or fringe benefits.

Stevens-NLRB settlement assailed

Organized labor announced its intention to continue boycotting J.P. Stevens & Co., despite the textile company's recent settlement with the National Labor Relations Board. (See *Monthly Labor Review*, July 1978, pp. 43–44) In a statement protesting the settlement, the Amalgamated Clothing and Textile Workers union said the April 28 agreement "is little cause for celebration among the vast majority of the company's 44,000 employees, but does provide grounds for labor law reform." The union added that the agreement "emphasizes that a lawless company can escape punishment by making an empty promise to a powerless NLRB, which is charged with enforcing a toothless law."

Jacob Sheinkman, secretary-treasurer of the union, said the agreement, which in theory ended proceedings for a nationwide injunction against Stevens, only dealt with a few of Stevens' many violations of labor laws—and those only on a temporary basis. According to Sheinkman, the settlement did not resolve unfair labor practices affecting employees in 30 Stevens plants, nor did it remedy 36 outstanding cases against Stevens involving 315 separate violations of the law.

The union charged that in not pursuing its suit for a court injunction on the basis of assurances from Stevens, "the NLRB has unfortunately chosen to abrogate its duty to enforce the act by failing to fully utilize its clearly mandated authority. . . ." The union claimed the only significant aspect of the agreement was the stipulation that the Government has the right to refile its injunction petition if Stevens breaches the agreement or further violates the National Labor Relations Act in other ways.

AFL-CIO President George Meany said the agreement was "the best argument I know for passage of labor law reform." He asserted that Stevens has found that it could deny workers their rights under the National Labor Relations Act, and could delay compliance with the law even after it has been found guilty by the Supreme Court.

In defense of the agency's action, NLRB Chairman John Fanning and General Counsel John Irving called the accusation that the Board had evaded its statutory duty "wholly unwarranted and irresponsible". In a letter to Sheinkman and union Executive Vice President William DuChessi, they said that Stevens had undertaken several programs designed to bringing it into compliance with the law, and that "while the effectiveness of those programs has not yet been finally demonstrated, it is our view that they should at least be given an opportunity to prove their efficacy." They informed the union that the injunction provisions of the act allow the Board to seek only "temporary, interim relief" and that even if the NLRB had pursued the injunction petition, any order granted by the court would have provided virtually the same relief as was obtained through the settlement agreement. They assured the union that the general counsel of the NLRB was continuing to prosecute unfair labor practices charges against Stevens and that the company's compliance with the settlement agreement would be monitored.

Contractors, unions sign cost-cutting pact

The AFL-CIO's Building and Construction Trades Department (BCTD) and the National Constructors Association (NCA) negotiated a 2-year agreement designed to reduce building time and costs in heavy construction projects and to enhance job prospects for union craftworkers. BCTD President Robert A. Georgine and NCA head Maurice L. Mosier said the agreement would help eliminate or reduce unnecessary strikes and lockouts while providing an orderly process for settlement of grievances, including the use of mandatory and binding arbitration, where necessary. They indicated that the agreement would also standardize overtime rates and shift work and establish "common sense" working conditions. Georgine said the agreement represents "another step in our efforts to halt the escalation of construction costs and to obtain more work for building tradesmen," and that stepped-up construction schedules would provide savings for contractors by cutting the time they are required to pay interest on construction loans.

Secretary of Labor Ray Marshall, who presided at the signing ceremony, noted that the goal of the agreement is to reduce construction costs on some industrial projects up to 14 percent through increased efficiency and productivity.

The pact covered eight construction unions—Asbestos Workers, Boilermakers, Carpenters, Operating Engineers, Iron Workers, Laborers, Plasterers and Cement Masons, and the Plumbers and Pipe Fitters. The States initially covered were Alabama, Georgia, Florida, Mississippi, North Carolina, South Carolina, Arkansas, Louisiana, Texas, Oklahoma, and Virginia, except for the Washington, D.C., vicinity.

The agreement created a joint administrative committee made up of the presidents of the signatory unions and the employer members—some 50 major engineering and construction firms specializing in building industrial facilities such as power and chemical plants, steel mills, and oil refineries. The committee is to meet at least quarterly to review operation of the agreement and study decisions issued on projects under the grievance procedure. The committee also will decide whether individual decisions apply to all parties in the agreement. There was provision for a special arbitrator to determine if work interruptions constitute a violation of the agreement, which rules out strikes, lockouts, picketing, work stoppages, or slowdowns. Local bargaining disputes are exempted from the ban on strikes and lockouts, but if an impasse occurs, the union or employer must give a 5-day notice before taking action.

GE discrimination complaint settled

The General Electric Co. agreed to spend millions over the next 5 years in settling a 1973 Government complaint accusing the company of discriminating against women and other minorities in hiring and promotions. An Equal Employment Opportunity Commission official called the agreement between the company and the Commission the most complicated case the agency ever handled because of the company's size and diversity. The settlement was also one of the largest in the Commission's history.

Both the Commission and the company said that the agreement did not signify an admission of guilt by General Electric. Frank P. Doyle, vice president for corporate employee relations, said the company agreed to the settlement "rather than becoming engaged in lengthy adversary proceedings." He said the 5-year pact formalized a number of affirmative action programs already effective in many of the company's operations and that the agreement "represents a thorough effort by General Electric to make certain that all of its personnel practices and employment procedures comply with the letter and spirit of the law."

Of the total package, $10.6 million was allocated for "promotion incentive" bonuses, with women and minority members promoted to certain jobs eligible to receive extra lump-sum payments of up to $800 to make up for past discrimination. An additional $9.9 million is to be spent for training programs for minorities and women, and $7.4 million—including $2.7 million for backpay—was allocated for higher wage rates for certain factory jobs held predominantly by women. An additional $3 million is to be used to implement an affirmative action plan for recruiting and promoting, and $1 million is to resolve pending charges of bias.

Commission chairperson Eleanor Holmes Norton said the agreement did not attempt to resolve all possible issues, and therefore did not deprive individuals of the right to seek relief from GE for alleged discrimination. ☐

Developments in Industrial Relations

Reported in *Monthly Labor Review*, September 1978.

Postal accord retains 'no layoff' clause

A tentative 3-year settlement was reached between the U.S. Postal Service and unions representing some 570,000 postal workers several hours after a July 20 strike deadline. The agreement featured the retention of the "no layoff" clause, and, if ratified by postal employees, will provide a maximum pay increase of 19.5 percent, including anticipated cost-of-living adjustments. Wages were increased 2 percent on July 22, and will rise 3 percent in July 1979 and 5 percent in July 1980. The 1979 and 1980 increases will be calculated on workers' base pay rates under the old contract.

The settlement provided for continuation of semiannual cost-of-living wage escalator adjustments, calculated at 1 cent an hour for each 0.4 point change in the Consumer Price Index. Adjustments will be limited to 73 cents an hour ($1,518 a year) over the term. The first adjustment is scheduled for September 1978.

Other provisions include a 100-percent pay bonus for work on Christmas day (was 50 percent), and 50 percent for the remaining 8 holidays, which had no prior premium. The Sunday premium was doubled to 50 percent, but now only applies to hours actually worked on Sunday. (Previously, if the shift started at 10 p.m. or later on Saturday, the worker would get a bonus for the entire 8 hours.) In addition, the uniform allowance was increased 10 percent.

Most of the postal workers are represented by the American Postal Workers, the Letter Carriers, and the Mail Handlers unions.

Railroads, four unions reach agreement

Tentative contracts have been reached between the Nation's major railroads and four unions for about 140,000 workers. The 39-month agreements provide for wage increases of 3 percent retroactive to April 1, 1978, 2 percent effective October 1,

1978, 4 percent July 1, 1979, and 5 percent July 1, 1980. Seminannual cost-of-living wage escalator reviews were continued, with the first adjustment on January 1, 1979. The formula provides for a 1-cent-an-hour adjustment for each 0.3-point rise in the Consumer Price Index (1967 = 100), up to an 8-percent index rise per year. In addition, the workers received 19 cents wage increases effective January 1, and July 1, 1978, representing the escalator adjustments that would have been paid if the sequence of reviews in the prior contract had been continued.

The settlements also included improved vacation, medical, and dental benefits. The unions reportedly agreed to some changes in work rules that will cut labor costs. One of the major issues, a management proposal for eliminating some jobs, will be handled on an individual carrier-union basis.

The four unions are the United Transportation Union, the Brotherhood of Locomotive Engineers, the Sheet Metal Workers, and the Brotherhood of Railroad Signalmen. Nine other unions are still negotiating.

State employees win wage increase

Some 76,000 Pennsylvania State employees, represented by the State, County and Municipal Employees, were covered by a 3-year agreement boosting wages 3 percent on July 1, 1978, 2½ percent on January 1, 1979, and 5½ percent on July 1 of 1980 and 1981. The settlement also provided for a 5-cent-an-hour increase (to 22 cents) in the State's contribution to the health and welfare fund, a 5-cent-an-hour increase (to 30 cents) in the shift differential, and an increase in mileage and meal allowances. The parties also revised contract language on coverage of seasonal employees, seniority provisions for furloughed employees, and the contracting out of work.

Philadelphia municipal employees end strike

Striking Philadelphia municipal employees have accepted a 2-year contract ending an 8-day walkout that interrupted numerous city service,

---

"Developments in Industrial Relations" is prepared by Leon Bornstein and other members of the staff of the Division of Trends in Employee Compensation, Bureau of Labor Statistics, and is largely based on information from secondary sources.

including the collection of trash. The 17,300 blue-collar and 2,300 white-collar workers, represented by the State, County and Municipal Employees, received a pay increase of 7 percent retroactive to July 1, and will also receive an increase on July 1, 1979, equal to the rise in the Philadelphia Consumer Price Index in the prior 12 months. The city also was to provide additional money on January 1, 1979, for optical care and prescription drug benefits. City officials estimated that the cost of the settlement, combined with that of earlier pacts reached for police and firefighters, would necessitate some layoffs. To minimize the number, the city agreed to reduce "where practical" contracts with outside trash collection and street repair firms, to replace uniformed police officers now in clerical jobs with the union's members, and to purge the city's payroll of "illegal nonresidence" workers who live outside the city. The union agreed to a reduction of overtime work and a ban on hiring during the coming year.

New York City police accept 'third' agreement

New York City police patrol officers, after rejecting two prior agreements, approved a settlement providing terms similar to those received by some 200,000 New York City municipal employees (*Monthly Labor Review*, August 1978, pp. 52–53). Reportedly, the 18,000 members of the Patrolmen's Benevolent Association (PBA) had objected to Mayor Edward I. Koch's proposal to gain more control of the use of sick leave and more flexibility in deploying officers. The Mayor announced the changes in the city's position on July 19. Citing estimates that "only" 350 officers might be sick-leave abusers, Koch said that the sick leave problem would be handled "administratively" by Police Commissioner Robert J. McGuire. He added that the deployment issue was "preempted" by a State law mandating that the commissioner "shall deploy his personnel as warranted by crime conditions and other police needs," and was not bargainable, although the union's cooperation had been and will be sought. Another major issue in the talks was resolved when parties agreed to changes in shift schedules that will give officers as much as 96 hours off between swings from one shift to another.

Guild, New York newspaper accord ends strike

A breakthrough in bargaining between three major New York City newspapers and 10 unions occurred when the Newspaper Guild and *The New York Daily News* agreed on a 3-year contract. Prior contracts between the unions and *The Daily News, The New York Times,* and *The New York Post* had expired March 30, but there was no work stoppage until the Newspaper Guild began a 4-day strike against *The Daily News* that ended with the settlement. The newspaper was able to maintain limited production during the first 3 days of the strike, but on the last day, lost the ability to distribute papers because members of the Newspaper and Mail Deliverers Union of New York and vicinity would no longer cross the picket lines. (The Mail Deliverers union had settled in April with the *News* and the *Times* on major contract provisions but negotiations were still continuing on some issues.)

The mid-June contract, which covered 1,350 news and commercial employees, provided for average salary increases totaling $68 a week—$23 retroactive to March 30, another $23 in March 1979, and $22 in March 1980. The newspaper had initially sought to have half of the value of all annual increases be subject to the approval of supervisors. There also was a provision for second- and third-year wage escalator adjustments equal to any rise in the Consumer Price Index in excess of 6 percent in each year. Starting minimum salaries for all job grades were not increased but could be increased in the second and third years, depending on the decision of a joint study committee. If the committee can not reach a decision, the issue will be settled by arbitration.

Management won several concessions, including a provision that the first 2 days of sick leave will now be without pay when an employee has already had 5 days of sick leave in the previous 12 months; a limit of 50 weeks severance pay for employees hired after the effective date of the agreement (current employees continue to be entitled to 2 weeks' severance pay for each year of service, without limit); a 15-year service requirement for assured protection from layoffs (was 10 years); and a provision permitting the imposition of a 4-day workweek, as long as the 35 hours of work are spread evenly among the 4 days and days off are consecutive (a 3-day workweek also could be instituted, with employee approval).

Delegates back merger. In Detroit, delegates to the 45th annual convention of the Newspaper Guild endorsed a call by President Charles A. Perlik, Jr., for completion of merger negotiations with the International Typographical Union before next year's convention. In the convention resolution, the delegates said a merger was necessary to help counter a concerted employer attempt to "destroy bargaining gains won over decades." The 227 delegates also expressed concern over government actions in the United States and Canada hampering news reporting, as well as over repressive policies against the press in the Soviet Union and South Africa.

Hospital league and union settle

The League of Voluntary Hospitals and Homes of New York City settled with the Retail, Wholesale and Department Store Union just hours before a scheduled walkout by 37,000 nonprofessional employees. The 2-year contract, which involved 61 private for–profit institutions, provided for wage increases of 7.5 percent on September 1, 1978, 4 percent on September 1, 1980, and for a percentage-point rise in the employers' pension fund contribution rate, bringing it to 8 percent of gross payroll.

League officials said that medicaid and insurance payments for hospital care would have to be increased about 11 percent to offset the cost increases resulting from the settlement. This would bring both types of payments to about $220 a day for each patient.

Plumbers' compensation surpasses $21 an hour

Plumbers and contractors in the San Francisco area negotiated a 75-month contract which will raise total compensation for the 1,500 employees to $21.18 an hour in the first year, with additional increases scheduled for each of the later years. The $1.53-an-hour increase in compensation in the first year included an 85-cent wage increase. The agreement between Local 38 and the Plumbing and Mechanical Contractors Association and three other associations superseded the balance of a 3-year agreement negotiated in 1977. The 1977 agreement had provided for deferred wage increases of 40 cents on April 1, 1978, and April 1, 1979, which were included in the new settlement package.

The subsequent annual increases in wage and benefit costs will equal any January-to-December rise in the Consumer Price Index, but the increases will not be implemented until the following July (beginning with July 1979) to aid employers in determining the cost portion of their bids on future projects.

One major concession of the union was the dropping of the "maintenance of differential" clause. This clause, adopted in 1975, first provided that the difference between Local 38 wages and benefits and those of other locals in the area as of March 31, 1975 (estimated to be 6 to 7 percent, in favor of Local 38), be maintained. In 1976, the formula was changed, which increased the differential to approximately 14 percent.

Hiring cuts begin in wake of 'Proposition 13'

California voters approved an iniative that limits the amount of real estate taxes local jurisdictions may impose. To offset the loss of revenue, the local government units began to cut or freeze employment and salaries, to cut services to the public, and to impose "user" fees.

Proposition 13 also had a substantial impact at the State government level. Governor Edmund G. Brown, Jr., cut nearly $400 million from the budget for the fiscal year beginning July 1. Among the items vetoed by the Governor was a 2.5-percent salary increase for 200,000 State employees that had been approved by the legislature.

In a message to the legislature, Governor Brown said, "Proposition 13 radically restructured the financing of government in California." He added that "during this transition year, local government will have its revenues reduced by $7 billion. To meet this unprecedented challenge and minimize human hardship, State government must share its funds. Accordingly, for this year I have frozen State hiring and salaries to provide maximum asssitance to local governments and minimize the layoffs, as well as to avoid cutting programs for the elderly and handicapped."

In addition to the cuts in tax revenue, the local governments were impelled to reduce labor costs by a new provision of State law requiring them to hold wage increases at or below those for State employees to be eligible for a share of the funds to be distributed by the State. As a result, some local lawmakers voted not to implement wage increases effective under previously negotiated labor contracts. This led some unions to file suits challenging the State's right to restrict wages of local government workers. □

Developments in Industrial Relations

Reported in *Monthly Labor Review*, October 1978.

Northwest pilots settle, ending walkout

Northwest Airlines and the Air Line Pilots Association settled in mid-August, ending a 108-day strike. The 3-year contract, covering 1,500 pilots, is retroactive to July 1, 1977, the date the previous contract expired. About 8,500 employees, other than pilots, were laid off as a result of the strike, which terminated virtually all Northwest service to about 40 cities in the United States and seven in the Far East.

Under the new agreement, pilots will receive pay increases averaging 7 percent. Pilots will also receive full pay (previously half pay) for "deadheading"—that is, flying from a home base to another base for an assigned flight. In addition, the contract provides for a "guaranteed line of flying" under which pilots will be paid for a monthly flight schedule once it has been assigned, even if the company cancels flights.

Pilots who were previously flight engineers will receive a $15-a-month increase in their pension for each year of such prior service. Previously, they did not receive pension credit for service as a flight engineer. The method for computing pension benefits was also improved.

Insurance agents end strike

A 22-day nationwide strike against the John Hancock Mutual Life Insurance Co. ended in mid-August when members of the Insurance Workers union ratified a 3-year contract. Terms, which applied to 5,500 district agents, included an immediate 11-percent increase in basic salaries, and 6 percent increases in the second and third years. The agents also received a lump-sum payment equal to 2½ weeks of basic salary and an improvement in one of the sales commission formulas. This was in lieu of a company-financed dental plan that would have been established under an earlier agreement that was rejected by the agents. Another provision included extension of health insurance to provide maternity benefits for the 557 female agents.

West Coast dockworkers settle

The International Longshoremen's and Warehousemen's Union and the Pacific Maritime Association negotiated a 3-year contract for about 11,500 west coast dockworkers, replacing one that expired on July 1. Under the new contract, straight-time hourly wages will rise by 85 cents each year for longshoremen who work 6 hours a day at straight-time pay and 2 hours at time and one-half. (Previously, the straight-time rate for these workers was $8.37.) A Relatively small number of workers who work 8 hours a day at straight-time pay will receive equivalent increases. As a result of the pay increases, the annual pay guarantee for fully registered longshoremen (those guaranteed 36 hours of straight-time pay per week) will rise from $15,700 to $17,300 in the first year of the contract, to $18,900 in the second, and to $20,400 in the third. Probationary longshoremen now have their weekly guarantee fixed at 24 hours (the amount previously allowed only if funds permitted) and their annual salary guarantee will also rise because of the pay increases.

Two additional paid holidays were provided, bringing the total to 11, and a 6th week of vacation was provided for workers with 25 years of service. Pension benefits for future retirees will be increased in each year of the contract and an increase in benefits for retirees is provided. Significant improvements also were made in hospitalization, life insurance, dental, and drug benefits.

AFL-CIO establishes safety department

At the summer meeting of the executive council, AFL-CIO President George Meany announced the creation of a Department of Occupational Safety and Health. The new department will coordinate union efforts to protect workers from work-related illness and injury by gathering and disseminating information on the economics of job safety and health, industrial hygiene, toxicology, and industrial engineering. George H. R. Taylor, executive

"Developments in Industrial Relations" is prepared by Leon Bornstein and other members of the staff of the Division of Trends in Employee Compensation, Bureau of Labor Statistics, and is largely based on information from secondary sources.

secretary of the AFL-CIO Standing Committee on Occupational Safety and Health, will head the new unit.

Among other actions, the council approved a Roofers' union request to change its name from the United Association of Slate, Tile & Composition Roofers, Damp and Waterproof Workers, to United Association of Roofers, Waterproofers and Allied Workers. The Council also adopted resolutions memorializing the Brotherhood of Sleeping Car Porters, which merged earlier in the year with the Railway and Airline Clerks, and mourning the death of C. L. Dennis, who died in August at the age of 70.

Dennis retired in 1976 as president of the Brotherhood of Railway and Airline Clerks after assuming the presidency in 1963. He had also served as an AFL-CIO vice president and in numerous union posts, including international vice president, prior to his ascension to the presidency. Fred J. Kroll, who succeeded him as president of the union, lauded Dennis' "enduring belief that working people are entitled to dignity and security on the job."

Convention activities

Letter Carriers oppose tentative contract. The Letter Carriers' 51st biennial convention recommended that union members reject the 3-year settlement reached with the U.S. Postal Service in July, contending that the contract provided "inadequate" wage increases, and insufficient work rules changes. For details of the tentative contract, see *Monthly Labor Review,* September 1978, p. 63.

The convention also approved an increase in the per capita payment, from $36 to $42 a year. The increase was voted after delegates rejected a proposal basing per capita on a percentage of pay and tied to rises in the cost of living. The 4,700 delegates from 663 local unions, representing over 220,000 letter carriers, also voted to establish a public relations fund to pay for a program to improve the union's public image. To finance the fund, 20 cents a year will be deducted from each per capita payment.

Sheet metal workers raise per capita taxes. At the 90th anniversary convention of the Sheet Metal Workers in St. Louis, Mo., 723 delegates, representing about 160,000 union members, reelected President Edward J. Carlough and Secretary–Treasurer David S. Turner to 4-year terms. Also reelected were 10 vice presidents, and Richard S. Dumancas will succeed retiring Vice President Curt Neidig.

The delegates voted to raise the per capita tax from $4.50 to $6 a month (beginning October 1), for its 120,000 building trade members, with additional 50-cent increases effective on January 1 of 1980 and 1981. The per capita increases for production, Federal, and railroad employees were to be raised by a total of $1 over the same period. In addition, the constitution was amended to provide annual per capita increases of 50 cents for building trade members, and 25 cents for others, beginning January 1, 1983, after the union's next scheduled convention. The executive council could defer any of the post-1983 increases if they found that additional funds were not needed to "maintain financial stability." The delegates approved a 20-percent pay increase for union officers and staff and endorsed a 10-point report backing the development of solar heating and cooling systems.

AFGE reelects top officers. In Chicago, 1,500 delegates to the American Federation of Government Employees' 25th biennial convention reelected top officers in closely contested elections. In weighted balloting, President Kenneth T. Blaylock was reelected over challenger Royal Sims, an AFGE vice president from the Philadelphia area, by a margin of 109,414 votes to 107,052. Secretary-Treasurer Nicholas J. Nolan won over William Nussbaum, a local union president from New Jersey. Louise Smothers, director of the union's Department of Women's Affairs, was also reelected. The contests were decided by runoff votes after other candidates were eliminated on the first ballot. Executive Vice President Joseph D. Gleason was the only national officer returned to office without opposition. The opposition to the incumbents apparently came from members who disagreed with Blaylock's support of civil service reform legislation submitted to Congress earlier in the year by President Carter. These members generally contended that the proposal would weaken employee job rights.

AFL-CIO President George Meany and other speakers criticized President Carter's declared intention to put a 5.5-percent "cap" on the scheduled October salary increase for Federal white-collar employees and members of the Armed Forces. The delegates then staged a protest march and adopted a resolution charging the President with breaking campaign promises to Federal employees. The resolution declared that the union was withdrawing its support of the civil service reorganization plan until President Carter abandons the pay ceiling and agrees to support stronger collective bargaining rights for Federal workers.

Typographical union endorses mergers. Merger proposals highlighted the International Typographical Union's (ITU) 120th convention in Springfield, Ill. The delegates approved and sent to membership referendum a plan for merger of the 3,000-member International Mailers' Union into the ITU. They also endorsed a timetable that would bring a merger proposal to the 1979 conventions of the ITU and the Newspaper Guild. (The Guild had endorsed the merger at its June 1978 convention.)

Leaders of the latter two unions launched a program of joint and coordinated bargaining 4 years earlier, and began meeting in October 1977 to draw up a plan for creation of a new industrial union. ITU President Joe Bigel told delegates of the 115,000-member union that traditional jurisdictional lines were becoming so blurred that "one union and one contract is the only reasonable solution for both workers and managements" in both the newspaper and commercial printing industries.

Bakery union completes merger. A merger of the 140,000-member Bakery and Confectionery Workers and the 32,000-member Tobacco Workers unions was completed at the 30th convention of the Bakery union, held in Las Vegas. The Tobacco Workers had endorsed the merger at a special convention the prior day.

Bakery Workers' President John De Concini told the convention that the merger is a natural outgrowth of a number of factors. He noted that the two organizations shared a common background, tradition, and philosophy, which served as a strong foundation for the merger, but that the impetus was the increasing tendency for tobacco companies to diversify and expand into the bakery and confectionery fields.

Under the merger agreement, the president and secretary-treasurer of the Bakery union would keep these positions in the new union. In addition to the three executive vice presidents provided by the Bakery union's constitution, the tobacco union would provide one additional executive vice president, two vice presidents, and nine general executive board members.

New York City adopts 'residency' law

New York City Mayor Edward I. Koch has signed a bill requiring municipal employees hired after November 1 to reside in the city. The new law, passed over the objections of the Patrolmen's Benevolent Association and other city unions, also stipulates that city employees now residing in the city must continue to do so. The city council had approved the measure, after unsuccessful attempts to persuade the State Legislature to end the State's exceptions to city residency requirements.

The new law covers employees who earn all or part of their salaries from the city, including teachers, police officers, firefighters, sanitation workers, and other groups exempted by the State. The courts were expected to be asked to rule on the conflict between the State law and the city's measure. Residency requirements also exist in other cities, including Chicago, Newark, Washington, D.C., Los Angeles, Detroit, Philadelphia, and Houston.

Paperworkers two officials indicted

Paperworkers union President Joseph P. Tonelli and Secretary-Treasurer Henry Segal took voluntary leaves of absence from their posts pending disposition of Federal indictments charging violations of criminal provisions of the Landrum-Griffin Act. Both were accused of embezzling $360,000 in union funds and accepting illegal payments to influence pension fund operations. They were indicted on July 20 in Federal District Court in New York City.

The leaves were announced at a special meeting of the union's 170-member executive board held in Washington, D.C., on July 31. The board elected Wayne Glenn of Little Rock, Ark., as temporary president and Nicholas C. Vrataric of Ann Arbor, Mich., as temporary secretary-treasurer. □

Developments in Industrial Relations

Reported in *Monthly Labor Review*, November 1978.

Arbitrator awards higher pay to postal workers

Arbitrator James J. Healy announced his binding decision on wages and layoff provisions for 527,000 U.S. Postal Service workers, after union and management negotiators had reached a stalemate on these issues.

The 3-year arbitration decision, made public September 15, provided for potentially larger total wage increases than the July 20 accord. (See *Monthly Labor Review*, September 1978, p. 63.) That accord was rejected by members of three unions—the American Postal Workers Union (representing 306,000 workers), the National Association of Letter Carriers (184,000), and the Mail Handlers Division of the Laborers' union (37,000). A fourth union, the Rural Letter Carriers which represents 43,000 employees, accepted the agreement.

The arbitrated award calls for a $500-increase in annual pay effective July 21, 1978, a 3-percent increase on July 21, 1979, and an additional $500 increase on July 21, 1980. These increases would raise the employee's average annual pay to about $17,400, about $100 less than would have resulted under the rejected contract. However, the award eliminated the "cap" on wage escalator adjustments, which would have limited the total increase in annual pay to $1,518 over the contract term. The parties estimated that specified and escalator increases combined would amount to about a 21.3-percent increase in pay, assuming a 6.5-percent annual rise in the Consumer Price Index. (Under the rejected contract, the maximum possible increase was 19.5 percent.) The escalator formula is a $20.80-increase in annual pay for each 0.4-point rise in the Consumer Price Index for Urban Wage Earners and Clerical Workers (1967 = 100).

Under the award, all regular employees on the payroll as of September 1, 1978, are not subject to layoff during their "work lifetime." New employees will also be protected after they attain 6 consecutive years of service, provided they work at least 20 pay periods in each year. The job protection clause in the rejected accord prohibited the layoff of regular employees, but this protection extended only for the life of the particular contract, rather than for each eligible employee's "work lifetime."

The events leading to Healy's decision to impose a settlement began in August, when leaders of the three unions announced the membership rejection of the July accord. Despite the fact that the Postal Reorganization Act of 1970 prohibits strikes by postal workers, there was an increasing possibility of at least scattered strikes, because the American Postal Workers and Letter Carriers were required by convention resolutions to strike if the postal service refused to reopen negotiations. Initially, Postmaster General William Bolger refused to bargain, contending that an arbitrator should decide all contract terms. At the end of August, the parties agreed to a 15-day period of bargaining on wage and job protection issues, with the arbitrator to decide the issues at the end of the period if the parties were unsuccessful.

Bolger and Healy said they viewed the dispute as closed, but union leaders expressed some dissatisfaction with Healy's decision and indicated that they would submit the terms to their members for ratification.

Conrail, UTU announce settlement

Consolidated Rail Corp. (Conrail) and the United Transportation Union (UTU) concluded negotiations on a contract that included provisions for reducing the number of brakemen on certain freight runs. Conrail later announced that it had also settled with the Brotherhood of Locomotive Engineers, ending negotiations that did not include a management proposal for a reduction in crew. The agreements provided for the same wage and benefit terms the UTU, the Locomotive Engineers, and the Brotherhood of Railroad Signalmen had negotiated with the National Railway Labor Conference, which represents most of the national major railroads. (*Monthly Labor Review*, September 1978, p. 63). Although Conrail is not a member of the Conference, there was a possibility that its settlement with the UTU on crew reductions could

"Developments in Industrial Relations" is prepared by Leon Bornstein and other members of the staff of the Division of Trends in Employee Compensation, Bureau of Labor Statistics, and is largely based on information from secondary sources.

lead to similar reductions at railroads that are members of the Conference. The Conference had sought crew reductions in its talks with the UTU but the final agreement specified that the issue would be resolved in separate negotiations between the union and the individual members of the Conference.

Under its contract with the UTU, Conrail will be permitted to reduce crews to one conductor and one brakeman on freight trains of 70 cars or less. The previous crew of one conductor and two brakemen for all trains will continue to apply to freight trains of more than 70 cars, except where the union agrees to a reduction. Union members will receive a special $4 allowance each time they operate as part of a reduced train service crew, and Conrail will contribute to a special "productivity fund" for each such occasion. The fund will be distributed among all train service employees. There will be no layoff of any of the 4,500 UTU members now working as "third members" of crews—reductions will be implemented through attrition.

The settlement also provides for adoption by September 1, 1979, of a single contract between the union and Conrail, replacing separate contracts Conrail inherited when it was formed to take over the operation of bankrupt railroads in the Northeast.

New study on job-related cancers

A study prepared by the National Cancer Institute and the National Institute of Environmental Health Sciences shows that at least 20 percent of all cancer deaths in the United States may be related to occupational exposure to carcinogens. (Previous estimates ranged from 1 to 5 percent.) A draft of the study was released in early September, during the AFL–CIO's first national conference on occupational safety and health.

According to the study, about 20 to 25 percent of those heavily exposed to asbestos die of lung cancer. An additional 8 to 9 percent die of gastrointestinal cancer, and 7 to 10 percent of plueral or peritoneal mesothelioma (a malignancy of the lining of the chest or abdominal cavities). The study predicts that in the next 30 to 35 years, about 17 percent of all cancers detected annually in the United States will be attributable to asbestos.

Past exposures indicate that eight other substances may contribute substantially to the incidence of cancer. The study projects that about 1 to 3 percent of the cancers occurring in a year will be

associated with arsenic, benzene, coal tar pitch volatiles, and coke oven emissions and that an estimated 3 to 18 percent will be related to chromium, iron oxide, nickel, and petroleum distillates.

Teacher strikes widespread

Teacher militancy in the face of inflation, combined with school districts attempting to limit budgets, led to a rash of strikes across the Nation. Hard-hit States included Pennsylvania, Connecticut, Ohio, Illinois, Michigan, and Louisiana. Among the cities affected were Philadelphia, where members of the Philadelphia Federation of Teachers struck for 7 days over salary demands, class size, preparation periods, and the June layoff of 2,200 teachers. The walkout ended with a 2-year agreement that provided for a 15-percent wage increase (in the second year of the contract), reduced class size, and reinstatement of the laid-off employees.

In New Orleans, the United Teachers of New Orleans struck for 11 days. The settlement provided for a 7-percent wage hike and an increased Board of Education contribution to the cost of hospitalization insurance (from 50 to 80 percent).

Meanwhile, a walkout continued against the Cleveland school system by 10,500 teachers who had not received a pay increase since 1975. The financially pressed Board of Education did not make a pay offer, but announced plans for a tax levy referendum in November.

Reportedly, nine locals of the American Federation of Teachers opened the school year with strikes, with three others walking out since Labor Day. The National Education Association had 45 strikes in progress when school began, and 15 more soon afterwards.

GM agrees to 'preferential hiring plan'

General Motors Corp. announced an agreement with the Auto Workers over the union's attempts to organize new GM plants in the South. Under the arrangement, "preferential consideration" would be given to UAW members currently employed by the automaker if they seek jobs in certain new GM plants. The UAW has contended that having its members in these plants would aid organizing efforts.

The UAW has organized only one of the dozen new GM plants located in the South. The union claims that GM opposition to unions is indicated by its "practice of building most of its new plants in the South, where unions have difficulty organizing workers. When this issue arose during the 1976 negotiations, GM agreed to a "neutrality pledge" under which it would not fight the UAW's organizing efforts. The UAW later claimed that GM was not abiding by its pledge.

A GM spokesman said the preferential hiring plan would cover 13 new GM plants, of which 11 are in the South. Also, GM agreed to recognize the union as the bargaining agent for workers at four of the facilities without going through election procedures. Under the terms of the 1976 national agreement, GM can take such a step if the new facility makes the same products as another GM plant already represented by the UAW. The plants, two in Michigan and one each in Alabama and Georgia, all manufacture auto parts.

UAW President Douglas Fraser said implementation of the agreement "will put behind us the problem of the 'southern strategy' the union has faced for a few years," and expressed confidence that the UAW would become the bargaining agent at all new GM plants. In 1977, a National Relations Board administrative law judge ruled that the automaker committed labor law violations in opposing UAW attempts to organize a GM auto battery plant in Fitzgerald, Ga. (*Monthly Labor Review,* December 1977, p. 73.)

Stevens, NLRB reach agreement

J.P. Stevens & Co. announced an informal settlement with the National Labor Relations Board of 47 alleged violations of the National Labor Relations Act. The allegations, filed by the Amalgamated Clothing and Textile Workers Union, contended that Stevens barred workers from organizing and discriminated against workers who engaged in union activities—practices that are illegal under the act. Stevens denied violations of the act, saying the agreement indicated the Board's recognition of Stevens' affirmative compliance program.

The agreement covered plants in Greenville, Piedmont, Great Falls, Pamplico, and Walterboro, S.C. (A previous agreement had excluded these plants. See *Monthly Labor Review,* July 1978, pp. 43–44.) Stevens agreed to cease the conduct covered by the complaint and provide remedial action, and also agreed to reinstate a discharged employee at the Pamplico plant. The Government can reopen the case if the company violates the agreement.

The union indicated that it agreed to the settlement because it was presented with "a fait accompli" and said it either had to sign or go through lengthy legal proceedings. A spokesman added, "Even though we don't like the settlement, it's still better than being in limbo for a long period of time."

Airlines reduce strike aid

Airlines participating in the Mutual Aid Agreement announced revisions of the pact which was established in 1958 to blunt the financial effect of strikes. The new provisions reduce the payments guaranteed to a struck carrier from 50 percent of its normal operating expenses in the first 2 weeks of a strike, to 35 percent. After 10 weeks of a strike, a carrier will receive nothing, compared to the 35 percent it received from the other member carriers under the old formula. The revisions were made to eliminate the possibility that an airline could show a profit while struck because of savings in wages and fuel bills. The agreement continues the provision under which airlines receiving increased business due to a strike will turn over resulting increase in net revenues to the struck airline.

Soccer players win union representation

Major league sports unionization spread to soccer, as players of the 22 American teams in the North American Soccer League (NASL) voted 271 to 94 to be represented by the North American Soccer League Players' Association. About 400 voters in 21 cities participated in the election conduced by the National Labor Relations Board. The Board had previously assumed jurisdiction over major league baseball, and in 1971 certified the National Football League Players Association as the representative of professional football players. Collective bargaining for players in the National Basketball Association and the National Hockey League exists through voluntary recognition.

The NASL had contended that leaguewide bargaining was inappropriate because each individual club franchise is an autonomous entity retaining control over its players. The Board, however, ruled that the league and its members are joint employers, even though the individual club franchises have a considerable degree of autonomy in daily relations with their employees. □

Developments in Industrial Relations

Reported in *Monthly Labor Review*, December 1978.

Carter Administration's anti-inflation plan

In an address to the Nation on October 24, President Carter announced a new plan to curb inflation. Rejecting the alternatives of mandatory controls or a "deliberate recession that would put millions out of work," the President's plan calls for cuts in Government spending and voluntary wage and price controls. (For details the Administration's proposal for wage and price restraints see *Monthly Labor Review,* March 1978, p. 53.)

Under the plan, employees are encouraged to limit requested wage increases to a maximum of 7 percent per year. Collective bargaining agreements negotiated after the announcement should not provide for an increase in compensation (pay and supplementary benefits) in excess of 8 percent in the first year of the contract, or more than 7 percent annually when all wage and benefit changes are averaged over the life of the contract. If the contract includes a cost-of-living wage escalator clause, the bargaining parties are to calculate the escalator portion of the overall wage and benefit package by assuming that the Consumer Price Index will rise at a 6-percent annual rate.

The general wage standard also applies to units of management and nonunion administrative and supervisory employees. However, there are some exceptions:

- units of employees can receive wage and benefits gains exceeding the standard if it is necessary to maintain a historical "tandem relationship" with related units that negotiated or were granted such increases prior to the controls program;

- increases in compensation can exceed the standard if warranted by changes in work rules and practices producing "improvements in productivity of equal or greater value";

- individual employees can receive increases in excess of the standard as long as the average for the unit conforms; and

- workers earning $4 and hour or less will not be subject to the standards.

"Developments in Industrial Relations" is prepared by Leon Bornstein and other members of the staff of the Division of Trends in Employee Compensation, Bureau of Labor Statistics, and is largely based on information from secondary sources.

The President will ask the Congress to enact what he termed "real wage insurance" designed to give workers "an additional incentive" to cooperate. Under this proposal, members of units conforming to the 7-percent wage standard would receive a tax rebate if the CPI rose more than 7 percent.

With regard to prices, the President said the basic target for "economywide price increases is 5–¾ percent." Individual firms are expected to limit price increases over the next year to 0.5 percentage point below their average annual rate of price increase during 1976–77.

Also, beginning January 1, 1979, the Government will require companies awarded contracts in excess of $5 million to "certify that they are observing the [wage and price] standards." If they are unable to do so, the contracts then would go to firms that are conforming to the standards. The Government also will attempt to induce compliance by publicizing the names of nonconforming companies, by relaxing certain import restrictions, and by asking regulatory agencies to "review rate levels and other rules in light of the standards."

The third major aspect of the anti-inflation plan would put a limit on Government spending. The President said that in fiscal 1980, which begins October 1, 1979, he plans to reduce the budget deficit "to $30 billion or less." This is about $10 billion less than the $40 billion deficit anticipated for fiscal 1979.

The President noted that the October 1978 salary increase for Federal employees and military personnel was limited to 5.5 percent, and Federal executives and military officers in the upper grades did not receive an increase. (Members of Congress, Federal judges, and various officials would have automatically received a matching 5.5-percent salary increase, but the Congress earlier had voted to suspend operation of the law for 1978.)

Alfred Kahn will chair the Council on Wage and Price Stability, which will direct and monitor the anti-inflation program. Kahn, an economist, had headed the Civil Aeronautics Board.

Volkswagen proposal modified after strike

Volkswagen of America, Inc., and the Auto Workers announced a first contract for the company's New Stanton, Pa., assembly plant, the first manufacturing facility in the United States operated by a foreign carmaker. Earlier, members of Local 2055 had rejected a settlement the parties said would have brought wage and benefit levels at the end of 3 years up to the levels prevailing at the "Big 3" auto makers—General Motors, Corp., Chrysler Corp., and Ford Motor Co.

Members of the local contended they should have immediate parity, saying that 1979 settlements with the "Big 3" companies would probably provide for gains that would further delay attainment of parity. Their dissatisfaction resulted in a 6-day walkout that ended prior to the revised agreement. The decision to return to work was influenced, to some extent, by a company announcement that it would "rearrange" the wage and benefit package, but could not increase its size because of the $250-million start up cost of the plant, which was not expected to become profitable until 1980.

The accepted agreement provided for a 6-month move up of each of the scheduled wage increases, in return for some concessions by the union. The union's concessions included a 1-year delay in the effective date of a new dental plan for new employees (available immediately for eligible employees already on the payroll); a longer wage-progression schedule for new employees; and a 37-month contract (instead of the 36-month contract originally proposed).

Under the new pay schedule, the pay rates for the various job classifications rose to a range of $7–$9.09 an hour (from $5.50–$8.09), effective immediately, and in two steps, to $8.20–$10.29 by Oct. 1, 1980. In addition, the Volkswagen employees will receive cost-of-living wage increases, beginning in December 1978. (October pay rates at the "Big 3" companies ranged from about $7.85 – $9.30 an hour, including the 84 cents escalator allowance.)

Other contract provisions, comparable to those at the "Big 3" companies, included a pension plan effective in the third year; 39 paid holidays and 9 paid absence days over the contract term; company-paid health insurance and group life and disability insurance; and a Supplemental Unemployment Benefits plan.

Brewery workers win backpay

Following a backpay settlement with members of Brewery Workers Local 366, Adolph Coors Co. requested the rescheduling of a previously postponed election to determine if the union will continue to act as bargaining agent for workers in the Golden, Colo., plant.

A decertification election to resolve a 14-month strike against Coors by union members had been indefinitely set aside by the National Labor Relations Board until the backpay issue could be decided. The $254,629 award to 111 employees stemmed from a 1976 company reorganization of production. The union claimed that the resulting downward reclassification for some employees violated the work contract.

About 1,500 workers walked off the job on Apr. 5, 1977 (their old contract had expired on Dec. 31, 1976). Employee rights and privacy were the primary issues in the negotiations, including the union's opposition to a lie-detector test for employees. Coors hired 350 permanent replacements in addition to the 945 strikers the company said had returned to work after the walkout began. The plant also employs 2,300 workers not represented by the Brewery Workers.

Steelworkers' income protection guidelines set

The United Steelworkers of America and the 10 Coordinating Committee Steel Companies announced guidelines for the "rule-of-65" pensions and other extended benefits of the Employment and Income Security Program established under the 1977 settlement in the basic steel industry. (See *Monthly Labor Review,* June 1977, pp. 62–63.) The guidelines were worked out by a Joint Task Force on Employment Security, which will resolve any future disputes over operation of the program. If the task force is unable to reach agreement, the disputes will be settled through binding arbitration.

Although the Employment and Income Security Program had been scheduled to go into effect on January 1, 1978, the effective date had been delayed because the benefits were to be available to laid-off or disabled employees only if the employer was unable to offer "suitable long-term employment," which had not been precisely defined by the parties. Under the definition negotiated by the task force, a job offered by a company is suitable if (1) the employee is physically able to perform the job and has the necessary skills or the ability to acquire the skills, (2) the job is of indefinite duration and is within the general type the employee had previously performed (such as production, salaried, plant protection), and (3) the new job is in a unit represented by the union and is in the employee's home plant. If a job is not available in the employee's home plant, the employee must accept a suitable job offered by the company from a list of "A" plants (those within commuting distance), or "B" plants (those involving a household move of under 120 miles), or "C" plants (those involving a move of somewhat greater distance). Employees moving to "B" or "C" plants will receive special temporary earnings guarantees higher than that for those moving to "A" plants, as well as supplemental relocation allowances.

The new regulations provide for retroactivity of benefits to Jan. 1, 1978. Some laid-off employees of Youngstown Sheet & Tube Co. and Bethlehem Steel Corp. will be immediately eligible for benefits under the program if the companies are unable to offer them "suitable" jobs. These employees were laid off prior to Jan. 1, 1978, but an arbitration panel has ruled that they should be covered, based on past negotiating practices in the industry. (See *Monthly Labor Review,* June 1978, pp. 56–57.)

ACTWU approves merger with Shoe Workers

In its first convention since the clothing and textile workers unions merged in June 1978, the Amalgamated Clothing and Textile Workers Union (ACTWU) vowed to continue to battle the flood of foreign imports, to organize J. P. Stevens, and fight against brown lung disease. ACTWU President Murray H. Finley indicated that the union would not stop fighting until "we stop the flood of imports which are robbing us of our decent jobs." Finley praised the Carter Administration for negotiating relief through bilateral agreements with other countries. But, he asserted that the agreements didn't work during the first 7 months of 1978, citing a 40-percent increase in textile and apparel imports over the 1977 rate. The delegates approved "in principle" plans to bring the 25,000-member United Shoe Workers into the 509,000-member ACTWU. The ACTWU expects to have a ratification vote on the merger through a secret ballot vote in local union halls. The Shoe Workers are scheduled to act on the merger at a special convention in December. In other actions, the delegates approved a 50-cent rise in the dues structure in each of the next 2 years, bringing a $10 monthly minimum by 1980, with the international's share of dues rising to $5.

Carpenters assail 'open shop' trend

The Carpenters' union's 33d convention in St. Louis expressed concern about the growing threat of nonunion competition. Union President William Sidell told the 2,300 delegates that "the open shop movement has invaded the construction industry to a point of grave concern" and job opportunities and wages and working conditions "stand in serious jeopardy." He further informed the delegates that it is difficult to win bargaining rights for workers because of cheap imports and products manufactured in nonunion shops. Sidell blamed the growth of the open shop on the serious recession of 1974–76, continuing inflation, and "the growth in the new right" in cooperation with big business with the objective of creating a "union-free environment."

The Carpenters' chief pointed out that since the union's last convention in 1974, membership has declined by 68,687 (59,868 of those in the construction industry), to a current total of 790,000. As a result, the convention adopted a major 15-point organizing program to be financed by a total of $1.50 in per capita increases spread over the next 3 years. The highlight of the program will be the creation of an industrial section in the union's organizing department.

The delegates also heard President Robert A. Georgine of the AFL–CIO Building and Construction Trades Department disclose that the department benefited from a pilot organizing drive in Los Angeles and, thus, has scheduled similar campaigns for Erie, Pa.; Baltimore, Md.; Washington, D.C.; and Phoenix, Ariz.

Union election results

Rene Rondou, age 51, was elected secretary-treasurer of the Bakery, Confectionary, and Tobacco Workers at a special meeting of the union's executive board, filling the vacancy created by the death of Gregory Oskian. Rondou was president of the Tobacco Workers until it merged with the Bakery and Confectionary Workers union in August (*Monthly Labor Review,* October 1978, p. 58).

The National Association of Letter Carriers elected Vincent R. Sombrotto as its new president, rejecting incumbent J. Joseph Vacca. Sombrotto, who headed Branch 36 in New York City, had been defeated for the post by Vacca in 1976.

Dennis Glavin was elected international president of the independent United Electrical, Radio, and Machine Workers of America at the union's 43d annual convention in Minneapolis. He succeeded Albert J. Fitzgerald, who retired after 37 years in office. Glavin, age 51, headed the union's national negotiating committee with Westinghouse.

Civil Service reorganization

A major part of President Carter's proposed legislative program, Civil Service reorganization, has become law. The Civil Service Reform Act of

1978 separates the Civil Service Commission into two agencies—the Merit Systems Protection Board, which is charged with ensuring adherence to merit principles, and the Office of Personnel Management, which will help the President manage the executive branch of the Government. In addition, the act provides for establishing an independent Federal Labor Relations Authority with functions similar to those of the National Labor Relations Board, which governs the private sector. The measure also

- provides machinery to deal with contract impasses;
- mandates arbitration of grievances;
- protects "whistle-blower" (those who report improper Government activities);
- creates a Senior Executive Service for top management officials (grades 16 to 18 of the General Schedule pay systems, plus certain officials covered by other systems), where performance will be the key to bonus rewards or demotions; and
- links pay raises to performance of supervisors in grades 13–15.

The President recalled that during the presidential campaign he promised to make "reorganization of the Government a top priority." He said the legislation was "a long step toward meeting that commitment," calling it "long overdue." (For an account of union's reaction to the measure, see "Civil Service reform proposal figures prominently in AFGE races," *Monthly Labor Review,* November 1978, pp. 30–32.)

In a separate action, the President signed the Federal Employees Flexible and Compressed Work Schedules Act of 1978, permitting Federal agencies to experiment with alternatives to the traditional 5-day, 40-hour week. The President noted that during his campaign he promised "to encourage the introduction of more flexible work alternatives to benefit, among others, persons with children, students, and the older or handicapped worker. Flexible time schedules will allow some Federal agencies to serve the public for a greater number of hours each day." The legislation also contains a provision allowing Federal employees to request compensatory time for hours of work lost because of religious beliefs.

Job safety task force report

Secretary of Labor Ray Marshall and Director of the Office of Management and Budget, James T. McIntyre, have announced 14 recommendations for improving Federal regulation of workplace safety and health. The recommendations are part of the First Recommendations Report released by the Interagency Task Force on Workplace Safety and Health, a presidential task force co-chaired by Marshall and McIntyre. Eleven of the proposals deal specifically with operations of OSHA. Included were proposals that OSHA increase accident investigations to obtain more data on injury causes and their relationship to standards and that OSHA permit abatement of cited safety violations by following standards or their "substantial equivalent."

Other proposals cover items such as developing standard-setting and enforcement criteria for determining which hazards are to be dealt with first; expanding the Small Business Administration-OSHA loan program; and developing publicity efforts to increase awareness of job hazards and their prevention at the local level. Three recommendations call for action by the Departments of Labor and Health, Education, and Welfare in improving the ability of participants enrolled in the Comprehensive Employment and Training Act and State vocational-educational programs to recognize hazards and follow safe practices.

Richard Bergman, executive director of the Task Force, said the First Recommendations Report would be followed by a final report which will expand these recommendations and add others. □

Developments in Industrial Relations

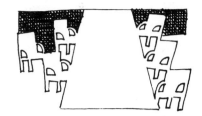

Reported in *Monthly Labor Review*, February 1979.

Administration's anti-inflation plan revised

The Carter Administration has announced revisions of its anti-inflation plan. (See *Monthly Labor Review*, January 1979, p. 59.) Alfred Kahn, chairman of the Council on Wage and Price Stability, said the changes were triggered by complaints from business and labor which termed the policy "too rigid." The Teamsters union, which began negotiations with the trucking industry on December 14, complained that the 7-percent limit would leave little room for improvements in pensions, as well as in wages and other benefits.

The revisions, announced in mid-December,

• exempt any cost increases needed to maintain existing levels of pension benefits from counting toward the 7-percent guideline limit for annual increases in compensation;

• specify that only the first 7 percent of any rise in health insurance premiums required to maintain benefits count toward the guideline;

• exempt from the 7-percent guideline increased labor costs mandated by Federal statutes (such as the new pregnancy-leave legislation and the law barring mandatory retirement for workers prior to age 70);

• suspend the 7-percent guideline when necessary to counter specific labor shortages;

• revise the method of assessing compensation increases for nonunion workers, making it similar to that for union-represented workers; and

• add a requirement that companies using the profit-margin approach to meet the price standard also must limit their dollar-profit increase to 6.5 percent during the year.

Meanwhile, the first legal test of the anti-inflation plan was moving toward an uncertain conclusion, as Federal District Court Judge Robert C. Belloni of Portland, Oreg., denied a request by the independent Association of Western Pulp and Paperworkers for a preliminary injunction barring the Government from enforcing the guidelines. However, Judge Belloni did order the Council on Wage and Price Stability to hold a hearing to determine if the union's coming settlements should be exempt from the guidelines, but the union indicated that it would not participate in the hearing. Union attorney Ronald Rosenberg said that during the court proceedings the Government had conceded that only contracts for sale to the Government of goods and services valued at $5 million or more would be denied a company exceeding the guidelines. According to Rosenberg, none of the companies with which the union was bargaining held or was in the process of bidding on contracts of that value.

Since July, 15,000 of the union's 22,000 members had been striking a number of pulp and paper concerns on the West Coast. The union was seeking a 10.75-percent raise in the first year and 10.5 percent in the second year, to parallel increases it won in 10 settlements earlier in 1978. The union claimed a "tandem relationship" with the earlier settlements, allowable under the anti-inflation plan, while the Council's position was that such a relationship did not exist.

One of the struck companies had informed its striking employees that agreeing to the settlement package could cause the company to lose Government sales contracts. This led to the union's suit which charged that the guidelines were mandatory to the extent they are enforced by the sales contract sanctions, and that mandatory controls are beyond the President's constitutional and statutory authority.

TWA and Machinists settle

The International Association of Machinists, which is bargaining with various airlines, has reached a 3-year agreement with Trans World Airlines (TWA) for 14,000 mechanics and other ground service employees. The contract provided for wage increases of 9.2 percent on November 1, 1978, 1.5 percent on July 1, 1979, 3.9 percent on January 1, 1980, 2 percent on July 1, 1980, 3.5 percent on January 1, 1981, and 5 percent on July 1, 1981. After the final increase, rates will range from $9.07 an hour for janitors to $14.82 for lead system technicians, with mechanics receiving $12.79. Under the prior agreement, the respective rates were $7.11, $11.60, and $10.03. The pay rates in the new contract are subject to additional increases of up to 17 cents in 1980 and 18 cents in 1981, depending on the rise in the Consumer Price Index for Urban Wage Earners and Clerical Workers. (Under the previous escalator clause, employees had received maximum adjustments of 12 cents in both 1977 and 1978.) The new agreement also provided that employees will receive a premium of 25 cents an hour (formerly, 15 cents) for each government airframe, engine, or radiotelephone license held, subject to a limit of 50 cents an hour (formerly, 30 cents).

Other terms included a seventh week of paid vacation after 35 years of service; a monthly pension rate of $17.50, $19, or $22 (varying by job classification) for each year of credited service, instead of the previous $12.50, $14, or $17; $250,000 annual major medical coverage, formerly $100,000); and a $2,000 increase in the schedule of life insurance coverage, bringing the maximum coverage to $26,000.

The agreement at TWA was attained under the new 90-day expedited bargaining procedure adopted in March 1977 with the approval of the National Mediation Board, which administers the provisions of the Railway Labor Act governing airlines bargaining. A 120-day schedule of deadlines for the various stages of bargaining applied at United Airlines, where the parties had not yet reached agreement. Bargaining also was continuing with Eastern Airlines and six smaller carriers. Including TWA, bargaining in the airlines industry covered 60,000 workers.

Shoe workers get 2-year contracts

About 20,000 employees of Brown Shoe Co. and International Shoe Co. are covered by recent settlements with the United Shoe Workers' union and the Retail Clerks' Boot and Shoe Workers Division, which bargained jointly with each of the companies. Employees of both companies work in Missouri, Arkansas, and Kentucky; Brown employees also are located in Mississippi and Tennessee and International Shoe employees, in Illinois.

The Brown accord was reached first and set the pattern for the International Shoe agreement. The 2-year contract provided for an initial wage increase of 25 cents an hour in November 1978, 13 cents in November 1979, and 12 cents in March 1980. The 10,000 Brown employees reportedly averaged $3.86 an hour under the prior contract. Other provisions included a rise in employer-financed life insurance to $5,000 (from $4,000); a 10th paid holiday, effective in the second year; and an increase in the monthly pension rate to $4.75 (from $4) for each year of credited service.

After the Brown and International Shoe settlements, the United Shoe Workers and the Florsheim Shoe Co., agreed on similar terms for 1,200 workers in Chicago. The union also was bargaining with shoe manufacturers in eastern Massachusetts, New York City, and Southern California.

Teachers open drive to organize nurses

The president of the American Federation of Teachers, Albert Shanker, announced that the union was launching an organizing campaign among nurses and other employees in the health care industry. The union, which claims about 500,000 members, plans to establish a new division called the American Federation of Nurses-AFT to direct the campaign.

The American Nurses Association, which represents about 100,000 nurses in collective bargaining relationships, called the plan "another attempt by an AFL-CIO affiliate to shore up their sagging membership." Barbara Nichols, president of the Association, said that if AFT "has difficulty representing teachers, I do not see how they can expect to represent nurses."

Shanker denied the AFT's membership was on the decline, but admitted that smaller student enrollments and fiscal cutbacks have slowed the union's growth rate, when compared with the 1960's and early 1970's. He asserted that nurses do not feel comfortable with some of the unions that bargain for health care workers because the unions represent nonprofessional as well as professional employees, and that his union was in a "unique position to do something" for the nurses, being experienced in dealing with certifying agencies at the State and Federal levels. □

Organized Labor in the United States

STRUCTURE OF
THE LABOR MOVEMENT

A total of 208 organizations—171 classified as unions and 37 as professional and state employee associations—are listed in this directory. AFL-CIO affiliates accounted for 106 of the unions; another 65 unions were unaffiliated. The 106 international unions in the American Federation of Labor and Congress of Industrial Organizations consist of more than 60,000 local unions with a combined membership of 13,600,000 workers as of January 1, 1978. The table included in this section shows the average membership based on the two-year period ending September 30, 1977. Membership figures for international unions in the directory itself are those available to the Bureau of Labor Statistics as of February 1978. These figures were made on the basis of an earlier study and because of differences in the method and basis of reporting, it is likely that the numbers in the table are more current and accurate than those in the listing.

THE AFL-CIO

The constitution of the American Federation of Labor and Congress of Industrial Organizations, adopted at its founding convention in 1955, established an organizational structure closely resembling that of the former AFL but vested more authority over affiliates in the new Federation. The chief members of the Federation continued to be the national and international unions, the trade departments, the State and local bodies, and the directly affiliated local unions. (See chart 1.)

The supreme governing body of the AFL-CIO is the biennial convention. Each union is entitled to convention representation according to the membership on which the per capita tax[1] has been paid.

Between conventions, the executive officers, assisted by the Executive Council and the General Board, direct the affairs of the AFL-CIO. In brief, the functions of the two top officers and of the two governing bodies are as follows:

Executive officers. The president, as chief executive officer, has authority to interpret the constitution between meetings of the Executive Council. He also directs the staff of the Federation. The secretary-treasurer is responsible for all financial matters.

Executive Council. The Executive Council, consisting of 33 vice-presidents and the two executive officers, is the governing body between conventions. It must meet at least three times each year by request of the president.

[1] 16 cents a month.

Responsibilities of the council include proposing and evaluating legislation of interest to the labor movement and safeguarding the Federation from corrupt or communist influence. To achieve the latter, the council has the right to investigate any affiliate accused of wrongdoing and, upon completion of the investigation, make recommendations or give directions to the affiliate involved.

Furthermore, by a two-thirds vote, the Executive Council may suspend a union found guilty on charges of corruption or subversion. The council also is given the right to (1) conduct hearings on charges against a council member of malfeasance or maladministration and report to the convention recommending the appropriate action; (2) remove from office or refuse to seat, by two-thirds vote, any executive officer or council member found to be a member or follower of a subversive organization; (3) assist unions in organizing activities and charter new national and international unions not in jurisdictional conflict with existing ones; and (4) hear appeals in jurisdiction disputes.

General Board. This body consists of all 35 members of the Executive Council and a principal officer of each affiliated international and national union and department. The General Board acts on matters referred to it by the executive officers or the Executive Council. It meets upon call of the president. Unlike members of the Executive Council, General Board members vote as representatives of their unions; voting strength is based on per capita payments to the Federation.

Standing committees and staff. The constitution authorizes the president to appoint standing committees to execute legislative, political, educational, and other activities. These committees operate under the direction of the president and are subject to the authority of the Executive Council and the convention. Fifteen standing committees are operating at present; staff departments are established as needed.

Department of Organization and Field Service. Meeting just prior to the opening of the 1973 general convention, the AFL-CIO's Executive Council revised the role and function of the Department of Organization, integrating the regional offices of the former department with all AFL-CIO operations and programs. Reflecting this expanded role, the name of the department was changed to the "Department of Organization and Field Services." The director of the department is appointed by the president,

STRUCTURAL ORGANIZATION
of the
AMERICAN FEDERATION OF LABOR AND CONGRESS OF INDUSTRIAL ORGANIZATIONS

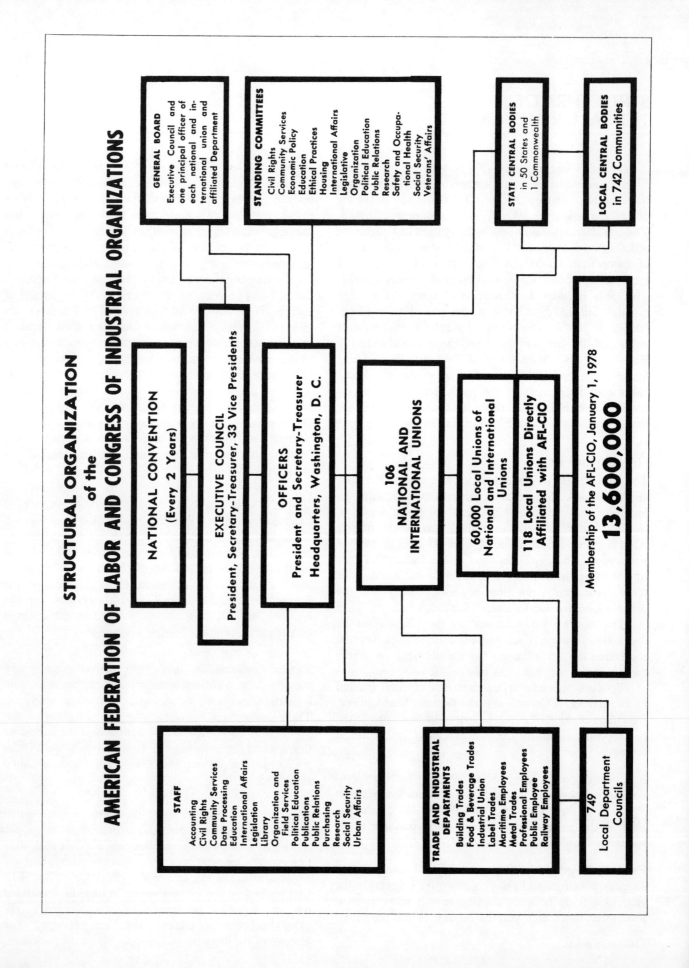

NATIONAL CONVENTION
(Every 2 Years)

EXECUTIVE COUNCIL
President, Secretary-Treasurer, 33 Vice Presidents

OFFICERS
President and Secretary-Treasurer
Headquarters, Washington, D. C.

106 NATIONAL AND INTERNATIONAL UNIONS

60,000 Local Unions of National and International Unions

118 Local Unions Directly Affiliated with AFL-CIO

Membership of the AFL-CIO, January 1, 1978
13,600,000

GENERAL BOARD
Executive Council and one principal officer of each national and international union and affiliated Department

STANDING COMMITTEES
Civil Rights
Community Services
Economic Policy
Education
Ethical Practices
Housing
International Affairs
Legislative
Organization
Political Education
Public Relations
Research
Safety and Occupational Health
Social Security
Veterans' Affairs

STATE CENTRAL BODIES
in 50 States and 1 Commonwealth

LOCAL CENTRAL BODIES
in 742 Communities

STAFF
Accounting
Civil Rights
Community Services
Data Processing
Education
International Affairs
Legislation
Library
Organization and Field Services
Political Education
Publications
Public Relations
Purchasing
Research
Social Security
Urban Affairs

TRADE AND INDUSTRIAL DEPARTMENTS
Building Trades
Food & Beverage Trades
Industrial Union
Label Trades
Maritime Employees
Metal Trades
Professional Employees
Public Employee
Railway Employees

749 Local Department Councils

subject to the approval of the Executive Council. The department has its own staff and other resources necessary to carry out its activities.

Trade and industrial departments. The AFL-CIO constitution provides for seven trade and industrial departments and others ". . . as may be established by the Executive Council or the Convention" (art. XI, sec. 1). An Industrial Union Department was added to the five departments which were carried over from the AFL. A department made up of unions in the food and beverage industry, chartered in 1961, was disbanded at the 1965 convention and reinstated in November 1976. On November 6, 1974, a charter was issued to another group, the Public Employee Department, which is composed of 29 members. The Convention in December of 1977 abolished the Council for Professional employees and created a new Professional Employees Department. Affiliation with departments is open to "all appropriate affiliated national and international unions and organizing committees" (art. XI, sec. 1). Affiliates are obligated to pay a department per capita tax which is determined by the number of members coming within their jurisdiction.

State and central bodies. Under the AFL-CIO constitution, the Executive Council is authorized to establish central bodies on a city, State, or other regional basis, composed of locals of national unions, organizing committees, and directly affiliated local unions. In 1975 there were 51 State bodies, including one for Puerto Rico. Approximately 745 local central bodies were in existence at this time.

Organizing committees. The Executive Council has the authority to issue charters to groups not eligible for membership in national unions and combine directly affiliated local unions into organizing committees. These committees have the same status as national unions, except that they are under control of the Federation. In February 1976 the only organizing committee was dissolved when the AFL-CIO Executive Council issued a union charter to the School Administrators and Supervisors Organizing Committee. The new union is known as the American Federation of School Administrators (AFL-CIO).

Directly affiliated local unions. At the time of the Federation's formation, local trade and federal labor unions (AFL) and local industrial unions (CIO) had a combined membership of 181,000. These local unions, having received charters from both federations, became directly affiliated local unions of the AFL-CIO and in October 1975 claimed approximately 57,000 members. Under the constitution of the merged Federation, the Executive Council of the AFL-CIO has responsibility for issuing charters and controlling the affairs of these locals. The council also is under obligation at the request of the locals to combine them into national unions, organizing committees, or national councils where appropriate.

Jurisdictional problems. Former AFL and CIO affiliates joined the Federation as fully autonomous unions and retained the same jurisdictional rights held before the merger. These principles are expressed as follows in article III, section 4 of the constitution: "The integrity of each . . . affiliate of this Federation shall be maintained and preserved." The concepts of autonomy and jurisdictional rights find further support in article III, section 7, which gives the Executive Council the right to issue charters to new organizations only if their jurisdiction does not conflict with that of present affiliates because "each affiliated national and international union is entitled to have its autonomy, integrity and jurisdiction protected and preserved." With respect to craft versus industrial form of organization—the issue primarily responsible for the 1935 split—the new constitution recognizes that "both craft and industrial unions are appropriate, equal, and necessary as methods of trade union organization . . ." (art. VIII, sec. 9). The constitution acknowledges the existence of overlapping jurisdictions which might invite conflict within the Federation. Affiliates are urged to eliminate such problems "through the process of voluntary agreement or voluntary merger in consultation with the appropriate officials of the Federation" (art. III, sec. 10).

New and enlarged machinery to replace those procedures previously provided for under the No-Raiding Agreement (art. III, sec. 4) were adopted at the 1961 convention and incorporated into a new section of the constitution, article XXI, Settlement of Internal Disputes, effective as of January 1, 1962 (art. XX in the 1975 constitution). Under the terms of this article, affiliates are required to respect both the established collective bargaining and the work relationships of every other affiliate. In a dispute, the case first goes to a mediator chosen from a panel "composed of persons from within the labor movement" (art. XX, sec. 8). Should the mediator be unable to settle the dispute within 14 days, it is then referred to an impartial umpire selected from a panel "composed of prominent and respected persons . . ." (art. XX, sec. 9), for a decision which is effected 5 days after it has been handed down, unless an appeal has been filed. An appeal case is first referred to a subcommittee of the Executive Council, which can either dismiss it or submit it to the full Executive Council for a final decision. A variety of sanctions are provided against noncomplying unions, including loss of the right to invoke the dispute settlement machinery and possible suspension. The Federation is further authorized to publicize the fact that a union has refused to comply with a decision and that it can extend "every appropriate assistance and aid" (art. XX, sec. 15) to an aggrieved union.

RAILWAY LABOR EXECUTIVES' ASSOCIATION

This Association is composed of the president of the Railway Employes' Department (AFL-CIO) and a major official from each of the 19 labor unions, of which all but one are affiliated with the AFL-CIO. Ten of these unions have virtually all of their membership in the railroad industry; the remaining nine are established principally in other industries.

In 1975, the unions affiliated with the Congress of Railway Unions agreed to dissolve the organization. All but one of the unions joined the Railway Labor Executives' Association (RLEA) on April 1 of that year. The Congress was formed in December 1969 after five unions withdrew from the RLEA over a dispute involving proposed compulsory retirement and pension benefit legislation. The reunification was suggested since those involved believed their functions could be more effectively handled as a united force. The RLEA is not a federation of unions, but rather functions as a policy-making body on legislative and other matters of material interest to railroad workers.

OTHER FEDERATIONS

Two organizations are listed which either act as a federation or have some of the characteristics of a federation, such as the issuance of charters to, and the maintenance of, a formal affiliation among autonomous labor organizations. The Assembly of Governmental Employees (AGE), founded in 1952 as the National Conference of Independent Public Employee Organizations, is made up of 45 State, county, and local affiliated organizations. The AGE is primarily concerned with the establishment and maintenance of the merit principle, although its affiliates have considerable autonomy on specific policy issues, including work stoppages. The 26 AGE affiliates that engage in collective bargaining or representational activities are listed individually in part II. The second organization listed is the National Federation of Independent Unions (NFIU). Unions affiliated with the NFIU which had negotiated agreements covering different employers in more than one State are included among the unaffiliated, or independent, unions discussed below.

UNAFFILIATED OR INDEPENDENT UNIONS

A total of 64 national or international unions not affiliated with the AFL-CIO were known to the Bureau. All of the unaffiliated unions (other than those organizing government employees) reported agreements covering different employers in more than one State.[2] The combined membership of these unions was 4.5 million, and included members of long-established and well-known organizations such as the Brotherhood of Locomotive Engineers and the United Mine Workers of America. Approximately four-fifths of the membership in unaffiliated national and international unions were in unions once affiliated with the AFL-CIO and the former CIO. These include the United Automobile Workers and expelled unions such as the International Brotherhood of Teamsters, the United Electrical Workers (UE), the Longshoremen's and Warehousemen's Union, and the Distributive Workers.

Unaffiliated local unions are generally confined to a single establishment, employer, or locality, and therefore do not meet the Bureau's definition of national unions used in compiling this directory. A 1967 Bureau survey showed about 475,000 members in 884 unaffilated local unions. According to the Bureau's finding, these local independent unions represented approximately 2.3 percent of the total union membership in the United States.

Internal Disputes Plan

The AFL-CIO Internal Disputes Plan was activated in January 1962. From that date through June 30, 1977, 1,794 complaints or claims of justification action were filed with the President's office. In the two-year period July 1, 1975 through June 30, 1977, 178 cases were filed.

Mediation, which is conducted by a member of a panel of mediators comprised of officers of international unions, continues to prove an effective means of settling disputes. Of the 1,794 cases filed, 1,008 (56 percent) have been settled through discussions between the organizations involved and mediation.

The four impartial umpires—David L. Cole, Howard W. Kleeb, Alexander B. Porter and D. Quinn Mills—hear and issue determinations on cases not settled at the mediation level, and 749 such determinations have been issued since 1962.

The following is a breakdown of the disposition of cases filed:

	7/1/75–6/30/77	1/1/62–6/30/77
Pending at start of period	34	—
Filed during period covered	178	1,794
	212	1,794
Mediation		
Settled in mediation	102	1,008
Pending 6/30/77	33	33
	135	1,041

---

[2] The requirement pertaining to collective bargaining agreements was waived for organizations of government workers. Since the issuance of Executive Orders 10988 and 11491, the Bureau has attempted to include those Federal Government unions holding exclusive bargaining rights. Organizations representing postal employees have been included. Some unaffiliated unions, interstate in scope, may have been omitted because adequate information as to their existence or scope was not available.

	7/1/75– 6/30/77	1/1/62– 6/30/77
Umpire's determinations		
Violations found	48	457
Not found	24	273
Pending	4	4
Justification Reports	1	19
	77	753
Appeals		
Pending at start of period	6	—
Filed	24	236
	30	236
Determinations sustained	13	167
Appeals withdrawn	6	39
Referred to Executive Council	5	24
Pending	6	6
	30	236
Executive Council Action on Appeals		
Determinations affirmed	—	15
Determinations set aside or modified	6	9
Appeals withdrawn	—	1
	6	25*
Non-compliance complaints		
Pending at start of period	12	—
Filed	17	128
	29	128
Compliance achieved	11	69
Non-compliance found	3	23
Withdrawn	4	25
Pending	11	11
	29	128

* The Executive Council has also issued 13 policy statements on the interpretation of Article XX.

Sanctions Imposed

In the period 1/1/62 through 6/30/77 13 affiliates have been found to have failed to comply with decisions of the impartial umpire, or directions of subcommittees in 23 cases. In 10 instances, compliance was later achieved and the affiliate's rights under Article XX were restored.

The following three organizations are presently under sanctions:

Air Line Pilots Association

International Typographical Union

Graphic Arts International Union

Professional and State Employee Associations

Thirty-seven associations were known to be engaged in collective bargaining activities as of late 1976 and are included in the listing section; this number is inclusive of changes in the status of two professional and State employee associations since the *Directory* questionnaire was distributed. The membership series, includes 37 associations with 2.6 million members.

American Federation of Labor and Congress of Industrial Organizations Paid Membership

The following table shows the average per capita membership paid to the AFL-CIO for the year 1955, and subsequent two-year periods thereafter. The 1977 figures are based on the two-year period ending September 30, 1977.

Organizations	Thousands of Members											
	1955	1957	1959	1961	1963	1965	1967	1969	1971	1973	1975	1977
Actors and Artistes of America, Associated	34	43	51	58	59	61	62	72	69	72	76	85
Agricultural Workers Organizing Committee, AFL-CIO				2*	2	2	w					
Agricultural Workers Union, National	4	4	4	a								
Air Line Dispatchers Association	1	1	1	1	1	1	1	1	1	1	1	uu
Air Line Pilots Association	9	14	18	18	17	18	23	32	39	40	47	44
Aluminum Workers International Union	20	22	18	18	19	22	25	27	25	25	27	26
Asbestos Workers, Int'l Association of Heat and Frost Insulators and	9	10	10	10	11	12	12	12	13	13	13	13
Automobile, Aerospace and Agricultural Implement Workers of America, International Union, United	1,260	1,216	1,060	1,019	1,033	1,150	1,325	x				
Automobile Workers of America, International Union, United	73	b										
Bakery and Confectionery Workers International Union, American			40*	69	71	75	79	83kk				
Bakery and Confectionery Workers International Union of America	136	137	gg									
Bakery and Confectionery Workers International Union of America										128	130	123	115
Barbers and Beauty Culturists Union of America	3	c										
Barbers, Hairdressers and Cosmetologists' International Union of America, The Journeymen	65	69	73	73	73	73	68	66	60	50	42	34
Bill Posters, Billers and Distributors of the United States and Canada, International Alliance of	2	2	2	2	1	2	2	1	1	mm		
Boiler Makers, Iron Ship Builders, Blacksmiths, Forgers and Helpers, International Brotherhood of	151	151	151	151	111	108	122	122	121	115	123	130
Bookbinders, International Brotherhood of	51	54	56	56	53	51	57	60	59	ll		
Boot and Shoe Workers' Union	40	40	40	40	40	40	40	40	38	35	34	vv
Brewery, Flour, Cereal, Soft Drink and Distillery Workers, International Union of, United	45	45	45	45	45	42	40	40	40	40	rr	
Bricklayers and Allied Crafsmen, International Union of	120	120	120	120	120	120	120	120	121	134	143	120
Brick and Clay Workers of America, The United	23	25	23	23	21	21	21	19	17	16	16	15
Broadcast Employees and Technicians, National Association of	4	4	4	4	4	4	5	5	5	5	5	5
Broom and Whisk Makers Union, International	1	1	1	1	d							
Building Service Employees International Union	205	222	235	261	279	305	328	y				
Carpenters and Joiners of America, United Brotherhood of	750	750	750	709	700	700	700	700	700	700	700	675
Cement, Lime and Gypsum Workers International Union, United	35	35	34	32	31	30	29	29	29	30	29	26
Chemical Workers Union, International	79	72	67	65	68	70	77	89	12*ii	70	58	51
Cigarmakers' International Union of America	9	8	7	6	5	4	4	3	3	2	ss	
Clerks, National Federation of Post Office	97	96	94	e								
Clothing and Textile Workers Union, Amalgamated												

Organizations	Thousands of Members											
	1955	1957	1959	1961	1963	1965	1967	1969	1971	1973	1975	1977
Clothing Workers of America, Amalgamated	210	273	288	290	288	288	288	285	270	257	232	ww
Commercial Telegraphers' Union, The	29	29	29	26	22	22	22	z				
Communications Workers of America	249	250	261	255	273	288	315	348	415	438	476	478
Coopers International Union of North America	3	4	4	3	3	2	3	3	2	2	2	1
Distillery, Rectifying, Wine and Allied Workers' Int'l Union of America	26	25	31	34	25	24	25	27	21	20	18	16
Dolls, Toys, Playthings, Novelties and Allied Products of the United States and Canada, AFL-CIO, International Union of	14	17	18	19	20	22	25	26	26	25	30	33
Electrical, Radio and Machine Workers, International Union of	271	314	280	274	262	265	304	313	283	227	255	238
Electrical Workers, International Brotherhood of	460	464	514	548	557	616	658	733	760	779	856	814
Elevator Constructors, International Union of	10	10	10	11	12	12	12	12	12	12	13	16
Engineers, International Union of Operating	200	200	241	270	270	270	296	300	300	300	300	300
Engravers and Marking Device Workers Union, International Metal	1	f										
Farm Workers of America, AFL-CIO, United							1*	2	11	20	14	12
Fire Fighters, International Association of	72	78	80	78	80	87	87	87	101	105	123	148
Firemen and Oilers, International Brotherhood of	57	57	54	48	45	44	41	42	42	40	40	38
Flight Engineers' International Association	1	2	3	3	1	1	1	2	2	2	2	2
Furniture Workers of America, United	34	39	35	32	32	32	33	31	32	30	28	26
Garment Workers of America, United	40	40	38	35	35	35	35	35	32	32	32	32
Garment Workers Union, International Ladies'	383	373	368	363	363	363	363	363	363	363	363	350
Glass and Ceramic Workers of North America, United	41	42	36	35	32	33	34	32	30	30	28	26
Glass Bottle Blowers' Association of the United States and Canada	47	52	52	53	58	65	67	70	72	74	75	75
Glass Cutters League of America, Window	2	2	2	1	1	1	1	1	1	1	1	xx
Glass Workers Union, American Flint	28	29	28	30	29	31	33	34	32	34	35	31
Gloce Workers Union of America, International	3	3	3	g								
Government Employees, American Federation of	47	56	56	68	97	132	196	263	286	270	255	254
Government and Civic Employees Organizing Committee	27	h										
Grain Millers, American Federation of	33	32	31	29	24	25	24	25	21	25	29	35
Granite Cutters International Association of America, The	4	3	3	3	3	2	2	2	2	1	1	1
Graphic Arts International Union										99	93	83
Hatters, Cap and Millinery Workers International Union, United	32	32	32	32	32	32	31	28	18	15	15	8
Hod Carriers, Building and Common Laborers Union of America, International	372	400	403	403	403	p						
Horse Shoers of United States and Canada, International Union of Journeymen	1	1	1	1	1	1	1	1	1	1	1	1
Hosiery Workers, American Federation of	15	10	6	5	5	q						
Hotel and Restaurant Employees' and Bartenders' Int'l Union	300	300	300	300	300	300	300	300	300	328	421	398
Industrial Workers of America, International Union, Allied		76	66	64	63	71	84	89	85	88	93	84
Insurance Agents International Union	13	12	i									
Insurance Workers of America	9	9	i									
Insurance Workers International Union, AFL-CIO			22	22	21	21	23	24	24	24	22	21
Iron Workers, International Association of Bridge and Structural	133	136	144	137	130	132	145	151	157	160	160	160
Jewelery Workers Union, International	20	22	17	13	13	14	14	12	10	10	10	9
Laborers' International Union of North America						403	422	468	475	475	475	475
Lathers, International Union of Wood, Wire and Metal	16	16	16	16	16	16	15	14	14	14	12	12
Laundry and Dry Cleaning International Union, AFL-CIO			15*	24	22	22	23	24	26	22	20	18
Leather Goods, Plastics and Novelty Workers Union, International	30	29	31	32	36	34	35	38	41	43	39	30
Leather Workers International Union of America	2	6	5	5	5	4	4	4	3	2	2	2
Letter Carriers, National Association of	100	100	100	108	128	130	130	138	151	151	151	151
Lithographers and Photoengravers International Union					r	30*	43	45	46	ll		
Lithographers of America, Amalgamated	28	28	j									
Locomotive Firemen and Enginemen, Brotherhood of		37	55	50	48	41	35	aa				
Longshoremen, International Brotherhood of	8	15	14	k								
Longshoremen's Association, AFL-CIO, International				46*	50	50	50	50	50	60	60	62
Machinists and Aerospace Workers International Association of	627	708	691	646	636	663	740	815	754	698	780	653
Maintenance of Way Employes, Brotherhood of	159	152	131	101	85	77	71	62	63	71	71	73
Marble, Slate and Stone Polishers, Rubbers and Sawyers, Tile & Marble Setters Helpers and Terazzo Helpers, Int'l Assn. of	6	8	8	8	8	8	8	8	8	8	8	yy
Marine and Shipbuilding Workers of America, Industrial Union of	27	34	34	30	28	22	30	31	27	21	22	23
Marine Engineers' Beneficial Association, National	9	8	8	8	8	9	9	9	9	14	20	23
Maritime Union of America, National	37	39	40	38	42	45	45	45	45	43	35	30
Masters, Mates and Pilots, International Organization of	9	9	9	9	9	9	9	9	10	nn		
Master Mechanics and Foremen of Navy Yards and Naval Stations, National Association of	1	1	1	1	1	s						
Meat Cutters and Butcher Workmen of No. America, Amalgamated	263	312	329	325	325	330	352	432	456	470	450	442
Mechanics Educational Society of America	49	49	41	38	37	37	37	37	33	26	23	15
Metal Polishers, Buffers, Platers and Allied Workers	15	16	14	13	11	11	11	10	9	9	9	6
Molders and Allied Workers Union, AFL-CIO, International	67	68	57	54	53	50	50	50	50	50	50	50
Musicians, American Federation of	250	255	255	247	233	225	224	237	236	204	215	187
Newspaper Guild, The	21	22	24	24	23	23	24	25	26	26	26	26
Office and Professional Employees International Union	44	45	46	48	50	52	57	63	67	68	74	77
Oil, Chemical and Atomic Workers International Union	160	165	159	151	146	140	142	146	149	145	145	145
Packinghouse, Food and Allied Workers, United	118	96	87	76	73	71	68	bb				
Painters and Allied Trades of the United States and Canada, International Brotherhood of	182	185	179	163	158	160	160	160	160	160	160	160
Paper Makers, International Brotherhood	60	1										
Paper Workers International Union, United										266	275	261
Paper Workers of America, United	40	1										
Papermakers and Paperworkers, United			110	116	121	122	121	120	124	125	oo	
Pattern Makers League of North America	11	11	11	11	10	10	10	10	10	10	10	10
Photo Engravers Union of North America, International	16	16	16	16	15	t						
Plasterers' and Cement Masons' International Association of the United States and Canada, Operative	60	60	65	68	68	68	68	68	68	68	55	50
Plumbing and Pipe Fitting Industry of the United States and Canada, United Association of Journeymen and Apprentices of the	200	200	200	215	217	217	221	226	228	228	228	228
Porters, Brotherhood of Sleeping Car	10	10	10	8	6	5	5	5	2	1	1	1
Post Office and General Service Maintenance Employees, National Association							5*	6	hh			
Post Office Mail Handlers, Watchmen, Messengers and Group Leaders, National Association of	1	1	1	1	1	1	9	cc				
Post Office Motor Vehicle Employees, National Federation of			2*	4	4	5	6	7	hh			
Postal Transport Association, National	22	21	19	e								
Postal Clerks, United Federation of				95	115	117	138	152	hh			
Postal Workers Union, AFL-CIO, American									169	234	249	254
Pottery and Allied Workers, International Brotherhood of	23	26	28	26	22	19	18	14	15	15	17	zz
Printers, Die Stampers & Engravers Union of North America, International Plate	1	1	1	1	1	1	1	1	1	1	1	1
Printing and Graphic Communications Union, International											105	99
Printing Pressmen's and Assistants' Union of North America, Int'l	87	92	96	99	100	100	102	106	107	104	tt	
Professional and Technical Engineers, International Federation of										13	14	14
Pulp, Sulphite and Paper Mill Workers of the United States and Canada, International Brotherhood of	154	161	164	142	137	135	135	142	120	oo		
Radio and Television Directors Guild	1	1	1	m								
Radio Association, American	2	2	2	2	2	2	2	2	1	1	1	1
Railroad Telegraphers, The Order of	30	30	30	30	30	u						
Railroad Trainmen, Brotherhood of		13*	128	121	104	98	96	aa				
Railway Carmen of the United States and Canada, Brotherhood	116	127	111	93	86	84	80	71	63	57	56	51
Railway, Airline and Steamship Clerks, Freight Handlers, Express and Station Employes, Brotherhood of	264	267	250	215	196	186	181	192	150	153	160	107
Railway Patrolmen's International Union	3	3	3	2	2	2	2	dd				

Organizations	Thousands of Members											
	1955	1957	1959	1961	1963	1965	1967	1969	1971	1973	1975	1977
Railway Supervisors Association American		1*	6	6	6	6	6	6	6	6	6	6
Retail Clerks International Union	259	291	315	340	364	410	472	525	558	582	602	646
Retail, Wholesale and Department Store Union	97	105	107	110	111	114	120	119	119	98	118	131
Roofers, Damp and Waterproof Workers Association, United Slate, Tile and Composition	18	20	21	21	21	22	23	24	25	26	27	27
Rubber, Cork, Linoleum and Plastic Workers of America, United	163	162	152	152	150	153	166	174	169	169	173	159
School Administrators, American Federation of									1*	5	7	10
Seafarers International Union of North America	42	52	58	69	77	80	80					94
Service Employees International Union, AFL-CIO								352	396	439	480	505
Sheet Metal Workers International Association	50	56	75	84	86	100	100	102	120	120	120	120
Shoe Workers of America, United	51	51	50	50	48	45	44	43	35	33	25	24
Siderographers, International Association of	1	1	1	1	1	1	1	1	1	1	1	1
Signalmen of America, Brotherhood Railroad	15	15	14	13	12	11	10	10	10	9	10	10
Special Delivery Messengers, The National Association of	2	2	2	2	1	1	2	2	hh			
Stage Employes and Moving Picture Machine Operators of the United States and Canada, International Alliance of Theatrical	46	50	50	50	50	50	50	50	50	50	50	50
State, County and Municipal Employees, American Federation of	99	147	173	188	212	237	297	371	458	545	647	685
Steelworkers of America, United	980	1,021	892	843	805	876	952	941	950	945	1,062	954
Stereotypers', Electrotypers', and Platemakers' Union, International	12	12	12	12	12	11	10	9	8	7	tt	
Stone and Allied Products Workers of America, United	11	13	12	12	11	11	12	11	jj			
Stonecutters Association of North America, Journeymen	2	2	2	2	2	2	2	ee				
Stove, Furnace and Allied Appliance Workers of North America	10	9	8	9	9	9	9	8	6	3	3	3
Street and Electric Railway Employes of America, Amalgamated Asso. of	139	129	124	116	110	v						
Switchmen's Union of North America	11	12	11	10	10	9	9	aa				
Teachers, American Federation of	40	48	50	57	65	97	125	145	194	254	396	420
Technical Engineers, American Federation of	10	12	13	13	11	11	13	13	pp			
Telegraph Workers, United								23	20	16	12	11
Textile Workers of America, United	49	43	37	34	33	36	37	38	37	37	36	31
Textile Workers Union of America	203	190	173	142	122	123	125	122	117	117	105	ww
Tile, Marble, Terrazzo, Finishers and Shopmen International Union, AFL-CIO												7
Tobacco Workers International Union	27	25	25	24	24	24	24	24	24	25	26	24
Train Dispatchers Association, American		1*	4	4	4	3	3	3	3	3	3	3
Transit Union, Amalgamated						98	90	87	82	87	90	89
Transport Service Employees of America, United	3	3	3	3	3	3	3	3	2	qq		
Transport Workers Union of America	80	80	80	80	80	80	80	80	93	95	95	93
Transportation-Communication Employees Union						29	27	ff				
Transportation Union, United								138	139	134	134	122
Typographical Union, International	78	78	79	81	86	87	90	89	87	81	73	61
Upholsterers' International Union of North America	51	52	50	50	50	50	50	50	50	50	50	46
Utility Workers Union of America	53	53	53	51	50	50	51	52	48	54	52	52
Wallpaper Craftsmen and Workers of North America, United	1	1	n									
Weavers Protective Association, American Wire	1	1	o									
Woodworkers of America, International	91	58	52	50	47	49	52	50	51	55	52	53
Yardmasters of America, Railroad	4	4	4	4	4	4	4	4	4	4	4	4
Sub-Totals	12,441	12,888	12,671	12,482	12,407	12,869	13,736	12,957	13,115	13,352	14,018	13,501
Directly Affiliated Local Unions	181	132	108	71	62	50	45	48	62	55	52	41
Grand Totals	12,622	13,020	12,779	12,553	12,469	12,919	13,781	13,005	13,177	13,407	14,070	13,542

NOTE: Affiliated Unions with a paid membership of less than 1,000 were credited with a paid membership of 1,000.
   a. Merged with Amalgamated Meat Cutters and Butcher Workmen of North America on August 16, 1960.
   b. Title changed to Industrial Workers of America, International Union, Allied, May 1, 1956.
   c. Reaffiliated with Barbers, Hairdressers and Cosmetologists' International Union of America, The Journeymen, July 1, 1956.
   d. Broom and Whisk Makers Union, International, disbanded August 1962.
   e. Merged with National Federation of Post Office Clerks on December 6, 1961. Title changed to United Federation of Postal Clerks.
   f. Merged with Machinists and Aerospace Workers, International Association of, September 1, 1956.
   g. Merged with Amalgamated Clothing Workers of America, December 6, 1961.
   h. Merged with State, County and Municipal Employees, American Federation of, August 1, 1956.
   i. Merged into Insurance Workers International Union, AFL-CIO, May 18, 1959.
   j. Disaffiliated, August 21, 1958.
   k. Merged into Longshoremen's Association, AFL-CIO, International, November 17, 1959.
   l. Merged into Papermakers & Paperworkers, United, March 6, 1957.
   m. Disaffiliated, January 1, 1960.
   n. Merged with Pulp, Sulphite and Papermill Workers of the United States and Canada, International Brotherhood of, April 29, 1958.
   o. Merged with Papermakers and Paperworkers, United, February 16, 1959.
   p. Title changed to Laborers' International Union of North America, September 20, 1965.
   q. Merged with Textile Workers Union of America, April 28, 1965.
   r. Reaffiliated with AFL-CIO by merging with Photo Engravers Union of North America, International, on September 7, 1964.
   s. Withdrew April 1, 1964.
   t. Merged into Lithographers and Photoengravers International Union, September 7, 1964.
   u. Title changed to Transportation-Communication Employees Union, February 25, 1965.
   v. Title changed to Transit Union, Amalgamated, February 25, 1965.
   w. Charter granted to Farm Workers Organizing Committee, United, August 23, 1966, bringing together Agricultural Workers Organizing Committee, AFL-CIO, and Independent National Farm Workers Association.
   x. Disaffiliated, July 1, 1968.
   y. Title changed to Service Employees International Union, AFL-CIO, February 19, 1968.
   z. Title changed to Telegraph Workers, United, February 19, 1968.
   aa. Merged into Transportation Union, United, December 16, 1968.
   bb. Merged with Meat Cutters and Butcher Workmen of North America, Amalgamated, July 9, 1968.
   cc. Merged with Laborers' International Union of North America, April 20, 1968.
   dd. Merged with Railway, Airline and Steamship Clerks, Freight Handlers, Express and Station Employees, Brotherhood of, January 1, 1969.
   ee. Merged with Laborers' International Union of North America, February 19, 1968.
   ff. Merged with Railway, Airline and Steamship Clerks, Freight Handlers, Express and Station Employees, Brotherhood of, February 21, 1969.
   gg. Expelled by convention, December 12, 1957, merged with American Bakery and Confectionery Workers' International Union, December 4, 1969 to form Bakery and Confectionery Workers International Union of America.
   hh. Merged to form Postal Workers' Union, American, July 1, 1971.
   ii. Charter revoked by Convention, October 3, 1969, charter reinstated by Executive Council, May 12, 1971.
   jj. Merged with Steelworkers of America, United, January 1, 1971.
   kk. Merged to form Bakery and Confectionery Workers, International Union of America, December 4, 1969.
   ll. Merged to form Graphic Arts International Union, September 4, 1972.
   mm. Charter surrendered, October 31, 1971.
   nn. Merged with Longshoremen's Association, AFL-CIO International, May 12, 1971.
   oo. Merged to form Paperworkers International Union, United, August 9, 1972.
   pp. Title changed to Professional and Technical Engineers, International Federation of, May, 1973.
   qq. Merged with Railway, Airline and Steamship Clerks, Freight Handlers, Express and Station Employees, Brotherhood of, October 1, 1972.
   rr. Certificate of affiliation revoked, AFL-CIO Convention, October 19, 1973.
   ss. Merged with Retail, Wholesale and Department Store Union, August 6, 1974.
   tt. Merged to form Printing and Graphic Communications Union, Int'l, October 17, 1973.
   uu. Dissolved April 1, 1977.
   vv. Merged with Retail Clerks International Union, September 1, 1977.
   ww. Merged to form Clothing and Textile Workers Union, Amalgamated, June 2, 1976.
   xx. Merged with Glass Bottle Blowers' Association of the United States and Canada, August 1, 1975.
   yy. Title changed to Tile, Marble, Terrazzo, Finishers and Shopmen International Union, AFL-CIO, February 20, 1976.
   zz. Affiliated with Seafarers International Union of North America, June 21, 1976.
   * Organization affiliated for only part of two-year period although membership shown is average for 24-month period.
The following unions (and Bakery and Confectionery Workers International Union of America as shown above, see gg) were expelled from the AFL-CIO at the Second Constitutional Convention in December 1957. Their paid membership for the years 1955 and 1957 were:

	1955	1957
Cleaning and Dye House Workers, International Association of	17	18
Laundry Workers International Union	72	72
Teamsters, Chauffeurs, Warehousemen and Helpers of America, International Brotherhood of	1,330	1,338
	1,419	1,428

LISTINGS FOR AMERICAN FEDERATION OF LABOR AND CONGRESS OF INDUSTRIAL ORGANIZATIONS

AFL-CIO Bldg., 815 16th St., N.W.
Washington, D.C. 20006
Phone: (202) 637-5000
GEORGE MEANY, President
LANE KIRKLAND, Secretary-Treasurer

Executive Council*

GEORGE MEANY, President.

LANE KIRKLAND, Secretary-Treasurer.

EMMET ANDREWS, President, American Postal Workers Union.

KENNETH T. BLAYLOCK, President, American Federation of Government Employees.

PETER BOMMARITO, President, United Rubber, Cork, Linoleum and Plastic Workers of America.

SOL C. CHAIKIN, President, International Ladies' Garment Workers' Union.

AL H. CHESSER, President, United Transportation Union.

C. L. DELLUMS, President, Brotherhood of Sleeping Car Porters.

MURRAY H. FINLEY, President, Amalgamated Clothing and Textile Workers Union.

DAVID J. FITZMAURICE, President, International Union of Electrical, Radio & Machine Workers.

ANGELO FOSCO, President, Laborers' International Union of North America.

THOMAS W. GLEASON, President, International Longshoremen's Association.

A. F. GROSPIRON, President, Oil, Chemical and Atomic Workers International Union.

MATTHEW GUINAN, President, Transport Workers Union of America.

PAUL HALL, President, Seafarers' International Union of North America.

ALVIN E. HEAPS, President, Retail, Wholesale & Department Store Union.

EDWARD T. HANLEY, President, Hotel and Restaurant Employees and Bartenders International Union.

GEORGE HARDY, President, Service Employees' International Union.

FRED J. KROLL, President, Brotherhood of Railway and Airline Clerks.

JOHN H. LYONS, President, International Association of Bridge and Structural Iron Workers.

LLOYD McBRIDE, President, United Steelworkers of America.

WILLIAM H. McCLENNAN, President, International Association of Fire Fighters.

FREDERICK O'NEAL, President, Associated Actors and Artistes of America.

CHARLES H. PILLARD, President, International Brotherhood of Electrical Workers.

HARRY R. POOLE, President, Amalgamated Meat Cutters & Butcher Workmen of North America.

S. FRANK RAFTERY, President, International Brotherhood of Painters and Allied Trades of the United States and Canada.

ALBERT SHANKER, President, American Federation of Teachers.

WILLIAM SIDELL, President, United Brotherhood of Carpenters and Joiners of America.

J. C. TURNER, President, International Union of Operating Engineers.

MARTIN J. WARD, President, United Association of Journeymen and Apprentices of the Plumbing and Pipe Fitting Industry of the United States and Canada.

GLENN E. WATTS, President, Communications Workers of America.

WILLIAM W. WINPISINGER, President, International Association of Machinists.

JERRY WURF, President, American Federation of State, County and Municipal Employees.

WILLIAM H. WYNN, President, Retail Clerks International Union.

Standing Committees and Chairmen

Civil rights: Frederick O'Neal.
Community services: Peter Bommarito.
Economic policy: I. W. Abel.
Education: Hunter P. Wharton.
Housing: William Sidell.

* Includes president, secretary-treasurer, and 33 vice presidents. The vice presidents are listed in alphabetical order. A current vacancy was created by the death of Hal C. Davis, President of the American Federation of Musicians, on January 11, 1978.

International affairs: Martin J. Ward.
Legislative: George Meany.
Organization: Paul Hall.
Political education: George Meany.
Research: (Vacant).
Safety and occupational health: A. F. Grospiron.
Social security: Floyd E. Smith.

Staff

Accounting: Harold H. Jack, Controller. Phone: 637-5250.
Civil rights: William E. Pollard, Director. Phone: 637-5270.
Community services: Leo Perlis, Director. Phone: 637-5189.
Education: Walter G. Davis, Director. Phone: 637-5141.
George Meany Center for Labor Studies: Fred K. Hoehler, Jr., Executive Director. Phone: (301) 431-6400.
International affairs: Ernest Lee, Director. Phone: 637-5050.
Publication: Free Trade Union News (monthly).
Inter-American representative: Andrew C. McLellan. Phone: 637-5060.
Legal: J. Albert Woll, General Counsel. Phone: 737-1717.
Legislative: Kenneth Young. Phone: 637-5075.
Library: Jean Webber, Librarian. Phone: 637-5297.
Organization and field services: Alan Kistler, Director. Phone: 637-5284.
Political education: Al Barkan, Director. Phone: 637-5101.
Publication: Political Memo from COPE (biweekly).
Publications: Saul Miller, Director. Phone: 637-5027.
Publication: AFL-CIO News (weekly).
Managing Editor: John M. Barry. Phone: 637-5038.
This office publishes on behalf of the Inter-American Regional Organization of Workers (ORIT) the following publication: Inter-American Labor Bulletin (monthly).
Editor: George Meany.
Publication: *AFL-CIO American Federationist* (monthly).
Associate Editor: Rex Hardesty. Phone: 637-5036.
Editor: George Meany.
Executive Editor: Saul Miller.
Public relations: Albert Zack, Director. Phone: 637-5010.
Purchasing and supplies: Joseph Evans, Director. Phone: 637-5045.
Research: Rudolph Oswald, Director. Phone: 637-5160.
Social security: Bert Seidman, Director. Phone: 637-5200.
Urban affairs: Henry B. Schechter, Director. Phone: 637-5310.
Convention held biennially. Constitution also provides for special conventions. The 1979 convention has not been scheduled.

Department of Organization and Field Services

ALAN KISTLER, Director
DONALD SLAIMAN, Deputy Director

Regional Directors

Region 1: Daniel J. Healy, O'Hare International Transportation Center, 6300 River Road, Suite 307, Rosemont, Ill. 60018
(Illinois, Indiana, Iowa, Michigan, Minnesota, Wisconsin)
Region 2: L. D. Porter, 208 Wilcox Bldg., 1241 S. Harvard, Tulsa, Okla. 74112.
(Oklahoma, Arkansas, Kansas, Missouri, Nebraska, North Dakota, South Dakota, Montana, Wyoming)
Region 3: Walter Waddy, 2701 W. Patapsco Ave., Baltimore, Md. 21230.
(Maryland, Delaware, District of Columbia, Kentucky, Ohio, Pennsylvania, Virginia, West Virginia)
Region 4: Nicholas Kurko, 360 Place Office Park, Suite 136, 1201 N. Watson Rd., Arlington, Tex. 76011.
(Texas, New Mexico, Colorado, Louisiana)
Region 5: James Sala, 157 Forsyth St., S.W., Atlanta, Ga. 30303.
(Georgia, Alabama, Florida, Mississippi, North Carolina, South Carolina, Tennessee)
Region 6: James E. Baker, 995 Market St., Room 1404, San Francisco, Calif. 94103
(California, Alaska, Arizona, Hawaii, Idaho, Nevada, Oregon, Utah, Washington)
Region 7: Michael Mann, 211 East 43rd St. (15th Floor), New York, N.Y. 10017.
(New York, New Jersey, Puerto Rico)
Region 8: John F. O'Malley, 6 Beacon St., Suite 1111, Boston, Mass. 02108.
(Massachusetts, Connecticut, Maine, New Hampshire, Rhode Island, Vermont)

Trade and Industrial Departments of the AFL-CIO

BUILDING AND CONSTRUCTION TRADES DEPARTMENT

AFL-CIO Bldg., 815 16th St., N.W.
Washington, D.C. 20006
Phone: (202) 347-1461

ROBERT GEORGINE, President
JOSEPH F. MALONEY, Secretary-Treasurer

Affiliated Organizations

Asbestos Workers; International Association of Heat and Frost Insulators and.
Boilermakers, Iron Ship Builders, Blacksmiths, Forgers and Helpers; International Brotherhood of.
Bricklayers, and Allied Craftsmen; International Union of.
Carpenters and Joiners of America; United Brotherhood of.
Electrical Workers; International Brotherhood of.
Elevator Constructors; International Union of.

Granite Cutters' International Association of America; The.

Iron Workers; International Association of Bridge and Structural.

Laborers' International Union of North America.

Lathers International Union; The Wood, Wire and Metal.

Operating Engineers; International Union of.

Painters and Allied Trades of the United States and Canada; International Brotherhood of.

Plasterers' and Cement Masons' International Association of the United States and Canada; Operative.

Plumbing and Pipe Fitting Industry of the United States and Canada; United Association of Journeymen and Apprentices of the.

Roofers, Damp and Waterproof Workers Association; United Slate, Tile and Composition.

Sheet Metal Workers' International Association.

Tile, Marble and Terrazzo Finishers and Shopmen International Union.

Convention

Held biennially in the same city as, and beginning immediately before, the AFL-CIO convention.

FOOD AND BEVERAGE TRADES DEPARTMENT

AFL-CIO Bldg., 815 16th St., N.W.
Washington, D.C. 20006
Phone: (202) 347-2640

DANIEL E. CONWAY, President
ROBERT F. HARBRANT, Secretary-Treasurer

Affiliated Organizations

Bakery and Confectionary Workers' International Union of America.

Distillery, Rectifying, Wine and Allied Workers' International Union of America.

Grain Millers; American Federation of.

Hotel and Restaurant Employees and Bartenders International Union.

Laundry and Dry Cleaning International Union.

Meat Cutters and Butcher Workmen of North America; Amalgamated.

Operating Engineers; International Union of.

Plumbing and Pipe Fitting Industry of the United States and Canada; United Association of Journeymen and Apprentices.

Retail Clerks International Association.

Retail, Wholesale and Department Store Union.

Seafarers' International Union of North America.

Service Employees' International Union.

Convention

Held in the same city as, and immediately before, the AFL-CIO convention.

INDUSTRIAL UNION DEPARTMENT

AFL-CIO Bldg., 815 16th St., N.W.
Washington, D.C. 20006
Phone: (202) 393-5581

JACOB CLAYMAN, President
Secretary-Treasurer (President)

Affiliated Organizations

Aluminum Workers International Union.

Bakery and Confectionery Workers' International Union of America.

Boilermakers, Iron Ship Builders, Blacksmiths, Forgers, and Helpers; International Brotherhood of.

Brick and Clay Workers of America; United.

Cement, Lime and Gypsum Workers International Union; United.

Chemical Workers Union; International.

Clothing and Textile Workers Union; Amalgamated.

Communications Workers of America.

Coopers' International Union of North America.

Electrical, Radio and Machine Workers; International Union of.

Electrical Workers; International Brotherhood of.

Firemen and Oilers; International Brotherhood of.

Furniture Workers of America; United.

Glass Bottle Blowers Association of the United States and Canada.

Glass and Ceramic Workers of North America; United.

Glass Workers' Union; American Flint.

Government Employees; American Federation of.

Grain Millers; American Federation of.

Graphic Arts International Union.

Industrial Workers of America; International Union of Allied.

Insurance Workers International Union.

Ladies' Garment Workers' Union; International.

Laborers' International Union of North America.

Machinists and Aerospace Workers; International Association of.

Marine and Shipbuilding Workers of America; Industrial Union of.

Maritime Union of America; National.

Meat Cutters and Butcher Workmen of North America; Amalgamated.

Mechanics Educational Society of America.

Metal Polishers, Buffers, Platers and Allied Workers International Union.

Molders' and Allied Workers' Union; International.

Newspaper Guild; The.

Oil, Chemical and Atomic Workers International Union.

Operating Engineers; International Union of.

Painters and Allied Trades of the United States and Canada; International Brotherhood of.

Paperworkers International Union; United.

Plumbing and Pipe Fitting Industry of the United States and Canada; United Association of Journeymen and Apprentices of the.

Printing and Graphic Communications Union; International.

Radio Association; American.

Railway Carmen of the United States and Canada; Brotherhood.

Retail, Wholesale and Department Store Union.

Rubber, Cork, Linoleum and Plastic Workers of America; United.

Service Employees International Union.

Sheet Metal Workers' International Association.

Shoe Workers of America; United.

Shoe Workers' Union; Boot and.

State, County and Municipal Employees; American Federation of.

Steelworkers of America; United.

Stove, Furnace and Allied Appliance Workers' International Union of North America.

Teachers; American Federation of.

Technical Engineers; International Federation of Professional and.

Telegraph Workers; United.

Theatrical Stage Employees and Moving Picture Machine Operators of the United States and Canada; International Alliance of.

Transit Union; Amalgamated.

Transport Workers Union of America.

Upholsterers' International Union of North America.

Utility Workers Union of America.

Woodworkers of America; International.

Convention

Held biennially.

Publications

Viewpoint (quarterly).
IUD Bulletin (bimonthly).
IUD Spotlight (quarterly).
Editor: (President).

Staff

Research director: Richard Prosten.
Director of occupational health, safety, and environmental affairs: Sheldon W. Samuels.
Coordinated collective bargaining director: Charles West.
Organizational director: Harold McIver.

MARITIME TRADES DEPARTMENT

AFL-CIO Bldg., 815 16th St., N.W.
Washington, D.C. 20006
Phone: (202) 628-6300

PAUL HALL, President
JEAN INGRAO, Administrator
JACK MCDONALD, Vice President

Affiliated Organizations

Barbers, Beauticians, and Allied Industries, International Association.

Boilermakers, Iron Ship Builders, Blacksmiths, Forgers and Helpers; International Brotherhood of.

Bricklayers, and Allied Craftsmen International Union of America.

Carpenters and Joiners of America; United Brotherhood of.

Cement, Lime and Gypsum Workers International Union; United.

Communications Workers of America.

Distillery, Rectifying, Wine and Allied Workers' International Union of America.

Electrical Workers; International Brotherhood of.

Elevator Constructors; International Union of.

Fire Fighters; International Association of.

Firemen and Oilers; International Brotherhood of.

Glass Bottle Blowers' Association of the United States and Canada.

Grain Millers; American Federation of.

Graphic Arts International Union.

Hotel and Restaurant Employees and Bartenders International Union.

Iron Workers; International Association of Bridge, and Structural.

Laborers' International Union of North America.

Laundry and Dry Cleaning International Union.

Leather Goods, Plastic and Novelty Workers Union; International.

Machinists and Aerospace Workers; International Association of.

Marine Engineers' Beneficial Association; National.

Marine and Shipbuilding Workers of America; Industrial Union of.

Meat Cutters and Butcher Workmen of North America; Amalgamated.

Office and Professional Employees International Union.

Oil, Chemical and Atomic Workers International Union.

Operating Engineers; International Union of.

Painters and Allied Trades of the United States and Canada; International Brotherhood of.

Paperworkers International Union; United.

Plasterers' and Cement Masons' International Association of the United States and Canada; Operative.

Plumbing and Pipe Fitting Industry of the United States and Canada; United Association of Journeymen and Apprentices of the.

Railway, Airline and Steamship Clerks, Freight Handlers, Express and Station Employees; Brotherhood of.

Retail Clerks International Association.

Retail, Wholesale and Department Store Union.

Rubber, Cork, Linoleum and Plastic Workers of America; United.

Seafarers' International Union of North America.

Sheet Metal Workers International Association.

State, County and Municipal Employees; American Federation of.

Telegraph Workers; United.

Textile Workers of America; United.

Toy, Playthings, Novelties and Allied Products of the United States and Canada; International Union of Dolls.

Variety Artists; American Guild of.

Convention

Held biennially in the same city as, and beginning immediately before, the AFL-CIO convention.

Publication

Maritime (monthly).

METAL TRADES DEPARTMENT

AFL-CIO Bldg., 815 16th St., N.W.
Washington, D.C. 20006
Phone: (202) 347-7255

PAUL J. BURNSKY, President
JOHN H. LYONS, First Vice President

Affiliated Organizations

Asbestos Workers; International Association of Heat and Frost Insulators and.
Boilermakers, Iron Ship Builders, Blacksmiths, Forgers and Helpers; International Brotherhood of.
Bricklayers, and Allied Craftsmen; International Union of.
Carpenters and Joiners of America; United Brotherhood of.
Chemical Workers; International Brotherhood of.
Electrical Workers; International Brotherhood of.
Elevator Constructors; International Union of.
Firemen and Oilers; International Brotherhood of.
Iron Workers; International Association of Bridge and Structural.
Laborers' International Union of North America.
Machinists and Aerospace Workers; International Association of.
Molders' and Allied Workers' Union of North America; International.
Office and Professional Employees International Union.
Operating Engineers; International Union of.
Painters and Allied Trades of the United States and Canada; International Brotherhood of.
Pattern Makers' League of North America.
Plasterers' and Cement Masons' International Association of the United States and Canada; Operative.
Plumbing and Pipe Fitting Industry of the United States and Canada; United Association of Journeymen and Apprentices of the.
Service Employees' International Union.
Sheet Metal Workers' International Association.
Stove, Furnace and Allied Appliance Workers' International Union of North America.
Technical Engineers; International Federation of Professional and.
Upholsterers' International Union of North America.

Convention

Held biennially in the same city as, and immediately before, the AFL-CIO convention.

Publication

Metaletter (monthly).
Editor: (President).

Staff

Research and education director: Saul S. Stein.
General representatives: Allen B. Coats, B. W. Hensley.

DEPARTMENT FOR PROFESSIONAL EMPLOYEES

(The Council of AFL-CIO Unions for Professional Employees has been chartered as the Department for Professional Employees.)
815 16th St., N.W.
Washington, D.C. 20006
Phone: (202) 638-0320

ALBERT SHANKER, President
HAL DAVIS (died Jan. 11, 1978), General Vice President
RODNEY A. BOWER, Treasurer
JACK GOLODNER, Director

Affiliated Organizations

Actors' Equity Association.
Broadcast Employees and Technicians; National Association of.
Chemical Workers Union; International.
Communications Workers of America.
Electrical, Radio and Machine Workers; International Union of.
Electrical Workers; International Brotherhood of.
Engineers; International Union of Operating.
Government Employees; American Federation of
Insurance Workers International Union.
Machinists and Aerospace Workers; International Association of.
Musicians; American Federation of.
Musical Artists; American Guild of.
Office and Professional Employees International Union.
Plumbing and Pipe Fitting Industry of the United States and Canada; United Association of Journeymen and Apprentices of the.
Railway, Airline and Steamship Clerks, Freight Handlers, Express and Station Employees; Brotherhood of.
Retail Clerks International Union.
Retail, Wholesale and Department Store Union.
Screen Actors Guild.
Seafarers' International Union of North America.
Service Employees International Union.
State, County and Municipal Employees; American Federation of.
Teachers; American Federation of.
Technical Engineers; International Federation of Professional and.
Television and Radio Artists; American Federation of.
Theatrical Stage Employees and Moving Picture Machine Operators of the United States and Canada; International Alliance of.

Convention

Held biennially in the same city as, and immediately before, the AFL-CIO convention.

Publication

Interface (quarterly).
Editor: Dick Moore.

PUBLIC EMPLOYEE DEPARTMENT
(The Government Employees Council has merged with the
Public Employee Department.)
AFL-CIO Bldg., 815 16th St., N.W.
Washington, D.C. 20006
Phone: (202) 393-2820

WILLIAM H. McCLENNAN, President
KENNETH T. BLAYLOCK, Treasurer
JOHN A. McCART, Executive Director

Affiliated Organizations
Chemical Workers Union; International.
Communications Workers of America.
Electrical, Radio and Machine Workers; International
  Union of.
Fire Fighters; International Association of.
Firemen and Oilers; International Brotherhood of.
Government Employees; American Federation of.
Graphic Arts International Union.
Iron Workers; International Association of Bridge and
  Structural.
Laborers' International Union of North America.
Laundry and Dry Cleaning International Union.
Letter Carriers, National Association of.
Marine Engineers' Beneficial Association; National.
Maritime Union of America; National.
Office and Professional Employees International Union.
Operating Engineers; International Union of.
Painters and Allied Trades of the United States and
  Canada; International Brotherhood of.
Plate Printers', Die Stampers' and Engravers' Union of
  North America; International.
Plumbing and Pipe Fitting Industry of the United States
  and Canada; United Association of Journeymen and
  Apprentices of the.
Postal Workers Union; American.
Printing and Graphic Communications Union; Interna-
  tional.
School Administrators; American Federation of.
Seafarers' International Union of North America.
Service Employees' International Union.
Sheet Metal Workers' International Association.
Teachers; American Federation of.
Technical Engineers; International Federation of Profes-
  sional and.
Transit Union; Amalgamated.
Transport Workers Union of America.
Typographical Union; International.
Utility Workers Union of America.

Convention
Held biennially. The 1979 convention is scheduled for
October in Washington, D.C.

Publication
In the Public Service (monthly).
Editor: Michael Grace.

Staff
Legislative director: John E. Cosgrove.
Research director: Rick M. Galleher.
Public relations director: (Editor).

RAILWAY EMPLOYES' DEPARTMENT
220 South State St.
Chicago, Ill. 60604
Phone: (312) 427-9546

JAMES E. YOST, President

Affiliated Organizations
Boilermakers, Iron Ship Builders, Blacksmiths, Forgers
  and Helpers; International Brotherhood of.
Electrical Workers; International Brotherhood of.
Firemen and Oilers; International Brotherhood of.
Railway Carmen of the United States and Canada; Broth-
  erhood.

Convention
Held every 4 years. The last convention was held April
6–7, 1976 in Las Vegas, Nevada.

Staff
Research director: James R. Ryden.

UNION LABEL AND SERVICE TRADES DEPARTMENT
AFL-CIO Bldg., 815 16th St., N.W.
Washington, D.C. 20006
Phone: (202) 628-2131

JOSEPH D. KEENAN, President
EARL D. McDAVID, Secretary-Treasurer

Affiliated Organizations
There are 87 organizations affiliated with this department.

Convention
Held biennially in the same city as, and immediately
before, the AFL-CIO convention.

Publication
Labeletter (monthly).
Editor: (Secretary-Treasurer).

RAILWAY LABOR EXECUTIVES' ASSOCIATION
400 First St., N.W.
Washington, D.C. 20001
Phone: (202) 737-1541

JOHN F. PETERPAUL, Chairman
CLARENCE M. McINTOSH, Executive Secretary-
  Treasurer
FRED J. KROLL, Vice Chairman

Affiliated Organizations

Boilermakers, Iron Ship Builders, Blacksmiths, Forgers and Helpers; International Brotherhood of.

Electrical Workers; International Brotherhood of.

Firemen and Oilers; International Brotherhood of.

Hotel and Restaurant Employees and Bartenders International Union.

Locomotive Engineers; Brotherhood of (Ind.).

Machinists and Aerospace Workers; International Association of.

Maintenance of Way Employees; Brotherhood of.

Marine Engineers' Beneficial Association; National.

Masters, Mates and Pilots; International Organization of.

Railroad Signalmen; Brotherhood of.

Railroad Yardmasters of America.

Railway Employees' Department.

Railway Carmen of the United States and Canada; Brotherhood.

Railway, Airline and Steamship Clerks, Freight Handlers, Express and Station Employees; Brotherhood of.

Railway and Airway Supervisors Association; The American.

Seafarers' International Union of North America.

Sheet Metal Workers' International Association.

Sleeping Car Porters; Brotherhood of.

Train Dispatchers Association; American.

Transport Workers Union of America.

Transportation Union; United.

Staff

Director of governmental affairs: D. S. Beattie.

OTHER NATIONAL FEDERATIONS OF UNIONS AND EMPLOYEE ASSOCIATIONS

ASSEMBLY OF GOVERNMENTAL EMPLOYEES

1730 Rhode Island Ave., N.W., Suite 611,
Washington, D.C. 20036.
Phone: (202) 347-5628.
President: Arthur N. Caple, Jr.
Secretary: Margaret E. Kovacs.
Treasurer: Joseph T. Pisano.
Executive director: James F. Marshall.
National administrative officer: Roy Fox.
Research director: Robert J. Pruim.
Legal: Robert J. McIntosh.
Public relations activities: (National administrative officer).
Government relations: (Executive director).
Convention: Annually.
Publications: *Coverage* (6 issues annually); *Hotline* (monthly).
Editor: (National administrative officer).
Membership: 700,000; affiliated associations, 50.

National Federation of Independent Unions (NFIU) (Ind. federation)
1625 Eye St., N.W., Suite 821, Washington, D.C. 20006.
Phone: (202) 659-1490.
President: Roger M. Rettig.
Secretary-treasurer: Alonzo Wheeler.
Organizing activities: (President).
Research director: Doris Fuller.
Legislative activities: John W. Shaughnessy, Jr.
Public relations activities: (President).
Convention: Annually.
Publication: News For Independent Unions (quarterly).
Editor: (National president).
Membership: 60,000; affiliated unions, 90.

Telecommunications International Union (Ind. federation)
P.O. Box 5462, Hamden, Conn. 16518.
Phone: (203) 288-2445.
President: John W. Shaughnessy, Jr.
Secretary-treasurer: Kay Dresler.
Recording secretary: Debra Slosberg.
Organizing activities: (President).
Research and education director: Martha Moret.

Legal: Mayer, Weiner & Mayer (Law firm).
19 West 44th St., New York, N.Y. 10036.
Legislative activities: Robert B. Leventhal.
Public relations activities: (Research and education director).
Publication: *News* (quarterly).
Editor: (President).
Membership: 65,000; affiliated unions, 15.

NATIONAL UNIONS AND EMPLOYEE ASSOCIATIONS

A total of 170 national labor unions and 35 professional and State employee associations as defined in the following paragraph are listed in this section. Listings of major subordinate or semiautonomous branches of unions are indented below the parent union or association.

106 AFL-CIO national unions are listed, in addition to 64 unions not affiliated with the AFL-CIO. Unions in the latter category were included if information indicated that they had negotiated contracts with different employers in more than one State or, in the case of Federal Government unions, exclusive bargaining rights under Executive Order 11491. Employee associations which represent their members in collective bargaining were included if they (a) reported membership in more than one State, or (b) represented members in two or more major cities of any individual State. The Assembly of Governmental Employees and the National Federation of Independent Unions are listed under Other Federations of National Unions and Employee Associations.

Unions and associations were asked to report their average annual dues-paying membership for 1975 and 1976, and the number of locals in operation at the end of 1976. If an organization did not report membership, the space for membership was left blank. For membership of nonreporting AFL-CIO affiliates, paid per capita membership as reported in the 1975 convention proceedings was used and is indicated by an asterisk. Membership totals of major subordinate of semiautonomous branches of labor organizations are reported separately and are not included in the figure shown for the parent organization with the exception of the Actors and Artistes (AFL-CIO), and the National Education Association (Ind.).

Wherever possible, each organization is listed alphabetically by the key word or words identifying the craft or industry organized by the union. For the convenience of those who customarily identify a union by its full title (e.g., International Association of Machinists and Aerospace Workers), a finding index begins on pages 2-18 to 2-21. Union affiliation is indicated by (AFL-CIO) for American Federation of Labor and Congress of Industrial Organizations, or (Ind.) for unaffiliated or independent unions. Affiliates of the National Federation of Independent Unions and of the Assembly of Governmental Employees are identified by footnotes.

Most unions and associations provided the necessary information for an adequate listing. For some, information was supplemented by reference to official union sources such as convention proceedings, officers' reports, or journals. In an effort to maintain current listings, all recent changes other than those related to membership and locals were incorporated wherever possible.

LISTING OF LABOR UNIONS
AND EMPLOYEE ASSOCIATIONS

Finding Index of Labor Unions and Employee Associations Listed in the Directory

Labor unions and professional associations are listed alphabetically by key words in the *Directory*. The listings below present the full official title of the organization with the key word or words (indicating where union may be found in the directory) appearing in boldface type.

Actors' Equity Association. See Associated **Actors** and Artistes of America (AFL-CIO).
Air Line Dispatchers Association (AFL-CIO).
Alabama State Employees Association (Ind.).
Alaska Public Employees Association (Ind.).
Aluminum Workers International Union (AFL-CIO).
Amalgamated **Clothing and Textile** Workers Union (AFL-CIO).
Amalgamated **Lace** Operatives of America (Ind.).
Amalgamated **Meat Cutters** and Butcher Workmen of North America (AFL-CIO).
Amalgamated **Transit** Union (AFL-CIO).
American Association of **Classified School Employees** (Ind.).
American Association of **School Administrators** (Ind.).
American Association of **University Professors** (Ind.).
American Federation of **Government** Employees (AFL-CIO).
American Federation of **Grain Millers** (AFL-CIO).
American Federation of **Musicians** (AFL-CIO).
American Federation of **State,** County and Municipal Employees (AFL-CIO).
American Federation of **Teachers** (AFL-CIO).
American Federation of Television and Radio Artists. See Associated **Actors** and Artistes of America (AFL-CIO).
American Flint **Glass** Workers' Union of North America (AFL-CIO).
American Guild of Musical Artists, Inc. See Associated **Actors** and Artistes of America (AFL-CIO).
American Guild of Variety Artists. See Associated **Actors** and Artistes of America (AFL-CIO).
American **Nurses** Association (Ind.).
American **Postal Workers** Union (AFL-CIO).
American **Radio** Association (AFL-CIO).
American **Train Dispatchers** Association (AFL-CIO).
American **Watch** Workers Union (Ind.).
Arizona Public Employees Association (Ind.).
Associated **Actors** and Artistes of America (AFL-CIO).
Associated **Trades and Crafts** National Construction Union (Ind.).
Association of Flight Attendants. See International **Air Line Pilots** Association (AFL-CIO).
Association of Western **Pulp and Paper** Workers (Ind.).
Atlantic, Gulf, Lakes and Inland Waters District. See **Seafarers'** International Union of North America (AFL-CIO).

Atlantic Independent Union (Ind.).
Bakery and Confectionary Workers' International Union of America (AFL-CIO).
Barbers, Beauticians, and Allied Industries International Association (AFL-CIO).
Boot and **Shoe** Workers' Union (AFL-CIO).
Brotherhood of **Locomotive** Engineers (Ind.).
Brotherhood of **Maintenance of Way** Employees (AFL-CIO).
Brotherhood of **Railroad Signalmen** (AFL-CIO).
Brotherhood of **Railway,** Airline and Steamship Clerks, Freight Handlers, Express and Station Employees (AFL-CIO).
Brotherhood of **Railway Carmen** of the United States and Canada (AFL-CIO).
Brotherhood of **Shoe** and Allied Craftsmen (Ind.).
Brotherhood of **Sleeping Car Porters** (AFL-CIO).
Brotherhood of **Utility** Workers of New England, Inc. (Ind.).
California State Employees Association (Ind.).
Christian Labor Association of the United States of America (Ind.).
Civil Service Employees Association, Inc. (NYS) (Ind.).
Civilian **Technicians** Association (Ind.).
Colorado Association of Public Employees (Ind.).
Communications Workers of America (AFL-CIO).
Congress of **Independent** Unions (Ind.).
Connecticut Employees Union (Ind.).
Connecticut State Employees Association (Ind.).
Coopers' International Union of North America (AFL-CIO).

Directors Guild of America, Inc. (Ind.).
Distillery, Rectifying, Wine and Allied Workers International Union of America (AFL-CIO).
Distributive Workers of America (Ind.).
Federal Plant **Quarantine** Inspectors National Association (Ind.).
Flight Engineers' International Association (AFL-CIO).
Fraternal Order of **Police** (Ind.).

Glass Bottle Blowers Association of the United States and Canada (AFL-CIO).
Graphic Arts International Union (AFL-CIO).
Great Lakes **Licensed Officers'** Organization (Ind.).

Hebrew Actors Union, Inc. See Associated **Actors** and Artistes of America (AFL-CIO).
Hotel and Restaurant Employees and Bartenders International Union (AFL-CIO).
Idaho State Employees Association (Ind.).
Illinois State Employees Association (Ind.).
Independent **Bakery** Employees Association (Ind.).

Independent **Minnesota** Association of Government Employees (Ind.).

Independent Union of Plant **Protection** Employees (Ind.).

Independent **Watchmen's** Association (Ind.).

Indiana State Employees Association (Ind.).

Industrial Union of **Marine and Shipbuilding Workers** of America (AFL-CIO).

Insurance Workers International Union (AFL-CIO).

International **Air Line Employees** Association. See International **Air Line Pilots** Association (AFL-CIO).

International **Air Line Pilots** Association (AFL-CIO).

International Alliance of **Theatrical Stage** Employees and Moving Picture Machine Operators of the United States and Canada (AFL-CIO).

International Association of Bridge, Structural **Iron Workers** (AFL-CIO).

International Association of **Fire Fighters** (AFL-CIO).

International Association of Heat and Frost Insulators and **Asbestos Workers** (AFL-CIO).

International Association of **Machinists** and Aerospace Workers (AFL-CIO).

International Association of **Siderographers** (AFL-CIO).

International Association of **Tool** Craftsmen (Ind.).

International Brotherhood of **Boilermakers**, Iron Ship Builders, Blacksmiths, Forgers and Helpers (AFL-CIO).

International Brotherhood of **Electrical Workers** (AFL-CIO).

International Brotherhood of **Firemen** and Oilers (AFL-CIO).

International Brotherhood of **Painters** and Allied Trades (AFL-CIO).

International Brotherhood of **Pottery** and Allied Workers. See **Seafarers'** International Union of North American (AFL-CIO).

International Brotherhood of **Teamsters**, Chauffeurs, Warehousemen and Helpers of America (Ind.).

International **Chemical** Workers Union (AFL-CIO).

International **Die Sinkers'** Conference (Ind.).

International Federation of Professional and **Technical Engineers** (AFL-CIO).

International **Guards** Union of America (Ind.).

International **Jewelry** Workers' Union (AFL-CIO).

International **Ladies' Garment** Workers' Union (AFL-CIO).

International **Leather** Goods, Plastic and Novelty Workers' Union (AFL-CIO).

International **Longshoremen's** Association (AFL-CIO).

International **Longshoremen's** and Warehousemen's Union (Ind.).

International **Mailers** Union (Ind.).

International **Molders'** and Allied Workers' Union of North America (AFL-CIO).

International Organization of Masters, Mates and Pilots (AFL-CIO). See International **Longshoremen's** Association (AFL-CIO).

International **Plate Printers'**, Die Stampers' and Engravers' Union of North America (AFL-CIO).

International **Printing** and Graphic Communications Union (AFL-CIO).

International **Typographical** Union (AFL-CIO).

International Union Allied **Industrial** Workers of America (AFL-CIO).

International Union of **Bricklayers** and Allied Craftsmen (AFL-CIO).

International Union of Dolls, **Toys**, Playthings, Novelties and Allied Products of the United States and Canada (AFL-CIO).

International Union of **Electrical**, Radio and Machine Workers (AFL-CIO).

International Union of **Elevator** Constructors (AFL-CIO).

International Union of Journeymen **Horseshoers** of the United States and Canada (AFL-CIO).

International Union of **Operating Engineers** (AFL-CIO).

International Union of Petroleum and Industrial Workers. See **Seafarers'** International Union of North America (AFL-CIO).

International Union, United **Automobile**, Aerospace and Agricultural Implement Workers of America (Ind.).

International Union, United **Plant Guard** Workers of America (Ind.).

International **Woodworkers** of America (AFL-CIO).

Italian Actors Union. See Associated **Actors** and Artistes of America (AFL-CIO).

Kentucky Career Employees Association (Ind.).

Laborers' International Union of North America (AFL-CIO).

Laundry and Dry Cleaning International Union (AFL-CIO).

Laundry, Dry Cleaning and Dye House Workers International Union. See International Brotherhood of **Teamsters**, Chauffeurs, Warehousemen and Helpers of America (Ind.).

Leather Workers International Union of America (AFL-CIO).

Machine Printers and Engravers Association of the United States (Ind.).

Maine State Employees Association (Ind.).

Major League **Baseball** Players Association (Ind.).

Major League **Umpires** Association (Ind.).

Marine Cooks and Stewards' Union. See **Seafarers'** International Union of North America (AFL-CIO).

Maryland Classified Employees Association (Ind.).

Massachusetts State Employees Association (Ind.).

Mechanics Educational Society of America (AFL-CIO).

Metal Polishers, Buffers, Platers and Allied Workers International Union (AFL-CIO).

Michigan State Employees Association (Ind.).

Montana Public Employees Association (Ind.).

National Alliance of **Postal and Federal Employees** (Ind.).

National Association of **Aeronautical Examiners** (Ind.).

National Association of **Aeronautical Production Controllers** (Ind.)

National Association of **Air Traffic Specialists** (Ind.).

National Association of **ASCS** County Office Employees (Ind.).

National Association of **Broadcast** Employees and Technicians (AFL-CIO).

National Association of Federal **Veterinarians** (Ind.).

National Association of **Government Employees** (Ind.).

National Association of **Government Inspectors** (Ind.).

National Association of **Letter Carriers** of the United States of America (AFL-CIO).

National Association of **Planners**, Estimators and Progressmen (Ind.).

National Association of **Postal** Supervisors (Ind.).

National **Basketball** Players Association (Ind.).

National Brotherhood of **Packinghouse and Industrial** Workers (Ind.).

National **Education** Association (Ind.).

National Federation of **Federal** Employees (Ind.).

National Federation of **Licensed** Practical Nurses (Ind.).

National **Football** League Players Association (Ind.).

National **Hockey** League Players' Association (Ind.).

National **Labor Relations Board** Professional Association (Ind.).

National **Labor Relations Board** Union (Ind.).

National League of **Postmasters** of the United States (Ind.).

National **Marine Engineers'** Beneficial Association (AFL-CIO).

National **Maritime** Union of America (AFL-CIO).

National **Operations Analysis** Association (Ind.).

National Organization of **Industrial Trade** Unions (Ind.).

National **Rural Letter Carriers' Association** (Ind.).

National **Treasury** Employees Union (Ind.).

Nebraska Association of Public Employees (Ind.).

New Hampshire State Employees Association (Ind.).

New Jersey State Employees Association (Ind.).

Newspaper and Mail Deliverers' Union of New York and Vicinity (Ind.).

North Carolina State Employees Association (Ind.).

North Carolina State **Government** Employee Association (Ind.)

Office and Professional Employees International Union (AFL-CIO).

Ohio Civil Service Employees Association (Ind.).

Oil, Chemical and Atomic Workers International Union (AFL-CIO).

Operative **Plasterers'** and Cement Masons' International Association of The United States and Canada (AFL-CIO).

Oregon State Employees Association (Ind.).

Overseas Education Association. See National **Education** Association (Ind.).

Pacific Coast Marine Firemen, Oilers, Watertenders and Wipers Association. See **Seafarers'** International Union of North America (AFL-CIO).

Patent Office Professional Association (Ind.).

Pattern Makers' League of North America (AFL-CIO).

Physicians National Housestaff Association (Ind.).

Professional Air Traffic Controllers Organization. See National **Marine Engineers'** Beneficial Association (AFL-CIO).

Railroad Yardmasters of America (AFL-CIO).

Retail Clerks International Association (AFL-CIO).

Retail, Wholesale and Department Store Union (AFL-CIO).

Sailors' Union of the Pacific. See **Seafarers'** International Union of North America (AFL-CIO).

Screen Actors Guild. See Associated **Actors** and Artistes of America (AFL-CIO).

Screen Extras Guild. See Associated **Actors** and Artistes of America (AFL-CIO).

Seafarers' International Union of North America (AFL-CIO).

Service Employees' International Union (AFL-CIO).

Sheet Metal Workers International Association (AFL-CIO).

Southern Labor Union (Ind.).

State of **Nevada** Employees Association (Ind.).

Stove, Furnace and Allied Appliance Workers' International Union of North America (AFL-CIO).

Telecommunications International Union (Ind.).

Textile Foremen's Guild, Inc. (Ind.).

The American **Railway** and Airway Supervisors Association (AFL-CIO).

The **Granite Cutters'** International Association of America (AFL-CIO).

The **Newspaper** Guild (AFL-CIO).

The Wood, Wire and Metal **Lathers** International Union (AFL-CIO).

Tile, Marble and Terrazzo Finishers and Shopmen International Union (AFL-CIO).

Tobacco Workers International Union (AFL-CIO).

Trademark Society, Inc. (Ind.).

Transport Workers' Union of America (AFL-CIO).

United **Allied** Workers International Union (Ind.).

United Association of Journeymen and Apprentices of the **Plumbing** and Pipe Fitting Industry of the United States and Canada (AFL-CIO).

United **Brick and Clay** Workers of America (AFL-CIO).

United Brotherhood of **Carpenters** and Joiners of America. (AFL-CIO).

United **Cement**, Lime and Gypsum Workers International Union (AFL-CIO).

United **Electrical**, Radio and Machine Workers of America (Ind.).

United **Farm Workers** of America (AFL-CIO).

United **Furniture** Workers of America (AFL-CIO).

United **Garment** Workers of America (AFL-CIO).

United **Glass and Ceramic** Workers of North America (AFL-CIO).

United **Hatters**, Cap and Millinery Workers International Union (AFL-CIO).

United **Mine** Workers of America (Ind.).

United **Paperworkers** International Union (AFL-CIO).

United **Retail** Workers Union (Ind.).

United **Rubber**, Cork, Linoleum and Plastic Workers of America (AFL-CIO).

United **Shoe** Workers of America (AFL-CIO).

United Slate, Tile and Composition **Roofers**, Damp and Waterproof Workers Association (AFL-CIO).

United **Steelworkers** of America (AFL-CIO).

United **Telegraph Workers** (AFL-CIO).

United **Textile** Workers of America (AFL-CIO).

United **Transportation** Union (AFL-CIO).

Upholsterers' International Union of North America (AFL-CIO).

Utah Public Employees Association (Ind.).

Utility Workers Union of America (AFL-CIO).

Vermont State Employees Association (Ind.).

Washington Public Employees Association (Ind.).

Western States Service Station Employees Union (Ind.).

West Virginia Public Employees Association (Ind.).

Writers Guild of America (Ind.).

Writers Guild of America, East, Inc. **See Writers** Guild of America (Ind.).

Writers Guild of America, West, Inc. **See Writers** Guild of America (Ind.)

Wyoming State Employees Association (Ind.).

ACTORS AND ARTISTES OF AMERICA; ASSOCIATED (AFL-CIO)

1500 Broadway, New York, N.Y. 10036.
Phone: (212) 869-0358.
President: Frederick O'Neal.
Executive secretary: Sanford I. Wolff.
Convention: Every 2 years; 1979.
Membership: 76,000; branches, 9.

ACTORS' EQUITY ASSOCIATION

1500 Broadway, New York, N.Y. 10036.
Phone: (212) 869-8530.
President: Theodore Bikel.
Executive secretary: Donald Grody.
Treasurer: Randy Phillips.
Organizing activities: (Executive secretary).
Research director: Dan Hogan.
Education director: Barbara Colton.
Social insurance: Thomas J. Mallon.
Legal: Jerome B. Lurie (Counsel).
Legislative activities: Jack Golodner.
Public Relations activities: Dick Moore.
Convention: Annually; 1978.
Publication: *Equity News* (9 times annually).
Editor: (Public relations activities).
Membership: ———; local unions ———.

AMERICAN FEDERATION OF TELEVISION AND RADIO ARTISTS

1350 Avenue of the Americas, 2nd floor, New York, N.Y. 10019.
Phone: (212) 265-7700.
President: Joseph Slattery.
Executive secretary: Sanford I. Wolff.
Organizing activities: Harold Kocin.
Research and education director: Walter Grinspan.
Social insurance: Arch Siegel.
Legal: Mortimer Becker (General counsel).
Legislative activities: (Executive secretary).
Public relations activities: Dick Moore.
Convention: Annually.
Publication: *AFTRA Magazine* (3 issues annually).
Editor: (Public relations activities).
Membership: 26,917; local unions, 32.

AMERICAN GUILD OF MUSICAL ARTISTS

1841 Broadway, New York, N.Y. 10023.
Phone: (212) 265-3687.
President: Gene Boucher.
Executive secretary: DeLloyd Tibbs.
Social insurance: Ellen Wagner.
Legal: Becker & London.
Convention: Upon membership call.
Publication: *MAGAZINE* (5 issues annually).
Editor: Sandra Munsell.
Membership: 4,000; local unions, 0.

AMERICAN GUILD OF VARIETY ARTISTS

1540 Broadway, New York, N.Y. 10036.
Phone: (212) 765-0800.
President: Penny Singleton.
Secretary-treasurer: Suzanne Barry.
Organizing activities: (President).
Research director: (President).
Social insurance: EAST Michiko Terajima.
Legal: Rains, Pogrebin & Scher.
1540 Broadway, 8th Floor, New York, N.Y. 10036.
Legislative activities: (Legal).
Convention: Every 4 years; 1980.
Publication: *AGVA Newsletter* (quarterly).
Editor: (Public relations).
Membership: ———; local unions, ———.

HEBREW ACTORS UNION, INC.

31 East 7th St., New York, N.Y. 10003.
Phone: (212) OR 4-1923.
President: Leon Liebgold.
Secretary-treasurer: Bernard Sauer.
Organizing activities: (President).
Research director: David Carrey.
Public relations activities: (Research director).
Membership: 190; local unions, 0.

ITALIAN ACTORS UNION

1674 Broadway, New York, N.Y. 10019.
Phone: (212) 582-6170.
President: Mimi Cecchini.
Executive Secretary: Sal Carollo.
Convention: Annually.
Membership: 75; local unions, 0.

SCREEN ACTORS GUILD

7750 Sunset Blvd., Hollywood, Calif. 90046.
Phone: (213) 876-3030.
President: Kathleen Nolan.
Executive secretary: Chester L. Midgen.
Recording secretary: Elizabeth Allen.
Treasurer: Gilbert Perkins.
Organizing activities: (Executive secretary).
Research Director: William Schallert.
Education Director: Judith Rheiner.
Social insurance: Richard Cline.
Legal: Paul Berger.
Legislative activities: Eugene Francis.
Public relations activities: (Education director).
Health and safety activities: Paulyne Golden (Controller).
Convention: Annually.
Publications: *Screen Actor Magazine* (quarterly).
Editor: (Public relations activities).
Membership: 29,797; local unions, 0.

SCREEN EXTRAS GUILD

3629 Chauenga Blvd., West, Hollywood, Calif. 90029.

Phone: (213) 851-4301.
President: Murray Pollack.
Executive secretary: H. O'Neil Shanks.
Organizing activities: (Executive secretary).
Social insurance: (Executive secretary).
Legal: Leo Geffner.
Convention: Annually.
Publication: *SEG News* (periodically).
Membership: 3,000; local unions, 2.

ACTORS EQUITY

See Actors and artistes of America; Associated (AFL-CIO)

AERONAUTICAL EXAMINERS, NATIONAL ASSOCIATION OF (IND.)

2178 18th Ave., San Francisco, Calif. 94116.
Phone: (415) 869-2474.
President: Claude T. Lawless.
Secretary-treasurer: Joe B. Puig, Jr.
Organizing activities: (President).
Convention: Every 2 years; 1980.
Membership: ———; local unions, 5.

AERONAUTICAL PRODUCTION CONTROLLERS, NATIONAL ASSOCIATION OF (IND.)

743 Red Mill Road, Norfolk, Virginia 23502.
Phone: (804) 461-3451.
President: Tommie Parker.
Secretary-treasurer: Bill Zuleger.
Organizing activities: Terry L. Cords.
3935 Wildwood Road, San Diego, Calif., 92107.
Research director: Jim DiFranco.
Education director: Robert J. Long.
Legal: Bill S. Walls.
Legislative activities: Larry L. Heck.
Public relations activities: John Dekonty.
Health & safety activities: Clayton A. Hooper.
Convention: Annually.
Membership: 725; local unions, 4.

AIR LINE DISPATCHERS ASSOCIATION (AFL-CIO)

(Merged with the Transport Workers Union, effective March 15, 1977).

AIR LINE PILOTS ASSOCIATION (AFL-CIO)

Pilot Division.
1625 Massachusetts Ave. N.W., Washington, D.C. 20036.
Phone: (202) 797-4000.
President: John J. ODonnell.
Secretary: Thomas Ashwood.
Treasurer: John J. Magee.
Organized activities: Michael R. Ferrara.
Research director: Michael E. Sparrough.
Education director: James V. Fergus.
Safety director: Roger Phaneuf.
Social insurance: John Buck.
Legal: Gary Green.
Legislative activities: Robert F. Bonitati.
Public relations activities: Walter Rossbach.
Convention: Every 2 years; 1980.
Publications: *Air Line Pilot* (monthly); *Pilot Report* (monthly).
Editor: C. V. Glines.
Membership: 27,707; local unions, 105.

ASSOCIATION OF FLIGHT ATTENDANTS

1625 Massachusetts Ave., N.W., Washington, D.C. 20036.
Phone: (202) 797-4075.

President: Patricia D. Robertson.
Secretary-treasurer: Fran Hay.
Organizing activities: E. A. Boyer.
Research director: Clydette Clayton.
Social insurance: John Buck.
Legal: Elizabeth Neumeier.
Legislative activities: Del Mott.
Public relations activities: Kenneth Crawley.
Health and safety activities: (Legislative activities).
Convention: Every 2 years; 1980.
Publication: *Flightlog* (bimonthly).
Editor: Kenneth Crawley.
Membership: 15,000; local unions, 61.

AIR LINE EMPLOYEES ASSOCIATION

5600 South Central Ave., Chicago, Ill. 60638.
Phone: (312) 767-3333.
President: Victor J. Herbert.
Secretary: Constance LaPare.
Treasurer: William A. Schneider.
Organizing activities: John P. Scott.
Research & education director: (Organizing activities).
Social insurance: Mort B. Wigderson.
Legal: Wyatt Johnson.
Legislative activities: (Legal).
Public relations activities: Edwin H. Roper.
Health and safety activities: (Social insurance).
Convention: Every 5 years; 1980.
Publication: *The Air Line Employee* (bimonthly).
Editor: Edwin H. Roper.
Membership: 10,000; local unions, 70.

> UNION OF PROFESSIONAL AIRMEN
> 1625 Massachusetts Avenue, N.W., Washington, D.C. 20036.
> Phone: (202) 797-4280.
> President: Charles Attardo.
> Secretary-Treasurer: Charles Holmes.
> Organizing activities: Michael R. Ferrara.
> Convention: Every 2 years; June 1979.
> Publication: *UPA News* (Seasonally).
> Membership: 220; local unions, 10.

AIR TRAFFIC SPECIALISTS, INC.; NATIONAL ASSOCIATION OF (IND.)

(Affiliated with the Professional Air Traffic Controllers of the Marine Engineers Beneficial Association (AFL-CIO) on July 20, 1976.)

ALABAMA STATE EMPLOYEES ASSOCIATION (IND.)

110 North Jackson St., Montgomery, Alabama 36104.
Phone: (205) 834-6965.
President: Vincent Mauser.
Secretary: Jo-Ellyn Norton.
Executive director: J. Victor Price, Jr.
Organizing activities: (Executive director).
Research director: (Executive director).
Public relations activities: (Executive director).
Legal: (Executive director).
Government relations: (Executive director).
Collective bargaining activities: (Executive director).
Convention: Annually.
Publication: *ASEA News* (monthly).
Editor: (Executive director).
Membership: 12,500; chapters, 88.

ALASKA PUBLIC EMPLOYEES ASSOCIATION (IND.)

130 Seward St., Juneau 99801.
Phone: (907) 586-2334.
President: Barry Jackson.
Secretary: Rose Anderson.

Executive director: Russell D. Mott.
Organizing activities: (Executive director).
Legal activities: Patrick Murphy.
Research director: Roy Dunn.
Public relations activities: Dianne Bergstrom.
Government relations: (Executive director).
Collective bargaining activities: (Executive director).
Convention: Annually
Publications: *Alaska Public Employee Reporter* (monthly);
APEA Eagle (weekly).
Editor: (Public relations activities).
Membership: 8,500; affiliates, 20.

ALLIED WORKERS INTERNATIONAL UNION; UNITED (IND.)
5506 Calumet Ave., Box 723, Hammond, Ind. 46320.
Phone: (219) 932-9400.
President: Norma J. Baggett.
Secretary-treasurer: George Dorsey.
Organizing activities: (Secretary-treasurer).
Research director: (President).
Education director: Rosemary Slack.
Legal: Irving M. Friedman (Attorney).
7 South Dearborn St., Suite 1734, Chicago, Ill. 60603.
Legislative activities: (President).
Public relations activities: Betty Dennehe.
Health and safety activities: (Secretary-treasurer).
Convention: Every 4 years; 1982.
Publication: *News and Views* (quarterly).
Editor: (President).
Membership: 200; local unions, 2.

ALUMINUM WORKERS INTERNATIONAL UNION (AFL-CIO)
Paul Brown Bldg., 818 Olive St., Suite 338, St. Louis, Mo. 63101.
Phone: (314) 621-7292.
President: Lawrence A. Holley.
Secretary-treasurer: H. Max Webster.
Organizing activities: John C. Black.
Research and education director: Allan Sutherland.
Social insurance: (Research and education director).
Legal: Anthony F. Cafferky (General counsel).
Legislative activities: Ernest LaBaff.
Public relations activities: (President).
Health and safety activities: (Research and education director).
Convention: Every 2 years; 1979.
Publications: *Aluminum Light* (bimonthly).
Editor: (President).
Membership: 32,000; local unions, 91.

AMERICAN FEDERATION OF TELEVISION AND RADIO ARTISTS
See Actors and Artistes of America; Associated (AFL-CIO)

AMERICAN GUILD OF MUSICAL ARTISTS
See Actors and Artistes of America; Associated (AFL-CIO)

AMERICAN GUILD OF VARIETY ARTISTS
See Actors and Artistes of America; Associated (AFL-CIO)

ARIZONA PUBLIC EMPLOYEES ASSOCIATION (IND.)
1820 West Washington, Phoenix 85007.
Phone: (602) 252-6501.
President: Ed Harvey.
Secretary: Judith Ann Barrette.
Treasurer: Ruben Medina.
Executive director: Al Palmer.
Organizing activities: Luis Arellano.

Research director: Gary Huish.
Social insurance: (Executive director).
Legal: Ron Logan.
Public relations: (Executive director).
Government relations: (Executive directors).
Collective bargaining activities: (Organizing activities).
Convention: Annually.
Publication: *Arizona Public Employee* (monthly).
Editor: (Executive Director).
Membership: 12,000; affiliates, 27.

ASBESTOS WORKERS; INTERNATIONAL ASSOCIATION OF HEAT AND FROST INSULATORS AND (AFL-CIO)
505 Machinists Bldg., 1300 Connecticut Ave. N.W., Washington, D.C. 20036.
Phone: (202) 785-2388.
President: Andrew T. Haas.
Secretary-treasurer: William G. Bernard.
Organizing activities: (President).
Research and education director: (President).
Social insurance: (President).
Legal: (President).
Legislative activities: (President).
Public relations activities: (President).
Health and safety activities: John Quinn.
Convention: Every 5 years; 1982.
Publication: *The Asbestos Worker* (quarterly).
Editor: (President).
Membership: 18,255; local unions, 119.

ASCS COUNTY OFFICE EMPLOYEES; NATIONAL ASSOCIATION OF (IND.)
P.O. Box 242, Gettysburg, Pa. 17325.
Phone: (717) 334-4216.
President: Wayne Taylor.
Secretary-treasurer: J. Glen Miller.
Organizing activities: (Secretary-treasurer).
Research and education director: (Secretary-treasurer).
Social insurance: H. Woodrow Jones.
P.O. Box 37, New Boston, Texas 75570.
Legal: (President.)
Legislative activities: (Social insurance).
Public relations activities: (Secretary-treasurer).
Health and safety activities: (Secretary-treasurer).
Convention: Annually.
Publication: *NASCOE News* (bimonthly).
Editor: (Secretary-treasurer).
Membership: 9,400; local unions, 46.

ATLANTIC, GULF, LAKES AND INLAND WATERS DISTRICT
See Seafarer's International Union of North America (AFL-CIO)

ATLANTIC INDEPENDENT UNION (IND.)
3207 U Centre Sq. E., 1500 Market St., Philadelphia, Pa. 19101.
Phone: (215) 564-3790.
President: Joseph A. Mullan.
Secretary: John J. Nussbaumer.
Treasurer: Anthony J. Dellaratta.
Organizing activities: (President).
Convention: Annually.
Publication: *AIU News* (quarterly).
Editor: Joseph Orlando.
Membership: 3,255; local unions, 7.

AUTOMOBILE, AEROSPACE AND AGRICULTURAL IMPLEMENT WORKERS OF AMERICA; INTERNATIONAL UNION, UNITED (IND.)

8000 East Jefferson Ave., Detroit, Mich. 48214.
Phone: (313) 926-5000.
President: Douglas A. Fraser.
Secretary-treasurer: Emil Mazey.
Organizing activities: Martin Gerber (Vice president).
Research director: Howard Young.
Education director: Carroll Hutton.
Social insurance: Melvin A. Glasser.
Legal: John Fillion (General counsel).
Legislative activities: Howard Paster.
1125 15th St., N.W., Washington, D.C. 20005.
Public relations activities: Don Stillman.
Health and safety activities: (Social insurance).
Convention: Every 3 years; April 1980.
Publication: *Solidarity* (monthly).
Editor: (Public relations activities).
Membership: 1,544,859; local unions, 1,580.

BAKERY, CONFECTIONERY AND TOBACCO WORKERS INTERNATIONAL UNION (AFL-CIO)

1828 L St., N.W., Suite 900, Washington, D.C. 20036.
Phone: (202) 466-2500.
President: John DeConcini.
Secretary-treasurer: Rene Rondou.
Organizing activities: Graydon E. Tetrick.
Research and education director: Vaughn Ball.
Social insurance: John Fleming.
Legal: Henry Kaiser (Attorney).
Legislative activities: John DeConcini (Executive vice president).
Public relations activities: Albert K. Herling.
Health and safety activities: (Research and education director).
Convention: Every 4 years; 1982.
Publication: *B & C News* (monthly).
Editor: (President).
Membership: 158,040; local unions, 195.

BAKERY EMPLOYEES UNION: INDEPENDENT (IND.)

P.O. Box 188, Alexandria, Louisiana 71301.
Phone: (318) 448-1600.
President: Eddie Franks.
Secretary-treasurer: Willis J. Guillory.
Organizing activities: (Legal).
Legal: Irving Ward-Steinman (General counsel).
Convention: Annually.
Membership: 287; local unions, 4.

BARBERS, BEAUTICIANS, AND ALLIED INDUSTRIES, INTERNATIONAL ASSOCIATION (AFL-CIO)

7050 West Washington Street, Indianapolis, Ind. 46214.
Phone: (317) 248-9221.
President: Richard A. Plumb.
Organizing activities: (President).
Education director: Frank Lilley.
Social insurance: Ada Dooley.
Legal: Edward Fillenwarth. (Attorney).
Legislative activities: (President).
Public relations activities: (President).
Convention: Every 5 years; 1983.
Publication: *Journeyman Barber* and *Beauty Culture* (monthly).
Editor: Gregory Croy.
Membership: 41,000; local unions, 702.

BASEBALL PLAYERS ASSOCIATION; MAJOR LEAGUE (IND.)

375 Park Ave., New York, N.Y. 10022.
Phone: (212) 752-0940.
Executive director: Marvin J. Miller.
Treasurers: Michael Marshall and William Lee.
Social insurance: (Executive director).
Legal: Richard M. Moss (General counsel).
Health and safety activities: (Treasurers).
Convention: Every 2 years; 1979.
Membership: 950; clubs, 24.

BASKETBALL PLAYERS ASSOCIATION; NATIONAL (IND.)

c/o Lawrence Fleisher, 15 Columbus Circle, New York, N.Y. 10023.
President: Paul Silas.
Secretary-treasurer: Robert Lanier.
Legal: Lawrence Fleisher (General counsel).
Convention: Annually.
Publication: *Time Out* (Monthly).
Editor: (Legal activities).
Membership: 216; clubs 18.

BOILERMAKERS, IRON SHIP BUILDERS, BLACKSMITHS, FORGERS AND HELPERS; INTERNATIONAL BROTHERHOOD OF (AFL-CIO)

New Brotherhood Bldg., 8th St. at State Ave., Kansas City, Kansas 66101.
Phone: (913) 371-2640.
President: Harold J. Buoy.
Secretary-treasurer: Charles F. Moran.
Organizing activities: (President).
Research and education director: William O. Kuhl.
Social insurance: (President).
Legal: John J. Blake (General counsel).
Legislative activities: H. Page Groton (Assistant to president).
814 Railway Labor Bld., 400 1st St., N.W., Washington, D.C. 20001.
Safety director: Michael Wood.
Public relations activities: (Safety director).
Convention: Every 4 years; 1981.
Publication: *Boilermakers-Blacksmiths Reporter* (monthly).
Editor: (President).
Membership: 138,000; local unions, 400.

BRICK AND CLAY WORKERS OF AMERICA; THE UNITED (AFL-CIO)

P.O. Box 809, 150 E. Mound St., Suite 308, Columbus, Ohio 43216.
Phone: (614) 464-2593.
President: Roy L. Brown.
Secretary-treasurer: Roy Lukens.
Organizing activities: (Secretary-Treasurer).
Research and education director: (Secretary-treasurer).
Social insurance: (Secretary-treasurer).
Legal: (President).
Legislative activities: (President).
Public relations activities: (Secretary-treasurer).
Health and safety activities (President).
Convention: Every 5 years; 1982.
Membership: 15,000; locals, 255.

BRICKLAYERS AND ALLIED CRAFTSMEN; INTERNATIONAL UNION OF (AFL-CIO)

815 15th Street, N.W., Washington, D.C. 20005.
Phone: (202) 783-3788.
President: Thomas F. Murphy.
Secretary: John T. Joyce.
Organizing activities: John M. Doyle.
Research director: L. Gerald Carlisle.

Education director: Noble B. Cain.
Social insurance: (Secretary).
Legal: (Secretary).
Legislative activities: (Education director).
Public relations: (Secretary).
Health and safety activities: (Secretary).
Convention: Every 2 years; 1979.
Publication: *Journal* (monthly).
Editor: (Secretary).
Membership: 147,715; local unions, 758.

BROADCAST EMPLOYEES AND TECHNICIANS; NATIONAL ASSOCIATION OF (AFL-CIO)
7101 Wisconsin Ave., Suite 1303, Bethesda, Md. 20012.
Phone: (301) 657-8420.
President: Edward M. Lynch.
Secretary-treasurer: Duane R. Corder.
Organizing activities: (President).
Research director: Lawrence D. MacLachlan.
Education director: Roy Davis.
Social insurance: (Secretary-treasurer).
Legal: Jerome Y. Sturm (General counsel).
Legislative activities: (President).
Convention: Every 4 years; 1982.
Publication: *NABET News* (bimonthly).
Editor: Ronald Chizever.
Membership: 6,600; local unions, 47.

CALIFORNIA STATE EMPLOYEES' ASSOCIATION (IND.)
1108 O St., Sacramento, Calif. 95814.
Phone: (916) 444-8134.
President: William A. Craib.
Secretary-treasurer: William D. Boyd.
Executive secretary: Dan L. Western (General manager).
Organizing activities: David Carnevale.
Research director: George Feinberg.
Social insurance: Robert L. Zenz.
Legal: Loren McMaster.
Government relations: Michael Douglas.
Public relations activities: (Social insurance).
Collective bargaining activities: (Social insurance).
Convention: Annually.
Publication: *The California State Employee* (monthly).
Editor: James Bald.
Membership: 106,000; affiliates, 191.

CARPENTERS AND JOINERS OF AMERICA; UNITED BROTHERHOOD OF (AFL-CIO)
101 Constitution Ave., N.W., Washington, D.C. 20001.
Phone: (202) 546-6206.
Secretary-treasurer: William Sidell.
First vice president: William Konyha.
Second vice president: Patrick J. Campbell.
Secretary: John S. Rogers.
Treasurer: Charles E. Nichols.
Organizing activities: James A. Parker.
Research and education director: Nicholas R. Loope.
Social insurance: Paul Connelley.
Legal: William A. McGowan (General counsel).
Legislative activities: (Treasurer).
Health and safety activities: (Social insurance).
Convention: Every 4 years; October 1978.
Publication: *The Carpenter* (monthly).
Editor: (Secretary).
Membership: 820,000; local unions, 2,301.

CEMENT, LIME AND GYPSUM WORKERS INTERNATIONAL UNION; UNITED (AFL-CIO)
7830 West Lawrence Ave., Chicago, Ill. 60656.
Phone: (312) 774-2217.

ORGANIZED LABOR IN THE UNITED STATES

President: Thomas F. Miechur.
Secretary-treasurer: Richard A. Northrip.
Organizing activities: J. C. Andrews.
Research and education director: Donald L. Spatz.
Social insurance: (President).
Legal: Lester Asher.
Legislative activities: (President).
Public relations activities: (President).
Health and safety activities: (Research and education director).
Convention: Every 2 years.
Publication: *Voice of the Cement, Lime, Gypsum and Allied Workers* (monthly).
Editor: Patricia Strandt.
Membership: 37,500; local unions, 327.

CHEMICAL WORKERS UNION; INTERNATIONAL (AFL-CIO)
1655 West Market St., Akron, Ohio 44313.
Phone: (216) 867-2444.
President: Frank D. Martino.
Secretary-treasurer: J. A. Thomas.
Organizing activities: (President).
Research and education director: Anne C. Green.
Social insurance: Edward D. Colvin.
Legal: Salvatore Falletta.
Legislative activities: (Research and education director).
Health and Safety director: Lawrence J. Ahern.
Public relations activities: Robert Kasen.
Community services director: George Freeman.
Convention: Every 2 years; 1980.
Publications: *Chemical Worker* (monthly).
Editor: (President).
Membership: 85,215; local unions, 450.

CHRISTIAN LABOR ASSOCIATION OF THE UNITED STATES OF AMERICA (IND.)
9820 Gordon Street, Box 65, Zeeland, Mich. 49464.
Phone: (616) 772-9153 or (616) 669-0360.
President: Don E. Leep.
Secretary: John Stobbe.
Treasurer: Murvel Lambers.
Convention: Annually.
Publication: *Christian Labor Herald* (quarterly).
Editor: (President).
Membership: ———; local unions, ———.

CIVIL SERVICE EMPLOYEES ASSOCIATION, INC. (NEW YORK STATE IND.)
[Merged into American Federation of State, County and Municipal Employees (AFL-CIO), April 1978.]

CLASSIFIED SCHOOL EMPLOYEES; AMERICAN ASSOCIATION OF (IND.)
1585 Liberty St., S.E., P.O. Box 3011, Salem, Ore. 97302.
Phone: (503) 588-0121.
President: John Brown.
Secretary: Pat Smith.
Treasurer: Richard C. Bartlett.
Convention: Annually.
Membership: 89,000; affiliates, 5.

CLOTHING AND TEXTILE WORKERS UNION; AMALGAMATED (AFL-CIO)
15 Union Square, New York, N.Y. 10003.
Phone: (212) 255-7800.
President: Murray H. Finley.

Secretary-treasurer: Jacob Sheinkman.
Research director: Dr. Vera Miller.
Education director: William Elkuss.
Social insurance: (President and secretary-treasurer).
Legal: Arthur M. Goldberg (General counsel).
Legislative activities: William DuChessi (Executive vice president).
815 16th Street N.W., Suite 310, Washington, D.C. 20006.
Public relations activities: Burt Beck.
Health and safety activities: George Perkel.
Convention: Every 2 years; 1980.
Publication: *ACTWU Labor Unity* (monthly).
Editor: Tom Harriman.
Membership: 517,000; local unions, 1,535.

COLORADO ASSOCIATION OF PUBLIC EMPLOYEES (IND.)

1390 Logan St., Room 200, Denver, Colo. 80203.
Phone: (303) 832-1001.
President: Russell W. Confer.
Secretary: Joyce Becker.
Executive director: Harry C. Reese.
Organizing activities: Byron F. Orr.
Social insurance: (Executive director).
Legal: James R. Gilsdorf (Attorney).
Public relations activities: Berth Jerde.
Government relations: (Executive director).
Convention: Annually.
Publication: *The Citizen* (every 3 weeks).
Editor: (Public relations activities).
Membership: 11,200; affiliates, 52.

COMMUNICATIONS WORKERS OF AMERICA (AFL-CIO)

1925 K St., N.W., Washington, D.C. 20006.
Phone: (202) 785-6700.
President: Glenn E. Watts.
Secretary-treasurer: Louis B. Knecht.
Organizing activities: James B. Booe.
Research director: Ronnie J. Straw.
Education director: John B. Kulstad.
Social insurance: John Abraham.
Legal: Charles V. Koons (General counsel).
Legislative activities: (Organizing activities).
Public relations activities: Lee M. White.
Health and safety activities: (Research director).
Convention: Annually.
Publication: *CWA News* (monthly).
Editor: Jeffery M. Miller.
Membership: 498,743; local unions, 874.

COMPOSERS & LYRICISTS GUILD OF AMERICA (IND.)

6565 Sunset Boulevard, Los Angeles, Calif. 90028.
Phone: (213) 462-6068.
President: Elmer Bernstein.
Secretary-treasurer: Lyn Murray.
Organizing activities: Nathan G. Scott (Vice president).
Research director: Angie Zajac.
Education director: Noema Corradi.
Legal activities: Abraham Marcus, Esq.
Public relations activities: Marilyn Bergman.
Convention: 5 times a year.
Membership: 363; local unions, 1.

CONNECTICUT EMPLOYEES UNION (IND.)

72 Court Street, Middletown, Conn. 06457.
Phone: (203) 344-0311.

President: Salvatore J. Perruccio.
Treasurer: Stephen Zadroga.
Organizing activities: (President).
Research director: Stephen J. Perruccio.
Social insurance: (President).
Legal: (President).
Government relations: (President).
Public relations activities: (President).
Collective bargaining activities: (President).
Convention: Annually.
Publication: *The Independent Union* (every 6 weeks).
Editor: (President).
Membership: 3,200; affiliates, 56.

CONNECTICUT STATE EMPLOYEES ASSOCIATION (IND.)

760 Capitol Ave., Hartford, Conn. 06106.
Phone: (203) 525-6614.
President: Al Marotta.
Secretary: Michelle Trombley.
Treasurer: Gilbert F. Thetreault.
Executive director: John W. Thompson.
Organizing activities: Edward Caffrey.
Research director: Henry Brown.
Social insurance: James Quinn.
Legal: Barry Scheinberg (Attorney).
Public relations activities: (Organizing activities).
Government relations: James Duffey.
Collective bargaining activities: (Legal).
Convention: Annually.
Publication: *Government News* (every 3 weeks).
Editor: Christopher Cosgrove.
Membership: 27,400; affiliates, 204.

COOPERS' INTERNATIONAL UNION OF NORTH AMERICA (AFL-CIO)

83 Mall Office Center, 400 Sherburn Lane, Louisville, Ky. 40207.
Phone: (502) 897-3274.
President: Ernest D. Higdon.
Secretary-treasurer: (President).
Organizing activities: (President).
Research and education director: (President).
Social insurance: Mabel Clark.
Legal: J. F. Souders.
Legislative activities: (President).
Public relations activities: (President).
Health and safety activities: (President).
Convention: Every 4 years; May 1979.
Publication: *Coopers Journal* (semiannually).
Editor: (President).
Membership: 1,700; local unions, 36.

DIE SINKERS' CONFERENCE; INTERNATIONAL (IND.)

One Erieview Plaza, Cleveland, Ohio 44114.
Phone: (216) 522-1050.
President: William E. Verderber.
Secretary-treasurer: James H. Anderson.
Organizing activities: (President).
Research director: Joseph J. Wnorowski.
Education director: (Secretary-treasurer).
Social insurance: (Secretary-treasurer).
Legal: (President).
Legislative activities: (President).
Public relations activities: (Secretary-treasurer).
Health and safety activities: (President).
Convention: Semiannually.
Publication: *News Flash* (monthly).
Editor: (President).
Membership: 3,690; local unions, 29.

DIRECTORS GUILD OF AMERICA, INC. (IND.)

7950 Sunset Blvd., Hollywood, Calif. 90046.
Phone: (213) 656-1220.
President: Robert Aldridge.
Secretary: Lionel Ephraim.
Treasurer: Sheldon Leonard.
Organizing activities: Joseph C. Youngerman (National executive secretary).
Social insurance: Gerald Wilson.
8201 Beverly Blvd., Los Angeles, Calif. 90048.
Legal: Gunther Schiff (General counsel).
Convention: Every 2 years; 1979.
Publication: *DGA Directory of Members* (annually).
Editor: Publications Committee.
Membership: 4,154; local unions, 0.

DISTILLERY, RECTIFYING, WINE AND ALLIED WORKERS' INTERNATIONAL UNION OF AMERICA (AFL-CIO)

66 Grand Ave., Englewood, N.J. 07631.
Phone: (201) 569-9212.
President: George J. Oneto.
Secretary-treasurer: George J. Orlando.
Organizing activities: (Secretary-treasurer).
Research and education director: Abe S. Weiss.
Social insurance: (President).
Legal: (President).
Legislative activities: (Research and education director).
Public relations activities: (Secretary-treasurer).
Health and safety activities: (Secretary-treasurer).
Convention: Every 2 years; 1980.
Publications: (1) *DWU Journal* (semiannually). (2) *DWU Newsletter* (quarterly).
Editors: (1) (Research and education director). (2) (Secretary-treasurer).
Membership: 31,000; local unions, 88.

DISTRIBUTIVE WORKERS OF AMERICA (IND.)

13 Astor Place, New York, N.Y. 10003.
Phone: (212) 673-5120.
President: Cleveland Robinson.
Secretary-treasurer: David Livingston.
Organizing activities: Frank Brown.
Social insurance: Esther Levitt.
Legal: Eisner, Levy & Steele (Attorneys).
Legislative activities: (President).
Health and safety activities: (Social insurance).
Convention: Every 4 years; April 1980.
Publication: *The Distributive Worker* (monthly).
Editor: Leo Wolfe.
Membership: 50,000; local unions, 40.

EDUCATION ASSOCIATION; NATIONAL (IND.)

1201 16th St., N.W., Washington, D.C. 20036.
Phone: (202) 833-4000.
President: John Edward Ryor.
Secretary-treasurer: John T. McGarigal.
Executive director: Terry Herndon.
Organizing activities: Gary D. Watts.
Social insurance: Arleigh Greenblat.
Legal: Robert H. Chanin.
Public relations activities: Susan Lowell.
Government relations: Stanley J. McFarland.
Collective bargaining activities: (Organizing activities).
Convention: Annually.
Publications: Today's Education (quarterly); *NEA Reporter* (monthly); *NEA NOW* (monthly); *NEA Advocate* (monthly).
Editors: Walter Graves, Marshall Donley, Patrice Gancie, Ann Kurzius.
Membership: 1,470,212; affiliates, 9,815.

OVERSEAS EDUCATION ASSOCIATION, INC.

1201 16th St., N.W., Room 210, Washington, D.C. 20036.
Phone: (202) 833-4276.
President: Lynne Holland.
Secretary: Karen Winingar.
Executive director: Carl D. Moore.
Organizing activities: (Executive director).
Research director: (Executive director).
Social insurance: (Executive director).
Legal: (Executive director).
Government relations: (President and Executive director).
Public relations: (President and Executive director).
Collective bargaining activities: (President and Executive director)
Convention: Annually.
Publication: *OEA Journal* (monthly).
Editor: Bill Hobbs.
Membership: 3,067; affiliates, 70.

ELECTRICAL, RADIO AND MACHINE WORKERS; INTERNATIONAL UNION OF (AFL-CIO)

1126 16th St., N.W. Washington, D.C. 20036.
Phone: (202) 296-1200.
President: David J. Fitzmaurice.
Secretary-treasurer: George Hutchins.
Organizing activities: Al Bilik.
Research director: Charles C. Kimble.
Education director: Gloria Johnson.
Social insurance: Rex Clifford.
Legal: Winn Newman (General counsel).
Legislative activities: George Collins.
Public relations activities: Jerry Borstel.
Health and safety activities: Jack Suarez.
Plaza 7, 1202 Troy-Sche Rd., Latham, N.Y. 12110.
Convention: Every 2 years; 1980.
Publication: *IUE News* (monthly).
Editor: (Public relations activities).
Membership: 298,231; local unions, 633.

ELECTRICAL, RADIO, AND MACHINE WORKERS OF AMERICA; UNITED (IND.)

11 East 51st St., New York, N.Y. 10022
Phone: (212) 753-1960.
President: Albert J. Fitzgerald.
Secretary-treasurer: Boris Block.
Organizing activities: Hugh J. Harley, Jr.
Research director: Nathan Spero.
Education director: Charles Kerns.
Social insurance: (Research director).
Legal: Frank Donner (General counsel).
Legislative activities: Millie Hedrick.
Health and safety activities: Howie Forman.
Public relations activities: (Education director).
Convention: Annually.
Publication: *UE News* (semimonthly).
Editor: James Lerner.
Membership: 163,000; local unions, 180.

ELECTRICAL WORKERS; INTERNATIONAL BROTHERHOOD OF (AFL-CIO)

1125 15th St., N.W., Washington, D.C. 20005.
Phone: (202) 833-7000.
President: Charles H. Pillard.
Secretary: Ralph A. Leigon.
Treasurer: Thomas P. Van Arsdale.
Organizing activities: (President).

Research and education director: Robert B. Wood.
Safety director: Charles H. Tupper.
Social insurance: (President).
Legal: (President).
Legislative activities: (Secretary).
Public relations activities: Robert W. McAlwee.
Convention: Every 4 years; 1982.
Publication: *IBEW Journal* (monthly).
Editor: (President).
Membership: 991,228; local unions, 1,583.

ELEVATOR CONSTRUCTORS; INTERNATIONAL UNION OF (AFL-CIO)
Suite 332, Clarke Building, 5565 Sterrett Place, Columbia, Md. 21044.
Phone: (301) 997-9000.
President: Everett A. Treadway.
Secretary-treasurer: John N. Russell.
Organizing activities: (President).
Education director: John J. O'Donnell.
Social insurance: Jerome A. Mullett.
Legal: (President).
Legislative activities: (President).
Health and safety activities: (President).
Convention: Every 5 years; July 1981.
Publication: (*The Elevator Constructor* (monthly).
Editor: (Social insurance).
Membership: 18,902; local unions, 109.

FARM WORKERS OF AMERICA; UNITED (AFL-CIO)
P.O. Box 62, Keene, Calif. 93531.
Phone: (805) 822-5571.
President: Cesar E. Chavez.
Secretary-treasurer: Gilber Padilla.
Organizing activities: Marshall Ganz.
Social insurance: Ralph Magana.
Legal: Jerome Cohen (General counsel).
P.O. Box 1049, Salinas, California 93901.
Legislative activities: Mack Lyons.
Public relations activities: Marc Grossman.
Convention: Every 2 years; 1979.
Membership: 12,000; local unions, 16.

FEDERAL EMPLOYEES; NATIONAL FEDERATION OF (IND.)
1016 16th St., N.W., Washington, D.C. 20036.
Phone: (202) 862-4400.
President: James M. Peirce.
Secretary-treasurer: Rita M. Hartz.
Organizing activities: Tom G. Black.
Research director: Thomas J. Trabucco.
Education director: Dennis N. Davis.
Social insurance: J. Gene Raymond.
Legal: Irving Geller (General counsel).
Legislative activities: Maureen Clancy.
Public relations activities: Frank Taylor.
Health and safety activities: (Social insurance).
Convention: Every 2 years; 1980.
Publication: *Federal Employee* (monthly).
Editor: (President).
Membership: 100,000; local unions, 1,700.

FIRE FIGHTERS; INTERNATIONAL ASSOCIATION OF (AFL-CIO)
1750 New York Ave., N.W., Washington, D.C. 20006.
Phone: (202) 872-8484.

President: William Howard McClennan.
Secretary-treasurer: Frank A. Palumbo.
Organizing activities: Daniel T. Delegato.
Research director: Walter Lambert.
Education director: Ross L. Atwood.
Legal: Edward J. Hickey (General counsel).
Legislative activities: Harold A. Schaitberger.
Public relations activities: Thomas W. Herz.
Convention: Every 2 years; 1980.
Publication: *The International Fire Fighter* (monthly).
Editor: (President).
Membership: 171,674; local unions, 1,798.

FIREMEN AND OILERS; INTERNATIONAL BROTHERHOOD OF (AFL-CIO)
VFM Bldg., 5th floor, 200 Maryland Ave., N.E., Washington, D.C. 20002.
Phone: (202) 547-7540.
President: John J. McNamara.
Secretary-treasurer: George J. Francisco.
Research director: Patricia J. Williams.
Social insurance: (Research director).
Legal: Clarence M. Mulholland.
Legislative activities: (President).
Health and safety activities: (Secretary-treasurer).
Convention: Every 5 years; July 1981.
Publication: *Firemen & Oilers Journal* (bimonthly).
Editor: (Secretary-treasurer).
Membership: 40,000; local unions, ———.

FLIGHT ENGINEERS' INTERNATIONAL ASSOCIATION (AFL-CIO)
905 16th St., N.W., Washington, D.C. 20006.
Phone: (202) 347-4511.
President: William A. Gill, Jr.
Secretary-treasurer: Karl F. Anderson.
Organizing activities: (President).
Research director: Jack A. Wahle.
Legal: Asher W. Schwartz (Legal counsel).
285 Madison Ave., New York, N.Y. 10017.
Legislative activities: (President).
Public relations activities: (President).
Health and safety activities: Donald F. Thielke.
Convention: Annually.
Membership: 4,291; local unions, 17.

FOOTBALL LEAGUE PLAYERS ASSOCIATION; NATIONAL (IND.)
1300 Connecticut Ave., N.W., Washington, D.C. 20036.
Phone: (202) 833-3335.
Research director: Stephen Koczak.
Education director: Arthur Kane.
Social insurance: (Secretary-treasurer).
Legal: Leo M. Pellerzi (General counsel).
Legislative activities: James Lynch.
Public relations activities: Greg Kenefick.
Health and safety activities: (Organizing activities).
Convention: Every 2 years; 1980.
Publications: (1) *The Government Standard* (monthly). (2) *The Washington Letter* (weekly).
Editors: (1) (Public relations activties). (2) Jeanette Abrams.
Membership: 300,000; local unions, 1,500.

GOVERNMENT EMPLOYEES; NATIONAL ASSOCIATION OF (IND.)
285 Dorchester Ave., Boston, Mass. 02127.
Phone: (617) 268-5002.
President: Kenneth T. Lyons.
Secretary-treasurer: Edmund J. Coan.
Organizing activities: Harry Breen (Vice president).
Research director: Richard Remmes.

Education director: Gerald Welcome.
Legal: Robert Canavan (General counsel).
Legislative activities: Alan J. Whitney (Executive director).
2139 Wisconsin Avenue, N.W., Washington, D.C. 20007.
Public relations activities: William Norton.
Health and safety activities: Frank Ward.
Convention: Every 3 years; 1980.
Publication: *FED News* (monthly).
Editor: Daniel Boyle.
Membership:153,527; local unions, 500.

GOVERNMENT INSPECTORS AND QUALITY ASSURANCE PERSONNEL; NATIONAL ASSOCIATION OF (IND.)

P.O. Box 13277, Chesapeake, Virginia 23325.
Phone: (804) 444-8851.
President: Charles D. Hadley.
Secretary-treasurer: Charles H. Wood.
Organizing activities: Charles Anderson.
Research director: Paul Whitehurst.
Education director: Harold Wilson.
Legal: (President).
Legislative activities: John Brice.
Public relations activities: (Education director).
Health and safety activities: Robert Chetister.
Convention: Annually.
Publication: *NAGI News* (quarterly).
Editor: (Secretary-treasurer).
Membership: 703; local unions, 9.

GRAIN MILLERS; AMERICAN FEDERATION OF (AFL-CIO)

4949 Olson Memorial Hwy., Minneapolis, Minn. 55422.
Phone: (612) 545-0211.
President: Roy O. Wellborn.
Secretary-treasurer: Harold P. Tevis.
Organizing activities: Joe Rajcevich.
Social insurance: (Secretary-treasurer).
Legal: (President).
Legislative activities: Frank T. Hoese.
Public relations activities: Shirley Wellborn.
Health and safety activities: (Public relations activities).
Convention: Every 2 years; 1979.
Membership: 35,000; local unions, 204.

GRANITE CUTTERS' INTERNATIONAL ASSOCIATION OF AMERICA; THE (AFL-CIO)

18 Federal Ave., Quincy, Mass. 02169.
Phone: (617) 472-0209.
President: Joseph P. Ricciarelli.
Secretary-treasurer: (President).
Organizing activities: (President).
Research and education director: (President).
Legal: (President).
Legislative activities: (President).
Public relations activities: (President).
Health and safety activities: (President).
Convention: Every 5 years; September 1981.
Publication: *The Granite Cutters' Journal* (quarterly).
Editor: (President).
Membership: 3,200; local unions, 17.

GRAPHIC ARTS INTERNATIONAL UNION (AFL-CIO)

1900 L St., N.W., Washington, D.C. 20036.
Phone: (202) 872-7900.
President: Kenneth J. Brown.
Secretary-treasurer: Joseph Hellman.
Organizing activities: Murray McKenzie (Vice president).
Research director: Sandra Wood.
Education director: John Stagg.
Social insurance: Leon Wickersham.

Legislative activities: Edward Donahue (Vice president).
Health and safety activities: William A. Schroeder (Vice president).
President: Richard Anderson.
Executive director: Edward Garvey.
Organizing activities: Gary Ballman.
Social insurance: (Organizing activities).
Legal: Richard Berthelsen.
Legislative activities: Ben Zelenko.
Public relations activities: (Executive director).
Convention: Annually.
Publications: *The Audible* (monthly); *The Checkoff* (weekly, July to January); *The Lawdible* (monthly).
Editors: Frank Woschitz. Bob Epstein. (legal).
Membership: ———; clubs, 26.

FURNITURE WORKERS OF AMERICA; UNITED (AFL-CIO)

700 Broadway, 4th floor, New York, N.Y. 10003.
Phone: (212) 533-1900.
President: Carl Scarbrough.
Secretary-treasurer: Lowell Daily.
Organizing activities: (President).
Research director: Meryl London.
Education director: (Secretary-treasurer).
Social insurance: George Rothman.
Legal: James Gill (General counsel).
Legislative activities: (Secretary-treasurer).
Public relations activities: (Research director).
Health and safety activities: (Secretary-treasurer).
Convention: Every 4 years; May 1980.
Publication: *Furniture Workers Press* (monthly).
Editor: (President).
Membership: 29,967; local unions, 106.

GARMENT WORKERS OF AMERICA; UNITED (AFL-CIO)

200 Park Ave., South, Suite 1610–1614, New York, N.Y. 10003.
Phone: (212) 677-0573.
President: William O'Donnell.
Secretary-treasurer: Catherine C. Peters.
Organizing activities: (President).
Resarch and education director: (President).
Legal: Richard H. Markowitz (Attorney).
Legislative activities: (President).
Public relations activities: (President).
Health and safety activities: (President).
Convention: Every 5 years; 1982.
Publication: *The Garment Worker* (monthly).
Editor: (Secretary-treasurer).
Membership: 25,000; local unions, 166.

GLASS BOTTLE BLOWERS ASSOCIATION OF THE UNITED STATES AND CANADA (AFL-CIO)

608 E. Baltimore Pike, Media, Pa. 19063.
Phone: (215) 565-5051.
President: James E. Hatfield.
Secretary-treasurer: Walter J. MacLuskie.
Organizing activities: Michael Martucci.
R.D. 2, Knox, Pennsylvania 16232.
Research and education director: Carl Legler.
Social insurance: (Research and education director).
Legal: Carl W. Lindner.
Legislative activities: Harry L. Moore (Legislative director).
Public relations activities: Francis Gildea.
Health and safety activities: (Legislative activities).

Convention: Every 4 years; 1981.
Publication: *GBBA Horizons* (monthly).
Editor: Harry Tulley.
Membership: 80,162; local unions, 244.

GLASS AND CERAMIC WORKERS OF NORTH AMERICA; UNITED (AFL-CIO)

556 East Town St., Columbus, Ohio 43215.
Phone: (614) 221-4465.
President: Joseph Roman.
Secretary-treasurer: Joseph Stanzione.
Organizing activities: (President).
Research and education director: H. Wayne Yarman.
Social insurance: (Secretary-treasurer).
Legal: David Clayman (Attorney).
Legislative activities: (Secretary-treasurer).
Public relations activities: (Research and education director).
Health and safety activities: (Research and education director).
Convention: Every 4 years; 1982.
Publication: *Glass Workers News* (bimonthly).
Editor: (Research and education director).
Membership: 38,500; local unions, 197.

GLASS WORKERS' UNION OF NORTH AMERICA; AMERICAN FLINT (AFL-CIO)

1440 South Byrne Road, Toledo, Ohio 43614.
Phone: (419) 385-6687.
President: George M. Parker.
Secretary-treasurer: Ivan T. Uncapher.
Research director: Harold Gibbons (2nd vice president).
Convention: Every 2 years; 1979.
Publication: *American Flint* (monthly).
Editor: R. W. Newell.
Membership: 35,000; local unions, 260.

GOVERNMENT EMPLOYEES; AMERICAN FEDERATION OF (AFL-CIO)

1325 Massachusetts Ave., N.W., Washington, D.C. 20005.
Phone: (202) 737-8700.
President: Kenneth T. Blaylock.
Secretary-treasurer: Nicholas J. Nolan.
Organizing activities: Ted Merrill.
Convention: Every 3 years; 1981.
Publication: *Graphic Arts Unionist* (bimonthly).
Editor: William Moody.
Membership: 100,000; local unions, 281.

GUARD UNION OF AMERICA; INTERNATIONAL (IND.)

1444 Gardiner Lane, Louisville, Kentucky 40213.
Phone: (303) 934-7360.
President: A. L. McLemore.
Secretary-treasurer: Raymond G. Curtis.
1070 South Knox Court, Denver, Colo. 80219.
Organizing activities: (Secretary-treasurer).
Research and education director: Roy Morrill.
2631 Birch Avenue, Richland, Washington 99352.
Legal: Charles R. Isenberg (Attorney).
Marion E. Taylor Bldg., Louisville, Kentucky 40202.
Legislative activities: (President).
Public relations activities: (Research and education director).
Convention: Every 4 years; 1981.
Publication: *Guards* (quarterly).
Editor: (Research and education director).
Membership: 3,250; local unions, 50.

GUARDS & WATCHMEN, INTERNATIONAL UNION OF (IND.)

452 Harrison Street, Room 213, San Francisco, Calif. 94105.
Phone: (415) 895-9905.
President: Melvin J. Roth.
Secretary-treasurer: Bruce G. Burt.
Organizing activities: (President).
Social insurance: (Secretary-treasurer).
Convention: Every 5 years; 1983.
Publication: *The Guard Watch* (bimonthly).
Editor: (Secretary-treasurer).
Membership: 3,500; local unions, 1.

HATTERS, CAP AND MILLINERY WORKERS INTERNATIONAL UNION; UNITED (AFL-CIO)

105 Madison Ave., New York, N.Y. 10016.
Phone: (212) 683-5200.
President: Nicholas Gyory.
Secretary-treasurer: Gerald R. Coleman.
Organizing activities: (Secretary-treasurer).
Education director: (Secretary-treasurer).
Social insurance: Irving Kaufman.
Legal: Marshall Rosenberg (General counsel).
Legislative activities: (Secretary-treasurer).
Public relations activities: (Secretary-treasurer).
Health and safety activities: (Secretary-treasurer).
Convention: Every 3 years; 1981.
Membership: 14,000; local unions, 54.

HEBREW ACTORS UNION, INC.

See Actors and Artistes of America; Associated (AFL-CIO)

HOCKEY LEAGUE PLAYERS' ASSOCIATION; NATIONAL (IND.)

Suite 1905, 80 Richmond St. W., Toronto, Ontario, Canada.
Phone: (416) 868-6574.
President: Robert Clarke.
Executive director: R. Alan Eagleson.
Organizing activities: (Executive director).
Legal: (Executive director).
Legislative activities: (Executive director).
Convention: Annually.
Membership: 396; clubs, 18.

HORSESHOERS OF THE UNITED STATES AND CANADA; INTERNATIONAL UNION OF JOURNEYMEN (AFL-CIO)

P.O. Box 504, Pleasanton, Calif. 94566.
Phone: (415) 846-2756.
President: Duke Bond, Jr.
Secretary-treasurer: Joe Young.
2917 S. Florida Ave., Caldwell, Idaho 83605.
Social insurance: (Secretary-treasurer).
Convention: Every 3 years; 1980.
Publication: *I.U.J.H. Newsletter* (quarterly).
Editor: (Secretary-treasurer).
Membership: 370; local unions, 25.

HOTEL AND RESTAURANT EMPLOYEES AND BARTENDERS INTERNATIONAL UNION (AFL-CIO)

120 East 4th St., Cincinnati, Ohio 45202.
Phone: (513) 621-0300.
President: Edward T. Hanley.
Secretary-treasurer: John Gibson.
Organizing activities: Charles A. Paulsen.
Research and education director: Phillip M. Valley.
Social insurance: (Secretary-treasurer).
Legal: John J. Reynolds (General counsel).
Legislative activities: Robert E. Juliano.
1666 K St., N.W., Suite 304, Washington, D.C. 20006.
Public relations activities: John P. Lavin.

Convention: Every 5 years; May 1981.
Publications: (1) *Catering Industry Employee* (monthly). (2) *Food for Thought* (monthly).
Editors: (1) (Secretary-treasurer). (2) (Research and education director).
Membership: 451,989; local unions, 386.

IDAHO PUBLIC EMPLOYEES ASSOCIATION (IND.)
430 North 9th Street, Boise, Idaho 83702.
Phone: (208) 336-2841.
President: M. Russell Bosch.
Secretary-treasurer: Phyllis K. Blunck.
Executive director: Stephen E. Swadley.
Organizing activities: James Broich.
Research director: Charles Murry, Jr.
Social insurance: (Executive director).
Legal: William C. Roden.
Public relations activities: Willard Abbott.
Government relations: (Executive director).
Collective bargaining activities: (Executive director).
Convention: Annually.
Publication: *I.P.E.A. News* (bimonthly).
Editor: (Executive director).
Membership: 4,200; chapters, 24.

ILLINOIS STATE EMPLOYEES ASSOCIATION (IND.)
2800 South Walnut St, Springfield 62704.
Phone: (217) 525-1944.
President: Joseph T. Pisano.
Secretary: Helen Peterson.
Treasurer: Willadene Hainline.
Executive director: Ivan Schraeder.
Organizing activities: (Executive director).
Legal: Ivan Schraeder.
Government relations: (Executive director).
Public relations activities: (Executive director).
Collective bargaining activities: (Legal).
Publication: *The Alerter* (monthly).
Editor: Pegg Warnick.
Membership: 13,000; chapters, ———.

INDEPENDENT UNIONS; CONGRESS OF (IND.)
303 Ridge St., Alton, Ill. 62002.
Phone: (618) 462-2447.
President: Truman Davis.
Secretary-treasurer: Ed Bickmore.
Organizing activities: (President).
Research director: John Hartshorn.
Education director: (Secretary-treasurer).
Social insurance: Clark Libhart (Executive vice president).
Legal: (Social insurance).
Legislative activities: Frank Eyles (Vice president).
Public relations activities: (Legislative activities).
Health and safety activities: Richard Davis.
Convention: Annually.
Publication: *Union Labor News Review* (monthly).
Editor: (Legislative activities).
Membership: 25,000; local unions, 10.

INDIANA STATE EMPLOYEES ASSOCIATION (IND.)
632 Illinois Bldg., 17 West Market St., Indianapolis 46204.
Phone: (317) 632-7254.
President: Jack Beckort.
Secretary: Helen Scheibner.
Treasurer: Paul Bender.
Executive director: Charles F. Eble.
Organizing activities: Ronald Gremore.
Social insurance: Valerie Zimmerman.
Legal: Ann Rybolt.
Public relations activities: (Vacant).
Government relations: (Executive director).

Collective bargaining activities: (Executive director).
Convention: Annually.
Publication: *ISEA Newsletter* (monthly).
Editor: (Organizing activities).
Membership: 4,500; local chapters, ———.

INDUSTRIAL TRADE UNIONS; NATIONAL ORGANIZATION OF (IND.)
148–06 Hillside Ave., Jamaica, N.Y. 11435.
Phone: (212) 291-3434.
President: Daniel Lasky.
Secretary-treasurer: Gerald Hustick.
Organizing activities: (President).
Social insurance: (President).
Convention: Every 4 years; October 1980.
Publication: *Union Craft* (quarterly).
Editor: Aaron Traqer.
Membership: 5,142; local unions, 10.

INDUSTRIAL WORKERS OF AMERICA; INTERNATIONAL UNION ALLIED (AFL-CIO)
3520 West Oklahoma Ave., Milwaukee, Wis. 53215.
Phone: (414) 645-9500.
President: Dominick D'Ambrosio.
Secretary-treasurer: Archie E. Robbins.
Organizing activities: (President).
Research director: Raymond MacDonald.
Education director: George Daitsman.
Social insurance: (Research director).
Legal: Goldberg, Previant and Uelmen (Attorneys).
Legislative activities: Kenneth Germanson (COPE director).
Public relations activities: (Legislative activities).
Health and safety activities: Thomas Ballanoff.
Convention: Every 2 years; 1979.
Publication: *Allied Industrial Worker* (monthly).
Editor: (President and legislative activities).
Membership: 96,817; local unions, 440.

INLAND BOATMEN'S UNION OF THE PACIFIC
See Seafarer's International Union of North America (AFL-CIO)

INDUSTRIAL WORKERS UNION; NATIONAL (IND.)
514 N. Main St., P.O. Box 1893, Lima, Ohio 45802.
Phone: (419) 223-8555.
President: Glen D. Wilkins.
Secretary-treasurer: Alonzo Wheeler.
Organizing activities: (Secretary-treasurer).
Convention: Annually.
Membership: 759; local unions, 11.

INSURANCE WORKERS INTERNATIONAL UNION (AFL-CIO)
1017 12th St., N.W., Washington, D.C. 20005.
Phone: (202) 783-1127.
President: Joseph Pollack.
Secretary-treasurer: Charles G. Heisel.
Organizing activities: (President).
Education director: William M. Gerhauser, Jr.
Legal: Isaac N. Groner (General counsel).
Legislative activities: (Education director).
Convention: Every 2 years; 1979.
Publication: *The Insurance Worker* (10 issues annually).
Editor: (President).
Membership: 21,896; local unions, 250.

INTERNATIONAL UNION OF PETROLEUM AND INDUSTRIAL WORKERS
See Seafarer's International Union of North America (AFL-CIO)

IRON WORKERS; INTERNATIONAL ASSOCIATION OF BRIDGE AND STRUCTURAL (AFL-CIO)

1750 New York Ave, N.W., Suite 400, Washington, D.C. 20006.
Phone: (202) 872-1566.
President: John H. Lyons.
Secretary: Juel D. Drake.
Treasurer: John McKean.
Organizing activities: (President) and A. S. Goodwin.
Research director: (President).
Social insurance: (President).
Legal: Harold Stern (General counsel).
Health and safety activities: Robert E. P. Cooney.
400 First St., N.W., Washington, D.C. 20001.
Convention: Every 5 years; 1981.
Publication: *The Ironworker* (monthly).
Editor: William M. Lawbaugh.
Membership: 181,647; local unions, 322.

ITALIAN ACTORS UNION

See Actors and Artistes of America; Associated (AFL-CIO)

JEWELRY WORKERS' UNION; INTERNATIONAL (AFL-CIO)

8 West 40th St., Room 501, New York, N.Y. 10018.
Phone: (212) 244-8793.
President and secretary-treasurer: Leon Sverdlove.
Social insurance: (President).
Convention: Every 3 years; 1980.
Membership: 10,000; local unions, 30.

LABORERS' INTERNATIONAL UNION OF NORTH AMERICA (AFL-CIO)

905 16th St., N.W., Washington, D.C. 20006.
Phone: (202) 737-8320.
President: Angelo Fosco.
Secretary-treasurer: W. Vernie Reed.
Organizing activities: (President).
Research director: James R. Sheets.
Education director: Joseph Short.
Social insurance: Howard Robinson.
Legal: Robert Connerton (General counsel).
Legislative activities: John Curran.
Public relations activities: Patrick Ziska.
Health and safety activities: (Secretary-treasurer).
Convention: Every 5 years; 1981.
Publications: *The Laborer* (monthly); *The Government Employee* (monthly); *Mailhandler Postal Review* (monthly); *The Mailhandler* (monthly).
Editor: (Public relations activities).
Membership: 650,000; local unions, 850.

LACE OPERATIVES OF AMERICA; AMALGAMATED (IND.)

4013 Glendale St., Philadelphia, Pa. 19124.
Phone: (215) 743-9358.
President: Reno G. Poli.
Secretary-treasurer: John Newton.
Organizing activities: (Secretary-treasurer).
Social insurance: (President).
297 Columbus Ave., Pautucket, R.I. 02861.
Convention: Every 5 years; June 1981.
Publication: *American Lace Worker* (bimonthly).
Editor: Frank J. Clark.
Membership: 1,500; local unions, 9.

LADIES' GARMENT WORKERS' UNION; INTERNATIONAL (AFL-CIO)

1710 Broadway, New York, N.Y. 10019.
Phone: (212) 265-7000.
President: Sol C. Chaikin.
Secretary-treasurer: (President).
Research director: Lazare Teper.
Education director: Gus Tyler.
Social insurance: Louis Rolnick.
Legal: Max Zimny (General counsel).
Legislative activities: Evelyn Dubrow.
Public relations activities: Michael Pollack.
Convention: Every 3 years; 1980.
Publications: *Justice* (semimonthly); *Giustizia* (Italian, monthly); *Justicia* (Spanish, monthly).
Editors: (1) (Public relations activities). (2) Lino Monocchia. (3) Tony Lespier.
Membership: 404,737; local unions, ———.

LATHERS; INTERNATIONAL UNION OF WOOD, WIRE AND METAL (AFL-CIO)

815 16th St., N.W., Washington, D.C. 20006.
Phone: (202) 628-0400.
President: Charles L. Brodeur.
Secretary-treasurer: Michael J. Brennan.
Organizing activities: (President).
Research and education director: (President).
Social insurance: Lillian Marsh and Helene Sullivan.
Legal: (President).
Legislative activities: (President).
Public relations activities: (President).
Health and safety activities: (President).
Convention: Every 3 years; August 1979.
Publication: *The Lather* (quarterly).
Editor: (Secretary-treasurer).
Membership: 14,428; local unions, 252.

LAUNDRY AND DRY CLEANING INTERNATIONAL UNION (AFL-CIO)

Carlton House, Suite 435, 550 Grant St., Pittsburgh, Pa. 15219.
Phone: (412) 471-4829.
President: Russell R. Crowell.
610 16th St., Rm. 421, Pacific Bldg., Oakland, Calif. 94612.
Secretary-treasurer: Sam H. Begler.
Organizing activities: Clem R. Regner.
Research director: (President).
Education director: (Secretary-treasurer).
Social insurance: (President).
Legal: Leo I. Shapiro (Legal consultant).
Legislative activities: (President).
Public relations activities: (Secretary-treasurer).
Health and safety activities: (President).
Convention: Every 5 years; 1983.
Publication: *AFL-CIO Laundry and Dry Cleaning Worker* (annually).
Editor: (Secretary-treasurer).
Membership: 19,543; local unions, 32.

LAUNDRY, DRY CLEANING AND DYE HOUSE WORKERS' INTERNATIONAL UNION

See Teamsters, Chauffeurs, Warehousemen, and Helpers of America; International Brotherhood of (Ind.)

LEATHER GOODS, PLASTIC AND NOVELTY WORKERS' UNION; INTERNATIONAL (AFL-CIO)

265 West 14th St., 14th floor, New York, N.Y. 10011.
Phone: (212) 675-9240.
President: Frank Casale.
Secretary-treasurer: Ralph Cennamo.
Organizing activities: Secretary-treasurer.
Research and education director: Abraham Weiss.

Social insurance: Charles R. Szabo.
Legal: Leonard Greenwald (General counsel).
Legislative activities: (Research and education director).
Public relations activities: (Research and education director).
Convention: Every 5 years; 1982.
Membership: 40,000; local unions, 97.

LEATHER WORKERS INTERNATIONAL UNION OF AMERICA (AFL-CIO)

11 Peabody Square, Peabody, Mass. 01960.
Phone: (617) 531-5605.
President: Arthur Z. Cecelski.
Secretary-treasurer: Joseph A. Duffy.
Organizing activities: Albano Quadros.
Social insurance: (Secretary-treasurer).
Legal: Angoff, Goldman, Manning (Legal counsel).
Public Relations activities: (President).
Convention: Every 5 years; 1982.
Membership: 3,000; local unions, ———.

LETTER CARRIERS OF THE UNITED STATES OF AMERICA; NATIONAL ASSOCIATION OF (AFL-CIO)

100 Indiana Ave., N.W., Washington, D.C. 20001.
Phone: (202) 393-4695.
President: Vincent R. Sombrotto.
Secretary-treasurer: Gustave J. Johnson.
Organizing activities: (Secretary-treasurer).
Research and education director: John Miller.
Social insurance: (President).
Legal: Mozart Ratner (General counsel).
Legislative activities: Tony R. Huerta (Executive vice president).
Public relations activities: John W. DiTolla.
Health and safety activities: (Secretary-treasurer).
Convention: Every 2 years; 1980.
Publication: *The Postal Record* (monthly).
Editor: (President).
Membership: 232,000; local unions, 5,600.

LICENSED OFFICERS' ORGANIZATION; GREAT LAKES (IND.)

P.O. Box 387, Ludington, Mich. 49431.
Phone: (616) 843-9543.
President: James E. Luke.
Secretary-treasurer: Willard D. Wissner.
Organizing activities: (Secretary-treasurer).
Social insurance: (Secretary-treasurer).
Legal: (Secretary-treasurer).
Legislative activities: (Secretary-treasurer).
Public relations activities: (Secretary-treasurer).
Health and safety activities: (Secretary-treasurer).
Convention: (Annual executive board meeting).
Membership: 42; local unions, 0.

LICENSED PRACTICAL NURSES; NATIONAL FEDERATION OF (IND.)

250 West 57th St., New York, N.Y. 10019.
Phone: (212) 246-6629.
President: E. Pauline Wright.
Secretary: Dorothy Thompson.
Executive director: Charles Hull.
Organizing activities: (Executive director).
Legal: Allan J. Parker.
Public relations activities: Robert Sanford.
Government relations: Paul Tendler.
Collective bargaining activities: Robert Merry.
Convention: Annually.
Publication: *NFLPN Newsletter* (in *Nursing Care* magazine) (monthly).
Editor: (Public relations activities).
Membership: 25,997; local associations, 38.

LOCOMOTIVE ENGINEERS; BROTHERHOOD OF (IND.)

1112 Brotherhood of Locomotive Engineers Bldg., Cleveland, Ohio 44114.
Phone: (216) 241-2630.
President: John F. Sytsma.
Secretary-treasurer: John D. Rinehart.
Organizing activities: (President).
Research and education director: Virgil F. Davis.
Social insurance: (President).
Legal: H. A. Ross (General counsel).
Legislative activities: (President).
Public relations activities: (President).
Health and safety activities: (President).
Convention: Every 5 years; 1981.
Publication: *Locomotive Engineer* (weekly).
Editor: W. A. Rice.
Membership: 39,245; local unions, 779.

LOG SCALERS ASSOCIATION, PACIFIC (IND.)

1675 Sixteenth St., North Bend, Ore. 97459.
Phone: (503) 759-4372.
President: Stanford D. Walton.
Secretary-treasurer: John E. Yoemans.
Health and safety activities: (Secretary-treasurer).
Convention: Semiannually.
Membership: 290; local unions, 3.

LONGSHOREMEN'S ASSOCIATION; INTERNATIONAL (AFL-CIO)

17 Battery Pl., Room 1530, New York, N.Y. 10004.
Phone: (212) 425-1200.
President: Thomas W. Gleason.
Secretary-treasurer: Harry R. Hasselgren.
Organizing activities: Fred F. Field, Jr.
Social insurance: Walter L. Sullivan (Welfare director).
Anthony Aurigemma (Pension director).
Legislative activities: Anthony Scotto.
Public relations activities: Lawrence G. Malloy.
Health and safety activities: Joseph Leonard.
Convention: Every 4 years; 1979.
Publication: *I.L.A. Longshore News* (periodically).
Editor: (Public relations activities).
Membership: 76,579; local unions, 367.

MASTERS, MATES AND PILOTS; INTERNATIONAL ORGANIZATION OF (ILA-MARINE DIVISION)

39 Broadway, New York, N.Y. 10006.
Phone: (212) 425-3860.
President: Capt. Frank T. Scavo.
Secretary-treasurer: Capt. Robert J. Lowen.
Organizing activities: (President).
Education director: Capt. William Rich.
Social insurance: Stephen P. Maher.
Legal: Marvin Schwartz (International counsel).
Legislative activities: Capt. Gene Laski.
Public relations activities: Maurice J. Weiss.
Health and safety activities: (Education director).
Convention: Every 2 years; 1979.
Publication: *The Master, Mate and Pilot* (monthly).
Editor: (Public relations activities).
Membership: 5,874; local unions, 4.

LONGSHOREMEN'S AND WAREHOUSEMEN'S UNION; INTERNATIONAL (IND.)

1188 Franklin St., San Francisco, Calif. 94109.
Phone: (415) 775-0533.

President: James R. Herman.
Secretary-treasurer: Curtis McClain.
Organizing activities: George Martin.
Research director: Barry Silverman.
Legislative activities: Pat Tobin.
417 Fourth Street, S.W., Washington, D.C. 20003.
Public relations activities: Daniel S. Beagle.
Convention: Every 2 years; April 1979.
Publication: *The Dispatcher* (semimonthly).
Editor: (Public relations activities).
Membership: 55,000; local unions, 76.

MACHINE PRINTERS AND ENGRAVERS ASSOCIATION OF THE UNITED STATES (IND.)

690 Warren Ave., E. Providence, R.I. 02914.
Phone: (401) 438-5849.
President: John T. Patton.
Secretary-treasurer: David J. Bernier.
Organizing activities: (President).
Social insurance: (President).
Convention: Annually.
Membership: 1,150; local unions, 14.

MACHINISTS AND AEROSPACE WORKERS; INTERNATIONAL ASSOCIATION OF (AFL-CIO)

1300 Connecticut Ave., N.W., Washington, D.C. 20036.
Phone: (202) 857-5200.
President: William W. Winpisinger.
Secretary-treasurer: Eugene Glover.
Organizing activities: Desford D. Smith.
Research director: Reginald Newell.
Education director: John Brumm.
Social insurance: E. Douglas Kuhns.
Legal: Plato Papps (Chief counsel).
Legislative activities: George Nelson.
Public relations activities: Robert Kalaski.
Health and safety activities: Angelo Cefalo.
Convention: Every 4 years; September 1980.
Publications: *The Machinist* (monthly); *Headquarters Report* (weekly).
Editor: (Public relations activities).

MAINE STATE EMPLOYEES ASSOCIATION (IND.)

65 State St., Augusta, Me. 04330.
Phone: (207) 622-3151.
President: Richard J. McDonaugh.
Secretary: Norma Arnold.
Executive director: James A. Monroe.
Organizing activities: (Executive director).
Research director: Arthur L. Valpey.
Legal: John J. Finn, Esq.
Government relations (Executive director).
Public relations activities: June Delano.
Collective bargaining activities: (Legal).
Convention: Annually.
Publication: *Maine Stater* (monthly).
Editor: (Executive director).
Membership: 8,917; chapters, 45.

MAINTENANCE OF WAY EMPLOYEES; BROTHERHOOD OF (AFL-CIO)

12050 Woodward Ave., Detroit, Mich. 48203.
Phone: (313) 868-0490.
President: Ole M. Berge.
Secretary-treasurer: B. L. Sorah, Jr.
Organizing activities: (President).

Research director: Geoffrey N. Zeh.
Education director: John Palloni.
Social insurance: (Research director).
Legal: (Research director).
Legislative activities: J. R. McGlaughlin.
Room 801, 400 First St., N.W., Washington, D.C. 20001.
Public relations activities: R. J. Williamson.
Health and safety activities: W. A. Hetherington.
Convention: Every 4 years; 1982.
Publications: *Brotherhood of Maintenance of Way Employees Journal* (monthly); *Scoreboard* (monthly); *Labor Newspaper* (biweekly).
Editors: (President); (President); Ruben Levin.
Membership: 119,184; local unions, 1,040.

MARINE COOKS AND STEWARD'S UNION
See Seafarer's International Union of North America (AFL-CIO)

MARINE ENGINEERS' BENEFICIAL ASSOCIATION; NATIONAL (AFL-CIO)

444 North Capitol Street, Room 800, Washington, D.C. 20001.
Phone: (202) 347-8585.
President: Jesse M. Calhoon.
Secretary-treasurer: C. E. DeFries.
Legal: Richard H. Markowitz (General counsel).
Legislative activities: Ben J. Man.
Convention: Every 2 years; 1980.
Publication: *The American Marine Engineer* (monthly).
Editor: Victor Rollo.
Membership: 9,150; districts, 2.

PROFESSIONAL AIR TRAFFIC CONTROLLERS ORGANIZATION

2100 M St., N.W., #706, Washington, D.C. 20037.
Phone: (202) 638-6500.
President: John F. Leyden.
Secretary-treasurer: Robert E. Poli.
Organizing activities: Michael J. Rock.
Research and education director: John F. Maher.
Social insurance: James E. Scott.
Legal: William Peer (General counsel).
Legislative activities: Allan Moskowitz.
Public relations activities: Arthur C. Kohler.
Convention: Annually.
Publication: *PATCO Newsletter* (biweekly).
Editor: (Public relations activities).
Membership: 12,535; local unions, 402.

MARINE AND SHIPBUILDING WORKERS OF AMERICA; INDUSTRIAL UNION OF (AFL-CIO)

1126-16th St., N.W., Washington, D.C. 20036.
Phone: (202) 223-0902.
President: Frank Derwin.
Secretary-treasurer: Arthur Batson, Jr.
Organizing activities: (Secretary-treasurer).
Social insurance: Barbara Tchipert.
Legal: Michael Brodie.
Legislative activities: John Bonner.
Health and safety activities: (President).
Convention: Every 2 years; 1980.
Publication: *The Shipbuilder* (bimonthly).
Editor: (President).
Membership: 25,000; local unions, 36.

MARITIME UNION OF AMERICA; NATIONAL (AFL-CIO)

346 West 17th Street, New York, N.Y. 10011.
Phone: (212) 924-3900.
President: Shannon J. Wall.
Secretary-treasurer: Thomas Martinez.
Organizing activities: James L. Martin (Vice president).
Research director: Eugene P. Spector.

Education director: Frank Boland.
Social insurance: Al Franco.
Legal: Ned Phillips (General counsel).
Legislative activities: Talmage E. Simpkins (Executive director).
AFL-CIO Maritime Committee, 100 Indiana Ave., N.W., Washington, D.C. 20001.
Public relations activities: Samuel Thompson.
Health and safety activities: Al Zeidel.
Convention: Every 4 years; October 1980.
Publication: *The Pilot* (monthly).
Editor: (Public relations activities).
Membership: 35,000; local unions, 0.

MARYLAND CLASSIFIED EMPLOYEES ASSOCIATION, INC. (IND.)

2113 North Charles St., Baltimore 21218.
Phone: (301) 685-7154.
President: Henry N. Williams.
Secretary: Thomas O. Jones.
Treasurer: Jerald P. Becker.
Executive director: Robert L. Jewell.
Organizing activities: Joseph H. Cook.
Research director: (Vacant).
Social insurance: Joni Shinsky.
Legal: J. Edward Davis (Attorney).
2503 Washington Ave., Towson, Md. 21204.
Public relations activities: Dennis Gring.
Government relations: (Executive director).
Collective bargaining activities: (Organizing activities).
Convention: Annually.
Publication: *MCEA News* (monthly).
Editor: (Public relations).
Membership: 29,000; chapters, 216.

MASSACHUSETTS STATE EMPLOYEES ASSOCIATION (IND.)

(Merged with National Association of Government Employees, effective January 1977).

MASTERS, MATES AND PILOTS; INTERNATIONAL ORGANIZATION OF (ILA-MARINE DIVISION)

See Longshoremen's Association; International (AFL-CIO)

MEAT CUTTERS AND BUTCHER WORKMEN OF NORTH AMERICA; AMALGAMATED (AFL-CIO)

2800 North Sheridan Rd., Chicago, Ill. 60657.
Phone: (312) 248-8700.
President: Harry Poole.
Secretary-treasurer: Samuel J. Talarico.
Organizing activities: Charles Hayes (Vice president).
Research director: James Wishart.
Education director: Helmuth F. Kern.
Social insurance: Frank Gemmato (Health); and Mark Jennings (Pensions).
Legal: (Social insurance).
Legislative activities: Arnold Mayer.
100 Indiana Ave., N.W., Room 505, Washington, D.C. 20001.
Public relations activities: Maurer, Fleisher, Zon & Anderson, Inc.
Health and safety activities: Nickolas M. Abondolo.
186-18 Hillside Avenue, Jamaica, N.Y. 11432.
Convention: Every 4 years; June 1980.
Publication: *Butcher Workman* (monthly).
Editor: Patrick E. Gorman.
Membership: 525,000; local unions, 461.

MECHANICS EDUCATIONAL SOCIETY OF AMERICA (AFL-CIO)

1421 First National Bldg., Detroit, Mich., 48226.
Phone: (313) 965-6990.
President: Alfred J. Smith.

Secretary-treasurer: Ernest E. Smith.
Organizing activities: (President).
Research director: (Secretary-treasurer).
Education director: Robert Wynne.
Legal: Thurlow Smoot (Attorney).
Legislative activities: (Education director).
Public relations activities: (Secretary-treasurer).
Health and safety activities: Robert Briggs.
Publication: *MESA Educator* (monthly).
Editor: (President).
Membership: 25,000; local unions, 29.

METAL POLISHERS, BUFFERS, PLATERS AND ALLIED WORKERS INTERNATIONAL UNION (AFL-CIO)

5578 Montgomery Rd., Cincinnati, Ohio 45212.
Phone: (513) 531-2500.
President: Jim Siebert.
Secretary-treasurer: (President).
Organizing activities: Glenn Holt.
Social insurance: (President).
Legal: Cedric Vogel (Attorney).
Convention: Every 3 years; 1980.
Membership: 10,000; local unions, 60.

MICHIGAN STATE EMPLOYEES ASSOCIATION (IND.)

Box 1154, Lansing, Mich. 48904.
Phone: (517) 372-9104.
President: James Johnson, Jr.
Secretary-treasurer: Billy G. Mohr.
Executive secretary: John R. Doyle.
Organizing activities: (Executive secretary).
Social insurance: (Executive secretary).
Legal: James R. Davis.
Fraser, Trebilcock, Davis & Foster.
Michigan National Tower, Lansing, Mich. 48933.
Government relations: (Executive secretary).
Public relations activities: John Strickler.
Collective bargaining activities: Fred Lapinski.
Convention: Annually.
Publication: *MSEA News* (bimonthly).
Editor: (Public relations activities).
Membership: 18,500; chapters, 158.

MINE WORKERS OF AMERICA; UNITED (IND.)

900 15th St., N.W., Washington, D.C. 20005.
Phone: (202) 638-0530.
President: Arnold R. Miller.
Secretary-treasurer: Willard A. Esselstyn.
Organizing activities: (President).
Research director: Steve Galati.
Education director: Mike Trulos.
Social insurance: Harry Huge.
2021 K St., N.W., Washington, D.C. 20006.
Legal: Harrison Combs (Chief counsel).
Legislative activities: Matt Miller.
Safety director: E. W. Gilbert.
Bridgeport, W.Va. 26332.
Convention: Every 4 years; 1980.
Publication: *United Mine Workers Journal* (semimonthly).
Editor: Harold Voyles.
Membership: 220,000; local unions, 850.

MINNESOTA ASSOCIATION OF GOVERNMENT EMPLOYEES; INDEPENDENT (IND.)

P.O. Box 3215, St. Paul, Minn. 55165.
Phone: (612) 291-1049.

President: K. Bruce MacMillan.
Secretary: Diane Uhlir.
Executive secretary: Bob Smith.
Organizing activities: Gerald D. Garski (Vice president).
Research director: (Executive secretary).
Social insurance: (Executive secretary).
Legal: Darel F. Swenson (Chief counsel).
Government relations: (President).
Public relations activities: (Executive secretary).
Collective bargaining activities: Everett Hedman.
Convention: Annually.
Publication: *IMAGE Mirror* (monthly).
Editor: (Executive secretary).
Membership: 460; chapters, 4.

MOLDERS' AND ALLIED WORKERS' UNION; INTERNATIONAL (AFL-CIO)

1225 East McMillan St., Cincinnati, Ohio 45206.
Phone: (513) 221-1525.
President: Carl W. Studenroth.
Secretary: William F. Cates.
Treasurer: Roland O. Belanger.
Organizing activities: (President).
Research and education director: James E. Wolfe.
Social insurance: (Secretary).
Legal: (President).
Legislative activities: (President).
Public relations activities: (President).
Health and safety activities: (President).
Convention: Every 4 years.
Publication: *International Molders' and Allied Workers' Union Journal* (monthly).
Editor: Edward F. Wulff.
Membership: 75,000; local unions, 247.

MONTANA PUBLIC EMPLOYEES ASSOCIATION (IND.)

P.O. Box 1184, Helena, Mont. 59601.
Phone: (406) 442-4600.
President: Ray Livingston.
Secretary-treasurer: Charles J. Stein, Jr.
Executive director: Thomas E. Schneider.
Organizing activities: Cordell R. Brown.
Research director: Robert Stephen.
Social insurance: (Executive director).
Legal: Ross W. Cannon and Barry Hjort.
Public relations activities: (Executive director).
Government relations: (Executive director).
Collective bargaining activities: (Organizing activities).
Convention: Annually.
Publication: *The Montana Public Employee* (bimonthly).
Editor: (Executive director).
Membership: 3,800; affiliates, 9.

MUSICIANS; AMERICAN FEDERATION OF (AFL-CIO)

1500 Broadway, New York, N.Y. 10036.
Phone: (212) 869-1330.
President: Victor W. Fuentealba.
Secretary-treasurer: J. Martin Emerson.
Research director: Dick Moore and Associates, Inc.
850 Seventh Avenue, New York, N.Y. 10019.
Social insurance: James Morrissey.
730 Third Avenue, New York, N.Y. 10017.
Legal: Henry Kaiser (Legal counsel).
Public relations activities: (Research director).
Convention: Annually.
Publication: *International Musician* (monthly).

Editor: (Secretary-treasurer).
Membership: 330,000; local unions, 620.

NATIONAL LABOR RELATIONS BOARD PROFESSIONAL ASSOCIATION (IND.)

1717 Pennsylvania Ave., N.W., Washington, D.C. 20006.
Phone: (202) 254-9312.
President: Carey Butsavage.
Secretary: Patrick Szymanski.
Treasurer: Margaret McCormick.
Membership: 125; local unions, 0.

NATIONAL LABOR RELATIONS BOARD UNION (IND.)

Rm. 238, Fed. Off. Bldg., 575 No. Penn St., Indianapolis, Ind. 46204.
Phone: (317) 269-7384.
President: Robert Droker.
Secretary: Ellen Hawks.
Organizing activities: William G. Kocal.
Room 881, Everett McKinley Dirksen Bldg., 219 South Dearborn St., Chicago, Ill. 60604.
Legislative activities: Donald L. Spooner, (District I Vice president).
Suite 4400, William J. Green Federal Bldg., 600 Arch St., Philadelphia, Pa. 19106.
Convention: Every 2 years, 1979.
Publication: *NLRBU Newsletter* (quarterly).
Editor: Stephen Appell.
Membership: 1,150; local unions, 33.

NEBRASKA ASSOCIATION OF PUBLIC EMPLOYEES (IND.)

521 South 14th St., Suite 310, Lincoln 68508.
Phone: (402) 432-5381.
President: Lyle C. Nelson.
Secretary: Fred Gunderson.
Executive director: Roger D. Schulz.
Organizing activities: (Executive director).
Research director: (Executive director).
Social insurance: Oliver Wolff.
Legal: Steven D. Burns.
Public relations activities: (Executive director).
Government relations: (Executive director).
Collective bargaining activities: (Legal).
Convention: Annually.
Publication: *The Watchdog* (monthly).
Editor: (Executive director).
Membership: 1,100; chapters, 12.

NEW HAMPSHIRE STATE EMPLOYEES ASSOCIATION (IND.)

Manchester St., Concord, N.H. 03301.
Phone: (603) 271-3411.
President: Damon A. Russell.
Secretary: Ethel MacKay.
Treasurer: William Moulton.
Executive director: Denis W. Parker.
Organizing activities: Thomas F. Hardiman.
Research director: Paul A. Worsowicz.
Social insurance: Thomas F. Manning.
Legal: Robert T. Clark (Attorney).
Public relations activities: Richard E. Molan (assistant executive director).
Government relations: (Executive director).
Collective bargaining activities: (Public relations activities).
Convention: Annually.
Publications: *SEA Newsletter* (bimonthly); *UNH Newsletter* (monthly); *Up-Date-Collective Bargaining* (monthly).
Editors: (Research director and public relations activities); (Public relations activities); (Public relations activities).
Membership: 4,177; affiliates, 52.

NEW JERSEY STATE EMPLOYEES ASSOCIATION (IND.)

15 W. State Street, Trenton, N.J. 08606.
Phone: (609) 394-8099.
President: Ben Lee.
Secretary: Philomena Severino.
Treasurer: Karen Sinnreich.
Executive director: Edgar G. Samman.
Organizing activities: (Executive director).
Legal: David Fox, Esq.
Government relations: Gerald Stoy.
Convention: Annually.
Publication: *The Spotlighter* (semimonthly).
Editors: Linda Holt and Valarie Caffee.
Membership: 8,000; chapters, 11.

NEWSPAPER GUILD; THE (AFL-CIO)

1125 15th St., N.W., Washington, D.C. 20005.
Phone: (202) 296-2990.
President: Charles A. Perlik, Jr.
Secretary-treasurer: Robert M. Crocker.
Organizing activities: J. William Blatz.
Research director: David J. Eisen.
Education director: Ellis T. Baker.
Social insurance: Richard J. Ramsey.
Legal: David S. Barr (General Counsel).
Public relations activities: (Research director).
Health and safety activities: Robert Dudnick.
Convention: Annually.
Publication: *The Guild Reporter* (22 issues annually).
Editor: James M. Cesnik.
Membership: 32,207; local unions, 84.

NEWSPAPER AND MAIL DELIVERERS' UNION OF NEW YORK AND VICINITY (IND.)

41–18 27th St., Long Island City, N.Y. 11101.
Phone: (212) 786-9565.
President: Douglas LaChance.
Secretary-treasurer: Dominic Percella.
Social insurance: Joe Baer.
Legal: Shea, Gould & Clemenko.
Public relations activities: Larry May (Vice president).
Publication: *Union Bulletin* (10 issues annually).
Editor: (Public relations activities).
Membership: 3,500; local unions, 0.

NORTH CAROLINA STATE EMPLOYEES ASSOCIATION (IND.)

P.O. Drawer 27727, Raleigh, N.C. 27602.
Phone: (919) 833-6436.
President: Dan Jones.
Treasurer: Jo Warren.
Executive director: Emmett W. Burden.
Public relations activities: Leonard W. Wilson.
Government relations: (Executive director).
Collective bargaining activities: (Executive director).
Convention: Annually.
Publication: *N.C. State Employee* (bimonthly).
Editor: (Public relations activities).
Membership: 25,000; affiliates, 20.

NORTH CAROLINA STATE GOVERNMENT EMPLOYEES ASSOCIATION (IND.)

3535 South Wilmington St., Suite 103, Raleigh, N.C. 27603.
Phone: (919) 772-1113.
President: G. P. Price.
Secretary: Alice Greene.
Treasurer: James F. Edgerton.
Executive director: Arch Laney.
Organizing activities: (Executive director).
Research director: Faye Godwin.
Social insurance: (Executive director).

Public relations activities: (Executive director).
Government relations: (Executive director).
Convention: Annually.
Publications: (1) *The Reporter* (bimonthly). (2) *Executive Newsletter* (bimonthly).
Editor: (Executive director).
Membership: 9,900; affiliates, 22.

NORTH DAKOTA STATE EMPLOYEES ASSOCIATION (IND.)

Post Office Box 1764, Bismarck, N.D. 58501.
Phone: (701) 223-1964.
President: Richard W. Blair.
Secretary: Muriel Dassinger.
Treasurer: Terry Dennis.
Executive Director: David Meyers.
Executive Secretary: Laura Ripplinger.
Organizing activities: (President).
Government relations: (President).
Negotiating activities: (Executive director).
Convention: Annually.
Publication: *Association Advocate* (monthly).
Editor: Jane Kemper.
Membership: 3,000; affiliates, 28.

NURSES' ASSOCIATION; AMERICAN (IND.)

2420 Pershing Rd., Kansas City, Mo. 64108.
Phone: (816) 474-5720.
President: Anne Zimmerman.
Secretary: Joan Guy.
Executive director: Myrtle Aydelotte.
Organizing activities: Wayne L. Emerson.
Research director: Harsh Thaker.
Legal: Edward W. Kriss (General counsel).
Public relations activities: James Loveless.
Government relations: Constance Holleran (Deputy executive director).
Collective bargaining activities: (Organizing activities).
Convention: Every 2 years; 1980.
Publication: *The American Nurse* (monthly).
Editor: Shirley Fondiller.
Membership: 196,499; affiliates, 53.

OFFICE AND PROFESSIONAL EMPLOYEES INTERNATIONAL UNION (AFL-CIO)

265 W. 14th St., Suite 610, New York, N.Y. 10011.
Phone: (212) 675-3210.
President: Howard Coughlin.
Secretary-treasurer: William A. Lowe.
Research director: William Reidy.
Social insurance: (Secretary-treasurer).
Legal: Joseph E. Finley (General counsel).
Legislative activities: (Secretary-treasurer).
815 16th St., N.W., Suite 606, Washington, D.C. 20006.
Public relations activities: (Research director).
Convention: Every 3 years; 1980.
Publication: *White Collar* (monthly).
Editor: (President).
Membership: 89,468; local unions, 245.

OHIO CIVIL SERVICE EMPLOYEES ASSOCIATION, INC. (IND.)

88 East Broad St., Suite 300, Columbus, Ohio 43215.
Phone: (614) 221-2409.
President: David Ehrhart.
Executive director: Patrick R. Sorohan.

Organizing activities: (President).
Social Insurance: William E. Smith.
Legal: James R. Davis.
Public relations activities: Thomas Daugherty.
Government relations: Arthur Evans.
Collective bargaining activities: John R. Kidwell, Jr.
Convention: Every 2 years; 1980.
Publications: (1) *Public Employee News* (monthly); (2) *This Week Bulletin* (biweekly).
Editors: (1) (Public relations activities); (2) (Government relations).
Membership: 33,000; affiliates, 150.

OIL, CHEMICAL AND ATOMIC WORKERS INTERNATIONAL UNION (AFL-CIO)

P.O. Box 2812, 1636 Champa St., Denver, Colo. 80201.
Phone: (303) 893-0811.
President: A. F. Grospiron.
Secretary-treasurer: A. C. Sabatine.
Organizing activities: Chic St. Croix.
Research and education director: Ray T. West.
Social insurance: (Research and education director).
Legal: John R. Tadlock (General counsel).
Legislative activities: Anthony Mazzocchi.
1126 16th St., N.W., Washington, D.C. 200036.
Public relations activities: James G. Archuleta.
Health and safety activities: (Legislative activities).
Convention: Every 2 years; 1979.
Publication: *Union News* (monthly).
Editor: (Public relations activities).
Membership: 177,433; local unions, 617.

OPERATING ENGINEERS; INTERNATIONAL UNION OF (AFL-CIO)

1125 17th St., N.W., Washington, D.C. 20036.
Phone: (202) 347-8560.
President: J. C. Turner.
Secretary-treasurer: Russell T. Conlon.
Organizing activities: Ralph Oswald.
Research director: Ray Stephens.
Education director: Reese Hammond.
Social insurance: (Secretary-treasurer).
Legal: Michael Fanning.
Legislative activities: John Brown.
Public relations activities: Alvin Silverman.
Health and safety activities: Alan Burck.
Convention: Every 4 years; April 1980.
Publication: *International Operating Engineer* (monthly).
Editor: (Secretary-treasurer).
Membership: 415,395; local unions, 255.

OREGON STATE EMPLOYEES ASSOCIATION (IND.)

1127-25th St., S.E., Salem, Ore. 97301.
Phone: (503) 581-1505.
President: Marie Grant.
Secretary-treasurer: Fred M. Tolleson.
Executive secretary: Morton H. Shapiro.
Organizing activities: (Executive secretary).
Research director: John Lund.
Social insurance: Kay Martens.
Legal: John S. Irvin (Attorney).
Public relations activities: Bentley B. Gilbert, Jr.
Government relations: William W. Wyatt.
Collective bargaining activities: Angelo Stephenson.
Convention: Annually.

Publication: *OSEA News* (monthly).
Editor: (Public relations activities).
Membership: 15,337; chapters, 83.

OVERSEAS EDUCATION ASSOCIATION, INC.

See Education Association; National (Ind.)

PACIFIC COAST MARINE FIREMEN, OILERS, WATERTENDERS AND WIPERS ASSOCIATION

See Seafarer's International Union of North America (AFL-CIO)

PACKINGHOUSE AND INDUSTRIAL WORKERS; NATIONAL BROTHERHOOD OF (IND.)

500 Adams St., Kansas City, Kan. 66105.
Phone: (913) 371-9076.
President: George Burton.
Secretary-treasurer: Bernie Ayala.
Organizing activities: Charles Markham (Vice president).
524 Browncut, Hurst, Texas 76053.
Legal: Henry A. Panethiere (Attorney).
Convention: Annually.
Membership: 2,000; local unions, 13.

PAINTERS AND ALLIED TRADES OF THE UNITED STATES AND CANADA; INTERNATIONAL BROTHERHOOD OF (AFL-CIO)

United Unions Bldg., 1750 New York Ave., N.W., Washington, D.C. 20006.
Phone: (202) 872-1444.
President: S. Frank Raftery.
Secretary-treasurer: Robert Petersdorf.
Organizing activities: Robert C. Welch.
Research director: Henry T. Wilson.
Education director: Thomas Gustine.
Social insurance: (Secretary-treasurer).
Legal: David Barr (General counsel).
Legislative activities: (Organizing activities).
Public relations activities: (President).
Health and safety activities: (Secretary-treasurer).
Convention: Every 5 years; 1979.
Publication: *Painters & Allied Trades Journal* (monthly).
Editor: (Secretary-treasuer).
Membership: 211,373; local unions, 904.

PAPERWORKERS INTERNATIONAL UNION; UNITED (AFL-CIO)

163–03 Horace Harding Expressway, Flushing, N.Y. 11365.
Phone: (212) 762-6000.
President: Wayne E. Glenn.
Secretary-treasurer: Nicholas C. Vrataric.
Research director: Henry Van Wie.
Education director: Frank Burger.
Social insurance: Leonard B. Comberiate.
Legal: (President).
Legislative activities: Louis H. Gordon.
434 Albee Sq., Brooklyn, N.Y. 11201.
Public relations activities: Richard A. Estep.
Health and safety activities: Vernon S. McDougall.
Convention: Every 4 years; October 1980.
Publication: *The Paperworker* (monthly).
Editor: William Berg.
Membership: 300,684; local unions, 1,322.

PATENT OFFICE PROFESSIONAL ASSOCIATION (IND.)

Patent Office, Washington, D.C. 20231.
Phone: (703) 557-2975.
President: Daren M. Stephens.
Secretary: Alan Douglas.
Treasurer: William Schulz.
Organizing activities: (Treasurer).
Education director: Norman Stack (Vice president).

Legal: (President).
Legislative activities: William Beha.
Public relations activities: Bruce Reynolds.
Health and safety activities: (Education director).
Convention: Annually.
Publication: *POPA Newsletter* (monthly).
Editor: Joe Brust.
Membership: 650; local unions, 1.

PATTERN MAKERS' LEAGUE OF NORTH AMERICA (AFL-CIO)

1000 Connecticut Ave., N.W., Suite 204, Washington, D.C. 20036.
Phone: (202) 296-3790.
President: Charles Romelfanger.
Secretary-treasurer: (President).
Convention: Every 5 years; 1982.
Publication: *Pattern Makers' Journal* (quarterly).
Editor: (President).
Membership: 10,912; local unions, 81.

PHYSICIANS NATIONAL HOUSESTAFF ASSOCIATION (IND.)

1625 L St., N.W., Washington, D.C. 20036.
Phone: (202) 452-0081.
President: Dr. Jay Dobkin.
Secretary: Dr. Patricia Stanahan.
Treasurer: Oliver Cameron.
Executive director: Stephen H. Diamond.
Organizing activities: Dr. Mike Gray.
Legal: Murray A. Gordon.
Legislative activities: (Executive director).
Public relations activities: Rea Tyler.
Convention: Annually.
Publications: (1) *Hospital Physician* (monthly); (2) *Special Update* (bimonthly).
Editors: (1) (Executive director); (2) (Public relations activities).
Membership: 5,000; local unions, 80.

PLANNER-ESTIMATORS AND PROGRESSMEN; NATIONAL ASSOCIATION OF (IND.)

3705 Forsyth Court, Chesapeake, Va. 23321.
Phone: (804) 444-7761.
President: Charles R. Zeiger.
928 Green Briar Lane, Springfield, Pa. 19064.
Secretary-treasurer: Lonnie M. Seaton.
Organizing activities: (President).
Legislative activities: (President).
Public relations activities: Alex Roos.
1032 Garrison Street, Port Orchard, Washington 98366.
Convention: Every 2 years, 1980.
Publication: *Quarterly Report* (quarterly).
Editor: (Secretary-treasurer).
Membership: 1,200; local unions, 16.

PLANT GUARD WORKERS OF AMERICA; INTERNATIONAL UNION, UNITED (IND.)

25510 Kelly Road, Roseville, Mich. 48066.
Phone: (313) 772-7250.
President: James C. McGahey.
Secretary-treasurer: Francis Fitzpatrick.
Organizing activities: Jack Russell.
303 South Preston Street, Groesbeck, Texas 76642.
Research and education director: Henry E. Applen (Vice president).
Legal: (Research and education director).
Legislative activities: (President).
Public relations activities: (President).
Convention: Every 5 years; May 1980.
Publication: *Guard News* (bimonthly).

Editor: Leon Rice.
Membership: 34,000; local unions, 150.

PLASTERERS' AND CEMENT MASONS' INTERNATIONAL ASSOCIATION OF THE UNITED STATES AND CANADA; OPERATIVE (AFL-CIO)

1125 17th St., N.W., Washington, D.C. 20036.
Phone: (202) 393-6569.
President: Joseph T. Power.
Secretary-treasurer: John J. Hauck.
Organizing activities: (President).
Research and education director: (Secretary-treasurer).
Social insurance: (Secretary-treasurer and Melvin H. Roots, Executive vice president).
Legal: (President).
Legislative activities: (President).
Public relations activities: (President).
Health and safety activities: (Social insurance).
Convention: Every 4 years; August 1979.
Publication: *The Plasterer and Cement Mason* (monthly).
Editor: (President).
Membership: 65,000; local unions, 450.

PLATE PRINTERS', DIE STAMPERS' AND ENGRAVERS' UNION OF NORTH AMERICA; INTERNATIONAL (AFL-CIO)

228 South Swarthmore Ave., Ridley Park, Pa. 19078.
Phone: (215) 521-2495.
President: Angelo LoVecchio.
Secretary-treasurer: James Donegan, Jr.
Organizing activities: (Secretary-treasurer).
Education director: (Secretary-treasurer).
Social insurance: (President).
Legislative activities: (President).
Public relations activities: (Secretary-treasurer).
Health and safety activities: Milton Tuckman (Vice president).
Convention: Every 2 years; May 1979.
Membership: 400; local unions, 10.

PLUMBING AND PIPE FITTING INDUSTRY OF THE UNITED STATES AND CANADA; UNITED ASSOCIATION OF JOURNEYMEN AND APPRENTICES OF THE (AFL-CIO)

901 Massachusetts Ave., N.W., Washington, D.C. 20001.
Phone: (202) 628-5823.
President: Martin J. Ward.
Secretary-treasurer: Joseph A. Walsh.
Convention: Every 5 years; 1981.
Publication: *United Association Journal* (monthly).
Editor: (Secretary-treasurer).
Membership: 228,000; local unions, ———.

POLICE; FRATERNAL ORDER OF (IND.)

G-3136 W. Pasadena Ave., Flint, Mich. 48504.
Phone: (313) 732-6330.
President: Robert H. Stark.
Secretary-treasurer: William R. Bannister.
Organizing activities: (President).
Social insurance: Francis Pilewski.
Legal: John Ruckleshause (Attorney).
Public relations activities: (President).
Government relations: Charles Bauman.
Convention: Every 2 years; 1979.
Publication: *The Journal* (bimonthly).
Editor: (Secretary-treasurer).
Membership: 147,000; affiliates, 1,036.

POSTAL AND FEDERAL EMPLOYEES; NATIONAL ALLIANCE OF (IND.)

1644 11th St., N.W., Washington, D.C. 20001.
Phone: (202) 332-4313.
President: Robert L. White.
Secretary-treasurer: Votie D. Dixon.
Organizing activities: Wesley Young (Vice president).
Social insurance: J. Leon Henderson.
Legal: Edward Welch and Belford Lawson (Attorneys).
Legislative activities: John W. White.
Public relations activities: T. Barry & Associates, Inc.
Health and safety activities: Eric R. Doyle.
Convention: Every 2 years; 1980.
Publication: *National Alliance* (monthly).
Editor: Jacquelyn C. Moore.
Membership: 20,000; local unions, 137.

POSTAL SECURITY POLICE, FEDERATION OF (IND.)

40-18 Bell Blvd., Bayside, N.Y. 11361.
Phone: (212) 631-0914.
President: John E. Alman.
Secretary-treasurer: Philip J. Mastrelli.
Organizing activities: Leo H. Ming, Jr. (Vice president).
Legal activities: Kenneth D. Hagood (Attorney).
Convention: Every 2 years; 1980.
Publication: *Federal News* (quarterly).
Editor: (Secretary-treasurer).

POSTAL SUPERVISORS; NATIONAL ASSOCIATION OF (IND.)

P.O. Box 23456 L'Enfant Plaza Station, Washington, D.C. 20024.
Phone: (202) 484-6070.
President: Donald N. Ledbetter.
Secretary: Rubin Handelman.
Organizing activities: (President).
Research director: M. J. Mo Twomey (Executive vice president).
Social insurance: (Executive vice president).
Legal activities: (President).
Legislative activities: (Research director).
Public relations activities: (President).
Convention: Every 2 years; 1980.
Publications: (1) *The Postal Supervisor* (monthly); (2) *NAPS letter* (biweekly).
Editors: (1) (President); (2) (Research director).
Membership: 35,000; local unions, 450.

POSTAL WORKERS UNION; AMERICAN (AFL-CIO)

817 14th St., N.W., Washington, D.C. 20005.
Phone: (202) 638-2304.
President: Emmet Andrews.
Secretary-treasurer: Chester Parrish.
Organizing activities: Benjamin Zemsky.
Research and education director: Ted Valliere.
Social insurance: John R. Dubay.
P.O. Box 967, Silver Spring, Md. 20904.
Legal: Daniel P. Jordan (General counsel).
Legislative activities: Patrick J. Nilan.
Public relations activities: C. Stanley Allen.
Health and safety activities: Forrest Newman.
Convention: Every 2 years; 1980.
Publications: *The American Postal Worker* (monthly); *APWU News Service Bulletin* (periodically).
Editors: (President); (Legislative activities).
Membership: 249,000; local unions, 4,900.

POSTMASTERS OF THE UNITED STATES; NATIONAL LEAGUE OF (IND.)

P.O. Box 23653, Washington, D.C. 20024.
Phone: (703) 892-2940.
President: Eugene Dalton.
Secretary-treasurer: Eleanor Monson.
Organizing activities: (President).
Social insurance: Hazel Berik.
Legal: Louis Ingram (Attorney).
Legislative activities: (President).
Public relations activities: (President).
Health and safety activities: (Social insurance).
Convention: Annually.
Publications: (1) *Postmasters Advocate* (monthly); (2) *Advocate Weekly* (weekly).
Editors: (1) Allen T. Lanier. (2) (President).
Membership: ———; local unions, 44.

POTTERY AND ALLIED WORKERS; INTERNATIONAL BROTHERHOOD OF

P.O. Box 988, East Liverpool, Ohio 43920.
Phone: (216) 386-5653.
President: Lester H. Null.
Secretary-treasurer: George R. Barbaree.
Organizing activities: (President).
Research director: (Secretary-treasurer).
Education director: Joseph Galvin (Vice president).
Social insurance: Lewis J. Richardson (Health insurance).
Sidney Braverman (Pension).
Legal: Joseph Finley (Attorney).
Legislative activities: Howard Chester.
Bender Bldg., Washington, D.C.
Public relations activities: Robert Duffy.
Health and safety activities: Richard Bratt.
Convention: Annually.
Publication: *The Potters Herald* (monthly).
Editor: (President).
Membership: 17,051; local unions, 112.

PRINTING AND GRAPHIC COMMUNICATIONS UNION; INTERNATIONAL (AFL-CIO)

1730 Rhode Island Ave., N.W., Washington, D.C. 20036.
Phone: (202) 293-2185.
President: Sol Fishko.
Secretary-treasurer: Burton F. Riley.
Organizing activities: (President).
Research and education director: William F. Martin.
Social insurance: (Secretary-treasurer).
Legal: John S. McLellan, Jr. (General counsel).
Health and safety activities: (Research and education director).
Convention: Every 4 years; September 1980.
Publication: *News and Views* (monthly).
Editor: Roy R. Reck.
Membership: 128,714; local unions, 785.

PROFESSIONAL AIR TRAFFIC CONTROLLERS ORGANIZATION

See Marine Engineers' Beneficial Association; National (AFL-CIO)

PROTECTION EMPLOYEES; INDEPENDENT UNION OF PLANT (IND.)

122 Pickard Drive, Mattydale, N.Y. 13211.
Phone: (617) 233-3529.
President: Edward Wolfe.
Secretary-treasurer: Charles A. Kelley.
Organizing activities: (President).
Legal: E. David Wanger (Attorney).
Convention: Annually.
Membership: 320; local unions, 14.

PULP AND PAPER WORKERS; ASSOCIATION OF WESTERN (IND.)

1430 Southwest Clay, Portland, Ore. 97201.
Phone: (503) 228-7486.
President: Farris H. Bryson.
Secretary-treasurer: Gene N. Hain.
Organizing activities: (President).
Research and education director: James A. Crook.
Social insurance: (President).
Legal: (President).
Legislative activities: (President).
Public relations activities: Robert J. Rodgers (Executive vice president).
Health and safety activities: (Secretary-treasurer).
Convention: Every 3 years; September 1979.
Publication: *The Rebel* (semimonthly).
Editor: (Public relations activities).
Membership: 20,781, local unions, 58.

QUARANTINE INSPECTORS NATIONAL ASSOCIATION; FEDERAL PLANT (IND.)

P.O. Box 592136, Miami, Fla. 31559.
Phone: (305) 522-1567.
President: Robert C. Peterson.
Secretary-treasurer: Edgar Ludwig.
Legal activities: Thomas F. Panza (Attorney).
Legislative activities: Grant Milner.
10109 Bayo, El Paso, Tex. 79925.
Health and safety activities: James Haley.
Convention: Annually.
Publication: *FPQINA Newsletter* (biquarterly).
Editor: Al Marulli.
Membership: 362; local unions, 30.

RADIO ASSOCIATION; AMERICAN (AFL-CIO)

270 Madison Ave., Room 207, New York, N.Y. 10016.
Phone: (212) 689-5754.
President: William R. Steinberg.
Secretary-treasurer: Bernard L. Smith.
Organizing activities: (President).
Research and education director: M. Harvey Strichartz.
Social insurance: (President).
Legal activities: Jay Darwin (General counsel-West Coast).
Edwin A. Steinberg, (General counsel-East Coast).
Legislative activities: (Secretary-treasurer).
Public relations activities: (Research and education director).
Health and safety activities: (Secretary-treasurer).
Convention: Every 4 years; 1982.
Publications: (1) *ARA Log* (quarterly); (2) *ARA FREE PRESS* (weekly).
Editors: (1) (President); (2) (Research and education director).
Membership: 618; local unions, 0.

RAILROAD SIGNALMEN; BROTHERHOOD OF (AFL-CIO)

601 West Golf Road, Mt. Prospect, Ill. 60056.
Phone: (312) 439-3732.
President: R. T. Bates.
Secretary-treasurer: W. D. Best.
Organizing activities: (President).
Research director: John E. Hansen.
Social insurance: (President).
Legal: (President).
Legislative activities: (President).
Public relations activities: (President).
Health and safety activities: (President).
Convention: Every 3 years; August 1979.
Publication: *The Signalman's Journal* (10 issues annually).
Editor: Robert W. McKnight.
Membership: 12,000; local unions, 205.

RAILROAD YARDMASTERS OF AMERICA (AFL-CIO)

1411 Peterson Ave., Room 202, Park Ridge, Ill. 60068.
Phone: (312) 696-2510.
President: A. T. Otto, Jr.
Secretary-treasurer: R. J. Culver.
Organizing activities: J. C. Thomas (Vice president).
1069 Mississippi Ave., Pittsburgh, Pa. 15216.
Research director: N. A. Erdody.
Education director: R. F. O'Leary.
268 Elmdorf Ave., Rochester, N.Y. 14619.
Social insurance: (President).
Legal: R. H. Kraushaar (General Counsel).
Legislative activities: (Secretary-treasurer).
Public relations activities: J. E. Waskey.
Health and safety activities: R. W. Berry (Vice president).
7923 Military Parkway, Dallas, Texas 75227.
Convention: Every 4 years; 1982.
Publication: *The Railroad Yardmaster* (8 issues annually).
Editor: (Secretary-treasurer).
Membership: 5,121; local unions, 75.

RAILWAY, AIRLINE AND STEAMSHIP CLERKS, FREIGHT HANDLERS, EXPRESS AND STATION EMPLOYEES; BROTHERHOOD OF (AFL-CIO)

3 Research Place, Rockville, Md. 20850.
Phone: (301) 948-4910.
President: Fred J. Kroll.
Secretary-treasurer: D. A. Bobo.
Organizing activities: R. J. Devlin (Vice president).
77 Forest Ave., Suite 100-B, Paramus, N.J. 07652.
Research and education director: Walter R. Williamson.
Social insurance: Gerald Toppen (Vice president).
Legal: W. J. Donlon (General counsel).
Legislative activities: J. J. Kennedy, Jr.
815 16th St., N.W., 5th Floor, Washington, D.C. 20006.
Public relations activities: D. S. Curry (Assistant editor).
Health and safety activities: (Social insurance).
Convention: Every 4 years; May 1979.
Publication: *Railway Clerk Interchange* (monthly).
Editor: (President).
Membership: 235,000; local unions, 980.

RAILWAY AND AIRWAY SUPERVISORS ASSOCIATION; THE AMERICAN (AFL-CIO)

4250 West Montrose Ave., Chicago, Ill. 60641.
Phone: (312) 282-9424.
President: Frank Ferlin, Jr.
Secretary-treasurer: Floyd R. Skendziel.
Convention: Every 2 years; 1980.
Publication: *The Supervisors Journal* (bimonthly).
Editor: (President).
Membership: 6,250; local unions, 53.

RAILWAY CARMEN OF THE UNITED STATES AND CANADA; BROTHERHOOD (AFL-CIO)

Carmen's Bldg., 4929 Main St., Kansas City, Mo. 64112.
Phone: (816) 561-1112.
President: Orville W. Jacobson.
Secretary-treasurer: Orville P. Channell, Jr.
Organizing activities: John J. DiGregorio (General vice president).
Education director: Charles W. Hauck.
Social insurance: (Secretary-treasurer).
Legal: (President).
Legislative activities: William D. Crawford (General vice president).

820 Railway Labor Building, 400 First St., N.W., Washington, D.C. 20001.
Public relations activities: (Education director).
Health and safety activities: (Legislative activities).
Convention: Every 5 years; 1983.
Publications: (1) *Railway Carmen's Journal* (monthly); (2) *Labor Paper* (triweekly).
Editors: (1) (Education director); (2) R. Levin.
Membership: 95,954; local unions, 661.

RETAIL CLERKS INTERNATIONAL UNION (AFL-CIO)

Suffridge Bldg., 1775 K St., N.W., Washington, D.C. 20006.
Phone: (202) 223-3111.
President: William H. Wynn.
Secretary-treasurer: Thomas G. Whaley.
Organizing activities: John E. Mara.
Research and education director: Richard C. McAllister (Vice president).
Social insurance: (Research and education director).
Legal: George Murphy (General counsel).
Legislative activities: James L. Huntley.
Public relations activities: Walter L. Davis.
Health and safety activities: (Research and education director).
Convention: Every 5 years; 1982.
Publication: *Retail Clerks Advocate* (bimonthly).
Editor: (President).
Membership: 728,200; local unions, 208.

RETAIL, WHOLESALE AND DEPARTMENT STORE UNION (AFL-CIO)

101 West 31st St., New York, N.Y. 10001.
Phone: (212) 947-9303.
President: Alvin E. Heaps.
Secretary-treasurer: Frank Parker.
Organizing activities: (President).
Research and education director: Leon L. Harris.
Social insurance: (President).
Legal: Martin L. Greenberg (General counsel).
Legislative activities: Lenore Miller.
Public relations activities: (Legislative activities).
Health and safety activities: (Research and education director).
Convention: Every 4 years; 1982.
Publication: *RWDSU Record* (monthly).
Editor: Tor Cedervall.
Membership: 180,000; local unions, 315.

RETAIL WORKERS UNION; UNITED (IND.)

9865 West Roosevelt Rd., Westchester, Ill. 60153.
Phone: (312) 681-1000.
Executive director: Fred A. Burki.
Secretary-treasurer: Frank Koukl.
Organizing activities: Tom Padgett.
Research and education director: Tom Walsh.
Social insurance: (Secretary-treasurer).
Legal: Tony Packard.
Legislative activities: (Executive director).
Public relations activities: Ed Jablonski.
Health and safety activities: Ron Powell.
Convention: Annually.
Publication: *URW News Digest* (bimonthly).
Editor: (Public relations activities).
Membership: 22,000; local unions, 4.

ROOFERS, DAMP AND WATERPROOF WORKERS ASSOCIATION; UNITED SLATE, TILE AND COMPOSITION (AFL-CIO)

1125 17th St., N.W., Washington, D.C 20036.
Phone: (202) 638-3228.

President: Roy E. Johnson.
Secretary-treasurer: Dale Zusman.
Organizing activities: (President).
Research and education director: (President).
Social insurance: (President).
Legal: (President).
Legislative activities: (President).
Public relations activities: (President).
Safety activities: Joseph E. Bissell.
Convention: Every 3 years; 1981.
Publication: *Journeyman Roofer & Waterproofer* (monthly).
Editor: (Secretary-treasurer).
Membership: 28,000; local unions, 205.

RUBBER, CORK, LINOLEUM AND PLASTIC WORKERS OF AMERICA; UNITED (AFL-CIO)

URWA Bldg., 87 South High St., Akron, Ohio 44308.
Phone: (216) 376-6181.
President: Peter Bommarito.
Secretary-treasurer: Donald C. Tucker.
Organizing activities: Robert G. Long.
Research director: C. Stephen Clem.
Education director: Robert M. Strauber.
Social insurance: George Marinich.
Legal: Harley M. Kastner (General counsel).
Legislative activities: Francis A. Maile (Director, Political Education Department).
Public relations activities: J. Curtis Brown.
Health and safety activities: Louis S. Beliczky.
Convention: Every 3 years; 1981.
Publication: *United Rubber Worker* (monthly).
Editor: (President).
Membership: 190,523; local unions, 565.

RURAL LETTER CARRIERS' ASSOCIATION; NATIONAL (IND.)

1750 Pennsylvania Ave., N.W., Washington, D.C. 20006.
Phone: (202) 393-5840.
President: Clifford E. Edwards.
Secretary-treasurer: Leland R. Sorteberg.
Organizing activities: (Secretary-treasurer).
Social insurance: Dean King (Vice president).
Legal: (President).
Legislative activities: (Vice president).
Public relations activities: (President).
Health and safety activities: (Secretary-treasurer).
Convention: Annually.
Publication: *National Rural Letter Carrier* (weekly).
Editor: (Social insurance).
Membership: 49,135; local unions, ———.

SAILORS' UNION OF THE PACIFIC

See Seafarer's International Union of North America (AFL-CIO)

SCHOOL ADMINISTRATORS; AMERICAN FEDERATION OF (AFL-CIO)

110 East 42nd Street, New York, N.Y. 10017.
Phone: (212) 697-5111.
President: Albert L. Morrison.
Secretary-treasurer: Martin Kalish.
Organizing activities: (President).
Legal: Max H. Frankle (General counsel).
Legislative activities: (President).
Public relations activities: Aaron Slotkin.
Convention: Every 3 years; 1979.
Publication: *AFSA News* (quarterly).
Editor: (Public relations activities).
Membership: 8,000; local unions, 32.

SCREEN ACTORS GUILD

See Actors and Artistes of America; Associated (AFL-CIO)

SCREEN EXTRAS GUILD

See Actors and Artistes of America; Associated (AFL-CIO)

SEAFARERS' INTERNATIONAL UNION OF NORTH AMERICA (AFL-CIO)
675 Fourth Ave., Brooklyn, N.Y. 11232.
Phone: (212) 499-6600.
President: Paul Hall.
Secretary-treasurer: Joseph DiGiorgio.
Organizing activities: Frank Drozak (Vice president).
Research director: Robert Vahey.
815-16th St., N.W., Washington, D.C. 20006.
Education director: Marietta Homayonpour.
192 20th St., Brooklyn, N.Y. 11232.
Social insurance: (Secretary-treasurer).
Legal: Howard Schulman (General counsel).
Legislative activities: David Dolgen.
Public relations activities: John Yarmola (Vice president).
815 16th St., N.W., Washington, D.C. 20006.
Health and safety activities: (Research director).
Convention: Every 3 years; 1981.
Membership: 80,000; affiliates, 27.

ATLANTIC, GULF, LAKES AND INLAND WATERS DISTRICT
675 Fourth Ave., Brooklyn, N.Y. 11232.
Phone: (212) 499-6600.
President: Paul Hall.
Secretary-treasurer: Joseph DiGiorgio.
Organizing activities: Frank Drozak (Vice president).
Research director: David Dolgen.
815 16th St., N.W., Washington, D.C. 20006.
Education director: Marietta Homayonpour.
192 20th St., Brooklyn, N.Y. 11232.
Social insurance: (Secretary-treasurer).
Legal: Howard Schulman (General counsel).
Legislative activities: (Research director).
Public relations activities: John Yarmola (Vice president).
815 16th St., N.W., Washington, D.C. 20006.
Health and safety activities: (Research director).
Publication: *Seafarers' Log* (monthly).
Editor: (Education director).
Membership: 25,000; port branches, ———.

INLAND BOATMEN'S UNION OF THE PACIFIC
1501 Norton Building, Seattle, Wash. 98104.
Phone: (206) 622-9736.
President: Merle D. Adlum.
Secretary-treasurer: Burrill L. Hatch.
Legal: William Roberts (General counsel).
Convention: Every 18 months; 1979.
Membership: 4,000; port branches, ———.

INTERNATIONAL UNION OF PETROLEUM AND INDUSTRIAL WORKERS
335 California Ave., Bakersfield, Calif. 93304.
Phone: (805) 327-1614.
President: Carroll G. Clark.
Secretary-treasurer: Earl W. Church.
Organizing activities: (President).
Convention: Every 3 years; 1980.
Publication: *IUPIW Views* (monthly).
Editor: (Secretary-treasurer).
Membership: 2,500; local unions, 17.

MARINE COOKS AND STEWARDS' UNION
(Merged into Atlantic Gulf Lakes District.)
Editor: (Research director).
Membership: 1,895; branches, 5.

PACIFIC COAST MARINE FIREMEN, OILERS, WATERTENDERS AND WIPERS ASSOCIATION
240 Second St., San Francisco, Calif. 94105.
Phone: (415) 362-4592.
President: Henry Disley.
Treasurer: Joel E. McCrum.

Organizing activities: (President).
Social insurance: (President).
Legal: (President).
Legislative activities: (President).
Public relations activities: (President).
Health and safety activities: (President).
Convention: Every 3 years; 1981.
Publication: *The Marine Fireman* (monthly).
Editor: (President).
Membership: ———; local unions, 5.

SAILORS' UNION OF THE PACIFIC
450 Harrison St., San Francisco, Calif. 94105.
Phone: (415) 362-8363.
President: Morris Weisberger.
Secretary-treasurer: (President).
Organizing activities: (President).
Social insurance: W. H. Clark (Administrator, Seamen's Security Funds).
522 Harrison St., San Francisco, Calif. 94105.
Legal: John P. Jennings (Attorney).
Legislative activities: (President).
Publication relations activities: (President).
Publication: *West Coast Sailors* (semimonthly).
Editor: John C. Hill.
Membership: 3,340; port branches, 6.

SERVICE EMPLOYEES' INTERNATIONAL UNION (AFL-CIO)
2020 K St., N.W., Washington, D.C. 20006.
Phone: (202) 452-8750.
President: George Hardy.
Secretary-treasurer: Anthony G. Weinlein.
Organizing activities: John B. Geagan.
Research and education director: Stanley Wisniewski.
Legal: Gerald Sommer.
Legislative activities: Richard E. Murphy.
Public relations activities: David Stack.
Convention: Every 4 years; 1980.
Publications: *Service Employee* (monthly); *SEIU Leadership News Update* (monthly.)
Editor: (Public relations activities).
Membership: 550,000; local unions, 360.

SHEET METAL WORKERS' INTERNATIONAL ASSOCIATION (AFL-CIO)
United Unions Bldg., New York Ave., N.W., Washington, D.C. 20006.
Phone: (202) 296-5880.
President: Edward J. Carlough.
Secretary-treasurer: David S. Turner.
Organizing activities: Lonnie A. Bassett.
Research and education director: Paul F. Stuckenschneider.
Legal: Timothy J. Lynch (Counsel).
Legislative activities: Frank J. Scaduto.
Health and safety activities: (Legislative activities).
Convention: Every 4 years; 1982.
Publications: (1) *Sheet Metal Workers' Journal* (monthly); (2) *The Scene Today* (semimonthly).
Editors: (1) (Secretary-treasurer); (2) (Research and education director).
Membership: 160,860; local unions, 436.

SHOE AND ALLIED CRAFTSMEN; BROTHERHOOD OF (IND.)
838 Main St., Brockton, Mass. 02401.
Phone: (617) 587-2606.

President: Kenneth W. Johnson.
Secretary-treasurer: Gerald N. Dufresne.
Organizing activities: (President).
Legal: Arthur Flamm (Attorney).
Convention: Periodically; February 1975.
Membership: 1,250; local unions, 17.

SHOE WORKERS OF AMERICA; UNITED (AFL-CIO)
(Merged with Clothing and Textile Workers Union.)

SHOE WORKERS' UNION; BOOT AND (AFL-CIO)
(Merged with the Retail Clerks International Association,
effective September 1, 1977).

**SIDEROGRAPHERS: INTERNATIONAL ASSOCIATION
OF (AFL-CIO)**
1134 Boulevard, New Milford, N.J. 07646.
Phone: (201) 836-9158.
President: James C. Small.
Secretary-treasurer: Harvey Henderson.
Organizing activities: (President).
Research director: (President).
Legal: (President).
Legislative activities: (Secretary-treasurer).
Public relations activities: (President).
Convention: Every 2 years; September 1979.
Membership: 18; local unions, 3.

**SLEEPING CAR PORTERS; BROTHERHOOD OF (AFL-
CIO)**
(Merged with Brotherhood of Railway and Airlines Clerks.)

SOUTHERN LABOR UNION (IND.)
Alberta Avenue & 2nd Street, Oneida, Tenn. 37841.
Phone: (615) 569-8335.
President: Noah Harris.
Secretary: Roger Wright.
Treasurer: Paul Byrge.
Social insurance: Teresa Spaulding (Pension fund) and Sandy
Roark (Welfare fund).
Legal: Ted Q. Wilson (General counsel).
Convention: Every 5 years; June 1979.
Publication: *Southern Labor News* (monthly).
Editor: (Executive Board).
Membership: 2,200; local unions, 54.

**STATE, COUNTY AND MUNICIPAL EMPLOYEES;
AMERICAN FEDERATION OF (AFL-CIO)**
1625 L St., N.W., Washington, D.C. 20036.
Phone: (202) 452-4800.
President: Jerry Wurf.
Secretary-treasurer: William Lucy.
Organizing activities: Thomas Fitzpatrick.
Research and education director: Donald S. Wasserman.
Social insurance: James Savarese.
Legal: A. L. Zwerdling (General counsel).
Legislative activities: William Welsh.
Public relations activities: Donovan McClure.
Health and safety activities: (Research and education director).
Convention: Every 2 years; 1980.
Publication: *The Public Employee* (monthly).
Editor: Marcia Silverman.
Membership: 957,000; local unions, 2,570.

STEELWORKERS OF AMERICA; UNITED (AFL-CIO)
Five Gateway Center, Pittsburgh, Pa. 15222.
Phone: (412) 562-2306.

President: Lloyd McBride.
Secretary: Lynn Williams.
Treasurer: Frank McKee.
Organizing activities: Elmer Chatak.
Research director: Otis Brubaker.
Education director: George Butsika.
Social insurance: Thomas Duzak.
Legal: Bernard Kleiman (General counsel).
Legislative activities: John Sheehan.
815–16th St., Suite 706, N.W., Washington, D.C. 20006.
Public relations activities: Raymond W. Pasnick.
Health and safety activities: Adolph Schwartz.
Convention: Every 2 years; 1980.
Publication: *Steel Labor* (monthly).
Editor: (Public relations activities).
Membership: 1,300,000; local unions, 5,300.

**STOVE, FURNACE AND ALLIED APPLIANCE WORK-
ERS' INTERNATIONAL UNION OF NORTH AMER-
ICA (AFL-CIO)**
2929 South Jefferson Ave., St. Louis, Mo. 63118.
Phone: (314) 664-3736.
President: George E. Pierson.
Secretary-treasurer: George E. Sodam.
Organizing activities: (President).
Social insurance: (Secretary-treasurer).
Research and education director: (Secretary-treasurer).
Legal: (President).
Legislative activities: (President).
Health and safety activities: (President).
Public relations activities: (President).
Convention: Every 3 years; 1980.
Publication: *Stove, Furnace and Allied Appliance Workers' Journal*
(quarterly).
Editor: (Secretary-treasurer).
Membership: 9,500; local unions, 45.

TEACHERS; AMERICAN FEDERATION OF (AFL-CIO)
11 Dupont Circle N.W., Washington, D.C. 20036.
Phone: (202) 797-4400.
President: Albert Sanker.
Secretary-treasurer: Robert Porter.
Organizing activities: Charles Richards.
Research director: Eugenia Kemble.
Education director: Marilyn Rauth.
Social insurance: (Secretary-treasurer).
Legal: (Secretary-treasurer).
Legislative activities: Carl Megel.
Public relations activities: Peter Laarman.
Health and safety actvities: Robert Ripperger.
Convention: Annually.
Publications: *American Teacher* (9 issues annually); *American
Educator* (quarterly).
Editor: Gail Miller.
Membership: 444,000; local unions, 1,938.

**TEAMSTERS, CHAUFFEURS, WAREHOUSEMEN AND
HELPERS OF AMERICA; INTERNATIONAL BROTH-
ERHOOD OF (IND.)**
25 Louisiana Ave., N.W., Washington, D.C. 20001.
Phone: (202) 624-6800.
President: Frank E. Fitzsimmons.
Secretary-treasurer: Ray Schoessling.
Organizing activities: (Secretary-treasurer).
Research director: Norman A. Weintraub.
Social insurance: (President).
Legal: Robert M. Baptiste (Labor counsel).
Legislative activities: David A. Sweeney.
Public relations activities: Allen Biggs.
Health and safety activities: R. V. Durham.

Convention: Every 5 years; 1981.
Publication: *International Teamster* (monthly).
Editor: (President).
Membership: 1,973,272; local unions, 805.

LAUNDRY, DRY CLEANING AND DYE HOUSE WORKERS' INTERNATIONAL UNION,
360 North Michigan Ave., Chicago, Ill. 60601.
Phone: (312) 726-9416.
President: John J. Fagan.
Secretary-treasurer: Mario A. Funcinari.
Organizing activities: Gus Sam Zapas.
Social insurance: (President).
Legal: Marvin Sacks (General counsel).
Convention: Every 5 years; 1980.
Membership: 33,284; local unions, 54.

TECHNICAL ENGINEERS; INTERNATIONAL FEDERATION OF PROFESSIONAL AND (AFL-CIO)
1126 16th St., N.W., Suite 200, Washington, D.C. 20036.
Phone: (202) 223-1811.
President: Rodney A. Bower.
Secretary-treasurer: John H. Dunne.
Organizing activities: (Secretary-treasurer).
Legal: David S. Barr (General counsel).
Legislative activities: James E. Lyons.
Convention: Every 2 years; July 1978.
Publication: *Outlook* (bimonthly).
Editor: (President).
Membership: 19,500; local unions, 78.

TECHNICIANS; ASSOCIATION OF CIVILIAN (IND.)
348A Hungerford Court, Rockville, Md. 20850.
Phone: (301) 762-5656.
President: Vincent J. Paterno.
Secretary: Donald E. Bean.
Treasurer: Gerald W. Titus.
Organizing activities: John T. Hunter (Executive vice president).
Research director: John W. Chapman.
Education director: James J. Walters.
250 Wick Road, Brentwood, N.Y. 11717.
Social insurance: John C. Giarrusso (Vice president).
38 Harris Ave., Johnston, R.I. 02919.
Legal: (President).
Legislative activities: (President).
Public relations activities: (Research director).
Health and safety activities: John J. Hernon (Vice president).
257 Claywood Drive, Brentwood, N.Y. 11717.
Convention: Semiannually.
Publication: *The Technician* (monthly).
Editor: (Secretary).
Membership: 5,500; Locals: 52.

TELEGRAPH WORKERS; UNITED (AFL-CIO)
701 Gude Drive, Rockville, Md. 20850.
Phone: (301) 762-4444.
President: Dan J. Beckstead.
Secretary-treasurer: Jerry Grim.
Organizing activities: (President).
Legal: (President).
Convention: Every 2 years; October 1979.
Publication: *Telegraph Workers Journal* (bimonthly).
Editor: (Secretary-treasurer).
Membership: 13,588; local unions, 90.

TEXTILE WORKERS OF AMERICA; UNITED (AFL-CIO)
420 Common St., Lawrence, Mass. 01842.
Phone: (617) 686-2901.
President: Francis Schaufenbil.

Secretary-treasurer: William Foley.
Organizing activities: Roy B. Groenert.
Isermann Bldg., 616-56th St., Rms. 11-12, Kenosha, Wisc. 53140.
Social insurance: (Secretary-treasurer).
Public relations activities: (President).
Convention: Every 4 years; 1980.
Publication: *Textile Challenger* (bimonthly).
Editor: (President).
Membership: 47,344; local unions, 275.

TEXTILE WORKERS UNION OF AMERICA (AFL-CIO)
(Merged into Clothing and Textile Workers Union, effective June 3, 1976).

THEATRICAL STAGE EMPLOYEES AND MOVING PICTURE MACHINE OPERATORS OF THE UNITED STATES AND CANADA; INTERNATIONAL ALLIANCE OF (AFL-CIO)
1515 Broadway, Suite 601, New York, N.Y. 10036.
Phone: (212) 730-1770.
President: Walter F. Diehl.
Secretary-treasurer: James R. Riley.
Organizing activities: (President).
Research and education director: (President).
Social insurance: (President).
Legal: (President).
Public relations activities: (President).
Health and safety activities: (President).
Convention: Every 2 years; 1980.
Publication: *Official Bulletin* (quarterly).
Editor: (Secretary-treasurer).
Membership: 61,471; local unions, 870.

TILE, MARBLE AND TERRAZZO FINISHERS AND SHOPMEN INTERNATIONAL UNION (AFL-CIO)
801 N. Pitt St., Suite 116, Alexandria, Va. 22314.
Phone: (703) 549-3050.
President: Pascal Di James.
Organizing activities: (President).
Social insurance: (President).
Legal: Maurice Abrams (General counsel).
Legislative activities: (President).
Public relations activities: (President).
Health and safety activities: (President).
Convention: Every 2 years; 1980.
Publication: *Bulletin* (monthly).
Editor (President).
Membership: 8,000; local unions, 107.

TOBACCO WORKERS INTERNATIONAL UNION (AFL-CIO)
(Merged with Bakery and Confectionery Workers.)

TOOL CRAFTSMEN; INTERNATIONAL ASSOCIATION OF (IND.)
3243 37th Ave., Rock Island, Ill. 61201.
Phone: (309) 788-9776.
President: Raymond K. Shaw.
Secretary-treasurer: Bert L. Fitzjohn.
128 Euclid Ave., Battle Creek, Mich. 49017.
Organizing activities: (President).
Social insurance: (Secretary-treasurer).
Legal: (President).
Legislative activities: (President).

Public relations activities: (President).
Health and safety activities: (President).
421 N. Mt. Carmel, Wichita, Kansas 67203.
Convention: Every 2 years; September 1979.
Publication: *The Craftsmen* (bimonthly).
Editor: James J. Ryan.
Membership: 496; local unions, 11.

TOOL, DIE AND MOLD MAKERS; INTERNATIONAL UNION OF (IND.)

71 Cherry St., Rahway, N.J. 07065.
Phone: (201) 388-3323.
President: Henry F. Schickling.
Secretary-treasurer: Julius Puchammer.
Organizing activities: Guenter Heim (Vice president).
Social insurance: Anthony Calello.
Legal: Harold Krieger (Legal counsel).
Legislative activities: (President).
Public relations activities: H. Walter Haase.
Convention: Annually.
Publications: (1) *The American Craftsmen* (quarterly); (2) *The Indicator* (quarterly).
Editors: (1) Raymond Shaw. (2) (Public relations activities).
Membership: 501; local unions, 4.

TOYS, PLAYTHINGS, NOVELTIES AND ALLIED PRODUCTS OF THE UNITED STATES AND CANADA; INTERNATIONAL UNION OF DOLLS (AFL-CIO)

147–149 East 26th St., New York, N.Y. 10010.
Phone: (212) 889-1212.
President: Julius Isaacson.
Secretary-treasurer: John Serpico.
Organizing activities: (President).
Research and education director: Abraham Weiss.
Legal: Joseph K. Reichbart (Attorney).
Legislative activities: (President).
Public relations activities: (Research and education director).
Convention: Every 5 years; May 1981.
Membership: 31,000; local unions, 23.

TRADEMARK SOCIETY INC. (IND.)

P.O. Box 2062, EADS Station, Arlington, Va. 22202.
Phone: (703) 557-3273.
President: Marc Bergsman.
Secretary: Hannah Fisher.
Treasurer: Joan Kupersmith.
Organizing activities: (President).
Legal: (President).
Legislative activities: David Sams.
Public relations activities: Mary Lou Donnelly (Vice president).
Membership: 48; local unions, 0.

TRAIN DISPATCHERS ASSOCIATION; AMERICAN (AFL-CIO)

1401 S. Harlem Ave., Berwyn, Ill. 60402.
Phone: (312) 795-5656.
President: Bernard C. Hilbert.
Secretary-treasurer: D. E. Collins.
Organizing activities: (President).
Research director: George J. Nixon, Jr.
Public relations activities: (Secretary-treasurer).
Convention: Every 4 years; October 1979.
Publication: *The Train Dispatcher* (8 issues annually).
Editor: (Secretary-treasurer).
Membership: 3,229; local unions, 79.

TRANSIT UNION; AMALGAMATED (AFL-CIO)

5025 Wisconsin Ave., N.W., Washington, D.C. 20016.
Phone: (202) 537-1645.
President: Dan V. Maroney.
Secretary-treasurer: Raymond C. Wallace.
Organizing activities: (President).
Research director: Elva Daniels.
Education director: Walter J. Bierwagen (Vice president).
Social insurance: (Education director).
Legal: Earle W. Putnam (General counsel).
Legislative activities: (Education director).
Public relations activities: (Education director).
Health and safety activities: (Education director).
Convention: Every 2 years; 1979.
Publication: *In Transit* (monthly).
Editor: Joseph Brady.
Membership: 140,000; local unions, 350.

TRANSPORT WORKERS UNION OF AMERICA (AFL-CIO)

1980 Broadway, New York, N.Y. 10023.
Phone: (212) 873-6000.
President: Matthew Guinan.
Secretary-treasurer: Roosevelt Watts.
Research director: Joseph Madison.
T.W.U., 100 Indiana Ave., N.W., Washington, D.C. 20001.
Education director: William Lindner.
Legal: John F. O'Donnell (General counsel).
Legislative activities: Herman Leonard (COPE director).
Public relations activities: John J. O'Connell.
Health and safety activities: (Education director).
Convention: Every 4 years; 1981.
Publication: *TWU Express* (monthly).
Editor: Joseph J. Kutch.
Membership: 150,000; local unions, 105.

TRANSPORTATION UNION; UNITED (AFL-CIO)

14600 Detroit Ave., Cleveland, Ohio 44107.
Phone: (216) 228-9400.
President: Al H. Chesser.
Secretary-treasurer: John H. Shepherd.
Research director: H. E. Nelson.
Organizing activities: George W. Legge (Manager of field services).
Education director: Dan W. Collins.
Social insurance: (President).
Legal: Robert L. Hart (General counsel).
Legislative activities: J. R. Snyder.
400 First St., N.W., Room 704, Washington, D.C. 20001.
Public relations activities: Lou Corsi.
Convention: Every 4 years; 1979.
Publication: *UTU News* (weekly).
Editor: Jim Turner.
Membership: 238,000; local unions, 1,211.

TREASURY EMPLOYEES UNION; NATIONAL (IND.)

1730 K St., N.W., Washington, D.C. 20006.
Phone: (202) 785-4411.
President: Vincent L. Connery.
Administrative controller: Blondell Ganey.
Organizing activities: Jerry Klepner.
Research director: James Spellane.
Education director: Frank Ferris.
Social insurance: Elaine Tager.
Legal: Robert M. Tobias (General counsel).
Legislative activities: Michael Goldman.
Public relations activities: (Organizing activities).
Convention: Every 2 years; August 1979.
Publication: *NTEU Bulletin* (every 3 weeks).
Editor: (Organizing activities).
Membership: 50,000; local unions, 130.

TYPOGRAPHICAL UNION; INTERNATIONAL (AFL-CIO)

P.O. Box 157, Colorado Springs, Colo. 80901.
Phone: (303) 636-2341.
President: Joseph Bingel.
Secretary-treasurer: Thomas W. Kopeck.
Organizing activities: Marvin DeWeerdt.
Research director: Robert L. Wartinger.
Education director: Kenneth Pratt.
Social insurance: Carl Hatton.
Legal: Ronald Rosenberg (Attorney).
Public relations activities: Horst A. Reschke.
Convention: Annually.
Publication: *The Typographical Journal* (monthly).
Editor: (Secretary-treasurer).
Membership: 138,000; local unions, 636.

UNION OF PROFESSIONAL AIRMEN

See Air Line Employees Association.

UNIVERSITY PROFESSORS; AMERICAN ASSOCIATION OF (IND.)

1 Dupont Circle, Suite 500, Washington, D.C. 20036.
Phone: (202) 466-8050.
President: Peter O. Steiner.
Secretary-treasurer: Sandra W. Phornton.
Executive secretary: Morton S. Baratz.
Organizing activities: Woodley B. Osborne.
Research director: Tom J. Truss, Jr.
Social insurance: William B. Woolf (Director, administration).
Legal: Matthew W. Finkin (General counsel).
Public relations activities: James G. Trulove.
Government relations: Alfred D. Sumberg.
Collective bargaining activities: (Organizing activities).
Convention: Annually.
Publications: (1) *Bulletin* (quarterly); (2) *Academe* (quarterly).
Editors: (1) Robert K. Webb, (2) (Public relations activities).
Membership: 72,265; chapters, 1,360.

UPHOLSTERERS' INTERNATIONAL UNION OF NORTH AMERICA (AFL-CIO)

25 North Fourth St., Philadelphia, Pa. 19106.
Phone: (215) 923-5700.
President: Sal B. Hoffman.
Treasurer: Paul W. Heaton.
Organizing activities: (President).
Research and education director: Ray M. Pudliner.
Social insurance: (President).
Legal: Richard S. Hoffman (Resident counsel).
Convention: Every 4 years; 1982.
Publication: *UIU Journal* (bimonthly).
Editor: (President).
Membership: 59,000; local unions, 170.

UTAH PUBLIC EMPLOYEES ASSOCIATION (IND.)

438 South 6th East, Salt Lake City 84102.
Phone: (801) 328-4995.
President: E. Woodrow Walton.
Secretary-treasurer: Richard B. Kinnersley.
Executive director: (Secretary-treasurer).
Organizing activities: (Secretary-treasurer).
Research director: J. Robert Brimhall.
Social insurance: (Research director).
Legal: J. Francis Valerga.
Public relations activities: Jerry W. Nelson.
Government relations: (Secretary-treasurer).
Collective bargaining activities: (Secretary-treasurer).
Convention: Annually.
Publications: *The Utah Public Employee* (monthly); *The Communicator* (periodically).
Editor: (Public relations activities).
Membership: 10,039; districts, 51.

UTILITY WORKERS OF NEW ENGLAND, INC.; BROTHERHOOD OF (IND.)

212 Union St., Providence, Rhode Island 02903.
Phone: (401) 751-6829.
President: John J. Earley.
159 Oxford St., Auburn, Mass. 01501.
Secretary-treasurer: Joseph R. Tracy.
73 Doric Ave., Cranston, R.I. 02910.
Organizing activities: George P. Forgarty.
133 Kentland Ave., N. Providence, R.I. 02908.
Research director: Donald R. Dolan.
21 Cherry St., Milford, Mass. 01757.
Education director: Paul F. Lepore, Jr.
378 Pleasant St., Marlboro, Mass. 01752.
Social insurance: Frank Simmons, Jr. (Regional vice president).
18 Speaker St., North Dartmouth, Mass. 02747.
Legal: (President).
Legislative activities: (Social insurance).
Public relations activities: (Secretary-treasurer).
Health and safety activities: (Education director).
Convention: Every 2 years; 1980.
Membership: 4,500; local unions, 19.

UTILITY WORKERS UNION OF AMERICA (AFL-CIO)

815 16th Street, N.W., Suite 605, Washington, D.C. 20006.
Phone: (202) 347-8105.
President: Harold T. Rigley.
Secretary-treasurer: Marshall M. Hicks.
Organizing activities: Clement J. Lewis.
Research and education director: (Organizing activities).
Social insurance: (Secretary-treasurer).
Legal: Donald Menagh (General counsel).
New York, N.Y. 10016.
Legislative activities: (Secretary-treasurer).
Public relations activities: (Secretary-treasurer).
Health and safety activities: (Organizing activities).
Convention: Every 2 years; 1979.
Publication: *Light* (monthly).
Editor: (Secretary-treasurer).
Membership: 60,000; local unions, 250.

VERMONT STATE EMPLOYEES ASSOCIATION, INC. (IND.)

79 Main St., Montpelier, Vt. 05602.
Phone: (802) 223-5247.
President: Laura M. Williams.
Treasurer: Helen M. Weed.
Executive director: Robert S. Babcock, Jr.
Organizing activities: (Executive director).
Research director: Rita Ricketson.
Social insurance: Steve Rising.
Legal: Alan Rome, Esq.
Government relations: (Executive director).
Collective bargaining activities: (Executive director).
Convention: Annually.
Publications: *VSEA Voice* (quarterly).
Editor: Beverly A. Ryan.
Membership: 3,700; chapters, 17.

WAREHOUSE INDUSTRIAL INTERNATIONAL UNION (IND.)

222 17 Northern Blvd., Bayside, N.Y. 11361.
Phone: (212) 776-5437.
President: Jack Adler.
Secretary-treasurer: Dennis Adler.

Organizing activities: (President).
Membership: 50; local unions, 0.

WASHINGTON PUBLIC EMPLOYEES ASSOCIATION (IND.)

124 West 10th St., Olympia 98501.
Phone: (206) 943-1121.
President: Les Johnson.
Secretary: Barbara Carr.
Executive director: Ann Quantock.
Organizing activities: (Executive director).
Social insurance: (Executive director).
Public relations activities: (Executive director).
Legal: Frank Dennis.
Government relations: (Executive director).
Collective bargaining activities: Bob Rakoz.
Convention: Annually.
Publications: *The Sentinel* (monthly); *Your Report* (monthly); *Legislative Report* (monthly during session).
Editor: (Executive director).
Membership: 4,000; chapters, 36.

WATCH WORKERS UNION; AMERICAN (IND.)

617 West Orange St., Lancaster, Pa. 17603.
Phone: (717) 397-1339.
President: Ralph F. Frey.
Secretary-treasurer: Charles H. Kirchner.
Organizing activities: (President).
Research director: (Secretary-treasurer).
Education director: Charles S. Koller (Vice president).
Legal: James H. Brock (Attorney).
Legislative activities: (President).
Public relations activities: (President).
Health and safety activities: (Education director).
Convention: Every 2 years; 1980.
Membership: 735; local unions, 2.

WATCHMEN'S ASSOCIATION; INDEPENDENT (IND.)

11 Broadway, New York, N.Y. 10004.
Phone: (212) 943-5880.
President: John J. Fanning.
Secretary-treasurer: Frank Mancini, Jr.
Organizing activities: Robert J. Clinton, Jr. and John Castelli, Jr.
Research and education director: (President).
Social insurance: George J. Drumm (Vice president).
Legal: Wilfred L. Davis (General counsel).
Legislative activities: (Secretary-treasurer).
Public relations activities: Robert J. Clinton, Jr.
Health and safety activities: John Castelli, Jr.
Convention: Every 5 years; June 1980.
Membership: 10,000; local unions, 14.

WESTERN STATES SERVICE STATION EMPLOYEES UNION (IND.)

703 Market Street, San Francisco, Calif. 94103.
President: Carl E. Anderson.
8015 South 130th St., Seattle, Wash. 98178.
Secretary-treasurer: George S. Rudelis.
5027 Zelzah Ave., Encino, Calif. 91316.
Organizing activities: (President).
Research and education director: (President).
Social insurance: (President).
Legal and legislative activities: (President).
Public relations activities: (Secretary-treasurer).
Health and safety activities: (President).

Convention: Every 3 years; 1981.
Publication: *WSSSEU "News"* (bimonthly).
Editor: (President).
Membership: 426; local unions, 14.

WOODWORKERS OF AMERICA; INTERNATIONAL (AFL-CIO)

1622 North Lombard St., Portland, Ore. 97217.
Phone: (503) 285-5281.
President: Keith W. Johnson.
Secretary-treasurer: Robert Gerwig.
Organizing activities: Fernie Viala (Vice president).
Research and education director: Roy A. Ockert.
Social insurance: R. Denny Scott.
Legal: James E. Youngdahl (Legal counsel).
Legislative activities: Bud Rahberger (Vice president).
Public relations activities: Richard E. Spahn.
Health and safety activities: (Social insurance).
Convention: Every 2 years; 1979.
Publications: (1) *Woodworker* (monthly); (2) *B. C. Lumberworker* (monthly).
Editors: (1) (Public relations activities); (2) Pat Kerr.
Membership: 107,966; local unions, 231.

WRITERS GUILD OF AMERICA

WRITERS GUILD OF AMERICA, EAST, INC. (IND.)
22 W. 48th St., New York, N.Y. 10036.
Phone: (212) 575-5060.
President: Loring Mandel.
Secretary-treasurer: Ken Gaughran.
Organizing activities: Leonard Wasser (Executive director).
Research and education director: Elihu Winer.
Social insurance: Jose V. Lim.
Legal: Hillel Gedrich.
Health and safety activities: Sylvia L. Williams.
Publication: *WGA Newsletter* (monthly).
Editor: (Research and education director).
Membership: 1,600; local unions, 0.

WRITERS GUILD OF AMERICA, WEST, INC. (IND.)
8955 Beverly Blvd., Los Angeles, Calif. 90048.
Phone: (213) 550-1000.
President: David W. Rintels.
Secretary-treasurer: William Ludwig.
Executive director: Michael H. Franklin.
Organizing activities: (Executive director).
Education director: (Executive director).
Social insurance: Leonard Chassman.
Legal: Paul P. Selvin and Elliott Williams.
Legislative activities: (Executive director).
Public relations activities: Allen Rivkin.
Convention: Annually.
Publication: *Newsletter* (monthly).
Editor: (Public relations activities).
Membership: 3,204; local unions, 0.

WYOMING STATE EMPLOYEES ASSOCIATION (IND.)

408 West 23rd St., Cheyenne 82001.
Phone: (307) 635-5633.
President: L. P. McGuire.
Secretary-treasurer: George Leckie.
Executive director: L. C. Case.
Research director: Dennis Smyth.
Legal: Ed Grant (Lawyer).
Government relations: (Research director).
Collective bargaining activities: (Research director).
Convention: Annually.
Publication: *Update* (monthly).
Editor: (Executive director).
Membership: 2,850; affiliates, 27.

AFL-CIO STATE LABOR ORGANIZATIONS

ALABAMA LABOR COUNCIL
23 West Valley Ave., Birmingham 35209.
Phone: (205) 942-5260.
President: Barney Weeks.
Secretary-treasurer: A. G. Trammell.
Other chief executive officer: Connie Entrekin (Executive vice
  president).
Research and education director: (Secretary-treasurer).
Legislative representative: (Secretary-treasurer).
Public relations director: (President).
Publication: *Alabama Labor Council News Letter* (weekly).
Editor: (President).

ALASKA STATE FEDERATION OF LABOR
4251 Warwick Drive, Anchorage 99504.
Phone: (907) 279-6311.
President: Dwayne Carlson.
Secretary-treasurer: Henry Hedberg.
Legislative representative: (President).
Public relations director: (President).

ARIZONA STATE AFL-CIO
520 West Adams St., Phoenix 85003.
Phone: (602) 258-3407.
President: Fred J. Brown.
Secretary-treasurer: Darwin Aycock.
Research director: (Secretary-treasurer).
Education director: Grace Carroll.
Legislative representative: (Secretary-treasurer).
Legal counsel: Herbert L. Ely.
Public relations director: (Secretary-treasurer).
Health and safety: (Secretary-treasurer).
Publication: *Arizona State AFL-CIO Legislative News Letter*
  (monthly).
Editor: (Secretary-treasurer).

ARKANSAS STATE AFL-CIO
1115 Bishop Street, Little Rock 72202.
Phone: (501) 375-9101.
President: J. Bill Becker.
Secretary-treasurer: E. J. Jacobs.
Research and education director: (President).
Legislative representative: (President).
Legal counsel: James E. Youngdahl.
Public relations director: (President).
Health and safety: (President).

CALIFORNIA LABOR FEDERATION
995 Market St., Suite 310, San Francisco 94103.
Phone: (415) 986-3585.
President: Albin J. Gruhn.
Executive secretary-treasurer: John F. Henning.
Other chief executive officer: Manuel Dias (General vice pres-
  ident).
Research director: Patrick F. Mason.
Education director: (President).
Legislative representative: (Secretary-treasurer).
Legal counsel: Charles P. Sculley.
Public relations director: Harry Finks.
Health and safety: (Secretary-treasurer).
Publication: *California AFL-CIO News* (weekly).
Editor: Glenn Martin.

COLORADO LABOR COUNCIL
360 Acoma St., Room 300, Denver 80223.
Phone: (303) 733-2401.
President: Norman N. Pledger.
Secretary-treasurer: Zelda Bransted.
COPE director: Kathy Oatis.
Legislative representative: Tim G. Flores.
Legal counsel: Edward J. Scheunemann and Douglas R.
  Phillips.

CONNECTICUT STATE LABOR COUNCIL, AFL-CIO
9 Washington Ave., Hamden 06518.
Phone: (203) 288-3591.
President: John J. Driscoll.
Secretary-treasurer: Walter M. O'Conner.
Other chief executive officers: Justin Ostro (Executive vice
  president) and Michael Ferruci, Jr. (Executive secretary).
Research director: Joseph Vehlein.
Legislative representative: (Secretary-treasurer).
Legal counsel: Norman Zolot.
Publication: *Call to Action* (quarterly).
Editor: (President).

DELAWARE STATE AFL-CIO
922 New Road, Elsmere, Wilmington 19805.
Phone: (302) 998-8801.
President: John A. Campanelli.
Secretary-treasurer: Thomas E. Watson.
Other chief executive officer: Norman L. Tyrie (Vice president).
Legislative representative: (President).

FLORIDA AFL-CIO
P.O. Box 1836, 135 South Monroe Street, Tallahassee 32302.
Phone: (904) 224-6926.
President: Daniel J. Miller, Jr.
Secretary-treasurer: William E. Allen.
Other chief executive officer: Art Hallgren (Executive vice
  president).
Education director: (Executive vice president).
Legislative representative: (President).
Legal counsel: Frank Hamilton.

GEORGIA STATE AFL-CIO
501 Pulliam St., Room 549, Atlanta 30312.
Phone: (404) 525-2793.
President: Herbert H. Mabry.
Secretary: Martha D. True.
Treasurer: Ronna Jones.
Other chief executive officer: M. J. Counihan (Executive vice
  president).
Legislative representative: (President).
Publication: *Journal of Labor* (weekly).
Editor: Theresa Koupas.

HAWAII STATE FEDERATION OF LABOR
547 Halekauwila St., Suite 216, Honolulu 96813.
Phone: (808) 536-4945.
President: Walter H. Kupau.
Secretary-treasurer: A. Van Horn Diamond.
Publication: *Hawaii AFL-CIO News* (bimonthly).
Editor: Ko Hayashi.

IDAHO STATE AFL-CIO
225 N. 16th, Boise 83706.
Phone: (208) 345-8582.
President: Robert W. Macfarlane.
Secretary-treasurer: James E. Kerns.
Other chief executive officer: Edward L. Johnson (Vice president).
Research and education director: (President).
Legislative representative: (President).
Legal counsel: George Greenfield.
Public relations director: (President).
Publication: *Idaho Labor Report* (monthly).
Editor: (President).

ILLINOIS STATE AFL-CIO
300 North State St., Chicago 60610.
Phone: (312) 222-1414.
President: Stanley L. Johnson.
Secretary-treasurer: Robert G. Gibson.
Research and education director: (President and Secretary-treasurer).
Legislative representative: (President and Secretary-treasurer).
Legal counsel: Asher, Greenfield, Goodstein, Pavalon & Segall, Ltd.
Public relations director: (President and Secretary-treasurer).
Health and safety: (President and Secretary-treasurer).
Publication: *Weekly News Letter*.
Editor: (President and secretary-treasurer).

INDIANA STATE AFL-CIO
P.O. Box 385, 1000 N. Madison Ave., Greenwood 46142.
Phone: (317) 881-6773.
President: Willis N. Zagrovich.
Secretary-treasurer: Max F. Wright.
Research and education director: (President).
Legislative representative: (President).
Publication: *News and Views* (monthly).
Editor: (President).

IOWA FEDERATION OF LABOR
2000 Walker St., Suite A, Des Moines 50317.
Phone: (515) 262-9571.
President: Hugh D. Clark.
Secretary-treasurer: James J. Wengert.
Other chief executive officer: Betty Talkington (Women's activities director).
Education director: (Secretary-treasurer).
Legislative representative: Allen J. Meier.
Public relations director: Joseph Poduska.
Publication: *Iowa AFL-CIO News* (monthly).
Editor: (Public relations director).

KANSAS STATE FEDERATION OF LABOR
110 W. 6TH, P.O. Box 1455, Topeka 66601.
Phone: (913) 357-0396.
President: John Overman.
Executive secretary-treasurer: Ralph McGee.
Other chief executive officer: H. J. Yount (Executive vice president).
Legislative representative: (Executive secretary-treasurer and executive vice president).

KENTUCKY STATE AFL-CIO
706 East Broadway, Louisville 40202.
Phone: (502) 584-8189.
President: Joseph B. Warren.
Secretary-treasurer: Leonard S. Smith.

Other chief executive officer: Robert T. Curtis (Executive vice president).
Research and education director: Ronald R. Cyrus.
Legislative representatives: (Secretary-treasurer) and Raymond Crider.
Publication: *Kentucky Labor News* (weekly).
Editor: Glenda Middlebrooks.

LOUISIANA AFL-CIO
P.O. Box 3477, 429 Government Street, Baton Rouge 70821.
Phone: (504) 383-5741.
President: Victor Bussie.
Secretary-treasurer: Emile J. Bourg, Sr.
Other chief executive officer: K. Gordon Flory (Executive vice president).
Legislative representative: (President and Executive vice president).
Legal counsel: John Avant (Law firm: Dodd, Avant, Wall & Thomas).
Public relations director: J. E. McCarthy.
Publication: *Louisiana AFL-CIO News* (monthly).
Editor: (Public relations director).

MAINE AFL-CIO
72 Center Street, Brewer 04412.
Phone: (207) 989-3630.
President: Charles O'Leary.
Secretary-treasurer: Gary B. Cook.
Other chief executive officer: Marvin W. Ewing (Vice president).
Research and education director: Kenneth F. Morgan.
Legislative representative: (President).
Legal counsel: Patrick Teague.
Public relations director: (Research and education director).
Publication: *Maine Labor News* (monthly).
Editor: (President).

MARYLAND STATE AND DISTRICT OF COLUMBIA AFL-CIO
305 West Monument St., Baltimore 21201.
Phone: (301) 727-7307.
President: Dominic N. Fornaro.
Secretary-treasurer: Edward Lanen.
Other chief executive officers: Edward Courtenay and Robert Peterson (Executive vice presidents).
Education director: (Secretary-treasurer).
Legislative representative: (President).

MASSACHUSETTS STATE LABOR COUNCIL
6 Beacon St., Suite 720, Boston 02108.
Phone: (617) 227-8260.
President: William J. P. Cleary.
Secretary-treasurer: James P. Loughlin.
Other chief executive officers: Arthur Osborn and John Prendergast (Executive vice presidents).
Education director: John A. Callahan.
Legislative representative: William A. Cashman.
Legal counsel: Robert M. Segal.
Public relations director: Gerard Kable.
Publication: *Newsletter* (quarterly).
Editor: (Public relations director).

MICHIGAN STATE AFL-CIO
419 South Washington Ave., Lansing 49806.
Phone: (517) 487-5966.
President: William C. Marshall.
Secretary-treasurer: George B. Watts.
Legislative representative: Simon Chapple.
Legal counsel: Theodore Sachs.
Public relations director: Aldo Vagnozzi.
Publication: *Michigan AFL-CIO News* (weekly).
Editor: (Public relations director).

MINNESOTA AFL-CIO
175 Auroro Avenue, St. Paul 55103.
Phone: (612) 227-7647.
President: David K. Roe.
Secretary-treasurer: Neil C. Sherburne.
Other chief executive officer: Leonard O. LaShomb (Executive vice president).
Research Director: Ronald G. Cohen.
Legal counsel: Roger Peterson.
Legislative representative: (President).
Public relations director: (Research director).
Publication: *Minnesota AFL-CIO News* (monthly).
Editor: (Research director).

MISSISSIPPI AFL-CIO
826 North West St., Jackson 39205.
Phone: (601) 948-0517.
President: Claude Ramsay.
Secretary-treasurer: Thomas Knight.
Education director: (Secretary-treasurer).
Legislative representative: (President).

MISSOURI STATE LABOR COUNCIL
P.O. Box 1086, 208 Madison St., Jefferson City 65101.
Phone: (314) 634-2115.
President: James E. Meyers.
Secretary-treasurer: ————.
Other chief executive officer: Emmett C. Mayer (Vice president).
Legislative representatives: (President, secretary-treasurer, and vice president).
Publication: *Newsletter* (monthly).
Editor: (President).

MONTANA STATE AFL-CIO
P.O. Box 1176, Lundy Shopping Center, Helena 59601.
Phone: (406) 442-1708.
President: Vincent Bosh.
Executive secretary: James W. Murry.
Other chief executive officer: Robert Kokoruda (Vice president).
Research director: Norma Tirrell.
Education director: Ernest Post.
Legislative representative: (Executive secretary).
Publication: *TAT Report* (monthly).
Editor: (Research director) and Candice Brown.

NEBRASKA STATE AFL-CIO
1821 California St., Omaha 68102.
Phone: (402) 345-2500.
President: William E. Brennan.
Secretary-treasurer: Victor G. Meyers.
Legislative representative: (Secretary-treasurer).
Legal counsel: Robert O'Connor.

NEVADA STATE AFL-CIO
P.O. Box 2999, Reno 89505.
Phone: (702) 329-1508.
President: Mark Tully Massagli.
Secretary-treasurer: Claude Evans.
Legislative representative: (Secretary-treasurer).
Legal counsel: John Anderson.

NEW HAMPSHIRE STATE LABOR COUNCIL
P.O. Box 1305, Portsmouth 03801.
Phone: (603) 625-8941.
President: Thomas J. Pitarys.
Secretary-treasurer: Saverio M. Giambalvo.
Other chief executive officer: Raymond Moran (Executive vice president).
Education director: (President).
Legislative representative: (Executive vice president).

NEW JERSEY STATE AFL-CIO
106 West State St., Trenton 08608.
Phone: (609) 989-8730.
President: Charles H. Marciante.
Secretary-treasurer: Edward B. Pulver.
Research director: Fred Mehelic.
Education director: (President).
Public relations director: (Research director).
Publication: *New Jersey State AFL-CIO News* (monthly).
Editor: (President).

NEW MEXICO STATE AFL-CIO
6303 Indian School Rd., N.E., Albuquerque 87110.
Phone: (505) 292-2911.
President: Toby Pacheco.
Secretary-treasurer: Neal Gonzalez.
Other chief executive officers: C. M. Norris (Vice president) and Mary Sue Gutierrez (COPE director).
Legislative representative: (Secretary-treasurer).
Legal counsel: Roland Kool.
Publication: *The Voice* (quarterly).
Editor: (COPE director).

NEW YORK STATE AFL-CIO
30 East 29th St., New York 10016.
Phone: (212) 689-9320.
President: Raymond R. Corbett.
Secretary-treasurer: E. Howard Molisani.
Research director: Ludwig Jaffe.
Legislative representative: (President).
Legal counsel: Herman A. Gray.
Public relations director: Joseph P. Murphy.
Publication: *The Federation* (monthly).
Editor: (Public relations director).

NORTH CAROLINA STATE AFL-CIO
P.O. Box 10805, Raleigh 27605.
Phone: (919) 833-6678.
President: Wilbur Hobby.
Secretary-treasurer: E. A. Britt.
Research and education director: Christopher Scott.
Legislative representative: (President).
Public relations director: (Research and education director).
Health and safety: (Secretary-treasurer).
Publication: *Carolina Labor News* (quarterly).
Editor: (Research and education director).

NORTH DAKOTA AFL-CIO
RR #1, Bismarck 58501.
Phone: (701) 223-0784.
President: James Gerl.
Secretary-treasurer: Robert A. Donegan.
Other chief executive officer: Ray Such (1st vice president).
Research and education director: (President).
Legislative representative: (President).
Public relations director: (President).
Health and safety: (President).
Publication: *News and Views* (periodically).
Editor: (President).

OHIO AFL-CIO
271 East State St., Columbus 43215.
Phone: (614) 224-8271.
President: Milan Marsh.
Secretary-treasurer: Warren J. Smith.
Legislative representative: (President).
Legal counsel: Clayman and Jaffy (Attorneys).

Public relations director: John R. Thomas.
Publications: *Focus* (8 times annually); *News & Views* (3 times monthly).
Editor: (Public relations director).

OKLAHOMA STATE AFL-CIO

501 N.E. 27th Street, Oklahoma City 73105.
Phone: (405) 528-2409.
President: Joe F. Johnson.
Secretary-treasurer: Ben Hutchinson.
Other chief executive officer: William H. Miller (Vice president).
Education director: (Secretary-treasurer).
Legislative representative: (President).
Publication: *AFL-CIO Oklahoma News* (monthly).
Editor: David Parrett.

OREGON AFL-CIO

530 Center St., Salem 97301.
Phone: (503) 585-6320.
President: Robert G. Kennedy.
Secretary-treasurer: Glenn E. Randall.
Legislative representative: Nellie Fox.

PENNSYLVANIA AFL-CIO

101 Pine St., Harrisburg 17101.
Phone: (717) 238-9351.
President: Harry Boyer.
Secretary: Harry Block.
Treasurer: Robert T. McIntyre.
Other chief executive officer: James Mahoney (Executive vice president).
Legislative representative: (Executive vice president).
Publication: *Pennsylvania AFL-CIO News* (monthly).
Editor: Stan Williams.

PUERTO RICO FEDERATION OF LABOR (AFL-CIO)

Avenida Central 274, Bajos, Hyde Park, Rio Piedras 00918.
Phone: (809) 764-4980.
President: Hipolito Marcano.
Secretary-treasurer: Clifford W. Depin.
Other chief executive officer: Manuel Huertos (1st vice president).
Legislative representative: (President).
Legal counsel: (President).

RHODE ISLAND AFL-CIO

357 Westminster St., Providence 02903.
Phone: (401) 751-7100.
President: Edward J. McElroy, Jr.
Secretary-treasurer: Edwin C. Brown.
Research and education director: (Secretary-treasurer).
Legislative representative: (Secretary-treasurer).
Public relations director: (Secretary-treasurer).
Health and safety: (Secretary-treasurer).

SOUTH CAROLINA LABOR COUNCIL, AFL-CIO

7420 North Main St., Columbia 29203.
Phone: (803) 754-8205.
President: James A. Johnson.
Secretary-treasurer: Melvin Burris.
Other chief executive officers: Tom Gibbons and James Johnson (Vice presidents).
Research director: Jean Dunham.
Education director: Tom Gibbons.
Legislative representative: H. Y. Landreth.
Legal counsel: James Bell.

Public relations director: (President).
Health and safety: (Legislative representative).

SOUTH DAKOTA STATE FEDERATION OF LABOR

515 South Dakota Ave., Room 6, Sioux Falls 57102.
Phone: (605) 338-3811.
President: Jack E. Dudley.
Secretary: Gary W. Ellsworth.
Legislative representative: (President).
Publication: *South Dakota AFL-CIO News Letter* (monthly).
Editor: (Secretary-treasurer).

TENNESSEE STATE LABOR COUNCIL

226 Capitol Blvd., Rm. 203, Nashville 37219.
Phone: (615) 256-5687.
President: Matthew Lynch.
Secretary-treasurer: Lee Case.
Research director: Ralph A. Franklin.
Education director: (President).
Legislative representative: (Secretary-treasurer).
Legal counsel: George E. Barrett.
Public relations director: (President).
Publication: *Tennessee State Labor Council Newsletter* (periodically).
Editors: (President).

TEXAS STATE AFL-CIO

1106 Lavaca St., Suite 200, P.O. Box 12727, Austin 78711.
Phone: (512) 477-6195.
President: Harry Hubbard Jr.
Secretary-treasurer: Sherman Fricks.
Research and education director: Ruth Ellinger.
Legislative representative: Harold Tate.
Legal counsel: Clinton & Richards (Attorneys).
Public relations director: A. Fred Cervelli.
Publication: *Labor News, Texas AFL-CIO* (monthly).
Editor: (Public relations director).

UTAH STATE AFL-CIO

2261 South Redwood Road, Salt Lake City 84119.
Phone: (801) 972-2771.
President and secretary-treasurer: Edward P. Mayne.
Research director: Louis Felice (Vice President).
Education director: Eugene Cullis.
Legislative representative: (President).
Legal counsel: A. Wally Sandack.
Public relations director: John Timothy Rice.

VERMONT STATE LABOR COUNCIL AFL-CIO

149 State St., Box 858, Montpelier 05602.
Phone: (802) 223-5229.
President: Robert E. Clark.
Secretary-treasurer: Ralph E. Crippen.
Other chief executive officer: Lindol Atkins, Jr. (Executive vice president).
Publication: *Vermont Labor Reporter* (quarterly).
Editors: (Executive vice president) and Lena Brown.

VIRGINIA STATE AFL-CIO

3315 West Broad St., Richmond 23230.
Phone: (804) 355-7444.
President: Julian F. Carper.
Secretary-treasurer: Rufus R. Foutz, III.
Other chief executive officer: Archie V. Iddings (Vice president).
Legislative representative: (President).
Publication: *News Hi-Lites* (monthly).
Editor: Brewster Snow.

WASHINGTON STATE LABOR COUNCIL, AFL-CIO

2701 First Ave., Room 300, Seattle 98121.
Phone: (206) 682-6002.

President: Joe Davis.
Secretary-treasurer: Marvin L. Williams.
Research director: Lawrence C. Kenney.
Education director: Louis O. Stewart.
Legislative representative: (President).
Health and safety: (Education director).
Publication: *Reports* (semimonthly).
Editor: (Research director).

WEST VIRGINIA LABOR FEDERATION, AFL-CIO
1018 Kanawha Blvd., East, Suite 1200, Charleston 25301.
Phone: (304) 344-3557.
President: Joseph W. Powell.
Secretary-treasurer: Lawrence Barker.
Research director: Lee Beard.
Legislative representative: (President).
Legal counsel: Stanley Hostler and S. Shinaberry.
Publication: *The Observer* (monthly).
Editor: (Research director).

WISCONSIN STATE AFL-CIO
6333 West Bluemound Rd., Milwaukee 53213.
Phone: (414) 771-0700.
President: John W. Schmitt.

Secretary-treasurer: Jack B. Reihl.
Other chief executive office: Joseph A. Gruber (Executive vice president).
Legislative representative: (Secretary-treasurer).
Legal counsel: Goldberg, Previant & Uelman.
Health and safety: Richard Sawicki.
Publication: *Labor News Review* (monthly).

WYOMING STATE AFL-CIO
1904 Thomes Aves., Cheyenne 82001.
Phone: (307) 635-5149.
President: H. P. "Paul" Johnson.
Executive secretary: L. Keith Henning.
Research and education director: (Executive secretary).
Legislative representative: (Executve secretary).
Public relations director: (Executive secretary).
Health and safety: (Executive secretary).
Publication: *State AFL-CIO News* (monthly).
Editor: (Executive secretary).

Labor organizations' fees and dues

A survey of national union and employee associations found wide variations in the size and type of initiation fees, monthly dues, and per capita taxes paid to headquarters

CHARLES W. HICKMAN

Although all members pay some dues or fees to their national labor organizations, the form and amount of these payments vary considerably. These fees are the principal source of income for most of these organizations. Many large unions and employee associations receive less than $6 from each member's monthly dues, for example, and others receive more than $16. Some set a single fee for all members; others permit locals a degree of choice by setting a minimum or maximum dues fee. Variations among initiation fees and per capita taxes are even greater, and some labor organizations do not require such payments.

The Bureau of Labor Statistics' biennial survey of national unions and employee associations gathered data on the level and distribution of members' fees by nationals for calendar year 1974.[1] The results (which may, of course, be out of date for some organizations[2]) do not include additional charges imposed by affiliates and locals. These charges are normally established by the organization's constitution and are often collected by employer deductions from members' wages through negotiated checkoff arrangements. The funds raised by these payments, the degree of authority given locals to increase member charges, and the spending policies that result from available revenue obviously help determine the activities and effectiveness of the organizations.

Dues and initiation fee policies may occasionally reflect issues broader than those implied by the treasury balance. Efforts to gain rank-and-file approval of dues increases (generally by delegate vote at national conventions) have in some instances become referenda on the overall performance of na-

Charles W. Hickman is an economist formerly with the Division of Industrial Relations, Bureau of Labor Statistics.

tional leaders. Varying levels of charges, particularly initiation fees, have also been used to attract or discourage increased membership.

Initiation fees

Most new union members have to pay initiation fees as their initial financial obligations. Of the 175 unions surveyed, only 25 (most of relatively small size) reported no initiation fee. On the other hand, only 3 of the 37 employee associations imposed any initiation fee, possibly reflecting the limited scope of collective bargaining activities historically performed by these associations. Overall, of the 212 labor organizations surveyed (representing more than 24 million members), 59 (representing 3.5 million) did not require such payments.

Initiation fees may be set by the national organization, or each local may set its own fee subject to upper or lower limits in the national constitution. In some cases, the national body sets no limits at all. Although most initiation fees are specific dollar amounts, a few are based on wages earned during a specified period or on some other measure not convertible to dollar terms. (See table 1.)

Of the 150 unions with initiation fees, 71 percent (representing 83 percent of the membership of these unions) permitted some local control over the size of the fee. And 11 of the 43 unions setting initiation fees solely at the national level did not have locals. A minimum and maximum both set by the national (29 percent of all unions with initiation fees), a single rate set by the national (21 percent), rates set entirely by the local (20 percent, including the Teamsters, International Brotherhood of Electrical Workers, Retail Clerks, and Service Employees), and a minimum set by the national (19 percent) were the most frequently reported practices. Larger unions tended to give locals some control over fees, whereas smaller organizations often set rates at the national level. Among unions permitting some local control of initiation fees, 36 percent had 100,000 members or more, compared with only 14 percent of unions setting rates solely at the national level. (Despite this pattern, two of the Nation's five largest unions—the Steelworkers and Machinists—set rates entirely at the national level.) More than a third of the unions that officially left fee levels to the locals in effect set a minimum payment by requiring locals to submit a fixed amount of the initiation fee to the national organization.[3]

Of the 89 unions with initiation fees that were identifiable in dollars (including both standard rates and national maximums, but excluding unions setting a national minimum only), 45—representing 74 percent of the membership of unions with these fees—charged less than $40. Major unions charging between $20 and $39 include the Auto Workers; State, County and Municipal Employees; Clothing Workers; and Paperworkers. The 29 unions (20 percent of membership) reporting payments of $100 or more tended to represent small numbers of specialized professional workers or craftworkers, such as the Elevator Constructors, Directors Guild, Football Players, and Radio Association (which charged $2,000). A few large unions, such as the Mine Workers and Iron Workers, also charged some new members $100 or more. (The use of maximum fees where no single level is set may overstate the actual amounts paid by individual union members.)

The division of funds between locals and the national body may indicate the relative influence of each level. Once fixed costs are met, the scope of activities and benefits of a local or national body can be affected by available funds. The following tabulation of the number of labor organizations re-

Table 1.   Initiation fees of national unions and employee associations, by type and amount, 1974

[Membership figures in thousands]

Fees	Total unions and associations		Unions						Employee associations	
			Total unions		AFL-CIO		Unaffiliated			
	Organizations	Membership	Organizations	Membership	Organizations	Membership	Organizations	Membership	Organizations	Membership
Total	212	24,190	175	21,580	111	16,879	64	4,701	37	2,610
Total imposing initiation fee	153	20,730	150	20,468	105	16,096	45	4,372	3	262
Fee set by national	44	3,514	43	3,425	24	3,108	19	317	1	89
Single rate	33	3,362	32	3,273	18	2,987	14	286	1	89
Less than $20	14	1,716	13	1,627	7	1,577	6	51	1	89
$20 to $39	5	387	5	387	5	387				
$40 to $59	4	9	4	9	1	3	3	6		
$60 to $79										
$80 to $99										
$100 and over	9	307	9	307	4	77	5	230		
Percent or fixed rate	1	943	1	943	1	943				
Varying rate[1]	11	151	11	151	6	120	5	31		
Less than $20	1	44	1	44	1	44				
$20 to $39	2	3	2	3	2	3				
$40 to $59	2	75	2	75	1	53	1	22		
$60 to $79	1	1	1	1			1	1		
$80 to $99										
$100 and over	5	28	5	28	2	20	3	8		
Percent or fixed rate										
Fee set by local	109	17,216	107	17,043	81	12,988	26	4,055	2	173
Minimum rate only set by national	28	2,422	28	2,422	21	2,357	7	65		
Less than $20	20	1,912	20	1,912	15	1,854	5	58		
$20 to $39	4	219	4	219	3	214	1	5		
$40 to $59	3	290	3	290	2	288	1	2		
$60 to $79										
$80 to $99										
$100 and over	1	(2)	1	(2)	1	(2)				
Percent or fixed rate									1	147
Maximum rate only set by national	7	1,339	6	1,192	4	1,037	2	155	1	147
Less than $20	3	273	2	125	1	25	1	100		
$20 to $39	3	1,053	3	1,053	2	998	1	55		
$40 to $59										
$60 to $79										
$80 to $99										
$100 and over										
Percent or fixed rate	1	14	1	14	1	14				
Minimum and maximum set by national[3]	43	6,341	43	6,341	37	4,592	6	1,749		
Less than $20	10	1,306	10	1,306	8	1,142	2	163		
$20 to $39	9	2,691	9	2,691	5	1,105	4	1,586		
$40 to $59	7	583	7	583	7	583				
$60 to $79	1	10	1	10	1	10				
$80 to $99										
$100 and over	15	1,591	15	1,591	15	1,591				
Percent or fixed rate	1	161	1	161	1	161				
No minimum or maximum set by national	31	7,114	30	7,088	19	5,002	11	2,086	1	26
No fee	59	3,461	25	1,113	6	784	19	329	34	2,348

[1] Rate varies according to skill level, or work experience, among other factors. Amount listed is maximum charged by 10 national unions, and the minimum charged by 1 other.

[2] Less than 500 members.

[3] Amount listed is maximum charged by national.

mitting part or all of the initiation fees to the national bodies illustrates the variations in relative responsibility among these organizations:

	Total organizations	All unions	AFL-CIO affiliates	Independent unions	Employee associations
Organizations surveyed	212	175	111	64	37
With initiation fee	153	150	105	45	3
Without initiation fee	59	25	6	19	34
Affiliates retaining entire fee	24	23	14	9	1
Affiliates remitting to national	100	100	68	32	0
Remitting 1 to 24 percent	18	18	11	7	0
Remitting 25 to 49 percent	17	17	12	5	0
Remitting 50 to 74 percent	29	29	21	8	0
Remitting 75 to 99 percent	4	4	3	1	0
Remitting 100 percent	32	32	21	11	0
Undetermined or no local unions	29	27	23	4	2

In dollar terms, most national unions (61 percent of those with an identifiable initiation fee, representing 72 percent of membership) received less than $10 from each member's initiation fee. Only 9 percent, representing 2 percent of membership, received $100 or more from the local affiliate as their share. Smaller organizations were strongly represented at both extremes, receiving no funds or substantial amounts from initiation fees.

Because most independent unions are relatively small, there were only limited differences between AFL-CIO and unaffiliated unions with respect to the amount received by national bodies from initiation fees. The impact of the Teamsters and Auto Workers (both extremely large independent unions) placed the bulk of unaffiliated membership with determinable fees in the 1-to-24-percent category of national receipts.

Monthly dues

Monthly dues payments, the principal source of continuing revenue for most labor organizations, were required by all 212 unions and employee associations surveyed. By directly setting dues levels or imposing a limit on the levels that locals may set,

Table 2. Monthly dues of national unions and employee associations, by type and amount, 1974
[Membership figures in thousands].

Dues	Total unions and associations		Unions						Employee associations	
			Total unions		AFL-CIO		Unaffiliated			
	Organizations	Membership	Organizations	Membership	Organizations	Membership	Organizations	Membership	Organizations	Membership
Total	212	24,190	175	21,580	111	16,879	64	4,701	37	2,610
Fee set by national[1]	101	6,193	68	4,042	34	3,610	34	432	33	2,151
Single rate	80	4,255	50	2,292	22	1,934	28	359	30	1,963
Less than $6	47	2,603	18	653	6	644	12	9	29	1,950
$6–$10	10	202	9	189	4	77	5	112	1	13
$11–$15	3	222	3	222	1	1	2	221		
$16 and over	7	7	7	7	1	1	6	6		
Percent or fixed rate	13	1,221	13	1,221	10	1,211	3	10		
Varying rate[2]	21	1,938	18	1,750	12	1,677	6	73	3	188
Less than $6	5	71	4	61	1	44	3	17	1	10
$6–$10	2	25	2	25	1	3	1	22		
$11–$15	1	35	1	35	1	35				
$16 and over	3	6	3	6	2	6	1	(3)		
Percent or fixed rate	10	1,801	8	1,623	7	1,589	1	34	2	178
Fee set by local	111	17,997	107	17,538	77	13,269	30	4,269	4	458
Minimum rate only set by national	67	13,758	64	13,447	47	9,396	17	4,051	3	311
Less than $6	39	5,734	36	5,423	23	4,895	13	527	3	311
$6–$10	24	6,207	24	6,207	21	4,228	3	1,979		
$11–$15	2	235	2	235	2	235				
$16 and over										
Percent or fixed rate	2	1,582	2	1,582	1	38	1	1,545		
Maximum rate only set by national	1	14	1	14	1	14				
Less than $6										
$6–$10										
$11–$15										
$16 and over	1	14	1	14	1	14				
Percent or fixed rate										
Minimum and maximum rate set by national[4]	16	1,292	15	1,145	9	1,069	6	76	1	147
Less than $6	1	147							1	147
$6–$10	10	418	10	418	6	385	4	33		
$11–$15	3	506	3	506	2	502	1	4		
$16 and over	1	182	1	182	1	182				
Amount not reported	1	39	1	39			1	39		
Percent or fixed rate										
No minimum or maximum rate set by national	27	2,933	27	2,933	20	2,791	7	143		

[1] Includes 17 unions that charge dues but do not have locals.
[2] Amount listed is maximum charged by 20 labor organizations, minimum charged by 1 national union.
[3] Less than 500 members.
[4] Amount listed is maximum limit established by national.

Table 3. Monthly per capita taxes for national unions, 1974 [Membership figures in thousands]						
Per capita taxes	All unions		AFL-CIO unions		Unaffiliated unions	
	Organi-zations	Member-ship	Organi-zations	Member-ship	Organi-zations	Member-ship
Organizations requiring per capita taxes	169	21,426	109	16,760	60	4,666
Less than $1	11	474	4	373	7	101
$1–$1.99	26	2,077	16	1,933	10	144
$2–$3.99	55	10,689	42	8,405	13	2,284
$4–$5.99	32	3,237	22	2,721	10	515
$6 and above	27	1,757	15	1,702	12	54
Undetermined	18	3,192	10	1,625	8	1,567
Organizations not requiring per capita taxes	6	155	2	120	4	35

NOTE: Totals include 17 unions that collect dues but do not have locals. In addition, 14 unions charged a varying per capita tax, based on total dues charged by the local, characteristics of individual affiliates and members, or other factors. The maximum possible amount remitted to the national is listed in all cases.

87 percent of the national organizations (representing 88 percent of membership) had some control over membership dues. (See table 2.) Because dues payments to some unions may include premiums for insurance, pensions, or other benefits, relative dues levels may be misleading; the authority granted many locals to set dues higher than a national minimum also limits the comparative value of the data.

Among unions, the maximum dues payment was usually delegated to local units; 64 unions set only a minimum rate at the national level. Most of the unions setting minimums only imposed a fee of less than $6 monthly, including the $5.15 minimum set by the State, County and Municipal Employees and the $5 minimums of the Service Employees and Hotel Employees. Another sizable group reported minimums of from $6 to $10, including the Teamsters ($8) and the Carpenters, Retail Clerks, and Laborers ($6 each). The Auto Workers' national minimum monthly dues were set at the equivalent of 2-hours' straight-time pay.

In contrast with these unions, the United Telegraph Workers set only a maximum national rate and 15 others set both a minimum and a maximum, thus providing some measure of authority to their locals. Of the 68 unions setting dues entirely at the national level, almost three-quarters established a single rate (usually less than $6) or a percentage of overall earnings. The remainder set charges varing with occupation, skill level, or other factors.[4]

As with initiation fees, dues differences between AFL-CIO and independent unions seem attributable primarily to membership size. Independent unions, many of which have relatively few members, often set rates entirely at the national level and tend to be highly represented at both ends of

the dues range. Larger independent unions reported dues patterns similar to those of large AFL-CIO unions, with shared responsibility between the national and local units and dues rates commonly less than $10 a month.

Reflecting the more limited geographical and occupational range of their members, employee associations reported dues procedures less varied than those of unions. Dues rates were set entirely by the parent body in 33 of the 37 organizations, with 29 of these setting a single monthly rate of less than $6 for all members. The National Education Association, which accounts for more than half of all employee association members, charged an annual fee of $25 ($2.08 per month). Of the four associations that allowed some local control of dues, three established only a minimum payment and the other set both a minimum and a maximum.

Three-quarters of the unions exempted unemployed members from dues payments, and slightly fewer exempted retirees, workers temporarily laid off, and apprentices. Larger unions were more likely to require dues from these workers and, except for unemployed members, these dues were usually the same as those paid by all other members. Employee associations were more liberal in granting reduction or waiver of dues, as shown by the following tabulation of the number of organizations granting special treatment to various groups:[5]

	Total organi-zations	All unions	AFL-CIO affili-ates	Independ-ent unions	Employee associa-tions
Organizations surveyed	212	175	111	64	37
Apprentices					
Dues required	73	66	47	19	7
Regular rate........	60	53	38	15	7
Special rate	13	13	9	4	0
No dues required	139	109	64	45	30
Retirees					
Dues required	71	49	39	10	22
Regular rate........	16	14	10	4	2
Special rate	55	35	29	6	20
No dues required	141	126	72	54	15
Unemployed					
Dues required	48	45	37	8	3
Regular rate........	25	24	19	5	1
Special rate	23	21	18	3	2
No dues required	164	130	74	56	34
Temporarily laid off					
Dues required	67	62	47	15	5
Regular rate........	56	53	40	13	3
Special rate	11	9	7	2	2
No dues required	145	113	64	49	32

Per capita taxes

Local affiliates of national unions are usually required to contribute to the parent organization a portion of monthly dues for each member. Only six national unions (representing less than 1 percent of total membership) do not require locals to forward a portion of dues. Table 3 provides the amount forwarded by the locals to the 169 national unions requiring such per capita taxes; among the six unions not requiring per capita taxes, most collected a percentage of earnings or wages for a fixed period of time. A third of all unions with per capita taxes (representing half the union members taxed) required from $2 to $3.99. Small unions tended to require extremely high or low per capita payments. Unlike monthly dues (which were allowed to fluctuate in 125 national unions), only 14 did not assess a specified per capita tax for all members. AFL-CIO and unaffiliated unions reported similar per capita tax patterns.

The common practice among employee associations is to collect dues directly from members; some distribute part of the funds to local affiliates.

All 169 unions receiving per capita payments from their locals directed some portion of the revenue to a general fund; 91 percent (representing 81 percent of the membership of these organizations) devoted more than half their per capita revenue to

Table 4.   Distribution of monthly per capita taxes received by national unions, by allocation to fund, 1974

[Membership figures in thousands]

Allocation	All unions		AFL-CIO unions		Unaffiliated unions	
	Organizations	Membership	Organizations	Membership	Organizations	Membership
General fund	169	21,426	109	16,760	60	4,666
1–5 percent						
6–15	2	991	1	991	1	(¹)
16–50	11	3,040	8	1,486	3	1,554
51–90	69	10,405	53	9,912	16	493
91–99	18	1,803	17	1,778	2	26
100	67	5,186	30	2,593	38	2,594
Strike fund	66	11,810	54	9,981	12	1,829
1–5 percent	6	1,132	5	1,132	1	(¹)
6–15	32	3,926	26	3,880	6	46
16–50	27	6,752	22	4,970	5	1,782
51–90	1	(¹)	1	(¹)		
91–99						
100						
Convention fund	31	3,936	23	3,752	8	184
1–5 percent	17	3,238	12	3,054	5	184
6–15	10	450	9	449	1	(¹)
16–50	3	248	2	248	1	(¹)
51–90	1	(¹)			1	(¹)
91–99						
100						
Union publications	19	4,860	15	3,177	4	1,683
1–5 percent	13	3,893	11	2,344	2	1,548
6–15	6	968	4	833	2	135
16–50						
51–90						
91–99						
100						
Education fund (including family)	7	2,029	3	314	4	1,715
1–5 percent	5	1,965	2	270	3	1,695
6–15	2	64	1	44	1	20
16–15						
51–90						
91–99						
100						
Retired members fund	8	3,533	8	3,533		
1–5 percent	2	560	2	560		
6–15						
16–50	5	1,982	5	1,982		
51–90	1	991	1	991		
91–99						
100						
Other	49	9,441	39	7,540	10	1,900
1–5 percent	12	2,649	9	841	3	1,808
6–15	15	3,021	11	2,941	4	80
16–50	20	3,627	18	3,618	2	9
51–90	1	140	1	140	1	4
91–99						
100						
Organizations not requiring per capita taxes	6	155	2	120	4	35

¹ Less than 500 members.

NOTE: Columns are nonadditive. Many organizations distribute payments to more than one fund. Totals include 17 unions that collect dues but do not have locals. In addition, 14 unions charged a varying per captia tax, based on total dues charged by the local, characteristics of individual affiliates and members, or other factors. The maximum possible percent remitted to the national is listed in all cases.

this fund. (See table 4.) Unaffiliated unions and those with comparatively small memberships were most likely to place all per capita revenue in the general fund. Strike funds received some per capita revenue in 39 percent of the unions, representing 55 percent of the membership. Unions supporting strike funds included the Auto Workers (which devoted 48 percent of per capita revenues to this fund), Plate Printers (highest at 68 percent), Coopers (50 percent), Rubber Workers (42 percent), and Machinists (23 percent). Though strikes by government workers are generally prohibited by Federal or State law, the Teachers (devoting 12 percent of per capita revenue) and Fire Fighters (6 percent) both allocated per capita revenue to strike funds. Half the AFL-CIO unions distributed some of this revenue to strike funds, a much higher proportion than for independent unions. The percentage of per capita revenue devoted to such funds is not, of course, a definitive measure of strike funds available, as the absolute size of the tax, membership, and availability of money from other sources (including assessments on employed members) may affect this total.[6] □

-----FOOTNOTES-----

[1] *Directory of National Unions and Employee Associations, 1975,* Bulletin 1937 (Bureau of Labor Statistics, 1977) (forthcoming).

[2] Published reports indicate that the comparative levels of fees, the manner of collection, and the percent of revenue devoted to various budget categories have remained essentially stable.

[3] These figures generally parallel those in a 1967 study, which found that 73 percent of unions charging initiation fees permitted some local control. In 1974, 28 percent of these unions permitted complete local control of initiation fees, up from 21 percent in 1967. See Edward R. Curtin, *Union Initiation Fees, Dues and Per Capita Tax—National Union Strike Benefits* (New York, Conference Board, 1968).

[4] Though no comprehensive data are available, published reports indicate that some unions have recently moved towards dues rates based on hourly wages or percentages of earnings in order to increase revenue in the face of sharply rising expenses. Some locals oppose the resultant decrease in control over dues; traditionally, dues increases have been approved by membership referendum or votes of delegates to national conventions. The use of dues levels not expressed in dollar amounts, particularly among larger unions setting rates solely at the national level, makes general comparisons of dues rates more difficult.

[5] The data in the tabulation are nonadditive; in many organizations, the dues charged various groups differ.

[6] For a discussion of strike expenditures and benefits, see Sheldon M. Kline, "Strike benefits of national unions," *Monthly Labor Review,* March 1975, pp. 17–23.

DECLINE IN LABOR UNION AND EMPLOYEE ASSOCIATION MEMBERSHIP

Membership in labor organizations headquartered in the United States declined for the first time since 1968 when professional and State employee associations were added to the union membership series, according to preliminary findings of the Bureau of Labor Statistics, U.S. Department of Labor. Total membership of labor unions and professional and State employees associations that engage in representational activities declined between 1974 and 1976 by 158,000 to 24.0 million (table 1). The total included members outside the United States, primarily in Canada. The total membership losses, centered in the private sector and the Federal government, were partially offset by gains in State and local government.

Over the 1974–76 period, the rolls of national and international unions were reduced by almost 600,000 members, the first decline since 1960–62. The 21.0 million union members reported in 1976 were, however, above the pre-1974 levels. Employee association membership contined to increase, and reached a new peak of 3.0 million, an increase of 400,000. About one-half of the 2-year increase was reported by the National Education Association, now the second largest labor organization in the United States, after the Teamsters.

TABLE 1

UNION AND ASSOCIATION MEMBERSHIP, 1974–76

	Total[1]		U.S. Membership[2]	
Year	Union and association membership	Union membership	Union and association membership	Union membership
1974	24,194,000	21,585,000	22,809,000	20,199,000
1976	24,036,000	21,006,000	22,463,000	19,432,000

[1] Includes membership outside the U.S., except members of locals directly affiliated with the AFL-CIO.
[2] Includes members of directly affiliated locals but excludes members in Canada and members of single firm unions.

Information on labor organization membership was provided to the Bureau by 177 unions and 35 professional and State employee associations for the "Directory of National Unions and Employee Associations, 1977."

UNION AND ASSOCIATION MEMBERSHIP

U.S. membership in labor organizations (excluding Canada) declined from 22.8 million in 1974 to 22.5 million in 1976 (Table 2). As a proportion of the total labor force, membership declined by more than 1 percentage point between 1974 and 1976 continuing the long term decline that had been briefly reversed in 1974. Membership in the U.S. represented 23.2 percent of the labor force in 1976 and 28.3 percent of employment in nonagricultural establishments.

TABLE 2

U.S. UNION AND ASSOCIATION MEMBERSHIP, 1970–1976*

		Total labor force		Employees in nonagricultural establishments	
Year	Total membership (thousands†)	Number (thousands)	Percent union members	Number (thousands)	Percent union members
1970	21,248	85,903	24.7	70,920†	30.0†
1971	21,327	86,929	24.5	71,222†	29.9
1972	21,657	88,991	24.3	73,714†	29.4
1973	22,239	91,040	24.4	76,896†	28.9
1974	22,809	93,240	24.5	78,413†	29.1
1975	22,298	94,793	23.5	77,051	28.9
1976	22,463	96,917	23.2	79,443	28.3

* Membership includes total reported membership excluding Canada. Also included are members of directly affiliated local unions. Members of single-firm unions are excluded.
† Revised

TABLE 3

UNION AND ASSOCIATION MEMBERSHIP BY EMPLOYMENT SECTOR, 1968–76[1]
(In thousands)

		Private sector			Government	
Year	Total	Manufacturing	Non-manufacturing	Total	Federal[2]	State and local
Unions and Associations						
1968	22,015	9,218	8,940	3,857	1,391	2,466
1970	22,558	9,173	9,305	4,080	1,412	2,668
1972	23,059	8,920	9,619	4,520	1,383	3,137
1974	24,194	9,144	9,705	5,345	1,433	3,911
1976	24,036	8,463	9,721	5,853	1,332	4,521
Associations						
1968	1,805	0	103	1,702	—	1,702
1970	1,869	0	107	1,762	—	1,762
1972	2,221	0	161	2,060	—	2,060
1974	2,610	0	185	2,425	—	2,425
1976	3,031	0	188	2,843	—	2,843

[1] Includes membership outside the United States, except members of locals directly affiliated with the AFL-CIO.
[2] Fewer than 50,000 were in the Federal government.

Membership in the public sector continued to increase with a 600,000 gain in State and local government, offsetting a 100,000 reduction in the number of Federal employees who belonged to labor organizations. As was true in earlier years, employee association members outnumbered union members at the State and local level.

Some 6.5 million union and association members were employed in white-collar occupations in 1976, a 579,000 member increase or about 10 percent. With the decrease in total membership of labor organizations, the proportion represented by white-collar members rose by 2.6 percentage points, to 26.9 percent. About three-fifths of all organized white-collar workers are members of unions.

The increasing number of women in labor organizations peaked in 1974 at slightly over 6 million or 25 percent of total membership. In 1976, women members of labor organizations declined by about 50,000 or 0.1 percent. This decline resulted from a 400,000 reduction in union rolls and a 350,000 gain in the number of new women members recruited by associations. Both constituted a significant proportion of the overall membership change in the two types of organizations: over two-thirds of the union loss and over four-fifths of the association increase.

TABLE 4

WHITE-COLLAR AND WOMEN UNION AND ASSOCIATION MEMBERSHIP, 1968–76

	Unions and Associations		Unions	
Year	Number (thousands)	Percent of total	Number (thousands)	Percent of total
White-collar members				
1968	—	—	3,176	15.7
1970	4,917	21.8	3,353	16.2
1972	5,202	22.6	3,434	16.5
1974	5,881	24.3	3,762	17.4
1976	6,460	26.9	3,857	18.4
Women				
1968	—	—	3,940	19.5
1970	5,398	23.9	4,282	20.7
1972	5,736	24.9	4,524	21.7
1974	6,038	25.0	4,600	.21.3
1976	5,991	24.9	4,201	20.0

Dashes indicate data are not available.

UNION MEMBERSHIP DEVELOPMENTS

For the first time since the 1960–62 period, the U.S. membership of unions declined, by 767,000 or about 4 percent from 1974 to 1976. Much of this decline is a reflection of the state of the economy, particularly in manufacturing and construction in 1975 and 1976 where average production work employment declined by approximately 1.4 million workers. However, the labor force and overall nonagricultural employment continued to grow. Thus, the union penetration rate declined from 21.7 percent of the labor force in 1974 to 20.1 percent in 1976. The nonagricultural union penetration rate fell from 25.8 percent to 24.5 percent over the same period.

TABLE 5

2-61
ORGANIZED LABOR
IN THE UNITED STATES

U.S. UNION MEMBERSHIP, 1960–74[1]

Year	Total membership[1] (thousands)	Total labor force		Employees in nonagricultural establishments	
		Number (thousands)	Percent union members	Number (thousands)	Percent union members
1960	17,049	72,142	23.6	54,234	31.4
1961	16,303	73,031	22.3	54,042	30.2
1962	16,586	73,442	22.6	55,596	29.8
1963	16,524	74,571	22.2	56,702	29.1
1964	16,841	75,830	22.0	58,331	28.9
1965	17,299	77,178	22.4	60,815	28.4
1966	17,940	78,893	22.7	63,955	28.1
1967	18,367	80,793	22.7	65,857	27.9
1968	18,916	82,272	23.0	67,951	27.8
1969	19,036	84,240	22.6	70,442	27.0
1970	19,381	85,903	22.6	70,920	27.3
1971	19,211	86,929	22.1	71,222	27.0
1972	19,435	88,991	21.8	73,714	26.4
1973	19,851	91,040	21.8	76,896	25.8
1974	20,199	93,240	21.7	78,413	25.8
1975	19,473	94,793	20.5	77,051	25.3
1976	19,432	96,917	20.1	79,443	24.5

[1] Membership includes total reported membership excluding Canada. Also included are members of directly affiliated local unions. Members of single-firm unions are excluded.

After an increase of more than 200,000 members in the U.S. and Canadian manufacturing industries between 1972 and 1974, total membership in the sector declined by 681,000 in 1976. This substantial decrease was somewhat offset by a small gain in nonmanufacturing industries and an 89,000 membership increment in government (table 6). Successful organizing drives at the State and local government levels increased membership by 181,000. Well over 100,000 of this gain was accounted for by American Federation of State, County, and Municipal Employees whose 1976 membership reached three-quarters of a million. Federal union membership declined by somewhat under 100,000.

TABLE 6

UNION MEMBERSHIP BY EMPLOYMENT SECTOR, 1968–1976[1]
(In thousands)

Year	Total	Private sector			Government	
		Manufacturing	Nonmanufacturing	Total	Federal	State and local
1968	20,210	9,218	8,837	2,155	1,351	804
1970	20,689	9,173	9,198	2,318	1,370	947
1972	20,838	8,920	9,458	2,460	1,355	1,105
1974	21,585	9,144	9,520	2,920	1,391	1,529
1976	21,006	8,463	9,533	3,009	1,300	1,710

[1] Includes membership outside the United States, except members of locals directly affiliated with the AFL-CIO.
NOTE: Because of rounding, sums of individual items may not equal totals.

Between 1974 and 1976, union white-collar membership continued its long-term upward trend, increasing by 95,000 to almost 3.9 million or 18.4 percent of all members in 1976. In 1974, white-collar members con-

stituted 17.4 percent of all members; in 1972, 16.5 percent.

After many years of growth, women union membership declined by 400,000 over the 2-year period. Women constituted 20.0 percent of all members in 1976, down from 21.3 percent in 1974 and 21.7 percent in 1972.

AFL-CIO affiliates reported 16.6 million members in 1976, compared with 16.9 million in 1974. The Federation represented 78 percent of all union members in 1976 and 1974, and 79 percent in 1972.

UNIONS WITH LARGEST GAINS IN MEMBERS OVER DECADE

Eight national and international unions increased their membership by 100,000 or more in the past decade, in contrast to 14 organizations that achieved that increase between 1964–74 and 13 between 1962–72. The Teamsters union, which reported the largest increase in the 1964–74 decade, was replaced as the most successful recruiter of new members by the State, County, and Municipal Employees (469,000) and the Teachers (321,000) unions. Three other unions reported 200,000 or more new members: Teamsters, Steelworkers, and Service Employees. A 257 percent increase in the Teachers' rolls was considerably higher than the percent increase recorded by any other union, as was the case in the previous 10 years (table 7). Two unions, down from three between 1964–74, more than doubled their membership over the decade—State, County and Municipal Employees, and Teachers.

Twelve large unions, those with 100,000 members or more, reported membership losses over the decade.

TABLE 7

UNIONS THAT GAINED 100,000 MEMBERS OR MORE, 1966–76

Union	Membership (in thousands)			Increase 1966–76[1]	
	1966	1974	1976	Number (in thousands)	Percent
State, County Employees	281	648	750	469	166.9
Teachers	125	444	446	321	256.8
Teamsters (Ind.)	1,651	1,973	1,889	238	14.4
Steelworkers	1,068	1,300	1,300	232	21.7
Service Employees	349	500	575	226	64.8
Retail Clerks	500	651	699	199	39.8
Communications Workers	321	499	483	162	50.0
Laborers	475	650	627	152	32.0

[1] Includes several unions where a portion of the membership gain was due to a merger with one or more other unions. Excludes merged unions where the membership of the smaller organization represented a significant proportion of the total and the combined membership did not increase 100,000.

TABLE 8

DISTRIBUTION OF MEMBERSHIP OF NATIONAL UNIONS AND EMPLOYEE ASSOCIATION BY INDUSTRY GROUP AND AFFILIATION, 1974

Industry group	Total unions and associations			Unions						Associations		
				AFL-CIO			Unaffiliated					
	Number[1]	Members[2]		Number[1]	Members[2]		Number[1]	Members[2]		Number[1]	Members[2]	
		Number (thousands)	Percent		Number (thousands)	Percent		Number (thousands)	Percent		Number (thousands)	Percent
Total[3]	212	24,194	100.0	111	16,879	100.0	64	4,705	100.0	37	2,610	100.0
Manufacturing	98	9,144	37.8	70	6,746	40.0	28	2,398	51.0	—	—	—
Ordnance and accessories	14	102	.4	7	91	.5	7	11	.2	—	—	—
Food and kindred products (including beverages)	26	908	3.8	17	570	3.4	9	338	7.2	—	—	—
Tobacco manufactures	6	43	.2	4	42	.2	2	1	(4)	—	—	—
Textile mill products	11	169	.7	6	158	.9	5	11	.2	—	—	—
Apparel and other finished products made from fabrics and similar materials	14	750	3.1	11	734	4.3	3	16	.3	—	—	—
Lumber and wood products, except furniture	18	261	1.1	10	254	1.5	8	7	.1	—	—	—
Furniture and fixtures	13	220	.9	8	190	1.1	5	29	.6	—	—	—
Paper and allied products	21	366	1.5	16	324	1.9	5	41	.9	—	—	—
Printing, publishing, and allied industries	19	359	1.5	13	339	2.0	6	20	.4	—	—	—
Chemicals and allied products	22	268	1.1	17	232	1.4	5	36	.8	—	—	—
Petroleum refining and related industries	10	82	.3	7	71	.4	3	11	.2	—	—	—
Rubber and miscellaneous plastics products	24	275	1.1	17	248	1.5	7	27	.6	—	—	—
Leather and leather products	16	128	.5	13	125	.7	3	4	.1	—	—	—
Stone, clay, glass, and concrete products	17	325	1.3	14	281	1.7	3	43	.9	—	—	—
Primary metals industries	14	817	3.4	11	691	4.1	3	126	2.7	—	—	—
Fabricated metal products, except ordnance, machinery, and transportation equipment . .	28	726	3.0	19	516	3.1	9	210	4.5	—	—	—
Machinery, except electrical	16	726	3.0	11	425	2.5	5	302	6.4	—	—	—
Electrical machinery, equipment, and supplies	14	1,074	4.4	10	820	4.9	4	254	5.4	—	—	—
Transportation equipment	16	1,144	4.7	10	319	1.9	6	825	17.5	—	—	—
Professional, scientific, and controlling instruments	12	65	.3	7	37	.2	5	28	.6	—	—	—
Miscellaneous manufacturing industries	40	338	1.4	30	282	1.7	10	56	1.2	—	—	—
Nonmanufacturing	104	9,705	40.1	73	7,687	45.5	28	1,833	39.0	3	185	7.1
Mining and quarrying (including crude petroleum and natural gas production) . . .	17	372	1.5	10	141	.8	7	231	4.9	—	—	—
Contract construction (building and special trade)	28	2,738	11.3	21	2,634	15.6	7	103	2.2	—	—	—
Transportation	37	2,343	9.7	28	1,297	7.7	9	1,046	22.2	—	—	—
Telephone and telegraph	11	672	2.8	9	606	3.6	2	65	1.4	—	—	—
Electric, gas, and sanitary services (including water)	11	243	1.0	9	234	1.4	2	8	.2	—	—	—
Wholesale and retail trade	22	1,329	5.5	13	1,066	6.3	9	263	5.6	—	—	—
Finance, insurance, and real estate	5	32	.1	4	31	.2	1	1	(4)	—	—	—
Service industries	48	1,850	7.6	27	1,571	9.3	18	94	2.0	3	185	7.1
Agriculture and fishing	9	36	.1	5	18	.1	4	18	.4	—	—	—
Nonmanufacturing (classification not available)	7	91	.4	6	88	.5	1	3	.1	—	—	—
Government	101	5,345	22.1	39	2,447	14.5	25	474	10.1	37	2,425	93.0
Federal	53	1,433	5.9	26	955	5.7	23	437	9.3	4	42	1.6
State	52	1,035	4.3	13	438	2.6	3	6	.1	36	592	22.7
Local	37	2,876	11.9	18	1,054	6.2	2	31	.7	17	1,791	68.6

[1] These columns are nonadditive; many organizations have membership in more than one industry group.
[2] Number of members computed by applying reported percentage figures to total membership, including membership outside the United States.
[3] 143 unions reported an estimated distribution by industry; for 32 unions, the Bureau estimated industrial composition.

Estimates were also made for 5 of the 37 employee associations. 3 employee associations have members not in government. The Bureau believed these to be in service industries.
[4] Less than 0.05 percent.

NOTE: Because of rounding, sums of individual items may not equal totals.

TABLE 9

DISTRIBUTION OF MEMBERSHIP OF NATIONAL UNIONS AND EMPLOYEE ASSOCIATIONS BY STATE AND AFFILIATION, 1974

State	Total union and association member-ship	Unions[1]				Associations			Total union and association membership as a percent of employees in non-agricultural establishments	
		Total	AFL-CIO	Unaffiliated		Total	Profes-sional and State associa-tions[3]	Municipal associa-tions[4]	Percent	Ranking
				National	Local unions[2]					
All States	23,408	20,566	15,639	4,453	475	2,842	2,607	235	29.9	—
Alabama[5]	278	223	199	23	1	55	55	([6])	23.9	26
Alaska.	45	32	24	7	([6])	13	13	—	37.2	7
Arizona[5]	156	118	98	20	([6])	38	37	1	21.1	32
Arkansas[5]	116	108	95	13	—	8	8	—	18.1	37
California	2,607	2,212	1,721	434	58	394	281	113	33.3	12
Colorado	220	181	152	28	([6])	39	38	1	23.0	29
Connecticut	382	317	235	76	6	65	63	2	30.3	19
Delaware	55	47	35	8	4	8	8	—	23.5	27
Florida	416	354	317	36	2	62	59	3	14.7	46
Georgia[5]	287	264	221	42	([6])	23	23	([6])	15.8	44
Hawaii	129	121	84	29	7	8	8	—	38.7	6
Idaho	54	40	30	9	1	13	13	([6])	20.6	34
Illinois	1,684	1,584	1,161	377	46	100	100	([6])	37.1	8
Indiana	729	670	448	211	11	59	59	—	36.2	10
Iowa[5]	251	212	152	59	1	39	38	1	25.1	24
Kansas[5]	137	110	95	13	2	27	27	([6])	17.5	41
Kentucky	309	269	184	80	4	41	41	—	28.9	20
Louisiana	211	194	169	21	3	17	17	—	17.7	39
Maine	83	59	50	7	3	24	23	1	22.8	30
Maryland-District of Columbia	545	462	375	72	15	83	78	5	25.5	23
Massachusetts	632	579	461	102	16	53	51	2	26.6	22
Michigan	1,388	1,255	599	649	7	133	126	7	42.4	2
Minnesota	421	375	293	75	7	46	46	([6])	28.3	21
Mississippi[5]	93	84	76	8	([6])	9	9	—	13.3	48
Missouri.	595	575	422	146	7	20	20	—	33.4	11
Montana	73	60	51	10	([6])	13	13	([6])	31.1	17
Nebraska[5]	99	83	72	11	([6])	15	15	—	17.8	38
Nevada[5]	81	71	59	12	([6])	10	10	([6])	31.4	16
New Hampshire . . .	58	46	37	6	2	12	12	([6])	19.0	36
New Jersey	898	786	590	165	31	112	101	11	32.3	13
New Mexico	63	51	41	10	([6])	12	12	—	17.6	40
New York	3,215	2,693	2,275	369	48	522	448	74	45.4	1
North Carolina[5] . .	201	140	116	24	([6])	61	61	—	9.8	50
North Dakota[5] . . .	38	29	19	10	([6])	9	9	—	19.7	35
Ohio	1,522	1,389	978	358	54	133	132	1	36.4	9
Oklahoma	148	132	111	19	2	16	16	—	16.8	42
Oregon	270	222	171	50	1	48	47	1	32.2	14
Pennsylvania	1,849	1,695	1,291	359	45	154	154	([6])	40.9	4
Rhode Island. . . .	111	101	81	19	1	11	11	([6])	30.3	18
South Carolina[5] . .	105	82	72	9	([6])	23	23	—	10.3	49
South Dakota[5] . . .	31	23	18	5	—	9	9	—	15.1	45
Tennessee[5]	328	295	244	48	3	34	33	1	20.9	33
Texas[5]	620	567	472	83	11	53	51	2	14.2	47
Utah[5]	94	65	51	14	([6])	29	28	1	21.5	31
Vermont	37	28	22	6	1	9	9	—	23.2	28
Virginia[5]	288	247	178	46	23	41	41	([6])	16.1	43
Washington	485	438	344	82	13	47	46	1	40.6	5
West Virginia	239	218	126	80	12	21	21	—	41.9	3
Wisconsin.	548	490	381	103	6	58	54	4	32.1	15
Wyoming[5]	33	25	20	4	([6])	8	8	([6])	24.3	25
Membership not classifiable[7]	149	146	121	4	20	4	4	—	—	—

[1] Based on reports from 129 national labor unions and estimates for 46. Also included are local unions directly affiliated with the AFL-CIO and members in single-firm and local unaffiliated unions.

[2] For source of membership in single-firm and local unaffiliated unions, see Unaffiliated Intrastate and Single-Employer Unions, 1967, Bulletin 1640 (Bureau of Labor Statistics, 1969).

[3] Includes members of 37 professional and State employee associations.

[4] Membership in municipal associations was reduced by 30,000 to eliminate duplication of professional members included in the previous column. Membership by State is based on unpublished data. For other statistics on municipal associations, see Municipal Public Employee Associations, Bulletin 1702 (Bureau of Labor Statistics, 1971).

[5] Has a right-to-work law.

[6] Less than 500 members.

[7] Includes local unions directly affiliated with the AFL-CIO.

NOTE: Because of rounding, sums of individual items may not equal totals.

TABLE 10

INTERVALS AT WHICH NATIONAL UNIONS AND EMPLOYEE ASSOCIATIONS HOLD CONVENTIONS

Interval between conventions	Total unions and associations		Unions				Associations
			Total		AFL-CIO	Unaffiliated	
	Number	Percent	Number	Percent			
All unions and associations	212	100.0	175	100.0	111	64	37
3 months	1	.5	1	.6	—	1	—
6 months . . . . ·	9	4.2	8	4.6	1	7	1
1 year	64	30.2	32	18.3	10	22	32
2 years . . . . · .	49	23.1	45	25.7	33	12	4
3 years	19	9.0	19	10.9	15	4	—
4 years	37	17.5	37	21.1	31	6	—
5 years	25	11.8	25	14.3	18	7	—
No convention	3	1.4	3	1.7	—	3	—
Information not available.	2	.9	2	1.1	1	1	—
Determined by referendum.	—	—	—	—	—	—	—
Other	3	1.4	3	1.7	2	1	—

NOTE: Because of rounding, sums of individual items may not equal totals.

UNION CONVENTIONS SCHEDULED FOR 1979

DATE	ORGANIZATION	PLACE	DATE	ORGANIZATION	PLACE
Apr. 22	Mechanics Educational Society	Niagara Falls, N.Y.	Sept. 10–14	Painters	Chicago
			Sept. 10–15	Amalgamated Transit Union	Los Angeles
May 14–18	Insurance Workers	Monticello, N.Y.	Sept. 12–13	Public Employee Dept.	Washington
May 14–19	Railway & Airline Clerks	Toronto	Sept. 14–16	Vermont	Burlington
May 22–25	Pennsylvania	Philadelphia	Sept. 16–20	Illinois	Springfield
June 4–15	Flint Glass Workers	New Orleans	Sept. 17–20	Florida	Hollywood
June 14	Actors & Artistes	New York	Sept. 17–22	Oregon	Coos Bay
June 18–20	Grain Millers	Minneapolis	Sept. 19–20	Industrial Union Dept.	San Francisco
June 20–23	Utility Workers	Washington	Sept. 21–22	Wyoming	Casper
June 25–27	Idaho	Pocatello	Sept. 24–26	Nebraska	Lincoln
July 2–6	Newspaper Guild	Providence, R.I.	Oct. 8	Telegraph Workers	Vancouver, B.C.
July 2–6	Teachers	San Francisco	Oct. 15–19	Woodworkers	St. Paul, Minn.
July 12–20	Coopers	Cleveland	Oct. 17–19	West Virginia	Charleston
July 16–20	Aluminum Workers	Kalispell, Mont.	Oct. 24–26	Georgia	Jekyll Island
July 16–20	Communications Workers	Detroit	Oct. 29–31	Train Dispatchers	Chicago
July 25–28	Texas	Austin	Nov. 1–3	Massachusetts	Boston
Aug. 6–10	Railroad Signalmen	Chicago	Nov. 11–14	International Labor Press Association	Washington
Aug. 13–17	Lathers	Atlanta			
Aug. 13–17	Oil, Chemical & Atomic Workers	Hollywood, Fla.	Nov. 12–13	Union Label & Service Trades Dept.	Washington
Aug. 13–17	Plasterers	New Orleans	Nov. 12–13	Maritime Trades Dept.	Washington
Aug. 16–18	Montana	Helena	Nov. 13–14	Dept. for Professional Employees	Washington
Aug. 18–24	Typographical Union	St. Paul, Minn.			
Aug. 26–31	Allied Industrial Workers	Atlanta	Nov. 28	Flight Engineers	Jerusalem, Israel
Sept. 9–12	Minnesota	Minneapolis	Nov. 28–30	Oklahoma	Tulsa

Labor on Politics and Foreign Affairs

EXCERPTS FROM THE SPEECH OF GEORGE MEANY AT THE OPENING OF THE 12th CONVENTION OF THE AFL-CIO

The greatest commitment this nation can make toward human rights at home is full employment. To us, unemployment is not only a waste—it is a denial of human rights.

Recently, President Carter announced his support for the Humphrey-Hawkins bill. We take that announcement as a solemn commitment. But a commitment is not enough.

Full employment promises must be backed up with comprehensive, effective programs that will meet that goal. Anything less is unacceptable because not only do the American people have a right to a job, they also have a human right to expect their government to fulfill its promises.

The 4 percent unemployment rate set forth in Humphrey-Hawkins is a realistic, achievable goal. The record proves that fact.

In January of 1969, when unfortunately Arthur Burns returned to Washington after eight years of absence, unemployment was 3.4 percent and inflation was 4.2 percent.

That was nine years ago—nine years filled with economic misery caused by the economic policies of Dr. Arthur F. Burns.

Enacting the Humphrey-Hawkins Full Employment and Balanced Growth Act and then providing policies and programs to make it work will set America back on the road toward full employment and toward alleviating the misery caused by widespread joblessness.

The election year of 1976 ended with an official unemployment rate of 7.9 percent. In reality, 10 million Americans who wanted and needed full-time jobs could not find them.

Today, the official unemployment rate has gone down to 6.9 percent. But there are still almost 10 million Americans who cannot find the full-time work they want and need.

Three million of these workers went the entire year without being able to find work. For them, the unemployment rate was 100 percent every day and every month of the year. About 20 million workers were out of work at least once during the year. Don't those statistics prove that something must be done?

What did it cost America not to have full employment in 1977?

In terms of budget deficits, a popular benchmark in the office of administration economic experts, it cost $61 billion—practically the entire budget deficit for the year.

In terms of the gross national product, unemployment cost more than $220 billion in lost output of goods and services, about $1,000 for every man, woman and child.

That is pure, unadulterated waste that is of itself a major contributing factor to inflation.

Consider the inflationary impact of keeping 14 percent of U.S. productive capacity idle. Firms with idle plant and equipment still pay for the machinery, pay property taxes, pay for maintenance and guards. Those costs are paid by all of us in higher prices for the products that were being produced.

For the unemployed and their families, the costs cannot even be estimated. There is no way to put a dollar value on human costs—like the mental anxiety that comes with unemployment, the fear of harassment over unpaid bills, idle hours, loss of self-esteem, stresses and strains on family relationships, lost physical health.

Continued high unemployment in America has created a new segregation between those who work and those who are always jobless. It is a segregation that is both brutal and dehumanizing.

Frankly, we must note that promises and speeches will not do the job. This bleak picture will only improve when there is strong action by the President and the Congress.

We hear a great deal of talk these days from economists inside and outside of government about an acceptable level of unemployment around 6 percent. What this really means is that we can live with a permanent rate of unemployment at that level.

The people who smugly decide that a 6 percent overall rate of unemployment is acceptable fail to spell out just what this actually means.

For example, 6 percent unemployment would mean approximately 32 percent permanent unemployment for black teenagers, 15 percent for white teenagers and 10 percent permanent unemployment for all of our black employables.

What would this mean in human terms? What would this mean in regard to the social structure of our nation for the future?

I am sure that the answers to these questions are obvious and frightening to anyone interested in the preservation of our American way of life.

We also hear these same voices stressing the importance of building up business confidence in the economic future of America.

This would be done by various concessions to business on tax relief, all designed to add to business profitability.

The same old trickle-down theory is advanced. If we make business more profitable, somehow or other those at the bottom of the economic ladder will benefit.

We believe the way to restore confidence throughout America is to set a goal of 4 million new jobs a year for the next four years. That is the only way unemployment is going to be reduced substantially.

That means 76,000 jobs a week for the next 208 weeks.

With that kind of commitment, the President would meet both of his major goals: full employment and a balanced budget.

Unless the Administration is honestly willing to make such a commitment and back it up with an economic stimulus program that won't be cut in half at the last minute neither goal will be met.

Real job-creating programs are what the economy needs. Tax cuts for business will not do the job.

Programs like an extra $5 billion in accelerated public works. In addition, funds should be provided for building the sewer and water systems and transportation facilities needed for a healthy economy.

Such a program would create more jobs than $10 billion in tax cuts. Of course, in addition, there is a return to the Treasury from taxes paid by people who go back to work.

So, the economists figure the net cost to the federal budget of $5 billion investment in public works would be about $2.75 billion, as opposed to a more than $7 billion net cost for $10 billion in tax cuts.

Three times President Carter's predecessor vetoed the public works program before we were able to secure passage of a $2 billion program. This year, the Congress increased the program to $4 billion, double President Carter's original proposal. An estimated 126,500 direct jobs at construction sites will be created by this program, plus an additional 66,000 indirect jobs in supplier industries. The so-called ripple effect will bring another 362,500 jobs, or a total of 555,000 jobs.

But, public works alone will not be enough.

America needs housing and housing construction can be the single most effective economic stimulus in terms of jobs and in terms of fighting inflation. Reducing home mortgage interest rates to 6 percent would lower monthly payments for an average house by more than $60 per month, enabling more families to buy homes.

Foreign trade is the guerrilla warfare of economics. And right now, the U.S. economy is being ambushed.

One by one, our manufacturing industries are being picked off. Now, the target is the steel industry.

What is most galling is that the imported steel is cheaper, not because U.S. wage rates are so much higher, but because foreign countries subsidize their steel industries so that they can undercut U.S. companies. When the U.S. steel industry is destroyed, the United States would become dependent on foreign sources and without a steel industry of our own, the foreign countries could charge whatever they want.

Obviously, economic blackmail doesn't just apply to oil.

The United States is playing the game of foreign trade by a different set of rules than most other nations. And we are losing the game badly.

The old rules about foreign trade no longer apply. In this era of closed economies and multinational corporations who operate like the Barbary pirates, the United States sticks stubbornly to old policies that are no longer appropriate or workable.

The situation is going from bad to worse.

While businesses are still exporting today's jobs, they are also exporting tomorrow's jobs.

When a U.S. firm sells the latest technology to a foreign country—technology that is not being introduced into U.S. plants—it is exporting the jobs that technology could produce right here at home.

A presidential commitment to full employment would be shallow if the Administration failed to take strong action to protect American industry from cutthroat and often illegal foreign competition.

The Administration negotiated what is called an orderly market agreement for color television sets with the Japanese, but it was too late to save the last color TV plant in the United States. And, as soon as the agreement was negotiated, the Japanese shifted production to microwave ovens and began flooding that U.S. market.

Will an "orderly market agreement" for microwave ovens be negotiated before or after the last U.S. plant closes? And what industry will be next?

America needs a new foreign trade policy. Without one, full employment will never be achieved. Imports must be regulated. Anti-dumping laws must be swiftly enforced. Tax breaks that encourage U.S. firms to go abroad must be cancelled.

The United States must make it clear to every other nation of the world: the use of tariff or non-tariff barriers to bar U.S. products will result in swift, retaliatory action by this government.

We are willing to buy goods from the rest of the world, but unless America has a productive base for its economy, there will be no paychecks to enable us to buy anything from anybody.

Government policy makers are quick to blame oil imports for the trade deficit. But oil is only part of the problem.

Japan and West Germany—both dependent on imported oil, like the United States—have huge trade surpluses.

Imports of manufactured goods rose by $2 billion, more than the rise in oil imports in the first half of 1977. Imports from low-wage countries are soaring as a result of zero tariffs on a host of goods.

Free trade is a joke and a myth. And, a government trade policy predicated on old ideas of "free trade" is worse than a joke; it is a prescription for disaster.

The answer is fair trade. Do unto others as they do to us—barrier for barrier, closed door for closed door.

Not here with us—their voices stilled by employer violations of their human rights—are the hundreds of thousands of American workers who want and need union representation. The freedom of workers to associate together in unions, a freedom essential to the survival of democracy, is regularly and repeatedly denied American workers through violations of the nation's labor law.

This year alone, more than 7,000 of these workers will be illegally fired by their employers and ultimately ordered reinstated by the National Labor Relations Board.

Each of these workers is used by employers as an example to all other employees of what happens to "union agitators." And, when it takes the law one, two, even 20 years or more to gain justice for these workers—that, too, is used as an example of what the future holds for workers who seek to exercise their right to union representation.

J. P. Stevens is outstanding in this area.

Business groups and trade associations will try to tell you that it is only J. P. Stevens that engages in such a reign of terror against unions and the workers that support unions.

Regrettably, that is not true.

Thousands of companies—big and small, blue chippers and those who aspire to be blue chippers—have decided it is cheaper to break the law and risk getting caught than it is to respect the legal and human rights of their employees.

That is a sad commentary on the state of the free enterprise system: break the law, it is cheaper.

And, when a law is proposed that would take the profit out of violating the law—a law that would only crack down on the violators—the response of a large segment of the business community is all-out opposition and a vitriolic attack on the labor movement unmatched since the days of the American Plan.

What has made the American economy great is the fact that workers are able to buy what they produce. They are able to do so because of collective bargaining. Yet, to circumvent collective bargaining, businesses use illegal tactics to fight union organization efforts.

Collective bargaining is a democratic institution. It provides millions of workers with a mechanism to have a say in their lives. Without it, the worker is weak and vulnerable to total domination by employers.

The attacks on the labor movement and collective bargaining are particularly disturbing when they come from many of the same businesses who look to the labor movement for support of their program. Particularly during Democratic administrations with Democratic congresses—which are supposedly more friendly to workers—businesses seek allies in the labor movement for pet programs to help their industry.

But today, business is out to gut labor law reform either through silent support for those who are breaking the law or through all-out opposition.

We won't hold our breath waiting for business support for this law-and-order legislation. The bill will be coming up in the Senate early next year and we are going to fight harder for this bill than any bill since the passage of the Wagner Act.

The opposition may resort to a filibuster or try to kill the bill by literally hundreds of amendments. We must be ready for both tactics. Just as unfair employers seek to use delay to defeat the hopes of workers for their own union, their allies seek to use delay to frustrate and defeat labor law reform.

But, all of their delaying tactics can not hide the facts:

■ A 115 percent increase in employer violations of the law since 1960.

■ More than double the number of workers illegally discriminated against by their employers.

■ A backlog of cases double that of 10 years ago.

■ A median delay of eight months from the time an election is requested until it is held.

■ A median delay of two years from the filing of a complaint about an unfair labor practice to court enforcement.

That is a pretty poor human rights records right here at home. A country that preaches human rights to Russia and Chile, should practice human rights in Roanoke Rapids and Charlotte.

For most Americans, the phrase "human rights" seems to bring to mind first the Soviet Union, where human rights are denied in a wholesale fashion.

This convention will hear from Vladimir Bukovsky, himself a living testimonial to the need for human rights.

His story is a story of oppression of human thought so brutal, so inhumane, so terrible, that it is hard to believe. Years in mental institutions which are really jails; torture, both physical and mental, deprivation, isolation and misery. And for what crime? The crime of thinking a different thought, of uttering a different word, of vocally yearning for freedom.

But this convention will not hear the voices of Andrei Sakharov, Nedezhda Mandelshtam, Aleksandr Podrabinek, Anatoli Marchenko, Vladimir Borison. Their voices will be silent here.

The Soviet Union denied them the right to come to Los Angeles and return home again. The fact of their silence here is truly a shout for human rights that echoes around the world.

Today, the Congress has made it "possible" to hear the voices of the oppressor—the so-called trade unionists of the Soviet Union—right here in our own land. But, it is not possible for us to hear the voices of Sakharov and the others we want to hear, the voices we asked to hear, the voices that remain locked behind the Iron Curtain.

By his strong statements in support of human rights, President Carter launched the greatest foreign policy initiative attempted in this half century. With that single action, he provided the American people with a foreign policy that reflected the greatness of their nation.

Yet, there are many who would like to see the President forget about human rights. The businessmen, who want to make more profitable deals with dictators of the right and the left are nervous about talk of human rights. After all, as they see it, there is no profit in that kind of talk.

And, then we have the so-called foreign policy experts who view diplomacy as a game or a ballet, forgetting that human rights are natural God-given rights and not barter for international wheeling and dealing.

Then, there are the Brezhnevs and the Pinochets, the Vorsters and the Amins—those who derive power from denial of human rights. They are worried about what such notions as liberty and freedom can do to an absolutist's regime. To them, a free mind is a dangerous thing.

We hope and pray that the President will continue to speak out on human rights.

It, truly, is the only policy the United States can pursue and remain true to its heritage.

Similarly, the President's new approaches toward relations with Africa and Latin America are heartening.

The strong U.S. support for majority rule in Rhodesia and South Africa is the only course a nation, based on democratic principles, can take. But it is evident that Rhodesia and South Africa will need more than prodding to eliminate the disgusting policy of apartheid.

In Europe, NATO needs to be strengthened and revitalized, and our allies encouraged to take an important role in the fight to encourage human rights.

And, the United States is still without a foreign policy for Asia in the aftermath of Vietnam.

In the Middle East, however, there are both positive and negative developments. The visit by President Sadat to Israel is hopefully the beginning of the only true process to achieving peace—face-to-face negotiations between the parties directly involved.

The visit constitutes de facto recognition of the State of Israel, a vital element to peace. All of Israel's neighbors must recognize and guarantee the right of Israel to exist or there will never be peace in that region.

The United States can best serve the cause of peace in the Middle East by strong and continuing support for Israel. Sudden shifts in administration positions only serve to increase the tension and the likelihood that Israel's neighbors will probe what they believe to be weakness in the U.S. support for Israel. The United States can help bring the parties together. But we can not, we must not, seek to impose a peace agreement on Israel.

Now is a time for strength, not vacillation. It is a time for courage, not a quick fix.

The American labor movement's enduring support for Israel is a product of our concern for human rights. While we have close ties with the Histadrut, our support is for Israel and her people.

And that support shall never waver or flinch.

THE AFL-CIO POSITIONS ON LEGISLATION IN THE SENATE

1. Minimum Wage (1)

President Carter signed into law in 1977 labor-backed legislation making significant improvements in the federal minimum wage law. During Senate debate, Sen. Peter Domenici (R-N.Mex.) tried to establish a subminimum wage rate for full-time young workers. Fearing that the youth subminimum wage rate would result in employers firing older workers to hire underpaid younger workers, the AFL-CIO opposed this amendment. By a 44-49 vote on Oct. 7 the Senate rejected this proposal.

For—Wrong.   Against—Right.

2. Minimum Wage (2)

Leading big business opposition to minimum wage legislation, Sen. John Tower (R-Tex.) tried to double the existing $250,000 annual sales volume test that exempts small businesses with earnings under this amount from paying a fair minimum wage. Tower's amendment would have removed 3.8 million workers from minimum wage protection. It was blocked when Sen. Dale Bumpers (D-

Ark.) countered with an amendment to increase the exemption in two steps to $325,000 by 1980. Tower's effort to table the Bumpers amendment failed by a 38–51 margin on Oct. 7.

For tabling—Wrong.   Against—Right.

3. Strip Mining Controls

President Carter signed into law in 1977 labor endorsed legislation establishing federal minimum standards for state strip mining control laws. The legislation had been twice vetoed by President Ford. During Senate debate, Sen. Bennett Johnston (D-La.) offered a crippling amendment designed to weaken enforcement of federal minimum standards. The Senate rejected it by a 39–51 vote on May 19.

For—Wrong.   Against—Right.

4. Food Stamps for Strikers

During Senate consideration of a major farm bill which included an extension of the food stamp program, Sen. Strom Thurmond (R-S.C.) attempted to deny strikers and their families food stamp benefits. Strikers are entitled to food stamp benefits if they meet the same stringent eligibility tests required of all other food stamp recipients. The Thurmond amendment was beaten 38–56 on May 24.

For—Wrong.   Against—Right.

5. Job Safety

A relic of the Ford Administration designed to delay implementation of occupational safety and health rules was an administrative requirement that any proposed OSHA job safety standard be accompanied by an impact statement assessing the economic effect of the proposed regulation. With the Carter Administration presently reviewing this time-consuming process, Sen. James McClure (R-Idaho) during debate on the Labor-HEW appropriations bill, offered an amendment to write the requirement into law. Strongly opposed by labor, McClure's amendment was defeated 41–47 on June 28.

For—Wrong.   Against—Right.

6. Public Service Jobs

To encourage economic recovery through lower unemployment the AFL-CIO in early 1977 recommended significant increases in federal funds for public service jobs programs. Higher funding levels were provided in an economic stimulus appropriations measure providing monies for a wide variety of jobs programs. During debate on the measure Sen. Richard Schweiker (R-Pa.) tried to slash public service jobs funds by $3.9 billion. This would have prevented a boost in public service employment from 310,000 to 750,000 jobs in 1977. The amendment was defeated 32–47 on May 2.

For—Wrong.   Against—Right.

7. Housing Funds (1)

Another component of labor's economic recovery plan was increased federal investment in government housing and community development programs. During debate on legislation setting tentative spending targets for various federal programs in fiscal 1978, the AFL-CIO supported an amendment by Senators William Proxmire (D-Wis.) and Edward Brooke (R-Mass.) to increase by $500 million community development aid for economically depressed cities, towns and counties. Without these funds community development activities underway in many jurisdictions would have been cut back. The amendment was approved by a 68–28 vote on May 4.

For—Right.   Against—Wrong.

8. Housing Funds (2)

Another Proxmire-Brooke amendment to the fiscal 1978 budget bill restored $6.2 billion in budget authority for assistance to low and middle income housing programs. Additional federal funds for low and middle income housing programs lessen the inflationary impact of higher housing costs resulting from housing shortages while at the same time creating many new job opportunities in housing construction. On May 4 the Senate also approved this amendment by a 57–39 vote.

For—Right.   Against—Wrong.

9. Water Projects

President Carter was rebuffed in his effort to trim federal spending by slashing funds for a number of water resource projects in various stages of construction throughout the United States. At a time of high unemployment and severe droughts in the West, the AFL-CIO strongly opposed this action. During debate on a public works jobs bill, Sen. Bennett Johnston (D-La.) offered an amendment prohibiting the President from withholding funds for 19 water projects. By a 65–24 vote on Mar. 10 the amendment was approved.

For—Right.   Against—Wrong.

10. Tax Breaks for Business

Direct federal job spending has proved more effective than tax breaks in reducing unemployment and thus stimulating economic recovery. Unfortunately, President Carter's 1977 economic recovery plan relied on tax breaks for business and individuals rather than direct federal job creating expenditures. During Senate consideration of tax cut legislation, the Carter Administration reversed directions and dropped its support of tax relief. Although the Senate then scrapped individual tax cuts, it refused to drop the $2.4 billion in tax giveaways to business. On

Apr. 21 the Senate defeated 20–74 a motion by Sen. Dale Bumpers (D-Ark.) to recommit the bill back to committee in order to eliminate the business tax breaks.

For recommittal—Right.   Against—Wrong.

11. Natural Gas Price Controls

The oil and gas lobby won a key victory in 1977 as the Senate voted to deregulate the price of new natural gas discovered after Jan. 1, 1977. Early in debate Sen. Henry Jackson (D-Wash.), leading labor and consumer opposition to deregulation, offered a motion to table an amendment aimed at ending federal price regulation of new natural gas. The Senate, however, rejected the tabling motion on a 46–52 vote on Sept. 22.

For tabling—Right.   Against—Wrong.

12. Emergency Gas Legislation

On the heels of 1976 winter gas shortages President Carter requested legislation, eventually approved, allowing for effective deregulation of natural gas prices for a period of six months. The AFL-CIO opposed this, urging instead legislation giving the President authority to divert gas from the unregulated intrastate market and allocate it to the interstate market where and as needed. An amendment to this effect by Sen. James Abourezk (D-S.D.) was defeated 31–58 on January 31.

For—Right.   Against—Wrong.

13. Nuclear Energy Development

Amid an intense anti-nuclear campaign by environmentalists, the Senate was forced to reduce from $150 million to $75 million the funds authorized for development of the Clinch River nuclear breeder reactor. This demonstration project is designed to test the feasibility of breeder reactor technology as a future source of electric power. The Carter Administration as part of its energy program had proposed termination of the Clinch River program—a recommendation which the AFL-CIO opposed. During debate on the legislation allocating funds for energy research programs, Sen. Dale Bumpers (D-Ark.) offered an amendment to reduce funds even further to a phase-out level of $33 million. The amendment was defeated 38–49 on July 11.

For—Wrong.   Against—Right.

14. Senate Reorganization

A proposal revising committee jurisdictions and making other changes to help the Senate streamline itself recommended elimination of the Post Office & Civil Service Committee. Its jurisdiction was to be transferred to other committees. The action effectively abolished the only

Senate forum available to federal and postal workers. The AFL-CIO urged that the committee be retained, but an amendment by Sen. Quentin Burdick (D-N.D.) to maintain the committee was tabled and thus killed by a 55–42 vote on Feb. 2.

For tabling—Wrong.   Against—Right.

15. Mine Safety

Legislation to improve federal mine safety laws by combining existing mine safety laws into one improved statute and transferring enforcement jurisdiction from the Interior Dept. to the Labor Dept. was signed into law by President Carter in 1977. Leading the industry opposition against the job safety bill, Sen. Orrin Hatch (R-Utah) during Senate debate offered a crippling amendment which would have retained separate weaker laws for coal and metal miners. His weakening amendment was rejected 30–66 on June 21.

For—Wrong.   Against—Right.

16. Congressional Election Financing

At present, federal financing is provided for Presidential candidates. The AFL-CIO supports legislation to extend public financing to congressional elections as well. In 1977, President Carter endorsed this election reform proposal. During debate on public financing legislation, the Senate was unable to overcome a Republican-led filibuster against the proposal. Three attempts by Majority Leader Robert Byrd (D-W.Va.) to invoke cloture and thus end debate were all defeated. The final key effort failed by a 52–46 vote on Aug. 2. Sixty votes are needed for cloture.

For cloture—Right.   Against—Wrong.

17. Union Political Rights (1)

During debate on the public financing bill, Sen. Jesse Helms (R-S.C.) led a right-wing, anti-union effort against union political rights. An amendment he offered to the bill would have prohibited labor unions from using funds collected under a union security agreement from being used for legitimate COPE-type activities such as non-partisan voter registration drives or get-out-the-vote efforts. No such restriction was applied to corporations under his amendment. On a tabling motion by Sen. Howard Cannon (D-Nev.), the Helms amendment was rejected by a 67–25 vote on Aug. 3.

For tabling—Right.   Against—Wrong.

18. Union Political Rights (2)

Conservatives made still another effort to handcuff union political activities. Sen Robert Griffin (R-Mich.) attempted to gag labor's political voice by denying to unions and other groups the use of reduced postal rates to which any nonprofit membership organization is entitled. The Senate on Aug. 3 blocked Griffin's amendment when it approved 54–37 a tabling motion by Sen. Howard Cannon (D-Nev.).

For tabling—Right. Against—Wrong.

19. Rhodesia Boycott

The AFL-CIO long supported renewed U.S. compliance with a United Nations embargo against the racist Rhodesian government. The United States had complied with the embargo until 1971 when Sen. Harry Byrd (Ind.-Va.) won Senate approval of a proviso prohibiting U.S. adherence to the trading ban involving strategic materials such as chromium ore. Although numerous attempts to reverse the Byrd amendment had failed previously the Senate by a 66–26 vote on Mar. 15 approved legislation repealing this provision.

For—Right. Against—Wrong.

20. Social Security

Legislation to stabilize the financing of the social security system while increasing employer-employee tax contributions for the first time shifted a higher portion of the tax responsibility to the employer. During Senate debate Sen. Carl Curtis (R-Nev.) offered an amendment to lower the increased employer taxes and thereby make employees pay a higher social security tax. Strongly opposed by the AFL-CIO, the Curtis amendment was defeated by a 40–50 vote on Nov. 3.

For—Wrong. Against—Right.

THE AFL-CIO POSITION ON LEGISLATION IN THE HOUSE OF REPRESENTATIVES

1. Labor Law Reform (1)

Conservatives were defeated in an attempt to sidetrack the Labor Law Reform bill and substitute for it an anti-union, employer-backed measure. By a 267–152 count on Oct. 4 the House, in a procedural vote, in effect upheld the rule which only allowed for debate on amendments germane to the substance of the Labor Law Reform legislation. Thus consideration of the anti-worker bill was blocked.

For the rule—Right. Against—Wrong.

2. Labor Law Reform (2)

In 1977 the House approved labor law reform legislation designed to better protect a worker's right to seek union representation. Endorsed by President Carter, the bill expedites the administration and procedures of the National Labor Relations Act while also strengthening penalties against labor law violators. The package of reforms contained in the legislation represents the most important revision in labor law since passage of the 1935 Wagner Act. Overcoming the concerted opposition of business and right-wing groups the House on Oct. 6 approved its version of the legislation by a 257–163 vote.

For—Right. Against—Wrong.

3. Minimum Wage (1)

The House rejected a move to establish a subminimum wage rate for non-student workers aged 18 or younger. An amendment offered by Rep. Robert Cornell (D-Wis.) would have allowed employers to pay these workers 85 percent of the minimum wage for the first six months. The AFL-CIO opposed the amendment on the basis that it would not relieve high teenage unemployment and would cause displacement of older workers by younger workers who could be paid less. The House rejected the amendment by a narrow 210–211 vote on Sept. 15.

For—Wrong. Against—Right.

4. Minimum Wage (2)

President Carter on Nov. 1 signed into law labor-backed minimum wage legislation. The final bill increased the minimum wage rate in four steps from the current $2.30 to $3.35 by 1981. The bill also made other significant improvements in the fair wage law. Despite strong opposition from business groups, the House on Oct. 20, approved the conference report on the bill by a 236–187 vote.

For—Right. Against—Wrong.

5. Situs Picketing Rights

House conservatives backed by some moderate Democrats helped defeat passage of labor-backed situs picketing. The legislation, a goal of organized labor for over a quarter of a century, would have reinstated equal rights for building trades workers to picket an entire job site—a right which industrial workers now have. By a 205–217 vote the House rejected the bill on March 23.

For—Right. Against—Wrong.

6. Hatch Act Reform

In debate on the Hatch Act Reform bill, Rep. John Ashbrook (R-Ohio) succeeded in securing House approval of an amendment to disallow unions from using funds for such legal political activities as non-partisan voter registration drives and get-out-the-vote efforts. Later, however, the House approved by a 266–139 vote on June 7 an amendment by Rep. Bill Clay (D-Mo.) effectively nullifying the anti-union Ashbrook amendment.

For—Right.   Against—Wrong.

7. Cargo Equity

To help rebuild the American Merchant Marine, protect the maritime environment and better assure the security of a portion of oil imports, the AFL-CIO backed legislation mandating that a percentage of U.S. oil be carried in American ships. With only 3 percent of oil imports now carried in American vessels, the bill would have boosted that percentage to 9.5 percent by 1981. The legislation would have created an estimated 20,000 maritime related jobs. The House, however, defeated the bill by a 165–257 vote on Oct. 19.

For—Right.   Against—Wrong.

8. Strip Mining Controls

The AFL-CIO endorsed legislation vetoed twice by President Ford providing for federal minimum standards for state strip mining control laws. This environmental bill was signed into law by President Carter in 1977. During House consideration, Rep. Robert Bauman (R-Md.) attempted to have the bill killed by recommitting it to committee. His effort failed by an 83–228 vote on Apr. 29.

For recommittal—Wrong.   Against—Right.

9. Food Stamps For Strikers

Striking workers and their families are entitled to food stamps as long as they comply with the stringent eligibility requirements under the program. During House consideration of a 1977 farm bill which included a four-year extension of the food stamp program, Rep. Richard Kelly (R-Fla.) offered an amendment to deny food stamps to strikers and their families. The House rejected the Kelly amendment by a 170–249 vote on July 27.

For—Wrong.   Against—right.

10. Job Safety

Every year since passage of the landmark job safety law, conservatives have attempted to weaken the Occupational Safety & Health Act. In 1977 Rep. Steven Symms (R-Idaho) tried to slash OSHA funding by $6.3 million for fiscal 1978. The House rejected this effort by a 162–231 vote on June 16.

For—Wrong.   Against—Right.

11. Economic Stimulus

Reacting to the need to provide more funds for economic recovery, the House, as part of its third budget resolution revising federal spending for fiscal year 1977, increased President Carter's proposed spending for jobs and local assistance. The extra monies were targeted to such programs as public works, public service jobs and youth employment. The conference report which added $3.4 billion for these economic stimulus programs was approved by a 226–173 vote on Mar. 4.

For—Right.   Against—Wrong.

12. Community Development Aid

In 1977 Congress completed action on legislation extending community development funding assistance to financially depressed cities and locales. During debate on the legislation an effort was made to delete a labor-backed spending formula giving priority to those urban areas most in need. The amendment offered by Rep. Mark Hannaford (D-Calif.) was defeated 149–261 on May 10.

For—Wrong.   Against—Right.

13. Aid to Cities and States

Congress approved legislation to extend and expand the program of counter-cyclical funds to help cities and state maintain public services and thus avoid massive layoff of public workers during periods of high unemployment. During House debate the AFL-CIO opposed an amendment by Rep. Les Aspin (D-Wis.) to rewrite the allocation formula so that a smaller share of the funds would have gone to areas with the highest unemployment. This amendment was beaten 127–216 on May 13.

For—Wrong.   Against—Right.

14. Water Projects

Federal funding of water resource projects has contributed significantly to the economic development of the nation in such areas as inland water transportation, energy power generation, flood control, water storage and irrigation. These projects have also provided thousands of job opportunities for American workers.

In early 1977, the Carter Administration announced its intention to terminate funding for a number of these projects. However, the House on June 14, during debate on a public works appropriations bill rejected 194–218 an Administration supported amendment by Rep. Silvio Conte (R-Mass.) and Butler Derrick (D-S.C.) to kill 16 water projects and cut back one other.

For—Wrong.   Against—Right.

15. Natural Gas Deregulation

Since the 1955 merger convention the AFL-CIO has fought efforts by the energy industry to deregulate federal price controls on natural gas. Deregulation would cost consumers billions of dollars and have a catastrophic effect on the economy. During House consideration of a national energy policy bill. Rep. Clarence Brown (R-Ohio) offered the industry's deregulation amendment which would cost consumers an estimated $71 billion by 1985. The House rejected Brown's amendment by a 199–227 vote on Aug. 3.

For—Wrong.   Against—Right.

16. Energy Tax Windfall

President Carter had recommended increased taxes on domestically produced oil in order to encourage conservation through higher prices. The AFL-CIO strongly opposed this rationing through higher taxes. During debate on House legislation which included the so-called crude oil equalization tax, Rep. James Jones (D-Okla.) tried to return a portion of these tax revenues to the oil industry rather than rebating all of the tax revenues to consumers. The AFL-CIO strongly opposed this amendment which was defeated by a 198–223 vote on Aug. 4.

For—Wrong.   Against—Right.

17. Nuclear Energy Development

To help meet the nation's energy demands the AFL-CIO has supported development of all energy resources to best determine their feasibility as future energy sources. As part of its energy program the Carter Administration proposed, however, that development of the Clinch River nuclear breeder reactor demonstration project be discontinued. During debate on Oct. 19 on a supplemental appropriations bill the House approved 252–165 an amendment by Rep. Tom Bevil (D-Ala.) restoring $80 million in funding for the Clinch River project.

For—Right.   Against—Wrong.

18. Mine Safety

Legislation to improve federal mine safety laws by consolidating and improving mine safety programs and transferring enforcement functions from the Interior Dept. to the Labor Dept. was signed into law by President Carter in 1977. During House debate on this bill Rep. Ronald Sarasin (R-Mass.) introduced a weaker substitute bill which would have maintained separate laws for hard rock and coal miners. The House rejected the Sarasin substitute by a 151–188 vote on July 15.

For—Wrong.   Against—Right.

19. Davis-Bacon Wages

President Carter's national energy program included recommendations to encourage energy conservation by authorizing funds for school, hopsital and public building insulation programs. During House debate on the legislation Rep. William Ford (D-Mich.) offered an amendment to extend the wage protections of the Davis-Bacon Act to workers installing insulation. His amendment

mandated the payment of the prevailing wage paid for similar work in their areas. By a 265–161 vote on Aug. 2 the House approved the Ford amendment.

For—Right.   Against—Wrong.

20. Social Security

In 1977 the Congress approved legislation to stabilize the financing of the social security system. During House consideration of the bill, Rep. William Ketchum (R-Calif.) offered a crippling amendment phasing out the present limitation on the outside earnings of a social security recipient thus increasing the number of eligible beneficiaries. An increase in employee payroll taxes would finance this provision. His amendment primarily benefits higher income beneficiaries working full time at the expense of higher taxes on low and middle income wage earners. The House approved the amendment by a 268–149 vote on Oct. 27.

For—Wrong.   Against—Right.

21. Education and Health Funding

During House consideration of 1978 Labor-HEW appropriations, Rep. Bob Michel (R-Ill.) attempted to slash $563.5 million in federal funds for 11 health, education and elderly programs. Opposed by labor, his amendment was beaten 72–334 on June 16.

For—Wrong.   Against—Right.

22. Rhodesia Boycott

In violation of a United Nations embargo against importing commodities from the racist Rhodesian government, the United States has been importing chromium ore since 1971. That year Sen. Harry Byrd (Ind-Va.) won Senate approval of a proviso prohibiting U.S. adherence to the boycott when it involved strategic materials such as chrome. In 1977, with the strong support of the Carter Administration, Congress approved legislation repealing the Byrd amendment. The House passed its version of the bill by a 250–146 vote on Mar. 14.

For—Right   Against—Wrong.

23. Aid to Consumers

Legislation to outlaw abusive tactics by bill collection agencies was passed by Congress in 1977 and signed into law by President Carter. The legislation curbed harassment of consumers at their workplace and disallowed such practices as late night phone calls and false representation. The House passed the consumer protection legislation by a narrow 199–198 vote on Apr. 4.

For—Right.   Against—Wrong.

DEFENSE AND DISARMAMENT

The AFL-CIO has historically been one of the strongest and most outspoken advocates of effective international disarmament, leading to world peace and a world in which scientific skills, technology and industrial capacities can be devoted solely to the attainment of a fuller and better life for all. Such disarmament must include, as the AFL-CIO's 9th Constitutional Convention said in 1971, "the prohibition of all weapons of mass destruction through an effective system of manned, on-site, international inspection, supervision and control."

Since World War II, the U.S. has taken the lead in both actions and proposals to achieve a reduction in arms and in international tensions, but progress has been slow. A drastic reduction in military forces following World War II was coupled with an offer to turn over nuclear resources to the UN, but both the UN's atomic energy control plan and President Eisenhower's atoms for peace plan were rejected by the Soviet Union.

In 1963, the AFL-CIO saluted President Kennedy for his role in the Anglo-American negotiations with the U.S.S.R. that resulted in the limited test-ban treaty on atmospheric blasts. The refusal of the Soviet Union to agree to international inspection, supervision and control resulted in the failure to prohibit underwater, space, and underground testing.

Also, in 1963, the AFL-CIO welcomed Congress' action establishing the Arms Control and Disarmament Agency "to provide impetus toward . . . an ultimate goal of the United States and a world which is free from the scourge of war and the dangers and burdens of armaments."

American labor has consistently supported international efforts to reduce tensions and remove the threat of a nuclear holocaust. A true, lasting peace and a reduction in tension and armaments must be reciprocal, balanced, in the mutual interest and guaranteed by some form of international inspection and control.

But the record of the Nixon-Ford-Kissinger years reflected a policy of appeasement and acquiescence to the publicly stated political and military objectives of the Soviet Union.

The SALT I agreement in 1972 granted the U.S.S.R. quantitative superiority in nuclear weapons over the U.S. While the agreement treated defensive weapons on the basis of equality—each country having the same number and size weapons—the interim five-year agreement on offensive weapons clearly gave the Soviet Union the advantage. It consigned U.S. land-based ICBM's to 65 percent of the Soviet level and U.S. nuclear submarines to 71 percent of the Soviet total, because of the U.S.

technological advantage and possession of MIRV's (multiple independently targetable warheads).

In addition to the strategic, offensive advantage given the USSR, the agreement encouraged the Soviets to continue their arms buildup and to expand weapons technology. Since then, the Soviet Union has developed a more advanced MIRV system than the U.S. and threatens to surpass the U.S. in military technological advantage.

At the same time, and while the U.S. has been decreasing its military expenditures at an annual rate of 3 percent, the Soviet Union continues to increase its military expenditures by an annual rate of 3 to 4 percent. This trend leads to a shift in the balance of military power and preparedness to the Soviet Union, which will constitute an unequaled threat to world peace and the viability of democratic governments, institutions and values throughout the world.

At its last convention, the AFL-CIO reaffirmed its commitment and belief in a defense establishment strong enough, but no stronger than necessary, to meet this nation's obligations. The AFL-CIO called "upon the government of the United States to provide for the common defense of this nation and of our allies with means sufficent not only to deter aggressive Soviet adventures, but to sustain the credibility of American leadership in the pursuit of world peace."

In February 1977, the Executive Council supported building the proposed B–1 bomber to maintain a strong national defense and a credible deterrent in the face of the growing sophistication of Soviet strategic abilities. The council said: "Like all Americans, we hope the new Administration is successful in its efforts to negotiate a workable and effective strategic arms limitation agreement. We believe the B–1 bomber program is essential if the United States is to have the best possible bargaining position in these talks, and thus hasten the day when major arms expenditures can be safely reduced."

While President Carter later decided to abandon the B–1 program—and it appears that Congress will make more efforts to restore funding for the program—the President expanded the promising Cruise missile program and continued development of the neutron bomb, which will be an important defensive weapon for NATO.

WESTERN EUROPE AND NATO

The AFL-CIO has always supported the concept of a strong Western alliance to ensure the security of the democratic societies within its boundaries.

In light of the increased violations of key sections of the Helsinki Agreement of 1975 by the Soviet Union and its satellites, the necessity for a unified and strengthened NATO is more apparent today than ever before.

Since the last convention of the AFL-CIO, we have witnessed with great concern the continued buildup of Warsaw Pact forces across central Europe, an escalation of provocative actions on the part of the Soviets on NATO's northern flank, and a serious weakening of NATO's capability on the southern flank.

These actions, linked with the growing strength and acceptance of "Euro-communism" in member states of the alliance, necessitate a greater emphasis on strengthening U.S. relations within the Atlantic community.

Developments on the Iberian Peninsula are encouraging for the free world, but continued weakness of the government in Italy is cause for concern.

EASTERN EUROPE

The Helsinki Accords on European Security and Cooperation have not brought from Eastern Europe the hoped for degree of cooperation with the West or provided them with more security against the political and military dominance of the Soviet Union. The Accords have seemingly made it easy for the Soviets to continue domination of Eastern Europe and use its people, territory and treasure as a base for the political subversion of Western Europe.

Secure behind boundaries guaranteed by the Western signatories at Helsinki, there are few indications that the USSR will change its policies, or come as serious participants to the Belgrade Conference.

The West's attempt to buy detente with Eastern Europe, through massive trade and technological gifts, may stir thoughts of independence but not overt acts of separation from Moscow. Overall, the trade and aid have brought handsome economic reward to Western traders with few, if any, benefits to the workers of the East or West. It has permitted the dictatorships of the East to piece together economies largely supportive of a military machine whose allegiance to Moscow cannot be doubted. This economic largess also helps the Soviet Union to support foreign political parties abroad, including the so-called national Communist parties in Western Europe.

We watch with concern the security provided Moscow and other East European tyrannies by Western policies. This gift provides Moscow and its satellites a wide latitude of options for increased trade with developing nations, usually reinforced by military missions.

ASIA

The March 1977 elections in India provide a ray of light and hope to millions of oppressed and exploited people, especially in the developing countries, in their struggle for dignity and a better life. The Executive Council pointed out in May that "the return of India to the fold of democratic nations may signal the reversal of a trend toward totalitarian rule that has grown for decades on a worldwide scale."

But the developments in India are, unfortunately, the lonely bright spot in a region where crushing poverty and massive populations are compounded by totalitarian rule, communist aggression and petty dictators busily enriching themselves through tyranny, exploitation, and repression. Authoritarian rules, whether military or civilian, continue to use and hide behind the facade of "development" and "social justice" to justify their denial of basic human rights and freedoms.

Labor movements throughout Asia, with few exceptions, suffer under government decrees denying them the right to strike and to organize and effectively represent their members. In some cases, authoritarian regimes attempt to use the labor movements in their countries to further their own designs for power and to control the growing industrial work forces demanding their rightful share.

The Executive Council in February 1976 noted that "economic and military assistance sought by the governments of those developing nations often serves to buttress despotic leadership and the inept management of bankrupt economies, rather than to alleviate human suffering or provide needed development assistance."

The AFL-CIO has consistently emphasized that the road to real development depends on the development of a strong and independent free trade union movement. The transition from subsistence economies and havens of exploitation for multinational corporations and autocratic rule will only be made when workers become consumers and truly benefit from their labor. But Asian workers will continue to be denied the only real hope of relief—through their own organizations—without the essential ingredient of freedom.

AFL-CIO President George Meany underlined this fact when he said, "Without freedom, there can be no free trade union movement. And since unions are the indispensable instrument for free workers to improve their standard of living, democracy is clearly the worker's staff of life."

Of particular importance to Asia will be the manner in which this administration will proceed with its stated intention of establishing full diplomatic relations with the People's Republic of China. The AFL-CIO congratulates President Carter in his selection of an outstanding trade unionist, Leonard Woodcock, as chief of liaison to Peking with the rank of ambassador.

But so-called "normalization" of this country's relations with Peking must not be pursued at the expense of Taiwan or this nation's commitment to human rights. As the Executive Council stated in February 1977, "human rights constitute the line at which diplomatic expediency must stop." The Peking regime is among the most repressive and oppressive, denying all forms of personal liberty.

U.S. relations with Japan cannot withstand further shockwaves, such as ex-President Nixon's sudden change in China policy or the disastrous wheat deal with the Soviets. Japan is one of this country's staunchest and most democratic allies.

The free world has largely shut its eyes to the atrocities and crimes against humanity being carried out under communist rule in Cambodia, Laos and Vietnam. The attitude of the countries of South and East Asia and of the Western World to the plight of the thousands of refugees who have risked and given their lives in attempts to flee the oppression of Indochina is shocking. These "boat people," impervious to the dangers of the sea, are being shunned, with the single and noteworthy exception of the U.S., by a world that no longer hears their pleas.

Since the last convention, the AFL-CIO was honored by an invitation from the Australian Council of Trade Unions for a delegation to visit Australia in celebration of the American Bicentennial. The AFL-CIO delegation that visited Australia in May 1976 was led by Vice President I. W. Abel and included Sheet Metal Workers' President Edward J. Carlough, Operative Plasterers' President Joseph T. Power and Pottery Workers' President Lester H. Null, Sr. ACTU President Robert Hawke, during a visit to the U.S. in June 1976, reported to President Meany the benefits of the AFL-CIO delegation in furthering and strengthening trade union ties between Australia and the U.S.

AFL-CIO relationships with Japanese unions continue to be mutually beneficial and friendly. The fraternal ties between the Japanese Confederation of Labor (DOMEI) and the AFL-CIO are particualrly strong, but exchanges and cooperation also exist with the General Council of Trade Unions of Japan (SOHYO), the National Federation of Industrial Organizations (SHINSAN-BETSU) and the Federation of Independent Unions (CHURITSUROREN). Additionally, many affiliates of the AFL-CIO have developed close and fraternal ties with their counterpart unions in Japan.

The AFL-CIO was represented at the DOMEI conventions in 1976 by Vice President Martin J. Ward and in 1977 by Vice President Murray H. Finley. Annual conferences between DOMEI and the AFL-CIO were held in Tokyo in March 1976 and in Washington, D.C. in May 1977.

Representing the AFL-CIO at the 1976 Tokyo meeting were Vice Presidents Ward and Joseph P. Tonelli and the international affairs director. Ernest S. Lee. At the 1977 Washington, D.C. AFL-CIO/DOMEI joint committee meeting, the AFL-CIO delegation was headed by President Meany and was comprised of Secretary-

Treasurer Lane Kirkland, Vice Presidents Charles Pillard and J. C. Turner, Sheet Metal Workers' President Carlough and then President-elect William Winpisinger of the Machinists.

The joint committee pledged continued efforts to improve living standards and working conditions of workers in both countries and to fight totalitarian threats to free workers in all parts of the world. In response to international and domestic economic problem, DOMEI and the AFL-CIO declared that "unemployment and poverty must be eradicated, not shifted from one country to another. Trade expansion must be based on fairness, reciprocity, and mutual benefit, especially to the workers of both nations."

The conferees expressed their "anxiety over the serious imbalance in international trade" and supported "the development and execution of international trade and investment policies which are fair and fully consistent with each nation's domestic needs for jobs and economic growth."

The meeting also welcomed "the adoption of the OECD code on multinational corporations as a first step toward regulating their behavior, while fully realizing that multilateral accords are only part of a larger program of national action to redress both imbalances in trade relations as well as abuses committed by multinational corporations."

Other areas of agreement outlined in the statement include:

■ AFL-CIO support of the application of Japanese union members for fishing rights in compliance with U.S. conservation and management measures under the new 200-mile coastal limit.

■ Reaffirmation of AFL-CIO support of DOMEI efforts for the return of northern island territories to Japan that the Soviet Union seized at the end of World War II.

■ A commitment to aid struggling trade union movements in Asia, in cooperation with other Asian trade union organizations, on a mutually agreeable, joint-sponsorship basis.

AFRICA

The AFL-CIO has long supported trade unionists in Africa in their struggle for polical freedom and economic justice and, beginning with the founding convention of the AFL-CIO in 1955, called for an end to all forms of colonialism at a time when the U.S. government was implicitly supporting certain European countries that sought to prolong colonial domination in Africa.

As early as 1958 the AFL-CIO spoke out concerning the denial of freedoms in Rhodesia and the inhuman and brutal racial policies of the government of South Africa and its illegal occupation of Namibia. We pledged to support democratic forces working to eliminate political tyranny and economic exploitation.

The AFL-CIO has repeatedly called upon this government to provide sufficient aid to the peoples of Africa. From 1945 to 1952 direct aid to Africa was less than $1 million. In the mid-1960s this increased to about $500 million, only to drop to half that amount in the 1970s. In a well-publicized dissent from the views expressed by the Clay report which led to the aid reduction, President Meany asked U.S. national leaders to support a Marshall Plan for Africa.

The poverty and despotism in Africa that prompted our deep concern unfortunately still exist today. Eighteen of the world's 28 least developed countries are located in Africa; 26 designated as among the most severely affected by fuel and food cost increases are found on that continent. Only 17 percent of the people are literate and schools are available for only 28 percent of school age children. Food production has not kept pace with population growth. While primarily rural, many countries are witnessing a 12 percent annual urban population growth rate as people move to the cities in the futile search for jobs.

The people of Africa have many distinct viewpoints bounded by family, lineage, group, ethnicity, language, culture, and religion. During any process of modernization there is frequently no shared vision of social purpose or justice, as new values are sought to replace the old. It is the profound belief of the AFL-CIO that worker organizations have a central role to play in the modernization process. Together with other elements in society, trade unions can mitigate more parochial concerns and help strengthen political and economic institutions.

While viable labor movements exist in many African countries, all face enormous problems in developing workable grievance procedures, in negotiating and enforcing collective bargaining agreements, and in dealing with contemporary problems of economic and social development. They need help in organizing, in providing their leaders with advanced training in industrial relations and research, in establishing vocational training schemes and social services for their members.

The AFL-CIO, however, has always recognized that African trade unions must develop their own style and dynamism. The 1961 convention reaffirmed its opposition "to any policy which might be construed as an attempt to impose on the workers of Africa any American or European pattern of trade union organization. The form of trade union organization in any country is determined not from the outside, but by the specific traditions and concrete conditions of each nation."

While not always happy with developments in Africa, the American labor movement has consistently demonstrated that it will be at the side of free unions in any legitimate dispute. The continued growth and success of African trade unionism and the future of many African nations will depend for a considerable period of time on the degree of the U.S. commitment to helping African nations to modernize.

The professed reshaping of U.S. government policy toward Africa brings to mind President Meany's repeated calls for an increase in bilateral assistance to Africa. His response to the Clay report is as true today as it was in 1962.

The situation in Southern Africa has not materially improved since the AFL-CIO first voiced its concerns in 1958. The Portuguese have departed from Angola and Mozambique, only to be replaced with Soviet-dominated dictatorships. "Stability" has been achieved, but at the expense of trade union rights and human freedoms. South Africa continues its immoral, adhorrent policy of apartheid and illegal occupation of Namibia. The de facto Smith regime in Rhodesia continues to exist.

The 1963 AFL-CIO convention said:

"The apartheid regime in South Africa is a permanent threat not only to the people of South Africa, but to every other country in Africa. It is a menace to the peace of the continent and the entire world. There can be no real peace and stability in Africa as long as the South African apartheid system continues . . . The political and racial character of apartheid . . . has provided fertile soil for attempts by totalitarian forces to take over some of the nationalist movements."

The truth of this statement has unfortunately been borne out by the communist governments in Angola and Mozambique.

Unfortunately, problems in Africa are not limited to the southern part of the continent. The council views with alarm the Soviet penetration in the strategic horn of Africa. The Soviet supported Marxist military regime in Ethiopia that has destroyed the trade union movement and subjected the people of that country to a reign of terror should be condemned by freedom-loving people everywhere.

Likewise, the existence of the deviant regimes in Uganda and the newly named Central African Empire stain the continent.

LATIN AMERICA

The Latin American foreign policy of both the Ford and Nixon administrations was shaped by a general lack of interest in the region and a failure to understand its political and economic concerns.

Kissinger-style diplomacy, with its concentration on major powers and "hot spots," prevented the development of a coherent policy toward the region based on the gradual resolution of long-standing sources of conflict. Both in Latin America and the U.S., there has long been an impression that U.S. policy-makers view Latin America as a region of only marginal importance to U.S. foreign policy.

Today there are only a few countries in Latin America and the Caribbean that can be described as democracies.

This has been the cause of much pessimism among U.S. policymakers, who sometimes use this fact alone as a reason for treating our neighbors to the south with neglect.

Yet, dictatorships, like democracies, do not endure forever in Latin America. Both Colombia and Venezuela, bastions of democracy today, were ruled by military autocrats not so long ago. Nor can we ignore the lack of interest of the U.S. in supporting faltering and weak constitutional governments, among which were the administrations of Belaunde of Peru, Ramon Cruz of Honduras, Velasco Ibarra of Ecuador and Silas of Bolivia, eventually taken over by military coups, while at the same time supporting dictatorships, as in Nicaragua, the Dominican Republic and Paraguay.

The human rights policy of the Carter administration and the passage in 1976 of the Arms Export Control Act with its human rights provisions, strongly supported by the AFL-CIO Executive Council, denying assistance to those dictatorial regimes which consistently violate universally accepted standards of human rights, has already had a favorable impact in Latin America. Three Latin republics presently under military rule have announced their intention of returning their countries to counstitutional governments. These are Honduras, Ecuador, and Peru.

Others, undoubtedly fearful of the consequences, have released political and trade union prisoners, many of whom had been incarcerated for years without ever having been brought to trial.

The AFL-CIO has repeatedly demanded the restoration of trade union rights and freedoms in Latin American republics where such rights are being denied or curtailed by repressive dictatorial regimes. The assassination, jailing, torturing and kidnapping of trade union leaders in Chile and Argentina is particularly repugnant, and vigorous AFL-CIO protests have been submitted to the U.S. State Department and the two military governments involved. Equally unacceptable is the holding of trade union leaders in jail indefinitely without trial.

In line with long-standing AFL-CIO policies in interAmerican affairs the Executive Council has strongly supported placing limitations on the quality and quantity of military assistance to Latin America. With equal vigor we have stressed the application of U.S. ethical values to the international arena, insisting that bilateral assistance be contingent on progress in human rights. Jointly with democratic trade unions in Latin America, the AFL-CIO has expressed its concern that the benefits of foreign assistance reach the large masses of the poor.

The AFL-CIO has sponsored and participated in a number of interAmerican trade union symposiums on the multinational corporations, where, by unanimous vote, codes of conduct for multinational corporations

have been called for, beginning with outlawing bribery and imposing sanctions on both the donor and the recipient, and the placing of constraints on the ability of these multinationals to influence national politics.

Our Latin colleagues share our deep preoccupation with nuclear proliferation, a grave threat to the region's historic peace, and one that demands immediate action before the nuclear arms race becomes a reality in Latin America.

Through the InterAmerican Regional Organization of Workers (ORIT) to which we are affiliated, the AFL-CIO has participated in regional forums seeking practical solutions for the control of illegal immigration, regional planning to combat unemployment and underemployment both here and in Latin America, and the effects of the impact of "runaway" shops in transformation industries, both in the U.S. and the Latin and Caribbean countries in which these plants are locating.

The AFL-CIO continues to support ORIT and its activities in the hemisphere, as well as the programs and activities of international trade secretariats in the region. Support is also given to the labor programs of the Organization of American States (OAS) with which we have been institutionally associated for many years.

Bilateral relations and contact are also maintained with all democratic trade union centers and peasant associations in Latin America and the Caribbean, and assistance has been rendered to many of these organizations through the AFL-CIO impact projects fund, in collaboration with the American Institute for Free Labor Development (AIFLD).

Two years ago an AFL-CIO/AIFLD jointly sponsored program known as "Operation Solidarity" was launched. Through this program, AFL-CIO delegations, consisting of two or three members of the Executive Council or their designees, visit three or four countries during a 10 to 12-day period. Annually six delegations visit a total of 18 or 20 countries. Meetings are held with democratic labor leaders, labor ministries, U.S. embassy personnel, leaders of counterpart unions and, where possible, representatives of international trade secretariats. Through interviews and frank exchanges of opinions and policies with labor leaders and government officials in the countries being visited, more cohesive bilateral and hemispheric programs are being developed and implemented through ORIT and the OAS.

After thirteen years of on-again, off-again negotiations between the governments of the United States and Panama, two treaties have been agreed to which radically alter the Panama Canal Treaty of 1903.

According to the Joint Chiefs of Staff, the treaties of 1977 provide for continuing freedom of action of the United States to maintain neutrality of the Canal and further guarantee U.S. access and rights to use all land and water areas and installations necessary for the defense of the Canal through the year 2000.

Job security and rights of workers in the Canal Zone, both U.S. and Panamanian, will be assured. Since 1949, the AFL has called for justice in the Canal Zone in arguing for equal pay for equal work, so that Panamanian citizens would not be exploited through a double standard of remuneration. Through the years, particularly during the long and arduous periods of negotiations groping toward a new treaty, the AFL-CIO has maintained a vigilant stance concerning workers' rights in the Canal Zone and the safe-keeping of the elements of U.S. defense inherent in the Panama Canal Agreement.

We are satisfied that the new treaties cover both considerations adequately. U.S. citizens now employed in the Canal Zone will be protected and remunerated as U.S. government employees and will be offered new benefits tailored to fit the new treaty characteristics. Based on these considerations, the AFL-CIO Executive Council on August 30, 1977 voted unanimously to support ratification of the treaties.

THE INTERNATIONAL LABOR ORGANIZATION

One month after our last convention, the United States served notice of its intent to withdraw from the International Labor Organization. The notice, in the form of a letter from Secretary of State Henry Kissinger to ILO Director General Francis Blanchard, dated November 5, 1976, was transmitted pursuant to Article 1, Paragraph 5 of the ILO constitution, which provides that a member may withdraw provided that a notice of intention to withdraw has been given two years earlier to the Director General.

Secretary Kissinger stated in the letter that, while the United States does not desire to leave the ILO, "we do intend to make every possible effort to promote the conditions which will facilitate our continued participation. If this should prove impossible, we are in fact prepared to depart." The letter went on to present four matters of "fundamental concern":

1. *"The Erosion of Tripartite Representation* . . . In particular, we cannot accept the workers' and employers' groups in the ILO falling under the domination of governments."

2. *"Selective Concern for Human Rights* . . . This strengthens the proposition that these human rights are not universally applicable, but rather are subject to different interpretations for states with different political systems."

3. *"Disregard of Due Process* . . . In recent years, sessions of the ILO Conference increasingly have adopted resolutions condemning particular member states which happen to be the political target of the moment, in utter disregard of the established procedures and machinery . . ."

4. *"The Increasing Politicization of the Organization* . . . Irrelevant political issues divert the attention of the ILO from improving the conditions of workers . . ."

In the two years since this letter was written, the United States government, at the urging of the AFL-

CIO, undertook a serious diplomatic effort to enlist our allies and other member nations in an effort to return the ILO to its original purposes. While some progress was made in securing the active support of the industrial democracies and a few of the developing countries, the 1977 Conference dealt a severe setback to the principle of due process by rejecting an American initiative that would have ruled out resolutions of condemnation which seek to bypass the ILO's established fact-finding machinery. Moreover, the persistence of a double standard on human rights was reinforced when the Conference rejected a report by the ILO's Committee on Applications of Conventions and Recommendations which found the Soviet Union in violation of the Conventions on Forced Labor and on Freedom of Association.

On Nov. 1, 1977, President Carter announced that the United States would withdraw from the ILO. At that time President Meany made the following statement:

"We support and endorse the decision of President Carter to stand by the notice of withdrawal by the United States from the International Labor Organization.

"The minimum objectives set forth in that notice, the attainment of which would have justified continued membership, were spurned and repudiated by the June Conference of the ILO, despite two years of intensive effort by American labor, management and the government.

"The AFL-CIO does, of course, strongly advocate and support the high ideals and principles set forth in the constitution and declarations of the ILO—tripartism, human rights, freedom of association and the pursuit of humane international standards of life and labor. We intend to continue and expand our work in the international arena, in furtherance of those aims and principles, through every effective channel that is available to us.

"We stand ready to cooperate and to work with the free trade union movements of the world, with our government and with management, to the end that the ILO might in the future return to its appropriate role in the promotion of its stated purposes. If and when significant progress in that direction is realized, the AFL-CIO will advocate rejoining that body."

COUNCIL RECOMMENDATION

The AFL-CIO believes that human rights must be a cardinal principle of U.S. foreign policy. We strongly endorse and commend the position and actions of President Carter in speaking out unequivocally on specific cases of oppression, as well as in general terms.

Abuses and threats to basic human rights are the most searching issues that divide the world today, and the clearest tests of American ideals and resolve. Where these issues are concerned, whether in Southern Africa, Chile, Uganda or the Soviet Union, "there are no longer any purely internal affairs."

Defense and Disarmament

The defense of the U.S. and her allies must be enhanced to the point where no aggressor will dare to test the determination of free people anywhere to remain free. To this end, regional alliances, such as the North Atlantic Treaty Organization, should receive the most critical review by our government to ensure the adequacy of forces and armaments sufficient to deter both conventional and nuclear attack.

The goals of disarmament and strategic arms limitation can only be met through a strong defense, trimmed of unnecessary waste, but able to meet all contingencies. Efforts to cut back military spending by fixed dollar or percentage amounts without reference to the adequacy of military forces to meet the real threats to peace should be rejected.

Western Europe and NATO

The AFL-CIO urges the U.S. government to more closely coordinate policy actions with America's Western allies. NATO should be transformed into a true partnership with joint responsibility among its member nations for maintenance of the alliance defenses. Major cuts in U.S. troop strength in Europe, however, must only be made on a mutual and balanced bias.

We view with regret the U.S. government's one-sided policy on the question of Cyprus which has caused both Greece and Turkey to reconsider their position as members of the Western alliance.

Spain's rapid moves toward a democratic form of government, after years of fascist domination, is to be applauded by the people of the free world. In light of these developments the U.S. should favorably view Spain's membership in NATO as an important and strengthening element for the alliance.

The economic and political survival of democratic forms of government rests with a vital, strong NATO that speaks and acts as one.

Eastern Europe

The AFL-CIO believes that only through continued U.S. government insistence on human rights will the peoples of Eastern Europe find hope and encouragement. We call upon the free nations of the world to insist on complete compliance by the Warsaw Bloc with the Helsinki Accords.

Those courageous individuals who have risked their lives to monitor compliance with the Accords must not be abandoned. Their voice is the voice of human rights, and it must not be stilled.

Middle East

The AFL-CIO vigorously reaffirms its historic support of the State of Israel and as vigorously rejects any so-called peace proposals which, in the guise of evenhandedness, would allow Israel's neighbors to evade an explicit acceptance of Israel's right to exist or deny Israel the practical means to secure that right. In our view, any American approach to the Middle East conflict that does not have this as its centerpiece is unlikely either to win the moral support of the American people or to remove the cause of the conflict.

Our support of Israel is not a function of which party is in power at a particular moment but rather is rooted in a deep respect for the extraordinary achievements of that small country, working through the democratic process, and in our conviction that the democratic road offers the best hope of progress and peace for all countries of that region. That Israel's achievements derive in large measure from the role of Histadrut in shaping Israeli society is, for us, an additional reason for support and identification.

The administration must resist oil blackmail and other pressures designed to isolate and undermine Israel. Capitulation to these pressures would not only harm Israel but would ultimately frustrate the legitimate aspirations of millions of Arabs oppressed by poverty and reactionary political regimes. Those aspirations can only be fulfilled within the framework of an enduring peace. And such a peace can only rest on an acceptance of Israel's right to be.

Africa

The AFL-CIO is encouraged by the Carter administration's professed desire to reshape U.S. policy toward Africa. A first step must be increased bilateral assistance to African countries rooted in humanitarianism and a sincere desire to help foster balanced economic development. If President Meany had been heeded in 1962, the need would not be so critical today.

The AFL-CIO also calls upon the U.S. government to place maximum political pressure on the governments of South Africa and Rhodesia to end the odious system of apartheid and immediately begin the process of transition to majority rule.

The U.S. government should demand that U.S. corporations with investments in Southern Africa immediately recognize bona fide trade union organizations, regardless of their racial composition, and begin treating their employees on an equal basis, commencing with such fundamental issues as wages and working conditions.

The International Affairs Committee of the AFL-CIO is directed to explore positive courses of action, such as selective boycotts against South Africa, to call attention to the plight of workers in that country.

The AFL-CIO pledges that—through influence on our government's foreign policy, through active participation in international trade secretariat activities, through greater education of our membership and utilization of our organizational strength and facilities such as the African-American Labor Center—we will strive to strengthen democracy, free trade unionism, economic development, and promote better conditions of work and life for all peoples of Africa.

Latin America

The AFL-CIO welcomes and encourages the Carter administration's new emphasis on improving relations with Latin America.

We believe that strengthening free labor movements in Latin America will be essential to a restoration of democracy in this hemisphere. The AFL-CIO, long committed to development of a free labor movement in Latin America, pledges its continued efforts to help train and assist the unionists who will sustain and nurture democracy in our neighbors to the South.

The AFL-CIO views the two Panama Canal Treaties guaranteeing the permanent neutrality of the Canal and the operation and defense of the Canal through the year 2000, as instruments worthy of support by U.S. citizens and their elected representatives. These new instruments constitute a just and enduring basis for harmony in the Western Hemisphere, and we support their ratification by the Senate.

Asia

The role that the United States can play and the assistance it can provide is crucial to the people of Asia. The American labor movement strongly rejects any policy of isolationism emerging from the debacle of Vietnam and urges our government to convey to the people of Asia the determination of the workers and citizens of this country to cooperate with them to preserve and strengthen human freedom, economic development and free trade unionism in the region.

We believe the U.S. government must maintain and strengthen ties with Japan as a true democracy and a nation committed to progress in Asia.

The difficult task of the Carter administration will be to convey to the authoritarian leaders in Asia the sentiments and the convictions of the American people. We will not tolerate the abridgment or denial of human rights, the use of terror or torture in squelching dissent, or the subjugation of trade union freedoms in the name of "security" or "development." At the same time, the United States must make it absolutely clear to the Communist dictators of the Soviet Union, China, North Korea and Indo-China that their imperialist designs and efforts will be resisted.

The government of Peking should be regarded by the United States as a repressive dictatorship, and should not be considered the inheritor of the free people of the Republic of China on Taiwan. Of great importance also is the apparent move to provide Peking with the technological basis for an industrial machine and the hardware to produce in competition with the Free World, using

a skilled but captive labor force in the process. So long as Peking entertains imperialist designs equal to that of the Soviet Union, it is foolhardy and destructive of democracy and freedom to aid that government to the detriment of the Free World.

Economic Trade and Aid

The AFL-CIO urges the U.S. government to more efficiently negotiate economic trade agreements with our free world trading partners to enhance the economic and employment opportunities of American workers. At the same time, the U.S. should reject trade concessions and technology transfers that provide obvious benefits to totalitarian states.

A concerted effort must be made to achieve the construction and maintenance of a merchant marine vital to the conduct of this nation's trade with others abroad and to preclude the further weakening of this element of national defense.

The AFL-CIO recognizes that the problem of aliens, illegally resident in the United States, is a manifestation of the poverty and deprivation they suffer abroad and that there is both a need to curtail their illegal entry as well as to aid the economies of nations in which they are citizens.

Attention should be given by the Agency for International Development, to the essential goal of creating and perfecting the democratic institutions and infrastructure which enable societies to provide the basis for economic, social and political security and individual well-being.

African-American Labor Center

The AFL-CIO has a long history of interest in African affairs, dating back to pre-independence days when African trade union movements provided the only channel for democratic participation and the training of indigenous leaders in the task of nation building. The contacts and support begun in this period were formalized in 1964 with the creation of the African-American Labor Center (AALC) to provide assistance to the new national trade union centers.

To date, the AALC has carried out 340 projects in 41 African countries in workers' education and leadership training, cooperatives and credit unions, medical services, the role of women in trade unions, research and development, economics and communications.

The AALC is governed by a board of directors with George Meany as chairman and president; Frederick O'Neal, secretary-treasurer, and Patrick J. O'Farrell, executive director. Other members of the board are top officers of leading trade unions in the United States.

Policy guidance is provided by the AFL-CIO and the African-American Consultative Committee, composed of four leading African trade unionists. Other internationally prominent union officals are often invited to contribute to meetings of the committee, which are held annually concomitant with the ILO conferences in Geneva, Switzerland. In 1976 the committee met for the first time in the United States where they had an opportunity to discuss African problems with American labor leaders and U.S. government officials.

The administrative structure of the AALC includes a staff of 16 based at the New York headquarters and 14 representatives and technical advisors in Africa. African nationals are employed as administrators, technicians and teachers in AALC-sponsored programs with the various national trade union centers.

The AALC works in close partnership with African trade unions and develops its programs at the invitation of and in cooperation with these unions and with the full endorsement of the host governments. All projects are geared to the eventual assumption of the complete administrative and financial responsibility by the various African labor movements.

In 1976, for example, the tailoring institute established by the AALC in Dakar a few years earlier passed totally into Senegalese hands. As a result of discussions held early this year between the Organization of African Trade Union Unity (OATUU) and the AALC, it is anticipated that OATUU will begin taking administrative responsibility for another AALC-sponsored institution, the Regional Economic Research and Documentation Center located in Lomé, Togo.

All of the AALC's programs are coordinated as far as possible with African missions to the United States, with the Economic Commission for Africa, OATUU, the Organisation of African Unity and the ILO.

Close relationships have also been developed between the AALC and many international trade secretariats, among them the International Federation of Commercial, Clerical and Technical Employees, the International Federation of Free Teachers Unions, the International Federation of Journalists and the Postal, Telegraph and Telephone International. Programs are developed with the various American affiliates of these trade secretariats. Since a substantial part of its programs take place in French-speaking Africa, the AALC has also cooperated with the French labor movement through the Force Ouvrière's Institut Syndical de Coopération.

Generalizations about present or future economic and political conditions of the nations of the African continent are difficult, if not hazardous, to make. Poverty is pervasive in most of Africa with only a few exceptions, yet growth rates in the first decade since independence have been impressive. The great drought of the early 1970s, the world recession and declining raw material prices have caused problems that have not yet been solved. Food and fuel price increases have severely hampered development.

All of this has contributed to political disruption within Africa and confrontation with the industrialized countries whose commitment to significant African economic development is yet to be demonstrated. In the southern third of the continent, the independence of Mozambique and Angola from Portuguese rule have drastically changed the outlook for Rhodesia, Namibia and ultimately for South Africa where apartheid is destined one day to disappear. A rational solution to these problems has not yet materialized, however.

It is not surprising, therefore, to see a trend in Africa toward one party states and/or direct military rule. Many African nations, despite their best efforts, are too poor to institute democracy as we in the U.S. understand it, but the seeds are there and must be nourished.

The trade union movement in Africa is strong and reasonably independent. Its members come from a group of people dedicated to participation in the economic development of their countries. They have created institutions that teach practical and functional democracy, serve as important channels of communication and provide badly needed social services to their community and its grass roots contacts. Their needs are great, and there is much that the American labor movement can offer to ensure that free trade unionism has a future in Africa.

The AALC, as a specialized institute of the AFL-CIO, has made a commitment to strengthen labor movements in Africa in their struggle for justice and economic advancement for the whole continent.

Asian-American Free Labor Institute

The Asian-American Free Labor Institute, created by the AFL-CIO Executive Council in 1968, sponsors programs in over 17 Asian countries designed to promote the growth of free and effective trade unions. The institute provides Asian trade unions with technical assistance in the fields of labor education, community projects, and cooperatives.

AAFLI has sponsored 30 regional seminars and 50 country educational organizing conferences as part of its union-to-union program in conjunction with AFL-CIO affiliates and their respective international trade secretariats in Asia. Participating in these programs have been the American Federation of Teachers, the Brotherhood of Railway and Airline Clerks, the International Alliance of Theatrical Stage Employees, the International Association of Machinists, the American Federation of Musicians, the United Steelworkers of America, the International Union of Electrical Workers, the Sheet Metal Workers' Union, the Retail Clerks International Union, the Amalgamated Clothing and Textile Workers Union and the International Ladies' Garment Workers Union.

Since its creation, AAFLI has sponsored over 1,100 educational programs attended by more than 42,000 trade unionists in Bangladesh, Fiji, India, Indonesia, Jordan, Korea, Lebanon, Malaysia, Nepal, Pakistan, Papua-New Guinea, the Philippines, Singapore, Sri Lanka, Thailand, Turkey, and Taiwan. Rank-and-file trade union members, as well as trade union leaders and staff members, have participated in programs dealing with labor-related subjects ranging from basic trade union administration to advanced labor economics.

AAFLI has published a wide range of materials for use in its own educational programs, as well as those sponsored by Asian trade unions. To date, over 50 books and pamphlets on labor subjects have been published and distributed. Materials have been translated into six Asian languages, and, in many instances, AAFLI materials are the only ones available in local languages.

In Korea, AAFLI and the Federation of Korean Trade Unions have launched a series of branch-level seminars which develop the skills and interests of rank-and-file workers. Specialized programs on arbitration and mediation techniques continue in the Philippines, and dozens of Turkish trade unionists have received intense training in job evaluation procedures. Other Asian trade unionists attended special seminars on a wide range of subjects including labor publications, educational methods, cooperative management, research, occupational safety, social security systems and collective bargaining. Under the auspices of the institute, Asian trade unionists have attended advanced training courses at the Harvard Trade Union Program and University of Wisconsin Center for Cooperatives.

Community projects sponsored by AAFLI have aided Asian labor unions in establishing a local presence, while helping to build the necessary infrastructure for future economic growth. The institute continued assistance to labor-supported medical facilities in Korea, Indonesia and the Philippines, and donated new mobile clinics to trade unions in the Philippines and Turkey. With help from AAFLI, these medical facilities have provided necessary service to thousands of Asian trade unionists at affordable fees.

The institute has also encouraged the development of labor-supported cooperatives and credit unions by making seed capital loans and technical assistance available to trade unions in Korea, Turkey, Indonesia and the Philippines. Through cooperatives, rank-and-file trade union members are able to expand the buying powers of their wages while strengthening the position of their trade union as an integral part of the community.

Emerging trade unions need material assistance to enable them to carry out the day-to-day tasks of organizing and servicing their members. AAFLI has assisted a number of trade unions in building community centers and headquarters facilities. Two community centers were opened in Thailand, and the institute has assisted trade unions in Sri Lanka, Malaysia and Korea in constructing various types of buildings. The institute has also donated

basic office equipment, such as typewriters and mimeograph machines, to several Asian trade unions.

The Asian Impact Project Fund, established in 1971 with a grant from the AFL-CIO impact project program, provides grants or interest-free loans for self-help projects to meet basic community and trade union needs. Projects undertaken during the last two years include assistance to a livestock cooperative in Korea, a new classroom building in Indonesia, vocational training projects in India and Sri Lanka, assistance to trade unions in war-torn Lebanon and renovated toilet facilities in Indonesia.

The institute's programs continue to grow, and while much has been accomplished, much remains to be done.

American Institute for Free Labor Development

Since 1961 the initiative and continuing interest of the AFL-CIO have been instrumental in providing technical assistance to free trade unions through the U.S. government's aid program in Latin America. These labor aid programs are implemented through the American Institute for Free Labor Development, which receives supplementary funding from the AFL-CIO and some U.S. corporations.

Despite increasing repression of free trade unionism by dictatorial governments in much of Latin America over the past two years, AIFLD has been able to maintain programs in 16 countries, strengthening free trade unionism in democratic countries and assisting movements to survive under dictatorships of varying degrees of severity. AIFLD's two main program areas are trade union education and social projects.

The education program consists mainly of short-term courses given throughout Latin America, in both cities and rural areas. Common topics are collective bargaining, labor legislation, organizing techniques, labor press and public relations, cooperatives, and parliamentary procedure. In both 1975 and 1976 AIFLD offered over 630 courses in 14 countries, training over 23,500 participants each year, of whom more than 3,700 were women.

AIFLD also offers two international education programs in the U.S. Near Front Royal, Va., AIFLD operates a residential education center which offers six programs annually to Latin American and Caribbean trade unionists drawn from the middle levels of union leadership. Each program has 40 participants, usually divided into two different courses.

AIFLD also sponsors a university-level program in Washington, D.C. for 15 trades unionists annually. In 1975 a regional program was presented for Central Americans, focusing on labor's role in the Central American Common Market. In 1976 a new university-level program was begun, devoting less class time to economics and statistics, and including comparative political philosophy, sociology, and international relations. This new program is designed as a mid-career course to prepare rising trade union officers for national level responsibilities.

AIFLD has continued an active social projects program. Under the impact projects program, funded privately by the AFL-CIO for projects costing $5,000 or less, 45 projects were approved over the past two years for unions in 13 countries. Of the total, nine were for shipments of medical supplies provided by the Direct Relief Foundation, ten were for building or equipping schools, six for construction of community centers, five for aid to vocational training, and five for aid to cooperatives.

AIFLD also administers an AID-funded Regional Revolving Loan Fund for larger projects involving up to $50,000 in loans. Over the past two years 16 projects in eight countries have been approved for RRLF funding, averaging $24,700 per loan. Among the 16 projects were four for disaster relief in Guatemala, two for agricultural cooperatives, two for rural health centers, and two for seed capital for credit unions.

On February 4, 1976 a disastrous earthquake hit Guatemala, affecting 15,000 families of union members. AIFLD coordinated an immediate relief effort for these families, using $55,000 donated by the AFL-CIO and over $44,000 given by 41 affiliated unions. The main effort was to provide materials and technical assistance so the workers could rebuild their homes before the rainy season began. Immediately after the earthquake, an AFL-CIO impact project funded the costs of distributing food donated to the trade union organizations by CARE and by unions in neighboring countries. For longer-range aid, the four disaster relief RRLF projects provided loans to families for replacement of homes and household utensils.

Over the last two years AIFLD's Agrarian Union Development Service has provided three main types of programs to rural unions in Latin America: funding of activists on union staffs, sponsorship of education courses for local rural union leaders, and organization of exchange visits between rural union leaders in various countries. During the 1976 contract year the AUDS offered 147 education courses in 11 countries. Twenty-four rural activists were supported in ten countries to organize new local unions, build up membership, conduct training, and advise on community projects, credit unions, and marketing cooperatives. Two exchange programs were conducted, one for 12 unionists from six countries to visit the Union Communal in El Salvador, and the other for 19 leaders from 10 countries to visit the FECAVE campesino in Venezuela.

A new organizing program has been carried out by AIFLD for the past two years with private-sector funding. Forty trade unionists each year have been trained in organizing techniques in courses at the Front Royal Institute and have then returned to their unions on scholarships for a year of full-time organizing work. In its first year this program resulted in the enrollment of over 31,000 new members and the formation or re-establishment of 147 unions in Latin America. Indications are that even greater success will be achieved by the second group of organizers, who graduated from Front Royal in mid-April 1977.

Through these and other projects, AIFLD pursues its goal of strengthening the trade union movement in Latin America as an effective force for democracy and social reform in societies long characterized by oligarchy and economic injustices. AIFLD believes that only through the power of organization can workers maintain their human rights and receive an equitable share of Latin America's wealth.

Free Trade Union Institute

Recognizing the need to establish closer relations with the European labor movement and in answer to requests made by a number of democratically oriented trade unions in several European countries, the AFL-CIO is in the process of establishing an institute vested with the responsibility of assisting free trade unions to strengthen their ranks and expand their organizations.

U.S. UNIONS AFFILIATED WITH INTERNATIONAL TRADE SECRETARIATS[1]

International Federation of Building and Woodworkers (IFBWW),
27-29, rue de la Coulouvreniere,
CH-1204 Geneva, Switzerland.
  Bricklayers and Allied Craftsmen; International Union of.
  Electrical Workers; International Brotherhood of (IBEW).
  Laborers' International Union of North America.
  Operating Engineers; International Union of.
    Painters and Allied Trades of the United States and Canada; International Brotherhood of.
    Plumbing and Pipe Fitting Industry of U.S. and Canada; United Alliance of Journeymen and Apprentices of the.
    Sheet Metal Workers' International Association.
    Upholsterers' International Union of North America.
    Woodworkers of America; International.
International Federation of Chemical and General Workers' Union (ICF),
58, rue de Moillebeau, P.O. Box 277,
CH-1211 Geneva 19, Switzerland.
  Cement, Lime and Gypsum Workers International Union; United.
  Chemical Workers Union; International.
  Distributive Workers of America (Ind.).
  Flint Glass Workers Union; American.
  Glass and Ceramic Workers of North America; United.
  Oil, Chemical and Atomic Workers International Union.
  Paperworkers International Union; United.
  Pottery and Allied Workers; International Brotherhood of.
  Rubber, Cork, Linoleum and Plastic Workers of America; United.
  Steelworkers of America; United.
  Teamsters, Chauffeurs, Warehousemen and Helpers of America; International Brotherhood of (Ind.).
International Federation of Commercial, Clerical and Technical Employees (FIET),
15, avenue de Balexert,
1211 Geneva-28, Switzerland.
  Insurance Workers International Union.
  Office and Professional Employees International Union.
  Retail Clerks International Association.
  Retail, Wholesale and Department Store Union.
International Secretariat of Entertainment Trade Unions (ISETU),
King's Court, 2 Goodge Street, 2nd Floor,
London WIP 2AE, England.
  American Federation of Television and Radio Artists.
  American Guild of Musical Artists.
  Electrical Workers; International Brotherhood of (IBEW).
  Musicians; American Federation of.
  Screen Actors Guild.
  Theatrical Stage Employees and Moving Picture Machine Operators of the U.S. and Canada; International Alliance of.
International Union of Food and Allied Workers' Association (IUF),
Rampe du Pont-Rouge 8,
CH-1213 Petit-Lancy, Switzerland.
  Bakery and Confectionery Workers International Union of America.

Distillery, Rectifying, Wine and Allied Workers International Union of America.
  Hotel and Restaurant Employees and Bartenders International Union.
  Meat Cutters and Butcher Workmen of North America; Amalgamated.
  Retail, Wholesale and Department Store Union.
  Tobacco Workers International Union.
International Graphical Federation (IGF),
Monbijoustrasse, 73,
CH-3007 Berne, Switzerland.
  Graphic Arts International Union.
International Federation of Journalists (IFJ),
Rue Duquesnoy, 14,
B-1000 Brussels, Belgium.
  Newspaper Guild; The.
International Metalworkers' Federation (IMF),
Route des Acacias, 54 bis,
1227 Geneva, Switzerland.
  Aluminum Workers International Union.
  Automobile, Aerospace and Agricultural Workers of America; International Union, United (Ind.).
  Boilermakers, Iron Ship Builders, Blacksmiths, Forgers and Helpers; International Brotherhood of.
  Electrical, Radio and Machine Workers; International Union of.
  Electrical Workers; International Brotherhood of (IBEW).
  Industrial Workers of America; Allied.
  Machinists and Aerospace Workers; International Association of.
  Sheet Metal Workers' International Association.
  Steelworkers of America; United.
International Federation of Plantation, Agricultural and Allied Workers (IFPAAW),
17, rue Necker,
1201 Geneva, Switzerland.
  Farm Workers of America; United.
  Meat Cutters and Butcher Workmen of North America; Amalgamated.
Postal Telegraph and Telephone International (PTTI),
36, avenue du Lignon,
CH-1211 Geneva, Switzerland.
  Communications Workers of America.
  Letter Carriers; National Association of.
  Postal Workers' Union; American.
  Telegraph Workers; United.
Public Services International (PSI),
Hallstrom House,
Central Way,
Feltham, Middlesex, Great Britain.
  State, County and Municipal Employees; American Federation of.
International Federation of Free Teachers' Unions (IFFTU),
111 Avenue G. Bergmann,
1050 Brussels, Belgium.
  Teachers; American Federation of.

[1] All unions not identified as independent (Ind.) are affiliated with the AFL-CIO. Listing compiled by the Bureau of Labor Statistics and the Department of International Affairs of the AFL-CIO.

International Textile and Garment Workers' Federation (ITGWF),
Rue Joseph Stevens, 8,
1000 Brussels, Belgium.
  Clothing and Textile Workers Union; Amalgamated.
  Ladies' Garment Workers' Union; International.
  Leather Goods, Plastics and Novelty Workers Union; International.
  Meat Cutters and Butcher Workmen of North America; Amalgamated.
  Shoe Workers of America; United.
  Textile Workers of America; United.
International Transportworkers' Federation (ITF),
Maritime House, Old Town,
Clapham, London, SW4 OJR, England.
  Airline Dispatchers Association.
  Flight Engineers' International Association.
  Hotel and Restaurant Employees and Bartenders International Union.
  Longshoremen's Association; International.
  Machinists and Aerospace Workers; International Association of.
  Maintenance of Way Employees; Brotherhood of.
  Marine Engineers' Beneficial Association; National.
  Maritime Union of America; National.
  Radio Association; American.
  Railway and Airline Clerks; Brotherhood of.
  Seafarers' International Union of North America.
  Telegraph Union; United.
  Transport Workers Union of America.
  Transportation Union; United.

Federal Legislation
Related to Labor

FEDERAL LEGISLATION RELATED TO LABOR RELATIONS

Sherman Antitrust Act (1890, as Amended)

SECTION 1. Every contract, combination in the form of trust or otherwise, or conspiracy, in restraint of trade or commerce among the several States, or with foreign nations, is hereby declared to be illegal: Provided, That nothing herein contained shall render illegal, contracts or agreements prescribing minimum prices for the resale of a commodity which bears, or the label or container of which bears, the trade mark, brand, or name of the producer or distributor of such commodity and which is in free and open competition with commodities of the same general class produced or distributed by others, when contracts or agreements of that description are lawful as applied to intrastate transactions, under any statute, law, or public policy now or hereafter in effect in any State, Territory, or the District of Columbia in which such resale is to be made, or to which the commodity is to be transported for such resale, and the making of such contracts or agreements shall not be an unfair method of competition under section 5, as amended and supplemented, of the Act entitled "An Act to create a Federal Trade Commission, to define its powers and, duties, and for other purposes," approved September 26, 1914: Provided further, That the preceding proviso shall not make lawful any contract or agreement, providing for the establishment or maintenance of minimum resale prices on any commodity herein involved, between manufacturers, or between producers, or between wholesalers, or between brokers, or between factors, or between retailers, or between persons, firms, or corporations in competition with each other. Every person who shall make any contract or engage in any combination or conspiracy hereby declared to be illegal shall be deemed guilty of a misdemeanor, and, on conviction thereof, shall be punished by fine not exceeding fifty thousand dollars, or by imprisonment not exceeding one year, or by both said punishments, in the discretion of the court.

SECTION 2. Every person who shall monopolize, or attempt to monopolize, or combine or conspire with any other person or persons, to monopolize any part of the trade or commerce among the several States, or with foreign nations, shall be deemed guilty of a misdemeanor, and, on conviction thereof, shall be punished by fine not exceeding fifty thousand dollars, or by imprisonment not exceeding one year, or by both said punishments, in the discretion of the court.

SECTION 3. Every contract, combination in form of trust or otherwise, or conspiracy, in restraint of trade or commerce in any Territory of the United States or of the District of Columbia, or in restraint of trade or commerce between any such Territory and another, or between any such Territory or Territories and any State or States or the District of Columbia, or with foreign nations, or between the District of Columbia and any State or States or foreign nations, is hereby declared illegal. Every person who shall make any such contract or engage in any such combination or conspiracy, shall be deemed guilty of a misdemeanor, and, on conviction thereof, shall be punished by fine not exceeding fifty thousand dollars, or by imprisonment not exceeding one year, or by both said punishments, in the discretion of the court.

SECTION 4. The several circuit courts of the United States are hereby invested with jurisdiction to prevent and restrain violations of this Act; and it shall be the duty of the several United States attorneys, in their respective districts, under the direction of the Attorney-General, to institute proceedings in equity to prevent and restrain such violations. Such proceedings may be by way of petition setting forth the case and praying that such violation shall be enjoined or otherwise prohibited. When the parties complained of shall have been duly notified of such petition the court shall proceed, as soon as may be, to the hearing and determination of the case; and pending such petition and before final decree, the court may at any time make such temporary restraining order or prohibition as shall be deemed just in the premises.

SECTION 5. Whenever it shall appear to the court before which any proceeding under section four of this Act may be pending, that the ends of justice require that other parties should be brought before the court, the court may cause them to be summoned, whether they reside in the district in which the court is held or not; and subpoenas to that end may be served in any district by the marshal thereof.

SECTION 6. Any property owned under any contract or by any combination, or pursuant to any conspiracy (and being the subject thereof) mentioned in section one of this act, and being in the course of transportation from one State to another, or to a foreign country, shall be forfeited to the United States, and may be seized and condemned by like proceedings as those provided by law for the forfeiture, seizure, and condemnation of property imported into the United States contrary to law.

SECTION 7. Any person who shall be injured in his business or property by any other person or corporation by reason of anything forbidden or declared to be unlawful by this Act, may sue therefor in any circuit court of the United States in the district in which the defendant resides or is found, without respect to the amount in controversy, and shall recover threefold the damages by him sustained, and the costs of suit, including a reasonable attorney's fee.★

SECTION 8. That the word "person," or "persons," wherever used in this Act shall be deemed to include corporations and associations existing under or authorized by the laws of either the United States, the laws of any of the Territories, the laws of any State, or the laws of any foreign country.

Clayton Antitrust Act (1914, as Amended)

SECTION 6. That the labor of a human being is not a commodity or article of commerce. Nothing contained in the antitrust laws shall be construed to forbid the existence and operation of labor, agricultural, or horticultural organizations, instituted for the purposes of mutual help, and not having capital stock or conducted for profit, or to forbid or restrain individual members of such organizations from lawfully carrying out the legitimate objects thereof; nor shall such organizations,

★ Section 7 was repealed by Public Law 137, 84th Congress, 1st Session, approved July 7, 1955, effective Jan. 7, 1956. Treble damage suits by private parties are now authorized under section 4 of the Clayton Act, (1914).

4-3

or the members thereof, be held or construed to be illegal combinations or conspiracies in restraint of trade, under the antitrust laws.

SECTION 20. That no restraining order or injunction shall be granted by any court of the United States, or a judge or the judges thereof, in any case between an employer and employees, or between employers and employees, or between employees or between persons employed and persons seeking employment, involving, or growing out of, a dispute concerning terms or conditions of employment, unless necessary to prevent irreparable injury to property, or to a property right, of the party making the application, for which injury there is no adequate remedy at law, and such property or property right must be described with particularity in the application, which must be in writing and sworn to by the applicant or by his agent or attorney.

And no such restraining order or injunction shall prohibit any person or persons, whether singly or in concert, from terminating any relations of employment, or from ceasing to perform any work or labor, or from recommending, advising or persuading others by peaceful means so to do; or from attending at any place where any such persons may lawfully be, for the purpose of peacefully obtaining or communicating information, or from peacefully persuading any person to work or to abstain from working; or from ceasing to patronize or to employ any party to such dispute, or from recommending, advising, or persuading others by peaceful and lawful means so to do; or from paying or giving to, or withholding from, any person engaged in such dispute, any strike benefits or other moneys or things of value; or from peaceably assembling in a lawful manner, and for lawful purposes; or from doing any act or thing which might lawfully be done in the absence of such dispute by any party thereto; nor shall any of the acts specified in this paragraph be considered or held to be violations of any law of the United States.

The Railway Labor Act (1926, as Amended)

SUMMARY AND DESCRIPTION

The Railway Labor Act governs the labor relations of railroads and airlines and their employees. The Act makes it the mutual duty of carriers and employees to make and maintain agreements, guarantees and provides for the exercise of labor's collective-bargaining rights, and prescribes methods for the settlement of various types of disputes.

The Act applies to all railroads, express companies and sleeping-car companies engaged in interstate commerce and their subsidiaries (such as refrigerator car companies, bridge companies, and others engaged in transport, transfer, or storage services) and to airlines engaged in interstate and foreign commerce and transportation of mail.

Two agencies administer the Act:

The National Mediation Board in Washington, D.C., composed of three members appointed by the President, with the advice and consent of the Senate, handles disputes concerning (1) designation of representatives for collective bargaining purposes, (2) negotiation of changes in rates of pay and new or revised collective bargaining agreements, and (3) interpretation of agreements reached through mediation.

The National Railroad Adjustment Board in Chicago, Illinois, is composed of 34 members, 17 of whom represent and are paid by the carriers, and 17 by the national railway labor organizations. Unlike the National Mediation Board, it has jurisdiction only over railway carriers and employees. It makes final and binding decisions in disputes growing out of grievances or the application and interpretation of existing agreements.

Rights of Employees

Section 2 of the Act states that: Employees shall have the right to organize and bargain collectively through representatives of their own choosing. Section 2 (3), (4), and (5) of the Act, outlined below, which protect this right, are made a part of every collective agreement.

In order to protect workers in exercising this right, carriers are forbidden to do any of the following acts:

a. To deny or question the right of their employees to organize or to interfere with their organization (sec. 2(4)).

b. To use funds of the carrier in maintaining any labor organization or to pay any employee representative (sec. 2(4)).

c. To influence employees to join or not to join any labor organization (sec. 2(4)).

d. To require employees to sign any agreement promising to join or not to join any labor organization (sec. 2(5)).

Determination of Collective Bargaining Representatives

Section 2(3) of the Act states that collective bargaining representatives shall be designated by the respective parties without interference, influence, or coercion by either party over the designation of representatives by the other; and neither party shall in any way interfere with, influence, or coerce the other in its choice of representatives.

It is specifically provided that employee representatives for collective bargaining shall not be required to be employees of the employer.

The Act states that the majority of any craft or class of employees shall have the right to determine who shall be the representative of the class or craft (sec. 2(4)). While the Board has no power to establish crafts or classes of employees, it may designate who may participate in representation elections. Such determinations are usually made in the light of accepted practice in employee self-organization over a period of years.

Where any labor organization, committee, or employee representative asserts that a dispute exists concerning representation of employees for the purposes of the Act, it is the duty of the National Mediation Board to investigate such a dispute and conduct an election by secret ballot or any other suitable method to determine who is the collective bargaining representative of the employees (sec. 2(9)). If a majority of the employees in a craft or class chooses an individual or a labor organization, the Board then issues a certification of that fact to the parties and the carrier.

The Act was amended in 1951 to specifically provide (sec. 2(11)) that carriers and labor organizations may negotiate union shop and checkoff agreements.

Interference by carriers in the designation of employee representatives is a misdeameanor. Employees may also appeal to the Federal courts for an injunction to restrain the carrier from violating the Act.

Duties of Carriers and Employees to Bargain Collectively

Section 2(1) states: It shall be the duty of all carriers, their officers, agents, and employees to exert every reasonable effort to make and maintain agreements concerning rates of pay, rules and working conditions, and to settle all disputes whether arising out of the application of such agreements or otherwise, in order to avoid any interruption to commerce or to the operation of any carrier growing out of any dispute between the carrier and the employees thereof.

Every carrier is required to file with the National Mediation Board a copy of every contract with its employees, as well as all changes when made.

Procedure in Making and Revising Agreements

The act provides for the following procedure in making and revising agreements:

a. *Notice.* Carriers and employees alike are required to give at least 30 days' notice of any intended change in their collective bargaining agreements regarding rates of pay, rules, or working conditions, and within 10 days the time and place for a conference shall be agreed upon.

b. *Mediation.* In case of a dispute not settled in conference, either party may request the mediation services of the National Mediation Board. The Board, at its discretion, may also proffer its services without a request.

c. *Arbitration.* If mediation is unsuccessful, the Board shall endeavor to induce the parties to submit their controversy to arbitration. However, the Act does not compel the parties to arbitrate. Arbitration boards, when agreed upon, may consist of 3 or 6 members, one-third of the number being appointed by each party to the dispute, who must then choose the remaining members. If they fail to do so within a time limit specified in the Act, the Board appoints the neutral members. At the request of either or both parties, any arbitration board so established shall also have authority to pass on any dispute over the meaning or application of its award.

d. *Emergency Boards.* Should arbitration be refused by either party and the dispute remain unsettled, and should it, in the judgment of the National Mediation Board, threaten substantially to interrupt interstate commerce to a degree such as to deprive any section of the country of essential transportation service (sec. 10), the National Mediation Board is required to notify the President. The President may then, at his discretion, appoint an Emergency Board to investigate and report within 30 days. During this period, and for 30 days after the Board has made its report to the President, no change may be made in the conditions which gave rise to the dispute except by mutual agreement of the parties.

Procedure in Disputes Arising Out of Existing Agreements on Railroads

The National Mediation Board, on request of either party, will give interpretations of agreements reached through mediation. The following procedure is prescribed for all other instances of dispute arising out of agreements.

a. When disputes arise growing out of grievances or out of the interpretation or application of agreements, they shall be handled through the regular grievance procedure in the contract, up to and including the chief operating officer of the carrier.

b. If no adjustment is reached, either or both parties may petition the appropriate division of the National Railroad Adjustment Board, submitting a full statement of the facts and supporting data. The Board is divided into four divisions, each representing the carriers and the labor organizations equally. Divisional jurisdictions are:

First Division—train, engine, and yard service employees.
Second Division—shop crafts.
Third Division—station, tower, telegraph, dispatching, clerical, store, maintenance-of-way, sleeping car, and dining car employees and signalmen.
Fourth Division—Marine service employees, and all other employees not included in the first three divisions.

c. The appropriate division may hold hearings if requested by either party and make an award.

d. If the division fails to agree and cannot itself agree on a referee, the National Mediation Board is required to appoint a referee to sit with the division and make an award.

e. Awards of the Adjustment Board are final and binding. If a carrier fails to comply with a money award, such as the payment of back pay, the employee or labor organization in whose favor it is made may apply to a U.S. district court for enforcement.

Procedure in Disputes Arising Out of Existing Agreements on Airlines

Airline carriers and their employees are required by the Act to establish machinery for the adjustment of grievances as a part of their collective agreements.

Maintenance of the Status Quo

While conferences on making or revising agreements are being held and while the National Mediation Board is acting in any dispute, the carrier may not alter rates of pay, rules, or working conditions.

Posting Notices

All carriers covered by the Act are required to post notices specified by the National Mediation Board stating that all disputes will be handled in accordance with the Act, and reprinting sections of the Act relating to the rights of employees.

Penalties

Violation by a carrier of the provisions outlined above regarding rights of employees, determination of collective bargaining representatives, giving notice of intended change of agreements, and posting notices, is a misdemeanor, punishable by a fine up to $20,000, imprisonment, or both. Claims of violations should be filed with the U.S. district attorney in the area where the violation occurred.

For further information write: National Mediation Board, Washington, D.C. 20572.

The Norris-La Guardia (Anti-Injunction) Act (1932)

SUMMARY AND DESCRIPTION

The Anti-Injunction Act declares it to be a public policy that the workers shall have full freedom of association, self-organization, and designation of representatives of his own choosing to negotiate the terms and conditions of his employment, free from employer interference in these or other concerted activities for mutual aid or protection.

The act defines and limits the powers of the Federal courts to issue injunctions in labor disputes, in conformity with this policy.

Yellow-Dog Contracts

Employment contracts whereby a worker agrees not to join a union, or to resign if he is a union member (yellow-dog contracts), are declared contrary to public policy and unenforceable in Federal courts.

When Injunctions May Not Be Issued

No Federal court may issue an injunction, temporary or permanent, in any case involving or growing out of a labor dispute, to prohibit any individual worker or group of workers acting in concert from doing any of the following acts, except as modified by the Labor-Management Relations Act.

1. Ceasing or refusing to work.

2. Joining or continuing membership in a union.

3. Aiding or refusing to aid financially or by other lawful means any person participating in or interested in a labor dispute.

4. Giving publicity to the existence of or the facts involved in any labor dispute whether by advertising, speaking, patrolling, or by any other method not involving fraud or violence.

5. Assembling peaceably to act or to organize to act in promotion of their interests in a labor dispute.

6. Advising or notifying any person of intent to do any of the above, agreeing or refusing to do any of the above, or inducing others to do any of the above acts, without fraud or violence.

The Act defines a labor dispute as any dispute over terms and conditions of employment or matters of employee representation in collective bargaining, even though the persons involved are not in the relation of employer and employee.

When Injunctions May Be Issued

Except as otherwise indicated below, a Federal court may issue a temporary or permanent injunction in cases involving or growing out of a labor dispute only after hearing the testimony of witnesses in open court with opportunity for cross-examination. Such hearings shall be held only after personal notice to all known persons involved including the public officers responsible for protecting the complainant's property.

The court must also find that:

1. Unlawful acts have been threatened and will be committed unless restrained or have been committed and will be continued unless restrained;

2. Substantial and irreparable property damage will follow;

3. Greater injury will result to the complainant from denying the injunction than to the defendant from granting it;

4. The complainant has no adequate remedy at law;

5. Public officers are unable or unwilling to furnish adequate protection;

6. The complainant has complied with every legal

obligation involved in the dispute and has made every reasonable effort to settle the dispute by negotiation or with the aid of available governmental machinery.

The injunction or temporary restraining order may be issued only against the person or persons, association, or organization making the threat or committing the unlawful act or actually authorizing or ratifying the act.

Exception: Under special circumstances a Federal court may issue a temporary restraining order for a maximum of 5 days without an open court hearing, on the basis of sworn testimony sufficient to sustain a temporary injunction issued on hearing after notice, and on condition that the complainant posts a bond.

Issuance of Injunctions in Special Cases

Temporary or permanent injunctions may be issued by Federal courts without regard to the above provisions of the Act, even though a labor dispute may exist, in the following instances: (1) Where an injunction is properly sought by the National Labor Relations Board pending the determination of an unfair labor practice proceeding, (2) in cases where the Board seeks to enforce an order issued by it or an aggrieved party desires to contest the Board's order, or (3) where, in the case of a threatened or actual strike affecting an industry engaged in interstate commerce which would imperil the national health or safety, the Attorney General of the United States requests an injunction. The Act does not affect the jurisdiction of Federal courts to issue injunctions in labor disputes between the United States and its employees.

For further information write to: Office of the Solicitor, U.S. Department of Labor, Washington, D.C. 20210.

Anti-Racketeering Act (Hobbs Act) (Act of 1934 as Amended)

SUMMARY AND DESCRIPTION

The Anti-Racketeering Law makes it a felony to obstruct, delay, or affect commerce, or the movement of any article or commodity in commerce, by robbery or extortion.

The Act also makes it a felony to act in concert with others to do anything in violation of the above, or to participate in any attempt at such violation, or to commit or threaten physical violence to any person or property in furtherance of any plan to commit such violation.

The provisions of the Anti-Injunction Act, Railway Labor Act, and National Labor Relations Act are specifically preserved.

The U.S. Department of Justice is charged with prosecuting violators, who are subject to a maximum fine of $10,000, imprisonment for a maximum of 20 years, or both.

Anti-Strike Breaker Law (Byrnes Act) (Act of 1934 as Amended)

SUMMARY AND DESCRIPTION

The Anti-Strikebreaker Law makes it a felony to transport in interstate commerce any person employed for the purpose of interfering by force or threats with:

a. Peaceful picketing by employees during any labor dispute affecting wages, hours, or working conditions; or

b. Exercise of employee rights of self-organization or collective bargaining.

The Act applies to persons who willfully transport others or cause others to be transported, and to persons knowingly transported for these purposes. It does not apply to common carriers.

The U.S. Department of Justice is charged with prosecuting violators, who are subject to a maximum fine of $5,000, imprisonment up to 2 years, or both.

A GUIDE TO BASIC LAW AND PROCEDURES
UNDER THE NATIONAL LABOR RELATIONS ACT

Summary of the Act

Purpose of the Act

It is in the national interest of the United States to maintain full production in its economy. Industrial strife among employees, employers, and labor organizations interferes with full production and is contrary to our national interest. Experience has shown that labor disputes can be lessened if the parties involved recognize the legitimate rights of each in their relations with one another. To establish these rights under law, Congress enacted the National Labor Relations Act. Its purpose is to define and protect the rights of employees and employers, to encourage collective bargaining, and to eliminate certain practices on the part of labor and management that are harmful to the general welfare.

What the Act provides

The National Labor Relations Act states and defines the rights of employees to organize and to bargain collectively with their employers through representatives of their own choosing. To ensure that employees can freely choose their own representatives for the purpose of collective bargaining, the Act establishes a procedure by which they can exercise their choice at a secret ballot election conducted by the National Labor Relations Board. Further, to protect the rights of employees and employers, and to prevent labor disputes that would adversely affect the rights of the public, Congress has defined certain practices of employers and unions as unfair labor practices.

How the Act is enforced

The law is administered and enforced principally by the National Labor Relations Board and the General Counsel acting through more than 45 regional and other field offices located in major cities in various sections of the country. The General Counsel and his staff in the Regional Offices investigate and prosecute unfair labor practice cases and conduct elections to determine employee representatives. The five-member Board decides cases involving charges of unfair labor practices and determines representation election questions that come to it from the Regional Offices.

How this material is organized

The rights of employees, including the rights to self-organization and collective bargaining that are protected by Section 7 of the Act, are presented first in this material. The Act's provisions concerning the union shop and the requirements for union-security agreements are covered in the same section which also includes a discussion of the right to strike and the right to picket. The obligations of collective bargaining and the Act's provisions for the selection of employee representatives are treated in the following section. Unfair labor practices of employers and of labor organizations are then presented in separate sections. The final section, entitled "How the Act Is Enforced," sets forth the organization of the NLRB; its authority and limitations; its procedures and powers in representation matters, in unfair labor practice cases, and in certain special proceedings under the Act; and the Act's provisions concerning enforcement of the Board's orders.

The Rights of Employees
The Section 7 Rights

The rights of employees are set forth principally in Section 7 of the Act, which provides as follows:

> Sec. 7. Employees shall have the right to self-organization, to form, join, or assist labor organizations, to bargain collectively through representatives of their own choosing, and to engage in other concerted activities for the purpose of collective bargaining or other mutual aid or protection, and shall also have the right to refrain from any or all of such activities except to the extent that such right may be affected by an agreement requiring membership in a labor organization as a condition of employment as authorized in section 8(a)(3).

Examples of the rights protected by this section are the following:

Examples of Section 7 rights

- Forming or attempting to form a union among the employees of a company.
- Joining a union whether the union is recognized by the employer or not.
- Assisting a union to organize the employees of an employer.
- Going out on strike to secure better working conditions.
- Refraining from activity in behalf of a union.

The Union Shop

The Act permits, under certain conditions, a union and an employer to make an agreement (called a union-security agreement) requiring all employees to join the union in order to retain their jobs (Section 8(a)(3)). However, the Act does not authorize such agreements in States where they are forbidden by state law (Section 14(b)).

Under certain circumstances an employee of a health care institution may not be required to pay dues or fees to a union where the employee has religious objections to the payment of such dues and fees.

A union-security agreement cannot require that applicants for employment be members of the union in order to be hired. The most that can be required is that all employees in the group covered by the agreement become members of the union within a certain period of time after the contract takes effect. This "grace period" cannot be less than 30 days except in the building and construction industry. New employees may be required to join the union at the end of a 30-day grace period after they are hired. The Act allows a shorter grace period of 7 full days in the building and construction industry (Section 8(f)). A union-security agreement that provides a shorter grace period than the law allows is invalid, and any employee discharged because of nonmembership in the union is entitled to reinstatement. *Union-security agreements*

For a union-security agreement to be valid, it must meet all of the following requirements:

1. The union must not have been assisted or controlled by the employer (see Section 8(a)(2) under "Unfair Labor Practices of Employers" on pages 19–24). *Requirements for union-security agreements*
2. The union must be the majority representative of the employees in the appropriate collective-bargaining unit covered by such agreement when made.
3. The union's authority to make such an agreement must not have been revoked within the previous 12 months by the employees in a Board election.
4. The agreement must provide for the appropriate grace period.

Section 8(f) of the Act allows an employer engaged primarily in the building and construction industry to sign a union-security agreement with a union without the union's having been designated as the representative of its employees as otherwise required by the Act. The agreement can be made before the employer has hired any employees for a project and will apply to them when they are hired. As noted above, new employees may be required to join the union *after* 7 full days. If the agreement is made while employees are on the job, it must allow nonunion employees the same 7-day grace period. As with any other union-security agreement, the union involved must be free from employer assistance or control. *Prehire agreements in the construction industry*

Agreements in the building and construction industry can include, as stated in Section 8(f), the following additional provisions:

1. A requirement that the employer notify the union concerning job openings.
2. A provision that gives the union an opportunity to refer qualified applicants for such jobs.
3. Job qualification standards based on training or experience.
4. A provision for priority in hiring based on length of service with the employer, in the industry, or in the particular geographic area. Such hiring provisions may lawfully be included in collective-bargaining agreements which cover employees in other industries as well.

The Right To Strike

Section 7 of the Act states in part, "Employees shall have the right . . . to engage in other concerted activities for the purpose of collective bargaining or other mutual aid or protection." Strikes are included among the concerted activities protected for employees by this section. Section 13 also concerns the right to strike. It reads as follows:

> Nothing in this Act, except as specifically provided for herein, shall be construed so as either to interfere with or impede or diminish in any way the right to strike, or to affect the limitations or qualifications on that right.

It is clear from a reading of these two provisions that the law not only guarantees the right of employees to strike, but also places limitations and qualifications on the exercise of that right. See, for example, restrictions on strikes in health care institutions, page 44.

The lawfulness of a strike may depend on the object, or purpose, of the strike, on its timing, or on the conduct of the strikers. The object, or objects, of a strike and whether the objects are lawful are matters that are not always easy to determine. Such issues often have to be decided by the National Labor Relations Board. The consequences can be severe to striking employees and struck employers, involving as they do questions of reinstatement and backpay. *Lawful and unlawful strikes*

It must be emphasized that the following is only a brief outline. A detailed analysis of the law concerning strikes, and application of the law to all of the factual situations that can arise in connection with strikes, is beyond the scope of this material. Employees and employers who anticipate being involved in strike action should proceed cautiously and on the basis of competent advice.

Employees who strike for a lawful object fall into two classes—"economic strikers" and "unfair labor practice strikers." Both classes continue as employees, but unfair labor practice strikers have greater rights of reinstatement to their jobs. *Strikes for a lawful object*

If the object of a strike is to obtain from the employer some economic concession such as higher wages, shorter hours, or better working conditions, the striking employees are called economic strikers. They retain their status as employees and cannot be discharged, but they can be replaced by their employer. If the employer has hired bona fide permanent replacements who are filling the jobs of the economic strikers when the strikers apply unconditionally to go back to work, the strikers are *not* entitled to reinstatement at that time. However, if the strikers do not obtain regular and substantially equivalent employment, they are entitled to be recalled to jobs for which they are qualified when openings in such jobs occur if they, or their bargaining representative, have made an unconditional request for their reinstatement.

Economic strikers defined

Employees who strike to protest an unfair labor practice committed by their employer are called unfair labor practice strikers. Such strikers can be neither discharged nor permanently replaced. When the strike ends, unfair labor practice strikers, absent serious misconduct on their part, are entitled to have their jobs back even if employees hired to do their work have to be discharged.

Unfair labor practice strikers defined

If the Board finds that economic strikers or unfair labor practice strikers who have made an unconditional request for reinstatement have been unlawfully denied reinstatement by their employer, the Board may award such strikers backpay starting at the time they should have been reinstated.

A strike may be unlawful because an object, or purpose, of the strike is unlawful. A strike in support of a union unfair labor practice, or one that would cause an employer to commit an unfair labor practice, may be a strike for an unlawful object. For example, it is an unfair labor practice for an employer to discharge an employee for lack of union membership where there is no union-security agreement in effect (Section 8(a)(3)). A strike to compel an employer to do this would be a strike for an unlawful object and, therefore, an unlawful strike. Strikes of this nature will be discussed in connection with the various unfair labor practices in a later section of this guide.

Strikes unlawful because of purpose

Furthermore, Section 8(b)(4) of the Act prohibits strikes for certain objects even though the objects are not necessarily unlawful if achieved by other means. An example of this would be a strike to compel Employer A to cease doing business with Employer B. It is not unlawful for Employer A voluntarily to stop doing business with Employer B, nor is it unlawful for a union merely to request that it do so. It is, however, unlawful for the union to strike with an object of forcing the employer to do so. These points will be covered in more detail in the explanation of Section 8(b)(4).

In any event, employees who participate in an unlawful strike may be discharged and are not entitled to reinstatement.

A strike that violates a no-strike provision of a contract is not protected by the Act, and the striking employees can be discharged or otherwise disciplined unless the strike is called to protest certain kinds of unfair labor practices committed by the employer. Also, an employee who is subject to a no-strike contract clause can be replaced for refusing to cross a picket line at the plant of another employer unless the contract specifically gives the employee the right not to cross a picket line. It should be noted that not all refusals to work are considered strikes and thus violations of no-strike provisions. A walkout because of conditions abnormally dangerous to health, such as a defective ventilation system in a spray-painting shop, has been held not to violate a no-strike provision.

Strikes unlawful because of timing —Effect of no-strike contract

Section 8(d) provides that where either party desires to terminate or change an existing contract, it must comply with certain conditions. (See page 7.) If these requirements are not met, a strike to terminate or change a contract is unlawful and participating strikers lose their status as employees of the employer engaged in the labor dispute. If the strike was caused by the unfair labor practice of the employer, however, the strikers are classed as unfair labor practice strikers and their status is not affected by failure to follow the required procedure.

Same—Strikes at end of contract period

Strikers who engage in serious misconduct in the course of a strike may be refused reinstatement to their former jobs. This applies to both economic strikers and unfair labor practice strikers. Serious misconduct has been held to include, among other things, violence and threats of violence. The U.S. Supreme Court has ruled that a "sitdown" strike, where employees simply stay in the plant and refuse to work, thus depriving the owner of property, is not protected by the law. Where an unfair labor practice by the employer involved provokes an unfair labor practice strike, this fact may be considered in the determination of whether misconduct by strikers will bar their reinstatement. Examples of serious misconduct that could cause the employees involved to lose their right to reinstatement are:

Strikes unlawful because of misconduct of strikers

- Strikers physically blocking persons from entering or leaving a struck plant.
- Strikers threatening violence against nonstriking employees entering a plant.
- Strikers attacking management representatives.

Likewise the right to picket is subject to limitations and qualifications. As with the right to strike, picketing can be prohibited because of its object or its timing, or misconduct on the picket line. In addition, Section 8(b)(7) declares it to be an unfair labor practice for a union to picket for certain objects whether the picketing accompanies a strike or not. This will be covered in more detail in the section on union unfair labor practices.

The Right To Picket

Collective Bargaining and Representation of Employees

Collective bargaining is one of the keystones of the Act. Section 1 of the Act declares that the policy of the United States is to be carried out "by encouraging the practice and procedure of collective bargaining and by protecting the exercise by workers of full freedom of association, self-organization, and designation of representatives of their own choosing, for the purpose of negotiating the terms and conditions of their employment or other mutual aid or protection."

Collective Bargaining

Collective bargaining is defined in the Act. Section 8(d) requires an employer and the representative of its employees to meet at reasonable times, to confer in good faith about certain matters, and to put into writing any agreement reached if requested by either party. The parties must confer in good faith with respect to wages, hours, and other terms or conditions of employment, the negotiation of an agreement, or any question arising under an agreement.

These obligations are imposed equally on the employer and the representative of its employees. It is an unfair labor practice for either party to refuse to bargain collectively with the other. The obligation does not, however, compel either party to agree to a proposal by the other, nor does it require either party to make a concession to the other.

Duty to bargain imposed on both employer and union

Section 8(d) provides further that where a collective-bargaining agreement is in effect no party to the contract shall end or change the contract unless the party wishing to end or change it takes the following steps:

1. The party must notify the other party to the contract in writing about the proposed termination or modification 60 days before the date on which the contract is scheduled to expire. If the contract is not scheduled to expire on any particular date, the notice in writing must be served 60 days before the time when it is proposed that the termination or modification take effect.

2. The party must offer to meet and confer with the other party for the purpose of negotiating a new contract or a contract containing the proposed changes.

Bargaining steps to end or change a contract

3. The party must, within 30 days after the notice to the other party, notify the Federal Mediation and Conciliation Service of the existence of a dispute if no agreement has been reached by that time. Said party must also notify at the same time any State or Territorial mediation or conciliation agency in the State or Territory where the dispute occurred.

4. The party must continue in full force and effect, without resorting to strike or lockout, all the terms and conditions of the existing contract until 60 days after the notice to the other party was given or until the date the contract is scheduled to expire, whichever is later.

(In the case of a health care institution, the requirement in paragraphs 1 and 4 is 90 days, and in paragraph 3 is 60 days. In addition, there is a 30-day notice requirement to the agencies in paragraph 3 when a dispute arises in bargaining for an initial contract.)

The requirements of paragraphs 2, 3, and 4, above, cease to apply if the NLRB issues a certificate showing that the employees' representative who is a party to the contract has been replaced by a different representative or has been voted out by the employees. Neither party is required to discuss or agree to any change of the provisions of the contract if the other party proposes that the change become effective before the provision could be reopened according to the terms of the contract.

When the bargaining steps are not required

As has been pointed out, any employee who engages in a strike within the notice period loses status as an employee of the struck employer. This loss of status ends, however, if and when that individual is reemployed by the same employer.

Section 9(a) provides that the employee representatives that have been "designated or selected for the purposes of collective bargaining by the majority of the employees in a unit appropriate for

The Employee Representative

such purposes, shall be the exclusive representatives of all the employees in such unit for the purposes of collective bargaining."

What is an appropriate bargaining unit

A unit of employees is a group of two or more employees who share common employment interests and conditions and may reasonably be grouped together for purposes of collective bargaining. The determination of what is an appropriate unit for such purposes is, under the Act, left to the discretion of the NLRB. Section 9(b) states that the Board shall decide in each representation case whether, "in order to assure to employees the fullest freedom in exercising the rights guaranteed by this Act, the unit appropriate for the purposes of collective bargaining shall be the employer unit, craft unit, plant unit, or subdivision thereof."

This broad discretion is, however, limited by several other provisions of the Act. Section 9(b)(1) provides that the Board shall not approve as appropriate a unit that includes both professional and nonprofessional employees, unless a majority of the professional employees involved vote to be included in the mixed unit.

Section 9(b)(2) provides that the Board shall not hold a proposed craft unit to be inappropriate simply because a different unit was previously approved by the Board, unless a majority of the employees in the proposed craft unit vote against being represented separately.

Section 9(b)(3) prohibits the Board from including plant guards in the same unit with other employees. It also prohibits the Board from certifying a labor organization as the representative of a plant guard unit if the labor organization has members who are nonguard employees or if it is "affiliated directly or indirectly" with an organization that has members who are nonguard employees.

How the appropriateness of a unit is determined

Generally, the appropriateness of a bargaining unit is determined on the basis of the common employment interests of the employees involved. Those who have the same or substantially similar interests concerning wages, hours, and working conditions are grouped together in a bargaining unit. In determining whether a proposed unit is appropriate, the following factors are also considered:

1. Any history of collective bargaining.
2. The desires of the employees concerned.
3. The extent to which the employees are organized. Section 9(c)(5) forbids the Board from giving this factor controlling weight.

Who can or cannot be included in a unit

A unit may cover the employees in one plant of an employer, or it may cover employees in two or more plants of the same employer. In some industries where employers are grouped together in voluntary associations, a unit may include employees of two or more employers in any number of locations. It should be noted that a bargaining unit can include only persons who are "employees" within the meaning of the Act. The Act excludes certain individuals, such as agricultural laborers, independent contractors, supervisors, and persons in managerial positions, from the meaning of "employees." None of these individuals can be included in a bargaining unit established by the Board. In addition, the Board, as a matter of policy, excludes from bargaining units employees who act in a confidential capacity to an employer's labor relations officials.

Duties of bargaining representative and employer

Once an employee representative has been designated by a majority of the employees in an appropriate unit, the Act makes that representative the exclusive bargaining agent for all employees in the unit. As exclusive bargaining agent it has a duty to represent equally and fairly all employees in the unit without regard to their union membership or activities. Once a collective-bargaining representative has been designated or selected by its employees, it is illegal for an employer to bargain with individual employees, with a group of employees, or with another employee representative.

Section 9(a) provides that any individual employee or a group of employees shall have the right at any time to present grievances to their employer and to have such grievances adjusted without the intervention of the bargaining representative provided:

1. The adjustment is not inconsistent with the terms of any collective-bargaining agreement then in effect.
2. The bargaining representative has been given the opportunity to be present at such adjustment.

How a Bargaining Representative Is Selected

Although the Act requires that an employer bargain with the representative selected by its employees, it does not require that the representative be selected by any particular procedure so long as the representative is clearly the choice of a majority of the employees. As one of the methods by which employees can select a bargaining representative the Act provides for the NLRB to conduct representation elections by secret ballot.

The NLRB can conduct such an election only when a petition has been filed requesting one. A petition for certification of representatives can be filed by an employee or a group of employees or any individual or labor organization acting on their behalf, or it can be filed by an employer. If filed by or on behalf of employees, the petition must be supported by a substantial number of employees who wish to be represented for collective bargaining and must state that their employer declines to recognize their representative. If filed by an employer, the petition must allege that one or more individuals or organizations have made a claim for recognition as the exclusive representative of the same group of employees. *Petition for certification of representatives*

The Act also contains a provision whereby employees or someone acting on their behalf can file a petition seeking an election to determine whether or not the employees wish to retain the individual or labor organization currently acting as their bargaining representative, whether the representative has been certified or voluntarily recognized by the employer. This is called a decertification election. *Petition for decertification election*

Provision is also made for the Board to determine by secret ballot whether the employees covered by a union-shop agreement desire to withdraw the authority of their representative to continue the agreement. This is called a union-shop deauthorization election and can be brought about by the filing of a petition signed by 30 percent or more of the employees covered by the agreement. *Union-shop deauthorization*

If you will refer to the "Types of Cases" chart on pages 24 and 25 of this booklet you may find it easier to understand the differences between the six types of petitions that can be filed under the Act.

The same petition form is used for any kind of Board election. When the petition is filed, the NLRB must investigate the petition, hold a hearing if necessary, and direct an election if it finds that a question of representation exists. The purpose of the investigation is to determine, among other things, the following: *Purpose of investigation and hearing*

1. Whether the Board has jurisdiction to conduct an election.
2. Whether there is a sufficient showing of employee interest to justify an election.
3. Whether a question of representation exists.
4. Whether the election is sought in an appropriate unit of employees.
5. Whether the representative named in the petition is qualified.
6. Whether there are any barriers to an election in the form of existing contracts or prior elections.

The jurisdiction of the NLRB to direct and conduct an election is limited to those enterprises that affect commerce. (This is discussed in greater detail at pages 45–49.) The other matters listed above will be discussed in turn. *Jurisdiction to conduct an election*

First, however, it should be noted that Section 8(b)(7)(C) provides, among other things, that when a petition is filed within a reasonable period, not to exceed 30 days, after the commencement of recognitional or organizational picketing, the NLRB shall "forthwith" order an election and certify the results. This is so if the picketing is not within the protection of the second proviso to Section 8(b)(7)(C). Where an election under Section 8(b)(7)(C) is appropriate, neither a hearing nor a showing of interest is required, and the election is scheduled sooner than under the ordinary procedure. *Expedited elections under Section 8(b)(7)(C)*

Regarding the showing of interest, it is the practice to require that a petitioner requesting an election for either certification of representatives or decertification show that at least 30 percent of the employees favor an election. The Act also requires that a petition for a union-shop deauthorization election be filed by 30 percent or more of the employees in the unit covered by the agreement for the NLRB to conduct an election for that purpose. The showing of interest must be exclusively by employees who are in the appropriate bargaining unit in which an election is sought. *Showing of interest required*

Section 9(c)(1) authorizes the NLRB to direct an election and certify the results thereof, provided the record shows that a question of representation exists. Petitions for certification of representatives present a question of representation if, among other things, they are based on a demand for recognition by the employee representative and a denial of recognition by the employer. The demand for recognition need not be made in any particular form; in fact, the filing of a petition by the representative itself is considered to be a demand for recognition. The NLRB has held that even a representative that is *Existence of question of representation*

4-13

currently recognized by the employer can file a petition for certification and that such petition presents a question of representation provided the representative has not previously been certified.

A question of representation is also raised by a decertification petition which challenges the representative status of a bargaining agent previously certified or currently recognized by the employer. However, a decertification petition filed by a supervisor does not raise a valid question of representation and must be dismissed.

Who can qualify as bargaining representative

Section 2(4) of the Act provides that the employee representative for collective bargaining can be "any individual or labor organization." A supervisor or any other management representative may not be an employee representative. It is NLRB policy to direct an election and to issue a certification unless the proposed bargaining agent fails to qualify as a bona fide representative of the employees. In determining a union's qualifications as bargaining agent, it is the union's willingness to represent the employees rather than its constitution and bylaws that is the controlling factor. The NLRB's power to certify a labor organization as bargaining representative is limited by Section 9(b)(3) which prohibits certification of a union as the representative of a unit of plant guards if the union "admits to membership, or is affiliated directly or indirectly with an organization which admits to membership, employees other than guards."

Bars to Election

Existing collective-bargaining contract

The NLRB has established the policy of not directing an election among employees presently covered by a valid collective-bargaining agreement except in accordance with certain rules. These rules, followed in determining whether or not an existing collective-bargaining contract will bar an election, are called the NLRB contract-bar rules. Not every contract will bar an election. Examples of contracts that would *not* bar an election are:

- The contract is not in writing, or is not signed.
- The contract has not been ratified by the members of the union, if such is expressly required.
- The contract does not contain substantial terms or conditions of employment sufficient to stabilize the bargaining relationship.
- The contract can be terminated by either party at any time for any reason.
- The contract contains a clearly illegal union-security clause.
- The bargaining unit is not appropriate.
- The union that entered the contract with the employer is no longer in existence or is unable or unwilling to represent the employees.
- The contract discriminates between employees on racial grounds.
- The contracting union is involved in a basic internal conflict with resulting unstabilizing confusion about the identity of the union.
- The employer's operations have changed substantially since the contract was executed.

Time provisions

Under the NLRB rules a valid contract for a fixed period of 3 years or less will bar an election for the period covered by the contract. A contract for a fixed period of more than 3 years will bar an election sought by a contracting party during the life of the contract, but will act as a bar to an election sought by an outside party for only 3 years following its effective date. A contract of no fixed period will not act as a bar at all.

When a petition can be filed if there is an existing contract

If there is no existing contract, a petition can bring about an election if it is filed before the day a contract is signed. If the petition is filed on the same day the contract is signed, the contract bars an election. Once the contract becomes effective as a bar to an election, no petition will be accepted until near the end of the period during which the contract is effective as a bar. Petitions filed not more than 90 days but over 60 days before the end of the contract-bar period will be accepted and can bring about an election. Of course, a petition can be filed after the contract expires. However, the last 60 days of the contract-bar period is called an "insulated" period. During this time the parties to the existing contract are free to negotiate a new contract or to agree to extend the old one. If they reach agreement in this period, petitions will not be accepted until 90 days before the end of the new contract-bar period.

Effect of certification

In addition to the contract-bar rules, the NLRB has established a rule that when a representative has been certified by the Board, the certification will ordinarily be binding for at least 1 year and a petition filed before the end of the certification year will be dismissed. In cases where the certified representative and the employer enter a valid collective-bargaining contract during the year, the contract becomes controlling, and whether a petition for an election can be filed is determined by the Board's contract-bar rules.

Section 9(c)(3) prohibits the holding of an election in any collective-bargaining unit or subdivision thereof in which a valid election has been held during the preceding 12-month period. A new election may be held, however, in a larger unit, but not in the same unit or subdivision in which the previous election was held. For example, if all of the production and maintenance employees in Company A, including draftsmen in the company engineering office, are included in a collective-bargaining unit, an election among all the employees in the unit would bar another election among all the employees in the unit for 12 months. Similarly, an election among the draftsmen only would bar another election among the draftsmen for 12 months. However, an election among the draftsmen would not bar a later election during the 12-month period among all the production employees including the draftsmen. *Effect of prior election*

It is the Board's interpretation that Section 9(c)(3) prohibits only the holding of an election during the 12-month period, but does not prohibit the filing of a petition. Accordingly, the NLRB will accept a petition filed not more than 60 days before the end of the 12-month period. The election cannot be held, of course, until after the 12-month period. If an election is held and a representative certified, that certification is binding for 1 year and a petition for another election in the same unit will be dismissed if it is filed during the 1-year period after the certification. If an election is held and no representative is certified, the election bars another election for 12 months. A petition for another election in the same unit can be filed not more than 60 days before the end of the 12-month period and the election can be held after the 12-month period expires. *When a petition can be filed if there has been a prior election*

Section 9(c)(1) provides that if a question of representation exists, the NLRB must make its determination by means of a secret ballot election. In a representation election employees are given a choice of one or more bargaining representatives or no representative at all. To be certified as the bargaining representative, an individual or a labor organization must receive a majority of the valid votes cast. **The Representation Election**

An election may be held by agreement between the employer and the individual or labor organization claiming to represent the employees. In such an agreement the parties would state the time and place agreed on, the choices to be included on the ballot, and a method to determine who is eligible to vote. They would also authorize the NLRB Regional Director to conduct the election. *Consent-election agreements*

If the parties are unable to reach an agreement, the Act authorizes the NLRB to order an election after a hearing. The Act also authorizes the Board to delegate to its Regional Directors the determination on matters concerning elections. Under this delegation of authority the Regional Directors can determine the appropriateness of the unit, direct an election, and certify the outcome. Upon the request of an interested party, the Board may review the action of a Regional Director, but such review does not stop the election process unless the Board so orders. The election details are left to the Regional Director. Such matters as who may vote, when the election will be held, and what standards of conduct will be imposed on the parties are decided in accordance with the Board's rules and its decisions. *Who determines election matters*

To be entitled to vote, an employee must have worked in the unit during the eligibility period set by the Board and must be employed in the unit on the date of the election. Generally, the eligibility period is the employer's payroll period just before the date on which the election was directed. This requirement does not apply, however, to employees who are ill, on vacation, or temporarily laid off, or to employees in military service who appear in person at the polls. The NLRB rules take into consideration the fact that employment is typically irregular in certain industries. In such industries eligibility to vote is determined according to formulas designed to permit all employees who have a substantial continuing interest in their employment conditions to vote. Examples of these formulas, which differ from case to case, are: *Who may vote in a representation election*

- In one case, employees of a construction company were allowed to vote if they worked for the employer at least 65 days during the year before the "eligibility date" for the election.

- In another case longshoremen who worked at least 700 hours during a specified contract year, and at least 20 hours in each full month between the end of that year and the date on which the election was directed, were allowed to vote.
- Radio and television talent employees and musicians in the television film, motion picture, and phonograph recording industries have been held eligible to vote if they worked in the unit 2 or more days during the year before the date on which the election was directed.

When strikers may be allowed to vote

Section 9(c)(3) provides that economic strikers who have been replaced by bona fide permanent employees may be entitled to vote in "any election conducted within 12 months after the commencement of the strike." The permanent replacements are also eligible to vote at the same time. As a general proposition a striker is considered to be an economic striker unless found by the NLRB to be on strike over unfair labor practices of the employer. Whether the economic striker is eligible to vote or not is determined on the facts of each case.

When elections are held

Ordinarily, elections are held within 30 days after they are directed. Seasonal drops in employment or any change in operations which would prevent a normal work force from being present may cause a different election date to be set. Normally an election will not be conducted when unfair labor practice charges have been filed except that, in certain cases, the Board may proceed to the election if the charging party so requests.

Conduct of elections

NLRB elections are conducted in accordance with strict standards designed to give the employee-voters an opportunity to freely indicate whether they wish to be represented for purposes of collective bargaining. Election details, such as time, place, and notice of an election, are left largely to the Regional Director who usually obtains the agreement of the parties on these matters. Any party to an election who believes that the Board election standards were not met may, within 5 days after the tally of ballots has been furnished, file objections to the election with the Regional Director under whose supervision the election was held. The Regional Director's rulings on these objections may be appealed to the Board for decision except in the case of elections that are held by consent of the parties, in which case the Regional Director's rulings are final.

An election will be set aside if it was accompanied by conduct that the NLRB considers created an atmosphere of confusion or fear of reprisals and thus interfered with the employees' freedom of choice. In any particular case the NLRB does not attempt to determine whether the conduct actually interfered with the employees' expression of free choice, but rather asks whether the conduct tended to do so. If it is reasonable to believe that the conduct would tend to interfere with the free expression of the employees' choice, the election may be set aside. Examples of conduct the Board considers to interfere with employee free choice are:

- Threats of loss of jobs or benefits by an employer or a union to influence the votes or union activities of employees.

- Misstatements of important facts in the election campaign by an employer or a union where the other party does not have a fair chance to reply.

- An employer firing employees to discourage or encourage their union activities or a union causing an employer to take such action.

- An employer or a union making campaign speeches to assembled groups of employees on company time within the 24-hour period before the election.

- The incitement of racial or religious prejudice by inflammatory campaign appeals made by either an employer or a union.

- Threats or the use of physical force or violence against employees by an employer or a union to influence their votes.

- The occurrence of extensive violence or trouble or widespread fear of job losses which prevents the holding of a fair election, whether or not caused by an employer or a union.

The unfair labor practices of employers are listed in Section 8(a) of the Act; those of labor organizations in Section 8(b). Section 8(e) lists an unfair labor practice that can be committed only by an employer and a labor organization acting together. The "Types of Cases" chart at pages 24–25 may be helpful in getting to know the relationship between the various unfair labor practice sections of the Act.

Unfair Labor Practices of Employers

Section 8(a)(1) forbids an employer "to interfere with, restrain, or coerce employees in the exercise of the rights guaranteed in section 7." Any prohibited interference by an employer with the rights of employees to organize, to form, join, or assist a labor organization, to bargain collectively, or to refrain from any of these activities, constitutes a violation of this section. This is a broad prohibition on employer interference, and an employer violates this section whenever it commits any of the other employer unfair labor practices. In consequence, whenever a violation of Section 8(a)(2), (3), (4), or (5) is committed, a violation of Section 8(a)(1) is also found. This is called a "derivative violation" of Section 8(a)(1.)

Section 8(a)(1)—Interference with Section 7 Rights

Employer conduct may of course independently violate Section 8(a)(1). Examples of such independent violations are:

Examples of violations of Section 8(a)(1)

- Threatening employees with loss of jobs or benefits if they should join or vote for a union.
- Threatening to close down the plant if a union should be organized in it.
- Questioning employees about their union activities or membership in such circumstances as will tend to restrain or coerce the employees.
- Spying on union gatherings, or pretending to spy.
- Granting wage increases deliberately timed to discourage employees from forming or joining a union.

Section 8(a)(2) makes it unlawful for an employer "to dominate or interfere with the formation or administration of any labor organization or contribute financial or other support to it." This section not only outlaws "company unions" that are dominated by the employer, but also forbids an employer to contribute money to a union it favors or to give a union improper advantages that are denied to rival unions.

Section 8(a)(2)—Domination or Illegal Assistance and Support of a Labor Organization

A labor organization is considered dominated within the meaning of this section if the employer has interfered with its formation and has assisted and supported its operation and activities to such an extent that it must be looked at as the employer's creation instead of the true bargaining representative of the employees. Such domination is the result of a combination of factors and has been found to exist where there is not only the factor of the employer getting the organization started, but also such other factors as the employer deciding how the organization will be set up and what it will do, or representatives of management actually taking part in the meetings and activities of the organization and trying to influence its actions and policies.

Domination

Interference that is less than complete domination is found where an employer tries to help a union that it favors by various kinds of conduct, such as giving the favored union improper privileges that are denied to other unions competing to organize the employees, or recognizing a favored union when another union has raised a real representation claim concerning the employees involved. Financial support of unions violates the noninterference provision of this section whether it is a direct payment to the assisted union or indirect financial aid.

Illegal assistance and support

An employer violates Section 8(a)(2) by:

Examples of violations of Section 8(a)(2)

- Taking an active part in organizing a union or a committee to represent employees.
- Bringing pressure on employees to join a union, except in the enforcement of a lawful union-security agreement.
- Allowing one of several unions, competing to represent employees, to solicit on company premises during working hours and denying other unions the same privilege.
- Soliciting and obtaining from employees and applicants for employment, during the hiring procedure, applications for union membership and signed authorizations for the checkoff of union dues.

1. CHARGES OF UNFAIR LABOR PRACTICES (C CASES)

Charge Against Employer		Charge Against Labor Organization		
Section of the Act **CA**	*Section of the Act* **CB**	*Section of the Act* **CC**	*Section of the Act* **CD**	

Charge Against Employer	Charge Against Labor Organization

Section of the Act CA

8(a)(1) To interfere with, restrain, or coerce employees in exercise of their rights under Section 7 (to join or assist a labor organization or to refrain).

8(a)(2) To dominate or interfere with the formation or administration of a labor organization or contribute financial or other support to it.

8(a)(3) By discrimination in regard to hire or tenure of employment or any term or condition of employment to encourage or discourage membership in any labor organization.

8(a)(4) To discharge or otherwise discriminate against employees because they have given testimony under the Act.

8(a)(5) To refuse to bargain collectively with representatives of its employees.

Section of the Act CB

8(b)(1)(A) To restrain or coerce employees in exercise of their rights under Section 7 (to join or assist a labor organization or to refrain).

8(b)(1)(B) To restrain or coerce an employer in the selection of its representatives for collective bargaining or adjustment of grievances.

8(b)(2) To cause or attempt to cause an employer to discriminate against an employee.

8(b)(3) To refuse to bargain collectively with employer.

8(b)(5) To require of employees the payment of excessive or discriminatory fees for membership.

8(b)(6) To cause or attempt to cause an employer to pay or agree to pay money or other thing of value for services which are not performed or not to be performed.

Section of the Act CC

8(b)(4)(i) To engage in, or induce or encourage any individual employed by any person engaged in commerce or in an industry affecting commerce, to engage in a strike, work stoppage, or boycott, or *(ii)* to threaten, coerce, or restrain any person engaged in commerce or in an industry affecting commerce, where in either case an object is:

(A) To force or require any employer or self-employed person to join any labor or employer organization or to enter into any agreement prohibited by Sec. 8(e).

(B) To force or require any person to cease using, selling, handling, transporting, or otherwise dealing in the products of any other producer, processor, or manufacturer, or to cease doing business with any other person, or force or require any other employer to recognize or bargain with a labor organization as the representative of its employees unless such labor organization has been so certified.

(C) To force or require any employer to recognize or bargain with a particular labor organization as the representative of its employees if another labor organization has been certified as the representative.

Section of the Act CD

(D) To force or require any employer to assign particular work to employees in a particular labor organization or in a particular trade, craft, or class rather than to employees in another trade, craft, or class, unless such employer is failing to conform to an appropriate Board order or certification.

Section of the Act CG

8(g) To strike, picket, or otherwise concertedly refuse to work at any health care institution without notifying the institution and the Federal Mediation and Conciliation Service in writing 10 days prior to such action.

Remedy in cases of domination differs from that in cases of illegal assistance and support

In remedying such unfair labor practices, the NLRB distinguishes between domination of a labor organization and conduct which amounts to no more than illegal assistance. When a union is found to be dominated by an employer, the Board has announced it will order the organization completely disestablished as a representative of employees. But, if the organization is found only to have been supported by employer assistance amounting to less than domination, the Board usually orders the employer to stop such support and to withhold recognition from the organization until such time as it has been certified by the Board as a bona fide representative of employees.

When an employer can pay employees for union activity during working hours

It should be noted in connection with the last example, above, that Section 8(a)(2) provides that an employer may permit employees to confer with it on union business during working hours without loss of pay. This means that both the employee and the union representative who goes along to discuss a grievance with the employer during working hours may do so without loss of pay.

Section 8(a)(3)—Discrimination Against Employees

Section 8(a)(3) makes it an unfair labor practice for an employer to discriminate against employees "in regard to hire or tenure of employment or any term or condition of employment" for the purpose of encouraging or discouraging membership in a labor organization. In general, the Act makes it illegal for an employer to discriminate in employment because of an employee's union or other group activity within the protection of the Act. A banding together of employees, even in the absence of a formal organization, may constitute a labor organization for purposes of Section 8(a)(3). It also prohibits discrimination because an employee has refrained from taking part in such union or group activity except where a valid union-shop agreement is in effect. Discrimination within the meaning of the Act would include such action as refusing to hire, discharging, demoting, assigning to a less desirable shift or job, or withholding benefits.

The union-shop exception to Section 8(a)(3)

As previously noted, Section 8(a)(3) provides that an employee may be discharged for failing to pay the required union initiation fees and dues uniformly required by the exclusive bargaining representative under a lawful union-shop contract. The section provides further, however, that no employer can justify any discriminatory action against an employee for nonmembership in a union if it has reason to believe that membership in the union was not open to the employee on the same

	Charge Against Labor Organization and Employer	2. PETITIONS FOR CERTIFCATION OR DECERTIFICATION OF REPRESENTATIVES (R CASES)	3. OTHER PETITIONS
		By or in Behalf of Employees	By or in Behalf of Employees

Section of the Act **CP**	*Section of the Act* **CE**	*Section of the Act* **RC**	*Section of the Act* **UD**
8(b)(7) To picket, cause, or threaten the picketing of any employer where an object is to force or require an employer to recognize or bargain with a labor organization as the representative of its employees, or to force or require the employees of an employer to select such labor organization as their collective-bargaining representative, unless such labor organization is currently certified as the representative of such employees: (A) where the employer has lawfully recognized any other labor organization and a question concerning representation may not appropriately be raised under Section 9(c), (B) where within the preceding 12 months a valid election under Section 9(c) has been conducted, or (C) where picketing has been conducted without a petition under 9(c) being filed within a reasonable period of time not to exceed 30 days from the commencement of the picketing; except where the picketing is for the purpose of truthfully advising the public (including consumers) that an employer does not employ members of, or have a contract with, a labor organization, and it does not have an effect of interference with deliveries or services.	8(e) To enter into any contract or agreement (any labor organization and any employer) whereby such employer ceases or refrains or agrees to cease or refrain from handling or dealing in any product of any other employer, or to cease doing business with any other person.	9(c)(1)(A)(i) Alleging that a substantial number of employees wish to be represented for collective bargaining and their employer declines to recognize their representative.* *Section of the Act* **RD** 9(c)(1)(A)(ii) Alleging that a substantial number of employees assert that the certified or currently recognized bargaining representative is no longer their representative.* **By an Employer** *Section of the Act* **RM** 9(c)(1)(B) Alleging that one or more claims for recognition as exclusive bargaining representative have been received by the employer.* *If an 8(b)(7) charge has been filed involving the same employer, these statements in RC, RD, and RM petitions are not required.	9(e)(1) Alleging that employees (30 percent or more of an appropriate unit) wish to rescind an existing union-security agreement. **By a Labor Organization or an Employer** *Board Rules* **UC** *Subpart C* Seeking clarification of an existing bargaining unit. *Board Rules* **AC** *Subpart C* Seeking amendment of an outstanding certification of bargaining representative.

Charges filed with the National Labor Relations Board are letter-coded and numbered. Unfair labor practice charges are classified as "C" cases and petitions for certification or decertification of representatives as "R" cases. This chart indicates the letter codes used for "C" cases, at left, and "R" cases, above, and also presents a summary of each section involved.

terms and conditions that apply to others, or if it has reason to believe that the employee was denied membership in the union for some reason other than failure to pay regular dues and initiation fees.

Even where there is a valid union-security agreement in effect, an employer may not pay the union the dues and fees owed by its employees. The employer may, however, deduct these amounts from the wages of its employees and forward them to the union for each employee who has *voluntarily* signed a dues "checkoff" authorization. Such checkoff authorization may be made irrevocable for no more than a year. But employees may revoke their checkoff authorizations after a Board-conducted election in which the union's authority to maintain a union-security agreement has been withdrawn.

This section does not limit an employer's right to discharge, transfer, or lay off an employee for genuine economic reasons or for such good cause as disobedience or bad work. This right applies equally to employees who are active in support of a union and to those who are not. However, the fact that a lawful reason for the discharge or discipline of employees may exist does not entitle an employer to discharge or discipline them when the true reason is the employees' union or other activities protected by the law.

The Act does not limit employer's right to discharge for economic reasons

An employer who is engaged in good-faith bargaining with a union may lock out the represented employees, sometimes even before impasse is reached in the negotiations, if it does so to further its position in bargaining. But a bargaining lockout may be unlawful if the employer is at that time unlawfully refusing to bargain or is bargaining in bad faith. It is also unlawful if the employer's purpose in locking out its employees is to discourage them in their union loyalties and activities, that is, if the employer is motivated by hostility toward the union. Thus, a lockout to defeat a union's efforts to organize the employer's employees would violate the Act, as would the lockout of only those of its employees who are members of the union. On the other hand, lockouts are lawful which are intended to prevent any unusual losses or safety hazards which would be caused by an anticipated "quickie" strike.

And a whipsaw strike against one employer engaged in multiemployer bargaining justifies a lockout by any of the other employers who are party to the bargaining.

Examples of illegal discrimination under Section 8(a)(3) include:

- Discharging employees because they urged other employees to join a union.
- Refusing to reinstate employees when jobs they are qualified for are open because they took part in a union's lawful strike.
- Granting of "superseniority" to those hired to replace employees engaged in a lawful strike.

Examples of violations of Section 8(a)(3)

- Demoting employees because they circulated a union petition among other employees asking the employer for an increase in pay.
- Discontinuing an operation at one plant and discharging the employees involved followed by opening the same operation at another plant with new employees because the employees at the first plant joined a union.
- Refusing to hire qualified applicants for jobs because they belong to a union. It would also be a violation if the qualified applicants were refused employment because they did not belong to a union, or because they belonged to one union rather than another.

Section 8(a)(4)—Discrimination for NLRB Activity

Section 8(a)(4) makes it an unfair labor practice for an employer "to discharge or otherwise discriminate against an employee because he has filed charges or given testimony under this Act." This provision guards the right of employees to seek the protection of the Act by using the processes of the NLRB. Like the previous section, it forbids an employer to discharge, lay off, or engage in other forms of discrimination in working conditions against employees who have filed charges with the NLRB, given affidavits to NLRB investigators, or testified at an NLRB hearing. Violations of this section are in most cases also violations of Section 8(a)(3).

Examples of violations of Section 8(a)(4) are:

Examples of violations of Section 8(a)(4)

- Refusing to reinstate employees when jobs they are otherwise qualified for are open because they filed charges with the NLRB claiming their layoffs were based on union activity.
- Demoting employees because they testified at an NLRB hearing.

Section 8(a)(5)—Refusal To Bargain in Good Faith

Section 8(a)(5) makes it illegal for an employer to refuse to bargain in good faith about wages, hours, and other conditions of employment with the representative selected by a majority of the employees in a unit appropriate for collective bargaining. A bargaining representative which seeks to enforce its right concerning an employer under this section must show that it has been designated by a majority of the employees, that the unit is appropriate, and that there has been both a demand that the employer bargain and a refusal by the employer to do so.

The duty to bargain covers all matters concerning rates of pay, wages, hours of employment, or other conditions of employment. These are called "mandatory" subjects of bargaining about which the employer, as well as the employees' representative, must bargain in good faith, although the law does not require "either party to agree to a proposal or require the making of a concession." These mandatory subjects of bargaining include but are not limited to such matters as pensions for present and retired employees, bonuses, group insurance, grievance procedure, safety practices, seniority, procedures for discharge, layoff, recall, or discipline, and the union shop. On "nonmandatory" subjects, that is, matters that are lawful but not related to "wages, hours, and other conditions of employment," the parties are free to bargain and to agree, but neither party may insist on bargaining on such subjects over the objection of the other party.

Required subjects of bargaining

Duty to bargain defined

An employer who is required to bargain under this section must, as stated in Section 8(d), "meet at reasonable times and confer in good faith with respect to wages, hours, and other terms and conditions of employment, or the negotiation of an agreement, or any question arising thereunder, and the execution of a written contract incorporating any agreement reached if requested by either party."

An employer, therefore, will be found to have violated Section 8(a)(5) if its conduct in bargaining, viewed in its entirety, indicates that the employer did not negotiate with a good-faith intention to reach agreement. However, the employer's good faith is not at issue where its conduct constitutes an out-and-out refusal to bargain on a mandatory subject. For example, it is a violation for an employer, regardless of good faith, to refuse to bargain about a subject which it believes is not a mandatory subject of bargaining, when in fact it is.

What constitutes a violation of Section 8(a)(5)

The duty of an employer to meet and confer with the representative of its employees includes the duty to deal with whoever is designated by the employees' representative to carry on negotiations. An employer may not dictate to a union its selection of agents or representatives and the employer must, in general, recognize the designated agent.

Duty to meet and confer

The employer's duty to bargain includes the duty to supply upon request information that is "relevant and necessary" to allow the employees' representative to bargain intelligently and effectively with respect to wages, hours, and other conditions of employment.

Duty to supply information

Where there is a history of bargaining between a union and a number of employers acting jointly, the employees who are thus represented constitute a multiemployer bargaining unit. Once such a unit has been established, any of the participating employers—or the union—may retire from this multiemployer bargaining relationship only by mutual assent or by a timely submitted withdrawal. Withdrawal is considered timely if unequivocal notice of the withdrawal is given near the termination of a collective-bargaining agreement but before bargaining begins on the next agreement. However, if the union agrees, an employer may also withdraw from a multiemployer unit and sign an individual contract with the union where there has been a breakdown in the multiemployer negotiations leading to an impasse and a resultant strike.

Multiemployer bargaining

Finally, the duty of an employer to bargain includes the duty to refrain from unilateral action, that is, taking action on its own with respect to matters concerning which it is required to bargain, and from making changes in terms and conditions of employment without consulting the employees' representative.

Duty to refrain from unilateral action

An employer who purchases or otherwise acquires the operations of another may be obligated to recognize and bargain with the union which represented the employees before the business was transferred. In general, these bargaining obligations exist—and the purchaser is termed a successor employer—where there is a substantial continuity in the employing enterprise despite the sale and transfer of the business. Whether the purchaser is a successor employer is dependent on several factors, including the number of employees taken over by the purchasing employer, the similarity in operations and product of the two employers, the manner in which the purchaser integrates the purchased operations into its other operations, and the character of the bargaining relationship and agreement between the union and the original employer.

Duty of successor employers

Examples of violations of Section 8(a)(5) are as follows:
- Refusing to meet with the employees' representative because the employees are out on strike.
- Insisting, until bargaining negotiations break down, on a contract provision that all employees will be polled by secret ballot before the union calls a strike.
- Refusing to supply the employees' representative with cost and other data concerning a group insurance plan covering the employees.
- Announcing a wage increase without consulting the employees' representative.
- Subcontracting certain work to another employer without notifying the union that represents the affected employees and without giving the union an opportunity to bargain concerning the change in working conditions of the employees.

Examples of violations of Section 8(a)(5)

Section 8(e), added to the Act in 1959, makes it an unfair labor practice for any labor organization and any employer to enter into what is commonly called a "hot cargo" or "hot goods" agreement. It may also limit the restrictions that can be placed on the subcontracting of work by an employer. The typical hot cargo or hot goods clause in use before the 1959 amendment to the Act provided that employees would not be required by their employer to handle or work on goods or materials going to, or coming from, an employer designated by the union as "unfair." Such goods were said to be "hot

Section 8(e)—Entering a Hot Cargo Agreement

cargo," thereby giving Section 8(e) its popular name. These clauses were most common in the construction and trucking industries.

Section 8(e) forbids an employer and a labor organization to make an agreement whereby the employer agrees to stop doing business with any other employer and declares void and unenforceable any such agreement that is made. It should be noted that a strike or picketing, or any other employee action, or the threat of it, to force an employer to agree to a hot cargo provision, or to force it to act in accordance with such a clause, has been held by the Board to be a violation of Section 8(b)(4). Exceptions are allowed in the construction and garment industries, and a union may seek, by contract, to keep within a bargaining unit work that is being done by the employees in the unit or to secure work which is "fairly claimable" in that unit.

What is prohibited

In the construction industry a union and an employer in the industry may agree to a provision that restricts the contracting or subcontracting of work to be done at the construction site. Such a clause contained in the agreement between the employer and the union typically provides that if work is subcontracted by the employer it must go to an employer who has an agreement with the union. A union in the construction industry may engage in a strike and picketing to obtain, but not to enforce, contractual restrictions of this nature. Similarly, in the garment industry an employer and a union can agree that work to be done on the goods or on the premises of a jobber or manufacturer, or work that is part of "an intergrated process of production in the apparel and clothing industry," can be subcontracted only to an employer who has an agreement with the union. This exception, unlike the previous one concerning the construction industry, allows a labor organization in the garment industry not only to seek to obtain, but also to enforce, such a restriction on subcontracting by striking, picketing, or other lawful action.

Exceptions for construction and garment industries

Unfair Labor Practices of Labor Organizations

Section 8(b)(1)(A)—Restraint and Coercion of Employees

Section 8(b)(1)(A) forbids a labor organization or its agents "to restrain or coerce employees in the exercise of the rights guaranteed in section 7." The section also provides that it is not intended to "impair the rights of a labor organization to prescribe its own rules" concerning membership in the labor organization.

Section 8(b)(1)(A) compared with Section 8(a)(1)

Like Section 8(a)(1), Section 8(b)(1)(A) is violated by conduct that independently restrains or coerces employees in the exercise of their Section 7 rights regardless of whether the conduct also violates other provisions of Section 8(b). But whereas employer violations of Section 8(a) (2), (3), (4), and (5) are held to be violations of Section 8(a)(1) too, the Board has held, based on the intent of Congress when Section 8(b)(1)(A) was written, that violations of Section 8(b)(2) through (7) do not also "derivatively" violate Section 8(b)(1)(A). The Board does hold, however, that making or enforcing illegal union-security agreements or hiring agreements that condition employment on union membership not only violates Section 8(b)(2) but also Section 8(b)(1)(A), since such action restrains or coerces employees in their Section 7 rights.

Union conduct which is reasonably calculated to restrain or coerce employees in their Section 7 rights violates Section 8(b)(1)(A) whether or not it succeeds in actually restraining or coercing employees.

A union may violate Section 8(b)(1)(A) by coercive conduct of its officers or agents, of pickets on a picket line endorsed by the union, or of strikers who engage in coercion in the presence of union representatives who do not repudiate the conduct.

What violates Section 8(b)(1)(A)

Unlawful coercion may consist of acts specifically directed at an employee such as physical assaults, threats of violence, and threats to affect an employee's job status. Coercion also includes other forms of pressure against employees such as acts of a union while representing employees as their exclusive bargaining agent (see Sec. 9(a), p. 10). A union which is a statutory bargaining representative owes a duty of fair representation to all the employees it represents. It may exercise a wide range of reasonable discretion in carrying out the representative function, but it violates Section 8(b)(1)(A) if, while acting as the employees' statutory bargaining representative, it takes or withholds action in connection with their employment because of their union activities or for any irrelevant or arbitrary reason such as an employee's race or sex.

Section 8(b)(1)(A) recognizes the right of unions to establish and enforce rules of membership and to control their internal affairs. This right is limited to union rules and discipline which affect the rights of employees as union members and which are not enforced by action affecting an employee's employment. Also, rules to be protected must be aimed at matters of legitimate concern to unions such as the encouragement of members to support a lawful strike or participation in union meetings. Rules which conflict with public policy, such as rules which limit a member's right to file unfair labor practice charges, are not protected. And a union may not fine a member for filing a decertification petition although it may expel that individual for doing so.

Examples of restraint or coercion that violate Section 8(b)(1)(A) when done by a union or its agents include the following:

- Mass picketing in such numbers that nonstriking employees are physically barred from entering the plant.
- Acts of force or violence on the picket line, or in connection with a strike.
- Threats to do bodily injury to nonstriking employees.
- Threats to employees that they will lose their jobs unless they support the union's activities.
- Statement to employees who oppose the union that the employees will lose their jobs if the union wins a majority in the plant.

Examples of violations of Section 8(b)(1)(A)

- Entering into an agreement with an employer which recognizes the union as exclusive bargaining representative when it has not been chosen by a majority of the employees.
- Fining or expelling members for crossing a picket line which is unlawful under the Act or which violates a no-strike agreement.
- Fining employees for conduct in which they engaged after resigning from the union.
- Fining or expelling members for filing unfair labor practice charges with the Board or for participating in an investigation conducted by the Board.

The following are examples of restraint or coercion that violate Section 8(b)(1)(A) when done by a union which is the exclusive bargaining representative:

- Refusing to process a grievance in retaliation against an employee's criticism of union officers.
- Maintaining a seniority arrangement with an employer under which seniority is based on the employee's prior representation by the union elsewhere.
- Rejecting an application for referral to a job in a unit represented by the union based on the applicant's race or union activities.

Section 8(b)(1)(B) prohibits a labor organization from restraining or coercing an employer in the selection of a bargaining representative. The prohibition applies regardless of whether the labor organization is the majority representative of the employees in the bargaining unit. The prohibition extends to coercion applied by a union to a union member who is a representative of the employer in the adjustment of grievances. This section is violated by such conduct as the following:

Section 8(b)(1)(B)—Restraint and Coercion of Employers

- Insisting on meeting only with a company's owners and refusing to meet with the attorney the company has engaged to represent the company in contract negotiations, and threatening to strike to force the company to accept its demands.
- Striking against several members of an employer association that had bargained with the union as the representative of the employers with resulting individual contracts being signed by the struck employers.

Examples of violations of Section 8(b)(1)(B)

- Insisting during contract negotiations that the employer agree to accept working conditions which will be established by a bargaining group to which it does not belong.
- Fining or expelling supervisors for the way they apply the bargaining contract while carrying out their supervisory functions.

Section 8(b)(2) makes it an unfair labor practice for a labor organization to cause an employer to discriminate against an employee in violation of Section 8(a)(3). As discussed earlier, Section 8(a)(3) prohibits an employer from discriminating against an employee in regard to wages, hours, and other conditions of employment for the purpose of encouraging or discouraging membership in a labor organization. It does allow, however, the making of union-security agreements under certain specified conditions.

Section 8(b)(2)—Causing or Attempting To Cause Discrimination

A union violates Section 8(b)(2), for example, by demanding that an employer discriminate against employees because of their lack of union membership where there is no valid union-shop agreement in effect. The section can also be violated by agreements or arrangements with employers that unlawfully condition employment or job benefits on union membership, on the performance of union membership obligations, or on arbitrary grounds. Union conduct affecting an employee's employment in a way which is contrary to provisions of the bargaining contract may likewise be violative of the section. But union action which causes detriment to an individual employee in that individual's employment does not violate Section 8(b)(2) if it is consistent with nondiscriminatory provisions of a bargaining contract negotiated for the benefit of the total bargaining unit or if it is for some other legitimate purpose.

What violates Section 8(b)(2)

To find that a union caused an employer to discriminate, it is not necessary to show that any express demand was spoken. A union's conduct, accompanied by statements advising or suggesting that action is expected of an employer, may be enough to find a violation of this section if the union's action can be shown to be a causal factor in the employer's discrimination.

Contracts or informal arrangements with a union under which an employer gives preferential treatment to union members are violations of Section 8(b)(2). It is not unlawful for an employer and a union to enter an agreement whereby the employer agrees to hire new employees exclusively through the union hiring hall so long as there is neither a provision in the agreement nor a practice in effect that discriminates against nonunion members in favor of union members or otherwise discriminates on the basis of union membership obligations. Both the agreement and the actual operation of the hiring hall must be nondiscriminatory; referrals must be made without reference to union membership or irrelevant or arbitrary considerations such as race. Referral standards or procedures, even if nondiscriminatory on their face, are unlawful when they continue previously discriminatory conditions of referral. However, a union may in setting referral standards consider legitimate aims such as sharing available work and easing the impact of local unemployment. It may also charge referral fees if the amount of the fee is reasonably related to the cost of operating the referral service.

Illegal hiring-hall agreements and practices

Union-security agreements that require employees to become members of the union after they are hired are permitted by this section as previously discussed. Union-security agreements that do not meet all the requirements listed on page 3 will not support a discharge. A union that attempts to force an employer to enter an illegal union-security agreement, or that enters and keeps in effect such an agreement, violates Section 8(b)(2), as does a union that attempts to enforce such an illegal agreement by bringing about an employee's discharge. Even when a union-security provision of a bargaining contract meets all statutory requirements so that it is permitted by Section 8(a)(3), a union may not lawfully require the discharge of employees under the provision unless the employees had been informed of the union-security agreement and of their specific obligation under it. And a union violates Section 8(b)(2) if it tries to use the union-security provisions of a contract to collect payments other than periodic dues and initiation fees uniformly required of members. Assessments, fines, and penalties may not be enforced by application of a union-security contract.

Illegal union-security agreements

Examples of violations of Section 8(b)(2) are:
- Causing an employer to discharge employees because they circulated a petition urging a change in the union's method of selecting shop stewards.
- Causing an employer to discharge employees because they made speeches against a contract proposed by the union.
- Making a contract that requires an employer to hire only members of the union or employees "satisfactory" to the union.
- Causing an employer to reduce employees' seniority because they engaged in antiunion acts.
- Refusing referral or giving preference on the basis of race or union activities in making job referrals to units represented by the union.
- Seeking the discharge of an employee under a union-security agreement for failure to pay a fine levied by the union.

Examples of violations of Section 8(b)(2)

Section 8(b)(3)—Refusal To Bargain in Good Faith

Section 8(b)(3) makes it illegal for a labor organization to refuse to bargain in good faith with an employer about wages, hours, and other conditions of employment if it is the representative of that employer's employees. This section imposes on labor organizations the same duty to bargain in good faith that is imposed on employers by Section 8(a)(5). Both the labor organization and the employer are required to follow the procedure set out in Section 8(d) before terminating or changing an existing contract (see pages 7 and 8).

A labor organization that is the employees' representative must meet at reasonable times with the employer or his designated representative, must confer in good faith on matters pertaining to wages, hours, or other conditions of employment, or the negotiation of an agreement, or any question arising under an agreement, and must sign a written agreement if requested and if one is reached. The obligation does not require the labor organization or the employer to agree to a proposal by the other party or make a concession to the other party, but it does require bargaining with an open mind in an attempt to reach agreement. So, while a union may try in contract negotiations to establish wages and benefits comparable to those contained in other bargaining agreements in the area, it may not insist on such terms without giving the employer an opportunity to bargain about the terms. Likewise, a union may seek *voluntary* bargaining on nonmandatory subjects of bargaining (p. 26), such as a provision for an industry promotion fund, but may not *insist* on bargaining about such subjects or condition execution of a contract on the reaching of agreement on a nonmandatory subject.

Where a union has been bargaining with a group of employers in a multiemployer bargaining unit, it may withdraw at any time from bargaining upon that basis and bargain with one of the employers individually if the individual employer and the multiemployer group agree to the union's withdrawal. And even in the absence of employer consent a union may withdraw from multiemployer bargaining by giving the employers unequivocal notice of its withdrawal near the expiration of the agreement but before bargaining on a new contract had begun. In some circumstances a union may withdraw after a breakdown in the multiemployer bargaining.

Section 8(b)(3) not only requires that a union representative bargain in good faith with employers, but also requires that the union carry out its bargaining duty fairly with respect to the employees it represents. A union, therefore, violates Section 8(b)(3) if it negotiates a contract which conflicts with that duty, such as a contract with racially discriminatory provisions, or if it refuses to handle grievances under the contract for irrelevant or arbitrary reasons.

Section 8(b)(3) is violated by any of the following:

- Insisting on the inclusion of illegal provisions in a contract, such as a closed shop or a discriminatory hiring hall.
- Refusing to negotiate on a proposal for a written contract.
- Striking against an employer who has bargained, and continues to bargain, on a multiemployer basis to compel it to bargain separately.
- Refusing to meet with the attorney designated by the employer as its representative in negotiations.
- Terminating an existing contract and striking for a new one without notifying the employer, the Federal Mediation and Conciliation Service, and the state mediation service, if any.
- Conditioning the execution of an agreement upon inclusion of a nonmandatory provision such as a performance bond.
- Refusing to process a grievance because of the race, sex, or union activities of an employee for whom the union is the statutory bargaining representative.

Examples of violations of Section 8(b)(3)

Section 8(b)(4) prohibits a labor organization from engaging in strikes or boycotts or taking other specified actions to accomplish certain purposes or "objects" as they are called in the Act. The proscribed action is listed in clauses (i) and (ii), the objects are described in subparagraphs (A) through (D). A union commits an unfair labor practice if it takes any of the kinds of action listed in clauses (i) and (ii) as a means of accomplishing any of the objects listed in the four subparagraphs.

Section 8(b)(4)—Prohibited Strikes and Boycotts

Clause (i) forbids a union to engage in a strike, or to induce or encourage a strike, work stoppage, or a refusal to perform services by "any individual employed by any person engaged in commerce or in an industry affecting commerce" for one of the objects listed in subparagraphs (A) through (D). The words "induce and encourage" are considered by the U.S. Supreme Court to be broad enough to include every form of influence or persuasion. For example, it has been held by the NLRB that a work stoppage on a picketed construction project was "induced" by a union through its business agents who, when they learned about the picketing, told the job stewards that they (the business agents) would not work behind the picket line. It was considered that this advice not only induced

Proscribed action: Inducing or encouraging a strike, work stoppage, or boycott

the stewards to leave the job, but caused them to pass the information on to their fellow employees, and that such conduct informed the other employees that they were expected not to work behind the picket line. The word "person" is defined in Section 2(1) as including "one or more individuals, labor organizations, partnerships, associations, corporations," and other legal persons. As so defined, the word "person" is broader than the word "employer." For example, a railroad company, although covered by the Railway Labor Act, is excluded from the definition of "employer" in the National Labor Relations Act and, therefore, neither the railroad company nor its employees are covered by the National Labor Relations Act. But a railroad company is a "person engaged in commerce" as defined above and, therefore, a labor organization is forbidden to "induce or encourage" individuals employed by a railroad company to engage in a strike, work stoppage, or boycott for any of the objects in subparagraphs (A) through (D).

Clause (ii) makes it an unfair labor practice for a union to "threaten, coerce, or restrain any person engaged in commerce or in an industry affecting commerce" for any of the proscribed objects. Even though no direct threat is voiced by the union, there may nevertheless be coercion and restraint that violates this clause. For example, where a union picketed a construction job to bring about the removal of a nonunion subcontractor in violation of Section 8(b)(4)(B), the picketing induced employees of several other subcontractors to stop work. When the general contractor asked what could be done to stop the picketing, the union's business agent replied that the picketing would stop only if the nonunion subcontractor were removed from the job. The NLRB held this to be "coercion and restraint" within the meaning of clause (ii).

Proscribed action: Threats, coercion, and restraint

Section 8(b)(4)(A) prohibits unions from engaging in clause (i) or (ii) action to compel an employer or self-employed person to join any labor or employer organization; or to force an employer to enter a hot cargo agreement prohibited by Section 8(e). Examples of violations of this section are:

Subparagraph (A)—Prohibited object: Compelling membership in an employer or labor organization or compelling a hot cargo agreement

Examples of violations of Section 8(b)(4)(A)

- In an attempt to compel a beer distributor to join a union, the union prevents the distributor from obtaining beer at a brewery by inducing the brewery's employees to refuse to fill the distributor's orders.
- In an attempt to secure for its members certain stevedoring work required at an employer's unloading operation, the union pickets to force the employer either to join an employer association with which the union has a contract or to hire a stevedoring firm that is a member of the association.
- A union pickets an employer (one not in the construction industry), or threatens to picket it, to compel that employer to enter into an agreement whereby the employer will only do business with persons who have an agreement with a union.

Section 8(b)(4)(B) contains the Act's secondary boycott provision. A secondary boycott occurs if a union has a dispute with Company A and in furtherance of that dispute causes the employees of Company B to stop handling the products of Company A, or otherwise forces Company B to stop doing business with Company A. The dispute is with Company A, called the "primary" employer, the union's action is against Company B, called the "secondary" employer, hence the term "secondary boycott." In many cases the secondary employer is a customer or supplier of the primary employer with whom the union has the dispute. In general, the Act prohibits both the secondary boycott and the threat of it. Examples of prohibited secondary boycotts are:

Subparagraph (B)—Prohibited object: Compelling a boycott or work stoppage

- Picketing an employer to force it to stop doing business with another employer who has refused to recognize the union.
- Asking the employees of a plumbing contractor not to work on connecting up air-conditioning equipment manufactured by a nonunion employer whom the union is attempting to organize.
- Urging employees of a building contractor not to install doors which were made by a manufacturer which is nonunion or which employs members of a rival union.
- Telling an employer that its plant will be picketed if that employer continues to do business with an employer the union has designated as "unfair."

Examples of violations of Section 8(b)(4)(B)

The prohibitions of Section 8(b)(4)(B) do not protect a secondary employer from the incidental effects of union action that is taken directly against the primary employer. Thus, it is lawful for a union to urge employees of a secondary supplier at the primary employer's plant not to cross a picket line there. Section 8(b)(4)(B) also does not proscribe union action to prevent an employer from contracting out work customarily performed by its employees, even though an incidental effect of such conduct might be to compel that employer to cease doing business with the subcontractor.

In order to be protected against the union action that is prohibited under this subparagraph the secondary employer has to be a neutral as concerns the dispute between the union and the primary employer. For secondary boycott purposes an employer is considered an "ally" of the primary employer and, therefore, not protected from union action in certain situations. One is based on the ownership and operational relationship between the primary and secondary employers. Here, a number of factors are considered, particularly the following: Are the primary and secondary employers owned and controlled by the same person or persons? Are they engaged in "closely integrated operations"? May they be treated as a single employer under the Act? Another test of the "ally" relationship is based on the conduct of the secondary employer. If an employer, despite its claim of neutrality in the dispute, acts in a way that indicates that it has abandoned its "neutral" position, the employer opens itself up to primary action by the union. An example of this would be an employer who, claiming to be a neutral, enters into an arrangement with a struck employer whereby it accepts and performs farmed-out work of that employer who would normally do the work itself, but who cannot perform the work because its plant is closed by a strike. *When an employer is not protected from secondary strikes and boycotts*

When employees of a primary employer and those of a secondary employer work on the same premises, a special situation is involved and the usual rules do not apply. A typical example of the shared site or "common situs" situation is where a subcontractor with whom a union has a dispute is engaged at work on a construction site alongside other subcontractors, with whom the union has no dispute. Picketing at a common situs is permissible if directed solely against the primary employer. But it is prohibited if directed against secondary employers regularly engaged at that site. To assist in determining whether picketing at a common site is restricted to the primary employer and therefore permissible, or directed at a secondary employer and therefore violative of the statute, the NLRB and the courts have suggested various guidelines for evaluating the object of the picketing, including the following: *When a union may picket an employer who shares a site with another employer*

Subject to the qualification noted below, the picketing would appear to be primary picketing, if the picketing is:

1. Limited to times when the employees of the primary employer are working on the premises.
2. Limited to times when the primary employer is carrying on its normal business there.
3. Confined to places reasonably close to where the employees of the primary employer are working.
4. Conducted so that the picket signs, the banners, and the conduct of the pickets indicate clearly that the dispute is with the primary employer and not with the secondary employer.

These guidelines are known as the *Moore Dry Dock* standards from the case in which they were first formulated by the NLRB. However, the NLRB has held that picketing at a common situs may be unlawful notwithstanding compliance with the *Moore Dry Dock* standards if a union's statements or actions otherwise indicate that the picketing has an unlawful objective.

In some situations a company may set aside, or reserve, a certain plant gate, or entrance to its premises, for the exclusive use of a contractor. If a union has a labor dispute with the company and pickets the company's premises, including the gate so reserved, the union may be held to have violated Section 8(b)(4)(B). The U.S. Supreme Court has stated the circumstances under which such a violation may be found as follows: *Picketing contractors' gates*

> There must be a separate gate, marked and set apart from other gates; the work done by the men who use the gate must be unrelated to the normal operations of the employer, and the work must be of a kind that would not, if done when the plant were engaged in its regular operations, necessitate curtailing those operations.

However, if the reserved gate is used by employees of both the company and the contractor, the picketing would be considered primary and not a violation of Section 8(b)(4)(B).

Section 8(b)(4)(B) also prohibits secondary action to compel an employer to recognize or bargain with a union that is not the certified representative of its employees. If a union takes action described in clause (i) or (ii) against a secondary employer, and the union's object is recognition by the primary employer, the union commits an unfair labor practice under this section. To establish *Subparagraph (B)—Prohibited object: Compelling recognition of an uncertified union* that the union has an object of recognition, a specific demand by the union for recognition need not be shown; a demand for a contract, which implies recognition or at least bargaining, is enough to establish an 8(b)(4)(B) object.

Subparagraph (C)—Prohibited object: Compelling recognition of a union if another union has been certified

Section 8(b)(4)(C) forbids a labor organization from using clause (i) or (ii) conduct to force an employer to recognize or bargain with a labor organization other than the one that is currently certified as the representative of its employees. Section 8(b)(4)(C) has been held not to apply where the picketing union is merely protesting working conditions which are substandard for the area.

Subparagraph (D)—Prohibited object: Compelling assignment of certain work to certain employees

Section 8(b)(4)(D) forbids a labor organization from engaging in action described in clauses (i) and (ii) for the purpose of forcing any employer to assign certain work to "employees in a particular labor organization or in a particular trade, craft, or class rather than to employees in another labor organization or in another trade, craft, or class." The Act sets up a special procedure for handling disputes over work assignments that will be discussed later in this material (see page 53).

The final provision in Section 8(b)(4) provides that nothing in Section 8(b)(4) shall be construed "to prohibit publicity, other than picketing, for the purpose of truthfully advising the public,

Publicity such as handbilling allowed by Section 8(b)(4)

including consumers and members of a labor organization, that a product or products are produced by an employer with whom the labor organization has a primary dispute and are distributed by another employer." Such publicity is not protected if it has "an effect of inducing any individual employed by any person other than the primary employer" to refuse to handle any goods or not to perform services. The Supreme Court has held that this provision permitted a union to distribute handbills at the stores of neutral food chains asking the public not to buy certain items distributed by a wholesaler with whom the union had a primary dispute. Moreover, it has also held that peaceful picketing at the stores of a neutral food chain to persuade customers not to buy the products of a struck employer when they traded in these stores was not prohibited by Section 8(b)(4).

Section 8(b)(5)—Excessive or Discriminatory Membership Fees

Section 8(b)(5) makes it illegal for a union to charge employees who are covered by an authorized union-security agreement a membership fee "in an amount which the Board finds excessive or discriminatory under all the circumstances." The section also provides that the Board in making its finding must consider among other factors "the practices and customs of labor organizations in the particular industry, and the wages currently paid to the employees affected."

Examples of violations of this section include:

Examples of violations of Section 8(b)(5)

- Charging old employees who do not join the union until after a union-security agreement goes into effect an initiation fee of $15 while charging new employees only $5.
- Increasing the initiation fee from $75 to $250 and thus charging new members an amount equal to about 4 weeks' wages when other unions in the area charge a fee equal to about one-half the employee's first week's pay.

Section 8(b)(6)—"Featherbedding"

Section 8(b)(6) forbids a labor organization "to cause or attempt to cause an employer to pay or deliver or agree to pay or deliver any money or other thing of value, in the nature of an exaction, for services which are not performed or not to be performed."

Section 8(b)(7)—Organizational and Recognitional Picketing by Noncertified Unions

Section 8(b)(7) prohibits a labor organization that is not currently certified as the employees' representative from picketing or threatening to picket with an object of obtaining recognition by the employer (recognitional picketing) or acceptance by his employees as their representative (organizational picketing). The object of picketing is ascertained from all the surrounding facts including the message on the picket signs and any communications between the union and the employer. "Recognitional" picketing as used in Section 8(b)(7) refers to picketing to obtain an employer's initial recognition of the union as bargaining representative of its employees or to force the employer, without formal recognition of the union, to maintain a specific and detailed set of working conditions. It does not include picketing by an incumbent union for continued recognition or for a new contract. Neither does it include picketing which seeks to prevent the employer from undermining area standards of working conditions by operating at less than the labor costs which prevail under bargaining contracts in the area.

Recognitional and organizational picketing are prohibited in three specific instances:

A. When the employer has lawfully recognized another union and a representation election would be barred by either the provisions of the Act or the Board's Rules, as in the case of a valid contract between the employer and the other union (8(b)(7)(A)). (A union is considered lawfully recognized when the employer's recognition of the union cannot be attacked under the unfair labor practice provisions of Section 8 of the Act.)

B. When a valid NLRB representation election has been held within the previous 12 months (8(b)(7)(B)).

C. When a representation petition is not filed "within a reasonable period of time not to exceed thirty days from the commencement of such picketing" (8(b)(7)(C)).

Publicity picketing

Subparagraph (C) is subject to an exception, called a proviso, which permits picketing "for the purpose of truthfully advising the public (including consumers)" that an employer does not employ union members or have a contract with a labor organization. However, such picketing loses the protection of this proviso if it has a substantial effect on the employer's business because it induces "any individual employed by any other person" to refuse to pick up or deliver goods or to perform other services.

If an 8(b)(7)(C) charge is filed against the picketing union and a representation petition is filed within a reasonable time after the picketing starts, subparagraph (C) provides for an election to be held forthwith. This election requires neither a hearing nor a showing of interest among the employees. As a consequence the election can be held and the results obtained faster than in a regular election under Section 9(c), and for this reason it is called an "expedited" election. Petitions filed more than a reasonable time after picketing begins and petitions filed during picketing protected by the 8(b)(7)(C) proviso, discussed above, are processed under normal election procedures and the election will not be expedited. The reasonable period in which to file a petition cannot exceed 30 days and may be shorter, when, for instance, picketing is accompanied by violence.

Expedited elections under Section 8(b)(7)(C)

Examples of violations of Section 8(b)(7) are as follows:

- Picketing by a union for organizational purposes shortly after the employer has entered a lawful contract with another union. (8(b)(7)(A))
- Picketing by a union for organizational purposes within 12 months after a valid NLRB election in which a majority of the employees in the unit voted to have no union. (8(b)(7)(B))
- Picketing by a union for recognition continuing for more than 30 days without the filing of a representation petition where the picketing stops all deliveries by employees of another employer. (8(b)(7)(C))

Examples of violations of Section 8(b)(7)

Section 8(e) makes it an unfair labor practice for an employer or a labor organization to enter a hot cargo agreement. This section applies equally to unions and to employers. The discussion of this section as an unfair labor practice of employers has been treated as a discussion of an unfair labor practice of unions as well. (See pages 28 and 29.)

Section 8(e)—Entering a Hot Cargo Agreement

Section 8(g) prohibits a labor organization from engaging in a strike, picketing, or other concerted refusal to work at any health care institution without first giving at least 10 days' notice in writing to the institution and the Federal Mediation and Conciliation Service.

Section 8(g)—Striking or Picketing a Health Care Institution Without Notice

---

The rights of employees declared by Congress in the National Labor Relations Act are not self-enforcing. To ensure that employees may exercise these rights, and to protect them and the public from unfair labor practices, Congress established the NLRB to administer and enforce the Act.

How the Act Is Enforced

Organization of the NLRB

The NLRB includes the Board, which is composed of five members with their respective staffs, the General Counsel and staff, and the Regional, Subregional, and Resident Offices. The General Counsel has final authority on behalf of the Board, in respect to the investigation of charges and issuance of complaints. Members of the Board are appointed by the President, with consent of the Senate, for 5-year terms. The General Counsel is also appointed by the President, with consent of the Senate, for a 4-year term. Offices of the Board and the General Counsel are in Washington, D.C. To assist in administering and enforcing the law, the NLRB has established 32 Regional and a number of other field offices. These offices, located in major cities in various States, are under the general supervision of the General Counsel.

The Board

The General Counsel

The Regional Offices

The Agency has two main functions: to conduct representation elections and certify the results, and to prevent employers and unions from engaging in unfair labor practices. In both kinds of cases the processes of the NLRB are begun only when requested. Requests for such action must be made in writing on forms provided by the NLRB and filed with the proper Regional office. The form used to request an election is called a "petition," and the form for unfair labor practices is called

Functions of the NLRB

a "charge." The filing of a petition or a charge sets in motion the machinery of the NLRB under the Act. Before discussing the machinery established by the Act, it would be well to understand the nature and extent of the authority of the NLRB.

Authority of the NLRB

The NLRB gets its authority from Congress by way of the National Labor Relations Act. The power of Congress to regulate labor-management relations is limited by the commerce clause of the United States Constitution. Although it can declare generally what the rights of employees are or should be, Congress can make its declaration of rights effective only in respect to enterprises whose operations "affect commerce" and labor disputes that "affect commerce." The NLRB, therefore, can direct elections and certify the results only in the case of an employer whose operations affect commerce. Similarly, it can act to prevent unfair labor practices only in cases involving labor disputes that affect, or would affect, commerce.

Enterprises whose operations affect commerce

"Commerce" includes trade, traffic, transportation, or communication within the District of Columbia or any Territory of the United States; or between any State or Territory and any other State, Territory, or the District of Columbia; or between two points in the same State, but through any other State, Territory, the District of Columbia, or a foreign country. Examples of enterprises engaged in commerce are:

What is commerce

- A manufacturing company in California that sells and ships its product to buyers in Oregon.
- A company in Georgia that buys supplies in Louisiana.
- A trucking company that transports goods from one point in New York State through Pennsylvania to another point in New York State.
- A radio station in Minnesota that has listeners in Wisconsin.

Although a company may not have any direct dealings with enterprises in any other State, its operations may nevertheless affect commerce. The operations of a Massachusetts manufacturing company that sells all of its goods to Massachusetts wholesalers affect commerce if the wholesalers ship to buyers in other States. The effects of a labor dispute involving the Massachusetts manufacturing concern would be felt in other States and the labor dispute would, therefore, "affect" commerce. Using this test, it can be seen that the operations of almost any employer can be said to affect commerce. As a result, the authority of the NLRB could extend to all but purely local enterprises.

When the operations of an employer affect commerce

Although the National Labor Relations Board could exercise its powers to enforce the Act in all cases involving enterprises whose operations affect commerce, the Board does not act in all such cases. In its discretion it limits the exercise of its power to cases involving enterprises whose effect on commerce is substantial. The Board's requirements for exercising its power or jurisdiction are called "jurisdictional standards." These standards are based on the yearly amount of business done by the enterprise, or on the yearly amount of its sales or of its purchases. They are stated in terms of total dollar volume of business and are different for different kinds of enterprises. The Board's standards in effect on July 1, 1976, are as follows:

The Board does not act in all cases affecting commerce

1. *Nonretail business:* Direct sales of goods to consumers in other States, or indirect sales through others (called outflow), of at least $50,000 a year; or direct purchases of goods from suppliers in other States, or indirect purchases through others (called inflow), of at least $50,000 a year.

2. *Office buildings:* Total annual revenue of $100,000 of which $25,000 or more is derived from organizations which meet any of the standards except the indirect outflow and indirect inflow standards established for nonretail enterprises.

NLRB jurisdictional standards

3. *Retail enterprises:* At least $500,000 total annual volume of business.

4. *Public utilities:* At least $250,000 total annual volume of business, or $50,000 direct or indirect outflow or inflow.

5. *Newspapers:* At least $200,000 total annual volume of business.

6. *Radio, telegraph, television, and telephone enterprises:* At least $100,000 total annual volume of business.

7. *Hotels, motels, and residential apartment houses:* At least $500,000 total annual volume of business.

8. *Privately operated health care institutions:* At least $250,000 total annual volume of business for hospitals; at least $100,000 for nursing homes, visiting nurses associations, and related facilities; at least $250,000 for all other types of private health care institutions defined in the 1974 amendments to the Act. The statutory definition includes: "any hospital, convalescent hospital, health maintenance organization, health clinic, nursing home, extended care facility,

or other institution devoted to the care of the sick, infirm, or aged person." Public hospitals are excluded from NLRB jurisdiction by Section 2(2) of the Act.

9. *Transportation enterprises, links and channels of interstate commerce:* At least $50,000 total annual income from furnishing interstate passenger and freight transportation services; also performing services valued at $50,000 or more for businesses which meet any of the jurisdictional standards except the indirect outflow and indirect inflow standards established for nonretail enterprises.

10. *Transit systems:* At least $250,000 total annual volume of business.

11. *Taxicab companies:* At least $500,000 total annual volume of business.

12. *Associations:* These are regarded as a single employer in that the annual business of all association members is totaled to determine whether any of the standards apply.

13. *Enterprises in the Territories and the District of Columbia:* The jurisdictional standards apply in the Territories; all businesses in the District of Columbia come under NLRB jurisdiction.

14. *National defense:* Jurisdiction is asserted over all enterprises affecting commerce when their operations have a substantial impact on national defense, whether or not the enterprises satisfy any other standard.

15. *Private universities and colleges:* At least $1 million gross annual revenue from all sources (excluding contributions not available for operating expenses because of limitations imposed by the grantor).

16. *Symphony orchestras:* At least $1 million gross annual revenue from all sources (excluding contributions not available for operating expenses because of limitations imposed by the grantor).

Through enactment of the 1970 Postal Reorganization Act, jurisdiction of the NLRB was extended to the United States Postal Service, effective July 1, 1971.

In addition to the above-listed standards, the Board asserts jurisdiction over gambling casinos in Nevada and Puerto Rico, where these enterprises are legally operated, when their total annual revenue from gambling is at least $500,000.

Ordinarily if an enterprise does the total annual volume of business listed in the standard, it will necessarily be engaged in activities that "affect" commerce. The Board must find, however, based on evidence, that the enterprise does in fact "affect" commerce.

The Board has established the policy that where an employer whose operations "affect" commerce refuses to supply the Board with information concerning total annual business, etc., the Board may dispense with this requirement and exercise jurisdiction.

Finally, Section 14(c)(1) authorizes the Board, in its discretion, to decline to exercise jurisdiction over any class or category of employers where a labor dispute involving such employees is not sufficiently substantial to warrant the exercise of jurisdiction, provided that it cannot refuse to exercise jurisdiction over any labor dispute over which it would have asserted jurisdiction under the standards it had in effect on August 1, 1959. In accordance with this provision the Board has determined that it will not exercise jurisdiction over racetracks, owners, breeders, and trainers of racehorses, and real estate brokers.

In addition to the foregoing limitations the Act states that the term "employee" shall include any employee *except* the following:

- Agricultural laborers.
- Domestic servants.
- Any individual employed by his parent or spouse.
- Independent contractors.
- Supervisors.
- Individuals employed by an employer subject to the Railway Labor Act.
- Government employees, including those employed by the U.S. Government, any Government corporation or Federal Reserve Bank, or any State or political subdivision such as a city, town, or school district.

The Act does not cover certain individuals

Supervisors are excluded from the definition of "employee" and, therefore, not covered by the Act. Whether an individual is a supervisor for purposes of the Act depends on that individual's authority over employees and not merely a title. A supervisor is defined by the Act as any individual who has the authority, acting in the interest of an employer, to cause another employee to be hired, transferred, suspended, laid off, recalled, promoted, discharged, assigned, rewarded, or disciplined, either by taking such action or by recommending it to a superior; or who has the authority responsibly to direct other employees or adjust their grievances; provided, in all cases, that the exercise of authority is not of a merely routine or clerical nature, but requires the exercise of independent judgment. For example, a foreman who determined which employees would be laid off after being directed by the job superintendent to lay off four employees would be considered a supervisor and would, therefore, not be covered by the Act; a "strawboss" who, after someone else determined which employees would be laid off, merely informed the employees of the layoff and who neither directed other employees nor adjusted their grievances would not be considered a supervisor and would be covered by the Act.

Supervisor defined

All employees properly classified as "managerial," not just those in positions susceptible to conflicts of interest in labor relations, are excluded from the protection of the Act. This was the thrust of a decision of the Supreme Court in 1974.

The term "employer" includes any person who acts as an agent of an employer, but it does *not* include the following:

The Act does not cover certain employers

- The United States or any State Government, or any political subdivision of either, or any Government corporation or Federal Reserve Bank.
- Any employer subject to the Railway Labor Act.

NLRB Procedure

The authority of the NLRB can be brought to bear in a representation proceeding only by the filing of a petition. Forms for petitions must be signed, sworn to or affirmed under oath, and filed with the Regional Office in the area where the unit of employees is located. If employees in the unit regularly work in more than one regional area, the petition may be filed with the Regional Office of any of such regions. Section 9(c)(1) provides that when a petition is filed, "the Board shall investigate such petition and if it has reasonable cause to believe that a question of representation affecting commerce exists shall provide for an appropriate hearing upon due notice." If the Board finds from the evidence presented at the hearing that "such a question of representation exists, it shall direct an election by secret ballot and shall certify the results thereof." Where there are three or more choices on the ballot and none receives a majority, Section 9(c)(3) provides for a runoff between the choice that received the largest and the choice that received the second largest number of valid votes in the election. After the election, if a union receives a majority of the votes cast, it is certified; if no union gets a majority, that result is certified. A union that has been certified is entitled to be recognized by the employer as the exclusive bargaining agent for the employees in the unit. If the employer fails to bargain with the union, it commits an unfair labor practice.

Procedure in representation cases

The procedure in an unfair labor practice case is begun by the filing of a charge. A charge may be filed by an employee, an employer, a labor organization, or any other person. Like petitions, charge forms, which are also available at Regional Offices, must be signed, sworn to or affirmed under oath, and filed with the appropriate Regional Office—that is, the Regional Office in the area where the alleged unfair labor practice was committed. Section 10 provides for the issuance of a complaint stating the charges and notifying the charged party of a hearing to be held concerning the charges. Such a complaint will issue only after investigation of the charges through the Regional Office indicates that an unfair labor practice has in fact occurred.

Procedure in unfair labor practice cases

In certain circumstances where an employer and union have an agreed-upon grievance arbitration procedure which will resolve the dispute and the charged party is willing to follow that procedure, the Board will defer processing an unfair labor practice case and await resolution of the issues through that grievance arbitration procedure. If the final disposition of the dispute by that process has afforded all parties an opportunity to be heard, if the process is fair and regular on its face, and if the result is not repugnant to the Act, the Board may accept the final resolution and defer to that decision. If the procedure fails to meet all of the Board standards for deferral, the Board may then resume processing of the unfair labor practice issues.

An unfair labor practice hearing is conducted before an NLRB administrative law judge in accordance with the rules of evidence and procedure that apply in the U.S. District Courts. Based on the hearing record, the administrative law judge makes findings and recommendations to the Board. All parties to the hearing may appeal the administrative law judge's decision to the Board. If the Board considers that the party named in the complaint has engaged in or is engaging in the unfair labor practices charged, the Board is authorized to issue an order requiring such person to cease and desist from such practices and to take appropriate affirmative action.

Section 10(b) provides that "no complaint shall issue based upon any unfair labor practice occurring more than six months prior to the filing of the charge with the Board and the service of a copy thereof upon the person against whom such charge is made." An exception is made if the charging party "was prevented from filing such charge by reason of service in the armed forces, in which event the six-month period shall be computed from the day of his discharge." It should be noted that the charging party must, within 6 months after the unfair labor practice occurs, file the charge with the Regional Office *and* serve copies of the charge on each person against whom the charge is made. Normally service is made by sending the charge by registered mail, return receipt requested.

The 6-month rule limiting issuance of complaint

If the Regional Director refuses to issue a complaint in any case, the person who filed the charge may appeal the decision to the General Counsel in Washington. Section 3(d) places in the General Counsel "final authority, on behalf of the Board, in respect of the investigation of charges and issuance of complaints." If the General Counsel reverses the Regional Director's decision, a complaint will be issued. If the General Counsel approves the decision not to issue a complaint, there is no further appeal.

Appeal to the General Counsel if complaint is not issued

To enable the NLRB to perform its duties under the Act, Congress delegated to the Agency certain powers that can be used in all cases. These are principally powers having to do with investigations and hearings.

Powers of the NLRB

As previously indicated, all charges that are filed with the Regional Offices are investigated, as are petitions for representation elections. Section 11 establishes the powers of the Board and the Regional Offices in respect to hearings and investigations. The provisions of Section 11(1) authorize the Board or its agents to

Powers concerning investigations

- Examine and copy "any evidence of any person being investigated or proceeded against that relates to any matter under investigation or in question."
- Issue subpenas, on the application of any party to the proceeding, requiring the attendance and testimony of witnesses or the production of any evidence.
- Administer oaths and affirmations, examine witnesses, and receive evidence.
- Obtain a court order to compel the production of evidence or the giving of testimony.

The National Labor Relations Act is not a criminal statute. It is entirely remedial. It is intended to prevent and remedy unfair labor practices, not to punish the person responsible for them. The Board is authorized by Section 10(c) not only to issue a cease-and-desist order, but "to take such affirmative action including reinstatement of employees with or without back pay, as will effectuate the policies of this Act."

The Act is remedial, not criminal

The object of the Board's order in any case is twofold: to eliminate the unfair labor practice and to undo the effects of the violation as much as possible. In determining what the remedy will be in any given case, the Board has considerable discretion. Ordinarily its order in regard to any particular unfair labor practice will follow a standard form that is designed to remedy that unfair labor practice, but the Board can, and often does, change the standard order to meet the needs of the case. Typical affirmative action of the Board may include orders to an employer who has engaged in unfair labor practices to:

Affirmative action may be ordered by the Board

- Disestablish an employer-dominated union.
- Offer certain named individuals immediate and full reinstatement to their former positions or, if those positions no longer exist, to substantially equivalent positions without prejudice to their seniority and other rights and privileges, and with backpay, including interest.
- Upon request, bargain collectively with a certain union as the exclusive representative of the employees in a certain described unit and sign a written agreement if an understanding is reached.

Examples of affirmative action directed to employers

Examples of affirmative action that may be required of a union which has engaged in unfair labor practices include orders to:

- Notify the employer and the employee that it has no objection to reinstatement of certain employees, or employment of certain applicants, whose discriminatory discharge, or denial of employment, was caused by the union.
- Refund dues or fees illegally collected, plus interest.

Examples of affirmative action directed to unions

• Upon request, bargain collectively with a certain employer and sign a written agreement if one is reached.

The Board's order usually includes a direction to the employer or the union or both requiring them to post notices in the employer's plant or the union's office notifying the employees that they will cease the unfair labor practices and informing them of any affirmative action being undertaken to remedy the violation. Special care is taken to be sure that these notices are readily understandable by the employees to whom they are addressed.

Special Proceedings in Certain Cases

Special proceedings are required by the Act in certain kinds of cases. These include the determination of jurisdictional disputes under Section 10(k) and injunction proceedings under Section 10(l) and (j).

Proceedings in jurisdictional disputes

Whenever it is charged that any person has engaged in an unfair labor practice in violation of Section 8(b)(4)(D), the Board must hear and determine the dispute out of which the unfair labor practice arises. Section 8(b)(4)(D) prohibits unions from striking or inducing a strike to compel an employer to assign particular work to employees in one union, or in one trade or craft, rather than another. For a jurisdictional dispute to exist, there must be real competition between unions or between groups of employees for certain work. In effect, Section 10(k) provides an opportunity for the parties to adjust the dispute during a 10-day period after notice of the 8(b)(4)(D) charge has been served. At the end of this period if the parties have not submitted to the Board satisfactory evidence that they have adjusted, or agreed on a method of adjusting, the dispute, the Board is "empowered and directed" to determine which of the competing groups is entitled to have the work.

The investigation of certain charges must be given priority

Section 10(l) provides that whenever a charge is filed alleging a violation of certain sections of the Act relating to boycotts, picketing, and work stoppages, the preliminary investigation of the charge must be given priority over all other types of cases in the Regional Office where it is filed. The unfair labor practices subject to this priority concerning the investigation are those defined in Section 8(b) (4)(A), (B), or (C), all three subparagraphs of Section 8(b)(7), and Section 8(e). Section 10(m) requires that second priority be given to charges alleging violations of Section 8(a)(3), the prohibition against employer discrimination to encourage or discourage membership in a union, and Section 8(b)(2), which forbids unions to cause or attempt to cause such discrimination.

Injunction proceedings under Section 10(l)

If the preliminary investigation of any of the first priority cases shows that there is reasonable cause to believe that the charge is true and that a complaint should issue, Section 10(l) further requires that the U.S. District Court be petitioned to grant an injunction pending the final determination of the Board. The section authorizes the court to grant "such injunctive relief or temporary restraining order as it deems just and proper." Another provision of the section prohibits the application for an injunction based on a charge of violation of Section 8(b)(7) (the prohibition on organizational or recognitional picketing in certain situations) if a charge against an employer alleging violation of Section 8(a)(2) has been filed and the preliminary investigation establishes reasonable cause to believe that such charge is true.

Injunction relief may be sought in other cases

Section 10(j) allows the Board to petition for an injunction in connection with any unfair labor practice after a complaint has been issued. This section does not require that injunctive relief be sought, but only makes it possible for the Board to do so in cases where it is considered appropriate.

Court Enforcement of Board Orders

If an employer or a union fails to comply with a Board order, Section 10(e) empowers the Board to petition the U.S. Court of Appeals for a court decree enforcing the order of the Board. Section 10(f) provides that any person aggrieved by a final order of the Board granting or denying in whole or in part the relief sought may obtain a review of such order in any appropriate circuit court of appeals.

In the U.S. Court of Appeals

When the court of appeals hears a petition concerning a Board order, it may enforce the order, remand it to the Board for reconsideration, change it, or set it aside entirely. If the court of appeals issues a judgment enforcing the Board order, failure to comply may be punishable by fine or imprisonment for contempt of court.

Review by the U.S. Supreme Court

In some cases the U.S. Supreme Court may be asked to review the decision of a circuit court of appeals particularly where there is a conflict in the views of different courts on the same important problem.

In this material the entire Act has been covered, but, of necessity, the coverage has been brief. **Conclusion**
No attempt has been made to state the law in detail or to supply you with a textbook on labor law.
We have tried to explain the Act in a manner intended to make it easier to understand what the basic
provisions of the Act are and how they may concern you. If it helps you to recognize and know your
rights and obligations under the Act, and aids in determining whether you need expert assistance
when a problem arises, its purpose will have been satisfied. More than that: the objective of the Act
will have been furthered.

The objective of the National Labor Relations Act, to avoid or reduce industrial strife and protect
the public health, safety, and interest, can best be achieved by the parties or those who may become
parties to an industrial dispute. Voluntary adjustment of differences at the community and local
level is almost invariably the speediest, most satisfactory, and longest lasting way of carrying out the
objective of the Act.

Efforts are being made in all our Regional Offices to increase the understanding of all parties
as to what the law requires of them. Long experience has taught us that when the parties fully understand their rights and obligations, they are more ready and able to adjust their differences voluntarily.
Seldom do individuals go into a courtroom, a hearing, or any other avoidable contest, knowing that
they are in the wrong and that they can expect to lose the decision. No one really likes to be publicly
recorded as a law violator (and a loser too). Similarly, it is seldom that individuals refuse to accept an
informal adjustment of differences that is reasonable, knowing that they can obtain no better result
from the formal proceeding, even if they prevail.

The consequences of ignorance in these matters—formal proceedings that can be time-consuming
and costly, and which are often followed by bitterness and antagonism—are economically wasteful,
and usually it is accurate to say that neither party really wins. It is in an attempt to bring about
more widespread awareness of the basic law and thus help the parties avoid these consequences that
this material has been prepared and presented as a part of a continuing program to increase understanding of the National Labor Relations Act.

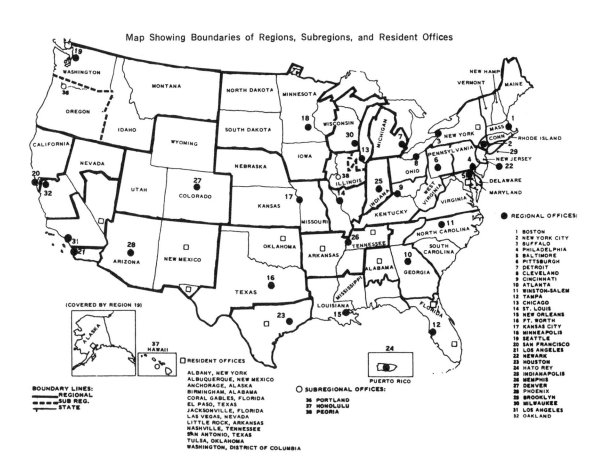

Map Showing Boundaries of Regions, Subregions, and Resident Offices

BOUNDARY LINES:
—— REGIONAL
- - - SUB REG.
— STATE

(COVERED BY REGION 19)

☐ RESIDENT OFFICES

ALBANY, NEW YORK
ALBUQUERQUE, NEW MEXICO
ANCHORAGE, ALASKA
BIRMINGHAM, ALABAMA
CORAL GABLES, FLORIDA
EL PASO, TEXAS
JACKSONVILLE, FLORIDA
LAS VEGAS, NEVADA
LITTLE ROCK, ARKANSAS
NASHVILLE, TENNESSEE
SAN ANTONIO, TEXAS
TULSA, OKLAHOMA
WASHINGTON, DISTRICT OF COLUMBIA

○ SUBREGIONAL OFFICES:

36 PORTLAND
37 HONOLULU
38 PEORIA

● REGIONAL OFFICES:

1 BOSTON
2 NEW YORK CITY
3 BUFFALO
4 PHILADELPHIA
5 BALTIMORE
6 PITTSBURGH
7 DETROIT
8 CLEVELAND
9 CINCINNATI
10 ATLANTA
11 WINSTON-SALEM
12 TAMPA
13 CHICAGO
14 ST. LOUIS
15 NEW ORLEANS
16 FT. WORTH
17 KANSAS CITY
18 MINNEAPOLIS
19 SEATTLE
20 SAN FRANCISCO
21 LOS ANGELES
22 NEWARK
23 HOUSTON
24 HATO REY
25 INDIANAPOLIS
26 MEMPHIS
27 DENVER
28 PHOENIX
29 BROOKLYN
30 MILWAUKEE
31 LOS ANGELES
32 OAKLAND

1 **Boston, Mass. 02110,** 12th Floor, Keystone Bldg., 99 High St.; *Telephone:* 617–223–3300. *Director:* Robert S. Fuchs; *Regional Attorney:* Harold M. Kowal.

2 New York, N.Y. 10007, 3614 Federal Bldg., 26 Federal Plaza; *Telephone:* 212–264–0300. *Director:* Winifred D. Morio; *Regional Attorney:* Edwin H. Bennett.

3 Buffalo, N.Y. 14202, 901 Federal Bldg., 111 W. Huron St.; *Telephone:* 716–842–3100. *Director:* Thomas W. Seeler; *Regional Attorney:* Richard L. De Prospero.

4 Philadelphia, Pa. 19106, 4400 William J. Green, Jr. Federal Bldg., 600 Arch St.; *Telephone:* 215–597–7601. *Director:* Peter W. Hirsch; *Regional Attorney:* Leonard Leventhal.

5 Baltimore, Md. 21201, 1019 Federal Bldg., Hopkins Plaza; *Telephone:* 301–962–2822. *Director:* William C. Humphrey; *Regional Attorney:* Charles B. Slaughter.

6 Pittsburgh, Pa. 15219, 10th Fl., Porter Bldg., 601 Grant St.; *Telephone:* 412–644–2977. *Director:* Henry Shore; *Regional Attorney:* Edward A. Grupp.

7 Detroit, Mich. 48226, 300 Patrick V. McNamara Bldg., 477 Michigan Ave.; *Telephone:* 313–226–3200. *Director:* Bernard Gottfried; *Regional Attorney:* Harry D. Camp.

8 Cleveland, Ohio 44199, 1695 Anthony J. Celebrezze Federal Bldg., 1240 E. 9th St.; *Telephone:* 216–522–3715. *Director:* Bernard Levine; *Regional Attorney:* John Koller.

9 Cincinnati, Ohio 45202, 3003 Federal Office Bldg., 550 Main St.; *Telephone:* 513–684–3686. *Director:* Emil C. Farkas; *Regional Attorney:* Thomas M. Sheeran.

10 Atlanta, Ga. 30308, 701 Peachtree Bldg., 730 Peachtree St. NE.; *Telephone:* 404–526–5760. *Director:* Curtis L. Mack; *Regional Attorney:* Gilbert Cohen.

11 Winston-Salem, N.C. 27101, 447 U.S. Courthouse and Fed. Bldg., Main and Second Sts.; *Telephone:* 919–761–3201. *Director:* Reed Johnston; *Regional Attorney:* Hugh F. Malone.

12 Tampa, Fla. 33602, 706 Federal Office Bldg., 500 Zack St.; *Telephone:* 813–228–2641. *Director:* Harold A. Boire; *Regional Attorney:* Joseph V. Moran.

13 Chicago, Ill. 60604, 881 Everett McKinley Dirksen Bldg., 219 S. Dearborn St.; *Telephone:* 312–353–7570. *Director:* Alex V. Barbour; *Regional Attorney:* Frederick C. Herzog.

38 (Subregion) Peoria, Ill. 61602, 10th Floor, Savings Center Tower, 411 Hamilton Blvd.; *Telephone:* 309–671–7080. *Officer-in-Charge:* Glenn A. Zipp.

14 St. Louis, Mo. 63101, Room 448, 210 N. 12th Blvd.; *Telephone:* 314–425–4167. *Director:* Joseph H. Solien; *Regional Attorney:* Gerard P. Fleischut.

15 New Orleans, La. 70113, 2700 Plaza Tower, 1001 Howard Ave.; *Telephone:* 504–589–6361. *Director:* Charles M. Paschal, Jr.; *Regional Attorney:* Fallon W. Bentz.

16 Fort Worth, Tex. 76102, 8A24 Federal Office Bldg., 819 Taylor St.; *Telephone:* 817–334–2921. *Director:* W. Edwin Youngblood; *Regional Attorney:* Hutton Brandon.

17 Kansas City, Kans. 66101, 616 Two Gateway Center, Fourth at State; *Telephone:* 816–374–4518. *Director:* Thomas C. Hendrix; *Regional Attorney:* Harry Irwig.

18 Minneapolis, Minn. 55401, 316 Federal Bldg., 110 S. 4th St.; *Telephone:* 612–725–2611. *Director:* Robert J. Wilson; *Regional Attorney:* Herbert S. Dawidoff.

19 Seattle, Wash. 98174, 29th Fl., Federal Bldg., 915 2d Ave.; *Telephone:* 206–442–4532. *Director:* Charles M. Henderson; *Regional Attorney:* Walter J. Mercer.

36 (Subregion) Portland, Oreg. 97205, 310 Six Ten Broadway Bldg., 610 SW Broadway; *Telephone:* 503–221–3085. *Officer-in-Charge:* Elwood G. Strumpf.

20 San Francisco, Calif. 94102, 13018 Federal Bldg., 450 Golden Gate Ave., Box 36047; *Telephone:* 415–556–3197. *Director:* Natalie P. Allen; *Regional Attorney:* Michael A. Taylor.

37 (Subregion) Honolulu, Hawaii 96813, 677 Ala Moana Blvd., Suite 914; *Telephone:* 808–546–5100. *Officer-in-Charge:* Dennis R. MacCarthy.

21 Los Angeles, Calif. 90014, Eastern Columbia Bldg., 849 S. Broadway; *Telephone:* 213–688–5200. *Director:* Wilford W. Johansen; *Regional Attorney:* James S. Scott.

22 Newark, N.J. 07102, 16th Fl., Federal Bldg., 970 Broad St.; *Telephone:* 201–645–2100. *Director:* Arthur Eisenberg; *Regional Attorney:* William A. Pascarell.

23 Houston, Tex. 77002, 920 One Allen Center, 500 Dallas Ave.; *Telephone:* 713–226–4296. *Director:* Louis V. Baldovin, Jr.; *Regional Attorney:* Arthur Safos.

24 Hato Rey, P.R. 00918, 591 U.S. Courthouse and Fed. Bldg., Avenue Carlos Chardon; *Telephone:* 809–763–6363. *Director:* Robert J. Cannella; *Regional Attorney:* Martin Arlook.

25 Indianapolis, Ind. 46204, 232 Federal Office Bldg., 575 N. Pennsylvania St.; *Telephone:* 317–269–7430. *Director:* William T. Little; *Regional Attorney:* George M. Dick.

26 Memphis, Tenn. 38103, 746 Clifford Davis Federal Bldg., 167 N. Main St.; *Telephone:* 901–521–3161. *Director:* Raymond A. Jacobson; *Regional Attorney:* John F. Harrington.

27 Denver, Colo. 80202, 260 U.S. Custom House, 721 19th St.; *Telephone:* 303–837–3555. *Director:* Francis Sperandeo; *Regional Attorney:* W. Bruce Gillis, Jr.

28 Phoenix, Ariz. 85014, La Torre Bldg., 6107 N. 7th St.; *Telephone:* 602–261–3717. *Director:* Milo V. Price; *Regional Attorney:* William L. Schmidt.

29 Brooklyn, N.Y. 11241, 4th Floor, 16 Court St.; *Telephone:* 212–330–7713. *Director:* Samuel M. Kaynard; *Regional Attorney:* Harold L. Richman.

30 Milwaukee, Wis. 53203, 2nd Floor, Commerce Bldg., 744 N. 4th St.; *Telephone:* 414–224–3861. *Director:* George F. Squillacote; *Regional Attorney:* Joseph A. Szabo.

31 Los Angeles, Calif. 90024, 12100 Federal Bldg., 11000 Wilshire Blvd.; *Telephone:* 213–824–7351. *Director:* Abraham Siegel; *Regional Attorney:* Roger W. Goubeaux.

32 Oakland, Calif. 94600, *Director:* Vacancy; *Regional Attorney:* Vacancy.

RESIDENT OFFICES:

Albany, N.Y. 12207
New Federal Bldg., Clinton Ave. at N. Pearl St.; *Telephone:* 518–472–2215.
Resident Officer: Thomas J. Sheridan.

Albuquerque, N. Mex. 87110
Patio Plaza Bldg., Upper Level, 5000 Marble Ave., NE.; *Telephone:* 505–766–2582.
Resident Officer: Peter N. Maydanis.

Anchorage, Alaska 99501
409 Hill Bldg., 632 W. 6th Ave.; *Telephone:* 907–265–5271.
Resident Officer: Paul H. Eggert.

Birmingham, Ala. 35203
2102 City Federal Bldg., 2026 2d Ave. North; *Telephone:* 205–254–1492.
Resident Officer: Donald E. Howard.

Coral Gables, Fla. 33146
410 Madruga Bldg., 1570 Madruga Ave.; *Telephone:* 305–350–5391.
Resident Officer: James L. Jeffers.

El Paso, Tex. 79902
Suite 307, Pershing Bldg., 4100 Rio Bravo St.; *Telephone:* 915–543–7737.
Resident Officer: Lloyd L. Porterfield.

Jacksonville, Fla. 32202
Federal Bldg., 400 W. Bay St.; *Telephone:* 904–791–3768.
Resident Officer: John C. Wooten.

Las Vegas, Nev. 98101
Room 4–503, 300 Las Vegas Blvd. S.; *Telephone:* 702–385–6416.
Resident Officer: Vacancy.

Little Rock, Ark. 72201
Suite 1120, 1 Union Plaza; *Telephone:* 501–378–6311.
Resident Officer: Robert K. Gentry.

Nashville, Tenn. 37203
A–702 Federal Bldg., U.S. Courthouse; *Telephone:* 615–749–5921.
Resident Officer: Bernard G. Aronstam.

San Antonio, Tex. 78206
Rm. 509A, Fed. Office Bldg., 727 E. Durango Blvd; *Telephone:* 512–225–5511.
Resident Officer: John C. Crawford.

Tulsa, Okla. 74135.
Skyline East Bldg., South Tower, 6128 E. 38th St.; *Telephone:* 918–664–1420.
Resident Officer: William N. Cates.

Washington, D.C. 20037
100 Gelman Bldg., 2120 L St., NW.; *Telephone:* 202–254–7612.
Resident Officer: Alexander T. Graham, Jr.

Anti-Kickback Law and Copeland Act (1934, as Amended)

SUMMARY AND DESCRIPTION

Persons and Employment Covered

These laws cover not only direct Federal public building and public work but also all work financed in whole or in part with Federal funds, loans, or grants.

Enforcement

The Government agencies that let the contracts are primarily responsible for obtaining compliance with these laws and the regulations of the Secretary of Labor.

Anti-Kickback Law

This law makes it punishable by a fine up to $5,000 or by imprisonment up to 5 years, or both, for anyone, by force, intimidation, threat of procuring dismissal from employment or by an other manner whatsoever, to induce an employee on work covered by the law to give up any part of the compensation to which he has a right under his contract of employment.

Copeland Act

This Act authorizes the Secretary of Labor to make reasonable regulations for contractors and subcontractors engaged in construction covered by the Act. These regulations show under what conditions deductions from wages are and are not permitted, require the contractors to present evidence that proposed deductions are proper ones, and require approval of the Department of Labor for such deductions. The Act also requires the contractors to file weekly statements with respect to the wages paid each employee during the preceding week. The regulations require payroll records showing the information needed to determine whether required wages are being paid. The requirements of these regulations are made a part of every contract for a Federal or Federal-aid job.

Labor-Management Reporting and Disclosure Act (Landrum-Griffin Act) (1959)

SUMMARY AND DESCRIPTION

This law is based upon congressional finding of a need "to eliminate or prevent improper practices on the part of labor organizations, employers, labor relations consultants, and their officers and representatives which distort and defeat the policies of the Labor Management Relations Act, 1947, as amended, and the Railway Labor Act, as amended."

The act is made up of seven titles, in addition to definitions, findings, and a statement of policy.

Title I is called the Bill of Rights of Members of Labor Organizations and sets forth certain basic rights which Congress believed should be guaranteed to members by Federal law. Members may enforce these rights by bringing suits in Federal district courts.

Titles II through VI deal primarily with the following: Reporting by labor organizations, by officers and employees of labor organizations, by employers, and by labor relations consultants; prevention of abuses in union trusteeships; standards for union elections; safeguards for labor organizations; and (in Title VI) certain miscellaneous provisions. The Secretary of Labor has varying administrative and enforcement responsibilities under these titles. In addition, Titles II through VI contain a number of criminal provisions which involve enforcement responsibilities of the U.S. Department of Justice.

Title VII and section 505 contain amendments to the Labor Management Relations Act, 1947, which involve matters administered by the National Labor Relations Board, an independent agency not part of the Department of Labor.

Where Government participation is provided for in Titles II through VI of the law, dealing with the administration of reporting requirements, regulation of union trusteeships and elections, and certain miscellaneous provisions, this function is performed generally by the Secretary of Labor. The Secretary exercises his authority through the Office of Labor-Management and Welfare-Pension Reports, headed by a Director. The Office is under the general direction and control of the Labor-Management Services Administrator.

Some of the previsions of the law depend for enforcement upon civil actions brought by the union members themselves; others upon criminal prosecution, or upon civil action brought by the Secretary of Labor. The Secretary has direct authority to investigate violations except of Title I (except section 104) and of the provisions amending other statutes.

Complaints Filed

Since the act authorizes the Secretary of Labor to make investigations of violations of Title II through Title VI (except for section 505), complaints involving noncompliance with those provisions should be brought to the attention of the U.S. Department of Labor. Complaints of violations of the Title I rights, except for the right to obtain copies of collective bargaining agreements, must be enforced by civil suits brought by the affected union members themselves. Complaints of violations of Title VII, which contains amendments to the National Labor Relations Act, should be made to the National Labor Relations Board. Complaints of violation of section 505 should be made to the local U.S. attorney.

Coverage

The first six titles of this act generally have broader coverage than the National Labor Relations Act. All labor organizations engaged in an industry affecting commerce (except those comprised solely of employees of Federal, State, and local governments or their subdivisions) are subject to these titles without regard to size. This includes conferences, committees, boards, or councils subordinate to national or international unions, and both railroad and airline unions. Unlike the National Labor Relations Act, the definition of "employee" in-

cludes railroad workers, certain agricultural workers, supervisors, and specifically, persons whose work has ceased because of a current labor dispute, of any unfair labor practice, or of exclusion or expulsion from a labor organization in any manner or for any reason inconsistent with the requirements of the act. Similarly, employers subject to the Railway Labor Act, and therefore not covered by the National Labor Relations Act, are subject to the pertinent provisions of the Labor-Management Reporting and Disclosure Act of 1959. Certain provisions of the act apply to labor relations consultants and others who receive compensation for advising or representing an employer or union in relation to organizing, bargaining, or other concerted activities.

Union Member Rights (Title I)

Title I of the law establishes for union members a Federal "Bill of Rights," which includes the following:

1. Equal rights to attend, participate in, and vote at meetings and elections, subject to reasonable union rules;

2. Freedom to meet and assemble with other members, to express any arguments or opinions, and to voice views upon candidates and business properly before a meeting. This freedom is subject to reasonable union rules pertaining to the conduct of union meetings and does not impair the right of a labor organization to assure responsible conduct of its members and responsible discharge of the organization's legal and contractual obligations;

3. Protection for increases in union dues or the imposition of assessments except where specified procedures are followed: i.e., in local unions by secret ballot of the membership either at a membership meeting or by means of a referendum; in national unions and intermediate bodies by majority vote of delegates at a convention, by secret ballot by members in a referendum, or, where authorized, by vote of the executive board or similar governing body;

4. Protection of the right to testify, to communicate with legislators, and to bring suit after using reasonable organizational remedies, for appropriate relief when unions infringe the rights of members;

5. The right to notice and a fair hearing before any disciplinary actions, except discipline for nonpayment of dues;

6. The right to obtain or inspect copies of collective bargaining agreements (this right extends to all employees affected by the agreement) and to be informed by the unions of the rights granted by this law. The right to obtain bargaining agreements is enforced by the Secretary of Labor as well as by the individual whose rights have been infringed; and

Existing rights under Federal and State laws are preserved for union members. Any person whose rights secured by Title I have been violated may bring an action for appropriate relief (including injunctions) in a U.S. district court.

Union reports

Title II requires each labor organization to adopt a constitution and bylaws, and to file a copy of these documents with the Secretary of Labor along with an organizational report. The labor organization must also submit annually to the Secretary a report covering its preceding fiscal year.

The law requires the inclusion of the following information in the initial organization report (Form LM-1, the "Labor Organization Information Report"):

1. Name of the organization, its mail address and any other address at which the organization maintains its principal office or keeps its records.

2. List of officers showing their names and their titles.

3. Initiation fees required, as well as fees charged to transferred members, and fees for work permits required by the organization.

4. Regular dues or other periodic payments required of members.

5. These specific details on the procedures of the organization and provisions made in its constitution and bylaws:

    a. What the qualifications and restrictions for membership are.

    b. How assessments are levied.

    c. What the provisions and procedures are for participation in insurance and other benefit plans.

    d. How the disbursement of union funds is authorized.

    e. What provisions and procedures the organization has for the audit of financial transactions.

    f. How regular and special meetings are called.

    g. How officers, stewards, executive board members, and any delegates to other bodies composed of labor organization representatives are selected.

    h. What method is used to discipline or remove officers or agents for breach of trust.

    i. How fines, and suspension or expulsion of members, are handled, including the grounds for such actions, and what the provisions and procedures are for hearings and appeals in such cases.

    j. How bargaining demands are authorized.

    k. How contract terms are ratified.

    l. How strikes are authorized.

    m. What the provisions and procedures are for issuing work permits.

Any change in this information as supplied in the initial labor organization information report must be submitted to the Secretary of Labor with the next annual report (Forms LM–2 or LM–3, the "Labor Organization Annual Report").

The annual report is due within 90 days after the end of the organization's fiscal year and must include this information about the reporting labor organization and its financial affairs during the previous fiscal year:

1. Assets and liabilities at the beginning and end of the fiscal year.

2. Listing of receipts of any kind and where they came from.

3. Salaries, allowances, and other direct or indirect payments (including reimbursed expenses) to each officer, irrespective of amounts, and also to each employee who received more than $10,000 in the aggregate during the year from the reporting organization and any other affiliated labor organization.

4. Listing of all loans (direct or indirect) made to any officer, employee, or member which aggregated more than $250 during the year to any one person. A statement must be included giving the purpose of each loan, the security furnished, if any, and what arrangements were made for repaying the loan.

5. Listing of all direct or indirect loans made to any business enterprise. A statement must be included giving the purpose of each loan, the security furnished, if any, and what arrangements were made for repayment.

6. Any other disbursements and the purposes for which they were made.

The above information is to be shown in the categories prescribed by the Secretary of Labor.

The Form LM–3 is a simplified version of the more detailed Form LM–2 and may be used by labor organizations having gross annual receipts totalling less than $30,000.

Reports of Union Officers and Employees

Every officer and employee (other than an employee performing exclusively clerical or custodial services) of a labor organization must file a signed report (Form LM–30, the "Labor Officer and Employee Report") with the Secretary of Labor listing the following "conflict of interest" transactions involving himself, his spouse or minor child:

1. Direct or indirect holdings of securities or other interests in a business whose employees his labor organization represents or actively seeks to represent and any income or other monetary benefit received from such business;

2. Transactions involving securities, loans to or from, or other interests in a business whose employees his labor organization represents or actively seeks to represent;

3. An interest in or income from a business which deals substantially with an employer whose employees his labor organization represents or actively seeks to represent;

4. An interest in or income from a business which has any commercial dealings with his labor organization or a trust in which his labor organization is interested;

5. Any business transaction or arrangement with an employer whose employees his organization represents or actively seeks to represent, except work performed and payments and benefits received as a bona fide employee and sales and services in the regular course of business at prices available to any of the employer's employees; and

6. Any payment from an employer or an employer's labor relations consultant except payments permitted by section 302 of the Labor Management Relations Act, 1947, as amended.

Paragraphs (1) through (5) above do not require any employee to disclose bona fide investments in securities traded on a securities exchange registered as a national securities exchange under the Securities Exchange Act of 1934, or in shares in an investment company registered under the Investment Company Act of 1940, or in securities or a public utility holding company registered under the Public Utility Holding Company Act of 1935, or to report any income derived therefrom.

An officer or employee is not required to file a "conflict of interest" report unless he or his spouse or minor child has engaged in a transaction described.

Report of Employers and Labor Consultants and Other Persons

Every employer must file with the Secretary of Labor a report (Form LM–10, the "Employer Report") within 90 days after the end of the employer's fiscal year under the following circumstances:

1. If he makes payments or loans of money, or other thing of value, including reimbursed expenses, or any promise or agreement for such payments or loans to any labor organization, union officer, agent, shop steward, or other union representative or employee. (Payments permitted under section 302(c) of the Labor Management Relations Act are excepted, as are payments or loans made by any national or State bank, credit union, insurance company, savings and loan association, or other credit institution.)

2. If he pays any of his employees, or any group or committee of his employees, to get them to persuade other employees to exercise or not to exercise, or how they shall exercise, the right to organize and bargain collectively through representatives of their own choosing, unless the payment was disclosed to the other employees before or at the same time as it was made.

3. If the object of any employer expenditure is to interfere with, restrain, or coerce any employees in the exercise of their right to organize and bargain collectively

through representatives of their own choosing; or is to obtain information about the activities of employees or of a labor organization concerning a labor dispute in which he is involved, except when the information is to be used only for an administrative or arbitration proceeding or a criminal or civil judicial proceeding.

4. If he makes an agreement or arrangement with a labor relations consultant or other independent contractor or organization covering activities where an object is to persuade employees to exercise or not to exercise, or how they shall exercise, the right to organize and bargain collectively through representatives of their own choosing; or whereby such labor relations consultant or similar person or organization undertakes to supply information about the activities of employees or of a labor organization in connection with a labor dispute involving the employer, except when the information is to be used only for an administrative or arbitration proceeding or a criminal or civil judicial proceeding.

5. If he makes any payment pursuant to any such agreements or arrangements.

Reports filed by employers must include:

1. A detailed statement of each covered payment, loan, promise, agreement or arrangement, showing its date and amount, and the name, address, and position, if any, in any firm or labor organization, of the person to whom it was made.

2. A full explanation of the circumstances of all such payments, and the terms of any agreement or understanding under which they were made.

Employers do not need to file reports concerning compensation paid to their regular officers, supervisors, or employees for their services as regular officers, supervisors, or employees. Also, employers are not required to file reports on the services of any person if such person *only* engaged or agreed to engage in the following activities: giving advice to the employer; representing the employer before a court, administrative agency, or arbitration tribunal; and engaging in collective bargaining on behalf of the employer with respect to wages, hours, or other conditions of employment.

Signed reports must also be filed with the Secretary of Labor by every person who agrees or arranges with an employer to undertake activities which have as an object, directly or indirectly:

1. To persuade employees to exercise, or not to exercise, or as to how they should exercise, the right to organize and bargain collectively through representatives of their own choosing.

2. To supply an employer with information on the activities of employees or a labor organization in connection with a labor dispute involving the employer, except information for use solely in conjunction with an administrative or arbitral proceeding or a criminal or civil judicial proceeding.

Form LM–20, the "Agreements and Activities Report," must be filed within 30 days after entering into the agreement or arrangement, and Form LM–21, the "Receipts and Disbursements Report," must be filed within 90 days after the end of the person's fiscal year.

The latter must report all receipts with their source, and all disbursements with the purpose thereof, in connection with any labor relations advice or services.

There are certain exceptions from these latter reporting requirements, as follows:

1. Reports are not required of regular officers, supervisors, or employees of any employer concerning the compensation they receive in connection with their work for such employer.

2. An attorney who is a member in good standing of the bar of any State need not report any information which is lawfully communicated to him in the course of a legitimate attorney-client relationship.

3. No person is required to make reports if he *only* engaged or agreed to engage in the following activities: giving advice to employers; representing employers before a court, administrative agency, or arbitration tribunal; and engaging in collective bargaining on behalf of employers with respect to wages, hours, or other conditions of employment.

Surety Company Reports

The Act contains bonding provisions. (See Title V, Safeguards for Labor Organizations, Section 502.) A 1965 amendment added a provision requiring surety companies to file annual reports with the Secretary of Labor describing their bonding experience under this Act and the Welfare and Pension Plans Disclosure Act. The Surety Company Annual Report, Form S–1, was developed for this purpose. It consists of four parts; I. Identification; II. Premium Data; III. Loss Data; and IV. Itemization of Losses Reported During Year.

Each surety company which has in force any LMRDA and/or WPPDA fidelity bonds, even though the volume of such bonds may be small, must file an S–1 report disclosing its annual totals of all such fidelity writings, indicating its experience separately for honesty and faithful discharge of contracts under each act. It need not submit an S–1 for each separate bond or class of bonds that it has written. A single report covering a group of companies is not acceptable.

A surety company is not required to indicate on the S–1 the number of persons bonded, bonds in force, or bonds on which direct losses were paid, and it need not name the defaulter when reporting a loss. However, it must include in Part IV each loss on which notice was received during the year, whether or not the involved labor union, trust or plan is insured under a contract reported in Parts II and III.

The data called for by the form do not show losses which were not claimed. Loss data are based on the amount of the loss or the amount of the bond coverage

available, whichever is less. Losses reported are not net losses; i.e., less salvage, which is applied to reduce losses in the year collected, regardless of when the loss was sustained.

Disclosure and Enforcement

All reports are public information. The Labor Department's Public Document Room, located at 8757 Georgia Avenue, Silver Spring, Md., just outside Washington, maintains copies of all reports for public disclosure. Area offices of the Labor-Management Services Administration, which are located in 24 cities, also have on file reports for unions within areas covered. They are subject to inspection by any person, and copies may be purchased by any person upon payment of a copying charge. Unions must make the reported information available to members, and permit members for just cause to examine any books and records necessary to verify the reports. Basic records to support all reports must be kept and preserved for at least 5 years. Criminal penalties are provided for willfully falsifying, withholding, or destroying reports or other required information. When it appears that any person has violated or is about to violate Title II, the Secretary of Labor may bring a civil action in the proper Federal district court for appropriate relief, including an injunction.

The filing requirements of former sections 9 (f) and (g) of the National Labor Relations Act are repealed since they have been replaced by the new requirements of this law.

For copies of the reporting forms and instructions, write to the Office of Labor-Management and Welfare-Pension Reports, U.S. Department of Labor, Washington, D.C. 20210.

Trusteeships (Title III)

Under the act trusteeships may be established over subordinate unions only in accordance with the constitution and bylaws of the labor organization imposing the trusteeship, and for one or more of the following purposes:

1. Correcting corruption or financial malpractice;

2. Assuring the performance of a collective bargaining agreement or other duties of a bargaining representative;

3. Restoring democratic procedures; or

4. Otherwise carrying out the legitimate objects of such labor organization.

Labor organizations imposing the trusteeship must file special reports within 30 days of the establishment of a trusteeship and must report semiannually thereafter.

In the initial report, these facts are to be included:

1. Name and address of the subordinate organization.

2. Date the trusteeship was established.

3. Detailed report of reason or reasons why the trusteeship was established or why it has been continued.

4. A statement of the extent to which members of the organization under trusteeship have any part in selecting delegates to represent them at union conventions or at other policymaking meetings and in electing the officers of the labor organization which has assumed the trusteeship.

5. A complete account of the financial status of the trusteed organization at the time the trusteeship went into effect.

Up-to-date information on matters included in the initial report (except the information listed under No. 5) must be reported to the Secretary of Labor in semiannual reports each 6 months after the initial report is filed, for so long as the trusteeship remains in effect.

In addition, the organization imposing a trusteeship must file on behalf of the subordinate organization the annual reports required by Title II and must use the form LM–2 for this purpose.

In administering a trusteeship two practices are specifically prohibited. First, it is unlawful to count votes of convention delegates from the subordinate organization unless they were elected by secret ballot in an election where all members in good standing could participate. Second, transfer of any funds from a subordinate to a supervisory organization, except normal per capita taxes and assessments payable by other subordinate bodies, is also unlawful. The act, however, does not prevent distribution of the subordinate union's assets in accordance with its constitution and bylaws upon its bona fide dissolution.

Generally, the means of enforcing trusteeship reporting requirements, and the criminal sanctions for improper reporting, parallel those available for the annual reports required by Title II. Civil suit to secure compliance with the trusteeship standards may be brought by any member, or by any subordinate body affected by violation of this title, as well as by the Secretary when he finds, as a result of a complaint in writing by a member of a subordinate organization or by a subordinate organization and after investigation, that there is probable cause to believe a violation has occurred. But when the Secretary files suit the court's jurisdiction is exclusive. A trusteeship is presumed valid for 18 months, from its establishment, after which the burden of proof is on the parent organization to justify its continuation.

Elections (Title IV)

This law requires national or international labor organizations, except federations of such organizations, to elect officers at least once every 5 years either by secret ballot among members in good standing, or at a convention of delegates chosen by secret ballot. Intermediate bodies are required to hold elections not less frequently than once every 4 years either by secret ballot among members in good standing or by officers representative of such members who were chosen by secret ballot. Local labor organizations must elect officers by secret ballot among members in good standing at least once every 3 years. The act includes the following standards for conducting elections of officers:

1. A candidate has a right, enforceable by pre-election private suit as well as by the Secretary of Labor, to distribution of campaign literature to the membership at his own expense, campaign literature must be distributed on equal terms for all candidates and no discriminatory use may be made of lists of members. Lists of members under union security agreements must be made available for inspection by candidates within 30 days prior to an election;

2. Adequate safeguards must be provided to insure a fair election, including the right of any candidate to have an observer at the polls and at the counting of ballots;

3. A reasonable opportunity to nominate candidates must be provided;

4. In an election conducted by secret ballot, each member in good standing is entitled to one vote;

5. Every member in good standing is eligible to be a candidate and to hold office, subject only to reasonable qualifications and the prohibitions on union officeholding in Title V of the Act, and to support the candidates of his choice without interference or reprisal;

6. Notice must be given by mail to each union member at his last known home address at least 15 days before a secret ballot election;

7. No member is subject to disqualification as a voter or candidate by reason of default or delay in paying dues checked off by an employer; and

Elections required by the act must be conducted in accordance with each organization's constitution and bylaws unless these provisions are inconsistent with the act.

Ballots and other election records must be preserved for one year. Use of union dues, assessments and similar levies by a labor organization and use of any moneys of an employer to promote the candidacy of any person is prohibited. If the Secretary finds, after a hearing upon application by a member, that the procedures in the labor organization's constitution or bylaws for removing an elected local union officer guilty of serious misconduct are inadequate, members may then, for cause shown and after notice and hearing, remove such officer in a secret ballot referendum conducted by the officers of the local union.

A member of a labor organization who has a complaint concerning an election or removal requirement must first use the remedies available within the union to secure relief. If these union remedies have been exhausted or a final decision has not been issued within three months after invoking such remedies, a complaint may be filed with the Secretary of Labor within one month. A challenged election is presumed valid until a final decision is made. If the Secretary, after investigation, finds probable cause to believe a violation has occurred, which has not been remedied, he may bring suit in the district court. If the court finds that an election has not been held within the prescribed time or that a violation occurred which may have affected the outcome of an election, the court shall direct the conduct of a new election under the supervision of the Secretary. The Secretary certifies the names of the persons elected, or the results of the removed vote, to the court, for entry of an appropriate order.

Safeguards for Labor Organizations (Title V)

Officers, agents, shop stewards or other representatives of labor organizations are declared by this law to occupy positions of trust in relation to such organizations and their members as a group. This requires them to hold and use money and property of the organization solely for the benefit of the members and in accordance with the constitution and bylaws of the organization. Whenever any person is alleged to have violated these duties and the union, upon request, fails to sue or secure appropriate relief within a reasonable time after the request, any member, upon leave of the court, may sue for an accounting or other appropriate relief, including the recovery of profits which might have been secured through activities in violation of fiduciary duties. The law also makes it a Federal crime for an officer or employee to embezzle, steal or convert to his own or another's use any funds of a labor organization.

Bonding Requirements

All officers, agents, and other representatives or employees of labor organizations, who handle funds or other property, must be bonded by a corporate surety in an amount equal to 10 percent of the funds handled during the preceding fiscal year but not in excess of $500,000. Persons serving in similar capacities in trusts in which a labor organization is interested are subject to the same requirement. Excepted from, the requirement are labor organizations whose property and annual financial receipts do not exceed $5,000 in value.

If the labor organization or the trust in which a labor organization is interested does not have a preceding fiscal year, the amount of the bond shall be, in the case of a local labor organization, not less than $1,000, and in case of any other labor organization or of a trust in which a labor organization is interested, not less than $10,000.

The bond is to provide protection against loss by reason of acts of fraud or dishonesty; prior to a 1965 amendment the Act required a faithful discharge of duties bond. Any person who is not covered by such bonds shall not be permitted to receive, handle, disburse, or otherwise exercise custody or control of the funds or other property of a labor organization or of a trust in which a labor organization is interested.

The corporate surety must hold a grant of authority from the Secretary of the Treasury under the Act of July 30, 1947 (6 U.S.C. 6–13), as an acceptable surety on Federal Bonds: *Provided*, That when in the opinion of the Secretary a labor organization has made other bonding arrangements which would provide the protection required by this section at comparable cost or less, he may exempt such labor organization from placing a bond through a surety company holding such grant of authority.

Making of Loans; Payment of Fines

The act also prohibits loans in an aggregate amount of more than $2,000 by a union to an officer or employee and prohibits unions and employers from paying the fine of any of their officers or employees convicted of willfully violating the act.

Prohibitions Against Certain Persons Holding Union Office

A person may not serve as a union officer, director, trustee, manager, business agent, organizer or other employee (other than as an employee performing exclusively clerical or custodial duties), as a labor relations consultant, or as an officer, agent or employee of a group or association of employers dealing with a union within 5 years after conviction or end of imprisonment for certain specified crimes, unless citizenship rights are restored or unless the Board of Parole of the Department of Justice has determined, in a hearing, the suitability of service by persons convicted of such crimes. In addition, the labor organization or its officers may not knowingly permit a person ineligible for these reasons to hold office.

Improper Payments and Fees

The Labor-Management Reporting and Disclosure Act tightens and clarifies the prohibition in section 302 of the Taft-Hartley Act concerning employer payments and loans to employee representatives.

Miscellaneous Provisions (Title VI)

1. The Secretary of Labor is granted express power, in order to determine whether any person has violated or is about to violate the provisions of the act except Title I and amendments to other statutes, to investigate, to inspect records, and to question persons in order to ascertain the facts. For the purpose of investigations provided for in the act, the provisions of sections 9 and 10 of the Federal Trade Commission Act (relating to attendance of witnesses, and production of documents) are made applicable to the jurisdiction, power and duties of the Secretary.

2. Criminal penalities are imposed for "extortionate picketing," i.e., picketing designed to extract money, other than for bona fide employee benefits, from an employer for the purpose of personal profit.

3. The obligations, rights, benefits, privileges or immunities under the Railway Labor Act, as amended, are not to be construed as impaired by the first six titles of the act. In addition, nothing contained in these titles (with the exception of section 505 amending section 302 of the National Labor Relations Act, as amended) shall be construed as conferring any rights, privileges or defenses upon employers, or to impair or affect the rights of any person under the National Labor Relations Act, as amended.

4. Nothing in this act, except as explicitly provided to the contrary, reduces or limits the responsibilities of any labor organization or any officer, agent, or other representative of a labor organization, or of any trust in which a labor organization is interested, under any other Federal law or State law. Similarly, nothing in the act is to be interpreted as barring the current remedies of union members under State or other Federal law.

5. It is a crime for any person by force or violence to coerce or intimidate union members for the purpose of interfering with rights under this law. It is unlawful for any labor organization to discipline its members for exercising rights under this law.

For further information write to: Labor Management Services Administration, U.S. Department of Labor, Washington, D.C. 20216.

Farm Labor Contractor Registration Act of 1963

SUMMARY AND DESCRIPTION

The Farm Labor Contractor Registration Act of 1963 authorizes the operation of a program designed to protect migrant workers and their families from exploitation by unscrupulous farm labor contractors. This Act requires certain farm labor contractors and their full-time regular employees to register on an annual basis with the Secretary of Labor and operate according to the provisions set forth in the Act. Authority for administration and enforcement of the act has been delegated to the Wage and Hour Division of the Employment Standards Administration. Responsibilities of the program include publicizing the requirements of the act and regulations pertaining to it, processing of applications for registration, recommending

issuance or denial of certificates of registration, investigating activities of crew leaders and the enforcement of violations of the Act.

For further information write to: Employment Standards Administration Wage and Hour Division, U.S. Department of Labor, Washington, D.C. 20210

Executive Order 11491—Labor-Management Relations in the Federal Service (1969, as amended)

WHEREAS the public interest requires high standards of employee performance and the continual development and implementation of modern and progressive work practices to facilitate improved employee performance and efficiency; and

WHEREAS the well-being of employees and efficient administration of the Government are benefited by providing employees an opportunity to participate in the formulation and implementation of personnel policies and practices affecting the conditions of their employment; and

WHEREAS the participation of employees should be improved through the maintenance of constructive and cooperative relationships between labor organizations and management officials; and

WHEREAS subject to law and the paramount requirements of public service, effective labor-management relations within the Federal service require a clear statement of the respective rights and obligations of labor organizations and agency management:

NOW, THEREFORE, by virtue of the authority vested in me by the Constitution and statutes of the United States, including sections 3301 and 7301 of title 5 of the United States Code, and as President of the United States, I hereby direct that the following policies shall govern officers and agencies of the executive branch of the Government in all dealings with Federal employees and organizations representing such employees.

General Provisions

SECTION 1. *Policy.* (a) Each employee of the executive branch of the Federal Government has the right, freely and without fear of penalty or reprisal, to form, join, and assist a labor organization or to refrain from any such activity, and each employee shall be protected in the exercise of this right. Except as otherwise expressly provided in this Order, the right to assist a labor organization extends to participation in the management of the organization and acting for the organization in the capacity of an organization representative, including presentation of its views to officials of the executive branch, the Congress, or other appropriate authority. The head of each agency shall take the action required to assure that employees in the agency are apprised of their rights under this section, and that no interference, restraint, coercion, or discrimination is practiced within his agency to encourage or discourage membership in a labor organization.

(b) Paragraph (a) of this section does not authorize participation in the management of a labor organization or acting as a representative of such an organization by a supervisor, except as provided in section 24 of this Order, or by an employee when the participation or activity would result in a conflict or apparent conflict of interest or otherwise be incompatible with law or with the official duties of the employee.

SECTION 2. *Definitions.* When used in this Order, the term—

(a) "Agency" means an executive department, a Government corporation, and an independent establishment as defined in section 104 of title 5, United States Code, except the General Accounting Office;

(b) "Employee" means an employee of an agency and an employee of a nonappropriated fund instrumentality of the United States but does not include, for the purpose of exclusive recognition or national consultation rights, a supervisor, except as provided in section 24 of this Order;

[Sec. 2(b) as amended by E.O. 11616, 36 F.R. 17319, Aug. 28, 1971]

(c) "Supervisor" means an employee having authority, in the interest of an agency, to hire, transfer, suspend, lay off, recall, promote, discharge, assign, reward, or discipline other employees, or responsibly to direct them, or to evaluate their performance, or to adjust their grievances, or effectively to recommend such action, if in connection with the foregoing the exercise of authority is not of a merely routine or clerical nature, but requires the use of independent judgment;

(d) "Guard" means an employee assigned to enforce against employees and other persons rules to protect agency property or the safety of persons on agency premises, or to maintain law and order in areas or facilities under Government control;

(e) "Labor organization" means a lawful organization of any kind in which employees participate and which exists for the purpose, in whole or in part, of dealing with agencies concerning grievances, personnel policies and practices, or other matters affecting the working conditions of their employees; but does not include an organization which—

(1) consists of management officials or supervisors, except as provided in section 24 of this Order;

(2) assists or participates in a strike against the Government of the United States or any agency thereof, or imposes a duty or obligation to conduct, assist, or participate in such a strike;

[Paragraph (2) revised by E.O. 11616, 36 F.R. 17319, Aug. 28, 1971]

(3) advocates the overthrow of the constitutional form of government in the United States; or

(4) discriminates with regard to the terms or conditions of membership because of race, color, creed, sex, age, or national origin.

(f) "Agency management" means the agency head and all management officials, supervisors, and other representatives of management having authority to act for the agency on any matters relating to the implementation of the agency labor-management relations program established under this Order;

(g) "Council" means the Federal Labor Relations Council established by this Order;

(h) "Panel" means the Federal Service Impasses Panel established by this Order; and

(i) "Assistant Secretary" means the Assistant Secretary of Labor for Labor-Management Relations.

SECTION 3. *Application.* (a) This Order applies to all employees and agencies in the executive branch, except as provided in paragraphs (b), (c) and (d) of this section.

(b) This Order (except section 22) does not apply to—

(1) the Federal Bureau of Investigation;

(2) the Central Intelligence Agency;

(3) any other agency, or office, bureau, or entity with an agency, which has as a primary function intelligence, investigative, or security work, when the head of the agency determines, in his sole judgment, thát the Order cannot be applied in a manner consistent with national security requirements and considerations; or

(4) any office, bureau or entity within an agency which has as a primary function investigation or audit of the conduct or work of officials or employees of the agency for the purpose of ensuring honesty and integrity in the discharge of their official duties, when the head of the agency determines, in his sole judgment, that the Order cannot be applied in a manner consistent with the internal security of the agency.

[Sec. 3(b) as amended by E.O. 11636, 36 F.R. 24910, Dec. 24, 1971]

(c) The head of an agency may, in his sole judgment, suspend any provision of this Order (except section 22) with respect to any agency installation or activity located outside the United States, when he determines that this is necessary in the national interest, subject to the conditions he prescribes.

(d) Employees engaged in administering a labor-management relations law or this Order shall not be represented by a labor organization which also represents other groups of employees under the law or this Order, or which is affiliated directly or indirectly with an organization which represents such a group of employees.

Administration

SECTION 4. *Federal Labor Relations Council.* (a) There is hereby established the Federal Labor Relations Council, which consists of the Chairman of the Civil Service Commission, who shall be chairman of the Council, the Secretary of Labor, the Director of the Office of Management and Budget, and such other officials of the executive branch as the President may designate from time to time. The Civil Service Commission shall provide administrative support and services to the Council to the extent authorized by law.

[Sec. 4(a) revised by E.O. 11616, 36 F.R. 17319, Aug. 28, 1971]

(b) The Council shall administer and interpret this Order, decide major policy issues, prescribe regulations, and from time to time, report and make recommendations to the President.

(c) The Council may consider, subject to its regulations—

(1) appeals from decisions of the Assistant Secretary issued pursuant to section 6 of this Order;

(2) appeals on negotiability issues as provided in section 11(c) of this Order;

(3) exceptions to arbitration awards; and

(4) other matters it deems appropriate to assure the effectuation of the purposes of this Order.

SECTION 5. *Federal Service Impasses Panel.* (a) There is hereby established the Federal Service Impasses Panel as an agency within the Council. The Panel consists of at least three members appointed by the President, one of whom he designates as chairman. The Council shall provide the services and staff assistance needed by the Panel.

(b) The Panel may consider negotiation impasses as provided in section 17 of this Order and may take any action it considers necessary to settle an impasse.

(c) The Panel shall prescribe regulations needed to administer its functions under this Order.

SECTION 6. *Assistant Secretary of Labor for Labor-Management Relations.*

(a) The Assistant Secretary shall—

(1) decide questions as to the appropriate unit for the purpose of exclusive recognition and related issues submitted for his consideration;

(2) supervise elections to determine whether a labor-organization is the choice of a majority of the employees in an appropriate unit as their exclusive representative, and certify the results;

(3) decide questions as to the eligibility of labor organizations for national consultation rights under criteria prescribed by the Council;

[(3) as amended by E.O. 11616, 36 F.R. 17319, Aug. 28, 1971]

(4) decide unfair labor practice complaints and alleged

violations of the standards of conduct for labor organizations; and

[(4) revised by E.O. 11616, 36 F.R. 17319, Aug. 28, 1971]

(5) decide questions as to whether a grievance is subject to a negotiated grievance procedure or subject to arbitration under an agreement.

[(5) added by E.O. 11616, 36 F.R. 17319, Aug. 28, 1971]

(b) In any matters arising under paragraph (a) of this section, the Assistant Secretary may require an agency or a labor organization to cease and desist from violations of this Order and require it to take such affirmative action as he considers appropriate to effectuate the policies of this Order.

(c) In performing the duties imposed on him by this section, the Assistant Secretary may request and use the services and assistance of employees of other agencies in accordance with section 1 of the Act of March 4, 1915, (38 Stat. 1084, as amended; 31 U.S.C. § 686).

(d) The Assistant Secretary shall prescribe regulations needed to administer his functions under this Order.

(e) If any matters arising under paragraph (a) of this section involve the Department of Labor, the duties of the Assistant Secretary described in paragraphs (a) and (b) of this section shall be performed by a member of the Civil Service Commission designated by the Chairman of the Commission.

Recognition

SECTION 7. *Recognition in general.* (a) An agency shall accord exclusive recognition or national consultation rights at the request of a labor organization which meets the requirements for the recognition or consultation rights under this Order.

(b) a labor organization seeking recognition shall submit to the agency a roster of its officers and representatives, a copy of its constitution and by-laws, and a statement of its objectives.

(c) When recognition of a labor organization has been accorded, the recognition continues as long as the organization continues to meet the requirements of this Order applicable to that recognition, except that this section does not require an election to determine whether an organization should become, or continue to be recognized as, exclusive representative of the employees in any unit or subdivision thereof within 12 months after a prior valid election with respect to such unit.

(d) Recognition of a labor organization does not—

(1) preclude an employee, regardless of whether he is in a unit of exclusive recognition, from exercising grievance or appellate rights established by law or regulations; or from choosing his own representative in a grievance or appellate action, except when presenting a grievance under a negotiated procedure as provided in section 13;

(2) preclude or restrict consultations and dealings between an agency and a veterans organization with respect to matters of particular interest to employees with veterans preference; or

(3) preclude an agency from consulting or dealing with a religious, social, fraternal, professional or other lawful association, not qualified as a labor organization, with respect to matters or policies which involve individual members of the association or are of particular applicability to it or its members. Consultations and dealings under subparagraph (3) of this paragraph shall be so limited that they do not assume the character of formal consultation on matters of general employee-management policy, except, as provided in paragraph (e) of this section, or extend to areas where recognition of the interests

of one employee group may result in discrimination against or injury to the interests of other employees.

[(d) revised by E.O. 11616, 36 F.R. 17319, Aug. 28, 1971]

(c) An agency shall establish a system for intra-management communication and consultation with its supervisors or associations of supervisors. These communications and consultations shall have as their purpose the improvement of agency operations, the improvement of working conditions of supervisors, the exchange of information, the improvement of managerial effectiveness, and the establishment of policies that best serve the public interest in accomplishing the mission of the agency.

(f) Informal recognition or formal recognition shall not be accorded.

[(f) revised by E.O. 11616, 36 F.R. 17320, Aug. 28, 1971]

SECTION 8. [Revoked.]

[Sec. 8 revoked by E.O. 11616, 36 F.R. 17320, Aug. 28, 1971]

SECTION 9. *National consultation rights.* (a) An agency shall accord national consultation rights to a labor organization which qualifies under criteria established by the Federal Labor Relations Council as the representative of a substantial number of employees of the agency. National consultation rights shall not be accorded for any unit where a labor organization already holds exclusive recognition at the national level for that unit. The granting of natural consultation rights does not preclude an agency from appropriate dealings at the national level with other organizations on matters affecting their members. An agency shall terminate national consultation rights when the labor organization ceases to qualify under the established criteria.

(b) When a labor organization has been accorded national consultation rights, the agency, through appropriate officials, shall notify representatives of the organization of proposed substantive changes in personnel policies that affect employees it represents and provide an opportunity for the organization to comment on the proposed changes. The labor organization may suggest changes in the agency's personnel policies and have its views carefully considered. It may confer in person at reasonable times, on request, with appropriate officials on personnel policy matters, and at all times present its views thereon in writing. An agency is not required to consult with a labor organization on any matter on which it would not be required to meet and confer if the organization were entitled to exclusive recognition.

(c) Questions as to the eligibility of labor organizations for national consultation rights may be referred to the Assistant Secretary for decision.

SECTION 10. *Exclusive recognition.* (a) An agency shall accord exclusive recognition to a labor organization when the organization has been selected, in a secret ballot election, by a majority of the employees in an appropriate unit as their representative.

(b) A unit may be established on a plant or installation, craft, functional, or other basis which will ensure a clear and identifiable community of interest among the employees concerned and will promote effective dealings and efficiency of agency operations. A unit shall not be established solely on the basis of the extent to which employees in the proposed unit have organized, nor shall a unit be established if it includes—

(1) any management official or supervisor, except as provided in section 24;

(2) an employee engaged in Federal personnel work in other than a purely clerical capacity;

(3) any guard together with other employees; or

(4) both professional and nonprofessional employees, unless a majority of the professional employees vote for inclusion

in the unit. Questions as to the appropriate unit and related issues may be referred to the Assistant Secretary for decision.

(c) An agency shall not accord exclusive recognition to a labor organization as the representative of employees in a unit of guards if the organization admits to membership, or is affiliated directly or indirectly with an organization which admits to membership, employees other than guards.

(d) All elections shall be conducted under the supervision of the Assistant Secretary, or persons designated by him, and shall be by secret ballot. Each employee eligible to vote shall be provided the opportunity to choose the labor organization he wishes to represent him, from among those on the ballot, or "no union." Elections may be held to determine whether—

(1) a labor organization should be recognized as the exclusive representative of employees in a unit;

(2) a labor organization should replace another labor organization as the exclusive representative; or

(3) a labor organization should cease to be the exclusive representative.

(e) When a labor organization has been accorded exclusive recognition, it is the exclusive representative of employees in the unit and is entitled to act for and to negotiate agreements covering all employees in the unit. It is responsible for representing the interests of all employees in the unit without discrimination and without regard to labor organization membership. The labor organization shall be given the opportunity to be represented at formal discussions between management and employees or employee representatives concerning grievances, personnel policies and practices, or other matters affecting general working conditions of employees in the unit.

Agreements

SECTION 11. *Negotiation of agreements.* (a) An agency and a labor organization that has been accorded exclusive recognition, through appropriate representatives, shall meet at reasonable times and confer in good faith with respect to personnel policies and practices and matters affecting working conditions, so far as may be appropriate under applicable laws and regulations, including policies set forth in the Federal Personnel Manual, published agency policies and regulations, a national or other controlling agreement at a higher level in the agency, and this Order. They may negotiate an agreement, or any question arising thereunder; determine appropriate techniques, consistent with section 17 of this Order, to assist in such negotiation; and execute a written agreement or memorandum of understanding.

(b) In prescribing regulations relating to personnel policies and practices and working conditions, an agency shall have due regard for the obligation imposed by paragraph (a) of this section. However, the obligation to meet and confer does not include matters with respect to the mission of an agency; its budget; its organization; the number of employees; and the numbers, types, and grades of positions or employees assigned to an organizational unit, work project or tour of duty; the technology of performing its work; or its internal security practices. This does not preclude the parties from negotiating agreements providing appropriate arrangements for employees adversely affected by the impact of realignment of work forces or technological change.

(c) If, in connection with negotiations, an issue develops as to whether a proposal is contrary to law, regulation, controlling agreement, or this Order and therefore not negotiable, it shall be resolved as follows:

(1) An issue which involves interpretation of a controlling agreement at a higher agency level is resolved under the procedures of the controlling agreement, or, if none, under agency regulations;

(2) An issue other than as described in subparagraph (1)

of this paragraph which arises at a local level may be referred by either party to the head of the agency for determination;

(3) An agency head's determination as to the interpretation of the agency's regulations with respect to a proposal is final;

(4) A labor organization may appeal to the Council for a decision when—

(i) it disagrees with an agency head's determination that a proposal would violate applicable law, regulation of appropriate authority outside the agency, or this Order, or

(ii) it believes that an agency's regulations, as interpreted by the agency head, violate applicable law, regulation of appropriate authority outside the agency, or this Order.

SECTION 12. *Basic provisions of agreements.* Each agreement between an agency and a labor organization is subject to the following requirements—

(a) in the administration of all matters covered by the agreement, officials and employees are governed by existing or future laws and the regulations of appropriate authorities, including policies set forth in the Federal Personnel Manual; by published agency policies and regulations in existence at the time the agreement was approved; and by subsequently published agency policies and regulations required by law or by the regulations of appropriate authorities, or authorized by the terms of a controlling agreement at a higher agency level;

(b) management officials of the agency retain the right, in accordance with applicable laws and regulations—

(1) to direct employees of the agency;

(2) to hire, promote, transfer, assign, and retain employees in positions within the agency, and to suspend, demote, discharge, or take other disciplinary action against employees;

(3) to relieve employees from duties because of lack of work or for other legitimate reasons;

(4) to maintain the efficiency of the Government operation entrusted to them;

(5) to determine the methods, means, and personnel by which such operations are to be conducted; and

(6) to take whatever actions may be necessary to carry out the mission of the agency in situations of emergency; and

(c) nothing in the agreement shall require an employee to become or to remain a member of a labor organization, or to pay money to the organization except pursuant to a voluntary, written authorization by a member for the payment of dues through payroll deductions.

The requirements of this section shall be expressly stated in the initial or basic agreement and apply to all supplemental, implementing, subsidiary, or informal agreements between the agency and the organization.

SECTION 13. *Grievance and arbitration procedures.*

(a) An agreement between an agency and a labor organization shall provide a procedure, applicable only to the unit, for the consideration of grievances over the interpretation or application of the agreement. A negotiated grievance procedure may not cover any other matters, including matters for which statutory appeals procedures exist, and shall be the exclusive procedure available to the parties and the employees in the unit for resolving such grievances. However, any employee or group of employees in the unit may present such grievances to the agency and have them adjusted, without the intervention of the exclusive representative, as long as the adjustment is not inconsistent with the terms of the agreement and the exclusive representative has been given opportunity to be present at the adjustment.

(b) A negotiated procedure may provide for the arbitration of grievances over the interpretation or application of the agreement, but not over any other matters. Arbitration may be invoked only by the agency or the exclusive representative. Either party may file exception to an arbitrator's award with the Council, under regulations prescribed by the Council.

(c) Grievances initiated by an employee or group of employees in the unit on matters other than the interpretation or application of an existing agreement may be presented under any procedure available for the purpose.

(d) Questions that cannot be resolved by the parties as to whether or not a grievance is on a matter subject to the grievance procedure in an existing agreement, or is subject to arbitration under that agreement, may be referred to the Assistant Secretary for decision.

(e) No agreement may be established, extended or renewed after the effective date of this Order which does not conform to this section. However, this section is not applicable to agreements entered into before the effective date of this Order.

[SECTION 13 revised by E.O. 11616, 36 F.R. 17320, Aug. 28, 1971]

SECTION 14. *Arbitration of grievances.*

[SECTION 14 revoked by E.O. 11616, 36 F.R. 17321, Aug. 28, 1971]

SECTION 15. *Approval of agreements.* An agreement with a labor organization as the exclusive representative of employees in a unit is subject to the approval of the head of the agency or an official designated by him. An agreement shall be approved if it conforms to applicable laws, existing published agency policies and regulations (unless the agency has granted an exception to a policy or regulation) and regulations of other appropriate authorities. A local agreement subject to a national or other controlling agreement at a higher level shall be approved under the procedures of the controlling agreement, or, if none, under agency regulations.

Negotiation Disputes and Impasses

SECTION 16. *Negotiation disputes.* The Federal Mediation and Conciliation Service shall provide services and assistance to Federal agencies and labor organizations in the resolution of negotiation disputes. The Service shall determine under what circumstances and in what manner it shall proffer its services.

SECTION 17. *Negotiation impasses.* When voluntary arrangements, including the services of the Federal Mediation and Conciliation Service or other third-party mediation, fail to resolve a negotiation impasse, either party may request the Federal Service Impasses Panel to consider the matter. The Panel, in its discretion and under the regulations it prescribes, may consider the matter and may recommend procedures to the parties for the resolution of the impasse or may settle the impasse by appropriate action. Arbitration or third-party fact finding with recommendations to assist in the resolution of an impasse may be used by the parties only when authorized or directed by the Panel.

Conduct of Labor Organizations and Management

SECTION 18. *Standards of conduct for labor organizations.*

(a) An agency shall accord recognition only to a labor organization that is free from corrupt influences and influences opposed to basic democratic principles. Except as provided in paragraph (b) of this section, an organization is not required to prove that it has the required freedom when it is subject to governing requirements adopted by the organization or by a national or international labor organization or federation of labor organizations with which it is affiliated or in which it

participates, containing explicit and detailed provisions to which it subscribes calling for—

(1) the maintenance of democratic procedures and practices, including provisions for periodic elections to be conducted subject to recognized safeguards and provisions defining and securing the right of individual members to participation in the affairs of the organization, to fair and equal treatment under the governing rules of the organization, and to fair process in disciplinary proceedings;

(2) the exclusion from office in the organization of persons affiliated with Communist or other totalitarian movements and persons identified with corrupt influences;

(3) the prohibition of business or financial interests on the part of organization officers and agents which conflict with their duty to the organization and its members; and

(4) the maintenance of fiscal integrity in the conduct of the affairs of the organization, including provision for accounting and financial controls and regular financial reports or summaries to be made available to members.

(b) Notwithstanding the fact that a labor organization has adopted or subscribed to standards of conduct as provided in paragraph (a) of this section, the organization is required to furnish evidence of its freedom from corrupt influences or influences opposed to basic democratic principles when there is reasonable cause to believe that—

(1) the organization has been suspended or expelled from or is subject to other sanction by a parent labor organization or federation of organizations with which it had been affiliated because it has demonstrated an unwillingness or inability to comply with governing requirements comparable in purpose to those required by paragraph (a) of this section; or

(2) the organization is in fact subject to influences that would preclude recognition under this Order.

(c) A labor organization which has or seeks recognition as a representative of employees under this Order shall file financial and other reports, provide for bonding of officials and employees of the organization, and comply with trusteeship and election standards.

(d) The Assistant Secretary shall prescribe the regulations needed to effectuate this section. These regulations shall conform generally to the principles applied to unions in the private sector. Complaints of violations of this section shall be filed with the Assistant Secretary.

SECTION 19. *Unfair labor practices.* (a) Agency management shall not—

(1) interfere with, restrain, or coerce an employee in the exercise of the rights assured by this Order;

(2) encourage or discourage membership in a labor organization by discrimination in regard to hiring, tenure, promotion, or other conditions of employment;

(3) sponsor, control, or otherwise assist a labor organization, except that an agency may furnish customary and routine services and facilities under section 23 of this Order when consistent with the best interests of the agency, its employees, and the organization, and when the services and facilities are furnished, if requested, on an impartial basis to organizations having equivalent status;

(4) discipline or otherwise discriminate against an employee because he has filed a complaint or given testimony under this Order;

(5) refuse to accord appropriate recognition to a labor organization qualifed for such recognition; or

(6) refuse to consult, confer, or negotiate with a labor organization as required by this Order.

(b) A labor organization shall not—

(1) interfere with, restrain, or coerce an employee in the exercise of his rights assured by this Order;

(2) attempt to induce agency management to coerce an employee in the exercise of his rights under this Order;

(3) coerce, attempt to coerce, or discipline, fine, or take other economic sanction against a member of the organization as punishment or reprisal for, or for the purpose of hindering or impending his work performance, his productivity, or the discharge of his duties owed as an officer or employee of the United States;

(4) call or engage in a strike, work stoppage, or slowdown; picket an agency in a labor-management dispute; or condone any such activity by failing to take affirmative action to prevent or stop it;

(5) discriminate against an employee with regard to the terms or conditions of membership because of race, color, creed, sex, age, or national origin; or

(6) refuse to consult, confer, or negotiate with an agency as required by this Order.

(c) A labor organization which is accorded exclusive recognition shall not deny membership to any employee in the appropriate unit except for failure to meet reasonable occupational standards uniformly required for admission, or for failure to tender initiation fees and dues uniformly required as a condition of acquiring and retaining membership. This paragraph does not preclude a labor organization from enforcing discipline in accordance with procedures under its constitution or by-laws which conform to the requirements of this Order.

(d) Issues which can properly be raised under an appeals procedure may not be raised under this section. Issues which can be raised under a grievance procedure may, in the discretion of the aggrieved party, be raised under that procedure or the complaint procedure under this section, but not under both procedures. Appeals or grievance decisions shall not be construed as unfair labor practice decisions under this Order nor as precedent for such decisions. All complaints under this section that cannot be resolved by the parties shall be filed with the Assistant Secretary.

[(d) revised by E.O. 11616, 36 F.R. 17321, Aug. 28, 1971]

Miscellaneous Provisions

SECTION 20. *Use of official time.* Solicitation of membership or dues, and other internal business of a labor organization, shall be conducted during the non-duty hours of the employees concerned. Employees who represent a recognized labor organization shall not be on official time when negotiating an agreement with agency management, except to the extent that the negotiating parties agree to other arrangements which may provide that the agency will either authorize official time for up to 40 hours or authorize up to one-half the time spent in negotiations during regular working hours, for a reasonable number of employees, which number normally shall not exceed the number of management representatives.

[Sec. 20 revised by E.O. 11616, 36 F.R. 11321, Aug. 28, 1971]

SECTION 21. *Allotment of dues.* (a) When a labor organization holds exclusive recognition, and the agency and the organization agree in writing to this course of action, an agency may deduct the regular and periodic dues of the organization from the pay of members of the organization in the unit of recognition who make a voluntary allotment for that purpose. Such an allotment is subject to the regulations of the Civil Service Commission, which shall include provision for the employee to revoke his authorization at stated six-month intervals. Such an allotment terminates when—

(1) the dues withholding agreement between the agency and the labor organization is terminated or ceases to be applicable to the employee; or

(2) the employee has been suspended or expelled from the labor organization.

(b) An agency may deduct the regular and periodic dues of an association of management officials or supervisors from

FEDERAL LEGISLATION
RELATED TO LABOR

the pay of members of the association who make a voluntary allotment for that purpose, when the agency and the association agree in writing to this course of action. Such an allotment is subject to the regulations of the Civil Service Commission.

[Sec. 21 revised by E.O. 11616, 36 F.R. 17321, Aug. 28, 1971]

SECTION 22. *Adverse action appeals.* The head of each agency, in accordance with the provisions of this Order and regulations prescribed by the Civil Service Commission, shall extend to all employees in the competitive civil service rights identical in adverse action cases to those provided preference eligibles under sections 7511–7512 of title 5 of the United States Code. Each employee in the competitive service shall have the right to appeal to the Civil Service Commission from an adverse decision of the administrative officer so acting, such appeal to be processed in an identical manner to that provided for appeals under section 7701 of title 5 of the United States Code. Any recommendation by the Civil Service Commission submitted to the head of an agency on the basis of an appeal by an employee in the competitive service shall be complied with by the head of the agency.

SECTION 23. *Agency implementation.* No later than April 1, 1970, each agency shall issue appropriate policies and regulations consistent with this Order for its implementation. This includes but is not limited to a clear statement of the rights of its employees under this Order; procedures with respect to recognition of labor organizations, determination of appropriate units, consultation and negotiation with labor organizations, approval of agreements, mediation, and impasse resolution; policies with respect to the use of agency facilities by labor organizations; and policies and practices regarding consultation with other organizations and associations and individual employees. Insofar as practicable, agencies shall consult with representatives of labor organizations in the formulation of these policies and regulations, other than those for the implementation of section 7(e) of this Order.

SECTION 24. *Savings clauses.* This order does not preclude—

(1) the renewal or continuation of a lawful agreement between an agency and a representative of its employees entered into before the effective date of Executive Order No. 10988 (January 17, 1962); or

(2) the renewal, continuation, or initial according of recognition for units of management officials or supervisors represented by labor organizations which historically or traditionally represent the management officials or supervisors in private industry and which hold exclusive recognition for units of such officials or supervisors in any agency on the date of this Order.

[Sec. 24 as amended by E.O. 11616, F.R. 17322, Aug. 28, 1971]

Editorial Note: In the amendment of Sec. 24, E.O. 11616, 36 F.R. 17322, Aug. 28, 1971, the designation "(a)" following the heading and subsections (b), (c), and (d) were deleted.

SECTION 25. *Guidance, training, review and information.*
(a) The Civil Service Commission, in conjunction with the Office of Management and Budget, shall establish and maintain a program for the policy guidance of agencies on labor-management relations in the Federal service and periodically review the implementation of these policies. The Civil Service Commission shall continuously review the operation of the Federal labor-management relations program to assist in assuring adherence to its provisions and merit system requirements; implement technical advice and information programs for the

agencies; assist in the development of programs for training agency personnel and management officials in labor-management relations; and, from time to time, report to the Council on the state of the program with any recommendations for its improvement.

[(a) revised by E.O. 11616, 36 F.R. 17322, Aug. 28, 1971]

(b) The Department of Labor and the Civil Service Commission shall develop programs for the collection and dissemination of information appropriate to the needs of agencies, organizations and the public.

SECTION 26. *Effective date*. This Order is effective on January 1, 1970 except sections 7(f) and 8 which are effective immediately. Effective January 1, 1970, Executive Order No. 10988 and the President's Memorandum of May 21, 1963, entitled Standards of Conduct for Employee Organizations and Code of Fair Labor Practices are revoked.

For further information write to: Assistant Secretary of Labor for Labor Management Relations, U.S. Department of Labor, Washington, D.C. 20210.

IMPLEMENTATION OF EXECUTIVE ORDER 11491

AUTHORITY: E.O. 11491 (1969) as last amended by E.O. 11838 (1975)

EXCLUSIONS: Employees whose participation would create a conflict of interest or be incompatible with duties. Also the F.B.I., C.I.A., other intelligence agencies, audit agencies, the foreign service, the State Department, U.S.I.A., A.I.D. and the T.V.A.

ADMINISTRATIVE AGENCY:
   Federal Labor Relations Council (202) 632-6878
   Room 7R48
   U.S. Civil Service Commission
   1900 E Street, N.W.
   Washington 20415

UNIT DETERMINATION: Asst. Sec. for Labor-Management Relations, U.S. Department of Labor

CRITERIA FOR UNIT DETERMINATION:
   plant, installation, craft, functional or other basis which insures a clear and identifiable community of interest and promotes effective dealings and efficient operations
   unit may not be based on extent of organization
   unit may not include supervisors, personnel employees (except clerical)
   professionals must vote for inclusion in nonprofessional units

RECOGNITION: Exclusive or National Consultation Rights. NCR is available where there is no exclusive representative and a union represents a significant number of employees. An election is required for exclusive recognition except where two or more units represented by a single union are consolidated

SCOPE OF BARGAINING: personnel practices, policies and matters affecting working conditions. Excludes agency mission, budget, organization, numbers and types of employees, technology and internal security practices

EMPLOYEE RIGHTS: to form, join and assist unions or to refrain from so doing

MANAGEMENT RIGHTS: to direct employees; to hire, promote, assign, discipline and discharge employees; to relieve employees for lack of work, to maintain efficiency, to determine methods, means and personnel; and to act in emergencies

TREATMENT OF SUPERVISORS: may not act as representatives of unions or participate in union management. Supervisors are excluded from the order unless they are members of units represented by unions of supervisors as of October 3, 1969

UNION SECURITY: dues deduction

EMPLOYER ULP's:
   Interfere, restrain or coerce employees
   Discriminate on account of union membership or testimony
   Dominate unions
   Refuse to recognize a qualified union
   Refuse to confer, consult or negotiate

UNION ULP's:
   Interfere, restrain or coerce employees
   Attempt to induce management to coerce an employee
   Coerce employee in order to hinder performance
   Strike or picket
   Discriminate on account of race, color, creed, sex, age or national origin
   Refuse to confer, consult or negotiate

MEDIATION: provided by the Federal Mediation and Conciliation Service. Federal Services Impasses Panel may recommend fact finding or arbitration if the mediator is unable to get a settlement

FACT FINDING: available only upon the recommendation of Federal Services Impasses Panel

ARBITRATION: available only upon the recommendation of Federal Services Impasses Panel

STRIKE POLICY: prohibited (5 U.S.C.A., Sec. 7311). Penalty is a fine of $1000 and/or imprisonment for up to one year and a day. (19 U.S.C.A., Sec. 1918)

GRIEVANCE PROCEDURE: a grievance procedure must be included in every agreement. Arbitration is permitted. Either party may file exceptions with the Council. The grievance procedure may not cover matters for which a statutory appeal procedure exists or which conflict with statue or the Order. The Assistant Secretary determines whether matters are subject to the grievance procedure

COVERAGE: U.S. Department of State, U.S. Information Agency, Agency for International Development

AUTHORITY: E.O. 11636 (36 F.R. 24901) (1971)

EXCLUSIONS: Management or confidential employees or those for whom coverage would create a conflict of interest. Also, alien clerks or employees

ADMINISTRATIVE AGENCY: Employee Management Relations Commission

RECOGNITION: exclusive. Election

BARGAINING RIGHTS: consultation

SCOPE OF BARGAINING: personnel policies and procedures. Excludes agency mission, budget or organization; number and grades of employees, technology, security

EMPLOYEE RIGHTS: to form, join or assist unions or to refrain from so doing

MANAGEMENT RIGHTS: to direct employees; to hire, promote, transfer, assign, retain, discharge or discipline employees; to relieve employees from duty; to maintain efficiency, to determine methods, means and personnel; to act in emergencies

UNION SECURITY: dues deduction

EMPLOYER ULP's:
   Interfere, restrain or coerce employees
   Discriminate on account of union membership or testimony
   Dominate unions
   Refuse to recognize a qualified union
   Refuse to consult

UNION ULP's:
   Interfere, restrain or coerce employees
   Cause employer to commit a ULP
   Coerce employee in order to hinder his performance
   Strike
   Discriminate on account of race, color, creed, sex, age or national origin
   Refuse to consult

ARBITRATION: Board of Foreign Service hears appeals from consultations which do not result in agreements. Agency head may overrule the Board

STRIKE POLICY: prohibited. (5 U.S.C.A. Sec. 7311). Penalty is a fine of $1000 and/or imprisonment for up to one year and a day. (19 U.S.C.A. Sec. 1918)

GRIEVANCE PROCEDURE: required

Postal Reorganization Act of 1970

SUMMARY AND DESCRIPTION

The Postal Reorganization Act established the United States Postal Service as an independent establishment in the Executive Branch of the United States Government, Title 39 of the United States Code was revised and reenacted by the Act, with Chapter 12 of the new Title 39 governing the employee-management relations of the Postal Service. The Act subjects the employee-management relations of the Postal Service to those provisions of the National Labor Relations Act, as amended, which are not inconsistent with the Postal Reorganization Act.

The Act provides that the National Labor Relations Board will determine the appropriate units for collective bargaining, and sets forth certain exclusions from the bargaining units. It establishes a petition and election process by which labor organizations may be accorded exclusive recognition by the Postal Service.

The Act further provides that any collective bargaining agreements between the Postal Service and any recognized bargaining representative shall be effective for not less than two years. Collective bargaining agreements may provide for procedures for the resolution of grievances and adverse actions including procedures culminating in binding third party arbitration. The Act does not remove the ban against strikes which applies to all Federal employees, including postal employees. Additionally, the inclusion of union security provisions other than dues check in any collective bargaining agreement is prohibited.

If the Postal Service and a labor organization with which it has a contract are unable to reach a new agreement at the appropriate time for contract modification or renegotiation, the Act provides a method for resolving such a dispute. The statutory processes for resolving contract negotiation impasse disputes provides for an investigation by a fact finding panel and a report issued no later than 45 days after the list of proposed panel members is submitted to the parties by the Federal Mediation and Conciliation Service. If no agreement is subsequently reached, the Act provides that an arbitration board be established, which, after affording the parties a hearing, shall issue a decision which will be conclusive and binding on the parties.

Similar procedures exist for the resolution of a collective bargaining dispute between the Postal Service and a recognized collective bargaining representative in the situation where no collective bargaining agreement exists.

The Postal Reorganization Act also provides that suits for violation of contract between the Postal Service and any labor organization, or between any labor organizations, may be brought in any United States district court having jurisdiction over the parties.

For further information write to: U.S. Postal Service, 12th and Pennsylvania Avenue, N.W., Washington D.C. 20260.

IMPLEMENTATION OF THE POSTAL REORGANIZATION ACT OF 1970

COVERAGE: U.S. Postal Service

AUTHORITY: 39 U.S.C.A. Ch. 12 (1970)

EXCLUSIONS: Supervisors, managerial personnel

ADMINISTRATIVE AGENCY:
National Labor Relations Board (202) 254-9102
1717 Pennsylvania Avenue, N.W.
Washington, D.C. 20570

UNIT DETERMINATION: board

CRITERIA FOR UNIT DETERMINATION:
No unit may contain management officials, supervisors, personnel employees other than non-confidential clerical employees
Professionals must vote for inclusion in nonprofessional unit
Guards must be in separate units represented by unions not admitting non-guards to membership

RECOGNITION: exclusive. Election

BARGAINING RIGHTS: duty to bargain. Consultation rights for supervisors

EMPLOYEE RIGHTS: to form, join or assist unions or to refrain from so doing

MANAGEMENT RIGHTS: to direct employees; to hire, promote, transfer, assign, retain, discharge or discipline employees; to relieve employees for lack of work; to maintain efficient operations; to determine methods, means and personnel; to prescribe uniforms; to act in emergencies; (39 U.S.C.A. Sec. 1001)

TREATMENT OF SUPERVISORS: consultation rights only

UNION SECURITY: dues deduction

EMPLOYER ULP's:
Interfere, restrain or coerce employees
Dominate unions
Discriminate on account of union membership or testimony
Refuse to bargain

UNION ULP's:
Restrain or coerce employees
Restrain or coerce employer choice of representative
Attempt to cause employer to discriminate
Refuse to bargain
Require excessive or discriminatory membership fees
Cause employer to pay for services not performed
Hot-cargo agreements
Secondary boycotts
Jurisdictional strikes

MEDIATION: by FMCS

FACT FINDING: if the parties have not agreed upon an impasse procedure, the Director of FMCS supplies each party with a list of names. Each party selects one panel member, those two select a chairman. Panel must issue its report within 45 days. Costs shared equally by the parties

ARBITRATION: If there is no agreement within 90 days of the expiration of the contract, each party selects one panel member. Those two select a chairman. Award due within 45 days of panel's appointment. Costs shared equally by the parties

STRIKE POLICY: prohibited (5 U.S.C.A. Sec. 7311 as applied by 39 U.S.C.A. Sec. 410) Penalty is a fine of $1000 and/or imprisonment for up to one year and a day. (19 U.S.C.A. Sec. 1918)

GRIEVANCE PROCEDURE: arbitration permitted

The Employee Retirement Income Security Act of 1974

The purpose of the Employee Retirement Income Security Act of 1974 (ERISA) is to protect the interests of workers and their beneficiaries who depend on benefits from employee pension and welfare plans. The law requires disclosure of plan provisions and financial information and establishes standards of conduct for trustees and administrators of welfare and pension plans. It sets up funding, participation, and vesting requirements for pension plans and makes termination insurance available for most pension plans.

The Department of Labor and the Internal Revenue Service share in the administration of the law. The pension plan termination insurance program is administered by the Pension Benefit Guaranty Corporation.

The law does not require a company to establish a welfare or pension plan. However, existing or new plans must meet certain minimum standards.

The law provides that any employee not covered by a pension plan, other than Social Security, may put aside a certain amount of his income tax-free to take care of retirement needs.

PLANS COVERED

The Act covers employee pension and welfare plans which are established or maintained (1) by any employer engaged in commerce or in any industry or activity affecting commerce or (2) by an employee organization or organizations representing employees engaged in commerce or in any industry or activity affecting commerce, or (3) by both, except those plans specifically exempted.

A pension plan is defined as any plan, fund, or program which provides retirement income to employees or results in a deferral of income by employees until the termination of employment or beyond.

A welfare plan is defined as any plan, fund, or program which provides medical, surgical, or hospital care or benefits, or benefits in the event of sickness, accident, disability, death or unemployment; or vacation benefits, apprenticeship or other training programs; or day care centers, scholarship funds, or prepaid legal services; or benefits under plans subject to Section 302(c) of the Labor Management Relations Act of 1947, other than pension benefits.

Plans not covered by the Act include:

■ Governmental plans

■ Certain church plans

■ Plans maintained solely to comply with workers' compensation, unemployment compensation, or disability insurance laws

■ Plans maintained outside the U.S. for the benefit of persons substantially all of whom are non-resident aliens

■ So-called "excess benefit" plans (plans which provide benefits or contributions in excess of those allowable for tax-qualified plans) which are unfunded

■ Certain other types of plans are expressly exempted from particular provisions of the Act

■ Certain covered plans have been exempted from specific requirements by the Secretary of Labor through regulation

The number of participants is not a factor in determining coverage, unlike the Welfare and Pension Plans Disclosure Act, which exempted plans covering fewer than 26 participants. The WPPDA was repealed by the new law. However, certain welfare plans covering fewer than 100 participants have been exempted by regulation from certain reporting and disclosure requirements.

Provisions for fiduciary standards and reporting and disclosure requirements apply to both pension and welfare benefit plans.

FIDUCIARY STANDARDS

A fiduciary is anyone who exercises discretionary control or authority over plan management or who controls assets. A fiduciary may include the plan administrator; or anyone who provides investment advice to a plan for a fee or other compensation, direct or indirect; or anyone with discretionary authority or responsibility in the administration of a plan.

The "administrator" of a plan is the person specifically designated by the plan instrument; or the plan sponsor. In case there is no designated administrator or identified sponsor, the administrator is such person as the Secretary of Labor may prescribe.

Under some circumstances, named fiduciaries may allocate some fiduciary responsibilities among themselves or delegate responsibilities to other persons, and thereby divest themselves, in part, of those responsibilities.

The Act imposes a federal "prudent man rule" on fiduciaries previously subject only to state fiduciary laws. The Act requires a fiduciary to discharge his duties solely in the interests of the participants and beneficiaries for

the exclusive purpose of providing them with the benefits and defraying the reasonable expenses of administering the plan. Fiduciaries are required to act with the care, skill, prudence, and diligence under the circumstances then prevailing that a prudent man acting in like capacity and familiar with such matters would use in conducting an enterprise of like character and aims. Fiduciaries must diversify plan investments in order to minimize the risk of large losses unless it is clearly prudent not to do so and must operate in accordance with the plan documents and instruments. Fiduciaries must take particular care NOT to engage in any transactions which are specifically prohibited.

A fiduciary may be paid for his services except that no person serving as fiduciary who ALREADY receives full-time pay from an employer or union whose employees or members are plan participants may receive more than reimbursement of properly incurred expenses.

Any plan fiduciary who breaches any of the responsibilities imposed by the Act is personally liable to make good to the plan any losses to the plan resulting from such breach and to restore to the plan any profits which may have been made by such a fiduciary through his improper use of the plan's assets. Fiduciaries are also subject to other equitable or remedial relief as a court may deem appropriate, including removal from the position of fiduciary.

A fiduciary may not:

■ Deal with plan assets for his own account or in his own interest.

■ Act in any capacity involving a plan on behalf of a party whose interests are adverse to the interests of the plan, its participants, or beneficiaries.

■ Receive any consideration for his personal account from any party dealing with the plan in connection with a transaction involving plan assets.

■ Cause a plan to engage in a transaction involving a party in interest if the transaction is a direct or indirect:

Sale, exchange or lease of property.
Lending of money or extending of credit.
Furnishing of goods, services or facilities.
Transfer of assets to or use of assets by a party in interest.
Cause a plan to acquire any employer security or real property in violation of special rules applicable to such security or property.

A party in interest is any administrator, officer, trustee, custodian, counsel, or employee of a plan or a fiduciary to the plan itself. Any person providing services to such a plan; the employer of covered employees; an employee organization whose members are covered; an owner, direct or indirect, of 50 percent or more of the company, or persons with a specified relationship to the plan which gives them an opportunity to influence its management. Certain relatives of specified parties in interest are also considered to be parties in interest. Exemptions to prohibited transactions may be made upon application.

The Secretary of Labor has established a joint procedure with the Commissioner of the Internal Revenue Service for granting such exemptions, upon application. In addition, the Act specifies certain exemptions, e.g., loans by the plan to parties in interest who are participants or beneficiaries if they are available on a non discriminatory basis, bear a reasonable rate of interest, are adequately secured, and are made in accordance with plan rules; arrangements with a party in interest for office space, or legal, accounting, or other services for the plan if no more than reasonable compensation is paid; loans to an employee stock ownership plan if the interest rate is reasonable and if it is primarily for the benefit of plan participants and beneficiaries; etc.

In general, the Act requires investment according to the "prudent man rule" and limits investment in the employer's securities or real property. As a rule, 10 percent of the assets of a plan may be invested in employer securities. Profit sharing, stock bonus, thrift or savings, employee stock ownership plans, and certain money purchase plans may be excepted from the 10 percent rule.

REPORTING AND DISCLOSURE

The following reports must be filed with the U.S. Department of Labor by the administrators of employee pension and welfare plans:

■ Plan description, 120 days after the plan is subject to the reporting and disclosure provisions.

■ Summary plan description, 120 days after the plan is subject to the reporting and disclosure provisions.

■ Any change in plan description or material modification to plan, 60 days after its adoption.

■ Updated plan description at such times as the Secretary of Labor may require but no more frequently than once every 5 years.

■ Annual report (joint form with IRS), by date prescribed by regulation.

■ Terminal reports for plans winding up their affairs, if prescribed by regulation.

■ Plan documents and other information, if requested by the Secretary of Labor.

The following reports for defined benefit pension plans covered by the termination insurance provisions must be filed with the Pension Benefit Guaranty Corporation:

■ Annual report, within 6 months after the end of plan year.

■ Intent to terminate plan, no later than 10 days before termination date.

■ Certain events which raise questions of the continued viability of a plan, within 30 days after plan administrator knows or had reason to know of their occurrence.

■ Such other reports as the Corporation may require from a plan administrator who has initiated termination proceedings.

■ Notice of withdrawal of a substantial employer from a plan to which more than one employer contributes or the closing of a facility which results in a decrease of 20 percent or more of the number of plan participants, within 60 days.

Pursuant to the Act's amendments to the Internal Revenue Code of 1954, reports which must be filed with the Internal Revenue Service include:

■ Annual Registration Statement, listing employees separated from service of plan, for plans subject to vesting standards, due as prescribed by regulation.

■ Notification of Change in Status, for plans subject to vesting standards, due as prescribed by regulations.

■ Annual Return for certain pension and deferred compensation plans (joint form with Department of Labor), by date prescribed by regulation.

■ Actuarial statement of valuation for certain pension and deferred compensation plans, not less than 30 days before merger, consolidation, or transfer of assets or liabilities.

■ Actuarial report for defined benefit plans for the first year that new funding requirements apply and every third year thereafter, or within time prescribed by regulation.

Unless exempted, administrators must disclose the following information to participants and beneficiaries:

■ Summary plan description, in easily understandable language, 90 days after a person becomes a participant or beneficiary or, if later, 120 days after plan is subject to reporting and disclosure provisions.

■ Summary of any change in the plan description or material modification in terms of the plan, 210 days after end of plan year in which change is adopted.

■ Updated summary plan description every 5 years integrating all amendments if there have been any; if not, every 10 years.

■ Summary of annual report, as prescribed by regulation.

■ Statement of nature, form, and amount of deferred vested benefits upon termination of employment, by date prescribed by regulation.*

■ Statement of total accrued benefits and the percentage vested upon termination of employment or one-year break in service, in accordance with the Secretary's regulations.*

■ If claim denied, explanation in writing.

■ A written explanation, before the annuity starting date, of the terms and conditions of any joint and survivor annuity and the effect of electing against such an option (applies only to plans subject to vesting provisions).

The following must be available at the principal office of the administrator and other places:

■ Plan description

■ Latest annual report

■ Documents under which the Plan was established or is operated

The following must be furnished upon written request by multiemployer plans:

■ Statements, not more than once in a 12-month period, of total benefits accrued, accrued benefits which are vested, if any, or earliest date on which accrued benefits will become vested.

Multiemployer plans must furnish upon written request at reasonable charge a copy of:

■ Latest updated summary plan description

■ Plan description

■ Latest annual report

■ Documents under which the plan was established or is operated

■ Terminal reports, if any

The plan description and the summary plan description both must include, among other things, the eligibility requirements for participation and for benefits; circumstances which may result in disqualification, ineligibility, loss, or denial of benefits; procedures for presenting claims for benefits; and remedies for redress of claims denied.

The annual report includes financial statements and schedules, showing the current value of plan assets and liabilities, receipts and disbursements, and employer contributions, schedules of assets held for investment purposes; uncollectable or defaulted loans and leases; detailed information on transactions with parties in interest and on those that exceed 3 percent of the value

* Applies to multiemployer plans only as prescribed in regulations, which may modify requirements.

of the plan assets; insurance data; an opinion of an independent qualified public accountant; actuarial information for certain plans and in such cases the opinion of an enrolled actuary.

To the extent needed for the annual report, insurance carriers which provide benefits or hold plan assets, banks which hold assets in trust or in a custodial account, and plan sponsors must furnish certified information to the plan administrator for inclusion in the annual report.

Records on matters for which disclosure or certification is required must be kept at least SIX years after the date the documents are due for filing (or would be due except for an exemption).

■ The Secretary may, by regulation, exempt any welfare plan from all or part of the reporting and disclosure requirements.

■ The Secretary may prescribe, by regulation, simplified annual reports for any pension plan which covers fewer than 100 participants, and simplified reports for welfare plans if the Secretary finds the reporting requirements are inappropriate as applied to welfare plans.

■ Under certain circumstances the Secretary may prescribe an alternate method of satisfying the reporting and disclosure requirements for pension plans.

PARTICIPATION, VESTING, AND FUNDING

The participation, vesting, funding and termination insurance requirements are applicable only to pension plans.

Generally, a pension plan must allow an employee to participate at age 25 and has completed one year of service. There are exceptions, e.g., any plan providing full and immediate vesting may require an employee to put in 3 years of service.

Once minimum age and service requirements are met, participation must begin at the start of the next plan year or 6 months after meeting the requirements, whichever is earlier.

A plan may not exclude an employee because of age. However, defined benefit and target benefit pension plans are permitted to exclude an employee who is within 5 years of the normal retirement age under the plan at the beginning of employment.

An employee can be required to put in a "year of service" defined as a 12-month period during which the employee has at least 1,000 hours of service. In the case of a seasonal industry, where the customary period of employment is less than 1,000 hours in a calendar year, the Secretary of Labor, by regulation, will determine the period necessary to qualify as a year of service. In the maritime industry, 125 days will be treated as a year of service.

Service with a predecessor employer will be counted if the successor employer continues to maintain the plan of the predecessor employer—and the successor employer cannot evade this requirement by nominally discontinuing the plan.

A break in service occurs in any year in which an employee has no more than 500 hours of service.

If an employee returns to his job after a break in service, certain rules apply. Generally, all service with the employer is to be taken into account for participation and vesting purposes. However, the plan may require a one-year waiting period before aggregating pre-break and post-break service. The only way a worker could lose previous pension credits is if he were not vested when he had a break in service AND his period of absence equalled or exceeded his years of service before the break. For example, if an employee works for 2 years, quits without being vested, and then returns to employment after a break of 2 years or more, the company need not give him credit for the initial two-year period.

Employees become eligible for participation in a pension plan when they start to earn credits towards a pension. After having worked a specified period of time with an employer under a pension plan, the Act requires that employees be given the right to certain pension benefits earned—even though the employee leaves that job before retirement. This right is called "vesting".
A pension plan covered by vesting provisions must provide full and immediate vesting of benefits derived from employee contributions. Employer contributions (except "class-year" plans) must vest at least as fast as provided under one of the following three schedules:

■ Full (100 percent) vesting after 10 years of service (with no vesting prior to completion of 10 years of service).

■ Graded vesting (5 to 15 years): 25 percent vesting after 5 years of service, plus 5 percent for each additional year of service up to 10 years (50 percent vesting after 10 years), plus an additional 10 percent for each year thereafter (100 percent vesting after 15 years of service).

■ Rule of 45 (based on age and service): 50 percent vesting for an employee with at least 5 years of service when his age and years of service add up to 45, plus 10 percent for each year thereafter.

Under any of the options an employee must be at least 50 percent vested after 10 years of service and 100 percent vested after 15 years of service, regardless of age. "Class-year" plans (profit sharing, stock bonus, and money purchase plans in which each year's contributions vest separately) must provide for 100 percent vesting not later than the end of the fifth year following the plan year for which contributions are made.

The vesting requirements will not take effect, in most cases, until plan years beginning after December 31, 1975. When they do go into effect, however, the requirements will take into account all of a worker's years of service with the employer. There are exceptions. Years of service before the plan is subject to the vesting provisions need not be counted if such service would have been disregarded under the plan's rules on break in service in effect on the applicable date. Service before 1971 must be recognized only if the employee earned credits for work in at least 3 years after 1970. Thus, some people who quit jobs in recent years could pick up permanent rights to pension credits earned in the past by returning to their former employer.

There are some pension plans covered by some parts of the Act but not by the vesting rules; for example, labor union plans which do not provide for employer contributions; certain trusts described in section 501(c)(18) of the Internal Revenue Code which were created before June 25, 1959 and are funded only by employee contributions; certain plans of fraternal benefit societies, orders, or associations which do not provide for employer contributions; plans which are unfunded and are maintained by an employer primarily for the purpose of providing deferred compensation for a select group of management or highly compensated employees, excess benefit plans, etc.

A plan may provide for suspension of a retiree's benefit payments for the period of reemployment if a retiree returns to work or, in the case of a multi-employer plan, during the period a retiree is employed in the same industry and trade or craft and in the same geographical area covered by the plan.

In the past many pension plans did not have a formal system under which employees built specific pension credits each year. The Act requires that plans permit employees to accumulate pension credits in a fair and orderly way and limits "backloading" (giving too little credit for early years of service).

The Act requires in general that funds be set aside in an orderly way so that sufficient money will be available to pay plan benefits.

Plans covered by these funding rules are generally, defined benefit and money purchase plans, with exceptions, such as most insurance contract plans and plans not providing for employer contributions after the law's enactment.

The Act requires employers to fund pension credits for current service as employees earn them. Formulas are established for funding over a specific period of time the costs of pension benefits earned in the past for which monies have not yet been set aside (past service liabilities) and for making up experience losses and changes in actuarial assumptions.

PENSION PLAN TERMINATION INSURANCE

The Act insures up to a maximum amount benefits of participants in covered defined benefit pension plans. A defined benefit pension plan is one which promises a future benefit which is stated in the plan before retirement or can be calculated according to a formula stated in the plan before retirement.

Insurance provisions are administered by the Pension Benefit Guaranty Corporation (PBGC), a corporation established within the U.S. Department of Labor.

The Corporation came into existence on enactment day, September 2, 1974, and is authorized to insure eligible pension plans terminating after July 1, 1974. Plans not covered by insurance provisions include:

■ Those plans exempt from the law's coverage, e.g., governmental plans, church plans, unfunded excess benefit plans, and plans maintained outside the U.S. for non-resident aliens.

■ Stock bonus, money purchase, and profit sharing plans.

■ Plans maintained exclusively for substantial owners.

■ Plans of professional service employers having fewer than 25 active participants.

■ Plans which do not provide for employer contributions.

■ Non-qualified deferred compensation plans established for a select group of management or highly compensated employees.

The insurance of basic benefits is mandatory.

The plans pay a premium for termination insurance. In addition the Corporation may borrow funds from the U.S. Treasury and has a right to recover from any employer the cost to the Corporation of paying benefits to participants or beneficiaries on its behalf, up to 30 percent of the employer's net worth.

The PBGC, generally, will pay monthly vested pension benefits up to a statutorily set maximum amount to a worker affected by a pension plan termination and then can attach up to 30 percent of a company's assets to cover its losses.

WIDOW-WIDOWERS' BENEFIT

When a pension plan provides that a plan participant receives benefits through an annuity upon retirement, it must also provide for a joint and survivor annuity, unless the participant elects, in writing, to give it up. A joint and survivor annuity in event of the death of either husband or wife supports the survivor. The survivor annuity must be at least one-half of the annuity payable to the participant while both are living.

Usually—the amount of the reduction depends on the plan provisions and the difference in ages between employee and spouse.

ENFORCEMENT

Criminal violations are set forth in the Act and penalties may be incurred. Key criminal violations are:

■ Any willful violation of the reporting and disclosure provisions of the Act is punishable by a maximum $5,000 fine or maximum one year's prison term or both. For organizations such as corporations, the penalty is a maximum $100,000 fine.

■ Embezzlement, kickback, false statements, and concealment of facts or any other related violations are punishable by a maximum $10,000 fine or maximum five year prison term or both.

■ Intentional violation of the office-holding prohibition is punishable by a maximum $10,000 fine or maximum one year prison term or both.

■ Willful interference with a participant's or beneficiary's rights through fraud or coercion is punishable by a maximum $10,000 fine or maximum one year prison term or both.

Depending on the circumstances, the Secretary of Labor, plan participants, plan beneficiaries, fiduciaries, plan administrators, the PBGC, and others may bring a civil action under the ERISA.

■ The Secretary of Labor can bring civil action when a fiduciary has breached any duty, obligation, or responsibility. Action can be taken for equitable or remedial relief, including removal from office.

■ When a party in interest is engaged in a prohibited transaction with a non-tax-qualified plan, such as a welfare plan, civil penalty can be sought.

■ To enjoin any act or practice violating any provisions under Title I, or to obtain other appropriate equitable relief to redress any such violation, or to enforce any provision of Title I. (Title I deals with the Secretary of Labor's responsibilities for reporting and disclosure, participation and vesting, funding, fiduciary responsibility, and administration and enforcement.) However, if the violation involves the participation, vesting, or funding provisions of a tax-qualified plan, the Secretary may take action only if he is requested to do so by the Secretary of the Treasury, or by one or more participants, beneficiaries, or fiduciaries, or if he finds that it relates to a participant's or beneficiary's claim for benefits.

■ To compel a plan administrator to furnish statements concerning accrued and vested benefits.

A participant or beneficiary may bring a civil action if his right to bring an action includes the following:

■ To compel an administrator to supply plan documents requested by the participant or beneficiary within 30 days after such request.

■ To enforce his rights under the plan and to recover benefits due.

■ To clarify his right to future benefits.

■ For appropriate relief from breach of fiduciary duty.

■ To enjoin any act or practice which violates any reporting, disclosure, participation, vesting, funding, fiduciary provision, or the terms of his plan, or to obtain other equitable relief.

■ To enforce his rights to receive the statement concerning his vested benefits upon termination of his employment.

■ To obtain review of a final action of the Secretary, to restrain or require him to take action.

■ To obtain review of any action adversely affecting him by the PBGC.

The Secretary may require the submission of books, reports, and records and the filing of data in connection with the conduct of an investigation to determine whether there is or is about to be a violation of any provision of the Act under his jurisdiction. However, he may not require any plan to submit books or records of the plan more than once in any 12-month period unless he has reasonable cause to believe there has been a violation. In addition, the Secretary may enter places to inspect the books and records of a plan and to interview those people he deems necessary to enable him to determine the facts relative to the investigation if he has reasonable cause to believe that there has been a violation or if the entry is pursuant to an agreement with the plan.

■ The Act does not require employers to offer pension plans—it does require those that do to meet certain minimum standards.

■ The Act does not guarantee a pension to every worker—only to workers who have satisfied plan requirements which are consistent with the minimum standards of the law.

■ It does not set specific amounts of money to be paid out as pensions and it does not deal with the adequacy of pension benefits—although it does require that a survivor benefit be at least 50 percent of the retirement benefit.

■ The Act does not guarantee benefits to all widows(ers)—it does not help widows(ers) whose spouses are already deceased or retired before enactment date, or widows(ers) whose spouses have refused the survivor option, or widows(ers) of participants who die before becoming eligible for the joint and survivor benefit.

■ Termination insurance does not cover all pension plans—only defined benefit pension plans (those that provide for a fixed pension benefit) which meet other specified standards, and only those which terminate after July 1, 1974.

■ The law does not provide that an employee can automatically transfer his pension if he changes jobs.

■ With few exceptions, the Act does not restore rights and benefits lost before its enactment.

For further information write to: Labor Management Services Administration, U.S. Department of Labor, Washington, D.C. 20216.

FEDERAL LEGISLATION RELATED TO LABOR STANDARDS AND EQUAL EMPLOYMENT OPPORTUNITY

Davis-Bacon Act (1931, as Amended)

SUMMARY AND DESCRIPTION

This act covers direct Federal construction, alteration, or repair of public buildings or public works, including

painting and decorating, where the contract is more than $2,000, and applies to all agencies of the Federal Government and the District of Columbia that directly make construction contracts.

The Davis-Bacon and related* Acts provide for minimum wages on construction work which shall be based upon the wages determined by the Secretary of

---

* The laws listed herein, among others, extend the Davis-Bacon Act to construction work, based on wage determinations by the Secretary of Labor: Federal-Aid Highway Act of 1956; United States Housing Act of 1937; Housing Act of 1949; Housing Act of 1950 (College Housing); Housing Act of 1959 (Housing for Elderly); National Housing Act (FHA); School Survey and Construction Act; Hospital Survey and Construction Act; Federal Airport Act; Federal Civil Defense Act of 1950; Federal Water Pollution Control Act; Delaware River Basin Compact; Health Professions Educational Assistance Act of 1963; Higher Education Facilities Act of 1963; Vocational Education Act of 1963; Mental Retardation Facilities and Community Mental Health Centers Construction Act of 1963; Airport and Airways Development Act of 1970; Postal Reorganization Act of 1970; National

Foundation on the Arts and Humanities Act; Clean Waters Restoration Act of 1966; Assistance to Local Educational Agencies for Education of Children of Low-Income Families; School Construction in Areas Affected by Federal Activities; Model Secondary School for the Deaf; Partnership for Health Amendments; Medical Library Assistance Extension Act; Health Research Facilities Act; Nurse Training Act; Demonstration Cities and Metropolitan Development Act; Air Quality Act; High Speed Ground Transportation Act; Urban Mass Transportation Act; Alcoholic and Narcotics Rehabilitation Amendments; Juvenile Delinquency Prevention and Control Act; Vocational Rehabilitation Act Amendments of 1968; Vocational Education Act of 1968; and Economic Opportunity Act of 1964.

Labor to be prevailing for the corresponding classes of workers on similar construction in the locality in which the work is to be performed.

These acts also provide for the determination of prevailing fringe benefits. These include medical care, pensions, unemployment benefits, life insurance, disability and sickness insurance, vacation and holiday pay, and costs of apprenticeship.

Money may be withheld from the contractor under the Davis-Bacon and related acts to pay underpaid workers. An employee who believes he is underpaid should complain to the contracting agency or to the Department of Labor. If an investigation confirms the underpayment, money is withheld from the contractor and the contractor is asked to make restitution. If the contractor refuses, funds withheld under the Davis-Bacon Act (but not under the related Acts) are forwarded to the Comptroller General where the employee may file a claim for the wages. Under the related acts the sponsoring agency processes the disbursement to employees.

If enough money has not been withheld to cover all underpayments to laborers or mechanics, a worker who does not receive all that is due him has the right to sue the contractor and the sureties on his bond under the Miller Act (see next page). It is no defense for the contractor that the worker has accepted or agreed to accept wages at rates less than the rates determined by the Secretary, or has refunded any of the wages voluntarily.

Wage Rates Incorporated in Contracts

The wage rates determined by the Secretary of Labor under the laws for each class of laborer or mechanic are made a part of the contract specifications such rates are minimum rates and the contractor may have to pay higher rates (at no increase in the contract price) if economic conditions so require. The schedule of wage rates determined by the Secretary of Labor must be posted by the contractor on the construction site and all laborers and mechanics working at the site must be paid their wages in full, without any unlawful deductions, at least once each week.

National Emergency

The President is authorized, in the event of a National Emergency, to suspend the provisions of the Davis-Bacon Act.

Enforcement

Enforcement of the laws is the duty of the Federal agency that makes the contract or furnishes Federal aid for the project. Under Reorganization Plan No. 14 of 1950, the Department of Labor has the legal duty to see that there is a coordinated and consistent enforcement of these laws by the responsible Federal agencies. Labor Department regulations provide what the contractors, subcontractors, and Federal agencies have to do.

Penalties

Regulations, Part 5, issued by the Secretary of Labor (29 CFR secs. 5.1–5.12a) provide that if the contractor or subcontractor fails to live up to any one of the contract provisions under the law, he has broken the contract and it may be cancelled and the work given to another contractor for completion. In addition, if a contractor has failed to pay required wages under these laws, the Federal Government may withhold or have withheld the full amount of any back wages due, from money that would otherwise be made available for payments to the contractor. Also, on written notice further payments or guarantees of funds may be suspended until violations have been corrected.

Contractors and subcontractors who disregard their obligations under any of these laws may be barred for a period of 3 years from receiving any further contracts to which the laws apply.

This law, while not a prevailing wage law or overtime pay law, is particularly important to laborers and mechanics who work on construction covered by the Davis-Bacon Act—that is, on construction contracts made directly by the Federal Government. Although the law does not apply to Federal-aid projects but only to direct Federal contracts, it is usual for Federal agencies administering grant-in-aid, loan, mortgage guarantee, and similar Federal-aid programs to require by regulation that contractors on construction under these programs execute a performance bond. Generally, the term of such bonds extends to 1 year after completion of the project.

Right to Sue

The Miller Act gives the worker a right to sue on the contractor's bond if he does not receive payment in full within 90 days after the day on which the last labor was performed. If the worker was employed by a subcontractor, he can sue the prime contractor and sureties on the bond for his unpaid wages, if he first gives written notice to the prime contractor within 90 days after the last labor was performed. This notice must be sent by registered mail, postage prepaid, in an envelope addressed to the contractor at any place he maintains an office or conducts his business; or it may be served in any other way that the U.S. marshal or the Federal district court for the district where the job is located is authorized to serve a summons.

Time and Manner for Bringing Suit

Suits to recover under the Miller Act must be commenced with 1 year after the date of final settlement of the contract and must be brought in the name of the United States, for the use of the person suing, in the U.S. district court in any district in which the contract was to be performed and executed. Suit is brought and prosecuted by the worker's own attorney.

For further information write to: Employment Standards Administration, Wage and Hour Division, U.S. Department of Labor, Washington, D.C. 20210.

Miller Act (1935, as Amended)

SUMMARY AND DESCRIPTION

Persons and Employments Covered

The Miller Act applies to every contract of over $2,000 for the construction, alteration, or repair of any public building or public work of the United States and provides that, before any contract covered by its provisions is awarded, the contractor must execute a payment bond with a surety or sureties to protect the wages of all persons supplying labor.

This law, while not a prevailing wage law or overtime pay law, is particularly important to laborers and mechanics who work on construction covered by the Davis-Bacon Act—that is, on construction contracts made directly by the Federal Government. Although the law does not apply to Federal-aid projects but only to direct Federal contracts, it is usual for Federal agencies administering grant-in-aid, loan, mortgage guarantee, and similar Federal-aid programs to require by regulation that contractors on construction under these programs executive a performance bond which require among its terms the payment of wages to laborers. Generally, the term of such bonds extends to 1 year after completion of the project.

Right to Sue

The Miller Act gives the worker a right to sue on the contractor's bond if he does not receive payment in full within 90 days after the day on which the last labor was performed. If the worker was employed by a subcontractor, he can sue the prime contractor and sureties on the bond for his unpaid wages, if he first gives written notice to the prime contractor within 90 days after the last labor was performed. This notice must be sent by registered mail, postage prepaid, in an envelope addressed to the contractor at any place he maintains an office or conducts his business; or it may be served in any other way that the U.S. marshal or the Federal district court for the district where the job is located is authorized to serve a summons.

Time and Manner for Bringing Suit

Suits to recover under the Miller Act must be commenced within 1 year after the date of final settlement of the contract and must be brought in the name of the United States, for the use of the person suing, in the U.S. district court in any district in which the contract was to be performed and executed. Suit is brought and prosecuted by the worker's own attorney.

For further information write to: Employment Standards Administration, Wage and Hour Division, U.S. Department of Labor, Washington, D.C. 20210.

Walsh-Healey Public Contracts Act (1936, as Amended)

SUMMARY AND DESCRIPTION

The Public Contracts Act sets basic labor standards for work done on United States Government contracts which exceed $10,000 in value for materials, supplies, articles, equipment, or naval vessels. In general, these standards apply to all persons engaged in the manufacture or furnishing, including the fabrication, assembling, handling, or shipping of the contracted items, except those in bona fide executive, administrative or professional positions, or those engaged in office, custodial, or maintenance work.

The act requires that the contractor be a manufacturer or regular dealer in the articles called for in the contract. Under special circumstances, as, for example, where it is the regular practice in an industry for the prime contractor to manufacture certain items, secondary contractors are covered.

Minimum Wage Rates

The Secretary of Labor is authorized to determine prevailing minimum wages for similar work in an industry on the basis of standards provided in the act. Such minimum wage determinations generally are issued by the Secretary after a public hearing. All workers engaged in performance of a contract let under the act must be paid not less than the minimum so set by the Secretary. Under current determinations, all covered employees must be paid not less than $2.00 effective January 1, 1975 and $2.30 an hour effective January 1, 1976, unless a higher rate is set for a particular industry.

Overtime

Covered workers must be paid at least one and one-half times their basic rate of pay for all hours worked in excess of 8 a day or 40 a week, whichever number of overtime hours is greater. Overtime is due on the basis of the total hours spent in all work, Government and non-Government, performed by the employee in any week in which covered work is performed.

Child Labor

The law prohibits employment of persons under 16 years of age.

Convict Labor

The law prohibits the employment of convict labor.

Safety and Health

The contract may not be performed nor the materials, supplies, articles, or equipment manufactured or furnished under working conditions which are unsanitary or hazardous or dangerous to the health and safety of employees engaged in the performance of the contract.

Compliance with the safety, sanitary, and factory inspection laws of the State in which the work is performed is prima facie but not conclusive evidence of compliance with this provision of the act.

Homework

Industrial homework is prohibited.

Beginners, Apprentices, and Handicapped Workers

Under specified conditions, wage determinations of the Secretary for some industries permit payment of less than the established minimum wage to beginners. When employed in accordance with special regulations, apprentices, student-learners, and handicapped workers may also be employed at less than the prevailing minimum wages.

Exemptions

The act specifically exempts certain types of contracts, including contracts for transportation by common carriers under published tariffs; utility services; perishable agricultural products; and rentals.

Exceptions

Upon a written finding of the head of the contracting agency that operations of the act will seriously impair the conduct of Government business, the Secretary of Labor is authorized to make exceptions in certain cases when justice or public interest will be served thereby.

Records: Posting Notices

Contractors are required to display a copy of the Public Contracts Act poster, with applicable attachment, wherever work is being performed under the act. Contractors also are required to keep specified records, including injury frequency rates, which are open for inspection by representatives of the Department of Labor.

Employer Liabilities

A contractor who violates the law is liable to the United States for:

A sum equal to the amount due employees under the law on account of underpayment of wages. Such sums recovered by the Government are paid directly to the employees to whom they are due.

Ten dollars per day for each minor under 16 or convict laborer knowingly employed on the contract.

Violations of the act may result in cancellation of the contract by the awarding agency, with any additional costs charged to the original contractor. Sums due the United States may be recovered by withholding payment of monies due or by court action.

No award of Government contracts may be made to the responsible person or firm within 3 years from the date on which the Secretary of Labor determines that a breach of contract occurred, unless the Secretary specifically recommends otherwise.

For further information write to: Employment Standards Administration, Wage and Hour Division, U.S. Department of Labor, Washington, D.C. 20210.

The Fair Labor Standards Act of 1938

The Fair Labor Standards Act establishes minimum wage, overtime pay, equal pay, recordkeeping, and child labor standards affecting more than 50 million full-time and part-time workers.

Basic Wage Standards

Covered non-exempt workers are entitled to a minimum wage of not less than

Beginning January 1, 1978
$2.65 an hour

Beginning January 1, 1979
$2.90 an hour

Beginning January 1, 1980
$3.10 an hour

Beginning January 1, 1981
$3.35 an hour

and overtime at not less than one and one-half times the employee's regular rate is due after 40 hours of work in the workweek

Wages required by the Act are due on the regular pay day for the pay period covered

Hospitals and residential care establishments may adopt, by agreement with the employees, a 14-day overtime period in lieu of the usual 7-day workweek, if the employees are paid at least time and a half their regular rate for hours worked over 8 in a day or 80 in a 14-day work period.

There are some exemptions from these basic provisions

Note: The FLSA does **not** require:
—vacation, holiday, severance, or sick pay
—a discharge notice or reason for discharge
—rest periods, holidays off, or vacations
—premium pay rates for weekend or holiday work
—pay raises or fringe benefits
—a limit on hours of work for employees 16 years of age or older

These are matters for agreement between the employer and the employees or their authorized representatives.

Who Is Covered?

All employees of certain enterprises having workers engaged in interstate commerce, producing goods for interstate commerce, or handling, selling, or otherwise working on goods or materials that have been moved in or produced for such commerce by any person are covered by the Act.

A covered enterprise is the related activities performed through unified operation or common control by any person or persons for a common business purpose and is —

(1) engaged in laundering or cleaning of clothing or fabrics; or
(2) engaged in the business of construction or reconstruction; or
(3) engaged in the operation of a hospital; an institution primarily engaged in the care of the sick, the aged, the mentally ill or defective who reside on the premises; a school for mentally or physically handicapped or gifted children; a preschool, an elementary or secondary school; or an institution of higher education (regardless of whether or not such hospital, institution or school is public or private or operated for profit or not for profit); or
(4) comprised exclusively of one or more retail or service establishments (as defined in the Act) whose annual gross volume of sales or business done is not less than —

$250,000

Beginning July 1, 1978
$275,000

Beginning July 1, 1980
$325,000

Beginning January 1, 1982
$362,500

(Any retail or service enterprise which has an annual gross volume of not less than $250,000 and which later ceases to be a covered enterprise as a result of increases in this dollar volume test must continue to pay its employees at least the minimum wage in effect at the time of the enterprise's removal from coverage, as well as overtime in accordance with the Act.) or

(5) any other type of enterprise having an annual gross volume of sales or business done of not less than $250,000.

The dollar volume standard mentioned above in (4) and (5) excludes excise taxes at the retail level which are separately stated.

Any establishment which has as its only regular employees the owner thereof or members of the owner's immediate family is not considered part of any enterprise.

Federal employees are subject to the minimum wage, overtime, child labor and equal pay provisions of the Act. Employees of State and local governments are subject to the same provisions, unless they are engaged in traditional governmental activities, in which case they are subject to the child labor and equal pay provisions only. The Supreme Court has indicated that such traditional governmental activities include schools, hospitals, fire prevention, police protection, sanitation, public health, parks and recreation.

Employees who are not employed in a covered enterprise may still be entitled to the Act's minimum wage, overtime pay, equal pay, and child labor protections if they are individually engaged in interstate commerce. These include —

(a) communication and transportation workers;
(b) employees who handle, ship, or receive goods moving in interstate commerce;
(c) clerical or other workers who regularly use the mails, telephone, or telegraph for interstate communication or who keep records on interstate transactions;

(d) employees who regularly cross State lines in the course of their work; and

(e) Employees of independent employers who perform clerical, custodial, maintenance, or other work for firms engaged in commerce or in the production of goods for commerce.

Domestic service workers such as maids, day workers, housekeepers, chauffeurs, cooks, or full-time baby sitters are covered if they (1) receive at least $100 in cash wages in a calendar year from their employer or (2) work a total of more than 8 hours a week for one or more employers.

Tipped Employees

Tipped employees are those who customarily and regularly receive more than $30 a month in tips. The employer may consider tips as part of wages, but such a wage credit must not exceed 50 percent of the minimum wage (beginning January 1, 1979, 45% is the maximum tip credit, and beginning January 1, 1980, 40% is the maximum tip credit).

The employer who elects to use the tip credit provision must inform the employee in advance and must be able to show that the employee receives at least the minimum wage when direct wages and the tip credit allowance are combined. Also, employees must retain all of their tips, except to the extent that they participate in a valid tip pooling or sharing arrangement.

Employer-Furnished Facilities

The reasonable cost or fair value of board, lodging, and other facilities provided by the employer may, as determined by the Wage and Hour Administrator, be considered part of wages.

Subminimum Wage Provisions

Learners, apprentices, and handicapped workers may, under certain circumstances, be paid less than the minimum wage, as well as full-time students in retail or service establishments, agriculture, or institutions of higher education. Special certificates issued by the Wage and Hour Administrator must be obtained by employers wishing to use these provisions.

Industry wage orders may set minimum rates below the generally applicable minimum wage under the Act for employees in Puerto Rico, the Virgin Islands, and American Samoa.

Equal Pay Provisions

The equal pay provisions of the FLSA prohibit wage differentials based on sex, between men and women employed in the same establishment on jobs that require equal skill, effort and responsibility and which are performed under similar working conditions.

Jobs need only be substantially equal — not identical — for comparison purposes. In addition, the comparison may be made in situations where employees of one sex are doing work formerly done by employees of the opposite sex.

Where a violation exists, an employer may not reduce the wage rate of an employee in order to eliminate the prohibited wage differential.

A wage differential based even in part on sex is prohibited. However, the law does permit differences based on factors other than sex (e.g., bona fide seniority or merit systems or systems that reward productivity).

In private employment, the equal pay provisions apply to most employees subject to the FLSA, including executive, administrative, professional and outside sales personnel. They apply not only to employers but to labor organizations. It is illegal for such organizations or their agents representing covered workers to cause or attempt to cause an employer to violate the law.

The Act's equal pay provisions also apply to Federal, state and local government employees.

Exemptions

Some employees are excluded from the minimum wage or overtime provisions, or both, by specific exemptions. Because each exemption is narrowly defined under the law, an employer should carefully check its exact terms and conditions before applying it. The following examples are illustrative only and do not spell out the conditions for each. Detailed information is available from local Wage-Hour offices.

Exemptions from Both Minimum Wage and Overtime

Executive, administrative, and professional employees (including teachers and academic administrative personnel in elementary or secondary schools) and outside sales persons (as defined in the Division's regulations);

Employees of certain individually owned and operated small retail or service establishments not part of a covered enterprise;

Employees of certain seasonal amusement or recreational establishments, employees of certain small newspapers, switchboard operators of small telephone companies, seamen employed on foreign vessels, and employees engaged in fishing operations;

Farm workers employed by anyone who used no more than 500 man-days of farm labor in any calendar quarter of the preceding calendar year;

Casual babysitters and persons employed as companions to the elderly or infirm.

Exemptions from Overtime Provisions Only

Certain highly-paid commission employees of retail or service establishments; auto, truck, trailer, farm implement, boat, or aircraft salesworkers, or partsmen and mechanics servicing autos, trucks or farm implements, and who are employed by nonmanufacturing establishments primarily engaged in selling these items to ultimate purchasers;

Employees of railroads and air carriers, taxi drivers, certain employees of motor carriers, seamen on American vessels, and local delivery employees paid on approved trip rate plans;

Announcers, news editors, and chief engineers of certain nonmetropolitan broadcasting stations;

Domestic service workers residing in the employers' residences;

Employees of motion picture theaters; and Farmworkers.

Partial Exemptions from Overtime

Employees of hotels and motels (other than maids or custodial employees) and restaurants must be paid overtime after 44 hours in a workweek effective January 1, 1978 and after 40 hours effective January 1, 1979. Maids and custodial employees of hotels and motels must be paid overtime after 40 hours in a workweek.

Partial overtime pay exemptions are provided for certain operations on agricultural commodities and for employees in certain bulk petroleum distribution.

Child Labor Provisions

The FLSA child labor provisions are designed to protect the educational opportunities of minors and prohibit their employment in jobs and under conditions detrimental to their health or well-being. The provisions include lists of hazardous occupation orders for both farm and nonfarm jobs banned by the Secretary of Labor as being too dangerous for minors to perform. Further information on prohibited occupations is available from local Wage-Hour offices.

Regulations governing youth employment in nonfarm jobs differ somewhat from those pertaining to agricultural employment. In nonfarm work, the permissible kinds and hours of work, by age, are:

18 years or older: any job, whether hazardous or not, for unlimited hours;

16 and 17 years old: any nonhazardous job, for unlimited hours;

14 and 15 years old: outside of school hours in various nonmanufacturing nonmining, nonhazardous jobs, under these conditions: no more than 3 hours on a school day, 18 hours in a school week, 8 hours on a nonschool day or 40 hours in a nonschool week. Also, work may not begin before 7 a.m., nor end after 7 p.m., except from June 1 through Labor Day, when evening hours are extended to 9 p.m.

Under a special provision, 14 and 15-year-olds enrolled in an approved Work Experience and Career Exploration Program (WECEP) may be employed for up to 23 hours in school weeks and 3 hours on school days (including during school hours).

Fourteen is the minimum age for most nonfarm work. However, at any age, youths may deliver newspapers, perform in radio, television, movie or theatrical productions, work for parents in their solely owned nonfarm business (except in manufacturing or on hazardous jobs), gather evergreens and make evergreen wreaths.

Permissible kinds and hours of work for youths employed in agriculture are:

16 years and older: any job, whether hazardous or not, for unlimited hours;

14 and 15 years old: any nonhazardous farm job outside of school hours;

12 and 13 years old: outside of school hours in nonhazardous jobs, either with parents' written consent or on the same farm as the parents;

Under 12 years old: jobs on farms owned or operated by parents or, with parents' written consent, outside of school hours in nonhazardous jobs on farms not covered by minimum wage requirements.

Local minors 10 and 11 years of age may work for no more than 8 weeks between June 1 and October 15 for employers who receive approval from the Secretary of Labor. This work must be confined to hand-harvesting short season crops outside school hours under very limited and specified circumstances prescribed by the Secretary of Labor.

Minors of any age may be employed by their parents at any time in any occupation on a farm owned or operated by their parents.

Recordkeeping

Employers are required to keep records on wages, hours and other items, as specified in the Division's record-keeping regulations. Most of the information is of the kind generally maintained by employers in ordinary business practice and in compliance with other laws and regulations. The records do not have to be kept in any

particular form and time clocks need not be used. With respect to an employee subject to both minimum wage and overtime pay provisions, the following records must be kept:

—Personal information, including employee's name, home address, occupation, sex, and birth date (if under 19 years of age)
—Hour and day when workweek begins
—Total hours worked each workday and each workweek
—Total daily or weekly straight-time earnings
—Regular hourly pay rate for any week when overtime is worked
—Total overtime pay for the workweek
—Deductions from or additions to wages
—Total wages paid each pay period
—Date of payment and pay period covered

Records required for exempt employees differ from those for nonexempt workers and special information is required on employees working under uncommon pay arrangements or to whom lodging or other facilities are furnished. Employers who have homeworkers must make entries in handbooks supplied by the Division.

Terms Used in the FLSA

Workweek

A workweek is a period of 168 hours during seven consecutive 24-hour periods. It may begin on any day of the week and any hour of the day established by the employer. For purposes of minimum wage and overtime payment, each workweek stands alone; there can be no averaging of two or more workweeks (except for hospital or nursing home employees on an "8 and 80" schedule or seamen on American vessels). Employee coverage, compliance with wage payment requirements and the application of most exemptions are determined on a workweek basis.

Hours Worked

Covered employees must be paid for all hours worked in a workweek. In general, "hours worked" includes all time an employee must be on duty, or on the employer's premises or at any other prescribed place of work. Also included is any additional time the employee is suffered or permitted to work.

Computing Overtime Pay

Overtime must be paid at a rate of at least 1-1/2 times the employee's regular pay rate for each hour worked in a workweek in excess of the maximum allowable in a given type of employment. Generally, the regular rate includes all payments made by the employer to or on behalf of the employee (excluding certain statutory exceptions). The following examples are based on a maximum 40-hour workweek:

1. Hourly rate (regular pay rate for an employee paid by the hour). If more than 40 hours are worked, at least 1-1/2 times the regular rate for each hour over 40 is due.

Example: An employee paid $3.80 an hour works 44 hours in a workweek. The employee is entitled to at least 1-1/2 times $3.80, or $5.70, for each hour over 40. Pay for the week would be $152 for the first 40 hours, plus $22.80 for the four hours of overtime — a total of $174.80.

2. Piece rate. The regular rate of pay for an employee paid on a piecework basis is obtained by dividing the total weekly earnings by the total number of hours worked in the same week. The employee is entitled to an additional 1/2 times this regular rate for each hour over 40, besides the full piecework earnings.

Example: An employee paid on a piecework basis works 45 hours in a week and earns $162. The regular pay rate for that week is $162 divided by 45, or $3.60 an hour. In addition to the straight time pay, the employee is entitled to $1.80 (half the regular rate) for each hour over 40.

Another way to compensate pieceworkers for overtime, if agreed to before the work is performed, is to pay 1-1/2 times the piece rate for each piece produced during overtime hours. The piece rate must be the one actually paid during non-overtime hours and must be enough to yield at least the minimum wage per hour.

3. Salaries — the regular rate for an employee paid a salary for a regular or specified number of hours a week is obtained by dividing the salary by the number of hours.

If, under the employment agreement, a salary sufficient to meet the minimum wage requirement in every workweek is paid as straight time for whatever number of hours are worked in a workweek, the regular rate is obtained by dividing the salary by the number of hours worked each week. To illustrate, suppose an employee's hours of work vary each week and the agreement with the employer is that the employee will be paid $200 a week for whatever number of hours of work are required. Under this pay agreement, the regular rate will vary in overtime weeks. If the employee works 50 hours, the regular rate is $4 ($200 divided by 50 hours). In addition to the salary, 1/2 the regular rate, or $2 is due for each of the 10 overtime hours, for a total of $220 for the week. If the employee works 54 hours, the regular rate will be $3.70 ($200 divided by 54). In that case, an additional $1.85 is due for each of the 14 overtime hours, for a total of $225.90 for the week.

In no case may the regular rate be less than the minimum wage required by the Act.

If a salary is paid on other than a weekly basis, the weekly pay must be determined in order to compute the regular rate and overtime. If the salary is for a half month, it must be multiplied by 24 and the product divided by 52 weeks to get the weekly equivalent. A monthly salary should be multiplied by 12 and the product divided by 52.

Enforcement

The Wage and Hour Division administers and enforces the law with respect to private employment, State and local government employment, and Federal employees of the Library of Congress, U.S. Postal Service, Postal Rate Commission, and the Tennessee Valley Authority. The Civil Service Commission is responsible for enforcement with regard to all other Federal employees.

The Wage-Hour Division's enforcement of the FLSA is carried out by compliance officers stationed across the U.S. As the Division's authorized representatives, they have the authority to conduct investigations and gather data on wages, hours, and other employment conditions or practices, in order to determine compliance with the Act. Where violations are found, they also may recommend changes in employment practices, in order to bring an employer into compliance with the law.

It is a violation of the FLSA to fire or in any other manner discriminate against an employee for filing a complaint or participating in a legal proceeding under the law.

Willful violations may be prosecuted criminally and the violator fined up to $10,000. A second conviction may result in imprisonment.

Violators of the child labor provisions are subject to a civil money penalty of up to $1,000 for each violation.

Recovery of Back Wages

The FLSA provides for the following methods of recovering unpaid minimum and/or overtime wages:

1. The Division may supervise payment of back wages.

2. The Secretary of Labor may bring suit for back wages and an equal amount as liquidated damages.

3. An employee may file a private suit for back pay and an equal amount as liquidated damages, plus attorney's fees and court costs.

4. The Secretary may obtain an injunction to restrain any person from violating the law, including the unlawful withholding of proper minimum wage and overtime compensation.

Any amount owed to an employee in violation of the equal pay provisions is deemed unpaid minimum wages or unpaid overtime compensation under the Act.

An employee may not bring suit if he or she has been paid back wages under the supervision of the Division or if the Secretary has already filed suit to recover the wages.

A two-year statute of limitations applies to the recovery of back pay, except in the case of willful violation, in which case a three-year statute applies.

The Wage and Hour Division

In addition to the FLSA, the Wage and Hour Division enforces and administers a number of other labor laws. Among these are:

- the Davis-Bacon Act (determines wage rates for Federally financed or assisted construction)

- the Walsh-Healey Public Contracts Act (determines wage rates for contracts to provide goods to the Federal government)

- the McNamara-O'Hara Service Contract Act (determines wage rates for contracts to provide services to the Federal government)

- the Contract Work Hours and Safety Standards Act (sets overtime standards for Federal contracts)

- the Age Discrimination in Employment Act (protects persons aged 40 to 65 (40 to 70, effective 1/1/79) from arbitrary employment discrimination based on age)

- the Farm Labor Contractor Registration Act (protects migrant farm workers by imposing certain restrictions and requirements on their crew leaders)

- the Wage Garnishment Law (limits amount of individual's income that may be legally garnished and prohibits the firing of an employee whose pay is garnished for payment of a single debt).

More detailed information on the FLSA and other laws administered by the Division is available from local Wage-Hour offices, which are listed in the white pages of most telephone directories under U.S. Government, Department of Labor, Employment Standards Administration, Wage and Hour Division.

The 1977 amendments
to the Federal minimum wage law

Roughly in line with estimated rates
under rejected indexing formula,
the minimum wage was increased
to $2.65 an hour on January 1
and will reach $3.35 by 1981

PEYTON ELDER

For the sixth time in its 40-year history, the Fair Labor Standards Act was amended to raise the minimum wage on January 1, 1978, as a result of legislation signed into law on November 1, 1977, by President Carter. The new rate is $2.65 an hour and covers approximately 52 million nonsupervisory workers (table 1). The rate will rise to $2.90 an hour on January 1, 1979, $3.10 on January 1, 1980, and $3.35 on January 1, 1981. With the 1981 increase, workers receiving the minimum wage will have annual gross earnings of more than $6,900 a year for full-time, year-round employment, compared with less than $4,800 last year.

The 1977 amendments culminated over 8 months of Congressional debate with regard to appropriate amounts and timing of minimum wage increases and their possible effects. For the first time in the history of the Fair Labor Standards Act, the Congress seriously considered instituting an indexing mechanism in the law, which would have provided automatic increases in the minimum wage to maintain it as a specific percentage of the average earnings of other higher paid workers. Although the indexing concept was rejected in the end, the minimum wage rates finally enacted are quite close to the rates which had been estimated by the U.S. Department of Labor

Peyton Elder is a labor economist in the Division of Legislative Analysis, Employment Standards Administration.

under the indexing formula recommended by the Carter Administration and adopted by committees in the House and the Senate.

Single rate established

Under the minimum wage levels established by the 1974 amendments to the Fair Labor Standards Act (FLSA), the minimum wage on November 1, 1977, was $2.30 an hour for eligible nonfarm workers and $2.20 an hour for eligible farm workers.[1] The farm worker minimum was scheduled to increase to $2.30 an hour on January 1, 1978. The 1977 amendments established a single minimum wage, initially $2.65 an hour, for both groups of workers beginning January 1, 1978.

Along with the increases in the Federal minimum wage, the amendments made a significant change in applying the mainland U.S. minimum wage levels to Puerto Rico and the Virgin Islands. As of January 1, 1978, all minimum wage rates in Puerto Rico and the Virgin Islands which were at the mainland level remain at the mainland rates and will not be subject to further review by the industry committees. (In the past, industry committees, composed of representatives of employees, employers, and the public, met in Puerto Rico or the Virgin Islands to review minimum wages applicable to various industries and increase them by "wage orders"—not to exceed the U.S. mainland minimum wage—as economic circumstances permitted.) Wage order rates in Puerto Rico and the Virgin Islands which were less than the mainland rates ($2.30 and $2.20) in effect on December 31, 1977, were increased automatically by specified amounts. The increases will continue each January 1 until the mainland rates are reached. At the same time, the industry committees are empowered to set additional increases over and above the automatic increases if they find that economic conditions in the affected industries warrant such action.

Tip credit provisions

In addition to raising the minimum wage, the 1977 amendments modify the extent to which employers of tipped employees may count the tips as a credit against their minimum wage obligations. Under the current tip credit provision, tips can be counted towards the minimum wage up to a maximum of 50 percent of the effective minimum wage rate or the amount of the tips actually received, whichever is lower. The 1977 amendments reduce the maximum 50-percent allowance to 45 percent beginning January 1, 1979, and to 40 percent beginning January 1, 1980, thus requiring employers to pay more of the minimum wage out of company funds. Previously, a tipped employee was defined as a worker who regularly and customarily receives more than $20 a month in tips. The amendments raised this amount to $30, effective January 1, 1978.

Modification in law's coverage

In a major shift from recent amendments to the act, the Congress included provisions that have the effect of removing several hundred thousand workers from coverage by the beginning of 1982. Currently, the act covers all employees in an enterprise which has the requisite links to interstate commerce and which has a gross annual volume of sales made or business done of at least $250,000. The amendments created a new category of coverage for enterprises consisting exclusively of one or more retail or service establishments. Such enterprises will be covered under the act if they have a gross annual volume of sales made or business done of at least $275,000 beginning on July 1, 1978, at least $325,000 beginning July 1, 1980, and at least $362,500 after December 31, 1981. Any retail or service enterprise which is removed from coverage on any of the above dates must continue to pay its employees in accordance with the overtime provisions and at least the minimum wage in effect at that time. An estimated 236,000 employees will be affected by this provision beginning July 1, 1978, 468,000 beginning July 1, 1980, and a cumulative total of 650,000 employees after December 31, 1981.

Impact of wage increases

The combination of increases in the Federal minimum wage and modification in the tip credit, while offset somewhat by the new enterprise coverage test, will obviously mean additional wage costs to employers. The January 1 wage provision required raises for about 4.5 million employees and will increase the annual wage bill of employers by more than $2.1 billion. Each of the three succeeding increases will affect more than 5 million workers, at costs of similar magnitude.

In response to the continuing controversy on the effects of the minimum wage, the Congress approved a provision under which an independent Minimum Wage Study Commission will be established to examine a number of issues related to the minimum wage. Consisting of eight members, two each appointed by the Secretaries of Labor; Health, Education, and Welfare; Commerce; and Agriculture, the commission will study, among a number of research topics (1) the effect of the minimum wage on reducing poverty, (2) the employment, price and indirect wage effects of minimum wages, (3) the youth minimum wage rate and minimum wage indexing issues, (4) the exemptions from the requirements of the Fair Labor Standards Act, (5) the degree of compliance with the provisions of the act, and (6) the demographic characteristics of minimum-wage workers. The final report by the Commission to the President and the Congress is to be made within 3 years.

Youth rate proposal

As has been the case in prior amendments, the Congress considered a number of proposals to establish special youth minimum wage rates for teenagers. All across-the-board proposals for youth rates were defeated. However, there were modifications made in

Table 1. Minimum wage rates and estimated coverage and costs, January 1, 1978, to January 1, 1981[1]

Effective date	Minimum wage rate		Tip allow- ance (percent)	Covered employ- ees (thou- sands[2])	Employees affected		Wage bill increase	
	Non- tipped employ- ees	Tipped employ- ees			Number (thou- sands)	Percent	Amount (millions)	Percent
January 1, 1978 . . .	$2.65	$1.33	50	51,875	4,530	8.7	$2,166	0.4
January 1, 1979 . . .	2.90	1.60	45	51,639	5,105	9.9	2,103	.4
January 1, 1980 . . .	3.10	1.86	40	51,639	5,198	10.1	1,917	.3
January 1, 1981 . . .	3.35	2.01	40	51,407	5,382	10.5	2,308	.4

[1] Covered employees as of September 1976; earnings levels were projected assuming an annual increase of 7 percent.

[2] Covered employees (as of September 1976) in enterprises within the range of the new annual sales volume tests of H.R. 3744: July 1, 1978 ($275,000)—236,000 employees; July 1, 1980 ($325,000)—468,000 employees; and December 31, 1981 ($362,500) 650,000 employees. Division of Evaluation and Research, Employment Standards Administration.

the current provisions for the issuance of special certificates by the Secretary of Labor for the employment of full-time students at 85 percent of the minimum wage. Specifically, the 1977 amendments raised from four to six the number of full-time students who may be employed by retailers and farmers at the 85 percent rate of the minimum wage without prior authorization by the Department of Labor. In addition, the amendments specify that employers applying for the authority to employ such students need only furnish their name, address, and type of business, the date the business began operations, and a statement certifying that the employment of the full-time students will not reduce the full-time employment opportunities of other individuals.

Other provisions

The Fair Labor Standards Act contains a number of exemptions from the minimum wage, overtime pay, and child labor requirements. Several modifications were made by the 1977 amendments. The most significant was the repeal by January 1, 1979, of the current overtime exemption for up to 46 hours per week for hotel, motel, and restaurant employees (maids and custodial employees of hotels and motels are already protected by the 40-hour workweek standard). An interim reduction in the maximum hours standard from 46 to 44 hours became effective January 1, 1978. About 2.4 million hotel, motel, and restaurant employees gain additional overtime pay protection as a result of this change.

Another change adds procedures authorizing the Secretary of Labor to waive the current prohibitions on the agricultural employment of children 10 and 11 years old. If an application sets forth objective data which meet the strict requirements necessary to qualify for a waiver, such youngsters can be employed outside of school hours for up to 8 weeks between June 1 and October 15 provided a number of other rigid conditions and qualifications established by the amendment are met. An estimated 83,000 individuals could be affected.

Four other exemptions were changed. The minimum wage and overtime exemption for seasonal amusement and recreational establishments was revised to include organized camps or religious or nonprofit educational conference centers. This exemption was also amended to exclude from its terms and conditions employees of concessioners in national parks and forests, and in the national wildlife refuge system, under contract with the Secretary of the Interior or the Secretary of Agriculture. However, employees of concessioners that provide skiing services and facilities continue to be exempt from the minimum wage, but not the overtime provisions of the law. A new overtime exemption for up to 56 hours per week was added for such private concessioners. An overtime exemption for certain agricultural employees engaged in specified shade-grown tobacco processing operations was repealed and a partial overtime exemption for certain cotton ginning and sugar processing employees was made less complex.

Finally, the amendments establish a new private right of action for employees who are discharged or discriminated against because they filed a complaint under the Fair Labor Standards Act or testified or otherwise cooperated with the Department of Labor in an enforcement action. Such retaliatory actions by employers were already prohibited, but suits for violations could be brought only by the Secretary of Labor. This modification, by providing additional protection of employee rights, is aimed at further encouraging employees to cooperate in the enforcement of the act. □

Portal to Portal Act of 1947

TEXT OF ACT

§ 251. Congressional findings and declaration of policy.

(a) The Congress finds that the Fair Labor Standards Act of 1938, as amended, has been interpreted judicially in disregard of long-established customs, practices, and contracts between employers and employees, thereby creating wholly unexpected liabilities, immense in amount and retroactive in operation, upon employers with the results that, if said Act as so interpreted or claims arising under such interpretations were permitted to stand, (1) the payment of such liabilities would bring about financial ruin of many employers and seriously impair the capital resources of many others, thereby resulting in the reduction of industrial operations halting of expansion and development, curtailing employment, and the earning power of employees; (2) the credit of many employers would be seriously impaired: (3) there would be created both an extended and continuous uncertainty on the part of industry, both employer and employee, as to the financial condition of productive establishments and a gross inequality of competitive conditions between employers and between industries; (4) employees would receive windfall payments, including liquidated damages, of sums for activities performed by them without any expectation of reward beyond that included in their agreed rates of pay; (5) there would occur the promotion of increasing demands for payment to employees for engaging in activities no compensation for which had been contemplated by either the employer or employee at the time they were engaged in; (6) voluntary collective bargaining would be interfered with and industrial disputes between employees and employers and between employees and employees would be created; (7) the courts of the country would be burdened with excessive and needless litigation and champertous practices would be encouraged; (8) the Public Treasury would be deprived of large sums of revenues and public finances would be seriously deranged by claims against the Public Treasury for refunds of taxes already paid; (9) the cost to the Government of goods and services heretofore and hereafter purchased by its various departments and agencies would be unreasonably increased and the Public Treasury would be seriously affected by consequent increased cost of war contracts; and (10) serious and adverse effects upon the revenues of Federal, State, and local governments would occur.

The Congress further finds that all of the foregoing constitutes a substantial burden on commerce and a substantial obstruction to the free flow of goods in commerce.

The Congress, therefore, further finds and declares that it is in the national public interest and for the general welfare, essential to national defense, and necessary to aid, protect, and foster commerce, that this chapter be enacted.

The Congress further finds that the varying and extended periods of time for which, under the laws of the several States, potential retroactive liability may be imposed upon employers, have given and will give rise to great difficulties in the sound and orderly conduct of business and industry.

The Congress further finds and declares that all of the results which have arisen or may arise under the Fair Labor Standards Act of 1938, as amended, as aforesaid, may (except as to liability for liquidated damages) arise with respect to the Walsh-Healey and Bacon-Davis Acts and that it is, therefore, in the national public interest and for the general welfare, essential to national defense, and necessary to aid, protect, and foster commerce, that this chapter shall apply to the Walsh-Healey Act and the Bacon-Davis Act.

(b) It is declared to be the policy of the Congress in order to meet the existing emergency and to correct existing evils (1) to relieve and protect interstate commerce from practices which burden and obstruct it; (2) to protect the right of collective bargaining; and (3) to define and limit the jurisdiction of the courts. (May 14, 1947, ch. 52, § 1, 61 Stat. 84.)

§ 252. Relief from certain existing claims under the Fair Labor Standards Act of 1938, as amended, the Walsh-Healey Act, and the Bacon-Davis Act.

(a) No employer shall be subject to any liability or punishment under the Fair Labor Standards Act of 1938, as amended, the Walsh-Healey Act, or the Bacon-Davis Act (in any action or preceeding commenced prior to or on or after May 14, 1947), on account of the failure of such employer to pay an employee minimum wages, or to pay an employee overtime compensation, for or on account of any activity of an employee engaged in prior to May 14, 1947, except an activity which was compensable by either—

1. an express provision of a written or nonwritten contract in effect, at the time of such activity, between such employee, his agent, or collective-bargaining representative and his employer; or

2. a custom or practice in effect, at the time of such activity, at the establishment or other place where such employee was employed, covering such activity, not inconsistent with a written or nonwritten contract, in effect at the time of such activity, between such employee, his agent, or collective-bargaining representative and his employer.

(b) For the purposes of subsection (a) of this section, an activity shall be considered as compensable under such contract provision or such custom or practice only when it was engaged in during the portion of the day with respect to which it was so made compensable.

(c) In the application of the minimum wage and overtime compensation provisions of the Fair Labor Standards Act of 1938, as amended, of the Walsh-Healey Act, or of the Bacon-Davis Act, in determining the time for which an employer employed an employee there shall be counted all that time, but only that time, during which the employee engaged in activities which were compensable within the meaning of subsections (a) and (b) of this section.

(d) No court of the United States, of any State, Territory, or possession of the United States, or of the District of Columbia, shall have jurisdiction of any action or proceeding, whether instituted prior to or on or after May 14, 1947, to enforce liability or impose punishment for or on account of the failure of the employer to pay minimum wages or overtime compensation under the Fair Labor Standards Act of 1938, as amended, under the Walsh-Healey Act, or under the Bacon-Davis Act, to the extent that such action or proceeding seeks to enforce any liability or impose any punishment with respect to an activity which was not compensable under subsections (a) and (b) of this section.

(e) No cause of action based on unpaid minimum wages, unpaid overtime compensation, or liquidated damages, under the Fair Labor Standards Act of 1938, as amended, the Walsh-Healey Act, or the Bacon-Davis Act, which accrued prior to May 14, 1947, or any interest in such case of action, shall hereafter be assignable, in whole or in part, to the extent that such cause of action is based on an activity which was not compensable within the meaning of subsections (a) and (b) of this section. (May 14, 1947, ch. 52, § 2, 61 Stat. 85.)

§ 253. Compromise of certain existing claims under the Fair Labor Standards Act of 1938, as amended, the Walsh-Healey Act, and the Bacon-Davis Act.

(a) Any cause of action under the Fair Labor Standards Act of 1938, as amended, the Walsh-Healey Act, or the Bacon-Davis Act, which accrued prior to May 14, 1947, or any action (whether instituted prior to or on or after May 14, 1947) to enforce such a cause of action, may hereafter be compromised in whole or in part, if there exists a bona fide dispute as to the amount payable by the employer to his employee; except that no such action or cause of action may be so compromised to the extent that such compromise is based on an hourly wage rate less than the minimum required under such Act, or on a payment for overtime at a rate less than one and one-half times such minimum hourly wage rate.

(b) Any employee may hereafter waive his right under the Fair Labor Standards Act of 1938, as amended, to liquidated damages, in whole or in part, with respect to activities engaged in prior to May 14, 1947.

(c) Any such compromise or waiver, in the absence of fraud or duress, shall, according to the terms thereof, be a complete satisfaction of such cause of action and a complete bar to any action based on such cause of action.

(d) The provisions of this section shall also be applicable to any compromise or waiver heretofore so made or given.

(c) As used in this section, the term "compromise" includes "adjustment", "settlement", and "release". (May 14, 1947, ch. 52, § 3, 61 Stat. 86.)

§ 254. Relief from certain future claims under the Fair Labor Standards Act of 1938, as amended, the Walsh-Healey Act, and the Bacon-Davis Act.

(a) Except as provided in subsection (b) of this section, no employer shall be subject to any liability or punishment under the Fair Labor Standards Act of 1938, as amended, the Walsh-Healey Act, or the Bacon-Davis Act, on account of the failure of such employer to pay an employee minimum wages, or to pay an employee overtime compensation, for or on account of any of the following activities of such employee engaged in on or after May 14, 1947—

1. walking, riding, or traveling to and from the actual place or performance of the principal activity or activities which such employee is employed to perform, and

2. activities which are preliminary to or postliminary to said principal activity or activities, which occur either prior to the time on any particular workday at which such employee commences, or subsequent to the time on any particular workday at which he ceases, such principal activity or activities.

(b) Notwithstanding the provisions of subsection (a) of this section which relieve an employer from liability and punishment with respect to an activity, the employer shall not be so relieved if such activity is compensable by either—

1. an express provision of a written or nonwritten contract in effect, at the time of such activity, between such employee, his agent, or collective-bargaining representative and his employer; or

2. a custom or practice in effect, at the time of such activity, at the establishment or other place where such employee is employed, covering such activity, not inconsistent with a written or nonwritten contract, in effect at the time of such activity, between such employee, his agent, or collective-bargaining representative and his employer.

(c) For the purposes of subsection (b) of this section, an activity shall be considered as compensable under such contract provision or such custom or practice only when it is engaged in during the portion of the day with respect to which it is so made compensable.

(d) In the application of the minimum wage and overtime compensation provisions of the Fair Labor Standards Act of 1938, as amended, of the Walsh-Healey Act, or of the Bacon Davis Act, in determining the time for which an employer employs an employee with respect to walking, riding, traveling, or other preliminary or postliminary activities described in subsection (a) of this section, there shall be counted all that time, but only that time, during which the employee engages in any such activity which is compensable within the meaning of subsections (b) and (c) of this section. (May 14, 1947, ch. 52, § 4, 61 Stat. 86.)

§ 255. Statute of limitations.

Any action commenced on or after May 14, 1947, to enforce any cause of action for unpaid minimum wages, unpaid overtime compensation, or liquidated damages, under the Fair Labor Standards Act of 1938, as amended, the Walsh-Healey Act, or the Bacon-Davis Act—

(a) if the cause of action accrues on or after May 14, 1947— may be commenced within two years after the cause of action accrued, and every such action shall be forever barred unless commenced within two years after the cause of action accrued, except that a cause of action arising out of a willful violation may be commenced within three years after the cause of action accrued;

(b) if the cause of action accrued prior to May 14, 1947— may be commenced within whichever of the following periods is the shorter: (1) two years after the cause of action accrued, or (2) the period prescribed by the applicable State statute of limitations; and, except as provided in paragraph (c) of this section, every such action shall be forever barred unless commenced within the shorter of such two periods;

(c) if the cause of action accrued prior to May 14, 1947, the action shall not be barred by paragraph (b) of this section if it is commenced within one hundred and twenty days after May 14, 1947 unless at the time commenced it is barred by an applicable State statute of limitations. (May 14, 1947, ch. 52, § 6, 61 Stat. 87; Sept. 23, 1966, Pub. L. 89–601, title VI, § 601 (b), 80 Stat. 844.)

(d) with respect to any cause of action brought under section 16(b) of the Fair Labor Standards Act of 1938 against a State or a political subdivision of a State in a district court of the United States on or before April 18, 1973, the running of the statutory periods of limitation shall be deemed suspended during the period beginning with the commencement of any such action and ending one hundred and eighty days after the effective date of the Fair Labor Standards Amendments of 1974, except that such suspension shall not be applicable if in such action judgment has been entered for the defendant on the grounds other than State immunity from Federal jurisdiction.

§ 256. Determination of commencement of future actions.

In determining when an action is commenced for the purposes of Section 255 of this title, an action commenced on or after

May 14, 1947 under the Fair Labor Standards Act of 1938, as amended, the Walsh-Healey Act, or the Bacon-Davis Act, shall be considered to be commenced on the date when the complaint is filed; except that in the case of a collective or class action instituted under the Fair Labor Standards Act of 1938, as amended, or the Bacon-Davis Act, it shall be considered to be commenced in the case of any individual claimant—

(a) on the date when the complaint is filed, if he is specifically named as a party plaintiff in the complaint and his written consent to become a party plaintiff is filed on such date in the court in which the action is brought; or

(b) if such written consent was not so filed or if his name did not so appear—on the subsequent date on which such written consent is filed in the court in which the action was commenced. (May 14, 1947, ch. 52, § 7, 61 Stat. 88.)

§ 257. Pending collective and representative actions.

The statute of limitations prescribed in section 255 (b) of this title shall also be applicable (in the case of a collective or representative action commenced prior to May 14, 1947 under the Fair Labor Standards Act of 1938, as amended) to an individual claimant who has not been specifically named as a party plaintiff to the action prior to the expiration of one hundred and twenty days after May 14, 1947. In the application of such statute of limitations such action shall be considered to have been commenced as to him when, and only when, his written consent to become a party plaintiff to the action is filed in the court in which the action was brought. (May 14, 1947, ch. 52, § 8, 61 Stat. 88.)

§ 258. Reliance on past administrative rulings, etc.

In any action or proceeding, commenced prior to or on or after May 14, 1947 based on any act or omission prior to May 14, 1947, no employer shall be subject to any liability or punishment for or on account of the failure of the employer to pay minimum wages or overtime compensation under the Fair Labor Standards Act of 1938, as amended, the Walsh-Healey Act, or the Bacon-Davis Act, if he pleads and proves that the act or omission complained of was in good faith in conformity with and in reliance on any administrative regulation, order, ruling, approval, or interpretation, of any agency of the United States, or any administrative practice or enforcement policy of any such agency with respect to the class of employers to which he belonged. Such a defense, if established, shall be a bar to the action or proceeding, notwithstanding that after such act or omission, such administrative regulation, order, ruling, approval, interpretation, practice, or enforcement policy is modified or rescinded or is determined by judicial authority to be invalid or of no legal effect. (May 14, 1947, ch. 52, § 9, 61 Stat. 88.)

§ 259. Reliance in future on administrative rulings, etc.

(a) In any action or proceeding based on any act or omission on or after May 14, 1947, no employer shall be subject to any liability or punishment for or on account of the failure of the employer to pay minimum wages or overtime compensation under the Fair Labor Standards Act of 1938, as amended, the Walsh-Healey Act, or the Bacon-Davis Act, if he pleads and proves that the act or omission complained of was in good faith in conformity with and in reliance on any written administrative regulation, order, ruling, approval, or interpretation, of the

agency of the United States specified in subsection (b) of this section, or any administrative practice or enforcement policy of such agency with respect to the class of employers to which he belonged. Such a defense, if established, shall be a bar to the action or proceeding, notwithstanding that after such act or omission, such administrative regulation, order, ruling, approval, interpretation, practice, or enforcement policy is modified or rescinded or is determined by judicial authority to be invalid or of no legal effect.

(b) The agency referred to in subsection (a) of this section shall be—

1. In the case of the Fair Labor Standards Act of 1938, as amended—the Administrator of the Wage and Hour Division of the Department of Labor:

2. In the case of the Walsh-Healy Act—the Secretary of Labor, or any Federal officer utilized by him in the administration of such Act; and

3. In the case of the Bacon-Davis Act—the Secretary of Labor.

(May 14, 1947, ch. 52, § 10, 61 Stat. 89.)

§ 260. Liquidated damages.

In any action commenced prior to or on or after the date of the enactment of this Act to recover unpaid minimum wages, unpaid overtime compensation, or liquidated damages, under the Fair Labor Standards Act of 1938, as amended, if the employer shows to the satisfaction of the court that the act or omission giving rise to such action was in good faith and that he had reasonable grounds for believing that his act or omission was not a violation of the Fair Labor Standards Act of 1938, as amended, the court may, in its sound discretion, award no liquidated damages or award any amount thereof not to exceed the amount specified in section 16 of such Act.

§ 261. Applicability of "area of production" regulations.

No employer shall be subject to any liability or punishment under the Fair Labor Standards Act of 1938, as amended, on account of the failure of such employer to pay an employee minimum wages, or to pay an employee overtime compensation, for or on account of an activity engaged in by such employee prior to December 26, 1946, if such employer—

1. was not so subject by reason of the definition of an "area of production", by a regulation of the Administrator of the Wage and Hour Division of the Department of Labor, which regulation was applicable at the time of performance of the activity even though at that time the regulation was invalid; or

2. would not have been so subject if the regulation signed on December 18, 1946 (Federal Register, Vol. 11, p. 14648) had been in force on and after October 24, 1938.

(May 14, 1947, ch. 52, § 12, 61 Stat. 89.)

§ 262. Definitions.

(a) When the terms "employer", "employee", and "wage" are used in this chapter in relation to the Fair Labor Standards Act of 1938, as amended, they shall have the same meaning as when used in such Act of 1938.

(b) When the term "employer" is used in this chapter in relation to the Walsh-Healey Act or Bacon-Davis Act it shall mean the contractor or subcontractor covered by such Act.

(c) When the term "employee" is used in this chapter in relation to the Walsh-Healey Act or the Bacon-Davis Act it shall mean any individual employed by the contractor or subcontractor covered by such Act in the performance of his contract or subcontract.

(d) The term "Walsh-Healey Act" means sections 35 to 45 of Title 41; and the term "Bacon-Davis Act" means sections 276a to 276a-5 of Title 40.

(e) As used in section 255 of this title the term "State" means any State of the United States or the District of Columbia or any Territory or possession of the United States. (May 14, 1947, ch. 52, § 13, 61 Stat. 90.)

Equal Pay Act of 1963

SUMMARY AND DESCRIPTION

The Fair Labor Standards Act, as amended by the Equal Pay Act of 1963, prohibits employers from discriminating on the basis of sex in the payment of wages for equal work. The equal pay standard applies to employees subject to the minimum wage requirements of the Act and employees who would be subject except for their status as executive, administrative, or professional employees.

The Equal Pay Act requires the employer to pay equal wages within the establishment to men and women doing substantially equal work on jobs requiring equal skill, effort, and responsibility which are performed under similar working conditions.

The Act does not prohibit payment of wages at lower rates to one sex than the other for equal work where the wage differential is based on a seniority system, a merit system, a system measuring earnings by quantity or quality of production, or on any other factor other than sex.

An employer who is paying a wage differential in violation of the equal pay provisions of the Act may not reduce the wage rate of any employee in order to comply with these provisions. Wages withheld in violation of the equal pay provisions have the status of unpaid minimum wages or unpaid overtime compensation under the Act, and back wages due under the equal pay provisions are subject to the same methods of recovery as any other wages due under the Act.

The law prohibits any labor organization, or its agents, representing employees of an employer having employees subject to the minimum wage provisions of the Act, from causing or attempting to cause the employer to discriminate against an employee in violation of the equal pay provisions.

For further information write to: Employment Standards Administration, Wage and Hour Division, U.S. Department of Labor, Washington, D.C. 20210.

Civil Rights Act of 1964

SUMMARY AND DESCRIPTION

Title VI

Title VI of the Civil Rights Act stipulates: "No person in the United States shall, on ground of race, color, or national origin be excluded from participation in, be denied the benefits of, or be subjected to discrimination under any program or activity receiving Federal financial assistance."

In essence, Title VI forbids discrimination on the basis of race, color, or national origin in any Federal or federally funded program. Each Federal agency sets up its own procedures and regulations to govern the implementation of these nondiscriminatory provisions. Title 29, Part 31 of the Labor Department Rules and Regulations sets up the provisions for the Department's enforcement of Title VI. The Office of Equal Opportunity oversees the efforts of the Department in the enforcement of these regulations. The Regional Offices of the Department under the jurisdiction of the Regional Manpower Administrators handle the day by day complaint investigation and compliance review evaluatory functions.

Title VI provides that voluntary efforts to achieve compliance should always precede mandatory legal steps.

Before an order suspending, terminating, or refusing to grant Federal financial assistance shall become effective, the following steps must have been taken:

1. The agency must advise the applicant or recipient of the failure to comply and of the agency's determination that compliance cannot be secured by voluntary means.

2. There must be an express finding on the record of a failure to comply after an opportunity for hearing.

3. There must be approval of the action terminating or suspending the Federal assistance by the head of the agency.

In any action ordering a suspension, termination, or refusal to grant Federal financial assistance, the head of the agency must file a full written report of the circumstances and grounds for such action with the Congressional committees that have jurisdiction over the program involved. Thirty days must have expired after the filing of the report before the action becomes effective.

Title VII

Title VII of the Civil Rights Act of 1964, "Equal Employment Opportunity," prohibits discrimination based on race, color, religion, sex, and national origin in all terms, conditions, and privileges of employment by employers, employment agencies, and labor unions.

Title VII established the Equal Employment Opportunity Commission (EEOC) to administer the Act. The Commission is composed of five members, serving five-year terms, who are appointed by the President, with the advice and consent of the Senate. The President designates one of the five Commissioners as Chairman, and another as Vice Chairman.

Among the principal operating units within the Commission are the following offices:

Compliance, which includes the Conciliation Division

General Counsel

Office of Technical Assistance

Office of Research

State and Community Affairs

Legislative Affairs

Public Affairs

The EEOC administers the Act through its headquarters office in Washington, D.C., and 13 regional offices located in major cities throughout the country. Each of the Commission's regional offices has an attorney who is available to assist private attorneys engaged in Title VII litigation.

Filing of Charges

Aggrieved Persons If a person believes that he or she is the victim of discrimination by an employer, employment agency, or labor union, that person may file a written charge or complaint at the Commission's Washington, D.C. headquarters or at any one of the regional offices located in major cities throughout the country.

A charge of employment discrimination may be filed by any person aggrieved by the conduct involved or by one of the EEOC's five Commissioners. A labor union which represents the bargaining unit involved has standing as an aggrieved person to file a charge of employment discrimination against the employer of that unit.

Instructions and charge forms are available at the Equal Employment Opportunity Commission, 1800 G Street, NW., Washington, D.C 20506, and at regional offices. While the use of the EEOC charge form is recommended, it is not required. A charging party may file his complaint in the form of a letter or written statement, which identifies the parties and describes generally the alleged unlawful conduct or practices.

The Act has certain requirements with regard to timeliness. Accordingly, it is essential that aggrieved persons file their charges within 90 days after the alleged unlawful employment practice occurred.

In those States that have a State fair employment practices commission with authority to provide relief in cases of employment discrimination, the aggrieved person must file a charge of discrimination with the State agency prior to filing a charge with the EEOC. In such a case the Federal charge should be filed with the EEOC within two hundred and ten days after the alleged unlawful employment practice occurred, or within thirty days after receiving notice that the State agency has terminated the proceedings, whichever is earlier.

Where an aggrieved person files a charge with the EEOC without first filing with the appropriate State agency, the EEOC will notify the State agency, and upon request afford them a reasonable time to act under the State law.

Commissioner's Charges An individual or a group of individuals may not themselves wish to file charges of employment discrimination because they want to remain anonymous; they are not themselves aggrieved by the conduct involved; or for some other reason. They may nonetheless bring a case of employment discrimination to the attention of the Commission. In such instances, the person or group involved may write to any one of the EEOC's five Commissioners, requesting that he file a Commissioner's Charge. At the discretion of the Commissioner, a Commissioner's Charge may then be filed. This charge would also have to be filed within ninety days after the alleged unlawful employment practice occurred.

Coverage

Inclusions Title VII prohibits discrimination by:

a. Employers, who have 8 or more employees.

b. Employment agencies, which regularly procure employees for an employer who is covered by Title VII. Covered employment agencies include the United States Employment Service and the system of State and local employment services receiving Federal assistance.

c. Labor unions, which have 8 or more members, or which operate a hiring hall or office.

Exclusions Certain categories of employers are excluded from the coverage of the Act, either completely or with regard to certain types of employees. Among the principal exemptions are the following:

a. Religious organizations, with respect to the employment of individuals whose work is connected with the organization's religious activities.

b. Educational institutions with religious affiliation, on the basis of religion with regard to all their employees.

Unlawful Employment Practices

Title VII prohibits discrimination in all terms, conditions, and privileges of employment. The Act covers the entire range of the employee/employer/employment agency/ union relationship. Thus, employees are entitled to be free of unlawful discrimination with regard to recruitment; classified advertising; job classification; hire; utilization of physical facilities; transfer; promotion; discharge; wages and salaries; seniority lines; testing; insurance coverage; pension and retirement benefits; referral to jobs; union membership; etc.

In addition, it is unlawful for an employer, employment agency, or labor union to discharge, discipline, harass, or otherwise retaliate against any person for filing a charge; for participating in an EEOC investigation, proceeding, or hearing; or for opposing any employment practice prohibited by Title VII.

Posters

Every employer, employment agency, and labor union covered by the Act is required to post in conspicuous places a notice setting forth a summary of Title VII and information about the filing of charges.

Compliance

Investigation, Decision, and Conciliation When an aggrieved person or a Commissioner files a charge of discrimination, the Commission conducts an investigation of that charge. In connection with its investigation, the Commission may require the testimony of witnesses under oath and the production of relevant documentary evidence. At the conclusion of the investigation, the Commission issues a decision determining whether or not there is reasonable cause to believe that the charge is true. If the Commission finds reasonable cause to believe that the charge is true, it endeavors to eliminate the alleged unlawful employment practice by the informal methods of conference, conciliation, and persuasion.

Enforcement

By Charging Party If within thirty days after a charge is filed or the time required after a charge is filed first in a local agency the Commission is unable to secure voluntary compliance with the Act through conciliation, it will so notify the parties. However the Commission may extend the period to no more than 60 days if it determines further efforts to secure voluntary compliance are warranted. Within 30 days after the receipt of such notice, the charging party or parties may institute suit in the appropriate federal district court. The charging party may institute such an action whether or not the Commission has found reasonable cause to believe that a violation of the Act has occurred, provided that the 30-day notice has been received.

The charging party or parties need not await the completion of the EEOC's case processing procedures prior to the institution of suit.

With regard to a civil action instituted under Title VII, the Act provides that the court, at its discretion, may appoint an attorney for the complainant and authorize the commencement of the action without the payment of fees costs, or security. At the conclusion of suit, the court may, in its discretion award a reasonable attorney's fee to the successful party.

The Act empowers the courts to order such relief as may be appropriate to remedy the unlawful employment practices found. Accordingly the court may require the

reinstatement or hiring of employees, the award of backpay, the elimination of discriminatory job classification and seniority systems, etc. Inasmuch as class relief is appropriate under Title VII, the relief ordered may affect not only the complaining parties but all other persons in the class.

By Attorney General Where there is a pattern of practice of employment discrimination, not only the charging party but also the Attorney General of the United States has the power to bring suit in the appropriate Federal district court. At the discretion of the court, the Attorney General may, moreover, intervene in suits brought by charging parties if he certifies that the case is of general public importance. The EEOC has the authority to refer matters to the Attorney General with recommendations for the institution of suits involving a pattern of practice of discrimination and for intervention in civil actions brought by aggrieved persons.

Other EEOC Activities: Research, Hearings, Reporting System, Cooperation with State Agencies Technical Assistance.

Some of the EEOC's most significant contributions to the understanding and elimination of employment discrimination have occurred not in the context of case processing but in the performance of its broader obligations under the Act, in meeting its responsibilities for dealing with employment discrimination on a "wholesale" basis, the EEOC has conducted and financed research and held hearings on significant occupational categories and major industries in areas where such occupations and industries are concentrated. Thus, the EEOC financed a report on the rubber industry in Ohio issued in September 1967; and conducted hearings on the textile industry in North and South Carolina in January 1967, in white-collar employment in New York City in January 1968, in the aerospace and communications industries in Los Angeles in March 1969, and in a number of industries, such as petroleum and chemicals in Houston in June 1970.

Beginning in 1966 for employers and 1967 for labor unions and joint labor-management apprenticeship committees, the EEOC has required annual reports on the employment of members of minority groups and women, with information on the types of jobs they hold, their union membership, their participation in job referral systems and apprenticeship programs, etc. In 1969, the EEOC published nationwide employment statistics on employment patterns as revealed by the 1966 employer reports in EQUAL EMPLOYMENT OPPORTUNITY REPORT NO. 1, *Job Patterns for Minorities and Women in Private Industry*, 1966 (1969).

The research activities of the EEOC are designed to improve the patterns of minority groups and women's

employment. For this reason, the Commission makes available, within the confidentiality restrictions of the Act, the information gained through research. Thus, a large number of State and local fair employment practices agencies have access to the reports filed with the Commission through data-sharing agreements.

The relationship between the EEOC and State and local anti-discrimination agencies goes far beyond the sharing of research information. Title VII gives the EEOC both the authority and the duty to work closely with and through these agencies to accomplish the common goal of eliminating employment discrimination. In this connection, the Commission plans and administers a program of grants and contracts to such agencies for services rendered to assist the EEOC in carrying out its responsibilities. The Commission focuses on "affirmative action" grants, whose purpose is to place minority group members and women in jobs previously unavailable to them.

The Act provides that the EEOC may furnish to those subject to the Act such "technical assistance" as they may request to further their compliance with Title VII. Accordingly, employers, employment agencies, and labor unions may call upon the resources and personnel of the Commission to assist them in voluntarily ending past patterns of discrimination, instituting fair employment practices, and developing "affirmative action programs" designed to increase opportunities for minorities and women.

In addition to responding to requests for aid, the EEOC also takes the initiative in developing key programs to eliminate discrimination. Some of these programs are directed at specific industries and unions, some concentrate on a particular geographical area, and some operate across the board with regard to one or more aspects of the employment process. Thus, Commission personnel have met with representatives of the drug and utilities industries; have worked with unions in expanding the "Operation Outreach" program, which seeks to provide opportunities for apprenticeship training for minority group youth; and have developed the "New Plants" program, designed to ensure the establishment of fair employment practices when a new plant is opened.

For further information write to: Office of the General Counsel, Equal Employment Opportunity Commission, 1800 G Street, N.W., Washington, D.C. 20506.

Urban Mass Transportation Act (Pertinent Provision)

SUMMARY AND DESCRIPTION

The Urban Mass Transportation Act of 1964 establishes a program to provide Federal assistance to States and local governments and agencies to finance improvements in urban mass transportation systems.

Section 3(e) requires that no Federal assistance may be provided unless the Secretary of Labor has certified that the requirements of Section 13(c) of the Act have been complied with.

Section 13(c) provides that the Secretary of Labor shall determine that fair and equitable arrangements are made to protect the interests of employees affected by such assistance.

Such protective arrangements shall include such provisions as may be necessary for:

1. The preservation of rights, privileges, and benefits (including continuation of pension rights and benefits) under existing collective bargaining agreements or otherwise;

2. The continuation of collective bargaining rights;

3. The protection of individual employees against a worsening of their positions with respect to their employment;

4. Assurance of employment to employees of acquired mass transportation systems and priority of re-employment of employees terminated or laid off;

5. Paid training or retraining programs.

Such arrangements shall include provisions protecting individual employees against a worsening of their positions with respect to their employment. The contract for the granting of any such assistance shall specify the terms and conditions of the protective arrangements.

In addition, section 13(a) makes the terms of the Davis-Bacon Act applicable to construction work assisted under this law.

For further information write to: Urban Mass Transportation Administration, Department of Transportation, 400 Seventh Street, S.W., Washington, D.C. 20590.

Implementation of Mass Transportation Bargaining Statutes

The following table indicates the provisions of the laws of those states which have statutorily guaranteed the collective bargaining rights of public mass transportation employees. Those rights are generally afforded to employees of formerly private systems which have been acquired by public bodies. The substantive protections set forth in these laws are reflective of the provisions in Federal statutes, particularly Section 13 (c) of the Urban Mass Transportation Act of 1964, as amended, 49 U.S.C. 1609(c).

	Alabama	Alameda	S. Cal. RTD	San Diego	W. Bay RT	Marin County	Stockton	Colorado	Connecticut	Delaware	District of Columbia[5]	Illinois (Chicago)	Indiana	Kentucky	Louisiana	Maine
Year	1971	1955	1964	1965	—	1964	1963	—	1961	—	1966	1945	1965	1970	1964	1966
Citation		Pub. Util. C. Sec. 25051	Pub. Util. C. Sec. 30750	Pub. Util. C. Sec. 90300		Pub. Util. C. Sec. 70120	Pub. Util. C. Sec. 50120	CRS 1963 Sec. 80-4	C.G.S.A. Sec. 7-273	2 Del. C. Sec. 1613	P.L. 89-774	S.H.A. Ch. III 2/3, Sec. 328a	Burns Ind. A. 19-5-2-23		23 West's LSARA 890	30 M.R.S.A. Sec. 4979
Continuation of Existing Bargaining Rights	X	X	X	X	X	X	X	X	X	X	X	X	X	X	X	X
Continuation of Existing Rights, Privileges, and Benefits	X							X	X	X	X	X	X		X	
Save Harmless Clause ("No Worsening of Conditions")	X		X	X	X	X	X		X	X	X			X		X
Protection of Employees' Seniority Rights	X	X		X				X	X	X	X	X		X	X	
Guarantee of Employment or Priority in Hiring	X	X	X	X	X	X	X	X	X	X	X	X	X	X	X	X
Retraining (if needed)	X							X				X				
Exclusive Administrative and Executive Employees From Act	X								X			X			X	X
Exclusion of Employees from Civil Service System	X															
Mediation of Bargaining Impasses								X								
Arbitration of Bargaining Impasses:	X	X	X	2	2	2	X	X	X	X		X			X	X
Tripartite	X	X	X	X	X	X	X						X		X	
Within Specified Time Limits				3	3	3										
Costs Shared Equally	X	X	X	X	X	X	X						X		X	
Strikes—Prohibited								X	X							
Strikes—Permitted								X								
Union Security Provided	1		1	1	1	1									1	

(Table continued on p. 4-78)

National Foundation on the Arts and Humanities Act—Secs. 5(j)–(k)

EXCERPT (LABOR STANDARDS APPLICABLE TO GRANTS-IN-AID BY NATIONAL ENDOWMENT FOR THE ARTS)

(j) It shall be a condition of the receipt of any grant under this section that the group or individual of exceptional talent or the State or State agency receiving such grant furnish adequate assurances to the Secretary of Labor that (1) all professional performers and related or supporting professional personnel (other than laborers and mechanics with respect to whom labor standards are prescribed in subsection (k) of this section) employed on projects or productions which are financed a whole or in part under this section will be paid, without subsequent deduction or rebate on any account, not less than the minimum compensation as determined by the Secretary of Labor to be the prevailing minimum compensation for persons employed in similar activities; and (2) no part of any project or production which is financed in whole or in part under this section will be performed or engaged in under working conditions which are unsanitary or hazardous or dangerous to the health and safety of the employees engaged in such project or production. Compliance with the safety and sanitary laws of the State in which the performance or part thereof is to take place shall be prima facie evidence of compliance. The Secretary of Labor shall have the authority to prescribe standards, regulations, and procedures as he may deem necessary or appropriate to carry out the provisions of this subsection.

(k) It shall be a condition of the receipt of any grant under this section that the group or individual of exceptional talent

	Maryland (Baltimore), Ann. Code 1957 Art. 64B	Massachusetts (Boston), M.G.L.A. Chap. 161B	Michigan, M.C.L.A. Sec. 124.413	Minnesota, M.S.A. Sec. 473.405	New Jersey, N.J.S.A. 40:37A-92	Ohio, R.C. Sec. 306.04	Oregon, Ore. Const. Art. XI, Sec. 13	Pennsylvania (Counties), 55 PPS Sec. 563.2	Pennsylvania (Cities), 53 PPS Sec. 39951	Rhode Island, G.L. Sec. 39-18-17	Tennessee, T.C.A. Sec. 6-3802	Utah, U.C.A. 1953 Sec. 11-20	Virginia, Va. C. Sec. 15.1-1357	Washington, Sec. 35.58.265 RCW	West Virginia, W. Va. C. Sec. 8-27-21	Wisconsin, W.S.A. 59.969
Year	1969	1973	1967	1969	1968	1970	1966	1959	1967	1964	1971	1969	1968	1965	1968	1973
Continuation of Existing Bargaining Rights	X	X	X	X	X	X		X	X	X	X	X	X	X	X	X
Continuation of Existing Rights, Privileges, and Benefits	X	X	X		X	X	X	X	X	X	X	X			X	X
Save Harmless Clause ("No Worsening of Conditions")	X	X	X	X	X	X		X	X	X	X	X	X	X	X	X
Protection of Employees' Seniority Rights	X	X	X	X	X			X	X			X	X	X		
Guarantee of Employment or Priority in Hiring	X	X	X	X	X			X	X	X	X	X	X	X	X	X
Retraining (if needed)	X	X		X							X	X	X		X	X
Exclusive Administrative and Executive Employees From Act	X			X	X		X	X								
Exclusion of Employees from Civil Service System																
Mediation of Bargaining Impasses																
Arbitration of Bargaining Impasses:	X	X		X	X	X		X	X	X	X	X	X		X	X
Tripartite	X				4			X	X	X	X	X	4		X	4
Within Specified Time Limits																
Costs Shared Equally	X			X				X	X	X		X			X	
Strikes—Prohibited	X											X				
Strikes—Permitted				X												
Union Security Provided																

1—dues deduction
2—arbitration or fact finding
3—for fact finding
4—single or tripartite
5—Washington Metropolitan Area Transportation Authority

or the State or State agency receiving such grant furnish adequate assurances to the Secretary of Labor that all laborers and mechanics employed by contractors or subcontractors on construction projects assisted under this section shall be paid wages at rates not less than those prevailing on similar construction in the locality as determined by the Secretary of Labor in accordance with the Davis-Bacon Act, as amended (40 U.S.C. 276a-276-5). The Secretary of Labor shall have with respect to the labor standards specified in this subsection the authority and functions set forth in Reorganization Plan Numbered 14 of 1950 (15 F.R. 3176; 5 U.S.C. 133z-15 and section 2 of the Act of June 13, 1934, as amended (40 U.S.C. 276c).

For further information write to: Employment Standards Administration, Wage and Hour Division U.S. Department of Labor, Washington, D.C. 20210.

Executive Order 11246—Equal Employment Opportunity (as Amended)

Under and by virtue of the authority vested in me as President of the United States by the Constitution and statutes of the United States, it is ordered as follows:

PART I—NONDISCRIMINATION IN GOVERNMENT EMPLOYMENT

Editorial Note: Part I as amended by EO. 11375, 32 F.R. 14303, Oct. 17, 1967, was superseded by E.O. 11478, 34 F.R. 12985, Aug. 12, 1969.

PART II—NONDISCRIMINATION IN EMPLOYMENT BY GOVERNMENT CONTRACTORS AND SUBCONTRACTORS

Subpart A—Duties of the Secretary of Labor

SECTION 201. The Secretary of Labor shall be responsible for the administration of Parts II and III of this Order and shall adopt such rules and regulations and issue such orders as he deems necessary and appropriate to achieve the purposes thereof.

Subpart B—Contractors' Agreements

SECTION 202. Except in contracts exempted in accordance with Section 204 of this Order, all Government contracting agencies shall include in every Government contract hereafter entered into the following provisions:

"During the performance of this contract, the contractor agrees as follows:

"(1) The contractor will not discriminate against any employee or applicant for employment because of race, color, religion, sex, or national origin. The contractor will take affirmative action to ensure that applicants are employed, and that employees are treated during employment, without regard to their race, color, religion, sex or national origin. Such action shall include, but not be limited to the following: employment, upgrading, demotion, or transfer; recruitment or recruitment advertising; layoff or termination; rates of pay or other forms of compensation; and selection for training, including apprenticeship. The contractor agrees to post in conspicuous places, available to employees and applicants for employment, notices to be provided by the contracting officer setting forth the provisions of this nondiscrimination clause.

"(2) The contractor will, in all solicitations or advertisements for employees placed by or on behalf of the contractor, state that all qualified applicants will receive consideration for employment without regard to race, color, religion, sex or national origin."

[Paragraphs (1) and (2) of the contract revised by E.O. 11375, 32 F.R. 14304, Oct. 17, 1967. Effective one year after October 13, 1967]

"(3) The contractor will send to each labor union or representative of workers with which he has a collective bargaining agreement or other contract or understanding, a notice, to be provided by the agency contracting officer, advising the labor union or workers' representative of the contractor's commitments under Section 202 of Executive Order No. 11246 of September 24, 1965, and shall post copies of the notice in conspicuous places available to employees and applicants for employment.

"(4) The contractor will comply with all provisions of Executive Order No. 11246 of Sept. 24, 1965, and of the rules, regulations, and relevant orders of the Secretary of Labor.

"(5) The contractor will furnish all information and reports required by Executive Order No. 11246 of September 24, 1965, and by the rules, regulations, and orders of the Secretary of Labor, or pursuant thereto, and will permit access to his books, records, and accounts by the contracting agency and the Secretary of Labor for purposes of investigation to ascertain compliance with such rules, regulations and orders.

"(6) In the event of the contractor's noncompliance with the nondiscrimination clauses of this contract or with any of such rules, regulations, or orders, this contract may be cancelled, terminated or suspended in whole or in part and the contractor may be declared ineligible for further Government contracts in accordance with procedures authorized in Executive Order No. 11246 of Sept. 24, 1965, and such other sanctions may be imposed and remedies invoked as provided in Executive Order No. 11246 of September 24, 1965, or by rule, regulation, or order of the Secretary of Labor, or as otherwise provided by law.

"(7) The contractor will include the provisions of Paragraphs (1) through (7) in every subcontract or purchase order unless exempted by rules, regulations, or orders of the Secretary of labor issued pursuant to Section 204 of Executive Order No. 11246 of Sept. 24, 1965, so that such provisions will be binding upon each subcontractor or vendor. The contractor will take such action with respect to any subcontract or purchase order as the contracting agency may direct as a means of enforcing such provisions including sanctions for noncompliance: *Provided, however,* That in the event the contractor becomes involved in, or is threatened with, litigation with a subcontractor or vendor as a result of such direction by the contracting agency, the contractor may request the United States to enter into such litigation to protect the interests of the United States."

SECTION 203. (a) Each contractor having a contract containing the provisions prescribed in Section 202 shall file, and shall cause each of his subcontractors to file, Compliance Reports with the contracting agency or the Secretary of Labor as may be directed. Compliance Reports shall be filed within such times and shall contain such information as to the practices, policies, programs, and employment policies, programs, and employment statistics of the contractor and each subcontractor, and shall be in such form, as the Secretary of Labor may prescribe.

(b) Bidders or prospective contractors or subcontractors may be required to state whether they have participated in any previous contract subject to the provisions of this Order, or any preceding similar Executive order, and in that event to submit, on behalf of themselves and their proposed subcontractors. Compliance Reports prior to or as an initial part of their bid or negotiation of a contract.

(c) Whenever the contractor or subcontractor has a collective bargaining agreement or other contract or understanding with a labor union or an agency referring workers or providing or supervising apprenticeship or training for such workers, the Compliance Report shall include such information as to such labor union's or agency's practices and policies affecting compliance as the Secretary of Labor may prescribe: *Provided,* That to the extent such information is within the exclusive possession of a labor union or an agency referring workers or providing or supervising apprenticeship or training and such labor union or agency shall refuse to furnish such information to the contractor, the contractor shall so certify to the contracting agency as part of its Compliance Report and shall set forth what efforts he has made to obtain such information.

(d) The contracting agency or the Secretary of Labor may direct that any bidder or prospective contractor or subcontractor shall submit, as part of his Compliance Report, a statement in writing, signed by an authorized officer or agent on behalf of any labor union or any agency referring workers or providing or supervising apprenticeship or other training, with which the bidder or prospective contractor deals, with supporting information, to the effect that the signer's practices and policies do not discriminate on the grounds of race, color, religion, sex or national origin, and that the signer either will affirmatively cooperate in the implementation of the policy and provisions of this order or that it consents and agrees that recruitment, employment, and the terms and conditions of employment under the proposed contract shall be in accordance with the purposes and provisions of the order. In the event that the union, or the agency shall refuse to execute such a statement, the Compliance Report shall so certify and set forth what efforts have been made to secure such a statement and such additional factual material as the contracting agency or the Secretary of Labor may require.

[Paragraph (d) revised by E.O. 11375, 32 F.R. 14304, Oct. 17, 1967. Effective one year after October 13, 1967]

SECTION 204. The Secretary of Labor may, when he deems that special circumstances in the national interest so require, exempt a contracting agency from the requirement of including any or all of the provisions of Section 202 of this Order in any specific contract, subcontract, or purchase order. The Secretary of Labor may, by rule or regulation, also exempt certain classes of contracts, subcontracts, or purchase orders (1) whenever work is to be or has been performed outside the United States and no recruitment of workers within the limits of the United States is involved; (2) for standard commercial supplies or raw materials; (3) involving less than specified amounts of money or specified numbers of workers; or (4) to the extent that they involve subcontracts below a specified tier. The Secretary of Labor may also provide, by rule, regulation, or order, for the exemption of facilities of a contractor which are in all respects separate and distinct from activities of the contractor related to the performance of the contract: *Provided,* That such an exemption will not interfere with or impede the effectuation of the purposes of this Order: *And provided further,* that in the absence of such an exemption all facilities shall be covered by the provisions of this Order.

Subpart C—Powers and Duties of the Secretary of Labor and the Contracting Agencies

SECTION 205. Each contracting agency shall be primarily responsible for obtaining compliance with the rules, regulations, and orders of the Secretary of Labor with respect to contracts entered into by such agency or its contractors. All contracting agencies shall comply with the rules of the Secretary of Labor in discharging their primary responsibility for securing compliance with the provisions of contracts and otherwise with the terms of this Order and of the rules, regulations, and orders of the Secretary of Labor issued pursuant to this Order. They are directed to cooperate with the Secretary of Labor and to furnish the Secretary of Labor such information and assistance as he may require in the performance of his functions under this Order. They are further directed to appoint or designate, from among the agency's personnel, compliance officers. It shall be the duty of such officers to seek compliance with the objectives of this Order by conference, conciliation, mediation, or persuasion.

SECTION 206. (a) The Secretary of Labor may investigate the employment practices of any Government contractor or subcontractor, or initiate such investigation by the appropriate contracting agency, to determine whether or not the contractual provisions specified in Section 202 of this Order have been violated. Such investigation shall be conducted in accordance with the procedures established by the Secretary of Labor and the investigating agency shall report to the Secretary of Labor any action taken or recommended.

(b) The Secretary of Labor may receive and investigate or cause to be investigated complaints by employees or prospective employees of a Government contractor or subcontractor which allege discrimination contrary to the contractual provisions specified in Section 202 of this Order. If this investigation is conducted for the Secretary of Labor by a contracting agency, that agency shall report to the Secretary what action has been taken or is recommended with regard to such complaints.

SECTION 207. The Secretary of Labor shall use his best efforts, directly and through contracting agencies, other interested Federal, State, and local agencies, contractors, and all other available instrumentalities to cause any labor union engaged in work under Government contracts or any agency referring workers or providing or supervising apprenticeship or training for or in the course of such work to cooperate in the implementation of the purposes of this Order. The Secretary of Labor shall, in appropriate cases, notify the Equal Employment Opportunity Commission, the Department of Justice, or other appropriate Federal agencies whenever it has reason to believe that the practices of any such labor organization or agency violate Title VI or Title VII of the Civil Rights Act of 1964 or other provision of Federal law.

SECTION 208. (a) The Secretary of Labor, or any agency, officer, or employee in the executive branch of the Government designated by rule, regulation, or order of the Secretary, may hold such hearings, public or private, as the Secretary may deem advisable for compliance, enforcement, or educational purposes.

(b) The Secretary of Labor may hold, or cause to be held, hearings in accordance with Subsection (a) of this Section prior to imposing, ordering, or recommending the imposition of penalties and sanctions under this Order. No order for debarment of any contractor from further Government contracts under Section 209(a) (6) shall be made without affording the contractor an opportunity for a hearing.

Subpart D—Sanctions and Penalties

SECTION 209. (a) In accordance with such rules, regulations, or orders as the Secretary of Labor may issue or adopt, the Secretary or the appropriate contracting agency may:

(1) Publish, or cause to be published, the names of contractors or unions which it has concluded have complied or have failed to comply with the provisions of this Order or of the rules, regulations, and orders of the Secretary of Labor.

(2) Recommend to the Department of Justice that, in cases in which there is substantial or material violation or the threat of substantial or material violation of the contractual provisions set forth in Section 202 of this Order, appropriate proceedings be brought to enforce those provisions, including the enjoining, within the limitations of applicable law, of organizations, individuals, or groups who prevent directly or indirectly, or seek to prevent directly or indirectly, compliance with the provisions of this Order.

(3) Recommend to the Equal Employment Opportunity Commission or the Department of Justice that appropriate proceedings be instituted under Title VII of the Civil Rights Act of 1964.

(4) Recommend to the Department of Justice that criminal proceedings be brought for the furnishing of false information to any contracting agency or to the Secretary of Labor as the case may be.

(5) Cancel, terminate, suspend, or cause to be cancelled, terminated, or suspended, any contract, or any portion or portions thereof, for failure of the contractor or subcontractor to comply with the nondiscrimination provisions of the contract. Contracts may be cancelled, terminated, or suspended absolutely or continuance of contracts may be conditioned upon a program for future compliance approved by the contracting agency.

(6) Provide that any contracting agency shall refrain from entering into further contracts, or extensions or other modifications of existing contracts, with any noncomplying contractor, until such contractor has satisfied the Secretary of Labor that such contractor has established and will carry out personnel and employment policies in compliance with the provisions of this Order.

(b) Under rules and regulations prescribed by the Secretary of Labor, each contracting agency shall make reasonable efforts within a reasonable time limitation to secure compliance with the contract provisions of this Order by methods of conference, conciliation, mediation, and persuasion before proceedings shall be instituted under Subsection (a) (2) of this Section, or before a contract shall be cancelled or terminated in whole or in part under Subsection (a)(5) of this Section for failure of a contractor or subcontractor to comply with the contract provisions of this Order.

SECTION 210. Any contracting agency taking any action authorized by this Subpart, whether on its own motion, or as directed by the Secretary of Labor, or under the rules and regulations of the Secretary, shall promptly notify the Secretary of such action. Whenever the Secretary of Labor makes a determination under this Section, he shall promptly notify the appropriate contracting agency of the action recommended. The agency shall take such action and shall report the results thereof to the Secretary of Labor within such time as the Secretary shall specify.

SECTION 211. If the Secretary shall so direct, contracting agencies shall not enter into contracts with any bidder or prospective contractor unless the bidder or prospective contractor has satisfactorily complied with the provisions of this Order or submits a program for compliance acceptable to the Secretary of Labor or, if the Secretary so authorizes, to the contracting agency.

SECTION 212. Whenever a contracting agency cancels or terminates a contract, or whenever a contractor has been debarred from further Government contracts, under Section 209 (a)(6) because of noncompliance with the contract provisions with regard to nondiscrimination, the Secretary of Labor, or the contracting agency involved, shall promptly notify the Comptroller General of the United States. Any such debarment may be rescinded by the Secretary of Labor or by the contracting agency which imposed the sanction.

Subpart E—Certificates of Merit

SECTION 213. The Secretary of Labor may provide for issuance of a United States Government Certificate of Merit to employers or labor unions, or other agencies which are or may hereafter be engaged in work under Government contracts, if the Secretary is satisfied that the personnel and employment practices of the employer, or that the personnel, training, apprenticeship, membership, grievance and representation, upgrading, and other practices and policies of the labor union or other agency conform to the purposes and provisions of this Order.

SECTION 214. Any Certificate of Merit may at any time be suspended or revoked by the Secretary of Labor if the holder thereof, in the judgment of the Secretary, has failed to comply with the provisions of this Order.

SECTION 215. The Secretary of Labor may provide for the exemption of any employer, labor union, or other agency from any reporting requirements imposed under or pursuant to this Order if such employer, labor union, or other agency has been awarded a Certificate of Merit which has not been suspended or revoked.

PART III—NONDISCRIMINATION PROVISIONS IN FEDERALLY ASSISTED CONSTRUCTION CONTRACTS

SECTION 301. Each executive department and agency which administers a program involving Federal financial assistance shall require as a condition for the approval of any grant, contract, loan, insurance, or guarantee thereunder, which may involve a construction contract, that the applicant for Federal assistance undertake and agree to incorporate, or cause to be incorporated, into all construction contracts paid for in whole or part with funds obtained from the Federal Government or borrowed on the credit of the Federal Government pursuant to such grant, contract, loan, insurance, or guarantee, or undertaken pursuant to any Federal program involving such grant, contract, loan, insurance, or guarantee, the provisions prescribed for Government contracts by Section 202 of this

Order or such modification thereof, preserving in substance the contractor's obligations thereunder, as may be approved by the Secretary of Labor, together with such additional provisions as the Secretary deems appropriate to establish and protect the interest of the United States in the enforcement of those obligations. Each such applicant shall also undertake and agree (1) to assist and cooperate actively with the administering department or agency and the Secretary of Labor in obtaining the compliance of contractors and subcontractors with those contract provisions and with the rules, regulations, and relevant orders of the Secretary, (2) to obtain and to furnish to the administering department or agency and to the Secretary of Labor such information as they may require for the supervision of such compliance, (3) to carry out sanctions and penalties for violation of such obligations imposed upon contractors and subcontractors by the Secretary of Labor or the administering department or agency pursuant to Part II, Subpart D, of this Order, and (4) to refrain from entering into any contract subject to this Order, or extension or other modification of such a contract with a contractor debarred from Government contracts under PART II, Subpart D, of this Order.

SECTION 302. (a) "Construction contract" as used in this Order means any contract for the construction, rehabilitation, alteration, conversion, extension, or repair of buildings, highways, or other improvements to real property.

(b) The provisions of Part II of this Order shall apply to such construction contracts, and for purposes of such application the administering department or agency shall be considered the contracting agency referred to therein.

(c) The term "applicant" as used in this Order means an applicant for Federal assistance or, as determined by agency regulation, other program participant, with respect to whom an application for any grant, contract, loan, insurance, or guarantee is not finally acted upon prior to the effective date of this Part, and it includes such an applicant after he becomes a recipient of such Federal assistance.

SECTION 303. (a) Each administering department and agency shall be responsible for obtaining the compliance of such applicants with their undertakings under this Order. Each administering department and agency is directed to cooperate with the Secretary of Labor, and to furnish the Secretary such information and assistance as he may require in the performance of his functions under this Order.

(b) In the event an applicant fails and refuses to comply with his undertakings, the administering department or agency may take any or all of the following actions: (1) cancel, terminate, or suspend in whole or in part the agreement, contract, or other arrangement with such applicant with respect to which the failure and refusal occurred; (2) refrain from extending any further assistance to the applicant under the program with respect to which the failure or refusal occurred until satisfactory assurance of future compliance has been received from such applicant; and (3) refer the case to the Department of Justice for appropriate legal proceedings.

(c) Any action with respect to any applicant pursuant to Subsection (b) shall be taken in conformity with Section 602 of the Civil Rights Act of 1964 (and the regulations of the administering department or agency issued thereunder), to the extent applicable. In no case shall action be taken with respect to an applicant pursuant to Clause (1) or (2) of Subsection (b) without notice and opportunity for hearing before the administering department or agency.

SECTION 304. Any executive department or agency which imposes by rule, regulation, or order requirements of nondiscrimination in employment, other than requirements imposed pursuant to this Order, may delegate to the Secretary of Labor by agreement such responsibilities would tend to bring the administration of such requirements into conformity with the administration of requirements imposed under this Order: *Provided*, That actions to effect compliance by recipients of Federal financial assistance with requirements imposed pursuant to Title VI of the Civil Rights Act of 1964 shall be taken in conformity with the procedures and limitations prescribed in Section 602 thereof and the regulations of the administering department or agency issued thereunder.

PART IV—MISCELLANEOUS

SECTION 401. The Secretary of Labor may delegate to any officer, agency, or employee in the Executive branch of the Government, any function or duty of the Secretary under Parts II and III of this Order, except authority to promulgate rules and regulations of a general nature.

SECTION 402. The Secretary of Labor shall provide administrative support for the execution of the program known as the "Plans for Progress."

SECTION 403. (a) Executive Orders Nos. 10590 (January 19, 1955), 10722 (August 5, 1957), 10925 (March 6, 1961), 11114 (June 22, 1963), and 11162 (July 28, 1964), are hereby superseded and the President's Committee on Equal Employment Opportunity established by Executive Order No. 10925 is hereby abolished. All records and property in the custody of the Committee shall be transferred to the Civil Service Commission and the Secretary of Labor, as appropriate.

(b) Nothing in this Order shall be deemed to relieve any person of any obligation assumed or imposed under or pursuant to any Executive Order superseded by this Order. All rules, regulations, orders, instructions, designations, and other directives issued by the President's Committee on Equal Employment Opportunity and those issued by the heads of various departments or agencies under or pursuant to any of the Executive orders superseded by this Order, shall to the extent that they are not inconsistent with this Order, remain in full force and effect unless and until revoked or superseded by appropriate authority. References in such directives to provisions of the superseded orders shall be deemed to be references to the comparable provisions of this Order.

SECTION 404. The General Services Administration shall take appropriate action to revise the standard Government contract forms to accord with the provisions of this Order and of the rules and regulations of the Secretary of Labor.

SECTION 405. This Order shall become effective thirty days after the date of this Order. [Dated: September 24, 1965]

Executive Order 11247—Providing for the Coordination by the Attorney General of Enforcement of Title VI of the Civil Rights Act of 1964 (1967)

WHEREAS the Departments and agencies of the Federal Government have adopted uniform and consistent regulations implementing Title VI of the Civil Rights Act of 1964 and, in cooperation with the President's Council on Equal Opportunity, have embarked on a coordinated program of enforcement of the provisions of that Title;

WHEREAS the issues hereafter arising in connection with

coordination of the activities of the departments and agencies under that Title will be predominantly legal in character and in many cases will be related to judicial enforcement; and

WHEREAS the Attorney General is the chief law officer of the Federal Government and is charged with the duty of enforcing the laws of the United States:

NOW, THEREFORE, by virtue of the authority vested in me as President of the United States by the Constitution and laws of the United States, it is ordered as follows:

SECTION 1. The Attorney General shall assist Federal departments and agencies to coordinate their programs and activities and adopt consistent and uniform policies, practices, and procedures with respect to the enforcement of Title VI of the Civil Rights Act of 1964. He may promulgate such rules and regulations as he shall deem necessary to carry out his functions under this Order.

SECTION 2. Each Federal department and agency shall cooperate with the Attorney General in the performance of his functions under this Order and shall furnish him such reports and information as he may request.

SECTION 3. Effective 30 days from the date of this Order, Executive Order No. 11197 of February 5, 1965, is revoked. Such records of the President's Council on Equal Opportunity as may pertain to the enforcement of Title VI of the Civil Rights Act of 1964 shall be transferred to the Attorney General.

SECTION 4. All rules, regulations, orders, instructions, designations and other directives issued by the President's Council on Equal Opportunity relating to the implementation of Title VI of the Civil Rights Act of 1964 shall remain in full force and effect unless and until revoked or superseded by directives of the Attorney General.

Service Contract Act of 1965, as Amended

SUMMARY AND DESCRIPTION

The Service Contract Act of 1965 provides labor standards for contracts (and any bid specification therefor) entered into by any agency or instrumentality of the United States or the District of Columbia which have as their principal purpose the furnishing of services in the United States through the use of service employees.

Examples of contracts which are principally for services subject to this act include laundry and dry cleaning, mail transportation, custodial, janitorial, maintenance and guard services, certain packing and crating services, cafeteria and food service, ambulance services, certain equipment and facility repair and maintenance services, linen supply services, lodging services, support services at military installations, and warehousing or storage services, stenographic reporting, and data processing. The act applies to service contracts, whether oral or written.

Services Employees

Many types of employees may be regarded as service employees under the act, including "guards, watchmen, and any person engaged in a recognized trade or craft, or other skilled mechanical craft, or in unskilled, semiskilled, or skilled manual labor occupations; and any other employee including a foreman or supervisor in a position having trade, craft, or laboring experience as the paramount requirement; and shall include all such persons regardless of any contractual relationship that may be alleged to exist between a contractor or subcontractor and such persons."

Employees who qualify for exemption as being employed in a bona fide executive, administrative, or professional capacity in accordance with regulations, 29 CFR Part 541, issued under the Fair Labor Standards Act, are not considered to be service employees under the Service Contract Act.

Labor Standards for Covered Contracts in Excess of $2,500

Contractors and subcontractors performing work under a Government service contract in excess of $2,500 must observe the following requirements:

Minimum Wage and Fringe Benefits A provision must be included in the contract specifying the minimum monetary wages and the fringe benefits to be given to the service employees as determined by the Secretary of Labor to be prevailing for such employees in the community. The Secretary of Labor shall give due consideration to the rates paid corresponding classifications of service employees under the Federal wage board system in arriving at the prevailing wage rates.

The obligation of a contractor to furnish any specified fringe benefits may be discharged by furnishing any equivalent combinations of benefits, or by making equivalent, or differential payments in cash.

The wage determination for employees who perform work under a covered contract cannot be less than the minimum wage required under section 6(a) (1) of the Fair Labor Standards Act, which is $2.00 effective May 1, 1974, $2.10 effective January 1, 1975, and $2.30 an hour effective January 1, 1976. The same wage applies in the absence of a wage determination.

Safe and Healthful Working Conditions Contractors and subcontractors are obligated to assure that no part of the services covered by the act will be performed in buildings or surroundings or under working conditions, provided by or under the control or supervision of the contractor or any subcontractor, which are unsanitary or hazardous or dangerous to the health or safety of service employees.

Minimum Wage for Covered Contracts Under $2,500 No wage or fringe benefit determinations are issued for contracts of $2,500 or less, nor are these contracts subject to the safety and health requirements of the Act. The minimum monetary rate specified in section 6(a) (1) of the Fair Labor Standards Act is applicable to employees engaged in the performance of such a contract.

Labor Standards for Other Employees of a Service Contractor Under section 6(e) of the Fair Labor Stand-

ards Act, other employees of contractor whose rate of pay is not governed by either the Service Contract Act or by section 6(a) (1) of the Fair Labor Standards Act must be paid a minimum wage of not less than $1.90 an hour, beginning May 1, 1974; $2.00 an hour, beginning January 1, 1975; $2.20 an hour, beginning January 1, 1976; and $2.30 an hour after December 31, 1976.

Overtime Pay Standards Although the Service Contract Act does not contain overtime standards, payment of time and one-half for all hours in excess of 40 in a workweek may be required by the Fair Labor Standards Act. Also, if the contract is in excess of $2,500, the Contract Work Hours and Safety Standards Act generally applies. The latter act requires time and one-half for all hours worked in the contract in excess of 40 in the workweek or 8 in any calendar day, whichever number of overtime hours is greater.

Notice to Employees In contracts in excess of $2,500, the contractor or subcontractor must provide a service employee, when he commences work on a contract subject to the act, with a notice of the compensation required by the act or shall post such notice in a location where it may be seen by all employees performing on the contract, using such posters as may be provided by the Department of Labor.

Recordkeeping Requirements

The contractor or subcontractor must make, and maintain for a period of 3 years from the completion of the work, certain records for each service employee performing work under the contract which are open for inspection and transcription by representatives of the Wage and Hour Division.

Notice in Subcontracts

Each contractor subject to the act is required to insert clauses relating to the Service Contract Act in all his subcontracts.

Exemptions

The Service Contract Act does not apply to the following:

1. Any contract for construction, alteration, and/or repair, including painting and decorating of public buildings or public works (contracts subject to the Davis-Bacon Act);

2. Any work required to be done in accordance with the provision of the Walsh-Healey Public Contracts Act.

3. Any contract for the carriage of freight or personnel by vessel, airplane, bus, truck, express, railway line, or oil or gas pipeline where published tariff rates are in effect or where such carriage is subject to rates covered by section 22 of the Interstate Commerce Act.

4. Any contract for the furnishing of services by radio, telephone, telegraph, or cable companies, subject to the Communications Act of 1934;

5. Any contract for public utility services, including electric light and power, water, steam, and gas;

6. Any employment contract providing for direct services to a Federal agency by an individual or individuals;

7. Any contract with the Post Office Department, the principal purpose of which is the operation of postal contract stations;

8. Any services to be furnished outside the United States as defined in the act; and

9. Any contract exempted by the Secretary of Labor under section 4(b) of the act. This section authorizes the Secretary to provide such reasonable limitations, variations, tolerances and exemptions to and from any or all provisions of the art (other than section 10) but only in special circumstances where he determines it may be necessary and proper in the public interest or to avoid serious impairment to the conduct of Government business.

Violations and Penalties

In the event of violations, the act authorizes the withholding of accrued payments due on the contract or any other contract between the same contractor and the Government to the extent necessary. The Government may also bring court action against the contractor, subcontractor, or surety to recover any remaining amount of the underpayment. In addition, the contract may be terminated because of violations and the contractor may be held liable for any resulting cost to the Government. Any persons or firms found to have violated the act shall not be awarded a contract for a period of 3 years from the date such name appears on the debarment list published by the Comptroller General, unless the Secretary of Labor recommends otherwise because of unusual circumstances.

Other Obligations

Observance of the labor standards of this act does not relieve the employer of any obligation he may have under any other laws or agreements providing for higher labor standards.

Successor-Predecessor Contracts

If a contract succeeds a contract, subject to the act, under which substantially the same services were furnished and service employees were paid wages and fringe benefits provided for in a collective bargaining agreement, then

neither the contractor nor any subcontractor under such a contract shall pay any service employee performing any of the contract work less than the wages and fringe benefits, provided for in such collective bargaining agreement, to which such employee would be entitled if employed under the predecessor contract, including accrued wages and fringe benefits and any prospective increases in wages and fringe benefits provided for under such agreement. No contractor or subcontractor may be relieved of the foregoing obligation unless the Secretary of Labor or his authorized representative determines that the collective bargaining agreement applicable to service employees employed under the predecessor contract was not entered into as a result of arms-length negotiations or finds, after a hearing that the wages and fringe benefits provided for in such agreement are substantially at variance with those which prevail for services of a character similar in the locality.

For further information write to: Employment Standards Administration, Wage and Hour Division, U.S. Department of Labor, Washington, D.C. 20210.

Executive Order 11375—Amending Executive Order No. 11246, Relating to Equal Employment Opportunity (1967)

It is the policy of the United States Government to provide equal opportunity in Federal employment and in employment by Federal contractors on the basis of merit and without discrimination because of race, religion, sex or national origin.

The Congress, by enacting Title VII of the Civil Rights Act of 1964, enunciated a national policy of equal employment opportunity in private employment, without discrimination because of race, color, religion, sex or national origin.

Executive Order No. 11246[1] of September 24, 1965, carried forward a program of equal employment opportunity in Government employment, employment by Federal contractors and subcontractors and employment under Federally assisted construction contracts regardless of race, creed, color or national origin.

It is desirable that the equal employment opportunity programs provided for in Executive Order No. 11246 expressly embrace discrimination on account of sex.

NOW, THEREFORE, by virtue of the authority vested in me as President of the United States by the Constitution and statutes of the United States, it is ordered that Executive Order No. 11246 of September 24, 1965, be amended as follows:

(1) Section 101 of Part I, concerning nondiscrimination in Government employment, is revised to read as follows:

"SEC. 101. It is the policy of the Government of the United States to provide equal opportunity in Federal employment for all qualified persons, to prohibit discrimination in employment because of race, color, religion, sex or national origin, and to promote the full realization of equal employment opportunity through a positive, continuing program in each executive department and agency. The policy of equal opportunity applies to every aspect of Federal employment policy and practice."

(2) Section 104 of Part I is revised to read as follows:

"SEC. 104. The Civil Service Commission shall provide for the prompt, fair, and impartial consideration of all complaints of discrimination in Federal employment on the basis of race, color, religion, sex or national origin. Procedures for the consideration of complaints shall include at least one impartial review within the executive department or agency and shall provide for appeal to the Civil Service Commission."

(3) Paragraphs (1) and (2) of the quoted required contract provisions in section 202 of Part II, concerning nondiscrimination in employment by Government contractors and subcontractors, are revised to read as follows:

"(1) The contractor will not discriminate against any employee or applicant for employment because of race, color, religion, sex, or national origin. The contractor will take affirmative action to ensure that applicants are employed, and that employees are treated during employment, without regard to their race, color, religion, sex or national origin. Such action shall include, but not be limited to the following: employment, upgrading, demotion, or transfer; recruitment or recruitment advertising; layoff or termination; rates of pay or other forms of compensation; and selection for training, including apprenticeship. The contractor agrees to post in conspicuous places, available to employees and applicants for employment, notices to be provided by the contracting officer setting forth the provisions of this nondiscrimination clause.

"(2) The contractor will, in all solicitations or advertisements for employees placed by or on behalf of the contractor, state that all qualified applicants will receive consideration for employment without regard to race, color, religion, sex or national origin." (4) Section 203 (d) of Part II is revised to read as follows:

"(d) The contracting agency or the Secretary of Labor may direct that any bidder or prospective contractor or subcontractor shall submit, as part of his Compliance Report, a statement in writing, signed by an authorized officer or agent on behalf of any labor union or any agency referring workers or providing or supervising apprenticeship or other training, with which the bidder or prospective contractor deals, with supporting information, to the effect that the signer's practices and policies do not discriminate on the grounds of race, color, religion, sex or national origin, and that the signer either will affirmatively cooperate in the implementation of the policy and provisions of this order or that it consents and agrees that recruitment, employment, and the terms and conditions of employment under the proposed contract shall be in accordance with the purposes and provisions of the order. In the event that the union, or the agency shall refuse to execute such a statement, the Compliance Report shall so certify and set forth what efforts have been made to secure such a statement and such additional factual material as the contracting agency or the Secretary of Labor may require."

The amendments to Part I shall be effective 30 days after the date of this order. The amendments to Part II shall be effective one year after the date of this order.

Age Discrimination in Employment Act of 1967

SUMMARY AND DESCRIPTION

The Age Discrimination in Employment Act of 1967, effective June 12, 1968, promotes the employment of the older worker based on ability rather than age; prohibits arbitrary age discrimination in employment; and helps employers and employees find ways to meet problems arising from the impact of age on employment. It protects most individuals who are at least 40 but less than 65 years of age from discrimination in employment based on age in matters of hiring, discharge, compensation, or

other terms, conditions, or privileges of employment. Responsibility for administration and enforcement of this Act rests with the Wage and Hour Division of the Department of Labor.

The Act applies to:

■ Most employers of 20 or more persons, including Federal, State and local governments.

■ Public and private employment agencies serving such employers.

■ Labor organizations with 25 or more members, or which refer persons for employment to covered employers, or which represent employees of employers covered by the Act.

Exceptions

The prohibitions of the Act do not apply:

1. where age is a bona fide occupational qualification reasonably necessary to the normal operations of the particular business;

2. where the differentiation is based on reasonable factors other than age;

3. where the differentiation is caused by observing the terms of a bona fide seniority system or any bona fide employee benefit plan which is not a subterfuge to evade the purposes of the Act;

4. where discharge of an individual is for good cause.

Exemptions

The Secretary of Labor is authorized to establish such reasonable exemptions to and from any or all provisions of the Act as he may find necessary and proper in the public interest.

Records: Posting Notices

Employers, employment agencies, and labor organizations, must post an officially approved notice in a prominent place where employees may see it, and maintain the records required by the Secretary of Labor.

Enforcement

The Act is enforced by the Secretary of Labor, who can make investigations, issue rules and regulations for administration of the law, and enforce its provisions by legal proceedings when voluntary compliance cannot be obtained.

Prohibited acts under the age discrimination law are to be deemed prohibited also by the Fair Labor Standards Act. Amounts owing to any person as a result of a violation are to be treated as unpaid compensation under the provisions of the Fair Labor Standards Act which authorize enforcement through civil actions in the courts.

The Secretary or any aggrieved person may bring suit under the act. Suits to enforce the act must be brought within 2 years after the violation, or in the case of a willful violation, within 3 years.

Before the Secretary begins court action, the act requires him to attempt to secure voluntary compliance by informal conciliation, conference, and persuasion. Before an individual brings court action, he must give the Secretary not less than 60 days' notice of his intention.

This notice must be filed within 180 days of the occurrence of the alleged unlawful practice except when a State has taken action in accordance with its own laws prohibiting age discrimination, then an individual must file within 300 days of the alleged violation. The law provides that after receiving such a notice, the Secretary will notify the prospective defendants and try to eliminate any alleged unlawful practice by informal conciliation, conference, and persuasion.

Following are methods to recover amounts owed which result from violations of this act:

1. The Secretary is authorized to supervise the payment of amounts owed;

2. In certain circumstances, the Secretary may bring suit upon written request of the individual, and in these cases may sue for additional liquidated damages up to an amount equal to the amount owed;

3. An individual may sue for payment, plus attorney's fees and court costs. In the case of willful violations, an additional amount up to the total of the amount owed, may be claimed as liquidated damages. (An employee may not bring suit if he has been paid the amount owed under the supervision of the Secretary, or if the Secretary has filed suit to enjoin the employer from retaining the amount due the employee.)

4. The Secretary may obtain a court injunction to restrain any person from violating the law, including the unlawful withholding of proper compensation.

The courts, in enforcement actions, are authorized to grant any relief appropriate to carry out the act's purposes, including among other things judgments compelling employment, reinstatement, or promotion.

Interference with representatives of the Secretary of Labor engaged in duties under the act may be prosecuted criminally and the violator subjected to a fine of not more than $500 or imprisonment, or both.

For further information write to: Employment Standards Administration, Wage and Hour Division, U.S. Department of Labor, Washington, D.C. 20210.

Consumer Credit Protection Act (Garnishment)

SUMMARY AND DESCRIPTION

Title III of the Consumer Credit Protection Act sets restrictions on the amount of an individual's earnings that may be deducted in any one week through garnishment proceedings, and on discharge from employment by reason of garnishment for any one indebtedness.

No court of the United States or of any State may make, execute, or enforce any order or process garnishing the aggregate disposable earnings of any individual for any workweek in an amount which is in excess of the lesser of the following restrictions:

1. 25 percent of the individual's disposable earnings for the workweek, or

2. the amount by which his disposable earnings for that week exceed 30 times the minimum wage under section 6(a) (1) of the Fair Labor Standards Act (presently $2.00 an hour. Effective January 1, 1975: $2.10 an hour; effective January 1, 1976: $2.30 an hour).

These restrictions do not apply in the case of (1) Court orders for the support of any person, (2) court orders under Chapter XIII of the Bankruptcy Act, and (3) any debt due for any State or Federal Tax.

"Disposable earnings" is compensation paid or payable for personal services less any amounts required to be withheld by law.

A section or provision of the State law that requires a larger amount to be garnished than the Federal law permits is considered preempted by the Federal law. On the other hand, the State law provision is to be applied if it results in a smaller garnishment amount.

Discharge Provisions

The law prohibits an employer from discharging any employee because his earnings have been subjected to garnishment for any one indebtedness. The term "One indebtedness" refers to a single debt, regardless of the number of levies made or creditors seeking satisfaction. Whoever willfully violates the discharge provisions of this law may be prosecuted criminally and fined up to $1,000, or imprisoned for not more than one year, or both.

For further information write to: Employment Standards Administration, Wage and Hour Division, U.S. Department of Labor, Washington, D.C. 20210.

Executive Order 11478—Equal Employment Opportunity in the Federal Government (as Amended)

It has long been the policy of the United States Government to provide equal opportunity in Federal employment on the basis of merit and fitness and without discrimination because of race, color, religion, sex, or national origin. All recent Presidents have fully supported this policy, and have directed department and agency heads to adopt measures to make it a reality.

As a result, much has been accomplished through positive agency programs to assure equality of opportunity. Additional steps, however, are called for in order to strengthen and assure fully equal employment opportunity in the Federal Government.

NOW, THEREFORE, under and by virtue of the authority vested in me as President of the United States by the Constitution and statutes of the United States, it is ordered as follows:

SECTION 1. It is the policy of the Government of the United States to provide equal opportunity in Federal employment for all persons, to prohibit discrimination in employment because of race, color, religion, sex, or national origin, and to promote the full realization of equal employment opportunity through a continuing affirmative program in each executive department and agency. This policy of equal opportunity applies to and must be an integral part of every aspect of personnel policy and practice in the employment, development, advancement, and treatment of civilian employees of the Federal Government.

SECTION 2. The head of each executive department and agency shall establish and maintain an affirmative program of equal employment opportunity for all civilian employees and applicants for employment within his jurisdiction in accordance with the policy set forth in section 1. It is the responsibility of each department and agency head, to the maximum extent possible, to provide sufficient resources to administer such a program in a positive and effective manner; assure that recruitment activities reach all sources of job candidates; utilize to the fullest extent the present skills of each employee; provide the maximum feasible opportunity to employees to enhance their skills so they may perform at their highest potential and advance in accordance with their abilities: provide training and advice to managers and supervisors to assure their understanding and implementation of the policy expressed in this Order; assure participation at the local level with other employers, schools, and public or private groups in cooperative efforts to improve community conditions which affect employability; and provide for a system within the department or agency for periodically evaluating the effectiveness with which the policy of this Order is being carried out.

SECTION 3. The Civil Service Commission shall provide leadership and guidance to departments and agencies in the conduct of equal employment opportunity programs for the civilian employees of and applicants for employment within the executive departments and agencies in order to assure that personnel operations in Government departments and agencies carry out the objective of equal opportunity for all persons. The Commission shall review and evaluate agency program operations periodically, obtain such reports from departments and agencies as it deems necessary, and report to the President as appropriate on overall progress. The Commission will consult from time to time with such individuals, groups, or organizations as may be of assistance in improving the Federal program and realizing the objectives of this Order.

SECTION 4. The Civil Service Commission shall provide for the prompt, fair, and impartial consideration of all complaints of discrimination in Federal employment on the basis of race, color, religion, sex, or national origin. Agency systems shall provide access to counseling for employees who feel aggrieved and shall encourage the resolution of employee problems on an informal basis. Procedures for the consideration of complaints shall include at least one impartial review within the executive department or agency and shall provide for appeal to the Civil Service Commission.

SECTION 5. The Civil Service Commission shall issue such regulations, orders, and instructions as it deems necessary and appropriate to carry out this Order and assure that the executive branch of the Government leads the way as an equal opportunity employer, and the head of each executive department and agency shall comply with the regulations, orders, and instructions issued by the Commission under this Order.

SECTION 6. This Order applies (a) to military departments as defined in section 102 of title 5, United States Code, and executive agencies (other than the General Accounting Office) as defined in section 105 of title 5, United States Code, and to the employees thereof (including employees paid from nonappropriated funds), and (b) to those portions of the legislative and judicial branches of the Federal Government and of the Government of the District of Columbia having positions in the competitive service and to the employees in those positions. This Order does not apply to aliens employed outside the limits of the United States.

SECTION 7. Part I of Executive Order No. 11246 of September 24, 1965, and those parts of Executive Order No. 11375 of October 13, 1967, which apply to Federal employment, are hereby superseded.

SECTION 8. This Order shall be applicable to the United States Postal Service and to the Postal Rate Commission established by the Postal Reorganization Act of 1970.

Contract Work Hours and Safety Standards Act (1969)

SUMMARY AND DESCRIPTION

Work Hours Standard

This act provides a uniform standard, namely, an 8-hour workday and a 40-hour workweek with overtime compensation of 1½ times the basic rate of pay for all work in excess of that standard performed under certain Federal and federally assisted contracts. It consolidates a series of "Eight Hour Laws" into a single statute with simplified provisions which apply in the same way to all contractors and subcontractors performing work coming within its terms.

The acts work hours standard applies to any contract involving the employment of laborers or mechanics, including watchmen and guards:

1. on a public work of the United States, of any Territory, or the District of Columbia,

2. to which the Federal Government (including any Federal agency or instrumentality), any Territory, or the District of Columbia is a party, or which is made for or on behalf thereof, or

3. which is financed in whole or in part by loans or grants from the Federal Government and to which Federal laws providing wage standards for such work apply. An exception is made to work where the assistance from the United States is only in the nature of a loan guarantee, or insurance.

The act makes clear that the contractor or subcontractor is liable to employees for unpaid overtime compensation. In addition, such an employer is liable to the Government for liquidated damages of $10 for each day an employee was permitted or required to work in excess of the work-hours standard without payment of overtime compensation. Criminal penalties are provided for intentional violations. The Secretary of Labor is given the authority and functions set forth in Reorganization Plan No. 14 of 1950, and pursuant to this plan an employer violating the act's work hours standard may be barred from receiving further Government contracts for a period of up to three years. The act also contains a provision making applicable in accordance with its terms, section 2 of the Copeland Act, as amended. (See p. 180.)

However, the Secretary of Labor is authorized to issue rules and regulations under which such adjustments may be made in the application of the act as he finds necessary and proper in the public interest to prevent injustice and serious impairment of the conduct of Government business.

The Federal contracting agency is directed to withhold sums necessary to satisfy liabilities for liquidated damages and unpaid overtime wages. If the amounts withheld are not sufficient to satisfy the liability for underpayment of wages, the employees must be paid an equitable proportion of the sums. Then they have a right of action against the employer for the balance and it is no defense that they have accepted less than the required amounts.

Construction Safety and Health Standards

This statute, which was originally entitled the "Contract Work Hours Standards Act of 1962," was amended by the Act of August 9, 1969 (76 Stat. 357) which changed its title to "Contract Work Hours and Safety Standards Act" and added at the end thereof a new section 107 (40 U.S.C. 333). The provisions added to the Act are designed to promote health and safety in the building trades and construction industry on all Federal, federally financed, and federally assisted construction projects in excess of $2,500. They specifically cover new construction and alterations and repair, including painting and decorating.

Standards, Reporting, and Compliance

The Secretary of Labor is authorized:

1. to promulgate safety and health standards;

2. to establish and supervise programs for the education and training of employers and employees in the recognition, avoidance, and prevention of unsafe working conditions;

3. to collect reports and data, and consult with and advise employers as to the best means of preventing injuries; and

4. to make inspections, hold hearings, issue orders, and make such decisions as are deemed necessary to gain compliance with the health and safety standards promulgated under the Act.

Under section 4(b)(2) of the Occupational Safety and Health Act of 1970, standards issued under this Act are deemed to be occupational safety and health standards issued under the Safety and Health Act. They may be superseded by standards promulgated under the Safety and Health Act.

Administration

Inspections, educational programs, reporting and data-collecting functions are conducted through regional and area offices located throughout the country. Copies of the Act, and the health and safety standards promulgated thereunder, are available at each of these offices.

Noncompliance

In the event, after an adjudicatory hearing, the Secretary determines noncompliance with the standards:

1. The government agency for which the contract work is done has the right to cancel the contract, and to enter into other contracts for the completion of the contract, charging any additional cost to the original contractors.

2. The U.S. district courts have jurisdiction to enforce compliance with the safety and health standards promulgated by the Secretary.

3. On findings of repeated willful or grossly negligent violations of the Act, the Secretary is authorized to transmit the name of such contractors or subcontractors to the Comptroller General. The Comptroller General will distribute such names to all agencies of the government, who must withhold awards of contract from them for a period of three years.

The Secretary may terminate the debarment before the end of the three-year period if the safety and health requirements are met to his satisfaction.

For further information write to: Employment Standards Administration, Wage and Hour Division, U.S. Department of Labor, Washington, D.C. 20210.

Rail Passenger Service Act of 1970 (Pertinent Provisions)

SUMMARY AND DESCRIPTION

The Rail Passenger Service Act of 1970 establishes a program to provide Federal assistance to certain railroads to permit the orderly transfer of railroad passenger service to a railroad passenger corporation.

Section 565(b) provides that no contract between a railroad and the corporation may be made unless the Secretary of Labor has certified that fair and equitable arrangements have been made to protect the interest of employees of such railroads.

The protective arrangements specified in section 565 of the Act are identical to those prescribed under the Urban Mass Transportation Act.

For further information write to: Federal Railroad Administration, Department of Transportation, 400 Seventh Street, S.W., Washington, D.C. 20590.

FEDERAL LEGISLATION RELATED TO EMPLOYEE TRAINING, BENEFITS, AND SAFETY AND HEALTH

Federal Employees' Compensation Act (1916, as Amended)

SUMMARY AND DESCRIPTION

The Federal Employees' Compensation Act provides workmen's compensation coverage to civilian employees of the United States for disability or death due to personal injury sustained while in the performance of duty or to employment related disease.

Persons and Employments Covered

The law covers three million individuals, including civilian employees of the United States Government; the District of Columbia Government; and such diverse groups as Peace Corps volunteers, enrollees in the Job Corps and the Neighborhood Youth Corps, Volunteers in Service to America (VISTA); and State and local law enforcement officers killed or injured under circumstances involving a crime against the United States. The Act also provides for the payment of benefits to dependents if the injury or disease causes the employee's death.

Injuries and Diseases Covered

Workers' compensation benefits are provided for accidental injuries sustained by employees while in the performance of duty and occupational disease proximately caused by the employment. Benefits cannot be paid if the injury or disease is caused by the willful misconduct of the employee or by the employee's intention to bring about the injury or death of himself or another, or if intoxication is the proximate cause of the injury or death.

Amount of Benefits

Compensation for total disability and death generally is payable at the rate of two-thirds of the employee's salary if he has not dependent; or three-fourths of his salary if he has one or more dependents. The minimum rate of compensation for total disability is three-fourths of the monthly pay of the lowest rate of basic pay for grade GS-2 of the General Schedule of the Classification Act of 1949, as amended, or the employee's full wages, whichever is less. The maximum compensation payable is three-fourths of the monthly pay of the highest rate of basic pay provided for grade GS-15 of the General Schedule.

Temporary Total Disability

Compensation for loss of wages is payable at the rate of two-thirds or three-fourths of the employee's salary after a 3-day waiting period, unless there is permanent injury or where the disability causing wage loss exceeds 21 days. If the disability lasts more than 21 days, compensation is paid for the waiting period.

Permanent Partial Disability

The law provides both scheduled benefits, and payments for nonscheduled disabilities based upon loss in wage-earning capacity for permanent effects of an injury. Scheduled benefits are awards for permanent impairment of certain members or functions of the body (such as loss or loss of use, either total or partial, of an eye, arm, hearing, etc.); or for serious disfigurement of the face, head or neck if of a character likely to handicap a person in securing or maintaining employment. Benefits for loss in wage-earning capacity due to an injury also may be paid after the scheduled award period has terminated. Compensation for loss in wage-earning capacity may be payable if the employee is unable to resume his regular work because of injury-related disability, and is paid on the basis of the difference between the employee's capacity to earn wages and the wages of the job he held when injured.

Permanent Total Disability

Loss, or loss of use, of both hands, or both arms, or both feet, or both legs, or both eyes or the sight thereof,

4-89

constitutes, prima facie, permanent total disability. Compensation for permanent total disability is payable for life on the basis of two-thirds or three-fourths of the employee's salary.

Death

Persons eligible for death compensation include a widow or wholly dependent widower, children under 18 years of age (or if over 18 the child is a student or incapable of self-support), and dependent parents, brothers, sisters, grandparents, and grandchildren. If there is no child eligible for benefits, the widow or wholly dependent widower's monthly compensation is 45 percent of the monthly pay of the deceased employee. If there is a child or children eligible for benefits, the widow or widower is entitled to 40 percent of the pay and each child is entitled to 15 percent. If children are the sole survivors, 35 percent is paid for one child and 15 percent additional for each additional child, shared equally. In no case, however, may the total monthly compensation paid be more than 75 percent of the employee's monthly pay, or 75 percent of the highest rate of monthly pay provided for grade GS-15 of the General Schedule.

Compensation to an employee's survivors terminates upon their death or marriage. Upon remarriage a widow will receive a lump sum equal to 24 times her monthly compensation.

Burial expenses not to exceed $800 are payable in an individual case. Transportation of the body to its former residence in the United States ir provided where an employee dies away from his home station.

Medical Care

All necessary medical care is provided for the effects of an injury, including medical, surgical and hospital services, appliances, and supplies prescribed or recommended by a qualified physician. Transportation expense is authorized if travel is necessary to secure treatment. Treatment must be obtained from United States medical officers and hospitals, if practicable. If these are not available, physicians designated by the Office of Workers' Cooperation Programs are to be used. Other qualified physicians may be used only if United States medical officers and hospitals or designated physicians are not available or if an emergency exists. The term "physician" includes surgeons and osteopathic practitioners, but not chiropractors, chiropodists, etc. Authorization for medical care must first be obtained from an employee's employing establishment or the Office before treatment can be obtained at Office expense.

Vocational Rehabilitation

The Office may direct a permanently disabled individual whose disability is compensable under this Act to undergo vocational rehabilitation, where necessary, and may provide for a maintenance allowance not to exceed $100 per month. Insofar as practicable, the Office uses the services or facilities of State agencies and corresponding agencies which cooperate in carrying out the purposes of the Vocational Rehabilitation Act, as amended.

Cost of Living Increases

In general, if benefits have been paid for more than a year, the law provides an automatic increase in benefit payments on the first day of the third month after any increase in the Consumer Price Index of at least 3 percent for three consecutive months over the price index for the most recent base month. The term "price index" means the Consumer Price Index (all items—United States city average) published by the U.S. Bureau of Labor Statistics. Each new "base month" is determined by subsequent adjustments.

Third Party Settlements

In instances where an employee's injury or death in the performance of duty is caused under circumstances creating a legal liability on some person other than the United States to pay damages, the cost of compensation and other benefits paid by the Office must be refunded from any settlement obtained. The Office will assist in obtaining a settlement, and the law guarantees that a certain proportion of the settlement (after any attorney fees and costs are first deducted) may be retained even when the cost of compensation and other benefits exceeds the amount of the settlement.

Administration

Responsibility for administration of this law is delegated to the Office of Workers' Compensation Programs of the U.S. Department of Labor, with headquarters at Washington, D.C. 20211. The Office's district offices adjudicate the claims arising within the areas of their respective jurisdictions. The Director of the Office is responsible for final decisions in respect to claims filed under the Act.

Hearing, Review, and Appeal Rights

If an employee or his survivors disagree with a final determination of the Office, a hearing may be requested where an opportunity will be afforded to present evidence in further support of the claim. After the hearing the Office will issue a new decision. There is also a provision for additional review by the Branch of Hearings and Review in the Office headquarters office. A claimant has the further right to appeal an Office decision to the Employees' Compensation Appeals Board, located in Washington, D.C.

Longshoremen's and Harbor Workers' Compensation Act (1927, as Amended)

SUMMARY AND DISPOSITION
The Longshoremen's and Harbor Workers' Compensation Act provides workers' compensation benefits for certain private employments subject to Federal jurisdiction.

Persons and Employments Covered
The law covers substantially all maritime employment in whole or in part on the navigable waters of the United States (including any adjoining pier, wharf, drydock, terminal, building way, marine railway, or other adjoining area customarily used by an employer in loading, unloading, repairing, or building a vessel), except the master or members of the crew of a vessel. The principal employments covered are longshoremen and ship repairmen. The law has been extended to other employments, including all private employment in the District of Columbia and employment outside the United States in the service of contractors with the United States at military, air, or naval bases or on public works, including employment on certain contracts made under the Mutual Security Act of 1954, as amended. Also certain employment on the Outer Continental Shelf lands and employment at post exchanges and other nonappropriated fund instrumentalities of the Armed Forces.

Injuries and Diseases Covered
The law provides workers' compensation benefits for accidental injury or death and diseases arising out of or occurring in the course of the employment.

Amount of Benefits
Compensation for disability and death is based on the average weekly wage of the injured worker. Maximum benefits may not exceed a specified percentage of the national average weekly wage. The percentage increases from 125 prior to September 30, 1973, to 200 beginning October 1, 1975. The minimum is 50% of the national average weekly wages or the employees' actual weekly wage, whichever is less.

Temporary Total Disability
The compensation rate is two-thirds of the employee's average weekly wage. There is a 3-day wating period, but if the disability lasts more than 14 days, compensation is paid for the waiting period. Benefits are paid during the period of such disability.

Permanent Partial Disability
Compensation for permanent partial disability is paid under a statutory schedule for the loss or loss of use of specified parts of the body or body functions, and for disfigurement, or upon the basis of two-thirds of a loss in wage earning capacity.

Permanent Total Disability
Compensation is payable for life at two-thirds of the employee's weekly wage.

Death
Burial expenses are provided up to a maximum of $1,000. Persons eligible for death compensation include a widow, children under 18 years, and those over 18 if incapable of self-support or if they are students, and dependent parents, brothers and sisters, grandparents, and grandchildren. The aggregate award to all beneficiaries may not exceed two-thirds of the average weekly wage.

Compensation to a widow is payable for life, or until remarriage. Upon remarriage, the widow receives 2 years' compensation.

Medical Treatment
All necessary medical care is authorized for the effects of an injury. The employer is required to provide necessary and reasonable medical care and treatment. The employee has an initial free choice of physicians. There is no limit on the cost or period of treatment.

Vocational Rehabilitation
Provision is made for the furnishing of vocational rehabilitation through appropriate State agencies and for the payment of not to exceed $25 per week for maintenance while undergoing such vocational training.

Second Injuries
The law sets up a special fund for payment of compensation in certain cases in which the employee suffers a permanent partial disability which, combined with a previous disability, causes permanent total disability. This fund is also available for payment of benefits in certain cases in which payments are in default by reason of the insolvency of the employer and his insurance carrier.

Administration
This law is administered by the Office of Worker's Compensation Programs of the U.S. Department of Labor, through Deputy Commissioners appointed to 16 Compensation Districts. Disputed claims are adjudicated by administrative law judges.

Appeals
The decision of an administrative law judge is subject to review by the Benefits Review Board, U.S. Department of Labor.

For further information write to: Office of Information Services, Occupational Safety and Health Administration, U.S. Department of Labor, Washington, D.C. 20210.

Federal Metal and Nonmetallic Mine Safety Act (1966)

SUMMARY AND DESCRIPTION

The main objectives of the Federal Metal and Nonmetallic Mine Safety Act are to reduce the frequency of disabling accidents and to prevent conditions that constitute hazards to the health of the workers in metal and nonmetal mines and associated plants. Such objectives are effected through inspections of mines and related plants; investigations of accidents, disasters, and unsafe health and safety conditions; publication of reports on findings; development of expanded programs for the education and training of employers and employees in recognition, avoidance, and prevention of accidents or unsafe or unhealthful working conditions in mines; and Federal enforcement of mandatory health and safety standards promulgated under the Act or enforcement under a "State Plan: agreement of State health and safety standards substantially as effective as the Federal mandatory standards. Part 55 of the standards applies to open pit mines; Part 56 applies to sand, gravel, and crushed stone operations; and Part 57 applies to underground mines. Those standards that are designated as mandatory become effective one year after publication. At least once each calendar year a Federal inspection shall be made of each underground mine subject to the Act. Federal inspections and investigations are also required for the purpose of evaluating the manner in which a State plan approved under Section 16 of the Act is being carried out.

Metal and nonmetal mine health and safety inspectors operate from strategically located field stations organized under six District Managers whose offices are situated in Pittsburgh, Pennsylvania; Birmingham, Alabama; Duluth, Minnesota; Dallas, Texas; Lakewood, Colorado; and Alameda, California.

For further information write to: Assistant Director, Metal and Nonmetal Mine Health and Safety, Bureau of Mines, U.S. Department of Interior, Washington, D.C. 20240.

Federal Coal Mine Health and Safety Act of 1969

SUMMARY AND DESCRIPTION

The main objective of the Federal Coal Mine Health and Safety Act is to protect the health and safety of the Nation's coal miners; and to improve and expand, in cooperation with the States and the coal mining industry, research and development and training programs aimed at preventing coal mine accidents and occupationally caused diseases in the industry. This is effected through frequent inspections by the Department of the Interior of mines and related plants for the purpose of obtaining, utilizing, and disseminating information related to health and safety conditions, the causes and diseases and physical impairments originating in such mines; gathering information with respect to mandatory health or safety standards, and determining whether or not there is compliance with the mandatory safety and health standards. Each coal mine, the products of which enter commerce, or the operation or products of which effect commerce; each operator of such mine, and every miner in such mine is subject to the provisions of the Act.

The Act establishes mandatory health and safety standards for such mines, which remain in effect until superseded in whole or in part by improved standards. The Secretary of Health, Education, and Welfare is required to develop and revise improved mandatory health standards, and the Secretary of the Interior is required to develop, promulgate, and revise mandatory safety standards.

Title IV of the Federal Coal Mine Health and Safety Act of 1969, as amended by the Black Lung Benefits Act of 1972:

GENERAL STATEMENTS

The Black Lung Benefits Act of 1972 improves Title IV of the Federal Coal Mine Health and Safety Act of 1969 with respect to coverage for additional beneficiaries, as well as easing evidentiary requirements of establishing total disability due to pneumoconiosis. Several other new provisions were added, which will materially aid the disabled coal miner, his family and survivors. Following is a discussion of the provisions of the new law.

DEPENDENT BENEFITS

Orphans

Orphaned children had no basis under title IV of the 1969 act for claiming benefits. The Black Lung Benefits Act of 1972 permits orphans to claim benefits and places them in the same position they would have been had they been covered since the date of the original 1969 act. That is, benefits are made retroactive to December 30, 1969, for children who file claims within 6 months after enactment (May 19, 1972), or for such retroactive period as they are eligible for benefits. Claims filed more than 6 months after enactment are payable for a period of twelve months preceding the date of filing, or for such portion of the 12 months a child is eligible for benefits.

Orphans are entitled to the amount of the miner's benefit, plus an additional 50 percent if there are two children, an additional 75 percent if there are three children, and an additional 100 percent if there are more than three children.

Other Dependents

Dependent parents, brothers, or sisters may be eligible for benefits as survivors of a miner. Such dependents are not eligible unless at the time of the miner's death the miner left no surviving widow or child. In such cases, if there is a surviving parent of the miner who was totally dependent on the miner for his or her support and lived in the miner's home for at least 1 year prior to the miner's death, such parent is entitled to benefits. If there is no surviving widow, child, or dependent parent, dependent brothers or sisters who meet the same requirements for eligibility as dependent parents are entitled to benefits.

Certification of Dependent Benefits

The Secretary of Health, Education, and Welfare may provide benefits directly to a dependent, or to a third person for the benefit of the dependent, where he determines it is in the dependent's interest to do so. Such cases may arise, for example, when a miner or widow refuses to ask for benefits for a dependent child, or where a miner estranged from his wife or children does not provide these dependents the black lung benefits to which they are entitled.

Widows' Claims

Before enactment of the 1972 law a widow of a miner could not claim black lung benefits unless her husband was receiving benefits at the time of his death, the miner had filed an application for benefits prior to his death, or died from pneumoconiosis or a respirable disease. Under the new law, in addition, a widow is entitled to benefits regardless of the cause of death if it is established that the miner was, under the law, totally disabled by pneumoconiosis at the time of his death.

EXPANSION OF COVERAGE

Denial of Claims Based on X-Rays

The 1972 law states that, determining the validity of claims for black lung benefits, denial of such claims shall not be based solely on the results of a chest roentgenogram. Many claims have in the past been denied either because there was no X-ray in the case of a deceased miner, or because the X-ray did not positively establish the existence of pneumoconiosis. Thus, under the new law the Social Security Administration and DOL must base the denial of a claim on evidence in addition to a negative X-ray. Persons who have filed claims under the old law and were denied benefits on this basis will have their cases reviewed under the 1972 act.

Rebuttable Presumption

A new rebuttable presumption of pneumoconiosis is established under the 1972 act, effective retroactively to December 30, 1969, under which a totally disabled coal miner who worked in an underground mine (or in conditions substantially similar to an underground mine) for 15 years, is considered totally disabled by pneumoconiosis if he has or had a totally disabling respiratory or pulmonary impairment but his chest X-ray (if any) has been interpreted as negative for pneumoconiosis. A

limitation is imposed on this presumption with respect to claims filed under part C of Title IV, discussed below. The presumption may be rebutted only by establishing that the miner does not, or did not, have pneumoconiosis, or that his respiratory or pulmonary impairment did not arise out of, or in connection with, his work in a coal mine.

Other Tests and Evidence

The Black Lung Benefits Act of 1972 provides that all relevant medical tests, such as blood gas studies, X-ray examination, electrocardiogram, pulmonary function studies, or physical performance tests, are to be considered in determining the validity of claims, as well as medical history, evidence submitted by the claimants' physician, and in the case of a deceased miner, affidavits of other persons with knowledge of his physical condition. Use of such additional tests, like the prohibition against denial of benefits solely on the basis of an X-ray and the rebuttable presumption just described, is made retroactive to December 30, 1969, so that previously denied or pending claims will be reviewed accordingly.

Total Disability Definition

The new law amends the definition of total disability to conform to the realities of the coal mining population. Thus, a coal miner will be considered totally disabled, for the purpose of determining eligibility for black lung benefits, when pneumoconiosis prevents him from gainful work which requires skills and abilities similar to those he used with some regularity and over a substantial period of time while working in the mines. The new definition is applicable retroactive to December 30, 1969, so that miners or their surviving dependents who filed claims under the 1969 act and were denied on the basis of the miner's not being totally disabled will have their claims reexamined.

Social Security Offset

The new black lung law states that the Federal black lung program is not to be considered a workmen's compensation law or plan for purposes of section 224 of the Social Security Act. Prior to enactment of the 1972 law where a claimant was receiving social security disability insurance benefits as well as black lung benefits, such social security payments were reduced to the extent that the combination of benefits exceeded 80 percent of the miner's prior earnings. Under the new law such reduction will be prohibited. Since this provision is made retroactive to December 30, 1969, beneficiaries whose social security disability benefits were reduced under the Social Security Administration's interpretation of 1969 law will be entitled to reimbursement by the Federal Government for the amount of the reduction.

Surface Miners

The 1969 act applied only to miners and dependents of miners who worked in underground coal mines. The 1972 Black Lung Benefits Act enlarges the coverage of the program to include coal miners (and their dependents, and survivors) who worked in coal mines other than underground mines. This was done by striking all references to "underground" in Title IV of the act. Surface miners may be eligible for benefits under the rebuttable presumption discussed above if the conditions during their 15 years of employment in a mine or mines were comparable to conditions in an underground mine. This provision is also effective retroactive to December 30, 1969.

PROTECTIONS, PROCEDURES, AND DATE CHANGES

Extension of Program

The 1972 act extends federal responsibility for payment of lifetime benefits by 18 months. Thus, claims filed on or before June 30, 1973, will, upon their approval, be paid by the Federal Government for the life of the beneficiaries, or for so long as such beneficiaries remain eligible for benefits.

Claims filed between July 1, 1973, and December 31, 1973, will be filed with the Social Security Administration district offices and at such other locations as provided in joint regulations of the Secretaries of Labor and Health, Education, and Welfare, and will be paid by the Secretary of Labor until December 31, 1973. All claims filed during this 6-month period, and all new claims filed after January 1, 1974, subsequently will be paid according to State workmen's compensation laws, if those laws comply with standards promulgated by the Secretary of Labor. In any State that does not have such a law the claim will be processed pursuant to Title IV of the Federal Coal Mine and Safety Act and will be paid either by the responsible operator or the Department of Labor.

The legislation also extends part C of Title IV, under which claims are filed pursuant to State workmen's compensation laws, from a termination date of 7 years following enactment of the 1969 act (December 30, 1976), to a termination date of 12 years following such enactment (December 30, 1981). Thus no new claims are payable after December 30, 1981. All claims filed under part C prior to that date, however will be paid under State workmen's compensation laws for the life of the beneficiaries, or for so long as such beneficiaries remain eligible for benefits.

Application of Part B to Part C

Amendments to Title IV of the Federal Coal Mine Health and Safety Act made by the Black Lung Benefits Act of 1972 to part B are also, to the extent appropriate, applicable to part C. Thus, all amendments to part B except the social security offset provision and the transition provision relating to claims filed between July 1, 1973, and December 31, 1973, apply to part C. There is, in addition, a limitation on the applicability under part C of the rebuttable presumption discussed previously. Under part C and part C only, no period of employment after June 30, 1971, shall be taken into account in establishing the 15 years' requirement of work in an underground mine or mines.

Discrimination in Employment

A new section of Title IV prohibits discrimination by an operator against any miner solely because such miner suffers from pneumoconiosis. Any miner who believes he has been discharged or otherwise discriminated against may within 90 days ask for a review consisting, as appropriate, of investigation, hearing and enforcement procedures conducted by the Secretary of Labor.

Notice to Claimants of Amendments

The 1972 act requires the Secretary of Health, Education, and Welfare to notify each person whose black lung claim has been denied or is pending of the changes to Title IV, and that his claim will be reviewed in light of the 1972 law. Also to be notified are those who may be entitled to retroactive benefits due to elimination of the social security offset provision. There will be no need for a claimant to file an application for review. Changes in the law will also be widely publicized in the various communications media by the Social Security Administration.

Limitation on Filing Certain Claims

With respect to claims filed under part C the validity of which rests on the new rebuttable presumption, these must be filed within 3 years after the miner's last exposed employment in a mine (for a living miner), and in the case of a deceased miner, such claims must be filed within 15 years after the miner's last exposed employment.

Medical Benefits

The new law requires employers under part C to provide medical benefits to their employees and requires State compensation laws to include such a requirement to qualify as adequate under part C.

Application of Social Security Act Procedures

The 1972 act makes applicable to Title IV certain procedural safeguards of the Social Security Act relating to hearing rights and procedures, judicial review, and limitation on attorneys' fees. Also included are provisions relating to subpoena authority and enforcement, overpayment and underpayment of claims, antigarnishment provisions, and criminal penalities for fraud.

The Black Lung Benefits Act of 1972 adds a new section to Title IV authorizing $10 million per year for 3 years to build and operate fixed site and mobile clinics for analysis, examination and treatment of respiratory and pulmonary impairments in both active and inactive coal miners. In addition, the new section directs that research be initiated to devise simple and effective tests to measure, detect and treat respiratory and pulmonary impairments.

For further information write to: Assistant Director, Coal Mine Health and Safety, Bureau of Mines, U.S. Department of the Interior, Washington, D.C. 20240.

Occupational Safety and Health Act of 1970

SUMMARY AND DESCRIPTION

Purpose of the Law

The declared Congressional purpose and policy of this Act is "to assure so far as possible every working man and woman in the Nation safe and healthful working conditions and to preserve our human resources."

Coverage

The law applies to every employer engaged in a business affecting commerce who has employees. It applies in all 50 States, the District of Columbia, Puerto Rico, the Virgin Islands, American Samoa, Guam, the Trust Territory of the Pacific Islands, Wake Island, the Outer Continental Shelf Lands, Johnston Island, and the Canal Zone. Federal, State and local government employees are specifically excluded from coverage, but may be covered by equally effective requirements.

In addition, the Act specifically provides that its terms shall not apply to working conditions protected under other Federal occupational safety and health laws (such as those under the Federal Coal Mine Health and Safety Act; and under the Atomic Energy Act of 1954, as amended, including State agreements under that Act).

Duties of Employers and Employees

Each *employer* under the Act has the general duty to furnish each of his employees employment and places of employment, free from recognized hazards causing, or likely to cause, death or serious physical harm; and the employer has the specific duty of complying with safety and health standards promulgated under the Act. Each *employee* has the duty to comply with these safety and health standards, and all rules, regulations, and orders issued pursuant to the Act which are applicable to his own actions and conduct.

Administration

Administration and enforcement of the Act are vested primarily in the Secretary of Labor and in a new agency, the Occupational Safety and Health Review Commission, a quasi-judicial board of three members appointed by the President. Research and related functions are vested in the Secretary of Health, Education, and Welfare whose functions will, for the most part, be carried out by the National Institute for Occupational Safety and Health established within HEW.

The Secretary of Labor is responsible for both promulgating and enforcing job safety and health standards. Occupational safety and health inspections are made by inspectors located in offices established in many communities throughout the country.

Occupational Safety and Health Standards

In general, job safety and health standards consist of rules for avoidance of hazards which have been proven by research and experience to be harmful to personal safety and health. They constitute an extensive compilation of wisdom which sometimes applies to *all* employees. An example of this would be fire protection standards. A great many standards, however, apply only to workers while engaged in *specific types of work*, such as handling compressed gas.

It is the obligation of all employers and employees to familiarize themselves with those standards which apply to them and to observe them at all times.

The Secretary of Labor is authorized, until April 28, 1973, to promulgate as occupational safety and health standards any existing Federal standards (such as those applying to Federal contractors under the Walsh-Healey Act) or any national consensus standards (such as those issued by the National Fire Protection Association), without complying with the rule-making requirements of the Administrative Procedure Act.

In addition, the Secretary of Labor may, upon the basis of information submitted by the Secretary of Health, Education, and Welfare, advisory committees and others, revise, modify or revoke existing standards as well as promulgate new ones. The promulgation of standards under this section of the Act must be done under the procedures set forth in the section itself, including various time limitations, and also under the procedures of the Administrative Procedure Act. Any person adversely affected by a standard issued by the Secretary may challenge its validity by petitioning the U.S. Court of Appeals within 60 days after its promulgation. Unless otherwise ordered by the Court, filing such a petition does not operate as a stay of the standard.

Also, the Act provides for the establishment of emergency temporary standards, effective immediately upon publication in the Federal Register, where it is found that employees are exposed to grave danger. The Act also contains provision for standards which may require:

■ That no employee dealing with toxic materials or harmful physical agents will suffer material impairment of health or functional capacity, even if such employee has regular exposure to the hazard dealt with by such standard for the period of his working life.

■ Development and prescription of labels or other appropriate forms of warning so that employees are made aware of all hazards to which they are exposed.

■ Prescription of suitable protective equipment.

■ Monitoring or measuring employee exposure to hazards as may be necessary for the protection of employees.

■ Prescription of the type and frequency of medical examinations or other tests for employees exposed to health hazards. At the request of an employee, the examination or test results shall be furnished to his physician.

The Secretary of Labor, after a hearing on an employer application therefor, is authorized to grant temporary variances from standards to give the employer sufficient time to come into compliance if he can show a need for certain time-extension and has a protective plan of action. Variances may be granted without time limits if the Secretary finds that an employer is using safety measures which are as safe as those required in a standard. Affected employees must be given notice of each such application and an opportunity for hearing.

Complaints of Violations

Any employees (or representative thereof) who believe that a violation of a job safety or health standard exists which threatens physical harm, or that an imminent danger exists, may request an inspection by sending a signed written notice to the Department of Labor. Such a notice shall set forth with reasonable particularity the grounds for the notice and a copy shall be provided the employer or his agent. The names of the complainants need not, however, be furnished to the employer. If the Secretary finds no reasonable grounds for the complaint and a citation is not issued, he is required to notify the complainants in writing of his determinations or final disposition of the matter. The Secretary is also required to set up procedures for informal review in a case where a citation is not issued.

Enforcement

In enforcing the standards, Labor Department safety insepctors may enter without delay, and at any reasonable times, any establishment covered by the Act to inspect the premises and all pertinent conditions, structures, machines, apparatus, devices, equipment, and materials therein, and to question privately any employer, owner, operator, agent, or employee. The Act permits the employer and a representative authorized by his employees to accompany the inspector during the physical inspection of any workplace for the purpose of aiding such inspection. The Secretary of Labor also has power, in making inspections and investigations to require the attendance and testimony of witnesses and the production of evidence under oath. The Secretary of Health, Education, and Welfare is also authorized to make inspections and question employers and employees in order to carry out those functions assigned to HEW under the Act.

Where an investigation reveals a violation, the employer is issued a written citation describing the specific nature of the violation. All citations shall fix a reasonable time for abatement of the violation, and each citation (or copies thereof) issued by the Department of Labor must be prominently posted at or near each place where a violation referred to in the citation occurred. Notices, in lieu of citations, may be issued for de minimis violations which have no direct or immediate relationship to safety or health.

No citation may be issued after the expiration of six (6) months following the occurrence of any violation.

Notification of Proposed Penalty Within a reasonable time after issuance of a citation for a job safety or health violation, the Labor Department shall notify the employer by certified mail of the penalty, if any, which is proposed to be assessed. The employer then has 15 working days within which to notify the Department that he wishes to contest the citation or proposed assessment of penalty. If the employer fails to so notify the Department, the citation and the assessment shall be final, provided no employee files an objection to the time allowed for abatement (see *below* "Time for Abatement of Hazards"). If the employer notifies the Department within such time that he does wish to contest, the Secretary of Labor will so advise the Occupational Safety and Health Review Commission which shall afford an opportunity for a hearing. The Commission will issue orders affirming, modifying or vacating the citation or proposed penalty, which orders are final 30 days after issuance. Review of Commission orders may be obtained in the U.S. Court of Appeals.

The Review Commission's rules of procedure shall provide affected employees (or representatives thereof) an opportunity to participate as parties to such hearings.

Time for Abatement of Hazards A citation issued by the Department shall prescribe a reasonable time for elimination or abatement of the hazard. This time limit may also be contested if notification is filed with the Department within 15 days. The time set by the Department for correcting a violation shall not begin to run until there is a final order of the Review Commission, if the review is initiated by the employer in good faith and not solely for delay or avoidance of penalties.

Employees (or representatives of employees) also have the right to object to the period of time fixed for the abatement of a violation. If, within 15 days after a citation is issued, an employee files a notice with the Department alleging that an unreasonable time was allowed for abatement, review procedures similar to those specified above apply.

Failure to Correct Violations Within Allowed Time Where time for correction of a violation is allowed, but the employer fails to abate within such time, the Secretary of Labor shall notify the employer by certified mail of such failure and of the proposed penalty. Such notice and assessment shall be final unless the employer contests the same by notice to the Secretary within 15 days.

Upon a showing by an employer of a good faith effort to comply with the abatement requirements of a citation, but that abatement has not been completed because of factors beyond his reasonable control, an opportunity for a hearing will be afforded, after which an order affirming or modifying the abatement requirement will be issued.

Penalties for Violations

Willful or repeated violations of the Act's requirements by employers may incur monetary penalties of up to $10,000 for each violation. Citations issued for serious violations incur *mandatory* monetary penalties of up to $1,000 for each violation, while penalties in the same amount *may* be incurred where non-serious violations are cited. A serious violation exists where there is a substantial probability that death or serious physical harm could result. Any employer who fails to correct a violation for which a citation has been issued within the period prescribed may be penalized up to $1,000 each day the violation persists.

A willful violation by an employer which results in the death of any employee is punishable by a fine of up to $10,000 or imprisonment for up to six months. A second conviction doubles these criminal penalties.

Criminal penalties are also established for making false official statements, and for giving unauthorized advance notice of any inspections to be conducted.

Recordkeeping Requirements

Employers are required to keep and make available to the Labor Secretary (and also to the HEW Secretary) records on certain employer activities. Employers are also required to maintain accurate records (and period reports) of work-related deaths, injuries and illnesses. Minor injuries requiring only first aid treatment need not be recorded, but a record must be made if it involves medical treatment, loss of consciousness, restriction of work or motion, or transfer to another job.

Employers can also be required to maintain accurate records of employee exposures to potentially toxic materials or harmful physical agents which are required to be monitored or measured and to promptly advise any employee of any excessive exposure and of the corrective action being undertaken. The Secretary of Labor, in

cooperation with the Secretary of Health, Education, and Welfare, is authorized to issue regulations in this area which shall provide employees or their representatives with an opportunity to observe such monitoring or measuring to have access to the records thereof and to such records as well indicate their own exposure to toxic materials or harmful physical agents.

For recordkeeping purposes, the Secretary's regulations may also require employers to conduct their own periodic inspections.

The Secretary is directed to issue regulations requiring employers to keep their employees informed of their protections and obligations through posting of notices or other appropriate means. The information which employers may be required to give their employees may also include the provisions of applicable standards.

Statistics

The Secretary of Labor, in consultation with the HEW Secretary, is required to develop and maintain an effective program of collection, compilation and analysis of statistics on work injuries and illnesses. In so doing he may make private grants or contracts and grants to States or political subdivisions thereof. The Secretary may also require employers to file such reports of work injuries and illnesses required to be kept as he shall deem necessary.

Existing agreements between the Department of Labor and a State for collection of occupational safety and health statistics are preserved until replaced by other arrangements under grants or contracts made under the Act.

General Notice Requirements

The Secretary of Labor is required to publish in the Federal Register a statement of his reasons for any action he takes with respect to the promulgation of any standard, the issuance of any rule, order or decision, the granting of any exemption or extension of time, as well as any action he takes to compromise, mitigate or settle any penalty assessed under the Act.

Imminent Danger

Any conditions or practices in any place of employment which are such that a danger exists which could reasonably be expected to cause death or serious physical harm immediately or before the imminence of such danger can be eliminated through normal enforcement procedures, may be restrained by order of a U.S. District Court upon petition of the Secretary of Labor. If the Secretary arbitrarily or capriciously fails to seek action to abate an imminent danger of such kind, a *mandamus* action to compel him to act may be brought in the U.S. District Court by any employee who may be injured by reason of such failure. A Labor Department safety inspector who concludes that such imminent-danger conditions or practices exist in any place of employment is obligated to inform the affected employees and employers of the danger and that he is recommending to the Secretary of Labor that relief be sought.

Protection Against Harassment

No person shall discharge or in any manner discriminate against any employee because he exercises any right under the Act or files a complaint or other proceeding or because he testifies or is about to testify in any proceeding under the Act. Any employee who believes that he has been discharged or otherwise discriminated against in violation of this provision may, within 30 days of such illegal action, file a complaint with the Secretary of Labor. The Secretary is authorized to investigate the matter and to bring action in the U.S. District Court for appropriate relief, including rehiring or reinstatement of the employee to his former job with back pay. The Secretary must notify the complainant of this action on the complaint within 90 days of its receipt.

State Participation

The Act encourages the States to assume the fullest responsibility for the administration and enforcement of their occupational safety and health laws by providing grants to the States for the purposes shown below. A specific disclaimer of Federal preemption is included in order to permit any State agency or court to assert jurisdiction under State law over any occupational safety or health issue with respect to which no Federal standard is in effect under this law.

In addition, any State may assume responsibility for the development and enforcement of occupational safety and health standards relating to any job safety and health issue covered by a standard promulgated under the Act, if such State submits an approved plan for so doing to the Secretary of Labor. The Secretary shall approve such a plan under the following conditions:

1. An agency, or agencies, of the State must be designated or created to carry out the plan.

2. The State standards (and enforcement thereof) must be at least as effective as the counterpart Federal standards in providing safe and healthful employment.

3. There must be effective provisions for rights of entry and inspection of workplaces, including a prohibition on advance notice of inspections.

4. Enforcement capacity must be demonstrated.

5. Adequate funds for administration and enforcement must be assured.

6. Effective and comprehensive job safety and health programs for all public employees within the State will be established to the extent permitted by the particular State's law.

7. The State, and employers within the State, will make such reports as may be required by the Secretary of Labor.

Following approval of a State plan for the development and enforcement of State standards, the Secretary of Labor may continue to exercise his enforcement authority with respect to comparable Federal occupational safety and health standards until he determines on the basis of actual operations that the criteria set forth above are being applied. Once he makes such determination (but he cannot do so during the first 3 years after the plan's approval), the Federal standards and the Secretary's enforcement of them become inapplicable with respect to issues covered under the plan.

The Secretary is required to make a continuing evaluation of the manner in which each State plan is being carried out and to withdraw his approval whenever there is a failure to comply substantially with any provision thereof. Such a plan shall cease to be in effect upon receipt of notice by the State of the Secretary's withdrawal of approval.

The Secretary of Labor is authorized, after consultation with the Secretary of Health, Education, and Welfare, to make grants to States for experimental and demonstration projects consistent with the objectives of the Act, for administering and enforcing approved programs, for assisting them in identifying their needs, or in developing their plans, in establishing systems for collection of information concerning the nature and frequency of occupational injuries and diseases, for developing and administering programs dealing with occupational safety and health statistics, and for improving the expertise of personnel or the administration and enforcement of State occupational safety and health laws consistent with the objectives of the Act.

If the Secretary of Labor rejects a State plan for development and enforcement of State standards, he shall afford the State submitting the plan due notice and opportunity for hearing before so doing. The subsequent withdrawal of an approved State plan or the rejection of a State's plan is subject to review in the U.S. Court of Appeals.

Education and Training Programs

The Act provides for programs to be conducted by the Secretary of Labor, in consultation with the Department of Health, Education, and Welfare, for the education and training of employers and employees in the recognition, avoidance, and prevention of unsafe and unhealthful working conditions, and in the effective means for preventing occupational injuries and illnesses. The Act also makes provision for educational and training programs to provide an adequate supply of qualified personnel to carry out the law's purposes and for informational programs on the importance of and proper use of adequate safety and health equipment to be conducted primarily by the Department of Health, Education, and Welfare, but also to some extent by the Secretary of Labor.

National Institute for Occupational Safety and Health

The Act establishes within HEW a National Institute For Occupational Safety and Health primarily for the purpose of carrying out the research and educational functions assigned to the HEW Secretary.

In addition to these functions, the Institute is authorized to develop and establish recommended occupational safety and health standards; to conduct research and experimental programs for developing criteria for new and improved job safety and health standards; and to make recommendations to the Secretaries of Labor and HEW concerning new and improved standards.

Among the HEW functions which may be carried out by the Institute is the one which calls for prescribing regulations requiring employers to measure, record, and make reports on the exposure of employees to potentially toxic substances or harmful physical agents which might endanger their safety and health. Employers required to do so may receive full financial or other assistance for the purpose of defraying any additional expense incurred. Also authorized are programs for medical examinations and tests as may be necessary to determine, for the purposes of research, the incidence of occupational illness and the susceptibility of employees to such illnesses. These examinations may also be at Government expense. The Secretary of HEW is required to publish annually a list of all known toxic substances and the concentrations at which toxicity is known to occur, and, at the written request of any employer or authorized representatives of employees, to make determinations whether any substance normally found in the place of employment has potentially toxic effects. Such determinations shall be submitted to both the employer and the affected employees as soon as possible. The HEW Secretary is also required to conduct and publish industry-wide studies on chronic- or low-level exposure to a broad variety of industrial materials, processes, and stresses on the potential for illness, disease, or loss of functional capacity in aging adults.

Information obtained by the Department of HEW and of Labor under the research provisions of the Act is to be disseminated to employers and employees and organizations thereof.

Workmen's Compensation

The Act does not in any manner affect any workmen's compensation law or enlarge or diminish or affect in any other manner the common law or statutory rights, duties, or liabilities of employers and employees under any law with respect to injuries, diseases, or death of employees

arising out of, or in the course of, employment. Provision is made in the law, however, for a 15-member National Commission on State Workmen's Compensation Laws to evaluate State workmen's compensation laws in order to determine if such laws provide an adequate, prompt, and equitable system of compensation for the injury or death arising out of or in the course of employment.

Assistance From Small Business Administration

The law includes amendments to the Small Business Act which provides for financial assistance to small firms for alterations in its equipment, facilities, or methods of operation to comply with standards established by the Department of Labor or by any State pursuant to the Act if the Small Business Administration determines that such a firm is likely to suffer substantial economic injury without such assistance.

Other Provisions

Advisory Committees The Act creates a 12-member National Advisory Committee to be appointed by the Secretary of Labor (including 4 designees of the Secretary of HEW) to advise, consult, and make recommendations on matters relating to the administration of the Act, and permits the establishment of *ad hoc* advisory committees to assist the Secretary of Labor in his standard-setting functions.

Nonobstruction Requirement Any information obtained by any agency under the Act shall be obtained with a minimum burden upon employers, especially those operating small businesses. Unnecessary duplication of efforts in obtaining information shall be reduced to the maximum extent feasible.

Occupational Safety and Health Review Commission The Act establishes a new independent Federal agency, called the Occupational Safety and Health Review Commission. This Commission is a quasi-judicial body whose functions are: (1) to hear and review cases of alleged violations brought before it by the Secretary of Labor; and, where warranted, (2) to issue corrective orders, and (3) to assess civil penalties. The Commission is composed of three members, appointed by the President (with approval of the Senate) to serve 6-year staggered terms, and chosen from among persons who are qualified by reason of training, education, or experience to perform their duties. One of the members shall be appointed by the President to serve as Chairman.

Labor Department Legal Representation The Solicitor of Labor is authorized to appear for and represent the Secretary in any civil litigation brought under the Act subject to the direction and control of the Attorney General.

Trade Secrets Any trade secrets revealed to Labor Department personnel during the course of their duties under the Act shall be considered confidential for the purpose of 18 U.S.C. 1905.*

National Defense Tolerances The Secretary of Labor may allow reasonable variations, tolerances, and exemptions from any and all of the Act's provisions, if he finds these necessary to avoid serious impairment of the national defense.

Federal Protection for Labor Department Inspectors The Act broadens the provisions of Title 18 of the United States Code, which makes it a Federal criminal offense to assault, kill, or otherwise interfere with certain law enforcement officials in the course of their assignments, by extending this protection to all employees of the Department of Labor assigned to perform investigative, inspection, or law enforcement functions.

Annual Reports Comprehensive annual reports on the Act must be prepared and submitted to the President for transmittal to the Congress by both the Secretary of Labor and the Secretary of Health, Education, and Welfare. Reports are also required from the Secretary of Labor on the grants program, from the Director of the National Institute for Occupational Safety and Health on the operations of that Institute, and from the Secretary of Labor on occupational safety and health programs for Federal employees.

New Assistant Secretary of Labor The law adds an additional Assistant Secretary in the Department of Labor, an Assistant Secretary for Occupational Safety and Health, who heads the new Occupational Safety and Health Administration within the Department. This Administration, established by Secretary's Order 12-71, effective April 28, 1971, has broad responsibilities to insure that employees have safe and healthful working conditions. In addition to administering the Williams-Steiger Occupational Safety and Health Act of 1970, the Administration also carries out the Department's safety and health functions under the Walsh-Healey Public Contraacts Act of 1936, as amended; the Service Contract Act of 1965; the Contract Work Hours and Safety Standards Act; the Longshoremen's and Harbor Workers'

Compensation Act; the National Foundation on the Arts and Humanities Act of 1965; Executive Order No. 11612, signed July 26, 1971 (July 28, 1971, 36 F.R. 13891), relating to occupational safety and health programs for Federal employees; and the Vocational Rehabilitation Act.

Addendum

Prior to establishment of the Occupational Safety and Health Administration, the Department's safety and health functions had been performed by the Bureau of Labor Standards. With creation of the new Administration, that Bureau was dissolved and its programs divided between two administrations within the Department. Safety and health functions were assimilated into the new Administration, except those responsibilities related to child labor provisions of the Fair Labor Standards Act, which remained within the Employment Standards Administration. Other programs of the Bureau, relating to technical assistance and information on subject matters other than safety, were absorbed into the Employment Standards Administration through continuance of two divisions.

The Division of Employment Standards and the Division of Workmen's Compensation help to improve employment standards for all workers through better legislation, administration, and practices. Upon request, technical advisory assistance and consultation are furnished to State labor agencies, unions, management, and others in the development and administration of improved standards. The divisions serve as a clearinghouse on State law and practice—the Division of Workmen's Compensation on the subject of workmen's compensation, and the Division of Employment Standards on such subjects as minimum wage, hours of work and overtime pay, wage garnishment, industrial relations, child labor, status of agricultural workers, employment discrimination, regulation of private employment agencies, and other matters affecting employment conditions. Better understanding of the need for and purposes of effective standards is promoted through issuance of publications and the provision of technical information services.

For further information write to: Office of Information Services, Occupational Safety and Health Administration, U.S. Department of Labor, Washington, D.C. 20210.

Executive Order 11612— Occupational Safety and Health Programs for Federal Employees (1971)

The Occupational Safety and Health Act of 1970 authorizes the development and enforcement of standards to assure safe and healthful working conditions for employees in the private sector. Section 19 of that Act makes each Federal agency head responsible for establishing and maintaining an effective and comprehensive occupational safety and health program which

---

* This section provides that any employee of any department or agency of the Federal Government who reveals any confidential information coming to him in the course of any examination or investigation, made or filed with such department or agency, which relates to trade secrets shall be fined not more than $1,000, or imprisoned for not more than 1 year or both, and removed from employment.

is consistent with the standards promulgated by the Secretary of Labor for businesses affecting interstate commerce.

Section 7902 of Title 5, United States Code, authorizes the President to establish by Executive Order a safety council composed of representatives of Federal agencies and of labor organizations representing employees to serve as an advisory body to the Secretary of Labor in carrying out a Federal safety program.

As the Nation's largest employer, the Federal Government has a special obligation to set an example for safe and healthful employment. It is appropriate that the Federal Government strengthen its efforts to assure safe and healthful working conditions for its own employees.

NOW, THEREFORE, by virtue of the authority vested in me by section 7902 of Title 5 of the United States Code, and as President of the United States, it is hereby ordered as follows:

Establishment of Occupational Safety and Health Programs in Federal Departments and Agencies

SECTION 1. The head of each Federal department and agency shall establish an occupational safety and health program (hereinafter referred to as a safety program) in compliance with the requirements of section 7902 of Title 5 of the United States Code and section 19(a) of the Occupational Safety and Health Act of 1970 (which Act shall hereinafter be referred to as the Safety Act). The programs shall be consistent with the standards prescribed by section 6 of the Safety Act. In providing safety programs for Federal employees, the head of each Federal department and agency shall—

1. Designate or appoint a qualified official who shall be responsible for the management of the safety program within his agency.

2. Establish (A) a safety policy; (B) an organization and a set of procedures, providing for appropriate consultation with employees, that will permit that policy to be implemented effectively; (C) a safety management information system; (D) goals and objectives for reducing and eliminating employee injuries and occupational illnesses; (E) periodic inspections of workplaces to ensure compliance with standards; (F) plans and procedures for evaluating the program's effectiveness; and (G) priorities with respect to the factors which cause occupational injury and illness so that appropriate countermeasures can be developed.

3. Correct conditions that do not meet safety and health standards.

4. Submit to the Secretary of Labor by April 1 of each year a report containing (A) the status of his agency's safety program in reducing injuries and occupational illnesses to personnel during the preceding calendar year as related to the goals and objectives established for that year; (B) goals and objectives for the current year; (C) a plan for achieving those goals and objectives; (D) any report required under section 7902(e) (2) of Title 5 of the United States Code; and (E) such other information as may be requested by the Secretary.

5. Cooperate with and assist the Secretary of Labor in the performance of the Secretary's duties under section 7902 of Title 5 of the United States Code and section 19 of the Safety Act.

Duties of the Secretary of Labor

SECTION 2. (a) The Secretary of Labor (hereinafter referred to as the Secretary), or his designee in the Department of Labor, shall—

1. By regulation, provide guidance to the heads of Federal

departments and agencies to assist them in fulfilling their occupational safety and health responsibilities;

2. evaluate the safety programs of Federal departments and agencies annually, and, with the consent of the head of the affected department or agency, the Secretary may conduct at headquarters or in the field such investigations as he deems necessary;

3. develop a safety management information system to accommodate the data requirements of the progarm;

4. submit to the President by June 1 of each year an analysis of the information submitted to him by the heads of the Federal departments and agencies. This analysis shall include the Secretary's evaluation of each agency's safety program and shall contain his recommendations for improving safety programs throughout the Federal service.

(b) By agreement, the Secretary may, to the extent permitted by law, extend the safety program provided for under this Order to Federal employees not covered under section 7902 of Title 5 of the United States Code and the Safety Act.

Federal Safety Advisory Council

SECTION 3. (a) A Federal Advisory Council on Occupational Safety and Health shall be established to advise the Secretary in carrying out his responsibilities under this Order. This Council shall consist of 15 members appointed by the Secretary and shall include representatives of Federal departments and agencies, and of labor organizations representing employees. At least three members shall be representatives of such labor organizations. The members shall serve for three-year terms, except that, for the first Council, one-third will serve for one year and one-third for two years.

(b) The Secretary, or his designee, shall serve as the Chairman of the Council, and shall prescribe such rules for the conduct of its business as he deems necessary and appropriate.

(c) The Council shall meet at the call of its Chairman. It may establish such subcommittees as it finds necessary.

(d) The Council may establish or continue field affiliates in such manner and to the extent it deems advisable to support the purposes of this Order.

Administrative and Budgetary Arrangements

SECTION 4. The Secretary shall make available necessary office space and furnish the Council necessary equipment, supplies, and staff services.

Effect on Other Powers and Duties

SECTION 5. Nothing in this Order shall be construed to impair or alter the powers and duties of the Secretary or the heads of other Federal departments and agencies pursuant to section 7902 of Title 5 of the United States Code, section 19 of the Safety Act, or any other provision of law.

Termination of Existing Order

SECTION 6. Executive Order No. 10990 of February 2, 1962, is hereby superseded.

Comprehensive Employment and Training Act (CETA)

The Comprehensive Employment and Training Act (CETA), signed into law on December 28, 1973, was designed to provide "job training and employment opportunities for economically disadvantaged, unemployed, and underemployed persons" to enable them to secure self-sustaining, unsubsidized employment. Unlike the federally administered program efforts of the preceding 12 years, however, CETA offers a flexible, decentralized system of comprehensive and decategorized training and employment programs, planned and operated by States and local units of government, subject to Federal agency oversight.

The act (as amended) contains the following seven titles:

■ Title I of CETA creates a decentralized program structure, placing the authority to plan and operate a flexible system of manpower services—including training, employment, counseling, testing, and placement—in the hands of prime sponsors. For the most part, the latter are States and units of local government in jurisdictions of 100,000 or more population.

■ Title II authorizes a program of developmental transitional public service employment for areas of "substantial unemployment" (defined as areas having 6.5 percent or more unemployment) to be administered in the same decentralized manner as programs carried out under Title I.

■ Title III authorizes the Secretary of Labor to provide additional employment and training services to such special groups as Indians, migrant and seasonal farmworkers, offenders, youth, and others whom the Secretary determines to have particular disadvantages in the labor market. This title also provides for research, demonstration, and evaluation programs to be administered by the Secretary.

■ Title IV contains continuing authority for the Job Corps, originally authorized under Title I–A of the Economic Opportunity Act of 1964.

■ Title V establishes a National Commission for Manpower Policy to serve as an independent policy advisory group with responsibility for examining manpower questions and suggesting to the Secretary of Labor and the Congress particular means of dealing with them.

■ Title VI (created by the Emergency Jobs and Unemployment Assistance Act of 1974) provides for a large temporary program of emergency public service employment specially designed to help ease the impact of the high unemployment.

■ Title VII contains definitions and administrative procedures necessary to assist in the orderly management of the act.

PROGRAM CONCEPTS

CETA was the result of over 12 years of national involvement in developing and operating programs that offered a variety of training, employment, and related services designed to help unemployed and underemployed persons, particularly the disadvantaged, secure and retain unsubsidized employment. The predecessors of CETA—the Area Redevelopment Act (ARA) of 1961, the Manpower Development and Training Act (MDTA) of 1962, the Economic Opportunity Act (EOA) of 1964, and the Emergency Employment Act (EEA) of 1971—provided specialized, nationally determined programs for target groups identified in the legislation (e.g., those persons experiencing structural unemployment, youth, minorities, older workers, and the economically disadvantaged). The proliferation of these efforts, which were administered by separate and often competing sponsors, produced a series of frequently overlapping and seldom coordinated program approaches and target group priorities.

Growing dissatisfaction with this extensive fragmentation and complexity resulted in the passage of CETA, which incorporates the following basic concepts:

■ First, the principal responsibility for the planning and operation of programs under CETA is decentralized and moved from Federal control to that of State and local elected officials designated as prime sponsors. This important change reflects the underlying assumption that local government officials, who are closer and more immediately accountable to the people requiring employment and training services, can best plan programs and set priorities geared to the needs of their particular areas.

■ Second, local program funding is consolidated and coordinated. The previous network of direct Department of Labor contracts with many diverse local sponsoring organizations, without any effective overall management for the local areas as a whole, has been largely replaced by a system of block grants to the chief elected officials at the State and local government levels, who are responsible for planning and managing the total program. These officials, becuase of their sensitivity to local conditions, have the capacity to minimize duplication and overlap and achieve greater coordination with other employment and training resources in the community.

■ Third, decategorized funding under CETA encourages localized, flexible responses to current or anticipated manpower needs. The individual prime sponsor may develop the full range of activities permitted under predecessor legislation—including classroom training, on-the-job training, work experience, public service employment, and such manpower and supportive services as counseling, direct placement, and child care—or may restrict the spectrum of program offerings in order to intensify services in response to local requirements.

It should be noted that most job placements and training for specific jobs in the United States occur in the private sector. This perspective must be kept in mind in considering the role of government in employment and training activities.

The three broad target groups to be served under

CETA—the unemployed, the underemployed, and the disadvantaged—were previously identified under MDTA (unemployed and underemployed), EOA (unemployed or having low income), and EEA (unemployed and underemployed). The Federal Government established priorities among these target groups and also mandated various levels of service for other special groups (e.g., veterans). Under CETA, prime sponsors, rather than the Federal Government, can now decide which activities will be available for which broad and special target groups within the framework of local needs, changing local labor market conditions, and the requirements of the act.

PRIME SPONSORS

Prime sponsors are units of State and local government that are responsible for operating CETA employment and training programs to serve the needs of their communities. Prime sponsors are generally one of the following: States; cities or counties with populations of at least 100,000; or combinations of units of government, called consortia, in which at least one member jurisdiction has a population of 100,000 or more. The Secretary of Labor may also designate additional sponsors if he determines that they have a special capacity for carrying out CETA programs within certain labor markets or rural areas with high unemployment.

Prime sponsors are responsible for determining local needs and providing programs designed to meet them through such activities as classroom training, on-the-job training, work experience, public service employment, counseling, testing, job development, child care, and other supportive services. Sponsors can arrange to provide these services directly or through contracts or subgrants with such organizations as the State employment service, vocational education agencies, community groups, or private firms. They are also responsible for monitoring and evaluating programs to insure that they meet local needs.

FUNDING AND ELIGIBILITY

Title I, section 103 of CETA prescribes that 80 percent of the appropriated funds be distributed to prime sponsors on the basis of the number of unemployed persons and the proportion of low-income families in each prime sponsor's area, as well as its proportionate share of employment and training funds received in the previous year. The remaining Title I funds are distributed as follows: 5 percent for grants to Governors for vocational training services; 4 percent to Governors for flexible State activities; 5 percent for incentives to encourage the formation of consortia; and the remaining 6 percent for the discretionary use of the Secretary of Labor.

Any person who is economically disadvantaged, unemployed, or underemployed is eligible to participate in a program offered under Title I. An economically disadvantaged person is defined as a member of a family

that receives cash welfare payments or whose annual income in relation to family size does not exceed the poverty level determined in accordance with criteria established by the Office of Management and Budget. An underemployed person is one who is working part time and seeking full-time work or is working full time but whose salary in relation to family size is below the officially determined poverty level.

Under Title II, 80 percent of the funds appropriated are distributed to prime sponsors who qualify under Title I in a manner that takes into account the number of unemployed persons residing in areas of substantial unemployment within their jurisdictions. The remaining 20 percent are distributed at the discretion of the Secretary of Labor, taking into account the severity of unemployment within eligible areas.

Any person living in an area of substantial unemployment who has been unemployed for at least 30 days, or is underemployed, is eligible to participate in Title II programs.

Under Title VI, 90 percent of the funds appropriated are distributed to prime sponsors on the basis of the number of unemployed persons living within the prime sponsor's jurisdiction and the number of such persons living within areas of substantial unemployment. The remaining 10 percent are distributed by the Secretary of Labor, taking into account changes in the rates of unemployment.

Any person who resides in the prime sponsor's jurisdiction and either has been unemployed for at least 30 days—15 days under certain conditions—or is underemployed is eligible to participate in a Title VI program.

THE LOCAL ROLE

Titles I, II, and VI of CETA are based on the assumption that elected officials at the State and local levels are more attuned to the needs of their communities than are Federal officials and are therefore better equipped to oversee the planning, development, and operation of employment and training programs in their jurisdictions. In addition to their roles as the grantees or responsible officials for a variety of other State or Federal programs, these officials are directly accountable, through the electoral process, to the people of the community.

The act requires each prime sponsor to establish a planning council with representation from all segments of the community, including (to the extent feasible) client groups and community-based organizations, the public employment service, education and training institutions, the business sector, labor, and where appropriate, agriculture.

The functions of the council are to submit recommendations regarding program plans, goals, policies, and procedures; to monitor and objectively evaluate employment and training programs in the prime sponsor's jurisdiction; and to provide for continuing analysis of employment and training needs.

THE STATE ROLE

The State role under CETA is multifaceted, encompassing the functions of program operator, coordinator, and evaluator. Governors may receive grants under titles I, II, and VI to provide services to the balance-of-State areas that do not fall within the jurisdictions of independent prime sponsors. In addition, there are special grants to Governors composed of 5 percent of Title I funds for vocational training services in prime sponsor jurisdictions, 4 percent for coordination and special statewide manpower services, and 1 percent for staffing and support of the State Manpower Services Council (SMSC's).

The State Manpower Services Council, whose chairperson and members are appointed by the Governor, is authorized to review both the plans of each prime sponsor and the plans of State agencies providing services to these prime sponsors. The SMSC is also charged with continuous monitoring of the operation of programs conducted by each prime sponsor and of the service of State agencies. The SMSC can make recommendations to prime sponsors, State agencies, and the Governor on ways to improve the effectiveness of such programs.

FEDERAL OVERSIGHT FUNCTIONS

The Federal oversight role as undertaken by the Department of Labor is based upon the legislative compromise position developed during the passage of CETA in 1973. On the basis of the act itself, the committee reports, and the floor debates, the legislative intent regarding Federal oversight can be summarized as follows: First, while there should be a strong and active Federal role at all stages of planning, review, and implementation, the Secretary of Labor should not attempt to "second guess" the good-faith judgment of the prime sponsor in developing and implementing a program to meet the needs of the sponsor's jurisdiction. Second, the Federal Government should not intrude in the day-to-day operations or decisionmaking process of the prime sponsor. Third, the Secretary of Labor may not rely on certification alone to insure that Federal funds are expended in accordance with the law but must exercise independent judgment. The Secretary is expected to look behind the sponsors' certifications of compliance, primarily through a process of regular auditing, spot checking, and followup on complaints of interested parties.

The four most significant elements of the Federal role therefore, are: Establishing national objectives, priorities, and performance standards; providing technical assistance; reviewing and approving plans; and assessing and evaluating performance.

First, there is a clear Federal role in interpreting national objectives and priorities and in establishing performance standards for employment and training programs. In Federal regulations and other issuances, the Department of Labor states the overall objectives of the act. In addition, the Department makes known, and works toward, specific goals that have been developed by the Congress through the appropriations and oversight process. Furthermore, the Department makes known priorities established by the executive branch to meet specific problems, such as special consideration for veterans. Finally, the Department works with sponsors and the public to develop objective standards for reviewing and assessing performance against plans.

Second, the broad responsibilities of prime sponsors under CETA for planning and operating programs often require technical assistance by the Department's Employment and Training Administration (formerly the Manpower Administration) in such areas as planning and financial management, both to improve the programs and to facilitate Federal Government review of sponsors' performance. Federal regional staff were given special training in CETA regulations and procedures prior to undertaking their new responsibilities for assisting prime sponsors to develop and operate their programs. A series of more than a dozen technical assistance guides on a variety of subjects ranging from fiscal activities to community-based-organizations has been issued by the Employment and Training Administration, and others are being developed. In addition, training centers are being established in each region to provide continuous training for Federal and prime sponsor staff.

Third, the Secretary of Labor is responsible for reviewing and approving prime sponsor plans to assure that they are in accordance with the purpose and provisions of the act and meet the conditions for Federal funding. As a condition of financial assistance, prime sponsors are required to submit a comprehensive manpower plan "in such detail as the Secretary deems necessary . . ." to satisfy various specifications of the act.

The regional offices of the Employment and Training Administration review sponsor plans and judge their adequacy on the basis of criteria set forth in the Federal regulations. Department of Health, Education, and Welfare regional office representatives are also provided plans for review, and they may make recommendations concerning their adequacy to Department of Labor officials. Plan disapproval is viewed only as a last step, when all efforts to resolve problems have been exhausted. To date, although plans have been returned to sponsors for corrections and mutually agreed-upon changes, no plans have been disapproved. Sponsors who disagree with the judgments and determinations of the Department of Labor have recourse to a public hearing and the judicial review process.

Fourth, the Federal role in assessing the performance of CETA prime sponsors involves three types of activities: Reviewing compliance; assessing performance in relation to the goals in the approved plan; and evaluating program impact or effectiveness.

Just as the plan approval process is intended to insure that the prime sponsor's plan is in compliance with the requirements of the act, programs must be reviewed to insure that operations are in accordance with the assurances and certifications made by the prime sponsor and that Federal funds are properly expended. Procedures adopted to carry out these responsibilities include onsite spot checking for compliance with assurances; investigation of allegations and complaints; audits by Department of Labor staff; review of recurring Federal reports; and special reports by the prime sponsor. Spot checking includes onsite inspections of such program aspects as equal employment opportunity activities, working and training conditions, and participant eligibility.

If the results of such procedures indicate noncompliance with assurances or inadequate financial management systems, the Department may require corrective action and, at the request of the prime sponsors, may provide technical assistance to remedy the problem. In extreme cases, the Secretary may revoke the plan, in whole or in part, and undertake direct operation of a program in the sponsor's jurisdiction. Such action has not been necessary to date, however.

Performance is assessed by comparing actual program accomplishments with the goals established for the grant period in the approved plan. The Employment and Training Administration requires quarterly reports and performs onsite reviews. At least once each quarter, representatives of the Employment and Training Administration discuss with the prime sponsors their performance against the plan for the preceding period.

Upon determination of inadequate performance, the Employment and Training Administration may require the prime sponsor to develop a corrective action plan that may include technical assistance from Federal staff or other sources. If continued performance reviews indicate that operating problems have not been resolved, the Secretary may take such further actions as reallocating funds or disapproving new funding. Of particular importance in taking such actions is the prime sponsor's responsiveness and readiness to modify the plan to accommodate changes in economic conditions in the area.

Effectiveness oversight is accomplished by continual reviews of both program activities and the use of grant funds. These reviews are based on recurring Federal reports submitted by the prime sponsor, special reports required of the prime sponsor from time to time, and special studies, in addition to onsite visits, conducted by the Department of Labor. To facilitate such reviews, the Department requires that the prime sponsor maintain specific records and information. In addition, the Department's evaluation staff is examining the experiences of a national sample of State and local sponsors. A long-term study of CETA effectiveness has also been undertaken through (a) the tracking of a national sample of participants in CETA programs under a Continuous Longitudinal Manpower Survey (CLMS), conducted by the U.S. Bureau of the Census, to determine impact on participants, particularly on their post-program employment and earnings; and (b) a study undertaken by a private contractor of the feasibility of developing consistent data on unit costs to enable cost effectiveness analyses.

Federal Agencies Related to Labor

The material in this section is drawn from the United States Government Manual, 1978–79* the official handbook of the Federal Government. It describes the purposes and programs of most Government agencies related to labor and lists top personnel. Summary paragraphs following personnel listing were prepared by the departments and agencies included. These paragraphs briefly describe the agencies role in the Federal Government.

DEPARTMENT OF LABOR

200 Constitution Avenue NW., Washington, D.C. 20210
Phone, 202-523-8165

Secretary of Labor	Ray Marshall.
Executive Assistant and Counselor to the Secretary	Paul H. Jensen.
Special Assistant to the Secretary	Walter Shapiro.
Special Assistant to the Secretary	Charles B. Knapp.
Special Assistant to the Secretary	Mary Ann Wyrsch.
Special Assistant to the Secretary	Jodie T. Allen.
Director, Office of Information, Publications, and Reports	John W. Leslie.
Director, Office of Special Investigations and Review	Rocco De Marco.
Director, Women's Bureau	Alexis Herman.
Under Secretary	Robert J. Brown.
Executive Assistant to the Under Secretary	Craig Berrington.
Special Assistant to the Under Secretary	Willis J. Nordlund.
Special Assistant to the Under Secretary	Joel Solkoff.
Special Assistant to the Under Secretary	Fred Romero.
Deputy Under Secretary for Evaluation	Peter Henle.
Chairman, Employees' Compensation Appeals Board	E. Gerald Lamboley, Acting.
Chairman, Benefits Review Board	Samuel J. Smith.
Chief Administrative Law Judge	H. Stephen Gordon.
Solicitor	Carin A. Clauss.
Deputy Solicitor	Alfred G. Albert.
Deputy Solicitor (Regional Operations)	(Vacancy).
Administrative Officer	J. J. Lafranchise.
Associate Solicitor, Division of General Legal Services	Ronald G. Whiting.
Associate Solicitor, Division of Employment and Training Legal Services	Nathaniel Baccus III.
Associate Solicitor, Division of Fair Labor Standards	Donald S. Shire.
Associate Solicitor, Division of Legislation and Legal Counsel	Seth D. Zinman.
Associate Solicitor, Division of Labor-Management Laws	Beate Bloch.
Associate Solicitor, Division of Employee Benefits	Laurie M. Streeter.
Associate Solicitor, Division of Occupational Safety and Health	Benjamin W. Mintz.
Associate Solicitor, Division of Labor Relations and Civil Rights	James D. Henry.
Associate Solicitor, Division of Plan Benefits Security	Monica Gallagher.
Associate Solicitor, Division of Mine Safety and Health	(Vacancy).
Deputy Under Secretary for Legislation and Intergovernmental Relations	Nik Edes.
Deputy Under Secretary for International Affairs	Howard D. Samuel.
Executive Assistant to the Deputy Under Secretary	Brian Turner.
Associate Deputy Under Secretary for International Affairs	Herbert N. Blackman.
Associate Deputy Under Secretary for Development Assistance	Darwin M. Bell.
Director, Office of Management, Administration and Planning	James F. Taylor.
Assistant Secretary for Policy, Evaluation, and Research	Arnold H. Packer.
Deputy Assistant Secretary for Economic Policy and Research	Donald Nichols.
Deputy Assistant Secretary for Policy, Evaluation and Research and Deputy Under Secretary for Economic Policy	Peter Henle.

* Published by Office of the Federal Register, National Archives and Records Service, and General Services Administration.

Assistant Secretary for Administration and Management ..... Alfred M. Zuck.
   Deputy Assistant Secretary .... Eckehard J. Muessig.
   Comptroller .... William R. Reise.
   Directorate of Audit and Investigations .... Frank A. Yeager
   Director, Office of Equal Employment Opportunity .... Velma M. Strode.
   Directorate of Administrative Programs and Services ..... W. Spence Filleman.
   Departmental Computer Center .... Eugene Wells.
   Directorate of Personnel Management .... Donald E. Lemmon.
   Office of Grants, Procurement and ADP Management Policy Walter C. Terry.
   Office of Labor-Management Relations .... Robert Hastings.
Assistant Secretary for Employment and Training .... Ernest G. Green.
   Deputy Assistant Secretary for Employment and Training .. Robert J. McConnon.
     Director of Information .... Larry R. Moen.
   Deputy Assistant Secretary for Veterans Employment ..... Roland R. Mora.
   Administrator, Office of Field Operations .... Lawrence W. Rogers.
   Administrator, Office of Policy, Evaluation, and Research .. William B. Hewitt.
   Administrator, Bureau of Apprenticeship and Training .... Hugh C. Murphy.
   Administrator, U.S. Employment Service .... William B. Lewis.
   Administrator, Office of Comprehensive Employment Development .... Robert Anderson.
   Administrator, Office of Youth Programs .... Robert Taggart.
   Administrator, Office of National Programs .... Lamond Godwin.
   Administrator, Unemployment Insurance Service .... Lawrence E. Weatherford, Jr.
   Administrator, Office of Administration and Management .. T. James Walker.
Assistant Secretary for Labor-Management Relations and Administrator, Labor-Management Services Administration ... Francis X. Burkhardt.
   Deputy Assistant Secretary and Deputy Administrator ..... Jack A. Warshaw.
   Administrator, Pension and Welfare Benefit Program ...... Ian D. Lanoff.
     Assistant Administrator for Field Operations .... (Vacancy).
     Director, Office of Labor-Management Standards Enforcement .... Carl H. Rolnick.
   Director, Office of Veterans Reemployment Rights ...... Joseph R. Beever.
   Director, Office of Labor-Management Relations Services Beatrice M. Burgoon.
   Director, Office of Labor-Management Policy Development August F. Cantfil.
   Director, Office of Federal Labor-Management Relations Louis S. Wallerstein.
   Director, Office of Planning Evaluation and Systems .... Ernest J. German.
   Director, Office of Administration and Management ..... Charles G. George.
Assistant Secretary for Employment Standards .... Donald E. Elisburg.
   Deputy Assistant Secretary .... John Mumford.
     Office of Information and Consumer Affairs .... Robert A. Cuccia.
   Wage and Hour Administrator .... Xavier M. Vela.
   Director, Office of Federal Contract Compliance Programs . Weldon J. Rougeau.
   Director, Office of Workers' Compensation Programs ...... Ralph M. Hartman.
   Director, Office of Program Development and Accountability (Vacancy).
   Director, Office of Administrative Management .... (Vacancy).
Assistant Secretary for Occupational Safety and Health ...... Eula Bingham.
   Deputy Assistant Secretary .... Basil J. Whiting.
   Director, Office of Information and Consumer Affairs ..... Frank Greer, Acting.
   Director, Office of Policy Analysis, Integration and Evaluation Suzie Nelson.
   Director, Office of Legislative and Interagency Affairs ..... Karen Mann, Acting.
   Director, Office of Field Coordination and Experimental Programs .... Donald MacKenzie.
   Director, Health Standards Programs .... Grover Wrenn.
   Director, Safety Standards Programs .... John Proctor.
   Director, Administrative Programs .... David C. Zeigler.
   Director, Federal Compliance and State Programs .... (Vacancy).
   Director, Training, Education, Consultation, and Federal Agency Programs .... Clinton Wright.
   Director, Technical Support .... Phil Brown, Acting.
Commissioner of Labor Statistics .... Julius Shiskin.
   Deputy Commissioner for Data Analysis .... Janet L. Norwood.
   Director, Program Evaluation .... Thomas W. Gavett.
   Associate Commissioner for Publications .... Henry Lowenstern.
   Associate Commissioner for Administrative Management ... Donald J. Keugh, Jr.
   Associate Commissioner for Statistical Operations .... William M. Eisenberg.

Assistant Secretary for Mine Safety and Health	Robert B. Lagather.
Deputy Assistant Secretary	(Vacancy).
Director, Office of Standards, Regulations, and Variances . .	(Vacancy).
Director, Office of Internal Affairs	(Vacancy).
Director of Assessments	(Vacancy).
Director of Education and Training	(Vacancy).
Director of Technical Support	(Vacancy).
Director of Administration and Support	(Vacancy).
Administrator for Coal Mine Safety and Health	(Vacancy).
Administrator for Metal and Nonmetal Mine Safety and Health	(Vacancy).

The purpose of the Department of Labor is to foster, promote, and develop the welfare of the wage earners of the United States, to improve their working conditions, and to advance their opportunities for profitable employment. In carrying out this mission, the Department administers more than 130 Federal labor laws guaranteeing workers' rights to safe and healthful working conditions, a minimum hourly wage and overtime pay, freedom from employment discrimination, unemployment insurance, and workers' compensation. The Depart-

ment also protects workers' pension rights; sponsors job training programs; helps workers find jobs; works to strengthen free collective bargaining; and keeps track of changes in employment, prices, and other national economic measurements. As the Department seeks to assist all Americans who need and want to work, special efforts are made to meet the unique job market problems of older workers, youths, minority group members, women, the handicapped, and other groups.

DEPARTMENT OF LABOR

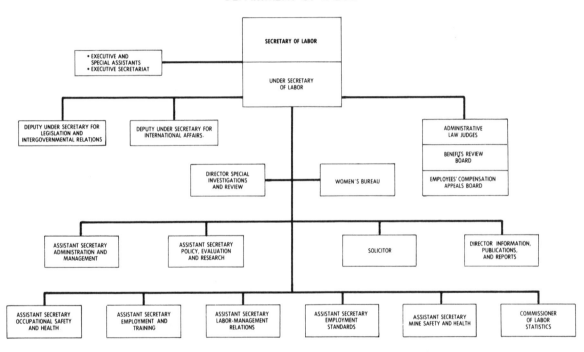

The Department of Labor, ninth executive department, was created by act approved March 4, 1913 (37 Stat. 736; 5 U.S.C. 611). A Bureau of Labor was first created by Congress in 1884 under the Interior Department. The Bureau of Labor later became independent as a Department of Labor without executive rank. It again returned to bureau status in the Department of Commerce and Labor which was created by act of February 14, 1903 (32 Stat. 827; 5 U.S.C. 591).

OFFICE OF THE SECRETARY OF LABOR

Secretary

The Secretary is the head of the Department of Labor and the principal adviser to the President on the development and execution of policies and the administration

and enforcement of laws relating to wage earners, their working conditions, and their employment opportunities.

Wage Appeals Board

The Wage Appeals Board acts on behalf of the Secretary of Labor in deciding appeals on questions of law and fact, taken in the discretion of the Board from wage determinations issued under the Davis-Bacon Act and its related prevailing wage statutes; debarments under the Department's regulations (29 CFR part 5), which implement Reorganization Plan 14 of 1950; under the Department's regulations, part 5, disputes concerning the payment of prevailing wage rates or proper classifications which involve significant sums of money, large groups of employees, or novel or unusual situations; and recommendations by Federal agencies for appropriate adjustments of liquidated damages which are assessed under the Contract Work Hours and Safety Standards Act.

Special Investigations and Review

The Director of the Office of Special Investigations and Review is responsible for planning, directing, and conducting a program of special assignments, reviews, sensitive investigations, audits, and inquiries into alleged and potential program abuse or fraud.

Public Information

The Director of Information, Publications and Reports advises the Secretary on public information matters and provides overall direction and guidance to the Department's public information and publications programs.

REGIONAL INFORMATION OFFICES—DEPARTMENT OF LABOR

Region	Regional Information Director
I. Boston, Mass. 02203 .... (John F. Kennedy Federal Bldg.)	Paul Neal.
II. New York, N.Y. 10036 .... (1515 Broadway)	Edward Weintraub.
III. Philadelphia, Pa. 19101 .... (3535 Market St.)	Jack Hord.
IV. Atlanta, Ga. 30309 .... (1371 Peachtree St. NE.)	Frances Ridgway.
V. Chicago, Ill. 60606 .... (230 S. Dearborn St.)	John Mellott.
VI. Dallas, Tex. 75202 .... (555 Griffin Sq. Bldg.)	Les Gaddie.
VII. Kansas City, Mo. 64106 .... (911 Walnut St.)	Neal Johnson.
VII. Denver, Colo. 80294 .... (1961 Stout St.)	Ernest Sanchez.
IX. San Francisco, Calif. 94102 .... (450 Golden Gate Ave.)	Joe Kirkbride.
X. Seattle, Wash. 98104............... (909 1st Ave.)	Jack Strickland.

WOMEN'S BUREAU

The Women's Bureau is responsible for formulating standards and policies which shall promote the welfare of wage earning women, improve their working conditions, increase their efficiency, advance their opportunities for professional employment, and investigate and report on all matters pertinent to the welfare of women in industry.

The Women's Bureau has regional offices established in 10 areas throughout the United States. Areas included within each region are indicated on the map in Appendix D.

REGIONAL OFFICES—WOMEN'S BUREAU
(Areas included within each region are indicated on the map on page 5-49.)

Region	Regional Administrator
I. Boston, Mass. 02203 .... (John F. Kennedy Federal Bldg.)	Vivian L. Buckles.
II. New York, N.Y. 10036 .... (1515 Broadway)	Mary E. Tobin.
III. Philadelphia, Pa. 19104 .... (3535 Market St.)	Kathleen Riordan.
IV. Atlanta, Ga. 30309 .... (1371 Peachtree St. NE.)	Gay Cobb.
V. Chicago, Ill. 60604 .... (230 S. Dearborn St.)	Eileen M. Schaeffler.
VI. Dallas, Tex. 75202 .... (555 Griffin Sq. Bldg.)	Rhobia C. Taylor.
VII. Kansas City, Mo. 64106 .... (911 Walnut St.)	Euphesenia Foster.
VIII. Denver, Colo. 80294 .... (1961 Stout St.)	Lynn Brown.
IX. San Francisco, Calif. 94102 .... (450 Golden Gate Ave.)	Madeline H. Mixer.
X. Seattle, Wash. 98104............... (909 1st Ave.)	Lazelle Johnson.

OFFICE OF THE UNDER SECRETARY OF LABOR

Under Secretary

The Under Secretary of Labor is the principal adviser to the Secretary. He serves as Acting Secretary in the Secretary's absence.

Employees' Compensation Appeals Board

The Employees' Compensation Appeals Board consists of three members appointed by the Secretary of Labor, one of whom is designated as Chairman and administrative officer. The function of the Board is to consider and decide appeals from final decisions in cases arising under the Federal Employees' Compensation Act (5 U.S.C. 8101). The decisions of the Board are final and not subject to court review.

Office of Administrative Law Judges

Administrative Law Judges preside over formal hearings to determine violations of minimum wage requirements, overtime payments, compensation benefits, and health and safety regulations set forth under the Walsh-Healey Public Contract Act, McNamara-O'Hara Service Contract Act, Longshoremen's and Harbor Workers' Compensation Act, Contract Work Hours and Safety Standards Act, Davis-Bacon Act, Occupational Safety and Health Act, Fair Labor Standards Act, Farm Labor Contractor Registration Act of 1963, Executive Order 11491, and the Black Lung Benefits Act. The Office of Administrative Law Judges also constitutes a permanent Board of Contract Appeals for the Department and provides the hearings and appeals system required by the Talmadge Amendments to the Social Security Act. The Administrative Law Judges evaluate all evidence, resolve credibility, and submit a report and recommendation to the Secretary of Labor or appropriate Assistant Secretary in accordance with applicable statutory and case law.

Benefits Review Board

[For the Benefits Review Board statement of organization, see Code of Federal Regulations, Title 20, Chapter VII, Part 801.103]

The Benefits Review Board is a three-member quasi-judicial body with exclusive jurisdiction to consider and decide appeals raising substantial questions of law or fact from decisions of Administrative Law Judges with respect to cases arising under the Longshoremen's and Harbor Workers' Compensation Act and its extensions and the Black Lung Benefits Act of 1972. The Board exercises the same review authority which the United States District Courts formerly held in these areas of the law prior to the 1972 amendments to both acts.

THE SOLICITOR OF LABOR

The Solicitor has responsibility for all the legal activities of the Department, its legislative program, and serves as legal adviser to the Secretary and other officials of the Department.

The Solicitor, through a subordinate staff of attorneys in Washington and 16 field offices, directs a broad scale litigation effort pertaining to the many statutes administered by the Department including institution and prosecution of Civil Court actions under the Fair Labor Standards Act, as amended, and the trial of cases under the Longshoremen's and Harbor Workers' Compensation Act, Employee Retirement Income Security Act of 1974, and the Farm Labor Contractor Registration Act; attorneys also represent the Department in administrative hearings under various statutes, including the Occupational Safety and Health Act. The cited litigation is conducted independently under an agreement and delegation of authority from the Department of Justice. Litigation under several other acts is carried out in cooperation with the Department of Justice.

Appellate litigation is conducted by attorneys in the national headquarters, whereas the large majority of litigation under various statutes is carried out by attorneys under the direction of the regional solicitors and attorneys who are the legal advisers to the Department officials in the field.

REGIONAL OFFICES—OFFICE OF THE SOLICITOR

Region	Regional Solicitor	Address
1. Maine, New Hampshire, Vermont, Rhode Island, Massachusetts, Connecticut.	Albert H. Ross	John F. Kennedy Federal Bldg. Boston, Mass. 02203.
2. New York, New Jersey	Francis V. LaRuffa	1515 Broadway, New York, N.Y. 10036.
3. Pennsylvania, Delaware, Maryland, District of Columbia, Virginia, West Virginia.	Marshall Harris	3535 Market St., Philadelphia, Pa. 19104.
4. Georgia, Florida, South Carolina, Alabama, Mississippi.	Bobbye Spears	1371 Peachtree St. NE., Atlanta, Ga. 30309.
Branch Office	George D. Palmer, Associate Regional Solicitor.	1929 9th Ave. S., Birmingham, Ala. 35205.
5. Michigan, Ohio, Illinois, Wisconsin, Indiana, Minnesota.	Herman Grant	230 S. Dearborn St., Chicago, Ill. 60604.
Branch Offices	William S. Kloepfer, Associate Regional Solicitor.	Federal Office Bldg., Cleveland, Ohio 44199.
	John C. Nangle, Associate Regional Solicitor.	234 State St., Detroit, Mich. 48226.
6. Texas, Oklahoma, New Mexico, Arkansas, Louisiana.	Ronald M. Gaswirth	555 Griffin Square, Dallas, Tex. 75202.
7. North Dakota, South Dakota, Kansas, Iowa, Missouri, Nebraska, Wyoming, Colorado, Utah, Montana.	Tedrick Housh	Federal Office Bldg., Kansas City, Mo. 64106.
Branch Office	Henry C. Mahlman, Associate Regional Solicitor.	Federal Office Bldg., Denver, Colo. 80294.
8. California, Washington, Oregon, Idaho, Nevada, Arizona, Alaska, Hawaii.	Daniel Teehan	450 Golden Gate Ave., San Francisco, Calif. 94102.
Branch Offices	John M. Orban, Associate Regional Solicitor.	Federal Bldg., Los Angeles, Calif. 90012.
	Robert A. Friel, Associate Regional Solicitor.	909 1st Ave., Seattle, Wash. 98104.
9. Tennessee, Kentucky, North Carolina	Marvin M. Tincher, Regional Attorney.	U.S. Courthouse Bldg., Nashville, Tenn. 37203.
10. Puerto Rico, Virgin Islands	Morton J. Marks, Regional Attorney	Federal Office Bldg., Hato Rey, P.R. 00918.

ADMINISTRATION AND MANAGEMENT

The Assistant Secretary for Administration and Management has responsibility for administrative policy; centralized management staff support and services to the Department's agencies in the areas of financial, organization, and personnel management; program review and audit; ADP systems development and services; administrative services; and equal employment opportunity.

POLICY, EVALUATION, AND RESEARCH

The Assistant Secretary for Policy, Evaluation, and Research is responsible for coordinating and providing leadership to the Department's activities in policy and program planning, program evaluation, and economic and social research, bearing on the welfare of all workers.

LEGISLATION AND INTERGOVERNMENTAL RELATIONS

The Deputy Under Secretary for Legislation and Intergovernmental Relations coordinates, supervises, and directs all legislative activities of the Department, including contacts with the Congress and presentation of legislative programs and views to the Congress. The Deputy also has responsibility for maintaining liaison with State and local officials and Federal agencies and relations with community, labor, minority, and business groups.

Regional representatives who report to the Deputy Under Secretary for Legislation and Intergovernmental Relations are located in the 10 standard Federal regions. They maintain liaison with local, State, and other Federal agencies and handle relations with community, labor, minority, and business groups and governmental bodies in their regions.

REGIONAL REPRESENTATIVES—LEGISLATION AND INTERGOVERNMENTAL RELATIONS
(Areas included within each region are indicated on the map on page 5-49.)

Region	Regional Representative
I. Boston, Mass. 02203. (John F. Kennedy Federal Bldg.)	Daniel Sullivan.
II. New York, N.Y. 10036 (1515 Broadway)	Frank R. Nero.
III. Philadelphia, Pa. 19107 (3535 Market St.)	J. Thomas Schranck.
IV. Atlanta, Ga. 30309 (1371 Peachtree St. NE.)	Kenneth English.
V. Chicago, Ill. 60604 (230 S. Dearborn St.)	Fran L. Ryan.
VI. Dallas, Tex. 75202 (Griffin Sq. Bldg.)	Gerald L. Brown.
VII. Kansas City, Mo. 64106 (911 Walnut St.)	James P. Mulvaney.
VIII. Denver, Colo. 80202 (1961 Stout St.)	John S. Mrozek.
IX. San Francisco, Calif. 94102 (450 Golden Gate Ave.)	Santiage Caudillo.
X. Seattle, Wash. 98104 (909 1st Ave.)	Sidney S. Stoddard.

International Affairs

The Department's international responsibilities are carried out under the direction of the Deputy Under Secretary for International Affairs and the Bureau of International Labor Affairs which he supervises. The Bureau assists in formulating international economic and trade policies affecting American workers. It also administers the trade adjustment assistance program under the Trade Act of 1974, which provides special benefits for workers adversely affected by import competition.

The Bureau also helps represent the U.S. in multilateral and bilateral trade negotiations and on such international bodies as the General Agreement on Tariffs and Trade (GATT), the International Labor Organization (ILO), and the Organization for Economic Cooperation and Development (OECD). The Bureau also helps provide direction to the U.S. Labor Attachés at Embassies abroad, carries out overseas technical assistance projects, and arranges trade union exchange and other programs for foreign visitors to the U.S.

Employment and Training Administration

The Employment and Training Administration (ETA) encompasses a group of offices and services which have been established to implement the responsibilities assigned to the Department of Labor for conduct of certain work-experience and work training programs; funding and overseeing of programs conducted under the provisions of the Comprehensive Employment and Training Act of 1973 by States and other authorized sponsors, administration of the Federal-State Employment Security System; and conduct of a continuing program of research, development, and evaluation. Administration of employment and training programs is directed by the Assistant Secretary and the Deputy Assistant Secretary for Veterans Employment.

EMPLOYMENT SERVICE

The United States Employment Service (USES), under the provisions of the Wagner-Peyser Act of 1933, provides assistance to States in establishing and maintaining a system of nearly 2,500 local public employment offices in the States and territories. The Federal-State employment service is responsible for providing job placement and other employment services to unemployed individuals and other jobseekers, providing employers and workers with job development, placement, recruitment, and similar assistance including employment, counseling, and special services to veterans, migrant and seasonal farmworkers, youth, women, older workers, and handicapped persons, and related supportive services. At the State and local levels, the Employment Service is also responsible for developing information on employment and unemployment, and on occupational demand and supply necessary for the planning and operation of job training and vocational education programs throughout the country.

USES efforts have been directed in recent years to improving the performance of State employment service agencies as labor market intermediaries through such programs as computerized job matching, local office relocation and redesign, establishment of local employer committees, and improvement of linkages with CETA and other employment and training programs.

Veterans

The Wagner-Peyser Act and subsequent legislation (most recently the Vietnam Era Veterans' Readjustment Assistance Act of 1974, the Emergency Jobs and Unemployment Assistance Act of 1974 and the Veterans Education and Employment Assistance Act of 1976) established and reaffirmed the legal basis for veterans priority and the preferential service to disabled veterans over other veterans, in placement, counseling, and referral to training activities of the USES and its affiliated State employment services. The Veterans Employment Service (VES), under the direction of the Deputy Assistant Secretary for Veterans Employment, is responsible for assuring that the legal mandate and the policies of the Secretary of Labor and the USES are carried out by the local public employment service offices. VES has a field staff of regional and State directors for veterans employment and their assistants who are responsible for providing functional supervision to State employment services helping to assure that legal and policy requirements for veterans services are maintained effectively. In addition, State employment services have local veterans employment representatives who are specialists in providing direct services to veterans. The USES and State employment services have cooperative agreements with the Veterans Administration for providing services to veterans.

Rural Area Workers

The USES develops policies and procedures to provide a complete placement service to workers and employers in rural areas. Migrant and seasonal farmworkers receive assistance to help them maintain year-round employment through the Federal-State employment services interstate clearance system. The USES is responsible for insuring that, in the interstate recruitment of farm and woods workers, applicable standards and the Secretary's regulations relating to transportation, wages, and other conditions are met.

Youth

The Employment Service provides special assistance to youth between 16 and 24 years of age through its cooperative school program and through specialized youth staff in local offices. The Cooperative School Program is a part of the overall youth program and is aimed at easing the transition from school to work by offering placement counseling and job finding services to prospective dropouts, graduates, and job-ready youth. Another youth service is the Summer Employment Program, through which school youths are referred to private and public summer jobs. In addition, special cooperative programs are developed with the U.S. Civil Service Commission, the National Alliance of Businessmen, and local prime sponsors under the Comprehensive Employment and Training Act for the referral of primarily disadvantaged youth to summer jobs and/or training opportunities in Federal establishments, with private employers, or to specially funded job or training opportunities.

STATE DIRECTORS FOR VETERANS EMPLOYMENT—VETERANS EMPLOYMENT SERVICE

State	Representative	Address
Alabama	James C. Gates	519 Industrial Relations Bldg., Montgomery, 36104.
Alaska	Edward P. Duckworth	118 S. Franklin St., P.O. Box 3–7000, Juneau, 99801.
Arizona	Marco A. Valenzuela	112 N. Central Ave., Phoenix, 85004.
Arkansas	Billy R. Threlkeld	203 Employment Security Bldg., P.O. Box 128, Little Rock, 72203.
California	Thomas Mitchell	800 Capitol Mall, Sacramento, 95814.
Colorado	Warren H. Hutchings	1210 Sherman St., Denver, 80203.
Connecticut	William F. Hill	200 Folly Brook Blvd., Wethersfield, 06115.
Delaware	Horace Best	801 West St., Wilmington, 19801.
District of Columbia	George Joiner	555 Pennsylvania Ave. NW., Washington, 20212.
Florida	Robert I. Clark	Department of Commerce Bldg., Rm. 317, Tallahassee, 32302.
Georgia	Eugene R. Wagner	501 Pulliam St. SW., Atlanta, 30302.
Hawaii	Henry S. Kuniyuki	1347 Kapiolani Blvd., Honolulu, 96811.
Idaho	William A. Hulet	317 Main St., P.O. Box 7189, Boise, 83707.
Illinois	(Vacancy)	910 S. Michigan Ave., Chicago, 60605.
Indian	Keith W. Collins	10 N. Senate Ave., Indianapolis, 46204.
Iowa	Howard J. Cloe	1000 E. Grand Ave., Des Moines, 50319.
Kansas	George L. Medlock	401 Topeka Blvd., Topeka, 66603.
Kentucky	Robert M. Barnes	State Office Bldg. Annex, Frankfort, 40601.
Louisiana	Merrick W. Swords	701 Loyola St., New Orleans, 70013.

STATE DIRECTORS FOR VETERANS EMPLOYMENT—VETERANS EMPLOYMENT SERVICE (*Continued*)

State	Representative	Address
Maine	Robert E. Fecteau	20 Union St., Augusta, 04330.
Maryland	John C. Bowers	1100 N. Eutaw St., Baltimore, 21201.
Massachusetts	Robert F. Murphy	506 John F. Kennedy Federal Bldg., Boston, 02203.
Michigan	William F. Wickstrom	7310 Woodward Ave., Detroit, 48202.
Minnesota	Anthony P. Caligiuri	390 N. Robert St., St. Paul, 55101.
Mississippi	Paul P. Smith	1520 W. Capitol St., Jackson, 39207.
Missouri	Jonas Matthews	421 E. Dunklin St., P.O. Box 59, Jefferson City, 65101.
Montana	Jess C. Fletcher	Employment Security Bldg., Rm. 412, Helena, 59601.
Nebraska	Robert T. Manifold	550 S. 16th St., P.O. Box 4600, Lincoln, 68509.
Nevada	Claude Shipley	1000 E. Williams, Capital Plaza Suite 101, Carson City, 89701.
New Hampshire	Emile Simard	55 Pleasant St., Concord, 03301.
New Jersey	Leon G. Scull	1106 Labor and Industry Bldg., Trenton, 08625.
New Mexico	Jacob Castillo	505 Marquette NW., Albuquerque, 87103.
New York	Clifford M. Johnson	State Office Bldg., Campus Bldg. 12, Albany, 12201.
North Carolina	S. Marvin Burton	507 Caswell Bldg., Raleigh, 27602.
North Dakota	Willard M. Williamson	1000 Divide Ave., Bismarck, 58501.
Ohio	Victor W. Smith	145 S. Front St., P.O. Box 1618, Columbus, 43216.
Oklahoma	Donald A. Davis	301 Will Rogers Memorial Office Bldg., Oklahoma City, 73105.
Oregon	Rex Newell	304 Labor and Industries Bldg., Salem, 97310.
Pennsylvania	Joseph F. Welsh	1114 Labor and Industry Bldg., Harrisburg, 17121.
Puerto Rico	José Mendin, Jr.	Barbosa Ave, 414, Hato Rey, P.O. Box 14337, Santurce, 00916.
Rhode Island	Daniel T. Martin	514 Federal Bldg., Providence, 02903.
South Carolina	William C. Plowden, Jr.	Suite 10B Jefferson Sq., Columbia, 29202.
South Dakota	Emil P. May	607 N. 4th St., P.O. Box 730, Aberdeen, 57401.
Tennessee	James E. Turner	301 James Robertson Pkwy., Nashville, 37201.
Texas	James H. Cornett	TEC Bldg., Congress and 15th Sts., Austin, 78767.
Utah	J. Dale Madsen	158 Social Hall Ave., Salt Lake City, 84111.
Vermont	Charles E. Healy	Green Mountain Dr., Montpelier, 05602.
Virginia	Fred C. Elliott, Jr.	703 E. Main St., Richmond, 23219.
Washington	Walter L. Nicholls, Jr.	212 Maple Park, P.O. Box 165, Olympia, 98501.
West Virginia	Andrew J. Trail	112 California Ave., Charleston, 25305.
Wisconsin	James D. Baird	201 E. Washington Ave., Madison, 53703.
Wyoming	Ernest E. Fender	100 W. Midwest Ave., Casper, 82601.

Other Services

The USES provides subsidiary services in addition to its primary labor exchange responsibilities. These include certifying aliens who seek to enter the United States for permanent employment as immigrants or as temporary workers; providing employment services and adjustment assistance to U.S. workers adversely affected by foreign imports under the Trade Act of 1974; providing job search guidance and aptitude-testing services to workers; giving specialized recruitment assistance to employers; providing labor market information to other Federal or State agencies to meet various program responsibilities and to the public on State and local employment conditions; providing guidance, counseling, referral, and placement in apprenticeship opportunities through Apprenticeship Information Centers located in selected State employment service offices; reviewing rural industrialization loan and grant certification applicants under the Rural Development Act of 1972; maintaining an occupational research program for the compilation of the "Dictionary of Occupational Titles"; and providing bonding assistance to individuals who have been unable to obtain it on their own.

COMPREHENSIVE EMPLOYMENT DEVELOPMENT PROGRAMS

The Office of Comprehensive Employment Development Programs (OCED) provides leadership in the development and improvement of nationwide work and training programs and delivery systems which will provide work training, work experience, and public service employment opportunities for disadvantaged, unemployed, and underemployed persons. The OCED has major responsibility for implementation of the Comprehensive Employment and Training Act (CETA) of 1973 and the Work Incentive Program (WIN).

Under CETA, the Secretary of Labor makes block grants to about 446 State and local units of government, the prime sponsors under the act. Prime sponsors identify employment and training needs in their areas and plan and provide the job training and other services required to meet those needs. The various types of programs, such as Institutional Training, On-the-Job Training, Operation Mainstream, Neighborhood Youth Corps, Public Service Careers, Job Corps, and the Concentrated Employment Program, may be provided by prime sponsors from their CETA grants. The goal of the programs provided under CETA is to encourage and develop the employment potential of disadvantaged, unemployed, and underemployed individuals to enable them to become self-sufficient, contributing participants in the economy.

CETA provides for services at the State and local level (title I), for public service programs (title II), for national programs (title III), for a special program for disadvantaged youth, Job Corps (title IV), for emergency public service jobs (title VI), and for a new program for youth, the Young Adult Conservation Corps (title VIII).

Comprehensive Manpower Services

The Comprehensive Manpower Services (title I) establishes a program of financial assistance to State and local governments for comprehensive manpower services. Among the purposes for which funds may be used are: recruitment, orientation, counseling, testing, placement, and followup services; classroom instruction in occupational skills and other job-related training, such as basic education; on-the-job training by public and private employers; allowances for persons in training; supportive services such as necessary medical care, child care, and help in obtaining bonding needed for employment; and transitional public employment programs.

The selection and array of manpower services provided under this broad umbrella are up to local and State governments acting as prime sponsors. A sponsor may choose to continue funding existing programs of demonstrated effectiveness or others which he feels are effective.

Groups to be served encompass the entire spectrum of the disadvantaged, unemployed, and underemployed. Programs may be developed for both in-school and out-of-school youth, older workers, members of minority groups, and others encountering special problems of labor market adjustment.

Public Employment Programs

The Public Employment Programs (title II) provide for programs of transitional public service employment in areas with a 6.5 percent or more unemployment rate for 3 consecutive months.

In their applications to the Secretary of Labor, program sponsors must specify detailed plans for a public service employment program to serve persons who have been unemployed at least 30 days. To the extent feasible, sponsors are to design programs which will develop new careers, open opportunities for career advancement, and enable people in the program to move into other public or private employment. The prime sponsor may also use title II funds to provide training and supportive services to individuals.

Special consideration is to be given to unemployed veterans who served in the Armed Forces in Indochina or Korea, welfare recipients, former manpower trainees, and the most severely disadvantaged in terms of length of unemployment. The prime sponsor must also serve

the significant segments in its jurisdiction on an equitable basis.

Emergency Job Programs

Under title VI (Emergency Job Programs), the Secretary of Labor enters into arrangements with eligible applicants to make financial assistance available for the purpose of providing temporary public service employment for unemployed and underemployed persons. When feasible, such persons may receive related training and services. The jobs are in such fields as environmental quality, health care, education, recreation, pollution control, conservation, and other areas of community service and improvement. They may include large, labor-intensive projects.

To provide sufficient job opportunities in areas of excessively high unemployment (7 percent or more), various provisions of the public employment program under title II of CETA are waived, thus permitting, if necessary: hiring persons who have been unemployed 15 days, rather than the usual 30 days; and hiring persons to work on community capital improvement projects that would not otherwise be carried out, due to lack of funds.

The Secretary of Labor, in cooperation with the Administrator of Veterans Affairs and the Secretary of Health, Education, and Welfare, provides an outreach and public information program to produce jobs and training for recently discharged veterans. In addition, a national veterans goal of 35 percent for filling public service employment positions has been set by the Secretary of Labor.

The Emergency Jobs Programs Extension Act of 1976, while permitting prime sponsors to continue title VI public service job levels as of June 30, 1976, provides that all funds beyond those needed to sustain these enrollment levels be used to undertake new projects and activities. Those eligible to sponsor projects and activities include local educational institutions, community-action agencies, community-based nonprofit organizations, and local units of government, including the prime sponsor's own jurisdiction. Prior to approval or disapproval of project applications, the prime sponsor must consider the recommendations of its planning council.

The Emergency Jobs Programs Extension Act mandates that all project participants and at least 50 percent of those hired to fill vacancies occurring in existing programs must meet new eligibility requirements. To meet these requirements, an individual must be from a family at or below 70 percent of the Bureau of Labor Statistics lower income living standard level (nationwide the 70 percent figure for an urban family of four was $6,700 in 1976), and either: (1) an Aid to Families with Dependent Children (AFDC) recipient; (2) receiving unemployment compensation for at least 15 weeks; (3)

be unemployed for 15 of 20 weeks, or have a combination of weeks unemployed and weeks receiving unemployment compensation totaling 15 weeks; or (4) an unemployment compensation exhaustee who is unemployed.

Summer Youth Employment Program

The Summer Youth Employment Program provides jobs for economically disadvantaged youth aged 14 to 21 during the summer months. The program is authorized under title 3A, Section 304(a) (3) of the Comprehensive Employment and Training Act of 1973, as amended.

The 1977 summer program provided 886,619 summer jobs for youth under title III and 95,085 under title I for a total of 981,704. The 1977 summer program, with an appropriation of $693 million, is expected to provide approximately 1 million job opportunities under title III.

Examples of jobs in which youth worked include: X-ray, laboratory, medical and dental technician; library, teacher, museum and legal aide; maintenance and operation crewmen; lifeguard, clerk-typist, coach/counselor; and trainee positions in such skills as sheetmetal shaping, boilerroom operation, and warehousing. These positions generally are at public or private nonprofit worksites.

Among the initiatives being taken to improve the summer program are: (1) improving outreach and selection techniques to ensure enrollment of all segments of the economically disadvantaged youth population; (2) providing a labor market orientation to participants in the summer program and emphasizing the need to provide skill training for those youth who can benefit from it; and (3) providing a design for vocational exploration in the private sector which includes adequate safeguards against subsidization of wages in the private sector.

Job Corps

The Job Corps, as authorized by the Comprehensive Employment and Training Act of 1973 provides leadership and overall direction and guidance for the administration of a nationwide training program offering comprehensive development for disadvantaged youth through centers with the unique feature of residential facilities for all or most enrollees. Its purpose is to prepare these youth for the responsibilities of citizenship and to increase their employability by providing them with education, vocational training, and useful work experience in rural, urban, or inner-city centers.

Enrollees may spend a maximum of 2 years in the Job Corps. However, a period of enrollment, from 6 months to a year, is usually sufficient to provide adequate training and education to improve employability to a substantial degree.

Job Corps recruiting is accomplished primarily through the State employment services. In certain areas, private organizations are the principal source of referrals. The State employment services and private, nonprofit organizations provide assistance to enrollees in locating jobs after completion of training.

Work Incentive Program

The Work Incentive Program (WIN) was authorized by the Social Security Amendments of 1967 and 1971. It is jointly administered by the Departments of Labor and Health, Education, and Welfare, and is designed to help persons receiving Aid to Families with Dependent Children (AFDC) become self-supporting. The 1971 amendments shifted the program emphasis from training to immediate employment.

All AFDC applicants and recipients are required, unless exempt by law, to register with the WIN sponsor, which is usually the State employment agency, for employment and manpower services as a condition of eligibility. WIN utilizes existing employment-related training programs and WIN-funded activities—both directed toward ultimate placements in unsubsidized jobs. In preparation for this, WIN offers such manpower services as on-the-job training (OJT) for the job—ready, or public service employment (PSE) arranged by prior agreement with public or private nonprofit organizations for individuals for whom unsubsidized jobs are not available. Manpower services are supplemented by necessary supportive social services, including day care for children, which are provided by or through a separate administrative unit (SAU) of the welfare agency.

The Revenue Act of 1971 provides employers with an incentive in the form of a tax credit for hiring WIN registrants. As an alternative, a welfare tax credit is also available to employers of WIN registrants under related legislation.

NATIONAL EMPLOYMENT AND TRAINING PROGRAMS

The Office of National Programs (ONP) is responsible for employment and training programs which, by law or reason, must be administered directly from the Employment and Training Administration's headquarters in Washington, D.C. These programs include the following:

Employment and Training Programs for Indians and Other Native Americans

These programs involve direct ETA grants to Indian tribes, bands, and groups, Alaskan Native villages, and public and private nonprofit agencies to support the provision of training, employment, and related services to Indians and other persons of Native American descent. The care of the program is found in the Comprehensive Employment and Training Act (CETA), section 302, which authorizes comprehensive employment and training programs directed specifically to the needs of Indian and Native American communities. However, sponsoring organizations also receive supplementary grants for public service employment programs funded from CETA titles II and VI, summer youth employment programs funded from CETA section 304, special programs for young persons funded from CETA title IIIC, and special programs for activities related to the economic development of Indian and Native American communities funded from recent economic stimulus measures.

Employment and Training Programs for Migrant and Seasonal Farmworkers

These programs, authorized principally by CETA section 303, provide a broad spectrum of training, employment-related services, and supportive services to migrant and other seasonally employed farmworkers. The programs are intended to assist farmworkers in preparing for more stable employment and to improve the general well-being of those who choose to remain in that work force. Under CETA section 302, project grants are made on a competitive basis to public agencies and private nonprofit organizations. Some project sponsors also receive supplementary funding for special youth programs authorized by CETA title IIC. In addition, ONP recently implemented a wide variety of employment-related proejcts for farmworkers with funds available from recent economic stimulus measures.

The Senior Community Service Employment Program

Authorized by title IX of the Older Americans Act, the Senior Community Service Employment Program (SCSEP) makes subsidized, part-time job opportunities in community service activities available to low-income persons aged 55 and above. Project grants are made to national-level public and private nonprofit agencies and to units of State government. The distribution of funds for spending within each State is governed by a statutory apportionment formula.

Hire

The HIRE Program (Help Through Industry Retraining and Employment) is funded from the discretionary provisions of CETA title I and involves reimbursements to private employers who hire and then provide on-the-job training to unemployed veterans and members of other eligible groups. The main emphasis is placed on job and training opportunities for disabled veterans and veterans of the Vietnam era. In order to qualify for reimbursements, employers must agree to hire and train at least 15 eligible persons. HIRE also includes a voluntary component under which employers can, as a public service, agree to hire and train eligible individuals without reimbursement.

Other National Programs

The Office of National Programs also administers several other programs funded from the discretionary provisions

of CETA title IIIA. The Apprenticeship Outreach Program (AOP) assists young persons, primarily minorities, to qualify for and obtain jobs in skilled trades. Many AOP projects also assist women to obtain what are commonly referred to as nontraditional jobs. The National On-the-Job Training Program (OJT) involves funding agreements mainly with national labor organizations and trade management associations under which they operate special training programs for unemployed and disadvantaged persons. Promotion and Development Programs (P&D) include those sponsored by the National Alliance of Businessmen and the AFL-CIO's Human Resources Development Institute. These two organizations work within the business community and the labor movement, respectively, to encourage involvement, understanding, and participation in federally sponsored employment and training activities.

APPRENTICESHIP AND TRAINING

The National Apprenticeship Act was passed in 1937 to enable the Department of Labor to formulate and promote the futherance of labor standards necessary to safeguard the welfare of apprentices and cooperate with the States in the promotion of such standards and to bring together employers and labor for the formulation of programs of apprenticeship.

Sponsors and potential sponsors are encouraged and assisted in the development, expansion, and improvement of apprenticeship and other forms of allied industrial training. Technical information on training methods, public training facilities, and successful systems are made available to industry. Through field representatives in each State, the Bureau of Apprenticeship and Training works closely with employers, labor unions, vocational schools, community planning groups, and others concerned with apprenticeship. Programs must meet standards established by the Bureau or a recognized State Apprenticeship Council to be registered. Field compliance reviews are conducted to determine conformity with Federal equal employment opportunity and other standards for apprenticeship and training. The program addresses national requirements for fully skilled workers as an essential component to continued economic growth and technological advances. Well planned, properly supervised apprenticeships provide craftworkers to meet present and future needs, ensure a supply of skilled workers to meet community needs, and help ensure the consuming public of those quality products and services that only trained hands and minds can provide.

UNEMPLOYMENT INSURANCE

The Unemployment Insurance Service (UIS) provides leadership and policy guidance to State Employment

Security agencies for the development, improvement, and operation of the Federal-State unemployment insurance program and related wage-loss income maintenance programs. The UIS reviews State unemployment insurance laws and their administration by the States to determine whether they are in conformity with Federal requirements. The UIS also establishes criteria for determining the amounts of money necessary for the proper and efficient administration of State unemployment insurance laws. The UIS maintains a continuing research program and provides technical assistance to States.

The Federal Unemployment Insurance Advisory Council, composed of representatives of employers, employees, and the public, advises the Secretary of Labor with respect to unemployment insurance problems. A special temporary advisory body, the National Commission on Unemployment Compensation, has been established to study and evaluate the present unemployment compensation system in order to assess long-range needs and recommend changes. The Commission's final report is due on July 1, 1979.

POLICY, EVALUATION AND RESEARCH

The Office of Policy, Evaluation and Research formulates and recommends Employment and Training Administration (ETA) policies, plans, and resource allocations; administers the ETA research and development program; develops and conducts ETA program evaluations and studies; provides leadership for and coordinates the development and review of all ETA legislative proposals and the implementation of employment and training program legislation; provides for the development, analysis, and dissemination of national, area, and local labor market information; encourages the development and extension of systems to provide occupational information to persons exploring occupational choices; and provides leadership to foreign employment activties of ETA in the development of U.S. policy positions on matters relating to employment in international forums such as the Organization for Economic Cooperation and Development, the Organization of American States, and appropriate U.S.-Mexican organizations.

REGIONAL OFFICES

Regional offices are established in 10 areas throughout the United States. The Office of Field Operations executes direct-line authority over ETA field activties (except the Bureau of Apprenticeship and Training and Veterans Employment Service), and provides a central point of contact at the headquarters level in connection with national office component dealings with regional staff.

Within its area of jurisdiction, each regional office is responsible for the planning, operation, and monitoring of comprehensive employment programs, in cooperation with State and local units of government and other contractor organizations within the region. Other public interest responsibilities include the coordination of Employment and Training Administration activities with Federal assistance programs of other agencies within the region; the implementation of employment training administrative policies on equal employment opportunity; and administrative and management assistance to State agencies and prime sponsors in reference to employment and training programs.

REGIONAL OFFICES—EMPLOYMENT AND TRAINING ADMINISTRATION
(Areas included within each region are indicated on the map on page 5-49.)

Region	Regional Administrator
I. Boston, Mass. 02203 (John F. Kennedy Federal Bldg.)	Luis F. Sepulveda.
II. New York, N.Y. 10036 (1515 Broadway)	Thomas C. Komarek, Acting.
III. Philadelphia, Pa. 19104 (P.O. Box 8796)	J. Terrell Whitsitt.
IV. Atlanta, Ga. 30309 (1371 Peachtree St. NE.)	David T. Duncan, Acting.
V. Chicago, Ill. 60604 (230 S. Dearborn St.)	Richard Gilliland.
VI. Dallas, Tex 75202 (555 Griffin Sq. Bldg.)	William S. Harris.
VII. Kansas City, Mo. 64106 (911 Walnut St.)	Richard G. Miskimins.
VIII. Denver, Colo. 80294 (1961 Stout St.)	Floyd E. Edwards.
IX. San Francisco, Calif. 94102 (450 Golden Gate Ave.)	William J. Hatigan.
X. Seattle, Wash. 98104 (909 1st Ave.)	Jess C. Ramaker.

Labor-Management Services Administration

The Assistant Secretary for Labor-Management Relations has responsibility for the Department's labor-management relations activties and serves as Administrator of the Labor-Management Services Administration.

The Labor-Management Services Administration (LMSA) administers three laws and major parts of a Presidential Executive order. It also provides assistance to collective bargaining negotiators and keeps the Secretary posted on development in labor-management disputes of national scope.

LMSA provides technical assistance to State and local governments in matters concerning public employee labor-relations and pursues research and policy development in the overall labor-management relations field.

Veterans Reemployment

Veterans reemployment rights are provided for in title 38, chapter 43 of the United States Code. LMSA helps veterans, reservists, national guardsmen, and rejectees exercise their reemployment rights, pertaining to the job, seniority, status, and rate of pay they would have achieved had they not been away.

General information is provided to veterans and their preservice employers at the time the veteran is released from the Armed Forces.

Technical assistance and more specific information is provided to veterans and employers, aimed at voluntary resolution of reemeployment problems. When such efforts are not successful, cases may be referred to the Department of Justice for legal action.

Pension and Welfare Plans

The Employee Retirement Income Security Act of 1974 (ERISA), approved September 2, 1974 (88 Stat. 629; 29 U.S.C. 1001 note), requires administrators of private pension and welfare plans to file copies of those plans with LMSA; to provide plan participants with easily understandable summaries of plans; and to report annually on the financial operation of the plans and bonding of persons charged with handling plan funds and assets. Such persons must also meet strict fiduciary responsibility standards administered by LMSA. Vesting, participation, and funding standards are administered by the Internal Revenue Service.

The Welfare and Pension Plans Disclosure Act (WPPDA) was repealed by ERISA on January 1, 1975, except that certain reporting provisions have been carried over by regulation.

Labor Organizations

The Labor Management Reporting and Disclosure Act calls upon labor organizations to file with LMSA copies of their constitutions and bylaws and annual financial reports of their transactions for public view.

The act also prescribes rules for election of union officers, administration of trusteeships by labor organizations, rights of union members, and the handling of union funds.

Through technical assistance in all these areas LMSA seeks to obtain voluntary compliance with provisions of the act. Enforcement through the Federal courts also is available under the law.

Federal Employee Organizations

Federal labor-management relations are governed by Executive Order 11491, as amended. The Assistant Secretary for Labor-Management Relations, under the order, decides appropriate bargaining units, supervises representation elections, rules on unfair labor practice complaints, and decides questions as to grievability and arbitrability.

As with labor organizations in the private sector, unions of Federal employees are required to file annual financial reports for disclosure to the public, and to observe standards of conduct in respect to election of union officers, administration of trusteeships, handling of money, and the rights of union members.

LMSA's emphasis in Federal labor-management relations matters, as it is with the laws it administers, is on voluntary compliance through technical assistance.

Labor-Management Relations Services

Services offered by LMSA cover a broad range. They include assistance to employers and unions in meeting long-range, complicated problems caused by major economic and technological change; reporting on current and potentially critical dispute situations, analyzing data for immediate use in specific collective bargaining situations; providing staff assistance to Presidential emergency boards and other ad hoc boards and commissions dealing with major disputes, such as in the transportation

REGIONAL OFFICES—LABOR-MANAGEMENT SERVICES ADMINISTRATION

Region	Regional Administrator	Address
NEW YORK—Maine, New Hampshire, Vermont, Rhode Island, Massachusetts, Connecticut, New York, New Jersey, Virgin Islands, Puerto Rico.	Robert Merchant, Acting	1515 Broadway, New York, N.Y. 10036.
PHILADELPHIA—Pennsylvania, Maryland, Delaware, Virginia, West Virginia.	Hillary Shepley	3535 Market St., Philadelphia, Pa. 19104.
ATLANTA—Kentucky, Tennessee, North Carolina, South Carolina, Mississippi, Alabama, Florida, Georgia.	Lem Bridges	1371 Peachtree St. NE., Atlanta, Ga. 30309.
CHICAGO—Illinois, Wisconsin, Indiana, Minnesota, Michigan, Ohio.	William Kane, Acting	230 S. Dearborn St., Chicago, Ill. 60604.
KANSAS CITY—Montana, Wyoming, Utah, Colorado, New Mexico, North Dakota, South Dakota, Nebraska, Kansas, Oklahoma, Texas, Iowa, Missouri, Arkansas, Louisiana.	Cullen Keough	911 Walnut St., Kansas City, Mo. 64106.
SAN FRANCISCO—Alaska, Hawaii, Idaho, Washington, Oregon, California, Nevada, Arizona.	Gordon M. Byrholdt	450 Golden Gate Ave., San Francisco, Calif. 94102.

industry; making sure under section 13(c) of the Urban Mass Transportation Act that protective arrangements exist so that the improvement of such systems with Federal funds shall not worsen the employment conditions of the workers; and exchanging information with, and giving technical assistance to, State and local governments and organizations of their employees to help them achieve sound labor-management relations.

Development, Research and Evaluation

Functions of LMSA in labor-management policy development and research include: review of collective bargaining performance and its contribution to meeting economic needs; development of policy for legislation of Executive orders; study of impact of private policies affecting collective bargaining; and coordination of labor-management relations research activities. The evaluation function is the review of LMSA programs to assess their effectiveness and efficiency.

Employment Standards Administration

The Assistant Secretary for Employment Standards has responsibility for administering and directing employment standards programs dealing with: minimum wage and overtime standards; equal pay; age discrimination in employment; registration of farm labor contractors; determining prevailing wage rates to be paid on Government contracts and subcontracts; promoting the economic and social status of women; nondiscirimination and affirmative action for minorities, women, veterans, and handicapped workers on Governmenment contracts and subcontracts; and workers' compensation programs for Federal and certain private employers and employees.

WAGE AND HOUR DIVISION

The Wage and Hour Administrator is responsible for planning, directing, and administering programs dealing with a variety of Federal labor legislation. These programs are designed to increase and protect low-wage incomes as provided by the minimum wage provisions of the Fair Labor Standards Act; safeguard the health and welfare of workers by discouraging excessively long hours of work through enforcement of the overtime provisions of the Fair Labor Standards Act; prevent curtailment of employment and earnings for students, trainees, and handicapped workers; eliminate discriminatory employment based on sex and age as prohibited by the Equal Pay Act and Age Discrimination in Employment Act; minimize losses of income and job rights caused by indebtedness; and direct a program of farm labor contractor registration designed to protect the health, safety, and welfare of migrant labor.

REGIONAL OFFICES—EMPLOYMENT STANDARDS ADMINISTRATION
(Areas included within each region are indicated on the map on page 5-49.)

Region	Regional Administrator
I. Boston, Mass. 02203 .... (John F. Kennedy Federal Bldg.)	Walter P. Parker.
II. New York, N.Y. 10036 .... (1515 Broadway)	Frank B. Mercurio.
III. Philadelphia, Pa. 19104 .... (3535 Market St.)	Charles M. Angell.
IV. Atlanta, Ga. 30309 .... (1371 Peachtree St. NE.)	James E. Patching.
V. Chicago, Ill. 60604 .... (230 S. Dearborn St.)	(Vacancy).
VI. Dallas, Tex. 75202 .... (555 Griffin Sq. Bldg.)	Bill A. Belt.
VII. Kansas City, Mo. 64106 .... (911 Walnut St.)	Doyle Loveridge.
VIII. Denver, Colo. 80294 .... (1961 Stout St.)	Higinio Costales, Jr.
IX. San Francisco, Calif. 94102 .... (450 Golden Gate Ave.)	Virginia Allee.
X. Seattle, Wash. 98104 .... (909 1st Ave.)	William C. Buhl.

REGIONAL OFFICES—WAGE AND HOUR DIVISION
(Areas included within each region are indicated on the map on page 5-49.)

Region	Assistant Regional Administrator
I. Boston, Mass. 02203 .... (John F. Kennedy Federal Bldg.)	William L. Smith.
II. New York, N.Y. 10036 .... (1515 Broadway)	Raymond G. Cordelli.
III. Philadelphia, Pa. 19104 .... (3535 Market St.)	John A. Craven.
IV. Atlanta, Ga. 30309 .... (1371 Peachtree St. NE)	Hugh B. Campbell.
(1931 9th Ave. S., Birmingham, Ala. 35205)	Sterling B. Williams.
V. Chicago, Ill. 60604 .... (230 S. Dearborn St.)	Donald H. Haack. Henry T. White.
VI. Dallas, Tex. 75202 .... (555 Griffin Sq. Bldg.)	Robert B. Snyder.
VII. Kansas City, Mo. 64106 .... (911 Walnut St.)	Rex L. Wayman.
VIII. Denver, Colo. 80294 .... (1961 Stout St.)	C. Lamar Johnson.
IX. San Francisco, Calif. 94102 .... (450 Golden Gate Ave.)	John M. Silver.
X. Seattle, Wash. 98104 .... (909 1st Ave.)	Loren E. Gilbert.

The Wage and Hour Division is also responsible for predetermination of prevailing wage rates for Federal construction contracts and federally assisted programs for construction, alteration and repair of public works subject to the Davis-Bacon and related acts, and a continuing program for determining wage rates under the Service Contract Act. The Division also has enforcement responsibility in ensuring that prevailing wages and overtime standards are paid in accordance with the provisions of the Davis-Bacon and related acts, Service Contract Act, Public Contracts Act, and Contract Work Hours and Safety Standards Act.

FEDERAL CONTRACT COMPLIANCE PROGRAMS

The Office of Federal Contract Compliance Programs is responsible for establishing policies and goals and providing leadership and coordination of the Government's program to achieve nondiscrimination in employment by Government contractors and subcontractors and in federally assisted construction programs; administering programs to assure affirmative action by government contractors to employ and advance in employment Vietnam era veterans and handicapped workers; coordinating with the Equal Employment Opportunity Commission and the Department of Justice matters relating to title VII of the Civil Rights Act of 1964 and maintaining liaison with other agencies having civil rights and equal employment opportunity activities.

Regional offices are established in 10 areas throughout the United States. Areas included within each region are indicated on the map in Appendix D.

REGIONAL OFFICES—FEDERAL CONTRACT COMPLIANCE
(Areas included within each region are indicated on the map on page 5-49.)

Region	Assistant Regional Administrator
I. Boston, Mass. 02203 (John F. Kennedy Federal Bldg.)	E. William Richardson.
II. New York, N.Y. 10036 (1515 Broadway)	George M. Hopkins.
III. Philadelphia, Pa. 19104 (3535 Market St.)	Bennett O. Staivey, Jr.
IV. Atlanta, Ga. 30309 (1371 Peachtree St. NE.)	Jodie G. Eggers.
V. Chicago, Ill. 60604 (230 S. Dearborn St.)	James T. Wardlaw.
VI. Dallas, Tex. 75202 (555 Griffin Sq. Bldg.)	Roberto Ornelas.
VII. Kansas City, Mo. 64106 (911 Walnut St.)	Bennie L. Daugherty, Jr.
VIII. Denver, Colo. 80294 (1961 Stout St.)	Jay Sauls.
IX. San Francisco, Calif. 94102 (450 Golden Gate Ave.)	Dola F. Miller.
X. Seattle, Wash. 98104 (909 1st Ave.)	James F. Warren.

OFFICE OF WORKERS' COMPENSATION PROGRAMS

The Office of Workers' Compensation Programs is responsible for the administration of the three basic Federal workers' compensation laws: the Federal Employees'

DISTRICT OFFICES—WORKERS' COMPENSATION PROGRAMS
(Administers both FECA and LHWCA, except as indicated.)

District	Deputy Commissioner
1. Boston, Mass. 02109 (147 Milk St.)	Stanley Wollaston.
2. New York, N.Y. 10036 (1515 Broadway at W. 44th St.)	John D. McLellan, Jr.
3. Philadelphia, Pa. 19104 (3535 Market St.)	Donald Frederick.
4. Baltimore, Md. 21201 (Federal Bldg.)	Bruno Disimons.[1]
5. Norfolk, Va. 23502 (3661 Virginia Beach Blvd. E.)	Basil Voltsides.[1]
6. Jacksonville, Fla. 32202 (400 W. Bay St.)	Robert Berjeron.
7. New Orleans, La. 70130 (Federal Bldg.)	Pablo Villalobos.
8. Houston, Tex. 77004 (2320 La Branch St.)	Robert Minors.
9. Cleveland, Ohio 44199 (1240 E. 9th St.)	John P. Traynor.
10. Chicago, Ill. 60604 (230 S. Dearborn St.)	Andrew J. Lang.
11. Kansas City, Mo. 64106 (911 Walnut St.)	Carol L. Fleschute.
12. Denver, Colo. 80294 (1961 Stout St.)	Robert Wedemeyer.
13. San Francisco, Calif. 94102 (450 Golden Gate Ave.)	Gerald Cullen.
14. Seattle, Wash. 98101 (909 First Ave.)	Willie L. Massey.
15. Honolulu, Hawaii 96850 (300 Alamoana Blvd.)	Edward F. Ducey, Jr.
16. Dallas, Tex. 75201 (555 Griffin Sq. Bldg.)	Lee H. Hollis.
17. Atlanta, Ga. 30309 (1371 Peachtree St. NE.)	Floyd Ansley.
25. Washington, D.C. 20211 (666 11th St. NW.)	Thomas Markey.[2]
40. Washington, D.C. 20211 (1717 K St. NW.)	Janice V. Bryant.[3]

[1] Administers LHWCA only.
[2] Administers FECA only.
[3] Administers DCCA only.

Compensation Act and related laws (the War Hazards Compensation Act and the War Claims Act), which provide workers' compensation for Federal employees and others; the Longshoremen's and Harbor Workers' Compensation Act and its various extensions (the Defense Base Act, Outer Continental Shelf Land Act, Nonappropriated Fund Instrumentalities Act, and District of Columbia Compensation Act), which provides benefits to employees in private enterprise while engaged in maritime employment on navigable waters in the United States, and which extends coverage to private employment in the District of Columbia; and the "Black Lung" benefit payment provisions of the Federal Coal Mine Health and Safety Act of 1969, as amended by the Black

Lung Benefits Acts of 1972 and 1977, which extend benefits to coal miners, and their survivors, who are totally disabled due to pneumoconiosis, a respiratory disease contracted after prolonged inhalation of coal dust.

The Office of Workers' Compensation Programs is also responsible for developing and recommending standards for improving State workers' compensation laws and providing technical advice and assistance to the States in implementing such standards.

Occupational Safety and Health Administration

The Assistant Secretary for Occupational Safety and Health has responsibility for occupational safety and health activities.

The Occupational Safety and Health Administration, established pursuant to the Occupational Safety and Health Act of 1970 (84 Stat. 1590), develops and promulgates occupational safety and health standards; develops and issues regulations; conducts investigations and inspections to determine the status of compliance with safety and health standards and regulations; and issues citations and proposes penalties for noncompliance with safety and health standards and regulations.

The Occupational Safety and Health Administration has regional offices established in 10 areas throughout the United States. Areas included within each region are indicated on the map in Appendix D.

REGIONAL OFFICES—OCCUPATIONAL SAFETY AND HEALTH ADMINISTRATION
(Areas included within each region are indicated on the map on page 5-49.)

Region	Regional Administrator
I. Boston, Mass. 02203 (JFK Federal Bldg.)	Gilbert J. Saulter.
II. New York, N.Y. 10036 (1515 Broadway)	Alfred Barden.
III. Philadelphia, Pa. 19104 (3535 Market St.)	David H. Rhone.
IV. Atlanta, Ga. 30309 (1375 Peachtree St. NE.)	(Vacancy).
V. Chicago, Ill. 60604 (230 S. Dearborn St.)	Barry J. White.
VI. Dallas, Tex. 75202 (555 Griffin Sq. Bldg.)	(Vacancy).
VII. Kansas City, Mo. 64106 (911 Walnut St.)	Vernon A. Strahm.
VIII. Denver, Colo. 80294 (1961 Stout St.)	Curtis Foster.
IX. San Francisco, Calif. 94102 (450 Golden Gate Ave.)	Gabriel J. Gillotti.
X. Seattle, Wash. 98104 (909 1st Ave.)	James W. Lake.

Mine Safety and Health Administration

The Assistant Secretary of Labor for Mine Safety and Health has responsibility for safety and health in the Nation's mines.

The Mine Safety and Health Administration (MSHA), formerly the Mining Enforcement and Safety Administration in the Department of the Interior, was established pursuant to the Federal Mine Safety and Health Amendments Act of 1977 (91 Stat. 1290; 30 U.S.C. 801). The Act of 1977 consolidates all provisions for mine safety and health under a single Federal law applicable to all types of mines—metal and nonmetal mines as well as coal mines.

The Mine Safety and Health Administration develops and promulgates mandatory safety and health standards, ensures compliance with such standards, assesses civil penalties for violations, investigates accidents, cooperates with and provides assistance to the States in the development of effective State mine safety and health programs, improves and expands training programs in cooperation with the States and the mining industry, and, in coordination with the Department of Health, Education, and Welfare and the Department of the Interior, contributes to the improvement and expansion of mine safety and health research and development. All of these activities are aimed at preventing and reducing mine accidents and occupational diseases in the mining industry.

The statutory responsibilities of the Mine Safety and Health Administration are administered by a headquarters staff located at Arlington, Virginia, reporting to the Assistant Secretary for Mine Safety and Health and by a field network of District and Subdistrict Offices, Penalty Assessment Field Offices, Training Centers, Technical Support Centers, the Health and Safety Analysis Center, the Approval and Certification Center, and Mining Equipment and Electrical Systems Laboratories.

For further information, contact the Mine Safety and Health Administration, Office of Information, Room 511, 4015 Wilson Blvd., Arlington, Va. 22203. Phone, 703-235-1452.

Labor Statistics

The Bureau of Labor Statistics (BLS) has responsibility for the Department's economic and statistical research activities. The Bureau is the Government's principal factfinding agency in the field of labor economics, particularly with respect to the collection and analysis of data on manpower and labor requirements, labor force, employment, unemployment, hours of work, wages and employee compensation, prices, living conditions, labor-management relations, productivity and technological developments, occupational safety and health, structure and growth of the economy, urban conditions and related

REGIONAL OFFICES—BUREAU OF LABOR STATISTICS

Region	Regional Commissioner	Address
BOSTON—Maine, New Hampshire, Vermont, Rhode Island, Massachusetts, Connecticut.	Wendell D. Macdonald	1603-B Federal Bldg., Boston, Mass. 02203.
NEW YORK—New York, New Jersey, Virgin Islands, Puerto Rico, Canal Zone.	Herbert Bienstock	1515 Broadway, New York, N.Y. 10036.
PHILADELPHIA—Pennsylvania, Maryland, Delaware, Virginia, West Vriginia, District of Columbia.	Alvin I. Margulis	3535 Market St., Philadelphia, Pa. 19104.
ATLANTA—Kentucky, Tennessee, North Carolina, South Carolina, Mississippi, Alabama, Florida, Georgia.	Donald Cruse	1371 Peachtree St. NE., Atlanta, Ga. 30309.
CHICAGO—Illinois, Wisconsin, Indiana, Minnesota, Michigan, Ohio.	William E. Rice	230 S. Dearborn St., Chicago, Ill. 60604.
KANSAS CITY—Montana, Wyoming, Utah, Colorado, North Dakota, South Dakota, Nebraska, Kansas, Iowa, Missouri.	Elliott A. Browar	Federal Office Bldg., 911 Walnut St., Kansas City, Mo. 64106.
DALLAS—New Mexico, Oklahoma, Texas, Arkansas, Louisiana.	W. Bryan Richey	555 Griffin Sq. Bldg., Dallas, Tex. 75202.
SAN FRANCISCO—American Samoa, Arizona, California, Guam, Hawaii, Nevada, Trust Territory of the Pacific Islands, Alaska, Idaho, Oregon, Washington.	Bruce B. Hanchett	450 Golden Gate Ave., San Francisco, Calif. 94102.

socio-economic issues, and international aspects of certain of these subjects.

It has no enforcement or administrative functions. Practically all of the basic data it collects from workers, businessmen, and from other governmental agencies are supplied by voluntary cooperation based on their interest in and need for the analyses and summaries which result. The research and statistical projects planned grow out of the needs of these groups, as well as the needs of Congress and the Federal and State governments. The information collected is issued in monthly press releases, in special publications, and in its official publication, the *Monthly Labor Review*. Other major periodicals of the Bureau include: the *Consumer Price Index, Wholesale Prices and Price Indexes, Employment and Earnings, Current Wage Developments, Occupational Outlook Handbook,* and *Occupational Outlook Quarterly*. BLS regional offices issue additional reports and releases usually presenting locality or regional detail.

Sources of Information

Reading Rooms

Department of Labor Library, Rooms N2439 and N2445, New Labor Building, 200 Constitution Ave. NW., Washington, D.C.

Labor-Management Services Administration maintains two Public Documents Rooms at 200 Constitution Ave. NW., Washington, D.C. Reports filed under WPPDA and ERISA provisions are available for public viewing in Room N4677, while LMRDA reports may be viewed in Room N5616. Interested persons should also consult the telephone directory for the nearest field office in their area.

Contracts

General inquiries may be directed to the Division of Procurement, OASAM, Room S1514, New Labor Building, 200 Constitution Ave NW., Washington, D.C. 20210.

Inquiries on doing business with the Job Corps should be directed to the appropriate Employment and Training Administration regional office.

Employment

Personnel Offices use lists of eligibles from the clerical, scientific and technical, and general examinations of the Civil Service Commission.

Inquiries and applications may be directed to the Reception and Correspondence Unit, Room S1318, Department of Labor, 200 Constitution Ave. NW., Washington, D.C. 20210, or the nearest regional office.

Speakers and Films

Private organizations, educational and civic groups, and recognized labor organizations may arrange for speakers and films through the regional offices or the main offices in Washington, D.C.

Publications

A subject listing, *Publications of the U.S. Department of Labor,* is available free at the Information Office, at the Department of Labor Building.

The Employment and Training Administration (ETA) publishes a wide variety of booklets, pamphlets, and reports on apprenticeship training, work experience, unemployment insurance, occupational analyses, and results of research. They are listed in the *Index to*

Publications of the Employment and Training Administration. One-page consumer fact sheets describe ETA's major programs. In addition to publishing Worklife Magazine, the agency's official monthly journal, ETA issues several other periodicals, including *Area Trends in Employment and Unemployment* and *Unemployment Insurance Statistics.* Foremost among the report required under the Comprehensive Employment and Training Act is the *Employment and Training Report of the President.* Single copies of most publications may be obtained from the Employment and Training Administration, Room 10225, 601 D St. NW., Washington, D.C. 20213.

The Bureau of Labor Statistics has an Information Office in Room 1539, General Accounting Office Building, 441 G St. NW., Washington, D.C. 20212. Publications are available both free and for sale. Inquiries may be directed to the Washington Information Office or to the Bureau's regional offices.

Publications of the Employment Standards Administration, such as *Handy Reference Guide to the Fair Labor Standards Act, Age Discrimination in Employment Act,* and *Affirmative Action for Equal Employment Opportunity* are available from the nearest area office. Single copies are free.

For further information concerning the Department of Labor, contact the Office of Information, Publications, and Reports, Room S1032, 200 Constitution Avenue NW., Washington, D.C. 20210. Phone, 202-523-7316.

INTERNATIONAL LABOR ORGANIZATION

International Labor Office: Geneva, Switzerland.

Director General.—Francis Blanchard.

Washington Branch: 1750 New York Ave. NW., Washington, D.C. 20006. Phone, 202-634-6335.

Director.—Edward B. Persons.

The International Labor Organization (ILO), a specialized agency associated with the United Nations, was created by the Treaty of Versailles in 1919 as a part of the League of Nations. The United States joined this autonomous intergovernmental agency in 1934 and is at present one of 132 member countries which finance its operations. Governments, workers, and employers share in making the decisions and shaping its policies. This tripartite representation gives the ILO its balance and much of its strength and makes it distinctive from all other international agencies.

The purpose of the ILO is to improve labor conditions, raise living standards, and promote economic and social stability as the foundation for lasting peace throughout the world.

The standards developed by the annual ILO Conference are guides for countries to follow and form an international labor code that covers such questions as employment, freedom of association, hours of work, migration for employment, protection of women and young workers, prevention of industrial accidents, workmen's compensation, other labor problems, conditions of seamen, and social security. The only obligation on any country is to consider these standards and no country is obligated to adopt, accept, or ratify them.

COUNCIL ON WAGE AND PRICE STABILITY

726 Jackson Place NW., Washington, D.C. 20506
Phone, 202-456-6757

Chairman	Charles L. Schultze, *Chairman, Council of Economic Advisers.*
Members:	
Secretary of the Treasury	W. Michael Blumenthal.
Secretary of State	Cyrus R. Vance.
Secretary of Commerce	Juanita M. Kreps.
Secretary of Labor	Ray Marshall.
Secretary of Housing and Urban Development	Patricia Roberts Harris.
Director, Office of Management and Budget	James T. McIntyre, Jr.
Assistant to the President for Domestic Affairs and Policy	Stuart E. Eizenstat.

Adviser Members:

Attorney General	Griffin B. Bell.
Secretary of Health, Education, and Welfare	Joseph A. Califano, Jr.
Secretary of the Interior	Cecil D. Andrus.
Special Representative for Trade Negotiations	Robert S. Strauss.

Staff:

Director, Council on Wage and Price Stability	Barry P. Bosworth.
General Counsel	Peter Lowry.
Assistant Director for Wage and Price Monitoring	Jack Meyer.
Assistant Director for Government Operations and Research	Thomas Hopkins.
Assistant Director for Public Affairs and Congressional Relations	Thomas H. Joyce.

The Council on Wage and Price Stability was established within the Executive Office of the President by act of August 24, 1974 (88 Stat. 750; 12 U.S.C. 1904 note), as amended by act of August 9, 1975 (89 Stat. 411).

The mission of the Council is to monitor the economy as a whole with respect to such key indicators as wages, costs, productivity, profits, and prices. It also has the responsibility to review and appraise the various programs, policies, and activities of the departments and agencies of the Federal Government for the purpose of determining the extent to which these programs and activities contribute to inflation.

FEDERAL MEDIATION AND CONCILIATION SERVICE

2100 K Street NW., Washington, D.C. 20427
Phone, 202-653-5300

Director	Wayne L. Horvitz.
Deputy Director	Kenneth E. Moffett.
General Counsel	Scott A. Kruse.
Director of Mediation Services	William P. Hobgood.
Director of Professional Development	Jerome T. Barrett.
Director of Arbitration Services	L. Lawrence Schultz.
Director of Administration	Robert P. Gajdys.
Director of Information	Norman O. Walker.

The Federal Mediation and Conciliation Service represents the public interest by promoting the development of sound and stable labor-management relationships; preventing or minimizing work stoppages by assisting labor and management to settle their disputes through mediation; advocating collective bargaining, mediation, and voluntary arbitration as the preferred processes for settling issues between employers and representatives of employees; developing the art, science, and practice of dispute resolution; and fostering constructive joint relationships of labor and management leaders to increase their mutual understanding and solution of common problems.

The Federal Mediation and Conciliation Service was created by the Labor Management Relations Act, 1947 (61 Stat. 153; 29 U.S.C. 172).

Activities

The Federal Mediation and Conciliation Service helps prevent disruptions in the flow of interstate commerce

REGIONAL OFFICES—FEDERAL MEDIATION AND CONCILIATION SERVICE

Region	Regional Director	Address
1. New York, N.Y. 10007	Paul Yager	26 Federal Plaza.
2. Philadelphia, Pa. 19106	Robert W. Donnahoo	4th and Chestnut Sts.
3. Atlanta, Ga. 30323	Tally R. Livingston	1422 W. Peachtree St. NW.
4. Cleveland, Ohio 44199	Edward F. O'Brien	1525 Superior Bldg.
5. Chicago, Ill. 60604	Richard D. Williams	219 S. Dearborn St.
6. St. Louis, Mo. 63105	Paul E. Bowers	120 S. Central.
7. San Francisco, Calif. 94102	Eugene J. Barry	50 Francisco St.
8. Seattle, Wash. 98121	James L. Macpherson	2615 4th Ave.

caused by labor-management disputes by providing mediators to assist disputing parties in the resolution of their differences. The Service can intervene on its own motion or by invitation of either side in a dispute. Mediators have no law enforcement authority and rely wholly on persuasive techniques. The Service also helps provide qualified third party neutrals as factfinders or arbitrators.

The mediator's efforts are directed toward the establishment of sound and stable labor-management relations on a continuing basis. Mediators of the Service assist representatives of labor and management in settling disputes about wages, hours, and other aspects of the employment relationship that arise in the course of negotiations. In this work the mediator has a more basic function: that of encouraging and promoting better day-to-day relations between labor and management. He thereby helps to reduce the incidence of work stoppages. Issues arising in negotiations may then be faced as problems to be settled through mutual effort rather than issues in dispute.

The Service offers its facilities in labor-management disputes in any industry affecting interstate commerce, either upon its own motion or at the request of one or more of the parties to the dispute, whenever it its judgment such dispute threatens to cause a substantial interruption of commerce. Under section 8(d) of the act, employers and unions are required to file with the Service a notice of every dispute affecting commerce not settled within 30 days after prior service of a notice to terminate or modify an existing contract. The Service is required to avoid the mediation of disputes which would have only a minor effect on interstate commerce if State or other conciliation services are available to the parties. The Service is directed to make its mediation and conciliation facilities available only as a last resort and in exceptional cases in the settlement of grievance disputes arising over the application or interpretation of existing collective bargaining agreements.

The Service, on the joint request of employers and unions, will also assist in the selection of arbitrators from a roster of private citizens who are qualified as neutrals to adjudicate matters in dispute.

The work of the Service is designed to strengthen the national labor-management relations policy favoring collective bargaining and responsible labor-management relations.

SOURCES OF INFORMATION

The Service has offices in 80 principal cities, with meeting facilities available for labor-management negotiations. Applications for employment from experienced negotiations practitioners may be sent to any of the listed regional offices, or the National Office in Washington. Inquiries regarding speakers and films may be made to the same offices.

For further information, contact the Office of Information, Federal Mediation and Conciliation Service, Washington, D.C. 20427. Phone, 202-653-5290.

COMMISSION ON CIVIL RIGHTS

1121 Vermont Avenue NW., Washington, D.C. 20425
Phone, 202-254-6758

Chairman	Arthur S. Flemming.
Vice-Chairman	Stephen Horn.
Commissioner	(Vacancy).
Commissioner	Frankie Muse Freeman.
Commissioner	Manuel Ruiz, Jr.
Commissioner	Murray Saltzman.
Staff Director	Louis Nunez, Acting.
Deputy Staff Director	John Hope III, Acting.
General Counsel	Richard Baca.
Assistant Staff Director for Program and Policy Review	Caroline Gleiter, Acting.
Assistant Staff Director for Federal Civil Rights Evaluation	Cynthia Graae.

EQUAL EMPLOYMENT OPPORTUNITY COMMISSION

2401 E Street NW., Washington, D.C. 20506
Phone, 202-634-6930

Chair	Eleanor Holmes Norton.
Special Assistant	Eve Wilkins.
Executive Assistant	Terry M. Banks.
Vice Chair	Daniel E. Leach.
Special Assistant	Beth Don.
Special Assistant	Judy Ellis.
Commissioner	Ethel B. Walsh.
Special Assistant	Ronnie Blumenthal.
Commissioner	(Vacancy).
Commissioner	(Vacancy).
Executive Director	Preston David.
Special Assistant	Betty R. Anderson.
Deputy Director	Alvin Golub.
Special Assistant	Sandy Padillo.
Director, Office of Policy Implementation	Peter Robertson.
Director, Office of Systemic Programs	Lowell D. Johnston.
Director, Office of Field Services	Charlotte Frank.
Director, Office of Management & Finance	Brooke Trent.
Director, Office of Government Employment Programs	Eduardo Pena.
Director, Office of Special Projects and Programs	Chris Roggerson.
Director, Office of Administration	Robert Amoruso.
Director, Office of Public Affairs	Daisy Voigt.
Director, Office of Internal Audit	Richard Huber.
Director, Office of Congressional Affairs	William F. Ware.
Director, Office of Equal Employment Opportunity	Terry M. Banks, Acting.
General Counsel	Abner W. Sibal.
Special Assistant	Sue E. Eisenberg.
Deputy General Counsel	Issie Jenkins.
Associate General Counsel, Appellate Division	Joseph Eddins.
Associate General Counsel, Legal Counsel Division	Constance Dupre.
Associate General Counsel, Trial Division	William Robinson.

The purposes of the Equal Employment Opportunity Commission (EEOC) are to end discrimination based on race, color, religion, sex, or national origin in hiring, promotion, firing, wages, testing, training, apprenticeship, and all other conditions of employment and to promote voluntary action programs by employers, unions, and community organizations to make equal employment opportunity an actuality.

The Equal Employment Opportunity Commission was created by title VII of the Civil Rights Act of 1964 (78 Stat. 241; 42 U.S.C. 2000a), and became operational July 2, 1965. Title VII was amended by the Equal Employment Opportunity Act of 1972 (86 Stat. 103).

The Commission's operations presently are being reorganized from a structure of five litigation centers, seven regional offices, and 32 district offices to a structure of 22 district offices and 37 smaller area offices which integrates the legal and compliance functions.

Activities

The Commission's field offices receive written charges of discrimination against public and private employers (exclusive of the Federal Government), labor organizations, joint labor-management apprenticeship programs, and public and private employment agencies. Members of the Commission also may initiate charges alleging that a violation of title VII has occurred. Charges of title VII violations must be filed with the Commission within 180 days of the alleged violation (or up to 300 days where a State or local fair employment practices agency initially was contacted), and the Commission is responsible for notifying persons so charged within 10 days of the receipt of a new charge. Before investigation, a charge must be deferred for 60 days to a local fair employment practices agency in States and municipalities where an enforceable fair employment practices law is in effect. The deferral period is 120 days for an agency which has been operating less than one year. Under a worksharing agreement, executed between the Commission and State and local fair employment practices agencies, the Commission routinely will assume jurisdiction over certain charges of discrimination and proceed with its investigation rather than wait for the expiration of the deferral period.

The Commission has instituted new procedural regulations which encourage settlement of charges of discrimination prior to a determination of decision by the agency on the merits of the charges. In addition, factfinding conferences may be required as a part of the investigation and may assist in establishing the framework for a negotiated settlement. After an investigation, if there is reasonable cause to believe the charge is true, the district or area office attempts to remedy the alleged unlawful practices through the informal methods of conciliation, conference, and persuasion.

Unless an acceptable conciliation agreement has been secured, the Commission may, after 30 days from the date the charge was filed, bring suit in an appropriate Federal district court. (The Attorney General brings suit when a State government, governmental agency, or a political subdivision is involved.) If the Commission or the Attorney General does not proceed in this manner, at the conclusion of the administrative procedures, or earlier at the request of the charging party, a Notice of Right to Sue is issued which allows the charging party to proceed within 90 days in a Federal district court. In appropriate cases the Commission may intervene in such civil action if the case is of general public interest. The investigation and conciliation of charges having an industrywide or national impact are coordinated or conducted by the Office of Systemic Programs.

Under the provisions of section 706(f)(2), as amended by section 5 of the Equal Employment Opportunity Act of 1972, if it is concluded after a preliminary investigation that prompt judicial action is necessary to carry out the purposes of the act, the Commission or the Attorney General, in a case involving a State government, governmental agency or political subdivision, may bring an action for appropriate temporary or preliminary relief pending final disposition of a charge.

The Commission participates in the development of the law of employment discrimination through issuance of guidelines, publication of significant Commission decisions, and involvement in litigation brought under title VII and related statutes.

The Commission has direct liaison with State and local governments, employer and union organizations, trade associations, civil rights organizations and other agencies and organizations concerned with employment of minority group members and women. The Commission engages in and contributes to the cost of research and other mutual interest projects with State and local agencies charged with the administration of fair employment practices laws. Furthermore, the Commission enters into worksharing agreements with the State and local agencies in order to avoid duplication of effort by identifying specific charges to be investigated by the respective agencies.

The Commission is also a major publisher of data on the employment status of minorities and women. Through six employment surveys (EEO–1 through EEO–6), covering private employers, apprenticeship programs, labor unions, State and local governments, elementary and secondary schools, and colleges and universities, the Commission tabulates and stores data on the ethnic, racial, and sex characteristics of employees at all job levels within the reported groups.

Research information thus collected is shared with selected Federal agencies, such as the Department of Health, Education, and Welfare, the Department of Labor, and others. It is also made available, in appropriate form, for public use.

SOURCES OF INFORMATION

Reading Room

Room 2303, 2401 E Street NW., Washington, D.C. 20506.

Employment

The Commission selects its employees from various examinations and registers, including the Professional and Administrative Career Examination (PACE), Mid-Level, and Senior Level registers; various secretarial, typing, and stenographic registers; and the Equal Opportunity Specialist register. Employment inquiries or applications for positions in the headquarters office should be directed to the Equal Employment Opportunity Commission, Personnel Office, Room 3214, 2401 E Street NW., Washington, D.C. 20506. Phone, 202-634-7002, or to the appropriate district office for district office positions. Applicants for attorney positions may apply directly to EEOC, Office of the General Counsel, 2401 E Street, NW., Washington, D.C. 20506.

For further information, contact the Director, Office of Public Affairs, Equal Employment Opportunity Commission, 2401 E Street NW., Washington, D.C. 20506. Phone, 202-634-6930.

DEPARTMENT OF HEALTH, EDUCATION, AND WELFARE

200 Independence Avenue SW., Washington, D.C. 20201
Phone, 202-245-7000

Secretary	Joseph A. Califano, Jr.
Executive Assistant to the Secretary	Ben W. Heineman, Jr.
Secretary to the Secretary	Kathy Backus.
Appointments Secretary	Muriel Hartley.
Executive Secretary to the Department	Frederick Bohen.
Deputy Executive Secretary	Richard Cotton.
Deputy Executive Secretary	James Pickman.
Under Secretary	Hale Champion.
Deputy Under Secretary for Intergovernmental Affairs	Eugene Eidenberg.
Executive Assistant to the Under Secretary	Leo J. Corbett.
Inspector General	Thomas D. Morris.
Deputy Inspector General	Charles F. C. Ruff.
Assistant Inspector General for Auditing	Edward Stepnick.
Assistant Inspector General for Investigations	Lawrence Lippe.
Assistant Inspector General for Health Care and Systems Review	Bryan Mitchell.
Director, Office for Civil Rights	David Tatel.
Deputy Director for Program Review	Wilbert Cheatham.
Deputy Director for Compliance and Enforcement	Cindy Brown.
Associate Director, Administration	Lafayette Walker.
Associate Director, Policy, Planning, and Research	Melvyn Leventhal.
Director, Office of Consumer Affairs	Lee Richardson, Acting.
Assistant Secretary (Public Affairs)	Eileen Shanahan.
Deputy Assistant Secretary (Public Affairs)	Cliff Sessions, Acting.
Deputy Assistant Secretary for Special Projects	Leroy V. Goodman, Acting.
Assistant Secretary (Legislation)	Richard Warden.
Deputy Assistant Secretary	Ken Levine.
Deputy Assistant Secretary (Health Legislation)	C. Grant Spaeth.
Deputy Assistant Secretary (Education Legislation)	William Blakey.
Deputy Assistant Secretary (Welfare Legislation)	Nancy Amidei.
Director (Congressional Liaison Office)	Dan Dozier.
Assistant Secretary (Planning and Evaluation)	Henry Aaron.
Executive Assistant to the Assistant Secretary	Gerald Bennett.
Deputy Assistant Secretary	Peter Schuck.
Deputy Assistant Secretary for Planning and Evaluation/Health	Karen Davis.
Deputy Assistant Secretary for Planning and Evaluation/Education	Michael O'Keefe.
Deputy Assistant Secretary for Program Systems	Gerald Britten.
Deputy Assistant Secretary/Income Security Policy	Michael Barth.
Director, Office of Special Concerns	Constance Downey, Acting.
Director, Office of Technical Support and Statistics	Wray Smith.
Director, Office of Social Services and Human Development	Edwin Marcus, Acting.
General Counsel	Peter Libassi.
Deputy General Counsel	Richard Beattie.
Deputy General Counsel Legal Counsel	Daniel Marcus.
Deputy General Counsel Regulation Review	James Hinchman.
Associate General Counsel (Regional Operations)	Inez Reid.
Assistant General Counsels:	
Business and Administrative Law Division	Bernard Feiner.
Civil Rights Division	Albert Hamlin.
Education Division	Theodore Sky.
Public Health Division	Richard Cooper.
Food and Drug Division	Sidney Edelman.
Health Care Financing and Human Development Services Division	Galen Powers.

Social Security Division	Joel Cohen.
Inspector General Division	Marjorie Knowles.
Legislation Division	Donald Hirsch.
Assistant Secretary for Management and Budget	Leonard D. Schaeffer.
Deputy Assistant Secretary	Charles Miller II.
Director, Office of the Secretary Budget Services	John Scully.
Deputy Assistant Secretary, Budget	Wilford J. Forbush.
Director, Division of Health Budget Analysis	Ellen Wormser.
Director, Division of Education Budget Analysis	William Dingeldein.
Director, Division of Welfare Budget Analysis	Michael L. Sturman.
Director, Division of Budget Review	Charles F. Kearney.
Deputy Assistant Secretary, Finance	David V. Dukes.
Deputy Assistant Secretary for Management	(Vacancy).
Deputy Assistant Secretary for Grants and Procurement	Paul A. Stone.
Deputy Assistant Secretary for Management Analysis and Systems	L. David Taylor, Acting.
Director, Office of Management Services	Edwin M. Sullivan.
Director, Office of Facilities Engineering	Robert D. Quinn.
Assistant Secretary for Personnel Administration	Thomas S. McFee.
Deputy Assistant Secretary for Personnel and Training	Raymond J. Sumser.
Executive Assistant	Thomas Shebby.
Director, Office of Equal Employment Opportunity	Samuel M. Hoston.
Director, Federal Women's Program	Florence Perman.
Director, Spanish Speaking Program	Manuel Carrillo.
Director, Grants Appeals Board	Malcolm Mason.

OFFICE OF HUMAN DEVELOPMENT SERVICES

200 Independence Avenue SW., Washington, D.C. 20201
Phone, 202-245-7246

Assistant Secretary for Human Development Services	Arabella Martinez.
Deputy Assistant Secretary for Human Development Services	T. M. Parham.
Director, Office of Policy and Management Control	Warren Master.
Director, Office of Planning, Research and Evaluation	Jerry Turem.
Director, Office of Administration and Management	Joseph Mottola.
Commissioner, Administration for Children, Youth and Families	Blandina Cardenas.
Commissioner, Administration on Aging	Robert C. Benedict.
Commissioner, Rehabilitation Services Administration	Robert R. Humphreys.
Commissioner, Administration for Native Americans	A. David Lester.
Commissioner, Administration for Public Services	Ernest Osborne, Acting.

EDUCATION DIVISION

Office of the Assistant Secretary for Education

200 Independence Avenue SW., Washington, D.C. 20202
Phone, 202-245-8430

Assistant Secretary for Education	Mary F. Berry.
Executive Assistant	Samuel H. Solomon.
Deputy Assistant Secretary for Education	Peter D. Relic.
Deputy Assistant Secretary for Education (Policy Development)	Joel S. Berke.
Deputy Assistant Secretary for Education (Management and Budget)	Domenic R. Ruscio.
Director, Fund for Improvement of Postsecondary Education	Ernest J. Bartell.
Administrator, National Center for Education Statistics	Marie D. Eldridge.
Director, Institute of Museum Services	Lee Kimche.

Office of Education

400 Maryland Avenue SW., Washington, D.C. 20202
Phone, 202-245-8795

Commissioner of Education	Ernest L. Boyer.
Executive Assistant	Martin H. Kaplin.
Assistant Commissioner for Executive Operations	Graeme Baxter.
Assistant Commissioner for Policy Studies	Marshall Smith.
Assistant Commissioner for Educational Community Liaison	Richard Whitford, Acting.
Assistant Commissioner for Legislation	Albert L. Alford.
Assistant Commissioner for Public Affairs	Margaret Rhoades.
Director, Bilingual Education	Thomas Burns, Acting.
Director, Career Education	Kenneth Hoyt.
Director, Teacher Corps	William L. Smith.
Executive Deputy Commissioner for Educational Programs	John Ellis.
Director, Right to Read	Gilbert Schiffman.
Assistant Commissioner for Regional Liaison	William E. McLaughlin.
Executive Deputy Commissioner for Support Services	William L. Pierce, Acting.
Director of Planning and Budgeting	Cora Beebe.
Deputy Commissioner for Administration	Edward T. York, Jr.
Associate Commissioner for Administration	Frank B. McGettrick.
Assistant Commissioner for Evaluation and Dissemination	John W. Evans.
Deputy Commissioner for Higher and Continuing Education	Alford L. Moye.
Associate Deputy Commissioner for Higher and Continuing Education	Leonard H. O. Spearman.
Associate Commissioner for Institutional Development and International Education	Robert Leestma.
Deputy Commissioner for Student Financial Assistance	Leo Kornfeld.
Deputy Commissioner for Education of the Handicapped	Edwin M. Martin.
Associate Deputy Commissioner for Education of the Handicapped	Robert B. Herman.
Deputy Commissioner for Elementary and Secondary Education	Thomas K. Minter.
Associate Commissioner/Director of Library and Learning Resources	Dick Hays.
Director, Environmental Education	Walter Bogan.
Associate Commissioner for Equal Education Opportunity Programs	Herman R. Goldberg.
Associate Commissioner for Compensatory Education Programs	John H. Rodriguez.
Associate Commissioner for State and Local Education Programs	John H. Rodriguez, Acting.
Deputy Commissioner for Indian Education	Gerald Gipp.
Associate Deputy Commissioner for Indian Education	John W. Tippeconnic.
Deputy Commissioner for Occupational and Adult Education	Charles H. Buzzell, Acting.
Associate Commissioner for Adult Vocational, Technical and Manpower Education	Howard F. Hjelm, Acting.
Associate Commissioner for Occupational Planning	Ann M. Martin.
Director, Consumers' Education	Dustin Wilson.

National Institute of Education

Brown Building, Nineteenth and M Streets NW., Washington, D.C. 20208
Phone, 202-254-5740

Director	Patricia Albjerg Graham.
Deputy Director	Michael P. Timpane.
Deputy Director for Management	Gladys Keith Hardy.
Chief, Office of Government and Public Affairs	Noel Vivaldi, Acting.
Chief, National Center for Educational Research Staff	Peter Gerber.
Associate Director for Planning, Budget and Program Analysis	John C. Christensen, Acting.
Associate Director for Administration and Management	John C. Christensen.
Associate Director for Basic Skills	Thomas Sticht.
Associate Director for Dissemination and Resources	Senta Raizen.

Associate Director for Finance and Productivity .... Arthur S. Melmed.
Associate Director for School Capacity for Problem Solving Marc S. Tucker.
Associate Director for Education and Work .... Corinne H. Rieder.
Associate Director for Educational Equity .... Vera Brown, Acting.

PUBLIC HEALTH SERVICE

Office of the Assistant Secretary for Health

200 Independence Avenue SW., Washington, D.C. 20201
Phone, 202-245-6296

5600 Fishers Lane, Rockville, Md. 20857
Phone, 301-443-2404

Assistant Secretary for Health (Surgeon General of the Public
   Health Service) .... Julius B. Richmond.
Deputy Assistant Secretary for Health/Programs .... Joyce C. Lashof.
Executive Officer .... Rupert Moure.
Deputy Executive Officer .... John C. Droke.
Deputy Assistant Secretary for Health Policy, Research and
   Statistics .... Ruth S. Hanft.
   Director, National Center for Health Services Research .... Gerald D. Rosenthal.
   Director, National Center for Health Statistics .... Dorothy P. Rice.
Deputy Assistant Secretary for Health (Special Health Initiatives) J. Michael McGinnis.
Deputy Assistant Secretary for National Health Insurance .... James J. Mongan.
Senior Advisor for External Relations .... James F. Dickson III.
Associate Director of Extramural Research and Training ..... Leon Jacobs, Acting.
Associate Director for Clinical Care .... Mortimer B. Lipsett.
Associate Director for Program Planning and Evaluation .... Joseph G. Perpich.
Associate Director for Administration .... Leon M. Schwartz.
Associate Director for Communications .... Storm Whaley.
Director, National Library of Medicine .... Martin M. Cummings.
Director, National Cancer Institute .... Arthur C. Upton.
Director, National Heart, Lung and Blood Institute .... Robert I. Levy.
Director, National Eye Institute .... Carl Kupfer.
Director, National Institute of Allergy and Infectious Diseases Richard M. Krause.
Director, National Institute of Arthritis, Metabolism, and Diges-
   tive Diseases .... G. Donald Whedon.
Director, National Institute of Child Health and Human De-
   velopment .... Norman Kretchmer.
Director, National Institute of Dental Research .... David B. Scott.

HEALTH CARE FINANCING ADMINISTRATION

330 C Street SW., Washington, D.C. 20201
Phone, 202-245-6726

Administrator .... Robert A. Derzon.
Deputy Administrator .... William D. Fullerton.
Chairman Provider Reimbursement Review Board .... Arthur P. Owens.
Attorney Advisor .... Erica L. Gosnell.
Director, Office of Policy, Planning and Research .... Clifton R. Gaus, Acting.
Director, Office of Management and Budget .... David N. Weinman, Acting.
Director, Office of Personnel .... John Berry, Acting.
Director, Office of Regional Affairs .... Rhoda M. Greenberg, Acting.
Director, Office of Congressional Affairs .... Cherry V. Tsutsumida, Act-
                                    ing.
Director, Office of Public Affairs .... Patricia Schoeni, Acting.
Director, Office of Systems and Organizational Integration ... (Vacancy).
Director, Medicare Bureau .... Thomas Tierney, Acting.
Director, Medicaid Bureau .... Paul R. Willging, Acting.

Director, Health Standards and Quality Bureau . . . . Helen Smits.
Director, Office of Reimbursement Practices and Cost Contain-
ment . . . . Robert O'Connor, Acting.
Director, Office of Program Integrity . . . . Donald Nicholson, Acting.

SOCIAL SECURITY ADMINISTRATION

6401 Security Boulevard, Baltimore, Md. 21235
Phone, 301-594-1234

Commissioner of Social Security . . . . Don I. Wortman, Acting.
  Deputy Commissioner of Social Security . . . . Don I. Wortman.
    Associate Commissioner for Management and Administra-
    tion . . . . Francis D. DeGeorge.
    Associate Commissioner for Program Operations . . . . Robert P. Bynum.
    Associate Commissioner for Program Policy and Planning Elmer Smith.
    Associate Commissioner for External Affairs . . . . Thomas C. Parrott.
    Director, Bureau of Hearings and Appeals . . . . Robert L. Trachtenberg.
    Director, Office of Advanced Systems . . . . E. R. Lannon.
  Associate Commissioner for Family Assistance . . . . Barry Van Lare.

OFFICE OF CHILD SUPPORT ENFORCEMENT

6401 Security Boulevard, Baltimore, Md. 21235
Phone, 301-594-1234

Director . . . . Don I. Wortman, Acting.
Deputy Director . . . . Louis B. Hays.

The Department of Health, Education, and Welfare (HEW) is the Cabinet-level department of the Federal executive branch most concerned with people and most involved with the Nation's human concerns. In one way or another—whether it is mailing out social security checks, or improving the quality of American education, or making health services more widely available—HEW touches the lives of more Americans than any other Federal agency. It is literally a department of people serving people, from newborn infants to our most elderly citizens.

The Department of Health, Education, and Welfare was created on April 11, 1953, under legislation proposed by President Eisenhower and approved by the Congress on April 1, 1953. That legislation abolished HEW's predecessor organization, the Federal Security Agency, and transferred all its functions to the new Department. In addition, it transferred all responsibilities of the Federal Security Administrator to the Secretary of Health, Education, and Welfare.

Office of the Secretary

The Secretary of HEW advises the President on health, education, welfare, and income security plans, policies, and programs of the Federal Government. The Secretary directs Department staff in carrying out the approved programs and activities of the Department and promotes general public understanding of the Department's goals, programs, and objectives. The Secretary administers these functions through the five Principal Operating Components (POC's) of the Department and the Office of the Secretary and through specialized units, such as the Office for Civil Rights. The Secretary also carries out certain Federal responsibilities for three federally aided corporations: American Printing House for the Blind, Gallaudet College, and Howard University.

The Under Secretary, the Assistant Secretaries, the General Counsel, and the heads of the POC's aid the Secretary in his overall management responsibilities.

Since the Secretary is accountable to the Congress and the public for the way the Department is spending taxpayers' money, the Secretary and his top staff spend a considerable amount of time testifying before committees of the Congress, meeting with groups of Congressmen, making speeches before national organizations, and meeting with the press and the public to explain HEW actions. They also prepare special reports on national problems which are available to the public through the Department and the Government Printing Office. In addition, the Secretary submits to the President and the Congress periodic reports required by law that further explain how tax money was spent, progress was achieved, or social problems have been resolved.

DEPARTMENT OF HEALTH, EDUCATION, AND WELFARE

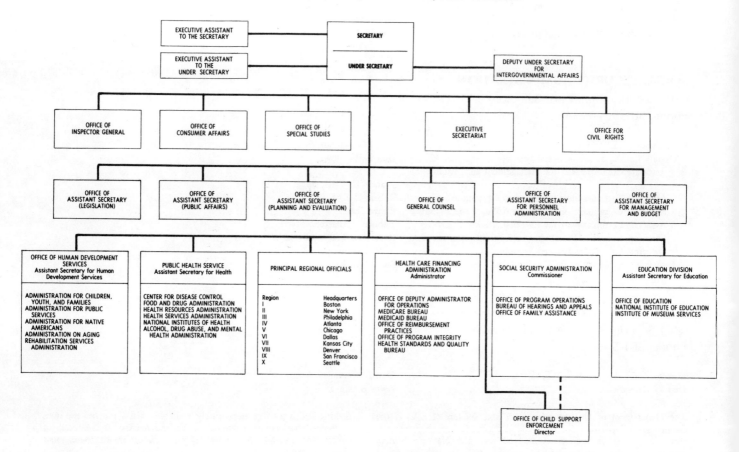

Under Secretary

The Under Secretary serves as Acting Secretary in the absence of the Secretary and performs on behalf of the Secretary such functions and duties as the Secretary may designate; coordinates regional and field activities; and coordinates Federal-State relations.

Inspector General

The Office of the Inspector General is responsible for conducting and supervising audits and investigations relating to programs and operations of the Department. The Office provides leadership and coordination for, and recommends policies and corrective actions concerning activities designed to promote economy and efficiency in the administration of, and prevent and detect fraud and abuse in the Department's programs and operation. The Office provides a means for keeping the Secretary and Congress fully and currently informed about problems and deficiencies relating to the administration of such programs and operations, and the necessity of corrective action.

Civil Rights

The Office for Civil Rights is responsible for the administration and enforcement of departmental policies under title VI of the Civil Rights Act of 1964 which prohibits discrimination with regard to race, color, or national origin in programs and activities receiving Federal financial assistance; titles VII and IX of the Education Admendments of 1972; sections 799A and 845 of the Comprehensive Health Manpower and Nurse Training Acts of 1971; section 504 of the Rehabilitation Act of 1973; and Executive Order 11246, as amended, which prohibits discrimination with regard to race, religion, color, sex, or national origin by employers holding Federal contracts.

Consumer Affairs

The Office of Consumer Affairs advises the Secretary on consumer-related policy and programs and constitutes the staff of the Special Assistant to the President for Consumer Affairs; analyzes and coordinates implementation of all Federal activities in the area of consumer protection; and recommends ways in which governmental consumer programs can be made more effective.

Public Affairs

The Assistant Secretary (Public Affairs) develops and coordinates public affairs policy for the Department; serves as principal public information officer for the

REGIONAL OFFICES—DEPARTMENT OF HEALTH, EDUCATION, AND WELFARE
(Areas included within each region are indicated on the map on page 5-49.)

Region	Principal Regional Official	Address	Phone
I	John Bean	John F. Kennedy Federal Bldg., Boston, Mass. 02203	617-223-6831.
II	Cesar A. Perales	26 Federal Plaza, New York, N.Y. 10007	212-264-4600.
III	James Mellody	3535 Market St., Philadelphia, Pa. 19101	215-596-6492.
IV	Sara Craig	50 7th St. NE., Atlanta, Ga. 30323	404-221-2442.
V	Chris Cohen	300 S. Wacker Dr., Chicago, Ill. 60606	312-353-5160.
VI	Eddie Bernice Johnson	1200 Main Tower Bldg., Dallas, Tex. 75202	214-655-3301.
VII	Thomas Higgins	601 E. 12th St., Kansas City, Mo. 64106	816-374-3436.
VIII	Wellington Webb	1961 Stout St., Denver, Colo. 80202	303-837-3373.
IX	Mike Murray	50 Fulton St., San Francisco, Calif. 94102	415-556-6746.
X	Bernard Kelly	1321 2d Ave., Seattle, Wash. 98101	206-442-0420.

Department; provides public affairs counsel in all departmental policy decisions; develops departmental public affairs objectives; reviews and evaluates agency public affairs structures, plans, and activities; develops departmental policy and administers the Freedom of Information Act; coordinates Department public affairs policies and activities with other cabinet departments and with the White House.

Legislation

The Assistant Secretary for Legislation serves as principal adviser to the Secretary in the development and implementation of the Department's legislative program and maintains liaison with the Members and committees of Congress and their staffs.

Planning and Evaluation

The Office of the Assistant Secretary (Planning and Evaluation) coordinates Department activities in economic and social analysis, program analysis and planning, and evaluation activities, and ensures that Department policy and program planning appropriately reflects the results of these activities.

General Counsel

The General Counsel furnishes legal advice to the Office of the Secretary and to the Principal Operating Components of the Department.

Management and Budget

The Assistant Secretary for Management and Budget provides advice and guidance to the Secretary on administrative and financial management, excluding personnel management, and provides for the direction and coordination of these activities throughout the Department on a day-to-day basis. The activities include overseeing the preparation of the departmental budget, maintenance of a department-wide system for developing and administrating financial operating plans, surplus real property utilization, health and education facilities, engineering and construction, and policy development and regulations for grants and procurement management.

Personnel Administration

The Assistant Secretary for Personnel Administration promotes effective personnel management and personnel administration in the Department. The Assistant Secretary advises and acts for the Secretary on personnel management and training matters, formulating policies and plans for broad programs under which the personnel and training functions will be carried out; maintains cognizance of such policies and programs; and represents the Department on personnel and training matters with the Civil Service Commission, other Federal agencies, the Congress, and the public. The Assistant Secretary for Personnel Administration also advises the Secretary on, and provides departmentwide leadership and guidance, to equal employment opportunity programs and activities and oversees the establishment, staffing, and operation of departmental advisory committees.

Regional Offices

The 10 principal regional officials of the Department of Health, Education, and Welfare are the Secretary's representatives in direct, official dealings with State and local government organizations. The regional officials provide a central focus in each region for departmental relations with Congress and promote general understanding of Department programs, policies, and objectives. They also advise the Secretary on the potential effects of decisions and provide administrative services and support to Department programs and activities in the regions.

Office of Human Development Services

The Office of Human Development Services (HDS) administers a broad range of social and rehabilitation services and human development programs designed to deal with the problems of specific populations, including the elderly, children of low-income families, persons with mental or physical handicaps, runaway youth, and Native Americans. HDS also serves as an advocate within the Department for the needs of these special groups. The Office is comprised of agencies and offices which ensure that the services to these groups are effective and well coordinated, and that the Department appropriately responds to their needs.

OFFICE OF THE ASSISTANT SECRETARY FOR HUMAN DEVELOPMENT SERVICES

The Office of the Assistant Secretary for Human Development Services provides executive leadership to HDS to focus the agency's planning and resources on the needs of its special constituencies and to coordinate efforts on their behalf. The Assistant Secretary for Human Development Services serves as the principal adviser to the Secretary on policies related to these special groups of Americans and is responsible for ensuring that issues concerning HDS constitutents are appropriately and effectively addressed within the Department.

MAJOR COMPONENTS

HDS agencies operate significant grant programs in addition to acting as advocates and coordinators of departmental or Government-wide services.

Administration on Aging

The Administration on Aging (AOA) is the principal Federal organization for identifying the needs, concerns, and interests of older persons and for carrying out the programs of the Older Americans Act. AOA is also the principal agency for promoting coordination of Federal resources available to meet the needs of older persons.

AOA administers three major grant programs: a Federal-State-local program which provides support for State agencies and area agencies on aging to establish comprehensive, coordinated service systems for older persons at the community level; the National Nutrition Program for the Elderly, designed to provide low-cost, nutritious meals to low-income persons age 60 and over; and a research, demonstration, and manpower development program which seeks to identify effective methods of helping older people, and to promote the preparation of teachers, researchers, and practitioners for the field of aging.

AOA maintains a National Clearinghouse on Aging and provides staff for the Federal Council on Aging.

Administration for Children, Youth, and Families

The Administration for Children, Youth, and Families (ACYF) consists of two principal program units: the Office of Services for Children and Youth and the Office of Developmental Services. The Office of Developmental Services emphasizes programs that maximize positive development of young children, especially those receiving out-of-home care during some portion of the day. The Office of Service for Children and Youth administers programs which provide social services to children and their families and serves as an advocate for the needs of children and youth. ACYF also serves as a coordination point for all Federal programs for children and their families and as an advocate for the children and youth of the Nation by bringing their needs to the attention of the Government and the public.

The Administration for Children, Youth, and Families operates federally funded programs for children, such as Head Start and Parent and Child Centers; administers the National Center on Child Abuse and Neglect and the Child Welfare Services program; and coordinates intradepartmental activities in the field of runaway youth. The Administration also awards grants for the training of child welfare workers and for research and demonstration projects in the fields of child, youth, and family services.

Administration for Native Americans

The Administration for Native American (ANA) provides a departmental focus for the special concerns of American Indians, Alaskan Natives, and Native Hawaiians. It assists Native Americans in achieving the goal of economic and social self-sufficiency by providing direct and flexible funding to Indian tribes and other organizations through which Native Americans establish their own priorities as well as control and direct the institutions and programs which affect their lives. A major goal of ANA is to strengthen the capability of Native American organizations and instruments of government, so that they can respond to the complex demands and increased responsibilities being placed upon them, provide community services, and obtain resources and benefits for which Native Americans are eligible as American citizens. In addition, ANA also has an advocacy responsibility to develop policy and legislative guidance, to advise the Secretary, and to provide liaison with other Federal agencies on Native American affairs. A primary mechanism for achieving this responsibility is the Intra-Departmental Council on Indian Affairs, which is chaired by the Commissioner, Administration for Native Americans.

Administration for Public Services

The Administration for Public Services (APS) provides leadership in the planning, development, management, and coordination of all social services programs authorized under title XX of the Social Security Act. It provides leadership for social services programs to improve the capability of eligible families and individuals to achieve self-support and self-sufficiency; to reduce institutionalization and institutionalized care; to strengthen family life for disadvantaged families and children; to assist in family planning; to improve the social functioning of disadvantaged individuals, including aged, blind, or permanently and totally disabled persons, drug addicts, and alcoholics; and to secure appropriate institutionalization and deinstitutionalization for eligible persons. The Administration also coordinates HEW programs and services designed to improve employment potential and job opportunities for Americans who are unemployed, underemployed, or in need of training; and works with other Federal agencies, such as the Department of Labor, in carrying out these functions.

The Administration works through HDS Regional Offices and other appropriate organizations to develop capability in State public welfare agencies to plan, manage, and evaluate the effective delivery of social services. Through its regional staff, the Administration also offers technical assistance to Comprehensive Employment and Training Act (CETA) grantees in planning their manpower strategies and in developing effective linkages with HEW manpower-related services.

The Administration for Public Services manages Federal training grant programs for social services training, and provides leadership in the planning, development, and management of programs which fund training to increase the competence of State and local agency and other social services manpower. APS advocates for the needs of rural Americans by identifying barriers to service delivery, recommending new service delivery systems, and coordinating with other Federal agencies to deliver services to target areas. The Administration also serves as an advocate for volunteer participation in HDS-funded programs.

Rehabilitation Services Administration

The Rehabilitation Services Administration (RSA) provides leadership in the planning, coordination, and development of services for handicapped individuals and advocates on their behalf. The Administration promotes effective utilization of the wide range of services available to aid handicapped persons; serves as a catalyst to stimulate the development and expansion of these services, especially for those with severe disabilities; and works to establish a coordinated network of services for handicapped citizens. RSA administers the State/Federal program of vocational rehabilitation and provides formula grants to the States and territories for planning, services, administration, and construction of facilities for the developmentally disabled.

The Administration supports research and demonstration programs to evolve new approaches toward more meaningful lives for handicapped individuals and directs and promotes a national training program to provide skilled manpower for working with those who are handicapped. It also funds project grants to demonstrate improved methods of providing services to the developmentally disabled and project grants to universities or affiliated facilities to provide partial support to interdisciplinary training programs for specialized personnel to serve the developmentally disabled.

The Administration provides support to the President's Committee on Mental Retardation (PCMR), which advises the President on mental retardation matters and coordinates with all departments and agencies throughout the Federal Government to further the goals of preventing retardation and reducing the institutionalization of mentally retarded people. The Committee publicizes means of preventing many of the specific causes of mental retardation and works with professional groups, the private sector, and the general public to improve services for mentally retarded people and to change misconceptions and prejudicial attitudes about them. RSA also coordinates with and supports the work of the Office for Handicapped Individuals, which is responsible for programs of research, evaluation, and training related to comprehensive services for handicapped individuals, and the Architectural and Transportation Barriers Compliance Board.

Architectural and Transportation Barriers Compliance Board

The Architectural and Transportation Barriers Compliance Board (A&TBCB) is composed of representatives from nine Federal agencies—Departments of HEW, Transportation, Housing and Urban Development, Defense, Labor, and Interior, the General Services Administration, Veterans Administration, and U.S. Postal Service. The Board's function is to ensure compliance with Federal standards of accessibility as specified under the Architectural Barriers Act and other Federal regulations, and to investigate and examine alternative approaches to architectural, transportation, and attitudinal barriers which impede the mobility of handicapped individuals.

Whenever Federal funds are used to support a building or facility, the Board has authority to ask questions about, and take action against, any barriers to handicapped individuals. The goal of the Board is to create a barrier-free environment. HEW is the chairing agency with the Assist Secretary for Human Development Services designated as Chairperson.

Office of Veterans Affairs

The Office of Veterans Affairs has the responsibility for the coordination of HEW-wide focus on veterans, and for establishing and directing an intradepartmental committee on veterans affairs to evaluate current programming directed towards veterans. The Office is also responsible for developing recommendations for increased veterans participation in services provided through program authorizations of HEW, and in preparing an HEW strategy for veterans through consultations with agencies within HEW, the private sector, and other Federal agencies.

Education Division

The Education Division was created by the Education Amendments of 1972 which were signed into law on June 23, 1972 (86 Stat. 327; 20 U.S.C. 1221e).

The Educational Division, under the direct supervision of the Assistant Secretary for Education who reports to the Secretary, is responsible for coordinating and generally supervising the education activities of the Department.

The Education Division consists of the Office of the Assistant Secretary for Education, the Office of Education, the National Institute of Education, and the Institute of Museum Services.

OFFICE OF THE ASSISTANT SECRETARY FOR EDUCATION

The Office of the Assistant Secretary for Education is responsible for the general direction and supervision of the Education Division. This Office provides leadership for the education activities of the Department, and serves as the key advocate for assuring that the Department provides professional and financial assistance to strengthen education in accordance with Federal laws and regulations.

National Center for Education Statistics

The National Center for Education Statistics collects and disseminates statistics and other data related to education in the United States and in other nations. The Center coordinates the information-gathering activities for education programs, and performs special analyses of and disseminates the statistical data so gathered.

Fund for the Improvement of Postsecondary Education

The Fund for the Improvement of Postsecondary Education is responsible for improving postsecondary educational opportunities by providing assistance to educational institutions and agencies to encourage a broad range of improvements and innovations.

INSTITUTE OF MUSEUM SERVICES

The Institute of Museum Services is responsible for assisting museums in their educational role to better serve all age groups, in modernizing their methods and facilities, and in easing the financial burden on museums which is a result of their increasing use by the public.

OFFICE OF EDUCATION

The Office of Education was created by act of March 2, 1867 (14 Stat. 434; 20 U.S.C. 1). In 1869 the Office of Education became a part of the Department of the Interior; it was transferred to the Federal Security Agency upon that Agency's creation in 1939; and it became a constituent agency of the Department of Health, Education, and Welfare upon the establishment of that Department in 1953.

The statutory function of the Office of Education is administration of programs of financial assistance to educational agencies, institutions, and organizations.

MAJOR COMPONENTS
Office of the Commissioner of Education

In addition to general responsibility for the Office of Education and its regional offices, the Office of the Commissioner administers the operations of the Teacher Corps, bilingual education, career education, and right-to-read programs.

Regional Offices

Each regional office administers the educational affairs of an HEW region. It serves as a center for dissemination of information and provides technical assistance to State and local educational agencies and other institutions and individuals having an interest in Federal education activities.

Management

The Office of Management plans, directs, and coordinates the activities of all segments of the Office having to do with management planning and evaluation, administrative and business management.

Planning

The Office of Planning directs and coordinates the activities of all segments of the Office having to do with program planning and evaluation, legislative planning, and Congressional liaison.

Elementary and Secondary Education

The Bureau of Elementary and Secondary Education is responsible for administration of a program of grants to State education agencies and local school districts, programs of financial and technical assistance to school districts to meet special needs incident to the elimination of racial segregation and discrimination, grants to States for development and construction of public library facilities and for acquisition of library resources, and technical assistance in the development, adoption, and implementation of plans for the desegregation of public schools.

Occupational and Adult Education

The Bureau of Occupational and Adult Education administers programs of grants, contracts, and technical assistance for vocational and technical education, occupational education, metric education, adult education, consumer education, education professions development, and community schools.

Education for the Handicapped

The Bureau of Education for the Handicapped assists States, colleges and universities, and other institutions and agencies in meeting the educational needs of the Nation's handicapped children who require special services. It administers programs such as support of training for teachers and other professional personnel; grants for research; financial aid to help States initiate, expand, and improve their resources; and media services and captioned films for the deaf.

Postsecondary Education

The Bureau of Postsecondary Education administers support and assistance programs directed to higher education, and assists in the improvement and expansion of American educational resources for international studies and services. It also administers a program of grants to improve instruction in crucial academic subjects.

Indian Education

The Office of Indian Education administers a program of financial assistance to local and educational agencies to meet the special educational needs of Indian students, and for special programs to improve educational opportunities for adult Indians and Indian children.

Student Financial Assistance

The Bureau of Student Financial Assistance administers programs of student financial assistance including Basic Educational Opportunity Grants, Supplemental Educational Opportunity Grants, Grants to States for State Student Incentives, Direct Loans to Students in Institutions of Higher Education, Work-Study, Cooperative Education, Insured Loans to Students in Health Professions Schools, and the Guaranteed Student Loan Program.

Incentive grants are available to the States for assistance to eligible students in attendance at institutions of higher education.

Students of exceptional financial need are assisted in pursuing postsecondary education by providing grant assistance for educational expenses. Programs are provided to promote part-time employment of students, particularly those with great financial need who require assistance. Also provided is a program to establish loan funds at eligible postsecondary education institutions to permit needy undergraduate and graduate students to complete their education. There is a program to provide long-term, low-interest-bearing loans to Cuban nationals who are attending eligible institutions and are in need of the funds to pursue their courses of study.

A very significant program consists of low-interest long-term insured loans for college and vocational students under which loans made by commercial and other lenders are insured, or reinsured, by the Federal Government and insured by State and nonprofit private agencies.

NATIONAL INSTITUTE OF EDUCATION

The National Institute of Education (NIE) was provided for as part of the Education Amendments of 1972 (86 Stat. 327; 20 U.S.C. 1221e).

The National Institute of Education was created to provide leadership in the conduct and support of scientific inquiry into the educational process, to provide more dependable knowledge about educational quality, and to improve education, including career education. These purposes are carried out through:

Helping to solve the problems of, and achieve the objectives of American education including equal opportunity;

Advancing the practice of education as an art, science, and profession;

Strengthening the scientific and technological foundations of education; and

Building an effective educational research and development system.

The National Institute of Education consists of a National Council on Educational Research, the Director and his Office, staff offices, and services elements. NIE has six major program thrusts, as follows:

Dissemination and resources: Improving the dissemination and use of knowledge for solving educational problems; and studying, evaluating, and improving the capabilities of institutions to produce and use knowledge in improving education.

Basic skills: Conducting research on the teaching and learning of basic subjects and on the measurement of student progress in these areas.

Finance and productivity: Improving the effectiveness and efficiency of our educational institutions through policy studies; research and development in finance, management, organization, and alternative delivery systems; and applying competency concepts.

School capacity for problem-solving: Identifying and understanding how school systems develop the capacity for problem-solving, and finding ways of helping other schools to do so.

Education and work: Improving the preparation of youth and adults for entering and progressing in careers.

Educational equity: Conducting research and development activities to assist schools in providing more adequate education for many students who have been limited in their choice of educational programs because of their home language, culture, ethnicity, sex, or economic status.

Health Care Financing Administration

The Health Care Financing Administration (HCFA) was created by the Secretary's reorganization of March 8, 1977, as a principal operating component of the Department. HCFA places under one Administration the oversight of the Medicare and Medicaid programs and related Federal medical care quality control staffs. The following major programs will be directed by HCFA.

Medicare

The Medicare program provides basic health benefits to recipients of social security and is funded through the Social Security Trust Fund. HCFA will be concerned with the development of policies, procedures, and guidance related to the program recipients, the providers of services such as hospitals, nursing homes, and physicians, the intermediaries who adjudicate claims, and the effective coordination with related Department programs, activities, and organizations which are closely related to the Medicare program.

Medicaid

The Medicaid program through grants to States provides medical services to the needy and the medically needy. HCFA is responsible for developing approaches toward meeting the needs of those who cannot afford adequate medical care; providing technical assistance to States and local organizations to extend the scope and content and improve the quality of medical care programs for the needy; and serves as the clearinghouse for information relating to the program.

Quality Assurance

An HCFA quality assurance focal point was established to carry out the quality assurance provisions of the Medicare and Medicaid programs (Titles XVIII and XIX, 79 Stat. 291 and 343; 42 U.S.C. 1395 and 1396), and maternal and child health legislation (Title V, 81 Stat. 921; 42 U.S.C. 701–731) of the Social Security Act, as amended. This responsibility includes implementation of the Professional Standards Review Organization (PSRO) program and the End–Stage Renal Disease (ESRD) program, both of which were authorized by the 1972 amendments to the Social Security Act (49 Stat. 620). It also includes the development and monitoring of health and safety standards for providers of health care services, which were authorized under earlier Medicare and Medicaid legislation.

As a means of meeting these national objectives, the PSRO provisions of section 249F of the Social Security Amendments of 1972 (86 Stat. 1429; 42 U.S.C. 1301) require that the Secretary of Health, Education, and Welfare establish and support a nationwide network of local, physician-sponsored PSROs. Through the application of ongoing peer review, the PSROs are expected to assure that quality inpatient health care services are provided to beneficiaries and recipients of Medicare, Medicaid, and Maternal and Child Health programs at a reasonable cost.

The provisions of section 299(I) of the Social Security Amendments of 1972 (86 Stat. 1463; 42 U.S.C. 426), known as the "Kidney Amendment," extend Medicare coverage under the Social Security Act to virtually all persons with a particular condition—End–Stage Renal Disease. The law authorizes the Secretary to limit reimbursement under Medicare to facilities that meet established standards.

The development and implementation of health safety standards for providers of care in Federal health programs dates from the 1965 Medicare amendments to the Social Security Act.

Long-Term Care

The Long-Term Care program is another aspect of the quality assurance effort. This programs serves as a focal point for Long Term Care (LTC) for the aged and the chronically ill and for nursing home affairs. This involves providing policy direction and coordination of LTC activities throughout the Department, the development, determination, and enforcement of LTC requirements and standards and the monitoring and coordination of LTC activities.

Social Security Administration

[For the Social Security Administration statement of organization, see Code of Federal Regulations, Title 20, Part 422]

The Social Security Administration (SSA) was established and its predecessor, the Social Security Board, was abolished by Federal Security Agency Reorganization Plan II, effective July 16, 1946.

By Reorganization Plan I, effective April 11, 1953, the Social Security Administration was transferred from the Federal Security Agency to the Department of Health, Education, and Welfare.

The Social Security Administration, under the direction of the Commissioner of Social Security, administers a national program of contributory social insurance whereby employees, employers, and the self-employed pay contributions which are pooled in special trust funds. When earnings stop or are reduced because the worker retires, dies, or becomes disabled, monthly cash benefits are paid to replace part of the earnings the family has lost.

Part of the contributions go into a separate hospital insurance trust fund, so that when workers and their dependents become 65 years old they will have help with their hospital bills. They may also elect to receive help with doctor bills and other medical expenses by paying a percentage of supplementary medical insurance premiums, while the Federal Government pays the remainder. Together these two programs are often referred to as "Medicare." Under certain conditions, Medicare protection is also provided to people who are receiving social security or railroad retirement monthly benefits based on a disability. The responsibility for the administration of the Medicare program has been transferred to the Health Care Financing Administration. By agreement with the Department of Labor, SSA is also involved in certain aspects of the administration of the black lung benefits provisions of the Federal Coal Mine Health and Safety Act of 1969, as amended (83 Stat. 793; 30 U.S.C. 901).

Effective January 1, 1974, SSA undertook administration of the supplemental security income program for the aged, blind, and disabled (SSI program). The basic Federal SSI payment program is financed out of general revenue, rather than a special trust fund. Some States, choosing to provide payments in supplementation of SSI benefits, have agreements with SSA under which SSA administers these supplementation payments for the States. The Social Security Administration is responsible for the administration of the income maintenance portion of grants to States under title IV, the Aid to Families with Dependent Children (AFDC) portion of the Social Security Act; and for financial aid to the needy aged, blind, and disabled in Puerto Rico, the Virgin Islands, and Guam, under other provisions of the act.

Sources of Information

OFFICE OF THE SECRETARY

Inquiries on the following information may be directed to the specified office, Department of Health, Education, and Welfare, Humphrey Building, 200 Independence Avenue SW., Washington, D.C. 20201.

Reading Room

Located in Information Center, Lobby of Humphrey Building. Phone, 202-245-6296.

Employment

Inquiries and application for employment and inquiries regarding the college recruitment program should be directed to the Office of the Secretary, Personnel Office. Phone, 202-245-6146.

Contract and Small Business Activities

Call or write the Director, Division of Contract and Grant Operation, concerning programs. Phone, 202-245-1946.

Consumer Activities

Call or write the Office of Consumer Affairs for information about consumer activities. Phone, 202-755-8875.

Publications

HEW—People Serving People is distributed free of charge at the Information Center.

Persons requiring a short history of HEW may request *A Common Thread of Service* from the Center.

Prenatal Care, Infant Care, Your Child from 1 to 6, Your Child From 6 to 12, No Smoking! Pamphlets for

Parents, Teenagers, Grade School Children, Thinking About Drinking, and many others are available at various prices from the Superintendent of Documents, Government Printing Office, Washington, D.C. 20402.

Telephone Directory

The Department of Health, Education, and Welfare telephone directory is available for sale by the Superintendent of Documents, Government Printing Office, Washington, D.C. 20402.

OFFICE OF HUMAN DEVELOPMENT SERVICES

General inquiries may be directed to the Office of Human Development Services, Department of Health, Education, and Welfare, Washington, D.C. 20201.

Information Center

Public Information Office, Room 322F, Humphrey Building.

Contracts

Contact the Grants and Contract Management Division.

Employment

The Office of Human Development Services uses various civil service examinations and registers in selecting new employees. Inquiries should be directed to the Personnel Division.

Mental Retardation

Call or write the Rehabilitation Services Administration for information on HEW mental retardation programs. Phone, 202-245-6644.

Publications

Year of Achievement: The Office of Human Development 1976 and *OHD—Mission—Programs—Approach* and many others are available free or at various prices from the Superintendent of Documents, Government Printing Office, Washington, D.C. 20402.

OFFICE OF EDUCATION

General inquiries may be directed to the Office of Education, Department of Health, Education, and Welfare, Washington, D.C. 20202.

Information Center

Office of Education Information Center, Room 1127.

Contracts

Contact the Grant and Procurement Management Division. Phone, 202-245-8160.

Employment

The Office of Education uses various civil service examinations and registers in selecting new employees. Inquiries should be directed to the Personnel and Training Division. Information on college recruitment programs is also available from the Personnel and Training Division, Room 1102. Phone, 202-245-8404.

Publications

The periodical, *American Education,* is available from the Superintendent of Documents, Government Printing Office, Washington, D.C. 20402.

NATIONAL INSTITUTE OF EDUCATION

Inquiries on the following subjects may be directed to the specified office, National Institute of Education, Department of Health, Education, and Welfare, Washington, D.C. 20208.

Contracts and Grants

Contact the Contracts and Grants Management Division, Room 720, 1832 M Street NW., Washington, D.C. 20208. Phone, 202-254-5620.

Employment

The National Institute of Education uses various civil service examinations and registers, as well as special appointment authorities in selecting new employees. Inquiries should be directed to the Personnel Division, Room 642, 1200 19th Street NW., Washington, D.C. 20208. Phone, 202-254-5450.

Other

All other inquiries should be directed to the Office of Public Information, Room 720, 1200 19th Street NW., Washington, D.C. 20208. Phone, 202-254-5800.

HEALTH SERVICES ADMINISTRATION

Inquiries on the following should be directed to the specified office, Health Services Administration, 6500 Fishers Lane, Rockville, Md. 20857.

Employment

The majority of HSA positions are in the Federal civil service. For positions in the Washington, D.C. metropolitan area, employment inquiries may be addressed to Office of Personnel, Room 4B-07.

Hiring in other areas is decentralized to the 17 field appointing authorities under HSA and to the Regional Health Director in each of the 10 HEW regional offices. The U.S. Government listings in the appropriate commercial telephone directories will provide specific addresses.

Publications

Single copies of most Health Services Administration publications are available, free of charge, from individual bureaus as listed above, or from the Executive Secretariat, Room 14A12, Parklawn Building. For a complete listing, request the catalog, *Publications of the Health Services Administration* from the Office of Communications and Public Affairs, Room 14A-55.

Bulk quantities of publications may be purchased from the Superintendent of Documents, Government Printing Office, Washington, D.C. 20402. Certain technical publications may be purchased from the National Technical Information Service, Department of Commerce, Springfield, Va. 22151.

HEALTH CARE FINANCING ADMINISTRATION

Inquiries on the following information may be directed to the Health Care Financing Administration, Department of Health, Education, and Welfare, 330 C Street SW., Washington, D.C. 20201.

Contracts and Small Business Activities

Contact the Chief, Contract Branch, Division of General Services.

Publications

For information on publications write to the Publications Distribution Section, Division of General Services.

Employment

Inquiries should be addressed to the Division of Personnel. For information on employment in an HCFA regional office, contact the Regional Personnel Officer in the Office of the Regional Director for that region.

SOCIAL SECURITY ADMINISTRATION

Inquiries on the following information may be directed to the specified office, Social Security Administration, 6401 Security Boulevard, Baltimore, Md. 21235.

Reading Rooms

Requests for information, for copies of records, or to inspect or copy records may be made at any of SSA's local offices or Room G-41.

Contracts and Small Business Activities

Contact the Office of Management and Administration, Room 800.

Publications

The Social Security Administration collects a substantial volume of economic, demographic, and other data in furtherance of its program mission. Basic data on employment and earnings, beneficiaries and benefit payments, utilization of health services and other items of program interest are published regularly in the *Social Security Bulletin,* its *Annual Statistical Supplement,* and in special releases and reports which appear periodically on selected topics of interest to the general public. Additional information may be obtained from the Publications Staff of SSA's Office of Research and Statistics, Room 1120, 1875 Connecticut Avenue NW., Washington, D.C. 20009.

The Office of Information has published numerous pamphlets relative to programs administered by SSA. Single copies may be obtained at any of SSA's over 1,300 local offices.

Employment

A variety of civil service registers and examinations are used in hiring new employees. Also, SSA has an extensive

college recruitment program. Specific employment information may be obtained from the Office of Human Resources.

Speakers and Films

It is SSA's policy to make speakers, films, and exhibits available to public or private organizations, community groups, schools, etc., throughout the Nation. Requests for this service should be directed to the nearest Social Security office or to the Office of External Affairs.

For further information concerning the Department of Health, Education, and Welfare, contact the Information Center, 200 Independence Avenue SW., Washington, D.C. 20201. Phone, 202-245-6295.

NATIONAL LABOR RELATIONS BOARD

1717 Pennsylvania Avenue NW., Washington, D.C. 20570
Phone, 202-655-4000

Chairman	John H. Fanning.
Member	Howard Jenkins, Jr.
Member	John A. Penello.
Member	Betty Southard Murphy.
Member	John C. Truesdale.
Executive Secretary	F. Robert Volger, Acting.
Solicitor	William A. Lubbers.
Chief Administrative Law Judge	Thomas N. Kessel.
Director of Information	Thomas W. Miller, Jr.

Office of the General Counsel

General Counsel	John S. Irving.
Deputy General Counsel	John E. Higgins, Jr.
Associate General Counsel, Division of Enforcement Litigation	Carl L. Taylor.
Associate General Counsel, Division of Operations Management	Joseph E. DeSio.
Associate General Counsel, Division of Advice	Harold J. Datz.
Director, Division of Administration	Ernest Russell.

[For the National Labor Relations Board statement of organization, see the Federal Register, Volume 32, page 9588, as amended at 37 FR 15956]

The National Labor Relations Board (NLRD) administers the Nation's

The National Labor Relations Board is an independent agency created by the National Labor Relations Act of 1935 (Wagner Act), as amended by the acts of 1947 (Taft-Hartley Act), 1959 (Landrum-Griffin Act), and 1974.

The act affirms the right of employees to self-organization and to bargain collectively through representatives of their own choosing or to refrain from such activities. The act prohibits certain unfair labor practices by employers and labor organizations or their agents and

laws relating to labor relations. The NLRB is vested with the power to safeguard employees' rights to organize, to determine through elections whether workers want unions as their bargaining representatives, and to prevent and remedy unfair labor practices.

authorizes the Board to designate appropriate units for collective bargaining and to conduct secret ballot elections to determine whether employees desire representation by a labor organization.

As of July 1, 1971, the Postal Reorganization Act (84 Stat. 719; 39 U.S.C. Prec. 101 note) conferred jurisdiction upon the Board over unfair labor practice charges and representation elections affecting U.S. Postal Service employees. As of August 25, 1974, jurisdiction over all privately operated health care institutions was conferred on the NLRB by an amendment to the act (29 U.S.C. 152 et seq.).

Functions and Activities

The Board has two principal functions under the act: preventing and remedying unfair labor practices by employers and labor organizations or their agents, and conducting secret ballot elections among employees in appropriate collective-bargaining units to determine whether or not they desire to be represented by a labor organization. The Board also conducts secret ballot elections among employees who have been covered by a union-shop agreement to determine whether or not they wish to revoke their union's authority to make such agreements; in jurisdictional disputes, decides and determines which competing group of workers is entitled to perform the work involved; and conducts secret ballot elections among employees concerning employers' final settlement offers in national emergency labor disputes.

The General Counsel in unfair labor practice cases has final authority to investigate charges, issue complaints, and prosecute such complaints before the Board. The General Counsel, on behalf of the Board, prosecutes injunction proceedings; handles courts of appeals proceedings to enforce or review Board orders; participates in miscellaneous court litigation; and obtains compliance with Board orders and court judgments. The General Counsel is responsible for the processing by field personnel of the several types of employee elections referred to above.

Under general supervision of the General Counsel, 32 regional directors and their staffs process representation, unfair labor practice, and jurisdictional dispute cases. (Some regions have subregional or resident offices.) They issue complaints in unfair labor practice cases; seek settlement of unfair labor practice charges; obtain compliance with Board orders and court judgments; and petition district courts for injunctions to prevent or remedy unfair labor practices. The regional directors also direct hearings in representation cases; conduct elections pursuant to agreement or the decision-making authority delegated to them by the Board, or pursuant to Board directions; and issue certifications of representatives when unions win or certify the results when unions lose employee elections. They process petitions for bargaining unit clarification, for amendment of certification, and for rescission of a labor organization's authority to make a union-shop agreement. They also conduct national emergency employee referendums.

The Board can act only when it is formally requested to do so. Individuals, employers, or unions may initiate cases by filing charges of unfair labor practices or petitions for employee representation elections with the Board field offices serving the area where the case arises.

In the event a regional director declines to proceed on a representation petition, the party filing the petition may appeal to the Board. Where a regional director declines to proceed on an unfair labor practice charge, the filing party may appeal to the General Counsel. For details concerning filing such appeals with those Washington, D.C., offices, parties may communicate with the field office most convenient to them. Field office addresses and telephone numbers are listed on page 597.

Administrative law judges conduct hearings in unfair labor practice cases, make findings, and recommend remedies for violations found. Their decisions are reviewable by the Board if exceptions to the decision are filed.

SOURCES OF INFORMATION

Speakers

To give the public and persons appearing before the Agency a better understanding of the act and its policies, the Board's procedures, and the services it provides, Washington and regional office personnel participate as speakers or panel members before bar associations, labor organizations, management groups, and educational, civic, and other groups. Requests for speakers or panelists may be made to Washington officials or to the appropriate regional director.

Publications

Anyone desiring to inspect formal case documents or read Agency publications may use facilities of the Washington or field offices. The Agency will assist in arranging reproduction of documents and ordering transcripts of hearings. The Board's offices offer free explanatory leaflets—*To Protect the Rights of the Public, Your Government Conducts an Election for You on the Job*, and *Jurisdiction Over Health Care Institutions*. The Superintendent of Documents, Government Printing Office, Washington, D.C. 20402, sells *A Guide to Basic Law and Procedures under the N.L.R.A.*, and *The N.L.R.B., What it is, What it does*, both of which are available in Spanish, and the *NLRB Casehandling Manual* (in three parts), a subscription service.

Contracts

Prospective suppliers of goods and services may inquire about Agency procurement and contracting practices by writing the Chief, Facilities and Services Branch, National Labor Relations Board, Washington, D.C. 20570.

Employment

The Board appoints administrative law judges from a register established by the Civil Service Commission. The Agency hires attorneys, stenographers, and typists for all its offices; field examiners for its field offices; and administrative personnel for its Washington office. In-

FIELD OFFICES—NATIONAL LABOR RELATIONS BOARD
(R.D.—Regional Director; O.C.—Officer-in-Charge; R.O.—Resident Officer)

Office	Director/Officer	Address	Telephone
Albany, N.Y. 12207	Thomas J. Sheridan, R.O.	New Federal Bldg.	518-472-2215
Albuquerque, N. Mex. 87110	Peter N. Maydanis, R.O.	5000 Marble Ave. NE	505-766-2508
Anchorage, Alaska 99501	Paul H. Eggert, R.O.	632 W. 6th Ave.	907-265-5271
Atlanta, Ga. 30303	Curtis L. Mack, R.D.	101 Marietta St. NW	404-221-2896
Baltimore, Md. 21201	William C. Humphrey, R.D.	Federal Bldg.	301-962-2822
Birmingham, Ala. 35203	C. Douglass Marshall, R.O.	City Federal Bldg.	205-254-1492
Boston, Mass. 02110	Robert S. Fuchs, R.D.	99 High St.	617-223-3300
Brooklyn, N.Y. 11241	Samuel M. Kaynard, R.D.	16 Court St.	212-596-3535
Buffalo, N.Y. 14202	Thomas W. Seeler, R.D.	Federal Bldg.	716-846-4931
Chicago, Ill. 60604	Alex V. Barbour, R.D.	219 S. Dearborn St.	312-353-7570
Cincinnati, Ohio 45282	Emil C. Farkas, R.D.	Federal Office Bldg.	513-684-3686
Cleveland, Ohio 44199	Bernard Levine, R.D.	Federal Bldg.	216-522-3715
Coral Gables, Fla. 33146	James L. Jeffers, R.O.	1570 Madruga Ave.	305-350-5391
Denver, Colo. 80202	Francis Sperandeo, R.D.	U.S. Custom House	303-837-3555
Detroit, Mich. 48226	Bernard Gottfried, R.D.	Federal Bldg.	313-226-3200
El Paso, Tex. 79902	Laureano A. Medrano, R.O.	4100 Rio Bravo St.	915-543-7737
Fort Worth, Tex. 76102	W. Edwin Youngblood, R.D.	Federal Office Bldg.	817-334-2921
Hato Rey, P.R. 00918	(Vacancy)	U.S. Courthouse	809-753-4347
Honolulu, Hawaii 96850	Dennis R. MacCarthy, O.C.	300 Ala Moana Blvd.	808-546-5100
Houston, Tex. 77002	Louis C. Baldovin, Jr., R.D.	500 Dallas Ave.	713-226-4296
Indianapolis, Ind. 46204	William T. Little, R.D.	Federal Office Bldg.	317-269-7430
Jacksonville, Fla. 32202	John C. Wooten, R.O.	Federal Bldg.	904-791-3768
Kansas City, Kans. 66101	Thomas C. Hendrix, R.D.	4th at State	816-374-4518
Little Rock, Ark. 72201	Robert K. Gentry, R.O.	1 Union National Plaza	501-378-6311
Las Vegas, Nev. 89101	Michael McReynolds, R.O.	300 Las Vegas Blvd. S.	702-385-6416
Los Angeles, Calif. 90024 Region 31	Abraham Siegel, R.D.	Federal Bldg.	213-824-7351
Los Angeles, Calif. 90014 Region 21	Wilford W. Johansen, R.D.	606 S. Olive St.	213-688-5200
Memphis, Tenn. 38104	Raymond A. Jacobson	1407 Union Ave.	901-222-2725
Milwaukee, Wis. 53203	George F. Squillacote, R.D.	744 N. 4th St.	414-224-3861
Minneapolis Minn. 55401	Robert J. Wilson, R.D.	Federal Bldg.	612-725-2611
Nashville, Tenn. 37203	William A. Molony, R.O.	Federal Bldg.	615-749-5921
Newark, N.J. 07102	Arthur Eisenberg, R.D.	Federal Bldg.	201-645-2100
New Orleans, La. 70113	Charles M. Paschal, Jr., R.D.	1001 Howard Ave.	504-589-6361
New York, N.Y. 10007	Winifred D. Morio, R.D.	Federal Bldg.	212-264-0300
Oakland, Calif. 94621	Michael Taylor, R.D.	7901 Oakport St.	415-632-9000
Peoria, Ill. 61602	Glen A. Zipp, O.C.	Savings Center Tower	309-671-7080
Philadelphia, Pa. 19106	Peter W. Hirsch, R.D.	Federal Bldg.	215-597-7601
Phoenix, Ariz. 85014	Milo V. Price, R.D.	6107 N. 7th St.	602-261-3717
Pittsburgh, Pa. 15219	Henry Shore, R.D.	601 Grant St.	412-644-2977
Portland, Oreg. 97205	Elwood G. Strumpf, O.C.	610 SW. Broadway	503-221-3085
St. Louis, Mo. 63101	Joseph H. Solien, R.D.	210 N. 12th Blvd.	314-425-4167
San Antonio, Tex. 78205	John C. Crawford, R.O.	Federal Office Bldg.	512-229-6140
San Diego, Calif. 92101	Claude Marston R.O.	940 Front St.	714-293-6184
San Francisco, Calif. 94102	Natalie P. Allen, R.D.	Federal Bldg.	415-556-3197
Seattle, Wash. 98174	Charles M. Henderson, R.D.	Federal Bldg.	206-442-4532
Tampa, Fla. 33602	Harold A. Boire, R.D.	Federal Office Bldg.	813-791-3768
Tulsa, Okla. 74135	William N. Cates, R.O.	6128 E. 38th St.	918-664-1420
Washington, D.C. 20037	Nicholas E. Karatinos, R.O.	2120 L St. NW	202-254-7612
Winston-Salem, N.C. 27101	Reed Johnston, R.D.	Federal Bldg.	919-761-3201

quiries about college and law school recruiting programs should be directed to the nearest regional office. Employment inquiries and applications may be sent to any regional office or the Washington personnel office.

For further information, contact the Division of Information, National Labor Relations Board, 1717 Pennsylvania Avenue NW., Washington, D.C. 20570. Phone, 202-254-9033.

NATIONAL MEDIATION BOARD

1425 K Street NW., Washington, D.C. 20572
Phone, 202-523-5920

Chairman	George S. Ives.
Member	David H. Stowe.
Member	Robert O. Harris.
Executive Secretary	Rowland K. Quinn, Jr.
General Counsel	William E. Fredenberger, Jr.
Staff Mediation Director	E. B. Meredith.

National Railroad Adjustment Board

220 South State Street, Chicago, Ill. 60604
Phone, 312-427-8383

Staff Director/Grievances	Roy J. Carvatta.

The National Mediation Board provides the railroad and airline industries with specific mechanisms for the adjustment of labor-management disputes; that is, the facilitation of agreements through collective bargaining, investigation of questions of representation, and the arbitration and establishment of procedures for emergency disputes.

The National Mediation Board was created on June 21, 1934, by an act of Congress amending the Railway Labor Act (48 Stat. 1185, 45 U.S.C. 151–58, 160–62). The act was further amended in April 1936 (49 Stat. 1189–91, 45 U.S.C. 1181–88); January 1951 (64 Stat. 1238: 45 U.S.C. 152); June 1966 (80 Stat. 208–9; 45 U.S.C. 153); and in April 1970 (84 Stat. 199–200; 45 U.S.C. 153).

The Board's major responsibilities are: (1) the mediation of disputes over wages, hours, and working conditions which arise between rail and air carriers and organizations representing their employees, and (2) the investigation of representation disputes and certification of employee organizations as representatives of crafts or classes of carrier employees.

Disputes growing out of grievances or out of interpretation or application of agreements concerning rates of pay, rules, or working conditions in the railroad industry are referable to the National Railroad Adjustment Board. This Board is divided into four divisions and consists of an equal number of representatives of the carriers and of national organizations of employees. In deadlocked cases the National Mediation Board is authorized to appoint a referee to sit with the members of the division for the purpose of making an award.

In the airline industry no national airline adjustment board has been established for settlement of grievances. Over the years the employee organizations and air carriers with established bargaining relationships have agreed to grievance procedures with final jurisdiction resting with a system board of adjustment. The National Mediation Board is frequently called upon to name a neutral referee to serve on a system board when the parties are deadlocked and cannot agree on such an appointment themselves.

The Board is assisted in its activities by the National Railroad Adjustment Board and other special boards of adjustment, which handle individual and group grievances arising under labor-management agreements.

Mediation Disputes

The Board is charged with mediating disputes between carriers and labor organizations relating to initial contract negotiations or subsequent changes in rates of pay, rules, and working conditions. When the parties fail to reach accord in direct bargaining either party may request the Board's services or the Board may on its own motion invoke its services. Thereafter, negotiations continue until the Board determines that its efforts to mediate have been unsuccessful, at which time it seeks to induce the parties to submit the dispute to arbitration. If either party refuses to arbitrate, the Board issues a notice stating that the parties have failed to resolve their dispute through mediation. This notice commences a 30-day cooling off period after which resort to self-help is normally available to either or both parties.

Employee Representation

If a dispute arises among a carrier's employees as to who is to be representative of such employees, it is the Board's duty to investigate such dispute and to determine by secret ballot election or other appropriate means whether or not and to whom a representation certification should be issued. In the course of making this determination, the Board must determine the craft or class in which the employees seeking representation properly belong.

Additional Duties

Additional duties of the Board are the interpretation of agreements made under its mediatory auspices; the appointment of neutral referees when requested by the National Railroad Adjustment Board; the appointment of neutrals to sit on System Boards and Special Boards of

Adjustments; and finally, the duty of notifying the President when the parties have failed to reach agreement through the Board's mediation efforts and the labor dispute, in the judgment of the Board threatens substantially to interrupt interstate commerce to a degree such as to deprive any section of the country of essential transportation service. In these cases, the President may, at his discretion, appoint an Emergency Board to investigate and report to him on the dispute. During the pendency of the Emergency Board investigation, resort to self-help is barred.

SOURCES OF INFORMATION

A booklet outlining the history and operations of the Board and the act (*Administration of the Railway Labor Act by the National Mediation Board 1934–70*) is available on request. Also available for public distribution are the following documents: *Determination of Craft Class* (5 volumes); *Interpretations Pursuant to Section 5, Second of the Act* (2 volumes); *Annual Reports of the National Mediation Board including the Report of the National Railroad Adjustment Board; The Railway Labor Act at Fifty*.

At the Board's headquarters in Washington, D.C., copies of collective-bargaining agreements between labor and management of various rail and air carriers, as well as copies of the awards and interpretations issued by the several divisions of the National Railroad Adjustment Board, are available for public inspection during office hours.

For further information, contact the Executive Secretary, National Mediation Board, 1425 L Street NW., Washington D.C. 20572. Phone, 202-523-5920.

OCCUPATIONAL SAFETY AND HEALTH REVIEW COMMISSION

1825 K Street NW., Washington, D.C. 20006
Phone, 202-634-7943

Chairman	Timothy F. Cleary.
Chief Legal Counsel	Thomas B. Flynn.
Commissioner	Frank R. Barnako.
Chief Legal Counsel	Joan M. Hollenbach.
Commissioner	Bertram R. Cottine.
Chief Legal Counsel	(Vacancy).

Administrative Law Judges

David H. Harris, *Chief Judge.*	Cecil L. Cutler, Jr.	James P. O'Connell.
F. Daley Abels.	Richard DeBennedetto.	David G. Oringer.
Edward V. Alfieri.	Jerome C. Ditore.	Henry K. Osterman.
Dee C. Blyth.	Paul E. Dixon.	George W. Otto.
Paul L. Brady.	Seymour Fier.	John S. Patton.
William E. Brennan.	Foster Furcolo.	Vernon G. Riehl.
Judd P. Brenton.	Abraham M. Gold.	Louis J. Rubin.
Harold O. Bullis.	Sidney J. Goldstein.	Erwin L. Stuller.
James D. Burroughs.	David J. Knight.	George O. Taylor, Jr.
John A. Carlson.	John J. Larkin.	Paul A. Tenney.
Joseph L. Chalk.	Louis G. LaVecchia.	Benjamin G. Usher.
Charles K. Chaplin.	Henry F. Martin, Jr.	Robert P. Weil.
Joseph Chodes.	Henry F. McQuade.	Alan M. Wienman.
James A. Cronin.	Jerry W. Mitchell.	Ben D. Worcester.
	John J. Morris.	Frank B. Zinn.

Executive Staff

Chairman	Timothy F. Cleary.
Executive Director	Ruth O. Robinson.
Chief Judge	David H. Harris.
Counsel for Appellate and Administrative Legal Services	(Vacancy).
Executive Secretary	Ray H. Darling, Jr.
Chief Review Counsel	Richard F. Schiffmann.
Director of Information and Publications	Linda P. Dodd.

The Occupational Safety and Health Review Commission (OSHRC) is concerned with providing safe and healthful working conditions. It adjudicates cases forwarded to it by the Department of Labor when disagreements arise over the results of safety and health inspection performed by the Department.

The Occupational Safety and Health Review Commission is an independent adjudicatory agency established by the Occupational Safety and Health Act of 1970 (84 Stat. 1590; 29 U.S.C. 651).

The act, enforced by the Secretary of Labor, is an effort to reduce the incidence of personal injuries, illnesses, and deaths among working men and women in the United States which result from their employment. The Review Commission was created to adjudicate enforcement actions initiated under the act when they are contested by employers, employees, or representatives of employees.

The principal office of the Review Commission is in Washington, D.C. There are also 9 offices where Review Commission judges are stationed:

REVIEW COMMISSION JUDGES—OCCUPATIONAL SAFETY AND HEALTH REVIEW COMMISSION

Address	Phone
Atlanta, Ga. 30309	
1365 Peachtree St. NE	404-881-4086.
Boston, Mass. 02110	
100 Summer St	617-223-3757.
Chicago, Ill. 60603	
55 E. Monroe St	312-353-2564.
Dallas, Tex. 75201	
Fidelity Union Life Bldg	214-749-7171.
Denver, Colo. 80265	
1050 17th St	303-837-2281.
Hyattsville, Md. 20782	
6525 Belcrest Rd	301-436-8870.
New York, N.Y. 10036	
1515 Broadway	212-399-5985.
Burlingame, Calif. 94010	
1818 Gilbreth Rd	415-876-9292.
St. Louis, Mo. 63101	
1114 Market St	314-425-5071.

Functions

The Commission's functions are strictly adjudicatory; it is, however, more of a court system than a simple tribunal, for within the Review Commission there are two levels of adjudication. All cases which require a hearing are assigned to a Review Commission judge who will decide the case. Each such decision is subject to discretionary review by the three members of the Review Commission upon themotion of any one of the three. However, approximately 90 percent of the decisions of the judges become final orders without any change whatsoever.

The Occupational Safety and Health Act covers virtually every employer in the country. It requires each employer to furnish to each of his employees employment and a place of employment which are free from recognized hazards that are causing or are likely to cause death or serious physical harm to his employees; and comply with occupational safety and health standards promulgated under the act.

The Secretary of Labor has promulgated a substantial number of occupational safety and health standards which, pursuant to the act, have the force and effect of law. He has also initiated a regular program of inspections in order to check upon compliance. A case for adjudication by the Commission arises when a citation is issued against an employer as the result of such an inspection and it is contested within 15 working days thereafter.

When a case is docketed, it is assigned for hearing to a Review Commission judge. The hearing will ordinarily be held in the community where the alleged violation occurred or close thereto. At the hearing, the Secretary of Labor will have the burden of proving his case.

After the hearing, the judge must issue a decision, based on findings of fact, affirming, modifying, or vacating the Secretary's citation or proposed penalty, or directing other appropriate relief. His decision will become a final order of the Commission 30 days thereafter unless, within such period, any Commission member directs that such decision shall be reviewed by the Commission itself. When that occurs, the members of the Commission will thereafter issue their own decision on the case.

Once a case is decided, any person adversely affected or aggrieved thereby, may obtain a review of such decision in the United States Court of Appeals.

SOURCES OF INFORMATION

To give the public and persons appearing before the Commission a better understanding of the act, and the Commission's procedures and decisions, members and officials participate as speakers or panel members before bar associations, safety councils, labor organizations, management associations, and educational, civic, and other groups. Requests for speakers or panelists may be made to the Commission's Washington office.

For further information, contact the Director of Information and Publications, Occupational Safety and Health Review Commission (OSHRC), 1825 K Street NW., Washington, D.C. 20006. Phone, 202-634-7943.

PENSION BENEFIT GUARANTY CORPORATION

2020 K Street NW., Washington, D.C. 20006
Phone, 202-254-4817

The Pension Benefit Guaranty Corporation (PBGC) guarantees basic pension benefits in covered private plans if they terminate with insufficient assets.

Title IV of the Employee Retirement Income Security Act of 1974 (ERISA), approved September 2, 1974 (88 Stat. 1003 et seq.; 29 U.S.C. 1301 et seq.), established the Pension Benefit Guaranty Corporation to guarantee payment of insured benefits if covered plans terminate without sufficient assets to pay such benefits.

The PBGC, a self-financing, wholly-owned Government corporation subject to the provisions of the Government Corporation Control Act (59 Stat. 597; 31 U.S.C. 846), is governed by a Board of Directors consisting of the Secretaries of Labor, Commerce, and the Treasury. The Secretary of Labor is Chairman of the Board and is responsible for administering the PBGC in accordance with policies established by the Board. A seven-member Advisory Committee, composed of two labor, two business, and three public members appointed by the President, advises the PBGC on various matters.

ACTIVITIES

COVERAGE

Title IV of ERISA provides for mandatory coverage of most private defined benefit plans. These are plans which provide a benefit, the amount of which can be determined from a formula in the plan, for example, based on factors such as age, years of service, average or highest salary, etc. At present, approximately 33 million participants in about 90,000 plans are covered.

INSURANCE PROGRAMS

Title IV of the act requires PBGC to establish two distinct but interrelated pension plan insurance programs and permits the PBGC to establish the terms and conditions of a third insurance program, as it determines to be appropriate. All of the PBGC insurance programs are restricted to the coverage of private pension plans. The insurance programs are:

Basic Benefits Insurance Program

Effective upon enactment and subject to the payment limitations described below, PBGC is required to guarantee the payment of all nonforfeitable basic benefits under the terms of a covered plan if the plan should terminate without sufficient assets to pay such benefits. Under this insurance program, PBGC guarantees the payment of the plan's basic benefits up to a maximum amount equal to the lesser of 100 percent of the average monthly earnings during the participant's highest paid consecutive 5-year period or the actuarial value of a life annuity of $750 per month beginning at age 65 for plans which terminated in 1974. The $750 per month limitation is adjusted whenever the Social Security Act contribution and benefit base is modified; and for plans terminating in 1978, the maximum figure is $1,005.68. A plan or plan amendment must be in force for five or more years prior to the plan's termination for its respective basic benefits to be fully insured. Lesser coverage is, however, provided on a time-phased basis for basic benefits which have been in force less than five years prior to a plan's termination.

PBGC is not required to guarantee benefits for covered multiemployer pension plans which terminate prior to July 1, 1979, but PBGC has discretionary authority to do so when it determines that such payment

PENSION BENEFIT GUARANTY CORPORATION

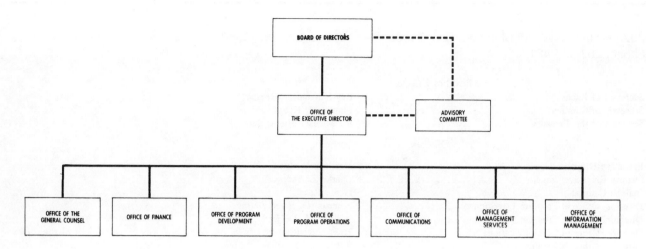

will not jeopardize its payment of like benefits after June 30, 1979, and certain other conditions are met.

Contingent Employer Liability Insurance Program

PBGC is also required to establish a contingent liability insurance program to insure any employer who maintains or contributes to a covered pension plan against his liability under ERISA (up to 30 percent of his net worth) in the event his plan terminates and assets are insufficient to pay the plan's guaranteed basic benefits.

If, in its determination, PBGC is able to develop satisfactory arrangements with private insurers within 36 months of ERISA's enactment to carry out the contingent liability insurance program in whole or in part, PBGC is authorized to require employers to elect coverage by such private insurers or by PBGC at such times and in such manner as PBGC determines necessary.

Non-Basic Benefits Insurance Program

As it determines to be appropriate, PBGC is authorized to establish insurance programs to guarantee the payment of other than basic plan benefits, as well as to establish when such other benefits are guaranteed.

The contingent employer liability insurance and non-basic benefits insurance programs are not yet in force.

PLAN TERMINATIONS

The plan administrator is required to notify PBGC at least 10 days prior to the proposed date of termination. The plan's assets and guaranteed benefit liabilities are then valued and a determination is made by PBGC regarding the sufficiency of assets to pay guaranteed benefits. In all plan terminations covered by title IV, plan assets must be allocated to participants as stipulated in the act.

PBGC also may institute termination proceedings when certain events specified in the act indicate that such action may be necessary.

PBGC is authorized to prescribe simplified procedures for small plans, and it may pool the assets of such plans. In addition, PBGC may purchase the assets of any plan it is terminating.

Whenever there is a change in conditions relating to a plan being terminated which makes termination no longer advisable, PBGC may take appropriate action to restore the plan.

In instances when PBGC determines that the withdrawal of any employer or employers from a plan under which more than one employer makes contributions will result in a significant reduction in contributions to a plan, it may terminate that portion of it attributable to the withdrawal and treat the remainder as a separate plan.

PREMIUM COLLECTION

All covered pension plans are required to pay prescribed premium rates to PBGC.

The annual premium rate has been set at $0.50 per plan participant for multiemployer pension plans and, effective for plan years starting on or after January 1, 1978, at $2.60 per plan participant for the single employer pension plans.

INDIVIDUAL RETIREMENT PROGRAMS

Pursuant to ERISA, PBGC provides advice and assistance to individuals on the economic desirability of establishing tax-qualified Individual Retirement Accounts (IRA's) or certain other individual retirement programs, and on transferring amounts to such IRA's or other programs from qualified pension plans when an employee receives a lump sum distribution.

For further information, contact the Office of Communications, Pension Benefit Guaranty Corporation, 2020 K Street NW., Washington, D.C. 20006. Phone, 202-254-4817.

RELATED TO LABOR

RAILROAD RETIREMENT BOARD

844 Rush Street, Chicago, Ill. 60611
Phone, 312-751-4500

Washington Liaison Office: Room 444, 425 Thirteenth Street NW., 20004
Phone, 202-724-0121

Member (Chairman)	William P. Adams.
Member (Labor)	C. J. Chamberlain.
Member (Management)	Earl Oliver.
Secretary of the Board	Richard F. Butler.
Chief Executive Officer	Kenneth J. Nolan.
General Counsel	Dale G. Zimmerman.
Director, Bureau of Research	Abraham Benjamin.
Chief Actuary	Robert E. Larson.
Director, Bureau of Management Control	W. V. Radesk.
Director, Bureau of Unemployment and Sickness Insurance	Eugene E. Koch.
Director, Bureau of Retirement Claims	Hubert P. Gibbons.
Director, Bureau of Data Processing and Accounts	Ralph A. Vicari.
Director, Bureau of Hearings and Appeals	George J. Baynes.
Director, Bureau of Budget and Fiscal Operations	John S. Suker.
Director, Bureau of Personnel	James J. Costello.
Director, Bureau of Supply and Service	David J. Langdon.
Washington Liaison Officer	Robert A. Russell.

The Railroad Retirement Board administers retirement-survivor and unemployment-sickness benefit programs provided by Federal laws for the Nation's railroad workers and their families. Under the Railroad Retirement Act, annuities are paid by the Board to rail employees with at least 10 years of service who retire because of age or disability and to their eligible wives. When other requirements are met, annuities are also provided to the surviving widows and children or parents of deceased employees. These retirement-survivor benefit programs are closely coordinated with social security benefit programs and include Medicare health insurance coverage. Under the Railroad Unemployment Insurance Act, biweekly benefits are payable by the Board to workers with qualifying railroad earnings who become unemployed or sick. About 100 field offices are maintained across the country.

The Railroad Retirement Board administers the Railroad Retirement and Railroad Unemployment Insurance Acts and participates in the administration of the Social Security Act and the Health Insurance for the Aged Act insofar as it affects railroad retirement beneficiaries.

The Board was established by the Railroad Retirement Act of 1935, approved August 29, 1935 (49 Stat. 967, as amended; 45 U.S.C. 215–228). It now derives statutory authority from the Railroad Retirement Act of 1974, approved October 16, 1974 (88 Stat. 1305, as amended; 45 U.S.C. 231–231t). The Board also derives authority from the Railroad Unemployment Insurance Act, approved June 25, 1938 (52 Stat. 1094, as amended; 45 U.S.C. 351–367).

The Board is composed of three members appointed by the President by and with the advice of the Senate— one upon recommendations of representatives of employees, one upon recommendations of carriers, and one, the Chairman, as a public member.

Field Organization

The Board maintains field offices located in centers of railroad population which are grouped into five regions, each under a regional director reporting directly to the Chief Executive Officer. Claimants for unemployment benefits register with designated employees of covered employers, and claimants for sickness benefits file their claims by mail with the Bureau of Unemployment and Sickness Insurance. Claims for benefits under the Railroad Retirement Act are received in all field offices as well as at headquarters.

Activities

The Railroad Retirement Act provides for the payment of annuities to individuals who have completed at least 10 years creditable service and have ceased compensated service upon their attainment of specified ages or at any age if permanently disabled for all employment. In some

RAILROAD RETIREMENT BOARD

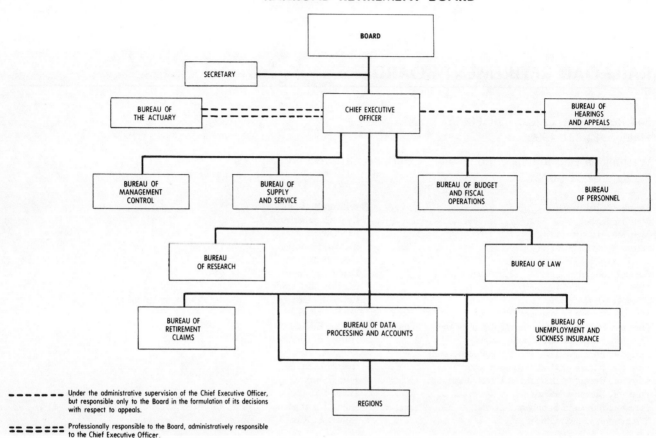

```
- - - - - -   Under the administrative supervision of the Chief Executive Officer,
              but responsible only to the Board in the formulation of its decisions
              with respect to appeals.

== == == ==   Professionally responsible to the Board, administratively responsible
              to the Chief Executive Officer.
```

circumstances occupational disability annuities or supplemental annuities are provided for longer term, or career, employees.

A spouse's annuity is provided, under certain conditions, for the wife or dependent husband of an employee annuitant.

Survivor annuities are awarded to the qualified widows, children and dependent widowers or parents, of deceased career employees. Two distinct lump sum benefits are provided in certain circumstances; for one of these there are no service requirements and the beneficiary may be designated by the employee.

The Railroad Retirement Act provides for extensive coordination with the Social Security Act in the computation, payment, and financing of railroad retirement annuities. Annuitants and members of their families also awarded social security benefits after 1974 receive the payment of such benefits through the Board. However, the responsibility for the adjudication of such benefits remains with the Social Security Administration.

Under the Health Insurance for the Aged Act, qualified railroad retirement beneficiaries are entitled to have payments made on their behalf for covered hospital, posthospital, and medical services.

Benefits are provided under the Railroad Unemployment Insurance Act to individuals who are unemployed in a benefit year, but who are ready and willing to work, and to individuals who are unable to work because of sickness or injury, based on qualifying railroad earnings in a preceding one-year period.

The Board maintains, through its field offices, a free employment service for railroad employees.

REGIONAL OFFICES—RAILROAD RETIREMENT BOARD

Region	Director	Address
Atlanta, Ga. 30308	Z. Jack Gyure	730 Peachtree St. NE.
Cleveland, Ohio 44199	Gene O. Wilson	1240 E. 9th St.
Kansas City, Mo. 64106	Walter W. Birch	601 E. 12th St.
New York, N.Y. 10007	Edmund J. Setaro	26 Federal Plaza.
San Francisco, Calif. 94102	Robert L. Livingston	450 Golden Gate Ave.

For further information, contact the Chief Executive Officer, Railroad Retirement Board, 844 Rush Street, Chicago, Ill. 60611. Phone, 312-751-4930.

Appendix: Standard Federal Regions

Standard Federal Administrative regions were established to achieve more uniformity in the location and geographic jurisdiction of Federal field offices as a basis for promoting more systematic coordination among agencies and between Federal-State-local governments and for securing management improvements and economies through greater interagency and intergovernmental cooperation. OMB circular A–105, *Standard Federal Regions*, provides further guidance on the policies and requirements governing standard administrative regions. Boundaries were drawn and regional office locations designated for 10 regions, and agencies are required to adopt the uniform system when changes are made or new offices established. A map showing the standard boundaries is printed below.

The regional structures of agencies not conforming to the uniform regional system can be found in the tables accompanying their descriptions, when provided by the agency.

Standard Federal Regions

Unemployment Insurance and the Employment Service

State unemployment insurance: changes during 1978

Many States amended or passed legislation that would help them repay funds previously borrowed from the Unemployment Insurance Fund; only 3 States increased weekly benefit amounts

DIANA RUNNER

Because of the significant improvements in 1977, there were relatively few major changes in State unemployment insurance laws in 1978. Many States amended their tax provisions to restore unemployment funds and to help permit the payment of advances borrowed from the Unemployment Trust Fund Account. Some States made their disqualification provisions more restrictive, and some made minor changes in their coverage provisions.

One of the more critical issues was the payment of borrowed funds to the Unemployment Trust Fund. Six States amended their tax provisions to help permit the payment of these advances. Twenty-five States borrowed money during 1975–77 for payment of benefits during a continuous rise in unemployment. As of December 1, 20 jurisdictions[1] were in debt to the fund and five States had repaid money borrowed from the fund.[2] It is projected that almost all the States will have paid the loans by 1981.

Three States—Kentucky, Maryland, and Virginia—increased their maximum weekly benefit amount. New Jersey decreased its maximum weekly benefit rate, overriding a decision of the legislature in 1977.

Five States amended their provisions covering public employees by specifying that if the U. S. court finds them unconstitutional under Federal law the provisions will be void.

Idaho and Tennessee will no longer cover children under age 18 in the employ of their father and mother. Minnesota now excludes children age 16 and under in agricultural work, unless the employer is covered under Federal law.

Nine States will deny benefits to professional and nonprofessional employees between terms or academic years or during established holiday or recess periods if the individual is under contract and plans to return to work when school reopens.

The disqualifying periods for benefits following the three major causes for disqualification—gross misconduct, refusal to accept or be referred to suitable work, and voluntary leaving without good cause—were increased in Colorado, Maryland and Rhode Island.

Following is a summary of some significant changes in State Unemployment Insurance laws in 1978.

Arizona

Coverage. Exempted from coverage are remuneration based solely on commission overrides, profits realized on sales from in-home solicitation of orders for sales of consumer goods in the home, and individuals who prepare tax returns on a commission basis unless employed by a covered employer.

California

Coverage. Claimants who have had a death in the family now will not be deemed ineligible for coverage if the death occurred outside the State in which the claimant resides

Benefits. A voluntary special work-sharing program will be established when agreed to by the employer and union. Under this program, persons will be eligible to receive shared-work unemployment benefits if their hours or days of work have been decreased as part of a plan to reduce employment and share the work.

Financing. Benefits paid inmates of State prisons and institutions will be charged to a special unemployment fund account. No new claim may be filed under the special program after November 1, 1983, and no claim may be based on wages the inmates earned after July 1,

Diana Runner is an unemployment insurance program specialist in the Office of Research, Legislation and Program Policies, Employment and Training Administration, U.S. Department of Labor.

1982. The balancing account will not be charged or credited with unemployment compensation and disability benefits paid to former State prisoners covered by a special California program.

Colorado

Disqualification. The provision requiring no benefit reduction for disqualification if the most recent employment paid base period wages of less than $500 was repealed.

The requirements for disqualifying individuals separated from their most recent employment was expanded from 6–12 weeks to 12–25 weeks. The agency will consider only the two most recent separations providing they did not occur more than 12 months before the filing of the initial claim. Benefits will be denied for 12 to 25 weeks if the claimant is disqualified because of separation from the next most recent employer. However, if the claimant's most recent employment lasted at least 6 months but less than 12 months, the disqualification period will be 6 to 12 weeks. The disqualification period for gross misconduct was changed from a variable 13–26 weeks to a uniform 26 weeks; for refusal to accept or be referred to suitable work, the disqualification period was changed from a variable 6–12 weeks to 20 weeks.

Financing. When an individual quits a job, benefits normally charged to the employer will be charged to the fund.

Connecticut

Penalties. The penalty for fraud will be considered a class A misdemeanor if the amount involved is $500 or less and will be considered a class D felony if more than $500.

Delaware

Disqualification. Aliens will not be eligible for benefits unless they were lawfully admitted to the United States or were legal U.S. residents at the time services were performed. Benefits will be denied to school personnel during established vacation periods and holiday recesses if the individual has reasonable assurances of performing those services when school reopens. Between-terms-denial was amended to apply to weeks of unemployment occurring after December 31, 1977, rather than to services performed after that date.

Financing. The penalty and interest rates charged to delinquent employers were increased from $5 to $15 and from 0.5 to 1 percent a month.

Florida

Disqualification. Suitable work was defined as any job which pays the minimum wage and is 120 percent or more of the individual's weekly benefit amount after the individual has received 25 weeks of benefits. Vacationing school personnel are disqualified if they have a reasonable assurance of performing the same services

when school reopens. The between-terms-denial disqualification was amended to apply for weeks of unemployment occurring after December 31, 1977.

Financing. The noncharging provisions of the law were limited to contributing employers.

Georgia

Disqualification. The penalty for fraud was changed from the forfeiture of all benefits for remainder of the quarter and the four following quarters to the forfeiture of all benefits for weeks of unemployment before the offense during the quarter and the four following quarters.

Coverage. If a U.S. court declares coverage of State and local government employees unconstitutional, those provisions of the law will be considered automatically repealed. The provision that no owner, part owner, or stockholder of a corporation will be considered an employee for the purposes of computing the number of farmworkers needed to meet the minimum size-of-firm criteria was deleted. Virgin Islands was included in definition of "State."

Disqualification. Benefits will be denied for any week that an employee participates in a picket line where last employed. Refusal-of-suitable-work disqualification was limited to the period following the claimant's filing of an otherwise valid claim.

Financing. Any employer who fails to pay contributions, interest, or penalties equal to or greater than $100 will be assigned the maximum tax rate. This rate will remain effective until the end of the quarter in which it was assigned. The provision exempting employers from paying taxes on an employee ineligible for benefits because of enrollment in an institution of higher education was removed. A new procedure was instituted for determining the contribution rate of employers whose charged benefits exceed their contributions; the deficit will be divided by the average annual payroll and the resulting percentage will be applied to the rate table.

Hawaii

Financing. Employers whose accounts have been chargeable for less than 12 months now must pay the maximum rate. Employer's rate will not be less than 0 or more than 4.5 percent. A fund solvency contribution rate for all experience-rated employers was added. The rate will be determined annually on the basis of the relationship between the most recent reserve fund and the most adequate reserve fund. Solvency rates will range from 0.5 to 2.4 percent.

Idaho

Disqualification. Benefits will be denied to nonprofessional employees of educational institutions between terms or academic years or during a period of paid established or customary vacation or holiday recess, if the individual performed services before the vacation or recess and has reasonable assurance to return to work.

The disqualification provision was modified to allow benefits to aliens legally in the United States for the purpose of working.

Coverage. A special eligibility provision which applied to individuals employed in a school district was deleted. Services performed by persons under age 18 in the employ of their mother or father were excluded from coverage, as were full-time students under age 22 and employed in a work-experience program (unless the services are performed in a program established for an employer or group of employers). Part-time services performed for nonprofit associations supplying cultural service to a community are no longer covered. The definition for an "educational institution" was amended to include preschool and kindergarten.

Financing. Reimbursable nonprofit employers are now liable for reimbursing to the fund one-half of extended benefits which were paid for services of persons in their employ through 1978. However, effective January 1, 1979, governmental agencies must reimburse the fund for the full amount of regular and extended benefits. School districts have the option of financing benefits either by contribution or by reimbursement.

Indiana

Disqualification. Benefits were denied employees of an educational institution if they worked prior to an established or customary vacation or recess and have reasonable assurances of returning when school re-opens.

Iowa

Financing. Any employer electing to make payments in lieu of contributions now will not be relieved of regular or extended benefit charges.

Kentucky

Benefits. The maximum weekly benefit amount was increased from 50 percent to 55 percent of the State's average weekly wage.

Louisiana

Eligibility: An individual now must be actively seeking work in order to qualify for unemployment benefits. Craftworkers who are union members are considered actively seeking work if (1) they report to the union hall once a week, (2) if they are partially employed in covered employment but remain available for reemployment at the last place of work, or (3) if temporarily laid off and available for reemployment. An offer of work will not be considered suitable if the rate of pay is below 80 percent of the highest rate of pay in the worker's base period, or below what the employer pays other employees; if the scale is below the wage in the employee's union agreement; or if a physician determines that the work would be hazardous to the claimant's health.

Maine

Disqualification. Benefits will be denied professional and nonprofessional employees between terms or academic years or during a customary holiday or vacation period if they have a contract or annual written assurance of returning to work when school reopens.

Maryland

Benefits. The weekly benefit amount was increased from $89 to $106.

Disqualification. The minimum disqualification for voluntary leaving without good cause and for discharge or suspension because of misconduct was increased from 1 week to 4 weeks.

Administration. The time limit for filing an appeal from a determination was extended from 7 days to 15 days.

Michigan

Benefits. Payment of benefits based on previously uncovered services to agricultural, domestic, and government employees and employees of a nonprofit educational institution are now permitted.

Financing. Benefits based on previously noncovered work now will not be charged to either contributing or reimbursing employers provided the State is reimbursed for those benefits by the Federal Government.

Minnesota

Coverage. Services performed by individuals age 16 and under in agricultural labor now will be excluded from coverage, unless the employer is covered under Federal law.

Disqualification. Benefits will be denied to employees of a developmental achievement center between terms or academic years, or during paid vacations or holiday recesses if there is a reasonable assurance they will return to work in the next period. Now exempted from the voluntary leaving and discharge for misconduct disqualification are claimants terminated by the employer within 4 weeks following a notice by the employee of intent to terminate the employment at some future date.

Mississippi

Coverage. Now excluded from the definition of employment are Comprehensive Employment and Training Act-Public Service Employment participants, and barbers and beauticians who lease work stations (but are free from direction and control by the lessor) and who are compensated directly by the patron.

New Jersey

Benefits. The weekly benefit rate was increased from one-half to two-thirds of claimant's average wage. The maximum weekly benefit rate was decreased from two-thirds to one-half of the State's average weekly wage.

New Mexico

Coverage. If a U.S. court declares coverage of public employees to be unconstitutional, the law providing such coverage is automatically repealed.

Disqualification. Nonprofessional employees of institutions of higher education are exempted from the between-terms disqualification. Disqualification of illegal aliens was modified to allow benefits to those legally in this country for the purpose of working.

Financing. Extended benefits now will not be non-charged to a government entity. Benefits paid after a voluntary quit without good cause or after discharge for work-related misconduct may not be noncharged to a reimbursing employer.

Ohio

Financing. A special fund was created in the State treasury for reimbursing school districts charged for payment of unemployment benefits.

Oklahoma

Coverage. A public school student working less than 30 hours per week is no longer exempted from coverage.

Disqualification. The disqualification of an individual receiving retirement pay was amended. Disqualification will not apply if based on wages paid subsequent to retirement, and if the annuity or pension does not exceed the average weekly wage as determined by the State agency. Full benefits will not be allowed if deductions are required as a condition for conformity to Federal requirements.

Rhode Island

Benefits. The definition of "credit week" was changed from $40 in earnings during a week to earnings of at least 20 times the legal minimum hourly wage.

Disqualification. The disqualification for voluntary leaving without good cause was changed from the duration of unemployment and earned wages of at least $20 per week in at least 4 weeks of work to wages of at least 20 times the minimum hourly wage in at least 4 weeks of work.

South Dakota

Coverage. If a U.S. court declares coverage of public employees unconstitutional, the law providing such coverage is automatically repealed.

Disqualification. An individual's weekly benefit amount for unemployment insurance will be reduced if the individual receives old-age and survivors insurance.

Tennessee

Coverage. If a U.S. court declares coverage of public employees unconstitutional, the law providing such coverage is automatically repealed. Exempted from coverage are individuals engaged in work-relief or work-training programs financed by a Federal agency, State, or political subdivision, unless such coverage is required as a condition of financing. Also excluded from coverage are services performed by children under age 18 in the employ of their father or mother.

Disqualification. During a customary vacation period or holiday recess, benefits will be denied to professional and nonprofessional employees of an educational institution (other than an institution of higher education) with the exception of nonprofessional employees who are paid an hourly rate. The disqualification for refusal of a prior job by a student or veteran enrolled in school was modified to apply only to a refusal of a job held immediately prior to entering school and then only if the job meet the criteria for suitable work. The disqualification provision on illegal aliens also was modified to allow benefits to an alien legally in this country for the purpose of working.

Financing. A higher rate than otherwise would be assigned (but not in excess of 4 percent) will be provided to employers who fail to file necessary payroll reports for determination of the reserve ratio.

Virginia

Benefits. The maximum weekly benefit amount was increased from $110 to $115 and minimum weekly benefit amount from $28 to $38.

Coverage. If a decision declares coverage of public employees unconstitutional, the law providing such coverage is automatically repealed. The seasonality provisions of the State law were repealed.

Financing. The provisions calling for a higher tax schedule were amended by reducing from 4 percent to 3.5 percent (3 percent beginning July 1, 1981) the fund balance required to trigger an adjustment factor to be added to the contribution rate of employers. The factor was changed from 25 percent of the difference between the fund balance and 5 percent of the average taxable payrolls to 40 percent of each employer contribution rate, calculated to the nearest 0.01 percent.

---FOOTNOTES---

[1] Alabama, Arkansas, Connecticut, Delaware, District of Columbia, Hawaii, Illinois, Maine, Massachusetts, Michigan, Minnesota, Montana, New Jersey, New York, Pennsylvania, Puerto Rico, Rhode Island, Vermont, Virgin Islands, Washington.

[2] Florida, Maryland, Nevada, Ohio, Oregon.

Significant Provisions of State Unemployment Insurance Laws, January 3, 1977

PREPARED FOR READY REFERENCE. CONSULT THE STATE LAW AND STATE EMPLOYMENT SECURITY AGENCY FOR AUTHORITATIVE INFORMATION

State	BENEFITS								COVERAGE	TAXES	
	Qualifying wage or employment (number x wba or as indicated) [1]	Waiting week [2]	Computation of wba (fraction of hqw or as indicated) [1,3]	Wba for total unemployment [4]		Earnings disregarded [5]	Duration in 52-week period		Size of firm (1 worker in specified time and/or size of payroll) [16]	1976 Tax rates (percent of wages) [9]	
							Proportion of base-period wages [6]	Benefit weeks for total unemployment [7]			
				Min.	Max.			Min [8]	Max.		Min.	Max.
Ala.	1-1/2 x hqw; not less than $522	0	1/26	$15	$90	$6	1/3	11+	26	20 weeks	[9]0.5	[9]4.0
Alaska	$750; $100 outside HQ	1	2.3-1.1% of annual wages, + $10 per dep. up to $30	18-23	90-120	Greater of $10 or 1/2 basic wba	[6]34-31%	14	28	Any time	[9]2.3	[9]4.8
Ariz.	1-1/2 x hqw; $375 in HQ	1	1/25	15	85	$15	1/3	12+	26	20 weeks	0.1	2.9
Ark.	30; wages in 2 quarters	1	1/26 up to 66-2/3% of State aww	15	100	2/5	1/3	10	26	10 days	0.5	4.4
Calif.	$750	1	1/24-1/31	30	104	$18	1/2	[7]12+-15	[7]26	Over $100 in any quarter	[9]1.4	[9]4.9
Colo.	30	1	60% of 1/13 of claimant's hqw up to 60% of State aww	25	116	1/4 wba	1/3	7+-10	26	20 weeks	0	3.6
Conn.	40	0	1/26, up to 60% of State aww + $5 per dep. up to 1/2 wba	15-20	116-174	1/3 wages	3/4	[7]26	[7]26	20 weeks	[9]1.6	[9]4.5
Del.	36	0	1/26, up to 60% of State aww 14/	20	125	Greater of $10 or 30% of wba	1/2	17	26	20 weeks	1.6	4.5
D.C.	1-1/2 x hqw; not less than $450; $300 in 1 quarter	1	1/23 up to 66-2/3% of State aww + $1 per dep. up to $3	13-14	[4]148	2/5 wba	1/2	17+	34	Any time	2.7	2.7
Fla.	20 weeks employment at average of $20 or more	1	1/2 claimant's aww	10	82	$5	1/2 weeks employment	10	26	20 weeks	0.7	4.5
Ga.	1-1/2 x hqw	[2]1	1/25+$1.00	27	90	$8	1/4	9	26	20 weeks	[9]0.05	[9]4.03
Hawaii	30; 14 weeks employment	[10]1	1/25 up to 66-2/3% of State aww	5	120	2	Uniform	[7]26	[7]26	Any time [17]	[9]3.0	[9]3.0

6-7

	BENEFITS								COVERAGE	TAXES	
State	Qualifying wage or employment (number x wba or as indicated)[1]	Waiting week[2]	Computation of wba (fraction of hqw or as indicated)[1,3]	Wba for total unemployment[4]		Earnings disregarded[5]	Duration in 52-week period			Size of firm (1 worker in specified time and/or size of payroll)[16]	1976 Tax rates (percent of wages)[9]	
							Proportion of base-period wages[6]	Benefit weeks for total unemployment[7]				
				Min.	Max.			Min.[8]	Max.		Min.	Max.
Idaho	1-1/4 x hqw; not less than $520.01; $416.01 in 1 quarter; wages in 2 quarters	1	1/26 up to 60% of State aww.	$17	$99	1/2 wba	Weighted schedule of bpw in relation to hqw	10	26	20 weeks or $300 in any quarter	[9]0.5	[9]3.6
Ill.	$1,000; $275 outside HQ	[10]1	½ claimant aww up to 50% of State aww[13]	15	110-135	$7	Uniform	26	26	20 weeks	0.1	4.0
Ind.	1-1/4 x hqw; not less than $500; $300 in last 2 quarters	1	1/25 up to $69[3]	35	69-115	20% of wba from other than BP employer	1/4	4+	26	20 weeks	0.3	3.3
Iowa	$600; $400 in 1 quarter and $200 in another	0	1/20 up to 66-2/3% of State aww	20	116	$15 + 1/2 wages	1/2	10	39	20 weeks	[9]0.7	[9]4.7
Kans.	30; wages in 2 quarters	1	1/25 up to 60% of State aww	25	101	$8	1/3	10	26	20 weeks	0	3.6
Ky.	1-3/8 x hqw; 8 x wba in last 2 quarters; $250 in 1 quarter	0	1/23 up to 50% of State aww	12	87	1/5 wages	1/3	15	26	20 weeks	0.4	4.2
La.	30	[10]1	1/20-1/25	10	120	1/2 wba	2/5	12	28	20 weeks	0.7	3.3
Maine	$900; $250 in each of 2 quarters	0	1/22 up to 52% of State aww +$5 per dep. to 1/2 wba	12-17	79-119	$10	1/2-1/3	11+-25	26	20 weeks	2.4	5.0
Md.	1-1/2 x hqw; $192.01 in 1 quarter; wages in 2 quarters	0	1/24 + $3 per dep. up to $12	10-13	[4]89	$10	Uniform	26	26	Any time	2.8	3.6
Mass.	30	1	1/21-1/26 up to 57.5% of State aww, + $6 per dep. up to 1/2 wba[3]	14-20	108-162	40% not less than $10 nor more than $30	36%	9+-30	30	13 weeks	3.9	5.1
Mich.	14 weeks employment at $25.01 or more	0	60% of claimant's aww up to $97 with variable max. for claimants with dep.[3]	[4]16-18	97-136	Up to 1/2 wba[5]	3/4 weeks employment	11	26	20 weeks or $1,000 in CY	[9]0.8	[9]6.6
Minn.	18 weeks employment at $30 or more	[10]1	13/	18	113	$25	7/10 weeks employment	13	26	20 weeks[17]	[9]0.9	[9]6.0
Miss.	36; $160 in 1 quarter; wages in 2 quarters	1	1/26	10	80	$5	1/3	12	26	20 weeks	1.3	2.7

State	Qualifying wage or employment (number x wba or as indicated)[1]	Waiting week[2]	Computation of wba (fraction of hqw or as indicated)[1,3]	Wba for total unemployment[4]		Earnings disregarded[5]	Duration in 52-week period				Size of firm (1 worker in specified time and/or size of payroll)[16]	1976 Tax rates (percent of wages)[9]	
							Proportion of base-period wages[6]	Benefit weeks for total unemployment[7]					
				Min.	Max.			Min.[8]	Max.			Min.	Max.
Mo.	30 x wba; $300 in 1 quarter; wages in 2 quarters	[10]1	1/20	$15	$85	$10	1/3	8-13+	26		20 weeks	[9]0.5	[9]3.2
Mont.	13 x wba outside HQ	[2]1	1/26 up to 60% of State aww	12	97	(2)	(6)	13	26		Over $500 in current or preceding year	[9]1.5	[9]3.1
Neb.	$600; $200 in each of 2 quarters	1	1/19-1/23	12	80	Up to 1/2 wba[5]	1/3	17	26		20 weeks	0.1	3.7
Nev.	1-1/2 x hqw	0	1/25, up to 50% of State aww	16	94	1/4 wages	1/3	11	26		$225 in any quarter	[9]1.1	[9]3.5
N.H.	$600; $100 in each of 2 quarters	0	2.3-1.2% of annual wages	14	95	1/5 wba	Uniform	26	26		20 weeks	2.4	4.15
N.J.	20 weeks employment at $30 or more; or $2,200	[10]1	66-2/3% of claimant's aww up to 50% of State aww	20	104	Greater of $5 or 1/5 wba	3/4 weeks employment	15	26		$1,000 in any year	[9]1.2	[9]6.2
N.Mex.	1-1/4 x hqw	1	1/26; not less than 10% nor more than 50% of State aww	17	83	1/5 wba	3/5	18+	30		20 weeks or $450 in any quarter	0.6	3.6
N.Y.	20 weeks employment at average of $30 or more[11]	[2,12]1	67-50% of claimant's aww	20	95	(12)	Uniform	26	26		$300 in any quarter	1.5	5.2
N.C.	1-1/2 x hqw; not less than $565.50; $150 in 1 quarter	0 (through 2-15-77)	1/26 up to 66-2/3% of State aww	15	105	1/2 wba	1/3 bpw	13	26		20 weeks	0.3	4.7
N.Dak.	40; wages in 2 quarters	1	1/26 up to 67% of State aww	15	107	1/2 wba	(6)	18	26		20 weeks	0.9	4.2
Ohio	20 weeks employment at $20 or more	[10]1	1/2 claimant's aww + d.a. of $1-$55 based on claimant's aww and number of dep. [3/18/]	10-16	102-161	1/5 wba	20 x wba + wba for each credit week in excess of 20	20	26		20 weeks	0.6	4.3
Okla.	1-1/2 x hqw; not less than $500 in BP; $4,200	1	1/26 up to 55% of State aww	16	93	$7	1/3	10+	26		20 weeks	1.2	2.7
Oreg.	18 weeks employment at average of $20 or more; not less than $700	1	1.25% of bpw up to 55% of State aww	28	102	1/3 wba	1/3	9	26		18 weeks or $225 in any quarter	[9]2.6	[9]4.0

State	BENEFITS								COVERAGE	TAXES	
	Qualifying wage or employment (number x wba or as indicated)[1]	Waiting week[2]	Computation of wba (fraction of hqw or as indicated)[1,3]	Wba for total unemployment[4]		Earnings disregarded[5]	Duration in 52-week period		Size of firm (1 worker in specified time and/or size of payroll)[16]	1976 Tax rates (percent of wages)[9]	
							Proportion of base-period wages[6]	Benefit weeks for total unemployment[7]			
				Min.	Max.			Min.[8]	Max.		Min.	Max.
Pa.	32 + -36; $120 in HQ; at least 20% of bpw outside HQ	0	1/20-1/25 up to 66-2/3% of State aww + $5 for 1 dep; $3 for 2d	$13-18	$133+41	Greater of $6 or 40% wba	Uniform	30	30	Any time	1.0	4.0
P.R.	21 + -30; not less than $150; $50 in 1 quarter; wages in 2 quarters	1	1/15-1/26; up to 60% of State aww	7	60	wba	Uniform	[7]20	[7]20	Any time	2.95	3.45
R.I.	20 weeks employment at $46 or more; or $2,760	[2]1	55% of claimant's aww up to 60% of State aww, + $5 per dep. up to $20	26-31	100-120	$5	3/5 weeks employment	12	26	Any time	[9]3.2	[9]5.0
S.C.	1-1/2 x hqw; not less than $300; $180 in 1 quarter	1	1/26 up to 66-2/3% of State aww	10	103	1/4 wba	1/3	10	26	20 weeks	1.3	4.1
S.Dak.	$400 in HQ; 10 x wba outside HQ	1	1/22 up to 62% of State aww	19	89	1/2 wages up to 1/2 wba	1/3	10+	26	20 weeks	0	2.7
Tenn.	36; $338.01 in 1 quarter	1	1/26	14	85	$20	1/3	12	26	20 weeks	0.4	4.0
Tex.	1-1/2 x hqw; not less than $500 or 2/3 FICA tax base	[10]1	1/25	15	63	Greater of $5 or 1/4 wba	27%	9	26	20 weeks	0.1	4.0
Utah	19 weeks employment at $20 or more; not less than $700	1	1/26 up to 65% of State aww	10	110	Lesser of $12 or 1/2 wba from other than regular employer	Weighted schedule of bpw in relation to hqw	10-22	36	$140 in CQ in current or preceding CY	[9]1.3	[9]2.8
Vt.	20 weeks employment at $30 or more	1	1/2 claimant's aww for highest 20 weeks up to 60% of State aww	15	96	$15 + $3 for each dep. up to $15	Uniform	26	26	20 weeks	1.0	5.0
Va.	36; wages in 2 quarters	[10]1	1/25	20	103	Greater of 1/3 wba or $10	1/3	12	26	20 weeks	0.55	2.7
Wash.	$1,550[15]/	1	1/25 of hqw up to 50% of State aww	17	102	$5 + 1/4 wages	1/3	8+-23+	30	Any time	[9]3.0	[9]3.0
W.Va.	$700	[2]1	1.9-0.8% of annual wages up to 66-2/3% of State aww	14	128	$25	Uniform	26	26	20 weeks	0	3.3

State	BENEFITS Qualifying wage or employment (number x wba or as indicated)[1]	Waiting week[2]	Computation of wba (fraction of hqw or as indicated)[1,3]	Wba for total unemployment[4] Min.	Max.	Earnings disregarded[5]	Proportion of base-period wages[6]	Benefit weeks for total unemployment[7] Min.[8]	Max.	COVERAGE Size of firm (1 worker in specified time and/or size of payroll)[16]	TAXES 1976 Tax rates (percent of wages)[9] Min.	Max.
Wisc.	17 weeks employment; average of $44.01 or more with 1 employer	1[10]	50% of claimant's aww up to 66-2/3% of State aww	$23	$126	Up to 1/2 wba[5]	8/10 weeks employment	1-13+	34	20 weeks	0.5[9]	5.2[9]
Wyo.	20 weeks employment with 20 hours in each week + $800 in bpw	1	1/25 up to 50% of State aww	10	95	$10	3/10	11-24	26	$500 in current or preceding CY	1.16	3.86

[1]Weekly benefit amount abbreviated in columns and footnotes as wba; base period, BP; base-period wages, bpw; high quarter, HQ; high-quarter wages, hqw; average weekly wage, aww; benefit year, BY; calendar quarter, CQ; calendar year, CY; dependent, dep.; dependents allowances, da.; minimum, min.; maximum, max.

[2]Unless otherwise noted, waiting period same for total or partial unemployment. N.Y., 2-4 weeks; W.Va., no waiting period required for partial unemployment. No partial benefits paid in Mont. but earnings not exceeding twice the wba and work in excess of 12 hours in any 1 week disregarded for total unemployment. Waiting period may be suspended if Governor declares State of emergency following disaster, N.Y., R.I. In Ga. no waiting week if claimant unemployed not through own fault.

[3]When States use weighted high-quarter, annual-wage, or average weekly-wage formula, approximate fractions or percentages figured at midpoint of lowest and highest normal wage brackets. When da provided, fraction applies to basic wba. In States noted variable amounts above max. basic benefits limited to claimants with specified number of dep. and earnings in excess of amounts applicable to max. basic wba. In Ind. da. paid only to claimants with earnings in excess of that needed to qualify for basic wba and who have 1-4 deps. In Mich. and Ohio claimants may be eligible for augmented amount at all benefit levels but benefit amounts above basic max. available only to claimants in dependency classes whose aww are higher than that required for max. basic benefit. In Mass. for claimant with aww in excess of $66 wba computed at 1/52 of 2 highest quarters of earnings or 1/26 of highest quarter if claimant had no more than 2 quarters work.

[4]When 2 amounts given, higher includes da. Higher for min. wba includes max. allowance for one dep.; Mich. for 1 dep. child or 2 dep. other than a child. In D.C. and Md., same max. with or without dep.

[5]In computing wba for partial unemployment, in States noted full wba paid if earnings are less than 1/2 wba; 1/2 wba if earnings are 1/2 wba but less than wba.

[6]With exception of Mont. and N.Dak., States noted have weighted schedule with percent of benefits based on bottom of lowest and highest wage brackets. In Mont., duration is 13, 20, and 26 weeks, depending on quarters of employment; in N.Dak., 18, 22, and 26 weeks, depending on amount of BP earnings.

[7]Benefits extended under State program when unemployment in State reaches specified levels: Calif., Hawaii, by 50%; Conn. by 13 weeks. In P.R. benefits extended by 32 weeks in certain industries, occupations or establishments when special unemployment situation exists. Benefits also may be extended during periods of high unemployment by 50%, up to 13 weeks, under Federal-State Extended Compensation Program and up to 26 additional weeks under the Federal Supplemental Benefits program.

[8]For claimants with min. qualifying wages and min. wba. When two amounts shown, range of duration applies to claimants with min. qualifying wages in BP; longer duration applies with min. wba; shorter duration applies with max. possible concentration of wages in HQ,; therefore highest wba possible for such BP earnings. Wis. determines entitlement separately for each employer. Lower end of range applies to claimants with only 1 week of work at qualifying wage; upper end to claimants with 17 weeks or more of such wages.

[9]Represents min.-max. rates assigned employers in CY 1975. Ala., Alaska, N.J., require employee taxes. Contributions required on wages up to $4,200 in all States except Mo., $4,500; Ala., Mont., R.I., $4,800; Mich., $5,400; N.J., $5,800; Ariz., Ark., Conn., Ga., Iowa, Wis., $6,000; Minn., Nev., $6,500; Calif., $7,000; Wash., $7,800; Oreg., $8,000; Idaho, $8,400; Utah, $8,800; Hawaii, $9,300; Alaska, $10,000; P.R., all wages.

[10]Waiting period compensable if claimant entitled to 12 consecutive weeks of benefits immediately following, Hawaii; unemployed at least 6 weeks and not disqualified, La.; after 9 consecutive weeks benefits paid, Mo.; when benefits are payable for third week following waiting period, N.J.; after benefits paid 4 weeks, Tex., Va.; after any 4 weeks in BY, Minn.; after 3d week unemployment, Ill.; after 3d week of total unemployment, Ohio; after 1 week, Wis.

[11]Or 15 weeks in last year and 40 weeks in last 2 years of aww of $30 or more, N.Y.

[12]For N.Y., waiting period is 4 effective days accumulated in 1-4 weeks; partial benefits 1/4 wba for each 1 to 3 effective days. Effective days: fourth and each subsequent day of total unemployment in week for which not more than $95 is paid.

[13]To 60% State aww if claimant has nonworking spouse; 66-2/3% if he had dep. child, Ill.; 60% of first $85, 40% of next $85, 50% of balance up to $105, Minn.

[14]July 1, 1977, 63%, July 1, 1978, 66-2/3%, Del.

[15]In addition to total wages of $1,550, claimant also must have either (1) 16 weeks of employment with wages of 15% of average wage or (2) 600 hours of employment.

[16]$1,500 in any CQ in current or preceding CY unless otherwise specified.

[17]Also covers employers of 20 or more agricultural workers in 20 weeks, Hawaii; covers 4 agricultural workers in 20 weeks, Minn.

[18]Max. amount adjusted annually by same percentage increase as occurs in State aww.

GPO.909.993

6-11

Benefit Data Under State Unemployment Insurance Programs, U.S. Totals for 1967-76 and by State for Fiscal Year 1976

(Figures through June 30, 1976)

Fiscal year and State	Initial claims [1]	Average weekly insured unemployment		Total number of beneficiaries [3]	Average weekly beneficiaries	Average weekly wage in covered employment	Average weekly benefit amount		Average duration (in weeks) all beneficiaries		Actual for exhaustees	Claimant exhaustion benefits	
		Number	Percent of covered employment [2]				Amount	Percent of average weekly (total) wages	Potential	Actual		Number	Percent of all beneficiaries [4]
1967	11,523,660	1,141,662	2.4	4,489,988	960,217	$117.10	$41.05	35.1	24.2	11.1	20.9	778,616	18.8
1968	10,959,972	1,158,716	2.4	4,335,810	977,852	122.62	42.10	34.3	24.5	11.7	21.1	893,686	19.3
1969	10,032,520	1,062,109	2.1	4,091,935	894,594	130.01	45.22	34.8	24.3	11.4	21.3	806,403	19.2
1970	12,701,116	1,376,748	2.6	5,306,745	1,152,295	137.27	48.23	35.1	24.6	11.3	21.6	933,323	22.1
1971	15,691,866	2,124,865	4.0	6,675,515	1,808,926	144.90	52.30	36.1	24.5	14.1	22.5	1,797,061	28.0
1972	14,800,165	2,029,185	3.8	6,117,016	1,690,762	149.04	55.36	37.1	24.4	14.5	22.8	1,975,349	30.2
1973	12,698,893	1,680,479	3.0	5,389,411	1,414,998	158.39	58.23	36.8	24.4	13.7	22.6	1,601,394	28.1
1974	14,784,734	1,879,299	3.0	6,222,500	1,578,607	168.67	61.46	36.4	24.4	13.2	22.3	1,600,224	30.0
1975	24,651,329	3,425,088	5.2	11,088,671	2,901,804	182.40	67.72	37.1	24.3	13.6	22.1	2,950,016	38.1
1976	20,803,817 [5]	3,317,817	5.0	8,675,265 [6]	2,746,433 [6]	188.96 [6][7]	73.61 [6]	39.0 [6][7]	24.1 [6]	16.5 [6]	22.8 [6]	4,063,988 [6]	36.4 [6]
Alabama	298,516	45,392	5.0	144,059	36,474	165.27	65.84	39.8	22.8	13.2	21.0	58,712	30.4
Alaska	64,126	8,502	8.2	35,088	10,053	405.89	79.74	19.6	27.7	14.9	27.4	5,760	21.6
Arizona	182,282	32,295	5.3	76,069	24,634	177.69	72.13	40.6	24.1	16.8	22.4	43,489	45.5
Arkansas	200,831	29,356	5.6	75,266	21,303	149.23	61.55	41.2	22.0	14.7	21.0	34,903	30.9
California	2,583,935	377,603	5.8	1,108,266	338,037	202.58	68.87	34.0	23.6	15.9	23.0	473,627	37.4
Colorado	163,416	22,871	3.0	63,254	14,841	184.77	83.18	45.0	21.1	12.2	19.9	31,988	59.4
Connecticut	488,709	75,755	6.4	252,657 [6]	79,918 [6]	198.06 [6]	76.41 [6]	38.6 [6]	26.0 [6]	16.5 [6]	25.9 [6]	92,860 [6]	36.7 [6]
Delaware	58,866	8,596	4.1	25,489 [6]	8,372 [6]	203.77 [6]	76.83 [6]	37.7 [6]	24.8	17.1 [6]	24.9	12,726	37.0
District of Columbia	51,657	13,541	3.8	33,488	14,005	212.98	95.90	45.0	30.6	21.7	28.3	17,309	48.1
Florida	586,166	114,356	4.4	263,510	80,224	171.38	63.27	36.9	20.7	15.8	20.1	167,071	51.5
Georgia	428,229	58,140	4.1	205,897	49,483	171.10	65.34	38.2	18.7	12.5	17.9	118,233	37.2
Hawaii	70,047	16,620	5.3	43,681	15,068	180.60	81.85	45.3	26.0	17.9	26.0	17,805	42.5
Idaho	83,052	10,666	4.9	34,054	7,295	165.24	68.09	41.2	19.1	11.1	16.6	10,590	28.8
Illinois	981,888	206,814	5.4	481,647	163,946	210.46	89.51	42.5	25.9	17.7	23.9	232,572	40.5
Indiana	476,265	53,671	3.3	166,414	46,494	193.07	63.63	33.0	20.1	14.5	18.7 [6]	97,322	34.4
Iowa	159,362	27,927	3.4	81,088	24,217	174.02	82.94	47.7	29.5	15.5	23.1	35,939	38.0
Kansas	108,535	17,875	2.9	59,089	15,583	168.99	66.59	39.4	22.6	13.7	21.6	23,470	33.1
Kentucky	266,864	40,077	4.7	118,396	32,506	169.29	66.00	39.0	22.8	14.3	21.8	49,484	30.8
Louisiana	201,101	40,010	3.9	99,795	30,744	177.09	64.86	36.6	24.6	16.0	22.8	41,385	34.5
Maine	174,474	18,831	6.7	68,849	15,267	151.84	59.90	39.4	20.0	11.5	17.7	25,843	30.0
Maryland	306,459	50,735	4.4	129,798	39,975	172.76	73.48	42.5	26.0	16.0	26.0	45,887	27.3
Massachusetts	604,940	129,893	6.6	279,862	102,395	184.59	75.28	40.8	26.3	19.0	25.9	144,268	40.0
Michigan	1,354,054	188,212	6.8	475,956	141,597	219.04	91.89	42.0	22.5	15.5	18.4	240,368	35.3
Minnesota	248,090	54,033	3.9	155,138	44,936	183.64	76.48	41.6	23.1	15.1	21.3	81,476	46.3
Mississippi	130,185	21,145	3.9	52,751	15,105	147.35	48.82	33.1	22.7	14.9	22.2	23,680	26.2
Missouri	545,720	66,052	4.6	182,141	51,529	182.13	72.44	39.8	20.8	14.7	19.8	92,286	38.7
Montana	67,215	9,776	5.6	26,568	7,656	163.94	62.78	38.3	22.2	15.0	21.4	11,110	37.6
Nebraska	82,431	13,677	3.1	41,587	12,034	160.54	67.46	42.0	22.1	15.0	19.2	21,152	39.2
Nevada	112,628	12,276	5.7	39,146	10,920	186.61	71.79	38.5	22.8	14.5	21.4	17,875	40.7
New Hampshire	82,905	12,137	4.8	39,631	9,706	160.75	64.21	39.9	26.0	12.7	25.9	8,225	12.2
New Jersey	787,924	151,515	6.7	401,178	141,992	206.63	76.86	37.2	24.1	18.4	21.9	220,547	46.3
New Mexico	67,229	12,724	4.9	26,093	9,266	161.43	57.73	35.8	29.1	18.5	27.1	11,172	35.0
New York	2,060,947	342,512	5.9	699,862	304,015	215.00	73.55	34.2	26.0	22.6	26.0	378,117	42.8
North Carolina	672,785	68,174	4.1	271,222	62,624	157.80	62.32	39.5	23.2	12.0	21.1	101,139	22.5
North Dakota	31,248	4,887	3.4	14,022	3,762	158.20	66.73	42.2	23.4	14.0	22.3	3,796	27.0
Ohio	931,495	138,291	3.7	333,397	113,104	197.39	81.33	41.2	25.6	17.6	25.5	165,667	30.5
Oklahoma	152,299	27,189	3.8	69,650	21,213	171.78	58.62	34.1	21.0	15.8	20.1	37,136	45.7
Oregon	349,963	47,872	6.3	126,008	36,328	186.40	67.30	36.1	25.4	15.0	25.1	41,923	28.1
Pennsylvania	1,600,604	249,597	6.6	619,480	221,727	193.00	85.29	44.2	30.0	18.6	30.0	222,823	30.9
Puerto Rico	271,515 [8]	69,940 [8]	13.4	126,769	41,353	119.50	41.60	34.8	20.0	17.0	20.0	95,436	68.7
Rhode Island	166,314	22,720	7.3	59,060	20,104	159.77	70.95	44.4	22.1	17.7	20.6	33,163	42.3
South Carolina	257,847	36,980	4.7	118,195	30,243	153.63	62.33	40.6	23.2	13.3	21.9	50,597	22.2
South Dakota	23,323	3,971	2.6	11,921	2,969	142.33	62.83	44.1	22.1	13.0	18.4	3,902	27.8
Tennessee	319,933	61,205	4.9	153,885	44,322	164.07	59.90	36.5	23.7	15.0	22.8	74,883	31.5
Texas	444,007	69,104	1.9	198,703	53,250	178.92	54.46	30.4	21.5	13.9	18.7	101,220	39.8
Utah	75,620	14,480	4.3	40,173	11,519	168.77	72.22	42.8	24.5	14.9	21.7	15,450	32.7
Vermont	51,011	9,380	7.2	21,512	7,442	158.47	67.76	42.8	26.0	18.0	26.0	9,009	36.1
Virginia	237,246	32,921	2.4	106,497	28,769	168.86	67.25	39.8	22.5	14.0	21.6	47,458	26.2
Virgin Islands	487	—	—	—	—	—	—	—	—	—	—	—	—
Washington	558,183	79,547	8.1	176,856	56,429	203.30	73.69	36.2	25.1	16.6	22.6	79,273	40.2
West Virginia	139,412	22,308	4.9	71,732	17,283	189.68	59.35	31.3	26.0	12.5	24.5	19,073	23.0
Wisconsin	427,110	73,087	4.6	160,198	52,413	183.43	81.43	44.4	23.7	17.0	25.2	72,051	32.5
Wyoming	14,367	2,199	2.1	10,218	1,993	185.91	68.55	36.9	18.9	10.1	15.9	2,738	29.1

[1] Excludes transitional claims.
[2] Based on average covered employment during the preceding fiscal year.
[3] Represents claimants receiving first payment in benefit year.
[4] Based on first payments for 12-month period ended December 31.
[5] Includes claims filed by interstate claimants in the Virgin Islands.
[6] Preliminary.
[7] Represents 12-month period ended December 31, 1975; weekly data for fiscal year are not available.
[8] Includes data under the program for Puerto Rican sugarcane workers.

THE EMPLOYMENT SERVICE IN 1977

The U.S. Employment Service (USES) was first established to provide a national capability for recruiting defense workers during World War I. Having accomplished this objective, however, the service almost disappeared as a result of the financial retrenchment policies of the postwar period. Not until the depression year of 1933, when unemployment had reached an estimated 13 million, was the present nationwide public employment service system established by the Wagner-Peyser Act. Section 3(a) of that act states, in part:

It shall be the province and duty of the bureau to promote and develop a national system of employment offices for men, women, and juniors who are legally qualified to engage in gainful occupations, including employment counseling and placement services for handicapped persons, to maintain a veterans' service to be devoted to securing employment for veterans, to maintain a farm placement service, and, in the manner hereinafter provided, to assist in establishing and maintaining systems of public employment offices in the several States and the political subdivisions thereof. . . .

Since 1933, the basic role of the employment service (ES) as a labor exchange has been both expanded and modified several times. The first expansion of responsibility came quickly when the Social Security Act of 1935 established the Federal-State unemployment insurance (UI) program. Under UI laws, availability for employment—generally called "the work test"—is a condition of eligibility for unemployment benefits. The employment service assists in the administration of this work test requirement. Throughout the 1930's, the employment service operated as a large-scale referral service for work relief programs. Immediately before and during World War II, the USES redirected its efforts to recruiting workers for defense and essential civilian work. During the postwar reconversion from 1946 to 1950, it aided in the massive national effort to assimilate nearly 12 million veterans into civilian life. The 1950's saw the development of special services for the handicapped, the expansion of services to employers, and the creation of a network of offices devoted to placement of professional workers. In the mid-1960's, the focus shifted to the special problems of the economically disadvantaged, and "employability development" of the hard-to-employ was stressed.

Today, in addition to its Wagner-Peyser Act mission, the USES and its affiliated State employment services are involved in the administration of 22 other laws, 17 Executive orders, and 14 agreements with various Federal agencies that require it to perform specific duties relating to special target groups. Among them are Vietnam-era veterans, the handicapped, older workers, youth, recipients of Aid to Families with Dependent Children (AFDC), food stamp recipients, and workers engaged in training and other activities under the Comprehensive Employment and Training Act (CETA). Beginning in 1972, the Department of Labor also moved to reemphasize placement of job-ready applicants, with a consequent need to develop more job openings with private employers.

The first section of this chapter examines the present-day operation of the employment service/job service [1] in some detail, with special attention to its primary statutory role as a labor exchange. The Federal-State structure, which now operates in 50 States, plus the District of Columbia, Guam, Puerto Rico, and the Virgin Islands and maintains

---

[1] Twenty-nine States now use "job service" as the designation statewide.

about 2,500 local employment offices, is described first. This is followed by further discussion of the ES role in terms of special applicant and employer services. This section of the chapter also contains information on efforts to develop a computerized job matching system. Next, information is presented on applicant characteristics, along with the kinds of services provided to various ES target groups. A fourth part of this section of the chapter offers data on the distribution of job openings and placements by occupation and industry, wage levels, and expected duration of employment. Enforcement and compliance activities are described next, followed by a discussion of ES support of the work test requirements for the Work Incentive (WIN), Food Stamp, and unemployment insurance programs.

The second and final section of the chapter deals with a number of current public policy issues, some of which stem from the varying missions and mandates under which the present-day employment service operates. Among the questions considered here are: What is the role of the ES in the labor market? Whom should it serve? What services should it provide? What should the role of the ES be in enforcement and compliance activities or in supporting agencies that administer work tests? What is the relationship of the ES to other programs? What are proper Federal-State relationships in the ES system? This discussion is not aimed at presenting specific solutions, but rather is part of an ongoing reassessment of the role of the Federal-State employment service system as it has evolved over the past four decades.

The ES System Today

A FEDERAL-STATE STRUCTURE

The Federal-State relationship that characterizes the public employment service program today is unique to the United States. In most other countries that have similar services, the ES program is controlled and operated by the central government, without much assistance from provincial or local governments. In the United States, responsibilities for the ES program are shared by the Federal Government and the States. The Federal Government assists in the establishment and maintenance of a system of public employment offices, including a veterans employment service, in the States. It is also responsible for setting procedures, standards, and guidelines for operation of the system. Actual operation of the employment service is the responsibility of State governments, although States are required to prepare plans for carrying out their responsibilities, which must be approved by the Secretary of Labor.

There is a growing tendency in many other countries toward completely separate organizations and financing for employment service and unemployment insurance functions. In the United States, however, the two systems are closely interrelated. Of the nearly 2,900 local offices in all 50 States, the District of Columbia, Puerto Rico, Guam, and the Virgin Islands which compose the employment security system, about 2,500 provide employment services. The remainder serve unemployment insurance claimants only.

A majority of local offices have fewer than 10 staff members, who provide a full range of ES and UI services. The larger offices, particularly the more than 400 that serve ES clients only, are generally located in the major urban centers. About 30,000 individuals are employed by the States to perform the various ES functions authorized by the Wagner-Peyser Act. An additional 14,000 State staff carry out ES responsibilities under other programs—such as CETA, WIN, and the Food Stamp Program. Federal funds appropriated for each program pay for this additional staff.

Federal obligations for State employment security agency (SESA) activities, including administration of the unemployment insurance system, totaled over $1.6 billion during fiscal 1976. Nearly 84 percent of this funding was provided in the form of grants to States. The remaining 16 percent was derived from other Department of Labor direct and indirect appropriations and from allocations made by other agencies, as shown below:

Sources of Federal funding for SESA's, fiscal 1976

[Thousands of dollars]

Type of funding	UI	ES	Total
Total funding, all sources	$894,057	$791,704	$1,685,761
Grants to States for UI and employment services	880,062	531,578	1,411,640
Employment and training assistance (CETA)	7,570	110,040	117,610
WIN Program	5,555	121,100	126,655
Food Stamp Program (Agriculture)	------	25,447	25,447
Statistical programs (Bureau of Labor Statistics)	------	3,189	3,189
Survey of Light and Sedentary Jobs (Health, Education, and Welfare, Social Security Administration)	------	350	350
Disaster relief (Housing and Urban Development)	870	------	870

ROLE OF THE EMPLOYMENT SERVICE

The basic role of the employment service, as defined by the Wagner-Peyser Act, is to act as a labor exchange for matching worker skills with job requirements. Depending upon the level of a worker's skills and interests and the availability of jobs, the local office may engage in any or all of the following functions:

—Interviewing jobseekers and identifying their various job skills, types of knowledge, and interests.

—Finding the agricultural and nonagricultural job openings in the area and obtaining information from employers on their hiring requirements.

—Matching job applications against openings and employer hiring requirements and referring qualified applicants to employers.

—Counseling and providing placement assistance to applicants who have not made, or have difficulty making, a choice of a field of work, who must or wish to change their occupations, or who have difficulty holding a job.

—Testing applicants who do not have a trade or occupational choice, or who have to make an occupational change, to help determine their skill levels and explore their potential for selected occupations.

—Providing labor market information on employment, unemployment, and job opportunities for individual areas, industries, or occupations.

Special Applicant Services

The labor exchange role of the public employment service encompasses more than a mechanical matching of available job opportunities with interested jobseekers. The public employment service provides special assistance for many groups of workers who have significant employment barriers to enable them to compete effectively in the labor market. Veterans by law are accorded preferential service. A court order requires the ES to assure equal access to available job opportunities for migrant and seasonal farmworkers. Other categories of jobseekers who are identified in USES guidelines for special attention include minorities, women, the economically disadvantaged, the handicapped, older workers, youth, and welfare recipients.

One of the various ES services directed at young people (aged 16 to 22 years) is career guidance. This service is aimed at helping high school and college graduates and/or dropouts find and enter suitable careers. As part of this effort, the Federal-State employment service system has developed a comprehensive program under CETA for compiling State and area occupational information for use in vocational education planning. At present, this program is designed to provide annual data on current employment by occupation for all States and all metropolitan areas within those States and annual occupational employment projections information for all States and all large metropolitan areas.

The employment service will participate in the multiagency effort led by the Department of Labor to address the school-to-work transition problem. Pilot projects are now being planned for some 20 areas. Major emphasis in these projects will be on the organization of local work and education councils whose primary purpose will be to bring about collaboration among various institutions in a community in order to smooth the transition process.

Employer Services

The primary objective and purpose of the employer service program in all ES local offices is to establish and maintain an effective and productive relationship with employers in order to generate sufficient job openings with the occupational variety necessary to satisfy the job needs of ES applicants. This program, which plays an important role in producing nearly 8 million job openings annually, includes several elements.

Basically, such a program serves as the central point of communication between ES local offices and employers. Technical assistance services are provided to employers in some areas to aid in the management of their inplant work force. Technical aids in this program include turnover and absenteeism studies, job analysis studies, preparation and analysis of staffing schedules, and upgrading.

As an incentive to employers to employ the disadvantaged, ES local offices issue appropriate certifications of eligibility under Defense Manpower Policy No. 4.[2] Certifications issued under this program provide for preferential consideration in the awarding of certain categories of Federal contracts to employers with establishments in high unemployment or other areas who agree to hire specific percentages of disadvantaged workers.

Contractors holding Federal contracts of $10,000 or over are legally required to list certain job openings with the State ES system. The Mandatory Listing Program is intended to provide additional job opportunities for Vietnam-era and disabled veterans. Employment service offices are required to give such veterans priority in referrals to job openings received under this program.

Assistance in job restructuring is another employer service offered by the ES. The employment service role in job restructuring activities tends to expand in periods of high employment and economic prosperity, such as the late 1960's. During such periods, when workers are often scarce in many areas and industries, employers may be more willing to modify their job specifications to take into account the skills of the available labor supply. ES occupational analysis techniques and technical services are used to assist employers to review their jobs for possible breakdown of tasks that can be performed by available jobseekers with lesser skills.

---

[2] The ES, under 29 CFR, pt. 8, is responsible for determining a contractor's initial and continuing eligibility for the program.

Automation of the Service

The Manpower Development and Training Act, as amended in 1968, called for a program using automated data processing technology to list job orders and match workers and jobs. This program began with the development of a job bank in Baltimore, Md., in 1968 and now comprises some 200 separate job banks in all States except Montana.

These job banks provide a daily computerized listing of all job openings on file with the employment service in a given area. The listings are made available to all ES interviewers and counselors, as well as to staff in cooperating community agencies. Copies may also be distributed to ES offices in other areas. Through the job bank system, a single job order can be exposed to a much larger pool of potential applicants and, conversely, each applicant may have a broader range of job possibilities than was possible under the manual system.

Computerized job listing led to the development of the Job Information Service (JIS), which now operates in approximately 1,000 of the employment service's nearly 2,500 local offices. Under the JIS, applicants may consult job bank books or microfiche viewers to make their own initial choice of job openings. This system saves time for both staff and clients by eliminating unnecessary services such as complete interviewing and counseling for applicants who are qualified for jobs and ready to make their own choices. The staff time saved can be used to provide more intensive services to applicants who actually need them.

The job bank system provides a computerized listing of employer job openings, but not of applicant files. Experiments involving computerized listings of both applicant and order files and use of automated data processing to match applicants with openings began in several States in the early 1970's. New computerized job matching projects were funded in fiscal 1976.

CLIENT SERVICES IN FISCAL 1976

In its role as a labor exchange, the employment service registered more than 15 million job applicants and made 5.2 million placements for nearly 3.4 million persons in fiscal 1976. Over 3 million of these placements were in nonagricultural jobs, of which 2.3 million were expected to last for more than 150 days. In addition, the ES counseled nearly 900,000 individuals, and administered over 1 million tests to nearly 700,000 persons.

Applicant Characteristics

Each year since 1958, more than 9 million persons have filed new applications for work with employment service offices throughout the country. In fiscal 1976, this number exceeded 12 million, and an additional 3 million renewed applications filed in previous years. The men and women served by the employment service have a wide variety of backgrounds and needs. Of every five applicants, three are high school graduates, and one of these three has had some college. The applicants include veterans, minorities, youth, older workers, the handicapped, women, and poor people with limited skills. Many have more than one of these characteristics. Others are persons in the prime working ages (22 to 44 years) with diverse skills and experience, who are temporarily unemployed.

Nearly one-fifth of all applicants are veterans, who get priority in job referrals and a full range of services to help them obtain employment and job training opportunities. Some 27 percent of the jobseekers are minority group members, and about 30 percent are youth under 22 years of age. As needed, applicants may get job counseling and testing, career guidance, and help in entering training and in finding a job. About 15 percent are older workers, aged 45 years or more.

Of all applicants, about 6 percent are people with mental or physical handicaps, who can often excel if placed in the right job. More than two-fifths of the total group are women—many seeking to reenter the labor force after considerable time away from it. Others are professionals. About one out of three are poor people with limited education and few job skills.

The composition of employment service job applicants varies according to the business cycle. In periods of high unemployment, a substantial proportion of these applicants tend to be experienced workers in the prime working age groups with strong labor market attachments. When unemployment is relatively low, ES job applicants are more likely to be young, inexperienced, economically disadvantaged, or older workers—categories that are hard to place.

Services Provided

Table 1 shows the number of individuals in each target group who received certain ES services during fiscal 1976. Compared with the number of clients who were counseled in the period from the early 1960's through fiscal 1973 (an annual average of over 1 million persons), the level of counseling service has declined considerably in recent years. This decline coincides with the change in emphasis from human resource development activities, primarily for the disadvantaged, in the late 1960's to the placement-oriented focus of the early and middle 1970's. During this period, a new performance-based resource allocation formula was introduced for use in determining the distribution of ES staff among the various States. The formula places a premium on placements (the final outcome) rather than such intermediate services as counseling. Another reason for the reduction of ES counseling activity has been the shift of employability development functions to CETA prime sponsors. The USES is taking administrative action to insure that applicants who can benefit most from counseling receive it.

The number of persons tested in fiscal 1976 also declined somewhat from previous years, apparently for the same reasons. Among specific target groups, however, large proportions of both women and youth receive testing services—women primarily because they are apt to seek clerical positions that require testing and youth because most are new labor force entrants who are given aptitude tests to assist them in making career choices.

There was a decline in the number of target group members enrolled in training through the employment service from 317,000 in fiscal 1975 to 192,000 in fiscal 1976. This change does not reflect a comparable change in the actual number of individuals enrolled in training. Under CETA, the ES is not the exclusive source of training referrals. The sponsors make their own selections among applicants from many sources for the available training slots. Those more frequently enrolled in training during fiscal 1976 were women, members of minority groups, the economically disadvantaged, and youth.

In accordance with the increasing emphasis on placements, the ES has continued to stress job development (contacting individual employers on behalf of specific applicants). Since fiscal 1971, there has been an annual increase in the level of

Chart 7

The number of individuals placed by ES, which declined during the economic downturn, moved upward again in fiscal 1976.

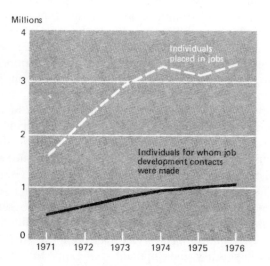

Source: U.S. Department of Labor.

have also shown a rather steady increase over this period, although higher unemployment levels resulting from recessionary conditions in 1974–75 caused a decline of about 6 percent, or 200,000, in the number of persons placed in fiscal 1975. During fiscal 1976, however, the number placed increased 7 percent.

The vast majority of the total number of persons placed in jobs is comprised of those placed in nonagricultural industries. In the main, these jobs tend to be of longer duration and pay higher wages than jobs in agricultural industries. The agricultural sector accounted for only about 6.3 percent of individuals placed during fiscal 1976.

JOB OPENINGS AND PLACEMENTS

Occupational Distribution

Of the close to 8 million job openings received by the public employment service system in fiscal 1976, nearly two-fifths were in industrial or other blue-collar categories, and more than one-fourth were in white-collar, chiefly clerical positions. Approximately 12 percent were in farm, forestry, and fishery jobs, and 21 percent in service occupations. Table 2 illustrates the distribution of job openings

these services, which totaled nearly 1.1 million actions in fiscal 1976. (See chart 7.) Job placements

TABLE 1. MEMBERS OF ES TARGET GROUPS WHO RECEIVED REPORTABLE SERVICES, ALL SOURCES OF FUNDING, FISCAL 1976

[Percent[1] distribution]

Selected services [2]	Total number [3] (thousands)	Veterans	Migrants [4]	Women	Minority members	Economically disadvantaged workers	Handicapped workers	Older workers (45 and older)	Youth (under 22)
Counseled	877	21.5	0.3	46.4	35.7	51.9	14.9	11.1	32.4
Tested	679	11.8	.2	63.9	31.2	28.0	7.3	6.2	43.0
Enrolled in training	192	13.5	.3	52.3	42.6	67.7	6.8	4.9	44.6
Received job development	1,078	27.5	.5	39.7	34.2	32.8	8.1	13.2	27.5
Placed:									
In all jobs	3,367	17.8	1.3	41.5	30.8	31.9	5.1	10.2	41.4
In nonagricultural industries	3,200	18.1	.4	42.4	30.5	31.5	5.2	10.0	41.2

[1] Percentages are based on the total new and renewal applications filed in local employment service offices from July 1, 1975, through June 30, 1976. Not included are those applications made earlier than July 1 that were still active during fiscal 1976. Because the same individual may be a member of more than one target group, the sum of percentages for a selected service will equal more than 100.

[2] Services reported under the Employment Security Automated Reporting System (ESARS).

[3] Figures are for all new and renewal applicants. Because the same individual may receive more than one service, the figures in this column add to a greater number than total applicants.

[4] Does not include nonmigrant seasonal farmworkers. Percentages represent only those farmworkers and food processing workers whose experience during the preceding 12 months required travel such that the worker was unable to return to his/her residence (domicile) in the same day.

TABLE 2. JOB OPENINGS RECEIVED AND INDIVIDUALS PLACED, BY OCCUPATIONAL GROUP, FISCAL YEARS 1974–76

[Percent distribution]

Occupational group	Job openings received			Individuals placed		
	Fiscal 1976	Fiscal 1975	Fiscal 1974	Fiscal 1976	Fiscal 1975	Fiscal 1974
Total: Number (thousands)	7,668	7,889	9,578	3,367	3,138	3,334
Percent	100.0	100.0	100.0	100.0	100.0	100.0
White collar:						
Professional, technical, and managerial	8.0	6.2	4.9	6.1	6.0	4.7
Clerical	15.0	13.4	12.4	17.2	17.7	16.8
Sales	5.0	4.5	4.2	5.2	5.4	5.3
Service:						
Domestic service	5.4	5.1	5.1	4.5	5.0	5.0
Other service	15.2	14.7	13.3	19.1	19.1	17.6
Farm, forestry, fishery	12.0	21.8	21.2	10.7	10.3	9.3
Blue collar:						
Processing	3.0	2.7	3.3	4.4	4.5	5.6
Machine trades	4.7	4.1	5.0	6.2	5.6	6.9
Benchwork	6.2	4.8	5.9	8.1	7.5	10.0
Structural work	10.4	8.9	9.2	13.7	13.7	13.4
Motor freight transportation	4.8	4.5	4.8	5.2	5.7	6.0
Packaging, materials handling	8.7	8.3	9.7	10.8	11.4	13.6
Other	1.1	1.0	1.0	1.6	1.6	1.7

NOTE: The sum of individuals placed in occupational groups exceeds the total since an individual may be placed in more than one occupation during a fiscal year. In addition, detail may not add to totals because of rounding.

and placements from fiscal 1974 through fiscal 1976.

Industry Distribution

No data on job openings by industry are currently available from ES automated reporting systems. Placement counts by industry are available but are limited to those jobs scheduled to last over 3 days.

Chart 8 gives the percent distribution by industry group of individuals placed in jobs expected to last over 3 days. Three industries (manufacturing, wholesale and retail trade, and services) each account for about one-fourth of the ES activity. Public administration represents an additional 15 percent, with the remainder distributed among five industry groups.

Wage Levels

The average hourly wage rate on all jobs available through the employment service in fiscal 1976 was $2.91. It ranged from a $2.27 average hourly wage for farmworkers to a $4.45 average for the professional, technical, and managerial occupations. In the same year, approximately 43 percent of ES openings were for jobs paying less than $2.50, about 43 percent were in the $2.50-to-$5 range, and the remaining 14 percent paid $5 and over or had no hourly wage equivalents. (See table 3.)

The relatively low level of these wage rates in comparison with the average hourly earnings of all American workers (about $4.65 for nonagricultural workers in the private sector) should be interpreted carefully. Average hourly earnings include such items as overtime pay and reflect the fact that a substantial share of employees have been on employer payrolls for some time. In the normal operations of the labor market, workers are hired at rates somewhat below the average wage or salary for their occupation and work up to or above the average over a period of service with the same employer.

Chart 8

Manufacturing, wholesale and retail trade, and service jobs accounted for most ES placement activity in fiscal 1976.

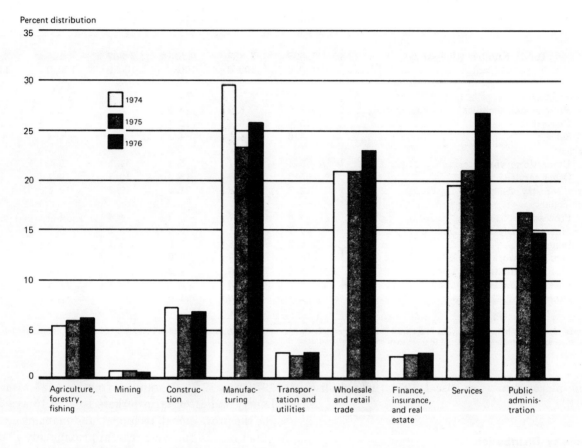

Source: U.S. Department of Labor.

Duration

A significant difference between agricultural and nonagricultural industries in duration of jobs is revealed by table 4.[3] Twelve percent or less of agricultural job openings are "long term" (over 150 days), and less than 25 percent of individuals placed in agricultural jobs are expected to stay in those jobs for more than 150 days. However, about 70 percent of nonagricultural job openings and individuals placed are for over 150 days. Nonagricultural placements account for over 90 percent of all individuals placed.

In fiscal 1976, 72 percent of the individuals placed in nonagricultural jobs went into "long term" jobs, expected to last over 150 days. Although comprehensive data are not available, findings from a limited special study indicated that most placements did not last that long. The study, conducted in six pilot areas[4] during 1974, found that only about one-fourth of a sample of persons placed in jobs listed as lasting over 150 days actu-

[3] Duration data reflect the expected length of jobs based on information supplied by employers on their job orders. The information is tabulated under three categories—3 days or less, over 3 days, and over 150 days. The third category is a subset of the second and identifies long-term jobs.

[4] The six areas included in this sample were Corpus Christi, Tex.; southwest Missouri; Topeka, Kans.; central Pennsylvania; Las Vegas, Nev.; and Portland, Oreg. There was a relatively narrow range of variation in the data reported for each of these areas, suggesting that the sample areas may have been generally representative of actual placement duration for the system as a whole.

ally stayed on the job for 150 days or longer. The findings also suggested that about three-fourths of those who left their jobs before 150 days were voluntary quits. More than 10 percent were laid off because of changing business needs or other reasons, and 13 percent were fired by employers.

ENFORCEMENT AND COMPLIANCE ACTIVITIES

When the Federal-State employment service system was instituted in the mid-1930's, few of the current protective workplace laws (Federal or State) existed. In the absence of protective legislation, the ES often seemed to be the logical vehicle by which to exercise Federal concern for the well-being of the worker.

As the need for certain worker protections became evident, it was often more expedient to broaden the responsibilities of the employment service to protect the worker than to seek new legislation or to set up a new protective mechanism. Most ES enforcement involvement in the agricultural sector—migrant housing inspection, prevailing wage, interstate clearance regulations,

and the complaint procedure—has developed as a result of the perceived gaps in protective legislation for agricultural workers. If prospective employers are not in compliance with these protective laws, the ES has a policy of refusing to make referrals to them.

Alien Employment Certification

The role of the U.S. Employment Service in alien employment certification derives from section 212(a)(14) of the Immigration and Nationality Act (INA). This law provides that certain categories of alien workers cannot be admitted for permanent entry into the United States on the basis of employment unless the Secretary of Labor certifies that there are not sufficient U.S. workers available for the jobs offered to these aliens and that the wages and working conditions meet prevailing standards.

The U.S. Employment Service also plays a role in the admission of temporary agricultural and nonagricultural alien workers. Although the appropriate INA provision places the sole authority for the admission of all nonimmigrants within the jurisdiction of the Department of Justice and its

TABLE 3. JOB OPENINGS RECEIVED AND INDIVIDUALS PLACED, BY JOB ORDER WAGE RATE, FISCAL YEARS 1974–76

[Percent distribution]

Wage rate	Job openings received			Individuals placed		
	Fiscal 1976	Fiscal 1975	Fiscal 1974	Fiscal 1976	Fiscal 1975	Fiscal 1974
Total: Number (thousands)	7,668	7,889	9,578	3,367	3,138	3,334
Percent	100.0	100.0	100.0	100.0	100.0	100.0
Under $2.10	12.5			11.3		
$2.10 to $2.29	16.7	45.4	54.2	20.2	51.6	60.3
$2.30 to $2.49	13.8			16.2		
$2.50 to $2.99	19.3	19.0		18.6	17.4	
$3.00 to $3.49	11.9	9.4		12.0	10.9	
$3.50 to $3.99	5.5	4.7	32.5	5.6	5.4	34.0
$4.00 to $4.49	3.9	3.1		3.8	3.3	
$4.50 to $4.99	2.4	6.2		1.8	4.9	
$5 and over	6.7	12.3	13.3	4.3	6.5	5.7
Other [1]	7.4			6.4		
Average	$2.91	$2.71	(2)	$2.83	$2.70	$2.43

[1] Includes all openings without equivalent hourly wage rates, such as wages derived exclusively from commissions or tips.

[2] Not available.

NOTE: Detail may not add to totals because of rounding.

TABLE 4. JOB OPENINGS RECEIVED AND INDIVIDUALS PLACED, BY EXPECTED DURATION OF EMPLOYMENT, FISCAL YEARS 1974–76

[Percent distribution]

Expected duration of employment	Job openings received			Individuals placed		
	Fiscal 1976	Fiscal 1975	Fiscal 1974	Fiscal 1976	Fiscal 1975	Fiscal 1974
Nonagricultural jobs:						
Total: Number (thousands)	7,013	6,338	7,719	3,200	2,967	3,172
Percent	100.0	100.0	100.0	100.0	100.0	100.0
3 days or less	14.6	15.0	14.6	10.5	10.4	10.4
Over 3 days	85.4	85.0	85.4	93.3	93.3	93.6
Over 150 days	68.6	70.1	72.4	72.0	74.6	76.7
Agricultural jobs:						
Total: Number (thousands)	655	1,551	1,859	212	215	214
Percent	100.0	100.0	100.0	100.0	100.0	100.0
3 days or less	30.4	58.1	54.0	20.6	19.1	19.2
Over 3 days	69.6	42.9	46.0	84.4	85.6	85.5
Over 150 days	11.9	6.1	8.0	24.0	21.4	23.8

NOTE: Because the same individual may be placed in a short-term as well as a longer term job, the sum of "over 3 days" and "3 days or less" is greater than the total. In addition, detail may not add to totals because of rounding.

Immigration and Naturalization Service, the Department of Labor is requested by Immigration Service regulations to provide advisory opinions concerning both the availability of resident workers for jobs offered to aliens and the adequacy of wages and working conditions offered.

During fiscal 1975 (the latest year for which complete data are available), the U.S. Employment Service processed some 37,500 applications for permanent admission and 22,000 were approved. Applications from 3,181 employers were received for temporary workers. Of these, 2,774 applications were approved for 11,024 workers.

Rural Loan Certification

Section 118 of the Consolidated Farm and Rural Development Act of 1972 assigns the Secretary of Labor responsibility for making sure layoffs will not result from rural industrialization grants and loans made by the Farmers Home Administration. The Labor Department investigates by publishing selected data from the application and by contacting competitors through the Federal-State employment service system. If any interested parties object—claiming that a competitor would have to lay off workers or that a company would reduce employment at the old location while opening a new branch—the applicant for the grant or loan is permitted to answer the objections. About 90 percent of the 1,200 applications received in fiscal 1976 were approved. Most of the other cases were closed (i.e., loans were not made) because the applicant did not reply when adverse comments were returned for rebuttal.

WORK TEST ROLE

An important ES function is the role it performs in support of agencies that administer work test requirements. The extensive labor exchange network of the States traditionally has been relied upon by the unemployment insurance system, welfare agencies, and the Department of Agriculture to determine the extent to which income transfer program [5] beneficiaries are seeking employment and whether employment is available.

---

[5] Defined as programs that provide public subsidies or unemployment insurance payments to individuals who must meet certain established criteria, such as low income, disability, or unemployment. Recipients of these benefits do not provide any current service in return.

Services to Transfer Payment Recipients

The number of ES applicants receiving transfer payments is determined largely by the eligibility of applicants for such payments in each year, since these individuals in most cases are required to register with ES as a condition for receipt of benefit payments. The proportion of all ES applicants who received transfer payments for fiscal 1974 through 1976 is indicated below:

Proportion of all ES applicants receiving transfer payments [1]

Program category	Fiscal 1976	Fiscal 1975	Fiscal 1974
Total ES new applicants and renewals:			
Number (thousands)	15,072	15,035	13,307
Percent	100.0	100.0	100.0
UI claimants	31.1	31.6	32.8
Food stamp recipients	11.7	11.7	7.2
WIN registrants	6.4	5.9	6.1
Other welfare	4.5	4.3	3.9

[1] There is some overlap among these populations; e.g., UI recipients may also receive food stamps, etc.

Table 5 shows the proportion of each program group that received counseling, testing, enrollment in training, job development, and/or job placement services compared with all ES applicants receiving these services.

Many UI claimants do not need significant amounts of service. They may be only temporarily unemployed, and may not desire referral or placement services, since they are already job attached. Food stamp recipients also receive limited services. However, in terms of a trend, the relative share of services to food stamp recipients appears to be increasing.

Compared with participants in the other two programs, WIN applicants receive a proportionately higher level of services in all categories except job placements, which lag slightly. ES services provided to other welfare recipients present a mixed picture. Non-WIN welfare recipients receive a proportionately larger share of counseling, training enrollment, and job development services than their share of the total ES applicant population. Their rate for testing, however, does not follow this pattern. While the specific cause for a lower proportion being tested is not known, it is likely that this reflects, at least in part, the mandatory registration of applicants who have serious barriers to employment.

TABLE 5. SELECTED ES SERVICES TO TRANSFER PAYMENT RECIPIENTS, AS A PERCENT OF ALL APPLICANTS SERVED, FISCAL 1974–76

[Percent distribution]

Selected services	UI claimants			Food stamp recipients			WIN applicants			Other welfare applicants		
	Fiscal 1976	Fiscal 1975	Fiscal 1974	Fiscal 1976	Fiscal 1975	Fiscal 1974	Fiscal 1976	Fiscal 1975	Fiscal 1974	Fiscal 1976	Fiscal 1975	Fiscal 1974
New applicants and renewals:												
Number (thousands)	4,686	4,758	4,368	1,767	1,673	954	962	890	811	673	647	517
Percent of all applicants served	31.1	31.6	32.8	11.7	11.7	7.2	6.4	5.9	6.1	4.5	4.3	3.9
Counseled	25.0	18.6	20.3	11.5	10.7	9.0	24.3	24.1	20.9	5.8	6.3	7.1
Tested	20.6	15.6	17.2	5.8	5.2	4.2	7.7	8.0	7.1	3.3	3.4	3.9
Enrolled in training	18.5	12.3	14.3	13.5	9.2	8.6	32.1	21.1	22.3	6.5	7.3	7.2
Job development performed	28.2	24.3	26.3	8.6	7.3	5.3	10.9	11.4	9.6	4.5	4.2	4.4
Placed in a job [1]	20.8	17.7	19.9	7.2	6.3	4.4	4.9	5.0	4.3	4.3	3.7	3.5

[1] The ES definition of a placement is more restrictive than definitions used by other employment and training programs. A placement is recorded after the employment office has completed all of the following steps: (a) Made prior arrangements with the employer for the referral of an individual or individuals; (b) referred an individual who has not been specifically designated by the employer; (c) verified from a reliable source, preferably the employer, that the individual has entered on the job; and (d) prepared a job order from prior referral and recorded the placement on the appropriate ES forms.

Work Test Requirements

The work test principle has been and continues to be one of the employment service's most challenging, and often controversial, areas of responsibility. The Department of Labor, through its many service delivery agents, is responsible for administering work requirements for three major programs, UI, WIN, and Food Stamps. The ES participates in all of these, in support of the benefit-determining agency.

The UI Work Requirement. In contrast to the WIN and Food Stamp work requirements, which are mandated by Federal legislation and, theoretically at least, are applied uniformly throughout the Nation, the UI work requirement varies among the States, according to their separate laws. Although the range is therefore broad, most States have common requirements.

The pertinent Federal guideline, the Secretary's Standard for Claim Filing, requires State claims personnel to "assure that each claimant is doing what a reasonable individual in his circumstances would do to obtain suitable work." The required active search for work is equated with making "such personal efforts to find work as are customarily made by persons in the same occupation who are genuinely interested in obtaining employment."

All States require that UI claimants be able and available to work and that they register with the ES when directed to do so. In addition, all but two States, either by law or administrative decision, require claimants to make an active search for work.

The WIN Work Requirement. Title IV of the Social Security Act was amended on December 28, 1971, to include mandatory registration for employment services, training, and work as a condition of eligibility for AFDC. Able-bodied AFDC recipients between the ages of 16 and 65, not statutorily exempt, are required to register for and accept appropriate work or training offered through WIN.

Joint regulations of the Departments of Labor and Health, Education, and Welfare require mandatory WIN registrants to accept any appropriate job or training offered, provided they receive the necessary employment and supportive services.

Registrants who fail to comply without good cause may lose their individual AFDC benefits.

When registrants are eligible for an income disregard, their wages must meet or exceed applicable Federal or State minimum wage laws or, when such laws are not applicable, must be not less than three-fourths of the Federal minimum wage. However, the wages of unemployed fathers, less certain allowable deductions for work-related expenses, must be equal to the family's cash grant, since the families of fathers employed more than 100 hours in a month are no longer eligible for AFDC.

WIN is jointly administered by the Departments of Labor and Health, Education, and Welfare. State and local operations are carried out by WIN Program sponsors, generally the State employment service,[6] and State welfare agencies. Local WIN sponsors administer the work requirement and provide appropriate job-related services, including employability planning and work training assignments. Local Separate Administrative Units (SAU's) of the welfare agency assist with appraisal and employability planning and provide or arrange for necessary self-support services, primarily child care.

New joint regulations, which became effective by March 16, 1976, shifted responsibility for registration from the welfare agency to the WIN sponsor and require, at a minimum, a personal interview with the WIN employability staff for each new registrant. However, registrants must meet no work test other than signing a registration form until they receive AFDC benefits and are also provided employment and training and social services.

The Food Stamp Work Requirement. The Food Stamp Act of 1964 was amended on January 11, 1971, to include a work requirement. Able-bodied food stamp registrants between the ages of 18 and 65, unless otherwise exempt, are required to register and to accept employment at not less than the applicable State or Federal minimum wage, or $1.30 per hour if there is no applicable minimum wage. Failure of an individual to comply without good cause results in loss of benefits for the whole family until such time as the individual complies.

---

[6] The State employment service is the WIN Program sponsor in all but two States—New Hampshire and West Virginia.

On the basis of an interagency agreement with the Department of Agriculture, the Department of Labor through the State employment service applies the work requirement provisions of the act. The local ES office receives food stamp registrations taken by the local welfare agency and offers the full range of services normally available to ES applicants. Of the approximately 19 million individuals receiving food stamps, about 1.8 million (14 percent) were required to register for work at the ES during fiscal 1976.

In addition to these three major program requirements, the ES agencies are required by law in many States to administer State-mandated requirements for both AFDC and general assistance recipients. The total number of mandatory registrants generated by the various work requirement programs is approaching 8 million.

Public Policy Issues

Currently, there are a number of major ES policy issues being addressed by the Department of Labor's U.S. Employment Service and its affiliated State ES agencies. The Department is conducting research and demonstration studies on several of these issues, which are of particular concern to the States, various administrative agencies, CETA prime sponsors, and the public at large. Six of the more significant issues are addressed below:

1. The focus of employment service programs and activities.
2. The employment service role in enforcement and compliance.
3. The relationship of the employment service to other Government-funded programs.
4. The employment service role in assisting in the administration of the work test.
5. Federal-State relationships.
6. Funding of the employment service and control of expenditures.

The discussion of these issues in this section of the chapter presents various viewpoints with no preferred solutions.

FOCUS OF ES PROGRAMS AND ACTIVITIES

The issue of the proper focus for ES programs and activities raises two questions: What clientele groups should the ES appropriately serve and which (if any) of these groups should be given priority attention?

Some observers have suggested limiting the ES clientele to those applicants who are receiving UI benefits, others to all the unemployed, and still others to those who are economically disadvantaged or who have special employability problems. Yet a fourth group believes that a balanced program of services to a broad spectrum of clients is in the best interest of both employers and jobseekers. It has been proposed also that the ES limit its employer contacts to those who employ certain categories of workers, usually in the low-skill, low-wage range. Those who favor this approach postulate that the employment service could be more successful in placing disadvantaged applicants in this manner and thus be of greater value to society.

The question of whether or not preferential treatment should be given to specific groups stems from the fact that present ES goals and objectives emphasize the need to assist *any* unemployed, underemployed, or employed worker. However, in the years since the ES was established, policies have been set forth providing for preferential service or special assistance to deal with particular categories of applicants for whom regular services might otherwise prove inadequate.

The number of identifiable groups that have been determined in the past to need such assistance is large, which has led some to criticize the ES for having so many priorities that the net result is in fact an absence of priorities. Presently, there are two binding legal requirements. The first, a statute, directs the ES to provide priority services to veterans. The second, a court order (NAACP vs. Brennan, U.S.D.C. of the District of Columbia, Civil Action No. 2010-72), requires the ES to assure equal access to available job opportunities for migrant and seasonal farmworkers. Other initiatives affecting special groups stem from a combination of related statutes, Executive orders, and public policy determinations.

A need to clarify this situation and to identify clearly the client groups entitled to priority service arises for several reasons. First, finite resources limit the ability of the public employment service system to carry out, simultaneously and to the degree that everyone might want, all of the many major assignments implicit in the various legislative mandates, Executive orders, and other directives affecting the operations of the system. Second, examination of clientele focus should be an ongoing concern, to insure that the system reflects the social and domestic policy needs of the Nation. Finally, it has been suggested that the public employment service may be more effective in serving some groups of clients than others.

ES ROLE IN ENFORCEMENT AND COMPLIANCE

At the time the employment service was established, there was little emphasis anywhere in government on the need for protective workplace laws. Later, as such laws began to be passed, the ES role was interpreted by the Department to be that of a coordinator, working with employers and whatever government agency was responsible for bringing about compliance. Other more definite enforcement and compliance functions have been stipulated by court orders. The issues are: What should be the role of the employment service in enforcement and compliance activities, and how do these activities affect its basic role as a labor exchange?

Today ES enforcement and compliance activities include immigration labor certification, equal employment opportunities, monitoring of agricultural housing and working conditions, and others. Since there are other agencies with responsibilities in these areas, some overlap of activities has developed. A systematic review is being made of the appropriateness of selected enforcement and compliance activities of the ES in the context of changes in the work environment, the roles of existing agencies having enforcement responsibilities and their relationships with the ES, and judicial mandates. Determinations will be made subsequently as to whether any of these enforcement functions might more appropriately be carried out by other agencies.

ES RELATIONSHIP TO OTHER PROGRAMS

CETA Programs

The Comprehensive Employment and Training Act (CETA) of 1973 altered the focus of operational control for employment and training activities. Instead of the Federal Government's requiring mandatory delivery of services by specific agencies such as the employment service, CETA authorizes units of State and local governments serving as prime sponsors to choose the appropriate service and service deliverer. The choice is based on local needs and an assessment of quality and cost of alternative services.

There are similarities between some of the missions of the employment service under the Wagner-Peyser Act and those of prime sponsors under CETA. Prime sponsors can fund separate and competing referral and placement systems if they so choose. To the extent they do, without satisfying the statute's criteria of assessing relative quality and cost, there is an issue of duplication between the two federally funded systems.

The Department of Labor's Employment and Training Administration is actively fostering cooperation and coordination between the ES and CETA prime sponsors. Improving CETA/ES linkages has been identified as a major goal for fiscal 1976 and 1977. Pilot projects have been initiated at nine sites throughout the country to demonstrate improved techniques for linking CETA prime sponsors and ES programs and activities. Models of successful linkages will be exported to State ES agencies and prime sponsors.

UI Program

The Federal-State unemployment insurance (UI) program has been a part of the employment security system since the enactment of social security legislation in 1935. Under laws establishing the unemployment compensation program, availability for employment is required as a precondition for eligibility to collect unemployment benefits. Placement activities provided by the ES have been used to determine availability for work required of unemployment compensation claimants. The issue here is: To what degree should the ES and UI Service be separated or integrated at the operational level?

In the years since the inception of the UI program, the organizational and administrative relationships between UI and ES have frequently come under review. The National Employers' Committee [7] recommended a complete separation of the two at the local level in its final report of June 1975. Department of Labor policy since the early 1960's has encouraged the separation of the ES and UI operations in large metropolitan areas.

While integration with UI has resulted in more stable financing available for ES operations, through funds authorized by title III of the Social Security Act, this advantage has been achieved at some cost in terms of the nature and quality of employment services. For example, some members of the public may still have the impression that the local public employment office is the "unemployment office," whose clients are primarily low-skilled, nonjob-attached workers or welfare recipients. With that image, the ES has lost the confidence of many prospective applicants, as well as employers interested in skilled and technical workers.

At the national level, the two services have always been housed under the same administration. Likewise, all State agencies have an administrator or commission over both ES and UI. Each service has had its own staff of technicians and specialists working under a separate director, although in many States, staffs engaged in such activities as reporting, researching, and personnel serve both UI and ES.

Organization and management practices at the State and local level differ. At the present time, States generally are permitted to determine the degree of autonomy they wish the services to have, both administratively and physically, at the local level. Some States maintain a completely separate chain of command for ES and UI, from a State director for each down through local office staff. Other States use combined field staff—ranging from field supervisors through local office managers.

THE ES AND WORK REQUIREMENTS

Separate work tests are prescribed by law for persons applying for and receiving benefits under the UI, WIN, and Food Stamp programs. The issue is: What is the appropriate role of the ES in administering these requirements?

The ES role in work test requirements is now limited to exposing to job openings those individuals who are job ready and receive UI benefits or are enrolled in publicly supported benefit programs. Many of these individuals also receive placement-related services from the ES. Actual enforcement of the work test is by the agency responsible for determining benefit amount and eligibility, although the determination may be based entirely on the ES report on the individual's willingness to accept job openings or to fulfill other job search requirements. The Department of Labor is conducting studies on ways to improve the work tests required for applicants to qualify for certain benefits or services.

The bulk of ES work requirement activity is related to UI and food stamps, while WIN comprises the smallest activity level. Of the total 15,072,000 new and renewal applicants for fiscal 1976, UI applicants comprised 31.1 percent of the total; food stamp applicants, 11.7 percent; and WIN applicants, 6.4 percent. The activity engendered by UI and food stamps is handled by regular ES staff, while WIN is administered through a WIN/ES substructure in all but two States.

A current research project is designed to measure the workload imposed upon the ES by mandatory registrants and to determine the impact of work test functions on overall ES performance and the deployment of ES resources. The results of this study should help to determine the appropriate organizational structure for administering the various programs.

FEDERAL-STATE RELATIONSHIPS

A key issue for ES policymakers is how to develop optimum relationships between Federal and State ES agencies in carrying out the responsibilities of the employment security system.

Implementation of policy objectives frequently requires the issuance by the Federal Government of regulations, policy directives, and guidelines designed to modify the program priorities and operational approaches of the State ES agencies. Obviously, however, the multitude of often-con-

---

[7] The National Employers' Committee was established in 1971 to recommend to the Department of Labor what could be done to improve the quality and relevance of ES service to employers.

flicting requirements on the ES have made it difficult to devise a complementary system for measuring performance against goals.

Until a few years ago, the primary procedure available to assure accountability by States to Federal objectives was to declare the State in noncompliance with applicable Federal law and regulations and to put an immediate halt to the entire employment service and unemployment insurance programs in that State. Because this remedy proved to be too drastic, it was never successfully used. More recently, a number of fiscal and administrative procedures have been devised that provide greater incentives to improve State performance and apply limited sanctions to those States in which performance is found to be below standard. A performance-based budget concept was used to allocate resources to the States in fiscal 1975 and 1976 under the Balanced Placement Formula and in fiscal 1977 under a revised allocation approach—the Resource Allocation Formula. A pool of discretionary funds has been created for each region to permit regional offices to make adjustments for any inequities resulting from application of the formula. In addition, the program monitoring and evaluation system has been expanded.

Several alternatives exist for modifying the present Federal-State relationship. One is to strengthen the authority of the Federal component of the ES system to establish program priorities and standards and to apply sanctions to assure conformity in implementing policies. A decentralized approach modeled on CETA operations is another alternative, which would delegate most of the responsibility for achieving program results to the States or to both States and localities and make State and local elected officials accountable to their electorates for the results achieved. A third alternative, occupying a middle ground, would be to provide Federal funding to the State employment service for a defined base level of specified activities and allow the States, at their own options, to fund the employment service beyond this level for their own high-priority activities. Finally, the existing relationships could be left in place while a goal structure and operational strategy for the ES were developed; in the meantime work would continue on improving present performance.

FUNDING

There are several issues related to the present method of funding the employment service system. The issues focus primarily on the questions, How can appropriate levels for employment service funding on a systemwide basis be determined, and how should available ES resources be allocated among the States?

State employment security agencies receive Federal funds from seven different appropriation accounts through the Department of Labor for their administration of unemployment insurance and employment service programs. During fiscal 1976, more than $1.6 billion was obligated from funds provided through these accounts. About 91 percent of these funds were from two direct appropriations to the Department of Labor: Grants to States under title III of the Social Security Act (83.7 percent) and employment and training assistance under CETA (7 percent).[8] Grants to States are provided directly to the State agencies, while CETA funding is derived by contractual agreement between the prime sponsor recipient and the State agency.

Of the amount derived from grants to States in fiscal 1976, about 85 percent of the total came from the Unemployment Trust Fund and 15 percent from general revenue. This financing system is based on the Employment Security Amendments of 1970, which changed section 901(c)(4) of the Social Security Act and required the President to make a determination of the proper proportion of the total cost of administering the employment service that should be charged to the Unemployment Trust Fund. The law indicates that the President's determination shall take into account such factors as the relationship between employment subject to State unemployment insurance laws and the total labor force, the number of claimants and the number of job applicants, and other relevant factors. The present 85/15 ratio was established in fiscal 1973, and a review is now underway to determine what changes should be made in the formula as a result of the additional unemployment insurance coverage enacted under the Unemployment Compensation Amendments of 1976 and other relevant changes.

---

[8] The remaining 9 percent of the funds were from an indirect appropriation (WIN) and four allocation accounts (Food Stamp Program, BLS statistical programs, Survey of Light and Sedentary Jobs, and disaster relief), with these funds being provided to the State agencies by grant agreements with the Department.

Primary emphasis in resource allocations to States since the early 1970's has been on placement performance results, although there was some adjustment for varying State unemployment levels in the first 2 years the Balanced Placement Formula was used. In fiscal 1977 the Resource Allocation Formula (RAF) attempts to compromise the issue by giving some added weight to the size of a State's labor force and external labor market factors influencing placement productivity. However, placement performance remains the primary consideration in the RAF.

One element of the current ES research program is aimed at developing factual data on "placement potential" as a guide to State allocation of budgetary resources. Information on alternative measures for budgetary allocation is also being developed as part of the overall research effort.

The Employment and Training Administration has initiated in the past few years a number of management studies, as well as expanded research and evaluation efforts, to develop more comprehensive information on both the costs and the benefits of the employment service system as a whole and of various component services. The findings will help provide appropriate base data for budgetary purposes. It is anticipated that these and other currently planned research and evaluation studies will provide tools to measure the net impact of the total employment service system on the economy and society as a whole, as well as the economic and social effects of various job placement and other services in relation to costs. Such information is expected to be useful in measuring the value of ES.

Workers' Compensation

Workers' compensation laws: major amendments in 1976

Benefits and services to injured workers
were improved in most of the 45 States
which amended compensation laws during 1976;
only 1 State meets 18 of the 19 standards
cited as essential by National Commission

AMY S. HRIBAL AND GERRI MINOR

Approximately 800 proposals relating to workers' compensation were introduced among 45 State legislatures in session during 1976. Approval of 153 of these proposals resulted in numerous administrative changes to State systems and some improvements in benefits and services for injured workers.

Objectives for the betterment of workers' compensation statutes to avoid federalization of State programs, and the creation of an Interdepartmental Workers' Compensation Task Force have encouraged State administrative agencies, legislators, and other interested parties to provide more equitable workers' compensation systems. Many important improvements have been made but to date no State has complied with all 19 recommendations cited as "essential" in the Report of the National Commission on State Workmen's Compensation Laws, although New Hampshire now fully meets 18.

Arkansas reduced its numerical exemption; and agricultural coverage was broadened in Iowa. Illinois, however, narrowed coverage of agricultural employees, postponed coverage of domestic workers, and repealed a provision that would have extended coverage to all businesses.

Coverage for certain public and private employments was established or improved in Arizona, California, Kentucky, Maryland, Michigan, Minnesota, South Carolina, Virginia, and Wyoming; but exempted or permitted to be waived in Idaho, Louisiana, Maine, and Tennessee.

Arkansas authorized full coverage of occupational diseases and deleted certain waivers and limitations relating to asbestosis or silicosis cases. Also, occupational disease coverage was improved in Kentucky, Pennsylvania, and South Dakota, but restricted in Illinois.

The percentage of an employee's average weekly wage, upon which disability or death benefits are based, increased in Arkansas and Vermont. Three States, South Carolina, South Dakota, and Vermont, whose maximum weekly benefit is based on a percentage of the State's average weekly wage, increased that percentage to 100 percent. Massachusetts also enacted legislation which increases, in two steps, its maximum weekly disability benefit and will change computation from a statutory amount to 100 percent of the State's average weekly wage, beginning October 1, 1978.

In Connecticut, the weekly compensation to a totally disabled employee for each dependent child was raised from $5 to $10; in Illinois, the maximum weekly benefit was limited to 100 percent of the State's average weekly wage (formerly that amount or 50 percent of the employee's wage, whichever was greater), and West Virginia increased compensation to persons receiving benefits under the Disabled Workmen's Relief Fund. (See table 1 for 1976 temporary total disability rate increases.)

Amy S. Hribal and Gerri Minor are labor standards advisers in the Division of State Workers' Compensation Standards, Interdepartmental Workers' Compensation Task Force.

Various statutorily prescribed maximum benefits (weekly and aggregate) were made in Arkansas, California, Indiana, and Mississippi.

Death benefits were extended to children beyond age 18 if incapable of self-support, or if full-time students in South Dakota; and in Arkansas to children until age 25 if in school. Allowances for burial expenses were increased in Mississippi, Missouri, South Dakota, and Virginia. Lump-sum awards payable upon remarriage in death cases were increased in Arkansas and limitations on these awards were removed in South Carolina. The waiting period for benefits eligibility was reduced in Iowa and Virginia.

Provisions for rehabilitating injured employees were improved in Arkansas, Vermont, and West Virginia. West Virginia also statutorily provided for full medical care; California, Iowa, and Louisiana enhanced medical care statutes.

Comprehensive amendments affected the administration of Ohio workers' compensation law; similarly, a number of other States enacted legislation to strengthen the administration of laws. References to "workman" were changed to "worker" in Arkansas, Iowa, Kansas, New Jersey, Ohio, and Wisconsin. Seven states (Alaska, Arkansas, California, Idaho, Illinois, Louisiana, and New Jersey) authorized studies of workers' compensation laws and Pennsylvania created an Advisory Council.

Amendments to State workers' compensation laws during 1976 are summarized below.

Alaska

An automatic adjustment of benefits for temporary total disability was restricted to those cases existing for more than 2 years. Provisions were enacted to facilitate the computation of workers' compensation benefits for a recipient who resides outside Alaska by basing benefits on such other State's average weekly wage. Benefits will be computed on the average weekly wage used under the Longshoremen's and Harbor Workers' Compensation Act in those States which do not publish an average weekly wage for workers' compensation purposes. Additionally, the maximum level of the Second Injury Fund was increased from $200,000 to $400,000.

The Director of Insurance was authorized to require workers' compensation insurance carriers to participate in assigned risk pools. The Department of Labor, rather than the Workmen's Compensation Board, will now make rules to carry out the provisions of the Workmen's Compensation Law and rules concerning medical care. However, these rules are effective only after approval by

---

Table 1. Jurisdictions which increased maximum weekly temporary total disability benefits during 1976[1]

Jurisdiction	Former maximum	New maximum	Jurisdiction	Former maximum	New maximum
Alabama	$102.00	$110.00	Nevada	$175.86	$185.64
Alaska[2]	$198.40 (80 percent of State's average weekly wage)	$357.59 (100 percent of State's average weekly wage)	New Hampshire	$147.00	$158.00
			New Jersey	$119.00	$128.00
Arkansas	$66.50	$77.00	New Mexico[2]	$90.00	$124.97 (78 percent of State's average weekly wage)
California	$119.00	$154.00 (effective January 1, 1977)			
			North Carolina	$146.00	$158.00
Colorado	$144.13	$152.53	North Dakota	$143.00[5]	$159.00[5]
Connecticut	$126.00[3]	$135.00[3]	Ohio	$119.00 (66-2/3 percent of State's average weekly wage)	$186.00 (100 percent of State's average weekly wage)
Delaware	$125.47	$135.55			
D.C.	$318.38	$342.54	Oregon	$180.17	$195.18
Florida	$105.00	$112.00	Pennsylvania	$171.00	$187.00
Hawaii	$155.00	$167.00	Rhode Island	$156.00[6]	$166.00[6]
Idaho	$82.80 to $124.20[4]	$90.00 to $135.00[4]	South Carolina	$95.35 (66-2/3 percent of State's average weekly wage)	$147.44 (100 percent of State's average weekly wage)
Illinois	$205.00	$231.42			
Indiana	$90.00	$104.00	South Dakota	$88.00 (66-2/3 percent of State's average weekly wage)	$107.00 (75 percent of State's aveerage weekly wage)
Iowa	$160.00	$174.00			
Kansas	$103.10	$112.67	Texas	$70.00	$77.00
Kentucky	$88.00	$96.00	Utah	$155.00	$169.00
Louisiana[2]	$65.00	$95.00	Vermont	$91.00 (60 percent of State's average weekly wage)	$127.00 (80 percent of State's average weekly wage)
Maine	$141.41	$151.84			
Maryland	$164.50	$175.86	Virginia	$149.00 $162.00	
Massachusetts	$95.00	$140.00 (effective January 1, 1977)	Washington	$138.45	152.31
			West Virginia	$173.00	$192.00
Michigan	$107.00 to $136.00[4]	$115.00 to $144.00[4]	Wisconsin	$108.00 (66-2/3 percent of State's average weekly Wage)	$176.00 (100 percent of State's average weekly wage)
Minnesota[2]	$135.00	$145.33			
Mississippi	$63.00	$84.00	Wyoming	$166.55	$183.73
Montana	$147.00	$162.00			

[1] Benefit increases are based on the applicable State, or national, average weekly wage. However, Arkansas, California, Indiana, Louisiana, Massachusetts, Mississippi, and Texas prescribe statutory amounts.

[2] Based on legislation enacted in a prior year.

[3] Plus $10 (formerly $5) for each dependent child but not to exceed 50 percent of the basic weekly benefit or 75 percent of the employee's average weekly wage.

[4] According to number of dependents.

[5] Plus $5 for each dependent child, but not to exceed worker's net wage after taxes and Social Security.

[6] Plus $6 for each dependent; aggregate not to exceed 80 percent of the worker's average weekly wage.

[7] Plus $5 for each dependent under 21 years of age.

a majority of the full Board. The Legislative Council was directed to study the feasibility of establishing a State Workmen's Compensation Insurance Fund.

Arizona

Coverage of certified ambulance drivers and attendants was broadened.

Arkansas

The numerical exemption for coverage in establishments was lowered from four to two employees. The maximum percentage of an employee's wage used in computing compensation for disabilities and death was increased from 65 to 66-2/3 percent. A three-step increase—from $66.50 to $87.50 by March 1, 1978—was provided for maximum weekly benefits for all disabilities and death; likewise, the aggregate maximum for temporary total and permanent partial disability was increased in three steps—from $29,000 to $39,375—by the same date. The period for basing the lump-sum payment to a widow upon remarriage increased from 52 to 104 weeks. Death benefits were extended to children to age 25 if in school full time. Also, the period during which vocational rehabilitation benefits are payable to an injured employee was increased from 40 to 60 weeks.

Full coverage of occupational diseases was provided, and the provision permitting an employee affected by silicosis or asbestosis to waive full compensation for aggravation resulting from continuing to work in a hazardous environment was eliminated. The 180-day limit during which an employee is entitled to medical care for silicosis or asbestosis, and the total maximum payable to an employee or dependents for uncomplicated silicosis or asbestosis, were eliminated.

References to "Workmen" were changed to "Workers" and the Arkansas Workers' Compensation Revision Commission was created to make a thorough study of various provisions in the State's law.

California

Coverage will now be extended to certain juvenile traffic offenders, juvenile probationers, and State prisoners.

The maximum average weekly earnings used in computing average annual earnings for temporary and permanent total disability and death was increased from $178.50 to $231; as a result the maximum weekly benefit rose from $119 to $154. The minimum average weekly earnings for permanent partial disability increased from $30 to $45, resulting in a rise (from $20 to $30) in the minimum benefit. Total maximum compensation payable to a widow without children was increased from $40,000 to $50,000, and to those with children, from $45,000 to $55,000.

A Disability Evaluation Bureau was established for evaluating permanent disabilities. Employers are now required to pay medical expenses incurred to prove contested claims within a specified time or pay additional compensation. The Administrative Director of the Division of Industrial Accidents is now required to adopt an official minimum medical fee schedule biannually.

The State Compensation Insurance Fund was authorized to insure California employers as fully as any private insurer, against liability occurring under the Longshoremen's and Harbor Workers' Compensation Act and other Federal or maritime laws. This authorization applies to operations carried on principally within California. Penalties for an employer's failure to obtain compensation insurance were stiffened considerably. Information relating to workers' compensation will now be made available to interested parties. The State Personnel Board was required to study counseling needs of employees with respect to workers' compensation and other benefits.

Connecticut

The weekly allowance payable to a totally disabled employee increased from $5 to $10 for each dependent child. The workmen's compensation commissioners were authorized to order depositions in compensation and other proceedings. Procedures were specified for handling employees complaints if an employer cancels health or life insurance coverage while the worker is eligible to receive, or is receiving, compensation payments; and a defendant employer, who is adjudged to have violated the law by canceling or withholding such insurance, will now be required to pay reasonable attorney fees and other costs involved in the suit. A fire, marine, or casualty insurance company will now be licensed to transact workers' compensation insurance within the State if the company's capital is at least $500,000.

Delaware

A supplementary appropriation of $417,830 to cover workers' compensation and other insurance was issued from the General Fund to the Insurance Commissioner.

Georgia

An amendment to the Georgia Constitution established a Subsequent Injury Workmen's Compensation Trust Fund; and the General Assembly was authorized to designate trustees and to provide for the administration of the Fund.

Hawaii

The maximum allowable monthly sum for services of an attendant for an injured employee was changed from $300 to an amount four times the effective maximum weekly benefit rate for total disability.

Idaho

An owner of a sole proprietorship was exempted from coverage. Local Boards of Trustees were authorized to supplement workers' compensation payments for schoolteachers. The Industrial Commission was required to adopt various rules pursuant to administrative procedures of the Idaho State Government and State Affairs Code; and the Legislative Council was directed to appoint a committee to review the implementation, operation and effectiveness of the 1971 recodification of the Workmen's Compensation Code.

Illinois

Several regressive changes were made. A provision was repealed which would have extended coverage in 1977 to those businesses with an annual payroll of $1,000 or less. Coverage of agricultural workers was narrowed by excluding employees of an employer with less than 500 days of labor per 3-month period (rather than 245 days a year); and the limited coverage of domestic workers was postponed from July 1, 1976, to July 1, 1980. Weekly compensation for disabilities and death was restricted to 100 percent of the State's average weekly wage in manufacturing industries (formerly that rate or 50 percent of the employee's wage, whichever was greater). An aggravation involving a compensable disease must now be directly related to employment, and must not be common to the general public.

Employers are now required to post notices revealing their workers' compensation insurance arrangements; and a limit of $2,500 was set on the $10-per-day penalty imposed on an employer, or carrier, who unreasonably delays payment of weekly benefits.

A five-member Special Committee on Medical Practices and a three-member Special Committee on Attorneys' Practices were created to investigate the fees charged by medical practitioners and providers, and attorneys, and the impact these fees have on the overall system of providing compensation to injured workers.

Indiana

The maximum weekly benefit for total disability and death was increased from $90 to $104 by increasing the maximum allowable average weekly wage from $135 to $156. The total maximum for all disabilities and death was increased from $45,000 to $52,000. Under the Occupational Diseases Act, the loss of more than one phalange of a thumb or toe will be considered a loss of the entire appendage, rather than one-half.

Iowa

Coverage of agricultural workers was broadened by including those working for a farm employer whose total cash payroll amounts to $1,000, rather than $2,500. The minimum weekly benefit for all disabilities and death was raised from $18 to $36. The period for receiving compensation for permanent partial (schedule) disabilities was lengthened as follows: for the loss of a hand, from 175 to 190 weeks; an eye, 125 to 140 weeks; an arm, 230 to 250 weeks; and a leg, 200 to 220 weeks.

The waiting period for eligibility of total disability benefits was reduced from 7 to 3 days, and compensation was made retroactive to the date of injury if the period of incapacity extends beyond the 14th day. An employee was authorized to choose his own medical care at the employer's expense only if an emergency and the employer cannot be reached immediately. Transportation expenses and dental services are now included in medical care. References to "workmen" were changed to "workers;" and the Industrial Commissioner was authorized to contract with any State agency in order to expeditiously, efficiently, and economically effectuate the purpose of

the Workers' Compensation Law, subject to approval by the executive council where required.

Kansas

A Division of Workers' Compensation, to be administered by the Director of Workers' Compensation, was created within the Department of Human Resources. Certain references to "workman" were changed to "worker."

Kentucky

Elective coverage was extended to an owner (or owners) of a business, including partnerships, whether or not any other person is employed. A Coal Miners' Pneumoconiosis Fund, to be administered jointly by the Executive Department for Finance and Administration and the Department of Labor, was created; and a claim for coalworker's pneumoconiosis or silicosis under the Kentucky law must now be filed and pursued in good faith under the Federal Coal Mine Health and Safety Act. "Noncoal worker's" silicosis was added in provisions relating to an employer's liability for compensation for certain occupational diseases. The Director of the Workmen's Compensation Board has authority to carry out all the administrative functions of the Division of Workmen's Compensation; and the Uninsured Employers' Fund is now administered by the attorney general instead of the Board.

Louisiana

Officers of corporations who own at least 10 percent of the stock, sole proprietors, or partnerships are now permitted to waive coverage by voluntary agreement. Provisions of the law were made inapplicable to uncompensated officers and members of the board of directors of certain bona fide nonprofit organizations.

A spinal fusion or the surgical removal of an intervertebral disc was added to the list of conditions which constitute permanent partial disability. An employer will now be liable for mileage traveled by an employee to obtain medical care; and may be subject to a civil penalty of $250, plus attorney fees, for failure to furnish an employee with results of a medical exam.

An employer or insurer is entitled to reimbursement from the Workmen's Compensation Second Injury Fund for death benefits paid over 175 weeks under specified conditions. The filing period in which an employer or insurer may apply for reimbursement from the Fund was extended from 10 days after the first payment of weekly compensation benefits to 180 days, and the Workmen's Compensation Board is authorized to extend that period.

Provisions relating to employees' exclusive rights or remedies, including rights to compensation in third-party actions, shall now apply to "an injury, or compensable sickness or disease" rather than "a personal injury." However, the immunity from civil liability afforded in provisions relating to employees' rights shall not extend to any officer, director, stockholder, partner, or employee not engaged in the normal course of employment at the time of the injury; or to any partner in a partnership formed for the purpose of evading any provisions of the law. A "principal" was newly defined.

The Senate and House Committees on Labor and Industrial Relations were authorized to establish a joint committee to study the effectiveness and possible misuse of the State unemployment compensation and workers' compensation laws. The Senate Committee was also authorized to study the Workmen's Compensation Law relative to the effect of prior existing conditions and disabilities.

Maine

Persons who operate as sternmen on lobster fishing boats were exempted from coverage. In cases where the employer is insured, the term "employer" shall now include the insurer except where contrary intent is apparent from the context or is inconsistent with the purposes of the law; and "private employer" was defined to include corporations, partnerships, and "natural persons."

The State was declared to have a legal interest in any claim of liability towards or against the Second Injury Fund, thereby requiring the attorney general to provide legal prosecution or defense of any claim (except those brought by the State) on behalf of the Fund. The Industrial Accident Commission was authorized to hire private counsel to defend State claims against the Fund.

Maryland

Compulsory coverage was extended to student teachers and student interns. The rate of compensation for disability and death, including vocational rehabilitation, is computed to the next highest dollar. Maximum compensation awardable for permanent partial disability (nonschedule) was changed to 500 weeks of compensation from a statutory amount of $17,500.

The Workmen's Compensation Commission was authorized to convert any benefit (except temporary disability) into a lump-sum payment. Lump sums were formerly restricted to costs of proceedings and attorneys' fees.

If the amount of Federal compensation payable to a member of the organized State militia for a work-connected injury is less than that provided under the Workmen's Compensation Law, the State and its insurer will furnish additional benefits to make up the difference.

Massachusetts

Effective January 1, 1977, maximum weekly benefits for all disabilities will increase from $95 to $140; the minimum weekly for total disability from $20 to $30; and the total maximum for temporary total and permanent partial disability from $23,750 to $35,000. On October 1, 1977, the maximum weekly for all disabilities will increase to $150, and the total maximum for temporary total and permanent partial disability to $37,500. However, beginning October 1, 1978, the maximum weekly benefit for disabilities will change to 100 percent of the State's average weekly wage, the minimum weekly for total disability to $40, and the total maximum for temporary total and permanent partial will increase to $45,000.

The Division of Industrial Accidents was authorized to determine a fair amount to be paid out of a lump-sum settlement when an employee and a lienholder (who has provided benefits to the employee) cannot agree on the amount.

Michigan

Coverage was extended to volunteer ambulance drivers and attendants employed by a county, city, village, or township.

Minnesota

Coverage was extended to a member of the military while in active service or on duty, when the service or duty is ordered by State authority.

Mississippi

The minimum weekly benefit for all disabilities and death was increased from $10 to $25. By July 1, 1977, maximum weekly benefits will increase, in two steps, from $63 to $91; total maximum from $21,000 and the combined total maximum recovery from $23,500, to $40,950. The burial allowance was raised from $500 to $1,000.

Missouri

The burial allowance was increased from $800 to $2,000.

New Jersey

Persons who become insane were exempted from the 2-year limitation within which applications for award modification must be filed; this limit resumes only when sanity has been restored.

A 12-member Commission on Income Maintenance was created to examine existing income maintenance programs, including workers' compensation, to determine the feasibility of consolidating two or more operations into a unified system. The Division of Workmen's Compensation, within the Department of Labor and Industry, is now known as the Division of Workers' Compensation.

New York

The Workmen's Compensation Board will pay benefits remaining unpaid due to default or insolvency of self-insurers; and is authorized to levy assessments under these circumstances. Additionally, the Board is authorized to make awards for physicians' fees remaining unpaid within 30 days from the time they are determined reasonable. Provisions pertaining to alternative liability and depositing future payments in the Aggregate Trust Fund were amended by referring to a "spouse" rather than the "husband" among those persons entitled to recover damages. To clarify coverage provisions, the term "newpaper carrier boy" was changed to "newspaper carrier."

Members of the State Insurance Fund were directed to ameliorate disastrous consequences of the State's financial crisis and restore financial integrity by investing in obligations of specified agencies. Although the investment schedule may be amended from time to time, the total amount of obligations held by the State Insurance Fund for investment shall not exceed $283 million.

Ohio

A comprehensive enactment designed to overhaul the State's administrative system authorized the attorney general to investigate any suspected illegal or improper conduct within the Industrial Commission and the Bureau of Workers' Compensation; the position of the workers' compensation administrator is no longer a part of the Governor's cabinet; rules, policy manuals, codes of ethics, and regulatory provisions were mandated; more frequent actuarial audits of the State insurance fund, as well as annual fiscal audits by the State's auditor, are now required; delineations of responsibility between the Commission and Bureau were established; an internal security committee was created to monitor overall administration; and the State's House and Labor committees were directed to review the progress of implementing these legislative directives and report to the General Assembly. References to "workmen" were changed to "workers."

Oklahoma

Employer discrimination against employees who participate in workers' compensation proceedings was prohibited; violation may result in liability for damage, including reinstatement to former position if discharge from employment occurs. The State district courts were given jurisdiction to restrain the occurrence of these violations.

Pennsylvania

Occupational disease coverage was extended to blood processors and fractionators whose employment involves exposure to tuberculosis, serum hepatitis, or infectious hepatitis.

A sum of $2,350,000 was appropriated from the General Fund to the Department of Labor and Industry for fiscal year beginning July 1, 1976, to implement increased compensation for benefit recipients on the rolls prior to 1968.

A Workmen's Compensation Administration Fund was created to finance the operating and administrative expenses of the Department of Labor and Industry (including the Workmen's Compensation Appeal Board and staff, but not the State's Insurance Fund) in the direct administration of the Workmen's Compensation and Occupational Disease Acts.

A nonsalaried Pennsylvania Workmen's Compensation Advisory Council was established to recommend changes in provisions and administration of the Workmen's Compensation and Occupational Disease Acts. The Secretary of the Department of Labor and Industry (who shall be an ex officio member) will appoint six additional members to represent employees, employers, and related interest groups. These council members shall serve 2-year terms and are authorized to hold hearings and solicit information necessary for compiling statistical data and developing surveys concerning the incidence of injury and occupational disease. Periodic reports will be made to the Secretary.

South Carolina

If actively engaged in the operation of the business, sole proprietors and business partners are permitted to elect coverage. Maximum compensation payable for total disability and death increased from 66-2/3 to 100 percent of the State's average weekly wage as computed each fiscal year; however, a 500-week limit remains. Lump-sum awards payable upon remarriage in death cases will no longer be limited to 2 years of compensation, but lump-sum settlements may be retroactive and not limited solely to those persons who remarry. (There is a $40,000 total maximum payable.) Additionally, when compensation claims are filed outside of the State, payments shall not exceed the maximum established under South Carolina statutes.

Employer or carrier responsibility for obtaining reimbursement from the Second Injury Fund was clarified and noncompliance with the procedure could bar recovery from the fund. Disbursement from the Second Injury Fund must be authorized by the Director via vouchers and other related data. Among changes relating to State appropriations, miscellaneous expenditures from the Workmen's Compensation Fund must be authorized by the Budget and Control Board.

South Dakota

Maximum benefits for disability and death were escalated in four steps, based on varying percentages of the State's average weekly wage, ranging from 66-2/3 to 100 percent by July 1, 1979. A surviving spouse (rather than a widow) if remarried, is now entitled to compensation for children over age 18 who are incapable of self-support, or to age 25 if attending school full time. Additionally, burial allowances were raised from $1,000 to $2,000.

Regarding occupational diseases, certain exposure requirements were eliminated for determining allowable claims for compensation due to "nondisabling silicosis" (caused by exposure to silicon dioxide) which does not prevent the employee from performing his usual work. A 10-year employment period formerly required for compensation eligibility due to silicosis was deleted, and the minimum period of injurious exposure to silica dust was reduced from 5 to 2 years. Without exception, claims for disability or death due to occupational disease must be filed with the Department of Labor within 2 years from the date of disablement or death.

Tennessee

Exemption from coverage now applies to any person performing voluntary services as a ski patrol who receives no compensation. For coverage purposes, a common carrier by motor vehicle operating pursuant to a certificate of convenience and necessity shall not be deemed the "employer" of a leased-operated or owner-operated motor vehicle under contract to said common carrier.

Vermont

Maximum benefits for disability and death were raised from 60 to 80 percent of the State's average weekly wage for the fiscal year beginning July 1, 1976, and to 100 percent beginning July 1, 1977; minimum benefits for that period increased from 30 to 40 percent, and thereafter to 50 percent. Death benefits increased from 50 to 66-2/3 percent of the decedent's average weekly wage for a surviving spouse without children; from 55 to 71-2/3 percent for one child; and for two children or more, from 60 to 76-2/3 percent. The Commissioner of Labor and Industry may now extend vocational rehabilitation services beyond a 1-year limit in unusual cases.

For firefighters, heart disease or injury is presumed to be work-related if occurring within 72 (formerly 24) hours from the date of last service in the line of duty.

Virginia

Coverage was extended to auxiliary or reserve police forces (if approved by political subdivisions for which they work), and in the event of injury, their average weekly wages shall be deemed sufficient to produce minimum compensation. Eligibility rules for extraterritorial coverage were relaxed by eliminating requirement that the employee be a resident of the State.

The waiting period was lowered from 6 to 3 weeks of continuing disability before compensation becomes payable from the first day of the disability. Further, compensation is now payable for severe disfigurement to any part of the body, rather than to the head and limbs. In death cases, burial expenses were increased from $800 to $1,000, and an additional payment not to exceed $300 is now permitted for expenses when transporting the deceased. Payments under the State's Supplemental Retirement System, which are reduced by amounts paid under the Workmen's Compensation Act, will continue to be reduced if compensation payments are withheld for refusal to work or accept medical attention.

In occupational pneumoconiosis cases, benefit disbursement up to $5,000 (formerly $2,500) may be paid to the estate when certain small sums are due persons upon whose estates there has been no settlement. Disability or death is now presumed to be work-related when members of the police force for the city of Richmond become disabled or die from hypertension or heart diseases, if previous examinations show they were free from these maladies. In death cases, a post mortem examination is required.

The Virginia legislature adopted a proposal urging Congress to promptly enact the Black Lung Benefits Reform Act of 1975 (HR 10760) designed to simplify benefits procedures.

West Virginia

Minimum weekly benefits for disability and death changed from $45 to 33-1/3 percent of the State's average weekly wage. A maximum of $7,500 payable for medical care was eliminated; however, the Workmen's Compensation Commissioner was previously authorized to extend treatment for as long as necessary based on competent medical evidence. The period within which bills may be submitted for payment of medical services and appliances was extended from 1 to 2 years from the date the services ceased or the appliances delivered; and the maximum amount payable for vocational rehabilitation was raised from $4,000 to $10,000.

Persons receiving benefits under the Disabled Workmen's Relief Fund are now being paid at the 1976 benefit levels. Monthly amounts of less than $210 to recipients of death benefits and $224 for permanent total disability, or any other specific amounts which are less than minimums established by statute, are currently considered eligibility factors for increased benefits under the Fund. Compensation is prohibited for occupational pneumoconiosis unless the employee was hazardously exposed for any 5 of 15 years immediately preceding the date of last exposure.

Upon receiving notice of injury, the Commissioner was directed to request from employers any wage information necessary to expedite payment of claims. If employers fail to comply within 15 days from the date of the request, the employee shall be paid maximum rates for temporary total disability with proper adjustments when the wage information is received. Noncomplying employers are not entitled to credits or refunds for any overpayments. In case of permanent partial or permanent total disability, the Commissioner shall require commencement of payments within 15 days from the date of the award. If the employer files a petition for review, payments shall continue until a final determination is made. In the event of overpayment, the employer shall be reimbursed or credited for the amount of overpayment; if the employee was not lawfully entitled to benefits, the Commissioner may recover by civil action or any other manner allowed under statute.

When there is a considerable difference in the degree of hazard caused by one subscriber in a particular employment category or group, the Commissioner may adjust that subscriber's premium rate based on review of his records over a 3-year period, rather than 1.

Wisconsin

Provisions formerly a part of the State's administrative code relating to payment of death benefits for dependents of firemen, law enforcement and correctional officers, were incorporated into workers' compensation statutes. Cases under the workers' compensation law must result from death occurring on or after January 1, 1973; however, no person may receive compensation who has also received payment under the administrative code prior to this enactment. References to "workmen" were changed to "workers" throughout much of the law.

Wyoming

Coverage was extended to volunteer ambulance service members, and for payment purposes, a salary of $50 monthly was established. □

Workers' compensation laws—significant enactments in 1977

*Although many of the 300 new laws
overhauled administrative machinery,
the States once again legislated
a myriad of benefit improvements*

AMY S. HRIBAL

The legislatures of 49 States in session during 1977 enacted more than 300 of approximately 1,700 proposals to alter workers' compensation statutes, the majority of which upgrade coverage, benefits, medical care, rehabilitation, and administration. Nevertheless, it is still true that no State fully meets the 19 essential recommendations of the National Commission on State Workmen's Compensation Laws issued in 1972.

In January, the policy group of the Interdepartmental Workers' Compensation Task Force submitted a report to the President and the Congress on the need for reform of State workers' compensation programs.[1] The report states that workers' compensation programs can be more effectively managed at the State level with the Federal Government monitoring progress and providing assistance. However, the study urges a reordering of priorities and a new mode of operation if workers' compensation is to achieve its traditional goals; for without these changes, workers' compensation is in jeopardy of becoming more expensive, less equitable, and less effective. Recommendations for reform and steps essential to get the reforms underway were outlined.

Significant 1977 enactments include an Oklahoma law which extends coverage to all employments in

---

Amy S. Hribal is a labor standards adviser in the Division of State Workers' Compensation Standards, Employment Standards Administration, U.S. Department of Labor.

which the employer meets a statutorily prescribed payroll minimum, and Nevada eliminated numerical exemptions for occupational disease coverage. California exempted certain household and casual employees who were previously covered; Nevada and Oregon narrowed coverage for casual employments.

Maryland, Texas, and Wyoming broadened the extraterritorial application of their laws. Tennessee authorized full coverage of occupational diseases; and such coverage was expanded in Oklahoma, Oregon, and South Carolina.

The maximum percentage of an employee's wage upon which death benefits are based in New Mexico increased to 66⅔ percent for a surviving spouse, or for dependent children if there is no surviving spouse; however, Alaska decreased its maximum percentage to 66⅔ percent. Minnesota's maximum weekly compensation will be based on 100 percent of the State's average weekly wage; and Oklahoma provided for an eventual increase to 66⅔ percent of the State's wage for total disability, 50 percent for permanent partial disability, and 75 percent for death. Illinois based benefits on the State's average weekly wage in covered industries under the Unemployment Insurance Act, rather than in manufacturing industries; and repealed the provision which would have further escalated the percentage of the State's wage for basing benefits. Statutorily prescribed dollar maximums were raised in Indiana, Nebraska, New

York, North Dakota, Oklahoma, Oregon, and Tennessee. The maximum period set on benefits for permanent total disability was eliminated in Oklahoma, but limitations were newly established in Alaska and Illinois. (See table 1 for temporary total disability rate increases.)

Payments for various benefits were equalized for widows or widowers in Connecticut, North Carolina, North Dakota, Oklahoma, and Utah; and lump sums were provided to surviving spouses upon remarriage under specified circumstances in Indiana, New Mexico, and Oklahoma. Death benefits were extended to children while in school full time until age 23 in New Mexico and Oklahoma. Compensation was extended to mentally or physically disabled children until age 21 in Wyoming, and the aggregate maximum set for such cases was eliminated.

Benefits to specific persons already receiving compensation were increased or established in Connecticut, Minnesota, New York, North Carolina, Utah, Washington, and West Virginia. Alaska, however, repealed the provision which adjusted benefits for temporary and permanent disability according to currently existing rates, and Oregon prohibited increases of temporary total disability benefits for certain claimants.

Statutes creating benefit offsets were enacted in the laws of Alaska, Florida, Maine, New Jersey, New

York, Oregon, and Wyoming; but similar provisions were repealed in Kansas.

Burial allowances were raised in Connecticut, Kansas, Maryland, Montana (under the Occupational Disease Act), North Dakota, and Texas; the maximum set under the Utah law can now be extended.

The periods for reporting injuries or filing claims were lengthened in Minnesota, Nebraska, North Dakota, and South Dakota (for occupational diseases). Oklahoma reduced the waiting period for benefits eligibility from 5 to 3 days; and California reduced the liability period of employers for certain claims relative to occupational diseases and cumulative injuries.

Full medical care was authorized in Missouri, Montana (for occupational diseases), New Mexico, and Tennessee; and 14 States (California, Florida, Illinois, Kansas, Louisiana, Maine, Minnesota, Missouri, Nevada, North Carolina, Oregon, Texas, Utah, and Washington) improved medical care statutes. Michigan, Mississippi, New Mexico, Oregon, and Washington improved provisions relating to rehabilitation of injured workers.

The laws of numerous States were amended to strengthen administration of the workers' compensation programs. Arkansas increased the membership of the Workers' Compensation Revision Commis-

---

Table 1. Jurisdictions which increased maximum weekly temporary total disability benefits during 1977[1]

Jurisdiction	Former maximum	New maximum	Jurisdiction	Former maximum	New maximum
Alabama	$110.00	$120.00	Minnesota[2]	$145.33	$197.00 (100 percent of State's average weekly wage)
Alaska[2]	$357.59 (100 percent of State's average weekly wage)	$551.86 (133-1/3 percent of State's average weekly wage)	Mississippi[2]	$84.00	$91.00
Arkansas[2]	$77.00	$84.00	Montana	$162.00	$174.00
California[2]	$119.00	$154.00	Nebraska	$100.00	$140.00
Colorado	$152.53	$161.42	Nevada[2]	$185.64	$198.22
Connecticut	$135.00[3]	$147.00[3]	New Hampshire	$158.00	$169.00
Delaware	$135.55	$144.00	New Jersey	$128.00	$138.00
District of Columbia	$342.54	$367.22	New Mexico[2]	$124.97 (78 percent of State's average weekly wage)	$142.59 (89 percent of State's average weekly wage)
Florida	$112.00	$119.00	North Carolina	$158.00	$168.00
Hawaii	$167.00	$179.00	North Dakota	$159.00[7]	$171.00[7]
Idaho	$90.00 to $135.00[4]	$99.00 to $148.50[4]	Ohio	$186.00	$198.00
Illinois[2]	$231.42 (100 percent of State's average weekly wage in manufacturing industries)	$304.21 (133-1/3 percent of State's average weekly wage)	Oregon	$195.18	$213.78
			Pennsylvania	$187.00	$199.00
			Rhode Island	$166.00[8]	$176.00[8]
Indiana	$104.00	$120.00	South Carolina	$147.44	$160.00
Iowa[2]	$174.00 (100 percent of State's average weekly wage)	$247.00 (133-1/3 percent of State's average weekly wage)	South Dakota[2]	$107.00 (75 percent of State's average weekly wage)	$130.00 (84 percent of State's average weekly wage)
			Tennessee	$85.00	$100.00
Kansas	$112.67	$120.95	Texas	$77.00	$91.00
Kentucky	$96.00	$104.00	Utah	$169.00	$183.00
Louisiana[2]	$95.00[5]	$95.00 (66-2/3 percent of State's average weekly wage)[5]	Vermont[2]	$127.00 (80 percent of State's average weekly wage)[9]	$170.00 (100 percent of State's average weekly wage)[9]
Maine[2]	$151.84 (100 percent of State's average weekly wage)	$220.93 (133-1/3 percent of State's average weekly wage)	Virginia	$162.00	$175.00
			Washington	$152.31	$163.38
			West Virginia	$192.00	$208.00
Maryland	$175.86	$188.00	Wisconsin	$176.00	$189.00
Massachusetts[2]	$95.00[6]	$150.00[6]	Wyoming	$183.73	$189.86
Michigan	$115.00 to $144.00[4]	$127.00 to $156.00[4]			

[1] Benefit increases are based on the applicable State or national average weekly wage. However, Arkansas, California, Indiana, Massachusetts, Mississippi, Nebraska, Tennessee, and Texas prescribe statutory amounts.
[2] The 1977 increase is a result of legislation enacted in a prior year.
[3] Plus $10 for each dependent child, aggregate not to exceed 50 percent of the basic weekly benefit or 75 percent of the employee's average weekly wage.
[4] Benefits are determined by number of dependents.

[5] Changed from a statutory amount to a percentage of the State's average weekly wage.
[6] Plus $6 for each total dependent, aggregate not to exceed worker's average weekly wage.
[7] Plus $5 for each dependent child, aggregate not to exceed worker's net wage after taxes and social security.
[8] Plus $6 for each dependent, aggregate not to exceed 80 percent of the worker's average weekly wage.
[9] Plus $5 for each dependent under 21 years of age.

sion; and additional positions were authorized for the Workmen's Compensation Commission. The Mississippi Workmen's Compensation Commission was authorized to increase the number of administrative judges; and Nevada established a position for an additional appeals officer in the Industrial Commission and created the Office of State Industrial Attorney to represent claimants unable to employ private counsel. The chairman of the North Carolina Industrial Commission was authorized to designate a deputy commissioner to take the place of a commissioner on review of any case. Oregon created a Department of Workers' Compensation to replace the Workers' Compensation Board, and a Field Services Division was established within the Board.

Georgia created a Subsequent Injury Trust Fund; Montana and Virginia established Uninsured Employers Funds; and New Mexico set up a $1 million Retention Fund to provide a reserve for payment of insurance premiums for State agencies. Studies of compensation laws were authorized in Louisiana, Minnesota, Nevada, New York, and Wyoming; and Connecticut continued a previously-established study. The term "workmen" was changed to "workers" in statutes of Illinois, Oklahoma, Oregon, Texas, and Washington; however, some States still use sex-stereotype language.

Following is a summary, by State, of important changes enacted during 1977.

Alaska

A total of $60,000 was set on benefits for permanent partial (nonschedule) disabilities. The maximum percentage of an employee's wage which is used in computing death benefits for a surviving spouse plus children was decreased from 90 percent to 66⅔ percent. Additionally, death benefits to a surviving spouse shall be reduced after 5 years, and again after 8 years, and shall be terminated after 10 years unless the worker was permanently and totally disabled at the time of death. However, such reductions will not apply after a spouse reaches age 52.

A provision which adjusted workers' compensation benefits for temporary and permanent disability according to currently existing rates was repealed; and offsets of social security benefits were established so that workers' compensation benefits for disability will be limited to a maximum of 80 percent of the employee's average weekly wage, and for death, workers' compensation benefits will be reduced by one-half of any Federal benefits.

Arizona

If an employee, or a dependent, files a compensation claim with the Industrial Commission in lieu of proceeding against an uninsured employer by civil action in court, any benefits awarded will be paid initially from a special fund, and the employer is liable to repay the fund for amount expended, plus a 10-percent penalty. Formerly, the employer had 10 days to pay such benefits before payment was made from the special fund.

Persons receiving permanent compensation benefits from the special fund are now required to report annual earnings to the Commission within 30 days of the anniversary date of the award, or benefits will be suspended.

Arkansas

The membership of the Arkansas Workers' Compensation Revision Commission was increased from 10 to 17 members, and additional positions were authorized for the Workmen's Compensation Commission.

For the continued payment of workers' compensation claims of city employees, $200,000 was appropriated from the Miscellaneous Revolving Fund to the Workmen's Compensation Commission. The $350,000-maximum set on funds transferable from the Municipal Aid Fund to the Revolving Fund was changed to such amount as the General Assembly may appropriate. However, State programs are now required to contribute equally into the Revolving Fund for costs of workers' compensation benefits charged to the State agencies operating such programs; the fund was formerly financed by the State.

California

The minimum weekly benefit for total disabilities and death was raised from $35 to $49. A regressive change was made exempting from coverage those household and casual employees who either work for an employer for less than 52 hours, or earn less than $100, during the 90 calendar days preceding the date of injury, or the date of last employment in an occupation exposing the employee to the hazards of an occupational disease. The provision was repealed which permits an insured who does not employ household and casual employees subject to the law to reject comprehensive personal liability coverage for such employees. Presumptions concerning dependency upon deceased employees shall now apply to aliens who are nonresidents of the United States at the time of injury.

Employees now have the right to be treated by the physician of their choice from the date of injury, rather than after 30 days, if they had previously notified the employer in writing that they had a personal physician. In addition, the definition of "physician" was broadened to include psychologists.

Employers' period of liability for compensation claims relating to occupational diseases and cumulative injuries filed on and after January 1, 1978, was reduced from 5 to 4 years. Beginning January 1, 1979, and thereafter on the first day of January for the next 2 years, the period of liability will be shortened by 1 additional year, so that by January 1, 1981, the liability period will be 1 year. Interested parties can now participate in the rulemaking process of the Workmen's Compensation Appeals Board by submitting written data or arguments, with opportunity for oral presentation.

Numerous proposals were enacted into law concerning insurance arrangements. Among these were amendments to enable certain local governmental entities to obtain insurance; and the requirement that the Insurance Commissioner approve or issue a classification of risks and premium rates under the Longshore Act with respect to operations carried on principally within California was eliminated.

Colorado

Compulsory coverage was extended to job trainees who are under any work training program sponsored by a joint apprenticeship and training committee; elective coverage was extended to certain members of volunteer police departments; coverage for officers of agricultural corporations was changed from compulsory to elective; and employees of passenger tramway operations were excluded from coverage if participating in recreational activity on their own initiative.

Connecticut

Death benefits to widows and widowers were equalized by deleting the 312-week limit on benefits to a widower, and annual cost-of-living adjustments will now be made to maximum weekly benefits payable to dependents. The burial allowance was raised from $1,000 to $1,500; and the requirement that death must occur within 6 years of the date of injury or the first symptom of an occupational disease before such burial expenses will be paid was repealed.

Employers must now provide lung function tests to employees who are exposed to hazardous materials as identified under the Occupational Safety and Health Act, if requested to do so by the Labor Commissioner. Also, the Commission established in 1975 to further study the recommendations of the National Commission on State Workmen's Compensation Laws was again continued.

Delaware

The tax on insurance carriers was changed from 4 percent of premiums to 2 percent plus additional assessments.

Florida

"Employee" was redefined to exclude real estate sales people who are paid solely by commission. Employers will now be liable for injured employees' transportation costs to obtain medical care. An offset of weekly benefits payable under the unemployment compensation law of any State against workers' compensation benefits for temporary total disability under the Florida Workmen's Compensation Law was established.

The liability of employers for future payments of compensation by advance payments will now be discharged when certain criteria are met; and attorney fees will now be based on a percentage of the amount of benefits secured, but may be increased or decreased if circumstances warrant such action.

Georgia

To encourage the employment of handicapped persons, a Subsequent Injury Trust Fund was established which protects employers from excess liability when an injury to a handicapped worker merges with a permanent impairment to cause a greater disability than would have resulted from the subsequent injury alone. Employers who refuse to insure the payment of compensation, or file evidence of their compliance after being notified of noncompliance, are now subject to a penalty not to exceed $50 per day.

Hawaii

Payments for funeral and burial expenses are now made directly to the surviving spouse or the decedent's estate if the deceased had a prepaid funeral and burial plan.

Idaho

Appeals to the Supreme Court from the Industrial Commission shall now be made according to rules prescribed by the Court, and the statutory sections, detailing former appeal procedures, were abolished. The State Insurance Fund may now voluntarily participate in pooling arrangements to insure employers against liability which results from injury to longshore and harbor workers, and governmental hospitals which are financed primarily by patient care revenue will not be required to insure liability for workers' compensation with the State fund.

Illinois

Maximum weekly benefits for disabilities and death will now be based on the State's average weekly wage in indusries covered by the Unemployment Insurance Act, rather than the average weekly wage in manufacturing industries. Scheduled increases in the maximum compensation rate to an eventual 200 percent of the State's average weekly wage by 1981 were eliminated, thereby stabilizing compensation at 133⅓ percent. Aggregate death benefits are now subject to a maximum of $250,000, or 20 years of benefits, whichever is greater. Increases in annual adjustments for disability awards will now be paid in the same manner as for payments made under the Second Injury Fund. A panel of physicians was established from which injured employees may choose a treating physician; but selection is not restricted to the panel.

The Industrial Commission was required to make and publish procedural rules for determining the extent of disability to employees injured in the course of employment. The Workmen's Occupational Diseases Act was designated as the Worker's Occupational Diseases Act, and other discriminatory language was eliminated.

Indiana

The maximum weekly benefit for permanent partial (schedule) disabilities was increased from $60 to $75, and for total disabilities and death, from $104 to $120; and the aggregate for all disabilities and death, from $52,000 to $60,000. In addition, a spouse who is the only surviving dependent is now entitled, upon remarriage, to a lump-sum settlement equal to benefits for 104 weeks or for the remainder of the compensation period, whichever is smaller. The Occupational Diseases Act was amended to conform with the Workmen's Compensation Act.

Iowa

The Director of the Department of Job Service, rather than the Employment Security Commission, will now determine the State's average weekly wage for computing benefits. Provisions of the Workmen's Compensation Act were amended to conform with the Administrative Procedures Act.

Kansas

Coverage was extended to duly authorized volunteer ambulance attendants and mobile intensive care technicians, and counties were required to provide coverage for specified district court officers and employees. Employers who do not expect to have a payroll in excess of $10,000 for the current calendar year will now be excluded from coverage if for the preceding calendar year they had a payroll of $10,000 or less, or if they had no payroll at all.

Provisions were repealed which terminate workers' compensation benefits for disabilities when injured employees are eligible for or receive benefits under the Social Security Act, and which offset workers' compensation death benefits by one-half of any periodic benefits payable under that act. The burial allowance was raised from $1,000 to $2,000. The maximum medical fee for which employers shall be liable in case employees consult a physician of their choice when dissatisfied with the employer-selected physician was increased from $100 to $150.

Louisiana

Coverage was extended to criminal deputy sheriffs for the parish of Orleans in the same manner as for public employees. In case there is no set term with respect to disability benefits for the lifetime of an employee, the amount claimed as compensation may now be commuted to a lump-sum settlement. Employers are now liable for reasonable and necessary transportation expenses incurred by employees to obtain medical services.

Reimbursements to employers from the Second Injury Fund for disability benefits are now limited to those payments occurring after the first 104 weeks of benefits. The filing period in which an employer may apply for reimbursement from the fund was extended from 180 days to 52 weeks after the first payment of weekly benefits; and mental retardation was added to the list of permanent partial disabilities which must exist and be certified prior to a subsequent injury for an employer to be eligible for reimbursement. A 2-year term of office was set for the fund chairman and vice chairman.

The Senate and House Committees on Commerce were directed to study, among other things, the feasibility of making the State a self insurer.

Maine

The definition of employee was broadened to include any person who regularly operates a business or practices a trade, profession, or occupation, whether individually or in partnership or association with other persons. Educational rehabilitation (including postsecondary, college, and university instruction) was authorized, which is in addition to vocational rehabilitation. Employers were prohibited from delaying or refusing benefits due an injured or diseased employee under an insured disability or medical payment plan because the employee has filed a work-

ers' compensation claim, but such benefits will be deducted from workers' compensation payments. The 5-percent discount on lump-sum payments was eliminated.

The Industrial Accident Commission was authorized to approve agreements between parties for a trial work period at specific jobs, not to exceed 3 months. Employees who have received compensation are now required to notify the Commission and the previous employer within 7 days of their return to work. Benefits are not to be suspended pending appeals to law courts; and the maximum fine for failure of the employer or insurance carrier to pay compensation was changed to $25 for each day of noncompliance (formerly a lump-sum payment of $500).

Maryland

Coverage was extended to certain volunteer, non-salaried and other persons in Dorchester County; and officers of corporations were permitted to waive coverage if the corporation maintains a health and accident insurance plan with benefits equivalent to those available under the Workmen's Compensation Law. Heart disease or hypertension resulting in disability or death of paid officers of Maryland's National Capital Park and Planning Commission will now be presumed work related. The maximum amount allowable for funeral expenses was increased from $750 to $1,200.

Extraterritorial coverage was broadened by specifying the State shall have jurisdiction over work-related injuries and occupational diseases if an employment contract is made in Maryland for work to be done entirely outside the United States. The Subsequent Injury Fund, in addition to the employer, was discharged from liability for compensation after due benefits are paid an employee, but subjected to liability for additional benefits to make up the difference between the actual benefit furnished by the employer and the similar benefit required by the Workmen's Compensation Law. Appealed decisions of the Workmen's Compensation Commission were permitted to be remanded from the courts to the Commission for further proceedings, and the Commission was authorized to assess each self insurer an annual sum of $250.

Massachusetts

Payments for examinations of injured employees will now be remitted directly to the attending physicians by respective insurers promptly upon receipt of the approved bills.

Michigan

Handicapped employees, working at incorporated non-profit work activities centers or sheltered workshops as part of their rehabilitation, may receive compensation less than for total disability, but not less than 25 percent of the State's average weekly wage or 100 percent of the employee's weekly earnings at the time of injury, whichever is less. Two or more public employers are permitted to pool their liabilities for the purpose of qualifying as self insurers. The assessment was changed on workers' compensation insurance carriers for financing operations of the Safety Education and Training Division relative to occupational health and safety.

Minnesota

Coverage was extended to members of the State legislature; to certain professional athletes, and voluntary uncompensated workers of the Minnesota historical society. However, nonprofit associations which do not pay more than $500 in salaries per year and officers of family farm corporations, were exempted. Coverage will now apply automatically to exempt owners of businesses or farms upon the procurement of workers' compensation insurance unless a written disclaimer is filed.

Maximum weekly benefits for disabilities and death were changed to 100 percent of the State's average weekly wage. Formerly, benefits for total disabilities and death were adjusted annually according to a specified formula of the State's wage; and for permanent partial disability, a statutory amount of $135 was prescribed for schedule disabilities, and $100 for nonschedule. The weekly minimum for total disabilities will be not less than 50 percent of the State's wage or the injured employee's actual wage, whichever is less; but the absolute weekly minimum of 20 percent of the State's wage was retained.

The proportion of the State's wage which is used for computing supplementary benefits was increased from 50 to 60 percent; and the period for notice of injury, from 90 to 180 days. Employers were required to alter or remodel the principal residence of a permanently disabled employee to allow free movement into and throughout the residence, as determined by the Division of Workers' Compensation or the Workers' Compensation Court of Appeals. If alteration or remodeling is not practicable, the employer is required to purchase or lease a residence. Expenses for this purpose are limited to prevailing costs in the respective community, not to exceed $30,000. A Workers' Compensation Study Commission was created to review various aspects of workers' compensation insurance and administrative procedures.

Mississippi

The Workmen's Compensation Commission was authorized to increase the number of administrative judges from 6 to 8 and to establish a Rehabilitation Unit, but the authority to establish the unit will be rescinded in mid-1979.

Missouri

Full medical care was authorized by the removal of the 180-day limit on medical treatment furnished injured employees by employers. References to "referees" were changed to "administrative law judges"; and judges of the Division of Workmen's Compensation may now be temporarily assigned to branch offices as necessary to insure proper administration of the law.

Montana

Certain students enrolled in vocational rehabilitation or other on-the-job training programs were excluded from coverage. Various provisions of the Occupational Disease Act were amended to conform with the Workers' Compensation Act. Maximum compensation increased from $5,000 to $10,000 for workers who are discharged from employment or transferred to a lower paying job or who cease employment because of an occupational disease that is not disabling, and the maximum funeral allowance was raised from $500 to $1,100. The Medical Panel was replaced with two panels—the Pulmonary Specialist Medical Panel and the Occupational Disease Medical Panel. Additionally, references to "silicosis" were changed to "pulmonary disease." Unlimited medical care was authorized for workers totally disabled from an occupational disease; and the maximum payable for medical treatment to employees who are able to continue working while receiving treatment was increased from $1,000 to $2,500. The provision was repealed which allowed employers, within a certain period, to require employees to submit to medical exams so that employers would not be liable for disabilities resulting from normal progression of existing diseases.

An Uninsured Employers Fund was created which provides the employees of uninsured employers the option of either suing the employer for damages or filing a claim against the newly created fund for benefits; and if an employee, or representative, elects to sue an employer, the common law defenses will not be available to the employer. Other enactments relating to insurance will strengthen penalties on, and encourage competition among, insurers.

Nebraska

Corporate executives, who own at least 25 percent of common stock, were permitted to waive coverage; however, coverage will apply automatically if a waiver is not filed. Maximum weekly benefits for disability and death were raised from $100 to $140. The period for filing claims and the statute of limitations were extended to 2 years.

Nevada

Coverage was extended to real estate brokers and salespeople who earn at least $900 monthly in wages or commissions; and numerical exemptions were eliminated for occupational disease coverage. "Casual employment" was redefined to mean that the work contemplated is to be completed in 20 (formerly 10) working days or parts thereof in a calendar quarter, at a total labor cost of $500 (formerly $100), regardless of number of employees. Certain voluntary ski patrolmen were excluded from coverage.

Circumstances were broadened for awarding lump sums in permanent partial disability cases; and a provision which limited the payment of benefits for hernias was repealed.

A position was added for another appeals officer in the Industrial Commission, and such officers now must be attorneys. In appeal cases, a final decision will be mandatory within 120 days after a hearing. An Office of State Industrial Attorney was created to represent claimants before appeals officers and the district court if they are financially unable to employ private counsel. Covered employers must report all accidents to the Commission within 6 days, and also must report when an injured employee is initially examined or treated by a physician, or subsequently receives medical care. The Commission was required to review each report to determine whether employers are adequately furnishing services. The Commission was further required to provide Statewide, tollfree telephone service to claimants. The legislative commission was directed to conduct a comprehensive study of the administrative procedures of the Industrial Commission and the desirability of permitting coverage to be provided through private carriers and self insurance.

New Hampshire

The Director of the Fish and Game Commission was authorized to organize a Deputy Conservation Officer Force with the same coverage as for State employees. Also, if a public employer chooses to self insure, the legislature is now required to appropriate sufficient funds to implement a self-insurance program based on actuarial amounts; any funds not encumbered at the end of the fiscal year may be transferred to the general fund of the employer.

New Jersey

Workers' compensation may now be reduced by the amount of a worker's disability pension benefits, but not by the amount of retirement pension benefits.

New Mexico

Death benefits were extended to dependent children until 23 years of age if they are full-time students in accredited schools; and the meaning of "dependent children" was broadened to include a grandchild, brother, or sister. Also, where there is no surviving spouse, payments to dependent children were increased from 35 to 66⅔ percent of the decedent's average weekly wage; however, the additional 15-percent compensation for each child in excess of two was eliminated. Payments to a surviving spouse were raised from 50 to 66⅔ percent. Although percentages to surviving spouses with children were reduced in certain cases, the overall maximum of 66⅔ percent of the decedent's average weekly wage was retained. A lump sum equal to 2 years of compensation (not to exceed an amount which equals the current 600-week limitation) will be awarded to a surviving spouse upon remarriage. Full medical benefits were authorized by eliminating the $40,000 maximum on medical and rehabilitation services. The Occupational Disease Disablement Law was modified to reflect these changes.

A Workmen's Compensation Retention Fund was established to pay coverage premiums for State employees. Procedures were altered for disqualifying judges in workers' compensation cases.

New York

Maximum weekly compensation for permanent total disability was increased to $125 to keep pace with the maximum currently payable for temporary total disability; on July 1, 1978, these benefits will increase to $180;

and on January 1, 1979, to $215. Benefits for permanent partial disability will rise to $105 weekly in early 1978. Supplemental benefits will now be paid for permanent total disabilities occurring before July 1 of 1974, rather than 1970; and total loss of use of the eyes and limbs was included in the meaning of such disability. The compensation of a surviving spouse, if also receiving social security benefits, can be reduced by an amount up to 50 percent of the social security benefits.

A system of uniform rates was developed for hospital services provided by employers under the law. A nine-member joint labor-management committee was created to study issues related to workers' compensation.

North Carolina

Coverage was extended to volunteer officers of the Board of Alcoholic Control. The aggregate maximum for serious disfigurement and loss of important organs or parts of the body was increased from $7,500 to $10,000. Permanent total disability compensation was increased for injuries occurring before July 1, 1973; and a formula was set up for computing the increase. "Widower" was redefined to also mean a husband who was dependent on the wife for support, or a husband who for justifiable cause was living apart from the wife at the time of her death. Benefits will now be paid in certain cases pending appeal.

The Forsyth County Hospital Authority, Inc., and the Wake County Hospital System, Inc., were authorized to purchase workers' compensation insurance or to self insure. Assessments on employers and carriers for financing the Second Injury Fund were augmented. The chairman of the Industrial Commission was authorized to designate a deputy commissioner to replace a commissioner on review of any case. Applications for award review must now be submitted to the Commission within 15 days from the date when the award notice is given (formerly 7 days).

North Dakota

The maximum weekly benefit was increased from $60 to $75; the lump sum payable to nondependent children when there are no other survivors, increased from $1,000 to $2,000; and the funeral allowance, from $750 to $1,000. Death benefits eligibility was extended to dependents of employees who died as a result of a work-related aggravation of a prior noncompensable injury or condition; and time for filing claims was increased from 60 days to 1 year from the date of the employee's injury or death. Benefits are now paid to surviving spouses, rather than widows only.

Oklahoma

During 1978, coverage will be extended to any employment not enumerated statutorily, if the employer had an annual payroll of more than $100,000 for the preceding calendar year. The list of covered public employments was expanded, but coverage for county officials and employees engaged in hazardous employment, except for county sheriffs and deputies, is now permissive, not mandatory.

The statutory maximum weekly benefit will increase from $50 to $110 for permanent total disabilities by January 1, 1980, and to $90 for permanent partial disabilities by January 1, 1981. However, maximum weekly benefits will change to 66⅔ percent of the State's average weekly wage for permanent total disabilities by 1981, and 50 percent for permanent partial disabilities by 1982. The 500-week period set on benefits for permanent total disability was eliminated; and the period of payment for certain permanent partial (schedule) injuries was increased. Effective July 1, 1978, the weekly benefit for temporary total disability will change from a statutory amount of $60 to 66⅔ percent of the State's wage. On that date, death benefits will be based on 75 percent of the State's wage; a 2-year lump sum will be payable to a surviving spouse upon remarriage; discrimination against widowers will be eliminated; and children will be eligible for compensation until age 23 if full-time students. The meanings of permanent impairment, permanent total disability, permanent partial disability, dependents, and occupational disease were broadened.

The waiting period for eligibility of benefits was reduced from 5 to 3 days. The Workmen's Compensation Law is now titled the Workers' Compensation Act.

Oregon

Volunteer emergency service personnel working part time were excluded from the provision exempting such personnel from mandatory coverage. "Casual employment" was redefined to mean work in any 30-day period without regard to number of employees at a total labor cost of less than $200, rather than $100. Certain amateur athletes were exempted from coverage; as were newspaper carriers and specific persons who engage in transportation of logs or poles by motor vehicle. Also, certain political subdivisions were permitted to elect to self insure.

The rate of compensation for permanent partial disability was increased from $70 to $85 per degree of rated disability. Increases of benefits, payable from the Retroactive Reserve, were prohibited to claimants whose injuries occurred on or after April 1, 1974. An offset of social security benefits against compensation was created. And presumptive conditions for disability of firemen due to occupational disease were broadened.

Disability prevention services were newly provided for injured employees to prevent injuries from causing long-term total disabilities, including physical restoration, psychological and psychiatric evaluation, counseling and vocational rehabilitation. However, employers are now permitted to petition the director of the State Accident Fund for an appropriate reduction of benefits if an employee fails to follow medical advice or refuses to participate in or complete physical restoration or vocational rehabilitation programs.

A Department of Workers' Compensation was created to replace the Workers' Compensation Board; and a Field Services Division was established within the Board to promptly contact and assist injured workers. Procedures governing appeals were altered; insurance arrangements were amended; penalties were stiffened; and references to "workmen" were changed to "workers" throughout the law.

South Carolina

The amount deemed to be the average weekly wage used in determining benefits for volunteer firefighters was increased from $40 to $84. Maximum weekly compensation for partial disability was increased from 66⅔ to 100 percent of the State's average weekly wage; and the 52-week period of payments for partial disability, due to occupational disease, was eliminated. The inhalation of fumes, as well as dust, resulting in pulmonary disease may now constitute a compensable claim; and the 1-year exposure requirement was deleted in all cases, except for byssinosis —which has a minimum 7-year exposure period. The Industrial Commission, rather than the Chief Insurance Commissioner, will now assess and collect taxes on self insurers.

South Dakota

The percentage of interest payable on lump-sum payments was raised from 3 to 5 percent per annum; and the 1-year statute of limitation for filing claims for disability or death due to occupational disease was eliminated.

Injured workers are now permitted to pursue recovery under the Workers' Compensation Law or the circuit court when employers have elected not to operate under that law—but benefits can be doubled. Statutes concerning exclusive rights and remedies of employees were clarified.

Tennessee

Epileptic employees were permitted to waive coverage for injury resulting from epilepsy, but remain subject to coverage for other injuries. The maximum weekly payments for disability and death were increased from $85 to $100; and the aggregate maximum, from $34,000 to $40,000. Full medical care was provided by the removal of the 3-year limit on employers' liability for medical benefits. In addition, full coverage of occupational diseases was authorized, and diseases of the heart or lung, and hypertension attributable to employment were deemed occupational diseases.

Texas

Coverage was extended to prisoners involved in work furlough programs. By a majority vote of the governing body, political subdivisions can now extend coverage to their elected officials, and self insure. Members of the State military forces and nonresidents performing services for a political subdivision of the State or Federal Government were exempted from coverage. Employees of specific agencies of the Board of Regents of Texas Tech University will now receive the same coverage as other State employees, rather than having coverage controlled by the Board.

Extraterritorial coverage was broadened by permitting Texas residents injured outside the State to file claims under the State's statutes if recruited for employment within the State.

The burial allowance was raised from $500 to $1,250. Repairs or replacements of artificial appliances will now be provided when needed, unless such need is due to improper care by the employee; and services of doctors of podiatric medicine were included within medical care. If a State agency fails to make timely payments, the claimant will be entitled to additional compensation; and $1,700,000 was appropriated from the General Revenue Fund for the payment of claims for State employees.

The term "workmen" was changed to "workers" throughout the statutes. Other laws were enacted relating to hearing procedures, third-party actions, liability for subsequent injuries, and assessments on insurers.

Utah

Employers of counties, cities, towns, and school districts were permitted to secure the payment of compensation in the same manner as other employers.

The minimum weekly benefit for permanent partial disability was increased from $35 to $45; and the weekly permanent total disability benefit for persons previously receiving payments was increased from $60 to $75. The issue of dependency must now be reviewed when wholly and partly dependent persons apply for a continuation of benefits; and discriminatory language relative to spouses was eliminated. Also, the weekly compensation rate is now rounded to the nearest dollar; and compensation payments were required to commence within 90 days of any final award of the Industrial Commission.

The Commission was authorized to order the payment of sums in excess of statutorily prescribed limitations for burial expenses and artificial appliance allowances, and to require an employer, or carrier, to maintain or replace worn out or obsolete artificial means or appliances.

Numerous provisions of the Occupational Disease Disability Law were changed to conform with the Workmen's Compensation Law.

Virginia

An Uninsured Employer's Fund was created to provide benefits for employees injured while employed by uninsured employers; the Industrial Commission will administer the fund. Penalties against employers for noncompliance with coverage requirements were stiffened. A review by the Commission for award adjustment, due to a change in claimant's condition, must be made within 24 months, (rather than 12 months) from the date of last payment of compensation. References to "firemen" were changed to "firefighters."

Washington

Elective coverage was extended to volunteer law enforcement officers, upon approval by the municipal corporation for which they work. However, jockeys will now be exempt while participating in or preparing horses for races licensed by the State Horse Racing Commission; and employers defined as sole proprietors, partners, or joint venturers are required to file notices with the Department of Labor and Industry if they wish to be included under the law.

Supplemental disability or death benefits will be provided to those persons on workers' compensation rolls between July 1, 1975, and July 1, 1977. Rehabilitation services will now include the cost of books, tuition, fees, supplies and transportation, up to an amount not to exceed $1,500 in any calendar year per employee; and the practice of reducing or suspending benefits for refusing rehabilitative treatment will not apply if an employee did so for good cause.

Penalty provisions were strengthened; procedures were amended relating to third-party actions; and the term "workmen" was changed to "workers" throughout the law.

West Virginia

The eligibility level of monthly payments to benefit recipients under the Disabled Workmen's Relief Fund was increased from $224 to $274 in permanent total disability cases; and from $210 to $260 in death cases. The provision which governs payment for hernia injuries was rescinded.

Wyoming

State officials were included within coverage provisions for State employees who are employed in occupations classified as extra hazardous. Extraterritorial coverage was broadened by permitting claims to be filed when employment is principally localized in the State; or a contract of hire was made in the State for work principally located elsewhere, including other States whose laws are not applicable to the employer or the injured employee. Also, awards made under other State statutes will not bar a worker's rights to, but will be credited against, benefits under the Wyoming law.

Benefits were extended to mentally or physically disabled children until they reach age 21, and the aggregate maximum of $20,000 payable in such cases was eliminated. Balance levels of the Reinsurance Fund were modified for suspension or resumption of assessments. A sum of $10,000 was appropriated from the Industrial Accident Reserve to retain an actuarial firm to develop and submit recommendations to a joint or select committee concerning an occupational premium rate system based on the accident experience of each employer; and the committee is to conduct an interim study relative to this subject and the adoption of an administrative adjudication system for the law. ☐

———FOOTNOTE———

[1] The report, *Workers' Compensation: Is There a Better Way?*, is based on the Task Force's findings but does not contain the results of technical assistance nor a complete summation of the research studies; reports are forthcoming on these details.

Workers' compensation laws— key State amendments of 1978

While coverage was slightly narrowed, all but four of the States increased temporary total disability benefits; many States streamlined procedures, and some added penalties for abuses

GERRI MINOR

It was a light year for legislative changes in workers' compensation. In 1978, States enacted 170 amendments, compared with more than 300 in 1977.

But there were signs 1979 may be busier. Dissatisfied with the present system, Florida decided to scrap its workers' compensation statute and start all over again. And Maryland and Rhode Island were taking hard looks at their systems, with an eye to overhauling them.

Six years after the report of the National Commission on State Workmen's Compensation Laws, no State had fully enacted its recommendations for reform.

All but four States did increase weekly payments for temporary total disability. Payments now range from $87.50 in Arkansas to $607.85 in Alaska. Because of the many State variables involved, such as average earnings and duration of benefits, it is difficult to compute a valid national median.

Several States also improved benefits for permanent disability. Twenty-five States placed emphasis on administrative changes designed to clarify or simplify the responsibilities of all parties involved

in a workers' compensation case. Additionally, penalties were established or strengthened to ensure that such responsibilities would be carried out. While some State efforts focused on better administration, important changes in coverage and benefits occurred.

For example, California extended coverage to in-home personnel who assist welfare recipients; however, volunteers working for certain nonprofit organizations were exempted. Colorado now covers members of the Civil Air Patrol and certain apprentices on a discretionary basis. Florida limited coverage to employment of three workers or more; formerly, no numerical exemption existed. Iowa provided coverage for penal inmates when working under State authority, while Minnesota, New Jersey, and Virginia extended coverage to certain court and law enforcement officers.

Tennessee now deems anyone who regularly operates a business an employee for coverage purposes. However, Minnesota applied limitations on coverage for certain corporate executives, and Mississippi exempted other forms of self-employment. Minnesota changed the definition of "family farm," raising the wage exemption for farmworkers from $2,000 to $4,000, thereby reducing employer liability based on payroll limitations. Missouri excluded from coverage, with certain exceptions,

Gerri Minor is a workers' compensation specialist in the Division of State Workers Compensation Standards, Employment Standards Administration, U.S. Department of Labor.

Table 1. Jurisdictions which increased maximum weekly temporary total disability benefits during 1978[1]

Jurisdiction	Former maximum	New maximum	Jurisdiction	Former maximum	New maximum
Alabama	$120.00	$128.00			
Alaska	$551.86	$607.85			
Arizona	$153.85, plus $2.30 for total dependents	$192.32			
Arkansas	$84.00	$87.50	Nebraska	$140.00	$155.00
Colorado	$161.42	$173.60	Nevada	$198.22	$212.02
Connecticut	$147.03, plus $10 for each dependent child not to exceed 75 percent of employee's wage	$160.00, plus $10 for each dependent child not to exceed 75 percent of employee's wage	New Hampshire	$169.00	$180.00
Delaware	$144.00	$154.50	New Jersey	$138.00	$146.00
District of Columbia	$367.22	$396.78	New Mexico	$142.59	$172.46
Florida	$119.00	$126.00	New York	$125.00	$180.00
Georgia	$95.00	$110.00	North Carolina	$168.00	$178.00
Hawaii	$179.00	$189.00	North Dakota	$171.00, plus $5 for each dependent child; aggregate not to exceed worker's net wage after taxes and social security	$180.00, plus $5 for each dependent child; aggregate not to exceed worker's net wage after taxes and social security
Idaho	$99.00 to $148.50, according to number of dependents	$109.80 to $164.70, according to number of dependents	Ohio	$198.00	$216.00
Illinois	$304.21	$321.50	Oklahoma	$121.00	$132.00
Iowa	$247.00	$265.00	Oregon	$213.78	$224.16
Kansas	$120.95	$129.06	Pennsylvania	$199.00	$213.00
Kentucky	$104.00	$112.00	Rhode Island	$166.00, plus $6 for each dependent; aggregate not to exceed 80 percent of worker's average weekly wage	$176.00, plus $6 for each dependent; aggregate not to exceed 80 percent of worker's average weekly wage
Louisiana	$95.00	$130.00	South Carolina	$160.00	$172.00
Maine	$220.93	$231.72	South Dakota	$130.00	$155.00
Maryland	$188.00	$202.00	Texas	$91.00	$105.00
Massachusetts	$150.00, plus $6 for each dependent; aggregate not to exceed worker's average weekly wage	$211.37, plus $6 for each dependent; aggregate not to exceed worker's average weekly wage	Utah	$183.00	$197.00
Michigan	$127.00 to $156.00, according to number of dependents	$142.00 to $171.00, according to number of dependents	Utah	$183.00	$197.00
			Vermont	$170.00, plus $5 for each dependent under 21 years of age	$181.00, plus $5 for each dependent under 21 years of age
Minnesota	$197.00	$209.00	Virginia	$175.00	$187.00
Missouri	$95.00	$115.00	Washington	$163.38	$175.30
Montana	$174.00	$188.00	West Virginia	$208.00	$224.00
			Wisconsin	$189.00	$202.00
			Wyoming	$189.86	$211.15

[1] Benefit increases are based on the applicable State's average weekly wage; and for the District of Columbia, the national average weekly wage. However, 10 States (Arizona, Arkansas, California, Georgia, Indiana, Mississippi, Missouri, Nebraska, New York, and Tennessee) prescribe statutory amounts; four (California, Indiana, Mississippi, and Tennessee) are not listed as no increases for temporary total disability were legislated during 1978.

occasional domestic help and any owner of a family farm corporation.

Connecticut increased the proportion of the State's average weekly production wage, upon which maximum benefits are based, from 66⅔ percent to 85 percent. West Virginia also amended its compensation formula, by increasing the percentage of the employee's wage, upon which compensation is based, from 66⅔ percent to 70 percent. Delaware changed the maximum weekly compensation payable for permanent partial disability from $75 to 66⅔ percent of the State's average weekly wage, and the minimum from $25 to 22⅖ percent. Kentucky eliminated a wage loss method of computing benefits and instituted a formula based on 66⅔ percent of the worker's wage subject to a maximum of 60 percent of the State's average weekly wage. (See table 1 for temporary total disability rate increases.) Rhode Island provided for cost-of-living increases based on the Consumer Price Index, while Louisiana and Florida established offsets against compensation.

Specific monetary amounts for workers' compensation were raised in Georgia, Nebraska, Massachusetts (death benefits), and Missouri; South Carolina eliminated a total amount of $40,000 previously set as the maximum payable.

Death benefits were improved in 12 States. West Virginia, for example, extended benefits to dependent children until 25 years of age if enrolled full time in accredited schools. This change complies, in part, with one of the key recommendations of the national commission. (Congressional hearings were held last year on a bill which proposes establishment of minimum compensation standards for the States.)

The Federal Interdepartmental Workers' Compensation Task Force, which, among other things, provided technical assistance to States for improved workers' compensation operations was dissolved. This responsibility was assigned to the Division of State Workers' Compensation Standards, Employment Standards Administration, U.S. Department of Labor.

Following is a summary, by State, of 1978 workers' compensation legislation.

Arizona

Employers are now entitled to direct payment, or a credit, for compensation benefits paid under a medical, wage loss, or disability benefits plan. Additionally, failure of employers or physicians to file certain required reports in workers' compensation cases is now considered a "petty offense."

California

Coverage was extended to homemakers and other in-home supportive personnel provided to recipients of public assistance by county welfare departments.

The status of certain vendors or carriers of newspapers or other periodicals shall not be affected by an employer's election to provide workers' compensation. Volunteers for tax-exempt, private, nonprofit organizations are exempted from coverage. In relation to the Longshoremen's and Harbor Workers' Compensation Act, the State Fund was authorized to provide insurance on a permanent basis; and a joint resolution was approved which urges the Congress to pass pending legislation which could alleviate certain problems of fish companies and boatyards.

"Temporary" total disability benefits are now payable for any period of incapacitation, rather than only the first 2 years; the amount payable shall be based on the current benefit level, rather than the level in effect at the time of injury. Burial allowances were increased from a maximum of $1,000 to $1,500.

Provisions prohibiting discrimination were strengthened by creating employee rights for reinstatement and reimbursement for lost wages and work benefits. Insurance carriers will be subject to misdemeanor penalties if they threaten, advise, or otherwise direct employers to discharge employees involved in these cases. Decisions of the Workmen's Compensation Appeals Board must be appealed within 45 days, rather than 30, after reconsideration is denied.

Regarding funding, the accounting practices of the General Fund now provide that in no-dependency death cases employers shall pay amounts which otherwise would have been payable as a death benefit. These payments will be credited as a reimbursement if the Fund pays for injuries involving other employees. The State appropriated $104,000 to the Department of Industrial Relations, as well as $700,000 from the General Fund, for payment of such injuries.

Colorado

Coverage was provided for members of the Colorado wing of the Civil Air Patrol. The Joint Apprenticeship and Training Committee may now, at its discretion, cover individuals receiving job training.

Connecticut

Maximum weekly benefits were increased from 66⅔ percent to 85 percent of the State's average weekly production wage. The waiting period for benefits to surviving spouses was eliminated in cases where payments were made to employees for more than 2 years.

The Vocational Rehabilitation Division was transferred from the Department of Human Resources to the State Board of Education. Physicians' fees for reporting occupational diseases were eliminated.

The method of payment for expenses of the Workmen's Compensation Commission by insurance carriers and self-insurers was changed from a quarterly to an annual billing with a year-end adjustment.

Additionally, employees who suffer injuries caused by employer violations of State or Federal safety regulations will be entitled to compensation at the rate of 75 percent of their average weekly wage (compensation is normally paid at the rate of 66⅔ percent).

Delaware

Maximum weekly benefits for permanent partial disability were changed from $75 to 66⅔ percent of the State's average weekly wage; and the minimum from $25 to 22²⁄₉ percent. Death benefits were liberalized to allow children over 18 years of age, who are mentally or physically disabled, to continue receiving benefits, providing the decedent was contributing to at least 50 percent of their support.

Employers will be required to replace or renew defective or worn prostheses for the life of an injured person without a new claim period.

A Workmen's Compensation Commission was established to study the status of insurance in the State and report to the governor and the General Assembly, on or before March 1, 1979.

Florida

Coverage under the Workmen's Compensation Act is limited to employment of three employees or more, and volunteers who serve in nonprofit private agencies are exempted. Immunity from common law suits filed by an injured worker was extended to fellow employees acting in furtherance of the employer's business, providing the latter are not assigned to work primarily unrelated to that performed by the injured worker.

In all cases of "unscheduled" permanent partial disability where the percentage of disability is 10 percent or less, the worker is entitled to compensation for a portion of 175 weeks; if disability is between 10 percent and 50 percent, compensation will be paid for a portion of 350 weeks; and if disability is between 50 percent and 99 percent, a portion of 525 weeks.[1] Compensation for total disability will now be reduced by the amount of unemployment compensation received by the worker.

The Division of Labor was authorized to adopt fee schedules for hospital treatment. The reporting time in which employers are required to report injuries or fatalities to their insurance carriers was extended from 7 to 10 days; and a penalty was established for employer failure to pay compensation within 14 days of the date it is due.

Claims based on diminution of wage-earning capacity now mature 90 days after the worker has reached maximum medical improvement and are to be based on the extent of the claimant's physical impairment, his or her education and work history, ability to compete in the labor market, and evidence of a good-faith work search.

Carriers are now required to make available, at the option of the employer, a policy containing a coinsurance provision whereby the carrier pays 80 percent, and the employer 20 percent, of the first $5,000 in medical benefits. Benefits above $5,000 are to be paid in full by the carrier and in the first instance the carrier pays all benefits, but shall be reimbursed by the employer to the extent of the coinsurance provision. If the employer cannot do so, the carrier is not required to offer coinsurance.

A joint legislative committee was established to review the Workers' Compensation Act and prepare recommendations to the Legislature on March 1, 1979. In recognition of the seriousness of the problems in the existing system and the urgent need for major reform, the entire Workmen's Compensation Act is repealed as of July 1, 1979.

Georgia

The word "workmen's" was changed to "workers" throughout the law. The maximum weekly benefit for total disability and death was increased from $95 to $110; and for temporary partial disability from $70 to $80. The number of weeks payable for the loss, or loss of use, of an arm was extended from 200 to 225 weeks. The percentage used in commuting lump-sum payments was raised from 5 percent to 7 percent; and partial lump-sum advance payments are no longer allowed. Permanent partial disability payments are prohibited when benefits for total or temporary partial disability are being paid.

Premature payments to an employee will now be deducted from any future compensation. Income benefits will be paid "periodically, promptly, and directly" to the eligible person without an award. When the employer denies liability, payments must be made no later than 14 days after the employer has knowledge of the injury. Thereafter, benefits will be paid weekly. Provides a 15-percent penalty for benefits 14 days overdue and a 20-percent penalty for late payments of awards.

A time requirement of 2 years was deleted in cases in which any award or settlement can be reviewed or modified because of a change in condition. The 1-year statute of limitations for filing claims was retained, but in case of payment for remedial treatment or weekly benefits by the employer, a claim may be filed within 1 year of last remedial treatment or within 2 years of the last payment of benefits. A fine of not less than $100 nor more than $1,000 will be assessed against any employer or insurer who willfully violates the filing and reporting procedures of the Board of Workers' Compensation, unless a written request for a hearing has been made within 10 days of the assessment date.

Hawaii

It is now unlawful for employers to suspend or discharge a worker solely because the employee suffers a work-related injury.

The Department of Labor and Industrial Relations was requested to coordinate with workers' compensation insurers and self-insurers in offering safety consultation services.

Idaho

Maximum burial allowances were raised from $750 to $1,500; and the section which had reduced compensation to a nonresident alien dependent was repealed. Employees must receive written notice within 15 days of any change of status which affects the level of benefits. Limitations will not run against a claim until the notice is filed. The Office of Manager of the Second Injury Fund was established in the Department of Administration; the manager will investigate claims, make agreements, and pay awards made against the fund. Employer liability shall be further reduced, as prior permanent physical impairment will be required to qualify under second injury law and the requirement for payment of $2,000 to the administration and second injury funds in no-dependency death cases was repealed.

Claims for disability due to occupational disease must now be filed within a year of disablement or manifestation of the disease.

In 1974, the Legislature enacted a law to provide, on an experimental basis, a program of physical and vocational rehabilitation for disabled workers. The temporary program expired July 1, 1977, but an amendment made it permanent.

Iowa

Coverage was extended to inmates while performing under State authority; immunity from civil liability was authorized for insurance companies when making safety inspections of the workplace; and additional funding was set for the Second Injury Fund through employer or carrier assessment.

Kentucky

Claimants are now permitted to be treated by a licensed chiropractor of their choice.

The wages loss method of computing compensation was eliminated; however, a new formula bases income benefits on 66⅔ percent of the employee's average weekly wage, multiplied by the percentage of disability, subject to a maximum of 60 percent of the State's average weekly wage. In cases where death is unrelated to the injury, income benefits continue to dependents during the compensable period or during the period of the decedent's normal life expectancy, whichever is shorter.

Additionally, if the Board finds as a fact that an employee remains incapacitated because of the work-related injuries or disabilities the employee may continue to receive compensation beyond the stated number of weeks. If a subsequent injury or occupational disease has resulted in additional permanent disability, the total of weekly benefits may not exceed 60 percent of the State's average weekly wage.

Assets of the Uninsured Employers' Fund were set at $50,000, by transfer of sufficient moneys from the Maintenance Fund to maintain the $50,000 threshold.

Louisiana

Permanent total disability benefits will be reduced for those recipients who are also receiving Federal Old Age, Survivors, and Disability Insurance Benefits. The reduction will be made only to the extent that the amount of the combined Federal and State workers' compensation benefits would otherwise cause, or result in, a reduction of the Federal benefits relating to Social Security Disability Insurance Benefits. Claimants may now be reimbursed for the actual cost of a physician's examination and report.

A joint Senate and House committee on governmental affairs was directed to study the feasibility of the State becoming a self-insurer in various areas of liability, including workers' compensation.

Maine

The name of the Industrial Accident Commission was changed to Workers' Compensation Commission; the Commission is now exempted from the State's Administrative Procedures Act, granting it more authority. Salaries were increased for the chairman of the Commission and for those members with more than 4 years of experience. The salary for each of the other members was set at $18,900. Additionally, Commission membership was raised from 6 to 8, with 6, rather than 4, being attorneys (formerly limited to men) who are members of the State's Bar Association.

Directs each State agency to cooperate fully with the Bureau of Labor in its efforts to compile labor and industrial statistics.

Notice procedures in cases before the Workers' Compensation Commission were simplified by directing commissioners to send hearing notices, decisions, finding of fact, rulings of law, and so on, to the attorney of record for each party, if not directly to all parties in interest; new appeal procedures, for use by the commissioners, were approved. In relation to employer/carrier penalties, the specification that all penalties collected shall be deposited with the State Treasurer was deleted from the law; and guilt for failure to secure compensation payments is now a Class D (more serious) crime. Additionally, statutes were deleted which provided that those persons guilty of willfully making false statements to obtain benefits shall be subject to a fine not exceeding $50, and shall forfeit all rights which they may have to compensation under the Workers' Compensation Act.

Claims for compensation for occupational deafness may no longer be filed until after the employee has been "separated from occupational noise" for at least 30 days; the last day of the period becomes the date of disability. The term "separation from occupational noise" was defined to mean the use of hearing protective devices or equipment, including noise attenuators and ear plugs.

Maryland

The period of payment for certain mutilation and disfigurement was extended from 100 to 156 weeks.

Accident leave with full pay was provided for State employees, but receipt of temporary total benefits is prohibited while collecting such full pay.

State firefighting instructors are now permitted to receive compensation for any condition or impairment of health caused by lung or heart diseases.

The Workmen's Compensation Commission is now required to make assessments against employers, to supplement the State Accident Fund; and to assess each insurer $150, payable to the Uninsured Employers Fund, for noncompliance with requirements concerning certification of insurance. Funds belonging to the State Accident Fund will now be invested by the State treasurer, rather than the Board of Public Works.

The governor was directed to appoint a study commission to consider the problem of industrial health and the adequacy of workers' compensation coverage and to report by December 1, 1978, with recommendations for any legislation deemed necessary.

Massachusetts

Benefits were increased for surviving spouses from $55 to $110 weekly; increases were also applied to compensation for dependent children. The total amount payable was raised from $16,000 to $32,000. These increases apply to cases occurring on or after November 1, 1978. Funeral benefits were increased from $1,000 to $2,000.

Conferences are now required in compensable cases to determine fees for attorneys and physicians when there is a disagreement between parties. Additionally, the requirement that one member of the 12-member Industrial Accident Board shall be a woman is now deleted. No more than six members maybe of the same political party.

Michigan

Professional athletes are now entitled to compensation only for those weeks in which all their earnings are less than 200 percent of the State average weekly wage. This will not apply to medical benefits, rehabilitation benefits, or payment for partial disability benefits. Additionally, a classified employee of the Michigan Department of State who is assaulted while on duty shall receive full wages until workers' compensation benefits begin. After the benefits begin, the employee shall receive, in addition to the worker's compensation benefits, a supplement from the Department which shall equal, but not exceed, his or her normal weekly wages at the time of the injury, up to 40 hours per week.

Cities, townships, counties, and villages are now considered public employers of the same type of unit and may form self-insurance groups. Private, nonprofit health care facility employers are also permitted to self-insure by joining public employee groups.

Minnesota

The definition of "family farm" was changed to increase the limit on wages for farm laborers from $2,000 to $4,000. Executive officers of closely held corporations are now specifically excluded from the act's definition of employee (thus, are excluded from automatic entitlement to the act's benefits), provided such officers both own at least 25 percent of the corporate stock and the corporation employed fewer than 11 full-time employees in the previous calendar year. The executive officers may, however, elect to come under the act by providing for the required insurance and are thus subject to the same provisions that govern farm owners and officers of family farm corporations. The Commissioner of Labor and Industry is authorized to approve "appropriate" pooling-of-liability agreements among employers for the purpose of their qualification as self-insurers.

Persons assisting law enforcement officials may now be eligible for benefits.

The limitation on the expense factor in setting workers' compensation insurance premiums was removed, and rates for expenses are now referred to the Workers' Compensation Study Commission. The 5-percent reduction of supplemental benefits is no longer applied when an employee does not receive the maximum benefits for which he or she is eligible under other governmental disability programs.

Mississippi

The Mississippi Department of Youth Services was authorized to acquire the liability insurance necessary to protect employees and others injured through the operation of its facilities. Exemption from coverage was applied to a buyer-seller or vendor-vendee when no employer-employee relationship exists.

The Workmen's Compensation Commission will now estimate expenses for administration annually, rather than semiannually. Every carrier and self-insurer will file a statement showing the gross compensation paid during the preceding year, on or before March 1, or be subject to a penalty of $20 per day for noncompliance.

Missouri

The definition of injury was expanded to include damage to artificial limbs and prostheses. Coverage is not applicable to occasional labor performed for and related' to a private household, or any one owning controlling interest in a family farm corporation, without special approval. The maximum weekly compensation for total disability and death was raised from $95 to $115; and for permanent partial disability, from $80 to $90. The weekly payment during rehabilitation was increased from $21 to $35.

Nebraska

The maximum weekly compensation for disability and death was increased from $140 to $155. Coverage was redefined to include surgery, plastic or reconstructive, when injury causes disfigurement. Dental appliances, hearings aids, eyeglasses if damage resulted from an accident, teeth, and other artificial members were also included without restriction.

Attorney fees may no longer be paid in a lump sum, but shall be paid out of each installment of compensation. Settlements and agreements to commute compensation to lump sums must now be verified by the respective parties, excepting petitions or answers to petitions. Stipulations between parties that claims will be heard in counties other than where the accident occurred must be filed at least 14 days before the hearing date.

New Hampshire

The exclusive remedy under the New Hampshire Workmen's Compensation Law shall now apply to the employer, the employer's insurance carrier, and any officer, director, agent, servant, or any other employee of the employer or insurance carrier. A spouse of an employee entitled to compensation shall have no right of action against any of these persons.

New Jersey

Those municipal police officers and investigators of the sheriff's office with statewide police powers now have all immunities and benefits, including workers' compensation coverage, while performing services in the employing municipality.

Reference to "workmen" was changed to "workers'" throughout the statutes.

New York

The title of the law was changed to the Workers' Compensation Law; and certain objectionable anachronistic terms such as "habitual drunkard" and "idiot" were replaced by such terms as "alcohol abuser" and "mentally ill."

The period of payment to dependent children was extended to age 23 if they are full-time students at an accredited school; the maximum amount payable for funeral expenses was increased from $750 to $1,250.

Wage expectancy may now be taken into account when determining the weekly basis for compensation for injured persons up to 25 years of age. Formerly, this consideration was extended to minors without an age limitation. The term "payroll," for assessment purposes, is limited to the first $6,000, rather than $4,200, of earnings for each employee during any calendar year.

Provisions to set rates and charges for workers' compensation hospital services were updated by allowing a one-year extension; and procedures for payment into the Vocational Rehabilitation Fund and the Special Fund for reopened no-dependency cases were revised.

Penalties for failure to secure compensation were increased. New penalties were established providing that any person, firm, or corporation (other than attorneys) attempting to represent claimants, and not duly authorized by the Workers' Compensation Board, shall be guilty of a misdemeanor.

Ohio

Authority was given to the Industrial Commission and Bureau of Workers' Compensation to use different methods to preserve necessary records and to make a supplemental appropriation for this purpose.

A limit on the amount of premium security deposit required of employers under workers' compensation was set; and a Premium Payment Security Fund was created to insure against any employer defaults in premium obligations.

Pennsylvania

Regulatory procedures were established relating to frequency of medical treatment rendered injured employees. Additionally, employers are now permitted to suspend compensation payments during the time the employee has returned to work at prior or increased earnings, providing a petition is filed to terminate or modify the compensation agreement or award within 15 days of the return to work.

The monthly compensation to workers totally disabled by reason of silicosis or asbestosis, whose claims are time-barred, was increased by $25, raising total monthly payments to $100.

Rhode Island

References to "workmen" were changed to "workers" throughout State statutes.

An annual cost-of-living increase was established for permanent total disability in accordance with the Consumer Price Index. However, eligibility for compensation benefits is now prohibited when injured employees become employed at an average weekly wage greater than that earned at the time of injury. The statute of limitations was extended from 2 to 3 years.

The name of the Medical Advisory Committee was changed to the Workers' Compensation Advisory Committee, which is charged with examining disputes. Other administrative changes occurred within the Workers' Compensation Commission relating to appointments and terms of commissioners; and appeal adjudication.

A resolution created a special legislative commission to study the State's workers' compensation laws. The commission will include members from the House of Representatives and Senate, the president of the Chamber of Commerce, and the president of the Rhode Island Chapter of the AFL-CIO. A report with recommendations is expected by the General Assembly on or before March 1, 1979.

South Carolina

A maximum limitation of $40,000 on workers'

compensation benefits was deleted from the law. Coverage for reserve police officers is now elective, rather than required.

Claims for pulmonary diseases shall now be referred to a medical doctor (in lieu of a medical panel) who specializes in pulmonary diseases and is employed by, or associated with, a medical university in the State, at the election of either party or the hearing commissioner. The 2-year limitation for filing claims for occupational disease commences from time of the physician's diagnosis and notification to the employee.

The membership of the Judicial Department of the Industrial Commission was increased from 6 to 7. Any person convicted of failing or refusing to comply with a commission subpoena shall be subject to imprisonment not to exceed 30 days as well as to a fine. The commission is now authorized to reduce the amount of the carriers' lien on proceeds from a third-party settlement or judgment between the third party and the injured employee, or the employee's representative, if the proceeds are less than the estimated value of the employee's damages as determined by the commission.

South Dakota

Any person performing labor incidental to his or her own occupation who has elected to come under the workers' compensation law may now be deemed an "employer" even if he or she has no employees.

Lump-sum settlements are eliminated in death cases except in the event of remarriage. Injured workers are permitted to recover for a subsequent permanent partial or total disability. The employer pays for the full disability and is reimbursed from the Second Injury Fund for any compensation paid in excess of the amount which would be payable for the last injury alone. If death results, the employer is reimbursed for compensation paid after the first 312 weeks.

Tennessee

A sole proprietor or a partner who devotes full time to a business may elect coverage by filing a notice with the Division of Workmen's Compensation at least 30 days before the occurrence of any injury or death. Occupational diseases arising out of or in the course of employment are now included within the definition of "injury" and "personal injury." The maximum burial allowance is increased from $750 to $1,250.

Additionally, notification is required by the director of the Division of Workmen's Compensation when an insurance carrier or employer makes first payment of benefits, stops or changes benefits for causes other than final settlement of a claim, or denies a claim after proper investigation. When the employer denies liability for compensation, a notice of controversy shall be filed within 15 days of the due date of the first omitted payment. Failure to make these notices is punishable by a fine of not more than $50. In these cases, prior payment by the employer shall not be considered a binding determination of obligations as to future payments, nor shall the acceptance of compensation be considered a binding determination of obligations as to future payments, nor the acceptance of compensation be considered a binding determination of the employee's rights.

Evidence of compliance with the workmen's compensation law by an employer or carrier must be filed with the Division of Workmen's Compensation within 30 days after procurement of suitable insurance or renewal of qualification as a self-insurer. A certificate of compliance must be conspicuously posted at the employer's place of business.

Vermont

Hearing aids are now included in medical coverage provisions. The employer penalty for failure to secure compensation was increased from $25 to $100 per day; survivor rights of widowers were equalized and limitations of rights to compensation were removed for widowers as well as widows in the event of remarriage. Allowance for funeral expenses was increased from $500 to $1,000. A 330-week restriction on payment of partial disability was eliminated, as well as a $7,000 maximum payable in silicosis and asbestosis cases.

Virginia

Supreme Court justices, circuit court judges, and other employees of the district courts are included within the definition of State employees, for coverage purposes. The secretary of administration and finance was authorized to initiate and implement a group workers' compensation insurance program (which accumulates maximum premium discounts on a state-wide basis) for all State employers after first determining that such a program will be less costly than the aggregate of individual agency policies.

"Preponderance of" was added to the meaning of competent evidence necessary to contradict the occupational disease presumption clause relating to death and disability from respiratory disease, hypertension or heart disease of specified firefighters and police officers.

West Virginia

The percentage of an employee's wage, upon which benefits are based, was increased from 66⅔ percent to 70 percent. The waiting period for commencement of payments was reduced from 14 to 7 days after first 3 days of disability. Benefits for hearing loss in one ear were raised from 15 to 25 percent, and loss in both ears from 45 to 65 percent. A 20-week entitlement to compensation was established for individuals who have occupational pneumoconiosis without measurable pulmonary impairment. Benefits to dependent children were extended from 23 to 25 years of age, providing they are full-time students in accredited schools. Employer rights to certain medical records were created, and new provisions were added which prohibit employer discrimination against employees who receive or attempt to receive workers' compensation. ☐

――――――FOOTNOTE――――――

[1] Unscheduled permanent partial disability is that physical impairment generally considered serious but not statutorily classified as the loss, or the loss of use, of a limb, loss of sight, hearing, and so on.

Research Summaries

Factors in more costly accidents drawn from compensated cases

HARVEY J. HILASKI

Medical and indemnity costs based on workers' compensation are frequently considered indicators of the severity of industrial accidents but are of limited value because they represent only a small portion of total costs. Ignored are the costs of lost or delayed production, to say nothing of the human costs of suffering.

Benefit amounts and the factors that affect the amount of compensation paid differ widely by State. Such factors include waiting-period differences, geographic variations in hospital costs, and varying legal influences in contested cases or out-of-court settlements. As a result, data among States are not comparable. Nevertheless, the study of compensated cases can help to delineate important causative factors, essential to the prevention or reduction of accidents and illnesses.[1]

The cases examined, all taken from a New York State study of cases occurring between 1966 and 1970,[2] were those in which payment of the claim was at least one and a half times greater than the average settlement of all compensated cases in New York.[3] In addition, the agency involved—the object, substance, or element of exposure—was clearly identified[4] (table 1).

Overall profile

The 72 specific agencies recorded 38,465 cases, or 6.5 percent of the cases covered in the New York study, and accounted for 15 percent of total costs ($1.1 billion). As shown in the following tabulation, 8 of the 72 agencies figured in more than two-thirds of the more costly cases:

Harvey J. Hilaski is a supervisory economist in the Office of Occupational Safety and Health Statistics, Bureau of Labor Statistics.

Agency	Number of cases	Average cost (in dollars)
Ladders	11,817	$3,039
Building in construction or demolition	4,445	3,323
Scaffolds and stagings	4,111	5,427
Shovel, spade	1,911	3,186
Contagious diseases, bacteria	1,165	3,190
Backhoe	1,014	3,840
Roofs	1,013	5,368
Fire engine, snow plow, utility	983	3,182

Specific agencies in the relatively few cases exceeding $10,000 were:

Specific agency	Number of cases	Average cost (in dollars)
Dyes, ink, paint	37	$11,382
Locomotive in motion	50	11,572
Parasites, bacteria	21	15,442
Metals, compounds	20	18,553
Heart attack	598	21,551
Plants and foods	82	21,891
Other noncorrosive dusts and particles	628	25,793

Ten of the 119 industries involved accounted for nearly 30 percent of the more costly cases:

Industry	Number of cases
Carpentry and wood flooring	486
Concrete work	599
General building contractors	4,387
Government hospitals	743
Heavy construction, except highway	964
Local government	1,021
Painting, paperhanging, decorating	1,017
Real estate operators and landlords	945
Roofing and sheetmetal work	733
Structural steel erection	547

Other frequently cited industries and the number of cases involved were:

Blast furnaces and basic steel manufacturing	79
Combination companies and systems	193
Excavation and foundation work	260
Fabricated structural metal products	273
Government transportation services	190
Highway, street construction	389
Plumbing, heating, and air conditioning	241
State government	81
Trucking, local and long distance	232

It is apparent from both lists of industries that construction accounted for a large number of the more costly cases. The Bureau of Labor Statistics' annual survey data indicate also that incidence rates for construction industries in general tend to be high.

Nature of injury

Fractures and concussions accounted for 70 percent of the cases. The proportion of fractures (67 percent) involved was triple the proportion in all accident cases. Fractures were generally associated

Table 1. Specific agencies involved in more costly accidents, by major agency of accident

Major agency	Location, type, or condition	Specific agency
Machines	Paper products	Die cutters
	Chemical goods	Rolls
	Stone, clay, glass	Drills, borers, lathes
	Laundry and dry cleaning	Rolls, ringer
		Rolls, mangle
	Farm and garden	Screens and separators
	Construction	Backhoe
		Pile drivers
		Road building and maintenance machines
	Mining, oil and ore refining	Drills and borers
	Metal briquettes	Baling presses
Elevators, hoists, conveyors	Freight elevator	Material hoist
	Hoists	Derrick
	Conveyor	Screw type
		Log jack
Hand tools	Hand and power tools	Pick axe
		Shovel, spade
		Ladle, skimmer
		Concrete vibrator
Vehicles	Motor in motion	Tractor
		Fire engine, plow, utility
	Railway vehicles	Subway and el train-moving
		Locomotive in motion
		Railroad car in motion
		Subway and el train at rest
	Aircraft	Airplane moving
	Other vehicle	Vehicle on track at rest
Boilers, electricity, explosives, chemicals	Boilers and pressure valves	Boiler, exploding furnace
		Cooking, processing
	Electrical apparatus	Third rail, trolley car
		Other transmission wire
		Other
	Explosives	Gases
		Organic solvents
		Dyes, ink, paint
		Other
	Chemicals	Gases
		Acids
		Organic solvents
		Dyes, ink, paint
		Metals, compounds
		Oils, resins
		Other
	Noncorrosive dusts and particles	Dyes, ink, paint
		Metals, compounds
		Plants, foods
		Other
	Parasites, bacteria	Contagious diseases, bacteria
		Other
Working surfaces	Special instances of working surfaces	Quarry, mine—from bench
	Floors, inside surface	Linoleum covered
	Platform, ramps	Scaffolds and stagings
		Runway, catwalk
		Plank over opening
	Roof openings, skylight	Roofs
	Fixed objects	Building in construction or demolition
		Window, wall opening
		Other building parts
		Other structures in construction or demolition
		Other structures not in construction or demolition
		Poles, trees
	Portable objects	Ladder
		Sawhorses
Miscellaneous objects	Stone, clay, glass stock, not elsewhere classified	Roof, wall—mine or quarry
	General aids to work	Compressed air
		Tires bursting
All other	Environmental conditions	Cold—frost bite
		Heat prostration
		Water, ice, snow, cold objects
	Positions assumed	Sitting
	General health conditions	Heart attack
		Drowning
		Other

with ladders, scaffolds and stagings, buildings in construction or demolition, roofs, backhoes, and other vehicles. The backhoe accounted for almost half of all construction machine injuries. Most cases of concussion occurred in falls from ladders and scaffolds. Blows, which accounted for the majority of all cases in the New York study, constituted fewer than 10 percent of the more costly cases.

Part of body affected

The trunk of the body was twice as likely to be involved in the injury and illness cases studied than any other part of the body. Upper body extremities and more than one part of the body, next highest in frequency, were about of equal relative importance.

Pattern differences

Although the distribution of costly cases by the nine major agencies of accident was appreciably different from that for all cases, the ranking by order of importance was markedly changed for only two major agencies—other miscellaneous objects[5] and boilers, electricity, explosives, and chemicals. Other miscellaneous objects accounted for 35 percent of all accident cases and ranked first among the nine agencies. Other miscellaneous objects accounted for slightly more than 3 percent of the more costly cases, ranking seventh among the nine agencies in terms of medical and indemnity costs. These objects figured prominently in cases involving materials handling, and although such cases were numerous, they were also less costly. Boilers, electricity, explosives, and chemicals accounted for about 4 percent of the 600,-000 cases (ranking seventh) but for 13 percent of the 38,000 cases studied (ranking second). Working surfaces were of relatively major importance in the incidence of the more costly cases and cases generally. The significance of ladders as working surfaces is most conspicuous in terms of cost, but they accounted for only about 2 percent of total cases.

Implications

There are various approaches to accident prevention efforts. One approach is to concentrate on areas of high incidence. From the employer's viewpoint, high incidence may be associated with accidents in particular plant departments, particular agencies such as saws or presses, or particular types of accident, such as falls. From the point of view of public policy, high incidence is usually associated with high-risk industries. An example of this is the Occupational Safety and Health Administration's early enforcement emphasis on five target industries,[6] under the "worst-first" principle.

Another approach is to concentrate on costly accidents, as suggested by this study. From the employer's viewpoint, the occurrence of costly accidents can adversely affect his experience rating and lead to increased insurance premiums. Unfortunately, the responsiveness of an employer is limited by his awareness of cost, which is all too often lacking or confused. Public policy can also be aimed at costly accidents and, if directed at the same time to those of highest incidence, can help achieve simultaneous benefits of cost reduction for the employer and of injury or illness reduction for the Nation's workers. □

---FOOTNOTES---

[1] For a study of employers' reports in compensation cases, see John Mazor, "How accurate are employers' illness and injury reports?" *Monthly Labor Review,* September 1976, pp. 26–31.

[2] See *Characteristics and Costs of Work Injuries in New York State, 1966–1970: Summary Tabulations,* 3 vols. (Ithaca, N.Y., Department of Labor, Division of Research and Statistics, 1972). Also see Arlen J. Slobodow, "Motor vehicles and occupational injuries in New York State," *Monthly Labor Review,* December 1974, pp. 57–61.

[3] The average cost for all cases was $1,918. Specific agencies were selected if the average cost of the cases involved was $3,000 or over. Other subcriteria: the specific agency had to be involved in at least 15 cases of injury or illness over the 5-year period; all cases were omitted where the agency was in the "Not indicated" category, even though the category met the average cost criterion; and, finally, for any specific agency the average cost criterion was applied to associated natures of injury, parts of the body affected, accident types, and industry to derive a profile of relatively high cost accidents by all these characteristics.

[4] The other major agency not represented in this report was "Prime movers and power transmission."

[5] The "Other miscellaneous objects" category includes such diverse materials as containers, packages, furniture, woodstock, metal stock, and so on, and general aids to work.

[6] The five target industries were roofing and sheet metal work; meat products; lumber and wood products; miscellaneous transportation equipment; and water transportation services.

State Labor Legislation

State labor legislation enacted in 1976

*The pace of new legislation protecting
workers slowed last year, but some States
did enact significant safeguards in
such areas as wages, job bias, and safety*

DEBORAH T. BOND

State legislatures were not as active in the labor field this year as in recent years, but in each major standards field—wage collection, employment on public works, job discrimination, and worker safety—there were some significant enactments to correct problems faced by workers.

The majority of the jurisdictions enacting laws or revising wage orders to increase the minimum wage rate matched or nearly matched the current $2.30 rate under the Fair Labor Standards Act (FLSA). In three jurisdictions the increased rates adopted in 1976 surpassed the FLSA rate: 50 cents more in the restaurant and hotel industry in the District of Columbia, 20 cents for all wage orders in California and in the retail industry in the District of Columbia, and 10 cents in all covered industries in New Jersey. Three other States—Alaska, Connecticut, and Hawaii—already have in effect rates higher than the FLSA rate. Illinois, along with increasing its minimum wage, enacted an overtime requirement for the first time. Rhode Island amended its Sunday and holiday overtime pay law and added a provision, among others, making work on such days voluntary on the part of the employee. Arkan-

Deborah T. Bond is a labor standards adviser in the Division of State Employment Standards, Employment Standards Administration, U.S. Department of Labor.

sas' overtime pay law for women was struck down by the court. Tip provisions in Ohio and Kentucky were made more stringent in favor of the worker.

Among the amendments to wage payment and collection laws was a California provision which protects earned vacation time by prohibiting contracts or policies that deprive employees of credit for that time on termination of employment. A Wisconsin law requires employers who anticipate changes in operations that would result in mass employee displacement to institute employee protection procedures. In Alaska, the limit on the wage claims assignable to the labor commission for collection was raised to $5,000.

The labor commissioner was given additional powers under prevailing wage laws in several States; for instance, in California the commissioner, instead of the awarding body, will determine prevailing wages; in Kentucky the commissioner will designate the geographic boundaries in which wages will be determined; and in Oklahoma the commissioner may now take wage assignments and halt work or bar contractors for violations. To insure that workers in Washington are paid all money due, a contractor must have labor department approval of wage records before requesting payment from a public agency.

For the most part, the laws amending wage garnishment provisions shored up protections against harsh garnishment consequences. Georgia put a limit on the amount of garnishable wages and Arizona increased the amount; California allowed a 100-percent exemption if employee claims wages are needed for self-support; Minnesota prohibited discharge for any garnishment and Alaska added such a provision in cases of garnishment under court-ordered dependency support.

The main thrust of child labor legislation was to provide additional opportunity for employment. Seven laws relaxed standards for jobs formerly considered hazardous, allowing some participation in such as volunteer fire and ambulance squads (in Pennsylvania), entertainment in mental institutions (in New York), employment in places where alcohol is sold for off premise use (in Alaska, Georgia, Michigan, and Missouri), on registered vessels as nautical trainees (in Louisiana), and in bowling alleys (in California). Hawaii established a special agency to coordinate all youth activities, with advice from such enforcement agencies as the labor department.

Three States enacted legislation specifically affecting agricultural labor. California covered such workers under the wage payment and collection law; Michigan added representation from farmworker ranks to its commission which was created to deal with problems of these workers; and South Carolina added a migrant labor division to the labor department. Illinois covered farmworkers under the minimum wage law for the first time, and minimum wage increases in California, Minnesota, New Jersey, and Ohio also were applicable to farmworkers.

Twenty-four States took action to eliminate some form of discriminatory practice. For instance, in Florida, State higher education institutions were required to begin a salary equalization program to eliminate sex bias; in Oklahoma retirement plans must have the same compulsory retirement age for men and women; and in Maryland a pilot program was started to assist displaced homemakers, usually women, who for one reason or other have lost the income of the major wage earner. Along with general legislation outlawing discrimination against the disabled, some specific problems were addressed: color blindness and color weakness (in California); unlawful preemployment inquiries about psychiatric conditions (in Maryland); and the use of guide dogs (in New York). Florida enacted an age discrimination law covering all public employees and among the provisions is a ban on mandatory retirement formerly required at age 65. Three States—Delaware, Massachusetts, and New Hampshire—

banned the knowing employment of unregistered aliens to improve job opportunities of U.S. citizens.

Three labor relations laws affected the private sector. New York extended the labor relations law to domestic workers hired by commercial firms; California made provisions for succession of contracts when management changes; and Louisiana made it unlawful for an employee to be required to become a union member as a condition of employment, the first such law a State legislature has passed since 1963 when Wyoming enacted a similar law.

Three States granted powers to municipal employers to act on bargaining procedures. Baltimore, Md., was empowered to adopt an ordinance to establish a collective bargaining structure for all municipal employees; Providence, R.I., was allowed to extend bargaining rights to certified school administrators below the rank of assistant superintendent and to all paid firefighters, instead of only paid uniform personnel; and the city and county of Honolulu, and the counties of Hawaii, Maui, and Kauai in Hawaii were authorized to extend bargaining rights to employees of the clerk's office. In other actions, nonunion members in exclusive bargaining units will be assessed specified amounts equivalent to dues in Alaska and Minnesota.

The laws on regulation of private employment agencies all were amendments of existing laws. For instance, Kentucky made several changes: It banned requirement of advance or registration fees from job applicants, set a ceiling on charges for an employee removed from a job without cause, and established a seven-member industry advisory council. California changed the composition of its advisory board to make it more public than industry oriented. New York modified some of its prohibited practices.

Twelve States enacted over two dozen laws—either new laws or amendments to existing laws—on safety standards for general industry or specifically for mines. Virginia was granted U.S. Department of Labor approval of its plan to assume responsibility for any safety and health issues addressed by Federal standards. A California law assigned all functions, standards, and regulations of carcinogens to the labor department and all violations under this law will be classified as serious. Hawaii amended its procedures for issuing temporary emergency standards to correct unforeseen grave dangers, granting variances when employees will receive comparable protection to that in an existing standard, setting penalties for offenses against State enforcement officers, and freeing trained first aid employees from civil damages. Employers in Louisiana who monitor toxic substances must now make the exposure level records available to employees. Mine safety laws were amended in Alabama, Kentucky, Ohio, and Pennsylvania.

This year, two States—Colorado and Florida—enacted "sunset laws," requiring periodic reexamination of all State agencies, rules, and regulations. These States began scheduling the termination of certain regulatory agencies. Kentucky has requested the U.S. Congress to refrain from passing duplicative standards and enforcement requirements. Large private firms and all public agencies in Minnesota will be eligible for grants to establish treatment and rehabilitation programs for employees with chemical dependency problems. In Michigan, public employers were banned from exerting pressure for political contributions. Resident contractors in New York now have preference on State contracts for materials, equipment, and supplies. Alaska strengthened its resident preference law by allowing an aggrieved person to take court action; making a lessee of natural resources lands liable for triple wages in case of violation of the preference provisions; and giving resident workers and contractors preference on State projects in determined economic disaster areas. Meetings, with certain exceptions, of all public agencies must be preceded by public notice and must be held in open session in Wisconsin. A bureau of labor statistics was recreated within the labor department in Connecticut. Rhode Island and Maryland gave employees the option to convert terminated group health plans to individual health plans.

The following is a summary by State of legislative action during 1976.

Alabama

Equal employment opportunity. The prohibition against the employment of women in coal mines was repealed; now any person over age 18 may be so employed.

Occupational safety and health. The coal mine safety law was amended to, among other things, allow employees to accompany inspectors on investigation tours, and to provide improvement of emergency medical services, ventilation systems, and maintenance and use of mechanical and electrical equipment.

Alaska

Wages. The labor commissioner was granted authority under the wage payment and collection law to take assignment of wages up to $5,000, an increase over the previous limit of $2,500. Employers now have 3 days to make final wage payments to employees terminated for any cause, such payment is to be made at the usual location or one agreed upon by the parties; and noncompliance with terminal pay provision makes an employer liable for payment of the employee's regular compensation from time of demand to time of payment or for 90 work-

ing days, whichever is less. Employees were permitted to make voluntary authorization for wage deductions for deposit in savings institutions.

The prevailing wage law was amended to expand the definition of public work to include onsite field surveying and to require that the current prevailing wage rate be that contained in the latest department of labor determination.

A wage garnishment order for child support was made binding on the employer. The employer was prohibited from discharging an employee because of such garnishment order, but will be allowed to deduct $1 for each payment made under the order.

Child labor. Newly required is a written work authorization from the labor commissioner for all minors under age 17 covered by the child labor law. Minors under age 18 will be permitted, with parental consent, in hotel or restaurant work not involving sale or delivery of alcoholic beverages; and in nonhazardous work at surface mines. The age for work in selling and serving alcoholic beverages was reduced from 21 to 19. The daily and weekly hours limitations for 16 to 18 years of age were removed, but the 6-day week was retained.

Equal employment opportunity. The age discrimination provisions will no longer apply to apprenticeship programs registered by the U.S. Department of Labor or meeting equivalent standards. The commission on human rights is being required to study the status of women in public and private employment, to identify barriers to full equality, and to report to the legislature by January 30, 1977.

Labor relations. Public employees whose religious convictions conflict with joining a labor organization will be exempt from such membership when required as a condition of employment, but the employee must pay the equivalent of dues or other assessments which the labor union shall contribute to a nonunion, nonsectarian charitable organization.

Occupational safety and health. Employers were required to report immediately, or within 24 hours, all job-related fatal injuries or all job-related illnesses requiring overnight hospitalization. The names of employees interviewed during health and safety inspections are to be kept confidential.

Other laws. Resident workers and resident contractors on State public work projects will be given preference on projects in determined economic disaster areas. An economic disaster fund will be administered by the department of commerce and economic development for making grants or loans to needy communities. Two strengthening provisions were added to laws requiring preference for resident workers on State public work projects and State leased natural resources lands: (1) an aggrieved person may now bring a court action to enforce the provision and the court may order denial of State funds to the contractor or other injunctive relief (formerly only the labor commissioner could institute punitive actions); and (2) a lessee violation will be subject to enforcement action by the labor commissioner, including requirement on the employer to pay triple wages.

Arizona

Wages. The amount of wages subject to garnishment was decreased from 50 percent of earnings to 25 percent of disposable weekly earnings or 30 times the Federal minimum wage, whichever is less; and the prejudgment garnishment of wages will be prohibited. For family support judgments, the wages subject to garnishment will now be 50 percent of disposable earnings.

Arkansas

Wages. Since the U.S. Supreme Court decision in *League of Cities v. Usery* has cast doubt on the legality of overtime payment to certain State employees, it was determined that for proper functioning of medical service institutions, State agencies may continue to pay overtime during the 1975-77 biennium.

Equal employment opportunity. The requirement for premium pay after 8 hours a day and on the seventh day for women only was struck down by the State supreme court.

Labor relations. Voters defeated an initiative that would have repealed the "right to work" law.

California

Wages. Minimum wage rates were increased to $2.50 for adults and $2.15 for minors under 18 in 14 wage orders, including an order for household occupations. For future increases to match the FLSA, the industrial welfare commission need only hold hearings in three cities, but for increases above the FLSA, the commission must follow the full wage board conference procedure. Overtime pay for men (for the first time) and women in nonfarmwork will be one and one-half times the regular rate after 8 hours a day and after 40 hours a week, with variations for other work schedules, and permission for four 10-hour days under very specific rules. Farmworkers will receive premium pay after 10 hours a day. At this writing 5 of the 14 wage orders are under court-issued stay orders. Petitioners asked for stay of overtime provisions in three orders—agricultural occupations, industries handling products after harvest, and industries preparing agricultural products for market on the farm. Orders covering the transportation industry, and amusement and recreation industry were stayed in their entirety.

An employment contract or employer policy was made invalid when such action results in an employee forfeiting earned vacation time upon termination of employment. Two amendments strengthened the authority and duties of the labor commissioner in enforcing wage payment and collection, mainly to make wage collection less burdensome for the worker. For instance, the commissioner may now accept complaints, investigate, and hold informal hearings in any action to recover wages, including making whole bad checks; when an employer fails to cooperate, the commissioner's orders or decisions may be based on the employee's evidence only, and such

order becomes final and enforceable as a judgment by the appropriate court. The commissioner may use the services of a bilingual person in hearings or investigations. The second law would allow a collective bargaining representative to file claims with the commissioner for all employees in the bargaining unit, instead of each individual taking action. As another enforcement aid, the employees' itemized wage statement must now also show gross and net wages earned.

Several amendments were made to the prevailing wage law. The labor commissioner, instead of the awarding body, will now be required to determine prevailing wages. Coverage was extended to hauling of refuse from a public worksite to an outside disposal location. Public works projects costing $500 or less are no longer covered. When a wage complaint has been filed with the commissioner or the awarding body, a public contractor will be required to file within 10 days a certified copy of payroll records. Payroll records must now contain work classification, daily and weekly straight time and overtime hours, and must be retained for 90 days after completion of a contract.

All earnings are exempt from wage garnishment if necessary for the support of a debtor. The exemption previously applied only to members of the debtor's family.

Child labor. Minors under age 16 will now be allowed to work in bowling alleys.

Agriculture. Coverage of the wage payment law was extended to workers on farms, with a requirement for bimonthly paydays and a 7-day holdover period for actual wage payment, the same as for most other employment covered by the law. Farm labor contractors are now required to pay employees at least once a week, instead of every 2; are required to furnish, upon request of a grower, a complete payroll list of all employees working for the grower; and are required to pay an increased licensing fee—up $25. The commissioner is required to deposit this amount in a special fund and to disburse money from the fund to employees for damages by the contractor when the damage exceeds the required bond.

A new law gives to agricultural workers who have harvested or transported farm products a lien on such severed crops, farm products, or on the proceeds for their sale, for unpaid wages up to a maximum of 2 weeks earnings. Such a lien would not be effective if an owner or his representative, or a contractor satisfies either of the following: deposits with the labor commissioner a bond of a surety company authorized to do business in the State, or a bank or trust time certificate payable to the order of the commissioner for every person employed. The commissioner was authorized to pursue such liens to their fulfillment either administratively or through the courts. The migratory labor housing code was amended to provide that after the first year of operating a permanent labor camp, without any violations of the code, an operator may apply for renewal of a housing permit every 5 years, instead of annually.

Two nonstatutory actions affected agricultural workers. The State supreme court upheld the constitutionality of the union access rule which gives union organizers the right to enter a grower's property before and after working hours and during lunch break. In the second action, the voters rejected a proposition to make the agricultural labor relations act and certain regulations of the agricultural labor relations board, created by the law, a part of the State constitution.

Equal employment opportunity. Wage differentials based on sex, which resulted from such former statutory restrictions for women as maximum hours, nightwork, and weightlifting, were prohibited. These and other special restrictions for women were removed from other laws to conform with a 1976 U.S. Supreme Court decision outlawing a discriminatory law in the State. The fair employment practices law now bans discrimination because of marital status, but the amendment specified that an employer could, for purposes of supervision, safety, security or morale, regulate the working of spouses in the same department or facility, or could provide additional or greater health benefits for employees with dependents than to those without or with fewer dependents. In correcting discriminatory employment practices among its own employees, the State prohibited biases because of color blindness or color weakness, and prohibited preemployment questions on marital status and sex; and it also banned differential treatment under State and local retirement systems, whether in rate of contributions or benefits. Contractors on State public works may not discriminate in employment on the basis of sex, marital status, religious creed, physical handicap, or medical condition.

The maximum age limit for entry into apprenticeship training programs was removed. Formerly, an association of employers, an organization of employees, or joint apprenticeship committee administering such a program could ban an applicant over age 31 from participation in an apprenticeship program. It is incumbent upon a joint apprenticeship committee to ensure equal employment and affirmative action in apprenticeship for women and minorities, so that contractors on public works have the benefit of qualified referrals from these groups.

Under a civil rights act, persons are guaranteed the right to freedom from violence in labor disputes irrespective of race, color, religion, ancestry, national origin, political affiliation, sex, or position.

The legislature expressed its opposition to any Federal proposal to permit contractual importation of foreign laborers to the disadvantage of American citizens and legal resident aliens.

Labor relations. When the management of a business changes and the previous employer had negotiated a successor clause, the succeeding employer is bound to the terms of the contract until its expiration, but in no instance for longer than 3 years from the effective date of the agreement.

Private employment agencies. The fee for new licenses was doubled to $100, and for renewals was reduced to $25. The advisory board composition was changed to three agency members and four public members.

Occupational safety and health. A number of laws relating to job safety were adopted. Among these, the labor department was assigned all regulation of the use of carcinogens and all violations will be designated as serious. The investigation period for nonserious violations under the general safety law has been extended to 14 days. Salvage of material will not be permitted while a building or other structure more than three stories high is being demolished.

Other laws. The composition of the industrial welfare commission was changed to be comprised of two union members who are not lawyers, two representatives of employers, and one representative of the general public, with the stipulation that membership be representative of both sexes.

Under a reorganization order, with legislative approval, a new division was created in the labor department. The division of labor standards enforcement replaces the divisions of labor law enforcement and industrial welfare. Successful vocational educational graduates of courses related to apprenticeable occupations taken in recognized State institutions may now receive credit toward a term of apprenticeship.

Colorado

Equal employment opportunity. Over the years, through various actions of government, a substantial number of agencies, programs, rules, and regulations have been created. A new "sunset law" intends to provide an orderly system for termination, continuation, or reestablishment of programs. Future termination dates of numerous agencies (including the division of civil rights, the civil rights commission, and the commission on the status of women—all slated for termination on July 1, 1979) have been set. The law, however, provides for public hearings prior to termination dates.

A proposal to repeal the equal rights section of the State constitution was defeated in the November 1976 election.

Connecticut

Wages. The exemption from wage garnishment under court-ordered dependent support was increased to $50 a week.

Equal employment opportunity. The clause against discrimination, required in all State contracts for public work, was expanded to cover age and marital status.

Other laws. A bureau of labor statistics was recreated within the labor department. (The former bureau was abolished in 1973.) An unlimited journeymen's license will now be issued to persons with at least 4 years of experience in the trade, instead of 5. Public and private employers were prohibited from using time card or other systems of recording an employee's hours of work, unless the system is synchronized with an easily visible clock.

Delaware

Wages. The wage garnishment law was amended to specify that wage attachments need be served only once and remain in force until the judgment is satisfied.

Equal employment opportunity. A new law was passed which would prohibit an employer from knowingly hiring an alien not entitled to lawful U.S. residency if such employment would have an adverse effect on lawful resident workers.

District of Columbia

Wages. In the wage order for hotel, restaurant, apartment building, and allied occupations, the minimum wage was increased to $2.80; in tipped occupations, the cash wage is now $1.35; for minors under age 18 the rate is $2.25. For retail trade the rate was increased to $2.50 per hour for adults and to $2.30 for minors under age 18.

Child labor. The city council approved a revision of the child labor law. The law repealed all unequal gender-based standards on minimum age, hours, and hazardous occupations for girls, and made the standards the same as for boys. This law conforms to a 1970 opinion of the corporation counsel that stated such provisions were discriminatory and therefore superseded by Title VII of the Civil Rights Act of 1964. The age of majority was set at 18, which, for most purposes, formerly was 21.

Equal employment opportunity. Another city council law extended to men the provisions requiring certain establishments to furnish seating facilities. The law further prohibits rules preventing employees from using the seats when not actively employed, and provides penalties for violations. The maximum hours limitations for women only were repealed to conform with a 1970 corporation counsel opinion. Each government agency head will be required to submit an affirmative action plan to the mayor and the city council. The law set as a goal representation in each agency of various ethnic groups equal to their representation in the work force.

Florida

Equal employment opportunity. The department of education was required to begin a program to achieve equal pay for State university faculty members. Each university is to determine the increases necessary to bring the salaries of women up to the level of men, retroactive to September 15, 1976, and annual reporting will be required on the number of women receiving increases and on salary inequality studies. An age discrimination law was enacted for State and local government employees, abolishing mandatory retirement at age 65, among other protections.

Labor relations. Two amendments clarified coverage under public sector collective bargaining law: school superintendents, supervisors, principals, and professional administrative assistants were classified as managerial employees and therefore excluded from the law, and an exclusion was added for employees of State legislatures.

Private employment agencies. As a part of a legislative program to reevaluate the regulation of business, the private employment agency law will be repealed on July 1, 1980, and the migrant labor camp regulation on July 1, 1982. One year before the repeal dates, a legislative committee will review the need for retaining such regulatory laws.

Georgia

Wages. The wage garnishment law was amended to, among other things, limit the amount of wages subject to garnishment to 25 percent of disposable weekly earnings or the excess of 30 times the Federal minimum, whichever is less, and to prohibit discharge of an employee for any one indebtedness.

Child labor. Persons under age 18 employed in supermarkets and specialty stores may now sell or handle alcoholic beverages used for off-premises consumption.

Hawaii

Wages. Resident staff members of tax-exempt seasonal youth camps are no longer subject to the minimum wage law.

Child labor. A separate office of children and youth was established to conduct research, coordinate, and evaluate youth programs, including child labor standards of the labor department.

Equal employment opportunity. When a government agency contracts for services, a 5-percent preference will be given to services performed by a nonprofit corporation or public agency operating a certified sheltered workshop for the physically or mentally handicapped.

The legislative committee on labor and public employment, in conjunction with the labor department and the attorney general, was requested to review the antidiscrimination law to, among other things, study the feasibility of giving the labor department authority to process class actions, conduct affirmative compliance reviews of public construction and nonconstruction contractors, apply the antidiscrimination law to these contractors, and exercise sanctions, such as termination and ineligibility for future contracts.

Labor relations. Collective bargaining rights were extended to employees of the clerk's office of the city and county of Honolulu, and the counties of Hawaii, Maui, and Kauai.

A study is to be conducted by an interagency committee, including the labor department and representatives of employee organizations, on the merits of compulsory binding arbitration for firefighters and police officers, and a report is due to the legislature by December 1, 1977.

Occupational safety and health. Several provisions were amended relating to issuing temporary emergency standards to correct unforeseen grave dangers, granting variances in standards when employees will receive protection comparable to that under an existing standard, protecting employees from retaliation for exercising rights accorded under the law, and setting criminal penalties, in addition to those in the existing penal code, for offenses against State employees during the course of employment. State employees were also exempt from civil liability for actions connected with administration or enforcement of the law. A trained and certified employee rendering first aid will not be liable for civil damages unless damages result from gross negligence.

Other laws. Under the election law an employer is prohibited from rescheduling normal work hours to avoid granting paid leave for voting. An employee may now request from an employer a waiver from the mandatory health care benefits plan, provided the employee has other adequate prepaid health care plan; employers must notify the labor commissioner of the receipt of a waiver request and may not coerce employees into making such waivers.

Idaho

Wages. The minimum wage rate was increased to $2, then to $2.20 on January 1, 1977, and $2.30 on July 1, 1977. Employers were prohibited from retaliating against employees who participate in any enforcement procedures. The labor commissioner was given new powers to enforce payment of unpaid minimum wages, for example, by use of authority under the wage payment and collection law, which requires the employer to pay three times the amount of unpaid wages. For students in secondary school work-experience programs, the labor commissioner may issue certificates for subminimum rates.

Equal employment opportunity. Veterans no longer need a year of State residency to qualify for preference in public employment, but the eligibility for preference will be limited to those whose military service spans more than 180 days. The minimum number of employees necessary for an employer to come under the fair employment practices law was increased from 4 to 10, and the criminal penalties were eliminated.

Illinois

Wages. The minimum wage for adults was increased to $2.20 and to $2.30 on January 1, 1977, and the current $1.75 for minors under 18, will increase to $1.95 on January 1, 1977. A new overtime standard was established requiring premium pay after 40 hours a week with certain exceptions and variations. Coverage was extended by making the law applicable to employers of four employees or more, instead of five or more, and by repealing the exemption for employment subject to the FLSA and for certain occupations in the motion picture industry. Newly set was a subminimum rate of $1.95 for full time students in certain motion picture theater occupations.

Equal employment opportunity. A position of equal employment opportunity officer was established and an advisory committee was created and the governor and each cabinet and agency head will be required to submit affirmative action plans. A Federal district court ruled that granting veterans preference points on police job qualification tests was not intended as a discriminatory act against women and nonveterans, and although such an act may hinder, it does not preclude, employment of these groups.

Indiana

Wages. A person may be ordered by the court to make a wage assignment for support payments and an employer will be obligated to accept such an assignment. An employee may not be discharged for a wage assignment for support payments.

Labor relations. A school district successfully challenged the 1975 law for public sector bargaining; the court declared the law unconstitutional on the grounds that it precludes judicial review of agency procedures for determining bargaining units. The issue is on appeal to the State supreme court.

Kansas

Wages. The minimum wage law was repealed to the extent it covered women, leaving the secretary of human resources with authority to issue wage orders only for learners, apprentices, and minors under age 18. At the time of repeal there were no wage rates in effect for anyone.

Labor relations. Instructional personnel of area vocational-technical schools will now have the right to collective bargaining.

Other laws. A department of human resources was created and the labor department's duties and functions were transferred to the new department, as were those of other agencies.

Kentucky

Wages. Employers will not be allowed to require employees to turn over tips, except for purpose of withholding taxes as required under Federal and State law. Taxi drivers, as defined by the FLSA, are now exempt from the weekly overtime provision.

Creditors may no longer serve two orders for wage garnishment on an employer against the same employee in the same pay period.

The labor commissioner was authorized to designate the geographic area in which prevailing wages are to be determined. Such locality may include one or more counties, but may not extend beyond a Federal congressional district. Formerly determinations were made primarily on a county basis.

Equal employment opportunity. Employers were prohibited from establishing employment practices in controvention of either an existing seniority system or collective bargaining agreement. A separate fair employment practices law was enacted to prohibit discrimination in employment against the physically handicapped. The law prohibits unfair labor practices by public or private employers with eight employees or more, labor organizations, and private employment agencies. The law also provides for administrative procedures, including authority for the labor commissioner to process complaints and institute civil action.

Industrial relations. The labor relations board, created in 1972 to administer the collective bargaining law for firefighters, was placed in the labor department for administrative purposes.

Private employment agencies. Among the changes in the private employment agency law were a prohibition against charging advance fees or registration fees, the institution of a placement fee ceiling of 20 percent of earnings of employees discharged without cause within 30 days of placement, and substantial increases in agency licensing fees and fines for violations. Practices made illegal included a requirement that applicants borrow from specific finance companies in order to pay fees, and referral of applicants to unlawful employment. A seven-member advisory committee was created with three representatives with private employment agency experience and four with experience in any sector of private industry.

Occupational safety and health. The reorganization law of 1974 was amended to include changes such as the abolition of the division of elevator inspection and placing the responsibility for administration of the elevator law at the department of labor level; making it discretionary for the labor department to enter into agreements with the department of human resources, and any other appropriate State agency, to conduct research, demonstrations, and the like on occupational safety and health issues; and designation of the department of human resources to monitor radioactive waste material sites and to be responsible for issuing regulations for licensing sources of handling and transportation of radioactive waste.

The mine safety law was amended to require, under ventilation standards, that 9,000 cubic feet of air be circulated per minute in specified work situations, instead of 6,000 as before, and to require more complete removal of dry coal dust and the watering or rock dusting of operating sections of all mines.

Other laws. The President and U.S. Congress were petitioned to cease passing and signing into law legislation requiring inspections and establishing standards which are duplicative of existing State laws and regulations.

Louisiana

Wages. The law governing the minimum wages, hours, and working conditions for women and girls was repealed. Among the working-conditions standards that were lost by this action were provisions for lunch and rest periods. The State did not have minimum wage rates in effect under the law.

A creditor must supply the employer of a debtor with a complete statement of the amount due under wage garnishment, and garnishment ceases when a worker's employment is terminated unless reinstated within 180 days.

Hours of work. Employees below the level of captain of a municipal police department will be eligible for overtime pay after 40 hours, instead of 48, at the rate of time and one-half the regular rate.

Child labor. Hours and nightwork restrictions were removed for minors age 16 and over; minors under age 18 will be allowed to work as helpers on vehicles; and the mandatory meal period was shortened. Another law will permit employment of minors age 16 and over on registered U.S. vessels if the minor is enrolled in a nautical training course.

Equal employment opportunity. Girls under age 18 were permitted to work in street trades on the same basis as boys.

Labor relations. It was made unlawful to require a person to become or remain a member of a labor organization as a condition of employment.

The authority to order intervention by State police in labor disputes was transferred from the governor to the superintendent of State police, and the authority may be used in case of threatened violence as well as actual violence.

Occupational safety and health. Employers who monitor the presence of toxic substances will be required to provide employees, upon request, access to records that indicate the employee's exposure to such substances.

Other laws. An employee's designation of beneficiary to benefits under a deferred compensation plan need not be in the form of a will and should not be affected by circumstances that would modify or invalidate a will.

Maine

Wages. The minimum wage laws was extended to employees on farms with more than 300,000 laying birds; other agricultural employment remains exempted.

Equal employment opportunity. All maximum hours restrictions and special requirements for women were repealed. Also repealed were the recordkeeping and posting requirements for women, but not for minors under age 16.

Labor relations. The University of Maine labor relations act was extended to employees of the Maritime Academy. A number of procedural changes were made in the public sector labor relations law: the executive director of the labor relations board may now administer oaths and issue subpoenas in unit determination proceedings; either party may petition for unit clarification; the filing period for election challenges was reduced from 15 to 5 days; upon request of the parties, the executive director may waive factfinding; procedures were added for prehearing conferences on prohibited practice complaints; and the executive director and legal and professional personnel employed by the labor relations board must be from the unclassified service. A new provision requires the appointment of three students to meet and confer with the University of Maine and they may also meet and confer with the bargaining agent prior to negotiations.

Other laws. A public or private employer will be required, upon written request, to make personnel folders available to both present and former employees during normal office hours.

Maryland

Wages. An employer will now be liable for an additional 20 percent of unpaid wages for each day that wages are illegally withheld, formerly the penalty was 10 percent of unpaid wages.

Dependents were permitted to petition the court for an order for wage deductions when support payments, in arrears over a 2-year period, equal 2 months' payments. Employers may deduct $1 for each payment made under such order, but may not dismiss an employee because of the order or retaliate in any other way.

Equal employment opportunity. The commission on human relations was directed to establish, as a pilot project, a multipurpose center for displaced homemakers and to furnish job counseling, training, job placement, and health care. A displaced homemaker was defined as a person over age 35 who has not been employed except as unpaid worker for the family, has depended on the family for income, and has suffered a loss of the major wage earner.

The labor commissioner was authorized to investigate and conciliate complaints regarding unlawful preemployment inquiries on psychiatric or psychological conditions or treatment, and upon verification of a violation, an applicant may seek injunctive or other relief, including money damages. Hereafter employers may receive criminal history record information for preemployment examination only if it is demonstrated that the activities of the applicant would call for close and sensitive contact with the public and the applicant is notified that a criminal record check will be made.

The Metropolitan Transit Authority will be required to provide free transportation to handicapped employees of sheltered workshops who receive less than the current Federal minimum wage. Enforcement procedures under the law prohibiting employer use of lie detector devices were strengthened by giving the labor commissioner power to receive and investigate complaints from job applicants, engage in informal mediation, or take action on behalf of the applicant to seek injunctive or other relief, including money damages.

Labor relations. The City of Baltimore was given the power to adopt an ordinance granting full collective bargaining rights to municipal employees. The legislature requested the creation of a task force which would include labor and management to study the feasibility of extending collective bargaining rights to State and local employees, instructing the task force to prepare a workable legislative proposal.

Private employment agencies. Theatrical managers will now be covered by the law. For license renewals, generally, agency operators no longer need resupply character references.

Occupational safety and health. Regulatory functions under the radiation control act were transferred to the department of health and mental hygiene from the State board of health.

Other laws. An employee insured under a group hospital and medical plan may, upon request, obtain an individual policy if the coverage under the group plan is terminated for any reason other than failure to pay the premium. The labor commissioner will be permitted to accept money grants for any program under the division of labor's jurisdiction from any Federal agency.

Massachusetts

Equal employment opportunity. The provision giving absolute preference in public employment to veterans and their families, based on the physical conditions of the veteran and the successful passing of a written test, was suspended, pending outcome of court challenge. In the interim veterans will be given preference by point credits added to test scores. The district court held that the veterans preference law was discriminatory against women, therefore unconstitutional. Without ruling on merits of veterans' preference, the U.S. Supreme Court remanded the case to the State supreme court for a ruling on a procedural question: whether the State attorney general has the authority to bring the decision of the district court to the Supreme Court over the objection of State officials who were ruled against by the lower court case.

The department of mental health was required to give major consideration to the development of employment opportunities for mentally ill and mentally retarded clients. It will be unlawful for an employer to knowingly employ an alien student or visitor, not admitted for permanent residence, unless the alien has a work permit or employment is authorized by the attorney general.

The electorate approved a constitutional amendment that guarantees equality under law on the basis of sex, color, creed, or national origin.

Michigan

Child labor. Minors 14 and 15 years of age will be permitted to work where alcoholic beverages are sold at retail, but not in the part of the establishment where such beverages are consumed.

Agriculture. The agricultural labor commission, created in the labor department to aid in the improvement of conditions for farmworkers, was enlarged; of the 11 members, four will now have to be farmworkers.

Equal employment opportunity. A law banning discrimination against handicapped persons was enacted. The law sets unfair labor practices by employers, labor organizations, employment agencies, and contractors on State projects. The antidiscrimination act of general application was amended to add marital status, height, and weight.

Labor relations. The labor relations agency was renamed the employment relations commission and was authorized to enforce both public and private labor relations acts. It was made unlawful for a member or agent of the employment relations commission to disclose confidential information received in course of labor dispute proceedings unless the information is about a criminal act.

The procedure for selection of arbitrators for resolving police and firefighter negotiation impasses was modified to allow the parties to choose from a panel of three provided by the employment relations commission, instead of being selected by the parties or appointed by the mediation board.

Occupational safety and health. The labor department was given the authority to enforce the new licensing and examination requirements for journeymen elevator installers and repairmen.

Other laws. The labor department was authorized to take complaints from public employees on coercive procedures used by public employers in soliciting political contributions. The department may hold hearings, issue orders which may require backpay and reinstatement, and seek injunctions for enforcement of orders.

Minnesota

Wages. The minimum wage was increased to $2.10 for adults and a rate of $1.89 was specified for minors under age 18, instead of 90 percent of the basic rate.

A person aggrieved by a final prevailing wage determination of the labor commissioner will now be allowed to petition the commissioner for reconsideration of the findings, and if not reconsidered, may then request a public hearing.

Employers were prohibited from discharging an employee because earnings have been subject to wage garnishment.

Equal employment opportunity. The labor commissioner was designated to administer the law prohibiting polygraph testing of employees or prospective employees. Voice stress analysis was added as a prohibited honesty-testing device. The persons who sell or interpret illegal testing devices or test results will now be subject to the provisions of the law.

The provision for the commissioner of human rights to issue within 10 days a nonappealable decision was repealed. The complainant now has 10 days to appeal, and the commissioner will have 20 more days to reconsider the appeal and 10 days for notification to the complainant of a final decision. Among other procedural changes, the commissioner is required to expedite charges of discrimination to prevent irreparable loss and to periodically notify complainant of the status of investigations.

Labor relations. A public employee who is a nonunion member in an exclusive bargaining unit may now be assessed 85 percent of the regular membership dues. (The other 15 percent of the dues is considered cost of benefits available only to union members.) Formerly the "fair share fee" was an unstipulated amount not to exceed the pro rata share of expenses for services rendered by the exclusive representative. A formal procedure for employee challenges of determinations of fair share fee assessments was established and made applicable to all fee challenges. Two other laws would allow provisions of public sector collective bargaining agreements to supersede inconsistent State personnel rules and regulations.

Private employment agencies. An agency which is exclusively engaged in job placements for teachers and nurses will no longer be subject to regulation as a private employment agency.

Other laws. Effective July 1, 1977, a department of vocational rehabilitation will assume the functions of the division of vocational rehabilitation and will have added responsibilities for technical assistance to sheltered workshops; the division was part of the department of education. For private employers of under 200 employees and all public employers, the public welfare department was given additional responsibility, including allocation of funds to such employers, to establish treatment and rehabilitation programs for employees with chemical dependency problems.

Mississippi

Occupational safety and health. A Statewide radiation protection program was instituted, to be administered by the board of health and a radiation advisory council. The law provides for licensing and registration of persons dealing in any way with radiation sources, authorizes onsite inspections, and requires that employees be furnished with copies of personal exposure records.

Missouri

Child labor. Young persons age 18 to 21 may now work in handling alcoholic beverages in distilleries, warehouses, and for wholesale distributorships, but may not be employed in dispensing such beverages for consumption or for retail sale.

Private employment agencies. By executive order, the administration of the private employment agency law was transferred from the labor department to the department of consumer affairs, regulation, and licensing.

Occupational safety and health. Commercial, industrial, and public buildings, among others, will be required to label any safety glazing material used in hazardous locations, and it will be unlawful to sell certain types of doors made of other than safety glazing material. Teachers, students, and visitors participating in courses where specified types of hazardous substances or processes are used will be required to use approved industrial quality eye-protective devices.

Nebraska

Other laws. To be eligible to become a trustee of employee's pension, disability, retirement, death benefit, or any such plan or fund, a person, in addition to being a State resident, must be qualified and licensed to do business in the State.

New Hampshire

Wages. Under the wage payment and wage collection law, an employee is now permitted to authorize employers to deposit wages through electronic fund transfer or other means to bank of employee's choice.

Equal employment opportunity. Citizenship requirements

cannot be used to deny lawful resident aliens the opportunity to seek and receive professional or occupational licenses, but it was made illegal for employers to hire persons known to be aliens not in possession of the proper documentation.

New Jersey

Wages. The minimum wage was increased to $2.40 an hour in November and to $2.50 on January 1, 1977.

New York

Wages. The salary threshold for exemption from the wage payment and wage collection law for executive, administrative, or professional employees was increased to $300 a week.

In New York City, an employee organization representing the majority of government employees in certain ungraded titles was given the right to file a single verified complaint under the prevailing wage law for all such employees it represents. Other employees on public works in other localities may complain about a wage determination but the decision applies only to the particular employee who filed the complaint.

Employees or retirees of a county or its political subdivision, and New York City or its boroughs may be subject to court-ordered wage, salary, or pension deductions when a petition by a dependent indicates support payments are three payments or more in arrears.

Child labor. The prohibition on employment of minors by institutions under the department of mental hygiene was modified to permit 14-year-olds to participate in volunteer recreational, social development, companionship, or entertainment programs in such institutions.

Equal employment opportunity. The human rights law was amended to add a provision to protect the rights of blind persons who have to use guide dogs in public or private employment.

It will now be an unfair discriminatory practice for a public agency to refuse an applicant any license, or for a public or private employer to bar employment because of one or more previous convictions for criminal offenses. A parole board may grant a certificate of good conduct to a person with one or more convictions for criminal offenses to relieve such person of any disability or to remove any bar to employment.

Labor relations. Collective bargaining rights were extended to domestic workers employed by a commercial household agency in business to supply workers for private homes.

Private employment agencies. Three laws modified the prohibited practices provision: the provision forbidding an agency from inducing employees to terminate present employment to accept a new offer was made inapplicable if the employee was not placed in the current job by the same agency and is offered an executive, administrative, or professional position paying at least $12,000 a year. Another law added a prohibition against use of information-gathering that makes distinctions between men and women, and the third repealed a prohibition against referral of women entertainers to places to engage in the selling of alcoholic beverages to patrons.

Occupational safety and health. The effective date of a law providing for industry work practices, procedures, and safety standards for employees working on energized high voltage lines was extended to 1980.

Other laws. An interagency job retention board was established and procedures were prescribed for giving preference in awarding State contracts for materials, equipment, and supplies to resident contractors with substantial economic ties in the State and with major effect on the level of employment opportunities for State residents. Among other criteria for selection, the bid must be within 10 percent of the lowest bid. The seven-member board, which will function until July 1, 1979, includes as members the governor and the labor commissioner.

North Dakota

Wages. Under a revised wage order for professional, technical, clerical, and similar occupations, the minimum wage was increased to $2.20 and to $2.30 on January 1, 1977. Overtime is now payable after 40 hours a week, instead of 48.

Ohio

Wages. The minimum wage was increased for nonfarmworkers in four steps to finally reach $2.30 on January 1, 1978, and in three steps to also reach $2.30 on January 1, 1978, for farmworkers. An employer must post a printed notice in a conspicuous place indicating the percentage of the minimum wage paid to tipped employees, and the employee must be notified that the employer will take a tip credit. For a limited time each year, a student in a cooperative vocational education program may be employed at the learner rate—80 percent of the minimum wage.

The threshold for coverage of public construction contracts under the prevailing wage law was increased to $4,000. Also under that law the labor commissioner may now take a wage assignment for underpayments, halt work on a finding of violations, and may bar contractors for 2 years from public works projects.

Equal employment opportunity. The antidiscrimination law was extended to protect the handicapped. The law will cover public and private employers of four or more. All contractors or subcontractors engaged in construction or rehabilitation of public housing will be required to give equal employment opportunity to the handicapped.

Private employment agencies. Management consultants and management executive recruiters were exempted from the law.

Occupational safety and health. The mine safety law was amended to make requirements for abatement of conditions constituting imminent and substantial threat to the health and safety of miners, and to expand regulation of such issues as transportation equipment, roof supports, firefighting equipment, and availability of emergency medical services.

Oklahoma

Wages. The minimum wage was increased to $1.85. A wage garnishment order before judgment will be allowed if an employee has been given notice of such action and has had the opportunity to request a hearing. Formerly, all prejudgment wage garnishments were disallowed.

Equal employment opportunity. Girls between 16 and 18 years of age may now work during hours of 7 a.m. and 6 p.m., the same as for boys of that age. Formerly, under the fair employment practices law a retirement plan could provide a younger retirement age for women than for men. This provision was repealed, but the provision for differences in annuity, death and survivors' benefits between widows and widowers was retained. Women are no longer barred from underground work in mines, and minors under age 16 will now be permitted to work aboveground in clerical and other office positions.

Pennsylvania

Child labor. Minors age 16 and 17 who are members of a volunteer ambulance corps or rescue squad will be permitted to participate in training and any other activity, but only those age 18 and over will be permitted to drive ambulances or other vehicles. Members of a volunteer fire company 16 or 17 years of age who answer a fire call may now remain on duty until excused by a fire department superior, without incurring a violation of the maximum hours requirement.

Labor relations. Under new procedures added to the public employee relations act, each party will pay for one arbitrator and the labor relations board will pay for the impartial arbitrator. The board of county commissioners was named as management negotiators with representatives of county employees for collective bargaining purposes.

Occupational safety and health. Within 2 years, all coal mine operators must provide opportunities for employees to get first-aid training, place trained medical technicians in hazardous work areas, and install a two-way communication system in the mine. Employees, in certain bakeries will be required to pass preemployment physical examinations, and annually thereafter, certifying freedom from communicable diseases and skin afflictions.

Other laws. With the stated aim to eventually abolish industrial homework, an amendment placed more stringent requirements on employers such as more than doubling most fees and fines, limiting the issuance of permits to persons who for various reasons are unable to work outside the home, and granting special permits to persons in the shoe and brush industries who had worked at least 6 months in such factories but are no longer able to continue factory work.

Rhode Island

Wages. The law requiring overtime pay at one and one-half times the employees' regular rate for work on Sunday and specified holidays was revised. For example, exemptions were added for such workers in agriculture, in medical care or maintenance, in a supervisory capacity as defined in FLSA, and in restaurants, hotel, motel, resort or other recreational facility (except health clubs); the permit for such overtime work that the employer is required to get from the labor commissioner will expire after a year; and employers are prohibited from discharging an employee who refuses Sunday or holiday overtime work, with provisions for backpay and reinstatement in case of violation.

Coverage of the prevailing wage law was extended to apprentices, teamsters, chauffeurs, and laborers engaged in transportation of gravel or fill to various sites of a public work project.

Labor relations. Certified administrators, below the rank of assistant superintendent, in the public school system of the City of Providence were granted collective bargaining rights. The law provided for impasse procedures, supervision of elections by the State labor relations board, and adoption of the same unfair labor practices as under the private employee relations act. All paid fire department personnel, instead of only paid uniformed members, will now benefit from the firefighters arbitration act.

Occupational safety and health. Two enactments amended or added procedures relating to receipt of complaints and conduct of investigations, requirement for employee representative to accompany a compliance officer on physical inspection of workplace, and procedures for granting variances from existing standards. A radiation control agency was created within the department of health.

Other laws. Until September 1, 1977, employees who are involuntarily laid off and surviving spouses of deceased employees will be allowed to continue group hospital, surgical, or medical insurance plans for up to 10 months.

South Carolina

Agriculture. A migrant labor division was added to the labor department. The labor commissioner, with the aid of a newly established commission, is to issue rules that will safeguard the health, safety, education, and welfare of migrant or seasonal farmworkers and to enter into agreements with other State and local agencies for services and for enforcement of rules and regulations.

South Dakota

Wages. Employers were prohibited from taking any retaliatory measures against employees who exercise their rights or cooperate in any proceedings under the minimum wage law.

Child labor. The age for work in any hazardous occupations was raised from 16 to 18 and a prohibition was added against exploitation of minors under 18, including imposing unreasonable wages, hours, and working conditions.

Equal employment opportunity. A proposed equal rights amendment to the State constitution, which was approved by the 1975 legislature, was rejected by the electorate on November 2, 1976.

Labor relations. The personnel commissioner was authorized to give final approval or rejection to all negotiated contracts for public employees without interim approval by agency heads, and the personnel policy board will make final decisions in grievances which are no longer appealable to the labor department.

Other laws. The department of manpower affairs and the division of labor and management relations were abolished, and all functions were transferred to the department of labor.

Tennessee

Child labor. The law was substantially amended to, among other changes, allow minors age 16 and 17 to work later on nights preceding nonschooldays; restrict the work hours of 14- and 15-year-old in-school youth to 3 a day and 18 a week; require a meal period after 4 hours, instead of 5, and a 15-minute rest period every 2 hours for all under 18. The amendments also greatly expanded the number of occupations considered hazardous and prohibited to those under age 18.

Equal employment opportunity. A women's maximum hours law was repealed. A law was enacted to prohibit public and private employers from discriminating against applicants based on physical, mental, or visual handicap. For public sector employees, the department of personnel was designated as the oversight agency with limited powers and duties, but no administrative agency was named for enforcement of new law for the private sector.

Utah

Labor relations. Several cities joined in a challenge of the 1975 firefighters' negotiation act. A district court ruled the law an unconstitutional delegation of legislative functions and also stated that the law created a commission (arbitration board) to perform municipal functions contrary to the State constitution.

Vermont

Equal employment opportunity. Under the fair employment practices act, an employer was prohibited from retaliation against employees for participating in any proceedings under the act; the attorney general and State's attorney were given specific authority for enforcement and the superior court was granted authority to order such actions as restitution of wages, reinstatement of an employee or class of employees, and imposition of penalties.

Labor relations. All of the public sector labor relations functions of the State employee relations board were transferred to the State labor relations board which formerly administered only the private sector law.

Virginia

Wages. The minimum wage was increased to $2.20; and coverage was extended to full-time students 18 and over.

The wage garnishment law was amended to make specific provision for procedures involving the U.S. Government as a garnishee to enforce court-ordered dependent support.

Child labor. With a special work permit issued by the court, minors 14 or 15 will be permitted to work up to 10 p.m., instead of 6 p.m.

School attendance. Parents' right to have a child excused from school attendance was limited to reasons of religious belief or training and to concern for the child's personal safety. School boards may now make determinations to grant excuses based on inability of child to benefit from further attendance; formerly this determination was made by the court.

Occupational safety and health. Various changes were made in the law, including changes relating to issuance of citations, employee participation in inspections, and confidentiality of trade secrets, and appeals to court, sitting without a jury. The State safety and health codes commission was empowered to adopt standards, with the proviso that they be at least as stringent as the Federal standards. The labor commissioner was directed to request the U.S. Department of Labor's approval of a plan for the State to assume responsibility for development and enforcement of any health and safety issue addressed by Federal standards. The plan was submitted and approved. The State became the 24th with an approved plan.

The mine safety law was amended to expand the reporting and record-keeping requirements for accidents not involving lost-time injuries and to require that copies of mine inspection and injury reports be given to employee safety committees. A coal mine safety and health commission was established to study the health and safety problems of coal miners, the current conditions of mines, and the State mine and safety law. The 10-member commission will include the chief of mines, a coal miner, and a coal mine operator.

Washington

Wages. Prior to submitting requests for payment to a public agency, public works contractors are now required to obtain the labor department's approval of statements on wages intended to be paid and wages paid. The public agency will be liable for unpaid wages if a contractor receives payment without having submitted the required wage statements.

Labor relations. Representatives of public employers and State uniformed personnel have 45 days to negotiate a contract before an impasse can be declared or an arbitration panel created. This 45-day period may now be modified by mutual written agreement of the parties.

Occupational safety and health. The department of ecology was designated to administer the new law on hazardous wastes, and among duties assigned was the adoption of standards and regulations for disposal of such wastes in consultation with and by technical assistance from other agencies, including the labor department.

Other laws. A department of veteran affairs was created and all duties, powers, functions, and services formerly in other statutory or nonstatutory agencies were transferred to the new department.

West Virginia

Wages. The minimum wage was increased to $2.20, and overtime will be payable after 42 hours instead of 44 as before.

Wisconsin

Wages. The daily overtime requirement, formerly applicable only to women, was dropped, but weekly overtime after 48 hours was retained and made applicable to men also.

The wage payment and wage collection law was substantially improved. For instance, wages now include such items as severance, holiday, and overtime pay, and coverage was extended to State and local governments and nonprofit organizations and institutions; the wage collection authority was broadened by the removal of the $500 limit on wage claims assigned to the labor commissioner; a new provision will require large employers who contemplate changes resulting in mass employee displacement, to notify the commissioner 60 days in advance and to pay all wages due within 24 hours of time of separation. Both the maximum liquidated damages due employees and maximum penalties were increased from $100 to $500.

Equal employment opportunities. A provision was added to the fair employment practices act to require all State contracting agencies to include a clause in contracts obligating contractors on public projects not to discriminate against employees because of physical condition or developmental disability and to take affirmative action to ensure equal employment opportunities for such persons. For general application, unfair labor practices against handicapped persons were enumerated for all employers, labor organizations, and licensing agencies; among the prohibited practices was a ban on an employer contributing less for fringe benefits (including life or disability insurance which was formerly permitted) for handicapped persons than for other employees.

Labor relations. The time period for public employee representatives to file petitions for bargaining unit or representation determinations was extended to 8 or 9 months, instead of 2 or 3 months, before the expiration of a contract. The first labor organization petitioning for a representation election must now show approval of at least 30 percent of the eligible voters in the unit and each additional petitioning labor organization must show at least 10-percent approval.

Other laws. Meetings of all State and local government bodies, with specified exceptions, must be preceded by public notice and must be held in open session. State and local agencies with rulemaking authority are now required to adopt procedures to ensure that economic values will be given proper consideration in the rulemaking process, along with environmental, social, health, and safety considerations. □

State labor legislation enacted in 1977

*Significant new legislation prohibits
mandatory retirement, discriminatory boycotts,
and employment of illegal aliens; some States
move to assist displaced homemakers*

RICHARD R. NELSON AND DAVID A. LEVY

The passage of labor legislation accelerated this year,[1] with enactment of new laws or amendments affecting each major standards field. Continued interest was shown in such traditional subjects as minimum wage rates and coverage, job discrimination, and child labor. At the same time, important new legislation reflected developing concern with such issues as mandatory retirement, undocumented workers, displaced homemakers, discriminatory boycotts, and reciprocal agreements for collection of unpaid wages.

Furthering traditional concerns

Minimum wage activity included both increased wage rates and broadened application of the laws. Kansas replaced a wage-board-type law that had no minimum rates with a law prescribing a minimum. Colorado extended its law to all workers; it formerly applied to women and minors only. Household workers now have minimum wage protection in Connecticut and Indiana, and tipped employees in Oregon who are subject to the Federal Fair Labor Standards Act (FLSA) are now also covered by State law, which bans any tip credit. Minimum wage rates were increased for some or all workers in Arkansas, California, Colorado, the District of Columbia, Indiana, Minnesota, North Carolina, and Oklahoma. In Nevada, the labor commissioner was given temporary authority to increase the rate within specified limits.

More than half of the States enacted legislation designed to eradicate various forms of employment discrimination. A comprehensive human rights act was passed in Florida, while North Carolina adopted a policy against many forms of discrimination. Administration of fair employment practices laws was strengthened in Connecticut, Hawaii, Maryland, and Nevada. Efforts to aid handicapped workers were the subject of legislation in 13 States. A new law in Minnesota makes age discrimination an unfair employment practice. Bans on discrimination in employment on public works contracts were initiated or broadened in Illinois, Kansas, and New York. In California, Colorado, Oregon, and Virginia, barriers to the employment or occupational licensing of persons with arrest or conviction records were eased.

In eight jurisdictions, amendments provided for wage garnishment or assignment for child support payments. As with other such provisions, the laws generally prohibited employers from discharging or disciplining employees for this reason. In New Hampshire, the wages of public employees were

Richard R. Nelson and David A. Levy are labor standards advisers in the Division of State Employment Standards, Employment Standards Administration, U.S. Department of Labor.

made subject to any assignment or garnishment permitted in the private sector.

Child labor legislation continued the trend toward easing restrictions and providing additional employment opportunities. In Arkansas, Hawaii, and Maryland, permissible nightwork was extended. Employment certificates are no longer required for certain minors in California, New Jersey, and Tennessee, and procedures for obtaining certificates were simplified in Indiana and North Carolina.

Breaking new ground

An emerging awareness of the valuable contributions of older workers and of the waste caused by arbitrary compulsory retirement based upon age has led to a reevaluation of such policies. Last year, Florida became the first State to prohibit mandatory retirement in the public sector. This year, California became the first State to prohibit mandatory retirement based on age in private employment, and public employees were granted the right to continue working after reaching the normal retirement age. Maine also prohibited the required retirement of public employees at a specified age and ordered a study followed by a phase-in of a similar prohibition in the private sector effective January 1, 1980. Los Angeles and Seattle eliminated compulsory retirement at age 65 for municipal workers.

The subject of undocumented, or illegal, alien workers has attracted considerable national attention, particularly as continued high unemployment has prompted concern that undocumented workers deprive American workers of jobs. This year, five States—Florida, Maine, Montana, Vermont, and Virginia—passed legislation banning the knowing employment of these workers. Such laws had previously been adopted in California, Connecticut, Delaware, Kansas, Massachusetts, and New Hampshire.

Nine states—Colorado, Illinois, Maine, Minnesota, Montana, New York, Ohio, Oregon, and Texas—passed legislation to help homemakers displaced because of dissolution of marriage or other loss of family income. Displaced homemaker laws were previously enacted in California, Florida, and Maryland. These laws direct the establishment of multipurpose centers or programs to provide employment services and other aid. Because of their age or lack of paid work experience, displaced homemakers often face difficulty in getting jobs. They are frequently ineligible for financial assistance from public sources. In addition, Rhode Island passed a resolution to study the feasibility of establishing a program for displaced homemakers. A few other States furnish similar services through projects such as those funded under the Federal Comprehensive Employment and Training Act (CETA).

Discrimination brought about by outside influences was prohibited in three States. Connecticut, North Carolina, and Washington made it illegal to participate in a discriminatory boycott or blacklist imposed by a foreign person, government, or international organization, which restricts business relationships and employment practices on such bases as race, color, creed, religion, sex, or national origin.

Kansas and Montana enacted legislation to remedy the problems caused by out-of-State employers who fail to pay wages and employers who move from the State without making payment. Their labor departments may now enter into agreements with other States to collect any wages due from these employers and to perform reciprocal services for such other States.

Legislation affecting agricultural workers included a comprehensive migrant labor law in Wisconsin that covers wages, hours of work, registration of labor contractors, and certification of labor camps. A council on migrant labor was created in the labor department. Colorado enacted a statute requiring farm labor contractors to register with the division of labor and to furnish migratory laborers with job-related information. Registration was formerly required by regulation.

"Sunset laws" requiring periodic reexamination of State agencies, rules, and regulations were enacted or amended in 15 States. The labor department was specifically assigned a termination date in Arkansas, Tennessee, and Texas and was reestablished in Alabama under the sunset law in that State. Private employment agency boards or other regulations on private employment agencies are scheduled for abolition or reassessment in Georgia, North Carolina, Oklahoma, Tennessee, Texas, and Washington. Similarly, the status of occupational and professional licensing and other boards or commissions will be reviewed in Alaska, Hawaii, Indiana, Nebraska, North Dakota, Oklahoma, Oregon, and Utah.

Court action invalidated public employee collective bargaining in two States. In Indiana, the public sector collective bargaining act was declared unconstitutional by the State supreme court, because the law excluded certain administrative determinations from judicial review. In Virginia, the State supreme court held that a county board and a school board do not have authority to negotiate or enter into collective bargaining agreements with their employees.

Indiana became the 35th State to ratify the proposed equal rights amendment to the U.S. constitution. If the amendment is to be approved, ratification by three additional States is necessary during 1978. The Nevada legislature provided for a nonbinding advisory referendum on the issue in November 1978.

The following is a summary by State of legislative action during 1977.

Alabama

Following a review and evaluation, as required under the 1976 sunset law, the continued existence of the department of labor and the department of industrial relations was authorized.

Centers offering such services as recruitment, counseling, pre–job and vocational training, family planning, and health and child care, will be established to aid economically disadvantaged, unemployed, and underemployed persons.

Alaska

Wages. Fish processors or primary fish buyers with less than $10,000 in lienable property in the State must file a $10,000 surety bond, or its equivalent, as security for collection of unpaid wages. The labor commissioner or an aggrieved person may sue against this bond.

Labor relations. Public employee collective bargaining agreements will now be required to include a pay plan with a cost-of-living differential between State resident and nonresident salaries. Nonresident salaries must remain constant until the differential reflects the difference in cost of living between Alaska and Seattle, Wash.

Other laws. A sunset law was enacted, setting future termination dates for certain boards, commissions, and agency programs and providing for periodic review and hearings to determine whether they should be terminated, continued, or reestablished.

It is now unlawful to dismiss, demote, suspend, lay off, or otherwise discipline a public employee for making public records or information available for public inspection as provided by law.

Arizona

Wages. A person may be ordered by the court to make a wage assignment for support payments. The assignment is binding on the employer, who may not discharge or discipline an employee for such assignment. If a writ of garnishment is not made permanent within 90 days, an employer must release to the employee any funds held (up to $200).

County boards of supervisors were authorized to pay county employees for overtime work and to develop pay plans incorporating classifications and conditions prescribed by the FLSA.

Occupational safety and health. Standards promulgated on employee exposure to hazardous substances must assure that no material impairment of health or function would occur if the employee were exposed to the hazard for his entire working life. Review board decisions on appeals from hearing officer decisions are binding, but the director of the occupational safety and health division is empowered to seek judicial review. Penalties are extended to cover violations of any provision of the act.

A comprehensive boiler safety law was enacted, to be administered by the industrial commission through the division of occupational safety and health.

Arkansas

Wages. The State minimum wage was increased from $2 to $2.10 per hour effective July 1, 1977, to $2.20 effective January 1, 1978, and to $2.30 effective January 1, 1979. Premium overtime pay, at one and one-half times the regular rate, is now required after 40 hours a week in nonagricultural employment, except in hotels, motels, and restaurants (48 hours). Tip credit allowances were increased to $1 effective July 1, 1977, $1.10 effective January 1, 1978, and $1.15 effective January 1, 1979.

An overtime policy was adopted for State employees, restricting payment for overtime to extreme emergencies. The agency must receive prior general authorization from the General Assembly.

A broad-coverage prohibition against sex-based pay discrimination was enacted, with a misdemeanor penalty for each day of violation. The State already has an equal pay law administered by the labor department.

Child labor. Minors age 16 and 17 may now work an extra hour—until 11 p.m.—preceding schooldays. There is no limit on nightwork preceding nonschooldays. Minors under 16 may be employed to perform in the same entertainment production as a parent, if they remain under parental supervision.

Labor relations. The Governor was requested to establish a tripartite commission to investigate and make recommendations to the legislature on teacher employment contracts, laws, and practices.

Private employment agencies. The private employment agency law was amended to exempt resumé services that do not make referrals to employment or are not financially connected with an employment agency.

Occupational safety and health. A new act provides for safeguards in the transportation of hazardous materials. It requires compliance with applicable Federal and State laws and regulations.

All companies, owners, lessees, or persons engaged in the installation, relocation, or alteration of elevators, dumbwaiters, or escalators must now be approved and registered by the department of labor. The fee structure for inspections and permits, and the examination and license fees for inspectors were revised.

Other laws. A sunset law was enacted, providing for periodic review of State agencies, departments, programs, boards, commissions, and institutions, to recommend termination, continuation, or reestablishment. A new law must be passed to reestablish an agency scheduled for termination. The department of labor is scheduled for termination on June 30, 1979.

State officers and employees will be protected against personal liability for actions taken while performing official duties. The State attorney general will participate in all trial and settlement proceedings and the State will pay court-awarded damages.

The law giving preference to resident firms in the purchase of goods by public agencies was amended to limit the preference to suppliers who have paid taxes within the State for 2 years prior to the bid. Penalties were established for violations of the law by public officials.

California

Wages. Student employees of organized camps were exempted from minimum wage and maximum hours orders if their pay, less the value of meals and lodging, is (1) at least $86 per week, regardless of the number of hours worked over 40 a week, or (2) at least $2.15 per hour, if working less than 40 hours. Unless extended by the legislature, this exemption will expire January 1, 1980.

Minors between age 16 and 18 who work more than 8 hours a day or 48 hours a week in handling products after harvest or preparing agricultural products on the farm for market must be paid at least the adult minimum wage rate for all hours worked, instead of the lower youth rate.

Minors under 18 who are high school graduates must be paid the adult minimum wage, rather than the youth rate, when they perform work equal to that of an adult.

The labor department was made responsible for enforcing the payment of prevailing wages for custodial and janitorial work contracted out by public utilities. Contractors and subcontractors are expressly mandated to pay the prevailing wage, which now specifically includes fringe benefits. Instead of using the wage determined by the U.S. Department of Labor, the prevailing wage will be determined by the State labor department.

Hours of work. If the chief of the division of labor standards enforcement determines that a hardship will result, he may exempt any employer or employees from any mandatory days-off requirement prescribed by the industrial welfare commission. Employers may not retaliate against employees who refuse to work hours beyond those permitted by the commission. Unless extended by the legislature, these provisions terminate June 30, 1979.

Child labor. High school graduates under age 18 are no longer subject to hours restrictions or to the work permit requirement otherwise applicable to this age group.

For days and weeks when minors between 16 and 18 are required by law to attend school, the new work limit in handling products after harvest, in preparing agricultural products on the farm for market, and in domestic labor is 6 hours a day and 20 hours a week.

Equal employment opportunity. In both private and public employment, mandatory retirement is now prohibited. Any employee in the private sector who wishes to continue working beyond the normal retirement date contained in a private pension or retirement plan may do so by written request to the employer. Such employment will continue as long as the employee performs the job adequately and the employer is satisfied with the quality of work.

The laws regulating the retirement systems for State, county, and municipal employees were amended to allow all public employees, except law enforcement workers and firefighters, to continue working beyond the normal age of employment—if certified as competent by the employing department or agency. Los Angeles also abolished mandatory retirement for city employees, but required older workers to take an annual physical examination.

In the past, existing limitations were set on employer inquiries about an arrest or detention not resulting in conviction. Now, public and private employers are also barred from asking job applicants for information concerning the applicant's referral to or participation in any pre-trial or post-trial diversion program.

The postsecondary education commission must submit biennial reports to the Governor and legislature on the representation and utilization of ethnic minorities and women among employees of the State University and Colleges, the University of California, and public community colleges.

Because foreign film companies and crews operate within the State, the President, the Congress, and the commissioner of Immigration and Naturalization were petitioned to protect the employment opportunities of U.S. workers in the entertainment industry.

Private employment agencies. Employer-retained agencies which charge fees exclusively to employers are now specifically exempted from regulations pertaining to contract provisions, receipts, and posting of fee schedules.

Occupational safety and health. The division of industrial safety was directed to enforce the law regulating the spraying of asbestos substances on buildings under construction, alteration, and repair. Employers will no longer be charged for the inspection for cancer-producing substances.

Other laws. The release of any medical information to an employer or union without the employee's authorization is now prohibited.

Prospective bidders on public works contracts may now be required to complete a questionnaire on their safety record. The transportation department was directed to begin a 3-year program of rating prospective bidders on the basis of their safety records.

Payment bonds from public works contractors are now required on contracts exceeding $15,000, rather than $10,000.

A Youth Employment and Development Act requires the employment development department to conduct youth on-the-job training programs, youth community service programs, and innovative demonstration projects to facilitate the transition from school to work.

The Governor was requested to provide legislative proposals for establishing a policy for employment rights of State citizens, a full employment program, and a permanent job creation system, and for creating a more favorable business climate.

Colorado

Wages. Minimum wage protection was extended to all workers instead of only women and minors, and a rate 15 percent below the full minimum was authorized for minors under 18. Under an administrative emergency order, a minimum rate of $1.90 was established in the public housekeeping, laundry, beauty service, and retail trade industries. Premium overtime pay is required after 40 hours a week generally, but after 46 hours for hotel, motel, and restaurant employees. Rest and meal periods are required, wage deductions for cash shortages are prohibited, and required uniforms must be furnished and maintained, free of charge, by the employer. The maximum tip credit is 50 percent. Employers are prohibited from taking their employees' tips, unless a public notice is posted.

Agriculture. Farm labor contractors must now register with the division of labor. Contractors must furnish migratory laborers with written information on the nature of work, transportation, housing, insurance, wages, charges by the contractor for his services, and any strikes at the place of contracted employment. The director of the division can conduct investigations; suspend, revoke, and refuse to renew registrations; and assess civil penalties. Retaliation against migratory laborers who file complaints or institute proceedings under the act is prohibited.

Equal employment opportunity. The antidiscrimination law was extended to protect the handicapped. An employer may no longer require a job applicant to disclose court-sealed arrest and criminal records information, and the employee may treat the event involved as nonexistent. The 1-year residency requirement was removed from the law that gives employment preference to State residents on public works projects. In determining such preference, sex and age are now prohibited bases of discrimination (in addition to race, creed, and color).

Labor relations. Under the Labor Peace Act, "all-union agreement" was redefined to include any type of union security agreement requiring employees' financial support or union membership. The definition had been limited to agreements requiring that all employees be union members. Procedures were established for ratification, certification, approval, and termination of "all-union agreements." These agreements were authorized in the building and construction industry, except those providing for agency or modified agency shops.

Displaced homemakers. The director of labor and employment was directed to establish multipurpose centers to provide training, counseling, and other services to displaced homemakers, to help them obtain jobs.

Other laws. The appointment and use of hearing officers was authorized in numerous State governmental activities, including hearings on charges of unfair labor practices under the Labor Peace Act and charges against certain certificated coal mine employees for failure to perform required duties.

The required minimum length of training under apprenticeship agreements was reduced from 2 years to 1 year.

Connecticut

Wages. Coverage of the minimum wage law was extended to domestic service employees (as defined in the FLSA) and babysitters were specifically exempted. As an alternative to basing his determinations of wage rates on public works contracts solely on information gathered at hearings in the locality of the project, the labor commissioner was authorized to use prevailing wage rate determinations made under the Federal Davis-Bacon Act.

Child labor. Minors 16 and older may now be licensed in all occupations at race tracks, jai alai frontons, and off-track betting establishments, rather than only in certain occupations.

Students between age 16 and 18 may be employed as ushers in nonprofit theaters until midnight during school vacations and on days preceding nonschooldays.

Equal employment opportunity. The human rights and opportunities commission was authorized to seek temporary injunctions against employers of 50 workers or more to prevent irreparable harm to a person alleging violation of the Fair Employment Practices Act. The commission was also authorized to receive and issue complaints alleging discriminatory activities by State agencies.

Starting July 1, 1978, it is unlawful to participate in a discriminatory boycott, which is defined as the entering into or performance of a contract or understanding with a foreign entity which restricts business relationships within the State (including ownership, management, employees, hiring practices, and customers) on the basis of race, color, creed, religion, sex, nationality, or national origin.

The legislature requested an investigation of several State agencies for compliance with nondiscrimination requirements.

Labor relations. Each party in public sector collective bargaining in all political subdivisions must furnish cost data for all provisions in proposed agreements submitted to arbitration panels. The legislative branch of government is no longer covered by the law authorizing and regulating collective bargaining for State employees.

The secretary of the State board of education must be notified of and considered to be an interested party to any hearings in injunctive proceedings resulting from a teachers' strike.

The legislature approved agreements negotiated between the State and unions representing various groups of State employees.

Private employment agencies. Registries conducted by hospitals for private duty placement of nurses employed by the hospital were exempted from the employment agency law.

Occupational safety and health. Effective July 1, 1978, the State safety and health law, which is currently part of an approved State plan under the Federal law, will cover only the public sector.

Employers will be required, upon employee request, to

furnish the employee with a written list of the hazardous substances with which the employee comes into contact. When required by the labor commissioner, voluntary, free lung function tests must be provided for each employee exposed to such substances.

Other laws. The labor commissioner was directed to establish a pre-employment and post-employment vocational and manpower training program to meet the labor requirements of specific employers in industrial projects. He must appoint a job training coordinator to develop training programs and incentives for apprenticeship programs in certain occupations. A job incentive fund was established to stimulate the creation and growth of jobs through incentive grants to businesses located in areas of high unemployment.

As part of a reorganization of State government, administration of provisions regulating the employment of minors in agriculture and establishing standards for living quarters provided for agricultural and migratory farmworkers was transferred from the commissioner of agriculture to the labor commissioner.

Delaware

Other laws. State officials responsible for making purchases or letting contracts are requested, wherever possible, to do business with State-based firms—to help them become economically viable and to employ unemployed residents of the State.

District of Columbia

Wages. The minimum wage for employees in clerical and semitechnical occupations was increased from $2.25 to $2.90 per hour for adults, and from $1.80 to $2.40 for minors under 18. This wage order also established a minimum of $2.55 an hour for teacher aides in child day care centers and authorized institutions of higher education to pay full-time student employees the minimum required by the FLSA, rather than the higher wage order rate.

Wages, annuities, and retirement and disability benefits of city employees are now subject to garnishment for child support, maintenance, or alimony payments.

Occupational safety and health. Comprehensive electrical and elevator codes were adopted.

Florida

Wages. Direct bank deposit of an employee's wages is permitted if the employee consents, but an employee may not be discharged for refusal to authorize such deposit.

Officials awarding public works contracts now have the option of exempting from the usual penal bond a person entering into a contract of $25,000 or less.

Child labor. Conforming changes were made in various provisions of the code by inserting the 18-year age of majority. For one, minors under 18 (instead of 21) who are employed by parents were exempted from the child labor law.

Equal employment opportunity. A comprehensive human rights act was enacted, replacing a limited provision applicable to public employees only. The new law, applicable to employers of 15 workers or more, prohibits discrimination in employment on the basis of age, handicap, and marital status, as well as race, sex, religion, and ancestry as enumerated before. It prescribes unfair labor practices for employers, labor organizations, employment agencies, and joint apprenticeship committees that will become effective July 1, 1978. The law expands the Governor-appointed membership of the human relations commission from 6 to 12. The commission is authorized to, among other duties, act upon complaints, issue subpoenas, hold hearings, and seek judicial remedies in cases of noncompliance.

Labor relations. Several changes were made in the public employee bargaining law. Members are now required to ratify contracts involving Statewide bargaining units; certified employee organizations are not required to process grievances for nonmembers; and dues checkoff will continue for as long as a union remains certified, rather than just for the duration of a collective bargaining agreement. Other provisions permit student representation in college negotiations, define good faith bargaining, authorize either party to declare a negotiation impasse, and specifically permit employees to engage in legal concerted activities for purposes of collective bargaining.

An amendment to the law regulating registration of unions and licensing of union business agents transferred administration from the department of business regulation to the division of labor in the department of commerce. The suspension, revocation, or denial of licenses or of registration can now be effected administratively, after a hearing, rather than only by the courts.

Undocumented workers. An employer is prohibited from knowingly hiring, recruiting, or referring an alien who is not authorized to work in the United States. A first violation, irrespective of the number of aliens employed, carries a civil penalty of up to $500; subsequent violations, each unauthorized alien constituting a separate offense, carry criminal penalties of up to $500.

Other laws. The occupational and professional licensing law was amended to permit resident aliens to receive these licenses, removing the requirement of U.S. citizenship or legal declaration of the intention of becoming a citizen.

The State labor department was authorized to enter into agreements to act as the registration agent for the Federal apprenticeship registration program. The same law prohibits the department from enforcing Federal apprenticeship requirements without first adopting necessary rules and regulations.

Counties, municipalities, school districts, and other political subdivisions of the State that let contracts for purchases of personal property are authorized to give preference to in-State businesses when the lowest bidder is from another State which grants a preference to its own residents, but only in an amount equal to that given by the other State.

Georgia

Wages. Employees are now permitted to assign their wages to the department of human resources to cover child support obligations, courts are permitted to require assignments for this purpose, and employers are barred from discharging an employee because of such assignment.

Equal employment opportunity. A resolution continues the study committee on services for the aged, directing it to study recommendations of the 1976 committee, including employment and mandatory retirement, and to report its findings and legislative proposals to the General Assembly by January 1, 1978.

Other laws. The State personnel board and commissioner of personnel administration were urged to rescind their recommendations for changes in or elimination of veterans preference in the State merit system. A sunset law repeals the private employment agency regulatory law, and the advisory council it created, as of July 1, 1978, and abolishes other regulatory agencies and boards on various dates. The law provides for public hearings to determine the need for continued existence. Legislative action is required to continue or reestablish these agencies.

Hawaii

Wages. Employers and employees may not set aside any provision of the wage and hour law by private agreement.

Amendments to the wage payment law make the employer civilly liable for twice the amount of unpaid wages, and criminally liable for discharging or discriminating against an employee for participating in enforcement procedures. In addition, withholding wages for cash shortages is prohibited if the employee is not given an opportunity to account for all monies received at the start and end of a shift, and employers are liable for any bank fees incurred by employees in negotiating paychecks not backed by sufficient funds.

A resolution requests the U.S. Department of Labor to accept Hawaii's determinations of prevailing wage rates on contracts involving Federal funds, contending that they are more current and more accurate than those determined under the Davis-Bacon Act.

Hours of work. The Governor and local officials were requested to initiate discussions about developing staggered or flexible work time programs during contract negotiations with public employee organizations. The Governor was given authority to modify the work hours of State government offices, schools, and other agencies to meet the need for public services, encourage energy conservation, and reduce traffic congestion.

Child labor. A change in nightwork restrictions permits 14- and 15-year-olds to work until 9 p.m., instead of 8 p.m., from June 1 through the day before Labor Day.

Equal employment opportunity. The labor department is now authorized to bring court action to enjoin unlawful discrimination and order affirmative action, including reinstatement and hiring of employees. If a judgment obtained under the act remains unsatisfied, the department may institute proceedings to compel violators to cease doing business.

The Governor's committee on employment of the handicapped was redesignated the commission on the handicapped, with responsibility for reviewing and assessing the problems and needs of the handicapped, including employment, and developing methods and goals for improvement.

Labor relations. The compensation, hours, conditions of employment, and other benefits of State, county, and school employees who are excluded from collective bargaining are to be adjusted to be not less than those granted to covered employees with equivalent or identical positions.

Occupational safety and health. The occupational safety and health law was amended to, among other things, strengthen worker protection against employer retaliation and clarify employer and labor department rights and duties in the employer appeal procedure. Penalties were established for criminal offenses committed against any State employee performing duties under this law.

Other laws. Subsidies for employment training programs were expanded to include all employers willing to participate, rather than only private employers. The "head of household" requirement was deleted from the criteria under which unemployed persons receive priority consideration for hiring in public service employment programs.

A sunset law was enacted, providing for a periodic assessment of existing professional and vocational regulation, setting policies concerning regulatory agencies, and establishing termination dates for several agencies (these can be reestablished by the legislature).

Several resolutions aimed at improving the employment situation in Hawaii were adopted. The Congress was petitioned to designate native Hawaiians and other minority groups in Hawaii as special target groups for CETA programs and to enact tax incentive language to promote private sector employment. Other resolutions requested the establishment of a task force to develop an employment program to create jobs and reduce unemployment; asked the State commission on manpower and full employment to assess short- and long-term manpower needs and policies and, together with other State agencies (including labor department) to study methods of increasing employment rates among teenagers and young adults; requested the State labor department to give high priority to implementing year-round occupational programs for youth; and requested the department of personnel services to study the feasibility of job sharing by public employees who may desire or need shorter hours.

Idaho

Wages. A new provision requires employers to abide by wage assignments made for court-ordered child support payments, with such assignments given priority over any other attachment, execution, or assignment. The limit on wage claims assignable to the labor commissioner for collection was increased from $450 to $1,000 for each employee.

Equal employment opportunity. Idaho's earlier ratification of the proposed equal rights amendment to the U.S. constitution was rescinded.

Labor relations. Changes in the firefighter collective bargaining law remove supervisors from coverage and eliminate a 1-year limit on contract duration. Ratification of all final offers in school district negotiations must now be made in open meetings, and records and minutes must be open for public inspection.

Other laws. A bid on a State printing contract to be performed outside of the State may now be accepted if it is at least 10 percent lower than that of an in-State bidder.

Illinois

Wages. Executive, administrative, and professional employees, who were not exempted from an overtime standard adopted last year that took effect August 22, 1976, were exempted by a law effective January 10, 1977. Employers may not recover any overtime payments made to such employees during this interval, or discharge or discipline an employee for refusal to return the money. Commission-paid employees and employees who have agreed to exchange worktime with each other were also exempted from the premium pay requirement this year.

Assignable wages, formerly restricted to 15 percent of gross weekly wages, are now restricted to that percentage or to the amount by which disposable weekly earnings exceed 30 times the Federal minimum hourly wage, whichever is less. This limitation applies irrespective of the place where compensation is earned or payable and the State where the employee resides.

Under the wage payment act, an employer may deposit wages into a bank chosen by the employee.

Child labor. The minimum age for work in mines was raised from 16 to 18.

Equal employment opportunity. Women will now be permitted to work in mines. Cities and towns may no longer ban employment of women in drawing, pouring, and mixing alcoholic beverages in retail establishments selling liquor.

Religion, sex, and national origin are added to the list of prohibited forms of discrimination which the attorney general is authorized to investigate and enforce. Sex, national origin, and physical or mental handicap unrelated to ability were added to prohibited forms of discrimination in employment by the Chicago transit board. Public works contractors and subcontractors under contract with the State or political subdivisions and war defense contractors are now prohibited from discriminating against an employee because of sex, religion, physical or mental handicap unrelated to ability, or national origin, in addition to race and color as before.

Sex discrimination in hours of work was eliminated by repealing hours limitations applicable to women only.

Occupational safety and health. A new act to assure safety in the transportation of hazardous materials over highways and in related loading and unloading operations gives the department of transportation regulatory and rulemaking authority. Conformance to or improvement on comparable Federal regulations is contemplated.

Within 2 years, coal mine operators will be required (1) to have a certified emergency medical technician on duty whenever 30 persons or more are working at the mine, (2) to provide two-way communication facilities to the outside, and (3) to provide all new employees with the opportunity for prescribed first-aid training and refresher training.

Displaced homemakers. A Displaced Homemakers Assistance Act directs the labor commissioner to establish multipurpose centers to provide displaced homemakers with counseling, training, education, and placement services to help them become gainfully employed. To the greatest extent possible, the centers will be staffed by displaced homemakers.

Indiana

Wages. The minimum wage law was amended to increase the minimum in steps to $2 by January 1, 1979 and to extend coverage to private household workers and 17-year-olds, formerly exempt. Minors under 17 continue to be exempt. Coverage of part-year workers was expanded.

Statutory overtime provisions for State employees were repealed, and the department of administration and the State personnel board were directed to develop overtime pay policies and procedures.

Child labor. The minimum age for agricultural employment was raised from 10 to 12. Proofs of physical fitness and schooling were deleted as requirements for obtaining employment certificates in covered occupations, only proofs of age and prospective employment are required.

Agriculture. The board of health must now inspect agricultural labor camps and issue operation permits before the camps are occupied each year.

Equal employment opportunity. The proposed equal rights amendment to the U.S. constitution was ratified.

The State commission on the aging and aged was reconstituted on a bipartisan basis. Its functions were enumerated comprehensively, with particular emphasis on its coordinating role in the delivery of services, including employment counseling.

Labor relations. The public employees' collective bargaining act was declared invalid in its entirety by the State supreme court, because the law prohibited judicial review of certain administrative determinations.

Occupational safety and health. Inspectors cannot be delayed from entering and inspecting work places at reasonable times. In establishments where there is no authorized employee representative, inspectors are now required to consult with a reasonable number of employees on safety and health matters, instead of merely being authorized to do so. The labor commissioner is now required to issue a notice of failure to correct a violation and to assess a penalty for continuing violations.

Other laws. Advance public notice must be given for meetings of all agencies of the State and political subdivisions, and information on the activities of the meetings must be made available to the public.

A legislative committee was established to evaluate State agencies and programs and to make recommendations on the need to continue the agencies and programs.

Kansas

Wages. A new minimum wage law was enacted, effective January 1, 1978, prescribing a rate of $1.60 an hour and premium pay at time and one-half the employee's regular rate, for work in excess of 46 hours per week. (Under a wage board law enacted in 1915, no minimum wage rates had been in effect.) Among the exemptions are employment subject to FLSA, agricultural and household workers, and persons of 18 or under or 60 and over who are employed in occasional or part-time work. The maximum tip credit is 40 percent of the minimum wage. Wage discrimination on the basis of sex is prohibited.

The secretary of human resources may enter into agreements with other States to collect unpaid wages from out-of-State employers and to reciprocate in Kansas for other States. The secretary is also authorized to investigate wage claims and make the final decision on wages and damages payable. Wage garnishment for court-ordered child support or alimony under specified circumstances is no longer subject to restrictions on garnishable amounts.

Equal employment opportunity. It is now unlawful for public works contractors with four employees or more or with contracts over $5,000 to discriminate in employment against handicapped persons when they are able to perform the work.

Labor relations. The collective bargaining law for teachers was amended to include, for the first time, employee, union, and management unfair labor practices. Also added were impasse procedures, including court review, mediation, and factfinding with nonbinding recommendations. Meetings between employee organizations and boards of education are now required to be public open meetings, except when they involve mediation or factfinding. Responsibility for overseeing bargaining unit determination and representation elections is transferred from the State board of education to the labor department.

Occupational safety and health. A new comprehensive boiler safety law, to be administered and enforced by the secretary of human resources, regulates the construction, installation, inspection, maintenance, and repair of boilers. All job health and safety provisions applicable to coal, underground rock, or limestone mines were repealed, because these are subject to Federal law; the only requirement retained was that the mine owner or operator prepare and submit to the secretary of human resources an accurate map of the mine.

Louisiana

Wages. The time within which an employer must pay wages upon discharge or resignation of an employee, and the time within which a suit for any unpaid wages must be filed by an employee after making the first demand following discharge or resignation were increased from 24 hours to 3 days. In case of a dispute over the amount due, the employer must pay the undisputed portion.

School attendance. A joint legislative committee was requested to study the compulsory school attendance law and the possible effects if the ages for required attendance were changed or dropped. The committee will report to the 1978 regular session of the legislature.

Equal employment opportunity. Physical barriers in new and existing public and government buildings are to be removed, giving the handicapped access to their places of employment and opportunity to secure employment.

The attorney general was requested to actively enforce all laws concerning discriminatory hiring practices and affirmative action programs, to ensure that all persons are given equal employment opportunity, especially during periods of high unemployment.

Labor relations. The antitrespass law was amended, removing the exemption for labor organizations conducting union activities such as picketing or lawful assembly.

Private employment agencies. Coverage of the law was enlarged by expanding the definition of employment agency to include persons furnishing employment information, providing names and addresses of employers, preparing resumés, determining applicants' qualifications, or recruiting applicants for referrals, where the applicant may be liable for a fee.

Occupational safety and health. Local governments will now be required to establish a fire prevention bureau to assume responsibility for certain fire inspection and prevention activities under the public health and safety law.

The legislature was requested to create a joint legislative committee to study and make recommendations on safety regulations for State employees, with a report and legislative proposals to be submitted prior to the 1978 legislative session.

Other laws. The department of health and human resources is solely responsible for implementing vocational rehabilitation programs for persons disabled in industry or otherwise, and must formulate a plan of cooperation with the labor department.

State and local government agencies will now be required to give preference to contractors residing within the State, except for contracts for construction maintenance or repair of highways and streets and contracts financed in whole or in part by Federal agencies.

The birthday of Dr. Martin Luther King, Jr. was added to the list of legal holidays.

Maine

Wages. When a person becomes unemployed because his employer is insolvent, claims for unpaid wages will include earned fringe benefits.

School attendance. Procedures were established for dealing with habitual truants and school dropouts under the compulsory school attendance law; a school committee was granted authority to require attendance or, if a child is at least 14 years old, waive the law. Pupils 14 or older may be excused for alternate programs of work, work study, or training, and a special work permit for employment in nonhazardous occupations may be issued to a child between 15 and 17 who is ineligible for a regular work permit.

Equal employment opportunity. Beginning July 1, 1978, public sector employers may not require employees to retire at or before a specified age or after completing a specified number of years of service. By January 31, 1979, the State planning office, in consultation with the committee on aging, is directed to present the legislature with recommendations for an orderly phase-in, no later than January 1, 1980, of a prohibition against mandatory retirement in private employment. Directors of mutual financial institutions will no longer be required to retire from board membership at age 72.

Labor organizations and employers can now adopt maximum ages for apprenticeship programs without violating the age discrimination prohibition of the fair employment practices law.

Labor relations. The collective bargaining law for employees of the University of Maine and the Maine Maritime Academy was extended to employees of State vocational-technical institutes and State schools for practical nursing.

Undocumented workers. It was made unlawful for any employer to knowingly hire an illegal alien. A good-faith written inquiry about the employee's status will constitute an affirmative defense. The commissioner of manpower affairs is directed to promulgate regulations specifying procedures to be followed by employers to assure compliance.

Displaced homemakers. A Displaced Homemakers Act directs the commissioner of manpower affairs to establish, by February 1, 1978, a program to provide displaced homemakers with counseling, training, education, and assistance in becoming gainfully employed. The program, a 2-year pilot project, will be staffed by displaced homemakers to the greatest extent possible.

Other laws. The prior criminal convictions which a State agency may consider in determining eligibility for an occupational license were spelled out in detail, replacing a general reference to convictions.

Until June 30, 1980, preference in awarding State contracts will be given to bidders whose principal place of business or branch thereof has been located in Maine for 2 years and who will employ at least 90 percent State residents on the contract—provided that the resident employer's bid is not more than 2 percent higher than the lowest bid and that he agrees to accept the contract at the amount submitted by the lowest bidder.

Beginning January 1, 1978, all State agency rules in effect or issued thereafter will automatically expire within 5 years, unless renewed by statute.

Maryland

Wages. The labor commissioner may no longer automatically accept a Federal subminimum wage certificate, in lieu of a State certificate, for handicapped persons employed in sheltered workshops or work activities centers who have completed a training program run by the center. The labor commissioner was authorized to use informal methods of mediation and conciliation to resolve unpaid wage claims before referral to the attorney general for court action. The list of exemptions from execution on a judgment were made inapplicable to wage attachments.

Child labor. A major revision of the law, strengthened some safeguards and relaxed others. For example, the law now bars employment of minors under age 18 in hazardous occupations banned by local, State, or Federal law and authorizes adoption of additional bans by reference to Federal law. Restrictions on part-time work by minors under 16 were eased; they may work until 8 p.m. instead of 7 p.m. and for 4 hours on schooldays rather than 3. Penalties for violation were stiffened substantially.

Equal employment opportunity. The Human Relations Act was amended to require the appointment of hearing examiners to conduct hearings and issue decisions on discrimination cases, with the human relations commission serving as a board of appeals. In deciding unlawful employment practice cases, specific authority is granted to order reinstatement or hiring, with or without back pay, or other appropriate remedies.

The same rules, procedures, powers, rights, and remedies applicable in private sector discrimination cases will apply in cases involving State agencies and employees, with the exception of the award of monetary relief and damages. In addition, State employees' complaints will not be acted on until all remedies under the code of fair practices have been exhausted.

Discrimination on the basis of a person's sexual orientation was prohibited.

Labor relations. A formal grievance procedure was established for employees of the executive branch of the State government. Persons subject to collective bargaining agreements containing other grievance procedures were exempted.

Private employment agencies. The labor commissioner was authorized to issue cease-and-desist orders to enforce the employment agency law. Provision was made for hearings on such action, and authority was granted to request court orders compelling compliance.

Occupational safety and health. Railroad sidetracks and switches may be immediately closed if the public service commission finds conditions which constitute a danger to the health and safety of railroad employees. The chief boiler inspector must investigate accidents and explosions involving boilers or pressure vessels.

Undocumented workers. The legislature expressed its support of Federal legislation that would penalize employers for employing illegal aliens.

Other laws. Contractors and subcontractors on public works projects are now permitted to refuse to hire residents of any State which enforces a law prohibiting employment of Maryland residents on public works in that State.

Massachusetts

Child labor. The law was amended to allow minors between the ages of 14 and 16 to work as volunteers in nonprofit hospitals until 8 p.m., rather than 6 p.m.

Equal employment opportunity. A qualified civil service applicant may not be discriminated against because he has had cancer, if his rights to cancer-related disability benefits are waived.

Labor relations. Coverage of the public sector bargaining law was extended to judicial employees. With certain exceptions, the right to appoint, promote, assign, and transfer employees was excluded from the scope of fire fighter arbitration.

The labor relations commission was given power to investigate petitions requesting decertification of an exclusive employee collective bargaining representative.

Private employment agencies. The fee limit for placement of models was changed from an applicant-paid maximum of 10 percent of wages to a maximum from all sources of 10 percent of wages. Certain types of model agencies may charge an employer for additional services, if the applicant is notified in writing of these additional services.

Other laws. The Governor may now appoint six persons to the energy facilities siting council, rather than five. The additional member will represent organized labor.

Minnesota

Wages. The minimum wage was increased to $2.30 per hour for adults and $2.07 for minors under 18. Tip credits were reduced from 25 percent to 20 percent of the minimum wage, and the dollar test for determining tipped occupations was increased from $20 to $35 per month. Employers may no longer require employees to pool tips, and tips are the sole property of those receiving them.

Deductions from wages are now prohibited for lost, stolen, or damaged property, or to recover any other claimed indebtedness, unless the employee voluntarily gives the employer written authorization or is held liable in court. If such deductions are allowed, they may not be in excess of the amount subject to wage garnishment, and the employer is liable for twice the amount of a deduction taken in violation.

Equal employment opportunity. Age discrimination against persons over 18 is now an unfair employment practice, with certain exceptions, such as a mandatory retirement age established by law or published policy, and apprenticeship programs. Women who are disabled by pregnancy, childbirth, and related conditions have the same rights as other employees, including disability or other fringe benefits. They may be given special safety consideration in duties which might be hazardous to the unborn child.

Labor relations. The commissioner of personnel is authorized to implement the wage provisions of collective bargaining agreements negotiated with the State and concluded as of May 15, 1977. Employees not covered by an agreement on this date (or in the future, May 15 of each odd-numbered year) will not receive the increased benefits provided by this law. Personnel rules are to be reviewed and those that are in conflict with negotiated agreements will be suspended.

Supervisory or confidential public employees may belong to the same employee organization as other public employees, but separate bargaining units of supervisory or confidential employees may not negotiate jointly with other employee units. The public employee collective bargaining law was amended to exempt unclassified managerial positions from bargaining units—for example, employees in State higher education institutions, bureau of mediation services, and personnel offices where employees have access to confidential collective bargaining information. The finance commissioner was authorized to pay awards resulting from grievance actions.

Private employment agencies. Employment agencies are now prohibited from requiring the payment of a fee, by any person, if a job applicant withdraws acceptance of a position within 3 days of notification, without having started the job.

Displaced homemakers. The executive director of the Governor's manpower office may enter into arrangements with existing organizations and agencies to provide counseling and training for displaced homemakers.

Other laws. An employee summoned for or serving jury duty will be protected from threat of discharge. An employer in violation is subject to a fine or imprisonment (or both), and a discharged employee may bring a civil action for reinstatement and recovery of up to 6 weeks in lost wages.

A new law prohibits mandatory participation of employees in a group life insurance plan covering more than five employees, unless the employer pays all costs, except where other provision is made in a collectively bargained contract.

Any agreement is now void which requires an employee to assign to an employer rights to an invention which was developed without use of the employer's time, equipment, supplies, facility, or trade secret information, and where such invention is unrelated to the employer's business.

The commissioner of public welfare is authorized to implement a mandatory work equity program for general assistance recipients in participating counties. Earned income will not be used to terminate a recipient's general assistance status or other incidental benefits.

A public employee appointed or elected to a full-time city or county office is now entitled to unpaid leave of absence with reemployment rights. Public employees who qualify as members of the U.S. team in international sports events will be given a paid leave of absence for up to 90 days a year.

The division of vocational rehabilitation was elevated to a department of the State government.

Missouri

Wages. Deductions from State employees' wages may now be made, with written authorization, for union dues or charitable contributions.

Equal employment opportunity. The Governor's committee on employment of the handicapped was statutorily assigned to the department of labor and industrial relations. The director of the department was given responsibility for appointing the members, except the chairman, who is appointed by the Governor.

Blind and visually handicapped persons are entitled to employment in all public services supported by public funds, under the same terms and conditions as able-bodied persons, when the disability does not impair job performance.

Private employment agencies. Several changes were made in the employment agency law. For example, agencies are required to give job applicants copies of contracts and specified job information and applicant-paid placement fees are limited to 25 percent of gross salary if employment terminates within 45 days, unless the applicant leaves voluntarily or is discharged for misconduct. Certain agency practices are prohibited, including inducing employees to quit their jobs or employers to discharge them, making referrals without bona-fide job orders, and splitting fees with employers.

Occupational safety and health. An 1891 requirement that every factory and workshop where dusty work is carried on and where women and children are employed be lime-washed or painted at least every 12 months was repealed.

Montana

Wages. The department of labor is authorized to enter into agreements with other States to collect unpaid wages from out-of-State employers and to reciprocate for such other States. Under these agreements, the department would either take court actions (if the agreeing State's laws permitted) in the other State or assign the claims to that State's labor department.

Child labor. A legislative proposal calls for a study of the child labor law, enacted in 1907, together with a report and draft legislation.

Occupational safety and health. Among changes affecting fire prevention and general safety, the office of the fire marshal was transferred from the supervision of the insurance commissioner to the justice department. As chief of the new fire marshal bureau, the marshal, will now be appointed by the attorney general. A labor safety study committee established in 1967 to recommend changes in safety codes was abolished.

The Congress was asked to review the Federal Occupational Safety and Health Act of 1970 (OSH Act) to eliminate those practices and procedures which the State believes violate the U.S. constitution.

Undocumented workers. Employers are now prohibited from knowingly employing aliens not authorized to accept employment. A maximum fine of $300 may be levied for violation of this law, and the labor department or an injured party may seek an injunction.

Displaced homemakers. Two multipurpose centers for displaced homemakers are to be established as a 2-year pilot program to offer job counseling, training, job referral, and placement. The appropriations are contingent upon receipt of Federal funds.

Other laws. The open meetings law was amended to allow public bodies to hold closed meetings when an open meeting would be detrimental to the agency—for example, on such matters as collective bargaining or litigation. Any open meeting may be made accessible to the press and photographed, televised, or tape recorded.

Two resolutions dealt with employment and training. One urges the governor's office and the Labor department to investigate all possible means of using Federal and State funds to employ unemployed persons, including youth, on maintenance, improvement of land resources, and conservation projects. The other resolution urges the Federal Bureau of Apprenticeship and Training and the State apprenticeship bureau to reexamine existing programs, to develop new ways for encouraging employers to train apprentices, and to encourage the participation of small businesses and the expansion and development of programs in occupations with a shortage of skilled craftsmen.

Nebraska

Wages. State employees are now granted either premium pay at one and one-half times their regular rate or compensatory time at one and one-half times the hours worked for work in excess of 40 hours per week. They previously received straight time pay or an equal number of hours of compensatory time off. Special overtime provisions are made for police, fire, and hospital employees who work irregular hours and duty shifts.

Equal employment opportunity. The prohibition against age discrimination was extended to employment agencies. In enforcing the age discrimination law, the State equal employment opportunity commission is authorized to seek access to evidence or records or to require the answering of interrogatories through the attorney general. Maximum age limitations of 30 and 35 years for employment in fire and police departments were removed.

Employers, employment agencies, and labor organizations may not discriminate in employment because of a person's marital status. However, a policy of not employing both husband and wife is permissible if applied equally to both sexes.

Labor relations. Contracts negotiated between the American Federation of State, County and Municipal Employees Council 32 and the departments of labor and public institutions were approved by the legislature in accordance with the public sector collective bargaining law.

Private employment agencies. Changes in the private employment agency law include requirements that agencies furnish applicants with copies of contracts and maintain files with specified information on job orders. The labor commissioner and the courts were directed to order refunds where agencies have engaged in unfair or deceptive practices. The types of licenses were consolidated from three to one, and a uniform $100 license fee and $10,000 surety bond were adopted.

Occupational safety and health. Responsibility for enforcing construction standards for public buildings was transferred from the State building division to the State fire marshal.

Other laws. A sunset law was enacted, establishing termination dates for several agencies, commissions, and occupational and professional licensing boards, unless the legislature reenacts the original enabling legislation.

Nevada

Wages. The labor commissioner was given temporary authority, until January 1, 1979, to increase the $2.30 minimum wage to $2.50 until July 1, 1978 and thereafter to $2.75 or the Federal minimum rate, whichever is less. The minimum for minors under 18 was changed from 15 cents below the adult hourly rate to 85 percent of that rate.

The prevailing wage law for public works projects was amended to authorize the labor commissioner to require public bodies to withhold from payments due contractors amounts equal to any valid wage claims. Each month, contractors are required to submit copies of payroll records to the labor commissioner.

Parents under court order to pay support for a minor child may be further ordered to assign their wages for support payments.

Hours of work. The standard 8-hour day, 40-hour week for public employees was amended to permit a 4-day, 40-hour week and variable 80-hour biweekly schedules, and to exempt executive, administrative, professional, and supervisory employees, as well as those covered by collective bargaining agreements which establish working hours.

Child labor. The law was amended to prohibit nonentertainment employment of minors under 18 in casino areas where there is gaming or where the sale of alcoholic beverages is the primary commercial activity. Minors under 14

may now be employed during school hours if they have been excused from attendance by the school district or by court order for purposes of employment.

School attendance. Minors of 16 may be excused by the juvenile division of the district court from compulsory school attendance, otherwise required until age 17, if they would benefit from employment and are under the court's supervision.

Equal employment opportunity. The State equal rights commission was empowered to issue cease-and-desist orders, to order restoration of all benefits including rehiring and backpay, and to seek temporary restraining orders and preliminary injunctions. The time limits for bringing action were substantially extended. A complaint may not be refiled with the labor commissioner or another administrative body after it has been decided by either, unless new facts or legal theory are introduced.

The age limits for apprenticeship programs were removed. A nonbinding advisory referendum on the proposed equal rights amendment to the U.S. constitution is to be submitted to the voters in November 1978. The Congress was urged to enact a tax credit for employers of newly-hired handicapped persons.

Labor relations. The use of a false union card to obtain employment was made a misdemeanor. A resolution calls for the appointment of a tripartite committee to study methods and develop plans for averting or resolving serious private sector labor disputes.

The local government employee-management relations board was authorized to dispense with hearings in deciding a case, if it adopts a previous decision as precedent. Among other changes, a 6-month limit was established for filing complaints or appeals with the board and employee representation elections may now be held by written agreement of the parties, without appeal to the board. Local government employers and their employees' unions are now required to promptly furnish each other with information relevant to the scope of mandatory bargaining, subsequent to the union's notification of its desire to bargain. In firefighter bargaining, mediation is required in cases of unresolved issues; separate procedures were established for factfinding and arbitration.

School district boards of trustees are authorized to negotiate sick leave and other types of leave.

Occupational safety and health. Permanent as well as temporary variances from standards adopted under the health and safety law may be granted.

Other laws. An employee may now serve as a juror without fear of job loss, because discharge for such reason has been made unlawful. If violations occur, employees have the right to sue for reinstatement and double lost wages.

New Hampshire

Wages. The wage and hour law was amended to require overtime pay for nursing home employees after 40 hours in a week, rather than after 8 hours in a day. The wages and retirement benefits of public employees are subject to assignment and garnishment to the same extent as those in the private sector. The welfare director was authorized to institute wage garnishment proceedings and to take wage assignments for the support of dependent children, in an amount up to 50 percent of disposable earnings. Discharge of an employee for garnishment or wage assignment was prohibited.

Child labor. The minimum age for entertainers in places where alcoholic beverages are sold was lowered to 17.

Equal employment opportunity. The Governor's committee on employment of the handicapped was reconstituted as a commission, with a requirement that half of its members be either handicapped themselves or parents or guardians of handicapped persons.

Labor relations. An office of negotiations was established to carry out duties assigned by the State negotiating committee, relating to State employee collective bargaining. These duties include doing background research, conducting negotiations, preparing recommendations to the committee, and maintaining official records.

Occupational safety and health. Enforcement of all laws concerning the sale, storage, handling, transportation, inspection, administration, and use of explosives was transferred from the State fire marshal to the State police.

Other laws. The law authorizing towns to require physically able welfare recipients to work for the town in any available job within the person's capability was amended to provide that earnings received will not affect the assistance received.

New Jersey

Wages. Employers are permitted to deduct from employees' wages payments authorized by the employees and approved by the employer for the rental or cleaning of work clothes or uniforms.

Child labor. When school is not in session, minors 14 years and older may now work for a 10-day period without an employment certificate in nonhazardous occupations at any agricultural fair or horse, dog, or farm show.

Equal employment opportunity. Discrimination in employment based upon an individual's nationality was prohibited, except that employment may be restricted to U.S. citizens where required by Federal law or where necessary to protect the national interest.

Labor relations. Procedures were established for the resolution of impasses in negotiations between public fire and police departments and representatives of their employees. These include mediation, factfinding, and various forms of arbitration, including limiting the award to a choice between the final offers of each party.

New Mexico

Wages. Residential employees of charitable, religious, or nonprofit group homes for mentally retarded or emotion-

ally or developmentally disturbed persons were excluded from minimum wage law coverage.

The legislative finance committee was requested to study the methods used by the labor commissioner to determine prevailing wage rates on public works contracts, particularly the use of Statewide rather than local rates.

Occupational safety and health. The coal mine safety law was amended to improve standards relating to ventilation and the use of safety lamps. The legislature directed the property control division of the department of finance and administration to examine the fire codes and the OSH Act for their impact on the cost of construction or renovation of State buildings, facilities, and higher education institutions. A report is due to the legislature in January 1978.

Other laws. Three new cabinet-status departments were created which affect labor functions. The human services department, headed by a Governor-appointed secretary, consolidates the functions of the labor and industrial commission, the employment security commission, several other commissions, and health and social services agencies. In addition, the human rights commission, the commission on the status of women, and the office of indian affairs were administratively attached to the new department by the Executive Reorganization Act. Among other changes, the chief of the labor and industrial bureau of the new department is designated as the labor commissioner.

The health and environment department assumes the health service functions of numerous agencies, boards, and commissions, including the environmental improvement agency, formerly responsible for administering the State's occupational safety and health program.

The commerce and industry department combines the functions of several State agencies. Its duties include regulating collection agencies, issuing contractor licenses and journeymen certificates, adopting building codes, and regulating the manufacture, storage, transportation, and sale of liquified petroleum gas.

New York

Wages. The prohibition against discharging an employee because of a wage assignment or income execution was extended to apply to any pending action or judgment for nonpayment of a contractual obligation.

Railroad corporations are now required to furnish each employee with an itemized statement each payday listing accrued total earnings and taxes to date, along with a separate listing of daily wages and how they were computed. A previous requirement for a statement listing gross wages, deductions, and net wages still stands.

Equal employment opportunity. An executive order of the Governor prohibits State contractors holding construction or nonconstruction contracts from discriminating against employees or applicants because of race, creed, color, national origin, sex, age, disability, or marital status, and requires contractors to undertake affirmative action programs. A contractor who does not comply may have his contract canceled or suspended or payments withheld and may be declared ineligible for future State contracts for a period of up to 2 years. An office of State contract compliance, within the division of human rights, was established to administer the order.

The civil service commission is authorized to find up to 200 positions with duties that can be performed by physically or mentally handicapped persons certified by the employee health service, and to fill the positions with such persons.

Labor relations. The position of director of labor-management relations was created in the New York City mayor's office, with responsibilities that include expediting the resolution of private sector labor disputes.

The public employee relations board may act to eliminate unfair labor practices by methods such as the reinstatement of an employee with or without back pay. The law on unfair labor practices was amended to state that good faith negotiations do not require any party to agree to a proposal or make a concession.

Public employee organizations may now negotiate for agency shop fee deductions, if they have a procedure for refunding, upon demand, that portion of an employee's deduction used for activities or causes not directly related to terms and conditions of employment.

Separate firefighter and police procedures for the resolution of impasses in collective bargaining negotiations were combined into a single procedure.

Private employment agencies. Agencies recruiting domestic workers from outside the United States must maintain copies of forms submitted in connection with immigration requirements, maintain copies of agency contracts with employers and employees, and notify the State labor department if an employment agreement is canceled by either the employee or employer prior to the employee's arrival in the country.

Occupational safety and health. Coverage of the State building conservation and fire prevention code was amended to include places subject to labor law. There will, however, be no infringement on the authority of the labor department to enforce safety and health standards in these work places.

Displaced homemakers. A Displaced Homemakers Act directs the industrial commissioner to establish, upon receipt of Federal funds, multipurpose service centers to provide job counseling, training, and placement; health education and counseling; and financial management, educational, outreach, and informational services. To the maximum extent possible, the centers will be staffed by displaced homemakers.

Other laws. The industrial commissioner may now issue judgments assessing civil penalties of up to $1,000 for each violation of the industrial homework law.

No person representing himself as being connected with show business may advertise or circulate statements relating to the availability of show business employment if an advance fee is a condition of such employment. He may not accept any fee from the public, except agreed commissions or repayment for advances or expenses.

The industrial commissioner must transmit labor market information to educational institutions, to facilitate career planning and planning by persons responsible for occupational education.

North Carolina

Wages. The minimum wage was increased from $2 to $2.30 an hour, with an increase to $2.50 to take effect the same day the Federal minimum equals or exceeds $2.50. Minimum wage coverage was extended to ushers, doormen, concession attendants, and cashiers in theaters who were formerly exempt, and a minimum hourly wage of $2 was set for seasonal employees of amusement, recreational, and religious assembly establishments. A definition of tipped employee was enacted for the first time: an employee making more than $20 a month in tips on a regular basis. Coverage of the wage payment law was extended to tips, requiring payment of tips to the persons for whom they were intended, but permitting tip pooling among employees.

Hours of work. Valentines Day and the preceding week were added to the holidays for which florist employees are exempt from maximum hours restrictions.

Child labor. Until July 1, 1979, the labor commissioner has discretionary authority to waive the child labor regulations and issue an employment certificate for a minor over 12 years—if the parent consents, the safety or health of the minor will not be adversely affected, and a permit from the department of social service specifies the type of work allowed.

Minors may now use a learner's permit or driver's license to verify their age for an employment certificate.

Equal employment opportunity. The Equal Employment Practices Act declared a public policy to protect all persons against employment discrimination based on race, religion, color, national origin, age, sex, or handicap, and authorized the human relations council to receive charges of discrimination from the Federal Equal Employment Opportunity Commission.

It was made unlawful for the State or any person doing business in the State to discriminate in employment based on race, color, creed, religion, sex, national origin, or foreign trade relationships pursuant to any contract or arrangement with a foreign government, person, or international organization. The attorney general may bring suit in case of violation, and the injured person may be awarded treble damages, court costs, and reasonable attorney fees.

A new law requires the State board of education and each local educational agency to make positive efforts to employ and promote qualified handicapped individuals.

Sex discriminatory provisions were eliminated from the child labor law by permitting girls to work in newspaper delivery, other street trades, and as messengers at the same age and hours of work as boys.

The Governor's council on employment of the handicapped and the Governor's advocacy council on children and youth were transferred from the department of human resources to the department of administration.

A Governor's jobs for veterans committee was created within the department of administration to, among other things, make certain that veterans receive employment preference with State agencies, ensure that the agencies list vacancies with public employment services, and aid employers in designing affirmative action plans for handicapped and Vietnam veterans.

A sex-based restriction on hours worked by an apprentice was eliminated and a provision dealing with approval of apprenticeship agreements was amended, giving either parent of a minor approval authority, rather than just the minor's father.

Occupational safety and health. The number of members on the State advisory council on occupational safety and health was increased from 7 to 11. One member was added from management, one from labor, and two from the public sector, with the provision that one of the public members have knowledge of migrant labor. Five members to represent the public were added to the mine safety and health advisory council, the three representatives for the mine operators and the workers were retained, and the member appointed to serve as chairman was eliminated.

A State fire commission was created in the department of crime control and public safety, composed of nine voting members and five nonvoting members, including the commissioner of labor.

The Congress was urged to amend a pending mine safety bill by restoring an existing provision for State-Federal agreements for administration of safety regulations. The State has such an agreement with the U.S. Department of Interior.[2]

Other laws. The types of outside work projects on which certain prison labor may be used under contract with the department of correction were clearly specified. The restriction that such projects be confined to work not normally performed by private industry was dropped.

The composition of the apprenticeship council was changed to provide for public representation. There will now be four employer, four union, and three public representatives and two ex-officio nonvoting members. The commissioner of labor, who appoints the voting members, will annually name one member as chairman.

An economic development board and a labor force development council were created within the department of commerce. The board will be concerned with expansion of existing industry and the travel and tourism industries; the council (aided by business, labor, and education leaders) will advise and assist in the development and utilization of the labor force to support industrial and economic expansion in the State.

A sunset law was enacted, setting termination dates for a number of regulatory agencies, including one that regulates private employment agencies and is scheduled to terminate July 1, 1979. A governmental evaluation commission was established to study each program or function and report to the General Assembly its recommendations to terminate, modify, or reestablish an agency by passage of a new law.

North Dakota

Equal employment opportunity. The legislative council was directed to study the feasibility of enacting comprehensive human rights legislation and the adequacy of present statutes and enforcement.

Labor relations. A new law allows payroll deduction of union dues for members of teachers' unions.

The President and the Congress were petitioned to refrain from enacting common situs picketing legislation, to refrain from repealing Section 14(b) of the Taft-Hartley Act, and to repeal the Landrum-Griffin Act.

Negotiation procedures were changed so that where new school districts are created and new school boards elected, the new board may negotiate with teachers prior to the assumption of its other duties.

Private employment agencies. Amendments to the law establish a uniform private employment agency license fee of $200 (replacing a fee schedule based upon the sex of persons placed), increase the required surety bond from $2,000 to $5,000, and exempt temporary help contractors from coverage.

Occupational safety and health. The Congress was requested to amend the OSH Act to eliminate administrative fines on the first inspection and to allow a 15-day grace period to correct violations on subsequent inspections, in cases where no imminent danger exists.

Other laws. All statutorily created boards, committees, commissions, and councils (other than occupational and professional licensing boards) will be reviewed, to consider their performance and responsiveness to the public, whether there are overlapping powers and duties, and whether any should be eliminated or consolidated. The open governmental meetings law was amended to include a penalty for those holding a meeting in violation of the law. A proposed constitutional amendment, which will be submitted to the voters in the 1978 general election, requires that, unless otherwise provided by law, all records of the State and political subdivisions be open to the public.

Ohio

Child labor. The child labor law was amended to exempt minors under 18 employed on a farm operated by a family member from prohibited hazardous occupations and maximum hours limits. These restrictions were made expressly applicable to minors residing in agricultural labor camps.

Displaced homemakers. A multipurpose center for displaced homemakers was established, as a pilot project, to educate, train, counsel, and assist such persons to become gainfully employed. The center will be operated by the Cuyahoga Community College district and staffed by displaced homemakers to the greatest extent possible.

Oklahoma

Wages. The minimum wage was increased from $1.85 to $2 an hour, and the wage collection law was amended to increase from $200 to $600 the limit on an employee suit to recover unpaid wages.

Private employment agencies. The maximum placement fee for employment terminating within 60 days was increased from 10 to 20 percent of earnings.

Other laws. A sunset law set termination dates for numerous agencies and commissions, including the wage and hour commission, the occupational health and safety standards commission, an advisory council to the department of labor concerning private employment agencies, the Governor's committee on the employment of the handicapped, and the public employees' relations board. Provision is made for review, public hearings, and recommendations to the legislature. These agencies can be reinstated by law.

The Open Meeting Act was adopted, providing that all meetings of public bodies must be preceded by a public notice and held in open session (except for certain executive sessions). All votes must be publicly cast and recorded.

Oregon

Wages. The exclusion from the minimum wage law of FLSA-regulated employees was modified by extending coverage to all tipped employees and extending the State ban against tip credits to tipped employees subject to FLSA. In addition, live-in employees performing managerial or maintenance duties in commercial multiunit lodging accommodations were exempted from the law, and the salary test for determining the exemption of administrative, executive, and professional employees was raised from $350 to $650 a month. The labor commissioner may bring a suit to recover unpaid minimum wages and overtime pay and to enjoin future nonpayment without an employee wage assignment.

The State overtime pay law for local government employees was amended to exempt those executive, administrative, professional, or supervisory employees, as defined by the labor commissioner or collective bargaining agreement, who are exempted by the local government.

All employees are now entitled to receive itemized wage deduction statements, rather than only those whose employers hire five or more employees. Employee safeguards were prescribed, such as requirements that deductions be for the employee's benefit and authorized in writing.

A $2,000 threshold was established for public works contracts covered by the prevailing wage law and the labor commissioner was authorized to adopt the federally determined rate where data for a locality are unavailable. A provision was added for debarring contractors or subcontractors from receiving a public contract (for up to 3 years) when there is evidence of intentional failure to pay the prevailing rate.

The amount of an employee's wage claim to be treated as a preferred debt in bankruptcy, liens, and similar situations was doubled to $600.

Equal employment opportunity. The general provision giving preference to veterans in public employment was repealed. The veteran's preference on civil service exams, except for disabled veterans, is now limited to only one use and to a position for which application is made within 15 years of discharge or release from service. Veterans whose active duty occurred entirely on or after October 15, 1976 may not use the preference unless their service occurred while the military services were engaged in armed conflict.

Amendments to the fair employment practices law prohibit discrimination because of expunged juvenile records and redefine sex discrimination to include pregnancy, childbirth, and related conditions. Also, a time limit of 1 year after an alleged violation was set for filing complaints. With certain exceptions, employers are now prohibited from refusing to hire or terminating the employment of an individual solely because a family member is a current employee.

The department of general services was instructed to encourage the sale of products and services of sheltered workshops and nonprofit activity centers for the handicapped. Contracts with these organizations may be entered into without competitive bidding. These provisions will expire on June 3, 1981.

The State's ratification of the proposed equal rights amendment to the U.S. constitution was reaffirmed. The Congress was urged to enact laws permitting the legal entry of aliens for seasonal labor based on the need in particular areas at particular times and to protect American jobs from unfair foreign competition.

Labor relations. The employment relations board was reduced from 5 to 3 members, of tripartite representation, who have training or experience in labor-management relations and labor law or the administration of the collective bargaining process. The new board may designate its own general counsel for litigation and other purposes, who may act independently of the attorney general. All former members' terms expire, to enable the governor to appoint members meeting the new qualifications.

Investigatory information relating to an unfair labor practice complaint is now exempt from public disclosure unless required in a particular instance by public interest.

Occupational safety and health. The term "willful" in the safety and health act was clarified to mean a violation committed knowingly by an employer or supervisory employee who, having a free will or choice, disobeys or recklessly disregards the requirements of any regulation.

The State personnel division must adopt rules restricting smoking in State offices and provide smoking and nonsmoking areas for employees.

Displaced homemakers. The director of human resources was directed to establish multipurpose service programs for displaced homemakers. The programs will be staffed to the maximum extent feasible by displaced homemakers and will include job counseling and training; health education and counseling services; and financial management, educational, outreach, and informational services.

Other laws. A 1,000-hour minimum of on-the-job work experience was prescribed for trainees in apprenticeable occupations requiring less than 2,000 hours of experience and a 2,000-hour work minimum was established for other occupations, instead of combined work and instruction. A State director of apprenticeship and training will be appointed by the commissioner of labor. The adoption of standards and policies by the State board of education is now mandatory instead of discretionary.

Community colleges operating preemployment or trade extension training programs in an apprenticeable occupation must appoint one employee member and one employer member of a local apprenticeship committee to the advisory committee for training.

Employers are required to provide employees with their personnel records, upon request, for inspection on the worksite. Employers must also retain records for 60 days after termination of employment and provide employees with certified copies at reasonable cost.

A member from organized labor will be appointed to the public contract review board when the next vacancy occurs or by July 1, 1979.

The budget and management division of the executive department was directed to use job sharing in State agencies during 1977–79, to improve management and increase employment opportunities. Afterwards, an evaluation will be submitted.

To promote employment in the State, a greater preference in determining the lowest bid for dry dock construction will be given to contractors who will work within the State rather than elsewhere. A preferred contractor who fails to pay wages in full is subject to a deduction from payment due him of the amount of the wage underpayment.

Debt collectors may not communicate or threaten to communicate with a debtor's employer concerning the debt, or attempt to collect the debt at his place of employment.

A sunset law was enacted providing for the termination of several State agencies—unless, following review by an interim committee, the agencies are reestablished by the legislature.

Pennsylvania

Wages. The wage payment and collection law was amended to define fringe benefits, to require employer notice to the employee of such benefits, and to reduce the permissible time interval for employer payment or remittance. Other changes strengthen labor department authority to collect unpaid wages and fringes by permitting on-site employee interviews, obligating employers to keep records open for inspection, giving labor organizations the same rights as employees for civil action and remedies, and increasing the amount of liquidated damages that can be collected. A declaration of bankruptcy will no longer exempt an employer from criminal penalties for willful violation.

Rhode Island

Wages. Legislation providing for regular paydays was extended to include employees of the State and its political subdivisions, and a requirement was enacted, for all covered employees, that a statement of earnings and deductions be furnished upon request.

Equal employment opportunity. Discrimination because of sex, age, or physical handicap was added to the bases on which a State employee may appeal personnel actions to the personnel appeal board.

Labor relations. A 1976 law granting collective bargaining and arbitration rights to city of Providence administrators below the level of assistant superintendent, not eligible for membership in other bargaining units, was repealed.

Occupational safety and health. New hazardous substances regulations were adopted, which govern labeling and inspection of the manufacturing, storage, and transportation of such goods.

Displaced homemakers. A legislative commission was created to study the feasibility of establishing a program to encourage the economic stability of displaced homemakers and to report to the General Assembly by January 1, 1978.

Other laws. The Congress was requested to grant tax exemptions for private pensions of persons age 62 and over and to declare Dr. Martin Luther King Jr.'s birthday a national holiday.

South Carolina

Labor relations. The law regulating State employee grievance procedures was amended to add layoffs and pay reductions to the list of grievable issues, and to provide that job classification and promotions may be grieved only on the basis of alleged discrimination. Exemptions from the grievance procedure were added, including inmate help in institutions, residents of rehabilitation facilities, and students employed in institutions of learning.

Other laws. The department of corrections was authorized to establish an extended work-release program for certain prisoners.

South Dakota

Child labor. The age at which minors may be employed in dangerous work was reduced from 18 to 16.

Equal employment opportunity. Certain constraints on the disclosure by the commission on human rights of information gathered in discrimination investigation were lifted.

Labor relations. The Congress and the President were asked not to modify or repeal Section 14(b) of the Taft-Hartley Act, and to refrain from enacting common situs picketing legislation, which would permit the picketing of an entire construction site.

Other laws. A department of rehabilitation was created and all vocational rehabilitation functions of the department of social services were transferred to the new department.

Tennessee

Wages. A contractor's payment bond is now required on all public works contracts over $10,000 (rather than $100), in an amount of 25 percent of the contract price over $10,000. This replaced a sliding scale of 50 to 25 percent on contracts ranging from $2,000 to $5,000 and over.

Child labor. A fine of $25 to $250 was established for employers or parents who violate the child labor law and for employers who obstruct the labor department's enforcement of the law. Minors age 16 and 17 who are not enrolled in school, and minors of 15 who have been exempted from compulsory school attendance for disciplinary reasons and for whom schooling is not of substantial benefit are no longer required to have an employment certificate.

Equal employment opportunity. When possible, State agencies are directed to purchase products from approved or State-operated workshops for the blind.

Labor relations. The Congress was asked to refrain from repealing Section 14(b) of the Taft-Hartley Act.

Private employment agencies. Several changes were made in the private employment agency law, including coverage amendments to include agencies charging fees to applicants or employers and to exempt musician booking agencies and nurses' registries. Agencies may not require applicants to contract with specific lenders to pay agency fees, or request information from applicants regarding arrest records not resulting in convictions, or give this information to prospective employers.

Occupational safety and health. Dual administration of the occupational safety and health law by the health and labor departments was eliminated by vesting sole authority in the labor department.

Other laws. A governmental commission was created to evaluate all functional areas of State government and political subdivisions, with emphasis on relationships between the State, local, and Federal governments, and to make recommendations and reorganization suggestions.

A sunset law was passed, setting effective dates for the abolition of the departments of labor and employment security, various safety boards and commissions, the private employment agency board, the prevailing wage commission, and other State agencies and boards. Following review, agencies may be continued, restructured, or reestablished by legislative action.

Texas

Equal employment opportunity. Employers, employment agencies, and labor organizations may not discriminate in employment because of mental retardation that would not significantly impair job performance. Blind, visually hand-icapped, and otherwise physically disabled persons must be employed by public employers and in other publicly supported employment on the same terms and conditions as the able-bodied, unless the disability prevents job performance.

Labor relations. All group life, accident, and health insurance policies, paid in whole or part by an employer, must provide for continuation of coverage during a work stoppage because of a labor dispute—if the employees pay all premiums, including the employer's contribution.

Private employment agencies. The private employment agency law was amended to exempt management search consultants who are paid by employers only (including payment of progress fees) to identify, appraise, and recommend individuals for executive or professional positions paying at least $20,000 per year and who engage in no other activities considered to be those of an employment agency.

Occupational safety and health. The Federal Occupational Safety and Health Administration was requested to suspend issuance of standards requiring the installation and operation of dust controls in cotton processing.

Under the boiler safety law, all boilers must now be registered with, certified, and inspected by the chief or deputy inspector of the labor department or by an authorized insurance company inspector.

Displaced homemakers. The rehabilitation commissioner was directed to establish two pilot multipurpose centers to perform job counseling, training, and other services for displaced homemakers, with one center to be located in the largest standard metropolitan area in the State and one in a small county.

Other laws. A commission was established to periodically review State agencies, commissions, and boards and determine the need for their termination, continuation, or reorganization. The office of the labor commissioner, scheduled for termination September 1, 1989, and the private employment agency regulatory board, scheduled for termination September 1, 1979, are among those to be abolished unless continued by the legislature.

An Employment Incentive Act was adopted which requires recipients of aid to families with dependent children (AFDC) to register for an employment program administered by the Texas employment commission. Beginning March 1, 1978, those individuals who are able to work will be required to apply for and accept suitable employment or become ineligible to receive AFDC payments. Also, an AFDC pilot project was established, administered by the department of public welfare, to educate and train eligible family members in skills and trades and to assist them in obtaining and retaining employment.

A State-funded apprenticeship system for the vocational education of adults was authorized, sponsored by the State board of vocational education, assisted by an advisory committee. Work and related instruction will be limited to occupations certified as apprenticeable by the Federal Apprenticeship Bureau.

A tripartite work-furlough committee was created to implement an employment program for eligible prisoners. Work-furlough conditions were amended to include provisions for deferred vacation time or vacation pay, workers' compensation coverage, and restrictions on the proportion of such persons in the work force, their use as strikebreakers, and their participation in union representation elections. When a prisoner asks to serve out his sentence on a work-release program, the trial judge is authorized to require him to request his employer, in writing, to voluntarily deduct from his wages an amount (determined by the court) to be used for such purposes as costs of maintenance in jail, support of any dependents, and installment payments on restitution, fines, and court costs. A person jailed for criminal nonsupport or for failure to make periodic payments for the support of a child may be required to have deductions made to be credited against such payments.

Utah

Wages. Employers are now permitted, with voluntary employee authorization, to deposit wages of employees in any Utah financial institution.

The law dealing with public support of children was amended to include wages, salaries, bonuses, commissions, and pension payments as earnings subject to garnishment for child support. The existing prohibition against discharging an employee because of such garnishment was strengthened by a prohibition against prejudicing the employee. An employer authorization to deduct $3 for each garnishment payment was repealed.

Equal employment opportunity. In conformance with the governor's code of fair practices, sex will not be a factor in employment for State employees and for peace officers in counties employing 130 or more nonmerit system employees.

The legislative judiciary study committee was instructed to expand its scope of study from sex discrimination only to all human rights legislation, and to prepare appropriate legislation. Another resolution called for the avoidance of gender-discriminatory language in legislative bills.

Other laws. Under a sunset act, legislative reauthorization is required every 6 years for the continued existence of numerous boards and agencies which regulate or license professions, occupations, or businesses.

Vermont

Wages. With written employee authorization, employers may now deposit wages by check, electronic fund transfer, or direct deposit to an employee's account in any financial institution.

Labor relations. The State Employee Labor Relations Law was amended to clarify bargaining unit membership and to add to the list of bargainable subjects such items as reduction in force, grievance procedures, and matters relating to employee financial participation in insurance programs. Mediation of impasses is now required prior to factfinding, and if the impasse continues after factfinding,

each party must submit a last best offer, one of which will be selected by the factfinding panel for submission for legislative approval.

Occupational safety and health. The department of health was directed to develop programs for the control of non-ionizing radiation and authorized to license and register sources of non-ionizing radiation.

Undocumented workers. Employers are subject to fines if they knowingly employ an illegal alien or one not authorized for employment. They are required to determine beforehand that aliens possess certification or authorization for employment.

Virginia

Wages. The minimum wage law now exempts from coverage any person in a work-study program or its equivalent who is enrolled full time in a secondary school, institution of higher learning, or trade school.

Child labor. Until July 1, 1979, those 16-year-olds who are engaged in an approved alternative education program will be exempt from the compulsory school attendance law, which requires attendance to age 17.

Equal employment opportunity. Employers may not subject prospective employees to polygraph tests dealing with sexual activities unless such activities have resulted in a criminal conviction in the State. Employers must destroy written records of polygraph tests or release them only with written permission of the tested employee.

Regulatory boards may not refuse to license a person because of a prior criminal conviction for an offense not directly related to the proposed occupation. Upon written request from a prospective employer, the central criminal records exchange must furnish conviction data on a job applicant who has consented to its release in writing. A new law allows expungement of certain arrest and criminal charge records and makes it unlawful for prospective employers and educational institutions to require information concerning any of these expunged records.

Labor relations. The Virginia supreme court held that a county board and a school board do not have the authority to negotiate or enter into collective bargaining agreements with their employees. Congress was asked to refrain from repealing Section 14(b) of the Taft-Hartley Act.

Occupational safety and health. New requirements mandate: (1) employment on each shift of at least one working coal miner who is certified as an emergency care attendant, (2) the availability of two-way voice equipment for communications outside of the mine, and (3) first aid training by the employer for each new employee requesting it. The fire marshal now has the same authority to issue citations and summons in case of violations as granted to the labor commissioner under agreed Federal-State enforcement procedures.

Undocumented workers. Employers, employment agencies, or unions may not knowingly refer or employ aliens who cannot document their eligibility for employment. All employment applications used after January 1, 1978 must ask prospective employees if they are legally eligible.

Other laws. A joint legislative commission was instructed to study possible sunset legislation which would require the legislature to periodically reaffirm the continuation of programs or agencies. A report is due in 1978.

Washington

Wages. The exempt status of volunteers under the minimum wage law is not affected by their receipt of out-of-pocket expenses or nominal compensation. Motion picture projectionists covered by union contracts which regulate hours of work and overtime pay, and seasonal employees working up to 14 days per year in concessions and recreational establishments at agricultural fairs, were exempted from the overtime pay requirement. Public works contractors and subcontractors owing wages under the prevailing wage law may no longer bid on any contract covered by the act until the wages have been paid. A second or subsequent violation within 5 years may now result in the contractor or subcontractor being prohibited for 1 year from bidding on any contract subject to the act.

Hours of work. The maximum consecutive hours that railroad employees engaged in or connected with the movement of trains may work was reduced from 16 to 12.

Agriculture. The migrant labor housing project in Yakima County, scheduled to end at the close of the 1975–77 biennium, was continued until December 1, 1978.

Equal employment opportunity. A State commission for the blind was created. It assumed those functions of the department of social and health services relating to services for the blind, including vocational rehabilitation and job placement.

Engaging in a discriminatory boycott or blacklist, which is defined as an agreement under which a foreign person or government imposes restrictions on a person's business relationships on the basis of race, color, creed, religion, sex, national origin, or lawful business relationships, was prohibited as an unfair trade practice.

A State women's commission was created in the Governor's office to replace the State women's council. The commission is directed to promote equal opportunity for women in government, education, economic security, employment, and services. In Seattle, a mayor's executive order abolished compulsory retirement on the basis of age from municipal employment, except for police and firefighters. Decisions on hiring, assignment, promotion, and discharge are to be made solely on the basis of functional capacity.

Private employment agencies. Applicant-paid placement fees are now limited to 20 percent of earnings if the employment ends within 60 days for any reason. Previously, the limit was 10 percent if the job terminated within 90 days without the employee being at fault.

Temporary domestic, household, babysitting, agricultural, or day labor workers may be charged 25 percent of the first full month's wages, or 25 percent of gross wages if employed for less than 1 month. Agencies are prohibited from requiring applicants to contract with any lending company to pay agency fees and are required to furnish applicants with job information before referrals for interviews.

Other laws. As part of a sunset law designed to provide a system for the termination, continuation, or modification of State agencies, including a scheduled review and evaluation of the agencies prior to such action, the employment agency advisory board is scheduled to be abolished on June 30, 1979.

The law requiring employment preference for State residents on public works projects was amended to exclude installation or repair of equipment for which a manufacturer's warranty is contingent upon the use of his own factory-trained personnel, and to make it clear that the existing preference is applicable to contracts let by all political subdivisions as well as the State.

West Virginia

Wages. The legislature reversed the legislative rule-making committee's disapproval of prevailing wage rates determined by the State department of labor, and approved the rates.

Equal employment opportunity. Employment preference in appointments to the department of public safety must, whenever possible, be given to veterans and State residents; employment discrimination in the department on the basis of religion or political conviction was prohibited; and the superintendent was directed to adhere to equal employment opportunity principles and to encourage applications from females and minorities in the State.

The commission on the status of women was abolished and reconstituted as the women's commission within the Governor's office. The commission was directed, among other things, to recommend methods of overcoming discrimination against women in public and private employment and to make surveys of labor laws and employment policies.

Labor relations. A 19-member labor-management advisory council was created, with 8 members each from industry and labor (appointed by the Governor); as ex-officio members, representatives of the economic development authority and the employment security commission; and, as chairman, the commissioner of labor. The council was directed to advise labor and management and to effect improved labor-management relations.

Occupational safety and health. Safety standards for miners were strengthened, including regulations for communication and alarm systems, required safety training and supervision of apprentices, and the employment of emergency medical personnel.

Other laws. Employees who are laid off must be permitted to continue their group accident and sickness insurance at the same rate and with the same coverage for up to 18 months.

Wisconsin

Wages. The labor department is prohibited from issuing daily overtime pay standards for 1 year.

Agriculture. A new comprehensive migrant labor law was enacted, to be enforced by the labor department. It establishes permissible hours of work, assures the payment of wages, and guarantees a minimum number of hours of work. Persons or their agents bringing migrant farmworkers into the State must give them a written work agreement setting forth terms of employment, including wage rates, approximate hours, place of employment, and kind of work available. Other provisions require registration of migrant labor contractors and set forth their duties and prohibited activities; establish requirements for the certification of migrant labor camps; mandate visitation rights to migrant workers; and permit workers to bring suit in cases of violation of the act, without retaliation by the employer or labor contractor. A council on migrant labor was created in the labor department.

Labor relations. The legislature ratified agreements negotiated under the Employment Labor Relations Act between the State and unions representing employees in various State agencies, such as the State attorney's association and the engineering association.

Other laws. The executive budget bill created a number of councils within the labor department, including a construction wage rate council, a fire prevention council, an apprenticeship council, and a labor standards council. Another change requires employers with State contracts to comply with nondiscrimination policies and affirmative action.

Wyoming

Equal employment opportunity. A proposal was adopted, to be voted on in a referendum at the next general election, for removing a constitutional provision that prohibits the employment of adult females in mines.

Other laws. A legislative management council was established to review administrative rules of all government agencies to determine if they are proper, and to report to the legislature, the Governor, and the agencies involved. The law further provides that prior to the adoption, amendment, or repeal of any rule in the future, agencies will be required to submit a draft of the proposed rule to the legislative service office for review. ☐

------FOOTNOTES------

¹ Kentucky was the only State where the legislature did not meet this year. The legislatures of Arkansas, California, Illinois, Massachusetts, Michigan, New Hampshire, New Jersey, New York, Ohio, and Pennsylvania were still in session at press time. Any further developments in these States will be reported in a later article.

² This bill, which also transfers administration of mine safety regulations from the U. S. Department of Interior to the U.S. Department of Labor, was signed into law Nov. 9, 1977. The provision for State-Federal agreements was not restored.

State labor legislation enacted in 1978

*Although it was a light legislative year,
17 States revised minimum wage rates; other
action included anti-discrimination laws,
easing of mandatory retirement rules, and
new programs to help displaced homemakers*

RICHARD R. NELSON

The volume of labor legislation enacted by State legislatures was less in 1978 than in recent years;[1] however, significant activity took place both in traditional standards fields, including minimum wage rates, child labor, and job discrimination, and in more recently emerging fields, including mandatory retirement, sunset laws, and help for displaced homemakers.

Much legislative activity concerned minimum wage rates, as increases provided for in the 1977 amendments to the Fair Labor Standards Act (FLSA) spurred State action. New legislation was enacted in 1978 or late 1977 in 17 jurisdictions. Also, minimum wage rates in several States were increased by prior law, wage order, or administrative action.

Twelve jurisdictions now have a minimum rate equal to the $2.65-an-hour Federal standard, and 11 of these will match the Federal increase to $2.90 on January 1, 1979, or later in the year. Alaska, Connecticut, and certain industries in the District of Columbia now have minimums higher than the Federal rate. In addition, in almost half the jurisdictions, the minimum wage for tipped employees was set higher than that payable under the FLSA.

Several States altered provisions of their wage laws. Michigan extended coverage of its law from employers of four or more to employers of two or more and removed the exemption for persons 65 years of age and over. The Oklahoma tripartite Wage and Hour Commission, formerly responsible for administering the minimum wage law, was abolished, and its powers were vested exclusively in the labor commissioner. In Kentucky, the wage payment sections of several laws were amended to enlarge the definition of wages for purposes of the minimum wage, prevailing wage, equal pay, and wage payment laws to include vested vacation pay, overtime, severance pay, bonuses, and other payments.

Wage garnishment or assignment continued to attract legislative attention, with laws enacted in 12 States. Most of these dealt with the amount of a person's earnings that may be garnished. Laws in six States specifically mentioned child support payments. Maryland required employers to honor multiple garnishments against the same employee in the order they are received.

Child labor legislation continued recent patterns of amendments to ease employment restrictions. Restrictions concerning nightwork and maximum hours were eliminated for 16- and 17-year-old minors in Ohio and Tennessee. Certificate requirements were eased in New York, Pennsylvania, and Virginia and were replaced in Tennessee by an employer obligation to require proof of age.

Richard R. Nelson is a labor standards adviser in the Division of State Employment Standards, Employment Standards Administration, U.S. Department of Labor.

Employment of minors in theatrical or other performances was the subject of legislation in Georgia, Louisiana, New Jersey, New York, and Oklahoma. Michigan's new child labor law retained most of the previous law's standards, but it eliminated a requirement that employers have occupational approval numbers, changed the farm work exemption from a total exemption to an exemption only for employment not in violation of department standards, and expanded the high school graduate exemption. Pennsylvania removed provisions that were more restrictive for female than for male workers.

Laws concerning arbitrary compulsory retirement based upon age were enacted in 10 States, some perhaps as a result of the 1978 amendments to the Federal Age Discrimination in Employment Act. Among other States, Arizona and Delaware raised the mandatory retirement age from 65 to 70 for State employees, and, effective June 1, 1980, Minnesota raised the retirement age similarly for most private and public sector employees. In Louisiana, administrative officers were asked to waive the 65-year mandatory retirement age of State and local employees prior to the effective date of the Federal law (Jan. 1, 1979), and an executive order, effective in November 1977, abolished mandatory retirement of State employees in Kansas.

Various forms of employment discrimination were addressed by legislation in 29 jurisdictions. Most notable were new comprehensive human rights laws for public employees in Georgia and for both public and private sector workers in Tennessee. Sex discrimination was addressed by legislation in 12 jurisdictions, including Alaska, which created a commission on the status of women, and the District of Columbia, which gave statutory status to a commission which previously existed by executive order. Legislation to aid handicapped workers was enacted in 12 States. The primary purpose of these laws was to prohibit employment discrimination on the basis of a handicap that is unrelated to ability to perform the job. In Ohio, any qualified person between 40 and 65 who is refused a job interview or discharged without cause may bring a civil action against the employer on the basis of age discrimination. Discrimination in the employment or occupational licensing of persons with arrest or conviction records was prohibited in Kentucky and Minnesota. As a result of legislative action in Iowa, employers who discriminate on any basis may lose public contracts.

Help for displaced homemakers has attracted considerable attention over the last few years, with the passage of several laws. During 1978, eight additional States—Delaware, Iowa, Kentucky, Massachusetts, New Mexico, Oklahoma, Rhode Island, and Wisconsin—passed legislation to help homemakers displaced because of dissolution of marriage or other loss of family income. Because of their age or lack of paid work experience, displaced homemakers often face difficulty in getting jobs and are frequently ineligible for financial assistance from public sources. Almost all of the new laws provide for the establishment of multipurpose centers to provide employment services and other aids.

A comprehensive law in Pennsylvania grants seasonal farmworkers important new protection. These workers now must be paid the State minimum wage, may not work in excess of specified hours, and are afforded numerous other or stronger protections governing child labor, equal pay, wage payment, the registration of farm labor contractors, and the certification of labor camps. In other legislation affecting agricultural workers, California required that unloaders of farm products in produce markets in three counties be registered by the State labor commissioner, who may investigate complaints and mediate disputes on the scale of charges. Virginia created a farmworkers commission.

Various other areas of labor standards were subjects of legislation in 1978. Kansas modified its illegal alien law to exempt from the ban on employment those aliens who are permitted to remain in the United States by Federal law, and Louisiana appointed a committee to study the relationship between unemployment and the employment of illegal aliens. Independent labor departments were established through the consolidation of previously separate boards in the District of Columbia and by the transfer of various divisions from other departments in Florida. "Sunset laws" requiring periodic reexamination of State agencies, rules, and regulations were enacted or amended in Florida, Georgia, and Kansas.

In Maryland, the labor commissioner was authorized to enter into reciprocal agreements with other States to collect unpaid wages due from out-of-State employers and employers who leave the State without making payment. An intergovernmental relations council was established in Rhode Island to study the relationship between and among the local, State, and Federal governments and to consider methods of fostering better relations; and, in South Carolina, a law was enacted permitting the exchange of employees between and among Federal, State, and local governments.

Labor relations issues were the subject of statutes, court action, and referenda. Collective bargaining was authorized by law for teachers in Tennessee and for employees of the California State Universities and Colleges and by a constitutional amendment for Michigan State Police. In Utah, the State supreme court held that the Labor Disputes Act, which recognizes labor's right to collective bargaining, does not apply to municipal employees. A "right-to-work" constitutional amendment was rejected by Missouri voters in the November general election.

No additional States ratified the proposed Equal Rights Amendment to the U.S. Constitution, but Congress extended the deadline for securing approval by the three additional States necessary for ratification to June 30, 1982. States will not be permitted to rescind prior ratification.

The following is a summary by jurisdiction of labor legislation during 1978:

Alaska

Wages. By prior law, which sets the minimum wage at 50 cents above the Federal rate, the State rate rose to $3.15 an hour in 1978 and will increase each year, reaching $3.85 on January 1, 1981.

Equal employment opportunity. The Commission on the Status of Women was created with authority to examine such issues as education, homemaking, civil and legal rights, and labor and employment. The commission, which will be terminated on June 30, 1983, is to make annual reports to the governor on its proceedings and recommendations.

The State personnel act was amended so that persons certified as severely handicapped may be granted employment preference without taking a competitive examination.

A resolution was adopted that urges the U.S. Department of Labor to conduct, with the State department of labor, an investigation of the labor certification of nonimmigrant aliens working in Alaska's fish processing industry and to consult the State about the availability of Alaskan workers for certain jobs before issuing work permits to nonimmigrant aliens.

Other laws. The name of the Governor's Committee on Employment of the Physically Handicapped was changed to the Governor's Committee on Employment of the Handicapped, and publicly-financed vocational rehabilitation services now are to be provided to all handicapped individuals, not just to those who require public assistance.

The U.S. Supreme Court held unconstitutional the "Alaska Hire" Act, which required hiring preference for State residents in all oil and gas leases, easements, right-of-way permits, and unitization agreements on the basis that it violated the privileges and immunities clause. This clause bars discrimination against citizens of other States.

Arizona

Wages. Prisoners under the prison industries program may now receive wages up to 50 cents per hour, instead of 35 cents; if the director of the Department of Corrections contracts with private parties to provide services or labor, prisoners may receive higher wages, not to exceed the minimum wage prescribed by law.

Equal employment opportunity. The mandatory retirement age was raised from 65 to 70 for State employees; provisions were made for continued employment after age 70 by annual requests if performance and other standards are met.

Discrimination based on race, color, religion, national origin, or sex was prohibited in all phases of apprenticeship employment and training.

Occupational safety and health. A new provision provides for inspection of boilers and heaters by the Industrial Commission and establishes safety conditions for elevators and similar conveyances.

Other laws. The number of hours required on-the-job work experience in apprenticeship programs was reduced from 4,000 to 2,000, and criteria were established for determining apprenticeable occupations.

California

Wages. A wage order increased the minimum wage rate from $2.50 an hour to $2.65 effective April 1, 1978, with a further increase to $2.90 scheduled on January 1, 1979.

An employee may designate in writing a representative to act for him in filing specified wage and other monetary claims with the labor commissioner for collection.

Retaliation against employees for filing bona fide complaints or claims under any of the provisions of the labor code within the jurisdiction of the labor commissioner was prohibited as was retaliation against an employee who has filed or intends to file a claim against an employer alleging an occupational injury.

An exemption from garnishment or attachment in bankruptcy proceedings for monies held in private retirement or profit-sharing plans was expanded to provide a total exemption from any garnishment or attachment of such funds.

An employee's earnings protection law was enacted to govern the procedures for wage garnishment. The Judicial Council was authorized to do all that is required by the U.S. Department of Labor to exempt the State from the earnings garnishment provisions of the Federal Consumer Credit Protection Act.

Child labor. The law permitting minors between 16 and 18 years old enrolled in approved work experience education programs to work as late as 12:30 a.m. was extended to minors in similar programs conducted by private schools.

Agriculture. All employees of the Agricultural Labor Relations Board now are specifically required to perform their duties in an objective and impartial manner without prejudice toward any party subject to the board's jurisdiction.

Separate provisions on regulating unloaders of farm products in produce markets were enacted for Alameda, San Francisco, and San Mateo counties. The labor commissioner will register unloaders, investigate complaints, and mediate disputes involving the establishment of a scale of charges.

Equal employment opportunity. To conform to the Federal Age Discrimination in Employment Act amendments of 1978, changes were made in State and local retirement systems to extend prohibitions against mandatory retirement prior to the age of 70 for public employees.

Inquiries into the physical condition or medical history of job applicants is permissible if directly related to the position.

The review authority of the Division of Fair Employment Practices, previously limited to public works contracts, was changed to a general authority to review and investigate employment policies and practices of all State contractors and subcontractors and to recommend appropriate sanctions.

State licensing boards, agencies, and authorities in the Department of Consumer Affairs were included within the coverage of the Fair Employment Practice Act, which states that it is unlawful to require an examination or qualification that is not job related and that discriminates because of an applicant's race, creed, color, national origin or ancestry, sex, age, medical condition, or physical handicap.

The ban on employment discrimination against pregnant women by district school boards was expanded to apply to all employers. Among other prohibitions, an employer may not refuse to promote or to select a pregnant employee for training if the training program can be completed at least 3 months before beginning maternity leave, nor can an employee be discharged for pregnancy. A pregnant employee must receive the same benefits as other employees, except that an employer is not required to grant disability leave for more than 6 weeks.

Labor relations. An employer-employee relations act, applicable to employees of the State college and university systems, was enacted, to be administered by the public employment relations board. Provision was made for mediation and factfinding in cases of impasses, and authority was given for agreements providing for binding arbitration.

Up to three representatives from each employee organization representing State college and university system employees are to be given reasonable time off during working hours to attend and make presentations at trustees meetings if a matter affecting conditions of employment is scheduled for consideration.

The name of the State Conciliation Service was changed to the State Mediation and Conciliation Service. The service is within the Department of Industrial Relations.

An employee organization alleging, in a petition to the public employment relations board, that the employees in an appropriate unit no longer wish to be represented by another employee organization may no longer use current dues deduction authorizations as evidence of support.

Private employment agencies. The requirement that agency counselors register with the Bureau of Employment Agencies was repealed, but agencies now must provide approved training for all new counselors. The exemption for management consultants now applies if they do not recommend individuals to positions having a starting salary of less than $25,000 per year, rather than the previous $20,000.

Regulation of musician booking agencies was transferred from the Department of Consumer Affairs to the labor department, where they, along with artists' managers, will be included within the provisions governing talent agencies.

Occupational safety and health. An employer cited for a first-instance occupational safety and health violation, resulting from an onsite inspection, will not be assessed a civil penalty unless the inspection finds 10 violations or more. This policy has been implemented by administrative regulations in effect since January 1, 1977.

The Department of Industrial Relations will be responsible for developing a long-range program for upgrading and expanding the State's resources in occupational health and medicine, including the creation of health centers that will train occupational health specialists, serve as referral centers for occupational illnesses, and engage in research on the causes, diagnosis, and prevention of occupational illnesses. The department is also to develop and maintain a repository of research information and data relating to toxic materials and harmful physical agents in use in places of employment.

A limited jurisdiction of the Division of Industrial Safety over workers employed in the construction and repair of railroad equipment was expanded to include jurisdiction over occupational safety and health problems of railroad employees.

Resolutions urged the Congress to amend the Occupational Safety and Health Act to allow the State program the administrative flexibility it needs to operate more effectively and to amend the Federal Mine Safety and Health Act to avoid duplication of efforts and conflicting laws, regulations, and penalties and to permit the State's Division of Industrial Safety to be the sole safety enforcement agency in the State.

Other laws. Discrimination against or discharge of an employee who is required to serve as a witness in court is prohibited provided reasonable notice is given to the employer. Discrimination of any type, rather than the previous discharge only, against an employee who serves as an inquest or trial juror is now unlawful.

The use of private investigators to provide employers with information concerning their employees was regulated. Among other provisions, employees now must receive copies of investigation reports prior to discipline or discharge, and the payment of bonuses to private investigators for discovering unfavorable information is prohibited.

A resolution urges the State and local governments, charitable and service organizations, and private employers to take volunteer work experience into account in job announcements, in application forms, and in the consideration of applicants for employment.

Connecticut

Wages. The hourly minimum wage increased to $2.66 on July 1, with further increases on January 1 of each year, to $2.91 in 1979, $3.12 in 1980, and $3.37 in 1981. The former wage differential was eliminated for farmworkers, who now are entitled to the same rate as others.

Employers' civil liability for unpaid wages was doubled to twice the amount of wages due along with costs and reasonable attorney fees, and the maximum fine for violation was increased from $200 to $1,000.

If an employer policy or collective bargaining agreement provides for payment of accrued fringe benefits to a discharged employee, the employer must pay for them in the form of wages.

The amount of wages exempt from garnishment for support payments was increased from $50 a week to the first $70 of disposable weekly earnings.

Equal employment opportunity. Provisions affecting involuntary retirement under the antidiscrimination law were conformed to the 1978 amendments to the Federal age discrimination act; however, termination of employment is now specifically permissible where age is a bona fide occupational qualification, such as in police work or firefighting.

It is now unlawful for an employer, employment agency, or labor organization to discriminate against mentally retarded persons, unless the disability prevents performance of the particular work involved.

Labor relations. The municipal collective bargaining law was amended to prohibit the inclusion of both supervisory and other employees in any new collective bargaining units.

Other laws. The number of hours of required training in approved apprenticeship programs was reduced from 4,000 to 2,000.

The Department of Corrections may contract with private nonprofit agencies to help prior offenders obtain employment, housing, transportation, and counseling.

Delaware

Wages. The State tax commissioner is now specifically authorized to issue a warrant to garnish wages of delinquent taxpayers after obtaining a judgment.

Child labor. The Alcoholic Beverage Control Act, which has a 20-year age minimum for liquor possession, was amended to permit liquor importers to employ persons 18 and 19 years old in occupations other than sales, and catering businesses and bowling alleys to employ 16-year-olds and over, provided the minors do not sell or serve liquor. Prior exemptions permit the employment of 16-year-olds in hotels, clubs, restaurants, and racetracks which have liquor licenses.

Equal employment opportunity. The mandatory retirement age for State employees was raised from 65 to 70 years.

A public employee will be guilty of a misdemeanor, if, in performing his official functions, he knowingly practices discrimination on the basis of race, creed, color, sex, or national origin.

Resolutions were adopted urging the congressional delegation to work for an extension of the deadline for ratification of the proposed Federal Equal Rights Amendment and to support legislation to establish a national office of the handicapped.

Displaced homemakers. A displaced homemakers act directs the State secretary of labor to establish and coordinate multipurpose service programs for displaced homemakers to provide job counseling, training, and placement as well as information on subjects such as financial management and health services.

District of Columbia

Wages. A revised wage order, effective April 15, 1978, increases the minimum wage for laundry and drycleaning industry employees from $2.40 to $3 an hour.

Equal employment opportunity. A new enactment gives statutory status to the Commission on Women, which previously existed by executive order of the mayor, and new procedures were adopted for the selection of future members and the appointment of a chairperson.

Other laws. The previously separate Minimum Wage and Industrial Safety Board, Unemployment Compensation Board, and Department of Manpower were abolished and their functions consolidated into a newly created Department of Labor.

Florida

Wages. The courts were authorized to award costs and reasonable attorney's fees in a civil action for unpaid wages. A continuing writ of garnishment, formerly issuable for child support payments, may now be issued also for periodic alimony payments.

Equal employment opportunity. The Human Rights Act was amended to conform provisions concerning involuntary retirement under seniority systems or employee benefit plans to the 1978 amendments to the Federal Age Discrimination in Employment Act.

Veterans' preference provisions in public employment were clarified to include certain spouses and unmarried widows and widowers under the privilege of preference in promotion or appointment to noncompetitive positions, formerly available only to veterans themselves.

Private employment agencies. The maximum period of employment during which employees are entitled to a refund of 75 percent of the fee they paid the agency, if they are discharged through no fault of their own, was increased from 14 to 30 days.

Other laws. The Divisions of Labor and of Employment Security were removed from the Department of Commerce and combined into a new Department of Labor and Employment Security. This department also includes commmissions on public employee relations, industrial relations, and unemployment appeals.

A sunset law was enacted to abolish certain statutory boards, committees, commissions, and councils that have not met since January 1, 1975, including the Employment Service Council, and setting an October 1, 1981, termination date for several others, unless reviewed and reestablished by the legislature. Some of those slated for review are the Private Employment Agencies Advisory Committee, State Apprenticeship Council, Industry Advisory Council, and Small Business Advisory Council.

Georgia

Child labor. Minors now may work in motion picture, theatrical, radio, or television productions or as photographic or advertising models with written consent of the labor commissioner. Employment of any minor for pornographic purposes is a felony.

Equal employment opportunity. A comprehensive fair employment practices law was enacted which prohibits employment discrimination against public employees on the basis of race, color, religion, national origin, sex, handicap, or age (between 40 and 65) and establishes an office of fair employment practices and a fair employment practices advisory board.

A resolution sustains the study committee on services for the aged and directs it to study recommendations of the 1977 committee, including employment and mandatory retirement, and to report its findings and legislative proposals to the general assembly by January 1, 1979.

Private employment agencies. The scheduled termination date of the employment agency regulatory law and advisory council under the sunset law was extended from July 1, 1978, to July 1, 1984.

Guam

Wages. The minimum wage rose to $2.65 an hour and will continue to increase each year to match Federal rates under a prior law which adopted the FLSA rates by reference.

Hawaii

Wages. The minimum wage rate was raised from $2.40

to $2.65 an hour effective July 1, 1978, with future increases to $2.90 on July 1, 1979, $3.10 on July 1, 1980, and $3.35 on July 1, 1981. These increases are identical to those under the Federal law.

The amount of wages subject to garnishment is computed on wages remaining after the withholding of deductions required by law.

Equal employment opportunity. It is now unlawful to discharge or suspend an employee for receiving or responding to a summons to serve as a witness or prospective witness. In case of violation, the employee may bring a civil action for reinstatement and for reimbursement for up to 6 weeks of lost wages and a reasonable attorney's fee.

Labor relations. The Public Employment Relations Board will help resolve bargaining impasses between firefighters and public employers by implementing special mediation and arbitration procedures.

The mandatory adjustment of compensation, hours, terms and conditions of employment, and other benefits applicable to public employees who are excluded from collective bargaining was extended to most court officers and employees.

Private employment agencies. All applicants for employment agency licenses are required to pass a certified employment consultant examination as designated by the director of the labor department.

Occupational safety and health. Several resolutions related to safety and health were adopted. The State's congressional delegation was requested to support efforts to gain Federal certification of its State occupational safety and health plan; labor unions and employers were urged to cooperate in the development and implementation of occupational safety and health programs with help from the legislature; and the State labor department was requested to cooperate with workers' compensation insurers to start employer safety consultation services.

Other laws. Hours of training required under apprenticeship agreements were changed from 4,000 hours to 2,000 hours or 12 months of reasonably continuous employment.

A 1-year residency requirement for public employment was replaced with a hiring preference for applicants who have filed resident income tax returns or who have been claimed as dependents on such returns.

A resolution urged the State's congressional delegation to work for passage of the Humphrey-Hawkins Full Employment and Balanced Growth Act.

Idaho

Wages. An exemption from the minimum wage law was added for seasonal employees of a nonprofit camping program.

Equal employment opportunity. A resolution was adopted delaying from February 2, 1978, to February 2, 1979, the effective date of amendments to the rules of the Human Rights Commission pertaining to the filing of discriminatory complaints, postfiling procedures, and orders issued by the commission.

Illinois

Agriculture. The effective date of the surety bond requirement for farm labor contractors was delayed until July 1, 1979. During this time, the director of the Deparment of Labor is to study the availability of surety bonds and other sources of financial assurance for such contractors and recommend continuance or discontinuance of the requirement.

Equal employment opportunity. The Department of Equal Employment Opportunity and the Equal Employment Opportunity Advisory Council were created to implement equal employment opportunity and affirmative action programs in State agencies.

Within 120 days after the filing of an unfair employment practices charge, the Fair Employment Practices Commission is to convene a factfinding conference to obtain evidence, identify issues in dispute, and explore the feasibility of negotiating a settlement prior to taking further action.

It was resolved that a special House Committee on equal employment opportunity be created to study and investigate discrimination in State employment against women, minorities, the handicapped, elderly, and persons with disabilities, to review the operations of the Department of Personnel and the EEO officer, and to determine the need for revisions in State law or additional financial aid and manpower to improve the State EEO program.

Private employment agencies. Administration of the private employment agencies act was strengthened by authorizing the labor director to issue orders to cease violating the law and to obtain court orders commanding agencies to comply, under penalty of contempt of court. Agency negligence, not only misconduct, will now be a basis for action against the surety bond.

Iowa

Wages. Court-ordered wage assignments for child support were made binding upon employers. "Disposable earnings" for purposes of garnishment limitation was redefined to mean earnings remaining after deductions required by law to be withheld or assigned instead of only withheld.

Equal employment opportunity. Several changes were made in the civil rights law including authorizing complainants to file court action if their complaints are not resolved by the Civil Rights Commission within 120 days and permitting the commission to designate local agencies as referral agencies for the disposition of complaints.

Other changes specifically exempt from the age discrimination provisions bona fide apprenticeship programs employees involved more than 45 years old, persons under 18 not legally considered adults, and State or Federal programs designed to benefit a specific age group. Also, employers may now lose public contracts if they discriminate on any basis.

A resolution proposes that an equal rights amendment to the State constitution be considered by the next general assembly.

Labor relations. The exemption from the open meetings law of public employer and employee negotiating sessions, strategy meetings, mediation, and arbitration deliberations was amended to require public meetings when parties present their initial bargaining positions.

Occupational safety and health. The position of State boiler inspector was eliminated and the labor commissioner was made responsible for inspections and enforcement of safety provisions for all boilers and unfired steam pressure vessels.

Displaced homemakers. Money was designated from the appropriation for adult and children services to fund displaced homemaker projects.

Kansas

Wages. Wage deductions were authorized for State employee organization membership dues at the employee's written request.

Limits were placed on the percentage of earnings which may be garnished to satisfy support payment orders.

Equal employment opportunity. Administrative regulations of the Commission on Civil Rights, pertaining to discrimination on public works contracts, were amended to reduce compliance requirements. For example, the commission may no longer require affirmative action programs but now must negotiate for their preparation and implementation, and contractors must no longer solicit bids from minority and female contractors but instead are prohibited from discriminatorily excluding such contractors from bidding.

An executive order effective November 23, 1977, abolished mandatory retirement at age 65 of State agency employees if they remain able to perform acceptable work.

Several changes were made in the civil service act, including the addition of a requirement that all personnel actions be made without regard to race, national origin or ancestry, religion, political affiliation, or other factors not relating to merit and shall not be based on sex, age, or physical disability except where sex, age, and physical requirements constitute a bona fide occupational qualification. Retaliation against an employee for using the appeals procedure is prohibited.

Occupational safety and health. Amendments to the law included extending coverage to State agencies and public works, broadening the scope of investigations to include additional factors such as job-related illness and occupant capacity, and prohibiting retaliation against employees for filing complaints or furnishing information.

Undocumented workers. The existing ban on employment of illegal aliens will not apply to the employment of aliens who have illegally entered the United States but who are permitted by Federal law to remain.

Other laws. A sunset law abolishes several regulatory agencies and boards on various dates. For example, the Commission on Civil Rights is scheduled for termination on July 1, 1981. The law also provides for public hearings to determine the need for continued existence with legislative action required to continue or reestablish these agencies.

Kentucky

Wages. The minimum wage rate was raised from $1.60 to $2 an hour, with a future increase to $2.15 on July 1, 1979.

Changes were made affecting the wage payment sections of several laws. The definition of wages for purposes of the minimum wage, prevailing wage, equal pay, and wage payment laws was enlarged to specifically include vested vacation pay, overtime, severance pay, bonuses, and other payments. The wage payment law was extended to include all employers instead of only corporations, and most State employees were exempted from the minimum wage law. Under the wage payment law, the labor commissioner was authorized to take assignment for collection rather than for minimum wage and overtime only and to enforce the prevailing wage law, including collecting of wages due and taking action against employers in violation. Employers may be barred from future public works contracts until they comply with the law's provisions.

It is now unlawful for any employer to withhold from an employee any part of an agreed upon wage (formerly the prohibition applied only to collectively bargained wage agreements). The exception for withholdings authorized by State or Federal law was extended to include local laws.

The definition of public authority in the prevailing wage law was amended to include any nonprofit corporation funded to act as a government agency in connection with the construction of public buildings.

Hours of work. Employers using continuous work scheduling are now exempt from the Sunday closing law, provided each employee receives 1 day of rest in each calendar week.

Equal employment opportunity. With the exception of those who practice law and of nonelective peace officers, it is now unlawful to deny public employment or an occupational license because of a prior conviction of a crime, except for crimes involving moral turpitude or relating directly to the employment or license sought.

Labor relations. Use of an injunction without a preliminary hearing is prohibited during a strike, picketing, or assembly, except when violence has occurred.

An 18-member labor-management advisory council composed of 8 management and 8 labor members was created. The commissioners of labor and commerce will be ex officio nonvoting members, with the commissioner of labor serving as chairman.

Occupational safety and health. Most safety legislation related to mining. Mine inspectors were authorized to enter and inspect any coal or clay mine at any reasonable time. It was made a felony to operate a validly closed mine. Procedures were expanded for corrective action when miners are deemed to be in imminent danger of bodily harm. Also, educational, training, and certification requirements for miners were strengthened.

Displaced homemakers. A new law permits the secretary of the Department for Human Resources to establish multipurpose service centers to provide job training and counseling, placement, health education, and financial and educational services to displaced homemakers. Whenever possible, staff positions will be filled by displaced homemakers.

Louisiana

Wages. The minimum amount of disposable income exempt from garnishment was increased from $70 per week to 30 times the Federal minimum hourly wage.

Child labor. An exemption from the law of any minor 14 or over in a concert or theatrical performance, with a permit granted by the commissioner of labor, was repealed. A new exemption was enacted permitting the participation by any minor, with written parental consent, in any theatrical or musical performance sponsored by a nonprofit private organization or public body, or in a commercial motion picture being produced or filmed in the State, with the written consent of the director of the film commission.

Equal employment opportunity. Age discrimination in employment against persons at least 40 but less than 70 years of age by employers of 20 employees or more, employment agencies, and labor organizations is now prohibited. The law previously prohibited such discrimination against persons under 50 by employers of at least 25 employees. Age discrimination in employment practices is prohibited by any State or local agency or political subdivision.

The Governor was authorized to establish an Office of Civil Rights to perform such duties as investigate and act on equal employment opportunity and discrimination complaints in State services.

A resolution requested administrative officers to waive mandatory retirement of State and local employees who reach age 65 before January 1, 1979, the effective date of the Federal law raising the mandatory retirement age to 70.

A bureau for handicapped persons was created within the Department of Health and Human Resources to administer and expand responsibilities formerly exercised by the Governor's Committee on Employment of the Physically Handicapped. Duties will include conducting programs to educate employers on the advantages of hiring the handicapped, Federal tax incentives, and Federal laws pertaining to employment, training, and advancement of handicapped persons.

Civil service entrance or promotion tests in cities with populations of more than 100,000 will be adapted for applicants with impaired sensory, manual, or speaking skills, unless such skills are a bona fide occupational qualification. Public notice will be given of the availability of such tests.

Undocumented workers. A joint legislative committee was created to study the relationship between unemployment in the State and the employment of illegal aliens. A report of findings and any proposed legislation are due prior to the 1979 regular session of the legislature.

Other laws. A work opportunity program was established which includes training, job placement, and public service employment, with participation mandatory for most welfare and unemployment insurance recipients.

The number of hours of required training in approved apprenticeship programs was reduced from 4,000 to 2,000.

Maine

Wages. The minimum wage was increased to $2.65 on January 1, 1978, and will increase to $2.90 a year later, under a prior law which mandated matching State increases to the Federal rate, up to a maximum $3 rate.

Labor relations. Attorneys employed in the office of the attorney general were excluded from coverage under the State Employees Labor Relations Act. Classified employees were removed as 1 of the 3 occupational bargaining units permitted for vocational-technical institutes and State schools under the University of Maine Labor Relations Act. The two other groups, faculty and instructors, and administrative staff remain covered.

Maryland

Wages. The minimum wage rose to $2.65 an hour and will continue to increase each year to match the Federal rate under a prior State law which adopted the FLSA rates by reference.

Farm machinery salesmen and employees of nonprofit organizations that furnish temporary home care services for the sick, aged, mentally ill, handicapped, or disabled are not exempt from overtime pay requirements.

The labor commissioner was authorized to enter into reciprocal agreements with other States to collect unpaid wages from out-of-State employers.

The time limit for bringing action under the equal pay law was extended from 1 to 3 years after the date of the alleged violation.

Employers must now honor garnishments against the same employee in the order they are received and must remit amounts withheld within 15 days of the close of the last pay period each month. Creditors are to furnish monthly statements of payments credited, and garnishment orders now lapse upon dismissal or resignation, unless the employee is reinstated within 90 days.

Child labor. The minimum consecutive hours of time off outside of school that minors of 16 and 17 must have in each 24-hour day were reduced from 9 to 8. The nightwork prohibition between 7 p.m. and 8 a.m. for those under 16 was retained.

Persons 18 or older now may be employed to stock alcoholic beverages in Anne Arundel County; however, persons under 21 continue to be prohibited from employment by the holder of a class D liquor license in the sale of alcoholic beverages.

Equal employment opportunity. The prohibition against the use of lie detector tests as a condition of employment was extended to State, county, and local government employment, except for employees of law enforcement agencies.

An employer cannot require an applicant to answer any question pertaining to a physical, psychological, or psychiatric illness, disability, handicap, or treatment that is not material to his fitness or capacity to perform the job. Previously, employers could not ask about any psychological or psychiatric condition or treatment.

Labor relations. State departments now are prohibited from awarding public contracts to persons found in contempt of court by a Federal Court of Appeals for failure to correct an unfair labor practice.

A formal five-step grievance procedure was established for classified employees of the University of Maryland.

Private employment agencies. Agencies knowingly charging or attempting to collect a higher fee than specified in the schedule previously filed with the administrator now forfeit their rights to any fee and must refund in full any previously collected fees. Agencies are no longer required to publish their address in all advertisements. The bond that they must deposit with the labor commissioner was increased from $5,000 to $7,000.

Occupational safety and health. Labor department investigators or inspectors who are authorized or required by law to inspect certain premises or property for occupational safety or health purposes may now apply to the District Court for administrative search warrants when, having made a proper request for entry, they are denied access.

The labor commissioner is authorized to issue regulations governing working conditions of employees working with high-voltage electrical lines.

Massachusetts

Wages. By an amendment adopted in late 1977, the minimum wage rate was increased to $2.65 an hour on

Minnesota

Wages. Workers under 18 in corn detasseling work are now protected by overtime pay and all other provisions of minimum wage law, except for the minimum rate itself. Before, minors in all types of farmwork were exempt from the law.

For employees of residential buildings who receive housing as full or partial payment, the minimum wage entitlement is to be computed for time actually worked and to exclude on-call time on the premises.

Under an explicit wage deduction, employees may agree in advance to deductions, either at regular intervals or upon termination, for purchases from the employer.

Equal employment opportunity. Effective June 1, 1980, mandatory retirement before age 70 will be prohibited for most private and public sector employees. The compulsory retirement age for most State employees is currently 65.

The Commissioner of Personnel was directed to institute an affirmative action program in the State civil service to eliminate underutilization of qualified women, handicapped persons, blacks, Hispanics, Asian or Pacific Islanders, American Indians, or Alaskan natives. A Council on Affairs of Spanish-Speaking People was created to advise the Governor and legislature on problems such as education, employment, human rights, health, housing, and social welfare and to serve as a liaison with the Spanish-speaking community. Retaliatory employment discrimination by employers or unions against present or former members of the legislature for comments made or beliefs held while serving was prohibited.

Labor relations. The public employee labor relations act was amended to clarify the definition of a public employee to include, in addition to the State and the board of regents of the University of Minnesota, the governing bodies of political subdivisions that have final budgetary approval authority with respect to employees. Also, physical and occupational therapists were added to the definition of teacher. Public employees covered by both union grievance procedures and civil service appeals procedures are now authorized to pursue redress through either, but not both, means.

Occupational safety and health. Corn detasselers who leave the worksite because of injury, illness, or discharge must be furnished transportation to the pick-up point and be paid for the time returning there. Employers of corn detasselers must provide an accessible water supply in the field and sanitary equipment for its use.

Other laws. Employers are prohibited from stopping or threatening to stop employee insurance coverage or pension benefits because of job performance, unless the employee has the opportunity to continue coverage by making the same contribution the employer would have made.

Missouri

Equal employment opportunity. Discrimination in employment based on a handicap that is unrelated to ability to perform the job was prohibited.

Labor relations. An attempt to enact a "right-to-work" constitutional amendment was rejected by voters in the November general election.

Nebraska

Equal employment opportunity. The authority of cities and villages to enact antidiscrimination ordinances was expanded to authorize discrimination bans on the basis of marital status, age, and disability.

Resolutions were adopted that authorize various studies: to investigate and propose legislation on such topics as job sharing, part-time employment, flexible hours, parental leave, and upward mobility; to facilitate the entrance of women into the job market; to determine actions that might be taken to identify and correct salary disparities in comparable jobs performed by men and women; and to examine and propose specific legislation dealing with the State's affirmative action efforts. The study committees are to report to the next regular session of the Legislature.

Occupational safety and health. The Department of Health was given authority to adopt regulations for the issuance of licenses to persons manufacturing, using, transporting, or possessing any source of radiation and to establish qualifications pertaining to the education and knowledge of radiation safety procedures for all users of radioactive materials. Penalties for violation include suspension, revocation, or limitation of a license.

Nevada

Wages. The labor commissioner, exercising specific authority given him in 1977, increased the minimum wage by regulation to $2.50 an hour on January 1, 1978, $2.65 on July 1, 1978, and $2.75 on January 1, 1979.

New Hampshire

Wages. The minimum wage rose to $2.65 an hour and will continue to increase each year to match Federal rates, under a prior State law which adopted the FLSA rates by reference.

New Jersey

Child labor. An 8-year minimum age for the professional employment of minors in theatrical productions was removed. Permit requirements now specify that minors not be endangered by the working conditions and that physical examinations of minors under age 8 include vision screening if practicable. The department of labor is to prescribe safeguards for the working conditions, supervision, and education of workers under 16 with special attention to those under 6. It will be unlawful to employ persons under 16 to perform an indecent or immoral exhibition.

January 1, 1978, and will increase to $2.90 on January 1, 1979, $3.10 on January 1, 1980, and $3.35 on January 1, 1981. An administrative regulation established subminimum rates for full-time students.

Equal employment opportunity. Age discrimination by dismissal or refusal to employ any person between 45 and 65 years of age is now subject to a fine of up to $500. A fine was not previously specified.

Labor relations. Advance notice must be posted alerting affected public employees to hearings being held by the labor relations commission to determine the exclusive representative for collective bargaining and for all elections.

Displaced homemakers. A new law directs the secretary of the Office of Economic Development and Manpower Affairs to establish multipurpose centers to provide displaced homemakers with counseling, training, education, and placement services to help them find employment. Whenever possible, the centers will be staffed by displaced homemakers.

Michigan

Wages. By an amendment adopted in late 1977, the minimum wage increased to $2.65 an hour on January 1, 1978, with future increases to $2.90 on January 1, 1979, $3.10 on January 1, 1980, and $3.35 on January 1, 1981. These increases equal those under the Federal law.

Coverage of the minimum wage law was extended from employers of four employees or more to employers of two or more at any time within a calendar year. The exemption for persons 65 years of age and over was removed.

Several changes were made in the wage payment law, including the following: authorizing the labor department rather than the county prosecutor to initiate action to enforce final agency orders; requiring written employee authorization for wage deductions; setting a time limit of 12 months after an alleged violation for filing a complaint; and establishing recordkeeping requirements. Other changes prohibit the kickback of wages as a condition of employment, prohibit retaliation against an employee for filing a complaint, and increase the penalties for violation.

The prevailing wage law now also applies to school construction.

Child labor. A revised child labor law made several changes: elimination of a requirement that employers have occupational approval numbers; a change from a total farmwork exemption to an exemption only for employment not in violation of department standards; and exemption from the law for 16-year-olds who have completed the requirements for graduation from high school and for 17-year-olds who have passed a general educational development test. Previously only 17-year-olds with high school diplomas were exempt.

A youth employment clearinghouse was created within the Department of Labor to assemble data on unemployed persons 14 through 23 years of age and to monitor, evaluate, and make recommendations concerning youth employment programs.

Equal employment opportunity. The prohibition against sex discrimination was expanded to include discrimination by reason of pregnancy, childbirth, or related conditions, exclusive of abortion not intended to save the life of the mother.

Labor relations. The right to petition the court for relief from an unfair labor practice, under the public employee collective bargaining law, was extended to any party with a complaint, rather than limited only to the Employment Relations Commission.

Special strike notice provisions for hospitals and public utilities were eliminated from the Labor Mediation Act. The same notice as for other employees is now required.

A constitutional amendment, passed in the 1978 general election, authorizes collective bargaining for the State police. As civil service employees, they did not previously have this right under the Public Employment Relations Act.

Private employment agencies. Applicants for employment agency licenses who are not of good moral character will be subject to rejection, suspension, revocation, or refusal to renew the license.

Occupational safety and health. The Fire Safety Board was authorized to issue rules for the storage, transportation, and handling of hazardous materials, and the State fire marshal is now required to inspect and certify each establishment and vehicle of firms engaged in transporting hazardous materials.

The Occupational Safety Standards Commission is no longer required to consult with an advisory committee that represents employee and employer interests in farm operations on the impact of any proposed safety regulations applicable to agriculture.

Any occupational safety and health board, commission, and committee is to conduct business at public meetings and is specifically required to give public notice of the time, date, and place of each meeting.

Other laws. A "right-to-know" law gives public and private employees the right to review their personnel files. It also establishes criteria both for the nature of material permitted to be kept on file or divulged to third parties and for procedures for correction or removal of false information.

The law governing occupational licensing of former offenders was amended to require the head of the licensing agency to screen criminal records prior to their use by the licensing board to insure that no prohibited information is included. The agency head is to set regulations for licensing boards to govern how they prescribe offenses that indicate an applicant is not likely to serve in the public interest.

Equal employment opportunity. It was made an unlawful employment practice to deny any blind person a job or promotion unless the blindness would prevent performance of the job.

A commission, composed of four legislative members, four public members, and the director of the Division on Women, was created to study sex discriminatory provisions in the statutes and to recommend necessary revisions to the Governor and legislature.

New Mexico

Displaced homemakers. The Office for Displaced Homemakers was created, within the Commission on the Status of Women, to research the problems of displaced homemakers and to plan job counseling, training, placement, and other programs for them.

Other laws. The apprenticeship council was placed in the Employment Services Division of the newly created Human Services Department, and a reduction from 4,000 to 2,000 was made in the required hours for an apprenticeship agreement in any given trade.

New York

Wages. The minimum wage rate for nonagricultural workers was increased from $2.30 to $2.65 an hour with additional increases to $2.90 on January 1, 1979, $3.10 on January 1, 1980, and $3.35 on January 1, 1981. Corresponding proportionate increases were made in allowances for tips, meals, lodging, and other specified rates in existing wage orders.

Procedures were clarified to establish that a hearing is not required before prevailing rates are determined or redetermined for public works but is necessary in an investigation of failure to pay prevailing rates.

Child labor. A minor applying for an employment certificate will now be issued a certificate of physical fitness if a physical examination has been made within 12 rather than 6 months. If a known health problem exists at the time of application, another examination may be required by the issuing authority.

The employment or exhibition of a person under 16 years of age as a rope walker, wire walker, horse rider, gymnast, or acrobat now will be permitted if the minor is protected by safety devices or protective equipment and has a child performer permit. The liquor authority may now issue permits to persons under age 18 to appear as entertainers on premises licensed for retail sales. Among other requirements, a parent or guardian must be present during the minor's appearance.

Equal employment opportunity. The industrial commissioner is to submit to the Governor and legislature an annual report on the status of older workers, including those over age 65. The report will include the employment needs of older workers, ability of the State employment service to deal with their problems, economic impact of unemployment among them, and need for affirmative action. It also will make recommendations for improved programs or changes in laws or regulations.

Labor relations. Public employees who violate the strike prohibition are no longer subject to the penalty of 1-year's probation with loss of tenure; other penalties were retained.

Jurisdiction over improper public employer and employee organization practices in New York City was transferred from the Public Employment Relations Board to the New York City Board of Collective Bargaining.

The civil service law was amended to permit employees to be represented by a union representative or counsel at disciplinary hearings, instead of only by counsel.

Police officers may not be penalized for failure to meet an established quota of traffic violations, other than parking, standing, or stopping.

State employees subject to agency shop deductions may now, in addition to demanding a refund of any portion of the deduction used for activities not directly related to terms and conditions of employment, also demand a refund for expenditures of a political or ideological nature.

Occupational safety and health. The industrial commissioner is to survey political subdivisions to determine the extent of capital expenditures required to conform to Federal OSHA standards and the availability of Federal funding for such projects. Findings are to be submitted to the Governor and legislature by February 15, 1979.

Work on an unsafe machine or in a dangerous area tagged as such by the industrial commissioner may not be resumed under any circumstances until reinspection by the commissioner and removal of the tag.

The Department of Environmental Conservation was given authority to regulate the transfer, storage, and disposal of hazardous wastes.

The time for municipalities to elect to enforce safety and health standards for places of public assembly, instead of the State labor department, was extended until July 1, 1979.

Other laws. The Administrative Regulations Review Commission, composed of eight legislators, was established to review the rules and regulations of State agencies for compliance with their legislative intent, their impact on the economy, on operations of the State and local governments, and on affected parties.

It is unlawful for an employer to conduct or require any employee or job applicant to submit to an examination to evaluate psychological stress. An employee discriminated against for filing a complaint or testifying in a proceeding relating to the use of such an examination may recover double the wages and benefits lost.

The Department of Correctional Services is to maintain a list of prison inmates who are eligible for release or parole and the vocational and training programs completed by them and to supply this list to approved prospective employers.

Promotion of business expansion for job creation and other purposes was the objective of three enactments. One enlarged the scope of financial assistance available under the economic development program of the Job Development Authority, another expanded the job incentive program through tax incentives to additional types of firms, and the third authorized the New York/New Jersey Port Authority to prepare and adopt a master development plan for the port district, taking such matters as unemployment into account.

North Carolina

Wages. An increase in the minimum wage to $2.50 an hour took effect January, 1, 1978. The State wage law authorized an increase to this amount when equaled or exceeded by the Federal rate.

Ohio

Wages. Calculation of time-and-one-half overtime pay for county employees who work over 40 hours is to be based on all "active-pay-status" hours, rather than hours actually worked, and county employees now may elect to receive compensatory time off on a time-and-one-half basis in lieu of overtime pay.

Minors participating in programs established under the Federal Young Adult Conservation Act of 1977 are to be paid in accordance with the State and Federal minimum wage laws.

Public works contractors are now required to furnish, on the first pay date, to each employee not covered by a collective bargaining agreement individual written notification of his or her job classification assignment and its prevailing hourly rate and fringe benefits as well as the identity of the prevailing wage coordinator. Other contractors and unions now may file complaints with the director of industrial relations alleging prevailing wage violations.

Child labor. Changes in the law included elimination of maximum hours and nightwork restrictions for 16- and 17-year-olds and conformance of restrictions for minors under age 16 to the Federal standards.

Equal employment opportunity. Any qualified person between the ages of 40 and 65 who is refused a job interview or is discharged without cause may bring a civil action against the employer on the basis of age discrimination, except where arbitration is available.

Labor relations. Use of successor employer clauses in private sector collective bargaining agreements will be permitted for employers not covered under the National Labor Relations Act or Railway Labor Act.

Private employment agencies. The required surety bond for employment agencies was increased from $1,000 to $5,000, and temporary help services meeting certain requirements were specifically exempted from the entire law.

Oklahoma

Wages. The tripartite Wage and Hour Commission, formerly responsible for rulemaking and administration of the minimum wage law, was abolished and its powers vested exclusively in the labor commissioner.

Prejudgment garnishment is now specifically permitted for support in divorce proceedings, and court-ordered garnishment of up to one-third of earnings for child support was authorized, with a 25-percent maximum otherwise applicable.

Child labor. A prohibition against work in theaters and bowling alleys by persons under age 14 was eliminated; any performer under age 15 must be accompanied by a parent who remains on stage during the performance.

Labor relations. The law establishing procedures for the recognition of professional organizations representing teachers was amended: separate petition and election procedures were established for school districts with an average daily attendance of 35,000 or more. Principals and assistant principals of school districts of this size will constitute separate collective bargaining units.

Occupational safety and health. A mining safety law, which specifies safety standards for miners, was enacted and will be administered by the State mining board. Standards included governing storage, transportation, and use of explosives; mine inspection; first aid; and certification of general managers, superintendents, mine foremen, shot firers, electricians, and repairmen. Certain provisions that required fire escapes on public and private buildings were repealed.

Displaced homemakers. A displaced homemakers act authorizes the Board of Vocational and Technical Education to establish a pilot multipurpose service center to provide job counseling, training, support, and educational services. The center will be operated in an area vocational-technical school and staffed whenever possible by displaced homemakers.

Other laws. Discharge of an employee because of jury service was made a misdemeanor punishable by a fine of up to $5,000, and the employer was made subject to civil action by the employee for damages.

Pennsylvania

Wages. The minimum wage rate was increased from $2.30 to $2.65 an hour, with future increases to $2.90 on January 1, 1979, $3.10 on January 1, 1980, and $3.35 on January 1, 1981. These increases are identical to those under the Federal law. The maximum tip credit was reduced to 45 percent of the minimum rate, with a further reduction to 40 percent on January 1, 1980. Hotel, motel, and restaurant employees will now receive overtime pay for work in excess of 44 hours a week, rather than 48, with a reduction to 40 hours scheduled for January 1, 1979.

When employees are paid, railroads must furnish each with a separate listing of daily wages and how they were computed or be subject to a monthly penalty of up to $200 per employee.

Child labor. A new physical examination to obtain each reissuance of an employment certificate is no longer required. Minors now need present only a promise of employment.

Constraints for girls, formerly more restrictive than for boys, were removed in street trades employment, in certain messenger work, and as caddies: all minors in such jobs are now subject to the same laws.

Agriculture. A new comprehensive, seasonal farm labor act was enacted. It establishes permissible hours of work, assures the payment of wages, provides for equal pay, and requires payment of the State minimum wage. Persons under 14 may not work as seasonal farmworkers, and those age 14 to 17 were made subject to the child labor law, including a prohibition against working during school hours. Other provisions require annual registration of farm labor contractors, set forth such contractor's duties and prohibited activities, establish requirements for the certification of labor camps, mandate visitation rights, and prescribe penalties for violation.

Equal employment opportunity. Sex-designated language was eliminated from numerous laws, such as those governing public appointments, entitlement to employment benefits, and employment rights.

Other laws. An employer may not dismiss or threaten to dismiss any employee because of required jury duty. In case of violation, the employee may sue for damages and may seek injunctive relief to secure reinstatement.

Rhode Island

Wages. The minimum wage law was amended to exempt from the overtime pay requirement any salaried employee of a nonprofit, national, voluntary health agency who chooses compensatory time off rather than overtime pay. A special legislative commission was established to study the feasibility of a special minimum wage for handicapped workers and to report to the general assembly by March 1, 1979.

Labor relations. The State labor relations board was expanded from 3 to 5 members by adding additional union and industry representatives.

Employers who willfully fail to make payments within 60 days to a health, welfare, or pension fund, as provided by a union contract, now are subject to a fine, imprisonment, or both. Prior law provided for a fine only with no time limit specified.

Displaced homemakers. A displaced homemakers act authorizes the director of community affairs to establish a pilot multipurpose service center to provide displaced homemakers with counseling, training, education, and placement services to help them find employment. The center is authorized until January 31, 1980.

Other laws. An intergovernmental relations council was established to study the relationships between and among the local, State, and Federal governments and to consider methods of fostering better relations among these three levels and among local governments.

A legislative commission will study the feasibility of creating and expanding flexible time, part-time, and job-sharing employment in State employment positions and of developing a program to encourage such job opportunities in the private sector.

South Carolina

Equal employment opportunity. The name of the Commission on the Status of Women was changed to the Commission on Women. Among other duties, the commission was empowered to receive and disburse State and Federal funds.

Private employment agencies. Agencies are now required to guarantee placed applicants a job lasting 90 days, with fees prorated over the 90-day period, if employment terminates for any reason. Applicants not reporting for work for any reason owe no fee.

Other laws. A law was enacted permitting the exchange of employees between and among Federal, State, and local governments with their consent and for a period of up to 4 years.

South Dakota

Wages. The minimum wage was increased from $2 to $2.30 an hour.

Labor relations. The public employee bargaining law was amended to exclude the following from all but the grievance provisions: elected officials, members of any board or commission, most administrators, students employed part time, temporary employees, the State National Guard, and judges and court employees.

Other laws. A resolution was adopted requesting the Legislative Research Council to study the feasibility of developing and financing a comprehensive vocational rehabilitation referral center.

Tennessee

Wages. The prevailing wage law was amended to require *annual* wage determinations for highway construction, but biennial determinations were retained for building construction. Also, the Prevailing Wage Commission is now authorized to make an adjustment of up to 6 percent in the determined wage to reflect changing economic conditions.

Withholdings from employee's pay for private pension and retirement plans are to be deposited into a separate trust fund which can be used only for providing benefits and administrative costs.

The amount of wages exempt from garnishment was increased from 50 percent of weekly earnings up to $50 for heads of household and 40 percent weekly up to $40 for other persons to 75 percent of disposable weekly earnings or 30 times the Federal minimum wage, whichever is greater, for all debtors.

Members of the general assembly will now be subject to wage garnishment in the same manner as are other public employees.

Child labor. Several significant changes were made in the child labor law, including replacement of employment certificate requirements with an employer obligation to require proof of age, elimination of maximum hours and nightwork restrictions for 16- and 17-year-olds, and easing nightwork restrictions for 14- and 15-year-olds.

Equal employment opportunity. A comprehensive antidiscrimination act was enacted covering both public employers and private employers of eight workers or more. The new law prohibits discrimination in employment by employers, labor organizations, employment agencies, and joint apprenticeship committees on the basis of race, creed, color, religion, sex, or national origin. The Commission for Human Development was given enforcement authority, including authority to order hiring, reinstatement, and back pay.

Labor relations. A new law provides for collective bargaining between boards of education and professional school employees. Good-faith bargaining is required by both parties, and strikes are prohibited. Negotiable items include wages, fringe benefits, grievance procedures, and working conditions. Impasse procedures consist of mediation, factfinding, and advisory arbitration.

Other laws. Employers of five employees or more now will be required to excuse from work any employees summoned to jury duty and to pay them their usual wages less any jury fees received. The Institute for Labor Studies within the labor department, and a Labor Educational Advisory Committee were established to develop an association between labor and higher education and to provide educational services to workers throughout the State.

Utah

Wages. By administrative action, minimum wage rates were increased for the retail trade, public housekeeping, restaurant, laundry, cleaning, dyeing and pressing industries, and the geographic rate zones were reduced in number. The new minimum in Salt Lake, Weber, Utah, and Davis counties and in all cities with a population of 5,000 or more was set for $2.30 an hour on April 1, 1978, with further increases to $2.45 on January 1, 1979, $2.60 on January 1, 1980, and $2.75 on January 1, 1981. The minimum for other areas was raised to $2.05 on April 1, 1978, with further increases scheduled on the above dates to $2.20, $2.35, and $2.50. The tip credit was increased from 25 to 30 percent of the minimum rate on April 1, 1978. The credit will return to 25 percent on January 1, 1980.

Labor relations. The State supreme court held that the Utah Labor Disputes Act, which recognizes labor's right to collective bargaining, was not intended to and does not, vest collective bargaining rights in municipal employees.

Vermont

Wages. The minimum wage rate was raised from $2.30 to $2.65 an hour, with future increases to $2.90 on January 1, 1979, $3.10 on January 1, 1980, and $3.35 on January 1, 1981. By wage order action, the maximum tip credits were also increased.

The wage payment law was amended: employer liability to employees for actual damages caused by failure to pay benefits required by a written agreement was established; any action for lack of payment of wages is required to be brought within 2 years of the cause of action; employers must pay discharged employees within 72 hours rather than immediately; and employees are permitted to authorize the deposit of their wages through electronic transfer to a bank of their choice.

Equal employment opportunity. The State commissioner of personnel is required to adopt rules and procedures to facilitate employment of the handicapped. He may waive certain requirements which exclude an otherwise qualified person to give him equal access to employment and may require certification that the applicant is physically qualified to do the work without hazard to himself or to others.

Other laws. To enhance employment opportunities in the State, the secretary of development and community affairs is authorized to contract with employers who, under specified conditions, will employ qualified State residents, recruited and trained by the secretary.

Elected municipal employees may now continue to serve and be elected to new terms of office after age 70 and will receive benefits accrued to the effective date of retirement.

Virginia

Wages. The minimum wage rate was increased from $2.20 per hour to $2.35 effective January 1, 1979.

Limits were placed on the percentage of earnings which may be garnished to satisfy support payment orders; previously there was no limit.

Child labor. Amendments to the child labor law eliminate time limits on the validity of employment and physical fitness certificates and exempt from the law, except for the certificate of physical fitness requirement, persons between ages 12 and 18 who are employed as pages or clerks in the State legislature.

A resolution requested that a joint legislative subcommittee be created to study and report on conflicts in State and Federal child labor laws and to recommend ways to resolve such conflicts and to end unnecessary employment restrictions.

Agriculture. A 15-member migrant and seasonal farmworkers commission was created as an advisory body to the Governor and general assembly. Membership will include representatives of growers, migrant and seasonal farmworkers, and crew leaders; government, public, and private agencies; and interest groups or citizens concerned with migrant and seasonal farmworkers.

Labor relations. Minimum criteria for State employees grievance procedures are to be established by the Department of Personnel and Training, and the Office of Employee Relations Counselors was created to furnish employees with information on grievance procedures and to investigate allegations of reprisal as a result of their use. Political subdivisions with more than 15 employees must conform their mandatory grievance procedures to standards established for State workers.

Private employment agencies. Administration of the act was transferred from the labor department to the newly created Department of Commerce, and the composition of the advisory board was changed from all agency representatives to include also representatives from consumer protection interest groups and a State official familiar with employment agency regulation. Rulemaking authority was delegated to the Board of Commerce, composed of nine citizens appointed by the Governor. Agency action against an applicant for a fee which the employer agreed to pay was barred, and agencies are prohibited from charging fees without a bona fide job order or without having made an appointment with the employer.

Occupational safety and health. Several changes were made in the mine safety law, including amendments to clarify required onsite emergency medical care, to provide for first aid training programs for mine employees, and to strengthen various provisions, including work assignments of inexperienced miners, use of cranes and hoists, storage and use of explosives, and noise levels. Other changes strengthened standards for safety lamps, roof supports, gas detection, two-way communications, and fire safety. In addition, ventilation and dust control requirements were expanded, and the employment of fire bosses is now required in all mines rather than only in those classed as "gaseous" or "gassy."

Other laws. The required period of on-the-job work experience for apprentices was reduced from 4,000 to 2,000 hours, "apprenticeable occupation" was defined, and the apprenticeship council was given authority to review decisions of local and State committees adjusting apprenticeship disputes and to initiate deregistration proceedings in appropriate instances.

The Department of Welfare was authorized to establish projects through any governmental unit or private, nonprofit agency to provide work experience for welfare recipients. Refusal to accept work experience will be grounds for denial of public assistance.

Both the Department and Board of Vocational Rehabilitation were reconstituted as the Department and Board of Rehabilitative Services, and the duties, responsibilities, and services of each were expanded.

West Virginia

Wages. As a result of pending litigation on the question of wage and hour law coverage of public safety department members, a law was passed explicitly exempting such members from the law but providing for supplemental payments to them in lieu of overtime pay. A similar law was enacted exempting State conservation officers following a State supreme court decision which deemed them subject to the wage and hour law.

Wisconsin

Wages. By administrative action, minimum hourly wage rates were increased from $2.10 to $2.55 effective August 1, 1978, with further increases on January 1 to $2.80 in 1979, $3 in 1980, and $3.25 in 1981. Differential minimums in farmwork and for workers under age 18 also were raised. Permissible tip credits, formerly set at 25 percent of the minimum wage, were converted to a rising scale of dollar amounts, reaching in 1981 the equivalent of a 40-percent credit, as in the Federal FLSA.

The wage payment law was amended to exempt from the frequency of payment provision school district employees who voluntarily request payment over a 12-month period and employees covered by collective bargaining agreements that establish different payment periods.

Equal employment opportunity. An employee who quits work because the employer made employment, compensation, promotion, or job assignments contingent upon consent to sexual contact or intercourse will not suffer loss of benefits. In addition, such activity by any employer, labor organization, or licensing agency now may be the basis for a complaint of sex discrimination.

Pilot grants are to be given to nonprofit employment facilities that employ the developmentally disabled in the manufacture of marketable products.

Displaced homemakers. A displaced homemakers act provides for the creation of a multipurpose center to provide counseling, training, education, and placement services to help displaced homemakers seeking employment. Whenever possible, the center will be staffed by displaced homemakers.

Other laws. An effort is to be made to place persons who are recipients of Aid to Families with Dependent Children (AFDC) and are registered with the work incentive program in part-time jobs that will provide training that may help them become self-supporting or where the earnings combined with child support payments will result in removal from the AFDC program. A mandatory work experience program was established for Indians receiving public assistance.

Employers now are required to grant employees a leave of absence without loss of time in service, seniority, or pay advancement while on jury duty. Public and private employers must grant employees serving as election officials time off without penalty, except deduction for time lost, for the entire 24-hour period on election day, if such employees give 7 days notice of application for such leave. ☐

————FOOTNOTES————

[1] The legislatures did not meet this year in Arkansas, Montana, Nevada, North Dakota, Oregon, and Washington. Sessions were held in Alabama, Colorado, Indiana, Mississippi, New Hampshire, North Carolina, Texas, Utah, and Wyoming; but no significant labor legislation was enacted. Puerto Rico and the Virgin Islands were not included in the study.

For a discussion of changes in workers' compensation, see Gerri Minor, "Workers' compensation laws—key State amendments of 1978," this issue, pp. 43-50.

Labor and the Courts

EARLY LANDMARK DECISIONS ON LABOR

1842: Massachusetts Supreme Court held that a worker in securing employment assumes the risks involved in that worker's job. (*Farwel v. Boston & Worcester RR*)

1842: Speaking for all his associates in a unanimous decision, Judge Lemuel Shaw ruled that "every free man, whether skilled laborer, mechanic, farmer or domestic servant, may work or not work, or work or refuse to work with any company or individual, at his own option, except so far as he is bound by contract." The case arose upon the complaint of a worker against the Bootmakers' Society in Boston that the Society had enforced a closed shop clause that deprived him of his right to work. Judge Shaw held, "to charge those who become members of an association with criminal conspiracy, it must be proved that the avowed object was criminal." (*Commonwealth v. Hunt— Massachusetts General Court*)

1894: In connection with a railroad strike originating in the Pullman Company, a blanket injunction was issued against the officers of the American Railway Union and "all other persons," enjoining them from interference with the mails and interstate commerce. In violation of this, Eugene Victor Debs, president of the union, was imprisoned for six months for contempt of court. This was the first important use of the injunction in a labor dispute. The Debs' appeal was denied by the U.S. Supreme Court. (*Debs Case; U.S. v. Debs*)

1898: United States Supreme Court upheld the constitutionality of a State of Utah law limiting miners and smelter operators to an 8-hour work day. (*Holden v. Hardy*)

1903: United States Supreme Court upheld the right of the government to limit the hours or workers employed by contractors with the government. (*Atkins v. Kansas*)

1905: United States Supreme Court struck down a New York State law (1897) limiting hours of work for bakery workers: "no foundation for holding this legislation necessary as a health measure . . . statute interferes with right of contract." (*Lochner v. New York*)

1908: United States Supreme Court held constitutional an Oregon law limiting to 10 hours a day the employment of women in a factory or laundry. "A woman's well being becomes an object of public interest and care in order to preserve the strength and vigor of the race." (*Muller v. Oregon*)

1908: An historic episode in labor annals with reference to the boycott and injunction. A strike of molders at the company resulted in the Bucks' Stove and Range Co. being placed on the "unfair list" by the American Federation of Labor. A sweeping injunction was violated and three officers of the Federation were sentenced to prison. After three years of litigation, the Supreme Court set aside this judgment. (*Bucks' Stove and Range Case*)

1902–1915: A boycott of the United Hatters' Union against a manufacturer in 1902 resulted in legal action against the union. In 1908 the Supreme Court declared the boycott illegal and authorized a suit for damages. In 1909 judgment for $230,000 was obtained against individual members of the union and confirmed by the Supreme Court in 1915. A general assessment was levied against organized workers throughout the country to relieve the individuals affected. (*Danbury Hatters Case; Lawlor v. Loewe*)

1908: United States Supreme Court declared Section 10 of the Erdman Act (1898) unconstitutional. Section 10 provided: ". . . any employer . . . who shall require any employee . . . to enter an agreement . . . not to become a member of any labor organization . . . is hereby declared to be guilty . . ." (*Adair v. United States*)

1911: United States Supreme Court upheld the right of a State to establish a minimum size crew to operate trains. (*Chicago, Rock Island and Pacific RR v. Arkansas*)

1912: An Illinois court ruled that workers had a right to strike to force the employer to discharge non-union employees and that an injunction against the union was improper. (*Kemp et al v. Division No. 241, Illinois*)

1915: United States Supreme Court held invalid a Kansas law outlawing the yellow-dog contract as violative of the Fourteenth Amendment. (*Coppage v. Kansas*)

1917: United States Supreme Court found unconstitutional a State of Washington law denying employment agencies the right to collect fees from employees. (*Adams v. Turner*)

1916: United States Supreme Court upheld the right of the State of Oregon to limit hours of work to 10 hours a day in mill and factories as a health measure. (*Bunting v. Oregon*)

1917: United States Supreme Court held constitutional a State of Iowa workmen's compensation law. It found neither denial of due process nor violation of equal protection of the laws. (*Hawkins v. Bleakly*)

1917: Supreme Court limited the right of a union to induce workers to violate a yellow-dog contract they had signed. The court held that "the purpose was not lawful" and that the means were not lawful and that the union was engaged in an unlawful conspiracy. (*Hitchman Coal and Coke v. Mitchell*)

1918: United States Supreme Court struck down the Keating-Owens Act of 1916, which prohibited the shipment in interstate commerce of goods produced by children, holding that manufacture was not commerce and thus only the states could regulate in this area. (*Hammer v. Dagenhart*)

1921: United States Supreme Court upheld an injunction issued against the International Association of Machinists restraining its officials from inducing their members not to install the equipment of the Duplex Printing Company of Battle Creek, Michigan, in the New York area. This decision nullified what had been considered the labor clauses of the Clayton Act. (*Duplex Printing v. Deering*)

1921: A Federal District Court in Indiana enjoined the United Mine Workers from organizing non-union plants in West Virginia and Kentucky. The activity was held in violation of the Sherman Antitrust Act. (*Borderland Coal Corp. v. United Mine Workers*)

1921: United States Supreme Court held that Section 20 of the Clayton Act, which provides for peaceful persuasion or picketing in labor disputes, must be judged on the basis of the circumstances in a particular case. It provided for free passage of strikebreakers and employees. It limited the number of pickets and restricted their right to observation, communication and persuasion. (*American Steel Foundries v. Tri-City Central Trades Council*)

1921: United States Supreme Court upheld the right of the State of Colorado to require publicity, mediation, and the use of legislative investigations in resolving labor disputes in essential industries, including coal mining. (*People v. United Mine Workers*)

1921: United States Supreme Court set aside an Arizona statute modelled after Section 20 of the Clayton Act, which prohibits injunctions in labor disputes. The prohibition of injunctions in the case of mass picketing was "a wrongful and highly injurious invasion of property rights." (*Truax v. Corrigan*)

1923: United States Supreme Court found unconstitutional an Act of Congress fixing minimum wages for women and children in the District of Columbia. (*Adkins v. Children's Hospital*)

1925: United States Supreme Court held the union liable for damages under the Sherman Antitrust Act. Of particular importance was the finding that unions could be sued as entities and subject to triple damages under the Sherman law. (*Coronado Coal v. United Mine Workers*)

1925: United States Supreme Court held unconstitutional the State of Arizona's minimum wage law. (*Murphy v. Sardell*)

1926: United States Supreme Court held there is no constitutional right to strike. (*Dorchy v. Kansas*)

1927: United States Supreme Court held the Stone Cutters Union in violation of the Sherman Antitrust Act for ruling that their members should not work on stone cut by non-union labor. (*Bedford Cut Stone Case*)

1927: The Court of Appeals of New York State held that a yellow-dog contract was not binding on either the signer of the contract or the union. (*Exchange Bakery v. Rifkin, N.Y.*)

1930: United States Supreme Court upheld an injunction against the railroad which had sought to bring in a company union in violation of the Railway Labor Act. The court ordered the railroad to bargain with the Railway Clerks rather than the company union. (*Texas and New Orleans Railway v. Brotherhood of Railway and Steamship Clerks*)

1934: United States Supreme Court denied petition by the State of Alabama for an injunction to restrain other states from stopping the sale of prison-made goods. (*Alabama v. Arizona*)

1932–34: Supreme Court denied certiorari which supported a circuit court decision upholding the constitutionality of the Norris-LaGuardia Act. The Bridge and Iron Workers Union had threatened a strike to enforce a closed shop. An injunction against the union was reversed. (*Levering and Garriques v. Morrin*)

1935: United States Supreme Court ruled the National Industrial Recovery Act unconstitutional. The NIRA provided for the setting up of codes of standards by the President. The court held: (1) the act was an illegal designation of legislative power; (2) the poultry in the case, because it was all consumed in New York, was not therefore subject to regulation by Congress. (*Schecter Poultry Corp. v. U.S.*)

1936: A New York Court ruled that a contract between a union and an employer preventing the employer from moving his shop to an area beyond the five-cent fare limit was legal and proper. (*Dubinsky v. Blue Dale Dress*)

1937: United States Supreme Court held that the National Labor Relations Board was within its power when it found that Jones and Loughlin had violated the NLRA by discriminating against workers for membership in a union. It ruled that Congress can regulate labor relations under its interstate commerce power. (*NLRB v. Jones and Loughlin Steel Co.*)

1937: United States Supreme Court upheld the minimum wage law of the State of Washington and denied that it was violative of the due process clause of the Fourteenth Amendment. This decision overruled the decision in the case of *Adkins v. Children's Hospital*. (*West Coast Hotel v. Parrish*)

1937: United States Supreme Court set aside the conviction of Angelo Herndon under an 1861 statute for "inciting to insurrection." Herndon, a union organizer in Atlanta, had been sentenced to 18 to 20 years on a chain gang. (*Herndon Case*)

1937: United States Supreme Court upheld the constitutionality of the Ashurst-Sumners Act of 1935, requiring the marking of prison-made goods with respect to origin, destination, and description. (*Kentucky Whip and Collar Co. v. Illinois Central Railway Company*)

1937: In the matter of Globe Machine and Stamping Company, the NLRB defended the right of employees to remain in their own unit if they indicated that preference to inclusion in a larger unit.

1937: United States Supreme Court reversed the conviction of DeJonge under the Oregon Criminal Syndicalism Statute which prohibited peaceable assembly: "The right of peaceable assembly is a cognate to those of free speech and free press and is equally fundamental." (*DeJonge v. Oregon*)

1938: United States Supreme Court upheld order of NLRB in disestablishing company-dominated unions. The decision specified that it was not necessary for the Board to issue an order against the union or permit the union to participate in the proceedings. (*NLRB v. Pennsylvania Greyhound Lines, Inc.*)

1938: United States Supreme Court supported the position of the NLRB that employees who go on strike do not thereby lose their status as employees. It held, however, that employees who had been replaced during the strike need not be recalled to work. The line was thus drawn between economic strikers and "unfair labor practice strikers." The refusal to reinstate an employee because of strike activity is an unfair labor practice. (*NLRB v. MacKay Radio and Telegraph Co.*)

1938: Supreme Court held that organizational picketing was protected by the Norris-LaGuardia Act and that an injunction to stop such picketing was in error. (*Lauf v. E. G. Shinner & Co.*)

1938: United States Supreme Court held that local law in Griffin County, Georgia, requiring permit for distribution of union organizing literature, was infringing on freedom of the press. (*Lovell v. City of Griffin*)

1939: Supreme Court held that the right to strike did not extend to the use of a sitdown strike. The discharged sitdown strikers had no reinstatement rights under the National Labor Relations Act. (*NLRB v. Fansteel Metallurgical Corp.*)

1939: The Third Circuit Court supported the power of the NLRB to order the reinstatement of strikers who were judged guilty of criminal conduct during a strike. The Board did deny reinstatement to those strikers who had been convicted of possession of explosives, malicious destruction of property in excess of $300, and possession of a bomb. (*Republic Steel v. NLRB*)

1939: United States Supreme Court held "void upon its face," an ordinance by city officials forbidding union members to hold meetings in streets and parks. (*Hague et al. v. CIO*)

1939: The NLRB ruled a single bargaining unit was appropriate for all six plants of a company. A finding of earlier unfair labor practices by the company was the basis of the decision. In 1941 the Supreme Court ruled that the NLRB had the authority to make such a determination. (*Pittsburgh Plate Glass Case*)

1940: Supreme Court limited the application of the Sherman Antitrust Act in labor disputes. Restraint of interstate commerce required a showing of actual or intended effect on competition for the employers products. (*Apex Hosiery v. Leader*)

1940: United States Supreme Court asserted that the right to picket in a labor dispute was protected by the First Amendment to the Constitution. (*Thornhill v. Alabama*)

1941: In 1941 the NLRB decided that a plant was a proper unit for collective bargaining. Prior to this, employer units were deemed the only proper unit, if the union had a majority in most plants of a company. (*Libbey-Owens Ford Case*)

1941: United States Supreme Court affirmed dismissal of indictment against Carpenters Union for conspiring to interfere with commerce by striking and picketing Anheuser-Busch Inc. See Allen-Bradley Case (1945), which limited such rights. (*United States v. Hutcheson*)

1941: United States Supreme Court held that the minimum wage and hours of provisions of Sections 6 and 7 of the Fair Labor Standards Act did not violate the due process clause of the Fifth Amendment. (*United States v. Darby Lumber Co.*)

1941: United States Supreme Court upheld decision of Illinois Supreme Court supporting an injunction against the union because of violence associated with picketing a rival union's establishment: "acts of violence may have a significance which neutralizes constitutional immunity." (*Milk Wagon Drivers' Union v. Meadow-Moor Dairies, Inc.*)

1941: United States Supreme Court upheld an order of the NLRB requiring the company to sign a contract with the union where there was no dispute as to wages, hours, and other conditions of employment. (*H. J. Heinz Co. v. NLRB*)

1941: Supreme Court ruled that the constitutional guarantee of freedom of discussion is infringed by the policy of a state to forbid picketing merely because there was no immediate labor-management dispute. (*American Federation v. Swing*)

1945: United States Supreme Court found action by a union in collaboration with employers to suppress competition to be in violation of the Eherman Act. (*Allen-Bradley Case*)

1948: U.S. Court of Appeals, 7th Circuit, upheld the NLRB ruling that the company was required to bargain with the union on retirement and pensions. (*Inland Steel Co. v. NLRB*)

1948: United States Supreme Court ruled that premium payments under a collective-bargaining agreement were to be considered in calculating overtime under the Fair Labor Standards Act. (*Bay Ridge v. Aaron*)

1950: The NLRB set forth the standards for determining the legality of common situs picketing: (1) Limited to times when the struck employer's workers are present at the site; (2) Picketing must be limited to places "reasonably close" to the operations of the struck employer; (3) The pickets show that the dispute is only with the struck employer; (4) The struck employer's workers must be engaged in the employer's normal business at the common site. (*Moore Drydock Case*)

1951: United States Supreme Court held that the picketing of a subcontractor at a construction project was illegal if it had the effect of inducing employers of the general contractor or other contractors to stop work. (*Denver Building Trades*)

1951: The NLRB ruled that an employer must give equal time to the union if it has made a presentation against the union to a captive audience of employees during working hours on the company's premises. (*Bonwit Teller Rule*)

1951: United States Court of Appeals for the District of Columbia upheld the NLRB order for the company to negotiate with the union despite the union's loss in a representation election. The election loss the Board held was caused by the company's refusal to bargain when the union did have a majority of the employees. (*Joy Silk Mills v. NLRB*)

1956: The NLRB ruled that a company or a union can be compelled to return dues to workers if a contract provided an illegal union security clause. (*Brown Olds Doctrine*)

1957: United States Supreme Court asserted the importance of arbitration in labor disputes and held that the arbitration clause in a contract was the *quid pro quo* given by an employer in return for the union's commitment not to strike during the life of a contract. (*Textile Workers v. Lincoln Mills*)

1958: United States Supreme Court enumerated three categories of bargaining under the Taft-Hartley Law: (1) illegal subjects: such as a closed shop; (2) mandatory subjects, such as wages, hours, working conditions, etc.; (3) voluntary subjects: neither 1 or 2 but areas such as sick leave and death in the family. (*Borg Warner Case*)

1961: Supreme Court held that the NLRB had no right to ban hiring halls. "There being no express ban of hiring halls in the provisions of the Taft-Hartley Act, those who add one, whether it be the Board or Courts, engage in a legislative act." (*Mountain Pacific Case: Local 357 IBT v. NLRB*)

1964: The NLRB ruled that the assertion of a union that it represented a majority of the employees of a company was not sufficient to warrant an election when a contract was in force with another union. Nor could such an assertion prevent another union from signing a contract. The assertion does not have a standing equal to a petition for certification.

1964: The NLRB held that "Boulwarism" was in violation of the principle of "good faith" bargaining required by the Taft-Hartley Act. The company's insistence on its "fair and firm" offer and its policy of communicating it to its employees was a "take it or leave it" attitude, not consistent with the requirement to bargain in good faith.

1964: United States Supreme Court held that the employer had an obligation to bargain with the maintenance workers on a decision to subcontract maintenance work. (*Fibreboard Paper Products Corp. v. NLRB*)

1964: United States Supreme Court held that a dispute concerning the assignment of work was subject to the process of arbitration. (*Carey v. Westinghouse*)

1965: Supreme Court held that a lockout by a company for the sole purpose of bringing economic pressure was not violative of the Taft-Hartley Act. (*American Ship Building Case*)

1965: United States Supreme Court held that an employer can terminate his business for any reason, including anti-union bias. An employer may not, however, move premises or operations to avoid a union. (*Textile Workers v. Darlington Mfg. Company*)

1965: United States Supreme Court held that Section 504 of the Landrum-Griffin Act was unconstitutional in that persons who are or had been members of the Communist Party were barred from union office. Section 504 was void as a bill of attainder. (*United States v. Archie Brown*)

1965: United States Supreme Court held that a union may for its own reasons impose terms on an employer that it had succeeded in winning from a multi-employer bargaining unit; but it may not be exempt from antitrust laws if it agrees with an employer to impose terms on another employer. (*United Mine Workers v. Pennington*)

Labor and the Supreme Court: significant decisions of 1976–77

*Last year, the High Court weakened
several of Title VII's job bias bans,
endorsed a new NLRB policy narrowing
the 'work preservation' doctrine,
and upheld public-sector agency shops*

In its 1976–77 term, the Supreme Court made a group of decisions that narrowly interpreted the statutory bans against employment discrimination. In two of these cases,[1] the Court broke a string of appeals court decisions, which had liberally interpreted the Title VII provisions of the 1964 Civil Rights Act and, in one,[2] rejected interpretive guidelines promulgated by the Equal Employment Opportunity Commission. In addition to the restrictive rulings in Title VII cases, the High Court clipped the meaning of the "work preservation" doctrine, endorsing a new interpretation by the National Labor Relations Board which limits a union's options in maintaining "traditional work."[3] Also endorsing a redefined NLRB policy, the Court narrowed the definition of "agricultural workers" who are exempt from National Labor Relations Act provisions.[4]

Public-sector labor relations did not command the Court's attention as it had in the previous term. In one of the few cases dealing with public employees, the Court upheld the right of unions to collect "bargaining fees" from nonunion employees under an agency-shop provision.[5] During its 9-month term, the Supreme Court also limited workers' eligibility for benefits related to employment[6] and went both ways on the handling of two sex-based benefit provi-

sions under the Social Security Act—striking one and upholding another.[7]

With the concurrence of at least six justices (Justices Thurgood Marshall, William Brennan, and, sometimes, John Paul Stevens registered dissents), the Court apparently limited the potential sweep of Title VII in the year's most controversial cases.[8] In its sometimes broad opinions, the Court restricted the statute's ban on discrimination based on sex or religion[9] and limited an employers' liability for the effects of prior discrimination.[10] Reflecting the impact of these Title VII decisions, one prominent law professor stated,[11] "[T]he Court's opinions leave little for civil rights proponents to cheer about; however, there are a few hopeful signs in some of the opinions—at least enough to suggest that we have not as yet seen the complete demise of the proscription against discrimination under Title VII."

Employment discrimination

In the 1976–77 term, the Supreme Court's first and most controversial Title VII decision, *General Electric Co. v. Gilbert*,[12] established the Court's year-long posture of narrowly interpreting the statute's prohibitions against employment discrimination. In a lengthy opinion written by Justice William Rehnquist, the Court rejected the Equal Employment Opportunity Commission's interpretive guidelines[13]—as well as the conclusions of six Federal appeals courts —in ruling that Title VII does not require employers

---

Gregory J. Mounts, an economist on the staff of the *Monthly Labor Review*, has been writing "Significant decisions in labor cases."

to include pregnancies in otherwise comprehensive disability plans.

In its landmark *Griggs v. Duke Power Co.* decision,[14] the Court held that Title VII violations can result from the discriminatory *effects* of a facially neutral classification.[15] In *Gilbert,* however, the majority seemed to deflate the application of this "effects test" and, instead, relied on a "minimal standard"[16] constitutional definition of sex discrimination, as applied in an earlier benefit-exclusion case.[17] Using this less-precise standard, (made possible, the Court said, because Title VII lacked any Congressional intent otherwise),[18] the majority concluded that the exclusion of pregnancies did not discriminate against women; it merely discriminated against "pregnant persons" as opposed to "nonpregnant persons." In the wake of this decision, labor unions and women's groups have taken the issue to Congress, hoping to amend Title VII to explicitly require pregnancy benefits under comprehensive disability programs.

Another case, *Trans World Airlines v. Hardison,*[19] invoked the Court's more restrictive interpretation of Title VII in the area of religious discrimination. The statute requires employers to "reasonably accommodate" the religious needs of their employees —as long as no "undue hardship" is imposed upon the employer. Deadlocked twice before on this issue,[20] the Court ruled, by a 7 to 2 margin, that employers are not required to violate the provisions of a valid seniority system or incur additional expenses such as overtime in order to allow employees to celebrate a Saturday Sabbath. To some observers, the Court's decision in Hardison effectively eliminated the adjective "undue" from the statute. In the observance of religious practices, as in other First Amendment guarantees, individual rights are normally protected. The Court's ruling in *Hardison,* however, reflected a traditional interpretation of national labor policy as embodied in the National Labor Relations Act (NLRA)—that in the context of collective bargaining, individual interests must yield to those of the group (the union). As in *Gilbert,* however, opponents of the decision are attempting to alter the effects of the ruling by amending Title VII to explicitly require more substantial accommodation on the part of employers to the religious needs of employees.

Although they did not receive the media attention accorded *Gilbert* or *Hardison,* two Supreme Court decisions involving the discriminatory impact of seniority systems may prove even more important to employee-plaintiffs under Title VII. In *Teamsters v. United States,*[21] the Court ruled that a seniority system is not unlawful merely because it perpetuates an employer's previous discriminatory policies. The majority found that Title VII protects "bona fide" seniority systems—those designed without discriminatory intent—even though they lock in the effects of illegal employment discrimination. The Congressional judgment, the Court said, was that Title VII should not "destroy or water down the vested seniority rights of employees simply because their employer had engaged in discrimination prior to the passage of the Act." Prior to the *Teamsters* ruling, eight Federal appeals courts were unanimous in holding that any seniority system that retained the effects of past discrimination was in violation of Title VII.[22] In these and many other lower court cases, the remedy was typically a total restructuring of the "illegal" systems. The effect of *Teamsters* on these prior rulings is unclear, although one law professor has speculated that a court-revised seniority system (such as those changed from "departmental" to "plant-wide") may now be seen as discriminatory against whites.[23] In addition to finding the seniority systems immune from attack under Title VII, the *Teamsters* ruling also held that proven victims of pre-Act discrimination were entitled to no relief; those discriminated against after the Act took effect may be granted seniority credit back to that date, but not before.

The other case involving seniority, *United Air Lines v. Evans,*[24] also limited an employer's liability for prior violations under Title VII. The Court ruled that an employee who was illegally discriminated against after Title VII took effect could lose her right to retroactive seniority if she fails to file charges within the specified period (now 180 days) after the violation occurred. Although the effects of the discrimination were perpetuated by the seniority system, there was no basis for her claim that the original unchallenged discrimination was a continuing violation of Title VII, the Court said.

In two other Title VII cases, the Court considered the applicability of statistical evidence in proving employment discrimination. In *Hazelwood School District v. United States,*[25] the Court held that statistical data showing racially discriminatory hiring practices may constitute the necessary evidence for a violation of Title VII. The justices added, however, that the employer must be given the opportunity to show that the statistically proven discrimination occurred prior to the Act's effective date and, therefore, is not a violation.[26] In *Dothard v. Rawlinson,*[27] the Court accepted statistical evidence as proof that minimum height and weight job requirements, although purportedly measurements of strength, constituted illegal sex discrimination because they automatically excluded more than 41 percent of all women but only 3 percent of all men in the country. This aspect of *Dothard* seemingly upholds Title VII's "effects test," feared impaired or even lost in the *Gilbert* ruling. The Court then went on to consider the legality of the Alabama Board of Corrections' gender-based hiring criterion for prison guards and noted, for the first time in a Title VII case, that "it is impermissible under Title VII to refuse to hire an individual woman or man on the basis of stereotyped characterizations of the sexes." Nevertheless, the Court concluded in *Dothard* that the State could bar women from the guard positions under the "bona fide occupational qualification" exception contained in Title VII.

Public sector employment

Claimed First Amendment freedoms of public schoolteachers—specifically, those of nonunion employees under collective bargaining agreements—were curtailed in one Supreme Court decision last year and strongly affirmed in another. A third developed a specific test for when an employee's "protected speech" may lawfully play a "substantial role" in the decision not to renew his contract.

In *Abood v. Detroit Board of Education,*[28] the High Court approved public-sector agency shops, requiring nonunion employees to pay a service fee equivalent to union dues. Interestingly, all nine justices agreed that the agency-shop provision in the union's contract infringed upon the First Amendment rights of nonunion employees; however, a six-justice majority found that this "impingement upon associational freedom" is permissible when the mandatory fees are used specifically for collective bargaining activity. Thus, the Court extended the long-established, private-sector concept of equal cost for equal representation, but it also ruled that nonunion employees may not be forced to support the union's "ideological activities." Therefore, the Court said, objecting nonunion employees are entitled to a partial refund to the extent that their money is being used to finance activities "unrelated to collective bargaining."

In the other case involving a conflict between collective bargaining activities and the First Amendment rights of public schoolteachers, the Court held that a union's right to exclusive representation does not prevent a nonunion teacher from discussing employment policies at an open meeting of the School Board. In *City of Madison Joint School District No. 8 v. Wisconsin Employment Relations Commission,*[29] the nonunion teacher addressed the Board during the "question and answer" period of a public meeting; he objected to certain bargaining demands made by the union. The union charged that this illegally interfered with its right as exclusive bargaining agent, because the action constituted "negotiation" between the teacher and the Board. The Court's ruling, upholding the employee's freedom of speech in the public meeting, reversed a decision by the Wisconsin Supreme Court.

In *Mt. Healthy City School District v. Doyle,*[30] the contract of a public schoolteacher was not renewed because of "a notable lack of tact in handling professional matters." On one occasion, he informed a local radio station of an official memorandum concerning teacher attire. Another time, he responded to disobedient students with obscene gestures. Agreeing with the lower court, the Supreme Court held that disclosing the memo was protected speech under the First Amendment and therefore could not constitutionally justify the nonrenewal of his contract. Because the disclosure played a "substantial role" in the employment decision, the lower court ruled that the teacher must be rehired. The High Court rejected this reasoning, however, and constructed an explicit causation test for this type of frequently alleged violation. Unanimously, the Court held that the teacher must be rehired only if his contract would have been renewed "but for" his exercise of free speech. This new standard provides greater leeway for public employers to rebut charges that their employment decisions result at least in part from unconstitutional motives.

'Traditional' labor law

The Supreme Court's decision in *NLRB v. Enterprise Association Steam Pipefitters*[31] was one of the year's most significant rulings involving organized labor. The decision, affirming the National Labor Relations Board's reinterpretation of the distinction between primary and secondary labor disputes, greatly limited the applicability of the "work preservation" doctrine established by the Supreme Court in *National Woodwork Manufacturers' Assn. v. NLRB.*[32] The union's contract in *Pipefitters* contained a work preservation clause, prohibiting the use of prefabricated products that reduced the amount of work performed by union members. However, the employer, a subcontractor, had accepted a contract with the general contractor that required the use of prefabricated products. As a result, the union refused to install the prefab devices. Under these circumstances, the union's work stoppage becomes an illegal secondary dispute the court ruled, because the union seeks to force the subcontractor to stop doing business with someone else (the general contractor). Thus, under the new, Court-approved NLRB standard, the "work preservation" doctrine, permitting unions to limit the introduction of labor saving technology, is restricted by a "right to control" test. In *Pipefitters,* the employer did not have control over the assignment of work sought by the union, even though he was aware of the job specifications before he signed the union agreement.

In the 1976–77 term, the Supreme Court extended the established policy of favoring arbitration in disputes arising under collective bargaining agreements. *Nolde Bros., Inc. v. Local 358, Bakery and Confectionery Workers*[33] provided a new twist, however, because the Court ruled that a dispute over severance pay must be arbitrated—even though the union's claim arose after the expiration of the contract. The 7 to 2 majority held that the contract's arbitration clause, providing for the arbitration of "any grievance," covered the dispute because the claim arose *under* the contract, although *after* its termination. *Nolde Bros.* was one of the few significant decisions organized labor applauded in last year's term; it requires arbitration of plausible union arguments that employees' "vested" rights have been violated after the expiration of (or during a lapse in) the collective bargaining agreement.

In *Bayside Enterprises, Inc. v. NLRB*,[34] the Supreme Court maintained its strong deference to the interpretations of the NLRB (as evidenced by its decision in *Pipefitters*[35]). The Court unanimously agreed with the Board that a group of truckdrivers in the vertically integrated poultry business were not "agricultural workers" (who are excluded from the scope of the NLRA). The decision, which affirmed the labor position, permits the drivers to organize and bargain under the Act. The NLRB's Court-approved interpretation, determining an employee's status by the specific work he performs for his employer, suggests that it might not be long before the only agribusiness employees exempted from the Act are those engaged in actual farming activities.

In *Walsh v. Schlect*,[36] the High Court followed its general rule of construing a labor contract to be legally sound, whenever possible. The Taft-Hartley amendments to the NLRA prohibit employer payments to any union fund with the exception of contractually created union-employer trust funds providing medical, retirement, vacation, or training funds to union employees and their dependents. The union's contract in *Walsh* required the general contractor to guarantee that payments would be made into the trust fund on an hours-worked basis, even with respect to the hours worked by a subcontractor's nonunion employees. Although these employees could not legally benefit from these payments, the Supreme Court ruled that the contractual provision was valid because the language specifically required payments based on the hours worked of all subcontractors' employees, rather than requiring that all workers actually benefit from those payments.

During last year's term, the Court availed itself of an opportunity to clarify certain aspects of Federal preemption in labor cases. Unanimously, the Court ruled in *Farmer v. United B'hd of Carpenters*[37] that, although Federal labor law preempts State jurisdiction over allegations of illegal employment practices,

it does not preempt State remedies for the claim of "intentional infliction of emotional distress" accompanying the alleged employment discrimination. Constructing a test from previous decisions,[38] the Court found that if the alleged conduct is not protected by the National Labor Relations Act, involves an "overriding State interest" for the protection of its aggrieved citizens, and has little risk of interfering with the administration of National labor policy it may be adjudicated by the State courts. The Court emphasized, however, that a State court must not consider whether there was an act of discrimination in *Farmer,* but rather only whether the alleged conduct occurred in an abusive manner. The case was then returned to California's State courts, allowing them to rule on the alleged "outrageous conduct" of union officers toward a member who sought to use the union's hiring hall.

The Labor-Management Reporting and Disclosure Act provides in part that a union member "in good standing" shall be able to run for union office subject to "reasonable qualifications uniformly imposed" by the union. In *United Steelworkers, Local 3489 v. Usery,*[39] the Supreme Court resolved a direct conflict between appeals courts[40] when it ruled that limiting eligibility for local union officeseekers to members that had attended at least one-half of the regular monthly meetings during the preceding 3 years was not "reasonable" and therefore illegal. The requirement, disqualifying 96.5 percent of the local's members, would "severely restrict the free choice of the membership in electing their leaders," the Court said. The decision had some aspects of an "effects test," but the Court was careful not to rule that any type of attendance criteria was unreasonable. The justices recognized that, by requiring some minimum attendance, the union was helping to ensure that members become familiar with the problems of running a union before they run for office.

Government benefits

Several cases involving employment-related social benefits were decided by the Supreme Court last term. A pair, *Ohio Bureau of Employment Services v. Hodory* and *Batterton v. Francis,*[41] provided opportunities for the Court to show a deference toward "States rights," when permitted by the construction of Federal statutes.

In *Hodory,* a unanimous Court upheld an Ohio law that denied unemployment compensation to workers who are jobless as a result of a strike, even if they do not participate in the dispute (which could occur at another location and involve another union). Neither the Social Security Act nor the Federal Unemployment Tax Act contains language that require States to disburse funds to the involuntarily unemployed, the Court ruled. Under the Fourteenth

Amendment's equal protection clause, the justices found the Ohio procedure rationally related to the legitimate State interests of protecting employers, discouraging labor disputes, and conserving funds. During the litigation, however, Ohio amended the statute to provide benefits in *Hodory*-type cases.

The question in *Batterton* was whether the term "unemployment" should be defined on the Federal or State level for purposes of eligibility for Federal welfare benefits. In 1968, after 7 years of State autonomy on the issue, Congress mandated a national definition of unemployment for disbursement of benefits under Aid to Families with Dependent Children—Unemployed Fathers, but it left the specific criterion to be proscribed by the Secretary of Health, Education, and Welfare. The Secretary, all but ignoring the Congressional intent, proceeded to construct a "national standard" that defined unemployment (and therefore benefit eligibility) "at the option of the State." As before, many States could and did deny unemployment status to strikers, those dismissed for cause, or those who would also be disqualified for unemployment compensation. The singular focus of the Supreme Court was whether the Secretary had exceeded his authority; the Fourth Circuit Court of Appeals ruled that he had. By a narrow 5 to 4 majority, the High Court reversed, relying on the concept of "cooperative Federalism" that Justice Harry Blackmun said allowed the Secretary to recognize "legitimate local policies in determining eligibility."

The differential treatment of the sexes under the Social Security Act was the subject of two cases before the Court last term; one of the sex-based benefit provisions was upheld. In *Califano v. Webster*,[42] the Court approved a benefit provision granting women, who reached the age of 62 before 1975, higher payments than men of the same age and earnings record. (After 1975, the benefit levels equalized for those newly qualified.) The majority reasoned that the differential treatment might have been intended to compensate women for the likelihood that they had been undercompensated (relative to men) during their working years. In *Califano v. Goldfarb*,[43] however, the Court struck down a provision of the Act that required widowers, but not widows, seeking survivors' benefits to prove that they had been dependent on the earnings of their spouses. A five-justice majority ruled the provision unconstitutional because similarly situated surviving spouses received unequal protection solely on the basis of sex. Four of the five justices (William Brennan, Byron White, Thurgood Marshall, and Lewis Powell) felt that the statute discriminated against women, providing less protection for their families than it provided for male workers. The fifth justice, John Paul Stevens, ruled the provision unconstitutional because it denied benefits for men unless they could prove that they had been dependent upon their wives' earnings.

New laws; veterans' rewards

When Congress enacts new laws, attempting to solve evolving social and economic problems, it frequently assigns factfinding and initial adjudicative functions to an administrative agency. In the 1976–77 term, the Supreme Court upheld the enforcement mechanisms of these agencies when it ruled that the administrative determination of violations under the Occupational Safety and Health Act is not prohibited by the Seventh Amendment's guarantee of a jury trial in civil actions. (*Atlas Roofing Co., Inc. v. Occupational Safety and Health Review Commission*.[44]) In a unanimous opinion, the Court held that where new "public rights" are created by statute, Congress has broad authority to place the responsibility for enforcing the law within the scope of administrative agencies.

Near the end of the 1976–77 term, the High Court provided rehired veterans with a fitting "reward" for their service to the country. In *Alabama Power Co. v. Davis*,[45] the Court ruled that employers who rehire a returning veteran are required to credit the employee's military service toward the calculation of their pension benefits. Justice Thurgood Marshall, writing for the unanimous Court, concluded that the Selective Service Act protects benefits of seniority that would have accrued with reasonable certainty had the veteran been continuously employed and are in the nature of a reward for length of service. These "two axes of analyses," developed by Marshall for determining whether a benefit is a "right of seniority" protected by the Act, dictated the award of higher pension benefits in *Alabama Power*.   □

————*FOOTNOTES*————

[1] *General Electric Co. v. Gilbert,* 45 U.S.L.W. 4031 (U.S. Dec. 7, 1976), see *Monthly Labor Review,* March 1977, pp. 73–74, and *Teamsters v. United States,* 45 U.S.L.W. 4506 (U.S. May 31, 1977), see *Monthly Labor Review,* August 1977, pp. 48–49.

[2] *General Electric Co. v. Gilbert,* 45 U.S.L.W. 4031 (U.S. Dec. 7, 1976).

[3] *NLRB v. Enterprise Association of Steam Pipefitters,* 45 U.S.L.W. 4144 (U.S. Feb. 22, 1977), see *Monthly Labor Review,* June 1977, pp. 57–58.

[4] *Bayside Enterprises, Inc. v. NLRB,* 45 U.S.L.W. 4086 (U.S. Jan. 11, 1977).

[5] *Abood v. Detroit Board of Education,* 45 U.S.L.W. 4473 (U.S. May 23, 1977), see *Monthly Labor Review,* August 1977, pp. 46–47.

[6] *Ohio Bureau of Employment Services v. Hodory,* 45 U.S.L.W. 4544 (U.S. May 31, 1977), and *Batterton v. Francis,* 45 U.S.L.W., 4768 (U.S. June 20, 1977). For a discussion of both of these cases, see *Monthly Labor Review,* September 1977, pp. 40–42.

[7] *Califano v. Webster,* 45 U.S.L.W. 3630 (U.S. Mar. 21, 1977); and *Calfiano v. Goldfarb,* 45 U.S.L.W. 4237 (U.S. Mar. 2, 1977), see *Monthly Labor Review,* May 1977, pp. 51–52.

[8] *General Electric v. Gilbert,* 45 U.S.L.W. 4031 (U.S. Dec. 7, 1976); *Trans World Airlines v. Hardison,* 45 U.S.L.W. 4672 (U.S. June 16, 1977), see *Monthly Labor Review,* September 1977, pp. 39–40; and *Teamsters v. United States,* 45 U.S.L.W. 4506 (U.S. May 31, 1977).

[9] *General Electric Co. v. Gilbert,* 45 U.S.L.W. 4031 (U.S. Dec. 7, 1976), and *Trans World Airlines v. Hardison,* 45 U.S.L.W. 4672 (U.S. June 16, 1977).

[10] *Teamsters v. United States,* 45 U.S.L.W. 4506 (U.S. May 31, 1977), and *United Air Lines v. Evans,* 45 U.S.L.W. 4566 (U.S. May 31, 1977).

[11] Harry T. Edwards, "The Coming Age of the Burger Court," 159 Daily Labor Report, Spec. Supp., p.2. Edwards, a professor of law at the University of Michigan, presented this analysis to the Annual Meeting of the American Bar Association in Chicago, Aug. 8, 1977.

[12] *General Electric Co. v. Gilbert,* 45 U.S.L.W. 4031 (U.S. Dec. 7, 1976).

[13] The rejection of the EEOC guidelines represented a clear retreat from the Court's attitude in earlier decisions—that they are entitled to "great deference." For a list of the six appeals court cases that had been decided differently, see *Monthly Labor Review,* March 1977, p. 76, footnote 3.

[14] *Griggs v. Duke Power Co.,* 401 U.S. 424 (1971).

[15] In *Griggs,* the Court held that, in a Title VII case, a facially neutral plan could be shown to be a prima facie violation of Title VII, irrespective of the lack of discriminatory motive, if it had the *effect* of discriminating against a protected class.

[16] In deciding cases under the Equal Protection Clause of the Fourteenth Amendment, the Court has several options. It can use a minimal standard of review, traditionally used to defer to the judgment of State legislatures in enacting laws. It may apply a more stringent standard, sometimes employed in sex-discrimination cases, which requires that a classification further a legitimate objective. The Court may also use a very strict scrutiny, declaring sex, for example, a suspect classification, to defeat some specific legislation.

[17] *Geduldig v. Aiello,* 417 U.S. 484 (1974). Using the minimal standard equal protection review, the Court ruled that the exclusion of pregnancy related benefits under a State disability insurance program was not sex discrimination, primarily because it restricted a specific physical condition (not women in general) and served the State's "legitimate interest" of maintaining the solvency and general equitability of the fund. For a discussion of the case, see *Monthly Labor Review,* October 1974, pp. 69–71.

[18] 97 S. Ct. at 407.

[19] *Trans World Airlines v. Hardison,* 45 U.S.L.W. 4672 (U.S. June 16, 1977).

[20] *Dewey v. Reynolds Metals Co.,* 402 U.S. 689 (1971); and *Parker Seal Co. v. Cummins,* 429 U.S. 65 (1976). The extent of the required accommodation was confronted in both cases, but both times the judgments of the Courts of Appeals were affirmed without opinion by an equally divided Court.

[21] *Teamsters v. United States,* 45 U.S.L.W. 4506 (U.S. May 31, 1977).

[22] In his dissent in *Teamsters,* Justice Thurgood Marshall lists more than 30 cases decided by eight Federal appeals courts. (Footnotes 3 and 4, 45 U.S.L.W. 4520.)

[23] Edwards, "The Coming of Age of the Burger Court," p. 3.

[24] *United Air Lines v. Evans,* 45 U.S.L.W. 4566 (U.S. May 31, 1977).

[25] *Hazelwood School District v. United States,* 45 U.S.L.W. 4882 (U.S. June 27, 1977).

[26] This principle was first enunciated in *Teamsters* when the Court held that, once a prima facie case has been established by statistical work force disparities, the employer must be given an opportunity to show that "the claimed discriminatory pattern is a product of pre-Act hiring rather than unlawful post-Act discrimination."

[27] *Dothard v. Rawlinson,* 45 U.S.L.W. 4888 (U.S. June 27, 1977), see *Monthly Labor Review,* October 1977, pp. 70–71.

[28] *Abood v. Detroit Board of Education,* 45 U.S.L.W. 4473 (U.S. May 23, 1977)

[29] *City of Madison, Joint School District No. 8 v. Wisconsin Employment Relations Commission,* 45 U.S.L.W. 4043 (U.S. Dec. 8, 1976), see *Monthly Labor Review,* April 1977, pp. 79–80.

[30] *Mt. Healthy School District v. Doyle,* 45 U.S.L.W. 4079 (U.S. Jan. 11, 1977), see *Monthly Labor Review,* March 1977, pp. 75–76.

[31] *NLRB v. Enterprise Association of Steam Pipefitters,* 45 U.S.L.W. 4144 (U.S. Feb. 22, 1977).

[32] *National Woodworks Manufacturers Assoc. v. NLRB,* 386 U.S. 612 (1967), see *Monthly Labor Review,* June 1967, pp. 65–66.

[33] *Nolde Bros., Inc. v. Local 358, Bakery and Confectionery Workers,* 45 U.S.L.W. 4251 (U.S. Mar. 7, 1977), see *Monthly Labor Review,* July 1977, pp. 46–47.

[34] *Bayside Enterprises, Inc. v. NLRB,* 45 U.S.L.W. 4086 (U.S. Jan. 11, 1977).

[35] *NLRB v. Enterprise Association of Steam Pipefitters,* 45 U.S.L.W. 4144 (U.S. Feb. 22, 1977).

[36] *Walsh v. Schlecht,* 45 U.S.L.W. 4126 (U.S. Jan. 18, 1977), see *Monthly Labor Review,* June 1977, pp. 58–59.

[37] *Farmer v. United B'hd. of Carpenters, Local 25,* 45 U.S.L.W. 4263 (U.S. Mar. 7, 1977), see *Monthly Labor Review,* July 1977, pp. 47–48.

[38] Expanding on its landmark opinion in *San Diego Building Trades Council v. Garmon,* 359 U.S. 236 (1959), the Court relied primarily upon its decision in *Linn v. Plant Guard Workers,* 383 U.S. 53 (1966).

[39] *United Steelworkers, Local 3489 v. Usery,* 45 U.S.L.W. 4089 (U.S. Jan. 12, 1977), see *Monthly Labor Review,* April 1977, p. 80.

[40] In *United Steelworkers,* the Seventh Circuit had held the attendance rule unconstitutional; however, the Sixth Circuit had held the same rule to be "reasonable" in *Brennan v. Local 5724, United Steelworkers of America,* 489 F.2d 884 (6th Cir. 1973).

[41] *Ohio Bureau of Employment Services v. Hodory,* 45 U.S.L.W. 4544 (U.S. May 31, 1977); and *Batterton v. Francis,* 45 U.S.L.W. 4768 (U.S. June 20, 1977).

[42] *Califano v. Webster,* 45 U.S.L.W. 3630 (U.S. Mar 21, 1977).

[43] *Califano v. Goldfarb,* 45 U.S.L.W. 4237 (U.S. Mar. 2, 1977).

[44] *Atlas Roofing Co., Inc. v. Occupational Safety and Health Review Commission,* 45 U.S.L.W. 4312 (U.S. Mar. 23, 1977).

[45] *Alabama Power Co. v. Davis,* 45 U.S.L.W. 4588 (U.S. June 6, 1977), see *Monthly Labor Review,* October 1977, p. 71.

Labor and the Supreme Court: significant decisions of 1977–78

Last term, the High Court consistently upheld NLRB positions, expanded business' constitutional rights, and raised more questions than it answered with rulings related to employment discrimination

GREGORY J. MOUNTS

At the end of the Supreme Court's 1977–78 term, the only clear winner in labor issues was the referee—the National Labor Relations Board. The High Court upheld the NLRB in every case where the Board was a party,[1] including a nonlabor case that shielded Board files from public scrutiny.[2] Employers also won significant victories in cases dealing with discrimination and with the relationship between unions and the workers they represent;[3] but they lost to unions in a pair of cases concerning leaflet distribution on employer property.[4]

On four occasions,[5] the Supreme Court considered employment questions that involved constitutional issues; in all four, employers received some advantage from new or restated interpretations of the Nation's legal lifeblood. In one of these cases, the Fourth Amendment was held to protect businesses from warrantless health and safety inspections.[6] In two others, the Court's interpretation of Article IV struck down State laws that impaired employers' contractual rights[7] and limited their hiring decisions.[8]

Employment discrimination cases received less attention last year, largely because they were overshadowed by the national furor over the *Bakke* decision striking down racial quotas in college admissions.[9] Schools must now consider race as only one factor, among many, in their admissions process. The imprecise nature of this requirement has created a sea of speculation about its potential impact on voluntary affirmative action programs in the employment area.

Answering one employment discrimination question—but again creating others—under Title VII of the 1964 Civil Rights Act, the High Court ended a long-standing insurance-industry practice by requiring men and women to pay equal amounts for equal pension benefits in employer-sponsored plans.[10] Other Title VII cases resolved by the Court granted employers some leeway to disprove discriminatory intent[11] and gave defendants procedural advantages in fighting class actions and in obtaining attorneys' fees after winning frivolous or unreasonable suits.[12] One other Title VII case eased the Court's restrictive stance on employment benefits for pregnant women.[13] But it, along with a pair of age-discrimination cases,[14] was rendered academic when Congress amended the relevant legislation.[15]

Gregory J. Mounts, an economist on the staff of the *Monthly Labor Review,* writes "Significant Decisions in Labor Cases."

Traditional labor law

Of the five Supreme Court cases pertaining to the National Labor Relations Act, perhaps the most significant—*Sears, Roebuck*[16]—did not, strictly speaking, "interpret" the act at all. Rather, the High Court ruled that courts may apply State trespass law to cases involving picketing that might either be protected or prohibited by the NLRA. This holding carved out an exception for the traditional rule of Federal preemption by permitting the application of State law in situations where an employer has no right to seek relief from the National Labor Relations Board if the union does not present the case to the Board.

Sears restates the traditional test for determining when Federal labor law preempts State statutes, as originally established in the 1959 case of *San Diego Building Trades v. Garmon*:[17] "When an activity is arguably subject to [the NLRA] the States as well as the Federal courts must defer to the exclusive competence of the National Labor Relations Board if the danger of State interference with national policy is to be averted." While leaving this basic formulation unchanged, *Sears* emphasizes the Court's new flexibility in interpreting the doctrine, as indicated by the 1977 case of *Farmer v. Carpenter*[18] (which permitted a State court to consider a harassment claim that occurred in the context of alleged hiring discrimination).

The Court recognized that this modification of the Federal preemption doctrine involved an increased risk of faulty State court interpretations of national labor laws. In his majority opinion, Justice John Paul Stevens argued, however, that unions will invoke Federal law—Board jurisdiction—when it offers needed protection, thereby avoiding State court interference. In cases where unions are unwilling to address the Board, Stevens reasoned that the resulting risk of erroneous State court decisions is not great enough to deny employers access to some judicial forum.

The underlying labor law issue in *Sears*—whether trespassory picketing by nonemployees adjacent to a retail establishment is protected activity under the Act—remains unresolved. In 1975, the NLRB held that striking *employees* could picket their employer on his property which was adjacent to his shopping-center retail outlet.[19] If and when the NLRB rules on the underlying issue, the question would be if *nonemployees* are entitled to the same protection by the Act.

In a pair of NLRA cases more in line with traditional labor analysis, the Supreme Court approved modest extensions of the NLRB's evolving formula for determining what written materials may be distributed on employers' premises, and where. In *Eastex, Inc.*,[20] the Court affirmed an NLRB ruling that union members have the right to distribute, on their employers' property, leaflets containing articles pertaining to political issues (such as right-to-work laws and minimum wages) as well as those directly connected to the union-employer relationship. The second case, *Beth Israel Hospital*,[21] upheld a Board determination that employees seeking to organize a bargaining unit of hospital employees could not be prohibited from distributing leaflets in a hospital cafeteria patronized predominantly by hospital employees. To a limited extent, the Court has given its approval to the Board's attempt to permit a substantial range for union communication to actual and potential members, provided such communication does not disrupt employers' business activities.

The Court also approved the NLRB's extension of another nascent doctrine—this one involving union discipline of members who are also supervisory employees—in *Writers Guild*.[22] Prior to this case, the Supreme Court's latest word on this subject had been its 1974 decision in *Florida Power & Light*,[23] which permitted unions to fine supervisor-members for performing bargaining-unit work during a strike. *Writers Guild* indicated, however, that such discipline is not permissible if the supervisor-members perform only their usual supervisory tasks. Thus, future cases involving union discipline against supervisory members will most likely turn on whether their tasks during a strike are judged "supervisory" or "nonsupervisory" by the NLRB.

Completing the NLRB's clean sweep of Supreme Court labor decisions this term was *Iron Workers*,[24] in which the Court accepted the Board's reasoning that, although the Taft-Hartley amendments to the NLRA authorize "pre-hire" agreements in construction (under which a union is not required to establish its majority status before bargaining with an employer), employers are nevertheless free to renounce the agreements at any time. Under the Board's ruling as affirmed by the Supreme Court, a pre-hire agreement is valid until an employer chooses to renounce it, at which time a union is limited to 30 days of recognitional picketing before it must either stop picketing or face an election to determine whether it represents a majority of the employees.

This decision, which severely limits the impact of pre-hire agreements, is especially significant in light of the nationwide trend for construction companies to operate without a union work force, at least on selected projects. Whenever an employer—even one that has signed a pre-hire agreement—feels that the union may lose an election, it can renounce the agreement and face a maximum of 30 days picketing. The decision could accelerate the growth of nonunion employment in the construction industry.

The NLRB scored one other victory during the 1977–78 term. In *Robbins Tire*,[25] the Supreme Court agreed with the Board that witness' statements in pending unfair labor practice cases are exempt from disclosure under the Freedom of Information Act. In overruling the Fifth Circuit, the Court rejected a limited case-by-case exemption for disclosure of this type of investigatory records, available only when their release would specifically "interfere with law enforcement proceedings." Instead, the Court endorsed the position of the Board and six other Circuits: Congress did not intend to prevent the Federal courts from determining that disclosure of particular kinds of investigatory records in pending cases would "generally interfere with enforcement proceedings."

Having justified this categorical exemption, the Supreme Court easily applied it to witness' statements in pending NLRB cases. The potential for employers and unions to intimidate or coerce workers who have given unfavorable statements—but who have yet to testify—constitutes the type of "interference" with NLRB enforcement proceedings that Congress intended to prevent, the Court concluded.

The Court's opinion in *Robbins Tire* precludes the use of the Freedom of Information Act as a discovery mechanism in Board hearings. At the same time, it suggests (in a concurrence by Justice Stevens) that the same general exemption from disclosure of investigatory records might also apply to other administrative enforcement proceedings. This would conflict with a recent Fourth Circuit ruling that Equal Employment Opportunity Commission records of statements from charging parties could only be exempted from disclosure following a review of the material by a Federal judge in each specific case.[26]

Constitutional issues

The concept of the Constitution as a living, evolving document was turned to business' advantage in two Supreme Court cases breaking new interpretative ground. In *Allied Structural Steel*,[27] the Court reinvigorated a little-used clause of Article IV (prohibiting States from impairing the obligations of contracts) to invalidate a Minnesota pension law. In *Barlow's*,[28] the Court interpreted the Fourth Amendment's prohibition on unreason-

able searches to impose a streamlined warrant requirement on Occupational Safety and Health Administration inspections.

In the pension case, Minnesota imposed a charge (sufficient to vest 10-year employees) on employers who terminated pension plans or closed Minnesota offices. Justice Potter Stewart's majority opinion held that this law violated Article IV's contract clause because it imposed extremely large, unexpected financial burdens on such employers. The law was not narrowly limited to emergency situations, he added, and was not justified by a State's traditional police power.

Barlow's imposed a warrant requirement on OSHA inspections because of the Fourth Amendment's ban on unreasonable searches and seizures. However, the Court ruled that such warrants do not require evidence establishing probable cause that a violation has occurred on the premises. Rather, a judge can issue an OSHA warrant upon a showing that the inspection follows a reasonable administrative or legislative plan for enforcing the Occupational Safety and Health Act.

In both these cases, the Court rejected more extreme alternatives. By establishing a warrant requirement of less than probable cause that a violation exists, the Court provided some Fourth Amendment protections to businesses without saddling OSHA with the burdensome requirement of meeting the traditional warrant standard. And, by striking down the Minnesota pension law on the basis of the contract clause rather than on due process or equal protection grounds, the Court left considerable room for other forms of State and Federal pension regulation. To achieve these goals, however, the Court brought a new focus to the Fourth Amendment and the contract clause, with possible implications in unrelated fields of law.

Constitutional interpretations also led to Supreme Court decisions striking down an Alaska law granting employment preferences to Alaskan residents for all oil-and-gas-related jobs and upholding a New York statute requiring State police to be U.S. citizens. In the first case, *Hicklin v. Orbeck*,[29] a unanimous Supreme Court held that sweeping employment preferences for State residents violate the constitutional requirement that States grant all U.S. citizens the same "privileges and immunities" granted to its own citizens. The second case, *Foley v. Connelie*,[30] demonstrated that the same requirement does not apply to aliens. Although earlier cases (notably the 1973 case of *Sugarman v. Dougall*,[31] which struck down a blanket prohibition against employment of aliens in State jobs) had emphasized the rights of aliens to have the chance to obtain employment, *Foley* expanded an earlier exception for "important nonelective . . . officers who participate directly in the formulation, execution, or review of broad public policy." According to the majority opinion by Chief Justice Warren Burger, State police exercise considerable discretion in executing the laws, and so a State may exclude aliens from such positions without unconstitutionally denying them equal protection of the laws.

In both these cases, the Supreme Court balanced a State's perceived economic and policy needs with a general constitutional prohibition against certain State conduct. In *Hicklin,* the Court decided that the limited economic justification (combatting unemployment among Alaskan residents) proposed for the Alaska Hire statute did not suffice to overcome the constitutional guarantee of equal "privileges and immunities" for residents of every State. In *Foley,* however, the general requirement of "equal protection" was ruled inapplicable for jobs that perform a vital function in governing— since governing is a privilege that may be constitutionally limited to U.S. citizens.

In recent years, the Supreme Court has been taking a new look at qualifications that may be imposed by Federal and State governments for both public and private jobs. In addition to *Hicklin* and *Foley,* for instance, the Court has since 1975 decided such cases as *Examining Board v. Flores de Otero*[32] (forbidding Puerto Rico from barring aliens from certain professions), *Elrod v. Burns*[33] (forbidding patronage firings in certain nonpolicy-making State jobs), and *Hampton v. Mow Sun Wong*[34] (striking down a sweeping ban on alien employment in the Federal Government, because of the way the ban was adopted). The Court is clearly seeking out a middle ground under which governments may impose requirements that may not be proven to be job-related (such as U.S. citizenship for State police) for important posts, but may not impose other such requirements (such as U.S. citizenship, State residency, or membership in a particular political party) for nonpolicymaking or private positions.

The 1977-78 term offered a rare Supreme Court event—the admission (and correction) of a 17-year-old error. In *Monell,*[35] a case with roots in the labor field, the Court overturned its earlier interpretation of the 1871 Civil Rights Act[36] and declared that cities and municipalities once again may be held liable when their official policies or customs violate a person's constitutional rights. Except for cases involving school boards,[37] local governments have enjoyed full immunity from such damage suits. The Court's latest interpretation of the Act, which arose from a challenge of a mandatory maternity leave policy once used by New York City, does not expose cities to liability for "torts" committed by public employees, however. The Court also suggested that cities may be eligible for some sort of limited immunity from large damage claims that could lead to bankruptcy.

Employment discrimination

Of the Supreme Court's discrimination decisions last term, *Regents of the University of California v. Bakke*[38] dominated public and media attention. The Court's decision, which struck down an affirmative action program at the University of California, Davis, Medical School, turned on a split vote invalidating a quota system while praising flexible affirmative action programs generally. Justice Lewis Powell, whose opinion announced the Court's ruling, because four justices wanted to uphold the plan and four others wanted to strike it down in more sweeping terms, based his decision solely on the terms of Title VI of the 1964 Civil Rights Act.

Title VI, the education section of the law, parallels Title VII's prohibition on discrimination in employment. Thus, *Bakke* will be cited again and again as the courts continue to confront the vexing issues of quotas, goals, and other forms of affirmative action. For example, in *Bakke,* Powell noted that the Court has "never approved preferential classifications in the absence of proven constitutional or statutory violations." Thus, voluntary affirmative action programs utilizing rigid numerical factors may be in jeopardy,[39] whereas court-imposed settlements involving these factors may still be permissible. (For instance, shortly before the end of its 1977-78 term, the Supreme Court left standing the Nation's largest consent decree, involving AT&T.[40])

One employment case decided shortly after *Bakke* concerned a voluntary affirmative action program that did not rely on numerical goals or quotas. In *Furnco,*[41] the employer had hired nearly three times the proportion of blacks as in the local labor market. Yet, because of the employer's method of hiring (refusing to hire at the gate), several black applicants were able to establish a prima facie case of discrimination based on earlier precedents.[42] In returning the case to the lower courts for further proceedings, the Supreme Court directed that the employer be given a chance to show "some legitimate nondiscriminatory reason" for the hiring method. In the course of these proceedings, the employer may rely, in part, on the racial composition of his work force to disprove the charge that his treatment of certain applicants (those who applied at the gate) was not racially motivated.

Another discrimination case with potentially sweeping implications is *Los Angeles v. Manhart* .[43] In an opinion by Justice John Paul Stevens, the Court ruled that Los Angeles violated Title VII by requiring female employees, based on their longer life expectancy, to make larger contributions than male employees to its pension plan. This arrangement, common in employer-managed pension plans since the 1840's, fell victim to Stevens' emphasis on considering each employee's individual situation. Stevens noted that Title VII forbids an employer "to discriminate against any *individual* with respect to his compensation . . . because of such individual's . . . sex." Classifying employees on the basis of sex to determine the amount of pension payments illegally discriminated against individual women (any of whom might die early despite their larger payments), Stevens ruled, sending tremors throughout the insurance industry and employee compensation departments across the country.

Manhart's implications have yet to be determined in full. Clearly, men and women can no longer be required to make differing payments into pension plans solely because of their sex (or because of differences in life expectancy based on sex). Separate rate schedules for optional pension or life insurance benefits may also be prohibited by Title VII. The fate of survivorship coverage (whose cost is often calculated with reference to the sex of the employee's spouse) is similarly uncertain.

Stevens' opinion also raises interesting questions about employment benefits other than pensions or life insurance—for instance, medical benefits. Just 2 years ago, Stevens dissented from the *Gilbert* decision,[44] in which the Court ruled that Title VII did not prohibit employers from offering otherwise comprehensive disability plans that excluded pregnancy. In that case (recently overturned by new legislation), the Court majority held that the exclusion of pregnancy did not discriminate against women, but only against "pregnant persons." One factor relied on by the Court in *Gilbert* was the greater actuarial value of comprehensive health plans (even excluding pregnancy) to women than to men. The discrepancy between relying on actuarial values in the health-plan field but prohibiting such reliance when dealing with pensions and (presumably) life insurance has not yet been dealt with by the Court.

In *Nashville Gas Co. v. Satty*,[45] the Supreme Court examined two other questions relating to the employment benefits of pregnant women. Consistent with *Gilbert,* the Court permitted the denial of sick pay during a pregnancy-related absence from work. However, the Court struck down an employer practice of denying accumulated seniority to women who returned to work following pregnancy leave. The critical distinction between the two practices, according to Justice William Rehnquist, Jr.'s, majority opinion, was that one—the denial of accumulated seniority—adversely affects a woman's "status as an employee." Both *Satty* and *Gilbert* have been effectively overturned by the 1978 amendments to Title VII. Essentially, Congress has required that pregnancy be treated the same as any other disability for employment purposes.

In two other Title VII cases, the Supreme Court made important procedural rulings that create new advantages for businesses in fighting class actions and in obtaining attorneys' fees after winning frivolous or unreasonable suits.

In *Gardner v. Westinghouse*,[46] a unanimous Court ruled that a district court's denial of class certification in a Title VII class action suit cannot be appealed immediately. Plaintiffs in this situation who seek to be designated as a class must now await a full decision by the district court. Because of the expense involved in litigating a Title VII claim, many cases where class certification has been denied (and individuals must bear the entire cost) will end at the district court level.

Attorneys' fees have always been available to successful plaintiffs in Title VII cases, based on the discretion of the district court. In *Christianburg Garment Co.*,[47] however, the Supreme Court ruled that because Title VII requires fees to be awarded to "the prevailing party," [48] Congress also intended to "protect defendants from burdensome litigation having no legal or factual basis." Based on the discretion of the district court, winning defendants in Title VII cases are now entitled to an award of attorneys' fees when "the plaintiff's action was frivolous, unreasonable, or without foundation, even though not brought in subjective bad faith."

Although the Supreme Court decided two bothersome questions under the Age Discrimination in Employment Act, both decisions were rendered moot when Congress revised the Act to extend its coverage up to age 70. Congress agreed with, and wrote into the statute, the Supreme Court's holding in *Lorillard v. Pons*[49] that plaintiffs were entitled to a jury trial such as that provided by the Fair Labor Standards Act (the procedural model for the age discrimination law). The new law overturned the Court's decision in *United Air Lines v. McMann,* [50] however. That case permitted involuntary retirement before age 65 (then the Act's age ceiling) if such retirement was required in accordance with the terms of a bona fide retirement plan—a result unambiguously prohibited by the 1978 amendments. ☐

————FOOTNOTES————

[1] *Eastex, Inc. v. NLRB,* 46 U.S.L.W. 4783 (U.S., June 22, 1978), see *Monthly Labor Review,* November 1978, p. 40; *Beth Israel Hospital v. NLRB,* 46 U.S.L.W. 4764 (U.S., June 22, 1978), see *Monthly Labor Review,* November 1978, p. 40; *NLRB v. Writers Guild of America, West, Inc.* 46 U.S.L.W. 4744 (U.S., June 21, 1978), see *Monthly Labor Review,* September 1978, pp. 60–61; and *NLRB v. Local 103, International Association of Bridge, Structural, and Ornamental Iron Workers, AFL-CIO,* 46 U.S.L.W. 4081 (U.S., Jan. 17, 1978), see *Monthly Labor Review,* March 1978, p. 48.

[2] *NLRB v. Robbins Tire & Rubber Co.,* 46 U.S.L.W. 4689 (U.S., June 15, 1978), see *Monthly Labor Review,* November 1978, pp. 41–42.

[3] *Furnco Construction Corp. v. Waters,* 46 U.S.L.W. 4966 (U.S., June 29, 1978); and *NLRB v. Writers Guild of America, West, Inc.,* 46 U.S.L.W. 4744 (U.S., June 21, 1978), see *Monthly Labor Review,* September 1978, pp. 60–61.

[4] *Eastex, Inc. v. NLRB,* 46 U.S.L.W. 4783 (U.S., June 22, 1978) and *Beth Israel Hospital v. NLRB,* 46 U.S.L.W. 4764 (U.S., June 22, 1978). For a discussion of both these cases, see *Monthly Labor Review,* November 1978, p. 40.

[5] *Marshall v. Barlow's, Inc.,* 46 U.S.L.W. 4483 (U.S., May 23, 1978), see *Monthly Labor Review,* July 1978, pp. 38–39; *Allied Structural Steel Co. v. Spannaus,* 46 U.S.L.W. 4887 (U.S., June 28, 1978), see *Monthly Labor Review,* November 1978, pp. 40–41; *Foley v. Connelie,* 46 U.S.L.W. 4237 (U.S., Mar. 22, 1978), see *Monthly Labor Review,* June 1978, p. 53; and *Hicklin v. Orbeck,* 46 U.S.L.W. 4763 (U.S., June 22, 1978), see *Monthly Labor Review,* October 1978, pp. 53–54.

[6] *Marshall v. Barlow's, Inc.,* 46 U.S.L.W. 4483 (U.S., May 23, 1978), see *Monthly Labor Review,* July 1978, pp. 38–39.

[7] *Allied Structural Steel Co. v. Spannaus,* 46 U.S.L.W. 4887 (U.S., June 28, 1978), see *Monthly Labor Review,* November 1978, pp. 40–41.

[8] *Hicklin v. Orbeck,* 46 U.S.L.W. 4763 (U.S., June 22, 1978), struck down a State law requiring private employers in Alaska's oil-and-gas-related industries to give State residents preference in hiring decisions. For a complete discussion of the case, see *Monthly Labor Review,* October 1978, pp. 53–54.

[9] *Regents of the University of California v. Allan Bakke,* 46 U.S.L.W. 4896 (U.S., June 28, 1978), see *Monthly Labor Review,* August 1978, p. 46.

[10] *City of Los Angeles, Department of Water and Power v. Manhart,* 46 U.S.L.W. 4347 (U.S., Apr. 25, 1978), see *Monthly Labor Review,* July 1978, p. 39.

[11] *Furnco Construction Corp. v. Waters,* 46 U.S.L.W. 4966 (U.S., June 29, 1978).

[12] *Christianburg Garment Co. v. Equal Employment Opportunity Comm'n,* 46 U.S.L.W. 4105 (U.S., Jan. 24, 1978, Justice Harry Blackmun took no part in the consideration of the case), see *Monthly Labor Review,* March 1978, pp. 49–50; and *Gardner v. Westinghouse Broadcasting Co.,* 46 U.S.L.W. 4762 (U.S., June 21, 1978), see *Monthly Labor Review,* September 1978, p. 61.

[13] *Nashville Gas Co. v. Satty,* 46 U.S.L.W. 4026 (U.S., Dec. 6, 1978), see *Monthly Labor Review,* February 1978, p. 58.

[14] *United Air Lines v. McMann,* 46 U.S.L.W. 4043 (U.S., Dec. 12, 1977), see *Monthly Labor Review,* February 1978, p.57; and *Lorillard v. Pons,* 46 U.S.L.W. 4150 (U.S., Feb. 22, 1978, Justice Harry Blackmun took no part in the consideration of the case), see *Monthly Labor Review,* April 1978, p. 51.

[15] In 1978, Congress amended both the Civil Rights Act of 1964, which includes Title VII, and the Age Discrimination in Employment Act of 1967.

[16] *Sears, Roebuck, & Co. v. San Diego County District Council of Carpenters,* 46 U.S.L.W. 4446 (U.S., May 15, 1978), see *Monthly Labor Review,* August 1978, pp. 46–47.

[17] *San Diego Building Trades v. Garmon,* 359 U.S. 236 (1959).

[18] *Farmer v. Bhd. of Carpenters, Local 25,* 430 U.S. 290 (1977), see *Monthly Labor Review,* July 1977, pp. 47–48.

[19] *Scott Hudgens,* 230 N.L.R.B. No. 73, 95 L.R.R.M. 1351 (1975).

[20] *Eastex, Inc. v. NLRB,* 46 U.S.L.W. 4783 (U.S., June 22, 1978), see *Monthly Labor Review,* November 1978, p. 40.

[21] *Beth Israel Hospital v. NLRB,* 46 U.S.L.W. 4764 (U.S., June 22, 1978), see *Monthly Labor Review,* November 1978, p. 40.

[22] *NLRB v. Writers Guild of America, West, Inc.,* 46 U.S.L.W. 4744 (U.S., June 21, 1978), *see Monthly Labor Review,* September 1978, pp. 60–61.

[23] *Florida Power & Light Co. v. International Bhd. of Electrical Workers, Local 641,* 417 U.S. 790 (1974), see *Monthly Labor Review,* September 1974, pp. 57–58.

[24] *NLRB v. Local 103, International Association of Bridge, Structural, and Ornamental Iron Workers, AFL-CIO,* 46 U.S.L.W. 4081 (U.S., Jan. 17, 1978), see *Monthly Labor Review,* March 1978, p. 48.

[25] *NLRB v. Robbins Tire & Rubber Co.,* 46 U.S.L.W. 4689 (U.S., June 15, 1978), see *Monthly Labor Review,* November 1978, pp. 41–42.

[26] *Charlotte-Mecklenberg Hospital v. Perry,* 571 F.2d 195 (4th Cir., Jan. 26, 1978).

[27] *Allied Structural Steel Co. v. Spannaus,* 46 U.S.L.W. 4887 (U.S., June 28, 1978), see *Monthly Labor Review,* November 1978, pp. 40–41.

[28] *Marshall v. Barlow's, Inc.,* 46 U.S.L.W. 4483 (U.S., May 23, 1978), see *Monthly Labor Review,* July 1978, pp. 38–39.

[29] *Hicklin v. Orbeck,* 46 U.S.L.W. 4763 (U.S., June 22, 1978), see *Monthly Labor Review,* October 1978, pp. 53–54.

[30] *Foley v. Connelie,* 46 U.S.L.W. 4237 (U.S., Mar. 22, 1978), see *Monthly Labor Review,* June 1978, p. 53.

[31] *Sugarman v. Dougall,* 413 U.S. 634 (1973), see *Monthly Labor Review,* October 1973, pp. 59–60, and February 1974, pp. 68–69.

[32] *Examining Board v. Flores de Otero,* 426 U.S. 572 (1976), see *Monthly Labor Review,* September 1976, p. 52.

[33] *Elrod v. Burns,* 427 U.S. 347 (1976), see *Monthly Labor Review,* October 1976, pp. 46–47.

[34] *Hampton v. Mow Sun Wong,* 426 U.S. 88 (1976) , see *Monthly Labor Review,* August 1976, pp. 43–44.

[35] *Monell v. Dept. of Social Services, New York City,* 46 U.S.L.W. 4569 (U.S., June 6, 1978), see *Monthly Labor Review,* October 1978, p. 53.

[36] *Monroe v. Pape,* 365 U.S. 167 (1961).

[37] For example, in *Cleveland Board of Education v. LaFleur,* 414 U.S. 632 (1974), *Tinker v. Des Moines Ind. School District,* 393 U.S. 503 (1969), *McNesse v. Board of Education,* 373 U.S. 668 (1971), *Cohen v. Chesterfield County School Board,* 414 U.S. 632 (1974), and others, the Court has permitted damage suits against school boards as local government entities.

[38] *Regents of the University of California v. Allan Bakke,* 46 U.S.L.W. 4896 (U.S., June 28, 1978), see *Monthly Labor Review,* August 1978, p. 46.

[39] One such voluntary affirmative action program adopted by the Detroit Police Department was struck down in *Detroit Police Officers Association v. Young,* 44 Daily Lab. Rep. D–1 (USDC EMich, Feb. 27, 1978). The case is currently on appeal to the 7th Circuit; for a discussion of the district court opinion, see *Monthly Labor Review,* May 1978, p. 65.

[40] *Communication Workers of America v. EEOC,* 46 U.S.L.W. 3801 (U.S., July 3, 1978, Review Denied), see *Monthly Labor Review,* August 1978, p. 46.

[41] *Furnco Construction Corp. v. Waters,* 46 U.S.L.W. 4966 (U.S., June 29, 1978).

[42] In *McDonnell-Douglas Corp. v. Green,* 411 U.S. 792 (1973), the Supreme Court established the standard for a prima facie showing of racially disparate treatment under Title VII of the 1964 Civil Rights Act.

[43] *City of Los Angeles, Department of Water and Power v. Manhart,* 46 U.S.L.W. 4347 (U.S., Apr. 25, 1978), see *Monthly Labor Review,* July 1978, p. 39.

[44] *General Electric Co. v. Gilbert,* 429 U.S. 125 (1976), see *Monthly Labor Review,* March 1978, pp. 73–74.

[45] *Nashville Gas Co. v. Satty,* 46 U.S.L.W. 4026 (U.S., Dec. 6, 1977), see *Monthly Labor Review,* February 1978, p. 58.

[46] *Gardner v. Westinghouse Broadcasting Co.,* 46 U.S.L.W. 4762 (U.S., June 21, 1978), see *Monthly Labor Review,* September 1978, p. 61.

[47] *Christianburg Garment Co. v. Equal Employment Opportunity Comm'n,* 46 U.S.L.W. 4105 (U.S., Jan. 24, 1978, Justice Harry Blackmun took no part in the consideration of the case), see *Monthly Labor Review,* March 1978, pp. 49–50.

[48] 42 U.S.C. Sec. 2000e–5(k) (1970).

[49] *Lorillard v. Pons,* 46 U.S.L.W. 4150 (U.S., Feb. 22, 1978, Justice Harry Blackmun took no part in the consideration of the case), see *Monthly Labor Review,* April 1978, p. 51.

[50] *United Air Lines v. McMann,* 46 U.S.L.W. 4043 (U.S., Dec. 12, 1977), see *Monthly Labor Review,* February 1978, p. 57.

Significant Decisions In Labor Cases

Pregnancy exclusion not sexually biased

Much of the battle in the hard-fought controversy concerning the exclusion of pregnancies from sick-leave and disability benefits programs has been about whether pregnancy is a "sickness" or a "disability;" the verbal fireworks on this issue have rivaled those over the terms of Title VII of the Civil Rights Act of 1964 itself, which forbids sex-based discrimination "with respect to. . . compensation, terms, conditions, or privileges of employment." Yet when, after having postponed its ruling until after the summer recess, the Supreme Court finally resolved a case challenging the exclusion of pregnancies from an otherwise comprehensive disability program, all the Justices assumed that pregnancy was indeed a disability. This classification didn't aid those attacking the program, however, for the Court went on to conclude by a 6 to 3 vote that exclusion of this one type of disability was not "discrimination based on sex" and so did not violate Title VII. (*General Electric Co. v. Gilbert.*[1])

In deciding the issue, Justice William Rehnquist's majority opinion cited *Geduldig v. Aiello,* a 1974 case holding that the exclusion of pregnancies from a disability program established by the State of California did not violate the equal protection clause of the Fourteenth Amendment.[2] In holding that the pregnancy exclusion was not discrimination based on sex, Justice Rehnquist's opinion in *Gilbert* quoted the following passage from the 1974 *Geduldig* decision:

> . . . [T]his case is . . . a far cry from cases . . . involving discrimination based upon gender as such. The California insurance program does not exclude anyone from benefit eligibility because of gender but merely removes one physical condition—pregnancy—from the list of compensable disabilities. While it is true that only women can become pregnant, it does not follow that every legislative classification concerning pregnancy is a sex-based classification. . . . Absent a showing that distinctions involving pregnancy are mere pretexts designed to effect an invidious discrimi-

nation against the members of one sex or the other, lawmakers are constitutionally free to include or exclude pregnancy from the coverage of legislation such as this on any reasonable basis, just as with respect to any other physical condition.

The lack of identity between the excluded disability and gender as such under this insurance program becomes clear upon the most cursory analysis. The program divides potential recipients into two groups—pregnant women and nonpregnant persons. While the first group is exclusively female, the second group includes members of both sexes.

Because earlier cases have held that a preliminary showing of discrimination under Title VII can be based solely upon the effects of an apparently neutral classification, Justice Rehnquist proceeded to consider the effects of excluding pregnancies from the disability program involved in the *Gilbert* case. He noted that General Electric's data indicate a higher benefit expenditure per female employee than per male employee in each of the years in question:

> . . . As there is no proof that the [benefit] package is in fact worth more to men than to women, it is impossible to find any gender-based discriminatory effect in this scheme simply because women disabled as a result of pregnancy do not receive benefits; that is to say, gender-based discrimination does not result simply because an employer's disability benefits plan is less than all inclusive. For all that appears, pregnancy-related disabilities constitute an *additional* risk, unique to women, and the failure to compensate them for this risk does not destroy the presumed parity of the benefits, accruing to men and women alike, which results from the facially evenhanded *inclusion* of risks. To hold otherwise would endanger the common-sense notion that an employer who has no disability benefits program at all does not violate Title VII even though the 'underinclusion' of risks impacts, as a result of pregnancy-related disabilities, more heavily upon one gender than upon the other.

The majority opinion then considered the effect of guidelines developed by the Equal Employment Opportunity Commission, one of which interpreted Title VII as forbidding exclusion of pregnancies from comprehensive disability programs. Justice

"Significant Decisions in Labor Cases" is written by Craig Polhemus, Office of Publications, Bureau of Labor Statistics.

Rehnquist noted that the guideline was interpretative rather than regulatory and that it was adopted 8 years after Title VII was enacted. He, therefore, rejected the EEOC's view and held that the exclusion of pregnancies was not illegal sex discrimination.

In a dissenting opinion joined by Justice Thurgood Marshall, Justice William Brennan complained that the majority opinion rejected not only the EEOC guidelines but also the decisions of all six Federal Courts of Appeals that had considered the issue.[3] Justice Brennan noted that those challenging the exclusion of pregnancies from disability plans saw the problem in a totally different framework from that adopted by the majority of the Justices:

> . . . By directing their focus upon the risks excluded from the otherwise comprehensive program, and upon the purported justifications for such exclusions, the Equal Employment Opportunity Commission, the woman plaintiffs, and the lower courts reason that the pregnancy exclusion constitutes a prima facie violation of Title VII. . . .
>
> The Court's framework is diametrically different. It views General Electric's plan as representing a gender-free assignment of risks in accordance with normal actuarial techniques. From this perspective the lone exclusion of pregnancy is not a violation of Title VII insofar as all other disabilities are mutually covered for both sexes. . . .
>
> . . . I believe that . . . the Court's assumption that General Electric engaged in a gender-neutral risk-assignment process is purely fanciful. . . . [T]he EEOC's interpretation that the exclusion of pregnancy from a disability insurance plan is incompatible with the overall objectives of Title VII has been unjustifiably rejected.

In a separate dissent, Justice John Stevens argued that the disability program's regulations placed pregnancies in a class by themselves and "by definition, such a rule discriminates on account of sex; for it is the capacity to become pregnant which primarily differentiates the female from the male."

Standing for the rights of others

Two recent appeals court decisions have authorized Title VII challenges to allegedly discriminatory employment practices brought by plaintiffs who have not been directly harmed by those practices. The Federal appeals court in the District of Columbia held that a black employee may challenge hiring practices even though he was never denied employment,[4] and the ninth circuit court of appeals allowed a white woman to bring suit against her employer challenging discrimination against black and Spanish-surnamed employees as well as against women.[5]

These cases reflect a liberal interpretation of the requirements of "standing," which allow courts to consider a dispute only if the plaintiff has a recognized interest in the result. Many suits are dismissed when courts find that the party bringing suit has not suffered any "injury in fact" because of the challenged practice.

In *Gray v. Greyhound Lines,* the appeals court in the District of Columbia rejected the employer's argument that because the plaintiff had been hired on his first application, he had not been harmed by the alleged discrimination in hiring. The court found that the employee had standing under his allegations that the hiring practices affected his treatment on the job and also affected his psychological well-being. Discriminatory discipline and route assignment resulting from biased hiring create an "injury in fact," the court said, and psychological interests should also be recognized to carry out the broad antidiscrimination purposes of Title VII.

The other case, *Waters v. Heublein, Inc.,* turned on interpretation of the Title VII clause granting standing to any "person claiming to be aggrieved" by illegal employment discrimination. Although the white woman plaintiff could clearly have been harmed by discrimination based on sex, the employer contended that she had no standing to bring charges of discrimination against black and Spanish-surnamed employees. In rejecting the employer's view, the appeals court cited the 1972 opinion of *Trafficante v. Metropolitan Life Ins. Co.,*[6] in which the Supreme Court held that tenants charging discriminatory housing policies could bring suit as persons aggrieved "by the loss of important benefits from interracial associations." The court of appeals in *Waters* applied the same reasoning to employment and held that Title VII gives employees standing to sue their employer for racial and ethnic discrimination directed against others.

In the court's words . . .

(*The following excerpt from the decision of the first circuit court of appeals in* Hochstadt v. Worcester Foundation for Experimental Biology[7] *deals with the scope of Title VII's protection against discharge for protesting allegedly discriminatory employment practices. An earlier case with the same name and factual background was discussed in the* Monthly Labor Review, *April 1976, pp. 51–52.*)

. . . Congress certainly did not mean to grant sanctuary to employees to engage in political activity for women's liberation on company time, and an employee does not enjoy immunity for discharge for misconduct merely by claiming that at all times she was defending the rights of her sex by "opposing" discriminatory practices. . . . On the other hand, [Title VII] clearly does protect an employee against discharge for filing complaints in good faith before Federal and State agencies and for registering grievances through channels appropriate in the particular employment setting.

It is less clear to what extent militant self-help activity falling between these two poles, such as particular types of on-the-job opposition to alleged discrimination, vociferousness, expressions of hostility to an employer or superior or the like, are protected. In the instant case, the issue is clouded by a sophisticated employment setting which lacks a rigid structure and within which it is not always easy to assess when an employee—in this case a highly educated senior scientist—clearly oversteps the bounds. . . .

Under the principles of [National Labor Relations Act] cases, the district court was entitled to conclude that Dr. Hochstadt's actions went beyond the scope of protected opposition because they damaged the basic goals and interests of the Foundation. An employer has a legitimate interest in seeing that its employees perform their work well. . . . In the employment setting at the Foundation, the employer had a particular interest in maintaining a harmonious and congenial working environment conducive to the interchange of ideas and the sharing of research. The district court was entitled to find that Dr. Hochstadt's constant complaints to colleagues damaged relationships among members of the cell biology group and sometimes even interfered with laboratory research. Even if justified, they occurred upon some occasions when the employer was entitled to expect her full commitment and loyalty. [Title VII] does not afford an employee unlimited license to complain at any and all times and places.

Dr. Hochstadt committed, moreover, acts of disloyalty to the Foundation, for which she cannot properly claim immunity. In this category were her assertions to others that the Foundation was in jeopardy of losing its Federal grant money—remarks that understandably aroused the concern of scientists at the Foundation because they raised the spectre of the sudden collapse of the institution for lack of funding. . . . The district court also observed that "her unauthorized disclosures of Foundation's confidential matters . . . injur(ed) the Foundation and jeopardiz(ed) its fund-raising efforts." . . .

Keeping in mind the legitimate interests both of Dr. Hochstadt and the Foundation, we face the ultimate question, whether the district court could properly on this record determine that Dr. Hochstadt "went too far" in her activities and deportment. We believe it could. . . .

. . . Although Dr. Hochstadt's actions were associated with a protected objective, the district court reasonably concluded that they constituted serious acts of disloyalty, which damaged the employer's interests and were of an excessive nature which was not warranted as a response to any conduct of the Foundation. Accordingly, the district court did not err in holding that the discharge had a sufficient and nondiscriminatory basis.

A 'but for' test of motivation

In a unanimous opinion written by Justice William Rehnquist, the Supreme Court adopted a new test for determining whether the nonrenewal of a public employee's employment contract violates the Constitution. Turning to the criminal-law field for analogy, the Court said that the Constitution required rehiring of an untenured teacher who had exercised his constitutional right of free speech only if the contract would have been renewed "but for" the protected speech. (*Mt. Healthy City School Dist. v. Doyle.*[8])

The *Doyle* case involved a teacher who was accused by the school board of "a notable lack of tact in handling professional matters." In particular, the board cited one incident in which the teacher had informed a radio station about a memorandum from the school principal concerning teacher dress and appearance, and a second incident when the teacher used obscene gestures to students who disobeyed his instructions.

The Supreme Court, like the lower courts that had considered the case, held that the first incident, contacting the radio station, was protected by the First and Fourteenth Amendments, and that the school board could not refuse to renew the teacher's contract because of it. The Court then considered the trial court's conclusion that the teacher should be rehired because the protected speech "played a substantial part in the decision not to renew" his contract.

Rejecting the "substantial part" test, the Supreme Court said:

> . . . A borderline or marginal candidate should not have the employment question resolved against him because of constitutionally protected conduct. But that same candidate ought not to be able, by engaging in such conduct, to prevent his employer from assessing his performance record and reaching a decision not to rehire on the basis of that record, simply be-

cause the protected conduct makes the employer more certain of the correctness of its decision.

Instead, the High Court sent the case back to the trial court to determine whether the school board would have reached the same decision if the teacher had not contacted the radio station. This new standard is similar to tests established in the criminal field for determining whether a coerced or unconstitutional confession "taints" a subsequent confession or plea of guilty; these tests reject the second confession or plea only if it would not have been made "but for" the impermissible prior confession.[9]

In brief

EQUAL PAY ACT AS APPLIED TO STATES UPHELD. Despite a challenge to its constitutionality (inspired by last year's Supreme Court decision in *National League of Cities v. Usery*[10] striking down minimum-wage and overtime restrictions on State governments), a Federal court of appeals upheld the Equal Pay Act's coverage of barbers and beauticians in State hospitals. The appeals court, citing several district court opinions upholding the application of the Equal Pay Act and the Age Discrimination in Employment Act to State and local employees,[11]

held that the Fourteenth Amendment empowered Congress to forbid sex discrimination in State employment. (*Allegheny County Institution District.*[12])

DUE PROCESS RIGHTS AT HEARINGS. A Federal court of appeals has affirmed a lower court ruling that police who participated in an illegal job action may not be disciplined differently according to whether they waived the right to counsel. The appeals court agreed that village officials had acted arbitrarily, illegally, and unconstitutionally in firing only those police who insisted on their right to counsel at disciplinary hearings. (*Village of Skokie.*[13])

RELIGIOUS BIAS CHARGES TO BE RECONSIDERED. Shortly after its 4 to 4 split (with Justice Stevens not participating) in *Cummins v. Parker Seal Co.,*[14] the Supreme Court agreed to again consider the extent to which employers must accommodate work practices to meet religious beliefs of their employees under Title VII of the Civil Rights Act of 1964. The High Court will review charges by a member of the World Wide Church of God, which observes a Saturday sabbath, that his employer and union illegally discriminated against him by refusing to allow him to rearrange his work schedule to be off on Saturdays. (*Hardison.*[15]) □

---FOOTNOTES---

[1] *General Electric Co. v. Gilbert,* 45 U.S.L.W. 4031 (U.S. Dec. 7, 1976); see *Monthly Labor Review,* July 1975, p. 55.

[2] 417 U.S. 484 (1974); see *Monthly Labor Review,* October 1974, p. 69.

[3] *Communications Workers v. A. T. & T. Co.,* 513 F.2d 1024 (2d Cir. 1975), petition for cert. pending, No. 74–1601; *Wetzel v. Liberty Mutual Ins. Co.,* 511 F.2d 199 (3rd Cir. 1975), vacated on juris. grounds, 424 U.S. 737 (1976) (see *Monthly Labor Review,* May 1974, pp. 76–77, June 1975, pp. 61–62, and June 1976, p. 54); *Gilbert v. General Electric Co.,* 519 F.2d 661 (4th Cir.), cert. granted, 423 U.S. 822 (1975); *Tyler v. Vickery,* 517 F.2d 1089, 1097–99 (5th Cir. 1975) (see *Monthly Labor Review,* December 1975, pp. 57–58, and September 1976, p. 52); *Satty v. Nashville Gas Co.,* 522 F.2d 850 (6th Cir. 1975), petition for cert. pending, No. 75–536; and *Hutchinson v. Lake Oswego School Dist.,* 519 F.2d 961 (9th Cir. 1975), petition for cert. pending, No. 75-1049 (see *Monthly Labor Review,* January 1976, p. 65).

[4] *Gray v. Greyhound Lines, East,* 209 DAILY LAB. REP. A-5 (D.C. Cir. Oct. 13, 1976) (Nos. 75–1159, 75-1631).

[5] *Waters v. Heublein, Inc.,* 225 DAILY LAB. REP. D-1 (9th Cir. Nov. 12, 1976) (Nos. 74-2870, 74-2871).

[6] 409 U.S. 205 (1972).

[7] *Hochstadt v. Worcester Foundation for Experimental Biology,* 203 DAILY LAB. REP. D-1 (1st Cir. Sept. 24, 1976) (No. 76–1019).

[8] *Mt. Healthy City School Dist. v. Doyle,* 691 GOV. EMP. RELATIONS REP. 24 (U.S. Jan. 11, 1977).

[9] See *Parker v. North Carolina,* 397 U.S. 790 (1970); *Lyons v. Oklahoma,* 322 U.S. 596 (1944).

[10] 44 U.S.L.W. 4974 (U.S. June 24, 1976); see *Monthly Labor Review,* September 1976, pp. 50–51.

[11] *Usery v. Board of Educ. of Salt Lake City,* 677 GOV. EMP. RELATIONS REP. E-1 (D. Utah Sept. 1, 1976) (No. C 75-510); *Usery v. Bettendorf Community School Dist.* (S.D. Iowa Sept. 1, 1976) (No. CA 76-7-D); *Usery v. Fort Madison Community School Dist.* (S.D. Iowa Sept. 1, 1976) (No. CA 75-62-1); *Usery v. Charleson City Community School Dist.* (N.D. Iowa Aug. 20, 1976) (No. CA 76-4024); *Christensen v. Iowa,* 617 GOV. EMP. RELATIONS REP. B-6 (N.D. Iowa Aug. 4, 1976) (No. CA 74-2030); *Riley v. University of Lowell* (D.Mass. July 22, 1976) (No. CA 76-1118-M). See *Monthly Labor Review,* December 1976, pp. 50–51.

[12] *Usery v. Allegheny C'ty Institution Dist.,* 682 GOV. EMP. RELATIONS REP. F-1 (3rd Cir. Oct. 28, 1976).

[13] *Olshock v. Village of Skokie,* 680 GOV. EMP. RELATIONS REP. B-3 (7th Cir. Sept. 17, 1976) (Nos. 76-1153 and 76-1191); see *Monthly Labor Review,* February 1976, pp. 49–50.

[14] 45 U.S.L.W. 4009 (U.S. Nov. 2, 1976); see *Monthly Labor Review,* September 1975, pp. 58–59, and January 1977, p. 38.

[15] *Trans World Airlines v. Hardison,* and *Machinists v. Hardison,* 45 U.S.L.W. 3363 (U.S. Nov. 15, 1976).

Warrantless safety inspections

The Fourth Amendment provides, in full, that "The right of the people to be secure in their persons, houses, papers, and effects, against unreasonable searches and seizures, shall not be violated, and no warrants shall issue, but upon probable cause, supported by oath or affirmation, and particularly describing the place to be searched, and the persons or things to be seized." The Occupational Safety and Health Act of 1970 states, in part, that safety inspectors may "enter without delay and at reasonable times any . . . workplace or environment where work is performed . . . and . . . inspect and investigate" working conditions. Recently, a three-judge Federal district court in Idaho decided that this passage violates the Fourth Amendment and issued an injunction against safety inspections under that section. In response, Justice William Rehnquist of the U.S. Supreme Court suspended the district court's order for most of the country pending appeal, leaving it in effect only for the employer involved in the case. (*Barlow's, Inc.*[1])

The district court based its decision on several Supreme Court cases dealing with what type of inspections constitute searches within the meaning of the Fourth Amendment. In *Camara v. Municipal Court,* the High Court held that a private residence cannot be inspected for housing code violations without the resident's consent.[2] A companion case, *See v. City of Seattle,* established that inspections of commercial premises not open to the public can also be required only through use of a warrant if the owners refuse permission.[3] Two later cases, *Colonnade Catering Corp. v. United States*[4] and *United States v. Biswell,*[5] upheld warrantless inspections of a liquor store and a firearms dealer on the grounds that both businesses had historically been subject to heavy regulation because of the type of goods they sold. The district court pointed out that the Occupational Safety and Health Act was not limited to such businesses:

> We simply cannot overlook the fact that in *Colonnade* and *Biswell* the Court dealt with an 'industry long subject to close supervision and inspection' . . .

and a 'pervasively regulated business.' . . . We believe that both of these cases fit into the *Camara* categorization of 'certain carefully defined classes of cases.' We have no such industry in this case. OSHA applies to all businesses that affect interstate commerce. . . . As such, it applies to a wide variety of over 6 million workplaces and does not focus on one particular type of business or industry. It cannot be questioned that this broad spectrum of businesses can be distinguished from the heavily regulated liquor and firearms industries encountered in *Colonnade* and *Biswell.* . . .

We, therefore, hold that the inspection provisions of OSHA which have attempted to authorize warrantless inspections of those business establishments covered by the act are unconstitutional as being violative of the Fourth Amendment.

Open covenants openly . . .

Under collective bargaining, an employer may not negotiate with an individual employee, only with a representative of an entire bargaining unit. This system, designed to ensure bargaining power on each side, led to a dispute in which the U.S. Supreme Court unanimously ruled that, because of the First Amendment's guarantee of free speech, a public employer may not be forced to exclude individual employees from public meetings concerned with issues subject to exclusive negotiation between the employer and a union. (*City of Madison, Joint School Dist. No. 8.*[6])

Because a State law provides that local school boards cannot negotiate with individual employees if they are in a bargaining unit represented by a union, the Wisconsin Employment Relations Commission had ruled that the Madison Board of Education improperly permitted a teacher to speak (at an open meeting) in opposition to a "fair share" proposal that would require all teachers to pay dues to the union to defray bargaining costs. The commission also ordered the Madison school board to "cease and desist from permitting employees, other than representatives of Madison Teachers, Inc. [the

"Significant Decisions in Labor Cases" is written by Craig Polhemus, Office of Publications, Bureau of Labor Statistics.

union], to appear and speak at Board of Education meetings, on matters subject to collective bargaining between it and Madison Teachers, Inc."

The Supreme Court, in an opinion by Chief Justice Warren E. Burger,[7] found that this order infringed on free speech and could not be justified by a concern for collective bargaining because, in the Court's view, the teacher had not "negotiated" at all. He had only expressed an opinion against the fair share proposal, the Court said, not sought a contract for himself or for other teachers. Burger also stressed that the meeting was open to the public:

> . . . [The teacher] addressed the school board not merely as one of its employees but also as a concerned citizen, seeking to express his views on an important decision of his government. . . . Where the State has opened a forum for direct citizen involvement, it is difficult to find justification for excluding teachers who make up the overwhelming proportion of school employees and are most vitally concerned with the proceedings. . . .
>
> . . . [W]hen the board sits in public meetings to conduct public business and hear the views of citizens, it may not be required to discriminate between speakers on the basis of their employment, or the content of their speech. . . .

Reasonable requirements for union office

The Labor-Management Reporting and Disclosure Act of 1959 (LMRDA) provides that all union members in good standing shall be eligible to run for local and national office, subject to "reasonable conditions uniformly imposed" by the union.[8] In 1968, the Supreme Court held that a rule requiring candidates for certain offices to have previously held elective union office (disqualifying 93.1 percent of the union's membership) was not reasonable.[9] And in 1977, the Court has added that a rule requiring candidates to have attended at least one-half of a local's regular meetings for the 3 years preceding the election (disqualifying 96.5 percent of the members) is similarly unreasonable and therefore illegal under the LMRDA. (*Local 3489, United Steelworkers*.[10])

Justice William Brennan's majority opinion emphasized that the LMRDA was designed to promote union democracy without unduly interfering with the internal affairs of unions:

> Applying these principles to this case, we conclude that . . . the anti-democratic effects of the meeting attendance rule outweigh the interests urged in its support. . . . [A]n attendance requirement that results in the exclusion of 96.5 percent of the members from candidacy for union office hardly seems to be a 'reasonable qualification' consistent with the goal of free and democratic elections. A requirement having that

result obviously severely restricts the free choice of the membership in selecting their leaders.

> . . . In the absence of a permanent 'opposition party' within the union, opposition to the incumbent leadership is likely to emerge in response to particular issues at different times, and member interest in changing union leadership is therefore likely to be at its highest only shortly before elections. Thus, it is probable that to require that a member decide upon a potential candidacy at least 18 months in advance of an election [to assure attendance at half the regular meetings over the 3-year period] when no issues exist to prompt that decision may not foster but discourage candidacies and to that extent impair the general membership's freedom to oust incumbents in favor of new leadership.

In dissent, Justice Lewis Powell (joined by Justices Potter Stewart and William Rehnquist) argued that the union rule was reasonable because it could encourage attendance at meetings, guarantee that candidates for office had a meaningful interest in the union, and assure that the candidates have a chance to become informed about union affairs. Powell charged that the case was being decided almost solely on the basis of a statistical test of the proportion of the membership disqualified, adding that these statistics had not convinced him that the rule itself was unreasonable.

Antipathy to women, or to a woman?

In a case turning primarily on the personalities of several Federal Government workers in the Midwest, the Federal district court in the District of Columbia recently ruled that promoting one woman over another can constitute sex discrimination prohibited by Title VII of the Civil Rights Act of 1964. Although it noted that discrimination based on sex usually involves preferential treatment for members of one sex over members of the other, the court held that the challenged promotion of one woman rather than another was illegal if it was based on a general "antipathy for women." (*Skelton v. Balzano*.[11])

The plaintiff in this case was Rita Skelton, who had been acting program director of ACTION (the agency that directs most government volunteer programs) for Ohio. Skelton claimed that her supervisor, Myron Kuropas, promised to support her for the position of permanent director but then later endorsed another woman, Anne Johnson, who in fact received the position.

In discussing this situation, the court listed earlier complaints of sex discrimination filed by Skelton and other women employees against Kuropas and then went on to consider whether his attitude toward women in general led to his decision not to support Skelton for the permanent directorship:

There is proof which the court accepts that Kuropas did not like 'pushy women,' and felt they needed to be handled firmly. Plaintiff was assertive and this annoyed Kuropas. . . .

But these insights are not enough. The question of whether Kuropas plotted to deny plaintiff the Ohio directorship because she was a woman, or whether he caused her removal because she proved not qualified for the job, hinges in part on the testimony of Charles Cain, a black and formerly one of Kuropas' deputies. Cain testified that he entered a conference where Kuropas was discussing Ohio with another deputy and some staff people, and heard Kuropas say he was planning to put another woman, Johnson, over Skelton. According to his own testimony, Cain laughed, and then objected when he found this was a serious proposal, commenting that it wouldn't work, that the women would devour each other. Cain testified that Kuropas said, 'Now you are beginning to use your head—that is the intent.'. . .

Defendant takes the position that there can be no sex discrimination as a matter of law when one woman is advanced over another. This proposition has superficial merit, but the inquiry must go deeper. It is enough to show by a preponderance of the evidence that if plaintiff had been a man she would not have been treated in the same manner, and at the very least would have been afforded genuine opportunity to advance to another State directorship, possibly one of those then available. If Kuropas was motivated by his antipathy for women in his mistreatment of plaintiff, this also will suffice to fall within the strictures of the act.

No arbitration of interest arbitration

In 1975, the National Labor Relations Board ruled that interest arbitration clauses (under which issues that are not resolved in the normal bargaining process are referred to an impartial arbitrator) are not mandatory subjects of bargaining.[12] This ruling meant that neither a union nor an employer could refuse to sign a collective bargaining contract if the only remaining issue between the parties was the inclusion of an interest arbitration clause. Recently, the case that evoked this NLRB ruling was discussed by a Federal appeals court, which agreed with the NLRB and enforced the Board's order against a union that refused to sign a contract omitting a traditional interest arbitration clause. (*Columbus Printing Pressmen.*[13])

Since 1947, every contract between the printer's union and the employer in this case had included an interest arbitration clause. During negotiations for the 1970–73 contract, the clause was included by order of an arbitrator who resolved the issue under a similar provision of the 1967–70 contract. In 1973, the parties were again unable to agree on the interest arbitration provision, and the union sought to have the dispute again submitted to arbitration

pursuant to the 1970–73 agreement. The employer successfully challenged the provision before the NLRB, and the appeals court's discussion of the dispute endorses the Board's decision:

> . . . Wages, hours, and other terms and conditions of employment are considered mandatory subjects of collective bargaining, and either party may insist upon . . . a clause relating to those subjects. . . . By the same token it is unlawful to insist upon the inclusion of a clause relating to matters as to which collective bargaining is not mandatory. . . .

> In assessing the Board's conclusion, we must keep in mind the Supreme Court's dictum that 'classification of bargaining subject as "terms (and) conditions of employment" is a matter concerning which the Board has special expertise.' . . .

> The Board's position is that new contract arbitration clauses are enforceable . . . insofar as the disputed terms are mandatory subjects of bargaining, leaving the negative implication that such clauses are not enforceable insofar as the disputed terms involve nonmandatory matters. We need not make such a wholesale determination. Rather, we decide only that a contract arbitration clause cannot be enforced in an attempt to obtain such a clause in a new contract. The Board's finding that insistence upon compliance with an existing clause is an unfair labor practice, therefore, does not conflict with the parties' enforceable contract obligations. □

———FOOTNOTES———

[1] *Alfred v. Barlow's, Inc.*, 18 DAILY LAB. REP. A-2 (U.S. No. A-600, Jan. 25 and Feb. 3, 1977) (Rehnquist, J.), modifying *Barlow's, Inc. v. Usery*, 1 DAILY LAB. REP. E-1 (D. Idaho Dec. 30, 1976).

[2] 387 U.S. 523 (1967).

[3] 387 U.S. 541 (1967).

[4] 397 U.S. 72 (1970).

[5] 406 U.S. 311 (1972).

[6] *City of Madison, Joint School Dist. No. 8 v. Wisconsin Employment Relations Commission*, 45 U.S.L.W. 4043 (U.S. Dec. 8, 1976).

[7] Justice William Brennan, Thurgood Marshall, and Potter Stewart concurred in the judgment but did not join the majority opinion.

[8] 29 U.S.C. sec. 481(e) (1970).

[9] *Wirtz v. Hotel Employees*, 391 U.S. 492 (1968) (see *Monthly Labor Review*, September 1968, pp. 58–59). See also *Wirtz v. Local Union No. 125, Laborers Int'l Union*, 389 U.S. 477 (1968) and *Wirtz v. Bottle Glass Blowers Assn.*, 389 U.S. 463 (1968) (both discussed in *Monthly Labor Review*, March 1968, p. 109).

[10] *Local 3489, United Steelworkers v. Usery*, 45 U.S.L.W. 4089 (U.S. Jan. 12, 1977).

[11] *Skelton v. Balzano*, 241 DAILY LAB. REP. D-1 (D.D.C. Dec. 7, 1976).

[12] *Columbus Printing Pressmen & Assistants' Union No. 252* and *R. W. Page Corp.*, 219 NLRB No. 54, July 23, 1975; see *Monthly Labor Review*, November 1975, pp. 73–74.

[13] *NLRB v. Columbus Printing Pressmen Union No. 252*, 244 DAILY LAB. REP. E-1 (5th Cir. Dec. 13, 1976).

Discrimination against whom?

The Social Security Act requires widowers seeking survivors' benefits based on their wives' former earnings to prove that they were dependent on those earnings; widows seeking survivors' benefits do not have to prove dependency. A majority of the U.S. Supreme Court recently struck down this unequal treatment as unconstitutional sex discrimination—four Justices holding that it discriminated against women wage earners, one that it discriminated against male survivors. Four other Justices felt the different treatment for men and women was constitutional. (Califano v. Goldfarb,[1])

The result in Goldfarb was foreshadowed by the Court's opinion in Weinberger v. Wiesenfeld, a 1975 case holding unconstitutional another part of the Social Security Act that granted benefits to widows with dependent children but denied benefits to similarly situated widowers.[2] Seven of the eight Justices who heard the case joined in the Court's opinion; even Justice William Rehnquist (who wrote the dissent in Goldfarb) concurred, stating simply that the exclusion of widowers "does not rationally serve any valid legislative purpose, including that for which [the section providing benefits to widows] was obviously designed [which was enabling] a child of a deceased contributing worker . . . to receive the full-time attention of the only parent remaining to it." The plurality opinion took a more sweeping approach, rejecting the argument that social patterns of male and female employment could constitutionally justify disparate treatment of surviving mothers and fathers:

> . . . [Although] the notion that men are more likely than women to be the primary supporters of their spouses and children is not entirely without empirical support, . . . such a gender-based generalization cannot suffice to justify the denigration of the efforts of women who do work and whose earnings contribute significantly to their families' support.
>
> [The statutory difference in treatment] clearly operates . . . to deprive women of protection for their fami-

lies which men receive as a result of their employment . . . [I]n this case social security taxes were deducted from [the mother's] salary during the years in which she worked. Thus, she not only failed to receive for her family the same protection which a similarly situated male worker would have received, but she also was deprived of a portion of her own earnings in order to contribute to the fund out of which benefits would be paid to others.

Given this approach to Wiesenfeld, it is not surprising that four Justices held in Goldfarb that it is unconstitutional discrimination against women to require widowers but not widows to prove that their spouses had provided at least half of their support. These four (Justices William Brennan, Byron White, Thurgood Marshall, and Lewis Powell) applied the same reasoning as in Wiesenfeld in concluding that the different treatment of men and women resulted in women's covered earnings providing less protection for their families than those of men.

In a dissenting opinion, Justice Rehnquist, joined by Justices Potter Stewart, Harry Blackmun, and Chief Justice Warren Burger, argued that the requirement that widowers but not widows prove dependency was constitutional. The four found two significant differences between Wiesenfeld and Goldfarb: (1) unlike the total exclusion of men in Wiesenfeld, widowers in the Goldfarb situation could receive benefits by proving dependency; and (2) the imposition of a dependency requirement on men but not women could reflect a desire to minimize the administrative cost of determining dependency for women, who were empirically more likely to be dependent. Justice Rehnquist also argued that the Supreme Court should scrutinize disparate treatment of men and women less strictly in social insurance legislation than in other areas, because such benefit systems deal with millions of people in various circumstances and do not award benefits on a strictly contractual basis; that is, benefits depend upon legislated procedures and are not "owed" to participants in strict proportion to their deducted contributions to the fund.

The most intriguing opinion in Goldfarb was Justice John Stevens' concurrence. Stevens agreed with

"Significant Decisions in Labor Cases" is written by Craig Polhemus, Office of Publications, Bureau of Labor Statistics.

Rehnquist that, because social security benefits are not a contractual right, working women are not unconstitutionally discriminated against simply because their contributions may in certain circumstances provide less protection to their families than contributions by similarly situated men. He also agreed that administrative convenience might in some circumstances justify this type of different treatment in requiring widowers but not widows to prove dependency. Using Rehnquist's own discussion of the relevant data, however, Stevens reasoned that the cost of providing benefits to widows who were not actually dependent would far outweigh the cost of requiring widows as well as widowers to establish dependency. He therefore concluded that Congress could not have set up the dual system for administrative convenience. He went on to consider other possible reasons for Congress to grant widowers survivors' benefits on stricter terms than widows:

> . . . It is fair to infer that habit, rather than analysis or actual reflection, made it seem acceptable to equate the terms 'widow' and 'dependent surviving spouse.' That kind of automatic reflex is far different from either a legislative decision to favor females in order to compensate for past wrongs [which might be constitutional], or a legislative decision that the administrative savings exceed the cost of extending benefits to nondependent widows.

> I am therefore persuaded that this discrimination against a group of males is merely the accidental by-product of a traditional way of thinking about females. I am also persuaded that a rule which effects an unequal distribution of economic benefits solely on the basis of sex is sufficiently questionable that 'due process requires that there be a legitimate basis for presuming that the rule was actually intended to serve (the) interest' put forward by the Government as its justification. See *Hampton v. Mow Sun Wong*, 426 U.S. 88, 103. In my judgment, something more than accident is necessary to justify the disparate treatment of persons who have as strong a claim to equal treatment as do similarly situated surviving spouses.

In the court's words . . .

(*On January 14, 1977, the Virginia Supreme Court ruled that State law does not permit local governing bodies and school boards to enter into collective bargaining agreements with public employee associations, voiding those agreements that had already been reached—by union estimates, covering at least 30,000 workers. The court's unanimous opinion is excerpted below.*[3])

The question for decision in this case is whether, absent express statutory authority, a local governing body or school board can recognize a labor organization as the exclusive representative of a group of public employees and can negotiate and enter into binding contracts with the organization concerning the terms and conditions of employment of the employees. . . .

. . . Upon the question of the extent of the boards' powers [with respect to dealing with employee representatives], the parties are in complete disagreement. The Attorney General contends on behalf of the Commonwealth that the question is to be determined by application of [Virginia's judicial] Dillon Rule of strict construction, *viz.*, that local public bodies may exercise only those powers conferred expressly or by necessary implication. On the other hand, the boards contend that the extent of their powers is to be determined not only by application of the Dillon Rule, but also by resort to another rule, *viz.*, that a general grant of power implies the necessary means for carrying into execution the power granted, and, accordingly, where a power is granted expressly but no mode or manner is specified for its execution, the public body, in its discretion, may select any reasonable method of exercising the power. . . .

There can be no question that Virginia long has followed, and still adheres to, the Dillon Rule of strict construction concerning the powers of local governing bodies. . . .

We have, however, recognized the 'reasonable selection of method' rule, relied upon by the boards, which permits local public bodies to exercise discretionary authority where a grant of power is silent upon its mode or manner of execution. . . . At first blush, the 'reasonable selection of method' rule would appear to be at odds with the Dillon Rule of strict construction or, at least, as the boards in the present case suggest, to permit a greater exercise of power than the Dillon Rule. But we do not believe either is the proper view of the two rules.

In the authorities we have consulted, the 'reasonable selection of method' rule always is stated in terms that there must be an express grant of power silent upon its mode or manner of execution before the rule comes into play. We perceive no reason, however, that the rule should not apply also, in a proper case, to a power which has been implied from an express grant. Given this application, the 'reasonable selection of method' rule can be made to harmonize with, rather than contradict, the Dillon Rule.

Thus, the Dillon Rule is applicable to determine in the first instance, from express words or by implication, whether a power exists at all. If the power cannot be found, the inquiry is at an end. On the other hand, where a power is found to exist but the question is whether it has been exercised properly, then the 'reasonable selection of method' rule may be applicable, and . . . the inquiry is directed to whether there may be implied the authority to exercise the power in the particular manner chosen. . . .

It is agreed that no statute expressly confers upon the boards the power to bargain collectively with labor organizations. We are concerned, therefore, with a question of implied power, and this is the question even when we consider the 'reasonable selection of method' rule. Indeed, this rule is premised upon the proposition that, because a grant of power is general in its terms, the necessary means for carrying into execution the power granted must be *implied* before the authority may be exercised. The real difference between the Dillon Rule and the 'reasonable selection of method' rule is that, under the former, any doubt is resolved against the existence of the power while, under the latter, the doubt is resolved in favor of the method selected to exercise the power.

Specifically, we are concerned in this case with the question whether, from the power conferred upon the boards in general language to enter into contracts and to hire employees and fix the terms and conditions of their employment, there may be implied the further power to bargain collectively with labor organizations. . . .

For this court to imply the power here sought, we would be required to find that because local governmental boards possess the power to enter into contracts and to hire employees and fix the terms and conditions of their employment, the boards also possess the authority to bargain collectively with labor organizations. But if the power cannot be found in this source, the boards in the present case then would have us find that, nonetheless, they possess the power to bargain collectively because they have discretionary authority to select any reasonable method of exercising a power expressly granted but silent upon its mode or manner of execution.

We cannot make either finding. To imply the contended for authority would constitute the creation of a power that does not exist or, at least, the expansion of an existing power beyond rational limits. To sanction the method of exercising authority which the boards have selected in this case, even given the selection the benefit of any doubt, would result in an unreasonable and strained application of the doctrine of implied powers. To approve the actions taken in this case would ignore the lack of any support for the proposition that collective bargaining by the boards is necessary to promote the public interest. And, finally but not least important, to imply the power asserted by the board would be contrary to legislative intent.

The powers vested in local boards to enter into contracts and to hire employees and fix the terms and conditions of their employment are of ancient origin, conferred at a time when the concept of collective bargaining in the public sector had not emerged as a debatable issue. While this fact is not controlling, because changing conditions may warrant different considerations of the extent of power, the recent Virginia history of public employee collective bargaining is persuasive, if not conclusive, that the General Assembly, the source of legislative intent, has never conferred upon local boards, by implication or otherwise, the power to bargain collectively and that express statutory authority, so far withheld, is necessary to confer the power. And when legislative intent is plain, our duty is to respect it and give it effect.

(*The following passage is excerpted from an opinion by the New Jersey Superior Court, Chancery Division, Salem County, in* Shimp v. New Jersey Bell Telephone Co., *a case filed by a telephone company employee seeking to bar cigarette smoking that she said was harmful to her health.*)

Such a rule imposes no hardship upon defendant New Jersey Bell Telephone Co. The company already has in effect a rule that cigarettes may not be smoked around the telephone equipment. The rationale behind the rule is that the machines are extremely sensitive and can be damaged by the smoke. Human beings are also very sensitive and can be damaged by cigarette smoke. Unlike a piece of machinery, the damage to a human is all too often irreparable. If a circuit or wiring goes bad, the company can install a replacement part. It is not so simple in the case of a human lung, eye, or heart. The parts are hard to come by, if indeed they can be found at all. □

———FOOTNOTES———

[1] *Califano v. Goldfarb,* 45 U.S.L.W. —— (U.S. Mar. 2, 1977).

[2] 420 U.S. 636 (1975).

[3] *Commonwealth v. County Bd.,* 693 GOV. EMP. RELATIONS REP. 32 (Va. Sup. Ct. Jan. 14, 1977).

Work preservation as secondary activity

The National Labor Relations Act forbids union members to seek to influence employers to cease doing business with another person or company; this prohibition has been interpreted to apply only to secondary disputes (those aimed at someone other than the members' own employer).[1] But what of strikes or boycotts intended to force an employer to stop purchasing prefabricated products that reduce the amount of work to be performed by union members? Is this type of dispute a legal primary job action (aimed at the union members' own employer) or an illegal secondary action (designed to force the employer to cease doing business with the producer of the prefabricated items)?

The Supreme Court recently reinterpreted the test used to resolve these questions, holding that even a valid work-preservation clause in a collective bargaining contract does not legitimize boycotts or other job actions whose purposes include a desire to persuade a subcontractor to cease doing business with a manufacturer of prefabricated construction products where the subcontractor's agreement with the general contractor specifies use of such products. (*NLRB v. Enterprise Association.*[2])

The three dissenting Justices (Brennan, Stewart, and Marshall) argued that the union in this case had simply sought to enforce a valid provision in the labor contract ensuring that members of the bargaining unit would cut and thread the internal piping in climate-control units to be installed in a construction project. They cited the Supreme Court's 1967 opinion in the *National Woodwork* case holding that a union could properly seek to prevent a contractor from using precut and prefitted doors in violation of the labor contract.[3] That case suggested that the proper standard for distinguishing between primary and secondary disputes in this area was "whether, under all the surrounding circumstances, the union's objective was preservation of work for [the subcontractor's] employees,

"Significant Decisions in Labor Cases" is written by Craig Polhemus, Office of Publications, Bureau of Labor Statistics.

or whether the agreements and boycott were tactically designed to satisfy union objectives elsewhere." The *National Woodwork* opinion went on to discuss the implications of this test in the work-preservation area:

. . . There need not be an actual dispute with the boycotted employer, here the door manufacturer, for the activity to fall within this [prohibited] category, so long as the tactical object of the agreement and its maintenance is that employer, or benefits to other than the boycotting employees or other employees of the primary employer thus making the agreement or boycott secondary in its aim. The touchstone is whether the agreement or its maintenance is addressed to the labor relations of the contracting employer *vis-a-vis* his own employees.

Applying this test to the *Enterprise Association* case, the dissenters concluded that the union was pursuing legal primary purposes. They argued that the subcontractor should not be insulated from this type of primary pressure just because it accepted a contract from a general contractor calling for prefabricated climate-control units. The dissent also charged that the National Labor Relations Board and the majority of the Supreme Court were altering the test of legality from the "totality of circumstances" standard of *National Woodwork* to a simplistic concern with whether the subcontractor faced with this sort of union pressure had the "right of control" over using prefabricated units.

The majority of the Court denied that it was changing the legal standard announced in *National Woodwork*. Although the NLRB, in finding that the dispute in this case was secondary, had emphasized the subcontractor's lack of discretion over whether to use prefabricated units, the Supreme Court majority stated that control was just one factor the Board had considered under the totality-of-the-circumstances test. The Court approved the Board's emphasis on control within the framework of this legal standard and discussed the resulting distinction between primary and secondary disputes involving valid work-preservation clauses:

. . . [T]he Board has [found] an unfair labor practice at least where the union employs a product boycott [of prefabricated items] to claim work that the immediate employer is not in a position to award, and it has declined to find a violation where the employer has such power, even if awarding the work might cause him to terminate contractual relations with another employer. In the latter circumstances, the cease-doing-business consequences are merely incidental to primary activity, but not in the former where the union, if it is to obtain work, must intend to exert pressure on one or more other employers [such as the general contractor who specified the prefabricated products].

Contract construction

Applying the general rule that contracts should, if possible, be construed in a manner that renders them valid and enforceable, the Supreme Court recently interpreted a collective bargaining agreement in the Oregon construction industry to fit within the terms of the Taft-Hartley Act's limitations on employer support of union activities. Those limitations prohibit employer payments to union funds, but they exempt payments required by a collective bargaining agreement into joint union-employer trust funds providing medical, retirement, vacation, apprenticeship, or other training benefits to signatory employers' employees and their dependents. Because this exemption applies only to funds benefiting workers employed by signatory employers, the Supreme Court had to determine whether the Oregon construction-industry contract illegally required employer payments designed to benefit employees of other, nonsignatory employers. (*Walsh v. Schlecht*.[4])

The labor contract in question obligated a signatory general contractor to ensure that payments were made with respect to employees of nonsignatory subcontractors:

If a contractor, bound by this Agreement, contracts or subcontracts, any work covered by this Agreement. . . the contractor shall require such subcontractor to be bound to all the provisions of this Agreement, or such contractor shall maintain daily records of the subcontractors employees jobsite hours and be liable for payment of the employees [sic] wages, travel, Health & Welfare, Pension, Vacation, Apprenticeship and CIAF [Construction Industry Advancement Fund] contributions in accordance with this agreement.

The question before the Supreme Court was whether this clause legally required payments *as measured by* hours worked by the subcontractor's employees or illegally required payments *for the benefit of* such employees, who would not actually be eligible to participate in the trust fund programs under the Taft-Hartley limitations. (The subcon-

tractor in this case had not signed the contract and so was not eligible to make payments into the funds, but its employees received additional wages equal to the amount of contributions that would otherwise have been made. The union then sought to have the general contractor make equivalent payments into the funds under the above "subcontractor's clause.")

In holding that the contract legitimately called for payments measured by noneligible employees' hours of work, the majority of the Supreme Court considered the purpose of the Taft-Hartley Act's limitations on employer support of union funds:

. . . The Subcontractor's Clause, although inartfully worded, lends itself to a construction that ties signatory employer contributions to the Trust Funds as measured both by hours worked by his own employees and hours worked by his nonsignatory subcontractor's employees, and, so construed, . . . not only is consistent with [the Taft-Hartley Act] but also does no disservice to the congressional purpose . . . to combat 'corruption of collective bargaining through bribery of employee representatives by employers . . . extortion by employee representatives, and . . . the possible abuse by union officials of the power which they might achieve if welfare funds were left to their sole control.'

In dissent, Justice White argued that the Court was distorting the natural meaning of the collective bargaining contract:

. . . Had the subcontractor been eligible to make these contributions, they surely would have been made for the benefit of his employees. The sensible inference from the contractual language is that the contractor, the petitioner, intended the same result. Common sense tells us that petitioner had no intention of making contributions with respect to employees who could never benefit.

As construed in this way, the provision is illegal because the employees of the noncontributing contractor may not be a beneficiary of the trust funds, even though the contributions are made with respect to them. But this would not be the first time that parties have drafted unenforceable contractual provisions, either by design, accident, or mistake.

I do not understand why the Court feels such compulsion to save the contract by construing it to mean that the payments at issue are not for the benefit of the contractor's employees at all and are not made on their behalf. The result of this construction is that in addition to the full contract price paid to the subcontractor, petitioner must pay into the trust funds 96 cents for each jobsite [hour] worked by the subcontractor's employees, these funds to be held for the employees of the contributing employers but excluding the subcontractor's employees. This is simply a penalty for employing a nonsignatory subcontractor, a penalty the Court creates in construing the contract as it does.

Catch 24(a)

Under section 706 of Title VII of the Civil Rights Act of 1964, suits charging employment discrimination may be brought by the Equal Employment Opportunity Commission or by an affected employee—but duplicative suits based on the same circumstances are not permitted.[5] If the EEOC decides to file suit against an employer based on an employee's complaint, the employee may intervene in the EEOC suit but may not file one of his own. Because Rule 24(a) of the Federal Rules of Civil Procedure requires that motions for intervention be "timely," a Federal court of appeals recently held that an employee who was not informed that the EEOC filed suit based on his complaint was not entitled either to sue his employer on his own behalf or to intervene in the EEOC suit, which had been settled through a consent decree. (*McClain v. Wagner Electric Corp.*[6])

Theophilus McClain, a black employee of Wagner Electric Corp., was never advised that the EEOC filed suit based on his complaint. (The Federal appeals court suggested that the lack of an EEOC policy of advising employees whether their charges would be acted upon was to blame for the difficulties McClain encountered in trying to obtain judicial recognition of his claims.) Had McClain sought to participate in the EEOC suit, he would have been entitled to intervene as a matter of law. By the time he filed his own suit, however, the EEOC's case had been settled. McClain was thus barred from pursuing his own case and could intervene in the EEOC case only if a Federal district judge reopened the matter and ruled his application "timely" under Rule 24(a).

The district judge ruled that McClain's motion was untimely. The Federal appeals court affirmed this ruling, in part because of the time lapse after the settlement between the EEOC and the employer and in part because McClain filed the intervention motion in his own case rather than in the EEOC case itself:

> The plaintiff, although represented by counsel, simply filed his motion in the wrong case. It is a legal anomaly for a person to file in one suit a motion for leave to intervene in an entirely different suit, and that is exactly what happened here. . . .

> It is unfortunate that this situation has arisen, but we do not feel free to ignore the fact that the situation exists or at liberty within the framework of this appeal to grant relief with respect to it.

In brief

DUE PROCESS HEARING UNNECESSARY. In an unsigned (*per curiam*) opinion, the Supreme Court held that a probationary police officer who claimed that his reputation had been injured by information in his personnel file was not entitled to a due process hearing under the Fourteenth Amendment because he did not dispute the truth of that information, so that the hearing could serve no constitutional purpose. (*Codd v. Velger.*[7])

NEW YORK BIAS BAN NOT FOR EXPORT. New York State's highest court, the Court of Appeals, held that New York City's administrative code forbidding the printing of advertisements directly or indirectly expressing employment limitations by race does not apply to discrimination in foreign countries such as South Africa, reversing a decision of the New York City Commission on Human Rights charging *The New York Times* with violating the code. "Without expressing disapproval of the goal of the complainants and without expressing approval of the invidious practices of the government of the Republic of South Africa, we conclude that a city agency was without jurisdiction to make and enforce its own foreign policy," the court said. (*The New York Times v. Commission on Human Rights.*[8]) □

-------FOOTNOTES-------

[1] The National Labor Relations Board and the Federal courts held the prohibition to apply only to secondary activities, and this interpretation was confirmed in 1959 by an amendment to the law specifically stating that primary activities were not thereby made illegal by the prohibition on influencing employers to cease doing business with other persons. See *National Woodwork Mfgs. v. NLRB*, 386 U.S. 612 (1967).

[2] *NLRB v. Enterprise Assn. Steamfitters, Local 638*, 45 U.S.L.W. 4144 (U.S. Feb. 22, 1977).

[3] 386 U.S. 612 (1967).

[4] *Walsh v. Schlecht*, 45 U.S.L.W. 4126 (U.S. Jan. 18, 1977).

[5] See *EEOC. v. Missouri Pacific R.R.*, 493 F.2d 71 (8th Cir. 1974). This ruling does not apply if the claims of the EEOC are broader than those of an individual employee or group of employees.

[6] *McClain v. Wagner Electric Corp.*, 54 DAILY LAB. REP. D-1 (8th Cir. Mar. 9, 1977).

[7] *Codd v. Velger*, 45 U.S.L.W. 4143 (U.S. Feb. 22, 1977). In dissent, Justices Brennan, Marshall, and Stevens argued that the discharged employee should not have to dispute the truth of the stigmatizing information; Justices Stewart and Stevens argued that the lower courts did not properly consider whether the employee had a "property interest" in his job under the due process clause; and Justice Stevens alone argued that the lower courts did not properly consider whether the employee had in fact been stigmatized by the information in his personnel folder.

[8] *The New York Times Co. v. New York Comm'n on Human Rights*, 39 DAILY LAB. REP. A-2 (N.Y.C.A. Feb. 10, 1977).

Death of a bakery

The Supreme Court recently extended the national policy favoring arbitration of labor disputes when it held that a severance-pay grievance arising from a bakery closing after termination of a union contract was arbitrable under the terms of the agreement. In so holding, the Court by a 7 to 2 vote, avoided ruling on the merits of the pay claim, leaving that decision to the arbitrator. *(Nolde Brothers, Inc.*[1]*)*

The dispute involved a 1970 contract between Nolde Brothers' bakery and the Bakery and Confectionary Workers Union. That contract, which authorized arbitration of any grievances arising under its terms, was to remain in effect until July 21, 1973, or 7 days after either party gave written notice of intent to terminate the agreement. On August 20, 1973, following 4 months of unsuccessful negotiations for a new contract, the union announced its intent to terminate the 1970 contract; 7 days later, the contract expired, although negotiations continued until August 31, when Nolde Brothers (faced with a strike threat from the union) permanently closed the bakery.

Nolde Brothers paid accrued wages and vacation pay under the cancelled contract, as well as wages earned between the contract termination on August 27 and the bakery closing on August 31. The company refused to pay severance wages that would have been required had the contract been in effect when the bakery was shut down, however; it also refused to submit the claim to arbitration.

According to Chief Justice Warren Burger's majority opinion, the only issue for decision when the case reached the Supreme Court was "whether a party to a collective-bargaining contract may be required to arbitrate a contractual dispute over severance pay pursuant to the arbitration clause of that agreement even though the dispute, although governed by the contract, arises after its termination." On this single legal question, the Court ruled in favor of arbitration:

> In arguing that Nolde's displaced employees were entitled to severance pay upon the closing of the Nor-

folk bakery, the union maintained that the severance wages provided for in the collective-bargaining agreement were in the nature of 'accrued' or 'vested' rights, earned by employees during the term of the contract on essentially the same basis as vacation pay, but payable only upon termination of employment. In support of this claim, the union noted that the severance pay clause is found in the contract under an article entitled 'Wages.' The inclusion within that provision, it urged, was evidence that the parties considered severance pay as part of the employees' compensation for services performed during the life of the agreement. In addition, the union pointed out that the severance pay clause itself contained nothing to suggest that the employees' right to severance pay expired if the events triggering payment failed to occur during the life of the contract. Nolde, on the other hand, argued that since severance pay was a creation of the collective-bargaining agreement, its substantive obligation to provide such benefits terminated with the union's unilateral cancellation of the contract.

. . . Of course, in determining the arbitrability of the dispute, the merits of the underlying claim for severance pay are not before us. However, it is clear that, whatever the outcome, the resolution of that claim hinges on the interpretation ultimately given the contract clause providing for severance pay. The dispute therefore, although arising *after* the expiration of the collective-bargaining contract, clearly arises *under* that contract.

Chief Justice Burger's opinion went on to dismiss the employer's claim that termination of the contract automatically ended all obligation to arbitrate grievances arising under it. "Carried to its logical conclusion that argument would preclude the entry of a post-contract arbitration order even when the dispute arose during the life of the contract but arbitration proceedings had not yet begun before termination," the Chief Justice said. "The same would be true if arbitration processes began but were not completed, during the contract's term." Because both parties were presumably aware of the national policy of deferring to arbitration wherever it is available, the Court held that (in the absence of clear evidence of a contrary intent) disputes arising under an expired bargaining agreement should be arbitrated according to the terms of the contract.[2]

In dissent, Justices Potter Stewart and William

"Significant Decisions in Labor Cases" is written by Craig Polhemus, Office of Publications, Bureau of Labor Statistics.

Rehnquist argued that the duty to arbitrate can only arise from—and should be limited to the scope of—an affirmative agreement to arbitrate specific issues. After the bakery was closed, they said, there was no bargaining relationship to preserve through arbitration and no current contract providing for such arbitration. Moreover, the dissenters added, the severance-pay dispute could have been settled much more swiftly if the Federal courts had confronted it directly instead of focusing solely on the arbitration question.

Union harassment and State law

Richard T. Hill, a member of the Carpenters Union, was elected vice president of his local in 1965. Shortly thereafter, he developed sharp disagreements with other union officials and, by Hill's account, the union began to discriminate against him in job referrals through its hiring hall. Hill also claimed that union officials conducted a campaign of personal abuse and harassment against him.

In April 1969, Hill filed suit in California's Superior Court for the County of Los Angeles, charging the union and its officials with discriminatory job referrals and with intentionally engaging in outrageous conduct, threats, and intimidation causing Hill grievous emotional distress resulting in bodily injury. State courts dismissed the job-referral discrimination claim, holding that it was preempted by the National Labor Relations Act; California's Court of Appeals held that the claim of outrageous conduct was also preempted because the "crux" of the action concerned employment relations. The U.S. Supreme Court recently heard Hill's case and unanimously held that State courts can hear "outrageous conduct" claims arising in employment contexts if they are either 1) unrelated to employment discrimination or 2) based on the particularly abusive manner in which the alleged employment discrimination is carried out, rather than on the nature of the discrimination itself. (*Farmer v. Carpenters.* [3])

The standard for determining whether a particular claim under State law is preempted by Federal labor law was established in the 1959 case of *San Diego Building Trades Council v. Garmon.* [4]

> When it is clear or may fairly be assumed that the activities which a State purports to regulate are protected by . . . the National Labor Relations Act, or constitute an unfair labor practice under [that act], due regard for the Federal enactment requires that State jurisdiction must yield. To leave the States free to regulate conduct so plainly within the central aim of Federal regulation involves too great a danger of conflict between power asserted by Congress and requirements imposed by State law.

The Court reaffirmed this basic standard while noting that certain exceptions have been recognized for issues only peripherally connected with labor relations or deeply rooted in local concerns. The prime example of a local issue that is generally not preempted by Federal labor law is violent, illegal conduct arising out of a labor dispute.

Hill's complaint of outrageous conduct by union officials was based on a State tort (civil action for infringement of rights) called intentional infliction of emotional distress. The Supreme Court's unanimous opinion addressed the relationship of Federal labor law and State tort law in the employment context:

> No provision of the National Labor Relations Act protects the 'outrageous conduct' complained of by petitioner Hill in the second count of his complaint. Regardless of whether the operation of the hiring hall was lawful or unlawful under Federal statutes, there is no Federal protection for conduct on the part of union officials which is so outrageous that 'no reasonable man in a civilized society should be expected to endure it.'
>
> . . . The State, on the other hand, has a substantial interest in protecting its citizens from the kind of abuse of which Hill complained. That interest is no less worthy of recognition because it concerns protection from emotional distress caused by outrageous conduct, rather than protection from physical injury, . . . or damage to reputation. . . . Although recognition of the tort of intentional infliction of emotional distress is a comparatively recent development in State law, . . . our decisions permitting the exercise of State jurisdiction in tort actions based on violence of defamation have not rested on the history of the tort at issue, but rather on the nature of the State's interest in protecting the health and well-being of its citizens.
>
> There is, to be sure, some risk that the State course of action for infliction of emotional distress will touch on an area of primary Federal concern. Hill's complaint itself highlights this risk. In those counts of the complaint that the trial court dismissed, Hill alleged discrimination against him in hiring hall referrals, which were also alleged to be violations of both the collective-bargaining agreement and the membership contract. These allegations, if sufficiently supported before the National Labor Relations Board, would make out an unfair labor practice. . . . The occurrence of the abusive conduct, with which the State tort action is concerned, in such a context of federally prohibited discrimination suggests a potential for interference with the Federal scheme of regulation.
>
> Viewed, however, in light of the discrete concerns of the Federal scheme and the State tort law, that potential for interference is sufficient to counterbalance the legitimate and substantial interest of the State in protecting its citizens. If the charges in Hill's complaint were filed with the [National Labor Relations] Board, the focus of any unfair labor practice proceeding would be on whether the statements or conduct on the part of union officials discriminated or threatened discrimination against him in employment referrals for reasons other

than failure to pay union dues. . . . Whether the statements or conduct of the respondents also caused Hill severe emotional distress and physical injury would play no role in the Board's disposition of the case, and the Board could not award Hill damages for pain, suffering, or medical expenses. Conversely, the State court tort action can be adjudicated without resolution of the 'merits' of the underlying labor dispute. Recovery for the tort of emotional distress under California law requires proof that the defendant intentionally engaged in outrageous conduct causing the plaintiff to sustain mental distress. . . . The State court need not consider, much less resolve, whether a union discriminated or threatened to discriminate against an employee in terms of employment opportunities. To the contrary, the tort action can be resolved without reference to any accommodation of the special interests of unions and members in the hiring hall context.[5]

In brief. . . .

CAPTAIN'S AUTHORITY UNABRIDGED. Overturning a recent National Labor Relations Board (NLRB) maritime decision, a Federal court of appeals reasoned, "During the course of a voyage, the normal employer-employee relationship is suspended . . . [The captain] is charged with the responsibility for the safety of the ship, cargo and crew. To discharge this responsibility Congress has seen fit to give him authority to maintain strict discipline."

Thus, the appeals court found that a seaman, charged with willful disobedience, can be required by the captain to attend a "logging" (a proceeding in which the seaman is given notice of entries in the ship's log relating to misconduct with which he is charged) without being accompanied by a union representative.

Although the NLRB based its ruling on the Supreme Court's *Weingarten* decision,[6] the Federal court ruled that this was not an "investigatory interview" (as was the case in *Weingarten*) but a proceeding mandated by law. (*Mt. Vernon Tanker Co.*[7])

RESTITUTION FOR RESCUE ON THE SEA. A maritime vessel, responding to a distress call from a ship with a crew member in need of medical attention, is entitled to compensation for its expenditure of time and fuel.

A Federal appeals court, reversing a lower court ruling, held that, because the rescue ship made known its intention to seek reimbursement before coming to the other ship's aid, the principles of quasi-contract require recovery.

The court believes that this rule will encourage operators of large vessels to perform their traditional moral obligations without fear of unreasonable expense. This action will not deter small ships from calling for aid, the court reasons, because ship captains already have a legal obligation to make reasonable efforts to secure medical aid for stricken crewmen. (*Peninsular & Oriental Steam Navigation Co.*[8]) ☐

---FOOTNOTES---

[1] *Nolde Bros., Inc. v. Local No. 358, Bakery Workers*, 45 U.S.L.W. 4251 (U.S. Mar. 7, 1977).

[2] The majority did not consider whether the arbitrator could find that the contract did not authorize arbitration of such disputes arising after its termination nor whether claims arising after contract termination could be pressed long after the expiration date.

[3] *Farmer v. United Bhd. of Carpenters*, Local 25, 45 U.S.L.W. 4263 (U.S. Mar. 7, 1977).

[4] 359 U.S. 236 (1959).

[5] Because the California trial on Hill's complaint did not properly separate his claim of discrimination from that of intentional infliction of mental distress, the Supreme Court sent the case back to the State courts for further proceedings.

[6] *NLRB v. J. Weingarten, Inc.*, 420 U.S. 251 (1975) (see *Monthly Labor Review*, May 1975, pp. 62–63).

[7] *Mt. Vernon Tanker Co. v. NLRB*, 45 U.S.L.W. 2471 (9th Cir. Mar. 4, 1977).

[8] *Peninsular & Oriental Steam Navigation Co. v. Overseas Oil Carriers, Inc.*, 45 U.S.L.W. 2526 (2d Cir. Apr. 25, 1977).

The agency shop in government agencies

A State cannot compel its employees to support the political activities of their collective bargaining representative, the Supreme Court recently ruled. All nine judges agreed that an agency-shop provision, requiring nonunion employees to pay "union dues," infringes on the First Amendment rights of public employees. However, a six-judge majority held that this "impingement upon associational freedom" is permissible when the mandatory fees paid by nonunion employees are used for activities specifically related to collective bargaining. In so holding, the Court extended the union-shop concept to public employment, reasoning that the same compelling governmental interest in private-sector industrial peace and stable labor-management relations applies because "[t]he desirability of labor peace is no less important in the public sector, nor is the risk of 'free riders' any smaller." (*Abood v. Detroit Board of Education.*[1])

The overriding issue—one decided for the private sector years ago—is whether all employees who benefit from union representation should share equally in the costs of that representation. The Supreme Court upheld the constitutionality of this principle, as defined by the union-shop provisions of the Railway Labor Act, with its decision in *Railway Employees' Dept. v. Hanson.*[2] The union-shop provision of the Act requires that, ". . . as a condition of continued employment, . . . within 60 days following the beginning of such employment . . . all employees shall become members of the labor organization representing their craft or class." In a subsequent decision involving union shops (*International Association of Machinists v. Street*[3]), the Court ruled, however, that fees collected by the union from employees that object to the ideological of political activities of the union cannot be used to support those activities. (The union-shop agreement differs from an agency-shop agreement only in the respect that employees are not required to become union members in an agency shop.)

In 1969, the Detroit Federation of Teachers negotiated a collective bargaining contract with the Detroit Board of Education which included an agency-shop clause. Nonunion teachers filed a class action suit, claiming that the agency-shop provision violated their First Amendment rights as well as the due process and equal protection guarantees of the Fourteenth Amendment to the Constitution. Following dismissal of their complaint by the trial court, the teachers appealed to the Michigan Court of Appeals. But while their case was pending the Michigan Supreme Court ruled that State law prohibited an agency shop in the public sector. While the teachers' case was then remanded to the lower court and, there, combined with a virtually identical case for further ajudication, the Michigan legislature amended its Public Employment Relations Act to expressly authorize an agency shop. The trial court upheld the constitutionality of the new amendment and applied it retroactively to the teachers' case. The teachers appealed, and the Michigan Court of Appeals also upheld the amendment but ruled that its retroactive application was invalid.

In its decision, the Appeals court recognized that the use of compulsory service fees for the union's political activities could impinge upon the teachers' constitutional rights; however, relying on the Supreme Court's ruling in *Street,* they reasoned that the teachers were not entitled to any relief because they had failed to notify the union that they objected to its political activities.

In their appeal to the High Court, the teachers argued that the Court has consistently ruled that public employment cannot be conditioned upon the surrender of First Amendment rights. They also argued that because collective bargaining in the public sector is inherently "political," requiring employees to contribute to a union represents "ideological conformity" which violates their constitutional rights.

Writing for the Court, Justice Potter Stewart agreed that, "To compel employees financially to support their collective bargaining representative has an impact upon their First Amendment rights. . . .

"Significant Decisions in Labor Cases" was written this month by Gregory J. Mounts, Office of Publications, Bureau of Labor Statistics.

But the judgment clearly made in *Hanson* and *Street* is that such interference as exists is constitutionally justified by the legislative assessment of the important contribution of the union shop to the system of labor relations established by Congress." Thus, the same governmental interests that prevailed in the private sector also rule here because, "Public employees are not basically different from private employees; on the whole, they have the same sort of skills, the same needs, and seek the same advantages."

Agreeing with the appeals court's interpretation of its ruling in *Street,* the Court found that a union may support ideological or political causes that a majority of its members endorse, but nonunion employees who must contribute can make known their objection to any union activities unrelated to collective bargaining and thus receive a proportional rebate of their mandatory contribution. The majority also held that the appeals court erred by ruling that, because they had not objected to *specific* union expenditures, the complaining teachers were not entitled to relief. The Court reasoned that to require an employee to make specific objections would result in a "considerable burden of monitoring all of the numerous and shifting expenditures made by the Union that are unrelated to its duties as exclusive bargaining representative." In remanding the case, the Court said that the teachers are entitled to "establish their right to appropriate relief" and suggested that a remedy may be provided through the use of an internal program already adopted by the union.

Although concurring with the majority's ruling that ". . . [a] State cannot constitutionally compel public employees to contribute to union political activities which they oppose," Justice Lewis Powell found a clear distinction between the statutory power of Congress to authorize a union shop agreement in the private sector and the statutory authority of a State to become an active party in such an agreement. Because of this "fundamental" distinction, Powell argued that, instead of placing the burden of litigation upon the employees by requiring an individual to make known his or her objection to a union activity, "[t]he State should bear the burden of proving that any dues or fees that it requires of nonunion employees are needed to serve paramount governmental interests."

Powell, in perceiving a greater constitutional issue, said that: "Before today it had been well established that when State law intrudes upon protected speech, the State itself must shoulder the burden of proving that its action is justified by overriding State interests. . . . The Court, for the first time in a First Amendment case, simply reverses this principle."

A victory for rhetoric

Declaring that employees no longer need "protection" from misleading campaign propaganda during union representation elections, the National Labor Relations Board recently overturned its long-established policy of investigating the truth or falsity of campaign statements. In a 3 to 2 decision, the Board ruled that it will no longer set aside elections based on the *substance* of alleged misrepresentations but only on the basis of the deceptive *manner* in which they were made. Thus, the Board will continue to intervene in cases involving the use of forged documents or other "deceptive campaign practices." (*Shopping Kart Food Market, Inc.* [4])

In addition to viewing employees as "mature individuals who are capable of recognizing campaign propaganda for what it is and discounting it," the Board concludes that its old policy, laid down in the *Hollywood Ceramics* decision,[5] has tended to frustrate the free choice of employees. According to the majority, the administration of the *Hollywood* standards has produced many ill effects, including "extensive analysis of campaign propaganda, restriction of free speech, variance of application as between the Board and the courts, increasing litigation, and a resulting decrease in the finality of election results."

Diagraming the reasoning behind their majority opinion, members John A. Penello and Peter D. Walther cite a recent law review article that has resulted from "an empirical study of NLRB elections."[6] The study, consisting of interviews with more than 1,000 employees who had participated in an NLRB election, reveals that "the votes of 81 percent of the employees could be correctly predicted from their pre-campaign intent and their attitudes toward working conditions and unions in general."

This finding, the two members reasoned, provides sufficient evidence that "the choices of these employees appear to be a product of attitudes formed on the basis of their everyday experiences in the industrial world" and that "employees are generally inattentive to the campaign." Thus, the Board concludes that to set aside an election because of an alleged campaign misrepresentation only causes a delay in the expression of the employees' free choice.

Betty Southard Murphy, since replaced by John H. Fanning as chairman, but still a member of the Board, concurred, stating, "The [*Hollywood*] ruling has been so expanded and misapplied as to have extended far from the original intent of the Board." Her "sole departure" from the majority ruling is that she would continue to set aside an election involving an "egregious mistake of fact" that interferes with an election in the "most extreme situations."

The almost complete reversal of the Board's policies in this area came in a case involving a statement made by a union representative the day before an election. The employees were told that the employer had profits of $500,000 during the previous year; they had actually amounted to only about $50,000. The Board discounted the statement and certified the union on the basis of the election results, agreeing with an earlier ruling by an NLRB regional director that "there was no evidence that [the union representative] had or could reasonably be perceived to have had knowledge concerning the employer's profits."

Although members John H. Fanning and Howard Jenkins, Jr., certified the election, they strongly disagreed with the abolition of the *Hollywood Ceramics* standards. They perceived a vital need to maintain election standards that "call a halt to misrepresentations considerably short of fraud." The two dissenters argued that any doubts as to the fairness of an election could have been properly resolved by the discarded standards, but now, without the Board's investigatory policy, there will be lingering doubt as to the fairness of elections—creating unstable collective bargaining relationships and, therefore, an unhealthy climate for industrial peace.

The dissenters contended that the number of elections investigated (300 to 400 per year) was an excellent investment in maintaining the tougher standards; the fact that roughly 7 percent of these cases result in second elections "can hardly be viewed as burdensome."

Fanning and Jenkins also refuted the empirical data cited by the majority,[7] terming it a "dubious proposition" that it constitutes a statistically significant sample. Even so, they stressed, the validity of the results are "surely limited to campaigns conducted in accordance with *Hollywood Ceramics* standards." They concluded that any relaxation of the standards will lead to an escalation in campaign charges and counter charges made with the assumption that the opposition will be less likely to challenge the validity of any statement. "As 'bad money drives out the good,' so misrepresentation, if allowed to take the field unchallengeable as to its impact, will tend to drive out the responsible statement."

'Bona fide' seniority and racial bias

A seniority system that may perpetuate the effects of an employer's previous discriminatory policies is not necessarily in violation of Title VII of the 1964 Civil Rights Act, the Supreme Court recently declared. The Court found that "bona fide" seniority systems, those designed without discriminatory intent, are specifically sanctioned by the legislative in-

tent of Section 703(h) of Title VII. The majority opinion, written by Justice Potter Stewart, states that "[e]ven where the employer's pre-Act discrimination resulted in whites having greater existing seniority rights than Negroes. . . . the congressional judgment was that Title VII should not. . . . destroy or water down the vested seniority rights of employees simply because their employer had engaged in discrimination prior to the passage of the Act." (*Teamsters v. United States* and *T.I.M.E.-D.C. v. United States.*[8])

Although the seniority system was held to be valid in this case, the Court was still confronted with the question of relief for the specific victims of discrimination. As in its decision in *Franks v. Bowman Transportation Co.,*[9] the High Court interpreted the "make whole" provision of Title VII to include the award of retroactive seniority to proven discriminatees. However, finding no "explicit reference in the legislative history" concerning employees who were discriminated against prior to the effective date of the act, the Court also reaffirmed its holding in *Franks* that retroactive seniority can only be awarded to those minorities discriminated against after the act took effect.

The Court's interpretation of the congressional intent embodied in Title VII was handed down in a case involving a nationwide trucking company and the union representing a large group of its employees. The Government brought a class action suit against both the company and the union, alleging that the company had engaged in a pattern or practice of discriminating against Negroes and Spanish-surnamed persons. The Government contended that minority members, hired in lower paying jobs were virtually denied advancement to higher paying jobs because of the effects of both the company's discriminatory policies and the union-maintained seniority system.

In the trucking industry, there exists a widespread practice of maintaining separate bargaining units for city drivers and line (long distance) drivers. As a result, a city driver loses his seniority if he transfers to a higher paying line driver job. Because almost all minority employees were hired as city drivers, the Government argued in this case that both the company's employment policy and the union's seniority system were in violation of Title VII.

The trial court found that the Government had produced a "preponderance of evidence" showing that the company had engaged in a "plan or practice" of employment discrimination. The court also found the seniority system to be in violation of Title VII and enjoined both the company and the union from using it in the future. The court then granted relief to all minorities, dividing the employees into three groups based on the severity of an individual's injury. The company and the union appealed the district court's decision, but the appeals court upheld the verdict and modified the relief in favor of the minority employees.

The Supreme Court also ruled against the company, but vacated the injunction against the union's seniority system. The Court also revised the extent to which relief should be granted, ruling that the "actual victims of the company's discriminatory policies" need to be determined on an individual basis. This, however, does not exclude those individuals who would have applied for a position as line driver but for the company's discriminatory policies. Thus, for the first time, the Court held that "an incumbent employee's failure to apply for a job is not an inexorable bar to an award of retroactive seniority. . . . When a person's desire for a job is not translated into a formal application solely because of his unwillingness to engage in a futile gesture he is . . . a victim of discrimination."

Justice Thurgood Marshall (concurring in part and dissenting in part) reasoned that, because the Court acknowledges that Congress never specifically addressed the problem posed by "pre-Act discriminatees already engaged in less desirable jobs," there is no basis for the Court to decide what the legislative intent might have been. Marshall decried the "devastating impact of today's holding" and does not believe that "the Congress that enacted Title VII would have agreed to postpone for one generation the achievement of economic equality."

In brief . . .

THE BAR OVERTURNED ON UNION REPRESENTATION. With the aid of the Supreme Court's ruling in *Goldfarb* v. *Virginia State Bar*,[10] the National Labor Relations Board ruled that law firms have a "direct and sufficient" impact upon interstate commerce to warrent the assertion of the Board's jurisdiction. (*Foley, Hoag & Eliot*.[11])

The unanimous decision, reversing a 1973 ruling,[12] grants a hearing on the petition filed by a union seeking to represent the file clerks and messengers of a Boston law firm. Although the Board recognizes that "in certain unusual situations" a unionized staff may conflict with the confidential attorney-client relationship, it finds no reason to treat law firm employees differently under the National Labor Relations Act. The Board will establish appropriate jurisdictional standards for law firms after the hearing is held. ☐

------FOOTNOTES------

[1] *Abood v. Detroit Board of Education*, 45 U.S.L.W. 4473 (U.S. May 23, 1977)

[2] 351 U.S. 225 (1956); see *Monthly Labor Review*, August 1956, pp. 941-45.

[3] 367 U.S. 740 (1961); see *Monthly Labor Review*, Sept. 1961, pp. 988-1005.

[4] *Shopping Kart Food Market, Inc.* and *Retail Clerks Union Local 99*, 228 NLRB No. 190, April 13, 1977.

[5] 140 NLRB 221 (1962).

[6] Getman and Goldberg, "The Behavioral Assumptions Underlying NLRB Regulation of Campaign Misrepresentations: An Empirical Evaluation," 28 *Standford Law Review* 263 (1976).

[7] Ibid.

[8] *International Brotherhood of Teamsters v. United States* and *T.I.M.E.-D.C. v. United States*, 45 U.S.L.W. 4506 (U.S. May 31, 1977).

[9] *Franks v. Bowman Transportaion Co.*, 424 U.S. 747 (1976). See *Monthly Labor Review*, June 1976, pp. 51-55.

[10] *Goldfarb v. Virginia State Bar*, 421 U.S. 773 (1975).

[11] *Foley, Hoag & Eliot and United File Room Clerks and Messengers of Foley, Hoag & Eliot*, 229 NLRB No. 80, May 8, 1977.

[12] *Bodle, Fogel, Julber, Reinhardt & Rothschild*, 206 NLRB 512 (1973).

Saturday services

In 1972, Congress amended Title VII of the 1964 Civil Rights Act to define "religion" in the context of employment discrimination. The amendment unequivocally affirmed an Equal Employment Opportunity Commission guideline that employers must "reasonably accommodate" the religious needs of their employees—as long as no "undue hardship" is imposed upon the employer. However, neither Congress nor the EEOC provided any specific examples as to how far an employer must go to satisfy his obligation.

The Supreme Court recently reduced this definitional void by ruling that an employer is not required to arrange Saturdays off for an employee so that he may observe his Sabbath, if in doing so the employer would incur more than minimal costs—such as overtime pay for a replacement. The Court also ruled that, if employees' work schedules are determined on the basis of seniority, an employer is not required to violate the seniority privileges of others so that an employee can observe a Saturday Sabbath. *(Trans World Airlines, Inc. v. Hardison.*[1]*)*

Larry Hardison, hired in 1967 as a clerk by Trans World Airlines, became active in the Worldwide Church of God in 1968. The religion observes a Saturday Sabbath whereby believers must refrain from any work between sunset Friday and sunset Saturday. Because he had accumulated some seniority (the basis for determining shift assignments), Hardison was able to arrange his work schedule so that he could observe his Sabbath. However, when he requested and received a transfer to another building, his seniority status at the new job was insufficient to enable him to take Saturdays off on a regular basis.

TWA gave his union permission to change Hardison's work assignments, but the union refused to do so because of the seniority provisions in its contract. In addition, the company would not allow Hardison to work a 4-day week; because it was crucial, the company said, his position would

"Significant Decisions in Labor Cases" was written this month by Gregory J. Mounts, of the *Monthly Labor Review* staff.

have had to be filled either by an employee from another area, which would have impaired the efficiency of that operation, or by someone not scheduled to work Saturdays, requiring the company to pay overtime.

Hardison, the company, and the union could reach no alternative solution. When he refused to report to work on Saturdays, Hardison was given a hearing and discharged for insubordination. He then filed suit in Federal court against both the company and the union, claiming that their actions violated Title VII's religious discrimination provisions. The District Court rejected his claim, holding that TWA had "satisfied its 'reasonable accommodation' obligations." Additionally, the trial court ruled that the union was not required to disregard its seniority system.

The Eighth Circut Court of Appeals reversed the favorable judgment for TWA, ruling that the company had not fulfilled its "accommodation" requirement. The court held that none of the possible solutions available to the company, involving overtime pay, loss of efficiency, or a breach of the seniority system provisions of the contract, imposed an "undue hardship" on TWA. However, because Hardison apparently failed to contest it, the court affirmed the judgment in favor of the union without ruling on its "substantive merits."

In reversing the Appeals Court, the Supreme Court ruled that TWA had met its obligation under Title VII. Thus, the Court avoided the question of whether the "reasonable accommodation" provision of the statute might be "an establishment of religion" contrary to the First Amendment to the Constitution.

The Court's decision reflected a concern that the rights of many should not be sacrificed for the rights of a few. The majority opinion, written by Justice Byron White, states:

> It is essential to TWA's business to require Saturday and Sunday work from at least a few employees even though most employees preferred those days off. Allocating the burdens of weekend work was a matter for collective bargaining. In considering criteria to govern this allocation, TWA and the union had two alternatives: adopt a neutral system, such as seniority, a lot-

tery, or rotating shifts; or allocate days off in accordance with the religious needs of its employees. TWA would have had to adopt the latter in order to assure Hardison and others like him of getting the days off necessary for strict observance of their religion, but it would have done so only at the expense of others who had strong, but perhaps nonreligious reasons for not working on weekends. There were no volunteers to relieve Hardison on Saturdays, and to give Hardison Saturdays off, TWA would have had to deprive another employee of his shift preference at least in part because he did not adhere to a religion that observed the Saturday Sabbath.

. . . . It would be anomalous to conclude that by "reasonable accommodation" Congress meant that an employer must deny the shift and job preference of some employees, as well as deprive them of their contractual rights, in order to accommodate or prefer the religious needs of others, and we conclude that Title VII does not require an employer to go that far.

White concluded that the same rationale applies to any additional costs an employer might have to pay in order to grant employees time off for religious observance. He reasoned: ". . . to require TWA to bear additional costs when no such costs are incurred to give other employees the days off that they want would involve unequal treatment of employees on the basis of their religion."

In dissent, Justices Thurgood Marshall and William Brennan, Jr., state that, in terms of social policy, the Court's decision is "deeply troubling." In Marshall's words, ". . . a society that truly values religious pluralism cannot compel adherents of minority religions to make the cruel choice of surrendering their religion or their job." He also felt that the majority had exceeded its judicial authority, "for the Court adopts the very position that Congress expressly rejected in 1972, as if we were free to disregard congressional choices that a majority of this Court thinks unwise . . . [D]espite Congress' best efforts, one of this Nation's pillars of strength—our hospitality to religious diversity—has been seriously eroded. All Americans will be a little poorer until today's decision is erased."

Layoff aid denied

A State can withhold jobless benefits from workers laid off as a result of a strike against their employer, the Supreme Court recently ruled, even when they are not involved in the strike because it occurs at another location. In an 8 to 0 decision, the Court determined that the "labor dispute disqualification" in Ohio's unemployment compensation statute does not conflict with Federal law, nor does it violate the due process and equal protection guarantees of the Fourteenth Amendment

to the Constitution. *(Ohio Bureau of Employment Services v. Hodory.* [2]*)*

In 1974, Leonard Hodory was employed as a millwright apprentice with United States Steel Corp. in Youngstown, Ohio. The manufacturing facilities operated with fuel produced by company-owned coal mines located throughout the country. As a result of a United Mine Workers' strike, however, fuel supplies dwindled, and the Youngstown plant was eventually forced to close.

After being laid off, Hodory filed for unemployment compensation, but his claim was denied because, at the time, State law disqualified persons who were unemployed "due to a labor dispute other than a lockout at any factory . . . owned or operated by the employer . . ." Hodory then filed a class action suit in Federal court, claiming that the statute violated the Federal laws that established—and continue to influence—the State-run unemployment compensation programs. Although the trial court did not resolve this statutory issue, it upheld Hodory's additional contention that the Ohio law violated his constitutional rights. The three-judge court reasoned that the State had no rational or legitimate interest in discriminating against "individuals who were unemployed through no fault of their own and neither participated in nor benefited from the labor dispute involving another union and their employer." [3]

In considering the case, the Supreme Court reviewed the issue of Federal pre-emption, which the trial court had left unresolved. The Court discounted Hodory's assertion that, in designing the scheme of unemployment compensation, the congressional intent was to award benefits to all "involuntarily unemployed" persons. The justices could find only one reference in the "voluminous legislative history of the Social Security Act" [4] that, "on its face," could possibly support his claim. However, they found that, when viewed in context, the single sentence "is only an expression of caution that funds should not be dispensed too freely, and is not a direction that funds must be dispensed."

After surveying the remaining Federal legislative history of unemployment compensation, Justice Harry Blackmun, writing for the Court, said:

"...when Congress wished to impose or forbid a condition for compensation, it was able to do so in explicit terms. . . The fact that Congress has chosen not to legislate on the subject of labor dispute disqualifications confirms our belief that neither the Social Security Act not the Federal Unemployment Tax Act intended to restrict the States' freedom to legislate in this area."

In reversing the lower court on the constitutional question, the High Court focused on whether the statute had a "rational relation to a legitimate State interest." In previous cases questioning legislative actions, the Court has acknowledged that the legislative task of creating distinctions is one where "[p]erfection . . . is neither possible nor necessary."[5]

Blackmun reasoned that, in legislating its unemployment compensation program, the State was compelled to consider the effects not only for the benefit recipients but for the contributors to the fund and for the fiscal integrity of the fund itself. Therefore, he found:

> Looking only at the face of the statute, an acceptable rationale immediately appears. The disqualification is triggered by "a labor dispute other than a lockout." In other words, if a union goes on strike the employer's contributions are not increased, but if the employer locks out, all his employees thus put out of work are compensated and the employer's contributions accordingly are increased. Although one might say that this system provides only "rough justice," its treatment of the employer is far from irrational.

The Court also affirmed the State's contention that, by limiting the number of recipients, the statute served a legitimate interest in protecting the fiscal integrity of the fund.

Although the lower court's decision in favor of Hodory was reversed, there was some consolation for him—and the class he represented. Acting before the trial court had delivered its verdict, the Ohio Legislature amended the contested statute to permit benefits for a person unemployed as a result of a strike at another location "if it is shown that he is not financing, participating in, or directly interested in such labor dispute."

Jobless fathers defined by State

Benefit eligibility was also the subject of another case recently decided by the Supreme Court. This time, the issue concerned welfare benefits for families of unemployed fathers, and, as it did in *Hodory,* the Court affirmed the authority of States to deny payments if the father is unemployed as a result of a strike. The close (5 to 4) decision upheld a Federal regulation that allows individual States to determine when a father is "unemployed" for purposes of receiving benefits. (*Batterton v. Francis*[6])

When the Aid to Families with Dependent Children—Unemployed Fathers program was established by Congress in 1961, States were given the authority to establish their own criteria for "unemployment." However, to eliminate variations in coverage, Congress amended the statute in 1968 so that the definition of "unemployment" would be "(as determined in accordance with the standards prescribed by the Secretary [of Health, Education, and Welfare])."

The HEW regulation that suddenly became the basis for a "uniform national standard" provided only an "hours-worked" criterion for unemployment. Thus, because Maryland continued to deny AFDC-UF benefits using more extensive criteria (unemployment due to a labor dispute other than a lockout, dismissal for misconduct, or voluntarily quitting a job), two jobless fathers who were denied benefits brought suit in the U.S. District Court. The Court's holding, summarily affirmed by the Supreme Court, was that the State law violated the national standards established by the Federal regulation. (*Francis v. Davidson.*)[7]

To "nullify the effect" of the judicial decision, HEW amended its regulation to give the States the option of denying benefits to families when the father's unemployment "results from participation in a labor dispute or . . . by reason of conduct or circumstances which would result in disqualification for unemployment compensation under the State's law."[8]

In *Davidson,* the District Court had enjoined Maryland from enforcing its own criteria for "unemployment," but, based on the amended HEW regulation, the State petitioned the court to lift the injunction. The court ruled that there was no longer a conflict between the Federal and State regulations, but it continued the injunction on the grounds that the amended Federal regulation conflicted with the congressional statute "because it delegated the question of coverage to the States without providing a uniform national standard." The State appealed, but the Fourth Circuit upheld the lower court's decision.

In the Supreme Court's decision, the central question was whether the Secretary of HEW had properly carried out the statutory responsibility delegated to him by Congress. Writing for the majority, Justice Harry Blackmun reasoned that, because the Federal regulation in this case has a "legislative effect, . . . [i]t can be set aside only if the Secretary exceeded his authority or if the regulation is 'arbitrary, capricious, an abuse of discretion, or not otherwise in accordance with law'." He found, however, that the regulation "does not even approach the limits of delegated authority."

Blackmun acknowledged that the congressional intent of the 1968 amendment was "to retract some of the authority previously delegated to the States," but he reasoned that this did not require the Secretary "to adopt a regulation that precludes any recognition of local policies." The majority declared that " . . . we have no quarrel with the statement in the legislative history that the Secretary is *authorized* to adopt such a uniform [national] definition; we simply hold that he is not *required* to do so."

In dissent, Justice Byron White, joined by Justices William Brennan, Jr., Thurgood Marshall, and John Stevens, claimed that "literally *all* of the relevant legislative history repeatedly and unequivocally affirms the strong congressional objective of creating a Federal definition of unemployment." White agreed with the majority that the Court should "defer to any reasonable definition given by the Secretary to the term 'unemployment'." However, he asserted, the effect of the present regulation is to circumvent the congressional intent by returning to the States the authority to define "unemployment."

In brief . . .

WHEN IN DEBT, IT HELPS TO BE A 'PERSON.' Found to have violated its contract by engaging in an unauthorized strike, Teamsters Local 600 in St. Louis, Mo., was faced with $6 million in damages. The union, seeking relief, successfully filed a petition for bankruptcy.

The employers, a group of more than 60 trucking companies, contested the bankruptcy court's ruling to no avail. However, the truckers took their case to District Court, and, there, the judge held that only a "person" is entitled to the benefits of voluntary bankruptcy. The definition of a "person" includes "corporations," but, the court said, "[u]nlike a corporation, a labor union does not pool capital for the purposes of investment and profit. Its assets are mainly its members who can collectively obtain bargaining leverage in labor-management negotiations. Its other financial functions are ancillary to this pur-

pose." (*Highway and City Freight Drivers, Dockmen, and Helpers.* [9])

In overruling the bankruptcy court, the Federal judge found that the legislative history of the Bankruptcy Act—amended in 1926 to provide the current definition of a corporation—indicates that Congress was "well aware" of labor union activity at the time. Thus, he ruled that, because unions are not specifically covered by the Act, the law should not be construed to include them.

NLRB EXTENDS SOVEREIGNTY. When they occur within the United States, commercial activities of foreign governments or their agents will now be subject to the full jurisdiction of the National Labor Relations Board. [10] Although the Board had consistently declined to assert its jurisdiction over such employers since 1967, the members unanimously agreed that the Chicago branch of the State Bank of India has a sufficient impact on interstate commerce and "meets the Board's present jurisdictional standards for the assertion of jurisdiction thereover."

The Board said that its decision is "reinforced" by the Foreign Sovereign Immunities Act of 1976. The Act stipulates that, in regards to commercial activity, foreign states will be treated in the same manner by the courts as any private individual within the territorial limits of the United States. Thus, the Board stated, ". . . we find that it will effectuate the purposes of the Act to assert jurisdiction herein."

The union involved in the case sought to represent the employees in the Chicago branch of the bank. The Board's decision, reversing the order of the regional director, provides for a secret-ballot election and requires all eligible employees to vote. ☐

------FOOTNOTES------

[1] *Trans World Airlines, Inc. v. Hardison,* 45 U.S.L.W. 4672 (U.S. June 16, 1977).

[2] *Ohio Bureau of Employment Services v. Hodory,* 45 U.S.L.W. 4544 (U.S. May 31, 1977).

[3] *Hodory,* 408 F. Supp. at 1022 (ND Ohio).

[4] Report of the Committee on Economic Security, as reprinted in Hearings on S. 1130 before the Committee on Finance of the United States Senate, 74th Cong., 1st Sess., pp. 1311–1328 (1935).

[5] From the opinion of the Court in *Dandridge v. Williams,* 397 U.S. at 485

[6] *Batterton v. Francis,* 45 U.S.L.W. 4768 (U.S. June 20, 1977)

[7] *Francis v. Davidson,* 340 F. Supp. 351 (Md.), affirmed 409 U.S. 904 (1972)

[8] 38 Fed. Reg. 49 (1973).

[9] *In the matter of Highway and City Freight Drivers, Dockmen, and Helpers, Local No. 600,* 127 DAILY LAB. REP. A-9 (E.D. Mo., In Bankruptcy No. 77–131 C(3), June 20, 1977).

[10] *State Bank of India* and *Chicago Joint Board, Amalgamated Clothing and Textile Workers Union, AFL-CIO,* 229 NLRB No. 137, May 26, 1977.

To guard or be guarded

Section 703(e) of Title VII permits sex-based discrimination "in those certain instances where . . . sex . . . is a bona fide occupational qualification reasonably necessary to the normal operation of that business or enterprise." Indicating that this amendment was intended to be an "extremely narrow exception to the general prohibition of discrimination on the basis of sex," the Supreme Court recently used it to uphold an Alabama regulation that prohibits the employment of women as prison guards in "contact positions" (requiring continual close physical proximity to inmates) within the State's correctional facilities. (*Dothard v. Rawlinson.*[1])

Dianne Rawlinson filed a class action suit in district court when she was denied employment as a prison guard for failing to meet the 120-pound minimum weight requirement of the position. The position also required a minimum height of 5 feet 2 inches. While her suit was pending, the Alabama Board of Corrections adopted a regulation that established gender criteria for hiring prison guards that, essentially, denied women employment in all "contact" positions. Rawlinson amended her complaint to include the new regulation, charging that both it and the physical requirements of the position were in violation of Title VII and the Equal Protection Clause of the Fourteenth Amendment to the Constitution.

The district court ruled that because the height and weight requirements would exclude more than 41 percent of all women and less than 3 percent of all men in the country, their use constituted unlawful sex discrimination. The court also held the new regulation to be in violation of Title VII, ruling that the "bona fide occupational qualification" defense offered by the State is valid in only the narrowest of exceptions.

Although agreeing with the lower court on the illegality of the physical requirements, the Supreme Court reversed the decision on Alabama's new regulation. Writing for the Court, Justice Potter Stewart explained:

> The environment in Alabama's penitentiaries is a peculiarly inhospitable one for human beings of whatever sex. Indeed, a Federal district court has held that the conditions of confinement in the prisons of the State, characterized by 'rampant violence' and a 'jungle atmosphere,' are constitutionally intolerable . . . . In the usual case, the argument that a particular job is too dangerous for women may appropriately be met by the rejoinder that it is the purpose of Title VII to allow the individual woman to make the choice for herself. More is at stake in this case, however, than an individual woman's decision to weigh and accept the risks of employment in a 'contact' position in a maximum security male prison.

> The essence of the correctional counselor's job is to maintain prison security. A woman's relative ability to maintain order in a male maximum security, unclassified penitentiary of the type Alabama now runs could be directly reduced by her womanhood. There is a basis in fact for expecting that sex offenders who have criminally assaulted women in the past would be moved to do so again if access to women were established within the prison. There would also be a real risk that other inmates, deprived of a normal heterosexual environment, would assault women guards because they were women. In a prison system where violence is the order of the day, where inmate access to guards is facilitated by dormitory living arrangements, where every institution is understaffed, and where a substantial portion of the inmate population is composed of sex offenders mixed at random with other prisoners, there are few visible deterrents to inmate assaults on women custodians. . . . The likelihood that inmates would assault a woman because she was a woman would pose a real threat not only to the victim of the assault but also to the basic control of the penitentiary and protection of its inmates and other security personnel. The employee's very womanhood would thus directly undermine her capacity to provide the security that is the essence of a correctional counselor's responsibility.

In a dissent joined by Justice William Brennan, Justice Thurgood Marshall found that the majority's opinion, allowing continued employment discrimination on the basis of sex, was formulated on the very same gender generalizations that Title VII was meant to abolish:

"Significant Decisions in Labor Cases" was written this month by Gregory J. Mounts, of the *Monthly Labor Review* staff. The summary of *Hoffman v. Dunlop* was prepared by Dudley E. Young, Assistant Commissioner, Office of Employment Structures and Trends, Bureau of Labor Statistics.

. . . [T]he fundamental justification for the decision is that women as guards will generate sexual assaults. With all respect, this rationale regrettably perpetuates one of the most insidious of the old myths about women —that women, wittingly or not, are seductive sexual objects. The effect of the decision, made I am sure with the best of intentions, is to punish women because their very presence might provoke sexual assaults. It is women who are made to pay the price in lost job opportunities for the threat of depraved conduct by prison inmates. Once again, '[t]he pedestal upon which women have been placed has . . . upon closer inspection, been revealed as a cage.' It is particularly ironic that the cage is erected here in response to feared misbehavior by imprisoned criminals.

Credit the vet

Employers who rehire a returning veteran are required to credit the employee's military service toward the calculation of pension benefits, the Supreme Court recently ruled. A unanimous Court concluded that "pension payments are predominantly rewards for continuous employment with the same employer," rather than deferred compensation for services rendered. Thus, the purpose of Section 9 of the Selective Service Act, as explained by Justice Thurgood Marshall for the Court, is to protect veterans "from the loss of such rewards when the break in their employment resulted from their response to the country's military needs." (*Alabama Power Co. v. Davis.*[2])

Section 9(b) of the Act not only requires an employer to rehire a returning veteran in his former position or "a position of like seniority, status, and pay," but also requires that any person restored to such a position:

shall be considered as having been on furlough or leave of absence during his period of training and service in the Armed Forces, shall be so restored without loss of seniority, shall be entitled to participate in insurance or other benefits offered by the employer . . . , and shall not be discharged from such position without cause within 1 year after such restoration.

Because neither the language nor the legislative history of the Act provides a definition of a veteran's protected "seniority," Marshall relies on prior Supreme Court rulings,[3] identifying "two axes of analysis" that provide a basis for deciding whether a benefit is a right of seniority protected by Section 9 of the act:

If the benefit would have accrued, with reasonable certainty, had the veteran been continuously employed by the private employer, and if it is in the nature of a reward for length of service, it is a 'perquisite of seniority.' If, on the other hand, the veteran's right to the benefit at the time he entered the military was subject to a significant contingency, or if the benefit is in the nature of short-term compensation for services rendered, it is not an aspect of seniority within the coverage of Section 9.

Employed by Alabama Power since 1936, Raymond E. Davis worked continuously on a full-time basis until March 1943, when he left to serve in the Armed Forces. Honorably discharged in October 1945, he was rehired by the company 1 week later and given his former position.

The company adopted its pension plan on July 1, 1944, giving employees credit for employment prior to that date. The plan is funded solely by the company, and all full-time regular employees (working at least 40 hours per week) are eligible for the plan. Those employees who have reached their 25th birthday and have completed 1 year of employment with the firm are covered. The usual retirement age is 65, but employees may retire at 55 and receive reduced benefits if they have 20 years of service with the company.

At the age of 61, Davis retired and was granted a pension of $198.95 per month. However, the company had not included his military service toward the computation of benefits; had it, his monthly payment would be $216.06.

In maintaining that Davis is entitled to the higher pension, Marshall reasoned that, had he not entered the military, he would "almost certainly have accumulated accredited service for the period." Marshall also concluded, using the "two axes of analysis," that because pension benefits are rewards for "length of service," the higher pension, calculated by including military service time, is a "seniority" right, protected under the Selective Service Act.

The Court's decision affirms the ruling by the Appeals Court, which had upheld the decision of the trial court.

New 'BLS method'—no loose change

Federal funds for several programs administered by the Departments of Labor, Commerce, and Treasury are allocated among the States and individual communities, in substantial part, by the number of unemployed and the rate of unemployment. The unemployment data used in making these allocations are compiled by the State employment security agencies in accordance with the instructions issued by the Bureau of Labor Statistics.

Responsibility for the methods used in the preparation of estimates of employment and unemployment for the States and local areas was transferred to BLS in 1972, and, in 1974, BLS began implementing a new procedure for gathering and preparing the unemployment data in the States. Prior to the implementation of the new "BLS method," data were gathered under the Manpower Administration statistical method (MA method). The new procedure uses the annual unemployment data derived from the Current Population Survey to adjust the estimates derived from Unemployment Insurance data and also provides a method for correcting current monthly data.

When the change in statistical techniques was made in New Jersey, the State found that the new method resulted in a potential loss of approximately $20 to $25 million in Federal funds provided through the Comprehensive Employment and Training Act of 1973 (CETA).

The Commissioner of Labor and Industry of the State of New Jersey, stating that the new "BLS method" was not being fully implemented in all 50 States, filed suit in Federal district court because the disparity in application, he said, "has acted to deny the citizens of New Jersey the equal protection of the law guaranteed by the due process clause of the Fifth Amendment" to the Constitution. The New Jersey commissioner also argued that the Secretary of Labor, in implementing the new method, exceeded his authority and acted in an arbitrary and capricious manner in violation of the Administrative Procedure Act. *(Hoffman v. Dunlop.*[4]*)*

Relying on the Supreme Court's decision in *Citizens to Preserve Overton Park v. Volpe,*[5] which noted that "a district court's function would not involve a *de novo* review of the administrative decision," the Federal judge found that the Secretary had not exceeded his authority:

> In resolving the question of whether the Secretary's challenged action was arbitrary and capricious, we must consider whether that 'decision was based on a consideration of relevant factors and whether there has been a clear error of judgment.' After a thorough consideration of all of the evidence presented by the parties, it is clear that both the BLS and MA methods are not statistically perfect. Nor do the proponents of each suggest that their method is infallible. Nevertheless, without deciding which system is the more accurate—for it would serve no useful purpose here to attempt to compare or evaluate the statistical virtues and shortcomings

of the sophisticated and complex methodologies championed by each of the parties—this Court concludes that the implementation of the BLS method was clearly not an action which could be described as either arbitrary or capricious. In short, the plaintiff failed to satisfy that burden of proof. The defendants' witnesses, all highly qualified and most credible as experts in the field of statistics and demography, testified to the careful preparation taken by the Department of Labor before instituting the BLS method. On the other hand, the plaintiff's experts concentrated on pointing out flaws in the BLS method but, importantly, did not provide the Court with even the slightest indication that the newer method was an arbitrary exercise of administrative power.

Finally, we conclude that the government's original implementation of the BLS method in certain States, including New Jersey, while retaining the MA method in other States does not contravene the requirement of equal protection as embodied in the Due Process Clause of the Fifth Amendment. Again, the concept of equal protection demands only that the government demonstrate a rational basis to support its actions.[6]

The facts reveal that New Jersey was in the original group of States which utilized the BLS method. These States were the 19 most heavily populated in the Nation, accounting for approximately 75 percent of the Nation's total population. At the time the BLS method was introduced, the government did not have adequate data available to permit the utilization of that method in the less populous States. However, as sufficient data becomes available to the government as to the less populous States, the government will and does employ the BLS method as to such States. Indeed, the government has projected that in 1977 the BLS method would be utilized in all 50 States.

This Court, therefore, is satisfied that the decision to implement the BLS method in New Jersey reflects the rational basis which is necessary to sustain its constitutionality.

In view of the large sums allocated on the basis of these data, more than $16 billion in 1977, the importance of this decision—firmly upholding the authority of the Bureau of Labor Statistics to prescribe methods for use in the compilation of statistics on unemployment by State employment security agencies—can hardly be overestimated. □

---FOOTNOTES---

[1] *Dothard v. Rawlinson,* 45 U.S.L.W. 4888 (U.S. June 27, 1977).

[2] *Alabama Power Co. v. Davis,* 45 U.S.L.W. 4588 (U.S. June 6, 1977).

[3] The following cases, involving an interpretation of the Military Selective Service Act, were the basis for Justice Marshall's "two axes of analysis" in the present case: *Fishgold v. Sullivan Drydock and Repair Corp.,* 328 U.S. 275 (1946); *McKinney v. Missouri-K.-T. R. Co.,* 357 U.S. 265 (1958); *Tilton v. Missouri Pac. R. Co.,* 376 U.S. 169 (1964); *Accardi*

v. Pennsylvania R. Co., 383 U.S. 225 (1966); and *Foster v. Dravo Corp.,* 420 U.S. 92 (1975).

[4] *Hoffman v. Dulop,* (D. N.J., filed June 1, 1977) (No. CA 74–330).

[5] 401 U.S. 402 (1971).

[6] Based on the Supreme Court's decision in *Mathews v. de Castro,* 45 U.S.L.W. 4049 (U.S. Dec. 13, 1976).

Statistical significance

In *Teamsters v. United States,*[1] the Supreme Court established that statistical evidence may be used to make out a prima facie case of a pattern or practice of employment discrimination under Title VII of the 1964 Civil Rights Act. The Court also held, however, that once a prima facie case has been established by statistical work force disparities, the employer must be given an opportunity to show "that the claimed discriminatory pattern is a product of pre-Act hiring rather than unlawful post-Act discrimination."

In one of its last decisions of the 1976–77 term, the Court applied the same reasoning to a case involving alleged employment discrimination on the part of a public school district in Missouri. Although the Government's statistical proof was held to constitute a prima facie case by the lower court, the Supreme Court remanded the case because the employer was not given the opportunity to show that the statistical evidence reflected only pre-Act employment practices.[2] Writing for the 8 to 1 majority, Justice Potter Stewart declared that a public employer did not violate Title VII if, from March 24, 1972 (when Title VII became effective for public employers), all of its employment decisions were made in a "wholly non-discriminatory way," even if it had "formerly maintained an all-white workforce by purposefully excluding Negroes." (*Hazelwood School District v. United States.*[3])

The Federal Government filed a "pattern or practice" suit against Hazelwood, citing a statistical disparity between the percentage of blacks on the school district's faculty and the percentage of teachers in the available area who were black. In addition, the Government also claimed that the school district had engaged in a history of alleged racially discriminatory policies, citing specific instances involving 55 unsuccessful black applicants.

The district court ruled that the Government, having the burden of proof, had failed in each instance. The court found that the statistics showing a disparity of black teachers on the faculty was insufficient because the percentage of black children in the district's school was similarly small.

Holding that the district court had made an irrelevant comparison of black teachers to pupils, the Eighth Circuit Court of Appeals reversed the decision. It contended that the proper comparison was between the percentage of Hazelwood teachers who were black (less than 2 percent) and the percentage of black teachers in the applicable labor market (about 15 percent). The applicable labor market, the court ruled, included the suburban county where the school district was located as well as the nearby City of St. Louis. The court reasoned that, although the percentage of black teachers in the surrounding area (outside St. Louis) was 5.7 percent, one-third of Hazelwood's teachers resided in the city at the time of their initial employment; therefore, both the city and the county should be included in the relevant labor market.

The appeals court found that 16 of the 55 unsuccessful black applicants had been discriminated against. This, the court said, "buttressed" the statistical proof, and, because the school district failed to rebut either the work force statistics or the specific instances of discrimination, the Government was awarded the decision.

The Supreme Court found that the Eighth Circuit was correct in rejecting the district court's statistical comparison; however, the Court ruled that the appeals court had erred by substituting its judgment for that of the district court and, more importantly, by totally disregarding "the possibility that this prima facie statistical proof in the record might at the trial level be rebutted by statistics dealing with Hazelwood's hiring after it became subject to Title VII."

The High Court noted that, during the 2 years after Title VII went into effect, 3.7 percent of the teachers hired by Hazelwood were black. If the relevant labor market does not include the city, as the school district argued, then the resulting statistical disparity "may be sufficiently small to weaken the government's other proof," Stewart acknowledged.

Stewart also faulted the appeals court because it "gave no consideration at all to the possibility that post-Act data as to the number of Negroes hired

"Significant Decisions in Labor Cases" was written this month by Gregory J. Mounts, of the *Monthly Labor Review* staff.

compared to the total number of Negro applicants may well tell a different story." In remanding the case to the district court, Stewart indicated that the relevant labor market should be determined and that applicant flow data should be used, if available.

The Board up against the 'wall'

The National Labor Relations Board was censured recently when it attempted to assert jurisdiction over secondary schools operated by the Roman Catholic Church. The Seventh Circuit Court of Appeals unanimously ruled that, by certifying unions to represent the lay faculty of seven parochial schools, the Board breached the "separation wall"—of church and state—provided by the Religion Clauses of the First Amendment to the Constitution. (*Catholic Bishop of Chicago v. NLRB.*[4])

As of 1975, the Board began accepting jurisdiction over parochial schools that were "merely religiously associated"—where the instruction was not limited to religious subjects.[5] It declined, however, to assert jurisdiction over schools that were "completely religious"—those devoted exclusively to teaching religion or religious subjects.

Based on this two-tiered jurisdictional standard, the Board ordered representation elections in five Indiana diocean high schools and two parochial secondary schools in Chicago. Following the union's success in the elections, the Board certified two bargaining units, one in Indiana and one in Chicago. The employers, however, refused to bargain; the Board issued summary judgments, holding the employers in violation of the Act. As they had hoped, the employers were then able to present their case in Federal court.

Initially, the appeals court addressed the Board's jurisdictional standard, finding it to be "a simplistic black or white, purported rule containing no borderline demarcation of where 'completely religious' takes over or, on the other hand, ceases . . . the dichotomous 'completely religious—merely religiously associated' standard provides no workable guide to the exercise of discretion." Judge Wilbur F. Pell, Jr., writing for the court, concluded that the Board's standard makes virtually all Catholic secondary schools subject to its jurisdiction:

> Under the rationale the Board has adopted, it is readily apparent that secondary schools operated by various dioceses of the Roman Catholic Church can never be characterized as 'completely religious.' Once the employer admits the fact that its schools are performing 'in part the secular function of educating children,' it becomes definitionally impossible under the Board's cases to establish that the institutions can be anything else but 'merely religiously associated' . . . The total

inability of the employers to overcome what appears to be an irrebuttable presumption . . . makes more understandable the complaint of the employers that the Board is cruelly whip-sawing their schools by holding that institutions too religious to receive governmental assistance are not religious enough to be excluded from its regulation.

After reviewing the Supreme Court decisions involving challenges to State aid for parochial schools,[6] the court found that religion permeates the entire curriculum, even the secular subjects such as mathematics and science. Thus, Pell concluded that the purpose of the parochial schools is "to carry out the teaching mission of the Catholic Church." Based on this, he determined that their classification as "merely religiously associated" constituted an "abuse of the Board's discretion." In response, the Board declared that it "would necessarily have to assert jurisdiction over all religious schools in view of the otherwise inclusive scope of the statute under which it operates."

The Board's assertion of such pervasive jurisdiction required the court to address the constitutional issue—whether the Board's interpretation of its authority under the National Labor Relations Act conflicts with the First Amendment. In resolving the question, Judge Pell found that "the very threshold act of certification of the union necessarily alters and impinges upon the religious character of all parochial schools. . . . As the Board recognizes, the Bishop [would] share 'some decision making' with the union and, as a practical matter, must consult the lay faculty's representative on all matters bearing upon the employment arrangement."

The court presented several paradigmatic situations, showing how the Board's bargaining order would infringe upon the rights of the religious community:

> If a bishop, for example, should refuse to renew all lay faculty teacher contracts because he believed that the union had adopted policies and practices at odds with the religious character of the institutions, or because he wanted to replace lay teachers with religious-order teachers who had become available, under ecclesiastical law he would have the right if not the duty to take such action. Yet, under the National Labor Relations Act, he might well be found guilty of an unfair labor practice.

In defending its position, the Board argued that it would be able to separate and thereby avoid any doctrinal issues involved in an investigation of an unfair labor practice. However, when the court hypothesized the discharge of a teacher-heretic and subsequent filing of charges with the Board, the Board's counsel indicated that "the Board would be required in that situation to take cognizance of the religious nature of the grounds for discharge" and, he said, it would be compelled to "try to make some reasonable accommodation to the religious purposes of the school." In considering the Board's argument, the court found that a "reasonable accommodation" would implicitly involve the "necessity of explanation and analysis, and probably verification and justification, of the doctrinal precept involved, all of which would itself erode the protective wall afforded by the constitutional right."

Judge Pell summarized the opinion of the court: "A church which chooses to educate its own young people in schools which it is required essentially to finance without governmental aid should because of the essentially religious permeation of its curriculum be equally freed of the obviously inhibiting effect and impact of the restriction of the National Labor Relations Act in conducting the teaching program of those schools."

Searching for 'probable cause'

Because the Fourth Amendment's "unreasonable search" prohibition applies to Occupational Safety and Health Administration inspections, the agency must show "probable cause" when it seeks to inspect the premises of an employer who does not consent to the inspection, the U.S. District Court for Northern Alabama recently ruled. The court also held that, to satisfy the probable cause requirement, OSHA must have reason to suspect violations in a specific company and not base its request for inspection merely on a reference to "some national accumulated group of statistics" for the industry. (*Marshall v. Shellcast Corp.*[7])

Under OSHA's 2-year-old National Emphasis Program, certain "target" industries are selected for compliance inspections based on the incidence of occupational illness and injury reported during a specific year. The iron and steel foundry industry, having an incidence rate three times higher than the national average in 1973, had thus been selected as a "target" industry.

When two foundries refused to comply with both an initial agency request and, then, inspection warrants issued by a U.S. magistrate, the agency filed charges in Federal court. Because one of the employers questioned the constitutionality of the statutory provision authorizing OSHA to obtain judicial enforcement for an inspection without having to show probable cause, the district judge addressed this issue first. Relying on the Supreme Court's decisions in *Camara v. Municipal Court* and *See v. Seattle*,[8] he reasoned that OSHA is also required by the Fourth Amendment to show probable cause under these circumstances; but the fact that Congress failed to include a procedure by which this can be accomplished does not render the entire statute unconstitutional. Judge Sam Pointer found that, because the statute does not prescribe a penalty for noncomplying employers prior to the matter being presented in some court, "the Court, in making a ruling, may quite appropriately incorporate the necessary provisions of the Fourth Amendment to assure that probable cause is given under the circumstances."

Applying the "probable cause" test to the present case, Pointer found that OSHA had failed to provide "any information to suggest that a particular violation or a particular hazard is likely to be found" on either of the employers' premises. Instead, the agency relied solely on aggregate industry statistics that are "unnecessary and inappropriate" because "the particular incident rate of a particular plant can be obtained if not already obtained," the court declared.

In its decision, the court also took into account the fact that one of the employers, Southern Foundry Corp., had been subjected to two prior OSHA investigations. The more recent of these, in 1975, reported no violations. "Indeed," Judge Pointer declared, "one would certainly raise the question as to whether in 1977, 2 years later, there was probable cause for still a third investigation, even granting the possibility that there had been improvement in the investigatory techniques of OSHA agents." □

———FOOTNOTES———

[1] *International Brotherhood of Teamsters v. United States*, 45 U.S.L.W. 4506 (U.S. May 31, 1977). See *Monthly Labor Review*, August 1977, pp. 48–49.

[2] It was not specifically stated in the opinion, but the Court implied that, because its ruling in *Teamsters* was subsequent to the lower court's decision in this case, the employer had no reason to know how to meet its burden of proof.

[3] *Hazelwood School District v. United States*, 45 U.S.L.W. 4882 (U.S. June 27, 1977).

[4] *Catholic Bishop of Chicago v. NLRB and Illinois Educational Assoc.*, and *Diocese of Fort Wayne—South Bend, Inc. v. NLRB*, 156 DAILY LAB. REP. D-1 (7th Cir., Aug. 3, 1977).

[5] The Board first asserted jurisdiction over parochial schools that were "merely religiously associated" with its decision in *Roman Catholic Archdiocese of Baltimore, Archdiocesan High Schools*, 216 NLRB 249 (1975).

[6] A few of the Supreme Court cases cited by the court included: *Meek v. Pettenger*, 421 U.S. 349 (1975); *Committee for Public Education v. Nyquist*, 413 U.S. 756 (1973); *Walz v. Tax Commission of the City of New York*, 397 U.S. 664 (1970); and *Lemon v. Kurtzman*, 403 U.S. 602 (1971).

[7] *Marshall v. Shellcast Corp.* and *Marshall v. Southern Foundry Corp.*, 155 DAILY LAB. REP. E-1 (USDC N.Ala., July 26, 1977).

[8] *Camara v. Municipal Court*, 387 U.S. 523 (1967); *See v. Seattle*, 387 U.S. 541 (1967).

Supreme Court opens new term

Opening its 1977–78 term on October 3, the U.S. Supreme Court issued summary rulings in 43 cases, agreed to consider arguments in 34 others, and rejected applications for consideration of 449 more. Approximately 60 labor and labor-related cases were denied review, leaving the rulings of lower courts in effect. (Denial of review does not technically affirm lower court holdings, however, because the Court is free to alter them by ruling in other cases raising the same issues.)

Of the labor cases denied review, one *Arado v. United States*,[1] provides a new dimension for judicial enforcement of Title VII discrimination remedies against State or local public employers. The High Court's dismissal left standing a circuit court ruling that Federal revenue sharing funds may be withheld from the City of Chicago because its police department did not comply with court-imposed mandatory hiring and promotion quotas for women and minorities.[2]

In 1974, a Federal district court found that, under Title VII standards, a test administered by the Chicago Police Department for hiring and promotions had a disproportionally adverse impact against women and minority applicants. After 2 years, the department had failed to take affirmative action to end this condition. Seeking a way to enforce its order, the court found that the majority of Chicago's Federal revenue sharing funds was used to pay police salaries. Because these funds are provided through the State and Local Fiscal Assistance Act, which prohibits employment discrimination using the same standards ordinarily applied under Title VII, the court held the city to be in violation of the Act and enjoined the Federal Government from paying all revenue sharing funds to the city. As of late November, the city stood to lose more than $76 million in Federal funds unless it complies with the hiring and promotion quotas.

Another case that was denied review, *NLRB v. Electrical Workers Local No. 388*,[3] has resulted in a new interpretation for a portion of the Taft-Hartley Act. The Seventh Circuit Court of Appeals ruled that the Act's pre-strike notification provision, requiring unions to give health care institutions 10 days notice of intent to strike or picket on their premises, applies only to unions that represent employees of the institution. Thus, the union employees of a contractor hired by the institution do not violate the Act when they picket their employer on the premises without prior notice.

The National Labor Relations Board had held in two earlier cases that the notification provision applied to any union activity against any employer on the premises of the institution. The appeals court, however, could find no reference in the legislative history of the health-care amendments to Taft-Hartley which pertained to the labor activities of other workers at the site.

In its second week of activity, the High Court issued a summary judgment that was particularly significant for public sector employment.[4] Last year, a three-judge Federal district court in Massachusetts ruled that the State's civil service statute, granting veterans priority consideration by ranking those with passing test scores above all other applicants, violated the Equal Protection Clause of the Fourteenth Amendment to the Constitution. (*Anthony v. Massachusetts.*[5]) The court found that the statute discriminated against women, depriving most women of the opportunity for civil service positions solely on the basis of their sex.

The court noted that throughout most of the period since World War II, Federal regulations have limited women to no more than 2 percent of the Armed Forces. Enlistment criteria for women also have been more stringent than those for men. These policies, the court reasoned, have excluded all but a few women from veterans' preference eligibility. Taken in conjunction with the civil service procedure of ranking veterans ahead of all other applicants, the effect is "a one-two punch that absolutely and permanently forecloses, on average, 98 percent of this State's women from obtaining significant civil service appointments," the court declared.

"Significant Decisions in Labor Cases" was written this month by Gregory J. Mounts of the *Monthly Labor Review* staff. Anne L. Jacobson, also of the *Review* staff, wrote the reports on *Ritz V. O'Donnell* and *Lowe V. Pate.*

Voting 6 to 3, the Supreme Court vacated the judgment and remanded the case to the district court with only one instruction—to review the case in light of the Supreme Court's decision in *Washington v. Davis.*[6] In *Washington,* the majority held, in part, that government statutes must have a discriminatory intent to be violative of constitutional rights.

The Court's summary judgment permits Massachusetts and, by implication, 45 other States to continue using veterans' preference in civil service employment. Arkansas, Mississippi, New Mexico, and South Carolina are the only States with no form of veterans' preference.

Lawful leverage

A State may influence the terms of a private collective bargaining contract by threatening to withhold subsidies from an employer who provides vital public services, the U.S. Court of Appeals for the Third Circuit recently held. (*Amalgamated Transit Union v. Byrne.*[7]) Ruling 5 to 4, the court affirmed a district court's dismissal of the suit because the union failed to state a claim on which relief could be granted.

In New Jersey, privately owned transportation companies are provided subsidies by the State to "assure the continuance of that portion of the bus and rail transit services which is essential."[8] When the bus companies began negotiating new contracts with union representatives in 1975, the Governor of New Jersey declared that any company that gave employees larger wage increases than State employees had received or retained unlimited cost-of-living increases in its contract with the union would no longer be subsidized by the State.

Faced with financial peril at the loss of subsidies, the companies presented the State's limiting conditions to the union at the bargaining table. The union strongly objected to the loss of the wage adjustment mechanism, negotiations reached an impasse, and strikes ensued. In Federal court, the union charged that the State interference violated the Supremacy Clause of the Constitution because it infringed on Federal labor policy as established by the National Labor Relations Act. Specifically, it relied on the Supreme Court's interpretation of the Act in *NLRB v. Nash-Finch Co.,*[9] which held that the substance of collective bargaining agreements should be determined by "the free play of economic forces."

In reaching its decision, the appeals court found that the NLRA does not address New Jersey's action in the present case and, therefore, no Federal jurisdiction is involved. The court reasoned that New Jersey's interest in the bargaining "is similar to that of any private purchaser of services which expresses an interest in the terms of a collective bargaining

agreement under consideration by the provider of the services. New Jersey, like a private consumer, is attempting to exert pressure on the parties to the collective bargaining negotiations in order to hold down the costs of purchasing the 'essential' transportation services these companies provide."

Writing for the court, Chief Judge Collins J. Seitz stated that New Jersey was merely establishing the conditions under which it will "spend its own money to insure that transportation services are provided to the public." The State's interest is providing the "essential" transportation services, "rather than regulating labor relations per se," Seitz concluded.

In a lengthy dissent, Judge Ruggero J. Aldisert found, in fundamental contrast to the majority, that the union's complaint did state a specific violation of the National Labor Relations Act. In fact, he, along with Judges Joseph F. Weis and James Hunter III, interpreted the union's charge as a contention that the State had "violated the keystone of our National labor policy." Aldisert cited several Supreme Court decisions[10] that have upheld the unrestricted nature of the collective bargaining process. He concluded that: "The power and authority of a State may not be invoked to disturb the balance of bargaining power existing between negotiating parties, nor may it be used to dictate the substantive terms of a collective bargaining agreement." When the State determines under what financial conditions it will subsidize the transit companies, and then makes these conditions prerequisites to continued subsidization, "the State has transformed these conditions into critical limitations on the terms of the collective bargaining agreement, and has moved beyond the pale of permissible activity," Aldisert declared.

'Employ me' ads may tell all

Pennsylvania jobseekers may once again place newspaper advertisements specifying their race, color, religion, ancestry, age, sex, or national origin. Although the State had barred this practice under its Human Relations Act, the Pennsylvania Commonwealth Court recently ruled that the interests of advertisers in obtaining a job outweighs the State's interest in eradicating employment discrimination.[11]

The Pittsburgh Press Co. was ordered by the State Human Relations Commission to stop publication of situation wanted advertisements such as: "White woman—desires day work, office cleaning;" and "College Grad—Born again Christian with Bachelor's Degree and 7 years sales and marketing management experience seeking work with Christian business or organization." The Commission claimed that such ads propose "purely commercial transactions" that are not protected by the First Amendment.

The Commission also argued that the Supreme Court's 1973 decision in *Pittsburgh Press Co. v. Pittsburgh Commission on Human Rights*[12] should govern this case. In the earlier case, the Court ruled that sex-based classification headings for help-wanted ads could be barred from publication by the Commission's guidelines. Constitutional freedom of the press would not be violated, they said, because the ads were commerical speech, whose publication is no more than a proposition of "a commercial transaction." In the present case, however, the court found that this interpretation of purely commercial speech has been virtually extinguished by more recent Supreme Court rulings.[13] The court noted that the earlier case, although not directly applicable, revealed a close relationship between the speech involved and illegal discrimination by employers. Therefore, the court declared that a balancing test was required to weigh the opposing governmental and First Amendment interests:

> The Commonwealth's asserted interest in the prevention of employment discrimination . . . is certainly a substantial one. Pitted against it is the jobseeker's interest in being able to fully, yet truthfully, utilize the press to 'advertise' himself or herself in that manner and by such terms as he or she believes will be most efficacious in producing the desired result. That this interest must not be minimized can be seen by looking at its component parts. As a pure matter of expression, there is a basic interest of the individual in being able to tell anyone who will listen just who and what the individual is: to be able to say 'I am black' as well as 'I am a college graduate' or 'I am male' as well as 'I am ambitious'. . . . We are dealing with the efforts of individuals to sell the only thing that they have to offer: their labor. For the users of the situation wanted column, often the least skilled and most desperate jobseekers, the quest for employment may cause the liveliest political or social controversy of the day to shrink to insignificance by comparison.

An alternative argument presented by the Commission was that the personal characteristics of the jobseekers would permit employers to discriminate readily in hiring. The court found this to be a simplistic analysis, pointing out that "a fair-minded employer may react in the negative to any ad that specifies race, religion, sex, or national origin." Alternatively, the court added, employers who subscribe to "Equal Opportunity" and "Affirmative Action" could use the descriptions to find more minority applicants to interview for a position.

In finding the balancing test to be weighted heavily in favor of the First Amendment, the court took note of the possible effects of the full implementation of the Commission's now unconstitutional rule. Referring to the range of occupational titles that are still commonly accepted, such as Salesman, Body man, Handyman, and Cleaning Lady, the court declared: "While it may very well be completely valid to require an employer-advertiser to substitute '-person' as the suffix of these words when used to describe a job, to compel an individual to describe himself or herself in such stilted and sterile language, or forgo speaking at all, smacks of the imposed linguistic conformity of an Orwellian nightmare."

Disciplinary latitude

Under Federal law, the courts will intervene in union disciplinary proceedings only in cases of "grievous unfairness." If there is some indication of equity, they will refuse to intercede. Furthermore, the safeguards normally accorded a defendant in a court proceeding, especially a criminal case, do not necessarily apply to a union trial. A case in point is a recent Air Lines Pilot Association trial. (*Ritz v. O'Donnell*.[14])

The controversy grew out of the 1972 merger of Northeast and Delta airlines, which resulted in the integration of the airlines' seniority lists. The Northeast pilots objected to their standing on the new roster. Through their union local, the pilots (led by Captain Karl F. Ritz) attacked the validity of the merged list—filing lawsuits against their national union. The pilots eventually organized a nonprofit corporation through which they collected funds to sustain the battle for their lost seniority rights.

In connection with the financing of this litigation, the union brought disciplinary charges against 10 pilots. The union hearing board dismissed all but one charge. Captain Ritz was convicted of refusing to provide the union with information concerning the funds that were raised for the legal fight on seniority rights, financial information required by the Department of Labor. Ritz had filed the information directly with the Department. The decision was upheld by the union's appeal board, which fined him $500.

Ritz contended that the disciplinary action resulted from his opposition to the union leadership and that he was denied a "full and fair hearing." Affirming the district court's decision, the appeals court found no proof that the union proceedings were a reprisal for Ritz's insurgency. It rejected each of Ritz's objections to the fairness of his trial. The court stressed that, under the Labor Management Reporting and Disclosure Act, its scope of inquiry in a union proceeding is limited to deciding whether there is "some evidence" to support the charges.

Dissenting Judge George E. MacKinnon acknowledged that the court should be reluctant to interfere but found that various procedural irregularities during the union hearing and internal appeal had precluded a just proceeding. For one, he noted, Ritz was required to appear without counsel. The charging parties did not appear at the disciplinary proceedings; they sent an uninformed representative, thus preventing Ritz from cross-examining his accusers. In addition, two members of the hearing board were employed by the same airlines as were two of the pilots who brought the charges. According to union rules, these board members should have been disqualified.

Judge MacKinnon warned, ". . . if the unions wish to continue to exercise the great power they possess over their members without more interference from courts, they should be doubly cautious."

On the waterfront

Assaulting a supervisor does not, in itself, justify dismissal—the attack must be considered "in light of all surrounding facts and circumstances." Reasoning thus, a U.S. court of appeals upheld a jury's verdict that a longshoreman was unfairly discharged and reversed a decision by the trial judge that overturned the jury verdict. (*Lowe v. Pate.*[15])

Presumably upset that he had not been called to work for several days because of a sprained ankle, John Lowe, who had been drinking, attacked his supervisor, knocking him to the ground. Lowe was subsequently eliminated from that supervisor's "gang," but he was allowed to work for other supervisors on jobs for the same employer—Pate Steve-doring Co. The International Longshoremen's Association refused Lowe's request to investigate the case.

Lowe filed a complaint, alleging that he was unjustifiably discharged and that the union had breached its duty of fair representation. A district court jury ruled in his favor. Lowe was awarded damages of $25,500, with the company responsible for one-third of the amount and the union for the rest.

The trial judge overturned the verdict. He stated that assaulting a supervisor was "universally recognized as constituting 'just cause' *per se*" for dismissal. To support his position, the judge cited three labor arbitration decisions. However, the appeals court found that even these cases recognized mitigating circumstances and other arbitration cases showed that an assault should be judged in relationship to surrounding conditions.

The court held that the jury verdict must be sustained if there was "substantial evidence" to support the verdict. No dispute existed over the occurrence of the assault. The court saw grounds for the jury determination, considering that the employee had a perfect record, the supervisor was not seriously hurt, and "knifings, shootings, and baseball bat beatings" were common on the wharves. It noted that even a defense witness had thought that the parties were just "horsing around."

Judge Peter T. Fay dissented, stating that if "unprovoked, malicious assault . . . is not universally recognized as constituting 'just cause' *per se,* it should be." He accused the majority of sanctioning criminal assault: ". . . John Lowe should be punished for the crime he admits committing. Instead, our judicial system rewards him with $25,500." □

———FOOTNOTES———

[1] *Arado v. United States,* 46 U.S.L.W. 3198 (Review denied, U.S. Oct. 3, 1977).

[2] *United States v. City of Chicago,* 13 DAILY LAB. REP. A-4 (7th Cir. Jan. 11, 1977).

[3] *NLRB v. Electrical Workers, Local No. 388,* 46 U.S.L.W. 3201 (Review denied, U.S. Oct. 3, 1977).

[4] *Massachusetts v. Feeney,* 46 U.S.L.W. 3240 (Judgment vacated, U.S. Oct. 11, 1977).

[5] *Anthony v. Massachusetts,* 44 U.S.L.W. 2495 (D. Mass. Mar. 29, 1976). Carol Anthony's claim was found moot when Massachusetts amended the statute, removing the position she sought, Counsel I, from the normal civil service procedures. However, her coplaintiff, Helen B. Feeney, was still subject to the veterans' preference procedures, whereupon the district court ruled in her favor.

[6] *Washington v. Davis,* 426 U.S. 229 (1976).

[7] *Amalgamated Transit Union v. Byrne,* 191 DAILY LAB REP. D-1 (3d Cir. Sept. 22, 1977).

[8] 27 N.J. Stat. Ann. Sec. 1A-28.7 (Supp. 1977).

[9] *NLRB v. Nash-Finch Co.,* 404 U.S. 138, 144 (1971).

[10] *Lodge 76, International Association of Machinists v. Wisconsin Employment Relations Commission,* 427 U.S. 132 (1976); *Teamsters Local 24 v. Oliver,* 358 U.S. 283 (1959); and *Hanna Mining Co. v. Marine Engineers,* 382 U.S. 181 (1965).

[11] *Pittsburgh Press Co. v. Commonwealth of Pennsylvania,* 161 DAILY LAB. REP. A-10 (PaCommwCt, No. 1275, July 21, 1977).

[12] *Pittsburgh Press Co. v. Pittsburgh Commission on Human Rights,* 413 U.S. 376 (1973). For a discussion of the case, see *Monthly Labor Review,* September 1973, pp. 80–83.

[13] For example, the court cited *Linmark Associates, Inc. v. Township of Willingsboro,* 45 U.S.L.W. 441 (U.S. May 2, 1977).

[14] *Ritz v. O'Donnell,* 180 DAILY LAB. REP. D-1 (D.D.C. Sept. 6, 1977).

[15] *Lowe v. Pate Stevedoring Co.,* 178 DAILY LAB. REP. E-1 (5th Cir. Sept. 1, 1977).

LABOR AND THE LAW

The Supreme Court, for the most part, has discretion to hear or not hear cases presented to it for review. Its selection of which issues to review, and which to leave to lower courts, can have as much impact upon the development of the law as the outcome in cases it does decide. Since the 1975 Labor and Law report there has been a sharp change in the labor law issues the Court is selecting, but no change in the Court's high interest in the field.

In the past, the Court's main emphasis has been on the "traditional" area of labor-management relations in the private sector of the economy. In the 1973 and 1974 terms, for example, 21 of 44 labor law cases—nearly 50 percent—concerned the National Labor Relations Act, its preemptive effect on state regulation, or the enforcement of collective agreements. In contrast, in the past two years, the Court decided 54 labor law cases but only 11—about 20 percent—involved private sector labor-management relations.

The decrease in NLRA cases has been more than offset by the Court's increased attention to two areas which in the past were given only intermittent glances—the rights of public employees and discrimination in employment based on race, sex, religion or national origin. The past two years have seen 19 cases dealing with state and federal employees, including several cases of major importance, and 19 civil rights employment discrimination cases, several of which have recast the law of employment discrimination as it had been developing in the lower courts since the 1964 Civil Rights Act was passed. Two years ago there were only 12 cases in these two areas combined.

In the labor-management relations area, decreased interest of the Supreme Court must be seen as helpful. For, the Court as presently constituted seems disposed, when it does decide important cases in this area, to decide against the union position. Of the 21 "traditional" labor cases discussed in the last report, for example, 12 were decided against the union position, and most of the remainder were either decided in a neutral fashion or were of minor importance. In the last two terms, however, only one labor-management case of major importance was lost. The other two setbacks in this area were encompassed in opinions which may ultimately prove useful to unions. And, while the majority of the eight victories in this area were in somewhat inconsequential cases, at least two were of importance.

Thus, it appears that the Court is able to take a more balanced view of labor-management relations than it has in the recent past, probably because it now views that area as the one best left, in large part, to the lower

courts and to the NLRB. This trend, however, may be deceptive. In declining to decide many cases in this area, the Court may simply have been reflecting approval of decisions by lower courts and an NLRB heavily influenced by Republican, pro-business appointments in the last few years. It is possible that the Court's interest in this area will revive if newly-constituted lower courts and a revitalized NLRB begin to decide more cases in favor of the union position in important areas. If that happens, the result may be not only that more cases will again go to the Supreme Court, but that its present disposition not to depart from established parameters in this area will change.

The grant of review in, and decisions upon, numerous cases involving the rights of public employees has resulted in a severe contraction of those rights as recognized by the lower courts. Nine of the 13 cases in this area in which the result clearly implicated the interests of unions or employees were decided against the union position. As a result, public employees no longer have the right to live where they please, work as long as they are able, wear their hair as they please or even to receive the federal minimum wage. They may be fired without a fair hearing in many instances, and they need not be given redress for employer dissemination of false or irrelevant information about themselves. The main function of many of these cases, most decided in the 1975 term, has been to put the brakes on the more expansive views taken by lower courts of constitutional rights generally. Public employees, that is, have lost in large part not so much because they are public employees but because they relied upon the federal constitution to establish their rights. For, this Court has taken a narrow view concerning judicial review of governmental decisions of any kind on the basis of constitutional rights of due process and free speech.

It is likely that the message that public bodies are usually not to be interfered with in making personnel decisions has been communicated with sufficient emphasis that the Supreme Court will not itself speak in this area as often in the future. The result is to put particular emphasis upon the need for collective bargaining for public employees, because only through bargaining, and not through the courts, can their right to fair treatment be established. For this reason, the one major union victory in the public employee area, upholding exclusive representation and agency shop clauses, takes on particular significance.

The Court has decided more cases in the equal employment area in the last two years than in the previous ten and has exhibited a late-blooming disquiet with the thrust of the lower courts' approach in this area. This disquiet has not been the result solely of changes in Court personnel; some of the very justices who wrote opinions in the past taking a broad view of the rights of plaintiffs in Title VII cases now seem to be uncomfortable with the resulting lower court decisions.

In one area of major interest to unions, this willingness to re-examine the roots of employment discrimination law has been beneficial. As to the relationship of seniority systems to employment discrimination, the union view appears to have prevailed: the Court's decisions indicate that persons who were actually discriminated against and complain in a timely manner are entitled to their "rightful place" on the seniority roster; but persons who were not themselves discriminated against, or were discriminated against before Title VII passed, or did not contest discrimination when it occurred, may not sue to entirely upset a seniority system. Thus, unions can no longer be held liable—and seniority systems which are designed to benefit all employees cannot be upset—because of long-ago discrimination for which neither the union nor the senior employees were responsible.

In other areas, however, the propensity to treat employment discrimination law as if years of lower court development had not occurred has resulted in upsetting long-established doctrines and created a situation in which even minor procedural issues cannot be considered settled until the Supreme Court has spoken. In particular, in those cases in which the Court has struck out in new directions, its opinions have often left enough loose ends so that it will be years before the precise rule to be applied in various situations is known. Had the Court paid more attention to the developing law of employment discrimination in its formative years, the present situation of confusion about rights and responsibilities could have been avoided.

TITLE VII SENIORITY DECISIONS

The Supreme Court's four decisions concerning the relationship between seniority systems and employment discrimination are significant not only for their results, but for what they reveal of the Court's apparent concern with the shape of employment discrimination law as it has evolved in the lower courts, and the Court's willingness to upset doctrines which many had regarded as firmly established.

The first Supreme Court decision addressing the impact of Title VII on seniority systems was *Franks* v. *Bowman Transportation Co.* In this case, a number of black applicants for employment with Bowman proved that their applications had been rejected because of their race. The lower courts directed that these individuals

should be given priority consideration for future hiring, but held that the company could not be required to credit them upon hire with the seniority they would have attained had they not been discriminatorily denied employment when they first applied. The Supreme Court reversed the lower courts' denial of seniority credits, and held that individuals who prove that they were discriminatorily denied employment after the effective date of Title VII should ordinarily be awarded the seniority they lost as a result.

The Court, in an opinion by Justice Brennan, reasoned that, like backpay, seniority lost by an individual due to discrimination should be restored so that victims of discrimination may be "made whole" for their losses. Justice Brennan emphasized that the plaintiffs were not contending that Bowman's seniority system was unlawful, or that the system should be modified in any way. Rather, the legal wrong the plaintiffs alleged was the operation of an unlawful hiring system, and they sought seniority credits only for identified victims of hiring discrimination. That point later proved decisive in the *Teamsters* case discussed below.

The *Franks* opinion shows also that the justices were troubled by the fact that incumbent employees, who were themselves innocent of any wrongdoing, would be adversely affected by the grant of retroactive seniority to the plaintiffs. While the Court concluded that the remedy sought should not be denied for that reason, again this concern proved pivotal in the *Teamsters* case.

Chief Justice Burger, in a short separate opinion, characterized the majority opinion as "robbing Peter to pay Paul," and contended that "front pay" rather than seniority credits should be awarded to victims of hiring discrimination. Justice Powell dissented, in an opinion joined by Justice Rehnquist and with which the Chief Justice expressed general agreement, contending that there should be no presumption in favor of an award of retroactive seniority.

The lower courts had reached varying results with respect to the question of retroactive seniority as a remedy decided in *Franks*. But on another question concerning the impact of Title VII on seniority systems, the decisions had been unanimous since 1968. That question involved situations in which an employer had in the past discriminated against minorities or women in determining the departments, units or jobs into which they were assigned upon hire, and the seniority system was based on departmental, unit or job service, so that an employee making a transfer would lose all seniority. Since this loss of seniority slowed advancement up the line of progression, the courts concluded that the seniority system perpetuated the employer's past discrimination, and violated Title VII.

The decisions of the lower courts in the departmental seniority cases gave remarkably short shrift to § 703(h) of Title VII, the provision which states that a bona fide seniority system does not violate the Act unless its purpose is to discriminate. The lower courts simply declared that a system which tends to perpetuate discrimination cannot be considered bona fide within the meaning of § 703(h), even if the system is neutral in form, operation and intent. Such an argument, of course, proves too much, since § 703(h) was obviously adopted for the purpose of protecting seniority systems which might otherwise be thought to violate Title VII by virtue of their effects. But the lower courts noted that while the legislative history of Title VII expressly indicated congressional concern that the act might be erroneously construed as prohibiting a date-of-hire seniority system where an employer had discriminated with respect to hire, there was no express mention of the effect Title VII might have on departmental seniority systems in cases where an employer had discriminated with respect to assignments. Because the legislative history did not expressly reject the dismantling of departmental seniority systems, the lower courts jumped to the unwarranted conclusion that § 703(h) extended no protection to such systems. Apart from the inference which the courts drew from Congress' silence, the only support which they cited for their conclusion was the belief that Congress could not possibly have meant to preserve departmental seniority systems which could be said to have the effect of perpetuating past discrimination.

In *Teamsters* v. *United States* the Court rejected the approach of the lower courts and held that a seniority system does not become illegal simply because it tends to perpetuate pre-act discrimination. The opinion for the Court by Justice Stewart (from which only Justices Marshall and Brennan dissented) did not enunciate precisely what would have to be shown in order to establish that a seniority system was not bona fide within the meaning of § 703(h), but noting that the seniority system at issue in *Teamsters* was rational, in accord with industry practice, consistent with NLRB precedents, and free from any illegal purpose, the Court declared it to be entirely bona fide.

In rejecting the unanimous view of the lower courts, the Supreme Court did not rely on any subtlety of legal analysis which had escaped those courts. Rather, where the lower courts had refused to accept the plain meaning of § 703(h) and indulged the view that Congress could not possibly have intended the result called for by the provision, the Supreme Court saw in § 703(h) a justifiable congressional decision that the seniority rights of innocent employees should not be discarded as a result of the adoption of Title VII. In *Teamsters* the Supreme Court's view of the proper balance between the interests of victims of discrimination and the interests of other innocent employees diverged entirely from the view that had prevailed in the lower courts. The disquiet exprssed by the dissenting justices in *Franks* bore fruit in *Teamsters*, and may also shape the Title VII law in several other contexts.

The *Teamsters* decision announced important rulings on several additional matters each plainly advantageous or at least not disadvantageous to Title VII plaintiffs.

First, the Court held that in order to prove a case of classwide discrimination, at least in a "pattern or practice" suit brought under § 707 of the Act, it must be shown that discrimination was the company's "standard operating procedure—the regular rather than the usual practice." In finding that the government had met this burden, the Court recognized the value of statistical evidence, but cautioned that the usefulness of statistics depends on all surrounding facts and circumstances.

The Court then reaffirmed and clarified a point which had been made in passing in *Franks*: that once a pattern or practice of discrimination is shown, each alleged individual discriminatee who unsuccessfully applied for a job will be presumed to have been rejected for discriminatory reasons, and the defendant has the burden of demonstrating that the denial was for lawful reasons.

The Court further held that even an individual who never made an application is entitled to that presumption upon proof that he would have applied were it not for the defendant's discriminatory practices. The Court did not define what form such proof should take, except to say that an individual who shows merely that he was aware of the discriminatory practices and that he presently desires the job in question has not carried his burden of proof.

Finally, several important questions are left open by the *Teamsters* decision. First, it is not clear under what circumstances a seniority system may be found not to be bona fide. Second, the Court did not define what types of rules and practices fall under the rubric of a "seniority system," as that term is used in § 703(h). The question is significant because Justice Stewart opened his opinion in *Teamsters* by suggesting that, were it not for § 703(h) a practice which perpetuates past discrimination would violate Title VII. Thus, for example, if a no-transfer rule is not regarded as part of a "seniority system," such a rule may well violate Title VII in circumstances where the employer has discriminated with respect to job assignments. Third, *Teamsters* does not discuss § 1981, the general reconstruction era civil rights statute which the Court held to apply to private employment discrimination in *Johnson* v. *Railway Express*, a 1975 case. *Johnson* did not discuss the substantive reach of § 1981, in relation to Title VII, and it seems sure that Title VII plaintiffs will argue that a seniority system which does not violate Title VII nonetheless violates § 1981.

In *United Air Lines* v. *Evans*, decided the same day as *Teamsters*, a female flight attendant, who had been separated from employment in violation of Title VII and subsequently rehired, alleged that United was committing a second violation by refusing to credit her with pre-separation seniority. The Court rejected this claim in a short and rather cryptic opinion by Justice Stevens. As in *Teamsters*, only Justices Brennan and Marshall dissented.

Justice Stevens noted the plaintiff had not filed a timely charge of discrimination following her separation from employment. It follows, he said, that United was entitled to treat that past act as lawful once the period for filing a charge had expired. Like a discriminatory act which occurred before Title VII was passed, an act as to which no timely charge is filed must be regarded as having no present legal consequences, even though it may be said to have a present effect.

A discriminatory discharge is not identical to a discriminatory assignment. And while the *Evans* opinion does not discuss when a charge of a misassignment must be filed in order to be timely, the *Teamsters* opinion, referring to and following *Evans*, states that "the operation of a seniority system is not unlawful under Title VII even though it perpetuates post-Act discrimination that has not been the subject of a timely charge by the discriminatee."

The *TWA* v. *Hardison* decision, written by Justice White, was the first in which the Court construed a provision in Title VII which requires employers to "reasonably accommodate" an employee's religious practices where to do so does not cause "undue hardship on the conduct of the employer's business." The Court held that where shift and workday assignments are determined by a seniority system, an employee whose religion does not permit him to work on a particular day has no right to insist on a change in his work schedule which would limit the superior rights of more senior employees.

In reaching its decision, the Court relied in part on § 703(h) and stated, even more strongly than in *Teamsters*, a seniority system cannot violate Title VII unless it has a discriminatory purpose. In a statement which would seem to foreclose the application of § 1981 in cases where a seniority system is lawful under Title VII, the Court said that without a "clear and express indication from Congress," the courts should not upset a collectively bargained seniority system. Another aspect of the *Hardison* decision which may indicate the Court's future direction on many Title VII issues is the emphasis placed by Justice White on the principle that Title VII prohibits discrimination against majorities as well as minorities. Arguing from that principle, the Court indicated that whenever the costs of accommodating an employee's religious practices are more than *de minimus*, the employer cannot be required to make the accommodation, and, indeed, the making of the accommodation might constitute impermissible discrimination in favor of a particular religion.

NATIONAL LEAGUE OF CITIES v. USERY

No recent decision concerning the rights of public employees has had more disturbing implications than the 5–4 ruling in *National League of Cities* v. *Usery*, where the Court struck down as unconstitutional the 1974 amendments to the Fair Labor Standards Act which had extended the FLSA's minimum wage and maximum hour provisions to almost all employees of states and their political subdivisions. In an opinion authored by Justice Rehnquist, the Court declared that the FLSA amendments impermissibly interfered with the integral governmental functions of state and local governments, and thereby exceeded the powers of Congress under the Commerce Clause.

Justice Rehnquist (joined by the Chief Justice and Justices Stewart and Powell) rested his analysis on a concept of "state sovereignty" as boundless as it is unjustified by precedent. Although he purported to consider the specific manner in which the FLSA amendments had an impact on the states, the crux of his opinion was that the amendments would "significantly alter or displace the States' abilities to structure employer-employee relationships." Obviously, that could be said of any legislation affecting public employment. And, *Fry* v. *United States*, the 1975 decision upholding the application of the Economic Stabilization Act of 1970 to temporarily freeze the wages of state and local government employees, was described by Justice Rehnquist in *League of Cities* as involving a temporary measure, adopted in emergency conditions, which did not significantly remake state or local policy choices. Thus, that decision upholding federal authority was sapped of vitality. Moreover, *Maryland* v. *Wirtz*, the 1968 decision upholding the extension of the FLSA wage and hour provisions to employees of state hospitals, institutions and schools, was overruled.

In a bitter dissent, Justice Brennan, joined by Justices Marshall and White, argued that the state sovereignty doctrine advanced by Justice Rehnquist is utterly without foundation in the Constitution. As Justice Brennan showed at length, the Court's prior decisions established that as long as Congress is regulating "commerce" and the regulation is not unreasonable, neither the Tenth Amendment nor any notion of inherent state sovereignty stands as a bar to Congress' action. The dissent also underscored the failure of the majority to demonstrate how the FLSA amendments in particular, and legislation affecting public employment in general, impinge upon state and local policymaking to any greater degree than countless federal regulatory statutes which have been upheld in their application to the States. Justice Stevens made essentially the same point in his brief separate dissent.

Thus, while the majority opinion embraced a doctrine of state sovereignty under which virtually any federal statute affecting the employment practices of state and local governments could be argued to be unconstitutional, four justices expressed a diametrically opposite view. The key to the future application of *League of Cities* may therefore lie with Justice Blackmun, who wrote a one-paragraph concurring opinion expressing the view that the state sovereignty doctrine espoused by the majority involves a balancing approach, which does not outlaw federal power in areas "where the federal interest is demonstrably greater [than in the case of the FLSA amendments] and where state facility compliance with imposed federal standard would be essential." Whether legislation dealing with other aspects of public employment might meet this test is impossible to determine from Justice Blackmun's opinion. For the only area of permissible federal power he mentioned is environmental protection; and it is possible that by citing that lone example Justice Blackmun meant to imply that the area of state and local government labor relations is not open to federal regulation, thereby aligning himself with Justice Rehnquist.

Whatever its immediate consequences, the hostility displayed in Justice Rehnquist's opinion toward federal legislation concerning state and local government employees is unmistakable. As Justice Brennan noted, the tone of Justice Rehnquist's opinion, as well as its mode of analysis, hearkens back to the language of Justice McReynolds and his colleagues in striking down social legislation in the early decades of this century. Unless checked by other members of the Court, Justice Rehnquist's open-ended notion of "state sovereignty" could serve the same ill purpose with regard to federal regulation in the public sector as "freedom of contract" once served for federal regulation of private enterprise.

NLRB v. PIPEFITTERS

The *Teamsters* and *League of Cities* decisions indicate the Supreme Court's willingness to make dramatic change in the status quo in cases involving civil rights and public employees. In contrast, the *Pipefitters* case illustrates the Court's comparative restraint when presented with an NLRA case in which the alternatives are to uphold an established rule of law comparatively favorable to unions, to overturn such a rule entirely, or to read the prior law narrowly. While the Court's preference for the third alternative results in the drawing of lines more nice than obvious, it also provides a measure of stability.

In *National Woodwork Manufacturers Assn.* v. *NLRB*, a 1967 case, which involved the legality of a collective agreement between a carpenters union and an employer requiring the employer to have certain work (the finishing and hanging of doors) done by his carpenter employees who had traditionally performed that task, the employer contended that the agreement was unlawful under section 8(e) of the NLRA (which prohibits "hot cargo" provisions), and that a strike to enforce the agreement was an unlawful secondary boycott. The Court, in an opinion by Justice Brennan, stated that since the "objective" of the agreement "was preservation of work traditionally performed by the jobsite carpenters * * * the Union's making of the * * * agreement was not a violation of section 8(e)" and that since the strike to enforce the agreement "related solely to preservation of the traditional tasks of the jobsite carpenters, * * * the Union's maintenance of the provision was not a violation of Section 8(b) (4) (B)." The Court emphasized that the "inquiry"

required by a Section 8(b) (4) (B) or Section 8(e) charge is "whether, under all the surrounding circumstances, the Union's objective was preservation of work for [the] employees [of the employer who signed the agreement and who is being struck] or whether the agreements and boycott were tactically calculated to satisfy Union objectives elsewhere." "The touchstone," said the Court "is whether the agreement or its maintenance is addressed to the labor relations of the contracting employer vis-a-vis his own employees."

National Woodwork and the *Pipefitters* case were identical except that in the former the employer, after agreeing that his employees should finish and hang doors, chose to buy finished doors, thereby depriving his carpenter employees of the opportunity to do their traditional work, while in the latter the employer, after signing a collective agreement providing that his pipefitter employees would do certain work (the cutting and threading of pipes) entered into a contract with a general contractor under which he agreed to install prepiped air conditioning units, thereby depriving his employees of the opportunity to do their traditional work. The Board, following its pre-*National Woodwork* decisions, and without attempting to reconcile them with the principles stated by the Supreme Court, concluded that this difference is a legally decisive distinction. A majority of the courts of appeals that considered the matter disagreed. In their view, under the test stated in *National Woodwork*, a strike by employees against their own employer to protest his failure to abide by the employees' agreed upon working conditions is not a secondary boycott but the clearest imaginable example of protected primary activity.

The illogic of this rationale is patent. It is normally true that collective agreements place limits on the employers' ability to do business with third persons. For example, the employer's promise to pay a certain wage means that he cannot accept contracts to do work at a price less than his labor costs. But that inevitable consequence has never been thought to make a strike by employees for better wages a secondary boycott. It confuses analysis, rather than clarifying the issue, to justify the *Pipefitters* result on the ground that the striking employees must have intended to affect the business relationships between their employer and others. Moreover, the 1947 Congress emphasized that the purpose of secondary boycott provisions is to assure that neutral employers are not enmeshed in labor disputes "that do not concern them at all." It follows that the court of appeals was correct when it said that when an employer makes a collective agreement guaranteeing his employees certain working conditions and then enters into a contract which requires him to break that agreement that the employer is not an innocent neutral caught in a labor dispute that "does not concern [him] at all."

It therefore appears that the Court reached the result

it did in *Pipefitters* because it felt greater sympathy for the subcontractor's economic situation than for that of the union, but that the Court was unable to develop a rationale for that result consistent with the *National Woodwork* principle to which it adhered because of its firm statutory support. As is often true in such situations, in order to ease its task, the Court characterized the *Pipefitters* case as one which "fall[s] within that category of situations in which the courts should defer to the agency's understanding of the statute which it administers," and scolded "the Court of Appeals [for] improperly substitut[ing] its own views of the facts for those of the Board." Such deference has been accorded by the Court more consistently when the Board has decided against unions than when it has decided against employers, and it will be interesting to see to what extent deferrence will be given to future decisions, if any, which read Section 8(a) of the Act more broadly.

"TRADITIONAL" LABOR LAW CASES

A. The National Labor Relations Act.

The 1976 term saw the demise of the Warren Court's 1968 decision in *Amalgamated Food Employees* v. *Logan Valley Plaza*. In *Logan Valley*, Justice Marshall declared that a suburban shopping center constitutes a "public forum" where citizens have a First Amendment right to engage in peaceful handbilling and picketing. Then, in *Hudgens* v. *NLRB*, Justice Stewart for a five-member majority ruled that *Logan Valley* had been wrongly decided and that the First Amendment has "no part to play in a case such as this." He reasoned that *Logan Valley* had been overruled by the Court's 1972 decision in *Lloyd Corp.* v. *Tanner*, a case in which Justice Stewart had dissented, and that he had no choice but to accept the Court's rejection of *Logan Valley's* rationale. While it is not unusual for a justice to acquiesce in a previous decision from which he had dissented and to apply the decision in subsequent cases, Justice Stewart's assertion that, even though it was not noticed at the time, *Lloyd* entailed the wholesale rejection of *Logan Valley* is to say the least most unusual. Indeed, Justice Powell, the author of the Court's opinion in *Lloyd*, wrote a concurrence in *Hudgens* in which he observed that *Lloyd* had not overruled *Logan Valley*, although he fully agreed with the decision to do so in *Hudgens*.

It may well be that the effect of *Hudgens* is to insure that labor picketing cases will be resolved primarily by the Board, rather than by First Amendment lawsuits. That result may not prove to be a serious setback for labor, even though the First Amendment right to picket established by *Logan Valley* was in some respects broader than any right the Board is likely to find in the NLRA.

For, upon remand in *Hudgens*, the Board reaffirmed its ruling that the company had violated the Section 7 rights of its employees by threatening them with arrest for trespass if they did not cease picketing. The Board regarded the case as an easy one under the NLRA precedents and rejected the company's arguments that those precedents should be distinguished in that they involved organizing activity while *Hudgens* involved an economic strike, or because the employees primary dispute in *Hudgens* was with one of the stores which leased space in the shopping center, rather than with the center which owned the property on which the picketing occurred. If the Board continues to analyze picketing cases as well as it did in *Hudgens*, the loss of the *Logan Valley* doctrine should not be of great significance.

Labor won a modest victory in *Oil, Chemical & Atomic Workers* v. *Mobile Oil Corp.*, where the Court held by a 7–2 vote that Texas right-to-work laws do not apply to seamen who work most of the time outside Texas, even though all the hiring was done in Texas, the employer's payroll office was in Texas, and a majority of the seamen resided in Texas.

The Court held that in determining whether Texas law or federal law should apply in this context, the job situs of the employees is the controlling consideration, as the union and the United States argued. The company contended that the whole employment relationship should be considered, and Justices Stewart and Rehnquist argued in dissent that the location at which the company's hiring took place should be the controlling factor. The approach adopted by the majority, while producing a favorable result in this case, was essentially based on neutral considerations concerning principles of conflicts-of-law, rather than on any traditional labor law concepts. Thus, the case does not imply a favorable Supreme Court attitude with respect to any other issues of concern to labor.

The Court decided only two other NLRA cases. In *South Prairie Construction Co.* v. *Local 627, Operating Engineers*, the Court held in a per curiam opinion that the court of appeals had impermissibly invaded the province of the Board when, after reversing the Board's ruling that two wholly-owned subsidiaries did not constitute a single employer, the court proceeded to determine that the employees of both subsidiaries comprised an appropriate unit for purposes of collective bargaining. The Board had not reached the unit-determination question, and the Supreme Court held that the court of appeals should have remanded that question to the Board rather than deciding it on its own.

In the remaining NLRA decision, *Bayside Enterprises* v. *NLRB*, the Court held that truck drivers employed by a vertically integrated poultry business, whose job consisted of trucking feed from the company's feed mill to the farms on which chickens were being raised, were "employees" within the meaning of the Act, rather than "agricultural laborers" excluded from coverage. The decision can be read to imply that a worker whose particular job duties are not of an agricultural nature is not an "agricultural laborer," regardless of the nature of the company for which he works. If so, the decision would forestall an unwarranted expansion of the agricultural exemption in the context of large vertically integrated agribusinesses.

B. Arbitration of Disputes Under Collective Agreements

The most significant labor victory in the "traditional" area of private labor-management relations over the past two years was *Buffalo Forge Co.* v. *Steelworkers*. The Court held that the Norris-LaGuardia Act prohibits a federal court from enjoining a sympathy strike pending an arbitrator's decision as to whether the strike is forbidden by the no-strike clause in the parties' collective bargaining agreement, where, as in the usual case, the sympathy strike is not over an arbitrable matter.

In *Buffalo Forge*, the question whether the sympathy strike violated the no-strike clause was an arbitrable issue, and therefore, as the Court observed, the employer would be entitled to an injunction compelling the union to arbitrate that question, should the union refuse to do so. But the strike itself was not over that issue, nor any other arbitrable issue, and thus could not be enjoined by the federal courts pending arbitration as to its lawfulness.

The 1970 decision in *Boys Markets* v. *Retail Clerks*, where the Court held for the first time that strikes in breach of contract can be enjoined by federal courts despite Norris-LaGuardia, had seemed to say that an injunction can be entered only where a strike is over an arbitrable grievance. In *Buffalo Forge*, the Court decided by a 5–4 vote that *Boys Markets* meant what it said. The Norris-LaGuardia ban on labor injunctions is lifted by *Boys Markets* only as to those disputes which the parties have agreed to submit to arbitration.

Although the opinion, written by Justice White, followed logically from *Boys Markets* and the underlying policies of Norris-LaGuardia, it may be that what actually carried the day in *Buffalo Forge* was the Court's desire to keep the federal courts clear of the preliminary injunction litigation which would have been fostered by an opposite result. The majority opinion referred with unusual frankness to the possibility of such litigation and to the Court's desire to avoid it.

The alignment of the justices in *Buffalo Forge* was extremely surprising. Justice White was joined in the majority by Justice Stewart, whose vote in labor cases is generally hard to predict, by Justices Rehnquist and Blackmun, and by Chief Justice Burger. Few would have expected those three Nixon Bloc votes. Justice Stevens wrote the dissent, joined by Justices Powell, Marshall and Brennan, who wrote for the Court in *Boys Markets*.

In *Nolde Brothers* v. *Local 358, Bakery & Confectionery Workers*, the Court issued another decision supporting arbitration, albeit one which, like *Buffalo Forge*, may have been motivated by a desire to clear the dockets of the federal courts rather than by any sympathy to labor

interests. The question in *Nolde Brothers* was whether a dispute over severance pay, which arose from events occurring after the union's termination of the collective bargaining agreement, was subject to arbitration under the agreement. Writing for the Court in the 7–2 decision, Chief Justice Burger answered in the affirmative.

The parties' agreement did not explicitly exclude from arbitration grievances which, while arising out of the contract, arose after its termination. The Chief Justice therefore concluded that, inasmuch as the parties must have been aware of the presumption of arbitrability under federal labor policy, their failure to exclude such grievances from arbitration should be construed as a decision to include them. *Nolde Brothers* concerned a claim for severance pay which had accrued while the contract was in effect. Thus, where a grievance concerns rights which did not accrue during the life of the contract, the decision may not be fully applicable.

Where a collective agreement provides for final and binding arbitration of disputes under the contract, the basic rule is that an employee who claims that he was improperly discharged may not sue in court to vindicate his position. In *Hines* v. *Anchor Motor Freight*, the Court held that such a suit will be allowed even though the arbitration panel's decision went against the individual if the union breached its duty of fair representation in prosecuting the aribtration case. This ruling, of course, cuts against the finality of arbitration decisions but was, nevertheless, to be expected in light of the 1967 decision in *Vaca* v. *Sipes*, holding that a union's breach of its fair representation obligation in determining whether to press a grievance to arbitration opens the way to a court suit by the affected employee to enforce the contract.

In *Hines*, the court of appeals had concluded that the employee could sue the union for its alleged failure to represent him properly before the arbitration panel, but that he could not sue the employer for the alleged improper discharge since there was no evidence of any misconduct during the arbitration proceedings "on the part of the employer." Justice White, speaking for a six-member majority, reinstated the contract claim against the employer stating "it was Anchor that originated the discharges * * * [i]f those discharges ere in error, Anchor has surely played its part in precipitating this dispute." Thus, said the Court, "we cannot believe that Congress intended to foreclose the employee from his § 301 remedy otherwise available against the employer if the contractual processes have been seriously flawed * * * ."

C. Preemption of State Regulation

Since the 1959 decision in *San Diego Building Trades Council* v. *Garmon*, the basic rule for determining whether state regulation of a matter is preempted by the NLRA is that activities which are either arguably protected by

§ 7 or arguably prohibited by § 8 are preempted. In the past two years the Supreme Court decided two preemption cases. In one, the Court held that state regulation was preempted even though the conduct at issue was neither arguably protected nor arguably prohibited by the NLRA. In the other, the Court held against preemption even though the conduct in question was arguably prohibited. Although the Court is prone to recast preemption law in each new decision, both of the recent opinions are likely to be of broad significance.

In Lodge 76, *Machinists* v. *Wisconsin Employment Relations Comm'n.*, the WERC had asserted jurisdiction over a claim that a concerted refusal by union members to work overtime in order to put pressure on an employer during contract negotiations violated Wisconsin law. The Supreme Court held, 6–3, that Wisconsin law was preempted in this context.

Justice Brennan concluded that the self-help activity engaged in by Lodge 76 constituted conduct which could be curtailed only at the expense of federal labor policy. Relying on his opinion for the Court in *NLRB* v. *Insurance Agents*, Justice Brennan stated that Congress has struck a balance between prohibited acts and the free play of economic forces, such that peaceful economic pressure exerted by a union, although not protected by § 7, must not be curtailed. The Court therefore held that the NLRA preempts state regulation of such activity. In so ruling, the Court overruled its 1949 decision in *UAW* v. *WERB* (*Briggs-Stratton*), which had sustained Wisconsin's power to enjoin a series of temporary work stoppages.

Justice Stevens, joined by Justices Stewart and Rehnquist, rejected the need to go outside the bounds of the *Garmon* rule, and disagreed with Justice Brennan's view of the extent to which Congress has meant to protect self-help activity which is not covered by § 7.

While the decision in *Local 76* must be regarded as highly beneficial to labor, the preemption ruling in *Farmer* v. *Carpenters, Local 25*, is more difficult to characterize. The question in *Farmer* was whether a state law cause of action for the intentional infliction of emotional distress should be regarded as preempted by federal labor law where the defendant is a union officer and the complaint refers, at least in part, to allegedly discriminatory hiring hall practices. While recognizing that the conduct of which the plaintiff complained included matters arguably prohibited by § 8 and hence within the literal sweep of *Garmon*, the Court ruled unanimously that the state cause of action was not preempted.

The opinion, by Justice Powell, observed that state regulation of "arguably prohibited" conduct had been held by the Court not to be preempted in certain contexts, primarily those involving picketline violence and mali-

cious libel. From those decisions Justice Powell fashioned a general exception to the *Garmon* preemption rule: a claim relating to conduct arguably prohibited by § 8 will not be preempted if (1) the underlying conduct is not protected by the NLRA, (2) there is an "overriding state interest" in protecting citizens from the type of conduct alleged, and (3) there is little risk that the state cause of action will interfere with the effective administration of national labor policy. With respect to the third criterion, the Court's main concern appeared to be that state courts should not be permitted to decide a question which could be taken to the Board in an unfair labor practice case.

Applying this tripartite test, the Court concluded in *Farmer* that the state cause of action was not preempted, but that a new trial was necessary because the state court had not adequately excluded from the case the labor law considerations which were not properly within the province of state law. The Court enunciated several rules designed to insulate issues pertaining to a labor dispute from consideration in a state-law tort case. The Court's efforts to forestall evasion by individual plaintiffs of the congressional determination that unfair labor practice cases are for the NLRB to decide displayed careful thought, and a more favorable resolution short of absolute preemption of the tort claim would have been difficult to fashion.

PUBLIC EMPLOYEES

A. Procedural Due Process Cases

In three cases during the past two years the Court demonstrated a growing antipathy to the procedural due process claims of public employees.

Perry v. *Sindermann*, decided in 1972, held that a public employee is entitled to a discharge hearing if he has either a "property" or "liberty" interest in continued employment. The past two terms saw a whittling away at the scope of these interests.

In *Bishop* v. *Wood*, a city ordinance enumerated the causes for which a nonprobationary employee could be discharged, and provided that a discharged employee was entitled to a written statement of reasons upon request. The Court, in an opinion written by Justice Stevens and joined by the Chief Justice and Justices Stewart, Powell, and Rehnquist, held that no property interst was created by the ordinance.

In essence, the Court reasoned that the question whether a property interest existed was one of state law, and that although there was no definite state court ruling on the point, the district judge had construed the ordinance to mean that a public employee held his position at the will and pleasure of the city, and the court of appeals had affirmed by an equally divided vote. This was enough, in the eyes of Justice Stevens, to foreclose independent examination of the issue by the Supreme Court. But as Justice Brennan pointed out in one of the three dissenting opinions, although property interests are defined by state law, the federal interest in due process in such that the Court is not justified in taking every pronouncement of a state court, let alone that of a federal judge residing in a particular state, as a dispositive definition of a person's property for due process purposes.

The plaintiff in *Bishop* also claimed a "liberty interest" on the basis of his allegations that the reasons which had been given for his discharge were false and of such a nature as to damage his reputation and hamper his efforts to find a new job. The Court held that inasmuch as the reasons for the discharge had not been made public except in the judicial proceedings, the employee could not claim damage to his reputation. But as Justice Brennan noted in dissent, nothing in the facts of *Bishop* indicated that the reasons for the employee's discharge would not be disclosed in the future to prospective employers.

Justice Stevens' closing comment in *Bishop*, that the due process clause "is not a guarantee against incorrect or ill-advised personnel decision," can only be regarded as an effort to make light of a constitutional right which is of paramount importance to public employees.

The damage done to both liberty and property interests in public employment by *Bishop* was, if anything, exceeded by the harm to liberty interests claims which could result from the decision in *Codd* v. *Velger*.

The plaintiff in *Codd*, a police officer, argued that he was entitled to a discharge hearing because material in his personnel file—information concerning an apparent suicide attempt involving a pistol—could reach prospective employers and could cost the plaintiff job opportunities. (Indeed, the lower courts found that he had already been turned down for a job due to the information in the file.)

Although the lower courts and the parties had focused on whether the plaintiff had been stigmatized and whether the defendant had made the incident public and thus was not protected by the holding of *Bishop*, the Supreme Court never reached those questions. Instead, in a *per curiam* opinion, the Court said that since it had not been alleged that the information concerning the suicide attempt was false, no claim had been stated. The Court stated that the sole purpose of a hearing in a "stigma" case is to enable the employee to clear his name, and therefore the hearing would be useless if the employee were not prepared to disprove the stigmatizing information. That analysis would imply that in a "stigma" case an employee has no right to a hearing on the question of whether the facts warrant discharge, and the Court proceeded to spell out that very point in *dicta*. Thus, the Court distinguished between the hearing required in "liberty" cases and that required in "property" cases, in a manner which the *Perry* court did not appear to contemplate.

Justices Stevens, Brennan and Marshall objected to both the rule of pleading established by the majority and the *dicta* regarding the purpose of a discharge hearing. Justice Blackmun wrote a one-paragraph concurrence

implying that there might be limits on a public employer's disclosure of "irrelevant" material, even if accurate, but that the case did not present the question. Justice Brennan, however, stated in his dissent that the decision in *Codd* was not particularly significant, apparently taking the view that the *dicta* was not fully considered by the Court. Therefore, this may not be the last battle in the Supreme Court over the purpose of a discharge hearing in liberty interest cases.

Much in the spirit of *Bishop* and *Codd* was *Hortonville Joint School District* v. *Hortonville Education Association*, where the Court held, 6–3, that school teachers discharged for participating in an unlawful strike were not entitled under the due process clause to a review of their discharges in the form of a trial de novo in state court, despite the claim that the school board which discharged the teachers was not an impartial decision-maker since the board had been involved in the negotiations which led up to the strike.

B. Employees' Substantive Rights

Claims of violations of substantive constitutional rights fared better than claims of violations of procedural due process in that they were not uniformly rejected.

In *Elrod* v. *Burns* a group of non-civil service employees in the Cook County, Ill. sheriff's office who had been discharged or threatened with discharge because they did not support the Democratic Party brought a broad-scale challenge to the county's patronage practices. Justice Brennan, joined by Justices White and Marshall, wrote the plurality opinion holding that patronage practices regarding non-policymaking positions violate the First Amendment. Justice Stewart concurred in an opinion joined by Justice Blackmun, which declined to assess the validity of hiring on a patronage basis but argued that a non-policymaking employee cannot be discharged on the sole ground of his political beliefs.

The Chief Justice dissented, as did Justices Powell and Rehnquist. Justice Stevens did not participate, but as a member of the Seventh Circuit he wrote an opinion holding that non-policymaking public employees may not be discharged for refusing to switch their political allegiance.

The unanimous decision in *Mt. Healthy School Board* v. *Doyle*, written by Justice Rehnquist, was, on balance, more favorable than might have been anticipated. The Court reaffirmed its 1968 decision in *Pickering* v. *Board of Education* that a teacher's criticism of his school board is protected by the First Amendment. In addition, the Court held that Ohio school boards are not arms of the state and hence cannot assert any Eleventh Amendment immunity from suit in the federal courts. And, at the urging of the teacher, the Court did not rule on the extremely important question whether an action arising under the Fourteenth Amendment may be brought directly under 28 U.S.C. § 1331, the general federal-question jurisdictional provision, by a plaintiff who cannot sue under 42 U.S.C. § 1983, the broad Reconstruction era civil rights statute.

The matter which most occupied the Court in *Mt. Healthy* was the standard of causation to be applied in "mixed motive" cases, where a public employee proves that a constitutionally-prohibited consideration was a factor in his dismissal, but the defendant claims that another factor was an independent ground. The lower courts had adopted approaches ranging from ordering reinstatement whenever an impermissible consideration was a "substantial" cause of the adverse decision, to denying reinstatement unless an impermissible factor was the "primary" cause. The Supreme Court took a middle ground, holding that a violation of constitutional rights is not established unless the court finds that the defendant would not have reached the same decision in the absence of constitutionally protected activity, but that once the employee shows that an impermissible consideration was a motivating factor in the decision, the burden is on the defendant to prove by a preponderance of the evidence that the same decision would have been reached independent of the consideration.

On the other hand, the remaining three cases in this category were clear defeats.

In *Kelley* v. *Johnson* the Court addressed the nature of the protection which the First Amendment confers on public employees in matters of personal appearance. Justice Rehnquist wrote for the Court in a 7–2 decision denying a policeman's claim that a hair regulation was unconstitutional. Only with the greatest reluctance did Justice Rehnquist concede that the First Amendment played any role in matters of personal appearance; and he declared that a regulation of the personal appearance of public employees does not run afoul of the amendment unless it is "so irrational that it may be branded 'arbitrary.'" The Court found sufficent evidence of the rationality of police grooming regulations in the fact that the overwhelming majority of state and local police are uniformed—a fact which implied to the Court that similarity in appearance of police officers is desirable, either to make the officers recognizable to the public or to promote esprit de corps.

The Court unanimously upheld a Philadelphia municipal regulation requiring employees of the city to reside there (*McCarthy* v. *Philadelphia Civil Service Commission*), and upheld with only one dissent a Massachusetts statute requiring mandatory retirement of uniformed state police officers at age 50 (*Massachusetts Board of Retirement* v. *Murgia*). Both *McCarthy* and *Murgia* were per curiam decisions which, like *Kelley*, required that the public employer show only a rational basis for the challenged regulations.

C. Public Employee Unions

Madison School District v. *Wisconsin Employment Relations Commission* presented the Court with its first case involving the relationship between freedom of speech and the principle of bargaining exclusivity in the public sector. The Court held that the WERC had violated the First Amendment by ordering the school board not to permit employees other than union representatives to speak on matters subject to collective bargaining at meetings open to the public. Since the Court concluded that the nonunion teacher who was denied the chance to speak had not sought to engage in actual "negotiations" with the Board, and inasmuch as the meeting was open to the general public, the Court's unanimous decision was not surprising.

More troubling was the failure of the Court's opinion, written by the Chief Justice, to indicate whether a school board can properly conduct closed negotiating sessions in which only union representatives are allowed to participate. The opinion of the Court specifically declared that question to be an open one, prompting Justice Brennan to file a separate concurrence stating that closed negotiating sessions with an exclusive bargaining representative of public employees in no way violates the Constitution.

Fortunately the question left open by the *Madison* decision was quickly answered correctly in *Abood* v. *Detroit Board of Education*. There the Court upheld, with certain restrictions, a Michigan statute authorizing agency shop agreements whereby public employees are required to pay their exclusive bargaining representative a "service fee" equal to the amount of union dues. In so doing Justice Stewart rejected the contention that such a requirement violates the First Amendment rights of employees who do not wish to support the union.

The opinion conceded that the activities of public employee unions may properly be described as "political," but stated that such a characterization "does not raise the ideas and beliefs of public employees onto a higher plane than the ideas and beliefs of private employees." The plurality therefore concluded that previous decisions under the Railway Labor Act, which had upheld the agency shop in the private sector against First Amendment challenges, called for the same result in *Abood*. The Court observed that agency shop provisions in the public sector advance the same governmental interests as in the private sector: avoiding the confusion and conflict that could arise if rival unions holding different views each sought to obtain the employer's agreement on disputed subjects of bargaining, and avoiding "free riders."

However, and again in conformity with the approach of the RLA cases, *Abood* held that the use of agency shop fees to support "ideological activities unrelated to collective bargaining" violates the First Amendment rights of employees who object to the ideological activities.

Justice Stevens joined the opinion of the Court, adding only that he did not read the opinion as foreclosing the contention that a union may be required to develop internal procedures designed to prevent unlawful "ideological" expenditures as a precondition to exacting an agency shop fee.

Justice Powell, joined by the Chief Justice and Justice Blackmun, concurred in the holding that public employees cannot be required to contribute to political activities which they oppose, but went on to dissent from the Court's holding that public sector agency shop provisions are constitutional.

Justice Rehnquist joined in the opinion and judgment of the Court, but only because of his agreement with Justice Powell's dissent in *Elrod* v. *Burns*. Justice Rehnquist's view was that the First Amendment precludes neither patronage discharges nor agency shop fees. Ironically, Justice Powell relied on the Court's decision in *Elrod* to support his conclusion in *Abood* that agency shop provisions in the public sector violate the First Amendment.

In *City of Charlotte* v. *Local 600, Firefighters* the Court held unanimously that the city's refusal to permit its firefighters to check off union dues did not violate the equal protection clause even though a check off could be authorized for other purposes. Since the Court viewed "a reasonably relaxed standard of reasonableness" as applicable, the result was predictable.

D. Public Employment of Aliens

The Court ruled in *Hampton* v. *Wong* that the Civil Service Commission had violated due process in promulgating a regulation excluding aliens from most federal jobs. But the opinion of the Court, written by Justice Stevens, indicated that such a regulation might well be constitutional if it were promulgated by Congress or the President. Justices Brennan and Marshall concurred in the result noting that they did not understand the Court's opinion to decide that an alien exclusion policy adopted by Congress or the President would necessarily be constitutional. Justice Rehnquist, joined in dissent by the Chief Justice and Justices White and Blackmun, would have upheld the regulation as issued by CSC. Since President Ford subsequently repromulgated the policy challenged in *Wong*, the issue may return.

In a second alien employment case, *DeCanas* v. *Bica*, the Court unanimously held that a California statute prohibiting employers from knowingly employing an alien not entitled to lawful residence in the U.S. "if such employment would have an adverse effect on lawful resident workers" was not preempted by federal regulation of immigration.

EMPLOYMENT DISCRIMINATION

A. Public Employees

The increased importance of both employment discrimination cases and public employee cases is reflected in the fact that four decisions of the Court involved both areas.

The most controversial was *Washington* v. *Davis*, in which the Court held that an employment practice of a public employer which has a racially disproportionate impact does not violate the Constitution unless a racially discriminatory purpose is shown. The lower courts had decided that in a constitutional challenge to employment practices in the public sector, it was appropriate to apply the 1971 decision in *Griggs* v. *Duke Power Co.* and the guidelines of the EEOC, under which a test having a disparate impact can be found to violate Title VII if the test has not been "validated," regardless of whether an intent to discriminate has been shown. The Court, in an opinion by Justice White, rejected that approach. The only dissenters were Justices Brennan and Marshall, although Justice Stevens emphasized in his concurring opinion that discriminatory purpose can be proved in many different ways.

The *Washington* decision also appeared to hold that discriminatory purpose must be proved in an action under § 1981, at least where a public employer is the defendant, but this aspect of the decision was not completely clear. Another element of uncertainty created by *Washington* was the Court's view that even under Title VII, the District of Columbia Police Department test at issue in the case would be valid because test scores bore a "positive relationship" to scores which police trainees achieved on another test given at the conclusion of their training program. The dissent argued that absent a showing that the training course scores were accurate predictors of a person's ability to do police work, the fact that the challenge test bore a relationship to training course scores would not suffice to validate the test under the EEOC guidelines, which had been approved in broad terms in *Griggs*. This aspect of *Washington*, coupled with the Court's newfound willingness to reject the views of the EEOC (in *Teamsters* and in *General Electric* v. *Gilbert*), may foreshadow a retreat, even in the private sector, from the wholesale approval of EEOC's testing guidelines which the Court had previously expressed.

A unanimous decision in *Fitzpatrick* v. *Bitzer* declared that the Eleventh Amendment in no way limits awards of monetary relief in Title VII actions against state governments. The opinion for the Court by Justice Rehnquist relied on the fact that Title VII was enacted pursuant to the Fourteenth Amendment, which limits the "principle of state sovereignty" embodied in the Eleventh Amendment to distinguish the *National League of Cities* opinion. In separate concurring opinions, Justices Stevens and Brennan observed that the 1972 amendments extending Title VII to the states rested on the commerce clause as well as the Fourteenth Amendment, and argued that the commerce clause provided a valid independent basis for Title VII actions seeking money damages against a state.

The Court in *Chandler* v. *Roudebush* unanimously

held that, under the 1972 amendments extending Title VII to federal employment, employees claiming discrimination have a right to a trial de novo in court rather than merely a review of the administrative record. Although the courts of appeals had split on the point, the issue would never have been in doubt except for one or two confused statements in the otherwise clear legislative history. In a related case, *Brown* v. *General Services Administration*, the Court settled the point that for federal employees the Title VII remedy is exclusive. Thus the Court rejected the plaintiff's reliance on § 1981 and other statutes in challenging an employment decision as discriminatory.

B. Sex Discrimination

After twice hearing argument, the Court held in *General Electric* v. *Gilbert* that the exclusion of pregnancy from the list of disabilities included in an otherwise comprehensive disability benefits plan does not violate Title VII. In so ruling, the Court rejected the unanimous views of the courts of appeal and the EEOC. The premise of Justice Rehnquist's opinion for the six-member majority was that the exclusion of pregnancy "is not a gender-based discrimination at all." The Court had previously adopted that view in *Geduldig* v. *Aiello*, a 1974 decision upholding California's exclusion of pregnancy from its disability insurance plan, where the Court stated that the classification of benefits on the basis of pregnancy constituted a difference in treatment between "pregnant women and nonpregnant persons," rather than between women and men. In the same vein, Justice Rehnquist applied in *Gilbert* the notion advanced by the Court in *Geduldig* that where a disability benefits plan has comparable economic value to women and to men, the fact that the plan is underinclusive with respect to risks peculiar to women does not render it discriminatory.

Considering the Court's difficulties in determining the proper mode of analysis in equal protection sex discrimination cases—particularly its uncertainty whether sex, like race, should be regarded as an inherently "suspect classification"—the unquestioning application of *Geduldig* in the *Gilbert* case was surprising. Even more surprising was Justice Rehnquist's broad assertion in *Gilbert* that the concept of discrimination under Title VII should be that derived from the equal protection clause. That view is inconsistent with *Grigg* v. *Duke Power Co.*, where the Court held that discriminatory purpose need not be proved in a Title VII case challenging a practice which has discriminatory effects, and *Washington* v. *Davis*, where the Court held that discriminatory purpose must be proved in an equal protection clause case. Indeed Justice Rehnquist's references to *Griggs* were so equivocal that Justices Stewart and Blackmun wrote separate one-paragraph concurrences rejecting any implication that

Griggs is not good law. Justices Brennan, Marshall and Stevens dissented.

The Court subsequently blunted Justice Rehnquist's veiled attack on *Griggs* by its decision in *Dothard* v. *Rawlinson*. The Court unanimously ruled in *Dothard* that Alabama's statutory height and weight requirements for prison guards, which tended to exclude women in disproportionate numbers, had not been shown to be job-related and therefore violated Title VII as construed in *Griggs*.

However, seven members of the Court upheld an Alabama regulation excluding women from "contact positions" in all-male maximum security penitentiaries, such as the job of prison guard. In an opinion by Justice Stewart the Court held that sex is a "bona fide occupational qualification" for that job. The basis for the Court's determination was its conclusion that the presence of women in "contact" positions would be likely to provoke sexual assaults by inmates, in what the Court described as the "jungle atmosphere" of Alabama's prisons.

Justice Marshall, joined by Justice Brennan, argued that Alabama should not be able to rely on the inhumane and unconstitutional condition of its prisons as a justification for denying employment to women, and contended that the Court's rationale "regrettably perpetuates one of the most insidious of the old myths about women—that women, wittingly or not, are seductive sexual objects."

C. "Reverse" Discrimination

In *McDonald* v. *Santa Fe Trail Transp. Co.*, a unanimous Court held that a white employee who has been discriminated against because of his race has a cause of action under Title VII. With two dissents, the Court also found a cause of action under § 1981. The claim in *Santa Fe Trail* was that white employees had been discharged for allegedly stealing company property while a black employee similarly charged in the same incident was not discharged. In a footnote the Court emphasized that the actions at issue in the case had not been taken pursuant to an affirmative action program, and that the Court was not considering in *Santa Fe Trail* the legality of such programs.

The Court subsequently relied on *Santa Fe Trail* to support its decision in *Hardison*, discussed earlier. Since disquiet at what has been called "reverse discrimination" was also evident in *Teamsters* and, to a lesser extent, *Franks*, and because the Court will hear argument in the coming term in *Regents of the University of California* v. *Bakke*, a case challenging the constitutionality of a preferential admissions program for minorities to state medical schools, whatever implications *Santa Fe Trail* and the seniority cases may contain for affirmative action programs in employment should soon become apparent.

D. Statistical Proof of Discrimination

The Supreme Court put a stamp of approval on the use of statistics in Title VII cases in *Hazelwood School District*

v. *United States*. The Court also spoke favorably of the use of statistics in *Teamsters* and *Dothard*.

In *Hazelwood* the Court refused to accept the argument that only statistics showing the actual percentage of white and black applicants hired by the school district, as opposed to statistics regarding the composition of the district's workforce, should be accepted as adequate to prove a prima facie case of discrimination. However, the Court recognized several limitations on the probative value of workforce data which had been ignored by some lower courts. In the first place, the Court stated in *Hazelwood* that where a job requires special qualifications, a comparison between the racial composition of the employees hired by the defendant for that job and the percentage of minorities in the general population would be misleading. The proper comparison would be with the percentage of qualified minorities in the population.

Second, both *Hazelwood* and *Teamsters* stressed that a defendant must be given an opportunity to show that statistics concerning the present composition of his workforce are misleading because they reflect pre-Act hiring or promotion practices rather than post-Act conduct. In *Hazelwood* the Court also recognized the importance of carefully defining the geographic labor market which is used in the statistics.

E. Procedure in Title VII Cases

The Court ruled on several significant issues of Title VII procedure. In *IUE* v. *Robbins & Myers* the Court held that the time limits on the filing of a charge of discrimination with the EEOC are not suspended by the processing of a grievance under a collective bargaining agreement. In *Occidental Life Ins. Co.* v. *EEOC,* the Court concluded that Title VII sets no statutory limits on the time within which EEOC may commence a lawsuit after receiving a charge, and rejected the argument that a state limitations period should be applied. In *United Airlines* v. *McDonald* the Court helt that if after final judgment a member of the asserted class moves promptly to intervene for purposes of appealing the denial of class certification, the motion should not be denied as untimely. In *East Texas Motor Freight* v. *Rodriguez* the Court held that the court of appeals had erred in certifying a class at the appellate stage of litigation, where it was clear as a result of the facts developed a trial that the named plaintiffs were not adequate class representatives.

F. Federal Agency Authority Over Employment Practices of Regulated Industries

The Court ruled unanimously in *NAACP* v. *Federal Power Commission* that the FPC is authorized to consider the consequences of discriminatory employment practices on the part of the companies it regulates insofar as such consequences bear directly on rate setting. But the Court held that the Commission had no authority to promulgate general directives prohibiting employment discrimination on the part of regulated companies.

LANDRUM-GRIFFIN ACT

In its only Landrum-Griffin decision of the past two years, *Steelworkers* v. *Usery*, the Court held by a 6–3 vote that a provision in the Steelworkers' constitution limiting eligibility for local union office to members who have attended at least one-half of the regular meetings of the local for three years previous to the election is not a "reasonable qualification" on the right to run for office. The Court emphasized that the provision resulted in the exclusion of over 90 percent of the local union members from eligibility, and the opinion by Justice Brennan indicated that the Court would not approve any eligibility rule having such an effect, absent extraordinary justifications.

TAFT-HARTLEY TRUSTS

Section 302(a)(1) of the Taft-Hartley Act prohibits agreements by employers to pay money into trust funds administered by a union unless the payments are "for the sole and exclusive benefit of the employees of such employer." In *Walsh* v. *Schlecht*, a general contractor agreed to pay contributions to certain trust funds measured by the number of hours of work performed by carpenters employed by a nonunion nonsignatory subcontractor. The Court held, 8–1, that inasmuch as only the employees of the general contractors were eligible for trust fund benefits, the fact that some of the general contractor's contributions were measured by reference to the hours worked by other employees did not render the contributions unlawful.

SOCIAL BENEFIT CASES

In *Kimball* v. *New Mexico* the Court summarily affirmed a ruling that the NLRA does not preempt state authority to grant unemployment benefits to strikers. Consistent with that view, in *Ohio Bureau of Employment Services* v. *Hodory*, the Court concluded that an Ohio statute disqualifying a worker from unemployment benefits where his unemployment is due to a labor dispute, other than a lockout, at any factory owned by his employer does not violate the due process or equal protection clauses, even where the employee had no connection with the dispute. In the third decision, *Batterton* v. *Francis*, the Court divided 5–4 on the question whether the Secretary of Health, Education, and Welfare had acted in accordance with the Social Security Act by promulgating a regulation authorizing the states, within their discretion, to exclude from eligibility under the program of Aid to Families with Dependent Children—Unemployed Fathers any father who is out of work due to participation in a labor dispute, or for any reason which would make him ineligible for unemployment compensation under state law. The majority, in an opinion by Justice Blackmun, upheld the regulation, in the face of a clear legislative direction to the Secretary to establish "a uniform definition of unemployment throughout the United States." The Court's efforts to explain away the legislative history, which it recognized to be "at some variance" with the statute, were wholly unconvincing.

Usery v. *Turner Elkhorn Mining Co.* was the Court's most favorable decision on an issue concerning social benefits programs. The Court upheld the Black Lung Benefits Act of 1972 against a claim that the Act violates due process by its retrospective application (i.e., requiring operators to compensate former employees who terminated their work in the industry before the Act was passed, and their survivors), and by virtue of the presumptions of disability and other evidentiary rules which govern the resolution of a claim under the Act.

Finally, in *Mathews* v. *Eldridge* the Court held that a recipient of Social Security disability benefit payments has no right to an evidentiary hearing prior to the termination of benefit payments. The Court distinguished *Goldberg* v. *Kelly*, the 1970 decision requiring such a hearing prior to the termination of AFDC welfare assistance, in a manner which indicates that *Goldberg* may only apply to welfare recipients.

OCCUPATIONAL SAFETY AND HEALTH ACT

In *Atlas Roofing Co.* v. *Occupational Safety and Health Review Commission* the Court rejected, without dissent, a contention that Congress violated the Seventh Amendment right to a jury trial by assigning to OSHRC the task of adjudicating alleged violations of the Occupational Safety and Health Act. In a broadly written opinion by Justice White, the Court reaffirmed the power of Congress to assign to an administrative agency the adjudication of new "public rights" created by Congress.

VETERANS' REEMPLOYMENT RIGHTS

A unanimous Court held in *Alabama Power Co.* v. *Davis* that, under § 9 of the Military Selective Service Act, an employer having a pension plan must give a veteran pension credit for the period in which his employment with the company was interrupted by military service.

FEDERAL EMPLOYEE RECLASSIFICATION

Without dissent, the Court held in *United States* v. *Testan* that neither the Classification Act nor the Back Pay Act creates a right to backpay for a federal employee who proves that he was wrongly classified at too low a grade of pay.

History of American Labor

1501: A Royal Ordinance by King Ferdinand and Queen Isabella of Spain provided for the importation of black slaves from Seville into the Spanish colonies in the New World.

1516: Charles V of Spain granted licenses to the Flemings to import blacks into the Spanish colonies in the New World.

1615: British Parliament allowed convicted felons to accept exile to colonies as indentured servants rather than suffer execution.

1619: London Common Council appointed "one hundred children out of the swarms that swarme in the place, to be sent to Virginia to be bound as apprentices for certain yeares." The Virginia Company was authorized to ship children out to America. Other indentured servants included criminals transported to finish their sentences, residents of debtors' prisons, and kidnapped persons. Other indentured servants came voluntarily and were sold into bondage by ship captains to provide the cost of passage. More than 50 percent of the immigrants in the middle colonies during the seventeenth century were indentured or bonded servants.

1619: A Dutch ship from the coast of Guinea sailed up the James River and sold its cargo of twenty black slaves to the planters of the Virginia Colony.

1630: The Massachusetts General Court imposed a 2-shilling-a-day wage ceiling for carpenters, joiners, bricklayers, sawyers, thatchers, and other artisans. Labor scarcity made enforcement impossible.

1645: An ordiance of the Lords and Commons assembled in Parliament provided a law to prevent the kidnapping of children for sale as indentured servants in the colonies: "For the Apprehending and bringing to condigne punishment, all such lewd persons as shall steale, sell, buy, inveigle, purloyne, convey, or receive any little Children. And for the strict and diligent search of all Ships and other Vessels on the River, or at the Downes."

1646: The Virginia Colony provided that two children from every county should be taught, at public cost, the arts of carding, knitting, and spinning.

1663: Black slaves and white indentured servants combined to rebel in Gloucester County, Virginia. The plot was exposed and its leaders beheaded.

1712: Black slaves in New York rebelled, killing nine whites. Twenty-one slaves were executed.

1741: In New York City, a combination of black slaves and white indentured servants was formed to revolt against their masters. The movement was crushed with the execution of thirty-five black and white leaders.

1768: Twenty journeymen tailors in New York City quit work because of a wage reduction and advertised their willingness to take private work in defiance of Masters (Employers) of the trade.

1778: Journeymen printers of New York City combined to demand an increase in wages. After the increase was granted, the organization was abandoned.

1786: The earliest authenticated strike of workers in the United States in a single trade occurred when Philadelphia printers gained a minimum wage of $6 a week.

1787: The Constitutional Convention provided, in Article 1, Section 9 of the new Constitution of the United States, against the importation of slaves after the year 1808: "The migration or importation of such persons as any of the States now existing shall think proper to admit shall not be prohibited by Congress prior to the year 1808. . . ."

1787: Congress, under the Articles of Confederation, abolished slavery in the Northwest Territory (later to be Wisconsin, Michigan, Ohio, Indiana, and Illinois).

1787: The Constitutional Convention, in Article 4, Section 2, provided for the return of runaway slaves: "No person held to Service or Labour in one State under the laws thereof, escaping into another . . . shall be delivered up on claim of the party to whom such Service or Labour may be due."

1791: Samuel Slater, who had British textile experience, constructed a copy of Richard Arkwright's spinning machine in Pawtucket, Rhode Island. Thus began the first modern American factory.

1791: Philadelphia carpenters struck unsuccessfully in May for a ten-hour day and additional pay for overtime. This was the first recorded strike of workers in the building trades.

1792: The first local craft union formed for collective bargaining was organized by Philadelphia shoemakers. It disbanded in less than a year.

1793: Eli Whitney's invention of the cotton gin increased the supply of American cotton and furthered industrialization.

1794: The Federal Society of Journeymen Cordwainers was formed in Philadelphia by the shoeworkers. It lasted until 1806, when it was tried and fined for conspiracy.

1794: The Typographical Society was organized in New York City by the printers. The Society remained in existence for 10½ years.

1799: The first paid walking delegate was hired by Philadelphia cordwainers to police conditions in the trade.

1805: A Journeymen Cordwainers' union in New York City included a closed-shop clause in its constitution.

1806: Members of the Philadelphia Journeymen Cordwainers were tried for criminal conspiracy after a strike for higher wages. The charges were (1) combination to raise wages and (2) combination to injure others. The union was found guilty and fined. Bankrupt as a result, the union disbanded. This was the first of several unions to be tried for conspiracy.

1809: New York cordwainers convicted of conspiracy to raise wages. The judge singled out the means they used to combine to raise wages, not simply the fact of their combination.

1818: Connecticut granted the right to vote to all who paid taxes and did militia duty.

1819: The United States suffered a steep depression; amidst widespread unemployment, many young labor unions dissolved.

1820: Massachusetts Republicans abolished the State freehold franchise, giving the vote to all adult males who payed taxes.

1820: The Missouri Compromise provided for admission to the United States of Maine as a free state, Missouri as a slave state, and no slavery north of 36 degrees, 30 minutes north latitude in any lands acquired in the Louisiana Purchase. By this time slavery had been abolished by State laws in Vermont (1770), Massachusetts (1780), New Hampshire (1789), and New York (1817). The States of Pennsylvania (1780), Connecticut (1789), Rhode Island (1784), and New Jersey (1804) had provided for gradual emancipation through which slave children would become free on reaching a specified age.

1821: New York State granted voting rights to all adult white males who payed taxes, performed work on public roads, or served in the militia.

1824: Female weavers of Pawtucket, Rhode Island, struck for higher wages and shorter hours.

1825: The United Tailoresses of New York, a trade union organization for women only, was formed in New York City.

1825: Strike by journeymen house carpenters in Boston for a ten-hour day ended in defeat.

1825: New York State granted universal manhood suffrage.

1827: New York City unions demanded a ten-hour day. Within one year the ten-hour day became universal in New York for skilled labor.

1827: The Mechanics' Union of Trade Associations, made up of unions of skilled craftsmen in different trades, was formed in Philadelphia. This was the first city central type of organization on record. Their program included: the ten-hour day, universal male suffrage, abolition of imprisonment for debt, a mechanics' lien law, abolition of all chartered monopolies, and equal universal compulsory education.

1828: The Workingmen's Party, including wage earners, craftsmen, and farmers, was organized in Philadelphia in July. It went out of existence in 1832.

1829: New York union activists and social reformers organized a local Workingmen's Party and elected one candidate to the State Assembly.

1831: Nat Turner, a black preacher and son of a free black man, led a revolt of slaves in Virginia. Scores of people, both black and white, were killed before the rebellion was put down.

1831: William Lloyd Garrison founded the abolitionist publication *The Liberator*. It became an effective voice of the abolitionist movement.

1833: Trade unions revived amidst the general economic prosperity. Within each city, union local's banded together in central labor bodies called Trades' Unions.

1834: The National Trades' Union was formed in New York City. This was the first attempt toward a national labor federation in the United States. It failed to survive the financial panic of 1837.

1834: Ely Moore, first President of the National Trades' Union and a journeyman printer, was elected to the U.S. Congress with the support of local New York unions and Tammany Hall.

1835: A New York Supreme Court judge ruled that, by combining to raise wages, New York cordwainers were guilty of conspiracy. The decision touched off widespread labor protest.

1835: Philadelphia journeymen successfully organized a city-wide strike for the ten-hour day. The movement spread to other cities.

1836: The National Cooperative Association of Cordwainers, the first national labor union of a specific craft, was formed in New York City. There is no further record of this organization after 1837. Other trades which formed national organizations within the next few years were the printers, combmakers, carpenters, and hand-loom weavers.

1836: Massachusetts enacted a child labor law, setting a minimum of fifteen years of age for employment of children in factories.

1837: The depression wiped out almost all trade unions.

1840: An Executive Order issued on March 31 by President Van Buren established a ten-hour day for Federal employees on public works without reduction in pay.

1841: The Brook Farm Colony, an experiment in Fourier socialism, was established near West Roxbury, Massachusetts. Everyone shared in the work and received equal pay. It was destroyed by fire in 1846.

1842: In the case of *Commonwealth v. Hunt*, the Massachusetts Court held that labor unions, as such, were legal organizations, and that "a conspiracy must be a combination of two or more persons, by some concerted action, to accomplish some criminal or unlawful purpose, or to accomplish some purpose not in itself criminal or unlawful by criminal or unlawful means." The decision also denied that an attempt to establish a closed shop was unlawful or proof of an unlawful aim.

1842: Irish immigrants began to displace native employees in New England textile mills.

1842: Massachusetts and Connecticut passed laws prohibiting children from working more than ten hours a day.

1843: Lowell factory operatives, then working twelve hours a day, began a five-year campaign for a ten-hour day in Massachusetts.

1844: Tailors and "tailoresses" of New York City and Boston unsuccessfully struck against reductions in piece rates.

1844: George Henry Evans organized the National Reform Association with hopes of sparking a working-class movement for land reform. He was joined by many labor leaders.

1845: Boston workers organized the Workmen's Protective Union, America's first consumer cooperative.

1845: In Lynn, Massachusetts, shoemakers organized a producers' cooperative shoe factory.

1845: More than 1,500 delegates attended the New England Workingmen's convention in Lowell, Massachusetts; land reformers and associations dominated the proceedings.

1846: The New England Workingmen's Association resolved that "American Slavery must be uprooted before the elevation sought by the laboring classes can be effected."

1846: The New York Irish laborers union struck for a wage increase. Employers defeated the strike by hiring newly arrived German immigrants.

1847: The first State law fixing ten hours as a legal workday was passed in New Hampshire.

1848: Pennsylvania passed a State child labor law, setting the minimum age for workers in commercial occupations at twelve years. In 1849 the minimum was raised to thirteen years.

1849: Discovery of gold in California touched off a westward migration of as many as 50,000 skilled workers.

1850: A new and strengthened Fugitive Slave law was passed by Congress and signed by President Millard Fillmore. The law provided for federal government assistance in the return of runaway slaves from the North. Thousands of runaways each year escaped through the underground railroad.

1850: Reviving New York City unions organized a citywide labor Congress. Trade unions of the 1850s confined themselves more to skilled workers and bread-and-butter issues than did labor organizations of previous decades.

1850: Thirteen hundred Fall River, Massachusetts, textile factory operatives struck against wage cuts, but failed after six months.

1850: The Typographical Union, the first national organization of workers to endure to the present day, was formed. Horace Greeley was its first elected president.

1852: The first law limiting working hours of women to ten hours a day was passed in Ohio.

1857: The U.S. Supreme Court, in its decision in the case of Dred Scott, ruled that Congress could not legally deprive slaveholders of their right to take human "articles of merchandise" into any part of the Nation. All antislave laws were thus unconstitutional.

1859: John Brown and a group of twenty followers raided the Federal arsenal at Harper's Ferry, Virginia. His purpose was to distribute arms to the slaves and spread revolt throughout the South. Troops under the command of Robert E. Lee captured Brown and his followers. Brown's two sons were killed during the skirmish. Brown and six others died on the gallows.

1859: The Iron Molders' Union, the forerunner of the present Molders' and Allied Workers' Union, was organized in Philadelphia.

1862: The Homestead Act opened Western land to settlers.

1862: The McKay sewing machine revolutionized the work of journeymen shoemakers.

1862: The "Molly Maguires," a secret society of Irish miners in the anthracite coal fields, first came to public attention. The "Mollies" were charged with acts of terrorism against mine bosses. They went out of existence in 1877, when fourteen of their leaders were imprisoned and ten were executed.

1863: President Lincoln issued the Emancipation Proclamation effective January 1, 1863: "All persons held as slaves within any State, or any designated part of a State, the people whereof shall then be in rebellion against the United States, shall be then, thenceforward, and forever free. . . ."

1863: The present-day Brotherhood of Locomotive Engineers was founded.

1863: Laws providing fines and imprisonment for strikers preventing other persons from working were passed in Illinois and Minnesota.

1864: The International Workingmen's Association (the First International) was founded by Karl Marx in Saint Martin's Hall in London.

1864: Cigarmakers, plasterers, ship carpenters, curriers, carpenters, bricklayers, painters, iron heaters, tailors, dry-goods clerks, and coachmakers held national organizing conventions.

1866: The National Labor Union, a national association of unions, was organized. A federation of trades' assemblies rather than of national craft organizations, it included radical and reform groups. Drifting into social rather than trade union endeavors, it lost craftsmen's support and went out of existence in 1872.

1866: Iron puddlers and their employers signed the first national trade agreement in United States history.

1867: The Knights of St. Crispin was organized on March 7 to protect journeymen shoemakers against the competition of

"green hands" and apprentices in the operation of newly introduced machinery in the shoe industry. The last vestige of the order disappeared in 1878.

1868: The United States and China signed the Burlingame Treaty, protecting the rights of Chinese to enter the United States. Congress violated this treaty by the first Oriental Exclusion Act of 1882.

1868: The first state labor bureau was established in Massachusetts.

1868: The first federal eight-hour-day law was passed by Congress. It applied only to laborers, workmen, and mechanics employed by or on behalf of the United States government.

1869: The Colored National Labor Union was formed in Washington, D.C., with a policy of cooperating with white workingmen "until the necessity for separate organizations shall be deemed unnecessary."

1869: The federal government adopted the eight-hour day for its employees, largely as a result of the agitation of the National Labor Union.

1869: The Noble Order of the Knights of Labor was organized in Philadelphia. It maintained extreme secrecy until 1878, then began organizing skilled and unskilled workers openly. By winning railroad strikes against the Gould lines, and advancing the program for the eight-hour day, it grew to over 700,000 members in 1886. It declined rapidly thereafter with the emergence of the AFL.

1869: The strike of the Knights of St. Crispin in Lynn, Massachusetts, succeeded. Manufacturers signed trade agreements; union membership soared to tens of thousands.

1869: The National Labor Union sent a delegate to the First International Workingmen's Association conference in Basel, Switzerland.

1870: The first written contract between coal miners and operators was signed on July 29. It provided for a sliding scale of pay based on the price of coal.

1873: The Brotherhood of Locomotive Firemen and Enginemen was organized.

1874: In the midst of the severe depression, New York City police attacked an unemployment demonstration; the incident is known as the Tompkins Square Riot.

1874: The Cigar Makers' International Union made first use of the union label.

1876: The Amalgamated Associates of Iron and Steel Workers was organized. Membership soon grew to 20,000, the largest in the country.

1876: The Socialist Labor Party was organized. At first, its emphasis was on trade unionism, but soon political action became paramount.

1876: Anarchists led by Johann Most organized the Workingmen's Party from the dissolved American branch of the International Workingmen's Association.

1877: A nationwide railroad strike over wage cuts erupted in violence, and gave rise to widespread fears of class war.

1878: The Greenback-Labor Party was organized by a fusion of the Greenback Party and the Workingmen's Party.

1881: The Federation of Organized Trades and Labor Unions (FOTLU), which later became the American Federation of Labor, was organized in Pittsburgh in November with 107 delegates present. Leaders of eight national unions attended, including Samuel Gompers, then president of the Cigar Makers' International Union.

1881: The United Brotherhood of Carpenters and Joiners, later to become one of the largest AFL unions, was organized.

1882: President Chester A. Arthur signed a bill prohibiting immigration of Chinese workers for ten years. The law was in response to agitation by California trade unionists.

1882: The first Labor Day celebration was held in New York City in September.

1883: The Brotherhood of Railroad Trainmen was organized.

1883: The International Working Peoples Association was formed by a combination of revolutionary socialists and anarchists in Pittsburgh with the demand for "the destruction of the existing Government by all means."

1883: Typographical Union 6 of New York City boycotted the *New York Tribune* over the discharge of union men. Boycotting became a major union weapon.

1884: The Federation of Organized Trades and Labor Unions proposed a campaign for the eight-hour day to begin May 1, 1886. At first, the Knights of Labor ignored the proposal.

1884: During the depression, the Knights of Labor won strikes against the Union Pacific Railway and three of Jay Gould's rail companies. The Knights of Labor became the leader of the American labor movement.

1884: The Knights of Labor and many trade unions adopted union labels to help boycott campaigns.

1884: The U.S. Congress passed a bill outlawing the importation of foreign workers on contract. The Knights of Labor had pressed for the bill after contract laborers had been used by employers to defeat several strikes.

1884: A Bureau of Labor was established in the U.S. Department of Interior. It later became independent as a Department of Labor without Cabinet rank. It then was absorbed into a new Department of Commerce and Labor, which was created in 1903, where it remained until the present Department of Labor was established in 1913.

1886: To defend themselves against antilabor assaults, New York City trade unionists nominated Henry George for mayor of New York. Widespread election fraud denied him victory, and the coalition that supported him soon broke up.

1886: As part of an employers' campaign against the Knights of Labor, lockouts were instituted against 5,000 Troy laundry workers, 20,000 Cohoes and Amsterdam, New York, knitters, and 20,000 Chicago packinghouse workers.

1886: Under the initiative of the Federation of Organized Trades and Labor Unions, some 340,000 workers participated in a movement for an eight-hour day.

1886: The Knights of Labor lost a two-month strike on Gould's Southwestern Railroad System after strikers refused to arbitrate.

1886: The general strike for an eight-hour day was smaller than expected because the Knights of Labor did not participate. Of 190,000 strikers, only 15,000 won the eight-hour day.

1886: The American Federation of Labor was organized at a convention in Columbus, Ohio, in December as successor to the Federation of Organized Trades and Labor Unions. Other trade unions and city councils that had failed to gain autonomy within the ranks of the Knights of Labor also joined the AFL.

1886: On May 4, at a meeting in Haymarket Square called by anarchists to protest the killing of four strikers at the McCormick Harvester Works in Chicago, a bomb was thrown, causing the immediate death of one policeman and the fatal wounding of seven others. The incident ended the fight for the eight-hour day and aroused public opinion against unionism and radicalism. The indictment and trial of the anarchists that followed resulted in the hanging of four, the suicide of one, and long prison terms for two others.

1887: The Brotherhood of Maintenance of Way Employees was organized.

1887: Four Chicago anarchists arrested for the Haymarket Square bombing were executed.

1888: The first federal labor relations law was enacted. It applied to railroads and provided for arbitration and presidential boards of investigation.

1888: The International Association of Machinists was organized in Atlanta, Georgia.

1890: The United Mine Workers was organized in Columbus, Ohio.

1890: The Sherman Antitrust Act was passed. Although the original target was industrial trusts, the first prosecution under the Act was aimed at Eugene V. Debs, head of the American Railway Union.

1891: The Stove Moulders Union and the employers' association signed a national trade agreement to regulate wages and arbitrate disagreements.

1892: The Populist Party nominated James B. Weaver for President. The platform contained many labor planks, but most trade unionists stayed aloof.

1892: State militia broke strikes of railroad switchmen in Buffalo, New York, and of coal miners around Tracy City, Tennessee.

1892: The Homestead strike by the Amalgamated Association of Iron, Steel & Tin Workers at the Carnegie steel mills in Homestead, Pennsylvania, resulted in the death of several strikers and Pinkerton guards. The strike failed and the union was ousted from most mills in the Pittsburgh area.

1892: Violence broke out in the Coeur d'Alene silver mining district in Idaho, as striking miners battled men hired to take their place. President Cleveland imposed martial law and sent in Federal troops, ending the strike.

1893: After their defeat at Coeur d'Alene, miners organized the Western Federation of Miners in Butte, Montana, and joined the American Federation of Labor. Violent dramatic strikes by mine operators and workers followed at Cripple Creek in 1894; Leadville in 1896; Salt Lake and again at Couer d'Alene in 1899; Telluride in 1901; Idaho Springs in 1903; and Cripple Creek again in 1903–1904.

1894: A strike of the American Railway Union led by Eugene V. Debs against the Pullman Company was defeated by the use of injunctions and by Federal troops sent into the Chicago area. Debs and several other leaders were imprisoned for violating the injunctions, and the union's effectiveness was destroyed.

1894: Coxey's Army marched on Washington to demand public works jobs for the unemployed.

1898: A general strike in the bituminous coal mining industry resulted in a trade agreement.

1898: Congress passed the Erdman Act, providing for mediation and voluntary arbitration on the railroads, and superseding the law of 1888. The Act also made it a criminal offense for railroads to dismiss employees or to discriminate against prospective employees because of their union membership or activity. This portion of the act was subsequently declared invalid by the U.S. Supreme Court.

1900: The International Ladies' Garment Workers' Union (AFL) was formed.

1901: The American Federation of Labor adopted the "Scranton Declaration," making craft autonomy the cornerstone of its organization.

1901: The Socialist Party of the United States was organized.

1901: The International Federation of Trade Unions (then the International Secretariat of National Trade Union Centers) was formed on August 21. The AFL affiliated in 1910, disaffiliated in 1921, and reaffiliated in 1937. It remained a member until the IFTU was formally dissolved in 1945.

1901: The Amalgamated Association of Iron, Steel & Tin Workers (AFL) lost fourteen union contracts after a three-month strike against the United States Steel Corporation.

1901: The United Textile Workers of America (AFL) was organized.

1902: On October 21, the United Mine Workers of America ended a five-month strike against anthracite operators, who agreed to arbitration by a commission after President Theodore Roosevelt threatened seizure of the mines. The Anthracite Coal Strike Commission, appointed on October 16, recommended on March 18, 1903, a 10 percent wage increase and conciliation machinery, but denied union recognition.

1903: The Department of Commerce and Labor was created by an act of Congress, and its Secretary was made a member of the Cabinet.

1903: Violence erupted during a strike at Cripple Creek, Colorado, over the eight-hour day. State militia entered the scene and the strike was defeated. This was a crushing blow to the Western Federation of Miners.

1903: Employers organized an antiunion campaign, with headquarters in Indianapolis. Unions adopted the union label and used boycotts as weapons of defense.

1904: The Amalgamated Meat Cutters strike against the Beef Trust was defeated. Employers instituted the open shop.

1904: The National Child Labor Committee was established. Within a decade, it succeeded in inducing most states to pass child labor legislation.

1905: The Industrial Workers of the World (IWW) was organized in Chicago by a combination of the Western Federation of Miners, other radical unions from the Midwest, and Eastern socialists. It adopted a preamble emphasizing "class struggle" as the philosophic basis of activity.

1905: The Supreme Court held that a maximum-hours law for bakery workers was unconstitutional under the due process clause of the Fourteenth Amendment (*Lochner v. New York*).

1905: The Supreme Court upheld a Kansas law setting maximum hours for men employed on public works.

1906: Frank Steunenberg, former governor of Idaho, was killed by a dynamite explosion. Western Federation of Miners leaders Moyer, Haywood, and Pettibone were indicted for conspiracy to murder, but were found not guilty.

1906: Three thousand electrical workers in Schenectady, New York, under the influence of the IWW, engaged in the first large sit-down strike on record.

1906: The International Typographical Union (AFL) struck successfully in book- and job-printing establishments for the eight-hour day, paving the way for extension of shorter hours in the printing trades.

1908: Section 10 of the Erdman Act, applying to railroad employees, whereby the yellow-dog contract was outlawed and an employer was forbidden to discharge a worker for union membership, was declared unconstitutional (*U.S. v. Adair*).

1908: The boycott by the United Hatters of Danbury, Connecticut, against D. E. Loewe and Co., was held to be in restraint of trade under the Sherman Antitrust Act. In January 1915, the individual union members were held responsible for the union's acts and were assessed damages and costs totaling $252,000. This was the first application of the treble-damage provision of the act to a labor union.

1909: The two-month strike of the International Ladies' Garment Workers' Union (AFL) was settled by providing preferential union hiring, a board of grievances, and a board of arbitration. This laid the foundation for the impartial chairman method of settling labor disputes.

1910: The Los Angeles Times building, owned by Harrison Gray Otis, a leading open-shop advocate, was blown up by a dynamite blast. The Ironworkers Union leaders pleaded guilty and the union disintegrated.

1910: Forty-one thousand workers in the men's garment industry won a strike and established the United Garment Workers Union.

1910: A strike of the International Ladies' Garment Workers Union in the cloakmaking industry won its "Protocals of Peace."

1911: The Supreme Court upheld an injunction ordering the AFL to eliminate the Bucks Stove and Range Company from its unfair list and to cease to promote an unlawful boycott. A contempt charge against union leaders, including AFL President Samuel Gompers, was dismissed on technical grounds. (*Gompers v. Bucks Stove and Range Co.*).

1911: The Triangle Waist Company fire in New York City on March 25, which caused the death of 146 workers, led to establishment of the New York Factory Investigating Commission on June 30, and eventual improvement in factory conditions.

1912: Massachusetts adopted the first minimum-wage act for women and minors.

1912: The IWW led a victorious strike of 25,000 mill hands at Lawrence, Massachusetts.

1912: The (Walsh) Commission on Industrial Relations was created to investigate industrial unrest. In 1916, it rendered a comprehensive series of reports on the status of labor-management relations.

1913: The IWW called a strike of textile workers in Paterson, New Jersey; starvation forced strikers back to work.

1913: The U.S. Department of Labor was established by law. It included the Bureau of Labor Statistics (created in 1884 as the Bureau of Labor), the Bureau of Immigration and Naturalization (created in 1891), and the Children's Bureau (created in 1912). Power was given the Secretary of Labor to "act as mediator and to appoint commissioners of conciliation in labor disputes." In 1918, the Conciliation Service was established as a separate division of the Department. William B. Wilson, a trade unionist and member of Congress, became the first Secretary of Labor.

1913: The Newlands Act set up a Board of Mediation and Conciliation to handle railroad disputes.

1914: The United States government established the eight-hour day for all Federal employees.

1914: On December 1, President Wilson appointed the Colorado Coal Commission, which investigated the Ludlow Massacre and labor conditions in the Colorado coal mines following an unsuccessful strike by the United Mine Workers.

1914: The Clayton Act was approved, limiting the use of injunctions in labor disputes and providing that picketing and other union activities shall not be considered unlawful.

1914: The Amalgamated Clothing Workers was formed by a seceding group of the United Garment Workers (AFL).

1915: The LaFollette Seamen's Act was approved, regulating conditions of employment for maritime workers.

1916: A federal child labor law was enacted (declared unconstitutional on June 3, 1918); followed by an act of February 24, 1919 (declared unconstitutional on May 15, 1922); followed by a proposed child labor amendment to the Constitution on June 2, 1924. Only twenty-eight of the necessary thirty-six states ratified the amendment.

1916: The Adamson Act, providing a basic eight-hour day on railroads, was enacted to eliminate a threatened nationwide railroad strike.

1917: The Supreme Court ruled that Oregon State law setting the ten-hour day for all manufacturing establishments was constitutional because it followed a customary and reasonable average.

1917: The Socialist Party declared its opposition to American entry into World War I. The IWW denounced the war as a capitalist plot.

1917: Congress passed the Espionage Act. Although the laws were originally aimed at opponents of the First World War, they were soon turned against socialists, wobblies, and labor militants.

1917: A strike led by the IWW in the copper mines of Bisbee, Arizona, was ended when the sheriff deported 1,200 strikers.

1917: The President appointed a mediation commission, headed by the Secretary of Labor, to adjust wartime labor difficulties.

1917: The yellow-dog contract was upheld, and union efforts to organize workers party to such contracts were held to be unlawful (*Hitchman Coal & Coke Co. v. Mitchell*).

1918: The federal government took control of the railroads from December 1917 until March 1, 1920, under existing federal legislation which provided for government railroad operation in wartime.

1918: The U.S. Supreme Court decided, in *Hammer v. Dagenhart,* that the federal child labor law was unconstitutional interference in interstate commerce.

1918: The President named the Secretary of Labor as War Labor Administrator on January 4.

1918: The President created the National War Labor Board on April 8 "to settle by mediation and conciliation controversies . . . in fields of production necessary for the effective conduct of the war." It went out of existence in May 1919.

1918: The minimum-wage law of the District of Columbia was approved September 19 (declared unconstitutional on April 9, 1923).

1919: The Socialist Party split over adherence to the Moscow-founded Third International. Two Communist Parties were organized.

1919: The United Mine Workers of America struck against bituminous coal operators on November 1. In December, the union agreed to arbitration by a Presidential commission. The Bituminous Coal Commission, appointed by the President on December 19, awarded a 27 percent wage increase, but denied the six-hour day and five-day week.

1919: Led by President Gompers of the AFL, a commission created by the Peace Conference at its second plenary session in January recommended the inclusion in the Peace Treaty of labor clauses creating an International Labour Organization.

1919: A Seattle general strike touched off national fear of American radicalism.

1919: A Boston police strike followed the discharge of two dozen policemen for joining a new AFL union. The State militia was called in and the strike ended in a defeat for the 1,117 strikers.

1920: The AFL Iron and Steel Organizing Committee ended an unsuccessful 3½-month strike in the steel industry on January 8 after most of the strikers had drifted back to work.

1920: In the midst of a nationwide "red scare," Attorney General A. Mitchell Palmer raided the homes of suspected radicals. More than 10,000 were arrested, 550 deported. The communist movement went underground.

1920: The Women's Bureau was established in the Department of Labor by an act of Congress.

1920: The Transportation Act provided for a tripartite Railroad Labor Board and terminated Federal control of railroads on March 1. Title III of the Act (Esch-Cummins) provided for settlement of labor disputes on interstate railroads by collective bargaining and arbitration.

1920: The Kansas Court of Industrial Relations provided the first experiment in compulsory arbitration in the United States (held unconstitutional in part in 1923).

1921: An act restricting the immigration of aliens into the United States and establishing the national-origin quota system was approved.

1921: The Supreme Court held that nothing in the Clayton Act legalized secondary boycotts or protected unions against injunctions brought against them for conspiracy in restraint of trade (*Duplex Printing Press v. Deering*).

1921: The International Seamen's Union (AFL) and Marine Engineers Beneficial Association (AFL) lost a fifty-two-day strike against wage reductions.

1921: The President's Conference on Unemployment placed the main responsibility for unemployment relief upon local communities.

1921: The Arizona law forbidding injunctions in labor disputes and permitting picketing was held unconstitutional under the Fourteenth Amendment (*Truax v. Corrigan*).

1922: The United Mine Workers was held not responsible for local strike action, and strike action was held not a conspiracy to restrain commerce within the Sherman Antitrust Act. Labor unions, however, were held suable for their acts (*Coronado Coal Co. v. UMWA*).

1924: Congress passed a restrictive Immigration Act approved by organized labor.

1924: Samuel Gompers, president of the AFL, died on December 13.

1924: Robert LaFollette ran for President on a ticket backed by American Federation of Labor and Socialist Party. He received nearly 5 million votes, which was one-sixth of the total. Six senators and twenty congressmen were elected as progressives.

1925: The Amalgamated Clothing Workers and Hart, Schaffner and Marx agreed to a productivity plan, touching off the union-management cooperation movement.

1926: The Railway Labor Act required employers to bargain collectively and not discriminate against their employees for joining a union. The act also provided for the settlement of railway labor disputes through mediation, voluntary arbitration, and fact-finding boards.

1927: The Longshoremen's and Harbor Workers' Compensation Act was enacted.

1927: Sacco and Vanzetti, two anarchists, were executed in Massachusetts for participation in an armored car holdup in what was widely regarded as a frame-up against foreign radicals.

1927: The Journeymen Stone Cutters' action in trying to prevent purchase of nonunion cut stone was held to be an illegal restraint of interstate commerce (*Bedford Cut Stone Co. v. Journeymen Stone Cutters' Association, et al.*).

1929: The Hawes-Cooper Act governing the shipment of convict-made goods in interstate commerce was approved.

1929: The Communist-inspired Trade Union Unity League was formed in September; it was dissolved in 1935.

1929: Socialists and trade union progressives, headed by A. J. Muste, organized the Conference for Progressive Labor Action, to convert the American Federation of Labor to industrial unionism and to organize the unskilled.

1929: A Communist-led strike of the South's textile center of Gastonia, North Carolina, was routed by mob action.

1930: The Railway Labor Act's prohibition of employer interference or coercion in the choice of bargaining representatives was upheld by the Supreme Court (*Texas & N.O.R. Co. v. Brotherhood of Railway Clerks*).

1931: The Davis-Bacon Act provided for the payment of prevailing wage rates to laborers and mechanics employed by contractors and subcontractors on public construction.

1932: The Anti-Injunction (Norris-LaGuardia) Act prohib-

ited federal injunctions in labor disputes, except as specified, and outlawed yellow-dog contracts.

1932: Wisconsin adopted the first unemployment insurance act in the United States.

1933: Frances Perkins became Secretary of Labor, the first woman named to the Cabinet.

1933: Section 7(a) of the National Industrial Recovery Act provided that every NRA code and agreement should guarantee the right of employees to organize and bargain collectively through their representatives without interference, restraint, or coercion by employers (Title I of the act was declared unconstitutional in *Schecter v. U.S.* on May 27, 1935).

1933: The Wagner-Peyser Act created the United States Employment Service in the Department of Labor.

1934: The first National Labor Legislation Conference was called by the Secretary of Labor to obtain closer Federal-State cooperation in working out a sound national labor legislation program. Annual conferences were held until 1955.

1934: The United States joined the International Labour Organization.

1934: Four hundred thousand textile workers struck, mainly in the South. Leaders called off the strike after President Roosevelt established a textile labor board.

1935: The Committee for Industrial Organization (later the Congress of Industrial Organizations) was formed on November 9 by several AFL international unions and officials to foster industrial unionism.

1935: The National Labor Relations (Wagner) Act established the first national labor policy of protecting the right of workers to organize and to elect their representatives for collective bargaining.

1935: The Bituminous Coal Conservation (Guffey) Act was passed to stabilize the industry and to improve labor conditions (labor relations provisions were declared unconstitutional on May 18, 1936).

1935: The Federal Social Security Act was approved August 14.

1936: In the first large sit-down strike, the United Rubber Workers (CIO) won recognition at Goodyear Tire & Rubber Co.

1936: The Anti-Strikebreaker (Byrnes) Act declared it unlawful "to transport or aid in transporting strikebreakers in interstate or foreign commerce."

1936: The Public Contracts (Walsh-Healey) Act established labor standards on Government contracts, including minimum wages, overtime compensation for hours in excess of eight a day or forty a week, child and convict labor provisions, and health and safety requirements.

1936: The CIO launched the Non-Labor Partisan League to work for Franklin D. Roosevelt's reelection.

1937: The General Motors Corporation agreed to recognize the United Automobile Workers (CIO) as the bargaining agent for its members, to drop injunction proceedings against strikers, not to discriminate against union members, and to establish grievance procedures.

1937: The Workers Defense League was organized.

1937: The United States Steel Corporation recognized the Steel Workers Organizing Committee as the bargaining agent for its members. A 10 percent wage increase and an eight-hour day and forty-hour week were negotiated.

1937: The National Labor Relations Act was held constitutional (*NLRB v. Jones & Laughlin Steel Corp.*).

1937: Ten people were killed and eighty wounded in a Memorial Day clash between police and the members of the Steel Workers Organizing Committee at the plant of the Republic Steel Company in South Chicago.

1937: The Railroad Retirement Act of 1937 was approved, followed by the Carriers Taxing Act of 1937. (Similar laws of June 27, 1934, and August 29, 1935, had been declared unconstitutional.)

1937: The five-week "Little Steel" strike was broken on July 1, when Inland Steel employees returned to work without union recognition or other gains.

1937: The National Apprenticeship Act was passed, establishing the Bureau of Apprenticeship in the U.S. Department of Labor.

1937: The railroads signed their first contract with the Brotherhood of Sleeping Car Porters, whose president was A. Philip Randolph.

1938: The Merchant Marine Act of 1936 was amended to provide a Federal Maritime Labor Board.

1938: The Fair Labor Standards Act provided a 25-cent minimum wage and time and one-half for hours over forty a week. Subsequent amendments raised the minimum wage, so that as of 1976 it was $2.30 an hour for most employees.

1938: The Railroad Unemployment Insurance (Crosser-Wheeler) Act was passed.

1940: A sit-down strike was held not to be an illegal restraint of commerce under the Sherman Antitrust Act in the absence of intent to impose market controls (*Apex Hosiery Co. v. Leader*).

1941: Actions by the Carpenters' Union in jurisdictional disputes were held to be protected by the Clayton Act from prosecution under the Sherman Antitrust Act. These actions were construed in light of Congress's definition of "labor dispute" in the Norris-LaGuardia Act.

1941: The UAW (CIO) won recognition at the Ford Motor Company after a ten-day strike. The union and the company signed a union-shop agreement—the first with a major automobile manufacturer.

1941: On December 24, the President announced a no-strike pledge by the AFL and CIO for the duration of the war.

1941: Philip Murray replaced John L. Lewis as President of the CIO after Lewis opposed President Roosevelt's bid for a third term.

1941: John L. Lewis called a strike to unionize "captive" coal mines. An arbitration panel granted a closed shop, but public reaction to the strike was negative.

1941: A. Philip Randolph organized a march on Washington, prompting President Roosevelt to form a Fair Employment Practices Committee. Executive Order No. 8802 banned discrimination in industries holding Government contracts.

1941: Sidney Hillman, president of the Amalgamated Clothing Workers Union, was appointed Director of Office of Production Management to plan war production.

1942: The United Steelworkers of America was organized. It replaced the Steel Workers Organizing Committee, which was first established by the CIO in 1936.

1942: The President established the National War Labor Board (NWLB) to determine procedures for settling disputes.

1942: The NWLB laid down the "Little Steel" formula for wartime wage adjustments (i.e., based on a 15 percent rise in living costs from January 1, 1941 to May 1, 1942).

1942: The Stabilization Act authorized the President to stabilize wages and salaries, as far as practicable, based on September 15, 1942 levels.

1943: The United Mine Workers Union struck for wage increases. When President Roosevelt ordered government seizure of the coal mines, the union went back to work and negotiations were resumed.

1943: The President created by an Executive Order a Committee on Fair Employment Practices, empowering it to "conduct hearings, make findings of fact, and take appropriate steps to obtain elimination" of "discrimination in the employment of any person in war industries or in Government by reason of race, creed, color, or national origin."

1943: The War Labor Disputes (Smith-Connally) Act, passed over the President's veto, authorized plant seizure, if needed to avoid interference with the war effort.

1944: The Railway Labor Act, authorizing a labor union chosen by a majority to represent a craft, was held to require union protection to the minority in that class. Discrimination against certain members on grounds of race was held enjoinable (*Steel v. Louisville & Nashville Railroad*).

1945: The CIO affiliated with the newly formed World Federation of Trade Unions. (It withdrew in 1949.) The AFL, which held that the labor organizations of Soviet Russia were not "free or democratic," did not affiliate with the WFTU.

1945: The President's National Labor-Management Conference convened in Washington, D.C., but produced few tangible results.

1946: The United Steelworkers (CIO) ended a one-month strike and established a "first round" wage pattern increase of 18½ cents an hour.

1946: The Employment Act of 1946 committed the government to take all practicable measures to promote maximum employment, production, and purchasing power.

1946: The United Automobile Workers (CIO) ended a 3½-month strike against the General Motors Corporation by negotiating an hourly wage increase of 18½ cents, after a presidential fact-finding board had recommended 19½ cents.

1946: Locomotive Engineers (Ind.) and Railroad Trainment (Ind.) ended a national two-day strike following an injunction and under threat of legislation to draft the workers. They accepted the 18½-cent-an-hour increase recommended by the President.

1946: The UMWA bituminous coal miners won a health and welfare fund from the federal government, which had seized the mines.

1946: Congress passed the Lea Act, directed against James Petrillo, president of the American Federation of Musicians.

1946: The President provided for the termination of all wartime wage and salary controls.

1947: The Norris-LaGuardia Act prohibition against issuance of injunctions in labor disputes was held inapplicable to the Government as an employer (*U.S. v. John L. Lewis*).

1947: The Portal-to-Portal Act was approved "to relieve employers and the Government from potential liability . . . in 'portal-to-portal' claims."

1947: The Labor Management Relations (Taft-Hartley) Act was passed (June 23) over the President's veto.

1947: The New York State legislature passed the Condon-Wadlin Act following a teachers' strike in Buffalo. The law provided for the discharge of all strikers. Should they be rehired, it would be on probation for five years with no pay increase for at least three years. The law was replaced with the milder Taylor Law in 1967.

1948: The General Motors Corporation and the United Automobile Workers (CIO) signed the first major contract with an "escalator" clause, providing for wage increases based on the Consumer Price Index.

1948: The President appointed the Commission on Labor Relations in the Atomic Energy installations, which, on April 18, 1949, recommended establishment of a panel to protect free collective bargaining in atomic plants.

1948: The federal government's first national conference on industrial safety met in Washington, D.C.

1949: An amendment to the Fair Labor Standards Act (1938) directly prohibited child labor for the first time.

1949: The Supreme Court, by denying review of a lower court's action, upheld a decision that the Labor Management Relations Act requires employers to bargain with unions on retirement plans (*Inland Steel Co. v. United Steelworkers of America*).

1949: Settlement of a steel industry-United Steelworkers (CIO) strike on the basis of noncontributory $100 monthly pensions at age sixty-five, plus death, sickness, and accident benefits, followed a recommendation by a presidential fact-finding board.

1949: The CIO anticommunist drive culminated in expulsion of two unions at its annual convention. Trial and expulsion of nine other unions followed early in 1950.

1949: The International Union of Electrical, Radio and Machine Workers was founded at the CIO convention following the expulsion of the United Electrical, Radio and Machine Workers.

1949: Free, democratic trade unions of various countries, including the CIO in the United States, withdrew from the World Federation of Trade Unions, which had become communist dominated.

1949: A new worldwide labor organization—the International Confederation of Free Trade Unions (ICFTU)—with the AFL, CIO, and United Mine Workers participating, was formed at a meeting in December at London, England, of labor representatives from fifty-one countries.

1950: A five-year contract with no reopening provisions was negotiated by the United Automobile Workers (CIO) and the General Motors Corporation. It provided for pensions, automatic cost-of-living wage adjustments, guaranteed annual increases, and a modified union shop.

1950: A United Labor Policy Committee, composed of representatives of the AFL, the CIO, and railroad unions, was formed in December for the purpose of presenting labor's views to the Government on problems arising from the national emergency. The AFL withdrew from the Committee in August 1951, thereby dissolving the group.

1950: The Defense Production Act authorized the President to curb inflation and promote defense production.

1951: The International Association of Machinists reaffiliated with the AFL in January after being independent since 1945 due to jurisdictional disputes. In August the American Federation of Hosiery Workers, formerly an affiliate of the AFL United Textile Workers, rejoined the AFL as a separate union.

1951: The Inter-American Regional Workers Organization (ORIT) of the International Confederation of Free Trade Unions was established at a meeting in Mexico City in January. It claimed to represent 17 million workers in North, South, and Central America.

1951: Labor representatives withdrew in February from all participation in the Government's mobilization and stabilization program in protest over what they felt was labor's secondary role in its operation. They voted to return in April after being given a stronger voice in policy making.

1951: The CIO participated with the AFL as part of the United States delegation to the International Labour Conference of the ILO for the first time since 1946.

1951: The first amendment to the Taft-Hartley Act, permitting negotiations of union-shop agreements without previous polls of employees, became law in October. The union shop for workers on the nation's railways and airlines had previously been approved under the National (Railway) Mediation Act in January.

1952: In February, a Presidential emergency board, recommended agreement on the union shop between the railroads and nonoperating railroad unions representing about 1 million workers.

1952: Three unions of railroad operating employees and the carriers reached an agreement on wage increases and working rules in May. Federal operation of the railroads was brought to an end after being in effect since August 1950.

1952: A strike of nearly eight weeks' duration ended in July when the United Steelworkers of America (CIO) signed agreements with basic steel producers employing about 500,000 workers. Following the companies' rejection of Wage Stabilization Board recommendations, the Government seized the steel industry. The strike began after a district court granted an injunction restraining the seizure order, but it was halted at the request of President Truman, pending review of the decision by the Supreme Court. The strike was resumed after the Supreme Court held that the President exceeded his constitutional powers when he ordered the seizure.

1952: The presidents of the principal labor federations, Philip Murray of the CIO and William Green of the AFL, died in November. The AFL Executive Council elevated George Meany, former secretary-treasurer of the Federation, to the presidency. Walter P. Reuther, president of the United Automobile Workers, was named president of the CIO by the CIO convention.

1953: The Supreme Court upheld the right of the International Typographical Union (AFFL) to compel a newspaper to pay for the setting of type not used, and of the American Federation of Musicians (AFL) to demand that a local "standby" orchestra be employed when a traveling orchestra was hired for an engagement. The Court said that neither practice violated the "featherbedding" ban in the Labor Management Relations (Taft-Hartley) Act.

1953: The AFL and CIO, meeting in their respective conventions, approved a no-raiding pact to extend for two years from January 1, 1954. The agreement was binding only upon those member unions accepting it. Both organizations hailed the pact as the first step towards organic unity.

1953: The convention of the AFL revoked the sixty-year-old charter of the International Longshoremen's Association, charging corruption within the union. A bitter struggle for representation in the East Coast longshore industry, between the old ILA and the newly chartered AFL union took place on the docks, in the courts, and in NLRB hearing rooms during the last three months of 1953. (Following a representation election, in which the AFL union was defeated, the unaffiliated ILA was certified by the NLRB in August 1954 as collective bargaining agent for the dock workers.)

1954: A no-raiding agreement was activated by the AFL and CIO in June. After a series of meetings, unity committees of the two federations agreed in October upon merger without resolving in advance the jurisdiction of competing AFL and CIO unions. (Unity committees and the executive boards of the AFL and CIO approved the terms of the merger in February 1955.)

1954: Proposals for guaranteed annual employment or wage plans were developed by the United Automobile Workers, the Steelworkers, the Electrical Workers, and the Rubber Workers.

1955: In June, the Ford Motor Company and the United Auto Workers (then CIO) negotiated a new three-year agreement which established a supplementary unemployment compensation plan financed by company contributions of 5 cents an hour. By the end of 1955, similar plans were negotiated for more than a million workers, including the remainder of the auto industry.

1955: The founding of the American Federation of Labor and the Congress of Industrial Organizations (AFL-CIO) on December 5, 1955, brought under one roof unions representing approximately 16 million workers, which was over 85 percent of the membership claimed by all unions in the United States. The last conventions of the separate organizations, held on December 1 and 2, approved the merger agreement, a new constitution, and an implementation agreement designed to combine the two federations without dissolving either organization. The first convention of the AFL-CIO elected its president (George Meany), secretary-treasurer (William F. Schnitzler), and twenty-seven vice presidents, of whom seventeen had been proposed by the AFL and ten by the CIO. Under the constitution, these twenty-nine officers constituted the Executive Council, the governing body between the biennial conventions.

Mergers among AFL-CIO affiliates, while encouraged, were not to be dictated by the Federation, conflicts among unions competing in the same field were likewise to be adjusted voluntarily. Existing State, territorial, and local bodies previously established by the CIO and the AFL were required to merge within 2 years. The constitution provided for an industrial union department to promote the interests of unions organized on an industrial basis. It was organized during the convention week with 69 affiliated unions, including 38 former AFL unions.

1956: In the first year of unity, former AFL and CIO State labor organizations merged in nineteen states. The Brotherhood of Locomotive Firemen and Enginemen—unaffiliated throughout its eighty-three-year history—joined the AFL-CIO in September. Although several international unions proposed and discussed mergers, only a few were carried out. On the other hand, a number of unions signed mutual assistance pacts or no-raiding agreements. The Federation's Ethical Practices Committee recommended to the Executive Council after hearings that three unions (the Allied Industrial Workers, the Laundry Workers, and the Distillery Workers) should show cause why they should not be suspended because of domination by "corrupt" influences in the administration of employee welfare funds.

1956: Amendments to the Federal Social Security Act provided that disabled industrial workers could qualify for disability benefits at age fifty, and women could retire at age sixty-two with reduced benefits. Railroad Retirement Act benefits were increased. Benefits were increased and the waiting period lowered for disabled workers coming under the Longshoremen's and Harbor Workers' Compensation Act. Benefits for Federal employees under the civil service retirement system were increased. Old-age and survivors' insurance benefits were extended to additional self-employed persons and the uniformed services.

1957: The Senate established the McClellan Committee to investigate racketeering in labor-management relations.

1957: The biennial convention of the AFL-CIO expelled the Teamsters, Bakery Workers, and Laundry Workers, which had a combined membership of approximately 1.6 million, on charges of domination by corrupt influences. This action followed upon a refusal on the part of the three unions to accept the corrective recommendation of the Executive Council.

1957: Three formerly independent railroad unions became affiliated with the AFL-CIO during 1957; the Brotherhood of Railroad Trainmen, the American Train Dispatchers Association, and the American Railway Supervisors Association.

1958: New York City adopted a system of labor relations designed to promote the type of "collective bargaining prevailing in industry."

1958: Federal legislation passed during 1958 included a Welfare and Pension Plans Disclosure Act, which required administrators of all health, insurance, pension, and supplementary unemployment compensation plans covering more than twenty-five workers (amended in 1962) to file with the Secretary of Labor descriptions and annual financial reports to be available for public inspection. Reports also had to be made available for plan participants. Other laws included one for optional Federal loans to states for a temporary 50 percent extension of unemployment payments to workers who had exhausted their benefits under Federal and State programs.

1959: The Labor-Management Reporting and Disclosure Act of 1959, designed to eliminate improper activities by labor or management, was signed by President Eisenhower on September 14. The act provided certain protection for the rights of labor organization memebers; provided for the fling of reports describing the organization, financial dealings, and business practices of labor organizations, their officers and employees, certain employers, labor relations consultants, and unions in trusteeship; safeguarded union election procedures; set standards for the handling of union funds; amended the Taft-Hartley law to eliminate the "no-man's land" in NLRB cases; closed previously existing loopholes in the protection against secondary boycotts; and limited organizational and jurisdictional picketing. The statute was to be administered by the Department of Labor, except for the provisions amending the Taft-Hartley Act, which were to be administered by the National Labor Relations Board.

1959: The longest major strike ever to take place in the steel industry began on July 15. Attempts to resolve the dispute through negotiation continued until October 21, when the national emergency provisions of the Taft-Hartley Act were invoked. After an unsuccessful attempt on the part of a board of inquiry to promote a settlement, a back-to-work injunction was issued. After a court battle over the constitutionality and applicability of the injunction, the Supreme Court upheld the injunction on November 7, the 116th day of the strike. Workers then returned to their jobs for the eighty-day "cooling off" period. (Negotiations were successfully completed and new contracts signed early in January 1960.)

1960: The nation's railroads and the five operating brotherhoods agreed to refer their long-standing dispute involving work rules and practices to a tripartite presidential commission for study and recommendations.

1960: An agreement which opened the way to relaxation of restrictive working rules and the increased use of labor-saving equipment on the waterfront was signed by the Pacific Maritime Association and the International Longshoremen's and Warehousemen's Union. In return for the union's acceptance of the changes, the association agreed to contribute $5 million a year to a fund to provide each of the 15,000 registered longshoremen $7,920 upon retirement at age sixty-five with twenty-five years of service, and to guarantee union members certain minimum weekly earnings and no layoffs as a result of decreased work opportunities under the new contract provisions. However, the fund would not protect longshoremen from reduced earnings resulting from a decline in business.

1961: Amendments to the Fair Labor Standards Act went into effect September 3, 1961, extending coverage to an additional 3.6 million workers, mostly in the retail trade and construction. The minimum-wage rates of workers already covered were increased. Newly covered workers were brought gradually under the overtime provisions of the act until they received time and one-half pay for any hours after forty per week by September 1965.

1961: The Southern Pacific Railroad and the Order of Railroad Telegraphers negotiated an agreement guaranteeing each telegrapher his job or equivalent wages during his lifetime.

1961: The fourth biennial convention of the AFL-CIO approved a constitutional amendment setting up a procedure for the peaceful resolution of jurisdictional disputes, a problem that had been disruptive since the 1955 merger. Constructive steps were also taken by the convention in the campaign to eliminate all vestiges of racial discrimination in the ranks of the AFL-CIO.

1962: The Manpower Development and Training Act was approved in March 15. It required the federal government to determine manpower requirements and resources and to "deal with the problems of unemployment resulting from automation and technological changes and other types of persistent unemployment." The act was to be administered by the Secretary of Labor and the Secretary of Health, Education, and Welfare.

1962: A citywide strike gained New York City's United Federation of Teachers its first contract.

1962: Federal employees' unions were granted the right to bargain collectively with Government agencies under an Executive Order signed January 17. The order guaranteed to unions of Federal workers certain rights of organization, consultation, and processing of grievances.

1963: The Equal Pay Act of 1963 was signed by President Kennedy on June 10. This act prohibited wage differentials based on sex for workers covered by the Fair Labor Standards Act.

1963: The March on Washington for Jobs and Justice drew 200,000 civil rights demonstrators.

1963: After negotiations to resolve the long-standing railroad dispute involving operating railroad workers failed to produce any concrete results, Congress passed legislation calling for arbitration of the two principal issues: the use of firemen on diesel locomotives in freight and yard service, and the makeup of train crews. The report of the arbitrators, issued on November 26, provided for the gradual elimination of firemen in 90 percent of freight and yard service. The crew-consist issue was returned to the unions and carriers for further negotiation, and arbitration, if necessary.

1964: The 4½-year dispute between the railroads and operating brotherhoods over work rules and other collective bargaining issues ended when final agreement was reached on all issues not resolved by the arbitration award of November 1963. The Brotherhood of Locomotive Firemen and Enginemen ratified the agreement on June 25, the last of the five operating unions to do so.

1964: The inability of the International Longshoremen's Association and the New York Shipping Association to agree on the terms of a new contract and the union's rejection of recommendations made by a special Board of Mediation on the basis of a Department of Labor study of labor utilization and job security led to a strike of all East Coast and Gulf Coast ports on October 1. The strike was immediately halted when the President invoked the eighty-day injunction provisions of the Taft-Hartley Act. This was the sixth application of the national emergency provisions of the act to East Coast longshoring.

1964: The Civil Rights Act of 1964 was signed on July 2 by President Johnson, to become effective a year later. Title VII—Equal Employment Opportunity"—barred discrimination on the basis of race, color, religion, sex, or national original in hiring, apprenticeship, compensation, and terms, conditions, or privileges of employment, and union membership. An Equal Employment Opportunity Commission was charged with investigating and adjudicating complaints under this title.

1964: The Economic Opportunity Act of 1964 was signed into law on August 20. The measure provided for work and education programs, loans to low-income farmers and business, and various other national community antipoverty programs.

1965: The United Farm Workers' Organizing Committee (AFL-CIO) was established, with Cesar Chavez as president.

1965: The longshore dispute erupted into a strike beginning January 11, after New York longshore workers voted down an agreement reached just before the injunction expired (see entry in 1964). The strike lasted about a month in major ports, but all East and Gulf Coast ports were not back to work until another month had elapsed.

1965: The enactment of the McNamara-O'Hara Service Contract Act on October 22 provided wage standards for employees performing work on Federal service contracts. These standards were similar to those long applicable to employees on Federal construction and supply contracts.

1965: Agricultural employers became subject to revised regulations governing applications for temporary foreign agricultural workers under the Immigration and Nationality Act of 1952. In addition to making a "reasonable effort" to recruit domestic workers, a grower was required to offer American workers minimum wages, varying by state, before foreign labor was permitted to be used. Beginning April 1, 1965, "nonadverse" higher wages became effective. The revised regulations were issued after expiration of the Mexican farm labor program.

1965: The Hosiery Workers Union was formally dissolved after fifty years of existence, and its members were absorbed by the Textile Workers Union of America (AFL-CIO). Once a union of 50,000 members, the Hosiery Workers Union had declined to around 5,000 members.

1965: Social security amendments of 1965 included the Medicare plan, which provided partial coverage, for those over sixty-five, for hospitalization, nursing home care, home nursing, and diagnostic expenses. An optional, supplementary plan provided coverage for most major medical expenses. Benefits became available on July 1, 1966.

1965: In November, the Industrial Union Department of the AFL-CIO arranged with ten insurance companies to underwrite a pooled pension plan for employees of small companies. The program was available in 1966 for employers having fewer than 100 workers.

1966: Delegates representing the United States trade union movement walked out of the fiftieth session of the International Labor Conference in Geneva when a delegate from Communist Poland was elected as presiding officer. The boycott led to an open argument between Walter Reuther, who protested the action, and George Meany, who defended it, over the international program of the AFL-CIO.

1966: Two transportation strikes tested the adequacy of legislation designed to prevent work stoppages. New York City's transit system was shut down for twelve days in violation of a State law banning public employee strikes. Union leaders were subsequently jailed for violating a court injunction. Five major airlines were struck on July 8, after the Machinists rejected the recommendations of an emergency board.

1966: The 1966 amendments to the Fair Labor Standards Act, the most far-reaching in the history of the act, extended minimum-wage protection to some 10 million workers previously excluded from the benefits of the law.

1966: Coalition bargaining, that is, the coordination of strategy and action among different unions having contracts with the same company, passed a major test when the General Electric Company negotiated a new agreement with the Electrical Workers (IUE) in the presence of representatives from ten other unions.

1967: Professional workers employed both their own independent associations and traditional trade unions during the year in increasing collective bargaining activity. AFL-CIO unions which organized professional workers moved toward closer cooperation. In March they formed the AFL-CIO Council of Scientific, Professional, and Cultural Employees (SPACE), dedicated to enhancing organizing, collective bargaining, legislative, and public relations activities for the member organizations.

1967: Early in the year, the unaffiliated Mine, Mill and Smelter Workers merged with the United Steelworkers. In mid-July the merged unions and twenty-five others joined in a strike against major copper producers, the strike continuing through the remainder of the year.

1967: A five-man arbitration board, established by Congress in July after a two-day railroad stoppage, imposed a two-year settlement within the framework of previous bargaining on the railroads and six shopcraft unions, when the parties were unable to reach agreement within the time limits specified in the legislation.

1967: A three-year agreement calling for higher wages, a greatly increased supplemental unemployment benefit (SUB) plan, and other benefits ended a nationwide walkout at the Ford Motor Company which idled 160,000 auto workers for seven weeks. Costs of the settlement were estimated at 90 cents an hour. Similar settlements were subsequently reached at General Motors and Chrysler without major shutdowns.

1967: At its biennial convention, the AFL-CIO explicitly rejected the application of guidepost formulas to collective bargaining and reiterated its support of double time as reimbursement for overtime. Earlier in the year, Auto Workers' President Walter P. Reuther and other top UAW officials resigned most of their AFL-CIO posts, protesting the "complacency" of the Federation's leadership.

1968: On June 12 the Age Discrimination in Employment Act, signed by President Johnson the previous December, went into effect. The act made it illegal for employers, unions, and employment agencies in interstate commerce to discharge, refuse to hire, or otherwise discriminate against persons aged forty to sixty-five. On November 27 the Secretary of Labor, in response to a requirement under the statute, recommended that no changes be made in these age limits.

1968: Provisions restricting wage garnishment—the practice of attaching portions of a debtor's salary or wage for satisfaction of creditors—were enacted as part of the Consumer Credit Protection ("truth in lending") Act of 1968.

1968: A major Fair Labor Standards Act case was decided by the Supreme Court in *Maryland v. Wirtz*. The Court held that coverage of employees of state and local government hospitals and schools was a valid exercise by the Congress of Article 1, Section 8 (the commerce clause) of the Constitution.

1968: The AFL-CIO created a new department to coordinate its urban rehabilitation programs, and pledged cooperation with business and government in placing the hardcore unemployed in jobs. The Federation's Building and Construction Trades Department announced a new program to facilitate minority-race entry into trades apprenticeships. A number of AFL-CIO affiliated and independent unions also announced programs to aid underprivileged groups.

1968: The United Mine Workers of America expelled its affiliate, District 50, in April, in a dispute over the latter's endorsement of atomic energy.

1968: In July the Amalgamated Meat Cutters and Butcher Workmen of America and the United Packinghouse, Food and

Allied Workers, with a combined membership of about 500,000, completed a merger.

1968: Following a long series of policy disputes and an earlier suspension, the United Automobile Workers formally disaffiliated from the AFL-CIO in July. The event marked the first major schism in the labor movement since 1957, when the AFL-CIO expelled the Teamsters and two other unions, charging corrupt practices. Shortly thereafter, the UAW and Teamsters formed the Alliance for Labor Action, to coordinate their efforts toward organizing, bargaining, community, and political goals. When other labor organizations were invited to join the new group, the AFL-CIO charged the two unions with attempting to set up a rival federation, and warned its affiliated unions that supporting or joining the ALA would be grounds for suspension. In November, following charges and counter-charges of raiding, the ALA stated that it would be willing to enter into negotiations for a no-raiding pact with the Federation.

1968: A two-week nationwide telephone strike, the first in twenty years, occurred when the Communications Workers rejected company offers under a wage reopener clause.

1968: The long copper strike, which had begun the previous July, was settled on a company-by-company basis, with the bulk of the workers finally returning to their jobs in late March, when the unions and larger cooper producers came to terms.

1968: Labor unrest among public employees, particularly in New York City, continued to mount. The city managed to avert a threatened transit strike, and to reach peaceful agreement with its nonuniformed employees (other than teachers), but experienced a nine-day garbage collectors' strike in February, a shorter strike by incinerator workers, and a bitter and prolonged walkout, beginning September 9, of its public school teachers over the issues of job security and school decentralization. The city and its teachers reached an uneasy truce on November 17. Teacher strikes also took place in Pittsburgh, Albuquerque, San Francisco, Hartford, and other cities. A nine-week garbage collectors' strike in Memphis ended shortly after the tragic death of Dr. Martin Luther King.

1969: The UAW–Teamster-sponsored Alliance for Labor Action held its first convention. The ALA resolved to "revitalize the labor movement," organize the unorganized, and campaign for social and political action, tax reform, national health insurance, urban renewal, and cuts in military spending.

1969: Four railroad brotherhoods—the Brotherhood of Railroad Trainmen, the Brotherhood of Locomotive Firemen and Enginemen, the Switchmen's Union of North America, and the Order of Railway Conductors and Brakemen—merged to form the United Transportation Union (AFL-CIO), having a combined membership of over 200,000. At the same time, the 2,500-member Railway Patrolmen's International Union merged with the 270,000-member Brotherhood of Railway, Airline and Steamship Clerks.

1969: The eighth biennial convention of the AFL-CIO voted to expel the 90,000-member Chemical Workers Union, which had joined the Alliance for Labor Action (considered by the AFL-CIO to be a rival federation) despite AFL-CIO warnings.

1969: In December the Bakery and Confectionary Workers, expelled from the AFL-CIO in 1957, returned to the Federation by merging with the American Bakery and Confectionary Workers' International Union (AFL-CIO).

1969: Joseph "Jock" Yablonsky was assassinated three weeks after he was defeated in a rigged election for president of the United Mine Workers Union.

1969: In February the AFL-CIO withdrew from the Inter-national Confederation of Free Trade Unions (ICFTU) in disapproval of ICFTU attitudes toward Soviet-bloc nations and for ICFTU failure to comply with AFL-CIO demands to reject admission of the United Auto Workers to the world labor organization.

1969: After expiration of an eighty-day Taft-Hartley injunction on December 20, East Coast dock-workers shut down major Atlantic and Gulf ports in a dispute over wages and benefits; "containerization" was a key issue. Settlement was reached in New York City in mid-January 1970, and strikes at other ports ended shortly afterward.

1969: A new Department of Labor drive to open construction jobs to minorities began; it focused first on the Philadelphia area. Builders were asked to submit specific minority hiring goals. The joint Department of Labor–National Alliance of Businessmen JOBS program announced expansion from 50 to 125 cities. The NAB reported in early 1969 that firms participating in JOBS had hired 120,000 hardcore unemployed. The program's goal was to hire 600,000.

1969: On October 29, President Johnson issued Executive Order No. 11491, Labor-Management Relations in the Federal Service, which replaced Executive Order No. 10988, Employee-Management Cooperation in the Federal Service, issued in 1962. Changes made by the new order included the establishment of a Federal Labor Relations Council to administer the program, and a Federal Service Impasse Panel to resolve disputes over new contract terms.

1970: Hawaii became the first state to allow state and local government employees the right to strike. Strikes were to be permitted only if efforts to reach an agreement failed and if the public health was not endangered.

1970: The first mass work stoppage in the 195-year history of the Post Office Department began March 18 with a walkout of letter carriers in Brooklyn and Manhattan, and soon involved nearly 750,000 postal employees, virtually paralyzing mail service in New York, Detroit, and Philadelphia, and affecting service in other major cities. Agreement was reached after two weeks, but not before President Nixon declared a state of national emergency, assigned military units to New York City post offices, and promised to begin discussions of all issues, including pay.

1970: On December 29 President Nixon signed the Occupational Safety and Health Act, which authorized the Secretary of Labor to establish occupational safety and health standards in the Nation's workplaces. Under provisions of this law, effective April 28, 1971, the Secretary and an independent review commission appointed by the President were given authority to impose civil penalties and fines. Criminal action was permitted in cases of willful violations that resulted in death and in certain other cases. The review commission was to hear appeals of citations and of proposed penalties for alleged violations. The party losing the appeal could seek further review by a United States court of appeals. The law also provided for state development and enforcement of occupational safety and health standards, subject to approval by the Secretary of Labor.

1970: After a 4½-year boycott of California table grapes, the United Farm Workers Organizing Committee (AFL-CIO) reached an agreement with most producers. In August the UFWOC and Teamsters signed a no-raiding pact, giving the UFWOC jurisdiction over all field workers, while the Teamsters retained the right to organize food processing and cannery workers.

1970: In December, following expiration of an emergency strike ban, a nationwide strike—the fourth since World War II—was called by four rail unions. The strike was ended after one day by issuance of a Federal injunction, and Congress hastily voted to extend the strike ban until March 1, 1971, and to increase retroactive pay.

1971: Five postal unions—the United Federation of Postal Clerks, the National Association of Post Office and General Services Maintenance Employees, the National Federation of Post Office Motor Vehicle Employees, the National Association of Special Delivery Messengers, and the National Postal Union (Ind.)—merged to form the American Postal Workers Union (AFL-CIO) having nearly 300,000 members.

1971: The Alliance for Labor Action, formed by the Auto Workers and Teamsters in 1968 to coordinate their organizing efforts and other common objectives, was disbanded in December.

1971: A federal court upheld the Philadelphia Plan (*Contractors Association of Eastern Pennsylvania v. Schultz*).

1972: On January 17 West Coast longshore workers resumed a strike that had been halted by a Taft-Hartley injunction issued in October 1971. The strike ended February 19, after 139 days, making it the longest dock strike in the Nation's history.

1972: Miners for Democracy, headed by Arnold Miller, took over the leadership of the United Mine Workers Union.

1972: One of the longest labor disputes in United States labor history was settled by a July agreement between the United Transportation Union and major railroad companies to gradually phase out firemen's jobs on diesel freight locomotives. The dispute began in 1937, and at various times involved arbitration boards, presidential panels, Congress, and the courts.

1972: Three mergers of major unions took place during the summer. District 50, Allied and Technical Workers, once a division of the Mine Workers, merged with the United Steelworkers, bringing the combined membership to more than 1.25 million. The United Papermarkers and Paperworkers Union combined with the International Brotherhood of Pulp, Sulphite and Paper Mill Workers to form the 345,000-member United Paper Workers International Union. The Lithographers and Photoengravers International Union and the International Brotherhood of Bookbinders combined to form the Graphic Arts International Union, with more than 120,000 members.

1973: The United Steelworkers and the Steel Industry Coordinating Committee, representing ten major steel producers, approved an "Experimental Negotiation Agreement" designed to avert crisis bargaining and stockpiling in the steel industry. Affecting 300,000 workers, the agreement provided for voluntary final and binding arbitration of unresolved issues in the 1974 negotiations.

1973: Under a law effective June 1, Washington became the first state to allow the union shop for civil servants.

1973: As a result of an agreement reached on June 1, the International Printing Pressmen and Assistants Union of North America and the International Stereotypers', Electrotypers', and Platemakers' Union of North America merged on October 2, forming the 135,000-member International Printing and Graphic Communications (AFL-CIO).

1973: On June 13, as a prelude to Phase IV, President Nixon announced a freeze of up to sixty days on prices. Wages, interest, and dividends continued to be exempt from controls. Phase IV, implemented on June 18, reaffirmed the wage standards of Phases II and III on a voluntary basis and required prenotification of price increases in key industries.

1973: The International Union of Brewery, Flour, Cereal, Soft Drink and Distillery Workers approved a leadership decision to merge with the International Brotherhood of Teamsters, ending a long-term rivalry between the two unions. Local unions representing about 25 percent of the Brewery Workers' 40,000 members rejected the merger, however, preferring direct affiliation with the AFL-CIO. The Federation had averted possible legal obstacles to direct affiliation by revoking the Brewery Workers' charter during the AFL-CIO Convention in October.

1973: President Nixon signed the Comprehensive Employment and Training Act of 1973, designed to consolidate and decentralize the numerous and sometimes overlapping federal employment programs. Under the law, the federal government was to provide funds to state and local governments, and the latter, as prime sponsors, were to determine the type of employment services to be provided within their jurisdictions. Additional Federal funds were to be made available to communities having disproportionately low earnings or high unemployment.

1974: On December 31, President Ford signed the Emergency Jobs and Unemployment Assistance Act of 1974. The act provided a special unemployment assistance program for individuals who have prior labor force attachment but are ineligible for unemployment insurance.

1974: On December 31, President Ford signed the Emergency Unemployment Compensation Act of 1974, which provided extended benefits of up to sixty-five weeks of unemployment compensation to workers whose rights to benefits would otherwise have expired.

1974: On January 3, President Ford signed amendments to the Social Security Act. The bill provided for automatic cost-of-living adjustments whenever the Consumer Price Index rose three percent. The bill also raised the taxable base from $10,800 to $13,200 in annual earnings effective January 1, 1974 (the taxable base had been scheduled to increase to $12,600).

1974: About 3,000 women unionists from fifty-eight labor organizations assembled in Chicago in late March to establish the Coalition of Labor Union Women. The Coalition was dedicated to promoting equal rights and better wages and working conditions for women workers. The organization was to work toward increasing union membership of women, greater participation by women in union affairs and policymaking, and favorable legislation affecting women workers.

1974: In May, *The New York Times* and the *New York Daily News* signed an eleven-year agreement with the International Typographical Union. The contract gave the newspapers the unrestricted right to introduce automated typesetting procedures in return for lifetime security for current employees. The companies were obligated to retrain employees displaced by new processes, and the work force could be reduced only through attrition. The papers agreed to encourage retirements through paid six-month productivity leaves (trial retirements) and retirement bonuses.

1974: On June 1, the Amalgamated Clothing Workers of America (AFL-CIO) called their first nationwide strike since 1921, involving 110,000 workers in thirty states. The union reached agreement with the Clothing Manufacturers Association on June 8.

1974: On June 4, the 2,500-member Cigar Makers' International Union of America (AFL-CIO) was merged into the Retail, Wholesale and Department Store Union (AFL-CIO). One of the oldest national unions, dating back to 1864, the Cigar Makers' once numbered Samuel Gompers, first president of the American Federation of Labor, among its members.

1974: On Labor Day, President Ford signed the Employee Retirement Income Security Act of 1974, which regulated all private pension plans and, to a much more limited extent, all private welfare plans.

1974: To assure workers that pension promises would not be broken, pension plans were required to observe certain funding standards to assure the payment of adequate contributions and to purchase termination insurance. The insurance, provided by the Pension Benefit Guaranty Corporation, headed by the Secretary of Labor, was to pay pensions up to $750 a month if a plan terminated without sufficient funds to pay all of its nonforfeitable benefits.

1974: A new Public Employee Department of the AFL-CIO was formed. It included twenty-four affiliated unions representing 2 million public employees, including those of the U.S. Postal Service. The thirty-year-old Government Employees Council was merged with the new organization.

1975: On January 2, President Ford signed the Trade Act of 1974. The Act was designed to help workers who lose their jobs because of imports, as well as to provide financial and technical assistance to companies and communities hurt by foreign competition. It provided displaced workers with up to fifty-two weeks of payments (seventy-eight weeks for workers sixty or older) and assistance in retraining, placement, and relocation.

1975: About two-thirds of the 3,000 physicians represented by the Committee of Interns and Residents struck twenty-two New York City hospitals for three days in March. Long working hours and other pressures associated with hospital training were at issue. A two-year agreement with the League of Voluntary Hospitals achieved improvements in hours, working conditions, salaries, and fringe benefits. The walkout was backed by the American Medical Association, which said it was the first by interns and residents in the Nation's history, excepting minor "job actions."

1975: The highest unemployment rates since 1941, reaching 9.2 percent in May, inspired considerable union criticism of administration policies. Heavy layoffs caused by declining auto sales resulted in the depletion of Chrysler's supplementary unemployment fund in March, and of General Motors' in May. The financial crises of city governments in New York and other major cities forced service cutbacks and widespread layoffs of municipal employees.

1975: Early in July, the nation witnessed the first large-scale strike of state employees, involving more than 80,000 employees of the State of Pennsylvania. The majority, represented by the American Federation of State, County and Municipal Employees, reached agreement and returned to work within a week, partly as a result of court injunctions claiming danger to the public. Employees represented by the Pennsylvania Social Services Unions and the Pennsylvania Nurses Association reached agreement later in the month.

1975: In August, California became the first state to pass legislation covering farm labor relations. Its Agricultural Relations Act provided for secret-ballot representation elections and established machinery to resolve unfair labor-practices complaints.

1975: In November, the United States gave the required two-year notice of its intention to withdraw from the ILO. This step would be taken unless the ILO reversed its increasing involvement in political issues.

1975: The Teamsters Union's General Executive Board canceled its mutual-aid and no-raiding pacts with twenty-two AFL-CIO unions. The action, revealed in the November 1975 issue of the *International Teamster*, followed a recent war of words between AFL-CIO President George Meany and Teamsters' head Frank Fitzsimmons. The dispute centered on the AFL-CIO's active support of the United Farm Workers Union in its continuing clash with the Teamsters over which union should represent agricultural workers.

1975: The American Medical Association went on record as favoring collective bargaining by physicians, reversing its previous position that group action by doctors is incompatible with good patient care. The AMA's new position was geared primarily toward the problems of interns and residents in dealing with the hospitals that employ them.

1975: A power struggle within the United Mine Workers Union surfaced on October 31, when a 14 to 6 majority of the International Executive Board adopted an otherwise routine report on pensioner affairs that concluded with a recommendation that a special convention be called to remove union president Arnold R. Miller from office. The dissident faction was led by Vice President Mike Trbovich.

1975: On November 11, the Railway, Airline and Steamship Clerks Union announced formation of a corporation that will bid for the operating rights of the bankrupt REA Express, Inc., which ceased operation earlier in the month. If it wins the rights, the union will reopen carrier operations and rehire the 7,000 terminated employees it represents.

1975: New York City's major commercial printing firms reached a ten-year agreement with Typographical Union No. 6, under which printers will receive job security in exchange for work-rule changes intended to increase productivity. The pact, ratified in late December, was similar to an agreement reached earlier in 1975 between the union and the city's major newspapers.

1975: Beginning in 1976, about 25 percent of the 78 million workers covered by social security contributed more to the system, to finance benefits. The tax rate—which remained at 5.85 percent for employees and for their employers—was levied on the first $15,300 of annual earnings, instead of the first $14,000, bringing the maximum yearly contribution to $895.05, from $824.85. The 7.9 percent tax rate for self-employed persons was also based on the higher earnings level.

1975: The longest strike by doctors in the nation's history ended November 13, when residents and interns at Chicago's only public hospital ratified a settlement with the Cook County Health and Hospital Governing Commission. The 500 doctors, represented by the hospital's House Staff Association, walked out October 27.

1975: The Screen Actors Guild gained its first woman president when Kathleen Nolan defeated four other candidates in a national referendum. She succeeded Dennis Weaver, who did not seek reelection but did accept election to a one-year term on the union's board of directors.

1975: At a December 3d press conference, Teamsters' President Frank Fitzsimmons pledged full cooperation with the

Department of Labor's investigation of the Teamsters' Central States Pension Fund, but attacked a proposed congressional inquiry into the fund's affairs.

1975: On December 4, the nation's railroads and four shop-craft unions reached tentative agreement on a new labor contract, averting a scheduled strike. When ratified by the 70,000 union members, the settlement concluded the round of railroad industry bargaining that began in February 1975. Terms were generally similar to those already accepted by the eleven other rail unions. They included wage increases of 10 percent on January 1, 1975, 5 percent on October 1, 1975, 3 percent on April 1, 1976, and 4 percent on July 1, 1977; a cost-of-living escalator clause providing for semiannual reviews beginning in January 1976; a tenth paid holiday; and an employer-financed dental plan.

1975: The Coalition of Labor Union Women, at their second convention held in Detroit in early December, reelected Olga Madar of the UAW as their national president. The 1,000 delegates, representing women members of sixty unions, also elected a slate of officers who declared their commitment to working for change by achieving more influence and power within their own unions. The coalition rededicated itself to work for ratification of the proposed Equal Rights Amendment to the U.S. Constitution.

1975: Workers at the Los Angeles *Herald Examiner* voted in favor of union representation in early December. The newspaper was staffed by nonunion workers from December 1967, when members of the Newspaper Guild walked out in a wage dispute. Other unions soon joined the union in the strike, which eventually became one of the longest in American newspaper history, and was never settled. A representative of the new independent union, the Employees for Better Working Conditions, said he expected quick certification of 177 to 92 vote by the National Labor Relations Board.

1975: On December 19, United Air Lines and the Machinists Union reached a three-year contract, ending a fourteen-day strike. The new agreement, covering some 17,000 mechanics, flight dispatchers, ramp service workers, and commissary workers, provided for wage increases of 5 percent on November 1, 1975, 4.7 percent on July 1, 1976, 2.8 percent on January 1, 1978, and 2.2 percent on July 1, 1978. Cost-of-living adjustments were scheduled for November 1976 and November 1977, with a maximum limit of 12 cents on each date.

1975: The Auto Workers Union filed the largest claim yet under the trade adjustment assistance provisions of the Trade Act of 1974. The claim, filed with the U.S. Department of Labor in mid-December, asked for special benefits for 70,000 workers who, the union said, suffered unemployment in 1975 because of increased automobile imports.

1975: The 175,000-member Brotherhood of Railway and Airline Clerks agreed with the Nation's railroads on a plan to modify seniority provisions of their labor contract to enhance job opportunities for minorities and women. The pact, reportedly the first of its kind in the railroad industry, was approved by key leaders of the union and by the National Railway Labor Conference, the bargaining arm for management.

1975: The New York State United Teachers' Board of Directors approved a resolution calling for the organization's disaffiliation from the National Education Association (NEA).

1975: The United Farm Workers Union (UFW) received 54 percent of all votes cast during the first four months of California's new farm labor law. The Teamsters' Union received 29 percent, and 17 percent went for no union representation. The UFW won elections at 185 farms for 18,000 workers, while the Teamsters had 110 victories covering 11,000 workers. The election wins did not guarantee labor contracts for the winning union; only exclusive bargaining rights for one year.

1976: Dunlop resigns as Secretary of Labor On January 14, Secretary of Labor John T. Dunlop announced his resignation. President Ford accepted the resignation with "great reluctance" while expressing appreciation for Dr. Dunlop's "enormous value" as Secretary of Labor and economic adviser. The resignation was effective February 1. Dr. Dunlop said that although he was not resigning in protest of the President's decision to veto the common situs bill for the construction industry, his departure was a direct consequence of that veto.

1976: Usery succeeds Dunlop On February 10, W. J. Usery, Jr., fifty-two, was sworn in as the fifteenth Secretary of Labor, succeeding Dr. Dunlop. President Ford had nominated Mr. Usery on January 22, and he was confirmed by a 79 to 7 Senate vote on February 4. Mr. Usery, when appointed, was Director of the Federal Mediation and Conciliation Service. He had been an Assistant Secretary of Labor in the Nixon Administration and, earlier, an official in the Machinists' Union.

1976: Settlement reached in apparel A forty-month agreement covering 55,000 workers was reached on February 2 between the International Ladies' Garment Workers' Union and five associations of dress manufacturers, jobbers, and contractors. The settlement, reached hours before a strike deadline, provided for wage increases of 5 percent on February 2, 1976, and June 7, 1976; 7 percent on June 6, 1977; and 6 percent on June 5, 1978. Guaranteed hourly minimums for pieceworkers were increased to $3.80 from $3.39 for operators, who constitute about 80 percent of the work force.

1976: "No-strike" plan adopted for airline In mid-February, National Airlines and the Air Line Employees Association agreed on a "no-strike plan to govern collective bargaining. Under the plan, any economic issues not resolved by a contract-termination date will go to binding arbitration, with the arbitrator's jurisdiction limited to two years from the contract-termination date. A minimum wage increase of 5 percent a year will be guaranteed if wage issues are arbitrated.

1976: Workers to receive federal aid to buy firm In mid-February, the U.S. Department of Commerce announced plans to give $13 million to the State of New Jersey to aid employees of the Okonite Company to buy the firm from Omega-Alpha, Inc. Omega-Alpha was involved in bankruptcy proceedings in a federal court in Dallas, Texas, and Okonite, a producer of wire and cable based in Ramsey, New Jersey, was its only operating subsidiary. Omega-Alpha's trustees had indicated a willingness to sell Okonite to the Employee Stock Ownership Trust for $38 million, if they could raise the money.

1976: Job security to be UAW theme United Auto Workers' (UAW) President Leonard Woodcock urged delegates to a special three-day convention in Detroit in March to make job security "the central theme" of the union's 1976 bargaining platform. The 3,000 delegates were at the special convention to prepare for upcoming September negotiations with the major automobile manufacturers. The adopted platform listed several "job security" goals, including a call for a reduction in work time.

1976: Settlements at *The Washington Post* At the end of March, three craft unions settled with *The Washington Post*, ending their participation in a 4½-month strike at the Nation's third largest morning newspaper. Only the pressmen, who began the violence-marred walkout October 1, remained on strike.

1976: Construction contract "below par" By the end of March, in an effort to spur activity and employment in their industry by minimizing cost increases and the possibility of strikes, twelve construction unions and twenty-two employer associations in Detroit, settled two months early on a two-year contract they described as "below par" on wage and benefit gains. The agreement, which became effective when the then existing contract expired, provided for a 3 percent boost in the combined cost of wages and benefits on that date (June 1), followed by a 3.5 percent increase on October 1, 1976, and 6.5 percent on June 1, 1977. Spokesmen for the bargainers indicated that the total increase would average $1.49 an hour for the trades involved and would bring average compensation to $13.74 an hour. Union officials said the wage moderation was necessary because about half of the 35,000 members in the covered trades were unemployed.

1976: Union merger in apparel and textile industries Two principal unions in the apparel and textile industries agreed to merge into a 500,000-member union. The executive boards of the Amalgamated Clothing Workers of America and the Textile Workers Union of America completed details of the merger agreement while meeting in New York City in mid-March. The agreement was subject to ratification in conventions to be held in the late spring.

The agreement was announced by Murray H. Finley and Jacob Sheinkman, president and secretary-treasurer of the Clothing Workers, and Sol Stetin and William M. Du Chessi, president and secretary-treasurer of the Textile Workers. Under the merger terms, Finley was expected to be president of the merged union, Sheinkman secretary-treasurer, Stetin senior vice president, and Du Chessi executive vice president. The merger was consummated on June 3, 1976.

1976: New York considers Social Security withdrawal New York City Mayor Abraham D. Beame announced that the city intended to pull out of the Social Security system on March 31, 1978. In formally notifying the federal government, Beame emphasized that the city could reverse its decision prior to the withdrawal date if further evaluation did not confirm a projected $200 million annual cost savings to the financially beleaguered city as a result of withdrawal. The required withdrawal notice only applied to about 112,000 workers in agencies directly controlled by the mayor, but Beame was pressing the other agencies to serve notices covering their 138,000 workers. City officials said the contemplated action would not have any impact on the portion of retirement income retirees receive from the existing city-operated pension plan. The city later withdrew its notice of withdrawal.

1976: Las Vegas strike ends A fifteen-day strike which closed down many of the gambling casinos and nightclubs on Las Vegas' "Strip" ended on March 26, when members of the Hotel and Restaurant Employees Union ratified a four-year contract. The new agreement applied to 11,000 culinary and bar employees. Several days later, 3,500 workers in the "downtown" establishments accepted the same terms. Together, the downtown establishments and those on the Strip comprise the Nevada Resort Association.

1976: New York teachers split with NEA The New York State United Teachers voted on March 5 to disaffiliate from the National Education Association (NEA). The 211,000-member state organization had been formed in 1972 as a result of a merger of state affiliates of the NEA and the American Federation of Teachers (AFT). Under the merger, both groups retained memberships in the national organizations.

1976: Leadership change at the IUE In mid-March, President Paul Jennings of the International Union of Electrical Workers announced he was retiring, effective June 1, for health reasons. The union's executive board backed Jennings' rec-

ommendation for a successor, naming David J. Fitzmaurice to complete the unexpired term of office. Jennings, fifty-eight, had headed the union since 1965, when he defeated former president James B. Carey, and moved up from executive secretary of IUE District 3.

1976: Interns and residents are not employees By a 4 to 1 margin, the National Labor Relations Board ruled in March that hospital interns and resident physicians are students rather than employees, and are therefore not covered by federal bargaining laws. The ruling, which could be appealed in federal court, came in a case in which the Board dismissed petitions for representation elections among the house staffs at Cedars-Sinai Medical Center in Los Angeles and St. Christopher's Hospital for Children in Philadelphia.

1976: Residency requirements allowed The Supreme Court upheld the right of cities to require municipal employees to live within a city's boundaries. In an unsigned opinion issued March 22, the Court stated that there was "no support in our cases" for a claim by a Philadelphia, Pennsylvania, municipal employee to "A constitutional right to be employed by the City of Philadelphia while he is living elsewhere."

1976: Ten-year rail strike ends The longest railroad dispute in United States history ended in April, when the United Transportation Union terminated its ten-year strike against the Florida East Coast Railway. The walkout began when the railroad eliminated some train-operating jobs it contended were unnecessary and asserted greater control over work schedules. Despite the end of the strike, a $22 million suit brought by the union against the railroad is still pending.

1976: New York State employees reach accord Members of the New York State Civil Service Employees Association ratified a two-year accord providing for no first-year wage increase. The agreement reached in April and which covered 136,000 of the state's 185,000 employees, called for an increase in the second year, the size to be determined at that time through collective bargaining. The union also gained clauses requiring that the state give six months' notice of any wide-ranging unit layoffs and that all temporary and provisional employees be dismissed before any permanent employees are laid off.

1976: Law firm agrees to job offer quota A major New York law firm settled a sex discrimination suit by agreeing that the percentage of the firm's job offers made to women will be at least 20 percent higher than the percentage of women in the graduating classes of the law schools from which it normally recruits. The consent judgment, made in April and which covered hirings over the succeeding three years, was signed by Judge Morris Lasker of the U.S. District Court for Southern New York. The agreement settled a class action suit against Rogers & Wells over the firm's refusal to hire Margaret Kohn, a graduate of Columbia Law School.

1976: New York Transit accord revised On May 19, the New York City Transit Authority and the Transport Workers announced that they had revised their April accord to meet the objections of the Emergency Financial Control Board. The Board had turned down the earlier settlement because it did not specify that the wage and benefit gains must be offset by improvements in productivity. In approving the revised accord, the Board also ruled that a similar productivity requirement would apply to some 200,000 municipal employees whose contracts would expire June 30.

1976: Mine workers have clean slate On May 18, the U.S. Department of Labor cleared top officals of the United Mine Workers' Union (UMW) of charges that they mismanaged union finances in violation of the Landrum-Griffin Act. The allegations had been made in November by UMW Vice President Mike Trbovich, and a majority of the union's executive board. They had charged that President Arnold Miller and other officials had spent union funds for illegal purposes.

1976: Auto workers get trade aid In May the Department of Labor certified an additional 10,800 laid-off auto workers as eligible for trade adjustment assistance. The workers, employed at Ford Motor Company plants in Los Angeles and San Jose, California, Metuchen, New Jersey, and Dearborn, Michigan, were deemed to have been laid off because of increased imports of full-sized, subcompact, and luxury small cars from Canada and overseas. These Ford employees are the third major group of auto workers certified by the Department in response to petitions filed in 1975 by the union. Workers ruled eligible for benefits can receive up to 70 percent of their weekly pay for up to fifty-two weeks, minus regular State unemployment benefits.

1976: San Francisco workers strike for 39 days A walkout of San Francisco municipal workers over proposed pay cuts ended May 8, when the Board of Supervisors approved a back-to-work agreement accepted earlier by union leaders. The agreement, which was not a final settlement, provided for the return to work of all city employees at current pay and without penalty in exchange for the removal form the June 8 primary ballot of two measures the unions opposed.

1976: Merged union approves boycott of J. P. Stevens Early in June, the Amalgamated Clothing and Textile Workers Union, a new 500,000-member union resulting from the merger of the Textile Workers Union and the Amalgamated Clothing Workers, approved a national boycott against J. P. Stevens & Company as part of a drive to organize 40,000 of the Southern-based firm's unorganized employees at eighty-five plants. In an address to the merged union's first convention, AFL-CIO President George Meany pledged the Federation's full support of the boycott.

1976: Teamsters reelect Fitzsimmons Delegates to the International Brotherhood of Teamsters' twenty-first convention, held in mid-June in Las Vegas, reelected top officers and raised their salaries amidst charges by union factions that the leadership was corrupt, dictatorial, and overpaid. This was the union's first convention since 1971. The 2,300 delegates unanimously reelected President Frank E. Fitzsimmons to another five-year term, and hiked his salary by 25 percent, to $156,250. Prior to this increase, the sixty-eight-year-old labor leader was the highest paid union president in the nation.

1976: Brokerage firm settles job-bias suit In June, Merrill Lynch, Pierce, Fenner & Smith, Inc., the nation's largest securities firm, agreed to liberalize its hiring and promotion practices for women and minority groups as part of a settlement with the Equal Employment Opportunity Commission (EEOC) of job-bias charges. The settlement, approved in June by Federal District Court Judge Barron P. McCune in Pittsburgh, was combined with the settlement of another case brought against Merrill Lynch by a Pittsburgh woman who charged that she was denied a sales job because of her sex.

1976: Farm workers merge with East Coast union In June, the United Farm Workers of America (UFW), headed by Cesar Chavez, announced a merger with an independent Puerto Rican farmworkers union based in Hartford, Connecticut. The 6,000-member Association da Trabajadores Agricolas (Association of Agricultural Workers) has members in New York, Connecticut, New Jersey, Massachusetts, Delaware, and Pennsylvania. Growers recruit the East Coast farmworkers in Puerto Rico, and the recruits enter the mainland under the Farm Labor Contractors Registration Act of 1963.

1976: San Francisco pay cuts take effect Late in June, the eleven-member San Francisco Board of Supervisors, after receiving three fact-finding committee reports, reaffirmed that pay reductions of up to 25 percent for 1,800 blue-collar municipal workers would take effect July 1. The pay cut proposals had led to a thirty-eight-day strike which ended May 8. As part of that settlement, five union leaders joined five supervisors and Mayor George Moscone on a committee to determine whether the officials were justified in cutting the wages of one-tenth of the city's craft employees while granting small wage increases to 16,000 other city workers. The supervisors had held that city voters mandated the cuts when they repealed a part of the city charter requiring the city to pay craftworkers the same amount as paid comparable workers in the private sector.

1976: End job bias, J. P. Stevens ordered On June 29, J. P. Stevens & Company, the Nation's largest textile producer, was ordered to end racial discrimination in employment at its plants in Roanoke Rapids, North Carolina, by Federal District Court Judge Franklin T. Dupree, Jr. Judge Dupree also directed the company to start compensatory hiring and training to put blacks into jobs previously closed to them, and reserved for the future any ruling on a request for damages.

1976: New York City hospitals struck A ten-day strike against fifty-seven hospitals and nursing homes in New York City ended on July 15, when management representatives bowed to state pressure and agreed to binding arbitration of bargaining differences with District 1199 of the National Union of Health Care Employees. District 1199, an affiliate of the Retail, Wholesale and Department Store Union, represents 35,000 employees, mostly nonprofessionals, at the hospitals and homes.

1976: Nonunion rubber employees get raises Goodyear Tire and Rubber Company and Firestone Tire and Rubber Company announced pay raises for their salaried employees who are not represented by the United Rubber Workers and have remained on the job during the union's three-month-old strike against these and other rubber companies. At Goodyear, the 13,000 salaried employees (except those paid commissions) earning less than $2,000 a month received a $130-a-month increase, and those earning $2,000 or more will receive various increases at various times, on a merit basis. The $130-a-month increase, effective July 1, was equivalent to the initial wage increase of 75 cents an hour included in the companies' latest offer to the striking hourly employees.

1976: J. P. Stevens ordered to bargain In a separate development, Reed Johnson, National Labor Relations Board regional director, said he would seek a "broad bargaining order" to counteract J. P. Stevens & Company's "demonstrated predisposition to violate" the Taft-Hartley Act. Johnson had issued an eleven-count complaint against the company on July 1. The order Johnson requested would require the company to bargain immediately with the union, currently certified to represent some workers, or any other labor organization that achieves certification in the future. A hearing on the complaint was scheduled to be held by an administrative law judge in Roanoke Rapids on August 23.

The complaint also charged that since June 1963, when the Textile Workers began organizing the Stevens' plants, the company "has engaged in a massive, multistate campaign to deny its employees their rights under the (National Labor

Relations) Act to seek collective bargaining representatives of their own choosing." The complaint added that in denying union representation, Stevens "committed unfair labor practices of unprecedented flagrancy and magnitude. . . ." It also stated that Stevens had continued its illegal practices despite NLRB and court orders issued against it.

1976: Pottery workers join Seafarers Early in July the International Brotherhood of Pottery and Allied Workers, at its eighty-second annual convention in Denver, accepted a charter to become an affiliate of the Seafarers International Union. The Pottery Workers had approved the action in a special convention in 1975, after President Lester H. Null, Sr., and other leaders of the 20,000-member union had warned that affiliation was necessary for the organization's survival and growth. Under the charter, the Pottery Workers' union retains its identity, autonomy, and constitutional structure. Null became a vice president of the Seafarers, whose membership now reportedly exceeds 100,000.

1976: Principals' union chartered A new union, the American Federation of School Administrators (AFSA) was chartered in July as an affiliate by the AFL-CIO, when 120 delegates convened in New York to adopt a constitution and elect officers. The union consists of 54 locals, representing nearly 10,000 principals and school executives across the nation. It grew out of the School Administrators and Supervisors Organizing Committee, established in 1971. The original locals were in New York, Chicago, San Francisco, and Washington, D.C.

1976: Women's Year panel issues report Late in July the National Commission on the Observance of International Women's Year presented its final report to President Ford. The study's 115 proposals for action by government as well as private parties included calls for creation of universally available day-care centers for the children of working parents, with fees based on the ability to pay, changes in inheritance, divorce, and social security laws; recognizing the economic contribution to marriages made by women who do not have paid jobs; revision of application for jobs, awards, and fellowships to end the disclosure of the sex of the applicant; and expansion of the "equal pay for equal work" concept to assure that skill and educational attainments are fully considered in setting pay levels.

1976: Rubber accord ends strike Full-scale production resumed in the rubber industry in early September, after four major firms reached agreements with the United Rubber Workers, ending the walkout that began April 21 when the previous agreements expired. The accords also led to a return to work by employees of smaller companies, who had joined the walkout as their contracts expired. At its peak, the walkout comprised 70,000 workers at more than fifty plants in twenty-one states.

The accords, which expire April 20, 1979, called for an initial general wage increase of 80 cents an hour, with additional increases at Firestone, Goodrich, and Uniroyal to eliminate differences in pay levels resulting from the 1973 bargaining. (In that round, Goodyear employees received a larger wage increase in exchange for a smaller increase in the normal pension rate.) The additional adjustments amounted to 8.8 cents an hour in wages at Firestone, 4.7 cents in wages at Goodrich, and about 10 cents in wages and benefits at Uniroyal.

1976: Wildcat coal strike comes to an end A month-long wildcat strike that idled up to 90,000 miners in seven states, virtually ended by mid-August. Among the miners returning to work were members of United Mine Workers (UMW) Local 1759 in West Virginia, where the strike began in mid-July over a job-posting dispute with the Cedar Coal Company. Federal District Judge Dennis R. Knapp assessed a $50,000 fine against

the local on the grounds that the wildcat walkout was a breach of contract, and he also warned that he would fine it $25,000 for each day the walkout continued.

1976: New York City hospitals struck Late in August New York City's hospitals were struck by 18,000 nonprofessional hospital workers, but continued emergency services during the four-day walkout. The strike was precipitated by the layoff of 1,350 workers represented by District Council 37 of the American Federation of State, County and Municipal Employees, the Teamsters Union, and the Practical Nurses Association. The strike ended when members of District Council 37 agreed to forego a $441 increase in annual salaries due under their cost-of-living clause. They also agreed to forego a possible adjustment in 1977, if necessary. In return, the 1,000 members of this union who were laid off regained their jobs, and the city agreed not to lay off any more employees through the end of the year. The other 350 laid-off workers may regain their jobs if their unions follow the lead of District Council 37 and give up cost-of-living adjustments.

1976: AFL-CIO Supports Carter In September the AFL-CIO Executive Council pledged "all-out support" for the Democratic ticket of Jimmy Carter for President and Walter F. Mondale for Vice President. The Council also called a meeting of the AFL-CIO General Board for August 31 in Washington "to prepare for the campaign and mobilize labor's full support for Carter and Mondale." The Council's endorsement was based on the "damage" done to America by the "Nixon-Ford Administration." AFL-CIO President George Meany said that Carter is a candidate "whose overall purpose is our purpose—to put America back to work." The endorsement returned the AFL-CIO to the Democratic fold after the Council had voted to remain neutral in the 1972 presidential race. Meany said the support would be delivered through the Federation's political arm, the Committee on Political Education.

1976: Farm Workers win 55 percent of elections The AFL-CIO Department of Organization and Field Services reported that the United Farm Workers (UFW) had concluded thirty-five new contracts with California growers since the State's farm labor law went into effect in August 1975. The pacts covered approximately 18,000 workers. In addition, the Farm Workers were in the process of negotiating more than 50 other contracts for an additional 20,000 workers, according to Don Slaiman, the department's deputy director. A survey by the California Agricultural Labor Relations Board, which oversees farm bargaining in California, showed by September that the United Farm Workers had won 55 percent of the more than 300 representation elections held under the act.

1976: United States Pay raised About 1.4-million Federal white-collar employees under the General Schedule (GS) pay system received a salary increase in October, ranging from 4.24 to 7.92 percent, and 2.5 million members of the Armed Forces, Foreign Service workers, and Veterans' Administration medical personnel received a comparable increase because their salary levels are linked by law to those of the GS employees. (The increase for military personnel was a flat 4.83 percent, and it applied to quarters and subsistence allowances, as well as salaries.) The increase did not apply to blue-collar employees, whose pay is based on local comparisons with trades in the private sector, or to postal workers, whose wages are set through collective bargaining.

1976: Sadlowski announces for steelworkers presi-

dency Late in August, Edward Sadlowski, thirty-eight, director of the Steelworkers' Chicago-area District 31, announced he would seek the union's presidency in the election to be held in February. Sadlowski criticized both current Steelworkers' President I. W. Abel, who, at sixty-eight, had reached the mandatory retirement age and planned to step down in June, and Lloyd McBride, sixty, the other announced candidate, who is running with Abel's backing. Sadlowski said, "We must retire them from business unionism, so that we can return to aggressive, effective labor unionism."

1976: Hiring quotas ordered in New York City A federal judge in September ordered two New York City construction union locals to increase the number of blacks and Puerto Ricans in their membership from a current 6 percent to 36 percent within five years. Blacks and Spanish-surnamed persons constitute 36 percent of the work force from which the locals draw their members. In addition to this goal, to be attained in annual steps, the locals must set up training programs for minority workers and provide back pay for those who can prove prior discrimination against them.

1976: Printing unions move toward merger Delegates to the forty-first convention of the International Printing and Graphic Communications Union, in September, approved a resolution calling on the union's board of directors to complete merger discussions with the United Paperworkers International Union and other unions in the graphics arts industry and to submit all contemplated mergers to a referendum vote of the membership. The action followed an address by Paperworkers' President Joseph P. Tonelli, in which he cited the common interests of the two unions and the advantages of a merger.

1976: New York agency plans to end Social Security coverage The New York City Transit Authority served notice in September of its intention to cancel social security coverage in two years for its 45,000 subway and bus employees. John G. de Roos, senior executive officer of the Transit Authority, said the decision was made at the insistence of the mayoral office of New York City, which had announced its planned withdrawal in March and asked other city agencies to do likewise. Transport Workers President Matthew Guinan and Ellis Van Riper, president of its largest local, sent a telegram to the Authority expressing "shock" that it has "surrendered to the blackmail tactics of the city administration." The Transit Authority later cancelled notice of withdrawal.

1976: Election moved up, Miller's Power cut Dissident forces at the United Mine Workers of America (UMW) convention held in Cincinnati succeeded in adopting a resolution advancing the union's scheduled November 1977 presidential election to June 1977. The resolution moving up the election stipulated that the winner serve as the union's chief bargainer in the fall 1977 bargaining to replace the soft coal agreement expiring December 6, 1977.

1976: Court of appeals holds J. P. Stevens in contempt J. P. Stevens & Company was held in civil contempt by the U.S. Court of Appeals for the Fifth Circuit, in New Orleans, for failing to comply with two prior Fifth Circuit decisions ordering the company to bargain with the Textile Workers. Asserting that Stevens' record at its Statesboro, North Carolina, plant "does not inspire a sense of approval," the court found that Stevens failed to bargain in good faith with the union by unilaterally granting merit and general wage increases, and failing to supply requested bargaining data to union negotiators. The circuit court had issued decrees ordering Stevens to bargain on March 22 and December 2, 1971. Subsequently, the company and the union met to bargain twenty-two times between January 1972 and June 1973. Following a petition filed by the union with the National Labor Relations Board that Stevens was not bargaining in good faith, the circuit court appointed a special master who found that the company had failed to meet its bargaining duty in three broad areas: the firm undertook unilateral changes in workload, work organization, and wages without giving the union an opportunity to negotiate the changes; it unreasonably delayed furnishing, or failed altogether to furnish, information needed by the union to negotiate a contract; and the company did not bargain in good faith over a union dues checkoff demand.

While agreeing with the first two, the court of appeals found that the Board did not meet its burden of proof on the issue of whether the company failed to bargain in good faith on a dues checkoff. Stevens had argued that it disapproved of paycheck deductions because the resulting reduction in take-home pay brought demands for higher wages. With regard to merit raises, Stevens contended that increases given to nine employees in a large bargaining unit like Statesboro did not violate the duty to bargain because they were "isolated instances not rising to the level of contempt." The appeals court rejected this argument, holding: "Apparently insignificant unilateral action that may constitute *de minimus* activity when undertaken by a company with a clean slate in labor law must be viewed more warily when committed by one who enjoys a record for intransigence like that of the J. P. Stevens Company."

1976: New York City teachers lose dues checkoff The United Federation of Teachers, the New York City affiliate of the American Federation of Teachers, lost its right to the automatic checkoff of dues when the State penalized the unit for a five-day strike in September 1975. The New York Public Employment Relations Board found the United Federation of Teachers guilty of striking against the city in violation of the State's Taylor Law, which prohibits walkouts by government workers, and ordered forfeiture of dues checkoff for two years or more. As a result, the union would have to collect its $190 annual dues from the 50,000 teachers on an individual and voluntary basis. Individual teachers who participated in the strike had already lost five days' pay for the unworked time and an additional five days' pay as a strike penalty. (In September 1975, a New York State Supreme Court judge found the union itself guilty of violating the Taylor Law, but he has not imposed a penalty.)

The Board provided a procedure for the conditional restoration of the checkoff after fourteen months (to be made permanent after twenty-four months) if the UFT demonstrates compliance with the law, affirms that it no longer asserts its right to strike, and declares it does not have a "no-contract, no-work" policy. The union has no formal right of appeal before the Board, according to a union representative, although it could ask for reargument of the case. American Federation of Teachers President Albert Shanker called the board's ruling "vengeful" and said no other city union had ever lost the checkoff for striking. The UFT had lost the checkoff for twenty-two months after strikes in 1967, and this cost it about $1 million in dues it was unable to collect on an individual basis.

1976: Auto Workers win more time off at Ford The Ford Motor Company and the Auto Workers reached an agreement October 5 on a national contract that led to an end to a strike that began September 14. The contract, which covers 170,000 workers and expires September 14, 1979, provided for additional paid time off, which the union hailed as a step toward its announced goal of a four-day workweek for the automobile industry. At Ford, the more immediate result was generally expected to be some improvement in job security, because more employees will be needed for a given level of output. Under the new Scheduled Paid Personal Holiday Plan, all employees with a year of seniority will receive five additional days off in the second contract year and seven in the final year. The time off will be taken in single-day units throughout the week. Employees will have an equal opportunity to take their time off on Mondays and Fridays. To be paid for the new days off, employees will be required to work the day before and the day after, and they will not be able to take days off during the summer vacation season, because of the increased difficulty of filling their jobs.

The agreement also added a regular paid holiday, July 3, 1978, bringing the total to thirty-seven regular holidays during the contract term, compared with thirty-nine during the prior contract. (The lower total resulted because of year-to-year fluctuations in the number of paid holidays required to comply with an existing provision that employees receive unbroken paid time off from Christmas through New Year's Day.) The employees also continue to receive one day of holiday pay each year for a Sunday in December that is not a regular workday.

General wage increases were 3 percent of base rates, plus 20 cents an hour, effective October 18, 1976, and 3 percent of base rates effective both September 19, 1977, and September 18, 1978. These increases amounted to 32.5 to 45, 16.5 to 30, and 17 to 31 cents per hour. Skilled workers received an additional 10 or 15 cents, depending on their pay group, on October 18 and 10 cents on September 19, 1977. The UAW said this special adjustment, the first of its type since 1967, was necessary to restore a proper differential between pay rates of skilled and production jobs. The compression of rates had resulted primarily because of the wage-escalator clause, under which all employees receive the same cents per hour adjustments, regardless of their job classification. Certain production and skilled workers will also receive wage-inequity adjustments, financed from an allocation of money equal to 1/2-cent-an-hour for each of the 170,000 workers.

Of the current $1.14-an-hour escalator allowance, $1.09 was incorporated into base rates, and the clause will continue to provide for quarterly cost-of-living adjustments (in March, June, September, and December) calculated at 1 cent an hour for each 0.3-point movement in a composite consumer price index (1967 = 100), derived from the official indexes issued by the United States and Canadian governments. (The 3 percent plus 20 cents wage increase was calculated on the base rates in effect immediately prior to the incorporation.) Part of the cost-of-living allowance will be temporarily diverted to help finance the one-time inflation bonus payment to retirees described below. This will be done by withholding 1 cent from the allowance paid in June 1977 and increasing the amount withheld by an additional cent each succeeding quarter, to a final maximum of 6 cents in September 1978. In December 1978, the allowance will be restored to the level that would have prevailed without the diversion and there will be no further diversions.

Although all eligible laid-off Ford workers continued to receive Supplemental Unemployment Benefit payments throughout the industry's 1974–1975 downturn, the company and union agreed to a number of financing changes to strengthen the fund. The company's payment into the fund was raised from 9 to 14 cents to a range of 13 to 23 cents an hour, depending on the level of the fund, effective January 1, 1978, and to a 14- to-24-cent range a year later. Employees with ten years of service or more gained additional protection as a result of the establishment of a "backup" SUB fund that will pay benefits only to these employees if the regular fund for all workers drops below the level required for payments to continue. Long-service workers at other auto companies had complained that they were unable to draw from the fund because laid-off employees with less seniority had depleted it.

Existing UAW pension agreements in the automobile industry do not expire until 1979, but Ford agreed to the one-time inflation bonus for retirees mentioned earlier. The bonus will be paid on January 1, 1978, to employees who retired prior to September 15, 1976. It will be based on length of service, and retirees with thirty years of service will receive a maximum payment of $600. Surviving spouses drawing benefits prior to the cutoff date will also receive bonuses, computed at lower rates.

Other economic terms of the agreement included the following.

■ Adoption of a company-financed vision care plan for employees with one year of service and for their dependents, effective October 1, 1977. It provides for eye examinations and free prescription glasses every two years, with the plan paying 80 percent of the cost.

■ Changes in the hospital-medical-surgical drug plan, including elimination of the requirement that any home care nursing services be preceded by a stay in a hospital or nursing home; full, rather than half, payment for such nursing care; coverage of additional surgical procedures; and a $3 charge to employees for each prescription, up from $2. The parties also agreed to a review of health care programs to hold down costs.

■ A $50-a-month increase, to $250, in the Transition Survivors Income Benefits for survivors receiving reduced social security benefits; a $25 increase, to $150, for those who are eligible for full social security benefits; and a $50 increase, to $250, in the Bridge Survivor Income Benefit.

■ Increased moving allowances to employees who relocate to other Ford plants after their jobs are terminated.

■ Improvements in the tuition refund program, bringing the maximum payment to $450 a year for business, trade, or vocational schools and $900 for colleges or universities.

■ Extension to certain skilled-trades foundry workers of a provision under which production foundry workers with twenty-five years or more of actual service receive 1.2 years of service credit for each year of actual service.

■ A 10-cents-an-hour increase (to 20 cents) in the premium paid to skilled workers on all seven-day-a-week operations except steel production.

In a change of particular importance to the skilled-trades workers, Ford agreed to retain all "new die machining, fabrication repair and repair work" in present plants "to the extent the company's program requirements can reasonably be met." Ford retained the right to make the final decision on contracting out such work to other firms or moving it to other Ford plants, but it will now be required to first discuss the situation with the UAW.

The union announced worker approval of the national accord on October 12, and Ford was able to resume production the next day at a few plants, but others remained closed pending settlement of local issues. By October 12, 68 of 99 units had reached agreements, and final local agreement was reached on November 1.

Production workers approved the national agreement by a vote of 35,192 to 22,026, but the vote for the skilled trades was only 8,957 in favor to 8,468 against. The UAW had announced that the settlement required approval by both groups, although Ford might have refused to resume negotiations if one of the groups turned down the settlement, but the combined vote favored the agreement. The close vote by the skilled workers apparently reflected their concern with the wage differential and subcontracting provisions, as well as some resentment against the union's implementing the 1973 settlement in the face of an unfavorable vote by the skilled workers.

After the Ford ratification was announced, talks were resumed with Chrysler Corporation and General Motors Corporation, where workers had remained on the job despite the fact that their contracts had also expired on September 14. This was in accord with the union's "divide and conquer" strategy of limiting walkouts to one of the major auto manufacturers, to exert economic pressure on that firm and to minimize the drain of strike benefits on the union's treasury. According to the UAW, an important issue at both companies was replenishing the Supplemental Unemployment Benefit funds, which were depleted as a result of the massive layoffs in 1974–1975. Another important issue at GM was the union's contention that the company had adopted a policy of resisting UAW attempts to organize its new facilities.

TWO HUNDRED YEARS
OF WORK IN AMERICA

Basic attitudes toward work have ranged from the idea that toil is an inevitable and lifelong punishment (Genesis 3:19) to the belief that work is ennobling and a way of serving God. More representative of the general attitude in America's last 200 years has been the view, expressed in the maxims of Benjamin Franklin's *Poor Richard's Almanack* and in Walt Whitman's lyrics, that work is—or should be—intrinsically satisfying to everyone. The idea that the many should labor so that the few could advance civilization has given way to the notion that work should be shared by all.

The ways in which people's needs for real income, security, and psychic satisfaction have been met by work in America over the last 200 years are the basic concerns of this Bicentennial chapter. A summary of its major themes would highlight the following:

European observers of the United States in the 19th century were quick to note the American worker's willingness to abandon one occupation for another or to engage in more than one occupation at a time. Multioccupation workers were not unknown in Europe; indeed, the farmer/miller was an important figure in many rural economies, just as the clergyman/schoolmaster was an essential part of the village social structure. Unique to the American experience, however, were the long-term shortages of skilled workers that appeared in both settled and new territories with each expansion of the frontier. Just as these skill shortages encouraged experimentation and versatility, the climate of opinion favored "progress," self-sufficiency, and upward mobility. American workers were readily distinguished from those elsewhere by their occupational flexibility and even more by their reluctance to accept Old World views of hereditary occupational status for themselves or their children. In the "shifting, unsteady, improving mass" described in one section of the chapter, it was not unusual to find such occupational combinations as sheriff/blacksmith, farmer/carpenter, or even salesman/phrenologist. Nor was it by any means uncommon for a newcomer to the country to pass from apprenticeship in a skilled trade, to farming, to commercial entrepreneurship. On the other hand, the "family business" involving successive generations in one occupational specialty was far more typical of upper income groups than of the large mass of earners.

With the closing of the frontier, the advent of the large corporation in the late 19th century, and its proliferation in the 20th, the American economic environment has become somewhat less hospitable to occupational experimentation. American workers are still relatively willing to move from job to job, but both blue- and white-collar workers are likely to find that each new position involves skill requirements similar or related to those of the previous one. For professional and technical workers who have been conditioned to think in terms of a "career," a change of occupational specialty usually requires some degree of risk and may require long-term investment in retraining. While the routes to upward mobility still exist, they now pass more frequently through the educational system or other sources of formal training or licensing than they did in the past. As a possible corollary of this greater emphasis on "credentialism," contemporary economic and educational institutions may have become less able to properly exploit the flexibility and responsiveness of a work force that remains, in both geographic and interindustry terms, highly mobile. This somewhat pessimistic observation should be balanced, however, by an acknowledgment of the many ways—volunteerism, community endeavors, do-it-yourself activities, to name just a few—in which American workers have resisted or compensated for the increased rigidity of today's occupational structure.

Another major theme of the chapter concerns the changing demographic composition of the labor force over the past two centuries. Once a significant source of low-paid, unskilled labor, child workers—or "small help" as they were once called—disappeared from the labor force at a pace reflecting the increasingly rigorous enforcement of laws regarding compulsory education, minimum working age, and minimum wages. The proportion of older men in the labor force has also declined, as the availability of social security, disability, and other benefits have made it possible for many to cease working at considerably earlier ages than 19th-century conditions permitted. Compensating for these declines has been the dramatic rise in female labor force participation, especially in the years following World War II. More than half of all women aged 18 to 55 years are now in the labor force, in marked contrast to a participation rate of 15 percent for women 16 and over in 1870.

Real incomes and the level of living for workers have improved several times over. Moreover, the length of life itself has been increased by better medical care, as well as by higher standards of living. This longer life has been made richer by education and advances in communications, transportation, and cultural and recreational facilities. All this has been accomplished while the amount of time available to enjoy life outside of work has been increased markedly—in each day and week, in the course of the year, and in the course of a lifetime. And insecurities that hang over the worker's head—about loss of income from unemployment, old age, illness, or industrial accident—have been mitigated. Increased income and security have given the worker more options, including opportunity to choose between additional work and income or more leisure—a choice inconceivable when wages were at a subsistence level. It cannot be emphasized too strongly that this summarization describes averages, obscuring the fact that a

considerable number of workers have only a small share in these benefits. Members of this latter sector of the labor force earn the lowest incomes, have the highest incidence of unemployment, get the least education, are least likely to be protected by some of the insurance programs—and, when protected, receive the lowest compensation.

While it is true that technology has done much to reduce brute, exhausting physical toil, some workers have achieved the productivity that has made higher incomes possible at the cost of doing work that is wholly repetitive and—in contemporary jargon—"dehumanizing." Division of labor in some large organizations may tend to deprive some workers of the pride in achievement they might get if they were solely responsible for the entire product. While the available evidence indicates that the overwhelming majority of workers are not dissatisfied with their jobs, there have been much research and debate on trends in this area. Some approaches now in use or being explored to address potential dissatisfaction are membership in unions and other employee organizations, worker participation in management decision-making, flexible working hours, and the like.

With respect to working conditions, the record is also equivocal. In comparison with earlier years, a much larger proportion of workers now work indoors, protected from the weather, and in offices and other reasonably comfortable surroundings; safety and health conditions in the workplace are promoted by State and Federal laws, and the accident rate has been reduced in the most dangerous industries; but pollution and new chemical hazards—little understood, but perhaps lethal—hang over some workers.

Finally, opportunities for promotion to higher paid jobs are shrinking for workers with limited education, but educational opportunities are greater. The increase in the number of part-time jobs has given workers—especially students and adult women—more options concerning the scheduling of work and time for nonwork activities.

In sum, the aspects of work that lead to intrinsic satisfaction have shown uneven progress in the past two centuries. Continuing efforts to produce improvements, however, are appropriate responses to the realization that expectations have risen: a better educated, better paid, more secure working population has raised its standards and will be seeking work of a different and higher quality in the future.

The Workers

The story of work in America properly begins with the workers themselves—their numbers, personal characteristics, education, and training. This section therefore describes the growth and changing composition of the population, the flows of immigrants, and where people have lived. It then turns to the composition of the labor force and the patterns of work activity of each group in the population. Finally, it reviews the education and training of American workers.

POPULATION GROWTH AND CHANGE

Population Increase and Migration

The most decisive mark of the prosperity of any country is the increase of the number of its inhabitants. In Great Britain, and most other European countries, they are not supposed to double in less than five hundred years. In the British colonies in North America, it has been found, that they double in twenty or five-and-twenty years. Nor in the present times is this increase principally owing to the continual importance of new inhabitants, but to the great multiplication of the species. Those who live to old age, it is said, frequently see there from fifty to a hundred, and sometimes many more, descendants from their own body. Labour is there so well rewarded that a numerous family of children, instead of being a burthen, is a source of opulence and prosperity to the parents. The labour of each child, before it can leave their house, is computed to be worth a hundred pounds clear gain to them. A young widow with four or five young children, who, among the middling or inferior ranks of people in Europe, would have so little chance for a second husband, is there frequently courted as a sort of fortune. The value of children is the greatest of all encouragements to marriage. We cannot, therefore, wonder that the people in North America should generally marry very young. Notwithstanding the great increase occasioned by such early marriages, there is a continual complaint of the scarcity of hands in North America. The demand for labourers, the funds destined for maintaining them, increase, it seems, still faster than they can find labourers to employ.

—Adam Smith, *The Wealth of Nations*, 1776

Today's ambivalence about population growth was not widely shared in the early years of the Republic. Concentrated for the most part on the edge of a vast and thinly populated continent, the 3 million Americans present at independence welcomed the larger work force and new markets that would result from population growth.

From the 3.9 million persons counted in the first census of 1790, the population grew by approximately one-third every 10 years until 1860, or at an annual average rate of about 3 percent. Thereafter, the annual growth rate slowed down, and from 1910 to 1970, it was only 1.3 percent.

Accompanying the growth of population was the westward movement toward vast areas of readily available land that constantly drew farm people from Europe and unemployed or dissatisfied workers from the Eastern States. The migration, documented in great detail in the decennial censuses, is illustrated by the movement of the calculated center of population. In 1790, the center of population was in the Chesapeake Bay east of Baltimore; every decade thereafter, it moved westward, sometimes in large jumps, sometimes in small; in 1970, it was just east of St. Louis and about to cross the Mississippi.

Over 90 percent of the black population was in the South in 1790 and remained just as heavily concentrated in that region until 1900. The large out-migration of blacks began after World War I, and by 1975, only about half were still in the South.[1]

Another kind of geographic movement has profoundly affected work in the United States—migration from rural to urban areas, and, more recently, from cities to the suburbs. In 1790, 95 percent of the population was in rural areas, and 80 percent of the population was still rural on the eve of the Civil War. Not until World War I did half the population live in cities, but by 1970, nearly three-quarters of the people lived in more than 7,000 urban areas.[2]

Concentration of population in urban areas has been accompanied by expansion in the suburban ring around each city, where most of the more recent metropolitan area growth has taken place. The central cities have grown more slowly. In fact, 54 of the 153 cities with 100,000 or more inhabitants suffered population decreases between 1960 and

---

[1] Figures on the black population were calculated from table AA-1 in the Bicentennial Supplement to the Statistical Appendix.
[2] Table AA-4 in the Bicentennial Supplement to the Statistical Appendix. (A change in definition of areas in 1950 added 4.4 percent of the population at that time to what was classified as urban.)

1970.[3] For millions of families, the move to the suburbs has meant a change in the material quality of life. For the individuals left behind, especially those in the deteriorating core of the cities, who are shouldering higher tax burdens, finding fewer job opportunities, and experiencing more residential segregation, the shift of population toward the suburbs has meant a loss.

The redistribution of population westward and into urban areas reflects migration in response to economic opportunity. Every census for the last hundred years reported that some 20 to 25 percent of the native-born people were living in States other than the ones in which they had been born. Most had moved to States at some distance from their home States, often in search of better jobs.[4] More recently, however, members of the middle and upper income population have begun moving into the Southern and Southwestern States, apparently for reasons more closely related to climate and lifestyle than to economics.

Immigration

In search of a greater measure of economic, political, or religious freedom came the greatest mass migration in history. It contributed to rapid growth in the labor force, bringing a wide spectrum of skills. But probably as significant as its economic contribution has been the cultural and ethnic diversity it has brought to the American scene.

Up to 1975, at least 47 million immigrants had arrived in this country, but since some later decided to leave, net immigration was closer to 36 million.[5] The major inflows were in the period from the late 1830's to the early 1920's (see chart 21). The peak decade was 1900–10, when net immigration was 5¼ millions. Immigration dropped off during wars in which the United States was involved and during nearly every extended depression. A more restrictive immigration policy reduced the flow in the 1920's, but it increased again after World War II. Net immigration accounted for about one-third of the population growth in the decades 1850–60, 1880–90, and 1900–10.

Immigration contributed even more to labor force growth than to total population increase. In the earlier years, a majority of the newcomers were men of working age, who emigrated before marriage or left their families at home. Foreign-born white workers amounted to one-fifth of all workers at each census year from 1870 to 1910; by 1930, their proportion had declined to 15 percent.[6]

Early immigration was preponderantly from Northern and Western Europe, but the balance swung toward Eastern and Southern Europe from 1900 to 1914 and in the first few years after World War I. Since World War II, major immigration flows have been from Latin America and the Caribbean (including a significant number of illegal entrants from these areas) and from Asia.[7]

Foreign-born workers have had more than their proportionate share of the unskilled, lower paying jobs in such industries as mining, construction, apparelmaking, and iron and steel. At the same time, an increasing number of skilled workers, farmers, businessmen, and professional and technical workers came into the country, primarily as a result of the more restrictive immigration policies adopted after World War I and the arrival of many relatively well-educated political refugees from Europe during the 1930's.[8] After World War II, some countries—both industrialized and "developing"—became

[3] *Statistical Abstract of the United States, 1971* (Washington: U.S. Department of Commerce, Bureau of the Census, 1971). pp. 21–23.

[4] Table AA–3 in the Bicentennial Supplement to the Statistical Appendix. This is a *minimum* measure of migration, since it does not take into account people moving within a State; and it counts each departure from the State of birth only once, no matter how many times the migrant moved.

[5] The statistical record of immigration is far from precise and needs much critical analysis. From 1790 to 1820—a period in which perhaps one-quarter of a million immigrants arrived—only fragmentary data were maintained. Thereafter, statistics were crude and incomplete for many years—ignoring departures of both foreign-born entrants and emigrating natives, omitting arrivals at Pacific coast ports and over the Mexican and Canadian borders, and even today missing illegal entrants. The data are described in *Historical Statistics of the United States: Colonial Times to 1957* (Washington: U.S. Department of Commerce, Bureau of the Census, 1960), pp. 48–49. A critical analysis and improved estimates are presented in Simon Kuznets and Ernest Rubin, *Immigration and the Foreign Born*, Occasional Paper 46

(New York: National Bureau of Economic Research, 1954). Recent immigration is described in *Immigrants and the American Labor Market*, Manpower Research Monograph No. 31 (Washington: U.S. Department of Labor, Manpower Administration. 1974). The data used here are based largely on Kuznets and Rubin, but a different method of estimating the contribution of immigration to population growth was used.

[6] Kuznets and Rubin, op. cit., p. 45; A. Ross Eckler and Jack Zlotnick, "Immigration and the Labor Force," in "Reappraising Our Immigration Policy," *Annals of the American Academy of Political and Social Science*, March 1949, pp. 92–101; and *Immigrants and the American Labor Market*, p. 5.

[7] *Historical Statistics*, pp. 62–69.

[8] Eckler and Zlotnick, op. cit., p. 97. Tables AA–6 and AA–7 in the Bicentennial Supplement to the Statistical Appendix.

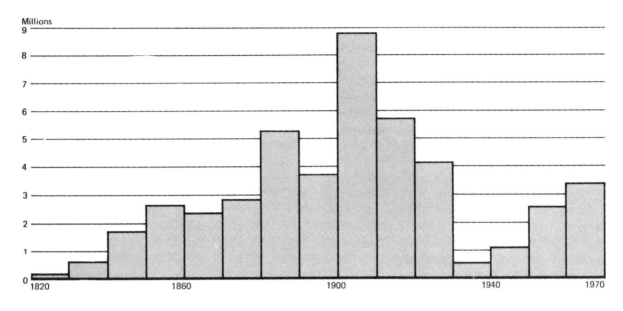

CHART 21

Immigrant arrivals peaked in the early years of this century.

Millions

Source: Immigration and Naturalization Service.

concerned about the "brain drain," the loss of their ablest and best educated people, many to the United States. For example, foreign medical graduates arriving between 1965 and 1973 amounted to 47 percent of all new physicians licensed in that period.[9]

The fact that so many Americans have been the children and grandchildren of immigrants has had a pronounced effect on labor force attitudes and expectations over the years. The improving fortunes of successive generations rode the general tide of rising real wages and the continuing occupational shift toward more high-status jobs. This experience helped create a general expectation of continued improvement.

Changing Composition of the Population

The population changed in its composition over the years. Its average age rose; the sex composition shifted slightly from preponderantly male to preponderantly female (mostly as a result of women's

greater longevity); the proportion of blacks at first declined, but then began to rise; the proportions of native-born and foreign-born—and the ethnic origins of the foreign-born—have changed; and the population has become better educated. All these changes were reflected in the working population as well.

A decline in birth and mortality rates has resulted in a population with fewer children and more older persons. The median age rose from 16.7 years in 1820 to 28.8 in 1975.

Since the increase in the proportion of older people has tended to offset the decline in younger ones, the proportion of the population that is supported by the work of others has remained fairly stable. In the past hundred years, the population aged 20 to 64 years—ages at which the bulk of society's work, both in the marketplace and in the home, is carried out—has remained about half the total.[10]

Black Americans have always been the largest racial minority group. They amounted to almost a fifth of the population in 1790, but their share

[9] Rosemary Stevens and others, "Physician Migration Reexamined," *Science*, Oct. 31, 1975, pp. 439–442.

[10] *Historical Statistics*, p. 10, and *Statistical Abstract, 1974* (Washington: U.S. Department of Commerce, Bureau of the Census, 1974), pp. 6 and 31.

decreased as large numbers of white immigrants arrived, accompanied somewhat later by significant numbers of immigrants from Oriental countries. By 1930, blacks were only about 10 percent of the population. Since then, as immigration decreased and their own birth rate remained higher than the national average, the black population increased to 24.5 million by 1975, or 11.5 percent of the total.[11]

The second largest racial minority is composed of the American Indians, of whom about 793,000 were counted in 1970. The Japanese (591,000 in 1970) and the Chinese (435,000) together account for 0.5 percent of the total. The population of Hispanic heritage, numbering about 10 million in 1970, while not comprising the largest minority group, has grown very rapidly in recent decades.

CHANGES IN THE LABOR FORCE

The labor force represents the human resources immediately available to the market economy. Economists distinguish between persons engaged in paid work done in the market economy and unpaid work done in the home or by volunteers. The distinction is useful, for example, in estimating the total number of people subject to unemployment in order to calculate an unemployment rate. But this distinction tends to downplay the significance of both the work done in the home and the large amount of volunteer work without which religious, charitable, political, and community organizations could hardly function.[12]

Early in the Nation's history, much of what the family consumed was produced in the home rather than in the market economy. Alexander Hamilton noted in his *Report on Manufactures* in 1791 that four-fifths of the clothing worn by the population was made at home. While this is not nearly true today, the work of the housewife is certainly crucial to the Nation's productivity, and references to women "working" in the market economy often really mean that they are taking on a job in addition to home and child-care responsibilities.

The historical perspective also needs to be taken into account in studying the work of men. Because there is always work to do on a family farm and much of it is done at the individual's option, labor force participation is usually closer to 100 percent for men living on such farms than for urban men, and unemployment (at least as it is measured today) is usually low. As residence patterns shift from predominantly rural to urban, unemployment increases, and labor force participation, particularly for older men, falls.

Growth of the Labor Force

The labor force, estimated at 1,900,000 in 1800, grew rapidly at an average annual rate of about 3 percent in every decade up to 1890, except during the Civil War period. (At this rate, it doubled every 24 years, on the average.) Growth slowed after 1890, however, and has averaged 1.6 percent in the 20th century.[13]

This rapid growth of available labor contributed greatly to the rate of economic growth in the 19th century. The slower labor force expansion of more recent years was accompanied by a substantial reduction in working hours, so that economic growth was less stimulated by the increase in labor input. (However, advances in technology, increased capital investment, and a more highly skilled work force resulted in a gross national product far exceeding the levels envisaged in earlier days, even though the proportion of this growth attributable to hours of labor declined.)

Slave Workers

In 1800, the 530,000 slaves of working age amounted to 28 percent of the labor force. Legal importation of slaves ended in 1808, but demand for slaves increased as cotton growing became more profitable following the invention of the cotton gin in 1793, and slave trafficking continued well into the 19th century. The number of slaves rose rapidly; they represented 32 percent of the labor force by 1810, but because of white immigra-

---

[11] U.S. Department of Commerce, Bureau of the Census, Current Population Reports, Series P–25, No. 614, pp. 2 and 6.

[12] *Americans Volunteer*, Manpower/Automation Research Monograph No. 10 (Washington: U.S. Department of Labor, Manpower Administration, April 1969).

[13] Stanley Lebergott, *Manpower in Economic Growth* (New York: McGraw-Hill Book Co., 1964), p. 510. The derivation of these estimates is described in the same author's paper, "Labor Force and Employment, 1800–1960," in *Output, Employment and Productivity in the United States After 1800*, Conference on Research in Income and Wealth. Studies in Income and Wealth, vol. 30 (New York: National Bureau of Economic Research, 1966), pp. 117 to 204. Subsequent page references are to *Manpower in Economic Growth*.

tion, their proportionate share of the work force declined in each subsequent decennial year, to 21 percent in 1860.[14]

This large segment of the labor force was, of course, in no position to demand money wages or go on strike. They were employed not only in agriculture but in skilled nonfarm jobs, including construction and crafts; indeed, some were rented out by their owners for such work.[15] Much of the opposition to extending slavery to new territories in the West—an issue that was the center of political controversy in the decades leading to the Civil War—arose from free farmers' and workers' fear of skilled slave labor competition.

Trends in Labor Force Participation

The size and composition of the labor force are determined not only by the size of the population but also by the participation rates of various groups. Trends in participation describe the changing style of life itself, since participation rates reflect the decisions of millions of people about how to spend their time—whether to invest in education or seek immediate income, whether to stay at home with the children or enter the labor force.

The quantitative results are clear: participation of older men has dropped, while that of women—including those with young children—has increased dramatically. Participation of children 10 to 15 years old has declined, but that of older youth, after dropping early in the present century, has risen, owing largely to higher participation by girls.

"Small Help." Children had always helped out on family farms and slave children were put to work on plantations, so that, as nonfarm industries developed, it seemed natural to use children in whatever kinds of work they could do. Power machinery, eliminating the need for physical strength in some industrial processes and calling only for dexterity, led to employment of children in mills and factories. In fact, one early 19th-century cotton mill was run entirely by children between the ages of 4 and 10, with one adult superintendent. In the 1820's and 1830's, children under 16 were reported to comprise one-third to one-half the factory labor force of New England and one-fifth that of Pennsylvania.[16]

Throughout most of the country's history, children were in demand for some types of work. In the 1860's, a Fall River man reported to a committee of the Massachusetts legislature:

Small help is scarce; a great deal of the machinery has been stopped for want of small help, so the overseers have been going round to draw the small children from the schools into the mills; the same as a draft in the army.[17]

Many children also worked in their homes on industrial tasks. Immigrant families, struggling to get a toehold in a new world, sought any chink or cranny in the economy—for example, collecting scraps of silk from dress factories and sewing them together to make linings for men's caps. The whole family and sometimes neighbors were involved. Home work in these "sweatshops" lent itself to abuse by the manufacturers; home workers could be played against each other and against the shop-workers, and contract prices could be squeezed down. Home workers were less able to organize unions, and there was no way to control the hours of work or the health conditions of the workplace.

Children's working conditions in factories did not meet particularly exacting legal or moral standards either. One factory overseer reported in 1870:

Six years ago I ran night work from 6:45 to 6 a.m. with forty-five minutes for meals, eating in the room. The children were drowsy and sleepy; have known them to fall asleep standing up at their work. I have had to sprinkle water in their faces to arouse them after having spoken to them till hoarse.[18]

Between 1870 and 1900, the proportion of children 10 to 15 years old who were gainful workers actually increased from 13 to 18 percent, and their share of all gainful workers rose slightly.[19] While there were laws as early as 1813 dealing with child labor in factories, enforcement was perfunctory. Some progress was made when a National Child Labor Committee was organized in 1904 to press for limitation of child labor, and from 1902 to

---

[14] Lebergott, op. cit., pp. 252 and 510.
[15] Kenneth M. Stampp, *The Peculiar Institution: Slavery in the Ante-Bellum South* (New York: Knopf, 1956), pp. 67–72.
[16] Lebergott, op. cit., p. 50.
[17] Edith Abbott, *Women in Industry: A Study in American Economic History* (New York: D. Appleton Co., 1910), p. 345.
[18] Ibid., p. 346.
[19] Alba M. Edwards, *Comparative Occupation Statistics for the United States, 1870 to 1940* (Washington: U.S. Department of Commerce, Bureau of the Census, 1943), pp. 91–92. In censuses through 1930, the economically active population included "gainful workers" 10 years of age or over; beginning in 1940, data were compiled on the "labor force" 14 years of age and over. The labor force includes only persons who were employed or seeking work in the current week, while the time reference for gainful workers is broader. The latter concept is therefore slightly more inclusive.

1909, some 43 States adopted laws setting minimum ages for school leaving and controlling hours and working conditions for children in businesses.[20]

The labor force participation rate of children aged 10 to 15 had decreased to 5 percent by 1930. Similarly, they made up a declining proportion of the "gainful workers"—decreasing from 6 percent in 1890 to less than 2 percent in 1930—with two-thirds of them in agriculture.[21]

The Fair Labor Standards Act in 1938 prohibited work of children under 16 in plants engaged in interstate commerce; under its provisions, regulations were issued prohibiting home work in certain industries.[22]

Women's Changing Role. The most remarkable change in labor force participation has been among adult women. In the earliest days, few women worked outside their homes. Private household work was the major area in which women found employment; in fact, many immigrant women got their first jobs in private homes.

When Secretary of the Treasury Alexander Hamilton urged the development of manufactures, he argued (to allay the farmers' fears that industry would rob them of labor) that factory workers could be recruited from among immigrants and the wives and children of farmers. "The husbandman himself," he wrote, "experiences a new source of profit and support from the increased industry of his wife and daughters, invited and stimulated by the demands of the neighboring manufactories."[23] Many women from rural families did enter the textile mills around Lowell and Fall River, Mass., and, by 1850, women constituted one-quarter of all factory workers.[24]

Nevertheless, the proportion of women participating in work outside their own homes continued to be low. For 1830, a rough estimate showed a participation rate below 10 percent for white women; virtually all black women, being slaves, were workers. By 1870, the participation rate for all women 16 and over was 15 percent.[25]

After 1870, women's labor force participation increased rapidly for 40 years, reaching 24 percent in 1910. There was little change for the next three decades, but many women went into warwork during World War II, and their participation increased remarkably thereafter, from 26 percent in 1940 to 46.4 percent in 1975.[26]

This dramatic increase reflects the changing patterns of women's life and the way they have dealt with their family responsibilities. The peak of women's participation has always occurred in their early twenties, before marriage or the birth of children. In earlier years, this peak was followed by a rapid drop in participation and a continued decline as women grew older (see chart 22). By 1960, however, the percent of women working, after decreasing in the late twenties, rose again at ages 35 to 44, as their children reached school age. Still another pattern had emerged by 1975: participation declined only slightly among those in their late twenties and thirties so that the participation rate remained above 50 percent from age 18 to age 55.

Throughout this whole period, there have been very large differences between labor force participation rates of white and black women, single and married women, and those with and without young children.

Black women have had a consistently higher participation rate than white ones, reflecting the lower income of their husbands and the larger proportion of them who were, and are, the sole support of their families. In 1890, for example, when 2.5 percent of married white women were in the labor force, 22.5 percent of minority group married women were workers.[27] The difference between white and black women's participation has, however, narrowed in recent years, as a rising proportion of white women have entered the labor market.

Participation rates for single and separated or divorced women have always been higher than that for married women. In 1890, 35 percent of the single white women, but only 2.5 percent of the married ones, were in the labor force; by 1960, the rate for single white women had risen to 46 percent, and that for married women had reached 30 percent. By 1975, rates for single women, re-

[20] William Miller, *A New History of the United States* (New York: George Braziller, Inc., 1958), p. 308.

[21] Edwards, op. cit., pp. 92 and 97.

[22] Youth aged 16 to 19 years, however, still encounter many problems in the form of restricted employment opportunities and high levels of unemployment. See the chapter on Employment and Unemployment: 1975 in Review in this report.

[23] Henry Pelling, *American Labor* (Chicago: University of Chicago Press, 1960), p. 23.

[24] Abbott, op. cit., p. 83.

[25] Lebergott, op. cit., p. 519, and Edwards, op. cit., pp. 98 and 129.

[26] Edwards, op. cit., pp. 13 and 92, and app. table A-1 in this report.

[27] Lebergott, op. cit., p. 519.

CHART 22

Patterns of labor force participation by women of different ages have altered remarkably over the years.

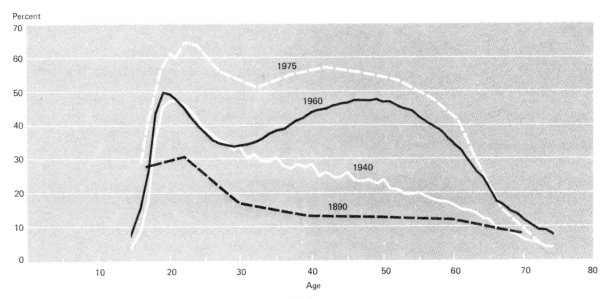

Sources: U.S. Department of Labor and U.S. Department of Commerce, Bureau of the Census.

gardless of color, in most age groups, had risen no further. Those for married women, however, had increased from 10 to 20 percentage points at each age. Women with young children have had the lowest rates, but their participation has also increased sharply in recent years; in 1948, only 11 percent of the married women with children under 6 years of age were in the labor force, in contrast to 36.6 percent in 1975.[28]

The rising participation rate of women is the reflection of vast social, economic, and cultural changes. Moving from farm to city gave women greater access to paid employment. Growth of white-collar occupations created demand for their services. Higher educational attainment opened more doors. Work-saving appliances in the home and the development of services (laundries, diaper services, convenience foods) lightened the burden of housework.[29] Declines in birth rates and the

wider availability of kindergartens and nursery schools reduced the child-care responsibility. More part-time jobs were created, partly as a result of expansion of the service sector, which accommodates such jobs more easily, partly in recognition of the fact that women who work outside the home may retain home responsibilities as well. (This is especially true of female family heads, of whom there were 6.8 million in 1974, in contrast to 3.7 million in 1950.) The desire of families for more income, not only to buy more material goods but also to support a longer period of education for children, was another important factor. Finally, there were changes in social attitudes toward work outside the home for married women, including those with children.

Older Men. Another marked change in labor force composition stems from the declining participation rate of men 65 and over, which has paralleled the population shift from rural to urban areas. In 1890, two-thirds of these older men were in the labor force, but by 1930, this proportion had dropped to only a little more than half. With the provision of benefits under social security in the 1930's, the proliferation of private pension plans

---

[28] Ibid. and app. tables B–2 and B–4 in this report.

[29] Women's participation increased despite a decline in the availability of workers willing to take over some of the household tasks. The number of private household workers has declined relative to the number of households—from 1 for every 10 households in 1900 to 1 for every 30 in 1960. See Valerie Kincade Oppenheimer, *The Female Labor Force in the United States,* Population Monograph Series, No. 5 (Berkeley: University of California, 1969), p. 36.

in the late 1940's and 1950's, and disability coverage under social security in the 1960's, the participation rate declined to 22 percent by 1975. This process was hastened, of course, by the imposition of mandatory retirement age requirements in both the private and public sectors. Among men 55 to 64 years of age, a decline began after World War II; from 90 percent in 1947, participation dropped to 76 percent by 1975.[30]

Changing Composition of the Labor Force

As a result of these diverse trends in participation, the composition of the labor force has changed. For example, the labor force, like the population, has been getting older.

The importance of women in the labor force has increased as a result of their higher participation rates. In 1870, the 1.9 million women who were gainful workers amounted to 14.8 percent of all such workers.[31] The number of women workers nearly doubled in the next two decades, and they made up 17 percent of gainful workers in 1890. The rate of increase has accelerated in the 20th century, especially during the two major wars. By 1975, there were about 37 million women in the labor force, representing almost 40 percent of all workers.

The implications for industry and for public policy of a work force in which 4 out of 10 workers are women have been immense. Employers have had to adjust their practices, unions their policies. Pressure has arisen for equal employment opportunities, training opportunities, and pay. Recent

interest in flexible working time has been stimulated in part by many women workers' need to carry on their home responsibilities. Perhaps most important in human terms, the greater dependence of the economy on women has been matched by the greater independence of women themselves.

Changing Patterns of Work in the Life Cycle

The place of work in the life cycle has altered greatly because of later entrance into the labor force for children, earlier retirement for men, and greater participation for women. This change can best be seen in relation to the lengthening of the lifespan itself.

A baby born in 1900 could expect, on the average, to live for some 50 years. In 1970, as a result of medical advances and healthier living conditions, a baby boy could expect to live about 19 years longer and a girl, 24 years longer (see table 1). From 1900 to 1970, however, men extended the average period in which they work by only 8 years, while their nonworking years—mainly for education and retirement—increased from 16 to 27. On the other hand, women's average working years rose from 6 to 23, while their nonworking years increased by less than 8 over the same seven decades. In other words, the average man has reduced his working years from two-thirds of his lifespan to about three-fifths; in contrast, the average woman has increased her working years from a little more than one-tenth to nearly one-third of her lifespan. These changes in the average work-life span have implications for education, family living, patterns of expenditure, the funding of pensions, leisure, and the quality of life itself.

[30] *Historical Statistics*, p. 71, and app. table A–2 in this report.
[31] Edwards, op. cit., pp. 122–129.

TABLE 1. LIFE AND WORKLIFE EXPECTANCY AT BIRTH, FOR MEN AND WOMEN, 1900–70

Year	Men			Women		
	Life expectancy	Worklife expectancy	Nonwork years	Life expectancy	Worklife expectancy	Nonwork years
1900	48. 2	32. 1	16. 1	50. 7	6. 3	44. 4
1940	61. 2	38. 1	23. 1	65. 7	12. 1	53. 6
1970	67. 1	40. 1	27. 0	74. 8	22. 9	51. 9

SOURCES: Seymour L. Wolfbein, *Changing Patterns of Working Life* (Washington: U.S. Department of Labor, Office of Manpower, Automation, and Training, 1963), and Howard J. Fullerton, Jr., and James J. Byrne, "Length of Working Life for Men and Women, 1970," *Monthly Labor Review*, February 1976, pp. 31–35.

EDUCATION AND TRAINING OF WORKERS

General Education

Education has played a major role in the qualitative development of the American work force. In addition to its traditional functions, the educational system has had three additional tasks thrust upon it: To help immigrants and their children learn the language and make up for educational deficiencies; to overcome the heritage of economic and social deprivation left by slavery; and to smooth the shift from an agricultural to an industrial and technical society.

Free public education was established in principle as early as 1647, when the Massachusetts Bay Colony passed a law requiring every community of 50 or more houses to contribute to the support of a teacher. Other colonies followed, but compliance was uneven. Through the first third of the 19th century, free public schools were reserved for the very poor; parents of other children had to find private schools.[32]

The demand for free, universal public education was raised by the unions in the 1820's. The Philadelphia Workingmen's Party in 1825 attacked the pauper system, urging free public education not only in the three R's but also in the knowledge needed for self-government and manual labor. Early public reactions were divided, however. The editor of the *Philadelphia National Gazette* wrote that "the scheme of Universal equal education at the expense of the state is virtually 'agrarianism,' an arbitrary division of the property of the rich with the poor." [33] But when the States did adopt laws setting up publicly supported schools open to all, budgets were low and instruction minimal for many years. Since children's help was needed on the farms, the number of days of schooling provided in a year was far lower than is common today.

The extension of high school education was a 20th-century development. In 1870, only 16,000 young people graduated from high school, or 2 percent of all youth of high school graduating age. Since a principal purpose of going to secondary school in those days was to prepare for higher education, more than half of the high school graduates of 1870 went on to graduate from college. The proportion of youth of high school age who were enrolled in high school rose gradually until the second decade of the 20th century, when it more than doubled—from 15 to 32 percent; by 1970, the proportion enrolled in high school reached 93 percent. While graduates of regular day high schools in 1910 amounted to 9 percent of the appropriate age group, they numbered 75 percent in 1974. Including graduates of night schools and persons getting high school equivalency certificates from State departments of education, about 80 percent of the population of high school age is currently completing high school or its equivalent.[34]

The extension of college education has lagged behind that of high school education by more than a generation. College graduates amounted to 2 percent of the population of college graduating age in 1910, but this figure had risen to about 25 percent by 1972.[35] This is only a partial measure of the extension of college education, however. The great expansion of community colleges, on the one hand, and of graduate education on the other has increased the proportion of youth served by colleges and universities. In 1973, 8.2 million students were enrolled in college, including 33 percent of all 18- and 19-year-olds and 29 percent of 20- and 21-year-olds. There were 1.9 million enrolled in 2-year institutions (compared with 222,000 in 1947) and 1.1 million graduate students enrolled in universities.[36]

The education of black youth has trailed far behind that of whites, but it has begun to catch up in recent years. In 1850, when slavery was at its peak, 56 percent of the whites aged 5 to 19 years were enrolled in school, but only 2 percent of the Negro and other races were enrolled; few of this small share were slave children. By 1880, 18 years after emancipation, black enrollment was up to 34 percent, and by 1970, 90 percent of black children were enrolled, about the same proportion

[32] H. G. Good, *A History of American Education*, 2d ed. (New York: Macmillan Co., 1962), p. 116.

[33] Good, op. cit., p. 122.

[34] *Digest of Educational Statistics, 1974* (Washington: U.S. Department of Health, Education, and Welfare, National Center for Educational Statistics, 1975), pp. 33, 54, and 101; *Educational Attainment in the United States: March 1973 and 1974*, Series P-20, No. 274 (Washington: U.S. Department of Commerce, Bureau of the Census, December 1974), p. 67.

[35] *Digest of Educational Statistics, 1974*, p. 101.

[36] *School Enrollment in the United States, October 1973*, Series P-20, No. 261 (Washington: U.S. Department of Commerce, Bureau of the Census, March 1974), p. 45; *Digest of Educational Statistics, 1974*, pp. 72 and 83.

as among white children. Blacks, however, are still far behind in college enrollment; 31 percent of the white youth aged 18 to 21 years were enrolled in college in October 1974, but only 21 percent of black youth. The enrollment rate for those of Spanish heritage was 22 percent. College enrollment differences between men and and women have narrowed in recent years; in 1974, 30 percent of the men and 29 percent of the women aged 18 to 21 years were enrolled.[37]

Vocational Education

Public vocational education in America goes back to 1646, when the Virginia Colony provided that two children from every county should be taught, at public cost, the arts of carding, knitting, and spinning.[38]

As interest in vocational education revived late in the 19th century, the proportion of high school graduates going on to complete college dropped from over half in 1870 to less than one-quarter in the 1920's. To meet the needs of those not intending to go to college, the schools broadened their curriculums to include vocational subjects. Youth in secondary schools were trained in agriculture, trade and industrial occupations, and home economics, and in 1917, the Federal Government began to provide financial support. Enrollments in federally aided classes had expanded to 2.3 million by 1940, and further rapid growth took place after the war. Federal funds were increased after a new Vocational Education Act was passed in 1963; by 1973, enrollments reached 12.3 million, of which 61 percent were in secondary school programs, 11 percent in postsecondary programs, and 28 percent in programs for adults.

Training by Employers

Despite the important contribution of the school and apprenticeship systems to skill acquisition, by far the greatest proportion of vocational training is provided on the job by employers in both the public and private sectors. While there are no accurate measures of the real extent of such training, since it exists in all occupational and industrial sectors, there is abundant evidence that a substantial proportion of larger firms (and many smaller ones) offer formal training to new employees to supplement the informal "breaking-in" process experienced by every job entrant. For many employees with longer job tenure, there are additional training programs linked to career progression ladders or tuition-support arrangements in which the employer assumes part or all of the cost of courses attended by the employee. While many tuition-support arrangements apply only to job-related courses, some employers are willing to assume general education costs as well, either for selected employees or on a companywide basis.

Apprenticeship

Although apprenticeship in the English tradition was brought over by craft workers in colonial times and retained moderate strength in some areas, it was not as readily accepted in the New World as in the Old; apprentices often dropped out, attracted by the chance to get a farm or a business as soon as they had acquired the rudiments of agriculture or a trade. Workers without formal training were free to enter crafts, and many did.

In 1937, the National Apprenticeship Act gave the Department of Labor responsibility for promoting apprenticeship. By 1972, there were 270,000 apprentices registered, more than half of them in the building trades, but with large numbers in metal and printing trades as well; 53,000 persons completed apprenticeships in that year, 0.5 percent of the number of craft workers employed at the time.[39] There are, in addition, over 100,000 workers in allied industrial training programs and an unknown number in apprenticeship programs not registered with the State apprenticeship councils or the Department of Labor.[40]

[37] *School Enrollment—Social and Economic Characteristics of Students: October 1974*, Series P–20, No. 278 (Washington: U.S. Department of Commerce, Bureau of the Census, February 1975), pp. 6 and 7. Population data for men corrected to include Armed Forces.

[38] Good, op. cit., p. 21.

[39] *1975 Manpower Report*, app. table A–15, p. 225, and app. table F–13, pp. 330–331, and Neal Rosenthal, "Projected Changes in Occupations," *Monthly Labor Review*, December 1973, p. 22.

[40] For a more extensive discussion of apprenticeship programs and a review of recent efforts to increase apprenticeship opportunities for minorities and women, see the chapters on Construction: The Industry and the Labor Force and National Program Developments in this report.

The Changing Nature of Work

In 1776, the most typical American worker was the farmer; in 1976, he—or she—is the white-collar worker. This section will review this and other changes in the nature of work that have taken place over 200 years: Shifts from a simple farming economy to a complex industrial one; changes in the way work is organized; changes in the kinds of work performed, as shown by the workers' occupations; and the changing conditions of work—including hours and days worked, health and safety in the workplace, and the extent of unionization.

ECONOMIC ACTIVITY

Farming, the predominant way of making a living when the Nation was founded, continued to occupy a majority of the work force for the first 100 years. In 1787, more than 89 percent of all employment was in farming.[41] Nonfarm industries began to grow more rapidly than agriculture, however, and between 1880 and 1890, the number of people engaged in nonfarm activity exceeded those in farming for the first time. The number of farmers and farmworkers reached a peak in the decade of World War I and then shrank by two-thirds to 3.4 million in 1975, or 3.6 percent of the total labor force.[42] This decline in employment did not mean a drop in production; on the contrary, farm output in the early 1970's was at a historic high.

Growth of Nonfarm Industries

In the early days of the 19th century, manufacturing was stimulated by the development of internal transportation—by roads, waterways, canals, and later railroads—that gave the factory a wider market and made large-scale production more feasible. The Constitution's provision prohibiting internal tariffs provided the legal framework for a single national market, and additional stimulus to the division of labor was supplied by Eli Whitney's introduction (in small arms manufacture in Connecticut) of standardized inter-changeable parts, which enabled mass production to supplant handicrafts.

By the eve of the Civil War, manufacturing production in the United States was second only to that of Great Britain. The war stimulated demand, starting a manufacturing boom that continued after the war. The railroads were extended rapidly; in the 8 years after 1865, 30,000 miles of track were laid, mostly in the East and Central States, but also across the continent; the golden spike signaling the creation of a transcontinental railroad system was driven in 1869. This, in turn, not only expanded markets but also stimulated the steel, lumber, and railroad car industries.

Growth of each new industry was rapid. Oil was struck in Pennsylvania in 1869; 3 years later, 40 million barrels were produced. The telephone was invented in 1876; 8 years later, the industry was so advanced that long-distance service was introduced, and by 1900, there were 1,350,000 telephones in service. Commercial manufacture of automobiles began in 1897; the Model T Ford was introduced in 1909, and a half-million cars were produced by 1914, creating new demand for steel, glass, rubber, petroleum, and roadbuilding.[43]

The Changing Industrial Distribution of Labor

The way in which rapid development of nonfarm industries profoundly changed the industrial distribution of the labor force can be highlighted by distinguishing among three broad industrial sectors: The extractive industries that develop the raw materials (agriculture, forestry, fisheries, and mining), the industries that convert the raw materials into forms for final use (manufacturing and construction), and the service-producing industries (trade, finance, transportation and public utilities, government, personal, professional, and business services, and private household employment).

A look at the changing allocation of the American labor force in these terms reveals the following: 84 percent were in the extractive industries in 1810; by 1840 (the first year for which the full

---

[41] Pelling, op. cit., p. 23.
[42] See app. table A–1 in this report.

[43] Miller, op. cit., pp. 264–294.

CHART 23

The preponderance of the labor force was in extractive industries until 1890 and has been in service activities since 1930.

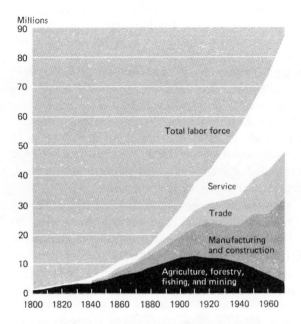

Sources: 1800-1960 from Stanley Lebergott, *Manpower in Economic Growth*, p. 510 (persons 10 years and older); 1970 data from Current Population Survey data supplied by the Bureau of Labor Statistics, covering persons 14 years and older.

comparison can be made), that sector was still dominant, with 64 percent of all workers, but manufacturing and construction had 14 percent and the services 22 percent of the total (see chart 23).

Growth of the latter two sectors accelerated through the second half of the 19th century; by 1890, extractive industries had less than half of the labor force, and more than half the workers were in services and trade industries by 1930. In 1970, these sectors claimed 64 percent of all workers, extractive industries only 5 percent, and manufacturing and construction 31 percent.[44]

In summary, the preponderance of the American work force was in extractive industries up to 1890 and has been in service activities since 1930. For

---

[44] Lebergott, op. cit., p. 510. These data include self-employed persons in the labor force of each industry; when only wage and salary workers are included, employment in service-producing industries does not exceed that in goods-producing industries until after 1950.

the past 100 years, about 1 worker in 4 has been in manufacturing and construction.

A closer look at the growth of nonfarm industries in the 20th century shows that the fastest growing sectors have been financial institutions and government, with average annual growth rates of about 3.5 percent from 1900 to 1974. Trade and service industries have grown annually at 2.6 and 2.8 percent respectively, manufacturing and construction at about 1.7 percent, and mining, after rapid growth early in the century, had returned to its 1900 level by 1970.[45]

Amidst the rapid growth of employment, some industries declined, with all that this meant in terms of unemployment and the need for their employees to shift into other lines of work. In addition to farming, industries with substantial employment declines include coal mining, which lost over half its jobs between World War I and the early 1970's, before expanding again in response to energy shortages; railroads, down by more than half since the mid-1920's; textiles, down by one-quarter since the early 1950's; shoes, down by nearly half in the same period; and many smaller industries. Shifts in consumer demand, competition from imports, and technological changes have taken their toll in these sectors.

ORGANIZATION OF WORK

The Large Organization

A major change in work over the past 200 years has been the rise of the large organization, which employs an increasing proportion of all workers, often on a transnational basis. In business, the prevalence of large firms increased in the second half of the 19th century. The "trust" form of corporate organization had its greatest growth toward the end of that century and in the early years of the 20th century. By 1951, 38 percent of all wage and salary workers in private industry were employed in firms that had 1,000 or more employees; 19 percent were in firms with 10,000 or more employees.[46]

Another area of employment in which the large organization is typical is government. In 1900,

---

[45] Lebergott, op. cit., pp. 514 and 516, and *1975 Manpower Report*, app. table C–1, p. 278.
[46] Betty C. Churchill, "Size Characteristics of the Business Population," *Survey of Current Business*, May 1954, pp. 15–24.

there were over a million civilian government employees, of whom only 22 percent were Federal and the rest State and local. Government employment rose to 14.8 million in the next 75 years, and increased its share of the total from 4 to 19 percent. The greatest growth has been in State and local government, where public education employs more than half the total.[47]

The military side of government employment has also grown. In the year the Constitution was adopted, the land forces available to back up this new venture amounted to 718 soldiers.[48] At the wartime peak of 1945, personnel on active duty numbered over 12 million. Then, with the assumption of a larger international role after World War II, the Armed Forces numbered 2.2 million in 1975. Washington's and Lincoln's peacetime Armed Forces were 0.3 percent of the labor force; now the Armed Forces are 2.3 percent.[49]

Self-Employment

In the early days of the Republic, self-employment—in farming—was the reality for a majority of all workers. Except in the plantation agriculture of the South and in the large holdings of the Hudson Valley and several other limited areas in the North, the family farm was typical. The availability of land made it relatively easy for the immigrant to establish a family holding after getting a stake and gaining experience by working as a hired laborer. In the towns, the prevalence of small handicrafts and stores made it possible for many to be self-employed. (Farming is still a major area for self-employment; half the farmworkers enjoy this status, as they have for the past 100 years.)[50]

In nonfarm enterprises, where 19 out of 20 workers are engaged, the number of self-employed increased up to the early 1960's but declined somewhat since then; as a proportion of all workers, however, the self-employed decreased drastically, from 27 percent of nonfarm workers in 1900 to 7 percent in 1975.[51] Some of this decline, of course,

reflects more frequent incorporation of small businesses, in which the former proprietor becomes an employee of the corporation. By and large, however, the chain store and the supermarket have grown; the "Mom and Pop" store and small businesses in general have not.

OCCUPATIONS

"A Shifting, Unsteady, Improving Mass"

Many observers of American experience in the early 19th century registered astonishment at the occupational flexibility of workers—their willingness and ability to shift among occupations and often to work at more than one occupation at a time. In addition to the large number who combined farming with other work, examples of multioccupation workers abounded: A judge who was also a butcher, fishermen who built ships, river boatmen who engaged in wholesale trade, flour millers who did blacksmiths' work on the side, and many others.[52] The quality of work may have suffered. Apprenticeship, as noted earlier, was ignored by many, and apprentices often skipped out before completing their training. Albert Gallatin, who was Secretary of the Treasury from 1801 to 1814, remarked that "every species of trade, commerce and professions [is] equally open to all without requiring a regular apprenticeship, admission or license," and a visiting British economist said: "The country is so vast and the temptation to other and easier pursuits so great, that there is no constancy to certain employment as in England. The laboring population in America is not stable; it is a shifting, unsteady, improving mass." Another European observer contrasted the high quality of British workers' skills with "the more general aptitude" of Americans.[53] And it can be argued that this willingness to try any work and the freedom to do so were among the wellsprings of the remarkable productivity of American industry.

Changing Occupational Employment Patterns

Comprehensive statistics tracing the changing occupational patterns of the American work force

[47] Lebergott, op. cit., p. 517; *Employment and Earnings*, January 1976, p. 165.
[48] *Historical Statistics*, pp. 736–737; Lebergott, op. cit., p. 510.
[49] See app. table A–1 in this report.
[50] Edwards, op. cit., p. 104; Lebergott, op. cit., p. 513; *Employment and Earnings*, January 1975, p. 150.
[51] Lebergott, op. cit., p. 513, and app. table A–17 in this report.
[52] Lebergott, op. cit., pp. 115–119.
[53] These quotations cited by Lebergott, op. cit., pp. 119–120.

go back only halfway through the country's history.[54] The major development since 1870 is the shift away from agricultural occupations, which engaged 53 percent of the gainful workers in that year. The gap was filled largely by white-collar occupations, which increased from 17.6 percent to 49.8 percent of the total between 1870 and 1975, and by service occupations, which increased from 9 to 13.7 percent.[55]

The growth of white-collar occupations was partly a result of the great expansion of service-producing industries, which employ many more white-collar than blue-collar workers. It was also generated by shifts in the composition of employment in each industry; in the mining, construction, and manufacturing industries (major employers of blue-collar workers), an increasing proportion of the workers are white-collar employees, as shown below:

	White-collar workers as a percent of total employment		
	1947	1974	1975
Mining	9	24	30
Construction	11	18	22
Manufacturing	17	27	31

The shift to white-collar work is dramatized in the story of clerical occupations, the fastest growing occupational field. The 1870 census found only 154 stenographers and typists in the Nation; 7 of them were women. A century later there were 1,153,000, as well as 2,770,000 secretaries, an occupation not separately identified in 1870. The business world got along with 1 clerical worker for every 20.6 nonfarm workers in 1900; in 1970 there was 1 for every 5.4 nonfarm workers. This growth is particularly impressive in view of the technological innovations designed to reduce labor requirements for office work—typewriters, copying machines, bookkeeping machines, calculators, electronic data processing, and many others.

Professional and technical occupations are the second-fastest growing group. One reason for this growth, the expansion of science and technology, is suggested by the increase in the number of engi-

neers from the 7,000 found by the 1870 census to 1,257,000 in 1970. Working with them in 1970 were 843,000 science and engineering technicians, an occupation not identified in 1870, and there were 246,000 natural scientists and mathematicians in 1970 (not including those teaching in colleges and universities), compared with 774 tallied in 1870.

A second reason for growth of the professional and technical occupations is the expansion of health services. In 1870, there were 73,000 physicians, dentists, and other health practitioners, backed up by 1,204 trained nurses, or one professional health worker for every 538 people in the United States. In 1970, there were 1,773,000 workers in the health professions; the 541,000 physicians, dentists, and other practitioners were backed up by 848,000 registered nurses and 384,000 health technicians—amounting to one health professional for every 115 people in the country.

A third reason for growth of professions is the expansion of education. There were 128,000 teachers at all levels in 1870, or one for every 136 persons aged 5 to 24 years (at a time when 2 percent of the youth were finishing high school).[56] In 1970, there were 3,280,000 teachers, one for every 23 persons aged 5 to 24 years, at a time when three-quarters of the population of appropriate age were finishing high school and one-quarter getting bachelor's degrees.

Sales and managerial occupations, the other white-collar fields, increased less rapidly, but both increased their shares of the total labor force—sales, from 4.5 percent in 1900 to 7 percent in 1970; managerial occupations, from 5.8 to 8.1 percent. Although self-employment in nonfarm industries has declined relative to total employment, salaried managerial workers have increased with the rise of the large firm.

While white-collar workers increased greatly as a proportion of the total economically active population, the proportion of blue-collar workers remained relatively steady between 1900 and 1970 (see chart 24). The least skilled "laborers" category declined from 12.6 to 4.7 percent, craft workers and supervisors gained from 10.5 to 13.5 percent, and operatives—the middle group in skill level—increased from 12.8 to 18.3 percent. Thus, the average skill level of blue-collar workers appears to have risen. Occupational content, however, has also changed over the years, and the

---

[54] Edwards, op. cit., and David L. Kaplan and M. Claire Casey, *Occupational Trends in the United States, 1900 to 1950*, Working Paper No. 5 (Washington: U.S. Department of Commerce, Bureau of the Census, 1958). Difficulties in tracing trends over time include changes in what is measured: "Gainful workers" up to 1930 and "labor force" beginning in 1940; workers 10 years old and over up to 1930, 14 and over since 1940, 16 and over since 1966; changes in the time of year in which the census was taken, affecting the nature of the work people were doing; and changes in the way in which occupations were classified.

[55] Bureau of the Census, 1870 Census of Population, *Occupational Characteristics*, Series PC(2)–7A, table 1, and app. table A–33 in this report.

[56] *Digest of Educational Statistics, 1974*, p. 54.

CHART 24

While the proportion of white-collar workers has increased substantially since 1900, that of blue-collar workers has remained about the same.

Percent of labor force

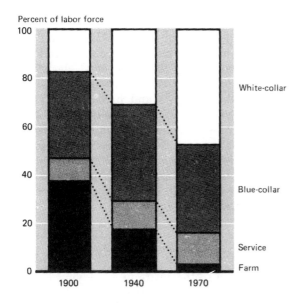

Sources: U.S. Department of Commerce, Bureau of the Census.

retention of traditional job titles in many crafts does not always reflect the narrowing or expansion of work content in step with technological changes.

The major change in the craft field is the general expansion of repair occupations, as the amount of mechanical equipment in industry, farms, and homes increased. Mechanics and repairers numbered 2,518,000 in 1970, 23 percent of all craft and kindred workers; they included 834,-000 automobile mechanics and 591,000 heavy equipment mechanics. The 1870 census did not list any repair occupations specifically. (In both years, members of many other crafts spent part of the time in repair work.) This growth in repair occupations accounts for the entire 3-percentage-point increase in the proportion of economically active workers who were in craft occupations.

None of the growth in service occupations was accounted for by service in private households. Private household workers were 5.4 percent of all workers in 1900 and only 1.5 percent in 1970. Despite the rise in the number of families that could afford such help and the increase in the proportion of women who worked outside the home and

therefore might have liked to hire someone to do the housework, the number of persons engaged in private household work was smaller in 1975 than in 1900—1.2 million compared with 1.5 million. This had been one of the main work opportunities for immigrant and black women, but as better paying jobs opened for them in other kinds of work, they left the field.

The shifts in the distribution of workers among occupations reflect, as noted earlier, changes in patterns of consumption, technology, and the way in which work is organized. Some occupations have declined in numbers of workers employed; among them are a few that have disappeared almost entirely, although this is rare, because few products or technologies disappear completely. Wagons, buggy whips, gold pens, and candles are still being made; more than a century and a half after the invention of the steamboat sealed the doom of the sailing ship, there are more sailmakers in the United States than ever—and sails, with their complex shapes, are now designed and cut by computer. (It should be noted, however, that these surviving "old-fashioned" occupations serve a clientele quite different from that of earlier years.)

While few occupations disappear, many new ones develop. George Washington never met a telegrapher, sewing machine operator, railroad engineer, linotype operator, or electric lineworker, let alone anyone in such 20th-century occupations as automobile mechanic, concrete finisher, inhalation therapist, air-conditioning repairer, nuclear physicist, fashion model, or computer programer.

Women's Occupational Distribution

Nearly half of all women who worked outside the home in 1870 were in private household work, but only 3.9 percent were so occupied a century later, when over 60 percent of working women were in white-collar jobs. This dramatic change in status has affected the worklife of women immensely: it has stimulated their educational aspirations and made working outside the home an attractive lifetime career for many.

More than half the white-collar women workers are in clerical jobs, but one-quarter are professional workers (primarily teachers and nurses)—slightly more than the proportion of white-collar men in professional jobs. Sales and managerial jobs and service occupations other than in private households have claimed a higher proportion of women workers since 1900, but a smaller proportion are in blue-collar occupations.

Women's share of white-collar jobs increased from 18.5 percent in 1900 to 48 percent in 1970. Their share of every type of white-collar job—in fact of every job category in nonfarm industry except operatives—rose, as shown below:

	Percent of women in job category	
	1900	1970
Professional and technical	25.6	40.1
Managerial	4.4	16.7
Clerical	24.2	73.8
Sales	17.4	40.1
Crafts, supervisors	2.5	4.9
Operatives	34.0	31.9
Laborers	3.8	8.2
Service, except private household	34.3	55.8

SOURCES: Kaplan and Casey, op. cit., table 5, and 1970 Census of Population, *Occupational Characteristics*, table 1.

A good part of the increase, however, was in the relatively low-paying clerical and sales fields, which helps account for the fact that average earnings of year-round full-time women workers are less than three-fifths those of men.

Black Workers' Occupational Status

Throughout the country's history, some blacks have been recorded in almost every occupation. The heritage of slavery, however, left black farm-workers with few of the skills required for jobs in the nonfarm sector that expanded so quickly after the Civil War.

Migration to southern cities and to the North brought black workers to places where nonfarm jobs were available. After finding their way into the steel mills, heavy industry, and service jobs, they encountered much greater difficulties in breaking into white-collar and craft jobs. But their rising educational level, together with training opportunities provided in the military, the civil rights movement, and enforcement of equal employment opportunity legislation, have since enabled them to enter a wider variety of jobs.

Most of the gains made by black workers in entering occupations involving higher skills, status, and pay in the 113 years since emancipation have been made in the years following the Supreme Court's 1954 decision on school segregation and the Civil Rights Act of 1964. Blacks have shifted out of private household service and farm and laborer jobs and have attained a larger

share of the white-collar and skilled jobs (see chart 25). One way to measure their gains in each occupation is to use as a rough yardstick their 11-percent share of the labor force. The small proportion of black workers in the higher level occupations in the past has been one indication of the extent of their disadvantage. In 1950, black workers had less than 4 percent of the professional, technical, and craft jobs and an even smaller share of the managerial, clerical, and sales positions, while they had more than half of private household jobs and high proportions of other service, labor, and farm jobs. An indication of their progress in the direction of occupational equality is the fact that their share of jobs in almost every field is now closer to their proportion in the labor force. (A disproportionate number, however, are still in the lower paying jobs in each category.)

Changes in the Content of Work

In addition to the shifts in employment among the various occupations, there have been profound changes in the content of occupations—the work that is done and skills required by each—and in the way in which workers enter occupations and advance in their careers.

Changes in the content of work have followed technological innovations or changes in the way work is organized, which reduced skill requirements in some fields and increased them in others. Since the Jacquard loom replaced the skilled hand weaver in weaving a design or pattern into cloth, the remaining loom tenders are less skilled; on the other hand, many electricians have taken special training in electronics arranged by their union in order to keep up with skill requirements.

Some occupations have lost out to technological change—the horseshoer, the boilermaker in railroad repair shops when the diesel locomotive came in—while others have made the new technology their own, like the coal miner who has abandoned pick and shovel for coal-digging machinery, or the construction craft worker who has increased productivity with power tools.

Extension of occupational scope has enriched the work of many. But the converse of this—and the more typical pattern as factory production supplanted handicrafts—is the narrowing of scope that occurred when the work was divided into many small tasks, each given to a different worker.

CHART 25

Blacks have obtained a rising share of white-collar and skilled jobs since 1950.

Percent of jobs held by blacks and other minority groups

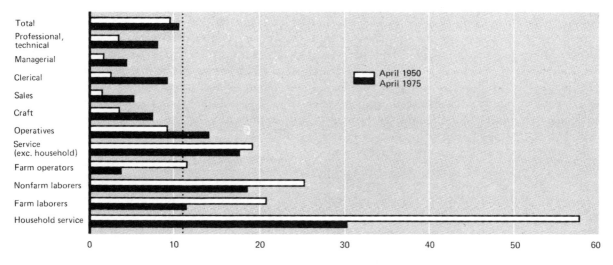

| | April 1950 |
| | April 1975 |

Total
Professional, technical
Managerial
Clerical
Sales
Craft
Operatives
Service (exc. household)
Farm operators
Nonfarm laborers
Farm laborers
Household service

0   10   20   30   40   50   60

Note: Dotted vertical line shows the percent of blacks and other minority group members in the labor force in 1950 and 1975.

Sources: U.S. Department of Labor and U.S. Department of Commerce, Bureau of the Census.

In place of the 18th-century cordwainer, there are now 135 shoe-producing occupations, each consisting of a single repetitive operation. This division of labor has contributed to great increases in productivity, which in their turn made possible higher real earnings—but at the sacrifice of variety in work and a sense of versatile proficiency.

Division of labor has not been confined to manual workers. The rise of the large firm creates specialization in managerial and clerical occupations as well. Titles on the doors of the executive suite include controller, accountant, personnel manager, purchasing agent, credit specialist, sales manager, public relations director, economist, traffic manager, and many others. The lone company bookkeeper has been supplemented by an army of file clerks, payroll clerks, accounts receivable clerks, keypunch operators, billing clerks, tabulating machine operators, and shipping clerks.

One of the most common changes in occupations associated with technology has been the craft worker's loss of responsibility for decisionmaking. Judging, from the color of the smelt, the moment when it was ready to be poured or knowing how thick a beam is needed to support a floor were traditional elements of craft wisdom, learned through training or long experience. But as the chemistry and physics underlying industrial processes have been mastered, the scientist and the engineer have taken over these decisions or provided precise (often computerized) instruments for measuring the process.

A significant trend in worklife has been the increasing complexity of rules governing entrance into occupations. Licensure, originally designed to protect the public against incompetent workers where health or safety are involved, has been used by those in many occupations to keep others out and reduce competition.[57] In other occupations, certification is used to identify workers who have gone through a training program. Unions in some crafts are selective in admitting workers to apprenticeship or membership. Employers give preference to workers with paper educational qualifications or administer screening tests of their own—a practice that has been discouraged, but not eliminated, by judicial recognition that such tests may have the effect of unlawfully discriminating against some minority groups.

[57] *Occupational Licensing and the Supply of Nonprofessional Manpower*, Manpower Research Monograph No. 11 (Washington: U.S. Department of Labor, Manpower Administration, 1969).

In general, credentialing and licensing have had the primary effect of raising the standards of training and the quality of workers in the protected occupations, but they have also had the secondary effects of reducing occupational mobility and limiting the supply of labor.

Another barrier to mobility is the way in which the roads to progression up the line have been changed. Many a corporation president of past years could boast of coming up the hard way. Even professional jobs could be learned by experience and independent study: a substantial proportion of the older engineers still in industry have no college degree. But, as a rising proportion of young people have gone to college, more and more companies have adopted the practice of recruiting executive trainees from among college graduates.

One result of these trends toward occupational rigidity is that "workers have jobs; middle and upper class people have careers." Manual, sales, and clerical workers not only earn less than professional and managerial workers, but they also reach an income peak earlier in their worklives, and the peak is not as high, relative to their starting rates, as that of workers in higher status occupations.

Another result of these trends is that young people feel they have to seek education to improve their competitive position. This has contributed to the great increase in the proportion of youth going to college—an increase that may have already produced a surplus of college graduates in relation to the number of jobs that have traditionally required college education.[58] It has also created balkanized labor markets, in which the less educated sector of the work force is restricted to a "secondary labor market" of undesirable, low-paid, and irregular jobs.

These accumulating rigidities are in marked contrast to the openness of access to occupations in early America.

WORKING CONDITIONS

Hours of Work

The issue of hours of work has been a major one for labor throughout American history, not only because time, in relation to pay, is at the heart of the bargaining process, but also because the length of the workday and workweek defines the time left to the worker for personal life.

In farming, the predominant activity at the Nation's beginning, worktime was generally from sunrise to sunset. This applied to independent farmers, hired hands, and slaves equally. In the early years, this pattern was adopted in nonfarm work, with a 6-day week. A little later, however, artificial light made possible a longer working day in factories and other indoor workplaces; while 12 and even 14 hours in the summer were common in construction and other outdoor work, textile mills worked up to 15 hours.[59]

Hours were a major issue pressed by workers' organizations, through both collective bargaining and labor laws. The early history of these groups is one of spotty gains followed by deterioration, as weak unions collapsed in depressions or as laws achieved with much effort failed to be enforced. The house carpenters in Boston struck for a 10-hour day in 1826, and again in 1832, this time joined by other outdoor trades. A 10-hour day was achieved generally by union workers in Philadelphia in 1835 and in other cities soon afterwards, with broad public support. The Federal Government established a 10-hour day in naval shipyards in 1836 and extended it to other Federal public works in 1840. But the gains were difficult to maintain. By 1840, 11 and 12 hours were still the most common worktimes in eastern factories, and mill girls in Lowell, Mass., regularly worked a 14-hour day as late as 1839.[60] Agitation continued, and by 1860 the average workday was 11 hours in most industries and 10 in the building trades and metal industries.[61]

The goal of unions shifted to an 8-hour day at about that time. Various State laws proclaiming 8 hours to be "a legal day's work" were enacted in the 1860's, but they were ineffective. A drive for an 8-hour day was launched nationwide in 1881, with massive parades on May 1 in New York, Chicago, San Francisco, Cincinnati, and Milwaukee. Among the participating groups was the Federation of Organized Trades and Labor Unions, forerunner of the American Federation of Labor. Employers of 185,000 workers conceded a 9-hour day soon thereafter. By 1890, the average workday in manufacturing was just under 10 hours, and build-

---

[58] Rosenthal, op. cit., pp. 18–26.

[59] Lebergott, op. cit., p. 47.
[60] Ibid.
[61] *Historical Statistics*, p. 90; Lebergott, op. cit., p. 48.

ing trades averaged 9.4.[62] And, in 1916, the Adamson Act awarded the 8-hour day to railroad workers, a key sector of the labor force at that time.

The campaign for the 8-hour day, continued during and after World War I, was aided by the depression of the 1930's, when shorter hours were seen as a way of spreading the work, and the average dropped as factories went on part time. In wholesale trades, an average of 41 to 43 hours was maintained, and in railroads, the 1939 average was 43.7.[63]

In 1938, the Fair Labor Standards Act established a flexible standard and required pay at time and a half after 44 hours (reduced to 42 in 1939 and then to 40 in 1940) for workers covered by the provisions of the act.

After a period of lengthened hours (often reflecting paid overtime) during World War II, an average of about 40 hours became general in all major industries. There are variations around the average, however. While a 35-hour week was achieved in women's apparel manufacturing as early as 1933, hours in papermills and some other continuous-process industries still average over 40.[64]

One of the factors making for shorter average hours is the increasing number of workers, mostly adult women and students, who work part time out of personal preference. The number of workers voluntarily on part-time schedules increased from about 5.4 million in 1955 to 12.1 million in 1975.[65]

Safety on the Job

For many years, the worker had little protection against industrial accidents or occupational disease. The history of workers' compensation is discussed in a later section; the point to be made here is that employers were motivated by the insurance feature of the laws passed in the early decades of the 20th century to pay more attention to safety and health standards. Some of the results show up in the statistics of industrial accidents, which are expressed by the number of disabling injuries in relation to the total number of hours worked. Since the early 1920's, rates of injury have been reduced by three-quarters in railroads, two-thirds in stone quarries, and more than half in manufacturing; since the early 1930's, rates in bituminous coal and in metal and nonmetallic mining have been cut by nearly half.[66]

Nevertheless, the risk is still there. In 1973, it was summarized in this way:

Preliminary estimates show that 3.1 million recordable occupational injuries and illnesses and nearly 4,300 work-related deaths occurred in the nonfarm sector during the reporting period [July–December 1971]. Injuries accounted for 95 percent of all recorded cases, illnesses the other 5 percent; the statistics, however, may not reflect all occupational illnesses since some illnesses of occupational origin may not have been recognized as such.[67]

Occupational disease, much more insidious and perhaps even more devastating in the long run than industrial accidents, has become the focus of great concern in recent years. This concern reflects increased public awareness of the potential size and seriousness of problems arising from exposure to chemical products used in industry. One of the earliest hazards recognized was phosphorus used to make matches; as early as 1838, it was observed that match factory workers contracted "phossy jaw," described as "the most loathsome of all industrial diseases." But it was not until 1912, and after bitter opposition by some of the manufacturers, that a Federal law placing a prohibitive tax on use of phosphorus in matches was passed.[68] In that year, the Bureau of Labor listed 54 industrial materials that were injurious to health, of which one alone, lead, was used in more than 150 trades.[69]

Initial attacks on industrial disease consisted of laws requiring reporting of the diseases (passed in 16 States between 1911 and 1916), laws prohibiting employment of children or women in work involving such hazards (passed in many States at about the same time), and prohibition of use of dangerous substances.

The problem is serious; new diseases keep

[62] *Historical Statistics*, pp. 90 and 91.

[63] Ibid., pp. 91 and 94; *Employment and Earnings Statistics for the United States, 1909–1972*, Bulletin 1312–9 (Washington: U.S. Department of Labor, Bureau of Labor Statistics, 1973), pp. xii and 527.

[64] *Employment and Earnings Statistics for the United States, 1909–1972*, p. xii.

[65] *Employment and Earnings*, January 1976, p. 139.

[66] *Historical Statistics*, p. 100, and *1962 Supplement*, p. 17.

[67] *The President's Report on Occupational Safety and Health, 1973* (Washington: U.S. Department of Labor, Occupational Safety and Health Administration, 1973), pp. 5–6. Based on a Bureau of Labor Statistics survey of a sample of approximately 60,000 employers in private nonfarm industry, about one-third of them manufacturers.

[68] John R. Commons and John B. Andrews, *Principles of Labor Legislation* (New York: Harper and Bros., 1916), pp. 325–326.

[69] *List of Industrial Poisons and Other Substances Injurious to Health Found in Industrial Processes*, Bulletin No. 100 (Washington: U.S. Department of Commerce and Labor, Bureau of Labor, May 1912).

appearing as thousands of new substances are introduced in industry every year. This fact, together with greater understanding of the physiological effects of chemicals and more advanced methods of detecting minute quantities of industrial poisons, makes it seem as if the problem is outrunning the capacity to deal with it. The Occupational Safety and Health Act of 1970 required the Department of Labor to investigate possible dangerous situations, issue safety standards, and enforce compliance with them.

Since then, the Occupational Safety and Health Administration (OSHA) has conducted a continuing review of safety and health hazards, in order to promulgate standards, including those applying to worksite exposure to asbestos, inorganic lead, carbon monoxide, beryllium, ultraviolet radiation, and noise. Onsite inspections by the OSHA field inspection force numbered more than 80,000 in 1975, and occupational injury and illness surveys in a sample of about 550,000 establishments have been conducted on an annual basis since 1972. (Prior to passage of the act, statistics on work-related injuries were based on the voluntary participation of about 150,000 employers with payrolls totaling some 15 million employees. Today, all employers subject to the act's provisions—with the exception of those employing fewer than 11 persons—are required to keep statistical records of work-related deaths, illnesses, and injuries other than those requiring only minor first aid. The recordkeeping system, which is administered by the Bureau of Labor Statistics, provides the field inspection force with onsite records for each establishment.)

Unionization

Among the most important conditions affecting the character of many workers' life on the job is the presence or absence of a union engaged in bargaining collectively for them. The fact of being represented, of having a right to object to unfair treatment—to "grieve," in the parlance of industrial relations—is perhaps as important to organized workers as the bread-and-butter gains in wages and fringe benefits unions have negotiated.

Although strikes of both masters and their employees occurred earlier, probably the first strike by wage earners against their employers was by the Philadelphia printers in 1786. The extent of 18th-century organization is suggested by the fact that 4,000 mechanics representing over 30 trades participated in the New York parade celebrating the ratification of the Constitution in 1788.[70] The main goals of workers' organizations in colonial times were social and philanthropic, but emphasis on economic issues soon developed; a Federated Society of Journeymen Cordwainers organized in Philadelphia in 1794 had as one of its aims protection from employers. Strikes in this period were mostly spontaneous, brief, and unorganized.

Broader organizations of local unions combined into workingmen's parties in various cities and in local federations of the separate trades in the 1820's and 1830's. By this time, economic issues, such as the 10-hour day, were paramount, but the workers' organizations were also pressing for universal free public education and abolition of imprisonment for debt.[71] This divided emphasis partly reflected an important legal problem: organizations of workers solely to gain higher wages and other benefits were considered conspiracies punishable by jail or fine. In 1842, however, Chief Justice Shaw of the Massachusetts Supreme Court issued the landmark decision that workers using lawful means to attain lawful ends were not acting illegally—thus legitimizing the labor movement.

In the 1850's, as unions grew and gained experience, concentration on economic issues increased. National unions were founded by the stonecutters, hat finishers, molders, machinists, printers, and locomotive engineers. The unions were less stable in those days; they had difficulty in surviving economic depressions when members could not afford to pay their dues or to forgo work at nonunion firms. A burst of organization during the Civil War and immediately afterward brought union membership to 300,000 by 1872, on the eve of the 1873 depression; membership dropped to 50,000 6 years later, but rebounded to 300,000 by 1885. The Knights of Labor, founded in 1869 as a secret organization and emphasizing educational and political methods of achieving gains rather than negotiation and strikes, claimed over 700,000 members by 1886. In that year, a group of unions led by Samuel Gompers of the cigarmakers and Peter McGuire of the carpenters founded the American Federation of Labor. While the Knights of Labor dropped to

[70] John R. Commons and others. *History of Labour in the United States*, vol. I (New York: Macmillan Co., 1936), p. 75.
[71] Ibid., pt. II.

100,000 members by 1890, the AFL steadily developed in strength.[72]

The Knights had been a national union open to skilled and unskilled workers. This organization of the unskilled as a political force conflicted directly with Gompers' concept of "business unionism." To him, the unions' primary emphasis was to be on negotiation. Only the skilled could have bargaining power, since their numbers were limited, placing them in short supply. On the other hand, there was a virtually unlimited supply of unskilled workers (including vast numbers of new immigrants). Organization of the unskilled was therefore delayed until the 1930's and the formation of the Congress of Industrial Organizations (CIO).

There were tensions reflecting diverse views among the unionists in those days; some emphasized the immediate issues of wages and working conditions, while others felt that socialism was the only way of achieving justice; some pushed for achieving improvements through the political process, while others put their trust primarily in collective bargaining. In spite of these tensions, American unions generally turned toward business or economic goals, at least to a greater degree than did their European counterparts. Among the many reasons for this choice of orientation was the fact that, in the absence of many of the political and class rigidities of European social systems, American unions could focus their energies to a greater extent on achieving economic goals.

By the opening of the 20th century, unions had nearly 800,000 members, about 8 percent of all potential members (defined as wage and salary workers in nonfarm enterprises, excluding self-employed persons and private household workers). Many employers vigorously opposed the growth of unions. The powerful large corporations refused to negotiate, forced workers to sign "yellow dog" contracts, fired and blacklisted active unionists, brought in strikebreakers, and pressed the government to intervene against strikes. In 1902, George F. Baer, president of the Reading Railroad, stated this view of unions when the company's coal mines were being struck: "The rights and interests of the laboring man will be cared for, not by labor agitators, but by the Christian

men to whom God in his infinite wisdom has given control of the property interests of this country." [73]

Nevertheless, workers flocked to the unions, raising their membership to over 2 million by 1904, 17 percent of potential membership. In 1914, the Clayton Act made it clear that "Nothing contained in the anti-trust laws shall be construed to forbid the existence and operation of labor organizations . . . instituted for the purpose of mutual help . . ."; and subsequent organizing efforts doubled union membership. By 1920, there were over 5 million members, 22 percent of the potential.

Membership dropped in the depressions of 1921 and the early 1930's. But then, aided by the anti-injunction provisions of the Norris-LaGuardia Act, the enactment of the statutory collective-bargaining structure of the National Labor Relations Act, and the CIO split with the AFL over the unionization of the unskilled, membership increased rapidly. Organizing drives in the steel, automobile, coal, and other mass production industries raised membership to 8.3 million by 1938—over 30 percent of the potential. World War II provided an even more supportive climate for union organization, and membership grew to nearly 15 million by 1945, nearly 40 percent of the potential. This was the high point in terms of the proportion of workers organized. The growing strength of labor after World War II prompted the 80th Congress in 1947 to amend the National Labor Relations Act through the Taft-Hartley provisions, to place some limitations on union practices. Although fairly steady membership gains were achieved in the postwar period, employment grew even faster, and by 1972 membership was down to 27.5 percent of the potential.

Over the years, the stance of Federal authorities toward union activities changed from that of strikebreaker (sometimes through the use of troops) to that of mediator. The change was first institutionalized by the elevation of the Bureau of Labor to a cabinet department in 1913 and is clearly embodied in the Federal Mediation and Conciliation Service, established in 1947.

In the 1950's, meanwhile, white-collar employment surpassed blue-collar employment, the traditional stronghold of organized labor. Between 1950 and 1974, white-collar employment rose by 20 million, blue-collar by 5 million. Government

[72] John M. Brumm, Theodore W. Reedy, and Witt Bowden, *Brief History of the American Labor Movement*, Bulletin No. 1000 (Washington: U.S. Department of Labor, Bureau of Labor Statistics, rev. 1957), pp. 8–14.

[73] Quoted in Miller, op. cit., p. 313.

employment, mostly white-collar, grew by 8 million in the same period. Some white-collar workers—musicians, performers, newspaper workers, and postal workers—had long been organized. Others resisted unionism, however, out of closer identification with the employer, a professional ethos, and, among many, relative satisfaction with their higher incomes. White-collar workers in government had an additional reason for not organizing—the traditions and laws prohibiting collective bargaining and strikes against the government by civil servants.

But these attitudes have been changing. More and more white-collar workers have found themselves in large organizations where personal contact with the employer is minimal. Teachers, police officers, firefighters, and hospital workers among government employees and employees in insurance and trade among other white-collar workers have begun to organize in large numbers in recent years, and many have gone on strike despite the existence of laws prohibiting such strikes. In fact, even some physicians began to organize in 1975.[74]

Earnings From Work

The real earnings of American workers have increased substantially over the past 200 years, but not at a steady pace, and there were long periods when real earnings did not rise at all.

Analysis of long-term trends in earnings is complicated by a number of significant cultural and economic changes. Supplements to wages—in the form of board and lodging or in the form of insurance premiums and holiday or vacation pay—have been an important but changing part of total compensation. Moreover, irregularity of employment, as well as changes in the workweek, must be taken into account in translating weekly or monthly wage rates into comparable terms for different periods. Finally, the changing impact and incidence of taxation affect the net earnings workers can spend at their own discretion; the obverse of this is, of course, the provision of services by government (education, for example) that workers no longer have to pay for out of earnings.

This section first discusses how earnings have been affected by both payments in kind and other supplements to wages, by occupational differentials, and by irregularity of employment. It then describes the trends in real earnings and the factors affecting those trends. Finally, changing standards of living and the distribution of income among families are discussed.

MONEY WAGES

In the early days of the Republic, a very substantial proportion of the people who worked received no money wages at all. They include not only the slaves, who were 28 percent of the labor force (omitting farmers, there were 80 slaves to every 100 free wage earners in 1800[75]), but also the many indentured workers who had bound themselves to work without pay for a period of years to pay their debts or to defray the costs of their passage from Europe.

For those workers who were paid money wages, the rates were higher than in Europe throughout the colonial period and well into the 19th century.[76] One reason for this was stated by Benjamin Franklin in 1751: "Till it is fully settled, Labor will never be cheap here, where no Man continues long a laborer for others, but gets a Plantation of his own, no Man continues long a Journeyman to a Trade, but goes among those new settlers and sets up for himself."[77]

Labor shortages and the resulting upward pressure on wage rates became so serious a problem for employers in early colonial times that the Plymouth and Massachusetts Bay Colonies adopted maximum wage legislation in 1630, and the Virginia Colony attempted wage fixing 20 years later. None of these laws were successfully enforced.[78]

---

[74] Mario F. Bognanno, James B. Dworkin, and Omotayo Fashoyin, "Physicians' and Dentists' Bargaining Organizations: A Preliminary Look," Monthly Labor Review, June 1975, pp. 33–35.

[75] Lebergott, op. cit., p. 19.

[76] History of Wages in the United States From Colonial Times to 1928, Bulletin 499 (Washington: U.S. Department of Labor, Bureau of Labor Statistics, October 1929), p. 27.

[77] Quoted in Pelling, op. cit., p. 15.

[78] History of Wages, pt. 1, pp. 9–11.

For the early years, there are no consistent and comparable wage data that permit a coherent description of levels or trends. Painstaking and imaginative researchers, however, have pieced together a rough picture of levels and changes in wage rates and in real wages for the early 19th century. One striking characteristic is the considerable variation in wage rates from place to place, a result of the imperfection of the labor market at a time when transportation was slow and difficult and there was little exchange of information concerning wage rates from one part of the country to another. A survey in 1832 showed wage rates of 40 cents a day for women textile workers in New Ipswich, N.H., and 63 cents in Peterborough, only 10 miles away. There is evidence, however, that patterns of migration among the States responded to wage rates.[79]

Occupational Differentials

Wage distinctions among skill levels and occupations were not so clearly made in the early years because of the relative ease with which workers could enter occupations and the lack of formal training on the part of so many workers. Scattered information suggests that skilled construction workers earned anywhere from 25 to 100 percent more than unskilled laborers in the period 1785 to 1808, the wide range possibly reflecting a disorganized labor market.[80] In 1832, the daily rates of blacksmiths in New England and the Middle Atlantic States averaged 46 percent above those of common laborers, which were 60 to 74 cents a day.[81]

Such differentials were generally greater early in the 20th century than later on. Wages of skilled manufacturing workers in 1907 were 2.05 times those of unskilled; the differential narrowed to 1.75 in 1918–19, and, after an increase when the Great Depression hit unskilled wages harder, declined further to 1.55 by 1945–47, partly as a result of wartime labor shortages. Organization of the unskilled by the newer industrial unions and the practice of negotiating flat cents-per-hour increases for a whole industry, common during World War II, tended to narrow the differentials. Other factors were increased demand for less

skilled workers, as production processes were simplified and routinized, minimum wage laws pushing up the bottom-level wages, and decreased immigration, reducing the downward pressure on rates for unskilled workers.[82]

A somewhat similar picture is shown for the skilled and unskilled workers in the building trades. Over the long term, the skilled-unskilled differential narrowed from 1.96 in 1907 to 1.32 in 1973. Wage scales for laborers have generally risen faster than those for craft workers during economic upswings and fallen behind or declined faster during downturns.[83]

Irregularity of Employment

The total income yielded by laborers' daily wage rates was very substantially affected by the irregularity of employment early in the 19th century. For outdoor work, such as construction, farming, logging, and shipbuilding, weather took its toll from the worker's income; as more work moved indoors, the effect of weather and seasons diminished. Aside from its impact on working time, of course, weather also affects farm crops, creating widespread ripples in an economy heavily dependent on income from agriculture. An undeveloped transportation system made shipment of materials, supplies, and finished products more chancy, and workers were subject to layoffs for lack of work. Business cycles and wars also cut into regularity of employment and therefore into income.

Supplements to Wages

In the early days, the most typical supplement to money wages was payment in kind; more recently, a complex of "fringe benefits" has become common.

Paying wages partly in cash and partly in kind was called "country pay." Room and board were commonly provided, since there were often no shops where earnings could be spent; in addition, the worker would sometimes be given a sack of

[79] Lebergott, op. cit., pp. 77–99, 132, and 257–352.
[80] History of Wages, ch. 4, and BLS Bulletin 604, a revision of Bulletin 499, with a supplement, 1929–1933, p. 58.
[81] Lebergott, op. cit., p. 547.

[82] Harry Ober, "Occupational Wage Differentials, 1907–47," Monthly Labor Review, August 1948, pp. 127–134.
[83] Arthur Rose, "Wage Differentials in the Building Trades," Monthly Labor Review, October 1969, pp. 14–17; and Martin E. Personick, "Wage Differentials Between Skilled and Unskilled Building Trades," Monthly Labor Review, October 1974, pp. 64–66.

flour, a bushel of rye, or whatever else was on hand and in surplus. For example, a worker in a Nashville brickyard in 1841 was paid off in bricks; for 5 months' work he had a heavy load to cart off, and he had to barter it for something edible.[84] Shipyard workers in Massachusetts received grog privileges as part of their remuneration until 1817, and canal workers were guaranteed a certain amount of rum.

More recently, however, different kinds of supplements to pay have come into the picture, and now they amount to a substantial part of the worker's total compensation. These supplements include pay for time not worked (holidays, vacations), premium pay for overtime or nightwork, and employer contributions for social security, private pensions, unemployment insurance, and life, accident, and health insurance. By 1972, pay for time actually worked accounted for only four-fifths of the total compensation of workers in the private nonfarm economy. The remaining fifth was devoted to supplements, including 7 percent of the total for retirement programs, 6 percent for paid leave, and 5 percent for life, accident, and health insurance benefits. Unionized workers generally receive a higher proportion of their compensation in supplementary pay than do nonunion workers.[85]

REAL EARNINGS

It is worth remembering in the mid-1970's that, historically, wage rates have gone down as well as up. The earliest record of wages for cabinetmakers (which first appeared as a distinct trade toward the end of the 18th century) shows that they were paid the exceptionally high rate of $2 a day for building furniture for the Massachusetts State House in 1797; 50 years later they were getting $1.50 for a 10-hour day in the District of Columbia. Successive "Books of Prices" for New York City cabinetmakers showed considerable declines from 1817 to 1834.[86] The question, of course, is what was happening to the prices of the things workers bought with their wages.

Before 1860, there is little in the way of consistent information on which to base a judgment about the movements of money wages in relation to consumer prices. Fitting together a mosaic of scraps of information, the most indefatigable student of this period suggests an increase of nearly 60 percent in real wages from 1800 to 1860.[87]

From 1860 on, the data improve. In these times of concern about inflation, it is instructive to recall the wide swings in consumers' prices in the past 100 years. During and immediately after the Civil War, a typical war-related pattern appeared: prices nearly doubled from 1860 to 1865. Thereafter, in contrast with recent experience, there was a long period of slowly declining prices, accelerating somewhat in depression periods, until consumers' prices were 46 percent below the 1865 peak at the end of the century and only 6 percent above the 1860 level. Prices shot up by 84 percent to a postwar peak in 1920. They fell in the 1921 depression and dropped 25 percent from 1929 to the depths of the depression in 1933. Controlled during World War II, consumers' prices jumped after the war and were 63 percent higher in 1948 than in 1941. Increases during the Korean war and in the period of inflation since 1967 brought the index to more than double the 1948 level in 1974. Altogether, consumers' prices were over six times higher than in 1860 and nearly three times their level in 1929.

Wage rises in the Civil War lagged behind the price increases; real wages of nonfarm employees dropped by 30 percent from 1860 to 1866 and did not return to their 1860 levels until 1883. They continued their slow rise for the remainder of the century (except in the 1894 depression) and, by 1900, were 25 percent above the 1860 level—an average annual increase of 0.6 percent. From 1900 to 1929, they rose by 57 percent, for an average annual increase of 1.6 percent. The real earnings of farmworkers trailed behind, however; at the end of the century, they were not much higher than in 1860.[88]

Real earnings declined during the depression of the 1930's; wage rates fell by nearly 5 percent from 1929 to 1934, but when allowance is made for unemployment (which affected as much as 25 per-

---

[84] Lebergott, op. cit., p. 146.
[85] *Employee Compensation in the Private Nonfarm Economy, 1972*, Bulletin 1873 (Washington: U.S. Department of Labor, Bureau of Labor Statistics, 1975).
[86] *History of Wages*, pp. 61–62.

[87] Lebergott, op. cit., p. 154.
[88] Lebergott, op. cit., pp. 528 and 539. Farmworkers' cash wages (in addition to board) were no higher when deflated by the Consumer Price Index for all items.

CHART 26

Real annual earnings of nonfarm workers have risen more rapidly since World War II than in earlier years.

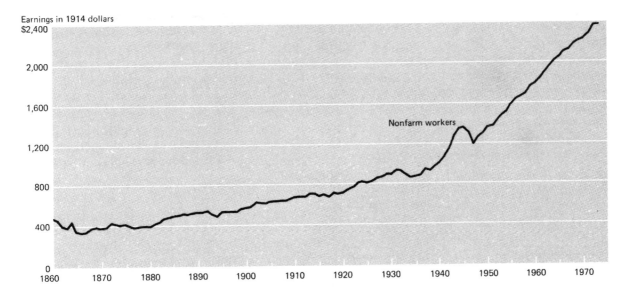

Earnings in 1914 dollars

Nonfarm workers

Sources: Stanley Lebergott, *Manpower in Economic Growth*, pp. 524 and 528, and U.S. Department of Labor.

cent of the civilian labor force) and for shorter hours, real earnings dropped by 34 percent from 1929 to the 1933 low. Following World War II and the rapid postwar price increases that set real earnings back for several years, real earnings resumed their uptrend, reaching a level in 1973 that was 2½ times that of 1929 (see chart 26). The average annual rate of increase from 1929 to 1973 was 2.2 percent. Today's nonfarm worker has annual real earnings about five times that of the nonfarm worker in 1860.

Reversing the 19th-century pattern, farmworkers' earnings grew faster than those of nonfarm workers in the 20th century, so that real earnings of all workers increased at an annual rate of 1.8 percent from 1900 to 1929 and at 2.4 percent from 1929 to 1973.[89]

The change in real earnings is dramatically illustrated in table FF–8 in the Bicentennial Supplement to the Statistical Appendix, which shows the number of hours of work required to buy several different commodities over the years from

1890 to 1973. For example, it took a factory worker 63 minutes to earn the price of a dozen eggs in 1890, 11 minutes in 1973.

Another insight into the change in levels of living can be gained by seeing what part of the consumer's dollar is spent on food, clothing, and shelter. In 1909, 64 percent of consumption expenditures went for these items; in 1974, only 44 percent. Among the items taking an increased share were medical care, recreation, and private education.[90]

Workers' Family Income

A more comprehensive view of the impact of wage changes on levels of living can be seen in the results of several attempts over the years to develop the cost of a minimal standard of living for a worker's family.

Matthew Carey, a Philadelphia economist, calculated in 1833 that the wages of a canal construction worker, even if he was employed throughout the year, were too low by $30 a year to support a

---

[89] Lebergott, op. cit., pp. 523–528 ; more recent data calculated from *Monthly Labor Review*, October 1975, p. 101, and *Survey of Current Business*, July issues 1961–74.

[90] Table FF–6 in the Bicentennial Supplement to the Statistical Appendix.

family of four on the most economical budget Carey could devise.[91]

Another account reports that, by the end of the 1880's, an annual income of roughly $500 was needed for a family of five in a middle-sized industrial town to enjoy any of life's amenities (newspapers, beer, lodge membership, outings, tobacco) without depriving themselves of the basic necessities. About 40 percent of working-class families earned less. Somewhat above this minimum level were the families of workers in such skilled occupations as molder, carpenter, machinist, coal miner, and mule skinner; they could have a four- or five-room house or flat and some amenities. The "aristocracy of labor"—iron rollers, locomotive engineers, patternmakers, and glass blowers, and others in the top 15 percent of the working class—earned $800 to $1,100 yearly and could have a parlor, carpets, curtains, and a piano bought on time.[92]

In 1906, John A. Ryan, taking inspiration from Pope Leo XIII's encyclical *Rerum novarum* of 1891, tried to find out what a worker's family needed to live on. He estimated that $600 ($650 to $800 in higher cost urban areas) was needed by an average family for a modest budget, including not only necessities but also medical care, insurance, education, and some savings.[93] In 1906, the average annual earnings for nonfarm employees working all year was $566.[94]

In 1974 a "poverty threshold" standard of living, as defined by a Federal interagency committee, was set at $5,038 a year for a nonfarm family of four. In that year, 5.1 million families (9 percent of the total) had incomes below the poverty level (adjusted for family size).[95]

The minimum budgets in these several studies are not consistently derived; what constitutes a minimum acceptable living standard at any time is difficult enough to establish, and differences in values and expectations over a century cannot be reconciled. The budgets also reflect different concepts, as well as the costs for families of different sizes.

Still, it is clear that a substantial proportion of 19th- and early 20th-century workers—even if they had been employed year round—received wages that would have afforded less than what contemporary budgetmakers considered a reasonable minimum standard of living. The proportion of workers with such low wages was much smaller in 1974, but it was still substantial. More than half of the 5.1 million families below the low-income level had at least one member working; in 1.2 million families the head had worked the entire year without earning enough to keep the family above a poverty level, and in another 1.5 million families the head was employed part of the year.[96]

Factors Behind the Increase in Real Earnings

The increase in real wages was made possible by a very substantial long-term gain in productivity. For most of the 19th century, there is no comprehensive measure of productivity, but there are limited data on labor requirements per unit of output. In 1900, the hours of labor required to produce what 100 hours had produced in 1800 were as follows:[97]

	Hours
Cotton textiles	16
Pig iron	4
Wheat	29
Corn	43
Cotton	47

For the period since 1890, there are more comprehensive measures of productivity change. In 1974, output per hour worked by persons employed in the private economy was nearly seven times as high as in 1889. The annual rate of growth was about 2 percent in the last part of the 19th century and in the first three decades of the 20th and 2.6 percent from 1929 to 1974.[98] These growth rates since 1900 do not differ greatly from those for real earnings, but in the period 1889–1900, the rate of

[91] Blanche D. Coll, *Perspectives in Public Welfare* (Washington: U.S. Department of Health, Education, and Welfare, 1969), pp. 34–35.

[92] In 1889, Lebergott estimates, average annual earnings for nonfarm employees working all year were $471.

[93] Coll, op. cit., pp. 65–66.

[94] The average earnings figure is from Lebergott, op. cit., p. 524.

[95] *Consumer Income: Characteristics of the Population Below the Poverty Line: 1974.* Series P–60, No. 102 (Washington: U.S. Department of Commerce, Bureau of the Census, January 1976), table E.

[96] *Consumer Income: Money Income and Poverty States of Families and Persons in the United States: 1974* (advance report), Series P–60, No. 99 (Washington: U.S. Department of Commerce, Bureau of the Census, July 1975), table 20.

[97] Lebergott, op. cit., p. 156.

[98] John W. Kendrick, *Productivity Trends in the United States* (New York: National Bureau of Economic Research, 1961), table A–XXII. Estimated by linking Kendrick's estimates for 1889 to 1909 to those published currently by the Bureau of Labor Statistics. *Handbook of Labor Statistics, 1975,* Bulletin 1865; *Trends in Output per Man-Hour in the Private Economy, 1909-1958,* Bulletin 1249, 1959.

productivity growth was twice as high as the rate of increase in real earnings.

In addition to the gains in productivity, a host of market and social factors impinged on wage levels. Among them were the availability of land for farming, immigration, the ending of slavery, the growth of unions, minimum wage and unemployment compensation laws, and the rising skill composition of the labor force.

While there is no consensus among economic historians as to how far into the 19th century the relatively easy availability of land offered an alternative to nonfarm employment and brought upward pressure on wages, this was certainly a factor in the early years.

That the heavy immigration of the late 19th century and early 20th century exerted a downward pressure on wages is generally conceded. The effect of the ending of slavery is not so obvious. Unions had opposed the extension of slavery partly on the grounds that it offered cheap competition to free labor; yet it appears likely that the ending of slavery had a depressing effect on wages. The price at which slave labor was offered by slave owners had to include not only the cost of maintaining the slaves but also a return on the owners' investments; and the owners, since they had some financial reserves, could hold out for their price. The freed slaves, however, were thrown on the labor market with every possible disadvantage and were barely able to earn their own maintenance. Wage-rate changes in the 1860's seem to support this assumption.[99]

Unions began to organize substantial segments of the labor force only in the 20th century; the proportion of nonfarm workers who were organized increased from 8 percent in 1900 to 17 percent in 1904, 22 percent in 1920, and about 36 percent in 1945. While there is some dispute among economists as to the direct effects of union organization on wage levels in unionized plants, the indirect effects (wage and other benefits granted to forestall unionization) and the gains unions achieved through the political process (e.g., State and Federal minimum wage laws) contributed to the rapid growth of real wages in the last 50 years. The Fair Labor Standards Act of 1938 introduced a 25-cents-an-hour minimum, which has been raised a number of times since, while coverage has been extended to a wider spectrum of industries. Each new minimum affected wages above the minimum,

as pressures built up to maintain skill differentials. And unemployment compensation, since it sustains workers for a period while they look for jobs as close as possible to their former occupational and wage levels, undoubtedly reduced downward pressure on wages.

The increasing proportion of high-paid professional, managerial, and craft workers in the labor force explains some of the increase in real wages. Occupational shifts from 1900 to 1970 account for a 20-percent increase in average real wage rates, reflecting returns on the higher investment in education of the 1970 labor force.[100]

Legal and social pressures against discrimination, together with improvement in educational attainment levels, have helped black workers enter higher paid occupations, as noted earlier. This gain has been reflected in some narrowing of the differential between the incomes of minority group members and those of whites. Median family income of the former was 51 percent of that of whites in 1947; in 1974, it was 62 percent of the white median income.[101]

Has the increase in real wages been accompanied by changes in income distribution? Are the poor getting a larger share of the pie? Data on the distribution of income among consumer units (families and unrelated individuals), available only for the last few decades, show that there was a substantial increase in the equality of distribution from the 1930's to the mid-1940's as the country came out of the depression and went through the wartime period of labor shortages. On the other hand, there has been no clear-cut trend in the postwar years. Some measures (such as family income) appear to show slightly greater equality of income distribution currently than just after the war, while others (such as earnings of individuals) show a perceptible decrease in equality.[102] The one-fifth of consumer units with the highest incomes have a smaller share of total income than in the early postwar years, while the second- and third-highest fifths gained a larger share. The share of the lowest fifth rose slightly (see table 2).

---

[99] Lebergott, op. cit., pp. 158–161.

[100] Calculated by applying the median earnings of full-year workers in 1969 to the occupational composition of the labor force in 1900 and 1970.

[101] Consumer Income, Series P–60, No. 99, p. 7.

[102] Various studies on this subject are summarized in Peter Henle, "Exploring the Distribution of Earned Income," Monthly Labor Review, December 1972, pp. 16–27; concepts and methods of estimating income distribution are described in Edward C. Budd, ed., Inequality and Poverty (New York: W. W. Norton and Co., Inc., 1967).

TABLE 2. PERCENT OF AGGREGATE INCOME RECEIVED BY EACH FIFTH OF CONSUMER UNITS,[1] SELECTED YEARS, 1929 TO 1974

Type of data and year	Income rank					
	Total	Highest fifth	Second highest fifth	Third highest fifth	Fourth highest fifth	Lowest fifth
PERSONAL INCOME SERIES[2]						
1929	100.0	54.4	19.3	13.8	9.0	3.5
1935-36	100.0	51.7	20.9	14.1	9.2	4.1
1941	100.0	48.8	22.3	15.3	9.5	4.1
1944	100.0	45.8	22.2	16.2	10.9	4.9
1947	100.0	46.0	22.0	16.0	11.0	5.0
1950	100.0	46.1	22.1	16.1	10.9	4.8
1954	100.0	45.2	22.5	16.4	11.1	4.8
1959	100.0	45.6	22.6	16.3	10.9	4.6
1962	100.0	45.5	22.7	16.3	10.9	4.6
CENSUS HOUSEHOLD SURVEY SERIES[2]						
1947	100.0	45.6	23.6	16.7	10.6	3.5
1950	100.0	45.0	24.1	17.3	10.5	3.1
1955	100.0	44.3	24.5	17.4	10.5	3.3
1959	100.0	43.9	24.7	17.7	10.6	3.2
1962	100.0	43.9	24.8	17.5	10.4	3.4
1965	100.0	43.6	24.8	17.5	10.6	3.6
1970	100.0	44.1	24.7	17.2	10.3	3.6
1974	100.0	44.4	24.8	16.9	10.1	3.8

[1] Families and unrelated individuals.

[2] The two series differ in method of compilation and in definition of income. The personal income series, prepared by the Bureau of Economic Analysis, U.S. Department of Commerce, is based on statistics from government agencies on funds received and paid out to individuals and includes various kinds of nonmoney income excluded from the Census definition (such as wages received in kind and the value of food and fuel produced and consumed on farms) which amount to about 4 percent of total personal income. The Census Bureau series, based on a survey of households, includes some types of income excluded from the personal income series (such as income received from boarders or roomers, support received from other family members, and employee contributions for social insurance) which altogether amount to less than the nonmoney items included in personal income.

NOTE: Detail may not add to totals because of rounding.

SOURCES: Personal income series: Edward C. Budd, ed., *Inequality and Poverty* (New York: W. W. Norton and Co., Inc., 1967), p. xiii, Census household survey series: 1947-70 from the *Historical Statistics of the United States—Colonial Times to 1970* (Washington: U.S. Department of Commerce, Bureau of the Census, 1974); 1974 from unpublished data of the Bureau of the Census.

The increase in the number of working wives has helped to bring their families into the higher income brackets; at the same time, the increasing availability of pensions has enabled more elderly persons to live apart from their families. In addition to the aging of the population, this latter development has raised the number of unrelated individuals more than twice as fast as the number of families in the postwar period. Since median income of unrelated individuals is one-third that of families, the effect of this trend is to make the income distribution for all consumer units taken together appear less equitable.

With the highest one-fifth of consumer units having a share of total income that is more than 10 times the share of the lowest one-fifth, the United States is far from equality in income distribution; nevertheless, a study by the International Labour Office found that the distribution of incomes in the United States was more equitable than in most non-Socialist countries in the 1960's.[103]

Three other comments should be made about the distribution of incomes among families. First, since the classification is based on income before taxes, it does not take into account any differences in amount of taxes paid by families at the various income levels, which affect the distribution of their spendable income. (Studies show that the percentage of incomes absorbed by all taxes—income, property, sales, etc.—is not very different

---

[103] *Money Income in 1973 of Families and Persons in the United States*, Series P-60, No. 97 (Washington: U.S. Department of Commerce, Bureau of the Census, January 1975), tables 10, 42, and 44; *Consumer Income*, Series P-60, No. 99, tables 1 and 4; and Felix Paukert, "Income Distribution at Different Levels of Development: A Survey of Evidence," *International Labor Review*, August-September 1973, pp. 97-105.

along the spectrum of incomes.[104]) Second, families at lower income levels may benefit more than those at higher levels from such government services as free public education, scholarships, medical care, food stamps, or skill retraining, a factor not reflected in the family income figures. Third, a worker's income generally rises with age, before reaching a plateau in the preretirement years. Distribution of lifetime income therefore shows a degree of disparity among families similar to distribution of income for given years.

In summary, the earnings of American workers, and the level of living they afford, have improved markedly over the past 200 years, with most of the improvement in the last quarter of this period. Moreover, there is evidence—in narrowing occupational wage differentials, in narrowing income differentials between white and black families, and in shifts in the distribution of income among families—that earnings are distributed somewhat more equally.

Work and Security

As the Nation's industrial economy developed, economic security became a major concern of workers. Weather is the principal source of economic insecurity in an agricultural society, but workers dependent on a weekly paycheck also have to fear loss of income from unemployment, sickness or injury, and old age. The record of employment and earnings insecurity and how American society has coped with it is the subject of this section.

Several general themes are woven through this history. One is the changing view of the responsibility for individual misfortunes—whether they result from personal sloth, improvidence, or negligence or arise out of social circumstances over which the individual has no control. A second is the shift from assistance as a form of charity to the concept that the worker has a right to it, embodied in the notion of insurance for which employees and/or employers pay premiums. A third theme is the change from completely local and often private assistance to assumption by the States and then the Federal Government of major roles in funding and administering security programs.

UNEMPLOYMENT

The Unemployment Experience

Even in the Nation's earliest years, when about 4 out of 5 workers were in farm employment, job-

lessness was a frequent problem in the nonfarm sector. Seasonal slack periods in construction, milling, and canal transportation left many workers jobless.[105] Joblessness among seamen had been a problem since the early days of the Revolution. Indeed, many of these seamen were active members of the "mobs" participating in patriotic demonstrations and later were among the privateers who harassed English shipping during the war. The Embargo of 1807 and the War of 1812 again stranded thousands of seamen along the east coast. Then a major business crisis struck in 1819, as British manufacturers tried to regain American markets lost during the Napoleonic wars by cutting into the business of infant American industries; in that year, New York and Philadelphia were each reported to have 20,000 unemployed and Baltimore, 10,000.[106]

Between 1834 and 1965, there were, by one estimate, 31 business cycles of 3 to 8 years' duration,[107] or an average of one every 4 years. Before the Civil War, unemployment, whatever its severity in particular cities, tended to be localized. But as communications and transportation improved, the country became a more integrated market across which economic events rippled with increasing speed. The long and deep depression of the 1870's affected the entire country, with 12 to 14 percent unemployment at its peak. In the depression of the 1890's, a peak of 4.6 million unemployed was reached in 1894—18 percent of the labor force—

[104] See, for example, Joseph A. Pechman and Benjamin A. Okner, *Who Bears the Tax Burden?* (Washington: The Brookings Institution, 1974).

[105] Lebergott, op. cit., p. 171.
[106] Commons, *History of Labour,* vol. I, p. 135.
[107] *Long Term Economic Growth 1860–1965* (Washington: U.S. Department of Commerce, Bureau of the Census, October 1966), p. 5.

and there were still over 3 million out of work 4 years later.[108]

Unemployment resulting from technological change or business failures has occurred repeatedly through America's history, going back to the mechanization of the shoe industry during the Civil War. And when the giant Amoskeag cotton mills of Manchester, N.H., closed down in 1936, a large majority of the 11,000 workers laid off found no jobs for more than a year.[109]

Finally, a certain amount of unemployment is endemic in the economy as a result of normal frictional joblessness, as well as seasonal and casual employment. Although great hopes were once held for the reduction of seasonal unemployment by action of business firms in spreading their operations more evenly over the year,[110] seasonal swings in unemployment are still extensive: an increase of 27 percent from the lowest to the highest month of the year is the average experience of recent years. Unemployment resulting from all causes (including frictional factors) affects a far larger share of the work force than the monthly figures indicate. When the average monthly unemployment rate is 5 percent, for example, about 15 million workers suffer some unemployment during the course of the year, one-third of them for more than 15 weeks.[111]

Measures To Alleviate Unemployment

"Continuous, Hard, and Underpaid." The way in which American society responded to distress caused by unemployment goes back to the Elizabethan poor laws and reflects a tension between two approaches, both of which were grounded in religious views. One was the impulse to charity and the other a work ethic that saw idleness as the reflection of faults of character, to be dealt with punitively. Cotton Mather thundered, "For those who indulge themselves in idleness, the express command of God is that we should let them starve." The fear that charity would corrode incentives to work was voiced early, as it is today. "Human nature is so constituted," said Josephine Shaw Lowell, head of the New York Charity Organization in the 1890's, "that no man can receive as a gift what he should own by his own labor without moral deterioration." [112] Even when the poor were given a chance to earn their bread by their own labor, through work relief, Ms. Lowell warned, "Relief work, to be a benefit and not an injury, must . . . be continuous, hard and underpaid." [113] In the late 19th century, this approach was bolstered by the social Darwinism of Herbert Spencer, who argued that "the unfit must be eliminated as nature intended."

On the other hand, there was no lack of compassion for the poor. Generous aid was given to refugees from frontier wars and to the Acadians who were forced to leave Nova Scotia in 1755 and resettle in the other colonies. George Washington wrote to his estate agent in 1775:

Let the hospitality of the house with respect to the poor be kept up. Let no one go away hungry. If any of this kind of people shall be in want, supply their necessities.[114]

The advent of large numbers of German and Catholic immigrants after the Revolutionary War hardened attitudes, however. The poorhouse commissioners of New York City complained of the "enormous and growing expense . . . not so much from the increase of our own poor, as from the prodigious influx of indigent foreigners in this city." [115]

Much of the burden of relief was assumed by private charities, some of them set up by ethnic or religious groups to take care of their own people, especially immigrants. While their most typical philosophy was that the poor needed "re-education, moral suasion and individual counseling, not relief," they did recognize their material needs, gave aid, and even tried to find them jobs.

The principal method by which aid was given in the earliest days derived from the Elizabethan poor laws. The recipients of public charity were housed in almshouses, and those who were able

---

[108] Lebergott, op. cit., p. 522.

[109] Daniel B. Creamer and C. W. Coulter, *Labor and the Shut-Down of the Amoskeag Textile Mills*, National Research Project, Report No. L-5 (Washington: Works Progress Administration, November 1939).

[110] Testimony of Isador Lubin before Senate Committee on Labor and Public Welfare, Mar. 1, 1929, reprinted in *History of Employ ment and Manpower Policy in the United States*, pts. I and II, vol. 5 of *Selected Readings in Employment and Manpower* (Washington: 89th Cong., 1st sess., U.S. Senate, Committee on Labor and Public Welfare, 1965), p. 1618.

[111] Computed from the seasonal adjustments and from recent annual work-experience surveys published by the Bureau of Labor Statistics.

[112] Walter I. Trattner, *From Poor Law to Welfare State* (New York: The Free Press, a division of Macmillan Co., 1974), p. 86.

[113] John R. Commons, Don D. Lescohier, and Elizabeth Brandeis, *History of Labour in the United States, 1896–1932*, vol. III (New York: Macmillan Co., 1935), p. 166.

[114] Trattner, op. cit., p. 52.

[115] Ibid.

were given work to do. Boston's almshouse inmates paved roads, built fortifications, did mending, and manufactured textiles and iron, and in 1774, the town of Providence built a meetinghouse to give work to unemployed carpenters.[116]

Public aid other than in almshouses—"outdoor relief"—was tried, but viewed with misgivings. When unemployment rose after the crisis of 1819, the chairman of a Massachusetts commission investigating public outdoor relief declared that this was "the most wasteful, the most expensive, and the most injurious to their morals and destructive to their industrious habits." In New York, an official investigating the same problem in 1824 recommended that no able-bodied person between the ages of 18 and 50 be given public assistance and that the old, the young, and the disabled be given relief only in institutions.[117]

When public officials did give work relief, it often had the character of work tests; the Overseers of the Poor in Massachusetts gave "outdoor relief" but, in 1875, installed a woodpile at each municipal center and required 2 hours of work before handing out a dinner. In time, rock crushing for roads and street cleaning or snow shoveling were introduced, as well as chair caning and other light work for the weaker clients.[118]

Whenever the numbers of unemployed rose in the severe depressions late in the 19th century, the primary methods of aid for the unemployed became soup kitchens, breadlines, grocery orders, and even some attempts to give work relief. New York City gave about 6 days' work at $1 a day to between 600 and 1,100 men to help build Central Park in 1858; in Philadelphia, culverts and reservoirs were built by the needy; and Chicago spent $30 million for work relief in 1890–92.[119] In the 1914–15 depression, work relief was used more extensively; over 100 cities throughout the country provided temporary part-time jobs on such public work as sewer building, street and road paving, quarrying, forestry, drainage, waterworks, painting buildings, and even clerical duties.[120] In the transition period after World War I, emergency public works programs, or the machinery for running them, were set up in 209 cities at the urging of the U.S. Department of Labor to conduct work that had been postponed during the war, financed in some cases by special bond issues.[121] Thus, there was a dawning perception of work relief as a possible countercyclical instrument.

Unemployment insurance began in the United States with private efforts by unions and employers. As early as 1831, the Typographical Association of New York paid benefits of $4 a week to unemployed members who were married.[122] The first employer plan was set up in 1916 by the Dennison Manufacturing Company of Framingham, Mass.; by 1929, 14 company plans, 13 set up by international unions, 24 joint employer-union plans, and more than a score of local union plans, the oldest type of unemployment benefits, had been established. Some were really guaranteed work plans and others true unemployment benefit plans, and the compensation varied from minimal to liberal.[123]

Depression of the 1930's. The depression of the 1930's was the worst in the Nation's history, awesome in its depth, severity, and duration. Banks failed, as many as 13 million workers—one-quarter of the total—were unemployed and many more had their hours and pay reduced, farm mortgages were foreclosed, and long breadlines formed. Local governments could not raise enough taxes to pay for relief, cash was so short that self-help groups were formed to barter work for each other, and hundreds of thousands of homeless jobseekers crowded the railway freight cars and bedded down in the jails.

This chilling disaster shook, but did not eradicate, the belief of some that individuals were wholly responsible for their own fate. A businessman explained to a conference on unemployment in December 1930 that the problem was that the workers had failed to save money while working to tide them over periods of unemployment, just as a prudent business firm tries to maintain a

[116] Steven J. Erlanger, *The Colonial Worker in Boston, 1775,* Regional Report 75–2 (Boston: U.S. Department of Labor, Bureau of Labor Statistics, New England Regional Office, 1975), p. 5.

[117] Trattner, op. cit., p. 55.

[118] Leah H. Feder, *Unemployment Relief in Periods of Depression* (New York: Russell Sage Foundation, 1936), pp. 66 and 174.

[119] Ibid., pp. 31–33, and Commons, Lescohier, and Brandeis, *History of Labour,* vol. III, p. 167.

[120] Commons and Andrews, *Principles of Labor Legislation,* p. 314.

[121] Commons, Lescohier, and Brandeis, *History of Labour,* vol. III, p. 173.

[122] John B. Andrews, "Trade Union Out-of-Work Benefits," in *Business Cycles and Unemployment* (New York: National Bureau of Economic Research, 1923), p. 294, and Commons, Lescohier, and Brandeis, *History of Labour,* vol. III, p. 259.

[123] Commons, Lescohier, and Brandeis, *History of Labour,* vol. III, pp. 260 and 286.

surplus: he saw the proper role of government as teaching thrift through the schools.[124]

A different view was, however, beginning to gain support. At the same conference another speaker said:

To care for the unemployed, the present agencies in the United States are charity, a disconnected system of employment bureaus, and a few new jobs created by a small extra amount of public and private works. . . . Charity will continue to some extent and in some form under any society. Now, however, public and private charity is used as a wholesale substitute for justice.[125]

It had become apparent that private charity could not handle the situation. Local governments tried, but they were swamped in the winter of 1930–31 by the combination of swelling needs and shrinking taxes; State governments tried to pick up the burden the following winter, but they, too, had insufficient resources and called for Federal help. Such help was justified not only by the financial plight of cities and States but also because residence requirements for local relief excluded hundreds of thousands of transients looking for work, who appeared to be a national, rather than a local, responsibility. In 1932, Congress authorized "advances" to the States by the Reconstruction Finance Corporation to give local relief and work relief, and in May 1933, a Federal Emergency Relief Administration was established. The Federal Government thus assumed a major role.[126]

A varied program of Federal aid was developed over the next few years. The Public Works Administration channeled funds for construction of public facilities to generate jobs in the private sector. The Work Projects Administration directly employed over 3 million workers at its peak (and 8.5 million in all) in work designed to meet a variety of public needs and employ workers with different skills—building roads, water and sewer systems, public buildings, and parks and also writing State guidebooks, painting murals in post offices, presenting concerts or plays, and providing mental health services to children in schools. National forest recreation areas were developed by youth working in the Civilian Conservation Corps, and students got part-time jobs through the National Youth Administration.[127]

A More Permanent Approach. While giving this immediate relief, the Federal Government began to move toward building a more permanent approach to security against unemployment and income loss. It included two elements: Income maintenance for persons directly affected and measures to stabilize the economy and help workers to find jobs. The Social Security Act of 1935 provided unemployment insurance, old-age pensions, and direct aid to the families of dependent children and to the blind. The Wagner-Peyser Act of 1933 established a Federal-State system of employment offices. A complex of measures to stabilize the banking system, industry, and agriculture and to stimulate homebuilding moved in the direction of setting up safeguards against severe depressions in the future. Unemployment insurance also had a stabilizing effect, since it cushioned declines in purchasing power. In short, out of many measures designed to serve different needs, the elements of a system of economic security began to emerge.

Important in this development was the Employment Act of 1946, which attempted to tie the diverse elements together. It declared as the explicit purpose of public policy the maintenance of "maximum employment." Noting that the Federal Government impinges on the economy in many ways—taxes, the Government's own payrolls and purchases, public works, monetary policies, the regulation and promotion of industries and agriculture, and tariffs, to name just a few—it established the policy that the actions of the separate Government agencies responsible for each be coordinated so that they contribute to, rather than unwittingly defeat, the major goal. The Council of Economic Advisers was created to advise the President and the Congress to this end.

The Nation's bicentennial year is the 30th anniversary of this act. In those three decades, an employment and income security system developed further. The earliest emphasis in administering the Employment Act of 1946 had been on establishing and maintaining levels of general demand for labor high enough to keep unemployment down.

[124] John E. Edgerton, president, National Association of Manufacturers, "Principles of Economic Security," at Conference on the Insecurity of Industry, Philadelphia, Dec. 5–6, 1930. *Annals of the American Academy of Political and Social Science*, March 1931, pp. 73–77. In fairness to Mr. Edgerton, it should be pointed out that this speech was made before all the savings banks closed down in the "Bank Holiday" of 1933.

[125] Rev. R. A. McGowan, assistant director, Department of Social Action, National Catholic Welfare Conference, *Annals of the American Academy of Political and Social Science*, March 1931, p. 42.

[126] Paul Webbink, "Unemployment in the United States, 1930–40," in *Selected Readings*, p. 2017.

[127] *1975 Manpower Report*, pp. 40 and 41, and *Selected Readings*, pp. 1961–68 and 2014–2029.

Economic downturns in 1949, 1954, 1958, and 1961 were not severe, but it appeared that unemployment was "sticking" at a higher level after each one. Observers questioned whether measures to maintain general demand were enough. Were "structural imbalances" between demand and supply—such as pockets of unemployment in local areas, geographic immobility of workers, shortages of some skills, displacement of workers by automation, and discrimination in employment—keeping people unemployed even when there was demand?

From this concern followed a series of measures—area redevelopment (aid to industry designed to create jobs in local areas with high unemployment), skill development (including training or retraining the unemployed and out-of-school youth and increased support for vocational education), equal employment opportunity legislation, and public employment. All are discussed in some detail in recent volumes of the annual *Manpower Report of the President*. Toward the end of its first 200 years, then, the United States was developing an arsenal of measures designed not only to relieve the effects of unemployment but also to reduce its causes.

The balance of this section briefly reviews two major elements of this system: Security against loss of income from accidents and sickness and security in old age. Other elements are discussed elsewhere in this report. (See the chapter on The Unemployment Insurance System: Past, Present, and Future and the section on the public employment service in the chapter on National Program Developments.)

ACCIDENTS AND SICKNESS

In earlier years, the worker suffering an injury at work was likely to experience a legalistic nightmare. The only recourse was to sue for damages through the courts under the common law. Negligence by the employer had to be proved and nonnegligence by the employee had to be demonstrated. Even so, the employer could still escape payment of damages if he or she could prove that the negligence of a fellow employee had brought on the accident or that the injured employee had known of the employer's negligence but had "assumed the risk" by continuing on the job; this defense applied even when the hazard was a violation of a safety law. The result was that not more than 15 percent of injured workers ever recovered damages under common law, and then only after long delays. In any event, much of what was awarded went to pay legal expenses.[128]

An 1856 Georgia statute was the first to temper the common law rules on employers' liability, and almost every State had followed suit by 1910. The first modern workers' compensation law, enacted in New York in that year, was declared invalid under the State constitution, but a majority of States had passed such laws by 1917, when the Supreme Court held them constitutional.[129] All States now have workers' compensation laws based on the insurance principle. About 83 percent of wage and salary workers are covered by such laws, the principal exemptions being those in small firms, farmworkers, private household and casual workers, and employees of religious or charitable organizations. The injured worker gets compensation regardless of fault or blame for the accident and with a minimum of delay and legal formality. An important feature of this system is that the premiums paid by many firms (in most States to private insurance companies, in a few to State funds) vary with the risk and are influenced by the hazard experience of the industry or occupation—sometimes by the experience of the individual employer. Premiums average a little over 1 percent of payroll but may go up to as high as 20 percent in extremely hazardous occupations. This can provide powerful motivation to maintain safety practices and has contributed to reduction in the accident rate.[130]

Workers' compensation is presently intended to cover only certain work-related conditions; occupational diseases, as distinct from injuries, are almost always treated separately, and the coverage is more limited; for example, only specified diseases are covered in nine States. To some extent, these limitations reflect the greater difficulty of establishing a causal link between many diseases and the worksite conditions experienced by the victims.

---

[128] Commons, Lescohier, and Brandeis, *History of Labour*, vol. III, pp. 564–573, and *Compendium on Workmen's Compensation* (Washington: National Commission on State Workmen's Compensation Laws, 1973), p. 3.

[129] Commons, Lescohier, and Brandeis, *History of Labour*, vol. III, pp. 575–576.

[130] *Social Security Programs in the United States* (Washington: U.S. Department of Health, Education, and Welfare, Social Security Administration, January 1973), pp. 72, 84–85, and *Compendium on Workmen's Compensation*, pp. 29 and 30.

Workers' compensation for temporary total disability replaces 40 to 44 percent of wage loss, on the average; in two States, it replaces less than 29 percent and in two others, from 60 to 64 percent. (In addition, the employer pays for medical care.) In 33 States, however, the maximum weekly cash benefit was below the poverty level in 1972.[131]

Disability not caused on the job is far more prevalent than occupational disability, but workers have less protection for this risk. A 1916–17 survey of 431 establishments in 31 States, employing approximately a million workers, found that "In nonhazardous industries some employers provided sickness care extending beyond occupational illnesses; others believed it inadvisable to do more than furnish first aid, leaving the balance of the medical care of the employee to his family and his own financial responsibility."[132]

The situation has improved since then. It was estimated that, in 1971, about two-thirds of the Nation's private wage and salary workers (or more than 70 percent, if government workers are included) had some protection against loss of earnings caused by short-term nonoccupational disability. This protection is achieved through group disability insurance or formal paid sick leave programs, through accident and sickness insurance policies purchased by the worker, or, in a few States, through compulsory public temporary disability insurance under State law. In addition, 70 percent of wage and salary workers had employee benefit plans covering hospital and surgical expenses, 67 percent had such plans covering regular medical expenses, and 73 percent had plans covering life insurance in 1973. Workers with long-term nonoccupational disabilities may be able to qualify, after 6 months, for coverage under the social security system's disability provisions, if they have enough work experience under the social security system.[133]

Finally, under the provisions of the Federal Coal Mine Health and Safety Act of 1969 (as amended in 1972), the coal industry is required to maintain respirable dust concentrations in the mines at acceptable levels. Title IV of that act created a program of "black lung" benefits, to be administered by the Departments of Labor and Health, Education, and Welfare, for coal miners who are suffering from pneumonconiosis ("black lung" disease) and for their survivors.

OLD AGE

Unlike earlier public attitudes toward the unemployed, those directed toward the elderly reflected sympathy. It was an industrial firm, the American Express Company, that established the first old age pension plan in the United States in 1875, with the company paying all the cost. The State of New Jersey's teachers' pension plan, set up in 1896, was the first plan for government employees. In the early 1900's, 72 railroads with two-thirds of the industry's employees had pension programs, and a number of local governments were setting up retirement plans for police officers, firefighters, and municipal employees generally. By 1929, 3.8 million workers in private industry—1 out of 7—were covered under plans, most of which were paid for entirely by employers. A major drawback was that the pensions could be earned only after more years of continuous service than most wage earners could attain.[134]

In the development of social security for the general population, however, the United States lagged behind other industrial nations. As early as 1907, Massachusetts appointed a commission to study the problem, but the first comprehensive old age pension law to be put into operation was passed in the Alaska Territory in 1915. By 1923, State laws had been passed in Montana, Nevada, and Pennsylvania, and by 1935, 35 States had enacted old age pension laws. A big selling point was that pensions were cheaper than supporting people in the poorhouse.[135]

The trend toward recognizing public responsibility for the general security of the population culminated in the passage of the Social Security Act of 1935, which authorized the employee-employer-financed old age pension system. In addition, the act provided Federal grants to the States for aid to the aged (those not covered by the newly

[131] Compendium on Workmen's Compensation, pp. 33, 119–120, and 122.

[132] Commons, Lescohier, and Brandeis, History of Labour, vol. III, pp. 364–365.

[133] Social Security Programs in the United States, pp. 87–88, and Alfred M. Skolnik, "Revised Coverage Estimates for Employee-Benefit Plan Series." Social Security Bulletin, October 1975, pp. 18–20.

[134] Commons, Lescohier, and Brandeis, History of Labour, vol. III, pp. 386–389.

[135] Ibid., pp. 611–616.

established insurance system), the blind, and dependent children and for various maternal and child health and welfare services, as well as vocational rehabilitation and public health services. Coverage of the contributory pension system was far from universal at first, but successive amendments have extended it to private household workers, self-employed persons, employees of nonprofit agencies, and State and local governments (inclusion being optional with the government in the last case). By 1975, 95 percent of all employed civilians were covered by the social security program or by retirement systems for government or railroad employees. The remaining noncovered workers are mainly those whose employment is casual or intermittent.[136]

The program has been extended in other ways, the most important being disability benefits and medicare. The former, first introduced in 1956, makes workers with a long-term disability (now defined as one expected to last for 12 months or more) eligible for benefits. A worker can qualify after being disabled for 5 months; thus, the social security program dovetails with various private and public programs to maintain income for the disabled. Medicare, a comprehensive health insurance program for older people, was introduced in 1965. It provides protection against the costs of hospital, convalescent, or nursing home care, funded by a tax on earnings, and a voluntary medical insurance plan financed by premiums paid by the elderly, matched by a Federal contribution.[137]

At the beginning of 1972, 112 million persons were insured—that is, they had worked long enough in covered employment to be eligible for the benefits when they reach appropriate age— and nearly 30 million persons were receiving benefits. Half of them were retired workers, 7 percent disabled workers, and the balance dependents. Average monthly benefits in December 1972 were $161.97 for retired workers and $179.22 for disabled workers.[138] In 1970, new beneficiaries received about 31 percent of their most recent preretirement earnings. Improvements in social security benefits raised this share to 35 percent in 1974.[139]

The retirement pension plans set up by employers were not abandoned as a result of the enactment of the Social Security Act. Far from it: they took a new lease on life during and after World War II. Under wartime wage controls, unions were free to negotiate for increases in deferred income, and many company pension plans were negotiated. Such plans, in conjunction with social security benefits, were aimed at providing workers with retirement benefits amounting to a very substantial proportion of the income they had been earning before retirement.

After World War II, the numbers of both private pension plans and workers covered rose rapidly. In 1950, 9.8 million workers were covered; by the end of 1973, there were 29 million (excluding self-employed and Federal, State, and local government workers), or about 44 percent of all private wage and salaried workers.[140] The proportion of workers with pension plans is greatest in the high-wage industries and occupations; as a result, proportionately more men than women and more whites than other races are covered.[141]

With both social security benefits and private pensions, older workers can come closer than such workers usually have to the level of living they had before retirement. Among workers retiring in 1970 who had both forms of coverage, men received benefits nearly half as high as their preretirement incomes, women a smaller fraction of former incomes. Husbands plus dependent wives also receiving benefits got about three-fifths of the men's previous earnings.

Only about 30 percent of newly retired men and 13 percent of newly retired women receive both types of pensions.[142] The minimum standards required by the Employee Retirement Insurance Security Act (ERISA) passed in 1974 (which established government standards for private pension plans for the first time) may in the long

[136] Susan Grad, "Economically Dependent Persons Without Pension Coverage in Old Age," *Social Security Bulletin*, October 1975, p. 13. To be covered, a worker must earn a minimum amount—$50 in a calendar quarter for nonfarm wage or salary workers, $50 in a quarter from one employer for farm or private household workers, and $400 a year for the self-employed.

[137] *Social Security Programs in the United States*, pp. 8–10.

[138] Ibid., p. 37.

[139] Alan Fox, *Earnings Replacement From Social Security and Private Pensions: Newly Entitled Beneficiaries, 1970*, Report No. 13 (Washington: U.S. Department of Health, Education, and Welfare, Social Security Administration, September 1974). Calculations of the proportion of earnings replaced by benefits are made on the basis of the average earnings in the worker's 3 best years; most commonly, they are the last 3 years before retirement.

[140] Skolnik, op. cit., pp. 19–20.

[141] *Coverage and Vesting of Full-Time Employees Under Private Retirement Plans: Findings From the April 1972 Survey* (Washington: U.S. Departments of Health, Education, and Welfare, Labor, and Treasury, September 1973), pp. 2 and 12.

[142] Fox, op. cit., pp. 5–7.

run increase the proportion of workers who benefit from private pensions.[143] Minimum requirements for participants under ERISA include an age threshold of 25 years and 1 year of job service.

Under the act's recordkeeping requirements, employers must provide the Federal Government with a yearly record of all departing employees with vested pension rights. When the retired worker applies for social security benefits, the Social Security Administration must notify the applicant of these private pension rights. Through the Pension Benefit Guaranty Corporation, the act also features a degree of protection against unexpected termination of private pension plans without payment of vested benefits. Private defined benefit plans pay the Corporation an annual premium intended to cover any deficit between a terminating plan's assets and the amount required to pay all vested benefits up to a set maximum.

In summary, a case can be made that any of the diverse elements of the present system of workers' security can be improved. For many workers, benefits are not adequate to maintain a reasonable level of living or one close enough to what they had before loss of their earning power. In the perspective of history, however, the system represents a substantial gain in the security of American workers: 95 percent of employed persons are covered by retirement pensions and are insured against medical costs and long-term disability; over 85 percent of wage and salary earners have unemployment insurance; 83 percent can draw workers' compensation; and over 70 percent have sickness or disability protection.

Conclusion

On November 12, 1775, the *Pennsylvania Evening Post* carried the following advertisement:

Just arrived from London, in the ship Hawke, Jacob Getsheus, master, and now lying off Market-street wharf, a few LIKELY HEALTHY SERVANTS, amongst whom are farmers, shoemakers, tailors, silversmiths, a jeweller, curriers, a plaisterer, clothier, butcher, hatter, cabinet maker, clerks and two young women, whose times (of indenture) are to be disposed of by STEPHEN and JOSEPH SHEWELL, WILLIAM CRAIG, or the master on board.

These workers, like many others, had indentured their services to pay their passage on a voyage lasting from 6 to 10 weeks from a secure home country to a string of colonies edging a wilderness. Some 8 months after the ship *Hawke*'s arrival, the same colonies proclaimed their independence and avowed their intention to secure certain rights which were, they asserted, inalienable.

Although the subsequent fate of the individual passengers aboard the *Hawke* is unknown to later historians, it can be assumed that, like those who preceded and followed them on similar voyages, they experienced rapid and repeated change in their working conditions and their social environment. Many (though not all) of these changes brought improvements in living standards, skill levels, and educational opportunity and were eagerly sought by the newcomers, either for themselves or for their children.

From this chapter's review of two centuries of working life in America, it is possible to extract this overriding theme of a generally sanguine commitment to positive change in the situation of the labor force—whether through the abolition of child and slave labor, through a long-term rise in industrial productivity and real earnings, through the extension of social security benefits to retirees and their families, or through a myriad of other mechanisms and procedures designed to enhance the situation of wage earners.

Economic and social institutions have become more complex over the years and correspondingly more resistant to change, but the labor force has remained responsive to new technological challenges, just as its individual members have retained a considerable measure of faith in their capacity to improve both the present and the future through their own efforts. While American history has been marked in the past two centuries by conflicting attitudes toward many issues, there has been widespread agreement that the Nation's course has been shaped by the disposition of a productive and striving labor force to take swift advantage of the possibilities latent in a generous physical environment.

---

[143] Peter Henle and Raymond Schmitt, "Pension Reform: The Long, Hard Road to Enactment," *Monthly Labor Review*, November 1974, pp. 3–12.

Labor in the Public Sector— State and Local

Binding arbitration laws for State and municipal workers

KEVIN J. CORCORAN AND DIANE KUTELL

By the end of 1977, 19 States had enacted some form of binding arbitration for public-sector bargaining disputes. Since the late 1960's when three States first passed such laws, other States have legislated broader statutes containing more sophisticated features. The spread of these laws has not been unchecked, however. They have been challenged in the courts of 14 States: nine have survived a constitutional test;[1] two have been found unconstitutional;[2] and three are still in litigation.[3]

The earliest statutes usually covered only disputes involving law enforcement and firefighter units, where disruption of services could jeopardize the community's safety. Of the States that currently mandate compulsory arbitration, eight still limit the practice to police and fire units only. Other State statutes include essential service personnel and other municipal and State employees.

Arbitration is regarded as the final step in the bargaining process and, under most statutes, is preceded by mediation. In some States, the appointment of a mediator is optional, based on whether one or both parties request assistance. The laws of Wyoming, Pennsylvania, and Rhode Island (police and fire) eliminate mediation altogether.

Some States include a mandatory factfinding step following mediation. Many others, however, provide for factfinding only if one or more of the parties request the procedure. In Iowa and Massachusetts, the factfinder's recommendations are one of three options open to the arbitrator in final-offer decisions. In Rhode Island, if mediation fails after 30 days, the mediator takes on the role of factfinder and issues his recommendations for settlement. Although these approaches illustrate how factfinding has been incorporated into the dispute settlement process, most States have deemphasized the factfinding function. In 1977, for example, New York eliminated the factfinding step when it amended its police and fire arbitration statutes.

Conventional arbitration, the traditional approach that does not restrict the decisionmaking authority of the arbitrator, is currently practiced in nine States. The other eight States, provide for varying forms of final-offer arbitration. Three of these (Massachusetts, Nevada, and Wisconsin) mandate final offer by package;[4] four permit the arbitrator to make his decisions on an issue-by-issue basis. New Jersey's law, the country's newest, provides for final-offer package arbitration on economic items and final-offer issue in the consideration of noneconomic items.

States that have chosen a final-offer package law reason that the fear of losing the complete package provides the strongest incentive for the parties to settle. Other States (Connecticut, Iowa, Michigan, and New Jersey) have opted for final offer by economic and noneconomic issues. Advocates of this approach suggest that settlements will be more equitable, even though there is less pressure to settle.

Legislation in Wisconsin (municipal employees other than police and fire) and Michigan mandate a mediation-arbitration scheme to resolve impasse disputes. A mutually selected neutral, in the event he or she is unsuccessful in mediating, has the authority to issue a final award. Under both procedures, further negotiation and mediation can continue throughout the arbitration process.

Nebraska's arbitration process differs from other States in that it follows a judicial approach. Five judges, appointed by the governor, preside over a labor court with individual cases decided by three-judge panels. Five State laws provide for tripartite arbitration; seven provide for single, neutral arbitrators; and in the remaining seven States, the parties are given the option to decide whether they prefer a single or tripartite arbitration process. The tripartite scheme facilitates mediation but, consequently, may be a more time-consuming and expensive process.

Kevin J. Corcoran, corporate personnel assistant with the Miller Brewing Co., and Diane Kutell, employee relations associate with the American Can Co., prepared this summary as graduate research assistants under the direction of professor James L. Stern at the Industrial Relations Research Institute, University of Wisconsin, Madison.

Ideally, arbitration is seen as a substitute to a strike. Except for Minnesota, Oregon, and Wisconsin, all States that have compulsory arbitration prohibit strikes or work actions. Nonessential employees in Minnesota are allowed to strike if an employer refuses to submit to arbitration or does not comply with the arbitrator's decision. In Oregon, nonessential employees have the right to strike, but if they are enjoined by a court, the court also must order arbitration. Wisconsin statutes provide that, if both parties withdraw their final offers, employees have the right to strike after giving 10 days notice.

Arbitration laws: A State summary

In recent years, a trend toward increasingly sophisticated arbitration schemes has emerged.[5] Final offer by issue or package, single or tripartite arbitration panels, and the mediation-arbitration structure are techniques that many of the following States have adopted for public sector impasse resolution.

Alaska

Passed in 1972, the Alaskan law requires arbitration for all law enforcement, fire, and hospital employees. In the event of a strike by other, less essential employees, arbitration may be ordered following a court injunction. Mediation is required, however, before a single, neutral arbitrator conducts conventional arbitration proceedings.

Connecticut

Recently, State Superior Court held that Connecticut's 1975 compulsory final-offer/issue arbitration statute violated the home-rule provisions of the State constitution.[6] The case is currently on appeal to the State Supreme Court, and, until a final decision, the law will remain in effect.

The statute's provisions cover all municipal employees, except teachers. Mediation and factfinding are mandatory; if the parties reject the factfinding report, they may request arbitration. In any case, if no agreement is reached within 90 days after a contract expires, the arbitration board can impose arbitration. Arbitration, itself, is performed by a tripartite board composed of one neutral arbitrator and two partisan representatives.

Iowa

All public employees are covered by Iowa's 1974 binding arbitration law. Mediation and factfinding are mandatory prior to actual arbitration; however, the parties may develop their own impasse procedure. Arbitration is conducted by a single person or a tripartite board, depending on the preference of the parties. This somewhat flexible law calls for a final-offer/issue conclusion, but, at the option of the parties, permits the factfinding report to be used as a sort of final-offer/package solution.

Maine

The Maine law, which went into effect in 1974, first had to survive a court test in 1973.[7] The following four categories of workers are covered by the statute: State; municipal; University of Maine; and all public employees except county workers. Mediation may be requested by the parties, or it may be ordered by the Labor Relations Board; either party may request factfinding. When the arbitration stage is reached the decision of a tripartite board (parties may agree on another form of arbitrator) is advisory on economic matters, but it is binding on all other matters.

Massachusetts

In 1974, Massachusetts passed its version of statutory interest arbitration covering only police and firefighters. Two years later, the law was upheld by the State's highest court.[8] During the dispute settlement process outlined by the law, either party may request mediation or factfinding. Arbitration consists of final offer by package under the direction of either a single arbitrator or a tripartite board. Although it is not provided for in the law, the arbitrator has been encouraged to mediate.

Under a 1977 amendment to the law, a joint labor-management committee is appointed by the governor to take jurisdiction over disputes. Now, once an impasse is reached, the committee may determine the form of arbitration.

Michigan

One of the early legislative efforts, the 1969 Michigan law covers police officers, firefighters, and emergency medical personnel. Mediation and factfinding may be used prior to final-offer arbitration on economic issues and conventional arbitration on other disputed areas. A single arbitrator or a tripartite board preside, and mediation at this stage is encouraged, although, as in Massachusetts, it is not specifically provided for in the law. The Michigan law has survived a court test.[9]

Minnesota

The 1975 Minnesota law requires arbitration for essential employees and makes it optional for others. Prior to conventional arbitration by either a tripartite board or a single, neutral arbitrator, either party may petition for mediation. The right to stike is available to nonessential employees if their employer refuses to submit to arbitration or comply with an arbitrator's decision. The law is currently being challenged in court.[10]

Nebraska

All public employees are covered by the 1974 Nebraska statute. Mediation may be used if both parties request; teachers, however, must use factfinding. The governor appoints five judges, from which three-judge panels are formed to decide cases. In settling a dispute, these courts first hold hearings to determine wages, hours, and conditions of employment. Strikes are prohibited by this law, which was upheld by a 1975 court decision.[11]

Nevada

In 1975, all local government employees became covered by Nevada's compulsory arbitration law. Mediation is mandatory; factfinding may be requested by either party. If factfinding is requested, both parties can agree that it be binding; the governor may order it binding at the request of either party, however, based on public interest, fiscal interest, or public safety. If a dispute continues to arbitration, it is handled by a single arbitrator in a conventional manner. In 1977, an amendment to the law created final-offer/package arbitration for firefighters only.

New Jersey

The State's law enforcement, fire, and correctional employees are covered by a 1977 binding arbitration statute. Under the New Jersey law, either party in a dispute may request mediation and factfinding; however, this step does not have to be completed before arbitration. Of all the State laws currently in effect, New Jersey's provides the greatest flexibility in the form of arbitration. The parties in a dispute have an option to design their own terminal procedure; if they do not, final offer by package on economic issues and final offer by issue on noneconomic items is implemented by a single arbitrator or a tripartite board. The law specifically encourages the arbitrator to mediate in the dispute.

New York

State police and fire department employees are covered by New York's 1974 law. Mediation occurs at the request of either party or by motion of the Public Employee Relations Board. Conventional arbitration is conducted by a tripartite

board; the board is encouraged to mediate, but it is not specifically called for in the law. A court decision in 1975 left the law intact.[12]

New York City. All city employees of mayoral agencies are covered by this complicated municipal law that dates back to 1972. The City's Board of Collective Bargaining first determines that an impasse in negotiations exists. Next, the director of the Board appoints an impasse panel; he may also appoint a mediation panel. The impasse panel issues a report with recommendations. If a party rejects the panel's positions, the Board of Collective Bargaining reviews the case and may affirm or modify, in whole or in part, the panel's recommendations.

The impasse panel is chosen by the parties to the dispute from a list of seven members of the Board's impasse panel register. The parties select as many of the seven that they can agree upon, or, in the absence of agreement, they must select the number of persons required by the director of the Board. The statute provides the impasse panel with the authority to mediate.

Oregon

One section of the 1973 Oregon law covers all public employees (State and municipal) except those in Home-Rule cities or counties.[13] The other section of the statute covers all police, fire, mental hospital, and correctional employees. Both sections provide for mediation and factfinding upon the request of either party, that conventional arbitration be used when necessary, and that a single arbitrator or a tripartite board conduct the proceedings. The all-public-employee section of the law permits workers to strike when there is no clear or present danger to public health, safety, or welfare. This section, but not the one covering essential employees, is currently being challenged in the courts.[14]

Eugene, Oregon. All city employees are covered. Strikes are permitted, but they may be enjoined when the public health and safety is threatened; public safety strikes are prohibited. When a strike is enjoined or prohibited, the arbitration procedure calls for final offer by package conducted by a tripartite board that is encouraged to mediate the dispute.

Pennsylvania

One of the first two State binding arbitration laws, Pennsylvania's 1968 statute covers police and fire department employees. After 30 days of bargaining, either party may request arbitration. A tripartite board then implements a conventional form of arbitration. The law survived an early court challenge in 1969.[15]

Rhode Island

Since 1970, there have been a half dozen laws enacted by Rhode Island that deal with binding arbitration for public employees; only one has been repealed. In 1970, both the police and firefighters were covered—each separately—by identical laws. All unresolved issues are submitted to arbitration after 30 days. Under a tripartite board, arbitration is conventional and binding on all issues. The firefighters statute was challenged in court and upheld 1 year before the law actually took effect.

In 1974, two more arbitration laws were added to the statute books; one for State employees, the other for municipal workers. For the State employees, disputes must be mediated after 30 days; a mediator, appointed by the State Labor Relations Board, issues a report with recommendations. If the dispute remains unresolved, a single arbitrator applies conventional arbitration; advisory on wages and binding on all other issues. The provisions of the law for municipal employees are similar, except that mediation is optional and arbitration is conducted by a tripartite board.

In 1975, the State's teachers were covered by a separate law. The provisions of the teachers' statute are identical to those for municipal employees enacted in 1974. Next, in 1976, the State passed a law covering certified administrators in the City of Providence public school system, who were not eligible for membership in any other unit. This law was short lived, however; it was repealed in 1977.

South Dakota

South Dakota passed a binding arbitration law covering fire and police department employees in 1975; the State Supreme Court struck it down as unconstitutional in the same year.[16] Under the provisions of the statute, a union was able to file a petition for arbitration. A tripartite board was then assembled to conduct conventional arbitration.

Utah

As in South Dakota, the Utah Legislature passed a binding arbitration law in 1975; here, however, the law stood for 2 years before a final decision of the State Supreme Court held it unconstitutional.[17] The law covered only firefighters and required that after 30 days of a dispute all unresolved issues be submitted to arbitration. A tripartite board conducted conventional arbitration.

Washington

Passed in 1975, this law covers all county police and police in cities with more than 15,000 persons; it also covers all firefighters in the State. Mediation is the first step in the dispute settlement process. If no agreement is reached after 45 days of negotiations, mediation begins and a tripartite factfinding panel may be appointed. If necessary, a tripartite board conducts conventional arbitration. The statute was upheld by a 1976 court decision.[18]

Wisconsin

The 1972 Wisconsin law covers all police and fire department employees, except those in cities with more than 500,000 or less than 2,500 persons. In a dispute settlement, mediation is used only if ordered by the Wisconsin Employment Relations Commission. A single, neutral arbitrator conducts final-offer/package arbitration; however, the parties may agree to use conventional arbitration.

In 1977, the State passed a second law, providing specifically for a mediation-arbitration scheme. This statute covers all other local government employees. A single arbitrator or a tripartite board conducts mediation and, if unsuccessful, final-offer/package arbitration. Unlike the 1972 law that prohibited strikes, the new statute allows a limited right to strike when both parties withdraw their final offers. (Employees must give 10 days notice that they intend to strike, however.)

Wyoming

The other State that shares the distinction of having the oldest binding arbitration law is Wyoming. Since 1968, the State's firefighters have been covered by a law that requires arbitration of a dispute that has lasted longer than 30 days. A tripartite board applies the conventional form of arbitration. This early law also withstood an early challenge in the courts—the State's highest Court upheld the law in 1968.[19]

———FOOTNOTES———

[1] The laws of the following States have survived challenges in the courts: Maine, *City of Biddeford v. Biddeford Teachers*, 304 A 2d 387, (Maine Sup. Ct., 1973); Massachusetts, *Arlington v. Board of Conciliation and Arbitration*, 352 NE 2d 914 (Mich. Sup. Ct., 1976); Michigan, *Dearborn Firefighters v. Dearborn*, 394 Mich. 229 (Mass. Supt. Ct., 1975); Nebraska, *Orleans Education Assn. v. School District of Orleans*, 193 Neb. 675 (Neb. Sup. Ct., 1975); New York, *City of Amsterdam v. Helsby*, 377 NY 2d 19 (N.Y. Ct. of Appeals, 1975); Pennsylvania, *Harney v. Russo*, 255 A 2d 560 (Pa. Sup. Ct., 1969); Rhode Island, *Warwick v. Warwick Reg. Firemen's Assn.*, 106 R.I. 109 (R.I. Sup. Ct., 1969); Washington, *Spokane v. Spokane Police Guild*, 87 Wash 2d 457 (Wash. Sup. Ct., 1976); and Wyoming, *State v. Laramie*,

437 P 2d 295, (Wyo. Sup. Ct., 1968).

[2] Binding arbitration laws were struck down in South Dakota, *Sioux Falls v. Sioux Falls Firefighters*, 239 N.W. 2d 35 (S.D. Sup. Ct., 1975), and Utah, *Salt Lake City v. Intn'l Assn. of Firefighters, Locals 1645, 593, and 2064*, Case No. 14689 (Utah Sup. Ct., 1977). South Dakota's arbitration statute was held unconstitutional on the basis of unlawful delegation of legislative powers; the State constitution prohibits the legislature from delegating powers that interfere with municipal functions. Interference with constitutional and home-rule powers has been a common ground for challenges in other States. For a discussion of the home-rule argument, see the decisions of New York's Court of Appeals in *Amsterdam v. Helsby*, 37 N.Y. 2d 19 (1975). The Utah Supreme Court found the Firefighters Act to be an unconstitutional delegation of authority from municipal governments to private arbitration panels. For a discussion of the illegal delegation of authority issue, see the Michigan Supreme Court's decision in *Dearborn Firefighters v. Dearborn*, 394 Mich. 229 (1975).

[3] The laws of the following States have been challenged and are presently under litigation: Connecticut, *Town of Berlin, et al. v. Santaquida*, (home-rule challenge); Oregon, several cases pending, and Minnesota, *City of Richfield v. Local 1215, International Firefighters* Case No. 48638 (illegal delegation of authority).

[4] For a discussion of the impact of the final-offer/package law in Massachusetts, see David B. Lipsky and Thomas A. Barocci, "Public employees in Massachusetts and final-offer arbitration," *Monthly Labor Review*, April 1978, pp. 34-36; and Lipsky and Barocci, "Final-offer arbitration and salaries of police and firefighters," *Monthly Labor Review*, July 1978, pp. 34–36.

[5] For example, the statutes enacted in Michigan (1972), Nevada (1977), New Jersey (1977), and Wisconsin (1977).

[6] *Town of Berlin, et al. v. Santaquida*, on appeal to Connecticut Supreme Court.

[7] *City of Biddeford v. Biddeford Teachers*, 304 A 2d 387 (Maine Sup. Ct., 1973).

[8] *Arlington v. Board of Conciliation and Arbitration*, 352 NE 2d 914 (Mass. Sup. Ct.,) 1976).

[9] *Dearborn Firefighters, v. Dearborn*, 394 Mich. 229 (Mich. Sup. Ct., 1969).

[10] *City of Richfield v. Local 1215, International Firefighters*, pending before the Minn. Sup. Ct.

[11] *Orleans Education Assn. v. School District of Orleans*, 193 Neb. 675 (Neb. Sup. Ct., 1975).

[12] *City of Amsterdam v. Helsby*, 337 N.Y. 2d 19 (N.Y. Ct. of Appeals, 1975).

[13] Home-rule cities and counties are jurisdictions which have enacted their own legislation governing municipal collective bargaining and impasse resolution.

[14] Several cases are presently pending before the Oregon Supreme Court.

[15] *Harney v. Russo*, 255 A 2d 560 (Pa. Sup. Ct., 1969).

[16] *Sioux Falls v. Sioux Falls Firefighters*, 239 N.W. 2d 35 (S.D. Sup. Ct., 1975).

[17] *Salt Lake City v. Intn'l Assn. of Firefighters, Locals 1645, 593, and 2064*, Case No. 14689 (Utah Sup. Ct., 1977).

[18] *Spokane v. Spokane Police Guild*, 87 Wash 2d 457 (Wash. Sup. Ct., 1976).

[19] *State v. Laramie*, 437 P 2d 295 (Wyo. Sup. Ct., 1968).

§ 200. Statement of policy.

The legislature of the state of New York declares that it is the public policy of the state and the purpose of this act to promote harmonious and cooperative relationships between government and its employees and to protect the public by assuring, at all times, the orderly and un-interrupted operations and functions of government. These policies are best effectuated by (a) granting to public employees the right of organization and repre-sentation, (b) requiring the state, local governments and other political subdivisions to negotiate with, and enter into written agreements with employee organiza-tions representing public employees which have been certified or recognized, (c) encouraging such public em-ployers and such employee organizations to agree upon procedures for resolving disputes, (d) creating a public employment relations board to assist in resolving dis-putes between public employees and public employers, and (e) continuing the prohibition against strikes by public employees and providing remedies for violations of such prohibition.

[Amended by L. 1969, c. 24, which inserted clause (c) and relettered other clauses.]

§ 201. Definitions.

As used in this article:

1. The term "board" means the public employment relations board created by section two hundred five of this article.

2. The term "membership dues deduction" means the obligation or practice of a government to deduct from the salary of a public employee with his consent an amount for the payment of his membership dues in an employee organization. Such term also means the ob-ligation or practice of a government to transmit the sums so deducted to an employee organization.

3. The term "chief legal officer" means (a) in the case of the state of New York or a state public authority, the attorney general of the state of New York, (b) in the case of a county, city, town, village or school dis-trict, the county attorney, corporation counsel, town attorney, village attorney or school district attorney, as the case may be, and (c) in the case of any such govern-ment not having its own attorney, or any other govern-ment or public employer, the corporation counsel of the city in which such government or public employer has its principal office, and if such principal office is not located in a city, the county attorney of the county in which such government or public employer has its principal office.

4. The term "terms and conditions of employment" means salaries, wages, hours and other terms and conditions of employment provided, however, that such term shall not include any benefits provided by or to be provided by a public retirement system, or payments to a fund or insurer to provide an income for retirees, or payment to retirees or their beneficiaries. No such retirement benefits shall be negotiated pursuant to this article, and any benefits so negotiated shall be void.

5. The term "employee organization" means an organization of any kind having as its primary purpose the improvement of terms and conditions of employment of public employees, except that such term shall not include an organization (a) membership in which is prohibited by section one hundred five of this chapter, (b) which discriminates with regard to the terms or conditions of membership because of race, color, creed or national origin, or (c) which, in the case of public employees who hold positions by appointment or employment in the service of the board and who are excluded from the application of this article by rules and regulations of the board, admits to membership or is affiliated directly or indirectly with an organization which admits to membership persons not in the service of the board, for purposes of any provision of this article other than sections two hundred ten and two hundred eleven of this article.

6. (a) The term "government" or "public employer" means (i) the state of New York, (ii) a county, city, town, village or any other political subdivision or civil division of the state, (iii) a school district or any governmental entity operating a public school, college or university, (iv) a public improvement or special district, (v) a public authority, commission, or public benefit corporation, or (vi) any other public corporation, agency or instrumentality or unit of government which exercises governmental powers under the laws of the state.

(b) Upon the application of any government, the board may determine that the applicant shall be deemed to be a joint public employer of public employees in an employer-employee negotiating unit determined pursuant to section two hundred seven of this chapter when such determination would best effectuate the purposes of this chapter.

7. (a) The term "public employee" means any person holding a position by appointment or employment in the service of a public employer, except that such term shall not include for the purposes of any provision of this article other than sections two hundred ten and two hundred eleven of this article, persons holding posi-

tions by appointment or employment in the organized militia of the state and persons who may reasonably be designated from time to time as managerial or confidential upon application of the public employer to the appropriate board in accordance with procedures established pursuant to section two hundred five or two hundred twelve of this article, which procedures shall provide that any such designations made during a period of unchallenged representation pursuant to subdivision two of section two hundred eight of this chapter shall only become effective upon the termination of such period of unchallenged representation. Employees may be designated as managerial only if they are persons (i) who formulate policy or (ii) who may reasonably be required on behalf of the public employer to assist directly in the preparation for and conduct of collective negotiations or to have a major role in the administration of agreements or in personnel administration provided that such role is not of a routine or clerical nature and requires the exercise of independent judgment. Employees may be designated as confidential only if they are persons who assist and act in a confidential capacity to managerial employees described in clause (ii).

(b) For the purpose of this article, assistant attorneys general shall be designated managerial employees and confidential investigators employed in the department of law shall be designated confidential employees.

8. The term "state public authority" means a public benefit corporation or public corporation, a majority of the members of which are (i) appointed by the governor or by another state officer or body, (ii) designated as members by virtue of their state office, or (iii) appointed or designated by any combination of the foregoing.

9. The term "strike" means any strike or other concerted stoppage of work or slowdown by public employees.

10. The term "chief executive officer" in the case of school districts, means the superintendent of schools in school districts employing their own superintendents, and in school districts under the jurisdiction of a district superintendent of schools, shall mean the principal of the district.

11. The term "legislative body of the government" in the case of school districts, means the board of education, board of trustees or sole trustee, as the case may be.

12. The term "agreement" means the result of the exchange of mutual promises between the chief executive officer of a public employer and an employee organization which becomes a binding contract, for the period set forth therein, except as to any provisions therein which require approval by a legislative body, and as to those provisions, shall become binding when the appropriate legislative body gives its approval.

[Amended by L. 1969, c. 24; L. 1971, c. 503 and c. 504; L. 1973, c. 382. L. 1969, c. 24 added subdivision 13 (now subdivision 12). L. 1971, c. 503 deleted subdivision 2, renumbered other subdivisions; changed definition of chief legal officer to include school district attorneys; added paragraph (b) to subdivision 6; and added material to subdivision 7 relating to managerial and confidential employees. L. 1971, c. 504 amended subdivision 7 with respect to managerial and confidential employees. L. 1972, c. 818 added paragraph (b) to subdivision 7. L. 1973, c. 382 excluded retirement benefits from definition of terms and conditions of employment in subdivision 4. They are now to be negotiated under the provisions of the Retirement and Social Security Law, §470 and L. 1973, c. 382, §70 as amended by L. 1973, c. 1046 §65.]

§ 202. Right of organization.

Public employees shall have the right to form, join and participate in, or to refrain from forming, joining, or participating in, any employee organization of their own choosing.

§ 203. Right of representation.

Public employees shall have the right to be represented by employee organizations to negotiate collectively with their public employers in the determination of their terms and conditions of employment, and the administration of grievances arising thereunder.

§ 204. Recognition and certification of employee organizations.

1. Public employers are hereby empowered to recognize employee organizations for the purpose of negotiating collectively in the determination of, and administration of grievances arising under, the terms and conditions of employment of their public employees as provided in this article, and to negotiate and enter into written agreements with such employee organizations in determining such terms and conditions of employment.

2. Where an employee organization has been certified or recognized pursuant to the provisions of this article, the appropriate public employer shall be, and hereby is, required to negotiate collectively with such employee organization in the determination of, and administration of grievances arising under, the terms and conditions of employment of the public employees as provided in this article, and to negotiate and enter into

written agreements with such employee organizations in determining such terms and conditions of employment.

§ 204-a. Argeements between public employers and employee organizations.

1. Any written agreement between a public employer and an an employee organization determining the terms and conditions of employment of public employees shall contain the following notice in type not smaller than the largest type used elsewhere in such agreement:

"It is agreed by and between the parties that any provision of this agreement requiring legislative action to permit its implementation by amendment of law or by providing the additional funds therefor, shall not become effective until the appropriate legislative body has given approval."

2. Every employee organization submitting such a written agreement to its members for ratification shall publish such notice, include such notice in the documents accompanying such submission and shall read it aloud at any membership meeting called to consider such ratification.

3. Within sixty days after the effective date of this act, a copy of this section shall be furnished by the chief fiscal officer of each public employer to each public employee. Each public employee employed thereafter shall, upon such employment, be furnished with a copy of the provisions of this section.

[Added by L. 1969, c. 24.]

§ 205. Public employment relations board.

1. There is hereby created in the state department of civil service a board, to be known as the public employment relations board, which shall consist of three members appointed by the governor, by and with the advice and consent of the senate from persons representative of the public. Not more than two members of the board shall be members of the same political party. Each member shall be appointed for a term of six years, except that of the members first appointed, one shall be appointed for a term to expire on May thirty-first, nineteen hundred sixty-nine, one for a term to expire on May thirty-first, nineteen hundred seventy-one, and one for a term to expire on May thirty-first, nineteen hundred seventy-three. The governor shall designate one member who shall serve as chairman of the board until the expiration

of his term. A member appointed to fill a vacancy shall be appointed for the unexpired term of the member whom he is to succeed.

2. Members of the board shall hold no other public office or public employment in the state. The chairman shall give his whole time to his duties.

3. Members of the board other than the chairman shall, when performing the work of the board, be compensated at the rate of one hundred dollars per day, together with an allowance for actual and necessary expenses incurred in the discharge of their duties hereunder. The chairman shall receive an annual salary to be fixed within the amount available therefor by appropriation, in addition to an allowance for expenses actually and necessarily incurred by him in the performance of his duties.

4. (a) The board may appoint an executive director and such other persons, including but not limited to attorneys, mediators, members of fact-finding boards and representatives of employee organizations and public employers to serve as technical advisers to such fact-finding boards, as it may from time to time deem necessary for the performance of its functions, prescribe their duties, fix their compensation and provide for reimbursement of their expenses within the amounts made available therefor by appropriation. Attorneys appointed under this section may, at the direction of the board, appear for and represent the board in any case in court.

(b) No member of the board or its appointees pursuant to this subdivision, including without limitation any mediator or fact-finder employed or retained by the board, shall, except as required by this article, be compelled to nor shall he voluntarily disclose to any administrative or judicial tribunal or at the legislative hearing, held pursuant to subparagraph (iii) of paragraph (e) of subdivision three of section two hundred nine, any information relating to the resolution of a particular dispute in the course of collective negotiations acquired in the course of his official activities under this article, nor shall any reports, minutes, written communications, or other documents pertaining to such information and acquired in the course of his official activities under this article be subject to subpoena or voluntarily disclosed; except that where the information so required indicates that the person appearing or who has appeared before the board has been the victim of, or otherwise involved in, a crime, other than a criminal contempt in a case involving or growing out of a violation of this article, said members of the board and its appointees may be required to testify fully in relation thereto upon any examination, trial, or other proceeding in which the commission of such crime is the subject of inquiry.

5. In addition to the powers and functions provided in other sections of this article, the board shall have the following powers and functions:

(a) To establish procedures consistent with the provisions of section two hundred seven of this article and after consultation with interested parties, to resolve disputes concerning the representation status of employee organizations.

(b) To resolve, pursuant to such procedures, disputes concerning the representation status of employee organizations of employees of the state and state public authorities upon request of any employee organization, state department or agency or state public authority involved.

(c) To resolve, pursuant to such procedures but only in the absence of applicable procedures established pursuant to section two hundred six of this article, disputes concerning the representation status of other employee organizations, upon request of any employee organization or other government or public employer involved.

(d) To establish procedures for the prevention of improper employer and employee organization practices as provided in section two hundred nine-a of this article, provided, however, that in case of a claimed violation of paragraph (d) of subdivision one or paragraph (b) of subdivision two of such section, such procedures shall provide only for the entry of an order directing the public employer or employee organization to negotiate in good faith. The pendency of proceedings under this paragraph shall not be used as the basis to delay or interfere with determination of representation status pursuant to section two hundred seven of this article or with collective negotiations. The board shall exercise exclusive nondelegable jurisdiction of the powers granted to it by this paragraph; provided, however, that this sentence shall not apply to the city of New York prior to March first, nineteen hundred seventy-three.

(e) To make studies and analyses of, and act as a clearing house of information relating to, conditions of employment of public employees throughout the state.

(f) To request from any government, and such governments are authorized to provide, such assistance, services and data as will enable the board properly to carry out its functions and powers.

(g) To conduct studies of problems involved in representation and negotiation, including, but not limited to (i) whether employee organizations are to be recognized as representatives of their members only or are to have exclusive representation rights for all employees in the negotiating unit, (ii) the problems of unit determination, (iii) those subjects which are open to negotiation in whole or in part, (iv) those subjects which require administrative or legislative approval of modifications agreed upon by the parties, and (v) those subjects which are for determination solely by the appropriate legislative body, and make recommendations from time to time for legislation based upon the results of such studies.

(h) To make available to employee organizations, governments, mediators, fact-finding boards and joint study committees established by governments and employee organizations statistical data relating to wages, benefits and employment practices in public and private employment applicable to various localities and occupations to assist them to resolve complex issues in negotiations.

(i) To establish, after consulting representatives of employee organizations and administrators of public services, panels of qualified persons broadly representative of the public to be available to serve as mediators, arbitrators or members of fact-finding boards.

(j) To hold such hearings and make such inquiries as it deems necessary for it properly to carry out its functions and powers.

(k) For the purpose of such hearings and inquiries, to administer oaths and affirmations, examine witnesses and documents, take testimony and receive evidence, compel the attendance of witnesses and the production of documents by the issuance of subpoenas, and delegate such powers to any member of the board or any person appointed by the board for the performance of its functions. Such subpoenas shall be regulated and enforced under the civil practice law and rules.

(l) To make, amend and rescind, from time to time, such rules and regulations, including but not limited to those governing its internal organization and conduct of its affairs, and to exercise such other powers, as may be appropriate to effectuate the purposes and provisions of this article.

6. Notwithstanding any other provisions of law, neither the president of the civil service commission nor the civil service commission or any other officer, employer, board or agency of the department of civil service shall supervise, direct or control the board in the performance of any of its functions or the exercise of any of its powers under this article; provided, however that nothing herein shall be construed to exempt employees of the board from the provisions of the civil service law.

[Amended by L. 1969, c. 24, c. 391 and c. 494; L. 1970, c. 32 and c. 1020; L. 1971, c. 13 and c. 503. L. 1969, c. 24 inserted paragraph (d) in subdivision 5 and relettered other paragraphs. L. 1969, c. 391 changed subdivision 1 with respect to the term of the chairman. L. 1969, c. 494 exempted New York City from paragraph (d) of subdivision 5 until March 1, 1970, L. 1970, c. 32 amended L. 1969, c. 494 to extend the exemption of the City of New York until March 1, 1971. L. 1970, c. 1020 amended subdivision 4 to authorize attorneys appointed by the Board to represent the Board in court. L. 1971, c. 13 amended L. 1970, c. 32 to extend the exemption of New York City to March 1, 1972. L. 1971, c. 503 added paragraph (b) of subdivision 4. L. 1972, c. 26 amended paragraph (d) of subdivision 5 to extend the exemption of New York City to March 1, 1973.]

§ 206. Procedures for determination of representation status of local employees.

1. Every government (other than the state or a state public authority), acting through its legislative body, is hereby empowered to establish procedures, not inconsistent with the provisions of section two hundred seven of this article and after consultation with interested employee organizations and administrators of public services, to resolve disputes concerning the representation status of employee organizations of employees of such government.

2. In the absence of such procedures, such disputes shall be submitted to the board in accordance with section two hundred five of this article.

§ 207. Determination of representation status

For purposes of resolving disputes concerning representation status, pursuant to section two hundred five or two hundred six of this article, the board or government, as the case may be, shall

1. define the appropriate employer-employee negoting unit taking into account the following standards:

(a) the definition of the unit shall correspond to a community of interest among the employees to be included in the unit;

(b) the officials of government at the level of the unit shall have the power to agree, or to make effective recommendations to other administrative authority or the legislative body with respect to, the terms and conditions of employment upon which the employees desire to negotiate; and

(c) the unit shall be compatible with the joint responsibilities of the public employer and public employees to serve the public.

2. ascertain the public employees' choice of employee organization as their representative (in cases where the parties to a dispute have not agreed on the means to ascertain the choice, if any, of the employees in the unit) on the basis of dues deduction authorization and other evidences, or, if necessary, by conducting an election.

3. certify or recognize an employee organization upon (a) the determination that such organization represents that group of public employees it claims to represent, and (b) the affirmation by such organization that it does not assert the right to strike against any government, to assist or participate in such strike, or to impose an obligation to conduct, assist or participate in such a strike.

§ 208. Rights accompanying certification or recognition.

1. A public employer shall extend to an employee organization certified or recognized pursuant to this article the following rights:

(a) to represent the employees in negotiations notwithstanding the existence of an agreement with an employee organization that is no longer certified or recognized, and in the settlement of grievances; and

(b) to membership dues deduction, upon presentation of dues deduction authorization cards signed by individual employees.

2. An employee organization certified or recognized pursuant to this article shall be entitled to unchallenged representation status until seven months prior to the expiration of a written agreement between the public employer and said employee organization determining terms and conditions of employment. For the purposes of this

subdivision, (a) any such agreement for a term covering other than the fiscal year of the public employer shall be deemed to expire with the fiscal year ending immediately prior to the termination date of such agreement, (b) any such agreement having a term in excess of three years shall be treated as an agreement for a term of three years and (c) extensions of any such agreement shall not extend the period of unchallenged representation status.

[Amended by L. 1971, c. 503, which inserted a clause beginning with "notwithstanding" in paragraph (a) of subdivision 1; repealed paragraph (c) of subdivision 1; added subdivision 2.]

§ 209. Resolution of disputes in the course of collective negotiations.

1. For purposes of this section, an impasse may be deemed to exist if the parties fail to achieve agreement at least one hundred twenty days prior to the end of the fiscal year of the public employer.

2. Public employers are hereby empowered to enter into written agreements with recognized or certified employee organizations setting forth procedures to be invoked in the event of disputes which reach an impasse in the course of collective negotiations. Such agreements may include the undertaking by each party to submit unresolved issues to impartial arbitration. In the absence or upon the failure of such procedures, public employers and employee organizations may request the board to render assistance as provided in this section, or the board may render such assistance on its own motion, as provided in subdivision three of this section.

3. On request of either party or upon its own motion, as provided in subdivision two of this section, and in the event the board determines that an impasse exists in collective negotiations between such employee organization and a public employer as to the conditions of employment of public employees, the board shall render assistance as follows:

(a) to assist the parties to effect a voluntary resolution of the dispute, the board shall appoint a mediator or mediators representative of the public from a list of qualified persons maintained by the board;

(b) if the impasse continues, the board shall appoint a fact-finding board of not more than three members, each representative of the public, from a list

of qualified persons maintained by the board, which fact-finding board shall have, in addition to the powers delegated to it by the board, the power to make public recommendations for the resolution of the dispute;

(c) if the dispute is not resolved at least eighty days prior to the end of the fiscal year of the public employer or by such other date determined by the board to be appropriate, the fact-finding board, acting by a majority of its members, (i) shall immediately transmit its findings of fact and recommendations for resolution of the dispute to the chief executive officer of the government involved and to the employee organization involved, (ii) may thereafter assist the parties to effect a voluntary resolution of the dispute, and (iii) shall within five days of such transmission make public such findings and recommendations;

(d) in the event that the findings of fact and recommendations are made public by a fact-finding board appointed by the board or established pursuant to procedures agreed upon by the parties under subdivision two of this section, and the impasse continues, the public employment relations board shall have the power to take whatever steps it deems appropriate to resolve the dispute, including (i) the making of recommendations after giving due consideration to the findings of fact and recommendations of such fact-finding board, but no further fact-finding board shall be appointed and (ii) upon the request of the parties assistance in providing for voluntary arbitration;

(e) in the event that either the public employer or the employee organization does not accept in whole or in part the recommendations of the fact-finding board, (i) the chief executive officer of the government involved shall, within ten days after receipt of the findings of fact and recommendations of the fact-finding board, submit to the legislative body of the government involved a copy of the findings of fact and recommendations of the fact-finding board, together with his recommendations for settling the dispute; (ii) the employee organization may submit to such legislative body its recommendations for settling the dispute; (iii) the legislative body or a duly authorized committee thereof shall forthwith conduct a public hearing at which the parties shall be required to explain their positions with respect to the report of the fact-finding board; and (iv) thereafter, the legislative body shall take such action as it deems to be in the public interest, including the interest of the public employees involved.

[Amended by L. 1969, c. 24; L. 1970, c. 414; L. 1971, c. 503. L. 1969, c. 24 changed subdivision 2 to allow parties to submit to arbitration; it changed paragraph (c) of subdivision 3 by altering the time requirements and by adding clause (ii). It changed paragraph (d) of subdivision 3 by adding clause (ii); changed paragraph (e) of subdivision 3 by altering time requirements and by adding clauses (iii) and (iv). L. 1970, c. 414 amended paragraph (d) of subdivision 3 by adding the phrase "appointed by the board". L. 1971, c. 503 amended subdivisions 1 and 3(c) to delete references to budget submission dates and to provide references to the fiscal year of a public employer; it inserted the word "public" in clause (iii) of paragraph (e) of subdivision 3.]

§ 209-a. Improper employer practices; improper employee organization practices; application.

1. Improper employer practices. It shall be an improper practice for a public employer or its agents deliberately (a) to interfere with, restrain or coerce public employees in the exercise of their rights guaranteed in section two hundred two for the purpose of depriving them of such rights; (b) to dominate or interfere with the formation or administration of any employee organization for the purpose of depriving them of such rights; (c) to discriminate against any employee for the purpose of encouraging or discouraging membership in, or participation in the activities of, any employee organization; or (d) to refuse to negotiate in good faith with the duly recognized or certified representatives of its public employees.

2. Improper employee organization practices. It shall be an improper practice for an employee organization or its agents deliberately (a) to interfere with, restrain or coerce public employees in the exercise of the rights granted in section two hundred two, or to cause, or attempt to cause, a public employer to do so; or (b) to refuse to negotiate collectively in good faith with a public employer, provided it is the duly recognized or certified representative of the employees of such employer.

3. Application. In applying this section, fundamental distinctions between private and public employment shall be recognized, and no body of federal or state law applicable wholly or in part to private employment, shall be regarded as binding or controlling precedent.

[Added by L. 1969, c. 24.]

§ 210. Prohibition of strikes.

1. No public employee or employee organization shall engage in a strike, and no public employee or employee organization shall cause, instigate, encourage, or condone a strike.

2. Violations and penalties; presumption; prohibition against consent to strike; determination; notice; probation; payroll deductions; objections; and restoration.

(a) Violations and penalties. A public employee shall violate this subdivision by engaging in a strike or violating paragraph (c) of this subdivision and shall be liable as provided in this subdivision pursuant to the procedures contained herein. In addition, any public employee who violates subdivision one of this section may be subject to removal or other disciplinary action provided by law for misconduct.

(b) Presumption. For purposes of this subdivision an employee who is absent from work without permission, or who abstains wholly or in part from the full performance of his duties in his normal manner without permission, on the date or dates when a strike occurs, shall be presumed to have engaged in such strike on such date or dates.

(c) Prohibition against consent to strike. No person exercising on behalf of any public employer any authority, supervision or direction over any public employee shall have the power to authorize, approve, condone or consent to a strike, or the engaging in a strike, by one or more public employees, and such person shall not authorize, approve, condone or consent to such strike or engagement.

(d) Determination. In the event that it appears that a violation of this subdivision may have occurred, the chief executive officer of the government involved shall, on the basis of such investigation and affidavits as he may deem appropriate, determine whether or not such violation has occurred and the date or dates of such violation. If the chief executive officer determines that such violation has occurred, he shall further determine, on the basis of such further investigation and affidavits as he may deem appropriate, the names of employees who committed such violation and the date or dates thereof. Such determination shall not be deemed to be final until the completion of the procedures provided for in this subdivision.

(e) Notice. The chief executive officer shall forthwith notify each employee that he has been found to have committed such violation the date or dates thereof and of his right to object to such determination pursuant to paragraph (h) of this subdivision; he shall also notify the chief fiscal officer of the names of all such employees and of the total number of days, or part thereof, on which it has been determined that such violation occurred. Notice to each employee shall be by personal service or by certified mail to his last address filed by him with his employer.

(f)   Probation. Notwithstanding any inconsistent provision of law, any public employee who has been determined to have violated this subdivision shall be on probation for a term of one year following such determination during which period he shall serve without tenure, provided, however, that the effect of probation hereunder with regard to teachers and others subject to the education law shall not exceed or differ from the effect of probation hereunder with regard to other public employees.

(g)   Payroll deductions. Not earlier than thirty nor later than ninety days following the date of such determination, the chief fiscal officer of the government involved shall deduct from the compensaton of each such public employee an amount equal to twice his daily rate of pay for each day or part thereof that it was determined that he had violated this subdivision; such rate of pay to be computed as of the time of such violation. In computing such deduction, credit shall be allowed for amounts already withheld from such employee's compensation on account of his absence from work or other withholding of services on such day or days. In computing the aforesaid thirty to ninety day period of time following the determination of a violation pursuant to subdivision (d) of paragraph two of this section and where the employee's annual compensation is paid over a period of time which is less than fifty-two weeks, that period of time between the last day of the last payroll period of the employment term in which the violation occurred and the first day of the first payroll period of the next succeeding employment term shall be disregarded and not counted.

(h)   Objections and restoration. Any employee determined to have violated this subdivision may object to such determination by filing with the chief executive officer, (within twenty days of the date on which notice was served or mailed to him pursuant to paragraph (e) of this subdivision) his sworn affidavit, supported by available documentary proof,

containing a short and plain statement of the facts upon which he relies to show that such determination was incorrect. Such affidavit shall be subject to the penalties of perjury. If the chief executive officer shall determine that the affidavit and supporting proof establishes that the employee did not violate this subdivision, he shall sustain the objection. If the chief executive officer shall determine that the affidavit and supporting proof fails to establish that the employee did not violate this subdivision, he shall dismiss the objection and so notify the employee. If the chief executive officer shall determine that the affidavit and supporting proof raises a question of fact which, if resolved in favor of the employee, would establish that the employee did not violate this subdivision, he shall appoint a hearing officer to determine whether in fact the employee did violate this subdivision after a hearing at which such employee shall bear the burden of proof. If the hearing officer shall determine that the employee failed to establish that he did not violate this subdivision, the chief executive officer shall so notify the employee. If the chief executive officer sustains an objection or the hearing officer determines on a preponderance of the evidence that such employee did not violate this subdivision, the chief executive officer shall forthwith restore to the employee the tenure suspended pursuant to paragraph (f) of this subdivision, and notify the chief fiscal officer who shall thereupon cease all further deductions and refund any deductions previously made pursuant to this subdivision. The determinations provided in this paragraph shall be reviewable pursuant to article seventy-eight of the civil practice law and rules.

3.   (a)   An employee organization which is determined by the board to have violated the provisions of subdivision one of this section shall, in accordance with the provisions of this section, lose the rights granted pursuant to the provisions of paragraph (b) of subdivision one of section two hundred eight of this chapter.

(b)   In the event that it appears that a violation of subdivision one of this section may have occurred, it shall be the duty of the chief executive officer of the public employer involved (i) forthwith to so notify the board and the chief legal officer of the government involved, and (ii) to provide the board and such chief legal officer with such facilities, assistance and data as will enable the board and such chief legal officer to carry out their duties under this section.

(c) In the event that it appears that a violation of subdivision one of this section may have occurred, the chief legal officer of the government involved, or the board on its own motion shall forthwith institute proceedings before the board to determine whether such employee organization has violated the provisions of subdivision one of this section.

(d) Proceedings against an employee organization under this section shall be commenced by service upon it of a written notice, together with a copy of the charges. A copy of such notice and charges shall also be served, for their information, upon the appropriate government officials who recognize such employee organization and grant to it the rights accompanying such recognition. The employee organization shall have eight days within which to serve its written answer to such charges. The board's hearing shall be held promptly thereafter and at such hearing, the parties shall be permitted to be represented by counsel and to summon witnesses in their behalf. Compliance with the technical rules of evidence shall not be required.

(e) In determining whether an employee organization has violated subdivision one of this section, the board shall consider (i) whether the employee organization called the strike or tried to prevent it, and (ii) whether the employee organization made or was making good faith efforts to terminate the strike.

(f) If the board determines that an employee organization has violated the provisions of subdivision one of this section, the board shall order forfeiture of the rights granted pursuant to the provisions of paragraph (b) of subdivision one of section two hundred eight of of this chapter, for such specified period of time, as the board shall determine, or, in the discretion of the board, for an indefinite period of time subject to restoration upon application, with notice to all interested parties, supported by proof of good faith compliance with the requirements of subdivision one of this section since the date of such violation, such proof to include, for example, the successful negotiation, without a violation of subdivision one of this section, of a contract covering the employees in the unit affected by such violation; provided, however, that where a fine imposed on an employee organization pursuant to subdivision two of section seven hundred fifty-one of the judiciary law remains wholly or partly unpaid, after the exhaustion of the cash and securities of the employee organization, the board shall direct that, notwithstanding such forfeiture,

such membership dues deduction shall be continued to the extent necessary to pay such fine and such public employer shall transmit such moneys to the court. In fixing the duration of the forfeiture, the board shall consider all the relevant facts and circumstances, including but not limited to: (i) the extent of any wilful defiance of subdivision one of this section (ii) the impact of the strike on the public health, safety, and welfare of the community and (iii) the financial resources of the employee organization; and the board may consider (i) the refusal of the employee organization or the appropriate public employer or the representative thereof, to submit to the mediation and fact-finding procedures provided in section two hundred nine and (ii) whether, if so alleged by the employee organization, the appropriate public employer or its representatives engaged in such acts of extreme provocation as to detract from the responsibility of the employee organization for the strike. In determining the financial resources of the employee organization, the board shall consider both the income and the assets of such employee organization. In the event membership dues are collected by the public employer as provided in paragraph (b) of subdivision one of section two hundred eight of this chapter, the books and records of such public employer shall be prima facie evidence of the amount so collected.

(g) An employee organization whose rights granted pursuant to the provisions of paragraph (b) of subdivision one of section two hundred eight of this article have been ordered forfeited pursuant to this section may be granted such rights after the termination of such forfeiture only after complying with the provisions of clause (b) of subdivision three of section two hundred seven of this article.

(h) No compensation shall be paid by a public employer to a public employee with respect to any day or part thereof when such employee is engaged in a strike against such employer. The chief fiscal officer of the government involved shall withhold such compensation upon receipt of the notice provided by paragraph (e) of subdivision two of section two hundred ten; notwithstanding the failure to have received such notice, no public employee or officer having knowledge that such employee has so engaged in such a strike shall deliver or cause to be delivered to such employee any cash, check or payment which, in whole or in part, represents such compensation.

4. Within sixty days of the termination of a strike, the chief executive officer of the government involved shall prepare and make public a report in writing, which shall contain the following information: (a) the circumstances surrounding the commencement of the strike, (b) the efforts used to terminate the strike, (c) the names of those public employees whom the public officer or body had reason to believe were responsible for causing, instigating or encouraging the strike and (d) related to the varying degrees of individual responsibility, the sanctions imposed or proceedings pending against each such individual public employee.

[Amended by L. 1969, c. 24 and c. 492; L. 1971, c. 503. L. 1969, c. 24 added "public employee" to subdivision 1, repealed old subdivision 2 and added subdivision 2; made changes in the language of paragraphs (c) and (d) of subdivision 3; changed paragraph (f) of subdivision 3 extensively with respect to the nature of penalties to be imposed upon employee organizations and the standards for the imposition of such penalties; made changes in the language of paragraph (g) of subdivision 3 and added paragraph (h) of subdivision 3; added the final two sentences of subdivision 4 (now §213) : and added subdivision 5 (now subdivision 4) . L. 1969, c. 492 added the final clause of paragraph (f) of subdivision 2. L. 1971, c. 503 inserted into paragraph (e) of subdivision 2 the clause "and of his right to object to such determination pursuant to paragraph (h) of this subdivision"; added the final sentence to paragraph (g) of subdivision 2; inserted references to subdivision 1 of §208 in paragraphs (a), (f) and (g) of subdivision 3; transferred old subdivision 4 to §213; and renumbered old subdivision 5 to be subdivision 4].

§ 211. Application for injunctive relief.

Notwithstanding the provisions of section eight hundred seven of the labor law, where it appears that public employees or an employee organization threaten or are about to do, or are doing, an act in violation of section two hundred ten of this article, the chief executive officer of the government involved shall (a) forthwith notify the chief legal officer of the government involved, and (b) provide such chief legal officer with such facilities, assistance and data as will enable the chief legal officer to carry out his duties under this section, and, notwithstanding the failure or refusal of the chief executive officer to act as aforesaid, the chief legal officer of the government involved shall forthwith apply to the su-

preme court for an injunction against such violation. If an order of the court enjoining or restraining such violation does not receive compliance, such chief legal officer shall forthwith apply to the supreme court to punish such violation under section seven hundred fifty of the judiciary law.

§ 212. Local government procedures.

1. This article, except sections two hundred one, two hundred two, two hundred three, two hundred four, paragraph b of subdivision four and paragraph d of subdivision five of section two hundred five, paragraph b of subdivision three of section two hundred seven, section two hundred eight, section two hundred nine-a, subdivisions one and two of section two hundred ten, section two hundred eleven, two hundred thirteen and two hundred fourteen, shall be inapplicable to any government (other than the state or a state public authority) which, acting through its legislative body, has adopted by local law, ordinance or resolution, its own provisions and procedures which have been submitted to the board by such government and as to which there is in effect a determination by the board that such provisions and procedures and the continuing implementation thereof are substantially equivalent to the provisions and procedures set forth in this article with respect to the state. 2. With respect to the city of New York, such provisions and procedures need not be related to the end of its fiscal year; and with respect to provisions and procedures adopted by local law by the city of New York no such submission to or determination by the board shall be required, but such provisions and procedures shall be of full force and effect unless and until such provisions and procedures, or the continuing implementation thereof, are found by a court of competent jurisdiction, in an action brought by the board in the county of New York for a declaratory judgment, not to be substantially equivalent to the provisions and procedures set forth in this article.

[Amended by L. 1969, c. 24; L. 1971, c. 503. L. 1969, c. 24 inserted cross-references in first sentence of subdivision 1 to paragraph (d) of subdivision 5 of §205 and §209-a and separated section into two subdivisions. L. 1971, c. 503 inserted cross-references in first sentence of subdivision 1 to paragraph (b) of subdivision 4 of §204 and to §§213 and 214; amended subdivision 2 to delete reference to budget submission dates and to provide a reference to the fiscal year of the city of New York.]

§ 213. Judicial review and enforcement.

(a) Orders of the board made pursuant to this article shall be deemed to be final against all parties to its proceedings and persons who have had an opportunity to be parties to its proceedings unless reversed or modified in proceedings for enforcement or judicial review as hereinafter provided. Such orders shall be (i) reviewable under article seventy-eight of the civil practice law and rules upon petition filed by an aggrieved party within thirty days after service by registered or certified mail of a copy of such order upon such party, and (ii) enforceable in a special proceeding, upon petition of such board, by the supreme court.

(b) Orders of the board or its agents made pursuant to subdivisions one and two of section two hundred seven of this chapter shall be reviewable only in a proceeding brought under article seventy-eight of the civil practice law and rules to review an order of the board made pursuant to subdivision three of section two hundred seven of this chapter.

(c) If a proceeding by the board for enforcement of its order is instituted prior to the expiration of the period within which a party may seek judicial review of such order, the respondent may raise in his answer the questions authorized to be raised by section seven thousand eight hundred three of the civil practice law and rules and thereafter the proceedings shall be governed by the provisions of article seventy-eight of the civil practice law and rules that are not inconsistent herewith, except that if an issue specified in question four of section seven thousand eight hundred three of the civil practice law and rules is raised, the proceeding shall be transferred for disposition to the appellate division of the supreme court. Where an issue specified in question four of section seven thousand eight hundred three of the civil practice law and rules is raised, either in a proceeding to enforce or review an order of the board, the appellate division of the supreme court, upon completion of proceedings before it, shall remit a copy of its judgment or order to the court in which the proceeding was commenced, which court shall have the power to compel compliance with such judgment or order.

(d) In a proceeding to enforce or review an order of the board, the court shall have power to grant such temporary relief or restraining order as it deems just and proper, and to make and enter a judgment or decree enforcing, modifying and enforcing as so modified, or setting aside in whole or in part the order of the board.

(e) The failure to perform the duties required by subdivisions two and three of section two hundred ten of this chapter and by section two hundred eleven of this chapter shall be reviewable in a proceeding under article seventy-eight of the civil practice law and rules by any taxpayer, as defined in section one hundred two of this chapter. Any such taxpayer shall also have standing to institute any action described in subdivisions one and two of section one hundred two of this chapter.

[Added by L. 1971, c. 503. Part of paragraphs (a) and (b) were derived from old paragraph 4 of §210; all the rest was new.]

§ 214. Management and confidential employees; membership and office in employee organizations.

No managerial or confidential employee, as determined pursuant to subdivision seven of section two hundred one of this article, shall hold office in or be a member of any employee organization which is or seeks to become pursuant to this article the certified or recognized representative of the public employees employed by the public employer of such managerial or confidential employee.

[Added by L. 1971, c. 503.]

* * * *

Chapter 503 of the Laws of 1971 as amended by Chapter 504 of the Laws of 1971 provides:

It is the intention of the Legislature that designations of employees as management or confidential pursuant to subdivision seven of section two hundred one of the civil service law as amended by this act reflect the extent to which a public employer has from time to time organized itself for collective negotiations. It is not the intention of the Legislature to destroy existing employer employee negotiating units such as principals or other school administrators who do not formulate policy or who do not have a significant role in employee relations as described in subdivision seven of section two hundred one of such law as amended by this act.

* * * *

The law amended section seven hundred fifty-one of the judiciary law as follows:

§ 751. Punishment for criminal contempts.

1. Except as provided in subdivisions (2) and (3), punishment for a contempt, specified in section seven hundred and fifty, may be by fine, not exceeding two hundred and fifty dollars, or by imprisonment, not exceeding thirty days, in the jail of the county where the court is sit-

ting, or both, in the discretion of the court. Where a person is committed to jail, for the nonpayment of such a fine, he must be dishcarged at the expiration of thirty days; but where he is also committed for a definite time, the thirty days must be computed from the expiration of the definite time.

Such a contempt, committed in the immediate view and presence of the court, may be punished summarily; when not so committed, the party charged must be notified of the accusation, and have a reasonable time to make a defense.

2. (a) Where an employee organization, as defined in section two hundred one of the civil service law, wilfully disobeys a lawful mandate of a court of record, or wilfully offers resistance to such lawful mandate, in a case involving or growing out of a strike in violation of subdivision one of section two hundred ten of the civil service law, the punishment for each day that such contempt persists may be by a fine fixed in the discretion of the court. In the case of a government exempt from certain provisions of article fourteen of the civil service law, pursuant to section two hundred twelve of such law, the court may, as an additional punishment for such contempt, order forfeiture of the rights granted pursuant to the provisions of paragraph (b) of subdivision one of section two hundred eight of such law, for such specified period of time, as the court shall determine or, in the discretion of the court, for an indefinite period of time subject to restoration upon application, with notice to all interested parties, supported by proof of good faith compliance with the requirements of subdivision one of this section since the date of such violation, such proof to include, for example, the successful negotiation, without a violation of subdivision one of this section, of a contract covering the employees in the unit affected by such violation; provided, however, that where a fine imposed pursuant to this subdivision remains wholly or partly unpaid, after the exhaustion of the cash and securities of the employee organization, such forfeiture shall be suspended to the extent necessary for the unpaid portion of such fine to be accumulated by the public employer and transmitted to the court. In fixing the amount of the fine and/or duration of the forfeiture, the court shall consider all the facts and circumstances directly related to the contempt, including, but not limited to: (i) the extent of the wilful defiance of or resistance to the court's mandate (ii) the impact of the strike on the public health, safety, and welfare of the community and

(iii) the ability of the employee organization to pay the fine imposed; and the court may consider (i) the refusal of the employee organization or the appropriate public employer, as defined in section two hundred one of the civil service law, or the representatives thereof, to submit to the mediation and fact-finding procedures provided in section two hundred nine of the civil service law and (ii) whether, if so alleged by the employee organization, the appropriate public employer or its representatives engaged in such acts of extreme provocation as to detract from the responsibility of the employee organization for the strike. In determining the ability of the employee organization to pay the fine imposed, the court shall consider both the income and the assets of such employee organization.

(b) In the event membership dues are collected by the public employer as provided in paragraph (b) of subdivision one of section two hundred eight of the civil service law, the books and records of such public employer shall be prima facie evidence of the amount so collected.

(c) (i) An employee organization appealing an adjudication and fine for criminal contempt imposed pursuant to subdivision two of this section, shall not be required to pay such fine until such appeal is finally determined.

(ii) The court to which such an appeal is taken shall on motion of any party thereto, grant a preference in the hearing thereof.

[Amended by L. 1967, c. 392; L. 1969, c. 24; L. 1971, c. 503. L. 1967, c. 392 added the first clause of the first sentence of subdivision 1 and paragraph (c) of subdivision 2. L. 1969, c. 24 made extensive amendments of subdivision 2 with respect to the penalty to be imposed upon an employee organization and the standards for the imposition of such penalties. L. 1971, c. 503 inserted reference to subdivision 1 of §208 in paragraphs (a) and (b) of subdivision 2.]

DIRECTORY OF PUBLIC EMPLOYMENT RELATIONS BOARDS AND AGENCIES

Preface

Thirty-seven States and a number of localities now have legislation providing for collective bargaining for all or some of their public employees. Of these, twenty-seven States and twenty-three localities provide an agency to administer the law or regulation. Most of the local boards are in New York and California.

These agencies come in a broad variety of forms. Some have responsibility for both the private and public sectors. Some share the responsibility with another agency such as a State board of mediation. Still others have additional, generally pre-existing, responsibilities such as State departments of labor, education commissions, or personnel boards.

Whatever their configuration the acronym PERB, for public employment relations board, has come into general usage as a generic term to describe this activity.

In the preparation of the directory, it was determined that complete information would be listed only for the primary PERB in each State and for local PERBs only when there was no State PERB. Other related agencies are listed in Appendix A. The remaining local PERBs are listed in Appendix B.

The directory was prepared by Beverly Lewis under the supervision of John Bonner, Chief, Division of Public Employee Labor Relations, Labor Management Services Administration.

California Public Employment Relations Board

Main Office
923-12th Street
Suite 300
Sacramento, California   95814
(916) 322-3088

Regional Offices
923-12th Street
Sacramento, California   95814
(916) 322-3198

3550 Welshire Boulevard
Suite 1700
Los Angeles, California   90010
(213) 736-3127

177 Post Street
9th floor
San Francisco, California   94108
(415) 557-1350

Statutory Authority
Sec. 3540 et. seg. West's Ann.
Government Code (1975)

Jurisdiction
School and State employees

Board
Consists of three full-time members appointed
for five-year terms.

Reginald Alleyne, chairman
Jerilou Cossack
Dr. Raymond Gonzales

Key Staff
Executive Director, Charles Cole
Assistant Executive Director, Robert Kingsley
General Counsel, William Smith
Assistant General Counsel, Terry Filliman
Assistant General Counsel, Sharrel Wyatt
Executive Assistant, Stephen Barber
Los Angeles Regional Director,
    Francis Kreiling
Sacramento Regional Director,
    William Brown
San Francisco Regional Director, James Tamm

Principal Responsibilities
o determines bargaining units
o determines negotiability
o conducts elections
o maintains lists of mediators, arbitrators
    and factfinders
o conducts studies relating to employer-
    employee relations
o hears and adjudicates improper labor-
    management practices
o decides contested matters involving recog-
    nition, certification or decertification

Decisions
Decisions are published in the *Public Employee
Reporter* by the Labor Relations Press, P.O.
Box 579, Fort Washington, Pennsylvania 19034.
The cost is $225 per year. Decisions may also
be purchased directly from the Board at a cost
of $100 per fifty decisions.

Budget
FY 1978 budget is $3,200,000.

Note
Local PERBs have been established in Los
Angeles City and County, San Diego County,
Napa County, Torence and San Bernardino.
PERBs in San Francisco and Fresno County
were abolished and their functions are now
performed by the Civil Service Commission.

Connecticut State Board of Labor Relations

Office
200 Folly Brook Boulevard
Hartford, Connecticut 06109
(203) 566-4398

Statutory Authority
Connecticut State Labor Relations Act
of 1945, Ch. 561, revised 1969

Jurisdiction
Private, State and municipal employees

Board
Consists of three part-time members
appointed for six-year terms.

       Fleming James, Jr., chairman
       Patricia Lowe
       Kenneth Stroble

Key Staff
Agent for the Board, John Kingston
    6 assistant agents
    6 clericals

Principal Responsibilities
o determines bargaining units
o conducts elections
o hears and adjudicates improper labor-
    management practices

Decisions
Decisions are $25 per year.

Budget
FY 1978 budget is $295,000.

District of Columbia Board of Labor Relations

Office
The Denrike Building
1010 Vermont Avenue, N.W.
Suite 821
Washington, D.C. 20005
(202) 629-5827

Statutory Authority
Executive Order No. 70-229, 6/70

Jurisdiction
Municipal employees including police,
firefighters and teachers

Board
Consists of five part-time members
appointed for three-year terms.

       James Harkless, chairman
       Eugene D. Carstater
       John N. Gentry
       Carolyn Jordan
       Iverson O. Mitchell

Key Staff
Executive Director, Bruce Waxman
    2 clericals

Principal Responsibilities
o determines bargaining units
o hears and adjudicates improper labor-
    management practices
o resolves impasses through factfinding or
    final and binding arbitration
o determines negotiability
o decides grievability
o conducts investigations, hears testimony
    and takes evidence under oath at
    hearings
o administers oaths or affirmations

Decisions
Decisions are available to those requesting
that their names be placed on the Board's
mailing list

Budget
FY 1978 budget is approximately $108,000.

Florida Public Employees Relations Commission

Office
2003 Apalachee Parkway
Suite 300
Tallahassee, Florida 32301
(904) 488-8641

Statutory Authority
Public Employee's Collective Bargaining Law.
Florida Statute Ch. 447, as amended L. 1976

Jurisdiction
State, county and municipal employees
including firefighters, police, teachers,
employees of special districts and the
state university system.

Commission
Consists of three full-time members
appointed for four-year terms.

      Leonard A. Carson, chairman
      Jean K. Parker
      Michael M. Parrish

Key Staff
Associate Commissioner, Thomas Lang
General Counsel, William E. Powers
Clerk-Editor, Anne M. Parker
Services Specialist, Millie J. Wynn
Supervisor of Elections, Charles Magalian

Principal Responsibilities
o determines bargaining units
o hears and adjudicates improper labor-
   management practices
o reviews and approves local option ordinances
o maintains panels of qualified persons to serve
   as Special Masters

Decisions
Decisions are published in *Florida Public
Employees Reporter* by the Labor Relations
Press, P.O. Box 579, Fort Washington,
Pennsylvania 19034.

Budget
FY 1978 budget is $1,004,000

Hawaii Public Employment Relations Board

Office
550 Halekauwila
Honolulu, Hawaii 96813
(808) 548-6267

Statutory Authority
Hawaii Revised Statutes, Ch. 89; L. 1970

Jurisdiction
State, county, municipal and school
district employees including employees
of the University System

Board
Consists of three full-time members appointed
for six-year terms. One member represents
labor, one management and one the public

      Mack Hamada, chairman
      James K. Clark
      John E. Milligan

Key Staff
Executive Officer, Sonia Faust
Hearing Officer, Carol Tukunaga
Legal Assistant, Lani Nakazawa
Research Analyst, Barbara Stanton
   3 clericals

Principal Responsibilities
o determines bargaining units
o resolves disputes concerning cost items
o supervises elections
o hears and adjudicates improper labor-
   management practices
o maintains lists of mediators, factfinders
   and arbitrators
o conducts studies on problems pertaining
   to public employee management relations

Decisions
Decisions may be requested from the PERB
for 25 cents per page plus postage.

Budget
FY 1958 budget is $358,000.

Illinois Office of Collective Bargaining

Main Office
525 West Jefferson
Springfield, Illinois 62702
(217) 782-3223

Regional Office
910 S. Michigan
18th floor
Chicago, Illinois 60605
(312) 793-2861

Statutory Authority
Executive Order No. 6 (9/4/73)

Jurisdiction
State employees

Board
Consists of three part-time members
who serve at the Governor's pleasure.

> John E. Cullerton, chairman
> Arthur A. Malinowski
> (one vacancy)

Key Staff
Executive Director, Jerry Berendt
Deputy Executive Director, David Loebach
Legal Advisor, Robert Sharpe
  2 investigators
  3 clericals

Principal Responsibilities
o   determines bargaining units
o   conducts elections
o   resolves negotiability disputes
o   hears and adjudicates improper labor-
    management practices
o   assists in process of impasse resolution

Decisions
Decisions are available upon request at no
charge

Budget
FY 1978 budget is $190,000.

Indiana Education Employment Relations Board

Office
9247 N. Meridian
Indianapolis, Indiana 46260
(317) 844-4161

Statutory Authority
I.C. 1971, 20 - 7.5.1

Jurisdiction
Teachers

Board
Consists of three members appointed for
four-year terms. Chairman is full time.

> Victor P. Hoehne, chairman
> William Faust
> George Gardner

Budget
FY 1978 budget is $1,281,000.

Key Staff
Director of Conciliation, Donald Russel
Director of Unfair Labor Practices,
  Richard Burdge
Director of Unit Determination, James Northway
Director of Statistics, Dan Smith
Administrative Assistant, William Selig

Principal Responsibilities
o   determines bargaining units
o   hears and adjudicates improper labor-
    management practices
o   assigns mediators
o   mediates disputes
o   collects statistics on public sector employ-
    ment relations
o   maintains lists of factfinders and aribtrators

Decisions
Decisions are published annually by the
Labor Relations Press, P.O. Box 579,
Fort Washington, Pennsylvania and may be
purchased for $32 per year.

Iowa Public Employment Relations Board

Office

507-10th Street
Des Moines, Iowa 50309
(515) 281-4414

Statutory Authority

Public Employment Relations Act
S.F. 531, Secs. 1 - 29, effective
July 1, 1974

Jurisdiction

State, county, municipal, school
district and other special purpose
district employees

Board

Consists of three full-time members
appointed for four-year terms. No
more than two may be of the same
political party

John E. Beemer, chairman
Vernon C. Cook
John Loihl

Key Staff

Executive Director, Peter Pashler
6 hearing officers/mediators
4 clericals
30 ad hoc mediators

Principal Responsibilities

o determines bargaining units
o conducts elections
o hears and adjudicates improper labor-
   management practices
o collects data and conducts studies relating
   to wages, hours, benefits and other
   terms and conditions of employment
o maintains lists of mediators, factfinders
   and arbitrators

Decisions

Decisions are available upon request from
the Board for a 10 cent fee per page. They
may also be requested from Fedlar and
Chambers, P.O. Box 3370, Davenport, Iowa
52808.

Budget

FY 1978 budget is $508,500.

Kansas Public Employee Relations Board

Office

535 Kansas Avenue
Room 1102
Topeka, Kansas   66612
(913) 296-3170

Statutory Authority

K.S.A. Sec. 75 - 4321, et. seq. (1971)

Jurisdiction

State, county, municipal, school
district and special district employees

Board

Consists of five part-time members
appointed for four-year terms. One
member represents public employers,
one represents public employees and
three represent the public. Not more
than three may belong to the same
political party. Chairman has not
been named.

Garold Been
Louisa Fletcher
E. Jay Rennick
Richard Rock
John Smith

Key Staff

Executive Director, Jerry Powell
Secretary, Twila Bloom

Principal Responsibilities

o determines bargaining units
o conducts elections
o hears and adjudicates improper labor-
     management practices
o assists in appointing mediators and
     factfinders

Decisions

Decisions are available upon request at 25
cents per page.

Budget

FY 1978 budget is $72,457

Kentucky Labor Relations Board

Main Office
Kentucky Department of Labor
Capitol Plaza Office Tower
Frankfort, Kentucky 40601
(502) 564-4912

Regional Office
Henry Tripplett
231 South Fifth Street
Louisville, Kentucky 40201
(502) 583-5581

Statutory Authority
K.R.S. Ch. 345.010 et. seq. (1972)

Jurisdiction
Firefighters

Board
Consists of three part-time members
appointed for four-year terms.

Henry Tripplett, chairman
George A. Lucas
William Siemens

Key Staff
The Board utilizes the staff of the
Kentucky Department of Labor

Principal Responsibilities
o determines bargaining units
o conducts elections
o hears and adjudicates improper labor-
  management practices

Decisions
Not available

Budget
Board members receive a standard fee plus
expenses when performing duties of the Board.
Other expenses come out of the Department
of Labor budget.

Maine Labor Relations Board

Office

State Office Building
Augusta, Maine 04330
(207) 289-2016

Statutory Authority

Municipal Public Employees Labor
Relations Law, M.R.S.A. Title 6,
Ch. 9-A, L. 1969.

Jurisdiction

State, municipal, school district, water
and sewer, the Maine Turnpike authority
and employees of the Maine University
system.

Board

Consists of three part-time members. The
chairman is neutral, one member represents
labor, the other represents management.
There are alternates for each position.

Walter Corey, chairman
Robert Curley, employer representative
Michael Schoonjans, employee representative

Key Staff

Executive Director, Parker Denaco
2 attorney/examiners
1 dispute resolution specialist
2 stenographers

Principal Responsibilities

o determines bargaining units
o accepts filings for units
o conducts representation and decertification elections
o hears and adjudicates improper labor-
management practices
o maintains lists of mediators, factfinders
and arbitrators

Decisions

Decisions are available on a case by case
basis from the Main Labor Relations Board
for a minimal reproduction fee. Decisions
are published by the Maine School Management Association.

Budget

FY 1978 budget is $159,935.

Massachusetts Labor Relations Commission

Office
100 Cambridge Street
Boston, Massachusetts   02202
(617) 727-3509

Statutory Authority
Massachusetts General Laws, Ch. 23,
Sec. 9-0, originally created the MLRC
to administer the private sector collective bargaining statute. Its authority
has since been expanded to include the
public sector.

Jurisdiction
Private, State, county and municipal
employees including firefighters, police
and teachers

Commission
Consists of three full-time **commissioners**
appointed for five-year terms.

James Cooper, chairman
Joan Dolan
Gary Wooters

Key Staff
Executive Secretary, Ann Da Dalt
7 staff attorneys
2 examiners

Principal Responsibilities
o determines bargaining units
o conducts elections
o hears and adjudicates improper labor-
   management practices

Decisions
Decisions are published in the *Massachusetts
Labor Relations Reporter* and the *Massachusetts
Labor Cases* printed by Joseph W. Ambash,
P.O. Box 48, Boston, Massachusetts   02101.
Cost for the Reporter is $70 per year; for
Labor Cases, $105.

Budget
FY 1978 budget is $490,000.

Michigan Employment Relations Commission

Main Office

State of Michigan
Plaza Building
14th floor
1200 Sixth Avenue
Detroit, Michigan   48226
(313) 256-3540

Regional Offices

Leonard Plaza Building
309 N. Washington
Lansing, Michigan   48909
(517) 373-3580

350 Ottawa Avenue, N.W.
Third floor
Grand Rapids, Michigan   49503
(616) 459-3531

Statutory Authority

Michigan Compiled Laws of 1948, Secs.
423.201 - 423.216; L. 1947

Jurisdiction

Private, municipal, county and
school district employees.

Commission

Consists of three part-time bipartisan
Commissioners appointed for three-year
terms.

Charles M. Rehmus, chairman
William M. Ellmann
Morris Milmet

Key Staff

Director, Robert Pisarski
    4 administrative law judges
   17 mediators
    3 election officers
    4 court reporters
    2 law clerks
   12 clericals

Principal Responsibilities

o   determines bargaining units
o   conducts elections
o   hears and adjudicates improper labor-
       management practices
o   appoints mediators, factfinders and
       arbitrators

Decisions

MERC decisions and orders are published
by the Opinions Press, P.O. Box 1095,
Big Rapids, Michigan   49307.

Budget

FY 1978 budget is $1,700,000.

Minnesota Public Employment Relations Board

Office

Space Center Building
Room 598
444 Lafayette Road
St. Paul, Minnesota 55101
(612) 296-8947

Statutory Authority

Public Employment Labor Relations
Act of 1971, as amended - Minn. Stat.
179.61 - 179.76.

Jurisdiction

State, county, municipal and school
district employees

Board

Consists of five part-time members appointed
for a term of four years. Two members are
representative of public employees, two are
representative of public employers, and one
is representative of the public at large.

George Seltzer, chairman
Peter Obermeyer, vice chairman
Don L. Bye
Lorraine T. Clark
Joseph E. Flynn

Key Staff

Executive Secretary, Claudia M. Hennen

Principal Responsibilities

o hears and decides issues relating to the
   meaning of the terms "supervisory
   employee", "confidential employee",
   "essential employee" and "professional
   "employee".
o hears and decides appeals from determinations of the Director of the Bureau
   of Mediation Services relating to the
   appropriateness of a unit
o hears and decides on the record from
   determinations of the Director of the
   Bureau of Mediation Services relating
   to a fair share fee challenge.
o maintains roster of qualified arbitrators
o provides for an independent review of public
   employee grievances.

Decisions

Decisions of the Board are printed and distri-
buted by the Documents Section of the Minnesota
Department of Administration, Room 140
Centennial Building, St. Paul, Minnesota 55155.
The cost for a yearly subscription is $20.80.

Budget

FY 1978 budget is $43,269.

Minnesota Bureau of Mediation Services

Office

Bureau of Mediation Services
Veterans Service Building
20 West 12th Street
St Paul, Minnesota 55155
(612) 296-2525

Statutory Authority

Minnesota Code Sec. 179-179.77.

Jurisdiction

Private, State, county, municipal and school
district employees

Key Staff

Director, Ernest Jones
   14 mediators
    4 court reporters
    1 office manager
    5 clericals

Principal Responsibilities

o determines bargaining units
o conducts elections
o provides mediation services

Decisions

Available upon request at cost

Budget

FY 1978 budget is $675,000.

Missouri State Board of Mediation

Office
207 Adams Street
Jefferson City, Missouri 65101
(314) 751-3614

Statutory Authority
Ch. 295; L. 1948

Jurisdiction
State and municipal employees

Board
Consists of five members appointed for
three-year terms. The Chairman is full-
time. Two members represent labor, two
represent employers, the fifth represents
the public.

> Michael Horn, chairman
> Stanley W. Cox
> Richard Mantia
> Robert Missey
> Harry R. Scott

Key Staff
Executive Secretary, Karen Conover

Principal Responsibilities
o determines bargaining units
o conducts elections
o requests assistance, services and data
   to enable Board to properly carry out
   its functions
o maintains lists of mediators, factfinders
   and arbitrators
o holds hearings and makes inquiries

Decisions
Decisions are available at 20 cents
per page.

Budget
FY 1978 budget is $35,000.

Montana Board of Personnel Appeals

Office
1417 Helena Avenue
Helena, Montana 59601
(406) 449-2890

Statutory Authority
Collective Bargaining for Public Employees,
R.C.M. Title 59, Ch. 16, Secs. 1601-1616,
as amended L. 1975.

Jurisdiction
State and local employees, including teachers
and college-level instructors

Board
Consists of five part-time members appointed
for six-year terms. Two represent management, two represent employees or employee
organizations and one is neutral.

> Brent Cromley, chairman
> George Heliker
> John Quinn
> Joseph Reber
> (one vacancy)

Key Staff
Administrator, Robert R. Jensen
Staff Attorney, Jerry Painter
   4 labor mediators and/or hearing examiners
   1 investigator
   1 grievance & appeals officer

Principal Responsibilities
o resolves disputes concerning representation
o determines bargaining units
o maintains panels of qualified arbitrators and
   factfinders
o hears classification appeals
o hears employee grievances
o hears and adjudicates improper labor-
   management charges.

Decisions
Decisions are available upon request at 10¢
per page.

Budget
FY 1978 budget is $251,615.

Nebraska Court of Industrial Relations

Office
301 Centennial Mall South
P.O. Box 94864
Lincoln, Nebraska 68509
(402) 471-2934

Statutory Authority
R.S. Nebraska, Ch. 48; L. 194

Jurisdiction
State and municipal employees
including those of public utilities

Court
Consists of five part-time members
appointed for six-year terms.

Benjamin Wall, Presiding Judge
Richard L. DeBacker
Dean G. Kratz
J. Patrick Green
Donald F. McGinley

Key Staff
Clerk of Court, Janet Stewart Arnold
2 assistants

Principal Responsibilities
o determines bargaining units
o conducts representation elections
o hears and adjudicates improper labor-
 management practices
o conducts studies concerning public sector
 collective bargaining
o maintains lists of mediators and arbitrators

Decisions
Decisions are published in the *NCIR Reporter,*
Initial fee for subscription is $145 plus tax.
Advanced sheets containing recent decisions
are published bi-monthly and cost $35 per year
plus tax.

Budget
FY 1978 budget is $112,965.

Nevada Local Government Employee Management Relations Board

Office
Bradley Building, Suite 201
2501 East Sahara Avenue
Las Vagas, Nevada 89158
(702) 385-0291

Statutory Authority
Local Government Employee-Management
Relations Act, NRS, Sec. 288.010 et. seg (1969).

Jurisdiction
Local employees including firefighters,
police and teachers

Board
Consists of three part-time members appointed for four-year terms. Not more than two
may be members of the same political party.

Dorothy Eisenberg, chairman
John T. Gojack, vice chairman
(one vacancy)

Key Staff
Commissioner, Sally S. Davis
1 clerical

Principal Responsibilities
o determines mandatory subjects of negotiations
o hears appeals in recognition disputes
o hears appeals from bargaining unit determi-
 inations
o hears and adjudicates improper labor-
 management practices

Decisions
All decisions of the Board are available, free of
charge, to those requesting that their names be
placed on the agency's mailing list.

Budget
FY 1978 budget is $64,919.

New Hampshire Public Employee Labor Relations Board

Office
1 Pillsbury Street *
Concord, New Hampshire   03301
(603) 271-3172

Statutory Authority
R.S.H. Ch. 273-A, 1975

Jurisdiction
State and municipal employees including
those of the State university system

Board
Consists of five part-time members
appointed for six-year terms. Two are
employee representatives, two are
management representatives and one,
the chairman, represents the public

Edward Hazeltine, chairman
Edward Allman, management representative
James Anderson, employee representative
Richard Cummings, management representative
Joseph Moriarty, employee representative

Key Staff
Clerk, Evelyn C. Lebrun

Principal Responsibilities
o   determines bargaining units
o   conducts elections
o   maintains a list of neutrals
o   conducts studies necessary to carry out
       functions
o   hears and adjudicates improper labor-
       management practices

Decisions
Decisions are $30 per year for those on the
mailing list or 20 cents per copy.

Budget
The estimated budget for FY 1978 is $48,000.

———————————————

*The Board is scheduled to move to a new
location, but at the time we went to print,
the new location had not been decided.

New Jersey Public Employment Relations Commission

Main Office
429 East State Street
Trenton, New Jersey   08625
(609) 292-6780

Regional Office
80 Mulberry Street
Newark, New Jersey
(201) 648-3425

Statutory Authority
New Jersey Employer-Employee Relations
Act, N.J.S.A. Title 34, Ch. 13-A; L. 1941,
Ch. 100, as amended L. 1974.

Jurisdiction
State, county, municipal and school district
employees

Commission
Consists of seven members appointed for
three-year terms. Of these, three are
public including the Chairman who is the
only full-time member. Of the remaining,
two are representative of public employee
organizations and two are representative
of public employers.

> Jeffrey B. Tener, chairman
> Francis A. Forst
> Bernard M. Hartnett, Jr.
> Federick L. Hipp
> Mark W. Hurwitz
> Charles H. Parcells
> (one vacancy)

Key Staff
General Counsel, Sidney H. Lehmann
Director of Conciliation & Arbitration,
   James W. Mastriani
Director of Unfair Practices & Represent-
ation, Carl Kurtzman
Special Assistant to the Chairman,

   Stephen B. Hunter
   5 mediators
   3 hearing examiners
   12 attorneys
   14 clericals

Principal Responsibilities
o maintains lists of mediators, factfinders and
      arbitrators
o administers interest arbitration statute
      covering firefighters and policemen
o renders determinations regarding scope of
      negotiations
o determines bargaining units
o conducts elections
o works with both professional neutrals and
      the parties in training and educational
      activities
o hears and adjudicates improper labor-
      management practices
o represents Commission in Appellate Division
      and Supreme Court when appeals are
      taken from Commission decisions.

Decisions
Decisions of the Commission are published in the
New Jersey Public Employee Reporter. These
decisions are published by Labor Relations
Press, P.O. Box 579, Ft. Washington, Pa.
19034 at an annual cost of $200.

Budget
FY 1978 budget is $1,139,498.

New York Public Employment Relations Board

Main Office
50 Wolfe Road
Albany, New York 06520
(518) 457-6483

Regional Offices
State Office Building
125 Main Street
Buffalo, New York 14203
Contact: Eric Lawson
Regional Representative
(716) 842-2357

342 Madison Avenue
New York, N. Y. 10017
Contact: Leon Applewhaite
Regional Representative
(212) 661-6970

Statutory Authority
New York Public Employee Fair Employment Act
(Taylor Law), Civil Services Law, Secs. 200-
214, L. 1967, Ch. 392 as amended

Jurisdiction
State, county, municipal, school district,
college, university, special district, public
authority, commission and public benefit
corporation employees. New York City
employees bargain under the NYC Collective
Bargaining Law administered by the NYC
Office of Collective Bargaining.

Board
Consists of three members appointed for six-year
terms. Chairman is full time, the others part
time. Not more than two may belong to the
same political party.

> vacant, chairman
> Joseph P. Crowley
> Ida Klaus

Key Staff
Deputy Chairman, Jerome Lufkowitz
Executive Director, Ralph D. Vatalaro
Director of Conciliation, Harold Newman
Director of Public Employment Practices and
  Representation, Harvey Mylow
General Counsel, Martin Barr
Director of Research, Thomas Joiner
Director of Public Information, Muriel Gibbons

2 administrative assistants	6 hearing officers
4 attorneys	9 mediators
19 clericals	4 researchers

Principal Responsibilities
o determines bargaining units
o conducts representation elections
o hears and adjudicates improper labor-
     management practices
o makes studies and acts as an information
     clearing house
o mediates disputes
o maintains panels of qualified factfinders
     and arbitrators

Decisions
*Official Decisions, Opinions and Related Mat-
ters, Public Employment Relations Board of
the State of New York,* printed by Lenz &
Riecker, Inc., 75 Varick Street, New York,
New York 10013. The cost is: Volumes 1-6,
$50; Volume 7, $65; Volume 8-10, $75.

Budget
FY 1978 budget is $1,800,000

Note
Mini-PERB's have been established in Delaware
County, Hempstead, Nassau County, North
Castle, Town of North Hempstead, Onandaga
County, Oyster Bay, Town of Rye, Suffolk
County, Syracuse City, Syracuse School
District, Tompkins County and Westchester
County.

New York City Office of Collective Bargaining

Office
250 Broadway
New York, New York 10007
(212) 566-3128

Statutory Authority
New York City Collective Bargaining Law,
NYC Code, Ch. 54, Sec. 1173-1.0; et. seq.

Jurisdiction
Municipal employees including police,
firefighters and teachers

Board
Consists of seven members serving three-year
terms. Two represent the City, two represent labor and three are impartial. The
Chairman is full-time.

Impartial Members:
    Arvid Anderson, chairman
    Walter L. Eisenberg
    Eric J. Schmertz

City of New York Members:
    Virgil B. Day
    Edward Silver

Labor Members:
    Edward F. Gray
    Harry Van Arsdale, Jr.

Key Staff
Deputy Chairman of Disputes, Thomas M. Laura
Deputy Chairman & General Counsel,
    Malcolm D. MacDonald
Executive Secretary & Director of
    Representation, John P. McNamara
        2 hearing officers
        2 researchers
        8 clericals

Principal Responsibilities
o determines questions regarding scope of
  bargaining
o determines arbitrability of grievances
o issues final and binding decisions of
  impasse panel report and recommendations
o determines bargaining units
o makes studies and acts as information
  clearing house
o requests assistance, services and data
  that will enable the Board to properly
  carry out its functions
o holds hearings and makes such inquiries as
  necessary to carry out its functions
o administers oaths and affirmations, examines
  witnesses and documents, takes testimony
  and receives evidence, compells the
  attendance of witnesses and the production of documents by the issuance of
  subpoenas
o conducts elections
o maintins lists of mediators, arbitrators and
  factfinders

Decisions
Decisions of the Boards are published by the
OCB and are also available in Summary Digest
Forms.

Budget
FY 1978 budget is $630,000.

Oklahoma Public Employee Relations Board

Office
556 W Street
First National Center
Oklahoma City, Oklahoma   73102
(405) 235-3331

Statutory Authority
11 O.S., Ch. 13F; L. 1971, Ch. 14;
amended L. 1972

Jurisdiction
Municipal employees including firefighters, police and school employees *

Board
Consists of three part-time members
appointed for five-year terms.

> Fred Boston, chairman
> Myrna Burman
> Terry West

Key Staff
None

Principal Responsibilities
o   determines bargaining units
o   conducts elections
o   conducts hearings
o   hears and adjudicates improper labor-
    management practices

Decisions
None

Budget
The Board has not been funded since the 1975
Supreme Court decision.

---

*The Oklahoma Supreme Court has declared
unconstitutional those sections of the statute
which extend coverage to municipal employees.

Oregon Public Employee Relations Board

Office

402 Capitol Tower Building
Salem, Oregon 97310
(503) 378-3807

Statutory Authority

Merit System Act, ORS Ch. 240

Jurisdiction

Private, State, counties, municipalities, community colleges, school districts, special districts and public and quasi-public corporations

Board

Consists of three full-time members appointed for four-year terms. The chairman is also the agency administrator

Melvin H. Cleveland, chairman
Steve Goldschmidt
Paul P. Tinning

Key Staff

State Conciliator, Kenneth E. Brown
Administrator of Representation - Improper Practices Division, Roy E. Edwards
Administrator of Merit System Division, Alfred H. Blogg
  5 hearing examiners
  7 mediators
 12 clericals
  1 other

Principal Responsibilities

o determines bargaining units
o maintains lists of qualified factfinders and arbitrators
o rules on petitions for review of classified state employees alleging actions affecting them were arbitrary or contrary to law or rules
o hears and rules on appeals of disciplined classified state employees
o mediates disputes
o hears and adjudicates improper labor-management practices
o conducts elections

Decisions

Decisions of the Board are published in the *Public Employer Collective Bargaining Reporter*, P.O. Box 1632, Lake Oswego, Oregon 97034. Cost for a subscription is $85 per year.

Budget

FY 1978 budget is $811,049.

Pennsylvania Labor Relations Board

Main Office

1617 Labor and Industry Building
Seventh & Forster Streets
Harrisburg, PA 17120
(717) 787-1091
(717) 787-4895

Regional Offices

801-8th and Arch Streets
Fifth Floor
Philadelphia, PA 19107
(215) 238-6781

State Office Building
Foom 1513
300 Liberty Avenue
Pittsburgh, PA 15122
(412) 565-5318

Statutory Authority

The Pennsylvania Labor Relations Act of
1937, P.L. 1168, No. 290 as amended, created
the Pennsylvania Labor Relations Board. In
1968, the Boards authority was extended to
include firemen and police, and in 1970, other
public employees.

Jurisdiction

Private, State, county, municipal,
school district, and special authority
employees

Board

Consists of three members appointed for six-
year terms. All members are part-time.

Kenneth F. Kahn, chairman
James H. Jones
Joseph J. Licastro

Key Staff

Executive Director, James F. Wildeman
Secretary, Earl G. Light
Chief Counsel, James L. Crawford
Philadelphia Regional Director,
    Irving W. Backman
Pittsburgh Regional Director,
    Isadore E. Binstock
Elections Coordinator, John E. Riley, Jr.
Public Information Officer, Robert E. Trump
    17 hearing officers   3 staff attorneys
    21 clericals

Principal Responsibilities

o resolves representation disputes
o determines bargaining units
o makes studies and analyzes information
      relating to public employment
o hears and adjudicates improper labor-
      management practices

Decisions

Decisions are published in the *Pennsylvania
Public Employe Reporter* by the Labor
Relations Press, P.O. Box 579, Fort
Washington, Pennsylvania 19034.
Subscription is $275 per year.

Budget

FY 1978 budget is approximately $1,100,000.

Phoenix Arizona Public Employment Relations Board

Office
17 South 2nd Avenue
Room 101
Phoenix, Arizona 85003
(602) 262-4081

Statutory Authority
Ordinance No. G. 1532 as codified in
Article XVII, Sec. 2-209 et. seq.

Jurisdiction
Municipal employees including firefighters, police and teachers

Board
Consists of three part-time members
appointed for three-year terms.

    Donald Daughton, chairman
    Karl Lind
    Raymond Wells

Key Staff
Executive Director, Harroliece Brown
    1 secretary

Principal Responsibilities
o determines bargaining units
o conducts elections
o hears and ajudicates improper labor-
   management practices

Decisions
None

Budget
FY 1978 budget is $80,000.

Prince Georges County Maryland Public Employee Relations Panel

Office
c/o American Arbitration Association
1730 Rhode Island Avenue, N.W.
Washington, D.C. 20036
(202) 296-8510

Statutory Authority
Prince George's County Code of
Ordinances and Resolutions, Ch. 13-A, 1973.

Jurisdiction
County employees including firefighters
and police

Board
Consists of nine part-time members composed of three panels of three members
each. There is no set term of office.

Representation panel:
    Howard Gamser, chairman
    Mollie Bowers
    Jacob Seidenberg

Impasse Panel:
    Walter Maggiolo, chairman
    Gilbert Seldin
    James Harkless

Unfair Practices Panel:
    Hugh Jascourt, chairman
    Howard Kleeb
    Lawrence Seibel

Key Staff
Executive Secretary, Thomas Colosi
Administrative Assistant, Linda Flick

Principal Responsibilities
o determines bargaining units
o hears and adjudicates improper labor-
   management practices.
o determines negotiability
o provides mediators and factfinders

Decisions
Decisions are not published but may be
requested.

Budget
FY 1978 budget is $61,320.

Rhode Island Labor Relations Board

Office
235 Promenade Street
Room 132
Providence, Rhode Island 02908
(401) 277-2752

Statutory Authority
R.I. General Laws, Title 28, Ch. 7;
L. 1956

Jurisdiction
Private, State and municipal employees including police, firefighters and teachers

Board
Consists of three part-time members appointed for six-year terms. One is a labor representative, one an industry representative, the third represents the general public

Samuel J. Azzinaro, chairman
Francis B. Brennan, represents industry
Raymond Petrarca, represents the public

Key Staff
Administrator, John H. Winter
General Counsel, Vincent F. Kane
Conciliator & Factfinder, Earl E. Bushman
Chief Field Investigator, Joseph Miragliuolo

2 clerical

Principal Responsibilities
o determines bargaining units
o conducts elections
o hears and adjudicates improper labor-management practices
o provides conciliation and factfinding
o administers oaths and affirmations, examines witnesses and documents, takes testimony and receives evidence.

Decisions
Decisions available to those on the mailing list

Budget
FY 1978 budget is $140,469.

Vermont Labor Relations Board

Office
12 Park Place
Brattleboro, Vermont 05301
(802) 254-2353

Statutory Authority
V.S.A. Title 3, Ch. 27; L. 1969, No. 113;
as last amended by L. 1976.

Jurisdiction
Private, State, state colleges and municipal employees

Board
Consists of three part-time members appointed for six-year terms. Not more than two may be members of the same political party.

John Burgess, chairman
Robert Brown
William Kensley

Key Staff
Secretary, Retha E. Wood

Principal Responsibilities
o determines bargaining units
o conducts elections
o appoints mediators
o prescribes a uniform procedure for the resolution of employee grievances submitted through the collective bargaining machinery (applies to state employees only)
o hears and adjudicates improper labor-management practices

Decisions
Annual report along with copies of decisions are filed with the Governor on an annual basis and becomes a part of the public records.

Budget
FY 1978 budget is $55,000.

Washington Public Employment Relations Commission

Office

603 Evergreen Plaza
Olympia, Washington, 98504
(206) 753-3444

Statutory Authority

R.C.W. Ch. 41.58; 1975, Ch. 296
as amended L. 1975, 2nd. Ex.s, Ch. 5.

Jurisdiction

Private, State, county, municipal, Port
District, State Ferry System and community
college employees are covered.

Board

Consists of three part-time members
appointed to five-year terms.

Mary Ellen Krug, chairman
Michael Beck
Paul Roberts

Key Staff

Executive Director, Marvin Schurke
Administrative Assistant, Beverly Westcott
    8 mediators
    2 secretaries

Principal Responsibilities

o   determines bargaining units
o   conducts elections
o   hears and adjudicates improper labor-
        management practices
o   mediates disputes

Decisions

Decisions are published in the Public
Employment Relations Reporter. The
decisions are published by the Book
Publishing Company, 2518 Western Avenue,
Seattle, Washington 98121. The cost is
$125 plus tax for original volume and six
months supplements.

Budget

1977-1979 budget is $840,000.

Wisconsin Employment Relations Commission

Main Office

30 West Mifflin Street
Room 910
Madison, Wisconsin 53703
(608) 266-1381

Regional Office

Milwaukee State Office Building
819 North Sixth Street, Room 560
Milwaukee, Wisconsin 53203
Contact: Marshall Gratz,
Staff Attorney
(414) 224-4597

Statutory Authority

The Wisconsin Employment Peace Act of 1939
created the Wisconsin Public Employment Relations Commission to administer the Private Sector Collective Bargaining Act. Its authority
was expanded to municipal employees in 1959,
and in 1966 to State employees.

Jurisdiction

Private, state and local employees, including
firefighters, police and teachers

Commission

Consists of three full-time commissioners
appointed for six-year terms.

Morris Slavney, chairman
Charles D. Hoornstra
Herman Torosian

Key Staff

General Counsel, George R. Fleischli
Staff Director, Byron Yaffe
    14 mediators (mediators perform the functions
        of hearing officers)
    8 clericals
    1 business manager
    4 court reporters
    1 elections supervisor

Principal Responsibilities

o determines bargaining units
o conducts representation elections
o conducts referenda for fair share and union
  agreements
o hears and adjudicates improper labor-
  management practices
o mediates and arbitrates disputes
o maintains panels of factfinders and
  arbitrators.

Decisions

Decisions are not in bound volumes but are
available on an individual basis from the
Commission. Digests of Decisions are available from the Commission.

Budget

FY 1978 budget is $897,600.

Appendix A

Agencies Other Than PERBs Having
Some Administrative Responsibility for
State Collective Bargaining Statutes

Alaska

State Personnel Board
Chairman, C. R. Hafling
Pouch C
Juneau, Alaska 99801
(907) 586-6500

Department of Labor
Commissioner, Henry Benson
P.O. Box 1149
Juneau, Alaska 99801
(907) 586-6500

California

Conciliation Service
Supervisor, Edward W. Allen
State Building
455 Golden Gate Avenue
San Francisco, California 94101
(415) 557-2426

Connecticut

Board of Mediation and Arbitration
Chairman, Dr. A. D. Joseph Emerzian
200 Folly Brook Boulevard
Hartford, Connecticut 06115
(203) 566-4394

Maryland

State Board of Education
Superintendent, James H. Sensenbough
P.O. Box 8717
Baltimore-Washington International Airport
Baltimore, Maryland 21240
(301) 796-8300

Delaware

State Department of Labor & Industrial Relations
Division of Industrial Affairs
Director, Leroy O'Neil
618 North Union Street
Wilmington, Delaware 19805
(302) 571-2877

State Department of Public Instruction
Superintendent, Kenneth C. Madden
Towsend Buklding
Dover, Delaware 19901
(302) 678-4601

Idaho

Department of Labor and Industry
Director, Robert Kinghorn
State House, room 400
317 Main Street
Boise, Idaho 83720
(208) 384-2327

Department of Education
Superintendent of Public Instruction,
  Roy Truby
Len B. Jordan Office Building
Boise, Idaho 83720
(208) 382-3300

Massachusetts

Board of Conciliation and Arbitration
Chairman, Helaine Knickerbocker
100 Cambridge Street
Boston, Massachusetts 02202
(617) 727-3470

Montana

Department of Labor and Industry
Labor Standards Division/Standards Bureau
Bureau Chief, Dick Kane
Box 202
Capitol Station
Helena, Montana 59601
(416) 449-3472

North Dakota

Education Factfinding Commission
Chairman, James Slocum
Members: Edward K. Lander,
    Calvin Lundberg
502 East Central
Bismark, North Dakota 58501
(701) 255-3129

New Mexico

State Personnel Board
130 South Capital
Santa Fe, New Mexico 87501

South Dakota

Department of Labor & Management Relations
Commissioner, William Miller
Foss Office Building, room 425
Pierre, South Dakota 57501
(605) 224-3681

Virgin Islands

Department of Labor
Commissioner, Richard Upton
P.O. Box 708
Christianated, St. Croix, Virgin Islands 00820

Appendix B

California

Los Angeles City Public Employee Relations
    Board
Room 1490, City Hall East
200 North Maine
Los Angeles, California 90012
Chairman, Leo Kotin

Los Angeles County Employee Relations
    Commission
374 Hall of Administration
500 West Temple Street
Los Angeles, California 90012
Chairman, David Ziskind

San Diego County Employee Relations Panel
1600 Pacific Highway
San Diego, California 92101
Chairman, Philip Tamoush

Torence Employee Relations Committee
3031 Torence Boulevard
Torence, California 90503
Chairman, William Applegate

Napa County Public Employee Relations Panel
c/o Napa County Personnel Department
1119 First Street
Napa County, California 94558
Chairman, vacant

San Bernardino County Employee Relations Panel
175 West Fifth Street
County Civic Building
San Bernardino, California 92415
Chairman, Bailey Dodson

New York

Delaware County PERB
Court House
Delhi, New York 13753
Chairman, Charles Mitchell

Syracuse School District Employment Relations
    Council
247 Sherbourne Road
Syracuse, New York 13224
Chairman, Paul Seifried

Tomkins County PERB
603 Cayuga Heights Road
Ithaca, New York 14850
Chairman, Harry C. Cornwall

Hempstead PERB
Town Hall
Hempstead, New York 11550
Chairman, Joel S. Kaplan

Nassau County PERB
1550 Franklin Avenue
Mineola, New York 11501
Chairman, John F. Coffey

Northcastle PERB
15 Bedford Road
Armonk, New York
Chairman, Schardlow E. Crawford

Towne of North Hempstead PERB
220 Plandone Road
Manhasset, New York 11030
Chairman, Donald J. Quinn

Onandago County PERB
247 Sherbourne Road
Syracuse, New York 13224
Chairman, Paul Seifried

Oyster Bay PERB
Town Hall Annex
65 Broadway
Hicksville, New York 11801
Chairman, Joseph P. Dole

Town of Rye PERB
10 Pearl Street
Portchester, New York 10573
Chairman, Dennis McKay

Suffolk County PERB
Veterans Memorial Highway
Hauppauge, New York 11787
Chairman, John F. Rogers

Syracuse City PERB
c/o Lemoyne College
Syracuse, New York 13210
Chairman, Reverend S. Oley Cutler

West Chester County PERB
County Office Building
Room 812
White Plains, New York 10601
Chairman, Robert L. Elis

UNION SECURITY PROVISIONS BY GOVERNMENT FUNCTION
(In State and local government agreements, July 1, 1975)

Government function	All agreements		Referring to union security									
			Total		Union shop		Modified union shop		Agency shop		Modified agency shop	
	Agreements	Workers	Agreements	Workers	Agreements	Workers	Agreements	Workers	Agreements	Workers	Agreements	Workers
All agreements	624	788,233	221	173,158	51	36,981	22	26,302	78	44,225	5	1,100
Agricultural services	2	175	—	—	—	—	—	—	—	—	—	—
Animal welfare services	1	50	1	50	—	—	—	—	1	50	—	—
Central administration	22	41,900	9	5,300	1	150	—	—	6	2,100	—	—
Central services	15	39,575	5	375	—	—	—	—	3	275	—	—
Correctional institutions	11	2,400	4	525	1	300	—	—	—	—	—	—
Courts	25	11,000	11	5,900	2	250	—	—	6	5,000	—	—
Fire protection	47	34,300	10	6,800	3	1,000	2	1,400	3	1,350	—	—
Health/medical	80	65,850	35	12,350	3	175	10	2,625	10	2,175	—	—
Law enforcement	91	54,025	21	10,175	1	200	—	—	15	7,575	—	—
Libraries	15	2,450	9	1,500	1	400	—	—	5	800	2	250
Parks and recreation	7	2,300	2	200	—	—	—	—	1	150	—	—
Public transportation	42	74,283	26	32,533	20	27,656	6	4,877	—	—	—	—
Public utilities	8	5,300	5	2,600	2	250	—	—	2	2,200	—	—
Public works	62	21,850	25	6,625	7	1,550	—	—	13	3,300	1	400
Regulatory agencies	4	6,650	1	3,200	—	—	—	—	—	—	—	—
Sanitation services	5	2,975	—	—	—	—	—	—	—	—	—	—
Social welfare	31	98,400	10	14,100	1	75	1	650	2	600	—	—
Urban development	14	8,800	6	1,075	3	325	1	600	1	50	—	—
All functions–except for protective services	6	15,650	1	700	1	700	—	—	—	—	—	—
All functions—Exceptions other than or in Addition to protective Services	78	178,400	19	44,350	2	2,100	1	15,750	5	5,900	2	450
All functions—No exceptions	58	121,900	21	24,800	3	1,850	1	400	5	12,700	—	—

Government function	Referring to union security (continued)								Sole bargaining	
	Maintenance of membership		Union shop and agency shop		Agency shop and maintenance of membership		Other [1]			
	Agreements	Workers	Agreements	Workers	Agreements	Workers	Agreements	Workers	Agreements	Workers
All agreements	44	53,625	10	7,725	8	1,400	3	1,800	403	615,075
Agricultural services	—	—	—	—	—	—	—	—	2	175
Central administration	1	50	1	3,000	—	—	—	—	13	36,600
Central services	2	100	—	—	—	—	—	—	10	39,200
Correctional institutions	3	225	—	—	—	—	—	—	7	1,875
Courts	2	575	—	—	1	75	—	—	14	5,100
Fire protection	1	2,800	—	—	1	250	—	—	37	27,500
Health/medical	8	5,750	4	1,625	—	—	—	—	45	53,500
Law enforcement	4	2,200	1	200	—	—	—	—	70	43,850
Libraries	1	50	—	—	—	—	—	—	6	950
Parks and recreation	—	—	1	50	—	—	—	—	5	2,100
Public transportation	—	—	—	—	—	—	—	—	16	41,750
Public utilities	1	150	—	—	—	—	—	—	3	2,700
Public works	2	975	1	350	—	—	1	50	37	15,225
Regulatory agencies	1	3,200	—	—	—	—	—	—	3	3,450
Sanitation services	—	—	—	—	—	—	—	—	5	2,975
Social welfare	3	10,200	1	2,400	2	175	—	—	21	84,300
Urban development	—	—	—	—	1	100	—	—	8	7,725
All functions—except for protective services	—	—	—	—	—	—	—	—	5	14,950
All functions—Exceptions other than or in Addition to protective services	8	19,700	—	—	1	450	—	—	59	134,050
All functions—No exceptions	7	7,650	1	100	2	350	2	1,750	37	97,100

[1] Includes 1 agreement with a combination of modified union shop and maintenance of membership; 1 with a combination of agency and modified agency shop, and 1 with a combination of modified agency shop and maintenance of membership.

SOURCE: Characteristics of Agreements in State and Local Governments BLS

CHECKOFF PROVISIONS BY GOVERNMENT FUNCTION
(In State and local government agreements, July 1, 1975)

Government function	All agreements		Type of checkoff — Total		Dues checkoff		Dues and assessments	
	Agreements	Workers	Agreements	Workers	Agreements	Workers	Agreements	Workers
All agreements	624	788,233	505	680,227	365	555,552	35	43,125
Agricultural services	2	175	2	175	2	175	—	—
Animal welfare services	1	50	1	50	—	—	—	—
Central administration	22	41,900	19	39,000	17	36,000	1	700
Central services	15	39,575	14	38,325	11	37,975	—	—
Correctional institutions	11	2,400	11	2,400	9	2,025	—	—
Courts	25	11,000	22	10,825	10	8,750	5	1,225
Fire protection	47	34,300	33	24,500	20	18,000	4	1,550
Health/medical	80	65,850	65	55,925	50	47,775	5	5,000
Law enforcement	91	54,025	61	36,525	48	27,325	3	650
Libraries	15	2,450	14	2,375	12	2,200	1	100
Parks and recreation	7	2,300	5	1,100	3	300	—	—
Public transportation	42	74,283	33	36,277	12	4,052	7	11,350
Public utilities	8	5,300	7	5,150	4	2,700	—	—
Public works	62	21,850	56	21,075	38	17,300	4	750
Regulatory agencies	4	6,650	4	6,650	3	3,450	—	—
Sanitation services	5	2,975	4	2,900	4	2,900	—	—
Social welfare	31	98,400	28	97,150	24	84,200	—	—
Urban development	14	8,800	11	8,525	9	7,525	—	—
All functions—except for protective services	6	15,650	4	9,950	3	8,950	—	—
All functions—Exceptions other than or in addition to protective services	78	178,400	68	168,900	53	141,450	5	21,800
All functions—No exceptions	58	121,900	43	112,450	33	102,500	—	—

Government function	Type of checkoff (*Continued*) — Dues and initiation fees		Dues, assessments, and initiation fees		Other [1]		No reference to checkoff	
	Agreements	Workers	Agreements	Workers	Agreements	Workers	Agreements	Workers
All agreements	80	42,200	21	24,325	4	15,025	119	108,006
Animal welfare services	1	50	—	—	—	—	—	—
Central administration	1	2,300	—	—	—	—	3	2,900
Central services	3	350	—	—	—	—	1	1,250
Correctional institutions	1	300	1	75	—	—	—	—
Courts	7	850	—	—	—	—	3	175
Fire protection	6	3,300	3	1,650	—	—	14	9,800
Health/medical	9	2,850	1	300	—	—	15	9,925
Law enforcement	6	1,800	4	6,750	—	—	30	17,500
Libraries	1	75	—	—	—	—	1	75
Parks and recreation	2	800	—	—	—	—	2	1,200
Public transportation	6	4,450	5	2,400	3	14,025	9	38,006
Public utilities	3	2,450	—	—	—	—	1	150
Public works	13	2,575	1	450	—	—	6	775
Regulatory agencies	1	3,200	—	—	—	—	—	—
Sanitation services	—	—	—	—	—	—	1	75
Social welfare	3	2,950	1	10,000	—	—	3	1,250
Urban development	1	600	1	400	—	—	3	275
All functions—except for protective services	—	—	—	—	1	1,000	2	5,700
All functions—Exceptions other than or in addition to effective services	6	3,350	4	2,300	—	—	10	9,500
All functions—No exceptions	10	9,950	—	—	—	—	15	9,450

[1] Includes 2 agreements specifying deductions of dues, assessments, and fines; 1 specifying dues, assessments, initiation fees, and fines; and 1 specifying "authorized deductions."

SOURCE: Characteristics of Agreements in State and Local Governments BLS

GRIEVANCE PROCEDURES BY LEVEL OF GOVERNMENT
(In State and local government agreements, July 1, 1975)

Procedure	All agreements		Level of government							
			State		County		Municipal		Special district	
	Agree-ments	Workers	Agree-ments	Workers	Agree-ments	Workers	Agree-ments	Workers	Agree-ments	Workers
All agreements	624	788,233	69	270,281	281	208,350	234	274,325	40	35,277
Total with reference to grievance procedure ...	538	740,758	68	269,781	236	177,075	197	261,375	37	32,527
Negotiated procedure	444	496,508	50	91,631	202	148,825	161	228,875	31	27,177
Agency procedure	26	30,250	1	450	6	6,100	18	22,650	1	1,050
Negotiated and agency procedure	45	192,675	17	177,700	16	5,925	11	6,650	1	2,400
Reference to procedure, no details given	23	21,325	—	—	12	16,225	7	3,200	4	1,900
No reference to grievance procedure	86	47,475	1	500	45	31,275	37	12,950	3	2,750

GRIEVANCE ARBITRATION PROCEDURES BY LEVEL OF GOVERNMENT
(In State and local government agreements, July 1, 1975)

Procedure	All agreements		Level of government							
			State		County		Municipal		Special district	
	Agree-ments	Workers	Agree-ments	Workers	Agree-ments	Workers	Agree-ments	Workers	Agree-ments	Workers
All agreements	624	788,233	69	270,281	281	208,350	234	274,325	40	35,277
Total with reference to arbitration	444	653,233	58	254,231	193	146,450	158	222,925	35	29,627
Advisory	35	42,800	—	—	27	21,900	7	19,100	1	1,800
Binding	351	516,683	53	244,831	133	66,725	132	177,375	33	27,752
Advisory and binding	33	57,075	—	—	26	51,025	7	6,050	—	—
Reference to arbitration, no details given	24	36,375	5	9,400	6	6,500	12	20,400	1	75
Other[1]	1	300	—	—	1	300	—	—	—	—
No reference to arbitration	180	135,000	11	16,050	88	61,900	76	51,400	5	5,650

[1] Includes 1 agreement in which the County Commissioners agree to binding arbitration only when the arbitrator's award does not exceed ¼ cent on the tax rate for a specific grievance or 1 cent on the tax rate in the aggregate.

WORK STOPPAGE PROVISIONS BY LEVEL OF GOVERNMENT
(In State and local government agreements, July 1, 1975)

Provision	All agreements		Level of government							
			State		County		Municipal		Special district	
	Agree-ments	Workers	Agree-ments	Workers	Agree-ments	Workers	Agree-ments	Workers	Agree-ments	Workers
All agreements	624	788,233	69	270,281	281	208,350	234	274,325	40	35,277
Total with reference to work stoppage or slow-down	425	645,508	59	259,631	168	129,200	166	224,450	32	32,227
Prohibited	230	287,858	22	47,631	87	53,875	104	171,500	17	14,852
Prohibited: union must work to end illegal stoppage	177	341,600	33	208,800	78	75,025	58	49,675	8	8,100
	18	16,050	4	3,200	3	300	4	3,275	7	9,275
Permitted under selected conditions [1]	199	142,725	10	10,650	113	79,150	68	49,875	8	3,050
No reference to work stoppage										

[1] Work stoppages would be permitted, for example, when the employer refuses to take a dispute to binding arbitration, when the employer rejects an arbitrator's award, or when a contract reopens.
SOURCE: Characteristics of Agreements in State and Local Governments BLS

NEGOTIATION IMPASSE PROCEDURES BY LEVEL OF GOVERNMENT
(In State and local government agreements, July 1, 1975)

Procedure	All agreements		Level of government							
			State		County		Municipal		Special district	
	Agree-ments	Workers	Agree-ments	Workers	Agree-ments	Workers	Agree-ments	Workers	Agree-ments	Workers
All agreements	624	788,233	69	270,281	281	208,350	234	274,325	40	35,277
Factfinding [1]	10	143,150	4	140,000	1	350	5	1,800	—	—
With recommendations	9	142,600	4	140,000	1	350	4	2,250	—	—
Without recommendations	1	550	—	—	—	—	1	550	—	—
Mediation [2]	18	8,150	2	1,400	4	2,000	12	4,750	—	—
Arbitration [3]	16	26,475	1	100	5	875	7	18,400	3	7,100

[1] *Factfinding* provisions authorize neutral third parties to investigate, assemble, and report the facts in labor disputes, sometimes with the power to make recommendations for settlement.
[2] *Mediation* provisions permit a third party to help negotiate or settle an impasse through suggestion, advice, or in other ways to stimulate agreement, short of dictating provisions.
[3] *arbitration* provisions permit a neutral third party (person or board) to hold hearings on the impasse and to render a decision. Arbitration can be advisory, binding, or of the final offer variety where the arbitrator chooses between the last proposals of the parties.
NOTE: Nonadditive.

Municipal pension plans: provisions and payments

Police and fire fighters received
higher benefits than other employees
in most of the 27 cities studied;
in several, the gap topped 50 percent

PHILIP M. DOYLE

Age and service requirements, benefit formulas, inflation escalators, and benefit options vary widely among the pension plans of the Nation's 27 largest cities. Monthly retirement benefits under the most generous plan were more than double those that would be paid to the same retiree under the least generous plan.

Comparisons between different occupational groups in the same city show that monthly benefit payments for fire fighters and police generally exceeded those for white- and blue-collar employees. For example, among employees retiring after 25 years of service with pension base earnings[1] of $10,000 per year, benefits for public safety officers were higher than those for other city employees in 38 of 46 comparisons; this advantage typically amounted to between 3 and 15 percent—although differences of more than 50 percent were noted in a few cities (table 1).

These findings are based on comparisons of 32 pension plans covering white- and blue-collar employees in 26 cities of 500,000 inhabitants or more, and 38 plans covering public safety officers in 27 cities.[2] The data are from municipal government wage surveys conducted by the Bureau of Labor Statistics from May 1975 through January 1977.[3] Surveys are conducted annually, although all 27 city governments have not been covered within a single year. The survey program includes all functions of each government studied (except schools and hospitals), but because municipal organization patterns vary, data may not represent the same governmental functions in each city. In some cities, local transit systems, sanitation and sewer services, and gas, electric, and water utilities may be integral parts of the municipal government; in others, separate commissions, special districts, or private industry may perform such functions.

Individual reports from the municipal government wage survey program summarize provisions of city-sponsored pension plans, provide salary data for workers in a variety of public safety and white- and blue-collar occupations, and supply information on selected work practices, pay plans, leave provisions, and health and insurance benefits. For this article, the individual reports were further condensed to highlight the major provisions common to most plans (table 2). A number of the plans contained exclusions, qualifications, or additional provisions which are not reported here.[4]

Coverage and financing

Typically, city governments reported two pension plans, one covering white- and blue-collar employees and the other covering public safety officers.[5] Signifi-

Philip M. Doyle is a labor economist in the Division of Occupational Wage Structures, Bureau of Labor Statistics.

cant exceptions were noted, however, in several cities. In Memphis, a single plan covered all workers identically; in Boston, a single plan provided different monthly benefits to the two basic groups. There were separate plans for fire fighters and separate plans for police in Chicago, Denver, Houston, Kansas City, New Orleans, New York, and St. Louis. Individual plans covered employees in the "labor service" in Chicago, Sewer Board employees in New Orleans, and sanitation workers in New York.

Workers in Cleveland and Columbus were covered by the same statewide plans—one for white- and blue-collar employees and another for public safety workers. In Indianapolis, only public safety employees were eligible for membership in a municipally sponsored pension plan.

Several cities provided different coverage and benefits for employees hired after a particular date. Such differences generally reflect a major revision in the pension plan, the merger of two or more plans, or the institution of a new plan. In this article, such variations by hiring date have been treated as separate plans.

In general, employees were eligible for participation in municipal pension systems immediately upon employment. The plans covering white- and blue-collar employees in Kansas City and Seattle, however, required 6 months of service prior to membership in the plan; in Atlanta, 3 months of service were required for all employees. San Diego's white- and blue-collar employees were eligible for enrollment only during their first 6 months of service. Restrictions on maximum age at the time of enrollment applied to all employees in Jacksonville (age 55 for white- and blue-collar workers, 40 for public safety

officers), to white- and blue-collar employees in St. Louis (60), and to fire fighters in Houston (30). In San Antonio, all employees had to meet age and service requirements before they could enroll in the pension system.

Nearly all of the plans studied were jointly financed by the cities and their employees. Employer and employee contributions varied considerably among the cities and between the two major occupational groups within each city. Percentage contributions based on salaries or payroll were almost universal. A number of the cities also raised pension funds from other sources, such as an annual budget appropriation, parking meter revenues, or proceeds from the sale of unclaimed property.

Normal retirement

Normal retirement provisions specify the minimum combination of age and service with which an employee may retire and receive the full amount of accrued benefits. These provisions also detail the formula for computing benefit amounts and the conditions and duration of benefit payments.

Age and service requirements. Under most of the white- and blue-collar plans studied, normal retirement benefits become available when the workers reach age 55 or 60, provided they have completed specified periods of service, such as 10, 20, or 30 years. Employees covered by 10 of the 32 plans, however, were eligible to retire at any age after meeting minimum service requirements of 20 to 32 years. Participants in 12 plans could retire after reaching a specified age without regard to service—55 in 3 plans, 60 in 3 plans, and 65 in 6 plans. Because nearly

Table 1. Distribution of municipal pension plans by monthly benefit payments at normal retirement

Monthly benefit	White-collar, trades, and laborers				Fire fighters and police			
	Assumed average annual earnings of—				Assumed average annual earnings of—			
	$10,000		$15,000		$10,000		$15,000	
	25 years of service	30 years of service	25 years of service	30 years of service	25 years of service	30 years of service	25 years of service	30 years of service
Total number of plans	30	30	30	30	38	38	38	38
Under $400	12	5	1	. . . .	1	1	. . . .	. . . .
$400 and under $450	10	4	2	1	19	3	1	. . . .
$450 and under $500	4	5	2	2	7	6	. . . .	. . . .
$500 and under $550	4	13	3	. . . .	9	13	. . . .	1
$550 and under $600	. . . .	1	4	1	. . . .	4	. . . .	. . . .
$600 and under $650	. . . .	2	11	4	1	7	18	3
$650 and under $700	. . . .	. . . .	2	2	1	2	6	2
$700 and under $750	. . . .	. . . .	1	4	. . . .	1	3	6
$750 and under $800	. . . .	. . . .	4	11	. . . .	. . . .	6	11
$800 and under $850	. . . .	. . . .	. . . .	2	. . . .	1	3	3
$850 and over	. . . .	. . . .	. . . .	3	. . . .	. . . .	1	12

NOTE: Assumed average annual earnings were selected to compare yields from pension formulas among cities. In some cities, these averages may not be currently earned by the majority of workers.

Data on monthly benefit amounts were not available for two plans covering white-collar, trades, and labor employees.

Table 2. Pension plan provisions in selected municipal governments

Item	White-collar, trades, and labor[1]			Fire fighters	Police	White-collar, trades, and labor	Fire fighters and police	
	Chicago					**Detroit**		
	Option A	*Option B*	*Option C*				*Entered service prior to 1969*	*Entered service after Jan. 1, 1969*
Payroll reference date of survey	June 1976	June 1976	June 1976	June 1976	June 1976	Jan. 1977	Jan. 1977	Jan. 1977
Normal retirement								
Age and/or service requirements	60 and 20	65 and 15	60 and none	53 and 23	53 and 23	None and 30 or 60 and 10	None and 25	55 and 25
Benefit base (years)	4	4	....	4	4	5	5	5
Minimum benefit (monthly)	⅜ final pay	20.5 percent of final pay	[2]$100	½ average pay	½ average pay	....		
Arithmetic summary of monthly benefit formula:								
Assumed pension base earnings of—								
$10,000 and 25 years service	$385	$260	(Not available)	$433	$433	$375	$417	$417
30 years service	473	313	(Not available)	475	475	448	500	417
Assumed pension base earnings of—								
$15,000 and 25 years service	$578	$365	(Not available)	$650	$650	$557	$625	$625
30 years service	709	438	(Not available)	713	713	666	750	625
Early retirement								
Age and/or service requirements	55 and 20		55 and 10 to 20	50 and 10	50 and 20	....		
Benefit options								
Normal and early retirement	Joint and survivor	Joint and survivor	Joint and survivor	Joint and survivor	Joint and survivor	Joint and survivor	Joint and survivor	Joint and survivor
Disability retirement								
Job-related:								
Minimum requirements as to age and/or service								
Benefit formula	¾ final pay plus dependent child allowance	¾ final pay plus dependent child allowance	¾ final pay plus dependent child allowance	¾ final pay plus dependent child allowance[3]	¾ final pay to age 63 then normal retirement	2/3 average pay plus annuity	2/3 final pay	2/3 final pay
Nonoccupational:								
Minimum requirements as to—								
Age								
Service	....					10	5	5
Benefit formula	½ final pay for up to 5 years	½ final pay for up to 5 years	½ final pay for up to 5 years	½ final pay for up to 5 years	Final pay for up to 5 years	Normal retirement benefit	Normal retirement benefit. (Cash refund if less than 5 years of service)	Normal retirement benefit. (Cash refund if less than 5 years of service)
Vesting								
Minimum requirements as to—								
Age	55	55	55	50	50	40	40	40
Service	10	10	10	10	10	8	8	8
Involuntary retirement								
Compulsory at age	....			63	63	65	60	60
Automatic at age	....			63	63	69	64	64
	Houston					**Los Angeles**		
Payroll reference date of survey	July 1976			July 1976	July 1976	Oct. 1976	Oct. 1976	
Normal retirement								
Age and/or service requirements	50 and 25; or 55 and 20; or 60 and 10			None and 20	None and 20	60 and 10	None and 20	
Benefit base (years)	3			3	5	1	Final pay	
Minimum benefit (monthly)	$8 times years			....		$60	$363	
Arithmetic summary of monthly benefit formula:								
Assumed pension base earnings of—								
$10,000 and 25 years service	$417			$417	$292	$450	$458	
30 years service	500			458	333	540	583	
Assumed pension base earnings of—								
$15,000 and 25 years service	$625			$625	$438	$675	$688	
30 years service	750			688	500	810	875	
Early retirement								
Age and/or service requirements	....			50 and 10	....	55 and 10 or none and 30	....	
Benefit options								
Normal and early retirement	....					Joint and survivor	....	
Disability retirement								
Job-related:								
Minimum requirements as to—								
Age								
Service						5		
Benefit formula	Normal retirement benefit or 1/5 final pay plus 1 percent per year of service to 20			Normal retirement benefit or ½ average pay	Normal retirement benefit (assume 20 years service)	1/70 average pay times years of service or 1/3 final pay	½ to 9/10 final pay	
Nonoccupational:								
Minimum requirements as to—								
Age						(Same provisions as job-related disability)	....	
Service	10						5	
Benefit formula	Normal retirement benefit			Normal retirement benefit or ¼ average pay plus 2.5 percent per year of service	....		2/5 final pay	

See footnotes at end of table.

Table 2. Pension plan provisions in selected municipal governments—Continued

Item	White-collar, trades, and labor[1]		Fire fighters	Police	White-collar, trades, and labor	Fire fighters and police
	Houston				Los Angeles	
Vesting						
Minimum requirements as to—						
Age	Under 50		(No vesting provision)	(No vesting provision)	5	(No vesting provision)
Service	[4]20					
Involuntary retirement						
Compulsory at age				65	70	65
Automatic at age				65		

Item	White-collar, trades, and labor		Sanitation workers	Fire fighters	Police	White-collar, trades, and labor	Fire fighters and police
	New York					Philadelphia	
	Plan I	*Plan II*					
Payroll reference date of survey	May 1975	May 1975	May 1975	May 1975	May 1975	November 1975	November 1975
Normal retirement							
Age and/or service requirements	55 and 25	55 and none	None and 20	None and 20	None and 20	55 and none	46 and none
Benefit base (years)	Final pay	Final pay	Final pay	Final pay	Final pay	3	Variable
Minimum benefit (monthly)							$250
Arithmetic summary of monthly benefit formula:							
Assumed pension base earnings of—							
$10,000 and 25 years service	$458	[5]$269	[6]$479	$486	[7]$486	$500	$521
30 years service	[8]529	[5]319	[6]542	556	[7]556	583	625
Assumed pension base earnings of—							
$15,000 and 25 years service	$688	[5]404	[6]$719	$729	[7]$729	$750	$781
30 years service	[8]794	[5]479	[6]813	833	[7]833	875	938
Early retirement							
Age and/or service requirements							
Benefit options							
Normal and early retirement	Joint and survivor, cash refund	Joint and survivor, cash refund	Joint and survivor, cash refund	Joint and survivor, cash refund	Joint and survivor, cash refund	Joint and survivor, cash refund	Joint and survivor, cash refund
Disability retirement							
Job-related:							
Minimum requirements as to age and/or service							
Benefit formula	¾ final pay plus annuity	¾ final pay plus annuity	¾ final pay plus annuity (additional benefit if over 20 yrs'. service)	¾ final pay (additional benefit if over 20 yrs'. service)	¾ final pay plus annuity	7/10 final pay plus cash refund	7/10 final pay plus cash refund
Nonoccupational:							
Minimum requirements as to—							
Age							
Service	10	10	5			10	Police—10[9]; Fire fighters—5.
Benefit formula	1.2 percent of final pay times service before 7/1/68 plus 1.53 percent of pay times service after 7/1/68 plus annuity	Same as normal retirement	1/3 to ½ final pay plus annuity	2.5 percent of final pay times service plus annuity	2.5 percent of final pay times service plus annuity	Normal retirement benefit	Normal retirement benefit
Vesting							
Minimum requirements as to—							
Age	55	55	(No vesting provision)				
Service	15	15		15	15	10	10
Involuntary retirement							
Compulsory at age	65	65	70	65	63	70	70
Automatic at age	70	70	80	65	65	72	72

[1] A separate plan covers employees in the "labor service" but offers nearly identical coverage. It allows vesting at age 60 with 5 years of service in addition to the provisions specified in this table.

[2] Until joint contributions are depleted.

[3] For employees incapacitated due to heart or lung disease, the plan provides ½ of final pay plus a dependent child allowance.

[4] Or, under age 60 and 15 years of service.

[5] Does not include additional payments based on employee's contribution and a pension based on city contributions.

[6] Does not include additional payments based on contributions made for service in excess of 25 years, or under a separate contractual agreement.

[7] Does not include additional payments based on city contributions made since January 1, 1976, employee contributions made for service in excess of 20 years, or payments made under a separate contractual agreement.

[8] Does not include additional payments based on contributions made for service in excess of 25 years.

[9] Service requirement is waived if employee is incapable of performing any job.

NOTE: In some cities, "pension base earnings" are limited to basic salary; in other cities additional payments, such as cost-of-living adjustments, shift premiums, longevity pay, and so on, are included in benefit calculations. Similar variations even occur within a single city in the earnings concept used to calculate normal and disability retirement benefits for individual occupational groups. A number of plans also specified minimum or maximum benefit levels for disability retirement and maximum payments for normal retirement which are not reported here. For these and other limitations and conditions, see the individual municipal government wage survey reports available from the Bureau of Labor Statistics.

Dollar amounts reported in this tabulation have been rounded to the nearest $1; percentage amounts have been rounded to the nearest one-tenth percent.

A tabulation providing similar summaries for each of the 27 cities included in the municipal government wage survey program is available from the Bureau of Labor Statistics.

one-half of the plans provided two or more eligibility options, some plans were counted more than once in the preceding analysis.

In most cities, retirement age and service requirements for public safety officers were more generous than those covering other municipal employees. Fire fighters or police (or both) could qualify for normal retirement by age 55 with 20 to 25 years of service under 15 of the 38 plans studied; 18 plans permitted normal retirement at any age with 16 to 25 years of service; and the balance stipulated ages ranging from 46 to 55 with 15 or fewer years of service. A number of plans also provided alternate age and service requirements.

Benefit formulas. Municipal pension plans used a variety of methods to calculate the level of benefits paid to retirees. The most common method, found in 25 of the 70 plans, was based on a specified percentage (usually 2 percent) of the employee's pension base earnings, multiplied by the number of years of service. In 30 other plans, the percentage varied as years of service increased. In Washington, D.C., for example, benefits amounted to 1.5 percent of pension base earnings times the first 5 years of service, 1.75 percent times the next 5 years, and 2 percent for all years over 10. In Philadelphia, however, the proportion of pension base earnings paid to white- and blue-collar employees declined after longer periods of service, falling from 2.5 percent for the first 20 years to 2.0 percent in subsequent years.

Benefit formulas under the remaining 15 plans differed considerably. In a number of plans, the proportion of base earnings paid as monthly benefits varied by age, date of employment, or level of earnings. In Indianapolis, the plan covering fire fighters and police did not base pension benefits on the employee's own salary. Instead, all payments amounted to one-half of the current salary for a specified job class (namely, first class private fire fighter or a police patrol officer with 11 years of service) plus an additional 2 percent for each year of service over 20.

The period used to compute a pension base varied among the plans. Such variations can result in different levels of monthly benefit payments for workers who retire with similar earnings histories under different pension plans. To illustrate, an employee whose annual salary had increased from $10,000 to $15,000 over the 5 years prior to retirement would report an average salary of $15,000 for the final year alone but $13,000 for the 5-year period—a difference of 13 percent. Individual plans studied had pension calculation bases ranging from "final salary" (pay at time of retirement) to 5-year averages. A 3-year base period, the most common provision, applied to

workers covered by about three-fifths of the white- and blue-collar plans and nearly two-fifths of the public safety plans. About one-fourth of the public safety plans specified base periods shorter than 3 years.

Two-fifths of the plans studied set a minimum level of benefits for employees meeting normal requirements for retirement. Most of these specified flat sums, generally less than $300 a month. Three cities (seven plans) set minimum limits based on a percentage of pay. In Chicago, white- and blue-collar employees under two different plans were guaranteed 20.5 percent or 37.5 percent of their final pay, compared with 50 percent of highest consecutive 4-year average for public safety officers. All workers in Memphis were protected with minimum payments of 20 percent of their final pay, while San Francisco fire fighters and police were guaranteed 55 percent of final pay.

Benefit levels. To facilitate comparison of benefit formulas among the various plans, monthly benefit amounts were calculated for specified conditions. These calculations assumed that the employee retired during the reference month of the wage survey, after meeting minimum age or service requirements, if any. Benefit amounts were determined for hypothetical employees having $10,000 or $15,000 as their pension base earnings and completing either 25 or 30 years of service.[6]

Monthly benefits under each of these assumptions covered a broad range. For both employment groups, however, the most common monthly yields computed on $10,000 were $417 after 25 years of service and $500 after 30 years; on $15,000, the corresponding yields were $625 and $750. Stated another way, the formulas commonly yield 50 and 60 percent of pension base earnings after 25 and 30 years of service, respectively.

In nearly all the cities, pension benefits paid to public safety officers equaled or exceeded those paid to white- and blue-collar employees with the same service and earnings history. In general, the differences favoring public safety officers were less than 30 percent, although they varied by length of service and pension base earnings (table 3). In Dallas, for example, public safety benefits exceeded those paid other retirees by 30 percent after 25 years of service, but by only 21 percent after 30 years of service—because after 25 years, the proportion of pension base earnings paid to retirees under the public safety plan decreased.

Pension escalators. Thirty-eight of the 70 pension plans contained provisions for periodic adjustments in the level of monthly benefits paid to retirees. These

Table 3. Distribution of municipal pension plans by difference between monthly benefits for white-collar, trades, and laborers and fire fighters and police in the same city

Normal retirement benefit difference	Assumed average annual earnings of—			
	$10,000		$15,000	
	25 years service	30 years service	25 years service	30 years service
Total number of comparisons[1]	46	46	46	46
Fire fighter and police benefits exceed other benefits by—				
Less than 5 percent.	11	5	10	8
5 and under 10 percent . . .	2	5	2	3
10 and under 20 percent . .	8	4	8	5
20 and under 30 percent . .	3	4	5	7
30 and under 40 percent . .	4	5	5	4
40 and under 50 percent . .	3	3	1	1
50 percent and over	7	5	7	5
Fire fighter and police benefits fall below other benefits by—				
Less than 10 percent.	. . . .	2	. . . .	2
10 percent and over	1	1	1	1
Benefits paid both groups are equal	7	12	7	10

[1] Where more than one plan was in effect for an occupational group in a city, comparisons were made for each individual plan.

escalator provisions covered all occupational groups in 10 cities, white- and blue-collar employees in 3 cities, all public safety officers in 5 cities and fire fighters in 1 city.[7]

Under 22 of the plans, adjustments were based on changes in the Consumer Price Index. These adjustments were usually made annually; in four plans they were equal to the actual change in the Consumer Price Index, but in 15 plans, they were limited to 5 percent or less. In Boston, adjustments equal to the change in the Consumer Price Index were made only to the first $6,000 in annual benefits. Prior to October 1976, each adjustment for white- and blue-collar retirees in Washington exceeded the actual change in the price index by 1 percent to compensate for the time lag between the increase in prices and the change in pension benefits.[8]

Under the remaining 16 plans containing escalator provisions, changes were not tied directly to increases in living costs. Instead, under 10 plans, annual changes of 1.5 to 6.0 percent were made automatically. Pension benefits under three plans were adjusted whenever the salary scale for active employees increased. In the other three plans, adjustments were made at the discretion of the plan's governing board.

Other retirement provisions

Four-fifths of the plans covering white- and blue-collar employees and two-fifths of those covering public safety officers provided benefit options. The two offered most frequently are discussed here. All plans containing benefit options included a "joint and survivor" option, which supplies a reduced lifetime benefit with a guarantee that after the retiree's death, payments will continue to a designated beneficiary. A "cash refund" option was available in one-third of the white- and blue-collar plans and almost one-fifth of the public safety plans. Under this option, if total benefits paid to a pensioner are less than the amount of the contributions made while working, the balance will be paid after the retiree's death to a designated beneficiary, in lieu of continuing pension payments.

Early retirement. Early retirement provisions, under which employees can retire before becoming eligible for normal benefits, were available to white- and blue-collar employees in slightly more than one-half of the plans studied. These provisions granted a reduced retirement benefit to employees meeting specified age or service requirements (or both)—commonly age 55 with 10 to 25 years of service.

Early retirement provisions were less common for public safety officers; they were found in only about one-fourth of the plans. As with normal retirement, such provisions in public safety plans were usually more liberal than those covering other municipal employees. For example, many allowed retirement at age 50 with 10 to 20 years of service, or at any age with 20 years of service.

Disability retirement. Each of the retirement pension plans studied provided benefits to employees who became permanently disabled while working. In three-fourths of the plans covering white- and blue-collar employees and in more than nine-tenths of those covering fire fighters and police, workers were eligible for disability benefits without meeting any age or service requirements. Where such prerequisites did exist, they generally amounted to no more than 5 years of service.

The most common provisions for job-related disabilities called for the payment of one-third to three-fourths of the employee's final or average salary. About three-fifths of the white- and blue-collar plans and nearly three-fourths of the public safety plans had such provisions. Normal retirement benefits—usually assuming a specified age or period of service as a basis for benefit computation—were paid to disabled employees under most of the remaining plans.

Most plans also paid disability pension benefits to employees who became permanently disabled away from work. Generally, however, more stringent eligibility requirements applied to nonoccupational disabilities than to those incurred on the job. One-half of the plans covering white- and blue-collar employees required at least 10 years of service, and one-half of the plans covering public safety officers required at least 5 years of service to qualify for benefits.

Benefits paid for nonoccupational disabilities tended to be the same or lower than those paid for job-related disabilities. For white- and blue-collar employees, benefits in the two cases were about the same in two-fifths of the plans, and lower for nonoccupational disability in one-fifth of the plans. About one-fifth of the public safety plans provided the same level of benefits, but nonoccupational benefits were lower than those for job-related disability in two-fifths of the plans. (The remaining plans for both groups could not be compared.)

Additional clauses. Vesting—a guarantee of pension rights to workers terminated from employment before retirement eligibility—was found in nearly all the plans covering white- and blue-collar employees and in two-thirds of those covering public safety officers. In the first instance, employees usually needed 5 to 10 years of service to gain vesting privileges; public safety officers, on the other hand, normally needed 10 to 20 years.

All of the vesting clauses provided deferred benefits for vested employees equal to those paid employees retiring normally with the same age, service, and earnings history. In general, deferred payments began when the vested employee attained the minimum age specified for normal retirement.

Most of the plans specified a "compulsory retirement age" at which time employees could be retired involuntarily. Typically, this was set at 65 or 70 years for white- and blue-collar employees and at 60 to 65 for public safety officers. In most cities where a compulsory retirement age was found, however, employers could retain white- and blue-collar employees until they reached an "automatic retirement age." This irrevocable maximum was generally 3 to 5 years later than the compulsory retirement age, but in a few cases the difference was as large as 10 years.

Virtually all of the plans covered the beneficiary of an employee who dies on the job. Typically, they provided a pension based on a proportion of the employee's final pay or normal retirement benefit. About one-fourth of the plans covering white- and blue-collar employees and two-thirds of those covering public safety employees provided an additional monthly allowance for dependent children. Some plans included payments to parents. Nearly three-fifths of the white- and blue-collar plans, and about three-fourths of the public safety plans provided for death benefits after retirement.

Social security coverage

In addition to the municipally sponsored plans, most cities also provided social security coverage for some or all of their employees. (Membership in the Federal system is mandatory for most establishments in private industry, but optional for State and local governments.) All municipal workers in New York City and Seattle and all white- and blue-collar employees in approximately one-half of the other city governments studied were covered by social security as well as a municipal plan.[9] In Memphis, members of the American Federation of State, County and Municipal Employees were covered only by social security, as were white- and blue-collar employees in Indianapolis. Jacksonville provided social security coverage for employees hired after age 55 or otherwise ineligible for membership in the municipal plan. In eight cities—Atlanta, Boston, Chicago, Cleveland, Columbus, Los Angeles, Phoenix, and Washington—pension benefits were limited to the city-sponsored plan. With a few exceptions, public safety officers were not eligible for social security benefits.

The social security system currently provides a minimum monthly benefit of $107.90 (upon retirement at age 62), death and disability benefits, and an allowance to dependent survivors of covered employees. The plan is jointly financed by employees and their employers; as of January 1, 1977, each contributes 5.85 percent of the first $16,500 of annual earnings.[10]

Federal pension plan

Full-time, permanent employees of the Federal Government are covered by the Civil Service Retirement System, which also provides pension benefits to white- and blue-collar employees of Washington, D.C. Under this plan, normal retirement benefits for white- and blue-collar employees were slightly below those paid under three-fifths of the municipal plans studied. Federal white- and blue-collar retirees receive 46 percent of pension base earnings after 25 years of service and age 60, and 56 percent after 30 years and age 55—compared with the 50 and 60 percent common to municipal plans. Federal retirement benefits are adjusted to reflect cost-of-living changes under the same formula described earlier for Washington, D.C.[11]

Other provisions of the Federal employees' plan were similar to those contained in many of the municipal plans. These provisions included a joint and survivor benefit option, death and disability benefits, and vesting rights after 5 years of service. Federal employees could retire as early as age 55 with 30 years of service, or at age 62 with 5 years of service. Voluntary early retirement is not available to white-

and blue-collar employees, although public safety officers and air traffic controllers have the option of retiring at age 50 after 20 years of service. Additionally, air traffic controllers may retire at any age with 25 years of service. The Civil Service Retirement System is financed equally by the employee and the Federal Government, each contributing 7 percent of the worker's salary for white- and blue-collar employees and 7.5 percent for public safety officers.

□

————FOOTNOTES————

[1] The employee's compensation, as defined in the various plans, used to compute retirement benefits.

[2] The 27 cities are: Atlanta, Baltimore, Boston, Chicago, Cleveland, Columbus, Dallas, Denver, Detroit, Houston, Indianapolis, Jacksonville, Kansas City, Los Angeles, Memphis, Milwaukee, New Orleans, New York, Philadelphia, Phoenix, Pittsburgh, St. Louis, San Antonio, San Diego, San Francisco, Seattle, and Washington, D.C. Population was based on the 1970 Census of Population. Atlanta was also included in the survey, although its population was slightly below 500,000.
For comparisons of municipal salary levels in 24 of the same cities, see Charles Field V and Richard L. Keller, "How salaries of large cities compare with industry and Federal pay," *Monthly Labor Review,* November 1976, pp. 23–28.

[3] Although the reference dates of the surveys cover a 20-month period, it is unlikely that such timing variations had a significant impact on the comparisons made in this article. Some provisions of individual plans changed slightly, but the major provisions summarized here tend to remain constant for extended periods.

[4] More complete information is contained in the individual municipal government wage survey reports, available from the Bureau of Labor Statistics or any of its regional offices.

[5] "White- and blue-collar employees" include professional, administrative, and technical employees; office clerical workers; data processing employees; and maintenance, custodial, trades, labor, and sanitation workers. "Public safety officers" include fire fighters and police.

[6] These pension base earnings were selected for comparing formula yields only. They do not necessarily reflect typical pension base earnings of employees covered by the individual plans.

[7] Escalator provisions covered all employees in Boston, Chicago, Dallas, Detroit, Los Angeles, Memphis, St. Louis, San Diego, San Francisco, and Washington; white- and blue-collar employees in Cleveland, Columbus, and Denver; public safety employees in Indianapolis, Kansas City, New Orleans, San Antonio, and Seattle; and fire fighters in Houston.

[8] In October 1976, this additional 1 percent adjustment was eliminated and the cost-of-living adjustment formula was amended to provide increases each March 1 and September 1 equal to the actual change in the Consumer Price Index during the preceding June-December and December-June periods. The earlier formula provided an automatic increase whenever the Consumer Price Index rose 3 percent or more and maintained that level for 3 consecutive months. When this occurred, percentage increases in pension benefits equaled the largest index change achieved during the 3-month period, plus 1 percent.

[9] Social security coverage, in addition to a municipal plan, applied to all white- and blue-collar employees in Baltimore, Dallas, Denver, Detroit, Houston, Kansas City, Milwaukee, New Orleans, Philadelphia, Pittsburgh, St. Louis, San Antonio, and San Diego. Social security coverage was available to most workers in San Francisco.

[10] The taxable limit was $15,300 during the period covered by this analysis of municipal government pension plans.

[11] See footnote 8.

COMPARISON OF AVERAGE SALARIES IN PRIVATE AND FEDERAL EMPLOYMENT

The survey was designed to provide a basis for comparing salaries under the General Schedule classification and pay system with salaries in private enterprise. To assure collection of pay data for work levels equivalent to the General Schedule grade levels, the Civil Service Commission, in cooperation with the Bureau of Labor Statistics, prepared the occupational work level definitions used in the survey. Definitions were graded by the Commission according to standards established for each grade level. The tables show the surveyed jobs grouped by work levels equivalent to General Schedule grade levels.

Comparison of average annual salaries in private industry with salary rates for Federal employees under the General Schedule

Occupation and level surveyed by BLS[1]	Average annual salaries in private industry,[2] March 1977	Grade[4]	Salary rates for Federal employees under the General Schedule, March 1977 and October 1977[3]										
			Average[5] Mar. 1977	Annual rates and steps[6]									
				1	2	3	4	5	6	7	8	9	10
Clerks, file I	$6,068	GS 1	$5,917	$5,810 (6,219)	$6,004 (6,426)	$6,198 (6,633)	$6,392 (6,840)	$6,586 (7,047)	$6,780 (7,254)	$6,974 (7,461)	$7,168 (7,668)	$7,362 (7,875)	$7,556 (8,082)
Messengers	7,166												
Clerks, file II	7,168	GS 2	6,775	6,572 (7,035)	6,791 (7,270)	7,010 (7,505)	7,229 (7,740)	7,448 (7,975)	7,667 (8,210)	7,886 (8,445)	8,105 (8,680)	8,324 (8,915)	8,543 (9,150)
Keypunch operators I	8,045												
Typists I	7,202												
Clerks, accounting I	8,138	GS 3	7,955	7,408 (7,930)	7,655 (8,194)	7,902 (8,458)	8,149 (8,722)	8,396 (8,986)	8,643 (9,250)	8,890 (9,514)	9,137 (9,778)	9,384 (10,042)	9,631 (10,306)
Clerks, file III	9,082												
Drafter-tracers	9,214												
Engineering technicians I	9,727												
Keypunch operators II	9,337												
Stenographers, general	9,086												
Typists II	8,585												
Clerks, accounting II	10,388	GS 4	9,259	8,316 (8,902)	8,593 (9,199)	8,870 (9,496)	9,147 (9,793)	9,424 (10,090)	9,701 (10,387)	9,978 (10,684)	10,255 (10,981)	10,532 (11,278)	10,809 (11,575)
Computer operators I	7,979												
Drafters I	10,354												
Engineering technicians II	11,355												
Secretaries I	9,329												
Stenographers, senior	10,178												
Accountants I	12,155	GS 5	10,567	9,303 (9,959)	9,613 (10,291)	9,923 (10,623)	10,233 (10,955)	10,543 (11,287)	10,853 (11,619)	11,163 (11,951)	11,473 (12,283)	11,783 (12,615)	12,093 (12,947)
Auditors I	12,570												
Buyers I	12,346												
Chemists I	12,872												
Computer operators II	9,463												
Drafters II	12,833												
Engineers I	14,613												
Engineering technicians III	13,151												
Secretaries II	10,100												
Computer operators III	10,529	GS 6	11,928	10,370 (11,101)	10,716 (11,471)	11,062 (11,841)	11,408 (12,211)	11,754 (12,581)	12,100 (12,951)	12,446 (13,321)	12,792 (13,691)	13,138 (14,061)	13,484 (14,431)
Secretaries III	11,159												

See footnotes at end of table.

Comparison of average annual salaries in private industry with salary rates for Federal employees under the General Schedule (Continued)

Occupation and level surveyed by BLS[1]	Average annual salaries in private industry,[2] March 1977	Grade[4]	Salary rates for Federal employees under the General Schedule, March 1977 and October 1977[3] — Annual rates and steps[6]										
			Average[5] Mar. 1977	1	2	3	4	5	6	7	8	9	10
Accountants II	$14,624	GS 7	$12,993	$11,523 (12,336)	$11,907 (12,747)	$12,291 (13,158)	$12,675 (13,569)	$13,059 (13,980)	$13,443 (14,391)	$13,827 (14,802)	$14,211 (15,213)	$14,595 (15,624)	$14,979 (16,035)
Auditors II	14,503												
Buyers II	15,099												
Chemists II	14,439												
Computer operators IV	12,557												
Drafters III	15,828												
Engineers II	16,221												
Engineering technicians IV	15,221												
Job analysts II	13,572												
Secretaries IV	12,138												
Computer operators V	14,099	GS 8	14,812	12,763 (13,662)	13,188 (14,117)	13,613 (14,572)	14,038 (15,027)	14,463 (15,482)	14,888 (15,937)	15,313 (16,392)	15,738 (16,847)	16,163 (17,302)	16,588 (17,757)
Secretaries V	13,407												
Accountants III	16,545	GS 9	15,761	14,097 (15,090)	14,567 (15,593)	15,037 (16,096)	15,507 (16,599)	15,977 (17,102)	16,447 (17,605)	16,917 (18,108)	17,387 (18,611)	17,857 (19,114)	18,327 (19,617)
Attorneys I	16,033												
Auditors III	17,108												
Buyers III	18,021												
Chemists III	17,600												
Computer operators VI	16,423												
Engineers III	18,696												
Engineering technicians V	17,237												
Job analysts III	17,016												
Accountants IV	$20,367	GS 11	$19,205	17,056 (18,258)	$17,625 (18,867)	$18,194 (19,476)	$18,763 (20,085)	$19,332 (20,694)	$19,901 (21,303)	$20,470 (21,912)	$21,039 (22,521)	$21,608 (23,130)	$22,177 (23,739)
Attorneys II	19,938												
Auditors IV	21,526												
Buyers IV	21,907												
Chemists IV	21,674												
Chief accountants I	22,558												
Directors of personnel I	19,062												
Engineers IV	22,072												
Job analysts IV	20,908												
Accountants V	25,042	GS 12	23,088	20,442 (21,883)	21,123 (22,612)	21,804 (23,341)	22,485 (24,070)	23,166 (24,799)	23,847 (25,528)	24,528 26,257	25,209 (26,986)	25,890 (27,715)	26,571 (28,444)
Attorneys III	25,460												
Chemists V	26,214												
Chief accountants II	25,320												
Director of personnel II	23,755												
Engineers V	25,620												

See footnotes at end of table.

11-61

Comparison of average annual salaries in private industry with salary rates for Federal employees under the General Schedule (Continued)

Occupation and level surveyed by BLS[1]	Average annual salaries in private industry,[2] March 1977	Grade[4]	Salary rates for Federal employees under the General Schedule, March 1977 and October 1977[3]											
			Average[5] Mar. 1977	Annual rates and steps[6]									
				1	2	3	4	5	6	7	8	9	10
Attorneys IV	$30,973	GS 13	$27,717	$24,308 (26,022)	$25,118 (26,889)	$25,928 (27,756)	$26,738 (28,623)	$27,548 (29,490)	$28,358 (30,357)	$29,168 (31,224)	$29,978 (32,091)	$30,788 (32,958)	$31,598 (33,825)
Chemists VI	30,526												
Chief accountants III	31,324												
Directors of personnel III	29,188												
Engineers VI	29,376												
Attorneys V	38,828	GS 14	32,677	28,725 (30,750)	29,683 (31,775)	30,641 (32,800)	31,599 (33,825)	32,557 (34,850)	33,515 (35,875)	34,473 (36,900)	35,431 (37,925)	36,389 (38,950)	37,347 (39,975)
Chemists VII	36,329												
Chief accountants IV	36,789												
Directors of personnel IV	37,785												
Engineers VII	32,999												
Attorneys VI	46,509	GS 15	38,956	33,789 (36,171)	34,915 (37,377)	36,041 (38,583)	37,167 (39,789)	38,293 (40,995)	39,419 42,201	40,545 (43,407)	41,671 (44,613)	42,797 (45,819)	43,923 (47,025)
Chemists VIII	44,642												
Engineers VIII	38,063												

[1] Occupational definitions in the collection of the salary data reflect duties and responsibilities in private industry; however, they are also designed to be translatable to specific General Schedule grades applying to Federal employees. Thus the definitions of some occupations and work levels were limited to specific elements that could be classified uniformly among establishments. The Bureau of Labor Statistics and the Civil Service Commission collaborated in the preparation of the definitions.
[2] Data collection was planned so that the data would reflect an average reference period of March 1977.
[3] The General Schedule rates that were in effect in March 1977, the reference data of the BLS PATC survey, are shown on the first line for each grade. The new rates, as adjusted in October 1977, are shown in parentheses.
[4] Corresponding grades in the General Schedule were supplied by the U.S. Civil Service Commission.

[5] Mean salary of all General Schedule employees in each grade as of March 31, 1977. Not limited to Federal employees in occupations surveyed by BLS.
[6] Section 5335 of title 5 of the U.S. Code provides for within-grade increases on condition that the employee's work is of an acceptable level of competence as defined by the head of the agency. For employees who meet this condition, the service requirements are 52 calendar weeks each for advancement to salary rates 2, 3, and 4; 104 weeks each for advancement to salary rates 5, 6, and 7; and 156 weeks each for advancement to salary rates 8, 9, and 10. Section 5336 provides that an additional within-grade increase may be granted within any period of 52 weeks in recognition of high quality performance above that ordinarily found in the type of position concerned.

Under Section 5303 of title 5 of the United States Code, higher minimum rates (but not exceeding the maximum salary rate prescribed in the General Schedule for the grade or level) and a corresponding new salary range may be established for positions or occupations under certain conditions. The conditions include a finding that the Government's recruitment or retention of well-qualified persons is significantly above the statutory pay salary rates in private industry are substantially above the salary rates of the statutory pay schedules. As of March 1977, special, higher salary ranges were authorized for professional engineers, accountants, and auditors at the entry grades (GS-5 and GS-7). Information on special salary rates, including the occupations and the areas to which they apply, may be obtained from the U.S. Civil Service Commission, Washington, D.C. 20415, or its regional offices.

Labor in Other Countries

An analysis of unemployment in nine industrial countries

*High unemployment rates, the result of
the international recession of 1974-75,
continued to plague the economies of
all of the nations surveyed in 1976,
with the exception of Sweden*

JOYANNA MOY AND CONSTANCE SORRENTINO

The economic recovery, which began in North
America in mid-1975 and then spread to Europe
and Japan, lost momentum in the second half of
last year. Consequently, unemployment rates remained high during 1976 in all countries studied
except Sweden. Labor markets were generally weak
even during the period when economic activity was
accelerating because of the extensive underutilization of the employed labor force during the recession. Working hours—cut sharply in 1975—increased first, thereby retarding the decline in
unemployment.

During 1975–76, postwar highs in unemployment were reached in the United States, Australia,
France, and Great Britain. German unemployment
rates were the highest since the mid-1950's, and
Japanese jobless rates reached the levels of 1959. In
1975, Sweden was the only country of the nine
studied in which unemployment declined.

During 1976, unemployment rates declined from
their 1975 averages in the United States but remained unchanged in Australia, Germany, and
Sweden. Although unemployment continued to rise
in the other five countries, only Great Britain experienced a significant increase. Last year's unemployment rates were above 6 percent in the United
States, Canada, and Great Britain. Australian,
French, German, and Italian jobless rates were between 3 and 5 percent, and Japanese and Swedish
rates were the lowest, averaging about 2 percent.

This article is the eighth in a series comparing
unemployment rates adjusted to U.S. concepts in
selected industrial countries.[1] Although the unemployment data have been adjusted for statistical
comparability, intercountry differences in unemployment rates reflect substantial differences in social and institutional arrangements, as well as in
economic performance. Differences in the demographic and sectoral composition of the labor force
also affect the unemployment rates.

Estimates of seasonally adjusted quarterly and
monthly unemployment rates appear in table 1, and
semiannual jobless rates are shown in chart 1. Table 2 and chart 2 contain average annual data for
1970-76. Employment–population ratios, adjusted

Joyanna Moy and Constance Sorrentino are economists in the Division
of Foreign Labor Statistics and Trade, Bureau of Labor Statistics.

to U.S. definitions, are examined in this article for the first time, and a short analysis of unemployment by age and sex is also included. Revisions of previously published estimates are discussed in the appendix.

Other labor market indicators

Because unemployment rates are by themselves incomplete measures of the underutilization of the labor force, other economic indicators such as employment, employment–population ratios, labor force participation rates, average hours, and migration have also been analyzed.

Employment. An indication of the extent and severity of the most recent economic downturn is that employment fell sharply in the United States, Australia, Japan, France, Germany, and Great Britain. Canadian and Italian employment fluctuated in 1974-75, but generally moved upward.

In 1975, Germany was the only country where the drop in employment greatly exceeded the rise in unemployment. Labor force withdrawals and foreign worker outflows resulted in the employment decline not being fully translated into unemployment. Employment declines were much smaller than the increases in unemployment in the United States, Australia, and Great Britain. In Japan and France, the decline in employment approximately equaled the rise in unemployment.

Employment growth rebounded sooner and more strongly in the United States than in other developed nations. U.S. employment began rising in the second quarter of 1975, and by December 1976 the number of employed persons had increased by more than 4 million from the recession low, recovering the entire cyclical loss and reaching a new high. In contrast, employment was still falling in France, Germany, and Great Britain in 1976 and rose only marginally in Italy and Sweden.

During the recession, employment opportunities for women were less severely affected than those for men in all countries except Japan. The explanation lies in the basic differences in employment patterns for each sex. Employment for women is heavily concentrated in the service sector, but men are employed predominantly in the goods-producing sector. Business downturns tend to be more severe in the manufacturing and construction industries than in the service industries. In most countries, employment gains in the service sector were relatively strong, but the recession adversely affected employment in the goods-producing sector. In Japan, the situation was different for men and women because of the lifetime employment system. Under this system, regular workers are protected against layoffs while temporary workers, mainly women, are let go.

Employment-population ratios. Another indicator of labor force utilization is the employment-population ratio. The ratio is derived by dividing civilian employment by the civilian working-age population. The employment-population ratio has several advantages over the unemployment rate.[2] Employment is a more precisely measurable condition than unemployment and, because it is much larger, it is subject to smaller relative statistical

Table 1. Seasonally adjusted unemployment rates, adjusted to U.S. concepts, 1974–76

Period	United States	Canada	Australia[1]	Japan	France[2]	Germany	Great Britain[2]	Italy[1]	Sweden
1974	5.6	5.4	2.3	1.4	3.1	1.7	3.2	3.2	2.0
I	5.0	5.3	1.7	1.3	3.0	1.3	3.0	3.3	2.2
II	5.1	5.2	1.8	1.2	2.8	1.5	3.0	2.9	2.1
III	5.6	5.3	2.4	1.4	2.9	1.9	3.2	3.2	2.0
IV	6.6	5.6	3.3	1.7	3.5	2.5	3.5	3.4	1.7
1975	8.5	6.9	4.4	1.9	4.3	[2]3.8	4.7	3.7	1.6
I	8.1	6.7	4.0	1.7	3.9	3.0	3.7	3.3	1.5
II	8.8	7.0	4.5	1.8	4.3	3.8	4.3	3.9	1.7
III	8.6	7.1	4.6	2.0	4.4	4.2	5.1	3.7	1.6
IV	8.4	7.1	4.6	2.2	4.6	4.0	5.7	3.8	1.7
1976	7.7	7.1	4.4	[2]2.1	4.6	[2]3.8	6.4	4.0	1.6
I	7.6	6.9	4.3	2.0	4.6	3.8	6.1	3.7	1.6
II	7.4	7.1	4.3	2.1	4.7	3.7	6.5	4.0	1.7
III	7.8	7.3	4.9	2.1	4.7	3.7	6.6	4.2	1.6
IV	7.9	7.4	4.2	2.1	4.6	3.6	6.6	4.1	1.6
October	7.9	7.4	....	2.1	4.6	3.6	6.5	4.1	1.7
November	8.0	7.3	4.2	2.1	4.6	3.6	6.7	....	1.4
December	7.8	7.5	....	2.0	4.6	3.5	6.7	....	1.6

[1] Quarterly rates for Australia refer to the second month of each quarter, and for Italy, the first month of each quarter.
[2] Preliminary estimates.

NOTE: Quarterly and monthly figures for France, Germany, Great Britain, and Italy are calculated by applying annual adjustment factors to current published data, and therefore, should be viewed as only approximate indicators of unemployment under U.S. concepts. Published data for Australia, Canada, Japan, and Sweden require little or no adjustment.

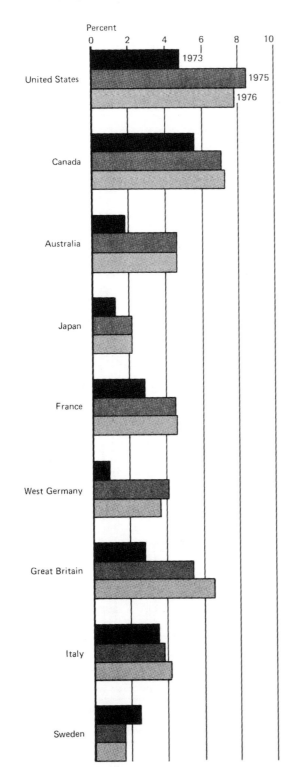

Chart 1. Unemployment rates in nine countries, for the second half of 1973, 1975, and 1976

(Seasonally adjusted)

Percent

United States
1973
1975
1976

Canada

Australia

Japan

France

West Germany

Great Britain

Italy

Sweden

error. Seasonal adjustment is less significant as seasonal changes are relatively small. Employment-population ratios for the 1970-76 period are shown in table 2.

In the short run, changes in the employment-population ratio are largely the result of fluctuations in economic activity. The ratio increases as economic activity increases and declines in periods of economic downturn. In the long run, structural factors such as trends toward increased schooling, earlier retirement, migration from rural to urban areas, and changing attitudes towards the role of working women in society account for the different employment-population ratios recorded in the nine countries.

Since 1960, the employment-population ratios for the United States and Australia have fluctuated within a narrow range, with increasing participation of women in the labor force offsetting declines in the participation rates for men. The Canadian and Swedish ratios have generally moved upward, as rapidly rising participation rates of women more than offset declining rates for men. Broadening of job opportunities for women, increased availability of part-time work and child care, and declining fertility rates have all contributed to the higher levels of employment for women.

In Japan, Italy, and Germany, in contrast, the participation of both men and women in the labor force has been declining, bringing about a long-term decline in the employment-population ratio. In Japan and Italy, the decline is partly attributable to a reduction in agricultural employment. As families move from rural to urban areas, employment of women initially declines, as those who were economically active as unpaid family workers withdraw from the labor force. In Germany, the labor force activity of women has been rising, but it has not been sufficient to make up for a sharp drop in participation by teenage girls brought about by the extension of schooling.

In 1976, almost 64 percent of Sweden's and 61 percent of Japan's civilian working-age population were employed. The United States, Canada, Australia, and Great Britain ranked next with ratios within the range of 56 to 59 percent. French and German employment ratios were slightly lower, around 53 percent, while Italy had the lowest ratio, 44 percent.

Participation rates. Several countries underwent recession-induced withdrawals from the labor force, causing a decline in participation rates, the ratio of the labor force to the civilian population of working age. This was particularly apparent in Japan, where

Table 2. Labor force, employment, and unemployment in nine countries, 1970–76

[Numbers in thousands]

Measure and year	United States	Canada	Australia	Japan	France	Germany	Great Britain	Italy	Sweden
	Data adjusted to U.S. concepts								
Civilian labor force:									
1970	82,715	8,399	5,381	50,730	21,040	26,240	24,270	19,090	3,884
1971	84,113	8,644	5,486	51,030	21,270	26,350	24,020	19,010	3,932
1972	86,542	8,920	5,589	51,140	¹21,490	26,310	24,240	18,800	3,939
1973	88,714	9,322	5,723	52,580	¹21,710	26,420	24,536	18,930	3,952
1974	91,011	9,706	5,869	52,040	¹21,900	26,220	¹24,610	19,230	4,013
1975	92,613	10,060	5,991	52,530	¹21,950	¹25,850	¹24,860	19,450	4,097
1976	94,773	10,308	6,075	¹53,070	¹22,000	¹25,580	¹25,120	¹19,660	¹4,130
Labor force participation rate:[2]									
1970	60.4	57.8	60.8	64.5	57.1	56.9	59.4	47.4	62.5
1971	60.2	58.1	60.7	64.2	57.1	56.4	59.1	47.1	62.8
1972	60.4	58.6	60.8	63.7	¹57.1	55.9	59.4	46.1	62.7
1973	60.8	59.7	61.1	64.0	¹57.1	55.5	60.8	45.9	62.7
1974	61.2	60.5	61.4	63.0	¹57.0	54.7	¹60.8	45.9	63.4
1975	61.2	61.1	61.6	62.4	¹56.7	¹54.2	¹61.1	46.0	¹64.5
1976	61.6	61.1	61.4	¹62.4	¹56.6	¹54.0	¹61.5	¹46.1	¹64.9
Employment:									
1970	78,627	7,919	5,306	50,140	20,460	26,040	23,520	18,430	3,830
1971	79,120	8,107	5,398	50,390	20,640	26,130	23,090	18,350	3,831
1972	81,702	8,363	5,464	50,410	¹20,840	26,090	23,230	18,050	3,832
1973	84,409	8,802	5,615	51,910	¹21,090	26,200	23,750	18,210	3,854
1974	85,936	9,185	5,736	51,700	¹21,220	25,770	¹23,830	18,630	3,933
1975	84,783	9,363	5,725	52,430	¹21,010	¹24,880	¹23,690	18,740	4,030
1976	87,485	9,572	5,807	¹51,950	¹20,980	¹24,620	¹23,510	¹18,870	¹4,063
Employment-population rate:[3]									
1970	57.4	54.5	60.0	63.8	55.6	56.5	57.5	45.8	61.6
1971	56.6	54.5	59.8	63.4	55.4	56.0	56.8	45.4	61.1
1972	57.0	54.9	59.4	62.8	¹55.4	55.4	56.9	44.2	61.0
1973	57.8	56.4	60.0	63.2	¹55.5	55.0	58.9	44.1	61.1
1974	57.8	57.3	60.0	62.0	¹55.3	53.8	¹58.8	44.5	62.2
1975	56.0	56.8	58.8	61.0	¹54.3	¹52.4	¹58.3	44.3	¹63.5
1976	56.8	56.7	58.7	¹60.9	¹54.0	¹51.9	¹57.6	¹44.2	¹63.8
Unemployment:									
1970	4,088	480	75	590	580	200	750	660	59
1971	4,993	538	87	640	630	220	930	660	101
1972	4,840	557	125	730	¹650	220	1,010	750	107
1973	4,304	520	108	670	¹620	220	780	720	98
1974	5,076	521	133	740	¹680	450	¹780	610	80
1975	7,830	697	266	1,000	¹940	¹970	¹1,170	710	67
1976	7,288	736	268	¹1,120	¹1,020	¹960	¹1,610	¹790	¹67
Unemployment rate:									
1970	4.9	5.7	1.4	1.2	2.8	.8	3.1	3.5	1.5
1971	5.9	6.2	1.6	1.3	3.0	.8	3.9	3.5	2.6
1972	5.6	6.2	2.2	1.4	¹3.0	.8	4.2	4.0	2.7
1973	4.9	5.6	1.9	1.3	¹2.9	.8	3.2	3.8	2.5
1974	5.6	5.4	2.3	1.4	¹3.1	1.7	¹3.2	3.2	2.0
1975	8.5	6.9	4.4	1.9	¹4.3	¹3.8	¹4.7	3.7	1.6
1976	7.7	7.1	4.4	¹2.1	¹4.6	¹3.8	¹6.4	¹4.0	¹1.6
	Data as originally published[4]								
Unemployment rate:									
1970	4.9	5.7	1.4	1.2	1.7	.7	2.5	3.2	1.5
1971	5.9	6.2	1.6	1.2	2.1	.8	3.4	3.2	2.5
1972	5.6	6.2	2.2	1.4	2.3	1.1	3.7	2.7	2.7
1973	4.9	5.6	1.9	1.3	2.1	1.2	2.6	3.5	2.5
1974	5.6	5.4	2.3	1.4	2.3	2.6	2.6	2.9	2.0
1975	8.5	6.9	4.4	1.9	4.1	4.8	4.1	3.3	1.6
1976	7.7	7.1	4.4	¹2.1	¹4.6	4.6	¹5.6	3.7	1.6

¹ Preliminary estimates based on incomplete data.
² Adjusted civilian labor force as a percent of civilian working age population.
³ Adjusted civilian employment as a percent of civilian working age population.
⁴ Published and adjusted data for the United States, Canada, and Australia are identical. For France, unemployment as a percent of the civilian labor force; for Japan, Italy, and Sweden, unemployment as a percent of the civilian labor force plus career military personnel; for Germany and Great Britain, registered unemployed as a percent of employed wage and salary workers plus the unemployed. With the exception of France, which does not publish an unemployment rate, these are the usually published unemployment rates for each country.

NOTE: Data for the United States relate to the population 16 years of age and over. Published data for France, Germany, and Italy relate to the population 14 years of age and over; for Sweden, to the population aged 16 to 74; and for Canada, Australia, Japan, and Great Britain, to the population 15 years of age and over. Beginning in 1973, published data for Great Britain relate to the population 16 years of age and over. The adjusted statistics have been adapted, insofar as possible, to the age at which compulsory schooling ends in each country. Therefore, adjusted statistics for France relate to the population 16 years of age and over, and for Germany to the population 15 years of age and over. The age limits of adjusted statistics for Canada, Japan, Great Britain, and Italy coincide with the age limits of the published statistics. Statistics for Sweden remain at the lower age limit of 16, but have been adjusted to include persons 75 years of age and over.

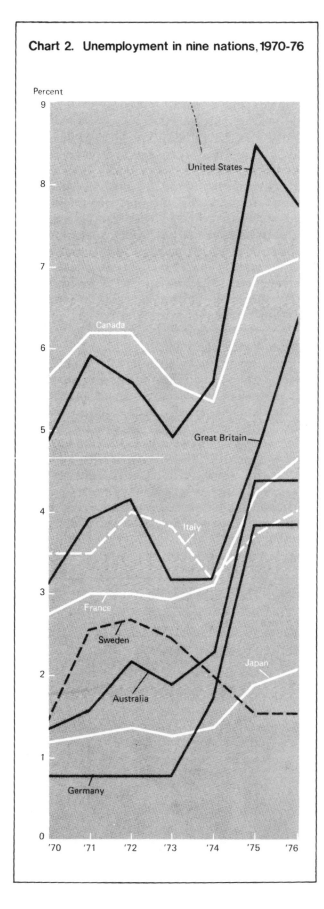

Chart 2. Unemployment in nine nations, 1970-76

Percent

United States

Canada

Great Britain

Italy

France

Sweden

Australia

Japan

Germany

'70 '71 '72 '73 '74 '75 '76

labor force growth came to a halt in 1974-75. Declining immigration also contributed to decreasing participation rates in France and Germany because a high proportion of migrants are economically active. Participation rates in the United States stabilized mainly because of the increased labor force participation of women. In 1976, participation in the labor force stabilized or rose in all countries, except Australia, France, and Germany.

Average hours. In France, Germany, Great Britain, Italy, and Japan, average weekly hours were reduced sharply during the recession to avoid layoffs. These countries all have systems for the payment of benefits during partial unemployment.[3] The decline in average hours in manufacturing in the United States, Canada, and Australia was small compared with most of the other nations.

Although higher in 1976 than in the previous year, average weekly hours in manufacturing in the United States did not return to pre-recession levels. Manufacturing hours were also above year-earlier levels in Canada, Japan, and Germany, and only Germany had not regained its pre-recession level. Hours worked did not increase to any significant extent in France and held steady in Great Britain in 1976.

Migration. In the past, the volume of migration in Western European countries tended to fluctuate with the business cycle. Foreign nationals flowed in when demand was high and left when it was low, without seriously affecting the recorded unemployment levels. This flexibility of labor supply acted as a cyclical shock absorber, helping to keep unemployment rates lower during recessions. However, in the 1974-75 recession, measures restricting immigration to Western Europe contributed to diminishing the cyclical outflow of migrants. Many foreign workers remained in the host countries, particularly in Germany, because they feared they would not be able to return when economic conditions improved. The existence of social benefits, such as unemployment compensation, which tend to be higher in the host country than in the home country, also encouraged many migrants not to repatriate. Consequently, Western European unemployment rolls were increased by the addition of unemployed foreign workers.

The "guestworker" phenomenon of Western European countries has no exact counterpart in the United States,[4] Canada, and Australia. These immigrant-receiving countries have traditionally taken the position that those who arrive from abroad to work may also become citizens; the legal foreign worker is usually granted immigrant status. However, Canada and Australia, countries which have traditionally encouraged immigration, both instituted more restrictive immigration policies during the recession.

Unemployment by age and sex

Table 3 presents 1974 unemployment rates by age and sex adjusted to U.S. concepts for the nine countries.[5] The lower age limit for teenagers has been adjusted to the age at which compulsory schooling ends in each country rather than to the U.S. lower age limit of 16. After an analysis of these data, unemployment trends by age and sex from late 1973 to late 1976 will be discussed. However, these trend data have not been adjusted to U.S. concepts because available statistics for most countries do not permit adjustment of partial-year data.

In the United States, unemployment rates vary widely by age and sex. Teenagers characteristically have the highest unemployment rate of any age group in the labor force, and older workers, age 55 and over, have relatively low jobless rates. Throughout the postwar period, U.S. women have had higher unemployment than men, and the gap has widened considerably since the 1950's. During recessionary periods, however, the gap usually narrows. The pattern of unemployment by age and sex in the other countries often parallels the U.S. experience, but there are some significant differences.

In all countries studied, teenagers had more difficulty than adults in securing jobs, but the degree of difficulty varied widely. In 1974, Italian teenagers had unemployment rates over 10 times as great as adults in the primary working ages of 25 to 54 (table 4). In the United States that year, the teenage unemployment rate was about four times the adult rate. This was lower than the differential in Australia, France, and Sweden, as well as in Italy. The youth-to-adult differential was narrowest in Japan.

Unlike the United States, older workers had higher unemployment rates than workers in the primary working ages (25-54) in Japan, France, Germany, Great Britain, and Sweden. In almost all countries studied, the unemployment rates for women were significantly higher than for men. The only exceptions were Great Britain, where men had a higher incidence of unemployment, and Japan, where the rates by sex were about equivalent.

Between late 1973 and late 1975, persons under age 25 experienced sharper increases in unemployment than persons 25 years and over in Canada, France, Germany, and Great Britain. In contrast, increases in joblessness among persons 25 years and over exceeded that of youths in the United States, Australia, and Japan. Older workers in all but Japan had smaller increases in unemployment than other age groups partially because of measures to protect older workers and to encourage earlier retirements.[6] Also, between late 1973 and late 1975, percentage increases in joblessness were higher for men than for women in the United States, Australia, Japan, France, and Germany, but Canadian, British, and Italian women experienced higher percent increases in unemployment than did the men of these countries.

Between late 1975 and late 1976 in Japan and

Table 3. Unemployment rates by age and sex adjusted to U.S. concepts in nine industrial countries, 1974[1]

Sex and age	United States	Canada	Australia	Japan	France	Germany	Great Britain	Italy	Sweden
BOTH SEXES									
All ages	5.6	5.4	2.3	1.4	3.0	0.7	3.2	3.2	2.0
Teenagers[2]	16.0	11.6	6.9	2.6	10.3	1.8	4.1	15.5	6.8
20 to 24 years	9.0	7.6	3.2	2.2	5.1	.8		9.9	3.4
25 to 54 years	3.8	[3]3.9	1.5	1.1	2.1	.5	2.7	1.5	1.3
55 and over	2.9	[3]4.0	.8	1.5	2.7	.8	4.1	.5	2.0
MEN									
All ages	4.8	4.8	1.8	1.4	1.7	.6	3.5	2.7	1.7
Teenagers[2]	15.5	12.2	6.1	3.2	7.0	1.7	4.4	15.6	6.0
20 to 24 years	8.7	7.9	2.9	2.1	3.5	.7		9.8	2.8
25 to 54 years	3.1	3.2	1.1	1.1	1.0	.4	2.8	1.4	1.1
55 and over	2.7	3.6	(4)	2.0	2.2	.8	4.9	.6	2.1
WOMEN									
All ages	6.7	6.4	3.2	1.3	4.9	.9	2.7	4.2	2.4
Teenagers[2]	16.5	10.9	7.7	2.1	14.7	1.8	3.8	15.3	8.0
20 to 24 years	9.5	7.3	3.8	2.2	6.8	.9		10.1	4.0
25 to 54 years	4.9	5.1	2.1	1.3	3.9	.8	2.5	1.7	1.6
55 and over	3.3		(4)		.7	3.4	1.0	1.9	(4)	2.3

[1] For France, data are for March 1974; for Germany, May 1973; for Great Britain, annual averages 1973.
[2] 16 to 19-year-old persons in the United States, France, Great Britain, and Sweden; 15 to 19-year old persons in Canada, Australia, Japan, and Germany; 14 to 19-year-old persons in Italy.
[3] Estimates by BLS based on new Canadian survey definitions.
[4] Not statistically significant.

Table 4. Ratio of teenage to adult unemployment rates[1] in eight industrial countries, 1974

Country	Both sexes	Men	Women
United States	4.2	5.0	3.4
Canada	3.0	3.8	(2)
Australia	4.6	5.5	3.7
Japan	2.4	2.9	1.6
France	4.9	7.0	3.8
Germany	3.6	4.3	2.3
Italy	10.3	11.1	9.0
Sweden	5.2	5.5	7.3

[1] Ratio of teenage unemployment rate to unemployment rate for 25 to 54-year-old persons.
[2] Not available.

Sweden, unemployment for women increased while joblessness for men declined. Unemployment rose for both sexes in Canada, France, Great Britain, and Italy, but the increase was far greater for women than for men in France and Great Britain. In Italy, the growth in unemployment for men exceeded that for women. In the United States and Germany, unemployment for men declined, while the number of jobless women remained about the same.

In late 1973, 1975, and 1976, unemployment rates for women were significantly higher than the rates for men in all countries except Japan and Great Britain. This was the same pattern indicated by the 1974 figures adjusted to U.S. concepts. In Japan, the impact of the recession was borne primarily by temporary workers, the majority of whom are women and older workers. Instead of looking for alternative employment, many laid-off Japanese women withdrew from the labor market and, thus, reduced the recorded jobless rates for women. Had these women remained in the labor force, the unemployment rate for women would have been higher than for men.

National developments

United States. During 1974 and 1975, the United States suffered from its worst economic downturn since the Depression of the 1930's. The recession began slowly after the energy crisis in the autumn of 1973 and rapidly gained momentum in late 1974 and early 1975. Unemployment increased substantially at the end of 1974, reaching a peak of 8.8 percent in the second quarter of 1975. By mid-1975, the American economy reached a turning point. Unemployment edged downward, averaging 8.5 percent for 1975. Joblessness continued declining to 7.4 percent in the second quarter of 1976, but by midyear began rising again. In the fourth quarter, the unemployment rate had reached an average of 7.9 percent because of the increasing numbers of both job losers and persons re-entering the labor force.

A decline in U.S. employment occurred in the fourth quarter of 1974 and the first quarter of 1975. Reductions in employment were sharpest in manufacturing and construction, whereas employment in the service sector remained relatively stable. The stability of service employment was partially the result of the federally funded public service jobs programs established to combat rising joblessness.[7] Employment growth resumed in the second quarter of 1975 and continued through August 1976. After a brief "pause" in the fall of 1976, employment reached a new high of 88.4 million in December.

Canada. Canada's most severe postwar recession began in the second quarter of 1974. Joblessness increased quite rapidly, moving from 5.3 percent in the third quarter of 1974 to 7.1 percent in the second half of 1975. In the fourth quarter of 1975, joblessness began to decline slowly, and in the first quarter of 1976, the recovery appeared to be well underway as the unemployment rate dropped to 6.9 percent. However, the rate rose to 7.1 percent in the very next quarter, and by December 1976, the unemployment rate had climbed to 7.5 percent—the highest since 1961.

Employment promotion and training schemes were stepped up in response to the recession. Total expenditures on the various programs doubled in relation to Gross National Product from 1970-71 to 1975-76. One scheme, the Local Initiatives Program, created 26,000 community level jobs in 1975. This program, introduced in the fall of 1971, is aimed at reducing seasonal and regional unemployment. With the aid of Federal funds, local governments and private organizations sponsor nonprofit, primarily labor intensive, community service projects to create jobs for unemployed persons. Priority is given to persons receiving unemployment insurance benefits or social assistance.

The growth rate of Canada's labor force tapered off from a 7-year high of 4.5 percent in 1973 to 3.6 percent in 1975 and 2.5 percent in 1976. The immigration law of 1974 tied immigration more closely to labor market needs, and, thus, contributed to the lower rate of growth.

Australia. The 1974-75 recession was also severe in Australia. Joblessness began rising sharply in the third quarter of 1974 and a year later had doubled, reaching a postwar high of 4.6 percent. In the first half of 1976, joblessness declined for the first time in over 2 years. In the third quarter, however, the unemployment rate increased by 0.6 percentage points to 4.9 percent.

Employment decreased from mid-1974 until the end of 1975. Selective measures were taken to protect employment, and immigration laws were modified to safeguard employment of Australians.[8] A National Employment and Training Scheme was introduced to upgrade the skill level of the labor force with priority accorded to jobless persons. A Regional Employment Development Scheme was established to create jobs in areas of high unemployment. Additional government funds were also authorized to expand the apprenticeship program.

Japan. During 1975, Japan was still in the midst of the severe recession which followed the 1974 "oil shock." The fourth quarter 1975 jobless rate of 2.2 percent, although low in comparison with other countries, was the highest rate recorded in Japan since 1959. By early 1976, the economy began to recover, and unemployment dropped to 1.9 percent in March. However, beginning in the second quarter, the jobless rate edged upward again, and the unemployment rate for 1976 averaged 2.1 percent.

As these low rates indicate, joblessness is not highly sensitive to the demand for labor in Japan. Employers, with their tradition of lifetime employment policies, prefer to reduce working hours, terminate contracts with part-time, seasonal, and temporary workers, reduce new hires of school leavers, and encourage "voluntary retirement." During the 1974-75 recession, Japanese employers also stepped up the practice of transferring employees from one job to another within the same company and setting up special education and training programs to avoid layoffs of permanent employees. In 1975, employment of regular workers increased by 0.5 percent, but employment of temporary workers and day laborers fell by over 5 percent. New hires of school leavers were reduced sharply as more than one-third of Japan's major businesses canceled plans to hire college and university graduates.

Most firms employing over 1,000 permanent workers solicited "voluntary retirements" by offering larger than normal lump sum retirement allowances. These programs were aimed specifically at younger women who tend to resign before their marriage and older workers with about 5 years left before mandatory retirement. The firms offered job placement guidance to those "voluntary retirees" who wished to continue working. Those not placed in new jobs are eligible to collect unemployment insurance benefits while jobseeking. Persons 55 years of age and over are eligible to collect benefits for up to 300 days.

Under the Employment Insurance Law of 1975, the Japanese government subsidized enterprises which kept employees on the payroll rather than laying them off. This employment adjustment grant enabled enterprises in industries designated as economically impacted by the Ministry of Labor to pay up to 90 percent of the workers' basic wage for 6 months with a 3-month additional extension. In small and medium-size firms, the government subsidy amounted to two-thirds of the workers' wage; in large-size firms, one-half of wage costs were covered. In several hard-pressed industries, the Ministry of Labor approved four consecutive 3-month extensions of this grant. Approximately one-third of all Japanese workers were eligible for such compensation during 1975.

France. Unemployment in France began to rise at the end of 1974. The jobless rate increased from 3.5 percent of the labor force to 4.6 percent between the fourth quarters of 1974 and 1975. During 1976, the jobless rate remained around 4.6 percent.

In response to the highest levels of unemployment recorded in the postwar period, the French government substantially raised unemployment benefits for certain workers. Beginning January 1, 1975, workers laid off for economic reasons were paid 90 percent of their former gross wage for up to 1 year unless they were re-employed. In mid-1976, about one out of every eight persons registered as unemployed was receiving this high benefit rate. The amount and duration of official assistance for workers on short-time schedules was also increased. The government subsidized 90 percent of the employer-paid supplementary assistance for workers on short time. The number of persons who were partially unemployed peaked at 385,000, and more than 1.4 million days were compensated for by unemployment assistance in November 1975. By August 1976, the number on short time had fallen sharply to 35,000, with 142,000 days paid for.

Financial incentives were provided to firms employing, for at least 1 year, persons under 25 years of age seeking their first job or persons unemployed more than 6 months. Training of unemployed 16- to 25-year-old persons for at least 6 months was encouraged via government subsidies of up to 100 percent of training costs plus the minimum wage.

Labor force participation declined from 57.0 percent in 1974 to 56.7 percent in 1975 and 56.3 in 1976, mainly because of the labor force withdrawal of women and a tendency for young people to continue their schooling rather than seek work. Also contributing to the fall were an increase in early retirements because of financial inducements[9] and a halting of immigration of foreign workers from outside the Common Market.

Germany. The average number of unemployed persons in Germany more than quadrupled between 1973 and 1975, approaching 1 million or averaging 3.8 percent of the civilian labor force. Joblessness peaked at 4.2 percent in the third quarter of 1975, and then declined slowly to 3.7 percent in the second quarter of 1976. By the end of 1976, German unemployment was 3.5 percent.

The large-scale outflow of foreign workers which took place in prior recessions did not occur during the 1974-75 recession. A November 1973 ban on recruitment of workers from countries outside the European Economic Community encouraged migrants from outside the community who lost their jobs to remain in Germany, fearing that they might not be able to return at a later date. In March 1975, over half of the employed migrant workers came from countries outside the European Community. Because there were few job opportunities elsewhere and unemployment compensation was usually higher in Germany than in their home countries, many unemployed foreigners chose to remain in Germany.

During the 1974-75 recession, approximately 10 percent of the migrant labor force left Germany, whereas during the 1966-67 recession, 25 percent returned home.[10] In 1975, 14 percent (151,500) of the registered unemployed were foreigners, compared to 3 percent (15,300) in 1967. By August 1976, the number of registered unemployed migrants had fallen from the April 1975 peak of 16.4 percent to 8 percent of total registrations. These figures probably understate foreign worker unemployment, because there were several hundred thousand migrants who were not entitled to unemployment benefits.[11] Additionally, a number of foreign workers, especially women, withdrew from the labor market but still remained in Germany.

In late 1974 and early 1975, the German government introduced measures to reduce the number of registered unemployed foreigners by requiring them to accept jobs which paid less than their former wages or unemployment compensation. If two such offers were refused, these workers could no longer collect unemployment compensation. Other efforts to limit employment of immigrants included the preferential hiring of German nationals, the denial of work permits to dependents of migrants, stiffer penalties for illegally employing aliens, and restrictions on the right of immigrants to settle in areas where foreigners constitute more than 12 percent of the population. The regional government of Baden-Wuerttemberg encouraged migrants to return home by offering them a lump-sum payment of their social security contributions.

Labor force programs initiated or expanded during the recession included wage subsidies to employers hiring additional workers, mobility allowances to aid workers who had to move to accept new jobs, special job creation activities directed toward older workers, youth, and the handicapped, and increased vocational education opportunities. Unemployment compensation and assistance, bad weather allowances for construction workers, and short-time work benefits were all increased.

In 1975, about 350,000 workers received financial assistance to relocate; wage subsidies paid to employers promoted the hiring of 79,000 workers; general employment subsidies involved the employment of 125,000 persons; and 84,000 persons participated in occupational training programs for the unemployed.[12]

Despite the more than 773,000 workers on short time, employment fell by 890,000 in 1975—which exceeded the increase in unemployment by 370,000. The decline affected all sectors of the economy, but was concentrated in the industrial sector. As of June 1976, employment was still falling, although at a greatly reduced rate, and the number of persons on short time had fallen to 320,000.

Great Britain. Unemployment in Great Britain has been rising almost steadily since the beginning of the oil crisis in the autumn of 1973. Between the fourth quarters of 1973 and 1975, joblessness rose from 2.7 percent to 5.7 percent. Unemployment continued to rise in 1976 and, in June, reached a new peak of 1.8 million persons or 7.2 percent. During the second half of 1976, joblessness leveled off at about 6.6 percent.

In 1975, the government undertook selective measures to limit unemployment and stimulate investment. The measures included: a grant to the Manpower Services Commission to create 15,000 jobs, particularly for young people in areas of high unemployment; a recruitment subsidy for the hiring of unemployed school leavers; the extension to the entire country of the temporary employment subsidy for retraining an employee who would otherwise be laid off; an additional grant for training programs with emphasis on apprenticeship schemes; and mobility allowances to encourage movement of unemployed persons to areas where jobs were available.

Employment fell by 160,000 in 1975, even though increased employment in the public sector, particularly for women, partially offset the decline in the private sector. Employees in manufacturing on short time peaked at 230,000 in the second quarter of 1975.

Italy. In Italy, the rise in joblessness was small relative to the decline in industrial output during the

1974-75 recession. Between the second quarters of 1974 and 1975, the unemployment rate rose from 2.9 percent to 3.9 percent, while industrial output fell by 12.5 percent. Averaging 3.7 percent in 1975, joblessness rose to 4.2 percent of the labor force in the third quarter of 1976. Employment increased in 1976 for the fourth consecutive year, reversing the general decline of the 1960's. The rising level of employment can be attributed partly to the extensive use of shortened workweeks and the rapid growth recorded in the service sector.[13]

Unemployment does not fully reflect the degree of labor force slack in Italy. Agreements reached between management and labor have helped to share the burden of recession by encouraging partial rather than full unemployment. The employer-financed Wage Supplement Fund allows industry or construction to reduce production, while maintaining employment by putting workers on shorter hours and paying supplements amounting to 80 percent of lost gross earnings. In 1975, over 350 million hours, more than double the 1974 level and approximately 11 percent of total hours worked, were compensated for by the fund. Consequently, the deterioration in the demand for labor in industry is initially reflected by a decline in working hours and a rise in the number of persons involuntarily working part time.

The number of persons working shorter hours for economic reasons in all sectors of the economy peaked at 520,000 in the second quarter of 1975 and averaged 446,000 for the year. In the first half of 1976, the number fell to 340,000. However, the number increased by 80,000 in the second half of the year.

In 1976, the Italian government set up a new scheme to promote the employment of young people who, because of their inexperience and newness to the labor market, are particularly hard to place. The plan provided funding for 300,000 positions in the private sector and 120,000 in the public sector. The government subsidized the minimum wages for each registered unemployed youth (age 15-26) hired on 1- or 2-year training contracts involving work and vocational training. During the period of the contract, the companies, which must have at least 20 employees, are not allowed to lay off workers.

Sweden. Labor market developments in Sweden differed markedly from the trend in other industrial countries during the recent international recession. Unemployment in 1975 remained low, falling to 1.6 percent from 2.0 percent in the previous year. Joblessness fluctuated within a narrow range in 1975 and 1976 partly because of expansionary economic policies adopted to maintain employment. The May 1976 unemployment rate of 1.4 percent was the lowest in almost 6 years, but the average unemployment rate for the year was the same as in 1975.

Although a decline in export demand caused a drop of more than 2 percent in industrial production, employment continued to expand in 1975 and 1976. The bulk of the increase occurred in the public sector with women the main beneficiaries. A tendency of Swedish enterprises to hoard labor in anticipation of the upturn in the world economy served to maintain employment.[14] The growth in aggregate hours worked, less than 1 percent, was not as strong as the growth of employment because of changes in overtime, shortened workweeks, and the increased employment of women who, on average, work shorter hours than men.

Among the stimulatory actions taken by the government were 25 special measures to maintain employment. To encourage industry to increase inventories instead of cutting production and employment, the government paid a 20-percent subsidy on stockpiles built up above normal levels. Subsidies were also paid to those enterprises which hired youths or trained workers who would otherwise have been laid off. Beginning in February 1976, a 75-percent wage subsidy was paid to those local authorities which gave additional training to current employees and at the same time employed a jobless person, preferably one under 25, to replace the trainee.

The Labor Market Board continued its expansive policies of training and public works programs for the unemployed and the handicapped during 1975. Close to 94,000 persons, nearly one and a half times the number of unemployed, were in job training programs or employed in public relief works, archive work, and sheltered workshops. ☐

------FOOTNOTES------

[1] See *Monthly Labor Review,* August 1962, pp. 857-64; March 1965, pp. 256-59; April 1967, pp. 18-20; September 1970, pp. 12-23; June 1972, pp. 29-33; January 1974, pp. 47-52; and June 1975, pp. 9-18.

[2] See James E. McCarthy, "Employment and Inflation in Major Industrial Countries," *The Conference Board Worldbusiness Perspectives,* August 1975, p. 4; and Julius Shiskin, "Employment and unemployment: the doughnut or the hole?" *Monthly Labor Review,* February 1976, pp. 3-10.

[3] See Constance Sorrentino, "Unemployment compensation in eight industrial nations." *Monthly Labor Review,* July 1976, pp. 18-24.

[4] In the United States, the number of illegal aliens is rapidly increasing. The Immigration and Naturalization Service estimates that there

are approximately 8 million illegal aliens currently in the United States.

[5] For an earlier analysis of unemployment by age and sex adjusted to U.S. concepts see Constance Sorrentino, "Unemployment in the United States and seven foreign countries," *Monthly Labor Review*, September 1970, pp. 12-23. Some of these data have subsequently been revised.

[6] Although compulsory retirement in Japan is at age 55, social security pensions are not payable until age 60. At the time of compulsory retirement, workers are given a lump-sum separation payment. However, the amount of this payment is generally not enough to allow for self-sufficiency before age 60. Therefore, most workers continue employment until 62 or 63.

[7] Stephen M. St. Marie and Robert W. Bednarzik, "Employment and unemployment during 1975," *Monthly Labor Review*, February 1976, pp. 11-20.

[8] *Economic Surveys: Australia* (Organization for Economic Cooperation and Development, July 1975), p. 40.

[9] As of July 1975, French manual workers engaged in more arduous kinds of labor and all women workers who have borne at least three children became eligible for early retirement at age 60 on the same pension as is normally given at age 65. Other workers age 60 and over are given "income guarantees" of about 70 percent of former earnings until eligible for pension.

[10] "Migrants: unemployed, they stay on," *ILO Information*, Vol. 4, No. 1, 1976, p. 11.

[11] "Slamming the Door on Europe's Guest Workers," *The Economist*, Aug. 9, 1975, p. 24.

[12] "Labor Market Assessment of the Federal Labour Institution," *What's New in Labor and Social Policy*, Vol. IV, No. 3 (April/May 1976), pp. 6-9.

[13] The high incidence of work done at home in Italy, which goes virtually unrecorded, is another element to consider when interpreting employment statistics. Partly as a result of legislation passed in 1973, home workers have been increasingly taking up recorded employment. See *Economic Surveys: Italy* (Organization for Economic Cooperation and Development, January 1976), p. 14.

[14] *The Swedish Economy, Preliminary National Budget* (Economic Department, Ministry of Finance, 1976), p. 97.

APPENDIX: Adjustment to U.S. data concepts

The basic labor force and unemployment statistics of the foreign countries studied, with the exceptions of Australia and Canada, require adjustments to bring them into closer comparability with U.S. data. Adjustments have been made for all known major definitional differences. The accuracy of the adjustments depends on the availability of relevant information, and, in some instances, it is necessary to make estimates based on incomplete data. Therefore, it is possible to achieve only approximate statistical comparability among countries. Nevertheless, the adjusted figures provide a better basis for international comparisons than the figures regularly published by each country.

The statistical incomparability of national figures on unemployment is attributable to two chief causes: (1) differences in the systems for collecting data, and (2) differences in concepts or definitions.

Statistical systems. Two systems for measuring unemployment are used by the countries studied by the Bureau of Labor Statistics. The United States, Canada, Australia, Japan, Italy, and Sweden depend on periodic (usually monthly) labor force sample surveys, whereas France, Germany, and Great Britain rely on monthly counts of registrants at employment exchanges. Labor force surveys generally yield the most comprehensive overall statistics, because they are designed to cover all persons seeking work, whether or not they register with employment exchanges. Also, changes in legislation and administrative regulations do not affect the continuity of the survey series, but may have a substantial impact on registration data.

Fortunately, all countries produce a good deal of supplementary information on unemployment in addition to the official unemployment rate. Such additional sources have been indispensable in adjusting the official data. For example, the three countries which use unemployment registrations as their official source of data also conduct periodic labor force surveys. BLS uses the results of these surveys to obtain adjustment factors to apply to the registered unemployed series. A problem arises from the fact that there is often a long time lag between data collection and survey publication (for example, the latest published survey for Great Britain is for 1973; for Germany, April 1975). Thus, BLS must occasionally make revisions to the comparative estimates when more recent surveys are published.

Concepts and definitions. Even when the same type of data collection method is used, definitions of unemployment and labor force may differ from country to country. Thus, labor force surveys may differ in regard to treatment of such groups as military personnel, students, unpaid family workers, discouraged workers, and persons on temporary layoff. Other areas of difference include criteria for seeking work, reference periods, age limits, and tests for current availability on the part of unemployed persons.

BLS is able to make adjustments of foreign country survey data to U.S. concepts for many of the differences noted above. However, there are certain conceptual differences for which it is not possible to make adjustments. For example, no adjustment can be made for differences in amount of time allowed for jobseeking activities. Since 1967, the U.S. survey has required active jobseeking within the past 4 weeks for a person to be counted as unemployed. Prior to 1967, the U.S. time period was vague and was probably interpreted by some jobseekers to refer only to the survey week. Special studies indicated that the effect of the change in definition in 1967 resulted in only a small increase in the number of persons enumerated as unemployed. In several foreign countries, the reference period for unemployment appears to be limited to the survey week. However, in practice, the reference period may be longer than the survey week because persons awaiting the results of previous job applications are generally counted as unemployed.

Revisions. Tables 1 and 2 include some revisions of the previously published estimates for Australia, Canada, France, Germany, and Great Britain. The revisions for Australia begin with 1975 and arise from modifications in the definition of unemployed persons. In February 1975, more comprehensive questions were added to the labor force survey, and the jobseeking period was extended from 1 to 4 weeks. Discouraged workers and persons who had looked for work in the survey week but would not have been able to start work that week, both formerly classified as unemployed, are now classified as not in the Australian labor force. Also, persons who had not looked for work during the survey week but had done so in the previous 3 weeks (formerly classified as not in the labor force) are now included in the unemployed. These changes have brought the Australian survey closer in concept to the U.S. survey, and therefore, no adjustments are necessary for comparability with U.S. definitions. The impact of these changes was to revise upward the 1975 unemployment rate from 4.2 percent to 4.4 percent. The revisions raise the unemployment rate by one-half of 1 percentage point for all women and by seven-tenths of 1 percentage point for married women. The increases in the jobless rates of men were marginal. Data for years prior to 1975 are still on the old definition, and the Australian Bureau of Statistics does not plan to make revisions for historical comparability.

In 1975, Canada revised its labor force survey to embrace a number of substantial statistical refinements, to collect new data, and to ask more specific questions on labor force status. The new survey is very close in concept to the U.S. survey, and, therefore, no adjustments are required for comparability with U.S. definitions. The revisions of the survey resulted in changes in levels and patterns of certain

series because of more precise identification of employment activities. Overall, unemployment rates were revised downward. While the total difference is slight (a downward revision of 0.1 percent in 1975), there are substantial differences in estimates by sex and region. In the revised survey, unemployment is significantly higher for women and lower for men. In 1975, the unemployment rate for women was 6.4 percent according to the old survey and 8.1 percent according to the new survey. Joblessness was formerly understated for women because they tended to respond to the question "What did . . . do last week?" in terms of household or other non-labor force activities. The more specific wording of the revised questionnaire revealed that some of these women were unemployed. Lower unemployment estimates for men (6.2 percent versus 7.4 percent) result from differences in the manner in which the new survey identifies and classifies persons who have not actively sought work.

Historical data have been revised on the basis of the new survey for 1966 and later years. Data for earlier years have not been revised because labor market conditions were believed to be too different in this earlier period to make estimates based on 1975 relationships.

The revisions in the data for France are based on the recently published detailed results of the 1971 and 1972 labor force surveys and the preliminary results of the 1973-76 surveys, which have been matched against the unemployment registration data. The revised French data also incorporate several new adjustments made possible by additional questions asked in the labor force surveys. The overall effect of these revisions has been to raise the adjusted French unemployment rates by less than three-tenths of 1 percentage point from 1970 through 1973. The average annual unemployment rate for 1974 remained the same as previously published, and the estimate for the first quarter of 1975 was reduced substantially because of the results of the April 1975 labor force survey. The 1975 survey indicated a sharp decline in the ratio of unemployment under U.S. concepts to unemployment from the registration statistics. This decline in the adjustment ratio was caused by the combined effect of: the further spread of the National Employment Agency to cover virtually the entire country; and the lengthening recession and increased unemployment benefits, which induced more unemployed persons to register.

The revisions in the data for Germany result from the incorporation of the 1975 labor force survey results and a new method of estimating average annual adjustment factors. Formerly, when the German labor force survey was conducted quarterly (one large sample-size survey and three much smaller surveys), BLS based its adjustments on the last year when data for all four quarters were available. Beginning in 1975, only the larger, more statistically reliable survey has been conducted. Therefore, BLS has revised its adjustments of German data so that they are now based on data from the large-sample labor force surveys, prorated from year to year These revisions lower unemployment rates slightly from those published previously.

Revisions for Great Britain stem from revised historical employment statistics and from the results of the 1972 and 1973 General Household Survey. The revised historical statistics were derived from the new establishment census. The household survey, providing annual unemployment rates under definitions quite similar to U.S. definitions, indicates that unemployed persons are now being registered more fully than during the 1960's. The effect of these revisions has been to slightly lower the adjusted British unemployment rates in some years.

Adjustment factors for 1974 have been assumed to be the same as in 1973 because the unemployment pattern was almost identical in both years. In 1975 and 1976, when unemployment rose substantially, adjustment factors from 1972 were used because that was a year of high unemployment. When results of the 1974 and later surveys are published, these estimates may require revision.

Adjustments by age and sex. The adjusted unemployment rates by age and sex for 1974 are less reliable than the overall adjusted unemployment rates. Whereas adjustments made to the overall unemployment rates are based on published statistics generally available each year, adjustments by age and sex have been partially estimated on the basis of data for years other than 1974. For instance, age distributions of career military personnel are often available only for census years.

Region and country	Year	Population[1] (thousands)	Labor force		Percent of labor force engaged[2] in—		Source of labor force data[4]
			Total (thousands)	Percent wage and salary workers[2]	Agriculture[3]	Manufacturing	
Africa:							
Ghana	1960	6,777	2,725	19.9	58.0	8.6	A
	1970	8,630	3,332	22.5	--------	--------	A
Morocco	1960	[5]11,626	3,254	34.7	56.3	8.2	A
	1971	15,830	3,981	37.2	50.6	9.7	A
South Africa	1951	12,708	4,593	--------	32.8	10.9	A
	1960	15,925	5,721	--------	29.5	11.3	A
	1970	21,830	7,986	--------	28.0	12.8	A
U.A.R. (Egypt)	1960	25,832	7,782	49.3	56.6	9.0	A
	1966	30,140	8,334	53.9	53.4	12.9	A
America:							
Argentina	1947	15,932	6,446	70.1	25.2	22.1	A
	1960	20,850	7,424	69.9	17.8	25.1	A[6]
	1970	23,210	9,011	70.8	14.8	19.7	A
Brazil	1950	[5]51,944	17,117	50.6	60.6	13.0	A[7]
	1960	69,730	22,651	48.0	54.1	12.4	A[7]
	1970	93,320	29,557	54.8	44.3	11.0	A
	1973	101,430	37,750	--------	--------	--------	B
Canada	1950	13,712	5,163	68.2	19.7	25.5	B[8]
	1960	17,909	6,411	75.5	10.7	22.9	B[8]
	1965	19,680	7,141	80.7	8.3	22.9	B[8]
	1970	21,320	8,374	81.7	6.1	21.4	B[8]
	1975	22,831	10,060	82.6	4.8	18.8	B[8]
	1976	--------	10,308	90.1	4.6	18.9	B[8]
Chile	1952	6,295	2,155	71.4	29.6	18.7	A
	1960	7,683	2,389	72.8	27.7	18.0	A
	1970	9,720	2,607	70.1	21.2	15.9	A
Colombia	1951	11,589	3,756	52.5	53.9	12.3	A[9]
	1964	17,462	5,134	57.3	47.2	12.8	B
	1970	21,120	6,226	--------	38.6	15.4	B
	1973	22,270	5,975	49.8	25.9	11.4	A
Dominican Republic	1960	3,036	821	44.1	61.4	8.2	A
	1970	4,060	1,241	38.2	44.3	8.1	A
Guatemala	1964	4,305	1,317	45.9	65.4	11.4	A
	1973	5,540	1,546	48.0	57.0	13.7	A
Jamaica	1960	1,629	655	54.6	36.1	13.7	B
	1975	2,030	869	44.6	29.0	10.4	B[10]
Mexico	1950	25,826	8,345	45.9	57.8	11.6	A[11]
	1960	36,046	11,332	64.1	54.2	13.7	A
	1970	50,690	12,955	62.2	39.5	16.7	A[12]
	1975	60,150	16,597	62.3	40.9	17.8	C
Peru	1961	10,320	3,125	48.1	49.7	13.2	A[13]
	1970	13,590	4,269	36.4	45.1	14.5	B[13]
	1972	14,460	3,786	48.2	40.6	12.7	A[13]
Puerto Rico	1950	2,211	597	80.8	36.8	17.2	A
	1960	2,362	594	80.2	23.0	17.2	A
	1970	2,720	684	--------	--------	--------	A[14]
	1975	3,090	870	84.6	7.8	18.8	B
	1976	--------	898	84.8	7.7	18.5	B
United States	1950	152,271	63,859	76.2	11.2	23.9	B[15]
	1960	180,671	72,143	80.0	7.6	23.3	B[15]
	1965	194,303	77,175	83.1	5.7	23.4	B[15]
	1970	204,878	85,903	85.9	4.0	22.5	B[15]
	1975	213,631	94,793	83.2	3.8	19.4	B[15]
	1976	214,955	96,917	84.1	3.4	19.6	B[15]
Venezuela	1950	4,976	1,706	54.0	41.3	10.1	A[16]
	1961	10,780	3,258	--------	20.3	18.6	A[16]
	1971	10,620	3,258	--------	20.3	18.6	B
	1975	11,990	3,172	62.3	18.6	15.4	B
Asia:							
China (Taiwan)	1956	9,240	2,993	33.1	50.1	10.9	A[17]
	1965	12,443	3,760	41.4	45.4	16.5	B[17]
	1970	14,512	4,654	50.0	36.1	20.0	B[17]
	1975	16,040	5,656	55.9	29.2	26.5	B[17]
	1976	16,343	5,748	57.5	28.7	28.0	B[17]
India	1951	[5]356,628	101,775	--------	70.6	9.0	A[18]
	1961	[5]439,235	188,676	12.8	72.9	9.5	A[19]
	1971	551,830	180,373	17.0	72.1	9.5	A[19]
Indonesia	1961	95,655	34,578	--------	68.0	5.4	A
	1965	104,880	36,543	27.1	67.2	5.6	B
	1971	117,890	40,100	31.7	62.2	7.4	A
Israel	1956	1,813	620	59.2	16.1	19.0	B[20]
	1961	2,185	752	64.3	12.8	21.9	A[20]
	1966	2,630	948	66.8	11.5	24.0	B[20]
	1970	2,910	1,001	70.8	8.6	23.8	B[20]
	1975	3,370	1,138	73.9	6.3	24.0	B[10, 20]

See footnotes at end of table.

POPULATION AND LABOR FORCE, SELECTED COUNTRIES

Region and country	Year	Population[1] (thousands)	Labor force		Percent of labor force engaged[2] in—		Source of labor force data[4]
			Total (thousands)	Percent wage and salary workers[2]	Agriculture[3]	Manufacturing	
Asia—Continued							
Japan	1955	89,000	41,940	41.5	34.3	17.9	B
	1960	93,210	45,110	51.9	27.6	21.0	B
	1965	97,952	47,870	59.9	21.6	24.0	B
	1970	104,340	51,530	64.2	16.3	26.7	B
	1975	110,570	53,230	68.4	11.6	25.3	B[21]
	1976	112,770	53,780	68.9	11.2	25.0	B
Korea, Republic of	1955	[5]21,526	8,073	12.1			A[14]
	1960	24,695	7,543	21.3	61.9	6.5	A[22]
	1965	28,327	8,859	29.7	54.3	8.7	B[22]
	1970	31,300	10,378	38.0	49.6	13.9	A[22]
	1975	34,660	12,340	38.9	44.0	17.9	B[22]
Pakistan	1951	76,602	22,393	15.9	76.5	6.3	A[23]
	1961	94,647	30,206	20.2	75.0	8.1	A[23]
	1965	102,876	39,591	34.8	67.6	9.6	B[23]
	1974	68,210	20,093	17.9	57.3	12.5	C[24]
Philippines	1948	19,144	7,416	40.3	65.7	6.1	A
	1960	27,410	8,536	27.2	60.5	9.8	A[17]
	1965	32,345	11,491	32.0	52.7	10.6	B[17]
	1970	36,850	12,297	39.9	51.5	11.4	A[17]
	1975	42,520	15,161	38.5	52.0	11.3	B[17]
Thailand	1954	19,925	10,249	6.7	88.0	2.1	C
	1960	26,392	13,837	11.8	82.0	3.4	A
	1970	36,210	16,850	15.4	78.2	4.1	A
	1973	39,790	17,117	19.9	71.8	7.0	B
Europe:							
Austria	1951	[5]6,934	3,347	61.9	32.3	28.3	A[25]
	1961	7,087	3,370	70.8	22.8	30.1	A
	1965	7,255	3,357		20.3	31.8	C
	1970	7,391	3,031	71.6	19.0	29.2	B
	1975	7,520	2,969	80.6	12.5	30.4	B
Belgium	1950	8,639	3,545	68.5	10.4	31.8	C
	1960	9,153	3,675	72.3	8.1	32.4	C
	1965	9,464	3,787	77.1	6.1	32.7	C
	1975	9,800	4,003	79.1	3.4	28.3	C
Czechoslovakia	1950	12,389	5,812	62.9	38.0	28.3	A
	1961	13,780	6,483	80.7	24.9	33.2	A
	1970	14,330	6,983	87.3	16.4	35.3	A[26]
Denmark	1950		2,063	75.6	25.1	26.1	A
	1955		2,136	73.8	22.9	25.7	A[10]
	1960	4,581	2,094	77.8	17.5	28.5	A
	1965	4,760	2,252	77.7	15.0	28.2	A[27]
	1970	4,930	2,313	80.2	10.6	25.9	B[27]
	1975	5,060	2,486	82.6	9.3	23.1	B[27]
France	1954	42,951	19,613	64.7	25.5	22.2	C
	1960	45,685	19,792	69.9	21.2	26.5	C
	1965	48,758	20,381	71.1	17.0	26.5	C
	1970	50,770	21,331	74.5	13.6	26.6	C
	1975	52,790	21,834	79.6	10.8	26.5	C
Germany, Democratic Republic	1971	17,060	8,214		11.7	37.6	A[28]
Germany, Federal Republic	1950	47,847	21,960	63.6	22.9	29.3	C
	1960	53,224	25,460	76.3	14.2	36.6	C

See footnotes at end of table.

Region and country	Year	Population[1] (thousands)	Labor force		Percent of labor force engaged[2] in—		Source of labor force data[4]
			Total (thousands)	Percent wage and salary workers[2]	Agriculture[3]	Manufacturing	
Europe—continued:							
Germany, Federal Republic and West Berlin-----------	1960	55,433	26,518	75.6	13.7	37.2	C
	1965	59,040	27,034	78.8	10.6	37.4	C
	1970	[29]60,650	26,817	81.1	8.4	38.4	C
	1975	61,830	26,424	79.1	6.9	34.8	C
	1976		26,164	79.3	6.8	34.7	C
Greece-----------	1951	7,646	2,840	36.8	48.2	15.9	A
	1961	8,398	3,639	33.5	53.9	13.4	A
	1971	8,850	3,284	41.8	40.5	16.4	A
Hungary-----------	1960	9,984	4,876	63.7	38.4	24.3	A
	1970	10,340	4,989	77.8	24.5	32.6	A
	1975	10,540	5,086	78.8	22.7	35.7	C[30]
Italy -----------	1951	46,996	19,693	----------	43.9	22.6	C[31]
	1960	49,642	20,972	56.4	31.3	25.3	B
	1965	51,940	19,717	61.7	24.9	27.5	B
	1970	53,570	19,302	66.5	18.8	30.3	B
	1975	55,810	19,650	71.4	15.1	31.2	B
	1976	56,190	19,858	71.5	14.8	31.0	B
Netherlands -----------	1947	9,629	3,866	68.4	19.3	23.9	A
	1960	11,480	4,232	74.8	11.0	27.4	C
	1965	12,292	4,538	78.4	8.6	28.2	C
	1970	13,030	4,752	80.4	6.9	25.3	C
	1973	13,439	4,790	80.0	6.5	23.4	C
Norway -----------	1950	3,279	1,388	71.1	25.9	25.8	A
	1960	3,581	1,406	78.0	19.5	25.5	A
	1965	3,723	1,448	76.4	17.4	25.7	C
	1970	3,880	1,509	79.7	13.8	26.5	A
	1975	4,010	1,734	82.4	9.9	24.9	B[32]
Poland-----------	1950	24,824	12,404	45.6	57.2	18.8	A[33]
	1960	29,703	13,907	51.9	47.7	23.3	A[33]
	1970	32,530	16,944	64.9	38.6	24.9	A[33]
	1974	33,690	17,507	69.0	34.6	30.2	A[33]
Portugal-----------	1950	8,405	3,289	69.8	48.4	18.8	A
	1960	8,826	3,424	71.9	42.3	20.3	A
	1970	[29]8,630	3,299	69.7	29.2	24.0	C[34]
Spain-----------	1950	27,868	10,793	65.7	48.8	17.6	A
	1960	30,303	11,817	59.3	41.1	22.1	A
	1965	32,060	12,177	59.5	32.6	25.2	C
	1970	33,780	12,732	62.6	28.8	26.5	C
	1975	35,470	13,388	----------	22.3	25.8	B
Sweden-----------	1950	7,014	3,105	76.8	20.3	31.5	A[35]
	1960	7,480	3,244	83.3	13.8	34.2	A[35]
	1965	7,734	3,742	84.8	11.1	32.1	B[35]
	1970	8,040	3,913	87.7	8.0	28.3	B
	1975	8,200	4,129	90.0	6.3	27.6	B
	1976	8,220	4,155	90.3	6.1	26.5	B

See footnotes at end of table.

POPULATION AND LABOR FORCE, SELECTED COUNTRIES

Region and country	Year	Population[1] (thousands)	Labor force		Percent of labor force engaged[2] in—		Source of labor force data[4]
			Total (thousands)	Percent wage and salary workers[2]	Agriculture[3]	Manufacturing	
Europe—continued							
Switzerland	1950	4,694	2,156	74.5	16.5	38.2	A
	1960	5,362	2,675	85.6	13.2	38.3	A[36]
	1970	6,190	2,996	85.0	7.7	37.7	A
	1974	6,440	2,943	---	7.6	---	C
Turkey	1955	[5]24,065	12,205	13.3	77.4	6.0	A
	1960	[5]27,755	12,993	18.8	75.0	6.8	A
	1965	31,150	13,614	22.5	71.8	7.1	A
	1970	35,605	15,119	27.6	67.6	8.5	A
U.S.S.R.	1959	210,484	108,995	60.4	35.2	33.6	A[37]
	1970	242,760	117,028	82.8	26.3	45.1	A[37]
United Kingdom	1951	50,562	22,610	87.8	5.1	37.4	A[38]
	1961	52,816	25,346	90.0	3.8	35.9	A[38]
	1965	54,218	25,504	90.5	3.7	34.0	C
	1970	55,421	25,293	88.8	3.1	33.4	C
	1975	55,962	25,834	87.9	2.6	29.8	C
	1976	---	26,084	86.2	2.5	28.7	C
Yugoslavia	1953	17,048	7,849	31.6	66.8	10.7	A[39]
	1961	18,607	8,340	42.3	56.9	11.9	A[39]
	1971	20,570	8,890	49.5	44.6	17.7	A[40]
Oceania:							
Australia	1954	[5]8,987	3,702	79.9	13.4	28.0	A[41]
	1961	[5]10,508	4,225	79.3	10.9	27.0	A[41]
	1965	11,390	4,745	81.6	9.7	29.5	B[42]
	1970	12,510	5,488	83.0	8.0	27.9	B[42]
	1975	13,500	5,991	81.9	6.6	22.0	B[29]
	1976	---	6,075	81.3	6.3	21.7	B
New Zealand	1951	[5]1,939	740	78.0	18.4	24.0	A[43]
	1961	2,420	895	83.9	14.4	25.0	A[43]
	1971	2,850	1,119	85.7	11.5	25.1	A[43]
	1975	3,070	1,199	---	12.0	23.5	C[43]

[1]Midyear estimates.

[2]Either experienced labor force or employed persons as percent of the total labor force. Data taken from population censuses usually relate to the experienced labor force; data taken from other sources, to employed persons.

[3]Includes forestry, hunting and fishing unless otherwise noted.

[4]Code:
  A—population census
  B—labor force sample survey
  C—official estimate

[5]Population census.

[6]Labor force excludes 99,445 persons 14 years of age.

[7]Indian jungle population (estimated at 150,000 persons in 1956) excluded. Agriculture includes mining and quarrying. Manufacturing includes construction in 1950 and 1960 and public utilities in 1950. Construction accounted for 3.5 percent of the labor force in 1960.

[8]Labor force excludes the Armed Forces (92,000 persons in 1970) and populations of the Yukon and Northwest Territories.

[9]Indian jungle population (128,000 persons) and the population of certain areas where the census was not carried out (191,500 persons) excluded.

[10]Manufacturing includes mining and quarrying.

[11]Percentages exclude 73,000 persons unemployed for 13 weeks or more.

[12]Labor force refers to persons who worked during 1969, regardless of the duration of work.

[13]Indian jungle population (estimated at 100,800 persons in 1961) excluded. Also, the population census data (1961 and 1972) do not include any adjustments for underenumeration (estimated at 412,800 persons in 1961).

[14]Labor Force excludes the unemployed.

[15]Alaska and Hawaii excluded in 1950. Agriculture excludes forestry and fishing. Manufacturing data are from an establishment survey and include wage and salary workers only.

[16]Indian jungle population (56,700 persons in 1950 and 31,800 persons in 1961) excluded.

[17]Armed Forces excluded.

[18]Kashmir-Jammu, the Jullundur area, and the tribal areas of Assam excluded. Labor force figures exclude family workers (37,937,200 persons).

[19]Parts of the North East Frontier Agency and Sikkim excluded. Labor force figures exclude unemployed persons.

[20]Armed forces excluded. In 1956, Bedouins in Negev also excluded. From 1970 onward, data include territories under occupation by Israeli military forces since June 1967.

[21]Beginning with 1973, data for Japan includes Okinawa (population of 990,000 persons and labor force of 370,000 persons in 1973).

[22]Military personnel in barracks excluded.

[23]Armed forces and persons living in certain frontier regions excluded. Data include Bangladesh.

[24]Persons living in Bangladesh, formerly a part of Pakistan, and certain frontier regions, and the unemployed excluded.

[25]Agriculture excludes hunting and fishing in 1951.

[26]Unpaid family workers excluded.

[27]Labor force excludes persons aged 75 years and over.

[28]Including East Berlin.

[29]Data not comparable with those for previous years.

[30]Labor force excludes persons seeking work for the first time. Manufacturing includes mining, quarrying, electricity, gas, and water.

[31]Military conscripts and unemployed excluded; permanent residents of institutions (300,000 persons) included. Percent engaged in manufacturing is not entirely comparable with 1960 and later data.

[32]Labor force excludes persons on compulsory military service [and persons aged 75 years and over]. Manufacturing includes mining, quarrying, electricity, gas, and water.

[33]Agriculture excludes sea fishing; manufacturing includes mining and quarrying, electricity and gas production, and sea fishing.

[34]Labor force relates to persons who worked at least 15 hours during the week preceeding the data of the census and include the Azores and Madeira Islands.

[35]Labor force excludes military conscripts in 1950 and 1960. Beginning in 1965, labor force data refer to persons age 16-74 years.

[36]Wage and salary workers include unpaid family workers.

[37]Manufacturing includes construction, transportation, and communications.

[38]Northern Ireland excluded. Wage and salary workers exclude the Armed Forces and unemployed.

[39]Residents of institutions included. For 1961, agriculture excludes hunting and fishing.

[40]Labor force excludes unemployed who at the date of the census declared themselves as being dependants.

[41]Full-blooded aborigines excluded.

[42]Manufacturing includes mining, electricity, gas, and water.

[43]Includes Maoris and excludes armed forces overseas.

NOTE: In so far as possible, the population estimates include national Armed Forces and diplomatic personnel and their dependents stationed outside the territory, and exclude alien Armed Forces, enemy prisoners of war, and alien diplomatic personnel and their dependents stationed inside the country.

The labor force data refer to the total of employed persons (including self-employed persons, wage and salary workers, and unpaid family workers) and unemployed persons, to the extent data are available. However, the figures are often not comparable because of differences between countries in the definitions used and methods of collection, e.g., differences in the minimum age for inclusion in the labor force; the extent to which family workers are included; the extent to which unemployed persons are included (particularly inexperienced new entrants into the labor force, who are frequently excluded from census data); and whether the count of persons in the labor force is based on usual employment status or actual status as of a particular day or other brief time period. The count of workers in agriculture is especially affected by the extent to which family workers are included and whether the count is based on usual or actual status. For similar reasons, the data for individual countries may not be comparable from one period to another, especially when the data are based on different sources, such as a census and a labor force survey.

SOURCE: **Demographic Yearbook** and **Monthly Bulletin of Statistics** (New York, Statistical Office of the United Nations), various issues; **Year Book of Labour Statistics** (Geneva, International Labour Office), various issues; Organization of Economic Co-operation and Development; and various individual country publications.

LABOR FORCE, EMPLOYMENT, AND UNEMPLOYMENT IN SELECTED INDUSTRIAL COUNTRIES

Year	United States[1]	Australia[1]	Canada[1]	Adjusted to U.S. concepts						As published					
				France	Germany, F.R. and West Berlin	Great Britain	Italy	Japan	Sweden	France	Germany, F.R. and West Berlin	Great Britain	Italy	Japan	Sweden
Civilian labor force[2] (in thousands)															
1967	77,347	4,958	7,748	20,160	25,850	24,600	19,290	48,810	3,743	20,118	26,409	24,542	19,525	49,830	3,774
1968	78,737	5,070	7,952	20,460	25,700	24,460	19,220	49,680	3,803	20,176	26,291	24,465	19,484	50,610	3,822
1969	80,734	5,213	8,195	20,720	25,970	24,400	19,030	50,140	3,815	20,434	26,535	24,468	19,266	50,980	3,840
1970	82,715	5,381	8,399	21,040	26,240	24,270	19,090	50,730	3,884	20,750	26,817	24,393	19,302	51,530	3,913
1971	84,113	5,486	8,644	21,270	26,350	24,020	19,010	51,030	3,932	20,958	26,910	24,160	19,254	51,780	3,961
1972	86,542	5,589	8,920	[3]21,490	26,300	24,240	18,800	51,140	3,939	21,155	26,901	24,414	19,028	51,820	3,969
1973	88,714	5,723	9,322	[3]21,710	26,410	24,530	18,930	52,580	3,952	21,388	26,985	24,686	19,169	53,260	3,977
1974	91,011	5,869	9,706	[3]21,900	26,210	24,610	19,230	52,440	4,013	21,601	26,797	24,772	19,458	53,100	4,043
1975	92,613	5,991	10,060	[3]21,950	[3]25,840	[3]24,860	19,450	52,530	4,097	21,649	26,424	25,012	19,650	53,230	4,129
1976	94,773	6,075	10,308	[3]22,000	[3]25,570	[3]25,120	19,660	53,100	4,123	[3]21,630	26,164	[3]25,148	19,858	53,780	4,155
Employment[2] (in thousands)															
1967	74,372	4,879	7,451	19,740	25,510	23,770	18,560	48,180	3,664	19,753	25,950	24,021	18,846	49,200	3,695
1968	75,920	4,992	7,593	19,880	25,300	23,660	18,480	49,080	3,718	19,749	25,968	23,916	18,800	50,020	3,737
1969	77,902	5,133	7,832	20,180	25,730	23,660	18,320	49,570	3,743	20,093	26,356	23,924	18,611	50,400	3,768
1970	78,627	5,306	7,919	20,460	26,040	23,520	18,430	50,140	3,830	20,394	26,668	23,811	18,693	50,940	3,854
1971	79,120	5,398	8,107	20,640	26,130	23,090	18,350	50,390	3,831	20,521	26,725	23,402	18,645	51,140	3,860
1972	81,702	5,464	8,363	[3]20,840	26,080	23,230	18,050	50,410	3,832	20,663	26,655	23,570	18,331	51,090	3,862
1973	84,409	5,615	8,802	[3]21,090	26,190	23,750	18,210	51,910	3,854	20,938	26,712	24,088	18,500	52,320	3,879
1974	85,936	5,736	9,185	[3]21,220	25,760	[3]23,830	18,630	51,700	3,933	21,100	26,215	24,176	18,898	52,370	3,963
1975	84,783	5,725	9,363	[3]21,010	[3]24,870	[3]23,690	18,740	51,530	4,030	20,764	25,350	24,042	18,996	52,230	4,062
1976	87,485	5,807	9,572	[3]20,980	[3]24,540	[3]23,510	18,870	52,020	4,057	[3]20,636	25,104	[3]23,843	19,127	52,700	4,089
Unemployment[4] (in thousands)															
1967	2,975	79	297	420	340	830	730	630	79	365	459	521	679	630	79
1968	2,817	78	359	580	400	800	740	590	85	427	323	549	684	590	85
1969	2,832	80	364	540	240	740	710	570	72	340	179	544	655	570	72
1970	4,088	75	480	580	200	750	660	590	59	356	149	582	609	590	59
1971	4,993	87	538	630	220	930	660	640	101	446	185	758	609	640	101
1972	4,840	125	557	[3]650	220	1,010	750	730	107	492	246	844	697	730	107
1973	4,304	108	520	[3]620	220	780	720	670	98	450	273	598	668	670	98
1974	5,076	133	521	[3]680	450	[3]780	610	740	80	501	582	596	560	740	80
1975	7,830	266	697	[3]940	[3]970	[3]1,170	710	1,000	67	885	1,074	970	654	1,000	67
1976	7,288	268	736	[3]1,020	[3]1,030	[3]1,610	790	1,080	66	[3]994	1,060	1,305	732	1,080	66
Unemployment rate[5]															
1967	3.8	1.6	3.8	2.1	1.3	3.4	3.8	1.3	2.1	1.8	2.1	2.2	3.5	1.3	2.1
1968	3.6	1.5	4.5	2.8	1.6	3.3	3.9	1.2	2.2	2.1	1.5	2.4	3.5	1.2	2.2
1969	3.5	1.5	4.4	2.6	.9	3.0	3.7	1.1	1.9	1.7	.9	2.4	3.4	1.1	1.9
1970	4.9	1.4	5.7	2.8	.8	3.1	3.5	1.2	1.5	1.7	.7	2.5	3.2	1.2	1.5
1971	5.9	1.6	6.2	3.0	.8	3.9	3.5	1.3	2.6	2.1	.8	3.4	3.2	1.2	2.5
1972	5.6	2.2	6.2	[3]3.0	.8	4.2	4.0	1.4	2.7	2.3	1.1	3.7	3.7	1.4	2.7
1973	4.9	1.9	5.6	[3]2.9	.8	3.2	3.8	1.3	2.5	2.1	1.2	2.6	3.5	1.3	2.5
1974	5.6	2.3	5.4	[3]3.1	1.7	[3]3.2	3.2	1.4	2.0	2.3	2.6	2.6	2.9	1.4	2.0
1975	8.5	4.4	6.9	[3]4.3	[3]3.8	[3]4.7	3.7	1.9	1.6	4.1	4.8	4.1	3.3	1.9	1.6
1976	7.7	4.4	7.1	[3]4.6	[3]4.0	[3]6.4	4.0	2.0	1.6	[3]4.6	4.6	5.6	3.7	2.0	1.6

[1]Published and adjusted data for the United States, Australia, and Canada are identical.
[2]Published figures for Germany, Italy, Japan, and Sweden include military personnel.
[3]Preliminary estimates based on incomplete data.
[4]Published figures for the United States, Australia, Canada, Italy, Japan, and Sweden refer to unemployment as recorded by sample labor force surveys; for France, to annual estimates of unemployment; and for Germany and Great Britain to the registered unemployed.
[5]Adjusted figures: as a percent of the civilian labor force. Published figures: for France, unemployment as a percent of the civilian labor force; for Italy, Japan, and Sweden, unemployment as a percent of the civilian labor force plus career military personnel; for Germany and Great Britain, registered unemployed as a percent of employed wage and salary workers plus the unemployed. With the excep-

tion of France, which does not publish an unemployment rate, these are the usually published rates for each country. Published rates shown for Germany and Great Britain cannot be computed from the data contained in this table.

NOTE: The adjusted statistics, insofar as possible have been adapted to the age at which compulsory schooling ends in each country. Therefore, the data for the United States and the adjusted data for France, Sweden, and beginning in 1973, Great Britain relate to the population 16 years of age and over; the data for Australia, Canada, Germany, Japan, and, prior to 1973, Great Britain relate to the population 15 years of age and over; and the data for Italy relate to the population 14 years of age and over.

ESTIMATED COMPENSATION PER HOUR WORKED OF PRODUCTION WORKERS IN MANUFACTURING, SELECTED COUNTRIES

Item and country	1967	1968	1969	1970	1971	1972	1973	1974	1975	1976[1]
Average hourly earnings in national currency:[2] [3]										
United States	2.83	3.01	3.19	3.36	3.57	3.81	4.08	4.41	4.81	5.19
Belgium	51.95	54.65	59.67	66.05	75.01	85.25	98.09	118.4	140.4	157.4
Canada	2.40	2.58	2.79	3.01	3.28	3.54	3.85	4.37	5.06	5.76
France	4.25	4.70	5.30	5.97	6.65	7.35	8.38	9.98	11.61	13.22
Germany	4.60	4.79	5.28	5.96	6.66	7.24	8.04	8.95	9.71	10.36
Italy	526	551	612	757	891	1,018	1,263	1,600	2,031	2,455
Japan	192	225	267	314	363	422	523	687	791	852
Netherlands	3.65	3.95	4.39	4.93	5.67	6.33	7.23	8.52	9.75	10.68
Sweden	9.28	9.85	10.60	12.01	12.90	14.83	16.05	17.81	20.45	24.08
United Kingdom	40.6	43.6	47.3	53.8	61.2	69.1	78.7	92.4	119.2	138.4
Total compensation per hour worked in national currency:[3] [4]										
United States	3.44	3.68	3.93	4.19	4.49	4.82	5.24	5.73	6.32	6.84
Belgium	78.08	82.90	91.35	103.2	119.2	140.1	164.0	199.6	242.9	273.4
Canada	2.84	3.07	3.33	3.60	3.95	4.29	4.69	5.37	6.26	7.22
France	6.98	7.73	8.47	9.57	10.71	11.93	13.68	16.39	19.37	22.21
Germany	6.36	6.68	7.42	8.48	9.66	10.72	12.13	13.93	15.38	16.66
Italy	744	780	868	1,054	1,244	1,412	1,742	2,246	2,886	3,506
Japan	217	255	303	355	411	480	592	778	904	974
Netherlands	5.50	6.09	6.86	7.73	8.99	10.14	11.92	14.26	16.36	17.80
Sweden	11.41	12.22	13.43	15.34	16.63	19.12	21.54	25.08	29.84	36.07
United Kingdom	45.8	47.3	53.8	61.9	70.9	81.2	93.2	110.5	144.6	168.3
Total compensation per hour worked in U.S. dollars:[4] [5]										
United States	3.44	3.68	3.93	4.19	4.49	4.82	5.24	5.73	6.32	6.84
Belgium	1.57	1.66	1.82	2.08	2.46	3.18	4.22	5.13	6.62	7.09
Canada	2.63	2.85	3.09	3.45	3.91	4.33	4.69	5.49	6.16	7.32
France	1.42	1.56	1.63	1.73	1.94	2.37	3.08	3.41	4.52	4.65
Germany	1.60	1.67	1.89	2.33	2.78	3.36	4.58	5.40	6.26	6.62
Italy	1.19	1.25	1.38	1.68	2.01	2.42	2.99	3.45	4.42	4.22
Japan	.60	.71	.84	.99	1.18	1.58	2.19	2.67	3.05	3.29
Netherlands	1.53	1.68	1.89	2.14	2.58	3.16	4.29	5.31	6.48	6.74
Sweden	2.21	2.36	2.60	2.96	3.26	4.02	4.95	5.66	7.20	8.27
United Kingdom	1.26	1.18	1.29	1.48	.1.73	2.03	2.28	2.59	3.21	3.04

[1]Preliminary.

[2]Published average hourly earnings do not include the same items of labor compensation in each country. Earnings generally include basic time and piece rates, overtime pay and shift differentials, regular bonuses and premiums, and cost of living adjustments. In some countries, earnings also include bonuses not paid regularly each pay period, private or contractual family allowances paid by the employer, and pay in kind. In general earnings are computed per hour paid and include pay for time not worked or else are computed per hour worked and exclude pay for time not worked. For Italy and Japan, however, earnings include pay for time not worked and are computed per hour worked. For all countries, earnings refer to gross payments made to the worker before payroll deductions for taxes and employee social insurance contributions.

[3]National currency units: United States, dollar; Belgium, franc; Canada, dollar; France, franc; Germany, mark; Italy, lira; Japan, yen; Netherlands, guilder; Sweden, Krona; and United Kingdom, pence.

[4]Total compensation includes all direct payments made to the worker (pay for time worked, pay for vacations, holidays, and other leave, all bonuses, and pay in kind) before payroll deductions of any kind, plus employer expenditures for legally-required insurance programs and contractual and private plans for the benefit of employees. In addition, compensation includes other significant taxes on payrolls or employment that are regarded as labor costs.

[5]Converted to U.S. dollars using the average daily exchange rate for the reference period.

SOURCE: Department of Labor, Bureau of Labor Statistics. Based on data from national and international statistical publications.

WORK STOPPAGES AND TIME LOST DUE TO INDUSTRIAL DISPUTES IN SELECTED COUNTRIES

Country	Number of industrial disputes	Workers involved[1] (thousands)	Working days lost (thousands)	Days lost per thousand employees[2]	Country	Number of industrial disputes	Workers involved[1] (thousands)	Working days lost (thousands)	Days lost per thousand employees[2]
UNITED STATES[3]					**FRANCE[9]**				
1967	4,595	2,870	42,100	649	1967	1,675	2,824	4,204	295
1968	5,045	2,649	49,018	737	1968[10]	1,103	464	423	29
1969	5,700	2,481	42,869	626	1969	2,480	1,444	2,224	150
1970	5,716	3,305	66,414	956	1970	3,319	1,160	1,742	114
1971	5,138	3,280	47,589	681	1971	4,358	3,235	4,388	282
1972	5,010	1,714	27,066	374	1972	3,464	2,721	3,755	237
1973	5,353	2,251	27,948	373	1973	3,731	2,246	3,915	241
1974	6,074	2,778	47,991	629	1974	3,381	1,564	3,380	204
1975	5,031	1,746	31,237	415	1975	3,888	1,827	3,869	237
1976	5,600	2,500	38,000	487	1976	(7)	(7)	(7)	(7)
AUSTRALIA[4]					**GERMANY[11]**				
1967	1,340	483	705	180	1967	(7)	60	390	19
1968	1,713	720	1,079	267	1968	(7)	25	25	1
1969	2,014	1,285	1,958	468	1969	(7)	90	249	12
1970	2,738	1,367	2,394	550	1970	(7)	184	93	4
1971	2,404	1,327	3,069	687	1971	(7)	536	4,484	207
1972	2,298	1,114	2,010	445	1972	(7)	23	66	3
1973	2,538	803	2,635	564	1973	(7)	185	563	26
1974	2,809	2,005	6,293	1,301	1974	(7)	250	1,051	49
1975	2,432	1,398	3,510	733	1975	(7)	36	69	3
1976	2,055	2,200	3,800		1976	(7)	169	534	26
BELGIUM[5]					**ITALY[12]**				
1967	58	38	182	65	1967	2,554	1,987	7,294	683
1968	71	29	364	130	1968	3,272	4,414	8,299	763
1969	88	25	162	56	1969	3,698	6,572	35,325	3,186
1970	151	108	1,432	484	1970	4,065	3,520	17,861	1,560
1971	184	87	1,241	411	1971	5,482	3,452	10,699	924
1972	191	67	354	117	1972	4,699	4,078	15,820	1,367
1973	172	62	866	281	1973	3,676	6,133	19,749	1,668
1974	235	56	580	184	1974	5,087	7,396	15,743	1,285
1975	243	86	610	194	1975	3,535	12,920	20,602	1,649
1976	266	108	886	281	1976	(7)	(7)	(7)	(7)
CANADA[6]					**JAPAN[13]**				
1967	522	252	3,975	641	1967	1,214	733	1,830	60
1968	582	224	5,083	787	1968	1,546	1,163	2,841	91
1969	595	307	7,752	1,170	1969	1,783	1,412	3,634	115
1970	542	262	6,540	950	1970	2,260	1,720	3,915	120
1971	569	240	2,867	406	1971	2,527	1,896	6,029	178
1972	598	706	7,754	1,056	1972	2,498	1,544	5,147	149
1973	724	348	5,776	740	1973	3,326	2,236	4,604	129
1974	1,216	592	9,255	1,135	1974		3,621	9,663	269
1975	1,054	482	10,894	1,311	1975	3,391	2,732	8,016	222
1976	(7)	(7)	(7)	(7)	1976	(7)	(7)	(7)	(7)
DENMARK[8]					**NETHERLANDS**				
1967	22	10	10	6	1967	8	2	6	2
1968	17	29	34	20	1968	11	5	14	4
1969	48	36	56	32	1969	28	12	22	6
1970	77	56	102	57	1970	99	52	263	70
1971	31	6	21	12	1971	15	36	97	26
1972	35	8	22	12	1972	31	20	134	36
1973	205	337	3,901	2,055	1973	7	58	584	155
1974	134	142	184	98	1974	14	3	7	2
1975	137	59	100	53	1975	5	(14)	1	(15)
1976	(7)	(7)	(7)	(7)	1976	(7)	(7)	(7)	(7)

See footnotes at end of table.

WORK STOPPAGES AND TIME LOST DUE TO INDUSTRIAL DISPUTES IN SELECTED COUNTRIES

Country	Number of industrial disputes	Workers involved[1] (thousands)	Working days lost (thousands)	Days lost per thousand employees[2]	Country	Number of industrial disputes	Workers involved[1] (thousands)	Working days lost (thousands)	Days lost per thousand employees[2]
SWEDEN					**UNITED KINGDOM**[17]				
1967	7	0.1	0.4	([15])	1967	2,116	734	2,787	122
1968	7	.4	1.2	([15])	1968	2,378	2,258	4,690	207
1969	41	9.0	112.4	35	1969	3,116	1,665	6,846	302
1970	134	26.7	155.7	48	1970	3,906	1,801	10,980	488
1971	60	62.9	839.0	250	1971	2,228	1,178	13,551	625
1972	44	7.1	10.5	3	1972	2,497	1,734	23,909	1,102
1973	48	4.3	11.8	4	1973	2,873	1,528	7,197	324
1974	85	17.5	57.6	16	1974	2,922	1,626	14,750	659
1975[16]	86	16.6	44.5	12	1975	2,282	809	6,012	270
1976	([7])	([7])	([7])	([7])	1976	1,990	661	3,286	149

[1]Workers are counted more than once if they were involved in more than 1 stoppage during the year.

[2]Per thousand persons with paid hours in nonagricultural industries. Days lost include all stoppages in effect.

[3]The number of stoppages and workers relate to those stoppages beginning in the year. Excludes disputes involving fewer than 6 workers and those lasting less than 1 full day or shift.

[4]Excludes disputes in which the time lost is less than 10 worker-days.

[5]Excludes workers indirectly affected.

[6]Excludes disputes in which the time lost is less than 10 worker-days. Excludes workers indirectly affected.

[7]Not available.

[8]Excludes political disputes and disputes in which the time lost is less than 100 worker-days.

[9]Excludes work stoppages in agriculture and public administration.

[10]May and June, the period of the national strike, excluded.

[11]Includes West Berlin. Excludes disputes lasting less than 1 day, except those involving a loss of more than 100 working days.

[12]Excludes work stoppages in agriculture, political strikes, and workers indirectly affected. Days lost computed from hours lost using 8 per day.

[13]Excludes workers indirectly affected and disputes lasting less than 4 hours.

[14]Less than 500.

[15]Less than 0.5 days.

[16]Excludes one dispute in agriculture involving 7,000 workers and 321,000 working days lost.

[17]Excludes disputes (a) not connected with terms of employment or conditions of labor, and (b) involving fewer than 10 workes or lasting less than 1 day, unless a loss of more than 100 working days is involved.

NOTE: 1975 Figures for the United States and the United Kingdom are preliminary. Figures shown for all other countries are based on data for 8 to 11 months converted to annual rates.

SOURCE: **Year Book of Labour Statistics** (Geneva, International Labour Office), various issues, and national publications.

Sample Contract Clauses in Labor Agreements

TITLE

AGREEMENT

By and Between

SPECIFIC PRODUCTS CORPORATION

and

INTERNATIONAL FEDERATION OF PRODUCTION WORKERS

LOCAL 365

For the Period

November 16, 1978 . . . . .November 15, 1980

PREAMBLE

regular form

This Agreement made and entered into this 16th day of November, 1978 by and between SPECIFIC PRODUCTS CORPORATION, located at Utopia, Ohio ("COMPANY") and INTERNATIONAL FEDERATION of PRODUCTION WORKERS ("UNION") and its Local 365.

WHEREAS, UNION is a labor organization which exists and is constituted, inter alia, for the purpose of collective bargaining and

WHEREAS, UNION has been certified by the National Labor Relations Board as the collective bargaining agent for all production and maintenance employees, excluding office clerical, professional technical employees, watchmen, guards and all supervisory employees as defined in the National Labor Relations Act, as amended; and

WHEREAS, the parties desire to enter into Agreement relating to wages, hours and conditions of employment, which will provide methods of harmonious cooperation between UNION and COMPANY and its employees, and to that extent, accomplish fair and peaceful adjustment of disputes which may arise without interruption of the business of COMPANY;

NOW, THEREFORE, the parties hereto, intending to be legally bound, hereby agree as follows:

short form

This Agreement is entered into by SPECIFIC PRODUCTS COMPANY, hereinafter referred to as the COMPANY, and Local 365, INTERNATIONAL FEDERATION of PRODUCTION WORKERS, hereinafter referred to as the UNION.

The parties agree as follows:

ARTICLE I
RECOGNITION

exclusive

The COMPANY recognizes the UNION as the sole and exclusive bargaining agent for the purpose of establishing salaries, wages, hours and other conditions of employment for:

(choose the appropriate one of the following:)

(1) all of its employees

(2) all of its employees in the following departments: _____ , _____ , _____
(example: production, maintenance, inspection)

(3) all of its employees with the exception of: _____
_____ , _____
(example: department heads, group leaders, foremen, temporary, seasonal employees)

(4) all of its employees with the exception of _____ , _____ , _____ ; in the following departments: _____ , _____ , _____ , _____

(5) all of its employees except those in the following departments:

_____ , _____
(Note: It may at times be necessary to specify a geographic location)

where COMPANY will only talk with UNION

The COMPANY recognizes the UNION and agrees to consult with the UNION in the formulation and implementation of personnel policies and practices and matters affecting the working conditions of its members.

where recognition is limited to UNION members

The COMPANY recognizes the UNION as the sole and exclusive bargaining agent for the purpose of establishing salaries, wages, hours and other conditions of employment for those employees who have designated the UNION as their representative.

ARTICLE II
UNION SECURITY

closed shop

The COMPANY will hire and retain as regular employees in the bargaining unit only members who are and maintain good standing in the UNION. When new employees are required, the COMPANY shall call the UNION to furnish such help. If the UNION is unable to fulfill the COMPANY'S requirements within ———— days, employees may be hired from other sources. All such employees, as well as temporary help added to the force, shall be given a work card by the UNION.

union shop

All present employees covered by this Agreement, shall, as a condition of employment, become and remain members of the UNION in good standing ———— days after the signing of this Agreement. All future employees shall be required to become and remain UNION members ———— calendar days after being employed. Employees who fail to comply with this requirement shall be discharged by the COMPANY within thirty days after receipt of written notice to the COMPANY from the UNION.

modified union shop

Each employee who, on the effective date of this Agreement, is a member of the UNION, shall, as a condition of employment, maintain his membership in the UNION. Each employee hired on or after the execution of this Agreement, shall, as a condition of employment, become a member of the UNION thirty days after his hiring date or the effective date of this agreement, whichever is later, and maintain membership in the UNION. Employees who fail to comply with this requirement shall be discharged by the COMPANY within 30 days after receipt of written notice to the COMPANY from the UNION.

agency shop

Any present or future employee who is not a UNION member and who does not make application for membership, shall, as a condition of employment, pay to the UNION each month a service charge as a contribution toward the administration of this Agreement in an amount equal to the regular monthly dues. Employees who fail to comply with this requirement shall be discharged by the COMPANY within 30 days after receipt of written notice to the COMPANY from the UNION. (*To make this clause effective, it may be combined with the modified union shop or maintenance of membership clauses.*)

ARTICLE III
DISCRIMINATION

The COMPANY and the UNION agree, that to the extent provided under applicable State and Federal laws and regulations, there will be no discrimination in hiring, training, promotions or discipline of employees because of race, color, creed, age, sex or national origin.

ARTICLE IV
CHECK-OFF

During the life of this Agreement, the COMPANY agrees to deduct UNION membership dues levied by the International Union or Local Union in accordance with the Constitution and By-Laws of the UNION, from the pay of each employee who executes or has executed the following "Authorization for Check-Off of Dues" form; provided, however, that the COMPANY will continue to deduct monthly membership dues from the pay of each employee for whom it has on file an unrevoked "Authorization for Check-Off of Dues" form.

AUTHORIZATION

FOR CHECK-OFF OF DUES

To The SPECIFIC PRODUCTS CORPORATION.
Date ————

I hereby assign to Local Union No. 365 from any wages earned or to be earned by me as your employee (in my present or in any future employment by you), such sums as the Financial Officer of said Local Union No. 365 may certify as due and owing from me as membership dues, including an initiation or reinstatement fee and monthly dues in such sum as may be established from time to time by said local union in accordance with the Constitution of the INTERNATIONAL FEDERATION OF PRODUCTION WORKERS but not less than $5.00 monthly. I authorize and direct you to deduct such amounts from my pay and to remit same to the UNION at such times and in such manner as may be agreed upon between you and the UNION at any time while this authorization is in effect.

This assignment, authorization and direction shall be irrevocable for the period of one (1) year from the date of delivery hereof to you, or until the termination of the collective agreement between the COMPANY and the UNION which is in force at the time of delivery of this authorization, whichever occurs sooner; and I agree and direct that this assignment, authorization and direction shall be automatically renewed, and shall be irrevocable for successive periods of one (1) year each or for the period of each succeeding applicable collective agreement between the COMPANY and the UNION, whichever shall be shorter, unless written notice is given by me to the COMPANY and the UNION, not more than twenty (20) days and not less than ten (10) days prior to the expiration of each period of one (1) year, or of each applicable collective agreement between the COMPANY and the UNION, whichever occurs sooner.

This authorization is made pursuant to the provisions of Section 302 (c) of the Labor-Management Relations Act of 1947 and otherwise.

_____
(Type or print name of Employee here)

_____
(Address of Employee)

_____
(City)   (State)

_____
(Signature of Employee here)

_____
(Date of Sign.)   (Emp. Clock No.)

_____
(Soc. Sec. No.)   (Date of Del. to Employer)

ARTICLE V
REPRESENTATION

SECTION 1   The employees shall be represented in the shop by Stewards and Shop Committeemen. There shall be a Shop Committee of not more than six (6) employees, one of whom may be the President of the Local Union. There shall not be more than one (1) Steward for each sixty (60) employees working in the bargaining unit, or major fraction thereof.

SECTION 2   The UNION shall furnish the COMPANY with current lists of the names of its Shop Committeemen and Stewards together with the area each represents. The COMPANY shall furnish the UNION with current lists of the names of its Shop Supervisors.

SECTION 3   (a) The President of the Local Union and the Chairman of the Shop Committee shall have access to any part of the Company plant, when their presence is required in settling disputes or grievances.

(b) If, in order to settle a grievance, in accordance with the Grievance Procedure, it becomes necessary for an International Representative to visit in the plant, arrangements for such visit shall be made with the Personnel Director.

SECTION 4   Committeemen and Stewards shall receive pay for time spent in the plant during their regular working hours only, for the sole purpose of investigating and settling grievances and for time spent in meetings with the COMPANY. However, each Committeeman

shall not be paid for more than 12 such hours per week, nor each Steward more than 3 such hours per week. The Chairman of the Shop Committee and the President of the Local Union may each be allowed up to 15 such hours per week. COMPANY-UNION meetings, including the regular weekly agenda meeting, held at the request of the Labor Relations Manager or his authorized representative, shall not, however, be counted in the accumulation of allowed Company-paid grievance time under this Section 4. The rate of pay for the Committeemen and Stewards shall be the rate of the job worked on at the time of leaving work to investigate or attend the meeting.

SECTION 5   Committeemen and Stewards shall handle grievances only within their respective areas. When leaving jobs to investigate or settle grievances, they shall report to their Foreman and secure a time stamped grievance pass. Upon return to their jobs, they shall again contact their Foreman who will time stamp their grievance pass. They shall record in writing on the grievance pass furnished by the COMPANY the information that the COMPANY shall require to control time spent on grievances.

ARTICLE VI
SETTLEMENT of DISPUTES
Grievance Procedure

SECTION 1   Grievances are defined as any alleged violation of the terms of this Agreement or differences of opinion as to its interpretation or application. Grievances, as defined herein, shall be settled promptly in the manner hereinafter set forth.

Step 1   A grievance, except one which is of a general or policy nature, must first be taken up orally with the Department Foreman by the Department Steward and the employee asserting the grievance. However, any individual employee or group of employees shall have the right to present grievances to the COMPANY at any time. In the event of a settlement, a UNION representative shall have the right to be present.

Step 2   If no satisfactory settlement of the grievance is reached in Step 1, the Steward will reduce it to writing in duplicate on a grievance form provided by the COMPANY and present it to the Department Foreman. No later than two working days following that on which the grievance was presented to the Foreman, a meeting shall be held for the purpose of a full investigation of all facts concerned with the grievance. Those present at this meeting may include the Labor Regulations Manager (or his designated representative), the Department Head, the Foreman, the aggrieved employee or employees, the Area Steward, the Shop Chairman (or his designated representative), the Area Committeeman, and any such other individual or individuals who have knowledge or information which would be pertinent to the discussion and settlement of the grievance. Within two working days following the conclusion of this meeting, the Department Head will answer the grievance and return it to the Area Committeeman. Failure to answer the grievance within the time limitation specified will automatically advance it to the next Step.

Step 3 If no satisfactory settlement of the grievance is reached in Step 2 above, the grievance shall be presented by the Shop Committee to the Labor Relations Manager (or his designated representative). The Labor Relations Manager (or his designated representative) shall meet with the Shop Committee once weekly at a designated time for the purpose of settling any grievances that may be referred to this Step. The International Representative of the UNION may participate in these meetings. The Labor Relations Manager (or his designated representative) shall give a written disposition to all grievances presented at this meeting within five (5) working days after this meeting. Failure to do so will automatically move the grievance to the next Step.

Step 4 In the event any grievance referred to the Third Step meeting of the Grievance Procedure, as provided herein, remains unsettled following discussion of the grievance in that meeting, it may be formally referred, in writing, by the UNION to the American Arbitration Association for the purpose of arbitrating the unsettled matter. In order to be valid, such formal written notification to the American Arbitration Association must be made within twenty-one (21) calendar days from the date a written answer is given following the Third Step grievance meeting and a copy of such notification shall be sent to the COMPANY. In the event such formal referral is not made within this twenty-one (21) calendar day limit, the grievance shall be considered settled on the basis of the last decision and not subject to further appeal. A grievance properly submitted to the American Arbitration Association shall be considered by an arbitrator who shall be selected, and arbitration shall proceed, under the Voluntary Labor Arbitration Rules then obtaining of the American Arbitration Association. The cost and expenses of the American Arbitration Association proceedings, including the compensation paid the arbitrator, shall be borne by the party losing the case. If the decision is not clear cut as to which party won or lost said case, the arbitrator shall decide which party shall be assessed the cost.

SECTION 2 Grievances of a general or policy nature may be initiated by the UNION in Step 3 of the Grievance Procedure, and if no satisfactory answer is given in Step

3, the UNION may refer the grievance through the balance of the Grievance Procedure, subject to the terms and conditions thereof.

SECTION 3 Minutes of the meetings provided for herein may be taken by either the COMPANY or the UNION.

ARTICLE VII
DISCIPLINE and DISCHARGE

SECTION 1 The COMPANY shall have the right to discharge or discipline employees for just and proper cause.

SECTION 2 In the event an employee or employees are subject to suspension or discharge, the Area Committeeman or the Shop Steward shall be contacted immediately and informed of the reason for such disciplinary action. The employee or employees disciplined under this Agreement may be required to leave the plant. However, depending upon conditions concerned with the discipline, a hearing will be held between COMPANY and UNION representatives immediately or not later than the next working day following that in which the discipline was given. At this meeting all relevant facts surrounding the discipline shall be reviewed and at the conclusion of the meeting the UNION shall be advised of the COMPANY'S position.

SECTION 3 Any grievance alleging unjust or improper discipline under this agreement shall enter the Grievance Procedure in the Third Step, provided, however, the grievance must be referred to the Labor Relations Manager within three (3) working days following that in which the COMPANY gave its answer, regarding such discipline, to the UNION.

Unless a written grievance is filed within the three (3) day time limitation, an employee or employees suspended or discharged shall have no right to object to such discipline or request any reimbursement. The COMPANY shall not be required to compensate any employee disciplined under this agreement for time lost from the point he may have been required to leave the plant or for time spent in the hearing provided above, unless and until it is determined that the suspension or discharge was improper under this Agreement.

SECTION 4 (a) Warnings, disciplinary actions and such notations as are to be made of record regarding an employee for possible later discipline, shall be in writing with a copy to the employee and the UNION. These records shall be effective for one (1) year, with the exception of cases of discharge. Prior to the time an employee is given a warning slip or subjected to other final disciplinary action, the foreman shall discuss the facts regarding the disciplinary action in a meeting limited to the employee together with the area Union Steward or, in his absence, the Area Committeeman. After one (1) year such warning slips shall be marked void and removed from the employee's jacket.

(b) The employee has the right to challenge such written warnings under the Grievance Procedure.

ARTICLE VIII
SENIORITY

SECTION 1   Seniority shall commence from the employee's date of last hire. If two or more employees are hired the same date, their seniority shall be determined alphabetically using the employee's last name.

SECTION 2   The COMPANY will give the UNION an up-to-date copy of the seniority list and employees date of hire each month.

SECTION 3   Seniority shall be determined by an employee's length of continuous service with the COMPANY and this seniority shall be exercised within his or her respective department.

SECTION 4   Employees shall lose seniority and employment shall cease for the following reasons:

(a) An employee quits.

(b) Employee is discharged and not reinstated through the Grievance Procedure.

(c) Employees on layoff shall retain and accumulate seniority for two (2) years or until the employee refuses a recall to work by the COMPANY. The employee shall have five (5) days (calendar days) to return to work unless physically unable after being notified by certified mail to do so and a copy of such certified mail shall be given to the UNION.

(d) Employee is absent for three (3) working days without notifying the COMPANY.

(e) Employee works at another job or for another Employer while on leave of absence.

SECTION 5   Probationary employees shall be laid off first. Further layoffs shall be made in accordance with plantwide seniority exercised within a department. Laid-off employees may exercise their plantwide seniority and displace the employee at the bottom of the seniority list (with the exception of skilled trades). In the event an employee is unable to displace the youngest employee because of a physical disability or because he does not have the present skill and ability to do the work involved, he may move up the plant seniority list to a job he is capable of doing. Employees will be placed as soon as possible but in no event later than five (5) working days.

(a) It is the intent of the parties that the youngest employee by the plant seniority list shall be separated from the payroll.

(b) Skilled trades shall consist of toolmaker, machinist, machinist mechanic, maintenance mechanic, electrician, and quality control inspectors. When a layoff occurs which affects the employees in these classifications, then the junior employee will be laid off in accordance with plant seniority and shall displace the employee at the bottom of the seniority list in accordance with the same procedure as above.

SECTION 6   The COMPANY will give reasonable notice to the UNION of the layoffs and the circumstances.

SECTION 7   When there is an increase in the working force after a layoff, the laid-off employee having the most plantwide seniority will be recalled to perform the available work provided he has the present skill and ability to do the work. However, this recall provision shall not limit or restrict the right of the COMPANY to hire skilled trades people as hereinbefore defined when there are no employees in a layoff status who have the present skill and ability to perform the work.

SECTION 8   Promoting to fill vacancies or new jobs or job openings on a permanent basis, when skill and ability to perform the job are relatively equal, shall be determined by an employee's length of continuous service with the COMPANY and exercised within the department. Employees placed on a job for which they must qualify shall be given a fair and reasonable trial on the job. If they are found to be not qualified, they shall return to their former job.

SECTION 9   In the event the job opening is not filled by an employee in the department, it shall be filled on a plantwide basis by the senior employee who has filed a job request form and who has the skills and ability to perform the work required. First preference will be given to the present employees in the bargaining unit who have the required skills and abilities, provided, however, that they shall not limit or restrict the right of the COMPANY to hire experienced employees when there are no employees who have the skill and ability to perform the work.

SECTION 10   Committeemen amd Officers of the UNION who are employees of the COMPANY shall have preferred seniority for layoffs and recalls only, provided, however, that such employees have the ability to do the available work. Stewards in their respective areas and shifts shall have preferred seniority for layoffs only, provided, however, that such employees have the ability to do the available work.

ARTICLE IX
LEAVES OF ABSENCE

SECTION 1   Union Representatives Attending Conferences: Union officers and delegated representatives of the UNION shall, for the purpose of attending conferences, be given a leave of absence without loss of seniority, providing the COMPANY is officially notified by the UNION within three (3) working days in advance of said conference.

SECTION 2 Union Representatives Leaves of Absence: Members of the UNION elected or appointed to an office in the UNION, National or International Union, which shall require him to be absent from work, shall be given an indefinite leave of absence without pay, and upon return shall be re-employed in accordance with their seniority, which shall accumulate during such absence.

SECTION 3 Personal Leave of Absence: A written leave of absence without pay for personal reasons shall be granted by mutual agreement between the UNION and the COMPANY without discrimination for the period of time the employee states. Failure of the employee to report for work on the first day following the expiration of the leave shall be considered as a resignation from the COMPANY, unless the employee not reporting has a reasonable excuse.

SECTION 4 An employee elected or appointed to a public office shall, upon receipt by the COMPANY of a request from such employee, receive a leave of absence for the term of the public office.

SECTION 5 When an employee covered by the terms of this Agreement is inducted into the Armed Forces of the United States, he shall continue to accumulate seniority and shall be reinstated to employment in accordance with applicable laws at the time of his discharge from the said Armed Forces.

SECTION 6 Funeral Pay: An employee who is absent from work in order to attend the funeral of a member of the employee's immediate family (Father, Mother, Father-in-law, Mother-in-law, Spouse, Child, Brother, Sister) shall receive pay for time lost from his regular work week not to exceed three (3) consecutive days of eight (8) hours each at his regular rate, the last day of which shall be the day of the funeral at which the employee is in attendance. Funeral pay shall be paid for regular work days only.

SECTION 7 Jury Duty: Employees who are working at the time they are called for jury duty shall be paid the difference between the amount received for jury duty and the amount they would have received at work, but in no event more than their regularly scheduled work week. Verification of the time and amount of pay received from the court will be required. The employee will notify the COMPANY as soon as he knows that he is listed for jury duty.

SECTION 8 Maternity Leave: Female employees with one (1) year or more of continuous service with the COMPANY shall be granted maternity leave providing they give the COMPANY prior written notice from their attending physician that such leave is necessary. Such leave shall be granted to the affected employee for a

period not to exceed six (6) months unless proof of unusual circumstances require an extension. Leave shall begin not less than three (3) months before the affected employee's physician estimates the date of delivery and end not more than three (3) months after birth. Where notice is given and leave of absence is granted employees affected shall accumulate continuous service credit or seniority during such leave of absence.

ARTICLE X
VACATIONS

SECTION 1 The COMPANY reserves the right to declare a shutdown in the plant during the period from June 1 to September 1, in which case employees eligible for vacations shall be required to take their vacations during such shutdown period. Notification of such shutdown shall be given by the COMPANY not less than sixty (60) days prior to each shutdown; provided that the COMPANY may postpone or cancel such shutdown at any time within the first thirty (30) days of said notice period. If no vacation period is scheduled by the COMPANY during a current year, vacations will, as far as possible, be granted at times most desired by employees, but the right to schedule an employee's vacation period is reserved by the COMPANY in order to insure the orderly and efficient operation of the plant or any department or section thereof. Seniority shall govern, as far as possible, in the selection of the weeks in which vacations are to be taken.

SECTION 2 The "vacation year" which shall be used in computing the amount of vacation time and payment shall be from June 1 to May 31, inclusive, of each year in which this Agreement continues in effect.

SECTION 3 The "vacation season" in which vacations may be granted for any vacation year during the term of this Agreement, if no plant shutdown has been scheduled by the COMPANY as outlined in Section 1 hereof, shall be from June 1 to May 31.

SECTION 4 Effective on and after June 1, 1979:
(a) All employees who have been on the payroll less than three (3) years and who have at least six (6) months' seniority as of May 31 of any year during the term of this Agreement shall receive one (1) week's vacation during the then current vacation season and shall receive vacation pay computed in the manner provided in the following Section 5 of this Article.
(b) All employees who have been on the payroll for three (3) years but less than five (5) years and who have at least six (6) months' seniority as of May 31 of any year during the term of this Agreement shall receive two (2) calendar weeks' vacation during the then current vacation season and shall receive vacation pay computed in the manner provided in the following Section 5 of this Article.
(c) All employees who have been on the payroll for five (5) years but less than ten (10) years and who

have at least six (6) months' seniority as of May 31 of any year during the term of this Agreement shall receive two (2) calendar weeks' vacation during the then current vacation season and shall receive vacation pay computed in the manner provided in the following Section 5 of this Article.

(d) All employees who have been on the payroll for ten (10) years but less than twenty (20) years and who have at least six (6) months' seniority as of May 31 of any year during the term of this Agreement shall receive three (3) calendar weeks' vacation during the then current vacation season and shall receive vacation pay computed in the manner provided in the following Section 5 of this Article.

(e) All employees who have been on the payroll for twenty (20) years or more and who have at least six (6) months' seniority as of May 31 of any year during the term of this Agreement shall receive four (4) calendar weeks' vacation during the then current vacation season and shall receive vacation pay computed in the manner provided in the following Section 5 of this Article.

(f) Employees who served in the Armed Forces of the United States shall be considered as being on "on the payroll" for the purpose of accumulating vacation eligibility provided such employees shall:

(1) Have an honorable discharge

(2) Still be qualified to perform the duties of their former or a comparable job, and

(3) Make application for reinstatement within ninety (90) days after being discharged from such service. Such employees shall be accorded status "on the payroll" only for the purpose of Section 4 of this Article. However, this vacation eligibility credit shall only apply to vacations for the year 1968 and thereafter.

(g) Effective as of July 18, 1969, any employee who quits, is discharged or loses his seniority for any reason except reduction in force, and who is subsequently rehired, shall begin accumulating time "on the payroll" for vacation purposes only from the date of last re-hire, and any time worked prior to such date of last re-hire shall be excluded in the computation of vacation eligibility.

SECTION 5   Vacation pay shall be computed by multiplying the employee's straight time hourly rate, including night shift premium and cost-of-living adjustment, if any, in effect on May 31 of the year in which the vacation is to be taken by forty (40) hours, if the employee is entitled to one (1) calendar week's vacation during the vacation season for the then current year, by sixty (60) hours, if the employee is then entitled to two (2) calendar weeks' vacation (three (3) but less than five (5) years' service) and by eighty (80) hours if the employee has five (5) but less than ten (10) years' service, by one hundred twenty (120) hours, if the employee is then entitled to three (3) calendar weeks' vacation or by one hundred

sixty (160) hours, if the employee is then entitled to four (4) calendar weeks' vacation, as the case may be.

However, if an eligible employee has not worked fourteen hundred (1400) hours of compensable time between June 1 of the preceding year and May 31 of the then current year, his vacation pay shall not be computed on the basis hereinbefore set forth but, in such case, the employee's vacation pay shall be an amount equal to two (2) percent of his gross earnings between June 1 of the preceding year and May 31 of the then current year, if he has been on the payroll less than three (3) years and has at least six (6) months' seniority as of May 31 of the then current year; an amount equal to three (3) percent of his gross earnings for the aforementioned period, if he has been on the payroll for three (3) years but less than five (5) years and has at least six (6) months' seniority as of the said May 31; an amount equal to four (4) percent of his gross earnings for the aforementioned period, if he has been on the payroll for five (5) years but less than ten (10) years and has at least six (6) months' seniority as of the said May 31; an amount equal to six (6) percent of his gross earnings for the aforementioned period, if he has been on the payroll for ten (10) years but less than twenty (20) years as of the said May 31; or an amount equal to eight (8) percent of his gross earnings for the aforementioned period, if he has been on the payroll for twenty (20) years or more and has at least six (6) months' seniority as of the said May 31, as the case may be.

SECTION 6   An eligible employee shall receive his vacation check the work day prior to the day he leaves for vacation, provided two (2) weeks' notice has been given of his selection of weeks and approval of such selection by the Foreman is obtained. In case of a vacation shutdown scheduled by the COMPANY, vacation checks will be delivered the last work day prior to the shutdown.

SECTION 7   (a) Vacations may not be accumulated from year to year, nor may a vacation be postponed from one vacation year to another.

(b) Eligible employees shall not take less than one (1) vacation at a time.

SECTION 8   Employees transferred from hourly to salary payroll or from salary to hourly payroll during the vacation year will receive vacation pay based on their status at the end of the vacation year.

SECTION 9   In the event that a vacation shutdown is not scheduled in accordance with Section 1 of this Article, any employee who is entitled to a vacation shall receive in lieu thereof a cash allowance computed in accordance with the applicable provisions of Section 5 of this Article.

(a) If, for reasons beyond his control, the employee has lost an excessive amount of time during the vacation year, and he elects to forego his vacation.

(b) If, because of production requirements, the COMPANY is unable to schedule a vacation period for employees required to perform necessary production operations.

(c) Employees referred to in (a) and (b) of this Section 9 may receive vacation checks, during the vacation season, upon two (2) weeks' notice to their Foreman.

SECTION 10   Employees who are laid off and not recalled to work, or who are serving in the Armed Forces as of the vacation qualifying date specified in Section 4 of this Article, and who are otherwise eligible to receive vacation pay shall be paid vacation pay in accordance with the provisions of this Article.

ARTICLE XI
HOLIDAY PAY

SECTION 1   Subject to the provisions of this Article, employees shall receive holiday pay for the following ten (10) holidays: (New Year's Day, Good Friday, Memorial Day, Independence Day, Labor Day, Election Day, Thanksgiving Day, Friday after Thanksgiving Day, the first day of the Deer Hunting Season, Christmas Day). For purposes of this Section 1, Election Day will be the first Tuesday after the first Monday in November of each year, and the first day of the Deer Hunting Season will be the first day of the period in each year during which the hunting of buckdeer with firearms is permitted under the laws of the State.

SECTION 2   Eligible employees shall receive eight (8) hours pay at the same rate that they earned and received the day before the holiday, including night shift premium, but excluding overtime premiums, for each such holiday provided:

(a) The employee has sixty (60) days' seniority as of the date of such holiday, and

(b) The employee works at least one regularly scheduled work day within the week in which the holiday or holidays occur, except as otherwise provided in Section 4 of this Article.

SECTION 3   In the event an employee is temporarily assigned to a lower rated job on the last day worked before a holiday, his holiday pay shall be computed on the basis of the rate of pay of his regular classification.

SECTION 4   An employee who is otherwise eligible but who fails to meet the requirements of Section 2 (b) of this Article, shall receive holiday pay for such holiday provided his absence from work is the result of:

(a) Personal illness or injury which is substantiated by satisfactory medical evidence provided such illness or injury commenced within one (1) calendar week prior to such holiday or on the first scheduled work day after such holiday.

(b) Temporary layoff, provided such layoff commenced within one (1) calendar week prior to such holiday or on the first scheduled work day after such holiday.

SECTION 5   Employees whose work comprises continuous seven (7) day operations, shall receive holiday pay in the event the holiday falls on one of their scheduled days off. However, if such an employee works on a holiday which falls on his scheduled day off, or when such employee is scheduled to work on a holiday and does work on such holiday, he shall receive eight (8) hours' pay for such holiday, plus double time for all hours worked. Such employees scheduled to work on any of the above holidays shall not receive holiday pay as provided herein if they absent themselves from such scheduled work on such holiday without reasonable and proper cause acceptable to Management.

SECTION 6   Other employees who may be requested to and do work on any of the aforementioned holidays, shall receive eight (8) hours' pay for such holiday, plus double time for all hours worked. However, employees who accept such holiday work assignments and then fail to report for and perform such work without reasonable and proper cause acceptable to Management, shall not receive pay for the holiday.

SECTION 7   If an employee, having less than sixty (60) days seniority, is requested to and does work on any of the above holidays he shall receive eight (8) hours' pay for such holiday, plus double time for all hours worked.

SECTION 8   When a holiday, specified in Section 1 of this Article, falls on Saturday, eligible employees shall receive pay for such holiday as provided herein.

SECTION 9   When a holiday, specified in Section 1 of this Article, falls on Sunday, it shall be celebrated on Monday and eligible employees shall receive pay for such holiday as provided herein.

SECTION 10   A holiday shall consist of twenty-four (24) consecutive hours, commencing with the first shift starting work after 10:59 P.M. of the day preceding such holiday.

ARTICLE XII
WAGES

SECTION 1   Effective November 16, 1978, all regular employees shall be paid at a minimum per the schedule listed below:

Labor Grade	Present Wage	Effective 11-16-78 15¢	Effective 11-16-79 5¢
1	3.85	4.00	4.05
2	4.30	4.45	4.50
3	4.50	4.65	4.70
4	5.10	5.25	5.30

SECTION 2 (a) Effective November 16, 1978, the minimum hiring rate of new employees shall be $3.85 per hour. At the end of the thirty (30) day probationary period, new employees shall receive $4.00 per hour.

(b) Effective May 16, 1979, the minimum hiring rate of new employees shall be $3.90 per hour. At the end of the thirty (30) day probationary period, new employees shall receive $4.05 per hour.

SECTION 3 When an employee is hired into Utility classification, after three (3) months he shall be reviewed and if the employee is performing his work in one of the higher labor grades, he will be changed to the higher labor grade and receive the rate of pay of that labor grade.

SECTION 4 Labor grades shall include the following classifications:

Labor Grade No. 1
Janitor-Fireman
Utility
Labor Grade No. 2
Forklift Operator
Truck Driver
Painter
Mechanic
Parts, Production and Sales
Shipping and Receiving Clerk
Machine Operator
Assembler
Labor Grade No. 3
Assembly Welder
Maintenance Man
Mechanic Welder
Labor Grade No. 4
Group Leader

SECTION 5 (a) A shift bonus of fifteen (15) cents per hour shall be paid to all employees working on the second shift during the first year of this Agreement.

(b) A shift bonus of twenty (20) cents per hour shall be paid to all employees working on the second shift effective November 16, 1979 of this Agreement.

ARTICLE XIII
COST-OF-LIVING

SECTION 1 There shall be a Cost-of-Living Allowance which will be determined in accordance with changes in the official Consumers Price Index, for urban wage earners and clerical workers (including single workers) published by the Bureau of Labor Statistics, U.S. Department of Labor (1957–1959 = 100) and hereinafter referred to as the BLS Consumer Price Index.

SECTION 2 Cost-of-Living Adjustments during the lifetime of this Agreement will be made as follows:

(1) Effective November 16, 1979, the Cost-of-Living Adjustment will be determined by the following table, based on the BLS Index for November 1978, subject to a minimum amount of three cents (3¢) per

hour and a maximum amount of eight cents (8¢) per hour:

BLS Consumer Price Index	Cost-of-Living Allowance In Addition to Wage Scale By Job Classification
193.2 or less	3¢ per hour
193.3–193.6	4¢ per hour
193.7–194.0	5¢ per hour
194.1–194.4	6¢ per hour
194.5–194.8	7¢ per hour
195.9 or more	8¢ per hour

SECTION 3 The amount of any Cost-of-Living Allowance in effect at the time shall be included in computing overtime premium, vacation payments, sick leave allowance, holiday payments, severance pay, jury duty pay and call-in pay.

SECTION 4 In the event the Bureau of Labor Statistics does not issue the Consumer Price Index on or before the beginning of the pay period referred to in Section 2, any adjustments required will be made at the beginning of the first pay period after receipt of the Index.

SECTION 5 No adjustments, retroactive or otherwise, shall be made due to any revision which may later be made in the published figures for the BLS Consumer Price Index for any base month.

SECTION 6 The parties of this Agreement agree that the continuance of the Cost-of-Living Allowance is dependent upon the availability of the official monthly BLS Consumer Price Index in its present form and calculated on the same basis as the Index for November 1978, unless otherwise agreed upon by the parties.

ARTICLE XIV
GROUP INSURANCE

SECTION 1 The COMPANY will pay the entire premium for an insurance policy or policies from an insurance carrier of its selection for each active employee who completes sixty (60) days' service providing the following coverage:

(a) Group Life Insurance in the amount of $4,000.00.
(b) Insurance for accidental death or dismemberment from accidental means in the amount of $4,000.00.
(c) Non-Occupational sickness and accident insurance paying weekly benefits of seventy (70) percent of the employee's straight time weekly earnings for a period of twenty (20) weeks beginning after the fourth day of absence from work.

SECTION 2 The COMPANY will pay the full cost of Blue Cross, 70 Day Special Program for employee and dependents. Benefits include:

(a) 70 Day semi-private rooms, drugs and medicine as provided in the plan.

(b) Laboratory tests unlimited.

(c) Maternity—Up to ten days for each pregnancy.

(d) Outpatient emergency accident, surgery, and radiation therapy treatment.

The foregoing list of benefits are set forth here for information purposes only. Full details of the benefits are as provided in the paln.

SECTION 3   The COMPANY will pay the full cost of Blue Shield prevailing fee "100" Plan for employee and dependents. Benefits include:

(a) Pay-in-full benefits for all subscribers, regardless of income, when covered services are performed by participating Doctors (except where certain maximums and deductibles are specified).

(b) Diagnostic X-ray Services (in or out of hospital).

(c) Diagnostic medical services (in or out of hospital).

(d) Employee only, home and office medical visits as provided in Plan.

The foregoing list of benefits are set forth here for information purposes only. Full details of the benefits are as provided in the Plan.

SECTION 4   The COMPANY will pay the full cost of Blue Cross–Blue Shield Major Medical Plan for employees and dependents.

During each calendar year eighty (80) percent of all covered medical expenses, subject to a $50.00 deductible, will be paid by the Plan. Maximum amount of coverage up to $5,000.00.

Full details of the benefits are as provided in the Plan.

ARTICLE XV
PENSION PLAN

The COMPANY will continue in full force and effect the Pension Plan which first became effective as of April 30, 1971. The entire Agreement with respect to the subject of Pensions will be contained in a separate Supplemental Agreement covering Pensions and will remain as a part of this Agreement.

ARTICLE XVI
HOURS of WORK and OVERTIME

SECTION 1   The work week shall begin at the start of each shift commencing work after 10:59 P.M. Sunday. (Schedule of regular working hours shall be posted.)

SECTION 2   The regular hours for the shifts shall be 7:00 A.M. TO 3:30 P.M. and 3:30 P.M. to Midnight. In the case of three shift operations, the regular hours

shall be 7:00 A.M. to 3:00 P.M., 3:00 P.M. to 11:00 P.M. and 11:00 P.M. to 7:00 A.M.

SECTION 3   The regular work week shall consist of five (5) consecutive eight-hour days, Monday to Friday, inclusive, except that this shall not apply to Power House.

SECTION 4   This Article shall not be construed as a guarantee of hours of work per day or per week.

SECTION 5   Employees on regular shifts shall be granted a thirty (30) minute lunch period. Employees on three-shift operations shall be granted a twenty (20) minute lunch period.

SECTION 6   Except as to Power House employees, time and one-half (1½) shall be paid for all work performed on Saturday and double (2) time shall be paid for all work performed on Sunday. Power House employees shall have two (2) consecutive "off-duty" days in each week, and time and one-half (1½) shall be paid for work performed on the first scheduled "off-duty," and double (2) time shall be paid for work performed on the second scheduled "off-duty" day.

SECTION 7   Time and one-half (1½) shall be paid to hourly rate employees for all hours worked in excess of eight (8) hours in any one day. A day shall consist of twenty-four (24) consecutive hours starting at the beginning of the regularly scheduled shift in which the employee starts to work, except that this determination shall not carry over from one regular work week into the next regular work week. No employee will be paid overtime twice for the same hours and no day shift employee shall be paid overtime and night premium for the same hours.

SECTION 8   The overtime provisions of the foregoing Section 7 shall not apply when an employee, at his request or at the request of the COMPANY, is transferred from one shift to another, provided such shifts are not consecutive.

SECTION 9   An employee called in for duty off schedule shall be credited with no less than four (4) hours' time at his regular straight time base rate, provided less than four (4) hours are earned. In the event that more than the equivalent of four (4) hours' straight time pay has been earned by the employee at applicable overtime rates, the guaranteed payment shall not be paid in addition to the employee's earnings.

SECTION 10   The COMPANY agrees that it will endeavor, to the best of its ability, taking into consideration production requirements, to equalize overtime among its employees by departments. Records of overtime work shall be kept in each department, and shall be posted therein.

Where an employee does not work overtime offered with adequate notice, such hours will be counted for equal distribution. When an employee works overtime in another department, such overtime work shall be recorded as overtime work in his own department.

Overtime work shall be assigned to the employee in the department having the least overtime recorded to his credit, provided that he is capable of performing the work required. When overtime is to be scheduled in a department, the department Foreman and the Steward or Committeeman will discuss the distribution of such overtime in advance. For the purpose of administering the provisions of this Section, the recording of overtime shall commence as of the effective date of this Agreement.

ARTICLE XVII
MANAGEMENT RIGHTS—ASSURANCES

The management of the plant and business and direction of the working forces and operations, including the hiring, promoting, the suspending, discharging or otherwise disciplining of employees, the laying off and calling to work of employees in connection with any reduction or increase in the working forces, the scheduling of work and the control and regulation of the use of all equipment and other property of the COMPANY are the exclusive functions of the management, it being understood, however, that this enumeration of management rights shall not be deemed to exclude other rights not herein enumerated; provided, however, that in the exercise of such functions the management shall not alter any of the provisions of this Agreement and shall not discriminate against any employee or applicant for employment because of his membership in or lawful activity on behalf of the UNION. However, the foregoing shall not be construed as preventing the UNION from questioning as a grievance in the manner herein prescribed any act of the COMPANY which is regarded by the UNION as a violation of this Agreement.

ARTICLE XVIII
STRIKES and LOCKOUTS

During the term of this Agreement neither the UNION nor any employee shall instigate, encourage, sanction or take part in any strike, slowdown or other stoppage, limitation or interference with or curtailment of work or production, and the COMPANY shall not engage in any lockout.

ARTICLE XIX
SUBCONTRACTING

The parties recognize that the job security of the employees is important; therefore the COMPANY agrees to continue its policy to utilize employees to the fullest practical extent, including laid-off employees.

Because of the nature of the Company's business, the parties recognize that subcontracting is necessary. However, it is understood that in the exercise of the Company's right to subcontract work, the COMPANY does not intend to cause layoffs of employees covered by this Agreement.

The COMPANY and the UNION shall meet monthly on the third Wednesday of each month, at which meeting there shall be a discussion concerning the reasons for subcontracting work out of the shop, including maintenance and construction work, during the preceding four (4) weeks and such plans as the COMPANY may have for subcontracting during the succeeding four (4) weeks, shall also be the subject of discussion.

ARTICLE XX
SAFETY COMMITTEE

The COMPANY and the UNION shall each designate two (2) representatives to a Safety Committee which shall meet monthly for the purpose of discussing and making recommendations with respect to safety conditions, practices and rules in the plant. The monthly meetings shall not be longer than two (2) hours and the COMPANY shall pay the employee-members of the Safety Committee for lost time from their scheduled work. In addition, up to two hours per month for safety investigation shall also be allotted. The Safety Committee shall have a chairman who shall be the Company Personnel Manager or his designee.

ARTICLE XXI
BULLETIN BOARDS

The COMPANY shall provide a centrally located bulletin board on which may be posted official notice of Union meetings and of other similar official Union business, provided, however, that before such notices are posted, the UNION shall first submit the same to the Personnel Manager of the COMPANY and receive his approval to post same. There shall be no other posting or distribution by employees of notices, pamphlets, advertising or political matter, or any kind of literature upon Company property unless prior written approval is obtained from the Personnel Manager.

ARTICLE XXII
REPORTING TIME

Call-in Pay

Any employee called to work or permitted to come to work without having been properly notified that there will be no work, shall receive a minimum of four (4) hours' pay at the regular hourly rate, except in cases of labor disputes, or other conditions beyond the control of the COMPANY.

ARTICLE XXIII
REST PERIODS

Employees shall be allowed two (2) rest periods during each shift, one (1) of fifteen (15) minutes and one (1) of ten (10) minutes, such periods to be taken at the times scheduled by the COMPANY.

ARTICLE XXIV
GENERAL PROVISIONS

SECTION 1 The COMPANY shall maintain sanitary conditions in the plants and proper safety devices, and agrees, insofar as possible, to eliminate any conditions hazardous to the health and welfare of the employees.

SECTION 2 Smoking shall be permitted at any time except in restricted areas, which shall be posted with "No Smoking" signs.

SECTION 3 Employees will be allowed a wash-up period not to exceed five (5) minutes immediately before the thirty (30) minute lunch period and immediately before the end of the shift.

SECTION 4 Foremen and Supervisors shall not perform any work or operations regularly performed by employees covered by this Agreement, except for the purpose of instructing employees. Clerical and other employees not in the bargaining unit shall not be permitted to perform any work normally performed by employees in the bargaining unit.

SECTION 5 The COMPANY shall have the right to publish factory rules and regulations from time to time and to post such rules and regulations on the Company's bulletin boards.

SECTION 6 The COMPANY agrees to send to the INTERNATIONAL FEDERATION of PRODUCTION WORKERS an IBM listing each six (6) months of names and addresses of all employees in the bargaining unit.

ARTICLE XXV
DURATION

SECTION 1 This Agreement constitutes the entire contract between the COMPANY and the UNION and settles all demands and issues with respect to all matters subject to collective bargaining. Therefore, the COMPANY and the UNION for the duration of this Agreement, waive the right, and each agrees that the other shall not be obligated to bargain collectively with respect to any subject or matter which is subject to collective bargaining whether or not such subject or matter is specifically referred to herein.

SECTION 2 (a) This Agreement shall become effective as of November 16, 1978, except as otherwise indicated herein, and shall remain in effect up to and including November 15, 1980, and shall automatically renew itself from year to year thereafter unless written notice to terminate or amend this Agreement is given by either party to the other at least sixty (60) days prior to November 15, 1980, or prior to the date of expiration of any annual renewal hereof.

(b) If notice of termination shall be given, negotiations for a new agreement shall take place during the sixty (60) days prior to the expiration of this Agreement.

SIGNATURES

IN WITNESS WHEREOF, the parties hereto have caused their names to be subscribed by their duly authorized officers and representatives, effective as of the day and year first above written.

SPECIFIC PRODUCTS CORPORATION

By _____
Personnel Director

_____
Asst. Personnel Director

_____

_____

_____

INTERNATIONAL FEDERATION of PRODUCTION WORKERS

By _____
International Representative

_____
Aerospace Representative

_____
Region 9, Director

and its Local Union No. 365
By _____
Chairman, Negotiating Committee

_____
President

_____

_____

_____

Glossary of Labor Terms

AAA: *See* American Arbitration Association.

Ability to Pay: Often a crucial criterion in wage negotiations, cited by either labor or management, or both. The National Labor Relations Board has held that where a company claims an inability to pay, the union may insist that the company offer documentation to that effect.

Able and Willing to Work: In many states, an eligibility criterion for the collection of benefits under unemployment insurance.

Absence Rate (A.R.): A statistical measure used by the Bureau of Labor Statistics. It is determined by the equation:

$$\frac{\text{work days lost (per month)}}{\text{work days worked } + \text{ work days lost}}$$

Absenteeism: Most commonly, the unjustified failure of workers to report to work when scheduled. In determining *rate of absenteeism*, however, it may apply to all absences, whether for justified (e.g., sickness) or unjustified reasons.

Absolute Majority: A vote in which more than 50 percent of those eligible to cast ballots vote in favor of or against a proposal. (*See* Majority.)

AC Case: Under NLRB procedures, a petition by a labor organization or an employer seeking amendment of an outstanding certification of a bargaining representative under subpart C of the rules of the National Labor Relations Board. (*See* Types of Cases.)

Access to Plant: *See* Right of Visitation.

Accession Rate (A.R.): A computation of employment trends determined as follows:

$$\frac{\text{Total additions to work force } \times 100}{\text{Number working during the period}}$$

Accident Frequency Rate: The statistical measure of the rate of accidents; expressed by the Bureau of Labor Statistics as the total number of disabling injuries per 1 million hours worked.

Accident and Sickness Benefits (Sick Benefits): Regular payments to workers who lose time from work because of off-the-job disabilities through accident or sickness, e.g., $50 a week for up to 26 weeks of disability. The benefits are usually insured and part of a private group health and insurance plan financed in whole or in part by the employer. (*See* Health and Insurance Plan; Temporary Disability Insurance; Workers' Compensation; Sick Leave.)

Accidental Death and Dismemberment Benefits: An extra lump-sum payment made under many group life insurance plans for loss of life, limb, or sight as a direct result of an accident. Coverage is usually for both occupational and non-occupational accidents, but may be limited to the latter. (*See* Life Insurance Plan; Workers' Compensation.)

Across-the-Board Increase: A general wage increase simultaneously affecting all, or most, employees in a plant, company, or industry, by way of a uniform cents-per-hour or percentage increase.

Act (Law): A statute enacted by a federal, state or local legislative body.

Action: An independent federal agency created under the provisions of the Reorganization Plan of 1971 to strengthen the impact and appeal of citizen participation programs. Included are the Peace Corps; Volunteers in Service to America (VISTA); Foster Grandparent Program; Retired Senior Volunteer Program (RSVP); Senior Companion Program; Youth Challenge Program (YCP). Action is an office directly under the President of the United States.

Active Employees: Employees at work, as distinguished from retired or laid-off employees.

Adamson Act (1916): The law providing for an 8-hour day for railroad employees engaged in interstate commerce. President Wilson urged passage of the proposed act following a threat of a national strike by the Railway Brotherhoods. Declared constitutional in *Wilson v. New* (1917).

Adequate Remedy at Law: In labor disputes when a union action can cause irreparable damage, a court injunction against such action often is sought. The basis for the granting of an injunction is often the absence of timely relief through judicial process or "adequate remedy at law."

Ad Hoc Arbitration: Single-case arbitration, as distinguished from cases that are handled by permanent arbitrators who have been named in contracts.

Adjusted Cases: As defined by the National Labor Relations Board: Cases are closed as "adjusted" when an informal settlement agreement is executed and compliance with its terms is secured. (*See* Informal Agreement.) In some instances, a written agreement is not secured but appropriate remedial action is taken so as to render further proceeding unnecessary. A central element in an "adjusted" case is the agreement of the parties to settle differences without recourse to litigation.

Administration on Aging: Established by the Secretary of HEW on Oct. 1, 1965, to carry out the provisions of the Older Americans Act of 1965 (79 Stat. 218; 42 U.S.C. 3001 note). Reassigned to the Social and Rehabilitation Service by Department reorganization of Aug. 15, 1967. Transferred to Office of the Assistant Secretary for Human Development by Secretary's Order of June 15, 1973.

Administrative Employee: A management-level worker who is denied protection of the Fair Labor Standards Act under the regulations of the Wage-Hour Administrator of the Employment Standards Administration of the Department of Labor.

Administrative Remedies: Procedures available within an agency charged with the administration of a statute. These procedures are often required before a court will accept jurisdiction of a case.

Advance: A payment of salary or wage made before it is due.

Advance Notice: In general, an announcement of an intention to carry out a certain action, given to an affected or interested party in sufficient time to prepare for it; for example, informing a union of planned changes in production methods or plant shutdown, notifying a worker of layoff on a certain future date, and notifying management of the union's intention to terminate or modify a collective bargaining agreement on its expiration date. (*See* Pay-in-Lieu-of-Notice.)

Advisory Arbitration: *See* Arbitration.

Advisory Committee on Federal Public Works: Established Oct. 5, 1955, pursuant to request of the President, to evaluate physical facilities needed to supply reasonable demands of a growing economy, and to coordinate Federal public works planning. Abolished by direction of the President, Mar. 12, 1961, and functions assigned to Director, Bureau of the Budget.

Advisory Council (NRA): Created by EO 7075 of June 15, 1935, to aid National Recovery Administration. Transferred to Department of Commerce by EO 7252 of Dec. 21, 1935, effective Jan. 1, 1936. By same order functions and duties of Advisory Council ordered terminated not later than Apr. 1, 1936. On Mar. 21, 1936, EO 7323 created Committee of Industrial Analysis with Secretary of Commerce as Chairman, to complete work of Advisory Council, effective Apr. 1, 1936.

Advisory Opinion Cases: *See* Types of Cases. Other Cases, AO.

Affecting Commerce: *See* Commerce Clause.

Affidavit: A written statement made upon oath before a notary public or another authorized person.

Affiliation: A limited connection between one trade union and another, or between one union and a group of unions. A local may be affiliated with a central labor union in its locality and also be a constituent part of its national union, which in turn is affiliated with the AFL-CIO.

Affirmative Order: A directive from the National Labor Relations Board or an administrative agency requiring a company or a union to perform a specific action to undo a committed wrong.

AFL: *See* American Federation of Labor.

AFL-CIO (American Federation of Labor and Congress of Industrial Organizations): A federation of approximately 105 autonomous national and international unions created by the merger of the American Federation of Labor (AFL) and the Congress of Industrial Organizations (CIO) in December 1955. More than 80 percent of union members in the United States come within the orbit of the AFL-CIO through their membership in affiliated unions. The initials AFL-CIO after the name of a union indicate that the union is an affiliate. (*See* Independent Union; AFL-CIO, Departments of.)

AFL-CIO, Cope: Formed, with the merger of the AFL and the CIO in 1955, as the successor to Labor's League for Political Education (AFL) and the Political Action Committee (CIO) to encourage trade unionists and their families to participate in the political life of the country and their communities.

AFL-CIO, Departments of: Associations of national and international unions within the AFL-CIO federation, working together to further mutual interests in their general fields of operation. The nine trade and industrial departments include the Building and Construction Trades, Food and Beverage Trades, Industrial Union, Maritime Trades, Metal Trades, Professional Employees, Public Employees, Railway Employees, and Union Label and Service Trades.

AFL-CIO, Executive Council: Consisting of twenty-seven vice-presidents, the secretary-treasurer, and the president of AFL-CIO, the Council is the highest authority of AFL-CIO when its convention is not in session.

AFL-CIO, General Board: Composed of all members of the Executive Council and a principal officer of each international union. It acts on all matters submitted to it by the Executive Council at its annual meeting.

Age Certificate: *See* Certificate of Age.

Age Discrimination in Employment Act of 1967: An act promoting the employment of older workers based on ability rather than age. It protects individuals who are at least 40 but less than 65 years of age from discrimination in employment based on age in matters of hiring, discharge, compensation, or other employment conditions.

Agency Shop: An employer who, in compliance with a provision in a collective bargaining agreement, requires that all employees in the bargaining unit who do not join the union pay a fixed amount monthly, usually the equivalent of union dues, as a condition of employment to help defray the union's expenses in acting as bargaining agent. Under some arrange-ments, the payments are allocated to the union's welfare fund or to a recognized charity. May operate in conjunction with a modified union shop. (*See* Union Shop.)

Agent: A person who acts in the interests of another but for whose activities the other may be held responsible.

Agent Provocateur: Someone hired or induced to discredit a union by stimulating it to commit outrageous behavior.

Agreement (Collective Bargaining Agreement; Union Contract): A written contract between an employer (or an association of employers) and a union (or unions), usually for a definite term, defining conditions of employment (wages, hours, vacations, holidays, overtime payments, working conditions, etc.), rights of workers and union, and procedures to be followed in settling disputes or handling issues that arise during the life of the contract.

Agreement of Parties: *See* Informal Agreement and Formal Agreement. The term *agreement* includes both types.

AIFLD: *See* American Institute for Free Labor Development.

ALA: *See* Alliance for Labor Action.

Alliance for Labor Action (ALA): A coalition formed in 1968 by the United Auto Workers and the International Brotherhood of Teamsters for common action to strengthen organization, collective bargaining, political involvement, and community service. It was dissolved in 1972.

Allied Printing Trades Council: A council of delegate bodies representative of separately organized printing trade workers established in areas where there is more than one national union.

Allowed Time: Total time allowed for completion of a task or an element thereof, including time for personal needs, rest, and unavoidable delays.

Amalgamated Local: A local union representing workers from different shops that are generally organized on an industrial basis. Often all units operate under a common contract.

Amalgamation: In trade union terminology, the merging of two or more unions into one integral body, with a single constitution, set of officers, plan of action, etc.

Amendment of Certification Cases: *See* Types of Cases: Other Cases, AC.

American Arbitration Association (AAA): A private non-profit organization established to aid professional arbitrators in their work through legal and technical services, and to promote arbitration as a method of settling commercial and labor disputes. Provides lists of qualified arbitrators to unions and employers on request.

American Federation of Labor (AFL): The national federation of autonomous trade unions formally organized in 1886, although tracing its origin to 1881. It merged with the Congress of Industrial Organizations in December 1955, thus ceasing to exist as a separate organization. (Thus, the term has no current application.)

American Federation of Labor and Congress of Industrial Organizations: *See* AFL-CIO.

American Institute for Free Labor Development (AIFLD): Founded by the Communications Workers of America in 1959 and supported by the AFL-CIO and private business organizations, the Institute trains Latin American labor leaders and assists in projects such as community development and housing.

American Labor Party: A New York expression of the Non-Partisan League of 1936, organized to support the election of

Franklin D. Roosevelt. In 1948 it opposed the Truman Administration and supported Henry Wallace, the Progressive Party candidate. A few years after that campaign, the American Labor Party disappeared.

American Liberty League: Formed by business and industry leaders to oppose the policies of Franklin Roosevelt. It opposed the Wagner Act and what it characterized as "radicalism." The American Liberty League is no longer active.

American Plan: A movement by employers in the 1920s to promote the open shop in American industry. It was supported by chambers of commerce, the National Association of Manufacturers, and the National Metal Trades Association.

Anarchism (Anarchosyndicalism): A social doctrine that all constituted authority is ethically wrong and antagonistic to the human's highest development. It is opposed to the state as the embodiment of the force employed in the government of the community. Anarchists played a significant role in the Haymarket riots and in the formation of Industrial Workers of the World.

Annual Earnings: *See* Earnings.

Annual Improvement Factor: As introduced in the 1948 agreement between General Motors Corp. and the United Automobile Workers, and since retained, this term designates wage increases granted automatically each contract year, in addition to cost-of-living adjustments. The provision was prefaced with the following words which set it apart from ordinary deferred wage increases: "The annual improvement factor provided herein recognizes that a continuing improvement in the standard of living of employees depends upon technological progress, better tools, methods, processes and equipment, and a cooperative attitude on the part of all parties in such progress. It further recognizes the principle that to produce more with the same amount of human effort is a sound economic and social objective." (*See* Deferred Wage Increase.)

Annual Wage or Employment Guarantee: *See* Guaranteed Annual Wage Plan.

Annuity: *See* Pension Plan.

Anti-Injunction Law (Norris-LaGuardia Act) (1932): The federal act regulating the issuance of injunctions by federal courts in labor disputes. The act also made yellow-dog contracts unenforceable. The Labor-Management Relations Act (1947) restored some injunctive powers to the courts. (*See* Yellow-Dog Contract.)

Anti-Kickback Law and the Copeland Act (1934): Laws covering all work financed in whole or in part with federal funds, loans, or grants. The Anti-Kickback Law makes it a crime to attempt to induce an employee to give up any part of the compensation described in that person's contract of employment. The Copeland Act authorizes the Secretary of Labor to regulate contractors and subcontractors engaged in construction covered by the act. It requires payroll records showing the information needed to determine whether stipulated wages are being paid.

Anti-Petrillo Act: *See* Lea Act.

Anti-Racketeering Law (Hobbs Act) (1934): A federal law making it a felony to obstruct, delay, or affect interstate commerce by robbery or extortion.

Anti-Strikebreaker Law (Byrnes Act) (1936): A federal law prohibiting the interstate transportation of strikebreakers.

Antitrust Act of 1890: *See* Sherman Antitrust Act.

Antitrust Act of 1914: *See* Clayton Antitrust Act.

AO Cases: *See* Types of Cases: Other Cases, AO.

AOP: *See* Apprenticeship Outreach Program.

Appeal: Removal of a cause from one jurisdiction to a higher one for purposes of review and retrial.

Apprentice: A person, usually young, who enters into agreement to learn a skilled trade and to achieve a journeyman status through supervised training and experience, usually for a specified period. Practical training is supplemented by related technical off-the-job instruction.

Apprentice Rates: The schedule of rates applicable to workers being given formal apprenticeship training. Usually set so as to permit a gradual rise to the journeyman rate.

Apprenticeship: The status of a learner in a craft prior to becoming a journeyman. The apprentice system originated in the late Middle Ages in Europe and was the source for the development of skilled workers (journeymen) to serve in the shops of the craft guilds. In 1937 Congress passed the Apprentice Training Service Act which provides for pay while learning in apprentice program.

Apprenticeship Outreach Program (AOP): A program of the Department of Labor to find and place minority youth in apprentice programs. (*See* Workers Defense League.)

Apprenticeship Section, Division of Labor Standards (Labor): Transferred to Federal Security Agency by EO 9139 of Apr. 18, 1942, where it functioned as Apprentice Training Service. Its organizational entity preserved by section 6 of the order. Transferred to War Manpower Commission by EO 9247 of Sept. 17, 1942, where it functioned within Bureau of Training. Returned to Department of Labor by EO 9617 of Sept. 19, 1945.

Appropriate Unit: A bargaining unit. The National Labor Relations Board has the responsibility of deciding in dispute cases the group of workers (department, plant, craft, company, etc.) appropriate for inclusion in the "exclusive bargaining agent" designation. Criteria are factors such as history of collective bargaining and organization of employees, their desires, interests, and interchangeability.

A.R.: *See* Absence Rate.

A.R.: *See* Accession Rate.

Arbiter: *See* Arbitrator.

Arbitrable: Subject to the process of arbitration.

Arbitrate: (1) To act as an arbitrator; (2) to submit to arbitration.

Arbitration (Voluntary, Compulsory, Advisory): A method of settling labor-management disputes through recourse to an impartial third party, whose decision is usually final and binding. Arbitration is *voluntary* when both parties agree to submit disputed issues to arbitration, and *compulsory* if required by law. (A court order to carry through a voluntary arbitration agreement is not generally considered as compulsory arbitration.) *Advisory arbitration*, as provided in federal government agreements, is arbitration without a final and binding award.

Arbitration Clause: The section of a labor contract providing for the settlement of disputes through arbitration.

Arbitration, Terminal: Generally the last step in the grievance procedure outlined in labor agreements.

Arbitration, Twilight: Arbitration involving the interpretation of a contract when the grievance does not specify the violated part or clause in the contract.

Arbitrator: An impartial third party to whom disputing parties submit their differences for decision (award). An *ad hoc* arbitrator is one selected to act in a specific case or a limited group of cases. A *permanent* arbitrator is one selected to serve for the life of the contract or a stipulated term, hearing all disputes that arise during this period. (*See* Impartial Chairperson.)

Area Development Act (1961): A federal act to stimulate the economic growth of distressed areas through loans for private and public projects, through technical assistance, and through occupational training and retraining (with subsistence allowances for trainees).

Area Redevelopment Administration: Established May 8, 1961, by Secretary of Commerce pursuant to Area Redevelopment Act (75 Stat. 47; 42 U.S.C. 2501) and Reorg. Plan 5 of 1950. Terminated Aug. 31, 1965, pursuant to terms of the act, as amended (79 Stat. 195; 42 U.S.C. 2525). Functions, personnel, and property transferred to Economic Development Administration in Department of Commerce by Department Order 4-A, effective Sept. 1, 1965 (*see* text).

Areawide Bargaining: Negotiations between labor and management on a contract applicable in a wide geographic area.

Aristocracy of Labor: A skilled artisan class represented by some craft unions; the term is usually applied in a pejorative sense.

Ashurst-Sumners Act (1935): A law forbidding the shipment of prison-made goods into states which forbid the sale of goods so made.

Assessment: A special charge levied by a union on its members to meet financial needs not covered by regular dues.

Assistance Payments Administration (HEW): Established by Secretary's reorganization of August 15, 1967, to administer assistance programs of certain State grants, Work Incentive Program, and for U.S. citizens returning from abroad and refugees. Transferred by Secretary's reorganization of Mar. 8, 1977 (42 FR 13262) from Social and Rehabilitation Service to Social Security Administration.

Association Agreement: An agreement with a union or unions, negotiated and signed by an employers' association on behalf of its members. (*See* Multiemployer Bargaining.)

Associationists: American followers of the French economist Charles Fourier (1772–1837), who sought to escape the evils of industrialism by forming independent, self-supporting communes where employers and workers would be indistinguishable and would share common interests. In 1841, the American group formed Brook Farm, where all shared in the work and received equal pay.

Atomic Energy Labor-Management Relations Panel: A board of impartial experts established in 1953 to assist the operating contractors of the Atomic Energy Commission and their unions in arriving at peaceful settlements of disputes over agreement terms. The parties are free to reject panel jurisdiction.

Attendance Bonus: Payment or another type of reward (e.g., a day off) for employees whose record of daily reporting for work, without absences, meets certain standards of excellence.

Attrition Arrangement: A process of relying upon voluntary quits, deaths, and retirements to reduce a company's labor force overtime instead of resorting to dismissal of workers.

Authorization Card: A statement signed by the worker authorizing a union to act as his or her representative in dealings with management, or authorizing the company to deduct union dues from his or her pay (checkoff). (*See* Card Check.)

Automatic Checkoff: The regular deduction of dues from the wages of workers by the employer and the forwarding of the sums withheld to the union.

Automatic Progression: A policy by which rates of pay of workers in jobs with established rate ranges are increased automatically at fixed time intervals. Also used to refer to automatic movement from a trainee rate to a job classification rate or to the minimum of a rate range.

Automatic Renewal: A clause in a collective bargaining agreement which provides for a continuation of an agreement after the date it would otherwise expire, unless either party notifies the other of its desire to terminate the contract and negotiate a new one.

Automatic Retirement: *See* Compulsory Retirement.

Automation: As used by engineers, the term designates one of several types of technical developments, including (1) a continuous-flow production process which integrates various mechanisms to produce a finished item with relatively few or no worker operations, usually through electronic control; (2) self-regulating machines that can perform highly precise operations in sequence; and (3) electronic computing machines. In common usage, however, the term is often used in reference to any type of advanced mechanization or as a synonym for technological change.

Autonomy: The right of self-government on the part of a trade union with respect to other unions or to a federation of unions. *Local autonomy* refers to such a right on the part of a local union with respect to its national union.

Average Hourly Earnings: *See* Earnings.

Award: The decision of an arbitrator setting forth the facts in the case and the reason for the judgment. It is almost always presented in writing.

B Standard: The required measure of output per minute under the Bedeaux system. (*See* Bedeaux System.)

Baby Wagner Acts: Laws passed in many states based on the National Labor Relations Act that are generally applicable to workers not under the jurisdiction of the National Labor Relations Board.

Backpay: Payment of part or all of the wages for a particular prior period of time, arising from arbitration, court, or board awards, grievance settlements, errors in computation of pay, misinterpretation of wage legislation, etc.

Backpay Hearing: As defined by the National Labor Relations Board, a supplementary hearing to receive evidence and testimony as to the amount of backpay due discriminatees under a prior National Labor Relations Board order or court decree.

Backpay Specification: As defined by the National Labor Relations Board: The formal document, a "pleading," that is served on the parties when the regional director and the respondent are unable to agree on the amounts of backpay due discriminatees pursuant to a Board order or court decree requiring payment of such backpay. It sets forth in detail the amount held by the regional director to be owing each discriminatee and the method of computation employed. The specification is accompanied by a notice of the backpay hearing and sets a date for it.

Back-to-Work Movement: Return of some or all striking workers to their jobs before the strike is ended.

Bargaining Agent: A union designated by an appropriate government agency, such as the National Labor Relations Board, or recognized voluntarily by the employer, as the exclusive representative of all employees in the bargaining unit for purposes of collective bargaining.

Bargaining Rights: Legally recognized rights of unions to represent workers in dealings with employers.

Bargaining Theory of Wages: A theory explaining the fluctuation in wages as the result of the law of supply and demand.

Bargaining Unit: A group of employees in a craft, department, plant, firm, or industry recognized by the employer or a group of employers, or designated by an authorized agency such as the National Labor Relations Board, as appropriate for representation by a union for purposes of collective bargaining.

Barth Premium Plan: A combination of time and productivity as a basis for wage payment.

Base Rate: Amount of pay for work performed during a unit of time, e.g., hour, day, week, month, or year, exclusive of overtime or incentive earnings. Under incentive systems, the term may refer to the amount paid for an established task or job standard, usually at a work level equivalent to a nonincentive pace.

BAT: *See* Bureau of Apprenticeship and Training.

Battle of the Overpass: The physical beating of Walter Reuther, Richard Frankenstein, and other organizers for the United Auto Workers while distributing organizational literature to Ford workers on May 26, 1937. The beating was administered by "service employees" of the Ford Company.

Bay Ridge Rule: A rule, laid down by the Supreme Court in *Bay Ridge Operating Company v. Aaron* (1948), requiring employers to pay "overtime on overtime" under the Fair Labor Standards Act. The act has since been amended so that such payments are no longer required.

Bedeaux System: A plan named after its sponsor, a French engineer, who introduced the time measurement of units of work as the basis of an incentive system.

Beginner Rate: *See* Learner Rate.

Belo Wage System: A system designed to overcome provisions of the Fair Labor Standards Act in situations where work hours are inherently irregular and a constant weekly wage is provided.

Benchmarks: *See* Peg Points.

Benefits Review Board: The Board, located in the Department of Labor, hears and determines certain appeals made by any interested party. Specifically, the appeals from decisions must raise a substantial question of law or fact with respect to claims of employees under the Longshoremen's and Harbor Workers' Compensation Act and its extensions, and the Black Lung Benefits Act of 1972.

Bereavement Pay: *See* Funeral Leave Pay.

Bergoff Technique: A method of antiunion activity which includes strikebreaking, importation of strikebreakers, and back-to-work movements when strikes occur.

Bidding: In plants where job openings are posted, the process by which employees express their desire ("bid") for a vacant job, which is then awarded on the basis of established criteria.

"Big Six": The common nickname for Typographical Union No. 6, the New York City branch of the International Typographical Union of North America, probably the oldest local union in the country.

"Big Steel": The U.S. Steel Corporation. (Cf. "Little Steel.")

Bindle Stiff or Bundle Stiff: An old-fashioned colloquial term for a migratory worker.

Bituminous Coal Division (Interior): Established July 1, 1939, by Secretary's Order 1394, of June 16, 1939 (amended by Order 1399, of July 5, 1939), pursuant to Reorg. Act of 1939 (53 Stat. 562; 5 U.S.C. 133t) and Reorg. Plan II, effective July 1, 1939. Administered, under supervision and direction of Secretary of the Interior, functions vested in National Bituminous Coal Commission by Bituminous Coal Act of 1937 (50 Stat. 72; 15 U.S.C. 828–851), which provided for stabilization of bituminous coal industry. This act by its terms was limited in operation to a period of 4 years from date of its enactment. Act extended to Aug. 24, 1943, on which date it expired.

The Bituminous Coal Division established minimum prices for bituminous coal; enforced compliance with established minimum prices and fair marketing rules prescribed by act; during wartime performed services for Solid Fuels Administration for War, Office of Price Administration, Navy Department, War Department, and other war agencies.

Bituminous Coal Labor Board: Established by act of July 12, 1921 (42 Stat. 140, 991; 15 U.S.C. 801–827), to mediate disputes between employees and employers in bituminous-coal industry. Abolished as result of Supreme Court decision, May 18, 1936, in the case of *Carter v. Carter Coal Company et al.*

Black Connery Bill: *See* Fair Labor Standards Act.

Black Death: The plague that decimated the populations of Europe and Great Britain in the winters of 1348 and 1349. The ensuing shortage of labor destroyed the manorial system and caused wages to rise rapidly. Legislation was successively introduced to halt the rise in wages. (*See* Statute of Labourers.)

Black Lung Benefits Act of 1972: Legislation that improves Title IV of the Federal Coal Mine Health and Safety Act of 1969 by authorizing coverage for additional beneficiaries, as well as by easing evidentiary requirements of establishing total disability due to pneumoconiosis. Several other new provisions were added, which will materially aid disabled coal miners, and their survivors.

Blackleg: A British term for scab.

Blacklist: (1) A list of names privately circulated among employers for the purpose of jointly refusing employment to union workers in general or to individual workers held in disfavor. (2) A list of contractors who have violated the Public Contracts (Walsh-Healy) Act specifications.

Blanket Injunction: An injunction prohibiting acts that have not been committed. Also, an injunction issued against persons unnamed and unknown.

BLS: *See* Bureau of Labor Statistics.

Blue-collar Workers: Manual workers, usually those employed in production, maintenance, and related occupations, and paid by the hour or on an incentive basis. (Cf. White-Collar Workers.)

Blue Cross: The independent nonprofit membership corporation providing protection against the costs of hospital care through an insurance plan. (*See* Hospitalization Benefits.)

Blue Shield: The independent nonprofit membership corporation providing payments for the costs of surgery and related medical care through an inusrance plan. (*See* Surgical Benefits.)

Blue-sky Bargaining: Negotiations in which either one or both of the parties make unreasonable demands and refuse to yield on any of the points they have presented.

BNA: *See* Bureau of National Affairs, Inc.

Board of Inquiry: A board appointed by the President of the United States, under the Labor-Management Relations Act, to examine and report on the facts and positions of the parties in a "national emergency" dispute. The term is often used for any board set up by a public agency to investigate a labor dispute. (*See* Fact-finding Board.)

Board of Inquiry for the Cotton Textile Industry: Created by EO 6840 of Sept. 5, 1934, to make a report not later than Oct. 1, 1934, through Secretary of Labor to the President, and to terminate upon completion of duties. Abolished by EO 6858 of Sept. 26, 1934.

Bogus Work: The term used in the printing industry to designate typesetting work which is not needed for printing but which is required by the collective bargaining agreement. Other terms for unused work are *reproduction, reset,* and *dead horse.*

Bonus Plan: A wage system that includes payment in addition to the regular or base wage for production exceeding the standard for the job, department, or plant. Sometimes used to indicate a piecework or wage-incentive system. The term *bonus* may also refer to any payment in addition to the regular wage (e.g., Christmas bonus).

Book Member: *See* Union Member.

Boondoggle: Unnecessary work that gives the appearance of productive effort.

Boring from Within: Engaging in a technique to gain control of an organization by becoming a fully participating member and endeavoring to mould its policies.

Boulwarism: A "negotiation" technique originated by Lemuel Boulware, a vice-president of General Electric. Using this technique, the company decides, before meeting with its union, what it will offer and then conveys that offer to its employees without consulting the union. During collective bargaining, even after the threat of a strike, GE's offer remained firm. In 1964 the National Labor Relations Board said that GE had thereby violated the "good faith" bargaining duty under the Taft-Hartley Act.

Boycott: Efforts by a union, usually in collaboration with other unions, to discourage the purchase, handling, or use of products of an employer with whom the union is in dispute. When such action is extended to another company doing business with the employer involved in the dispute, it is termed a *secondary boycott.* (*See* Hot-Cargo Clause.)

Break Time: *See* Rest Period.

Break-in Time: The time necessary for a worker or a group of workers to adjust to a new job under an incentive plan.

Bridge Benefits: *See* Survivors' Benefits.

British Trade Union Congress (TUC): Britain's counterpart to the AFL-CIO, with similar interests, similar authority, and similar scope.

Broadbanding: The consolidation of job titles by placing many job classifications under one common title.

Brookwood Labor College: Formed as the first resident workers college in the United States at a meeting of trade union leaders in New York in 1921, and established at Katonah, New York. It no longer exists.

Brotherhood: A word used frequently in the names of earlier unions, notably those of railway workers that started as fraternal benefit organizations.

Bug: *See* Union Label.

Building and Construction Trades Department: *See* AFL-CIO, Departments of.

Building Trades: Those occupations involved in construction, such as carpenters, bricklayers, painters, and lathers.

Bumping (Rolling): The practice that allows a senior employee (in seniority ranking or length of service) to displace a junior employee in another job or department during a layoff or reduction in force. (*See* Seniority.)

Bureau of Apprenticeship and Training (BAT): Created under the National Apprenticeship Act of 1937 and located within the Department of Labor, the Bureau is responsible for promoting the apprenticeship and training program among employers and for protecting the welfare of apprentices through its support of high labor standards. It works in conjunction with state apprenticeship councils to approve and register local programs and to provide employers with technical assistance. BAT has approved state councils in thirty-two states.

Bureau of Employees' Compensation: Transferred from Federal Security Agency to Department of Labor by Reorg. Plan 19, effective May 24, 1950. On Mar. 13, 1972, functions of the Bureau were absorbed by the Employment Standards Administration.

Bureau of Employment Security (Labor): Transferred from the Federal Security Agency by Reorg. Plan 2 of 1949, effective Aug. 20, 1949. Abolished by Secretary's order of Mar. 14, 1969 and functions transferred to the Manpower Administration. *See also* United States Employment Service.

Bureau of Family Services (HEW): Created Jan. 1, 1962, by Secretary's order. Functions redelegated to the Social and Rehabilitation Service by Secretary's reorganization of Aug. 15, 1967.

Bureau of Immigration and Naturalization: Bureau of Immigration established by act of Mar. 3, 1891 (26 Stat. 1085; 5 U.S.C. 342), as a branch of Treasury Department, and transferred to Department of Commerce and Labor by act of Feb. 14, 1903 (32 Stat. 827; 5 U.S.C. 342a). By act of June 29, 1906 (34 Stat. 596; 8 U.S.C. 357), naturalization duties made a part of its functions, and it became Bureau of Immigration and Naturalization. Bureau made separate divisions after Department of Labor was created by act of Mar. 4, 1913 (37 Stat. 736; 5 U.S.C. 611). Consolidated into Immigration and Naturalization Service, Department of Labor, by section 14 of EO 6166 of June 10, 1933. Transferred to Department of Justice by Reorg. Plan V, effective June 14, 1940.

Bureau of International Labor Affairs: The agency that coordinates and directs the international activities of the Department of Labor, participating in the formulation of international economic policy through the Secretary of Labor's membership on the Council on International Economic Policy. Its responsibilities under the Trade Act of 1974 include participation in trade negotiations and administration of trade adjustment assistance for workers; and provision of assistance in the management of the U.S. Foreign Service and the U.S. Labor

Attaché program through membership on the Board of the Foreign Service.

Bureau of Labor Standards (Labor):   Established by departmental order in 1934 to safeguard the Nation's work force by administering Federal occupational safety and health laws and by promoting safety programs in the States and in industry and to improve employment conditions for all workers through legislation. Functions absorbed by the Occupational Safety and Health Administration in May 1971.

Bureau of Labor Statistics (BLS):   The agency that has responsibility for the Department of Labor's economic and statistical research activities. It is the federal government's principal fact-finding agency in the field of labor economics, particularly with respect to the collection and analysis of data on workpower and labor requirements, labor force, employment, unemployment, hours of work, wages and employee compensation, prices, living conditions, labor-management relations, productivity and technological developments, occupational safety and health, structure and growth of the economy, urban conditions and related socioeconomic issues, and international aspects of certain of these subjects.

Bureau of Mines: Created in Department of the Interior by act of May 16, 1910 (36 Stat. 369; 30 U.S.C. 1 and note). Transferred to Department of Commerce July 1, 1925, by EO 4239 of June 4, 1925. Transferred from Department of Commerce to Department of the Interior by EO 6611 of Feb. 22, 1934, effective Apr. 23, 1934.

Bureau of National Affairs, Inc. (BNA):   A commercial nongovernmental organization engaged in providing various types of reports and services dealing with industrial relations and labor affairs. It is located at 1231 25th St. N.W., Washington, D.C. 20037.

Bureau of Work-Training Programs (Labor):   Abolished by reorganization of the Manpower Administration, effective Mar. 17, 1969, and functions assigned to U.S. Training and Employment Service.

Business Agent (Union Representative):   Generally a full-time paid employee or official of a local union whose duties include day-to-day dealing with employers and workers, adjustment of grievances, enforcement of agreements, and similar activities. (Cf. International Representative.)

Business Unionism ("Bread-and-Butter" Unionism):   The union policy that places primary emphasis on securing higher wages and better working conditions for its members through collective bargaining rather than through political action or radical reform of society. The term has been widely used to characterize the objectives of the trade union movement in the United States.

Button: The insignia worn by members of a union to indicate membership therein.

Bylaws: Generally, provisions supplementing the charter or constitution of a union or other organization and setting forth the rules for the organization.

Byrnes Act: *See* Anti-Strikebreaker Law.

C Case: *See* Types of Cases: C Cases.

Callback Pay   *See* Call-in Pay.

Ca'canny: Scottish word meaning to "go easy" and to slow down production by means not readily apparent to the employer.

CA Case: Under the National Labor Relations Board procedures, a charge against an employer for committing any of the acts in the following paragraphs of Section 8 of the National Labor Relations Act:

8(a)(1)   To interfere with, restrain, or coerce employees in exercise of their rights under Section 7 (to join or assist a labor organization or to refrain).

8(a)(2)   To dominate or interfere with the formation or administration of a labor organization or contribute financial or other support to it.

8(a)(3)   By discrimination in regard to hire or tenure of employment or any term or condition of employment, to encourage or discourage membership in any labor organization.

8(a)(4)   To discharge or otherwise discriminate against employees because they have given testimony under the Act.

8(a)(5)   To refuse to bargain collectively with representatives of its employees.
(*See* Types of Cases.)

Call-in Pay (Callback Pay):   Amount of pay guaranteed to a worker recalled to work after completing the regular work shift. Call-in pay is often used as a synonym for reporting pay. (*See* Reporting Pay.)

Captive Audience: A group of workers in a plant who are asked to assemble during working hours to listen to an employer's side of a controversy with the workers or with a potential union.

Captive Mine: A coal mine owned by a company that uses the entire product of that mine.

Card Check: The procedure whereby signed union authorization cards are checked against a list of workers in a prospective bargaining unit to determine whether the union has majority status. The employer may recognize the union on the basis of this check without the necessity of a formal election. Often conducted by an outside party, e.g., a respected member of the community. (*See* Authorization Card.)

Card Men: Members of a labor organization who carry dues cards as proof of membership in good standing.

Case: As defined by the National Labor Relations Board: A "case" is the general term used in referring to a charge or petition filed with the Board. Each case is numbered and carries a letter designation indicating the type of case. (*See* Types of Cases.)

Casual Workers: Workers who have no steady employer, but who shift from employer to employer. Also used in longshoring to refer to workers not regularly attached to a particular work group. Sometimes applied to temporary employees.

Catastrophe Insurance: *See* Major-Medical Expense Benefit.

CB Case: Under National Labor Relations Board procedures, a charge against a labor organization for commission of any of the following acts described in the paragraphs indicated below of Section 8 of the National Labor Relations Act:

8(b)(1)(A)   To restrain or coerce employees in exercise of their rights under Section 7 (to join or assist a labor organization or to refrain).

8(b)(1)(B)   To restrain or coerce an employer in the selection of its representatives for collective bargaining or adjustment of grievances.

8(b)(2)   To cause or attempt to cause an employer to discriminate against an employee.

8(b)(3)   To refuse to bargain collectively with employer.

8(b)(5)   To require of employees the payment of excessive or discriminatory fees for membership.

$8(b)(6)$ To cause or attempt to cause an employer to pay or agree to pay money or other thing of value for services which are not performed or not to be performed.
(*See* Types of Cases.)

CC Case: Under National Labor Relations Board procedures, a charge against a labor organization for commission of the following acts as described in Section 8 of the National Labor Relations Act:

$8(b)(4)(i)$ To engage in, or induce or encourage any individual employed by any person engaged in commerce or in an industry affecting commerce to engage in, a strike, work stoppage, or boycott, or (*ii*) to threaten, coerce, or restrain any person engaged in commerce or in an industry affecting commerce, where in either case an object is:

(*A*) To force or require any employer or self-employed person to join any labor or employer organization or to enter into any agreement prohibited by Sec. 8(e).

(*B*) To force or require any person to cease using, selling, handling, transporting, or otherwise dealing in the products of any other producer, processor, or manufacturer, or to cease doing business with any other person, or force or require any other employer to recognize or bargain with a labor organization as the representative of its employees unless such labor organization has been so certified.

(*C*) To force or require any employer to recognize or bargain with a particular labor organization as the representative of its employees if another labor organization has been certified as the representative.
(*See* Types of Cases.)

CCH: *See* Commerce Clearing House, Inc.

CD Case: Under National Labor Relations Board procedures, a charge against a labor organization for commission of the following acts defined in Section 8(b)(4)(i)(D) of the National Labor Relations Act:

$8(b)(4)(i)(D)$ To engage in, or induce or encourage any individual employed by any person engaged in commerce or in an industry affecting commerce to engage in, a strike, work stoppage, or boycott, or (*ii*) to threaten, coerce, or restrain any person engaged in commerce or in an industry affecting commerce, where in either case an object is:

To force or require any employer to assign particular work to employees in a particular labor organization or in a particular trade, craft, or class, rather than to employees in another trade, craft, or class, unless such employer is failing to conform to an appropriate Board order or certification.
(*See* Types of Cases.)

CDC: *See* Community Development Corporation.

CE Case: Under National Labor Relations Board procedures, a charge against a labor organization and an employer for commission of the following behavior, as outlined in the Section 8(e) of the National Labor Relations Act:

$8(e)$ To enter into any contract or agreement (any labor organization and any employer) whereby such employer ceases or refrains, or agrees to cease or refrain, from handling or dealing in any product of any other employer, or to cease doing business with any other person.
(*See* Types of Cases.)

Central Labor Council (City Central Body): An AFL-CIO organization, formed by association of local unions in a community or other geographical area, to further union interests and activities.

Certificate of Age (Age Certificate): A certificate issued by governmental authorities in connection with laws authorizing the employment of minors.

Certification: Formal designation by a government agency, such as the National Labor Relations Board, of the union selected by the majority of the employees in a supervised election to act as exclusive bargaining agent for all employees in the bargaining unit.

Certified Employee Organization: The organization officially recognized as the employees' bargaining agent.

CETA: *See* Comprehensive Employment and Training Act.

CG Case: Under National Labor Relations Board procedures, a charge against a labor organization for the commission of certain behaviors outlined in Section 8(g) of the National Labor Relations Act:

$8(g)$ To strike, picket, or otherwise concertedly refuse to work at any health care institution without notifying the institution and the Federal Mediation and Conciliation Service in writing 10 days prior to such action.
(*See* Types of Cases.)

Challenges: As defined by the National Labor Relations Board: The parties to an NLRB election are entitled to challenge any voter. At the election site, the challenged ballots are segregated and not counted when the other ballots are tallied. Most frequently, the tally of unchallenged ballots determines the election and the challenged ballots are insufficient in number to affect the result of the election. The challenges in such a case are never resolved, and the certification is based on the tally of (unchallenged) ballots.

When challenged ballots may determine the result, a decision as to whether they are to be counted rests with the regional director in the first instance, subject to possible appeal to the Board. Often, however, the "determinative" challenges are resolved informally by the parties by mutual agreement. No record is kept of nondeterminative challenges or of determinative challenges which are resolved by agreement prior to issuance of the first tally of ballots.

Changeover Time: Working time lost while a company changes from one model to another, as in the automobile industry.

Chapel: In the International Typographical Union, a sublocal of the members in a particular shop. So called because the first printing press was set up (by William Caxton) in an unused chapel of Westminster Abbey.

Chapter: *See* Local Union.

Charge: As defined by the National Labor Relations Board, a document filed by an employee, an employer, a union, or an individual alleging that an unfair labor practice has been committed. *See* Types of Cases, C Cases.

Charter: The written authorization to establish a subordinate or affiliated body of a union.

Checkoff: A practice whereby the employer, by agreement with the union (and upon written authorization from each employee where required by law or agreement), regularly withholds union dues from employees' wages and transmits these funds to the union. Checkoff is a common practice in organized establishments and does not depend on the existence of a formal union security clause. The arrangement may also provide for deductions of initiation fees and assessments. (*See* Union Security.)

Checkweighman: A person designated and paid by miners to check the weighing of coal by the company to protect the interests of the miners. This practice was followed in union-organized mines when miners were paid on the basis of weight produced rather than time spent on the job.

Children's Bureau: Created by act of Apr. 9, 1912 (37 Stat. 79, as amended; 42 U.S.C. 191 et seq.), and was placed in Department of Labor by act of Mar. 4, 1913 (37 Stat. 737; 5 U.S.C. 616). Transferred, with exception of child labor functions under Fair Labor Standards Act, to Federal Security Agency pursuant to Reorg. Plan 2 of 1946, where it functioned under Social Security Administration. Continued under this Administration when FSA functions were assumed by Department of Health, Education, and Welfare. Reassigned to the Welfare Administration by Department reorganization on Jan. 28, 1963. Reassigned to the Social and Rehabilitation Service by Department reorganization on Aug. 15, 1967. Reassigned to the Office of Child Development by Department reorganization order of Sept. 17, 1969.

Chinese Overtime: A rate of pay calculated, under the Fair Labor Standards Act, by dividing wages of salaried employees by hours worked in excess of 40 per week.

CIM (Comisión Interamericana de Mujeres): *See* Inter-American Commission of Women.

CIO: *See* Committee for Industrial Organization and Congress of Industrial Organization.

Citizens' Advisory Council on the Status of Women: Established in 1963 by Executive Order No. 11126, it is the oldest federal advisory group in the field of women's rights. Its members, appointed by the President, stimulate action on the part of private organizations and individuals in areas of special concern to women.

City Central Body: *See* Central Labor Council.

Civil Rights Act of 1964: The act contains two highly significant titles. Title VI stipulates: "No person in the United States shall, on ground of race, color, or national origin, be excluded from participation in, be denied the benefits of, or be subjected to discrimination under any program or activity receiving Federal financial assistance."

Under Title VII, employers, unions, and employment agencies are required to treat all persons equally, regardless of race, color, religion, sex, or national origin, in all phases of employment, including hiring, promotion, compensation, firing, apprenticeship, job assignments, and training. The Equal Employment Opportunity Commission was created to assist in carrying out this section of the act.

Civil Rights Division: The Division established in 1957 in the office of the Attorney General in response to the need to secure effective federal enforcement of civil rights. Headed by an assistant attorney general, the Division is responsible for enforcing federal civil rights laws which prohibit discrimination on the basis of race, color, religion, or national origin in the areas of voting, education, employment, and housing, in the use of public facilities and public accommodations, and in the administration of federally assisted programs. With respect to employment, housing, and education, sex discrimination is also prohibited. The congressional statutes enforced by the Division are the Civil Rights Acts of 1957, 1960, 1964, 1968, the Voting Rights Act of 1965, and their amendments.

Civilian Conservation Corps: Created by act approved June 28, 1937 (50 Stat. 319; 16 U.S.C. 584), as amended, to succeed Emergency Conservation Work (appendix A) as amended. Was made a part of Federal Security Agency by Reorg. Plan I, effective July 1, 1939. Established to provide employment, as well as vocational training, for youthful citizens of the United States who were unemployed and, to a limited extent, for war veterans and Indians, through performance of useful public work in connection with conservation and development of

natural resources of the United States, its Territories and insular possessions. In May 1940 the Corps began converting to defense work on military reservations and forest protection. The Labor-Federal Security Appropriation Act, 1943 (56 Stat. 569), provided for liquidation of the CCC not later than June 30, 1943.

Civilian Production Administration: Established within Office for Emergency Management by EO 9638 of Oct. 4, 1945, to assume functions of War Production Board terminated by same order, effective Nov. 3, 1945, to further swift and orderly transition from wartime production to maximum peacetime production in industry free from wartime Government controls, with due regard for stability of prices and costs. Consolidated with other agencies to form Office of Temporary Controls by EO 9809 of Dec. 12, 1946.

Class Consciousness: Awareness of the identity of interests of those whose economic relationship and status are similar—such as workers, employers, landlords, slaves, slave owners, feudal lords, and serfs—with such awareness giving rise to "class solidarity" and "class antagonism."

Classification: The grouping of workers in a single plant or industry according to the grade or kind of work they perform as the basis for fixing wage scales.

Classification Act Employees: Federal government employees, typically professional, administrative, technical, and clerical, whose salary rates and certain other conditions of employment are determined by Congress. (Cf. Wage Board Employees.)

Clayton Antitrust Act (1914): Legislation designed to prevent the use of the Sherman Antitrust Act against unions and to limit the jurisdiction of the courts to issue injunctions in labor disputes. The labor sections of the Clayton Act were nullified by the Supreme Court in 1921 in the *Duplex Printing v. Dearing* case.

Cleanup Time (Washup Time): Paid time allowed to workers to clean their workplaces or tools or to wash up before leaving the plant at the close of the workday or for lunch. (*See* Clothes-changing Time.)

Cleavage: The difference between a union and a previously disestablished company union. It is a policy of the National Labor Relations Board that this difference be clear not only in form but in substance.

Closed Shop: A form of union security provided in an agreement which binds the employer both to hire and to retain only union members in good standing. In a closed shop, membership in the union is a required condition before hiring. The key distinction between a closed shop and a union shop lies in the hiring restriction, which was prohibited by the Labor-Management Relations Act, 1947. Legal closed shops may be found outside the scope of this act (which applies to employers and employees in industries affecting interstate commerce) and outside of states with right-to-work laws.

Closed Union: A union which bars new members or makes membership acquisition difficult (e.g., by very high initiation fees) in order to protect job opportunities for its present members, or for other reasons. Some unions accept only children of present members. (Cf. Open Union.)

Clothes-changing Time: Time allotted within the paid workday for changing from street wear to working clothes or from working clothes to street wear, or both. (*See* Cleanup Time.)

Clothing Allowance: A monetary allowance for clothing and/or its upkeep, granted by an employer to employees who are required to wear special clothing, such as uniforms or safety garments, in the performance of their work.

CLUW: *See* Coalition of Labor Union Women.

Coalition of Labor Union Women (CLUW): Convened in Chicago in March 1974 with 3200 delegates representing over fifty-eight labor unions and resolved to work within the labor movement. The trade union women (nonunion women are ineligible to join) defined several goals: (1) to encourage the 30 million nonunion working women to take advantage of the tangible economic benefits of unionists by joining unions; (2) to increase women's participation within unions; (3) to seek affirmative action on the parts of unions against employers' discriminatory practices; and (4) to press for legislative action which would further women's interests, such as child care assistance and the passage of the Equal Rights Amendment (ERA).

Coal Mines Administration: Established July 1, 1943, by Secretary of the Interior to supervise operation of coal mines taken over by the Federal Government under EO 9340 of May 1, 1943, and EO 9393 of Nov. 1, 1943. Administration abolished by Secretary's Order 1977 of Aug. 16, 1944, as amended by Order 1982 of Aug. 31, 1944. Functions assumed by Solid Fuels Administration for War. Administration reestablished within Interior Department by EO 9728 of May 21, 1946. Ceased to exist upon expiration of the Second War Powers Act on June 30, 1947.

Codes of Ethical Practices: The rules adopted by the AFL-CIO in 1956–1957, setting standards of behavior for unions and their officers.

Coffee Breaks: *See* Rest Period.

Collective Bargaining: A method whereby representatives of the employees (the union) and the employer determine the conditions of employment through direct negotiation, normally resulting in a written contract setting forth the wages, hours, and other conditions to be observed for a stipulated period (e.g., 2 years). The term is also applied to union-management dealings during the term of the agreement. (*See* Agreement.)

Collective Bargaining Agreement: *See* Agreement.

Collective Bargaining Committee in Construction: Established by EO 11849 of Apr. 1, 1975, to encourage and facilitate collective bargaining process at local and area levels, assist in providing data bank of wage and benefit information, and seek to resolve disputes that could not otherwise be reasonably resolved. Inactive since Jan. 7, 1976.

Combined Apprenticeship and Journeyman Outreach Program: Established under Title I of the Comprehensive Employment and Training Act (CETA), this program is designed to recruit, motivate, and guide primarily minority youth toward entrance into apprenticeship programs operated by labor and management, mainly in the construction trades.

Comisión Interamericana de Mujeres: *See* Inter-American Commission of Women.

Commerce Clause (Commerce Power): The clause in Article I, Section 8, of the United States Constitution that grants the power to the Congress "to regulate commerce with foreign nations and among the several states . . . ." This clause is the basis for much labor legislation and for the involvement of the federal government in labor matters.

Commerce Clearing House, Inc. (CCH): A private publisher of a wide range of material in the field of labor-management relations.

Commission on Civil Rights: Created by the Civil Rights Act of 1964, the Commission encourages constructive steps toward equal opportunity for minority groups and women. It investigates complaints, holds public hearings, and collects and studies information on denials of equal protection under the laws because of race, color, religion, sex, or national origin. Voting rights, administration of justice, and equality of opportunity in education, employment, and housing are among the many topics of specific Commission interest.

Commission Earnings: Compensation, based on a predetermined percentage of the value of sales, paid to salespeople. It may be an addition to a guaranteed salary rate or may constitute total pay.

Commissioner of Immigration (Labor): Offices of commissioner of immigration of the several ports, created by act of 1894, abolished by section 6 of Reorg. Plan III, functions to be administered by the Commissioner of Immigration and Naturalization through district directors of immigration and naturalization, effective June 30, 1940. *See* Bureau of Immigration and Naturalization.

Committee for Industrial Organization (CIO): The committee organized by unions within the American Federation of Labor in 1935 that were committed to organize industrial workers on an industrial basis. These unions were expelled from the American Federation of Labor and changed the name of their group to Congress of Industrial Organization in 1938.

Committee on Political Education: *See* AFL-CIO, COPE.

Committee on Government Contract Compliance: Established by EO 10308 of Dec. 3, 1951, to improve means for obtaining compliance with nondiscrimination provisions of Federal contracts. Abolished by EO 10479 of Aug. 13, 1953.

Committee on Economic Security: Created by EO 6757 of June 29, 1934, pursuant to provisions of National Industrial Recovery Act (48 Stat. 195), to study the problem of economic and social security and to develop an appropriate legislative program. The Social Security Act and 1939 amendments are the result of its work. Terminated as a formal agency in April 1936, as provided in section 2(c) of act as amended. Continued informally for some time thereafter.

Committee on Fair Employment Practice: Established within Office of Production Management by EO 8802 of June 25, 1941, and transferred to War Manpower Commission by Presidential letter effective July 30, 1942. Committee ceased to exist upon establishment of the Committee on Fair Employment Practice within Office for Emergency Management by EO 9346 of May 27, 1943. Purpose was to promote fullest utilization of all available manpower and to eliminate discriminatory employment practices. Terminated June 30, 1946, by National War Agencies Appropriation Act of 1946 (59 Stat. 473).

Committee Person: A worker designated by the union to act within the plant in the settlement of grievances and to further the administrative and organizational goals of the union. In most cases, the committee person ranks higher in the union hierarchy than the steward.

Common Labor: The general term used to designate unskilled workers, usually men, performing heavy labor. In specific plants, it may refer to unskilled workers not assigned to a particular job. The latter use is probably now the more frequent one.

Communism: A worldwide revolutionary movement based on the doctrines of Karl Marx (as interpreted by V. I. Lenin and current leaders of the Communist Party of the Soviet Union and the People's Republic of China). It seeks the abolition of private ownership of the means of production, distribution, and exchange. Communism differs from democratic Marxist movements (socialism) in its insistence on the "dictatorship of the proletariat" and in its skepticism of democracy as a means of achieving goals.

Communist International: Formed in Moscow in 1919 to "unite all revolutionary parties in the world proletariat" in opposition to the then existing Socialist International; and to overthrow capitalism and set up a "dictatorship of the proletariat." Also known as the "Bolshevik" or "Red" Internationale.

Community Development Corporation (CDC): A program under the Community Services Administration which includes industrial parks, improved housing, job training, and ownership opportunities for low-income residents of economically deprived and physically blighted communities. It operates mainly through Community Development Corporations (CDCs) by building a solid economic base through the creation of new businesses and jobs. Established by act of December 31, 1970 (42 U.S.C. 4501, et seq). Name changed to New Community Development Corporation on May 18, 1976, by act of August 22, 1974 (88 Stat. 725).

Community Services Administration (CSA): Established by the Headstart, Economic Opportunity, and Community Partnership Act of 1974 as the successor to the Office of Economic Opportunity (OEO). The programs transferred (in 1975) from OEO are those of Community Action, Economic Development, and Legal Services.

Company Man: Used by workers as a pejorative term to describe a person who is more concerned for the employer's interests than for those of fellow workers. It is used in a nonpejorative sense to describe someone who holds a position in a supervisory capacity.

Company Spy: Someone hired by an employer to report on union activities among employees.

Company Store: A store, generally in a company-owned town that sells goods at noncompetitive prices set by the company. Goods and supplies are sometimes advanced on the basis of the worker's future earnings or on payment of scrip money.

Company Town: An industrial community in which the employer is the sole or main proprietor of land, improvements, homes, stores, churches, public halls, etc.

Company Union: A labor organization that is organized, financed, or dominated by the employer and is thus suspected of being an agent of the company rather than of the workers. This practice is prohibited under the Labor-Management Relations Act, 1947. The term also survives as a derogatory charge leveled against a union suspected of being ineffectual. (*See* Single-Company Union.)

Companywide Bargaining: *See* Multiplant Bargaining.

Compensable Injury: A work injury for which compensation indemnity benefits are payable to the injured worker or that person's beneficiary under workers' compensation laws.

Compensation: *See* Earnings.

Compensatory Time Off: Time away from a job permitted a worker in lieu of extra financial compensation due to him or her for overtime work, holiday work, etc.

Complaint: As defined by the National Labor Relations Board, the document which initiates "formal" proceedings in an unfair labor practice case. It is issued by the regional director who concludes, on the basis of a completed investigation, that any of the allegations contained in the charge has merit and adjustment or settlement has not been achieved by the parties.

The complaint sets forth all allegations and information necessary to bring a case to hearing before an administrative law judge pursuant to due process of law. The complaint contains a notice of hearing, specifying the time and place of hearing.

Compliance: As defined by the National Labor Relations Board: the carrying out of remedial action as agreed upon by the parties in writing (*see* Formal Agreement, Informal Agreement); as recommended by the administrative law judge in his or her decision; as ordered by the Board in its decision and order; or as decreed by the court.

Comprehensive Employment Development Programs: *See* Comprehensive Employment and Training Act.

Comprehensive Employment and Training Act (CETA): Signed into law in 1973, designed to provide "job training and employment opportunities for economically disadvantaged, unemployed and underemployed persons." The act (as amended) contains seven titles: Title I creates a decentralized structure in the hands of prime sponsors (usually states and units of local government with populations of at least 100,000).

Title II authorizes programs in areas of substantial unemployment (6.5 percent or more).

Title III provides employment to special groups, such as Indians and migrant farm workers.

Title IV provides continuing authority for the Job Corps.

Title V establishes the National Commission for Manpower Policy to advise the Secretary of Labor and the Congress.

Title VI (created by the Emergency Jobs and Unemployment Assistance Act of 1974) provides for a large temporary program of emergency public service employment to ease the impact of high unemployment.

Title VII contains definitions and describes administrative procedures necessary to assist in the orderly management of the act.

Comprehensive Manpower Services: The program of financial assistance to state and local governments for comprehensive manpower services, established under Title I of the Comprehensive Employment and Training Act.

Compulsory Arbitration: *See* Arbitration.

Compulsory Retirement (Automatic Retirement): Involuntary separation from employment in a company upon reaching a specified age (e.g., 65 or 68). In precise pension terms, a distinction is usually made between compulsory and automatic retirement. The age of compulsory retirement is that point at which the worker loses the right to decide whether to retire or to continue on the job. The age of automatic retirement is the age beyond which no employee may continue to work under the terms of the pension plan. In other words, an employee may work beyond the *compulsory* retirement age if the employer consents, but *automatic* retirement rules out the option on both sides.

Conciliation: *See* Mediation.

Condon-Wadlin Law: The law covering labor relations in public employment in New York State. It was repealed in 1967 and replaced by the Taylor Law.

Conference Board, The: The fact-finding organization (formerly named the National Industrial Conference Board) that serves as a clearinghouse and agency for the dissemination of information on employer-employee relations, business economics, and business management.

Congress of Industrial Organizations (CIO): The federation of national and international unions formally established in 1938 by industrial unions, many of which had been affiliated with the American Federation of Labor. Merged with the AFL in December 1955, to form the AFL-CIO, and is thus extinct as a separate organization. (*See* AFL-CIO.)

Consent Decree: An order issued to parties in a dispute after an agreement has been reached between them.

Conspiracy Doctrine: A doctrine having its roots in the common law which made it illegal for a group to do what would be regarded as legal if done by a single person. It was applied in the early nineteenth century against combinations of workers asking for a pay increase or striking to achieve such an increase.

Constitution: The fundamental law set forth in a written document, approved at a convention outlining the organizational structure and the designation of authority within the institution.

Construction Industry Stabilization Committee: *See* Economic Stabilization Program.

Constructive Discharge: The action of an employer to make conditions so unbearable that a given worker will quit the job.

Consultation: A procedure, frequently provided for by agreement that management has an obligation to consult the union on particular issues (e.g., contracting-out) in advance of taking action. What consultation actually means in each situation is what the parties want it to mean. In general, the process of consultation lies between notification to the union, which may amount simply to providing information, and negotiation, which implies agreement on the part of the union before the action can be taken.

Consumer Credit Protection Act (Garnishment): A law that, in its Title III, sets restrictions (1) on the amount of an individual's earnings that may be deducted in any week through garnishment proceedings, and (2) on discharge from employment because of garnishment for any one indebtedness.

Consumer Price Index (CPI): A government index, issued monthly by the Bureau of Labor Statistics, which measures the average change in prices of goods and services purchased by urban wage-earner and clerical-worker families. The "new series," begun in 1967, covers all urban wage-earner and clerical-worker consumers, including single workers living alone as well as families of two or more persons. The CPI measures price change only, describing shifts in the purchasing power of the consumer's dollar. It is often incorrectly referred to as a cost-of-living index. (*See* Cost-of-Living Adjustment; Escalator Clause.)

Contempt of Court: An action that obstructs the administration of justice by a court; also, an action that tends to detract from the dignity of a court. In labor disputes, often the failure of a union to obey an injunction.

Continuous Bargaining Committees (Interim Committees): Committees established by management and union in a collective bargaining relationship to keep the agreement under constant review, and to discuss possible contract changes, long in advance of the contract expiration date. It may provide for third-party participation. (*See* Human Relations Committees; Crisis Bargaining.)

Continuous Operations (Round-the-Clock Operations): Necessary plant operations (powerhouse, maintenance, protection, etc.) that must continue to function on a 24-hour, 7-day basis. (*See* Continuous Process.)

Continuous Process: A process which, once begun, must continue without interruption for a long period, making the use of multiple shifts necessary. Often applied to a service (e.g., electric utility) needed continuously.

Continuous Service: Uninterrupted employment. Participation in an economic strike may be held to constitute a break in continuous service.

Contract: *See* Agreement.

Contract Bar: A denial of the request for a representation election, based on the existence of an agreement. Such an election will not be conducted by the National Labor Relations Board if there is a current written agreement which is binding upon the parties, has not been in effect for more than a "reasonable" time, and the terms of which are consistent with the National Labor Relations Act.

Contract Work Hours and Safety Standards Act: An act to promote health and safety in the building trades and construction industry on all federal, federally financed, and federally assisted construction projects in excess of $2500. It specifically covers new construction and alterations and repair, including painting and decorating.

This Act amends the Contract Work Hours Standards Act of 1962 by adding at the end thereof Section 107, for the above purpose, and changing the title of the 1962 Act to "Contract Work Hours and Safety Standards Act."

The Act, as amended, also provides for an 8-hour day and a 40-hour week, with overtime compensation of 1½ times the basic rate for all work in excess of that standard.

Contracting-out (Subcontracting; Farming Out): The practice of having certain steps in a manufacturing process, plant maintenance, or other work functions performed by outside contractors using their own work forces.

Convention: *See* Union Convention.

Cooling-off Period: A period of time which must elapse before a strike or lockout can begin or be resumed, by agreement or by law. The term derives from the hope that the tensions of unsuccessful negotiation will subside in time and that a work stoppage will be averted. (*See* National Emergency Dispute.)

COPE (Committee on Political Education): *See* AFL-CIO, COPE.

Copeland Act: *See* Anti-Kickback Law.

Core Time: *See* Flexitime.

Corridor: *See* Deductible.

Cost-of-Living Adjustment: The rise or decrease in wages or salaries in accordance with changes in the cost of living as measured by a designated index; in collective bargaining agreements, usually the Bureau of Labor Statistics Consumer Price Index. (*See* Escalator Clause.)

Cost of Living Council: *See* Economic Stabilization Program.

Cost-of-Living Allowance (FLOAT): Regular cents-per-hour or percentage payments made to workers through the operation of escalator clauses or other types of cost-of-living adjustments. *Float* is a cost-of-living allowance not incorporated into base rates.

Cost of Living Council Committee on Food: *See* Economic Stabilization Program.

Cost of Living Council Committee on Health: *See* Economic Stabilization Program.

Cost-of-Living Index: A term often used incorrectly, to designate the Bureau of Labor Statistics Consumer Price Index. (*See* Consumer Price Index.)

Cotton Textile National Industrial Relations Baord: Created by section XVII of original Code of Fair Competition for the Cotton Textile Industry as amended July 10, 1934. Abolished by EO 6858 of Sept. 26, 1934.

Cotton Textile Work Assignment Board: The President, by EO 6876 of Oct. 16, 1934, approved amendments to Code of Fair Competition for Cotton Textile Industry which authorized Textile Labor Relations Board to appoint a Cotton Textile Work Assignment Board to develop a plan for regulation of work assignments. Expired June 15, 1935, having completed work for which it was established.

Council of Economic Advisers: The small federal government agency, established under the terms of the Employment Act of 1946, that advises the President on economic developments, appraises government economic policies, recommends to the President policies for economic growth and stability, and assists in the preparation of the President's annual economic report to the Congress.

Council on Economic Policy: Established by President's memorandum of Feb. 2, 1973, to help ensure better coordination in the formation and execution of economic policy and to perform such functions relating to economic policy as the President or the Chairman of the Council might specify. Inactive. Functions absorbed by the President's Economic Policy Board, Sept. 30, 1974.

Council on Wage and Price Stability: Established within the Executive Office of the President by law on August 24, 1974. The mission of the Council is to monitor the economy as a whole with respect to such key indicators as wages, costs, productivity, profits, and prices. It also has the responsibility to review and appraise the various programs, policies, and activities of the federal departments and agencies in order to determine the extent to which these programs and activities contribute to inflation.

Covered Job: A work classification subject to the rules of a contract or an applicable state or federal law.

Covered Title: *See* Covered Job.

CP Case: Under National Labor Relations Board procedures, a charge against a labor organization for commission of the following activities as outlined in Section 8 of the National Labor Relations Act:

8(b)(7) To picket, cause, or threaten the picketing of any employer where an object is to force or require an employer to recognize or bargain with a labor organization as the representative of its employees, or to force or require the employees of an employer to select such labor organization as their collective-bargaining representative, unless such labor organization is currently certified as the representative of such employees:

(A) where the employer has lawfully recognized any other labor organization and a question concerning representation may not appropriately be raised under Section 9(c),

(B) where within the preceding 12 months a valid election under Section 9(c) has been conducted, or

(C) where picketing has been conducted without a petition under 9(c) being filed within a reasonable period of time not to exceed 30 days from the commencement of the picketing; except where the picketing is for the purpose of truthfully advising the public (including consumers) that an employer does not employ members of, or have a contract with, a labor organization, and it does not have an effect of interference with deliveries or services. (*See* Types of Cases.)

CPI: *See* Consumer Price Index.

Craft: Usually, a skilled occupation requiring a thorough knowledge of processes involved in the work, the exercise of considerable independent judgment, usually a high degree of manual dexterity, and, in some instances, extensive responsibility for valuable product or equipment.

Craft-conscious: Identifying with a particular craft rather than with the working class in general.

Craft Union: A labor organization that limits membership to workers having a particular craft or skill or working at closely related trades. In practice, many so-called craft unions also enroll members outside the craft field; some come to resemble industrial unions in all major respects. The traditional distinction between craft and industrial unions has therefore been substantially blurred. The International Typographical Union is an example of a craft union. (Cf. Industrial Union.)

Craft Unit: A bargaining unit composed solely of workers having a recognized skill; for example, electricians, machinists, or plumbers.

Credited Service: Years of employment counted for retirement, severance pay, seniority, etc. The definition of a credited year of service varies among companies and plans.

Criminal Conspiracy: *See* Conspiracy Doctrine.

Crisis Bargaining: Characteristically, collective bargaining taking place under the shadow of an imminent strike deadline, as distinguished from extended negotiations in which both parties enjoy ample time to present and discuss their positions. (*See* Continuous Bargaining Committees; Strike Deadline.)

Cross-check: A determination of employee interests in a union by a comparison of signed authorization cards and the company payroll list. (*See* Authorization Card.)

CSA: *See* Community Services Administration.

Custodial Employees: Guards and security officers. They are not subject to the provisions of the Public Contracts (Walsh-Healey) Act.

Cyclical Unemployment: Unemployment brought about by the periodic fluctuations of the economy.

Danbury Injunction: An injunction, overwhelmingly antilabor, that provides for the seizure of workers' homes to satisfy a judgment resulting from a labor dispute. The name derives from the court-issued injunction in the Danbury Hatters' case in 1908.

DARG: A Scottish word meaning a day's work or a definite task. In some mining areas, "darg" implies a limitation on output and a maximum not to be exceeded.

Daughters of Saint Crispin: Organized in 1869 as the Women's Auxiliary of the Knights of Saint Crispin (1867–1873). A secret labor organization of female shoe workers that existed for a few years following the Civil War.

Davis-Bacon Act: *See* Prevailing Wage Law.

Day Laborer: An unskilled worker hired on a daily basis.

Daywork: Usually work for which pay is computed on an hourly rate or on a per-day basis, in contrast to piecework or incentive work.

Dead-end Job: A job with no promotional opportunities.

Dead-Horse Rule: *See* Bogus Work.

Dead Time: *See* Downtime.

Deadheading: The movement of empty buses, trucks, or trains. Also, an individual riding without paying fare.

Deadheading Pay: Special payment to a transportation worker who is required to report for work at a point far removed from the home terminal or to return without passengers or freight after completing a run.

Deadwork: Nonproductive work in mining, such as the removal of debris or waste matter.

Death Benefit: The payment, usually a lump sum, provided to a designated beneficiary in the event of a worker's death. May be provided by a pension plan, another type of employer-sponsored welfare plan, or by a union to its members. When insured, the more common term is life insurance. (*See* Life Insurance Plan.)

Deauthorization Election: A procedure under the National Labor Relations Board to decertify a union by a majority vote of the workers participating.

Decasualization: The process of eliminating or barring casual workers in order to regularize employment. (*See* Casual Workers.)

Decertification: Withdrawal by a government agency, such as the National Labor Relations Board, of a union's official recognition as exclusive bargaining representative.

Deductible (Corridor): In major-medical insurance plans, that portion of covered hospital and medical charges which the insured worker must pay before the plan's benefits begin. If the worker also has basic health insurance protection, the worker's liability is often referred to as the corridor because it lies between two insured areas. (*See* Major-Medical Expense Benefit.)

Deductions: Money withheld from wages and salaries by the employer to cover social security payments, union dues, etc.

Defense Manpower Administration (Labor): Created by Secretary of Labor (General Order 48, as amended) pursuant to authority of EO 10161 of Sept. 9, 1950, and Reorg. Plan 6, effective May 24, 1950, to develop plans, policies, and programs for meeting defense manpower requirements. General Order 48 revoked by General Order 63 of Aug. 25, 1953, which established the Office of Manpower Administration within the Department.

Deferred Wage Increase: The general term for negotiated wage changes that are not to become effective until some specified date in the future, e.g., a year later. (*See* Annual Improvement Factor.)

Delay Time: *See* Downtime.

Delinquent Member: A union member who has not paid her or his dues.

De Minimis Doctrine: The concept that law is not concerned with trifles, and that enforcement of federal regulations will not apply where trifling sums are involved.

Demotion: *See* Downgrading.

Department of Health, Education, and Welfare: *See* Health, Education, and Welfare Department.

Department of Housing and Urban Development: *See* Housing and Urban Development Department.

Department of Labor: *See* Labor Department.

Dependent Unionism: *See* Company Union.

Deposit Administration: *See* Pension Plan.

Differential Piece Rates: A plan under which piece rates vary at different levels of output.

Direct Action: A union's substitution of the strike or slowdown in place of negotiations.

Direct Labor: Usually, workers engaged in productive occupations, e.g., an essential step in a manufacturing process. *Indirect labor* usually includes employees whose jobs cannot be associated directly with a specific product or process. The precise meaning of these terms varies from company to company.

Directly Affiliated Unions: *See* Federal Labor Unions.

Disability: Any injury or illness, temporary or permanent, that prevents a worker from carrying on his or her usual occupation.

Disability Insurance: Compensation for loss of wages incurred because of illness or disability under state Workmens' Compensation laws.

Disability Retirement: Retirement because of physical inability to perform the job. (*See* Permanent and Total Disability.)

Disaffiliation: Withdrawal of a local union from membership in a national or international union, or of a national or international union from a federation.

Discharge: Dismissal of a worker from employment. The term implies discipline for unsatisfactory performance and is thus usually limited to dismissals for cause relating to the individual, e.g., insubordination, absenteeism, inefficiency.

Disciplinary Layoff: The temporary layoff of an employee because of an infraction of a company rule.

Discipline: The action of an employer to punish an employee or to correct his or her behavior.

Discrimination: Prejudice against, or unequal treatment of, workers in hiring, employment, pay, or conditions of work because of race, national origin, creed, color, sex, age, union membership or activity, or any other characteristic not related to ability or job performance.

Disestablishment: A procedure of the National Labor Relations Board to terminate a labor organization, usually because it has been found to be company-dominated.

Dismissal Pay or Allowance: *See* Severance Pay.

Dismissed Cases: As defined by the National Labor Relations Board, cases the prosecution of which is judged to be unnecessary or unjustified. Cases may be dismissed at any stage. They are dismissed informally when, following investigation, the regional director concludes that there has been no violation of the law, that there is insufficient evidence to support further action, or for a variety of other reasons. Before the charge is dismissed, however, the charging party is given the opportunity to withdraw the charge voluntarily. (*See* also Withdrawn Cases.) Cases may also be dismissed by the administrative law judge, by the Board, or by the courts through their refusal to enforce orders of the Board.

Disposable Income: *See* Spendable Earnings.

Dispute (Labor Dispute): Any disagreement between union and management which requires resolution in one way or another; e.g., inability to agree on contract terms, an unsettled grievance.

District Commissioner of Immigration and Naturalization (Labor): Offices of district commissioner of immigration and naturalization, created by an act of 1894, abolished by section 6 of Reorg. Plan III, effective June 30, 1940, their functions to be administrated by Commissioner of Immigration and

Naturalization, Department of Justice, through district directors of immigration and naturalization.

District Council: The organization of two or more locals of the same national union when they exist in the same geographical area; common among carpenters, painters, public workers, and other unions.

Division of Business Cooperation (National Recovery Administration): Created by EO 7075 of June 15, 1935, to aid in voluntary maintenance, by trade and industrial groups, of standards of fair competition, and in elimination of unfair competition in employment of labor or in trade practices. Transferred to Department of Commerce by EO 7252 of Dec. 21, 1935, effective Jan. 1, 1936. By same order, functions and duties of Division of Business Cooperation ordered terminated by Apr. 1, 1936. On Mar. 21, 1936, EO 7323 created Committee of Industrial Analysis with Secretary of Commerce as chairman, to complete work of Division of Business Cooperation, effective Apr. 1, 1936.

Division of Work: *See* Work Sharing.

Docking: The practice of making deductions from a worker's pay because of faulty output, tardiness, unexplained absence, or other reasons.

DOL: *See* Labor Department.

Dole: Welfare payments or relief provided by a public authority.

Double Time: Penalty or premium rate (e.g., for overtime work, for work on Sundays and holidays) amounting to twice the employee's regular rate of pay for each hour worked.

Downgrading (Demotion): Reassignment of a worker to a task or job requiring lower skills and drawing a lower rate of pay.

Downtime (Dead Time; Delay Time; Waiting Time): A brief period during which workers are unable to perform their tasks while waiting for materials, repair, setup, or adjustment of machinery. Under incentive wage systems, the term may refer to payment made to employees for such lost time.

Drawing Account: Usually, an allowance given to salespeople working on a straight commission as an advance against commission payments.

Dual Pay System: As used in transportation industries, a system under which road employees are paid on a combined mileage and hours basis.

Dual Unionism: The charge leveled at a union member or officer who seeks or accepts membership or a position in a rival union, or who otherwise attempts to undermine a union by helping its rival. This is usually a punishable offense.

Dues: *See* Union Dues.

Early Retirement: *See* Retirement.

Earnings (Hourly, Daily, Weekly, Annual, Average, Gross, Straight-Time; Compensation): In general, the remuneration (pay, wages) of a worker or group of workers for services performed during a specific period of time. The term invariably carries a defining word or a defining phrase, e.g., "straight-time average hourly earnings." Since a statistical concept is usually involved in the term and its variations, the producers and users of earnings figures have an obligation to define them. In the absence of such definition, the following may serve as rough guides: (1) *Hourly, daily, weekly, annual,* the period of time to which earnings figures, as stated or computed, relate. The context in which annual earnings (sometimes weekly earnings) are used may indicate whether the reference includes

earnings from one employer only or from all employment plus other sources of income; (2) *average,* usually the arithmetic mean; that is, total earnings (as defined) of a group of workers (as identified) divided by number of workers in the group; (3) *gross,* usually total earnings, including, where applicable, overtime payments, shift differentials, production bonuses, cost-of-living allowances, commissions, etc.; (4) *straight-time,* usually gross earnings excluding overtime payments and (with variations at this point) shift differentials and other monetary payments. The Bureau of Labor Statistics, in its wage surveys, defines straight-time earnings so as to exclude premium pay (for overtime and for work on weekends and holidays) and shift differentials; (5) *Compensation* is a concept sometimes used to encompass the entire range of wages and benefits, both current and deferred, which workers receive out of their employment.

Economic Action: Activity in the economic, rather than the political, sphere; sometimes, a synonym for a strike.

Economic Opportunity Act of 1964: An act "to mobilize the human and financial resources of the Nation to combat poverty in the United States." An important part of the act, the work-training program (administered by the U.S. Department of Labor) is directed to encouraging young unemployed persons (age 16 to 21, inclusive) to stay in school or to obtain job experience that will prepare them for meaningful work careers. Its function was absorbed by the Comprehensive Employment and Training Act in 1973.

Economic Stabilization Agency: Established by EO 10161 of Sept. 9, 1950, as amended, issued under authority of Defense Production Act of 1950 (64 Stat. 798; 50 U.S.C. App. 2071 note), as amended, and EO 10276 of July 31, 1951, as amended, issued under Housing and Rent Act of 1947, as amended (61 Stat. 196; 50 U.S.C. App. 1891 et seq.), to control inflation and maintain stabilization of national economy. Terminated, except for liquidation purposes, Apr. 30, 1953, pursuant to EO 10434 of Feb. 6, 1953, and provisions of Defense Production Act Amendments of 1952 and 1953 (66 Stat. 296, 67 Stat. 131; 50 U.S.C. App. 2166, 2071 note). Liquidation completed Oct. 31, 1953, pursuant to EO 10480 of Aug. 14, 1953.

Economic Stabilization Board: Established by EO 9250 of Oct. 3, 1942, to advise Director of Economic Stabilization. Transferred by EO 9620 of Sept. 20, 1945, to Office of War Mobilization and Reconversion to advise and consult with Director of War Mobilization and Reconversion. Returned to Office of Economic Stabilization upon its reestablishment by EO 9699 of Feb. 21, 1946, EO 9762 of July 25, 1946, returned Board to Office of War Mobilization and Reconversion. Functions terminated by EO 9809 of Dec. 12, 1946.

Economic Stabilization Program: Authorized by the Economic Stabilization Act of 1970 (84 Stat. 799), as amended, Aug. 15, 1970, to stabilize the economy, reduce inflation, minimize unemployment, improve the competitive position in world trade, and protect the purchasing power of the dollar. Statutory authority expired Apr. 30, 1974.

Agencies set up to carry out the program were:

Cost of Living Council: Established by EO 11615 of Aug. 15, 1971; abolished by EO 11788 of June 18, 1974, effective July 1, 1974.

Pay Board: Established by EO 11627 of Oct. 15, 1971; abolished by EO 11695 of Jan. 11, 1973.

Price Commission: Established by EO 11627 of Oct. 15, 1971; abolished by EO 11695 of Jan. 11, 1973.

Rent Advisory Board: Established by EO 11632 of Nov. 22, 1971, and continued under EO 11640 of Jan. 26, 1972; abolished by EO 11695 of Jan. 11, 1973.

Committee on the Health Service Industry: Established by EO 11627 of Oct. 15, 1971; abolished by EO 11695 of Jan. 11, 1973.

Committee on State and Local Government Cooperation: Established as a presidential advisory panel pursuant to EO 11627 of Oct. 15, 1971, and continued pursuant to EO 11640 of Jan. 26, 1972; abolished by EO 11695 of Jan. 11, 1973.

Health Industry Advisory Committee: Established by EO 11695 of Jan. 11, 1973; abolished by EO 11781 of May 1, 1974, effective May 31, 1974.

Food Industry Advisory Committee: Established by EO 11627 of Oct. 15, 1971, abolished by EO 11781 of May 1, 1974.

Committee on Interest and Dividends: Established by EO 11695 of Jan. 11, 1973; and continued by EO 11695 of Jan. 11, 1973; abolished by EO 11781 of May 1, 1974.

Construction Industry Stabilization Committee: Established by EO 11588 of Mar. 29, 1971, and continued by EO 11695 of Jan. 11, 1973; abolished by EO 11788 of June 18, 1974, effective July 1, 1974.

Cost of Living Council Committee on Health: Established by EO 11695 of Jan. 11, 1973; abolished by EO 11788 of June 18, 1974, effective July 1, 1974.

Cost of Living Council Committee on Food: Established by EO 11695 of Jan. 11, 1973; abolished by EO 11788 of June 18, 1974, effective July 1, 1974.

Labor-Management Advisory Committee: Established by EO 11695 of Jan. 11, 1973; abolished by EO 11788 of June 18, 1974, effective July 1, 1974.

Economic Strikes: Union-authorized strikes to bring about changes in wages, hours, working conditions, or health, pension, and other benefits, usually associated with contract negotiations.

EEOC: *See* Equal Employment Opportunity Commission.

EFMS: *See* Emergency Food and Medical Services.

Eight-hour (8-hour) Movement: Activity by labor organizations in the nineteenth century to limit working time to 8 hours per day.

Election: *See* Representation Election.

Election, Board-Directed: As defined by the National Labor Relations Board, an election conducted by the regional director pursuant to a decision and direction of election by the Board. Postelection rulings are made by the regional director or by the Board.

Election, Consent: As defined by the National Labor Relations Board, an election conducted by the regional director pursuant to an agreement signed by all parties concerned. The agreement provides for the waiving of a hearing, the establishment of the appropriate unit by mutual consent, and the final determination of all postelection issues by the regional director.

Election, Expedited: As defined by the National Labor Relations Board, an election conducted by the regional director pursuant to a petition filed within 30 days of the commencement of picketing in a situation in which a meritorious, charge under Section 8(b)(7)(C) of the National Labor Relations Act has been filed. The election is conducted under priority conditions and without a hearing unless the regional director believes the proceeding raises questions that cannot be decided without a hearing.

Postelection rulings on objections and/or challenges are made by the regional director and are final and binding unless the Board grants an appeal on application by one of the parties.

Election, Regional Director-Directed: As defined by the National Labor Relations Board, an election conducted by the regional director pursuant to a decision and direction of election issued by the regional director after a hearing. Postelection rulings are made by the regional director or by the Board.

Election, Rerun: As defined by the National Labor Relations Board, an election held after an initial election has been set aside either by the regional director or by the Board.

Election, Runoff: As defined by the National Labor Relations Board: an election conducted by the regional director after an initial election, having three or more choices on the ballot, has turned out to be inconclusive (none of the choices receiving a majority of the valid votes cast). The regional director conducts the runoff election between the choices on the regional ballot which received the highest and the next highest number of votes.

Election, Stipulated: As defined by the National Labor Relations Board: an election held by the regional director pursuant to an agreement signed by all the parties concerned. The agreement provides for the waiving of hearing and the establishment of the appropriate unit by mutual consent. Postelection rulings are made by the Board.

Eligibility Date: The hiring date as an eligibility criterion for permission to vote in a National Labor Relations Board election.

Eligibility List: A list used in city, state, or Federal civil service as a roster of those eligible for jobs.

Eligible Voters: As defined by the National Labor Relations Board, employees within an appropriate bargaining unit who were employed on a fixed date prior to an election, or are otherwise qualified to vote under the Board's eligibility rules.

Emergency Board: Under the Railway Labor Act, the board that the President, upon notification by the National Mediation Board that a contract negotiation dispute threatens seriously to interrupt interstate commerce, may appoint to investigate and report within 30 days. During this period, and for 30 days after the Board reports, no change may be made in the conditions underlying the dispute except by agreement of the parties. This is the last formal step in the act's procedures regarding contract disputes.

Emergency Conservation Work: Created by EO 6101 of Apr. 5, 1933, under authority of act approved Mar. 31, 1933 (48 Stat. 22), to relieve acute conditions of distress and unemployment in the United States and to provide for restoration of the country's natural resources and advancement of an orderly program of extensive public works. Succeeded by Civilian Conservation Corps.

Emergency Disputes: Industrial conflicts that may imperil the national health or safety referred to in the Railway Labor and Taft-Hartley Acts.

Emergency Food and Medical Services (EFMS): A program under the Community Services Administration that provides funds to assist local communities in their efforts to combat conditions of hunger and malnutrition among the poor.

Emergency Job Program: Under Title VI (Emergency Job Program) of the Comprehensive Employment and Training Act, the Secretary of Labor enters into arrangements with eligible applicants (generally a state or a unit of local government) to make financial assistance available for the purpose of providing temporary public service employment for unemployed and underemployed persons, with preferential consideration being given to the unemployed.

Employee: An employed wage earner or salaried worker. The word is used interchangeably with "worker" in the context of a work situation, but a "worker" is not an "employee" when no longer on the payroll.

Employee Benefit Plan: *See* Welfare Plan.

Employee Handbook: A book or pamphlet given to new employees to orient them with respect to the history and policies of a company. It may or may not refer to an existing union contract outlining the rights and obligations of union members.

Employee Representation Plans: Plans that are generally organized as substitutes for unions but which give employees the opportunity to meet with management on the solution of common problems.

Employee Retirement Income Security Act of 1974 (ERISA): An act to protect the interests of workers and their beneficiaries who depend on benefits from employee welfare and pension plans. The act requires disclosure of plan provisions and financial information and establishes standards of conduct for trustees and administrators. It sets up funding, participation, and vesting requirements. [*See* Labor-Management Services Administration (LMSA); also Pension Benefit Guaranty Corporation.]

Employees' Compensation Appeals Board: The Board consists of three members appointed by the Secretary of Labor, one of whom is designated as chairperson and administrative officer. The Board's function is to consider and decide appeals from final decisions in cases arising under the Federal Employees' Compensation Act. Transferred from Federal Security Agency to Department of Labor by Reorg. Plan 19, effective May 24, 1950.

Employer: The general term for any individual, corporation, or other operating group that hires workers (employees). The terms *employer* and *management* are often used interchangeably when there is no intent to draw a distinction between owners and managers.

Employment Act of 1946 (Full Employment Act): This act sets forth a broad policy for the federal government" . . . to coordinate and utilize all its plans, functions, and resources for the purpose of creating and maintaining, in a manner calculated to foster and promote free competitive enterprise and the general welfare, conditions under which there will be afforded useful employment opportunities, . . . and to promote maximum employment, production, and purchasing power."

Employment Standards Administration: This agency, headed by the Assistant Secretary for Employment Standards of the Department of Labor, has responsibility for administering and directing employment standards programs dealing with minimum wage and overtime standards; equal pay; age discrimination in employment; promotion of women's welfare; standards to improve employment conditions other than safety, nondiscrimination, and affirmative action in government contracts and subcontracts and in federally assisted construction; and workers' compensation programs for federal and certain private employers and employees.

Employment and Training Administration (ETA): A group of offices and services that have been established to implement the responsibilities assigned to the Department of Labor for conduct of certain work-experience and work-training programs; for the funding and overseeing of programs conducted under the provisions of the Comprehensive Employment and Training Act of 1973 by states and other authorized operators;

for administration of the Federal-State Employment Security System; and for conduct of a continuing program of research, development, and evaluation.

Employers' Association: A voluntary membership organization of employers established to deal with problems common to the group. It may be formed specifically to handle industrial relations and to negotiate with a union or unions. (*See* Association Agreement.)

Engel's Law: A theory that the percentage of income spent on food and necessities is greater in low-income families than in high-income families.

English Workweek: A workweek of 5½ days.

Enjoin: To prohibit by court order.

Entrance Rate: The hourly rate at which new employees are hired, at times referred to as a probationary or hiring rate. It may apply to the establishment as a whole or to a particular occupation.

Equal Employment Opportunity Act (1972): Legislation outlawing certain discriminatory practices by private employers of fifteen or more persons, public and private employment agencies, labor unions with fifteen or more members, public and private educational institutions, and state and local governments. Not covered are private membership clubs and Indian tribes. Unlawful practices, based on sex, race, color, religion, or national origin include (1) discrimination by an employer in hiring or firing, wages and salaries, promotions, or any terms, conditions, or privileges of employment; (2) discrimination by a labor union in membership, classification, or referrals for employment, or actions or attempts to cause an employer to discriminate; (3) discrimination by an employment agency in classifying or referring for employment; and (4) discrimination by any employer, labor union, or joint labor-management committee in training, retraining, or apprenticeship, or in printing or publishing advertisements indicating discriminatory preference or limitation.

Equal Employment Opportunity Commission: Created under the Civil Rights Act of 1964, a presidentially appointed, five-member commission to administer that part of the Equal Employment Opportunity Act that makes it unlawful to discriminate in employment against any individual by reason of race, color, religion, sex, or national origin.

Equal Pay Act of 1963: An amendment to the Fair Labor Standards Act prohibiting wage discrimination solely because of sex. (*See* Fair Labor Standards Act.)

Equal Pay for Equal Work: A policy denoting, or a demand for, payment of equal compensation to all employees in an establishment performing the same kind or amount of work, regardless of race, sex, or other characteristics of the individual workers not related to ability or performance.

Equal Rights Amendment (ERA): A proposed amendment to the U.S. Constitution, approved by the House of Representatives on October 12, 1971, and the Senate on March 22, 1972, by overwhelming majorities, and submitted to the states for ratification. The amendment reads: "Equality of rights under the law shall not be denied or abridged by the United States or by any State on account of sex.
"The Congress shall have the power to enforce, by appropriate legislation, the provisions of this article.
"This amendment shall take effect two years after the date of ratification.

"To become part of the Constitution, it must be ratified by three-fourths of the States within seven years of its submission." By the end of 1978, 35 states of the 38 necessary had ratified the proposed amendment. The deadline for ratification was postponed to June 1982.

ERA: *See* Equal Rights Amendment.

Erdman Act (1898): The act, replacing the Arbitration Act of 1888, established machinery for the settlement of industrial disputes between management and employees of railroads engaged in interstate commerce. It also provided for mediation and arbitration and outlawed the yellow-dog contract. The act was declared unconsitutional in 1908 in the case of *Adair v. United States*. It was superseded by the Newlands Act of 1913, which also forbade the yellow-dog contract.

ERISA: *See* Employee Retirement Income Security Act of 1974.

Escalator Clause (Wage Escalation): A provision in an agreement stipulating that wages are to be automatically increased or reduced periodically according to a schedule related to changes in the cost of living, as measured by a designated index, or, occasionally, to another standard, e.g., an average earnings figure. The term may also apply to any tie between an employee benefit and the cost of living, as in a pension plan. (*See* Consumer Price Index.)

Escape Clause: A general term signifying release from an obligation. One example is the maintenance-of-membership arrangement which gives union members an "escape period" during which they may resign from membership in the union without forfeiting their jobs.

Esch-Cummins Act: *See* Transportation Act of 1920.

Escrow Agreement: An agreement between two parties to put a sum of money in the hands of a third party to be kept until certain conditions are met.

ETA: *See* Employment and Training Administration.

Excelsior Rule (1966): A requirement by the National Labor Relations Board that an employer provide to the Board a list of employees eligible to participate in a union representation election 7 days prior to such an election.

Exclusive Bargaining Rights: The right and obligation of a union designated as majority representative to bargain collectively for all employees, including nonmembers, in the bargaining unit.

Executive Board: A constitutional union administrative body composed of elected officials and other elected or appointed members, generally responsible for overseeing union operations and carrying out union policies.

Executive Council, AFL-CIO: *See* AFL-CIO, Executive Council.

Executive Order No. 10988: Titled "Employee-Management Cooperation in the Federal Service," this federal order, issued by the President in 1962, guarantees the right of employees of the executive branch of the government to join unions. The order also defines the scope of participation by unions in the determination of personnel policies and working conditions not established by statute.

Executive Order No. 11478: An order establishing equal employment opportunities in the federal government, to be achieved through affirmative programs in each executive department and agency.

Executive Order No. 11491: An order providing for labor-management relations in the federal service. (*See* Labor-Management Services Administration.)

Executive Order No. 11612: An order decreeing that each federal department and agency shall establish an occupational safety and health program protecting their own employees.

Exhaustion of Remedies: The doctrine under which a court refuses to take jurisdiction until all remedial procedures available under an administrative agency or a union constitution are completed.

Ex Parte Injunction: An injunction granted on behalf of an applicant without the opposing party's being present.

Experience Rating: The process of basing tax rates or insurance premiums on the employer's own record—as in maintaining workers' compensation, unemployment insurance, and commercially insured health and insurance programs—so that the employer may benefit from a good record.

Expiration Date: The formal termination date established in a collective bargaining agreement, or the earliest date at which the contract may be terminated.

Extended Leave Plan: In general, a plan allowing a worker to take extended, unpaid leave without loss of job or seniority, such leave being usually granted for a limited number of specific reasons.

Extended Vacation Plan: A plan providing extra-long paid vacations (e.g., 10 to 13 weeks) to qualified (long-service) workers at regular intervals (e.g., every 5 years), supplementing an annual paid vacation plan.

Fabianism: Politically, the doctrine of "making haste slowly"; also, a school of British socialist thought committed to this doctrine. The name is derived from that of the Roman general Quintus Fabius Maximus, noted for his cautious and dilatory tactics.

Face-to-Face Pay: In mining, wages paid for work performed only at the place where the mine is worked.

Fact-finding Board: A group of individuals appointed under government authority to investigate, assemble, and report the facts in a labor dispute, sometimes with authority to make recommendations for settlement. (*See* Board of Inquiry.)

Fair Employment Board (Civil Service Commission): Established by Civil Service Commission pursuant to EO 9980 of July 26, 1948. Primarily concerned with actions affecting equality of economic opportunity among Federal employees and applicants. Abolished by EO 10590 of Jan. 18, 1955, which established President's Committee on Government Employment Policy. Records retained by Civil Service Commission.

Fair Employment Practice Committee (FEPC): A committee set up by an Executive order of President Roosevelt in 1941 to investigate complaints with respect to discrimination in employment because of race, creed, color, or national origin.

Fair Employment Practice Laws: Laws that forbid discrimination in hiring, promotion, discharge, or conditions of employment on the basis of race, creed, color, national origin, and in some cases, sex and age. Such laws exist at federal, state, and local levels. (*See* Civil Rights Act of 1964.)

Fair Labor Standards Act of 1938 (FLSA; Wage-Hour Law): A federal law which prohibited oppressive child labor and established a minimum hourly wage and premium overtime pay for hours in excess of a specific level (now time and one-half after 40 hours per week) for all workers engaged in, or producing goods for, interstate commerce. The minimum wage and the coverage of the act have been modified several times since 1938. (Originally known as the Black Connery Bill.)

Fair List: Published by trade unionists, a roster of employers (in a town or area) who abide by union regulations and comply with union conditions.

Farm Labor Contractor Registration Act of 1963: Legislation authorizing the operation of a program designed to protect migrant workers and their families from exploitation by unscrupulous farm labor contractors.

Farm Workers Organizing Committee, United (AFL-CIO): A committee formed in 1966 by a merger of the Agricultural Workers Organizing Committee of the AFL and the National Farm Workers Association led by Cesar Chavez.

Farming-Out: *See* Contracting-out.

"Favored Nations" Clause: An agreement provision indicating that one party to the agreement (employer or union) shall have the opportunity to share in more favorable terms negotiated by the other party with another employer or union.

Featherbedding (Make-Work): A derogatory term applied to a practice, working rule, or agreement provision which limits output or requires employment of excess workers and thereby creates or preserves soft or unnecessary jobs; or to a charge or fee levied by a union upon a company for services which are not performed or not to be performed.

Federal Advisory Council (Federal Security Agency): Established pursuant to act of June 6, 1933 (48 Stat. 116, as amended; 29 U.S.C. 49j (a)). Consists of outstanding representatives of labor management and the public who are especially familiar with employment problems. Transferred to Department of Labor by Reorg. Plan 2, effective Aug. 20, 1949.

Federal Board for Vocational Education: Created by Smith-Hughes Act of Feb. 23, 1917 (39 Stat. 929; 20 U.S.C. 11–28), for promotion of vocational education in the States. EO 6166 of June 10, 1933, transferred functions to Department of the Interior. Functions assigned to Commissioner of Education on Oct. 10, 1933. Office of Education, with all its functions, transferred from Department of the Interior to Federal Security Agency by Reorg. Plan I, effective July 1, 1939. Board abolished by Reorg. Plan 2, effective July 16, 1946.

Federal Civil Works Administration: Established Nov. 9, 1933, by EO 6420–B, to provide regular jobs on public works for 4 million unemployed men and women. Function of employment expired March 1934. Function of settling claims continued under Works Progress Administration.

Federal Coal Mine Health and Safety Act of 1969: Legislation designed to protect the health and safety of the nation's coal miners; and, in cooperation with the states and the coal mining industry, to improve and expand research, development, and training programs aimed at preventing coal mining accidents and occupationally caused diseases.

Federal Coal Mine Safety Board of Review: Established by act of July 16, 1952, as amended by act of Mar. 26, 1966 (66 Stat. 697, 80 Stat. 84; 30 U.S.C. 475), to hear and determine applications by coal mine operators for annulment or revision of, and temporary relief from, orders of Federal coal mine inspectors of the Director of the United States Bureau of Mines, issued under the authority granted by the Federal Coal Mine Safety Act, as amended. Became inactive after Mar. 30, 1970, pursuant to Federal Coal Mine Health and Safety Act of 1969 (83 Stat. 803), which repealed the Federal Coal Mine Safety Act, as amended.

Federal Committee on Apprenticeship: Previously known as Federal Committee on Apprentice Training, established by EO 6750–C of June 27, 1934, to aid in interpretation and

application of certain labor provisions of codes of fair competition as they affect apprenticeship training programs in industry. Functioned as part of Division of Labor Standards in Department of Labor, as provided by Federal Apprenticeship Act of 1937 (50 Stat. 664; 29 U.S.C. 50), to promote furtherance of labor standards to safeguard welfare of apprentices. Transferred to Office of Administrator of Federal Security Agency by EO 9139 of Apr. 18, 1942. Transferred to War Manpower Commission by EO 9247 of Sept. 17, 1942, where it functioned within Bureau of Training. Returned to Department of Labor by EO 9617 of Sept. 19, 1945.

Federal Corrupt Practices Act (Hatch Act): Section 304 of the Labor Management Relations Act of 1947 restricts political contributions by corporations and labor unions.

Federal Emergency Administration of Public Works: Established pursuant to act approved June 16, 1933 (48 Stat. 200; 15 U.S.C. 701–712; 40 U.S.C. 401–414). Subsequent legislation continued its operation, and Public Works Administration Appropriation Act of 1938 (52 Stat. 816), as amended, authorized continuance of those operations to June 30, 1942. Reorg. Plan I, effective July 1, 1939, consolidated Federal Emergency Administration of Public Works into Federal Works Agency to be administered as Public Works Administration, to promote and stabilize employment and purchasing power by encouraging construction of useful public works projects through making of loans and/or grants to non-Federal public bodies and, to a limited extent, by financing construction of Federal projects; also to promote interest in long-range planning in public works. Independent Offices Appropriation Act for fiscal year 1943 extended Public Works Administration to June 30, 1943. EO 9357 of June 30, 1943, transferred functions to office of Federal Works Administrator. *See* Federal Works Agency.

Federal Emergency Relief Administration: Created by act approved May 12, 1933 (48 Stat. 55), to cooperate with States, Territories, and District of Columbia in relieving hardships caused by unemployment and drought. Expired June 30, 1938, having been liquidated by Works Progress Administrator in accordance with provisions of Emergency Relief Appropriation Act of 1937 (50 Stat. 352). *See* Works Progress Administration.

Federal Employees' Compensation Act: A law providing workers compensation coverage to civilian employees of the United States government for disability or death due to personal injury sustained while in the performance of duty or to employment-related disease.

Federal Employment Stabilization Board: Employment Stabilization Act of 1931 (46 Stat. 1085), established Board, composed of Secretaries of Commerce, Agriculture, Labor, and Treasury, to advise the President of trend of employment and business activity and existence or approach of period of business depression and unemployment. Abolished by EO 6166 of June 10, 1933. Abolishment deferred by EO 6623 of Mar. 1, 1934, until functions of Board, together with funds, personnel, and records, could be transferred to Federal Employment Stabilization Office in Department of Commerce, which office was established by same order.

Federal Employment Stabilization Office: Abolished, and functions and personnel transferred from Department of Commerce to National Resources Planning Board in Executive Office of the President by Reorg. Plan I, effective July 1, 1939.

Federal Labor Unions (Directly Affiliated Unions): Local unions affiliated directly with the AFL-CIO rather than with an affiliated national or international union.

Federal Mediation and Conciliation Service (FMCS): An independent U.S. government agency which provides mediators to assist the parties involved in negotiations, or in a labor dispute, in reaching a settlement; provides lists of suitable arbitrators on request; and engages in various types of "preventive mediation." Mediation services are also provided by several state agencies.

Federal Metal and Nonmetallic Mine Safety Act: A law to reduce the frequency of disabling accidents and to prevent conditions that constitute hazards to the health of the workers in metal and nonmetal mines and associated plants.

Federal Personnel Council: Established as Council of Personnel Administration, Feb. 1, 1939, by EO 7916 of June 24, 1938. By EO 8467 of July 1, 1940, became unit within Civil Service Commission. Effective May 1, 1947, name was changed to Federal Personnel Council by EO 9830 of Feb. 24, 1947. Functioned as an advisory body to promote through study and discussion the application, interpretation, and development of Federal personnel policies and practices. Council abolished by First Independent Offices Appropriations Act, 1954 (67 Stat. 300), and its personnel, files, and records transferred on June 30, 1953, to office of Executive Director, Civil Service Commission.

Federal Salary Act of 1967: A law creating pay comparability of the federal service with that of the private sector.

Federal Security Agency: Created by Reorg. Plan I, effective July 1, 1939, grouping under one administration those agencies whose major purposes were to promote social and economic security, educational opportunity, and health of the citizens of the Nation; namely, Office of Education, Public Health Service, Social Security Board, U.S. Employment Service, Civilian Conservation Corps, and National Youth Administration. Other units were added to FSA by subsequent acts and Reorganization Plans. FSA abolished by Reorg. Plan I, effective Apr. 11, 1953, which plan established a Department of Health, Education, and Welfare, and transferred to it functions and units of Federal Security Agency, including Food and Drug Administration, Office of Education, Office of Vocational Rehabilitation, Public Health Service, Saint Elizabeths Hospital, and Social Security Administration.

Federal Women's Program (FWP): Established in 1967 by the Civil Service Commission, it requires all federal agencies to have an FWP coordinator or committee to advise the head of the agency on matters involving the employment of women.

Federal Works Agency: Created by Reorg. Plan I of 1939 to consolidate agencies of the Government dealing with public works not incidental to the normal work of other departments, and which administered Federal grants or loans to State and local governments or other agencies for construction purposes. Abolished by act approved June 30, 1949 (63 Stat. 380; 5 U.S.C. 630b), and functions transferred to General Services Administration.

Federation: An association of unions formed to promote common interests. The major federation is the AFL-CIO (formed by the merger of two federations).

Federation of Organized Trades and Labor Unions of the United States and Canada (FOOTALU): A predecessor organization to the American Federation of Labor, started by Samuel Gompers and Adolph Strasser as a craft organization in opposition to the Knights of Labor in 1881. Its name was changed to the American Federation of Labor in 1886.

Fees, Dues, and Fines: As defined by the National Labor Relations Board: The collection by a union or an employer of dues, fines, and referral fees from employees may be found to be an unfair labor practice under Section 8(b) (1)(A) or (2) or 8(a) (1) and (2) or (3) of the National Labor Relations Act, where, for instance, such moneys were collected pursuant to an illegal hiring hall arrangement, or an invalid or unlawfully applied union-security agreement; where dues were deducted from employees' pay without their authorization; or, in the case of fines, where such fines restrained or coerced employees in the exercise of their rights. The remedy for such unfair labor practices usually requires the reimbursements of such moneys to the employees.

Fellow-Servant Doctrine: In common law, the doctrine that an employer is not responsible to an employee for injury caused by the employee's or fellow employee's negligence. This doctrine has been virtually abrogated in all states by workers' compensation laws.

FEPC: *See* Fair Employment Practice Committee.

Fiduciary: With respect to welfare and pension programs, anyone who exercises discretionary control or authority over funds.

Field Examiners: Employees of the National Labor Relations Board who handle representation and dispute cases.

Filing Requirements: Under the Landrum-Griffin Act, the requirement that union officials file financial reports with the Labor Department.

Fink: *See* Strikebreaker.

First International: An organization (sometimes spelled "Internationale") founded in London in 1864 by British trade unionists and a number of political refugees from the European continent as the International Workingmen's Association. Its first constitution and declaration of principles were drafted by Karl Marx. All important European countries were represented. It was disrupted by defeat of the Paris Commune in 1871 and the disagreement between socialists and anarchists. Dissolved in Philadelphia in 1876, it was succeeded by the Second Internationale, founded in Brussels in 1891.

Flagged Rate: *See* Red-Circle Rate.

Flags of Convenience: Shipping licenses granted to many American shipping companies by other countries, such as Panama, Honduras, the Philippines, and Liberia. The American companies thus avoid United States safety and wage regulations.

Flexitime: An alternative to the traditional 5-day, 40-hour week that was introduced early in the 1970s. It permits the worker to choose, within limits, the starting and finishing times of his or her day's work. Under most programs, there is a designated "core time" of 4 to 6 hours when all employees are expected to work.

Float: *See* Cost-of-Living Allowance.

Floater: A worker who moves from job to job.

FLSA: *See* Fair Labor Standards Act of 1938.

Flying Squad: A group of multiskilled employees who are used in various jobs on an emergency basis. Also, a group of workers loyal to the union sent out on organizing drives or to assist in strike situations.

FMCS: *See* Federal Mediation and Conciliation Service.

FOOTALU: *See* Federation of Organized Trades and Labor Unions of the United States and Canada.

Form Agreement: *See* Standard Agreement.

Formal Action: As defined by the National Labor Relations

Board: Formal actions may be documents issued or proceedings conducted when the voluntary agreement of all parties regarding the disposition of all issues in a case cannot be obtained, and where dismissal of the charge or petition is not warranted. Formal actions are, further, those in which the decision-making authority of the Board (the regional director in representation cases), as provided in Sections 9 and 10 of the National Labor Relations Act, must be exercised in order to achieve the disposition of a case or the resolution of any issue raised in a case. Thus, formal action takes place when a Board decision and consent order is issued pursuant to a stipulation, even though the stipulation constitutes a voluntary agreement.

Formal Agreement (in Unfair Labor Practice Cases): As defined by the National Labor Relations Board: a written agreement between the Board and the other parties on an unfair labor practice case in which hearing is waived and the specific terms of a Board order agreed upon. The agreement may also provide for the entry of a consent court decree enforcing the Board order.

Foster Grandparent Program: Created in 1965, the program offers to older men and women opportunities for working closely with children with special or exceptional needs. Older Americans can thus continue serving their communities and themselves in an active and meaningful capacity. (*See* Action.)

Fourierism: A socialist scheme of cooperative ownership named after F. C. M. Fourier (1772–1837). The scheme called for organizing society into phalanxes composed of 1600 people, each of whom would be part worker, capitalist, producer, and consumer. Conflicts inherent in the class nature of society could thus be resolved. Many such communities were set up in the United States in the mid-nineteenth century.

Free Labor Market: Theoretically, a place where employers are free to hire and workers are free to compete for available jobs.

Free Riders: A derogatory term applied by unions to non-members who, because of being in the bargaining unit, share in benefits resulting from union activities without paying dues.

Free-Speech Fights: For several years, a technique of the Industrial Workers of the World in the western United States. Following the arrest of union organizers in small communities, hundreds of foot-loose IWW members would flock to the scene and provoke their own arrests, thus becoming guests of the communities and clogging the judicial process.

Freedom of Contract: A theory of law, often invoked in opposition to early labor legislation, that interference in labor relations was invalid under the due-process clause of the Fifth Amendment to the United States Constitution.

Frictional Unemployment: Unemployment brought about by the personal desire of workers to leave jobs or by other temporary or transitional conditions.

Fringe Benefits: Generally, supplements to wages received by workers at a cost to employers. The term encompasses a host of practices (paid vacations, pensions, health and insurance plans, etc.) that usually add to something more than a "fringe," and it is sometimes applied to a practice that may constitute a dubious "benefit" to workers. No agreement prevails as to the list of practices that merit inclusion in this term, with the chief areas of disagreement arising at the juncture of "wages" and "fringes" and, at the other end, of "fringes" and company personnel practices. Differences of opinion also occur regarding the inclusion of legally required benefits. Other terms often substituted for fringe benefits include *wage extras, hidden payroll, nonwage labor costs,* and *supplementary wage practices.* The Bureau of Labor Statistics avoids the pitfalls of the term *fringe benefits* by use of the phrase "selected supplementary compensation (or remuneration) practices," which is then defined for survey pruposes.

Frozen Seniority: Seniority that does not accumulate during a period of layoff but is retained intact throughout the period.

Full-Crew Law or Rule: Generally, the laws or regulations of several states which require a minimum number of workers having specified skills for each railway train, e.g., engineer, firemen, conductors, brakemen, and flagmen, and for women designated to do these jobs.

Full Employment Act: *See* Employment Act of 1946.

Functus Officio: A designated task performed by an official, such as by an arbitrator who has rendered his decision.

Fund (Trust Fund): In general, money and investments set aside in a separate account, usually administered by trustees, to provide for the payment of pensions, supplemental unemployment benefits, strike benefits, etc. Also used as a verb, i.e., to set up a fund; to set aside adequate reserves.

Funded Pension Plan: A plan in which reserves are set aside so that the plan will be solvent for the future.

Funeral Leave Pay (Bereavement Pay): Pay to a worker, usually for a limited period (e.g., 3 days), for time lost because of the death and funeral of a member of his or her immediate family.

Future Service Benefits: Accumulated credits earned while working under a pension plan.

FWP: *See* Federal Women's Program.

Gaffer: *See* Gang Boss.

Gang Boss: The person in charge of a small group of workers.

Garnishment: The legal attachment of an employee's wages to pay a debt owned by the employee to someone other than the employer.

GAW: *See* Guaranteed Annual Wage Plan.

General Board, AFL-CIO: *See* AFL-CIO, General Board.

General Counsel: Appointed by the President of the United States for a term of 4 years as legal officer of the National Labor Relations Board. As counsel, he or she has final authority under the Labor Management Relations Act of 1947 with respect to the investigation of charges and the issuance of complaints in labor disputes.

General Strike: *See* Strike.

General Wage Changes: Wage adjustments that affect large numbers of workers in a similar manner at the same time.

Gentleman's Agreement: An unenforceable agreement, usually oral, based upon an understanding between two parties.

GI Bill of Rights: The Servicemen's Readjustment Act of 1944, which provides allowances for educational opportunities and other financial assistance to war veterans.

Globe Doctrine: A policy of the National Labor Relations Board, outlined in the case of the Globe Machine and Stamping Company, permitting employees to determine the form of the bargaining unit when more than one unit is appropriate.

Going Rate: *See* Prevailing Rate.

Goldbricking: Loafing while pretending to work.

Goldfish Bowl Bargaining: Collective bargaining sessions that are open to the press and the public.

Good-faith Bargaining: As defined in the Tafe-Hartley Act, the "obligation to meet at reasonable times and confer in good faith, with respect to wages, hours and other terms and conditions of unemployment."

Good Standing: The status of a union member whose payment of dues is up to date and who is in compliance with all the requirements of membership.

Goon: Slang term for a person hired by either management or union during a labor dispute to make trouble and intimidate the opposition by violence or the threat of violence.

Gradualism: The policy of Samuel Gompers of "making haste gradually." (*See* Fabianism.)

Graveyard Shift: *See* Shift.

Grievance: A complaint by an employee or a union alleging a violation of a collective bargaining agreement, a past practice, or an appropriate federal, state or local law, or a violation of the rights of an individual in an employment relationship. Grievances may sometimes be filed by an employer. Details of the procedures for the resolution of grievances are usually detailed in a collective bargaining agreement.

Grievance Communittee: *See* Shop Committee.

Grievance Procedure (Grievance Machinery): Typically a formal plan, specified in the agreement, which provides a channel for the adjustment of grievances through discussions at progressively higher levels of authority in company and union, usually culminating in arbitration if necessary. Formal plans may also be found in nonunion companies, with the important difference that there is no union to represent workers.

Grievance Steps: The regular steps in a grievance procedure by which a grievance dispute moves from one level of authority in the company and union to the next higher level. The steps are usually specified in the agreement.

Group Annuity Plan: *See* Pension Plan.

Group Incentive Plan: Payment of incentive earnings based on the output of a group of workers (team, gang, department, etc.) rather than on the output of the individual worker.

Group Leader: A supervisor of a group of workers who generally does the same work that they do.

Guaranteed Annual Wage Plan (Annual Wage or Employment Guarantee): A plan whereby employees meeting certain qualifications are assured wage income or employment for a full year or the greater part of a year. Such plans are not common. (*See* Supplemental Unemployment Benefit Plans.)

Guaranteed Time: The rate of hourly or weekly pay guaranteed to a worker under an incentive system. It may differ from the base rate. Also a term sometimes used for weekly wage or employment guarantees (e.g., a guarantee of 36 hours' work for employees called to work on the first day of the workweek.)

Guild: Historically, an association of craftsmen and merchants in a particular trade or craft exercising a monopoly in a community. Guild functions included the fixing of wages, prices, standards of quality, and rules of apprenticeship. The system was almost wholly ended by the rise of the large-factory method of production and the improvement in the means of transportation of goods and services.

Hatch Act: *See* Federal Corrupt Practices Act.

Hawes-Cooper Act (1929): Legislation permitting states to regulate the sale of prison-made goods within their borders.

Haymarket Riot: A demonstration and meeting in Haymarket Square in Chicago on May 4, 1886, to protest the killing of strikers at the McCormick factory. The meeting was interrupted by police, a bomb was thrown, a policeman was killed. Altogether, ten persons were killed and fifty were injured. Eight anarchists were tried for this offense, four were executed, one committed suicide, and three received long prison sentences but were granted unconditional pardons later by Governor Altgeld.

Hazard Pay: Extra payments to workers engaged in dangerous occupations or in work where the chances of injury are greater than normal. (*See* High Time.)

Headstart: A program under the Economic Opporunity Act of 1964 which provides child care services and pre-school education.

Health, Education, and Welfare Department (HEW): Created under legislation proposed by President Eisenhower and approved by Congress on April 1, 1953. The legislation abolished HEW's predecessor, the Federal Security Agency, transferred all FSA functions to the new department, and assigned all responsibilities of the Federal Security Administrator to the Secretary of HEW. The Department is the Cabinet-level arm of the federal government most involved with people and the nation's human concerns.

Health and Insurance Plan (Welfare Plan): A program of providing financial protection to workers and their families against death, illness, accidents, and other risks, in which the costs are borne in whole or in part by the employer. One or more of the following major benefits may be provided for workers and, frequently, their dependents: life insurance, accidental death and dismemberment benefits, accident and sickness benefits, hospitalization benefits, surgical and medical benefits, and major medical expense benefits. (*See* entries for each item.) Although sometimes self-insured in whole or in part, these programs usually consist of insurance purchased from Blue Cross, Blue Shield, and commercial insurance companies. Some plans provide for health centers or clinics.

HEW: *See* Health, Education, and Welfare, Department of.

High Time: Extra pay for workers engaged in a job high above ground and therefore dangerous or uncomfortable, as in construction. Sometimes also applied to work below ground level with extra dangers or discomforts for the worker. (*See* Hazard Pay.)

Hiring Hall: An office maintained by a union, or jointly by employers and union, for referring workers to jobs or for the actual hiring operation. Common in the maritime industry.

Hiring Rate: *See* Entrance Rate.

"Hit the Bricks": Slang for "go on strike."

Hobbs Act: *See* Anti-Racketeering Law (1934).

Hold-back Pay: Money due a worker for services performed which has not been paid to the worker by the employer.

Holiday Premium Pay: Pay to workers at premium rates (e.g., double time) for work on holidays. (*See* Paid Holidays.)

Homestead Strike (1892): Organized by the Amalgamated Iron & Steel Workers in a dispute with the Carnegie Steel Company in Homestead, Pennsylvania. The strike was defeated by the violence of Pinkerton agents acting against the strikers. It was a serious setback to the organization of steel workers.

Homework: The production of industrial goods by workers in their homes from materials supplied by the employer.

Honeymoon Period: The time immediately after the settlement of an agreement following a dispute, when each side is eager to please the other.

Horizontal Union: A union which includes only workers in a single craft or skill, or closely related skills, such as carpenters or electricians, usually cutting across industry lines. Use of the term is declining. (*See* Craft Union.)

Hospitalization Benefits: A plan that provides workers, and in many cases their dependents, with hospital room and board (e.g., semiprivate room) or cash allowances toward the cost of such care (e.g., $15 to $20 per day) for a specified number of days (21 to 365), plus the full cost of specified services. Usually part of a more inclusive health and insurance program. (*See* Health and Insurance Plan; Blue Cross.)

Hot-Cargo Clause: An agreement provision stipulating that employees covered by the agreement cannot be required to handle or use goods shipped from, or bound to, an employer who is involved in a strike with a union. (*See* Struck Work.)

Hot Goods: Goods shipped in interstate commerce that were produced under conditions in violation of the Fair Labor Standards Act. Also, goods produced under nonunion conditions or in a plant where workers are on strike.

Hourly Rate: Usually, the rate of pay, expressed in dollars and cents per hour, for manual and other workers paid on a time basis. The term is also used at times to designate the earned rate per hour under incentive methods of wage payment.

Housing and Urban Development, Department of (HUD): Established in 1965. HUD is the principal federal agency responsible for programs concerned with housing needs and with improving and developing the nation's communities.

HUD: *See* Housing and Urban Development, Department of.

Human Relations: The broad area of managerial effort and research dealing with the social and psychological relationships among people at work. Bringing into play the insights and techniques of several of the social sciences, it concentrates upon workers and supervisors as individuals, all with personal problems and personality differences, and all with both psychic and material satisfactions to be fulfilled. Its practical application at the work level includes improving personal relationships, reducing friction, and improving organization, and thereby enhancing efficiency.

Human Relations Committees: Continuing committees of union and management set up by agreement to study problems and to make joint recommendations to negotiators for contract improvements. The term originated in the steel industry. (*See* Continuous Bargaining Committees.)

IACW: *See* Inter-American Commission of Women.

IFTU: *See* International Federation of Trade Unions.

Illegal Purpose Doctrine: The determination of courts as to which objectives of a union are proper and legal, or improper and illegal.

Illegal Strike: A strike against the law, against the contract, or against the wishes of the parent union.

ILO: *See* International Labor Organization.

Immigration and Naturalization Service (Labor): *See* Bureau of Immigration and Naturalization.

Impartial Chairperson (Umpire): An arbitrator employed jointly by a union and an employer, usually on a long-term basis, to serve as the impartial party on a tripartite arbitration board and to decide all disputes or specific kinds of disputes arising during the life of the contract. The functions of an impartial chairperson often expand with experience and the growing confidence of the parties, and this person alone may constitute the arbitration board in practice.

Impasse: A deadlock in bargaining between an employer and a union.

Improper Practice: An action by a union or by an employer in violation of the National Labor Relations Act.

Improvement Factor: *See* Annual Improvement Factor.

Incentive Wage System: The general term for methods of wage payment which relate earnings of workers to their actual production, individually or as a group. (*See* Group Incentive Plan; Piecework.)

Indentured Service: The system common in the seventeenth and eighteenth centuries under which labor was bound by a written agreement (indenture) to serve a master in a colony for a specified number of years until passage had been paid, or to finish a term of prison imposed in the mother country. Indentured servants were sometimes kidnapped and sold by ship masters upon arrival in the colonies.

Independent Local: A lcoal union not affiliated with any parent body.

Independent Union (Unaffiliated Union): The term applied to local, national, and international unions not affiliated with the AFL-CIO (e.g., Mine Workers, Teamsters). *Unaffiliated union* is perhaps the better term, but it is used less frequently.

Indirect Labor: *See* Direct Labor.

Individual Rates: Rates paid to workers in establishments without a standardized wage-rate system. It may also be used to indicate the rate paid to an individual worker, as distinguished from the standard job rate.

Industrial Action: A euphemism for a strike or boycott and, more specifically, for economic, rather than political, activity.

Industrial Democracy: Commonly applied to the concept of majority rule established in the workplace either through collective bargaining or through workers' sharing in those decisions now reserved to management.

Industrial Engineering Techniques: Outside of specialized literature, a general term covering application of systematic procedures, such as time-and-motion studies, to production or work processes in order to increase production or decrease costs, to set incentive rates of pay, etc. Industrial engineering is a recognized profession, with professional standards, etc., but union representatives often must become involved in such procedures without benefit of professional training.

Industrial Relations: A general term covering matters of mutual concern to employers and employees; the relationships, formal and informal, between employer and employees or their representatives; government actions and law bearing upon these relationships; an area of specialization in a company; a field of study whose scope is suggested by this glossary.

Industrial Relations Research Association: One of the professional associations in the social sciences, attracting academicians and practitioners of similar interests. Researchers and users of industrial relations research findings in universities, business, unions, and government participate in this association.

Industrial Revolution: Changes that took place in the methods of production and transportation and the consequent adjustment in class relationships from the middle of the 1700s to the modern day.

Industrial Union (Vertical Union): A union that represents all, or most, production, maintenance, and related workers, both skilled and unskilled, in an industry or company. It may also include office, sales, and technical employees of the same companies. The United Automobile Workers and United Steelworkers of America are examples of industrial unions. (Cf. Craft Union.)

Industrial Union Department: *See* AFL-CIO, Departments of.

Industrial Workers of the World (IWW): Organized in 1905 in Chicago by labor groups hostile to the American Federation of Labor, it was, despite its activity in Lawrence, Massachusetts, and Paterson, New Jersey, confined largely to the Midwest and the western part of the United States. It was an expression of militant Marxism, with a membership in excess of 100,000, chiefly among migrant workers in agriculture and lumbering. It declined rapidly at the end of World War I and is presently a very small organization.

Industrywide Bargaining: Negotiations between an employers' group and a union resulting in an agreement covering an entire "industry" or a substantial part thereof, e.g., all class I railroads. Ordinarily, the term *industry* in this connection is not consistent with standard statistical definitions, nor does *industrywide* necessarily imply nationwide coverage. It is usually safe to assume that in whatever way "industry" is used, it does not include every establishment.

Ineligible List: A roster of employees not legally entitled to participate in a union election. Also, a list of contractors who have been found to be in violation of the Walsh-Healey Public Contracts Act and are prohibited from bidding on government contracts.

Inequity: A disadvantageous condition, real or alleged, generally relating to wage rates or benefits, usually the former, that are substantially lower than those prevailing elsewhere in the plant, company, locality, or industry for the same or comparable work.

Informal Agreement (in unfair labor practice cases): As defined by the National Labor Relations Board: a written agreement entered into by the party charged with committing an unfair labor practice, the regional director, and (in most cases) the charging party requiring the charged party to take certain specific remedial action as a basis for the closing of the case. Cases closed in this manner are considered "adjusted" cases.

Informational Picketing: Picketing the immediate purpose of which is not to gain recognition but to notify the public that an employer does not have a contract with the union, or is unfair to it.

Initiation Fee: Payment to the union required of a worker when joining, usually as set forth in the union's constitution. The Labor-Management Relations Act of 1947 prohibits excessive or discriminatory fees where workers are required to join the union to remain employed, as in a union shop.

Injunction (Labor Injunction): A court order restraining one or more persons, corporations, or unions from performing some act which the court believes would result in irreparable injury to property or other rights.

Injunction Petitions: As defined by the National Labor Relations Board: petitions filed by the Board with respective U.S. district courts for injunctive relief under Section 10(j) or Section 10(e) of the Labor Management Relations Act of 1947, pending hearing and adjudication of unfair labor practice charges before the Board. Also, petitions filed with the U.S. court of appeals under Section 10(e) of the act.

Insurance Plan: *See* Health and Insurance Plan.

Inter-American Commission of Women (IACW) (Comisión Interamericana de Mujeres, CIM): The first official regional body (established in 1928) to promote the rights of women. It became a permanent specialized organization of the Organization of American States (OAS) in 1953. The Commission has assumed the responsibility for lessening the gap between de jure and de facto situations of women in South and Central American countries.

Interim Agreement: An agreement designed to maintain a truce until issues in a dispute can be resolved.

Interim Committees: *See* Continuous Bargaining Committees.

Intermediate Body: A term sometimes used to classify a union office or department performing certain functions between the local union level and the national union level, e.g., a regional or district office.

International: Often, the central governing authority of many unions; in this sense, the same as "National" or "Brotherhood." (*See* First International.)

Interdepartmental Committee on the Status of Women: Established by EO 11126 of Nov. 1, 1963, as amended by EO 11221 of May 6, 1965, to maintain a continuing review and evaluation of the progress of Federal departments and agencies in advancing the status of women. Terminated by EO 12050 of Apr. 4, 1978.

International Confederation of Free Trade Unions (ICFTU): An international organization of labor movements or federations of non-Communist nations, with which the AFL-CIO is affiliated. It was founded in 1949 after the predecessor organization, the World Federation of Trade Unions, became Communist-dominated.

International Federation of Trade Unions (IFTU): Established in 1913, it was, up to 1945, an international organization composed of national trade unions organized to advance the position of organized labor through education and the publication of material on labor. Following World War II, it was replaced by the World Federation of Trade Unions.

International Labor Office: The permanent staff and officials of the International Labor Organization stationed in Geneva.

International Labor Organization (ILO): This autonomous intergovernmental agency, associated with the United Nations, was created by the Treaty of Versailles in 1919 as a part of the League of Nations. The United States joined in 1934 and is at present one of 128 member countries which finance its operations. Governments, workers, and employers share in making its decisions and shaping its policies. This tripartite representation gives the ILO its balance and much of its strength and distinguishes it from all other international agencies. The purpose of the ILO is to improve labor conditions, raise living standards, and promote economic and social stability as the foundation for lasting peace throughout the world. The United States joined this autonomous intergovernmental agency in 1934. U.S. membership terminated Nov. 1, 1977, at the direction of the President.

International Representative (National Representative): Generally, a full-time employee of a national or international union whose duties include assisting in the formation of local unions, dealing with affiliated local unions on union business, assisting in negotiations and grievance settlements, settling disputes within and between locals, and similar activities. (Cf. Business Agent.)

International Trade Secretariats: Organizations comprising unions from the same industries and in different countries, and meeting regularly to discuss common problems. The International Metalworkers' Federation is one of eighteen such organizations.

International Union: A union claiming jurisdiction both within and outside the United States (usually in Canada). Sometimes the term is loosely applied to all national unions; that is, "international" and "national" are used interchangeably.

International Workingmen's Association: See First International.

Interstate Association of Commissions on the States of Women: See National Association of Commissions for Women.

Interstate Commerce: Trade, traffic, commerce, transportation, or communication among the several states, upon which federal labor legislation often rests. The Fair Labor Standards Act of 1938, for example, applies to employees who are engaged in interstate commerce and to those engaged in the production of goods for such commerce. Authority to regulate interstate commerce is reserved to the federal government by the Constitution of the United States.

Intrastate Commerce: Commerce within a state.

Iron Law of Wages: The subsistence theory that wages cannot in the long run be more than just enough to provide for the barest necessities for workers and their families. Although thoroughly refuted and discredited, the "law" exerts an influence on many.

IUD (Industrial Union Department): See AFL-CIO, Departments of.

IWW: See Industrial Workers of the World.

Jack of All Trades: Someone skilled in a variety of crafts.

Jim Crow: Attitudes and actions harmful to black people; racial discrimination.

Job Action: A slowdown or a strike.

Job Analysis: The systematic study of a job to discover its specifications, its mental, physical, and skill requirements, its relation to other jobs in the plant, etc., usually for wage setting or job simplification purposes. (See Job Description.)

Job Classification: Arrangement of tasks in an establishment or industry into a limited series of jobs or occupations, rated in terms of skill, responsibility, experience, training, and similar considerations, usually for wage-setting purposes. This term, or the term job class, may also be used in reference to a single cluster of jobs of approximately equal "worth."

Job Corps: Authorized by the Comprehensive Employment and Training Act of 1973, the Corps provides leadership and overall direction and guidance for the administration of a nationwide training program offering comprehensive development for disadvantaged youth through centers with the unique feature of residential facilities for all or most enrollees.

Job Description: A written statement listing the elements of a particular job or occupation, e.g., purpose, duties, equipment used, qualifications, training, physical and mental demands, and working conditions.

Job Dilution: Division of a skilled craft into small unskilled operations and assignment of these operations to unskilled workers.

Job Evaluation (Job Grading; Job Rating): Determination of the relative importance or ranking of jobs in an establishment, for wage-setting purposes, by systematically rating them on the basis of selected factors, such as skill, responsibility, and experience. Ordinarily used as a means of determining relative levels, not the actual rate structure as a whole.

Job Family: A group of jobs with common attributes, such as use of the same tools or same skills. It is sometimes the basis of applying seniority or length of service criteria for promotions or layoffs within such groups.

Job Opportunities in the Business Sector (JOBS): A federal program to stimulate the private sector into hiring, training, and retraining disadvantaged, unemployed persons and to upgrade the skills of those already employed.

Job Posting: Listing of available jobs, usually on a bulletin board, so that employees may bid for promotion or transfer.

Job Study: Collection of information about a particular job and use of the data for job descriptions, specifications, and the application of wage rates. It is used as a basis for time-study.

JOBS: See Job Opportunities in the Business Sector.

Joint Apprenticeship Council: A labor-management committee to administer an apprenticeship program.

Joint Bargaining: Usually indicates two or more unions joining forces in negotiating an agreement with a single employer.

Joint Board (or Council): A delegate body composed of representatives of locals of a single national or international union in a particular area, working together to further the interests of the union. When more than one union is involved, the term trade council may be used.

Joint Lockout: See Lockout.

Joint and Survivor Option (Survivor's Option): A pension plan provision under which the pensioner may elect to receive a reduced benefit with a guarantee that, if he or she dies while the worker's beneficiary is living, payments of a predetermined proportion of the reduced benefit will be continued to that beneficiary for life.

JOP: *See* Jobs Optional Program.

Journeyman: A fully qualified craftworker, generally one who has mastered his or her trade by serving an apprenticeship.

Journeyman Rate: The rate of pay for a fully qualified worker in a skilled trade or craft, usually as distinguished from apprentice rate, helpers' rate, probationary rate, etc.

Jurisdiction: Among unions, the right or claim to represent workers within specified occupations, industries, or geographical boundaries.

Jurisdictional Dispute: A conflict between two or more unions over the organization of a particular establishment or over the performance of a certain type of work by members of one union or another.

Jurisdictional Strike: A work stoppage resulting from a jurisdictional dispute. (*See* Jurisdictional Dispute.)

Jury-Duty Pay: The pay or allowance granted an employee by the employer for working time spent on jury duty, usually in addition to fees paid by the court.

Just Cause: Good or fair reasons for discipline. The term is commonly used in agreement provisions safeguarding workers from unjustified discharge or a lesser punishment. When defined in agreements, it usually includes such offenses as insubordination, fighting, and inefficiency.

Justiciable Arbitration: Arbitration that involves the interpretation or the applicability of the contract.

Kaiser Steel Long-range Sharing Plan: Negotiated by the Kaiser Steel Corporation and the United Steelworkers in 1963, this highly publicized plan guarantees employees against loss of jobs or income caused by technological change and provides for sharing savings in materials or labor costs.

Kickback: A coercive, illegal, or secret return of wages, fees, etc., as when a worker returns a portion of his or her pay to an employer or a supervisor as a bribe for obtaining or retaining a certain job.

Knights of Labor: Founded in 1869 by Uriah Stevens, the organization adopted the name of "Noble Order of the Knights of Labor." First an organization of tailors, it spread rapidly to include workers of every craft, both skilled and unskilled, both black and white. The Knights of Labor was a secret organization and reached its height in 1886 when the reaction to the Haymarket violence and the competition with the new American Federation of Labor caused a rapid decline from a membership of 700,000. It no longer exists.

Knights of Saint Crispin: A secret organization of shoe workers (1867–1973); once the most powerful labor organization in the United States, with about 40,000 members.

Knocked Off: Discharged, fired.

Label: *See* Union Label.

Label Trades: Trades in which unions attach insignia to the product indicating that it is union-made.

Labor: A term whose varied meanings and uses (in addition to "work") are given full scope in dictionaries and economics textbooks. Readers probably will most often see it used as a synonym for organized workers, the AFL-CIO, a particular union, or any union.

Labor Agreement: *See* Agreement.

Labor Area: *See* Labor Market Area.

Labor Contract: *See* Agreement.

Labor Day: The day set aside to honor the interests of workers and celebrated on the first Monday in September. Founded by the carpenter Peter Maguire of the Knights of Labor in 1882, the holiday was designated by Congress in 1894. In Europe, May 1 has been celebrated as Labor Day since 1890.

Labor Department (DOL): The Department established by Act of Congress in 1913 to "foster, promote, and develop the welfare of the wage earners of the United States, to improve their working conditions, and to advance their opportunities for profitable employment." The Department also has important functions in the field of international labor affairs. Its major bureaus and offices include the Bureau of Apprenticeship and Training, Bureau of Employment Security, Bureau of Labor Standards, Bureau of Labor Statistics, Wage and Hour and Public Contracts Divisions, Women's Bureau, Bureau of International Labor Affairs, Office of Manpower, Automation and Training, Office of the Solicitor, Neighborhood Youth Corps, Labor-Management Services Administration, and Manpower Administration. The Secretary of Labor heads the Department.

Labor Dispute: *See* Dispute.

Labor Economics: The area of general economics that is concerned with employment, wages, hours, working conditions, health and security, etc.

Labor Force (Work Force): In census terms, all persons age 14 or over, employed or unemployed (but looking for work). *Total labor force* includes members of the armed forces; *civilian labor force* excludes them. The term is often used to designate the entire roll of employees of a particular company or industry.

Labor Grades: One of a series of rate steps (single rate or a range of rates) in the wage structure of an establishment. Labor grades are typically the outcome of some form of job evaluation, or of wage-rate negotiations, by which different occupations are grouped, so that occupations of approximately equal "value" or "worth" fall into the same grade and thus command the same rate of pay. (*See* Job Classification; Job Evaluation.)

Labor Injunction: *See* Injunction.

Labor Law: The branch of the law and the statutes in local, state, and federal governments dealing with labor relations, the employment of children, wages, and working conditions.

Labor Lobby: Persons who, on behalf of labor, seek to promote legislation favorable to labor. The term is generally used in a pejorative sense.

Labor-Management Advisory Committee: *See* Economic Stabilization Program.

Labor-Management Relations Act (Taft-Hartley Act) (1947): The federal law, amending the National Labor Relations Act (Wagner Act), 1935, which, among other changes, defined and made illegal a number of unfair labor practices by unions. It preserved the guarantee of the right of workers to organize and bargain collectively with their employers or to refrain from such activities, and retained the definition of unfair labor practices as applied to employers. The act does not apply to employees in a business or industry where a labor dispute would not affect interstate commerce. Other major exclusions are: employees subject to the Railway Labor Act, agricultural workers, employees of government and nonprofit hospitals, domestic servants, and supervisors. Amended by the Labor-Management Reporting and Disclosure Act of 1959. (*See* National Labor Relations Act; National Labor Relations Board; Unfair Labor

Practices; Section 14(b), Labor-Management Relations Act, 1947.)

Labor-Management Reporting and Disclosure Act of 1959 (Landrum-Griffin Act): The federal law designed "to eliminate or prevent improper practices on the part of labor organizations, employers," etc. Its seven titles include a bill of rights to protect members in their relations with unions; regulations of trusteeships; standards for elections; and fiduciary responsibility of union officers. The Labor-Management Relations Act, 1947, was amended in certain respects by this act. Among other changes, hot-cargo clauses in contracts were forbidden, except for apparel and construction industries. Restrictions were placed on secondary boycotts and picketing.

Labor-Management Services Administration (LMSA): In the Department of Labor, LMSA has administrative responsibilities with respect to the Employment Retirement Income Security Act of 1974 (ERISA); the Labor-Management Reporting and Disclosure Act (LMRD); Title 38, chapter 43, of the United States Code on veterans reemployment rights; Section 13(c) of the Urban Mass Transportation Act; and Executive Order No. 11491, as amended. It also provides technical assistance to state and local governments in matters concerning labor relations with public employees.

Labor Market Area (Labor Area): A general term often used to mean a geographical area from which workers may be recruited, surrounding a concentration of establishments. Usually a metropolitan area, consisting of a central city and its suburbs. In 1978, however, the U.S. Department of Labor favored the use of "labor area" rather than "labor market area."

Labor Mobility: In general, the extent to which workers can, are willing to, or do move from job to job, employer to employer, or place to place to find employment or work of their choice.

Labor Monopoly: Control exercised by labor unions over jobs and conditions of work; a term generally used pejoratively.

Labor Movement: The economic, political, and social expression of workers unified by their common status as wage earners to improve their position relative to that of other economic classes in the community. It includes the total intersests of the trade unions including economic activity, political involvement, and social, cultural, and educational institutions.

Labor Organization: A group of workers in continuous organization for the purpose of improving their wages, hours, and working conditions through negotiations with employers and through social legislation.

Labor Organizer: An employee of a labor union whose prime responsibility is to persuade workers to become members of the union.

Labor Racketeer: A dishonest union official or employee who, through force or threats of force, extorts moneys from employers or wage earners.

Labor Relations: The relationship between employers and workers, usually involving problems—especially those of collective bargaining and the administration of labor contracts.

Labor Relations Boards: Official agencies of the state, local, and federal governments concerned with labor-management problems.

Labor Skate: Slightly humorous, slightly friendly, slightly pejorative slang term for a union official or union employee.

Labor Solidarity: The understanding of the common status and objectives of wage earners irrespective of classification, race, color, national origin, or sex.

Labor Spy: A person hired by an employer to report on matters with respect to employee activity and interest in a union.

Labor Theory of Value: A theory explaining the determination of the exchange value (price) of commodities, formulated by Adam Smith in the eighteenth century and later developed by David Ricardo and Karl Marx. Central to Marxist economics, the theory holds that the exchange value of a commodity is determined by the amount of socially necessary labor embodied in its production.

Labor Turnover (Turnover): The movement of workers into and out of employment in a company or industry through hiring, layoffs, recall, quits, etc. *Labor turnover rates* are usually expressed as the number of accessions and separations during a given period per 100 employees.

Labor Union: The continuous organization of working people to improve their wages, hours, and working conditions through collective bargaining and/or political and social action.

Labor's League for Political Education (LLPE): The unit established in 1948 by the America Federation of Labor as the vehicle through which it expressed itself politically. It was succeeded by the Committee on Political Education (COPE) in 1955. (*See* AFL-CIO, COPE.)

Laches: Unreasonable delay in the assertion of rights. Arbitrators have held that the failure to assert a right within a reasonable time can mean the loss of the right.

Laissez Faire Doctrine: The concept that enlightened self-interest—without government interference—will best serve the needs of all.

Landrum-Griffin Act: *See* Labor-Management Reporting and Disclosure Act of 1959.

Layoff (Reduction in Force): Involuntary separation from employment for a temporary or an indefinite period, without prejudice, that is, resulting from no fault of the workers. Although *layoff* usually implies eventual recall, or at least an intent to recall workers to their jobs, the term is occasionally used for separations plainly signifying permanent loss of jobs, as in plant shutdowns. *Reduction in force* usually signifies permanent layoff.

Layoff Allowance: *See* Severance Pay.

Lea Act (1946) (Anti-Petrillo Act): A law making it a criminal offense to threaten force or other means to compel any radio station to employ, or agree to employ, more employees than are needed, or to make any extra payment in place of hiring additional employees.

Leadman: A subforeman who works with a group of employees and is responsible for job performance within the group. Leadmen and foremen are now referred to as supervisors.

Leaf-Raking: *See* Boondoggle.

League for Industrial Democracy (LID): An association organized in the 1920s to urge a socialist outlook on organized labor. The League urged the development of cooperatives, labor education, and more intense involvement in politics.

Leap-Frogging: A situation that may arise when an employer is dealing with many unions, particularly those with contracts expiring during the same period. The settlement with the first union becomes a goal to be surpassed by the second union, that settlement becomes a further goal for the third union, and so on.

Learner: Generally, a beginner learning a job for which extensive technical training or experience is not required. (*See* Apprentice.)

Learner Rate (Beginner Rate): A rate or, more frequently, schedule of rates applicable to workers inexperienced in the job for which they are employed, until they attain the necessary competence. (*See* Entrance Rate.)

Learner's Certificates: Certificates issued by the U.S. Department of Labor, under provisions of the Fair Labor Standards Act of 1938, which permit employers to pay rates below the statutory minimum to learners, messengers, apprentices, and handicapped workers so as not to curtail opportunities for their employment.

Leave of Absence: Generally, excused time (unpaid) away from work, usually for a week or more, without loss of job or seniority.

Left-Wing: Commonly, belonging to the most radical section or group within a movement.

Legally Required Benefits: Employee-benefit programs to which employers must contribute or insurance that they must purchase for employees according to law. The benefits include social security, unemployment compensation, workers' compensation, and, to a lesser extent, state temporary disability insurance, and the special programs for railroad workers.

Level Income Option: *See* Social Security Adjustment Option.

Liaison Office for Personnel Management: Established by EO 8248 of Sept. 8, 1939, to assist the President with respect to personnel management. Abolished by EO 10452 of May 1, 1953, and functions delegated to Chairman of the Civil Service Commission.

LID: *See* League for Industrial Democracy.

Life Insurance Plan: Group term insurance coverage for employees, paid for in whole or in part by the employer, providing a lump-sum payment to a worker's beneficiary in the event of the worker's death. (*See* Health and Insurance Plan; Death Benefit.)

Liquidated Damages: A sum agreed upon in advance as the payment to be made in the event of a breach of contract.

"Little Steel": The large steel companies, excepting the United States Steel Corporation. They include Bethlehem, Republic, Inland, Youngstown Sheet and Tube, and Jones & Loughlin. (U.S. Steel is known as "Big Steel.")

"Little Steel" Formula: Enunciated July 16, 1942, by the National War Labor Board as the settlement of the labor dispute between the United Steelworkers of America and the "Little Steel" companies. The formula became applicable to all industry and permitted wage increases of up to 15 percent between January 1941 and May 1942.

Living Document: As used by unions, the belief that the terms of an agreement, particularly a long-term agreement, should be subject to review and renegotiation by the parties if conditions change or unforeseen events come about, despite the absence of a reopening clause.

LLPE: *See* Labor's League for Political Education.

LMRA: *See* Labor-Management Relations Act.

LMRDA: *See* Labor-Management Reporting and Disclosure Act.

LMSA: *See* Labor-Management Services Administration.

Local Autonomy: Authority vested in a local union as distinguished from that held by a national union.

Local Union (Local, Chapter, Lodge): A labor organization comprising the members of a union within a particular area or establishment, which has been chartered by, and is affiliated with, a national or international union.

Lockout (Joint Lockout): A temporary withholding of work or denial of employment to a group of workers by an employer during a labor dispute in order to compel a settlement at, or close to, the employer's terms. A *joint lockout* is such an action undertaken at the same time by a group of employers. Technically, the distinction between a strike and a lockout turns on which party actually initiates the stoppage. One, however, can develop into the other. (*See* Work Stoppage.)

Lodge: The term for local union used in some Railroad Brotherhoods and in the International Association of Machinists.

Longshoremen's and Harbor Workers' Compensation Act: The law providing workers' compensation benefits for certain private employments subject to federal jurisdiction.

Long-term Contract: Generally, a collective bargaining agreement with a duration of 2 or 3 years or longer, as distinguished from a 1-year agreement (the standard term up to a decade or so ago).

Loose Rate: *See* Runaway Rate.

Lost Time: Time away from work for which the employee is paid wages by either the employer or the union. Such "lost time" may be used for union activity, education, training, etc.

Luddites: Riotous bands of workers in England in 1811 through 1816 who went about destroying textile machinery and factories that were built and introduced to displace labor.

Ludlow Massacre: During the United Mine Workers strike against the Colorado Fuel and Iron Corporation in Ludlow in 1913, the state militia fired on the tents of the strikers and their families. Two women and eleven children died, including those who had dug holes to escape the line of fire and were killed when the militia poured oil on the tents and set them afire.

M of M: *See* Maintenance-of-Membership Clause.

McNamara Case: The case on which J. J. McNamara, an official of the Bridge and Structural Iron Wrokers Union, and his brother J. B. McNamara were indicted and tried, in 1911 on a charge of dynamiting the *Los Angeles Times* building. They were defended by Clarence Darrow and supported by wide sections of the labor movement who believed that the "boys were being framed." The defendants confessed and were sentenced to long prison terms.

Made Work: *See* Featherbedding.

Maintenance-of-Membership Clause (M of M): An arrangement provided for in a collective bargaining agreement whereby employees who are members of the union at the time the agreement is negotiated, or who voluntarily join the union subsequently, must maintain their membership for the duration of the agreement or possibly for a shorter period, as a condition of continued employment. (*See* Union Security.)

Major-Medical Expense Benefits (Catastrophe Insurance): A plan designed to insure workers against the heavy medical expenses resulting from catastrophic or prolonged illness or injury. If the benefit supplements the benefit payable by a basic health insurance plan (hospital, medical, or surgical), it is called a *supplementary* plan; otherwise, it is called a *comprehensive* plan. (*See* Deductible; Health and Insurance Plan.)

Majority: A vote in which more than 50 percent of those voting support or oppose a proposal. (*See* Absolute Majority.)

Make Whole: To undo a wrong to an individual or to a group of individuals. It may take the form of back pay or continued seniority.

Make-Work: *See* Featherbedding.

Makeup Pay: The difference between actual piecework earnings and earnings at guaranteed rates or statutory minimum rates. The term is also associated with the practice of permitting employees to earn a full week's wages by making up for lost time.

Man-days of Strike Idleness: A key measure of strike activity regularly compiled by the Bureau of Labor Statistics, reflecting working time lost because of strikes and lockouts. The figures on strike idelness do not include secondary idleness—that is, the effects of a work stoppage on other establishments or industries whose employees may be made idle as a result of material or service shortages.

Management: The employer and his or her representatives or the corporation executives who are responsible for the administration and direction of an enterprise. (*See* Employer.)

Management Clause: The clause in a labor agreement outlining the rights of management under the contract. They generally include statements setting the hours of work, fixing prices, and deciding what goods are to be produced.

Management Prerogatives: As used in union-management relationships, the rights reserved to management, which may be expressly noted as such in a collective bargaining agreement. They usually include the rights to schedule production, to determine the process of manufacture, to maintain order and efficiency, and to hire.

Managerial Employees: Employees who have supervisory responsibilities or whose status is so close to that of top management that they are properly excluded from the bargaining unit.

Manning Table: A listing of the positions, or the number of workers, to be used in the operation of a particular machine or process.

Manpower: Generally, all persons (male and female) able and willing to work, that is, the available labor force. The term is sometimes used in reference to a more limited group, e.g., company, industry, community, or workers with particular skills.

Manpower Administration (Labor): Name changed to Employment and Training Administration by order of the Secretary of Labor, as of Nov. 12, 1975.

Manpower Development and Training Act of 1962 (MDTA): A federal act designed to provide an opportunity for unemployed workers and workers otherwise not qualified to fulfill new job demands to learn new skills, by providing vocational, basic education, on-the-job, and other training programs, with allowances to trainees under certain circumstances. The act also called for a broad program of research into employment needs, causes of unemployment, impact of automation and technological change, and labor mobility. MDTA functions have been absorbed into CETA. (*See* Comprehensive Employment and Training Act.)

Manual Workers: *See* Blue-collar Workers.

Maritime Advisory Committee: Established by EO 11156

of June 17, 1964, to consider matters of Federal maritime policy, including those policies and practices which may be followed by labor, management, or the Government for strengthening the trade, national defense, manpower, and labor relations of the maritime industry. Terminated by EO 11427 of Sept. 4, 1968.

Maritime Labor Board: Authorized by Merchant Marine Act of 1936, as amended (52 Stat. 968, 55 Stat. 259; 46 U.S.C. 1251–1262), to encourage maritime employers and their employees to make and maintain written collective agreements to settle disputes and to receive and file contracts between employers and employees in maritime and related industries. Mediatory duties abolished by law June 1941; title expired June 22, 1942.

Maritime Trades Department: *See* AFL-CIO, Departments of.

Marxism: The social and economic policies of Karl Marx and Friedrich Engels, developed from 1842 to 1893. They include a critique of capitalism and the concepts of class struggle, theories of value, and theories of surplus value. Marxism has formed the basis of most radical thought and activity during the last 125 years throughout the world.

Master: The calling of a fully skilled craftsman during the days of the guild system; usually an owner of an establishment who employed and supervised the training of apprentices within his shop.

Master Agreement: A single or uniform collective bargaining agreement covering a number of plants of a single employer or the members of an employers' association. (*See* Multiplant Bargaining; Multiemployer Bargaining.)

Masterpiece: Work, demonstrating one's skill, presented by a journeyman in a craft to the Masters in a guild when seeking admittance to the guild as a Master.

Maternity Benefits: Health and insurance plan benefits payable to women workers absent because of pregnancy and childbirth, and to workers' wives where such dependents' benefits are provided. The benefits provide for hospital, surgical, and medical costs related to maternity.

MDTA: *See* Manpower Development and Training Act.

Mealtime: *See* Paid Lunch Period.

Mechanics Lien: The prior claim of a worker upon a building or land up to the amount of wages for labor performed on such building or land.

Mechanics Union of Trade Associations: The association formed following a strike of carpenters in Philadelphia in 1827, which gained the support of other unions. The first association in America of workers from many trades, it can be called the first labor movement. Beginning in 1828, it published the first labor newspaper, *The Mechanics Free Press*.

Mediation (Conciliation): An attempt by a third party to help in negotiations or in the settlement of a dispute between employer and union through suggestion, advice, or other ways of stimulating agreement, short of dictating its provisions (a characteristic of arbitration). Most of the mediation in the United States is undertaken through federal and state mediation agencies. *Mediator* is the term used to designate the person who undertakes mediation of a dispute. *Conciliation,* in practice, is synonymous with mediation; the term lives on mainly in the name of the chief mediation agency. (*See* Federal Mediation and Conciliation Service.)

Medical Benefits: Plans which provide workers, and in many cases their dependents, with specified medical care (other than that connected with surgery) or a cash allowance toward the cost of doctors' visits. Generally part of a health and insurance program. (*See* Health and Insurance Plan; Health Center.)

Member in Good Standing: *See* Union Member.

Members-Only Contract: A clause in a labor agreement providing coverage only for members of the union.

Memorial Day Massacre: The deaths that resulted from an attack by the police on the strikers during the "Little Steel" strike, Memorial Day, 1937.

Merchant Guilds: Organizations during the Middle Ages that set down rules protecting their trade by limiting the number of people who could enter the trade and by fixing prices.

Merger, AFL-CIO: *See* AFL-CIO.

Merit Increase: An increase in the wage rate of a worker, usually given on the basis of certain criteria of worth, e.g., efficiency and performance.

Merit Progression: *See* Wage Progression.

Merit Rating: The system under the federal-state unemployment insurance program in which many states permit employers who have a stable workforce to pay less money into the Unemployment Insurance fund than do employers with frequent turnover. Seasonal industries therefore pay more money into the fund.

MESA: *See* Mining Enforcement and Safety Administration.

Metal Trades Department: *See* AFL-CIO, Departments of.

Migrant Health Act: A federal law providing for grants to public and other nonprofit agencies and institutions for paying part of the costs of establishing and operating family health service clinics for domestic agricultural migratory workers and their families. It is administered by the Department of Health, Education, and Welfare.

Migratory Workers: Persons whose principal income is earned from temporary employment (usually in farming) and who, in the course of a year, move one or more times, often through several states.

Military Leave: Excused leave of absence for military service, reserve training, National Guard duty, etc. Time lost may be paid for by the employer in whole or in part.

Miller Act: Legislation requiring that on alterations or repair of any public building, the contractors must execute a payment bond with a surety or sureties to protect the wages of all persons supplying labor.

Minimum Wage: The rate of pay, established by law or through collective bargaining, below which workers cannot be employed. Exceptions are frequently made for learners and handicapped workers. It is usually expressed as an hourly rate.

Minimum-Wage Determination: The minimum wage in an area, determined by the Secretary of Labor as authorized by the Walsh-Healey Public Contracts Act. All those working for contractors with the United States government may be paid no less than this minimum.

Minimum-Wage Law: *See* Fair Labor Standards Act.

Mining Enforcement and Safety Administration (MESA):   Established on May 7, 1973, by the Secretary of the Interior; the Administration became operative on July 16, 1973. The Secretary assigned to the Administrator the responsibility for administering the enforcement provisions of the Federal Coal Mine Health and Safety Act of 1969 and the Federal Metal and Nonmetallic Mine Safety Act. Terminated by departmental directive Mar. 9, 1978, and functions transferred to Labor Department's Mine Safety and Health Administration established by act of Nov. 9, 1977 (91 Stat. 1319; 29 U.S.C. 557a).

Minority Union: A union that does not enjoy majority status and therefore is denied exclusive bargaining rights.

Modified Closed Shop: A union security clause generally providing that older employees need not be in the union, but requiring that all new employees be members of the union prior to their employment.

Modified Union Shop: *See* Union Shop.

Mohawk Valley Formula: A technique of fighting unions developed by the Remington Rand Corporation. It includes discrediting a union in its members' eyes and involving all members of the community in antiunion activity. Sometimes called the Rand formula.

Molly Maguires: A secret organization using violence to protect the rights of miners in the eastern Pennsylvania coal fields during the 1870s. The association was ended by the activity of a Pinkerton agent, with the exposure, conviction, and hanging of Molly Maguire leaders in 1877.

Money-Purchase Plan: *See* Pension Plan.

Monitorship: Supervision or surveillance of a union by an outside party, usually for a limited time, imposed by order of a court or parent union organization.

Monthly Labor Review: A magazine devoted to general economic and labor matters, issued by the Department of Labor, Bureau of Labor Statistics.

Moonlighting: The simultaneous holding of more than one paid employment by a worker, e.g., a full-time job and a second supplementary job with another employer, or self-employment.

Most Favored Nation Clause: An article in a labor agreement granting the employer the advantages of any contract terms the union may negotiate with another employer.

Motor Carriers Act: A statute, passed in 1935, bringing truckers in interstate commerce under the regulation of the Interstate Commerce Commission.

Moving Allowance: *See* Relocation Allowance.

Multicraft Union: A labor union having workers of different crafts among its members and under its jurisdiction.

Multiemployer Bargaining: Collective bargaining between a union or unions and a group of employers, usually represented by an employers association, resulting in a uniform or master agreement.

Multiplant Bargaining (Companywide Bargaining):   Collective bargaining between a company and the union or unions representing workers in more than one of its plants, usually resulting in a master agreement. If all or most plants are involved, the term *companywide* is appropriately used.

NAB: *See* National Alliance of Businessmen.

NACW: *See* National Association of Commissions for Women.

NAM: *See* National Association of Manufacturers.

National Alliance of Businessmen (NAB): An organization of employers formed in 1969 to work with the government to provide jobs and training for the unemployed. Subsidies for training are provided by the federal government.

National Apprenticeship Act: A law, enacted in 1937, to enable the Department of Labor (1) to formulate and promote the labor standards necessary to safeguard the welfare of apprentices; (2) to cooperate with the states in the promotion of such standards; and (3) to bring together employers and labor for the formulation of apprenticeship programs.

National Association of Commissions for Women (NACW): The association known until March 1975 as the Interstate Association of Commissions on the Status of Women, organized in 1970. It is not a governmental agency, although its membership consists entirely of the official commissions established in the states and local jurisdictions. The Association fosters a closer relationship and fuller exchange of ideas among members to further equal legal, social, political, economic, and educational opportunity for men and women.

National Association of Manufacturers (NAM): Organized by manufacturers in 1895, NAM consistently opposed unions and their political objectives. The Association believes in "working on a constructive and problem-solving basis to improve the industrial climate in this country."

National Bituminous Coal Commission: Created under authority of Bituminous Coal Conservation Act of 1935 (49 Stat. 992; 15 U.S.C. 801). Organized on Sept. 21, 1935, to conserve bituminous coal resources of the United States; to stabilize bituminous coal mining industry and to promote interstate commerce; to promulgate a bituminous coal code; and to study and report upon problems confronting bituminous coal industry. Abolished by Reorg. Plan II of 1939 and functions transferred to Bituminous Coal Division, Department of the Interior effective July 1, 1939.

National Commission on Technology, Automation, and Economic Progress: A temporary fourteen-member public body, established by Act of Congress in August 1964, to study the effects and pace of technological change in the United States and to make recommendations for public and private action to promote technological improvement and to facilitate adjustments thereto.

National Consumers League: Formed in the early twentieth century, the League fought for minimum-wage laws, strict enforcement of factory laws, and the outlawing of sweatshops.

National Council on Indian Opportunity: Established by EO 11399 of Mar. 6, 1968, as amended by act of Nov. 26, 1969 (83 Stat. 220; 25 U.S.C. prec. 1 note), EO 11551 of Aug. 11, 1970, and EO 11688 of Dec. 1, 1972, to encourage and coordinate the use of Federal programs to benefit the American Indian population, to appraise the impact and progress of such programs, and to suggest ways to improve them to fit the needs and desires of the Indian population. Terminated on Nov. 26, 1974, under the provisions of section 2 of the act.

National Defense Mediation Board: Established by EO 8716 of Mar. 19, 1941, to settle labor disputes which threatened to obstruct production or transportation of equipment or materials essential to national defense. Ceased to exist upon creation of National War Labor Board by EO 9017 of Jan. 12, 1942.

National Emergency Dispute: A term used in the Labor-Management Relations (Taft-Hartley) Act to designate an actual or threatened strike or lockout which may imperil the national health or safety. If such a possibility exists in the opinion of the President, he may appoint a board of inquiry to investigate the issues in the dispute. Upon receiving a report from the board, the President may direct the Attorney General to petition the appropriate district court for an 80-day injunction, during which time the board of inquiry and the National Labor Relations Board have certain functions to perform. If no settlement is reached during this cooling-off period, the parties are free to resume their dispute, and the President may recommend appropriate action to the Congress.

National Enforcement Commission (ESA): Established by General Order 18 of Economic Stabilization Administrator, effective July 30, 1952, to enforce wage or salary regulations promulgated pursuant to Defense Production Act of 1950, as amended (65 Stat. 131; 50 U.S.C. App. 2071 note). Functions transferred to the Director, Office of Defense Mobilization, and the Attorney General by EO 10494 of Oct. 14, 1953.

National Federation of Independent Unions: Formed by the merger of the Confederated Unions of America and the National Independent Union Council in 1963, this federation promotes independent unions and a loose form of affiliation among its member organizations.

National Foundation on the Arts and Humanities Act: Section 5(j) and (k) of the act provide for fair labor standards applicable to grants-in-aid by the National Endowment for the Arts.

National Indian and Native American Program: The program, under Title III of the Comprehensive Employment and Training Act, provides job training and employment opportunities for economically disadvantaged, unemployed, and underemployed Indians and others of native American descent.

National Industrial Conference Board: *See* Conference Board, The.

National Industrial Recovery Act (NIRA): Enacted early in the Roosevelt administration, June 16, 1933, the NIRA attempted to codify industry practices. Section 7A provided for the right of employees to organize and gave impetus to many organizational drives. It was declared unconstitutional in 1935.

National Industrial Recovery Board: Created by EO 6859 of Sept. 27, 1934, under authority of National Industrial Recovery Act, to exercise functions formerly conferred by Executive orders upon Administrator for Industrial Recovery. Terminated by EO 7075 of June 15, 1935.

National Institute of Labor Education (NILE): A privately financed organization conducting off-campus programs of concern to labor.

National Labor Board: Organized as an agency in 1933 to administer Section 7A of the Nationa Industrial Recovery Act.

National Labor and Reform Party: Formed in 1872 as an outgrowth of the National Labor Union (1866), the Party set up a lobby in Washington and agitated for the 8-hour day until 1886.

National Labor Relations Act (Wagner Act) (1935): The basic federal act guaranteeing workers the right to organize and bargain collectively through representatives of their own choosing. It also defined "unfair labor practices" as regards employers. It was amended by the Labor-Management Relations Act of 1947 and the Labor-Management Reporting and Disclosure Act of 1959.

National Labor Relations Board (NLRB): The agency was created by the National Labor Relations Act, 1935, and continued through subsequent amendments. Its functions are to define appropriate bargaining units, to hold elections to determine whether a majority of workers want to be represented by a specific union or no union, to certify unions to represent employees, to interpret and apply the act's provisions prohibiting certain employer and union unfair practices, and otherwise to administer the provisions of the act. (*See* Labor-Management Relations Act.)

National Labor Union: Organized immediately following the Civil War, the Union made the 8-hour day its central goal. It urged a public bureau of labor statistics. Composed of representatives from various labor organizations, the Union at one time represented 600,000 workers.

National Longshoremen's Labor Board: EO 6748 of June 26, 1934, created Board in Department of Labor to deal with longshoremen's strike on Pacific coast. Abolished by Proc. 2120 of Mar. 11, 1935.

National Mediation Board: An agency established by the Railway Labor Act, 1926, to provide aid in settling disputes between railway and airline companies and unions over union representation, negotiation of changes in agreements, and interpretation of agreements reached through mediation.

National Migrant Worker Program: The program, defined in Title III of the Comprehensive Employment and Training Act, authorizes a broad spectrum of employment training and supportive services to help provide migrant and seasonal farm workers with year-round employment.

National Older Worker Program: A program providing work experience and training for adults with poor employment prospects. Designed for rural areas and towns, its projects concentrate on work experience and training activities. Its activities are defined in Title III of the Comprehensive Employment and Training Act.

National On-the-Job Training Program (NAT-OJT): This nationwide program, defined in Title III of the Comprehensive Employment and Training Act, is designed to develop job skills in the unemployed and underemployed, with emphasis on training the disadvantaged and Vietnam-era veterans. Contracts are made with organizations that operate on a nationwide or multiregional basis, such as trade associations, national or international labor unions, and industrial corporations.

National Planning Board (Federal Emergency Administration of Public Works): Established by Administrator of Public Works, July 30, 1933, to advise on preparation of comprehensive program of public works, through development of regional plans, surveys and research, and correlation of effort among Federal, State, and local agencies. Abolished by EO 6777 of June 30, 1934, which created National Resources Board.

National Railroad Adjustment Board (NRAB): The federal agency, established in 1934, that functions as a board of arbitration, handing down final and binding decisions on disputes arising out of grievances, or the application or interpretation of agreements, in the railroad industry (airline industry not covered). The Board is composed of thirty-four members, seventeen of whom represent and are paid by the carriers, and seventeen by national railway labor organizations.

National Railway Labor Panel: Established by EO 9172 of May 22, 1942, from which railroad emergency boards were selected to investigate and report to the President recommen-

dations for settlement of disputes between carriers and employees during war emergency. EO 9172 revoked by EO 9883 of Aug. 11, 1947.

National Recovery Administration: Established by the President on June 16, 1933, by authority of title I, National Industrial Recovery Act (48 Stat. 194) to administer industrial recovery provisions of that title. All provisions of title I of National Industrial Recovery Act, delegating powers to the President to approve or prescribe codes of fair competition and providing for enforcement of such codes, repealed by Public Resolution 26, approved June 14, 1935 (49 Stat. 375). The resolution also provided for extension of NRA in skeletonized form until Apr. 1, 1936.

Office of Administrator, National Recovery Administration, created by EO 7075 of June 15, 1935, to provide for continuing administration of title I, National Industrial Recovery Act. National Recovery Administration and Office of Administrator terminated by EO 7252 of Dec. 21, 1935, which transferred Division of Review, Division of Business Cooperation, and Advisory Council of NRA to Department of Commerce, directing Secretary of Commerce to terminate their functions and duties by Apr. 1, 1936. The order also transferred Consumers' Division of NRA to Department of Labor.

National Recovery Review Board: Established by EO 6632 of Mar. 7, 1934, to report to the President whether any code of fair competition approved under authority of title I of National Industrial Recovery Act was designed to promote monopoly or to eliminate small enterprise, and to recommend to the President changes in approved codes which would rectify or eliminate such results. Abolished by EO 6771 of June 30, 1934, having completed functions for which established.

National Representative: *See* International Representative.

National Resources Planning Board: By virtue of a public resolution approved June 7, 1939 (53 Stat. 813; 5 U.S.C. 133s note, 133t note), National Resources Planning Board was established in Executive Office of the President, effective July 1, 1939, by Reorg. Plan I, which abolished National Resources Committee and Federal Employment Stabilization Office in the Department of Commerce and transferred all functions, personnel (except members of National Resources Committee), property, and records of the two agencies to new Board. EO 8248, of Sept. 8, 1939, authorized Board to collect, prepare, and make available to the President, with recommendations, such plans, data, and information as may be helpful to a planned development and use of national resources. EO 8455, of June 26, 1940, imposed on Board certain duties in cooperation with Bureau of the Budget for development of the 6-year program of Federal public works. Act approved June 26, 1943 (57 Stat. 169; 5 U.S.C. 133t note), abolished National Resources Planning Board, effective Aug. 31, 1943, and authorized Director to wind up affairs by Jan. 1, 1944.

National Right-to-Work Committee: A private organization in opposition to the union shop, it promotes state right-to-work laws and supports Section 14(b) of the Taft-Hartley Act.

National Summer Youth Sports Program: A program under the Community Services Administration that provides disadvantaged youth opportunities to participate in sports activities on college and university campuses during the summer.

National Union: Ordinarily, a union composed of a number of affiliated local unions. The Bureau of Labor Statistics, in its union directory, defines a national union as one with agreements with different employers in more than one state, or an affiliate of the AFL-CIO, or a national organization of government employees. (Cf. International Union.)

National Urban League: Formed in 1918 with primary

emphasis on the problems of black workers, the League urges pertinent legislation against job discrimination and works for programs eliminating race barriers to employment and promotional opportunities.

National Wage Stabilization Board: Established within Department of Labor by EO 9672 of Dec. 31, 1945, which terminated National War Labor Board. Functions included stabilization of wages and salaries and settlement of certain labor disputes. Terminated by EO 9809 of Dec. 12, 1946, effective Feb. 24, 1947, and functions transferred to Secretary of Labor and Department of the Treasury.

National War Labor Board: Established within Office for Emergency Management by EO 9017 of Jan. 12, 1942, to assume duties of National Defense Mediation Board, established by EO 8716 of Mar. 19, 1941. Empowered to act as final arbiter of wartime labor disputes and to control adjustments of wages and of salaries under $5,000 a year, with certain exceptions. EO 9617 of Sept. 19, 1945, transferred Board to Department of Labor to be administered as an organizational entity under supervision of Secretary of Labor. Terminated Dec. 31, 1945, by EO 9672, which established the National Wage Stabilization Board.

National Youth Administration: Established within Works Progress Administration by EO 7086 of June 26, 1935, under authority of Emergency Relief Appropriation Act of 1935 (48 Stat. 115), to provide work training for unemployed youth and part-time employment for needy students. Transferred to Federal Security Agency by Reorg. Plan I, effective July 1, 1939. Transferred to War Manpower Commission by EO 9247 of Sept. 17, 1942, where it functioned within Bureau of Training. Act approved July 12, 1943 (57 Stat. 539; 15 U.S.C. 728, par. 26), provided for liquidation of National Youth Administration.

NAT-OJT: *See* National On-the-Job Training Program.

Needle Trades: The trades involved in the manufacture of clothing, including suits, dresses, coats, undergarments, millinery, lace, embroidery, skirts, and caps.

Negative Income Tax: A proposed measure to supplement family incomes that are below a fixed level. Families at a poverty or zero level would pay no income tax; families with incomes below this zero level would receive some income from the federal government.

Negotiation: *See* Collective Bargaining.

"Neither" Vote: A vote indicating that the voter wants to reject both of two unions seeking to represent workers under an appropriate law. The voter casts his or her ballot by checking the box marked "Neither" on the ballot.

Nepotism: The granting of favors to relatives in regard to employment or promotion.

New Careers: The concept for change that calls for permanent upward mobility as an essential part of manpower development programs.

New Deal: A term describing the changes instituted during the early years of the Roosevelt Administration.

New Harmony: A socialist utopian community established by Robert Owen in 1825 at New Harmony, Indiana.

New Lanark: The model community of textile workers established by Robert Owen in Scotland at the beginning of the nineteenth century, widely known for their excellent working and living conditions as well as their high wages.

Newlands Act (1913):   The statute that created the United States Board of Mediation and Conciliation for the settlement of disputes between employers an employees engaged in inter-

state transportation. The Newlands Act replaced the Erdman Act of 1898.

NICB: *See* Conference Board, The.

Night Premium: Extra compensation paid for work done during evening and night shifts.

Night Shift: *See* Shift.

NILE: *See* National Institute of Labor Education.

NIRA: *See* National Industrial Recovery Act.

NLRA: *See* National Labor Relations Act.

NLRB: *See* National Labor Relations Board.

No-Contract Policy: The policy of a union whose members refuse to work following the expiration of a contract, even though negotiations for a new contract are still continuing.

No-Man's Land: The area of labor relations that falls between the jurisdiction of federal and state agencies and/or laws.

No-Raiding Agreement: *See* Raiding.

Nonoperating Union: In the railroad industry, a labor organization of those workers who do not directly operate the railroads, such as porters, clerks, and telegraphers.

Nonproduction Bonus: An extra payment to employees which depends on factors other than the output of the individual worker, such as profit-sharing, safety, attendance, and Christmas bonuses. (See Bonus Plan; Production Bonus.)

Normal Retirement: *See* Retirement.

Normal Retirement Age: In technical terms, the earliest age at which a worker under a pension plan may retire voluntarily and receive the full amount of benefits to which he or she is entitled under the normal benefit formula of the plan. In most plans and under social security, this age is 65 years.

Norris-LaGuardia Act: *See* Anti-Injunction Law.

No-Strike, No-Lockout Clause: A provision in a collective bargaining agreement through which the union agrees not to strike and the employer agrees not to lock out employees for the duration of the contract. These pledges may be hedged by certain qualifications, e.g., the union may strike if the employer violates the agreement.

No-Suit Clause: A clause in a labor agreement committing the employer not to file a lawsuit against the union during the life of the contract.

NRAB: *See* National Railroad Adjustment Board.

OASDHI: *See* Old-Age Survivors, Disability, and Health Insurance.

Objections: As defined by the National Labor Relations Board: Any party to an election may file objections alleging that the conduct either of the election or of a party to the election failed to meet the Board's standards. An election will be set aside if eligible employee-voters have not been given an adequate opportunity to cast their ballots in secrecy and without hindrance from fear or other interference with the expression of their free choice.

OCB: *See* Office of Collective Bargaining.

Occupational Rates: Wage rates (single or rate ranges) for particular occupations in an establishment, industry, or area.

Occupational Safety and Health Act of 1970: *See* Occupational Safety and Health Administration.

Occupational Safety and Health Administration (OSHA): This federal agency, established pursuant to the Occupational Safety and Health Act of 1970, develops and promulgates occupational safety and health standards; develops and issues regulations; conducts investigations and inspections to determine the status of compliance with safety and health standards and regulations; and issues citations and proposes penalties for noncompliance with safety and health standards and regulations.

Occupational Safety and Health Review Commission: An independent adjudicatory agency established by the Occupational Safety and Health Act of 1970 to adjudicate enforcement actions initiated under the act that are contested by employers, employees, or employees' representatives.

Office of Aging (HEW): Established by Secretary on June 2, 1955, as Special Staff on Aging to conduct review and analysis of program needs, activities, and accomplishments in the field of aging. Abolished Sept. 30, 1965, and functions assumed by the Administration on Aging.

Office for Civil Rights: The bureau, in the Department of Health, Education, and Welfare, is responsible for the administration and enforcement of departmental policies under title VI of the Civil Rights Act of 1964, which prohibits discrimination with regard to race, color, or national origin in programs and activities receiving Federal financial assistance; titles VII and IX of the Education Amendments of 1972; sections 799A and 845 of the Comprehensive Health Manpower and Nurse Training Acts of 1971; section 504 of the Rehabilitation Act of 1973; and Executive Order 11246, as amended, which prohibits discrimination with regard to race, religion, color, sex, or national origin by employers holding Federal contracts.

Office of Collective Bargaining (OCB): An agency of the City of New York, created by agreement between the City and the major unions of the City's employees. It operates through the Board of Collective Bargaining and the Board of Certification to supervise labor relations between the City and its employees.

Office of Comprehensive Employment Development (OCED): The office that provides leadership in the development and improvement of nationwide programs and delivery systems designed to provide work training and work experience opportunities for disadvantaged, unemployed, and underemployed persons. The OCED has major responsibility for implementation of the Comprehensive Employment and Training Act and the Work Incentive Program.

Office of Economic Opportunity (OEO): Established within the Executive Office of the President in 1964. In 1973, most OEO programs were transferred by administrative action to other federal agencies. (See Department of Health, Education, and Welfare, Department of Labor, and Department of Housing and Urban Development.) The three programs, the Community Action Program, the Economic Development Program, and the Legal Services Program, were transferred to the Community Services Administration in 1975.

Office of Economic Stabilization: Established within Office for Emergency Management by EO 9250 of Oct. 3, 1942, to control so far as possible inflationary tendencies and vast dislocations attendant thereon which threatened military effort and domestic economic structure. Abolished by EO 9620 of Sept. 20, 1945, and functions transferred to Office of War Mobilization and Reconversion. Reestablished within Office for Emergency Management by EO 9699 of Feb. 21, 1946. Transferred by EO 9762 of July 25, 1946, to Office of War Mobilization and Reconversion. Functions of Director transferred to Director of War Mobilization and Reconversion. Consolidated with other agencies to form Office of Temporary Controls by EO 9809 of Dec. 12, 1946.

Office of Federal Contract Compliance: The federal agency responsible for establishing policies and goals and providing leadership and coordination of the government's program to achieve nondiscrimination in employment by government contractors and subcontractors and in federally assisted construction programs.

Office of Human Development (OHD): The unit in the Department of Health, Education, and Welfare that is responsible for coordination with the Labor Department in the implementation of Comprehensive Employment and Training Administration programs and policies. It has direct responsibility for the Office of Native American Programs; the Office for Handicapped Individuals; Rehabilitation Services; and Out-of-School Programs.

Office of Manpower: The unit that coordinates HEW programs and services designed to improve employment potential and job opportunities for persons who are unemployed, underemployed, or in need of training. HEW activities that are coordinated with manpower programs of other organizations and government agencies (federal, state, and local) include vocational education, vocational rehabilitation, adult education, health manpower, paraprofessional training, and support services, including child care and health care.

Office of Native American Programs (ONAP): This office provides a departmental focus for the special concerns of American Indians, Alaskans, and native Hawaiians and helps these native Americans to achieve the goal of economic and social self-sufficiency.

Office of Price Administration: Office of Price Administration and Civilian Supply was created by EO 8734 of Apr. 11, 1941, combining Price and Consumer Divisions of National Defense Advisory Commission, to avoid inflation by stabilization of prices and rents, prevent speculation, profiteering, hoarding, and manipulation by regulating prices and pricing practices. Name changed to Office of Price Administration by EO 8875 of Aug. 28, 1941, which transferred Civilian Allocation Division to Office of Production Management. Additional legislation delegated other powers to agency, such as rationing of scarce commodities to consumers. Consolidated with other agencies into Office of Temporary Controls by EO 9809 of Dec. 12, 1946, except Financial Reporting Division, which was transferred to Federal Trade Commission.

Office of Price Stabilization (ESA): Created by General Order 2 of Economic Stabilization Administrator on Jan. 24, 1951. Director of Price Stabilization was provided for in EO 10161 of Sept 9, 1950, issued pursuant to Defense Production Act of 1950 (64 Stat. 798; 50 U.S.C. App. 2071 note). Office served to establish price ceilings to stabilize cost of living and cost of production, both civilian and military, to eliminate and prevent profiteering, hoarding, manipulation, speculation, and other disruptive practices. Terminated Apr. 30, 1953, pursuant to EO 10434 of Feb. 6, 1953, and provisions of Defense Production Act Amendments of 1952 and 1953 (66 Stat. 296, 67 Stat. 131; 50 U.S.C. App. 2166, 2071 note).

Office of Salary Stabilization (ESA): *See* Salary Stabilization Board.

Office of Vocational Rehabilitation: Created to administer the expended program of State-Federal vocational rehabilitation provided by the act of July 6, 1943 (57 Stat. 374; 29 U.S.C. 31 note). Other duties were delegated pursuant to the Vocational Rehabilitation Amendments of 1954 (68 Stat. 652) and of 1965 (79 Stat. 1282); International Health Research Act (74 Stat. 364; 22 U.S.C. 2101 note); and the Agricultural Trade Development and Assistance Act of 1954 (68 Stat. 454; 7 U.S.C. 1691 note). Redesignated Vocational Rehabilitation Administration on Jan. 28, 1963.

Office of Workers' Compensation Programs: This unit of the Department of Labor is responsible for administration of the three basic laws that provide workers' compensation for federal employees: the Federal Employees' Compensation Act, the War Hazards Compensation Act, and the War Claims Act.

OHD: *See* Office of Human Development.

OJT: *See* National On-the-Job Training Program.

Old-Age Survivors, Disability, and Health Insurance (OAS-DHI): Authorized under Title II of the Social Security Act, the program provides monthly cash benefits to retired or disabled insured workers and their dependents and to the survivors of insured workers. Within the specifications of the law, retirement benefits are payable to an aged insured worker; an insured worker's aged spouse or his spouse at any age caring for his child who is under age 18 or totally disabled; and to his child who is under age 18, totally disabled, or a full-time student under age 22. Aged workers become eligible for full benefits at age 65, although they may elect reduced benefits up to 3 years earlier; their spouses are under the same limitations. Under certain conditions, survivor benefits are payable to dependents of an insured worker, including his aged widow or his widow at any age caring for his child who is under age 18 or totally disabled; his child who is under age 18, totally disabled, or a full-time student under age 22; and his aged parents. Disability benefits are payable to insured workers under age 65 with a prolonged disability that meets the definition in the act and to their dependents on the same basis as dependents of retired workers. A lump-sum benefit is also payable on the death of an insured worker. Since July 1966, health insurance is being provided under two coordinated plans for nearly all persons age 65 or over: A hospital insurance plan which covers hospital and related services, and a voluntary supplementary medical insurance plan which covers physicians' services and related medical services. Since July 1973, the same health insurance is provided to certain severely disabled persons. Retirement, survivors, disability, and hospital insurance benefits are paid for by the contributions of workers, employers, and the self-employed on annual earnings up to a maximum taxable limit. Hospital benefits are financed out of federal general revenues for persons 65 and over with specified amounts of social security coverage less than that required for cash-benefit eligibility. The voluntary medical insurance plan is financed by premiums paid by eligible persons who choose to enroll in the plan, and by contributions by the federal government from general revenues. The money collected is deposited in federal trust funds.

Oligopoly: Control by a few sellers of the quantity and price of goods or services made available to many buyers.

Oligopsony: Control of a market by a few buyers with the power to influence the demand for goods or services.

Ombudsman: An agent of the people, a role established in Sweden over 150 years ago to represent the interests of individuals in a geographic area in their relationship with the government.

ONAP: *See* Office of Native American Programs.

On-call Time Pay: Wages paid for being ready to work (on call) rather than actually at work.

One Big Union: A concept that originated with the Western Federation of Miners at the beginning of the twentieth century, calling for the inclusion of all working people in one labor organization; an idea later adopted by the Industrial Workers of the World.

One-Thousand-Hour (1000-Hour) Clause: *See* Thousand-hour Clause.

One-Year Rule: A provision in the Taft-Hartley Act that an election for representation can be held only once in a 12-month period.

Open-end Agreement: A collective bargaining agreement with no definite termination date, usually subject to reopening for negotiations or to termination at any time upon proper notice by either party.

Open Shop: An establishment with a policy of not recognizing or dealing with a labor union. The term may sometimes be applied to an organized establishment where union membership is not a condition of employment. (*See* Union Security.)

Open Union: A union which will admit any qualified person to membership, usually upon payment of reasonable initiation fees. (Cf. Closed Union.)

Operating Union: In the railroad industry, a union of workers engaged in the physical movement of trains and cars.

Organizational Picketing: Picketing that seeks to induce an employing company to recognize a union as the bargaining agent for its employes.

Organizer (Union Organizer): The employee of a union or federation (usually paid but sometimes a volunteer) whose duties involve recruiting new members for the union, assisting in forming unions in nonunion companies, assisting in campaigns for recognition, etc.

OSHA: *See* Occupational Safety and Health Administration.

Out-of-line Rate: *See* Red-Circle Rate.

Out-of-work Benefits: Usually, payments made by a union to unemployed members.

Outlaw Strike: *See* Strike.

Output per Work-hour: *See* Productivity.

Outside Agitator: A pejorative term to describe a union organizer who is not an employee of the plant being organized.

Overtime: Work performed in excess of the basic workday or workweek, as defined by law, collective bargaining agreement, or company policy. Sometimes applied to work performed on Saturdays, Sundays, and holidays at premium rates.

Overtime-on-Overtime: Premium pay rates for Saturday, Sunday, and holiday work that were calculated into the regular rate of pay for determining the time-and-one-half provisions of the Fair Labor Standards Act (FLSA) prior to 1949. This requirement for "overtime on overtime" was upheld by the Supreme Court (*See* Bay Ridge Rule). In 1949, an amendment to the FLSA denied such calculation as the basis for overtime pay.

Overtime Pay (Premium Overtime Pay): Payment at premium rates (e.g., time and one-half, double time) for work defined as overtime. (*See* Overtime.)

Package Settlement: The total money value (usually quoted in cents per hour) of a change in wages and supplementary benefits negotiated by a union in a contract renewal or reopening.

Pact: *See* Agreement.

Paid-Absence Allowance: Payment for lost working time available to workers for various types of leave not otherwise compensated for, e.g., excused personal leave.

Paid Holidays: Days that have been established by agreement or by company policy for which workers receive their full daily pay without working. Half-day holidays are also common. Such days are those of special religious, cultural, social, or patriotic significance in which work or business ordinarily ceases.

Paid Lunch Period (Mealtime): Time allowed for eating lunch (or the mid-shift meal on late shifts), commonly 20 or 30 minutes, counted as part of the paid workday. Usually practiced where employees cannot leave their workplaces for meals (e.g., coal mining). Agreements sometimes also require the company to furnish meals when workers remain in the plant for overtime work.

Paid Vacations: Excused leave of absence of a week or more, with full pay, granted to workers annually for purposes of rest and recreation. Paid vacations are provided in private industry by collective bargaining agreements or company policy, not by law. Vacations are frequently graduated by length of service, e.g., 1 week of vacation after 1 year's service; 2 weeks after 5 years; 3 weeks after 15 years; and 4 weeks after 25 years. (*See* Extended Vacation Plan.)

Panels of Arbitrators: Lists of qualified arbitrators maintained by the American Arbitration Association, the Federal Mediation and Conciliation Service, and various state mediation boards.

Paper Locals: Local unions which exist only "on paper" (charter) with no actual membership.

Parent Union: A national or international union with which a local union is affiliated.

Parliamentary Procedure: Rules for the democratic conduct of a meeting; established to maintain order and to assist in the routine business of an organization.

Part-time Employee: A worker employed on a temporary or regular basis for a workweek substantially shorter than the scheduled week for full-time employees.

Past Practice: Existing practices in the plant or company that are sanctioned by use and acceptance. Then are not specifically included in the collective bargaining agreement, except, perhaps, by reference to their continuance.

Past Service: Under a pension plan, years of employment or credited service prior to the establishment of the plan or a change in the plan's benefits.

Patent Assignment: An agreement that the rights to a patent for any new process will belong to the employer and not to the individual who developed the patent.

Paternalism: A derogatory terms to describe the fatherly interest of an employer in his or her workers.

Pattern Bargaining: Follow-the-leader negotiating practices in an industry. (*See* Wage Pattern.)

Pay-as-you-go: *See* Unfunded Plan.

Pay Board: *See* Economic Stabilization Program.

Pay-in-Lieu-of-Notice: The payment which, by prior agreement on giving advance notice of layoff, the employer is required to pay workers for the full notice period as a penalty for failure to give notice, or which permits the employer the choice of giving notice or making payment.

Payment in Kind: Also known as the *truck system*. Payment of wages in goods or services, rather than money. Mainly associated with the company store and company housing, where the employer owns the store from which all employees are required to purchase their food, clothing, and supplies, or owns houses in which they are required to live.

Payment by Results: *See* Incentive Wage System.

Payroll Deductions: Amounts withheld from employees' earnings by the employer for social security, federal income taxes, and other governmental levies; they also may include union dues, group insurance premiums, and other authorized wage assignments.

Payroll Period: Frequency with which workers' wages are calculated and paid, usually weekly, biweekly, or semimonthly.

PBGC: *See* Pension Benefit Guaranty Corporation.

Peace Corps: Established as an agency of the Department of State by EO 10924 of Mar. 1, 1961, and continued in existence under the Peace Corps Act (75 Stat. 612; 22 U.S.C. 2501 et seq.) pursuant to EO 11041 of Aug. 6, 1962. Functions, powers, and responsibilities transferred to ACTION by Reorg. Plan 1 of 1971, effective July 1, 1971.

Peg Points (Benchmarks): Occupational rates for key unskilled, semiskilled, or skilled jobs, used to establish wage rates for other jobs by comparison.

Penalty Rate: Extra rate paid for particularly hazardous or onerous work. The term is at times applied to any premium or overtime rate. (*See* Hazard Pay; Premium Pay.)

Pension Benefit Guaranty Corporation (PBGC): A federal agency, established under Title IV of the Employee Retirement Income Security Act of 1974 (ERISA), approved September 2, 1974, to guarantee payment of insured benefits if covered plans terminate without sufficient assets to pay such benefits.

Pension Office: The act of Mar. 2, 1833 (4 Stat. 668) provided for a Commissioner of Pensions. Continued by act of Mar. 3, 1835 (4 Stat. 779), and other acts as the Office of the Commissioner of Pensions until the act of Mar. 3, 1849 (9 Stat. 395; 5 U.S.C. 481), established the Department of the Interior and transferred the Office of the new Department where it became a bureau. EO 5398 of July 21, 1930, consolidated the Bureau of Pensions along with other bureaus and agencies to form the Veterans Administration.

Pension Plan (Retirement Plan; Group Annuity Plan; Annuity): Any plan whose primary purpose is to provide regular payments for life to employees upon retirement. Additional benefits are often provided. The term *private pension plans* is often used to distinguish voluntary plans from the social security system. If the employee shares in the cost, the plan is *contributory;* if the cost is borne entirely by the employer, the plan is *noncontributory.* A *group annuity plan* is a pension plan underwritten and administered by an insurance company. A *trusteed plan* is noninsured; contributions are deposited with a bank, trust company, or board of trustees that administers the program. *Deposit administration* means that the insurance company assumes the role of trustee, as above. With a *money-purchase plan,* fixed contributions are made to the worker's account, with the pension thus determined by the amount contributed.

Permit Card (Work Permit): A card issued by a union permitting a nonmember to accept or retain employment on a temporary basis in a union shop or on a union job.

Perquisites: Food, lodging, or other services and merchandise regularly given to workers by an employer in addition to monetary compensation.

Personal Leave: Excused leave granted for reasons important to the individual worker, e.g., for getting married, but not otherwise provided for.

Personalized Rate: *See* Red-Circle Rate.

Personnel Administration: The area of management in which an employer, public or private, works to achieve the most effective use of employees and materials.

Pertrillo Act: *See* Lea Act.

Petroleum Labor Policy Board: On Oct. 10, 1933, Planning and Coordination Committee recommended in a letter to Secretary of the Interior, who was Administrator of Code of Fair Competition for Petroleum Industry, that a bipartisan labor advisory board be established to aid him in supervision and enforcement of labor provisions of petroleum code. Administrator approved the recommendation and established a board of seven members. Acting on recommendation of Solicitor of Department of the Interior, Administrator on Dec. 19, 1933, reorganized Petroleum Labor Policy Board by making it nonpartisan. By order of Mar. 8, 1935, Administrator confirmed creation of this board. Terminated on Mar. 31, 1936, when Petroleum Administrative Board was abolished by EO 7076 of June 15, 1935.

Philadelphia Plan: Issued in 1967 pursuant to Executive Order No. 11246, the plan required employers with government contracts to submit an acceptable affirmative action program for the employment of minorities in the construction industry.

Picketing: Patrolling near the employer's place of business by union members (pickets) to publicize the existence of a labor dispute, persuade workers to join the union or the strike, discourage customers from buying or using the employer's goods or service, etc. *Organizational picketing* is picketing carried on by the union for the purpose of persuading employees to join the union or authorize the union to represent them. *Recognitional picketing* is picketing to compel the employer to recognize the union as the exclusive bargaining agent for employees. *Informational picketing* is picketing directed toward informing the public that an employer does not employ members of, or have a contract with, a union.

Piece Rate: A predetermined amount paid per unit of output to workers under a piecework incentive plan.

Piecework: A method of wage payment based on the number of units produced, or any work for which piece rates are paid.

Pinkerton: An employee of the Pinkerton Detective Agency. Established in the 1870s, the agency in its early years was an antiunion strikebreaking company. It now supplies plant police to protect industrial property.

Plans for Progress: *See* President's Committee on Equal Employment Opportunity.

Plant Unit: A bargaining unit of the employees within a single plant.

Plumb Plan: A program put forward in 1919 by the Railroad Brotherhoods for the government ownership and control of the railroad industry.

Plurality: In an election, an excess of votes over those cast for any other candidate for the same office, especially over those cast for the closest opponent.

P.M. (Premium Money; Push Money): An additional payment to induce retail sales people to push the sale of items on which the profit is large, to dispose of slow-moving items, or to stimulate a sales promotion campaign.

Pork-chopper: A sometimes humorous or pejorative word used to describe a paid employee of a union.

Portable Pension: An arrangement under which credits earned toward a pension can be carried from company to company, so that workers who have had more than one employer will have all their years of service credited toward their pensions.

Portal-to-Portal Act of 1947: A statute setting limits on the claims of workers arising under the Fair Labor Standards Act of 1938 as amended, the Walsh-Healey Act, or the Davis-Bacon Act.

Portal-to-Portal Pay: Payment for time spent in traveling to and from the plant or mine entrance to the working site, or, conceptually, for all time in the plant rather than merely time at the workplace.

Postal Reorganization Act of 1970: A law subjecting the employee-management relations of the U.S. Postal Service to those provisions of the National Labor Relations Act, as amended, which are not inconsistent with the Postal Reorganization Act.

Posting: *See* Job Posting.

Preferential Hiring: An agreed-upon arrangement whereby the employer gives preference in hiring to union members, to applicants with previous training and experience in the industry, to workers displaced from another plant or from another part of a particular plant, or, by order of the National Labor Relations Board, to employees found to be discriminatorily discharged.

Preferential Shop: An establishment which, by agreement with a union, gives preference in hiring to union members over equally qualified nonunion members.

Premium Overtime Pay: *See* Overtime Pay.

Premium Pay: Compensation at more than the regular rate. The term may refer to overtime, shift differentials, or penalty rates.

Prentice-Hall, Inc.: A major private publisher with an information-gathering service covering developments in the field of labor and management relations.

President's Advisory Committee on Labor-Management Policy: A committee established by Executive Order No. 10918 of February 16, 1961, to study, and to advise and make, recommendations to the president on policies that might be followed by labor, management, or the public which would promote free and responsible collective bargaining, industrial peace, sound wage and price policies, higher standards of living, and increased productivity. Abolished by Executive Order No. 11710 in 1973.

President's Commission on the Status of Women: Established by EO 10980 of Dec. 14, 1961, to review progress and make recommendation for constructive action to overcome discrimination in Government and private employment on the basis of sex. Submitted its final report to the President on Oct. 11, 1963.

President's Committee on Employment of the Handicapped: A long-standing federal government committee whose purpose is to encourage the development of maximum employment opportunities for the handicapped. Established by EO 10640 of Oct. 10, 1955, continuing the Committee established pursuant to act of July 11, 1949 (63 Stat. 409), to facilitate development of maximum employment opportunities for physically and mentally handicapped. Superseded by President's Committee on Employment of the Handicapped established by EO 10994 of Feb. 14, 1962.

President's Committee on Equal Employment Opportunity (Plans for Progress): A committee set up by President Kennedy in March 1961 to study employment practices of the U.S. government and to recommend steps to be taken by executive departments and agencies to promote nondiscrimination in employment in the federal government, with government contractors, and on federally assisted construction projects. *Plans for Progress* is a program under which participating companies actively engage in increasing opportunities for equal employment, going beyond the requirements of the Executive orders enforced by the Committee. Abolished and functions transferred to Department of Labor and U.S. Civil Service Commission by EO 11246 of Sept. 24, 1965.

President's Committee on Government Employment Policy: Established by EO 10590 of Jan. 18, 1955, to advise the President concerning conformity of department and agency personnel practices with nondiscrimination policy specified by order. Abolished by EO 10925 of Mar. 6, 1961, and functions transferred to President's Committee on Equal Employment Opportunity.

President's Committee on Manpower: Established by EO 11152 of Apr. 15, 1964, to assist in carrying out Federal functions under the Manpower Development and Training Act of 1962 (76 Stat. 23; 42 U.S.C. 2571), as amended. Terminted by EO 11515 of Mar. 13, 1970.

President's Committee on Migratory Labor: Appointed by letter of the President, Aug. 26, 1954; formally established by EO 10894 of Nov. 15, 1960, to assess needs of migratory workers and stimulate programs toward improving their living and working conditions. Terminated Jan. 6, 1964, by the Secretary of Labor, by letter to the members, with approval of the President.

President's Council on Aging: Established by EO 11022 of May 14, 1962, to maintain a continuing review and coordination of Federal activities on aging. Inactive.

President's Council on Equal Opportunity: Established by EO 11197 of Fab. 5, 1965, to assist Federal departments and agencies to coordinate civil rights programs and activities, and to recommend to the President policies, programs, actions, and changes in law as will promote the purposes of the Civil Rights Acts of 1957 and 1964 and other Federal laws relating to civil rights. Abolished by EO 11247 of Sept. 24, 1965, and functions transferred to the Attorney General.

President's Council on Youth Opportunity: Established by EO 11330 of Mar. 5, 1967, to coordinate youth opportunity programs of employment, education, recreation, and health services. Inactive as of June 30, 1971.

Prevailing Rate (Going Rate): The term has no precise statistical meaning in ordinary usage. It may refer to average level of wages paid by employers for specific occupations in a community or area; or rate most commonly paid; or rate paid to most workers; or rate established by union contracts.

Prevailing Wage Law (Davis-Bacon Act), 1931: A federal act requiring the payment of prevailing wage rates in the locality on construction, alteration, or repair of public buildings, or public works performed under contract with the federal government. The law was amended in 1964 to include certain payments for fringe benefits as part of the prevailing rate.

Preventive Mediation: A function of the Federal Mediation and Conciliation Service involving the development of procedures by union and management designed to anticipate and to study potential problems. This function may take the form of early entry into labor disputes before a strike threatens.

Price Commission: *See* Economic Stabilization Program.

Price List: A listing of piece prices or rates to be paid for piecework, usually established by company-union negotiation.

Prima Facie Evidence: Evidence which on its first appearance is sufficient to establish a fact.

Primary Boycott: A boycott against a particular establishment without involving its customers or other organizations with which it has a relationship.

Probationary Period: Usually a stipulated period of time (e.g., 30 days) during which a newly hired employee is on trial prior to establishing seniority or otherwise becoming a regular employee. Sometimes used in relation to discipline, e.g., a period during which a regular employee, gulity of misbehavior, is on trial. *A probationary employee* is a worker in a probationary period. Where informal probation is the practice, a worker who has not yet attained the status of regular employee may be called a *temporary employee*. (Cf. Regular Employee.)

Probationary Rate: A trial rate of pay for an experienced and otherwise qualified worker during the initial period of employment on a new job or in a new plant.

Proceeding: As defined by the National Labor Relations Board, one or more cases included in a single litigated action. A proceeding may be a combination of C (unfair labor practice) and R (representation) cases consolidated for the purposes of a hearing.

Production Bonus: Extra payment directly related to the output of an individual worker or a group of workers. (Cf. Bonus Plan; Nonproduction Bonus.)

Production Standards: Usually, the expected output of a worker or group of workers that is consistent with the quality of work, efficiency of operations, and the reasonable working capacities of normal operators.

Production Workers: Usually, employees directly involved in manufacturing or operational processes, as distinguished from supervisory, sales, executive, and office employees. The term *production and related workers* as used in federal government statistics is usually specifically defined for survey purposes.

Productivity (Output per Man-Hour): A measurement of efficiency of production; in technical terms, as in measuring rate of change, usually stated as a ratio of units of output to a unit of input, e.g., 10 units per labor hour.

Productivity Factor: *See* Annual Improvement Factor.

Professional Employee: An employee whose work is non-repetitive and demands a high degree of discretion and judgment. The professional status is generally the result of formal education.

Profit-sharing Plan: Any procedure under which an employer pays the firm's employees, in addition to their regular pay, a share of the profits of the business as a whole. Under a *deferred profit-sharing plan*, a share of profits is set aside in a fund to be distributed at some later date, usually when the employee retires (a form of retirement plan).

Progression System: *See* Wage Progression.

Protocol: The treaty of peace between the manufacturers and the International Ladies Garment Workers Union following a severe strike in 1919 in New York City. The treaty provided for a 50-hour week, preferential shop, final arbitration of disputes by a board of arbitration composed of one member chosen from each side and an impartial chairmperson selected by both parties.

Public Contracts Act (Walsh-Healey Act), (1936): The act prescribing basic labor standards for work done on U.S. government contracts exceeding $10,000 in value for materials, articles, supplies, equipment, and naval vessels. The Secretary of Labor is authorized to determine prevailing minimum wages in the industry. The act, among other stipulations, provides for daily and weekly overtime and health and safety standards.

Public Employee: One working for federal, state, or local government.

Public Employees' Fair Employment Act (Taylor Law): Passed in New York State on April 21, 1967, the law regulates labor relations between unions and public employers in the state. Strikes are prohibited, with penalties to be levied against the employees and the unions in the event of strikes.

Public Employment Program (PEP): A program under Title II of the Comprehensive Employment and Training Act, which is designed to provide unemployed and underemployed persons with transitional employment in needed public service jobs during periods of high unemployment. The program allows state and local governments to fulfill public needs that cannot be met without federal assistance because of lack of local funds.

Public Review Boards: Institutions set up in the United Automobile Workers Union and in the American Federation of Teachers. The boards are composed of prestigious individuals who are not connected with the union but who exercise authority in any complaint made by a member against a local or the international union.

Public Works Administration (PWA): Established in June 1933 under the National Industrial Recovery Act, with $3 billion for the construction of highways, waterways, public building, hospitals, public housing projects, and other projects. The PWA operated through private contractors and functioned until 1939.

Pull: A slang word for influence.

Pullman Strike (1894): The strike begun by employees of the Pullman Car Company in Pullman, Illinois, to resist wage cuts and layoffs and supported by the American Railway Union, which refused to handle Pullman cars or equipment. Federal troops were called in over the objection of Illinois Governor Altgeld and an injunction was granted against the union and its president, Eugene Victor Debs. Debs was jailed and the strike was broken. This strike marked the first use of the labor injunction in a major labor dispute under the Sherman Antitrust Law.

PWA: *See* Public Works Administration.

Pyramiding: Double payment of overtime rates for overtime work. It may result from paying both daily and weekly overtime rates for the same hours of work; sometimes applied to any premium added to another premium rate.

Quickie Strike: *See* Strike.

Quit: Voluntary termination of employment initiated by an employee, as distinguished from a dismissal or layoff which is involuntary.

Quit Rate: A statistical term expressing the ratio of quits to the number of employees during a stated period.

Quorum: The number of persons necessary at a meeting before business can be legally conducted; the precise number (or ratio) is usually stated in local union bylaws.

Quota: The production necessary to earn a base rate of wages for an individual or a group.

R Cases: *See* Types of Cases.

Racial Discrimination: A policy of hiring, promoting, disciplining, laying off, or maintaining differentials in pay or work assignment based upon race.

Racketeering: In labor, the use of extortion or bribery to maintain labor peace; the use of a union office to enrich oneself.

Radius Clause: An agreement of an individual entering a training program not to work for other employers in a specified geographical area.

Raiding (No-Raiding Agreement): A union's attempt to enroll members belonging to another union or already covered by a collective bargaining agreement negotiated by another union, with the intent to usurp the union's bargaining relationship. A *no-raiding agreement* is a written pledge, signed by two unions or more, to abstain from raiding; applicable only to signatory unions.

Rail Passenger Service Act of 1970: An act that established a program to provide federal assistance to certain railroads to permit the orderly transfer of railroad passenger service to a railroad passenger corporation. Among its pertinent provisions, Section 565(b) specifies that no contract between a railroad and the corporation may be made unless the Secretary of Labor has certified that fair and equitable arrangements have been made to protect the interest of employees of such railroads. The protective arrangements specified in Section 565 of the act are identical to those prescribed under the Urban Mass Transportation Act.

Railroad Adjustment Board: *See* National Railroad Adjustment Board.

Railroad and Airline Wage Board: Established by General Order 7, of Sept. 27, 1951, as revised, of the Economic Stabilization Administrator, pursuant to section 403 of Defense Production Act of 1950, as amended (64 Stat. 816, as amended; 50 U.S.C. App. 2061), to determine substantive policies necessary to carry out wage and salary stabilization program with respect to employees subject to Railway Labor Act, as amended. Terminated Apr. 30, 1953, pursuant to EO 10434 of Feb. 6, 1953, and Defense Production Act Amendments of 1952 and 1953 (66 Stat. 296, 67 State. 131, 50 U.S.C. App. 2166, 2071 note).

Railroad Brotherhoods: The major labor unions in the railroad industry.

Railroad Retirement Act of 1935: A federal act establishing a nationwide program providing railroad employees with retirement benefits (old-age, disability, and survivors' benefits) based on the individual worker's earnings and length of service in the railroad industry. Railroad workers are not covered by the Social Security Act.

Railroad Retirement Board: The Board administers retirement-survivor and unemployment-sickness benefit programs provided by federal laws for the nation's railroad workers and their families. Under the Railroad Retirement Act, annuities are paid by the Board to rail employees with at least 10 years of service who retire because of age or disability and to their eligible spouses. When other requirements are met, annuities are also provided to the survivors of deceased employees. These retirement-survivor benefit programs are closely coordinated with social security benefit programs and include Medicare health insurance coverage. Under the Railroad Unemployment Insurance Act, biweekly benefits are payable by the Board to workers with qualifying railroad earnings who become unemployed or sick. About 100 field offices are maintained across the country.

Railway Employees Department: *See* AFL-CIO, Departments of.

Railway Labor Act: The act governing the labor relations of railroads and airlines and their employees; it provides for the establishment of the National Mediation Board and the National Railroad Adjustment Board. The act, pased in 1926, was amended in 1934, 1936, 1940, 1951, 1964, and 1966.

Rand Award: The award handed down by the Canadian Supreme Court in 1946 in a dispute between the Ford Motor Company and its workers. It granted an agency shop.

Rand Formula: *See* Mohawk Valley Formula.

Rand School of Social Science: A school for workers' education founded in New York City in 1906 under an endowment by Carrie A. Rand. Its courses, including subject matter of interest to trade unionists and Marxism, reflected the democratic socialism of its directors, the American Socialist Society. It ceased to exist in the late 1940s.

Rank and File: Members of an organization exclusive of officers and employees of the organization.

Rat: A pejorative term to describe a worker whose activties are inimical to those of the union in its relationship with management.

Rate Cutting: A reduction by management of established incentive or time wage rates in the absence of comparable changes in job content, or any actions by companies in reducing wages.

Rate Range: Two rates of pay or more for the same job, with the specific rates of individual workers at or between the bottom and the top rates determined by merit, length of service, or a combination of the two.

Rate Setting: The process of establishing wage or piece rates for a job or operation.

Ratification: Formal approval of a newly negotiated agreement by vote of the union members affected.

RC Case: Under National Labor Relations Board procedures, a petition by, or in behalf of, employees under Section 9(c)(1)(A)(i) of the National Labor Relations Act:

9(c)(1)(A)(i) Alleging that a substantial number of employees wish to be represented for collective bargaining and their employer declines to recognize their representative. (*See* Types of Cases.)

RD Case: Under National Labor Relations Board procedures, a petition by, or in behalf of, employees under Section 9(c)(1)(A)(ii) of the National Labor Relations Act:

9(c)(1)(A)(ii) Alleging that a substantial number of employees assert that the certified or currently recognized bargaining representative is no longer their representative. (*See* Types of Cases.)

Real Wages: The purchasing power of money wages, or the amount of goods and services that can be acquired with money wages. An index of real wages takes into account changes over time in earnings levels and in price levels as measured by an appropriate index, e.g., the Consumer Price Index.

Recall: The process of bringing laid-off employees back to work, usually based on the same principles that governed the order of layoff in inverse order (e.g., last worker laid off is first to be recalled). In union affairs, recall is a procedure for removing (disciplining) an officer by means of a membership vote.

Recognition: *See* Union Recognition.

Recognition Picketing: Picketing with the purpose of forcing the employer to acknowledge that the union represents the employees and to bargain with it on wages and working conditions.

Red-Circle Rate (Out-of-Line Rate; Personalized Rate; Flagged Rate): A rate of pay higher than the contractual, or formally established, rate for a job. The special rate is usually attached to the incumbent worker, not to the job as such. This procedure is commonly used to protect long-service workers from a decline in earnings through no fault of their own.

Red International of Labor Unions (RILU): An organization formed in 1920 by communist-dominated unions in the Soviet Union and Western Europe to act as the political arm of the Third International (Communist International).

Red Union: One dominated by communists.

Reduction in Force: *See* Layoff.

Referee: An arbitrator permanently assigned to resolve disputes between an employer and a union.

Referendum: A process by which all members of a union vote, usually as individuals, for the election of officers, changes in union constitution, etc., as distinguished from decision making through delegates assembled in convention.

Refusal to Bargain: A finding that either party to contract negotiations has not carried out its obligations under the Labor-Management Relations Act to bargain collectively in good faith.

Regional Director: An official of a federal agency or a labor union having jurisdiction and/or administrative responsibilities in a specified geographic area.

Registration Requirements: Regulations under the Labor-Management Reporting and Disclosure Act of 1959 requiring unions and employers to file specified information.

Regular Employee: Usually, a full-time employee who has fulfilled formal or informal probationary requirements, as distinguished from seasonal, part-time, probationary, and temporary employees. (*See* Probationary Period.)

Regular Rate: Usually, basic rate of pay or the straight-time rate. The Fair Labor Standards Act defines "regular rate of pay" for overtime pay computations; collective bargaining agreements also usually define the term for calculation purposes (vacation pay, overtime, etc.).

Rehabilitation Services Administration (RSA): A component in the Social and Rehabilitation Service in the Department of Health, Education, and Welfare since 1967. Primarily, RSA supports the state-federal program of vocational rehabilitation services. It provides leadership in the planning, coordination, and development of programs of services for the handicapped, including disabled social security applicants.

Rehire: As a verb, to reemploy a worker previously separated. As a noun, a former employee returned to his or her job as a new employee.

Relief Time (Spellout): Time during which a worker is permitted to leave his or her workplace, usually for personal needs, with that place being taken by a substitute when necessary. (*See* Rest Period.)

Relocation Allowance (Moving Allowance): Payment to workers of all or part of their expenses in moving to a new location, or a fixed allowance to be used for this purpose.

Renewal Clause: In a labor agreement, a provision that the contract is to continue automatically beyond an anniversary date unless notice to reopen is given by one of the participants.

Reopening Clause (Wage Reopener): A clause in a collective bargaining agreement stating the time or the circumstances under which negotiations can be requested prior to the expiration of the contract. Reopenings are usually restricted to wage issues and, perhaps, other specified economic issues, not to the contract as a whole.

Reporting Pay: Minimum pay guaranteed to a worker who is scheduled to work, reports for work, and finds no work available, or less work than can be done in the guaranteed period (usually 4 hours). Sometimes identified as *call-in pay*. (*See* Call-in Pay.)

Representation Cases: As defined by the National Labor Relations Board, cases designated as RC, RM, or RD. (*See* R Cases under Types of Cases, this glossary, for specific definitions of these terms.) All three types of cases are included in the term *representation*, which deals generally with the problem of which union, if any, shall represent employees in negotiations with their employer. The cases are initiated by the filing of a petition by a union, an employer, or a group of employees.

Representation Election: As defined by the National Labor Relations Board: an election by secret ballot conducted by the Board among the employees in an appropriate collective bargaining unit to determine whether the employees wish to be represented by a particular labor organization for purposes of collective bargaining.

Representation Hearing: Procedures for the determination of whether a union represents sufficient employees in a bargaining unit to warrant its recognition as the bargaining agent.

Rerum Novarum: An encyclical issued in 1891 by Pope Leo XIII expressing the attitude of the church on labor-management questions.

Rest Period (Coffee Break; Break Time): A brief interruption in the workday, usually of 5 to 15 minutes' duration, during which the worker rests, smokes, or takes refreshments without loss of pay. (*See* Relief Time.)

Retired Senior Volunteer Program (RSVP): A program creating a variety of meaningful opportunities for persons of retirement age to participate, through volunteer service, more fully in community life. RSVP projects are planned, organized, and operated at the local level, and developed under the auspices of an established organization able to generate local financial support. (*See* Action.)

Retirement: Withdrawal from working life or from a particular employment because of old age, disability, etc. *Normal retirement* is retirement for age, usually at age 65 or later. *Early retirement* is retirement prior to the normal retirement age. *Disability retirement* is retirement prior to the normal retirement age because of poor health or injury disabling the worker. *Special early retirement* is retirement with extra early retirement benefits provided under specified circumstances, e.g., involuntary separation. (*See* Pension Plan; Social Security Act.)

Retirement Plan: *See* Pension Plan.

Retraining: Development of new skills for workers through a definite program, thus enabling them to qualify for new or different work.

Retraining and Reemployment Administration: Created by EO 9427 of Feb. 24, 1944, and by title III of War Mobilization and Reconversion Act of 1944 (58 Stat. 788; 50 U.S.C. 1661 note), to have general supervision and direction of activities of all existing executive agencies (except Veterans Administration and Administrator of Veterans Affairs) relating to retraining, reemployment, vocational education, and vocational rehabilitation of persons discharged or released from the armed services or other war work. Transferred from Office of War Mobilization and Reconversion to Department of Labor by EO 9617 of Sept. 19, 1945. Section 603 of War Mobilization and Reconversion Act of 1944 provided for termination of the Administration on June 30, 1947.

Retroactive Pay: Wages due for past services, frequently required when wage increases are made effective as of an earlier date, or when contract negotiations are extended beyond the expiration date. (*See* Back Pay.)

Revolutionary Unionism: An approach concerned more with the overthrow of capitalism than with winning the immediate demands of workers for higher wages, shorter hours, better working conditions, etc.

Right-to-Work Law: A state law which prohibits any contractual requirement that a worker join a union in order to get or keep a job, thus banning provisions in agreements requiring employees to become and remain union members (otherwise permissible under the Labor-Management Relations Act). (See Section 14(b), Labor-Management Relations Act.)

Right of Visitation (Access to Plant): A clause in a labor agreement giving a union official access to the premises of an employer for purposes of collection of dues and/or the administration and enforcement of a contract.

RILU: *See* Red International of Labor Unions.

Ringed Rate: *See* Red-Circle Rate.

Rival Unionism: Two or more unions actively competing to represent workers in the same craft or in the same industry.

RM Case: Under National Labor Relations Board procedures, a petition by an employer under Section 9(c)(1)(B) of the National Labor Relations Act, as follows:

Alleging that one or more claims for recognition as exclusive bargaining representative have been received by the employer. (*See* Types of Cases.)

Rolling: *See* Bumping.

Rotating Shift: *See* Shift.

Round-the-Clock Operations: *See* Continuous Operations.

Royalty: As used by some unions, a term for employer payments to health, welfare, or retirement funds. For professional workers, royalties are payments for work based upon a percentage of the return on the sale of the final product (an invention, book, piece of music, etc.).

RSA: *See* Rehabilitation Services Administration.

RSVP: *See* Retired Senior Volunteer Program.

Rule of Three: The practice, in various federal, state, and local civil service commissions, used in selecting one of the three highest persons on an eligibility list for appointment to a job.

Runaway Rate (Loose Rate): A piece rate or other incentive rate which, because of changed technology or faulty rate setting, yields earnings that are substantially higher than earnings on other jobs with similar work requirements.

Runaway Shop: The term used by unions to characterize a business establishment which moves to evade a union or state labor laws, or to reap a competitive advantage from low wage standards in another area, dismissing all or most of its regular employees in the process.

Runoff Election: A second election conducted after the first produces no winner according to the rules. If more than two contenders were in the first contest, the runoff may be limited to the two highest. (*See* Representation Election.)

Sabbatical: A recurring period of rest; extended time off for a member of the teaching faculty; recently applied to long vacations provided in steelworkers' contracts.

Sabotage: Any process by which an employee, while remaining at work, deliberately damages the interest of the employer. It may vary from mere malingering to willful destruction of property.

Safety Committee: A group appointed by management and labor within a plant to be responsible for the establishment and maintenance of sound safety practices.

Salami Tactics: A method of making progress in small stages not readily perceived as significant.

Salaried Employee: An employee paid on a weekly or monthly rather than an hourly basis, a common practice in the employment of office and supervisory personnel.

Salary Stabilization Board (ESA): Established May 10, 1951, by General Order 8 of Economic Stabilization Administrator, to be responsible for salary stabilization functions pursuant to title IV of Defense Production Act of 1950 (64 Stat. 803, as amended; 50 U.S.C. App. 2101–2110). Stabilization program administered by Office of Salary Stabilization. Terminated Apr. 30, 1953, pursuant to EO 10434 of Feb. 6, 1953, and Defense Production Act Amendments of 1952 and 1953 (66 Stat. 296, 67 Stat. 131; 50 U.S.C. App. 2166, 2071 note).

Salary Rate: For workers hired on a weekly, monthly, or annual basis (e.g., clerical, technical, managerial employees), the rate of pay normally expressed in terms of dollars per week, month, or year.

Sanctions: Economic and social pressure used by faculty personnel as a technique other than striking or picketing to win objectives.

Sandhog: A person who works in tunnels under compressed air, as in the pneumatic-caisson method.

Savings Clause: A clause in a contract or law which protects the body of the document even though a section of it is found to be invalid.

Savings Plan: *See* Thrift Plan.

Scab: Among trade unionists, the word "scab" is applied to anyone guilty of disloyalty to a union. More specifically, it describes a worker who crosses a picket line to take the place of a worker out on strike. It includes those who normally were workers in the struck premises and outsiders who replace those on strike. Although the word goes back to the late 1500s as meaning a "low, scurvy fellow," since 1811 Americans have used it to mean a workman who refuses to join an organized movement on behalf of his trade.

Scale: *See* Union Rate.

Scanlon Plan: A formal program whose general objectives are the reduction of labor costs through increased efficiency and the sharing of the resultant savings among workers. The scope and details of the few plans bearing this name vary considerably.

"Scissorbill": A slang term used mainly by Industrial Workers of the World members to designate a worker who holds aloof from the class-conscious labor movement.

Scope of Bargaining: The range of the included subject matter of negotiations.

Scranton Declaration: The declaration made in 1901 by the convention of the United Mine Workers that the union had jurisdiction over all workers in the mines irrespective of craft.

Scrip: Token money valid only in a company store or with some merchants willing to accept it. A form of wage payment common in isolated mining and lumbering establishments; now illegal in many states.

Seasonal Employment: Employment during part of the year only, arising out of the seasonal character of an industry. Agricultural, cannery, construction, and lumber workers are examples of persons subject to seasonal employment.

Seasonal Tolerance Clause: A clause in some collective bargaining agreements that permits waiving overtime after 40 hours during peak production periods; sometimes permissible under the Fair Labor Standards Act.

Second International: A group formed in 1889 by European labor and socialist parties in Paris and directed against militarism. It collapsed in 1914 at the beginning of World War I.

Secondary Boycott: *See* Boycott.

Secondary Picketing: Picketing of an establishment not involved in a dispute so that the establishment will prevail upon a party to the dispute to yield to the demands of the picketers.

Section 14(b), Labor-Management Relations Act, 1947: This section of the Taft-Hartley Act provides the opening through which states may enact right-to-work laws. It reads as follows: "Nothing in this act shall be construed as authorizing the execution or application of agreements requiring membership in a labor organization as a condition of employment in any State or Territory in which such execution or application is prohibited by State or Territorial law." (*See* Right-to-Work Law.)

Section 7(a) of the National Industrial Recovery Act: A statute asserting the right of workers to organize, thus serving as an incentive to unionization following passage of the act in 1933. The act was declared unconstitutional.

Section 10(j) of the Taft-Hartley Act: The section permitting the National Labor Relations Board to seek injunctive relief when it is necessary to effect the policies of the act.

Sellout: A labor contract whose terms are so bad for the workers that the union's negotiating officials are assumed to have taken a bribe.

Senior Companion Program: A program providing meaningful part-time opportunities for low-income older volunteers to render, in a mutually beneficial relationship, supportive person-to-person services to adults (21 years and over), with special needs in health, education, and welfare-related settings. (*See* Action.)

Senior Opportunities and Services (SOS): A program under the Community Services Administration that initiates projects that provide a wide range of local services for and with the elderly poor.

Seniority: A term used to designate an employee's status relative to other employees, as in determining order of promotion, layoff, vacations, etc. *Straight seniority* is seniority acquired solely through length of service. *Qualified seniority* includes other factors, such as ability, along with length of service. *Departmental or unit seniority* is seniority applicable in a particular section of a plant, rather than in the entire establishment. *Plantwide or companywide seniority* is seniority applicable throughout the plant or company. A *seniority list* ranks individual workers in order of seniority. (*See* Superseniority.)

SEOOs: *See* State Economic Opportunity Offices.

Separability Clause: *See* Savings Clause.

Separation Pay or Allowance: *See* Severance Pay.

Serfdom: A peasant's state of obligation to the landowner in a feudal society.

Service Contract Act of 1965: The law establishing labor standards for contracts, entered into by any United States agency, which have as their principal purpose the provision of services by service employees.

Service Credit: Seniority, or more specifically, years of service to be counted in determining the amount of a future pension.

Service Fee: The fee required by unions to be paid by nonmembers applying for employment in union hiring halls, as a condition of referral to employment.

Setup Time: The time allowed under an incentive system for a machine operator to set up equipment prior to running a job.

Severance Pay (Dismissal Pay or Allowance; Termination Pay; Separation Pay; Layoff Allowance): The monetary allowance paid by an employer to displaced employees, generally upon permanent termination of employment with no chance of recall, but often upon indefinite layoff with recall rights intact. The plans usually graduate payments by length of service.

Shakedown: A bribe.

Shakedown Time: The time allowed under a new incentive system for work on a new project until normal production is achieved.

Shapeup: A system of hiring work gangs from groups of workers assembled to seek employment. Used in longshore work in some ports and in the hiring of migratory farm workers.

Share-the-Work: *See* Work Sharing.

Sheltered Workshop: An employment establishment for handicapped workers.

Sherman Antitrust Act of 1890: A law forbidding all combinations in restraint of interstate and foreign trade. Although directed toward industry, the act was widely used against unions. Under a Supreme Court decision in the Danbury

Hatters' case, the act was held to apply against unions. This liability was removed to a degree by the Clayton Act in 1914.

Shift (Tour of Duty; Stint; Trick; Turn): The daily working schedule of a plant or its employees. The *day shift* usually works the daylight hours; the *evening shift* ends at or near midnight; the *night (graveyard) shift* starts at or near midnight. With a *fixed shift,* scheduled hours remain the same, week after week, for each group of workers. *Rotating shift* is the practice whereby crews change their hours at periodic intervals. With a *split shift,* the daily work schedule is divided into two parts or more. The *swing shift* is the fourth or rotating shift used on continuous 7-day or round-the-clock operations.

Shift Differential (Shift Premium): Additional compensation (cents per hour or percentage of the day rate) paid to workers employed at other than regular daytime hours.

Shipbuilding Stabilization Committee (Labor): Originally organized by National Defense Advisory Commission in 1940. In August 1942 established by War Production Board to aid in stabilization of basic wage rates and certain working conditions in shipbuilding industry, EO 9656 of Nov. 15, 1945, transferred Committee to Department of Labor from Civilian Production Administration, successor agency to War Production Board. Dissolved June 30, 1947.

Shop Chairperson: The chief officer of a shop committee, elected either by the committee members or by all the stewards in a plant.

Shop Committee (Grievance Committee; Negotiating Committee): A group of workers selected by fellow employees, usually union members, to represent them in their dealings with management.

Shop Rules (Working Rules): Either regulations established by an employer dealing with day-to-day conduct in the plant—operations, safety, hygiene, records, etc.—or working rules set forth in collective bargaining agreements and in some union constitutions.

Shop Steward (Union Steward): A local union's representative in a plant or department elected by union members (or sometimes appointed by the union) to carry out union duties, adjust grievances, collect dues, and solicit new members. Usually a fellow employee.

Short-Workweek Benefit: As part of a supplemental unemployment benefit plan, payment to a worker for the difference between a specified level of weekly hours and the hours actually worked or paid for.

Sick Benefits: *See* Accident and Sickness Benefits.

Sick Leave: Period of time during which a worker may be absent without loss of job or seniority if unable to work because of illness or accident. A *paid sick-leave plan* provides for full or partial pay for such absence, usually up to a stipulated maximum. Sick-leave plans differ from accident and sickness benefits principally in that the former cover shorter periods of absence, usually provide higher pay, and are uninsured. (*See* Accident and Sickness Benefits.)

Silk Textile Work Assignment Board: The President, in EO 6875 of Oct. 16, 1934, approved amendments to Code of Fair Competition for Silk Textile Industry which provided that Textile Labor Relations Board appoint a Silk Textile Work Assignment Board to develop a plan for regulation of work assignments. Expired June 15, 1935, having completed work for which it was established.

Single-Company Union: An independent or unaffiliated union of employees of one company, usually with no formal ties to any other labor organization.

Single Rate: The rate of pay which is the same for all workers in the same job or job classification.

Sitdown Strike: *See* Strike.

Situs Picketing: Picketing at the work site when it is other than the establishment of the employer. Common in building construction when craftworkers of one union picket at the work place and appeal to other workers not to cross their picket line.

Sixty-Day (60-Day) Notice: A provision in the Labor Management Relations Act of 1947 requiring parties to a labor agreement to give notice of their intention to modify or terminate a labor contract.

Slave Driver: A supervisor who makes unreasonable work demands on the employees.

Slave-Labor Law: A pejorative term used by trade unionists to describe the Labor-Management Relations Act of 1947 (the Taft-Hartley Act).

Slowdown: *See* Strike.

Smith-Connally Act: *See* War Labor Disputes Act.

Smith-Hughes Act (1917): A law authorizing federal matching grants with states to develop programs for vocational education.

SMSC: *See* State Manpower Services Council.

Social Security Act of 1935: The law setting up a national insurance program and the Social Security Administration. The original law has been amended and broadened and now includes unemployment insurance, old-age retirement insurance, workers' compensation and disability insurance, hospitalization insurance for those over 65 (Medicare), supplementary medical insurance for those over 65 (Medicaid), assistance to the blind and the needy aged, aid to the crippled and the permanently disabled, and vocational and health programs.

Social Security Adjustment Option (Level-Income Option): A pension plan provision under which a worker eligible for an early retirement benefit may elect to get a larger plan benefit than is actually due up to the time the social security benefit is payable, and a smaller benefit thereafter, so that a level income is maintained throughout retirement.

Social Security Administration (SSA): Under the direction of the Commissioner of Social Security, SSA administers a national program of contributory social insurance whereby employees, employers, and the self-employed pay contributions which are pooled in special trust funds. When earnings stop or are reduced because the worker retires, dies, or becomes disabled, monthly cash benefits are paid to replace part of the earnings the family has lost.

Social Security Board: Established under provisions of Social Security Act (49 Stat. 620; 42 U.S.C. 301 et seq.), and became part of Federal Security Agency in accordance with Reorg. Plan I, effective July 1, 1939. Responsibilities included general determination of policies and specific action in administering a system of old-age and survivors' insurance benefits, providing for grants by Federal Government to States for old-age assistance, aid to dependent children, and aid to needy blind; supervising State administration of unemployment compensation. Abolished by Reorg. Plan 2, effective July 16, 1946, and functions transferred to Federal Security Administrator.

Social Security Offset: Under some pension plans, the amount of social security benefit to which a retiring worker is entitled that is to be deducted from the private plan benefit, as computed, to obtain the actual benefit payable. The offset or deduction may be all or part of the social security benefit.

Social Security Taxes: Taxes levied on employers and employees through payroll deductions and on the self-employed through self-employment taxes. The tax revenues are used to finance benefits under social security regulations.

Socialism: A term with many definitions depending on the writer or the country described. In the United States, some will agree that it is a movement of the working class favoring the abolition of the private ownership of the means of production, distribution, and exchange and its replacement by common ownership of the social means of production—land, factories, railroads, mines, banks, etc.—by the people.

Socialist Labor Party: Organized in 1877 as the Workingmen's Party of America, it was for nearly a quarter-century the leading socialist party in the United States. Its members favored industrial rather than craft unions, believed in direct action, and had little faith in political democracy as a means of achieving goals. The Party's declaration of war on the American Federation of Labor brought a split in its ranks and was in a great measure the cause of its decline. Its leaders helped in founding the Industrial Workers of the World. Party candidates for political office on a national level and on some state levels are still in the political arena.

Socialist Trades and Labor Alliance: Organized in 1895 as a dual union to the American Federation of Labor by Daniel DeLeon, it went out of existence about 1902.

Soldiering: Loafing.

Sole Bargaining Rights: The exclusive right to represent all workers in a unit recognized by the National Labor Relations Board or an appropriate state or local agency.

Solidarity of Labor: Awareness by workers of the identity of interests of wage earners.

SOS: *See* Senior Opportunities and Services.

Special Unemployment Assistance (SUA): A temporary program under Title II of the Emergency Jobs and Unemployment Assistance Act of 1974, designed to provide temporary assistance during periods of high unemployment for individuals who are not eligible for unemployment benefits under any state or federal law.

Speedup: A workers' term for conditions which force them to increase effort or production within a given time without a compensating increase in earnings. (*See* Stretchout.)

Spellout: *See* Relief Time.

Spendable Earnings (Disposable Income): In general, earnings available for spending. As used by the Bureau of Labor Statistics, gross average weekly earnings less the estimated amount of the workers' social security and income tax liability. (*See* Take-Home Pay.)

Split Shift: *See* Shift.

Spread-the-Work: *See* Work Sharing.

Standard Agreement (Form Agreement): A collective bargaining agreement prepared by a national or international union for use by, or guidance of, its local unions, designed to produce standardization of practices within the union's bargaining relationships. A *form agreement* is a uniform agreement signed by individual members of an employers' association and often by employers in the same line of work but outside the association.

Standard Rate: Usually, a uniform rate of pay established for an occupation or craft in an area or industry through collective bargaining or by law.

Standby: A person who is available for work in an emergency situation but who normally is not required to work. The required presence of a standby is sometimes characterized as featherbedding.

State Economic Opportunity Offices (SEOOs):   A program under the Community Services Administration to advise the state governors, to mobilize resources, and to advocate for the poor within the respective states.

State Federation of Labor: An organization of the AFL-CIO on a statewide basis to advance workers' interests. It has no collective bargaining responsibilities.

State Industrial Union Council: Under the former CIO, such councils were organized on a statewide basis to represent the interests of workers in political and community activities.

State Labor Relations Act: *See* Baby Wagner Act.

State Manpower Services Council (SMSC):   A state agency authorized to review and monitor plans of program sponsors and state agencies under the Comprehensive Employment and Training Act.

Statute of Labourers (1351):   The statute by which the British Parliament attempted to control a sharp rise in wages caused by a decline in workers following the Great Plague of 1348 and 1349. The legislation prevented laborers from demanding an increase in wages and employers from granting increases. Under a later Statute of Labourers (1563), justices of the peace in each locality were empowered to fix wages.

Statute of Limitations: A law fixing the period of time within which an action in law can be instituted.

Stay-in Strike: A sitdown strike.

Step Rates: Fixed levels between the minimum and maximum rates for an occupation in a wage progression system. (*See* Wage Progression.)

Stint: *See* Shift.

Stock Option Plan: A plan allowing employees or officers the privilege of purchasing company stock (shares) at a certain price at a time of their own choosing.

Stock Purchase Plan: A plan enabling employees to purchase stock (shares) in the company, with or without employer contributions, generally under more favorable terms than are available on the open market.

Stool Pigeon: A labor spy.

Straight Time: Time worked at the regular rate, as distinguished from overtime. (*See* Earnings; Overtime.)

Stranger Picketing: Picketing of an establishment by individuals not employed there.

Straw Boss: A worker in charge of other workers in a small group.

Stretchout: A term used by workers when they are required to tend more machines or assume additional duties within a given time without a corresponding increase in earnings. (*See* Speedup.)

Strike (Wildcat, Outlaw, Quickie, Slowdown, Sympathy, Sitdown, General):   A temporary stoppage of work by a group of employees (not necessarily members of a union) to express a grievance, enforce a demand for changes in the conditions of employment, obtain recognition, or resolve a dispute with management. A *wildcat or outlaw strike* is a strike not sanctioned by a union and one which violates an agreement. A *quickie strike* is a spontaneous or unannounced strike. A *slowdown* is a deliberate reduction of output without an actual strike in order to force concessions from the employer. The *sympathy strike* is a strike of workers not directly involved in a dispute, but who wish to demonstrate worker solidarity or bring additional pressure upon the company involved. A *sitdown strike* is a strike during which workers stay inside the plant or workplace, but refuse to work or allow others to do so. A *general strike* is a strike involving all organized workers in a community or country (rare in the United States). A *walkout* is the same as a strike.

Strike Benefits: Union payments made to members who are on strike.

Strike Committee: A group set up by a union to conduct and administer a strike.

Strike Deadline: The time set by the union for beginning a strike if a satisfactory settlement is not reached. Typically, this is at midnight of the last day of the contract term or the start of the next day's first shift.

Strike Duty: Obligations of an individual during a strike; they may include picketing, fund raising, providing food, and other supportive activties.

Strike Fund: Money allocated by a union or set aside in a separate account to pay strike benefits and to defray other expenses of strikes.

Strike Insurance: Payment by companies in an association to a fund or for the purchase of insurance, to reimburse a struck member company for lost business.

Strike Notice: A formal notice of an intention to strike, presented by the union to the employer, or to the appropriate federal government agency, e.g., the Federal Mediation and Conciliation Service.

Strike Vote: A vote conducted among union members to determine whether or not a strike should be called.

Strikebreaker (Scab; Fink):   A worker or person on hire who accepts employment or continues to work in a plant where an authorized strike is in process, filling the job of a striker and knowingly assisting in defeating the strike. (*See* Anti-Strikebreaker Law.)

Struck Work or Goods: Goods produced or services performed by a firm while a strike of its employees is in progress. (*See* Hot-Cargo Clause.)

Structural Unemployment: Unemployment that is caused by changes in the nature of the economy, or the development of new industry and the obsolescence of others.

SUB: *See* Supplemental Unemployment Benefit Plans.

Subcontracting: *See* Contracting-Out.

Subsistence Allowance: Payment to a worker for expenses of meals and lodging (and sometimes transportation) while traveling for the employer; or reimbursement of living expenses required by the nature of the job.

Substandard Rate: A rate of pay below the established plant or occupational minimum, allowed for workers who are physically or otherwise unable to meet the production quota; also, rates below federal or state minimum wages, "prevailing" levels, or union scales.

Successor Union: A union which replaces another union, and often claiming the rights of its predecessor under the contract.

Suggestion System: A plan whereby employees' ideas that may increase efficiency or improve operations or safety are channeled to the attention of management; usually combined with a system of rewards for acceptable ideas.

Superannuated Workers: A term sometimes applied to employees who are unable to perform their jobs, or any job, at the normal level because of advanced age and its attendant infirmities. A *superannuated rate* is a rate of pay below the regular level, set especially for superannuated workers.

Superseniority: A position on the seniority list ahead of what the employee would acquire solely on the basis of length of service or other general seniority factors. Usually such favored treatment is reserved to union stewards or other workers entitled to special consideration in connection with layoff and recall to work.

Supplemental Unemployment Benefit Plans (SUB): Introduced by agreement between the Ford Motor Company and the United Automobile Workers in mid-1955 and subsequently adopted by other companies in the automobile, steel, and related industries, these plans provide regular weekly payments to laid-off workers receiving state unemployment insurance, through funds financed by the employer. Other benefits (e.g., short-workweek benefits and severance pay) were added to many plans.

Supplementary Benefits: *See* Fringe Benefits.

Surgical Benefits: Plans which provide workers, and in many cases their dependents, with specified surgical care or a cash allowance toward the cost of such care, usually in accordance with a schedule of surgeon's fees. Generally part of a health and insurance program. (*See* Health and Insurance Plan; Blue Shield.)

Surplus Value, Theory of: The theory developed by Karl Marx that the exchange value of commodities is determined by the amount of labor socially necessary for its production; that labor power is a commodity and its value (wages) is thus only sufficient for the working class to reproduce itself, and that hours worked beyond those necessary for workers to sustain themselves are accrued to the advantage of the employing class and become the basis of new capital investment.

Survivors' Benefits (Transition Benefits; Bridge Benefits; Widow's Allowance): Payments to dependents of employees who die prior to retirement, financed in whole or in part by the employer. They may be in the form of payments for a fixed period (e.g., 24 months) supplementing regular life insurance benefits, a benefit for life out of a pension program, a lump-sum payment, etc.

Survivor's Option: *See* Joint and Survivor Option.

Suspension: A form of disciplinary action of a temporary nature, as in removing a worker from her or his job for a stipulated time with the consequent loss of pay as punishment, or in removing a union official from office until the official's affairs are checked or put into order.

Sweatshop: A term of contempt applied to an establishment employing workers for long hours at low wages under unfavorable working conditions.

Sweetheart Agreement: A derogatory term for a union contract exceptionally favorable to a particular employer, in comparison with other contracts, implying less favorable employment conditions than could be obtained under a legitimate collective bargaining relationship.

Swing Shift: *See* Shift.

Sympathy Strike: *See* Strike.

Syndicalism: The central doctrine of syndicalism is that the workers should control the conditions of work; industry should be managed solely by the producers organized in industrial unions. In the United States, the Industrial Workers of the World were an expression of this point of view.

Taft-Hartley Act: *See* Labor Management Relations Act.

Take-Home Pay: Generally, earnings for a payroll period, less deductions (legal and authorized); the amount of cash the worker "takes home."

Taylor Law: *See* Public Employees' Fair Employment Act.

Taylor System: A "science of industrial conservation and a technique for increasing output and lowering production costs," formulated by an American engineer, Frederick W. Taylor. Urges individual selection of persons to fit the job, training of workers, positive control over all operations, and the conscious stimulation of the workers to maximum efforts by means of a bonus for superior accomplishment.

Technocracy: A theory of government, in vogue during Franklin Roosevelt's first administration, that called for the management of society by engineers and technicians.

Technological Change: Change brought about by improved methods in the means of production, distribution, transportation, and record keeping; a continuing part of the industrial revolution.

Technological Unemployment: The displacement of workers caused by, or attributed to, the installation of laborsaving methods or mechinery.

Temporary Disability Insurance: A provision, enacted into law in some states, providing payments for a limited time to workers suffering loss of wages because of sickness or disability incurred off the job.

Temporary Employee: *See* Probationary Period.

Temporary Rates: Wage or piece rates set tentatively on new work, sometimes called *experimental* or *trial* rates.

Temporary Restraining Order: *See* Injunction.

Tennessee Valley Authority (TVA): Established early in the New Deal in 1933, TVA was the first major program for the development of a river valley. It provides flood control, power, and recreational facilities. Although a government authority, the TVA from its very earliest days has dealt with unions of its employees.

Termination Clause: A clause in a labor agreement, indicating its expiration date.

Termination Pay or Allowances: *See* Severance Pay.

Textile National Industrial Relations Board: Created by administrative order of June 28, 1934. Abolished by EO 6858 of Sept. 26, 1934, which created Textile Labor Relations Board in connection with Department of Labor. Textile Labor Relations Board ceased to exist July 1, 1937, and functions were absorbed by United States Conciliation Service in the Department of Labor.

Theory of Surplus Value: *See* Surplus Value, Theory of.

Third International: Organized in Moscow in 1919 at the close of World War I, the group urged the establishment of Communist parties throughout the world and called for a workers' revolution. It rejected the admission of all democratic socialist parties, and is sometimes referred to as the Communist International.

Thousand-Hour (1000-Hour) Clause: A clause in Section 7 of the Fair Labor Standards Act that provides an exception to the requirement of time-and-one-half payments after 40 hours of work in one week. Under a union contract, workers in seasonal industries may work more than 40 hours in a week without penalty, provided that they not work more than 1040 hours during any period of 26 consecutive weeks.

Thrift Plan (Savings Plan): An arrangement under which payroll deductions are made, with the worker's consent, for investment and saving, to which plan the employer contributes. The accumulated amounts (contributions plus earnings on the contributions) become available to the worker, usually after certain conditions are met.

Tie Up: To strike.

Time Limit: A requirement in most union agreements that a grievance to be processed must be called to management's attention within a set time after the grievant has become aware of his or her complaint.

Time Lost on Grievances: Time lost by a union official while engaged in settling workers' grievances that arise in the plant. Union contracts provide for the official's reimbursement at the regular pay rate.

Time-and-Motion Study: An industrial engineering function involving a study of the time required and the motions involved in the performance of a job. The purpose may be to establish standards of performance, the best way of doing a job, or incentive wage rates.

Time and One-Half: A premium rate consisting of one and one-half times the employee's regular rate. For example, if a worker's regular rate is $3 an hour, an hour's work at time and one-half would yield $4.50, of which $1.50 is the premium.

Time-Study Expert: An individual in a plant operated under a system of scientific management who conducts time-and-motion studies involving the use of a split-second timing device.

Timework: *See* Daywork.

Tip: A gratuity common in the service industries, such as restaurants, hotels, and taxis. The word stems from the initial letters of "to insure promptness."

Tonnage Rate: Pay on the basis of tons of material handled, common in the basic iron and steel industries and coal mining.

Tool Allowance: The allowance to an employee, paid by the employer, as reimbursement for the cost of tools and their upkeep, where the employee furnishes the necessary tools or is responsible for their maintenance.

Tooling-up Period: The time required in many mass-production industries to prepare dies, tools, and forms for new models.

Tour of Duty: *See* Shift.

Trade Council: *See* Joint Board.

Trade Expansion Act (1962): The federal act, whose purposes include that of expanding foreign markets for U.S. goods, providing assistance to firms and workers to adjust to possible adverse effects of increased imports. Aid to workers includes

special weekly unemployment benefits, counseling and retraining, and in some cases, relocation allowances.

Trade Union: A continuous association of wage earners for the purpose of maintaining or improving the conditions of their working lives. Although there were similar organizations earlier, the name "Trades' Union" first appeared in England and the United States in the 1830s. (*See* Union.)

Trade Union Educational League (TUEL): Organized in 1920 to propagandize for revolutionary communist activity and leadership in the American trade union movement. It was a predecessor of the Trade Union Unity League.

Trade Union Unity League: A league organized in 1929 as an expression of the new international communist policy of withdrawing the most militant sections from the American labor movement to set up militant revolutionary unions.

Trainee: A worker receiving formal on-the-job training.

Training and Technical Assistance (T & TA): A program under the Community Services Administration that includes training of Community Services Administration and grantee staffs to upgrade management skills and to support programs in specific functional areas.

Tramping Committee: In the nineteenth century, groups of union workers who walked from plant to plant, work site to work site, to see that union conditions were being met.

Transfer Card: The card issued by a local union to a member in good standing, certifying his or her eligibility to join local of the same union in a different location.

Transition Benefits: *See* Survivors' Benefits.

Transportation Act of 1920 (Esch-Cummins Act): The act setting up the Railroad Labor Board with three members each from the employers, the employees, and the public, with authority to resolve all unresolved disputes including wages. The Board was abolished in 1926 with the passage of the Railway Labor Act.

Travel Time: Time spent traveling to and from a designated point and the work site. Such time may be paid for as portal-to-portal pay in mining, deadheading on railroads, and out-of-town work in construction.

Traveling Card: A card issued to a trade unionist whose work requires traveling to various parts of the country. The card shows that the holder is a member of a union and permits him or her to obtain employment with an employer organized by another local of the same union.

Trial Examiner: A person designated under the rules of the Labor Management Relations Act of 1947 to act as a judge following a complaint by the General Counsel of the N.L.R.B.

Trial Period: The probationary period following employment, during which time the worker has no recourse to the grievance procedure and can be discharged with or without cause.

Trick: *See* Shift.

Truck System: *See* Payment in Kind.

Trust Fund: *See* Fund.

Trustee: A person, bank, or trust company who administers and takes responsibility for a trust fund, or a person who is a member of a board of trustees. (*See* Fund.)

Trusteeship: In union affairs, the taking of direct control of a local union by the national or international union, generally to correct mismanagement or illegal practices on the part of local officers, to prevent secession, or to strengthen the local. Control of the local is returned to members or officers after the cause for trusteeship has been corrected. (*See* Monitorship.)

T & TA: *See* Training and Technical Assistance.

Tube-bending Formula: A policy of the National Labor Relations Board permitting employers to speak to their employees against the union, provided no coercion or threatening action is indicated.

TUC: *See* British Trade Union Congress.

TUEL: *See* Trade Union Educational League.

Tuition Payment Plan: A plan providing for payment by the employer of part or all of the costs of job-related training courses undertaken by an employee.

Turn: *See* Shift.

Turnout: A strike.

Turnover: *See* Labor Turnover.

TVA: *See* Tennessee Valley Authority.

Twilight Zone: Labor relations problems not clearly under the jurisdiction of either a federal or a state agency.

Two-Thousand-Hour (2000-Hour) Clause: A clause in section 7 of the Fair Labor Standards Act providing an exception to the requirement of time-and-a-half payments after 40 hours of work in one week. Under a union contract, overtime provisions do not apply if the worker works up to 12 hours in one day or 56 hours in a week, as long as no employee is required to work more than 2080 hours in a period of 52 consecutive weeks. Up to 2240 hours is permitted without overtime penalty, if the contract calls for a guaranty for a specified number of hours of employment.

Two-Year (2-Year) Rule: A regulation of the National Labor Relations Board that the first 2 years of a labor contract is a period during which claims by a rival union will not be considered.

Types of Cases: As defined by the National Labor Relations Board:

General: Letter designations are given to all cases depending upon the subsection of the National Labor Relations Act allegedly violated or otherwise describing the general nature of each case. Each of the letter designations appearing below is descriptive of the case with which it is associated.

C Cases (unfair labor practice cases)

A case number which contains the first letter designation C, in combination with another letter, i.e., CA, CB, etc., indicates that it involves a charge that an unfair labor practice has been committed in violation of one or more subsections of Section 8.

CA: A charge that an employer has committed unfair labor practices in violation of Section 8(a) (1), (2), (3), (4), or (5), or any combination thereof.

CB: A charge that a labor organization has committed unfair labor practices in violation of Section 8(b) (1), (2), (3), (5), or (6), or any combination thereof.

CC: A charge that a labor organization has committed unfair labor

practices in violation of Section 8(b)(4)(i) and/or (ii)(A), (B), or (C), or any combination thereof.

CD: A charge that a labor organization has committed an unfair labor practice in violation of Section 8(b)(4)(i) or (ii)(D). Preliminary actions under Section 10(k) for the determination of jurisdictional disputes are processed as CD cases. (See Jurisdictional Disputes.)

CE: A charge that either a labor organization or an employer, or both jointly, have committed an unfair labor practice in violation of Section 8(e).

CG: A charge that a labor organization has committed unfair labor practices in violation of Section 8(g).

CP: A charge that a labor organization has committed unfair labor practices in violation of Section 8(b)(7) (A), (B), or (C), or any combination thereof.

R Cases (representation cases)

A case number which contains the first letter designation R, in combination with another letter, i.e., RC, RD, RM, indicates that it is a petition for investigation and determination of a question concerning representation of employees, filed under Section 9(c) of the act.

RC: A petition filed by a labor organization or an employee alleging that a question concerning representation has arisen and seeking an election for the determination of a collective bargaining representative.

RD: A petition filed by employees alleging that the union previously certified or currently recognized by the employer as their collective bargaining representative no longer represents a majority of the employees in the appropriate unit and seeking an election to determine this.

RM: A petition filed by an employer alleging that a question concerning representation has arisen and seeking an election for the determination of a collective bargaining representative.

Other Cases

AC: (Amendment of Certification cases): A petition filed by a labor organization or an employer for amendment of an existing certification to reflect changed circumstances, such as changes in the name or affiliation of the labor organization involved or in the name or location of the employer involved.

AO: (Advisory Opinion cases): As distinguished from the other types of cases described above, which are filed in and processed by regional offices of the Board, AO or "advisory opinion" cases are filed directly with the Board in Washington and seek a determination as to whether the Board would or would not assert jurisdiction, in any given situation on the basis of its current standards, over the party or parties to a proceeding pending before a state or territorial agency or a court. (See subpart H of the Board's Rules and Regulations, Series 8, as amended.)

UC: (Unit Clarification cases): A petition filed by a labor organization or an employer seeking a determination as to whether certain classifications of employees should or should not be included within a presently existing bargaining unit.

UD: (Union Deauthorization cases): A petition filed by employees pursuant to Section 9(e)(1) requesting that the Board conduct a referendum to determine whether a union's authority to enter into a union-shop contract should be rescinded.

UC Case: Under National Labor Relations Board procedures, a petition by either a labor organization or an employer seeking clarification of an existing bargaining unit under subpart C of the rules of the National Labor Relations Board. (*See* Types of Cases.)

UD Case: Under National Labor Relations Board procedures, a petition by or in behalf of employees under Section 9(e)(1) of the National Labor Relations Act:

9(e)(1) Alleging that employees (30 percent or more of an appropriate unit) wish to rescind an existing union-security agreement.
(*See* Types of Cases.)

UI: *See* Unemployment Insurance.

UIS: *See* Unemployment Insurance Service.

Umpire: *See* Impartial Chairperson.

Unaffiliated Union: *See* Independent Union.

UNCSW: *See* United Nations Commission on the Status of Women.

Under the Hat Agreement: *See* Sweetheart Contract.

Unemployed Persons: As defined by the Bureau of Labor Statistics, all persons who did not work during the BLS survey week, who had made specific efforts to find a job within the past 4 weeks, and who were available for work during the survey week except for temporary illness. Also included as unemployed are those who did not work at all, were available for work, and (1) were waiting to be recalled to a job from which they had been laid off, or (2) were waiting to report to a new wage or salary job within 30 days.

Unemployment Benefits: Money available to those out of work under state unemployment insurance programs.

Unemployment Insurance (Unemployment Compensation): The joint federal-state program, established in 1935 under the Social Security Act and subject to the standards set forth in the Federal Unemployment Tax Act, under which state-administered funds obtained through payroll taxes provide payments to eligible unemployed persons for specified periods. Levels of benefits and tax rates are established by each state. Generally excluded groups include, among others, railroad workers (covered by the Railroad Unemployment Insurance Act), agricultural workers, state and municipal employees, and workers in nonprofit institutions. The federal part of the program is administered by the Labor Department.

Unemployment Insurance Service (UIS): A federal unit providing leadership and policy guidance to state employment security agencies for the development, improvement, and operation of the federal-state unemployment insurance program and related wage-loss income maintenance programs.

Unfair Labor Practice: Action by either an employer or a union which violates the provisions of national or state labor relations acts, such as refusal to bargain in good faith. An *unfair labor practice strike* is a strike caused, at least in part, by an employer's unfair labor practice.

Unfair Labor Practice Cases: *See* Types of Cases: C Cases.

Unfair List: A union list of employers designated as unfair to organized labor.

Unfunded Plan (Pay-as-You-Go): A plan (e.g., pension plan) under which benefits are paid, like wages, directly from an employer's general assets, often as a payroll item, as distinguished from a fund irretrievably segregated from the firm's general assets and separately administered. Some pension plans are funded in part and unfunded with regard to certain benefits.

Unilateral Action: Activity by one party to an agreement without either consultation or approval of the second party.

Union (Trade Union, Labor Union, Labor Organization): Any organization in which workers participate as members and which exists for the purpose of dealing with employers con-

cerning grievances, wages, hours, and conditions of employment. Unions are voluntary organizations and need no license from the government to operate. They may incorporate if they wish.

Union Agreement: *See* Agreement.

Union Contract: *See* Agreement.

Union Convention: An assembly of delegates meeting periodically (e.g., every 2 years) to act on union problems, elect officers, and determine policies. The convention is typically the chief governing body of the union in constitutional terms.

Union Deauthorizing Cases: *See* Types of Cases: Other Cases, UD.

Union Dues Fee paid periodically, usually monthly, by members of a union, typically as a condition of continued membership. Each union sets its own dues requirements. (*See* Checkoff.)

Union Label (Bug): A tag, imprint, or design attached to an article as evidence that it was produced by union labor.

Union Label and Service Trades Department: *See* AFL-CIO, departments of.

Union Leave: Paid or unpaid, but excused, leave for union representatives, shop stewards, etc., to attend to union business, e.g., to participate in union conventions.

Union-Management Cooperation: The voluntary joint participation of union and management in solving problems such as production and safety, or in engaging in certain outside activities, such as community or charitable work. The term is usually reserved to joint actions outside of the process of collective bargaining itself.

Union Member: In broad terms, a worker who has met the union's qualifications for membership, has joined the union, and has maintained her or his membership rights. Each union usually determines its own qualifications. In general, *dues-paying members* are those who pay dues to the union on a regular basis. *Members in good standing* include dues-paying members and members exempted for various reasons (unemployed, on strike, ill, etc.) but still carried on the union rolls as full-fledged members. *Book members* are those listed on the union rolls, dues-paying or not.

Union Organizer: *See* Organizer.

Union Rate (Scale): The minimum rate (hourly or weekly) paid to qualified workers in a specific occupation or trade under the terms of a union agreement. (*See* Standard Rate.)

Union Recognition: Employer acceptance of a union as the representative of the firm's employees, the first step in the establishment of a collective bargaining relationship.

Union Representative: *See* Business Agent.

Union Security: Protection of a union's status by a provision in the collective bargaining agreement establishing a closed shop, union shop, agency shop, or maintenance-of-membership arrangement. In the absence of such a provision, employees in the bargaining unit are free to join or support the union at will, and thus, in union reasoning, are susceptible to pressures to refrain from joining or to the inducement of enjoying a "free ride."

Union Shop: The relationship obtaining with the provision in a collective bargaining agreement that all employees become membrs of the union within a specified time after hiring (typically, 30 days), or after a new provision is negotiated, and remain members of the union as a condition of continued employment. The term *modified union shop* contains variations on the union shop. Certain employees may be exempted, e.g., those already employed at the time the provision was negotiated who had, up until then, not joined the union.

Union Steward: *See* Shop Steward.

Unit, Appropriate Bargaining: As defined by the National Labor Relations Board: a grouping of employees in a plant, firm, or industry that is recognized by the employer, agreed upon by the parties to a case, or designated by the Board or its regional director as appropriate for the purposes of collective bargaining.

United Labor Party: The political expression of the single-tax movement sponsored by Henry George in 1886.

United Nations Commission on the Status of Women (UNCSW): A commission established in 1946 to prepare recommendations and reports to the Economic and Social Council (ECOSOC) of the United Nations.

United States Board of Mediation: Board of Mediation was provided for by act of May 20, 1926 (44 Stat. 577; 45 U.S.C. 153). Abolished by act approved June 21, 1934 (48 Stat. 1193; 45 U.S.C. 154), and superseded by National Mediation Board, July 21, 1934.

United States Civil Service Commission: Title of President of the United States Civil Service Commission, office of Executive Director and Chief Examiner, and office of Secretary of the Commission abolished by Reorg. Plan 5, effective Aug. 20, 1949. The Plan provided for a chairman and an Executive Director.

United States Conciliation Service (Labor): Established pursuant to section 8 of act creating Department of Labor, approved Mar. 4, 1913 (29 U.S.C. 51), to bring about peaceful settlements of industrial disputes arising in various sections of the country between employers and employees. Functions transferred to Federal Mediation and Conciliation Service, established by act of June 23, 1947 (sec. 202, 61 Stat. 153; 29 U.S.C. 172).

United States Employees' Compensation Commission: Created by act approved Sept. 7, 1916 (39 Stat. 742; 5 U.S.C. 751 et seq.), to administer provisions of act which provided for workmen's compensation benefits for civil employees of the United States suffering personal injuries while on duty. Further legislation increased scope of Commission to cover private employment within jurisdiction of the Government. Commission abolished by Reorg. Plan 2, effective July 16, 1946, and functions transferred to Federal Security Administrator (*see* Federal Security Agency).

United States Employment Service: Government participation in placement of workers originated with creation in 1907 of Division of Information, Bureau of Immigration and Naturalization, in Department of Commerce and Labor; Employment Service established as a unit in Department of Labor in 1918 by departmental order; existing Service abolished and created as a bureau with same name by act approved June 6, 1933 (48 Stat. 113; 29 U.S.C. 49). Functions consolidated with unemployment compensation functions of Social Security Board in Bureau of Employment Security and transferred to Federal Security Agency as provided in Reorg. Plan I, effective July 1, 1939, and Office of Director abolished.

EO 9247 of Sept. 17, 1942, transferred U.S. Employment Service from Social Security Board to War Manpower Commission and became part of Bureau of Placement.

Returned to Department of Labor by EO 9617 of Sept. 19, 1945, to be administered as an organizational entity. Transferred to Federal Security Agency, effective July 1, 1948, by act of June 16, 1948 (62 Stat. 443), to function as part of Bureau of Employment Security in Social Security Administration. Bureau of Employment Security (*see* appendix A), including U.S. Employment Service, transferred to Department of Labor by Reorg. Plan 2, effective Aug. 20, 1949. Abolished by reorganization of the Manpower Administration, effective Mar. 17, 1969, and functions assigned to U.S. Training and Employment Service. (*See* Wagner-Peyser Act.)

United States Training and Employment Service (USTES): Established within the Manpower Administration in 1969 and abolished by the Secretary's letter of December 6, 1971, its functions are now carried by the Office of Employment Development Programs and the reestablished United States Employment Service.

Unlicensed Personnel: Seafarers not required to have an official license, such as deckhands, stewards, firemen, etc., as distinguished from licensed masters, mates, and engineers.

Unpaid Holidays: Holidays observed by an establishment only to the extent of providing premium pay for work on that day. Paid time off is not provided. (Cf. Paid Holidays.)

Upgrading: The process of raising the pay level of a job relative to other jobs or of advancing workers to jobs with higher skills and rates of pay.

Urban Mass Transportation Act. A law passed in 1964 whose pertinent provisions include establishment of a program providing federal assistance to states and local governments and agencies to finance improvements in urban mass transportation systems. Protective arrangements for labor are identical to those prescribed under the Rail Passenger Service Act of 1970.

USES: *See* United States Employment Service.

VA: *See* Veterans Administration.

Vacation Pay: Wages received by an employee for his or her vacation period. (*See* Paid Vacations.) *Pay-in-lieu-of-vacation* is vacation pay to workers who do not take the actual time off, paid in addition to wages for time worked.

Valid Vote: As defined by the National Labor Relations Board, a secret ballot on which the choice of the voter is clearly shown.

Vertical Union: *See* Industrial Union.

Vestibule Training: Training that prepares an individual for the world of work in a factory, office, or service trade.

Vesting (Vested Rights): As commonly used in connection with pension plans, a guarantee to workers of their equity in the plan, based on contributions by the employer on their behalf, should their employment terminate before they become eligible for retirement. The worker usually must meet specified minimum age (e.g., 40 or 45) and service (e.g., 10 or 15 years) requirements for qualification. Vested workers receive the pensions they have earned when they reach retirement age, wherever they are then employed.

Veterans Administration (VA): The federal agency that administers a thorough system of benefits for veterans and their dependents. The benefits include compensation payments for disabilities or death related to military service; pensions based on financial need for totally disabled veterans or certain survivors for disabilities or death not related to military service; education and rehabilitation; home-loan guaranty; burials, including cemeteries, markers, and flags; and a comprehensive medical program involving a widespread system of nursing homes, clinics, and more than 170 hospitals.

Veterans Placement Service Board: Created by title IV of Servicemen's Readjustment Act of 1944 (58 Stat. 293; 38 U.S.C. 695), to cooperate with and assist U.S. Employment Service in providing an effective job counseling and employment service for veterans. Abolished by Reorg Plan 2, and functions transferred to Secretary of Labor, effective Aug. 20, 1949.

Veterans Reemployment Rights: Veteran rights provided for in Title 38, Chapter 43, of the United States Code. The Labor-Management Services Administration helps veterans, reservists, National Guard members, and rejectees to exercise their reemployment rights pertaining to the job, seniority, status, and rate of pay they would have achieved had they not been in the armed forces. (*See* Labor-Management Services Administraion.)

Villienage: Serfdom.

Vocational Rehabilitation Administration: Known as the Office of Vocational Rehabilitation until January 28, 1963. It became the Rehabilitation Services Administration on reorganization of the Department of Health, Education, and Welfare on August 15, 1967. (*See* Rehabilitation Services Administration.)

Voluntarism: A policy, held by Samuel Gompers, against any government involvement in labor-management relations.

Voluntary Arbitration: Arbitration that comes about as the result of the will of the participants in a dispute. It is required neither by law nor by a relevant contract.

Voluntary Checkoff: Required under Section 302 of the Labor-Management Relations (Taft-Hartley) Act.

Volunteers in Service to America (VISTA): Established by act of Nov. 8, 1966 (80 Stat. 1472; 42 U.S.C. 2991–2994e), to provide volunteers to work in domestic poverty areas to help the poor break the poverty cycle and administered by the Office of Economic Opportunity. Functions transferred to ACTION by Reorg. Plan 1 of 1971, effective July 1, 1971.

Wage Adjustment Board: Created May 29, 1942, by Secretary of Labor by direction of the President on May 14, 1942, to accomplish purpose of act of Mar. 3, 1931, as amended by act of Aug. 30, 1935 (46 Stat. 1494, 49 Stat. 1011; 40 U.S.C. 276a), and of section I(a) of the act of Jan. 30, 1942 (56 Stat. 23; 50 U.S.C. App. 901), as amended, and to investigate and act upon adjustment of wage rates, under Wage Stabilization Agreement of May 22, 1942, in building and construction industry. Disbanded upon termination of National Wage Stabilization Board.

Wage Assignments: The voluntary transfer by a worker of some of his or her earned wages to another party, e.g., for the payments of purchases or debts, union dues or assessments, or charity contributions.

Wage Board Employees: Federal government employees, typically manual workers, whose rates of pay are determined on the basis of prevailing rates for comparable work in the area. (Cf. Classification Act Employees.)

Wage Deductions: Money withheld from a worker's earnings by the employer to pay sums authorized by the employee or required by law. Social Security taxes, income taxes, and union dues may be included in such deductions.

Wage Determination: The process of establishing wage rates and wage structures through collective bargaining, employer determinations, arbitration, or other methods.

Wage Differentials: Differences in wages among occupations, plants, areas, industries, types of worker, etc. A more precise definition is usually attached to the term, e.g., sex differentials, geographic differentials.

Wage Drift: Generally, the differential change in average earnings levels over time as measured against negotiated changes. The difference between the level of actual earnings, which is influenced by many factors, and the level at which earnings would be if formal general wage changes alone are taken into account is thus likened to an upward drift.

Wage Escalation: *See* Escalator Clause.

Wage-Hour Law: *See* Fair Labor Standards Act.

Wage Leadership: The influence of the wage settlement reached by a large firm or group of firms on other negotiations in the same industry or area.

Wage Pattern: A wage change negotiated by a major company which is followed by similar increases in other companies in the same industry or area.

Wage Payments in Contracts for Public Construction: Section 2 of act of June 13, 1934 (48 Stat. 948; 40 U.S.C. 276c), requires Secretary of the Treasury and Secretary of the Interior jointly to make reasonable regulations for contractors or subcontractors on any public building or public work, or building or work financed in whole or in part by loans or grants from the United States. Functions transferred to Secretary of Labor by Reorg. Plan IV, effective June 30, 1940.

Wage Progression: A plan providing within-grade pay increases, generally at specified time intervals or on a merit basis, for workers in occupations having established minimum and maximum wage rates. (*See* Automatic Progression; Step Rates.)

Wage-Push Inflation: Increases in prices brought about by increases in wages.

Wage Rate: The monetary compensation for a given unit of time or output, exclusive of premium payments for overtime or other extras.

Wage Reopener: *See* Reopening Clause.

Wage Scale (Wage Schedule): A schedule specifying the pay structure for an establishment, industry, or locality. May also refer to a single rate. (*See* Union Rate.)

Wage Stabilization Board (ESA): Created by EO 10161 of Sept. 9, 1950, amended by EO 10233 of Apr. 21, 1951, to administer wage stabilization functions pursuant to title IV of Defense Production Act of 1950, EO 10161, and General Order 3 of Economic Stabilization Administrator; also labor dispute functions defined in EO 10233. Board reconstituted by EO 10377 of July 25, 1952. Terminated Apr. 30, 1953, pursuant to EO 10434 of Feb. 6, 1953, and provisions of Defense Production Act Amendments of 1952 and 1953 (66 Stat. 296, 67 Stat. 131; 50 U.S.C. App. 2071 note, 2166).

Wage Structure: The total of various elements and considerations that characterize the schedule of compensation in an establishment, industry, or area. Such elements are (1) relationship among rates for occupations of different skill requirements; (2) sex differentials, if any; (3) provisions for shift differentials, overtime, etc.; (4) interarea, interregional, and union-nonunion differentials; (5) methods of pay; (6) provisions for lunch and rest periods; and (7) supplementary benefits, such as vacations, sick leave, insurance, and health and welfare plans.

Wagner Act: *See* National Labor Relations Act (1935).

Wagner-Connery Act: *See* National Labor Relations Act.

Wagner-Peyser Act: Passed by Congress in 1933, the act provided for the establishment of the United States Employment Service, to be jointly administered and financed by matching federal and state funds.

Waiting Time: *See* Downtime.

Walking Delegate: The term, almost obsolete, for a union representative who is responsible for visiting employer establishments to see that the prevailing conditions are in accord with the contract and union conditions. (*See* Business Agent.)

Walkout: *See* Strike.   **Walsh-Healey Act:**

Walsh-Healey Act: *See* Public Contracts Act.

War Labor Disputes Act (Smith-Connally Act) (1943): Passed by Congress over President Roosevelt's veto, the act provided that strikes would be permitted only following a vote conducted by the National Labor Relations Board during a cooling-off period. Seizure of struck plants, criminal penalties for those advocating strikes, and a ban against union contributions to political campaigns were also authorized by the act. The act ended at the close of World War II.

War Manpower Commission: Established within Office for Emergency Management by EO 9139 of Apr. 18, 1942, to assure the most effective mobilization and utilization of the Nation's manpower for war. Terminated by EO 9617 of Sept. 19, 1945, and functions, except Procurement and Assignment Service transferred to Department of Labor.

Washington Job Protection Agreement: Negotiated in the railroad industry in 1936 and still in effect, this plan provides displacement and severance allowances to employees required to accept a new position or separated from employment because of unification, consolidation, merger, or pooling of separate facilities, operations, or services.

Washup Time: *See* Cleanup Time.

Watch: The shift or work period for a worker aboard ship.

WDL: *See* Workers Defense League.

Welfare Administration (HEW): Created by Secretary's reorganization of Jan. 28, 1963. Components consisted of Bureau of Family Services, Children's Bureau, Office of Juvenile Delinquency and Youth Development, and the Cuban Refugee Staff. These functions reassigned to the Social and Rehabilitation Service by Department reorganization on Aug. 15, 1967.

Welfare Plan (Employee-Benefit Plan): A general term usually covering health and insurance plans and other types of employee-benefit plans. The Welfare and Pension Plans Disclosure Act specifically defines welfare plans for purposes of compliance, but the term is often used loosely outside of the law.

Wetback: A Mexican worker, so designated in the southwestern part of the United States; used chiefly in contempt.

WFTU: *See* World Federation of Trade Unions.

Whipsawing: A union tactic of negotiating with one employer at a time, using each negotiated gain as a lever against the next employer.

White-Collar Workers: Office, clerical, administrative, sales, professional, and technical employees as distinguished from production and maintenance employees, who are usually referred to as blue-collar workers.

Wholesale Price Index: The index issued by the Bureau of Labor Statistics, U.S. Department of Labor, indicating changes in wholesale prices over stated time intervals.

Widow's Allowance: *See* Survivors' Benefits.

Wildcat Strike: *See* Strike.

"Willing and Able" Clause: A provision in a labor agreement which attempts to protect the union from lawsuits in the event of a strike. The contract is so written that only those "willing and able" to work are represented by the union. The term had its origin in the United Mine Workers contract of 1947.

WIN: *See* Work Incentive Program.

Withdrawn Cases: As defined by the National Labor Relations Board: Cases are closed as "withdrawn" when the charging party or petitioner, for whatever reasons, requests withdrawal of the charge or the petition and such request is approved.

Wobbly: The nickname of members of the Industrial Workers of the World.

Women's Bureau: Established in 1920 as part of the Department of Labor and charged specifically with formulating standards and policies that would promote the welfare of wage-earning women, improve their working conditions, increase their efficiency, and advance their opportunities for profitable employment. The Bureau, with ten regional offices throughout the United States, investigates and reports on all matters pertinent to the welfare of women in industry.

Women's Trade Union League: Organized by social workers and trade unionists in Boston in 1903 to promote trade union education among women and protective legislation for women in industry. Its activities included organizing women workers, picketing in labor disputes, and publicizing the need for improved working conditions. The League instrumental in setting up and running the Bryn Mawr Summer School for Working Women from 1921 to 1939. It ceased to exist in 1955.

Wool Textile Work Assignment Board: Created by EO 6877 of Oct. 16, 1934, to administer paragraph 2 of section 3 of Code of Fair Competition for Wool Industry. Expired June 15, 1935, having completed its work.

Work Force: *See* Labor Force.

Work Incentive Program (WIN): Funded through the Social Security Act since 1967, the program provides a broad range of employment and related services to welfare recipients who are receiving payments under Aid to Families with Dependent Children. Its objective is to enable qualifying and able recipients to become self-supporting and to reduce the welfare rolls. Jointly administered by the Departments of Labor and Health, Education, and Welfare through state employment services, other manpower agencies, and welfare agencies.

Work Permit: *See* Permit Card.

Work Projects Administration (Federal Work Agency): *See* Works Progress Administration.

Work Sharing (Division of Work; Share-the-Work; Spread-the-Work): An arrangement to avoid layoffs whereby available work during slack periods is spread as evenly or as equitably as possible among regular employees by reducing each worker's daily or weekly hours. Sometimes arranged on a week-on, week-off basis.

Work Stoppage: A temporary halt to work, initiated by workers or an employer, in the form of a strike or lockout. The term was adopted by the Bureau of Labor Statistics to replace "strikes and lockouts." In aggregate figures, "work stoppages" usually means "strikes and lockouts, if any"; as applied to a single stoppage, it usually means strike *or* lockout unless one or the other is clearly indicated. The difficulties in terminology arise largely from the inability of the Bureau of Labor Statistics (and, often, the parties) to distinguish between strikes and lockouts, since the initiating party is not always evident.

Workers' Compensation: A system of insurance required by state law and financed by employers which provides payment to workers or their families for occupational illness, injuries, or fatalities resulting in loss of wage income.

Workers Defense League (WDL): A New York City organization whose program is to find qualified minority youth and offer them sufficient preparation and counseling to enable them to compete effectively for apprenticeship openings. The program became the prototype for efforts by the federal government. The federal program under the Department of Labor is called the Apprenticeship Outreach Program.

Working Rules: *See* Shop Rules.

Working Stiff: Slang expression denoting an ordinary worker.

Workload: The amount of work to be performed by an employee, or output expected, in a given time period.

Work-to-Rule: A technique, developed by European workers in the railroad industry, of adhering very strictly to all the employer's safety rules and regulations in order to slow down operations. A mild form of sabotage against which the employer is almost helpless.

Works Progress Administration: Established by EO 7034 of May 6, 1935, under authority of Emergency Relief Appropriation Act of 1935, and continued by subsequent yearly Emergency Relief Appropriation Acts, to operate a program of useful public works projects, and to aid employable needy persons by providing work on such projects. Name changed to Work Projects Administration on July 1, 1939, by Reorg. Plan I, which provided for consolidation of Works Progress Administration into Federal Works Agency. Letter of the President to Federal Works Administrator, Dec. 4, 1942, authorized its liquidation.

Workweek: Usually, the expected or actual period of employment for the week, generally expressed in number of hours.

Some uses of the term may relate to the outside dimensions of a week (e.g., 7 consecutive days).

World Federation of Trade Unions (WFTU): Organized in September 1945 in Paris by delegates from fifty-six countries, the Federation was subjected to the dominance of Russian, French, and Italian Communists. In 1948 the British Trade Union Congress and the Congress of Industrial Organizations broke relations with the WFTU, and in cooperation with the American Federation of Labor, set up the International Confederation of Free Trade Unions.

Wrap-up Clause: A clause in a labor agreement that states that the contract itself is complete and sets forth all the terms and conditions of employment.

Written Grievance: A grievance reduced to writing.

YCP: *See* Youth Challenge Program.

Yearbook of Labor Statistics: Issued annually by the International Labor Office, indicating the comparative status of labor movements and labor conditions throughout the world.

Yellow-Dog Contract: An employment agreement whereby a worker agrees not to join a union, or to resign if already a member. Such contracts are unenforceable in federal courts since the passage of the Norris-LaGuardia Act. The act specifically says that yellow-dog contracts "shall not be enforceable in any court of the United States and shall not afford any basis for the granting of legal or equitable relief by any such court . . . ."

Youth Challenge Program (YCP): A program offering young people (ages 14 to 21) meaningful opportunities to provide volunteer service to poverty communities and to work toward the solution of poverty-related problems. Schools, colleges, and other public and nonprofit organizations that qualify as eligible sponsors develop YCP projects in conjunction with organizations that can use young workers in supplementing their efforts to eliminate poverty problems. It is YCP's intent that young volunteers be granted academic credit or recognition, such as released time from their school studies, so that they can provide their services. (*See* Action.)

Zipper Clause: An agreement provision specifically barring any attempt to reopen negotiations during the term of the agreement. (*See* Reopening Clause; Living Document.)

Indexes of the *Monthly Labor Review*

ABSENTEEISM

Absence from work--a look at some national data. 1973 July 24–30.
Unscheduled absence from work--an update. 1975 Aug. 36–39.

ACCIDENTS (See Work injuries.)

AFL-CIO

AFL-CIO convention, 1971. 1972 Jan. 67–69.
AFL-CIO focus: economy, farmworkers, and women's rights. 1975 Dec. 42–46.
ILO accomplishments--organized labor's view. 1975 May 37–39.
National politics dominates AFL-CIO convention. 1973 Dec. 59–60.

AGRICULTURE

ALF-CIO focus: economy, farmworkers, and women's rights. 1975 Dec. 42–46.
Collective farms in Communist China. 1973 Mar. 45–50.
Employment in agriculture: a profile. 1974 Apr. 28–32.
Green revolution in Latin America: Income effects, policy decisions. 1972 Mar. 20–27.
Unemployment insurance for farm workers. 1973 July 43.

AMERICAN ASSEMBLY

Papers from 43d meeting, November 1973. 1974 Feb. 57–59.

AMERICAN ECONOMIC ASSOCIATION

Papers from annual meeting, December 1973. 1974 Mar. 42–44.
Rethinking the allocation of resources in social research. 1974 June 36–39.
Social experiments: their uses and limitations. 1974 June 28–35.

AMERICAN FEDERATION OF GOVERNMENT EMPLOYEES

American Federation of Government Employees 23d convention. 1972 Nov. 51–53.
Finances and constitution are AFGE convention issues. 1974 Nov. 51–52.

AMERICAN FEDERATION OF STATE, COUNTY AND MUNICIPAL EMPLOYEES

Harmony prevails at AFSCME convention. 1974 Aug. 54–56.
State, County and Municipal Employees convention, 1972. 1972 Aug. 38–39.

AMERICAN FEDERATION OF TEACHERS

American Federation of Teachers endorses merger talks with NEA. 1973 Oct. 43–44.
American Federation of Teachers 56th annual convention. 1972 Oct. 55–56.

APPRENTICESHIP (See Education and training.)

ARBITRATION (See also Collective bargaining.)

Arbitration: the steel industry experiment. 1972 Nov. 7–10.
Attitudes toward mediation: U.S., Great Britain, and Ireland. 1975 Jan. 55–59.
Bargaining and arbitration in British civil service. 1973 Aug. 61–63.
Bargaining in 1975: oil, maritime, postal talks top light agenda. 1974 Dec. 24–33.
Binding arbitration in the public sector. 1975 Apr. 53–56.
Canada's discontent with strikes prompts interest in arbitration. 1973 Aug. 63–64.
Compulsory arbitration: The Australian experience. 1972 May 45–48.
Effect of the Gardner-Denver case on Title VII disputes. 1975 Mar. 46–48.
Expedited arbitration of labor grievances. 1975 Apr. 51–53.
Exploring alternatives to the strike--A special section. 1973 Sept. 59–66.
   A more activist approach by mediators.
   Some successful uses of interest arbitration.
   Combining mediation and arbitration.
   Mediation-arbitration: a trade union view.
   Mediation-arbitration: reactions from rank and file.
Final offer arbitration--initial experience in Wisconsin. 1974 Sept. 39–43.
Final-offer arbitration: the Indianapolis experience. 1973 May 20–25.
FMCS and arbitration: problems and prospects. 1971 Apr. 40–53.
Grievance and arbitration patterns in the Federal service. 1972 Nov. 23–30.
How other nations deal with emergency disputes. 1972 May 37–43.
Improving arbitration: roles of parties and agencies. 1972 Nov. 15–22.
Is a 'final offer' ever final? 1974 Sept. 43–45.
Mediation-arbitration from the employer's standpoint. 1973 Dec. 52–53.
Need for conciliation under Title VII, The. 1975 Mar. 48–50.
On improving arbitration: the transcript trauma. 1974 June 47–50.
Playboy Club International, Inc., Detroit Div. and Hotel, Motel and Restaurant Employees, Local 705. (FMCS case.) 1973 Jan. 69–70.
Some attempts to reduce arbitration costs and delays. 1972 Nov. 3–6.
Some ways to control arbitration costs: an arbitrator's view. 1975 June 31–33.
Transcripts as chastening rods in labor arbitration. 1974 Oct. 55–56.
Using two new arbitration techniques. 1972 Nov. 11–14.
Why few arbitrators are deemed acceptable. 1975 Sept. 27–30.

ASIA

Education levels and unemployment in Asian countries. 1973 Nov. 58–59.

ASSEMBLY OF GOVERNMENTAL EMPLOYEES

Assembly of Governmental Employees stresses professionalism. 1973 Nov. 56–57.

AUSTRALIA

Australian industrial relations--a system in transition? 1975 Apr. 65–67.

Compulsory arbitration: The Australian experience. 1972 May 45–48.

Unemployment in nine industrial nations, 1973-75. 1975 June 9–18.

Unemployment in the United States and eight foreign countries. 1974 Jan. 47–52.

AUSTRIA

Pension supplements based on need in five European countries. 1974 Mar. 48.

Wage agreements in Austria. 1974 Jan. 69.

What happens when everyone organizes? 1972 Apr. 27–32.

AUTOMATION (See Technological change.)

AUTO WORKERS (UAW)

United Automobile Workers' 23d constitutional convention. 1972 July 32–34.

BARGAINING (See Collective bargaining.)

BELGIUM

European experience: linking wages to cost-of-living indexes. 1975 Sept. 53–56.

Pension supplements based on need in five European countries. 1974 Mar. 48.

BENEFITS (See Supplemental benefits.)

BLUE-COLLAR WORKERS

Blue-collar/white-collar pay trends. 1971 June 3–36.
    Changing attitudes and patterns.
    Analysis of occupational wage differences.
    Earnings and family income.
    Compensation per man-hour and take-home pay.
    Comment on the findings.
Discontented blue-collar workers--a case study. 1971 Apr. 25–32.
Employment characteristics of low-wage workers. 1972 July 9–14.
Further look at the blue-collar blues. 1971 Nov. 40.
Has the blue-collar worker's position worsened? 1971 Sept. 23–29.

BRAZIL

Brazil raises its minimum wage levels. 1973 Nov. 59.

BUDGETS

Family budgets and geographic differences in price levels. 1975 Apr. 8–15.
Retired couple's budget updated to:
    Autumn 1971. 1972 July 39–36.
    Autumn 1972. 1973 Oct. 45–50.
    Autumn 1973. 1974 Oct. 57–61.
    Autumn 1974. 1975 Oct. 42–46.
Setting national priorities: the 1973 budget--a review essay. 1972 Sept. 33–37.
Spring 1970 cost estimates for urban family budgets. 1971 Jan. 59–61.
Urban family budgets updated to:
    Autumn 1971. 1972 June 46–50.
    Autumn 1972. 1973 Aug. 70–76.
    Autumn 1973. 1974 Aug. 57–62.
    Autumn 1974. 1975 June 42–48.

CANADA

Canada and the 4-day week. 1972 July 42–43.

Canada: Appraisal of expected economic trends to 1980. 1973 Jan. 65–66.

Canada's discontent with strikes prompts interest in arbitration. 1973 Aug. 63–64.

Canadian ministry studies use of layoff notice. 1973 Sept. 80.

How other nations deal with emergency disputes. 1972 May 37–43.

Labor union membership in Canada, 1971. 1972 June 54.

Productivity and unit labor costs in the United States and abroad. 1975 July 28–32.

Public sector bargaining: the Canadian experience. 1973 May 34–36.

Training completion: U.S. and Canada. 1972 July 39–40.

Unemployment in nine industrial nations, 1973-75. 1975 June 9–18.

Unemployment in the United States and eight foreign countries. 1974 Jan. 47–52.

Wage differentials between U.S. and Canada. 1975 Apr. 67–68.

CIVIL SERVANTS (See Public employees.)

CHINA

Administrative and technical workers in China. 1973 July 51–52.

Collective farms in Communist China. 1973 Mar. 45–50.

COLLECTIVE BARGAINING (See also Arbitration.)

Analysis of wage gains in 1974, An. 1975 Apr. 3–7.

Australian industrial relations--a system in transition? 1975 Apr. 65–67.

Autos, trucking head increased 1976 bargaining activity. 1975 Dec. 11–21.

Bargaining in 1975: oil, maritime, postal talks top light agenda. 1974 Dec. 24–33.

Binding arbitration in the public sector. 1975 Apr. 53–56.

Calendar of wage increases and negotiations:
    1971. 1971 Jan. 31–44.
    1972. 1972 Jan. 3–14.
    1973. 1973 Jan. 3–16.
    1974. 1974 Jan. 3–8.
    1975. 1974 Dec. 24–33.
    1976. 1975 Dec. 11–21.

City employee representation and bargaining policies. 1972 Nov. 43–50.

Collective bargaining and the media. 1974 Apr. 2.

Collective bargaining in higher education. 1973 May 33–34.

Collective bargaining settlements. 1975 Mar. 2.

Effect of escalators on wages in major contracts expiring in 1974. 1974 July 27–32.

Emergency disputes and public policy. 1971 Aug. 42–45.

Employee rights under an agreement: A current evaluation. 1971 Aug. 52–56.

Factfinding in public employee negotiations. 1972 Feb. 60–64.

Factfinding in teacher disputes: the Wisconsin experience. 1974 Oct. 47–51.

Government intervention in railroad disputes. 1971 Dec. 27–34.

How other nations deal with emergency disputes. 1972 May 37–43.

Inflation policies and collective bargaining. 1971 Aug. 48–52.

Institute of Collective Bargaining and Group Relations, Collective Bargaining Forum, June 7-8, 1973, Papers from. 1973 Sept. 33–66.

Layoff and recall provisions in major agreements. 1971 July 41–46.

Negotiated health programs: the California experience. 1975 Apr. 37–42.

NLRB remedies for unfair labor practices. 1971 Mar. 53–57.

NLRB's regulation of union job control. 1971 Mar. 59–62.

On improving aribtration: the transcript trauma. 1974 June 47–50.

Physicians' and dentists' bargaining organizations: a preliminary look. 1975 June 33–35.

Public sector strikes--legislative and court treatment. 1974 Sept. 19–22.

Recognition, negotiation, and work stoppages in hospitals. 1971 May 54–58.

Review of wage gains in 1973, A. 1974 Apr. 17-20.
Scheduled wage increases and escalator provisions in 1975. 1975 Jan. 43-48.
Seniority administration in major agreements. 1972 Dec. 36-39.
Social cost of bargaining: A European perspective. 1971 Aug. 56-59.
Some ways to control arbitration costs: an arbitrator's view. 1975 June 31-33.
Strike benefits of national unions. 1975 Mar. 17-23.
Transcripts as chastening rods in labor arbitration. 1974 Oct. 55-56.
Wage changes and bargaining gains in 1972. 1973 Apr. 17-20.

COMPREHENSIVE EMPLOYMENT AND TRAINING ACT OF 1973

Intergovernmental relations under the new manpower act. 1974 June 10-16.

CONFERENCES AND CONVENTIONS

Conferences

American Assembly, Papers from 43d meeting, November 1973. 1974 Feb. 57-59.
American Economic Association. Papers from annual meeting, December 1973. 1974 Mar. 42-44.
Assembly of Governmental Employees. 21st annual meeting. 1973 Nov. 56-57.
Industrial Relations Research Association. Papers from:
    23d annual meeting, December 1970. 1971 Mar. 51-62, Apr. 60-64.
    24th annual meeting, December 1971. 1972 Apr. 15-26.
    25th annual meeting, December 1972. 1973 Apr. 49-60, May 26-40.
    26th annual meeting, December 1973. 1974 Mar. 31-42, Apr. 41-52.
    27th annual meeting, December 1974. 1975 Mar. 35-50, Apr. 37-56, May 35-48.
Institute of Collective Bargaining and Group Relations. Papers from 3d annual Collective Bargaining Forum, May 1971. 1971 Aug. 42-59.
International Labor Conference:
    55th, October 1970. 1971 Feb. 49-54.
    56th, June 1971. 1971 Sept. 30-37.
    57th, June 1972. 1972 Sept. 38-46.
    58th, June 1973. 1973 Oct. 28-33.
    59th, June 1974. 1974 Sept. 55.
North American Conference on Labor Statistics. Papers from annual meeting, June 1971. 1971 Sept. 38-50.

Conventions

American Federation of Government Employees:
    23d biennial convention. 1972 Nov. 51-53.
    24th biennial convention. 1974 Nov. 51-52.
AFL-CIO:
    9th biennial constitutional convention, November 1971. 1972 Jan. 67-69.
    10th biennial convention, October 1973. 1973 Dec. 59-60.
    11th biennial convention, October 1975. 1975 Dec. 42-46.
International Association of Fire Fighters 31st annual convention, August 1972. 1972 Oct. 52-55.
International Brotherhood of Teamsters, Chauffeurs, Warehousemen and Helpers of America (Ind.), 20th constitutional convention, July 1971. 1971 Sept. 54-55.
International Longshoremen's and Warehousemen's Union (Ind.), 19th biennial convention, April 1971. 1971 Aug. 60-62.
International Longshoremen's Association (AFL-CIO), 42d convention, July 1971. 1971 Oct. 72.
International Union of District 50, Allied and Technical Workers of the United States and Canada, 4th constitutional convention, August 1971. 1971 Oct. 74.
National Education Association:
    51st, June 1972. 1972 Sept. 55-56.
    111th, July 1973. 1973 Sept. 67-68.

    112th, July 1974. 1974 Sept. 46-47.
United Automobile Workers:
    23d constitutional convention, April 1972. 1972 July 32-34.
    24th constitutional convention, June 1974. 1974 Aug. 52-54.
United Steelworkers of America:
    16th biennial convention, September 1972. 1972 Nov. 53-54.
    17th biennial convention, September 1974. 1974 Dec. 47-48.

CONSTRUCTION

Comment on wage-price restraints in construction. 1972 Jan. 70.
Construction manpower needs by 1980. 1971 July 12-18.
Discrimination, monopsony, and union power in the building trades. 1972 Apr. 24-26.
Labor and material requirements for apartment construction. 1975 Jan. 70-73.
Labor and materials required for highway construction. 1973 June 40-45.
Labor requirements for:
    Construction of single-family houses. 1971 Sept. 12-14.
    Federal highway construction. 1975 Dec. 31-36.
    Public housing. 1972 Apr. 40-42.
Minorities in construction referral unions--revisited. 1973 May 43-46.
Minority workers in construction referral unions. 1972 May 17-26.
Pension plan provisions in construction industry, 1973. 1975 Mar. 63-64.
Prefabricated construction: Developments abroad. 1972 May 27-36.
Productivity in the ready-mixed concrete industry. 1973 May 12-15.
Programs for providing winter jobs in construction. 1971 Feb. 24-32.
Surveying the gaps in construction statistics. 1971 Feb. 33-37.
Wage differentials between skilled and unskilled building trades. 1974 Oct. 64-66.
Wage-price restraints in construction. 1971 Sept. 46-47.
What subcontractors pay construction workers. 1972 Sept. 57-59.

CONSUMER PRICE INDEX (See also Prices.)

Determining the effects of quality change on the CPI. 1971 May 27-32.
Measuring regional price change in urban areas. 1973 Oct. 34-38.
New consumer price indexes by size of city. 1972 Aug. 3-8.
New CPI by size of city shows larger increases in big areas. 1973 Mar. 55-57.
Price indexes by size of city:
    1973 Mar. 55-57, June 54-55, Sept. 73-74, Dec. 65-67.
South and smaller areas led 1973 regional and city-size CPI's. 1974 May 59-64.
Southern cities again paced consumer price rise in 1974. 1975 May 53-57.
Updating the Consumer Price Index--an overview. 1974 July 3-20.

CONTROLS

Comment on wage-price restraints in construction. 1972 Jan. 70.
Indexing: the Brazilian solution and the U.S. economy. 1974 Nov. 57-58.
Minimizing the effect of controls. 1974 Mar. 39-42.
Pay Board assessment of wage controls. 1973 Apr. 21-23.
Problems in formulating a general pay standard. 1974 Mar. 31-34.
Reconciling Labor Department and stabilization agency wage data. 1973 Apr. 24-30.
Wage and price controls during the American revolution. 1973 Sept. 3-10.
Wage-price controls and incomes policies. 1974 Mar. 34-39.
Wage-price restraints in construction. 1971 Sept. 46-47.

COST OF LIVING

Adjusting wages to living costs: a historical note. 1974 July 21-26.
Cost-of-living escalation of pensions. 1972 June 21-24.
Cost-of-living indexes for Americans living abroad:
    1972 Apr. 46-47; July 41-42; Oct. 65.
    1973 Jan. 66; Apr. 69; July 48-49; Oct. 56.

1974 Jan. 69; Apr. 63; July 61; Oct. 62.
1975 Feb. 76; July 49; Nov. 71.
Employment and personal consumption expenditures. 1972 Mar. 39–47.
Exploring the distribution of earned income. 1972 Dec. 16–27.
Factors affecting trends in real spendable earnings. 1973 May ·16–19.
Family budgets and geographic differences in price levels. 1975 Apr. 8–15.
Retired couple's budget updated to:
    Autumn 1971. 1972 July 35–36.
    Autumn 1972. 1973. Oct. 45–50.
    Autumn 1973. 1974 Oct. 57–61.
    Autumn 1974. 1975 Oct. 42–46.
Spring 1970 cost estimates for urban family budgets. 1971 Jan. 59–61.
Tax effects in measures of economic well-being. 1974 Nov. 45–50.
Two measures of purchasing power contrasted. 1971 Apr. 3–14.
Urban family budgets updated to:
    Autumn 1971. 1972 June 46–50.
    Autumn 1972. 1973 Aug. 70–76.
    Autumn 1973. 1974 Aug. 57–62.
    Autumn 1974. 1975 June 42–48.
Usual weekly earnings of American workers. 1972 Mar. 28–38.

DEFENSE

Defense engineers: Do they have special reemployment problems? 1971 July 52–54.
Employment effects of reduced defense spending. 1971 Dec. 3–11.
Occupational impact of defense expenditures. 1971 Dec. 12–15.

DENMARK

European experience: linking wages to cost-of-living indexes. 1975 Sept. 53–56.
Problems in measuring unemployment. 1975 Aug. 3–10.
Universal sick pay coverage adopted in Denmark. 1973 July 49–50.

DISCRIMINATION (See Equal Employment Opportunity.)

EARNINGS AND WAGES

General

Adjusting wages of living costs: a historical note. 1974 July 21–26.
Amendments to the Federal minimum wage law, The 1974. 1974 July 33–37.
Analysis of wage gains in 1974, An. 1975 Apr. 3–7.
Annual earnings of household heads. 1975 Aug. 14–21.
Area sample changes in the area wage survey program. 1975 May 49–50.
Area wage survey test focuses on part-timers. 1974 Apr. 60–62.
Brazil raises its minimum wage levels. 1973 Nov. 59.
Calendar of wage increases and negotiations:
    1971. 1971 Jan. 31–44.
    1972. 1972 Jan. 3–14.
    1973. 1973 Jan. 3–16.
    1974. 1974 Jan. 3–8.
    1975. 1974 Dec. 24–33.
    1976. 1975 Dec. 11–21.
Changes in employee compensation, 1966 to 1972. 1975 Mar. 10–16.
Comparability wage programs. 1971 Sept. 38–43.
Developing a general wage index. 1971 Mar 3–8.
Differences in hourly earnings between men and women. 1971 May 9–15.
Differences in reporting family income. 1973 Apr. 46–48.
Differentials and overlaps in earnings of blacks and whites. 1971 Dec. 16–26.
Economic situation of Spanish Americans. 1973 Apr. 3–9.
Effect of changes in payment system on productivity in Sweden. 1973 Mar. 51–52.
Effect of escalators on wages in major contracts expiring in 1974. 1974 July 27–32.

Employment and Earnings Inadequacy: A measure of worker welfare. 1973 Oct. 19–27.
Employment characteristics of low-wage workers. 1972 July 9–14.
Exploring the distribution of earned income. 1972 Dec. 16–27.
Factors affecting trends in real spendable earnings. 1973 May 16–19.
Health and the education-earnings relationship. 1973 Apr. 61–63.
Impact of health on earnings and labor market activity. 1972 Oct. 46–49.
Improved area wage survey indexes. 1975 May 30–34.
Improving area wage survey indexes. 1973 Jan. 52–57.
Income policy and the price system. 1971 Aug. 45–48.
Manpower training and earnings. 1975 Apr. 46–48.
Measures of change in real wages and earnings. 1972 Feb. 48–53.
Measuring union-nonunion earnings differences. 1974 Dec. 3–9.
New measures of wage-rate change. 1974 Dec. 10–15.
Occupational rankings for men and women by earnings. 1974 Aug. 34–51.
Older workers: income and employment. 1972 Jan. 71.
Pay Board assessment of wage controls. 1973 Apr. 21–23.
Pay differences between men and women in the same job. 1971 Nov. 36–39.
Purchasing power of workers in the Soviet Union. 1971 May 39–45.
Quantitative research on the minimum wage. 1975 Apr. 44–46.
Recent trends in retirement benefits related to earnings. 1972 June 12–20.
Reconciling Labor Department and stabilization agency wage data. 1973 Apr. 24–30.
Report on self-employed Americans in 1973. 1975 Jan. 49–54.
Review of wage gains in 1973, A. 1974 Apr. 17–20.
Rise of prices and pay adjustments in Italy. 1973 July 47–48.
Romanian earnings data. 1972 Oct. 62–64.
Scheduled wage increases and escalator provisions in 1975. 1975 Jan. 43–48.
Tax effects in measures of economic well-being. 1974 Nov. 45–50.
Trends in overtime hours and pay, 1969-74. 1975 Feb. 45–52.
Trends in weekly earnings: an analysis. 1975 Aug. 22–32.
Two measures of purchasing power contrasted. 1971 Apr. 3–14.
Usual weekly earnings of American workers. 1972 Mar. 28–38.
Wage and price controls during the American Revolution. 1973 Sept. 3–10.
Wage changes and bargaining gains in 1972. 1973 Apr. 17–20.
Wage differentials between U.S. and Canada. 1975 Apr. 67–68.
Women's earnings: recent trends and long-run prospects. 1974 May 23–26.
Young workers and their earnings. 1971 July 3–11.

Specified industries

Airlines, August 1970. 1971 Dec. 68–72.
Analyzing earnings differentials in industry wage surveys. 1974 June 56–59.
Apparel:
    Dresses, August 1971. 1973 Mar. 57–58.
    Hosiery manufacturing:
        1969. Oct. 61.
        September 1970. 1972 Jan. 71–72.
        September 1973. 1975 Mar. 56–58.
    Separate trousers, men's and boys', January 1971. 1972 Mar. 53–54.
    Separate trousers, men's and boys', June 1974. 1975 Nov. 63–65.
    Shirts, men's and boys', July 1974. 1975 Sept. 48–50.
    Shirts, men's and boys', October 1971. 1973 Jan. 60–61.
    Suits and coats, men's and boys', April 1970. 1971 June 76–77.
    Suits and coats, men's and boys', April 1973. 1974 May 69–72.
    Suits and coats, women's and misses', August 1970. 1971 Nov. 58–59.
Auto dealer repair shops, June 1973. 1975 Sept. 45–48.
Banking, November 1969. 1971 Apr. 57–59.
Building trades, skilled and unskilled, July 1973. 1974 Oct. 64–66.
Candy manufacturing, August 1970. 1971 Nov. 59–60.

Chemical plants, June 1971. 1972 Oct. 57–58.
Cigarette manufacturing, May-June 1971. 1972 Mar. 54–55.
Cigar plants, March 1972. 1973 June 56–57.
Comment on wage-price restraints in construction. 1972 Jan. 70.
Commercial and savings banks, November 1973. 1975 May 59–61.
Communications, December 1973. 1975 Jan. 73–74.
Comparing municipal salaries with industry and Federal pay. 1971 Oct. 46–50.
Comparing union and nonunion wages in manufacturing. 1971 May 20–26.
Construction, 1969. 1972 Sept. 57–59.
Construction, September 1972. 1974 Aug. 71–75.
Contract cleaning, July 1971. 1973 Mar. 53–55.
Department stores, September 1973. 1975 Apr. 61–64.
Earnings differences in machinery manufacturing. 1974 July 38–47.
Electric and gas utilities, November 1972. 1974 Nov. 53–54.
Electronic data processing, February 1973. 1975 Mar. 51–56.
Fertilizer plants, April 1971. 1972 Aug. 40–41.
Flour mills, May 1972. 1973 Oct. 51–52.
Footwear, March 1971. 1973 June 57–58.
Foundries, nonferrous, June 1970. 1971 Sept. 56–57.
Furniture, October 1971. 1973 June 58–60.
Glassware manufacturing, May 1970. 1971 June 77.
Grocery stores, July 1971. 1973 May 47–49.
Grocery workers, July 1973. 1975 Feb. 72–74.
Hospitals, State and local government, August 1972. 1974 Apr. 56–57.
Hotels and motels, June 1973. 1975 Mar. 60–63.
Leather tanning, March 1973. 1974 Dec. 61–62.
Life insurance, December 1971. 1973 Aug. 66–68.
Machinery, nonelectrical, winter 1970-71. 1972 July 37–39.
Meat industry, March 1974. 1975 Dec. 53–55.
Metal mining, September 1972. 1974 Apr. 59–60.
Milk industry, November 1973. 1975 May 57–59.
Nonelectrical machinery, February 1973. 1974 Nov. 55–57.
Paint and varnish manufacturing, November 1970. 1972 Feb. 65–66.
Paperboard container and box plants, March 1970. 1971 Aug. 63–64.
Papermaking, November 1972. 1974 Apr. 58–59.
Petroleum and gas, August 1971. 1973 August 68–69.
Petroleum refining, April 1971. 1972 May 54–55.
Printing industry, July 1974 1975 Sept. 43–45.
Printing trades, July 1973. 1975 Feb. 69–71.
Restaurants and hotels, March 1970. 1971 July 47–51.
Steel foundries, November 1973. 1975 Nov. 62–63.
Steel industry, September 1972. 1974 Aug. 75–77.
Synthetic fibers manufacturing, December 1970. 1971 Nov. 55–56.
Textile dyeing and finishing, December 1970. 1972 Apr. 42–43.
Textile mills, August 1971. 1972 Sept. 59–60.
Wage differences among manufacturing establishments. 1971 May 16–19.
Wage-price restraints in construction. 1971 Sept. 46–47.
Where women work--an analysis by industry and occupation. 1974 May 3–13.

Specified occupations

Blue-collar/white-collar pay trends. 1971 June 3–36.
    Changing attitudes and patterns.
    Analysis of occupational wage differences.
    Earnings and family income.
    Compensation per man-hour and take-home pay.
    A comment on the findings.
Firemen and policemen, January 1972. 1972 Oct. 59–60.
Measuring annual earnings of household heads in production jobs. 1974 Apr. 3–11.
Nursing home, May 1973. 1975 Mar. 58–60.
Pay for police and firefighters. 1975 Oct. 55.
Telephone and telegraph workers:
    December 1969. 1971 Jan. 61–62.
    December 1970. 1972 Aug. 43–44.
    December 1972. 1974 July 57–58.
Transit employees, July 1973. 1974 July 55–56.

Transit employees, July 1974. 1975 July 47–48.
Truckdrivers, July 1973. 1974 Sept. 53–54.
Truckdrivers, July 1974. 1975 Sept. 50–51.
TV and appliance technicians, September 1972. 1974 July 53–55.
Where women work--an analysis by industry and occupation. 1974 May 3–13.
White-collar workers:
    1971 Jan. 53–56, 57–59.
    1972 Jan. 72–74, Dec. 39–41.
    1973 Oct. 53–55.
    1974 Oct. 63–64.
    1975 Oct. 52–54.

ECONOMIC DEVELOPMENT AND GROWTH

Economic growth and ecology--a biologist's view. 1971 Nov. 3–13.
Economic growth and ecology--an economist's view. 1971 Nov. 14–21.
Helping underdeveloped countries tackle unemployment. 1971 May 60–61.
Job-creating potential of Federal spending. 1975 Nov. 66–68.
Regional development of Japan. 1972 June 53–54.

ECONOMIC POLICIES AND PROGRAMS

AFL-CIO focus: economy, farmworkers, and women's rights. 1975 Dec. 42–46.
Economic indicators issued by States. 1971 Sept. 47–50.
Economic policy and inflation in the 1960's--a review essay. 1973 Nov. 49–52.
Economics and politics. 1974 Feb. 2.
Emergency disputes and public policy. 1971 Aug. 42–45.
Has the potential output of the U.S. economy been misstated? 1974 Dec. 34–42.
Indexing: the Brazilian solution and the U.S. economy. 1974 Nov. 57–58.
Internal and external functions of the Council of Economic Advisers. 1974 Mar. 42–43.
Labor and the economy in:
    1970. 1971 Jan. 3–13.
    1971. 1972 Jan. 15–27.
    1972. 1973 Jan. 17–26.
    1973. 1974 Jan. 9–21.
    1974. 1975 Jan. 3–16.
Labor markets and manpower policies in perspective. 1972 Sept. 22–28.
Maximum efficient rate of recovery. 1974 Mar. 2.
Numeraire. 1974 Mar. 2.
Problems in formulating a general pay standard. 1974 Mar. 31–34.
Quantitative research on the minimum wage. 1975 Apr. 44–46.
Rethinking the allocation of resources in social research. 1974 June 36–39.
Setting national priorities: the 1973 budget--a review essay. 1972 Sept. 33–37.
Social experiments: their uses and limitations. 1974 June 28–35.
State and local government spending in 1975. 1971 Aug. 19–28.
Statistical needs for setting policy. 1971 Sept. 43–45.
Three pitfalls for presidential advisers. 1974 Mar. 43–44.
United States economy in 1985, The. 1973 Dec. 3–42.
    An overview of BLS projections.
    Population and labor force projections.
    Projected changes in occupation.
    Projections of GNP, income, output, and employment.
Wage-price controls and incomes policies. 1974 Mar. 34–39.

EDUCATION AND TRAINING

A further view on laboratory education. 1971 Mar. 63–65.
American Federation of Teachers 56th annual convention. 1972 Oct. 55–56.
BLS pilot survey of training in industry, The. 1974 Feb. 26–32.
Breadth of training in apprenticeship. 1975 May 46–47.
Collective bargaining in higher education. 1973 May 33–34.
Developing reliable data on training in industry. 1974 Feb. 33–37.
Education Amendments of 1972. 1973 Jan. 50–51.
Educational attainment of workers:

March 1971. 1971 Nov. 30–35.
March 1972. 1972 Nov. 38–42.
March 1973. 1974 Jan. 58–62.
March 1974. 1975 Feb. 64–69.
Education and job training of scientists and engineers. 1973 Nov. 54–55.
Education and labor market tightness. 1974 Oct. 51–53.
Education levels and unemployment in Asian countries. 1973 Nov. 58–59.
Education of workers: projections to 1990. 1973 Nov. 22–31.
Employer and union reactions to foreign training practices. 1974 Feb. 65–66.
Faculty unionism in institutions of higher education. 1974 Apr. 48–51.
Going back to school at 35. 1973 Oct. 39–42.
Going back to school at 35 and over. 1975 Dec. 47–50.
Health and the education-earnings relationship. 1973 Apr. 61–63.
How union leaders view job training programs. 1971 Apr. 65–66.
Investment in human capital and black-white unemployment. 1975 July 13–21.
Job Corps experience with manpower training. 1975 October 3–11.
Job training programs in urban poverty areas. 1971 Aug. 36–41.
Labor market 'twist,' 1964–69, The. 1971 July 26–36.
Lessons for American apprenticeship from foreign innovations. 1975 May 47–48.
Manpower evaluations: vulnerable but useful. 1975 Apr. 51.
Manpower programs for criminal offenders. 1972 Aug. 17–24.
Manpower training and earnings. 1975 Apr. 46–48.
Manpower training and lifetime employment in Japan. 1974 Nov. 43–45.
Manpower training in Japan. 1973 Sept. 16–24.
Measurement and analysis of work training. 1975 Sept. 19–26.
National Education Association's 51st convention. 1972 Sept. 55–56.
Recurrent education and manpower training in Great Britain. 1975 Sept. 30–34.
Role of on-the-job training in a clinical laboratory. 1971 Mar. 65–69.
Statistical effect of work-training programs on the unemployment rate. 1972 Sept. 7–13.
Training completion: U.S. and Canada. 1972 July 39–40.
'Vocational training revolution' in France, The. 1974 Jan. 69.
Where women work--an analysis by industry and occupation. 1974 May 3–13.
Women in professional training. 1974 May 41–43.
Women in professional training--an update. 1975 Nov. 49–51.

EMERGENCY EMPLOYMENT ACT

Emergency Employment Act: An interim assessment. 1972 June 3–11.

EMPLOYMENT (See also Labor force; Unemployment.)

A 25-year look at employment as measured by two surveys. 1973 July 14–23.
Comparing employment shifts in 10 industrialized countries. 1971 Oct. 3–11.
Defense engineers: Do they have special reemployment problems? 1971 July 52–54.
Effect of the energy crisis on employment. 1974 Aug. 8–16.
Emergency Employment Act: An interim assessment. 1972 June 3–11.
Employment among the poor of six central cities. 1973 Oct. 52–53.
Employment and earnings inadequacy: a measure of worker welfare. 1973 Oct. 19–27.
Employment and exports, 1963–72. 1973 Aug. 16–27.
Employment and personal consumption expenditures. 1972 Mar. 39–47.
Employment and unemployment among Americans of Spanish origin. 1974 Apr. 12–16.
Employment and unemployment in:
    1970. 1971 Feb. 12–23.
    1971. 1972 Feb. 20–28.
    1972. 1973 Feb. 24–34.
    1973. 1974 Feb. 3–14.
    First half of 1974. 1974 Aug. 3–7.
    1974. 1975 Feb. 3–14.
    First half of 1975. 1975 Aug. 11–13.
Employment characteristics of low-wage workers. 1972 July 9–14.
Employment Cost Index: a measure of change in the 'price of labor.' 1975 July 3–12.
Employment developments in the first half of 1973. 1973 Sept. 25–28.
Employment effects of reduced defense spending. 1971 Dec. 3–11.
Employment in agriculture: a profile. 1974 Apr. 28–32.
Employment in manufacturing during the '69–'71 downturn. 1972 June 34–40.
Employment in the atomic energy field:
    1970. 1971 Oct. 51–54.
    1971. 1972 Sept. 47–49.
    1973. 1974 Sept. 23–27.
Employment of high school graduates and dropouts:
    October 1970. 1971 May 33–38.
    October 1971. 1972 May 49–53.
    October 1972. 1973 June 26–32.
    October 1973. 1974 Sept. 48–52.
    October 1975. 1975 Aug. 33–36.
Employment of recent college graduates:
    October 1971. 1973 Feb. 41–50.
    October 1972. 1974 Oct. 33–40.
Employment of school-age youth:
    October 1970. 1971 Aug. 13–18.
    October 1971. 1972 Aug. 25–30.
    October 1972. 1973 Sept. 11–15.
    October 1973. 1974 Oct. 66–67.
Employment of scientists and engineers in 1970. 1972 Apr. 43–44.
Employment situation of Vietnam-era veterans:
    1971 Sept. 3–11.
    1972 Dec. 7–15.
    1974 Aug. 17–26.
Enlarging the concept of a labor reserve. 1975 Apr. 20–28.
Exploring the adequacy of employment. 1973 Oct. 3–9.
Factors affecting the job status of workers with Spanish surnames. 1973 Apr. 10–16.
Federal employment standards legislation. 1973 Jan. 50–51.
France curbs its temporary work agencies. 1972 Nov. 55–56.
How employers screen disadvantaged job applicants. 1972 Sept. 14–21.
Industrial use of petroleum: effect on employment. 1974 Mar. 3–8.
Involuntary part-time work: a cyclical analysis. 1975 Sept. 12–18.
Jobs for veterans. 1973 Feb. 2.
Job situation of Vietnam-era veterans. 1974 Aug. 17–26.
Labor and the economy in:
    1970. 1971 Jan. 3–13.
    1971. 1972 Jan. 15–27.
    1973. 1974 Jan. 9–21.
    1974. 1975 Jan. 3–16.
Labor force growth and the return to full employment. 1972 Feb. 29–39.
Labor force participation of men, 25–54, by race. 1975 July 40–42.
Labor in a year of economic stabilization. 1973 Jan. 17–26.
Managerial jobseeking: methods and techniques. 1972 Dec. 29–30.
Manpower impact of Federal pollution control expenditures. 1975 June 54–56.
Manpower programs for criminal offenders. 1972 Aug. 17–24.
Marital and family characteristics of the labor force:
    March 1970. 1971 Mar. 46–50.
    March 1971. 1972 Apr. 4–8.
    March 1972. 1973 Apr. 31–36.
    March 1973. 1974 Apr. 21–27.
    March 1974. 1975 Jan. 60–64.
    March 1975. 1975 Nov. 52–56.
Multiple jobholding:
    1970 and 1971. 1971 Oct. 32–45.
    May 1973. 1974 May 64–69.
    May 1974. 1975 Feb. 60–64.
    May 1975. 1975 Nov. 56–62.

New Federal-State occupational employment statistics program. 1971 Oct. 12–17.

Occupational employment survey in printing and publishing. 1971 Nov. 56–58.

Older workers: income and employment. 1972 Jan. 71.

Open issues in public employment programs. 1975 May 29.

Pension provisions affecting the employment of older workers. 1973 Apr. 41–45.

Plunge of employment during the recent recession, The. 1975 Dec. 8–10.

Professional manpower: the job market turnaround. 1972 Oct. 9–15.

Regional differences in employment and unemployment, 1957–72. 1974 Mar. 15–24.

Removing roadblocks to minority hiring. 1972 Apr. 23–24.

Report on self-employed Americans in 1973, A. 1975 Jan. 49–54.

Role of the Job Bank in the placement process. 1972 Dec. 28–29.

Students and summer jobs. 1971 Feb. 55–62.

Students, graduates, and dropouts in the labor market, October 1974. 1975 Aug. 33–36.

Supplemental measures of labor force underutilization. 1975 May 13–23.

Trends in Federal employment, 1958–72. 1974 Oct. 17–25.

U.S. and U.S.S.R. civilian employment in government. 1972 Aug. 44–46.

Women in the labor force:
 The early years. 1975 Nov. 3–9.
 The middle years. 1975 Nov. 10–16.
 The later years. 1975 Nov. 17–24.

Work experience of the population:
 1969. 1971 Jan. 45–52.
 1970. 1971 Dec. 35–44.
 1972. 1974 Feb. 48–56.
 1973. 1974 Dec. 49–53.
 1974. 1975 Oct. 47–52.

Young workers: in school and out. 1973 Sept. 11–15.

ENERGY REQUIREMENTS

Effect of the energy crisis on employment. 1974 Aug. 8–16.

Effect of the energy crisis on employment in 172 industries. 1974 June 60.

Industrial use of petroleum: effect on employment. 1974 Mar. 3–8.

Labor and the economy in 1974. 1975 Jan. 3–16.

ENGINEERS

Attitudes of Federal scientists and engineers toward unions. 1975 Apr. 57–60.

Characteristics of jobless engineers. 1972 Oct. 16–21.

Defense engineers: Do they have special reemployment problems? 1971 July 52–54.

Education and job training of scientists and engineers. 1973 Nov. 54–55.

Employment in the atomic energy field:
 1970. 1971 Oct. 51–54.
 1971. 1972 Sept. 47–49.
 1973. 1974 Sept. 23–27.

Employment of scientists and engineers in 1970. 1972 Apr. 43–44.

Mobility of unemployed engineers: a case study. 1973 May 41–43.

Persons in engineering, scientific, and technical occupations. 1974 Feb. 66.

Projected demand for and supply of Ph. D. manpower, 1972–85. 1975 Dec. 52–53.

Reemployment assistance for engineers, scientists, and technicians. 1974 May 72–73.

EQUAL EMPLOYMENT OPPORTUNITY

Consent decree on seniority in the steel industry. 1975 Mar. 43–46.

Discrimination, monopsony, and union power in the building trades. 1972 Apr. 24–26.

Effect of the Gardner-Denver case on Title VII disputes. 1975 Mar. 46–48.

Equal Employment Opportunity Act of 1972. 1973 Jan. 50–51.

Evaluating the success of the EEOC compliance process. 1973 May 26–29.

Federal employment standards legislation. 1973 Jan. 50–51.

Labor and the economy in 1974. 1975 Jan. 3–16.

Labor market changes for black men since 1964. 1975 Apr. 42–44.

Minority workers in construction referral unions. 1972 May 17–26.

Need for conciliation under Title VII, The. 1975 Mar. 48–50.

Proposed revision of sex discrimination guidelines. 1974 May 58.

Sex stereotyping: its decline in skilled trades. 1974 May 14–22.

Working women and their membership in labor unions. 1974 May 27–33.

ESCALATOR CLAUSES

Analysis of wage gains in 1974, An. 1975 Apr. 3–7.

Calendar of wage increases and negotiations:
 1971. 1971 Jan. 31–44.
 1972. 1972 Jan. 3–14.
 1973. 1973 Jan. 3–16.
 1974. 1974 Jan. 3–8.
 1975. 1974 Dec. 24–33.
 1976. 1975 Dec. 11–21.

Does inflation ride escalators? Not yet, Pay Council study finds. 1975 Nov. 65–66.

Effect of escalators on wages in major contracts expiring in 1974. 1974 July 27–32.

Escalators and wage change: more comparisons. 1974 Oct. 54–55.

Escalators and wage change: the business cycle. 1974 Oct. 54.

Scheduled wage increases and escalator provisions in 1975. 1975 Jan. 43–48.

EUROPE

Comparing employment shifts in 10 industrialized countries. 1971 Oct. 3–11.

European experience: linking wages to cost-of-living indexes. 1975 Sept. 53–56.

European workers' participation in management. 1973 Feb. 9–15.

How other nations deal with emergency disputes. 1972 May 37–43.

Programs for providing winter jobs in construction. 1971 Feb. 24–32.

Regulation of private pension plans in Europe. 1971 Apr. 33–39.

Social security for migrant workers in the European communities. 1972 Oct. 65.

Turkish labor and the European Economic Community. 1972 June 52–53.

Unit labor costs in eleven countries. 1971 Aug. 3–12.

EXPORTS (See Foreign trade.)

FAIR LABOR STANDARDS ACT

Federal employment standards legislation. 1973 Jan. 50–51.

FARMING (See Agriculture.)

FEDERAL EMPLOYEES (See Public employees.)

FEDERAL MEDIATION AND CONCILIATION SERVICE

FMCS and arbitration: problems and prospects. 1971 Apr. 40–45.

Playboy Club International, Inc., Detroit Div. and Hotel, Motel and Restaurant Employees, Local 705. (FMCS case.) 1973 Jan. 69–70.

FINLAND

Pension supplements based on need in five European countries. 1974 Mar. 48.

FOREIGN TRADE

Contrasting experiences with trade adjustment assistance. 1975 June 25–30.

Employment and exports, 1963–72. 1973 Aug. 16–27.

Trade adjustment assistance to workers displaced by imports, fiscal 1963–73. 1974 Jan. 63–65.

Trends in U.S. export prices and OPEC oil prices. 1975 Nov. 36–43.

Unions, devaluation, and foreign trade. 1972 Apr. 15–18.

FRANCE

European experience: linking wages to cost-of-living indexes. 1975 Sept. 53–56.

France curbs its temporary work agencies. 1972 Nov. 55–56.

Improving working life--the role of European unions. 1974 Sept. 3–11.

Pension supplements based on need in five European countries. 1974 Mar. 48.

Productivity and unit labor costs in the United States and abroad. 1975 July 28–32.

Unemployment in nine industrial nations, 1973-75. 1975 June 9–18.

Unemployment in the United States and eight foreign countries. 1974 Jan. 47–52.

'Vocational training revolution' in France, The. 1974 Jan. 69.

FRINGE BENEFITS (See Supplemental benefits.)

GERMANY

European experience: linking wages to cost-of-living indexes. 1975 Sept. 53–56.

German retirement pensions made more flexible. 1973 Oct. 57.

Improving working life--the role of European unions. 1974 Sept. 3–11.

Productivity and unit labor costs in the United States and abroad. 1975 July 28–32.

Unemployment in the United States and eight foreign countries. 1974 Jan. 47–52.

GOVERNMENT WORKERS (See Public employees.)

GREAT BRITAIN (See United Kingdom.)

HEALTH AND SAFETY

Black Lung Benefits Act of 1972. 1973 Jan. 50–51.

Dental care added to Sweden's national health program. 1973 Oct. 57.

Determining eligibility for black-lung compensation. 1974 Mar. 25–30.

Effect of health on duration of unemployment, The. 1974 Apr. 53–54.

Enforcing job safety: a managerial view. 1975 Mar. 36–39.

Enforcing job safety: a union view of OSHA. 1975 Mar. 39–41.

Federal role in job safety and health, The. 1973 Aug. 28–55.
    Forging a partnership with the States.
    Inspection and enforcement at the workplace.
    If a citation is appealed.
    Research to determine what's dangerous.
    The new survey of occupational injuries and illnesses.

Health and the education-earnings relationship. 1973 Apr. 61–63.

How auxiliaries increase productivity of dentists. 1971 Apr. 63–64.

Impact of health on earnings and labor market activity. 1972 Oct. 46–49.

Improvements in employee health care benefits. 1972 Aug. 31–34.

Motor vehicles and occupational injuries in New York State. 1974 Dec. 57–61.

Negotiated health programs: the California experience. 1975 Apr. 37–42.

New approach to occupational safety and health statistics. 1972 Mar. 14–19.

OSHA and State job safety plans. 1974 Apr. 44–46.

Physician's assistants and the licensing issue. 1971 Apr. 62–63.

Physician's role in hospital management. 1971 Apr. 60–62.

Role of on-the-job training in a clinical laboratory. 1971 Mar. 65–69.

Safety and health provisions before and after OSHA. 1975 Sept. 40–43.

Setting priorities for NIOSH research. 1974 Mar. 41–43.

Three years of OSHA: the view from within. 1975 Mar. 35–36.

Union report slow rise in health, insurance, and pension coverage. 1975 Jan. 67–70.

Worker health and safety: an area of conflicts. 1975 Sept. 3–11.

HEALTH AND INSURANCE PLANS

Changes in employee compensation, 1966 to 1972. 1975 Mar. 10–16.

Changes in selected health care plans. 1975 Dec. 22–26.

Dental care added to Sweden's national health program. 1973 Oct. 57.

Employer expenditures for private retirement and insurance plans. 1972 July 15–19.

Health benefits and job loss. 1975 Apr. 2.

Sweden changes maternity benefit to parent insurance. 1973 Aug. 78.

Unions report slow rise in health, insurance, and pension coverage. 1975 Jan. 67–70.

HOSPITALS

Hospital and surgical insurance coverage. 1972 July 40.

Physician's role in hospital management. 1971 Apr. 60–62.

Recognition, negotiation, and work stoppages in hospitals. 1971 May 54–58.

Wage differences narrow between government and private hospitals. 1974 Apr. 56–57.

HOURS OF WORK

A look at the 4-day workweek. 1971 Oct. 33–37.

Canada and the 4-day week. 1972 July 42–43.

How many days make a workweek? 1975 Apr. 29–36.

Involuntary part-time work: a cyclical analysis. 1975 Sept. 12–18.

Measuring productivity under a 4-day week. 1974 Apr. 55–56.

New patterns for working time. 1973 Feb. 3–8.

Recent trends in overtime hours and premium pay. 1971 Aug. 29–35.

Seven-day production week proposed in India. 1973 June 64.

Trends in labor and leisure. 1971 Feb. 3–11.

Trends in overtime hours and pay, 1969-74. 1975 Feb. 45–52.

Work schedules and the rush hour. 1975 July 43–47.

HOUSING (See Construction.)

IMMIGRATION

Immigrant Mexicans and the U.S. work force. 1975 May 44–46.

Impact of immigration on the labor force. 1975 May 41–44.

IMPORTS (See Foreign trade.)

INCENTIVE PLANS

Analysis of Michigan's experience with work incentives. 1971 Sept. 15–22.

Time and incentive pay practices in urban areas. 1971 Dec. 53–56.

INCOME (See Earnings and wages.)

INDEXES (See also Prices.)

Comparing the behavior of two measures of price change. 1973 Aug. 66.

Consumer Expenditure Survey, The 1972-73. 1974 Dec. 16–23.

Cost-of-living indexes for Americans living abroad:
    1972 Apr. 46–47; July 41–42; Oct. 65.
    1973 Jan. 66; Apr. 69; July 48–49; Oct. 56.
    1974 Jan. 69; Apr. 63; July 61; Oct. 62.
    1975 Feb. 76; July 49; Nov. 71.

Determining the effects of quality change on the CPI. 1971 May 27–32.

Developing a general wage index. 1971 Mar. 3–8.

Does inflation ride escalators? Not yet, Pay Council study finds. 1975 Nov. 65–66.

Employment Cost Index: a measure of change in the 'price of labor.' 1975 July 3–12.

European experience: linking wages to cost-of-living indexes. 1975 Sept. 53–56.

Family budgets and geographic differences in price levels. 1975 Apr. 8–15.
Improved area wage survey indexes. 1975 May 30–34.
Improvements in the industrial price program. 1975 May 51–52.
Indexing: the Brazilian solution and the U.S. economy. 1974 Nov. 57–58.
Introducing price indexes for railroad freight. 1975 June 19–24.
Measuring regional price change in urban areas. 1973 Oct. 34–38.
New consumer price indexes by size of city. 1972 Aug. 3–8.
New hourly earnings index. 1971 Dec. 66–67.
Pension adjustment using wage and price indexes. 1974 Sept. 55–56.
Price indexes by size of city:
   1973 Mar. 55–57, June 54–55, Sept. 73–74, Dec. 65–67.
Toward comprehensive measurement of prices. 1971 Mar. 9–22.
Two measures of purchasing power contrasted. 1971 Apr. 3–14.
Southern cities again paced consumer price rise in 1974. 1975 May 53–57.
Statistical characteristics of major BLS series. 1974 July 48–52.
Subemployment: exclusion and inadequacy indexes. 1975 May 3–12.
Supplemental measures of labor force underutilization. 1975 May 13–23.
Updating the Consumer Price Index--an overview. 1974 July 3–20.

INDIA

Seven-day production week proposed in India. 1973 June 64.

INDUSTRIAL RELATIONS (See Labor-management relations.)

INDUSTRIAL RELATIONS RESEARCH ASSOCIATION

Papers from annual meeting:
   23d, December 1970. 1971 Mar. 51–62, Apr. 60–64.
   24th, December 1971. 1972 Apr. 15–26.
   25th, December 1972. 1973 Apr. 49–60, May 26–40.
   26th, December 1973. 1974 Mar. 31–42, Apr. 41–52.
   27th, December 1974. 1975 Mar. 35–50, Apr. 37–56, May 35–48.
Papers from spring meeting, May 1973. 1973 Aug. 56–64.

INFLATION (See also Prices.)

Inflation policies and collective bargaining. 1971 Aug. 48–52.
Inflation versus unemployment: another view of the trade-off. 1971 Nov. 49–54.
Inflation versus unemployment: the worsening trade-off. 1971 Feb. 68–71.
Manpower approach to the unemployment-inflation dilemma. 1971 May 51–54.

INSTITUTE OF COLLECTIVE BARGAINING AND GROUP RELATIONS

Papers from Collective Bargaining Forum:
   3d annual, May 1971. 1971 Aug. 42–59.
   5th annual, June 1973. 1973 Sept. 33–66.

INTERNATIONAL ASSOCIATION OF FIRE FIGHTERS

International Association of Fire Fighters convention. 1972 Oct. 52–55.

INTERNATIONAL BROTHERHOOD OF TEAMSTERS, CHAUFFEURS, WAREHOUSEMEN AND HELPERS OF AMERICA (Ind.)

International Brotherhood of Teamsters convention. 1971 Sept. 54–55.

INTERNATIONAL LABOR ORGANIZATION

ILO accomplishments--organized labor's view. 1975 May 37–39.
ILO accomplishments--the U.S. employers' view. 1975 May 40–41.
ILO conference adopts standard on carcenogenic substances. 1974 Sept. 55.
ILO plan for solving the job crisis in Colombia. 1971 Mar. 32–40.

Results of the 1972 International Labor Conference. 1972 Sept. 38–46.
Results of the 1973 International Labor Conference. 1973 Oct. 28–33.
Seamen and modernization of merchant shipping. 1971 Feb. 49–54.
Tripartism reaffirmed by the 1971 International Labor Conference. 1971 Sept. 30–37.
U.S. participation in the ILO: a political dimension. 1975 May 35–37.

IRELAND

Attitudes toward mediation: U.S., Great Britain, and Ireland. 1975 Jan. 55–59.
European experience: linking wages to cost-of-living indexes. 1975 Sept. 53–56.

ISRAEL

Israeli manpower in perspective. 1974 Aug. 63–66.
Israel's labor federation: a look at its current status. 1975 Nov. 69–71.
What happens when everyone organizes? 1972 Apr. 27–32.

ITALY

European experience: linking wages to cost-of-living indexes. 1975 Sept. 53–56.
Improving working life--the role of European unions. 1974 Sept. 3–11.
Rise of prices and pay adjustments in Italy. 1973 July 47–48.
Unemployment in nine industrial nations, 1973-75. 1975 June 9–18.
Unemployment in the United States and eight foreign countries. 1974 Jan. 47–52.

JAPAN

Computerizing labor market information in Japan. 1974 Feb. 60–64.
Japan's labor economy--prospect for the future. 1972 Oct. 3–8.
Japan's net national welfare provisionally computed. 1973 July 50.
Japan's public workers seek to regain the right to strike. 1973 Feb. 53.
Manpower training and lifetime employment in Japan. 1974 Nov. 43–45.
Manpower training in Japan. 1973 Sept. 16–24.
Productivity and unit labor costs in the United States and abroad. 1975 July 28–32.
Regional development of Japan. 1972 June 53–54.
Unemployment in nine industrial nations, 1973-75. 1975 June 9–18.
Unemployment in the United States and eight foreign countries. 1974 Jan. 47–52.
Union membership in Japan edged upward in 1972. 1973 July 51.
Workers' morale in Japan. 1975 June 49–53.

JOB SATISFACTION

Absence from work--a look at some national data. 1973 July 24–30.
Adapting jobs to people: experiments at Alcan. 1973 Apr. 49–51.
Asking the right questions on job satisfaction. 1973 Apr. 51–52.
Determining who are the 'hidden unemployed.' 1973 Mar. 27–30.
Discontented blue-collar workers--a case study. 1971 Apr. 25–32.
Discouraged workers and changes in unemployment. 1973 Mar. 8–16.
Discouraged workers and unemployment. 1974 Sept. 28–30.
Evaluating working conditions in America. 1973 Nov. 32–41.
Government approaches to the humanization of work. 1973 Apr. 52–54.
How *do* workers view their work in America? 1973 June 46–48.
How employers screen disadvantaged job applicants. 1972 Sept. 14–21.
How many days make a workweek? 1975 Apr. 29–36.
Improving working life--the role of European unions. 1974 Sept. 3–11.

Job enrichment: a union view. 1973 Apr. 54–56.

Job redesign, reform, enrichment--exploring the limitations. 1973 July 35–41.

Middle-aged job changers. 1973 June 60–61.

Six American workers assess job redesign at Saab-Scania. 1975 Sept. 52–53.

What's wrong with work in America?--a review essay. 1973 Mar. 38–44.

Worker dissatisfaction: a look at the causes. 1974 Feb. 57–58.

Worker dissatisfaction: a look at the economic effects. 1974 Feb. 58–59.

Working conditions survey as a source of social indicators. 1971 Apr. 15–24.

JOBSEEKING METHODS

Jobseeking methods used by American workers. 1975 Aug. 39–42.

Jobseeking methods used by unemployed workers. 1973 Feb. 35–40.

Methods of looking for work in Philadelphia's inner city. 1973 May 49–51.

JOB VACANCIES (See also Quit rate.)

Job tenure of workers, January 1973. 1974 Dec. 53–57.

Job vacancies, hires, quits, and layoffs in manufacturing, 1972. 1973 Apr. 66–67.

Job vacancies in manufacturing, 1969-73. 1974 Aug. 27–33.

Job vacancies in 1970. 1971 Feb. 20–21.

LABOR COSTS (See Unit labor cost.)

LABOR FORCE

General

Area wage survey test focuses on part-timers. 1974 Apr. 60–62.

Changes in the occupational structure of U.S. jobs. 1975 Mar. 24–34.

Disabled and the decline in men's labor force participation, The. 1973 Nov. 53.

Employment and unemployment among Americans of Spanish origin. 1974 Apr. 12–16.

Employment and unemployment in:
   1970. 1971 Feb. 12–23.
   1971. 1972 Feb. 20–28.
   1972. 1973 Feb. 24–34.
   1973. 1974 Feb. 3–14.
   First half of 1974. 1974 Aug. 3–7.
   1974. 1975 Feb. 3–14.
   First half of 1975. 1975 Aug. 11–13.

Employment in agriculture: a profile. 1974 Apr. 28–32.

Enlarging the concept of a labor reserve. 1975 Apr. 20–28.

Immigrant Mexicans and the U.S. work force. 1975 May 44–46.

Impact of immigration on the labor force. 1975 May 41–44.

Involuntary part-time work: a cyclical analysis. 1975 Sept. 12–18.

Job losers, leavers, and entrants: traits and trends. 1973 Aug. 3–15.

Labor force developments. 1974 Nov. 2.

Labor force developments, first quarter 1973. 1973 May 19.

Labor force participation of men, 25-54, by race. 1975 July 40–42.

Manpower decentralization. 1974 June 2.

Manpower evaluations: vulnerable but useful. 1975 Apr. 51.

Manpower impact of Federal pollution control expenditures. 1975 June 54–56.

Manpower impact of purchases by State and local governments. 1973 June 33–39.

Manpower programs for criminal offenders. 1972 Aug. 17–24.

Manpower revenue sharing. 1973 Apr. 2.

Migration and the labor force. 1974 Sept. 12–16.

New type of working life table for men. 1972 July 20–27.

Occupational migration, discrimination, and the central labor force. 1971 Dec. 57–61.

Occupational mobility of workers. 1975 Feb. 53–59.

On the decline of male labor force participation. 1972 Oct. 44–49.

Professional manpower: the job market turnaround. 1972 Oct. 9–15.

Profile of the temporary help industry and its workers. 1974 May 44–49.

Seasonal adjustment of labor force series. 1973 May 52.

Sex stereotyping: its decline in skilled trades. 1974 May 14–22.

Supplemental measures of labor force underutilization. 1975 May 13–23.

Unutilized manpower in poverty areas of six U.S. cities. 1971 Dec. 45–52.

Work experience of the population:
   1969. 1971 Jan. 45–52.
   1970. 1971 Dec. 35–44.
   1972. 1974 Feb. 48–56.
   1973. 1974 Dec. 49–53.
   1974. 1975 Oct. 47–52.

Characteristics

Analysis of unemployment by household relationship. 1972 Aug. 9–16.

Marital and family characteristics of workers:
   March 1970. 1971 Mar. 46–50.
   March 1971. 1972 Apr. 4–8.
   March 1972. 1973 Apr. 31–36.
   March 1973. 1974 Apr. 21–27.
   March 1974. 1975 Jan. 60–64.
   March 1975. 1975 Nov. 52–56.

Multiple jobholding:
   1970 and 1971. 1971 Oct. 32–45.
   May 1973. 1974 May 64–69.
   May 1974. 1975 Feb. 60–64.
   May 1975. 1975 Nov. 56–62.

Occupational characteristics of urban workers. 1971 Oct. 21–32.

Report on self-employed Americans in 1973, A. 1975 Jan. 49–54.

Education

Educational attainment of workers:
   March 1971. 1971 Nov. 30–35.
   March 1972. 1972 Nov. 38–42.
   March 1973. 1974 Jan. 58–62.
   March 1974. 1975 Feb. 64–69.

Education of workers: projections to 1990. 1973 Nov. 22–31.

Projections

Construction manpower needs by 1980. 1971 July 12–18.

Education of workers: projections to 1990. 1973 Nov. 22–31.

Future of work: Three possible alternatives. 1972 May 3–11.

Labor force growth and the return to full employment. 1972 Feb. 29–39.

On the accuracy of labor force projections. 1972 Oct. 22–29.

Projected demand for and supply of Ph. D. manpower, 1972-85. 1975 Dec. 52–53.

United States economy in 1985, The. 1973 Dec. 3–42.
   An overview of BLS projections.
   Population and labor force projections.
   Projected changes in occupation.
   Projections of GNP, income, output, and employment.

U.S. labor force: projections to 1990. 1973 July 3–13.

Women

Changes in the labor force status of women. 1973 Aug. 76.

Children of working mothers:
   March 1970. 1971 July 19–25.
   March 1972. 1973 Apr. 37–40.
   March 1973. 1974 May 50–58.
   March 1974. 1975 Jan. 64–74.

Labor force activity of married women. 1973 Apr. 31–36.

Occupations of women and black workers, 1962-74. 1975 Nov. 25–35.

Where women work--an analysis by industry and occupation. 1974 May 3–13.

Women in professional training. 1974 May 41–43.

Women in the labor force:
   The early years. 1975 Nov. 3–9.
   The middle years. 1975 Nov. 10–16.

The later years. 1975 Nov. 17–24.

Women in the professions, 1890-1970. 1974 May 34–39.

Women's earnings: recent trends and long-run prospects. 1974 May 23–26.

Working women and the division of household tasks. 1972 Apr. 9–14.

Youth

College students and the meaning of work. 1973 Nov. 42.

Employment of high school graduates and dropouts:
    October 1970. 1971 May 33–38.
    October 1971. 1972 May 49–53.
    October 1972. 1973 June 26–32.
    October 1973. 1974 Sept. 48–52.

Employment of recent college graduates. 1973 Feb. 41–50.

Employment of school-age youth:
    October 1971. 1972 Aug. 25–30.
    October 1973. 1974 Oct. 66–67.

High school class of 1972: more at work, fewer in college. 1973 June 26–32.

Students and summer jobs. 1971 Feb. 55–62.

Students, graduates, and dropouts in the labor market, October 1974. 1975 Aug. 33–36.

Young workers: in school and out. 1973 Sept. 11–15.

Young workers and their earnings. 1971 July 3–11.

LABOR HISTORY

Black studies in the Department of Labor, 1897-1907. 1974 June 17–27.

Coal strike of 1902--turning point in U.S. policy. 1975 Oct. 21–28.

Creation of the Bureau of Labor Statistics, The. 1975 Feb. 25–31.

Furor over working children and the Bureau of Labor, A. 1975 Oct. 34–36.

Origin of the U.S. Department of Labor. 1973 Mar. 3–7.

Selection of the first U.S. Commissioner of Labor, The. 1975 Apr. 16–19.

Senator's reaction to report on working women and children, A. 1975 Oct. 36–38.

Who is the father of Labor Day? 1972 Sept. 3–6.

LABOR LAW

Amendments to the Federal minimum wage law, The 1974. 1974 July 33–37.

Changes in State labor laws:
    1970. 1971 Jan. 14–21.
    1971. 1972 Jan. 29–39.
    1972. 1973 Jan. 27–36.
    1973. 1974 Jan. 22–31.
    1974. 1975 Jan. 17–29.

Changes in worker's compensation:
    1971. 1972 Jan. 51–55.
    1972. 1973 Jan. 45–49.
    1973. 1974 Jan. 32–38.
    1974. 1975 Jan. 30–37.

Federal employment standards legislation. 1973 Jan. 50–51.
    Longshoremen's and Harbor Workers' Compensation Act.
    Black Lung Benefits Act of 1972.
    Service Contract Act Amendments of 1972.
    Education Amendments of 1972.
    Equal Employment Opportunity Act of 1972.

Intergovernmental relations under the new manpower act. 1974 June 10–16.

Labor and the economy:
    1971. 1972 Jan. 15–27.
    1972. 1973 Jan. 17–26.
    1973. 1974 Jan. 9–21.
    1974. 1975 Jan. 3–16.

Measuring total and State insured unemployment. 1971 June 37–48.

Report on State unemployment insurance laws:
    1971 Jan. 22–30.
    1972 Jan. 40–50.
    1973 Jan. 37–44.

    1974 Jan. 39–46.
    1975 Jan. 38–42.

LABOR-MANAGEMENT RELATIONS

Attitudes toward mediation: U.S., Great Britain, and Ireland. 1975 Jan. 55–59.

Australian industrial relations--a system in transition? 1975 Apr. 65–67.

Autos, trucking head increased 1976 bargaining activity. 1975 Dec. 11–21.

Binding arbitration in the public sector. 1975 Apr. 53–56.

Consent decree on seniority in the steel industry. 1975 Mar. 43–46.

Developing language on alcoholism in labor-management contracts. 1975 June 57.

Dispute settlement in the electrical contracting industry. 1972 Apr. 21–23.

Effect of the Gardner-Denver case on Title VII disputes. 1975 Mar. 46–48.

European workers' participation in management. 1973 Feb. 9–15.

Expedited arbitration of labor grievances. 1975 Apr. 51–53.

Exploring alternatives to the strike--A special section. 1973 Sept. 33–66.
    Is the strike outmoded?
    The search for industrial peace.
    Basic steel's experimental negotiating agreement.
    In the public sector:
        Factfinding with binding recommendations.
        Variations in third-party decisionmaking.
        The unreal distinction between public and private sectors.
        Why teachers need the right to strike.
        Mutual anxiety: A California proposal.
    In the private sector:
        Replacing economic weapons with reason.
        Stretching out the duration of labor contracts.
        Partisan mediation by the central labor council.
        Limitations of arms-length or adversary arbitration.
        There is no alternative to the right to strike.
    Techniques:
        A more activist approach by mediators.
        Some successful uses of interest arbitration.
        Combining mediation and arbitration.
        Mediation-arbitration: a trade union view.
        Mediation-arbitration: reactions from rank and file.

Ford Motor Company as a multinational employer. 1973 Aug. 58–61.

Government intervention in railroad disputes. 1971 Dec. 27–34.

Industrial Relations Act tested in Britain. 1973 Jan. 64–65.

Intergovernmental relations under the new manpower act. 1974 June 10–16.

Japan's labor economy—prospect for the future. 1972 Oct. 3–8.

Labor and the economy in 1970. 1971 Jan. 3–13.

Labor and the economy in 1971. 1972 Jan. 15–27.

Legalism in U.S. industrial relations. 1971 Mar. 51–53.

Mediation-arbitration from the employer's standpoint. 1973 Dec. 52–53.

Need for conciliation under Title VII, The. 1975 Mar. 48–50.

New legal framework for Britain's industrial relations. 1972 Mar. 48–52.

Public employee labor relations in other democracies—a review essay. 1972 Oct. 37–43.

Public sector strikes--legislative and court treatment. 1974 Sept. 19–22.

Strike benefits of national unions. 1975 Mar. 17–23.

What happens when everyone organizes? 1972 Apr. 27–32.

LABOR MARKET

Additional thoughts on the dual labor market. 1972 Apr. 37–39.

Computerizing labor market information in Japan. 1974 Feb. 60–64.

Dual labor market and manpower policy, The. 1971 Nov. 45–48.

Education and labor market tightness. 1974 Oct. 51–53.

Enlarging the concept of a labor reserve. 1975 Apr. 20–28.

Geographic structure of unemployment rates, The. 1975 Mar. 3–9.

Immigrant Mexicans and the U.S. work force. 1975 May 44–46.
Impact of health on earnings and labor market activity. 1972 Oct. 46–49.
Impact of immigration on the labor force. 1975 May 41–44.
Job tenure of workers, January 1973. 1974 Dec. 53–57.
Labor market changes for black men since 1964. 1975 Apr. 42–44.
Labor market experience of recent college graduates. 1974 Oct. 33–40.
Labor markets and manpower policies in perspective. 1972 Sept. 22–28.
Professional manpower: the job market turnaround. 1972 Oct. 9–15.
Profile of the temporary help industry and its workers. 1974 May 44–49.
Quantitative research on the minimum wage. 1975 Apr. 44–46.
Subemployment: exclusion and inadequacy indexes. 1975 May 3–12.
Supplemental measures of labor force underutilization. 1975 May 13–23.
Unemployment in nine industrial nations, 1973-75. 1975 June 9–18.

LABOR ORGANIZATIONS

Attitudes of Federal scientists and engineers toward unions. 1975 Apr. 57–60.
Changes in employee compensation, 1966 to 1972. 1975 Mar. 10–16.
Emergence of urban low-wage unionism, The. 1974 Apr. 51–52.
Faculty unionism in institutions of higher education. 1974 Apr. 48–51.
How union leaders view job training programs. 1971 Apr. 65–66.
Improving working life--the role of European unions. 1974 Sept. 3–11.
Job enrichment: a union view. 1973 Apr. 54–56.
Labor and the economy in 1971. 1972 Jan. 15–27.
Labor and the economy in 1973. 1974 Jan. 9–21.
Labor in a year of economic stabilization. 1973 Jan. 17–26.
Labor union membership in Canada, 1971. 1972 June 54.
Mediation-arbitration: a trade union view.
Membership in labor unions and employee associations, 1972. 1974 Aug. 67–69.
Multinational corporations and trade unions. 1973 Aug. 56–58.
Public employee developments in 1971. 1972 Jan. 56–66.
Soviet Trade Union Congress urged to increase members' productivity. 1972 Aug. 49–50.
Strike benefits of national unions. 1975 Mar. 17–23.
Union and nonunion pay patterns in construction, September 1972. 1974 Aug. 71–75.
Union membership in Japan edged upward in 1972. 1973 July 51.
Union merger pace quickens. 1971 June 63–70.
Unions and local government: A review essay. 1972 Apr. 33–36.
Unions, devaluation, and foreign trade. 1972 Apr. 15–18.
What happens when everyone organizes? 1972 Apr. 27–32.
Women in labor unions. 1971 Feb. 42–48.
Women's participation in labor organizations. 1974 Oct. 3–9.
Working women and their membership in labor unions. 1974 May 27–33.

LABOR REQUIREMENTS

Labor and material requirements for apartment construction. 1975 Jan. 70–73.
Labor and materials required for highway construction. 1973 June 40–45.
Labor requirements for construction of single-family houses. 1971 Sept. 12–14.
Labor requirements for Federal highway construction. 1975 Dec. 31–36.

LATIN AMERICA

Green revolution in Latin America: Income effects, policy decisions. 1972 Mar. 20–27.

LEISURE

A look at the 4-day workweek. 1971 Oct. 33–37.
Trends in labor and leisure. 1971 Feb. 3–11.

LONGSHORE WORKERS

International Longshoremen's and Warehousemen's Union (Ind.). 19th biennial convention, April 1971. 1971 Aug. 60–62.
International Longshoremen's Association (AFL-CIO). 42d convention, July 1971. 1971 Oct. 72.
Longshoremen's and Harbor Workers' Compensation Act. 1973 Jan. 50–51.

LUXEMBOURG

Compensation for unemployment due to bad weather. 1972 July 42.

MALAYSIA

Malaysia strives for ethnic equality. 1972 Apr. 47.

MANPOWER DEVELOPMENT AND TRAINING ACT

Manpower evaluations: vulnerable but useful. 1975 Apr. 51.
Manpower training and earnings. 1975 Apr. 46–48.

MANUFACTURING

Comparing union and nonunion wages in manufacturing. 1971 May 20–26.
Earnings differences in machinery manufacturing. 1974 July 38–47.
Employment in manufacturing during the '69-'71 downturn. 1972 June 34–40.
Job vacancies, hires, quits, and layoffs in manufacturing, 1972. 1973 Apr. 66–67.
Job vacancies in manufacturing, 1969-73. 1974 Aug. 27–33.
Manufacturing labor costs in 1973 rose faster abroad than in U.S. 1974 July 60–61.
Manufacturing quit rates revisited: a cyclical view of women's quits. 1973 Dec. 53–56.
Manufacturing quit rates revisited: secular changes and women's quits. 1973 Dec. 56–58.
More on the causes of quits in manufacturing. 1973 June 48–49.
Prevalence of private retirement plans in manufacturing. 1973 Sept. 29–33.
Quits in manufacturing: a study of their causes. 1972 Nov. 31–37.
Unit labor costs in eleven countries. 1971 Aug. 3–12.
Wage differences among manufacturing establishments. 1971 May 16–19.

MARITIME

Collective bargaining in the maritime industry. 1973 Jan. 63.
Seamen and modernization of merchant shipping. 1971 Feb. 49–54.

MEDIATION

Attitudes toward mediation: U.S., Great Britain, and Ireland. 1975 Jan. 55–59.
Exploring alternatives to the strike--A special section. 1973 Sept. 59–66.
  A more activist approach by mediators.
  Some successful uses of interest arbitration.
  Combining mediation and arbitration.
  Mediation-arbitration: a trade union view.
  Mediation-arbitration: reactions from rank and file.
Mediation-arbitration from the employer's standpoint. 1973 Dec. 52–53.

MEDICAL CARE

Medical care spending since medicare. 1972 Aug. 47.

MEXICO

Immigrant Mexicans and the U.S. work force. 1975 May 44–46.

MINORITY WORKERS

Asian Americans in the labor market. 1975 July 33–38.

Black and white unemployment: the dynamics of the differential. 1974 Feb. 38–47.

Black studies in the Department of Labor, 1897-1907. 1974 June 17–27.

Consent decree on seniority in the steel industry. 1975 Mar. 43–46.

Differentials and overlaps in earnings of blacks and whites. 1971 Dec. 16–26.

Economic situation of Spanish Americans. 1973 Apr. 3–9.

Educational attainment of workers, March 1974. 1975 Feb. 64–69.

Effect of the Gardner-Denver case on Title VII disputes. 1975 Mar. 46–48.

Employment and unemployment among Americans of Spanish origin. 1974 Apr. 12–16.

Employment and unemployment in 1974. 1975 Feb. 3–14.

Enlarging the concept of a labor reserve. 1975 Apr. 20–28.

Factors affecting the job status of workers with Spanish surnames. 1973 Apr. 10–16.

Gathering data on residents of poverty areas. 1975 Feb. 38–44.

High school class of 1972: more at work, fewer in college. 1973 June 26–32.

Immigrant Mexicans and the U.S. work force. 1975 May 44–46.

Investment in human capital and black-white unemployment. 1975 July 13–21.

Jobs Puerto Ricans hold in New York City, The. 1975 Oct. 12–16.

Labor market changes for black men since 1964. 1975 Apr. 42–44.

Minorities in construction referral unions--revisited. 1973 May 43–46.

Minority workers in construction referral unions. 1972 May 17–26.

Need for conciliation under Title VII, The. 1975 Mar. 48–50.

Occupations of women and black workers, 1962-74. 1975 Nov. 25–35.

On the stability of relative black-white unemployment. 1973 May 30–32.

Persons of Spanish origin: education, income, employment. 1971 May 59–60.

Persons of Spanish origin: number and characteristics. 1975 Oct. 56.

Removing roadblocks to minority hiring. 1972 Apr. 23–24.

Women in the labor force:
  The early years. 1975 Nov. 3–9.
  The middle years. 1975 Nov. 10–16.
  The later years. 1975 Nov. 17–24.

MOBILITY

Commuting patterns of inner-city residents. 1973 Nov. 43–48.

Middle-aged job changers. 1973 June 60–61.

Migration and the labor force. 1974 Sept. 12–16.

Occupational migration, discrimination, and the central city labor force. 1971 Dec. 57–61.

Occupational mobility of workers. 1975 Feb. 53–59.

Social security for migrant workers in the European communities. 1972 Oct. 76.

MULTINATIONAL CORPORATIONS

Employment and payroll costs of multinational companies. 1974 Jan. 66–67.

Ford Motor Company as a multinational employer. 1973 Aug. 58–61.

Multinational corporations and trade unions. 1973 Aug. 56–58.

MULTIPLE JOBHOLDERS

Multiple jobholding:
  1970 and 1971. 1971 Oct. 38–45.
  May 1973. 1974 May 64–69.
  May 1974. 1975 Feb. 60–64.
  May 1975. 1975 Nov. 56–62.

NATIONAL LABOR RELATIONS BOARD (See also Decisions, pp. 21-24.)

Job reinstatement under section 8(a)(3) of the NLRA. 1971 Mar. 57–59.

NLRB petitions that are dismissed or withdrawn. 1971 June 71–72.

NLRB remedies for unfair labor practices. 1971 Mar. 53–57.

NLRB's regulation of union job control. 1971 Mar. 59–62.

NATIONAL EDUCATION ASSOCIATION

National Education Association again focuses on merger issue. 1973 Sept. 67–68.

National Education Association's 51st convention. 1972 Sept. 55–56.

NEA convention proposes new federation. 1974 Sept. 46–47.

NEW ZEALAND

Broad accident compensation law enacted in New Zealand. 1973 Aug. 77–78.

NONFINANCIAL CORPORATIONS

Measuring the productivity of nonfinancial corporations. 1974 Nov. 21–34.

NORWAY

New manpower program in Norway. 1972 Aug. 51–52.

Partial retirement plan enacted in Norway. 1974 Apr. 63–64.

OCCUPATIONAL SAFETY AND HEALTH

BLS reports first annual data on work injuries and illnesses. 1974 Mar. 45.

Determining eligibility for black-lung compensation. 1974 Mar. 25–30.

Enforcing job safety: a managerial view. 1975 Mar. 36–39.

Enforcing job safety: a union view of OSHA. 1975 Mar. 39–41.

Federal role in job safety and health, The. 1973 Aug. 28–55.
  Forging a partnership with the States.
  Inspection and enforcement at the workplace.
  If a citation is appealed.
  Research to determine what's dangerous.
  The new survey of occupational injuries and illnesses.

First results of new BLS survey of occupational injuries and illnesses. 1973 Mar. 58–59.

New approach to occupational safety and health statistics. 1972 Mar. 14–19.

Occupational injuries and illnesses. 1973 July 2.

Occupational safety and health. 1975 Feb. 2.

OSHA and State job safety plans. 1974 Apr. 44–46.

Safety and health provisions before and after OSHA. 1975 Sept. 40–43.

Setting priorities for NIOSH research. 1974 Mar. 41–43.

Three years of OSHA: the view from within. 1975 Mar. 35–36.

Worker health and safety: an area of conflicts. 1975 Sept. 3–11.

OCCUPATIONS

Bank unionization: status and prospects. 1975 Oct. 38–41.

Changes in the occupational structure of U.S. jobs. 1975 Mar. 24–34.

Experimental survey of occupations in metalworking. 1971 Oct. 18–20.

New Federal-State occupational employment statistics program. 1971 Oct. 12–17.

Occupational characteristics of urban workers. 1971 Oct. 21–32.

Occupational employment survey in printing and publishing. 1971 Nov. 56.

Occupational impact of defense expenditures. 1971 Dec. 12–15.

Occupational mobility of workers. 1975 Feb. 53–59.

Occupations of women and black workers, 1962-74. 1975 Nov. 25–35.

Projected changes in occupations. 1973 Dec. 18–26.

Regional pay differentials in white-collar occupations. 1971 Jan. 53–56.

Removal of sex stereotyping in census occupational classification. 1974 Jan. 67–68.
Salary profile of electronic data processing occupations. 1975 Mar. 51–56.
Trends in overtime hours and pay, 1969-74. 1975 Feb. 45–52.
Wage gains in hosiery manufacturing, 1970-73. 1975 Mar. 56–58.
Wages and tips in hotels and motels. 1975 Mar. 60–63.
Where women work--an analysis by industry and occupation. 1974 May 3–13.
White-collar workers:
    June 1969. 1971 Jan. 53–56.
    June 1970. 1971 Jan. 57–59.
    June 1971. 1972 Jan. 72–74.
    March 1972. 1972 Dec. 39–41.
    March 1973. 1973 Oct. 53–55.
    March 1974. 1974 Oct. 63–64.
    March 1975. 1975 Oct. 52–54.

OLDER WORKERS

Managerial jobseeking: methods and techniques. 1972 Dec. 29–30.
Older workers: income and employment. 1972 Jan. 71.
Pension provisions affecting the employment of older workers. 1973 Apr. 41–45.

PENSIONS (See also Supplemental benefits.)

Cost-of-living escalation of pensions. 1972 June 21–24.
Employer expenditures for private retirement and insurance plans. 1972 July 15–19.
German retirement pension made more flexible. 1973 Oct. 57.
Growth of benefits in a cohort of pension plans. 1971 May 46–50.
Key changes in major pension plans. 1975 July 22–27.
Multiemployer pension plan provisions in 1973. 1974 Oct. 10–16.
Pension formula summarization: an emerging research technique. 1971 Apr. 49–56.
Pension plan provisions in construction industry, 1973. 1975 Mar. 63–64.
Pension provisions affecting the employment of older workers. 1973 Apr. 41–45.
Pension reform: the long, hard road to enactment. 1974 Nov. 3–12.
Regulation of private pension plans in Europe. 1971 Apr. 33–39.
Survivor's pensions: an emerging employee benefit. 1973 July 31–34.
Unions report slow rise in health, insurance, and pension coverage. 1975 Jan. 67–70.

POPULATION

Population and labor force projections. 1973 Dec. 8–17.

POVERTY (See also Unemployment.)

Employment among the poor of six central cities. 1973 Oct. 52–53.
Gathering data on residents of poverty areas. 1975 Feb. 38–44.
How poverty area residents look for work. 1971 Mar. 41–45.
Job training programs in urban poverty areas. 1971 Aug. 36–41.
Measuring subemployment in poverty areas of large U.S. cities. 1973 Oct. 10–18.
Policy options for welfare reform. 1971 Mar. 23–31.
Unutilized manpower in poverty areas of six U.S. cities. 1971 Dec. 45–52.

PRICES

Anatomy of price change:
    1971 Feb. 38–41; June 73–75; Oct. 55–58; Dec. 62–65.
    1972 Feb. 40–47; June 41–45; Sept. 50–54; Dec. 31–36.
    1973 Feb. 16–23; June 50–54; Sept. 69–74; Dec. 61–65.
    1974 Feb. 15–25; June 51–55; Sept. 34–38; Dec. 43–46.
    1975 Feb. 15–24; June 36–41; Sept. 35–39; Dec. 37–41.
Comment on wage-price restraints in construction. 1972 Jan. 70.
Determining the effects of quality change on the CPI. 1971 May 27–32.
Family budgets and geographic differences in price levels. 1975 Apr. 8–15.

Food and fuel prices continue to increase in third quarter. 1975 Dec. 37–41.
Improvements in the industrial price program. 1975 May 51–52.
Introducing price indexes for railroad freight. 1975 June 19–24.
Labor and the economy:
    1970. 1971 Jan. 3–13.
    1971. 1972 Jan. 15–27.
    1973. 1974 Jan. 9–21.
    1974. 1975 Jan. 3–16.
Measuring regional price change in urban areas. 1973 Oct. 34–38.
Minimizing the effect of controls. 1974 Mar. 39–42.
Other early efforts at price control. 1974 Feb. 64.
Price change in 1971: rate of inflation slows down. 1972 Feb. 40–7.
Price changes in 1973--an analysis. 1974 Feb. 15–25.
Price increases slow down in first quarter of 1975. 1975 June 36–41.
Prices for food and fuels accelerate in second quarter. 1975 Sept. 35–39.
Prices in 1972: An analysis of changes during Phase 2. 1973 Feb. 16–23.
Problems in formulating a general pay standard. 1974 Mar. 31–34.
Purchasing power of workers in the Soviet Union. 1971 May 39–45.
Rise of prices and pay adjustments in Italy. 1973 July 47–48.
South and smaller areas led 1973 regional and city-size CPI's, The. 1974 May 59–64.
Southern cities again paced consumer price rise in 1974. 1975 May 53–57.
Toward comprehensive measurement of prices. 1971 Mar. 9–22.
Trends in U.S. export prices and OPEC oil prices. 1975 Nov. 36–43.
Value of quality changes in 1973 model passenger cars. 1972 Oct. 58.
Wage and price controls during the American Revolution. 1973 Sept. 3–10.
Wage-price restraints in construction. 1971 Sept. 46–47.

PRODUCTIVITY

Analyzing 'Productivity trends in intercity trucking.' 1974 Oct. 41–45.
Changes in productivity and unit labor costs--a yearly review. 1971 May 3–8.
Effects of changes in payment system on productivity in Sweden. 1973 Mar. 51–52.
First annual decline in labor productivity. 1975 Mar. 2.
How auxiliaries increase productivity of dentists. 1971 Apr. 63–64.
Measuring the productivity of nonfinancial corporations. 1974 Nov. 21–34.
Measuring productivity in the Federal Government. 1974 Nov. 13–20.
Measuring productivity under a 4-day week. 1974 Apr. 55–56.
New technology in laundry and cleaning services. 1972 Feb. 54–59.
Popularizing productivity. 1973 May 2, 112.
Problems in formulating a general pay standard. 1974 Mar. 31–34.
Problems of measuring railroad productivity. 1974 Oct. 26–32.
Productivity and cost movements in 1971. 1972 May 12–16.
Productivity and costs in perspective. 1975 Nov. 44–48.
Productivity and costs in the private economy:
    1972. 1973 May 3–7.
    1973. 1974 June 3–9.
    1974. 1975 June 3–8.
Productivity and unit labor costs in the United States and abroad. 1975 July 28–32.
Productivity and unit labor costs in 12 industrial countries. 1973 Nov. 14–21.
Productivity in:
    Bakery products industry 1947-71. 1972 June 25–28.
    Copper rolling and drawing industry, 1974. 1975 Dec. 27–30.
    Gasoline stations, 1958-73. 1975 Feb. 32–37.
    Hotels and motels, 1958-73. 1975 May 24–28.
    Intercity trucking, 1954-72. 1974 Jan. 53–57.
    Intercity trucking: a rejoinder. 1974 Oct. 45–47.

Metal cans industry, 1947-71. 1972 July 28–31.
Nonfinancial corporations. 1973 July 2.
Paints and allied products industry, 1958-72. 1973 Nov. 10–13.
Petroleum pipelines industry. 1971 Apr. 46–48.
Pharmaceutical industry, 1963-72. 1974 Mar. 9–14.
Ready-mixed concrete industry, 1958-71. 1973 May 12–15.
Selected industries:
    1970. 1971 Oct. 59–60.
    1971. 1972 Aug. 41–43.
    1972. 1973 July 43–45.
    1973. 1974 Aug. 69–71.
    1974. 1975 Dec. 50–52.
Steel foundries industry, 1954-71. 1973 May 8–11.
Structural clay products, 1958-74. 1975 Oct. 29–33.
Telephone communications, 1951-72. 1973 Nov. 3–9.
Progress in measuring productivity in government. 1972 Dec. 3–6.
Reflections on a productivity rule for a university's budget. 1974 Sept. 30–33.
Soviet Trade Union Congress urged to increase members' productivity. 1972 Aug. 49–50.
Unit labor costs in the U.S. and 10 other nations, 1960-71. 1972 July 3–8.

PROJECTIONS

Canada: Appraisal of expected economic trends to 1980. 1973 Jan. 65–66.
Construction manpower needs by 1980. 1971 July 12–18.
Education of workers: projections to 1990. 1973 Nov. 22–31.
Future of work: Three possible alternatives. 1972 May 3–11.
Labor force growth and the return to full employment. 1972 Feb. 29–39.
On the accuracy of labor force projections. 1972 Oct. 22–29.
Professional manpower: the job market turnaround. 1972 Oct. 9–15.
State and local government spending in 1975. 1971 Aug. 19–28.
United States economy in 1985, The. 1973 Dec. 3–42.
    An overview of BLS projections.
    Population and labor force projections.
    Projected changes in occupation.
    Projections of GNP, income, output, and employment.

PUBLIC EMPLOYEES

American Federation of Government Employees 23d convention. 1972 Nov. 51–53.
American Federation of Teachers endorses merger talks with NEA. 1973 Oct. 43–44.
American Federation of Teachers 56th annual convention. 1972 Oct. 55–56.
Attitudes of Federal scientists and engineers toward unions. 1975 Apr. 57–60.
Bargaining and arbitration in British civil service. 1973 Aug. 61–63.
Binding arbitration in the public sector. 1975 Apr. 53–56.
City employee representation and bargaining policies. 1972 Nov. 43–50.
Comparing municipal salaries with industry and Federal pay. 1971 Oct. 46–50.
Emergency disputes and public policy. 1971 Aug. 42–45.
Exploring alternatives to the strike--A special section. 1973 Sept. 43–52.
    Factfinding with binding recommendations.
    Variations in third-party decisionmaking.
    The unreal distinction between public and private sectors.
    Why teachers need the right to strike.
    Mutual anxiety: a California proposal.
Factfinding in public employee negotiations. 1972 Feb. 60–64.
Factfinding in teacher disputes: the Wisconsin experience. 1974 Oct. 47–51.
Federal employment standards legislation. 1973 Jan. 50–51.
Final-offer arbitration: the Indianapolis experience. 1973 May 20–25.
Grievance and arbitration patterns in the Federal service. 1972 Nov. 23–30.

Harmony prevails at AFSCME convention. 1974 Aug. 54–56.
International Association of Fire Fighters convention. 1972 Oct. 52–55.
Japan's public workers seek to regain the right to strike. 1973 Feb. 53.
Labor requirements for Federal highway construction. 1975 Dec. 31–36.
Measuring productivity in the Federal Government. 1974 Nov. 13–20.
Meeting the rising cost of public sector settlements. 1973 May 38–40.
National Education Association's 51st convention. 1972 Sept. 55–56.
Open issues in public employment programs. 1975 May 29.
Pay for police and firefighters. 1975 Oct. 55.
Public employee developments in 1971. 1972 Jan. 56–66.
Public employee labor relations in other democracies—a review essay. 1972 Oct. 37–43.
Public sector bargaining: the Canadian experience. 1973 May 34–36.
Public sector strikes--legislative and court treatment. 1974 Sept. 19–22.
State, County and Municipal Employees convention, 1972. 1972 Aug. 38–39.
Trends in Federal employment, 1958-72. 1974 Oct. 17–25.
Unions and local government: A review essay. 1972 Apr. 33–36.
U.S. and U.S.S.R. civilian employment in government. 1972 Aug. 44–46.
White collar pay increases. 1975 Aug. 2.
White-collar workers:
    June 1969. 1971 Jan. 53–56.
    June 1970. 1971 Jan. 57–59.
    June 1971. 1972 Jan. 72–74.
    March 1972. 1972 Dec. 39–41.
    March 1973. 1973 Oct. 53–55.
    March 1974. 1974 Oct. 63–64.
    March 1975. 1975 Oct. 52–54.

QUALITY CHANGE

Determining the effects of quality change on the CPI. 1971 May 27–32.
Value of quality changes in 1973 model passenger cars. 1972 Oct. 58.

QUIT RATE

Job vacancies, hires, quits, and layoffs in manufacturing, 1972. 1973 Apr. 66–67.
Manufacturing quit rates revisited: a cyclical view of women's quits. 1973 Dec. 53–56.
Manufacturing quit rates revisited: secular changes and women's quits. 1973 Dec. 56–58.
More on the causes of quits in manufacturing. 1973 June 48–49.
Quits in manufacturing: a study of their causes. 1972 Nov. 31–37.

REHABILITATION

Manpower programs for criminal offenders. 1972 Aug. 17–24.

RETIREMENT (See also Pensions.)

Coverage and vesting under private retirement plans. 1974 Jan. 65–66.
Employer expenditures for private retirement and insurance plans. 1972 July 15–19.
German retirement pensions made more flexible. 1973 Oct. 57.
Incidence of private retirement plans. 1971 July 37–40.
Partial retirement plan enacted in Norway. 1974 Apr. 63–64.
Prevalence of private retirement plans. 1975 Oct. 17–20.
Prevalence of private retirement plans in manufacturing. 1973 Sept. 29–33.
Recent trends in retirement benefits related to earnings. 1972 June 12–20.
Retired couple's budgets updated to:
    Autumn 1971. 1972 June 46–50.
    Autumn 1972. 1973 Aug. 70–76.

Autumn 1973. 1974 Aug. 57–62.
Autumn 1974. 1975 June 42–48.

ROMANIA

Romanian earnings data. 1972 Oct. 62–64.

RUSSIA (See U.S.S.R.)

SAFETY (See Health and safety.)

SALARIES (See Earnings and wages.)

SCIENTISTS

Attitudes of Federal scientists and engineers toward unions. 1975 Apr. 57–60.
Education and job training of scientists and engineers. 1973 Nov. 54–55.
Employment in the atomic energy field:
    1970. 1971 Oct. 51–54.
    1971. 1972 Sept. 47–49.
    1973. 1974 Sept. 23–27.
Employment of scientists and engineers in 1970. 1972 Apr. 43–44.
Projected demand for and supply of Ph. D. manpower, 1972-85. 1975 Dec. 52–53.
Reemployment assistance for engineers, scientists, and technicians. 1974 May 72–73.

SENIORITY

Consent decree on seniority in the steel industry. 1975 Mar. 43–46.
Seniority administration in major agreements. 1972 Dec. 36–39.

SOCIAL SECURITY

Children's allowances in five countries. 1972 Nov. 56–58.
Recent trends in retirement benefits related to earnings. 1972 June 12–20.
Social security for migrant workers in the European communities. 1972 Oct. 65.
Women and social security in five nations. 1973 Sept. 79.

SOCIAL WELFARE

Federal standards and social welfare. 1974 Apr. 41–43.
Malaysia strives for ethnic equality. 1972 Apr. 47.
Manpower programs for criminal offenders. 1972 Aug. 17–24.
Problems of measurement in areas of social concern. 1974 Sept. 17–18.
Social and welfare programs for the handicapped abroad. 1972 Aug. 50–51.
Social cost of bargaining: a European perspective. 1971 Aug. 56–59.
Tax effects in measures of economic well-being. 1974 Nov. 45–50.
Using experiments for social research and planning. 1972 Feb. 16–19.
Working conditions survey as a source of social indicators. 1971 Apr. 15–24.

SOUTH AFRICA

South Africa seeks to improve work conditions for black workers. 1974 July 59–61.

SOUTH AMERICA

ILO plan for solving the job crisis in Colombia. 1971 Mar. 32–40.

SPECIAL LABOR FORCE REPORTS

Analysis of unemployment by household relationship, An. 1972 Aug. 9–16.
Changes in employment and unemployment in 1970. 1971 Feb. 12–23.
Children of working mothers:
    March 1970. 1971 July 19–25.
    March 1972. 1973 Apr. 37–40.
    March 1973. 1974 May 50–58.

    March 1974. 1975 Jan. 64–74.
Educational attainment of workers:
    March 1971. 1971 Nov. 30–35.
    March 1972. 1972 Nov. 38–42.
    March 1973. 1974 Jan. 58–62.
    March 1974. 1975 Feb. 64–69.
Education of workers: projections to 1990. 1973 Nov. 22–31.
Employment and unemployment in:
    1970. 1971 Feb. 12–23.
    1971. 1972 Feb. 20–28.
    1972. 1973 Feb. 24–34.
    1973. 1974 Feb. 3–14.
    First half of 1974. 1974 Aug. 3–7.
    1974. 1975 Feb. 3–14.
    First half of 1975. 1975 Aug. 11–13.
Employment of high school graduates and dropouts:
    October 1970. 1971 May 33–38.
    October 1971. 1972 May 49–53.
    October 1972. 1973 June 26–32.
    October 1973. 1974 Sept. 48–52.
    October 1974. 1975 Aug. 33–36.
Employment of recent college graduates:
    October 1971. 1973 Feb. 41–50.
    October 1972. 1974 Oct. 33–40.
Employment of school-age youth:
    October 1970. 1971 May 13–18.
    October 1971. 1972 Aug. 25–30.
    October 1972. 1973 Sept. 11–15.
    October 1973. 1974 Oct. 66–67.
Employment situation of Vietnam-era veterans:
    1971 Sept. 3–11.
    1972 Dec. 7–15.
    1974 Aug. 17–26.
Going back to school at 35. 1973 Oct. 39–42.
Going back to school at 35 and over. 1975 Dec. 47–50.
Investment in human capital and black-white unemployment. 1975 July 13–21.
Job losers, leavers, and entrants: traits and trends. 1973 Aug. 3–15.
Jobseeking methods used by unemployed workers, 1970-71. 1973 Feb. 35–40.
Job situation of Vietnam-era veterans. 1974 Aug. 17–26.
Job tenure of workers, January 1973. 1974 Dec. 53–57.
Labor force activity of married women. 1973 Apr. 31–36.
Labor market experience of recent college graduates. 1974 Oct. 33–40.
Labor market 'twist,' 1964-69, The. 1971 July 26–36.
Marital and family characteristics of the labor force:
    March 1970. 1971 Mar. 46–50.
    March 1971. 1972 Apr. 4–8.
    March 1972. 1973 Apr. 31–36.
    March 1973. 1974 Apr. 21–27.
    March 1974. 1975 Jan. 60–64.
    March 1975. 1975 Nov. 52–56.
Multiple jobholding:
    1970 and 1971. 1971 Oct. 38–45.
    May 1973. 1974 May 64–69.
    May 1974. 1975 Feb. 60–64.
    May 1975. 1975 Nov. 56–62.
Occupational characteristics of urban workers. 1971 Oct. 21–32.
Occupational mobility of workers. 1975 Feb. 53–59.
Recent trends in overtime hours and premium pay. 1971 Aug. 29–35.
Report on self-employed Americans in 1973. 1975 Jan. 49–54.
Students and summer jobs. 1971 Feb. 55–62.
Students, graduates, and dropouts in the labor market, October 1974. 1975 Aug. 33–36.
Trends in overtime hours and pay, 1969-74. 1975 Feb. 45–52.
U.S. labor force: projections to 1990. 1973 July 3–13.
Usual weekly earnings of American workers. 1972 Mar. 28–38.
Where women work--an analysis by industry and occupation. 1974 May 3–13.
Work experience of the population:
    1969. 1971 Jan. 45–52.

1970. 1971 Dec. 35-44.
1972. 1974 Feb. 48-56.
1973. 1974 Dec. 49-53.
1974. 1975 Oct. 47-52.
Young workers: in school and out. 1973 Sept. 11-15.

STATE GOVERNMENT

Economic indicators issued by States. 1971 Aug. 47-50.
Manpower impact of purchases by States and local governments. 1973 June 33-39.
Negro jobs in southern State and local governments. 1973 June 63.
New Federal-State occupational employment statistics program. 1971 Oct. 12-17.
State and local government spending in 1975. 1971 Aug. 19-28.

STATISTICS

Area sample changes in the area wage survey program. 1975 May 49-50.
Consumer Expenditure Survey, The 1972-73. 1974 Dec. 16-23.
Manpower programs and unemployment statistics. 1973 Apr. 63-65.
Measures of variability for seasonally adjusted series. 1972 Feb. 66-67.
New approach to occupational safety and health statistics. 1972 Mar. 14-19.
New benchmarks introduced. 1975 Nov. 100.
New developments in labor statistics. 1972 Mar. 3-13.
New Federal-State occupational employment statistics program. 1971 Oct. 12-17.
New type of working life table for men. 1972 July 20-27.
Pension formula summarization: an emerging research technique. 1971 Apr. 49-56.
Problems of measurement in areas of social concern. 1974 Sept. 17-18.
Report of the Commission on Federal Statistics. 1972 Sept. 29-32.
Revisions in SMSA's reflect 1970 census data. 1973 July 42-43.
Statistical characteristics of major BLS series. 1974 July 48-52.
Statistical needs for setting policy. 1971 Sept. 43-45.
Statistics and analysis. 1973 Jan. 58-59.
Surveying the gaps in construction statistics. 1971 Feb. 33-37.
Table of expected working life for men, 1968. 1971 June 49-55.
Unemployment statistics and what they mean. 1971 Nov. 22-29.

STEELWORKERS

Arbitration: the steel industry experiment. 1972 Nov. 7-10.
Steelworkers review constitution, remove dues ceiling. 1974 Dec. 47-48.
United Steelworkers of America convention. 1972 Nov. 53-54.

STRIKES (See Work stoppages.)

SUBEMPLOYMENT (See Employment; Unemployment.)

SUPPLEMENTAL BENEFITS

Benefits in Great Britain for the 'working poor.' 1972 July 43.
Changes in employee compensation, 1966 to 1972. 1975 Mar. 10-16.
Children's allowances in five countries. 1972 Nov. 56-58.
Determining eligibility for black-lung compensation. 1974 Mar. 25-30.
Disabled widow's annuities under the Railroad Retirement Act. 1972 Sept. 61.
Employer expenditures for private retirement and insurance plans. July 15-19.
Federal standards and social welfare. 1974 Apr. 41-43.
Fringe benefits of urban workers. 1971 Nov. 41-44.
Growth of benefits in a cohort of pension plans. 1971 May 46-50.
Incidence of private retirement plans. 1971 July 37-40.
Pension plan provisions in construction industry, 1973. 1975 Mar. 63-64.
Pension provisions affecting the employment of older workers. 1973 Apr. 41-45.

Pension supplements based on need in five European countries. 1974 Mar. 48.
Prevalence of private retirement plans in manufacturing. 1973 Sept. 29-33.
Recent trends in retirement benefits related to earnings. 1972 June 12-20.
Salary profile of electronic data processing occupations. 1975 Mar. 51-56.
Survivor's pensions: an emerging employee benefit. 1973 July 31-34.
Universal sick pay coverage adopted in Denmark. 1973 July 49-50.

SURVEY METHODS

BLS revises procedures for estimating area unemployment. 1974 Jan. 65.
Development and uses of Table Producing Language, The. 1975 Feb. 74-75.
How useful is the cross-section sample survey? 1972 Feb. 3-10.
Improved area wage survey indexes. 1975 May 30-34.
Improvements in the industrial price program. 1975 May 51-52.
Longitudinal surveys: prospects and problems. 1972 Feb. 11-15.

SWEDEN

Dental care added to Sweden's national health program. 1973 Oct. 57.
Effects of changes in payment system on productivity in Sweden. 1973 Mar. 51-52.
Improving working life--the role of European unions. 1974 Sept. 3-11.
Sweden changes maternity benefit to parent insurance. 1973 Aug. 78.
Unemployment in nine industrial nations, 1973-75. 1975 June 9-18.
Unemployment in the United States and eight foreign countries. 1974 Jan. 47-52.
What happens when everyone organizes? 1972 Apr. 27-32.

SWITZERLAND

Pension supplements based on need in five European countries. 1974 Mar. 48.

TEACHERS

American Federation of Teachers endorses merger talks with NEA. 1973 Oct. 43-44.
American Federation of Teachers 56th annual convention. 1972 Oct. 55-56.

TECHNOLOGICAL CHANGE

Green revolution in Latin America: Income effects, policy decisions. 1972 Mar. 20-27.
Modernization and manpower in textile mills. 1973 June 18-25.
New technology in laundry and cleaning services. 1972 Feb. 54-59.
Technology and manpower in nonelectrical machinery. 1971 June 56-62.

TRADE EXPANSION ACT OF 1962

Contrasting experiences with trade adjustment assistance. 1975 June 25-30.
Trade adjustment assistance to workers displaced by imports, fiscal 1963-73. 1974 Jan. 63-65.

TRADE UNIONS (See Labor organizations.)

TRAINING (See Education and training.)

TURKEY

Turkish labor and the European Economic Community. 1972 June 52-53.

UNDEREMPLOYMENT (See Employment; Unemployment.)

UNEMPLOYMENT (See also Employment; Labor force.)

Analysis of unemployment by household relationship. 1972 Aug. 9–16.

Black and white unemployment: the dynamics of the differential. 1974 Feb. 38–47.

BLS revised procedures for estimating area unemployment. 1974 Jan. 65.

British jobless rate shows sharp decline. 1973 Sept. 80.

Characteristics of jobless engineers. 1972 Oct. 16–21.

Contrasting experiences with trade adjustment assistance. 1975 June 25–30.

Defense engineers: Do they have special reemployment problems? 1971 July 52–54.

Determining who are the 'hidden unemployed.' 1973 Mar. 27–30.

Discouraged workers and changes in unemployment. 1973 Mar. 8–16.

Discouraged workers and unemployment. 1974 Sept. 28–30.

Economic situation of Spanish Americans. 1973 Apr. 3–9.

Economics of might have been, The. 1974 Nov. 40–42.

Economics that never was, The. 1975 July 39–40.

Education levels and unemployment in Asian countries. 1973 Nov. 58–59.

Effect of health on duration of unemployment, The. 1974 Apr. 53–54.

Employment and unemployment among Americans of Spanish origin. 1974 Apr. 12–16.

Employment and unemployment in:
    1970. 1971 Feb. 12–23.
    1971. 1972 Feb. 20–28.
    1972. 1973 Feb. 24–34.
    1973. 1974 Feb. 3–14.
    First half of 1974. 1974 Aug. 3–7.
    1974. 1975 Feb. 3–14.
    First half of 1975. 1975 Aug. 11–13.

Enlarging the concept of a labor reserve. 1975 Apr. 20–28.

Estimating the number of 'hidden unemployed.' 1973 Mar. 17–26.

Gathering data on residents of poverty areas. 1975 Feb. 38–44.

Geographic structure of unemployment rates, The. 1975 Mar. 3–9.

Helping underdeveloped countries tackle unemployment. 1971 May 60–61.

Hidden unemployment and related issues (a bibliography). 1973 Mar. 31–37.

How poverty area residents look for work. 1971 Mar. 41–45.

ILO plan for solving the job crisis in Colombia. 1971 Mar. 32–40.

Inflation versus unemployment: another view of the trade-off. 1971 Nov. 49–54.

Inflation versus unemployment: the worsening trade-off. 1971 Feb. 68–71.

Investment in human capital and black-white unemployment. 1975 July 13–21.

Involuntary part-time work: a cyclical analysis. 1975 Sept. 12–18.

Job losers, leavers, and entrants: a cyclical analysis. 1974 Nov. 35–39.

Job losers, leavers, and entrants: traits and trends. 1973 Aug. 3–15.

Jobseeking methods used by unemployed workers. 1973 Feb. 35–40.

Job vacancies in manufacturing, 1969-73. 1974 Aug. 27–33.

Managerial jobseeking: methods and techniques. 1972 Dec. 29–30.

Manpower approach to the unemployment-inflation dilemma. 1971 May 51–54.

Manpower programs and unemployment statistics. 1973 Apr. 63–65.

Measuring subemployment in poverty areas of large U.S. cities. 1973 Oct. 10–18.

Measuring total and State insured unemployment. 1971 June 37–48.

Measuring unemployment in States and local areas. 1974 June 40–46.

Mobility of unemployed engineers: a case study. 1973 May 41–43.

On the stability of relative black-white unemployment. 1973 May 30–32.

Plunge of employment during the recent recession, The. 1975 Dec. 8–10.

Problems in measuring unemployment. 1975 Aug. 3–10.

Regional differences in employment and unemployment, 1957-72. 1974 Mar. 15–24.

Role of the Job Bank in the placement process. 1972 Dec. 28–29.

Statistical effect of work-training programs on the unemployment rate. 1972 Sept. 7–13.

Subemployment: exclusion and inadequacy indexes. 1975 May 3–12.

Supplemental measures of labor force underutilization. 1975 May 13–23.

Unemployment in nine industrialized countries. 1972 June 29–33.

Unemployment in the United States and eight foreign countries. 1974 Jan. 47–52.

Unemployment in nine industrial nations, 1973-75. 1975 June 9–18.

Unemployment statistics and what they mean. 1971 Nov. 22–29.

Where unemployment was heaviest in 1972. 1973 Aug. 65–66.

Work experience of the population:
    1969. 1971 Jan. 45–52.
    1970. 1971 Dec. 35–44.
    1972. 1974 Feb. 48–56.
    1973. 1974 Dec. 49–53.
    1974. 1975 Oct. 47–52.

UNEMPLOYMENT INSURANCE

Changes in State unemployment insurance legislation. 1974 Jan. 39–46.

Compensation for unemployment due to bad weather. 1972 July 42.

Measuring total and State insured unemployment. 1971 June 47–48.

Report on State unemployment insurance laws. 1972 Jan. 40–50.

State unemployment insurance changes in 1974. 1975 Jan. 38–42.

State unemployment insurance laws: status report. 1973 Jan. 37–44.

Status report on State unemployment insurance laws. 1971 Jan. 22–30.

Strike benefits of national unions. 1975 Mar. 17–23.

Unemployment insurance: its economic performance. 1974 Apr. 33–40.

Unions report slow rise in health, insurance, and pension coverage. 1975 Jan. 67–70.

U.S. impact on jobless aid and workmen's compensation. 1974 Apr. 46–48.

Work requirements in welfare and unemployment insurance. 1973 Apr. 56–57.

UNION MEMBERSHIP

Attitudes of Federal scientists and engineers toward unions. 1975 Apr. 57–60.

Changes in union membership. 1973 Oct. 2.

Labor membership. 1975 Oct. 2.

Labor union membership in Canada, 1971. 1972 June 54.

Physicians' and dentists' bargaining organizations: a preliminary look. 1975 June 33–35.

Portrait of union members. 1973 Jan. 2.

Trends in overtime hours and pay, 1969-74. 1975 Feb. 45–52.

Union membership in Japan edged upward in 1972. 1973 July 51.

Women in labor unions. 1971 Feb. 42–48.

Women's participation in labor organizations. 1974 Oct. 3–9.

Working women and their membership in labor unions. 1974 May 27–33.

UNION REPRESENTATION ELECTIONS

City employee representation and bargaining policies. 1972 Nov. 43–50.

NLRB petitions that are dismissed or withdrawn. 1971 June 71–72.

What factors influence union representation elections? 1972 Oct. 49–51.

UNIONS (See Labor organizations.)

UNIT LABOR COST

Changes in productivity and unit labor costs--a yearly review. 1971 May 3–8.
Employment Cost Index: a measure of change in the 'price of labor.' 1975 July 3–12.
Manufacturing labor costs in 1973 rose faster abroad than in U.S. 1974 July 60–61.
Productivity and costs in the private economy.
    1971. 1972 May 12–16.
    1972. 1973 May 3–7.
    1973. 1974 June 3–9.
    1974. 1975 June 3–8.
Productivity and unit labor costs in 12 industrial countries. 1973 Nov. 14–21.
Productivity and unit labor costs in the United States and abroad. 1975 July 28–32.
Unit labor costs in eleven countries. 1971 Aug. 3–12.
Unit labor costs in the U.S. and 10 other nations, 1960–71. 1972 July 3–8.

UNITED AUTOMOBILE WORKERS

Internal affairs hold the spotlight at the UAW convention. 1974 Aug. 52–54.

UNITED KINGDOM

Attitudes toward mediation: U.S., Great Britain, and Ireland. 1975 Jan. 55–59.
Bargaining and arbitration in British civil service. 1973 Aug. 61–63.
Benefits in Great Britain for the 'working poor.' 1972 July 43.
British coal mine strike of 1972. 1972 Oct. 30–36.
British jobless rate shows sharp decline. 1973 Sept. 80.
European experience: linking wages to cost-of-living indexes. 1975 Sept. 53–56.
Improving working life--the role of European unions. 1974 Sept. 3–11.
Industrial Relations Act tested in Britain. 1973 Jan. 64–65.
New legal framework for Britain's industrial relations. 1972 Mar. 48–52.
Productivity and unit labor costs in the United States and abroad. 1975 July 28–32.
Recurrent education and manpower training in Great Britain. 1975 Sept. 30–34.
Unemployment in nine industrial nations, 1973-75. 1975 June 9–18.
Unemployment in the United States and eight foreign countries. 1974 Jan. 47–52.

UNITED STEELWORKERS OF AMERICA

Consent decree on seniority in the steel industry. 1975 Mar. 43–46.
Steelworkers' convention reviews constitution, removes dues ceiling. 1974 Dec. 47–48.

U.S.S.R.

Purchasing power of workers in the Soviet Union. 1971 May 39–45.
Soviet Trade Union Congress urged to increase members' productivity. 1972 Aug. 49–50.
U.S. and U.S.S.R. civilian employment in government. 1972 Aug. 44–46.
U.S.S.R. economic and labor data for 1971. 1972 Oct. 61–62.

URBAN EMPLOYMENT SURVEYS

Employment among the poor of six central cities. 1973 Oct. 52–53.

VETERANS

Employment situation of Vietnam-era veterans:
    June 1971. 1971 Sept. 3–11.
    June 1972. 1972 Dec. 7–15.
Jobs for veterans. 1973 Feb. 2.
Job situation of Vietnam-era veterans. 1974 Aug. 17–26.
Labor force developments. 1974 Nov. 2.

WAGE CALENDAR

Calendar of wage increases and negotiations:
    1971. 1971 Jan. 31–44.
    1972. 1972 Jan. 3–14.
    1973. 1973 Jan. 3–16.
    1974. 1974 Jan. 3–8.
    1975. 1974 Dec. 24–33.
    1976. 1975 Dec. 11–21.

WAGE-PRICE POLICY

Comment on wage-price restraints in construction. 1972 Jan. 70.
Comparability wage programs. 1971 Sept. 38–43.
Income policy and the price system. 1971 Aug. 45–48.
Inflation policies and collective bargaining. 1971 Aug. 48–52.
Wage-price freeze and incomes policy, 1971. 1972 Apr. 18–21.
Wage-price restraints in construction. 1971 Sept. 46–47.

WAGES (See Earnings and wages.)

WELFARE PLANS

Social and welfare programs for the handicapped abroad. 1972 Aug. 50–51.
Welfare mothers and the work ethic. 1972 Aug. 35–37.

WELFARE REFORM

Federal standards and social welfare. 1974 Apr. 41–43.
Multiemployer pension plan provisions in 1973. 1974 Oct. 10–16.
Policy options for welfare reform. 1971 Mar. 23–31.
Welfare reform should mean the welfare of children. 1973 Apr. 57–59.
Work ethic is not enough. 1973 Apr. 59–60.
Work requirements in welfare and unemployment insurance. 1973 Apr. 56–57.

WEST GERMANY

German retirement pensions made more flexible. 1973 Oct. 57.
Unemployment in nine industrial nations, 1973-75. 1975 June 9–18.

WHITE-COLLAR WORKERS

Blue-collar/white-collar pay trends. 1971 June 3–36.
    Changing attitudes and patterns.
    Analysis of occupational wage differences.
    Earnings and family income.
    Compensation per man-hour and take-home pay.
    Comment on the findings.
Regional pay differentials in white-collar occupations. 1971 Jan. 53–56.
White-collar pay increases. 1975 Aug. 2.
White-collar pay in private industry. 1972 Dec. 39–41.
White-collar pay rises 9 percent. 1975 Oct. 52–54.
White-collar pay up 5.4 percent. 1973 Oct. 53–55.
White-collar pay up 6.6 percent. 1972 Jan. 72–74.
White-collar salaries rise 6.2 percent. 1971 Jan. 57–59.
White-collar salaries rise 6.4 percent. 1974 Oct. 63–64.

WHOLESALE PRICE INDEX (See Prices.)

WOMEN

AFL-CIO focuses on economic woes, farmworkers, and women's rights. 1975 Dec. 42–46.
Changes in the labor force status of women. 1973 Aug. 76.
Changes in the occupational structure of U.S. jobs. 1975 Mar. 24–34.
Children of working mothers:
    March 1970. 1971 July 19–25.
    March 1972. 1973 Apr. 37–40.

March 1973. 1974 May 50–58.
March 1974. 1975 Jan. 64–74.
Differences in hourly earnings between men and women. 1971 May 9–15.
International Women's Year ... More women focus on a career. 1975 Nov. 2.
Labor force activity of married women. 1973 Apr. 31–36.
Occupational rankings for men and women by earnings. 1974 Aug. 34–51.
Occupations of women and black workers, 1962-74. 1975 Nov. 25–35.
Pay differences between men and women in the same job. 1971 Nov. 36–39.
Profile of the temporary help industry and its workers. 1974 May 44–49.
Sex stereotyping: its decline in skilled trades. 1974 May 14–22.
Where women work--an analysis by industry and occupation. 1974 May 3–13.
Women and social security in five nations. 1973 Sept. 79.
Women in labor unions. 1971 Feb. 42–48.
Women in professional training. 1974 May 41–43.
Women in professional training--an update. 1975 Nov. 49–51.
Women in the economy. 1974 Jan. 2.
Women in the labor force:
    The early years. 1975 Nov. 3–9.
    The middle years. 1975 Nov. 10–16.
    The later years. 1975 Nov. 17–24.
Women in the professions, 1870-1970. 1974 May 34–39.
Women's earnings: recent trends and long-run prospects. 1974 May 23–26.
Women's participation in labor organizations. 1974 Oct. 3–9.
Working women and the division of household tasks. 1972 Apr. 9–14.
Working women and their membership in labor unions. 1974 May 27–33.

WORKERS' COMPENSATION

Broad accident compensation law enacted in New Zealand. 1973 Aug. 77–78.
Changes in employee compensation, 1966 to 1972. 1975 Mar. 10–16.
Changes in workmen's compensation:
    1971. 1972 Jan. 51–55.
    1972. 1973 Jan. 45–49.
    1973. 1974 Jan. 32–38.
    1974. 1975 Jan. 30–37.
Compromise agreements as a means of work injury settlement. 1971 Sept. 51–53.
Prevalence of private retirement plans. 1975 Oct. 17–20.
U.S. impact on jobless aid and workmen's compensation. 1974 Apr. 46–48.

WORKING LIFE

Table of expected working life for men, 1968. 1971 June 49–55.
New type of working life table for men. 1972 July 20–27.

WORK INJURIES AND ILLNESSES

BLS reports first annual data on work injuries and illnesses. 1974 Mar. 45.
Compromise agreements as a means of work injury settlement. 1971 Sept. 51–53.
Enforcing job safety: a managerial view. 1975 Mar. 36–39.
Enforcing job safety: a union view of OSHA. 1975 Mar. 39–41.
First results of new BLS survey of occupational injuries and illnesses. 1973 Mar. 58–59.
Setting priorities for NIOSH research. 1974 Mar. 41–43.
Three years of OSHA: the view from within. 1975 Mar. 35–36.
Work injuries in atomic energy establishments. 1972 June 50–51.

WORK MOTIVATION

Analysis of Michigan's experience with work incentives. 1971 Sept. 15–22.

WORK STOPPAGES

British coal mine strike of 1972. 1972 Oct. 30–36.
Canada's discontent with strikes prompts interest in arbitration. 1973 Aug. 63–64.
Exploring alternatives to the strike--A special section. 1973 Sept. 33–66.
Public sector strikes--legislative and court treatment. 1974 Sept. 19–22.
Recognition, negotiation, and work stoppages in hospitals. 1971 May 54–58.
Strike benefits of national unions. 1975 Mar. 17–23.
Work time lost decreased sharply in 1972. 1973 Feb. 2.

YOUTH (See Labor force, youth.)

INDEX OF VOLUME 99
JANUARY 1976 THROUGH DECEMBER 1976

AGRICULTURE

California's farm labor elections: an analysis of the initial results. 1976 Dec. 25–30.

AMALGAMATED CLOTHING AND TEXTILE WORKERS UNIONS

Textile and clothing unions merge, aim at organizing the South. 1976 Aug. 32–33.

AMERICAN POSTAL WORKERS UNION (AFL-CIO)

Postal Workers denounce working conditions, 'waste'. 1976 Oct. 34–35.

ARBITRATION

The supply of arbitrators: prospects for the 1980's. 1976 Oct. 27–29.
Use of arbitration to speed EEO adjudication. 1976 May 37–39.

BARGAINING (See Collective bargaining.)

BENEFITS (See Supplemental benefits.)

BUDGETS

Retired couple's budgets updated to autumn 1975. 1976 Oct. 36–37.
Urban family budgets updated to autumn 1975. 1976 July 40–44.

CANADA

Fair comparison criteria in public sector bargaining. 1976 July 50–51.
Unemployment compensation in eight industrial nations. 1976 July 18–24.

CIVIL SERVANTS (See Public employees.)

COLLECTIVE BARGAINING

Bargaining calendar to be heavy in 1977. 1976 Dec. 14–24.
Faculty representation: the vote at Cincinnati. 1976 Mar. 44–48.
Fair comparison criteria in public sector bargaining. 1976 July 50–51.
Labor and the economy during 1975. 1976 Jan. 3–16.
Resolution of impasses in public employee bargaining. 1976 Jan. 57–58.
Students and bargaining at public and private colleges. 1976 Apr. 31–33.
The supply of arbitrators: prospects for the 1980's. 1976 Oct. 27–29.
Why the slowdown in faculty bargaining? 1976 Mar. 43–44.

CONFERENCES AND CONVENTIONS

Amalgamated Clothing and Textile Workers Union, June 1975. 1976 Aug. 32–33.
American Postal Workers Union, 3d annual convention, August 1976. 1976 Oct. 34–35.

Industrial Relations Research Association, 28th annual meeting, December 1975. 1976 Mar. 37–48, Apr. 23–33, May 36–40.
International Brotherhood of Teamsters, Chauffeurs, Warehousemen and Helpers of America (Ind.), 21st convention, June 1976. 1976 Sept. 41–43.
United Steelworkers of America 18th biennial constitutional convention. 1976 Nov. 44–46.

CONSTRUCTION

Decline noted in hours required to erect Federal office buildings. 1976 Oct. 18–22.

CONSUMER PRICE INDEX (See also Prices.)

Food prices helped ease inflation during the third quarter of 1976. 1976 Dec. 40–45.
Rate of inflation eases in first quarter. 1976 June 31–36.
West, small cities led increase in consumer prices during 1975. 1976 July 35–37.

COST OF LIVING

Cost-of-living indexes for Americans living abroad. 1976 Jan. 63; July 52; Oct. 43.
Family expenditures by level of income. 1976 June 50.
Retired couple's budgets updated to autumn 1975. 1976 Oct. 36–37.
Urban family budgets updated to autumn 1975. 1976 July 40–44.

DECISIONS, COURT

Age Discrimination in Employment Act of 1967

Hodgson v. Approved Personnel Serv., Inc. 1976 Feb. 50–51.
National League of Cities v. Usery. 1976 Dec. 50–51.
Rogers v. Exxon Research & Eng'r Co. 1976 Feb. 51.

Back Pay Act

United States v. Testan. 1976 May 47.

Bankruptcy Act

Brotherhood of Railway Clerks v. REA Express, Inc. 1976 Jan. 66–67; Apr. 52.

Civil Rights Act of 1866

McDonald v. Sante Fe Trail Transportation Co. 1976 Nov. 53.

Civil Rights Act of 1871

Jones v. Pitt County Bd. of Educ. 1976 Apr. 51.

Civil Rights Act of 1964

Brown v. General Services Administration. 1976 Aug. 42–43.
Chandler v. Roudebush. 1976 Aug. 42–43.
EEOC v. Enterprise Assn. Steamfitters Local 638. 1976 Dec. 51.
EEOC v. Sheet Metal Workers, Local 28. 1976 June 52.
Fitzpatrick v. Bitzer. 1976 Sept. 51.

Franks v. Bowman Transp. Co. 1976 June 51–52.
Gonzalez v. Shanker. 1976 July 54–55.
Guy v. Robbins & Myers, Inc. 1976 Feb. 50.
Harper v. Trans World Airlines, Inc. 1976 Feb. 52.
Hochstadt v. Worcester Foundation for Experimental Biology, Inc. 1976 Apr. 51–52.
Hutchinson v. Lake Oswego School Dist. No. 7. 1976 Jan. 65.
Kirkland v. New York State Dep't of Correctional Services. 1976 Dec. 49–50.
Lewis v. Cohen. 1976 June 54.
Liberty Mutual Ins. Co. v. Wetzel. 1976 June 54.
McDonald v. Sante Fe Trail Transportation Co. 1976 Nov. 53.
Smith v. Troyan. 1976 Sept. 52.
Tyler v. Vickery. 1976 Sept. 52.
Voyles v. Ralph K. Davies Medical Center. 1976 Feb. 51–52.
Washington v. Davis. 1976 Aug. 41–42.
Williams v. Saxbe. 1976 July 55.

Classification Act

United States v. Testan. 1976 May 47.

Constitutional issues

Anthony v. Massachusetts. 1976 July 55–56.
Bishop v. Wood. 1976 Oct. 46.
Buckley v. Valeo. 1976 Apr. 48–49.
Cannon v. Guste. 1976 Feb. 49.
C.D.R. Enterprises, Inc. v. Board of Education. 1976 July 56.
Charlotte v. Local 660, International Association of Firefighters. 1976 Oct. 45–46.
Christensen v. Iowa. 1976 Dec. 50–51.
Kirkland v. New York State Dep't of Correctional Services. 1976 Dec. 49–50.
Dan J. Sheehan Co. v. OSAHRC. 1976 Jan. 66; June 54–55.
DeCanas v. Bica. 1976 May 45–46.
Doe v. Martin. 1976 Feb. 52.
Elrod v. Burns. 1976 Oct. 46–47.
Examining Board v. Flores de Otero. 1976 Sept. 52.
Fitzpatrick v. Bitzer. 1976 Sept. 51.
Godwin v. OSHRC. 1976 Nov. 54.
Hampton v. Mow Sun Wong. 1976 Aug. 43–44.
Hortonville Joint School District No. 1 v. Hortonville Education Association. 1976 Oct. 46.
Hudgens v. NLRB. 1976 May 46–47.
Hutchinson v. Lake Oswego School Dist. No. 7. 1976 Jan. 65.
Kelly v. Johnson. 1976 June 53–54.
Lavine v. Milne. 1976 May 45.
Lewis v. Cohen. 1976 June 54.
McCarthy v. Philadelphia Civil Serv. Comm'n. 1976 June 54.
Massachusetts Board of Retirement v. Murgia. 1976 Oct. 44.
Mathews v. Diaz. 1976 Aug. 43–44.
Mathews v. Eldridge. 1976 May 44–45.
National League of Cities v. Usery. 1976 Sept. 50–51; Dec. 50–51.
New Orleans v. Dukes. 1976 Oct. 45.
Olschock v. Village of Skokie. 1976 Feb. 49–50.
Pandol & Sons v. Agricultural Labor Relations Bd. 1976 Dec. 49.
Tennessee v. Dunlap. 1976 Nov. 54.
Turner v. Department of Employment Security. 1976 Jan. 64–65.
Tyler v. Vickery. 1976 Sept. 52.
United States v. Testan. 1976 May 47.
Usery v. Board of Educ. of Salt Lake City. 1976 Dec. 50–51.
Usery v. Turner Elkhorn Mining Co. 1976 Oct. 44–45.
Washington v. Davis. 1976 Aug. 41–42.

Controlled Substances Act

United States v. Moore. 1976 Apr. 52.

Equal Pay Act

University of Nebraska v. Dawes. 1976 Jan. 69; May 48.

Fair Labor Standards Act

Christensen v. Iowa. 1976 Dec. 50–51.
Leone v. Mobil Oil Corp. 1976 Apr. 52.
National League of Cities v. Usery. 1976 Sept. 50–51; Dec. 50–51.

Federal Coal Mine Health and Safety Act of 1969

National Coal Operator's Assn. v. Kleppe. 1976 Apr. 49–50.
Usery v. Turner Elkhorn Mining Co. 1976 Oct. 44–45.

Federal Election Campaign Act of 1971

Buckley v. Valeo. 1976 Apr. 48–49.

Freedom of Information Act

Chassen Bakers, Inc. v. NLRB. 1976 Mar. 50–51.
Climax Molybdenum Co. v. NLRB. 1976 Mar. 50–51.
Deering Milliken, Inc. v. Nash. 1976 Mar. 50–51.
Department of the Air Force v. Rose. 1976 July 53 54.
NLRB v. Hardeman Garment Corp. 1976 Mar. 50–51.
Poss v. NLRB. 1976 Mar. 50–51.
Title Guarantee Co. v. NLRB. 1976 Mar. 50–51; Dec. 49–50.

Labor-Management Reporting and Disclosure Act of 1959

Auto Workers v. National Right to Work Legal Defense & Educ. Foundation, Inc. 1976 Apr. 52.

National Guard Technicians Act of 1968

Tennessee v. Dunlap. 1976 Nov. 54.

National Labor Relations Act

Aetna Freight Lines, Inc. v. NLRB. 1976 May 48.
Buffalo Forge Co. v. United Steelworkers. 1976 Nov. 52–53.
Communications Workers, Local 1104 v. NLRB. 1976 Apr. 52.
Deboles v. Trans World Airlines, Inc. 1976 Feb. 50.
Local 14055, Steelworkers v. NLRB. 1976 Apr. 50–51; Dec. 49.
Local 627, Operating Eng'rs. v. NLRB. 1976 Jan. 69.
Lodge 76, IAM v. Wisconsin Employment Relations Commission. 1976 Sept. 51–52.
NLRB v. Bausch & Lomb, Inc. 1976 Mar. 51–52.
NLRB v. Bernard Gloekler North East Co. 1976 Nov. 53–54.
NLRB v. Martin A. Gleason, Inc. 1976 June 52–53.
Oil Workers v. Mobil Oil Corp. 1976 Sept. 52.
South Prairie Construction Co. v. Local No. 627, Operating Engineers. 1976 Aug. 44.
Teamsters v. Eazor Express, Inc. 1976 May 48.

Norris-LaGuardia Act

Buffalo Forge Co. v. United Steelworkers. 1976 Nov. 52–53.

Occupational Safety and Health Act of 1970

Accu-Namics, Inc. v. Secretary of Labor. 1976 June 55.
Dan J. Sheehan Co. v. OSAHRC. 1976 Jan. 66; June 54–55.
Godwin v. OSAHRC. 1976 Nov. 54.
Horne Plumbing & Heating Co. v. OSAHRC. 1976 June 54.
Leone v. Mobil Oil Corp. 1976 Apr. 52.

Railway Labor Act

Brotherhood of Railway Clerks v. REA Express, Inc. 1976 Jan. 66–67; Apr. 52.

State laws

Anthony v. Massachusetts. 1976 July 55–56.
Cannon v. Guste. 1976 Feb. 49.
C.D.R. Enterprises, Ltd. v. Board of Education. 1976 July 56.
DeCanas v. Bica. 1976 May 45–46.
Edgeley Educ. Assn. v. Edgeley Public School Dist. No. 3. 1976 Jan. 67–68.
Illinois v. Federal Tool & Plastics. 1976 Jan. 68–69.
Lavine v. Milne. 1976 May 45.
Massachusetts Board of Retirement v. Murgia. 1976 Oct. 44.
Nelson v. Miwa. 1976 July 54.
Pandol & Sons v. Agricultural Labor Relations Bd. 1976 Dec. 49.

Other court decisions

Dohrer v. Wakeman. 1976 Jan. 69.
EEOC v. Georgia-Pacific Corp. 1976 Mar. 51.

DECISIONS, NLRB

Glaziers Local 1621 and Glass Management Assn. 1976 Mar. 49–50.
Graphic Acts Int'l Union and Kable Printing Co. 1976 Apr. 50.

DISCRIMINATION

Unions and Title VII of the Civil Rights Act of 1964. 1976 Apr. 34–37.

EARNINGS AND WAGES

General

Bargaining calendar to be heavy in 1977. 1976 Dec. 14–24.
Earnings and jobs of ex-offenders. 1976 Dec. 31–39.
Federal pay procedures and the comparability survey. 1976 Aug. 27–31.
How type of employment affects earnings differences by sex. 1976 July 25–30.
Income, poverty in 1975. 1976 Nov. 2.
Long workweeks and premium pay. 1976 Apr. 7–12.
Occupational pay differences among metropolitan areas. 1976 May 29–35.
Scheduled wage increases and escalator provisions in 1976. 1976 Jan. 42–48.
200 years of earnings. 1976 Sept. 2.
Union wage trends in building trades. 1976 Jan. 59–60.
Wage gains in 1975: a summary analysis. 1976 Apr. 3–6.
Wages of communications workers double in decade. 1976 Jan. 61–62.
White-collar pay survey. 1976 Aug. 2.

Specified industries and occupations

Building trades, July 1, 1975. 1976 July 38–40.
Contract cleaning workers, July 1974. 1976 June 42–44.
Fabricated structural steel, November 1974. 1976 Aug. 36–38.
Furniture industry, November 1974. 1976 Apr. 46–47.
Glassware industry, May 1975. 1976 Sept. 47–49.
Grocery store workers, July 1975. 1976 Oct. 37–38.
How salaries of large cities compare with industry and Federal pay. 1976 Nov. 23–28.
Labor and materials requirements for sewer works construction. 1976 Nov. 38–41.
Miscellaneous plastics products industry, September 1974. 1976 June 44–45.
Printing trades, July 1975. 1976 Aug. 34–36.
Production workers at automobile manufacturers, April 1974. 1976 June 45–47.
Transit operating employees, July 1975. 1976 Apr. 44–45.
Trucking industry, July 1975. 1976 Sept. 45–47.
Women's dress manufacturing, August 1974. 1976 July 44–47.

ECONOMIC DEVELOPMENT AND GROWTH

Economic and political issues in population redistribution. 1976 Apr. 25–27.
Future labor supply for lower level occupations. 1976 Mar. 22–31.
Revised industry projections to 1985. 1976 Nov. 3–9.
Revised projections of the U.S. economy to 1980 and 1985. 1976 Mar. 9–21.

ECONOMIC POLICIES AND PROGRAMS

Evaluation of BLS 1970 economic and employment projections. 1976 Aug. 13–26.
Labor and the economy during 1975. 1976 Jan. 3–16.

EDUCATION AND TRAINING

Educational and occupational goals of men and women at black colleges. 1976 June 10–16.
Start-up training and rural industrial location. 1976 Apr. 23–25.
Students, graduates, and dropouts in the labor market, October 1975. 1976 June 37–41.

EMPLOYMENT

Demographic influences on labor force rates of black males. 1976 Nov. 42–43.
Employment and unemployment during 1975. 1976 Feb. 11–20.
Employment and unemployment in the first half of 1976. 1976 Aug. 9–12.
Employment and unemployment: the doughnut or the hole? 1976 Feb. 3–10.
Evaluation of BLS 1970 economic and employment projections. 1976 Aug. 13–26.
Labor and materials requirements for sewer works construction. 1976 Nov. 38–41.
New labor force projections to 1990. 1976 Dec. 3–13.
Revised industry projections to 1985. 1976 Nov. 3–9.
Revised occupational projections to 1985. 1976 Nov. 10–22.
Seasonally adjusted employment data. 1976 Mar. 2.
Work experience of the population, 1975. 1976 Nov. 47–51.
Workweeks and leisure: an analysis of trends, 1948-75. 1976 Aug. 3–8.
Youth in the labor force: an area study. 1976 July 3–9.

EQUAL EMPLOYMENT OPPORTUNITY

Cost-sharing in gaining equal employment opportunity. 1976 May 39–40.
Defining the labor market for equal employment standards. 1976 Mar. 32–36.
Unions and Title VII of the Civil Rights Act of 1964. 1976 Apr. 34–37.
Use of arbitration to speed EEO adjudication. 1976 May 37–39.

ESCALATOR CLAUSES

Bargaining calendar to be heavy in 1977. 1976 Dec. 14–24.

FARMING (See Agriculture.)

FEDERAL EMPLOYEES (See Public employees.)

FEDERAL MEDIATION AND CONCILIATION SERVICE

Federal mediation in the public sector. 1976 Feb. 41–45.

FRANCE

Unemployment compensation in eight industrial nations. 1976 July 18–24.

GERMANY

Unemployment compensation in eight industrial nations. 1976 July 18–24.

GOVERNMENT WORKERS (See Public employees.)

GREAT BRITAIN (See United Kingdom.)

HEALTH AND SAFETY

How accurate are employers' illness and injury reports? 1976 Sept. 26–31.
Occupational injuries. 1976 Jan. 2.

HOLLAND

U.S. longshoremen evaluate work conditions in Rotterdam. 1976 Aug. 39–40.

HOURS OF WORK

Decline noted in hours required to erect Federal office buildings. 1976 Oct. 18–22.
Experience with flexible hours of work. 1976 May 41–42.
Long workweeks and premium pay. 1976 Apr. 7–12.
Workweeks and leisure: an analysis of trends, 1948-75. 1976 Aug. 3–8.

HOUSING (See Construction.)

IMMIGRATION

Why Puerto Ricans migrated to the United States in 1947-73. 1976 Sept. 7–18.

INCENTIVE PLANS

New work theories and compensation problems. 1976 Mar. 41–42.

INCOME (See Earnings and wages.)

INDEXES (See also Prices.)

Cost-of-living indexes for Americans living abroad. 1976 Jan. 63, July 52, Oct. 43.
Updating the weights in indexes of wholesale, industry prices. 1976 Sept. 19–25.
Wholesale Price Index weights updated. 1976 Apr. 41–43.

INDUSTRIAL RELATIONS (See Labor-management relations.)

INDUSTRIAL RELATIONS RESEARCH ASSOCIATION

Papers from 28th annual meeting, December 1975. 1976 Mar. 37–48, Apr. 23–33, May 36–40.

INTERNATIONAL BROTHERHOOD OF TEAMSTERS, CHAUFFEURS, WAREHOUSEMEN AND HELPERS OF AMERICA (Ind.)

Dissidents criticized, leadership strengthened at Teamster convention. 1976 Sept. 41–43.

ITALY

Unemployment compensation in eight industrial nations. 1976 July 18–24.

JAPAN

Unemployment compensation in eight industrial nations. 1976 July 18–24.

JOBSEEKING METHODS

Effectiveness of rural job search methods. 1976 Apr. 27–30.

LABOR COSTS (See Unit labor cost.)

LABOR FORCE

Americans of Spanish origin in the labor force: an update. 1976 Sept. 3–6.
Demographic influences on labor force rates of black males. 1976 Nov. 42–43.
Educational attainment of workers, March 1975. 1976 Feb. 46–48.
Families and the rise of working wives--an overview. 1976 May 12–19.
Labor force participation of recently disabled adults. 1976 Apr. 45–46.
Length of working life for men and women, 1970. 1976 Feb. 31–35.
New labor force projections to 1990. 1976 Dec. 3–13.
Students, graduates, and dropouts in the labor market, October 1975. 1976 June 37–41.
Women who head families: a socioeconomic analysis. 1976 June 3–9.
Work experience of the population, 1975. 1976 Nov. 47–51.
Youth in the labor force: an area study. 1976 July 3–9.
Youth unemployment in the 1974-75 recession. 1976 Jan. 49–56.

LABOR HISTORY

A Bicentennial look at the early days of American labor. 1976 May 20–28.
American labor, 1865-1902: the early industrial era. 1976 July 10–17.
Expansion of unionization in the early 20th century. 1976 Sept. 32–35.
Labor from the Revolution to the Civil War. 1976 June 17–24.

Labor movement after World War II, The. 1976 Nov. 34–37.
Public policy and the American worker, 1933-45. 1976 Oct. 11–17.

LABOR LAW

State labor legislation enacted in 1975. 1976 Jan. 17–29.
Unemployment insurance--State changes in 1975. 1976 Jan. 37–41.
Workers' compensation--1975 enactments. 1976 Jan. 30–36.

LABOR-MANAGEMENT RELATIONS

California's farm labor elections: an analysis of the initial results. 1976 Dec. 25–30.
Labor-management cooperation: a report on recent initiatives. 1976 Apr. 13–22.
Union-management committees in the Federal sector. 1976 Oct. 30–32.

LABOR MARKET

Defining the labor market for equal employment standards. 1976 Mar. 32–36.

LABOR ORGANIZATIONS

California's farm labor elections: an analysis of the initial results. 1976 Dec. 25–30.
Expansion of unionization in the early 20th century. 1976 Sept. 32–35.
Labor movement after World War II, The. 1976 Nov. 34–37.
Unions and Title VII of the Civil Rights Act of 1964. 1976 Apr. 34–37.

LABOR REQUIREMENTS

Decline noted in hours required to erect Federal office buildings. 1976 Oct. 18–22.
Labor and materials requirements for sewer works construction. 1976 Nov. 38–41.

MEDIATION

Federal mediation in the public sector. 1976 Feb. 41–45.

MIGRATION

Why Puerto Ricans migrated to the united States in 1947-73. 1976 Sept. 7–18.

MINORITY WORKERS

Americans of Spanish origin in the labor force: an update. 1976 Sept. 3–6.
Demographic influences on labor force rates of black males. 1976 Nov. 42–43.
Earnings and jobs of ex-offenders. 1976 Dec. 31–39.
Inverse seniority as an aid to disadvantaged groups, 1976. May 36–37.
Why Puerto Ricans migrated to the United States in 1947-73. 1976 Sept. 7–18.

NATIONAL LABOR RELATIONS BOARD (See Decisions.)

NETHERLANDS

Industrial democracy in the Netherlands. 1976 July 48–49.

OCCUPATIONAL SAFETY AND HEALTH ACT

A penalty system to discourage OSHA violations. 1976 Apr. 30–31.

OCCUPATIONS

Dispersion tendencies in occupational unemployment rates. 1976 Apr. 38–41.
Future labor supply for lower level occupations. 1976 Mar. 22–31.
Revised occupational projections to 1985. 1976 Nov. 10–22.

POPULATION

Economic and political issues in population redistribution. 1976 Apr. 25–27.

PRICES

Food prices helped ease inflation during the third quarter of 1976. 1976 Dec. 40–45.

Price changes in 1975--an analysis. 1976 Feb. 21–30.

Rate of inflation eases in first quarter. 1976 June 31–36.

Turnaround in food, energy fueled second-quarter retail price rise. 1976 Sept. 36–40.

Updating the weights in indexes of wholesale, industry prices. 1976 Sept. 19–25.

West, small cities led increase in consumer prices during 1975. 1976 July 35–37.

Wholesale Price Index weights updated. 1976 Apr. 41–43.

PRODUCTIVITY

New sector definitions for productivity series. 1976 Oct. 40–42.

Productivity and costs, first quarter 1976. 1976 July 31–34.

Productivity and costs in the private economy, 1975. 1976 May 3–11.

Productivity and costs in the second quarter, 1976. 1976 Oct. 23–26.

Productivity and costs in the third quarter. 1976 Feb. 36–40.

Productivity in the nonmetallic minerals industry, 1954-75. 1976 June 25–30.

PROJECTIONS

Evaluation of BLS 1970 economic and employment projections. 1976 Aug. 13–26.

Future labor supply for lower level occupations. 1976 Mar. 22–31.

New labor force projections to 1990. 1976 Dec. 3–13.

Revised BLS projections to 1980 and 1985: an overview. 1976 Mar. 3–8.

Revised industry projections to 1985. 1976 Nov. 3–9.

Revised occupational projections to 1985. 1976 Nov. 10–22.

Revised projections of the U.S. economy to 1980 and 1985. 1976 Mar. 9–21.

PUBLIC EMPLOYEES

Faculty union strike activity: reasons and measures, 1967-75. 1976 Oct. 32–33.

Fair comparison criteria in public sector bargaining. 1976 July 50–51.

Federal mediation in the public sector. 1976 Feb. 41–45.

Federal pay procedures and the comparability survey. 1976 Aug. 27–31.

How salaries of large cities compare with industry and Federal pay. 1976 Nov. 23–28.

Resolution of impasses in public employee bargaining. 1976 Jan. 57–58.

Students and bargaining at public and private colleges. 1976 Apr. 31–33.

Union-management committees in the Federal sector. 1976 Oct. 30–32.

White-collar pay survey. 1976 Aug. 2.

SAFETY (See Health and safety.)

SALARIES (See Earnings and wages.)

SENIORITY

Inverse seniority as an aid to disadvantaged groups. 1976 May 36–37.

SOCIAL WELFARE

Altering the social structure in coal mining: a case study. 1976 Oct. 3–10.

SPECIAL LABOR FORCE REPORTS

Educational attainment of workers, March 1975. 1976 Feb. 46–48.

Families and the rise of working wives--an overview. 1976 May 12–19.

Length of working life for men and women, 1970. 1976 Feb. 31–35.

New labor force projections to 1990. 1976 Dec. 3–13.

Students, graduates, and dropouts in the labor market, October 1975. 1976 June 37–41.

Women who head families: a socioeconomic analysis. 1976 June 3–9.

Work experience of the population, 1975. 1976 Nov. 47–51.

Youth unemployment in the 1974-75 recession. 1976 Jan. 49–56.

STATISTICAL METHODS

New sector definitions for productivity series. 1976 Oct. 40–42.

STEELWORKERS (See United Steelworkers of America.)

STRIKES (See Work stoppages.)

SUBEMPLOYMENT (See Employment; Unemployment.)

SUPPLEMENTAL BENEFITS

Do benefits cause unemployed to hold out for better jobs? 1976 Mar. 37–38.

SWEDEN

Unemployment compensation in eight industrial nations. 1976 July 18–24.

TEAMSTERS (See International Brotherhood of Teamsters, Chauffeurs, Warehousemen and Helpers of America.)

TRADE UNIONS (See Labor organizations.)

TRAINING (See Education and training.)

UNDEREMPLOYMENT (See Employment; Unemployment.)

UNEMPLOYMENT (See also Employment; Labor force.)

Dispersion tendencies in occupational unemployment rates. 1976 Apr. 38–41.

Do benefits cause unemployed to hold out for better jobs? 1976 Mar. 37–38.

Employment and unemployment during 1975. 1976 Feb. 11–20.

Employment and unemployment in the first half of 1976. 1976 Aug. 9–12.

Employment and unemployment: the doughnut or the hole? 1976 Feb. 3–10.

Unemployment compensation: its effect on unemployment. 1976 Mar. 39–41.

Workers on layoff: a comparison of two data series. 1976 Nov. 29–33.

Youth in the labor force: an area study. 1976 July 3–9.

Youth unemployment in the 1974-75 recession. 1976 Jan. 49–56.

UNEMPLOYMENT INSURANCE

Unemployment compensation in eight industrial nations. 1976 July 18–24.

Unemployment insurance--State changes in 1975. 1976 Jan. 37–41.

UNIONS (See Labor organizations.)

UNIT LABOR COST

New sector definitions for productivity series. 1976 Oct. 40–42.

Productivity and costs, first quarter 1976. 1976 July 31–34.

Productivity and costs in the second quarter, 1976. 1976 Oct. 23–26.

Productivity and costs in the third quarter. 1976 Feb. 36–40.

UNITED KINGDOM

Unemployment compensation in eight industrial nations. 1976 July 18–24.

UNITED STEELWORKERS OF AMERICA

Abel-dominated convention endorses no-strike policy, seeks job guarantee. 1976 Nov. 44–46.

WAGE CALENDAR

Bargaining calendar to be heavy in 1977. 1976 Dec. 14–24.

WAGES (See Earnings and wages.)

WHITE-COLLAR WORKERS

Federal pay procedures and the comparability survey. 1976 Aug. 27–31.
How salaries of large cities compare with industry and Federal pay. 1976 Nov. 23–28.
White-collar pay survey. 1976 Aug. 2.

WHOLESALE PRICE INDEX (See Prices.)

WOMEN

Families and the rise of working wives--an overview. 1976 May 12–19.
How type of employment affects earnings differences by sex. 1976 July 25–30.
Length of working life for men and women, 1970. 1976 Feb. 31–35.
Women who head families: a socioeconomic analysis. 1976 June 3–9.

WORKER'S COMPENSATION

Unemployment compensation in eight industrial nations. 1976 July 18–24.
Workers' compensation--1975 enactments. 1976 Jan. 30–36.

WORKING LIFE

Altering the social structure in coal mining: a case study. 1976 Oct. 3–10.
Length of working life for men and women, 1970. 1976 Feb. 31–35.

WORK INJURIES AND ILLNESSES

How accurate are employers' illness and injury reports? 1976 Sept. 26–31.
Labor force participation of recently disabled adults. 1976 Apr. 45–46.
Occupational injuries. 1976 Jan. 2.

WORK MOTIVATION

Labor-management cooperation: a report on recent initiatives. 1976 Apr. 13–22.

WORK STOPPAGES

Faculty union strike activity: reasons and measures, 1967-75. 1976 Oct. 32–33.

YOUTH

Youth in the labor force: an area study. 1976 July 3–9.
Youth unemployment in the 1974-75 recession. 1976 Jan. 49–56.

DEPARTMENTS (regular features)

Anatomy of Price Change. June, September, December.
Book Reviews. Each issue. (See list of Book Reviews by author of book.)
Communications. January, April, October, November.
Conference Papers. March, April, May.
Conventions. August, September, October, November.
Current Labor Statistics. Each issue.
Developments in Industrial Relations. Each issue.
Foreign Labor Developments. January, July, August, October.
Labor Month In Review. Each issue except May.
Major Agreements Expiring Next Month. Each issue.
Productivity Reports. July, October.
Research Summaries. Each issue except March and November.
Significant Decisions in Labor Cases. Each issue. (See list of cases under Decisions, Court, and Decisions, National Labor Relations Board.)
Special Labor Force Report--Summaries. June, November.
Technical Notes. April, October.

BOOK REVIEWS (listed by author of book)

Asbell, Bernard and Clair F. Vough. *Tapping the Human Resource: A Strategy for Productivity.* 1976 Feb. 59–60.
Ashford, Nicholas A. *Crisis in the Workplace: Occupational Disease and Injury--A Report to the Ford Foundation.* 1976 Nov. 61–62.

Baron, Jean J. and Frank H. Cassell. *Collective Bargaining in the Public Sector: Cases in Public Policy.* 1976 May 58–59.
Barsby, Steve L. and Dennis R. Cox. *Interstate Migration of the Elderly.* 1976 Jan. 77–78.
Bell, Daniel. *The Cultural Contractions of Capitalism.* 1976 Dec. 57–58.
Blake, Robert and Jane Srygley Mouton. *Diary of an O.D. Man.* 1976 Sept. 61–62.
Break, George F. and Joseph A. Pechman. *Federal Tax Reform: The Impossible Dream?* 1976 June 65.
Burns, Scott. *HOME, INC.: the Hidden Wealth and Power of the American Household.* 1976 Aug. 55.

Calkins, Susannah E., Richard P. Nathan, Allen D. Manvel. *Monitoring Revenue Sharing.* 1976 Feb. 58–59.
Cassell, Frank H. and Jean J. Baron. *Collective Bargaining in the Public Sector: Cases in Public Policy.* 1976 May 58–59.
Committee on Department of Labor Manpower Research and Development, Assembly of Behavioral and Social Sciences, National Research Council. *Knowledge and Policy in Manpower: A Study of the Manpower Research and Development Program in the Department of Labor.* 1976 Aug. 50–51.
Cornuelle, Richard. *De-Managing America: The Final Revolution.* 1976 June 67–68.
Cox, Dennis R. and Steve L. Barsby. *Interstate Migration of the Elderly.* 1976 Jan. 77–78.

Davis, Joseph S. *The World Between the Wars, 1919-39: An Economist's View.* 1976 Jan. 81.
Davis, Karen. *National Health Insurance: Benefits, Costs and Consequences.* 1976 June 68–69.
Day, Dawn and Dorothy K. Newman. *The American Energy Consumer.* 1976 May 57–58.
Dutka, Anna B. and Miriam Ostow. *Work and Welfare in New York City.* 1976 Sept. 62–63.

Finley, Joseph E. *White Collar Union: The Story of the OPEIU and Its People.* 1976 Aug. 53.
Fleuter, Douglas L. *The Workweek Revolution: A Guide to the Changing Workweek.* 1976 Jan. 77.
Flynn, Ralph J. *Public Work, Public Workers.* 1976 Mar. 57–58.
Friedlander, Peter. *The Emergence of a UAW Local, 1936-1939: A Study in Class and Culture.* 1976 Aug. 52–53.

Gies, Joseph and Melvin Kranzberg. *By the Sweat of Thy Brow.* 1976 Jan. 80–81.
Ginzberg, Eli. *The Human Economy.* 1976 Dec. 60.
Gordon, Richard L. *U.S. Coal and The Electric Power Industry.* 1976 May 63–64.

Harris, Seymour E. *The Economics of Health Care.* 1976 Apr. 58–59.

International Bank for Reconstruction and Development. *Population Policies and Economic Development.* 1976 Jan. 78–79.
International Council for Educational Development. *Attacking Rural Poverty: How Nonformal Education Can Help.* 1976 May 62–63.

Jantscher, Gerald R. *Bread Upon the Waters: Federal Aids to the Maritime Industries.* 1976 July 62–63.

Johnston, William B., Robert Taggart, Sar A. Levitan. *Minorities in the United States: Problems, Progress and Prospects.* 1976 June 65–67.

Klein, Lisl. *New Forms Of Work Organization.* 1976 Oct. 56–57.

Kornblum, William. *Blue Collar Community.* 1976 Apr. 59–60.

Kranzberg, Melvin and Joseph Gies. *By the Sweat of Thy Brow.* 1976 Jan. 80–81.

Kushner, Sam. *Long Road to Delano.* 1976 Aug. 65–66.

Levitan, Sar A. and Robert Taggart. *The Promise of Greatness.* 1976 Nov. 62–63.

——, William B. Johnston, Robert Taggart. *Minorities in the United States: Problems, Progress and Prospects.* 1976 June 65–67.

Lloyd, Cynthia B., ed. *Sex, Discrimination, and the Division of Labor.* 1976 Aug. 64.

Lopez, Felix M. *Personnel Interviewing: Theory and Practice.* 1976 Aug. 55–56.

Manvel, Allen D., Susannah E. Calkins, Richard P. Nathan. *Monitoring Revenue Sharing.* 1976 Feb. 58–59.

Martin, George. *Madam Secretary: Frances Perkins.* (*A biography of America's first woman cabinet member.*) 1976 Nov. 63–65.

Masters, Stanley H. *Black-White Income Differentials: Empirical Studies and Policy Implications.* 1976 Dec. 59–60.

Mills, Daniel Quinn. *Government, Labor, and Inflation: Wage Stabilization in the United States.* 1976 Aug. 51–52.

Minsky, Hyman P. *John Maynard Keynes.* 1976 June 63–65.

Mouton, Jane Srygley and Robert Blake. *Diary of an O.D. Man.* 1976 Sept. 61–62.

Nakayama, Ichiro. *Industrialization and Labor-Management Relations in Japan.* 1976 Sept. 60–61.

Nathan, Richard P., Allen D. Manvel, Susannah E. Calkins. *Monitoring Revenue Sharing.* 1976 Feb. 58–59.

Newman, Dorothy K. and Dawn Day. *The American Energy Consumer.* 1976 May 57–58.

Okun, Arthur M. *Equality and Efficiency: The Big Tradeoff.* 1976 Sept. 54.

Ostow, Miriam and Anna B. Dutka. *Work and Welfare in New York City.* 1976 Sept. 62–63.

Pechman, Joseph A. and George F. Break. *Federal Tax Reform: The Impossible Dream?* 1976 June 65.

Pechman, Joseph A. and P. Michael Timpane, eds. *Work Incentives and Income Guarantees: The New Jersey Negative Income Tax Experiment.* 1976 May 60–61.

Poole, Michael. *Workers' Participation in Industry.* 1976 Mar. 58–59.

Rehmus, Charles M., ed. *Public Employment Labor Relations: An Overview of Eleven Nations.* 1976 Mar. 57–58.

Rivlin, Alice M. and P. Michael Timpane, eds. *Ethical and Legal Issues of Social Experimentation.* 1976 Aug. 54–55.

Rosen, George. *Peasant Society in a Changing Economy: Comparative Development in Southeast Asia and India.* 1976 Jan. 76–77.

Ross, Heather L. and Isabel V. Sawhill. *Time-of-Transition: The Growth of Families Headed by Women.* 1976 Sept. 63–64.

Ryan, Joseph A., ed. *White Ethnics, Their Life in Working-Class America.* 1976 Mar. 60–61.

Sawhill, Isabel V. and Heather L. Ross. *Time-of-Transition: The Growth of Families Headed by Women.* 1976 Sept. 63–64.

Schultz, Theodore W., ed. *Economics of the Family: Marriage, Children and Human Capital.* 1976 Apr. 60–61.

Seiden, Martin H. *Who Controls the Mass Media? Popular Myths and Economic Realities.* 1976 Mar. 60–61.

Starr, Roger. *Housing and the Money Market.* 1976 June 69–70.

Stern, James L. and others. *Final-Offer Arbitration: The Effects on Public Safety Employee Bargaining.* 1976 May 61–62.

Sundquist, James J. *Dispersing Population: What America Can Learn From Europe.* 1976 Aug. 63.

Taggart, Robert, Sar A. Levitan, William B. Johnston. *Minorities in the United States: Problems, Progress and Prospects.* 1976 June 65–67.

Taylor, Ronald B. *Chavez and the Farm Workers.* 1976 Aug. 65–66.

Thurow, Lester C. *Generating Inequality: Mechanisms of Distribution in the U.S. Economy.* 1976 Oct. 55–56.

Tilove, Robert. *Public Employee Pension Funds.* 1976 Oct. 54–55.

Timpane, P. Michael and Alice M. Rivlin, eds. *Ethical and Legal Issues of Social Experimentation.* 1976 Aug. 54–55.

—— and Joseph A. Pechman, eds. *Work Incentives and Income Guarantees: The New Jersey Negative Income Tax Experiment.* 1976 May 60–61.

Trolander, Judith Ann. *Settlement Houses and the Great Depression.* 1976 Aug. 56–57.

Tussing, A. Dale. *Poverty in a Dual Economy.* 1976 Jan. 75–76.

Tyler, Gus, ed. *Mexican-Americans Tomorrow: Educational and Economic Perspectives.* 1976 July 64–65.

Vough, Clair F. and Bernard Asbell. *Tapping the Human Resource: A Strategy for Productivity.* 1976 Feb. 59–60.

Wabe, J. S., ed. *Problems in Manpower Forecasting.* 1976 May 59–60.

Wilber, George L., ed. *Poverty: A New Prospective.* 1976 Jan. 79–80.

—— and others. *Minorities in the Labor Market: Vol. I, Spanish Americans and Indians in the Labor Market; Vol. II, Orientals in the American Labor Market.* 1976 June 65–67.

Williamson, Jeffrey G. *Late Nineteenth-Century American Development: A General Equilibrium History.* 1976 Feb. 60–61.

Wirtz, Willard and the National Manpower Institute. *The Boundless Resource: A Prospectus for an Education-Work Policy.* 1976 June 62–63.

AUTHORS

Adams, Larry T. Abel-dominated convention endorses no-strike policy, seeks job guarantee. 1976 Nov. 44–46.

Adler, James N. Use of arbitration to speed EEO adjudication. 1976 May 37–39.

Alexander, Robert J. Book review. 1976 Aug. 52–53.

Andrews, Emily S. Book review. 1976 July 64.

Aussieker, Bill. Faculty union strike activity: reasons and measures, 1967–75. 1976 Oct. 32–33.

——. Students and bargaining at public and private colleges. 1976 Apr. 31–33.

Baldwin, Stephen E. and Robert S. Daski. Occupational pay differences among metropolitan areas. 1976 May 29–35.

Ball, Robert and Joseph T. Finn. Labor and materials requirements for sewer works construction. 1976 Nov. 38–41.

Barbash, Jack. The labor movement after World War II. 1976 Nov. 34–37.

Barnum, Darold T. and John M. Gleason. A penalty system to discourage OSHA violations. 1976 Apr. 30–31.

Barsky, Carl. Container plants top pay scale in glassware manufacturing. 1976 Sept. 47–49.

——. Pay relationships in the furniture industry. 1976 Apr. 46–47.

——. Union wage trends in building trades. 1976 Jan. 59–61.

Bednarzik, Robert W. Book review. 1976 Jan. 77.

—— and Stephen M. St. Marie. Employment and unemployment during 1975. 1976 Feb. 11–20.

Bell, Winifred. Book review. 1976 May 60–61.

Bernstein, Irving. Public policy and the American worker, 1933-45. 1976 Oct. 11–17.

Bolton, Lena. Bargaining calendar to be heavy in 1977. 1976 Dec. 14–24.

Bond, Deborah T. State labor legislation enacted in 1975. 1976 Jan. 17–29.

Bond, M. E. Book review. 1976 July 63.

Bowman, Charles T. and Terry H. Morlan. Revised projections of the U.S. economy to 1980 and 1985. 1976 Mar. 9–21.

Bradshaw, Thomas F. and Janet L. Scholl. Workers on layoff: a comparison of two data series. 1976 Nov. 29–33.

Briggs, Vernon M., Jr. Book review. 1976 July 64–65.

Broad, Michael and Clyde Huffstutler. Productivity in the non-metallic minerals industry, 1954-75. 1976 June 25–30.

Brown, Gary D. How type of employment affects earnings differences by sex. 1976 July 25–30.

Bumstead, Dennis C., Robert T. Lund, Sheldon Friedman. Inverse seniority as an aid to disadvantaged groups. 1976 May 36–37.

Byrne, James J. and Howard N Fullerton, Jr. Length of working life for men and women, 1970. 1976 Feb. 31–35.

Carey, Max L. Revised occupational projections to 1985. 1976 Nov. 10–22.

Cook, Alice H. Book review. 1976 Sept. 63–64.

Cormier, Gerard H. and John Early. Updating the weights in indexes of wholesale, industry prices. 1976 Sept. 19–25.

Couturier, Jean J. Book review. 1976 May 58–59.

Cowan, G. K. Fair comparison criteria in public sector bargaining. 1976 July 50–51.

D'Angelo, Rocco. Book review. 1976 Aug. 56–57.

Darmstadter, Joel. Book review. 1976 May 57–58.

Daski, Robert S. and Stephen E. Baldwin. Occupational pay differences among metropolitan areas. 1976 May 29–35.

Davidson, Paul. Book review. 1976 June 63–65.

Defina, Catherine C. Labor and the economy during 1975. 1976 Jan. 3–16.

Doyle, Philip M. Wages at auto assembly plants top those at parts factories. 1976 June 45–47.

——. Wages, employment rise in plastics manufacturing. 1976 June 44–45.

——. Wages of communications workers double in decade. 1976 Jan. 61–62.

Dresch, Stephen P. Book review. 1976 Feb. 58–59.

Dyer, Lee. New work theories and compensation problems. 1976 Mar. 41–42.

Early, John and Gerard H. Cormier. Updating the weights in indexes of wholesale, industry prices. 1976 Sept. 19–25.

Ehrenberg, Ronald G. and Ronald L. Oaxaca. Do benefits cause unemployed to hold out for better jobs? 1976 Mar. 37–39.

Feldstein, Martin. Unemployment compensation: its effect on unemployment. 1976 Mar. 39–41.

Fellman, Gordon. Book review. 1976 Mar. 60–61.

Feuille, Peter. Book review. 1976 May 61–62.

Field, Charles V and Richard L. Keller. How salaries of large cities compare with industry, Federal pay. 1976 Nov. 23–28.

Finn, Joseph T. and Robert Ball. Labor and materials requirements for sewer works construction. 1976 Nov. 38–41.

Fitzpatrick, June. Book review. 1976 Apr. 62–63.

Flaim, Paul O. and Howard N Fullerton, Jr. New labor force projections to 1990. 1976 Dec. 3–13.

Foltman, Felician F. Book review. 1976 June 67–68.

Franklin, Paula. Book review. 1976 Aug. 54–55.

Friedland, William H. Book review. 1976 Jan. 76–77.

Friedman, Bernard. Book review. 1976 June 68–69.

Friedman, Sheldon, Dennis C. Bumstead, Robert T. Lund. Inverse seniority as an aid to disadvantaged groups. 1976 May 36–37.

Fulco, Lawrence J. and J.Randolph Norsworthy. New sector definitions for productivity series. 1976 Oct. 40–42.

—— and J. Randolph Norsworthy. Productivity and costs, first quarter 1976. 1976 July 31–34.

—— and J. Randolph Norsworthy. Productivity and costs in the private economy, 1975. 1976 May 3–11.

—— and J. Randolph Norsworthy. Productivity and costs in the second quarter, 1976. 1976 Oct. 23–26.

—— and J. Randolph Norsworthy. Productivity and costs in the third quarter. 1976 Feb. 36–40.

Fuller, Varden and W. H. Segur. California's farm labor elections: an analysis of the initial results. 1976 Dec. 25–30.

Fullerton, Howard N, Jr., and James J. Byrne. Length of working life for men and women, 1970. 1976 Feb. 31–35.

—— and Paul O. Flaim. New labor force projections to 1990. 1976 Dec. 3–13.

Gastwirth, Joseph L. and Sheldon E. Haber. Defining the labor market for equal employment standards. 1976 Mar. 32–36.

Gaylord, Carolyn and Patricia Gurin. Educational and occupational goals of men and women at black colleges. 1976 June 10–16.

Ginzberg, Eli. Book review. 1976 Aug. 50–51.

Gleason, John M. and Darold T. Barnum. A penalty system to discourage OSHA violations. 1976 Apr. 30–31.

Goldberg, Joseph P. Book review. 1976 July 62–63.

Goldin, Claudia Dale. Book review. 1976 Feb. 60–61.

Grossman, Michael. Book review. 1976 Apr. 58–59.

Gurin, Patricia and Carolyn Gaylord. Educational and occupational goals of men and women at black colleges. 1976 June 10–16.

Haber, Sheldon E. and Joseph L. Gastwirth. Defining the labor market for equal employment standards. 1976 Mar. 32–36.

Hammerman, Herbert. Book review. 1976 Sept. 64–65.

—— and Marvin Rogoff. Unions and Title VII of the Civil Rights Act of 1964. 1976 Apr. 34–37.

Hartley, Jo. Experience with flexible hours of work. 1976 May 41–42.

Hayghe, Howard. Families and the rise of working wives--an overview. 1976 May 12–19.

——. New data series on families shows most jobless have working relatives. 1976 Dec. 46–48.

Hedges, Janice Neipert. Long workweeks and premium pay. 1976 Apr. 7–12.

——. Youth unemployment in the 1974-75 recession. 1976 Jan. 49–56.

Henle, Peter. Book review. 1976 Oct. 54 55.

Herman, E. Edward and Gordon S. Skinner. Faculty representation: the vote at Cincinnati. 1976 Mar. 44–48.

Hickey, Joseph A. Unemployment insurance--State changes in 1975. 1976 Jan. 37–41.

Hickman, Charles W. Postal Workers denounce working conditions, 'waste.' 1976 Oct. 34–35.

Hill, C. Russell. Book review. 1976 Apr. 60–61.

Hribal, Amy S. and G. M. Minor. Workers' compensation--1975 enactments. 1976 Jan. 30–36.

Huffstutler, Clyde and Michael Broad. Productivity in the non-metallic minerals industry, 1954-75. 1976 June 25–30.

Hurd, Richard W. Book review. 1976 Jan. 75–76.

Jones, James E., Jr. Cost-sharing in gaining equal employment opportunity. 1976 May 39–40.

Jones, Lamar B. Book review. 1976 July 65–66.

Kahley, William J. Book review. 1976 Jan. 78–79.

Kanterman, Frances E. Dissidents criticized, leadership strengthened at Teamster convention. 1976 Sept. 41–43.

Keller, Richard L. and Charles Field, V. How salaries of large cities compare with industry, Federal pay. 1976 Nov. 23–28.

King, Allan G. and Ralph White. Demographic influences on labor force rates of black males. 1976 Nov. 42–43.

King, Sandra L. Occupational pay of contract cleaning workers. 1976 June 42–44.

——. Wage relationships in women's dress manufacturing. 1976 July 44–47.

Klein, Deborah Pisetzner. Employment and unemployment in the first half of 1976. 1976 Aug. 9–12.

Klein, Lawrence R. Book review. 1976 Dec. 57–58.

Krislov, Joseph. The supply of arbitrators: prospects for the 1980's. 1976 Oct. 27–30.

Kuhmerker, Peter. Scheduled wage increases and escalator provisions in 1976. 1976 Jan. 42–48.

Kutscher, Ronald E. Revised BLS projections to 1980 and 1985: an overview. 1976 Mar. 3–8.

Leab, Daniel J. Book review. 1976 Mar. 59–60.

Leggett, John C. Book review. 1976 Apr. 59–60.

Levine, Solomon B. Book review. 1976 Sept. 60–61.

Lewin, David. Book review. 1976 Mar. 57–58.

Lockhart, Madelyn. Book review. 1976 Jan. 77–78.

Lubin, Isador. Book review. 1976 Nov. 63–65.

Lund, Robert T., Sheldon Friedman, Dennis C. Bumstead. Inverse seniority as an aid to disadvantaged groups. 1976 May 36–37.

McCraw, M. Louise. Retired couple's budget updated to autumn 1975. 1976 Oct. 36–37.
McEaddy, Beverly Johnson. Women who head families: a socioeconomic analysis. 1976 June 3–9.
McKay, Roberta V. Americans of Spanish origin in the labor force: an update. 1976 Sept. 3–6.
Maclachlan, Gretchen. Book review. 1976 Jan. 79–80.
Maldonado, Rita M. Why Puerto Ricans migrated to the United States in 1947-73. 1976 Sept. 7–18.
Marshall, Ray and Roy Van Cleve. Start-up training and rural industrial location. 1976 Apr. 23–25.
Martin, James E. Union-management committees in the Federal sector. 1976 Oct. 30–32.
Mazor, John. How accurate are employers' illness and injury reports? 1976 Sept. 26–31.
Miller, Floyd John. Book review. 1976 Aug. 53.
Mills, Ted. Altering the social structure in coal mining: a case study. 1976 Oct. 3–10.
Minor, G. M. and Amy S. Hribal. Workers' compensation--1975 enactments. 1976 Jan. 30–36.
Mitchell, Daniel J. B. Book review. 1976 Aug. 52–53.
Monson, Paul. West, small cities led increase in consumer prices during 1975. 1976 July 35–37.
—— and Toshiko Nakayama. Food prices helped ease inflation during the third quarter of 1976. 1976 Dec. 40–45.
—— and Toshiko Nakayama. Price changes in 1975--an analysis. 1976 Feb. 21–30.
—— and Toshiko Nakayama. Rate of inflation eases in first quarter. 1976 June 31–36.
—— and Toshiko Nakayama. Turnaround in food, energy fueled second-quarter retail price rise. 1976 Sept. 36–40.
Montgomery, David. American labor, 1865-1902: the early industrial era. 1976 July 10–17.
Mooney, Thomas J. and John H. Tschetter. Revised industry projections to 1985. 1976 Nov. 3–9.
Morlan, Terry H. and Charles T. Bowman. Revised projections of the U.S. economy to 1980 and 1985. 1976 Mar. 9–21.
Morris, Richard B. A Bicentennial look at the early days of American Labor. 1976 May 20–28.
Morton, Herbert C. Book review. 1976 Nov. 61–62.
Murphey, Janice D. Wage gains in 1975: a summary analysis. 1976 Apr. 3–6.
Musser, Wesley N. Economic and political issues in population redistribution. 1976 Apr. 25–27.

Nakayama, Toshiko and Paul Monson. Food prices helped ease inflation during the third quarter of 1976. 1976 Dec. 40–45.
—— and Paul Monson. Price changes in 1975--an analysis. 1976 Feb. 21–30.
—— and Paul Monson. Rate of inflation eases in first quarter. 1976 June 31–36.
—— and Paul Monson. Turnaround in food, energy fueled second-quarter retail price rise. 1976 Sept. 36–40.
Niemi, Beth. Book review. 1976 Oct. 55–56.
Norsworthy, J. Randolph and Lawrence J. Fulco. New sector definitions for productivity series. 1976 Oct. 40–42.
—— and Lawrence J. Fulco. Productivity and costs, first quarter 1976. 1976 July 31–34.
—— and Lawrence J. Fulco. Productivity and costs in the private economy, 1975. 1976 May 3–11.
—— and Lawrence J. Fulco. Productivity and costs in the second quarter, 1976. 1976 Oct. 23–26.
—— and Lawrence J. Fulco. Productivity and costs in the third quarter. 1976 Feb. 36–40.

Oaxaca, Ronald L. and Ronald G. Ehrenberg. Do benefits cause unemployed to hold out for jobs? 1976 Mar. 37–39.
Olsen, John G. Decline noted in hours required to erect Federal office buildings. 1976 Oct. 18–22.
Owen, John D. Workweeks and leisure: an analysis of trends, 1948-75. 1976 Aug. 3–8.

Pak, Chong M. Book review. 1976 Sept. 61–62.
Parnes, Herbert S. Book review. 1976 Dec. 60.
Patten, Thomas H., Jr. Book reviews. 1976 Feb. 59–60, Mar. 58–59.
Pavlov, Yosef. Book review. 1976 Aug. 55–56.
Perry, Herbert A. U.S. longshoremen evaluate work conditions in Rotterdam. 1976 Aug. 39–40.
Personick, Valerie A. and Robert A. Sylvester. Evaluation of BLS 1970 economic and employment projections. 1976 Aug. 13–26.
Pessen, Edward. Labor from the Revolution to the Civil War. 1976 June 17–24.

Raines, John C. Book review. 1976 Aug. 55.
Ray, Robert N. Dispersion tendencies in occupational unemployment rates. 1976 Apr. 38–41.
Riche, Martha Farnsworth. Book review. 1976 Jan. 80–81.
Rieg, Mary Kay. Transit wage gains in large cities. 1976 Apr. 44–45.
——. Union wage rates in printing trades. 1976 Aug. 34–36.
Rogoff, Marvin and Herbert Hammerman. Unions and Title VII of the Civil Rights Act of 1974. 1976 Apr. 34–37.
Rosenblum, Marc. Book review. 1976 June 65–67; Dec. 59–60.
Ross, Jerome H. Federal mediation in the public sector. 1976 Feb. 41–45.
Rungeling, Brian, Lewis H. Smith, Loren C. Scott. Effectiveness of rural job search methods. 1976 Apr. 27–30.

Schilling, Eric D. Southern cities register top grocery wage gains. 1976 Oct. 37–38.
——. Trucking wages vary by type of hauling. 1976 Sept. 45–47.
Scholl, Janet L. and Thomas F. Bradshaw. Workers on layoff: a comparison of two data series. 1976 Nov. 29–33.
Schramm, Carl J. Why the slowdown in faculty bargaining? 1976 Mar. 43–44.
Scott, Loren C., Brian Rungeling, Lewis H. Smith. Effectiveness of rural job search methods. 1976 Apr. 27–30.
Segur, W. H. and Varden Fuller. California's farm labor elections: an analysis of the initial results. 1976 Dec. 25–30.
Seidman, Bert. Book review. 1976 Nov. 62–63.
Shiskin, Julius. Employment and unemployment: the doughnut or the hole? 1976 Feb. 3–10.
Sieling, Mark. Union wage rates in building trades. 1976 July 38–40.
Skinner, Gordon S. and E. Edward Herman. Faculty representation: the vote at Cincinnati. 1976 Mar. 44–48.
Smith, Lewis H., Loren C. Scott, Brian Rungeling. Effectiveness of rural job search methods. 1976 Apr. 27–30.
Smith, William M. Federal pay procedures and the comparability survey. 1976 Aug. 27–31.
——. White-collar pay rises 7 percent. 1976 Sept. 44–45.
Sorrentino, Constance. Unemployment compensation in eight industrial nations. 1976 July 18–24.
Steinberg, Edward. Book review. 1976 June 65; Aug. 54.
——. Labor force participation of recently disabled adults. 1976 Apr. 45–46.
Stephens, Elvis C. Resolution of impasses in public employee bargaining. 1976 Jan. 57–58.
St. Marie, Stephen M. and Robert W. Bednarzik. Employment and unemployment during 1975. 1976 Feb. 11–20.
Striner, Herbert E. Book review. 1976 June 62–63.
Struyk, Raymond J. Book review. 1976 June 69–70.
Sveikauskas, Leo. Book review. 1976 May 59–60.
Sylvester, Robert A. and Valerie A. Personick. Evaluation of BLS 1970 economic and employment projections. 1976 Aug. 13–26.

Taft, Philip. Expansion of unionization in the early 20th century. 1976 Sept. 32–35.
Tibbetts, Thomas R. Wholesale Price Index weights updated. 1976 Apr. 41–43.
Tschetter, John H. and Thomas J. Mooney. Revised industry projections to 1985. 1976 Nov. 3–9.

Uri, Noel D. Book review. 1976 May 63–64.

Van Cleve, Roy and Ray Marshall. Start-up training and rural industrial location. 1976 Apr. 23–25.
Verrochi, Peter C. Textile and clothing unions merge, aim at organizing the South. 1976 Aug. 32–33.

Watford, Warren T. Book review. 1976 Oct. 56–57.
Weinberg, Arthur S. Industrial democracy in the Netherlands. 1976 July 48–49.
Weinberg, Edgar. Labor-management cooperation: a report on recent initiatives. 1976 Apr. 13–22.
Weir, Paula E. Urban family budgets updated to autumn 1975. 1976 July 40–44.
Westcott, Diane N. Youth in the labor force: an area study. 1976 July 3–9.
White, Ralph and Allan G. King. Demographic influences on labor force rates of black males. 1976 Nov. 42–43.

Whitmore, Bob. Educational attainment of workers, March 1975. 1976 Feb. 46–48.
Williams, Harry B. Occupational pay structure in structural steel fabrication. 1976 Aug. 36–38.
Winegarden, C. R. Book review. 1976 Sept. 62–63.
Witte, Ann Dryden. Earnings and jobs of ex-offenders: a case study. 1976 Dec. 31–39.
Woodruff, William. Book review. 1976 Jan. 81.
Wool, Harold. Future labor supply for lower level occupations. 1976 Mar. 22–31.

Young, Anne McDougall. Work experience of the population, 1975. 1976 Nov. 47–51.
——. Students, graduates, and dropouts in the labor market, October 1975. 1976 June 37–41.

INDEX OF VOLUME 100
JANUARY 1977 THROUGH DECEMBER 1977

ABSENTEEISM

Absence from work--measuring the hours lost. 1977 Oct. 16–23.
Job absence and turnover: a new source of data. 1977 Oct. 24–31.

AGRICULTURE

Agricultural labor relations laws in four States--a comparison. 1977 May 14–18.

ARBITRATION (See Collective bargaining.)

AUSTRALIA

An analysis of unemployment in nine industrial countries. 1977 Apr. 12–24.

AUSTRIA

Incomes policy in Austria under a voluntary partnership. 1977 Aug. 13–17.

AUTO INDUSTRY

Technology and labor in automobile production. 1977 Oct. 32–35.

AUTO WORKERS

UAW elects its last Reuther-generation president. 1977 Aug. 36–37.

BARGAINING (See Collective bargaining.)

BELGIUM

Productivity and unit labor costs in 12 industrial countries. 1977 July 11–17.

BENEFITS (See Supplemental benefits.)

BUDGETS

Budgets for retired couples rose moderately in 1976. 1977 Oct. 53–56.
Family budget costs continued to climb in 1976. 1977 July 35–39.

CANADA

An analysis of unemployment in nine industrial countries. 1977 Apr. 12–24.
Canadian efforts to stabilize collective bargaining in construction. 1977 Apr. 76–78.
Employment ratio as an indicator of aggregate demand pressure. 1977 Apr. 25–32.
Productivity and unit labor costs in 12 industrial countries. 1977 July 11–17.
Regional unemployment and job search in Canada. 1977 Oct. 42–43.

CIVIL SERVANTS (See Public employees.)

COLLECTIVE BARGAINING

American labor's stake in a changing world economy. 1977 Mar. 34–50.
  Labor's interests vital in setting trade policies
  Establishing international fair labor standards
  Problems facing international collective bargaining
  Economic relations between developed and developing countries
  Aid to developing countries: a Third World trade unionist view
  Development of Third World would affect U.S. supply of raw materials
  Trade adjustment assistance: should it be modified?
  'Rentier' economy would threaten manufacturing jobs
  Building a counterforce to multinational corporations
  America's improving competitiveness promotes export growth
  Labor content of imports and exports
Bargaining calendar to be light in 1978. 1977 Dec. 34–43.
Canadian efforts to stabilize collective bargaining in construction. 1977 Apr. 76–78.
Effects of collective bargaining as measured for men in blue-collar jobs, The. 1977 Apr. 46–49.
European union agreements provide framework for public policies. 1977 Jan. 62–64.
Forces working to reshape collective bargaining. 1977 Feb. 60–61.
Handling prison grievances: the 'labor model' in practice. 1977 Mar. 53–56.
Has collective bargaining altered the salary structure of baseball? 1977 Mar. 51–52.
How final-offer arbitration affects baseball bargaining. 1977 Mar. 52–53.
Industrial relations in 1976: highlights of key settlements. 1977 Jan. 27–35.
Industrial Relations Research Association. Papers from 29th annual meeting, September 1976. 1977 Feb. 52–61; Mar. 51–57; Apr. 44–60.
Organization behavior as an aid to labor impasse resolution. 1977 Apr. 49–52.
Process of work restructuring, and its impact on collective bargaining, The. 1977 Apr. 52–55.
Scheduled wage increases and escalator provisions in 1977. 1977 Jan. 20–26.
Significant labor decisions--an analysis. 1977 Jan. 36–41.
Wage gains smaller during 1976. 1977 Apr. 3–6.

CONFERENCES AND CONVENTIONS

Carnegie Endowment for International Peace, the New York State School of Industrial and Labor Relations of Cornell University, and the University of the State of New York, December 1976. 1977 Mar. 34–50.
Industrial Relations Research Association. Papers from 29th annual meeting, September 1976. 1977 Feb. 52–61; Mar. 51–57; Apr. 44–60.

North American Conference on Labor Statistics. Papers from 34th annual meeting, June 1977. 1977 Oct. 42–48.

United Automobile, Aerospace and Agricultural Implement Workers of America, 25th constitutional convention, May 15-19, 1977. 1977 Aug. 36–37.

United Mine Workers of America, 47th constitutional convention, Sept. 23-Oct. 2, 1976. 1977 Jan. 58–61.

CONSTRUCTION

Canadian efforts to stabilize collective bargaining in construction. 1977 Apr. 76–78.

European experience with rent controls. 1977 June 21–28.

CONSUMER PRICE INDEX (See also Prices.)

Anatomy of price change--the sharp first-quarter rise. 1977 June 3–8.

A new role for economic indicators. 1977 Nov. 3–5.

Inflation rate high in second quarter, but prices of raw materials declined. 1977 Sept. 29–33.

Inflation slowed markedly during the third quarter. 1977 Dec. 49–52.

CONTROLS

European experience with rent controls. 1977 June 21–28.

COST OF LIVING

Budgets for retired couples rose moderately in 1976. 1977 Oct. 53–56.

Changes in the distribution of consumer spending. 1977 Sept. 33–34.

Cost-of-living indexes for Americans living abroad. 1977 Jan. 64; Apr. 78; Sept. 38; Oct. 69.

DECISIONS, COURT (See also Significant labor decisions--an analysis. 1977 Jan. 36–41.)

Administrative Procedure Act

Hoffman v. Dunlop. 1977 Oct. 71–72.

Bankruptcy Act

In the matter of Highway and City Freight Drivers, Dockmen and Helpers, Local No. 600. 1977 Sept. 42.

Civil Rights Act of 1964

Arado v. United States. 1977 Dec. 66.
Dothard v. Rawlinson. 1977 Oct. 70–71.
General Electric Co. v. Gilbert. 1977 Mar. 73–74.
Gray v. Greyhound Lines. 1977 Mar. 74.
Hazelwood School District v. United States. 1977 Nov. 51–52.
Hochstadt v. Worcester Foundation for Experimental Biology. 1977 Mar. 74–75.
McClain v. Wagner Electric Co. 1977 June 59.
Skelton v. Balzano. 1977 Apr. 80–81.
Teamsters v. United States. 1977 Aug. 48–49.
Trans World Airlines v. Hardison. 1977 Mar. 76; Sept. 39–40.
Waters v. Heublein, Inc. 1977 Mar. 74.

Constitutional issues

Abood v. Detroit Board of Education. 1977 Aug. 46–47.
Alfred v. Barlow's, Inc. 1977 Apr. 79.
Califano v. Goldfarb. 1977 May 51–52.
Catholic Bishop of Chicago v. NLRB. 1977 Nov. 52–53.
City of Madison, Joint School Dist. No. 8 v. Wisconsin Employment Relations Comm'n. 1977 Apr. 79–80.
Codd v. Velger. 1977 June 59.
Dothard v. Rawlinson. 1977 Oct. 70–71.
Hoffman v. Dunlop. 1977 Oct. 71–72.
Marshall v. Shellcast Corp. 1977 Nov. 53.
Massachusetts v. Feeney. 1977 Dec. 66.
Mt. Healthy City School Dist. v. Doyles. 1977 Mar. 75–76.
Ohio Bureau of Employment Services v. Hodory. 1977 Sept. 40–41.

Olshock v. Village of Skokie. 1977 Mar. 76.
Pittsburgh Press Co. v. Commonwealth of Pennsylvania. 1977 Dec. 68.
Usery v. Allegheny C'ty Institution Dist. 1977 Mar. 76.

Equal Pay Act

Usery v. Allegheny C'ty Institution Dist. 1977 Mar. 76.

Labor-Management Reporting and Disclosure Act

Local 3489, United Steelworkers v. Usery. 1977 Apr. 80.
Ritz v. O'Donnell. 1977 Dec. 68–69.

National Labor Relations Act

Amalgamated Transit Union v. Byrne. 1977 Dec. 67.
Catholic Bishop of Chicago v. NLRB. 1977 Nov. 52–53.
Farmer v. Bhd. of Carpenters, Local 25. 1977 July 47–48.
Mt. Vernon Tanker Co. v. NLRB. 1977 July 48.
NLRB v. Columbus Printing Pressmen. 1977 Apr. 81.
NLRB v. Enterprise Association. 1977 June 57–58.

Occupational Safety and Health Act of 1970

Alfred v. Barlow's, Inc. 1977 Apr. 79.
Marshall v. Shellcast Corp. 1977 Nov. 53.

Selective Service Act

Alabama Power Co. v. Davis. 1977 Oct. 71.

Social Security Act

Batterton v. Francis. 1977 Sept. 41–42.
Califano v. Goldfarb. 1977 May 51–52.
Ohio Bureau of Employment Services v. Hodory. 1977 Sept. 40–41.

State and Local Fiscal Assistance Act

Arado v. United States. 1977 Dec. 66.

State laws

Abood v. Detroit Board of Education. 1977 Aug. 46–47.
Batterton v. Francis. 1977 Sept. 41–42.
City of Madison, Joint School Dist. No. 8 v. Wisconsin Employment Relations Comm'n. 1977 Apr. 79–80.
Commonwealth v. County Bd. 1977 May 52–53.
Dothard v. Rawlinson. 1977 Oct. 70–71.
Farmer v. Bhd. of Carpenters, Local 25. 1977 July 47–48.
Massachusetts v. Feeney. 1977 Dec. 66.
Ohio Bureau of Employment Services v. Hodory. 1977 Sept. 40–41.
Pittsburgh Press Co. v. Commonwealth of Pennsylvania. 1977 Dec. 68.
Shimp v. New Jersey Bell Telephone Co. 1977 May 53.

Taft-Hartley Act

NLRB v. Electrical Workers Local No. 388. 1977 Dec. 66.
Walsh v. Schlecht. 1977 June 58–59.

Other court decisions

Lowe v. Pate. 1977 Dec. 69.
Nolde Bros., Inc. v. Local No. 358, Bakery Workers. 1977 July 46–47.
The New York Times v. New York City Comm'n on Human Rights. 1977 June 59.

DECISIONS, NLRB

Foley, Hoag & Eliot and United File Room Clerks and Messengers of Foley, Hoag & Eliot. 1977 Aug. 49.
Shopping Kart Food Market, Inc., and Retail Clerks Union, Local 99. 1977 Aug. 47–48.
State Bank of India and Chicago Joint Board, Amalgamated Clothing and Textile Workers Union, AFL-CIO. 1977 Sept. 42.

DENMARK

Productivity and unit labor costs in 12 industrial countries. 1977 July 11–17.

DISCRIMINATION (See Equal Employment Opportunity.)

EARNINGS AND WAGES

General

Bargaining calendar to be light in 1978. 1977 Dec. 34–43.

Earnings of men and women. 1977 Jan. 2.

Effect on women's earnings of enforcement in Title VII cases, The. 1977 Mar. 56–57.

Effects of collective bargaining as measured for men in blue-collar jobs, The. 1977 Apr. 46–49.

Experienced professionals lead white-collar pay rise. 1977 Nov. 48–49.

How racial bias and social status affect the earnings of young men. 1977 Apr. 44–46.

Impact of the winter of 1977 on payroll employment, The. 1977 Aug. 43–45.

Lifetime jobs and wage security: vintage wine in new containers? 1977 Sept. 27–28.

Measuring income inequality with extended earnings periods. 1977 June 29–31.

New approaches to statistics on the family. 1977 July 31–34.

Scheduled wage increases and escalator provisions in 1977. 1977 Jan. 20–26.

Slowdown in real wages: a postwar perspective, The. 1977 Aug. 7–12.

Wage gains smaller during 1976. 1977 Apr. 3–6.

Workers on long hours and premium pay, May 1976. 1977 May 42–45.

Work injuries and earnings of partially disabled men in California. 1977 Apr. 58–60.

Year-round full-time earnings in 1975. 1977 June 36–41.

Specified industries and occupations

Airlines flight deck personnel, November 1975. 1977 Nov. 49–50.

Cigarette manufacturing, May 1976. 1977 Sept. 36.

Communications workers, December 1975. 1977 May 49-50.

Corrugated and solid fiber box industry, March 1976. 1977 Sept. 36.

Leather footwear manufacturing, April 1975. 1977 June 53–54.

Nonelectrical machinery workers, winter 1974-75. 1977 Apr. 73–75.

Nonferrous foundries, May 1975. 1977 June 49–51.

Nursing homes, May 1976. 1977 Aug. 45.

Petroleum refineries, April 1976. 1977 June 54–56.

Private hospitals, January 1976. 1977 May 46–47.

Shipbuilders, September 1976. 1977 Sept. 35–36.

Suit and coat fabrication, April 1976. 1977 Oct. 65–67.

Textile dyeing and finishing plants, June 1976. 1977 Sept. 35.

Textile mills, May 1975. 1977 June 51–53.

TV-radio and appliance repairers, November 1975. 1977 May 48–49.

ECONOMIC POLICIES AND PROGRAMS

Demographic change, government transfers, and income distribution. 1977 Apr. 7–11.

Employment ratio as an indicator of aggregate demand pressure. 1977 Apr. 25–32.

European union agreements provide framework for public policies. 1977 Jan. 62–64.

Incomes policy in Austria under a voluntary partnership. 1977 Aug. 13–17.

Recent immigration and current data collection. 1977 Oct. 36–41.

Reducing unemployment. 1977 Feb. 2.

EDUCATION AND TRAINING

Academic degrees for labor studies--a new goal for unions. 1977 June 15–20.

Educational attainment of workers, March 1976. 1977 Mar. 62–65.

Educational attainment of workers, March 1977. 1977 Dec. 53–57.

Education, work, and leisure: must they come in that order? 1977 July 3–10.

Employment prospects brighten a bit for some teachers in California. 1977 Oct. 49–52.

Going back to school at 35 and over. 1977 July 43–45.

Labor force trends: a synthesis and analysis. 1977 Oct. 3–12.

Military as an employer: past performance and future prospects, The. 1977 Nov. 19–23.

National standardization of educational statistics. 1977 Oct. 46–47.

Relevance of recurrent education to worker satisfaction, The. 1977 Apr. 62–64.

Students, graduates, and dropouts in the labor market, October 1976. 1977 July 40–43.

EMPLOYMENT

Employment and unemployment during the first half of 1977. 1977 Aug. 3–6.

Employment and unemployment in 1976. 1977 Feb. 3–13.

Employment problems of disabled persons. 1977 Mar. 3–13.

Employment prospects brighten a bit for some teachers in California. 1977 Oct. 49–52.

Establishment of a new Employment Statistics Review Commission. 1977 Mar. 14–20.

Labor force participation of married women, March 1976. 1977 June 32–36.

Multiple jobholding rate remained unchanged in 1976. 1977 June 44–48.

Nuclear energy employment measured in 1975 survey. 1977 Sept. 36–37.

Occupational mobility in the American labor force. 1977 Jan. 3–19.

Supply of Federal physicians and dentists found adequate. 1977 May 50.

Work experience of the population, 1976. 1977 Nov. 43–47.

ENERGY

Nuclear energy employment measured in 1975 survey. 1977 Sept. 36–37.

The impact of the winter of 1977 on payroll employment. 1977 Aug. 43–45.

ENGINEERS

Nuclear energy employment measured in 1975 survey. 1977 Sept. 36–37.

Scientists, engineers, and unions, revisited. 1977 Nov. 32–33.

Supply of Federal physicians and dentists found adequate. 1977 May 50.

EQUAL EMPLOYMENT OPPORTUNITY

Effect on women's earnings of enforcement in Title VII cases, The. 1977 Mar. 56–57.

How racial bias and social status affect the earnings of young men. 1977 Apr. 44–46.

State and local governments found to underemploy women and minorities. 1977 Sept. 37.

ESCALATOR CLAUSES

Bargaining calendar to be light in 1978. 1977 Dec. 34–43.

Industrial relations in 1976: highlights of key settlements. 1977 Jan. 27–35.

Scheduled wage increases and escalator provisions in 1977. 1977 Jan. 20–26.

Wage gains smaller during 1976. 1977 Apr. 3–6.

FARMING (See Agriculture.)

FEDERAL EMPLOYEES (See Public employees.)

FINLAND

European union agreements provide framework for public policies. 1977 Jan. 62–64.

FIRE FIGHTERS

Unions and public sector supervisors: the case of fire fighters. 1977 Dec. 44–48.

FRANCE

An analysis of unemployment in nine industrial countries. 1977 Apr. 12–24.
Productivity and unit labor costs in 12 industrial countries. 1977 July 11–17.

GERMANY

An analysis of unemployment in nine industrial countries. 1977 Apr. 12–24.
Productivity and unit labor costs in 12 industrial countries. 1977 July 11–17.

GOVERNMENT WORKERS (See Public employees.)

GREAT BRITAIN (See United Kingdom.)

HEALTH AND SAFETY

Factors in more costly accidents drawn from compensated cases. 1977 Aug. 41–43.
ILO tightens standards for maritime safety. 1977 July 25–30.

HOSPITALS

Private hospitals nearing wage levels in State, local government hospitals. 1977 May 46–47.

HOURS OF WORK

Absence from work--measuring the hours lost. 1977 Oct. 16–23.
Changes in the number of days in the workweek, 1973-76. 1977 Apr. 72–73.
Easing the constraints of time-oriented work. 1977 Feb. 58–59.
End of the 12-hour day in the steel industry, The. 1977 Sept. 21–26.
Full and part time: a review of definitions. 1977 Mar. 21–28.
How blue-collar workers on 4-day workweeks use their time. 1977 Aug. 18–26.
Special flexitime reports. 1977 Feb. 62–74.
   Flexible schedules: problems and issues
   Drug company workers like new schedules
   Reaction at computer firm: more pluses than minuses
   Concept wins converts at Federal agency
Workers on long hours and premium pay, May 1976. 1977 May 42–45.
Work-sharing initiatives at home and abroad. 1977 Sept. 16–20.

HOUSING (See Construction.)

IMMIGRATION

Analyzing Puerto Rican migration: problems with the data and the model. 1977 Aug. 29–35.
Recent immigration and current data collection. 1977 Oct. 36–41.

INCOME (See Earnings and wages.)

INCOME PAYMENTS AND TRANSFERS

A new role for economic indicators. 1977 Nov. 3–5.
Demographic change, government transfers, and income distribution. 1971 Apr. 7–11.

INDEXES

Cost-of-living indexes for Americans living abroad. 1977 Jan. 64; Apr. 78; Sept. 38; Oct. 69.
Developing an index to measure female labor force attachment. 1977 May 35–38.

INDUSTRIAL RELATIONS (See Labor-management relations.)

INDUSTRIAL RELATIONS RESEARCH ASSOCIATION

Papers from 29th annual meeting, September 1976. 1977 Feb. 52–61; Mar. 51–57; Apr. 44–60.

INFLATION

The slowdown in real wages: a postwar perspective. 1977 Aug. 7–12.

ITALY

An analysis of unemployment in nine industrial countries. 1977 Apr. 12–24.
Productivity and unit labor costs in 12 industrial countries. 1977 July 11–17.

JAPAN

An analysis of unemployment in nine industrial countries. 1977 Apr. 12–24.
Productivity and unit labor costs in 12 industrial countries. 1977 July 11–17.

JOB SATISFACTION

Criteria for job satisfaction: is interesting work most important? 1977 May 30–35.
Education, work, and leisure: must they come in that order? 1977 July 3–10.
Relevance of recurrent education to worker satisfaction, The. 1977 Apr. 61–64.
White-collar unions and the work humanization movement. 1977 May 9–13.

JOB SEARCH

Extent of job search by employed workers, The. 1977 Mar. 58–62.
Job search of the unemployed, May 1976. 1977 Nov. 39–43.
Regional unemployment and job search in Canada. 1977 Oct. 42–43.

JOBSEEKING METHODS

Extent of job search by employed workers, The. 1977 Mar. 58–62.

LABOR COSTS (See Unit labor cost.)

LABOR FORCE

Almost half of all children have mothers in the labor force. 1977 June 41–44.
Another look at working-age men who are not in the labor force. 1977 June 9–14.
Developing an index to measure female labor force attachment. 1977 May 35–38.
Educational attainment of workers, March 1977. 1977 Dec. 53–57.
Employment and unemployment during the first half of 1977. 1977 Aug. 3–6.
Employment and unemployment in 1976. 1977 Feb. 3–13.
Employment prospects brighten a bit for some teachers in California. 1977 Oct. 49–52.
Female labor force participation: why projections have been too low. 1977 July 18–24.
How blue-collar workers on 4-day workweeks use their time. 1977 Aug. 18–26.
Labor force participation of married women, March 1976. 1977 June 32–36.
Labor force patterns of divorced and separated women, The. 1977 Jan. 48–53.
Labor force trends: a bibliography. 1977 Oct. 12–15.

Labor force trends: a synthesis and analysis. 1977 Oct. 3–12.

More than half of women who work part time have pre-school children. 1977 Sept. 37.

Multiple jobholding rate remained unchanged in 1976. 1977 June 44–48.

Nuclear energy employment measured in 1975 survey. 1977 Sept. 36–37.

Occupational mobility in the American labor force. 1977 Jan. 3–19.

Regional unemployment and job search in Canada. 1977 Oct. 42–43.

Sources of growth of the female labor force, 1971-75. 1977 Aug. 27–29.

LABOR HISTORY

End of the 12-hour day in the steel industry, The. 1977 Sept. 21–26.

Lifetime jobs and wage security: vintage wine in new containers? 1977 Sept. 27–28.

LABOR LAW

State labor legislation enacted in 1976. 1977 Feb. 25–38.

State labor legislation enacted in 1977. 1977 Dec. 3–24.

State unemployment insurance: legislative changes in 1976. 1977 Feb. 46–51.

Workers' compensation laws: major amendments in 1976. 1977 Feb. 39–45.

LABOR-MANAGEMENT RELATIONS

Agricultural labor relations laws in four States--a comparison. 1977 May 14–18.

Industrial relations in 1976: highlights of key settlements. 1977 Jan. 27–35.

Organization behavior as an aid to labor impasse resolution. 1977 Apr. 49–52.

Process of work restructuring, and its impact on collective bargaining, The. 1977 Apr. 52–55.

Significant labor decisions--an analysis. 1977 Jan. 36–41.

LABOR MARKET

American labor's stake in a changing world economy. 1977 Mar. 34–50.

    Labor's interest vital in setting trade policies

    Establishing international fair labor standards

    Problems facing international collective bargaining

    Economic relations between developed and developing countries

    Aid to developing countries: a Third World trade unionist view

    Development of Third World would affect U.S. supply of raw materials

    Trade adjustment assistance: should it be modified?

    'Rentier' economy would threaten manufacturing jobs

    Building a counterforce to multinational corporations

    America's improving competitiveness promotes export growth

    Labor content of imports and exports

Employment ratio as an indicator of aggregate demand pressure, The. 1977 Apr. 25–32.

Going back to school at 35 and over. 1977 July 43–45.

Measuring the supply of scientific personnel. 1977 Oct. 47–48.

Military as an employer: past performance and future prospects, The. 1977 Nov. 19–23.

Students, graduates, and dropouts in the labor market, October 1976. 1977 July 40–43.

LABOR ORGANIZATIONS

Academic degrees for labor studies--a new goal for unions. 1977 June 15–20.

American labor's stake in a changing world economy. 1977 Mar. 34–50.

    Labor's interests vital in setting trade policies

    Establishing international fair labor standards

    Problems facing international collective bargaining

    Economic relations between developed and developing countries

    Aid to developing countries: a Third World trade unionist view

    Development of Third World would affect U.S. supply of raw materials

    Trade adjustment assistance: should it be modified?

    'Rentier' economy would threaten manufacturing jobs

    Building a counterforce to multinational corporations

    America's improving competitiveness promotes export growth

    Labor content of imports and exports

Industrial relations in 1976: highlights of key settlements. 1977 Jan. 27–35.

Labor organizations' fees and dues. 1977 May 19–24.

Significant labor decisions--an analysis. 1977 Jan. 36–41.

Unions and public sector supervisors: the case of fire fighters. 1977 Dec. 44–48.

White-collar unions and the work humanization movement. 1977 May 9–13.

LEISURE

Education, work, and leisure: must they come in that order? 1977 July 3–10.

MARITIME

ILO tightens standards for maritime safety. 1977 July 25–30.

MINE WORKERS (See United Mine Workers of America.)

MINORITY WORKERS

Black women in the professions, 1890-1970. 1977 May 38–41.

Employment and unemployment in 1976. 1977 Feb. 3–13.

Employment patterns of women and minorities. 1977 Nov. 50.

Employment problems of disabled persons. 1977 Mar. 3–13.

In black and white. 1977 Oct. 2.

Labor force participation of married women, March 1976. 1977 June 32–36.

State and local governments found to underemploy women and minorities. 1977 Sept. 37.

Work experience of the population, 1976. 1977 Nov. 43–47.

Year-round full-time earnings in 1975. 1977 June 36–41.

MOBILITY

Interstate occupational migration: an analysis of data from 1965-70. 1977 Apr. 64–67.

Occupational mobility in the American labor force. 1977 Jan. 3–19.

Occupational mobility of health workers. 1977 May 25–29.

MONETARY AND FISCAL POLICY

Allocating Federal funds through local unemployment rates. 1977 Oct. 45–46.

NATIONAL LABOR RELATIONS BOARD (See Decisions, NLRB.)

NETHERLANDS

Productivity and unit labor costs in 12 industrial countries. 1977 July 11–17.

NONFINANCIAL CORPORATIONS

Productivity and costs in the second quarter. 1977 Nov. 34–38.

NORWAY

European union agreements provide framework for public policies. 1977 Jan. 62–64.

OCCUPATIONS

Occupational data program yielding big dividends. 1977 Oct. 44–45.

Occupational mobility in the American labor force. 1977 Jan. 3–19.

Occupational mobility of health workers. 1977 May 25–29.

PENSIONS (See also Retirement; Supplemental benefits.)

Forced retirement: how common is it? 1977 Dec. 60–61.
Municipal pension plans: provisions and payments. 1977 Nov. 24–31.

POPULATION

Work experience of the population, 1976. 1977 Nov. 43–47.

PRICES

Anatomy of price change--the sharp first-quarter rise. 1977 June 3–8.
Inflation rate high in second quarter, but prices of raw materials declined. 1977 Sept. 29–33.
Inflation slowed markedly during the third quarter. 1977 Dec. 49–52.
Price changes in 1976--an analysis. 1977 Feb. 14–24.
Trouble in steel. 1977 Nov. 2.
Users find industrial price data satisfactory but urge some changes. 1977 Dec. 58–59.

PRODUCTIVITY

Federal employees see increase in productivity. 1977 Feb. 66.
New-car dealers experience long-term gains in productivity. 1977 Mar. 29–33.
Productivity and costs:
  Third quarter, 1976. 1977 Feb. 75–79.
  Fourth quarter. 1977 Apr. 68–71.
  First quarter, 1977. 1977 Aug. 38–40.
  Second quarter. 1977 Nov. 34–38.
Productivity and costs in the private economy, 1976. 1977 Sept. 3–8.
Productivity and new technology in eating and drinking places. 1977 Sept. 9–15.
Productivity and unit labor costs in 12 industrial countries. 1977 July 11–17.
Productivity in:
  Grain mill products, 1963-75. 1977 Apr. 38–43.
  Sawmills, 1958-75. 1977 Apr. 33–37.
Productivity rates rose in 1976 for almost all industries surveyed. 1977 Oct. 57–60.
Productivity slowdown and the outlook to 1985, The. 1977 May 3–8.
Report on productivity gains in selected industries. 1977 Feb. 80–83.
Slowdown in real wages: a postwar perspective, The. 1977 Aug. 7–12.
Technology and labor in automobile production. 1977 Oct. 32–35.

PROJECTIONS

Female labor force participation: why projections have been too low. 1977 July 18–24.
Productivity slowdown and the outlook to 1985, The. 1977 May 3–8.

PUBLIC EMPLOYEES

European union agreements provide framework for public policies. 1977 Jan. 62–64.
Experienced professionals lead white-collar pay rise. 1977 Nov. 48–49.
Federal employees see increase in productivity, 1977 Feb. 66.
Military as an employer: past performance and future prospects, The. 1977 Nov. 19–23.
Municipal pension plans: provisions and payments. 1977 Nov. 24–31.
Private hospitals nearing wage levels in State, local government hospitals. 1977 May 46–47.
Reshaping a statistical program to meet legislative priorities. 1977 Nov. 6–11.
Scientists, engineers, and unions, revisited. 1977 Nov. 32–33.

Supply of Federal physicians and dentists found adequate. 1977 May 50.
Unions and public sector supervisors: the case of fire fighters. 1977 Dec. 44–48.
White-collar unions and the work humanization movement. 1977 May 9–13.

PUERTO RICO

Analyzing Puerto Rican migration: problems with the data and the model. 1977 Aug. 29–35.

RETIREMENT

Forced retirement: how common is it? 1977 Dec. 60–61.
Labor force trends: a synthesis and analysis. 1977 Oct. 3–12.
Military as an employer: past performance and future prospects, The. 1977 Nov. 19–23.
Municipal pension plans: provisions and payments. 1977 Nov. 24–31.

SAFETY (See Health and safety.)

SALARIES (See Earnings and wages.)

SCIENTISTS

Nuclear energy employment measured in 1975 survey. 1977 Sept. 36–37.
Scientists, engineers, and unions, revisited. 1977 Nov. 32–33.
Supply of Federal physicians and dentists found adequate. 1977 May 50.

SOCIAL SECURITY

Future funding of social security and the total dependency ratio. 1977 Feb. 53–55.
Generational equity and social security. 1977 Feb. 52–53.
Social security reform: a look at the problems. 1977 Feb. 55–58.

SOCIAL WELFARE

Employment problems of disabled persons. 1977 Mar. 3–13.

SPECIAL LABOR FORCE REPORTS

Absence from work--measuring the hours lost. 1977 Oct. 16–23.
Almost half of all children have mothers in the labor force. 1977 June 41–44.
Educational attainment of workers, March 1976. 1977 Mar. 62–65.
Educational attainment of workers, March 1977. 1977 Dec. 53–57.
Extent of job search by employed workers, The. 1977 Mar. 58–62.
Going back to school at 35 and over. 1977 July 43–45.
Job search of the unemployed, May 1976. 1977 Nov. 39–43.
Labor force participation of married women, March 1976. 1977 June 32–36.
Labor force patterns of divorced and separated women, The. 1977 Jan. 48–53.
Students, graduates, and dropouts in the labor market, October 1976. 1977 July 40–43.
Year-round full-time earnings in 1975. 1977 June 36–41.
Multiple jobholding rate remained unchanged in 1976. 1977 June 44–48.
Workers on long hours and premium pay, May 1976. 1977 May 42–45.
Work experience of the population, 1976. 1977 Nov. 43–47.

STATE GOVERNMENT

Efforts to improve estimates of State and local unemployment. 1977 May 12–18.
Reshaping a statistical program to meet legislative priorities. 1977 Nov. 6–11.
State and local governments found to underemploy women and minorities. 1977 Sept. 37.
State labor legislation enacted in 1976. 1977 Feb. 25–38.
State labor legislation enacted in 1977. 1977 Dec. 3–24.

Workers' compensation laws: major agreements in 1976. 1977 Feb. 39–45.

Workers' compensation laws--significant enactments in 1977. 1977 Dec. 25–33.

STATISTICAL PROGRAMS AND METHODS

Allocating Federal funds through local unemployment rates. 1977 Oct. 45–46.

A method to measure flow and duration as unemployment rate components. 1977 Mar. 71–72.

A new role for economic indicators. 1977 Nov. 3–5.

Employment ratio as an indicator of aggregate demand pressure. 1977 Apr. 25–32.

Establishment of a new Employment Statistics Review Commission. 1977 Mar. 14–20.

Job absence and turnover: a new source data. 1977 Oct. 24–31.

Measuring income inequality with extended earnings periods. 1977 June 29–31.

New approaches to statistics on the family. 1977 July 31–34.

Reshaping a statistical program to meet legislative priorities. 1977 Nov. 6–11.

STATISTICS

Analyzing Puerto Rican migration: problems with the data and the model. 1977 Aug. 29–35.

Efforts to improve estimates of State and local unemployment. 1977 May 12–18.

Federal-State approach to labor statistics, The. 1977 Oct. 43–44.

Measuring the supply of scientific personnel. 1977 Oct. 47–48.

National standardization of educational statistics. 1977 Oct. 46–47.

Occupational data program yielding big dividends. 1977 Oct. 44–45.

STEELWORKERS

End of the 12-hour day in the steel industry, The. 1977 Sept. 21–26.

Lifetime jobs and wage security: vintage wine in new containers? 1977 Sept. 27–28.

SUBEMPLOYMENT (See Employment; Unemployment.)

SUPPLEMENTAL BENEFITS

Noninsured death benefits under union and company programs. 1977 Oct. 61–63.

Work-sharing initiatives at home and abroad. 1977 Sept. 16–20.

SWEDEN

An analysis of unemployment in nine industrial countries. 1977 Apr. 12–24.

European union agreements provide framework for public policies. 1977 Jan. 62–64.

Productivity and unit labor costs in 12 industrial countries. 1977 July 11–17.

SWITZERLAND

Productivity and unit labor costs in 12 industrial countries. 1977 July 11–17.

TEACHERS

Employment prospects brighten a bit for some teachers in California. 1977 Oct. 49–52.

TECHNOLOGICAL CHANGE

Productivity and new technology in eating and drinking places. 1977 Sept. 9–15.

Technology and labor in automobile production. 1977 Oct. 32–35.

TRADE UNIONS (See Labor organizations.)

TRAINING (See Education and training.)

TURNOVER RATES

Job absence and turnover: a new source of data. 1977 Oct. 24–31.

UNDEREMPLOYMENT (See Employment; Unemployment.)

UNEMPLOYMENT (See also Employment; Labor Force.)

An analysis of unemployment in nine industrial countries. 1977 Apr. 12–24.

A new role for economic indicators. 1977 Nov. 3–5.

Efforts to improve estimates of State and local unemployment. 1977 May 12–18.

Employment and unemployment during the first half of 1977. 1977 Aug. 3–6.

Employment and unemployment in 1976. 1977 Feb. 3–13.

Factors affecting unemployment. 1977 July 2.

Job search of the unemployed, May 1976. 1977 Nov. 39–43.

Outcome of a spell of unemployment, The. 1977 Jan. 54–57.

Reducing unemployment. 1977 Feb. 2.

Regional unemployment and job search in Canada. 1977 Oct. 42–43.

Reshaping a statistical program to meet legislative priorities. 1977 Nov. 6–11.

Work experience of the population, 1976. 1977 Nov. 43–47.

Youth unemployment. 1977 Sept. 2.

UNEMPLOYMENT INSURANCE

Efforts to improve estimates of State and local unemployment. 1977 May 12–18.

State unemployment insurance: legislative changes in 1976. 1977 Feb. 46–51.

UNEMPLOYMENT RATES

Allocating Federal funds through local unemployment rates. 1977 Oct. 45–46.

UNIONS (See Labor organizations.)

UNIT LABOR COST

Output per unit of labor input in the retail food store industry. 1977 Jan. 42–47.

Productivity and costs:
    Third quarter, 1976. 1977 Feb. 75–79.
    Fourth quarter. 1977 Apr. 68–71.
    First quarter. 1977 Aug. 38–40.
    Second quarter. 1977 Nov. 34–38.

Productivity and costs in the private economy, 1976. 1977 Sept. 3–8.

Productivity and unit labor costs in 12 industrial countries. 1977 July 11–17.

UNITED KINGDOM

An analysis of unemployment in nine industrial countries. 1977 Apr. 12–24.

European union agreements provide framework for public policies. 1977 Jan. 62–64.

Productivity and unit labor costs in 12 industrial countries. 1977 July 11–17.

UNITED MINE WORKERS OF AMERICA

Internal politics splits Mine Workers convention. 1977 Jan. 58–61.

WAGE CALENDAR

Bargaining calendar to be light in 1978. 1977 Dec. 34–43.

WAGES (See Earnings and wages.)

WHITE-COLLAR WORKERS

Experienced professionals lead white-collar pay rise. 1977 Nov. 48–49.

White-collar unions and the work humanization movement. 1977 May 9–13.

WHOLESALE PRICE INDEX (See Prices.)

WOMEN

Almost half of all children have mothers in the labor force. 1977 June 41–44.

Black women in the professions, 1890-1970. 1977 May 38–41.

Developing an index to measure female labor force attachment. 1977 May 35–38.

Earnings of men and women. 1977 Jan. 2.

Effect on women's earnings of enforcement in Title VII cases, The. 1977 Mar. 56–57.

Employment patterns of women and minorities. 1977 Nov. 50.

Female labor force participation: why projections have been too low. 1977 July 18–24.

Labor force participation of married women, March 1976. 1977 June 32–36.

Labor force patterns of divorced and separated women, The. 1977 Jan. 48–53.

Labor force trends: a synthesis and analysis. 1977 Oct. 3–12.

More than half of women who work part time have pre-school children. 1977 Sept. 37.

Scheduled wage increases and escalator provisions in 1977. 1977 Jan. 20–26.

Sources of growth of the female labor force, 1971-75. 1977 Aug. 27–29.

State and local governments found to underemploy women and minorities. 1977 Sept. 37.

WORKERS' COMPENSATION

Efforts to improve estimates of State and local unemployment. 1977 May 12–18.

Factors in more costly accidents drawn from compensated cases. 1977 Aug. 41–43.

Will workers' compensation standards be mandated by Federal legislation? 1977 Apr. 55–57.

Workers' compensation compared with other disability programs. 1977 Apr. 57–58.

Workers' compensation laws: major amendments in 1976. 1977 Feb. 39–45.

Workers' compensation laws--significant enactments in 1977. 1977 Dec. 25–33.

WORKING AGE

Another look at working-age men who are not in the labor force. 1977 June 9–14.

WORKING LIFE

A look at factors affecting the quality of working life. 1977 Oct. 64–65.

WORK INJURIES AND ILLNESSES

Factors in more costly accidents drawn from compensated cases. 1977 Aug. 41–43.

Work injuries and earnings of partially disabled men in California. 1977 Apr. 58–60.

Workers' compensation compared with other disability programs. 1977 Apr. 57–58.

WORK MOTIVATION

Education, work, and leisure: must they come in that order? 1977 July 3–10.

WORK SHARING

Work-sharing initiatives at home and abroad. 1977 Sept. 16–20.

YOUTH

How racial bias and social status affect the earnings of young men. 1977 Apr. 44–46.

In black and white. 1977 Oct. 2.

Youth unemployment. 1977 Sept. 2.

DEPARTMENTS

Anatomy of Price Change. September, December.

Book Reviews. Each issue. (See Book Reviews by author of book.)

Communications. April, May, August, September, October, November.

Conference Papers. February, March, April, October.

Conventions. January and August.

Current Labor Statistics. Each issue.

Developments in Industrial Relations. Each issue except January.

Family Budgets. July, October.

Foreign Labor Developments. January, April, September, October, December.

Labor Month in Review. Each issue except April, May.

Major Agreements Expiring Next Month. Each issue.

Productivity Reports. February, April, August, October, November.

Research Summaries. Each issue except January, February, July.

Significant Decisions in Labor Cases. Each issue except January, February. (See list of cases under Decisions, Court, and Decisions, National Labor Relations Board.)

Special Flexitime Reports. February.

Special Labor Force Reports--Summaries. March, May, June, July, November, December.

Technical Note. March.

BOOK REVIEWS (listed by author of book)

Aaron, Benjamin and others. *The Future of Labor Arbitration in America.* 1977 Sept. 51.

Alderman, Karen Cleary and Sar A. Levitan. *Child Care & ABC's Too.* 1977 Jan. 67–68.

Alexander Hamilton Institute editors and Eugene J. Benge. *Elements of Modern Management.* 1977 Oct. 78–79.

Andreasen, Alan R. *The Disadvantaged Consumer.* 1977 Mar. 82–83.

Arble, Meade. *The Long Tunnel: A Coal Miner's Journal.* 1977 Aug. 56.

Arnold, Selma and Bertrand B. Pogrebin, eds. *Basic Labor Relations.* 1977 Nov. 60–61.

Barkin, Solomon, ed. *Worker Militancy and Its Consequences, 1965-75: New Directions in Western Industrial Relations.* 1977 Mar. 83–85.

Benge, Eugene J. and the editors of Alexander Hamilton Institute. *Elements of Modern Management.* 1977 Oct. 78–79.

Bennett, Dudley *TA and the Manager.* 1977 July 56–57.

Brandes, Stuart D. *American Welfare Capitalism, 1880-1940.* 1977 June 67–68.

Caire, Guy. *Freedom of Association and Economic Development.* 1977 Aug. 57–58.

Carter, Allan M. *Ph. D's and the Academic Labor Market.* 1977 June 68–69.

Caves, Richard E. and Masu Uekusa. *Industrial Organization in Japan.* 1977 July 58.

Chapman, Jane Roberts, ed. *Economic Independence for Women: The Foundation for Equal Rights.* 1977 June 66–67.

Dickson, Paul. *The Future of the Workplace: The Coming Revolution in Jobs.* 1977 Apr. 87.

Dubinsky, David and A. H. Raskin. *David Dubinsky: A Life With Labor.* 1977 Nov. 58.

Follman, Joseph F., Jr. *Alcoholics and Business: Problems, Costs, Solutions.* 1977 Jan. 68–69.

Form, William H. *Blue-Collar Stratification: Autoworkers in Four Countries.* 1977 Apr. 86–87.

Freeman, Richard B. *The Overeducated American.* 1977 July 55–56.

INDEX OF VOLUME 101
JANUARY 1978 THROUGH DECEMBER 1978

AFGE

Civil Service reform proposal figures prominently in AFGE races. 1978 Nov. 30–32.

AFL-CIO

Meany attacks U.S. trade policy, demands more jobs, labor law reform. 1978 Mar. 35–37.

AFSCME

AFSCME attacks Proposition 13, endorses new dues structure. 1978 Sept. 43–45.

ARBITRATION (See also Collective bargaining.)

Binding arbitration laws for State and municipal workers. 1978 Oct. 36–40.

Final-offer arbitration and salaries of police and firefighters. 1978 July 3⁴ ·36.

Public employees in Massachusetts and final-offer arbitration. 1978 Apr. 34–37.

Resolution of job bias cases through mediation and arbitration, The. 1978 Apr. 43–45.

AUTO INDUSTRY

Heavy bargaining returns in 1979. 1978 Dec. 15–24.

BARGAINING (See Collective bargaining.)

BELGIUM

Productivity and unit labor costs in 11 industrial countries, 1977. 1978 Nov. 11–17.

BENEFITS (See Supplemental benefits.)

BLACK LUNG BENEFITS REVENUE ACT OF 1977

Amendments to the black lung benefits law, The 1977. 1978 May 25–29.

BUDGETS

Medical care costs lead rise in 1976-77 family budgets. 1978 Nov. 33–36.

CANADA

Canadian strike activity--is centralization the solution? 1978 Apr. 40–42.

Productivity and unit labor costs in 11 industrial countries, 1977. 1978 Nov. 11–17.

CIVIL RIGHTS ACT OF 1964, TITLE VII

Resolution of job bias cases through mediation and arbitration, The. 1978 Apr. 43–45.

CIVIL SERVANTS (See Public employees.)

CIVIL SERVICE REFORM

Civil Service reform proposal figures prominently in AFGE races. 1978 Nov. 30–32.

COLLECTIVE BARGAINING

Attitudes of college faculties toward unions: two case studies. 1978 May 42–45.

Heavy bargaining returns in 1979. 1978 Dec. 15–24.

Housestaff physicians and interns press for bargaining rights. 1978 Aug. 30.

Industrial relations in 1977: highlights of key developments. 1978 Feb. 24–31.

Labor and the Supreme Court: significant decisions of 1976-77. 1978 Jan. 12–17.

Scheduled wage increases and escalator provisions in 1978. 1978 Jan. 3 8.

Some determinants of bargaining in Government enterprises. 1978 Apr. 32–34.

Unions and bargaining among employees of State prisons. 1978 Mar. 10–16.

Which side 'learns' faster in the bargaining process. 1978 May 36–38.

CONFERENCES AND CONVENTIONS

AFL-CIO, 12th biennial convention, December 1977. 1978 Mar. 35–37.

American Economic Association and allied societies. Brief excerpts from 4 papers presented at annual meeting. 1978 Feb. 2.

American Federation of Government Employees (AFGE), 26th biennial convention. 1978 Nov. 30–32.

American Federation of State, County and Municipal Employees, 23d biennial convention, June 1978. 1978 Sept. 43–45.

Industrial Relations Research Association. Papers from 39th annual meeting, December 1977. 1978 Mar. 29–34; Apr. 28–42; May 30–46.

Physicians National Housestaff Association, 7th national assembly, May 1978. 1978 Aug. 30.

United Steelworkers of America, 19th biennial constitutional convention. 1978 Dec. 65–69.

CONSTRUCTION

Construction wage gains taper off in the mid-1970's. 1978 Dec. 72.

Safety and health record in the construction industry, The. 1978 Mar. 3–9.

CONSUMER PRICE INDEX (See also Prices.)

CPI revision. 1978 Mar. 2.

Medical care services in the Consumer Price Index. 1978 Aug. 35–39.

Price changes in 1977--an analysis. 1978 Feb. 3–11.

COST OF LIVING

Cost-of-living indexes for Americans living abroad. 1978 Jan. 39; Apr. 50; July 37; Oct. 51–52.

Medical care costs lead rise in 1976-77 family budgets. 1978 Nov. 33–36.

DECISIONS, COURT (See also Labor and the Supreme Court: significant decisions of 1976-77. 1978 Jan. 12–17.)

Administration Procedure Act

Batterton v. Marshall. 1978 Apr. 52.

Age Discrimination in Employment Act of 1967

Evans v. Oscar Meyer & Co. 1978 June 54.

Gabriele v. Chrysler Corp. 1978 June 54.

Lorillard v. Pons. 1978 Apr. 51.

McDonnell Douglas Corp. v. Houghton. 1978 Feb. 57.

Polstorff v. Fletcher. 1978 June 54.

United Air Lines v. McMann. 1978 Feb. 57.

Civil Rights Act of 1866

Johnson v. Ryder Truck Lines. 1978 July 39–40.

Civil Rights Act of 1871

Monell v. Department of Social Services of N.Y.C. 1978 Oct. 53.

Civil Rights Act of 1964

Associated General Contractors of California v. Kreps. 1978 Aug. 46.

Christianburg Garment Co. v. EEOC. 1978 Mar. 49–50.

City of Los Angeles v. Manhart. 1978 July 39.

Communication Workers of America v. EEOC. 1978 Aug. 46.

Condit v. United Air Lines. 1978 July 40–41.

County of Los Angeles v. Davis. 1978 Aug. 48.

Cramer v. Virginia Commonwealth University. 1978 Aug. 48.

Detroit Police Officers Assn. v. Young. 1978 May 65.

Gardner v. Westinghouse Broadcasting Co. 1978 Sept. 61.

Nashville Gas Co. v. Satty. 1978 Feb. 58.

Regents of the University of California v. Allan Bakke. 1978 Aug. 46.

United States v. South Carolina. 1978 Mar. 50.

Weber v. Kaiser Aluminum and United Steel Workers of America. 1978 Aug. 48.

Comprehensive Employment and Training Act of 1973

Batterton v. Marshall. 1978 Apr. 52.

Constitutional issues

Allied Structural Steel Co. v. Spannaus. 1978 Nov. 40–41.

Associated General Contractors of California v. Kreps. 1978 Aug. 46.

Atkins v. United States. 1978 Mar. 48–49.

Beth Israel Hospital v. NLRB. 1978 Nov. 40.

Communication Workers of America v. EEOC. 1978 Aug. 46.

County of Los Angeles v. Davis. 1978 Aug. 48.

Cramer v. Virginia Commonwealth University. 1978 Aug. 48.

Detroit Police Officers Assn. v. Young. 1978 May 65.

Eastex, Inc. v. NLRB. 1978 Nov. 40.

Federal Employees For Non-Smokers Rights v. United States. 1978 July 40.

Foley v. Connelie. 1978 June 53.

Gault v. Garrison. 1978 Apr. 51–52.

Hicklin v. Orbeck. 1978 Oct. 53–54.

Marshall v. Barlow's, Inc. 1978 July 38–39.

Monell v. Department of Social Services of N.Y.C. 1978 Oct. 53.

Regents of the University of California v. Allan Bakke. 1978 Aug. 46.

United States v. South Carolina. 1978 Mar. 50.

Weber v. Kaiser Aluminum and United Steel Workers of America. 1978 Aug. 48.

Executive Order 11246

Mississippi Power & Light Co. v. U.S. 1978 Oct. 54.

New Orleans Public Service, Inc. v. U.S. 1978 Oct. 54.

Federal Salary Act

Atkins v. United States. 1978 Mar. 48–49.

Freedom of Information Act

NLRB v. Robbins Tire and Rubber Co. 1978 Nov. 41–42.

National Labor Relations Act

Beth Israel Hospital v. NLRB. 1978 Nov. 40.

Eastex, Inc. v. NLRB. 1978 Nov. 40.

J. P. Stevens & Co. v. NLRB. 1978 Apr. 51.

NLRB v. Gray-Grimes Tool Co. 1978 June 54.

NLRB v. Robbins Tire and Rubber Co. 1978 Nov. 41–42.

Sears, Roebuck and Co. v. San Diego County Carpenters. 1978 Aug. 46–47.

NLRB v. Writers Guild of America. 1978 Sept. 60–61.

United Telegraph Workers v. NLRB. 1978 May 64.

Occupational Safety and Health Act of 1970

American Iron and Steel Inst. v. OSHA. 1978 June 53–54.

Federal Employees For Non-Smokers Rights v. United States. 1978 July 40.

Marshall v. Barlow's, Inc. 1978 July 38–39.

State laws

Allied Structural Steel Co. v. Spannaus. 1978 Nov. 40–41.

Evans v. Oscar Meyer & Co. 1978 June 54.

Foley v. Connelie. 1978 June 53.

Gabriele v. Chrysler Corp. 1978 June 54.

Gault v. Garrison. 1978 Apr. 51–52.

Sears, Roebuck and Co. v. San Diego County Carpenters. 1978 Aug. 46–47.

Hicklin v. Orbeck. 1978 Oct. 53–54.

United States v. South Carolina. 1978 Mar. 50.

DENMARK

Productivity and unit labor costs in 11 industrial countries, 1977. 1978 Nov. 11–17.

DISCOURAGED WORKERS

Discouraged workers' link to jobless rate reaffirmed. 1978 Oct. 40–42.

Improving our information on discouraged workers. 1978 Sept. 15–25.

DISCRIMINATION (See Equal Employment Opportunity.)

EARNINGS AND WAGES

General

Amendments to the Federal minimum wage law, The 1977. 1978 Jan. 9–11.

Black-white pay gap narrows as skill levels converge. 1978 Aug. 45.

Discrimination and pay disparities between white men and women. 1978 Mar. 17–22.

Fair Labor Standards Act of 1938: maximum struggle for a minimum wage. 1978 June 22–30.

How occupational mix inflates regional pay differentials. 1978 Feb. 45–49.

Scheduled wage increases and escalator provisions in 1978. 1978 Jan. 3–8.

Sharp rise in 1978 white-collar pay characterized by wide variations. 1978 Nov. 37–39.

Viva la difference? 1978 Oct. 2.

Wage developments during 1977. 1978 Apr. 3–6.

Why part-time workers tend to be in low-wage jobs. 1978 June 11–14.

Working a long week and getting premium pay. 1978 Apr. 46–48.

Specified industries and occupations

Building trades, July 1977. 1978 Dec. 72.
Communications workers, December 1976. 1978 Sept. 59.
Hosiery mills, July 1976. 1978 Aug. 44–45.
Local transit industry, July 1977. 1978 Oct. 46–48.
Paints and varnishes industry, November 1976. 1978 June 48–51.
Police and firefighters in Massachusetts, June 1977. 1978 July 34–36.
Printing trades workers, July 1976. 1978 Apr. 48–49.
Synthetic fiber plants, August 1976. 1978 Feb. 55.

ECONOMIC AND SOCIAL STATISTICS

Federal Indian policy and labor statistics--a review essay. 1978 Apr. 22–27.
Financial resources of Federal employee unions, The. 1978 Feb. 49–50.
Marital and family characteristics of workers, March 1977. 1978 Feb. 51–54.

ECONOMIC DEVELOPMENT AND GROWTH

Changing patterns of demand: BLS projections to 1990. 1978 Dec. 47–55.
Japanese economic growth and industrial accidents. 1978 Sept. 50–53.
Labor force projections to 1990: three possible paths. 1978 Dec. 25–35.
Transnational bargaining--problems and prospects. 1978 Mar. 33–34.
U.S. economy to 1990: two projections for growth, The. 1978 Dec. 36–47.

ECONOMIC POLICIES AND PROGRAMS

Employment policies that deal with structural unemployment. 1978 May 30 32.
Federal Indian policy and labor statistics--a review essay. 1978 Apr. 22–27.

EDUCATION AND TRAINING

Attitudes of college faculties toward unions: two case studies. 1978 May 42–45.
Entry jobs for college graduates: the occupational mix is changing. 1978 June 51–52.
Occupational opportunities for college-educated workers, 1950-75. 1978 June 15–21.
Paid educational leave: who reaps the benefits? 1978 May 40–41.
Structure, cost, and performance of the Job Opportunities Program. 1978 Aug. 40–43.
Students, graduates, and dropouts in the labor market, October 1977. 1978 June 44–47.

EMPLOYEE OWNERSHIP

Employee-owned companies: is the difference measurable? 1978 July 23–28.

EMPLOYMENT

Average workweek: two surveys /Current Employment Statistics program and the Current Population Survey/ compared. 1978 July 3–8.
Children of working mothers, March 1977. 1978 Jan. 30–33.
Divorced and separated women in the labor force--an update. 1978 Oct. 43–45.
Employment and prices at midwinter. 1978 Apr. 2.
Employment and unemployment during the first half of 1978. 1978 Aug. 3–7.
Employment and unemployment--trends during 1977. 1978 Feb. 12–23.
Employment policies that deal with structural unemployment. 1978 May 30–32.
Employment Service graded with new quantitative test. 1978 May 32–33.

Estimating employment potential in U.S. energy industries. 1978 May 10–13.
How benefits will be incorporated into the Employment Cost Index. 1978 Jan. 18–26.
Moonlighting increased sharply in 1977, particularly among women. 1978 Jan. 27–30.
More public services spur growth in government employment. 1978 Sept. 3–7.
Older men--the choice between work and retirement. 1978 November 3–10.
Oversupply of Ph. D.'s to continue through 1985, The. 1978 Oct. 48–50.
Productivity and cost during recession and recovery. 1978 Aug. 31–34.
Productivity and technology in the electric motor industry. 1978 Aug. 20–25.
Productivity growth below average in the household furniture industry. 1978 Nov. 23–29.
Profile of women on part-time schedules, A. 1978 Oct. 3–12.
Rural employment programs: the case for remedial policies. 1978 Apr. 30–32.
Technology and labor in electric power and gas industry. 1978 Nov. 18–22.
Two methods of projecting occupational employment. 1978 May 57–58.
Viva la difference? 1978 Oct. 2.
Women who head families, 1970-77: their numbers rose, income lagged. 1978 Feb. 32–37.

ENERGY

Changing patterns of demand: BLS projections to 1990. 1978 Dec. 47–55.
Estimating employment potential in U.S. energy industries. 1978 May 10–13.
Rural employment programs: the case for remedial policies. 1978 Apr. 30–32.

EQUAL EMPLOYMENT OPPORTUNITY

Labor and the Supreme Court: significant decisions of 1976-77. 1978 Jan. 12–17.
Minorities and women still lagging in private industry jobs, EEOC finds. 1978 Feb. 55–56.
Minority membership improves in job-referral unions. 1978 Feb. 56.
Resolution of job bias cases through mediation and arbitration, The. 1978 Apr. 43–45.
Specifying the labor market for individual firms. 1978 Aug. 26–29.

ESCALATOR CLAUSES

Heavy bargaining returns in 1979. 1978 Dec. 15–24.
Scheduled wage increases and escalator provisions in 1978. 1978 Jan. 3–8.
Wage developments during 1977. 1978 Apr. 3–6.

FAIR LABOR STANDARDS ACT OF 1938

Fair Labor Standards Act of 1938: maximum struggle for a minimum wage. 1978 June 22–30.

FARMWORKERS

Estimating the cost of extending jobless insurance to farmworkers. 1978 May 18–24.

FEDERAL EMPLOYEES (See Public employees.)

FRANCE

Productivity and unit labor costs in 11 industrial countries, 1977. 1978 Nov. 11–17.

GERMANY

Productivity and unit labor costs in 11 industrial countries, 1977. 1978 Nov. 11–17.
Unions in the military: three European cases. 1978 Apr. 39–40.

Worker participation in West German industry. 1978 May 59–63.

GOVERNMENT WORKERS (See Public employees.)

GREAT BRITAIN (See United Kingdom.)

HEALTH AND SAFETY

Amendments to the black lung benefits law, The 1977. 1978 May 25–29.

Changes in health plans reflect broader benefit coverage. 1978 Sept. 57–59.

Housestaff physicians and interns press for bargaining rights. 1978 Aug. 30.

Japanese economic growth and industrial accidents. 1978 Sept. 50–53.

Maternity benefits available to most health plan participants. 1978 May 53–56.

Medical care costs lead rise in 1976-77 family budgets. 1978 Nov. 33–36.

Medical care services in the Consumer Price Index. 1978 Aug. 35–39.

Providing more information on work injury and illness. 1978 Apr. 16–21.

Safety and health record in the construction industry, The. 1978 Mar. 3–9.

HISPANIC AMERICANS

New data on Hispanics. 1978 July 2.

Profile of Hispanics in the U.S. work force, A. 1978 Dec. 3–14.

HOURS OF WORK

Average workweek: two surveys /Current Employment Statistics program and the Current Population Survey/ compared. 1978 July 3–8.

How many hours of work do the unemployed want? 1978 Dec. 70–71.

Moonlighting increased sharply in 1977, particularly among women. 1978 Jan. 27–30.

Working a long week and getting premium pay. 1978 Apr. 46–48.

HOUSING (See Construction.)

INCOME (See Earnings and wages.)

INDEXES

Amendments to the Federal minimum wage law, The 1977. 1978 Jan. 9–11.

Cost-of-living indexes for Americans living abroad. 1978 Jan. 39; Apr. 50; July 37; Oct. 51–52.

Employment Cost Index: a review of the statistics. 1978 Jan. 22–23.

How benefits will be incorporated into the Employment Cost Index. 1978 Jan. 18–26.

Improving the measurement of producer price change. 1978 Apr. 7–15.

Productivity and technology in the electric lamp industry. 1978 Aug. 15–19.

Productivity and technology in the electric motor industry. 1978 Aug. 20–25.

Productivity growth below average in the household furniture industry. 1978 Nov. 23–29.

INDUSTRIAL RELATIONS (See Labor-management relations.)

INDUSTRIAL RELATIONS RESEARCH ASSOCIATION

Papers from 30th annual meeting, December 1977. 1978 Mar. 29–34; Apr. 28–42; May 30–46.

INTERNATIONAL ECONOMICS

A labor response to multinationals: coordination of bargaining goals. 1978 July 9–13.

ITALY

Productivity and unit labor costs in 11 industrial countries, 1977. 1978 Nov. 11–17.

JAPAN

Japanese economic growth and industrial accidents. 1978 Sept. 50–53.

Japanese industrial relations--is one economic 'miracle' enough? 1978 Mar. 31–33.

Productivity and unit labor costs in 11 industrial countries, 1977. 1978 Nov. 11–17.

JOB OPPORTUNITIES PROGRAM

Structure, cost, and performance of the Job Opportunities Program. 1978 Aug. 40–43.

JOB SECURITY

Problem of job obsolescence: working it out at River Works, The. 1978 July 29–32.

JOBSEEKING METHODS

Employment Service approved by users, but placements often fail to keep jobs. 1978 Jan. 35–36.

How welfare recipients find jobs: a case study in New Jersey. 1978 Feb. 43–45.

LABOR COSTS (See Unit labor cost.)

LABOR FORCE

Children of working mothers, March 1977. 1978 Jan. 30–33.

Discouraged workers' link to jobless rate reaffirmed. 1978 Oct. 40–42.

Divorced and separated women in the labor force--an update. 1978 Oct. 43–45.

Employment and unemployment during the first half of 1978. 1978 Aug. 3–7.

Employment and unemployment--trends during 1977. 1978 Feb. 12–23.

Global efforts to obtain equality for women workers. 1978 Oct. 48.

Improving our information on discouraged workers. 1978 Sept. 15–25.

Labor force projections to 1990: three possible paths. 1978 Dec. 25–35.

Longitudinal labor market surveys: asking 'how come,' not 'how many.' 1978 Sept. 8–14.

Marital and family characteristics of workers, March 1977. 1978 Feb. 51–54.

More public services spur growth in government employment. 1978 Sept. 3–7.

Older men--the choice between work and retirement. 1978 November 3–10.

Profile of Hispanics in the U.S. work force, A. 1978 Dec. 3–14.

Profile of women on part-time schedules, A. 1978 Oct. 3–12.

Sexual equality in the Swedish labor market. 1978 Oct. 31–35.

U.S. economy to 1990: two projections for growth, The. 1978 Dec. 36–47.

Voluntary part-time workers: a growing part of the labor force. 1978 June 3–10.

Women's labor force participation--a look at some residential patterns. 1978 Mar. 38–41.

Women who head families, 1970-77: their numbers rose, income lagged. 1978 Feb. 32–37.

Young adults: a transitional group with changing labor force patterns. 1978 May 3–9.

LABOR HISTORY

Fair Labor Standards Act of 1938: maximum struggle for a minimum wage. 1978 June 22–30.

Work stoppage in Government: the postal strike of 1970. 1978 July 14–22.

LABOR LAW

Binding arbitration laws for State and municipal workers. 1978 Oct. 36–40.

State labor law activity in 1977--an update. 1978 May 50–53.

LABOR-MANAGEMENT RELATIONS

Attitudes of college faculties toward unions: two case studies. 1978 May 42–45.

Employee-owned companies: is the difference measurable? 1978 July 23–28.

Housestaff physicians and interns press for bargaining rights. 1978 Aug. 30.

How some European nations avoided U.S. levels of industrial conflict. 1978 Apr. 37–39.

Industrial relations in 1977: highlights of key developments. 1978 Feb. 24–31.

Japanese industrial relations--is one economic 'miracle' enough? 1978 Mar. 31–33.

Labor and the Supreme Court: significant decisions of 1976-77. 1978 Jan. 12–17.

Labor-management panel seeks to help laid-off State workers. 1978 May 38–40.

Perceptions of participants in a joint productivity program, The. 1978 July 33–34.

Problem of job obsolescence: working it out at River Works, The. 1978 July 29–32.

Scheduled wage increases and escalator provisions in 1978. 1978 Jan. 3–8.

Some determinants of bargaining in Government enterprises. 1978 Apr. 32–34.

State and local government employees in labor organizations. 1978 Aug. 43–44.

Which side 'learns' faster in the bargaining process. 1978 May 36–38.

Worker participation in West German industry. 1978 May 59–63.

Work stoppage in Government: the postal strike of 1970. 1978 July 14–22.

LABOR MARKET

Entry jobs for college graduates: the occupational mix is changing. 1978 June 51–52.

Longitudinal labor market surveys: asking 'howw come,' not 'how many.' 1978 Sept. 4.

Moonlighting increased sharply in 1977, particularly among women. 1978 Jan. 27–30.

Sexual equality in the Swedish labor market. 1978 Oct. 31–35.

Specifying the labor market for individual firms. 1978 Aug. 26–29.

Students, graduates, and dropouts in the labor market, October 1977. 1978 June 44–47.

LABOR ORGANIZATIONS

A labor response to multinationals: coordination of bargaining goals. 1978 July 9–13.

Financial resources of Federal employee unions, The. 1978 Feb. 49–50.

State and local government employees in labor organizations. 1978 Aug. 43–44.

Union mergers in the 1970's: a look at the reasons and the results. 1978 Oct. 13–23.

Unions and bargaining among employees of State prisons. 1978 Mar. 10–16.

Women in labor organizations: their ranks are increasing. 1978 Aug. 8–14.

LABOR REQUIREMENTS

Technology and labor in electric power and gas industry. 1978 Nov. 18–22.

U.S civil works construction shows decrease in required labor. 1978 Oct. 24–30.

LEISURE

Preferences on worklife scheduling and work-leisure tradeoffs. 1978 June 31–37.

MIGRATION

Occupational change among U.S. immigrants. 1978 Mar. 29–31.

MINORITY WORKERS

Black and rural accents found to lessen job opportunities. 1978 May 35–36.

Black-white pay gap narrows as skill levels converge. 1978 Aug. 45.

Federal Indian policy and labor statistics--a review essay. 1978 Apr. 22–27.

Management perceptions of older employees. 1978 May 33–35.

Minorities and women still lagging in private industry jobs, EEOC finds. 1978 Feb. 55–56.

Minority membership improves in job-referral unions. 1978 Feb. 56.

New data on Hispanics. 1978 July 2.

Profile of Hispanics in the U.S. work force, A. 1978 Dec. 3–14.

Specifying the labor market for individual firms. 1978 Aug. 26–29.

Women in labor organizations: their ranks are increasing. 1978 Aug. 8–14.

Women who head families, 1970-77: their numbers rose, income lagged. 1978 Feb. 32–37.

MULTINATIONAL BARGAINING

Transnational bargaining--problems and prospects. 1978 Mar. 33–34.

MULTINATIONAL CORPORATIONS

A labor response to multinationals: coordination of bargaining goals. 1978 July 9–13.

NETHERLANDS

Productivity and unit labor costs in 11 industrial countries, 1977. 1978 Nov. 11–17.

NORWAY

Unions in the military: three European cases. 1978 Apr. 39–40.

OCCUPATIONS

How occupational mix inflates regional pay differentials. 1978 Feb. 45–49.

Occupational opportunities for college-educated workers, 1950-75. 1978 June 15–21.

Oversupply of Ph. D.'s to continue through 1985, The. 1978 Oct. 48–50.

Sexual equality in the Swedish labor market. 1978 Oct. 31–35.

OLDER WORKER

Management perceptions of older employees. 1978 May 33–35.

Older men--the choice between work and retirement. 1978 Nov. 3–10.

OCCUPATIONAL SAFETY AND HEALTH

Providing more information on work injury and illness. 1978 Apr. 16–21.

PART-TIME WORK

A profile of women on part-time schedules. 1978 Oct. 3–12.

Voluntary part-time workers: a growing part of the labor force. 1978 June 3–10.

Why part-time workers tend to be in low-wage jobs. 1978 June 11–14.

PENSIONS (See Retirement; Supplemental benefits.)

PHYSICIANS

Housestaff physicians and interns press for bargaining rights. 1978 Aug. 30.

POSTAL REORGANIZATION ACT OF 1970

Work stoppage in Government: the postal strike of 1970. 1978 July 14–22.

POSTAL WORKERS

Work stoppage in Government: the postal strike of 1970. 1978 July 14–22.

PRICES

Anatomy of price change:
    First quarter. 1978 June 38–43.
    Second quarter. 1978 Sept. 38–42.
    Third quarter. 1978 Dec. 56–60.
CPI revision. 1978 Mar. 2.
Double-digit inflation returns in second quarter. 1978 Sept. 38–42.
Employment and prices at midwinter. 1978 Apr. 2.
Food prices lead acceleration of inflation in first quarter. 1978 June 38–43.
Medical care services in the Consumer Price Index. 1978 Aug. 35–39.
Price changes in 1977--an analysis. 1978 Feb. 3–11.
Slowdown in food prices curbs inflation in third quarter. 1978 Dec. 56–60.

PRODUCER PRICE INDEX

Improving the measurement of producer price change. 1978 Apr. 7–15.

PRODUCTIVITY

Laundry and cleaning services pressed to post productivity gains. 1978 Feb. 38–42.
Pattern of productivity in the lighting fixtures industry, The. 1978 Sept. 31–37.
Perceptions of participants in a joint productivity program, The. 1978 July 33–34.
Productivity and costs during recession and recovery. 1978 Aug. 31–34.
Productivity and costs in the first quarter of 1978. 1978 Sept. 46–49.
Productivity and costs in the second quarter. 1978 Dec. 61–64.
Productivity and costs in the third quarter. 1978 Mar. 42–44.
Productivity and technology in the electric lamp industry. 1978 Aug. 15–19.
Productivity and technology in the electric motor industry. 1978 Aug. 20–25.
Productivity and unit labor costs in 11 industrial countries, 1977. 1978 Nov. 11–17.
Productivity center has failed to meet key goals, GAO finds. 1978 Nov. 39.
Productivity growth below average in the household furniture industry. 1978 Nov. 23–29.
Productivity increased during 1977 in a majority of selected industries. 1978 Sept. 54–57.
U.S. civil works construction shows decrease in required labor. 1978 Oct. 24–30.
Veneer and plywood industry: above average productivity gains, The. 1978 Sept. 26–30.

PROFIT SHARING

Employee-owned companies: is the difference measurable? 1978 July 23–28.
Technology and labor in electric power and gas industry. 1978 Nov. 18–22.

PROJECTIONS

Changing patterns of demand: BLS projections to 1990. 1978 Dec. 47–55.
Estimating employment potential in U.S. energy industries. 1978 May 10–13.
Labor force projections to 1990: three possible paths. 1978 Dec. 25–35.
Oversupply of Ph. D.'s to continue through 1985, The. 1978 Oct. 48–50.
Two methods of projecting occupational employment. 1978 May 57–58.
U.S. economy to 1990: two projections for growth, The. 1978 Dec. 36–47.

PUBLIC EMPLOYEES

Attitudes of college faculties toward unions: two case studies. 1978 May 42–45.
Binding arbitration laws for State and municipal workers. 1978 Oct. 36–40.
Civil Service reform proposal figures prominently in AFGE races. 1978 Nov. 30–32.
Final-offer arbitration and salaries of police and firefighters. 1978 July 34–36.
Financial resources of Federal employee unions, The. 1978 Feb. 49–50.
Labor and the Supreme Court: significant decisions of 1976-77. 1978 Jan. 12–17.
Labor-management panel seeks to help laid-off State workers. 1978 May 38–40.
More public services spur growth in government employment. 1978 Sept. 3–7.
Pay for police and firefighters. 1978 Jan. 36.
Public employees in Massachusetts and final-offer arbitration. 1978 Apr. 34–37.
Public service jobs of little help in cutting unemployment, GAO says. 1978 Jan. 36.
Some determinants of bargaining in Government enterprises. 1978 Apr. 32–34.
State and local government employees in labor organizations. 1978 Aug. 43–44.
Union mergers in the 1970's: a look at the reasons and the results. 1978 Oct. 13–23.
Unions and bargaining among employees of State prisons. 1978 Mar. 10–16.
Work stoppage in Government: the postal strike of 1970. 1978 July 14–22.

QUALITY OF WORKLIFE (See Working life.)

RETIREMENT

Economic status of black retirees. 1978 Jan. 37.
Older men--the choice between work and retirement. 1978 November 3–10.

SAFETY (See Health and safety.)

SALARIES (See Earnings and wages.)

SERVICES

Laundry and cleaning services pressed to post productivity gains. 1978 Feb. 38–42.

SOCIAL CHANGE

Sexual equality in the Swedish labor market. 1978 Oct. 31–35.

SOCIAL WELFARE

How welfare recipients find jobs: a case study in New Jersey. 1978 Feb. 43–45.

SPECIAL LABOR FORCE REPORTS

Children of working mothers, March 1977. 1978 Jan. 30–33.

Marital and family characteristics of workers, March 1977. 1978 Feb. 51–54.

Moonlighting increased sharply in 1977, particularly among women. 1978 Jan. 27–30.

Students, graduates, and dropouts in the labor market, October 1977. 1978 June 44–47.

Young adults: a transitional group with changing labor force patterns. 1978 May 3–9.

STATE GOVERNMENT

Binding arbitration laws for State and municipal workers. 1978 Oct. 36–40.

Unemployment insurance covers additional 9 million workers. 1978 May 14–17.

State labor law activity in 1977--an update. 1978 May 50–53.

STATISTICAL PROGRAMS AND METHODS

Discrimination and pay disparities between white men and women. 1978 Mar. 17–22.

How benefits will be incorporated into the Employment Cost Index. 1978 Jan. 18–26.

How occupational mix inflates regional pay differentials. 1978 Feb. 45–49.

Improving the measurement of producer price change. 1978 Apr. 7–15.

New computer system improves display of statistical tables. 1978 Mar. 45–47.

Providing more information on work injury and illness. 1978 Apr. 16–21.

Two methods of projecting occupational employment. 1978 May 57–58.

STATISTICS

Average workweek: two surveys /Current Employment Statistics program and the Current Population Survey/ compared. 1978 July 3–8.

Employment Cost Index: a review of the statistics. 1978 Jan. 22–23.

Employment statistics. 1978 June 2.

Federal statistics. 1978 Sept. 2.

Improving our information on discouraged workers. 1978 Sept. 15–25.

Longitudinal labor market surveys: asking 'how come,' not 'how many.' 1978 Sept. 14.

More public services spur growth in government employment. 1978 Sept. 3–7.

Specifying the labor market for individual firms. 1978 Aug. 26–29.

Statistics for policy. 1978 Aug. 2

STEELWORKERS

Steelworkers laud import restrictions, ban outsiders' election contributions. 1978 Dec. 65–69.

SUBEMPLOYMENT (See Employment; Unemployment.)

SUPPLEMENTAL BENEFITS

Changes in health plans reflect broader benefit coverage. 1978 Sept. 57–59.

Estimating the cost of extending jobless insurance to farmworkers. 1978 May 18–24.

How benefits will be incorporated into the Employment Cost Index. 1978 Jan. 18–26.

Maternity benefits available to most health plan participants. 1978 May 53–56.

Unemployment compensation and labor supply. 1978 May 47–50.

Unemployment insurance covers additional 9 million workers. 1978 May 14–17.

SWEDEN

Productivity and unit labor costs in 11 industrial countries, 1977. 1978 Nov. 11–17.

Sexual equality in the Swedish labor market. 1978 Oct. 31–35.

Unions in the military: three European cases. 1978 Apr. 39–40.

TECHNOLOGICAL CHANGE

Pattern of productivity in the lighting fixtures industry, The. 1978 Sept. 31–37.

Problem of job obsolescence: working it out at River Works, The. 1978 July 29–32.

Productivity and technology in the electric lamp industry. 1978 Aug. 15–19.

Productivity and technology in the electric motor industry. 1978 Aug. 20–25.

Productivity growth below average in the household furniture industry. 1978 Nov. 23–29.

Technology and labor in electric power and gas industry. 1977 Nov. 18–22.

U.S. civil works construction shows decrease in required labor. 1978 Oct. 24–30.

Veneer and plywood industry: above average productivity gains, The. 1978 Sept. 26–30.

TRADE UNIONS (See Labor organizations.)

TRAINING (See Education and training.)

UNDEREMPLOYMENT (See Employment; Unemployment.)

UNEMPLOYMENT (See also Employment; Labor force.)

Changing patterns of demand: BLS projections to 1990. 1978 Dec. 47–55.

Discouraged workers' link to jobless rate reaffirmed. 1978 Oct. 40–42.

Divorced and separated women in the labor force--an update. 1978 Oct. 43–45.

Employment and unemployment during the first half of 1978. 1978 Aug. 3–7.

Employment and unemployment--trends during 1977. 1978 Feb. 12–23.

Employment policies that deal with structural unemployment. 1978 May 30–32.

How many hours of work do the unemployed want? 1978 Dec. 70–71.

Improving our information on discouraged workers. 1978 Sept. 15–25.

Structure, cost, and performance of the Job Opportunities Program. 1978 Aug. 40–43.

UNEMPLOYMENT INSURANCE

Estimating the cost of extending jobless insurance to farmworkers. 1978 May 18–24.

Unemployment compensation and labor supply. 1978 May 47–50.

Unemployment insurance covers additional 9 million workers. 1978 May 14–17.

UNION MEMBERSHIP (See also Labor organizations.)

A profile of women on part-time schedules. 1978 Oct. 3–12.

Labor organizations report membership declined in 1974-76. 1978 Jan. 37–38.

Minority membership improves in job-referral unions. 1978 Feb. 56.

Women in labor organizations: their ranks are increasing. 1978 Aug. 8–14.

UNION MERGERS (See also Labor organizations.)

Union mergers in the 1970's: a look at the reasons and the results. 1978 Oct. 13–23.

UNITED KINGDOM

Productivity and unit labor costs in 11 industrial countries, 1977. 1978 Nov. 11–17.

UNIT LABOR COST

Productivity and costs during recession and recovery. 1978 Aug. 31–34.

Productivity and costs in the first quarter of 1978. 1978 Sept. 46–49.

Productivity and costs in the second quarter. 1978 Dec. 61–64.

Productivity and costs in the third quarter. 1978 Mar. 42–44.

Productivity and unit labor costs in 11 industrial countries, 1977. 1978 Nov. 11–17.

URBAN AND RURAL STUDIES

Rural employment programs: the case for remedial policies. 1978 Apr. 30–32.

Welfare reform and the plight of the poor in the rural South. 1978 Apr. 28–30.

Women's labor force participation--a look at some residential patterns. 1978 Mar. 38–41.

WAGE CALENDAR

Scheduled wage increases and escalator provisions in 1978. 1978 Jan. 3–8.

WAGES (See Earnings and wages.)

WELFARE REFORM

Welfare reform and the plight of the poor in the rural South. 1978 Apr. 28–30.

WEST GERMANY (See Germany.)

Unions in the military: three European cases. 1978 Apr. 39–40.

WHITE-COLLAR WORKERS

Sharp rise in 1978 white-collar pay characterized by wide variations. 1978 Nov. 37–39.

WHOLESALE PRICE INDEX (See Prices; Producer Price Index.)

WOMEN

Children of working mothers, March 1977. 1978 Jan. 30–33.

Civil Service reform proposal figures prominently in AFGE races. 1978 Nov. 30–32.

Discrimination and pay disparities between white men and women. 1978 Mar. 17–22.

Divorced and separated women in the labor force--an update. 1978 Oct. 43–45.

Global efforts to obtain equality for women workers. 1978 Oct. 48.

Maternity benefits available to most health plan participants. 1978 May 53–56.

Minorities and women still lagging in private industry jobs, EEOC finds. 1978 Feb. 55–56.

Minority membership improves in job-referral unions. 1978 Feb. 56.

Profile of women on part-time schedules, A. 1978 Oct. 3–12.

Sexual equality in the Swedish labor market. 1978 Oct. 31–35.

Viva la difference? 1978 Oct. 2.

Women in labor organizations: their ranks are increasing. 1978 Aug. 8–14.

Women's labor force participation--a look at some residential patterns. 1978 Mar. 38–41.

Women who head families, 1970-77: their numbers rose, income lagged. 1978 Feb. 32–37.

WORKERS' COMPENSATION

Amendments to the black lung benefits law, The 1977. 1978 May 25–29.

WORKING LIFE

Dynamics of establishing cooperative quality-of-worklife projects. 1978 Mar. 23–28.

Preferences on worklife scheduling and work-leisure tradeoffs. 1978 June 31–37.

WORK INJURIES AND ILLNESSES

Providing more information on work injury and illness. 1978 Apr. 16–21.

Safety and health record in the construction industry, The. 1978 Mar. 3–9.

WORK STOPPAGES

Canadian strike activity--is centralization the solution? 1978 Apr. 40–42.

Industrial relations in 1977: highlights of key developments. 1978 Feb. 24–31.

Strike impact. 1978 May 2.

Work stoppage in Government: the postal strike of 1970. 1978 July 14–22.

WORLD AUTO COUNCILS

A labor response to multinationals: coordination of bargaining goals. 1978 July 9–13.

YOUTH

Students, graduates, and dropouts in the labor market, October 1977. 1978 June 44–47.

Young adults: a transitional group with changing labor force patterns. 1978 May 3 9.

DEPARTMENTS

Anatomy of Price Change. June, September, December.

Book Reviews. Each issue (See Book Reviews by author of book.)

Communications. February, March, April, July, August, October.

Conference Papers. March, April, May.

Conventions. March, August, September, November, December.

Current Labor Statistics. Each issue.

Developments in Industrial Relations. Each issue except February.

Family Budgets. November.

Foreign Labor Developments. January, April, May, July, September, October.

Labor Month in Review. Each issue.

Major Agreements Expiring Next Month. Each issue.

Productivity Reports. March, August, September, December.

Research Summaries. Each issue except February.

Significant Decisions in Labor Cases. Each issue except January and December

Special Labor Force Reports--Summaries. January, February, June, October.

Technical Note. May, August.

BOOK REVIEWS (listed by author of book)

Aaron, Henry J. *Politics and the Professors: The Great Society in Perspective*. 1978 Oct. 59–60.

American Indian Policy Review Commission. *American Indian Policy Review Commission, Final Report*. 1978 Apr. 22–27.

Ansari, Javed A. and Hans W. Singer. *Rich and Poor Countries*. 1978 Aug. 56.

Bailey, Richard. *Energy: The Rude Awakening*. 1978 Nov. 47–48.

Belous, Richard S. and Sar A. Levitan. *Shorter Hours, Shorter Weeks: Spreading the Work to Reduce Unemployment*. 1978 June 59.

Blanpain, Roger, ed. *International Encyclopedia for Labour Law and Industrial Relations*. 1978 Oct. 60–61.

Brittain, John A. *The Inheritance of Economic Status*. 1978 July 47–48.

Cheek, Logan M. *Zero-Base Budgeting Comes of Age: What It Is and What It Takes to Make It Work*. 1978 Jan. 47–48.

Couturier, Jean J. and Richard P. Schick. *The Public Interest in Government Labor Relations*. 1978 Jan. 46–47.

D'Aprix, Roger M. *The Believable Corporation*. 1978 July 48.

Dix, Samuel. *Energy: A Critical Decision for the United States Economy*. 1978 Nov. 48–50.

Hill, Herbert. *Black Labor and the American Legal System: Race, Work, and the Law*. 1978 May 72–73.

Hirsch, Fred. *Social Limits to Growth*. 1978 May 78.

Johnston, Denis F., comp. *Social Indicators 1976.* 1978 July 46–47.

Kagan, Robert A. *Regulatory Justice: Implementing a Wage-Price Freeze.* 1978 Dec. 79–80.
Krendel, Ezra S. and Bernard L. Samoff, eds. *Unionizing the Armed Forces.* 1978 Jan. 49–50.

Levitan, Sar A. and Richard S. Belous. *Shorter Hours, Shorter Weeks: Spreading the Work to Reduce Unemployment.* 1978 June 59.
Loftis, Anne and Dick Meister. *A Long Time Coming: The Struggle to Unionize America's Farm Workers.* 1978 Mar. 57.

Mangum, Garth L. *Employability, Employment, and Income: A Reassessment of Manpower Policy.* 1978 Sept. 67–68.
Meister, Dick and Anne Loftis. *A Long Time Coming: The Struggle to Unionize America's Farm Workers.* 1978 Mar. 57.

Noble, David F. *America by Design: Science, Technology, and the Rise of Corporate Capitalism.* 1978 Mar. 55–57.

Palm, Goran. *The Flight From Work.* 1978 Nov. 47.

Reisler, Mark. *By The Sweat of Their Brow: Mexican Immigrant Labor in the United States, 1900-1940.* 1978 Jan. 46.

Sabrosky, Alan Ned., ed. *Blue Collar Soldiers: Unionization and the U.S. Military.* 1978 Sept. 66–67.
Samoff, Bernard L. and Ezra S. Krendel, eds. *Unionizing the Armed Forces.* 1978 Jan. 49–50.
Schick, Richard P. and Jean J. Couturier. *The Public Interest in Government Labor Relations.* 1978 Jan. 46–47.
Schlagheck, James L. *The Political, Economic and Labor Climate in Brazil.* 1978 Feb. 61.
Schneider, Stephen A. *The Availability of Minorities and Women for Professional and Managerial Positions, 1970-1985.* 1978 Apr. 59–60.
Schramm, Carl J., ed. *Alcoholism and Its Treatment in Industry.* 1978 Apr. 61.
Schrank, Robert. *Ten Thousand Working Days.* 1978 Dec. 78–79.
Shafritz, Jay M. and others. *Personnel Management in Government: Politics and Process.* 1978 Aug. 55–56.
Simon, Julian L. *The Economics of Population Growth.* 1978 Apr. 60–61.
Singer, Hans W. and Javed A. Ansari. *Rich and Poor Countries.* 1978 Aug. 56.
Snedeker, Bonnie B. and David M. Snedeker. *CETA: Decentralization on Trial.* 1978 Sept. 68–69.
Staudohar, Paul D. *Grievance Arbitration in Public Employment.* 1978 June 59–60.
Stein, Leon, ed. *Out of the Sweat Shop: The Struggle for Industrial Democracy.* 1978 Feb. 61–62.

Taylor, William J. and others, eds. *Military Unions: U.S. Trends and Issues.* 1978 Sept. 66–67.

Wertheimer, Barbara Mayer. *We Were There: The Story of Working Women in America.* 1978 Jan. 48–49.

AUTHORS

Anderson, John C. and Robert N. Stern. Canadian strike activity--is centralization the solution? 1978 Apr. 40–42.
Andreassen, Arthur. Changing patterns of demand: BLS projections to 1990. 1978 Dec. 47–55.
Andrews, Mary A. Housestaff physicians and interns press for bargaining rights. 1978 Aug. 30.
Appleyard, Dennis R. Book review. 1978 Aug. 56.
Aurand, Harold W. Book review. 1978 Jan. 46.
Ayres, Mary Ellen. Federal Indian policy and labor statistics--a review essay. 1978 Apr. 22–27.

Bain, Trevor and Myron D. Fottler. Sources of occupational information used by Alabama high school seniors. 1978 May 45–46.
Barocci, Thomas A. and David B. Lipsky. Final-offer arbitration and salaries of police and firefighters. 1978 July 34–36.

—— and David B. Lipsky. Public employees in Massachusetts and final-offer arbitration. 1978 Apr. 34–37.
——, Bennett Harrison, Robert Jerrett III. Structure, cost, and performance of the Job Opportunities Program. 1978 Aug. 40–43.
Becker, Eugene H. Steelworkers laud import restrictions, ban outsiders' election contributions. 1978 Dec. 65–69.
Bednarzik, Robert W. How many hours of work do the unemployed want? 1978 Dec. 70–71.
—— and Carol Leon. A profile of women on part-time schedules. 1978 Oct. 3–12.
Bendiner, Burton B. A labor response to multinationals: coordination of bargaining goals. 1978 July 9–13.
Best, Fred. Preferences on worklife scheduling and work-leisure tradeoffs. 1978 June 31–37.
Bingham, Barbara J. U.S. civil works construction shows decrease in required labor. 1978 Oct. 24–30.
Blair, Larry M. and Hugh S. Conner. Black and rural accents found to lessen job opportunities. 1978 May 35–36.
Bognanno, Mario F. and James B. Dworkin. Which side 'learns' faster in the bargaining process. 1978 May 36–38.
Bolton, Lena W. Heavy bargaining returns in 1979. 1978 Dec. 15–24.
Bornstein, Leon. Industrial relations in 1977: highlights of key developments. 1978 Feb. 24–31.
Braddock, Douglas. The oversupply of Ph. D.'s to continue through 1985. 1978 Oct. 48–50.
Brand, Horst. Book review. 1978 Mar. 55–57.
—— and James York. Productivity and technology in the electric motor industry. 1978 Aug. 20–25.
Briggs, Vernon M., Jr., Brian Rungeling, Lewis H. Smith. Welfare reform and the plight of the poor in the rural South. 1978 Apr. 28–30.
Brown, Gary D. Discrimination and pay disparities between white men and women. 1978 Mar. 17–22.
Brown, Scott Campbell. Moonlighting increased sharply in 1977, particularly among women. 1978 Jan. 27–30.
—— and William V. Deutermann, Jr. Voluntary part-time workers: a part of the labor force. 1978 June 3–10.
Burdetsky, Ben. Book review. 1978 Jan. 47–48, Aug. 55–56.

Carnes, Richard B. Laundry and cleaning services pressed to post productivity gains. 1978 Feb. 38–42.
——. Productivity and technology in the electric lamp industry. 1978 Aug. 15–19.
Chapman, Jane Roberts. Book review. 1978 Jan. 48–49.
Chenoweth, Lillian and Elizabeth Maret-Havens. Women's labor force participation--a look at some residential patterns. 1978 Mar. 38–41.
Chiswick, Barry R. Occupational change among U.S. immigrants. 1978 Mar. 29–31.
Clague, Ewan. Book reviews. 1978 May 73; Dec. 79–80.
Conner, Hugh S. and Larry M. Blair. Black and rural accents found to lessen job opportunities. 1978 May 35–36.
Conte, Michael and Arnold S. Tannenbaum. Employee-owned companies: is the difference measurable? 1978 July 23–28.
Cook, Carvin. The 1977 amendments to the black lung benefits law. 1978 May 25–29.
Corcoran, Kevin J. and Diane Kutell. Binding arbitration laws for State and municipal workers. 1978 Oct. 36–40.
Critchlow, Robert W. Technology and labor in electric power and gas industry. 1978 Nov. 18–22.

Daly, Keith and Arthur Neef. Productivity and unit labor costs in 11 industrial countries, 1977. 1978 Nov. 11–17.
Denenberg, Tia Schneider. Book review. 1978 June 59–60.
Deuterman, William V., Jr., and Scott Campbell Brown. Voluntary part-time workers: a growing part of the labor force. 1978 June 3–10.
Devens, Richard M., Jr. The average workweek: two surveys compared. 1978 July 3–8.
——, Bob Whitmore, Gloria P. Green. Employment and unemployment--trends during 1977. 1978 Feb. 12–23.
Drexler, John A., Jr., and Edward E. Lawler III. Dynamics of establishing cooperative quality-of-worklife projects. 1978 Mar. 23–28.

15-49

Driscoll, James W. Attitudes of college faculties toward unions: two case studies. 1978 May 42–45.

Dworkin, James B. and Mario F. Bognanno. Which side 'learns' faster in the bargaining process. 1978 May 36–38.

Early, John F. Improving the measurement of producer price change. 1978 Apr. 7–15.

Elder, Peyton. The 1977 amendments to the Federal minimum wage law. 1978 Jan. 9–11.

Elterich, G. Joachim. Estimating the cost of extending jobless insurance to farmworkers. 1978 May 18–24.

Evans, Robert, Jr. Japanese economic growth and industrial accidents. 1978 Sept. 50–53.

Farnell, James E. and Elaine Pitzalis. How welfare recipients find jobs: a case study in New Jersey. 1978 Feb. 43–45.

Farris, Mary Robinson. The veneer and plywood industry: above-average productivity gains. 1978 Sept. 26–30.

Finegan, T. Aldrich. Improving our information on discouraged workers. 1978 Sept. 15–25.

Fisher, David T. Worker participation in West German industry. 1978 May 59–63.

Fisher, Robert W. Book review. 1978 Dec. 78–79.

Fishkind, Henry and R. Blaine Roberts. Two methods of projecting occupational employment. 1978 May 57–58.

Flaim, Paul O. and Howard N Fullerton, Jr. Labor force projections to 1990: three possible paths. 1978 Dec. 25–35.

Fottler, Myron D. and Trevor Bain. Sources of occupational information used by Alabama high school seniors. 1978 May 45–46.

Froomkin, Joseph and A. J. Jaffe. Occupational opportunities for college-educated workers, 1950-75. 1978 June 15–21.

Fulco, L. J. and J. R. Norsworthy. Productivity and costs during recession and recovery. 1978 July 31–34.

—— and J. R. Norsworthy. Productivity and costs in the first quarter of 1978. 1978 Sept. 46–49.

—— and J. R. Norsworthy. Productivity and costs in the second quarter. 1978 Dec. 61–64.

—— and J. R. Norsworthy. Productivity and costs in the third quarter. 1978 Mar. 42–44.

Fullerton, Howard N, Jr., and Paul O. Flaim. Labor force projections to 1990: three possible paths. 1978 Dec. 25–35.

Gastwirth, Joseph L. and Shelton E. Haber. Specifying the labor market for individual firms. 1978 Aug. 26–29.

Ginsburg, Daniel H. Medical care services in the Consumer Price Index. 1978 Aug. 35–39.

Ginsburg, Helen. Book review. 1978 Sept. 67–68.

Goldoff, Anna C. The perceptions of participants in a joint productivity program. 1978 July 33–34.

Gomberg, William. Unions in the military: three European cases. 1978 Apr. 39–40.

Green, Gloria P., Richard M. Devens, Bob Whitmore. Employment and unemployment--trends during 1977. 1978 Feb. 12–23.

Grossman, Allyson Sherman. Children of working mothers, March 1977. 1978 Jan. 30–33.

——. Divorced and separated women in the labor force--an update. 1978 Oct. 43–45.

Grossman, Jonathan. Book review. 1978 Feb. 61–62.

——. Fair Labor Standards Act of 1938: maximum struggle for a minimum wage. 1978 June 22–30.

Haber, Sheldon E. and Joseph L. Gastwirth. Specifying the labor market for individual firms. 1978 Aug. 26–29.

Hammerman, Herbert. The resolution of job bias cases through mediation and arbitration. 1978 Apr. 43–45.

Hanna, James S. Employment Service graded with new quantitative test. 1978 May 32–33.

Harrison, Bennett, Robert Jerrett III, Thomas A. Barocci. Structure, cost, and performance of the Job Opportunities Program. 1978 Aug. 40–43.

Hayghe, Howard. Marital and family characteristics of workers, March 1977. 1978 Feb. 51–54.

Henneberger, J. Edwin. Productivity growth below average in the household furniture industry. 1978 Nov. 23–29.

Herman, Arthur S. Productivity increased during 1977 in a majority of selected industries. 1978 Sept. 54–57.

Hickey, Joseph A. Unemployment insurance covers additional 9 million workers. 1978 May 14–17.

Hilaski, Harvey J. and Chao Ling Wang. The safety and health record in the construction industry. 1978 Mar. 3–9.

Holloway, Thomas M. Book review. 1978 Sept. 68–69.

Howell, Craig and Toshiko Nakayama. Slowdown in food prices curbs inflation in third quarter. 1978 Dec. 56–60.

——, Paul Monson, Toshiko Nakayama. Double-digit inflation returns in second quarter. 1978 Sept. 38–42.

——, Paul Monson, Toshiko Nakayama. Food prices lead acceleration of inflation in first quarter. 1978 June 38–43.

——, Paul Monson, William Thomas, Toshiko Nakayama. Price changes in 1977--an analysis. 1978 Feb. 3–11.

Jaffe, A. J. and Joseph Froomkin. Occupational opportunities for college-educated workers, 1950-75. 1978 June 15–21.

Janus, Charles J. AFSCME attacks Proposition 13, endorses new dues structure. 1978 Sept. 43–45.

——. Union mergers in the 1970's: a look at the reasons and results. 1978 Oct. 13–23.

Jerrett, Robert III, Thomas A. Barocci, Bennett Harrison. Structure, cost, and performance of the Job Opportunities Program. 1978 Aug. 40–43.

Jick, Todd. Labor-management panel seeks to help laid-off State workers. 1978 May 38–40.

Job, Barbara Cottman. More public services spur growth in government employment. 1978 Sept. 3–7.

Johnson, Beverly L. Women who head families; 1970-77: their numbers rose, income lagged. 1978 Feb. 32–37.

Jonung, Christina. Sexual equality in the Swedish labor market. 1978 Oct. 31–35.

Kalachek, Edward. Longitudinal labor market surveys: asking 'how come,' not 'how many.' 1978 Sept. 8–14.

Kassalow, Everett M. How some European nations avoided U.S. levels of industrial conflict. 1978 Apr. 37–39.

Kemp, Homer R., Jr. Book review. 1978 June 59.

Kipps, John. Cost-of-living indexes for Americans living abroad. 1978 Jan. 39; Apr. 50; July 37; Oct. 51–52.

Kittner, Dorothy R. Changes in health plans reflect broader benefit coverage. 1978 Sept. 57–59.

——. Maternity benefits available to most health plan participants. 1978 May 53–56.

Kohler, Daniel M. The Employment Cost Index: a review of the statistics. 1978 Jan. 22–23.

Kutell, Diane and Kevin J. Corcoran. Binding arbitration laws for State and municipal workers. 1978 Oct. 36–40.

Kutscher, Ronald E. Book review. 1978 Nov. 48–50.

Lawler, Edward E. III and John A. Drexler, Jr. Dynamics of establishing cooperative quality-of-worklife projects. 1978 Mar. 23–28.

LeGrande, Linda H. Women in labor organizations: their ranks are increasing. 1978 Aug. 8–14.

Leon, Carol. Young adults: a transitional group with changing labor force patterns. 1978 May 3–9.

Leone, Richard. Book review. 1978 Apr. 59–60.

LeRoy, Douglas. Scheduled wage increases and escalator provisions in 1978. 1978 Jan. 3–8.

Lipsky, David B. and Thomas A. Barocci. Final-offer arbitration and salaries of police and firefighters. 1978 July 34–36.

—— and Thomas A. Barocci. Public employees in Massachusetts and final-offer arbitration. 1978 Apr. 34–37.

Loewenberg, J. Joseph. Book review. 1978 Jan. 46–47.

——. Some determinants of bargaining in Government enterprises. 1978 Apr. 32–34.

Lowe, Eugene Theus. Book review. 1978 May 72–73.

McCaffrey, David and Norman Root. Providing more information on work injury and illness. 1978 Apr. 16–21.

McCall, Jim, Victor G. Stotland, Gregory O'Connell. New computer system improves display of statistical tables. 1978 Mar. 45–47.

McCollum, James K. Book review. 1978 Sept. 66–67.

McCraw, M. Louise. Medical care costs lead rise in 1976-77 family budgets. 1978 Nov. 33–36.

McCullough, George B. Transnational bargaining--problems and prospects. 1978 Mar. 33–34.

McFarland, Dalton E. Book review. 1978 July 48.

Maret-Havens, Elizabeth and Lillian Chenoweth. Women's labor force participation--a look at some residential patterns. 1978 Mar. 38–41.

Marshall, Ray. Employment policies that deal with structural unemployment. 1978 May 30-32.

Martin, Philip L. Rural employment programs: the case for remedial policies. 1978 Apr. 30–32.

Mellor, Earl F. Working a long week and getting premium pay. 1978 Apr. 46–48.

Merrick, Thomas W. Book review. 1978 Apr. 60–61.

Monson, Paul, Toshiko Nakayama, Craig Howell. Double-digit inflation returns in second quarter. 1978 Sept. 38–42.

——, Toshiko Nakayama, Craig Howell. Food prices lead acceleration of inflation in first quarter. 1978 June 38–43.

——, William Thomas, Toshiko Nakayama, Craig Howell. Price changes in 1977--an analysis. 1978 Feb. 3–11.

Morton, Herbert C. Book review. 1978 July 46–47.

Mounts, Gregory J. Labor and the Supreme Court: significant decisions of 1976-77. 1978 Jan. 12–17.

Mumford, John and Willis J. Nordlund. Estimating employment potential in U.S. energy industries. 1978 May 10–13.

Murphey, Janice D. Wage developments during 1977. 1978 Apr. 3–6.

Nakayama, Toshiko and Craig Howell. Slowdown in food prices curbs inflation in third quarter. 1978 Dec. 56–60.

——, Craig Howell, and Paul Monson. Double-digit inflation returns in second quarter. 1978 Sept. 38–42.

——, Craig Howell, Paul Monson. Food prices lead acceleration of inflation in first quarter. 1978 June 38–43.

——, Craig Howell, Paul Monson, and William Thomas. Price changes in 1977--an analysis. 1978 Feb. 3–11.

Neef, Arthur and Keith Daly. Productivity and unit labor costs in 11 industrial countries, 1977. 1978 Nov. 11–17.

Nelson, Richard R. State labor law activity in 1977--an update. 1978 May 50–53.

Newman, Morris J. A profile of Hispanics in the U.S. work force. 1978 Dec. 3–14.

Nilsen, Sigurd R. How occupational mix inflates regional pay differentials. 1978 Feb. 45–49.

Nollen, Stanley D. Paid educational leave: who reaps the benefits? 1978 May 40–41.

Nordlund, Willis J. and John Mumford. Estimating employment potential in U.S. energy industries. 1978 May 10–13.

Norsworthy, J. R. and L. J. Fulco. Productivity and costs during recession and recovery. 1978 July 31–34.

—— and L. J. Fulco. Productivity and costs in the first quarter of 1978. 1978 Sept. 46–49.

—— and L. J. Fulco. Productivity and costs in the second quarter. 1978 Dec. 61–64.

—— and L. J. Fulco. Productivity and costs in the third quarter. 1978 Mar. 42–44.

O'Connell, Gregory, Jim McCall, Victor G. Stotland. New computer system improves display of statistical tables. 1978 Mar. 45–47.

Ondeck, Carol M. Discouraged workers' link to jobless rate reaffirmed. 1978 Oct. 40–42.

Otto, Phyllis Flohr. The pattern of productivity in the lighting fixtures industry. 1978 Sept. 31–37.

Owen, John D. Why part-time workers tend to be in low-wage jobs. 1978 June 11–14.

Perlis, Leo. Book review. 1978 Apr. 61.

Pitzalis, Elaine and James E. Farnell. How welfare recipients find jobs: a case study in New Jersey. 1978 Feb. 43–45.

Roberts, R. Blaine and Henry Fishkind. Two methods of projecting occupational employment. 1978 May 57–58.

Robock, Stefan H. Book review. 1978 Feb. 61.

Rones, Philip L. Employment and unemployment during the first half of 1978. 1978 Aug. 3–7.

——. Older men--the choice between work and retirement. 1978 Nov. 3–10.

Root, Norman and David McCaffrey. Providing more information on work injury and illness. 1978 Apr. 16–21.

Rosen, Benson. Management perceptions of older employees. 1978 May 33–35.

Rungeling, Brian, Lewis H. Smith, Vernon M. Briggs, Jr. Welfare reform and the plight of the poor in the rural South. 1978 Apr. 28–30.

Sandver, Marcus Hart. The financial resources of Federal employee unions. 1978 Feb. 49–50.

Saunders, Norman C. The U.S. economy to 1990: two projections for growth. 1978 Dec. 36–46.

Schlein, David. Civil Service reform proposal figures prominently in AFGE races. 1978 Nov. 30–32.

Scholl, Janet L. Book review. 1978 July 47–48.

Shannon, Stephen C. Work stoppage in Government: the postal strike of 1970. 1978 July 14–22.

Sheifer, Victor J. How benefits will be incorporated into the Employment Cost Index. 1978 Jan. 18–26.

Sieling, Mark S. Occupational earnings differences narrow in paint manufacturing. 1978 June 48–51.

Smith, Lewis H., Vernon M. Briggs, Jr., Brian Rungeling. Welfare reform and the plight of the poor in the rural South. 1978 Apr. 28–30.

Solon, Gary. Unemployment compensation and labor supply. 1978 May 47–50.

Staudohar, Paul D. Book review. 1978 Jan. 49–50.

Steinberg, Edward. Book review. 1978 Oct. 59–60.

Stern, Robert N. and John C. Anderson. Canadian strike activity--is centralization the solution? 1978 Apr. 40–42.

Stieber, Jack. Book review. 1978 Oct. 60–61.

Stotland, Victor G., Gregory O'Connell, Jim McCall. New computer system improves display of statistical tables. 1978 Mar. 45–47.

Taira, Koji and Solomon B. Levine. Japanese industrial relations--is one economic 'miracle' enough?

Tannenbaum, Arnold S. and Michael Conte. Employee-owned companies: is the difference measurable? 1978 July 23–28.

Thomas, William, Toshiko Nakayama, Craig Howell, Paul Monson. Price changes in 1977--an analysis. 1978 Feb. 3–11.

Thornton, Robert J. Book review. 1978 Mar. 57.

Tillery, Winston. Meany attacks U.S. trade policy, demands more jobs, labor law reform. 1978 Mar. 35–37.

Uri, Noel D. Book review. 1978 Nov. 47–48.

Van Auken, Kenneth, Jr. Book review. 1978 Nov. 47.

Wang, Chao Ling and Harvey J. Hilaski. The safety and health record in the construction industry. 1978 Mar. 3–9.

Whitmore, Bob, Gloria P. Green, Richard M. Devens. Employment and unemployment trends during 1977. 1978 Feb. 12–23.

Williams, Harry B. Cost-of-living adjustments keep transit wages on track. 1978 Oct. 46–48.

Wynne, John M., Jr. Unions and bargaining among employees of State prisons. 1978 Mar. 10–16.

York, James and Horst Brand. Productivity and technology in the electric motor industry. 1978 Aug. 20–25.

Young, Anne McDougall. Students, graduates, and dropouts in the labor market, October 1977. 1978 June 44–47.

Zager, Robert. The problem of job obsolescence: working it out at River Works. 1978 July 29–32.

Zoltek, Robin. Sharp rise in 1978 white-collar pay characterized by wide variations. 1978 Nov. 37–39.

Labor Education

Academic degrees for labor studies —a new goal for unions

Forty-seven colleges and universities
offer a 'major' or concentration in labor studies,
but high dropout rates and the fiscal crunch
in higher education may threaten the programs;
most graduates take on increased union responsibilities

LOIS S. GRAY

The role of academics has been a controversial and largely unresolved issue in the history of American labor education. Union officials viewed with suspicion early efforts on the part of individual intellectuals, many with academic connections, to provide workers education. Brookwood Labor School, the first year-round labor college, was officially condemned as "radical" by the American Federation of Labor in 1928 and subsequently went out of business.

When universities entered the field, mostly after World War II, their credentials and commitment were questioned by unionists who considered institutions of higher education to be management dominated, a belief reinforced in 1948 by General Motors Corporation's successful effort to abolish the University of Michigan's labor education program.[1] Today universities are well established as active providers of labor education. There are more than 40 year-round programs serving almost all industrial sectors of the United States. Nonetheless, the role of universities with respect to unions in labor education has never been fully resolved. Although detente, and even entente, has been achieved through the establishment of labor advisory committees,[2] considerable overlap and even rivalry, continues between programs offered by universities and those organized by the unions. On college campuses, labor programs are marginal, both in academic status and funding,[3] in marked contrast to programs for business and agriculture which have achieved academic respectability and international renown[4] with a solid financial backing from their respective constituencies.

In the 1960's, partly in an effort to carve out a unique role which would be accepted by both their academic colleagues and their allies in unions, university labor centers began to develop long-term courses of leadership training. These varied in format, from 3- to 4-month residential programs to 2- to 4- year sequences of evening courses for part-time students, and in content, from narrowly focused professional training in collective bargaining and administration (the Harvard University Graduate School of Business model) to liberal arts subjects. Common characteristics of university advanced labor studies programs were the following: (1) sequential courses aimed toward progression, (2) reading and writing requirements, (3) in-depth treatment of subject matter, and (4) certificates awarded on the basis of performance—all characteristics normally associated with academic credit and degree programs. It is not surprising, therefore, that participants began to demand credit for credit equivalent work.

Lois S. Gray is Associate Dean for Extension and Public Service, New York State School of Industrial and Labor Relations, Cornell University. This article is based on a paper presented at a seminar for Directors of Centres for Advanced Labour Studies, conducted by the International Institute for Labour Studies, International Labour Office, in Geneva, Switzerland, in September 1976.

Proliferation of credit courses

Labor studies for college credit have registered phenomenal growth in the 8 years since 1968, when the first such degree program was established at Rutgers University. According to the latest available information, 47 U.S. colleges and universities offered a major or concentration in labor studies.[5] (See exhibit 1.) In addition to labor studies, a specialized program catering to incumbent or aspiring union officers, a growing number of technical and liberal arts degree programs are planned in cooperation with unions and aimed at part-time worker students. For example, building trade unions promote dual enrollment programs in community colleges through which apprentices receive college credit for skill training offered by their union.[6] Liberal arts for labor is the focus of the Weekend College of Wayne State University in Detroit, which enrolls more than 3,000 worker students in programs of liberal studies delivered through television and supplemented by discussion meetings in union halls. College credit education for labor is a whole new development not only for the United States, but for the western world, where higher education has generally been the prerogative of middle and upper income groups.[7]

What accounts for the spread of labor-based college degree programs? It is interesting to note that the demand for credit courses comes from unions and their members and that the skepticism is on the college and university side.[8] In earlier efforts to popularize long-term certificate courses for labor, the roles were reversed. Universities, in some cases with the financial backing of philanthropic organizations, planned and promoted courses which were designed to "upgrade" union professionals and "broaden" labor's point of view. These, although moderately successful in attracting labor students, met with union resistance, and few were able to make it on their own without foundation assistance. Now the shoe is on the other foot. Unions are pushing for credit programs, and institutions of higher education dragging their feet. Why?

For unions and their members, higher education may be viewed as (1) an investment in skills which pays off in jobs, wage rates, or psychic income or (2) a consumption good which is highly valued in American society. Manpower training for occupational upgrading, which has received increasing emphasis in collective bargaining, is one impetus for labor-based degree programs. For example, interest in college credits among workers in the public sector stems from the credential requirements of civil service for upgrading to higher level jobs. Another push for advanced labor studies comes from within the labor movement, in which there is growing recognition of the need for professional-level leadership training. As the responsibilities of union officials have become more complex with changing legal requirements and as the scope of functions has broadened with increasing union involvement in political, social, and economic decisionmaking, aspiring and incumbent leaders must seek advice from professionals such as lawyers, accountants, and actuaries, and specialized training at the professional level.[9] As a result, academic credentials increase in value.

In addition to its market value, education is valued as a consumer good competing with automobiles, travel, and homes in the suburbs in bringing enjoyment and conferring status. The pressure of invidious comparison with neighbors, friends, and even one's own children is strong in an education-conscious society. Worker pursuit of both of these goals—investment and consumption—is increasingly possible in the United States by virtue of the rising average family income of unionized workers (estimated at $14,000 per year in 1975 according to the AFL-CIO) and, even more important, through collectively bargained educational benefit plans which underwrite tuition for approved courses. The underutilization of these plans[10] and the fact that college credit is a requirement for eligibility are additional reasons for converting labor education to the credit mode.

Characteristics of degree programs

Diversity characterizes the rapidly expanding labor studies degree programs in U.S. colleges and universities. No single pattern has emerged. However, most programs have the following in common: (1) adult union members as a target student body, (2) the active role of labor unions as sponsors or advisors, (3) a mix of labor-related subjects with liberal arts offerings, and (4) the policy of "open admissions" (that is the waiver of test scores normally required for enrollment in American colleges and universities). Within this broad framework, the programs vary in structure, content, and focus.

A few are directly sponsored by unions for their own members. Outstanding is the George Meany AFL-CIO Labor Studies Center–Antioch College external degree designed exclusively for union staff. In New York City, three colleges to date bear a union label. One is State financed and supported by the Central Labor Council. This is the "Labor College," a cooperative undertaking of two units of the State university, Empire State College, and the New York State School of Industrial and Labor Rela-

Exhibit 1. Colleges and universities which offer a labor studies concentration for college credit toward a degree or certificate

Institution	Degree or certificate	Institution	Degree or certificate
Antioch College/AFL-CIO Labor Studies Center Silver Spring, Md.	B.A.	College of New Rochelle/D.C. Campus-AFSCME/Cornell-ILR New York, N.Y.	B.A.
Black Hawk College Moline, Ill.	A.A.S.	New York State School of Industrial & Labor Relations-Cornell University In Albany, Buffalo, Long Island, New York, Rochester, and Westchester New York, N.Y.	Certificate
Brockport-SUNY/Cornell-Industrial and Labor Relations (ILR) Rochester Labor Studies Program Rochester, N.Y.	B.L.S.	Niagara College of Applied Arts and Technology Institute of Labour and Labour-Management Studies Welland, Ont.	Certificate
Bucks County Community College Newtown, Pa.	Certificate	Northern Kentucky State College Associate Degrees and Evening Program Highland Heights, Ky.	A.A.
Charles Stewart Mott Community College Flint, Mich.	A.A., A.G.S., and Certificate	Olive Harvey College Chicago, Ill.	A.A.
Delta College/Michigan State University Labor Relations Specialist Program University Center, Mich.	A.A.	The Pennsylvania State University Department of Labor Studies University Park, Pa.	A.A., B.A.
Dundalk Community College Labor Studies Program Dundalk, Md.	A.A.	Prairie State College Illinois Jr. College District 515 Chicago Heights, Ill.	A.A.S.
Eastern Michigan University Ypsilanti, Mich.	B.A.	Roosevelt University Labor Education Division Chicago, Ill.	A.A.S.
El Camino College Torrance, Cal.	A.A.		
Empire State College/Cornell-ILR Center for Labor Studies New York, N.Y.	A.S., A.A. B.S., B.A.	Russell Sage College/Cornell-ILR Russell Sage Evening Division Albany, N.Y.	B.A.
Essex County College Newark, N.J.	A.A., A.A.S.	Rutgers University Labor Studies Department New Brunswick, N.J.	B.A., M.A., M.Ed. and Ed.D.
Federal City College Labor Studies Center Washington, D.C.	M.A.	St. Clair College of Applied Arts and Technology Windsor, Ont.	Certificate
Florida International University Institute for Labor Research and Studies Miami, Fla.	B.A.	San Francisco Community College San Francisco, Cal.	A.A.
Forest Park Community College St. Louis, Mo.	Certificate	San Jose City College San Jose, Cal.	A.A.
Greater Hartford Community College/University of Connecticut Hartford, Conn. Labor Education Center, University of Connecticut Storrs, Conn.	Certificate	Schoolcraft College Public and Human Services Garden City, Mich.	A.A.
Houstatonic Community College/University of Connecticut Bridgeport, Conn.	A.A.	Shoreline Community College Seattle, Wash.	A.A.
Indiana University School for Continuing Studies Bloomington, Ind.	A.S.	South Central Community College/University of Connecticut New Haven, Conn. Labor Education Center, University of Connecticut Storrs, Conn.	Certificate
Iowa University/Community Colleges in Cedar Rapids, Des Moines, Estherville, Clinton Center for Labor and Management Iowa City, Ia.	A.A.	Tarrant County Junior College Hurst, Tex.	A.A.S.
Jackson Community College Jackson, Mich.	A.A.	Weekend College[1] Wayne State University Detroit, Mich.	B.A.
Lewis and Clark Community College Godfrey, Ill.	A.A.	West Virginia Institute of Technology Division of Social Sciences School of Human Studies Montgomery, W.Va.	B.S.
Macomb County Community College Warren, Mich.	A.A.S.	West Virginia Northern Community College Wheeling, W.Va.	A.A.
University of Massachusetts Labor Relations Research Center Amherst, Mass.	M.A.	University of Puerto Rico Labor Relations Institute Rio Piedras, P.R.	B.A.
Merritt College/University of California Berkeley, Cal.	A.A.	Westchester Community College/Cornell-ILR Valhalla, N.Y.	Certificate
Monroe City Community College Monroe, Mich.	A.A.		
Monteith College/Wayne State University[1] Division of Labor Education and Services Institute of Labor and Industrial Relations Detroit, Mich.	B.A.		

[1] Does not presently offer a major in Labor Studies.

NOTE: B.A. indicates Bachelor of Arts; B.S., Bachelor of Science; A.A. Associate in Arts; A.S., Associate in Sciences; B.L.S., Bachelor of Labor Studies; A.G.S., Associate of General Studies; A.A.S., Associate in Applied Science.

tions (often referred to as ILR). The other two are sponsored by individual unions in cooperation with private colleges. These are District Council 37 of the American Federation of State, County and Municipal Employees in cooperation with the College of New Rochelle and District 65 of the Distributive Workers Union in cooperation with Hofstra University.

The fantastic range of course offerings and degree requirements in the United States is reflected in the burgeoning labor studies degree movement. Even though 4-year State universities have been dominant as providers of labor education, local community colleges (2-year institutions) are the major suppliers of labor studies degrees.[11] Labor studies credits earn certificates and apply toward associate, bachelor's and master's degrees. Typical students are married white men over age 35 and active in their unions. Women and ethnic minorities are underrepresented except in a few programs with specific outreach to these groups.[12]

Core content of a labor studies major aims to cover the body of skills and knowledge required for effective functioning in a union—collective bargaining, union administration, labor history, labor law, and communications. Additional degree requirements vary by institution but tend to give heavy weight to the social sciences. One baccalaureate, two Master's, and one Ph. D. program specialize in labor education, preparing graduates as professionals in this field. In addition to the AFL-CIO– Antioch College degree, a few aim to prepare unionists for professional full-time employment in the labor movement. The others seem to be aimed at a more generalized educational objective, building on the labor interest of worker students.[13] Although, it is generally agreed that all subject areas should be oriented toward capitalizing on union experience, outlook, and role in society, the best mix of labor and liberal arts content is yet to be decided.

Finding qualified faculty and administrators is a major problem. With rapid growth of programs and position openings has come a shortage of experienced labor educators. Whether to retool existing faculty for teaching labor subjects to worker students or to recruit practitioners as teachers is another dilemma. Unions press for the latter, but academic institutions emphasize formal education as essential to maintaining standards in credit programs. Ideally, labor studies faculty and administrators have both academic credentials and union experience. In practice, this combination is hard to come by, particularly for community colleges which are newcomers to the labor education field.

The vast majority of labor studies credit programs are traditional in format. Classroom instruction is the primary mode. Even in programs in which opportunities for independent study are available, labor students prefer a group experience. For example, Empire State College, founded by the State of New York to provide nontraditional college education for adults through individual study, was pressured by labor students to convert its delivery system to traditional classroom teaching. And the AFL-CIO– Antioch program offers structure to its "university without walls" through periodic meetings at its Silver Spring, Md. center. This preference for interaction and structure is consistent with the experience and life style of workers.

Expected results

What do students expect to achieve through pursuing a degree in labor studies? In a society which tends to view education as an avenue to upward mobility, the first question about a new degree program is "What is its market value?" [14] Purveyors of labor studies degrees wonder whether they can place their graduates. With our limited experience we really do not know whether labor studies students expect to obtain better jobs or higher incomes as a result of their studies or whether they pursue a degree in order to become more effective in their union and community responsibilities with psychic rather than monetary income rewards. An in-depth study of Cornell's labor studies programs found that students did not enroll with the primary goal of advancing themselves in their jobs.[15] Their stated objectives were increased understanding of labor problems and greater effectiveness in their unions. Evaluated in these terms, the program was judged successful. The majority of the graduates took on new and increased union responsibilities and expressed the belief that the program made them better and more effective in their union. Although graduates felt that this educational experience also helped them on the job, a minority actually received promotions. The major payoff, according to the independent researchers who interviewed graduates, union officials, and employers, was increased self-esteem.[16] This parallels findings from a study of business executive training[17] and is generally consistent with research on the long-term impact of higher education in the United States.[18]

Outlook

The big question with respect to labor studies degree programs is whether they will survive. Earlier efforts to enlist labor students in long-term study both inside and outside the unions met with initial enthusiasm but eventually went out of business either as a result of conflict between the sponsors and union officials or declining interest and enrollment.[19]

Danger signals include the following: (1) relatively high student dropout rates, (2) critical reaction of many labor educators both in unions and universities, and (3) pressure for academic institutions to combine or drop new programs in a fiscal crunch.

Like those in other "open admissions" programs, students in labor studies encounter difficulties in keeping up with course requirements. About half drop out before completing the proscribed sequence of courses.[20] This rate is comparable to the record of community colleges and the City University of New York under open admissions.[21] Competing time demands for working adults who are active in union and community activities present formidable obstacles to regular attendance. In addition, home and family responsibilities are cited as reasons for dropping out, particularly for women. Needed for student retention in this type of program is a continuing follow-up by sympathetic counselors and tutoring for those who lack proficiency in reading, writing, and study skills. Because labor studies degree programs tend to be underfinanced and consequently understaffed, these needs are rarely met. Time frame is another crucial component. Few programs offer credit for knowledge acquired through experience, a controversial innovation in U.S. higher education. If academic institutions are interested in sustained participation of worker students, they must create new arrangements which facilitate progress, grant credit for knowledge acquire through experience, and recognize accomplishment through certificates and associate degrees as milestones along the way to a bachelor's degree.

Many labor educators resist the rapid spread of credit and degree links for labor education because they see "credentialism" as a distortion and even corruption of traditional labor values. For several years, annual meetings of the University and College Labor Education Association have featured debates on this subject. National union education directors have also expressed serious reservations reminiscent of the old suspicion of academicians in labor education.[22] The fact that many university labor education centers have opted out of the credit trend has resulted in a shift of labor studies to community and private colleges, which have no previous experience in labor education. In a few States, university labor education centers play a partnership role with local community colleges. In many, union education directors serve as advisors. From programs launched *de novo* have emanated a number of horror stories about total inexperience in planning curriculum and employment of teachers with antiunion reputations. The lack of solid support from experienced labor educators is a point of vulnerability for labor studies degrees. Needed is a national center for curriculum planning, development of course materials, and exchange of experience.

If labor studies degree programs have tenuous support from labor students and educators, the fiscal crisis facing higher education in the United States may be their undoing. Since World War II, colleges and universities have been expanding with ever increasing budgetary support from public and private sources. A downturn in the economy and decline in the traditional college-age population has brought expansion to a screeching halt. In a time of cutbacks, new programs are the first to go.

Will labor studies degree programs survive? Certainly the institutionalization of advanced labor studies in the universities and the unions is long overdue. Whether it will take college degree form is still to be decided. □

--------FOOTNOTES--------

[1] For history and characteristics of labor education in the United States, see Alice H. Cook and Agnes M. Douty, *Labor Education Outside the Unions* (Ithaca, New York, New York State School of Industrial and Labor Relations, Cornell University, 1958); T.A. Adams, *The Workers Road to Learning* (New York, American Association for Adult Education, 1940); J.B.S. Hardman and Maurice Neufeld, *House of Labor* (New York, Prentice Hall, 1951); Lois S. Gray, "American Way in Labor Education," *Industrial Relations*, February 1966, pp. 53–66; Lawrence Rogin and Marjorie Rachlin, *Labor Education in the United States* (Washington, National Institute of Labor Education, 1968); and *Workers Education* (Oxford, University of Oxford Extra-Mural Delegacy, 1965).

[2] For further information about university-union relations, see Irving Kerrison, *Worker Education at the University Level* (New Brunswick,

N.J., Rutgers University Press, 1951); Caroline Ware, *Labor Education in Universities* (New York, American Labor Education Service, 1946); Jack Barbash, *Universities and Unions in Workers' Education* (New York, Harper and Row, 1955); Harry R. Blaine and Fred A. Teller, "Union Attitudes Toward University Participation in Labor Education," *Labor Law Journal*, April 1967; Rogin and Rachlin, *Labor Education;* and Herbert A. Levine, "Union-University Cooperation in Workers Education in the United States," in *The Role of Universities in Workers Education* (Geneva, Switzerland, International Labor Organization, 1974), pp. 172–97.

[3] For international comparisons on this question, see *The Role of Universities in Workers Education*, pp. 1–216.

[4] Leading business sources in Western Europe credit university training with providing the cutting edge to U.S. business in competition

with other countries, and the U.S. model of promoting agricultural education has been exported and widely emulated throughout the world.

[5] Lois S. Gray, "Labor Studies—A Growth Sector of Higher Education," *Labor Studies Journal*, May 1976, pp. 34–51.

[6] For a description of this type of program developed by the Operating Engineers, see Reese Hammond, "A Degree and a Union Card," *Technical Education Reporter*, May-June 1974, pp. 5–8.

[7] Even in such nontraditional programs as the British Open University and the U.S. University Without Walls, blue-collar workers are estimated at only 5 percent of enrollment. Released-time courses and residential schools attached to colleges and universities in Great Britain are exceptions to the generalization that blue-collar and low-paid white-collar workers are generally outside the reach of higher education in Western Europe and the United States.

[8] "Forty Year Old Freshman," *ILR Report*, Summer 1972.

[9] For an analysis of the need for professional training of union leadership and a description of efforts to provide it, see Lois S. Gray, "Training of Labor Union Officials," *Labor Law Journal*, August 1975, pp. 472–77.

[10] Herbert A. Levine, "Negotiating Educational Opportunities for Employees and Their Families," New Brunswick, N. J., Rutgers University, 1972, unpublished.

[11] For discussion of the growing community college role, see *Organized Labor and Community Colleges*, report of the American Association of Community and Junior Colleges-UAW-AFL-CIO Assembly, Dec. 8–10, 1975. Washington, D.C. American Association of Community and Junior Colleges.

[12] Lois S. Gray, "Labor Studies," p. 39.

[13] John Miller, "UCLEA Curriculum Survey," unpublished paper, George Meany AFL-CIO Labor Studies Center, August 1976.

[14] For an analysis of the link between education and income, see Gary S. Becker, *Human Capital* (New York, National Bureau of Economic Research, 1964).

[15] Larry R. Matlock and Charles L. Wright, *The Non-Traditional Programs of Higher Education for Union Members*, report to the Carnegie Corporation of New York (Philadelphia, University of Pennsylvania, The Wharton School, Industrial Research Unit, 1975).

[16] Matlock and Wright, *The Non-Traditional Programs*, p. 228.

[17] Leo Gruenfeld, "Selection of Executives for a Training Program," Ph. D. dissertation, Purdue University.

[18] *A Degree and What Else? Consequences and Correlates of College Education*. Carnegie Commission on Higher Education (McGraw Hill Book Company, 1971.)

[19] For a description of the history of union staff training, see Lois S. Gray, "Training of Labor Union Officials," pp. 472–76.

[20] See Matlock and Wright, *The Non-Traditional Programs*, for an analysis of dropout rates for Cornell University and for the degree program sponsored by District Council 37 of the American Federation of State, County and Municipal Employees with the College of New Rochelle. Peter Guidry, Director of the University of California (Berkeley) labor program reports about the same experience. (Unpublished report to Ford Foundation, 1976.)

[21] Dropout rates for the City University of New York following "open admissions" averaged 45 percent, a significant increase over its record before open admissions. See Kenneth Libo and Edward Stewart, "Open Admissions: An Open-and-Shut Case?" *Saturday Review*. Dec. 9, 1972. A recent survey reported that more than 50 percent of community college freshman enrolled in programs designed to enable them to enter baccalaureate programs drop out before completion. See Edward Kiester, Jr., "Community Colleges: Innovation or Gimmickery?" *Saturday Review/World*, Feb. 9, 1974.

[22] University and union educators' views on credit and degree programs are reported in *Proceedings* of the AFL-CIO Education Conference (Washington, D.C., 1976), and in *Organized Labor and Community Colleges*.

GEORGE MEANY CENTER FOR LABOR STUDIES

Since the last convention, the Executive Council has renamed the AFL-CIO Labor Studies Center as the George Meany Center for Labor Studies. The work of reconstructing and enlarging the facilities on the 47-acre campus at 10000 New Hampshire Avenue, Silver Spring, Md., has been completed and the center is now operating at near capacity.

Campus facilities include 130 beds in 100 guests rooms, with private baths, a pleasant cafeteria, seven classrooms and several smaller breakout rooms, a 200-seat auditorium with a stage for live theatrical presentations and a 27-acre recreation area that includes tennis, volleyball, softball and plety of hiking room. Ping-pong, billiards and an exercise room are also available.

The center is equipped with the latest electronic teaching aids: television cameras for video taping, TV monitors, cassette players, overhead projector, 35mm motion picture projector and 16mm carousel slide projectors.

More than 3,000 full-time officers, representatives and staff members of AFL-CIO unions have studied on this campus since the 1975 convention, attending the multi-union institutes, workshops and programs or participating in leadership training programs and staff conferences conducted by their own union.

During the last two years, 22 unions have used the center for their own training program. Twelve AFL-CIO departments and one state central body have conducted their own programs on the campus. The only cost beyond room and board to AFL-CIO unions using the center is for out-of-pocket expenses incurred in running their programs. On request, the center has assisted in program planning and provided instructors.

The center's academic program includes institutes, workshops and programs on 28 union-relation subjects. Most run from Sunday evening to Friday noon.

A special two-week course is offered for newly-appointed staff members or newly-elected representatives of any AFL-CIO union. Its purpose is to help new full-timers understand and adjust to their new responsibilities and status.

One three-week course is available in advanced labor studies. Its purpose is to help the development of key staff members by giving them the opportunity to study society as a whole away from their work-a-day world and looking ahead at expected changes that will influence future union programs and activities.

Institutes, workshops and programs are offered on 26 other subjects. They are open to all full-time officers, representatives and staff members of AFL-CIO affiliates. No tuition is charged to participants in these programs.

Collective bargaining and grievance arbitration are the most popular subjects at the George Meany Center. Nine institutes are offered on various aspects of collective bargaining and four others on grievance arbitration. The curriculum includes nine programs on leadership development and four on organizing.

The center sponsors special programs for executive officers, civil rights designees, safety directors, building trades business agents, research economists, union editors and women leaders.

Grants from the National Endowment for the Arts help to finance the center's fine arts and performing arts programs, and the center offers a continuing series of art exhibits, paintings, sculpture and photography by American artists.

Evening activities at the center include lectures by union leaders, live entertainment by union artists in the campus theater and trips to nearby sports arenas for professional basketball and hockey in season.

The George Meany Center also offers union leaders a unique opportunity to study for a college degree without interrupting their union work. In fact, some college credits are given for competence gained through experience in the labor movement. The program leads to a Bachelor of Arts degree in labor studies from Antioch College.

Following action by the Executive Council in 1969, a committee of AFL-CIO vice-presidents studied the feasibility of establishing a labor archives on the campus. Their report stressed the need for the systematic collection and preservation of labor movement records. Unless this is done, the committee found, irreplaceable records will be discarded and valuable chapters in the history of the American labor movement will be lost forever.

COUNCIL RECOMMENDATION

The George Meany Center for Labor Studies has developed into one of the great adult learning centers in the country. It has a dedicated, union-oriented faculty. Its facilities and its services are available to every AFL-CIO affiliate. We urge them to make full use of the campus, its instructors and facilities.

The AFL-CIO has an important interest in encouraging an accurate accounting of the role that the American trade union movement has played in the development of this nation. As soon as it is feasible, the AFL-CIO should establish a national labor archival project at the George Meany Center which will not only assure the preservation of valuable historial files of the AFL-CIO, but provide the needed resources and leadership to affiliated unions in the preservation of their files.

Directory of International Labor Press Association

GENERAL INFORMATION

INTERNATIONAL LABOR PRESS ASSOCIATION
AFL-CIO/CLC
815 Sixteenth Street, N.W., Washington, D.C. 20006
(202) 637-5068 and 347-5564

PRESIDENT

Albert K. Herling
B & C News
Washington, D.C.

**SECRETARY-TREAS-
URER**

Allen Y. Zack
AFL-CIO Public Relations
Dept.
Washington, D.C.

VICE PRESIDENTS

Jerry Archuleta
OCAW Union News
Denver, Colorado

Charles L. Borsari
Ohio AFL-CIO focus
Columbus, Ohio

Joe Brady
In Transit
Washington, D.C.

James M. Ccsnik
The Guild Reporter
Washington, D.C.

Diane S. Curry
Railway Clerk/interchange
Rosemont, Illinois

Russell Gibbons
Steel Labor
Pittsburgh, Pennsylvania

Neville S. Hamilton
Canadian Paperworker Jour-
nal
Montreal, Que., Canada

Gene Klare
Oregon Labor Press
Portland, Oregon

Sal Perrotta
Los Angeles Citizen
Los Angeles, California

Mel Stack
Retail Clerks Advocate
Washington, D.C.

Bernard Stephens
Public Employee Press,
AFSCME, 37
New York, N.Y.

Patricia Strandt
CLGW Voice
Chicago, Illinois

Allen R. Williams
Aero Facts, IAM, Dist. 837
Hazelwood, Missouri

Stan Williams
Pennsylvania AFL-CIO
News
Harrisburg, Pennsylvania

Patrick J. Ziska
The Machinist
Washington, D.C.

EX-OFFICIO

Saul Miller
AFL-CIO Dept. of Publica-
tions
Washington, D.C.

PAST PRESIDENT

Raymond W. Pasnick
Steel Labor
Pittsburgh, Pennsylvania

Address mail for officers and members of the ILPA to their addresses in the directory, not to the association's address.

Address ILPA correspondence to: Allen Y. Zack, Secretary-Treasurer, International Labor Press Association, 815 16th St., N.W., Washington, D.C. 20006.

INTRODUCTION

In this directory, you will find a complete list of ILPA affiliated, their sponsors, and locations. International and national publications are grouped, alphabetically, under the name of their organizations. The other journals are listed state by state, initially alphabetized by city, and then by their publication titles.

EDITORIAL SERVICES

Periodicals issued by AFL-CIO affiliates are eligible to receive the AFL-CIO News Service free of charge. News copy is mailed twice weekly and pictures once a week. The service basically consists of material that will appear in that week's AFL-CIO News. To order, write: Saul Miller, director of publications, 815 16th St., N.W., Washington, D.C. 20006. Please enclose a copy of your publication.

A supplementary labor news and picture service is available from Press Associates, Inc., 806 15th St., N.W., Suite 632, Washington, D.C. 20005. Available are hard news, in-depth analysis, columns, features, comment and humor, with prices set according to the size and needs of the publication. Special materials are available for local union newsletters.

Four other news services are available to union publications by writing ILPA. These include:

AFL-CIO Legislative News Service A monthly packet of news and artwork about labor's key legislative goals developed particularly for mimeographed publications.

Union Label News Service A variety of line art, fillers, short editorials and other material with the emphasis on where to buy union made products and services. Each month the service spotlights one union of the AFL-CIO and the products or services its members make or provide. Sponsored by ILPA and the Union Label and Service Trades Department.

PED News Service Hard news, cartoons, editorials and features mailed monthly by the Public Employee Department of the AFL-CIO. Public employee issues are featured, but the emphasis is on increased trade union movement understanding among workers in the public and private sector.

Interface Clipsheet A two-page insert in the quarterly newsletter of the Council of AFL-CIO Unions of Professional Employees, this editor's clipsheet provides news and information about professional employees and their unions.

DEFINITIONS

National union: An organization embracing workers within the same jurisdiction throughout the country. An international union is one that covers Canada as well.

Local union: A unit of a national or international union, usually comprising the workers in a single plant or, where many small units are involved, a single city.

Local central body: An organization of the local unions within a city or county. A state central body is the larger equivalent.

Joint council: A geographical grouping of local unions in the same national union, also called a joint board in some cases. Variations include building trades councils, which bring together the local unions of various building craftsmen in the same area.

ABBREVIATIONS

The full names of some national and international unions are so long that they are awkward typographically; even some shorter titles are more familiar as initials. Abbreviations have been used in identifying the affiliation of these local unions:

ACTWU	Amalgamated Clothing and Textile Workers Union
AFGE	American Federation of Government Employees
AFSCME	American Federation of State, County and Municipal Employees
SEIU	Service Employees International Union, AFL-CIO
HREBIU	Hotel and Restaurant Employees and Bartenders International Union
IAFF	International Association of Fire Fighters
IATSE	International Alliance of Theatrical Stage Employees and Moving Picture Machine Operators of the United States and Canada
IBEW	International Brotherhood of Electrical Workers
ILGWU	International Ladies' Garment Workers' Union
IUE	International Union of Electrical, Radio and Machine Workers
OPEIU	Office and Professional Employees International Union
RWDSU	Retail, Wholesale and Department Store Union
SIU	Seafarers International Union
TWU	Transport Workers Union of America
UA	United Association of Journeymen and Apprentices of the Plumbing and Pipe Fitting Industry of the United States and Canada

OFFICIAL AFL-CIO PUBLICATIONS

American Federationist
815 16th St., N.W., Washington, D.C. 20006
(202) 637-5036
Editor: George Meany; Executive Editor: Saul Miller; Associate
   Editor: Rex Hardesty
Monthly magazine. Circulation 130,000

AFL-CIO News
815 16th St., N.W., Washington, D.C. 20006
(202) 637-5032
Editor: Saul Miller; Man. Editor: John M. Barry
Weekly newspaper. Circulation 60,000

Official Canadian Labour Congress Publication

Canadian Labour
2841 Riverside Drive, Ottawa, Ont.
(613) 521-3400
Editor and Pub. Rel. Director: Charles Bauer
Monthly magazine. (French Section) Circulation 4,800

AFL-CIO Departmental Publications

Building & Construction Trades Department

Building Trades Bulletin
815 16th St., N.W., Washington, D.C. 20006
(202) 637-5073
Editor: Robert Georgine
Circulation 5,000

Committee on Political Education

Political Memo from COPE
815 16th St., N.W., Washington, D.C. 20006
(202) 637-5114
Editor: Ben Albert
Bi-weekly newsletter. Circulation 50,000

Industrial Union Department

VIEWPOINT
815 16th St., N.W. Washington, D.C. 20006
(202) 393-5582
Editor: Jacob Clayman
Quarterly magazine. Circulation 21,234

IUD BULLETIN
815 16th St., N.W., Washington, D.C. 20006
(202) 393-5582
Editor: Jacob Clayman
Quarterly newsletter. Circulation 15,000

IUD Spotlight on Health and Safety
815 16th St., N.W., Washington, D.C. 20006
(202) 393-5582
Editor: Jacob Clayman
Quarterly newsletter. Circulation 15,000

Maritime Trades Department

Maritime
815 16th St., N.W., Washington, D.C. 20006
(202) 637-5040
Administrator: O. William Moody
Monthly magazine. Circulation 55,000

Metal Trades Department

Metaletter
815 16th St., N.W., Washington, D.C. 20006
(202) 347-7255
Editor: Paul Burnsky
Monthly newsletter. Circulation 2,500

Public Employee Department

In Public Service
815 16th St., N.W., Washington, D.C. 20006
(202) 393-2820

Editor: Michael Grace
Twice a month tabloid. Circulation 3,500

Scientific, Professional & Cultural Employees, Council of AFL-CIO Unions for

Interface
815 16th St., N.W., Washington, D.C. 20006
(202) 638-0320
Editor: Dick Moore; Correspondence to: Jack Golodner
Quarterly newsletter. Circulation 10,500

Union Label & Service Trades Department

Labeletter
815 16th St., N.W., Washington, D.C. 20006
(202) 637-5249
Editor: Earl D. McDavid
Monthly bulletin. Circulation 7,000

International Affairs Department

The Free Trade Union News
815 16th St., N.W., Washington, D.C. 20006
(202)637-5304
Editor: Tom Kahn
Monthly newsletter. Circulation 9,500

AFL-CIO NATIONAL AND INTERNATIONAL PUBLICATIONS
(Listed alphabetically by key word in union name)

Actors Equity Association

Equity News
1500 Broadway, New York, N.Y. 10036
(212) 757-7660
Editor: Dick Moore
Monthly newspaper. Circulation 19,500

American Federation of Television & Radio Artists

AFTRA
850 7th Ave., Suite 1103, New York, N.Y. 10019
(212) 265-0610
Editor: Dick Moore
Quarterly magazine. Circulation 26,500

Asian-American Free Labor Institute

AAFLI News
815 16th St., N.W., Room 406, Washington, D.C. 20006
(202) 737-3000
Editor: Morris Paladino; Man. Editor: Michael Kerper
Monthly newsletter.

Air Line Pilots Association

Air Line Pilot
1625 Massachusetts Ave., N.W., Washington, D.C. 20036
(202) 797-4000
Editor: C. V. Glines
Monthly magazine. Circulation 41,000

The Air Line Employee
5600 S. Central Ave., Chicago, Ill. 60638
(312) 767-3333
Editor: E. H. Roper
Bi-monthly magazine. Circulation 9,000

Aluminum Workers International Union

Aluminum Light
Suite 338, 818 Olive St., St. Louis, Mo. 63101
(314) 621-7292
Editor: Vernon E. Kelly; Man. Editor: L. A. Holley
Monthly magazine. Circulation 25,000

Bakery and Confectionery Workers Intl. Union of America

B & C News
1828 L St., N.W., Suite 900, Washington, D.C. 20036
(202) 466-2500
Editor: Daniel E. Conway; Man. Editor: Albert K. Herling
Monthly newspaper. Circulation 150,890

Barbers, Beauticians & Allied Industries Intl. Association

The Journeyman Barber and Beauty Culture
7050 W. Washington St., Indianapolis, Ind. 46241
(317) 248-9221

Editor: Richard A. Plumb
Monthly magazine. Circulation 53,000

Boilermakers, Iron Ship Builders, Blacksmiths, Forgers and Helpers; Intl. Brotherhood of

Boilermakers-Blacksmiths Reporter
592 New Brotherhood Building, Kansas City, Kansas 66101
(913) 371-2640
Editor: Harold J. Buoy: Asst. Editor: Leona Nichols; Managing
   Ed.: Michael Wood
Monthly Newspaper. Circulation 133,500

Bricklayers and Allied Craftsmen; Intl. Union of

Journal
815 15th St., N.W., Washington, D.C. 20005
(202) 783-3788
Editor: John T. Joyce
Monthly magazine. Circulation 58,861

Broadcast Employees and Technicians; National Association of

NABET News
80 E. Jackson Blvd., Chicago, Ill. 60604
(312) 922-2462
Editor: Ronald Chizever; Canadian Editor: Jiacomo Papa
Bi-monthly newspaper. Circulation 8,100

Carpenters and Joiners of America; United Brotherhood of

The Carpenter
101 Constitution Ave., N.W., Washington, D.C. 20001
(202) 546-6206
Editor: R. E. Livingston; Assoc. Ed.: Roger A. Sheldon
Monthly magazine. Circulation 700,000

Cement, Lime and Gypsum Workers International Union; United

VOICE of the Cement, Lime, Gypsum and Allied Workers
7830 W. Lawrence Ave., Chicago, Ill. 60656
Editor: Thomas F. Miechur; Man. Editor: Pat Strandt
Monthly magazine. Circulation 15,200

Chemical Workers Union, International

The International Chemical Worker
1655 West Market St., Akron, Ohio 44313
(216) 867-2444
Editor: Frank D. Martino
Monthly newspaper. Circulation 86,000
Canadian edition: Published in French and English

Clothing and Textile Workers Union, Amalgamated

ACTWU Labor Unity
15 Union Square, New York, N.Y. 10003
(212) 255-7800
Editor: Tom Herriman; Asst. Editors: Anne Rivera, Bert
   Schwartz; Designer: Ed Schneider
Monthly newspaper. Circulation 368,000

Communications Workers of America

The CWA News
1925 K St., N.W., Washington, D.C. 20006
(202) 785-6743
Editor: Jeffrey Miller
Monthly newspaper. Circulation 410,000

Electrical, Radio and Machine Workers; International Union of

IUE News
1126 16th St., N.W., Washington, D.C. 20036
(202) 296-1200
Editor: David J. Fitzmaurice; Man. Editor: Gerry Borstel
Monthly newspaper. Circulation 300,000

Electrical Workers; International Brotherhood of

IBEW Journal
1125 15th St., Washington, D.C. 20005
(202) 833-7000
Editor: Charles H. Pillard; Man. Editor: Robert W. McAlwee
Monthly magazine. Circulation 1,000,000

Elevator Constructors; International Union of

The Elevator Constructor
Clarks Bldg., Suite 332, 5565 Sterrett Place, Columbia, Md.
   21044
(301) 997-9000
Editor: Edward R. Smith
Monthly magazine. Circulation 12,000

Engineers; International Federation of Professional & Technical

Engineer's Outlook
1126 16th St., N.W., Room 200, Washington, D.C. 20036
(202) 223-1811
Editor: Rodney A. Bower
Monthly newspaper. Circulation 25,000

Engineers; International Union of Operating

International Operating Engineer
1125 16th St., N.W., Washington, D.C. 20036
(202) 347-8560
Editor: J. C. Turner
Monthly magazine. Circulation 336,000

Farm Workers National Union, United

El Malcriado
P.O. Box 62, Kenne, California 93531
(805) 822-5571
Semi-monthly newspaper. Circulation 22,000

Fire Fighters, International Association of

International Fire Fighter
1750 New York Ave., Washington, D.C. 20006
(202) 872-8484
Editor: William H. McClennan; Man. Editor: William Slusher
Monthly magazine. Circulation 150,000

Firemen and Oilers; International Brotherhood of

Firemen and Oilers Journal
VFW Building
200 Maryland Ave., N.E., Washington, D.C. 20002
(202) 547-7540

President & Editor: John J. McNamara; Man. Ed.: John B. Curan
Bi-monthly magazine. Circulation 45,000

Furniture Workers of America; United

Furniture Workers Press
700 Broadway, New York, N.Y. 10003
(212) 533-1900
Editor: Carl Scarbrough; Man. Editor: Ms. Meryl London
Monthly newspaper. Circulation 40,000

Garment Workers of America, United

Garment Worker
200 Park Ave., S. Suite 1610–1614, New York, N.Y. 10003
(212) 677-0573–4–5
Editor: Miss Catherine Peters
Monthly newspaper. Circulation 32,192

Garment Workers' Union, International Ladies'

JUSTICE (English)
1710 Broadway, New York, N.Y. 10019
(212) 265-7000
Editor: Michael Pollack; Man. Editor: Meyer Miller
Semi-monthly newspaper. Circulation 450,000

JUSTICIA (Spanish)
Editor: Tony Lespier
Monthly newspaper

GIUSTIZIA (Italian)
Editor: Lino Manocchia
Monthly newspaper

Glass Bottle Blowers Association of the U.S. and Canada

GBBA Horizons
608 East Baltimore Pike, P.O. Box 607
Media, Pa. 19063
(215) 565-5051
Editor: Harry A. Tulley; Man. Editor: Lon Vallery
Monthly magazine. Circulation 78,000

Glass & Ceramic Workers of N.A.; United

United Glass Workers News
556 East Town St., Columbus, Ohio 43215
(614) 221-4465
Editor: H. Wayne Yarman
Bi-monthly newspaper. Circulation 50,000

Glass Workers Union; American Flint

American Flint
1440 S. Byrne Road, Toledo, Ohio 43614
(419) 385-6687
Editor: Robert W. Newell
Monthly magazine. Circulation 22,000

Government Employees; American Federation of

The Government Standard
1325 Massachusetts Ave., N.W., Washington, D.C. 20005
(202) 737-8700
Editor and Public Relations Director: Greg Kenefick
Monthly newspaper. Circulation 300,000

Graphic Arts International Union

Graphic Arts Unionist
1900 L St., N.W., Washington, D.C. 20036

(202) 872-7900
Man. Editor: William Moody
Monthly magazine. Circulation 121,500

Hotel & Restaurant Employees and Bartenders International Union

Catering Industry Employee
1666 K St., N.W., Suite 304, Washington, D.C. 20006
(202) 785-4220
Editor: John P. (Jack) Lavin
Monthly magazine. Circulation 450,000

Human Resources Development Institute, AFL-CIO

HRDI Manpower Advisory
815 16th St., N.W., Room 405, Washington, D.C. 20006
(202) 638-3912
Man. Editor: Charles Bradford
10 issues annually; newspaper. Circulation 3,000

Industrial Workers of America, Allied

Allied Industrial Worker
3520 West Oklahoma Ave., Milwaukee, Wisc. 53215
(414) 645-9500
Editor: Dominick D'Ambrosio; Man. Editor: Ken Germanson
Monthly newspaper. Circulation 115,000

Insurance Workers International Union

The Insurance Worker
1017 12th St., N.W., Washington, D.C. 20005
(202) 783-1127
Editor: Joseph Pollack
Monthly newspaper. Circulation 29,000

Iron Workers, International Association of Bridge, Structural and Ornamental

The Ironworker
1750 New York Ave., N.W., Suite 400, Washington, D.C. 20006
(202) 872-1566
Editor: John H. Lyons; Man. Editor: Bill Lawbaugh
Monthly magazine. Circulation 116,277

Laborers International Union

The Laborer
905 16th St., N.W., Washington, D.C. 20006
(202) 737-8320
Editor: Angelo Fosco
Monthly magazine. Circulation 600,000

The Government Employee
905 16th St., N.W., Washington, D.C. 2006
(202) 737-8320
Editor: Vic Adamus
Monthly newspaper. Circulation 35,000

The Mailhandler
905 16th St., N.W., Washington, D.C. 20006
(202) 737-8066
Editor: Vic Adamus
Monthly newspaper. Circulation 35,000

Longshoremen's Association, International

The Longshore News
17 Battery Place, New York, N.Y. 10004
(212) 425-1200
Editor: Lawrence G. Malloy
Monthly newspaper. Circulation 60,000

Machinists and Aerospace Workers; International Association of

The Machinist
1300 Connecticut Ave., N.W., Washington, D.C. 20036
(202) 785-2525
Editor: Dean K. Ruth; Assoc. Editors: Jane Stokes,
Robert Kalaski, Jerry Rollings, Victor Vaschi, Mary Ellen
  Twombly, Frank Sis, Patrick J. Ziska
Monthly newspaper. Circulation 754,000

The Machinist Canadian Edition
80 Argyle Ave., Ste. 302, Ottawa, Ont. K2P 1B5
(613) 236-9761
Editor: Joseph Hanafin
Monthly newspaper. Circulation 50,000

Maintenance of Way Employes; Brotherhood of

Brotherhood of Maintenance of Way Employes Railway Journal
12050 Woodward Ave., Detroit, Mich. 48203
(313) 868-0492
Editor: H. C. Crotty; Assoc. Editor: R. J. Williamson
Monthly magazine. Circulation 140,000

Marine Cooks & Stewards Union

Stewards News
350 Fremont St., San Francisco, Calif. 94105
(415) 543-5855
Editor: Don L. Rotan
Semi-monthly newspaper. Circulation 8,000

Maritime Union of America; National

The NMU Pilot
346 W. 17th St., New York, N.Y. 10011
(212) 924-3900
Editor and Dir. of Publications: Samuel Thompson
Monthly magazine. Circulation 41,000

Masters, Mates and Pilots; Intl. Organization of

Master, Mate & Pilot
39 Broadway, New York, N.Y. 10006
(212) 944-8505
Editor: Thomas F. O'Callaghan; Dir. of Public Affairs: Maurice
  J. Weiss
Quarterly magazine. Circulation 30,000

Meat Cutters and Butcher Workmen of N.A.; Amalgamated

The Butcher Workman
2800 Sheridan Road, North, Chicago, Ill. 60657
(312) 248-8700
Editor: Samuel J. Talarico; Man. Editor: Raymond Dickow
Monthly magazine. Circulation 450,000

Molders and Allied Workers Union; International

Molders' Journal
1225 E. McMillan St., Cincinnati, Ohio 45206
(513) 221-1526
Editor: Edward F. Wulf
Monthly magazine. Circulation 50,000

Musicians; American Federation of

International Musician
1500 Broadway, New York, N.Y. 10036
(212) 869-1330
Editor: J. Marton Emerson; Assoc. Editor: Annemarie F.
  Woletz
Monthly newspaper. Circulation 282,672

Newspaper Guild, The

Guild Reporter
1125 15th St., N.W. Washington, D.C. 20005
(202) 296-2990
Editor: James M. Cesnik
Semi-monthly newspaper. Circulation 31,500

Office and Professional Employees Intl. Union

White Collar
815 16th St., N.W., Suite 606, Washington, D.C. 20006
(202) 393-4464
Editor: Howard Coughlin
Monthly newspaper. Circulation 62,000

Oil, Chemical and Atomic Workers Intl. Union

Oil, Chemical & Atomic Union News
P.O. Box 2812, 1636 Champa St., Denver, Colo. 80201
(303) 893-0811
Editor: Jerry Archuleta
Monthly newspaper. Circulation 165,000

Painters & Allied Trades, Intl. Brotherhood of

Painters & Allied Trades Journal
1750 New York Ave., N.W., Washington, D.C. 20006
(202) 872-1444
Editor: Robert J. Petersdorf
Monthly magazine. Circulation 200,000

Paperworkers International Union; United

The Paperworker
163-03 Horace Harding Blvd., Flushing, N.Y. 11365
(212) 762-6000
Editor: William R. Berg; Assoc. Editor: Chic Maglione
Monthly newspaper. Circulation 350,000

Plasterers' and Cement Masons' Intl. Association; Operative

The Plasterer and Cement Mason
1125 17th St., N.W., Washington, D.C. 20036
(202) 393-6569
Editor: Joseph T. Power
Monthly magazine. Circulation 65,000

Plumbing and Pipe Fitting Industry of the U.S. and Canada; United Association of Journeymen and Apprentices of the

UA Journal
901 Massachusetts Ave., N.W., Washington, D.C. 20001
(202) 628-5823

Editor: Joseph A. Walsh
Monthly magazine. Circulation 313,000

Postal, Telegraph and Telephone International (Trade Secretariat)

UNITY
Box 10037, Centro Colon 3 er. Piso, Costa Rica, CA.
22-04-77/22-09-44
Editor: Louis E. Moore; Man. Ed.: Lucrecia J. Lobaton H.
Monthly newsletter. Circulation 1,250

Postal Workers Union, American

The American Postal Worker
817 14th St., N.W., Washington, D.C. 20005
(202) 638-2304
Editor: Emmet Andrews; Assoc. Editor: Patrick J. Nilan
Monthly magazine. Circulation 275,000

Printing & Graphic Communications Union

News and Views
1730 Rhode Island Ave., N.W., Washington, D.C. 20036
(202) 293-2185
Editor: Sol Fishko
Monthly newspaper. Circulation 115,000

Railroad Signalmen; Brotherhood of

Signalman's Journal
601 W. Golf Road, Mt. Prospect, Ill. 60056
(312) 439-3732
Editor: Robert W. McKnight
Monthly magazine. Circulation 15,400

Railroad Yardmasters of America

The Railroad Yardmaster
1411 Peterson Ave., Park Ridge, Ill. 60068
(312) 696-2510
Editor: R. J. Culver
Monthly magazine. Circulation 5,100

Railway Carmen of America, Brotherhood of

Railway Carmen's Journal
4929 Main St., Kansas City, Mo. 64112
(816) 561-8449
Editor: Charles W. Hauck
Monthly magazine. Circulation 123,000

Railway Labor Organizations

LABOR Newspaper
400 First St., N.W., Washington, D.C. 20001
(202) 628-9260
Editor: Ruben Levin, Sec.-Treas.: Richard C. Howard
Bi-weekly newspaper. Circulation 350,000

Canadian Railwayman
130 Albert St., Suite 513, Varette Bldg.
KIP5G4 Ottawa, Ontario
Monthly newspaper. Circulation 55,000

Railway, Airline and Steamship Clerks, Freight Handlers, Express and Station Employes; Brotherhood of

Railway Clerk/Interchange
6300 River Road, Rosemont, Ill. 60018
(312) 692-7711

Editor: Fred J. Kroll; Asst. Editor: Diane S. Curry
Monthly magazine. Circulation 275,000

Canadian Interchange/Exchange
550 Sherbrooke St., W., Suite 690
Montreal, Quebec, Canada
(514) 842-8676
Editor: Robert Douglas
Monthly magazine. Circulation 22,000

Retail Clerks, Intl. Association of

Retail Clerks Advocate
1775 K St., N.W., Washington, D.C. 20006
(202) 223-3111
Editor: James T. Housewright; Asst. Editor: Mel Stack
Monthly magazine. Circulation 650,000

Retail, Wholesale and Dept. Store Union

RWDSU Record
101 W. 31st. St., New York, N.Y. 10001
(212) 947-9303
Managing Editor: Tor Cedervall
Semi-monthly newspaper. Circulation 205,000

Roofers, Damp and Waterproof Workers Association; United Slate, Tile and Composition

The Journeyman Roofer & Waterproofer
1125 17th St., N.W., Washington, D.C. 20036
(202) 638-3228
Editor: Dale Zusman
Monthly magazine. Circulation 21,000

Rubber, Cork, Linoleum & Plastic Workers; United

United Rubber Worker
87 South High St., Akron, Ohio 44308
(216) 376-6181
Editor: Peter Bommarito; Man. Editor: J. Curtis Brown
Monthly newspaper. Circulation 210,000

Screen Actors Guild

Screen Actor
7750 Sunset Blvd., Hollywood, Calif. 90046
(213) 876-3030
Editor: Judith Rheiner
Quarterly magazine. Circulation 26,000

Seafarers International Union

Seafarers Log
675 Fourth Ave., New York, N.Y. 11232
(212) 499-6600
Editor: Marietta Homayonpour
Monthly newspaper. Circulation 60,000

Industrial Workers Union, United (Seafarers)

UIW Newsletter
675 Fourth Ave., Brooklyn, N.Y. 11232
(212) 499-6600 x242
Editor-in-Chief: Marietta Homayonpour; Editor: James
   Gannon
Monthly newspaper. Circulation 10,000

Pottery & Allied Workers, Intl. Brotherhood of (Seafarers)
Potters Herald
Box 988, East Liverpool, Ohio 43929
(216) 385-0507
Editor: L. H. Null; Assoc. Editor: George Barbaree
Weekly newspaper. Circulation 16,000

Service Employees International Union
Service Employee
2020 K St., N.W., Washington, D.C. 20006
(202) 452-8750
Director of Publications: David Stack
Monthly newspaper. Circulation 490,000

Sheet Metal Workers International Union
Sheet Metal Workers Journal
1750 New York Ave., N.W., Washington, D.C. 20006
(202) 296-5880
Editor: David S. Turner
Monthly magazine. Circulation 160,000

Shoe Workers of America; United
The United Shoe Worker
120 Boylston St., Suite 222, Boston, Mass. 02116
(617) 523-6121
Editor: George O. Fecteau; Man. Editor: Kenneth Fiester
Bi-monthly newspaper. Circulation 35,000

Stage Employes and Moving Picture Machine Operators of the U.S. and Canada; Intl. Alliance of Theatrical
IATSE Official Bulletin
1515 Broadway, 6th Floor, New York, N.Y. 10036
(212) 730-1770
Editor: John A. Forde; Assoc. Editor: Rene L. Ash
Quarterly magazine. Circulation 60,850

State, County and Municipal Employees, American Federation of
The Public Employee
1625 L St., N.W., Washington, D.C. 20036
(202) 452-4800
Director of Public Affairs: Mike Dowling
Editor: Marcia Silverman
Monthly newspaper. Circulation 600,000

Steelworkers of America, United
Steel Labor
Five Gateway Center, Pittsburgh, Pa. 15222
(412) 562-2666
Editor: Raymond W. Pasnick; Asst. Editor: Russell Gibbons
Monthly newspaper. Circulation 1,550,000

Steel Labor Regional Editorial Offices
Midwest Edition, Gary Hubbard
1900 Engineering Bldg., 205 W. Wacker Dr., Chicago, Ill. 60606
(312) 782-3126

Western Edition, Cass Alvin

720 Airport Imperial Towers, El Segundo, Calif. 90245
(213) 640-0433

Southern Edition, William T. Edwards
409 North 21st St., Suite 202, Birmingham, Ala. 35203
(205) 251-3486

Canadian Edition, Merl Day
55 Eglinton Ave., East, Toronto 12, Ontario
(416) 487-1571

French-Canadian Edition, Jean-Marc Carle
1290 St. Denis, Montreal 129, Quebec
(514) 288-7200

Teachers; American Federation of
American Teacher
11 Dupont Circle, 5th Floor, Washington, D.C. 20036
(202) 797-4400
Editor: Gail Miller
Monthly newspaper. Circulation 200,000

Telegraph Workers; United
Telegraph Workers Journal
701 Gude Drive, Rockville, Maryland 20850
(301) 424-7877
Editor: Jerry Grim
Monthly newspaper. Circulation 28,000

Textile Workers of America; United
Textile Challenger
420 Common St., Lawrence, Mass. 01840
(617) 686-2901
Editor: Francis Schaufenbil
Bimonthly newspaper. Circulation 47,000

Tobacco Workers International Union
Tobacco Worker
1522 K St., N.W., Washington, D.C. 2005
(202) 659-1366
Co-Editors: Rene Rondou and Homer Cole
Bi-monthly newspaper. Circulation 25,500

Train Dispatchers Association; American
Train Dispatcher
1401 S. Harlem Avenue, Berwyn, Ill. 60402
(312) 795-5656
Managing Editor: D. E. Collins
Magazine (8 yearly issues). Circulation 4,500

Transit Union, Amalgamated
In Transit
5025 Wisconsin Ave., N.W., Washington, D.C. 20016
(202) 537-1645
Director of Publications: Joe Brady
Monthly newspaper. Circulation 133,000

Transport Workers Union of America
TWU Express
1980 Broadway, New York, N.Y. 10023
(212) 873-6000
Editor: Joseph J. Kutch
Monthly newspaper. Circulation 110,000

Transportation Union, United
UTU News
14600 Detroit Ave., Cleveland, Ohio 44107
(216) 228-9400
Editor: Lou Corsi
Weekly newspaper. Circulation 146,886

Typographical Union, International
Typographical Journal
P.O. Box 2341, Colorado Springs, Colo. 80901
(303) 471-2460
Editor: Thomas W. Kopeck; Assoc. Editor: Ralph O. Johns
Monthly magazine. Circulation 106,348

ITU Review
301 South Union Blvd, P.O. Box 157
Colorado Springs, Colo. 80901
(303) 636-2341
Editor: A. Sandy Bevis; Man. Editor: Horst A. Reschke
Newspaper. Circulation 36,000

Upholsterers' International Union of North America
UIU Journal
25 N. 4th St., Philadelphia, Pa. 19106
(215) 923-5700

Editor: Sal B. Hoffmann
Monthly newspaper. Circulation 55,000

Utility Workers Union of America
Light
815 16th St., N.W., Room 605, Washington, D.C. 20006
(202) 347-8105
Editor: Marshall Hicks
Monthly newspaper. Circulation 70,000

Wood, Wire and Metal Lathers Intl. Union
The Lather
815 16th St., N.W., Room 401, Washington, D.C. 20006
(202) 628-0400
Editor: Michael J. Brennan
Quarterly magazine. Circulation 12,000

Woodworkers of America; International
International Woodworker
1622 N. Lombard, Portland, Ore. 97217
(503) 285-5281
Acting Editor: Dick Spohn
Semi-monthly newspaper. Circulation 56,800

AFL-CIO STATE AND LOCAL CENTRAL BODY PUBLICATIONS; U.S. LOCAL UNION PUBLICATIONS
(Listed Alphabetically by State and City)

ALABAMA
Alabama Labor Council News Letter
231 W. Valley Ave., Birmingham, Ala. 35209
(205) 870-5260
Owned by: Alabama Labor Council
Editor: Barney Weeks
Weekly newsletter. Circulation 1,000

ARIZONA
Arizona State AFL-CIO Legislative Newsletter
520 West Adams, Phoenix, Ariz. 85003
(602) 258-3407
Owned by: Arizona State AFL-CIO
Editor: Darwin Aycock
Weekly newsletter. Circulation 200

Engineers News Report
1426 N. 1st St., Phoenix, Arizona 85004
(602) 254-5226
Owned by: Local 428, Intl. Union of Operating Engineers
Editor: Larry Dugan, Jr.
Monthly newspaper. Circulation 4,000

The Labor Journal
5818 N. 7th St., Room 200, Phoenix, Arizona 85014
(602) 263-5460
Owned by: The Central Arizona Labor Council
Editor: Jim White
Monthly newspaper. Circulation 30,000

Local Level
2475 E. Water St. Tucson, Arizona 85719
(602) 793-9476
Owned by: United Assoc. of Plumbers & Steamfitters Local 741
Editor: Howard Shaw
Weekly newsletter. Circulation 850

Southern Arizona Central Labor Council Newsletter
606 South Plumer, Tucson, Arizona 85719
(602) 882-2168
Owned by: Southern Arizona Central Labor Council
Editor: Grace Carroll
Weekly newsletter. Circulation 250

Union Dispatch
606 South Plumer, Tucson, Ariz. 85713
(602) 624-5551
Owned by: District Council of Carpenters
Editor: Ted W. Clark
Weekly newsletter. Circulation 1,500

CALIFORNIA

The Labor Journal
200 W. Jeffrey, Bakersfield, Calif. 93305
(805) 323-4409
Owned by: Kern, Inyo and Mono Counties Central Labor
  Councils
Editor: Will Powers
Monthly newspaper. Circulation 6,000

Viewpoint
P.O. Box 1808, Bakersfield, Calif. 93303
(805) 327-4481
Owned by: Retail Clerks Union Local 137
Editor: Mel Rubin
Quarterly newsletter. Circulation 1,300

University Guardian
2527 Dwight Way, Berkeley, Calif. 94704
(415) 841-1750
Owned by: University Council-American Federation of Teachers
Editor: Paul Goodman; Man. Editor: Sam Bottone
Bi-monthly newspaper.

Local 324 Reporter
8530 Stanton Ave., Buena Park, Calif. 90620
(714) 527-8811
Owned by: Local 324, Retail Clerks
President: John C. Sperry
Monthly newspaper. Circulation 18,000

American Aeronaut
2600 W. Victory Blvd. Burbank, Calif. 91503
(213) 845-7401
Owned by: Dist. 727, Machinists
Editor: Neil Vandercook
Monthly newspaper. Circulation 23,000

California Teacher
2412 W. Magnolia Blvd. Burbank, Calif. 91506
(213) 843-8226
Owned by: California Federation of Teachers
Assoc. Man. Editor: Ralph Lloyd
Monthly newspaper. Circulation 50,000

Trade Winds
1511 Rollins Road, Burlingame, Calif. 94010
(415) 697-8716
Owned by: Machinists Lodge 1781
Editor: Colin A. Cooke
Monthly newspaper. Circulation 7,500

Union Reporter
12944 E. 166th St., Cerritos, Calif. 90701
(213) 926-2132
Owned by: IBEW Local 47
Editor: H. D. Higginbotham
Monthly newspaper. Circulation 6,000

Desert Edge and Desert
190 West G St., P.O. Box 539, Colton, Calif. 92324
(714) 825-1310
Owned by: Retail Clerks Local 1167
Editor: William I. Brooks
Monthly newspaper. Circulation 2,650

1288 Grapevine
265 N. Fresno St., Fresno, Calif. 93701
(209) 442-1288

Owned by: RCIA Local 1288
Editor: Art Smith; Asst. Editor: Bob McGrath, Jerry Lench
  & Associates, Inc.
Monthly newspaper. Circulation 5,000

Orange Empire News
12311 Chapman Ave., #207, Garden Grove, Calif. 96240
(714) 530-1981
Owned by: CWA Local 11510
Editor: Michael Drake
Monthly newspaper. Circulation 4,200

Reflections
14810 #7 Halldale, Gardena, Calif. 90247
(213) 532-4719
Owned by: GBBA Local 19
Editor: Gerald Brown
Monthly newsletter. Circulation 200–300

The 899 Good Land
7190 Hollister Ave., Goleta, Calif. 93017
(805) 968-2501
Owned by: RCIA Local 899
Editor: Dick Warren; Asst. Editors: Jerry Lench and Chuck
  Conyers
Monthly newspaper. Circulation 5,000

The Overture
817 Vine St., Hollywood, Calif. 90038
(213) 462-2161
Owned by: Musicians Local 47
Editor: Marl Young
Monthly newspaper. Circulation 17,500

Serving America
532 E. 4th St., Long Beach, Calif. 90812
(213) 432-6423
Owned by: Culinary Alliance, Local 681, HREBIU
Editor: James T. Stevens
Bi-monthly magazine. Circulation 7,000

Coffee Break
2411 W. 8th, Suite 201, Los Angeles, Calif. 90057
(213) 389-1158
Owned by: OPEIU Local 30
Editor: Gwen Newton
Monthly newsletter. Circulation 2,350

Communique
2404 Wilshire Blvd., Suite 504, Los Angeles, Calif. 90057
(213) 385-5555
Owned by: Local 660, SEIU
Editor: Shiela Anderson
Monthly newspaper. Circulation 54,000

County Employee
2404 Wilshire Blvd, Los Angeles, Calif. 90057
(213) 385-5555
Owned by: Local 660, SEIU
Editor: Pamela Allison
Semi-monthly newspaper. Circulation 40,000

The Los Angeles Firefighter
1539 Beverly Blvd., Los Angeles, Calif. 90026
(213) 489-1300
Owned by: IAFF Local 112
Editor: Michael J. Kaemerer
Bi-monthly newspaper. Circulation 4,500

Guildsman
1543 W. Olympic Blvd., Suite 337, Los Angeles, Calif. 90015
(213) 386-2068
Owned by: Los Angeles Newspaper Guild Local 69
Monthly newspaper. Circulation 1,558

Local 11 News Calendar
321 South Bixel St., Los Angeles, Calif. 90017
(213) 482-9800
Owned by: HREBIU Local 11
Editor: Paul E. Greenwood; Man. Editor: Andrew Allan;
  Assoc. Editor: Harry Weisman
Monthly newsletter. Circulation 9,000

Local 37 News
1040 S. Grand Ave., Los Angeles, Calif. 90015
(213) 748-0013
Owned by: Bakers Union Local 37
Editor: Allan D. Bryan; Man. Editor: Eleanor J. Moore
Monthly newspaper. Circulation 7,500

535 Newsletter
2300 West 7th St., Los Angeles, Calif. 90057
(213) 385-9321
Owned by: Social Services Union, Local 535, SEIU
Executive Director: David D. Crippen
Bi-monthly newspaper. Circulation 6,500

Los Angeles Citizen
2130 W. 9th St., Los Angeles, Calif. 90006
(213) 381-5611
Owned by: County Federation of Labor
Editor: Sal Perrotta
Weekly newspaper. Circulation 42,800

Protective Order of Dining Car Waiters Local 465 Newsletter
3911 Westside Ave., Los Angeles, Calif. 90008
(213) 293-2030
Owned by: Protective Order of Dining Car Waiters Local 465
President & Editor: Robert E. Weir
Monthly newsletter.

Service Union Reporter
1247 W. 7th St., Los Angeles, Calif. 90017
(213) 680-9567
Owned by: California State Council of Bldg. Service Unions,
  SEIU
Editor: Robert Crain
Monthly newspaper. Circulation 105,500

The Voice of '94'
214 S. Loma Drive, Los Angeles, Calif. 90026
(213) 483-6630
Owned by: Machinists District Lodge 94
Editor: Dan Swinton; Man. Editor: Charles E. Edwards
Secretary-Treasurer: Ted Neima
Monthly newspaper. Circulation 14,000

United Teacher
2511 West Third St., Los Angeles, Calif. 90057
(213) 487-5560
Owned by: United Teachers Los Angeles
Editor: Robert M. Sanders
Weekly newspaper. Circulation 35,000

Voice of 770
3055 Wilshire Blvd., Suite 410, Los Angeles, Calif. 90010
Owned by: Local 770, Retail Clerks
Editor: Jerry Lench & Assoc.
Monthly newspaper. Circulation 30,000

CASE Reporter
5236 Claremont Ave., Oakland, Calif. 94618
(415) 547-2912
Owned by: Clerical & Allied Service Employees, AFSCME
  Local 909
Editor: Judy Baston
Monthly newspaper. Circulation 6,000

Local 390 News
522 Grand Ave., Oakland, Calif. 94610

(415) 465-0120
Owned by: United Public Employees, Local 390, SEIU
Editor: Paul Varacalli
Monthly newspaper. Circulation 5,000

1428 Message
1716 West Holt Ave., Pomona, Calif. 91766
(714) 623-1687
Owned by: Retail Clerks Union Local 1428
President: Ira Van Valkenburgh
Monthly newspaper. Circulation 5,300

Electranews
1775 Broadway, Redwood City, Calif. 94063
(415) 369-3369
Owned by: Local 1969 IBEW
Editor: John Knezevich; Man. Editor: Elsie M. Smith
Monthly newspaper. Circulation 3,500

Sacramento Valley Union Labor Bulletin
2525 Stockton Blvd., Sacramento, Calif. 95817
(916) 456-4728
Owned by: Sacramento Labor Council, Sacto-Yolo Building
  Trades Council and Sacto Allied Printing Trades Council
Editor: Thomas P. Kenny
Weekly newspaper. Circulation 18,646

San Diego Labor Leader, The
2232 El Cajon Blvd., San Diego, Calif. 92104
(714) 291-4870
Official publication of San Diego-Imperial Counties Labor
  Council
Editor: Jim Price
Semi-monthly newspaper.

Broadcaster
2090 Beach St., #208, San Francisco, Calif. 94123
(415) 982-2100
Owned by: BRAC Feather River Lodge #248
Editor: William P. Thompson
Monthly newspaper. Circulation 450

California AFL-CIO News
995 Market St., San Francisco, Calif. 94103
(415) 986-3585
Owned by: California Labor Federation
Editor: Glenn Martin
Weekly newsletter. Circulation 5,200

Engineers News
474 Valencia St., San Francisco, Calif. 94103
(415) 431-1568
Owned by: Operating Engineers Local 3
Editor: Dale Marr; Man. Editor: Kenneth Erwin
Monthly newspaper. Circulation 35,000

MSTU Seafarer
1321 Mission St., San Francisco, Calif. 94103
(415) 626-5676
Owned by: Military Sea Transport Union, SIU
Editor: Roy A. Mercer
Monthly newspaper. Circulation 2,000

Pipe Lines
1621 Market St., Room 102, San Francisco, Calif. 94103
(415) 626-2000
Owned by: Plumbers & Steamfitters, Local 38
Editor: Ernest Rae
Monthly newspaper. Circulation 3,000

Public Employee News
474 Valencia St., San Francisco, Calif. 94103
(415) 431-1568
Owned by: Operating Engineers Local 3
Editor: Dale Marr; Man. Editor: Kenneth Erwin
Monthly newspaper. Circulation 5,000

Northern California Labor
3068 16th St., San Francisco, Calif. 94103
(415) 863-7011
Published jointly by: San Francisco & Santa Clara Central Labor
  Councils
Editor: David F. Selvin
Monthly newspaper. Circulation 54,000

The Spotlight
P.O. Box 9006, Presidio of San Francisco, Calif. 94129
(415) 561-4871
Owned by: Local 1457, AFGE
Editor: Gordon Dudley
Monthly newsletter. Circulation 500

Toll Reporter
1485 Bayshore Blvd., San Francisco, Calif. 94124
(415) 467-3414
Owned by: IBEW Local 1011
Editor: Kenneth L. Leavitt
Monthly newspaper. Circulation 2,900

Vote Views
474 Valencia St., San Francisco, Calif. 94103
(415) 431-1568
Owned by: Operating Engineers Local 3
Editor: Dale Marr; Man. Ed.: John McMahon
Monthly newspaper. Circulation 5,000

Labor Union Gazette
2102 Almaden Road, San Jose, Calif. 95125
(408) 265-6280
Published by: Los Gatos Times-Saratoga Observer
Endorsed by: Bldg. Const. Trades Council of Santa Clara & San
  Benito Counties
Editor: Betty L. Dravis
Monthly newspaper. Circulation 8,000

The Retail Employee
240 S. Market St., San Jose, Calif. 95113
(408) 298-0500
Owned by: Retail Store Employees Union Local 428
Monthly newspaper. Circulation 9,000

The Score
2050 South Main St., Santa Ana, Calif. 92707
(714) 546-3647
Owned by: American Federation of Musicians Local 7
Editor: Ansell Hill; Man. Editor: Bob Karg
Monthly newspaper. Circulation 1,600

Retail Clerks Union, Local 1442 News
1410 Second St. Santa Monica, Calif. 90401
(213) 395-9977
Owned by: Retail Clerks Union, Local 1442
Editor: Michael S. Straeter
Bi-monthly newspaper. Circulation 5,700

The Eye Opener
9222 Pioneer Blvd., Santa Fe Springs, Calif. 90670
(213) 692-3031
Owned by: USWA Local 1502

Editor: Jose L. C. Arevalo; Man. Editor: Frank J. Diaz
Monthly newsletter. Circulation 400

IAM District 720 Report
19626 S. Normandie Ave., Torrance, Calif. 90502
(213) 396-3161
Owned by: IAM District Lodge 720
Editor: E. M. Smith; Secretary-Treasurer: Ted Neima
Monthly newspaper. Circulation 10,000

The Mail Call
14362 Oxnard St. Van Nuys, Calif. 91401
Owned by: N.A.L.C. Branch 2462
Editor: Lee Fenstermacher
Monthly newsletter. Circulation 475

Butcher's 532 Review
441 Nebraska St., Vallejo, Calif. 94590
(707) 552-7270
Owned by: Meatcutters Local 532
Editor: Preston T. Epperson
Monthly newsletter. Circulation 850

Utility Reporter
P.O. Box 4790, Walnut Creek, Calif. 94596
(415) 933-6060
Owned by: IBEW Local 1245
Exec. Editor: L. L. Mitchell; Editor: Kenneth O. Lohre
Monthly newspaper. Circulation 18,500

COLORADO

Colorado Labor Advocate
35 W. 4th Ave., Denver, Colo. 80223
(303) 744-1731
Endorsed by: Colorado Labor Council; Denver Labor Council
  & Colo. Springs Labor Council
Editor: William F. Payne
Monthly newspaper. Circulation 22,500

The Hot Line
2320 Mountview Dr., Pueblo, Colo. 81008
(303) 545-9015
Owned by: IAFF, Local 3
Editor: Kenneth W. Jones; Man. Editor: Robert F. McCabe
Monthly newsletter. Circulation 300

Steel News
P.O. Box 2006, Pueblo, Colo. 81004
(303) 544-3085
Owned by: USWA Local 2102
Editor: Ted T. Lopez
Monthly magazine. Circulation 2,500

CONNECTICUT

The Union Speaks
2889 Fairfield Ave., Bridgeport, Conn. 06605
(203) 334-7929
Owned by: USWA Local 7528
Editor: John Del Vecchio
Monthly newsletter.

BFT Union Teacher
90 Jewel St., Bristol, Conn. 06010
(203) 583-3472
Owned by: Bristol, Federation of Teachers AFT 1464
Editor: Barbara Y. Doyle
Weekly newsletter.

IAM Shop Talk
357 Main St., East Hartford, Conn. 06118

(203) 568-3000
Owned by: IAM Lodge 91
Editor: Lou Kiefer
Monthly newspaper. Circulation 18,000

The Union Teacher
639 Oakwood Ave., West Hartford, Conn. 06110
(203) 278-5093
Owned by: Connecticut State Federation of Teachers
Editor: Irving Leskowitz
8–10 issues yearly, newspaper. Circulation 7,500

DISTRICT OF COLUMBIA

Local 25's Two-bit's Worth
1003 K St., N.W., Washington, D.C. 20001
(202) 737-2225
Owned by: HREBIU Local 25
Editor: Ron Richardson; Man. Editor: Hank Beardsley
Monthly newspaper. Circulation 8,500

Local 82 Union Talk
6135 Kansas Ave., N.E., Washington, D.C. 20011
(202) 882-2666
Owned by: SEIU, Local 82
Editor & Pres.: Arlene M. Neal; Man. Editor: Henry Beardsley
Monthly newsletter. Circulation 5,200

The Guardian
633 Indiana Ave., N.W., Room 786, Washington, D.C. 20531
(202) 376-3897
Owned by: AFSCME Local 2830
Editor: Marilyn Marbrook; Man. Editor: Laurie Maxwell
Monthly newsletter. Circulation 625

The Prompter
Chevy Chase Center Bldg., Ste. 210, 35 Wisconsin Circle, Washington, D.C. 20015
(202) 657-2560
Owned by: AFTRA, Washington-Baltimore Local
Editor: Donald B. Gaynor
Quarterly newsletter. Circulation 2,000

Trades Unionist
1126 16th St., N.W., Washington, D.C. 20036
(202) 296-0057
Owned by: Greater Washington Central Labor Council
Editor: Steve Estroff; Ad Man.: Ann K. Helmick
Weekly newspaper. Circulation 14,500

FLORIDA

Steelworkers Speak
506 Hedge Row Road, Brandon, Fla. 33511
(813) 689-3700
Owned by: USWA Local 4939
Editor: Ethel W. Trice
Monthly newspaper. Circulation 500

Venice of America Newsletter
200 N.W. 22nd Ave., Ft. Lauderdale, Fla. 33311
(305) 581-7023
Owned by: National Assn. of Letter Carriers, Branch 2550
Editor: Mrs. B. B. Aultz
Monthly newspaper. Circulation 1,100

Relay 53
P.O. Box 7001, Jacksonville, Fla. 32210
(305) 771-3130
Owned by: National Assn. of Letter Carriers, Branch 53
Monthly newsletter. Circulation 760

South Florida AFL-CIO News
Everglades Hotel, Rm. 302, 244 Biscayne Blvd. Miami, Fla. 33132
(305) 358-5315
Owned by: South Florida AFL-CIO
Editor: Hank Greenberg
Monthly newspaper. Circulation 10,000

UTD Today
1809 Brickell Ave., Miami, Fla. 33129
(305) 854-0220
Owned by: United Teachers of Dade County
Editor: Pat L. Tornillo, Jr.
Monthly newspaper. Circulation 55,000

AFSCME, Local 1363 News
2171 N.W. 22 Court, Miami, Fla. 33142
(305) 634-2727
Owned by: L. 1363 AFSCME
Editor: Lee Tafel
Monthly newspaper. Circulation 6,000

Palm Beach County Labor News
929 Belvedere Rd., West Palm Beach, Fla. 33405
(305) 833-8571
Owned by: Palm Beach County Federation of Labor
Editor: Jacob Aronson; Pres.: Lee Fornari
Monthly newspaper.

The United Teacher
208 West Pensacola St., Tallahassee, Fla. 32304
(904) 224-1161
Owned by: United Florida Education Association
Editor: Peter Boespflug
Monthly newspaper. Circulation 35,000

GEORGIA

The Journal of Labor
Electric Plaza Bldg., 501 Pulliam St., S.W., Atlanta, Ga. 30312
(404) 524-7903
Owned by: Georgia State AFL-CIO
Editor: Therese A. Koupas
Weekly newspaper. Circulation 13,400

GUAM

Union
P.O. Box 2301, Agana, Guam 96910
Owned by: Guam Federation of Teachers
Editor: Robert W. Cole
Monthly newspaper. Circulation 2,000

HAWAII

Hawaii AFL-CIO News, Inc.
547 Halekauwila St., Rm. 216, Honolulu, Hawaii 96813
(808) 536-4945
Owned by: Hawaii State Federation of Labor, AFL-CIO
Editor: A. Van Horn Diamond
Monthly newspaper. Circulation 51,000

HFT Reporter
547 Halekauwila St., Rm. 217, Honolulu, Hawaii 96813
(808) 523-1634

Owned by: Hawaii Federation of Teachers L. 1127
Editor: Jessica Kirk
Monthly newsletter. Circulation 2,000

The Hawaii Carpenter
311 Houghtailing St., Honolulu, Hawaii 96817
(808) 847-5761
Owned by: Carpenters Local 745
Editor: Jean C. Cote'
Monthly newsletter. Circulation 7,000

IDAHO

Idaho Labor Report
225 N. 16th, Boise, Idaho 83706
(208) 345-8582
Owned by: Idaho State AFL-CIO
Editor: Robert Macfarlane
Monthly newsletter. Circulation 2,400

ILLINOIS

Belleville Labor News
606 Bornman St., Belleville, Ill. 62221
(618) 233-6501
Endorsed by: Belleville Trades & Labor Assembly
Editor: Harold A. Wright
Monthly newspaper. Circulation 4,000

Aluminum Workers' News
5722 W. 63rd St., Chicago, Ill. 60638
(312) 587-3098
Owned by: USWA Local 3911
Editor: James Dixon; Asst. Editor: Robert Pryor
Monthly newspaper. Circulation 2,000

CCTU in Action
19 S. LaSalle St., Chicago, Ill. 60603
(312) 332-3007
Owned by: Cook County College Teachers Union in Action
Editor: Norman G. Swanson
Monthly newsletter. Circulation 1,800

Chicago Teacher
201 N. Wells St., Chicago, Ill. 60606
(312) 346-1828
Owned by: Chicago Teachers Union, Local 1, AFT
Editor: Lester Davis
Monthly newspaper. Circulation 29,000

College Union Voice
19 South LaSalle St., Chicago, Ill. 60603
(312) 322-3007
Owned by: Cook County College Teachers Union, Local 1600, AFT
Editor: Leon Novar; Asst. Editor: Joanne Kitch
Monthly newspaper. Circulation 2,500

Craftsman
204 S. Ashland Blvd., Chicago, Ill. 60607
(312) 226-4424
Owned by: Graphic Arts International Union Local 245
Editor: George K. Gundersen; Man. Editor: Harry E. Conlon
Bi-monthly newspaper. Circulation 8,000

Federation News
300 N. State St., Chicago, Ill. 60610
(312) 222-1000
Owned by: Chicago Federation of Labor & Industrial Union Council
Editor: Robert L. Kite
Monthly newspaper. Circulation 54,000

Illinois Teacher
201 N. Wells St., Chicago, Ill. 60606
(312) 346-1828
Owned by: Chicago Teachers Union
Editor: Mary Dunea
Bi-monthly magazine. Circulation 31,000

Inside Track
844 N. Rush St., 1st Floor, Chicago, Ill. 60611
(312) 944-5500
Owned by: AFGE Local 375
Editor: Jolanta M. Jarosz
Monthly newspaper. Circulation 2,500

Local 165 Communicator
201 N. Wells St., Room 1730, Chicago, Ill. 60606
(312) 236-5511
Owned by: IBEW Local 165
Editor: Lawrence F. Biehl
Monthly newspaper. Circulation 4,200

Local 73 Journal
1640 North Wells, Chicago, Ill. 60614
(312) 787-5868
Owned by: SEIU Local 73
Editor: Irving Kurasch
Bi-monthly newspaper. Circulation 12,000

Midwest News
333 South Ashland Blvd., Chicago, Ill. 60607
(312) 421-4100
Owned by: Midwest Regional Jt. Bd., ACTWU
Editor: Libby Saries
Quarterly newspaper. Circulation 18,500

News & Views of Local 1478
5744 S. Western Ave., Chicago, Ill. 60636
(312) 476-0882
Owned by: USWA Local 1478
Editor: William Nelson
Monthly newspaper. Circulation 2,500

Local 25 Voice
509 Wabash Ave., Chicago, Ill. 60606
(312) 922-8873
Owned by: Local 25, SEIU
Editor: Linda Chalk
Monthly newspaper. Circulation 13,000

65 News
9350 S. Chicago Ave., Chicago, Ill. 60617
(312) 731-6500
Owned by: USWA Local 65
Editor: Ben Valadez; Asst. Ed.: Frank Paluch; Director of Public Relations: Otis Harlan
Monthly newspaper. Circulation 10,000

1033 News & Views
11731 Ave. O, Chicago, Ill. 60617
(312) 646-0800
Owned by: USWA Local 1033
Editor: Adam Kwiatkowski
Monthly newspaper. Circulation 6,000

The Chicago Police Officer
127 N. Dearborn St., Suite 1544, Chicago, Ill. 60602
(312) 346-3453

Owned by: United Paperworkers Local 1975
Editor: James O'Neill
Monthly newsletter. Circulation 10,000

Weekly News Letter
300 N. State St., Chicago, Ill. 60610
(312) 222-1414
Owned by: Illinois State AFL-CIO
Editors: Stanley L. Johnson, Robert G. Gibson
Weekly newspaper. Circulation 7,000

Local 150 Engineer
6140 Joliet Rd., Countryside, Ill. 60525
(312) 482-9610
Owned by: IUOE Local 150
Man. Editor: Ray Johnson
Monthly newspaper. Circulation 13,000

The Banner
100 Old Higgins Road, Des Plaines, Ill. 60018
(312) 686-0440
Owned by: Council 12, Air Line Pilots Assn.
Editor: David H. Friend
Monthly newspaper. Circulation 2,100

The Galesburg Labor News
193 North Cherry St., Galesburgh, Ill. 61401
(309) 342-4219
Endorsed by: Local Unions
Editor: Fred W. Emery
Weekly newspaper. Circulation 6,070

The Local 148 Guage
148 Wilma Drive, P.O. Box 396, Maryville, Ill. 62062
(314) 421-1252
Owned by: Operating Engineers Local 148
Editor: Charles C. Oliver
Quarterly newsletter. Circulation 2,900

McLean County Union News
400 N.E. Jefferson, Peoria, Ill. 61603
(309) 674-3148
Owned by: Unions of McLean
Published by: Peoria Labor News
Editor: John Penn, Marketing Dir.: Jerry Pelka
Bi-monthly newspaper. Circulation 6,000

Peoria Labor News
400 NE. Jefferson, Peoria, Ill. 61603
(309) 674-3148
Owned by: Peoria Labor Temple Assn. (45 local unions)
Marketing Director: Jerry Pelka
Weekly newspaper. Circulation 16,000

The Labor News
331 Hampshire St., Quincy, Ill. 62301
(217) 223-0803
Endorsed by: Quincy Trades & Labor Assembly
Editor: W. R. Spratt
Weekly newspaper. Circulation 5,593

Tri-City Labor Review
311 21st St., Rock Island, Ill. 61201
(309) 786-6439
Endorsed by: Quad-City Federation of Labor
Editor: Ernest Paustian
Monthly newspaper. Circulation 6,000

INDIANA

Local 1010 Steelworker
3211 Grand Blvd. Highland, Ind. 46322
Owned by: USWA Local 1010

Editor: Martin Connelly; Pres.: Henry J. Lopez
Monthly newspaper. Circulation 18,000

The Record
1803 Broadway East Chicago, Ind. 46312
(219) 398-3150
Owned by: USWA Local 1011
Editor: Mike Schnake
Monthly newspaper. Circulation 10,000

The Banner
100 East Fifth Ave., Room 107, Gary Ind. 46402
(219) 886-1569
Owned by: USWA Local 1066
Editor: Jerome W. Watson; Asst. Editor: John Neagu
Quarterly newspaper. Circulation 5,000

Local 2483 Monthly News
3520 Burr St., Gary, Ind. 46408
(219) 838-1708
Owned by: USWA Local 2483
Editor: Raymond Wyckoff
Monthly bulletin. Circulation 250

Amplifier
3518 East Michigan, Indianapolis, Ind. 46201
(317) 356-7284
Owned by: IBEW Local 1048
Editor: Aubrey Armour; Man. Editor: Harold E. Purcell
Monthly newspaper. Circulation 6,000

Local 1150 News
218 S. Addison St., Indianapolis, Ind. 46222
(317) 639-1479
Owned by: USWA Local 1150
Editor: Charles Mulligan
Quarterly newsletter. Circulation 3,000

News and Views
1000 N. Madison Ave., Greenwood, Ind. 46142
(317) 881-6773
Owned by: Indiana State AFL-CIO
Editor: Willis Zagrovich
Semi-monthly newsletter. Circulation 8,000

Telephone Line
6501 Massachusetts Ave., Indianapolis, Ind. 46226
(317) 546-4884
Owned by: IBEW Local 1504
Editor: Paul R. Jarboe
Monthly newspaper. Circulation 9,000

Coffee Break News
2111 W. Lincoln Highway, Merrillville, Ind. 46410
769-5373
Owned by: USWA Local 12775
Editor: Art White
Monthly newspaper. Circulation 3,500

Labor Beacon
205 E. Garfield St., Michigan City, Ind.
(219) 872-1545
Endorsed by: LaPorte County Labor Council
Publisher: Michael Joseph; Editor: Marcelle Joseph
Weekly newspaper. Circulation 13,000

fac sheet
Department of Journalism, Ball State Univ., Muncie, Ind.
47306
(317) 285-6848

Owned by: AFT Local 3153
Editor: Dr. Mark Popovich
Monthly newspaper. Circulation 1,200

IOWA

AMC & BW News
116 14th Ave., S.E., Cedar Rapids, Iowa 52401
(319) 365-2053
Owned by: AMC & BW Local P-3
Editor: George T. Tresnak
Monthly newspaper. Circulation 2,200

Cereal Workers World
P.O. Box 4233, Cedar Rapids, Iowa 52407
(319) 363-4525
Owned by: RWDSU Local 110
Editor: Robert Ryan
Monthly newsletter.

Harmony Highlights
3224 1st Ave., N.E., Cedar Rapids, Iowa 52402
(319) 364-2459
Owned by: Machinists Lodge 831
Editor: Clarence F. Dunn
Monthly newspaper. Circulation 2,700

Farmer-Labor Press
1316 6th Ave., Council Bluffs, Iowa 51501
(712) 328-3663
Endorsed by: Southwest Iowa Labor Council
Editor: Stanley Bruner
Weekly newspaper. Circulation 1,100

Iowa AFL-CIO News
2000 Walker St., Des Moines, Iowa 50317
(515) 262-9571
Owned by: Iowa Federation of Labor
Editor: Joe Poduska
Monthly newspaper. Circulation 70,000

Dubuque Leader
1154 Iowa St., Dubuque, Iowa 52001
(319) 582-7859
Endorsed by: Dubuque Federation of Labor
Editor: William J. Ryder
Weekly newspaper. Circulation 5,300

Talking Union
1346 West Airline Highway, Waterloo, Iowa 50701
(319) 234-4891
Owned by: IAM District 134
Editor: Laurie Graham
Monthly newspaper. Circulation 2,200

KENTUCKY

The Voice of 1865
734 Carter Ave., Ashland, Kentucky 44101
(606) 325-1950, 325-4415
Owned by: USWA Local 1865
Editor: Charles Green; Asst. Editor: Marvin Scaff
Monthly newsletter. Circulation 4,500

Kentucky Labor News
706 E. Broadway, Louisville, Kentucky 40202
(502) 584-8182

Owned by: Kentucky State AFL-CIO
Editor: Glenda A. Middlebrooks
Weekly newspaper. Circulation 10,000

Stand by
P.O. Box 13085, Louisville, Kentucky 40213
(502) 368-2568
Owned by: IBEW Local 369
Editor: Dan Burke
Monthly newspaper. Circulation 2,300

The Way the Wind Blows
824 S. Second St., Louisville, Kentucky 40203
(502) 587-1557
Owned by: IAM Lodge 681
Editor: Ava Rose Barton
Monthly newspaper. Circulation 3,300

LOUISIANA

Delgado Federationist
P.O. Box 1130, New Orleans, La. 70119
(504) 482-4677
Owned by: United Fed. of College Teachers AFT Local 1130
Editor: William M. Painter
Monthly newsletter. Circulation 500

MAINE

Maine State Labor News
72 Center St., Brewer Maine 04412
(207) 989-3630
Owned by: Maine AFL-CIO
Editor: Benjamin J. Dorsky; Man. Editor: Kenneth F. Morgan
Monthly newspaper. Circulation 18,600

MARYLAND

The Baltimore Fire Fighter
305 W. Monument St., Baltimore, Md. 21201
(301) 837-4043
Owned by: Baltimore Fire Fighters Local 734
Editor: Charney L. Harris, Sr., Man. Editor: Richard Hammen
Monthly newsletter. Circulation 2,800

The ILG'er
1 N. Howard St., Baltimore, Md. 21201
(301) 685-0884
Owned by: Upper South Dept., ILGWU
Editors: Betsy Raymond, Jay Levine
Newspaper. Circulation 13,000

Retail Reporter
305 W. Monument St., Baltimore, Md. 21201
(301) 837-8500
Owned by: Retail Clerks Local 692
Editor: Alvin Akman
Monthly newspaper. Circulation 15,500

Union Leader
7801 Old Branch Ave., Clinton, Md. 20735
(301) 868-7500
Published by: Retail Store Employees L. 400
Editor: Richard B. Lewis; Man. Editor: Thomas McNutt
Monthly newspaper. Circulation 16,000

Shipjack
Harry Lundeberg School, Piney Pt., Md. 20674
(301) 944-0010
Owned by: Harry Lundeberg School

Endorsed by: Seafarers International Union
Editor: Hazel Brown; Man. Editor: Kathleen Kneeland
Circulation 15,000

2108 News
10 Old Post Office Rd., Silver Spring, Md. 20910
(301) 585-4084
Owned by: CWA Local 2108
Editor: Gerard A. Belanger; Man. Editor: Victor O. Musick, Jr.
Monthly newsletter. Circulation 2,000

The Union Response
P.O. Box 9228, Suitland, Md. 20023
(301) 763-2454
Owned by: AFGE, Local 2782
Editor: Michael Adams
Monthly newspaper. Circulation 3,000

MASSACHUSETTS

Local 26 Reporter
58 Berkeley St., Boston, Mass. 02116
(617) 267-0441
Owned by: HREBIU
Editor: Rita A. Matthews
Quarterly bulletin. Circulation 2,000

Local 509 News
14 Beacon St., Room 803, Boston, Mass. 02108
(617) 227-3350
Owned by: SEIU Local 509
Editor: Kenneth P. Trevett
Monthly newspaper. Circulation 4,000

Massachusetts State Labor Council Newsletter
6 Beacon St., Boston, Mass. 02108
(617) 227-8260
Owned by: Massachusetts State Labor Council, AFL-CIO
Editor: Gerard Kable
Monthly newsletter. Circulation 8,000

Local 2 Union Newsletter
220 Forbes Road, Braintree, Mass. 02184
Owned by: Meat Cutters Local 2
Editor: Gerald J. O'Leary
Quarterly newsletter. Circulation 3,000

The Bulletin
907 Westminster Hill Road, Fitchburg, Mass. 01420
Owned by: USWA Local 7896
Editor: Richard G. DeLisle
Monthly newsletter. Circulation 550

Massachusetts Union Teacher
114 Western Ave., Lynn, Mass. 01904
(617) 599-6800
Owned by: Massachusetts Federation of Teachers
Editor: E. Alison Long
Monthly newspaper. Circulation 13,000

Federation News
880 Boston Road, Box 176, Pinehurst, Mass. 01866
(617) 667-5151
Owned by: Billerica Federation of Teachers
Editor: Edmund J. Silvestri
Quarterly newsletter. Circulation 750

MICHIGAN

Huron Valley News
245 Murray St., Ann Arbor, Mich.

Owned by: Michigan AFL-CIO News
Endorsed by: Huron Valley Central Labor Council
Editor: Fred J. Veigel; Asst. Editor: James Schaefer
Monthly newspaper. Circulation 2,706

Detroit Building Tradesman
10800 Puritan Ave., Detroit, Mich. 48238
(313) 345-8200
Owned by: Detroit Bldg. Trades Council
Editor: Don M. Constantineau
Weekly newspaper. Circulation 75,000

Detroit Labor News
2310 Cass At Montcalm, Detroit, Mich. 48201
(313) 963-5012
Owned by: Wayne County AFL-CIO Council
Editor: Thomas Turner
Weekly newspaper. Circulation 20,000

The Detroit Teacher
7451 Third, Detroit, Mich. 48202
(313) 875-3500
Owned by: Detroit Federation of Teachers
Editor: Lois Vagnozzi
Bi-monthly during school year. Circulation 20,500

Hard Hat
14333 Livernois Ave., Detroit, Mich. 48238
(313) 931-2200
Owned by: Riggers Local 575, Ironworkers
Editor: Paul C. Allen; Man. Editor: Hal DeLong
Monthly newspaper. Circulation 2,200

Hotel-Bar-Restaurant Review
100 Selden St., Detroit, Mich. 48201
(313) 833-3905
Owned by: Hotel, Motel, Restaurant Employees, Cooks & Bartenders Union, Local 24
Editor: Herbert Triplett; Assoc. Editor: Francis R. Dixon
Monthly newspaper. Circulation 15,000

Local 876
2550 West Grand Blvd., Detroit, Mich. 48208
(313) 896-2600
Owned by: Retail Store Employees Union, Retail Clerks
Editor: Horace Brown
Monthly newspaper. Circulation 18,000

Michigan AFL-CIO News
2310 Cass Ave., Detroit, Mich. 48201
(313) 963-1783
Owned by: Michigan State AFL-CIO
Editor: Aldo Vagnozzi; Man. Editor: Joan Kelley
Weekly newspaper. Circulation 60,000

The Scoop
13020 Puritan, Detroit, Mich. 48227
(313) 869-3333
Owned by: Operating Engineers Local 547
Editor: Herbert J. Corcoran; Man. Editor: Robert Ross
Monthly newsletter. Circulation 1,500

Service Employees News
2604 Fourth St., Detroit, Mich. 48201
(313) 965-4950
Owned by: SEIU Local 79
Editor: Richard W. Cordtz
Monthly newspaper. Circulation 9,400

Michigan Council 12
1034 N. Washington, Lansing, Mich. 48906
(517) 487-5081
Owned by: AFSCME Council 12
Monthly newspaper. Circulation 25,000

Lansing Labor News
342 S. Clare St., Lansing, Mich. 48917
(517) 484-7408
Endorsed by: Greater Lansing Labor Council
Editor: Dick Holmes
Semi-monthly newspaper. Circulation 26,000

Western Michigan AFL-CIO News
490 W. Western Ave., Muskegon, Mich. 49444
(616) 722-7361
Endorsed by: Muskegon Labor Council
Editor: Claudia Dyga
Weekly newspaper. Circulation 12,000

MINNESOTA

Local News, USWA 4757
52 Balsam Circle, Babbitt, Minn. 55706
(218) 826-5555
Owned by: USWA 4757
Monthly newsletter. Circulation 1,600

Labor World
2002 London Rd., Room 300, Duluth, Minn. 55812
(218) 727-2931
Owned by: Duluth AFL-CIO Central Body
Editor: James A. Cran
Weekly newspaper. Circulation 11,000

Minneapolis Labor Review
312 Central Avt., Suite 318, Minneapolis, Minn. 55414
(612) 332-7446
Owned by: Minneapolis Central Labor Council
Editor: Richard Viets
Weekly newspaper. Circulation 40,000

Minnesota AFL-CIO News
175 Aurora Ave., St. Paul, Minn. 55103
(612) 227-7647
Owned by: Minnesota AFL-CIO
Editor: Ronald G. Cohen
Monthly newspaper. Circulation 3,000

Minnesota Public Employee
236 E. Plato Blvd., St. Paul, Minn. 55107
(612) 291-1020
Owned by: Minn. State Employees Union Council 6, AFSCME
Editor: Robert J. Currie
Monthly newspaper. Circulation 9,500

Union Advocate
440 W. Minnehaha Avt., St. Paul, Minn. 55103
(612) 488-6747
Owned by: St. Paul Trades & Labor Assembly
Editor: Gordon Spielman
Weekly newspaper. Circulation 58,000

Voice of Local 1938
307 First St., North, Virginia, Minn. 55792
(218) 741-0887
Owned by: USWA Local 1938
Editor: Donald Wavernack
Monthly newsletter. Circulation 3,230

MISSOURI

Aero Facts
212 Utz Lane, Hazelwood, Mo. 63042
(314) 731-0603
Owned by: IAM District 837
Editor: Allen R. Williams
Semi-monthly newspaper. Circulation 12,000

Kansas City Labor Beacon
1015 Central, Kansas City, Mo. 64105
(816) 221-5660
Endorsed by: Central Labor Councils of Kansas City, Mo. and
   Kans. Building & Construction Trades Council of Greater
   Kansas City
Editor: David Peery; Publisher: Meyer L. Goldman
Weekly newspaper. Circulation 46,000

Over the Counter
4010 Washington, 4th Floor, Kansas City, Mo. 64111
(816) 561-8472
Owned by: Retail Store Employees Union L. 782
Editor: Craig Williams
Monthly newspaper. Circulation 6,000

Viewpoint
5539 Oak, Kansas City, Mo. 64113
(816) 471-0589
Owned by: CWA Local 6450
Editor: John Tull
Monthly newspaper. Circulation 1,009

District 6 Newsline
2334 Olive St., St. Louis, Mo. 63103
(314) 421-2211
Owned by: CWA Dist. 6
Editor: Stanley Hubbard
Monthly newspaper. Circulation 7,500

Hospital Employee
706 Chestnut, Room 210, St. Louis, Mo. 63101
(314) 231-0460
Published by: Service & Hospital Employees L. 50
Editor: Thomas E. Tecklenburg
Monthly newspaper. Circulation 5,000

St. Louis Labor Tribune
7777 Bonhomme Ave., Suite 1000, St. Louis, Mo. 63105
(314) 863-0660
Endorsed by: St. Louis Labor Council
Editor: Jim Templeton; Man. Ed.: Edward M. Finkelstein
Weekly newspaper. Circulation 97,000

South Illinois Labor Tribune
7777 Bonhomme, Suite 1000, St. Louis, Mo. 63105
(314) 863-0660
Endorsed by: Greater East St. Louis, Ill. Central Labor Council
Editor: Jim Templeton; Man. Editor: Edward M. Finkelstein
Weekly newspaper. Circulation 14,100

Ten/Twenty News
9191 West Florissant, St. Louis, Mo. 63136
(314) 524-1222
Owned by: CWA Locals 6310 & 6320
Editor: J. M. Templeton; Man. Editor: Ed Finkelstein
Monthly newsletter. Circulation 3,500

Union Labor Record
442 South Campbell St., Springfield, Mo. 65806
(417) 831-3301
Owned by: James L. Vandeventer; Endorsed by: Springfield
   Building Trades Council
Editor: James L. Vandeventer
Weekly newspaper. Circulation 9,000

MONTANA

TAT Report
2737 Airport Rd., Helena, Montana 59601
(406) 442-9597
Published by: Montana State AFL-CIO
Editor: James W. Murry
Semi-monthly newsletter. Circulation 1,100

NEBRASKA

District Record
1210 Douglas St., Omaha, Neb.
Owned by: AMC & BW, Local 271
Correspondence to: Virgil Talbot, Man. Ed.
Rt. 4, Siloam Springs, Arkansas 72761
Editor: Robert Parker
Bi-monthly newspaper. Circulation 2,000

The Short Circuit
13306 Stevens St., Omaha, Neb. 68137
(402) 895-4080
Owned by: IBEW Local 1974
Editor: Don Wieczorek
Monthly newspaper. Circulation 6,000

Nebraska State Ass'n. Newsletter
3326 S. 56 St. Omaha, Neb. 68106
(402) 554-1439
Owned by: Neb. State Ass'n./NALC
Editor: John T. Tillson
Monthly newspaper. Circulation 1,700

The Unionist
1309 N. W. Radial Hwy., Omaha, Neb. 68132
(402) 341-9573
Endorsed by: Nebraska State AFL-CIO
Editor: Larry L. Maupin
Monthly newspaper. Circulation 10,000

NEW JERSEY

1245 News
791 Passaic Ave., Clifton, N.J. 07012
(201) 471-2380
Owned by: Retail Clerks Local 1245
Editor: Frank De Vito; Man. Editor: Vincent Puglisi
Monthly newspaper. Circulation 5,000

1262 Banner
1389 Broad St., Clifton, N.J. 07013
(201) 777-3700
Owned by: Retail Clerks Local 1262
Editors: Sam Kinsora, John Lyons
Monthly newspaper. Circulation 22,000

Local 1470 Journal
2 Central Ave., Kearny, N.J. 07032
(201) 623-3605
Owned by: IBEW Local 1470
Editor: Frank W. Cerra
Monthly magazine. Circulation 12,500

1049 Showcase
744 Broad St., Newark, N.J. 07102
(201) 623-6291
Owned by: Retail Clerks Local 1049
Editor: Ira Berkeley
Monthly newspaper. Circulation 2,000

Local 21 Guide
21 Deerfield Ave., Piscataway, N.J. 08854

(201) 623-3188
Owned by: Retail Clerks Dept. Store Employees Local 21
Editor: George Meisler
Monthly newspaper. Circulation 4,500

NJSFT IN Action
152 S. Bridge St., Apt 6-B, Somerville, N.J. 08876
(201) 964-8950
Owned by: N. J. St. Fed. of Teachers
Editor: Jim Auerback
Monthly newsletter. Circulation 5–8,000

Beacon
690 Whitehead Road, Trenton, N.J. 08638
(609) 396-3707
Owned by: AFSCME Council 1
Editor: Al Wurf; Man. Editor: Michael Scott
Monthly newspaper. Circulation 12,000

NEW MEXICO

The RCIA 1564 Report
130 Alvarado Drive, Northeast, Albuquerque, N.M. 87108
(505) 255-8617
Owned by: Retail Clerks Union Local 1564
Editor: Louise G. Olguin
Quarterly newsletter.

NEW YORK

Union Catholic Teacher
24-36 26th St., Astoria, N.Y. 11102
(212) 932-2574
Owned by: AFT, Local 2092
Editor: Harold J. T. Isenberg
Monthly newsletter. Circulation 1,200

American Maritime Officer
650 4th Ave., Brooklyn, N.Y. 11232
(212) 788-0209
Owned by: MEBA Dist. 2
Editor: Roger Allaway
Monthly newspaper. Circulation 28,000

Brooklyn Longshoreman
343 Court St., Brooklyn, N.Y. 11231
(212) 858-7777
Owned by: ILA Local 1814
Editor: Jonathan Visel
Monthly newspaper. Circulation 17,500

Western N.Y. Federation of Labor News
1686 Ellicott Sq. Bldg., Buffalo, N.Y. 14203
(716) 853-2023
Owned by: Buffalo AFL-CIO Council
President: George Wessel
Semi-monthly newspaper. Circulation 25,000

Local 220 Reporter
91-31 Queens Blvd. Elmhurst, N.Y. 11373
(212) 672-9130
Owned by: L. 220 Cannery & Misc. Workers Union AMC &
   BW of N.A.
Editor: Mike Scott; President: Harold Wilkerson
Quarterly newspaper. Circulation 950

Electrical Union World
158-11 Jewel Ave. Flushing, N.Y. 11365
(212) 591-4000
Owned by: IBEW Local 3
Editor: George J. Schuck, Jr.; Assoc. Editor: Frank Vivert
Semi-monthly newspaper. Circulation 46,000

Greenburgh Action Bulletin
67 Chaucer St., Hartsdale, N.Y. 10530
(914) 761-5959
Owned by: Greenburgh Teachers Federation
Editor: Mildred Zimmerman
Monthly newsletter. Circulation 400

The Ten 49er
745 Kings Highway, Hauppauge, N.Y. 11787
(212) 234-1800
Owned by: IBEW Local 1049
Editor: George H. Fisher, Jr.; Man. Editor: Philip Fulco
Monthly newsletter. Circulation 3,500

Local 342 Forefront
186-18 Hillside Ave., Jamaica, N.Y. 11432
(212) 479-5000
Owned by: Amalgamated Meat Cutters, Local 342
Editor: Irving Stern
Semi-monthly newspaper. Circulation 13,500

Local 3 Bakery Workers News
41-07 Crescent St., Long Island City, N.Y. 11101
(212) 784-3476
Owned by: B & C Local 3
Editor: Michael Sandroff
Monthly newspaper. Circulation 6,000

Clarion
25 West 43rd St., Suite 620, New York, N.Y. 10036
(212) 354-1252
Owned by: Professional Staff Congress/City Univ. of N.Y. AFT
Editor: Aaron Alexander
Monthly newspaper. Circulation 10,000

Dining Room Employee
140 W. 43rd St., New York, N.Y. 10036
(212) 695-3456
Owned by: HREBIU Local 1
Editor: David Siegal
Monthly newspaper. Circulation 10,000

888 Leader
229 Park Ave. South, New York, N.Y. 10003
(212) 673-8888
Owned by: RCIA Local 888
Editor: Sidney Heller
Bi-monthly newspaper. Circulation 15,000

FLM Joint Board Tempo
109 W. 26th St., New York, N.Y. 10001
(212) 242-5450
Owned by: Jt. Bd. Fur, Leather & Machine Workers' Unions
Editor: Henry Foner; Man. Editor: Michael Scott
Bi-monthly newspaper. Circulation 6,500

1199 News
310 W. 43rd St., New York, N.Y. 10036
(212) 582-1890
Owned by: Natl. Union of Hospital & Nursing Home Emp. RWDSU
Exec. Editor: Moe Foner; Editor: Dan North
Monthly magazine. Circulation 70,000

Frontpage
133 W. 44th St., New York, N.Y. 10036
(212) 582-0530
Owned by: Newspaper Guild Local 3
Editor: Dona Fowler Kaminsky
Monthly newspaper. Circulation 9,000

Jewelry Workers Bulletin
133 W. 44th St., New York, N.Y. 10036
(212) 246-2335
Owned by: JWU Local 1
Editor: Joseph Tarantola
Monthly newspaper. Circulation 4,000

Labor Chronicle
386 Park Ave. South, New York, N.Y. 10016
(212) 685-9552
Owned by: N.Y. City Central Labor Council
Editor: Harry Avrutin; Man. Editor: Sally Genn
Monthly newspaper. Circulation 5,000

Local 50 News
799 Broadway, New York, N.Y. 10003
(212) 777-9350
Owned by: B & C Local 50
Editor: Martin T. Hullah
Monthly newspaper. Circulation 5,000

Local 1-S News
140 West 31st St., New York, N.Y. 10001
(212) 594-6190
Owned by: RWDSU Local 1-S
Editor: Charles E. Boyd
Monthly newspaper. Circulation 10,000

Local 30 Recorder
817 Broadway, New York, N.Y. 10003
(212) 777-3200
Owned by: Operating Engineers L. 30
Editor: Charles Flynn
Quarterly newspaper. Circulation 3,200

Local 144 News
233 W. 49th St., New York, N.Y. 10019
Owned by: Hotel Nursing Home & Allied Health Services Union L. 144 SEIU
Trustee: John Kelly
Bi-monthly newspaper. Circulation 12,000

Local 174 News
120 E. 16th St., New York, N.Y. 10003
(212) 533-8800
Owned by: Butcher Workmen Local 174
Editor: Michael Dolan
Bi-monthly newspaper. Circulation 18,000

Local 223 News
147 E. 26th St., 1st Floor, New York, N.Y. 10010
(212) 889-8180
Owned by: Doll, Toy & Plastic Novelty & Allied Workers L. 223
Editor: Harry O. Damino; Man. Editor: Andrew Arcuri
Bi-monthly newspaper. Circulation 10,000

Local 234 Bulletin
37 Union Square West, New York, N.Y. 10003
(212) 255-7440
Owned by: Hebrew Butcher Workers Local 234, Meat Cutters
Editor: William Bein
Quarterly magazine. Circulation 2,000

The Federation
30 E. 29th St., New York, N.Y. 10016
(212) 689-9320
Owned by: New York State AFL-CIO

Editor: Joseph P. Murphy
Monthly newspaper. Circulation 4,000

The New York Teacher
260 Park Ave. South, New York, N.Y. 10010
(212) 777-7500 or 533-6300
Owned by: The New York Congress of Teachers AFT/NEA
Editor: Matthew F. Doherty; Editor-in-chief: Ted Bleecker
Weekly newspaper in two editions: New York State & New
    York City
Circulation 200,000

On the Truck
27 Union Square West, New York, N.Y. 10003
(212) 255-3400
Owned by: Meat Cutters, Provision Salesman & Distributors
    L. 627
Editor: Morris N. Horn
Monthly newspaper. Circulation 2,500

The Overseas Teacher
Overseas Federation of Teachers, Vicenza America High School
    APO, New York, N.Y. 09221
Owned by: Overseas Federation of Teachers, AFL-CIO
Editor: Sy Hakim
Newspaper—6 issues per school year. Circulation 6,500

Project Rehab Newsletter
386 Park Ave. South, New York, N.Y. 10016
(212) 679-5250
Owned by: Community Services-Labor Rehabilitation Liaison
    Project N.Y. City Central Labor Council
Editor: Gerald R. Waters
Monthly newsletter. Circulation 3,000

Public Employee Press
140 Park Place, New York, N.Y. 10007
(212) 766-1000
Owned by: AFSCME Dist. Council 37
Editor: Bernard Stephens; Man. Editor: Walter Balcerak
Newspaper every three weeks. Circulation 117,000

Reel
551 Fifth Ave., New York, N.Y. 10017
(212) 687-4623
Owned by: Screen Actors Guild-N.Y. Branch
Publications Committee: John Connell, Chairman; Lee Zim-
    merman, Vice Chairman; Elizabeth Pennell, Editorial Con-
    sultant
Quarterly magazine. Circulation 9,500

The Record
386 Park Ave. South, New York, N.Y. 10016
(212) 532-7110
Owned by: Utility Workers Local 1-2
Editor: John J. McMahon
Monthly newspaper. Circulation 25,000

Stand By!
850 7th Ave., New York, N.Y. 10019
(212) 265-0610
Owned by: Am. Fed. of Television & Radio Artists, N.Y.
    Local
Editor: Dick Moore
Monthly magazine. Circulation 9,500

The 340 Leader
147 W. 42nd St., New York, N.Y. 10036
(212) 563-6175
Owned by: ACTWA Local 340
Editor: Hyman Nemser
Bi-monthly newspaper. Circulation 3,500

32B-32J
1 East 35th St., New York, N.Y. 10016
(212) 679-1288
Owned by: SEIU Local 32B
Editor: Richard Strunsky
Bi-monthly magazine. Circulation 43,000

Taxi Drivers Voice
386 Park Ave. South, New York, N.Y. 10016
(212) 679-2600
Owned by: N.Y. City Taxi Drivers Local 3036
Managing Editors: Ben Goldberg and Robert Pancaldo
Bi-weekly newspaper. Circulation 25,000

338 News
1790 Broadway at 58th, New York, N.Y. 10019
(212) 947-7364
Owned by: RWDSU Local 338
Editor: Mary C. Allen
Monthly magazine. Circulation 11,500

The Storeworker
101 West 31st St., New York, N.Y. 10001
(212) 239-6100
Owned by: The United Storeworkers Locals 2, 3 and 5
Editor: Doris Loewi
Monthly newspaper. Circulation 10,000

The Unionist
817 Broadway, New York, N.Y. 10003
(212) 677-3900
Owned by: Social Service Employees Union Local 371, AFSCME
Vice Pres. Publicity: Robert S. Pfefferman
Bi-weekly newspaper. Circulation 13,000

Typographical Union No. 6 Bulletin
817 Broadway, New York, N.Y. 10003
(212) 533-2000
Owned by: N. Y. Typographical Union No. 6
Editor: Bertram A. Powers; Man. Editor: Gunnar Janger
Monthly magazine. Circulation 11,350

*Union Label and Services Trades NEWS & UNION CON-
    SUMER*
119 E. 27th St., New York, N.Y. 10016
(212) 889-6070
Owned by: New York State Union Label and Service Trades
    Dept.
Editor: Harry Avrutin
Monthly newsletter. Circulation 6,000

Voice of 1707
50 W. 23rd St., 5th Floor, New York, N.Y. 10010
(212) 924-2662
Owned by: Community & Social Agency Employees L. 1707,
    AFSCME
Editor: Eric Strong
Monthly newspaper. Circulation 9,000

Local 1500
221-10 Jamaica Ave., Queens Village, N.Y. 11428
(212) 479-8700
Owned by: Local 1500 RCIA
Editor: Arthur Wolfson
Quarterly newspaper. Circulation 14,500

Local 301 News
121 Erie Blvd. Schenectady, N.Y. 12305
(518) 393-1386

Editor: John A. Martucci
Monthly newspaper. Circulation 13,000

Local 345 Courier
40 West Ave., Rochester, N.Y. 14611
(716) 328-1340
Owned by: Retail Clerks Union Local 345
Editor: Robert G. Smith
Quarterly newspaper. Circulation 2,700

News and Opinions
Smithtown Classroom Teachers Assn. 215 E. Main St. Smithtown, N.Y. 11787
(516) 265-4218
Owned by: Smithtown Classroom Teachers Assn.
Editor: Stephen Weitzman
Monthly newsletter. Circulation 1,000

Rochester AFL-CIO Labor News
131 Powers Bldg., Rochester, N.Y. 14614
(716) 232-3478
Endorsed by: Rochester AFL-CIO Council
Editor: Alex Gaby
Weekly newspaper. Circulation 18,500

Voice of Local 1
106 Memorial Parkway, Utica, N.Y. 13501
(315) 733-4696
Owned by: District Union Local 1, Meat Cutters
Editor: Samuel J. Talarico
Quarterly magazine. Circulation 7,700

Local 17 News
10th Ave. & 25th St., Watervliet, N.Y. 12181
(518) 273-8255
Owned by: L. 17 UPIU
Editor: Raymond A. Holobaski
Monthly newspaper. Circulation 2,000

Norta News
34 Van Houten Fields, W. Nyack, N.Y. 10994
(914) 358-7934
Owned by: North Rockland Teachers Assn.
Editor: Patricia Sweet
Bi-monthly newsletter. Circulation 1,700

In Contact
258 N. Main St., Spring Valley, N.Y. 10977
(914) 634-4941
Owned by: Clarkstown Teachers Assn.
Editor: Mike McNally
Bi-monthly newspaper. Circulation 700

The Yonkers Teacher
35 East Grassy Sprain Rd., Yonkers, N.Y.
(914) 793-0200
Owned by: Yonkers Federation of Teachers
Editor: Muriel Weintraub
Bi-monthly newsletter. Circulation 1,800

NORTH CAROLINA
NCFT Teacher
2310-B Ardmore Terrace, Winston-Salem, N.C.
Owned by: North Carolina Federation of Teachers
Editor: Barbara Brown
Semi-monthly newspaper. Circulation 15,000

OHIO
Labor Education News
116 Oakdale, Akron, Ohio 44302
Owned by: AFT Local 189
Editor: Joan Suarez
Newsletter. Circulation 1,000

Local 2 News
3 Goodyear Blvd., Akron, Ohio 44305
(216) 733-6204
Owned by: United Rubber Workers Local 2
Editor: John Nardella; Man. Editor: Don Wolfe
Monthly newspaper.

Retail Clerks 698 Star
106 N. Main St. Akron, Ohio 44308
(216) 376-4186
Owned by: Retail Clerks Union, Local 698
Editor: Doris L. Poe
Monthly newspaper. Circulation 7,400

Shop and Other Talk
125 Warhurst Road, Campbell, Ohio 44405
(216) 755-2189
Owned by: L. 1418 USWA
President: Mike Carney, Editor: Nadene Vrabel

Golden Lodge News
1234 Harrison Ave., S.W., Canton, Ohio 44706
(216) 454-6137
Owned by: USWA Local 1123
Editor: James F. Ragazino; Assoc. Ed.: Jack Fernandez
Monthly newspaper. Circulation 8,500

The Chronicler
1015 Vine St., Suite 706, Cincinnati, Ohio 45202
(216) 421-1846
Owned by: Cincinnati AFL-CIO Labor Council
Editor: Joe Minster; Man. Editor: W. P. Sheehan
Semi-monthly newsletter. Circulation 1,500

RCIA Local 1099 Memo
2562 North Bend Rd., Cincinnati, Ohio 45239
(513) 681-4000
Owned by: RCIA Local 1099
Editor: James M. Connolly
Monthly newspaper. Circulation 5,600

The Critique
602 Engineers Blvd., Cleveland, Ohio 44114
(216) 861-7676
Owned by: Cleveland Teachers Union
Editor: Janet Binder
Newspaper (6 issues per year.) Circulation 7,500

Compass
1221 Superior Bldg., Cleveland, Ohio 44114
(216) 241-7407
Owned by: Local 5000, USWA
Editor: William H. Greenlee
Monthly newspaper. Circulation 2,500

District Union 427 Voice
2605 Detroit Ave., Cleveland, Ohio 44113
(216) 781-8161
Owned by: District Union 427, Meat Cutters & Butcher Workmen
Editor: Frank Cimino; Man. Editor: Ray DeSantis
Monthly newspaper. Circulation 6,200

Local 880 News and Views
2828 Euclid Ave., Cleveland, Ohio 44115
(216) 241-5931
Owned by: Retail Clerks Local 880

Editor: David McDonald; Man. Editor: Charles R. Baker
Monthly newspaper. Circulation 3,000

Ohio-Kentucky News
3233 Euclid Ave., Cleveland, Ohio 44115
(216) 391-1765
Owned by: Ohio-Kentucky Region ILGWU
Editor: Barbara Janis
Quarterly newspaper. Circulation 5,000

Focus
271 E. State St., Columbus, Ohio 43215
(614) 224-8271
Owned by: Ohio AFL-CIO
Editor: Charles L. Borsari
Monthly magazine. Circulation 750,000

Federal Bulletin
3250 Euclid Ave., Room 250, Cleveland, Ohio 44115
(216) 781-5650
Owned by: Cleveland AFL-CIO Federation of Labor
Monthly newspaper. Circulation 2,300

News-Tribune
5 E. Long St., Suite 1005, Columbus, Ohio 43215
(614) 224-3442
Owned by: The Columbus-Franklin County AFL-CIO
Editor: C. D. Anstead
Bi-monthly newspaper. Circulation 23,407

News & Views
271 East State St., Columbus, Ohio 43215
(614) 224-8271
Owned by: Ohio AFL-CIO
Editor: Charles L. Borsari
Weekly newsletter. Circulation 16,000

Tele-Time
555 E. Rich St., Columbus, Ohio 43215
(614) 224-4993
Owned by: CWA Local 4320
Editor: John P. Haignere
Monthly newspaper. Circulation 1,700

Newscope
1860 Radio Road, Dayton, Ohio 45431
(513) 254-2608
Owned by: Retail Clerks Union, L. 1552
Editor: Kenneth V. Mitchell
Monthly newsletter. Circulation 4,000

Lorain Labor Leader
2501 Broadway, Lorain, Ohio 44052
(216) 244-1358
Owned by: USWA Local 1104
Editor: James W. Gedling; Man. Editor: Tony Zampieri
Weekly newspaper. Circulation 9,800

Nips and Chips
727 Lime City Road, Rossford, Ohio 43460
(419) 666-0437
Owned by: United Glass Workers, Local 9
Editor: Daniel C. Cole
Monthly newsletter.

Local 717 News
406 Bank St., Warren, Ohio 44483
(216) 393-0971
Owned by: IUE Local 717
Editor: George Bucan
Monthly newspaper. Circulation 12,500

Brier Hill Unionist
1343 Belmont Ave., Youngstown, Ohio 44504

(216)746-6309
Owned by: USWA Local 1462
Editor: Gerald Dickey
Monthly newspaper. Circulation 1,700

Ohio Works Organizer
1080 Salt Spring Rd., Youngstown, Ohio 44509
(216) 799-3281
Owned by: USWA Local 1330
Editor: Sam DoCompo
Bi-monthly newspaper. Circulation 3,800

OREGON

Local 701 News Report
1529 S. W. 12th Ave., Portland, Ore. 97201
(503) 226-3551
Owned by: Operating Engineers L. 701
Editor: Russ Joy
Monthly newsletter. Circulation 6,000

Oregon Labor Press
207 Portland Labor Center, 201 S.W. Arthur St., Portland, Ore.
  97201
(503) 222-1791
Owned by: 21 AFL-CIO Unions & Councils in Oregon
Editor: Gene Klare
Weekly newspaper. Circulation 64,000

Portland Restaurant, Bar Hotel News
306 Willamette Bldg. 534 S. W. 3rd, Portland, Oregon 97204
(503) 222-1763
Owned by: Local Jt. Bd. of Hotel & Restaurant Employees
  & Bartenders International Union
Editor: Dick A. Samuels
Monthly newspaper. Circulation 6,600

The Union Register LSW-UBA & J
812 S. W. Washington, Portland, Oregon 97205
(503) 228-0780
Owned by: Western Council of Lumber & Sawmill Workers
  (Carpenters); Southern Council, Lumber & Plywood Workers
Editor: Merle A. Reinikka
Weekly newspaper. Circulation 25,000

PENNSYLVANIA

The Local 1211 Steelworker
501 Franklin Ave., Aliquippa, Pa. 15001
(412) 375-6631
Owned by: USWA Local 1211
Editor: Felice DiPietrantonio; Asst. Editor: Dave Forse
Monthly newspaper. Circulation 13,000

AFT News
1643 W. Union St., Allentown, Pa. 18102
(215) 433-4691
Owned by: Allentown Federation of Teachers
Editor: Herbert L. Martin, Jr.
Monthly newsletter. Circulation 1,000

Lehigh Valley Labor Herald
809 North 4th St., Allentown, Pa. 18102
(215) 432-7511
Endorsed by: Union Councils of Lehigh, Northampton (Pa.)
  and Warren, N.J.

Editor: R. E. Uhler; Asst. Editor: M. L. Montgomery
Bi-monthly newspaper. Circulation 13,250

Needle News
1017 Hamilton St., Allentown, Pa. 18101
(215) 433-7445
Owned by: ILGWU L. 111
Editor: Al Baldwin; Man. Editor: Pete Nadash
Bi-monthly newspaper. Circulation 9,200

The Gomper's Gazette
P. O. Box A, Beaver, Pa. 15009
(412) 843-0571
Owned by: Beaver County Labor Council
Editor: Wally Lavery; Asst. Editor: James Macry
Monthly newsletter. Circulation 2,000

Union Lite Review
217 Sassafras Lane, Beaver, Pa. 15009
(412) 774-6958
Owned by: IBEW Local 201
Editor: Julia Frank
Monthly newspaper. Circulation 2,300

Inside Local 1082
828 7th Ave., Beaver Falls, Pa. 15010
(412) 846-2450
Owned by: USWA Local 1082
Editor: James Ciganik
Semi-monthly newspaper. Circulation 4,500

Newsletter Local Union 2600
53 E. Lehigh St., Bethlehem, Pa. 18018
(215) 867-3772
Owned by: Local Union 2600, USWA
Editor: John Sabo
Monthly newsletter. Circulation 3,000

1557 Labor Journal
332 State St., Clairton, Pa. 15025
(412) 233-5672
Owned by: USWA Local 1557
Editor: Nick Maffeo
Monthly magazine. Circulation 2,000

Fairless Union News
920 Trenton Rd., Fairless Hills, Pa. 19030
(215) 945-2930
Owned by: USWA Local 4889
Editor: Joseph Gaughan
Quarterly newspaper. Circulation 7,000

Pointer
5399 Peach Drive, Gibsonia, Pa. 15044
(412) 562-2641
Owned by: USWA Local 3657
Editor: Jerry Sokolow; Man. Editor: Donald T. Dalena
Bi-monthly newsletter. Circulation 475

AFSCME Public Employee Press
City Towers Bldg. 5th Floor, 301 Chestnut St., Harrisburg,
   Pa. 17101
(717) 233-3812
Owned & Published by: AFSCME Council 13
Monthly newspaper. Circulation 55,000

Central Pennsylvania Garment Worker
2926 N. 7th St., Harrisburg, Pa. 17110
(717) 236-7979

Owned by: Central Pa. District Garment Workers ILGWU
Editor: Robert Hostetter
Bi-monthly newspaper. Circulation 7,000

Pennsylvania AFL-CIO-COPE Newsletter
101 Pine St., Harrisburg, Pa. 17101
(717) 238-9351
Owned by: Pennsylvania AFL-CIO
Editor: Irwin Aronson

Pennsylvania AFL-CIO News
101 Pine St. Harrisburg, Pa. 17101
(717) 238-9351
Owned by: Pennsylvania AFL-CIO
Editor: Stan Williams
Monthly newspaper. Circulation 15,000

Pennsylvania Service Employee
2903A North 7th St., Harrisburg, Pa. 17110
(717) 234-4113
Owned by: Pennsylvania Jt. Council #45 SEIU
Quarterly newspaper. Circulation 30,000

Re:union
2903A North 7th St., Harrisburg, Pa. 17110
(717) 234-4113
Owned by: Pa. Social Services Union, SEIU, L. 668
Monthly newspaper. Circulation 6,000

Central Pennsylvania Labor News
P. O. Box 639, Harrisburg, Pa. 17108
(717) 233-4581
Endorsed by: Central Labor Council
Editor: R. Stearl Sponaugle; Man. Editor: Marcus M. Kob
Weekly newspaper. Circulation 11,500

The Informer
P.O. Box 503, Harrisburg, Pa.
Owned by: Local 2551, CWA
Editor: Vincent R. Miller, Jr.
Monthly newsletter. Circulation 200

Sewing Circle
626 Main St., Johnstown, Pa. 15901
(814) 536-3594
Owned by: Western Pa. Dist. Council ILGWU
Editor: Blaine E. Pynkala
Newspaper. Circulation 6,000

Clear Vision
20 Greenfield Rd., Lancaster, Pa. 17602
(717) 394-5201
Owned by: IBEW Local 1666
Monthly newspaper. Circulation 2,000

Spotlight
202 W. Liberty St., Lancaster, Pa. 17602
(717) 394-7544
Owned by: Rubber Workers Local 285
President: Benedict F. Cicero
Monthly newspaper. Circulation 2,500

West Branch Labor News
P.O. Box 101, Mill Hall, Pa. 17751
(717) 748-2586
Owned by: Clinton County Central Labor Union
Recording Secretary: Jeanne M. Neff
Newsletter. Circulation 2,500

Labor Lines
1945 Lincoln Highway, North Versailles, Pa. 15137
Owned by: USWA District 15
Editor: Joseph Odorcich
Monthly newsletter. Circulation 1,600

Current Lines
2827 West Ridge Pike, Norristown, Pa. 19401
(215) 539-0200
Owned by: IBEW Local 126
Editor: Howard Grabert
Monthly newsletter. Circulation 3,000

PET—Public Employee Tattler
R.D. 1, Oil City, Pa. 16301
Owned by: Polk State School
Published by: Local 1050, AFSCME
Editor: Terry Spatharas
Monthly newsletter. Circulation 1,000

Dialogue
210 E. Courtland St., Philadelphia, Pa. 19120
(215) 457-5200
Owned by: Retail Clerks Local 1357
Ex. Editor: Wendell Young
Monthly newspaper. Circulation 6,000

The Pandora
Benjamin Franklin Hotel, Ste 258,
Chestnut at 9th, Philadelphia, Pa. 19105
(215) 627-3464
Owned by: Firemen & Oilers Local 1201
Editor: William McDevitt
Monthly newsletter. Circulation 4,000

The PFT Reporter
1816 Chestnut St., Philadelphia, Pa. 19103
(215) 567-1300
Owned by: Phila. Federation of Teachers Local 3
Editor: Henry Maurer
Monthly newspaper. Circulation 16,000

The Quaker City Carrier
8040 Roosevelt Blvd., Room 202, Philadelphia, Pa. 19152
(215) 335-0580
Owned by: National Assn. of Letter Carriers, Branch 157
Editor: James M. Jackson
Monthly newspaper. Circulation 3,400

590 News
500 Center Bldg., 201 Penn Center Blvd, Pittsburgh, Pa. 15235
(412) 244-1820
Owned by: Amalgamated Food Employees Local 590, Meat Cutters
Editor: Clifton C. Caldwell; Man. Editor: Adolph Conte
Monthly newspaper. Circulation 12,000

The Sentinel
1007 Laclair St., Pittsburgh, Pa. 15218
(412) 462-2522–23
Owned by: USWA Local 1397
Editor: Andy Poklemba
Bi-monthly newspaper. Circulation 6,500

New Era
245 N. 5th St., Reading, Pa. 19603
(215) 373-0688
Endorsed by: Reading & Berks County United Labor Council;
   Pottsville, Hazleton & Delaware Counties Central Labor
   Unions
Editor: Robert R. Gerhart Jr.
Bi-weekly newspaper. Circulation 8,000

The Pennsylvania Teacher
431 Wyoming Ave., Scranton, Pa. 18503
(717) 343-3911
Owned by: Pennsylvania Federation of Teachers
Editor: James J. Loftus
Monthly newspaper. Circulation 30,000

2227 News
1301 Philip Murray Road, West Mifflin, Pa. 15122
(412) 469-0100
Owned by: USWA Local 2227
Editor: Paul Baran
Monthly newspaper. Circulation 4,500

The Voice of 1319
67 Public Square, IBEW Bldg. Room 1217, Wilkes-Barre, Pa. 18701
(717) 823-2078
Owned by: IBEW Local 1319
Editor: Anthony Harzinski
Monthly newsletter. Circulation 1,200

RHODE ISLAND

328 News Digest
278 Silver Spring St., Providence, R.I. 02904
(401) 861-0300
Owned by: Meat Cutters Local 328
Editor: Romeo Caldarone; Man. Editor: Prentice Witherspoon
Quarterly newspaper. Circulation 6,000

WTG News
28 Main St., Woonsocket, R.I. 02895
769-5320
Owned by: Woonsocket Teachers' Guild
Editor: Richard DiPardo; Pres.: Tom Flood
Monthly newsletter. Circulation 575

TENNESSEE

The Labor World
3616 Conner St., Chattanooga, Tenn. 37411
(615) 899-0134 or (615) 266-1725
Owned by: Chattanooga Area Labor Council
Editor: J. R. (Bob) Watkins
Monthly newspaper. Circulation 10,250

Memphis Union News
2881 Lamar, Suite 116, Memphis, Tenn. 38114
(901) 525-6481
Owned by: Memphis AFL-CIO Labor Council
Editor: James L. Burt
Monthly newspaper. Circulation 30,000

Trades & Labor News
631 N. First St., Nashville, Tenn. 37207
(615) 255-4002
Owned by: Central Labor Council of Nashville & Middle Tenn.
Chairman, Board of Control: Eddie Byran

TEXAS

Texas AFL-CIO News
P.O. Box 12727, Austin, Texas 78711
(512) 477-6195
Owned by: Texas State AFL-CIO
Editor: Harry Hubbard; Dir. of PR: A. Fred Cervelli
Monthly newspaper. Circulation 168,000

Dallas Craftsman
1710 S. Harwood, St., Dallas, Texas 75215
(214) 428-8385
Endorsed by: Dallas AFL-CIO

Editor: Mrs. Wallace C. Reilly
Weekly newspaper. Circulation 27,000

The Unioneer
1414 N. Washington, Dallas, Texas 75204
(214) 826-6215
Owned by: CWA Local 6215
Editor: E. B. McMenamy
Monthly newspaper. Circulation 4,900

Insight
12821 Industrial Road, Houston, Texas 77015
(713) 453-7181
Owned by: USWA Local 2708
Editor: Charles Pearson
Quarterly newsletter. Circulation 3,500

Professional Fire Fighter
1907 Freeman St., Houston, Texas 77009
(713) 223-9166
Owned by: IAFF Local 341
Editor: R. Wayne Dees
Monthly newspaper. Circulation 2,600

The Star Bulletin
4615 North Freeway, Ste. 300, Northline Plaza, Houston, Texas
    77022
(713) 694-5541
Owned by: Retail Clerks Local 455
Editor: Ray B. Wooster; Assoc. Editor: Alexander Hieken
Bi-monthly newsletter. Circulation 5,000

The Stretch
Route 11, Box 258, Tyler, Texas 75701
Owned by: Rubber Workers Local 746
Editor: Jim Duncan
Monthly newspaper. Circulation 1,500

UTAH

Labor's News and Views
1847 South Columbia Lane, Orem, Utah 84057
(801) 225-1010
Owned by: USWA Local 2701
Editor: Lynn J. Bellows, Asst. Editor: Paul Wilkey
Monthly newspaper. Circulation 4,200

VIRGINIA

Local 593's Allied Progress Report
5240 Port Royal Road, Springfield, Va. 22151
(703) 321-7711
Owned by: Meat Cutters Local 593
Editor: William Sellars; Man. Editor: Henry Beardsley
Monthly newsletter. Circulation 5,000

Typofax
P.O. Box 192, Norfolk, Va. 23510
Owned by: ITU Local 32
Editor: Tom Patten
Monthly newsletter. Circulation 5,000

WASHINGTON

Northwestern Washington Labor News
203 W. Holly St., Box 1174, Bellingham, Wash. 98225
Owned by: Watcom County Central Labor Council
Monthly newspaper. Circulation 7,000

Washington State Employee
201 W. 5th, Room 401, Olympia, Wash. 98501
(206) 352-7603
Owned by: Washington Federation of State Employees, AFL-
    CIO
Editor: Worth Hedrick
Monthly newspaper. Circulation 20,000

Inlandboatman of the Pacific
4210 S. W. Oregon St., Seattle, Wash 98116
(206) 937-5550
Owned by: Inlandboatmen's Union of the Pacific District
    Union, Seafarers Intl. Union
Editor: Merle D. Adlum
Monthly newspaper. Circulation 5,200

Northwestern States SEIU News
107 S. Main, Seattle, Wash. 98104
Owned by: Northwestern States SEIU Council #14
Monthly newspaper. Circulation 14,000

The Retail Outlook
2819 1st Ave., Seattle, Wash. 98121
(206) 624-3630
Owned by: Jt. Coun. of Retail Clerks Unions, Seattle and
    Vicinity
Editor: Bill McCarthy
Monthly newspaper. Circulation 18,000

The Scanner and King County Labor News
2800 1st Ave., No. 208, Seattle, Wash. 98121
(206) 682-7102
Owned by: AFL-CIO King County Labor Council
Editor: John Van Devanter
Monthly newspaper. Circulation 65,000

Washington State Labor Council Reports
2701 1st Ave., Seattle, Wash. 98121
(206) 682-6002
Owned by: Wash. State Labor Council
Editor: Joseph Davis
Semi-monthly newsletter. Circulation 1,700

Tacoma Labor Advocate
950 Fawcett Avt., Room 1, Tacoma, Washington 98402
(206) 572-7513
Endorsed by: Pierce County Center Labor Council
Editor: Paul Anderson
Bi-weekly newspaper. Circulation 21,978

WEST VIRGINIA

The Appalachian Voice
1018 Kanawha Blvd., East. Ste. 1200, Charleston, W.V. 25301
(304) 342-4138
Owned by: AFL-CIO Appalachian Council
Monthly newspaper. Circulation 3,000

The West Virginia AFL-CIO Observer
1018 Kanawha Blvd., East, Charleston, W.V. 25301
(304) 344-3557
Owned by: W. Va. Labor Federation, AFL-CIO
Editor: Lee Beard; President; Joseph W. Powell
Monthly newspaper. Circulation 69,000

WISCONSIN

The Kenosha Labor
1008 56 St., Kenosha, Wisc. 53140 ·
(414) 657-6116
Owned by: Kenosha Unions
Editor: Roger Wyosnick; Publisher: Joseph Schackelman
Weekly newspaper. Circulation 17,800

LaCrosse Union Herald
P. O. Box 626, LaCrosse, Wisc. 54602
(608) 784-4810
Owned by: Nine local unions
Editor: Louis Youngman
Monthly newspaper. Circulation 5,800

Local 1401 Newsletter
3010 E. Washington Ave., Madison, Wisc. 53704
(608) 241-1526
Owned by: RCIA Local 1401
Editor: William A. Moreth
Monthly newsletter. Circulation 2,300

Union Labor News
1406 Emil St., P. O. Box 9510, Madison Wisc. 53715
(608) 255-0778
Endorsed by: Madison Federation of Labor, Janesville Central
    Labor Union, Sauk Co. Federation of Labor
Editor: Marvin Brinkson
Monthly newspaper. Circulation 23,000

AFL-CIO Milwaukee Labor Press
633 S. Hawley Rd., Milwaukee, Wisc. 53214
(414) 771-7070
Owned by: Milwaukee County Labor Council
Editor: Ray W. Taylor. Bus. Man.: Bud Frederick
Weekly newspaper. Circulation 115,000

Keeping Score with Local 444
4850 W. Fond du Lac Ave., Milwaukee, Wisc. 53216
(414) 871-8150
Owned by: Retail Store Employees Union Local 444
Editor: Michael J. Burtak
Monthly newsletter. Circulation 7,000

Labor News Review
6333 W. Blue Mound Rd., Milwaukee, Wisc. 53213
(414) 771-0700

Owned by: Wisconsin State AFL-CIO
Editor: John W. Schmitt
Monthly newsletter. Circulation 4,000

Local 139 Wisconsin News
7283 W. Appleton Ave., Milwaukee, Wisc. 53216
(414) 461-8060
Owned by: Operating Engineers Local 139
Editor: Joseph J. Goetz
Quarterly newsletter. Circulation 4,200

19806 Chronicle
3651 N. 27th St., Milwaukee, Wisc. 53216
Owned by: Smith Steel Workers D.A.L.U. 19806
Editor: Robert Poplawski
Monthly newspaper.

Newsletter
Wittman Field, Oshkosh, Wisc. 54901
(414) 233-0499
Owned by: Retail Store Employees Union L. 214
Editor: Richard P. Eiden
Monthly newsletter.

The Racine Labor
1337 Washington Ave., Racine, Wisc. 53403
(414) 634-7186
Owned by: Local unions under name of Union Publishing Co.
Editor: Dick Olson
Weekly newspaper. Circulation 14,300

WYOMING

Wyoming State AFL-CIO News
1904 Thomes, Cheyenne, Wyoming 82001
(307) 635-5149
Owned by: Wyoming State AFL-CIO
Editor: L. Keith Henning
Monthly newspaper. Circulation 10,000

CANADIAN LABOUR PUBLICATIONS
(Listed alphabetically by City and Province)

Official Canadian Labour Congress Publication

Canadian Labour
2841 Riverside Drive, Ottawa, Ont.
(613) 521-3400
Director of Public Relations: Charles Bauer
Monthly magazine (French section). Circulation 12,000

The Provincial
4911 Canada Way, Burnaby, B.C. V5G 3W3
291-9611
Owned by: B.C. Government Employees Union
Editor: Bruce McLean
Monthly newspaper. Circulation 18,000

The Steel Gauntlet
19 Elizabeth Dr. Thompson, Man.
(204) 677-4511

Owned by: USWA Local 6166
Editor: Brooke Sundin, Asst. Ed: Dick Martin
Monthly newspaper. Circulation 5,000

Labour Review
15 Gervaise Dr., Suite 202, Don Mills, Ont.
429-2731
Owned by: Ontario Federation of Labour
Editor: Ed Cosgrove
Monthly newspaper. Circulation 5,000

ACTION
1308 Portage Ave., Winnipeg, Man. R3G 2E1
(204) 774-1984
Owned by: Retail Store Employees Union L. 832
Editor: Bernard Christophe
Monthly newspaper. Circulation 4,000

Argus-Journal
233 Gilmour St., Ottawa K2P OP1 Ont.
(613) 236-9931
Owned by: Public Service Alliance of Canada, CLC
Editor: Bonnie Mewdell
Monthly newspaper. Circulation 110,000

Civil Service Review
233 Gilmour, Ottawa K2P OP1 Ont.
(613) 236-9931
Owned by: Public Service Alliance of Canada, CLC
Editor: Bonnie Mewdell
Quarterly magazine. Circulation 16,000

Weekly Newsletter
233 Gilmour, Ottawa K2P OP1 Ont.
(613) 236-9931
Owned by: Public Service Alliance of Canada, CLC
Editor: Bonnie Newdell
Circulation 20,000

Canadian Railwayman
130 Albert St., Ste. 513, Ottawa K1P 5G4, Ont.
(613) 236-7231
Owned by: 18 International rail unions
Semi-monthly newspaper. Circulation 65,000

The Circlet
330 McLeod St., Ottawa 4, Ont.
(613) 232-3541

Owned by: Union of National Defense Employees CLC
Editor: Bruce Stirling; Man. Editor: A. K. Green
Weekly newspaper. Circulation 4,000

The Machinist Canadian Edition
80 Argyle Ave., Ste. 302, Ottawa K2P 1B5 Ont.
(613) 236-9761
Editor: Joseph Hanafin
Monthly newspaper. Circulation 52,000

The Searcher
92 Frood Road, Sunburg, Ont.
Owned by: USWA Local 6500
Editor: Guy Arseneault
Monthly newspaper. Circulation 22,000

Steel Labor Canadian Edition
55 Eglinton Ave., E. Toronto M4P 1B5, Ont.
487-1571
Owned by: United Steelworkers of America
Editor: Merl Day, Director of PR: Kenneth (Robbie) Robinson
Monthly newspaper. Circulation 175,000

Canadian Interchange/Echange Canadien
550 Sherbrooke St., W. Ste. 690, Montreal, Quebec
(514) 842-8676
Owned by: Brotherhood of Railway & Airline Clerks
Editor: Robert Douglas
Monthly magazine. Circulation 22,000

Canadian Paperworker Journal
1155 Sherbrooke St. W. Suite 1501, Montreal H3A 2N3, Quebec
(514) 842-8931
Owned by: The Canadian Paperworkers Union
Editor: Neville S. Hamilton
Monthly newspaper. Circulation 50,000

ASSOCIATE MEMBERS

Martin Bartos
Lorain Labor Leader, USWA L. 1104
2501 Broadway
Lorain, Ohio 44052

Burt Beck, Dir.
Public Relations
Amalgamated Clothing & Textile Workers Union
15 Union Square
New York, N.Y. 10003

John G. Blair, Dir.
Information Services
National Council of Senior Citizens
1511 K St., N.W.
Washington, D.C. 20005

Diane S. Curry
CLUW News
Coalition of Labor Union Women
6300 River Road
Rosemont, Ill. 60018

Max W. Fine, Exec. Dir.
Committee for National Health Insurance
5124 Wickett Terrace
Bethesda, Md. 20014

Ed Finkelstein, President
Union Communications, Corporation

7777 Bonhomme Ave., Ste. 1001
St. Louis, Missouri 53105

Les Finnegan
Press Associates Inc.
805 15th St., N.W., Suite 314
Washington, D.C. 20005

Janice Garrett
Retail Store Employees Union, Local 782
4010 Washington
Kansas City, Missouri 64111

William A. Gillen
Assistant Director
George Meany Center for Labor Studies
10000 New Hampshire Ave.
Silver Spring, Md. 20903

Irv Gitlin
Retail Store Employees Union Local 880
2828 Euclid Ave.
Cleveland, Ohio 44115

Rochelle D. Hart, Director
Public Relations and Publications
Chicago Teachers Union
201 North Wells St.
Chicago, Ill. 60606

Morden Lazarus, Managing Editor
Co-operative Press Associates
P.O. Box 174 Station R
Toronto M4G 3G2 Canada

Ron Lipker
USWA, Local 2116
3814 Gallia St.
New Boston, Ohio 45662

Lawrence G. Molloy
International Longshoremen's Assn.
17 Battery Place
New York, N.Y. 10004

Jeff McAlravey
IBEW Local Union 212
801 B West 8th St.
Cincinnati, Ohio 45203

Edwin Palenque
American Institute for Free Labor Development
1015 20th St., N.W.
Washington, D.C. 20036

Bernard Raskin
Direct Communications
424 Stratford Court
Del Mar, California 92014

Carl Schlesinger
New York Typographical Union Bulletin No. 6
39 Myrtle St.
Rutherford, N.J. 07070

Martin Tomasic
Lorain Labor Leader, USWA L. 1104
2501 Broadway
Lorain, Ohio 44052

Marion Wells, Research Director
American Physical Fitness Research Institute
824 Moraga Dr.
West Los Angeles, Calif. 90025

Philip G. Yunger
Media Coordinator
George Meany Center for Labor Studies
10000 New Hampshire Ave.
Silver Spring, Md. 20903

REGIONAL AND INDUSTRIAL ASSOCIATIONS

Amalgamated Press Association
Robert Sexton, President
Ray DeSantis, Secretary-Treasurer
2800 N. Sheridan Road
Chicago, Ill. 60657

Connecticut Labor Press Council
Saul Nesselroth, President
The University of Connecticut
Storrs, Conn. 06268
Joseph H. Soifer, Treasurer
630 Oakwood Ave, Ste. 317
West Harford, Conn. 06110

Michigan Labor Press
Joan Kelley, President
419 S. Washington
Lansing, Michigan 48933
Greg Wheeler, Secretary-Treasurer
812 Leith St.
Flint, Michigan 48458

Midwest Labor Press Association
James F. Ragazino, President
1234 Harrison Ave.
Canton, Ohio 44706
Allen Williams, Executive Secretary
212 Utz Lane
Hazelwood, Missouri 63042
George B. Thorp, Secretary-Treasurer
912 W. Stadium
Ann Arbor, Michigan 48103

Missouri State Labor Press Association
Meyer Goldman, President
1015 Central
Kansas City, Missouri 64105
(816) 221-5660

Edward M. Finkelstein, Secretary Treasurer
7777 Bonhomme Ave., Ste. 1000
St. Louis, Mo. 63105
(314) 863-0012

New Jersey Labor Press Council
Max Wolf, President
11 Hill St
Newark, N.J. 07102
Hugh Dunlop, Secretary Treasurer
Shephards Lane
Totowa Boro, N.J. 07512

Labor Press Council of Metropolitan New York
Matthew Doherty, President
Barry Rock, Secretary
Eric Strong, Treasurer
119 East 27th St.
New York, N.Y. 10016

Ohio Labor Press Association
George Bucan, President
Charles L. Borsari, Secretary Treasurer
271 E. State St.
Columbus, Ohio 43215

Pennsylvania Labor Press Association
Emrich Stellar, President
118 Keene St.—Afton Village
Center Valley, Pennsylvania 18034
Stan Williams, Secretary-Treasurer
101 Pine St.
Harrisburg, Pa. 17101

APWU Postal Press Association
Hank Greenberg, President
Box 560606
Miami, Florida 33156

United Steelworkers Press Association
Ted Lopez, President
William V. Scoggins, Secretary Treasurer
Five Gateway Center
Pittsburgh, Pa. 15222

Union Teacher Press Association
Ted Bleecker, President
260 Park Ave., S.
New York, N.Y. 10010
Joseph H. Soifer, Treasurer
630 Oakwood Ave., Ste. 317
W. Hartford, Conn. 06110

Western Labor Press Association
Kenneth O. Lohre, President
c/o Utility Reporter, IBEW, L. 1245
P.O. Box 4790
Walnut Creek, Calif. 94596
Sal Perrotta, Secretary Treasurer
2130 W. 9th St.
Los Angeles, Ca. 90006

OFFICE OF INFORMATION, PUBLICATIONS AND REPORTS
Room S1032
New Department of Labor Building
Third and Constitution Ave., N.W.
Washington, D.C. 20210

Director:
John W. Leslie   Office: 202/523-7316
   Home: 202/484-6342

Assistant Director:
Dorothy J. Dunkle   Office: 202/523-7343
   Home: 202/338-3563

Chief, Division of Media & Editorial Services:
Donald S. Smyth   Office: 202/523-7316
   Home: 301/933-8112

Chief, Division of Field Services:
Charles A. Caldwell   Office: 202/523-7334
   Home: 703/356-8284

Chief, Division of Graphic Services:
Donald L. Berry   Office: 202/961-3051
   Home: 301/997-9145

EMPLOYMENT AND TRAINING ADMINISTRATION (ETA)
Functions of the ETA include:

- U.S. Employment Service—Job Bank
- Comprehensive Employment and Training Act and manpower programs for public service employment, classroom and on-the-job training, older workers, migrant workers, Indians, offenders, etc.
- Research and Development
- Work Incentive (WIN) program
- Youth Programs
- Unemployment insurance
- Veterans Employment
- Apprenticeship
- Job Corps

Office of Information
Room 10406
Patrick Henry Building
6th & D Sts., N.W.
Washington, D.C. 20213

Larry R. Moen, Director   Office 202/376-6270   Home 703/938-6879

Jack Hashian, Media Contact   Office 202/376-6905   Home 703/938-2343

OCCUPATIONAL SAFETY AND HEALTH ADMINISTRATION (OSHA)
Functions of OSHA include:

- Industrial safety and health standards
- Inspections of workplaces for compliance with standards
- Education, training and information programs to promote safe and healthful work practices and encourage voluntary compliance

Office of Information
Room N3641
New Department of Labor Building
Third and Constitution Ave., N.W.
Washington, D.C. 20210

Joe Mancias, Jr., Director   Office 202/523-8148   Home 703/354-7695

James Foster, Media Contact   Office 202/523-8151   Home 703/941-6798

EMPLOYMENT STANDARDS ADMINISTRATION (ESA)
Functions of ESA include:

- Minimum wage and special rates for youths and sheltered workshop employees
- Overtime
- Equal pay
- Employer recordkeeping
- Farm labor contractor registration
- Worker's compensation for longshoremen and harbor workers, federal employees
- Black lung benefits for coal miners

■ Women's programs

■ Equal employment opportunity for minorities and women in federal contract work

■ Equal opportunity for the mentally and physically handicapped

■ Equal opportunity for Vietnam-era and disabled veterans

■ Age discrimination

■ Standards for employees working on government service, supply and manufacturing contracts (Walsh-Healey and McNamara-O'Hara)

■ Prevailing minimum wages on federally assisted construction projects (Davis-Bacon)

■ Wage garnishment provisions of the Consumer Credit Protection Act.

Office of Information
Room C4331
New Department of Labor Building
Third and Constitution Ave., N.W.
Washington, D.C. 20210

Robert A. Cuccia,	Office	202/523-8743
Director	Home	703/525-6943
Ledford Day,	Office	202/523-8743
Media Contact	Home	703/620-4367

BUREAU OF LABOR STATISTICS (BLS)
Functions of BLS include:

■ Consumer Price Index

■ Wholesale Price Index

■ Employment Situation

■ Wages and hours of work

■ Industrial relations

■ Work Stoppages

■ Family Budgets

■ Consumer expenditures

■ Labor turnover

■ Productivity

■ Economic growth

■ Occupational safety and health statistics

■ Occupational outlook

Office of Publications
Room 2029
General Accounting Office Building
441 G St., N.W.
Washington, D.C. 20212

Henry Lowenstern,	Office	202/523-1327
Associate Commissioner	Home	703/560-3899
Kathryn Hoyle,	Office	202/523-1913
Media Contact	Home	202/333-1384

WOMEN'S BUREAU
Functions of the Women's Bureau include:

■ Developing policies and programs promoting the welfare of women in the labor force

■ Encouraging better utilization of women in the work force

■ Providing information and assistance to state and community leaders and other nations regarding women and work

■ Promoting the elimination of sex discrimination in employment and training

Information Office
Room S3319
New Department of Labor Building
Third and Constitution Ave., N.W.
Washington, D.C. 20210

Eleanor Coakley,	Office	202/523-6652
Director	Home	202/484-6061

LABOR-MANAGEMENT SERVICES ADMINISTRATION (LMSA)
Functions of LMSA include:

■ Veterans' reemployment rights

■ Executive Order governing labor-management relations in federal government

■ Pension reform

■ Labor-management reporting and disclosure act

■ Labor-management relations services—providing technical assistance to employers and unions, keeping track of collective bargaining disputes, etc.

Office of Information
Room N5637
New Department of Labor Building
Third and Constitution Ave., N.W.
Washington, D.C. 20210

Thomas J. Cosgrove,	Office	202/523-7408
Director	Home	202/966-4813
Chip Walker,	Office	202/523-7408
Media Contact		

BUREAU OF INTERNATIONAL LABOR AFFAIRS (ILAB)

Functions of the ILAB include:

- Trade adjustment assistance

- Technical assistance to developing countries

- Assistance to U.S. foreign affairs agencies with their international labor activities

- Assistance in administration of the Foreign Service

- Represents interests of American workers in trade and tariff matters

Office of Information

Room S5214
New Department of Labor Building
Third and Constitution Ave., N.W.
Washington, D.C. 20210

Mac Shields,   Office   202/523-6259
Director   Home   703/671-0385

U.S. DEPARTMENT OF LABOR REGIONAL INFORMATION OFFICES

Paul Neal
Public Information Director, Region I
U.S. Department of Labor
JFK Federal Building, Room E-308
Boston, Mass. 02203
   Office   617/223-6767
   Home   617/233-0832

Edward I. Weintraub
Public Information Director, Region II
U.S. Department of Labor
1515 Broadway, Room 3570
New York, N.Y. 10036
   Office   212/971-5477
   Home   212/352-1086

Jack Hord
Public Information Director, Region III
U.S. Department of Labor
3535 Market St., Room 2460
Philadelphia, Pa. 19104
   Office   215/596-1139
   Home   609/784-9016

Frances Ridgway
Public Information Director, Region IV
U.S. Department of Labor
1371 Peachtree St., N.E., Room 317
Atlanta, Ga. 30309
   Office   404/881-4495
   Home   404/325-3117

John D. Mellott
Public Information Director, Region V
U.S. Department of Labor
230 South Dearborn St., Room 737
Chicago, Ill. 60606
   Office   312/353-6976
   Home   312/246-3509

Les Gaddie
Public Information Director, Region VI
U.S. Department of Labor
555 Griffin Sq. Bldg., Room 220
Dallas, Tx. 75202
   Office   214/749-2308
   Home   214/239-9868

Neal Johnson
Public Information Director, Region VII
U.S. Department of Labor
911 Walnut St., Room 2509
Kansas City, Mo. 64106
   Office   816/374-5481
   Home   816/363-0855

Ernest Sanchez
Public Information Director, Region VIII
U.S. Department of Labor
1961 Stout St., Room 4010
Denver, Co. 80202
   Office   303/837-4234
   Home   303/237-8986

Joe Kirkbride
Public Information Director, Region IX
U.S. Department of Labor
450 Golden Gate Ave., Room 10007
Fed. Building & U.S. Courthouse
San Francisco, Ca. 94102
   Office   415/556-3423
   Home   415/897-8903

Frank W. Terry
Public Information Officer, Region IX
U.S. Department of Labor
Federal Building, Room 3261
300 North Los Angeles St.
Los Angeles, Ca. 90012
   Office   213/688-4970
   Home   213/291-7631

Jack Strickland
Public Information Director, Region X
U.S. Department of Labor
Federal Office Building Room 8001
909 First Avenue
Seattle, Washington 98174
   Office   206/442-7620
   Home   206/842-6532

Current ILPA Publications

JOIN ILPA—A general introduction to the organization . . . its goals and how it operates to help develop a bigger, broader labor press. Single copy free.

ILPA PRESS RELATIONS GUIDE—A working manual, designed to help the local editor, his president and other union officials deal effectively with the mass communications media—the press radio and television. 50 cents.

ILPA LOCAL PUBLICATIONS GUIDE—A booklet developed to help the working editor launch a labor paper—or improve one that is already being published—including hints on preparing copy, kinds of stories to look for, explanation of the various printing processes available and discussion of ways a local can finance the local paper. 50 cents.

ILPA ADVERTISING GUIDE—How to get it, what to charge, what it will—and will not—do for the labor press. 35 cents.

SPEAKING OF LABOR UNIONS—A glossary of terms used in stories about labor, a listing of abbreviations by which unions are known, plus their full, formal names, and a summary of the major federal laws relating to organized labor. 50 cents.

POSTAGE DUE (and how to avoid it)—A booklet providing guidelines and hints for maintenance of clean and accurate mailing lists—the most vital link between your membership and your union. Points discussed: 1) computer maintained lists; 2) addressplate lists; 3) proper usage of Form 3579; 4) other aids for cost control. 1 to 10 copies, 50 cents; 11 to 50 copies, 40 cents; 50 to 99 copies, 35 cents; more than 100 copies, 30 cents.

COORDINATED BARGAINING . . . What? . . . Why? An examination of a vital development in labor-management relations. Free.

THE TEN COMMANDMENTS OF THE LABOR PRESS—An exhaustive interpretation of ILPA's Code of Ethics. Free.

TOWARD COMMON GOALS—The need for unity among trade unionists, blacks and the young, by Michael Barrington. Free.

VOTERS IN THE 70s—An analysis from the nation's premier student of voter motivation. By Richard M. Scammon. Free.

TELL IT LIKE/AS IT IS—A witty, sharply-pointed exposition on language as it is written—or ought to be, by Roy H. Copperud. 30 cents.

REACHING THEM—A searching examination of communications needs, especially bridging gaps to youth and minorities. 50 cents.

A QUESTION OF RELEVANCY—Fifth Liebling memorial lecture; in this Liebling lecture a press critic laments the unfruitful nature of press criticism, by Richard L. Hardwood. Free.

LABOR AND THE PRESS—Seventh Liebling memorial lecture; in this Liebling lecture AFL-CIO Secretary-Treasurer, Lane Kirkland said, "the labor press—from the smallest mimeographed newsletter to the slickest magazine—is the vital communications link that helps to hold the labor movement together". Free.

The Work Force

EMPLOYMENT STATUS OF THE NONINSTITUTIONAL POPULATION 16 YEARS AND OVER, 1947 TO DATE
(Numbers in thousands)

Year and month	Total noninstitutional population	Total labor force		Civilian labor force						Not in labor force
				Total	Employed			Unemployed		
		Number	Percent of population		Total	Agriculture	Nonagricultural industries	Number	Percent of labor force	
Annual averages										
TOTAL										
1947.........	103,418	60,941	58.9	59,350	57,038	7,890	49,148	2,311	3.9	42,477
1948.........	104,527	62,080	59.4	60,621	58,343	7,629	50,714	2,276	3.8	42,447
1949.........	105,611	62,903	59.6	61,286	57,651	7,658	49,993	3,637	5.9	42,708
1950.........	106,645	63,858	59.9	62,208	58,918	7,160	51,758	3,288	5.3	42,787
1951.........	107,721	65,117	60.4	62,017	59,961	6,726	53,235	2,055	3.3	42,604
1952 [1]......	108,823	65,730	60.4	62,138	60,250	6,500	53,749	1,883	3.0	43,093
1953 [1]......	110,601	66,560	60.2	63,015	61,179	6,260	54,919	1,834	2.9	44,041
1954.........	111,671	66,993	60.0	63,643	60,109	6,205	53,904	3,532	5.5	44,678
1955.........	112,732	68,072	60.4	65,023	62,170	6,450	55,722	2,852	4.4	44,660
1956.........	113,811	69,409	61.0	66,552	63,799	6,283	57,514	2,750	4.1	44,402
1957.........	115,065	69,729	60.6	66,929	64,071	5,947	58,123	2,859	4.3	45,336
1958.........	116,363	70,275	60.4	67,639	63,036	5,586	57,450	4,602	6.8	46,088
1959.........	117,881	70,921	60.2	68,369	64,630	5,565	59,065	3,740	5.5	46,960
1960 [1]......	119,759	72,142	60.2	69,628	65,778	5,458	60,318	3,852	5.5	47,617
1961.........	121,343	73,031	60.2	70,459	65,746	5,200	60,546	4,714	6.7	48,312
1962 [1]......	122,981	73,442	59.7	70,614	66,702	4,944	61,759	3,911	5.5	49,539
1963.........	125,154	74,571	59.6	71,833	67,762	4,687	63,076	4,070	5.7	50,583
1964.........	127,224	75,830	59.6	73,091	69,305	4,523	64,782	3,786	5.2	51,394
1965.........	129,236	77,178	59.7	74,455	71,088	4,361	66,726	3,366	4.5	52,058
1966.........	131,180	78,893	60.1	75,770	72,895	3,979	68,915	2,875	3.8	52,288
1967.........	133,319	80,793	60.6	77,347	74,372	3,844	70,527	2,975	3.8	52,527
1968.........	135,562	82,272	60.7	78,737	75,920	3,817	72,103	2,817	3.6	53,291
1969.........	137,841	84,240	61.1	80,734	77,902	3,606	74,296	2,832	3.5	53,602
1970.........	140,182	85,903	61.3	82,715	78,627	3,462	75,165	4,088	4.9	54,280
1971.........	142,596	86,929	61.0	84,113	79,120	3,387	75,732	4,993	5.9	55,666
1972 [1]......	145,775	88,991	61.0	86,542	81,702	3,472	78,230	4,840	5.6	56,785
1973 [1]......	148,263	91,040	61.4	88,714	84,409	3,452	80,957	4,304	4.9	57,222
1974.........	150,827	93,240	61.8	91,011	85,935	3,492	82,443	5,076	5.6	57,587
1975.........	153,449	94,793	61.8	92,613	84,783	3,380	81,403	7,830	8.5	58,655
1976.........	156,048	96,917	62.1	94,773	87,485	3,297	84,188	7,288	7.7	59,130
1977.........	158,559	99,534	62.8	97,401	90,546	3,244	87,302	6,855	7.0	59,025
1978.........	161,058	102,537	63.7	100,420	94,373	3,342	91,031	6,047	6.0	58,521
Monthly data, seasonally adjusted [2]										
1977:										
December..	159,736	100,877	63.2	98,748	92,561	3,304	89,257	6,187	6.3	58,860
1978:										
January...	159,937	101,336	63.4	99,215	92,923	3,363	89,560	6,292	6.3	58,601
February..	160,128	101,263	63.2	99,139	93,047	3,280	89,767	6,092	6.1	58,865
March....	160,313	101,557	63.3	99,435	93,282	3,334	89,948	6,153	6.2	58,755
April....	160,504	101,885	63.5	99,767	93,704	3,274	90,430	6,063	6.1	58,619
May.......	160,713	102,222	63.6	100,109	93,953	3,243	90,710	6,156	6.1	58,492
June......	160,928	102,602	63.8	100,504	94,640	3,424	91,216	5,864	5.8	58,326
July......	161,148	102,738	63.8	100,622	94,446	3,377	91,069	6,176	6.1	58,410
August....	161,348	102,785	63.7	100,663	94,723	3,351	91,372	5,940	5.9	58,563
September.	161,570	103,097	63.8	100,974	95,010	3,406	91,604	5,964	5.9	58,473
October...	161,829	103,199	63.8	101,077	95,241	3,374	91,867	5,836	5.8	58,630
November..	162,033	103,745	64.0	101,628	95,751	3,275	92,476	5,877	5.8	58,288
December..	162,250	103,975	64.1	101,867	95,855	3,387	92,468	6,012	5.9	58,275

[1] Not strictly comparable with data for prior years.
[2] Because seasonality, by definition, does not exist in population figures, data for "total noninstitutional population" are not seasonally adjusted.

EMPLOYMENT STATUS OF THE NONINSTITUTIONAL POPULATION 16 YEARS AND OVER BY SEX, 1967 TO DATE
(Numbers in thousands)

Year, month, and sex	Total noninsti- tutional popula- tion	Total labor force		Civilian labor force							Not in labor force
		Number	Percent of popula- tion	Total	Employed			Unemployed			
					Total	Agri- culture	Nonagri- cultural indus- tries	Number	Percent of labor force		
MALES					Annual averages						
1967.........	64,316	52,398	81.5	48,987	47,479	3,164	44,315	1,508	3.1		11,919
1968.........	65,345	53,030	81.2	49,533	48,114	3,157	44,957	1,419	2.9		12,315
1969.........	66,365	53,688	80.9	50,221	48,818	2,963	45,855	1,403	2.8		12,677
1970.........	67,409	54,343	80.6	51,195	48,960	2,861	46,099	2,235	4.4		13,066
1971.........	68,512	54,797	80.0	52,021	49,245	2,790	46,455	2,776	5.3		13,715
1972[1]......	69,864	55,671	79.7	53,265	50,630	2,839	47,791	2,635	4.9		14,193
1973[1]......	71,020	56,479	79.5	54,203	51,963	2,833	49,130	2,240	4.1		14,541
1974.........	72,253	57,349	79.4	55,186	52,518	2,900	49,618	2,668	4.8		14,904
1975.........	73,494	57,706	78.5	55,615	51,230	2,801	48,429	4,385	7.9		15,788
1976.........	74,739	58,397	78.1	56,359	52,391	2,716	49,675	3,968	7.0		16,341
1977.........	75,981	59,467	78.3	57,449	53,861	2,639	51,222	3,588	6.2		16,514
1978.........	77,169	60,535	78.4	58,542	55,491	2,681	52,810	3,051	5.2		16,634
				Monthly data, seasonally adjusted[2]							
1977:											
December..	76,541	60,079	78.5	58,068	54,922	2,690	52,232	3,146	5.4		16,463
1978:											
January..	76,636	60,251	78.6	58,248	54,992	2,734	52,258	3,256	5.6		16,385
February.	76,725	60,171	78.4	58,164	54,943	2,604	52,339	3,221	5.5		16,555
March....	76,811	60,278	78.5	58,277	55,042	2,641	52,401	3,235	5.6		16,533
April....	76,901	60,277	78.4	58,280	55,184	2,598	52,586	3,096	5.3		16,624
May......	77,000	60,396	78.4	58,404	55,372	2,636	52,736	3,032	5.2		16,604
June.....	77,102	60,555	78.5	58,582	55,766	2,745	53,021	2,816	4.8		16,546
July.....	77,206	60,492	78.4	58,502	55,531	2,718	52,813	2,971	5.1		16,715
August...	77,301	60,510	78.3	58,517	55,580	2,695	52,885	2,937	5.0		16,792
September	77,407	60,552	78.2	58,559	55,594	2,739	52,855	2,965	5.1		16,855
October..	77,546	60,717	78.3	58,725	55,754	2,707	53,047	2,971	5.1		16,829
November.	77,643	61,006	78.6	59,019	56,096	2,614	53,482	2,923	5.0		16,636
December.	77,746	61,095	78.6	59,116	56,072	2,702	53,370	3,044	5.1		16,651
FEMALES					Annual averages						
1967.........	69,003	28,395	41.2	28,360	26,893	680	26,212	1,468	5.2		40,608
1968.........	70,217	29,242	41.6	29,204	27,807	660	27,147	1,397	4.8		40,976
1969.........	71,476	30,551	42.7	30,513	29,084	643	28,441	1,429	4.7		40,924
1970.........	72,774	31,560	43.4	31,520	29,667	601	29,066	1,853	5.9		41,214
1971.........	74,084	32,132	43.4	32,091	29,875	598	29,277	2,217	6.9		41,952
1972[1]......	75,911	33,320	43.9	33,277	31,072	633	30,439	2,205	6.6		42,591
1973[1]......	77,242	34,561	44.7	34,510	32,446	619	31,827	2,064	6.0		42,681
1974.........	78,575	35,892	45.7	35,825	33,417	592	32,825	2,408	6.7		42,683
1975.........	79,954	37,087	46.4	36,998	33,553	579	32,973	3,445	9.3		42,868
1976.........	81,309	38,520	47.4	38,414	35,095	582	34,513	3,320	8.6		42,789
1977.........	82,577	40,067	48.5	39,952	36,685	605	36,080	3,267	8.2		42,510
1978.........	83,890	42,002	50.1	41,878	38,882	661	38,221	2,996	7.2		41,888
				Monthly data, seasonally adjusted[2]							
1977:											
December..	83,195	40,798	49.0	40,680	37,639	614	37,025	3,041	7.5		42,397
1978:											
January..	83,301	41,084	49.3	40,967	37,931	629	37,302	3,036	7.4		42,217
February.	83,403	41,092	49.3	40,975	38,104	676	37,428	2,871	7.0		42,311
March....	83,501	41,280	49.4	41,158	38,240	693	37,547	2,918	7.1		42,222
April....	83,603	41,608	49.8	41,487	38,520	676	37,844	2,967	7.2		41,995
May......	83,714	41,826	50.0	41,705	38,581	607	37,974	3,124	7.5		41,888
June.....	83,826	42,047	50.2	41,922	38,874	679	38,195	3,048	7.3		41,779
July.....	83,941	42,246	50.3	42,120	38,915	659	38,256	3,205	7.6		41,695
August...	84,047	42,276	50.3	42,146	39,143	656	38,487	3,003	7.1		41,772
September.	84,162	42,545	50.6	42,415	39,416	667	38,749	2,999	7.1		41,618
October...	84,283	42,482	50.4	42,352	39,487	667	38,820	2,865	6.8		41,801
November..	84,390	42,738	50.6	42,609	39,655	661	38,994	2,954	6.9		41,652
December..	84,504	42,880	50.7	42,751	39,783	685	39,098	2,968	6.9		41,624

[1] Not strictly comparable with data for prior years.
[2] Because seasonality, by definition, does not exist in population figures, data for "total noninstitutional population" are not seasonally adjusted.

EMPLOYMENT STATUS OF THE NONINSTITUTIONAL POPULATION BY SEX, AGE, AND RACE
(Numbers in thousands)

Sex, age, and race	Total labor force		Civilian labor force				Not in labor force				
	Number	Percent of population	Total	Employed	Unemployed		Total	Keeping house	Going to school	Unable to work	Other reasons
					Number	Percent of labor force					
MALES											
16 years and over	60,671	78.0	58,692	55,668	3,024	5.2	17,075	323	4,560	1,709	10,483
16 to 21 years	8,512	66.8	7,843	6,726	1,117	14.2	4,237	23	3,794	31	389
16 to 19 years	5,048	59.7	4,757	3,955	803	16.9	3,409	17	3,133	16	243
16 to 17 years	2,018	48.0	1,996	1,585	410	20.6	2,189	8	2,066	5	110
18 to 19 years	3,030	71.3	2,762	2,369	392	14.2	1,220	9	1,067	11	133
20 to 64 years	53,679	89.8	51,991	49,841	2,149	4.1	6,107	130	1,427	1,230	3,319
20 to 24 years	8,761	86.0	8,010	7,317	693	8.7	1,428	9	1,083	44	292
25 to 54 years	37,757	94.7	36,821	35,539	1,282	3.5	2,125	66	339	630	1,093
25 to 29 years	8,510	95.1	8,141	7,713	428	5.3	436	12	208	47	169
30 to 34 years	7,651	96.5	7,407	7,165	241	3.3	274	10	78	55	131
35 to 39 years	6,207	96.5	6,013	5,842	172	2.9	225	8	19	77	122
40 to 44 years	5,228	95.1	5,138	4,991	146	2.8	270	4	17	76	173
45 to 49 years	5,087	93.2	5,054	4,921	134	2.6	369	13	11	127	217
50 to 54 years	5,075	90.2	5,068	4,906	162	3.2	553	18	7	247	283
55 to 64 years	7,161	73.7	7,160	6,986	174	2.4	2,553	56	5	557	1,935
55 to 59 years	4,397	82.5	4,396	4,294	102	2.3	932	18	3	311	599
60 to 64 years	2,764	63.0	2,764	2,692	72	2.6	1,622	38	3	246	1,336
65 years and over	1,944	20.5	1,944	1,872	72	3.7	7,558	175	--	463	6,921
65 to 69 years	1,146	30.5	1,146	1,097	49	4.3	2,616	42	--	177	2,397
70 years and over	798	13.9	798	775	23	2.9	4,942	133	--	286	4,523
White											
16 years and over	53,936	78.7	52,347	49,976	2,371	4.5	14,585	264	3,672	1,372	9,278
16 to 21 years	7,473	68.9	6,947	6,089	858	12.4	3,373	22	3,040	19	292
16 to 19 years	4,471	62.4	4,242	3,605	637	15.0	2,700	16	2,484	9	191
16 to 17 years	1,826	51.4	1,808	1,464	344	19.0	1,724	8	1,622	3	91
18 to 19 years	2,645	73.0	2,434	2,141	293	12.1	976	8	862	6	100
20 to 64 years	47,720	90.4	46,360	44,680	1,679	3.6	5,074	97	1,188	992	2,796
20 to 24 years	7,602	86.7	7,015	6,520	496	7.1	1,170	9	910	38	213
25 to 54 years	33,609	95.4	32,837	31,812	1,024	3.1	1,624	45	272	482	825
25 to 34 years	14,308	96.5	13,809	13,283	526	3.8	518	15	228	72	204
35 to 44 years	10,206	96.7	9,968	9,705	262	2.6	351	10	30	97	214
45 to 54 years	9,095	92.3	9,060	8,824	236	2.6	755	20	15	313	407
55 to 64 years	6,509	74.1	6,507	6,348	160	2.5	2,279	43	5	472	1,758
55 to 59 years	3,996	83.2	3,995	3,905	90	2.3	808	15	3	264	526
60 to 64 years	2,512	63.1	2,512	2,443	70	2.8	1,471	28	3	208	1,232
65 years and over	1,745	20.4	1,745	1,691	55	3.1	6,812	151	--	371	6,291
Black and other											
16 years and over	6,735	73.0	6,345	5,692	653	10.3	2,489	59	888	337	1,205
16 to 21 years	1,039	54.6	896	637	259	28.9	865	2	754	12	97
16 to 19 years	577	44.8	515	350	166	32.1	710	2	649	7	52
16 to 17 years	192	29.2	188	121	67	35.6	465	--	444	2	19
18 to 19 years	385	61.2	327	229	99	30.1	244	2	205	5	33
20 to 64 years	5,960	85.2	5,632	5,162	469	8.3	1,034	34	239	238	523
20 to 24 years	1,159	81.8	994	797	197	19.8	258	--	172	6	79
25 to 54 years	4,148	89.2	3,985	3,726	258	6.5	501	21	66	148	267
25 to 34 years	1,853	90.6	1,738	1,596	143	8.2	191	7	58	30	96
35 to 44 years	1,228	89.5	1,183	1,128	56	4.7	144	2	6	56	80
45 to 54 years	1,067	86.5	1,063	1,003	60	5.6	166	12	2	61	90
55 to 64 years	653	70.4	653	638	14	2.2	275	12	--	85	177
55 to 59 years	401	76.4	401	390	12	2.9	124	3	--	47	73
60 to 64 years	252	62.5	252	249	3	1.1	151	9	--	38	104
65 years and over	198	21.0	198	181	18	8.9	746	24	--	92	630

EMPLOYMENT STATUS OF THE NONINSTITUTIONAL POPULATION BY SEX, AGE, AND RACE (Continued)
(Numbers in thousands)

Sex, age, and race	Total labor force		Civilian labor force				Not in labor force				
					Unemployed						
	Number	Percent of population	Total	Employed	Number	Percent of labor force	Total	Keeping house	Going to school	Unable to work	Other reasons
FEMALES											
16 years and over	43,069	51.0	42,940	40,239	2,701	6.3	41,435	32,444	4,197	1,056	3,737
16 to 21 years	7,272	58.2	7,220	6,302	919	12.7	5,217	1,336	3,532	25	324
16 to 19 years	4,446	53.7	4,426	3,782	644	14.6	3,830	614	2,987	20	209
16 to 17 years	1,864	45.8	1,863	1,546	318	17.0	2,210	167	1,968	6	69
18 to 19 years	2,582	61.5	2,562	2,236	326	12.7	1,620	447	1,019	14	140
20 to 64 years	37,487	59.8	37,379	35,353	2,026	5.4	25,191	21,947	1,206	470	1,568
20 to 24 years	7,019	69.0	6,952	6,365	587	8.4	3,155	2,057	828	24	246
25 to 54 years	25,890	62.2	25,849	24,560	1,290	5.0	15,761	14,381	369	254	760
25 to 29 years	6,080	66.7	6,051	5,635	416	6.9	3,033	2,682	142	16	194
30 to 34 years	4,992	61.4	4,984	4,738	246	4.9	3,140	2,902	105	28	105
35 to 39 years	4,244	62.7	4,241	4,031	210	5.0	2,520	2,319	61	36	103
40 to 44 years	3,642	62.6	3,641	3,487	155	4.2	2,177	2,021	30	42	84
45 to 49 years	3,482	60.5	3,482	3,336	145	4.2	2,276	2,072	18	49	137
50 to 54 years	3,450	56.9	3,450	3,332	118	3.4	2,616	2,385	13	82	137
55 to 64 years	4,578	42.2	4,578	4,428	150	3.3	6,275	5,510	9	192	563
55 to 59 years	2,860	48.8	2,860	2,776	83	2.9	2,995	2,656	3	84	250
60 to 64 years	1,718	34.4	1,718	1,652	66	3.9	3,280	2,854	6	108	313
65 years and over	1,135	8.4	1,135	1,104	31	2.7	12,414	9,883	4	567	1,960
65 to 69 years	709	15.0	709	696	13	1.9	4,007	3,380	2	104	520
70 years and over	425	4.8	425	408	17	4.1	8,407	6,502	2	463	1,440
White											
16 years and over	37,311	50.6	37,209	35,158	2,051	5.5	36,366	29,091	3,308	805	3,161
16 to 21 years	6,392	60.7	6,351	5,671	680	10.7	4,140	1,107	2,780	18	235
16 to 19 years	3,960	56.9	3,943	3,456	487	12.4	3,005	495	2,340	14	156
16 to 17 years	1,691	49.4	1,690	1,430	260	15.4	1,728	142	1,524	6	56
18 to 19 years	2,269	64.0	2,254	2,026	228	10.1	1,276	352	816	8	100
20 to 64 years	32,345	59.4	32,266	30,722	1,538	4.8	22,083	19,489	965	358	1,271
20 to 24 years	6,036	70.0	5,983	5,582	401	6.7	2,581	1,723	669	16	173
25 to 54 years	22,202	61.6	22,170	21,150	1,021	4.6	13,851	12,749	289	195	618
25 to 34 years	9,416	63.7	9,388	8,878	510	5.4	5,375	4,924	188	32	231
35 to 44 years	6,736	61.9	6,733	6,441	292	4.3	4,145	3,869	73	55	148
45 to 54 years	6,051	58.3	6,050	5,831	218	3.6	4,331	3,956	28	108	240
55 to 64 years	4,106	42.1	4,106	3,991	115	2.8	5,651	5,016	7	147	480
55 to 59 years	2,571	49.0	2,571	2,506	64	2.5	2,673	2,399	3	58	212
60 to 64 years	1,536	34.0	1,536	1,485	51	3.3	2,978	2,617	4	89	268
65 years and over	1,006	8.2	1,006	980	26	2.6	11,278	9,108	3	434	1,733
Black and other											
16 years and over	5,758	53.2	5,731	5,081	650	11.3	5,069	3,353	889	251	577
16 to 21 years	879	44.9	870	630	239	27.5	1,077	229	752	7	89
16 to 19 years	486	37.1	483	326	156	32.4	825	120	647	6	52
16 to 17 years	174	26.5	174	116	58	33.4	482	25	444	--	12
18 to 19 years	312	47.7	309	210	99	31.9	343	94	203	6	40
20 to 64 years	5,142	62.3	5,119	4,630	489	9.6	3,108	2,459	241	111	297
20 to 24 years	983	63.2	969	783	186	19.2	573	333	159	7	73
25 to 54 years	3,688	65.9	3,679	3,410	269	7.3	1,910	1,632	80	58	141
25 to 34 years	1,656	67.5	1,648	1,496	152	9.2	798	660	58	12	68
35 to 44 years	1,150	67.6	1,150	1,077	72	6.3	551	471	18	23	39
45 to 54 years	882	61.1	882	837	45	5.1	561	501	3	23	34
55 to 64 years	472	43.0	472	437	34	7.3	624	494	2	45	83
55 to 59 years	289	47.3	289	270	19	6.7	322	257	--	26	38
60 to 64 years	182	37.6	182	168	15	8.2	302	237	2	19	45
65 years and over	129	10.2	129	125	4	3.2	1,136	774	1	134	227

December 1978

EMPLOYMENT STATUS OF THE NONINSTITUTIONAL POPULATION 16 YEARS AND OVER BY SEX, 1947 TO DATE
(Numbers in thousands)

Year, month, and sex	Total noninstitutional population	Total labor force		Civilian labor force						Not in labor force
		Number	Percent of population	Total	Employed			Unemployed		
					Total	Agriculture	Nonagricultural industries	Number	Percent of labor force	
MALES										
1947.........................	50,968	44,258	86.8	42,686	40,995	6,643	34,352	1,692	4.0	6,710
1948.........................	51,439	44,729	87.0	43,286	41,725	6,358	35,367	1,559	3.6	6,710
1949.........................	51,922	45,097	86.9	43,498	40,925	6,343	34,583	2,572	5.9	6,825
1950.........................	52,352	45,446	86.8	43,819	41,578	6,002	35,576	2,239	5.1	6,906
1951.........................	52,788	46,063	87.3	43,001	41,780	5,534	36,246	1,221	2.8	6,725
1952.........................	53,248	46,416	87.2	42,869	41,682	5,390	36,293	1,185	2.8	6,832
1953[1]......................	54,248	47,131	86.9	43,633	42,430	5,253	37,177	1,202	2.8	7,117
1954.........................	54,706	47,275	86.4	43,965	41,619	5,200	36,418	2,344	5.3	7,431
1955.........................	55,122	47,488	86.2	44,475	42,621	5,265	37,356	1,854	4.2	7,634
1956.........................	55,547	47,914	86.3	45,091	43,379	5,040	38,339	1,711	3.8	7,633
1957.........................	56,082	47,964	85.5	45,197	43,357	4,824	38,532	1,841	4.1	8,118
1958.........................	56,640	48,126	85.0	45,521	42,423	4,596	37,827	3,098	6.8	8,514
1959.........................	57,312	48,405	84.5	45,886	43,466	4,532	38,934	2,420	5.2	8,907
1960[1]......................	58,144	48,870	84.0	46,388	43,904	4,472	39,431	2,486	5.4	9,274
1961.........................	58,826	49,193	83.6	46,653	43,656	4,298	39,359	2,997	6.4	9,633
1962[1]......................	59,626	49,395	82.8	46,600	44,177	4,069	40,108	2,423	5.2	10,231
1963.........................	60,627	49,835	82.2	47,129	44,657	3,809	40,849	2,472	5.2	10,792
1964.........................	61,556	50,387	81.9	47,679	45,474	3,691	41,782	2,205	4.6	11,169
1965.........................	62,473	50,946	81.5	48,255	46,340	3,547	42,792	1,914	4.0	11,527
1966.........................	63,351	51,560	81.4	48,471	46,919	3,243	43,675	1,551	3.2	11,792
1967.........................	64,316	52,398	81.5	48,987	47,479	3,164	44,315	1,508	3.1	11,919
1968.........................	65,345	53,030	81.2	49,533	48,114	3,157	44,957	1,419	2.9	12,315
1969.........................	66,365	53,688	80.9	50,221	48,818	2,963	45,855	1,403	2.8	12,677
1970.........................	67,409	54,343	80.6	51,195	48,960	2,861	46,099	2,235	4.4	13,066
1971.........................	68,512	54,797	80.0	52,021	49,245	2,790	46,455	2,776	5.3	13,715
1972[1]......................	69,864	55,671	79.7	53,265	50,630	2,839	47,791	2,635	4.9	14,193
1973[1]......................	71,020	56,479	79.5	54,203	51,963	2,833	49,130	2,240	4.1	14,541
1974.........................	72,253	57,349	79.4	55,186	52,518	2,900	49,618	2,668	4.8	14,904
1975.........................	73,494	57,706	78.5	55,615	51,230	2,801	48,429	4,385	7.9	15,788
1976.........................	74,739	58,397	78.1	56,359	52,391	2,716	49,675	3,968	7.0	16,341
1977.........................	75,981	59,467	78.3	57,449	53,861	2,639	51,222	3,588	6.2	16,514
1978[1]......................	77,169	60,535	78.4	58,542	55,491	2,681	52,810	3,051	5.2	16,634
FEMALES										
1947.........................	52,450	16,683	31.8	16,664	16,045	1,248	14,797	619	3.7	35,767
1948.........................	53,088	17,351	32.7	17,335	16,617	1,271	15,346	717	4.1	35,737
1949.........................	53,689	17,806	33.2	17,788	16,723	1,315	15,409	1,065	6.0	35,883
1950.........................	54,293	18,412	33.9	18,389	17,340	1,159	16,181	1,049	5.7	35,881
1951.........................	54,933	19,054	34.7	19,016	18,181	1,193	16,988	834	4.4	35,879
1952.........................	55,575	19,314	34.8	19,269	18,568	1,111	17,458	698	3.6	36,261
1953[1]......................	56,353	19,429	34.5	19,382	18,749	1,006	17,743	632	3.3	36,924
1954.........................	56,965	19,718	34.6	19,678	18,490	1,006	17,486	1,188	6.0	37,247
1955.........................	57,610	20,584	35.7	20,548	19,551	1,184	18,366	998	4.9	37,026
1956.........................	58,264	21,495	36.9	21,461	20,419	1,244	19,175	1,039	4.8	36,769
1957.........................	58,983	21,765	36.9	21,732	20,714	1,123	19,591	1,018	4.7	37,218
1958.........................	59,723	22,149	37.1	22,118	20,613	990	19,623	1,504	6.8	37,574
1959.........................	60,569	22,516	37.2	22,483	21,164	1,033	20,131	1,320	5.9	38,053
1960[1]......................	61,615	23,272	37.8	23,240	21,874	986	20,887	1,366	5.9	38,343
1961.........................	62,517	23,838	38.1	23,806	22,090	902	21,187	1,717	7.2	38,679
1962[1]......................	63,355	24,047	38.0	24,014	22,525	875	21,651	1,488	6.2	39,308
1963.........................	64,527	24,736	38.3	24,704	23,105	878	22,227	1,598	6.5	39,791
1964.........................	65,668	25,443	38.7	25,412	23,831	832	23,000	1,581	6.2	40,225
1965.........................	66,763	26,232	39.3	26,200	24,748	814	23,934	1,452	5.5	40,531
1966.........................	67,829	27,333	40.3	27,299	25,976	736	25,240	1,324	4.8	40,496
1967.........................	69,003	28,395	41.2	28,360	26,893	680	26,212	1,468	5.2	40,608
1968.........................	70,217	29,242	41.6	29,204	27,807	660	27,147	1,397	4.8	40,976
1969.........................	71,476	30,551	42.7	30,513	29,084	643	28,441	1,429	4.7	40,924
1970.........................	72,774	31,560	43.4	31,520	29,667	601	29,066	1,853	5.9	41,214
1971.........................	74,084	32,132	43.4	32,091	29,875	598	29,277	2,217	6.9	41,952
1972[1]......................	75,911	33,320	43.9	33,277	31,072	633	30,439	2,205	6.6	42,591
1973[1]......................	77,242	34,561	44.7	34,510	32,446	619	31,827	2,064	6.0	42,681
1974.........................	78,575	35,892	45.7	35,825	33,417	592	32,825	2,408	6.7	42,683
1975.........................	79,954	37,087	46.4	36,998	33,553	579	32,973	3,445	9.3	42,868
1976.........................	81,309	38,520	47.4	38,414	35,095	582	34,513	3,320	8.6	42,789
1977.........................	82,577	40,067	48.5	39,952	36,685	605	36,080	3,267	8.2	42,510
1978[1]......................	83,890	42,002	50.1	41,878	38,882	661	38,221	2,996	7.2	41,887

[1] Because seasonality, by definition, does not exist in population figures, data for "total noninstitutional population" are not seasonally adjusted.

EMPLOYMENT STATUS OF THE NONINSTITUTIONAL POPULATION BY SEX, AGE, AND RACE (ANNUAL AVERAGES)
(numbers in thousands)

Sex, age, and race	1978										
	Total labor force		Civilian labor force				Not in labor force				
					Unemployed						
	Number	Percent of population	Total	Employed	Number	Percent of labor force	Total	Keeping house	Going to school	Unable to work	Other reasons
MALES											
16 years and over	60,535	78.4	58,542	55,491	3,051	5.2	16,634	335	3,713	1,724	10,862
16 to 21 years	8,924	70.0	8,242	7,100	1,141	13.8	3,833	20	3,029	34	750
16 to 19 years	5,383	63.5	5,078	4,279	799	15.7	3,093	15	2,494	14	569
16 to 17 years	2,208	52.2	2,185	1,767	418	19.2	2,024	9	1,654	5	356
18 to 19 years	3,175	74.8	2,893	2,512	381	13.2	1,069	6	840	9	213
20 to 64 years	53,229	89.8	51,541	49,370	2,171	4.2	6,070	138	1,218	1,251	3,463
20 to 24 years	8,811	87.1	8,063	7,330	733	9.1	1,309	12	890	47	360
25 to 54 years	37,330	94.4	36,392	35,149	1,243	3.4	2,201	69	325	667	1,140
25 to 29 years	8,405	94.9	8,033	7,619	415	5.2.	452	6	201	47	198
30 to 34 years	7,495	96.3	7,251	7,010	241	3.3	291	14	68	70	139
35 to 39 years	6,074	96.4	5,880	5,710	170	2.9	224	5	21	75	123
40 to 44 years	5,196	95.1	5,106	4,968	138	2.7	269	10	16	99	143
45 to 49 years	5,103	93.0	5,071	4,934	137	2.7	387	17	12	148	210
50 to 54 years	5,058	89.7	5,051	4,908	143	2.8	579	17	6	229	327
55 to 64 years	7,088	73.5	7,087	6,892	195	2.7	2,560	57	3	537	1,963
55 to 59 years	4,390	82.9	4,389	4,266	123	2.8	904	26	2	282	594
60 to 64 years	2,698	62.0	2,698	2,626	72	2.7	1,656	31	1	255	1,369
65 years and over	1,923	20.5	1,923	1,842	81	4.2	7,471	182	1	458	6,830
65 to 69 years	1,120	30.1	1,120	1,068	52	4.7	2,607	53	--	169	2,385
70 years and over	803	14.2	803	774	29	3.6	4,864	129	1	290	4,444
White											
16 years and over	53,867	79.1	52,258	49,893	2,365	4.5	14,204	276	2,980	1,397	9,550
16 to 21 years	7,849	72.3	7,308	6,451	857	11.7	3,015	16	2,414	23	562
16 to 19 years	4,767	66.3	4,525	3,916	609	13.5	2,427	13	1,970	10	435
16 to 17 years	1,988	55.6	1,969	1,637	332	16.9	1,588	8	1,295	4	281
18 to 19 years	2,779	76.8	2,556	2,279	277	10.8	839	5	675	6	153
20 to 64 years	47,375	90.4	46,008	44,319	1,690	3.7	5,039	109	1,009	1,010	2,909
20 to 24 years	7,688	88.1	7,100	6,560	540	7.6	1,038	8	737	34	258
25 to 54 years	33,232	95.1	32,454	31,472	983	3.0	1,724	53	270	522	879
25 to 34 years	14,074	96.1	13,570	13,064	505	3.7	572	14	224	92	241
35 to 44 years	10,033	96.4	9,794	9,545	249	2.5	375	11	30	136	198
45 to 54 years	9,125	92.2	9,091	8,862	228	2.5	777	28	16	294	439
55 to 64 years	6,455	73.9	6,454	6,287	167	2.6	2,277	49	3	453	1,773
55 to 59 years	3,993	83.6	3,992	3,889	102	2.6	781	22	2	235	522
60 to 64 years	2,463	62.2	2,462	2,398	65	2.6	1,496	27	1	218	1,251
65 years and over	1,725	20.4	1,725	1,658	67	3.9	6,738	154	1	378	6,206
Black and other											
16 years and over	6,667	73.3	6,284	5,599	686	10.9	2,430	59	733	326	1,312
16 to 21 years	1,074	56.8	934	649	285	30.5	818	4	615	11	188
16 to 19 years	616	48.0	553	363	190	34.4	666	3	524	4	134
16 to 17 years	220	33.5	216	130	87	40.0	436	1	359	1	75
18 to 19 years	396	63.2	337	233	104	30.8	230	1	165	3	60
20 to 64 years	5,854	85.0	5,533	5,052	481	8.7	1,033	29	208	242	554
20 to 24 years	1,124	80.5	963	770	193	20.0	272	4	153	13	102
25 to 54 years	4,098	89.6	3,938	3,678	261	6.6	478	16	55	145	262
25 to 34 years	1,826	91.4	1,714	1,564	150	8.8	171	5	45	25	96
35 to 44 years	1,236	91.3	1,192	1,134	59	4.9	118	4	8	38	68
45 to 54 years	1,035	84.6	1,031	979	52	5.0	188	6	2	82	98
55 to 64 years	632	69.1	632	605	28	4.4	283	8	1	84	190
55 to 59 years	397	76.5	397	376	20	5.1	122	4	--	47	71
60 to 64 years	236	59.4	236	228	8	3.2	161	5	--	37	119
65 years and over	198	21.3	198	184	14	7.1	732	28	--	80	624

EMPLOYMENT STATUS OF THE NONINSTITUTIONAL POPULATION BY SEX, AGE, AND RACE (ANNUAL AVERAGES) (*Continued*)
(numbers in thousands)

Sex, age, and race	Total labor force		Civilian labor force				Not in labor force				
					Unemployed						
	Number	Percent of population	Total	Employed	Number	Percent of labor force	Total	Keeping house	Going to school	Unable to work	Other reasons
FEMALES											
16 years and over	42,002	50.1	41,878	38,882	2,996	7.2	41,887	32,788	3,626	1,042	4,432
16 to 21 years	7,293	58.4	7,243	6,161	1,082	14.9	5,204	1,458	3,021	21	704
16 to 19 years	4,482	54.0	4,462	3,702	760	17.0	3,814	725	2,523	14	553
16 to 17 years	1,866	45.5	1,865	1,502	363	19.5	2,233	218	1,676	5	333
18 to 19 years	2,616	62.3	2,597	2,200	397	15.3	1,582	507	848	8	219
20 to 64 years	36,401	58.5	36,296	34,103	2,193	6.0	25,798	22,342	1,095	458	1,903
20 to 24 years	6,926	68.5	6,860	6,168	692	10.1	3,181	2,122	740	24	295
25 to 54 years	25,007	60.5	24,968	23,609	1,359	5.4	16,300	14,734	345	241	581
25 to 29 years	5,804	64.3	5,777	5,372	405	7.0	3,224	2,852	156	26	190
30 to 34 years	4,776	59.8	4,769	4,471	298	6.2	3,215	2,941	79	26	168
35 to 39 years	4,035	60.9	4,032	3,820	212	5.3	2,593	2,365	48	33	146
40 to 44 years	3,610	62.5	3,609	3,439	169	4.7	2,169	1,967	33	38	130
45 to 49 years	3,463	59.8	3,462	3,319	143	4.1	2,331	2,113	21	45	151
50 to 54 years	3,319	54.5	3,319	3,188	131	3.9	2,770	2,494	9	72	195
55 to 64 years	4,469	41.4	4,468	4,325	144	3.2	6,316	5,486	13	193	627
55 to 59 years	2,825	48.6	2,825	2,738	87	3.1	2,994	2,636	6	92	259
60 to 64 years	1,643	33.1	1,643	1,587	56	3.4	3,323	2,850	4	101	367
65 years and over	1,120	8.4	1,120	1,077	43	3.8	12,275	9,721	7	571	1,976
65 to 69 years	699	14.9	699	668	31	4.4	3,993	3,334	2	102	554
70 years and over	421	4.8	421	409	12	2.8	8,283	6,387	5	469	1,422
White											
16 years and over	36,298	49.6	36,198	33,943	2,255	6.2	36,920	29,430	2,877	818	3,795
16 to 21 years	6,414	60.8	6,373	5,578	795	12.5	4,136	1,178	2,397	16	546
16 to 19 years	3,981	57.0	3,965	3,396	569	14.4	3,008	575	1,991	11	430
16 to 17 years	1,684	48.9	1,683	1,396	287	17.1	1,759	173	1,313	5	268
18 to 19 years	2,297	64.8	2,281	2,000	282	12.4	1,249	402	678	6	163
20 to 64 years	31,330	57.9	31,247	29,597	1,650	5.3	22,749	19,908	880	343	1,617
20 to 24 years	5,958	69.5	5,906	5,418	488	8.3	2,615	1,771	597	18	229
25 to 54 years	21,375	59.7	21,344	20,302	1,042	4.9	14,426	13,141	274	176	834
25 to 34 years	8,931	61.1	8,904	8,385	519	5.8	5,690	5,169	182	40	299
35 to 44 years	6,518	60.8	6,515	6,219	296	4.5	4,211	3,856	68	52	234
45 to 54 years	5,926	56.7	5,925	5,699	226	3.8	4,525	4,115	24	85	301
55 to 64 years	3,997	41.2	3,997	3,878	119	3.0	5,707	4,995	9	149	554
55 to 59 years	2,528	48.5	2,528	2,456	72	2.8	2,689	2,388	5	69	228
60 to 64 years	1,469	32.7	1,469	1,422	48	3.2	3,018	2,608	4	80	326
65 years and over	986	8.1	986	950	36	3.7	11,164	8,947	6	464	1,748
Black and other											
16 years and over	5,705	53.5	5,679	4,938	741	13.1	4,967	3,358	748	224	637
16 to 21 years	879	45.1	870	583	286	32.9	1,068	280	624	5	158
16 to 19 years	500	38.3	497	306	191	38.4	807	150	532	2	122
16 to 17 years	182	27.7	182	106	76	41.7	474	45	363	--	66
18 to 19 years	319	48.9	315	200	115	36.5	333	105	170	2	56
20 to 64 years	5,070	62.4	5,048	4,505	544	10.8	3,049	2,435	215	114	285
20 to 24 years	967	63.1	954	750	204	21.3	566	351	143	6	66
25 to 54 years	3,632	66.0	3,624	3,307	317	8.7	1,875	1,592	71	65	146
25 to 34 years	1,649	68.8	1,642	1,458	183	11.2	749	624	52	12	60
35 to 44 years	1,127	67.2	1,126	1,041	85	7.6	551	476	13	20	42
45 to 54 years	856	59.8	856	808	48	5.6	575	492	6	32	45
55 to 64 years	472	43.6	472	447	24	5.1	609	491	1	44	73
55 to 59 years	297	49.4	297	282	15	5.2	305	249	1	23	32
60 to 64 years	174	36.4	174	166	9	5.0	304	242	--	21	41
65 years and over	134	10.7	134	127					1	168	229

EMPLOYEES ON NONAGRICULTURAL PAYROLLS BY INDUSTRY DIVISION, 1919 TO DATE
(Numbers in thousands)

Year and month	Total	Goods-producing				Service-producing									
		Total	Mining	Construction	Manufacturing	Total	Transportation and public utilities	Wholesale and retail trade			Finance, insurance, and real estate	Services	Government		
								Total	Wholesale trade	Retail trade			Total	Federal	State and local
1919	27,078	12,828	1,133	1,036	10,659	14,250	3,711	4,514	-	-	1,096	2,253	2,676	-	-
1920	27,340	12,760	1,239	863	10,658	14,580	3,998	4,467	-	-	1,160	2,352	2,603	-	-
1925	28,766	12,489	1,089	1,461	9,939	16,277	3,826	5,576	-	-	1,218	2,857	2,800	-	-
1926	29,806	12,911	1,185	1,570	10,156	16,895	3,942	5,784	-	-	1,290	3,033	2,846	-	-
1927	29,962	12,738	1,114	1,623	10,001	17,224	3,895	5,908	-	-	1,352	3,154	2,915	-	-
1928	29,986	12,618	1,050	1,621	9,947	17,368	3,828	5,874	-	-	1,420	3,251	2,995	-	-
1929	31,324	13,301	1,087	1,512	10,702	18,023	3,916	6,123	-	-	1,494	3,425	3,065	533	2,532
1930	29,409	11,958	1,009	1,387	9,562	17,451	3,685	5,797	-	-	1,460	3,361	3,148	526	2,622
1931	26,635	10,272	873	1,229	8,170	16,363	3,254	5,284	-	-	1,392	3,169	3,264	560	2,704
1932	23,615	8,647	731	985	6,931	14,968	2,816	4,683	-	-	1,326	2,918	3,225	559	2,666
1933	23,699	8,965	744	824	7,397	14,734	2,672	4,755	-	-	1,280	2,861	3,166	565	2,601
1934	25,940	10,261	883	877	8,501	15,679	2,750	5,281	-	-	1,304	3,045	3,299	652	2,647
1935	27,039	10,893	897	927	9,069	16,146	2,786	5,431	-	-	1,320	3,128	3,481	753	2,728
1936	29,068	11,933	946	1,160	9,827	17,135	2,973	5,809	-	-	1,373	3,312	3,668	826	2,842
1937	31,011	12,936	1,015	1,127	10,794	18,075	3,134	6,265	-	-	1,417	3,503	3,756	833	2,923
1938	29,194	11,401	891	1,070	9,440	17,793	2,863	6,179	-	-	1,410	3,458	3,883	829	3,054
1939	30,603	12,297	854	1,165	10,278	18,306	2,936	6,426	1,762	4,664	1,447	3,502	3,995	905	3,090
1940	32,361	13,221	925	1,311	10,985	19,140	3,038	6,750	1,835	4,914	1,485	3,665	4,202	996	3,206
1941	36,539	15,963	957	1,814	13,192	20,574	3,274	7,210	1,960	5,250	1,525	3,905	4,660	1,340	3,320
1942	40,106	18,470	992	2,198	15,280	21,636	3,460	7,118	1,906	5,212	1,509	4,066	5,483	2,213	3,270
1943	42,434	20,114	925	1,587	17,602	22,320	3,647	6,982	1,822	5,160	1,481	4,130	6,080	2,905	3,174
1944	41,864	19,328	892	1,108	17,328	22,536	3,829	7,058	1,845	5,213	1,461	4,145	6,043	2,928	3,116
1945	40,374	17,507	836	1,147	15,524	22,867	3,906	7,314	1,949	5,365	1,481	4,222	5,944	2,808	3,137
1946	41,652	17,248	862	1,683	14,703	24,404	4,061	8,376	2,291	6,085	1,675	4,697	5,595	2,254	3,341
1947	43,857	18,509	955	2,009	15,545	25,348	4,166	8,955	2,471	6,484	1,728	5,025	5,474	1,892	3,582
1948	44,866	18,774	994	2,198	15,582	26,092	4,189	9,272	2,605	6,667	1,800	5,181	5,650	1,863	3,787
1949	43,754	17,565	930	2,194	14,441	26,189	4,001	9,264	2,602	6,662	1,828	5,240	5,856	1,908	3,948
1950	45,197	18,506	901	2,364	15,241	26,691	4,034	9,386	2,635	6,751	1,888	5,357	6,026	1,928	4,098
1951	47,819	19,959	929	2,637	16,393	27,860	4,226	9,742	2,727	7,015	1,956	5,547	6,389	2,302	4,087
1952	48,793	20,198	898	2,668	16,632	28,595	4,248	10,004	2,812	7,192	2,035	5,699	6,609	2,420	4,188
1953	50,202	21,074	866	2,659	17,549	29,128	4,290	10,247	2,854	7,393	2,111	5,835	6,645	2,305	4,340
1954	48,990	19,751	791	2,646	16,314	29,239	4,084	10,235	2,867	7,368	2,200	5,969	6,751	2,188	4,563
1955	50,641	20,513	792	2,839	16,882	30,128	4,141	10,535	2,926	7,609	2,298	6,240	6,914	2,187	4,727
1956	52,369	21,104	822	3,039	17,243	31,265	4,244	10,858	3,018	7,840	2,389	6,497	7,277	2,209	5,069
1957	52,853	20,964	828	2,962	17,174	31,889	4,241	10,886	3,028	7,858	2,438	6,708	7,616	2,217	5,399
1958	51,324	19,513	751	2,817	15,945	31,811	3,976	10,750	2,980	7,770	2,481	6,765	7,839	2,191	5,648
1959[1]	53,268	20,411	732	3,004	16,675	32,857	4,011	11,127	3,082	8,045	2,549	7,087	8,083	2,233	5,850
1960	54,189	20,434	712	2,926	16,796	33,755	4,004	11,391	3,143	8,248	2,629	7,378	8,353	2,270	6,083
1961	53,999	19,857	672	2,859	16,326	34,142	3,903	11,337	3,133	8,204	2,688	7,620	8,594	2,279	6,315
1962	55,549	20,451	650	2,948	16,853	35,098	3,906	11,566	3,198	8,368	2,754	7,982	8,890	2,340	6,550
1963	56,653	20,640	635	3,010	16,995	36,013	3,903	11,778	3,248	8,530	2,830	8,277	9,225	2,358	6,868
1964	58,283	21,005	634	3,097	17,274	37,278	3,951	12,160	3,337	8,823	2,911	8,660	9,596	2,348	7,248
1965	60,765	21,926	632	3,232	18,062	38,839	4,036	12,716	3,466	9,250	2,977	9,036	10,074	2,378	7,696
1966	63,901	23,158	627	3,317	19,214	40,743	4,158	13,245	3,597	9,648	3,058	9,498	10,784	2,564	8,220
1967	65,803	23,308	613	3,248	19,447	42,495	4,268	13,606	3,689	9,917	3,185	10,045	11,391	2,719	8,672
1968	67,892	23,732	606	3,350	19,776	44,160	4,318	14,099	3,779	10,320	3,337	10,567	11,839	2,737	9,102
1969	70,384	24,361	619	3,575	20,167	46,023	4,442	14,705	3,907	10,798	3,512	11,169	12,195	2,758	9,437
1970	70,880	23,578	623	3,588	19,367	47,302	4,515	15,040	3,993	11,047	3,645	11,548	12,554	2,731	9,823
1971	71,214	22,935	609	3,704	18,623	48,278	4,476	15,352	4,001	11,351	3,772	11,797	12,881	2,696	10,185
1972	73,675	23,668	628	3,889	19,151	50,007	4,541	15,949	4,113	11,836	3,908	12,276	13,334	2,684	10,649
1973	76,790	24,893	642	4,097	20,154	51,897	4,656	16,607	4,277	12,329	4,046	12,857	13,732	2,663	11,068
1974	78,265	24,794	697	4,020	20,077	53,471	4,725	16,987	4,433	12,554	4,148	13,441	14,170	2,724	11,446
1975	76,945	22,600	752	3,525	18,323	54,345	4,542	17,060	4,415	12,645	4,165	13,892	14,686	2,748	11,937
1976	79,382	23,352	779	3,576	18,997	56,030	4,582	17,755	4,546	13,209	4,271	14,551	14,871	2,733	12,138
1977	82,256	24,288	809	3,833	19,647	57,968	4,696	18,492	4,697	13,795	4,452	15,249	15,079	2,727	12,352
1978ᵖ	85,760	25,381	837	4,213	20,331	60,380	4,858	19,392	4,897	14,496	4,676	15,976	15,478	2,754	12,723
1977:															
Dec	84,464	24,568	682	3,896	19,990	59,896	4,773	19,568	4,797	14,771	4,533	15,540	15,482	2,724	12,758
1978:															
Jan	82,724	24,018	669	3,507	19,842	58,706	4,706	18,806	4,768	14,038	4,526	15,316	15,352	2,711	12,641
Feb	82,962	23,996	668	3,464	19,864	58,966	4,720	18,615	4,780	13,835	4,550	15,482	15,599	2,720	12,879
Mar	83,897	24,356	686	3,675	19,995	59,541	4,759	18,801	4,815	13,986	4,577	15,678	15,726	2,725	13,001
Apr	85,075	24,973	858	4,014	20,101	60,102	4,808	19,053	4,843	14,210	4,609	15,866	15,766	2,739	13,027
May	85,796	25,262	870	4,183	20,209	60,534	4,842	19,267	4,870	14,397	4,642	15,975	15,808	2,756	13,052
June	86,799	25,839	895	4,462	20,482	60,960	4,920	19,499	4,934	14,565	4,712	16,138	15,691	2,802	12,889
July	85,925	25,712	900	4,572	20,240	60,213	4,856	19,469	4,930	14,539	4,746	16,213	14,929	2,815	12,114
Aug	86,134	25,997	902	4,633	20,462	60,137	4,870	19,519	4,930	14,589	4,754	16,235	14,759	2,793	11,966
Sept	86,688	26,131	894	4,586	20,651	60,557	4,908	19,634	4,932	14,702	4,724	16,159	15,132	2,744	12,388
Oct	87,303	26,161	897	4,601	20,663	61,142	4,952	19,701	4,970	14,731	4,732	16,201	15,556	2,746	12,810
Nov.ᵖ	87,779	26,150	903	4,516	20,731	61,629	4,970	19,967	4,987	14,980	4,761	16,228	15,703	2,746	12,957
Dec.ᵖ	88,043	25,976	896	4,347	20,733	62,067	4,990	20,378	5,004	15,374	4,774	16,215	15,710	2,755	12,955

[1] Data include Alaska and Hawaii, beginning in 1959. This inclusion has resulted in an increase of 212,000 (0.4 percent) on the nonagricultural total for the March 1959 benchmark month.

p = preliminary

EMPLOYED PERSONS BY DETAILED OCCUPATION, SEX, AND RACE
(Numbers in thousands)

Occupations	1978 Total employed	Percent of total — Female	Percent of total — Black and other
Total, 16 years and over	94,373	41.2	11.2
White-collar workers	47,205	52.1	8.1
Professional and technical	14,245	42.7	8.7
Accountants	975	30.1	7.5
Architects	69	5.8	5.8
Computer specialists	428	23.1	6.5
Computer programmers	247	26.7	6.5
Computer systems analysts	152	21.1	7.2
Engineers	1,265	2.8	5.5
Aeronautical and astronautical engineers	59	--	3.4
Civil engineers	160	1.9	8.1
Electrical and electronic engineers	329	1.8	6.4
Industrial engineers	206	8.7	5.3
Mechanical engineers	216	.9	5.1
Foresters and conservationists	58	6.9	3.4
Lawyers and judges	499	9.4	2.6
Lawyers	479	9.4	2.7
Librarians, archivists, and curators	202	80.7	6.9
Librarians	187	84.5	7.0
Life and physical scientists	273	17.9	9.2
Biological scientists	58	37.9	12.1
Chemists	118	14.4	11.9
Operations and systems researchers and analysts	129	21.7	6.2
Personnel and labor relations workers	405	43.7	12.3
Physicians, dentists and related practitioners	756	10.4	7.3
Dentists	117	1.7	4.3
Pharmacists	136	16.9	6.6
Physicians, medical and osteopathic	424	11.3	9.7
Nurses, dieticians, and therapists	1,351	92.9	11.7
Registered nurses	1,112	96.7	11.7
Therapists	189	70.4	9.0
Health technologists and technicians	498	70.9	12.9
Clinical laboratory technologists and technicians	208	73.6	14.4
Radiologic technologists and technicians	97	67.0	9.3
Religious workers	325	14.8	8.9
Clergy	262	3.8	3.1
Social scientists	255	33.7	7.8
Economists	118	22.9	8.5
Psychologists	106	48.1	8.5
Social and recreation workers	505	61.0	19.2
Social workers	385	62.3	19.0
Recreation workers	121	57.0	20.7
Teachers, college and university	562	33.8	7.1
Teachers, except college and university	2,992	71.0	9.8
Adult education teachers	81	49.4	11.1
Elementary school teachers	1,304	84.0	10.6
Prekindergarten and kindergarten teachers	299	96.5	15.7
Secondary school teachers	1,154	51.6	8.8
Teachers except college and university, n.e.c	224	75.9	4.5
Engineering and science technicians	985	13.4	7.5
Chemical technicians	76	21.1	6.6
Drafters	296	11.1	5.4
Electrical and electronic engineering technicians	227	7.9	11.0
Surveyors	82	2.4	2.4
Technicians, except health, engineering and science	173	17.3	5.8
Airplane pilots	69	1.4	1.4
Radio operators	53	47.2	9.4
Vocational and educational counselors	171	52.6	14.6
Writers, artists, and entertainers	1,193	35.5	5.1
Athletes and kindred workers	101	40.6	4.0
Designers	161	27.3	6.8
Editors and reporters	184	42.4	4.9
Musicians and composers	149	30.9	7.4
Painters and sculptors	186	44.6	2.2
Photographers	93	14.0	5.4
Public relations specialists and publicity writers	131	40.5	4.6
Research workers, not specified	122	32.0	10.7
All other professional and technical workers	54	37.0	11.1
Managers and administrators, except farm	10,105	23.4	5.0
Bank officials and financial managers	573	30.4	4.4
Buyers and purchasing agents	370	30.5	4.6
Buyers, wholesale and retail trade	170	40.0	5.3
Credit and collection managers	49	36.7	2.0
Health administrators	184	46.2	7.6
White-collar workers—Continued			
Managers and administrators—Continued			
Inspectors, except construction and public administration	98	15.3	7.1
Managers and superintendents, building	157	50.3	6.4
Office managers, n.e.c	370	65.1	2.4
Officials and administrators; public administration n.e.c.	420	24.8	9.0
Officials of lodges, societies, and unions	121	27.3	7.4
Restaurant, cafeteria, and bar managers	589	33.8	8.7
Sales managers and department heads, retail trade	343	37.3	5.0
Sales managers, except retail trade	330	7.0	1.9
School administrators, college	108	32.4	10.7
School administrators, elementary and secondary	275	35.6	12.4
All other managers and administrators	6,118	16.6	4.2
Sales workers	5,951	44.8	5.0
Advertising agents and sales workers	96	35.4	2.1
Demonstrators	96	94.8	4.2
Hucksters and peddlers	203	80.8	5.4
Insurance agents, brokers, and underwriters	548	20.3	6.8
Newspaper carriers and vendors	93	29.0	6.5
Real estate agents and brokers	555	45.0	2.7
Stock and bond sales agents	109	.2	3.7
Sales workers and sales clerks, n.e.c	4,247	46.4	5.2
Sales representatives, manufacturing industries	386	14.5	3.1
Sales representatives, wholesale trade	840	9.4	3.8
Sales clerks, retail trade	2,338	71.5	6.4
Sales workers, except clerks, retail trade	513	17.5	2.9
Sales workers, services and construction	169	43.2	7.7
Clerical workers	16,904	79.6	10.5
Bank tellers	449	91.5	8.0
Billing clerks	168	88.1	7.7
Bookkeepers	1,830	90.7	5.0
Cashiers	1,403	87.1	10.6
Clerical supervisors, n.e.c	204	63.2	11.3
Collectors, bill and account	78	57.7	11.5
Counter clerks, except food	377	77.2	10.1
Dispatchers and starters, vehicle	97	30.9	9.3
Enumerators and interviewers	53	75.5	15.9
Estimators and investigators, n.e.c	451	53.4	11.2
Expediters and production controllers	224	32.1	8.0
File clerks	273	85.7	23.4
Insurance adjusters, examiners, and investigators	169	51.5	11.2
Library attendants and assistants	172	80.8	11.0
Mail carriers, post office	256	11.7	9.4
Mail handlers, except post office	162	49.4	19.1
Messengers and office helpers	87	28.7	20.7
Office machine operators	827	74.2	15.4
Bookkeeping and billing machine operators	45	86.7	13.3
Computer and peripheral equipment operators	393	58.3	13.2
Key punch operators	273	95.6	18.3
Payroll and timekeeping clerks	241	75.5	7.1
Postal clerks	267	32.2	24.7
Receptionists	588	96.9	9.5
Secretaries	3,590	99.2	6.2
Secretaries, legal	162	99.4	3.1
Secretaries, medical	83	98.8	7.2
Secretaries, n.e.c	3,345	99.2	6.3
Shipping and receiving clerks	461	22.8	14.8
Statistical clerks	377	76.1	11.1
Stenographers	94	90.4	10.6
Stock clerks and storekeepers	507	31.2	12.8
Teachers aides, except school monitors	342	92.1	11.4
Telephone operators	311	94.2	12.5
Ticket, station, and express agents	128	40.6	11.7
Typists	1,044	96.6	16.2
All other clerical workers	1,674	41.9	14.3
Blue-collar workers	31,531	18.3	12.4
Craft and kindred workers	12,386	5.6	7.5
Carpenters	1,253	1.0	5.3
Brickmasons and stonemasons	204	--	15.2
Cement and concrete finishers	83	--	36.1
Electricians	590	.8	4.4
Excavating, grading, and road machinery operators	425	--	8.5
Painters, construction and maintenance	484	5.2	9.1

(Numbers in thousands)

Occupations	1978 Total employed	Percent of total — Females	Percent of total — Black and other
Blue-collar workers—Continued			
Craft and kindred workers—Continued			
Plumbers and pipefitters	428	.7	7.0
Structural metal craft workers	78	--	3.8
Roofers and slaters	114	.9	10.5
Blue-collar worker supervisors, n.e.c	1,671	9.9	7.0
Machinists and job setters	591	3.0	6.6
Job and die setters, metal	98	3.1	7.1
Machinists	493	3.1	6.5
Metal craft workers, excluding mechanics, machinists, and job setters	622	2.7	6.8
Millwrights	95	--	4.2
Molders, metal	54	13.0	20.4
Sheetmetal workers and tinsmiths	153	1.3	5.2
Tool and die makers	182	1.1	2.2
Mechanics, automobiles	1,209	.6	8.9
Automobile body repairers	184	1.1	9.8
Automobile mechanics	1,024	.6	8.7
Mechanics, except automobiles	2,126	2.0	6.6
Air conditioning, heating, and refrigeration mechanics	210	1.0	4.8
Aircraft mechanics	132	3.0	8.3
Data processing machine repairers	63	4.8	7.9
Farm implement mechanics	62	--	3.2
Heavy equipment mechanics, including diesel	950	1.6	6.5
Household appliance and accessory installers and mechanics	145	2.1	8.3
Office machine repairers	63	1.6	11.1
Radio and television repairers	131	3.1	5.3
Railroad and car shop mechanics	49	--	14.3
Printing craft workers	417	21.8	7.9
Compositors and typesetters	181	28.7	9.4
Printing press operators	169	10.1	7.7
Bakers	128	48.4	10.2
Cabinetmakers	78	2.6	5.1
Carpet installers	68	1.5	7.4
Crane, derrick, and hoist operators	156	2.6	16.7
Decorators and window dressers	125	70.4	6.4
Electric power line and cable installers and repairers	111	.9	3.6
Inspectors, n.e.c	139	8.6	11.5
Locomotive engineers	54	1.9	3.7
Stationary engineers	179	1.1	6.7
Tailors	45	31.1	11.1
Telephone installers and repairers	297	6.7	5.4
Telephone line installers and repairers	77	2.6	3.9
Upholsterers	59	23.7	11.9
All other craft workers	575	15.3	8.0
Operatives, except transport	10,875	39.7	15.0
Assemblers	1,164	52.1	16.4
Bottling and canning operatives	56	44.6	17.9
Checkers, examiners, and inspectors; manufacturing	736	48.8	11.8
Clothing ironers and pressers	126	80.2	42.9
Cutting operatives, n.e.c	263	31.9	14.4
Dressmakers, except factory	116	97.4	12.1
Drillers, earth	51	3.9	5.9
Dry wall installers and lathers	105	1.0	10.5
Filers, polishers, sanders, and buffers	129	29.5	12.4
Furnace tenders, smelters, and pourers, metal	61	4.9	24.6
Garage workers and gas station attendants	416	4.8	9.4
Laundry and dry cleaning operatives, n.e.c	174	67.8	26.4
Meat cutters and butchers, except manufacturing	204	6.4	9.8
Meat cutters and butchers, manufacturing	114	28.9	19.3
Mine operatives, n.e.c	177	2.3	5.1
Mixing operatives	85	3.5	20.0
Packers and wrappers, excluding meat and produce	675	62.5	17.6
Painters, manufactured articles	182	14.8	13.7
Photographic process workers	96	50.0	12.5
Precision machine operatives	386	11.1	7.5
Drill press operatives	64	23.4	7.8
Grinding machine operatives	129	7.8	8.5
Lathe and milling machine operatives	125	8.8	5.6
Punch and stamping press operatives	156	30.1	14.7
Sawyers	138	10.1	17.4
Sewers and stitchers	814	94.8	17.4

Occupations	1978 Total employed	Percent of total — Females	Percent of total — Black and other
Blue-collar workers—Continued			
Operatives, except transport—Continued			
Shoemaking machine operatives	78	76.9	7.7
Furnace tenders and stokers, except metal	71	1.4	14.1
Textile operatives	374	59.9	25.7
Spinners, twisters, and winders	151	66.2	29.1
Welders and flame cutters	679	6.0	11.0
Winding operatives, n.e.c	68	54.4	13.2
All other operatives, except transport	3,181	33.4	14.8
Transport equipment operatives	3,541	7.3	14.9
Busdrivers	337	45.1	21.1
Delivery and route workers	579	6.6	8.1
Fork lift and tow motor operatives	363	2.8	19.8
Railroad switch operators	52	--	9.6
Taxicab drivers and chauffeurs	172	9.9	24.4
Truck drivers	1,923	1.9	13.9
All other transport equipment operatives	115	2.6	20.0
Nonfarm laborers	4,729	10.4	17.7
Animal caretakers	83	51.8	9.6
Construction laborers including carpenters' helpers	953	2.7	18.6
Freight and material handlers	798	8.5	19.9
Garbage collectors	79	5.1	32.9
Gardeners and grounds keepers, except farm	614	5.9	17.1
Timber cutting and logging workers	90	1.1	26.7
Stockhandlers	915	23.5	10.9
Vehicle washers and equipment cleaners	199	12.6	17.6
Warehouse laborers, n.e.c	262	4.2	14.9
All other nonfarm laborers	736	8.4	22.0
Service workers	12,839	62.6	19.8
Private households	1,162	97.7	33.0
Child care workers	486	98.1	7.6
Cleaners and servants	530	97.0	52.5
Housekeepers	118	99.2	44.1
Service workers, except private households	11,677	59.1	18.5
Cleaning workers	2,430	35.3	28.1
Lodging quarters cleaners	179	97.2	40.8
Building interior cleaners, n.e.c	862	53.6	32.3
Janitors and sextons	1,389	16.0	24.0
Food service workers	4,283	68.9	13.7
Bartenders	282	39.4	6.4
Waiters' assistants	215	20.9	13.5
Cooks	1,186	57.2	20.2
Dishwashers	240	34.2	17.1
Food counter and fountain workers	463	85.7	11.4
Waiters	1,383	90.5	7.2
Food service workers, n.e.c	514	74.7	20.6
Health service workers	1,846	89.9	23.6
Dental assistants	130	98.5	3.8
Health aides, excluding nursing	276	86.2	19.6
Nursing aides, orderlies, and attendants	1,037	87.0	27.6
Practical nurses	402	97.0	22.4
Personal service workers	1,760	74.0	15.3
Attendants	306	57.2	13.1
Barbers	121	9.1	14.0
Child care workers	425	94.8	15.3
Hairdressers and cosmetologists	542	89.1	9.2
Housekeepers, excluding private households	135	68.1	19.3
Welfare service aides	96	87.5	34.4
Protective service workers	1,358	8.5	13.5
Fire fighters	221	.5	7.2
Guards	548	9.7	20.1
Police and detectives	475	5.9	9.9
Sheriffs and bailiffs	60	5.0	5.0
Farm workers	2,798	18.2	9.2
Farmers and farm managers	1,480	8.9	3.4
Farmers (owners and tenants)	1,445	8.9	3.5
Farm laborers and supervisors	1,318	28.6	15.7
Farm laborers, wage workers	972	17.2	20.2
Farm laborers, unpaid family workers	299	69.6	2.7

NOTE: N.E.C. is an abbreviation for "not elsewhere classified" and designates broad categories of occupations which cannot be more specifically identified.

EMPLOYED PERSONS BY DETAILED INDUSTRY, SEX, AND RACE
(Numbers in thousands)

Industries	Total employed (1978)	Percent of total — Females	Percent of total — Black and other
Total, 16 years and over	94,373	41.2	11.2
Agriculture, forestry, and fisheries	3,501	19.6	9.2
Agricultural production	2,850	18.9	9.0
Agricultural services, except horticultural	245	40.8	8.2
Horticultural services	247	8.5	12.6
Forestry	87	21.8	5.7
Fisheries	73	8.2	13.7
Mining	828	11.7	3.9
Metal mining	93	7.5	2.2
Coal mining	226	3.1	1.8
Crude petroleum and natural gas extraction	381	18.1	4.2
Nonmetallic mining and quarrying, except fuel	128	10.9	8.6
Construction	6,043	6.8	8.1
General building contractors	1,762	6.0	7.4
General contractors, except building	1,106	7.1	10.4
Special trade contractors	2,858	7.0	7.2
Not specified construction	316	9.8	11.4
Manufacturing	21,497	30.5	11.2
Durable goods	12,821	24.2	10.7
Lumber and wood products, except furniture	724	12.0	17.4
Logging	165	3.0	27.9
Sawmills, planing mills, and mill work	428	12.1	13.3
Miscellaneous wood products	130	23.1	17.7
Furniture and fixtures	554	31.0	9.9
Stone, clay, and glass products	679	20.5	13.0
Glass and glass products	223	32.3	14.8
Cement, concrete, gypsum, and plaster products	240	7.9	13.3
Miscellaneous nonmetallic mineral and stone products	147	21.1	8.8
Primary metal industries	1,220	11.5	14.2
Blast furnaces, steelworks, rolling and finishing mills	467	7.7	13.1
Other primary iron and steel industries	340	10.6	17.4
Primary aluminum industries	188	14.9	9.0
Other primary nonferrous industries	224	18.3	16.5
Fabricated metal products	1,444	20.7	9.4
Cutlery, hand tools and other hardware	158	32.9	8.9
Fabricated structural metal products	531	14.7	8.9
Screw machine products	100	26.0	7.0
Metal stamping	177	24.3	8.5
Miscellaneous fabricated metal products	476	21.2	10.9
Machinery, except electrical	2,485	18.7	6.2
Engines and turbines	117	15.4	4.3
Farm machinery and equipment	174	16.7	8.0
Construction and material handling machines	391	12.5	6.1
Metalworking machinery	356	16.3	3.4
Office and accounting machines	121	26.4	8.3
Electronic computing equipment	333	31.2	8.7
Machinery, except electrical, n.e.c	991	17.8	6.0
Electrical machinery, equipment, and supplies	2,144	41.5	9.9
Household appliances	177	37.9	7.9
Radio, T.V., and communication equipment	553	39.1	11.0
Electrical machinery, equipment, and supplies, n.e.c	1,409	42.9	9.7
Transportation equipment	2,230	15.1	13.7
Motor vehicles and motor vehicle equipment	1,247	15.9	15.1
Aircraft and parts	560	16.6	7.7
Ship and boat building and repairing	265	8.7	22.6
Mobile dwellings and campers	78	15.4	2.6
Professional and photographic equipment, and watches	560	42.5	7.1
Scientific and controlling instruments	160	40.6	5.6
Optical and health services supplies	231	51.5	6.9
Photographic equipment and supplies	137	26.3	8.0
Ordnance	190	24.2	7.4
Miscellaneous manufacturing industries	591	48.4	10.7
Nondurable goods industries	8,676	39.8	12.0
Food and kindred products	1,874	28.8	13.1
Meat products	423	30.7	16.3
Dairy products	211	15.2	7.1
Canning and preserving fruits, vegetables, and seafood	271	46.9	14.0
Grain-mill products	142	24.6	9.2
Bakery products	273	26.4	11.7
Confectionery and related products	94	55.3	20.2
Beverage industries	255	15.3	11.4
Miscellaneous food preparation and kindred products	203	25.1	14.3

Industries	Total employed (1978)	Percent of total — Females	Percent of total — Black and other
Nondurable goods industries—Continued			
Tobacco manufactures	73	31.5	30.1
Textile mill products	871	47.0	17.8
Knitting mills	196	64.3	10.2
Yarn, thread, and fabric mills	514	44.6	21.2
Miscellaneous textile mill products	60	38.3	13.3
Apparel and other fabricated textile products	1,285	77.4	16.4
Apparel and accessories	1,128	79.6	16.7
Miscellaneous fabricated textile products	157	61.8	14.6
Paper and allied products	705	22.8	10.2
Pulp, paper, and paperboard mills	291	12.0	7.2
Miscellaneous paper and pulp products	209	34.4	12.0
Paperboard containers and boxes	205	26.8	12.7
Printing, publishing, and allied industries	1,429	39.0	6.6
Newspaper publishing and printing	469	37.7	4.9
Printing, publishing, and allied industries, except newspapers	960	39.7	7.5
Chemicals and allied products	1,189	24.1	11.2
Industrial chemicals	434	14.7	9.7
Plastics, synthetics and resins, except fibers	87	17.2	9.2
Synthetic fibers	80	26.3	12.5
Drugs and medicines	185	38.4	10.8
Soaps and cosmetics	143	42.0	11.2
Paints, varnishes, and related products	75	20.0	14.7
Agricultural chemicals	68	20.6	20.6
Miscellaneous chemicals	116	22.4	10.3
Petroleum and coal products	242	17.4	10.3
Petroleum refining	209	17.7	9.6
Rubber and miscellaneous plastic products	708	36.3	8.2
Rubber products	328	26.2	7.9
Miscellaneous plastic products	379	45.1	8.4
Leather and leather products	283	62.5	9.2
Footwear, except rubber	189	69.8	7.4
Leather products, except footwear	68	58.8	5.9
Transportation, communications, and other public utilities	6,162	23.4	12.3
Transportation	3,548	18.7	12.7
Railroads and railway express service	582	6.7	10.5
Street railways and bus lines	506	36.2	21.7
Taxicab service	121	9.1	28.9
Trucking service	1,343	9.7	9.5
Warehousing and storage	159	24.5	12.6
Water transportation	177	11.9	17.5
Air transportation	468	28.4	12.0
Services incidental to transportation	177	58.8	5.1
Communications	1,311	44.8	11.2
Radio broadcasting and television	185	29.2	10.8
Telephone (wire and radio)	1,065	48.3	11.5
Telegraph and miscellaneous communications services	60	33.3	8.3
Utilities and sanitary services	1,303	14.7	12.2
Electric light and power	510	14.5	9.6
Electric-gas utilities	171	17.0	8.8
Gas and steam supply systems	170	21.2	8.2
Water supply	165	17.6	10.9
Sanitary services	244	4.9	25.0
Wholesale and retail trade	19,253	45.5	8.1
Wholesale trade	3,616	24.9	7.2
Motor vehicles and equipment	267	21.3	6.4
Drugs, chemicals, and allied products	194	26.8	6.2
Dry goods and apparel	91	40.7	8.4
Food and related products	557	22.4	10.8
Farm products—raw materials	122	22.1	4.9
Electrical goods	224	28.1	6.3
Hardware, plumbing, and heating supplies	157	24.2	6.4
Machinery equipment and supplies	770	24.7	4.9
Metals and minerals, n.e.c	107	21.5	6.5
Petroleum products	169	21.3	6.5
Scrap and waste materials	110	10.9	13.6
Alcoholic beverages	108	17.6	8.3
Paper and its products	105	24.8	4.8
Lumber and construction materials	149	18.8	7.4
Wholesalers, n.e.c	479	34.2	7.9
Retail trade	15,636	50.3	8.4
Lumber and building material retailing	461	21.5	7.2
Hardware and farm equipment stores	297	29.3	3.7
Department and mail order establishments	2,030	68.4	9.8

See footnotes at end of table.

EMPLOYED PERSONS BY DETAILED INDUSTRY, SEX, AND RACE (*Continued*)
(Numbers in thousands)

Industries	Total employed (1978)	Percent of total — Females	Percent of total — Black and other	Industries	Total employed (1978)	Percent of total — Females	Percent of total — Black and other
Wholesale and retail trade—Continued				Service industries—Continued			
Retail trade—Continued				Business and repair services—Continued			
Limited price variety stores	160	76.9	8.1	Automobile services, except repair	200	23.0	15.0
Vending machine operators	76	39.5	6.6	Automobile repair and related services	672	8.3	9.4
Direct selling establishments	350	71.1	5.1	Electrical repair shops	137	12.4	2.9
Miscellaneous general merchandise stores	218	71.1	6.9	Miscellaneous repair services	353	13.0	6.5
Grocery stores	2,055	42.8	8.7	Personal services	3,826	74.4	21.5
Dairy products stores	62	62.9	9.7	Private households	1,396	87.2	31.1
Retail bakeries	140	65.7	5.0	Hotels and motels	693	61.2	22.1
Food stores, n.e.c.	168	48.2	9.5	Lodging places, except hotels and motels	382	30.9	9.4
Motor vehicle dealers	953	15.8	5.8	Laundering, cleaning, and other garment services	363	63.6	26.4
Tire, battery, and accessory dealers	294	16.0	5.4	Beauty shops	553	89.0	9.2
Gasoline service stations	622	12.5	6.3	Barber shops	122	12.3	13.9
Miscellaneous vehicle dealers	126	19.8	.8	Dressmaking shops	41	97.6	7.3
Apparel and accessory stores, except shoe stores	674	76.6	8.8	Miscellaneous personal services	252	45.2	9.9
Shoe stores	132	45.5	5.3	Entertainment and recreation services	1,018	37.3	8.2
Furniture and home furnishings stores	463	32.8	5.6	Theaters and motion pictures	324	32.1	6.8
Household appliances, T.V., and radio stores	293	28.0	4.8	Bowling alleys, billiard and pool parlors	82	40.2	6.1
Eating and drinking places	4,015	60.7	11.2	Miscellaneous entertainment and recreation services	612	39.7	9.2
Drug stores	473	59.8	7.4	Professional and related services	18,327	65.1	13.3
Liquor stores	138	29.0	12.3	Offices of physicians	753	67.2	4.8
Farm and garden supply stores	158	25.9	1.9	Offices of dentists	360	67.2	3.3
Jewelry stores	133	57.9	6.0	Hospitals	3,781	75.8	19.4
Fuel and ice dealers	102	19.6	3.9	Convalescent institutions	1,009	88.1	19.2
Retail florists	148	66.2	4.1	Offices of health practitioners, n.e.c.	83	57.8	--
Miscellaneous retail stores	883	57.4	6.9	Health services, n.e.c.	687	68.9	15.1
				Legal services	650	48.5	2.6
Finance, insurance, and real estate	5,406	55.6	9.0	Elementary and secondary schools	5,180	70.6	13.2
Banking	1,442	70.9	10.3	Colleges and universities	1,996	49.1	11.4
Credit agencies	441	65.1	7.0	Libraries	167	81.4	11.4
Security, commodity brokerage, and investment companies	270	36.3	5.6	Educational services, n.e.c.	277	67.1	10.1
Insurance	1,776	53.8	9.1	Museums, art galleries, and zoos	67	47.8	9.0
Real estate, including real estate-insurance-law offices	1,478	43.3	8.6	Religious organizations	618	42.4	8.4
				Welfare services	788	70.9	23.5
Service industries	31,682	56.6	14.1	Residential welfare facilities	119	60.5	20.2
Business and repair services	3,490	30.7	10.3	Nonprofit membership organizations	464	53.0	11.6
Advertising	173	39.3	3.5	Engineering and architectural services	469	18.8	5.1
Services to dwellings and other buildings	348	34.5	23.0	Accounting, auditing, and bookkeeping services	445	44.9	3.6
Commercial research, development, and testing labs	157	25.5	7.6	Miscellaneous professional and related services	370	42.4	5.4
Employment and temporary help agencies	188	70.7	16.0				
Business management and consulting services	268	51.5	6.0	Public administration	5,020	33.6	15.5
Computer programming services	156	40.4	7.7	Postal service	700	22.6	20.0
Detective and protective services	213	13.1	18.3	Federal public administration	1,601	36.7	17.4
Business services, n.e.c.	623	50.7	7.1	State public administration	882	39.0	11.6
				Local public administration	1,838	32.6	14.0

NOTE: N.E.C. is an abbreviation for "not elsewhere classified" and designates broad categories of occupations which cannot be more specifically identified.

Effective wage adjustments going into effect in major collective bargaining units, 1972 to date

[In percent]

Sector and measure	Average annual changes						Average quarterly changes							
	1972	1973	1974	1975	1976	1977	1976	1977				1978ᵖ		
							IV	I	II	III	IV	I	II	III
Total effective wage rate adjustment, all industries	6.6	7.0	9.4	8.7	8.1	8.0	1.5	1.2	2.9	2.7	1.1	1.3	2.6	2.5
Change resulting from—														
Current settlement	1.7	3.0	4.8	2.8	3.2	3.0	.9	.3	1.0	1.3	.5	.5	.6	.5
Prior settlement	4.2	2.7	2.6	3.7	3.2	3.2	.4	.5	1.4	1.0	.3	.6	1.4	1.1
Escalator provision	.7	1.3	1.9	2.2	1.6	1.7	.3	.3	.6	.5	.3	.3	.5	.9
Manufacturing	5.6	7.3	10.3	8.5	8.5	8.4	2.4	1.2	2.9	2.7	1.4	1.4	2.1	2.7
Nonmanufacturing	7.4	6.7	8.6	8.9	7.7	7.6	.8	1.1	2.9	2.7	.8	1.3	2.9	2.4

NOTE: Because of rounding and compounding, the sums of individual items may not equal totals.

Work stoppages, 1947 to date

Month and year	Number of stoppages		Workers involved		Days idle	
	Beginning in month or year	In effect during month	Beginning in month or year (thousands)	In effect during month (thousands)	Number (thousands)	Percent of estimated working time
1947	3,693		2,170		34,600	.30
1948	3,419		1,960		34,100	.28
1949	3,606		3,030		50,500	.44
1950	4,843		2,410		38,800	.33
1951	4,737		2,220		22,900	.18
1952	5,117		3,540		59,100	.48
1953	5,091		2,400		28,300	.22
1954	3,468		1,530		22,600	.18
1955	4,320		2,650		28,200	.22
1956	3,825		1,900		33,100	.24
1957	3,673		1,390		16,500	.12
1958	3,694		2,060		23,900	.18
1959	3,708		1,880		69,000	.50
1960	3,333		1,320		19,100	.14
1961	3,367		1,450		16,300	.11
1962	3,614		1,230		18,600	.13
1963	3,362		941		16,100	.11
1964	3,655		1,640		22,900	.15
1965	3,963		1,550		23,300	.15
1966	4,405		1,960		25,400	.15
1967	4,595		2,870		42,100	.25
1968	5,045		2,649		49,018	.28
1969	5,700		2,481		42,869	.24
1970	5,716		3,305		66,414	.37
1971	5,138		3,280		47,589	.26
1972	5,010		1,714		27,066	.15
1973	5,353		2,251		27,948	.14
1974	6,074		2,778		47,991	.24
1975	5,031		1,746		31,237	.16
1976	5,648		2,420		37,859	.19
1977	5,506		2,040		35,822	.17
1977: December	133	485	200	308	5,029	.28
1978: January	217		62		5,286	.30
February	247		45		4,802	.30
March	287		90		4,842	.25
April	395		118		2,097	.12
May	484		130		2,670	.14
June	475		114		2,579	.13
July	467		177		3,071	.18
August	439		198		3,714	.18
September	453		448		4,446	.25
October	389		106		2,277	.12
November	290		63		1,776	.10
December	157		49		1,440	.08

Hours and Earnings

STATISTICS ON COMPENSATION CHANGES

Definition of Terms

Average hourly compensation—The series measures changes in wages and salaries plus supplements (according to National Income Accounts definitions) per hour paid for. Data for all persons in the private business sector include compensation of employees and imputed labor compensation of self-employed. Data for employees in the nonfarm business sector include employees of government enterprises. Data in 1967 dollars adjust current-dollar series for price changes.

Average hourly and weekly earnings—The basic series consist of regular hourly or weekly payroll expenditures before deductions, that is, straight-time earnings plus premium and incentive pay. Weekly earnings in 1967 dollars adjust earnings for price changes, while real spendable earnings adjust for price and Federal income and social security tax changes. Data for the private nonfarm economy cover production and related workers in mining and manufacturing, construction workers in contract construction, and nonsupervisory workers in all other industries; data for Federal executive branch employees include supervisory and nonsupervisory employees.

Hourly Earnings Index—This series adjusts average hourly earnings data (as described above) to exclude effects of two types of changes that are unrelated to underlying wage-rate developments: Fluctuations in overtime premiums in manufacturing (the only sector for which overtime data are available) and the effects of changes in the proportion of workers in high-wage and low-wage industries. In addition, the seasonal adjustment eliminates the effect of changes that normally occur at the same time and in about the same magnitude each year.

Union scales, building trades—Underlying data consist of wage rates and selected benefits as of the first workday in January, April, July, and October paid to unionized workers in seven building trades in continental cities of 100,000 population or more: Bricklayers, laborers, carpenters, electricians, painters, plasterers, and plumbers. Compensation is, in the case of "hourly wage rates," minimum wage rates (excluding premium pay for overtime, or for work on weekends, holidays, or late shifts) agreed upon in collective bargaining; in the case of "wages and selected benefits," it is wage rates, as defined above, plus employer payments to health and welfare, pension, and vacation funds.

Wage rates, hired farm labor—Data refer to wages paid during the week which includes January 12, April 12, July 12, and October 12. The series covers cash payments to workers and excludes perquisites such as room or board. Hired farmworkers are defined as those working only for wages for 1 hour or more on farm during the survey week. The data are obtained by the U.S. Department of Agriculture and are published by the agency (without seasonal adjustment) in *Farm Labor*.

Employment Cost Index—The statistics are changes in straight-time average hourly earnings between the survey periods including the 12th of the months of March, June, September, and December. These statistics are computed from occupational wage and salary data collected from a sample of approximately 2,000 respondents, representing with certain exclusions (such as, self-employed and private household workers), the occupational employment composition of the private nonfarm economy. The occupational pay for this sample of respondents, matched every quarter, is weighted up into industry averages, using essentially employment weights derived from, a 1974 survey. These industry pay averages are aggregated with fixed employment weights from the 1970 census, and compared over successive quarters. The percent changes are thus free of the effect of employment shifts among industries, occupations, and establishments.

They are not annualized or adjusted for seasonal influences. Data on the cost of benefits, as well as wages and salaries, will be added in the future. Work is also under way to extend the measure to include the public as well as the private sector.

Average wage-rate adjustments effective in major collective bargaining units—Data refer to general wage-rate adjustments made effective during reference period under private nonfarm industry bargaining agreements covering 1,000 workers or more. The data combine newly negotiated adjustments, those negotiated earlier, and cost-of-living escalator adjustments. Wage-rate changes are expressed as a percent of straight-time hourly earnings. Average adjustments are affected by workers receiving no change as well as by those receiving increases or decreases. Averages are worker-weighted, and all workers affected by an action are entered at the average for the group. The data are limited to production and related workers in manufacturing and to nonsupervisory workers in nonmanufacturing industries.

Wage and benefit adjustments, major collective bargaining settlements—Data apply to private nonfarm industry collective bargaining settlements affecting 1,000 workers or more (5,000 workers or more for wages and benefits). They are further limited to production and related workers in manufacturing and to nonsupervisory workers in nonmanufacturing industries. Measures are recorded in the quarter in which the settlement was reached regardless of effective dates of adjustment. Changes over the life of agreements refer to total agreed-upon changes, expressed as an average annual rate of change. First-year adjustments refer to changes to go into effect within the first 12 months after the effective date of agreement. Wage-rate changes are expressed as a percent of straight-time hourly earnings, while wage and benefit (package) changes are expressed as a percent of total compensation, including legally required employer contributions for social insurance. Averages are worker-weighted, and all workers affected by an action are entered at the average for the group. Data cover all settlements, including those increasing, decreasing, and making no change in pay.

Wage-rate increases in manufacturing—Data apply to decisions in manufacturing industry establishments that make general wage changes and are limited to production and related workers. Changes shown are the general wage-rate increases to go into effect within 12 months of the decision date and are recorded in the quarter of decision.

Wage-rate changes are expressed as a percent of straight-time hourly earnings. Averages are worker weighted, and all workers affected by an action are entered at the average for the group. Data average only decisions to increase wages.

Earnings changes, selected occupational groups in metropolitan areas—The percent increases presented are based on changes in average straight-time hourly earnings for establishments reporting the trend jobs in both the current and previous year. The trends are not affected by changes in average earnings resulting from employment shifts among establishments or turnover of establishments included in survey samples, but they are affected by hirings, layoffs, and employee turnover within establishments that have a range of wage rates for individual jobs. The data are based on the Bureau's annual surveys of earnings in over 75 Standard Metropolitan Statistical Areas for selected occupations common to six broad industry groups. Establishments employing 50 workers or more are studied in manufacturing; transportation, communication, and other public utilities; wholesale trade; retail trade; finance, insurance, and real estate; and selected services. In 13 of the largest areas, the minimum is 100 workers in manufacturing; transportation, communication, and other public utilities; and retail trade. Dashes indicate no data or data that do not meet publication criteria.

SELECTED OVERALL MEASURES OF COMPENSATION (ANNUAL DATA)

Measure	1967	1968	1969	1970	1971	1972	1973	1974	1975	1976	1977
In dollars											
Average hourly earnings, private nonfarm sector[1]											
Current dollars	$2.68	$2.85	$3.04	$3.23	$3.45	$3.70	$3.94	$4.24	$4.53	$4.86	$5.24
1967 dollars	2.68	2.74	2.77	2.78	2.84	2.95	2.96	2.87	2.81	2.85	2.89
Average weekly earnings, private nonfarm sector[1]											
Current dollars	101.84	107.73	114.61	119.83	127.31	136.90	145.39	154.76	163.53	175.45	188.64
1967 dollars	101.84	103.39	104.38	103.04	104.95	109.26	109.23	104.78	101.45	102.90	103.93
Spendable average weekly earnings, private nonfarm sector (worker and 3 dependents):[1]											
Current dollars	90.86	95.28	99.99	104.90	112.43	121.68	127.38	134.61	145.65	155.87	169.66
1967 dollars	90.86	91.44	91.07	90.20	92.69	97.11	95.70	91.14	90.35	91.42	93.48
Indexes, 1967=100											
Average hourly compensation:											
All persons, private business sector:											
Current dollars	100.0	107.6	114.9	123.1	131.4	139.7	151.1	164.8	181.2	197.0	213.0
1967 dollars	100.0	103.2	104.7	105.8	108.3	111.5	113.5	111.6	112.4	115.5	117.4
All employees, nonfarm business sector:											
Current dollars	100.0	107.2	114.1	121.6	129.9	138.2	149.0	162.4	178.6	193.3	209.0
1967 dollars	100.0	102.9	103.9	104.5	107.1	110.3	112.0	110.0	110.8	113.4	115.1
Hourly Earnings Index[1]											
Current dollars	100.0	106.2	113.2	120.7	129.2	137.5	146.0	157.5	170.7	183.0	196.8
1967 dollars	100.0	101.9	103.1	103.8	106.5	109.7	109.7	106.6	105.9	107.3	108.4

[1] Production and nonsupervisory workers.

SELECTED OVERALL MEASURES OF COMPENSATION (MONTHLY DATA, UNLESS OTHERWISE NOTED)

Measure	1977		1978										
	Nov.	Dec.	Jan.	Feb.	Mar.	Apr.	May	June	July	Aug.	Sept.	Oct. [P]	Nov. [P]
Data before seasonal adjustment													
In dollars													
Average hourly earnings, private nonfarm sector[1]													
Current dollars	$5.40	$5.40	$5.47	$5.49	$5.52	$5.59	$5.62	$5.65	$5.69	$5.71	$5.82	$5.86	$5.87
1967 dollars	2.91	2.90	2.92	2.91	2.91	2.92	2.91	2.89	2.89	2.89	2.92	2.92	(*)
Average weekly earnings, private nonfarm sector[1]													
Current dollars	193.86	195.48	192.00	193.80	197.62	200.12	200.63	204.53	206.55	206.70	209.52	210.37	210.15
1967 dollars	104.56	105.04	102.62	102.87	104.18	104.56	103.79	104.73	105.01	104.55	105.23	104.82	(*)
Spendable average weekly earnings, private nonfarm sector (worker and 3 dependents):[1]													
Current dollars	176.53	177.80	171.86	173.25	176.16	178.03	178.41	181.34	182.85	182.96	185.08	185.71	185.55
1967 dollars	95.22	95.54	91.85	91.96	92.86	93.01	92.30	92.85	92.96	92.54	92.96	92.53	(*)
Indexes, 1967=100													
Hourly Earnings Index[1]													
Current dollars	202.1	203.2	206.1	206.5	207.3	209.5	210.3	211.3	213.3	213.7	216.6	217.9	218.5
1967 dollars	109.0	109.2	110.2	109.6	109.3	109.4	108.8	108.2	108.4	108.1	108.8	108.6	(*)
Data after seasonal adjustment													
In dollars													
Average hourly earnings, private nonfarm sector[1]													
Current dollars	$5.39	$5.41	$5.46	$5.49	$5.54	$5.61	$5.62	$5.66	$5.71	$5.73	$5.77	$5.82	$5.86
1967 dollars	2.91	2.91	3.01	2.91	2.91	2.90	2.90	2.90	2.91	2.90	2.90	2.90	(*)
Average weekly earnings, private nonfarm sector[1]													
Current dollars	194.04	194.22	193.83	195.99	199.44	202.52	201.76	203.19	204.99	205.13	206.57	208.36	210.37
1967 dollars	104.77	104.42	103.38	103.86	104.86	105.59	104.21	104.04	104.43	103.92	103.91	103.97	(*)
Spendable average weekly earnings, private nonfarm sector (worker and 3 dependents):[1]													
Current dollars	176.67	176.81	173.27	174.93	177.52	179.83	179.26	180.33	181.68	181.78	182.86	184.21	185.71
1967 dollars	95.39	95.06	92.41	92.70	93.33	93.76	92.59	92.33	92.55	92.09	91.98	91.92	(*)
Indexes, 1967=100													
Average hourly compensation (quarterly data):													
All persons, private business sector:													
Current dollars	218.8	–	–	225.2	–	–	229.6	–	–	235.3	–	–	(*)
1967 dollars	118.2	–	–	119.3	–	–	118.6	–	–	119.0	–	–	(*)
All employees, nonfarm business sector:													
Current dollars	214.6	–	–	220.9	–	–	225.3	–	–	230.4	–	–	(*)
1967 dollars	115.9	–	–	117.0	–	–	116.4	–	–	116.6	–	–	(*)
Hourly Earnings Index[1]													
Current dollars	202.4	203.5	206.0	206.6	208.3	210.3	211.0	212.3	214.1	214.6	216.2	217.9	218.9
1967 dollars	109.3	109.4	109.9	109.5	109.5	109.6	109.0	108.7	109.0	108.7	108.7	108.7	(*)

[1] Production and nonsupervisory workers.
(*) Not available.
p=preliminary.

SELECTED MEASURES OF COMPENSATION, BY INDUSTRY, CURRENT DOLLARS (ANNUAL DATA)

Measure	1967	1968	1969	1970	1971	1972	1973	1974	1975	1976	1977
In dollars											
Average hourly earnings, private nonfarm economy[1]	$2.68	$2.85	$3.04	$3.23	$3.45	$3.70	$3.94	$4.24	$4.53	$4.86	$5.24
Mining	3.19	3.35	3.60	3.85	4.06	4.44	4.74	5.23	5.95	6.46	6.94
Contract construction	4.11	4.41	4.79	5.24	5.69	6.06	6.41	6.81	7.31	7.70	8.09
Manufacturing	2.83	3.01	3.19	3.35	3.57	3.82	4.09	4.43	4.83	5.22	5.67
Transportation and public utilities	3.23	3.42	3.63	3.85	4.21	4.65	5.02	5.41	5.88	6.45	6.99
Wholesale and retail trade	2.25	2.41	2.56	2.72	2.88	3.05	3.23	3.48	3.73	3.97	4.27
Wholesale trade	2.88	3.05	3.23	3.44	3.67	3.85	4.07	4.38	4.72	5.03	5.39
Retail trade	2.01	2.16	2.30	2.44	2.57	2.75	2.91	3.14	3.36	3.57	3.85
Finance, insurance, and real estate	2.58	2.75	2.93	3.07	3.22	3.36	3.53	3.77	4.06	4.27	4.54
Services	2.29	2.42	2.61	2.81	3.04	3.27	3.47	3.75	4.02	4.31	4.65
Indexes, 1967=100											
Hourly Earnings Index, private nonfarm economy[1]	100.0	106.2	113.2	120.7	129.2	137.6	146.1	157.7	170.9	183.3	196.8
Mining	100.0	105.3	113.3	119.9	126.8	147.0	147.0	163.0	183.2	198.6	214.7
Contract construction	100.0	107.2	116.5	127.2	138.0	145.9	153.8	163.6	175.3	184.7	194.2
Manufacturing	100.0	106.1	112.4	119.4	127.3	135.4	143.6	156.0	171.4	184.6	199.4
Transportation and public utilities	100.0	105.2	111.8	118.6	129.6	142.3	153.4	165.3	179.8	196.7	213.2
Wholesale and retail trade	100.0	106.9	113.8	120.9	128.0	134.7	142.6	154.0	165.4	176.1	189.5
Wholesale trade	100.0	105.7	112.1	119.3	127.3	134.9	142.8	153.7	165.5	176.0	188.7
Retail trade	100.0	107.5	114.7	121.7	128.4	134.6	142.5	154.1	165.4	176.1	190.0
Finance, insurance, and real estate	100.0	105.8	112.2	118.9	124.5	130.0	136.5	149.9	161.2	169.9	180.7
Services	100.0	105.6	113.5	121.6	131.0	139.7	148.2	159.7	171.2	193.9	197.9
Average hourly earnings, all Federal executive branch employees	100.0	106.5	115.7	128.9	139.5	150.0	161.1	(*)	(*)	199.5	214.1

[1] Production and nonsupervisory workers.
(*) Not available.

SELECTED MEASURES OF COMPENSATION, BY INDUSTRY, CURRENT DOLLARS (MONTHLY DATA, UNLESS OTHERWISE NOTED)

Measure	1977 Nov.	1977 Dec.	1978 Jan.	Feb.	Mar.	Apr.	May	June	July	Aug.	Sept.	Oct.[P]	Nov.[P]
Data before seasonal adjustment													
In dollars													
Average hourly earnings, private nonfarm economy[1]	$5.40	$5.40	$5.47	$5.49	$5.52	$5.59	$5.62	$5.65	$5.69	$5.71	$5.82	$5.86	$5.87
Mining	7.19	6.77	6.91	6.93	6.95	7.62	7.64	7.69	7.82	7.79	7.94	7.97	8.07
Contract construction	8.26	8.29	8.34	8.32	8.40	8.39	8.52	8.56	8.63	8.72	8.87	8.89	8.90
Manufacturing	5.85	5.92	5.97	5.98	6.00	6.03	6.07	6.11	6.17	6.16	6.28	6.33	6.37
Transportation and public utilities	7.25	7.29	7.34	7.37	7.34	7.45	7.45	7.47	7.53	7.63	7.73	7.73	7.72
Wholesale and retail trade	4.38	4.38	4.54	4.54	4.56	4.60	4.61	4.62	4.6	4.67	4.74	4.78	4.79
Finance, insurance, and real estate	4.63	4.67	4.76	4.76	4.76	4.84	4.85	4.89	4.93	4.91	4.97	5.03	5.02
Services	4.78	4.80	4.89	4.91	4.91	4.95	4.95	4.93	4.95	4.94	5.06	5.11	5.13
Wage rates, hired farm labor (quarterly data)	-	-	3.40	-	-	3.22	-	-	3.06	-	-	3.34	-
Indexes, 1967=100													
Hourly Earnings Index, private nonfarm economy[1]	202.1	203.2	206.1	206.5	207.3	209.5	210.3	211.3	213.3	213.7	216.6	217.9	218.5
Mining	221.2	218.4	220.3	221.5	222.5	236.9	237.1	239.3	243.8	243.7	248.3	248.8	250.3
Contract construction	198.3	198.2	198.4	198.3	200.6	201.5	204.6	206.4	207.9	210.1	213.4	213.9	213.6
Manufacturing	205.5	207.3	209.0	209.7	210.8	211.9	213.0	214.3	216.0	216.8	219.1	220.9	222.3
Transportation and public utilities	221.4	222.6	224.0	224.9	224.0	227.3	227.6	227.8	229.7	232.6	235.2	236.1	235.9
Wholesale and retail trade	194.3	195.3	200.4	200.2	201.2	203.8	204.4	205.2	207.5	207.6	210.4	211.6	212.1
Wholesale trade	194.3	196.5	198.4	198.3	199.3	202.3	202.5	203.6	207.0	207.4	210.8	212.4	212.5
Retail trade	194.2	194.5	201.4	201.2	202.2	204.6	205.4	206.0	207.7	207.7	210.2	211.2	211.9
Finance, insurance, and real estate	184.3	185.6	189.2	189.2	189.3	192.3	192.6	194.2	196.3	195.2	197.6	199.7	199.4
Services	202.4	203.5	207.4	207.8	208.5	210.3	210.6	211.1	213.0	212.0	215.7	216.9	217.5
Average hourly earnings, all Federal executive branch employees	225.9	227.0	227.8	227.3	226.2	225.4	225.4	225.4	(*)	(*)	(*)	(*)	(*)
Average union scales, 7 building trades (quarterly data):													
Wages and selected benefits	-	-	234.6	-	-	235.3	-	-	246.1	-	-	247.6	-
Hourly wage rates	-	-	212.7	-	-	213.3	-	-	225.5	-	-	223.6	-
Data after seasonal adjustment													
In dollars													
Average hourly earnings, private nonfarm economy[1]	$5.39	$5.41	$5.46	$5.49	$5.54	$5.61	$5.62	$5.66	$5.71	$5.73	$5.77	$5.82	$5.86
Mining	7.18	6.75	6.84	6.92	6.94	7.63	7.66	7.71	7.85	7.88	7.88	7.99	8.05
Contract construction	8.20	8.24	8.30	8.35	8.47	8.47	8.59	8.65	8.66	8.72	8.75	8.78	8.84
Manufacturing	5.85	5.88	5.93	5.98	6.01	6.05	6.08	6.12	6.18	6.20	6.25	6.33	6.37
Transportation and public utilities	7.21	7.28	7.34	7.38	7.40	7.49	7.50	7.52	7.53	7.58	7.65	7.67	7.68
Wholesale and retail trade	4.39	4.42	4.51	4.50	4.55	4.60	4.60	4.63	4.67	4.70	4.73	4.77	4.80
Finance, insurance, and real estate	4.66	4.68	4.72	4.71	4.75	4.84	4.84	4.89	4.95	4.92	4.98	5.04	5.05
Services	4.76	4.78	4.86	4.87	4.90	4.95	4.94	4.96	5.01	5.02	5.05	5.09	5.11
Wage rates, hired farm labor (quarterly data)	-	-	(*)	-	-	(*)	-	-	(*)	-	-	(*)	-
Indexes, 1967=100													
Hourly Earnings Index, private nonfarm economy[1]	202.4	203.5	206.0	206.6	208.3	210.3	211.0	212.3	214.1	214.6	216.2	217.9	218.9
Mining	221.2	217.7	219.7	221.0	222.5	237.1	237.3	239.8	244.3	244.5	247.1	249.8	250.0
Contract construction	196.7	197.4	198.8	200.1	203.0	203.5	206.0	207.6	207.9	209.2	209.9	210.7	211.9
Manufacturing	205.3	206.5	208.1	209.4	211.0	212.2	213.5	214.7	216.7	217.5	218.9	220.8	222.2
Transportation and public utilities	220.2	222.1	223.8	224.9	225.6	228.4	229.2	229.6	230.4	231.2	233.3	234.2	234.7
Wholesale and retail trade	194.6	195.9	199.9	199.7	201.5	203.5	204.0	205.2	207.6	208.3	209.9	211.4	212.5
Wholesale trade	193.9	195.9	197.6	198.1	199.9	202.3	202.5	204.5	207.8	208.3	210.4	211.7	212.1
Retail trade	195.0	195.9	201.2	200.6	202.4	204.1	204.8	205.6	207.5	208.3	209.6	211.2	212.8
Finance, insurance, and real estate	185.4	186.0	187.7	187.3	188.9	192.3	192.4	194.6	196.9	196.0	198.2	199.9	200.6
Services	202.6	203.5	207.0	206.7	208.7	210.5	210.4	211.5	213.2	212.9	214.8	217.1	217.7
Average union scales, 7 building trades (quarterly data):													
Wages and selected benefits	-	-	235.3	-	-	238.4	-	-	243.4	-	-	246.6	-
Hourly wage rates	-	-	213.3	-	-	216.1	-	-	220.1	-	-	222.7	-

[1] Production and nonsupervisory workers.
* Not available.

p=preliminary.

GROSS HOURS AND EARNINGS OF PRODUCTION OR NONSUPERVISORY WORKERS ON PRIVATE NON-AGRICULTURAL PAYROLLS BY INDUSTRY DIVISION, 1957 TO DATE

Year and month	Average												
	Total private[1]			Mining			Construction			Manufacturing			
	Weekly earnings	Weekly hours	Hourly earnings	Weekly earnings	Weekly hours	Hourly earnings	Weekly earnings	Weekly hours	Hourly earnings	Weekly earnings	Weekly hours	Hourly earnings	Hourly earnings excl. overtime
1957	$73.33	38.8	$1.89	$98.25	40.1	$2.45	$100.27	37.0	$2.71	$81.19	39.8	$2.04	$1.98
1958	75.08	38.5	1.95	96.08	38.9	2.47	103.78	36.8	2.82	82.32	39.2	2.10	2.05
1959[2]	78.78	39.0	2.02	103.68	40.5	2.56	108.41	37.0	2.93	88.26	40.3	2.19	2.12
1960	80.67	38.6	2.09	105.04	40.4	2.60	112.67	36.7	3.07	89.72	39.7	2.26	2.19
1961	82.60	38.6	2.14	106.92	40.5	2.64	118.08	36.9	3.20	92.34	39.8	2.32	2.25
1962	85.91	38.7	2.22	110.70	41.0	2.70	122.47	37.0	3.31	96.56	40.4	2.39	2.31
1963	88.46	38.8	2.28	114.40	41.6	2.75	127.19	37.3	3.41	99.23	40.5	2.45	2.37
1964	91.33	38.7	2.36	117.74	41.9	2.81	132.06	37.2	3.55	102.97	40.7	2.53	2.43
1965	95.45	38.8	2.46	123.52	42.3	2.92	138.38	37.4	3.70	107.53	41.2	2.61	2.50
1966	98.82	38.6	2.56	130.24	42.7	3.05	146.26	37.6	3.89	112.19	41.4	2.71	2.59
1967	101.84	38.0	2.68	135.89	42.6	3.19	154.95	37.7	4.11	114.49	40.6	2.82	2.71
1968	107.73	37.8	2.85	142.71	42.6	3.35	164.49	37.3	4.41	122.51	40.7	3.01	2.88
1969	114.61	37.7	3.04	154.80	43.0	3.60	181.54	37.9	4.79	129.51	40.6	3.19	3.05
1970	119.83	37.1	3.23	164.40	42.7	3.85	195.45	37.3	5.24	133.33	39.8	3.35	3.23
1971	127.31	36.9	3.45	172.14	42.4	4.06	211.67	37.2	5.69	142.44	39.9	3.57	3.45
1972	136.90	37.0	3.70	189.14	42.6	4.44	221.19	36.5	6.06	154.71	40.5	3.82	3.66
1973	145.39	36.9	3.94	200.98	42.4	4.74	235.89	36.8	6.41	166.46	40.7	4.09	3.91
1974	154.76	36.5	4.24	219.14	41.9	5.23	249.25	36.6	6.81	177.20	40.0	4.43	4.25
1975	163.53	36.1	4.53	249.31	41.9	5.95	266.08	36.4	7.31	190.79	39.5	4.83	4.67
1976	175.45	36.1	4.86	273.90	42.4	6.46	283.36	36.8	7.70	209.32	40.1	5.22	5.02
1977	188.64	36.0	5.24	301.20	43.4	6.94	295.29	36.5	8.09	228.50	40.3	5.67	5.44
1978ᵖ	203.34	35.8	5.68	330.27	43.4	7.61	316.35	36.7	8.62	248.86	40.4	6.16	5.90
1977:													
Dec	195.48	36.2	5.40	289.08	42.7	6.77	299.27	36.1	8.29	243.31	41.1	5.92	5.67
1978:													
Jan	192.00	35.1	5.47	289.53	41.9	6.91	275.22	33.0	8.34	234.02	39.2	5.97	5.73
Feb	193.80	35.3	5.49	297.30	42.9	6.93	287.87	34.6	8.32	236.81	39.6	5.98	5.73
Mar	197.62	35.8	5.52	301.63	43.4	6.95	304.92	36.3	8.40	242.40	40.4	6.00	5.75
Apr	200.12	35.8	5.59	332.23	43.6	7.62	310.43	37.0	8.39	243.61	40.4	6.03	5.79
May	200.63	35.7	5.62	331.58	43.4	7.64	312.68	36.7	8.52	245.23	40.4	6.07	5.82
June	204.53	36.2	5.65	336.05	43.7	7.69	324.42	37.9	8.56	249.29	40.8	6.11	5.85
July	206.55	36.3	5.69	337.82	43.2	7.82	329.67	38.2	8.63	248.65	40.3	6.17	5.92
Aug	206.70	36.2	5.71	338.09	43.4	7.79	330.49	37.9	8.72	248.86	40.4	6.16	5.90
Sept	209.52	36.0	5.82	345.39	43.5	7.94	332.63	37.5	8.87	255.60	40.7	6.28	5.99
Oct	210.37	35.9	5.86	348.29	43.7	7.97	336.55	37.9	8.88	256.59	40.6	6.32	6.04
Nov.ᵖ	210.15	35.8	5.87	351.35	43.7	8.04	323.60	36.4	8.89	260.53	40.9	6.37	6.09
Dec.ᵖ	212.40	36.0	5.90	352.59	43.8	8.05	328.99	36.8	8.94	265.74	41.2	6.45	6.16

Year and month	Transportation and public utilities			Wholesale and retail trade			Finance, insurance, and real estate			Services		
	Weekly earnings	Weekly hours	Hourly earnings	Weekly earnings	Weekly hours	Hourly earnings	Weekly earnings	Weekly hours	Hourly earnings	Weekly earnings	Weekly hours	Hourly earnings
1957	-	-	-	$59.60	38.7	$1.54	$67.53	36.7	$1.84	-	-	-
1958	-	-	-	61.76	38.6	1.60	70.12	37.1	1.89	-	-	-
1959[2]	-	-	-	64.41	38.8	1.66	72.74	37.3	1.95	-	-	-
1960	-	-	-	66.01	38.6	1.71	75.14	37.2	2.02	-	-	-
1961	-	-	-	67.41	38.3	1.76	77.12	36.9	2.09	-	-	-
1962	-	-	-	69.91	38.2	1.83	80.94	37.3	2.17	-	-	-
1963	-	-	-	72.01	38.1	1.89	84.38	37.5	2.25	-	-	-
1964	$118.78	41.1	$2.89	74.66	37.9	1.97	85.79	37.3	2.30	$70.03	36.1	$1.94
1965	125.14	41.3	3.03	76.91	37.7	2.04	88.91	37.2	2.39	73.60	35.9	2.05
1966	128.13	41.2	3.11	79.39	37.1	2.14	92.13	37.3	2.47	77.04	35.5	2.17
1967	130.82	40.5	3.23	82.35	36.6	2.25	95.72	37.1	2.58	80.38	35.1	2.29
1968	138.85	40.6	3.42	87.00	36.1	2.41	101.75	37.0	2.75	83.97	34.7	2.42
1969	147.74	40.7	3.63	91.39	35.7	2.56	108.70	37.1	2.93	90.57	34.7	2.61
1970	155.93	40.5	3.85	96.02	35.3	2.72	112.67	36.7	3.07	96.66	34.4	2.81
1971	168.82	40.1	4.21	101.09	35.1	2.88	117.85	36.6	3.22	103.06	33.9	3.04
1972	187.86	40.4	4.65	106.45	34.9	3.05	122.98	36.6	3.36	110.85	33.9	3.27
1973	203.31	40.5	5.02	111.76	34.6	3.23	129.20	36.6	3.53	117.29	33.8	3.47
1974	217.48	40.2	5.41	119.02	34.2	3.48	137.61	36.5	3.77	126.00	33.6	3.75
1975	233.44	39.7	5.88	126.45	33.9	3.73	148.19	36.5	4.06	134.67	33.5	4.02
1976	256.71	39.8	6.45	133.79	33.7	3.97	155.43	36.4	4.27	143.52	33.3	4.31
1977ᵖ	278.90	39.9	6.99	142.19	33.3	4.27	165.26	36.4	4.54	153.45	33.0	4.65
1978ᵖ	301.60	40.0	7.54	152.85	32.8	4.66	178.85	36.5	4.90	163.67	32.8	4.99
1977:												
Dec	293.06	40.2	7.29	146.29	33.4	4.38	169.99	36.4	4.67	158.40	33.0	4.80
1978:												
Jan	289.20	39.4	7.34	146.19	32.2	4.54	173.26	36.4	4.76	160.39	32.8	4.89
Feb	294.80	40.0	7.37	146.64	32.3	4.54	173.26	36.4	4.76	160.56	32.7	4.91
Mar	294.33	40.1	7.34	149.11	32.7	4.56	172.79	36.3	4.76	161.05	32.8	4.91
Apr	296.51	39.8	7.45	150.42	32.7	4.60	177.14	36.6	4.84	162.36	32.8	4.95
May	297.26	39.9	7.45	150.75	32.7	4.61	176.06	36.3	4.85	161.37	32.6	4.95
June	301.04	40.3	7.47	153.38	33.2	4.62	178.49	36.5	4.89	162.69	33.0	4.93
July	301.20	40.0	7.53	157.04	33.7	4.66	180.93	36.7	4.93	164.84	33.3	4.95
Aug	307.49	40.3	7.63	156.45	33.5	4.67	179.71	36.6	4.91	164.01	33.2	4.94
Sept	309.94	40.2	7.71	155.47	32.8	4.74	180.91	36.4	4.97	165.46	32.7	5.06
Oct	309.57	40.1	7.72	156.31	32.7	4.78	183.73	36.6	5.02	167.42	32.7	5.12
Nov.ᵖ	309.20	40.0	7.73	156.48	32.6	4.80	182.59	36.3	5.03	167.24	32.6	5.13
Dec.ᵖ	312.76	40.2	7.78	158.07	33.0	4.79	183.32	36.3	5.05	168.22	32.6	5.16

[1] For coverage of series, see footnote 1, table B-2.
[2] Data include Alaska and Hawaii beginning 1959.
[3] Prior to January 1956, data were based on the application of adjustment factors to gross average hourly earnings. (See Explanatory Note.)

p = preliminary.

1972 SIC Code	Industry	Average weekly earnings					Average hourly earnings				
		Nov. 1977	Dec. 1977	Oct. 1978	Nov. 1978p	Dec. 1978p	Nov. 1977	Dec. 1977	Oct. 1978	Nov. 1978p	Dec. 1978p
–	TOTAL PRIVATE	$193.86	$195.48	$210.37	$210.15	$212.40	$5.40	$5.40	$5.86	$5.87	$5.90
–	MINING	317.80	289.08	348.29	351.35	352.59	7.19	6.77	7.97	8.04	8.05
10	METAL MINING	309.10	318.37	360.29	364.04	–	7.67	7.69	8.64	8.73	–
101	Iron ores	331.67	309.60	371.60	379.38	–	7.47	7.74	8.89	8.99	–
102	Copper ores	296.29	311.64	367.69	371.96	–	7.88	7.95	8.86	8.92	–
11, 12	COAL MINING	374.41	270.68	397.13	412.57	–	8.49	8.08	9.83	9.87	–
12	BITUMINOUS COAL AND LIGNITE MINING ...	375.29	269.10	399.33	413.82	–	8.51	8.13	9.86	9.90	–
13	OIL AND GAS EXTRACTION	293.40	294.54	326.95	323.73	–	6.52	6.56	7.17	7.21	–
131, 2	Crude petroleum, natural gas, and natural gas liquids	299.21	307.23	336.58	336.15	–	7.28	7.35	8.13	8.10	–
138	Oil and gas field services	290.78	289.54	323.74	318.08	–	6.20	6.24	6.83	6.87	–
14	NONMETALLIC MINERALS, EXCEPT FUELS ...	269.25	261.76	302.15	298.88	–	6.01	5.99	6.54	6.54	–
142	Crushed and broken stone	262.48	250.13	302.10	294.51	–	5.82	5.75	6.32	6.32	–
–	CONSTRUCTION	298.19	299.27	336.55	323.60	328.99	8.26	8.29	8.88	8.89	8.94
15	GENERAL BUILDING CONTRACTORS	279.00	276.02	300.82	293.59		7.75	7.71	8.31	8.27	
152	Residential building construction	262.43	263.16	284.76	277.02	–	7.31	7.31	7.91	7.87	–
153	Operative builders	243.89	240.08	259.19	253.82	–	6.87	6.84	7.24	7.17	–
154	Nonresidential building construction ...	304.08	298.21	327.57	319.34	–	8.40	8.33	8.95	8.92	–
16	HEAVY CONSTRUCTION CONTRACTORS	286.48	287.28	350.70	324.87	–	7.66	7.56	8.35	8.33	–
161	Highway and street construction	271.32	262.39	348.83	301.09	–	7.14	6.78	7.91	7.76	–
162	Heavy construction, except highway ...	294.57	298.21	352.97	336.57	–	7.94	7.91	8.63	8.63	–
17	SPECIAL TRADE CONTRACTORS	314.16	316.48	349.65	339.97	–	8.80	8.89	9.45	9.47	–
171	Plumbing, heating, air conditioning	328.19	340.86	367.10	360.96	–	8.87	8.97	9.61	9.60	–
172	Painting, paper hanging, decorating ...	275.22	278.56	312.02	305.01	–	8.24	8.34	8.74	8.79	–
173	Electrical work	365.02	373.16	403.01	400.14	–	9.76	9.82	10.55	10.53	–
174	Masonry, stonework, and plastering ...	292.56	285.36	325.33	314.50	–	8.63	8.70	9.19	9.25	–
175	Carpentering and flooring	274.92	268.60	305.09	293.94	–	7.90	7.90	8.57	8.52	–
176	Roofing and sheet metal work	247.62	234.96	277.70	269.78	–	7.69	7.78	8.12	8.25	–
–	MANUFACTURING	238.10	243.31	256.59	260.53	265.74	5.85	5.92	6.32	6.37	6.45
24, 25, 32-39	DURABLE GOODS	258.75	265.86	279.19	283.30	290.07	6.25	6.33	6.76	6.81	6.89
20-23, 26-31	NONDURABLE GOODS	208.03	211.47	222.78	226.46	229.43	5.24	5.30	5.64	5.69	5.75
	DURABLE GOODS										
24	LUMBER AND WOOD PRODUCTS	208.95	210.80	233.11	228.05	227.48	5.25	5.27	5.77	5.73	5.73
241	Logging camps and logging contractors ...	258.00	255.13	321.30	287.47	–	6.88	6.84	7.56	7.39	–
242	Sawmills and planing mills	222.77	226.19	243.54	240.17	–	5.46	5.49	5.94	5.93	–
2421	Sawmills and planing mills, general ...	234.36	238.71	257.70	252.72	–	5.73	5.78	6.27	6.24	–
2426	Hardwood dimension and flooring ...	151.10	155.74	165.64	166.87	–	3.74	3.78	4.04	4.10	–
243	Millwork, plywood, and structural members	207.08	211.70	224.07	225.44	–	5.19	5.24	5.63	5.65	–
2431	Millwork	196.12	197.78	209.91	211.62	–	4.94	4.92	5.41	5.44	–
2434	Wood kitchen cabinets	180.69	183.74	201.17	205.65	–	4.73	4.81	5.08	5.18	–
2435	Hardwood veneer and plywood	171.74	176.35	182.96	184.68	–	4.23	4.27	4.54	4.56	–
2436	Softwood veneer and plywood	273.97	282.63	290.90	292.93	–	6.57	6.65	7.13	7.11	–
244	Wooden containers	146.69	150.15	161.20	162.86	–	3.85	3.85	4.22	4.23	–
245	Wood buildings and mobile homes	188.07	182.57	211.68	207.90	–	4.81	4.83	5.40	5.40	–
2451	Mobile homes	187.89	185.65	207.13	203.52	–	4.83	4.86	5.38	5.37	–
249	Miscellaneous wood products	176.14	177.80	188.47	189.81	–	4.36	4.39	4.70	4.71	–
25	FURNITURE AND FIXTURES	177.91	182.66	189.29	189.21	194.57	4.47	4.51	4.78	4.79	4.84
251	Household furniture	164.30	170.91	176.46	176.79	–	4.17	4.22	4.49	4.51	–
2511	Wood household furniture	154.33	158.62	166.38	168.00	–	3.82	3.85	4.17	4.20	–
2512	Upholstered household furniture	172.97	184.86	187.11	187.60	–	4.54	4.61	4.81	4.86	–
2514	Metal household furniture	167.35	171.35	174.65	171.97	–	4.28	4.36	4.56	4.49	–
2515	Mattresses and bedsprings	185.96	190.81	196.21	193.67	–	4.83	4.88	5.07	5.07	–
252	Office furniture	209.99	213.27	212.05	212.98	–	5.06	5.09	5.21	5.22	–
253	Public building and related furniture ...	205.42	205.13	211.04	212.22	–	5.11	5.09	5.16	5.24	–
254	Partitions and fixtures	216.00	215.60	230.00	227.26	–	5.40	5.39	5.75	5.71	–
259	Miscellaneous furniture and fixtures ...	198.58	198.00	205.80	208.69	–	4.82	4.95	5.25	5.27	–

See footnotes at end of table.

1972 SIC Code	Industry	Average weekly hours					Average overtime hours				
		Nov. 1977	Dec. 1977	Oct. 1978	Nov. 1978 P	Dec. 1978 P	Nov. 1977	Dec. 1977	Oct. 1978	Nov. 1978 P	Dec. 1978 P
--	TOTAL PRIVATE	35.9	36.2	35.9	35.8	36.0	–	–	–	–	–
–	MINING	44.2	42.7	43.7	43.7	43.8	–	–	–	–	–
10	METAL MINING	40.3	41.4	41.7	41.7	–	–	–	–	–	–
101	Iron ores	44.4	40.0	41.8	42.2	–	–	–	–	–	–
102	Copper ores	37.6	39.2	41.5	41.7	–	–	–	–	–	–
11, 12	COAL MINING	44.1	33.5	40.4	41.8	–	–	–	–	–	–
12	BITUMINOUS COAL AND LIGNITE MINING	44.1	33.1	40.5	41.8	–	–	–	–	–	–
13	OIL AND GAS EXTRACTION	45.0	44.9	45.6	44.9	–	–	–	–	–	–
131, 2	Crude petroleum, natural gas, and natural gas liquids	41.1	41.8	41.4	41.5	–	–	–	–	–	–
138	Oil and gas field services	46.9	46.4	47.4	46.3	–	–	–	–	–	–
14	NONMETALLIC MINERALS, EXCEPT FUELS	44.8	43.7	46.2	45.7	–	–	–	–	–	–
142	Crushed and broken stone	45.1	43.5	47.8	46.6	–	–	–	–	–	–
–	CONSTRUCTION	36.1	36.1	37.9	36.4	36.8	–	–	–	–	–
15	GENERAL BUILDING CONTRACTORS	36.0	35.8	36.2	35.5	–	–	–	–	–	–
152	Residential building construction	35.9	36.0	36.0	35.2	–	–	–	–	–	–
153	Operative builders	35.5	35.1	35.8	35.4	–	–	–	–	–	–
154	Nonresidential building construction	36.2	35.8	36.6	35.8	–	–	–	–	–	–
16	HEAVY CONSTRUCTION CONTRACTORS	37.4	38.0	42.0	39.0	–	–	–	–	–	–
161	Highway and street construction	38.0	38.7	44.1	38.8	–	–	–	–	–	–
162	Heavy construction, except highway	37.1	37.7	40.9	39.0	–	–	–	–	–	–
17	SPECIAL TRADE CONTRACTORS	35.7	35.6	37.0	35.9	–	–	–	–	–	–
171	Plumbing, heating, air conditioning	37.0	38.0	38.2	37.6	–	–	–	–	–	–
172	Painting, paper hanging, decorating	33.4	33.4	35.7	34.7	–	–	–	–	–	–
173	Electrical work	37.4	38.0	38.2	38.0	–	–	–	–	–	–
174	Masonry, stonework, and plastering	33.9	32.8	35.4	34.0	–	–	–	–	–	–
175	Carpentering and flooring	34.8	34.0	35.6	34.5	–	–	–	–	–	–
176	Roofing and sheet metal work	32.2	30.2	34.2	32.7	–	–	–	–	–	–
–	MANUFACTURING	40.7	41.1	40.6	40.9	41.2	3.6	3.7	3.8	3.8	3.9
24, 25, 32-39	DURABLE GOODS	41.4	42.0	41.3	41.6	42.1	3.9	4.0	4.1	4.1	4.3
20-23, 26-31	NONDURABLE GOODS	39.7	39.9	39.5	39.8	39.9	3.3	3.3	3.4	3.3	3.4
	DURABLE GOODS										
24	LUMBER AND WOOD PRODUCTS	39.8	40.0	40.4	39.8	39.7	3.6	3.6	4.0	3.7	–
241	Logging camps and logging contractors	37.5	37.3	42.5	38.9	–	3.4	3.5	5.7	4.0	–
242	Sawmills and planing mills	40.8	41.2	41.0	40.5	–	4.4	4.5	4.8	4.5	–
2421	Sawmills and planing mills, general	40.9	41.3	41.1	40.5	–	4.5	4.6	5.0	4.8	–
2426	Hardwood dimension and flooring	40.4	41.2	41.0	40.7	–	3.8	4.2	3.9	3.6	–
243	Millwork, plywood, and structural members	39.9	40.4	39.8	39.9	–	3.3	3.5	3.3	3.4	–
2431	Millwork	39.7	40.2	38.8	38.9	–	2.6	2.8	2.3	2.3	–
2434	Wood kitchen cabinets	38.2	38.2	39.6	39.7	–	2.3	2.5	2.4	2.6	–
2435	Hardwood veneer and plywood	40.6	41.3	40.3	40.5	–	4.0	4.3	3.8	3.9	–
2436	Softwood veneer and plywood	41.7	42.5	40.8	41.2	–	4.9	5.0	5.0	5.3	–
244	Wooden containers	38.1	39.0	38.2	38.5	–	2.8	3.2	3.1	3.1	–
245	Wood buildings and mobile homes	39.1	37.8	39.2	38.5	–	2.5	2.1	2.7	2.4	–
2451	Mobile homes	38.9	38.2	38.5	37.9	–	2.5	2.2	2.1	1.9	–
249	Miscellaneous wood products	40.4	40.5	40.1	40.3	–	3.6	3.5	3.6	3.7	–
25	FURNITURE AND FIXTURES	39.8	40.5	39.6	39.5	40.2	2.9	3.1	2.8	2.7	–
251	Household furniture	39.4	40.5	39.3	39.2	–	2.8	3.1	2.8	2.6	–
2511	Wood household furniture	40.4	41.2	39.9	40.0	–	3.4	3.5	3.4	3.4	–
2512	Upholstered household furniture	38.1	40.1	38.9	38.6	–	2.1	2.8	2.2	1.9	–
2514	Metal household furniture	39.1	39.3	38.3	38.3	–	1.7	1.6	1.8	1.5	–
2515	Mattresses and bedsprings	38.5	39.1	38.7	38.2	–	2.8	3.4	3.2	2.1	–
252	Office furniture	41.5	41.9	40.7	40.8	–	3.6	3.8	2.7	2.8	–
253	Public building and related furniture	40.2	40.3	40.9	40.5	–	3.3	3.3	2.6	2.9	–
254	Partitions and fixtures	40.0	40.0	40.0	39.8	–	2.9	2.8	3.4	2.9	–
259	Miscellaneous furniture and fixtures	41.2	40.0	39.2	39.6	–	2.8	2.3	2.2	2.3	–

See footnotes at end of table.

GROSS HOURS AND EARNINGS OF PRODUCTION OR NONSUPERVISORY WORKERS ON PRIVATE NON-AGRICULTURAL PAYROLLS, BY INDUSTRY (Continued)

1972 SIC Code	Industry	Average weekly earnings					Average hourly earnings				
		Nov. 1977	Dec. 1977	Oct. 1978	Nov. 1978ᴾ	Dec. 1978ᴾ	Nov. 1977	Dec. 1977	Oct. 1978	Nov. 1978ᴾ	Dec. 1978ᴾ
32	STONE, CLAY, AND GLASS PRODUCTS	$249.37	$249.00	$274.10	$274.72	$275.14	$5.98	$6.00	$6.48	$6.51	$6.52
321	Flat glass	327.82	345.80	357.47	372.86	–	7.40	7.60	8.18	8.36	–
322	Glass and glassware, pressed or blown	250.88	252.10	272.83	273.78	–	6.21	6.24	6.72	6.76	–
3221	Glass containers	261.39	261.79	286.71	284.72	–	6.47	6.48	7.01	7.03	–
3229	Pressed and blown glass, nec	236.34	238.36	254.47	259.20	–	5.85	5.90	6.33	6.40	–
323	Products of purchased glass	243.79	248.21	276.68	279.72	–	5.99	6.01	6.51	6.49	–
324	Cement, hydraulic	345.56	342.32	377.40	404.36	–	8.15	8.17	8.88	9.19	–
325	Structural clay products	198.65	199.55	214.61	220.06	–	4.81	4.82	5.26	5.29	–
326	Pottery and related products	195.42	198.97	209.22	212.53	–	4.91	5.05	5.27	5.30	–
327	Concrete, gypsum, and plaster products	256.71	247.63	287.30	277.56	–	5.97	5.91	6.50	6.47	–
3271	Concrete block and brick	236.03	228.11	263.14	258.98	–	5.34	5.38	5.90	5.94	–
3272	Concrete products, nec	231.63	224.35	245.23	243.49	–	5.45	5.38	5.77	5.77	–
3273	Ready-mixed concrete	277.02	264.71	324.27	302.57	–	6.58	6.52	7.19	7.17	–
329	Misc. nonmetallic mineral products	247.87	254.40	272.00	278.21	–	5.93	6.00	6.40	6.44	–
3291	Abrasive products	239.78	248.40	255.19	261.02	–	5.75	6.00	6.27	6.32	–
3292	Asbestos products	271.06	276.95	293.26	293.91	–	6.26	6.28	6.59	6.59	–
33	PRIMARY METAL INDUSTRIES	319.19	325.14	352.80	360.82	364.23	7.71	7.76	8.42	8.51	8.55
331	Blast furnace and basic steel products	352.15	357.69	400.75	412.16	–	8.76	8.81	9.68	9.79	–
3312	Blast furnaces and steel mills	359.00	365.52	411.18	423.19	–	9.02	9.07	9.98	10.10	–
3317	Steel pipe and tubes	313.34	312.28	326.70	331.33	–	7.39	7.40	7.76	7.87	–
332	Iron and steel foundries	294.68	308.62	315.78	319.60	–	6.95	7.03	7.43	7.52	–
3321	Gray iron foundries	306.16	326.31	322.06	324.28	–	7.17	7.30	7.56	7.63	–
3322	Malleable iron foundries	305.14	308.45	331.64	336.20	..	7.30	7.14	8.03	8.20	–
3325	Steel foundries, nec	267.07	269.19	300.48	308.02	..	6.42	6.44	7.07	7.18	–
333	Primary nonferrous metals	343.48	339.04	370.86	374.36	–	8.12	8.15	8.83	8.85	–
3334	Primary aluminum	365.44	362.64	397.71	390.31	–	8.87	8.91	9.38	9.36	–
335	Nonferrous rolling and drawing	296.34	295.64	322.07	329.18	–	6.94	6.94	7.49	7.55	–
3351	Copper rolling and drawing	259.79	277.76	300.40	301.53	–	6.23	6.40	6.89	6.90	–
3353	Aluminum sheet, plate, and foil	358.09	363.10	391.19	399.81	–	8.27	8.29	9.14	9.17	–
3357	Nonferrous wire drawing and insulating	279.97	269.21	299.34	310.03	..	6.65	6.55	7.06	7.16	–
336	Nonferrous foundries	247.70	256.88	262.26	264.16	–	5.94	6.03	6.35	6.35	–
3361	Aluminum foundries	257.46	266.45	272.33	276.05	–	6.13	6.24	6.61	6.62	–
34	FABRICATED METAL PRODUCTS	251.10	257.04	266.09	270.10	277.62	6.08	6.12	6.49	6.54	6.61
341	Metal cans and shipping containers	304.38	320.68	354.75	357.40	–	7.37	7.51	8.25	8.37	–
3411	Metal cans	311.88	331.27	365.93	368.94	–	7.57	7.74	8.51	8.62	–
342	Cutlery, hand tools, and hardware	248.53	247.38	249.27	251.53	–	5.96	5.89	6.17	6.18	–
3423, 5	Hand and edge tools, and hand saws and blades	225.50	232.39	237.60	240.99	–	5.50	5.52	5.94	5.98	–
3429	Hardware, nec	267.13	262.48	260.89	260.71	–	6.33	6.22	6.41	6.39	–
343	Plumbing and heating, except electric	210.94	222.09	226.46	230.35	–	5.30	5.43	5.69	5.73	–
3432	Plumbing fittings and brass goods	199.68	208.55	222.56	227.26	–	5.12	5.24	5.55	5.57	–
3433	Heating equipment, except electric	208.24	220.37	221.43	224.53	–	5.18	5.31	5.62	5.67	–
344	Fabricated structural metal products	235.48	239.61	249.46	252.32	–	5.80	5.83	6.19	6.23	–
3441	Fabricated structural metal	244.22	248.05	264.55	271.58	–	6.03	6.05	6.50	6.56	–
3442	Metal doors, sash, and trim	184.00	189.72	195.92	195.22	–	4.60	4.65	4.96	4.98	–
3443	Fabricated plate work (boiler shops)	263.49	266.85	273.78	276.76	–	6.38	6.43	6.76	6.80	–
3444	Sheet metal work	239.99	244.22	252.49	251.70	–	5.97	6.03	6.36	6.34	–
3446	Architectural metal work	228.83	230.74	241.38	246.65	–	5.65	5.56	6.08	6.09	–
345	Screw machine products, bolts, etc.	246.67	251.87	263.34	269.19	–	5.71	5.79	6.11	6.16	–
3451	Screw machine products	230.37	232.09	242.65	247.66	–	5.37	5.41	5.75	5.80	–
3452	Bolts, nuts, rivets, and washers	262.74	271.83	284.89	290.55	–	6.04	6.15	6.46	6.50	–
346	Metal forgings and stampings	300.04	310.31	318.02	326.40	–	7.11	7.15	7.59	7.68	–
3462	Iron and steel forgings	329.22	350.47	350.65	356.87	–	7.82	8.02	8.27	8.28	–
3465	Automotive stampings	362.90	374.40	382.12	396.20	–	8.42	8.32	8.97	9.15	–
3469	Metal stampings, nec	222.73	227.27	237.56	239.29	–	5.38	5.45	5.78	5.78	–
347	Metal services, nec	204.50	203.53	211.93	212.74	–	5.00	4.94	5.22	5.24	–
3471	Plating and polishing	192.78	195.23	203.52	205.74	–	4.76	4.75	5.05	5.08	–
3479	Metal coating and allied services	232.41	224.93	232.37	231.65	–	5.56	5.42	5.64	5.65	–
348	Ordnance and accessories, nec	236.34	248.05	256.94	257.44	–	5.85	5.92	6.36	6.42	–
3483	Ammunition, exc. for small arms, nec	218.44	229.77	231.00	233.55	–	5.53	5.51	6.00	6.13	–
349	Misc. fabricated metal products	237.31	243.02	251.94	255.23	–	5.76	5.80	6.16	6.18	–
3494	Valves and pipe fittings	261.01	269.18	270.17	277.53	–	6.07	6.09	6.51	6.53	–
3496	Misc. fabricated wire products	207.36	210.83	219.35	221.65	–	5.12	5.18	5.47	5.50	–
35	MACHINERY, EXCEPT ELECTRICAL	272.61	281.22	291.48	297.50	305.86	6.46	6.54	6.94	7.00	7.08
351	Engines and turbines	330.17	338.34	344.42	351.90	–	7.59	7.76	8.22	8.28	–
3511	Turbines and turbine generator sets	288.23	294.89	320.46	316.58	–	7.03	7.21	7.63	7.61	–
3519	Internal combustion engines, nec	348.33	354.57	353.64	364.23	–	7.81	7.95	8.44	8.51	–
352	Farm and garden machinery	279.30	302.45	308.33	315.18	–	7.00	7.15	7.67	7.65	–
3523	Farm machinery and equipment	284.57	309.94	316.76	324.21	–	7.15	7.31	7.86	7.85	–
353	Construction and related machinery	290.37	298.78	316.30	317.90	–	6.93	7.03	7.46	7.48	–

See footnotes at end of table.

1972 SIC Code	Industry	Average weekly hours					Average overtime hours				
		Nov. 1977	Dec. 1977	Oct. 1978	Nov. 1978P	Dec. 1978P	Nov. 1977	Dec. 1977	Oct. 1978	Nov. 1978P	Dec. 1978P
32	STONE, CLAY, AND GLASS PRODUCTS	41.7	41.5	42.3	42.2	42.2	4.6	4.4	5.2	4.9	–
321	Flat glass	44.3	45.5	43.7	44.6	–	7.2	6.7	5.8	6.4	–
322	Glass and glassware, pressed or blown	40.4	40.4	40.6	40.5	–	4.1	4.1	4.2	4.1	–
3221	Glass containers	40.4	40.4	40.9	40.5	–	4.5	4.7	4.8	4.5	–
3229	Pressed and blown glass, nec	40.4	40.4	40.2	40.5	–	3.6	3.3	3.4	3.5	–
323	Products of purchased glass	40.7	41.3	42.5	43.1	–	3.7	3.7	5.6	6.1	–
324	Cement, hydraulic	42.4	41.9	42.5	44.0	–	4.2	4.0	4.4	3.9	–
325	Structural clay products	41.3	41.4	40.8	41.6	–	4.3	4.5	4.4	4.2	–
326	Pottery and related products	39.8	39.4	39.7	40.1	–	2.8	2.6	2.9	3.0	–
327	Concrete, gypsum, and plaster products	43.0	41.9	44.2	42.9	–	6.0	5.3	7.2	6.2	–
3271	Concrete block and brick	44.2	42.4	44.6	43.6	–	6.5	5.6	7.7	7.0	–
3272	Concrete products, nec	42.5	41.7	42.5	42.2	–	5.2	4.7	6.0	5.6	–
3273	Ready-mixed concrete	42.1	40.6	45.1	42.2	–	6.1	5.1	7.7	6.0	–
329	Misc. nonmetallic mineral products	41.8	42.4	42.5	43.2	–	3.9	4.3	4.6	4.7	–
3291	Abrasive products	41.7	41.4	40.7	41.3	–	3.5	3.8	3.6	3.9	–
3292	Asbestos products	43.3	44.1	44.5	44.6	–	4.2	4.7	5.3	4.7	–
33	PRIMARY METAL INDUSTRIES	41.4	41.9	41.9	42.4	42.6	3.8	4.1	4.3	4.4	–
331	Blast furnace and basic steel products	40.2	40.6	41.4	42.1	–	2.4	2.8	3.6	3.6	–
3312	Blast furnaces and steel mills	39.8	40.3	41.2	41.9	–	2.2	2.6	3.5	3.5	–
3317	Steel pipe and tubes	42.4	42.2	42.1	42.1	–	4.4	4.2	4.4	4.4	–‍
332	Iron and steel foundries	42.4	43.9	42.5	42.5	–	5.4	6.0	5.2	5.3	–
3321	Gray iron foundries	42.7	44.7	42.6	42.5	–	5.9	6.6	5.6	5.7	–
3322	Malleable iron foundries	41.8	43.2	41.3	41.0	–	4.9	4.9	5.1	5.1	–
3325	Steel foundries, nec	41.6	41.8	42.5	42.9	–	4.2	4.7	4.4	4.7	–
333	Primary nonferrous metals	42.3	41.6	42.0	42.3	–	3.8	3.7	3.6	3.7	–
3334	Primary aluminum	41.2	40.7	42.4	41.7	–	4.6	4.3	3.8	3.9	–
335	Nonferrous rolling and drawing	42.7	42.6	43.0	43.6	–	5.2	5.1	5.6	5.7	–
3351	Copper rolling and drawing	41.7	43.4	43.6	43.7	–	4.0	5.0	6.1	5.1	–
3353	Aluminum sheet, plate and foil	43.3	43.8	42.8	43.6	–	7.5	7.2	7.1	7.3	–
3357	Nonferrous wire drawing and insulating	42.1	41.1	42.4	43.3	–	4.4	4.0	4.8	5.4	–
336	Nonferrous foundries	41.7	42.6	41.3	41.6	–	3.8	4.4	3.8	3.9	–
3361	Aluminum foundries	42.0	42.7	41.2	41.7	–	4.0	4.4	3.9	4.3	–
34	FABRICATED METAL PRODUCTS	41.3	42.0	41.0	41.3	42.0	3.8	4.0	3.9	3.9	–
341	Metal cans and shipping containers	41.3	42.7	43.0	42.7	–	3.2	3.7	4.2	4.3	–
3411	Metal cans	41.2	42.8	43.0	42.8	–	2.9	3.4	3.8	4.0	–
342	Cutlery, hand tools, and hardware	41.7	42.0	40.4	40.7	–	4.2	3.8	3.3	3.3	–
3423, 5	Hand and edge tools, and hand saws and blades	41.0	42.1	40.0	40.3	–	3.3	4.1	3.1	2.9	–
3429	Hardware, nec	42.2	42.2	40.7	40.8	–	4.8	3.7	3.6	3.4	–
343	Plumbing and heating, except electric	39.8	40.9	39.8	40.2	–	2.7	3.4	3.1	3.0	–
3432	Plumbing fittings and brass goods	39.0	39.8	40.1	40.8	–	1.7	2.3	3.2	3.5	–
3433	Heating equipment, except electric	40.2	41.5	39.4	39.6	–	3.4	3.9	2.9	2.6	–
344	Fabricated structural metal products	40.6	41.1	40.3	40.5	–	3.4	3.5	3.2	3.2	–
3441	Fabricated structural metal	40.5	41.0	40.7	41.4	–	3.2	3.4	3.9	4.1	–
3442	Metal doors, sash, and trim	40.0	40.8	39.5	39.2	–	3.2	3.5	2.7	2.6	–
3443	Fabricated plate work (boiler shops)	41.3	41.5	40.7	40.7	–	3.8	3.8	3.0	3.1	–
3444	Sheet metal work	40.2	40.5	39.7	39.7	–	3.5	3.5	3.5	3.1	–
3446	Architectural metal work	40.5	41.5	39.7	40.5	–	2.6	2.5	2.3	2.3	–
345	Screw machine products, bolts, etc.	43.2	43.5	43.1	43.7	–	5.1	5.4	5.7	5.8	–
3451	Screw machine products	42.9	42.9	42.2	42.7	–	5.2	5.3	5.7	5.8	–
3452	Bolts, nuts, rivets, and washers	43.5	44.2	44.1	44.7	–	5.0	5.4	5.8	5.9	–
346	Metal forgings and stampings	42.2	43.4	41.9	42.5	–	4.9	5.0	5.0	5.2	–
3462	Iron and steel forgings	42.1	43.7	42.4	43.1	–	5.1	5.7	5.7	6.0	–
3465	Automotive stampings	43.1	45.0	42.6	43.3	–	6.2	5.8	5.8	6.2	–
3469	Metal stampings, nec	41.4	41.7	41.1	41.4	–	3.4	3.8	3.7	3.7	–
347	Metal services, nec	40.9	41.2	40.6	40.6	–	3.9	4.2	3.9	3.9	–
3471	Plating and polishing	40.5	41.1	40.3	40.5	–	4.0	4.2	3.7	3.7	–
3479	Metal coating and allied services	41.8	41.5	41.2	41.0	–	3.8	4.3	4.6	4.5	–
348	Ordnance and accessories, nec	40.4	41.9	40.4	40.1	–	2.5	3.3	2.9	3.0	–
3483	Ammunition, exc. for small arms, nec	39.5	41.7	38.5	38.1	–	2.0	2.9	1.6	1.5	–
349	Misc. fabricated metal products	41.2	41.9	40.9	41.3	–	3.2	3.7	3.6	3.6	–
3494	Valves and pipe fittings	43.0	44.2	41.5	42.5	–	4.1	4.8	3.7	4.0	–
3496	Misc. fabricated wire products	40.5	40.7	40.1	40.3	–	2.7	2.9	3.3	3.2	–
35	MACHINERY, EXCEPT ELECTRICAL	42.2	43.0	42.0	42.5	43.2	4.2	4.7	4.4	4.5	–
351	Engines and turbines	43.5	43.6	41.9	42.5	–	4.5	4.8	4.2	4.3	–
3511	Turbines and turbine generator sets	41.0	40.9	42.0	41.6	–	4.1	5.2	5.2	4.5	–
3519	Internal combustion engines, nec	44.6	44.6	41.9	42.8	–	4.6	4.7	3.8	4.2	–
352	Farm and garden machinery	39.9	42.3	40.2	41.2	–	2.8	3.5	4.2	4.4	–
3523	Farm machinery and equipment	39.8	42.4	40.3	41.3	–	2.9	3.5	4.4	4.5	–
353	Construction and related machinery	41.9	42.5	42.4	42.5	–	3.5	4.2	4.1	3.9	–

See footnotes at end of table.

1972 SIC Code	Industry	Average weekly earnings					Average hourly earnings				
		Nov. 1977	Dec. 1977	Oct. 1978	Nov. 1978 P	Dec. 1978 P	Nov. 1977	Dec. 1977	Oct. 1978	Nov. 1978 P	Dec. 1978 P
	MACHINERY, EXCEPT ELECTRICAL—Continued										
3531	Construction machinery	$317.95	$324.73	$345.69	$346.94	–	$7.68	$7.75	$8.29	$8.30	–
3532	Mining machinery	269.12	274.73	315.66	310.60	–	6.58	6.75	7.29	7.24	–
3533	Oil field machinery	277.93	290.70	300.56	303.70	–	6.36	6.46	6.80	6.84	–
3535	Conveyers and conveying equipment	249.95	253.73	256.85	264.15	–	5.84	5.97	6.13	6.23	–
3537	Industrial trucks and tractors	255.22	267.97	279.75	279.60	–	6.24	6.32	6.79	6.77	–
354	Metalworking machinery	296.59	305.10	316.24	324.56	–	6.68	6.75	7.22	7.31	–
3541	Machine tools, metal cutting types	311.21	321.08	332.57	339.14	–	6.87	6.98	7.44	7.47	–
3542	Machine tools, metal forming types	293.78	304.23	322.39	335.16	–	6.88	6.93	7.48	7.60	–
3544	Special dies, tools, jigs, and fixtures	328.19	334.54	347.08	357.63	–	7.15	7.21	7.73	7.86	–
3545	Machine tool accessories	261.97	271.39	275.14	281.39	–	6.05	6.14	6.52	6.59	–
3546	Power driven hand tools	221.08	232.52	230.77	238.71	–	5.34	5.42	5.67	5.78	–
355	Special industry machinery	256.43	266.79	271.17	279.30	–	6.12	6.19	6.55	6.65	–
3551	Food products machinery	266.80	275.18	286.35	295.96	–	6.46	6.49	6.90	7.03	–
3552	Textile machinery	210.63	216.06	220.19	226.74	–	5.10	5.12	5.41	5.49	–
3555	Printing trades machinery	269.24	284.27	274.90	287.22	–	6.38	6.52	6.79	6.79	–
356	General industrial machinery	268.36	275.80	285.52	292.74	–	6.42	6.52	6.88	6.97	–
3561	Pumps and pumping equipment	275.18	284.00	283.04	289.82	–	6.49	6.62	6.87	6.95	–
3562	Ball and roller bearings	268.55	274.49	291.35	295.26	–	6.44	6.52	6.97	7.03	–
3563	Air and gas compressors	286.89	292.03	301.75	311.61	–	6.58	6.76	7.10	7.18	–
3564	Blowers and fans	237.86	242.78	248.44	258.54	–	5.83	5.85	6.18	6.26	–
3566	Speed changers, drives, and gears	284.50	309.32	322.51	326.92	–	6.79	7.03	7.36	7.43	–
3568	Power transmission equipment, nec	252.56	268.98	283.75	289.49	–	6.16	6.27	6.74	6.86	–
357	Office and computing machines	225.06	227.81	235.00	241.38	–	5.41	5.45	5.69	5.72	–
3573	Electronic computing equipment	227.94	230.54	233.19	240.54	–	5.44	5.45	5.66	5.70	–
358	Refrigeration and service machinery	245.86	255.26	258.08	260.65	–	5.91	5.95	6.31	6.42	–
3585	Refrigeration and heating equipment	253.98	261.87	263.86	266.59	–	5.99	6.02	6.42	6.55	–
359	Misc. machinery, except electrical	260.18	266.02	285.24	288.77	–	6.18	6.23	6.68	6.70	–
3592	Carburetors, pistons, rings, valves	309.64	312.18	325.71	336.93	–	7.39	7.26	7.61	7.71	–
3599	Machinery, except electrical, nec	250.92	257.30	277.98	280.36	–	5.96	6.04	6.51	6.52	–
36	**ELECTRIC AND ELECTRONIC EQUIPMENT**	226.44	233.35	240.78	243.39	$249.48	5.55	5.65	5.96	5.98	$6.07
361	Electric distributing equipment	229.45	238.05	243.41	247.64	–	5.61	5.75	6.01	6.04	–
3612	Transformers	210.71	214.20	230.52	235.15	–	5.19	5.25	5.65	5.68	–
3613	Switchgear and switchboard apparatus	245.55	258.10	254.87	258.62	–	5.96	6.16	6.34	6.37	–
362	Electrical industrial apparatus	231.24	238.21	244.22	251.93	–	5.64	5.74	6.01	6.10	–
3621	Motors and generators	238.79	248.89	250.70	256.88	–	5.81	5.94	6.19	6.25	–
3622	Industrial controls	208.15	213.46	229.39	237.06	–	5.23	5.31	5.65	5.74	–
363	Household appliances	220.70	225.84	233.63	231.48	–	5.49	5.59	5.87	5.89	–
3632	Household refrigerators and freezers	237.80	249.99	255.10	247.29	–	5.80	5.91	6.33	6.39	–
3633	Household laundry equipment	245.36	271.88	266.81	267.88	–	6.44	6.68	6.93	6.94	–
3634	Electric housewares and fans	189.54	190.24	203.00	203.00	–	4.68	4.78	5.00	5.00	–
364	Electric lighting and wiring equipment	209.56	218.48	223.51	226.95	–	5.20	5.29	5.56	5.59	–
3641	Electric lamps	226.32	230.16	247.61	251.40	–	5.52	5.60	6.01	6.00	–
3643	Current-carrying wiring devices	198.13	204.26	206.92	210.94	–	4.88	4.91	5.16	5.17	–
3644	Noncurrent-carrying wiring devices	221.81	218.70	224.80	228.42	–	5.41	5.40	5.62	5.64	–
3645	Residential lighting fixtures	161.83	161.68	168.66	166.73	–	4.27	4.30	4.45	4.47	–
365	Radio and TV receiving equipment	204.53	210.48	216.78	214.82	–	5.05	5.21	5.53	5.48	–
3651	Radio and TV receiving sets	202.27	214.12	219.63	216.55	–	5.16	5.38	5.69	5.61	–
366	Communication equipment	264.13	269.22	280.71	284.28	–	6.38	6.41	6.83	6.85	–
3661	Telephone and telegraph apparatus	268.51	273.46	278.20	283.91	–	6.47	6.48	6.99	7.01	–
3662	Radio and TV communication equipment	260.19	265.85	281.82	284.01	–	6.30	6.36	6.71	6.73	–
367	Electronic components and accessories	185.78	190.88	201.40	205.22	–	4.61	4.69	5.01	5.03	–
3671-3	Electronic tubes	248.67	253.73	263.96	266.49	–	5.81	5.97	6.33	6.30	–
3674	Semiconductors and related devices	208.69	217.35	226.70	230.33	–	5.09	5.25	5.57	5.55	–
3679	Electronic components, nec	169.49	175.77	185.07	190.01	–	4.28	4.34	4.65	4.68	–
369	Misc. electrical equipment and supplies	282.32	292.58	292.74	294.28	–	6.69	6.82	7.14	7.16	–
3691	Storage batteries	305.27	305.06	313.96	306.71	–	6.86	6.84	7.37	7.32	–
3694	Engine electrical equipment	313.83	330.48	321.18	325.19	–	7.49	7.65	7.95	7.99	–
37	**TRANSPORTATION EQUIPMENT**	323.24	337.48	350.57	355.18	367.00	7.57	7.67	8.21	8.26	8.36
371	Motor vehicles and equipment	359.86	379.86	389.39	395.60	–	8.16	8.24	8.87	8.91	–
3711	Motor vehicles and car bodies	381.33	400.76	412.83	422.55	–	8.55	8.60	9.34	9.39	–
3713	Truck and bus bodies	260.00	272.30	277.60	279.05	–	6.50	6.53	6.94	6.89	–
3714	Motor vehicle parts and accessories	357.58	380.94	391.16	394.26	–	8.09	8.21	8.81	8.84	–
3715	Truck trailers	214.52	224.13	222.66	224.62	–	5.39	5.48	5.68	5.88	–
372	Aircraft and parts	302.60	309.60	329.45	335.91	–	7.12	7.20	7.77	7.83	–
3721	Aircraft	305.11	311.58	337.50	345.40	–	7.23	7.28	7.96	8.07	–
3724	Aircraft engines and engine parts	309.33	319.27	334.05	340.00	–	7.33	7.53	8.03	8.00	–
3728	Aircraft equipment, nec	288.61	293.05	302.40	306.24	–	6.65	6.63	7.00	7.04	–
373	Ship and boat building and repairing	245.07	245.78	267.30	(*)	–	6.22	6.27	6.75	(*)	–
3731	Shipbuilding and repairing	257.68	257.40	283.14	(*)	–	6.54	6.60	7.15	(*)	–
3732	Boat building and repairing	198.29	201.39	212.51	213.55	–	5.02	5.06	5.38	5.42	–
374	Railroad equipment	309.37	324.66	329.11	336.36	–	7.62	7.73	8.29	8.43	–

See footnotes at end of table.

1972 SIC Code	Industry	Average weekly hours					Average overtime hours				
		Nov. 1977	Dec. 1977	Oct. 1978	Nov. 1978p	Dec. 1978p	Nov. 1977	Dec. 1977	Oct. 1978	Nov. 1978p	Dec. 1978p
	MACHINERY, EXCEPT ELECTRICAL—Continued										
3531	Construction machinery	41.4	41.9	41.7	41.8	–	3.0	3.7	3.2	3.0	–
3532	Mining machinery	40.9	40.7	43.3	42.9	–	3.1	2.7	3.8	3.3	–
3533	Oil field machinery	43.7	45.0	44.2	44.4	–	4.8	5.9	5.9	5.5	–
3535	Conveyers and conveying equipment	42.8	42.5	41.9	42.4	–	4.8	4.5	4.1	4.2	–
3537	Industrial trucks and tractors	40.9	42.4	41.2	41.3	–	3.1	4.2	3.9	3.8	–
354	Metalworking machinery	44.4	45.2	43.8	44.4	–	6.2	6.6	5.9	6.3	–
3541	Machine tools, metal cutting types	45.3	46.0	44.7	45.4	–	6.4	7.0	6.8	7.2	–
3542	Machine tools, metal forming types	42.7	43.9	43.1	44.1	–	5.2	6.1	5.9	6.7	–
3544	Special dies, tools, jigs, and fixtures	45.9	46.4	44.9	45.5	–	7.8	7.8	6.8	7.2	–
3545	Machine tool accessories	43.3	44.2	42.2	42.7	–	4.6	5.3	4.9	5.2	–
3546	Power driven hand tools	41.4	42.9	40.7	41.3	–	3.9	4.7	3.3	3.7	–
355	Special industry machinery	41.9	43.1	41.4	42.0	–	3.8	4.8	4.0	4.2	–
3551	Food products machinery	41.3	42.4	41.5	42.1	–	3.4	3.8	3.5	3.8	–
3552	Textile machinery	41.3	42.2	40.7	41.3	–	2.8	3.6	3.0	3.1	–
3555	Printing trades machinery	42.2	43.6	41.4	42.3	–	4.3	5.8	4.3	4.5	–
356	General industrial machinery	41.8	42.3	41.5	42.0	–	3.9	4.6	4.4	4.5	–
3561	Pumps and pumping equipment	42.4	42.9	41.2	41.7	–	4.4	4.8	4.1	4.2	–
3562	Ball and roller bearings	41.7	42.1	41.8	42.0	–	4.6	4.6	5.2	5.2	–
3563	Air and gas compressors	43.6	43.2	42.5	43.4	–	4.6	5.8	4.1	4.3	–
3564	Blowers and fans	40.8	41.5	40.2	41.3	–	3.0	3.9	3.5	3.7	–
3566	Speed changers, drives, and gears	41.9	44.0	43.7	44.0	–	3.5	5.4	5.1	5.2	–
3568	Power transmission equipment, nec	41.0	42.9	42.1	42.2	–	3.7	5.1	4.8	4.8	–
357	Office and computing machines	41.6	41.8	41.3	42.2	–	3.4	3.7	3.2	3.3	–
3573	Electronic computing equipment	41.9	42.3	41.2	42.2	–	3.7	3.9	3.1	3.4	–
358	Refrigeration and service machinery	41.6	42.9	40.9	40.6	–	3.6	3.7	3.2	3.1	–
3585	Refrigeration and heating equipment	42.4	43.5	41.1	40.7	–	4.0	3.7	3.3	3.3	–
359	Misc. machinery, except electrical	42.1	42.7	42.7	43.1	–	4.8	4.9	5.1	5.2	–
3592	Carburetors, pistons, rings, valves	41.9	43.0	42.8	43.7	–	3.4	3.9	4.0	4.7	–
3599	Machinery, except electrical, nec	42.1	42.6	42.7	43.0	–	5.0	5.1	5.3	5.3	–
36	**ELECTRIC AND ELECTRONIC EQUIPMENT**	40.8	41.3	40.4	40.7	41.1	2.9	3.1	2.9	3.1	–
361	Electric distributing equipment	40.9	41.4	40.5	41.0	–	2.7	3.4	2.9	3.1	–
3612	Transformers	40.6	40.8	40.8	41.4	–	2.3	2.6	3.0	3.2	–
3613	Switchgear and switchboard apparatus	41.2	41.9	40.2	40.6	–	3.0	4.0	2.9	3.0	–
362	Electrical industrial apparatus	41.0	41.5	40.5	41.3	–	3.1	3.6	3.1	3.3	–
3621	Motors and generators	41.1	41.9	40.5	41.1	–	3.4	4.0	3.2	3.4	–
3622	Industrial controls	39.8	40.2	40.6	41.3	–	2.2	2.5	2.5	2.9	–
363	Household appliances	40.2	40.4	39.8	39.3	–	2.4	2.3	2.3	2.2	–
3632	Household refrigerators and freezers	41.0	42.3	40.3	38.7	–	1.1	1.5	1.6	1.5	–
3633	Household laundry equipment	38.1	40.7	38.5	38.6	–	1.3	2.7	.8	1.6	–
3634	Electric housewares and fans	40.5	39.8	40.6	40.6	–	2.9	2.3	3.4	2.8	–
364	Electric lighting and wiring equipment	40.3	41.3	40.2	40.6	–	2.6	2.8	3.0	3.1	–
3641	Electric lamps	41.0	41.1	41.2	41.9	–	2.3	2.2	2.9	3.3	–
3643	Current-carrying wiring devices	40.6	41.6	40.1	40.8	–	2.8	3.3	3.0	3.0	–
3644	Noncurrent-carrying wiring devices	41.0	40.5	40.0	40.5	–	2.5	2.3	3.0	3.1	–
3645	Residential lighting fixtures	37.9	37.6	37.9	37.3	–	1.9	1.9	2.2	2.0	–
365	Radio and TV receiving equipment	40.5	40.4	39.2	39.2	–	2.7	2.4	2.4	2.2	–
3651	Radio and TV receiving sets	39.2	39.8	38.6	38.6	–	1.5	2.1	1.8	1.6	–
366	Communication equipment	41.4	42.0	41.1	41.5	–	3.1	3.3	3.0	3.3	–
3661	Telephone and telegraph apparatus	41.5	42.2	39.8	40.5	–	3.1	3.3	2.9	3.4	–
3662	Radio and TV communication equipment	41.3	41.8	42.0	42.2	–	3.0	3.3	3.1	3.3	–
367	Electronic components and accessories	40.3	40.7	40.2	40.8	–	2.6	2.9	2.8	3.0	–
3671-3	Electronic tubes	42.8	42.5	41.7	42.3	–	2.7	2.8	2.1	2.7	–
3674	Semiconductors and related devices	41.0	41.4	40.7	41.5	–	3.6	3.6	3.6	3.8	–
3679	Electronic components, nec	39.6	40.5	39.8	40.6	–	2.3	2.7	2.7	2.9	–
369	Misc. electrical equipment and supplies	42.2	49.9	41.0	41.1	–	4.3	4.3	4.0	3.9	–
3691	Storage batteries	44.5	44.6	42.6	41.9	–	5.2	5.4	5.4	5.0	–
3694	Engine electrical equipment	41.9	43.2	40.4	40.7	–	4.7	4.5	3.8	3.9	–
37	**TRANSPORTATION EQUIPMENT**	42.7	44.0	42.7	43.0	43.9	5.3	5.0	5.5	5.6	–
371	Motor vehicles and equipment	44.1	46.1	43.9	44.4	–	6.5	5.9	7.0	7.2	–
3711	Motor vehicles and car bodies	44.6	46.6	44.2	45.0	–	7.2	5.9	7.4	7.9	–
3713	Truck and bus bodies	40.0	41.7	40.0	40.5	–	3.2	3.0	3.7	3.5	–
3714	Motor vehicle parts and accessories	44.2	46.4	44.4	44.6	–	6.5	6.4	7.2	7.2	–
3715	Truck trailers	39.8	40.9	39.2	38.2	–	2.7	3.5	2.7	3.1	–
372	Aircraft and parts	42.5	43.0	42.4	42.9	–	4.4	4.6	4.6	4.7	–
3721	Aircraft	42.2	42.8	42.4	42.8	–	3.4	3.7	4.0	4.0	–
3724	Aircraft engines and engine parts	42.2	42.4	41.6	42.5	–	5.0	5.0	5.2	5.3	–
3728	Aircraft equipment, nec	43.4	44.2	43.2	43.5	–	5.5	5.9	5.6	5.9	–
373	Ship and boat building and repairing	39.4	39.2	39.6	(*)	–	2.7	3.0	2.8	(*)	–
3731	Ship building and repairing	39.4	39.0	39.6	(*)	–	2.8	3.1	2.8	(*)	–
3732	Boat building and repairing	39.5	39.8	39.5	39.4	–	2.5	2.4	2.8	2.4	–
374	Railroad equipment	40.6	42.0	39.7	39.9	–	3.7	4.4	3.6	3.6	–

See footnotes at end of table.

1972 SIC Code	Industry	Average weekly earnings					Average hourly earnings				
		Nov. 1977	Dec. 1977	Oct. 1978	Nov. 1978 P	Dec. 1978 P	Nov. 1977	Dec. 1977	Oct. 1978	Nov. 1978 P	Dec. 1978 P
	TRANSPORTATION EQUIPMENT—Continued										
376	Guided missiles, space vehicles, parts	$296.94	$315.25	$335.82	$346.84	–	$7.35	$7.56	$7.72	$7.83	–
3761	Guided missiles and space vehicles	299.02	323.75	331.55	346.80	–	7.57	7.82	7.97	8.16	–
379	Miscellaneous transportation equipment	217.49	213.88	223.91	224.87	–	5.52	5.47	5.64	5.65	–
3792	Travel trailers and campers	188.86	181.28	196.72	192.53	–	4.97	4.86	5.07	5.04	–
38	**INSTRUMENTS AND RELATED PRODUCTS**	222.63	227.56	237.39	240.20	$247.28	5.43	5.51	5.79	5.83	$5.93
381	Engineering and scientific instruments	242.76	252.59	261.69	260.53	–	5.78	5.82	6.10	6.13	–
382	Measuring and controlling devices	224.81	227.00	241.13	245.14	–	5.51	5.55	5.91	5.95	–
3822	Environmental controls	208.43	216.36	224.87	231.13	–	5.25	5.29	5.58	5.61	–
3823	Process control instruments	234.92	233.79	254.28	260.15	–	5.62	5.62	6.04	6.05	–
3825	Instruments to measure electricity............	234.60	236.64	249.48	250.48	–	5.75	5.80	6.16	6.20	–
383	Optical instruments and lenses	256.36	261.22	271.92	280.86	–	5.80	5.87	6.18	6.34	–
384	Medical instruments and supplies	186.80	189.41	201.10	201.80	–	4.67	4.70	4.99	5.02	–
3841	Surgical and medical instruments	179.45	184.26	197.41	195.50	–	4.42	4.44	4.78	4.78	–
3842	Surgical appliances and supplies............	192.06	193.16	204.46	207.36	–	4.85	4.89	5.15	5.21	–
385	Ophthalmic goods	168.60	169.60	179.41	185.50	–	4.29	4.36	4.66	4.72	–
386	Photographic equipment and supplies	291.21	306.56	306.68	307.52	–	6.82	7.08	7.25	7.27	–
387	Watches, clocks, and watchcases	170.83	174.84	176.71	178.75	–	4.26	4.36	4.44	4.48	–
39	**MISCELLANEOUS MANUFACTURING**										
	INDUSTRIES	176.12	177.51	186.51	188.64	193.25	4.47	4.54	4.77	4.80	4.88
391	Jewelry, silverware, and plated ware	192.98	191.70	191.69	197.20	–	4.65	4.71	4.89	4.93	–
3911	Jewelry, precious metal	196.88	193.66	184.89	191.58	–	4.71	4.77	4.84	4.85	–
393	Musical instruments	173.32	175.85	184.61	187.78	–	4.29	4.31	4.65	4.73	–
394	Toys and sporting goods	154.31	158.50	168.58	168.52	–	4.05	4.16	4.39	4.40	–
3942, 4	Dolls, games, toys, and children's vehicles ...	142.09	144.08	160.40	160.40	–	3.83	3.98	4.21	4.21	–
3949	Sporting and athletic goods, nec	164.58	167.38	176.79	176.33	–	4.22	4.27	4.58	4.58	–
395	Pens, pencils, office and art supplies	186.05	191.32	198.05	201.06	–	4.56	4.61	4.89	4.94	–
396	Costume jewelry and notions	149.77	148.14	156.15	155.45	–	3.89	3.94	4.12	4.08	–
3961	Costume jewelry	139.43	137.27	144.20	140.21	–	3.65	3.70	3.94	3.81	–
399	Miscellaneous manufactures	198.69	198.35	213.07	217.74	–	5.03	5.06	5.34	5.43	–
3993	Signs and advertising displays	216.46	212.31	222.61	229.20	–	5.48	5.43	5.65	5.73	–
	NONDURABLE GOODS										
20	**FOOD AND KINDRED PRODUCTS**	222.31	225.68	235.60	239.20	241.80	5.53	5.60	5.89	5.98	6.03
201	Meat products	228.10	228.23	238.60	243.79	–	5.66	5.72	6.01	6.11	–
2011	Meat packing plants	286.62	285.02	301.07	309.33	–	6.76	6.77	7.22	7.33	–
2013	Sausages and other prepared meats	261.23	265.58	267.34	272.52	–	6.45	6.59	6.82	6.83	–
2016	Poultry dressing plants	134.23	132.11	145.88	146.49	–	3.57	3.59	3.89	3.97	–
202	Dairy products	231.26	234.34	247.39	250.06	–	5.48	5.54	5.99	6.04	–
2022	Cheese, natural and processed	215.97	216.63	226.63	225.50	–	5.13	5.22	5.68	5.68	–
2026	Fluid milk	241.79	246.78	258.07	263.08	–	5.61	5.66	6.13	6.19	–
203	Preserved fruits and vegetables	181.16	184.02	199.25	195.58	–	4.73	4.83	5.07	5.08	–
2032	Canned specialties	218.51	224.17	245.27	255.09	–	5.24	5.35	5.91	5.96	–
2033	Canned fruits and vegetables	174.19	178.00	183.05	186.90	–	4.67	4.85	4.95	4.88	–
2037	Frozen fruits and vegetables	176.79	173.45	195.62	177.88	–	4.58	4.65	4.94	4.86	–
204	Grain mill products	264.72	270.50	286.18	284.68	–	6.03	6.12	6.46	6.47	–
2041	Flour and other grain mill products	305.28	295.22	335.12	340.82	–	6.40	6.39	7.07	7.16	–
2048	Prepared feeds, nec	206.35	216.23	228.51	225.85	–	4.81	4.87	5.17	5.18	–
205	Bakery products	228.10	228.49	237.39	242.35	–	5.76	5.77	6.15	6.23	–
2051	Bread, cake, and related products	225.98	227.34	236.31	240.24	–	5.75	5.77	6.17	6.24	–
2052	Cookies and crackers	235.89	234.67	241.35	248.00	–	5.81	5.78	6.11	6.20	–
206	Sugar and confectionery products	201.50	208.82	227.03	228.97	–	5.18	5.26	5.69	5.71	–
2061-3	Cane and beet sugar	230.88	256.80	261.62	277.55	–	5.86	6.00	6.59	6.64	–
2065	Confectionery products	176.87	174.55	200.30	193.44	–	4.63	4.63	5.02	4.96	–
207	Fats and oils	251.43	259.45	268.32	278.13	–	5.65	5.74	6.14	6.25	–
208	Beverages	269.99	274.03	282.40	286.63	–	6.65	6.70	7.06	7.13	–
2082	Malt beverages	380.61	390.28	395.65	410.73	–	8.79	8.87	9.65	9.71	–
2086	Bottled and canned soft drinks	189.47	194.39	205.15	201.76	–	4.96	5.01	5.22	5.20	–
209	Misc. foods and kindred products	184.99	188.57	193.91	200.31	–	4.83	4.86	5.13	5.23	–
21	**TOBACCO MANUFACTURES**	226.69	224.46	224.63	238.55	246.91	5.71	5.80	5.99	6.18	6.38
211	Cigarettes	279.10	277.11	273.04	288.79	–	6.96	6.98	7.46	7.56	–
22	**TEXTILE MILL PRODUCTS**	168.51	169.33	178.13	180.67	182.78	4.12	4.14	4.42	4.45	4.48
221	Weaving mills, cotton	177.57	176.73	190.81	194.84	–	4.31	4.30	4.62	4.65	–
222	Weaving mills, synthetics	181.38	182.23	195.67	198.34	–	4.36	4.37	4.67	4.70	–
223	Weaving and finishing mills, wool	172.03	177.57	184.87	187.32	–	4.29	4.31	4.52	4.58	–
224	Narrow fabric mills	153.95	157.67	162.37	167.27	–	3.82	3.84	4.09	4.13	–
225	Knitting mills	150.11	147.44	155.90	157.06	–	3.81	3.80	4.06	4.09	–

See footnotes at end of table.

1972 SIC Code	Industry	Average weekly hours					Average overtime hours				
		Nov. 1977	Dec. 1977	Oct. 1978	Nov. 1978p	Dec. 1978p	Nov. 1977	Dec. 1977	Oct. 1978	Nov. 1978p	Dec. 1978p
	TRANSPORTATION EQUIPMENT—Continued										
376	Guided missiles, space vehicles, parts	40.4	41.7	43.5	44.3	–	3.3	3.3	5.4	5.8	–
3761	Guided missiles and space vehicles	39.5	41.4	41.6	42.5	–	3.0	3.0	4.0	4.5	–
379	Miscellaneous transportation equipment	39.4	39.1	39.7	39.8	–	2.3	2.3	2.3	2.1	–
3792	Travel trailers and campers	38.0	37.3	38.8	38.2	–	2.0	2.1	2.2	1.9	–
38	**INSTRUMENTS AND RELATED PRODUCTS**	41.0	41.3	41.0	41.2	41.7	2.6	2.8	2.9	2.8	–
381	Engineering and scientific instruments	42.0	43.4	42.9	42.5	–	3.2	3.6	3.7	3.5	–
382	Measuring and controlling devices	40.8	40.9	40.8	41.2	–	2.4	2.7	2.5	2.6	–
3822	Environmental controls	39.7	40.9	40.3	41.2	–	1.8	2.5	1.6	2.2	–
3823	Process control instruments	41.8	41.6	42.1	43.0	–	3.1	3.3	3.7	3.7	–
3825	Instruments to measure electricity	40.8	40.8	40.5	40.4	–	2.1	2.4	2.0	2.0	–
383	Optical instruments and lenses	44.2	44.5	44.0	44.3	–	3.8	4.3	3.5	4.0	–
384	Medical instruments and supplies	40.0	40.3	40.3	40.2	–	2.1	2.1	3.2	2.6	–
3841	Surgical and medical instruments	40.6	41.5	41.3	40.9	–	1.9	2.0	4.3	3.2	–
3842	Surgical appliances and supplies	39.6	39.5	39.7	39.8	–	2.5	2.4	2.4	2.2	–
385	Ophthalmic goods	39.3	38.9	38.5	39.3	–	1.4	1.5	1.8	1.9	–
386	Photographic equipment and supplies	42.7	43.3	42.3	42.3	–	3.4	3.7	3.5	3.5	–
387	Watches, clocks, and watchcases	40.1	40.1	39.8	39.9	–	2.3	2.3	2.4	2.1	–
39	**MISCELLANEOUS MANUFACTURING INDUSTRIES**	39.4	39.1	39.1	39.3	39.6	2.7	2.5	2.8	2.5	–
391	Jewelry, silverware, and plated ware	41.5	40.7	39.2	40.0	–	4.6	4.0	3.2	3.7	–
3911	Jewelry, precious metal	41.8	40.6	38.2	39.5	–	5.3	4.6	2.8	3.8	–
393	Musical instruments	40.4	40.8	39.7	39.7	–	2.0	2.3	2.1	2.1	–
394	Toys and sporting goods	38.1	38.1	38.4	38.3	–	1.8	1.8	2.3	1.8	–
3942, 4	Dolls, games, toys, and children's vehicles	37.1	36.2	38.1	38.1	–	1.4	1.3	2.8	1.8	–
3949	Sporting and athletic goods, nec	39.0	39.2	38.6	38.5	–	2.1	2.1	1.9	1.8	–
395	Pens, pencils, office and art supplies	40.8	41.5	41.5	40.7	–	3.3	3.3	2.6	2.9	–
396	Costume jewelry and notions	38.5	37.6	37.9	38.1	–	3.0	2.5	3.1	2.7	–
3961	Costume jewelry	38.2	37.1	36.6	36.8	–	3.2	2.6	3.1	2.3	–
399	Miscellaneous manufactures	39.5	39.2	39.9	40.1	–	2.6	2.3	2.9	2.6	–
3993	Signs and advertising displays	39.5	39.1	39.4	40.0	–	2.9	2.6	2.8	2.6	–
	NONDURABLE GOODS										
20	**FOOD AND KINDRED PRODUCTS**	40.2	40.3	40.0	40.0	40.1	4.1	4.1	4.1	4.0	–
201	Meat products	40.3	39.9	39.7	39.9	–	4.4	4.2	4.0	4.0	–
2011	Meat packing plants	42.4	42.1	41.7	42.2	–	5.1	5.1	5.0	4.8	–
2013	Sausages and other prepared meats	40.5	40.3	39.2	39.9	–	3.6	4.0	3.2	3.4	–
2016	Poultry dressing plants	37.6	36.8	37.5	36.9	–	3.9	3.0	3.1	3.2	–
202	Dairy products	42.2	42.3	41.3	41.4	–	4.0	4.2	4.0	3.9	–
2022	Cheese, natural and processed	42.1	41.5	39.9	39.7	–	4.8	4.4	3.9	3.3	–
2026	Fluid milk	43.1	43.6	42.1	42.5	–	4.2	4.5	4.2	4.3	–
203	Preserved fruits and vegetables	38.3	38.1	39.3	38.5	–	3.1	3.0	4.1	3.4	–
2032	Canned specialties	41.7	41.9	41.5	42.8	–	4.3	4.8	5.9	7.2	–
2033	Canned fruits and vegetables	37.3	36.7	39.0	38.3	–	3.3	2.6	4.7	3.4	–
2037	Frozen fruits and vegetables	38.6	37.3	39.6	36.6	–	2.9	2.8	3.9	2.4	–
204	Grain mill products	43.9	44.2	44.3	44.0	–	6.4	6.3	6.9	6.3	–
2041	Flour and other grain mill products	47.7	46.2	47.4	47.6	–	7.8	6.7	8.6	8.2	–
2048	Prepared feeds, nec	42.9	44.4	44.2	43.6	–	6.3	6.8	6.8	5.9	–
205	Bakery products	39.6	39.6	38.6	38.9	–	3.6	3.6	3.3	3.4	–
2051	Bread, cake, and related products	39.3	39.4	38.3	38.5	–	3.8	3.8	3.5	3.7	–
2052	Cookies and crackers	40.6	42.4	39.5	40.0	–	2.8	2.8	2.4	2.2	–
206	Sugar and confectionery products	38.9	39.7	39.9	40.1	–	3.7	3.7	3.6	3.6	–
2061-3	Cane and beet sugar	39.4	42.8	39.7	41.8	–	5.5	6.1	5.0	5.2	–
2065	Confectionery products	38.2	37.7	39.9	39.0	–	2.7	2.3	3.0	2.9	–
207	Fats and oils	44.5	45.2	43.7	44.5	–	6.5	6.6	6.1	6.1	–
208	Beverages	40.6	40.9	40.0	40.2	–	4.2	4.0	4.0	3.8	–
2082	Malt beverages	43.3	44.0	41.0	42.3	–	5.9	5.1	4.8	5.7	–
2086	Bottled and canned soft drinks	38.2	38.8	39.3	38.8	–	3.1	3.5	3.4	2.8	–
209	Misc. foods and kindred products	38.3	38.8	37.8	38.3	–	3.7	3.6	3.4	3.7	–
21	**TOBACCO MANUFACTURES**	39.7	38.7	37.5	38.6	38.7	2.8	2.7	1.5	2.1	–
211	Cigarettes	40.1	39.7	36.6	38.2	–	2.9	3.0	1.3	2.2	–
22	**TEXTILE MILL PRODUCTS**	40.9	40.9	40.3	40.6	40.8	3.7	3.6	3.6	3.8	–
221	Weaving mills, cotton	41.2	41.1	41.3	41.9	–	4.2	4.1	4.1	4.7	–
222	Weaving mills, synthetics	41.6	41.7	41.9	42.2	–	3.8	3.6	4.2	4.5	–
223	Weaving and finishing mills, wool	40.1	41.2	40.9	40.9	–	3.6	3.9	4.0	3.8	–
224	Narrow fabric mills	40.3	40.8	39.7	40.5	–	3.4	3.6	3.1	3.0	–
225	Knitting mills	39.4	38.8	38.4	38.4	–	2.9	2.6	2.8	2.7	–

See footnotes at end of table.

1972 SIC Code	Industry	Average weekly earnings					Average hourly earnings				
		Nov. 1977	Dec. 1977	Oct. 1978	Nov. 1978P	Dec. 1978P	Nov. 1977	Dec. 1977	Oct. 1978	Nov. 1978P	Dec. 1978P
	TEXTILE MILL PRODUCTS—Continued										
2251	Women's hosiery, except socks	$142.91	$139.91	$153.22	$152.86	–	$3.52	$3.56	$3.84	$3.86	–
2252	Hosiery, nec	141.02	134.17	141.26	140.84	–	3.57	3.54	3.87	3.88	–
2253	Knit outerwear mills	144.02	141.75	147.17	147.50	–	3.80	3.79	4.01	4.03	–
2254	Knit underwear mills	139.32	137.92	143.25	144.02	–	3.60	3.62	3.75	3.78	–
2257	Circular knit fabric mills	170.05	170.10	184.91	187.58	–	4.23	4.20	4.51	4.52	–
226	Textile finishing, except wool	184.29	189.16	189.88	194.68	–	4.43	4.43	4.70	4.76	–
2261	Finishing plants, cotton	191.56	194.79	194.25	199.48	–	4.55	4.53	4.82	4.83	–
2262	Finishing plants, synthetics	191.27	194.54	200.64	202.46	–	4.62	4.61	4.87	4.95	–
227	Floor covering mills	177.66	183.18	189.28	193.28	–	4.21	4.30	4.55	4.58	–
228	Yarn and thread mills	159.01	158.26	168.90	168.87	–	3.85	3.86	4.16	4.18	–
2281	Yarn mills, except wool	162.39	162.09	168.90	169.30	–	3.83	3.85	4.16	4.17	–
2282	Throwing and winding mills	147.73	142.86	162.78	163.61	–	3.74	3.73	3.98	4.07	–
229	Miscellaneous textile goods	187.65	188.58	198.77	200.16	–	4.50	4.49	4.86	4.87	–
23	**APPAREL AND OTHER TEXTILE PRODUCTS**	133.93	135.74	142.76	145.44	$146.52	3.71	3.76	4.01	4.04	$ 4.07
231	Men's and boys' suits and coats	161.82	164.16	175.29	180.68	–	4.52	4.51	4.91	4.95	–
232	Men's and boys' furnishings	122.28	123.08	128.88	131.77	–	3.35	3.40	3.61	3.65	–
2321	Men's and boys' shirts and nightwear	118.13	119.68	127.76	131.38	–	3.21	3.27	3.51	3.57	–
2327	Men's and boys' separate trousers	123.53	122.85	131.65	132.38	–	3.47	3.51	3.74	3.75	–
2328	Men's and boys' work clothing	121.32	121.51	126.73	131.38	–	3.27	3.32	3.53	3.57	.
233	Women's and misses' outerwear	126.79	125.74	134.06	136.40	–	3.74	3.72	3.99	4.00	–
2331	Women's and misses' blouses and waists	121.09	120.01	128.00	129.80	–	3.52	3.54	3.71	3.73	–
2335	Women's and misses' dresses	124.69	124.64	132.43	135.88	–	3.79	3.80	4.10	4.13	–
2337	Women's and misses' suits and coats	135.96	133.17	140.48	141.14	–	4.12	4.06	4.27	4.29	–
2339	Women's and misses' outerwear, nec	126.73	126.02	135.14	137.45	–	3.59	3.58	3.85	3.85	–
234	Women's and children's undergarments	123.50	121.61	130.68	131.77	–	3.32	3.35	3.61	3.63	–
2341	Women's and children's underwear	121.60	118.74	128.16	128.52	–	3.26	3.28	3.56	3.57	–
2342	Brassieres and allied garments	131.01	131.40	143.23	146.65	–	3.56	3.60	3.84	3.89	–
236	Children's outerwear	121.66	125.15	127.09	131.77	–	3.37	3.41	3.58	3.63	–
2361	Children's dresses and blouses	122.64	120.55	126.38	130.31	–	3.36	3.33	3.54	3.57	–
238	Misc. apparel and accessories	134.25	133.56	142.40	143.93	–	3.58	3.60	3.88	3.89	–
239	Misc. fabricated textile products	167.42	181.35	183.22	186.05	–	4.26	4.50	4.71	4.71	–
2391	Curtains and draperies	126.44	120.41	129.48	134.82	–	3.31	3.30	3.49	3.52	–
2392	House furnishing, nec	145.36	146.92	157.97	162.41	–	3.68	3.71	4.03	4.05	–
2396	Automotive and apparel trimmings	274.03	341.42	316.92	315.40	–	6.92	7.39	7.60	7.60	–
26	**PAPER AND ALLIED PRODUCTS**	265.31	272.06	285.90	292.28	296.24	6.17	6.24	6.68	6.75	6.81
261, 2,6	Paper and pulp mills	315.06	322.08	347.85	351.72	–	7.08	7.11	7.73	7.73	–
262	Paper mills, except building paper	315.58	323.05	350.49	354.49	–	7.06	7.10	7.72	7.74	–
263	Paperboard mills	327.52	336.26	356.80	363.78	–	7.23	7.31	8.00	8.12	–
264	Misc. converted paper products	226.87	234.92	242.13	248.95	–	5.48	5.58	5.92	5.97	–
2641	Paper coating and glazing	269.24	284.21	294.19	298.28	–	6.35	6.43	6.81	6.81	–
2642	Envelopes	208.79	212.16	221.05	232.25	–	5.13	5.20	5.54	5.61	–
2643	Bags, except textile bags	221.01	231.12	234.48	235.75	–	5.30	5.40	5.65	5.64	–
265	Paperboard containers and boxes	232.94	237.28	253.80	257.98	–	5.52	5.57	6.00	6.07	–
2651	Folding paperboard boxes	245.10	251.41	264.12	268.55	–	5.70	5.74	6.20	6.26	–
2653	Corrugated and solid fiber boxes	246.96	251.12	271.10	274.34	–	5.77	5.84	6.29	6.38	–
2654	Sanitary food containers	216.83	222.79	226.55	236.70	–	5.25	5.33	5.58	5.69	–
27	**PRINTING AND PUBLISHING**	237.88	239.51	248.72	251.56	255.46	6.26	6.27	6.58	6.62	6.67
271	Newspapers	232.49	234.20	232.90	242.55	–	6.70	6.73	6.79	6.93	–
272	Periodicals	214.70	219.82	232.02	237.68	–	5.85	5.80	5.98	6.11	–
273	Books	220.09	225.48	232.85	232.07	–	5.53	5.54	5.91	5.89	–
2731	Book publishing	218.59	216.68	223.47	222.87	–	5.52	5.39	5.73	5.70	–
2732	Book printing	221.05	233.60	241.38	240.37	–	5.54	5.67	6.08	6.07	–
274	Miscellaneous publishing	217.40	205.42	209.20	213.58	–	5.49	5.42	5.86	5.90	–
275	Commerical printing	251.41	253.09	266.85	267.93	–	6.43	6.44	6.86	6.87	–
2751	Commerical printing, letterpress	236.90	239.34	247.42	246.79	–	6.09	6.09	6.46	6.41	–
2752	Commerical printing, lithographic	259.23	261.86	278.64	280.13	–	6.63	6.68	7.09	7.11	–
276	Manifold business forms	244.08	254.66	258.96	262.29	–	5.91	5.95	6.24	6.26	–
278	Blankbooks and bookbinding	189.21	189.44	197.73	198.74	–	4.79	4.87	5.07	5.07	–
279	Printing trade services	308.32	310.01	331.58	332.35	–	8.05	7.99	8.68	8.61	–
28	**CHEMICALS AND ALLIED PRODUCTS**	279.05	283.58	301.26	304.26	305.95	6.66	6.72	7.19	7.21	7.25
281	Industrial inorganic chemicals	308.13	309.64	334.54	339.40	–	7.25	7.32	7.89	7.93	–
2819	Industrial inorganic chemicals, nec	305.41	307.33	328.22	333.06	–	7.22	7.30	7.89	7.93	–
282	Plastics materials and synthetics	273.84	279.03	299.20	302.87	–	6.52	6.55	7.04	7.06	–
2821	Plastics materials and resins	307.98	310.87	335.92	342.66	–	7.08	7.13	7.74	7.77	–
2824	Organic fibers, noncellulosic	246.22	255.97	273.19	274.03	–	6.02	6.08	6.52	6.54	–
283	Drugs	254.61	261.24	271.00	271.00	–	6.21	6.22	6.53	6.53	–
2834	Pharmaceutical preparations	246.04	251.93	262.22	262.17	–	6.09	6.10	6.38	6.41	–

See footnotes at end of table.

1972 SIC Code	Industry	Average weekly hours					Average overtime hours				
		Nov. 1977	Dec. 1977	Oct. 1978	Nov. 1978 P	Dec. 1978 P	Nov. 1977	Dec. 1977	Oct. 1978	Nov. 1978 P	Dec. 1978 P
	TEXTILE MILL PRODUCTS—Continued										
2251	Women's hosiery, except socks	40.6	39.3	39.9	39.6	–	3.4	2.7	3.1	2.9	–
2252	Hosiery, nec	39.5	37.9	36.5	36.3	–	2.7	1.7	2.3	2.1	–
2253	Knit outerwear mills	37.9	37.4	36.7	36.6	–	2.5	2.2	1.9	1.9	–
2254	Knit underwear mills	38.7	38.1	38.2	38.1	–	2.1	2.2	2.1	2.2	–
2257	Circular knit fabric mills	40.2	40.5	41.0	41.5	–	3.5	3.5	4.6	4.6	–
226	Textile finishing, except wool	41.6	42.7	40.4	40.9	–	4.5	4.6	3.7	4.0	–
2261	Finishing plants, cotton	42.1	43.0	40.3	41.3	–	5.4	5.1	3.8	4.0	–
2262	Finishing plants, synthetics	41.4	42.2	41.2	40.9	–	4.4	4.4	4.2	4.7	–
227	Floor covering mills	42.2	42.6	41.6	42.2	–	4.3	5.0	4.3	4.6	–
228	Yarn and thread mills	41.3	41.0	40.6	40.4	–	3.9	3.7	3.7	3.4	–
2281	Yarn mills, except wool	42.4	42.1	40.6	40.6	–	4.4	4.2	3.8	3.6	–
2282	Throwing and winding mills	39.5	38.3	40.9	40.2	–	3.1	2.8	3.7	3.5	–
229	Miscellaneous textile goods	41.7	42.0	40.9	41.1	–	4.1	3.8	4.2	3.7	–
23	**APPAREL AND OTHER TEXTILE PRODUCTS**	36.1	36.1	35.6	36.0	36.0	1.5	1.3	1.4	1.4	–
231	Men's and boys' suits and coats	35.8	36.4	35.7	36.5	–	.8	.9	1.0	.9	–
232	Men's and boys' furnishings	36.5	36.2	35.7	36.1	–	1.2	1.0	1.0	1.0	–
2321	Men's and boys' shirts and nighwear	36.8	36.6	36.4	36.8	–	1.2	1.0	1.1	1.1	–
2327	Men's and boys' separate trousers	35.6	35.0	35.2	35.3	–	1.2	1.0	.7	.7	–
2328	Men's and boys' work clothing	37.1	36.6	35.9	36.8	–	1.1	.8	.9	1.1	–
233	Women's and misses' outerwear	33.9	33.8	33.6	34.1	–	1.3	1.2	1.2	1.2	–
2331	Women's and misses' blouses and waists	34.4	33.9	34.5	34.8	–	1.1	1.0	1.0	1.2	–
2335	Women's and misses' dresses	32.9	32.8	32.3	32.9	–	1.2	1.2	1.2	1.2	–
2337	Women's and misses' suits and coats	33.0	32.8	32.9	32.9		1.3	1.3	.9	.8	–
2339	Women's and misses' outerwear, nec	35.3	35.2	35.1	35.7	–	1.5	1.1	1.4	1.4	–
234	Women's and children's undergarments	37.2	36.3	36.2	36.3	–	1.5	1.0	1.3	1.1	–
2341	Women's and children's underwear	37.3	36.2	36.0	36.0	–	1.5	1.0	1.3	1.1	–
2342	Brassieres and allied garments	36.8	36.5	37.3	37.7	–	1.3	1.1	1.1	1.1	–
236	Children's outerwear	36.1	36.7	35.5	36.3	–	1.5	1.4	1.2	1.4	–
2361	Children's dresses and blouses	36.5	36.2	35.7	36.5	–	2.0	1.9	1.8	1.6	–
238	Misc. apparel and accessories	37.5	37.1	36.7	37.0	–	1.9	1.4	1.7	1.7	–
239	Misc. fabricated textile products	39.3	40.3	38.9	39.5	–	2.6	2.6	2.8	2.8	–
2391	Curtains and draperies	38.2	37.7	37.1	38.3	–	2.2	1.3	1.7	2.2	–
2392	House furnishings, nec	39.5	39.6	39.2	40.1	–	2.7	2.5	2.6	2.8	–
2396	Automotive and apparel trimmings	39.6	46.2	41.7	41.5	–	2.9	4.3	5.1	4.6	–
26	**PAPER AND ALLIED PRODUCTS**	43.0	43.6	42.8	43.3	43.5	4.9	5.2	5.3	5.3	–
261, 2, 6	Paper and pulp mills	44.5	45.3	45.0	45.5	–	6.5	6.6	6.9	6.9	–
262	Paper mills, except building paper	44.7	45.5	45.4	45.8	–	6.5	6.6	7.0	7.1	–
263	Paperboard mills	45.3	46.0	44.6	44.8	–	6.9	7.6	7.4	7.5	–
264	Misc. converted paper products	41.4	42.1	40.9	41.7	–	3.7	4.0	4.0	4.1	–
2641	Paper coating and glazing	42.4	44.2	43.2	43.8	–	5.1	5.8	5.8	5.5	–
2642	Envelopes	40.7	40.8	39.9	41.4	–	2.8	3.0	3.4	3.6	–
2643	Bags, except textile bags	41.7	42.8	41.5	41.8	–	3.9	4.6	3.8	4.0	–
265	Paperboard containers and boxes	42.2	42.6	42.3	42.5	–	3.9	4.0	4.5	4.3	–
2651	Folding paperboard boxes	43.0	43.8	42.6	42.9	–	4.1	4.5	4.9	4.4	–
2653	Corrugated and solid fiber boxes	42.8	43.0	43.1	43.0	–	4.5	4.5	5.2	4.8	–
2654	Sanitary food containers	41.3	41.8	40.6	41.6	–	2.7	3.0	3.1	3.4	–
27	**PRINTING AND PUBLISHING**	38.0	38.2	37.8	38.0	38.3	3.0	3.2	3.3	3.2	–
271	Newspapers	34.7	34.8	34.3	35.0	–	2.1	2.1	2.2	2.3	–
272	Periodicals	36.7	37.9	38.8	38.9	–	3.0	3.4	3.6	3.0	–
273	Books	39.8	40.7	39.4	39.4	–	3.6	4.2	3.9	3.7	–
2731	Book publishing	39.6	40.2	39.0	39.1	–	3.0	3.3	2.1	2.1	–
2732	Book printing	39.9	41.2	39.7	39.6	–	4.1	5.0	5.6	5.2	–
274	Miscellaneous publishing	39.6	37.9	35.7	36.2	–	2.9	2.1	2.5	2.4	–
275	Commercial printing	39.1	39.3	38.9	39.0	–	3.5	3.8	3.9	3.7	–
2751	Commerical printing, letterpress	38.9	39.3	38.3	38.5	–	3.2	3.3	3.2	2.9	–
2752	Commercial printing, lithographic	39.1	39.2	39.3	39.4	–	3.7	4.1	4.2	4.1	–
276	Manifold business forms	41.3	42.8	41.5	41.9	–	3.9	4.9	3.9	4.0	–
278	Blankbooks and bookbinding	39.5	38.9	39.0	39.2	–	2.4	2.3	2.5	2.4	–
279	Printing trade service	38.3	38.8	38.2	38.6	–	3.1	3.2	3.9	3.4	–
28	**CHEMICALS AND ALLIED PRODUCTS**	41.9	42.2	41.9	42.2	42.2	3.2	3.4	3.7	3.6	–
281	Industrial inorganic chemicals	42.5	42.3	42.4	42.8	–	3.6	3.7	4.0	4.0	–
2819	Industrial inorganic chemicals, nec	42.3	42.1	41.6	42.0	–	3.3	3.3	3.4	3.3	–
282	Plastics materials and synthetics	42.0	42.6	42.5	42.9	–	3.0	3.2	3.5	3.6	–
2821	Plastics materials and resins	43.5	43.6	43.4	44.1	–	4.5	4.4	4.9	5.0	–
2824	Organic fibers, noncellulosic	40.9	42.1	41.9	41.9	–	2.0	2.4	2.2	2.2	–
283	Drugs	41.0	42.0	41.5	41.5	–	2.9	3.0	2.9	3.0	–
2834	Pharmaceutical preparations	40.4	41.3	41.1	40.9	–	2.7	2.9	2.9	2.9	–

See footnotes at end of table.

1972 SIC Code	Industry	Average weekly earnings					Average hourly earnings				
		Nov. 1977	Dec. 1977	Oct. 1978	Nov. 1978 P	Dec. 1978 P	Nov. 1977	Dec. 1977	Oct. 1978	Nov. 1978 P	Dec. 1978 P
	CHEMICALS AND ALLIED PRODUCTS—Cont'd										
284	Soap, cleaners, and toilet goods	$260.35	$261.58	$271.62	$275.95	–	$6.35	$6.38	$6.74	$6.78	–
2841	Soap and other detergents	349.80	353.22	378.44	376.28	–	8.06	8.12	8.66	8.69	–
2842, 3	Polishing, sanitation, and finishing preparations	228.42	229.80	245.43	244.42	–	5.64	5.66	6.09	6.08	–
2844	Toilet preparations	210.00	210.79	212.42	218.23	–	5.33	5.35	5.59	5.61	–
285	Paints and allied products	247.61	252.34	264.27	268.51	–	6.01	6.11	6.43	6.47	–
286	Industrial organic chemicals	324.19	334.19	359.54	365.04	–	7.61	7.79	8.44	8.45	–
2865	Cyclic crudes and intermediates	307.55	315.92	322.63	329.30	–	7.07	7.33	7.70	7.73	–
2861, 9	Gum, wood, and industrial organic chemicals, nec	329.94	340.26	372.36	378.01	–	7.80	7.95	8.70	8.71	–
287	Agricultural chemicals	268.60	272.84	300.61	300.33	–	6.38	6.45	7.04	7.05	–
289	Miscellaneous chemical products	262.06	266.07	280.06	282.66	–	6.21	6.29	6.70	6.73	–
29	**PETROLEUM AND COAL PRODUCTS**	340.92	348.00	384.08	384.12	$388.07	7.91	8.00	8.67	8.73	$8.86
291	Petroleum refining	367.65	371.95	407.09	411.65	–	8.55	8.61	9.38	9.42	–
295	Paving and roofing materials	268.62	277.86	333.20	313.72	–	6.05	6.08	6.87	6.82	–
30	**RUBBER AND MISC. PLASTICS PRODUCTS**	215.78	218.48	233.76	236.55	244.76	5.25	5.29	5.66	5.70	5.80
301	Tires and inner tubes	313.54	314.08	362.37	372.22	–	7.36	7.39	8.18	8.29	–
302	Rubber and plastics footwear	141.31	142.72	148.61	150.93	–	3.68	3.65	3.84	3.87	–
303, 4	Reclaimed rubber, and rubber and plastics hose and belting	277.10	223.31	238.71	245.53	–	5.42	5.46	5.78	5.86	–
306	Fabricated rubber products, nec	205.41	209.99	221.40	221.40	–	5.01	5.06	5.40	5.40	–
307	Miscellaneous plastics products	196.32	199.26	210.12	210.94	–	4.80	4.86	5.15	5.17	–
31	**LEATHER AND LEATHER PRODUCTS**	138.37	138.01	146.17	147.66	148.40	3.68	3.69	3.94	3.98	4.00
311	Leather tanning and finishing	199.79	200.29	202.93	205.27	–	4.97	4.97	5.19	5.21	–
314	Footwear, except rubber	132.77	132.79	139.85	140.91	–	3.55	3.56	3.79	3.85	–
3143	Men's footwear, except athletic	141.66	142.43	148.97	148.14	–	3.67	3.69	3.91	3.94	–
3144	Women's footwear, except athletic	122.82	123.84	132.10	135.66	–	3.45	3.44	3.69	3.80	–
316	Luggage	138.70	127.97	156.46	160.76	–	3.80	3.72	4.24	4.31	–
317	Handbags and personal leather goods	132.30	130.50	138.73	145.54	–	3.50	3.48	3.78	3.81	–
–	**TRANSPORTATION AND PUBLIC UTILITIES**	291.45	293.06	309.57	309.20	312.76	7.25	7.29	7.72	7.73	7.78
	RAILROAD TRANSPORTATION:										
4011	Class I railroads [2]	337.57	330.81	357.21	(*)	–	7.62	7.64	8.10	(*)	–
41	**LOCAL AND INTERURBAN PASSENGER TRANSIT**	177.14	180.58	196.31	196.18	–	5.21	5.28	5.74	5.67	–
411	Local and suburban transportation	263.74	272.90	289.95	286.86	–	6.48	6.64	6.97	6.83	–
413	Intercity highway transportation	270.82	263.77	312.42	313.01	–	7.44	7.43	8.20	8.13	–
42	**TRUCKING AND WAREHOUSING**	294.19	304.79	320.76	318.39	–	7.30	7.38	7.92	7.94	–
421, 3	Trucking and trucking terminals	301.38	311.74	328.45	324.81	–	7.46	7.53	8.09	8.10	–
422	Public warehousing	207.90	211.60	218.12	225.10	–	5.25	5.29	5.55	5.67	–
46	**PIPE LINES, EXCEPT NATURAL GAS**	337.43	348.19	368.40	376.74	–	8.23	8.31	8.92	8.97	–
48	**COMMUNICATION**	289.98	285.68	302.91	301.36	–	7.16	7.16	7.63	7.61	–
481	Telephone communication	301.84	295.07	313.98	311.24	–	7.38	7.34	7.83	7.82	–
4817	Switchboard operating employees [3]	231.25	222.12	222.33	220.38	–	6.25	6.17	6.52	6.52	–
4818	Line construction employees [4]	413.52	404.50	426.82	424.65	–	8.97	8.89	9.57	9.50	–
483	Radio and television broadcasting	234.32	240.41	256.36	257.26	–	6.15	6.36	6.80	6.77	–
49	**ELECTRIC, GAS, AND SANITARY SERVICES**	305.24	308.28	326.51	329.80	–	7.32	7.34	7.83	7.89	–
491	Electric services	306.29	312.80	327.76	333.80	–	7.31	7.36	7.86	7.91	–
492	Gas production and distribution	279.48	281.26	302.91	299.80	–	6.85	6.86	7.37	7.33	–
493	Combination utility services	341.51	341.90	365.43	370.44	–	8.17	8.16	8.68	8.82	–
495	Sanitary services	251.39	256.22	269.03	262.89	–	5.86	5.89	6.33	6.35	–
–	**WHOLESALE AND RETAIL TRADE**	144.10	146.29	156.31	156.48	158.07	4.38	4.38	4.78	4.80	4.79
50, 51	**WHOLESALE TRADE**	215.34	218.79	236.34	236.51	239.68	5.55	5.61	6.06	6.08	6.13
50	**WHOLESALE TRADE-DURABLE GOODS**	218.51	222.39	239.55	239.55	–	5.56	5.63	6.08	6.08	–
501	Motor vehicles and automotive equipment	198.39	205.27	217.32	219.61	–	5.10	5.21	5.63	5.66	–
502	Furniture and home furnishings	185.37	190.88	206.72	209.34	–	4.93	5.01	5.44	5.48	–
503	Lumber and construction materials	221.20	221.82	243.97	244.16	–	5.60	5.63	6.13	6.15	–
504	Sporting goods, toys, and hobby goods	220.96	229.46	230.49	231.48	–	5.83	5.96	6.13	6.14	–

See footnotes at end of table.

1972 SIC Code	Industry	Average weekly hours					Average overtime hours				
		Nov. 1977	Dec. 1977	Oct. 1978	Nov. 1978 P	Dec. 1978 P	Nov. 1977	Dec. 1977	Oct. 1978	Nov. 1978 P	Dec. 1978 P
	CHEMICALS AND ALLIED PRODUCTS—Cont'd										
284	Soap, cleaners, and toilet goods	41.0	41.0	40.3	40.7	–	3.0	3.1	3.3	3.0	–
2841	Soap and other detergents	43.4	43.5	43.7	43.3	–	4.7	4.8	5.4	4.9	–
2842, 3	Polishing, sanitation, and finishing preparations	40.5	40.6	40.3	40.2	–	2.5	2.8	3.5	2.9	–
2844	Toilet preparations	39.4	39.4	38.0	38.9	–	1.9	1.9	1.8	1.7	–
285	Paints and allied products	41.2	41.3	41.1	41.5	–	2.9	2.9	3.4	3.2	–
286	Industrial organic chemicals	42.6	42.9	42.6	43.2	–	3.3	3.8	3.9	3.8	–
2865	Cyclic crudes and intermediates	43.5	43.1	41.9	42.6	–	4.2	4.3	3.9	4.0	–
2861, 9	Gum, wood, and industrial organic chemicals, nec	42.3	42.8	42.8	43.4	–	3.0	3.6	3.9	3.7	–
287	Agricultural chemicals	42.1	42.3	42.7	42.6	–	4.5	4.6	5.4	4.8	–
289	Miscellaneous chemical products	42.2	42.3	41.8	42.0	–	3.4	3.4	3.8	3.7	–
29	**PETROLEUM AND COAL PRODUCTS**	43.1	43.5	44.3	44.0	43.8	4.1	4.1	4.8	4.4	–
291	Petroleum refining	43.0	43.2	43.4	43.7	–	3.7	3.7	3.7	3.7	–
295	Paving and roofing materials	44.4	45.7	48.5	46.0	–	5.7	6.2	8.9	6.9	–
30	**RUBBER AND MISC. PLASTICS PRODUCTS**	41.1	41.3	41.3	41.5	42.2	3.5	3.5	4.0	3.8	–
301	Tires and inner tubes	42.6	42.5	44.3	44.9	–	4.2	4.4	6.1	5.8	–
302	Rubber and plastics footwear	38.4	39.1	38.7	39.0	–	1.9	2.4	2.3	2.1	–
303, 4	Reclaimed rubber, and rubber and plastics hose and belting	41.9	40.9	41.3	41.9	–	4.3	4.0	4.4	4.7	–
306	Fabricated rubber products, nec	41.0	41.5	41.0	41.0	–	3.1	3.2	3.6	3.5	–
307	Miscellaneous plastics products	40.9	41.0	40.8	40.8	–	3.5	3.4	3.6	3.5	–
31	**LEATHER AND LEATHER PRODUCTS**	37.6	37.4	37.1	37.1	37.1	2.0	1.9	1.7	1.6	–
311	Leather tanning and finishing	40.2	40.3	39.1	39.4	–	3.4	3.1	2.8	2.8	–
314	Footwear, except rubber	37.4	37.3	36.9	36.6	–	1.8	1.8	1.4	1.2	–
3143	Men's footwear, except athletic	38.6	38.6	38.1	37.6	–	2.0	2.2	1.3	1.1	–
3144	Women's footwear, except athletic	35.6	36.0	35.8	35.7	–	1.3	1.5	1.6	1.4	–
316	Luggage	36.5	34.4	36.9	37.3	–	1.9	1.3	2.0	2.1	–
317	Handbags and personal leather goods	37.8	37.5	36.7	38.2	–	2.1	1.8	2.3	2.6	–
–	**TRANSPORTATION AND PUBLIC UTILITIES**	40.2	40.2	40.1	40.0	40.2	–	–	–	–	–
	RAILROAD TRANSPORTATION:										
4011	Class I railroads [2] **	44.3	43.3	44.1	(*)	–	–	–	–	–	–
41	**LOCAL AND INTERURBAN PASSENGER TRANSIT**	34.0	34.2	34.2	34.6	–	–	–	–	–	–
411	Local and suburban transportation	40.7	41.1	41.6	42.0	–	–	–	–	–	–
413	Intercity highway transportation	36.4	35.5	38.1	38.5	–	–	–	–	–	–
42	**TRUCKING AND WAREHOUSING**	40.3	41.3	40.5	40.1	–	–	–	–	–	–
421, 3	Trucking and trucking terminals	40.4	41.4	40.6	40.1	–	–	–	–	–	–
422	Public warehousing	39.6	40.0	39.3	39.7	–	–	–	–	–	–
46	**PIPE LINES, EXCEPT NATURAL GAS**	41.0	41.9	41.3	42.0	–	–	–	–	–	–
48	**COMMUNICATION**	40.5	39.9	39.7	39.6	–	–	–	–	–	–
481	Telephone communication	40.9	40.2	40.1	39.8	–	–	–	–	–	–
4817	Switchboard operating employees [3]	37.0	36.0	34.1	33.8	–	–	–	–	–	–
4818	Line construction employees [4]	46.1	45.5	44.6	44.7	–	–	–	–	–	–
483	Radio and television broadcasting	38.1	37.8	37.7	38.0	–	–	–	–	–	–
49	**ELECTRIC, GAS, AND SANITARY SERVICES**	41.7	42.0	41.7	41.8	–	–	–	–	–	–
491	Electric services	41.9	42.5	41.7	42.2	–	–	–	–	–	–
492	Gas production and distribution	40.8	41.0	41.1	40.9	–	–	–	–	–	–
493	Combination utility services	41.8	41.9	42.1	42.0	–	–	–	–	–	–
495	Sanitary services	42.9	43.5	42.5	41.4	–	–	–	–	–	–
–	**WHOLESALE AND RETAIL TRADE**	32.9	33.4	32.7	32.6	33.0	–	–	–	–	–
50, 51	**WHOLESALE TRADE**	38.8	39.0	39.0	38.9	39.1	–	–	–	–	–
50	**WHOLESALE TRADE-DURABLE GOODS**	39.3	39.5	39.4	39.4	–	–	–	–	–	–
501	Motor vehicles and automotive equipment	38.9	39.4	38.6	38.8	–	–	–	–	–	–
502	Furniture and home furnishings	37.6	38.1	38.0	38.2	–	–	–	–	–	–
503	Lumber and construction materials	39.5	39.4	39.8	39.7	–	–	–	–	–	–
504	Sporting goods, toys, and hobby goods	37.9	38.5	37.6	37.7	–	–	–	–	–	–

See footnotes at end of table.

1972 SIC Code	Industry	Average weekly earnings					Average hourly earnings				
		Nov. 1977	Dec. 1977	Oct. 1978	Nov. 1978 P	Dec. 1978 P	Nov. 1977	Dec. 1977	Oct. 1978	Nov. 1978 P	Dec. 1978 P
	WHOLESALE TRADE-DURABLE GOODS—Continued										
505	Metals and minerals, except petroleum	$254.40	$256.48	$272.55	$274.91	–	$6.36	$6.38	$6.90	$6.89	–
506	Electrical goods	221.55	230.08	243.04	240.17	–	5.71	5.81	6.20	6.19	–
507	Hardware, plumbing, and heating equipment	210.06	211.62	222.53	220.99	–	5.40	5.44	5.78	5.77	–
508	Machinery, equipment, and supplies	230.62	233.42	254.87	254.23	–	5.78	5.85	6.34	6.34	–
509	Miscellaneous durable goods	184.42	187.79	202.01	205.67	–	4.79	4.84	5.22	5.22	–
51	**WHOLESALE TRADE-NONDURABLE GOODS**	210.31	213.71	230.95	232.64	–	5.52	5.58	6.03	6.09	–
511	Paper and paper products	233.68	235.69	265.35	266.45	–	6.35	6.37	7.28	7.28	–
512	Drugs, proprietaries, and sundries	219.82	223.29	238.13	238.08	–	5.68	5.74	6.25	6.20	–
513	Apparel, piece goods, and notions	182.16	183.32	203.69	207.75	–	5.06	5.05	5.55	5.63	–
514	Groceries and related products	215.81	219.82	232.86	235.78	–	5.62	5.68	6.08	6.14	–
516	Chemicals and allied products	237.93	243.57	271.55	267.53	–	6.18	6.31	6.84	6.79	–
517	Petroleum and petroleum products	248.22	252.49	284.40	288.29	–	6.30	6.36	7.20	7.28	–
518	Beer, wine, and distilled beverages	248.16	258.70	262.22	273.33	–	6.60	6.79	7.03	7.25	–
519	Miscellaneous nondurable goods	175.10	176.78	190.96	190.12	–	4.62	4.64	4.96	4.99	–
52-59	**RETAIL TRADE**	122.53	124.58	131.82	131.58	$133.42	3.94	3.93	4.28	4.30	$4.29
52	**BUILDING MATERIALS AND GARDEN SUPPLIES**	166.50	166.50	181.54	181.71	–	4.44	4.44	4.79	4.82	–
521	Lumber and other building materials	185.72	185.50	201.60	202.29	–	4.69	4.72	5.04	5.07	–
525	Hardware stores	129.18	132.85	136.46	136.96	–	3.67	3.67	3.99	4.04	–
53	**GENERAL MERCHANDISE STORES**	109.88	115.18	118.90	117.50	–	3.75	3.68	4.10	4.08	–
531	Department stores	114.95	120.26	123.83	122.11	–	3.91	3.83	4.27	4.24	–
533	Variety stores	84.92	91.79	97.41	95.50	–	2.99	2.99	3.43	3.41	–
539	Misc. general merchandise stores	89.40	92.65	94.28	94.72	–	2.97	2.96	3.24	3.20	–
54	**FOOD STORES**	158.72	159.71	169.69	172.36	–	4.96	4.96	5.37	5.42	–
541	Grocery stores	165.38	165.89	176.96	179.68	–	5.12	5.12	5.53	5.58	–
546	Retail bakeries	107.53	110.70	116.51	117.56	–	3.67	3.69	3.99	4.04	–
55	**AUTOMOTIVE DEALERS AND SERVICE STATIONS**	171.75	173.50	187.62	188.00	–	4.58	4.59	4.99	5.00	–
551, 2	New and used car dealers	212.46	212.62	231.39	231.17	–	5.49	5.48	6.01	6.02	–
553	Auto and home supply stores	172.60	176.35	183.56	184.50	–	4.09	4.13	4.51	4.50	–
554	Gasoline service stations	119.71	122.15	130.59	131.67	–	3.48	3.51	3.71	3.73	–
56	**APPAREL AND ACCESSORY STORES**	104.02	110.45	112.99	110.87	–	3.55	3.54	3.83	3.81	–
561	Men's and boys' clothing and furnishings	128.79	137.16	140.51	139.00	–	4.05	4.07	4.31	4.29	–
562	Women's ready-to-wear stores	92.30	99.10	97.65	95.63	–	3.25	3.26	3.50	3.49	–
565	Family clothing stores	95.37	101.99	109.56	106.86	–	3.30	3.29	3.64	3.61	–
566	Shoe stores	114.27	120.26	124.68	121.80	–	3.90	3.93	4.27	4.20	–
57	**FURNITURE AND HOME FURNISHINGS STORES**	158.10	167.61	172.48	173.68	–	4.53	4.63	4.90	4.92	–
571	Furniture and home furnishings	165.90	173.88	175.90	179.01	–	4.74	4.83	5.04	5.10	–
572	Household appliance stores	173.26	172.89	185.13	188.27	–	4.67	4.68	5.10	5.13	–
573	Radio, television, and music stores	128.54	148.01	155.67	150.77	–	3.86	4.10	4.41	4.32	–
58	**EATING AND DRINKING PLACES**[5]	81.35	81.87	88.29	87.25	–	2.98	3.01	3.27	3.28	–
59	**MISCELLANEOUS RETAIL**	125.00	129.31	133.66	133.56	–	3.87	3.86	4.19	4.20	–
591	Drug stores and proprietary stores	111.81	114.98	120.26	120.96	–	3.69	3.65	3.93	3.94	–
594	Miscellaneous shopping goods stores	110.72	118.19	121.37	118.04	–	3.56	3.56	3.89	3.87	–
596	Nonstore retailers	152.06	155.22	164.22	163.68	–	4.32	4.36	4.83	4.80	–
598	Fuel and ice dealers	206.52	222.71	216.61	221.43	–	5.15	5.29	5.54	5.62	–
599	Retail stores, nec	123.00	123.70	131.88	132.72	–	3.82	3.76	4.20	4.20	–
–	**FINANCE, INSURANCE, AND REAL ESTATE**[6]	168.53	169.99	183.73	182.59	183.32	4.63	4.67	5.02	5.03	5.05
60	**BANKING**	146.00	146.73	156.65	155.73	–	4.00	4.02	4.28	4.29	–
602	Commercial and stock savings banks	142.72	143.45	153.72	152.82	–	3.91	3.93	4.20	4.21	–
61	**CREDIT AGENCIES OTHER THAN BANKS**	152.99	153.35	166.05	163.80	–	4.18	4.19	4.50	4.50	–
612	Savings and loan associations	146.25	145.89	157.98	153.51	–	4.04	4.03	4.34	4.30	–
614	Personal credit institutions	148.27	149.41	162.80	162.58	–	4.04	4.06	4.40	4.43	–
63	**INSURANCE CARRIERS**	185.13	186.74	198.97	199.60	–	4.99	5.02	5.32	5.38	–
631	Life insurance	186.48	187.45	196.31	197.25	–	5.04	5.08	5.32	5.36	–
632	Medical service and health insurance	179.55	180.78	191.52	195.56	–	4.75	4.77	5.04	5.16	–
633	Fire, marine, and casualty insurance	185.61	187.73	202.54	202.76	–	5.03	5.06	5.43	5.48	–

See footnotes at end of table.

GROSS HOURS AND EARNINGS OF PRODUCTION OR NONSUPERVISORY WORKERS ON PRIVATE NON-AGRICULTURAL PAYROLLS, BY INDUSTRY (Continued)

1972 SIC Code	Industry	Average weekly hours					Average overtime hours				
		Nov. 1977	Dec. 1977	Oct. 1978	Nov. 1978 P	Dec. 1978 P	Nov. 1977	Dec. 1977	Oct. 1978	Nov. 1978 P	Dec. 1978 P
	WHOLESALE TRADE-DURABLE GOODS—Continued										
505	Metals and minerals, except petroleum	40.0	40.2	39.5	39.9	–	–	–	–	–	–
506	Electrical goods	38.8	39.6	39.2	38.8	–	–	–	–	–	–
507	Hardware, plumbing, and heating equipment	38.9	38.9	38.5	38.3	–	–	–	–	–	–
508	Machinery, equipment, and supplies	39.9	39.9	40.2	40.1	–	–	–	–	–	–
509	Miscellaneous durable goods	38.5	38.8	38.7	39.4	–	–	–	–	–	–
51	**WHOLESALE TRADE-NONDURABLE GOODS**	38.1	38.3	38.3	38.2	–	–	–	–	–	–
511	Paper and paper products	36.8	37.0	36.3	36.6	–	–	–	–	–	–
512	Drugs, proprietaries, and sundries	38.7	38.9	38.1	38.4	–	–	–	–	–	–
513	Apparel, piece goods, and notions	36.0	36.3	36.7	36.9	–	–	–	–	–	–
514	Groceries and related products	38.4	38.7	38.3	38.4	–	–	–	–	–	–
516	Chemicals and allied products	38.5	38.6	39.7	39.4	–	–	–	–	–	–
517	Petroleum and petroleum products	39.4	39.7	39.5	39.6	–	–	–	–	–	–
518	Beer, wine, and distilled beverages	37.6	38.1	37.3	37.7	–	–	–	–	–	–
519	Miscellaneous nondurable goods	37.9	38.1	38.5	38.1	–	–	–	–	–	–
52-59	**RETAIL TRADE**	31.1	31.7	30.8	30.6	31.1	–	–	–	–	–
52	**BUILDING MATERIALS AND GARDEN SUPPLIES**	37.5	37.5	37.9	37.7		–	–	–	–	
521	Lumber and other building materials	39.6	39.3	40.0	39.9	–	–	–	–	–	
525	Hardware stores	35.2	36.2	34.2	33.9	–	–	–	–	–	–
53	**GENERAL MERCHANDISE STORES**	29.3	31.3	29.0	28.8	–	–	–	–	–	–
531	Department stores	29.4	31.4	29.0	28.8	–	–	–	–	–	–
533	Variety stores	28.4	30.7	28.4	28.3	–	–	–	–	–	–
539	Misc. general merchandise stores	30.1	31.3	29.1	29.6	–	–	–	–	–	–
54	**FOOD STORES**	32.0	32.2	31.6	31.8	–	–	–	–	–	–
541	Grocery stores	32.3	32.4	32.0	32.2	–	–	–	–	–	–
546	Retail bakeries	29.3	30.0	29.2	29.1	–	–	–	–	–	–
55	**AUTOMOTIVE DEALERS AND SERVICE STATIONS**	37.5	37.8	37.6	37.6	–	–	–	–	–	–
551, 2	New and used car dealers	38.7	38.8	38.5	38.4	–	–	–	–	–	–
553	Auto and home supply stores	42.2	42.7	40.7	41.0	–	–	–	–	–	–
554	Gasoline service stations	34.4	34.8	35.2	35.3	–	–	–	–	–	–
56	**APPAREL AND ACCESSORY STORES**	29.3	31.2	29.5	29.1	–	–	–	–	–	–
561	Men's and boys' clothing and furnishings	31.8	33.7	32.6	32.4	–	–	–	–	–	–
562	Women's ready-to-wear stores	28.4	30.4	27.9	27.4	–	–	–	–	–	–
565	Family clothing stores	28.9	31.0	30.1	29.6	–	–	–	–	–	–
566	Shoe stores	29.3	30.6	29.2	29.0	–	–	–	–	–	–
57	**FURNITURE AND HOME FURNISHINGS STORES**	34.9	36.2	35.2	35.3	–	–	–	–	–	
571	Furniture and home furnishings	35.0	36.0	34.9	35.1	–	–	–	–	–	
572	Household appliance stores	37.1	37.1	36.3	36.7	–	–	–	–	–	
573	Radio, television, and music stores	33.3	36.1	35.3	34.9	–	–	–	–	–	
58	**EATING AND DRINKING PLACES** [5]	27.3	27.2	27.0	26.6	–	–	–	–	–	
59	**MISCELLANEOUS RETAIL**	32.3	33.5	31.9	31.8	–	–	–	–	–	–
591	Drug stores and proprietary stores	30.3	31.5	30.6	30.7	–	–	–	–	–	–
594	Miscellaneous shopping goods stores	31.1	33.2	31.2	30.5	–	–	–	–	–	–
596	Nonstore retailers	35.2	35.6	34.0	34.1	–	–	–	–	–	–
598	Fuel and ice dealers	40.1	42.1	39.1	39.4	–	–	–	–	–	–
599	Retail stores, nec	32.2	32.9	31.4	31.6	–	–	–	–	–	–
–	**FINANCE, INSURANCE, AND REAL ESTATE** [6]	36.4	36.4	36.6	36.3	36.3	–	–	–	–	–
60	**BANKING**	36.5	36.5	36.6	36.3	–	–	–	–	–	–
602	Commercial and stock savings banks	36.5	36.5	36.6	36.3	–	–	–	–	–	–
61	**CREDIT AGENCIES OTHER THAN BANKS**	36.6	36.6	36.9	36.4	–	–	–	–	–	–
612	Savings and loan associations	36.2	36.2	36.4	35.7	–	–	–	–	–	–
614	Personal credit institutions	36.7	36.8	37.0	36.7	–	–	–	–	–	–
63	**INSURANCE CARRIERS**	37.1	37.2	37.4	37.1	–	–	–	–	–	–
631	Life insurance	37.0	36.9	36.9	36.8	–	–	–	–	–	–
632	Medical service and health insurance	37.8	37.9	38.0	37.9	–	–	–	–	–	–
633	Fire, marine, and casualty insurance	36.9	37.1	37.3	37.0	–	–	–	–	–	–

See footnotes at end of table.

GROSS HOURS AND EARNINGS OF PRODUCTION OR NONSUPERVISORY WORKERS ON PRIVATE NON-AGRICULTURAL PAYROLLS, BY INDUSTRY (*Continued*)

1972 SIC Code	Industry	Average weekly earnings					Average hourly earnings				
		Nov. 1977	Dec. 1977	Oct. 1978	Nov. 1978 P	Dec. 1978 P	Nov. 1977	Dec. 1977	Oct. 1978	Nov. 1978 P	Dec. 1978 P
–	SERVICES	$157.26	$158.40	$167.42	$167.24	$168.22	$4.78	$4.80	$5.12	$5.13	$5.16
	HOTELS AND OTHER LODGING PLACES:										
701	Hotels, motels, and tourist courts	104.38	105.10	116.24	114.20	–	3.40	3.48	3.69	3.72	
	PERSONAL SERVICES:										
721	Laundry, cleaning, and garment services	121.45	122.48	131.86	132.86	–	3.51	3.54	3.80	3.84	–
723	Beauty shops	121.28	121.27	119.45	120.65	–	3.79	3.72	3.78	3.83	–
73	**BUSINESS SERVICES**	160.06	162.68	170.69	170.17	–	4.88	4.90	5.22	5.22	–
731	Advertising	245.07	247.20	259.17	259.55	–	6.77	6.81	7.28	7.17	–
734	Services to buildings	119.14	118.44	124.85	124.12	–	4.24	4.20	4.59	4.53	–
737	Computer and data processing services	199.65	202.58	219.25	215.62	–	5.44	5.49	6.04	5.94	–
75	**AUTO REPAIR, SERVICES, AND GARAGES** ...	176.06	178.29	188.47	189.30	–	4.72	4.78	5.08	5.13	–
753	Automotive repair shops	201.61	205.65	212.14	215.95	–	5.13	5.18	5.51	5.58	–
76	**MISCELLANEOUS REPAIR SERVICES**	230.84	236.70	251.54	254.82	·	5.80	5.83	6.15	6.20	
78	**MOTION PICTURES**	179.76	179.47	208.03	200.44	–	6.22	6.21	7.51	7.21	–
781	Motion picture production and services	321.86	311.71	401.94	376.09	–	8.77	8.54	10.69	10.11	–
79	**AMUSEMENT AND RECREATION SERVICES** ..	138.15	137.86	148.15	148.35		4.50	4.52	4.81	4.88	
80	**HEALTH SERVICES**	147.93	148.91	161.53	161.70	–	4.51	4.54	4.88	4.90	–
801	Offices of physicians	155.57	157.74	168.81	170.01		4.70	4.78	5.10	5.09	–
802	Offices of dentists	132.31	134.21	138.36	136.59	–	4.61	4.66	4.69	4.71	–
805	Nursing and personal care facilities	102.28	103.56	113.20	113.15	–	3.31	3.33	3.64	3.65	–
806	Hospitals	161.90	162.10	176.64	177.14		4.79	4.81	5.18	5.21	–
81	**LEGAL SERVICES**	203.65	205.71	218.32	217.90	–	5.92	5.98	6.44	6.39	–
89	**MISCELLANEOUS SERVICES**	264.65	266.81	281.96	280.42	–	6.91	6.93	7.42	7.36	–
891	Engineering and architectural services	287.17	288.75	301.84	302.64	–	7.27	7.31	7.84	7.78	–
893	Accounting, auditing, and bookkeeping	226.42	227.02	245.05	239.14	–	5.99	5.99	6.50	6.36	–

[1] For coverage of series, see footnote 1, table B-2.

[2] Beginning January 1978, data relate to line haul railroads with operating revenues of $50,000,000 or more.

[3] Data relate to employees in such occupations in the telephone industry as switchboard operators; service assistants; operating room instructors; and pay-station attendants. In 1977, such employees made up 20 percent of the total number of nonsupervisory employees in establishments reporting hours and earnings data.

[4] Data relate to employees in such occupations in the telephone industry as central office craft persons; installation and exchange repair craft persons; line, cable and conduit craft persons; and laborers. In 1977, such employees made up 37 percent of the total number of nonsupervisory employees in establishments reporting hours and earnings data.

[5] Money payments only; tips, not included.

[6] Data for nonoffice sales agents excluded from all series in this division.

* Not availbale.

p=preliminary.

** Data for class I Railroads (SIC 4011) are: August 1978—$342.27, $7.64 and 44.8. September 1978—$324.41, $8.01 and 40.5.

1972 SIC Code	Industry	Average weekly hours					Average overtime hours				
		Nov. 1977	Dec. 1977	Oct. 1978	Nov. 1978^P	Dec. 1978^P	Nov. 1977	Dec. 1977	Oct. 1978	Nov. 1978^P	Dec. 1978^P
–	SERVICES	32.9	33.0	32.7	32.6	32.6	–	–	–	–	–
701	HOTELS AND OTHER LODGING PLACES: Hotels, motels, and tourist courts	30.7	30.2	31.5	30.7	–	–	–	–	–	–
721	PERSONAL SERVICES: Laundry, cleaning, and garment services	34.6	34.6	34.7	34.6	–	–	–	–	–	–
723	Beauty shops	32.0	32.6	31.6	31.5	–	–	–	–	–	–
73	BUSINESS SERVICES	32.8	33.2	32.7	32.6	–	–	–	–	–	–
731	Advertising	36.2	36.3	35.6	36.2	–	–	–	–	–	–
734	Services to buildings	28.1	28.2	27.2	27.4	–	–	–	–	–	–
737	Computer and data processing services	36.7	36.9	36.3	36.3	–	–	–	–	–	–
75	AUTO REPAIR, SERVICES, AND GARAGES	37.3	37.3	37.1	36.9	–	–	–	–	–	–
753	Automotive repair shops	39.3	39.7	38.5	38.7	–	–	–	–	–	–
76	MISCELLANEOUS REPAIR SERVICES	39.8	40.6	40.9	41.1	–	–	–	–	–	–
78	MOTION PICTURES	28.9	28.9	27.7	27.8	–	–	–	–	–	–
781	Motion picture production and services	36.7	36.5	37.6	37.2	–	–	–	–	–	–
79	AMUSEMENT AND RECREATION SERVICES ...	30.7	30.5	30.8	30.4	–	..	–	–	–	–
80	HEALTH SERVICES	32.8	32.8	33.1	33.0	–	–	–	–	–	–
801	Offices of physicians	33.1	33.0	33.1	33.4	–	–	–	–	–	–
802	Offices of dentists	28.7	28.8	29.5	29.0	–	–	–	–	–	–
805	Nursing and personal care facilities	30.9	31.1	31.1	31.0	–	–	–	–	–	–
806	Hospitals	33.8	33.7	34.1	34.0	–	–	–	–	–	–
81	LEGAL SERVICES	34.4	34.4	33.9	34.1	–	–	–	–	–	–
89	MISCELLANEOUS SERVICES	38.3	38.5	38.0	38.1	–	–	–	–	–	–
891	Engineering and architectural services	39.5	39.5	38.5	38.9	–	–	–	–	–	–
893	Accounting, auditing, and bookkeeping	37.8	37.9	37.7	37.6	–	–	–	–	–	–

EMPLOYMENT, HOURS, AND INDEXES OF EARNINGS IN THE EXECUTIVE BRANCH OF THE FEDERAL GOVERNMENT
(Employment in thousands—includes both supervisory and nonsupervisory employees)

Item	1977			1978									
	Oct.	Nov.	Dec.	Jan.	Feb.	Mar.	Apr.	May	June	July	Aug.	Sept.	Oct.
Executive Branch													
Total employment	2,662.5	2,664.3	2,673.1	2,659.5	2,668.2	2,672.9	2,686.7	2,702.9	2,747.5	2,760.3	2,738.5	2,691.9	2,694.5
Average weekly hours	39.8	39.4	40.0	39.6	39.9	39.9	39.6	39.5	39.6	39.8	39.7	39.5	39.9
Average overtime hours ...	1.2	1.1	1.6	1.2	1.2	1.1	1.1	1.1	1.1	1.2	1.2	1.3	1.3
Indexes (1967=100):													
Average weekly earnings ..	226.9	225.9	230.5	229.0	230.2	227.4	226.5	226.0	226.5	227.7	226.8	230.0	242.0
Average hourly earnings ...	224.6	225.9	227.0	227.8	227.3	226.2	225.4	225.4	225.4	225.4	225.1	229.5	238.9
Department of Defense													
Total employment	907.8	909.8	907.7	906.4	906.0	905.6	905.4	911.3	924.8	927.1	918.6	905.4	905.8
Average weekly hours	39.9	39.8	40.0	39.9	40.1	40.0	40.1	40.0	40.0	40.1	40.1	39.7	39.9
Average overtime hours ...	.9	.9	.8	.7	.8	.9	.9	.9	1.0	.9	1.0	1.2	1.0
Indexes (1967=100):													
Average weekly earnings ..	217.4	220.9	220.4	221.8	222.3	221.5	222.1	222.0	221.5	220.4	221.2	223.3	232.5
Average hourly earnings ...	219.6	223.7	222.1	224.0	223.4	223.2	223.2	223.7	223.2	221.5	222.3	226.7	234.9
Postal Service													
Total employment	649.2	650.2	668.2	645.6	646.9	647.6	647.9	648.3	648.3	647.5	649.0	651.9	646.9
Average weekly hours	41.2	39.8	41.8	41.1	41.5	40.4	40.1	39.9	40.0	40.2	39.9	39.7	41.5
Average overtime hours ...	2.0	1.5	3.5	2.5	2.1	1.7	1.5	1.5	1.6	1.8	1.5	1.8	2.3
Indexes (1967=100):													
Average weekly earnings ..	259.0	253.4	271.7	253.9	266.5	258.5	256.2	254.3	259.7	261.9	260.3	259.3	278.7
Average hourly earnings ...	242.7	245.7	250.9	249.9	247.9	247.0	246.6	246.0	250.6	251.5	251.8	252.1	259.5
Other Agencies													
Total employment	1,105.5	1,104.3	1,097.2	1,107.5	1,115.3	1,119.7	1,133.4	1,143.3	1,174.4	1,185.7	1,170.9	1,134.6	1,141.8
Average weekly hours	38.8	38.9	38.8	38.5	38.9	38.8	38.9	38.8	39.0	39.3	39.3	39.1	39.0
Average overtime hours ...	1.1	1.1	1.0	.9	1.0	1.0	1.0	1.0	1.0	1.1	1.2	1.2	1.1
Indexes (1967=100):													
Average weekly earnings ..	216.6	215.4	216.1	216.6	217.6	215.1	214.1	213.4	212.0	214.6	213.4	218.3	229.1
Average hourly earnings ...	216.6	214.9	216.1	218.3	217.1	215.1	213.6	213.4	210.9	211.9	210.6	216.6	228.0

NOTE: The hours and earnings averages presented in this table have been computed using data collected by the U.S. Civil Service Commission from agencies with 2500 or more employees in the Executive Branch of the Federal Government; the data cover both salaried workers and hourly paid wage-board employees. Since these averages relate to hours and earnings of all workers both supervisory and nonsupervisory, they are not comparable to similar data presented in table C-2 which relate only to production or nonsupervisory workers. The total employment levels shown include all workers in the Executive Branch regardless of the size of the agency.

AVERAGE HOURLY EARNINGS EXCLUDING OVERTIME OF PRODUCTION WORKERS ON MANUFACTURING PAYROLLS BY INDUSTRY

Major industry group	Average hourly earnings excluding overtime [1]				
	Nov. 1977	Dec. 1977	Oct. 1978	Nov. 1978[p]	Dec. 1978[p]
MANUFACTURING	$5.60	$5.67	$6.04	$6.09	$6.16
DURABLE GOODS	5.97	6.04	6.44	6.49	6.56
Lumber and wood products	5.03	5.04	5.49	5.47	-
Furniture and fixtures	4.32	4.35	4.61	4.64	-
Stone, clay, and glass products	5.67	5.70	6.11	6.16	-
Primary metal industries	7.37	7.40	8.01	8.09	-
Fabricated metal products	5.81	5.84	6.19	6.24	-
Machinery, except electrical	6.15	6.20	6.60	6.64	-
Electric and electronic equipment	5.36	5.44	5.75	5.76	-
Transportation equipment	7.13	7.26	7.71	7.75	-
Instruments and related products	5.26	5.33	5.59	5.64	-
Miscellaneous manufacturing industries	4.32	4.40	4.60	4.65	-
NONDURABLE GOODS	5.03	5.09	5.41	5.46	5.52
Food and kindred products	5.25	5.33	5.61	5.69	-
Tobacco manufactures	5.51	5.61	5.87	6.02	-
Textile mill products	3.94	3.96	4.23	4.25	-
Apparel and other textile products	3.63	3.70	3.94	3.95	-
Paper and allied products	5.84	5.89	6.29	6.36	-
Printing and publishing	(2)	(2)	(2)	(2)	-
Chemicals and allied products	6.41	6.46	6.89	6.92	-
Petroleum and coal products	7.56	7.63	8.23	8.32	-
Rubber and misc. plastics products	5.03	5.08	5.40	5.45	-
Leather and leather products	3.59	3.60	3.85	3.90	-

[1] Derived by assuming that overtime hours are paid at the rate of time and one-half.

[2] Not available as average overtime rates are significantly above time and one-half. Inclusion of data for the group in the nondurable goods total has little effect.

p=preliminary.

ANNUAL PERCENT INCREASE IN AVERAGE HOURLY EARNINGS FOR SELECTED OCCUPATIONAL GROUPS IN METROPOLITAN AREAS, ADJUSTED FOR EMPLOYMENT SHIFTS

Area	Year ending	Office clerical	Electronic data processing	Industrial nurses	Skilled maintenance	Unskilled plant
United States	Oct. 77	7.1	7.2	8.2	8.9	8.1
Northeast	Oct. 77	6.5	7.0	8.0	8.3	7.5
Albany-Schenectady-Troy	Sept. 77	5.8	–	6.5	7.1	7.7
Boston	Aug. 78	6.0	6.7	8.7	7.3	7.1
Buffalo	Oct. 77	7.6	5.9	8.3	8.3	7.4
Hartford	Mar. 78	5.6	7.3	9.7	8.5	5.8
Nassau-Suffolk	June 78	5.0	5.7	7.7	7.6	6.9
Newark	Jan. 78	7.3	8.4	8.8	8.3	8.3
New York	May 78	5.8	5.3	6.6	7.1	5.8
Northeast Pennsylvania	Aug. 78	6.8	6.2	7.8	8.0	8.5
Paterson-Clifton-Passaic	June 78	6.0	7.9	3.6	5.5	5.5
Philadelphia	Nov. 77	7.1	7.4	8.7	8.1	7.2
Pittsburgh	Jan. 78	7.7	7.8	10.2	11.2	9.7
Portland	Dec. 77	9.0	–	–	7.4	8.7
Poughkeepsie	June 78				–	2.6
Providence-Warwick-Pawtucket	June 78	7.7	7.2	9.3	7.1	9.9
Trenton	Sept. 77	6.7	7.2	8.1	11.7	8.5
Utica-Rome	July 78	7.0	6.8	4.9	6.8	8.1
Worcester	Apr. 78	7.2	11.0	6.9	9.0	8.8
York	Feb 78	8.8	–	8.0	7.5	8.2
South	Oct. 77	7.1	7.1	8.6	9.3	7.4
Atlanta	May 78	6.5	9.4	9.4	8.1	9.8
Baltimore	Aug. 78	8.1	7.6	8.6	8.8	10.7
Birmingham	Mar. 78	7.0	8.2	5.7	5.5	10.4
Chattanooga	Sept. 78	6.5	10.7	–	6.7	9.1
Corpus Christi	July 78	–	–	–	8.2	13.2
Dallas-Fort Worth	Oct. 77	7.0	6.6	8.3	8.9	5.9
Daytona Beach	Aug. 77	–	–	–	–	6.1
Gainesville	Sept. 77	–	–	–	–	–
Greensboro-Winston-Salem-High Point	Aug. 78	6.2	6.7	5.8	9.0	9.6
Greenville-Spartanburg	June 78	8.0	8.6	5.6	6.1	7.2
Houston	Apr. 78	9.1	12.1	9.9	10.4	–
Huntsville	Feb. 78	8.1	–	–	–	10.3
Jackson	Jan. 78	6.9	7.1	–	9.3	12.1
Jacksonville	Dec. 77	6.8	6.3	10.5	8.9	7.8
Louisville	Nov. 77	6.3	8.9	9.2	8.7	6.7
Memphis	Nov. 77	7.5	7.6	10.4	8.3	5.8
Miami	Oct. 77	7.0	8.5	–	9.5	5.4
New Orleans	Jan. 78	7.1	10.0	–	10.3	11.5
Norfolk-Virginia Beach-Portsmouth	May 78	7.7	–	–	9.2	8.2
Norfolk-Virginia Beach-Portsmouth and Newport News-Hampton	May 78	7.6	7.1	7.7	8.5	8.1
Oklahoma City	Aug. 78	8.9	7.8	–	10.2	11.2
Richmond	June 78	6.9	8.0	7.3	9.8	8.8
San Antonio	May 78	7.8	6.9	–	6.5	9.9
Washington	Mar. 78	7.9	5.5	8.7	7.9	4.8
North Central	Oct. 77	7.6	7.5	8.3	9.2	9.2
Akron	Dec. 77	8.3	7.6	9.7	8.4	8.2
Canton	May 78	7.6	6.7	8.0	8.2	9.1
Chicago	May 78	7.1	7.6	8.7	8.6	8.7
Cincinnati	July 78	6.9	7.2	8.7	8.2	9.1
Cleveland	Sept. 78	7.6	7.5	8.2	7.5	8.3
Columbus	Oct. 77	7.1	6.5	11.0	10.4	7.4
Davenport-Rock Island-Moline	Feb. 78	11.2	9.4	10.1	11.8	9.2
Dayton	Dec. 77	6.6	8.0	6.1	9.4	8.6
Detroit	Mar. 78	6.5	6.8	8.1	8.3	7.9
Green Bay	July 78	7.8	–	–	10.3	9.5
Indianapolis	Oct. 77	7.0	5.8	11.4	11.3	8.2
Kansas City	Sept. 78	8.8	9.3	8.5	8.3	8.1
Milwaukee	Apr. 78	7.8	8.6	8.6	8.4	10.0
Minneapolis-St. Paul	Jan. 78	8.0	7.3	6.8	8.2	8.1
Omaha	Oct. 77	7.9	11.4	–	9.2	6.5
Saginaw	Nov. 77	6.7	–	–	–	7.4
St. Louis	Mar. 78	6.9	7.6	8.8	8.2	8.6
South Bend	Aug. 78	8.8	6.2	8.3	8.9	8.7
Toledo	May 78	9.4	8.6	11.0	9.1	9.3
Wichita	Apr. 78	7.8	7.6	6.8	8.1	9.2
West	Oct. 77	7.4	7.4		8.6	7.3
Anaheim-Santa Ana-Garden Grove	Oct. 77	7.7	6.3	7.7	8.0	5.5
Billings	July 78	7.6	–	–	6.8	6.4
Denver-Boulder	Dec. 77	7.7	7.4	7.6	8.6	9.5
Fresno	June 78	6.8	–	–	6.2	7.0
Los Angeles-Long Beach	Oct. 77	7.4	6.6	7.4	8.8	6.7
Portland	May 78	8.5	8.5	–	7.1	7.7
Sacramento	Dec. 77	8.8	–	–	8.4	7.8
Salt Lake City-Ogden	Nov. 77	7.4	9.5	–	7.4	8.0
San Diego	Nov. 77	5.6	7.2	–	7.3	5.9
San Francisco-Oakland	Mar. 78	6.9	7.9	11.7	9.2	8.0
San Jose	Mar. 78	7.2	7.0	6.6	7.4	7.5
Seattle-Everett	Dec. 77	8.8	6.5	13.7	10.4	8.9

NOTE: Dashes indicate data do not meet publication criteria.

Union Wage Rates for Building Trades Workers Advance 0.5 Percent in Third Quarter of 1978

Union wage rates for building trades workers in large cities increased an average of 0.5 percent in the third quarter of 1978. (See table 1.) The third quarter gain, which raised the Bureau's index of wage rates for these workers to 225.2 (1967=100), was slighly less than the 0.7 percent recorded for the same period last year. About a sixth of the union members in cities covered by the survey (all cities with 100,000 inhabitants or more) were in bargaining units for which rate changes became effective in the third quarter of 1978—about the same proportion as a year ago.

Over the 12 months ended October 2, 1978, the wage increase was 5.8 percent—slightly more than the pace of 1 year earlier. (See table A.) Excluding the 1973 wage controls period, 1977 and 1978 saw the smallest 12-month increases for the third quarter since October 1967, when 5.7 percent was recorded.

The 12-month increases for wage rates declined sharply from a peak of 12.3 percent in the first quarter of 1971 to 4.4 percent in the fourth quarter of 1973. They rose rapidly to double that rate by the fourth quarter of 1974- and the first quarter of 1975 and then declined steadily— staying in the 5.5-6.0 percent range since mid-1976.

Percentage increases in wage rates plus benefits followed a similar path at somewhat higher levels.

Wage-rate increases averaged 3.6 percent for those bargaining units for which adjustments were effective in the third quarter of 1978; the corresponding average adjustment was 4.5 percent in 1977. Of those surveyed, slightly over one-third of the union members whose rates increased in the third quarter of 1978 had wage gains of between 1 and 3 percent; another third, between 3 and 5 percent; and about one-fifth, scattered between 5 and 9 percent.

Union wage rates in the building trades averaged $10.69 an hour on October 2. (See table 1.) The addition of employer payments for health, welfare, pension, and vacation plans raised the average to $13.09—up 0.6 percent in the third quarter and 6.3 percent over the year. (See table 2.) In 1977, the corresponding increases were 0.9 and 6.6 percent.

The proportion of employer labor costs for employee benefits has more than doubled since the Bureau first developed such data in 1965. At that time, employer contributions equaled 7.1 percent of the wage-and-benefit package, compared with 18.4 percent on October 2, 1978.

Table A. 12-month percentage increases in wage rates and wage rates plus benefits of building trades workers, 1969-78

Period	1969	1970	1971	1972	1973	1974	1975	1976	1977	1978
	Wage rates only									
First quarter	7.8	9.1	12.3	10.4	5.8	4.5	9.2	8.0	5.8	5.3
Second quarter	8.8	11.8	11.4	6.5	4.9	7.4	8.8	6.7	5.8	5.9
Third quarter	8.7	11.6	11.2	7.1	4.9	7.6	8.3	6.1	5.6	-
Fourth quarter	9.4	11.9	10.2	7.1	4.4	9.0	8.0	5.9	5.5	-
	Wage rates plus benefits[1]									
First quarter	9.0	10.2	13.5	11.8	7.0	5.6	9.9	8.8	7.0	6.4
Second quarter	9.9	12.9	12.2	7.3	6.0	8.2	9.8	7.9	6.7	6.7
Third quarter	9.6	12.9	12.7	8.2	6.2	8.2	9.6	7.4	6.6	-
Fourth quarter	10.6	13.0	11.6	8.2	5.5	9.6	9.1	7.1	6.6	-

[1] Benefits include employer payments for insurance, pensions, and vacations.

The wage rates plus benefits shown in table 3 were payable under labor-management contracts in force on October 2 and include all negotiated or deferred changes put into effect between July 3, 1978, and October 2, 1978. Among the 830 bargaining units reported in the 121 cities studied, nearly one-half of the third-quarter increases resulted from newly negotiated contracts. Slightly more than two-fifths of the units with rate increases during the quarter also had one or more rate advances during the preceding 2 quarters.

Scope and method of survey

Union wage rates are the basic (minimum) rates agreed upon through collective bargaining and reported to the Bureau by local union officials. The rates do not reflect those for apprentices or premium rates for overtime or for work on weekends, holidays, or late shifts.

Information on employer contributions to insurance (health and welfare), pension, and vacation funds, as provided in labor-management contracts, is presented for the various trades. These contributions are expressed in cents per hour or percent of basic rates. Payments to other funds, such as those for holidays and supplementary unemployment benefits, are also indicated in table 3. The latter payments are not included in the computation of "union wage rates plus employer payments to specified worker benefit funds."

The "average wage rates" apply to all cities that had 100,000 inhabitants or more in the 1970 census. Sixty-six of the 121 cities in the survey were appropriately weighted to represent the 153 cities of this size.

The "average wage rates," developed by applying percentage changes that occurred on a quarterly basis since July 1, 1977, to averages recorded in the Bureau's annual survey relating to that date, are designed to show current levels. They are not for precise quarter-to-quarter or year-to-year comparisons. Fluctuations in union membership (the weighting factor used to obtain average wage rates) among the various crafts and areas studied may cause differences in the average regardless of wage-rate changes.

"Changes in average union wage rates" are computed by weighting the rates for comparable situations in each year or quarter by a fixed membership count, developing averages for each period using the fixed membership, and recording differences in these averages. Thus, the averages used in this computation are not necessarily identical with published "average wage rates."

This is the first time that averages from the Bureau's July 1, 1977, annual study are being used to develop average wage rates on a quarterly basis. This benchmarking procedure, which occurs annually, does not affect the cents-per-hour or percentage changes presented in this or earlier releases but does affect the averages in the current report. Thus, the averages in this release may differ from those obtained by applying the cents-per-hour or percentage changes to the averages contained in earlier quarterly releases.

Table 1. Union wage rates in the building trades in cities of 100,000 inhabitants or more

| Trade or occupation | Hourly average, Oct. 2, 1978 | Change to Oct. 2, 1978 from:[1] | | | |
| | | July 3, 1978 | | Oct. 2, 1977 | |
		Cents	Percent	Cents	Percent
All trades	$10.69	5.8	0.5	57.9	5.8
Bricklayers	11.05	8.0	.7	57.2	5.5
Building laborers	8.42	3.3	.4	46.4	5.8
Carpenters	10.91	3.9	.4	57.4	5.6
Electricians	11.83	10.3	.9	68.3	6.1
Painters	10.53	5.7	.6	61.3	6.3
Plasterers	10.68	6.5	.6	55.6	5.5
Plumbers	11.64	9.4	.8	65.0	6.0

[1] In computing changes in wage rates, increases in each trade were averaged among all workers in the trade, including those that did not receive wage rate increases.

Table 2. Union wage rates plus employer payments to specified worker benefit funds in the building trades in cities of 100,000 inhabitants or more

| Trade or occupation | Hourly average, Oct. 2, 1978 | Change to Oct. 2, 1978 from:[1] | | | |
| | | July 3, 1978 | | Oct. 2, 1977 | |
		Cents	Percent	Cents	Percent
All trades	$13.09	7.7	0.6	76.7	6.3
Bricklayers	13.41	8.7	.7	72.6	5.8
Building laborers	10.47	5.3	.5	62.3	6.3
Carpenters	13.32	4.6	.3	77.6	6.2
Electricians	14.47	13.1	.9	90.4	6.7
Painters	12.27	8.1	.7	75.8	6.6
Plasterers	12.74	8.8	.7	73.3	6.1
Plumbers	14.61	15.2	1.1	85.5	6.3

[1] See footnote 1, table 1.

Table 3. Union hourly wage rates and employer insurance, pension, vacation, and other fund payments for selected building trades in 121 cities. Oct. 2, 1978

	BRICKLAYERS					CARPENTERS				
	EMPLOYER CONTRIBUTIONS FOR SELECTED BENEFITS‡					EMPLOYER CONTRIBUTIONS FOR SELECTED BENEFITS‡				
CITY	BASIC RATE¹	INSUR- ANCE²	PENSION	VACATION PAY	OTHER³	BASIC RATE¹	INSUR- ANCE²	PENSION	VACATION PAY	OTHER³
AKRON OH............	$11.290	$0.880	$0.550	⁴$1.000	$0.100	$12.150	$0.550	$0.900	–	$0.060
ALBANY NY...........	†10.400	.700	.750	–	††.200	9.800	.700	.700	⁴$0.750	.120
ALBUQUERQUE NM......	9.260	.670	.500	1.000	.120	9.800	1.000	1.050	.650	.040
ANCHORAGE AK.......	⁴16.680	.900	2.450	–	.060	⁴16.510	⁴.900	⁴1.750	–	.050
ATLANTA GA.........	†8.950	.550	.500	⁴.650	.080	9.650	†.450	–	–	–
BALTIMORE MD.......	9.830	.700	.500	.500	.030	9.550	.750	.690	.250	.030
BIRMINGHAM AL......	⁴10.150	⁴.400	⁴.500	–	.050	⁴9.550	.550	⁴.400	–	.030
BOISE ID...........	11.150	.750	1.100	–	–	10.150	.750	.700	.650	.080
BOSTON MA..........	⁴10.550	.850	1.400	–	.090	10.750	.900	1.000	–	.020
BUFFALO NY.........	12.880	–	1.400	–	.820	11.330	†⁵1.650	†1.800	–	.100
BURLINGTON VT......	8.300	.750	.200	–	.010	8.620	.650	.500	–	–
BUTTE MT...........	11.500	–	.550	–	.050	9.400	.700	1.000	.750	–
CHARLESTON SC......	7.200	.250	–	–	.010	7.650	.450	.300	–	–
CHARLESTON WV......	⁴12.020	.650	⁴.250	–	⁴.760	10.920	.500	.500	1.000	–
CHARLOTTE NC.......	7.200	.250	.250	–	.010	8.250	.450	.300	–	–
CHATTANOOGA TN.....	10.500	.450	.300	–	.020	9.330	.500	.500	–	.020
CHEYENNE WY........	10.550	–	.300	–	.200	9.730	.650	.650	.750	2.00% ⁴$0.050
CHICAGO IL.........	11.710	.900	.850	–	.070	11.500	.980	1.080	–	–
CINCINNATI OH......	11.845	.650	.350	⁴1.000	.185	†12.200	.600	.650	–	.035
CLEVELAND OH.......	11.280	1.050	1.200	⁴1.250	.070	11.870	.850	1.250	⁴1.000	.040
COLUMBIA SC........	⁶–	⁶–	⁶–	⁶–	–	⁴8.100	–	–	.650	–
COLUMBUS OH........	⁴11.290	.800	⁴1.000	–	.010	10.790	.580	.850	–	.040
CORPUS CHRISTI TX..	9.060	.280	.300	–	.060	⁴8.240	.510	.300	–	–
DALLAS TX..........	9.850	.450	.500	–	.040	⁷10.200	.500	⁷.400	–	–
DAYTON OH..........	10.710	.850	.750	⁴.370	.110	10.950	.800	1.100	–	.070
DENVER CO..........	10.140	.850	.950	⁴.500	.310	10.065	.800	.900	.750	–
DES MOINES IA......	11.275	.800	.750	–	.200	10.180	.600	.750	–	–
DETROIT MI.........	12.270	.950	8.00% ⁴$0.200	11.00%	.200	11.790	.950	11.00%	11.00%	.030
DULUTH MN..........	11.020	.400	.300	.500	.050	9.900	.400	.500	.750	–
EL PASO TX.........	7.700	.400	.200	–	.080	8.170	.670	–	–	–
ERIE PA............	12.210	.700	.400	–	.050	10.970	.600	.580	–	.030
EVANSVILLE IN......	10.530	1.000	.500	⁴.500	.040	10.600	.650	.750	.500	.030
FARGO ND...........	10.650	.600	.300	.300	.050	9.510	–	.300	–	–
FLINT MI...........	10.950	.850	1.300	⁴.500	.060	⁴10.480	.600	⁴.700	⁴.610	.020
FORT WORTH TX......	10.100	.450	.500	–	.040	10.200	.500	.400	–	–
FREMONT CA.........	12.500	1.500	1.250	⁴1.000	.300	12.700	1.575	1.810	⁸1.000	.120
FRESNO CA..........	⁴11.650	1.200	1.000	1.000	.150	12.700	1.575	1.810	⁸1.000	.120
GRAND RAPIDS MI....	9.050	.700	.250	⁴.400	.070	9.500	.600	.700	⁴.450	.020
HAMMOND IN.........	12.200	.900	.550	⁴.500	.060	11.780	.650	.670	⁴1.000	.010
HARTFORD CT........	⁴10.300	.750	.750	–	⁴.150	10.350	.900	.650	–	–
HONOLULU HI........	10.180	1.300	1.700	.600	.120	⁴10.500	⁴1.240	⁴1.850	1.000	.020
HOUSTON TX.........	11.360	.630	.600	–	.160	10.600	.850	.800	–	–
HUNTSVILLE AL......	10.100	–	–	–	–	8.100	.400	.300	–	–
INDIANAPOLIS IN....	11.140	.500	.550	⁴.500	.120	11.850	.750	.750	⁴.500	.050
JACKSON MS.........	⁴9.100	.250	.100	–	.030	⁴8.400	.400	.300	–	.050
JACKSONVILLE FL....	9.270	.450	.500	–	†.010	9.170	.620	.500	–	.050
KANSAS CITY MO.....	⁹11.025	⁷.800	1.000	1.000	–	11.750	.500	.300	–	.060
KNOXVILLE TN.......	⁴10.617	–	–	–	.020	†8.940	–	.500	–	.020
LANSING MI.........	11.280	–	.900	⁴.250	0.39% ⁴$0.040	10.580	.600	.700	⁴.650	.020
LAS VEGAS NV.......	12.270	.700	.600	–	.100	11.960	.850	1.100	1.000	.020
LITTLE ROCK AR.....	9.100	.600	.350	–	.020	9.060	.450	.350	–	.030
LONG BEACH CA......	⁴11.850	1.150	1.450	⁴.500	.250	10.770	1.590	2.070	⁸1.000	.110
LOS ANGELES CA.....	⁴11.850	1.150	1.450	⁴.500	.250	10.770	1.590	2.070	⁴1.000	.110
LOUISVILLE KY......	10.940	.500	.400	⁴.500	.080	10.350	.450	.450	–	.020
LUBBOCK TX.........	9.600	–	.300	–	–	⁴9.200	.480	.500	–	–
MADISON WI.........	9.840	.750	.700	⁴.500	.010	10.270	.500	.600	⁴.500	–
MANCHESTER NH......	8.890	.800	.600	–	.060	8.620	.650	.500	–	.010
MEMPHIS TN.........	⁴†10.650	.530	.300	⁴.250	.200	9.800	.600	.500	–	–
MIAMI FL...........	10.150	.700	.540	⁴.250	.020	⁴9.450	.800	.550	–	–
MILWAUKEE WI.......	11.410	1.120	1.100	.560	.150	10.860	.900	.900	⁴.510	.040
MINNEAPOLIS MN.....	10.760	.655	.530	.560	.050	10.460	.650	.500	.500	–
MOBILE AL..........	10.110	–	1.700	–	.060	9.970	.400	.500	–	.050
MONTGOMERY AL......	9.100	–	–	–	–	9.500	.500	.300	–	–
NASHVILLE TN.......	9.250	–	.500	–	–	10.000	–	.250	–	.020
NEW BEDFORD MA.....	⁴10.600	1.200	1.000	–	.100	10.500	.600	–	–	.020
NEW HAVEN CT.......	⁴10.300	.750	.750	–	–	10.100	.900	.650	–	–
NEW ORLEANS LA.....	10.890	.450	.300	–	†.020	10.260	.500	.350	.160	–
NEW YORK NY........	⁴11.040	⁹1.480	⁹3.380	⁹.300	⁹.060	11.800	1.500	1.780	.850	†.040
NEWARK NJ..........	11.250	.920	1.000	.500	⁴.020	11.700	8.00%	7.00%	–	–
NORFOLK VA.........	9.330	.600	.200	–	.020	⁴9.000	.400	.350	–	.020
OAKLAND CA.........	12.500	1.500	1.250	⁴1.000	.300	12.700	1.575	1.810	⁸1.000	.120
OKLAHOMA CITY OK...	10.470	.500	.500	.500	†.150	9.650	.450	⁴.600	–	.010
OMAHA NE...........	10.450	.670	.670	.750	.190	⁴10.960	⁴.670	.550	–	.050
PEORIA IL..........	11.200	.700	1.000	.500	.040	11.760	.400	.750	–	.050
PHILADELPHIA PA....	⁴11.380	1.100	1.000	.450	.090	10.370	2.330	1.350	–	.080
PHOENIX AZ.........	11.770	.650	.900	–	.210	10.235	1.045	1.055	⁴.250	–
PITTSBURGH PA......	10.500	.750	1.400	–	1.450	11.150	6.00%	8.00%	–	6.00% + .250
PORTLAND ME........	8.800	.400	.500	–	.010	8.200	.550	.600	–	.020
PORTLAND OR........	12.690	.850	.850	⁴.250	.210	11.280	.600	.950	.500	–
PROVIDENCE RI......	⁴10.350	1.000	1.000	–	.030	10.000	.650	.900	⁴.250	.030
RALEIGH NC.........	7.200	.250	.250	–	.010	8.200	.500	.300	–	–
READING PA.........	⁴9.800	⁴.850	.750	–	.050	9.480	.720	.450	–	–
RICHMOND VA........	9.500	.550	.300	–	.050	9.000	.400	.350	–	.010
RIVERSIDE CA.......	11.750	1.300	1.650	⁴.500	.250	10.770	1.590	2.070	⁴1.000	.110
ROCHESTER NY.......	11.770	.750	.850	–	†.180	10.950	.850	1.060	–	.430
ROCK ISLAND IL¹⁰...	⁴10.700	.550	1.000	⁴.750	.060	11.110	.600	.900	–	.050
ROCKFORD IL........	11.100	.550	.600	⁴.450	.030	10.850	.550	1.000	⁴.200	.050
SACRAMENTO CA......	⁴12.480	⁴1.300	1.210	1.000	⁴.200	12.700	1.575	1.810	⁸1.000	.120
SALT LAKE CITY UT..	11.260	.450	⁴.420	⁴.350	.170	10.250	.550	.650	–	†–
SAN ANTONIO TX.....	10.020	.450	–	.250	.050	⁴9.340	⁴.480	–	⁴.400	.010
SAN DIEGO CA.......	11.590	1.130	1.340	⁴.500	.300	11.710	.710	1.200	.800	.170
SAN FRANCISCO CA...	⁴12.420	1.500	⁴1.370	⁸⁴1.180	⁴.430	12.700	1.575	1.810	⁴1.000	.120
SANTA ANA CA.......	⁴11.850	1.150	1.450	⁴.500	.250	10.770	1.590	2.070	⁸1.000	.110
SANTA FE NM........	10.260	.670	.500	1.000	.120	⁴10.450	1.000	1.050	.650	.040
SAVANNAH GA........	⁴9.300	⁴.400	.200	–	.010	⁴9.050	.500	–	–	–
SCHENECTADY NY.....	⁴10.900	.700	⁴.750	–	⁴.200	9.800	.700	.700	⁴.750	.100
SCRANTON PA........	⁴10.500	.850	.900	.500	.460	10.670	.640	.500	–	.100
SEATTLE WA.........	11.860	.800	1.150	⁴.550	.200	11.680	.600	.800	⁴.200	.020
SHREVEPORT LA......	9.900	.400	.450	–	–	⁴9.550	.400	.350	–	.020
SIOUX FALLS SD.....	10.850	.450	.400	⁴.500	–	9.960	–	.200	⁴.250	–
SOUTH BEND IN......	10.840	1.000	.900	–	⁴.570	10.550	.600	.850	⁴.350	.050
SPOKANE WA.........	11.440	⁴.800	.700	–	.550	11.090	.780	.850	⁴.500	.095
SPRINGFIELD MA.....	10.050	.700	.950	–	.090	10.000	.600	1.000	–	.020
ST LOUIS MO........	10.600	.720	.700	.900	.200	10.660	.700	.800	⁴.500	.070
ST PETERSBURG FL...	⁴9.650	.450	.500	–	¹¹.040	9.210	.500	.400	–	–
ST. PAUL MN........	10.760	.655	.530	.560	.050	10.460	.650	.500	.500	–
STAMFORD CT........	⁴10.820	.830	⁴.250	–	–	9.700	.900	.650	⁴.350	.100
SYRACUSE NY........	10.590	.750	1.060	–	–	10.320	.850	1.200	–	.100
TAMPA FL...........	9.650	.450	.500	–	¹¹.040	⁴9.210	.500	.400	–	–
TOLEDO OH..........	12.355	1.060	1.300	–	.200	12.240	1.060	.750	⁴.750	.050
TOPEKA KS..........	⁴10.690	.400	.250	–	.020	⁴9.600	.400	.350	–	–
TRENTON NJ.........	10.900	.800	1.000	–	.040	10.850	.700	1.400	⁴.500	.050
TULSA OK...........	10.440	.600	.400	.330	.060	9.680	.450	.750	–	–
WASHINGTON DC......	11.550	⁴1.100	⁴.850	–	⁴.100	10.450	.800	.600	–	–
WICHITA KS.........	⁴10.530	.500	.500	–	–	⁴9.800	.500	–	–	†.100
WILMINGTON DE......	10.600	.950	.850	–	.050	⁴10.700	1.290	⁴1.000	–	⁴.080
WORCESTER MA.......	10.000	.950	1.150	–	.050	11.000	.650	1.000	–	.020
YORK PA............	9.690	.450	.450	–	–	9.890	.650	.450	–	–
YOUNGSTOWN OH......	⁴11.210	.700	1.000	⁴.500	.110	10.340	.920	1.100	⁴.600	.360

See footnotes at end of table.

Table 3. Union hourly wage rates and employer insurance, pension, vacation, and other fund payments for selected building trades in 121 cities, Oct. 2, 1978—Continued

CITY	ELECTRICIANS					PAINTERS				
	EMPLOYER CONTRIBUTIONS FOR SELECTED BENEFITS[4]					EMPLOYER CONTRIBUTIONS FOR SELECTED BENEFITS[4]				
	BASIC RATE[1]	INSURANCE[2]	PENSION	VACATION PAY	OTHER[3]	BASIC RATE[1]	INSURANCE[2]	PENSION	VACATION PAY	OTHER[3]
AKRON OH	$11.142	$0.740	6.00% +$0.650	–	†$1.258	$10.790	$0.930	$0.600	–	–
ALBANY NY	*12.100	*.750	*3.00% + .600	–	1.00%	10.380	–	.350	*$0.250	$0.020
ALBUQUERQUE NM	10.556	.600	3.00% + .700	7.00%	–	9.320	.500	.200	–	.040
ANCHORAGE AK	18.950	1.050	3.00% + 3.000	–	1.00% +$0.150	18.000	.700	2.000	–	.200
ATLANTA GA	*†10.258	†9.00%	11.00%	–	4 8.00%	†9.450	*.550	†.750	–	–
BALTIMORE MD	10.500	.800	3.00% + .900	$0.400	–	8.850	1.000	.550	.500	–
BIRMINGHAM AL	11.050	.550	3.00% + .400	–	1.00%	10.050	–	.700	–	.050
BOISE ID	11.350	.700	3.00% + .750	–	–	9.140	.560	.350	.200	–
BOSTON MA	10.980	.750	3.00% + 1.550	4.500	41.00% + .500	*10.460	.820	*1.200	–	.050
BUFFALO NY	11.988	1.000	123.00% + 1.450	.902	.050	11.205	.625	.500	–	.760
BURLINGTON VT	8.800	.500	3.00%	–	1.00% + .101	5.750	–	–	–	–
BUTTE MT	11.350	.600	3.00% + .500	4.300	1.00%	*9.230	*.420	*.350	–	–
CHARLESTON SC	*8.250	*.550	*3.00% + .250	–	1.00%	7.000	.400	.300	–	–
CHARLESTON WV	11.700	.500	3.00% + .270	.270	–	*9.940	.550	–	–	–
CHARLOTTE NC	7.900	.550	3.00% + .250	–	1.00%	7.000	.400	.300	–	–
CHATTANOOGA TN	9.548	.700	†9.00%	4 2.50%	3.50%	8.150	.450	.350	–	–
CHEYENNE WY	10.590	.720	3.00% + .500	45.00%	1.00%	10.400	.760	1.000	.750	–
CHICAGO IL	12.250	1.090	3.00% + 1.139	.800	.061	10.000	.575	.650	–	†.200
CINCINNATI OH	11.500	.500	3.00% + .600	41.000	.200	11.600	–	.250	4.500	–
CLEVELAND OH	12.400	.600	3.00% + .480	41.000	4.250	11.710	.670	1.000	4.500	.050
COLUMBIA SC	7.750	.400	*3.00% + .250	–	1.00%	7.000	.400	.300	–	–
COLUMBUS OH	12.180	.400	3.00% + 1.020	–	1.00%	10.690	.650	.650	–	–
CORPUS CHRISTI TX	†10.550	.600	3.00%	–	1.00%	*8.100	*.550	.250	–	–
DALLAS TX	10.589	6.00%	7.00%	4.00%	41.00%	9.525	.450	.500	–	–
DAYTON OH	12.030	.750	3.00% + 1.000	–	–	11.970	–	.600	–	–
DENVER CO	10.940	.700	3.00% + 1.250	44.00%	43.40%	10.400	.700	1.000	.750	–
DES MOINES IA	12.030	.400	3.00% + .800	4.500	1.75%	10.550	–	.400	.250	.020
DETROIT MI	12.148	1.400	3.00% + 1.060	41.202	1.00% + .250	11.350	.920	1.150	1.100	–
DULUTH MN	11.430	4.00%	8.00%	11.00%	1.00%	10.810	.400	.400	–	–
EL PASO TX	9.600	.300	3.00%	–	†1.00%	7.700	.380	–	–	–
ERIE PA	12.300	4.50%	7.00%	.750	1.00%	9.300	.600	.500	–	.050
EVANSVILLE IN	†12.350	.500	3.00%	4†.700	†1.00%	9.264	.650	.300	4.386	–
FARGO ND	10.650	.400	3.00%	–	3.00%	9.300	–	–	–	–
FLINT MI	11.600	.500	3.00% + 1.250	4.500	–	9.050	.500	.700	4.600	.010
FORT WORTH TX	10.462	.600	7.00%	6.00%	–	10.395	–	.200	–	–
FREMONT CA	14.644	1.300	3.00% + 1.650	10.00%	1.70%	12.740	1.100	1.500	.400	.420
FRESNO CA	12.110	.950	3.00% + 1.150	412.00%	1.00% + .050	11.260	.610	.200	41.250	.070
GRAND RAPIDS MI	10.478	.500	3.00% + .350	45.00%	–	8.270	.500	.250	.280	–
HAMMOND IN	12.096	6.50%	8.30%	44.00%	1.00%	10.500	.640	.500	–	–
HARTFORD CT	11.300	1.500	3.00% + .800	–	1.00%	10.200	.950	.700	–	–
HONOLULU HI	*11.260	*1.020	15.00% + 1.740	411.20%	*5.00% + .530	9.350	.790	3.000	*.750	.100
HOUSTON TX	10.951	.550	*10.00%	6.00%	*.010	10.605	.565	.450	.400	–
HUNTSVILLE AL	10.600	†1.500†	3.00% + .450	–	1.00%	8.250	.400	.250	–	–
INDIANAPOLIS IN	11.732	4.00%	7.00%	45.00%	–	10.030	.780	4.340	.400	–
JACKSON MS	9.450	.350	3.00% + .500	–	1.00%	7.500	1.150	–	–	–
JACKSONVILLE FL	9.550	.500	3.00% + .810	.810	1.00%	†8.700	.400	.600	–	.020
KANSAS CITY MO	*12.770	.540	3.00% + .510	.700	1.00% + .250	10.850	.550	.700	–	–
KNOXVILLE TN	9.710	.500	3.00% + .500	–	1.00%	*8.200	.400	.400	–	–
LANSING MI	11.313	.500	3.00% + 1.000	410.00%	1.00%	10.890	.550	.400	.500	.003
LAS VEGAS NV	13.250	*.980	3.00% + 1.300	412.00%	1.00%	12.140	.750	.350	1.500	.030
LITTLE ROCK AR	10.213	.500	3.00% + .350	5.00%	5.00%	*8.500	–	.400	–	–
LONG BEACH CA	12.258	1.150	3.00% + 2.150	10.00%	1.00% + .120	12.050	.710	.900	.600	.120
LOS ANGELES CA	12.258	1.150	3.00% + 2.150	10.00%	1.00% + .120	12.050	.710	.800	.600	.120
LOUISVILLE KY	*12.800	.500	*3.00% + .600	4.500	1.00%	9.020	.350	.200	–	–
LUBBOCK TX	9.729	.600	3.00%	6.00%	–	*8.100	–	–	–	–
MADISON WI	11.040	.840	3.00%	6.00%	2.00%	9.710	.700	.300	.400	.130
MANCHESTER NH	11.250	.500	4.00%	–	1.00%	7.550	.500	–	–	–
MEMPHIS TN	10.930	.750	3.00% +	–	1.00%	9.400	.500	.450	–	–
MIAMI FL	11.250	5.00%	5.50%	4.500	1.00%	9.150	.550	.500	–	.020
MILWAUKEE WI	12.000	1.000	3.00% + .350	7.00%	–	10.000	1.060	.900	.500	.040
MINNEAPOLIS MN	*11.350	*7.00%	6.00%	46.30%	6.15%	10.260	.550	.300	4.400	.100
MOBILE AL	*11.620	*.550	*3.00% + .400	13–	1.00%	8.910	.400	.350	41.000	–
MONTGOMERY AL	*9.025	.500	3.00%	5.00%	1.39%	*7.500	–	*.500	–	–
NASHVILLE TN	*10.200	.550	3.00%	4.250	1.00%	8.150	.400	.500	–	–
NEW BEDFORD MA	10.080	.900	3.00% + .850	4.00%	1.00%	9.250	.700	.650	–	.050
NEW HAVEN CT	†10.800	1.000	*3.00% + .520	–	1.00%	9.450	.500	.600	–	.020
NEW ORLEANS LA	11.068	.350	3.00% + .300	5.00%	–	8.965	.425	.400	–	†–
NEW YORK NY	12.850	4.60%	5.40% + .571	6.00%	140.50% + .571	*10.040	*9.50%	*9.50% +$0.714	3.00%	1.00%
NEWARK NJ	12.040	9.00%	12.00%	10.00%	15 15–	10.300	.700	.600	.300	–
NORFOLK VA	9.750	6.00%	6.00%	–	4.00%	8.050	–	.400	–	.010
OAKLAND CA	14.644	1.300	3.00% + 1.650	10.00%	1.70%	12.740	1.100	1.500	.400	.420
OKLAHOMA CITY OK	10.166	.500	3.00% + .500	80.00%	†1.00%	8.950	.500	.350	.350	–
OMAHA NE	†11.923	.780	3.00% + .750	4 6.00%	4 3.50%	9.850	–	.500	4.600	–
PEORIA IL	11.830	.500	3.00% + .750	4.00%	1.00%	11.300	.550	.300	–	.050
PHILADELPHIA PA	*13.030	6.00%	*9.00%	4.00%	.075	10.345	1.125	.400	.400	.050
PHOENIX AZ	*15.280	.960	3.00% + .880	–	2.50% + .100	10.500	.600	.400	–	.220
PITTSBURGH PA	12.850	.450	3.00% + .400	.600	–	11.480	.700	.400	–	–
PORTLAND ME	10.300	.650	4.00% + .250	–	1.00% + .023	6.400	–	–	–	–
PORTLAND OR	13.386	.900	3.00% + 1.000	48.00%	1.00% + .050	10.820	.550	.700	4.500	.140
PROVIDENCE RI	10.500	.750	3.00% + 1.650	.300	1.00% + .020	9.550	.600	.900	4.250	–
RALEIGH NC	8.600	.550	3.00% + .250	–	1.00%	7.000	.400	.300	–	–
READING PA	*11.690	.780	3.00% + .200	–	–	9.350	.700	.650	–	–
RICHMOND VA	10.910	5.00%	3.00%	–	–	*8.550	–	–	–	–
RIVERSIDE CA	13.760	.850	3.00% + 1.650	–	1.00%	11.580	1.380	1.280	.750	.240
ROCHESTER NY	11.600	1.000	3.00% + 1.350	–	1.25%	9.600	1.230	.620	–	.380
ROCK ISLAND IL[10]	*11.606	.550	7.50%	44.00%	4.00%	10.270	.550	.850	–	.140
ROCKFORD IL	11.670	.550	3.00% + .600	45.00%	10.00%	10.450	.550	–	4.500	–
SACRAMENTO CA	14.080	.950	3.00% + .850	45.00%	475.00% + .063	12.740	1.100	1.500	.400	.420
SALT LAKE CITY UT	†10.904	†.700	3.00% + .750	4 6.00%	11.55%	9.200	.510	.300	4.500	.030
SAN ANTONIO TX	*10.174	*.600	5.00%	5.00%	2.00%	*8.800	–	.200	–	–
SAN DIEGO CA	12.540	.700	3.00% + 1.710	41.390	1.00% + .090	11.580	1.380	1.280	.750	.240
SAN FRANCISCO CA	14.661	1.360	3.00% + 1.255	44.00%	8.00% + .270	12.610	1.100	1.500	.400	.400
SANTA ANA CA	*14.790	.810	3.00% + 1.450	–	1.00% + .020	11.580	1.380	1.280	.750	.240
SANTA FE NM	10.556	.600	3.00% + .700	7.00%	.020	8.950	.350	.200	–	.040
SAVANNAH GA	*9.900	.600	*3.00% + .650	–	1.00%	8.100	–	–	–	–
SCHENECTADY NY	*11.600	.700	*3.00% + 1.200	–	.030	10.630	–	.350	–	–
SCRANTON PA	10.450	.500	3.00% + .500	.500	.100	9.000	–	1.200	–	–
SEATTLE WA	13.660	.850	3.00% + .900	46.00%	1.00% + .050	11.770	.610	.700	–	.080
SHREVEPORT LA	*11.184	1.150	3.00%	4.00%	–	*9.200	.400	.300	–	–
SIOUX FALLS SD	10.400	.400	3.00% + .500	4.00%	3.50%	8.400	–	–	–	–
SOUTH BEND IN	11.380	4.80%	7.00%	44.00%	1.00%	9.590	–	.400	–	–
SPOKANE WA	*12.990	*.830	3.00% + .400	48.00%	1.00%	11.220	.400	.900	–	.080
SPRINGFIELD MA	10.880	.750	3.00% + .300	–	1.00%	9.170	.880	.550	–	.040
ST LOUIS MO	11.600	.700	3.00% + .640	.810	3.00% + .990	10.640	.480	.300	4.500	.100
ST PETERSBURG FL	10.200	5.00%	10.00%	–	1.00%	8.650	.350	.400	–	.100
ST. PAUL MN	11.200	5.75%	5.88%	411.25%	1.00%	10.140	.550	.250	4.700	–
STAMFORD CT	12.000	6.00%	9.50%	10.00%	1.00% + 1.020	8.800	.500	*.750	4.300	–
SYRACUSE NY	12.700	.770	3.00% + .950	–	.050	10.020	.800	.880	–	.050
TAMPA FL	10.200	5.50%	6.00%	4.00%	1.00%	8.650	.350	.400	–	.100
TOLEDO OH	13.800	.650	3.00% + .550	–	1.00%	10.280	1.060	1.100	41.000	–
TOPEKA KS	*11.985	.450	3.00% + .500	46.00%	1.00%	10.400	.500	–	–	–
TRENTON NJ	*13.870	7.00%	3.00% + .600	–	451.00%	10.300	.700	†.600	.300	–
TULSA OK	11.500	*.580	*3.00% + .510	–	–	10.400	–	.400	–	–
WASHINGTON DC	11.400	*.650	3.00% + .800	–	–	10.610	.860	1.100	–	.040
WICHITA KS	10.340	.600	3.00% + .500	46.00%	2.00%	10.070	.100	.300	–	–
WILMINGTON DE	11.380	†.50%	9.00%	–	–	*9.470	.950	.550	–	–
WORCESTER MA	10.790	8.00%	$0.890	–	1.00%	*10.460	.820	*1.000	–	.050
YORK PA	10.900	.450	3.00% + .150	–	–	7.800	.450	.150	–	.070
YOUNGSTOWN OH	11.880	.750	7.00%	–	48.00%	10.500	.750	1.000	41.000	.070

See footnotes at end of table.

Table 3. Union hourly wage rates and employer insurance, pension, vacation, and other fund payments for selected building trades in 121 cities, Oct. 2, 1978— Continued

CITY	PLASTERERS — EMPLOYER CONTRIBUTIONS FOR SELECTED BENEFITS‡					PLUMBERS — EMPLOYER CONTRIBUTIONS FOR SELECTED BENEFITS‡				
	BASIC RATE[1]	INSURANCE[2]	PENSION	VACATION PAY	OTHER[3]	BASIC RATE[1]	INSURANCE[2]	PENSION	VACATION PAY	OTHER[3]
AKRON OH	$10.410	$¹.600	$0.750	⁴$1.000	–	$12.150	$0.850	$1.000	–	$0.150
ALBANY NY	†10.400	.700	.750	–	†⁴$0.700	10.929	.800	1.020	⁴$0.571	.170
ALBUQUERQUE NM	*9.410	.670	.550	.500	.080	11.200	.630	1.420	.500	.080
ANCHORAGE AK	16.500	.700	2.400	–	.100	18.650	.730	1.900	–	.050
ATLANTA GA	†9.170	.400	*¹.800	–	.100	*10.650	.650	.500	⁴.500	.060
BALTIMORE MD	8.950	.600	.400	.500	–	10.300	.790	.830	–	.070
BIRMINGHAM AL	*9.220	.500	–	–	.030	*11.100	.580	.850	⁴.500	.040
BOISE ID	*9.670	*.840	*.550	*.800	–	11.120	.790	1.100	1.200	.100
BOSTON MA	†9.900	.850	–	–	1.650	*12.050	1.020	1.280	⁴.400	.050
BUFFALO NY	12.710	–	–	–	–	†12.850	.830	1.110	†–	.150
BURLINGTON VT	*8.300	.750	.200	–	*.100	9.200	.600	.500	–	.240
BUTTE MT	9.700	1.000	.500	1.000	–	11.750	.700	.850	⁴1.000	–
CHARLESTON SC	7.200	.250	–	–	.010	*9.400	◊.500	*.400	–	–
CHARLESTON WV	11.820	–	–	–	–	*12.440	.650	*.800	–	*1.020
CHARLOTTE NC	7.030	.250	–	–	–	*9.400	.400	.500	–	–
CHATTANOOGA TN	9.650	–	–	–	–	10.500	.500	.550	–	.070
CHEYENNE WY	10.340	.400	–	⁴.500	.200	9.720	.750	.600	1.500	–
CHICAGO IL	10.870	.875	.920	–	.150	12.000	.756	.820	–	*.550
CINCINNATI OH	11.345	–	.750	⁴1.500	.235	11.970	.700	1.200	⁴.850	.430
CLEVELAND OH	12.000	.880	–	⁴2.000	.130	11.710	.900	1.100	⁴1.000	⁴.250
COLUMBIA SC	⁶–	⁶–	⁶–	⁶–	⁶–	9.540	.350	.350	–	–
COLUMBUS OH	10.590	.600	.300	⁴.500	–	12.000	.730	.820	⁴1.000	.220
CORPUS CHRISTI TX	10.150	–	–	–	.080	*9.840	◊.450	.350	–	–
DALLAS TX	*9.740	.450	–	.500	.080	†9.980	.430	1.000	.250	.040
DAYTON OH	10.850	–	–	1.250	–	11.460	.800	1.050	⁴1.000	.040
DENVER CO	10.340	.400	–	⁴.500	.200	11.170	.800	1.050	.750	.180
DES MOINES IA	10.635	–	⁴.800	–	–	11.650	.600	1.050	⁴.500	.300
DETROIT MI	12.200	.850	.750	1.000	.060	11.310	1.250	*1.510	*1.900	.090
DULUTH MN	10.850	.400	–	.450	–	10.660	.400	.750	1.500	.150
EL PASO TX	8.250	.670	–	–	.080	8.490	.590	.440	⁴.600	.040
ERIE PA	9.960	.600	1.000	–	.030	11.620	.550	.500	–	.020
EVANSVILLE IN	10.880	–	–	⁴.500	–	11.790	.600	.900	*1.310	–
FARGO ND	10.300	–	–	–	–	10.140	.850	.420	⁴1.000	–
FLINT MI	9.670	.600	.500	⁴1.010	.100	11.000	1.000	1.200	◊1.000	◊.470
FORT WORTH TX	10.710	–	–	–	.080	9.980	.430	1.000	.250	.040
FREMONT CA	10.740	1.100	2.200	⁴1.000	.210	▴13.900	*1.400	*2.390	⁴⁸1.500	†.190
FRESNO CA	10.010	1.100	1.500	1.250	.150	13.100	1.590	2.350	⁴.750	.370
GRAND RAPIDS MI	10.680	.600	.500	⁴1.000	.100	10.850	.900	.900	◊1.240	.230
HAMMOND IN	9.960	1.000	.600	⁴.750	.010	11.220	1.000	1.150	⁴1.000	.100
HARTFORD CT	*10.300	.750	.750	–	.050	*11.010	*1.100	*1.390	–	.140
HONOLULU HI	10.020	1.300	2.000	.600	.170	*11.000	†1.050	2.050	◊.891	◊.909
HOUSTON TX	10.775	.870	.300	.525	.080	⁷10.540	.650	.700	⁷1.000	.035
HUNTSVILLE AL	9.600	–	–	–	–	10.000	.500	.550	⁴.500	–
INDIANAPOLIS IN	9.900	.800	–	⁴1.000	.383	11.400	.500	.800	⁴1.000	.060
JACKSON MS	7.800	.250	.500	–	.050	10.030	1.050	1.000	–	–
JACKSONVILLE FL	7.330	.400	.300	–	–	*†10.450	.550	.550	¹⁸.750	.070
KANSAS CITY MO	12.500	–	–	–	.100	11.826	.850	1.050	–	*1.534
KNOXVILLE TN	9.450	–	–	–	–	9.950	.400	.700	.300	.100
LANSING MI	9.560	.600	.500	⁴1.120	.100	11.160	.750	1.250	◊1.000	.140
LAS VEGAS NV	10.980	1.000	1.000	1.200	–	12.630	1.250	2.320	2.000	.150
LITTLE ROCK AR	*9.700	–	–	–	–	◊10.300	.540	*.750	–	.500
LONG BEACH CA	12.335	.980	1.850	⁴.650	.250	13.120	10.00%	16.00%	⁸13.00%	2.00%
LOS ANGELES CA	12.335	.980	1.850	⁴.650	.250	13.120	10.00%	16.00%	⁸13.00%	2.00%
LOUISVILLE KY	*10.100	–	–	–	¹⁹.850	▴12.060	*.800	*1.240	.750	²⁰.080
LUBBOCK TX	10.000	–	–	–	.040	9.450	.500	.450	.500	–
MADISON WI	9.100	.750	.800	⁴1.000	–	11.040	.600	1.000	.850	1.00%
MANCHESTER NH	8.890	.800	.600	–	.060	10.750	.680	.550	–	.020
MEMPHIS TN	10.250	–	–	–	.280	11.770	.750	.300	⁴.500	–
MIAMI FL	10.150	.700	.540	–	.020	*8.820	.920	1.050	⁴.600	–
MILWAUKEE WI	10.180	1.150	.900	.850	.060	11.820	1.050	1.100	.560	.150
MINNEAPOLIS MN	10.600	.500	.450	.700	.150	11.090	.530	.500	1.350	.050
MOBILE AL	10.470	.400	.500	–	.050	10.350	◊.600	1.100	⁴1.000	.050
MONTGOMERY AL	*7.850	–	–	–	–	*8.250	◊.600	◊.400	–	–
NASHVILLE TN	8.250	.550	.200	¹.250	.070	10.340	.600	1.000	–	.070
NEW BEDFORD MA	*10.600	1.200	1.000	–	.100	10.850	.950	1.270	–	.200
NEW HAVEN CT	*10.300	.750	.750	–	–	10.100	.750	.700	–	4.50% +$0.166
NEW ORLEANS LA	*8.830	*.600	◊.250	.550	.080	10.500	.450	.750	.500	.060
NEW YORK NY	*9.900	*1.350	1.540	.900	²¹.250	*11.050	²²3.720	–	.720	1.870
NEWARK NJ	11.250	.920	1.000	⁴.500	.020	12.895	1.000	1.080	–	.325
NORFOLK VA	10.510	–	–	–	.010	◊9.300	*.700	◊.650	⁴.500	.010
OAKLAND CA	10.740	1.100	2.200	⁴1.000	.210	*13.900	*1.400	*2.390	⁴⁸1.500	†.190
OKLAHOMA CITY OK	10.500	–	–	–	–	10.920	.600	.850	.750	.080
OMAHA NE	10.700	.670	.500	⁴.500	.200	†11.500	.850	.950	⁴†.740	.300
PEORIA IL	11.200	.800	.900	–	.050	11.550	.660	1.300	⁴.750	.050
PHILADELPHIA PA	*12.650	.930	–	.500	–	10.270	.810	1.300	1.250	.080
PHOENIX AZ	11.020	.950	1.300	–	.050	*13.240	.750	1.350	–	◊.140
PITTSBURGH PA	9.990	.700	1.400	–	1.140	*11.800	.920	*1.260	–	.980
PORTLAND ME	7.700	.400	–	–	–	9.650	.450	.450	–	.020
PORTLAND OR	10.420	.600	⁴2.000	⁴.450	.120	13.070	1.500	1.600	⁴1.250	.190
PROVIDENCE RI	*9.600	.900	.450	–	–	10.510	.900	1.950	.150	.120
RALEIGH NC	7.030	.250	–	–	–	9.400	.400	.550	–	–
READING PA	9.180	–	1.030	–	1.00%	*12.770	.810	1.300	–	◊.080
RICHMOND VA	9.700	–	–	–	.010	*11.050	.450	.600	–	–
RIVERSIDE CA	13.558	–	–	2.033	.359	13.120	10.00%	16.00%	⁸13.00%	2.00%
ROCHESTER NY	11.770	.750	.850	–	.180	11.510	.705	1.160	.550	2.140
ROCK ISLAND IL[10]	13.000	–	–	–	–	²¹11.160	.540	1.290	⁵.00%	.120
ROCKFORD IL	9.780	.550	.750	⁴.750	.040	11.580	.540	.600	⁴.750	.100
SACRAMENTO CA	12.440	1.040	1.820	⁴1.000	.140	12.440	1.450	2.000	*2.780	.170
SALT LAKE CITY UT	10.400	.550	.650	–	–	*11.250	.660	1.000	⁴.250	.130
SAN ANTONIO TX	10.450	–	–	–	.060	10.580	*.550	.550	.750	.170
SAN DIEGO CA	10.460	.650	2.250	⁴1.250	.100	13.120	10.00%	16.00%	13.00%	2.00%
SAN FRANCISCO CA	11.700	1.000	2.650	⁸.750	1.010	13.450	2.235	2.150	⁸.610	2.735
SANTA ANA CA	12.335	.980	1.850	⁴.650	.250	13.120	10.00%	16.00%	13.00%	²⁴2.00%
SANTA FE NM	*9.668	.670	*.550	.600	.080	†11.200	.630	1.420	⁸.500	.080
SAVANNAH GA	7.250	–	–	–	–	*10.700	.450	.600	–	–
SCHENECTADY NY	*10.900	.700	*.750	–	*.200	*11.350	.750	1.000	–	.120
SCRANTON PA	11.630	–	–	–	.050	11.240	.800	1.250	–	.100
SEATTLE WA	10.720	.700	1.100	⁴1.000	.120	13.900	.890	1.510	1.250	.120
SHREVEPORT LA	9.750	–	–	1.000	–	10.540	.500	.600	.950	.080
SIOUX FALLS SD	9.960	–	–	–	–	10.000	.550	.450	⁴.430	–
SOUTH BEND IN	9.490	.850	.900	⁴.750	.050	10.600	.480	.950	⁴.500	.080
SPOKANE WA	10.730	.750	1.000	–	.100	13.940	.850	1.260	1.250	.080
SPRINGFIELD MA	10.050	.700	.950	–	.090	10.300	1.010	1.100	–	.220
ST LOUIS MO	9.945	.780	.800	⁴1.000	.150	11.755	.800	.800	.500	.700
ST PETERSBURG FL	8.650	.450	.500	–	.100	10.730	.600	1.000	–	–
ST. PAUL MN	10.650	.700	.250	.650	.070	10.920	.540	.500	.670	.880
STAMFORD CT	10.820	.830	.250	.250	–	11.200	.750	.700	4.00%	.020
SYRACUSE NY	9.700	.800	1.210	–	.025	11.430	1.170	.870	–	.130
TAMPA FL	8.650	.450	.500	–	.100	10.310	.800	.900	⁴1.000	.100
TOLEDO OH	13.050	.600	–	⁴.750	.060	11.830	1.100	1.100	–	1.440
TOPEKA KS	*10.500	–	–	–	–	10.680	.800	.650	⁴1.500	.110
TRENTON NJ	10.900	.800	1.000	–	.040	12.210	1.040	.900	⁴1.000	.160
TULSA OK	10.150	–	–	–	–	11.220	.550	.750	–	.350
WASHINGTON DC	10.400	*.600	.750	–	.030	11.320	1.050	1.000	–	.030
WICHITA KS	9.750	–	–	–	–	10.920	*.800	.850	⁴.750	.040
WILMINGTON DE	*10.620	.900	–	.500	◊.080	10.950	1.150	1.000	9.00%	–
WORCESTER MA	10.000	.950	1.150	–	.050	10.830	*1.150	.450	–	–
YORK PA	*9.300	.450	.350	†1.250	–	11.300	.700	.800	–	–
YOUNGSTOWN OH	11.350	.600	–	–	⁴1.070	10.790	1.070	.800	⁴1.500	.080

See footnotes at end of table.

19-31

Table 3. Union hourly wage rates and employer insurance, pension, vacation, and other fund payments for selected building trades in 121 cities, Oct. 2, 1978—Continued

CITY	BUILDING LABORERS EMPLOYER CONTRIBUTIONS FOR SELECTED BENEFITS‡					CITY	BUILDING LABORERS EMPLOYER CONTRIBUTIONS FOR SELECTED BENEFITS‡				
	BASIC RATE[1]	INSUR-ANCE[2]	PENSION	VACATION PAY	OTHER[3]		BASIC RATE[1]	INSUR-ANCE[2]	PENSION	VACATION PAY	OTHER[3]
AKRON OH	$10.270	$0.700	$0.700	-	$0.160	MINNEAPOLIS MN	8.750	.600	.450	.400	-
ALBANY NY	8.920	.900	1.100	-	.220	MOBILE AL	6.450	.400	.500	-	.050
ALBUQUERQUE NM	*7.160	.430	*.720	-	*.040	MONTGOMERY AL	4.750	.200	.100	-	-
ANCHORAGE AK	13.770	.700	2.750	-	.400	NASHVILLE TN	6.700	.250	.270	-	.020
ATLANTA GA	*†6.400	*†.250	.330	-	.050	NEW BEDFORD MA	8.250	.600	.750	-	.170
BALTIMORE MD	6.750	.300	.500	$0.300	.105	NEW HAVEN CT	7.950	*.600	*.750	-	†.150
BIRMINGHAM AL	*6.650	*.350	*.400	-	.060	NEW ORLEANS LA	7.650	.250	.270	-	.050
BOISE ID	8.110	†.850	†1.120	.400	.100	NEW YORK NY	*9.700	*1.620	1.510	-	*.080
BOSTON MA	8.250	.600	.750	-	.170	NEWARK NJ	8.000	.750	.950	-	.070
BUFFALO NY	8.955	1.100	1.400	-	†.650	NORFOLK VA	*5.950	.200	.150	-	.070
BURLINGTON VT	6.100	.750	.600	-	.100	OAKLAND CA	*9.225	1.300	1.750	†1.000	*.210
BUTTE MT	7.960	.600	.500	†.750	.050	OKLAHOMA CITY OK	7.650	.300	.400	-	.010
CHARLESTON SC	6_	6_	6_	6_	6_	OMAHA NE	7.960	.670	.450	-	†.380
CHARLESTON WV	8.720	.400	.400	-	.030	PEORIA IL	10.650	.500	.600	-	.035
CHARLOTTE NC	4.900	.150	.150	-	.050	PHILADELPHIA PA	9.000	.900	.650	-	.080
CHATTANOOGA TN	6.600	.250	.300	-	.020	PHOENIX AZ	8.110	.920	.980	†.250	.100
CHEYENNE WY	6.970	.330	.400	1.000	.300	PITTSBURGH PA	9.530	.860	.710	-	.050
CHICAGO IL	9.200	.570	1.100	-	-	PORTLAND ME	*6.200	.600	.750	-	.100
CINCINNATI OH	10.500	.700	.700	-	.100	PORTLAND OR	8.400	.950	1.050	†.700	.150
CLEVELAND OH	10.520	1.070	1.400	-	.340	PROVIDENCE RI	8.250	.600	.800	-	.180
COLUMBIA SC	6_	6_	6_	6_	6_	RALEIGH NC	4.900	.150	.150	-	.050
COLUMBUS OH	8.040	.700	.700	-	†.600	READING PA	7.600	.450	.350	-	*.080
CORPUS CHRISTI TX	5.970	.280	.130	-	-	RICHMOND VA	5.600	.200	.200	-	.020
DALLAS TX	6.320	.275	.400	-	†.020	RIVERSIDE CA	*8.480	1.150	2.450	.700	*.230
DAYTON OH	8.790	.700	.700	-	.100	ROCHESTER NY	8.350	1.050	1.040	-	.770
DENVER CO	7.670	.520	.600	-	.100	ROCK ISLAND IL[10]	9.720	.400	1.000	-	.075
DES MOINES IA	9.335	.300	.800	-	-	ROCKFORD IL	9.800	.550	.600	-	.050
DETROIT MI	9.530	.900	.900	.850	.070	SACRAMENTO CA	9.225	1.300	1.750	†1.000	.210
DULUTH MN	8.650	.400	.450	.500	-	SALT LAKE CITY UT	7.770	.500	†.350	-	.040
EL PASO TX	5.410	.530	.400	-	-	SAN ANTONIO TX	*5.910	*.380	.400	-	*.060
ERIE PA	8.840	.800	.600	-	.030	SAN DIEGO CA	8.350	.770	2.050	.750	.230
EVANSVILLE IN	8.300	.700	.500	-	.120	SAN FRANCISCO CA	9.225	1.300	1.750	†1.000	.210
FARGO ND	7.040	.350	-	-	-	SANTA ANA CA	*8.480	1.150	2.450	.700	*.230
FLINT MI	8.440	.650	.650	†.500	.040	SANTA FE NM	7.160	.430	.720	-	.040
FORT WORTH TX	6.320	.275	.400	-	†.020	SAVANNAH GA	*5.420	.150	.130	-	.100
FREMONT CA	9.225	1.300	1.750	†1.000	.210	SCHENECTADY NY	9.170	.800	1.000	-	.170
FRESNO CA	9.225	1.300	1.750	†1.000	.210	SCRANTON PA	9.300	.480	.590	-	.050
GRAND RAPIDS MI	7.010	.650	.350	†.550	.050	SEATTLE WA	9.920	.950	1.100	†.250	.100
HAMMOND IN	8.700	.700	.550	-	.120	SHREVEPORT LA	6.500	.200	.100	-	.020
HARTFORD CT	*7.950	*.600	*.750	-	.150	SIOUX FALLS SD	7.500	-	-	-	.120
HONOLULU HI	8.110	.840	1.210	8.480	.100	SOUTH BEND IN	8.250	.700	.500	-	.120
HOUSTON TX	7.840	.450	.600	-	-	SPOKANE WA	8.750	.820	.900	-	25.780
HUNTSVILLE AL	5.210	.300	.450	-	-	SPRINGFIELD MA	8.250	.600	.750	-	.170
INDIANAPOLIS IN	7.950	.700	.500	-	.120	ST LOUIS MO	9.575	.450	1.000	.500	†.040
JACKSON MS	*5.450	.150	.200	-	*.070	ST PETERSBURG FL	6.650	.500	.200	-	.025
JACKSONVILLE FL	5.570	.200	.200	-	-	ST. PAUL MN	8.750	.600	.450	.400	-
KANSAS CITY MO	9.150	.450	.400	†.500	.210	STAMFORD CT	7.950	*.600	*.750	-	.150
KNOXVILLE TN	6.200	.200	.200	-	.010	SYRACUSE NY	8.450	.750	1.150	-	.050
LANSING MI	†8.125	.650	.350	†.625	.050	TAMPA FL	6.650	.500	.200	-	.025
LAS VEGAS NV	9.950	.660	1.530	1.000	-	TOLEDO OH	10.360	.700	.700	†.500	.160
LITTLE ROCK AR	*6.250	*.330	*.600	-	*.030	TOPEKA KS	*7.000	.400	.500	-	.200
LONG BEACH CA	8.480	1.150	2.450	.700	.230	TRENTON NJ	8.500	.400	.800	-	.070
LOS ANGELES CA	*8.480	1.150	2.450	.700	*.230	TULSA OK	7.650	.300	.400	-	-
LOUISVILLE KY	7.930	.350	.470	-	.020	WASHINGTON DC	8.460	.600	.450	-	-
LUBBOCK TX	*5.525	.275	.270	-	-	WICHITA KS	†7.200	.500	*.350	-	†.200
MADISON WI	9.380	.450	.400	-	.020	WILMINGTON DE	8.500	.900	.600	-	.080
MANCHESTER NH	7.270	.600	.800	-	.100	WORCESTER MA	8.250	.600	.750	-	.170
MEMPHIS TN	6.975	.300	.350	-	.070	YORK PA	6.850	*.500	*.570	-	-
MIAMI FL	†6.800	†1.020	†.550	-	†.050	YOUNGSTOWN OH	8.780	.700	.700	-	†1.160
MILWAUKEE WI	9.790	.900	.900	.500	.070						

[1] These rates represent the minimum wage rates (excluding holiday and vacation payments regularly made or credited to the worker each pay period) agreed upon through collective bargaining between employers and trade unions.

[2] Includes life insurance, hospitalization, and other types of health and welfare benefits.

[3] Includes all other nonlegally required employer contributions, except those for apprenticeship fund payments, as indicated in individual agreements.

[4] Part of negotiated rate not included in basic rate shown. Amount may be included in computation of overtime and other premium rates.

[5] Includes contributions for insurance and supplementary unemployment benefits; separate data not available.

[6] No union wage rate in effect on survey date.

[7] Part of the basic rate transferred to insurance, pension, and/or vacation plans.

[8] Includes contributions for vacation and holidays; separate data are not available.

[9] New rate in negotiation on survey date.

[10] Includes Rock Island and Moline, Illinois and Davenport, Iowa.

[11] Discontinued.

[12] Percentage based on negotiated rate of $12.89.

[13] Fund has been discontinued.

[14] Employer pays employee's share of Social Security taxes; in addition, agreement also provides for 9 paid holidays.

[15] In addition to legally required contributions, employer pays employee's share of Temporary Disability Insurance.

[16] In addition, employer contributes to NEIF as follows: 0.8% of first $50,000 monthly gross payroll; 0.7% of second $50,000; and 0.2% of remaining monthly gross payroll.

[17] 5% deferred pay is part of the negotiated rate; not included in basic rate shown.

[18] To be included in basic scale.

[19] Includes 75 cents Savings Fund Contribution; part of negotiated rate, not included in basic rate shown.

[20] Includes 2 cents contribution to holiday fund; part of negotiated rate, not included in basic rate shown.

[21] Industry promotion fund discontinued.

[22] Includes contributions for insurance and pension, separate data not available.

[23] The following rates are applicable to plumbers in Davenport, Iowa: Basic rate, $11,250; insurance, 61 cents; pension, 95 cents; vacation,[4] 50 cents; and other, 10 cents.

[24] Includes $1.00 Security Savings Contribution which is part of negotiated rate; not included in basic rate shown.

[25] 70 cents credit union savings is part of the negotiated rate; not included in basic rate shown.

* Represents either a newly negotiated or deferred change which became effective during the quarter.

† Revision of data previously reported.

‡ Unless otherwise indicated, employer benefit contributions are shown in dollar and cent amount.

NOTE: Information on employer contributions to insurance (welfare), pension, vacation pay, and other fund payments, as provided in labor-management contracts, is presented as cents-per-hour or as percent of basic rate; in actual practice, however, some employer payments are calculated on the basis of total hours worked or gross payroll. These variations in the method of computation are not indicated in the above tabulation. Payments directly to worker each pay period for, or in lieu of, benefits, are footnoted.

Some contracts also provide for employer contributions to an apprenticeship fund. Information on payments to this fund was not collected.

Scheduled wage increases and escalator provisions in 1979

Deferred increases will average 5.1 percent, equal to the previous year's gain, while scheduled escalator reviews may affect wage rates of 4.1 million workers during 1979

BETH A. LEVIN

At least 5.2 million workers will receive wage-rate increases averaging 5.1 percent during 1979, under the provisions of major collective bargaining settlements concluded in previous years. These agreements cover 1,000 workers or more in the private nonfarm sector of the economy.[1] Of the workers receiving deferred wage increases, 2.8 million also will be among the 4.1 million workers whose total wage gains in 1979 may be affected by scheduled cost-of-living reviews.

While the average deferred increase of 5.1 percent in 1979 is identical to that for the preceding year, the 1978 figure covered substantially more workers.[2] This difference in coverage is attributable to the cyclical nature of negotiations within the major bargaining units. Eighty-three percent of the workers in such units are under 3-year contracts; therefore, a pattern has resulted in which 2 years of heavy bargaining are followed by a third with substantially fewer expirations and reopeners. In the pattern's lighter bargaining years, such as 1978, a maximum number of deferred wage changes take effect.

Because 1979 will be a relatively heavy bargaining year in some key industries, the total wage change for the year will be influenced greatly by immediate adjustments agreed upon in the negotiations. More than 3.8 million workers are covered by contracts that will expire or be reopened during the year. Some 746,000 workers in transportation equipment will negotiate new contracts in 1979, including those working for the three major auto companies. Another large group with expiring agreements are 400,000 members of the Teamsters union covered by the National Master Freight Agreement, among a total 589,000 workers with expirations in the entire transportation industry. Workers in the construction (436,000), apparel (366,000), electrical machinery (300,000), retail trade (259,000), food (204,000), and machinery except electrical (148,000) industries will also account for large segments of 1979 bargaining.[3]

The data in this article are derived from information available to the Bureau of Labor Statistics in early November 1978. Of the 9.6 million workers in major collective bargaining units, the data exclude some 690,000 workers whose contracts expired later in 1978, had unspecified expiration dates, or had already expired but

Beth A. Levin is an economist in the Division of Trends in Employee Compensation, Bureau of Labor Statistics. Douglas R. LeRoy, a labor economist in the Division, helped in the preparation of the tables.

had not been renegotiated or the settlement terms were unknown.[4]

Deferred increases

The 5.1-percent average deferred increase amounts to an hourly hike of 43.4 cents. (See table 1.) Of the 5.2 million workers affected, the largest group of workers, 3.1 million, will receive an average increase of 4.5 percent in 1979 as a result of 1977 negotiations. About 1.9 million workers whose new contracts were settled in the first 10 months of 1978 will gain an average 6.1 percent. The average 1979 deferred increase for nearly 125,000 workers whose agreements were negotiated in 1976 is 3.6 percent. For 28,000 workers whose agreements were made prior to that year, the average is 5.2 percent.

Approximately 248,000 workers will receive a deferred increase in 1979 before their contracts expire later in the year. No negotiated wage increase or cost-of-living review is scheduled during the year for nearly 397,000 workers, although their contracts expire after 1979. Another 74,000 workers with post-1979 expirations will have an escalator review but no deferred increase in 1979.

By industry. As table 1 shows, out of a total 1.8 million workers receiving deferred increases in 1979 in the manufacturing sector, the largest single block of workers (1.1 million) is in the metalworking industries. The average gain in these industries—3.4 percent—is the same as in 1978. In the nonmanufacturing sector, over 1 million construction industry workers will receive an average gain of 6.7 percent, up somewhat from 6.5 percent in 1978.[5] The nonmanufacturing sector as a whole continues to have a higher average deferred

Table 1. Workers receiving deferred wage increases in 1979, by major industry group and size of increase

[Workers in thousands]

Average hourly increase	Number of contracts	All private non-agricultural industries	Manufacturing						Nonmanufacturing					
			Total¹	Food and kindred products	Apparel	Paper and allied products	Stone, clay, and glass products	Metal-working	Total²	Contract construc-tion	Trans-portation	Commu-nications, gas, and electric utilities	Ware-housing, wholesale and retail trade	Services
Total	1,208	5,153	1,769	104	118	53	83	1,140	3,384	1,059	445	842	556	214
CENTS PER HOUR														
Under 15 cents	51	210	131	---	1	---	8	109	79	---	22	---	46	11
15 and under 20	72	225	68	5	6	---	2	52	158	6	32	85	18	18
20 and under 25	177	1,239	529	11	90	---	---	375	710	5	7	600	24	40
25 and under 30	141	677	493	14	13	---	7	430	184	10	43	34	29	49
30 and under 35	79	250	104	17	6	---	10	41	146	11	12	4	46	23
35 and under 40	67	287	62	9	---	2	2	26	225	11	145	12	15	40
40 and under 45	89	309	100	18	---	---	39	23	209	86	51	9	58	5
45 and under 50	43	88	34	12	---	1	---	11	53	18	6	7	20	2
50 and under 60	149	579	104	17	3	11	12	39	474	138	3	26	285	21
60 and under 70	107	339	103	---	---	15	3	28	235	133	23	64	13	1
70 and under 80	69	328	32	---	---	18	---	4	296	129	2	---	---	5
80 and under 90	73	273	8	---	---	7	---	---	265	213	52	---	---	---
90 and over	91	350	2	---	---	---	---	2	349	299	47	---	3	---
Mean increase	---	43.4	30.3	36.0	22.0	67.8	38.4	25.9	50.2	75.6	53.5	26.6	41.0	31.0
With escalators	---	31.5	25.4	33.8	21.0	0.0	32.7	24.4	36.4	78.5	42.8	23.4	43.4	40.6
Without escalators	---	59.7	44.7	37.7	26.0	67.8	41.7	43.1	63.6	75.2	97.5	55.3	36.5	30.6
Median increase	---	33.0	25.9	37.5	20.0	68.9	43.0	25.0	44.2	75.0	37.1	21.8	50.0	25.4
PERCENT³														
Under 3 percent	204	926	746	6	1	---	10	708	180	27	63	---	57	1
3 and under 4	179	1,303	394	16	85	---	2	230	909	53	108	719	10	1
4 and under 5	126	478	102	15	1	---	9	52	376	135	118	6	42	74
5 and under 6	143	429	98	20	8	---	3	50	331	183	10	---	71	30
6 and under 7	175	623	104	22	14	---	20	23	518	142	11	27	264	66
7 and under 8	178	766	133	10	9	3	36	20	634	244	36	71	88	26
8 and under 9	111	390	112	5	---	7	4	36	278	184	59	11	20	4
9 and under 10	36	128	24	10	---	4	---	8	104	66	28	1	3	5
10 and under 11	37	57	43	---	---	37	---	1	14	7	5	---	---	2
11 and over	19	53	14	---	---	2	---	12	39	19	6	7	1	5
Mean increase	---	5.1	4.3	5.7	4.3	9.7	6.1	3.4	5.5	6.7	5.1	3.6	5.9	5.9
With escalators	---	3.9	3.3	4.8	3.9	---	4.6	3.1	4.4	6.7	4.5	3.2	5.9	6.3
Without escalators	---	6.7	7.0	6.4	5.7	9.7	6.9	7.1	6.6	6.7	7.3	7.4	5.8	5.8
Median increase	---	4.6	3.0	5.7	3.6	10.0	6.8	3.0	5.7	6.9	4.0	3.0	6.3	6.0

¹Includes workers in the following industry groups for which separate data are not shown: Ordnance (19,000); tobacco (28,000); textiles (22,000); lumber (52,000); furniture (14,000); printing (40,000); leather (30,000); chemicals (34,000); and instruments and miscellaneous manufacturing (29,000).

²Includes 216,000 workers in mining and 52,000 in finance, insurance, and real estate for which separate data are not shown.

³Percent of straight-time average hourly earnings.

NOTE: Workers are distributed according to the average adjustment for all workers in each bargaining unit considered. Deferred wage increases include guaranteed minimum adjustments under cost-of-living escalator clauses. The number of workers affected in each industry is based on data available in early November 1978 and, thus, may understate the number of workers receiving deferred wage increases. Only bargaining units in the private, nonagricultural economy covering 1,000 workers or more are considered in this table. Because of rounding, sums of individual items may not equal totals. Dashes indicate there are no workers having wage increases that fall within that stated range.

increase than the manufacturing industries. This dominance is true for both percentage increases and hourly wage gains: nonmanufacturing averages 5.5 percent and 50.2 cents, and manufacturing averages 4.3 percent and 30.3 cents.

Workers in the paper industry will have the largest percent deferred gains of any group, an average 9.7 percent. Construction workers will get the largest hourly raise, 75.6 cents. Workers in retail and wholesale trade, a group that accounts for a substantial portion of all those receiving deferred increases in 1979, will gain an average 5.9 percent or 41.0 cents; employees of retail food stores make up a large number of these workers. Another large group, workers in the transportation field, will receive an average wage-rate hike of 5.1 percent (53.5 cents).

Table 2 shows when in 1979 workers will receive deferred increases. The heavy concentration of increases in August largely reflects changes scheduled for 708,000 workers under agreements with the American Telephone and Telegraph operating companies and 303,000 workers under basic steel industry contracts.

For contracts covering 5,000 workers or more, the 1979 average increase in the cost of both deferred wages and benefits is 4.7 percent. (See table 3.) This average represents a decline from the 1978 average of 5.3 percent and from the 1977 average of 5.9 percent.

An important influence on the negotiation of deferred increases implemented over the term of a contract is the possibility of any additional wage gains under escalator provisions. The likelihood of wage changes based on the inflation rate tends to hold down the amount of the guaranteed deferred increases. This tendency is evident in 1979, as in previous years, in an average 6.7-percent deferred

Table 2. Workers receiving deferred increases in 1979 in bargaining units covering 1,000 workers or more, by month

[Workers in thousands]

Effective month	Principal industries affected	Workers covered
Total[1]		5,153
January	Construction; transportation; food stores	447
February	Primary metals	570
March	Mining; food stores	420
April	Construction; stone, clay, and glass; food stores	377
May	Construction	473
June	Construction	676
July	Construction; railroads	701
August	Primary metals; communications	1,437
September	Food stores; services	244
October	Apparel; transportation equipment	433
November	Construction; transportation equipment	179
December	Construction	123

[1]This total is smaller than the sum of individual items because 928,000 workers will receive more than one increase. This total is based on data available as of Nov. 1, 1978, and, thus, may understate the number of workers receiving deferred increases for the entire year.

Table 3. Workers receiving deferred wage and benefit increases in 1979 in bargaining units covering 5,000 workers or more, by size of increase

[Workers in thousands]

Percentage increase	Workers covered
All settlements providing deferred changes[1]	2,909
Under 3 percent	819
3 and under 4	466
4 and under 5	467
5 and under 6	158
6 and under 7	609
7 and under 8	159
8 and under 9	168
9 and under 10	52
10 and under 11	5
11 percent and over	6
Mean increase (percent)	4.7
Median increase (percent)	4.1

[1]This total excludes workers covered by contracts expiring in 1979 who receive a deferred benefit change only.
NOTE: Only bargaining units in the private, nonagricultural economy are considered in this table. Because of rounding, sums of individual items may not equal totals.

increase for those contracts without a cost-of-living clause versus only a 3.9-percent gain in contracts with such provisions.

Cost-of-living reviews

If the inflation rate continues to rise as it did during the first 9 months of 1978, cost-of-living escalator reviews, covering 4.1 million workers, are likely to have a large impact on the total wage change effective this year. If the Consumer Price Index continues rising at the 8.2-percent rate experienced from September 1977 to September 1978, compared to 6.6 percent for the same period a year earlier, and 5.5 percent 2 years previously, workers may receive substantially larger escalator increases in 1979.[6]

Workers covered by cost-of-living reviews in the major collective bargaining sector dropped in both number and percent in 1978 for the second straight year. Much of last year's change was a result of the elimination in March 1978 of escalator reviews in the new contract between the Bituminous Coal Operators Association and the United Mine Workers. Also, such coverage decreased in the printing and publishing industry and in finance, insurance, and real estate. The following tabulation shows the number of workers (in millions) under cost-of-living clauses on January 1 of each year, 1968–79:[7]

Year	Workers	Year	Workers
1968	2.5	1974	4.0
1969	2.7	1975	5.3
1970	2.8	1976	6.0
1971	3.0	1977	6.0
1972	4.3	1978	5.8
1973	4.1	1979	5.6

Table 4. Prevalence of escalator clauses in major collective bargaining agreements, November 1978

[Workers in thousands]

Industry	2-digit standard industrial classification (SIC)	All contracts		Contracts with escalator clauses		Percent of workers covered by escalator clauses
		Workers covered	Number of contracts	Workers covered	Number of contracts	
Total		9,567	2,109	5,580	850	58.3
Metal mining	10	56	14	53	12	94.1
Anthracite mining	11	2	1	---	---	0.0
Bituminous coal and lignite mining	12	160	1	---	---	0.0
Building construction general contractors	15	672	194	26	8	3.8
Construction other than building construction	16	486	114	66	10	13.5
Construction — special trade contractors	17	496	208	74	24	14.9
Ordnance and accessories	19	31	14	25	10	81.7
Food and kindred products	20	341	116	122	46	35.7
Tobacco manufacturers	21	29	8	28	7	94.9
Textile mill products	22	51	16	12	2	24.5
Apparel and other textile products	23	483	52	187	10	38.6
Lumber and wood products	24	58	20	1	1	2.0
Furniture and fixtures	25	30	20	14	10	47.4
Paper and allied products	26	105	70	---	---	0.0
Printing and publishing	27	64	37	19	10	29.4
Chemical and allied products	28	99	51	30	15	29.9
Petroleum refining and related industries	29	57	26	---	---	0.0
Rubber and plastic products	30	96	21	86	16	89.9
Leather and leather products	31	54	20	1	1	1.8
Stone, clay, and glass products	32	97	40	34	17	35.4
Primary metal industries	33	514	124	493	112	95.9
Fabricated metal products	34	83	38	66	26	79.4
Machinery, except electrical	35	285	98	258	80	90.3
Electrical equipment	36	469	107	429	86	91.6
Transportation equipment	37	1,072	110	998	89	93.1
Instruments and related products	38	32	16	13	7	39.8
Miscellaneous manufacturing industries	39	23	12	4	2	18.7
Railroad transportation	40	429	19	429	19	100.0
Local and urban transit	41	118	33	107	28	91.2
Motor freight transportation	42	559	27	548	21	98.1
Water transportation	44	99	17	36	7	36.4
Transportation by air	45	161	43	112	24	69.8
Transportation services	47	2	1	2	1	1.00.0
Communications	48	765	47	716	31	93.7
Electric, gas, and sanitary services	49	233	78	48	13	20.7
Wholesale trade	50	70	27	44	14	63.0
Retail trade – general merchandise	53	88	22	21	5	24.3
Food stores	54	566	106	424	67	75.0
Automotive dealers and service stations	55	19	11	2	1	7.9
Apparel and accessory stores	56	15	7	1	1	7.2
Eating and drinking places	58	74	24	---	---	0.0
Miscellaneous retail stores	59	18	7	8	3	43.5
Finance, insurance, and real estate	60–65	84	14	30	6	36.0
Services	70–89	319	78	12	8	3.7

NOTE: Because of rounding, sums of individual items may not equal totals, and percentages may not reflect shown ratios. Dashes indicate absence of cost-of-living coverage.

The percent of workers covered by contracts with escalator clauses dropped from 60.6 percent in November 1976 to 60.2 percent a year later and to 58.3 percent in November 1978. (See table 4.) Only 40.3 percent of all major contracts have cost-of-living clauses. However, nearly 60 percent of all workers are covered by such clauses; therefore, escalator provisions tend to be included most often in contracts that cover the largest number of workers. In fact, some of the larger contracts expiring in 1979 are among the largest contracts that provide cost-of-living coverage. These contracts include agreements between the Auto Workers and General Motors, Ford, and Chrysler and the trucking industry's contract with the Teamsters. Two other large groups of workers with escalator protection whose contracts expire in later years are the Communications Workers with the Bell System and the Steelworkers with major steel producers. Following are listed on a union-by-union basis the approximate number of members (in thousands) covered under cost-of-living clauses in major bargaining units:

Union	Workers
Auto Workers	987
Teamsters	603
Communications Workers	585
Steelworkers	537
Retail Clerks	326
Machinists	273
Electrical Workers (IBEW)	213
Clothing Workers	189
Electrical Workers (IUE)	166
Meat Cutters	131
Railway Clerks	122
United Transportation Union	120
All others	1,328

Adjustment formulas. The actual rate of inflation is only one of many factors that determine the amount of any increase or decrease granted under the provisions of an escalator clause. One possible limit on any change is the presence of a "ceiling" or maximum increase. Of the 5.6 million workers under cost-of-living clauses as of November 1978, 1.3 million are under contracts with such "ceilings" or "caps." Another half million are guaranteed some minimum amount of adjustment, even if the contract formula yields a lesser amount.[8]

The popularity of specific formulas used to calculate a cost-of-living increase or decrease shifted within the last year. As of November 1978, even more workers than in the previous year fell under agreements which have a formula of a 1-cent hourly wage increase for each 0.3-point rise in the CPI—a total of slightly less than 2.1 million workers, up from 1.9 million as of November 1977. The elimination of an escalator clause from the bituminous coal miners' agreement explains most of the drop in the number of workers with a 1-cent for each 0.4-point change formula—down to 592,000 workers from 726,000 workers in 1977. The number of workers whose escalator adjustments are based on a 1-cent wage change for each 0.3- or 0.4-*percent* CPI change is up to more than 372,000 from 300,000 workers in this category in late 1977.

More than 2.5 million workers are covered by escalator provisions that provide adjustments based on some formula other than the ones mentioned. For example, the American Telephone and Telegraph contracts grant across-the-board increases of 50 cents per week plus 0.6 percent on each employee's weekly rate for each 1-percent rise in the CPI. Some contracts in the construction industry give percent-for-percent increases based on any rise in the CPI above the amount of any deferred increase scheduled for the year.

Review timing and indexes. The timing of reviews has an impact on the size of individual changes under an escalator clause. As table 5 shows, more than half of all workers will come under quarterly review. Of course, the frequency of review in any year is also affected by agreement expirations during the year.

The year 1967 = 100 is the most common CPI base year for escalator formulas and is specified as such in contracts with over 3.9 million workers. The 1957–59 = 100 base is the second most common, occurring in 94 contracts covering 909,000 workers. A very small group, less than 6,000 workers, still uses the 1947–49 = 100 base. The balance of workers with cost-of-living provisions uses some other base. For example, in the contract between the trucking companies and the Teamsters, the base year was switched from 1957–59 to 1967 during the second review of the agreement. For 1979, the percent of total coverage for each base year is essentially unchanged from 1978.

The national, all-cities index continues to be the most prevalent trigger in escalator provisions: nearly 87 percent of the clauses designate that index. Specific city indexes are used in the remaining clauses, except for 11 agreements in the transportation equipment industry that use a weighted average of the U.S. and Canadian indexes.

One new factor in the consideration of cost-of-living provisions in 1979 are the new and revised indexes introduced by the Bureau of Labor Statistics in February 1978. Parties negotiating

Table 5. Timing of 1979 cost-of-living reviews in major contracts, by year of contract expiration and frequency of review

[Workers in thousands]

Type of contract, by expiration and frequency of escalator review	First quarter		Second quarter		Third quarter		Fourth quarter		Full year[1]	
	Number of contracts	Workers covered	Number of contracts	Workers covered	Number of contracts	Workers covered	Number of contracts	Workers covered	Number of contracts	Workers covered
ALL CONTRACTS										
Total	445	2,606	420	2,261	420	2,400	327	1,306	669	4,107
Quarterly	359	2,058	339	2,022	297	1,092	275	1,021	365	2,068
Semiannual	52	364	26	79	44	342	31	104	89	492
Annual	34	184	55	160	79	966	21	181	191	1,494
Other[2]	...	...	...	...	...	...	...	...	24	53
CONTRACTS EXPIRING IN 1979[3]										
Total	117	1,184	76	1,048	38	155	1	1	138	1,253
Quarterly	82	1,027	62	989	20	59	1	1	82	1,027
Semiannual	27	119	4	21	17	95	...	...	31	141
Annual	8	38	10	37	1	1	...	...	20	78
Other[2]	...	...	...	...	...	...	...	...	5	7
CONTRACTS EXPIRING IN LATER YEARS										
Total	328	1,422	344	1,214	382	2,245	326	1,305	531	2,854
Quarterly	277	1,031	277	1,033	277	1,033	274	1,020	283	1,041
Semiannual	25	245	22	58	27	248	31	104	58	352
Annual	26	146	45	123	78	965	21	181	171	1,416
Other[2]	...	...	...	...	...	...	...	...	19	46

[1] Contracts that have at least one review in the year.
[2] Includes monthly, combinations of annual and quarterly, combinations of annual and semiannual, other, and reviews dependent upon levels of the Consumer Price Index.

[3] Includes only those reviews through the termination of the present agreements; it does not assume the continuation of existing reviews after contract expiration dates.

NOTE: Because of rounding, sums of individual items may not equal totals. Dashes indicate that there is no coverage for a particular review in the quarter.

now will have a choice between the revised Consumer Price Index for Urban Wage Earners and Clerical Workers (CPI–W) or the new CPI for All Urban Consumers (CPI–U). In addition, current agreements will have to be reevaluated to determine which of the two indexes will replace the discontinued CPI for Urban Wage Earners and Clerical Workers. Contracts for which a decision has already been made have predominantly been changed to incorporate the CPI–W. □

————FOOTNOTES————

[1] They include multiplant or multifirm agreements covering 1,000 workers or more, even though individual units may be smaller. Although approximately 1 American worker in 5 is a union member, only about 1 in 9 is included in an agreement covering 1,000 workers or more in the private nonfarm sector.

[2] For an analysis of the 1978 data, see Douglas LeRoy, "Scheduled wage increases and escalator provisions in 1978," *Monthly Labor Review,* January 1978, pp. 3–8.

[3] For an analysis of the bargaining schedule for 1979, see Lena W. Bolton, "Heavy bargaining returns in 1979," *Monthly Labor Review,* December 1978, pp. 15-24.

[4] Information was not available for 50 agreements that expired between Nov. 1, 1978, and Dec. 31, 1978, covering 119,000 workers; 132 agreements that expired earlier in the year but for which negotiations were continuing or terms of the new agreement were not yet available, covering 521,000 workers; and 14 agreements with no specified expiration date, covering 51,000 workers.

[5] About 659,000 of these construction workers will receive deferred increases under settlements in which the parties agreed to a total wage and benefit package, with the ultimate allocation between wages and benefits to be determined by the union. Because the final division was not known at the time this article was prepared, the entire amount has been treated as a wage increase and may be expected to change as the data become available.

[6] Price changes for September 1977 through September 1978 were the latest data available at the time this article was prepared.

[7] At the end of 1977, about 1.1 million workers under smaller union contracts and 89,000 workers in nonunion manufacturing plants also were covered by escalators. The 5.6 million workers in major contracts include those under expired contracts containing such clauses, in which new agreements had not been negotiated at the time this article was prepared. This discussion excludes 53,000 workers whose contracts provide for possible reopeners based on increases in the Consumer Price Index.

[8] Guaranteed minimum cost-of-living increases are treated as scheduled wage increases and are included in tabulations for deferred increases in 1979. Some 366,000 workers have both minimum and maximum constraints.

Section **20**

Consumer Price Index

PRICE DATA

PRICE DATA are gathered by the Bureau of Labor Statistics from retail and primary markets in the United States. Price indexes are given in relation to a base period (1967 = 100, unless otherwise noted).

Definitions

The **Consumer Price Index** is a monthly statistical measure of the average change in prices in a fixed market basket of goods and services. Effective with the January 1978 index, the Bureau of Labor Statistics began publishing CPI's for two groups of the population. One index, a new CPI for All Urban Consumers, covers 80 percent of the total noninstitutional population; and the other index, a revised CPI for Urban Wage Earners and Clerical Workers, covers about half the new index population. The All Urban Consumers index includes, in addition to wage earners and clerical workers, professional, managerial, and technical workers, the self-employed, short-term workers, the unemployed, retirees, and others not in the labor force.

The CPI is based on prices of food, clothing, shelter, fuel, drugs, transportation fares, doctor's and dentist's fees, and other goods and services that people buy for day-to-day living. The quantity and quality of these items is kept essentially unchanged between major revisions so that only price changes will be measured. Prices are collected from over 18,000 tenants, 24,000 retail establishments, and 18,000 housing units for property taxes in 85 urban areas across the country. All taxes directly associated with the purchase and use of items are included in the index. Because the CPI's are based on the expenditures of two population groups in 1972-73, they may not accurately reflect the experience of individual families and single persons with different buying habits.

Though the CPI is often called the "Cost-of-Living Index," it measures only price change, which is just one of several important factors affecting living costs. Area indexes do not measure differences in the level of prices among cities. They only measure the average change in prices for each area since the base period.

Producer Price Indexes measure average changes in prices received in primary markets of the United States by producers of commodities in all stages of processing. The sample used for calculating these indexes contains about 2,800 commodities and about 10,000 quotations per month selected to represent the movement of prices of all commodities produced in the manufacturing, agriculture, forestry, fishing, mining, gas and electricity, and public utilities sectors. The universe includes all commodities produced or imported for sale in commercial transactions in primary markets in the United States.

Producer Price Indexes can be organized by stage of processing or by commodity. The stage of processing structure organizes products by degree of fabrication (that is, finished goods, intermediate or semifinished goods, and crude materials). The commodity structure organizes products by similarity of end-use or material composition.

To the extent possible, prices used in calculating Producer Price Indexes apply to the first significant commercial transaction in the United States, from the production or central marketing point. Price data are generally collected monthly, primarily by mail questionnaire.

Most prices are obtained directly from producing companies on a voluntary and confidential basis. Prices generally are reported for the Tuesday of the week containing the 13th day of the month.

In calculating Producer Price Indexes, price changes for the various commodities are averaged together with implicit quantity weights representing their importance in the total net selling value of all commodities as of 1972. The detailed data are aggregated to obtain indexes for stage of processing groupings, commodity groupings, durability of product groupings, and a number of special composite groupings.

Price indexes for the output of selected SIC industries measure average price changes in commodities produced by particular industries, as defined in the *Standard Industrial Classification Manual 1972* (Washington, U.S. Office of Management and Budget, 1972). These indexes are derived from several price series, combined to match the economic activity of the specified industry and weighted by the value of shipments in the industry. They use data from comprehensive industrial censuses conducted by the U.S. Bureau of the Census and the U.S. Department of Agriculture.

Notes on the data

Beginning with the May issue of the *Review*, regional CPI's cross classified by population size, were introduced. These indexes will enable users in local areas for which an index is not published to get a better approximation of the CPI for their area by using the appropriate population size class measure for their region. The cross-classified indexes will be published bimonthly. (See table 24.)

For further details about the new and the revised indexes and a comparison of various aspects of these indexes with the old unrevised CPI, see *Facts About the Revised Consumer Price Index,* a pamphlet in the Consumer Price Index Revision 1978 series. See also *The Consumer Price Index : Concepts and Content Over the Years.* Report 517, revised edition (Bureau of Labor Statistics, May 1978).

For interarea comparisons of living costs at three hypothetical standards of living, see the family budget data published in the *Handbook of Labor Statistics, 1977,* Bulletin 1966 (Bureau of Labor Statistics, 1977), tables 122-133. Additional data and analysis on price changes are provided in the *CPI Detailed Report* and *Producer Prices and Price Indexes,* both monthly publications of the Bureau.

As of January 1976, the Wholesale Price Index (as it was then called) incorporated a revised weighting structure reflecting 1972 values of shipments. From January 1967 through December 1975, 1963 values of shipments were used as weights.

For a discussion of the general method of computing consumer, producer, and industry price indexes, see *BLS Handbook of Methods for Surveys and Studies,* Bulletin 1910 (Bureau of Labor Statistics, 1976), chapters 13-15. See also John F. Early, "Improving the measurement of producer price change," *Monthly Labor Reveiw,* April 1978, pp. 7–15. For industry prices, see also Bennett R. Moss, "Industry and Sector Price Indexes," *Monthly Labor Review,* August 1965, pp. 974–82.

Consumer Price Index for Urban Wage Earners and Clerical Workers, annual averages and changes, 1967–77

[1967 = 100]

Year	All items		Food and beverages		Housing		Apparel and upkeep		Transportation		Medical care		Entertainment		Other goods and services	
	Index	Percent change	Index	Percent change	Index	Percent change	Index	Percent change	Index	Percent change	Index	Percent change	Index	Percent change	Index	Percent change
1967	100.0	-----	100.0	-----	100.0	-----	100.0	-----	100.0	-----	100.0	-----	100.0	-----	100.0	-----
1968	104.2	4.2	103.6	3.6	104.0	4.0	105.4	5.4	103.2	3.2	106.1	6.1	105.7	5.7	105.2	5.2
1969	109.8	5.4	108.8	5.0	110.4	6.2	111.5	5.8	107.2	3.9	113.4	6.9	111.0	5.0	110.4	4.9
1970	116.3	5.9	114.7	5.4	118.2	7.1	116.1	4.1	112.7	5.1	120.6	6.3	116.7	5.1	116.8	5.8
1971	121.3	4.3	118.3	3.1	123.4	4.4	119.8	3.2	118.6	5.2	128.4	6.5	122.9	5.3	122.4	4.8
1972	125.3	3.3	123.2	4.1	128.1	3.8	122.3	2.1	119.9	1.1	132.5	3.2	126.5	2.9	127.5	4.2
1973	133.1	6.2	139.5	13.2	133.7	4.4	126.8	3.7	123.8	3.3	137.7	3.9	130.0	2.8	132.5	3.9
1974	147.7	11.0	158.7	13.8	148.8	11.3	136.2	7.4	137.7	11.2	150.5	9.3	139.8	7.5	142.0	7.2
1975	161.2	9.1	172.1	8.4	164.5	10.6	142.3	4.5	150.6	9.4	168.6	12.0	152.2	8.9	153.9	8.4
1976	170.5	5.8	177.4	3.1	174.6	6.1	147.6	3.7	165.5	9.9	184.7	9.5	159.8	5.0	162.7	5.7
1977	181.5	6.5	188.0	6.0	186.5	6.8	154.2	4.5	177.2	7.1	202.4	9.6	167.7	4.9	172.2	5.8

Consumer Price Index for All Urban Consumers and revised CPI for Urban Wage Earners and Clerical Workers, U.S. city average—general summary and groups, subgroups, and selected items

[1967 = 100 unless otherwise specified]

General summary	All Urban Consumers							Urban Wage Earners and Clerical Workers (revised)						
	1977	1978						1977	1978					
	Nov.	June	July	Aug.	Sept.	Oct.	Nov.	Nov.	June	July	Aug.	Sept.	Oct.	Nov.
All items	185.4	195.3	196.7	197.8	199.3	200.9	202.0	185.4	195.3	196.7	197.7	199.1	200.7	201.8
Food and beverages	191.2	208.5	209.7	210.1	210.3	211.6	212.5	191.2	208.3	209.5	210.0	210.1	211.5	212.4
Housing	191.4	202.0	203.8	205.2	207.0	209.5	210.6	191.4	204.8	203.5	204.8	207.0	209.1	210.1
Apparel and upkeep	158.5	159.9	158.0	159.6	161.9	163.3	164.1	158.5	159.9	158.2	159.7	161.9	163.6	164.0
Transportation	178.7	185.5	187.2	188.1	188.7	189.7	191.4	178.7	185.9	187.7	188.7	189.2	190.3	191.9
Medical care	208.1	217.9	219.4	221.4	222.6	224.7	227.0	208.1	217.8	219.5	221.3	222.8	224.9	226.8
Entertainment	170.4	176.2	177.0	177.4	178.3	179.3	179.5	170.4	175.4	176.2	176.5	177.4	178.3	178.8
Other goods and services	177.2	181.0	183.1	184.0	187.8	188.3	188.8	177.2	181.4	183.7	184.3	187.1	187.6	188.2
Commodities	177.9	187.5	188.6	189.3	190.5	191.8	192.9	177.9	187.5	188.7	189.4	190.4	191.8	192.9
Commodities less food and beverages	169.1	175.4	176.5	177.3	178.9	180.2	181.4	169.1	175.4	176.6	177.4	178.7	180.0	181.2
Nondurables less food and beverages	172.2	175.6	176.1	177.3	179.1	180.1	181.1	172.2	175.6	176.2	177.5	179.2	180.2	181.2
Durables	165.5	173.9	175.3	175.9	177.2	178.8	180.0	165.5	174.0	175.5	175.9	177.0	178.5	179.8
Services	199.5	209.9	211.7	213.4	215.6	217.6	218.6	199.5	209.8	211.6	213.1	215.2	217.3	218.3
Rent, residential	157.0	163.6	164.2	165.1	166.4	167.4	168.5	157.0	163.5	164.2	165.1	166.3	167.4	168.4
Household services less rent	219.0	233.9	236.7	239.3	241.8	244.3	245.0	219.0	233.8	236.7	239.1	241.7	244.2	244.8
Transportation services	192.0	196.2	196.9	197.3	198.7	200.4	202.0	192.0	196.3	197.0	197.5	198.8	200.7	202.5
Medical care services	223.0	233.5	235.4	237.7	239.1	241.5	244.1	223.0	233.3	235.3	237.5	239.2	241.6	243.6
Other services	176.8	183.1	184.0	185.0	188.9	189.9	190.5	176.8	183.9	184.5	185.1	188.4	189.8	190.5
Special indexes:														
All items less food	182.5	190.6	192.0	193.3	195.1	196.7	197.8	182.5	190.5	191.9	193.1	194.8	196.4	197.5
All items less mortgage interest costs	183.0	192.3	193.4	194.2	195.5	196.9	197.9	183.0	192.3	193.4	194.2	195.4	196.7	197.7
Commodities less food	168.1	174.4	175.4	176.3	177.8	179.1	180.3	168.1	174.4	175.5	176.3	177.7	179.0	180.1
Nondurables less food	170.1	173.7	174.1	175.4	177.1	178.1	179.1	170.1	173.7	174.3	175.5	177.2	178.3	179.2
Nondurables less food and apparel	178.6	183.8	185.5	186.6	188.0	c188.8	190.0	178.6	183.7	185.4	186.5	188.0	188.9	190.1
Nondurables	182.4	192.7	193.6	194.4	195.4	196.6	197.5	182.4	192.7	193.7	194.6	195.5	196.7	197.6
Services less rent	207.2	218.3	220.4	222.2	224.6	226.7	227.8	207.2	218.2	220.2	221.9	224.2	226.4	227.4
Services less medical care	195.7	206.0	207.8	209.4	211.7	213.6	214.5	195.7	205.9	207.6	209.1	211.3	213.2	214.2
Domestically produced farm foods	180.9	203.6	204.5	204.3	203.9	205.1	205.9	180.9	203.4	204.5	204.2	203.7	204.9	205.8
Selected beef cuts	166.8	217.7	214.5	213.1	211.1	212.6	213.7	166.8	218.9	216.1	215.3	212.0	213.4	215.6
Energy	211.2	220.7	222.4	223.7	225.1	226.5	225.9	211.2	220.4	222.0	223.4	224.9	226.4	226.0
All items less energy	183.6	193.6	195.0	196.1	197.6	199.2	200.4	183.6	193.7	195.0	196.0	197.4	199.0	200.2
All items less food and energy	179.9	188.0	189.3	190.5	192.4	194.0	195.3	179.9	187.9	189.2	190.3	192.1	193.7	195.0
Commodities less food and energy	164.2	170.7	171.5	172.2	173.7	175.1	176.2	164.2	170.7	171.7	172.3	173.6	174.9	175.9
Energy commodities	205.9	210.8	213.2	215.4	217.1	218.0	220.0	205.9	210.7	213.1	215.5	217.3	218.3	220.5
Services less energy	198.0	207.8	209.7	211.6	213.9	215.8	217.4	198.0	207.6	209.5	211.3	213.5	215.5	217.1
Purchasing power of the consumer dollar, 1967 = $1	$0.539	$0.512	$0.508	$0.506	$0.502	$0.498	$0.495	$0.539	$0.512	$0.508	$0.506	$0.502	$0.498	0.496

[1967 = 100 unless otherwise specified]

General summary	All Urban Consumers							Urban Wage Earners and Clerical Workers (revised)						
	1977	1978						1977	1978					
	Nov.	June	July	Aug.	Sept.	Oct.	Nov.	Nov.	June	July	Aug.	Sept.	Oct.	Nov.
FOOD AND BEVERAGES	191.2	208.5	209.7	210.1	210.3	211.6	212.5	191.2	208.3	209.5	210.0	210.1	211.5	212.4
Food	195.6	213.8	215.0	215.4	215.6	216.8	217.8	195.6	213.5	214.8	215.4	215.4	216.7	217.7
Food at home	193.0	213.9	214.7	214.5	214.1	215.4	216.1	193.0	213.5	214.5	214.3	213.8	215.1	215.9
Cereals and bakery products	187.1	199.6	201.3	203.1	203.8	205.1	206.6	187.1	200.5	202.0	203.9	204.3	206.0	207.6
Cereal and cereal products¹	....	107.8	109.4	110.3	110.5	110.5	110.6	.....	108.5	109.9	110.8	110.7	110.6	110.6
Flour and prepared flour mixes¹	....	107.9	109.7	111.4	111.7	111.8	111.0	.....	109.0	110.2	111.8	112.1	112.1	111.8
Cereal¹	....	105.8	107.6	108.5	109.0	109.2	109.6	.....	106.2	108.0	109.0	109.4	109.5	109.6
Rice, pasta, and cornmeal¹	....	110.4	111.6	111.9	111.4	111.3	111.7	.....	110.9	112.0	112.3	111.2	110.7	110.9
Bakery products¹	....	104.9	105.6	106.5	106.9	107.9	108.9	.....	105.3	105.9	106.9	107.3	108.5	109.6
White bread	162.3	174.4	174.7	176.6	176.5	178.0	181.1	162.3	173.8	174.2	175.9	175.5	178.9	181.7
Other breads¹	....	104.7	105.9	106.6	107.3	108.5	109.7	.....	106.3	106.8	108.8	108.5	110.0	111.0
Fresh biscuits, rolls, and muffins¹	....	105.7	106.0	106.8	107.4	108.7	109.3	.....	106.1	106.8	107.1	107.7	108.6	109.8
Fresh cakes and cupcakes¹	....	104.3	105.1	104.7	106.2	107.4	107.9	.....	104.8	105.6	105.4	106.4	108.2	108.6
Cookies¹	....	103.7	104.2	105.2	105.9	106.8	107.8	.....	105.2	105.6	106.3	107.1	107.9	108.9
Crackers and bread and cracker products¹	....	104.1	105.0	107.0	107.4	107.5	107.2	.....	103.5	104.1	106.9	107.0	107.6	107.3
Frozen and refrigerated bakery products and fresh pies, tarts, and turnovers¹	....	104.7	106.7	108.3	108.8	109.9	109.7	.....	103.5	105.7	107.7	108.6	108.7	109.9
Meats, poultry, fish, and eggs	180.0	210.6	210.8	210.4	209.9	211.7	214.0	180.0	210.0	210.4	210.5	209.4	211.1	213.9
Meats, poultry, and fish	181.9	216.6	216.1	214.4	214.0	216.1	218.0	181.9	216.0	215.6	214.5	213.5	215.5	217.8
Meats	177.5	216.5	214.5	213.2	212.7	215.3	217.6	177.5	216.0	214.3	213.7	212.3	214.8	217.5
Beef and veal	166.0	216.0	213.0	211.6	209.7	211.3	212.5	166.0	217.2	214.6	213.7	210.6	212.0	214.4
Ground beef other than canned	156.8	213.7	210.9	211.0	209.1	210.5	212.2	156.8	214.2	212.4	212.4	209.7	211.3	213.9
Chuck roast	167.1	216.2	213.6	214.0	208.4	213.0	215.1	167.1	223.1	220.7	219.8	214.8	216.7	221.5
Round roast	158.6	201.3	194.8	193.6	190.8	192.0	193.0	158.6	202.0	194.1	193.4	189.9	192.8	194.7
Round steak	165.4	208.6	203.1	199.8	200.1	202.6	200.5	165.4	204.2	201.5	198.4	197.2	200.2	201.6
Sirloin steak	168.2	221.9	217.5	214.2	212.9	212.1	214.9	168.2	223.9	220.7	217.5	212.4	212.7	213.8
Other beef and veal¹	..	125.7	125.0	123.6	123.1	123.7	124.2	.....	126.2	125.5	125.1	123.5	123.9	124.9
Pork	193.8	215.8	214.4	212.4	213.7	218.7	222.6	193.8	214.9	213.5	212.0	213.2	217.9	221.5
Bacon	194.8	232.8	220.5	218.8	219.1	220.5	222.1	194.8	233.3	221.7	219.9	220.8	222.8	222.1
Pork chops	183.3	200.8	202.5	197.8	200.5	207.5	209.7	183.3	200.8	201.9	197.9	200.8	207.0	208.9
Ham other than canned¹	....	97.4	96.4	96.6	98.0	103.2	108.8	.....	97.9	96.1	97.4	98.0	103.9	108.3
Sausage	226.7	266.3	267.2	266.1	265.0	265.3	269.8	226.7	262.4	265.3	263.8	263.6	262.9	266.3
Canned ham	199.8	219.6	218.1	217.8	218.4	223.9	227.8	199.8	216.4	214.4	214.3	213.0	219.9	226.4
Other pork¹	....	116.8	118.9	117.3	117.9	120.2	120.7	.....	116.1	118.1	116.5	117.4	118.3	120.1
Other meats	180.0	214.4	214.3	215.2	215.7	216.7	219.4	180.0	211.5	211.9	213.8	213.1	214.6	216.6
Frankfurters	164.4	212.6	210.7	213.3	210.9	210.9	215.1	164.4	209.3	208.3	211.6	209.7	210.0	214.6
Bologna, liverwurst, and salami¹	....	118.4	118.5	119.6	119.5	120.6	122.2	.....	116.9	117.4	118.9	118.3	119.4	120.3
Other lunchmeats¹	....	110.3	111.7	111.7	113.0	113.2	113.9	.....	108.8	109.9	110.4	110.7	111.6	111.7
Lamb and organ meats¹	....	117.2	115.5	114.9	115.8	116.9	118.5	.....	116.4	115.6	115.8	115.2	116.5	117.7
Poultry	157.4	178.4	185.2	179.1	177.9	177.3	176.0	157.4	176.3	183.1	178.0	175.5	174.9	174.9
Fresh whole chicken	157.7	185.1	194.4	182.0	180.6	177.6	175.5	157.7	180.7	190.3	179.7	175.4	173.8	172.6
Fresh and frozen chicken parts¹	....	114.2	118.1	113.8	111.7	112.4	112.3	.....	114.4	118.1	114.8	112.0	111.7	112.3
Other poultry¹	....	107.8	110.7	113.1	116.6	117.2	116.3	.....	109.2	111.6	113.7	115.3	115.8	116.4
Fish and seafood	262.4	273.5	275.6	277.2	280.0	281.7	285.4	262.4	270.9	273.3	273.9	278.7	279.6	282.5
Canned fish and seafood¹	....	104.4	104.5	104.8	104.9	105.8	107.3	.....	103.9	104.2	105.0	105.7	106.6
Fresh and frozen fish and seafood¹	....	104.1	105.3	106.0	107.7	108.2	109.5	.....	102.8	104.1	104.4	106.9	107.0	108.2
Eggs	157.9	137.0	146.5	164.1	161.9	159.1	167.0	157.9	135.0	145.7	163.1	161.4	159.1	167.8
Dairy products		184.8	185.3	186.1	188.8	191.1	193.2	176.5	184.8	185.4	186.3	189.5	191.7	193.5
Fresh milk and cream¹	....	104.6	104.8	105.1	106.5	107.8	108.9	.....	104.4	104.5	105.1	106.6	107.9	108.8
Fresh whole milk	163.8	171.4	171.7	172.1	174.2	176.5	178.4	163.8	11.1	171.3	172.2	174.6	176.8	178.3
Other fresh milk and cream¹	....	104.2	104.5	105.1	106.6	107.6	108.5	.....	103.5	104.2	104.7	106.6	107.8	108.4
Processed dairy products¹	....	104.3	104.7	105.3	107.0	108.3	109.7	.....	104.5	105.2	105.7	107.8	109.0	110.2
Butter	166.9	175.8	176.5	180.7	187.0	189.3	190.7	166.9	176.1	177.1	181.5	187.9	189.9	191.1
Cheese¹	....	104.0	104.4	104.8	106.7	107.8	109.4	.....	103.2	104.1	104.5	106.9	108.1	109.6
Ice cream and related products¹	....	104.9	104.8	105.5	106.4	108.0	109.4	.....	106.0	107.3	107.3	108.4	109.9	110.7
Other dairy products¹	....	103.8	105.0	105.1	105.4	107.0	107.7	.....	104.5	105.2	104.7	106.0	107.1	108.0
Fruits and vegetables	188.7	223.5	225.6	221.4	216.2	216.3	210.4	188.7	223.0	225.4	219.9	214.6	214.0	208.2
Fresh fruits and vegetables	185.0	240.1	242.5	233.8	222.5	221.5	207.7	185.0	239.1	242.1	231.2	219.9	217.9	205.0
Fresh fruits	186.7	235.8	241.4	252.8	248.2	244.4	215.9	186.7	234.5	239.9	251.8	248.4	241.4	212.4
Apples	164.0	284.5	300.3	305.9	246.4	195.3	197.4	164.0	279.1	296.2	297.2	245.8	197.6	192.2
Bananas	167.8	178.0	179.5	178.5	168.2	181.4	175.4	167.8	178.9	180.2	181.6	168.0	181.5	176.3
Oranges	208.6	230.2	235.0	263.5	297.1	312.9	274.5	208.6	218.5	222.6	258.0	285.4	296.6	261.2
Other fresh fruits¹	....	120.2	121.5	126.8	130.0	132.4	109.1	.....	121.2	121.7	127.3	133.0	133.0	109.5
Fresh vegetables	183.9	244.2	243.5	216.1	198.5	200.1	200.1	183.9	243.3	244.2	212.7	194.3	196.8	198.4
Potatoes	179.6	240.6	283.9	262.9	221.1	198.5	191.3	179.6	239.4	289.2	260.4	216.4	196.2	191.8
Lettuce	179.2	292.9	209.9	185.9	180.2	202.6	223.2	179.2	287.0	211.1	187.0	174.2	195.6	221.0
Tomatoes	179.5	191.3	205.6	166.2	154.4	159.5	182.7	179.5	193.8	207.8	166.6	152.5	163.5	181.9
Other fresh vegetables¹	....	133.1	136.2	120.7	114.1	116.5	110.0	.....	133.3	135.0	118.3	112.0	114.1	108.4
Processed fruits and vegetables	194.2	207.0	208.8	209.7	211.2	212.5	215.3	194.2	206.9	208.6	209.1	210.5	211.5	213.6
Processed fruits¹	....	104.8	105.7	106.1	106.7	107.9	110.5	.....	105.1	106.2	106.3	107.2	108.1	110.4
Frozen fruit and fruit juices¹	....	106.6	107.0	107.2	107.1	108.0	110.5	.....	107.3	107.7	107.6	107.1	107.3	110.1
Fruit juices and other than frozen¹	....	105.0	105.7	105.7	106.5	107.0	108.5	.....	105.6	106.6	106.4	107.3	107.9	109.3
Canned and dried fruits¹	....	103.1	104.7	105.5	106.6	108.8	112.7	.....	102.8	104.5	105.2	107.1	108.8	111.9
Processed vegetables¹	....	103.1	104.0	104.5	105.3	105.5	105.7	.....	102.8	103.4	103.8	104.4	104.5	104.5
Frozen vegetables¹	....	103.2	103.6	104.0	105.0	105.4	106.0	.....	103.2	103.8	103.9	104.9	104.8	105.3

General summary	All Urban Consumers							Urban Wage Earners and Clerical Workers (revised)						
	1977	1978						1977	1978					
	Nov.	June	July	Aug.	Sept.	Oct.	Nov.	Nov.	June	July	Aug.	Sept.	Oct.	Nov.
FOOD AND BEVERAGES—Continued														
Food—Continued														
Food at home—Continued														
Fruits and vegetables—Continued														
Cut corn and canned beans except lima[1]	....	103.8	105.8	106.9	107.6	108.2	108.0	.....	103.8	105.5	106.4	106.9	107.1	106.7
Other canned and dried vegetables[1]	....	102.7	103.4	103.5	104.4	104.3	104.5	.....	102.0	102.2	102.4	102.9	103.1	103.1
Other foods at home	241.9	252.0	253.0	253.8	253.9	254.5	255.9	241.9	251.7	252.7	253.3	253.5	254.7	255.4
Sugar and sweets	236.3	259.0	260.4	262.0	261.8	262.3	263.8	236.3	259.3	261.0	261.6	261.9	262.2	263.4
Candy and chewing gum[1]	....	108.1	108.9	109.6	109.8	110.1	110.9	.....	108.3	109.2	109.5	110.0	110.4	111.1
Sugar and artificial sweeteners[1]	....	110.9	111.1	111.2	110.5	110.5	110.8	.....	111.7	112.0	111.9	110.9	110.5	110.8
Other sweets[1]	....	104.8	105.3	106.6	106.5	106.9	107.5	.....	103.7	104.6	105.1	105.7	105.9	106.4
Fats and oils[1]	....	210.9	213.5	214.5	215.4	216.3	216.9	.....	211.7	214.0	214.5	216.6	217.1	217.1
Margarine	214.3	230.1	231.8	230.9	231.9	231.6	232.1	214.3	230.8	230.9	230.0	232.6	232.2	232.1
Nondairy substitutes and peanut butter[1]	....	102.9	104.7	106.0	107.0	107.4	107.6	.....	103.0	105.0	106.0	107.4	107.6	107.2
Other fats, oils, and salad dressings[1]	....	108.7	110.1	110.9	111.1	111.9	112.3	.....	109.3	110.7	111.0	111.9	112.5	112.7
Nonalcoholic beverages	337.4	341.6	341.6	340.7	339.8	340.4	340.9	337.4	340.4	340.9	340.0	338.7	341.0	339.8
Cola drinks, excluding diet cola	208.2	216.8	219.4	220.4	221.4	223.4	224.0	208.2	216.9	218.3	219.7	220.0	223.1	222.9
Carbonated drinks, including diet cola[1]	....	106.9	107.6	108.2	108.9	109.1	109.8	.....	105.3	106.3	106.7	107.0	108.2	107.3
Roasted coffee	464.4	415.6	408.5	388.8	377.7	371.8	370.6	464.4	415.8	407.9	387.7	376.1	372.0	369.9
Freeze dried and instant coffee	384.2	359.9	356.6	354.2	349.6	346.7	345.0	384.2	360.1	356.3	353.4	348.6	346.4	344.7
Other noncarbonated drinks[1]	....	106.3	106.8	107.9	107.9	108.5	108.5	.....	105.9	106.4	107.4	107.5	108.3	108.0
Other prepared foods	179.9	189.0	190.2	192.0	192.6	193.2	195.6	179.9	189.1	190.0	191.8	192.6	193.3	195.6
Canned and packaged soup[1]	....	102.3	102.5	103.2	103.6	103.9	105.0	.....	102.6	102.7	103.4	103.7	103.4	104.9
Frozen prepared foods[1]	....	106.0	106.0	107.0	108.1	107.9	110.3	.....	105.5	106.0	106.5	108.0	107.5	110.3
Snacks[1]	....	102.3	102.9	104.0	103.7	104.1	105.2	.....	102.7	103.0	103.9	103.8	104.6	105.6
Seasonings, olives, pickles, and relish[1]	....	105.3	105.9	107.6	108.3	109.1	110.8	.....	105.2	105.6	107.2	107.7	108.9	110.7
Other condiments[1]	....	105.3	105.5	106.4	106.8	107.0	107.7	.....	106.0	106.0	107.1	107.3	107.8	107.7
Miscellaneous prepared foods[1]	....	105.2	107.5	107.7	107.8	108.3	109.3	.....	105.0	106.7	107.4	107.7	108.4	109.6
Other canned and packaged prepared foods[1]	....	105.2	105.8	107.3	107.7	108.0	109.3	.....	105.2	105.6	106.9	107.3	107.8	108.8
Food away from home	205.4	217.8	219.9	221.7	223.2	224.6	225.9	205.4	217.5	219.5	221.9	223.2	224.5	226.0
Lunch[1]	....	105.7	106.9	107.9	108.6	109.4	110.1	.....	105.2	106.5	108.0	108.5	109.1	110.0
Dinner[1]	....	105.6	106.4	107.4	108.1	108.8	109.4	.....	105.7	106.2	107.2	108.0	108.8	109.5
Other meals and snacks[1]	....	105.7	106.8	107.3	180.0	108.6	109.1	.....	105.0	106.9	107.8	108.4	108.8	109.2
Alcoholic beverages	153.2	159.5	160.1	161.0	162.0	163.1	163.9	153.2	159.7	160.5	161.3	162.6	163.8	164.3
Alcoholic beverages at home[1]	....	103.9	104.1	104.6	105.3	106.0	106.5	.....	104.2	104.6	105.2	106.1	107.0	107.2
Beer and ale	147.6	153.0	154.0	155.1	156.8	158.1	158.6	147.6	153.7	154.5	155.7	157.5	159.1	159.5
Whiskey	118.8	122.6	122.7	122.7	122.9	123.4	123.9	118.8	122.8	123.5	123.7	124.0	124.3	124.6
Wine	166.3	177.5	176.7	177.8	179.8	180.9	182.7	166.3	179.7	180.2	180.9	183.0	185.9	186.1
Other alcoholic beverages[1]	....	102.5	101.9	102.2	102.5	102.7	103.5	.....	102.0	101.5	101.8	102.1	102.3	102.7
Alcoholic beverages away from home[1]	....	105.1	106.2	107.1	107.4	108.2	108.8	.....	104.0	105.1	105.5	106.2	106.6	107.1
HOUSING	191.4	202.0	203.8	205.2	207.5	209.5	210.6	191.4	201.8	203.5	204.8	207.0	209.1	210.1
Shelter	196.9	208.9	211.3	213.3	216.2	218.6	220.1	196.9	208.7	211.2	213.0	216.0	218.5	220.0
Rent, residential	157.0	163.6	164.2	165.1	166.4	167.4	168.5	157.0	163.5	164.2	165.1	166.3	167.4	168.4
Other rental costs	192.3	207.1	209.6	212.7	212.0	213.8	215.1	192.3	207.1	209.3	212.3	211.9	213.5	214.9
Lodging while out of town	192.3	212.5	216.0	220.5	218.5	220.3	221.9	192.3	212.1	215.2	219.5	218.0	219.7	221.2
Tenants' insurance[1]	....	101.2	101.4	101.7	102.4	103.5	103.7	.....	101.3	101.5	101.9	102.4	103.5	103.8
Homeownership	211.5	225.3	228.3	230.6	234.2	237.0	238.8	211.5	225.1	228.3	230.4	234.1	237.1	238.7
Home purchase	184.8	195.3	197.4	197.9	201.2	203.4	204.8	184.8	195.2	197.3	197.7	201.1	203.4	204.6
Financing, taxes, and insurance	235.7	254.7	259.3	264.1	268.9	272.4	274.7	235.7	254.9	259.6	264.3	269.4	273.1	275.4
Property insurance[1]	....	105.4	105.8	105.9	106.2	106.4	106.6	.....	105.2	105.6	105.9	106.1	106.3	106.5
Property taxes	185.9	192.9	193.0	194.8	195.2	195.4	196.3	185.9	193.3	193.4	195.3	195.6	196.0	197.0
Contracted mortgage interest[1] cost	....	108.8	111.5	114.0	116.8	118.8	120.0	.....	108.7	111.4	113.8	116.7	118.8	119.9
Mortgage interest rates	140.2	144.9	147.0	149.9	151.0	152.1	152.8	140.2	144.9	147.0	149.9	151.0	152.2	152.8
Maintenance and repairs	220.4	231.9	234.4	236.1	237.5	240.7	242.3	220.4	230.3	233.3	234.3	235.4	238.6	240.1
Maintenance and repair services	236.6	250.8	254.0	255.3	256.9	260.2	261.9	236.6	248.5	253.2	253.8	254.5	258.0	259.4
Maintenance and repair commodities	183.1	187.8	188.5	191.2	192.2	195.0	196.7	183.1	189.0	188.7	190.4	192.4	194.8	196.3
Paint and wallpaper, supplies, tools, and equipment[1]	....	100.9	101.1	103.9	104.7	106.3	107.2	.....	102.1	101.5	103.1	104.9	106.1	106.6
Lumber, awnings, glass, and masonry[1]	....	104.3	105.4	105.5	106.5	107.4	108.5	.....	104.9	105.3	105.9	106.8	108.4	109.7
Plumbing, electrical, heating, and cooling supplies[1]	....	100.9	101.1	101.8	102.4	103.4	104.4	.....	100.9	100.9	102.5	103.5	104.0	105.0
Miscellaneous supplies and equipment[1]	....	102.7	102.7	103.1	102.9	104.9	106.0	.....	102.2	102.6	101.5	101.5	103.8	104.1
Fuel and other utilities	207.4	217.5	218.0	218.1	218.8	220.1	218.5	207.4	217.8	218.1	218.2	218.9	220.3	218.7
Fuels	234.8	250.2	250.7	250.4	251.5	254.0	250.6	234.8	250.4	250.6	250.3	251.3	253.9	250.8
Fuel oil, coal, and bottled gas	289.9	295.1	294.5	294.2	295.7	300.1	306.1	289.9	295.2	294.7	294.3	295.8	300.3	306.4
Fuel oil	286.6	293.3	293.0	293.0	295.1	c300.1	307.2	286.6	293.4	293.1	293.0	295.1	300.2	307.4
Other fuels[1]	....	98.6	98.0	97.4	96.7	97.1	97.3	.....	98.6	98.1	97.4	97.0	97.4	97.5
Gas (piped) and electricity	219.5	236.5	237.2	236.9	237.9	240.0	234.9	219.5	236.8	237.1	236.8	237.7	239.9	235.0
Electricity	191.1	209.6	210.7	209.7	209.4	207.7	201.9	191.1	210.3	210.9	209.8	209.6	208.1	202.2
Utility (piped) gas	250.0	261.5	261.4	262.8	266.3	276.2	273.3	250.0	261.0	260.8	262.4	265.5	275.0	272.8

[1967 = 100 unless otherwise specified]

General summary	All Urban Consumers							Urban Wage Earners and Clerical Workers (revised)						
	1977	1978						1977	1978					
	Nov.	June	July	Aug.	Sept.	Oct.	Nov.	Nov.	June	July	Aug.	Sept.	Oct.	Nov.
HOUSING—Continued														
Fuel and other utilities—Continued														
Other utilities and public services	155.4	159.7	158.4	159.1	159.2	158.9	159.7	155.4	157.9	158.5	159.1	159.3	159.0	159.6
Telephone services	132.0	132.7	132.9	133.2	133.3	133.0	133.0	132.0	132.7	132.9	133.3	133.4	133.0	133.1
Local charges¹	....	101.1	101.4	101.8	101.9	101.4	101.5	.....	101.2	101.4	101.9	102.0	101.5	101.6
Interstate toll calls¹	....	99.1	99.1	99.1	99.1	99.1	99.2	.....	99.1	99.1	99.1	99.1	99.2	99.2
Intrastate toll calls¹	....	100.2	100.1	100.3	100.4	100.3	100.3	.....	100.1	100.0	100.2	100.2	100.2	100.1
Water and sewerage maintenance	219.9	230.6	233.4	235.2	235.5	235.9	240.4	219.9	231.0	233.8	235.5	235.7	236.0	240.2
Household furnishings and operations	170.2	177.6	178.1	178.9	180.5	181.9	183.0	170.2	177.1	177.3	177.8	179.0	180.5	181.8
Housefurnishings	149.5	154.4	154.1	154.7	156.4	157.7	158.3	149.5	154.0	153.8	154.1	155.1	156.6	157.5
Textile housefurnishings	158.5	163.2	162.3	160.7	166.2	167.9	167.1	158.5	162.8	160.7	160.2	165.7	167.9	167.7
Household linens¹	....	100.5	98.3	98.0	102.6	103.5	102.9	.....	100.3	98.0	98.1	102.0	103.1	103.6
Curtains, drapes, slipcovers, and sewing materials¹	....	103.0	104.3	102.5	104.7	105.8	105.5	.....	102.8	102.8	109.1	104.8	106.4	105.7
Furniture and bedding	160.2	166.5	165.0	165.6	168.9	170.7	171.9	160.2	165.9	165.2	165.2	166.9	168.9	170.2
Bedroom furniture¹	....	104.7	104.6	104.8	105.4	107.9	108.6	.....	103.5	103.4	103.3	104.0	105.9	106.8
Sofas¹	....	102.8	101.3	101.6	104.2	104.0	104.3	.....	103.7	102.9	102.0	103.3	103.9	104.7
Living room chairs and tables¹	....	101.5	997	100.2	102.4	103.0	103.2	.....	100.8	99.9	100.1	101.1	102.8	102.8
Other furniture¹	....	104.4	103.6	104.4	107.1	108.2	109.7	.....	104.3	104.1	104.7	106.2	106.7	108.2
Appliances including TV and sound equipment	127.1	130.5	130.5	131.5	131.7	132.6	133.1	127.1	130.2	130.2	130.9	131.1	132.1	132.5
Television and sound equipment¹	....	101.4	101.5	102.0	102.6	102.8	103.3	.....	101.2	101.3	101.2	101.6	101.7	102.2
Television	101.5	101.2	101.3	101.5	101.9	102.1	102.4	101.5	100.7	100.7	100.3	100.7	101.2	101.4
Sound equipment¹	....	102.6	102.7	103.6	104.2	104.6	105.1	.....	102.6	102.8	103.0	103.3	103.2	103.8
Household appliances	142.1	147.7	147.7	149.1	148.8	150.4	150.8	142.1	147.4	147.3	148.8	148.7	150.7	151.0
Refrigerators and home freezer	142.2	146.9	147.4	147.7	147.9	150.1	149.5	142.2	148.8	149.1	150.0	151.1	153.3	152.9
Laundry equipment¹	....	103.4	103.5	104.3	104.4	105.5	105.7	.....	103.0	103.6	104.2	104.1	105.2	105.7
Other household appliances¹	....	104.0	103.8	105.2	104.6	105.7	106.3	.....	103.0	102.6	104.1	103.6	105.1	105.3
Stoves, dishwashers, vacuums, and sewing machines¹	....	105.2	104.4	106.2	106.1	107.3	108.1	.....	104.0	102.7	104.7	104.3	105.9	106.3
Office machines, small electric appliances, and air conditioners¹	....	102.5	103.1	104.1	102.9	103.8	104.3	.....	102.0	102.4	103.3	102.8	ᶜ104.1	104.0
Other household equipment¹	....	103.1	103.6	104.2	104.5	105.2	105.8	.....	102.8	103.6	103.6	103.3	103.9	105.3
Floor and window coverings, infants' laundry cleaning and outdoor equipment¹	....	101.7	103.0	103.4	103.5	104.9	105.2	.....	97.9	99.9	98.0	97.9	100.3	100.9
Clocks, lamps, and decor items¹	....	101.9	102.6	103.3	102.8	102.9	102.7	.....	102.0	103.3	104.0	103.6	103.5	104.0
Tableware, serving pieces, and nonelectric kitchenware¹	....	105.5	106.1	106.4	107.6	107.7	108.6	.....	105.9	105.9	106.2	106.1	105.3	107.5
Lawn equipment, power tools, and other hardware¹	....	101.5	101.2	102.3	102.3	103.7	104.6	.....	102.2	102.9	103.7	103.0	104.5	105.9
Housekeeping supplies	197.0	205.9	207.3	207.9	208.9	210.0	212.0	197.0	205.8	206.4	206.6	208.0	209.3	211.0
Soaps and detergents	188.6	197.7	198.6	200.4	200.1	202.0	206.9	188.6	196.9	197.5	198.6	199.0	201.2	204.8
Other laundry and cleaning products¹	....	102.8	103.6	104.7	105.6	106.6	107.3	.....	102.4	103.0	104.2	105.0	105.9	107.1
Cleansing and toilet tissue, paper towels and napkins¹	....	106.7	107.6	108.1	108.2	108.5	109.5	.....	106.7	107.6	108.2	109.0	109.7	110.1
Stationery, stationery supplies, and gift wrap¹	....	102.3	103.0	103.1	102.9	103.2	103.7	.....	103.3	103.3	103.3	103.3	103.2	103.7
Miscellaneous household products¹	....	104.1	104.9	105.4	106.5	107.3	107.5	.....	104.2	104.3	103.7	105.1	105.8	106.0
Lawn and garden supplies¹	....	102.8	103.5	102.9	102.0	102.7	103.6	.....	102.2	102.0	100.0	100.8	101.1	101.7
Housekeeping services	212.0	226.3	228.3	230.2	231.6	233.7	235.7	212.0	226.5	228.1	229.7	231.4	233.2	235.3
Postage	225.6	257.3	257.3	257.3	257.3	257.3	257.3	225.6	257.2	257.2	257.2	257.2	257.2	257.2
Moving, storage, freight, household laundry, and drycleaning services¹	....	104.2	105.5	106.4	106.6	107.6	108.3	.....	105.0	105.9	106.4	107.0	107.8	109.0
Appliance and furniture repair¹	....	103.0	103.2	103.5	103.6	104.2	105.2	.....	102.4	102.4	103.0	103.3	103.9	104.7
APPAREL AND UPKEEP	158.5	159.9	158.0	159.6	161.9	163.3	164.1	158.5	159.9	158.2	159.7	161.9	163.6	164.0
Apparel commodities	155.9	156.1	153.9	155.5	157.9	159.3	160.0	155.9	156.2	154.2	155.8	158.1	159.6	160.0
Apparel commodities less footwear	155.1	154.7	152.5	154.1	156.5	157.7	158.4	155.1	155.0	152.8	154.5	156.8	158.2	158.4
Men's and boys'	158.0	157.8	156.3	156.7	158.7	159.1	160.1	158.0	157.7	156.9	157.0	159.3	159.8	160.5
Men's¹	....	100.2	99.2	99.5	100.8	100.9	101.5	.....	100.4	99.9	100.0	101.4	101.7	102.1
Suits, sport coats, and jackets¹	....	100.3	97.9	98.2	100.4	100.3	100.1	.....	100.2	96.9	96.8	99.7	99.8	99.0
Coats and jackets¹	....	98.7	97.9	98.3	99.9	99.7	99.6	.....	99.6	100.1	100.9	101.8	101.8	101.3
Furnishings and special clothing¹	....	101.7	101.5	101.5	102.2	103.4	104.1	.....	101.3	100.8	101.2	102.2	103.1	103.9
Shirts¹	....	101.1	100.7	100.7	101.1	100.9	103.1	.....	102.2	102.7	101.7	102.3	102.6	104.6
Dungarees, jeans, and trousers¹	....	99.2	98.6	99.1	100.2	100.6	100.8	.....	99.2	99.6	100.3	101.4	101.7	102.0
Boys'¹	....	99.0	98.3	98.4	99.7	100.4	101.3	.....	98.4	97.9	97.8	99.4	99.9	100.5
Coats, jackets, sweaters, and shirts¹	....	95.7	94.5	94.6	96.7	96.3	96.9	.....	94.8	93.4	93.9	96.0	95.6	96.0
Furnishings¹	....	101.7	101.6	101.2	101.7	104.1	106.0	.....	101.1	101.2	100.6	101.2	103.1	104.7
Suits, trousers, sport coats, and jackets¹	....	100.4	100.0	100.2	101.3	102.1	102.8	.....	100.1	100.1	99.7	101.3	101.9	102.3
Women's and girls'	151.4	150.0	146.4	149.1	152.3	154.0	154.1	151.4	150.1	146.3	149.2	152.1	154.0	153.8
Women's¹	....	100.1	97.4	99.1	101.4	102.6	102.8	.....	100.7	97.9	99.6	101.5	102.7	102.6
Coats and jackets	168.4	171.3	164.9	168.9	172.0	172.5	169.7	168.4	175.7	165.5	170.4	173.1	172.8	172.0
Dresses	158.1	157.6	153.0	157.1	159.7	165.2	167.7	158.1	157.8	155.2	157.4	160.6	165.9	166.8
Separates and sportswear¹	....	99.2	95.5	97.7	100.6	101.2	101.3	.....	97.9	95.9	97.4	99.9	100.2	99.9
Underwear, nightwear, and hosiery¹	....	101.0	101.8	102.5	102.5	102.6	102.7	.....	101.5	102.1	102.8	102.8	103.1	103.4
Suits¹	....	96.2	90.3	94.1	97.3	99.4	98.5	.....	98.8	88.3	91.7	96.0	99.7	98.0

[1967 = 100 unless otherwise specified]

General summary	All Urban Consumers							Urban Wage Earners and Clerical Workers (revised)					
	1977	1978						1977	1978				
	Nov.	June	July	Aug.	Sept.	Oct.	Nov.	Nov.	June	July	Aug.	Sept.	Oct.	Nov.
APPAREL AND UPKEEP—Continued													
Apparel commodities—Continued													
Apparel commodities less footwear—Continued													
Girls'¹	....	98.3	97.1	99.3	101.1	101.5	101.2	.....	96.0	94.7	97.5	99.9	101.2	100.9
Coats, jackets, dresses, and suits¹		98.1	98.4	102.2	101.7	101.2	99.7		95.4	93.9	97.1	98.4	99.2	98.8
Separates and sportswear¹		97.8	94.9	96.5	100.8	101.6	101.9		94.4	92.4	96.8	101.0	103.0	102.5
Underwear, nightwear, hosiery, and accessories¹		99.4	98.9	99.7	101.0	102.0	102.4		99.5	100.0	99.2	100.5	101.5	101.8
Infants' and toddlers'	216.4	216.5	216.4	219.3	220.4	220.0	220.9	216.4	216.1	215.3	217.7	217.8	219.3	219.1
Other apparel commodities	154.5	157.6	157.8	159.0	159.6	161.9	163.4	154.5	160.0	159.8	161.2	162.1	164.1	164.7
Sewing materials and notions¹		98.1	98.0	99.2	98.0	99.4	98.7		97.9	97.3	98.6	97.7	99.0	98.3
Jewelry and luggage¹		103.6	103.7	104.4	105.4	107.0	108.6		106.0	106.1	106.8	108.1	109.4	110.3
Footwear	159.9	163.8	162.1	163.5	165.7	167.8	169.1	159.9	162.6	161.9	163.0	164.7	167.0	168.4
Men's¹		102.2	101.7	103.3	104.2	105.9	106.7		102.7	102.4	104.2	105.0	105.6	106.2
Boys' and girls'¹		102.5	101.7	102.4	102.7	103.8	104.7		102.5	102.7	102.4	102.2	104.6	106.1
Womens'¹		103.0	101.4	101.8	104.2	105.4	106.2		100.7	99.6	100.2	102.3	103.9	104.5
Apparel services	174.2	184.9	185.6	186.9	188.3	190.1	191.3	174.2	184.2	184.9	185.8	187.1	190.2	191.1
Laundry and drycleaning other than coin operated¹		106.1	106.6	107.0	107.9	109.2	109.8		106.1	106.4	106.9	107.9	109.8	110.4
Other apparel services¹		104.1	104.3	105.6	106.3	106.9	107.6		103.2	103.7	104.3	104.7	106.2	106.5
TRANSPORTATION	178.7	185.5	187.2	188.1	188.7	189.7	191.4	178.7	185.9	187.7	188.7	189.2	190.3	191.9
Private	178.0	185.0	186.8	187.7	188.3	189.4	191.1	178.0	185.4	187.2	188.2	188.8	189.8	191.5
New cars	148.2	153.5	153.9	153.8	153.5	155.5	158.5	148.2	153.2	153.6	153.6	153.1	155.1	158.1
Used cars	175.0	191.5	195.9	196.7	195.9	195.4	194.7	175.0	191.5	195.8	196.7	195.9	195.4	194.7
Gasoline	189.8	194.4	197.2	199.8	201.5	201.9	203.5	189.8	194.3	196.9	199.6	201.4	202.0	203.7
Automobile maintenance and repair	208.6	219.5	220.9	222.5	224.4	226.4	228.2	208.6	220.0	221.3	222.9	224.8	226.8	228.4
Body work¹		104.5	105.5	106.2	107.1	107.8	108.6		105.2	106.3	106.8	107.4	108.3	109.2
Automobile drive train, brake, and miscellaneous mechanical repair¹		105.3	106.1	106.7	107.4	108.4	109.4		106.1	106.9	107.6	108.3	109.1	110.1
Maintenance and servicing¹		104.0	104.5	105.0	105.7	106.5	108.4		103.8	104.2	105.0	106.1	107.1	107.7
Power plant repair¹		103.8	104.5	105.3	106.2	107.1	107.8		104.1	104.6	105.5	106.3	107.3	108.2
Other private transportation	180.8	183.4	183.9	184.3	185.3	186.9	189.0	180.8	183.6	184.2	184.6	185.7	187.2	189.5
Other private transportation commodities	154.4	158.8	159.8	161.2	160.8	161.2	162.9	154.4	160.1	161.3	162.6	163.3	162.9	165.8
Motor oil, coolant, and other products¹		102.3	102.5	103.3	103.6	104.2	104.5		101.4	102.2	103.1	103.6	104.8	104.9
Automobile parts and equipment¹		102.7	103.4	104.3	104.0	104.2	105.4		103.8	104.6	105.4	105.8	105.4	107.5
Tires	138.6	141.9	142.7	144.0	143.2	143.0	144.9	138.6	143.4	144.7	146.0	146.2	144.7	148.4
Other parts and equipment¹		102.7	103.7	104.5	104.9	105.8	106.8		103.8	104.3	104.9	105.8	107.0	107.7
Other private transportation services	189.6	191.7	192.1	192.2	193.7	195.5	197.7	189.6	191.6	192.1	192.3	193.5	195.4	197.7
Automobile insurance	214.6	214.4	214.9	214.9	217.0	218.7	220.6	214.6	214.6	215.1	215.1	217.2	218.8	220.5
Automobile finance charges¹		102.9	103.3	103.2	104.0	105.0	107.6		102.3	102.7	102.8	102.6	104.6	107.0
Automobile rental, registration, and other fees¹		101.5	101.5	101.8	103.0	103.5	103.8		101.7	101.8	102.0	102.9	103.5	104.1
State registration	142.2	143.0	143.0	143.0	143.7	143.8	143.8	142.2	142.9	143.0	143.0	143.5	143.5	143.6
Drivers' license¹		103.5	103.7	103.7	104.0	104.1	104.5		103.3	103.5	103.5	103.8	103.9	104.3
Vehicle inspection¹		110.3	109.8	109.9	109.3	109.5	110.2		111.7	111.3	110.2	110.6	110.8	111.4
Other vehicle related fees¹		101.7	101.9	102.7	104.9	106.1	106.8		102.4	102.8	103.5	105.3	106.9	108.5
Public	184.7	187.2	187.7	187.6	188.2	189.3	189.7	184.7	187.1	187.9	187.9	188.5	190.2	190.4
Airline fare	184.3	191.1	190.0	189.6	189.6	189.5	190.0	184.3	190.6	189.6	189.2	189.1	189.1	189.6
Intercity bus fare	232.2	240.8	241.4	241.8	242.6	243.7	244.0	232.2	240.8	241.4	241.6	242.7	244.1	244.2
Intracity mass transit	179.5	180.0	181.7	181.6	182.9	185.4	185.6	179.5	180.1	181.6	181.5	182.6	185.3	185.4
Taxi fare	195.3	201.4	204.1	205.0	205.3	206.7	207.8	195.3	203.4	206.7	207.9	208.1	210.9	211.9
Intercity train fare	186.4	195.1	198.9	202.7	201.8	195.1	193.1	186.4	195.1	198.9	202.0	201.1	194.9	193.0
MEDICAL CARE	208.1	217.9	219.4	221.4	222.6	224.7	227.0	208.1	217.8	219.5	221.3	222.8	224.9	226.8
Medical care commodities	137.3	143.4	144.0	144.5	145.1	145.9	147.9	137.3	143.8	144.5	145.0	145.5	146.6	147.6
Prescription drugs	125.3	131.3	131.9	132.5	132.9	134.0	134.9	125.3	131.6	132.5	133.1	133.6	134.7	135.7
Anti-infective drugs¹		104.2	104.0	104.6	104.6	105.4	106.4		104.3	104.8	105.2	105.6	106.4	107.4
Tranquillizers and sedatives¹		104.5	105.0	105.1	105.4	106.5	109.0		104.7	105.3	105.6	105.4	106.6	108.7
Circulatories and diuretics¹		102.4	103.1	103.6	104.0	104.6	104.5		102.9	103.6	104.1	104.5	105.6	105.4
Hormones, diabetic drugs, biologicals, and prescription medical supplies¹		107.7	108.1	109.2	109.9	110.8	111.2		108.1	108.7	109.8	110.7	111.7	111.7
Pain and symptom control drugs¹		104.2	104.6	104.8	105.6	106.3	106.4		104.0	104.9	105.1	105.5	106.5	107.2
Supplements, cough and cold preparations, and respiratory agents¹		103.1	104.1	104.3	104.6	105.3	105.7		103.6	104.4	104.9	105.1	105.8	106.4
Nonprescription drugs and medical supplies¹		103.6	104.0	104.3	104.8	105.2	106.0		104.0	104.4	104.7	105.0	105.7	106.4
Eyeglasses¹		102.1	102.4	102.6	103.3	103.5	103.8		102.4	102.6	102.5	103.2	103.5	104.1
Internal and respiratory over-the-counter drugs	151.6	159.1	159.6	160.5	161.1	161.9	162.9	151.6	159.5	159.8	160.6	161.2	162.4	163.4
Nonprescription medical equipment and supplies¹		103.3	103.7	103.7	104.1	104.5	106.0		104.2	105.0	105.1	104.9	105.7	106.5
Medical care services	223.0	233.5	235.4	237.7	239.1	241.5	244.1	223.0	233.3	235.3	237.5	239.2	241.6	243.6
Professional services	199.3	207.7	208.7	210.5	211.7	213.7	215.5	199.3	208.0	209.2	210.7	212.5	214.3	215.7
Physicians' services	211.9	221.8	223.2	225.0	226.7	228.1	230.0	211.9	222.3	223.7	225.3	227.1	228.4	230.1
Dental services	190.4	197.2	197.8	199.8	200.6	202.9	203.9	190.4	197.7	198.6	200.3	202.2	204.5	205.7
Other professional services¹		103.4	103.8	104.4	105.0	106.4	108.7		102.5	103.1	103.9	104.8	105.8	106.2
Other medical care services	251.8	264.8	267.6	270.6	272.2	275.2	278.7	251.8	264.0	267.0	270.1	271.6	274.8	277.8
Hospital and other medical services¹		104.9	106.2	107.6	108.1	109.4	110.9		104.5	105.9	107.4	107.9	109.3	110.6
Hospital room	307.9	327.5	332.1	337.1	338.3	343.7	349.4	307.9	326.1	330.9	336.5	337.6	343.7	348.2
Other hospital and medical care services		104.8	106.0	107.2	107.9	108.7	109.9		104.5	105.8	106.9	107.6	108.5	109.7

Continued—Consumer Price Index—U.S. city average

[1967 = 100 unless otherwise specified]

General summary	All Urban Consumers							Urban Wage Earners and Clerical Workers (revised)						
	1977	1978						1977	1978					
	May	June	July	Aug.	Sept.	Oct.	Nov.	Nov.	June	July	Aug.	Sept.	Oct.	Nov.
ENTERTAINMENT	170.4	176.2	177.0	177.4	178.3	179.3	179.5	170.4	175.4	176.2	176.5	177.4	178.3	178.8
Entertainment commodities	171.8	177.7	178.3	178.4	178.9	179.7	180.0	171.8	175.9	176.8	177.1	177.7	178.4	178.7
Reading materials¹	....	102.2	102.7	103.7	104.4	104.3	104.3	.....	102.0	102.5	103.4	104.1	104.0	104.1
Newspapers	196.1	199.9	200.4	201.3	202.2	202.1	203.3	196.1	199.5	199.9	200.8	201.8	201.7	202.9
Magazines, periodicals, and books¹	....	102.8	103.6	105.2	106.1	106.0	105.3	.....	102.8	103.6	105.3	106.2	106.0	105.3
Sporting goods and equipment¹	....	103.2	103.3	102.8	102.6	103.4	103.6	.....	99.9	100.4	100.2	100.3	101.1	101.4
Sport vehicles¹	....	103.7	103.8	102.7	102.1	103.1	103.2	.....	99.2	99.9	99.3	99.4	100.3	100.7
Indoor and warm weather sport equipment¹	....	102.0	102.3	102.8	103.0	103.3	104.0	.....	100.2	100.3	100.2	100.3	101.5	101.6
Bicycles	147.6	151.4	151.3	152.8	153.7	154.1	154.1	147.6	150.7	150.8	152.4	152.2	152.7	152.4
Other sporting goods and equipment¹	....	101.9	101.8	101.7	101.9	102.7	103.0	.....	100.3	100.2	100.1	100.7	101.3	101.7
Toys, hobbies, and other entertainment¹	....	102.9	103.2	103.1	103.4	104.1	104.2	.....	102.6	103.3	103.3	103.6	104.1	104.2
Toys, hobbies, and music equipment¹	....	103.6	103.8	103.3	103.6	104.6	104.8	.....	103.1	103.6	102.6	102.7	103.2	103.7
Photographic supplies and equipment¹	....	103.3	103.7	104.0	103.7	103.9	103.9	.....	102.9	103.2	103.6	104.3	104.4	104.0
Pet supplies and expense¹	....	101.2	101.8	102.1	102.9	103.4	103.4	.....	101.8	102.8	104.2	105.0	105.4	105.3
Entertainment services	168.7	174.3	175.5	176.3	177.9	179.1	179.3	168.7	175.6	176.1	176.5	177.7	178.9	179.7
Fees for participant sports¹	....	102.7	103.4	103.8	105.0	106.0	106.1	.....	103.9	103.8	104.1	105.3	106.4	106.9
Admissions¹	....	105.3	106.1	106.4	107.1	107.5	107.4	.....	105.8	106.9	107.1	107.4	107.9	108.3
Other entertainment services¹	....	102.3	103.0	104.1	104.9	105.4	105.8	.....	101.9	101.9	101.9	102.6	102.9	103.4
OTHER GOODS AND SERVICES	177.2	181.0	183.1	184.0	187.8	188.3	188.8	177.2	181.4	183.7	184.3	187.1	187.6	188.2
Tobacco products	172.8	174.9	179.9	180.6	180.8	181.0	180.9	172.8	174.9	180.3	180.5	180.8	180.8	180.7
Cigarettes	175.5	177.1	182.5	183.2	183.5	183.5	183.5	175.5	177.2	183.0	183.3	183.6	183.5	183.3
Other tobacco products and smoking accessories¹	....	103.8	104.7	104.9	105.3	106.4	105.8	.....	103.6	104.5	104.6	104.9	105.3	105.8
Personal care	175.5	181.1	182.4	183.1	184.9	185.6	186.8	175.5	181.7	182.7	183.1	184.2	185.0	186.3
Toilet goods and personal care appliances	171.4	175.2	176.5	177.7	179.5	180.1	181.1	171.4	175.8	176.9	177.7	178.2	179.0	180.6
Products for the hair, hairpieces, and wigs¹	....	103.1	101.9	103.1	104.4	103.9	105.0	.....	100.7	101.7	101.8	102.0	102.0	103.8
Dental and shaving products¹	....	103.2	102.4	104.0	105.8	106.2	106.5	.....	104.5	104.1	104.1	105.0	105.9	106.2
Cosmetics, bath and nail preparations, manicure and eye makeup implements¹	....	100.5	102.4	102.8	104.0	104.7	104.8	.....	100.8	101.7	102.8	103.3	103.7	104.2
Other toilet goods and small personal care appliances¹	....	102.6	103.2	102.9	102.8	103.7	104.6	.....	103.6	104.1	104.5	104.4	104.9	106.0
Personal care services	179.7	186.8	188.2	188.5	190.3	191.0	192.5	179.7	187.6	188.6	188.7	190.2	191.1	192.2
Beauty parlor services for women	181.3	188.6	189.8	190.1	191.9	192.5	194.0	181.3	190.3	191.0	191.1	192.2	193.2	194.6
Haircuts and other barber shop services for men¹	....	103.9	104.9	105.1	106.1	106.6	107.4	.....	103.5	104.3	104.3	105.5	106.0	106.2
Personal and educational expenses	190.6	194.1	194.4	195.7	205.7	206.3	206.5	190.6	194.3	194.6	196.0	205.9	206.5	206.6
School books and supplies	177.8	180.7	180.7	181.1	187.3	187.8	187.8	177.8	181.2	181.2	181.7	189.1	189.7	189.7
Personal and educational services	194.1	197.7	198.1	199.6	210.4	211.0	211.1	194.1	197.9	198.3	199.9	210.3	210.9	211.1
Tuition and other school fees¹	....	100.8	100.9	101.5	108.2	108.4	108.4	.....	100.8	100.8	101.5	108.1	108.3	108.3
College tuition¹	....	100.9	101.0	101.6	108.3	108.6	108.6	.....	100.9	101.0	101.6	108.3	108.6	108.6
Elementary and high school tuition¹	....	100.6	100.6	101.2	107.4	107.5	107.5	.....	100.4	100.4	101.0	107.3	107.4	107.4
Personal expenses¹	....	103.8	104.5	105.9	106.7	107.4	107.8	.....	104.0	104.8	105.9	106.8	107.5	108.0
Special indexes:														
Gasoline, motor oil, coolant and other products	188.4	193.0	195.7	198.3	200.0	200.4	201.9	188.4	192.9	195.5	198.1	199.9	200.5	202.1
Insurance and finance	218.4	231.8	235.0	238.2	241.9	244.9	247.1	218.4	231.3	234.5	237.6	241.2	244.3	246.5
Utilities and public transportation	191.7	200.7	201.3	201.4	202.0	203.0	201.1	191.7	201.0	201.5	201.6	202.2	203.3	201.4
Housekeeping and home maintenance services	230.7	245.3	248.0	249.6	251.2	254.0	255.9	230.7	244.0	247.5	248.5	249.6	252.5	254.3

¹ December 1977 = 100.
c = Corrected.

Index

INDEX

Absenteeism, turnover rates and, chart, 11-61
Accidents, 10-59 to 10-60
  covered under workmen's compensation, 7-29 to 7-31
Actors and Artistes of America, Associated, listings for, 2-21 to 2-22
Actors' Equity Association:
  listings for, 2-21
  publication of, 17-5
  (*See also* Actors and Artistes of America, Associated)
Administration and Management, Office of, 5-7 to 5-8
Administrative Law Judges, 5-6 to 5-7
Adolph Coors Co., settlement with Brewery Workers, 1-76
Aeronautical Examiners, National Association of, listings for, 2-22
Aeronautical Production Controllers, National Association of, listings for, 2-22
AFL-CIO:
  Building and Construction Trades Department, settlement with NCA, 1-64 to 1-65
  Department of Organization and Field Services of, 2-3, 2-5
    listings for, 2-11
  directly affiliated local unions and, 2-5
  executive council of, 1-54, 2-3
    listings for, 2-10
  executive officers of, 2-3
  general board of, 2-3
  Internal Disputes Plan of, 2-6 to 2-7
    sanctions imposed by, 2-7
  jurisdictional problems of, 2-5
  membership of, table, 2-7 to 2-9
  position on Africa, 3-14 to 3-15, 3-19 to 3-20
  position on Asia, 3-13 to 3-14, 3-19
  position on Carter's economic program, 1-22, 1-59 to 1-60
  position on defense and disarmament, 3-12, 3-18
  position on Eastern Europe, 3-13, 3-18
  position on economic trade and aid, 3-19
  position on House legislation, 3-9 to 3-11
  position on ILO, 3-17
  position on Latin America, 3-15 to 3-17, 3-20
  position on Middle East, 3-18
  position on Senate legislation, 3-6 to 3-9
  position on Western Europe and NATO, 3-12 to 3-13, 3-18

AFL-CIO (*Cont.*):
  priorities of, 1-34 to 1-35
  professional employees organized by, 1-47
  publications of, 17-4 to 17-5
    national and international, 17-5 to 17-11
    state and local, 17-11 to 17-29
  reactivation of Food and Beverage Trades Department by, 1-6
  RLEA and, 2-6
  safety department established by, 1-69 to 1-70
  shoe tariffs and, 1-18
  standing committees and staff of, 2-3
    listings for, 2-10 to 2-11
  state and central bodies of, 2-5
  state labor organizations of, 2-49 to 2-53
  structural organization of, chart, 2-4
  trade and industrial departments of, 2-5
    listings for, 2-11 to 2-16
  UAW rejects reaffiliation with, 1-37
Africa, AFL-CIO position on, 3-14 to 3-15, 3-19 to 3-20
African-American Labor Center (AALC), 3-19 to 3-20
AFSCME (*see* State, County and Municipal Employees, American Federation of)
Age:
  labor force composition and, 10-33 to 10-34
  of retirement, 1-55, 1-58
  unemployment and, 12-8 to 12-9
Age Discrimination in Employment Act of 1967, 4-85
  enforcement of, 4-85 to 4-86
  exceptions under, 4-85
  exemptions under, 4-85
  records and posting of notices under, 4-87
Agency shop, sample contract clause and, 13-4
Aging, Administration on (AOA), 5-32
Agreements:
  disputes arising out of, under Railway Labor Act, 4-5 to 4-6
  under Executive Order 11491, 4-47 to 4-48
  hot cargo, under National Labor Relations Act, 4-21 to 4-22, 4-29
  making and revising, under Railway Labor Act, 4-5
Air Line Dispatchers Association, listings for, 2-22
Air Line Employees Association, listings for, 2-22

Air Line Pilots Association, 2-7
  listings for, 2-22
  publication of, 17-5
  settlement with Eastern Airlines, 1-19
  settlement with Northwest Airlines, 1-69
Air Traffic Specialists, Inc., National Association of, listings for, 2-22
Airmen, Union of Professional:
  listings for, 2-22
  (*See also* Air Line Employees Association, listings for)
Alabama State Employees Association, listings for, 2-22
Alaska Public Employees Association, listings for, 2-22 to 2-23
Aliens:
  employment certification of, 6-21 to 6-22
  as public employees, 9-63
Allied Workers International Union, United, listings for, 2-23
Aluminum Company of America, settlement with Steelworkers, 1-23 to 1-24
Aluminum Workers International Union:
  listings for, 2-23
  publication of, 17-5
American Federation of Labor (*see* AFL-CIO)
American Institute for Free Labor Development (AIFLD), 3-21 to 3-22
American Motors Corp., contract with UAW, 1-11, 1-37
Anti-Kickback Law, 4-37
Anti-Racketeering Act, 4-7
Anti-Strike Breaker Law, 4-7
Antitrust legislation:
  Clayton Antitrust Act, 4-3 to 4-4
  Sherman Antitrust Act, 4-3
Apprenticeship, 10-36 to 10-37
Apprenticeship Act, National, 5-13
Apprenticeship Outreach Program (AOP), 5-13
Arbitration under collective agreements, 9-59
Architectural and Transportation Barriers Compliance Board (A&TBCB), 5-23
Arizona Public Employees Association, listings for, 2-23
Asbestos Workers, International Association of Heat and Frost Insulators and, listings for, 2-23
ASCS County Office Employees, National Association of, listings for, 2-23
Asia, AFL-CIO position on, 3-13 to 3-14, 3-19

Asian-American Free Labor Institute (AAFLI), 3-20 to 3-21
publication of, 17-5
Assault of supervisor, 9-52
Atlantic, Gulf, Lakes and Inland Waters District:
listings for, 2-43
(See also Seafarer's International Union of North America)
Atlantic Independent Union, listings for, 2-23
Auto Workers, United (UAW), 1-8 to 1-9
agreement with GM, 1-73 to 1-74
contract with American Motors, 1-11, 1-37
contract with McDonnell Douglas, 1-58
Fraser elected president of, 1-20
legal service plan of, 1-28
rejects reaffiliation with AFL-CIO, 1-37
settlement with Caterpillar, 1-4 to 1-5
settlement with Volkswagen, 1-76
wins representation at Monroe, 1-50
Automobile, Aerospace and Agricultural Implement Workers of America, International Union, United, listings for, 2-24

Bakery, Confectionery and Tobacco Workers International Union, 1-77
listings for, 2-24
Bakery and Confectionery Workers International Union of America, publication of, 17-5
Bakery and Confectionery Workers Union:
merger with Tobacco Workers, 1-71
settlements reached by, 1-24 to 1-25, 1-34
Bakery Employees Union, Independent, listings for, 2-24
Barbers, Beauticians, and Allied Industries, International Association:
listings for, 2-24
publication of, 17-5 to 17-6
Baseball Players Association, Major League, listings for, 2-24
Basketball Players Association, National, listings for, 2-24
Benefits Review Board, 5-7
Benzene standards of OSHA, 1-20, 1-53 to 1-54
Bituminous Coal Operators Association (BCOA), settlement with UMW, 1-52 to 1-53
Black Lung Benefits Reform Act, 1-53
Blacks, occupational status of, 10-42
BLS (see Labor Statistics, Bureau of)
Boeing Co., settlement reached by, 1-39
Boilermakers, Iron Ship Builders, Blacksmiths, Forgers and Helpers,

Boilermakers continued
International Brotherhood of:
listings for, 2-24
publication of, 17-6
Bonding under Landrum-Griffin Act, 4-43
Boot and Shoe Workers, merger with Retail Clerks, 1-30
Boycotts, prohibited, under National Labor Relations Act, 4-25 to 4-28
Brewery Workers, backpay won by, 1-76
Brick and Clay Workers of America, The United, listings for, 2-24
Bricklayers and Allied Craftsmen, International Union of:
listings for, 2-24 to 2-25
pay cut accepted by, 1-42
publication of, 17-6
Bridges, Harry, 1-20
Broadcast Employees and Technicians, National Association of:
listings for, 2-25
publication of, 17-6
Building trades:
hiring of women in, 1-32 to 1-33, 1-60
wage rates for workers in, 19-26 to 19-32
Byrnes Act, 4-7

California State Employees' Association, listings for, 2-25
Canada, labour publications of, 17-29 to 17-30
Cancer, job-related, 1-73
Carcinogens, OSHA policy on, 1-40 to 1-41
Cargo equity, AFL-CIO position on, 3-10
Carpenters and Joiners of America, United Brotherhood of:
listings for, 2-25
publication of, 17-6
Carrier Management, Inc. (CMI), 1-38
merges with TEI, 1-62
Carter, Jimmy:
anti-inflation plan of, 1-17 to 1-18, 1-46, 1-75
revision of, 1-79
economic program of, AFL-CIO position on, 1-22, 1-59 to 1-60
Caterpillar Tractor Co., Auto Workers' settlement with, 1-4 to 1-5
Cement, Lime and Gypsum Workers International Union, United:
listings for, 2-25
publication of, 17-6
settlement with cement companies, 1-58
Central States Pension Fund, resignation of trustees of, 1-12
Checkoff provisions:
sample contract clause and, 13-4 to 13-5
table, 11-51
Chemical Workers Union, International:
listings for, 2-25
publication of, 17-6

Child Support Enforcement, Office of, listings for, 5-29
Children, Youth, and Families, Administration for (ACYF), 5-32
Children in labor force, 10-31 to 10-32
Christian Labor Association of the United States of America, listings for, 2-25
Chrysler Corp., legal service plan of, 1-28
Cities, aid to, AFL-CIO position on, 3-10
Civil Rights, Commission on, 5-22
Civil Rights, Office for, 5-30
Civil Rights Act of 1964, 4-73 to 4-74
compliance under, 4-75
coverage under, 4-74
enforcement of, 4-75 to 4-76, 4-82
filing of charges under, 4-74
posters under, 4-75
unlawful employment practices under, 4-74 to 4-75
Civil Service Commission, job testing and hiring guidelines of, 1-5
Civil Service Employees Association, Inc.:
merges with AFSCME, 1-60
(See also State, County and Municipal Employees, American Federation of)
Civil Service Reform Act of 1978, 1-77 to 1-78
Classified School Employees, American Association of, listings for, 2-25
Clayton Antitrust Act, 4-3 to 4-4
Closed shop, sample contract clause and, 13-4
Clothing and Textile Workers Union, Amalgamated (ACTWU), 1-21
listings for, 2-25 to 2-26
merger with Shoe Workers, 1-77
publication of, 17-6
wage increase won by, 1-27
[See also Garment Workers of America, United; Garment Workers Union, International Ladies' (ILGWU)]
Clothing Manufacturers Association of the U.S.A., wage increase granted by, 1-27
Coke emission standards, 1-3 to 1-4
Cole, David L., 2-6
Collective bargaining:
lawful leverage and, 9-50
under National Labor Relations Act, 4-11 to 4-16
open negotiations and, 9-23 to 9-24
under Railway Labor Act, 4-4 to 4-5
under Taylor law, 11-8 to 11-9
Colorado Association of Public Employees, listings for, 2-26
Communications Workers of America:
listings for, 2-26
pay increases won by, 1-29
publication of, 17-6
settlement reached by, 1-31 to 1-32
Community Development aid, AFL-CIO position on, 3-10

Compensation:
  average hourly, defined, **19**-3
  measures of, tables, **19**-4 to **19**-6
  (*See also* Earnings; Salaries; Wages)
Compensation:
  unemployment [*see* Unemployment
    insurance (compensation)]
  workers' (*see* Workers' compensation)
Composers & Lyricists Guild of
  America, listings for, **2**-26
Comprehensive Employment and
    Training Act (CETA), **1**-7, **4**-101
    to **4**-102
  federal oversight functions and, **4**-104
    to **4**-105
  funding and eligibility for, **4**-103
  local role of, **4**-103 to **4**-104
  prime sponsors of, **4**-103
  program concepts, **4**-102 to **4**-103
  relationship to USES, **6**-28
  state role of, **4**-104
Comprehensive Employment
    Development Programs, Office of
    (OCED), **5**-10 to **5**-12
Comprehensive Manpower Services, **5**-
  11
Congress of Industrial Organizations
    (CIO):
  United Electrical Workers (UE)
    expelled by, **1**-8
  (*See also* AFL-CIO)
Connecticut Employees Union, listings
  for, **2**-26
Connecticut State Employees
    Association, listings for, **2**-26
Consolidated Rail Corp., settlement
  with UTU, **1**-72 to **1**-73
Constructors Association, National
    (NCA), settlements reached by, **1**-
    25, **1**-64 to **1**-65
Consumer Affairs, Office of, **5**-30
Consumer Credit Protection Act, **4**-86
  discharge provisions of, **4**-86
Consumer Price Index:
  annual averages and changes in,
    table, **20**-4
  cross-classification of, table, **20**-10
  defined, **20**-3
  U.S. city averages of, table, **20**-4 to
    20-9, **20**-11
Consumers, aid to, AFL-CIO position
  on, **3**-11
Contract Work Hours and Safety
    Standards Act:
  administration of, **4**-88
  construction safety and health
    standards of, **4**-88
  noncompliance under, **4**-88
  standards, reporting, and compliance
    under, **4**-88
  work hours standard of, **4**-87 to **4**-88
Coopers' International Union of North
  America, listings for, **2**-26
Copeland Act, **4**-37
Cost of living, sample contract clause
  and, **13**-11
Court decisions on, **9**-3 to **9**-66
  agency shop in government agencies
    and, **9**-35 to **9**-36

Court decisions on (*Cont.*):
  antipathy for women and, **9**-21 to **9**-
    25
  assault of supervisor and, **9**-52
  authority of captains and, **9**-34
  bargaining by local governing bodies
    and school boards and, **9**-27 to
    9-28
  Bureau of Labor Statistics and, **9**-44
    to **9**-45
  "but for" test of motivation and, **9**-
    21 to **9**-22
  campaign propaganda and, **9**-36 to **9**-
    37
  cities' foreign policy and, **9**-31
  constitutional issues and, **9**-14 to **9**-15
  contract construction and, **9**-30 to **9**-
    31
  definition of a person and, **9**-42
  discriminatory practices and, **9**-6 to
    9-8, **9**-15 to **9**-17, **9**-20 to **9**-22,
    9-26 to **9**-27, **9**-43 to **9**-44
  due process and, **9**-22, **9**-31
  "employ me" ads and, **9**-50 to **9**-51
  equal pay and, **9**-22
  government benefits and, **9**-9 to **9**-10
  interest arbitration and, **9**-25
  jobless fathers and, **9**-41 to **9**-42
  lawful leverage and, **9**-50
  layoff aid and, **9**-40 to **9**-41
  NLRB and parochial school and, **9**-
    47 to **9**-48
  open negotiations and, **9**-23 to **9**-24
  pregnancy exclusion and, **9**-19 to **9**-20
  public sector employment and, **9**-10
    to **9**-11, **9**-15
  rescue at sea and, **9**-34
  safety inspections and, **9**-23, **9**-48
  Saturday services and, **9**-39 to **9**-40
  scope of state labor laws, **9**-9 to **9**-10
  seniority and racial bias and, **9**-37 to
    9-38
  severance pay and, **9**-32 to **9**-33
  sovereignty and, **9**-42
  standing for rights of others and, **9**-
    20
  statistical evidence and, **9**-46 to **9**-47
  traditional labor law and, **9**-15 to **9**-
    16, **9**-68 to **9**-69
  union conduct during strikes, **9**-9
  union disciplinary hearings and, **9**-51
    to **9**-52
  union harassment and, **9**-33 to **9**-34
  union office requirements and, **9**-24
  union representation and, **9**-38
  veterans' pensions and, **9**-44
  veterans' rewards and, **9**-17
  work preservation and, **9**-29 to **9**-30

Davis, Hal C., **1**-47
Davis-Bacon Act, **4**-58 to **4**-59
  AFL-CIO position on, **3**-11
  enforcement of, **4**-59
  national emergency and, **4**-59
  penalties under, **4**-59
  suing under, **4**-59 to **4**-60
  wage rates under, **4**-59
Deere & Co., Auto Workers' settlement
  with, **1**-4

Defense, AFL-CIO position on, **3**-12,
  3-18
Die Sinkers' Conference, International,
  listings for, **2**-26
Directors Guild of America, listings for,
  2-27
Disarmament, AFL-CIO position on, **3**-
  12, **3**-18
Discharge, sample contract clause and,
  13-6 to **13**-7
Discipline, sample contract clause and,
  13-6 to **13**-7
Distillery, Rectifying, Wine and Allied
    Workers' International Union of
    America:
  listings for, **2**-27
  settlement of, **1**-42 to **1**-43
Distributive Workers of America,
  listings for, **2**-27
Due process, public employees and, **9**-
  60 to **9**-61
Dues (*see* Labor organizations, dues of)

Earnings:
  average hourly and weekly, defined,
    19-3
  of federal employees, table, **19**-24
  increases in, table, **19**-25
  of production or nonsupervisory
    workers, table, **19**-7 to **19**-23,
    19-24
  real, history of, **10**-50 to **10**-55
  (*See also* Compensation; Salaries;
    Wages)
Eastern Airlines:
  settlement with Air Line Pilots
    Association, **1**-19
  wages of mechanics of, **1**-27 to **1**-28
Economic activity, changing nature of
  work and, **10**-37 to **10**-38
Economic stimulus, AFL-CIO position
  on, **3**-10
Education:
  funding for, AFL-CIO position on,
    3-11
  in labor studies, **16**-3 to **16**-9
  of workers, **10**-35 to **10**-36
Education, Assistant Secretary for, **5**-34
  listings for, **5**-26
Education, Commissioner of, **5**-34
Education, National Institute of (NIE),
  5-35
  listings for, **5**-27 to **5**-28
  sources of information on, **5**-38
Education, Office of, **5**-34 to **5**-35
  listings for, **5**-27
  sources of information on, **5**-37 to **5**-
    38
Education Association, National
    (NEA):
  listings for, **2**-27
  settlement with AFSCME, **1**-6
Education Statistics, National Center
  for, **5**-34

EEOC (*see* Equal Employment
Opportunity Commission)
Election financing, AFL-CIO position
on, 3-8
Elections under Landrum-Griffin Act,
4-42 to 4-43
Electrical, Radio and Machine
Workers, International Union of:
listings for, 2-27
publication of, 17-6
Electrical, Radio, and Machine
Workers of America, United, 1-77
listings for, 2-27
Electrical Workers, International
Brotherhood of (IBEW):
listings for, 2-27 to 2-28
settlements reached by, 1-31 to 1-32,
1-62 to 1-63
Electrical Workers, International Union
of (IUE), 1-8
publication of, 17-6
Electrical Workers, United (UE), 1-8
Elementary and Secondary Education,
Bureau of, 5-34
Elevator Constructors, International
Union of:
listing for, 2-28
publication of, 17-6
Emergency Job Programs, 5-11 to 5-12
Employee associations (*see* Labor
organizations)
Employee representative under National
Labor Relations Act, 4-11 to 4-16
Employee Retirement Income Security
Act of 1974 (ERISA), 4-52, 5-15
enforcement of, 4-57 to 4-58
fiduciary standards under, 4-53 to 4-
54
participation, nesting, and funding
under, 4-55 to 4-56
pension plan termination insurance
under, 4-56 to 4-57
plans covered by, 4-52 to 4-53
reporting and disclosure under, 4-54
to 4-55
widow-widowers' benefit under,
4-57
Employee rights:
under National Labor Relations Act,
4-8 to 4-9
under Railway Labor Act, 4-4
Employees' Compensation Appeals
Board, 5-6
Employment:
advertising for, 9-50 to 9-51
data on, tables, 18-3 to 18-4
by federal government, 9-11
table, 19-24
irregularity of, wages and, 10-49
labor force and unemployment and,
table, 12-20
in public sector, 9-8
by states, 9-10 to 9-11
unemployment and, 12-4 to 12-5
(*See also* Unemployment)

Employment and Training
Administration (ETA), 5-8 to 5-14
listings for, 17-32
publications of, 5-19 to 5-20
regional offices of, 5-14
Employment Cost Index, 19-3
Employment discrimination:
against handicapped, 1-29
by law firm, 1-22
public employees and, 9-63 to 9-64
sample contract clause and, 13-4
Supreme Court decisions on, 9-6 to
9-8, 9-15 to 9-17
(*See also* Equal Employment
Opportunity Commission)
Employment Service (*see* United States
Employment Service)
Employment Standards Administration
(ESA), 5-16 to 5-18
Federal Contract Compliance
Program, 5-17
regional offices of, 5-17
listings for, 17-32 to 17-33
Office of Workers' Compensation
programs, 5-17
district offices of, 5-17
regional offices of, 5-16
Wage and Hour Division, 5-16
regional offices of, 5-16
Energy tax windfall, AFL-CIO position
on, 3-11
Engineers, International Federation of
Professional and Technical,
publication of, 17-6
Engineers, International Union of
Operating, publication of, 17-6
Equal employment opportunity (*see*
Executive Order 11246; Executive
Order 11478)
Equal Employment Opportunity
Commission (EEOC), 5-23 to 5-24
discrimination criteria of, 1-54
job testing and hiring guidelines and,
1-5 to 1-6
sources of information on, 5-24
Equal Pay Act of 1963, 4-73
ERISA (*see* Employee Retirement
Income Security Act of 1974)
Europe:
Eastern, AFL-CIO position on, 3-13,
3-18
Western, AFL-CIO position on, 3-12
to 3-13, 3-18
Executive Order 11246, 4-79 to 4-82
amendment to, 4-84 to 4-85
Executive Order 11247, 4-82
Executive Order 11375, 4-84 to 4-85
Executive Order 11478, 4-86 to 4-87
Executive Order 11491, 4-44
administration of, 4-45 to 4-46
agreements under, 4-47 to 4-48
conduct of labor organizations and
management under, 4-48 to 4-49
general provisions of, 4-44 to 4-45
implementation of, 4-50
in foreign service, 4-51
miscellaneous provisions of, 4-49 to
4-50
negotiation disputes and impasses
under, 4-48

Executive Order 11491 (*Cont.*):
recognition under, 4-46 to 4-47
Executive Order 11612, 4-100 to 4-101

Fair Labor Standards Act of 1938, 4-61
to 4-66
child labor provisions of, 4-64
cost of employee-furnished
employees, 4-63
coverage of, 4-62 to 4-63
definitions of terms used in, 4-64 to
4-65
enforcement of, 4-65
equal pay provisions of, 4-64
exemptions under, 4-63 to 4-64
1977 amendments to, 4-67 to 4-69
recovery of back pay under, 4-65
recordkeeping unkder, 4-64
special provisions of, 4-65 to 4-66
tipped employees, 4-63
wage and hour standards of, 4-62, 4-
63
Farm Labor Contractor Registration
Act, 4-44
Farm Workers National Union, United,
publication of, 17-6
Farm Workers of America, United
(UFW):
agreement with Teamsters, 1-12 to 1-
13
boycott ended by, 1-46
convention of, 1-35
grape and citrus settlements of, 1-25,
1-59
listings for, 2-28
Farmworkers, seasonal, employment
and training programs for, 5-13
Fatalities, job-related, 1-4
Federal Coal Mine Health and Safety
Act of 1969, 4-92
clinical facilities and research under,
4-95
dependent benefits under, 4-92 to 4-
93
expansion of coverage under, 4-93 to
4-94
protections, procedures, and date
changes under, 4-94
Federal Employees, National
Federation of, listings for, 2-28
Federal Employees' Compensation Act,
4-89
administration of, 4-90
amount of benefits under, 4-89
cost of living increases under, 4-90
death under, 4-90
hearing, review, and appeal rights
under, 4-90
injuries and diseases covered by, 4-89
medical care under, 4-90
permanent partial disability under, 4-
89
permanent total disability under, 4-89
to 4-90
persons and employment covered by,
4-89
temporary total disability under, 4-89
third party settlements under, 4-90
vocational rehabilitation under, 4-90

Federal Metal and Nonmetallic Mine
  Safety Act, 4-92
Federal Mine Enforcement Safety and
  Health Act of 1977, 1-40
Fire Fighters, International Association
  of:
  listings for, 2-28
  publication of, 17-6
Firefighters and police, wage rates for,
  11-78 to 11-81
Firemen and Oilers, International
  Brotherhood of:
  listings for, 2-28
  publication of, 17-6 to 17-7
Fitzmaurice, David J., as president of
  IUE, 1-8
Fitzsimmons, Frank, quits pension
  fund, 1-12
Flight Engineers' International
  Association, listings for, 2-22, 2-28
Food stamps:
  for strikers, AFL-CIO position on, 3-
    7, 3-10
  work requirement and, 6-24 to 6-25
Football League Players Association,
  National, listings for, 2-28
Foreign trade:
  AFL-CIO position on, 3-19
  Meany's remarks about, 3-4 to 3-5
  unions affiliated with international
    trade secretariats, table, 3-23 to
    3-24
Fraser, Douglas A., 1-20
  endorsement by Auto Workers
    leaders, 1-8 to 1-9
Furniture Workers of America, United:
  listings for, 2-29
  publication of, 17-7

Garment Workers of America, United:
  listings for, 2-29
  publication of, 17-7
Garment Workers Union, International
  Ladies' (ILGWU):
  contract with Vanity Fair, 1-41 to 1-
    42
  election of, 1-25 to 1-26
  listings for, 2-32
  publications of, 17-7
General Counsel, 5-31
General Electric Co., discrimination
  charged against, 1-43, 1-65
General Motors Corp.:
  labor law violations by, 1-38
  preferential hiring plan of, 1-73 to 1-
    74
George Meany Center for Labor
  Studies, 16-9
Gimbels Bros., Inc., settlement reached
  by, 1-28
Glass and Ceramic Workers of North
  America, United:
  listings for, 2-30
  publication of, 17-7
  wage increase won by, 1-41
Glass Bottle Blowers Association of the
  United States and Canada:
  listings for, 2-29 to 2-30
  publication of, 17-7

Glass Bottle Blowers Association of the
  United States and Canada (Cont.):
  settlement with Owens-Illinois Inc.,
    1-15
Glass Workers' Union of North
  America, American Flint:
  listings for, 2-30
  publication of, 17-7
Glossary of labor terms, 14-1 to 14-56
Goodrich, B. F., Co.:
  binding arbitration plan of, 1-14
  no-strike plan proposed by, 1-50 to
    1-51
Government Employees, American
  Federation of:
  convention of, 1-70
  listings for, 2-30
  organization of military vetoed by, 1-
    33
  publication of, 17-7
Government Employees, National
  Association of, listings for, 2-28 to
    2-29
Government Inspectors and Quality
  Assurance Personnel, National
  Association of, listings for, 2-29
Governmental Employees, Assembly of
  (AGE), 2-6
  listings for, 2-16
Grain Millers, American Federation of,
  listings for, 2-29
Granite Cutters' International
  Association of America, The,
  listings for, 2-29
Graphic Arts International Union, 2-7
  listings for, 2-29
  publication of, 17-7
Grievance procedures:
  for public employees, table, 11-52
  sample contract clause and, 13-5 to
    13-6
Group Health Association Physicians
  Association, 1-47
Guard Union of America, International,
  listings for, 2-30
Guards and Watchmen, International
  Union of, listings for, 2-30
Gulf Oil Corp. settlement with OCAW,
  1-8

Handicapped, Bureau of Education for,
  5-35
Handicapped workers, discrimination
  against, 1-29
Hatch Act Reform, AFL-CIO position
  on, 3-9 to 3-10
Hatters, Cap and Millinery Workers
  International Union, United,
  listings for, 2-30
Health, Education, and Welfare,
  Department of (HEW):
  Education Division, 5-34 to 5-35
  Health Care Financing
    Administration [see Health Care
    Financing Administration
    (HCFA)]
  listings for, 5-25 to 5-29
  Office of Human Development
    Services [see Human

Health, Education, and Welfare,
  Department of (HEW) (Cont.):
  Development Services, Office of
    (HDS)]
  Office of the Secretary of, 5-29 to 5-
    31
  organizational chart, 5-30
  regional offices, 5-31
  Social Security Administration [see
    Social Security Administration
    (SSA)]
  sources of information on, 5-37 to 5-
    39
Health, funding for, AFL-CIO position
  on, 3-11
Health Care Financing Administration
  (HCFA), 5-35 to 5-36
  listings for, 5-28 to 5-29
  sources of information on, 5-38
Health Services Administration (HSA),
  sources of information on, 5-38
Hebrew Actors Union, Inc.:
  listings for, 2-21
  (See also Actors and Artistes of
    America, Associated)
Herman, James R., 1-26
HEW (see Health, Education, and
  Welfare, Department of)
HIRE, 1-7, 5-13
Hiring guidelines, 1-5 to 1-6
History:
  of labor organizations, 10-46 to 10-48
  of unemployment, 10-55 to 10-59
  of wages (see Wages, history of)
  of work (see Work, history of)
Hobbs Act, 4-7
Hockey League Players' Association,
  National, listings for, 2-30
Holidays, sample contract clause and,
  13-10
Horseshoers of the United States and
  Canada, International Union of
  Journeymen, listings of, 2-30
Hospitals and Homes of New York
  City, League of Voluntary,
  settlement with union, 1-68
Hot cargo agreements under National
  Labor Relations Act, 4-21 to 4-22,
  4-29
Hotel and Restaurant Employees and
  Bartenders International Union:
  listings for, 2-30 to 2-31
  publication of, 17-7
Hourly Earnings Index, 19-3
Hours:
  of federal employees, table, 19-24
  history of, 10-44 to 10-45
  of production or nonsupervisory
    workers, table, 19-7 to 19-23
  sample contract clause and, 13-12 to
    13-13
  unemployment and, 12-7
Housewright, James T., 1-35
Housing funds, AFL-CIO position on,
  3-7

Human Development Services, Office of (HDS), 5-31 to 5-33
listings for, 5-26
sources of information on, 5-37
Human Resources Development Institute, AFL-CIO, publication of, 17-7
Humphrey-Hawkins bill, Meany's remarks about, 3-3

IBEW (*see* Electrical Workers, International Brotherhood of)
Idaho Public Employees Association, listings for, 2-31
ILA (*see* Longshoreman's Association, International)
ILGWU (*see* Garment Workers Union, International Ladies')
Illinois State Employees Association, listings for, 2-31
Illnesses, job-related, 1-4
Immigration, labor force and, 10-28 to 10-29
Independent Unions, Congress of, listings for, 2-31
Indian Education, Office of, 5-35
Indiana State Employees Association, listings for, 2-31
Industrial Associations, listing of, 17-31 to 17-32
Industrial Trade Unions, National Organization of, listings for, 2-31
Industrial Workers of America, Allied:
listings for, 2-31
merger with Molders, 1-38
publication of, 17-7
Industrial Workers Union, National, listings for, 2-31
Industrial Workers Union, United, publication of, 17-9
Inflation, Carter's program to combat, 1-17 to 1-18, 1-46, 1-75
revision of, 1-79
Information, Publications and Reports, Office of, 5-6
listings for, 17-32
regional offices of, table, 5-6
Initiation fees of labor organizations, 2-54 to 2-56
table, 2-55
Injunctions under Norris-La Guardia Act, 4-6 to 4-7
Injuries, job-related:
asbestos and, 1-56
decline in, 1-4
Inland Boatmen's Union of the Pacific:
listings for, 2-43
(*See also* Seafarers' International Union of North America)
Inspector General, Office of, 5-30
Insurance:
PBGC and, 5-43 to 5-44
sample contract clause and, 13-11 to 13-12

Unemployment Insurance Service (UIS), 5-13 to 5-14
[*See also* Unemployment insurance (compensation)]
Insurance Workers International Union:
listings for, 2-31
publication of, 17-7
settlement with John Hancock, 1-69
Interest arbitration, 9-25
International Affairs, Office of, 5-8
International Harvester Co., Auto Workers' settlement with, 1-4
International Labor Affairs, Bureau of (ILAB), 5-8
listings for, 17-34
International Labor Organization (ILO), 3-17, 5-20
termination of U.S. membership in, 1-33, 1-41
International Labor Press Association, 17-3 to 17-4
Iron Workers, International Association of Bridge, Structural and Ornamental:
listings for, 2-32
publication of, 17-7
Italian Actors Union:
listings for, 2-21
(*See also* Actors and Artistes of America, Associated)

Jewelry Workers' Union, International, listings for, 2-32
Job bank, 6-16
Job Corps, 5-12
Job Information Service (JIS), 6-16
Job safety, AFL-CIO position on, 3-7, 3-10
Job testing guidelines, 1-5 to 1-6
John Hancock Mutual Life Insurance Co., settlement with Insurance Workers, 1-69
Justice, Department of, job testing and hiring guidelines of, 1-5

Kansas City Construction Committee, 1-57
Kennecott Copper Corp., settlements reached by, 1-27
Kleeb, Howard W., 2-6

Labor, Department of:
Administration and Management, 5-7 to 5-8
Bureau of Labor Statistics [*see* Labor Statistics, Bureau of (BLS)]
Employment and Training Administration [*see* Employment and Training Administration (ETA)]
International Affairs, 5-8
investigation of Steelworkers' election by, 1-25
job testing and hiring guidelines of, 1-5
labor management [*see* Labor-Management Services

Labor, Department of (*Cont.*):
Administration (LMSA)]
listings for, 5-3 to 5-5
Mine Safety and Health Administration, 5-18
Occupational Safety and Health Administration [*see* Occupational Safety and Health Administration (OSHA)]
organization chart, 5-5
Policy, Evaluation and Research, 5-8, 5-14
regional information offices of, 17-34
Secretary of, 5-5
office of, 5-5 to 5-6
Solicitor of Labor, 5-7
regional offices of, 5-7
sources of information on, 5-19 to 5-20
Under Secretary of, 5-6
office of, 5-6 to 5-7
Women's Bureau, 5-6
listings for, 17-33
Labor agreements, sample contract clauses in, 13-3 to 13-14
Labor force:
changes in, 10-30 to 10-34
children in, 10-31 to 10-32
education and training of, 10-35 to 10-36
employment and unemployment and, table, 12-20
population and, tables, 10-27 to 10-30, 12-16 to 12-19
women in, 9-49 to 9-50, 10-32 to 10-33
Labor legislation:
in 1976, 8-3 to 8-16
in 1977, 8-17 to 8-38
in 1978, 8-39 to 8-55
(*See also* Law, labor and)
Labor Management Relations Act (*see* Taft-Hartley Act)
Labor management relations in federal service (*see* Executive Order 11491)
Labor Management Reporting and Disclosure Act, 5-15
(*See also* Landrum-Griffin Act)
Labor-Management Services Administration (LMSA), 5-14 to 5-16
listings for, 17-33
regional offices of, 5-15
Labor organizations:
affiliated with international trade secretariats, table, 3-23 to 3-24
conventions scheduled for 1979, 2-64
disciplinary proceedings of, latitude in, 9-51 to 9-52
dues of, 2-54, 2-56 to 2-57
under National Labor Relations Act, 4-28
table, 2-56
employer opposition to, 3-5
harassment by, 9-33 to 9-34
history of, 10-46 to 10-48
initiation fees of, 2-54 to 2-56
table, 2-55
Labor Management Reporting and

Labor Organizations (*Cont.*):
  Disclosure Act and, 5-15
  listings of, 2-16 to 2-53
  membership of, 2-59 to 2-60
    developments in, 2-60 to 2-61
    gains in, 2-61
    tables, 2-59 to 2-64
  per capita taxes of, 2-58 to 2-59
    table, 2-57, 2-58
  of physicians, 1-47
  political rights of, AFL-CIO position
    on, 3-8 to 3-9
  for professional employees, 1-47
  public employees and (*see* Public
    employees, unions and)
  representation for, 9-38
    sample contract clause and, 13-5
  requirements for office in, 9-24
  safeguards for, under Landrum-
    Griffin Act, 4-43
  security and, sample contract clause
    and, 13-4
  unaffiliated and independent, 2-6
Labor Statistics, Bureau of (BLS), 5-
  18 to 5-19
  listings for, 17-33
  publications of, 5-19
  regional offices, 5-19
  statistical techniques of, 9-44 to 9-45
Labor studies, 16-3 to 16-9
Laborers' International Union of North
  America:
  listings for, 2-32
  publications of, 17-7
  settlement reached by, 1-25
Lace Operatives of America,
  Amalgamated, listings for, 2-32
Landrum-Griffin Act, 4-37 to 4-38, 4-
  43 to 4-44, 9-65
  bonding requirement of, 4-43
  complaints under, 4-38
  coverage of, 4-38
  disclosure and enforcement under, 4-
    41
  elections under, 4-42 to 4-43
  improper payments and fees under,
    4-43
  loans and fines under, 4-43
  prohibitions against holding union
    office under, 4-43
  reporting requirement under, 4-39
  reports of employers, labor
    consultants, and other persons
    under, 4-40 to 4-41
  reports of union officers and
    employees under, 4-39 to 4-40
  safeguards for labor organizations
    under, 4-43
  surety company reports under, 4-41
  trusteeships under, 4-41 to 4-42
  union member rights under, 4-38
Lathers, International Union of Wood,
  Wire and Metal, listings for, 2-32
Latin America, AFL-CIO position on,
  3-15 to 3-17, 3-20
Laundry, Dry Cleaning and Dye House
  Workers' International Union:
  listings for, 2-45
  (*See also* Teamsters, Chauffeurs,

Laundry, Dry Cleaning and Dye House
  Workers' International Union:
  (*Cont.*):
    Warehousemen, and Helpers of
    America, International
    Brotherhood of)
Laundry and Dry Cleaning
  International Union, listings for, 2-
  32
Law, labor and, 9-53 to 9-54
  AFL-CIO position on reform of, 3-9
  arbitration under collective
    agreements and, 9-59
  employment discrimination and, 9-63
    to 9-65
  federal employee reclassification and,
    9-66
  Landrum-Griffin Act and, 9-65
  Occupational Safety and Health Act
    and, 9-66
  Pipefitters case and, 9-57 to 9-58
  preemption of state regulation and, 9-
    59 to 9-60
  public employees and, 9-60 to 9-63
  seniority decisions and, 9-54 to 9-56
  social benefit cases and, 9-65 to 9-66
  Taft-Hartley Act and, 9-65
  veterans' reemployment rights and,
    5-15, 9-66
  wages and hours of public employees
    and, 9-56 to 9-57
  (*See also* National Labor Relations Act)
Layoffs by steel companies, 1-36
  (*See also* Unemployment)
Leather Goods, Plastic and Novelty
  Workers' Union, International,
  listings for, 2-32 to 2-33
Leather Workers International Union of
  America, listings for, 2-33
Leaves of absence, sample contract
  clause and, 13-7 to 13-8
Legislation, Assistant Secretary for, 5-31
Legislation and Intergovernmental
  Relations, Office of, 5-8
Letter Carriers of the United States of
  America, National Association of,
  1-77
  convention of, 1-70
  listings for, 2-33
Libby-Owens-Ford settlement with
  Glass and Ceramic Workers, 1-41
Licensed Officers' Organization, Great
  Lakes, listings for, 2-33
Licensed Practical Nurses, National
  Federation of, listings for, 2-33
Life cycle, place of work in, 10-34
Loans, rural, certification of, 6-22
Lockouts, sample contract clause and,
  13-13
Locomotive Engineers, Brotherhood of,
  listings for, 2-33
Log Scalers Association, Pacific,
  listings for, 2-33
Longshoremen's and Harbor Workers'
  Compensation Act, 4-91
  administration of, 4-91
  amount of benefits under, 4-91
  appeals under, 4-91
  death under, 4-91

Longshoremen's and Harbor Workers'
  Compensation Act (*Cont.*):
  injuries and diseases covered under,
    4-91
  medical treatment under, 4-91
  permanent partial disability under, 4-
    91
  permanent total disability under, 4-91
  persons and employments covered
    by, 4-91
  second injuries under, 4-91
  temporary total disability under, 4-91
  vocational rehabilitation under, 4-91
Longshoremen's and Warehousemen's
  Union, International, 1-20
  contract with sugar companies, 1-44
  election of, 1-26
  listings for, 2-33 to 2-34
  settlement with Pacific Maritime
    Association, 1-69
Longshoremen's Association,
  International (ILA):
  dock container dispute and, 1-21
  listings for, 2-33
  publication of, 17-8
  settlement ending strike, 1-44
Long-Term Care (LTC), 5-36

McBride, Lloyd, 1-10
McDonnell Douglas Corp., contract
  with Auto Workers, 1-58
Machine Printers and Engravers
  Association of the United States,
  listings for, 2-34
Machinists and Aerospace Workers,
  International Association of:
  aerospace settlements of, 1-61
  listings for, 2-34
  publications of, 17-8
  settlements reached by, 1-39, 1-79 to
    1-80
Machinists union (IAM), 1-11
Magma Copper Co., settlement reached
  by, 1-27
Maine State Employees Association,
  listings for, 2-34
Maintenance of Way Employees,
  Brotherhood of:
  listings for, 2-34
  publication of, 17-8
Management, rights of, sample contract
  clause and, 13-13
Management and Budget, Assistant
  Secretary for, 5-31
Management and Budget, Office of, 5-34
Marine and Shipbuilding Workers of
  America, Industrial Union of,
  listings for, 2-34
Marine Cooks and Stewards Union:
  publication of, 17-8
  (*See also* Atlantic, Gulf, Lakes and
    Inland Waters District;
    Seafarers' International Union of
    North America)

Marine Engineers' Beneficial
  Association, National, listings for,
  2-34
Maritime Service Committee, 1-61
Maritime Union of America, National:
  listings for, 2-34 to 2-35
  publication of, 17-8
  settlement with East and Gulf Coast
    seamen, 1-61 to 1-62
Marshall, F. Ray, 1-7
  identifies OSHA problems, 1-14 to 1-
    15
  plan to create jobs for Vietnam
    veterans, 1-7 to 1-8
Maryland Classified Employees
  Association, Inc., listings for,
  2-35
Massachusetts State Employees
  Association (see Government
  Employees, National Association
  of)
Masters, Mates, and Pilots,
  International Organization of:
  listings for, 2-33
  publication of, 17-8
Meany, George:
  on foreign trade, 3-4 to 3-5
  George Meany Center for Labor
    Studies, 16-9
  on Humphrey-Hawkins bill, 3-3
  opposition to prenotification of wage
    increases, 1-10
  resignation called for, 1-45
Meat Cutters and Butcher Workmen of
  North America, Amalgamated:
  listings for, 2-35
  publication of, 17-8
  settlement of, 1-42
Mechanics Educational Society of
  America, listings for, 2-35
Mediation and Conciliation Service,
  Federal, 5-21 to 5-22
  regional offices, 5-21
Medicaid, 5-6
Medicare, 5-36
Membership (see Labor organizations,
  membership of)
Men, discrimination against, 9-26 to 9-
  27
Metal Polishers, Buffers, Platers and
  Allied Workers International
  Union, listings for, 2-35
Metropolitan New York Nursing Home
  Association, agreement with
  Service Employees' Local 144, 1-
  19
Michigan State Employees Association,
  listings for, 2-35
Middle East, AFL-CIO position on, 3-
  18
Migrant workers, employment and
  training programs for, 5-13
Migration:
  labor force and, 10-27 to 10-28
  unemployment and, 12-7 to 12-8

Miller, Arnold, 1-24
Miller Act:
  persons and employments covered
    by, 4-60
  suing under, 4-60
Mills, D. Quinn, 2-6
Mine safety, AFL-CIO position on, 3-
  8, 3-11
Mine Safety and Health Administration
  (MSHA), 5-18
Mine Workers of America, United
  (UMW), 1-9
  election of, 1-38
  listings for, 2-35
  Miller as president of, 1-24
  settlement with BCOA, 1-52 to 1-53
  Taft-Hartley invoked against, 1-48 to
    1-49
Minnesota Association of Government
  Employees, Independent, listings
  for, 2-35 to 2-36
Molders' and Allied Workers' Union,
  International:
  listings for, 2-36
  merger with AIW, 1-38
  publication of, 17-8
Monroe Auto Equipment Co., UAW
  wins representation at, 1-50
Montana Public Employees Association,
  listings for, 2-36
Monthly Labor Review:
  index of volumes 94–98 (January
    1971–December 1975), 15-3 to
    15-22
  index of volume 99 (January
    1976–December 1976), 15-23 to
    15-32
  index of volume 100 (January
    1977–December 1977), 15-33 to
    15-40
  index of volume 101 (January
    1978–December 1978), 15-41 to
    15-51
Museum Services, Institute of, 5-34
Musical Artists, American Guild of:
  listings for, 2-21
  (See also Actors and Artistes of
    America, Associated)
Musicians, American Federation of, 1-
  47
  listings for, 2-36
  publication of, 17-8

Nabisco, Inc., settlement with Bakery
  and Confectionery Workers, 1-34
National Broadcasting Co. (NBC),
  settlement of sex-bias suit against,
  1-15
National Federation of Independent
  Unions (NFIU), 2-6
  listings for, 2-16
National Foundation on the Arts and
  Humanities Act, 4-79 to 4-80
National Labor Relations Act, 4-8
  boycotts prohibited under, 4-25 to 4-
    28
  cases heard under, 9-52
  collective bargaining under, 4-11 to
    4-16
  decisions under, 9-58 to 9-59

National Labor Relations Act (*Cont.*):
  employee rights under, 4-8 to 4-9
  enforcement of, 4-29 to 4-35
  hot cargo agreements under, 4-21 to
    4-22, 4-29
  right to picket under, 4-11, 4-28 to 4-
    29
  right to strike under, 4-9 to 4-11
  unfair labor practices under, 4-17 to
    4-29
  cases, 4-19
National Labor Relations Board
  (NLRB), 5-39 to 5-40
  agreement with Stevens, 1-58 to 1-
    59, 1-74
  labor's opposition to, 1-64
  authority of, 4-30 to 4-32
  court enforcement of orders of, 4-34
  field offices, 5-41
  listings for, 5-39
  organization of, 4-29 to 4-30
  parochial schools and, 9-47 to 9-48
  powers of, 4-33 to 4-34
  procedures of, 4-32 to 4-34
  regional directory of, 4-36
  regional offices of, map, 4-35
  requests injunction against Stevens,
    1-46 to 1-47
  sources of information on, 5-40 to 5-
    41
National Labor Relations Board
  Professional Association, listings
  for, 2-36
National Labor Relations Board Union,
  listings for, 2-36
National Mediation Board, 5-42 to 5-43
  listings for, 5-42
  sources of information on, 5-43
National Programs, Office of (ONP), 5-
  12 to 5-13
Native Americans, Administration for
  (ANA), 5-32
Native Americans, employment and
  training programs for, 5-12 to 5-13
NATO, AFL-CIO position on, 3-12 to
  3-13, 3-18
Natural gas:
  deregulation of, AFL-CIO position
    on, 3-10 to 3-11
  emergency legislation for, AFL-CIO
    position on, 3-8
  price controls on, AFL-CIO position
    on, 3-8
  shortages of, 1-7
Nebraska Association of Public
  Employees, listings for, 2-36
Negotiation, impasse procedures for,
  table, 11-53
New Hampshire State Employees
  Association, listings for, 2-36
New Jersey State Employees
  Association, listings for, 2-37
New York City:
  employees of, wages of, 1-32, 1-63
  keeps social security coverage, 1-9
New York City Board of Education,
  agreement with UFT, 1-13 to 1-14
New York City schools, job bias
  charges against, 1-5

Newspaper and Mail Deliverers' Union of New York and Vicinity, listings for, 2-37

Newspaper Guild, The:
contract with *New York Daily News*, 1-67 to 1-68
listings for, 2-37
publication of, 17-8

NLRB (*see* National Labor Relations Board)

Norris-La Guardia Act, 4-6 to 4-7

North Carolina State Employees Association, listings for, 2-37

North Carolina State Government Employees Association, listings for, 2-37

North Dakota State Employees Association, listings for, 2-37

Northwest Airlines, settlement with Air Line Pilots, 1-69

Nuclear energy, development of, AFL-CIO position on, 3-8, 3-11

Nurses Association, American, 1-80
listings for, 2-37

Occupational and Adult Education, Bureau of, 5-34

Occupational Safety and Health Act of 1970 (OSHA), 4-102, 9-66
administration of, 4-95
advisory committees under, 4-99
annual reports of, 4-100
assistance from Small Business Administration under, 4-99
Assistant Secretary of Labor under, 4-100
coverage under, 4-95
duties of employers and employees under, 4-95
education and training programs under, 4-98 to 4-99
enforcement of, 4-96
general notice requirements under, 4-97
imminent danger under, 4-97 to 4-98
inspections by, 9-48
Labor Department legal representation and, 4-99 to 4-100
national defense tolerances and, 4-100
National Institute under, 4-99
nonobstruction requirement of, 4-99
notification of proposed penalty under, 4-96
protection against harassment under, 4-98
protection for Labor Department inspectors under, 4-100
purpose of, 4-95
recordkeeping requirements under, 4-97
Review Commission of, 4-99
standards of, 4-95 to 4-96
state participation in, 4-99
statistics under, 4-97
time for abatement of hazards under, 4-96 to 4-97
trade secrets and, 4-100
violations under: complaints of, 4-96

Occupational Safety and Health Act of 1970 (OSHA), violations under (*Cont.*):
failure to correct within allowed time, 4-97
penalties for, 4-97
workmen's compensation under, 4-99

Occupational Safety and Health Administration (OSHA), 5-18
benzene standards of, 1-20, 1-53 to 1-54
coke emission standards of, 1-3 to 1-4
cotton dust standards of, 1-62
listings for, 17-32
policy on carcinogens, 1-40 to 1-41
problems in, 1-14 to 1-15
regional offices of, 5-18
reporting forms of, 1-29

Occupational safety and health programs for federal employees, 4-100 to 4-101
establishment of, 4-101

Occupational Safety and Health Review Commission (OSHRC), 5-43 to 5-44
listings for, 5-43
review commission judges for, 5-44
sources of information on, 5-44

Occupations, 10-39
of blacks, 10-42
changing patterns in, 10-39 to 10-41
(*See also* Work, history of)
content of work and, 10-42 to 10-44
employment data for, tables, 18-11 to 18-14
wage differentials and, 10-49
of women, 10-41 to 10-42

Office and Professional Employees International Union:
listings for, 2-37
publication of, 17-8

Ohio Civil Service Employees Association, Inc., listings for, 2-37 to 2-38

Oil, Chemical and Atomic Workers International Union (OCAW):
listings for, 2-38
publication of, 17-8
settlement with petroleum refining companies, 1-8

Old age, history of work and, 10-60 to 10-62

On-the-Job Training Program, National (OJT), 5-13

Operating Engineers, International Union of, listings for, 2-38

Oregon State Employees Association, listings for, 2-38

Organization of African Trade Union Unity (OATUU), 3-20

OSHA (*see* Occupational Safety and Health Act of 1970; Occupational Safety and Health Administration)

Overseas Education Association, Inc., listings for, 2-27

Overtime, sample contract clause and, 13-12 to 13-13

Owens-Illinois Inc., agreement with Glass Bottle Blowers union, 1-15

Pacific Coast Marine Firemen, Oilers, Watertenders and Wipers Association:
listings for, 2-43
(*See also* Seafarers' International Union of North America)

Pacific Maritime Association, settlement with Longshoremen, 1-69

Packinghouse and Industrial Workers, National Brotherhood of, listings for, 2-38

Painters and Allied Trades of the United States and Canada, International Brotherhood of:
listings for, 2-38
publication of, 17-8

Paperworkers International Union, United:
indictment of officials of, 1-71
listings for, 2-38
publication of, 17-8
settlement reached by, 1-28 to 1-29

Patent Office Professional Association, listings for, 2-38 to 2-39

Patrick, Harry, 1-9

Patrolmen's Benevolent Association (PBA), agreement accepted by, 1-67

Pattern Makers' League of North America, listings for, 2-39

Pension Benefit Guaranty Corporation (PBGC), 5-45 to 5-47
listings for, 5-45
organizational chart, 5-46

Pension plans, 5-15
federal, 11-60 to 11-61
municipal, 11-54 to 11-61
"rule-of-65," 1-55 to 1-56
sample contract clause and, 13-12
termination insurance for, under Employee Retirement Income Security Act of 1974, 4-56 to 4-57

Personnel Administration, Assistant Secretary for, 5-31

Petroleum and Industrial Workers, International Union of:
listings for, 2-43
(*See also* Seafarers' International Union of North America)

Petroleum industry, settlement with OCAW, 1-8

Physicians National Housestaff Association, listings for, 2-39

Picketing:
under National Labor Relations Act, 4-11, 4-28 to 4-29
situs picketing rights, AFL-CIO position on, 3-9

Planner-Estimators and Progressmen, National Association of, listings for, 2-39

Planning, Office of, 5-34

Planning and Evaluation, 5-31

Plant Guard Workers of America, International Union, United, listings for, 2-39

Plasterers' and Cement Masons' International Association of the United States and Canada, Operative:
listings for, 2-39
publication of, 17-8

Plate Printers', Die Stampers' and Engravers' Union of North America, International, listings for, 2-39

Plumbing and Pipe Fitting Industry of the United States and Canada, United Association of Journeymen and Apprentices of the:
labor law and Pipefitters case, 9-57 to 9-58
listings for, 2-39
publication of, 17-8 to 17-9
wages reduced by, 1-34

Police, Fraternal Order of, listings for, 2-39

Policy, Evaluation, and Research, Office of, 5-8, 5-14

Population:
growth and change of, 10-27 to 10-30
labor force and, tables, 10-27 to 10-30, 12-16 to 12-19

Portal to Portal Act of 1947, 4-72 to 4-75

Porter, Alexander B., 2-6

Postal, Telegraph and Telephone International, publication of, 17-9

Postal and Federal Employees, National Alliance of, listings for, 2-40

Postal Reorganization Act of 1970, 4-51
implementation of, 4-52

Postal Security Police, Federation of, listings for, 2-40

Postal Service (see United States Postal Service)

Postal Supervisors, National Association of, listings for, 2-40

Postal Workers Union, American:
listings for, 2-40
publication of, 17-9

Postmasters of the United States, National League of, listings for, 2-40

Postsecondary Education, Bureau of, 5-35

Postsecondary Education, Fund for the Improvement of, 5-34

Pottery and Allied Workers, International Brotherhood of:
listings for, 2-40
publication of, 17-10

Pregnancy under sick benefits, 9-19 to 9-20

Prenotification of wage increases, 1-10

Price controls on natural gas, AFL-CIO position on, 3-8

Price indexes, defined, 20-3

Printing and Graphic Communications Union, International:
listings for, 2-40
publication of, 17-9

Producer Price Indexes, defined, 20-3

Professional and state employee associations, 2-7

Professional Air Traffic Controllers Organization (PATCO):
job reclassifications for, 1-5
listings for, 2-34

Professional Standards Review Organization (PSRO), 5-36

Promotion and Development Programs (P&D), 5-13

Proposition 13, 1-68

Protection Employees, Independent Union of Plant, listings for, 2-40

Public Affairs, 5-30 to 5-31

Public Employee Organizations, National Conference of Independent, 2-6

Public employees:
aliens as, 9-63
employment discrimination and, 9-63 to 9-64
pension plans of, 11-54 to 11-61
procedural due process cases and, 9-60 to 9-61
reclassification of, 9-66
residency requirements for, 1-71
substantial constitutional rights of, 9-61 to 9-62
under Taylor law, 11-4 to 11-14
unions and, 5-15, 9-62 to 9-63
checkoff provisions and, table, 11-51
grievance procedures and, table, 11-52
negotiation impasse procedures and, table, 11-53
security provisions and, table, 11-50
under Taylor law, 11-4 to 11-14
wages and hours of, 9-56 to 9-57
federal, 1-36 to 1-37, 1-56
work stoppage provisions and, table, 11-52

Public Employment Programs, 5-11

Public employment relations boards (PERBs), directory of, 11-15 to 11-49

Public Health Service, listings for, 5-28

Public service jobs, AFL-CIO position on, 3-7

Public Services, Administration for (APS), 5-32 to 5-33

Pulp and Paper Workers, Association of Western, listings for, 2-41

Quarantine Inspectors National Association, Federal Plant, listings for, 2-41

Radio Association, American, listings for, 2-41

Rail Passenger Service Act of 1970, 4-89

Railroad Adjustment Board, National, 5-42

Railroad Retirement Board, 5-47 to 5-49
listings for, 5-45
organizational chart, 5-48

Railroad Signalmen, Brotherhood of:
listings for, 2-41
publication of, 17-9

Railroad Yardmasters of America:
listings for, 2-41
publication of, 17-9

Railway, Airline and Steamship Clerks, Freight Handlers, Express and Station Employees, Brotherhood of:
listings for, 2-41
merger with Porters, 1-54
publications of, 17-9

Railway and Airway Supervisors Association, The American, listing for, 2-41

Railway Carmen of the United States and Canada, Brotherhood of:
listings for, 2-41 to 2-42
publication of, 17-9

Railway Labor Act, 4-4 to 4-6

Railway Labor Executives' Association (RLEA), 2-6

Railway Labor Organizations, publications of, 17-9

Railway Unions, Congress of, 2-6

Recognition, sample contract clause and, 13-3 to 13-4

Reemployment rights of veterans, 5-16, 9-66

Regional associations, listing of, 17-31 to 17-32

Regulated industries, employment practices of, 9-65

Rehabilitation Services Administration (RSA), 5-33

Retail, Wholesale and Department Store Union:
listings for, 2-42
publication of, 17-9
settlement with hospital league, 1-68

Retail Clerks International Association (RCIA):
merger of Boot and Shoe workers with, 1-30
publication of, 17-9

Retail Clerks International Union, 1-35
listings for, 2-42

Retail Workers Union, United, listings for, 2-42

Retirement:
age of, 1-55, 1-58
(See also Pension plans)

"Reverse" discrimination, 9-64

Rhodesia boycott, AFL-CIO position on, 3-9, 3-11

Roofers, Damp and Waterproof Workers Association, United Slate, File and Composition:
listings for, 2-42
publication of, 17-9

Rubber, Cork, Linoleum and Plastic
Workers of America, United:
listings for, 2-42
publication of, 17-9
Rubber Workers, United, 1-14
no strike plan and, 1-50 to 1-51
Rural area workers, employment
services for, 5-9
Rural Letter Carriers' Association,
National listings for, 2-42

Sadlowski, Edward, 1-50
Safety, on-the-job, history of, 10-45 to
10-46
Safety Advisory Council, Federal, 4-
103
Sailors' Union of the Pacific:
listings for, 2-43
(*See also* Seafarers' International
Union of North America)
Salaries:
in private and federal employment,
compared, table, 11-62 to 11-65
(*See also* Compensation; Earnings;
Wages)
School Administrators, American
Federation of, listings for, 2-42
Screen Actors Guild:
listings for, 2-21
publication of, 17-9
(*See also* Actors and Artistes of
America, Associated)
Screen Extras Guild:
listings for, 2-21 to 2-22
(*See also* Actors and Artistes of
America, Associated)
Seafarers' International Union of North
America:
listings for, 2-43
publication of, 17-9
Seasonal farmworkers, employment and
training programs for, 5-13
Self-employment, 10-39
Senate reorganization, AFL-CIO
position on, 3-8
Senior Community Service
Employment Program (SCSEP),
5-13
Seniority:
legal decisions on, 9-54 to 9-56
sample contract clause and, 13-7
Service Contract of 1965, 4-82
exemptions under, 4-83 to 4-84
labor standards under, 4-83
minimum wage and fringe benefits
under, 4-83
notice in subcontracts under, 4-83
notice to employees under, 4-83
other obligations under, 4-84
overtime pay standards of, 4-83
recordkeeping requirements under, 4-
83
services employees under, 4-82 to 4-
83
successor-predecessor contracts
under, 4-84
violations and penalties under, 4-84
working conditions under, 4-83

Service Employees International Union:
agreement with Metropolitan New
York Nursing Home
Association, 1-19
listings for, 2-43
publication of, 17-10
strike averted, 1-51
Sex, unemployment and, 12-8 to 12-9
Sex discrimination, 1-15, 9-64
(*See also* Employment discrimination;
Women)
Sheet Metal Workers' International
Association:
convention of, 1-70
listings for, 2-43
publication of, 17-10
Sherman Antitrust Act, 4-3
Shoe and Allied Craftsmen,
Brotherhood of, listings for, 2-43
to 2-44
Shoe industry, tariffs and, 1-18
Shoe Workers of America, United, 1-
80
merger with ACTWU, 1-77
publication of, 17-10
(*See also* Clothing and Textile
Workers Union, Amalgamated)
Shoe Workers' Union, Boot and (*see*
Retail Clerks International
Association)
Sickness, 10-59 to 10-60
Siderographers, International
Association of, listings for, 2-44
Situs picketing rights, AFL-CIO
position on, 3-9
Slave workers, 10-30 to 10-31
Sleeping Car Porters, Brotherhood of:
merger with BRASC, 1-54
(*See also* Railway, Airline and
Steamship Clerks, Freight
Handlers, Express and Station
Employees, Brotherhood of)
Soccer League, North American
(NASL), 1-74
Social benefits, 9-65 to 9-66
Social security:
AFL-CIO position on, 3-9, 3-11
coverage of, 11-60
discrimination against men under, 9-
26 to 9-27
New York City employees and, 1-9
tax increased for, 1-44 to 1-45
Social Security Administration (SSA),
5-36 to 5-37
listings for, 5-29
sources of information on, 5-38 to 5-
39
Southern Labor Union:
listings for, 2-44
trustees resign from, 1-26
Special Investigations and Review,
Office of, 5-6
Stage Employees and Moving Picture
Machine Operators of the U.S.
and Canada, International Alliance
of Theatrical, publication of,
17-10
Standard Federal (Administrative)
Regions, 5-49

State, County and Municipal
Employees, American Federation
of (AFSCME):
CSEA merges with, 1-60
listings for, 2-44
Philadelphia strike ended by, 1-66 to
1-67
publication of, 17-10
settlement with NEA, 1-6
wage increase won by, 1-66
State and Local Fiscal Assistance Act,
9-49
State Employment Security Agencies
(SESAs), sources of federal
funding for, table, 6-17
States:
aid to, AFL-CIO position on, 3-10
regulation by, preemption of, 9-59 to
9-60
Steelworkers of America, United
(USWA), 1-10 to 1-11
bias charged by, 1-43
elections of, 1-50
investigation of, 1-25
gain employment security, 1-16 to 1-
17
income protection guidelines of, 1-76
to 1-77
listings for, 2-44
publication of, 17-10
settlement with ALCOA, 1-23 to 1-
24
settlement with can companies, 1-39
to 1-40
win shipyard vote, 1-49 to 1-50
Stevens, J. P., & Co.:
injunction requested against, 1-46 to
1-47
settlement with NLRB, 1-58 to 1-59,
1-74
labor's opposition to, 1-64
Storeworkers, United, settlement
reached by, 1-28
Stove, Furnace and Allied Appliance
Workers' International Union of
North America, listings for, 2-44
Strikes:
against airlines, 1-74
prohibited, under National Labor
Relations Act, 4-25 to 4-29
right to, under National Labor
Relations Act, 4-9 to 4-11
sample contract clause and, 13-13
under Taylor law, 11-9 to 11-12
by teachers, 1-73
union conduct during, 9-9
(*See also* Work stoppages)
Strip mining controls, AFL-CIO
position on, 3-7, 3-10
Student Financial Assistance, Bureau
of, 5-35
Subcontracting, sample contract clause
and, 13-13
Substantive rights of public employees,
9-61 to 9-62

Summer Youth Employment Program, 5-12

Supplemental Security Income (SSI), 5-37

Taft-Hartley Act, 9-49, 9-65
  invoked to end coal strike, 1-48 to 1-49

Tanker Service Committee, 1-61

Tax breaks, for business, AFL-CIO position on, 3-7 to 3-8

Taxes, per capita, of labor organizations, 2-58 to 2-59
  table, 2-57, 2-58

Taylor law of New York State, 11-3 to 11-14

Teachers, American Federation of (AFT):
  attempt to organize nurses, 1-80
  listings for, 2-44
  publication of, 17-10

Teachers, United Federation of (UFT), agreement with New York City Board of Education, 1-13 to 1-14

Teamsters, Chauffeurs, Warehousemen, and Helpers of America, International Brotherhood of:
  agreement with Farm Workers, 1-12 to 1-13
  listings for, 2-44 to 2-45
  pension fund of, 1-12, 1-51
  settlement with United Parcel, 1-3

Technical Engineers, International Federation of Professional and, listings for, 2-45

Technicians, Association of Civilian, listings for, 2-45

Telecommunications International Union:
  listings for, 2-16
  settlement reached by, 1-31 to 1-32

Telegraph Workers, United:
  listings for, 2-45
  publication of, 17-10

Television and Radio Artists, American Federation of:
  listings for, 2-21
  publication of, 17-5
  (See also Actors and Artistes of America, Associated)

Textile Workers of America, United:
  listings for, 2-45
  publication of, 17-10
  (See also Clothing and Textile Workers Union, Amalgamated)

Theatrical Stage Employees and Moving Picture Machine Operators of the United States and Canada, International Alliance of, listings for, 2-45

Tile, Marble and Terrazzo Finishers and Shopmen International Union, listings for, 2-45

Tobacco Workers International Union, 1-13
  merger with Bakery Workers, 1-71
  publication of, 17-10
  (See also Bakery and Confectionary Workers Union)

Tool, Die and Mold Makers, International Union of, listings of, 2-46

Tool Craftsmen, International Association of, listings for, 2-45 to 2-46

Toys, Playthings, Novelties and Allied Products of the United States and Canada, International Union of Dolls, listings for, 2-46

Trademark Society, Inc., listings for, 2-46

Train Dispatchers Association, American:
  listings for, 2-46
  publications of, 17-10

Training of workers, 10-36

Trans World Airlines (TWA), settlement with Machinists, 1-79 to 1-80

Transit Union, Amalgamated:
  listings for, 2-46
  publication of, 17-10

Transport Workers Union of America (TWU):
  convention of, 1-43
  listings for, 2-46
  publication of, 17-10
  settlement with NYC Transit Authority, 1-63 to 1-64

Transportation Union, United:
  listings for, 2-46
  publication of, 17-11
  settlement with Conrail, 1-72 to 1-73

Treasury Employees Union, National, listings for, 2-46

Trucking Employers, Inc. (TEI), 1-38
  merger with CMI, 1-62

Trusteeships under Landrum-Griffin Act, 4-41 to 4-42

Turnover rates, absenteeism and, chart, 11-61

TWU (see Transport Workers Union of America)

Typographical Union, International (ITU), 2-7
  convention of, 1-71
  listings for, 2-47
  merger panel appointed by, 1-35
  publications of, 17-11

UAW (see Auto Workers, United)

UFW (see Farm Workers of America, United)

UMW (see Mine Workers of America, United)

Unemployment, 12-3 to 12-4
  by age and sex, 12-8 to 12-9
  history of, 10-55 to 10-59
  labor force and employment and, table, 12-20

Unemployment (Cont.):
  Meany's remarks about, 3-3 to 3-4
  national developments and, 12-9 to 12-12
  other labor market indicators and, 12-4 to 12-8
  statistics for, 12-13 to 12-15
  (See also Layoffs by steel companies)

Unemployment insurance (compensation):
  benefit data under, table, 6-14
  coverage under, 6-3 to 6-6
  qualifying for, 6-3
  relationship to USES, 6-26 to 6-27
  significant provision of, table, 6-7 to 6-11
  work requirement of, 6-4

Unemployment Insurance Service (UIS), 5-13 to 5-14

Unfair labor practices under National Labor Relations Act, 4-17 to 4-29
  cases, 4-19

Union shop, sample contract clause and, 13-4

Unions (see Labor organizations)

United Auto Workers (see Auto Workers, United)

United Parcel, Teamsters' settlement with, 1-3

United States Employment Service (USES), 5-8 to 5-10, 6-13 to 6-14
  client services of, 6-16 to 6-18
  enforcement and compliance activities of, 6-21 to 6-22, 6-26
  Federal-State relationship and, 6-14 to 6-15, 6-27 to 6-28
  focus of programs and activities of, 6-25 to 6-26
  funding of, 6-28 to 6-29
  job openings and placements under, 6-18 to 6-21
  relationship to other programs, 6-26 to 6-27
  role of, 6-15 to 6-16
  work requirement activities of, 6-27
  work test role of, 6-22 to 6-25

United States Postal Service:
  labor violations charged against, 1-56
  no-layoff agreement of, 1-66
  wage increase granted by, 1-72

United States Supreme Court:
  significant decisions of 1976–77, 9-6 to 9-11
  significant decisions of 1977–78, 9-12 to 9-18

University Professors, American Association of, listings for, 2-47

Upholsterers' International Union of North America:
  listings for, 2-47
  publication of, 17-11

Urban Mass Transportation Act, 4-76
  implementation of bargaining statutes under, 4-76 to 4-78

USES (see United States Employment Service)

USWA (see Steelworkers of America, United)

Utah Public Employees Association, listings for, 2-47

Utility Workers of New England, Inc., Brotherhood of, listings for, 2-47
Utility Workers Union of America:
listings for, 2-47
publication of, 17-11
UTU (*see* Transportation Union, United)

Vacations, sample contract clause and, 13-8 to 13-10
Vanity Fair, contract with ILGWU, 1-41 to 1-42
Variety Artists, American Guild of:
listings for, 2-21
(*See also* Actors and Artistes of America, Associated)
Vermont State Employees Association, Inc., listings for, 2-47
Veterans, reemployment of, 5-15, 9-66
Veterans Affairs, Office of, 5-33
Veterans Employment Service (VES), 5-9
state directors for, table, 5-9 to 5-10
Volkswagen of America, Inc., settlement with UAW, 1-76

Wage and Price Stability, Council on, 5-20 to 5-21
Wage Appeals Board, 5-5 to 5-6
Wage rates for building trades workers, 19-26 to 19-32
Wages:
cuts accepted by Florida Plumbers, 1-21
Davis-Bacon, AFL-CIO position on, 3-11
history of, 10-48 to 10-49
irregularity of employment and, 10-49
occupational differentials in, 10-49
supplements and, 10-49 to 10-50
increases in, prenotification of, 1-10
minimum, 1-41
AFL-CIO position on, 3-6 to 3-7, 3-9
1977 amendments to law, 4-67 to 4-69
under Walsh-Healey Public Contracts Act, 4-60
of public employees, 9-56 to 9-57
federal, 1-36 to 1-37, 1-56

Wages (*Cont.*):
sample contract clause and, 13-10 to 13-11
scheduled increases in for 1979, 19-33 to 19-38
in selected countries, table, 12-21
at Southern textile firms, 1-20 to 1-21
in textile industry, 1-62
under USES, 6-19
Wagner Act (*see* National Labor Relations Act)
Wagner-Peyser Act, 6-13
Walsh-Healey Public Contracts Act, 4-60
child labor under, 4-60
convict labor under, 4-61
employer liabilities under, 4-61
exceptions under, 4-61
exemptions under, 4-61
homework under, 4-61
minimum wage under, 4-60
overtime under, 4-60
posting notices under, 4-61
Warehouse Industrial International Union, listings for, 2-47 to 2-48
Washington (D.C.) Building Trades Council, pact with George Hyman Construction Co., 1-11
Washington Public Employees Association, listings for, 2-48
Washington (D.C.) Star, The, wage increases and, 1-14
Watch Workers Union, American, listings for, 2-48
Watchmen's Association, Independent, listings for, 2-48
Water projects, AFL-CIO position on, 3-7, 3-10
Welfare and Pension Plans Disclosure Act (WPPDA), 5-15
Western States Service Station Employees Union, listings for, 2-48
Winpisinger, William W., 1-11
Women:
antipathy toward, 9-24 to 9-25
in building trades, 1-32 to 1-33, 1-60
in labor force, 9-49 to 9-50, 10-32 to 10-33
occupation patterns of, 10-41 to 10-42
promotion and hiring of, NBC's agreement on, 1-15
(*See also* Employment discrimination)
Women's Bureau, 5-6
listings for, 17-33

Wood, Wire and Metal Lathers International Union, publication of, 17-11
Woodworkers of America, International:
listings for, 2-48
publication of, 17-11
Work, history of, 10-25 to 10-26
accidents and sickness and, 10-59 to 10-60
changes in labor force and, 10-30 to 10-34
economic activity and, 10-37 to 10-38
education and training of workers and, 10-35 to 10-36
money wages and, 10-48 to 10-50
occupations and, 10-39 to 10-44
old age and, 10-60 to 10-62
organization of work and, 10-38 to 10-39
population growth and change and, 10-27 to 10-30
real earnings and, 10-50 to 10-55
unemployment and, 10-55 to 10-59
working conditions and, 10-44 to 10-48
Work Incentive Program (WIN), 5-12
work requirement of, 6-24
Work-rule concessions by construction unions, 1-11
Work stoppages:
by public employees, provisions for, table, 11-52
time lost due to, table, 12-22 to 12-23
(*See also* Strikes)
Work tests under USES, 6-24 to 6-27
Workers' (workmens') compensation:
accidents covered under, 7-29 to 7-31
1976 amendments to, 7-3 to 7-9
1977 enactments for, 7-10 to 7-18
1978 amendments to, 7-19 to 7-26
Working conditions, history of, 10-44 to 10-48
Writers Guild of America, listings for, 2-48
Wyoming State Employees Association, listings for, 2-48

Yellow-dog contracts under Norris-La Guardia Act, 4-6
Youth, employment services for, 5-9